College Board AP® Topic Outline Macroeconomics

B. Loanable funds market

C. Central bank and control of the money supply

V. Stabilization Policies (20–30%)

A. Fiscal and monetary policies

B. The Phillips curve

VI. Economic Growth (5–10%)

A. Definition of economic growth

B. Determinants of economic growth

C. Growth policy

VII. Open Economy: International Trade and Finance (10–15%)

A. Balance of payments accounts

B. Foreign exchange market

C. Imports, exports, and financial capital flows

D. Relationships between international and domestic financial and goods markets

Krugman's Economics f
2nd edition

Module 25 Banking and Money Creation

Module 28 The Money Market

Module 29 The Market for Loanable Funds

Module 26 The Federal Reserve System: History and Structure

Module 27 The Federal Reserve: Monetary Policy

Section 6: Inflation, Unemployment, and Stabilization Policies

Module 30 Long-Run Implications of Fiscal Policy: Deficits and the Public Debt

Module 31 Monetary Policy and the Interest Rate

Module 32 Money, Output, and Prices in the Long Run

Module 33 Types of Inflation, Disinflation, and Deflation

Module 34 Inflation and Unemployment: The Phillips Curve

Module 35 History and Alternative Views of Macroeconomics

Module 36 Consensus and Conflict in Modern Macroeconomics

Section 7: Economic Growth and Productivity

Module 37 Long-Run Economic Growth

Module 38 Productivity and Growth

Module 39 Growth Policy: Why Economic Growth Rates Differ

Module 40 Economic Growth in Macroeconomic Models

Section 8: The Open Economy: International Trade and Finance

Module 41 Capital Flows and the Balance of Payments

Module 42 The Foreign Exchange Market

Module 43 Exchange Rate Policy and Macroeconomic Policy

Module 41 Capital Flows and the Balance of Payments

Module 44 Barriers to Trade

Module 45 Putting It All Together

College Board AP® Topic Outline Microeconomics	Krugman's Economics for AP® 2nd edition
I. Basic Economic Concepts (8–14%)	**Section 1: Basic Economic Concepts**
A. Scarcity, choice, and opportunity cost	Module 1 The Study of Economics
B. Production possibilities curve	Module 3 The Production Possibilities Curve Model
C. Comparative advantage, absolute advantage, specialization, and trade	Module 4 Comparative Advantage and Trade
D. Economic systems	Module 1 The Study of Economics
E. Property rights and the role of incentives	Module 1 The Study of Economics
F. Marginal analysis	Module 1 The Study of Economics
II. The Nature and Function of Product Markets (55–70%)	**Section 2: Supply and Demand**
A. Supply and Demand	
1. Market equilibrium	Module 5 Supply and Demand: Introduction and Demand
	Module 6 Supply and Demand: Supply
	Module 7 Supply and Demand: Equilibrium
2. Determinants of supply and demand	Module 8 Supply and Demand: Price Controls (Ceilings and Floors)
3. Price and quantity controls	Module 9 Supply and Demand: Quantity Controls
	Section 9: Behind the Demand Curve: Consumer Choice
4. Elasticity	Module 46 Income Effects, Substitution Effects, and Elasticity
	Module 47 Interpreting Price Elasticity of Demand
	Module 48 Other Important Elasticities
5. Consumer surplus, producer surplus, and allocative efficiency	Module 49 Consumer and Producer Surplus
6. Tax incidence and deadweight loss	Module 50 Efficiency and Deadweight Loss
B. Theory of consumer choice	Module 51 Utility Maximization
C. Production and costs	**Section 10: Behind the Supply Curve: Profit, Production, and Costs**
1. Production functions: short and long run	Module 54 The Production Function
2. Marginal product and diminishing returns	Module 54 The Production Function
3. Short-run costs	Module 55 Firm Costs
4. Long-run costs and economies of scale	Module 56 Long-Run Costs and Economies of Scale
5. Cost minimizing input combination and productive efficiency	Module 72 The Cost-Minimizing Input Combination
D. Firm behavior and market structure	Module 57 Introduction to Market Structure
1. Profit	Module 52 Defining Profit
	Module 53 Profit Maximization
	Section 11: Market Structures: Perfect Competition and Monopoly
2. Perfect competition	Module 58 Introduction to Perfect Competition
	Module 59 Graphing Perfect Competition
	Module 60 Long-Run Outcomes in Perfect Competition

College Board AP® Topic Outline Microeconomics	Krugman's Economics for AP® 2nd edition	
3. Monopoly	Module 61	Introduction to Monopoly
	Module 62	Monopoly and Public Policy
	Module 63	Price Discrimination
	Section 12: Market Structures: Imperfect Competition	
4. Oligopoly	Module 64	Introduction to Oligopoly
	Module 65	Game Theory
	Module 66	Oligopoly in Practice
5. Monopolistic competition	Module 67	Introduction to Monopolistic Competition
	Module 68	Product Differentiation and Advertising
III. Factor Markets (10–18%)	**Section 13: Factor Markets**	
A. Derived factor demand	Module 69	Introduction and Factor Demand
B. Marginal revenue product	Module 69	Introduction and Factor Demand
C. Hiring decisions in the markets for labor and capital	Module 70	The Markets for Land and Capital
	Module 71	The Market for Labor
D. Market distribution of income	Module 73	Theories of Income Distribution
IV. Market Failure and the Role of Government (12–18%)	**Section 14: Market Failure and the Role of Government**	
A. Externalities	Module 74	Introduction to Externalities
	Module 75	Externalities and Public Policy
B. Public goods	Module 76	Public Goods
C. Public policy to promote competition	Module 77	Public Policy to Promote Competition
D. Income distribution	Module 78	Income Inequality and Income Distribution

TEACHER'S EDITION

Dianna Miller
Florida Virtual Schools

Margaret Pride
St. Louis University High School (retired)

Leslie Paige Wolfson
Association of Corporate Counsel, New Jersey

to accompany

Krugman's Economics for AP®
Second Edition

Krugman's Macroeconomics for AP®
Second Edition

Margaret Ray
University of Mary Washington

David Anderson
Centre College

Adapted from *Economics*, Third Edition
by Paul Krugman and Robin Wells

bfw
WORTH

Publisher: Ann Heath
Sponsoring Editor: Janie Pierce-Bratcher
Development Editor: Karen Misler
Editorial Assistant: Rachel Chlebowski
Marketing Manager: Julie Comforti
Marketing Assistant: Nont Pansringarm
Photo Editor: Cecilia Varas
Photo Researcher: Cecilia Varas
Director of Design, Content Management: Diana Blume
Cover Designer: Joseph DePinho
Interior Designer: Tamara Newnam
Managing Editor: Lisa Kinne
Project Editor: Andrew Roney
Production Managers: Barbara Seixas/Stacey Alexander
Illustrations: Matt McAdams
Composition: TSI evolve
Printing and Binding: King Printing Co., Inc.
Cover Photos: Kivilcim Pinar/Getty Images (market photo);
Petr Vaclavek/Shutterstock (puzzle pieces);
upixa/iStock/Getty Images Plus (wood background)

Library of Congress Control Number: 2015930275

ISBN-10: 1-4641-5579-8
ISBN-13: 978-1-4641-5579-6

Printed in the United States of America

Second Printing

BFW/Worth Publishers
41 Madison Ave.
New York, NY 10010

highschool.bfwpub.com/KrugmanAP2e

What's Included in This Teacher's Edition

About the Teacher's Edition

Welcome to the Teacher's Edition for *Krugman's Economics for AP®* and *Krugman's Macroeconomics for AP®*, Second Editions. This first-of-its-kind resource brings expert advice on how to teach an outstanding AP® economics course for both new and experienced teachers. To that end, we have created this Teacher's Edition in the familiar wrap-around style, with materials to help you teach, focus, and assess your students; resources to help you easily flip your classroom; and references to the most useful activities and teacher demonstrations in the Teacher's Resource Materials (TRM).

The Teacher's Edition includes:

- An AP® Economics Primer that offers guidance on how to initiate, prepare, and teach an AP® Economics course successfully.
- The complete student text with wrap-around content including teaching tips, AP® Exam Tips, video suggestions, activities, demonstrations, graphing exercises, and more—many of which are connected to the TRM.
- "Blue Pages" that precede the wrap-around student pages at the beginning of each section and provide an in-depth guide to the section content and support materials, including:
  - A section overview with link to a Professional Development video to support your teaching of the section
  - An alignment to the AP® Economics Course Descriptions, highlighting the percentage at which each section is represented on the AP® Economics exam
  - A module-by-module Pacing Guide for both regular and block classes
  - A list of resources that are available in the TRM for the section
  - Suggestions for using external resources, such as those developed by the education division of the St. Louis Federal Reserve Bank
- Answers to all the end-of-module "Tackle the Test" Multiple-Choice Questions and Practice FRQs, with graphs, as appropriate.
- Answers to all end-of-section AP® Exam Practice Questions, including full sample rubrics to the FRQs and sample student graphs.

How to Use the Teacher's Edition

This Teacher's Edition was developed with the goal of being your ultimate teaching tool. Every tip, activity, and reference was written with one thing in mind: to provide guidance and activities that are pertinent and helpful and will support you in leading your students to success in AP® Economics. By using this Teacher's Edition and accompanying Teacher's Resource Materials, you will have at your fingertips everything you need to be the most effective and efficient AP® Economics teacher possible.

Look at What We Offer

Pay special attention to the "Blue Pages" that precede the wrap-around student pages at the beginning of each section. These pages provide an in-depth guide to the chapter content and support materials.

SECTION 2

Supply and Demand

PD Section 2 Overview:

Watch the video overview of Section 2 (for teachers), which is accessible through the Teacher's ... drive, or the book's website, bcs.worthpublishers.com/krugmanap2e (teacher log-in required).

Section 2 introduces supply and demand, a fundamental economic model. The supply and demand model is used to understand how price and quantity sold are determined in a market. The demand for a good or service is determined by consumers who are trying to maximize their satisfaction, and the supply of a good or service is determined by businesses seeking to maximize profits. The interaction of supply and demand determines the equilibrium market price and quantity sold. The supply and demand model can be used to identify how a relevant change will affect the equilibrium price and quantity in a market.

Topics that your students will study in Section 2 include:

- defining a competitive market.
- how a demand curve is constructed.
- the determinants ... to shift.
- how a supply cu...
- the determinants ... shift.
- how equilibrium ...
- how changes to ... equilibrium in th...
- the difference be... supply/quantity supplied.
- the effect of a price ceiling and a price floor on a market.
- the effect of a quantity control in a market.
- the effect of government controls on market efficiency.

Section Overview
Each section begins with a concise overview of its key ideas, along with concrete takeaways for the students, so that you know exactly what to expect. The PD button PD indicates that a professional development video featuring an interview with Dave Anderson or Margaret Ray is available for you on the Teacher's Resource Flash Drive (TRFD), book companion site (bcs), or edAPtext TE-book.

Alignment to AP® Economics Course Description

Macroeconomics I. Basic Economic Concepts: 8–12%

AP® Outline	Module
A. Scarcity, choice, and opportunity costs	(Section 1)
B. Production possibilities curve	(Section 1)
C. Comparative advantage, specialization, and exchange	(Section 1)
D. Demand, supply, and market equilibrium	5: Supply and Demand: Introduction and Demand 6: Supply and Demand: Supply and Equilibrium 7: Supply and Demand: Changes in Equilibrium
E. Macroeconomic issues: Business cycle, unemployment, inflation, growth	(Section 1)

Microeconomics II. The Nature and Function of Product Markets: 55–70%

AP® Outline	Module
A. Supply and demand (15–20%)	5: Supply and Demand: Introduction and Demand 6: Supply and Demand: Supply and Equilibrium 7: Supply and Demand: Changes in Supply and Demand 8: Supply and Demand: Price Controls 9: Supply and Demand: Quantity Controls
B. Theory of consumer choice	(Sections 9, 10)
C. Production and costs	(Section 10)
D. Firm behavior and market structure	(Sections 10, 11, 12)

Alignment to Course Description
We let you know how much weight each section carries in the College Board's AP® Economics Course Outline and correlate the outlines to the modules within the section.

48a **Section 2** Supply and Demand

Pacing Guide

Module	Standard Teaching Days	Block Teaching Days
5	1	½*
6	1	½*
7	1	½*
8	1	½*
9	1	½*
Section 2 Assessment	1	½*
Total	**6**	**3**

*Those students on a block schedule will have more time to spend on activities and TRM materials in class.

Pacing Guide
Whether you're new to teaching AP® Economics or a seasoned veteran, this Pacing Guide will help you plan your course by offering suggestions for how much time to devote to each module for both block and standard schedules.

Introductory Note on Assessments

AP® Macroeconomic students will only need to study Modules 5, 6, and 7. The topics found in Modules 8 and 9 are only a part of the AP® Microeconomics Outline.

TRM Section Resources

All section resources may be accessed through the Teacher's e-Book, the TR-flash drive, or the book's website, bcs.worthpublishers.com/krugmanap2e *(teacher log-in required).*

Section 2 PD Video (for teachers)

Explained (2 of 2)
Worksheet 6.2: Market Changes in Supply

Worksheet 6.3: Changes in Supply
t 6.4: Supply Summary Study
t 6.5: Veterinary Shortages
Module 6
7
Sample Lecture
t 7.1: Simple Supply and Demand
t 7.2: Equilibrium Questions
t 7.3: Changes to Markets
t 7.4: Shifting Supply and
d
t 7.5: Simultaneous Shifts
t 7.6: Graphing Equilibrium
t 7.7: Supply and Demand
Exit Slip: Module 7

Module 8
Module 8 Sample Lecture
Worksheet 8.1: Analyzing Figures 8.1 and 8.2
Worksheet 8.2: Price Ceilings
Worksheet 8.3: Analyzing Figures 8.3 and 8.4
Worksheet 8.4: Price Floors
Worksheet 8.5: Price Floors and Ceilings
Exit Slip: Module 8

Module 9
Module 9: Sample Lecture
Worksheet 9.1: Graphing Quotas
Worksheet 9.2: Graphing Quotas—Peanuts!
Exit Slip: Module 9
Section 2 Review Video (for students)

Section Resources
By using this book, you'll never be short on great activities, projects, and teacher demonstrations. We've made it easy for you to find what you need for each module by listing all the worksheets at the beginning of the unit. Each worksheet is referenced in the wrap-around text and noted with a TRM icon TRM to help you use it at the most appropriate point in the lesson.

St. Louis Federal Reserve Bank Resources

Many of the Federal Reserve Banks have educational departments that offer helpful resources for studying economics. Members of the Educators Advisory Board of the St. Louis Federal Reserve Bank have handpicked some of their best resources for use with your AP® Economics students. References to these resources are included in the margin notes. A complete list of the St. Louis Fed resources for each section with the corresponding URL (as of fall 2014) can be found in the TRM.

NOTE We have included a number of links to useful videos and articles in the margin notes in this sec- tion. Although all are active at the time of publication, we know that some may expire over the next few years. If a link is no longer active, you may wish to search for a similar article or video to illustrate the point. We may also periodically refresh resources on the book's companion website.

St. Louis Federal Reserve Bank Resources
There are a wealth of resources on the Federal Reserve Bank of St. Louis's website. To help you find the information you need when you need it, their Educators Advisory Board has handpicked the best resources, and we reference them on the appropriate pages to help you and your students delve more deeply into the content.

In this text, you will find the complete student text with wrap-around content written by experienced AP® Economics teachers. Look for key instructions and materials, including teaching tips, videos, activities, demonstrations, graphing exercises, and more.

OPEN & CLOSE Start Here

To introduce Module 5, hold up an item that many students will want (like a candy bar). Ask each student how much he or she would pay for the item, and then write the p
Based on the recorded pri
is likely to get the candy b
room auction and what th
to be. Explain whether you
the candy for that price a
cost you and whether you
With your class, discuss v
price for the item. Ask stu
price of the candy bar mig
even 30 bars were being a
one. What if all students a
to bid in the auction, not j
class? Use this discussion
and demand model as a v
how prices are determine
changes in the market af

TEACH Teach It

It is important th
ference between
and a change in
changes, the qua
well. This concep
movement to a n
or a new point on
schedule and de
we just moved to
table/curve. We r
demanded, and c
caused *only* by a
is the variable or
When the en
is called a chan
demand result f
than price and
table/point on the curve to change.

FOCUS Graph It

Looking at Figure 5.2, ask:

- At the price of $1.25, what is the quantity demanded in 2012 and 2013? *9, 11*
- What are some of the factors that might have brought about greater demand for cotton in 2013 than in 2012? *Increased income, people's tastes and preferences, prices of other goods*
- If students in 2014 started to wear only moisture-wicking gym clothes and stopped purchasing cotton athletic clothes, how would you expect the demand curve for cotton to react in 2014? *Shift to the left*

Wrap-around Tips
Find guidance in the margins of this edition from teachers who have been in your shoes. These tips will help you engage students with pertinent material at the point of application.

TRM Connections
When you see the TRM icon TRM before a tip, you know that additional support material exists. All TRM resources may be accessed in digital format from the book companion website (bcs), the Teacher's Resource Flash Drive (TRFD), or opened at the point of use in the edAPtext TE-book.

FOCUS Active Learning

TRM Assign **Worksheet 7.5 (Simultaneous Shifts)** from the TRM for students to get practice graphing situations with simultaneous changes in demand and supply and to determine the effects on price and quantity.

FOCUS Flip It

TRM Have students watch Jacob Clifford's video "Micro 2.2 Supply and Demand" (see econextras video list with hyperlinks on the bcs and TRFD). This video will assist in cementing the concepts of supply, demand, equilibrium, and disequilibrium; it also explains surpluses and shortages.

Assign **Worksheet 7.7 (Supply and Demand)** from the TRM for related questions.

Flip Your Instruction
Look for opportunities to flip your instruction with support from Jacob Clifford and his ACDC Economics videos on YouTube. Instead of asking you to type in ridiculously long URLS, we compiled all video links into a single, clickable document found on our book companion site (bcs). Most Flip It videos have an associated TRM worksheet.

Answers to Student Edition Assessments

Find answers to all "Check Your Understanding" module review questions, end-of-module "Tackle the Test" questions, and end-of-section AP® Exam Practice questions in the margin next to the assessments in the student text. Answers to the complete AP® Practice Exams can also be found in the margins of this Teacher's Edition. When appropriate, answer graphs are included.

Check Your Understanding

1. Explain whether each of the following events represents (i) a *change in* supply or (ii) a *movement along* the supply curve.
   a. During a real estate boom that causes house prices to rise, more homeowners put their houses up for sale.
   b. Many strawberry farmers open temporary roadside stands during harvest season, even though prices are usually low at that time.
   c. Immediately after the school year begins, fewer young people are available to work. Fast-food chains must raise wages, which represent the price of labor, to attract workers.
   d. Many construction workers temporarily move to areas that have suffered hurricane damage, lured by
   e. Since new technologies have made it possible to build larger cruise ships (which are cheaper to run per passenger), Caribbean cruise lines have offered more cabins, at lower prices, than before.
2. After each of the following events, will the supply curve for the good that is mentioned shift to the left, shift to the right, or remain unchanged?
   a. The coffee berry borer beetle destroys large quantities of coffee berries.
   b. Consumers demand more bike helmets than ever.
   c. The number of tea producers increases.
   d. The price of leather, an input in wallet production,

Answers to Module 6 Review Questions

Check Your Understanding

1. a. The quantity of houses supplied rises as a result of an increase in prices. This is a *movement along* the supply curve.
   b. The quantity of strawberries supplied is higher at any given price. This is an *increase in* supply, which shifts the supply curve to the right.
   c. The quantity of labor supplied is lower at any given wage when school is in session. This is a *decrease in* supply, which shifts the supply curve to the left.
   d. The quantity of labor supplied rises in response to a rise in wages. This is a *movement along* the supply curve.
   e. The quantity of cabins supplied is higher at any given price. This is an *increase in* supply, which shifts the supply curve to the right.
2. a. The supply curve shifts to the left.
   b. The supply curve remains unchanged.
   c. The supply curve shifts to the right.
   d. The supply curve shifts to the left.

rve

SECTION 2

Tackle the Test: Multiple-Choice Questions

1. Which of the following would increase demand for a normal good? A decrease in
   a. price
   b. income
   c. the price of a substitute
   d. consumer taste for a good
   e. the price of a complement
2. A decrease in the price of butter would most likely decrease the demand for
   a. margarine.
   b. bagels.
   c. jelly.
   d. milk.
   e. syrup.
3. If an increase in income leads to a decrease in demand, the good is
   a. a complement.
   b. a substitute.
   c. inferior.
   d. abnormal.
   e. normal.
4. Which of the following will occur if consumers expect the price of a good to fall in the coming months?
   a. The quantity demanded will rise today.
   b. The quantity demanded will remain the same today.
   c. Demand will increase today.
   d. Demand will decrease today.
   e. No change will occur today.
5. Which of the following will increase the demand for disposable diapers?
   a. a new "baby boom"
   b. concern over the environmental effect of landfills
   c. a decrease in the price of cloth diapers
   d. a move toward earlier potty training of children
   e. a decrease in the price of disposable diapers

Tackle the Test: Multiple-Choice Questions

1. e
2. a
3. c
4. d
5. a

Tackle the Test: Free-Response Questions

1. Create a table with two hypothetical prices for a good and two corresponding quantities demanded. Choose the prices and quantities so that they illustrate the law of demand. Using your data, draw a correctly labeled graph showing the demand curve for the good. Using the same graph, illustrate an increase in demand for the good.

Rubric for FRQ 1 (6 points)

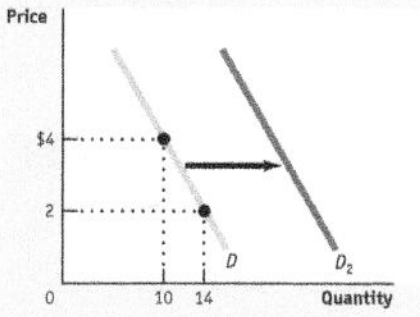

Price	Quantity
$4	10
2	14

1 point: Table with data labeled "Price" (or "*P*") and "Quantity" (or "*Q*")
1 point: Values in the table show a negative relationship between *P* and *Q*
1 point: Graph with "Price" on the vertical axis and "Quantity" on the horizontal axis
1 point: Negatively sloped curve labeled "Demand" or "*D*"
1 point: Demand curve correctly plots the data from the table
1 point: A second demand curve (with a label such as D_2) shown to the right of the original demand curve

2. Draw a correctly labeled graph showing the demand for apples. On your graph, illustrate what happens to the demand for apples if a new report from the Surgeon General finds that an apple a day really *does* keep the doctor away.
(3 points)

Tackle the Test: Free-Response Question

Rubric for FRQ 2 (3 points)

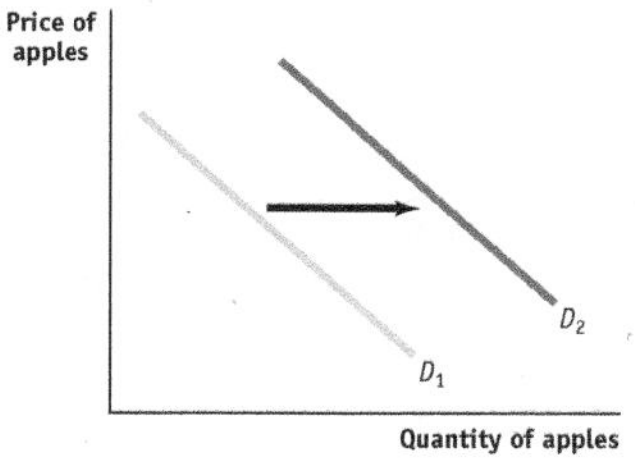

1 point: The vertical axis is labeled "Price" and the horizontal axis is labeled "Quantity."
1 point: The original demand curve is downward-sloping and labeled.
1 point: The new demand curve is labeled, downward-sloping, and to the right of the original demand curve.

Answers to Section 2 AP® Exam Practice Questions

Multiple-Choice Questions

1. e
2. e
3. a

AP® Exam Practice Questions

Multiple-Choice Questions

1. Which of the following changes will most likely result in an increase in the demand for hamburgers in your hometown?
   a. The price of hotdogs decreases.
   b. The price of drinks sold at hamburger restaurants increases.
   c. Income in your town decreases and hamburgers are a normal good.
   d. The local newspaper publishes a story on health problems caused by red meat.
   e. The number of vegetarians in your town decreases and the population size remains the same.
2. Which of the following changes will most likely result in a decrease in the supply of guitars?
   a. The popularity of guitar music increases.
   b. Consumer incomes decrease.
   c. A new firm enters the guitar industry.
   d. The guitar-making process is reengineered to be more efficient.
   e. The wages of guitar makers increase.
3. Which of the following will most likely result in a decrease in the quantity of lemons demanded?
   a. an increase in the price of lemons
   b. an increase in the price of limes
   c. an increase in the price of lemonade
   d. an increase in the number of lemonade stands
   e. a decrease in consumer income

Assess your students' understanding of concepts with ease using the multitude of quizzes and practice problems in this book program.

FOCUS Test It

How will each of the following changes affect the equilibrium price and quantity in the market for ham? Use a graph to determine your answer.

- An increase in the price of eggs (if people eat ham and eggs together). *Demand for ham decreases, equilibrium price and quantity of ham decrease.*
- An increase in the price of pig feed. *Supply of ham decreases, equilibrium price increases, quantity decreases.*
- A simultaneous increase in the price of pig feed and eggs. *Equilibrium quantity decreases (note that it decreased in both examples above), equilibrium price is indeterminate (note that price went up in one example above and down in the other—we don't know which change was larger).*

Assessment Support

"Test It" and "Exit Slip" activities allow you to quiz your students on the concepts you just covered. Answers to these assessments appear within the corresponding tip.

OPEN & CLOSE Exit Slip

TRM *Please see **Exit Slip: Module 7** in the TRM for formative multiple-choice questions to ask before finishing your lesson. These questions will help you quickly assess whether your students have mastered the module's concepts before moving on.*

Answers to the Exit Slip Questions

1. C
2. D
3. B

Additional Resources in the Program

In addition to the support provided in the Teacher's Edition, there are many resources available for use with *Krugman's Economics for AP®*, Second Edition. To see a sample of most of these supplements, contact your BFW sales representative.

For Teachers

edAPtext TEACHER'S EDITION (TE-BOOK)

Powered by COPIA

This innovative new digital text offers the accessibility you want and the flexibility you expect. The edAPtext TE-Book gives you full access to the Teacher's Edition for *Krugman's Economics for AP®*, Second Edition, when and where you want it. The TE-Book offers page fidelity so that it matches the print Teacher's Edition exactly. You may review the downloaded content, take notes on your computer at school, and then pick up where you left off on your home computer, your iPad, or your Android tablet. Your notes will sync once you log in and are connected to the Internet.

Your edAPtext TE-Book is the ultimate integrator for all your *Krugman's Economics for AP®* resources. While you are in the connected mode, you may access all the videos, TRM resources, and other links at the point of use. If you want to provide assignments or notes, or give quizzes to the entire class, you may do so using the social media function of edAPtext and the teacher dashboard. The edAPtext TE-Book is designed to make classroom management and communication easier, so you can focus on teaching.

TEACHER'S RESOURCE FLASH DRIVE (TRFD)

ISBN: 1-4641-5580-1

The Teacher's Resource Flash Drive includes all text figures and tables (in JPEG and PPT formats) and the entirety of the Teacher's Resource Materials (TRM) in PDF form. The TRM, compiled by Margaret Pride in collaboration with Dianna Miller and Leslie Wolfson, includes:

- Sample lectures written by Eric Dodge.
- Teacher demonstrations.
- Classroom and homework activities (worksheets) for students.
- The Federal Reserve Bank of St. Louis resource links.
- Econextras, links to videos referenced in the wrap-around material of this Teacher's Edition. (*Note:* We will include this on the TRFD, but you will want to check the book's companion site periodically for updates.)
- PD Professional Development (PD) videos: These brief section overviews by Jacob Clifford with David Anderson and Margaret Ray offer advice on what to emphasize in a given section, how to anticipate and overcome common pitfalls, as well as tips for helping students realize success in the course and on the AP® exam.
- PowerPoint® lecture slides that closely follow the text. These enhanced slides are designed to assist teachers with lecture preparation and presentations. The slides contain graphs, figures, data tables, links, and explanations of key concepts suitable for lecture presentation. They may be customized by adding personalized data, questions, and additional lecture slides and notes.
- The Image PowerPoint slides and JPG Image Bank.

Look for the Teacher's Resource Materials TRM icon throughout the Teacher's Edition for reminders about available resources.

BOOK COMPANION SITE **bcs.worthpublishers.com/krugmanap2e**

The companion website offers valuable tools for both instructors and students. Here's a sample of what you can access:

- The entirety of the Teacher's Resource Flash Drive
- Professional Development videos
- Student Edition and Teacher's Edition errata

EXAMVIEW® ASSESSMENT SUITE TEST BANK
ISBN: 1-4641-5575-5

The Test Bank, written by Eric Dodge, is available exclusively within the ExamView® Assessment Suite software. With more than 5,000 5-distracter multiple-choice and AP®-style free-response questions, you'll never be at a loss for great assessment options. The questions have been checked for correlation with the text and the AP® topic outline, as well as for overall usability and accuracy. You may select from the provided questions or use the step-by-step tutorial to write your own. Questions can be sorted according to various metadata fields and scrambled to create different versions of tests. Tests may be printed or administered online using the ExamView® Player.

For Students

Please see the Student Edition preface starting on page xxxvi for more information on these innovative supplements for students:

- *Krugman's Economics for AP®*, Second Edition, text and e-Book
- *Strive for a 5: Preparing for the AP® Macroeconomics Examination* and *Strive for a 5: Preparing for the AP® Microeconomics Examination*
- Book companion site, including
  - Flashcards
  - Self-test quizzes
  - Section Review videos
  - Econextras, links to videos referenced in the wrap-around material of this Teacher's Edition
  - Activities and worksheets
- edAPtext powered by CopiaClass, which accompanies *Krugman's Economics for AP®*, Second Edition, is a premium digital tool that offers an e-Book and much more. Students may:
  - Access edAPtext from up to four devices. Download the text to their home PC or Mac computer, iPad or Android tablet, and use it on the computer at school.
  - Take advantage of the social networking feature to communicate with their teacher and classmates. Form study groups and share notes.
  - Access videos and assignments, questions, and assessments from their teacher while connected.
  - Work anywhere, anytime and not worry about losing their work. All notes, highlights, and other communication will sync automatically once connected to the Internet.

Your AP® Economics Primer

Before You Begin Teaching AP® Economics

Teaching AP® Economics can be a tremendously rewarding experience, but it takes a lot of preparation. If you are like most teachers of AP® Economics, you probably took few, if any, economics courses in college. And even if you took some, they were probably very different from the AP® course.

Don't worry! This Teacher's Edition includes an abundance of resources to help you teach AP® Macroeconomics and Microeconomics. There are also many other resources available from the College Board and other groups to make your life easier.

Here is a list of things you should do before you start teaching the course, if possible:

1. Attend a College Board–approved workshop. Ideally, you should attend a one-week summer institute. These institutes are held all over the country and are led by College Board–endorsed consultants, including the authors of and many of the contributors to the *Krugman's Economics for AP®* Student and Teacher's Editions. College Board–endorsed consultants are seasoned veterans who have attended many readings where the exams are scored but they, too, were once new to AP® Economics just like you. Other alternatives include one- and two-day workshops offered by the College Board during the school year as well as AP®-specific workshops sponsored by regional Federal Reserve Banks, the Foundation for Teaching Economics, and state and national Councils for Economic Education. Some of these workshops are free and offer materials that will greatly support and enhance your teaching efforts.
2. Download and read the AP® Course Description found on the Macro and Micro course home pages at AP® Central (**apcentral.collegeboard.com**). Combined into a single document for Macro and Micro, the course description contains key information about the two courses, including an introduction, course overviews, course standards, plus information about the AP® exams with sample questions.

3. Download and read the AP® Economics Teacher's Guide, authored by Margaret Pride, who is also one of the supplement authors for this textbook program. You can find the Teacher's Guide on the Macro and Micro course pages on AP® Central. Designed specifically to help teachers who are new to AP® Economics, this document includes several sample syllabi and advice for the AP® Audit for each course.
4. Participate in the AP® Teacher Community, an online forum for AP® Macro and Micro teachers found at **apcommunity.collegeboard.org**. Here you can ask questions, get advice, give suggestions, and share resources. If you are like most other AP® Economics teachers, you are the only teacher at your school who is charged with AP® Economics. The AP® Teacher Community is a great remedy for this problem. Plus, this book's authors and supplement authors are regular contributors.
5. Complete the AP® Course Audit. See the AP® Coordinator at your school or go to **www.collegeboard.com/html/apcourseaudit** for more information. A Sample Syllabus and Pacing Guide are included in the Teacher's Resource Materials.

TRM **Sample Syllabus**

Sequencing and Pacing

With one possible exception (see below), it would be best to go through the modules and sections of this text in order. The decisions about the arrangement of topics in this Second Edition were made after careful thought and discussion, and they reflect the preferences of not only the authors, but also many other current users of *Krugman's Economics for AP®*. You will notice that this text covers the basic principles of economics in Sections 1 and 2, which is covered in both courses. Macro topics are then covered in Sections 3–8, followed by the Micro topics in Sections 9–14. Thus, if you are teaching both courses, simply cover Sections 1–14. If you are teaching just Macro, you will teach Sections 1–8 in order. If you are teaching Micro only, you should cover Sections 1 and 2, and then skip to Sections 9–14.

Alternate Organization

Some experienced teachers choose to assign Appendix 1: Graphs in Economics (found at the end of Section 1) at the beginning of the school year because students need to use these models throughout both courses. Some teachers choose to assign the appendix as homework and/or quiz students on the material to get a baseline of their understanding or, depending on the students, spend a complete class period having students work through the problems.

Starting with the appendix also sends a clear message to students that this isn't a typical social studies class —there is more reading, writing, calculating, graphing, and interpretation than they might be accustomed to. For students who add the AP® Economics course during the first few weeks of school, it would be wise to assign this module as homework to be sure they have the requisite math skills to tackle the course. Regardless of when you use it, don't skip Appendix 1!

Pacing

Pacing is one of the biggest challenges for new (and experienced) teachers of AP® Economics, and the organization of this text is designed to help you meet that challenge. The sections in this text are comparable to a standard chapter. The modules within each section are small chunks of information purposefully created to allow you to cover one module per class meeting. However, depending on your schedule and when your course starts, you may not have sufficient time to work at that pace before the AP® exams are given in early May. A good rule of thumb is to plan backwards, leaving at least one full week before AP® exam week begins (the first week in May), and to use the pacing guides at the beginning of each section in this text to plan your calendar accordingly. Complete pacing guides may also be found in the Teacher's Resource Materials included in this book program. Also be mindful of the percentage indicated for each section, so you don't get bogged down on material that will not be heavily tested on the AP® exam. Using frequent formative assessment, such as the Exit Slips provided in this Teacher's Edition, will let you know if your students are ready to move on.

TRM **Pacing Guide**

TRM **Pacing Guide (Block Schedule)**

Preparing Students for the AP® Exam

Unfortunately, there is no foolproof way to prepare students for success on the AP® exam. By choosing *Krugman's Economics for AP®*, however, you are off to a good start; it was written and reviewed by instructors who are experienced AP® Economics teachers and have expertise in the nuances of the AP® Economics exam. Here are some of the features designed specifically to help students excel on the AP® exam:

- Every topic on the official AP® Microeconomics and Macroeconomics Topic Outline is covered in detail in the textbook.
- For each section, you may access a Professional Development video featuring Jacob Clifford's interview with Dave Anderson or Margaret Ray that offers you an insider's view of the most important issues in the section. Each video provides an overview of the section, with suggestions for tackling tough topics and/or addressing misconceptions. Look for the PD icon throughout the Teacher's Edition. PD
- Created by Jacob Clifford and denoted by the green play button in the student text, short Section Review Videos present key ideas in the section using lots of visuals, down-to-earth language, and a little humor.

Section Review Video

- In addition, students can access short video clips that provide "just in time" instruction on key concepts throughout the modules. These videos are referenced in the wrap-around material of this Teacher's Edition and are available in the econextras list on our book companion site at **bcs.worthpublishers.com/krugmanap2e**.

- Throughout the student text, you will find AP® Exam Tips that provide helpful advice on what students should read closely and what common pitfalls they can avoid. This Teacher's Edition offers AP® Exam teaching tips that extrapolate on such advice and often include activities for further teaching of tough topics.
- At the end of each module in the student textbook, a "Tackle the Test" section offers five practice multiple-choice and two free-response-style questions (FRQ). These short, focused FRQ-style problems help students develop the skills necessary to answer the full FRQs on the AP® Exam. The first FRQ in each module includes a rubric to help train students on how to answer an FRQ. The second FRQ is for each student to practice on his or her own. Answers to these questions appear in the margins of this Teacher's Edition.
- Each section of the Student Edition now concludes with a more comprehensive set of AP® Exam Practice Questions that covers the entire section.
- Finally, two complete AP® practice exams (one Macro and one Micro) now appear at the end of the Student Edition to help students get ready for the real thing. Answers to AP® Exam Practice Questions and the Practice Tests, with appropriate graphs, appear in the margins of this Teacher's Edition.
- Additional helpful tools in the Teacher's Resource Materials include Sample Lectures for the teacher, Open and Close suggestions for each topic, Focus activities for active learning and real-world applications, worksheets that can be used in class or for homework, Exit Slips for formative assessment (consider using these with clickers if you have them), and links to videos and lessons from many different sources, including the St. Louis Federal Reserve Bank.
- Each section also links to chapters in David Anderson's reader *Economics by Example*. The discussion questions after each chapter of the supplemental reader are excellent for class seminars and discourse. Students need to practice argumentation using economic reasoning and these questions work well for this type of lesson.

TRM **Sample Lectures**

TRM **Activities and Worksheets**

Use as many of the tools this book program provides as possible to support you and your students.

Here are some additional strategies for preparing students for the AP® exam:

- Early in the year, give students a copy of the AP® Topic Outline and get in the habit of alerting students when you have finished one topic and are starting another. For convenience, you can find the AP® Topic Outline in the front endpapers of the Student Edition and this Teacher's Edition, including the module and section correlation.
- Have students use an AP® preparation book, such as *Strive for a 5*, which was written specifically for *Krugman's Economics for AP®*, Second Edition, by Melanie Fox.
- Make reading and writing an integral part of your course—on the AP® exam, students are often surprised at how little they actually need to calculate. The majority of questions involve quite a bit of reading, making connections, and linkages. Make sure your students get plenty of practice throughout the year and show them previous AP® questions so that they understand the high expectations of AP® Readers.
- Keep in mind that students may not use calculators on the exam, so be sure to practice basic math skills in class without calculators! It is important for them to be able to add, subtract, multiply, divide, find percentage change, read and interpret a graph, and use decimals and fractions. This might sound derisive, but given our reliance on technology, those basic arithmetic skills are rusty. Sadly, there are students who lose points on the exam because they can't find the area of a triangle or can't divide .20 into 1!
- Also, emphasize the correct use of economics vocabulary—remind students to read the AP® Exam Tips in each module that coach them to focus on unique economic meanings for common words, models they must use, and critical understanding.
- Graph, graph, and graph again! Using mini whiteboards can help you quickly assess if your students are drawing and labeling graphs correctly.
- Make sure your students understand the structure of the AP® exam.
  - On the current exam, Section I consists of 60 multiple-choice questions to be answered in 70 minutes. This section accounts for two-thirds of the exam score. There is no penalty for guessing, so make sure your students answer every question.
  - Section II consists of three free-response questions to be answered in 60 minutes. This section accounts for one-third of the exam score. The first question should take about 30 minutes and accounts for half of the Section II score. The second and third questions should be answered in the remaining 30 minutes and are equally weighted to account for the second half of the Section II score. The first question in both courses is often cumulative and will bring in graphing, calculations, and critical thinking applications of numerous topics in the course.
- Shortly before taking the actual AP® exam, have students come in after school or on the weekend to complete a full-length AP® exam for practice, such as the one offered at the end of the student text. It is beneficial for students to experience a real exam, given under real conditions, so they can get a sense of how fast they need to work and what topics they need to review. If you teach both courses, consider finishing Macro at mid-term such that the mid-term exam can be an AP® Macroeconomics practice test. Use the AP® Macroeconomics Practice Exam in the back of the student text or pull multiple-choice questions and select three free-response questions from published College Board Exams. Provide students with the scoring rubrics and the diagnostic, and grade the exam using the most recent point distribution to let students know if they are likely to

score a 5, 4, 3, 2, or 1 on the exam. Making the assessment high-stakes gives students a realistic expectation of their future performance on the AP® exam. Currently, the complete 2000, 2005, and 2010 AP® exams are available for purchase from the College Board. Also, the international versions of the exam in recent years are available through your AP® audit account (look for the link to "Secure Documents" after logging in). These forms are indeed secure, so students can't find them at AP® Central. Please help keep the forms secure by only using them in class and collecting them when you are done! *Note:* The international version of the exam is different from the version administered to the majority of students in the United States and Canada. However, it is comparable both in quality and difficulty to other versions.

- Use as many actual AP® questions as possible. There are a number of ways to incorporate previous free-response questions into your course. Some teachers include one or two AP® free-response questions on each test. Other teachers assign them for homework or in cooperative groups during class, having small groups present their answers to FRQs to the class. I frequently use the short FRQs as a timed test (I allow 15 minutes for each question). If you assign the questions for homework, be aware that students can access the solutions online. However, because there are more than 100 released free-response questions, it's probably safe to include one or two on an exam.

Assessments

Although you will find a multitude of assessments and test items with this book program, you probably won't have time to use all of them. How each teacher assesses students is a matter of personal preference. Some teachers find time for quizzes, while many teachers only formally assess their students at the end of each section. I like to give short quizzes allowing students to work in pairs; these are three- to five-question multiple-choice quizzes after each module or topic, and we debrief them right away. If you are new to teaching AP® Economics, it is probably better to err on the side of fewer assessments, so you have more time to cover the content. This will also save you time grading! Here are some additional suggestions for assessments:

- Give challenging assessments that mimic the AP® exam. Be sure to include multiple-choice and free-response questions and don't be afraid to ask difficult questions. Also, don't be afraid to grade with a firm hand—the rubrics on the real AP® exam are often quite strict.
- Scale the test scores like they do on the real AP® exam. Experience will help you know how much to adjust them, but remember that obtaining a raw score of 72 out of 90 will almost certainly earn a student a 5 on the AP® exam. Alternatively, you can use tests as formative assessments—don't scale the test but encourage students to earn points for doing test corrections.
- Give cumulative assessments. Some teachers include cumulative questions on each exam, while others give cumulative exams every couple of chapters. The review questions at the end of each module and section, as well as the cumulative AP® Practice Tests in the text, will help.

Included in this book program are test items in the ExamView® Assessment Suite. This makes it easy to develop your own assessments. ExamView® is an easy-to-use resource for creating multiple-choice tests or cumulative assessments to help students prepare for the AP® exam. You can make multiple versions of the same test and an alternate that is more challenging as a makeup exam.

IMPORTANT: *Please do not post any of the questions or solutions online, as some students search online for questions and answers to cheat. The publisher receives many e-mails and complaints from teachers who have discovered that their students found answers online. Once posted, they are readily available to all AP® students with access to the Internet.*

Homework

The number of problems, worksheets, and activities available in the textbook should greatly exceed the number you would need to assign in any given school year. In fact, as teachers get more experience with AP® Economics, they tend to assign fewer and fewer homework problems. It is better to have students spend time doing a few problems in depth rather than giving shallow answers to a large set of problems. Students consistently say that reading the modules slowly and carefully is critical to understanding, so provide incentives to encourage such reading. Open notes quizzes using the exercises from the text are an efficient way to check on students' grasp of the material.

Finally, there is no consensus on how best to grade and count homework. Some teachers collect homework daily, while others collect it only occasionally and at random. Some teachers grade homework problems for correctness, while others grade it only for effort. Often, this decision is based on your own preferences and school culture. I frequently assign the discussion questions in *Economics by Example* for a homework grade because they require much more individualized responses. I then use each section's AP® Exam Practice Questions as practice homework, giving an effort grade. Another useful technique is to assign the homework and give one of the assigned questions as an impromptu in-class quiz.

Activities and Projects

One of the best parts about teaching AP® Economics is that there are a number of simulations and activities that allow students to apply the concepts. Activities and projects are often the best way to help students learn, hands-on, the important concepts in AP® Economics.

To emphasize the importance of activities, the Focus tips in the margins of this Teacher's Edition provide suggestions and resources for enhancing your lecture with videos/visuals, discussions, and graphing activities. Although you may feel overwhelmed trying to make it through the content, experienced teachers agree that getting students engaged in activities is time well spent.

Projects are a great way to have students put their knowledge to work. Although it is probably not possible to assign a project for each section, many teachers try to assign one project per semester. For Micro, students can collect articles in a journal—applying what they've learned about supply/demand and externalities and the role of government—and use graphs to show the changes. In Macro, many teachers assign indicators to students who then prepare PowerPoint® presentation slides to demonstrate the current state of the economy. You might also want to assign reading to your students on economists and economic thought, and require students to present their findings to the class. Experienced teachers often find that they can give students more independence once the pacing has been established.

Current Events

Another great aspect of teaching AP® Economics is that there is no shortage of real-life applications—in fact, this is perhaps the most valuable aspect of the course. Every day, newspaper articles describe current events, policies, or data that you can discuss with your students. When students see that the concepts they are learning can be applied to the world around them, their motivation is sure to increase! (In fact, I'm so confident of the ubiquity of economics that each semester I offer $5.00 to any AP® Econ student who can bring in *the front page* of a newspaper that includes absolutely no economics. I've only had to pay up three times in twenty years!) If you don't have time to read the newspaper cover to cover looking for articles, join the AP® Economics Teacher Community (see Before You Begin Teaching AP® Economics above). Several times a week, someone posts a link to an article that can be used in class. Alternatively, you can offer extra credit to students for bringing in articles related to class concepts.

One helpful way to engage students in discussion is through blogging. See Jason Welker's "Economics in Plain English" at **welkerswikinomics.com/blog** for a masterful example of blogs in economics. Other teachers maintain a class home page on Facebook to post articles and other links. Also, check out NPR's Marketplace and Paul Solman's "Making Sense" for short news briefs you can discuss in class—in fact, you will find many references to these websites in the margins of this Teacher's Edition. Starting each class with a 3-minute news piece—an article or a podcast, such as those from Planet money—can engage your students and enhance the meaning of the models and concepts studied in the text.

Technology

Access to technology is helpful in the AP® Economics class, and real-time data and policy announcements can make your classroom come alive. Websites and simulations to enhance your classroom can be found in the margins throughout this Teacher's Edition. Don't be afraid to go digital or flip a lesson, if not your whole classroom. But don't forget, also, that you can have an effective and exciting class with mini whiteboards and poster paper as well!

Movies, TV, and music are excellent resources for economic topics. Basically any movie scene you can think of has been uploaded to YouTube. Just be sure that you view the clip in its entirety before showing it to your class or requiring students to watch it—sometimes you will find rude and/or inappropriate voice-overs on a rather innocuous clip. Also, ask your students for examples; they make fun and entertaining connections that you had not considered, but that you can use nonetheless. Your ability to infuse AP® Economics concepts with real-life examples, current events, and your students' favorite medium (media!) is limitless. One small word of caution, however: be sure to stay on pace to cover all topics and have time to review before the exam in May.

What to Do After the AP® Exam

If you still have class time left with your students after the AP® exam, there are several options:

1. **Teach the enrichment modules at the end of the student text.** Because some schools are in session until the end of June, you might have quite a bit of time to fill. Consider teaching the "Enrichment Modules" found at the back of the book. These modules are a combination of topics that range from simple student interest to material that might one day be folded into the AP® curriculum:

   Module A: Financial Markets and Crises

   Module B: Behavioral Economics

   Module C: The Economics of Information

   Module D: Indifference Curves and Consumer Choice
2. **Teach personal finance.** The "Financial Literacy Handbook," included at the end of the student text, was written by Laura Adams (*The Money Girl* from **quickanddirtytips.com**) and offers excellent personal finance support. Pair this with Laura's podcasts from Quick and Dirty Tips and your students will be entertained while learning key life lessons. Alternatively, the St. Louis Fed has a wonderful online course that students can work on at their own pace. I also recommend the movie *Maxed Out*, which fits into a discussion on credit card debt.
3. **Have your students do a project.** This is an ideal time for students to bring together all of the topics from the course. Have them pose a question about environmental, domestic, or international policies that have multiple perspectives and involve many trade-offs.
4. **Show full-length films.** We don't have the luxury of watching full movies in AP® Economics, but after the exam students can enjoy and really understand the movies *Inside Job* or *Enron: The Smartest Guys in the Room* and discuss them with clarity.
5. **Have a debate.** Economic theories can be argued as to what each school of economic thought would do about a certain problem, such as Japan's economic recession or the national debt in the United States. Students can discuss the economic rationale for raising the minimum wage, adjusting the interest rate on college loans, or public financing for domestic sports stadiums. Other possible topics: immigration, Social Security, and health care reform. Show your students the value of the economic reasoning they have learned.

6. **Bring in guest speakers.** Now is the time for you to relax and ask someone else to speak to your students. Suggestions for guest speakers:
   a. A local banker
   b. A small business owner
   c. Someone from a Federal Reserve branch (if one is nearby)
   d. A local broker or your credit union representative
   e. Former students
7. **Take a field trip.** Many Federal Reserve branches employ one or more individuals devoted to education—contact a local branch to organize a tour.
8. **Introduce trade books.** Economics is a popular topic. Have your students form a book club in which each group reads a book by Thomas Friedman, Jeffrey Sachs, Tim Harford, or another economist. Make the assignment into a project by having the groups present to the class on the topics they learned.

   Here is a brief list of books your students may enjoy:
   - Niall Ferguson's *The Ascent of Money*
   - Michael Lewis's *The Big Short*
   - Greg Ip's *The Little Book of Economics: How the Economy Works in the Real World*
   - Pietra Rivoli's *The Travels of a T-shirt in the Global Economy*
   - Tim Harford's *The Undercover Economist*
   - John McMillan's *Reinventing the Bazaar*
   - Steven Levitt and Stephen Dubner's *Think Like a Freak* or *Superfreakonomics*
   - Naomi Klein's *This Changes Everything*
   - the fun Marshall Jevons novels

Recruiting Students for Next Year

In many cases, students have no idea what an economics class is all about. It is your job to promote the hands-on learning and real-world applications that make AP® Economics a class worth taking! One way to do this is to visit upper-level math classes like Algebra II and above and give them a short presentation about the class. Even though economics is a social studies class, students who enjoy math often state that this is the first social studies class they have enjoyed. When I talk to potential students, I try to hit three main themes:

1. **It is a fresh start.** This isn't a typical social studies class. This doesn't mean the class will be easy, as you will still need to use critical thinking and communication skills. But it will be much more relevant to everyday events.
2. **It is great preparation for college.** Many majors require students to take an economics course and be familiar with the methods of analysis in AP® Economics.
3. **You will never ask, "When will we ever use this?"** Economics is on the front page of newspapers and popular magazines every day! In my class, we will read articles from current newspapers and magazines, and learn how to evaluate and understand the economic impact of events and decisions.

I also try to give prospective students an example or two of the topics we study. For example: Will raising the minimum wage be good for the economy? Or, what's so good about falling gas prices?

Many students will ask you how AP® Economics compares to regular economics (which is required in roughly half the states in the United States). I present such students with the following questions of my own:

1. *What college major do you plan to pursue?* If you are going into business, economics will be required. However, the principles course is often a large lecture or taught by a T.A., and this is an opportunity to study the subject in high school, where I will be available to help you. All social science degrees will also require economics.
2. *Are you planning to obtain a science or STEM degree?* If so, this may be your only opportunity to take an economics course, which impacts your life in more ways than you can imagine.
3. *Do you want to make good life decisions?* Students will avoid the class if they are math phobic. I show them the simple models we use (for example, supply and demand) and some easy formulas, but then I explain that economics is about more than math and money. It's also about learning decision-making skills that can positively impact the rest of their lives.
4. *Do you want to sign up for an AP® class, but don't know which one to take?* This is a class in which everyone can succeed if you (the teacher) provide support. There are no prerequisites, and the topics are varied and interesting once we help students get over their initial fears of models and numbers.

Additional Internet Resources

In addition to the links found in this Teacher's Edition, the book's website **bcs.worthpublishers.com/krugmanap2e**, the AP® Central home page, and the AP® Teacher Community at **apcommunity.collegeboard.org**, there are a wealth of Internet sources for you to explore.

Economic Conditions—Where would economics students be without data? Listed below are links to current economic data, historical data archives, financial data, and social statistics:

- **http://research.stlouisfed.org//fred2/**. The St. Louis Federal Reserve website is rich with data, interactive lessons, and videos.
- **http://www.census.gov/**. Students can spend a good amount of time here. Design a quick data lesson for the income distribution in Micro using the real data to construct a Lorenz curve.
- **http://stats.bls.gov/eag/eag.us.htm**. At the Bureau of Labor and Statistics website, send students to the Occupational Outlook Handbook to discover job requirements and current demand.

News and Politics—Economic knowledge and insight affect every aspect of society, from its news to its politics.

- **http://www.economist.com/**. Students can access some *Economist* articles online even without a subscription.

- **http://www.businessweek.com/**. Bloomberg's *Business Week* articles are clear and easily searchable.
- **http://online.wsj.com/home-page**. Find some *Wall Street Journal* articles without a subscription.
- **http://www.nytimes.com/pages/topics/**. In addition to daily articles, *The New York Times* topics are a treasure trove of in-depth collections of articles on a single topic.
- **http://www.swcollege.com/bef/econ_debate.html**. This is a wonderful site for after-the-AP® exam debate topics.
- **http://www.heritage.org/Research/**. Heritage Foundation materials are easily searchable.

Teaching Resources

- **http://dirkmateer.com/**. This is a very thorough site with many links to media for both Micro and Macro.
- **http://www.youtube.com/watch?v=7Z16Gb3jkpl**. This is the adorable Glen Hubbard video students made in response to Ben Bernanke's selection as Fed Chair. Hilarious.
- **http://yadayadayadaecon.com/**. Great Seinfeld clips that relate to economics—many would be appropriate to Micro.
- **http://econstories.tv/**. The well-known Keynes-Hayek video.
- **http://www.huffingtonpost.com/2011/06/21/robert-reich-solves-economy_n_881479.html**. Robert Reich fixes the economy in 2 minutes.
- **http://www.whitenova.com/thinkEconomics/index.html**. Through interactive graphs, ThinkEconomics illustrates basic economic principles that are taught in a college-level introductory economics course.
- **http://www.bos.frb.org/education/econedpubs.htm**. Link to publications from the Federal Reserve of Boston.
- **http://www.lerner.udel.edu/centers/ceee/online-resources**. The University of Delaware Center for Economic Education & Entrepreneurship provides teacher links and resources as well as personal finance lessons from Practical Money Skills for Life.
- **http://www.counciloreconed.org/**. This is the national Council for Economic Education home page.
- **http://web.centre.edu/econed/**. David Anderson, co-author of this text, offers activities for your classroom as well as other helpful resources for teachers.
- **http://www.fee.org/**. You will find the Foundation for Economic Education a particularly useful resource.
- **http://www.businessbookmall.com/Economics%20Videos.htm**. Use this resource for all types of economics videos.

Student Tutorials and Lectures

Krugman's Economics for AP®, Second Edition, includes a book companion site with abundant resources—find them at **bcs.worthpublishers.com/krugmanap2e.** But there are often students who ask for additional lectures and tutorials. Here is a brief list of some of the many resources available online:

- **http://reffonomics.com/reff/index.html**. One of the first and best online tutorials for students and teachers.
- **http://www.econclassroom.com/**. Jason Welker's lectures can stand in for your own.
- **https://www.youtube.com/user/ACDCLeadership**. We have vetted many of these links from Jacob Clifford and correlated them to topics in the text, but this is the full archive.
- **https://www.youtube.com/user/mjmfoodie**. Similarly, we reference several of Dr. Mary Glasson's videos in this text, but this is her full archive.

Note: For the complete list of videos referenced in the margins of this Teacher's Edition, please see the econextras list at **bcs.worthpublishers.com/krugmanap2e**.

Good luck with your AP® Economics course!

Patti Brazill

Irondequoit High School, Rochester, New York

About the Authors

University of Mary Washington

Margaret Ray is Professor of Economics and Director of the Center for Economic Education at the University of Mary Washington, where she specializes in teaching introductory economics. She received her BS in Economics from Oklahoma State University and her PhD in Economics from the University of Tennessee. In 2012 she received her MEd in Curriculum and Instruction and became certified to teach K-12 Social Studies. She has taught AP® Economics at several high schools in Virginia and has received the Council on Economic Education's Excellence in Teaching Economics award. She has been involved in the AP® Economics program since 1992, serving as a reader and question leader, writing test items, overseeing the AP® course audit, writing College Board "Special Focus" articles, and editing the Council on Economic Education's AP® Macroeconomics resource. She has been a College Board® Endorsed Consultant for economics since 2001, and she conducts several professional development workshops and institutes each year. Her favorite hobby is showing hunter-jumper horses adopted from racehorse rescue organizations. She lives on a farm in Spotsylvania, Virginia with her two daughters.

Donna Anderson

David Anderson is the Paul G. Blazer Professor of Economics at Centre College. He received his BA in Economics from the University of Michigan and his MA and PhD in Economics from Duke University. Anderson has been involved in the AP® Economics program for two decades. For five years he led the grading of one or both of the AP® Economics exams, and he speaks regularly at AP® conferences and workshops. He has authored dozens of scholarly articles and many books, including *Cracking the AP® Economics Exam, Economics by Example, Favorite Ways to Learn Economics, Environmental Economics and Natural Resource Management, Economics in Modules*, and *Explorations in Economics*. His research is primarily on economic education, environmental economics, law and economics, and labor economics. Anderson teaches courses in each of these fields and loves teaching introductory economics. His favorite hobby is running, and he competes in marathons and triathlons. He lives in Danville, Kentucky, with his wife and two children.

Ligaya Franklin

Paul Krugman, recipient of the 2008 Nobel Memorial Prize in Economic Sciences, recently moved from Princeton University, where he taught for 14 years, to the Graduate Center of the City University of New York. In his new position, he is associated with the Luxembourg Income Study, which tracks and analyzes income inequality around the world. He received his BA from Yale and his PhD from MIT. Before Princeton, he taught at Yale, Stanford, and MIT. He also spent a year on the staff of the Council of Economic Advisers (1982–1983). His research has included pathbreaking work on international trade, economic geography, and currency crises. In 1991, Krugman received the American Economic Association's John Bates Clark medal. In addition to his teaching and academic research, Krugman writes extensively for nontechnical audiences. He is a regular op-ed columnist for the New York Times. His bestselling trade books include *The Return of Depression Economics and the Crisis of 2008*, a history of recent economic troubles and their implications for economic policy, and *The Conscience of a Liberal*, a study of the political economy of economic inequality and its relationship with political polarization from the Gilded Age to the present. His earlier books, *Peddling Prosperity* and *The Age of Diminished Expectations*, have become modern classics.

Robin Wells was a Lecturer and Researcher in Economics at Princeton University. She received her BA from the University of Chicago and her PhD from the University of California at Berkeley; she then did postdoctoral work at MIT. She has taught at the University of Michigan, the University of Southampton (United Kingdom), Stanford, and MIT.

Key Contributors and Advisors

Brian Held

Section Review Questions

Brian Held teaches AP® Economics at Loyola High School in Los Angeles, his alma mater. He holds an MA in Economics from California State University of Los Angeles. He has served as an AP® Macroeconomics reader for the past 10 years, including six as a Table Leader. In 2010, the California Council on Economic Education, CCEE, recognized Held with its Teacher of the Year Award. His students won CCEE's Capital Markets Contest in 2007.

Laura Adams

Financial Literacy Handbook

Laura Adams is an award-winning personal finance author. She earned a BS from the University of the South and an MBA from the University of Florida. She received the Excellence in Financial Literacy Education (EIFLE) Award from the Institute for Financial Literacy for her book *Money Girl's Smart Moves to Grow Rich*. Adams is the author of several e-Books and audiobooks and hosts the "Money Girl" podcast, a top-10 Internet show on iTunes that has been downloaded more than 45 million times.

Melanie Fox

Strive For a 5: Preparing for the AP® Macroeconomics Examination

Strive For a 5: Preparing for the AP® Microeconomics Examination

Melanie Fox currently teaches economics at the University of Louisville after serving as Chair of the Department of Economics and Business Administration at Austin College. She earned her BA and PhD from the University of Houston. Fox has been an AP® Macroeconomics Reader and Table Leader since 2007.

Margaret Pride

Teacher's Edition, Teacher's Resource Materials

Peggy Pride holds BA degrees in History and Economics and an MA in Business Education from Southern Illinois University. She taught AP® Economics for 35 years at St. Louis University High School. Her involvement with AP® Economics was long and varied, having served as Table Leader and Question Leader for Micro for 12 years and on the Test Development Committee for AP® Economics from 1999 to 2004. In addition, Pride was the primary author of the College Board publication *Advanced Placement Economics Teacher's Guide*. She received the GATE Teacher of the Year Award in 2005.

Richard Rankin

Section Review Questions

Dick Rankin teaches at Iolani School in Honolulu, Hawaii. He holds a BA in Economics from Virginia Military Institute and an MA in Economics from the University of Texas at Austin. Rankin is a former member and College Board Advisor to the AP® Economics Development Committee. He has been a Reader, Table Leader, and Question Leader for the AP® Economics Exams for the past 17 years, has taught AP® Economics for 20 years, and was Course Director for the Principles of Economics Course at the US Military Academy at West Point. Rankin is the 2014 Stephen L. Jackstadt Economics Award Winner.

Eric Dodge

ExamView® Assessment Suite Questions

Eric Dodge is Professor of Economics and Business Administration at Hanover College in Indiana. He received his BA from the University of Puget Sound and his MA and PhD from the University of Oregon. Dodge has been involved with AP® Economics for more than 10 years and has served as Reader, Table Leader, and Question Leader.

Dianna Miller

Teacher's Edition, Teacher's Resource Materials

Dianna Miller earned her BA in Social Studies Education and an MA in History from the University of North Florida. She currently teaches AP® Economics for Florida Virtual School, an online public school in Florida. She was a finalist for the National Online Teacher of the Year Award in 2010 and was the 2011 Florida Council for the Social Studies Trimble Award Winner. Miller has been active in AP® Economics since 2005 as a Reader and Table Leader.

Leslie Paige Wolfson

Teacher's Edition, Teacher's Resource Materials

Leslie Paige Wolfson holds a Certificate in Character Education and a Masters in Economics and Finance. She taught AP® Economics for 18 years at The Pingry School in New Jersey, and was the coordinator and instructor for its Financial Literacy program. Wolfson was awarded the Research Fellowship Award and the Woodruff English Faculty Honor Award.

Accuracy Reviewers

Darcy Brodison, Coronado High School, TX
Patricia Brazill, Irondequoit High School, NY
Dixie Dalton, Southside Virginia Community College, VA
David Frank, Bartram Trail High School, FL
Brian Heggood, Stanton College Prep, FL
Holly Jones, The Pennington School, NJ
Rachael Sharpe, Florida Virtual School, FL
James Watson, Independent Contractor, FL

Brief Contents

*Glosario available on Book Companion Site at bcs.worthpublishers.com/KrugmanAP2e

Contents

*Glosario available on Book Companion Site at bcs.worthpublishers.com/KrugmanAP2e

To the Student

How to Get the Most from This Program

The AP® Economics course represents a wonderful opportunity for high school students to be challenged by the rigor of a college-level course, while learning life-relevant concepts from the discipline of economics. We understand the unique challenges of teaching and learning AP® Economics and have designed this book and its support program to be the most effective possible resources to help you succeed in AP® Economics.

Intent on promoting the efficiency and effectiveness of AP® Economics courses, we started with the best available college-level introduction to economics—Krugman and Wells' *Economics*, second and third editions. We knew these would be the best foundation for an AP® adaptation. Our goal was to retain the features of *Economics* that make it a winner, while crafting it to closely follow the AP® syllabus and speak to a high school audience. *Krugman's Economics for AP®*, second edition, is designed to be easy to read and easy to use. Our hope is that you will find our explanations clear and concise, and that you will enjoy reading the book.

What's New in this Edition?

This book is your ultimate tool for success in the AP® Economics courses. With this in mind, the second edition features improvements to the organization and presentation of content, as well as to our system of supporting student learning and preparation for the AP® Exam. For a visual walk-through of the features of the book, please see page xxiv.

More AP®-focused elements and study aids

- **AP® exam tips**, found in the margin throughout the text, provide invaluable advice on where you should focus, how to avoid pitfalls, and how to be successful in the course and on the exam. These "on-the-spot" reminders help you avoid common mistakes.
- More **AP® exam practice** is provided through an increased number of multiple-choice and free-response questions (FRQs) at the end of each module and section. These assessments not only test you on the material you learned in the module, but also mimic AP® questions to train you on what you will see on the exam. The open-ended, conceptual FRQs help familiarize you with the kind of synthesis skills you'll need to master the exam.
- **Full-length AP®-style practice examinations** are included at the end of the text to ensure you have nailed down the content and are ready to tackle the real test in May.

New video clips to help you study and review

Economics videos available on the Internet can be both entertaining and educational. For a complete list of these videos, look for econextras video links on the Book Companion Site at bcs.worthpublishers.com/KrugmanAP2e.

- **Module "Flip It" Concept Videos** are short, concise videos that explain a key concept covered in a module, such as the Production Possibilities Curve in Module 3 and Comparative Advantage in Module 4. Each video is short, focused, and funny. These Internet videos offer simple examples to underscore the concepts and give lots of practice in reading and interpreting graphs—skills that are important on the AP® Exam.
- **Section Review Videos** provide a great review of the key concepts in a section. These longer videos focus on explaining the big picture ideas, key graphs, and common mistakes/pitfalls for the section. Watching the Section Review Video is a smart way to make sure you understand the key ideas in the section.

What Continues?

Perhaps the most important feature is what has been left unchanged from the first edition. We adhere to the general approach of Krugman's balanced and proven *Economics* text:

> "To achieve deeper levels of understanding of the real world through economics, students must learn to appreciate the kinds of trade-offs and ambiguities that economists and policy makers face when applying their models to real-world problems. We believe this approach will make students more insightful and more effective participants in our common economic, social, and political lives."

Alignment with the College Board® Topic Outline

We have organized the book to match up with the College Board's Topic Outlines for AP® Macroeconomics and Microeconomics, so you can be sure you are receiving the best possible preparation for the AP® exam. Where the outline has recommended coverage within specific sections, you can be sure that you will find that coverage. You can find a guide correlating each module with its equivalent College Board course description topic on the front endpaper of this text.

A flexible modular approach

This book is arranged by sections that correspond to the AP® Topic Outline. Each section is divided into four to seven modules. Each module breaks the course material into a pedagogically appropriate unit that is designed to be covered in one class period. This organization takes you through the required AP® course material in a sequence and at a pace designed for optimal success.

Effective study aids

- **Learning Objectives** establish measurable goals for each module and help you direct your reading.
- **Module Reviews** allow you to practice what you've learned with AP®-style questions. These reviews help you determine your mastery of each module so you can decide if you're ready to move on or need more study.
- **Section Reviews** include detailed summaries of each module as well as page-referenced Key Terms and AP®-style multiple-choice and free-response questions.

Additional Resources to Optimize Productivity

- **Downloadable e-Book**
  This PDF-style e-Book matches the printed book page for page and is optimized for use on Windows or Apple computers, laptops, and tablets.
- **Strive for a 5: Preparing for the AP® Macroeconomics and Microeconomics Exams**
  The *Strive for a 5* guides are designed for use with *Krugman's Economics for AP®*, second edition. They are written to help you evaluate your understanding of the material covered in the textbook, reinforce the key concepts, develop conceptual understanding and graphing skills, and prepare you to succeed on the AP® Macroeconomics and Microeconomics Exams. The guides are divided into two sections: a study guide and a test preparation section. The study guides are written to be used throughout the course, while the prep section offers additional AP® test strategies and includes two full-length AP®-style practice exams—each with 60 multiple-choice questions and three free-response questions.

Turn the page for a tour of the text. Once you know how to use the book properly, you will be more likely to realize success in the course and on the AP® exam!

Each section and its modules are structured around a common set of features designed to help you learn the concept and practice for the AP® Exam. By putting all of the pieces together as you work through the text, you will complete the entire puzzle by the end of the course.

Use the features to help you study economics and prepare for the exam.

Each unit is designed with a different color so that you may easily determine which AP® exam topic you are studying. For example, Section 1 is blue and Section 2 is magenta.

Review the **Learning Objectives** for an overview of the critical concepts you will be tackling in the module. Focus on mastering these skills as you work through the module.

Read the **Opening Story**. Each section opens with a compelling story that often extends through the modules. The opening stories illustrate important concepts, to build intuition with realistic examples that are designed to pique your interest as you prepare to learn about the economic concepts in the modules.

Pay attention to the **AP® Exam Tip** boxes. They provide helpful advice on what to read closely and what common pitfalls to avoid so you can ace the AP® exam.

Watch for the blue **Key Term** boxes, which highlight the vocabulary you'll need to master to realize success on the AP® exam. The terms are repeated in the Section Review and in the Glossary at the end of the book, as well as the Glosario on the Book Companion Site.

Study the graphs and figures. To succeed, you must be able to interpret and draw graphs correctly.

Figure 7.1 Market Equilibrium

Market equilibrium occurs at point *E*, where the supply curve and the demand curve intersect. In equilibrium, the quantity demanded is equal to the quantity supplied. In this market, the equilibrium price is $1 per pound and the equilibrium quantity is 10 billion pounds per year.

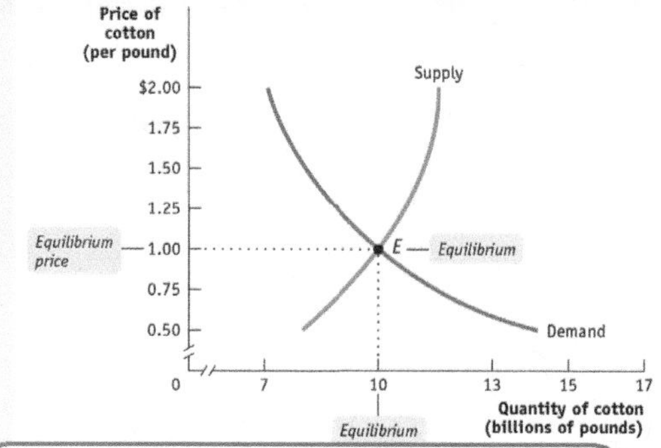

Figure 10.1 The Circular-Flow Diagram

This diagram represents the flows of money, factors of production, and goods and services in the economy. In the markets for goods and services, households purchase goods and services from firms, generating a flow of money to the firms and a flow of goods and services to the households. The money flows back to households as firms purchase factors of production from the households in factor markets.

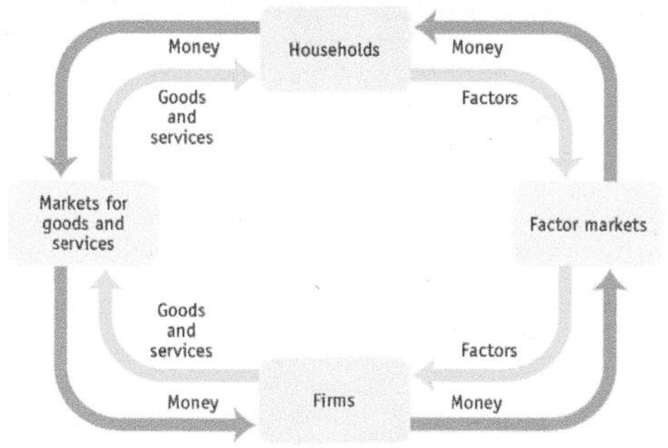

Figures and **graphs** hold volumes of information. Study them carefully and read the captions. Mastering the creation and interpretation of economic models is important to realizing success on the AP® exam. Color is used consistently to distinguish between demand (blue) and supply (red) curves.

econextras

Video List

to accompany

Krugman's Economics for AP® Second Editio

Section	Module	Name of Video	Link
Section 1			
	Module 1	Econ Overview	https://www.youtube.com/watch?v=Np-d2Sdzymk&feature=c4-overview-vl&list=PL15D
		Keynesian Theory in 6 Minutes	https://www.youtube.com/watch?v=KJ_gcvp10B4
	Module 2	The Business Cycle	https://www.youtube.com/watch?v=DmXvUJ0gAtw&feature=youtu.be
	Module 3	Scarcity, Opportunity Cost, and the PPC	https://www.youtube.com/watch?v=kmjgg8_tUJ8&feature=youtu.be
		The Law of Increasing Opportunity Cost and the PPC Model	https://www.youtube.com/watch?v=m1hY3-y0-dM&feature=youtu.be
		Production Possibilities Curve and Opportunity Cost	https://www.youtube.com/watch?feature=player_detailpage&v=SJO56vJoy3Y&list=PL
	Module 4	Milton Friedman - I, Pencil	https://www.youtube.com/watch?v=67tHtpac5ws&feature=youtu.be
		Comparative Advantage	https://www.youtube.com/watch?v=FpTBjR8iKss&list=PLD5BC72708462542S&index=3

Watch the **econextras** module video clips that provide "just in time" instruction on key concepts in each module. You can watch the videos as many times as needed to make sure that you understand the material. See the econextras list with hyperlinks to recommended videos on the book companion website, bcs.worthpublishers.com/krugmanap2e.

FYI The Price of Admission

The market equilibrium, so the theory goes, is pretty egalitarian because the equilibrium price applies to everyone. That is, all buyers pay the same price—the equilibrium price—and all ... rice. But is ... ckets is ... ontradict ... e at the ... her price ... he same ... e people ... sell them. ... ay. For ex- ... fice price ... n Miami, ... price ... n: $88.50

Puzzling as this may seem, there is no contradiction once we take opportunity costs and tastes into account. For major events, buying tickets from the box office means waiting in very long lines. Ticket buyers who use Internet resellers have decided that the opportunity cost of their time is too high to spend waiting in line. And tickets for major events being sold at face value by online box offices often sell out within minutes. In this case, some people who want to go to the concert badly but have missed out on the opportunity to buy cheaper tickets from the online box office are willing to pay the higher Internet reseller price.

Not only that—perusing the StubHub.com website, you can see that markets really do move to equilibrium. You'll notice that the prices quoted by different sellers for seats close to one another are also very close: $184.99 versus $185 for seats on the main floor of the Drake concert. As the competitive market model predicts, units of the same good end up selling for the same price. And prices move in response to demand and supply. According to an article in the *New York Times*, tickets on StubHub.com can sell for less than the face value for events with little appeal, but prices can skyrocket for events that are in high demand. (The article quotes a price of $3,530 for a Madonna concert.) Even StubHub.com's chief executive says his site is "the embodiment of supply-and-demand economics."

So the theory of competitive markets isn't just speculation. If you want to experience it for yourself, try buying tickets to a concert.

The competitive market model determines the price you pay for concert tickets.

Need a break? Read the **FYI boxes** for short but compelling applications of the major economic concepts just covered in the module. You can connect the content you're reading with these real-life examples to deepen your understanding of the concepts. Exercise your synthesis skills with these boxes!

Practice makes perfect!

Practice what you've learned at the end of each module with **Multiple-Choice Questions** and skill-building practice **Free-Response Questions**.

MODULE 4 Review

Check Your Understanding

1. In Italy, an automobile can be produced by 8 workers in one day and a washing machine by 3 workers in one day. In the United States, an automobile can be produced by 6 workers in one day, and a washing machine by 2 workers in one day.
   a. Which country has an absolute advantage in the production of automobiles? In washing machines?
   b. Which country has a comparative advantage in the production of washing machines? In automobiles?
   c. What type of specialization results in the greatest gains from trade between the two countries?
2. Refer to the story of Tom and Hank illustrated by Figure 4.1 in the text. Explain why Tom and Hank are willing to engage in a trade of 1 fish for 1½ coconuts.

Tackle the Test: Multiple-Choice Questions

Refer to the graph below to answer the following questions.

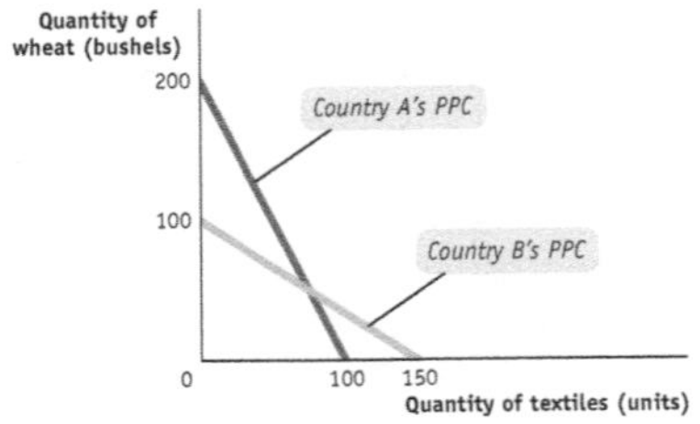

1. Use the graph to determine which country has an absolute advantage in producing each good.

	Absolute advantage in wheat production	*Absolute advantage in textile production*
a.	Country A	Country B
b.	Country A	Country A
c.	Country B	Country A
d.	Country B	Country B
e.	Country A	Neither country

30 Section 1 Basic Economic Concepts

Check Your Understanding questions at the end of each module allow you to immediately test your understanding of the content. If you're having a hard time with these questions, you'll know to go back and re-read the module.

Tackle the Test: Free-Response Questions

1. Refer to the graph below to answer the following questions.

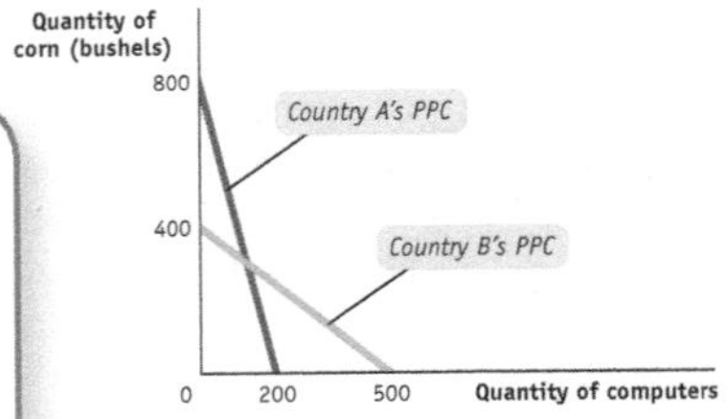

   a. What is the opportunity cost of a bushel of corn in each country?
   b. Which country has an absolute advantage in computer production? Explain.
   c. Which country has a comparative advantage in corn production? Explain.
   d. If each country specializes, what good will Country B import? Explain.
   e. What is the minimum price Country A will accept to export corn to Country B? Explain.

Rubric for FRQ 1 (9 points)

1 point: Country A, ¼ computer; Country B, 1¼ computers
1 point: Country B
1 point: Because Country B can produce more computers than Country A (500 versus 200)
1 point: Country A
1 point: Because Country A can produce corn at a lower opportunity cost (¼ versus 1¼ computers)
1 point: Corn
1 point: Country B has a comparative advantage in the production of computers, so it will produce computers and import corn (Country A has a comparative advantage in corn production, so it will specialize in corn and import computers from Country B).
1 point: ¼ computer
1 point: Country A's opportunity cost of producing corn is ¼ computer, so that is the lowest price it will accept to sell corn to Country B.

2. Refer to the table below to answer the following questions. These two countries are producing textiles and wheat using equal amounts of resources.

	Weekly output per worker	
	Country A	**Country B**
Bushels of wheat	15	10
Units of textiles	60	60

   a. What is the opportunity cost of producing a bushel of wheat for each country?
   b. Which country has the absolute advantage in wheat production?
   c. Which country has the comparative advantage in textile production? Explain.
   (5 points)

Tackle the Test presents five AP®-style multiple-choice questions to help you become comfortable with the types of questions you'll see in the multiple-choice section of the AP® exam.

In addition, two **AP®-style free-response questions** are provided. A sample grading rubric is given for the first FRQ to show you how questions are graded and to help you learn how to write thoughtful answers. The second problem asks you try a "mini FRQ" for yourself. These short, focused FRQ-style questions are one small piece of the puzzle.

Watch the review video and work through cumulative questions at the end of each section.

Start your review of each section by watching the special Section Review Video, indicated by the green play button. These reviews present the key ideas in the section using lots of visuals, down-to-earth language, and a little humor.

Read the **Section Review** and study the **Key Terms** at the end of each section.

SECTION 1 Review

Section 1 Review Video

Module 1

1. Everyone has to make choices about what to do and what *not* to do. **Individual choice** is the basis of **economics**—if it doesn't involve choice, it isn't economics. The **economy** is a system that coordinates choices about production and consumption. In a **market economy**, these choices are made by many firms and individuals. In a **command economy**, these choices are made by a central authority. **Incentives** are rewards or punishments that motivate particular choices, and can be lacking in a command economy where producers cannot set their own prices or keep their own profits. **Property rights** create incentives in market economies by establishing ownership and granting individuals the right to trade goods and services for mutual gain. In any economy, decisions are informed by **marginal analysis**—the study of the costs and benefits of doing something a little bit more or a little bit less.
2. The reason choices must be made is that **resources**—anything that can be used to produce something else—are **scarce**. The four categories of resources are **land**, **labor**, **capital**, and **entrepreneurship**. Individuals are
3. Because you must choose among limited alternatives, the true cost of anything is what you must give up to get it—all costs are **opportunity costs**.
4. Economists use economic models for both **positive economics**, which describes how the economy works, and for **normative economics**, which prescribes how the economy *should* work. Positive economics often involves making forecasts. Economics can determine correct answers for positive questions, but typically not for normative questions, which involve value judgments. Exceptions occur when policies designed to achieve a certain prescription can be clearly ranked in terms of preference.
5. There are two main reasons economists disagree. One, they may disagree about which simplifications to make in a model. Two, economists may disagree—like everyone else—about values.
6. **Microeconomics** is the branch of economics that studies how people make decisions and how those decisions interact. **Macroeconomics** is concerned with the overall ups and downs of the economy, and focuses on **economic aggregates** such as the unemployment ...domestic product, that summarize data ...fferent markets.

Key Terms

Economics, p. 2	Economic aggregates, p. 5	Model, p. 14
Individual choice, p. 2	Positive economics, p. 6	Other things equal (*ceteris paribus*) assumption, p. 14
Economy, p. 2	Normative economics, p. 6	Trade-off, p. 16
Market economy, p. 2	Business cycle, p. 11	Production possibilities curve, p. 17
Command economy, p. 2	Depression, p. 11	Efficient, p. 18
Incentives, p. 3	Recessions, p. 11	Productive efficiency, p. 18
Property rights, p. 3	Expansions, p. 11	Allocative efficiency, p. 18
Marginal analysis, p. 3	Employment, p. 11	Technology, p. 21
Resource, p. 3	Unemployment, p. 11	Trade, p. 24
Land, p. 3	Labor force, p. 12	Gains from trade, p. 24
Labor, p. 3	Unemployment rate, p. 12	Specialization, p. 24
Capital, p. 3	Output, p. 12	Comparative advantage, p. 27
Entrepreneurship, p. 3	Aggregate output, p. 12	Absolute advantage, p. 27
Scarce, p. 3	Inflation, p. 13	Terms of trade, p. 28
Opportunity cost, p. 4	Deflation, p. 13	
Microeconomics, p. 5	Price stability, p. 13	
Macroeconomics, p. 5	Economic growth, p. 13	

AP® Exam Practice Questions

Multiple-Choice Questions

1. In a market economy, most choices about production and consumption are made by which of the following?
   a. politicians
   b. many individuals and firms
   c. the government
   d. managers
   e. economists
2. Which of the following pairs indicates a category of resources and an example of that resource?

	Category	*Example*
a.	money	investment
b.	capital	money
c.	capital	minerals
d.	land	factory
e.	land	timber

3. You can either go to a movie or study for an exam. Which of the following is an opportunity cost of studying for the exam?
   a. a higher grade on the exam
   b. the price of a movie ticket
   c. the cost of paper, pens, books, and other study materials
   d. the enjoyment from seeing the movie
   e. the sense of achievement from learning

Free-Response Question

The Hatfield family lives on the east side of the Hatatoochie River and the McCoy family lives on the west side. Each family's diet consists of fried chicken and corn on the cob, and each is self-sufficient, raising its own chickens and growing its own corn.

Assume the Hatfield family has a comparative advantage in the production of corn.

1. Draw a correctly labeled graph showing a hypothetical production possibilities curve for the McCoy family.
2. Which family has the comparative advantage in the production of chickens? Explain.
3. Assuming that each family is producing efficiently, how can the two families increase their consumption of both chicken and corn?
(5 points)

Test yourself at the end of each section by tackling the **AP® Exam Practice Questions**. Here's your chance to prove that you've mastered the Economics content *and* the types of questions you'll see on the AP® exam!

The final pieces of the puzzle...Putting It All Together and the comprehensive AP® Practice Test

MODULE
45
Putting It All Together

In this Module, you will learn to:

- Use macroeconomic models to conduct policy analysis
- Improve your approach to free-response macroeconomics questions

Having completed our study of the basic macroeconomic models, v analyze scenarios and evaluate policy recommendations. In this n a step-by-step approach to macroeconomic analysis. You can adap problems involving any macroeconomic model, including models of and supply, production possibilities, money markets, and the Phillip of this module you will be able to combine mastery of the principles ics with problem solving skills to analyze a new scenario on your ow

A Structure for Macroeconomic A

Putting It All Together The final module in macroeconomics, 45, teaches you how to use what you have learned to answer comprehensive, "real-world" questions about the macroeconomy, like the type you will see in the long section FRQ on the AP® Exam.

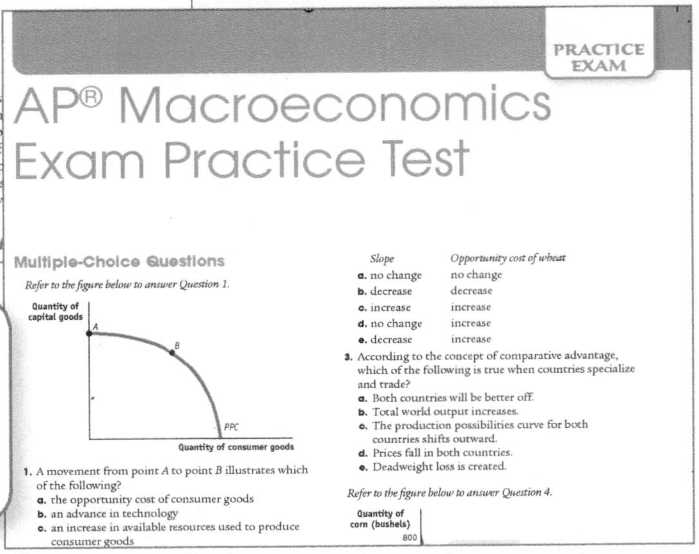

PRACTICE EXAM

AP® Macroeconomics Exam Practice Test

Multiple-Choice Questions

Refer to the figure below to answer Question 1.

1. A movement from point *A* to point *B* illustrates which of the following?
   a. the opportunity cost of consumer goods
   b. an advance in technology
   c. an increase in available resources used to produce consumer goods

	Slope	*Opportunity cost of wheat*
a.	no change	no change
b.	decrease	decrease
c.	increase	increase
d.	no change	increase
e.	decrease	increase

3. According to the concept of comparative advantage, which of the following is true when countries specialize and trade?
   a. Both countries will be better off.
   b. Total world output increases.
   c. The production possibilities curve for both countries shifts outward.
   d. Prices fall in both countries.
   e. Deadweight loss is created.

Refer to the figure below to answer Question 4.

Quantity of corn (bushels)
800

Test your knowledge and readiness for the AP® exam by taking the end-of-book **AP®-Style Practice Exams**, which include 60 multiple-choice questions and three FRQs per exam, just like the official tests. Time yourself to simulate the actual exams.

Interesting reading for after the Exam

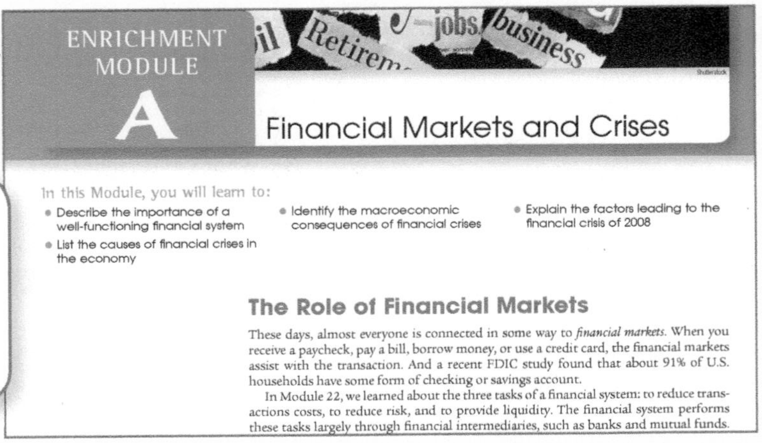

ENRICHMENT MODULE
A
Financial Markets and Crises

In this Module, you will learn to:

- Describe the importance of a well-functioning financial system
- List the causes of financial crises in the economy
- Identify the macroeconomic consequences of financial crises
- Explain the factors leading to the financial crisis of 2008

The Role of Financial Markets

These days, almost everyone is connected in some way to *financial markets.* When you receive a paycheck, pay a bill, borrow money, or use a credit card, the financial markets assist with the transaction. And a recent FDIC study found that about 91% of U.S. households have some form of checking or savings account.

In Module 22, we learned about the three tasks of a financial system: to reduce transactions costs, to reduce risk, and to provide liquidity. The financial system performs these tasks largely through financial intermediaries, such as banks and mutual funds.

Learning about Economics doesn't stop after you take the exam in May. Continue your study of Economics with **Enrichment Modules** and the **Financial Literacy Handbook** to help round out the course and to prepare you for further Economics study in college and beyond.

For additional help...

Use the **Strive for a 5 Guide** companions to this text. Each Guide was written to work hand-in-glove with the text and includes a study guide followed by tips and advice on taking the exam and two more full AP® practice exams per guide.

Study when and where you want...

Take the e-Book with you anywhere! Download the text to your home computer or tablet so you can stay up to date on reading assignments.

SECTION 1

Basic Economic Concepts

PD Section 1 Overview:

Watch the video overview of Section 1 (for teachers), which is accessible through the Teacher's e-Book, the TR-flash drive, or the book's website, bcs.worthpublishers.com/krugmanap2e *(teacher log-in required).*

Welcome to the study of AP® Economics! This first unit of the course will open the doors to the new vocabulary and way of economic thinking that are central to AP® Economics. Section 1 kicks off both macroeconomics and microeconomics courses.

Topics that your students will study in Section 1 are:

- scarcity and choice, the foundation of the economic problems that we will solve in this course.
- the production possibilities curve, which is used to model the concept of opportunity cost.
- the concepts of comparative advantage and terms of trade that will define the basis of trade.
- how countries choose an economic system to determine the answers to the basic economic questions.
- the mixed market economic system with incentives and property rights as two major elements of the mixed market model.
- marginal thinking as a central idea of microeconomics.
- introductory topics to macroeconomic ideas.

Alignment to AP® Economics Course Description

Macroeconomics I. Basic Economic Concepts: 8–12%

AP® Outline	Module
A. Scarcity, choice, and opportunity costs	1: The Study of Economics
B. Production possibilities curve	3: The Production Possibilities Curve Model
C. Comparative advantage, specialization, and exchange	4: Comparative Advantage and Trade
D. Demand, supply, and market equilibrium	**(Section 2)**
E. Macroeconomic issues: business cycle, unemployment, inflation, growth	1: The Study of Economics 2: Introduction to Macroeconomics

Microeconomics I. Basic Economic Concepts: 8–14%

AP® Outline	Module
A. Scarcity, choice, and opportunity cost	1: The Study of Economics
B. Production possibilities curve	3: The Production Possibilities Curve Model
C. Comparative advantage, absolute advantage, specialization, and trade	4: Comparative Advantage and Trade
D. Economic systems	1: The Study of Economics
E. Property rights and the role of incentives	1: The Study of Economics
F. Marginal analysis	1: The Study of Economics

Pacing Guide

Module	Standard Teaching Days	Block Teaching Days
1	1	½
2	1	½
3	1	½
4	2	1
Section 1 Exam	1	½
Total	**6**	**3**

Introductory Note on Assessments

To help your students perform well on the AP® Economics exams, it is important that they learn to recognize the language used in the free-response questions (FRQs) and to understand how the grading rubric works. Gaining familiarity with the style and form of the FRQs will help them to answer the questions correctly and thoroughly, thereby raising their AP® Economics exam scores. Throughout this book, you will find practice FRQs with AP®-specific language that students should master. The following list provides both insights into the most frequent language used and tips to share with your students on how to answer each type of question:

(1) **Show:** Literally draw a visual, generally a graph. Label graphs properly and thoroughly to receive full credit. Keep graphs neat and clear. Label each line and each equilibrium point as shown in the example below.

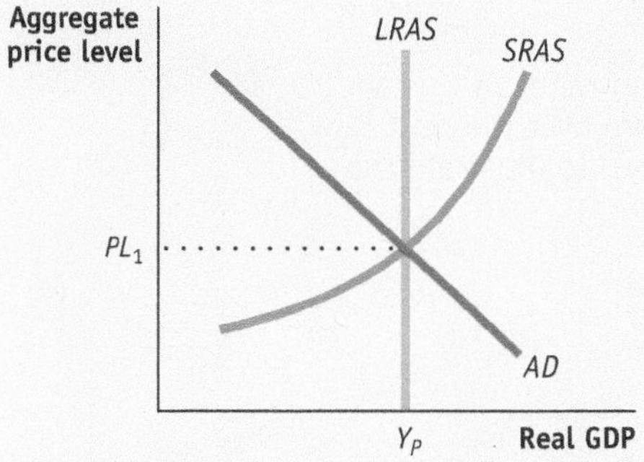

(2) **Explain:** Clearly articulate each step in your thinking process. Link economic concepts and explain your reasoning. Lists and graphs are acceptable as part of your explanation. Long essays are not suggested in economics FRQs.

(3) **Identify:** Merely state an answer. No details are necessary. Writing complete sentences in response to an "Identify" question will not result in a higher score.

(4) **Calculate:** Use math that concludes with a numeric answer to the question. Be sure to show your work as the calculations are considered as part of your answer. Calculators are not allowed on the exam, so the math will be simple. If your answer is complex, you probably did the math wrong.

To help your students succeed, you should graph early and often throughout the course. The more students practice graphing, the more comfortable and successful they will be when taking the AP® exam. Have them graph answers both to multiple-choice questions, when appropriate, and also to free-response questions. Drawing a graph is frequently the most efficient way to determine which distractor is the correct choice in an MC question.

When going over problems in class, practice "Identify" and "Explain" questions orally with students. Using the language of the AP® exam with your students will make it easier for them to recognize how to answer the questions on the exam. For example, when studying inflation, draw a graph showing inflation on the board, and ask students to *identify* the problem shown in the graph or *identify* one fiscal policy tool that might be used to correct the problem in the economy. Then follow up with an "Explain" step. That is, students should *explain* how aggregate demand will be impacted by the fiscal policy action you just identified. Ensure that students answer the "Identify" part of the question in one or two words; the "Explain" question, on the other hand, should include all the links in the process to shift aggregate demand.

Finally, require students to show their work when doing all calculations in the course. Do not accept answers without the calculations, so they realize they must do the same thing on the AP® exam.

TRM Section Resources

All section resources may be accessed through the Teacher's e-Book, the TR-flash drive, or the book's website bcs.worthpublishers.com/krugmanap2e *(teacher log-in required).*

Section 1 PD Video (for teachers)

Module 1

Module 1 Sample Lecture

Activity 1.1: Build a Zoo!

Worksheet 1.2: Economic Concepts

Worksheet 1.3: Questions for "Keynesian Theory" Video

Exit Slip: Module 1

Module 2

Module 2 Sample Lecture

Worksheet 2.1: Questions for "The Business Cycle" Video

Worksheet 2.2: The Business Cycle

Exit Slip: Module 2

Module 3

Module 3 Sample Lecture

Activity 3.1: Widgets and Whatsits

Worksheet 3.2: Questions for "Scarcity, Opportunity Cost, and the *PPC*" Video

Worksheet 3.3: Shifting the *PPC*

Worksheet 3.4: Production Possibilities Curves

Exit Slip: Module 3

Module 4

Module 4 Sample Lecture

Activity 4.1: Haves and Have-Nots

Activity 4.2: Two States

Worksheet 4.3: Comparative Advantage: Input & Output

Worksheet 4.4: Comparative Advantage

Exit Slip: Module 4

Section 1 Review Video (for students)

St. Louis Federal Reserve Bank Resources

Many of the Federal Reserve Banks have educational departments that offer helpful resources for studying economics. Members of the Educators Advisory Board of the St. Louis Federal Reserve Bank have handpicked some of their best resources for use with your AP® Economics students. References to these resources are included in the margin notes. A complete list of the St. Louis Fed resources for each section with the corresponding URL (as of fall 2014) can be found in the TRM.

NOTE We have included a number of links to useful videos and articles in the margin notes in this section. Although all are active at the time of publication, we know that some may expire over the next few years. If a link is no longer active, you may wish to search for a similar article or video to illustrate the point. We may also periodically refresh resources on the book's companion website.

SECTION 1

Basic Economic Concepts

istockphoto.com (Young man looking up, Movie tickets, Orange Converse sneakers); Thinkstock (iPod Touch); Shutterstock (Rayban sunglasses)

Common Ground

The annual meeting of the American Economic Association draws thousands of economists, young and old, famous and obscure. There are booksellers, business meetings, and quite a few job interviews. But mainly the economists gather to talk and listen. During the busiest times, 60 or more presentations may be taking place simultaneously, on questions that range from the future of the stock market to who does the cooking in two-earner families.

What do these people have in common? An expert on the stock market probably knows very little about the economics of housework, and vice versa. Yet an economist who wanders into the wrong seminar and ends up listening to presentations on some unfamiliar topic is nonetheless likely to hear much that is familiar. The reason is that all economic analysis is based on a set of common principles that apply to many different issues.

Some of these principles involve *individual choice*—for economics is, first of all, about the choices that individuals make. Do you choose to work during the summer or take a backpacking trip? Do you download a new album or go to a movie? These decisions involve *making a choice* from among a limited number of alternatives—limited because no one can have everything that he or she wants. Every question in economics at its most basic level involves individuals making choices.

But to understand how an economy works, you need to understand more than how individuals make choices. None of us lives like Robinson Crusoe, alone on an island—we must make decisions in an environment that is shaped by the decisions of others. Indeed, in our global economy even the simplest decisions you make—say, what to have for breakfast—are shaped by the decisions of thousands of other people, from the banana grower in Costa Rica who decided to grow the fruit you eat to the farmer in Iowa who provided the corn in your cornflakes. And because each one of us depends on so many others—and they, in turn, depend on us—our choices interact. So, although all economics at a basic level is about individual choice, in order to understand behavior within an economy we must also understand economic *interaction*—how my choices affect your choices, and vice versa.

Many important economic interactions can be understood by looking at the markets for individual goods—for example, the market for corn. But we must also understand economy-wide interactions in order to understand how they can lead to the ups and downs we see in the economy as a whole.

In this section we discuss the study of economics and the difference between microeconomics and macroeconomics. We also introduce the major topics within macroeconomics and the use of models to study the macroeconomy. Finally, we present the production possibilities curve model and use it to understand basic economic activity, including trade between two economies. Because the study of economics relies on graphical models, an appendix on the use of graphs follows the end of this section.

PD Section 1 Overview

Watch the video overview of Section 1 (for teachers), which is accessible through the Teacher's e-Book, the TR-flash drive, or the book's companion website bcs.worthpublishers.com/krugmanap2e (teacher log-in required).

TEACH Teach It

As part of their supplies for this course, ask students to buy a personal whiteboard and dry eraser markers. They are inexpensive and will enable students to practice content while allowing you to provide immediate feedback to those who are struggling. You can also go to a hardware store and buy a piece of shower board. Have the shower board cut to the size you would like the whiteboards to be. We recommend 16″ × 16″.

FOCUS Active Learning

Students can read Chapter 1 of *Economics by Example* to discover many real-world applications of the economic way of thinking.

TEACH Teach It

Graph early and often! Have students use the whiteboards to practice; have them work in pairs to correct each other's work. Another idea is to assign students to draw graphs in poster format to display inside or outside your classroom so they will see them every time they pass by. Getting your students to practice and understand graphing will enable them to better understand key concepts and perform well on the AP® exam.

PD To prepare for teaching this lesson, you may want to consult the **Module 1 Sample Lecture** in the TRM.

OPEN & CLOSE Start Here

TRM Complete **Activity 1.1 (Build a Zoo!)** from the TRM as a group activity to help students understand scarcity and choice.

TEACH Teach It

Make sure students recognize the types of economies noted in the text but don't spend a great deal of time on the subject. Help them to understand that it is unlikely there will be a pure market economy operating in today's world because some type of government control is always present.

FOCUS Active Learning

Show "EconMovies—Episode 1: *Star Wars*" (see econextras video list with hyperlinks on the bcs and TRFD). Ask students to identify five basic economic concepts presented in the short clip.

- *People make decisions based on their own self-interests.*
- *People make decisions based on costs and benefits.*
- *There is voluntary exchange between buyers and sellers.*
- *Free markets are more efficient than command economies.*
- *The invisible hand works to regulate markets.*

What did Obi-Wan Kenobi say about economics at the end of the video clip? "It surrounds us, penetrates us, and binds us together."

© 13/Tony Hopewell/Ocean/Corbis

MODULE 1 The Study of Economics

In this Module, you will learn to:

- Explain how scarcity and choice are central to the study of economics
- Discuss the importance of opportunity cost in individual choice and decision making
- Explain the difference between positive economics and normative economics
- Identify areas of agreement and disagreement among economists
- Distinguish between microeconomic concepts and macroeconomic concepts

Economics is the study of scarcity and choice.

Individual choice is decisions by individuals about what to do, which necessarily involve decisions about what not to do.

An **economy** is a system for coordinating a society's productive and consumptive activities.

In a **market economy**, the decisions of individual producers and consumers largely determine what, how, and for whom to produce, with little government involvement in the decisions.

In a **command economy**, industry is publicly owned and a central authority makes production and consumption decisions.

Individual Choice: The Core of Economics

Economics is the study of scarcity and choice. Every economic issue involves, at its most basic level, **individual choice**—decisions by individuals about what to do and what *not* to do. In fact, you might say that it isn't economics if it isn't about choice.

Step into a big store such as Walmart or Target. There are thousands of different products available, and it is extremely unlikely that you—or anyone else—could afford to buy everything you might want to have. Besides, there's only so much space in your room. Given the limitations on your budget and your living space, you must choose which products to buy and which to leave on the shelf.

The fact that those products are on the shelf in the first place involves choice—the store manager chose to put them there, and the manufacturers of the products chose to produce them. The **economy** is a system that coordinates choices about production with choices about consumption, and distributes goods and services to the people who want them. The United States has a **market economy**, in which production and consumption are the result of decentralized decisions by many firms and individuals. There is no central authority telling people what to produce or where to ship it. Each individual producer makes what he or she thinks will be most profitable, and each consumer buys what he or she chooses.

An alternative to a market economy is a **command economy**, in which industry is publicly owned and there *is* a central authority making production and consumption decisions. Command economies have been tried, most notably in the Soviet Union between 1917 and 1991, but they didn't work very well. Producers in the Soviet Union

TEACH Teach It

Students may feel they are already familiar with many of the key terms in the course, but explain to them that an economist may have different or extended meanings for words they believe they already know. They should therefore study each key term carefully, using the flash cards provided for free on the Book Companion Site.

St. Louis Federal Reserve Bank Resources

"Factors of Production,"
The Economic Lowdown Podcast Series,
Episode 2

This episode presents the building blocks of the economy, the factors of production.

routinely found themselves unable to produce because they did not have crucial raw materials, or they succeeded in producing but then found that nobody wanted what the central authority had them produce. Consumers were often unable to find necessary items—command economies are famous for long lines at shops.

At the root of the problem with command economies is a lack of **incentives**, which are rewards or punishments that motivate particular choices. In market economies, producers are free to charge higher prices when there is a shortage of something, and to keep the resulting profits. High prices and profits provide incentives for producers to make more of the most-needed goods and services and to eliminate shortages.

In fact, economists tend to be skeptical of any attempt to change people's behavior that doesn't change their incentives. For example, a plan that calls on manufacturers to reduce pollution voluntarily probably won't be effective; a plan that gives them a financial incentive to do so is more likely to succeed.

Property rights, which establish ownership and grant individuals the right to trade goods and services with each other, create many of the incentives in market economies. With the right to own property comes the incentive to produce things of value, either to keep, or to trade for mutual gain. And ownership creates an incentive to put resources to their best possible use. Property rights to a lake, for example, give the owners an incentive not to pollute that lake if its use for recreation, serenity, or sale has greater value.

In any economy, the decisions of what to do with the next ton of pollution, the next hour of free time, and the next dollar of spending money are *marginal decisions.* They involve trade-offs at the margin: comparing the costs and benefits of doing a little bit more of an activity versus a little bit less. The gain from doing something one more time is called the *marginal benefit.* The cost of doing something one more time is the *marginal cost.* If the marginal benefit of making another car, reading another page, or buying another latte exceeds the marginal cost, the activity should continue. Otherwise, it should not. The study of such decisions, known as **marginal analysis**, plays a central role in economics because the formula of doing things until the marginal benefit no longer exceeds the marginal cost is the key to deciding "how much" to do of any activity.

All economic activities involve individual choice. Let's take a closer look at what this means for the study of economics.

Resources Are Scarce

You can't always get what you want. Almost everyone would like to have a beautiful house in a great location (and help with the housecleaning), two or three luxury cars, and frequent vacations in fancy hotels. But even in a rich country like the United States, not many families can afford all of that. So they must make choices—whether to go to Disney World this year or buy a better car, whether to make do with a small backyard or accept a longer commute in order to live where land is cheaper.

Limited income isn't the only thing that keeps people from having everything they want. Time is also in limited supply: there are only 24 hours in a day. And because the time we have is limited, choosing to spend time on one activity also means choosing not to spend time on a different activity—spending time studying for an exam means forgoing a night at the movies. Indeed, many people feel so limited by the number of hours in the day that they are willing to trade money for time. For example, convenience stores usually charge higher prices than larger supermarkets. But they fulfill a valuable role by catering to customers who would rather pay more than spend the time traveling farther to a supermarket where they might also have to wait in longer lines.

Why do individuals have to make choices? The ultimate reason is that *resources are scarce.* A **resource** is anything that can be used to produce something else. The economy's resources, sometimes called *factors of production,* can be classified into four categories: **land** (including timber, water, minerals, and all other resources that come from nature), **labor** (the effort of workers), **capital** (machinery, buildings, tools, and all other manufactured goods used to make other goods and services), and **entrepreneurship** (risk taking, innovation, and the organization of resources for production). A resource is **scarce**

Incentives are rewards or punishments that motivate particular choices.

Property rights establish ownership and grant individuals the right to trade goods and services with each other.

Marginal analysis is the study of the costs and benefits of doing a little bit more of an activity versus a little bit less.

A **resource** is anything that can be used to produce something else.

Land refers to all resources that come from nature, such as minerals, timber, and petroleum.

Labor is the effort of workers.

Capital refers to manufactured goods used to make other goods and services.

Entrepreneurship describes the efforts of entrepreneurs in organizing resources for production, taking risks to create new enterprises, and innovating to develop new products and production processes.

A **scarce** resource is not available in sufficient quantities to satisfy all the various ways a society wants to use it.

AP® Exam Tip

Students of microeconomics should pay close attention to *marginal analysis,* as it is often tested on the AP® exam. Any time you see "additional," think "marginal."

AP® Exam Tip

Be careful when you see key terms you think you already know, because economists have special meanings for many terms. For example, *scarcity* is about more than just a limited amount of a good. For an economist, scarcity involves trying to satisfy unlimited consumer wants with limited resources. The difference is the relationship to unlimited consumer wants.

FOCUS Active Learning

Have students watch Jacob Clifford's video "Economic Systems: Why is Communist China Doing So Well?"(see econextras video list with hyperlinks on the bcs and TRFD) to get a current example of the mix of command and market economic systems.

TEACH Teach It

If you are teaching Micro, *marginal analysis* is a key concept that must be thoroughly taught and understood. Stress that in the context of economics, the term *marginal* is associated with additional, be it resources, utility, or benefit.

TEACH Teach It

Students really struggle to understand the various meanings of the term *capital.* The capital discussed in this module is physical capital—manufactured goods used to make other goods. Contrast that idea with financial capital, which is funds from savings that are available for investment spending. If students hear a news story about a firm's capital being depleted during a recession, this means the firm now has less money with which to expand the business. It does not mean the firm is losing its machinery. Later in the book, students will learn about human capital, which is the improvement in labor created by education and knowledge. If the term *capital* appears on the AP® exam without a modifier, tell students to pay attention to the context, but in this case, the term most likely refers to machinery and equipment.

TEACH Teach It

You may see *resources* and *factors of production* used interchangeably. Ensure that students know both terms.

TEACH Teach It

This is a good place to discuss the difference between needs and wants. Ask students to generate a list of needs and write them on the board as they list them. Do the same for wants. Then, ask if any items appear in the needs column that should not be there. Help students see that some of the items on the needs list are really wants. Needs are things like clean air, clean water, food, clothing, and shelter.

TEACH Teach It

Show students a grocery store ad that has a buy one, get one free offer. Ask if the good being offered is really free. If students answer yes, challenge them to explain why. If they say no, they are correct. There is always an opportunity cost because the resources used to produce the free goods could have been used to produce other goods.

FOCUS Active Learning

Ask students to list and then write on their whiteboards all the things they could do tonight if you don't assign homework. Ask each of them to write the opportunity cost of not having homework on his or her whiteboard or a piece of paper, and hold it up. (Students should only write one thing on the board.) Use this as an opportunity to talk about the differences between trade-offs and opportunity costs as well as the personalized nature of opportunity costs.

FOCUS Active Learning

Ask students if college athletes should get paid to play their sport. Use this as a jumping-off point for a discussion on opportunity cost. Should college athletes be required to obtain a degree or spend a certain number of years in college prior to turning pro? What is the opportunity cost of such a requirement?

AP® Exam Tip

Questions on the AP® exam generally use the term *capital* to refer to the category of factors of production made up of manufactured goods used to make other goods and services. Don't confuse this type of capital with *financial capital* such as money, stocks, and bonds.

when there is not enough of it available to satisfy the various ways a society wants to use it. For example, there are limited supplies of oil and coal, which currently provide most of the energy used to produce and deliver everything we buy. And in a growing world economy with a rapidly increasing human population, even clean air and water have become scarce resources.

Just as individuals must make choices, the scarcity of resources means that society as a whole must make choices. One way for a society to make choices is simply to allow them to emerge as the result of many individual choices. For example, there are only so many hours in a week, and Americans must decide how to spend their time. How many hours will they spend going to supermarkets to get lower prices rather than saving time by shopping at convenience stores? The answer is the sum of individual decisions: each of the millions of individuals in the economy makes his or her own choice about where to shop, and society's choice is simply the sum of those individual decisions.

For various reasons, there are some decisions that a society decides are best not left to individual choice. For example, two of the authors of this book live in an area that until recently was mainly farmland but is now being rapidly built up. Most local residents feel that the community would be a more pleasant place to live if some of the land were left undeveloped. But no individual has an incentive to keep his or her land as open space, rather than sell it to a developer. So a trend has emerged in many communities across the United States of local governments purchasing undeveloped land and preserving it as open space. Decisions about how to use scarce resources are often best left to individuals, but sometimes should be made at a higher, community-wide, level.

The real cost of an item is its **opportunity cost**: what you must give up in order to get it.

Opportunity Cost: The Real Cost of Something Is What You Must Give Up to Get It

Charles D. Winters

Suppose it is the last term before you graduate from high school and you must decide which college to attend. You have narrowed your choices to a small liberal arts college near home or a large state university several hours away. If you decide to attend the local liberal arts college, what is the cost of that decision? Of course, you will have to pay for tuition, books, and housing no matter which college you choose. Added to the cost of choosing the local college is the forgone opportunity to attend the large state university, your next best alternative. Economists call the value of what you must give up when you make a particular choice an **opportunity cost.**

Opportunity costs are crucial to individual choice because, in the end, all costs are opportunity costs. That's because with every choice, an alternative is forgone—money or time spent on one thing can't be spent on another. If you spend $15 on a pizza, you forgo the opportunity to spend that $15 on a steak. If you spend Saturday afternoon at the park, you can't spend Saturday afternoon doing homework. And if you attend one school, you can't attend another.

The park and school examples show that economists are concerned with more than just costs paid in dollars and cents. The forgone opportunity to do homework has no direct monetary cost, but it is an opportunity cost nonetheless. And if the local college and the state university have the same tuition and fees, the cost of choosing one school over the other has nothing to do with payments and everything to do with forgone opportunities.

Now suppose tuition and fees at the state university are $5,000 less than at the local college. In that case, what you give up to attend the local college is the ability to attend the state university *plus* the enjoyment you could have gained from spending $5,000 on other things. So the opportunity cost of a choice includes all the costs—whether or not they are monetary costs—of making that choice.

The choice to go to college *at all* provides an important final example of opportunity costs. High school graduates can either go to college or seek immediate employment. Even with a full scholarship that would make college "free" in terms of monetary costs, going to college would still be an expensive proposition because most young people,

© ZUMA Press, Inc./Alamy

LeBron James understood the concept of opportunity cost.

St. Louis Federal Reserve Bank Resources

"Opportunity Cost," ***The Economic Lowdown Podcast Series*****, Episode 1**

This episode introduces choice, scarcity, and opportunity cost.

if they were not in college, would have a job. By going to college, students forgo the income they could have earned if they had gone straight to work instead. Therefore, the opportunity cost of attending college is the value of all necessary monetary payments for tuition and fees *plus* the forgone income from the best available job that could take the place of going to college.

For most people the value of a college degree far exceeds the value of alternative earnings, with notable exceptions. The opportunity cost of going to college is high for people who could earn a lot during what would otherwise be their college years. Basketball star LeBron James bypassed college because the opportunity cost would have included his $13 million contract with the Cleveland Cavaliers and even more from corporate sponsors Nike and Coca-Cola. Facebook co-founder Mark Zuckerberg, Microsoft co-founder Bill Gates, and actor Matt Damon are among the high achievers who decided that the opportunity cost of completing college was too much to swallow.

Microeconomics Versus Macroeconomics

We have presented economics as the study of choices and described how, at its most basic level, economics is about individual choice. The branch of economics concerned with how individuals make decisions and how those decisions interact is called **microeconomics**. Microeconomics focuses on choices made by individuals, households, or firms—the smaller parts that make up the economy as a whole.

Macroeconomics focuses on the bigger picture—the overall ups and downs of the economy. When you study macroeconomics, you learn how economists explain these fluctuations and how governments can use economic policy to minimize the damage they cause. Macroeconomics focuses on **economic aggregates**—economic measures such as the unemployment rate, the inflation rate, and gross domestic product—that summarize data across many different markets.

Table 1.1 lists some typical questions that involve economics. A microeconomic version of the question appears on the left, paired with a similar macroeconomic question on the right. By comparing the questions, you can begin to get a sense of the difference between microeconomics and macroeconomics.

Microeconomics is the study of how individuals, households, and firms make decisions and how those decisions interact.

Macroeconomics is concerned with the overall ups and downs of the economy.

Economic aggregates are economic measures that summarize data across many different markets.

Table 1.1 Microeconomic Versus Macroeconomic Questions

Microeconomic Questions	Macroeconomic Questions
Should I go to college or get a job after high school?	How many people are employed in the economy as a whole this year?
What determines the salary that Citibank offers to a new college graduate?	What determines the overall salary levels paid to workers in a given year?
What determines the cost to a high school of offering a new course?	What determines the overall level of prices in the economy as a whole?
What government policies should be adopted to make it easier for low-income students to attend college?	What government policies should be adopted to promote employment and growth in the economy as a whole?
What determines the number of iPhones exported to France?	What determines the overall trade in goods, services, and financial assets between the United States and the rest of the world?

As these questions illustrate, microeconomics focuses on how individuals and firms make decisions, and the consequences of those decisions. For example, a school will use microeconomics to determine how much it would cost to offer a new course, which includes the instructor's salary, the cost of class materials, and so on. By weighing the costs and benefits, the school can then decide whether or not to offer the course. Macroeconomics, in contrast, examines the *overall* behavior of the economy—how the actions of all of the individuals and firms in the economy interact to produce a particular economy-wide level of economic performance. For example,

FOCUS In the News

Before examining newspaper articles, discuss the definitions of macroeconomics and microeconomics with your students. Display two recent newspaper stories, one that illustrates a micro topic and one that focuses on a macro topic. Challenge students to identify which one highlights a macro idea and which one highlights a micro idea. This could also be a homework assignment: Ask each student to bring several articles to class and explain why the articles illustrate micro or macro topics, or maybe both.

FOCUS Active Learning

Now that students understand the difference between macroeconomics and microeconomics, place them in groups of two or three. Ask each group to develop a list of five questions that would be classified as macroeconomics and five questions that would be classified as microeconomics. Have each group share one or two questions without revealing to the other students how the question is classified, and then discuss with the class the question's appropriate placement. Students should be able to justify the proper placement of the question.

Module 1 The Study of Economics 5

FOCUS Active Learning

TRM Have students complete **Worksheet 1.2 (Economic Concepts)** from the TRM in class or as homework. The first section of the worksheet asks students to define whether a concept is related to micro- or macroeconomics, and the second section asks them to differentiate between positive and normative economics.

TEACH Teach It

When economists use models, they assume the only thing changing is the variable being measured. One error that students often make is to change many variables at the same time. Get them to try to stop this tendency to overthink questions by practicing and explaining only the first thing that changes in the question being asked.

macroeconomics is concerned with the general level of prices in the economy and how high or low they are relative to prices last year, rather than with the price of a particular good or service.

Positive Versus Normative Economics

Positive economics is the branch of economic analysis that describes the way the economy actually works.

Normative economics makes prescriptions about the way the economy should work.

Economic analysis, as we will see throughout this book, draws on a set of basic economic principles. But how are these principles applied? That depends on the purpose of the analysis. Economic analysis that is used to answer questions about the way the economy works, questions that have definite right and wrong answers, is known as **positive economics**. In contrast, economic analysis that involves saying how the economy *should* work is known as **normative economics**.

Imagine that you are an economic adviser to the governor of your state and the governor is considering a change to the toll charged along the state turnpike. Below are three questions the governor might ask you.

1. How much revenue will the tolls yield next year?
2. How much would that revenue increase if the toll were raised from $1.00 to $1.50?
3. Should the toll be raised, bearing in mind that a toll increase would likely reduce traffic and air pollution near the road but impose some financial hardship on frequent commuters?

AP® Exam Tip

In economics, positive statements are about *what is*, while normative statements are about *what should be*.

There is a big difference between the first two questions and the third one. The first two are questions about facts. Your forecast of next year's toll revenue without any increase will be proved right or wrong when the numbers actually come in. Your estimate of the impact of a change in the toll is a little harder to check—the increase in revenue depends on other factors besides the toll, and it may be hard to disentangle the causes of any change in revenue. Still, in principle there is only one right answer.

But the question of whether or not tolls should be raised may not have a "right" answer—two people who agree on the effects of a higher toll could still disagree about whether raising the toll is a good idea. For example, someone who lives near the turnpike but doesn't commute on it will care a lot about noise and air pollution but not so much about commuting costs. A regular commuter who doesn't live near the turnpike will have the opposite priorities.

John Green/Loop Images/Corbis

Should the toll be raised?

This example highlights a key distinction between the two roles of economic analysis and presents another way to think about the distinction between positive and normative analysis: positive economics is about description, and normative economics is about prescription. Positive economics occupies most of the time and effort of economists.

Looking back at the three questions the governor might ask, it is worth noting a subtle but important difference between questions 1 and 2. Question 1 asks for a simple prediction about next year's revenue—a forecast. Question 2 is a "what if" question, asking how revenue would change if the toll were to increase. Economists are often called upon to answer both types of questions. Economic *models*, which provide simplified representations of reality using, for example, graphs or equations, are especially useful for answering "what if" questions.

The answers to such questions often serve as a guide to policy, but they are still predictions, not prescriptions. That is, they tell you what will happen if a policy is changed, but they don't tell you whether or not that result is good. Suppose that your economic model tells you that the governor's proposed increase in highway tolls will raise property values in communities near the road but will tax or inconvenience people who currently use the turnpike to get to work. Does that information make this proposed toll increase a good idea or a bad one? It depends on whom you ask. As we've just seen, someone who is very concerned with the communities near the road will support the increase, but

6 Section 1 Basic Economic Concepts

someone who is very concerned with the welfare of drivers will feel differently. That's a value judgment—it's not a question of positive economic analysis.

Still, economists often do engage in normative economics and give policy advice. How can they do this when there may be no "right" answer? One answer is that economists are also citizens, and we all have our opinions. But economic analysis can often be used to show that some policies are clearly better than others, regardless of individual opinions.

Suppose that policies A and B achieve the same goal, but policy A makes everyone better off than policy B—or at least makes some people better off without making other people worse off. Then A is clearly more beneficial than B. That's not a value judgment: we're talking about how best to achieve a goal, not about the goal itself.

For example, two different policies have been used to help low-income families obtain housing: rent control, which limits the rents landlords are allowed to charge, and rent subsidies, which provide families with additional money with which to pay rent. Almost all economists agree that subsidies are the preferable policy. (In a later module we'll see why this is so.) And so the great majority of economists, whatever their personal politics, favor subsidies over rent control.

When policies can be clearly ranked in this way, then economists generally agree. But it is no secret that economists sometimes disagree.

When and Why Economists Disagree

Economists have a reputation for arguing with each other. Where does this reputation come from? One important answer is that media coverage tends to exaggerate the real differences in views among economists. If nearly all economists agree on an issue—for example, the proposition that rent controls lead to housing shortages—reporters and editors are likely to conclude that there is no story worth covering, and so the professional consensus tends to go unreported. But when there is some issue on which prominent economists take opposing sides—for example, whether cutting taxes right now would help the economy—that does make a good news story. So you hear much more about the areas of disagreement among economists than you do about the many areas of agreement.

It is also worth remembering that economics, unavoidably, is often tied up in politics. On a number of issues, powerful interest groups know what opinions they want to hear. Therefore, they have an incentive to find and promote economists who profess those opinions, which gives these economists a prominence and visibility out of proportion to their support among their colleagues.

Although the appearance of disagreement among economists exceeds the reality, it remains true that economists often *do* disagree about important things. For example, some highly respected economists argue vehemently that the U.S. government should replace the income tax with a *value-added tax* (a national sales tax, which is the main source of government revenue in many European countries). Other equally respected economists disagree. What are the sources of this difference of opinion?

One important source of differences is in values: as in any diverse group of individuals, reasonable people can differ. In comparison to an income tax, a value-added tax typically falls more heavily on people with low incomes. So an economist who values a society with more social and income equality will likely oppose a value-added tax. An economist with different values will be less likely to oppose it.

A second important source of differences arises from the way economists conduct economic analysis. Economists base their conclusions on models formed by making simplifying assumptions about reality. Two economists can legitimately disagree about which simplifications are appropriate—and therefore arrive at different conclusions.

TEACH Teach It

All economies must answer three basic questions:

- What to produce?
- How will resources be used to produce goods and services?
- For whom will goods and services be produced?

Although a nation's market system plays a big role in determining how these questions will be answered, differing economic viewpoints impact the strategies used to answer them. As you move through the course, remind students of the differing viewpoints of economists and why they might disagree.

FOCUS Active Learning

TRM If time allows, show the video titled "Keynesian Theory in 5 Minutes" (see econextras video list with hyperlinks on the bcs and TRFD). I would suggest muting the music as your students watch it. Suggested questions on this video may be found in **Worksheet 1.3 (Questions for "Keynesian Theory" Video)** from the TRM.

OPEN & CLOSE Exit Slip

TRM *Please see **Exit Slip: Module 1** in the TRM for formative multiple-choice questions to ask before finishing your lesson. These questions will help you quickly assess whether your students have mastered the module's concepts before moving on.*

Answers to the Exit Slip Questions

1. E
2. C
3. C

FYI When Economists Agree

"If all the economists in the world were laid end to end, they still couldn't reach a conclusion." So goes one popular economist joke. But do economists really disagree that much?

Not according to a classic survey of members of the American Economic Association, reported in the May 1992 issue of the *American Economic Review*. The authors asked respondents to agree or disagree with a number of statements about the economy; what they found was a high level of agreement among professional economists on many of the statements. At the top of the list, with more than 90% of the economists agreeing, were the statements "Tariffs and import quotas usually reduce general economic welfare" and "A ceiling on rents reduces the quantity and quality of housing available." What's striking about these two statements is that many noneconomists disagree: tariffs and import quotas to keep out foreign-produced goods are favored by many voters, and proposals to do away with rent control in cities like New York and San Francisco have met fierce political opposition.

So is the stereotype of quarreling economists a myth? Not entirely. Economists do disagree quite a lot on some issues, especially in macroeconomics, but they also find a great deal of common ground.

Suppose that the U.S. government was considering a value-added tax. Economist A may rely on a simplification of reality that focuses on the administrative costs of tax systems—that is, the costs of monitoring compliance, processing tax forms, collecting the tax, and so on. This economist might then point to the well-known high costs of administering a value-added tax and argue against the change. But economist B may think that the right way to approach the question is to ignore the administrative costs and focus on how the proposed law would change individual savings behavior. This economist might point to studies suggesting that value-added taxes promote higher consumer saving, a desirable result. Because the economists have made different simplifying assumptions, they arrive at different conclusions. And so the two economists may find themselves on different sides of the issue.

Most such disputes are eventually resolved by the accumulation of evidence that shows which of the various simplifying assumptions made by economists does a better job of fitting the facts. However, in economics, as in any science, it can take a long time before research settles important disputes—decades, in some cases. And since the economy is always changing in ways that make old approaches invalid or raise new policy questions, there are always new issues on which economists disagree. The policy maker must then decide which economist to believe.

MODULE 1 Review

Check Your Understanding

1. Provide an example of a resource from each of the four categories of resources.
2. What type of resource is each of the following?
   a. time spent flipping hamburgers at a restaurant
   b. a bulldozer
   c. a river
3. You make $45,000 per year at your current job with Whiz Kids Consultants. You are considering a job offer from Brainiacs, Inc., which would pay you $50,000 per year. Is each of the following elements an opportunity cost of accepting the new job at Brainiac, Inc.? Answer yes or no, and explain your answer.
   a. the increased time spent commuting to your new job
   b. the $45,000 salary from your old job
   c. the more spacious office at your new job
4. Identify each of the following statements as positive or normative, and explain your answer.
   a. Society should take measures to prevent people from engaging in dangerous personal behavior.
   b. People who engage in dangerous personal behavior impose higher costs on society through higher medical costs.

Answers to Module 1 Review Questions

Check Your Understanding

1. Possible examples of the four categories of resources include fisheries (land), time spent working on a fishing boat (labor), fishing nets (capital), and the opening of a new seafood market (entrepreneurship).

2. a. time spent flipping hamburgers at a restaurant: labor

b. a bulldozer: capital

c. a river: land

3. a. No. The increased time spent commuting is a direct cost you will incur if you accept the new job.

b. Yes. One of the benefits of the new job is that you will be making $50,000. But if you take the new job, you will have to give up your current job; that is, you have to give up your current salary of $45,000.

c. No. A more spacious office is an additional benefit of your new job and does not involve forgoing something else, so it is not an opportunity cost.

4. a. This is a normative statement because it stipulates what *should* be done. Your answer involves a value judgment. For example, should people be prevented from all dangerous personal behavior if they enjoy that behavior—like skydiving? Your answer will depend on your point of view.

b. This is a positive statement because it is a description of fact.

Tackle the Test: Multiple-Choice Questions

1. Which of the following is an example of a resource?
   I. petroleum
   II. a factory
   III. a cheeseburger dinner
   a. I only
   b. II only
   c. III only
   d. I and II only
   e. I, II, and III
2. Which of the following is not an example of resource scarcity?
   a. There is a finite amount of petroleum in the world.
   b. Farming communities are experiencing droughts.
   c. There are not enough physicians to satisfy all desires for health care in the United States.
   d. Cassette tapes are no longer being produced.
   e. Teachers would like to have more instructional technology in their classrooms.
3. Suppose that you prefer reading a book you already own to watching TV and that you prefer watching TV to listening to music. If these are your only three choices, what is the opportunity cost of reading?
   a. watching TV and listening to music
   b. watching TV
   c. listening to music
   d. sleeping
   e. the price of the book
4. Which of the following statements is/are normative?
   I. The price of gasoline is rising.
   II. The price of gasoline is too high.
   III. Gas prices are expected to fall in the near future.
   a. I only
   b. II only
   c. III only
   d. I and III only
   e. I, II, and III
5. Which of the following questions is studied in microeconomics?
   a. Should I go to college or get a job after I graduate?
   b. What government policies should be adopted to promote employment in the economy?
   c. How many people are employed in the economy this year?
   d. Has the overall level of prices in the economy increased or decreased this year?
   e. What determines the overall salary levels paid to workers in a given year?

Tackle the Test: Free-Response Questions

1. Define the term *resources*, and list the four categories of resources. What characteristic of resources results in the need to make choices?

Rubric for FRQ 1 (6 points)

1 point: Resources are anything that can be used to produce something else.

1 point each: The four categories of the economy's resources are land, labor, capital, and entrepreneurship.

1 point: The characteristic that results in the need to make choices is scarcity.

2. In what type of economic analysis do questions have a "right" or "wrong" answer? In what type of economic analysis do questions not necessarily have a "right" answer? On what type of economic analysis do economists tend to disagree most frequently? Why might economists disagree? Explain.
(5 points)

Tackle the Test: Multiple-Choice Questions

1. d
2. d
3. b
4. b
5. a

Tackle the Test: Free-Response Question

Rubric for FRQ 2 (5 points)

1 point: Positive economics (the answers are based on facts)

1 point: Normative economics (the answers involve value judgments)

1 point: Normative economics (because opinions and value judgments differ)

1 point: Economists disagree about models.

1 point: Economists might disagree because of differences in values and in the assumptions they find appropriate when constructing models.

PD To prepare for teaching this lesson, you may want to consult the **Module 2 Sample Lecture** in the TRM.

OPEN & CLOSE Start Here

Project the employment data table (Table A-9, Selected Employment Indicators) found at http://www.bls.gov/news.release/empsit.t09.htm. Post the following questions for discussion:

1. Are more teen boys or girls employed? Why? Remind students that this table does not give the *why* answer; it only gives us the numbers.
2. Use the ranges for 20 to 24, 25 to 54, and 55 years and over to describe how employment changes as men and women age. How would you explain the reason for this?

Answers: Students' answers will be dependent on the data pull, which is changed monthly. They may talk about college, starting families, retirement ages, or family situations.

FOCUS Active Learning

TRM Have students watch Jason Welker's video "The Business Cycle" (see econextras video list with hyperlinks on the bcs and TRFD). This video offers a good explanation of the business cycle and the goal of macroeconomic policy. Suggested questions on this video may be found in **Worksheet 2.1 (Questions for "The Business Cycle" Video)** from the TRM.

FOCUS Active Learning

TRM Have students complete **Worksheet 2.2 (The Business Cycle)** from the TRM as you explain each part of the cycle.

American Stock/Getty Images

MODULE 2 Introduction to Macroeconomics

In this Module, you will learn to:

- Explain what a business cycle is and why policy makers seek to diminish the severity of business cycles
- Describe how employment and unemployment are measured and how they change over the business cycle
- Define aggregate output and explain how it changes over the business cycle
- Define inflation and deflation and explain why price stability is preferred
- Explain how economic growth determines a country's standard of living
- Summarize the crucial role of models—simplified representations of reality—in economics

Today many people enjoy walking, biking, and horseback riding through New York's beautiful Central Park. But in 1932 there were many people living there in squalor. At that time, Central Park contained one of the many "Hoovervilles"—the shantytowns that had sprung up across America as a result of a catastrophic economic slump that had started in 1929. Millions of people were out of work and unable to feed, clothe, and house themselves and their families. Beginning in 1933, the U.S. economy would stage a partial recovery. But joblessness stayed high throughout the 1930s—a period that came to be known as the Great Depression.

Why the name "Hooverville"? These shantytowns were named after President Herbert Hoover, who had been elected president in 1928. When the Depression struck, people blamed the president: neither he nor his economic advisers seemed to understand what had happened or to know what to do to improve the situation. At that time, the field of macroeconomics was still in its infancy. It was only after the economy was plunged into catastrophe that economists began to closely examine how the macroeconomy works and to develop policies that might prevent such disasters in the future. To this day, the effort to understand economic slumps and find ways to prevent them is at the core of macroeconomics.

In this module, we will begin to explore the key features of macroeconomic analysis. We will look at some of the field's major concerns, including business cycles, employment, aggregate output, price stability, and economic growth.

St. Louis Federal Reserve Bank Resources

The Great Depression Curriculum Unit

The St. Louis Fed's *Great Depression* curriculum unit is designed to provide teachers with economic lessons that they can share with their students so that they can understand this significant experience in U.S. history. The six lessons take students through measuring the Great Depression (using GDP and CPI), dealing with the Great Depression, and discussing whether it could happen again.

The Great Depression Online Course

The St. Louis Fed's *Great Depression* curriculum unit can also be accessed as a web-based interactive unit.

The Business Cycle

The alternation between economic downturns and upturns in the macroeconomy is known as the **business cycle**. A **depression** is a very deep and prolonged downturn; fortunately, the United States hasn't had one since the Great Depression of the 1930s. Instead, we have experienced less prolonged economic downturns known as **recessions**, periods in which output and employment are falling. These are followed by economic upturns—periods in which output and employment are rising—known as **expansions** (sometimes called *recoveries*). According to the National Bureau of Economic Research there have been 11 recessions in the United States since World War II. During that period the average recession lasted 11 months, and the average expansion lasted 58 months. The average length of a business cycle, from the beginning of a recession to the beginning of the next recession, has been 5 years and 8 months. The shortest business cycle was 18 months, and the longest was 10 years and 8 months. The most recent economic downturn started in December 2007 and ended in June 2009. **Figure 2.1** shows the history of the U.S. unemployment rate since 1989 and the timing of business cycles. Recessions are indicated in the figure by the shaded areas.

The business cycle is an enduring feature of the economy. But even though ups and downs seem to be inevitable, most people believe that macroeconomic analysis has guided policies that help smooth out the business cycle and stabilize the economy.

What happens during a business cycle, and how can macroeconomic policies address the downturns? Let's look at three issues: employment and unemployment, aggregate output, and inflation and deflation.

The **business cycle** is the alternation between economic downturns, known as *recessions*, and economic upturns, known as *expansions*.

A **depression** is a very deep and prolonged downturn.

Recessions are periods of economic downturns when output and employment are falling.

Expansions, or recoveries, are periods of economic upturns when output and employment are rising.

AP® Exam Tip

Be prepared to identify the different phases of the business cycle so you can relate each phase to changes in employment, output, and growth.

Figure 2.1 The U.S. Unemployment Rate and the Timing of Business Cycles, 1989–2013

The unemployment rate, a measure of joblessness, rises sharply during recessions (indicated by shaded areas) and usually falls during expansions.

Source: Bureau of Labor Statistics.

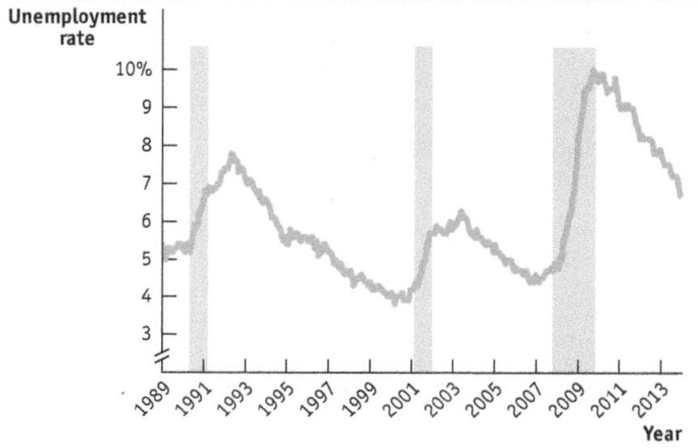

Employment, Unemployment, and the Business Cycle

Although not as severe as a depression, a recession is clearly an undesirable event. Like a depression, a recession leads to joblessness, reduced production, reduced incomes, and lower living standards.

To understand how job loss relates to the adverse effects of recessions, we need to understand something about how the labor force is structured. **Employment** is the total number of people who are currently working for pay, and **unemployment** is the total

Employment is the number of people who are currently working for pay in the economy.

Unemployment is the number of people who are actively looking for work but aren't currently employed.

TEACH Teach It

Students probably assume that a recession begins at the bottom of the business cycle when business activity (i.e., production and income) is at its lowest levels. In fact, the recession commences at the peak of the business cycle, where business activity begins to fall and the unemployment rate is likely starting to rise. Recall this from the Welker video cited on page 10.

TEACH Teach It

If you would like to give students current data, they can visit www.bls.gov/cps/cps_htgm.htm for additional information on how the government measures unemployment. Unemployment will be covered in detail later in the course.

St. Louis Federal Reserve Bank Resources

"Why Scarce Resources Are Sometimes Unemployed," *Page One Economics Classroom Edition*

The unemployment rate always seems to be in the news, but students may not realize that there are different types of unemployment. There is the natural rate of unemployment; cyclical, frictional, and structural unemployment; plus underemployment. Have students read this article to learn the differences.

TEACH Teach It

Introduce the following terms, and make students familiar with them. The labor force is not the same as the number of employed workers, nor is it the same as the overall population. The labor force (LF) is simply the total number of employed workers (E) plus the number of those who are unemployed and actively seeking work (U). The unemployment rate does not tell us the fraction of the nation that is without work; it is the fraction of the labor force that is unemployed and *seeking* work. Using the notation above, the unemployment rate is $U/(E + U) = U/LF$. Stress that to be considered unemployed, an individual must be actively looking for a job.

TEACH Teach It

Point out to students that the total production of goods and services produced in an economy during a given time period—the aggregate output—moves in the opposite direction from unemployment. When unemployment is high, aggregate output is low. When unemployment is low, output is high. Show this relationship using the peaks and troughs of the business cycle.

TEACH Teach It

Stress that inflation and deflation are associated with general changes in the overall prices of goods and services throughout the economy. Neither is good for the economy as both cause a decrease in consumer spending. With inflation, a dollar doesn't buy as much as it once did. With deflation, consumers hold onto their dollars, waiting for prices to go even lower. Stress that when prices of specific goods change, this changes the opportunity cost of purchasing such goods but is not a sign of inflation or deflation.

FYI Defining Recessions and Expansions

Some readers may be wondering exactly how recessions and expansions are defined. The answer is that there is no exact definition!

In many countries, economists adopt the rule that a recession is a period of at least two consecutive quarters (a quarter is three months), during which aggregate output falls. The two-consecutive-quarter requirement is designed to avoid classifying brief hiccups in the economy's performance, with no lasting significance, as recessions.

Sometimes, however, this definition seems too strict. For example, an economy that has three months of sharply declining output, then three months of slightly positive growth, then another three months of rapid decline, should surely be considered to have endured a nine-month recession.

In the United States, we try to avoid such misclassifications by assigning the task of determining when a recession begins and ends to an independent panel of experts at the National Bureau of Economic Research (NBER). This panel looks at a variety of economic indicators, with the main focus on employment and production, but ultimately, the panel makes a judgment call.

Sometimes this judgment is controversial. In fact, there is lingering controversy over the 2001 recession. According to the NBER, that recession began in March 2001 and ended in November 2001, when output began rising. Some critics argue, however, that the recession really began several months earlier, when industrial production began falling. Other critics argue that the recession didn't really end in 2001 because employment continued to fall and the job market remained weak for another year and a half.

Finding a job was difficult in 2009.

number of people who are actively looking for work but aren't currently employed. A country's **labor force** is the sum of employment and unemployment.

The **unemployment rate**—the percentage of the labor force that is unemployed—is usually a good indicator of what conditions are like in the job market: a high unemployment rate signals a poor job market in which jobs are hard to find; a low unemployment rate indicates a good job market in which jobs are relatively easy to find. In general, during recessions the unemployment rate is rising, and during expansions it is falling. Look again at Figure 2.1, which shows the unemployment rate from 1989 through 2013. The graph shows significant changes in the unemployment rate. Note that even in the most prosperous times there is some unemployment. A booming economy, like that of the late 1990s, can push the unemployment rate down to 4% or even lower. But a severe recession, like the one that began in 2007, can push the unemployment rate into double digits.

The **labor force** is equal to the sum of employment and unemployment.

The **unemployment rate** is the percentage of the labor force that is unemployed.

Output is the quantity of goods and services produced.

Aggregate output is the economy's total production of goods and services for a given time period.

Aggregate Output and the Business Cycle

Rising unemployment is the most painful consequence of a recession, and falling unemployment the most urgently desired feature of an expansion. But the business cycle isn't just about jobs—it's also about **output**: the quantity of goods and services produced. During the business cycle, the economy's level of output and its unemployment rate move in opposite directions. At lower levels of output, fewer workers are needed, and the unemployment rate is relatively high. Growth in output requires the efforts of more workers, which lowers the unemployment rate. To measure the rise and fall of an economy's output, we look at **aggregate output**—the economy's total production of goods and services for a given time period, usually a year. Aggregate output normally falls during recessions and rises during expansions.

Inflation, Deflation, and Price Stability

In 1970 the average production worker in the United States was paid \$3.40 an hour. By October 2013 the average hourly earnings for such a worker had risen to \$19.65. Three cheers for economic progress!

St. Louis Federal Reserve Bank Resources

The Story of Unemployment Online Course

How do we know how many people are unemployed? Why are they unemployed? What can be done to get people back to work? Students get the answers to these and other questions in *The Story of Unemployment*, including why education might be the best way to avoid unemployment in their futures.

But wait—American workers were paid much more in 2013, but they also faced a much higher cost of living. In 1970 a dozen eggs cost only about \$0.58; by October 2013 that was up to \$1.93. The price of a loaf of white bread went from about \$0.20 to \$1.36. And the price of a gallon of gasoline rose from just \$0.33 to \$3.43. If we compare the percentage increase in hourly earnings between 1970 and October 2013 with the increases in the prices of some standard items, we see that the average worker's paycheck goes just about as far today as it did in 1970. In other words, the increase in the cost of living wiped out many, if not all, of the wage gains of the typical worker from 1970 to 2013. What caused this situation?

Between 1970 and 2013, the economy experienced substantial **inflation**, a rise in the overall price level. The opposite of inflation is **deflation**, a fall in the overall price level. A change in the prices of a few goods changes the opportunity cost of purchasing those goods but does not constitute inflation or deflation. These terms are reserved for more general changes in the prices of goods and services throughout the economy.

A rising overall price level is **inflation**.

A falling overall price level is **deflation**.

Both inflation and deflation can pose problems for the economy. Inflation discourages people from holding on to cash, because if the price level is rising, cash loses value. That is, if the price level rises, a dollar will buy less than it would before. As we will see later in our more detailed discussion of inflation, in periods of rapidly rising prices, people stop holding cash altogether and instead trade goods for goods.

Deflation can cause the opposite problem. That is, if the overall price level falls, a dollar will buy more than it would before. In this situation it can be more attractive for people with cash to hold on to it rather than to invest in new factories and other productive assets. This can deepen a recession.

In later modules we will look at other costs of inflation and deflation. For now, note that economists have a general goal of **price stability**—meaning that the overall price level is changing only slowly if at all—because it avoids uncertainty about prices and helps to keep the economy stable.

The economy has **price stability** when the overall price level is changing only slowly if at all.

Economic Growth

In 1955 Americans were delighted with the nation's prosperity. The economy was expanding, consumer goods that had been rationed during World War II were available for everyone to buy, and most Americans believed, rightly, that they were better off than citizens of any other nation, past or present. Yet by today's standards Americans were quite poor in 1955. For example, in 1955 only 33% of American homes contained washing machines, and hardly anyone had air conditioning. If we turn the clock back to 1905, we find that life for most Americans was startlingly primitive by today's standards.

20th Century Advertising/Alamy

Why are the vast majority of Americans today able to afford conveniences that many lacked in 1955? The answer is **economic growth**, an increase in the maximum possible output of an economy. Unlike the short-term increases in aggregate output that occur as an economy recovers from a downturn in the business cycle, economic growth is an increase in productive capacity that permits a sustained rise in aggregate output over time. **Figure 2.2** on the next page shows annual figures for U.S. real gross domestic product (GDP) per capita—the value of final goods and services produced in the U.S. per person—from 1900 to 2013. As a result of this economic growth, the U.S. economy's aggregate output per person was more than eight times as large in 2013 as it was in 1900.

Economic growth is fundamental to a nation's prosperity. A sustained rise in output per person allows for higher wages and a rising standard of living. The need for economic growth is urgent in poorer, less developed countries, where a lack of basic necessities makes growth a central concern of economic policy.

As you will see when studying macroeconomics, the goal of economic growth can be in conflict with the goal of hastening recovery from an economic downturn. What is good for economic growth can be bad for short-run stabilization of the business cycle, and vice versa.

We have seen that macroeconomics is concerned with the long-run trends in aggregate output as well as the short-run ups and downs of the business cycle. Now that

Economic growth is an increase in the maximum amount of goods and services an economy can produce.

FOCUS Active Learning

Show students how much prices have changed over time. Use the inflation rate calculator found at www.usinflationcalculator.com to show the difference in common items such as gasoline, hamburgers, and blue jeans. The US Inflation Calculator measures the buying power of the dollar over time. To use the calculator, enter any two dates between 1913 and the present year, an amount for the good or service you want to check, and then click "Calculate." Students will need to research the cost of the good in the initial year to determine the answer.

Inflation Calculator

If in [1955] (enter year)

I purchased an item for \$ [0.40]

then in [2014] (enter year)

that same <u>**item would cost**</u>: **\$3.49**

Cumulative rate of inflation: **772.8%**

FOCUS In the News

If you have time, look for current news articles on inflation at www.usinflationcalculator.com under Inflation News. These can be assigned as homework reading or used in a class discussion.

FOCUS In the News

If you like Twitter, you and your students can track the news on economic growth by following the Twitter user @EconomicGrowth (twitter.com/EconomicGrowth). Even the president's perspective can be found here!

TEACH Teach It

Economic growth is not the same as the recovery phase of the business cycle, although they are both shown on the upward portion of the business cycle graph. Recovery from a recession is a short-term return to a nation's current level of productive capacity. Economic growth is a long-term concept that describes an increase in the nation's total productive capacity.

St. Louis Federal Reserve Bank Resources

"Inflation," *The Economic Lowdown Podcast Series*, Episode 4

This episode discusses three aspects of inflation: what it is, what causes it, and how it is measured. The episode also addresses related topics such as deflation, disinflation, and the role of the Federal Reserve in monitoring inflation.

Module 2 Introduction to Macroeconomics 13

FOCUS Active Learning

Note: At the beginning of this class, hand a student a piece of paper, and ask him or her to create a paper airplane. Hold the paper airplane up and ask the class, "What is this?" Someone will usually say, "It's a plane." But, is it a plane? No, the paper airplane is a model of an actual plane. It has some general characteristics of a plane (tapered nose, wings), but it is certainly not a plane. It is a very simple model of something much more complex.

Is the paper airplane a good model of a real plane? How will we test it? Will it fly? We don't know; we need to test it. Have someone in the class test the plane. What if it doesn't fly? Then we need to modify it. What if it never flies? Maybe we need to scrap it. Assure the class that economic models are developed, tested, and modified in much the same way. Sometimes they don't work very well and must be rethought.

TEACH AP® Exam Tip

Make sure students understand that economists use models to test their hypotheses about the economy. Typically, only one variable will be changed at a time while holding all other factors constant. This is the *ceteris paribus* assumption. By only changing one factor at a time, it is easier to see what has had an impact in the market. A common mistake students make on the AP® Economics exam is trying to change multiple factors when answering questions. Have students practice providing only the answer that is requested without going beyond it.

Figure 2.2 Growth, the Long View

Over the long run, growth in real GDP per capita has dwarfed the ups and downs of the business cycle. Except for the recession that began the Great Depression, recessions are almost invisible.

Sources: Angus Maddison, "Statistics on World Population, GDP and Per Capita GDP, 1-2006 AD," http://www.ggdc.net/maddison; Jutta Bolt and Jan Luiten van Zanden, "The First Update of the Maddison Project; Re-estimating Growth Before 1820;" Bureau of Economic Analysis.

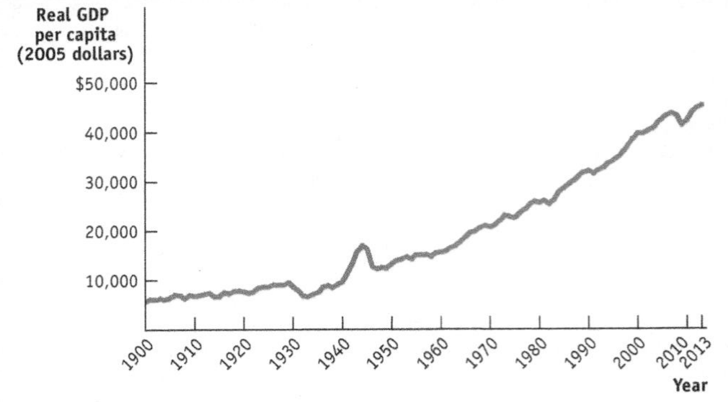

AP® Exam Tip

Economic growth is an increase in the economy's potential output. Changes in real GDP (output) do not necessarily indicate economic growth. Temporary fluctuations in economic conditions often alter real GDP when there has been no change in the economy's potential output.

we have a general understanding of the important topics studied in macroeconomics, we are almost ready to apply economic principles to real economic issues. To do this requires one more step—an understanding of how economists use *models*.

The Use of Models in Economics

In 1901, one year after their first glider flights at Kitty Hawk, the Wright brothers built something else that would change the world—a wind tunnel. This was an apparatus that let them experiment with many different designs for wings and control surfaces. These experiments gave them knowledge that would make heavier-than-air flight possible. Needless to say, testing an airplane design in a wind tunnel is cheaper and safer than building a full-scale version and hoping it will fly. More generally, models play a crucial role in almost all scientific research—economics included.

A **model** is a simplified representation used to better understand a real-life situation.

A **model** is any simplified version of reality that is used to better understand a real-life situation. But how do we create a simplified representation of an economic situation? One possibility—an economist's equivalent of a wind tunnel—is to find or create a real but simplified economy. For example, economists interested in the economic role of money have studied the system of exchange that developed in World War II prison camps, in which cigarettes became a universally accepted form of payment, even among prisoners who didn't smoke.

Another possibility is to simulate the workings of the economy on a computer. For example, when changes in tax law are proposed, government officials use *tax models*—large mathematical computer programs—to assess how the proposed changes would affect different groups of people. Models can also be depicted by graphs and equations. Starting in the next module you will see how graphical models illustrate the relationships between variables and reveal the effects of changes in the economy.

The **other things equal assumption** means that all other relevant factors remain unchanged. This is also known as the *ceteris paribus* assumption.

Models are important because their simplicity allows economists to focus on the influence of only one change at a time. That is, they allow us to hold everything else constant and to study how one change affects the overall economic outcome. So when building economic models, an important assumption is the **other things equal assumption**, which means that all other relevant factors remain unchanged. Sometimes the Latin phrase *ceteris paribus*, which means "other things equal," is used.

But it isn't always possible to find or create a small-scale version of the whole economy, and a computer program is only as good as the data it uses. (Programmers have a

St. Louis Federal Reserve Bank Resources

"Economic Growth," *The Economic Lowdown Podcast Series*

Have you encountered mobile payment systems like mobile credit card readers? They are pretty cool, and this kind of innovation can be good for the economy. From micro to macro, in this episode of the *Economic Lowdown* podcast series, we'll take a look at economic growth, at how innovation and technological progress can make things happen for the economy over time by organizing the factors of production to be, well, more productive.

saying: garbage in, garbage out.) For many purposes, the most effective form of economic modeling is the construction of "thought experiments": simplified, hypothetical versions of real-life situations. And as you will see throughout this book, economists' models are very often in the form of a graph. In the next module, we will look at the *production possibilities curve*, a model that helps economists think about the choices every economy faces.

MODULE 2 Review

Check Your Understanding

1. Describe two types of models used by economists.
2. Describe who gets hurt in a recession and how they are hurt.

Tackle the Test: Multiple-Choice Questions

1. During the recession phase of a business cycle, which of the following is likely to increase?
   a. the unemployment rate
   b. the price level
   c. economic growth rates
   d. the labor force
   e. wages
2. The labor force is made up of everyone who is
   a. employed.
   b. old enough to work.
   c. actively seeking work.
   d. employed or unemployed.
   e. employed or capable of working.
3. Which of the following provides a long-term increase in the productive capacity of an economy?
   a. an expansion
   b. a recovery
   c. a recession
   d. a depression
   e. economic growth
4. Which of the following is the most likely result of inflation?
   a. falling employment
   b. a dollar will buy more than it did before
   c. people are discouraged from holding cash
   d. price stability
   e. low aggregate output per capita
5. The other things equal assumption allows economists to
   a. avoid making assumptions about reality.
   b. focus on the effects of only one change at a time.
   c. oversimplify.
   d. allow nothing to change in their model.
   e. reflect all aspects of the real world in their model.

Tackle the Test: Free-Response Questions

1. Define an expansion and economic growth, and explain the difference between the two concepts.

Rubric for FRQ 1 (3 points)

1 point: An expansion is the period of recovery after an economic downturn.

1 point: Economic growth is an increase in the productive capacity of the economy.

1 point: An expansion can occur regardless of any increase in the economy's long-term potential for production, and it only lasts until the next downturn, while economic growth increases the economy's ability to produce more goods and services over the long term.

2. Define inflation, and explain why an increase in the price of donuts does not indicate that inflation has occurred. **(2 points)**

OPEN & CLOSE Exit Slip

TRM *Please see **Exit Slip: Module 2** in the TRM for formative multiple-choice questions to ask before finishing your lesson. These questions will help you quickly assess whether your students have mastered the module's concepts before moving on.*

Answers to the Exit Slip Questions

1. A
2. B
3. B

Answers to Module 2 Review Questions

Check Your Understanding

1. Types of models include real but simplified economies, computer programs that simulate the workings of a large economy, and graphs or equations that illustrate relationships between variables.

2. Recessions inflict a great deal of pain across the entire society. They cause large numbers of workers to lose their jobs and make it difficult for workers to find new jobs. Recessions reduce the standard of living of many families and are usually associated with a rise in the number of people living below the poverty line, an increase in the number of people who may lose their houses because they can no longer afford their mortgage payments, and a fall in the percentage of Americans with health insurance. Recessions also reduce the profits of firms.

Tackle the Test: Multiple-Choice Questions

1. a
2. d
3. e
4. c
5. b

Tackle the Test: Free-Response Question

Rubric for FRQ 2 (2 points)

1 point: Inflation is an overall increase in the price of goods and services throughout an economy.

1 point: If inflation occurs, the price of donuts may increase, but an increase in the price of one good does not necessarily indicate inflation. For example, the price of donuts might have increased due to an increase in the price of sugar, while the prices of most other goods in the economy have remained unchanged.

PD To prepare for teaching this lesson, you may want to consult the **Module 3 Sample Lecture** in the TRM.

OPEN & CLOSE Start Here

TRM Start class with **Activity 3.1 (Widgets and Whatsits)** from the TRM to introduce students to production possibilities curves. This activity will allow students to create production possibilities and graph their outcomes to form a curve.

TEACH AP® Exam Tip

The production possibilities curve (*PPC*) is often difficult for students to understand. Take the time to practice it often as you move through the course. Students will need to draw and interpret this graph for the AP® exam.

TEACH Teach It

Ask students what they are giving up to attend your class. They will come up with a variety of answers. Explain that each of these options is a trade-off for sitting in class.

20th Century Fox/Dreamworks/The Kobal Collection

MODULE 3 The Production Possibilities Curve Model

In this Module, you will learn to:

- Explain the importance of trade-offs in economic analysis
- Describe what the production possibilities curve model tells us about efficiency, opportunity cost, and economic growth
- Explain why increases in the availability of resources and improvements in technology are the two sources of economic growth

A good economic model can be a tremendous aid to understanding. In this module, we look at the *production possibilities curve*, a model that helps economists think about the *trade-offs* every economy faces. The production possibilities curve helps us understand three important aspects of the real economy: efficiency, opportunity cost, and economic growth.

Trade-offs: The Production Possibilities Curve

The 2000 hit movie *Cast Away*, starring Tom Hanks, was an update of the classic story of Robinson Crusoe, the hero of Daniel Defoe's eighteenth-century novel. Hanks played the role of a sole survivor of a plane crash who was stranded on a remote island. As in the original story of Robinson Crusoe, the Hanks character had limited resources: the natural resources of the island, a few items he managed to salvage from the plane, and, of course, his own time and effort. With only these resources, he had to make a life. In effect, he became a one-man economy.

You make a **trade-off** when you give up something in order to have something else.

One of the important principles of economics we introduced in Module 1 was that resources are scarce. As a result, any economy—whether it contains one person or millions of people—faces trade-offs. You make a **trade-off** when you give up something in order to have something else. For example, if a castaway devotes more resources to catching fish, he benefits by catching more fish, but he cannot use those same resources to gather coconuts, so the trade-off is that he has fewer coconuts.

St. Louis Federal Reserve Bank Resources

"Production Possibilities Frontier"

In this lesson, students develop the production possibilities frontier model while discussing the value of models in general in explaining complex ideas. They see what movement along the production possibilities curve entails—on both the constant-cost curve and on a bowed curve indicating increasing costs. They discuss ways a society can consume beyond the limits of its production possibilities through specialization and trade, as well as through an increase in resources, capital investment, and technological advances.

16 Section 1 Basic Economic Concepts

To think about the trade-offs necessary in any economy, economists often use the **production possibilities curve** model. The idea behind this model is to improve our understanding of trade-offs by considering a simplified economy that produces only two goods. This simplification enables us to show the trade-offs graphically.

Figure 3.1 shows a hypothetical production possibilities curve for Tom, a castaway alone on an island, who must make a trade-off between fish production and coconut production. The curve shows the maximum quantity of fish Tom can catch during a week *given* the quantity of coconuts he gathers, and vice versa. That is, it answers questions of the form, "What is the maximum quantity of fish Tom can catch if he also gathers 9 (or 15, or 30) coconuts?"

The **production possibilities curve** illustrates the trade-offs facing an economy that produces only two goods. It shows the maximum quantity of one good that can be produced for each possible quantity of the other good produced.

Figure 3.1 The Production Possibilities Curve

The production possibilities curve illustrates the trade-offs facing an economy that produces two goods. It shows the maximum quantity of one good that can be produced, given the quantity of the other good produced. Here, the maximum quantity of coconuts that Tom can gather depends on the quantity of fish he catches, and vice versa. His feasible production is shown by the area *inside* or *on* the curve. Production at point *C* is feasible but not efficient. Points *A* and *B* are feasible and *productively efficient*, but point *D* is not feasible.

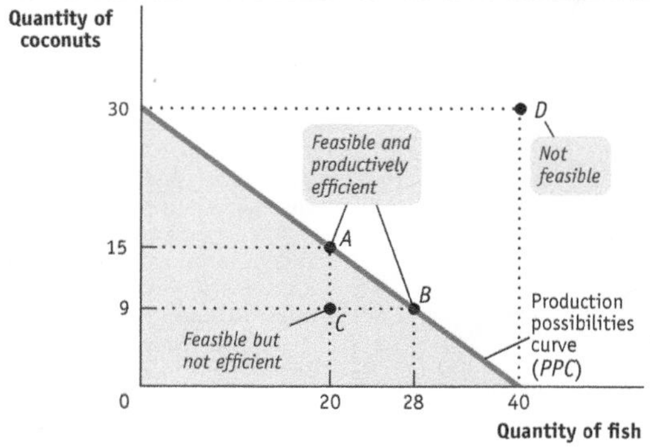

There is a crucial distinction between points *inside* or *on* the production possibilities curve (the shaded area) and points *outside* the production possibilities curve. If a production point lies inside or on the curve—like point *C*, at which Tom catches 20 fish and gathers 9 coconuts—it is feasible. After all, the curve tells us that if Tom catches 20 fish, he could also gather a maximum of 15 coconuts, so he could certainly gather 9 coconuts. However, a production point that lies outside the curve—such as point *D*, which would have Tom catching 40 fish and gathering 30 coconuts—isn't feasible.

In Figure 3.1 the production possibilities curve intersects the horizontal axis at 40 fish. This means that if Tom devoted all his resources to catching fish, he would catch 40 fish per week but would have no resources left over to gather coconuts. The production possibilities curve intersects the vertical axis at 30 coconuts. This means that if Tom devoted all his resources to gathering coconuts, he could gather 30 coconuts per week but would have no resources left over to catch fish. Thus, if Tom wants 30 coconuts, the trade-off is that he can't have any fish.

The curve also shows less extreme trade-offs. For example, if Tom decides to catch 20 fish, he would be able to gather at most 15 coconuts; this production choice is illustrated by point *A*. If Tom decides to catch 28 fish, he could gather at most 9 coconuts, as shown by point *B*.

Thinking in terms of a production possibilities curve simplifies the complexities of reality. The real-world economy produces millions of different goods. Even a castaway on an island would produce more than two different items (for example, he would need clothing and housing as well as food). But in this model we imagine an economy that produces only two goods, because in a model with many goods, it would be much harder to study trade-offs, efficiency, and economic growth.

AP® Exam Tip

Be prepared to draw a correctly labeled production possibilities curve and use it to identify opportunity cost, efficient points, inefficient points, and unattainable points. Unemployment results in production at a point below the production possibilities curve. Most production possibilities curves are concave to the origin, as shown in Figure 3.2 on page 19, due to the specialization of resources.

FOCUS Active Learning

Use Jacob Clifford's video "The Production Possibilities Curve" to reinforce Figure 3.1 (see econextras video list with hyperlinks on the bcs and TRFD).

FOCUS Graph It

In considering Figure 3.1, ask your class the following:

- What goods is this economy producing? *Fish and coconuts.* How do you know? *Those are the labels on the axes.*
- Why isn't point *C* efficient? *The economy can produce more of either one or both goods because it has unused resources.*
- Why is point *D* not feasible? *There aren't enough resources to produce 30 coconuts and 40 fish.*

Using their whiteboards or notebook paper, have students draw a constant-cost (straight) production possibilities curve for an economy producing cell phones and bread that is similar to the one in Figure 3.1. Some students won't know how to label the axes so take time to explain this in class. Have them identify a point of efficient production, inefficient production, and unattainable production. Once they finish, have them hold up their work to see if each student correctly labeled the graph. Draw the correct graph on the board.

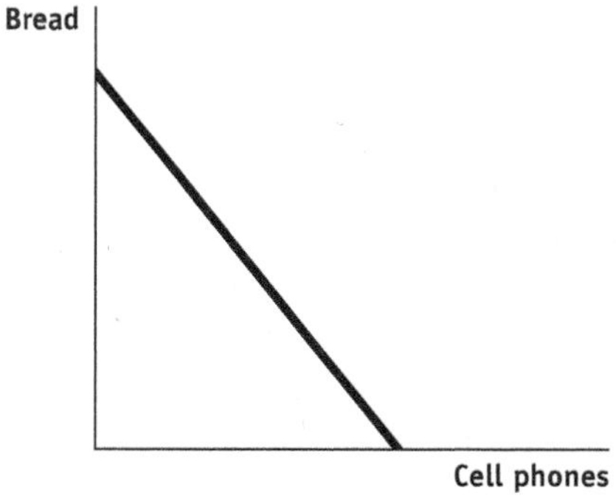

Module 3 The Production Possibilities Curve Model 17

TEACH Teach It

Every point on the curve is efficient in production. Each society has a different point on the curve where it would be allocatively efficient. What is efficient in allocation for one society will be a different point on the curve from what is efficient in allocation for another society based on which good is valued more. So, productive efficiency is achieved at any point on the curve where resources are used to produce as much of each good as the society can manage, given the quantity of the other good, and allocative efficiency is achieved at some point on the curve based on the wants and needs of society.

FOCUS Active Learning

TRM Show Jason Welker's "Scarcity, Opportunity Cost, and the *PPC*" video (see econextras video list with hyperlinks on the bcs and TRFD). Welker does a great job of explaining each of these concepts. Suggested questions on this video may be found in **Worksheet 3.2 (Questions for "Scarcity, Opportunity Cost, and the PPC" Video)** from the TRM.

FOCUS Test It

Using the graph below, identify the most efficient point(s) of production, the unattainable point, and the inefficient point of production. Explain your answer.

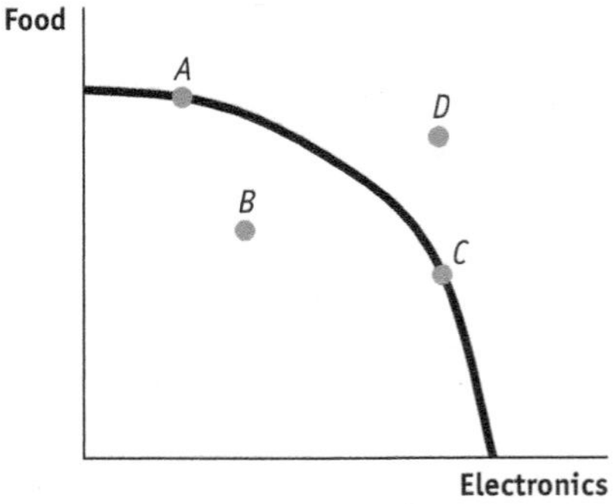

Answer: Points A *and* C *are the most efficient points of production because they are on the frontier of the* PPC. *Point* D *is unattainable and Point* B *reflects unemployed resources.*

Efficiency

An economy is **efficient** if there is no way to make anyone better off without making at least one person worse off.

An economy achieves **productive efficiency** if it produces at a point on its production possibilities curve.

An economy achieves **allocative efficiency** if it produces at the point along its production possibilities curve that makes consumers as well off as possible.

The production possibilities curve is useful for illustrating the general economic concept of efficiency. An economy is **efficient** if there are no missed opportunities—meaning that there is no way to make some people better off without making other people worse off. For example, suppose a course you are taking meets in a classroom that is too small for the number of students—some may be forced to sit on the floor or stand—despite the fact that a larger classroom nearby is empty during the same period. Economists would say that this is an *inefficient* use of resources because there is a way to make some people better off without making anyone worse off—after all, the larger classroom is empty. The school is not using its resources efficiently. When an economy is using all of its resources efficiently, the only way one person can be made better off is by rearranging the use of resources in such a way that the change makes someone else worse off. So in our classroom example, if all larger classrooms were already fully occupied, we could say that the school was run in an efficient way; your classmates could be made better off only by making people in the larger classroom worse off—by moving them to the room that is too small.

Returning to our castaway example, as long as Tom produces a combination of coconuts and fish that is on the production possibilities curve, his production is efficient. At point *A*, the 15 coconuts he gathers are the maximum quantity he can get *given* that he has chosen to catch 20 fish; at point *B*, the 9 coconuts he gathers are the maximum he can get *given* his choice to catch 28 fish; and so on. If an economy is producing at a point on its production possibilities curve, we say that the economy has achieved **productive efficiency**.

Alamy RF

A crowded classroom reflects inefficiency if switching to a larger classroom would make some students better off without making anyone worse off.

But suppose that for some reason Tom was at point *C*, producing 20 fish and 9 coconuts. Then this one-person economy would definitely not be productively efficient and would therefore be inefficient: it is missing the opportunity to produce more of both goods.

Another example of inefficiency in production occurs when people in an economy are involuntarily unemployed: they want to work but are unable to find jobs. When that happens, the economy is not productively efficient because it could produce more output if those people were employed. The production possibilities curve shows the amount that can *possibly* be produced if all resources are fully employed. In other words, changes in unemployment move the economy closer to, or further away from, the production possibilities curve (*PPC*). But the curve itself is determined by what would be possible if there were no unemployment in the economy. Greater unemployment is represented by points farther below the *PPC*—the economy is not reaching its possibilities if it is not using all of its resources. Lower unemployment is represented by points closer to the *PPC*—as unemployment decreases, the economy moves closer to reaching its possibilities.

Although the production possibilities curve helps clarify what it means for an economy to achieve productive efficiency, it's important to understand that productive efficiency is only *part* of what's required for the economy as a whole to be efficient. Efficiency also requires that the economy allocate its resources so that consumers are as well off as possible. If an economy does this, we say that it has achieved **allocative efficiency**. To see why allocative efficiency is as important as productive efficiency, notice that points *A* and *B* in Figure 3.1 both represent situations in which the economy is productively efficient, because in each case it can't produce more of one good without producing less of the other. But these two situations may not be equally desirable. Suppose that Tom prefers point *B* to point *A*—that is, he would rather consume 28 fish and 9 coconuts than 20 fish and 15 coconuts. Then point *A* is inefficient from the point of view of the economy as a whole: it's possible to make Tom better off without making anyone else worse off. (Of course, in this castaway economy there isn't anyone else; Tom is all alone.)

Creasy Studio Heinemann/Getty Images

This example shows that efficiency for the economy as a whole requires *both* productive and allocative efficiency. To be efficient, an economy must produce as much of each good as it can, given the production of other goods, and it must also produce the mix of goods that people want to consume.

Opportunity Cost

The production possibilities curve is also useful as a reminder that the true cost of any good is not only its price, but also everything else in addition to money that must be given up in order to get that good—the *opportunity cost*. If, for example, Tom decides to go from point *A* to point *B*, he will produce 8 more fish but 6 fewer coconuts. So the opportunity cost of those 8 fish is the 6 coconuts not gathered. Since 8 extra fish have an opportunity cost of 6 coconuts, 1 fish has an opportunity cost of $\frac{6}{8} = \frac{3}{4}$ of a coconut.

Is the opportunity cost of an extra fish in terms of coconuts always the same, no matter how many fish Tom catches? In the example illustrated by Figure 3.1, the answer is yes. If Tom increases his catch from 28 to 40 fish, an increase of 12, the number of coconuts he gathers falls from 9 to zero. So his opportunity cost per additional fish is $\frac{9}{12} = \frac{3}{4}$ of a coconut, the same as it was when his catch went from 20 fish to 28. However, the fact that in this example the opportunity cost of an additional fish in terms of coconuts is always the same is a result of an assumption we've made, an assumption that's reflected in the way Figure 3.1 is drawn. Specifically, whenever we assume that the opportunity cost of an additional unit of a good doesn't change regardless of the output mix, the production possibilities curve is a straight line.

Moreover, as you might have already guessed, the slope of a straight-line production possibilities curve is equal to the opportunity cost—specifically, the opportunity cost for the good measured on the horizontal axis in terms of the good measured on the vertical axis. In Figure 3.1, the production possibilities curve has a *constant slope* of $-\frac{3}{4}$, implying that Tom faces a *constant opportunity cost* per fish equal to $\frac{3}{4}$ of a coconut. (A review of how to calculate the slope of a straight line is found in the Section 1 Appendix.) This is the simplest case, but the production possibilities curve model can also be used to examine situations in which opportunity costs change as the mix of output changes.

Figure 3.2 illustrates a different assumption, a case in which Tom faces *increasing opportunity cost*. Here, the more fish he catches, the more coconuts he has to give up to catch an additional fish, and vice versa. For example, to go from producing zero fish to producing 20 fish, he has to give up 5 coconuts. That is, the opportunity cost of those 20 fish is 5 coconuts. But to increase his fish production from 20 to 40—that is, to produce an additional 20 fish—he must give up 25 more coconuts, a much higher opportunity cost. As you can see in Figure 3.2, when opportunity costs are increasing

AP® Exam Tip

Opportunity Cost = Opportunity Lost (The financial or nonfinancial cost of a choice not taken.)

Figure 3.2 Increasing Opportunity Cost

The bowed-out shape of the production possibilities curve reflects increasing opportunity cost. In this example, to produce the first 20 fish, Tom must give up 5 coconuts. But to produce an additional 20 fish, he must give up 25 more coconuts.

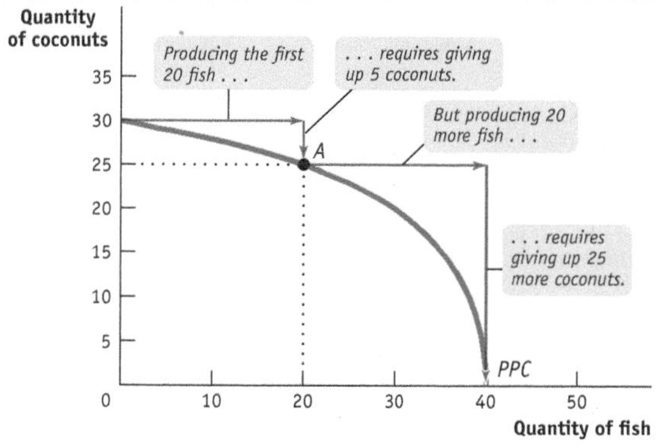

TEACH Teach It

The opportunity cost of the good graphed on the *x*-axis is always the slope of the *PPC*. The opportunity cost of the good graphed on the *y*-axis is always the inverse of the slope of the *PPC*. Stress that the bowed out shape means increasing opportunity costs exist. Demonstrate this to be true.

FOCUS Active Learning

Have students watch Jason Welker's video "The Law of Increasing Opportunity Cost and the *PPC* Model" (see econextras video list with hyperlinks on the bcs and TRFD). Welker explains why opportunity costs increase as resources are not completely adaptable to alternative uses. Ask students to explain why opportunity costs increase as more of a good is produced.

Answer: Resources are not perfectly suited for the production of both goods.

TEACH Teach It

The law of increasing opportunity costs is an important concept. Ensure that students understand that opportunity costs increase because economic resources are not completely adaptable to alternative uses. Therefore, if a society wants to produce more of one good, it must be willing to give up an increasing amount of the other good it produces. Do not let students assume that outputs are the same as resources.

FOCUS Graph It

In considering Figure 3.2, ask your class the following:

- Why is point *A* an efficient level of production? *The economy is using all of its resources to produce coconuts and fish.*
- What is the opportunity cost of changing from point *A* to a point where 20 coconuts and 30 fish are produced? *5 coconuts*
- What is the opportunity cost of changing from point *A* to a point where 20 coconuts and 20 fish are produced? *This point is inefficient because it is inside the curve. More of either good can be produced. The economy is giving up 5 of the coconuts it produced beforehand while still producing the same number of fish, so that is the opportunity cost of this decision.*

St. Louis Federal Reserve Bank Resources

Opportunity Cost Online Course for Teachers and Students

In under 12 minutes, your students can complete this course, which points to an important concept in economics—namely, that every choice we make has a cost, an opportunity cost. Some costs are small and relatively short-term. Others are significant. Recognizing the opportunity costs of your decisions can help you make more informed choices. This short course is designed to help you apply the idea of opportunity cost to the decisions you make.

Additional St. Louis Fed resources on these topics are provided in the St. Louis Fed resource list in the TRM.

FOCUS Graph It

Using their whiteboards or notebook paper, have students draw a constant-cost *PPC* and an increasing-cost *PPC* for an economy producing clothing and food so they can see the difference. These are the two graphs they will see on the AP® exam. To really determine if students understand the material, challenge them to calculate the constant opportunity cost of each good in the first graph and the increasing opportunity cost of one of the goods at two points on the second graph.

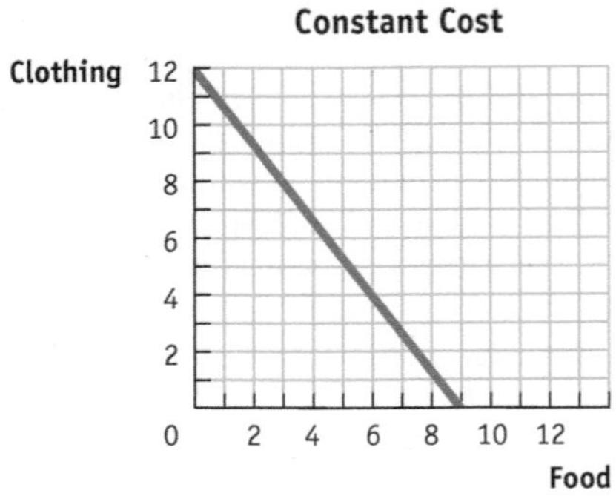

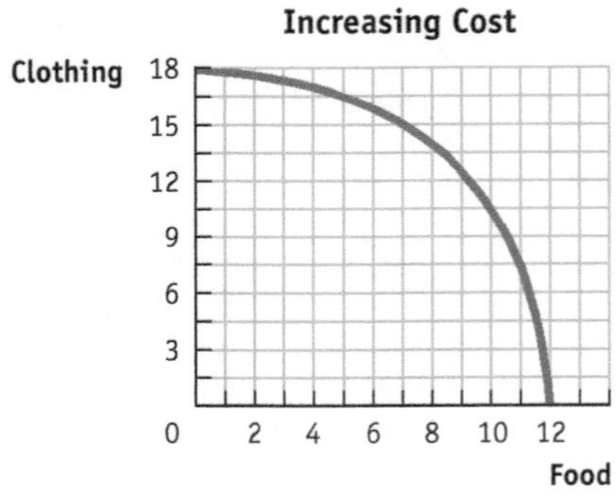

FOCUS Flip It

TRM For reinforcement and review, have students watch Jacob Clifford's "Shifting the Production Possibilities Curve" (see econextras video list with hyperlinks on the bcs and TRFD). Suggested questions may be found in the **Worksheet 3.3 (Shifting the PPC)** from the TRM.

FOCUS Test It

Assume that a nation is currently experiencing a recession. It produces high-tech products and wheat with increasing costs. Draw a correctly labeled *PPC* for the nation. Using the graph you drew, show a point that could represent the current output combination for the nation and label it *A*.

rather than constant, the production possibilities curve is a bowed-out curve rather than a straight line.

Although it's often useful to work with the simple assumption that the production possibilities curve is a straight line, economists believe that in reality, opportunity costs are typically increasing. When only a small amount of a good is produced, the opportunity cost of producing that good is relatively low because the economy needs to use only those resources that are especially well suited for its production. For example, if an economy grows only a small amount of corn, that corn can be grown in places where the soil and climate are perfect for growing corn but less suitable for growing anything else, such as wheat. So growing that corn involves giving up only a small amount of potential wheat output. Once the economy grows a lot of corn, however, land that is well suited for wheat but isn't so great for corn must be used to produce corn anyway. As a result, the additional corn production involves sacrificing considerably more wheat production. In other words, as more of a good is produced, its opportunity cost typically rises because well-suited inputs are used up and less adaptable inputs must be used instead.

Economic Growth

Finally, the production possibilities curve helps us understand what it means to talk about *economic growth*. We introduced the concept of economic growth in Module 2, saying that it allows *a sustained rise in aggregate output*. We learned that economic growth is one of the fundamental features of the economy. But are we really justified in saying that the economy has grown over time? After all, although the U.S. economy produces more of many things than it did a century ago, it produces less of other things—for example, horse-drawn carriages. In other words, production of many goods is actually down. So how can we say for sure that the economy as a whole has grown?

The answer, illustrated in **Figure 3.3**, is that economic growth means an *expansion of the economy's production possibilities:* the economy *can* produce more of everything. For example, if Tom's production is initially at point *A* (20 fish and 25 coconuts), economic growth means that he could move to point *E* (25 fish and 30 coconuts). Point *E* lies outside the original curve, so in the production possibilities curve model, growth is shown as an outward shift of the curve. Unless the *PPC* shifts outward, the points beyond the *PPC* are unattainable. Those points beyond a given *PPC* are beyond the economy's possibilities.

Figure 3.3 Economic Growth

Economic growth results in an *outward shift* of the production possibilities curve because production possibilities are expanded. The economy can now produce more of everything. For example, if production is initially at point *A* (20 fish and 25 coconuts), it could move to point *E* (25 fish and 30 coconuts).

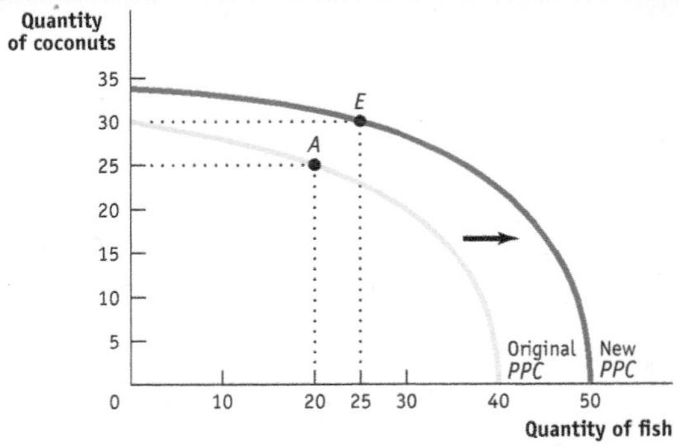

Answer:

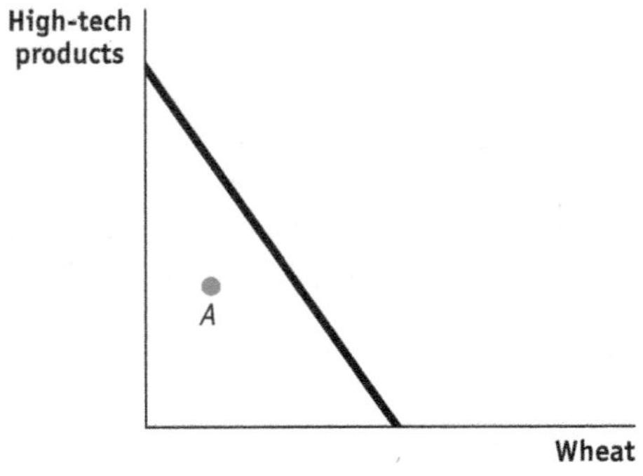

Point out to students that to earn points on the AP® exam, the reader must see:

- labels on each axis that match those given in the question (1 point).
- a point labeled "*A*" placed inside the curve to show unemployed resources (1 point).
- a bowed out line to show that increasing costs exist (1 point).

On past AP® exams, many students correctly placed the point but failed to label it, costing them 1 point for not following directions.

What can cause the production possibilities curve to shift outward? There are two general sources of economic growth. One is an increase in the resources used to produce goods and services: labor, land, capital, and entrepreneurship. To see how adding to an economy's resources leads to economic growth, suppose that Tom finds a fishing net washed ashore on the beach. The fishing net is a resource he can use to produce more fish in the course of a day spent fishing. We can't say how many more fish Tom will catch; that depends on how much time he decides to spend fishing now that he has the net. But because the net makes his fishing more productive, he can catch more fish without reducing the number of coconuts he gathers, or he can gather more coconuts without reducing his fish catch. So his production possibilities curve shifts outward.

The other source of economic growth is progress in **technology**, the technical means for the production of goods and services. Suppose Tom figures out a better way either to catch fish or to gather coconuts—say, by inventing a fishing hook or a wagon for transporting coconuts. Either invention would shift his production possibilities curve outward. However, the shift would not be a simple outward expansion of every point along the *PPC*. Technology specific to the production of only one good has no effect if all resources are devoted to the other good: a fishing hook will be of no use if Tom produces nothing but coconuts. So the point on the *PPC* that represents the number of coconuts that can be produced if there is no fishing will not change. In real-world economies, innovations in the techniques we use to produce goods and services have been a crucial force behind economic growth.

Again, economic growth means an increase in what the economy *can* produce. What the economy actually produces depends on the choices people make. After his production possibilities expand, Tom might not choose to produce both more fish and more coconuts; he might choose to increase production of only one good, or he might even choose to produce less of one good. For example, if he gets better at catching fish, he might decide to go on an all-fish diet and skip the coconuts, just as the introduction of motor vehicles led most people to give up horse-drawn carriages. But even if, for some reason, he chooses to produce either fewer coconuts or fewer fish than before, we would still say that his economy has grown, because he *could* have produced more of everything. If an economy's production possibilities curve shifts inward, the economy has become smaller. This could happen if the economy loses resources or technology (for example, if it experiences war or a natural disaster).

The production possibilities curve is a very simplified model of an economy, yet it teaches us important lessons about real-life economies. It gives us our first clear sense of what constitutes economic efficiency, it illustrates the concept of opportunity cost, and it makes clear what economic growth is all about.

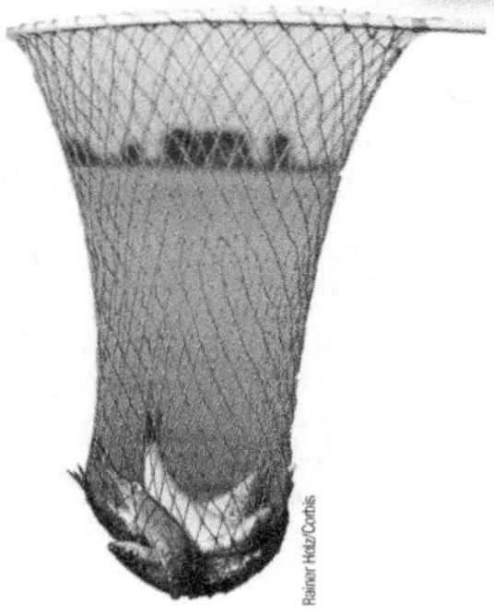

Technology is the technical means for producing goods and services.

TEACH Teach It

Economic growth frequently shows up on the FRQ portion of the AP® exam. An *expansion of the economy's production possibilities* means that economic growth is possible. With new and enhanced resources, the economy *can* produce more of what society wants and needs. Changes in productivity (which can result from changes in education and technology) and new resources (which can result from increased investments in capital) cause changes in economic growth. Demonstrate how changes in productivity and resource availability affect the *PPC*.

The top graph shows the effect of an increase in the availability of resources that can be used to produce both ice cream and automobiles. The bottom graph shows the effect of an improvement in technology that only applies to automobile production.

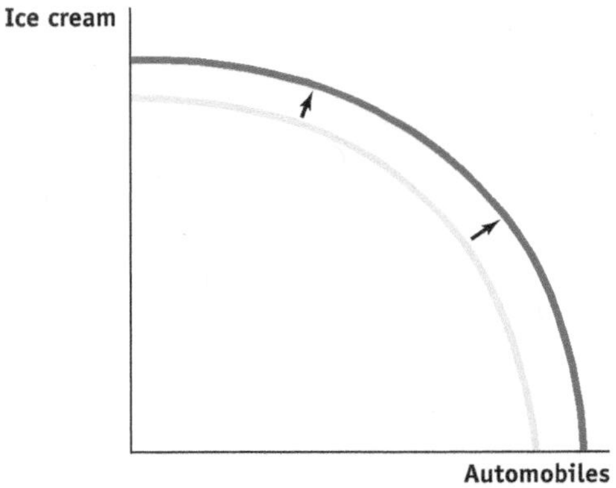

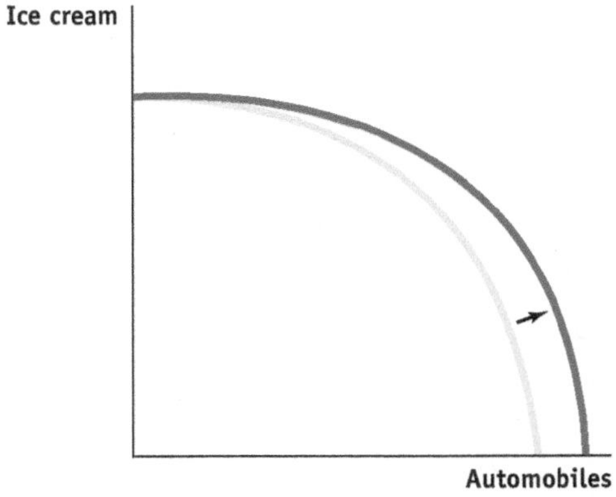

FOCUS Active Learning

TRM Graphing practice is essential at all stages of economics. Assign **Worksheet 3.4 (Production Possibilities Curves)** from the TRM in class or as homework. In this activity, students will practice labeling production possibilities curves. They will be given a scenario reflecting unemployment, economic growth, or reallocation of resources to graph, as well as questions about opportunity cost that must be answered based on the graphs given in the activity.

OPEN & CLOSE Exit Slip

TRM *Please see **Exit Slip: Module 3** in the TRM for formative multiple-choice questions to ask before finishing your lesson. These questions will help you quickly assess whether your students have mastered the module's concepts before moving on.*

Answers to the Exit Slip Questions

1. C
2. B
3. B

Module 3 The Production Possibilities Curve Model 21

MODULE 3 Review

Check Your Understanding

1. True or false? Explain your answer.
   a. An increase in the amount of resources available to Tom for use in producing coconuts and fish does not change his production possibilities curve.
   b. A technological change that allows Tom to catch more fish relative to any amount of coconuts gathered results in a change in his production possibilities curve.
   c. Points inside a production possibilities curve are efficient and points outside a production possibilities curve are inefficient.

Tackle the Test: Multiple-Choice Questions

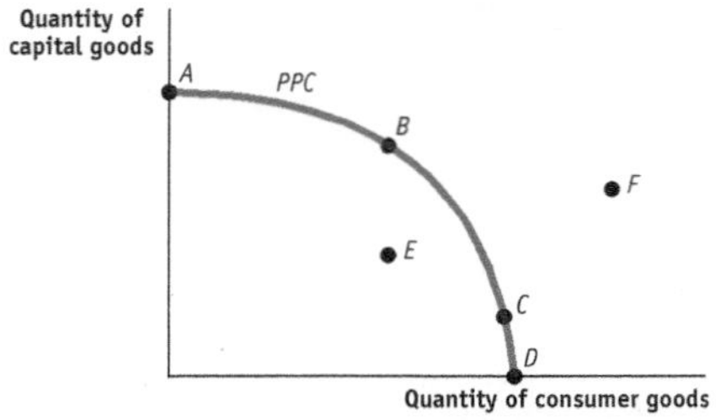

Refer to the graph above to answer the following questions.

1. Which point(s) on the graph represent productive efficiency?
   a. *B* and *C*
   b. *A* and *D*
   c. *A, B, C,* and *D*
   d. *A, B, C, D,* and *E*
   e. *A, B, C, D, E,* and *F*
2. For this economy, an increase in the quantity of capital goods produced without a corresponding decrease in the quantity of consumer goods produced
   a. cannot happen because there is always an opportunity cost.
   b. is represented by a movement from point *E* to point *A*.
   c. is represented by a movement from point *C* to point *B*.
   d. is represented by a movement from point *E* to point *B*.
   e. is only possible with an increase in resources or technology.
3. An increase in unemployment could be represented by a movement from point
   a. *D* to point *C*.
   b. *B* to point *A*.
   c. *C* to point *F*.
   d. *B* to point *E*.
   e. *E* to point *B*.
4. Which of the following might allow this economy to move from point *B* to point *F*?
   a. more workers
   b. discovery of new resources
   c. building new factories
   d. technological advances
   e. all of the above
5. This production possibilities curve shows the trade-off between consumer goods and capital goods. Since capital goods are a resource, an increase in the production of capital goods today will increase the economy's production possibilities in the future. Therefore, all other things equal (*ceteris paribus*), producing at which point today will result in the largest outward shift of the *PPC* in the future?
   a. *A*
   b. *B*
   c. *C*
   d. *D*
   e. *E*

Answers to Module 3 Review Questions

Check Your Understanding

1. a. False. An increase in the resources available to Tom for use in producing coconuts and fish changes his production possibilities curve by shifting it outward, because he can now produce more fish and coconuts than before. In the accompanying graph, the line labeled "Tom's original *PPC*" represents Tom's original production possibilities curve, and the line labeled "Tom's new *PPC*" represents the new production possibilities curve that results from an increase in resources available to him.

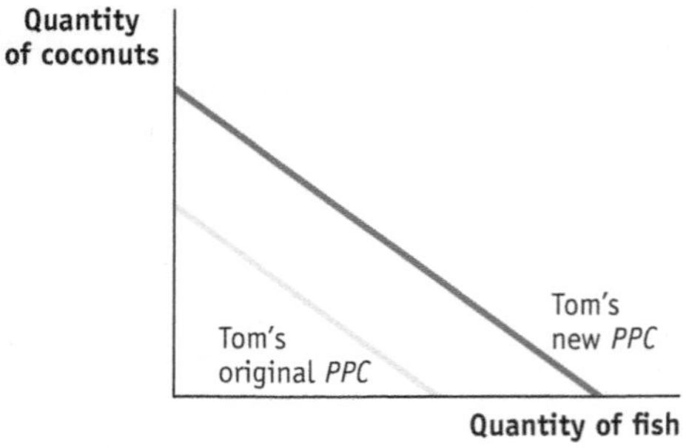

b. True. A technological change that allows Tom to catch more fish for any amount of coconuts gathered results in a change to his production possibilities curve. This is illustrated in the accompanying graph. The new production possibilities curve is represented by the line labeled "Tom's new *PPC*," and the original production possibilities curve is represented by the line labeled "Tom's original *PPC*." Since the maximum quantity of coconuts that Tom can gather is the same as before, the new production possibilities curve intersects the vertical axis at the same point as the old curve. But since the maximum possible quantity of fish is now greater than before, the new curve intersects the horizontal axis to the right of the old curve.

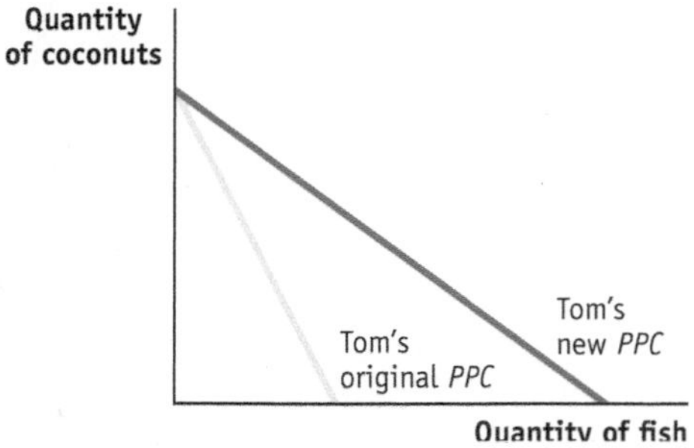

c. False. Productive efficiency is achieved at points along a production possibilities curve, but every point inside a *PPC* is inefficient because more of either good could be produced without producing less of the other. Points outside the *PPC* are simply unobtainable.

Tackle the Test: Multiple-Choice Questions

1. c
2. d
3. d
4. e
5. a

22 Section 1 Basic Economic Concepts

Tackle the Test: Free-Response Questions

1. Refer to the graph below. Assume that the country is producing at point *C*.

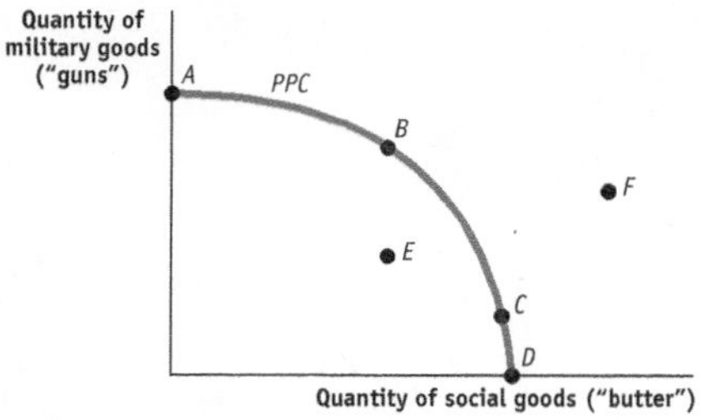

a. Does this country's production possibilities curve exhibit increasing opportunity costs? Explain.
b. If this country were to go to war, the most likely move would be from point *C* to which point? Explain.
c. If the economy entered into a recession, the country would move from point *C* to which point? Explain.

Rubric for FRQ 1 (6 points)

1 point: Yes

1 point: The *PPC* is concave (bowed outward), so with each additional unit of butter produced, the opportunity cost in terms of gun production (indicated by the slope of the line) increases. Likewise, as more guns are produced, the opportunity cost in terms of butter increases.

1 point: *B*

1 point: The country would choose an efficient point with more (but not all) military goods with which to fight the war. Point *A* would be an unlikely choice because at that point there is no production of any social goods, some of which are needed to maintain a minimal standard of living.

1 point: *E*

1 point: A recession, which causes unemployment, is represented by a point below the *PPC*.

2. Assume that an economy can choose between producing food and producing shelter at a constant opportunity cost. Draw a correctly labeled production possibilities curve for the economy. On your graph:
a. Use the letter *E* to label one of the points that is productively efficient.
b. Use the letter *U* to label one of the points at which there might be unemployment.
c. Use the letter *I* to label one of the points that is not feasible.
(5 points)

Tackle the Test: Free-Response Question Rubric for FRQ 2 (5 points)

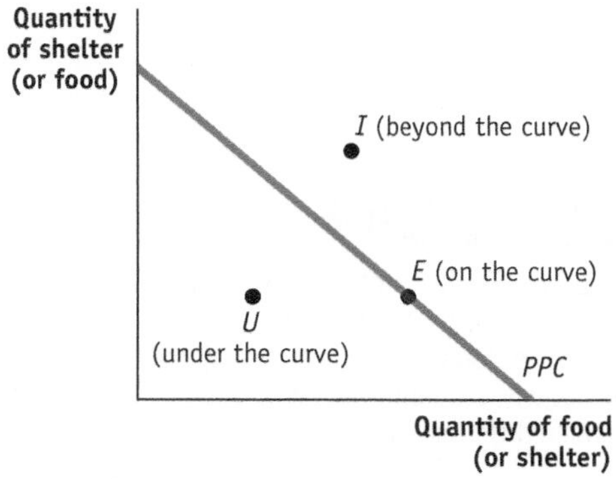

1 point: The graph has "Quantity of shelter" and "Quantity of food" labeled on the axes.

1 point: The production possibilities curve is a downward-sloping, straight line.

1 point: *E* is labeled on the production possibilities curve.

1 point: *U* is labeled below the production possibilities curve.

1 point: *I* is labeled beyond the production possibilities curve.

Module 3 The Production Possibilities Curve Model 23

PD To prepare for teaching this lesson, you may want to consult the **Module 4 Sample Lecture** in the TRM.

OPEN & CLOSE Start Here

TRM Assign **Activity 4.1 (Haves and Have-Nots)** from the TRM to help students connect previous lessons to the content in Module 4. In this activity, students will be placed in groups and provided differing levels of resources to create products. As part of this activity, some students will figure out they can *trade* for resources that they need but don't have. During the debriefing, make sure you discuss this concept.

TEACH Teach It

Ask students how many of them think they could make a pencil. Count the number and write it on the board, complimenting the students on their ability to do so. Show students this short clip of Milton Friedman talking about how a pencil is made in "I, Pencil"(see econextras video list with hyperlinks on the bcs and TRFD). Ask how many students still believe they could make a pencil. Lead a discussion on how people benefit from trade and why nations benefit at a variety of levels.

Chris Fertnig/Getty Images

MODULE 4 Comparative Advantage and Trade

In this Module, you will learn to:

- Explain how trade leads to gains for an individual or an economy
- Explain the difference between absolute advantage and comparative advantage
- Describe how comparative advantage leads to gains from trade in the global marketplace

Gains from Trade

A family could try to take care of all its own needs—growing its own food, sewing its own clothing, providing itself with entertainment, and writing its own economics textbooks. But trying to live that way would be very hard. The key to a much better standard of living for everyone is **trade**, in which people divide tasks among themselves and each person provides a good or service that other people want in return for different goods and services that he or she wants.

The reason we have an economy, rather than many self-sufficient individuals, is that there are **gains from trade**: by dividing tasks and trading, two people (or 7 billion people) can each get more of what they want than they could get by being self-sufficient. Gains from trade arise, in particular, from this division of tasks, which economists call **specialization**—a situation in which different people each engage in a different task.

The advantages of specialization, and the resulting gains from trade, were the starting point for Adam Smith's 1776 book *The Wealth of Nations*, which many regard as the beginning of economics as a discipline. Smith's book begins with a description of an eighteenth-century pin factory where, rather than each of the 10 workers making a pin from start to finish, each worker specialized in one of the many steps in pin-making:

> One man draws out the wire, another straights it, a third cuts it, a fourth points it, a fifth grinds it at the top for receiving the head; to make the head requires two or three distinct operations; to put it on, is a particular business, to whiten the pins is another; it is even a trade by itself to put them into the paper; and the important business of making a pin is, in this manner, divided into about eighteen distinct operations. . . . Those ten persons, therefore, could make among them upwards of forty-eight thousand pins in a day. But if they had all wrought separately and independently, and without any of them having been educated to this particular business, they certainly could not each of them have made twenty, perhaps not one pin a day. . . .

In a market economy, individuals engage in **trade**: they provide goods and services to others and receive goods and services in return.

There are **gains from trade**: people can get more of what they want through trade than they could if they tried to be self-sufficient. This increase in output is due to **specialization**: each person specializes in the task that he or she is good at performing.

AP® Exam Tip

Take note! The content in this module frequently shows up in the free-response and multiple-choice sections of the AP® exam.

St. Louis Federal Reserve Bank Resources

"The Global Economy: It's a Small World After All," *Page One Economics Classroom Edition*

To understand why people trade, suppose you were limited to consuming only items you could find within walking distance of your house—or, perhaps even worse, only items you could produce yourself. For most of us, this restriction would severely diminish the variety of goods and services we enjoy on a daily basis. Therefore, the simplest answer to the question is that people (or entire countries) trade because they will enjoy a wider variety of goods.

24 Section 1 Basic Economic Concepts

The same principle applies when we look at how people divide tasks among themselves and trade in an economy. The economy, as a whole, can produce more when each person *specializes* in a task and *trades* with others.

The benefits of specialization are the reason a person typically focuses on the production of only one type of good or service. It takes many years of study and experience to become a doctor; it also takes many years of study and experience to become a commercial airline pilot. Many doctors might have the potential to become excellent pilots, and vice versa, but it is very unlikely that anyone who decided to pursue both careers would be as good a pilot or as good a doctor as someone who specialized in only one of those professions. So it is to everyone's advantage when individuals specialize in their career choices.

Markets are what allow a doctor and a pilot to specialize in their respective fields. Because markets for commercial flights and for doctors' services exist, a doctor is assured that she can find a flight and a pilot is assured that he can find a doctor. As long as individuals know that they can find the goods and services that they want in the market, they are willing to forgo self-sufficiency and are willing to specialize.

Comparative Advantage and Gains from Trade

The production possibilities curve model is particularly useful for illustrating gains from trade—trade based on *comparative advantage*. Let's stick with Tom being stranded on his island, but now let's suppose that a second castaway, who just happens to be named Hank, is washed ashore. Can Tom and Hank benefit from trading with each other?

It's obvious that there will be potential gains from trade if the two castaways do different things particularly well. For example, if Tom is a skilled fisherman and Hank is very good at climbing trees, clearly it makes sense for Tom to catch fish and Hank to gather coconuts—and for the two men to trade the products of their efforts.

But one of the most important insights in all of economics is that there are gains from trade even if one of the trading parties isn't especially good at anything. Suppose, for example, that Hank is less well suited to primitive life than Tom; he's not nearly as good at catching fish, and compared to Tom, even his coconut-gathering leaves something to be desired. Nonetheless, what we'll see is that both Tom and Hank can live better by trading with each other than either could alone.

For the purposes of this example, let's go back to the simple case of straight-line production possibilities curves. Tom's production possibilities are represented by the production possibilities curve in panel (a) of **Figure 4.1** on the next page, which is the same as the production possibilities curve in Figure 3.1 (page 17). According to this *PPC*, Tom could catch 40 fish, but only if he gathered no coconuts, and he could gather 30 coconuts, but only if he caught no fish. Recall that this means that the slope of his production possibilities curve is $-3/4$: his opportunity cost of 1 fish is $3/4$ of a coconut.

Panel (b) of Figure 4.1 shows Hank's production possibilities. Like Tom's, Hank's production possibilities curve is a straight line, implying a constant opportunity cost of fish in terms of coconuts. His production possibilities curve has a constant slope of -2. Hank is less productive all around: at most he can produce 10 fish or 20 coconuts. But he is particularly bad at fishing: whereas Tom sacrifices $3/4$ of a coconut per fish caught, for Hank the opportunity cost of a fish is 2 whole coconuts. **Table 4.1** on the next page summarizes the two castaways' opportunity costs of fish and coconuts.

Now, Tom and Hank could go their separate ways, each living on his own side of the island, catching his own fish and gathering his own coconuts. Let's suppose that they start out that way and make the consumption choices shown in Figure 4.1: in the absence of trade, Tom consumes 28 fish and 9 coconuts per week, while Hank consumes 6 fish and 8 coconuts.

Roderick Chen/Getty Images

TEACH Connect It

Draw a *PPC* on the board. Put a point on the graph just outside the curve and ask students what the point represents. Ask them under what circumstances they can reach that point. Earlier you had mentioned that such points could be achieved if more or better resources were made available, but now students should also talk about trade, especially if you completed the opening activity for this section.

TEACH Teach It

TRM Students struggle with the math to determine who has the comparative advantage in production. Use **Activity 4.2 (Two States)** from the TRM to work out a second problem similar to the one in the book. Take the activity all the way through to show how a comparative advantage is determined.

St. Louis Federal Reserve Bank Resources

Comparative Advantage Online Course for Teachers and Students

In this course, you will meet Jack Of All Trades, a most awesome superhero. In all tasks, Jack can do everything better and faster (he has an absolute advantage), but does that mean he must do everything while the rest of the people stand around helplessly? Find out if justice is served when a formerly idle citizen, Andy, wades through the depths of opportunity cost and the benefits of comparative advantage.

TEACH AP® Exam Tip

TRM It is essential to help your students understand comparative advantage calculations as they will encounter them on the AP® exam. Please use **Worksheet 4.3 (Comparative Advantage: Input & Output)** from the TRM to help students work through the content more quickly.

FOCUS Flip It

For reinforcement and review, have students watch Jacob Clifford's "Comparative Advantage and Terms of Trade" video (see econextras video list with hyperlinks on the bcs and TRFD).

Figure 4.1 Production Possibilities for Two Castaways

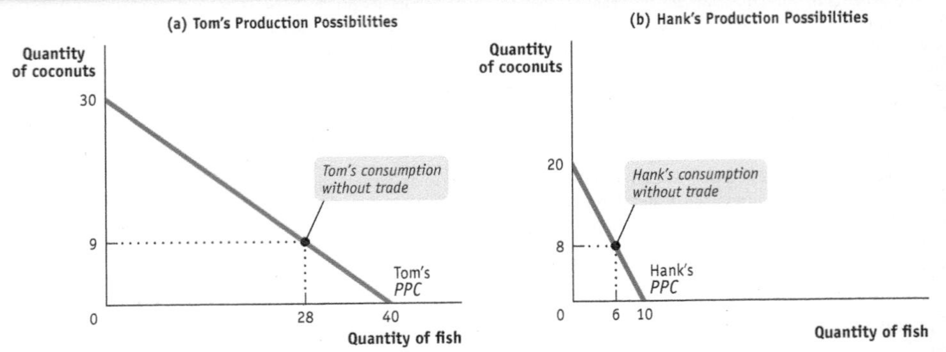

Here, each of the two castaways has a constant opportunity cost of fish and a straight-line production possibilities curve. In Tom's case, each fish has an opportunity cost of ¾ of a coconut. In Hank's case, each fish has an opportunity cost of 2 coconuts.

Table 4.1 Tom's and Hank's Opportunity Costs of Fish and Coconuts

	Tom's Opportunity Cost	Hank's Opportunity Cost
One fish	3/4 coconut	2 coconuts
One coconut	4/3 fish	1/2 fish

But is this the best they can do? No, it isn't. Given that the two castaways have different opportunity costs, they can strike a deal that makes both of them better off. **Table 4.2** shows how such a deal works: Tom specializes in the production of fish, catching 40 per week, and gives 10 to Hank. Meanwhile, Hank specializes in the production of coconuts, gathering 20 per week, and gives 10 to Tom. The result is shown in **Figure 4.2**. Tom now consumes more of both goods than before: instead of 28 fish and 9 coconuts, he consumes 30 fish and 10 coconuts. Hank also consumes more, going from 6 fish and 8 coconuts to 10 fish and 10 coconuts. As Table 4.2 also shows, both Tom and Hank experience gains from trade: Tom's consumption of fish increases by two, and his consumption of coconuts increases by one. Hank's consumption of fish increases by four, and his consumption of coconuts increases by two.

So both castaways are better off when they each specialize in what they are good at and trade with each other. It's a good idea for Tom to catch the fish for both of them, because his opportunity cost of a fish is only ¾ of a coconut not gathered versus 2 coconuts for Hank. Correspondingly, it's a good idea for Hank to gather coconuts for both of them.

Or we could describe the situation in a different way. Because Tom is so good at catching fish, his opportunity cost of gathering coconuts is high: ⁴⁄₃ of a fish not caught for every coconut gathered. Because Hank is a pretty poor fisherman, his opportunity cost of gathering coconuts is much less, only ½ of a fish per coconut.

Table 4.2 How the Castaways Gain from Trade

		Without Trade		With Trade		Gains from Trade
		Production	Consumption	Production	Consumption	
Tom	Fish	28	28	40	30	+2
	Coconuts	9	9	0	10	+1
Hank	Fish	6	6	0	10	+4
	Coconuts	8	8	20	10	+2

An individual has a **comparative advantage** in producing something if the opportunity cost of that production is lower for that individual than for other people. In other words, Hank has a comparative advantage over Tom in producing a particular good or service if Hank's opportunity cost of producing that good or service is lower than Tom's. In this case, Hank has a comparative advantage in gathering coconuts and Tom has a comparative advantage in catching fish.

Notice that Tom is actually better than Hank at producing both goods: Tom can catch more fish in a week, and he can also gather more coconuts. This means that Tom has an **absolute advantage** in both activities: he can produce more output with a given amount of input (in this case, his time) than Hank can. It might seem as though Tom has nothing to gain from trading with less competent Hank. But we've just seen that Tom can indeed benefit from a deal with Hank, because *comparative*, not *absolute*, advantage is the basis for mutual gain. It doesn't matter that it takes Hank more time to gather a coconut; what matters is that for him the opportunity cost of that coconut in terms of fish is lower. So, despite his absolute disadvantage in both activities, Hank has a comparative advantage in coconut gathering. Meanwhile Tom, who can use his time better by catching fish, has a comparative disadvantage in coconut gathering.

An individual has a **comparative advantage** in producing a good or service if the opportunity cost of producing the good or service is lower for that individual than for other people.

An individual has an **absolute advantage** in producing a good or service if he or she can make more of it with a given amount of time and resources. Having an absolute advantage is not the same thing as having a comparative advantage.

Figure 4.2 Comparative Advantage and Gains from Trade

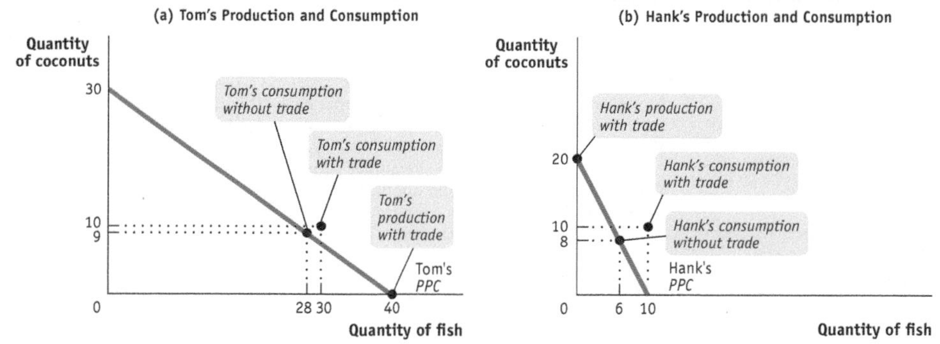

By specializing and trading, the two castaways can produce and consume more of both goods. Tom specializes in catching fish, his comparative advantage, and Hank—who has an *absolute* disadvantage in both goods but a *comparative* advantage in coconuts—specializes in gathering coconuts. The result is that each castaway can consume more of both goods than either could without trade.

FOCUS Graph It

In considering Figure 4.2, ask your students the following:

- What are Tom and Hank's consumption levels without trade? *Tom: 9 coconuts and 28 fish; Hank: 8 coconuts and 6 fish.*
- We know that Tom should specialize in catching fish and Hank should specialize in producing coconuts. Why wouldn't Tom produce both goods since he can produce the most? *Because he has a lower opportunity cost to produce fish.*
- Why would Tom be willing to trade 10 fish to Hank for 10 coconuts? *It costs Tom 4/3 of a fish to get a coconut. Through trade, it only costs him 1 fish for a coconut. As a result, he can have more fish and more coconuts through trade (10 coconuts and 30 fish).*

TEACH Teach It

TRM Students really struggle to determine terms of trade that are mutually beneficial to both parties. Terms of trade are set *after* comparative advantage is determined. Reuse the example in **Worksheet 4.2 (Two States)** from the TRM to talk about terms of trade with your students. Begin by drawing the production possibilities curves for each state on the board. We already learned that Oregon will export timber and Washington will export apples. Since each state would like some of both goods, they will now have to trade.

You may need to review how to calculate comparative advantage using the worksheet. Explain that the original cost conditions in each state will limit the terms of trade. In Washington, 1 apple = .25 timber, so Washington must obtain more than .25 timber for each 1 unit of apples exported, or it will not benefit from export. In Oregon, 1 apple costs 4 timber, so Oregon will not give up more than 4 timber to get 1 apple. The rate of exchange will be somewhere between .25 and 4 timber for each apple. Suppose a trade is negotiated whereby Washington sends 20 apples to Oregon in exchange for 20 timber.

Consumption after trade:

Oregon: 20 timber and 20 apples

Washington: 20 timber and 20 apples

Show these points outside of both *PPCs*. Stress to the students that without trade, each state is constrained by the *PPC*. But with trade, each is well beyond the *PPC*.

Module 4 Comparative Advantage and Trade 27

TEACH Teach It

Students often confuse absolute and comparative advantage. Ensure they understand that the nation with the absolute advantage can produce the good more efficiently using the same resources. You can tell who has the absolute advantage by looking to see who can produce more of the good overall. One nation can have the absolute advantage in more than one good. Trade is based on comparative advantage and two nations can't have a comparative advantage in the production of the same good. If the *PPCs* of two nations have the same slope, then neither country has a comparative advantage in either good, although one might have an absolute advantage in making both goods.

FOCUS Test It

Give students Question 3 from the 2003 released AP® exam located on AP® Central. Give them 12.5 minutes to answer the question, just as they would have on the AP® exam. Then work the question yourself or show them Jason Welker's "Determining Comparative Advantage Using *PPCs*" video with the solution to the question (see econextras video list with hyperlinks on the bcs and TRFD).

FOCUS Active Learning

Comparative advantage can be calculated by focusing on using the inputs or the output. Use Jacob Clifford's video "Comparative Advantage Practice: Output and Input Questions" (see econextras video list with hyperlinks on the bcs and TRFD) to help students understand the differences in calculating comparative advantage.

Mutually Beneficial Terms of Trade

The **terms of trade** indicate the rate at which one good can be exchanged for another.

The **terms of trade** indicate the rate at which one good can be exchanged for another. In our story, Tom and Hank traded 10 coconuts for 10 fish, so each coconut traded for 1 fish. Why not some other terms of trade, such as 3/4 fish per coconut? Indeed, there are many terms of trade that would make both Tom and Hank better off than if they didn't trade. But there are also terms that Tom or Hank would certainly reject. For example, Tom would not trade 2 fish per coconut, because he only gives up 4/3 fish per coconut without trade.

To find the range of mutually beneficial terms of trade for a coconut, look at each person's opportunity cost of producing a coconut. *Any price per coconut between the opportunity cost of the coconut producer and the opportunity cost of the coconut buyer will make both sides better off than in the absence of trade.* We know that Hank will produce coconuts because he has a comparative advantage in gathering coconuts. Hank's opportunity cost is 1/2 fish per coconut. Tom, the buyer of coconuts, has an opportunity cost of 4/3 fish per coconut. So any terms of trade between 1/2 fish per coconut and 4/3 fish per coconut would benefit both Tom and Hank.

To understand why, consider the opportunity costs summarized in Table 4.1. When Hank doesn't trade with Tom, Hank can gain 1/2 fish by giving up a coconut, because his opportunity cost of each coconut is 1/2 fish. Hank will clearly reject any deal with Tom that provides him with less than 1/2 fish per coconut—he's better off not trading at all and getting 1/2 fish per coconut. But Hank benefits from trade if he receives more than 1/2 fish per coconut. So the terms of 1 fish per coconut, as in our story, are acceptable to Hank.

When Tom doesn't trade with Hank, Tom gives up 4/3 fish to get a coconut—his opportunity cost of a coconut is 4/3 fish. Tom will reject any deal that requires him to pay more than 4/3 fish per coconut. But Tom benefits from trade if he pays less than 4/3 fish per coconut. The terms of 1 fish per coconut are thus acceptable to Tom as well. Both islanders would also be made better off by terms of 3/4 fish per coconut or 5/4 fish per coconut or any other price between 1/2 fish and 4/3 fish per coconut. The islanders' negotiation skills determine where the terms of trade fall within that range.

So remember, Tom and Hank will engage in trade only if the "price" of the good each person obtains from trade is less than his own opportunity cost of producing the good. The same is true for international trade. Whenever two parties trade voluntarily, for each good, the terms of trade are found between the opportunity cost of the producer and the opportunity cost of the buyer.

The story of Tom and Hank clearly simplifies reality. Yet it teaches us some very important lessons that also apply to the real economy. First, the story provides a clear illustration of the gains from trade. By agreeing to specialize and provide goods to each other, Tom and Hank can produce more; therefore, both are better off than if each tried to be self-sufficient. Second, the story demonstrates a key point that is often overlooked in real-world arguments: as long as people have different opportunity costs, *everyone has a comparative advantage in something, and everyone has a comparative disadvantage in something, so everyone can benefit from trade.*

AP® Exam Tip

The producer with the *absolute advantage* can produce the largest quantity of the good. However, it is the producer with the *comparative advantage*, and not necessarily the one with the absolute advantage, who should specialize in the production of that good to achieve mutual gains from trade.

The idea of comparative advantage applies to many activities in the economy. Perhaps its most important application is in trade—not between individuals, but between countries. So let's look briefly at how the model of comparative advantage helps in understanding both the causes and the effects of international trade.

Comparative Advantage and International Trade

Look at the label on a manufactured good sold in the United States, and there's a good chance you will find that it was produced in some other country—in China or Japan or even in Canada. On the other hand, many U.S. industries sell a large portion of their output overseas. (This is particularly true for the agriculture, high technology, and entertainment industries.)

Should we celebrate this international exchange of goods and services, or should it cause us concern? Politicians and the public often question the desirability of international trade, arguing that the nation should produce goods for itself rather than buy them from foreigners. Industries around the world demand protection from foreign competition: Japanese farmers want to keep out American rice, and American steelworkers want to keep out European steel. These demands are often supported by public opinion.

Economists, however, have a very positive view of international trade. Why? Because they view it in terms of comparative advantage. **Figure 4.3** shows, with a simple example, how international trade can be interpreted in terms of comparative advantage. Although the example is hypothetical, it is based on an actual pattern of international trade: American exports of pork to Canada and Canadian exports of aircraft to the United States. Panels (a) and (b) illustrate hypothetical production possibilities curves for the United States and Canada, with pork measured on the horizontal axis and aircraft measured on the vertical axis. The U.S. production possibilities curve is flatter than the Canadian production possibilities curve, implying that producing one more ton of pork costs fewer aircraft in the United States than it does in Canada. This means that the United States has a comparative advantage in pork and Canada has a comparative advantage in aircraft.

Although the consumption points in Figure 4.3 are hypothetical, they illustrate a general principle: just like the example of Tom and Hank, the United States and Canada can both achieve mutual gains from trade. If the United States concentrates on producing pork and sells some of its output to Canada, while Canada concentrates on aircraft and sells some of its output to the United States, both countries can consume more than if they insisted on being self-sufficient. For example, the United States could trade 1 million tons of pork for 1,500 aircraft from Canada. This would allow both countries to consume at a point outside of their production possibilities curves.

Moreover, these mutual gains don't depend on each country's being better at producing one kind of good. Even if one country has, say, higher output per person-hour in both industries–that is, even if one country has an absolute advantage in both industries–there are still mutual gains from trade.

Figure 4.3 Comparative Advantage and International Trade

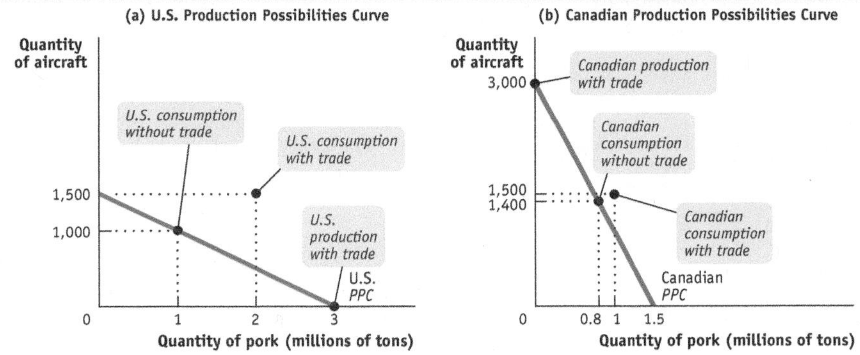

In this hypothetical example, Canada and the United States produce only two goods: pork and aircraft. Aircraft are measured on the vertical axis and pork on the horizontal axis. Panel (a) shows the U.S. production possibilities curve. It is relatively flat, implying that the United States has a comparative advantage in pork production. Panel (b) shows the Canadian production possibilities curve. It is relatively steep, implying that Canada has a comparative advantage in aircraft production. Just like two individuals, both countries gain from specialization and trade.

FOCUS Active Learning

TRM Assign **Worksheet 4.4 (Comparative Advantage)** from the TRM to ensure that students fully understand and can determine comparative advantage and calculate terms of trade.

FOCUS Flip It

For review and practice in calculating comparative advantage and terms of trade, have students watch Jacob Clifford's videos "Question 10—Comparative Advantage" and "Question 11—Terms of Trade" (see econextras video list with hyperlinks on the bcs and TRFD).

OPEN & CLOSE Exit Slip

TRM *Please see **Exit Slip: Module 4** in the TRM for formative multiple-choice questions to ask before finishing your lesson. These questions will help you quickly assess whether your students have mastered the module's concepts before moving on.*

Answers to the Exit Slip Questions

1. A
2. D
3. B

Answers to Module 4 Review Questions

Check Your Understanding

1. a. The United States has an absolute advantage in automobile production because it takes fewer workers (6) to produce a car in one day than it takes in Italy (8). The United States also has an absolute advantage in washing machine production because it takes fewer workers (2) to produce a washing machine in one day than it takes in Italy (3).

b. Creating a table with the data will help students as they tackle this question. In Italy, the opportunity cost of a washing machine in terms of an automobile is $\frac{3}{8}$. In other words, $\frac{3}{8}$ of a car can be produced with the same number of workers and in the same time it takes to produce 1 washing machine. In the United States, the opportunity cost of a washing machine in terms of an automobile is $\frac{2}{6} = \frac{1}{3}$. In other words, $\frac{1}{3}$ of a car can be produced with the same number of workers and in the same time it takes to produce 1 washing machine. Since $\frac{1}{3} < \frac{3}{8}$, the United States has a comparative advantage in the production of washing machines: to produce a washing machine, only $\frac{1}{3}$ of a car must be given up in the United States but $\frac{3}{8}$ of a car must be given up in Italy. This means that Italy has a comparative advantage in automobiles, which can be checked as follows. The opportunity cost of an automobile in terms of a washing machine in Italy is $\frac{8}{3}$, equal to $2\frac{2}{3}$. In other words, $2\frac{2}{3}$ washing machines can be produced with the same number of workers and in the time it takes to produce 1 car in Italy. And the opportunity cost of an automobile in terms of a washing machine in the United States is $\frac{6}{2}$, equal to 3. In other words, 3 washing machines can be produced with the same number of workers and in the time it takes to produce 1 car in the United States. Since $2\frac{2}{3}$ is less than 3, Italy has a comparative advantage in automobiles.

Number of workers	Italy	United States
Car	8	6
Washing Machine	3	2

c. The greatest gains are realized when each country specializes in producing the good for which it has a comparative advantage. Therefore, based on this example, the United States should specialize in washing machines and Italy should specialize in automobiles.

2. In a trade of 1 fish for $1\frac{1}{2}$ coconuts, Hank gives up less for a fish than he would if he were producing fish himself—that is, he gives up less than 2 coconuts for 1 fish. Likewise, Tom gives up less for a coconut than he would if he were producing coconuts himself—with trade, a coconut costs $\frac{2}{3}$ of a fish, less than the $\frac{4}{3}$ of a fish he must give up if he does not trade.

Tackle the Test: Multiple-Choice Questions

1. a
2. a
3. a
4. d
5. d

FYI — Rich Nation, Poor Nation

Try taking off your clothes—at a suitable time and in a suitable place, of course—and take a look at the labels inside that say where the clothes were made. It's a very good bet that much, if not most, of your clothing was manufactured overseas, in a country that is much poorer than the United States is—say, in El Salvador, Sri Lanka, or Bangladesh.

Why are these countries so much poorer than the United States? The immediate reason is that their economies are much less *productive*—firms in these countries are just not able to produce as much from a given quantity of resources as comparable firms in the United States or other wealthy countries. Why countries differ so much in productivity is a deep question—indeed, one of the main questions that preoccupy economists. But in any case, the difference in productivity is a fact.

If the economies of these countries are so much less productive than ours, how is it that they make so much of our clothing? Why don't we do it for ourselves?

The answer is "comparative advantage." Just about every industry in Bangladesh is much less productive than the corresponding industry in the United States. But the productivity difference between rich and poor countries varies across goods; there is a very great difference in the production of sophisticated goods such as aircraft but not as great a difference in the production of simpler goods such as clothing. So Bangladesh's position with regard to clothing production is like Hank's position with respect to coconut gathering: he's not as good at it as his fellow castaway is, but it's the thing he does comparatively well.

Although Bangladesh is at an absolute disadvantage compared with the United States in almost everything, it has a comparative advantage in clothing production.

Although less productive than American workers, Bangladeshi workers have a comparative advantage in clothing production.

This means that both the United States and Bangladesh are able to consume more because they specialize in producing different things, with Bangladesh supplying our clothing and the United States supplying Bangladesh with more sophisticated goods.

MODULE 4 Review

Check Your Understanding

1. In Italy, an automobile can be produced by 8 workers in one day and a washing machine by 3 workers in one day. In the United States, an automobile can be produced by 6 workers in one day, and a washing machine by 2 workers in one day.
   a. Which country has an absolute advantage in the production of automobiles? In washing machines?
   b. Which country has a comparative advantage in the production of washing machines? In automobiles?
   c. What type of specialization results in the greatest gains from trade between the two countries?
2. Refer to the story of Tom and Hank illustrated by Figure 4.1 in the text. Explain why Tom and Hank are willing to engage in a trade of 1 fish for $1\frac{1}{2}$ coconuts.

Tackle the Test: Multiple-Choice Questions

Refer to the graph below to answer the following questions.

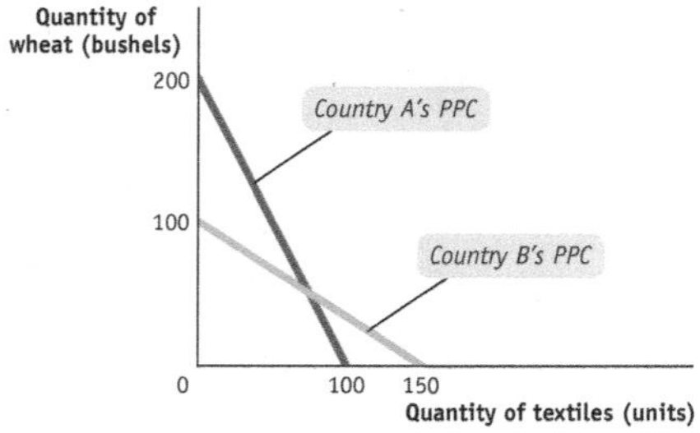

1. Use the graph to determine which country has an absolute advantage in producing each good.

	Absolute advantage in wheat production	*Absolute advantage in textile production*
a.	Country A	Country B
b.	Country A	Country A
c.	Country B	Country A
d.	Country B	Country B
e.	Country A	Neither country

2. For Country A, the opportunity cost of a bushel of wheat is
   a. ½ unit of textiles.
   b. ⅔ unit of textiles.
   c. 1⅓ units of textiles.
   d. 1½ units of textiles.
   e. 2 units of textiles.

3. Use the graph to determine which country has a comparative advantage in producing each good.

	Comparative advantage in wheat production	*Comparative advantage in textile production*
a.	Country A	Country B
b.	Country A	Country A
c.	Country B	Country A
d.	Country B	Country B
e.	Country A	Neither country

Tackle the Test: Free-Response Questions

1. Refer to the graph below to answer the following questions.

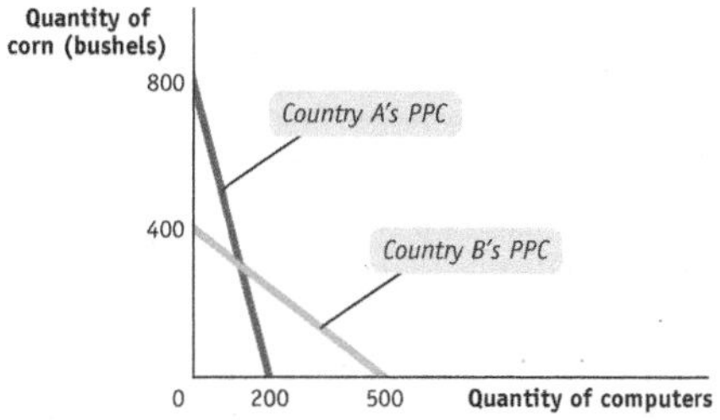

   a. What is the opportunity cost of a bushel of corn in each country?
   b. Which country has an absolute advantage in computer production? Explain.
   c. Which country has a comparative advantage in corn production? Explain.
   d. If each country specializes, what good will Country B import? Explain.
   e. What is the minimum price Country A will accept to export corn to Country B? Explain.

Rubric for FRQ 1 (9 points)

1 point: Country A, ¼ computer; Country B, 1¼ computers

1 point: Country B

1 point: Because Country B can produce more computers than Country A (500 versus 200)

1 point: Country A

1 point: Because Country A can produce corn at a lower opportunity cost (¼ versus 1¼ computers)

1 point: Corn

1 point: Country B has a comparative advantage in the production of computers, so it will produce computers and import corn (Country A has a comparative advantage in corn production, so it will specialize in corn and import computers from Country B).

1 point: ¼ computer

1 point: Country A's opportunity cost of producing corn is ¼ computer, so that is the lowest price it will accept to sell corn to Country B.

4. If the two countries specialize and trade, which of the choices below describes the countries' imports?

	Import wheat	*Import textiles*
a.	Country A	Country A
b.	Country A	Country B
c.	Country B	Country B
d.	Country B	Country A
e.	Neither country	Country B

5. What is the highest price Country B is willing to pay to buy wheat from Country A?
   a. ½ unit of textiles
   b. ⅔ unit of textiles
   c. 1 unit of textiles
   d. 1½ units of textiles
   e. 2 units of textiles

2. Refer to the table below to answer the following questions. These two countries are producing textiles and wheat using equal amounts of resources.

	Weekly output per worker	
	Country A	Country B
Bushels of wheat	15	10
Units of textiles	60	60

   a. What is the opportunity cost of producing a bushel of wheat for each country?
   b. Which country has the absolute advantage in wheat production?
   c. Which country has the comparative advantage in textile production? Explain.
   (5 points)

Tackle the Test: Free-Response Question Rubric for FRQ 2 (5 points)

1 point: Country A: opportunity cost of 1 bushel of wheat = 4 units of textiles.

1 point: Country B: opportunity cost of 1 bushel of wheat = 6 units of textiles.

1 point: Country A has an absolute advantage in the production of wheat. With the same resources, Country A can produce more bushels of wheat (15) than can Country B (10).

1 point: Country B has the comparative advantage in textile production.

1 point: Country B has a lower opportunity cost of producing textiles:

Country A: opportunity cost of 1 unit of textiles = $\frac{1}{4}$ bushel of wheat

Country B: opportunity cost of 1 unit of textiles = $\frac{1}{6}$ bushel of wheat

Alternate answer: Country B has the comparative advantage in the production of textiles because Country A has a comparative advantage in the production of wheat based on opportunity costs shown in part a.

Module 4 Comparative Advantage and Trade 31

FOCUS **Flip It**

Encourage your students to watch the **Section 1 Review Video**, which was created as a special student review tool and is linked into the e-Book or can be found on the book's companion website.

SECTION 1 Review

Section 1 Review Video

Module 1

1. Everyone has to make choices about what to do and what *not* to do. **Individual choice** is the basis of **economics**—if it doesn't involve choice, it isn't economics. The **economy** is a system that coordinates choices about production and consumption. In a **market economy**, these choices are made by many firms and individuals. In a **command economy**, these choices are made by a central authority. **Incentives** are rewards or punishments that motivate particular choices, and can be lacking in a command economy where producers cannot set their own prices or keep their own profits. **Property rights** create incentives in market economies by establishing ownership and granting individuals the right to trade goods and services for mutual gain. In any economy, decisions are informed by **marginal analysis**—the study of the costs and benefits of doing something a little bit more or a little bit less.
2. The reason choices must be made is that **resources**—anything that can be used to produce something else—are **scarce.** The four categories of resources are **land**, **labor**, **capital**, and **entrepreneurship**. Individuals are limited in their choices by money and time; economies are limited by their supplies of resources.
3. Because you must choose among limited alternatives, the true cost of anything is what you must give up to get it—all costs are **opportunity costs**.
4. Economists use economic models for both **positive economics**, which describes how the economy works, and for **normative economics**, which prescribes how the economy *should* work. Positive economics often involves making forecasts. Economics can determine correct answers for positive questions, but typically not for normative questions, which involve value judgments. Exceptions occur when policies designed to achieve a certain prescription can be clearly ranked in terms of preference.
5. There are two main reasons economists disagree. One, they may disagree about which simplifications to make in a model. Two, economists may disagree—like everyone else—about values.
6. **Microeconomics** is the branch of economics that studies how people make decisions and how those decisions interact. **Macroeconomics** is concerned with the overall ups and downs of the economy, and focuses on **economic aggregates** such as the unemployment rate and gross domestic product, that summarize data across many different markets.

Module 2

7. Economies experience ups and downs in economic activity. This pattern is called the **business cycle**. The downturns are known as **recessions;** the upturns are known as **expansions**. A **depression** is a long, deep downturn.
8. Workers are counted in **unemployment** figures only if they are actively seeking work but aren't currently employed. The sum of **employment** and unemployment is the **labor force**. The **unemployment rate** is the percentage of the labor force that is unemployed.
9. As the unemployment rate rises, the output for the economy as a whole—the **aggregate output**—generally falls.
10. A short-term increase in aggregate output made possible by a decrease in unemployment does not constitute **economic growth**, which is an increase in the maximum amount of output an economy can produce.
11. Rises and falls in the overall price level constitute **inflation** and **deflation**. Economists prefer that prices change only slowly if at all, because such **price stability** helps keep the economy stable.
12. Almost all economics is based on **models**, "thought experiments" or simplified versions of reality, many of which use analytical tools such as mathematics and graphs. An important assumption in economic models is the **other things equal (*ceteris paribus*) assumption**, which allows analysis of the effect of change in one factor by holding all other relevant factors unchanged.

Module 3

13. One important economic model is the **production possibilities curve**, which illustrates the **trade-offs** facing an economy that produces only two goods. The production possibilities curve illustrates three elements: opportunity cost (showing how much less of one good must be produced if more of the other good is produced), **efficiency** (an economy achieves **productive efficiency** if it produces on the production possibilities curve and **allocative efficiency** if it produces the mix of goods and services that people want to consume), and economic growth (an outward shift of the production possibilities curve).
14. There are two basic sources of growth in the production possibilities curve model: an increase in resources and improved **technology**.

32 Section 1 Basic Economic Concepts

Module 4

15. There are **gains from trade**: by engaging in the **trade** of goods and services with one another, the members of an economy can all be made better off. Underlying gains from trade are the advantages of **specialization**, of having individuals specialize in the tasks they are comparatively good at.

16. **Comparative advantage** explains the source of gains from trade between individuals and countries. Everyone has a comparative advantage in something—some good or service in which that person has a lower opportunity cost than everyone else. But it is often confused with **absolute advantage**, an ability to produce more of a particular good or service than anyone else. This confusion leads some to erroneously conclude that there are no gains from trade between people or countries.

17. As long as a comparative advantage exists between two parties, there are opportunities for mutually beneficial trade. The **terms of trade** indicate the rate at which one good can be exchanged for another. The range of mutually beneficial terms of trade for a good are found between the seller's opportunity cost of making the good and the buyer's opportunity cost of making the same good.

Key Terms

Economics, p. 2
Individual choice, p. 2
Economy, p. 2
Market economy, p. 2
Command economy, p. 2
Incentives, p. 3
Property rights, p. 3
Marginal analysis, p. 3
Resource, p. 3
Land, p. 3
Labor, p. 3
Capital, p. 3
Entrepreneurship, p. 3
Scarce, p. 3
Opportunity cost, p. 4
Microeconomics, p. 5
Macroeconomics, p. 5
Economic aggregates, p. 5
Positive economics, p. 6
Normative economics, p. 6
Business cycle, p. 11
Depression, p. 11
Recessions, p. 11
Expansions, p. 11
Employment, p. 11
Unemployment, p. 11
Labor force, p. 12
Unemployment rate, p. 12
Output, p. 12
Aggregate output, p. 12
Inflation, p. 13
Deflation, p. 13
Price stability, p. 13
Economic growth, p. 13
Model, p. 14
Other things equal (*ceteris paribus*) assumption, p. 14
Trade-off, p. 16
Production possibilities curve, p. 17
Efficient, p. 18
Productive efficiency, p. 18
Allocative efficiency, p. 18
Technology, p. 21
Trade, p. 24
Gains from trade, p. 24
Specialization, p. 24
Comparative advantage, p. 27
Absolute advantage, p. 27
Terms of trade, p. 28

AP® Exam Practice Questions

Multiple-Choice Questions

1. In a market economy, most choices about production and consumption are made by which of the following?
   a. politicians
   b. many individuals and firms
   c. the government
   d. managers
   e. economists

2. Which of the following pairs indicates a category of resources and an example of that resource?

	Category	*Example*
a.	money	investment
b.	capital	money
c.	capital	minerals
d.	land	factory
e.	land	timber

3. You can either go to a movie or study for an exam. Which of the following is an opportunity cost of studying for the exam?
   a. a higher grade on the exam
   b. the price of a movie ticket
   c. the cost of paper, pens, books, and other study materials
   d. the enjoyment from seeing the movie
   e. the sense of achievement from learning

Answers to Section 1 AP® Exam Practice Questions

Multiple-Choice Questions

1. b
2. e
3. d

4. d	7. d	10. b
5. c	8. c	11. a
6. a	9. a	12. c

4. Which of the following situations is explained by increasing opportunity costs?
   a. More people go to college when the job market is good.
   b. More people do their own home repairs when hourly wages fall.
   c. There are more parks in crowded cities than in suburban areas.
   d. Convenience stores cater to busy people.
   e. People with higher wages are more likely to mow their own lawns.

5. Which of the following is a normative statement?
   a. The unemployment rate is expected to rise.
   b. Individuals purchase more of a good when the price rises.
   c. The government should increase the minimum wage.
   d. An increase in the tax rate on wage earnings reduces the incentive to work.
   e. Public education generates greater benefits than costs.

6. Falling output in an economy is consistent with which of the following?
   a. a recession
   b. an expansion
   c. a recovery
   d. falling unemployment
   e. long-term economic growth

7. Which of the following is a goal for the macroeconomy?
   a. declining labor force
   b. inflation
   c. deflation
   d. rising aggregate output
   e. rising unemployment rate

Refer to the following table and information for Questions 8–11.

Suppose that Atlantis is a small, isolated island in the South Atlantic. The inhabitants grow potatoes and catch fish. The following table shows the maximum annual output combinations of potatoes and fish that can be produced.

Maximum annual output options	Quantity of potatoes (pounds)	Quantity of fish (pounds)
A	1,000	0
B	800	300
C	600	500
D	400	600
E	200	650
F	0	675

8. Atlantis can produce which of the following combinations of output?

	Pounds of potatoes	*Pounds of fish*
a.	1,000	675
b.	600	600
c.	400	600
d.	300	800
e.	200	675

9. If Atlantis is efficient in production, what is the opportunity cost of increasing the annual output of potatoes from 600 to 800 pounds?
   a. 200 pounds of fish
   b. 300 pounds of fish
   c. 500 pounds of fish
   d. 675 pounds of fish
   e. 800 pounds of fish

10. As Atlantis produces more potatoes, what is true about the opportunity cost of producing potatoes?
   a. It stays the same.
   b. It continually increases.
   c. It continually decreases.
   d. It increases and then decreases.
   e. It decreases and then increases.

11. Which of the following combinations of output is efficient?

	Pounds of potatoes	*Pounds of fish*
a.	1,000	0
b.	600	600
c.	400	500
d.	500	400
e.	0	0

Refer to the following information for Questions 12–13.

In the ancient country of Roma, only two goods—spaghetti and meatballs—are produced. There are two tribes in Roma, the Tivoli and the Frivoli. By themselves, in a given month, the Tivoli can produce 30 pounds of spaghetti and no meatballs, 50 pounds of meatballs and no spaghetti, or any combination in between. In the same month, the Frivoli can produce 40 pounds of spaghetti and no meatballs, 30 pounds of meatballs and no spaghetti, or any combination in between.

12. Which tribe has a comparative advantage in meatball and spaghetti production?

	Meatballs	*Spaghetti*
a.	Tivoli	Tivoli
b.	Frivoli	Frivoli
c.	Tivoli	Frivoli
d.	Frivoli	Tivoli
e.	neither	both

13. In A.D. 100, the Frivoli discovered a new technique for making meatballs and doubled the quantity of meatballs they could produce each month. After the discovery of this new technique in Frivoli only, which tribe had an absolute advantage in meatball production and which had a comparative advantage in meatball production?

	Absolute advantage	*Comparative advantage*
a.	Tivoli	Tivoli
b.	Frivoli	Frivoli
c.	Tivoli	Frivoli
d.	Frivoli	Tivoli
e.	Frivoli	both

14. Which of the following is a basic source of economic growth in the production possibilities model?
    a. specialization
    b. efficiency
    c. opportunity cost
    d. trade-offs
    e. improved technology

15. Comparative advantage explains which of the following?
    a. a country's ability to produce more of a particular good or service
    b. when production is considered efficient
    c. why the production possibilities curve is bowed outward
    d. the source of gains from trade
    e. why the production possibilities curve shifts outward

Free-Response Question

The Hatfield family lives on the east side of the Hatatoochie River and the McCoy family lives on the west side. Each family's diet consists of fried chicken and corn on the cob, and each is self-sufficient, raising its own chickens and growing its own corn.

Assume the Hatfield family has a comparative advantage in the production of corn.

1. Draw a correctly labeled graph showing a hypothetical production possibilities curve for the McCoy family.
2. Which family has the comparative advantage in the production of chickens? Explain.
3. Assuming that each family is producing efficiently, how can the two families increase their consumption of both chicken and corn?
   (5 points)

13. d
14. e
15. d

Rubric for Free-Response Question

1 point: A graph with axes labeled "Quantity of chickens" and "Quantity of corn"

1 point: A negatively-sloped production possibilities curve

1 point: A statement that the McCoy family has the comparative advantage in the production of chickens

1 point: An explanation that the McCoy family must have the comparative advantage in the production of chickens because the Hatfield family has the comparative advantage in the production of corn

1 point: The Hatfields specialize in corn, and the McCoys specialize in chicken. The two families can increase their consumption of both chicken and corn through specialization and trade.

Please see page SG-1 for sample student graphs for this Free-Response Question.

TEACH Teach It

Use this section if you have students whose graphing skills are weak. Make sure all students understand that in a graph of supply and demand, price is the independent variable and on the vertical axis, while quantity will always be on the horizontal axis.

TEACH Teach It

TRM Depending on the needs of your students, you can either assign this appendix as homework, or you can spend a class period working with students on these essential graphing skills.

SECTION 1 APPENDIX

Graphs in Economics

In this Appendix, you will learn to:

- Recognize the importance of graphs in studying economics
- Describe the basic components of a graph
- Explain how graphs illustrate the relationship between variables
- Explain how to calculate the slope of a line or curve and discuss what the slope value means
- Describe how to calculate areas represented on graphs
- Explain how to interpret numerical graphs

Getting the Picture

Whether you're reading about economics in the *Wall Street Journal* or in your economics textbook, you will see many graphs. Visual presentations can make it much easier to understand verbal descriptions, numerical information, or ideas. In economics, graphs are the type of visual presentation used to facilitate understanding. To fully understand the ideas and information being discussed, you need to know how to interpret these visual aids. This module explains how graphs are constructed and interpreted and how they are used in economics.

Graphs, Variables, and Economic Models

A **variable** is a measure that can take on more than one value.

One reason to attend college is that a bachelor's degree provides access to higher-paying jobs. Additional degrees, such as MBAs or law degrees, increase earnings even more. If you were to read an article about the relationship between educational attainment and income, you would probably see a graph showing the income levels for workers with different levels of education. This graph would depict the idea that, in general, having more education increases a person's income. This graph, like most graphs in economics, would depict the relationship between two economic variables. A **variable** is a measure that can take on more than one value, such as the number of years of education a person has, the price of a can of soda, or a household's income.

As you learned in this section, economic analysis relies heavily on *models*, simplified representations of real situations. Most economic models describe the relationship between two variables, simplified by holding constant other variables that may affect the relationship. For example, an economic model might describe the relationship between the price of a can of soda and the number of cans of soda that consumers will buy, assuming that everything else that affects consumers' purchases of soda stays constant. This type of model can be depicted mathematically, but illustrating the relationship in a graph makes it easier to understand. Next we show how graphs that depict economic models are constructed and interpreted.

How Graphs Work

Most graphs in economics are based on a grid built around two perpendicular lines that show the values of two variables, helping you visualize the relationship between them. So a first step in understanding the use of such graphs is to see how this system works.

Two-Variable Graphs

Figure A.1 shows a typical two-variable graph. It illustrates the data in the accompanying table on outside temperature and the number of sodas a typical vendor can expect to sell at a baseball stadium during one game. The first column shows the values of outside temperature (the first variable) and the second column shows the values of the number of sodas sold (the second variable). Five combinations or pairs of the two variables are shown, denoted by points *A* through *E* in the third column.

Figure A.1 Plotting Points on a Two-Variable Graph

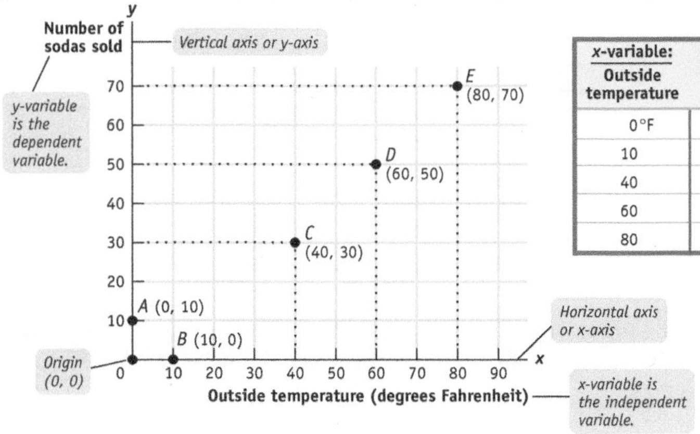

x-variable: Outside temperature	y-variable: Number of sodas sold	Point
0°F	10	*A*
10	0	*B*
40	30	*C*
60	50	*D*
80	70	*E*

The data from the table are plotted where outside temperature (the independent variable) is measured along the horizontal axis and number of sodas sold (the dependent variable) is measured along the vertical axis. Each of the five combinations of temperature and sodas sold is represented by a point: *A*, *B*, *C*, *D*, or *E*. Each point in the graph is identified by a pair of values. For example, point *C* corresponds to the pair (40, 30)—an outside temperature of 40°F (the value of the *x*-variable) and 30 sodas sold (the value of the *y*-variable).

Now let's turn to graphing the data in this table. In any two-variable graph, one variable is called the *x*-variable and the other is called the *y*-variable. Here we have made outside temperature the *x*-variable and number of sodas sold the *y*-variable. The solid horizontal line in the graph is called the **horizontal axis** or ***x*-axis**, and values of the *x*-variable—outside temperature—are measured along it. Similarly, the solid vertical line in the graph is called the **vertical axis** or ***y*-axis**, and values of the *y*-variable—number of sodas sold—are measured along it. At the **origin**, the point where the two axes meet, each variable is equal to zero. As you move rightward from the origin along the *x*-axis, values of the *x*-variable are positive and increasing. As you move up from the origin along the *y*-axis, values of the *y*-variable are positive and increasing.

The solid horizontal line on a graph is called the **horizontal axis** or ***x*-axis**.

The solid vertical line on a graph is called the **vertical axis** or ***y*-axis**.

The two axes meet at the **origin**.

You can plot each of the five points *A* through *E* on this graph by using a pair of numbers—the values that the *x*-variable and the *y*-variable take on for a given point. In Figure A.1, at point *C*, the *x*-variable takes on the value 40 and the *y*-variable takes on the value 30. You plot point *C* by drawing a line straight up from 40 on the *x*-axis and a horizontal line across from 30 on the *y*-axis. We write point *C* as (40, 30). We write the origin as (0, 0).

Looking at point *A* and point *B* in Figure A.1, you can see that when one of the variables for a point has a value of zero, it will lie on one of the axes. If the value of the *x*-variable is

Appendix Graphs in Economics 37

A **causal relationship** is one in which the value taken by one variable directly influences or determines the value taken by the other variable.

In a causal relationship, the determining variable is called the **independent variable** and the determined variable is called the **dependent variable**.

A line on a graph is called a **curve**, regardless of whether it is a straight line or a curved line.

If a curve that shows the relationship between two variables is a straight line, or linear, the variables have a **linear relationship**.

When a curve is not a straight line, or nonlinear, the variables have a **nonlinear relationship**.

zero, the point will lie on the vertical axis, like point *A*. If the value of the *y*-variable is zero, the point will lie on the horizontal axis, like point *B*. (The location of point *B* was chosen to illustrate this fact and not because soda sales will really decrease when the temperature rises.)

Most graphs that depict relationships between two economic variables represent a **causal relationship**, a relationship in which the value taken by one variable directly influences or determines the value taken by the other variable. In a causal relationship, the determining variable is called the **independent variable**; the variable it determines is called the **dependent variable**. In our example of soda sales, the outside temperature is the independent variable. It directly influences the number of sodas that are sold, which is the dependent variable in this case.

By convention, we put the independent variable on the horizontal axis and the dependent variable on the vertical axis. Figure A.1 is constructed consistent with this convention: the independent variable (outside temperature) is on the horizontal axis and the dependent variable (number of sodas sold) is on the vertical axis. An important exception to this convention is in graphs showing the economic relationship between the price of a product and quantity of the product: although price is generally the independent variable that determines quantity, it is always measured on the vertical axis.

Curves on a Graph

Panel (a) of **Figure A.2** contains some of the same information as Figure A.1, with a line drawn through the points *B, C, D,* and *E*. Such a line on a graph is called a **curve**, regardless of whether it is a straight line or a curved line. If the curve that shows the relationship between two variables is a straight line, or linear, the variables have a **linear relationship**. When the curve is not a straight line, or nonlinear, the variables have a **nonlinear relationship**.

Figure A.2 Drawing Curves

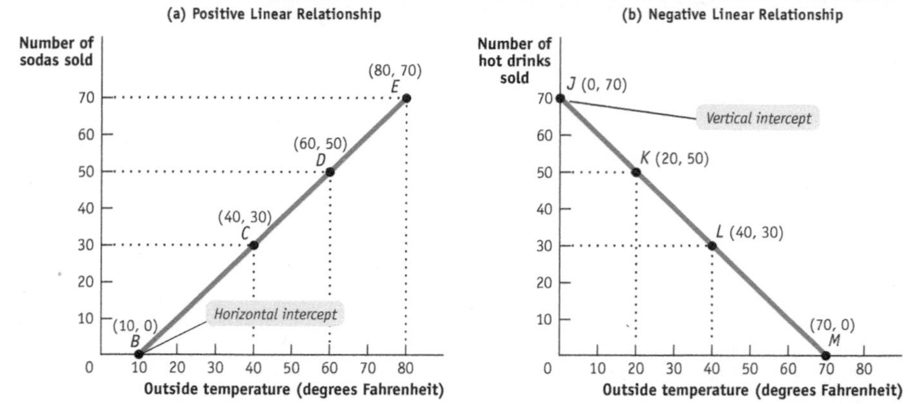

The curve in panel (a) illustrates the relationship between the two variables, outside temperature and number of sodas sold. The two variables have a positive linear relationship: positive because the curve has an upward tilt, and linear because it is a straight line. The curve implies that an increase in the *x*-variable (outside temperature) leads to an increase in the *y*-variable (number of sodas sold). The curve in panel (b) is also a straight line, but it tilts downward. The two variables here, outside temperature and number of hot drinks sold, have a negative linear relationship: an increase in the *x*-variable (outside temperature) leads to a decrease in the *y*-variable (number of hot drinks sold). The curve in panel (a) has a horizontal intercept at point B, where it hits the horizontal axis. The curve in panel (b) has a vertical intercept at point *J*, where it hits the vertical axis, and a horizontal intercept at point *M*, where it hits the horizontal axis.

38 Section 1 Basic Economic Concepts

A point on a curve indicates the value of the y-variable for a specific value of the x-variable. For example, point D indicates that at a temperature of 60°F, a vendor can expect to sell 50 sodas. The shape and orientation of a curve reveal the general nature of the relationship between the two variables. The upward tilt of the curve in panel (a) of Figure A.2 suggests that vendors can expect to sell more sodas at higher outside temperatures.

When variables are related in this way—that is, when an increase in one variable is associated with an increase in the other variable—the variables are said to have a **positive relationship**. It is illustrated by a curve that slopes upward from left to right. Because this curve is also linear, the relationship between outside temperature and number of sodas sold illustrated by the curve in panel (a) of Figure A.2 is a positive linear relationship.

When an increase in one variable is associated with a decrease in the other variable, the two variables are said to have a **negative relationship**. It is illustrated by a curve that slopes downward from left to right, like the curve in panel (b) of Figure A.2. Because this curve is also linear, the relationship it depicts is a negative linear relationship. Two variables that might have such a relationship are the outside temperature and the number of hot drinks a vendor can expect to sell at a baseball stadium.

Return for a moment to the curve in panel (a) of Figure A.2, and you can see that it hits the horizontal axis at point B. This point, known as the **horizontal intercept**, shows the value of the x-variable when the value of the y-variable is zero. In panel (b) of Figure A.2, the curve hits the vertical axis at point J. This point, called the **vertical intercept**, indicates the value of the y-variable when the value of the x-variable is zero.

When an increase in one variable is associated with an increase in the other variable, the variables are said to have a **positive relationship**.

When an increase in one variable is associated with a decrease in the other variable, the two variables are said to have a **negative relationship**.

The **horizontal intercept** indicates the value of the x-variable when the value of the y-variable is zero.

The **vertical intercept** indicates the value of the y-variable when the value of the x-variable is zero.

The **slope** of a curve is a measure of how steep it is; the slope indicates how sensitive the y-variable is to a change in the x-variable.

A Key Concept: The Slope of a Curve

The **slope** of a curve is a measure of how steep it is; the slope indicates how sensitive the y-variable is to a change in the x-variable. In our example of outside temperature and the number of cans of soda a vendor can expect to sell, the slope of the curve would indicate how many more cans of soda the vendor could expect to sell with each 1° increase in temperature. Interpreted this way, the slope gives meaningful information. Even without numbers for x and y, it is possible to arrive at important conclusions about the relationship between the two variables by examining the slope of a curve at various points.

The Slope of a Linear Curve

Along a linear curve the slope, or steepness, is measured by dividing the "rise" between two points on the curve by the "run" between those same two points. The rise is the amount that y changes, and the run is the amount that x changes. Here is the formula:

$$\frac{\text{Change in } y}{\text{Change in } x} = \frac{\Delta y}{\Delta x} = \text{slope}$$

In the formula, the symbol Δ (the Greek uppercase delta) stands for "change in." When a variable increases, the change in that variable is positive; when a variable decreases, the change in that variable is negative.

The slope of a curve is positive when the rise (the change in the y-variable) has the same sign as the run (the change in the x-variable). That's because when two numbers have the same sign, the ratio of those two numbers is positive. The curve in panel (a) of Figure A.2 has a positive slope: along the curve, both the y-variable and the x-variable increase. The slope of a curve is negative when the rise and the run have different signs. That's because when two numbers have different signs, the ratio of those two numbers is negative. The curve in panel (b) of Figure A.2 has a negative slope: along the curve, an increase in the x-variable is associated with a decrease in the y-variable.

Figure A.3 on the next page illustrates how to calculate the slope of a linear curve. Let's focus first on panel (a). From point A to point B the value of the y-variable changes from 25 to 20 and the value of the x-variable changes from 10 to 20. So the slope of the line between these two points is

$$\frac{\text{Change in } y}{\text{Change in } x} = \frac{\Delta y}{\Delta x} = \frac{-5}{10} = -\frac{1}{2} = -0.5$$

Appendix Graphs in Economics **39**

Figure A.3 Calculating the Slope

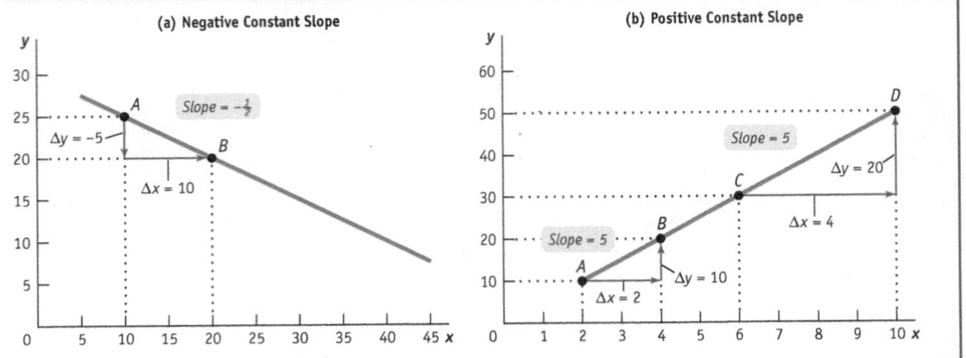

Panels (a) and (b) show two linear curves. Between points A and B on the curve in panel (a), the change in *y* (the rise) is −5 and the change in *x* (the run) is 10. So the slope from *A* to *B* is $\frac{\Delta y}{\Delta x} = \frac{-5}{10} = -\frac{1}{2} = -0.5$, where the negative sign indicates that the curve is downward sloping. In panel (b), the curve has a slope from *A* to *B* of $\frac{\Delta y}{\Delta x} = \frac{10}{2} = 5$. The slope from *C* to *D* is $\frac{\Delta y}{\Delta x} = \frac{20}{4} = 5$. The slope is positive, indicating that the curve is upward sloping. Furthermore, the slope between *A* and *B* is the same as the slope between *C* and *D*, making this a linear curve. The slope of a linear curve is constant: it is the same regardless of where it is calculated along the curve.

Because a straight line is equally steep at all points, the slope of a straight line is the same at all points. In other words, a straight line has a constant slope. You can check this by calculating the slope of the linear curve between points *A* and *B* and between points *C* and *D* in panel (b) of Figure A.3.

$$\frac{\Delta y}{\Delta x} = \frac{10}{2} = 5$$

$$\frac{\Delta y}{\Delta x} = \frac{20}{4} = 5$$

Horizontal and Vertical Curves and Their Slopes

When a curve is horizontal, the value of *y* along that curve never changes—it is constant. Everywhere along the curve, the change in *y* is zero. Now, zero divided by any number is zero. So regardless of the value of the change in *x*, the slope of a horizontal curve is always zero.

If a curve is vertical, the value of *x* along the curve never changes—it is constant. Everywhere along the curve, the change in *x* is zero. This means that the slope of a vertical line is a ratio with zero in the denominator. A ratio with zero in the denominator is equal to infinity—that is, an infinitely large number. So the slope of a vertical line is equal to infinity.

A vertical or a horizontal curve has a special implication: it means that the *x*-variable and the *y*-variable are unrelated. Two variables are unrelated when a change in one variable (the independent variable) has no effect on the other variable (the dependent variable). To put it a slightly different way, two variables are unrelated when the dependent variable is constant regardless of the value of the independent variable. If, as is usual, the *y*-variable is the dependent variable, the curve is horizontal. If the dependent variable is the *x*-variable, the curve is vertical.

40 Section 1 Basic Economic Concepts

The Slope of a Nonlinear Curve

A **nonlinear curve** is one along which the slope changes. Panels (a), (b), (c), and (d) of **Figure A.4** show various nonlinear curves. Panels (a) and (b) show nonlinear curves whose slopes change as you follow the line's progression, but the slopes always remain positive. Although both curves tilt upward, the curve in panel (a) gets steeper as the line moves from left to right in contrast to the curve in panel (b), which gets flatter. A curve

A **nonlinear curve** is one along which the slope changes.

Figure A.4 Nonlinear Curves

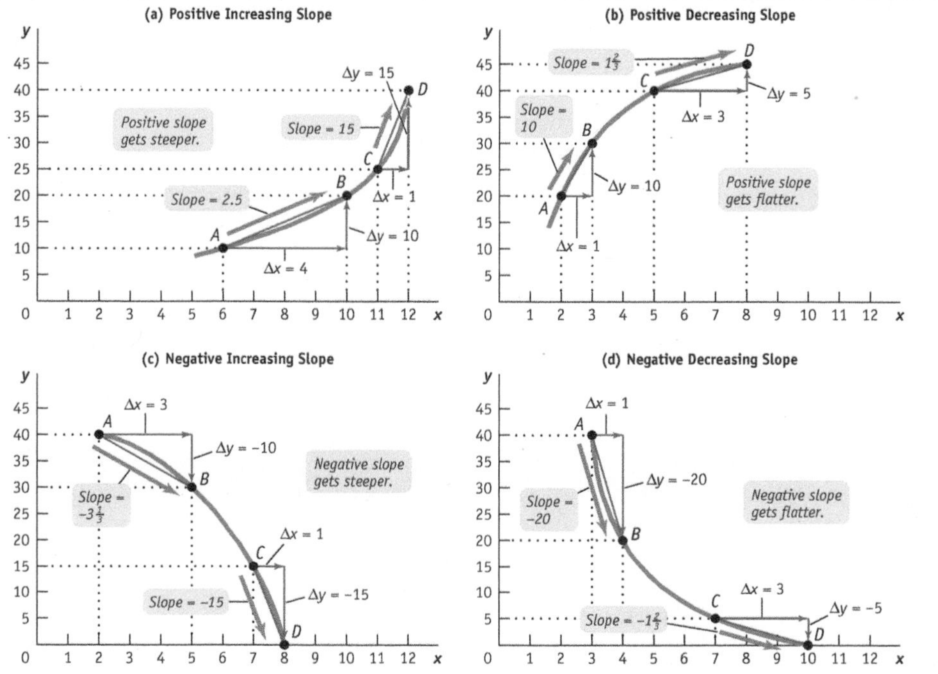

In panel (a) the slope of the curve from A to B is $\frac{\Delta y}{\Delta x} = \frac{10}{4} = 2.5$, and from C to D it is $\frac{\Delta y}{\Delta x} = \frac{15}{1} = 15$. The slope is positive and increasing; it gets steeper as it moves to the right. In panel (b) the slope of the curve from A to B is $\frac{\Delta y}{\Delta x} = \frac{10}{1} = 10$, and from C to D it is $\frac{\Delta y}{\Delta x} = \frac{5}{3} = 1\frac{2}{3}$. The slope is positive and decreasing; it gets flatter as it moves to the right. In panel (c) the slope from A to B is $\frac{\Delta y}{\Delta x} = \frac{-10}{3} = -3\frac{1}{3}$, and from C to D it is $\frac{\Delta y}{\Delta x} = \frac{-15}{1} = -15$. The slope is negative and increasing; it gets steeper as it moves to the right. And in panel (d) the slope from A to B is $\frac{\Delta y}{\Delta x} = \frac{-20}{1} = -20$, and from C to D it is $\frac{\Delta y}{\Delta x} = \frac{-5}{3} = -1\frac{2}{3}$. The slope is negative and decreasing; it gets flatter as it moves to the right. The slope in each case has been calculated by using the *arc method*—that is, by drawing a straight line connecting two points along a curve. The average slope between those two points is equal to the slope of the straight line between those two points.

Appendix Graphs in Economics **41**

that is upward sloping and gets steeper, as in panel (a), is said to have *positive increasing* slope. A curve that is upward sloping but gets flatter, as in panel (b), is said to have *positive decreasing* slope.

When we calculate the slope along these nonlinear curves, we obtain different values for the slope at different points. How the slope changes along the curve determines the curve's shape. For example, in panel (a) of Figure A.4, the slope of the curve is a positive number that steadily increases as the line moves from left to right, whereas in panel (b), the slope is a positive number that steadily decreases.

The **absolute value** of a number is the value of that number without a minus sign, whether or not the number was negative to begin with.

The slopes of the curves in panels (c) and (d) are negative numbers. Economists often prefer to express a negative number as its **absolute value**, which is the value of the negative number without the minus sign. In general, we denote the absolute value of a number by two parallel bars around the number; for example, the absolute value of -4 is written as $|-4| = 4$. In panel (c), the absolute value of the slope steadily increases as the line moves from left to right. The curve therefore has *negative increasing* slope. And in panel (d), the absolute value of the slope of the curve steadily decreases along the curve. This curve therefore has *negative decreasing* slope.

Maximum and Minimum Points

The slope of a nonlinear curve can change from positive to negative or vice versa. When the slope of a curve changes from positive to negative, it creates what is called a *maximum* point of the curve. When the slope of a curve changes from negative to positive, it creates a *minimum* point.

The point along a curve with the largest value of *y* is called the **maximum** of the curve.

Panel (a) of **Figure A.5** illustrates a curve in which the slope changes from positive to negative as the line moves from left to right. When x is between 0 and 50, the slope of the curve is positive. When x equals 50, the curve attains its highest point—the largest value of y along the curve. This point is called the **maximum** of the curve. When x exceeds 50, the slope becomes negative as the curve turns downward. Many important curves in economics, such as the curve that represents how the profit of a firm changes as it produces more output, are hill-shaped like this one.

Figure A.5 Maximum and Minimum Points

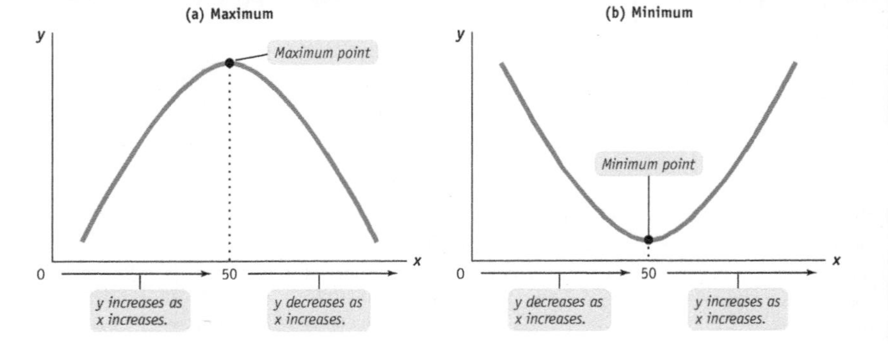

Panel (a) shows a curve with a maximum point, the point at which the slope changes from positive to negative. Panel (b) shows a curve with a minimum point, the point at which the slope changes from negative to positive.

42 Section 1 Basic Economic Concepts

In contrast, the curve shown in panel (b) of Figure A.5 is U-shaped: it has a slope that changes from negative to positive. When x equals 50, the curve reaches its lowest point—the smallest value of y along the curve. This point is called the **minimum** of the curve. Various important curves in economics, such as the curve that represents how a firm's cost per unit changes as output increases, are U-shaped like this one.

The point along a curve with the smallest value of y is called the **minimum** of the curve.

Calculating the Area Below or Above a Curve

Sometimes it is useful to be able to measure the size of the area below or above a curve. To keep things simple, we'll only calculate the area below or above a linear curve.

How large is the shaded area below the linear curve in panel (a) of **Figure A.6**? First, note that this area has the shape of a right triangle. A right triangle is a triangle in which two adjacent sides form a 90° angle. We will refer to one of these sides as the *height* of the triangle and the other side as the *base* of the triangle. For our purposes, it doesn't matter which of these two sides we refer to as the base and which as the height. Calculating the area of a right triangle is straightforward: multiply the height of the triangle by the base of the triangle, and divide the result by 2. The height of the triangle in panel (a) of Figure A.6 is 10 – 4 = 6. And the base of the triangle is 3 – 0 = 3. So the area of that triangle is

Figure A.6 Calculating the Area Below and Above a Linear Curve

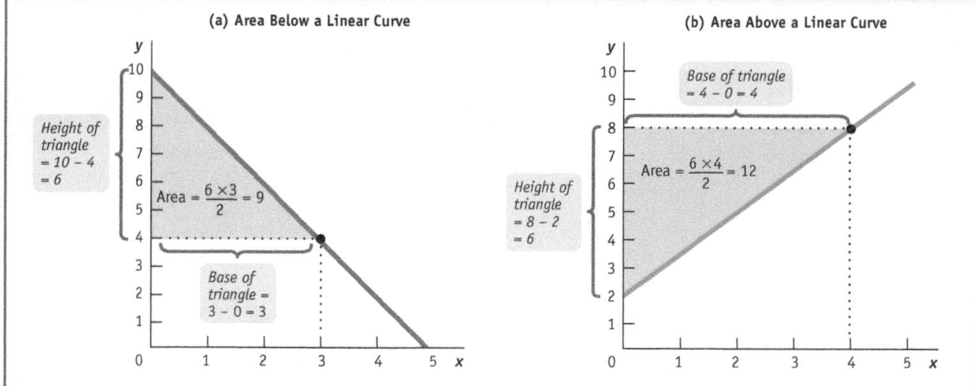

The area below or above a linear curve forms a right triangle. The area of a right triangle is calculated by multiplying the height of the triangle by the base of the triangle, and dividing the result by 2. In panel (a) the area of the shaded triangle is 9. In panel (b) the area of the shaded triangle is 12.

$$\frac{6 \times 3}{2} = 9$$

How about the shaded area above the linear curve in panel (b) of Figure A.6? We can use the same formula to calculate the area of this right triangle. The height of the triangle is 8 – 2 = 6. And the base of the triangle is 4 – 0 = 4. So the area of that triangle is

$$\frac{6 \times 4}{2} = 12$$

Appendix Graphs in Economics **43**

Graphs That Depict Numerical Information

Graphs can also be used as a convenient way to summarize and display data without assuming some underlying causal relationship. Graphs that simply display numerical information are called *numerical graphs*. Here we will consider four types of numerical graphs: *time-series graphs, scatter diagrams, pie charts,* and *bar graphs*. These are widely used to display real empirical data about different economic variables, because they often help economists and policy makers identify patterns or trends in the economy.

Types of Numerical Graphs

A **time-series graph** has successive dates on the horizontal axis and the values of a variable that occurred on those dates on the vertical axis.

You have probably seen graphs in newspapers that show what has happened over time to economic variables such as the unemployment rate or stock prices. A **time-series graph** has successive dates on the horizontal axis and the values of a variable that occurred on those dates on the vertical axis. For example, **Figure A.7** shows the unemployment rate in the United States from 1989 to late 2013. A line connecting the points that correspond to the unemployment rate for each month during those years gives a clear idea of the overall trend in unemployment during that period. Note the two short diagonal lines toward the bottom of the *y*-axis in Figure A.7. This *truncation sign* indicates that a piece of the axis—here, unemployment rates below 4%—was cut to save space.

Figure A.7 Time-Series Graph

Time-series graphs show successive dates on the *x*-axis and values for a variable on the *y*-axis. This time-series graph shows the seasonally adjusted unemployment rate in the United States from 1989 to late 2013.
Source: Bureau of Labor Statistics.

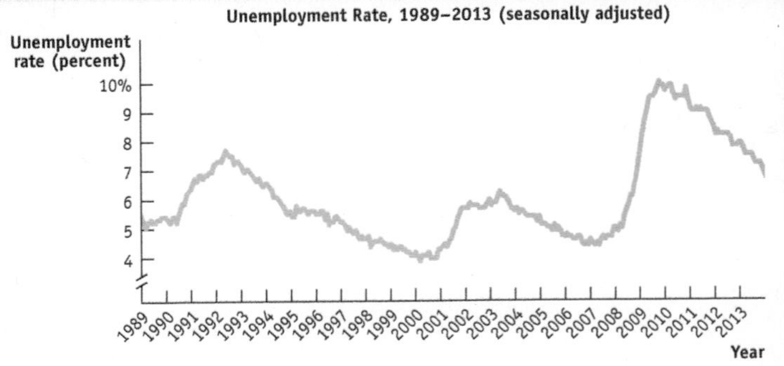

Figure A.8 is an example of a different kind of numerical graph. It represents information from a sample of 168 countries on average life expectancy and gross national product (GNP) per capita—a rough measure of a country's standard of living. Each point in the graph indicates an average resident's life expectancy and the log of GNP per capita for a given country. (Economists have found that the log of GNP rather than the simple level of GNP is more closely tied to average life expectancy.) The points lying in the upper right of the graph, which show combinations of high life expectancy and high log of GNP per capita, represent economically advanced countries such as the United States. Points lying in the bottom left of the graph, which show combinations of low life expectancy and low log of GNP per capita, represent economically less advanced countries such as Afghanistan and Sierra Leone. The pattern of points indicates that there is a positive relationship between life expectancy and log of GNP per capita: on the whole, people live longer in countries with a higher standard of living. This type

44 Section 1 Basic Economic Concepts

Figure A.8 Scatter Diagram

In a scatter diagram, each point represents the corresponding values of the *x*- and *y*-variables for a given observation. Here, each point indicates the observed average life expectancy and the log of GNP per capita of a given country for a sample of 168 countries. The upward-sloping fitted line here is the best approximation of the general relationship between the two variables.

Source: World Bank (2012).

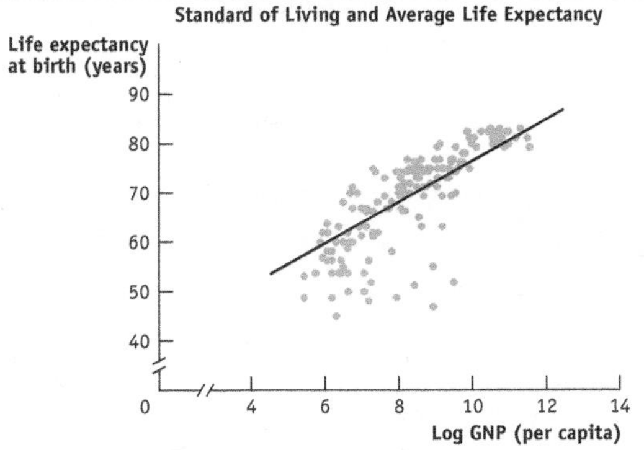

of graph is called a **scatter diagram**, a diagram in which each point corresponds to an actual observation of the *x*-variable and the *y*-variable. In scatter diagrams, a curve is typically fitted to the scatter of points; that is, a curve is drawn that approximates as closely as possible the general relationship between the variables. As you can see, the fitted curve in Figure A.8 is upward-sloping, indicating the underlying positive relationship between the two variables. Scatter diagrams are often used to show how a general relationship can be inferred from a set of data.

Each point on a **scatter diagram** corresponds to an actual observation of the *x*-variable and the *y*-variable.

A **pie chart** shows the share of a total amount that is accounted for by various components, usually expressed in percentages.

A **pie chart** shows the share of a total amount that is accounted for by various components, usually expressed in percentages. For example, **Figure A.9** is a pie chart that depicts the various sources of revenue for the U.S. government budget in 2012, expressed in percentages of the total revenue amount, $2,663 billion. As you can see, social insurance receipts (the revenues collected to fund Social Security, Medicare, and unemployment insurance) accounted for 35% of total government revenue, and individual income tax receipts accounted for 43%.

Figure A.9 Pie Chart

A pie chart shows the percentages of a total amount that can be attributed to various components. This pie chart shows the percentages of total federal revenues received from each source.

Source: Office of Management and Budget.

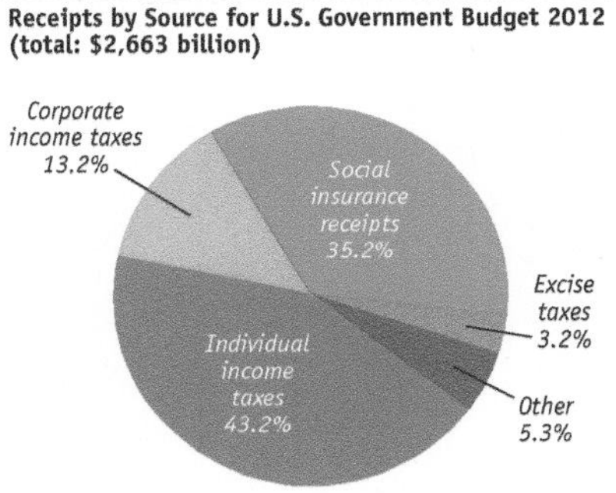

Appendix Graphs in Economics 45

A **bar graph** uses bars of various heights or lengths to indicate values of a variable.

A **bar graph** uses bars of various heights or lengths to indicate values of a variable. In the bar graph in **Figure A.10**, the bars show the percent change in the number of unemployed workers in the United States from 2012 to 2013, indicated separately for White, Black or African-American, and Asian workers. Exact values of the variable that is being measured may be written at the end of the bar, as in this figure. For instance, the number of unemployed Asian workers in the United States decreased by 15% between 2012 and 2013. But even without the precise values, comparing the heights or lengths of the bars can give useful insight into the relative magnitudes of the different values of the variable.

Figure A.10 Bar Graph

A bar graph measures a variable by using bars of various heights or lengths. This bar graph shows the percent change in the number of unemployed workers between 2012 and 2013, indicated separately for White, Black or African-American, and Asian workers.

Source: Bureau of Labor Statistics.

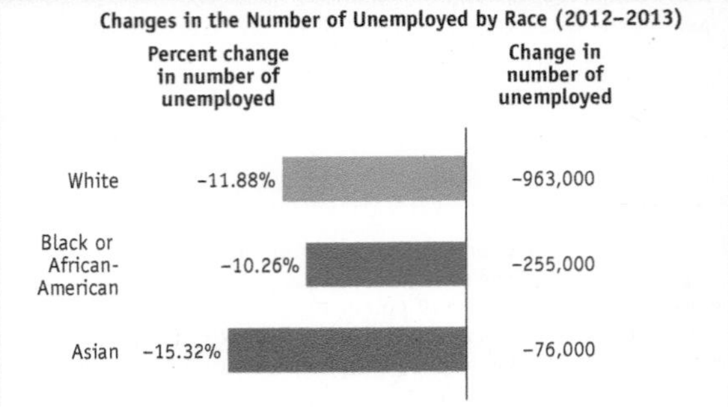

46 Section 1 Basic Economic Concepts

Check Your Understanding

1. Study the four accompanying diagrams. Consider the following statements and indicate which diagram matches each statement. For each statement, tell which variable would appear on the horizontal axis and which on the vertical. In each of these statements, is the slope positive, negative, zero, or infinity?

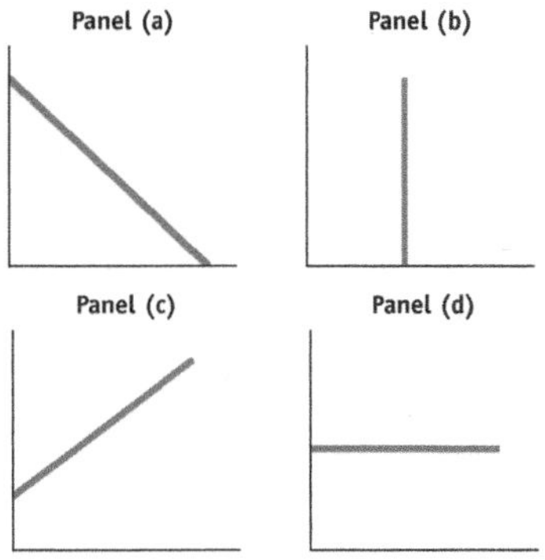

   a. If the price of movies increases, fewer consumers go to see movies.
   b. Workers with more experience typically have higher incomes than less experienced workers.
   c. Regardless of the temperature outside, Americans consume the same number of hot dogs per day.
   d. Consumers buy more frozen yogurt when the price of ice cream goes up.
   e. Research finds no relationship between the number of diet books purchased and the number of pounds lost by the average dieter.
   f. Regardless of its price, there is no change in the quantity of salt that Americans buy.

2. During the Reagan administration, economist Arthur Laffer argued in favor of lowering income tax rates in order to increase tax revenues. Like most economists, he believed that at tax rates above a certain level, tax revenue would fall (because high taxes would discourage some people from working) and that people would refuse to work at all if they received no income after paying taxes. This relationship between tax rates and tax revenue is graphically summarized in what is widely known as the Laffer curve. Plot the Laffer curve relationship, assuming that it has the shape of a nonlinear curve. The following questions will help you construct the graph.
   a. Which is the independent variable? Which is the dependent variable? On which axis do you therefore measure the income tax rate? On which axis do you measure income tax revenue?
   b. What would tax revenue be at a 0% income tax rate?
   c. The maximum possible income tax rate is 100%. What would tax revenue be at a 100% income tax rate?
   d. Estimates now show that the maximum point on the Laffer curve is (approximately) at a tax rate of 80%. For tax rates less than 80%, how would you describe the relationship between the tax rate and tax revenue, and how is this relationship reflected in the slope? For tax rates higher than 80%, how would you describe the relationship between the tax rate and tax revenue, and how is this relationship reflected in the slope?

Key Terms

Variable, p. 36
Horizontal axis/x-axis, p. 37
Vertical axis/y-axis, p. 37
Origin, p. 37
Causal relationship, p. 38
Independent variable, p. 38
Dependent variable, p. 38
Curve, p. 38
Linear relationship, p. 38
Nonlinear relationship, p. 38
Positive relationship, p. 39
Negative relationship, p. 39
Horizontal intercept, p. 39
Vertical intercept, p. 39
Slope, p. 39
Nonlinear curve, p. 41
Absolute value, p. 42
Maximum, p. 42
Minimum, p. 43
Time-series graph, p. 44
Scatter diagram, p. 45
Pie chart, p. 45
Bar graph, p. 46

Answers to Section 1 Appendix Review Questions

Check Your Understanding

1. a. Panel (a) illustrates this relationship. The higher price of movies causes consumers to see fewer movies. The relationship is negative, and the slope is therefore negative. The price of movies is the independent variable, and the number of movies seen the dependent variable.

However, there is a convention in economics that if price is a variable, it is measured on the vertical axis. So, the quantity of movies is measured on the horizontal axis.

b. Panel (c) illustrates this relationship. Since it is likely that firms would pay more to workers with more experience, then years of experience is the independent variable that would be shown on the horizontal axis, and the resulting income, the dependent variable, would be shown on the vertical axis. The slope is positive.

c. Panel (d) illustrates this relationship. With the temperature on the horizontal axis as the independent variable, and the consumption of hot dogs on the vertical axis as the dependent variable, we see that no change occurs in hot dog consumption regardless of the temperature. The slope is zero.

d. Panel (c) illustrates this relationship. When the price of ice cream goes up, this causes consumers to choose a close alternative, frozen yogurt. The price of ice cream is the independent variable and the consumption of frozen yogurt the dependent variable. However, there is a convention in economics that if price is a variable, it is measured on the vertical axis. The quantity of frozen yogurt that consumers buy is on the horizontal axis. The slope is positive.

e. Panel (d) illustrates this relationship. Because the intent is for diet books to influence the number of pounds lost, the number of diet books is the independent variable and belongs on the horizontal axis. The number of pounds lost is the dependent variable measured on the vertical axis. The absence of a discernible relationship between the number of diet books purchased and the weight loss of the average dieter results in a horizontal curve. The slope is zero.

f. Panel (b) illustrates this relationship. Although price is the independent variable and salt consumption the dependent variable, by convention the price appears on the vertical axis and the quantity of salt on the horizontal axis. Since salt consumption does not change regardless of the price, the curve is a vertical line, and the slope is infinity.

2. a. The income tax rate is the independent variable and is measured on the horizontal axis. Income tax revenue is the dependent variable and is measured on the vertical axis.

b. If the income tax rate is 0% (there is no tax), tax revenue is zero.

c. If the income tax rate is 100% (all of your income is taxed), you will have no income left after tax. Since people are unwilling to work if they receive no income after tax, no income will be earned. As a result, there is no income tax revenue.

d. For tax rates less than 80%, tax rate and tax revenue are positively related, so the Laffer curve has a positive slope. For tax rates higher than 80%, the relationship between tax rate and tax revenue is negative, so the Laffer curve has a negative slope. Therefore, the Laffer curve looks like the accompanying graph with a maximum point at a tax rate of 80%.

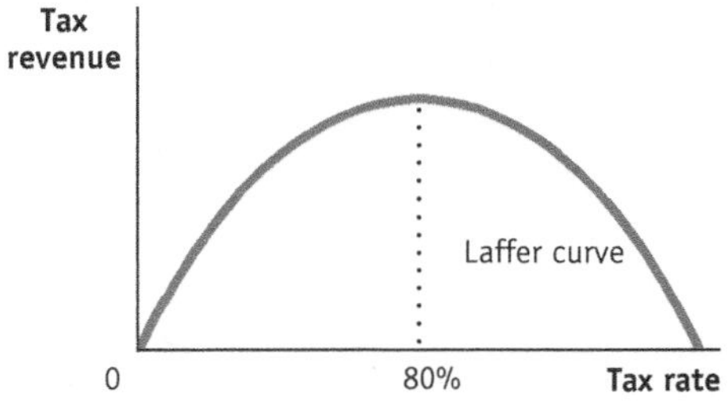

SECTION 2

Supply and Demand

Section 2 Overview:

Watch the video overview of Section 2 (for teachers), which is accessible through the Teacher's e-Book, the TR-flash drive, or the book's website, bcs.worthpublishers.com/krugmanap2e *(teacher log-in required).*

Section 2 introduces supply and demand, a fundamental economic model. The supply and demand model is used to understand how price and quantity sold are determined in a market. The demand for a good or service is determined by consumers who are trying to maximize their satisfaction, and the supply of a good or service is determined by businesses seeking to maximize profits. The interaction of supply and demand determines the equilibrium market price and quantity sold. The supply and demand model can be used to identify how a relevant change will affect the equilibrium price and quantity in a market.

Topics that your students will study in Section 2 include:

- defining a competitive market.
- how a demand curve is constructed.
- the determinants of demand that will cause a demand curve to shift.
- how a supply curve is constructed.
- the determinants of supply that will cause a supply curve to shift.
- how equilibrium is determined in a market.
- how changes to the determinants of supply or demand affect equilibrium in the market.
- the difference between demand/quantity demanded and supply/quantity supplied.
- the effect of a price ceiling and a price floor on a market.
- the effect of a quantity control in a market.
- the effect of government controls on market efficiency.

Alignment to AP® Economics Course Description

Macroeconomics I. Basic Economic Concepts: 8–12%

AP® Outline	Module
A. Scarcity, choice, and opportunity costs	**(Section 1)**
B. Production possibilities curve	**(Section 1)**
C. Comparative advantage, specialization, and exchange	**(Section 1)**
D. Demand, supply, and market equilibrium	5: Supply and Demand: Introduction and Demand 6: Supply and Demand: Supply 7: Supply and Demand: Equilibrium
E. Macroeconomic issues: Business cycle, unemployment, inflation, growth	**(Section 1)**

Microeconomics II. The Nature and Function of Product Markets: 55–70%

AP® Outline	Module
A. Supply and demand (15–20%)	5: Supply and Demand: Introduction and Demand 6: Supply and Demand: Supply 7: Supply and Demand: Equilibrium 8: Supply and Demand: Price Controls (Ceilings and Floors) 9: Supply and Demand: Quantity Controls
B. Theory of consumer choice	**(Sections 9, 10)**
C. Production and costs	**(Section 10)**
D. Firm behavior and market structure	**(Sections 10, 11, 12)**

Pacing Guide

Module	Standard Teaching Days	Block Teaching Days
5	1	½*
6	1	½*
7	1	½*
8	1	½*
9	1	½*
Section 2 Assessment	1	½*
Total	**6**	**3**

*Those students on a block schedule will have more time to spend on activities and TRM materials in class.

Introductory Note on Assessments

AP® Macroeconomic students will only need to study Modules 5, 6, and 7. The topics found in Modules 8 and 9 are only a part of the AP® Microeconomics Outline.

TRM Section Resources

All section resources may be accessed through the Teacher's e-Book, the TR-flash drive, or the book's website, bcs.worthpublishers.com/krugmanap2e *(teacher log-in required).*

Section 2 PD Video (for teachers)

Module 5

Module 5 Sample Lecture

Worksheet 5.1: Demand and Supply Explained (1 of 2)

Worksheet 5.2: Change in Demand vs. Change in Quantity Demanded

Worksheet 5.3: Starbucks Tea

Worksheet 5.4: Market Changes in Demand

Worksheet 5.5: Demand Summary Study Guide

Exit Slip: Module 5

Module 6

Module 6 Sample Lecture

Worksheet 6.1: Demand and Supply Explained (2 of 2)

Worksheet 6.2: Market Changes in Supply

Worksheet 6.3: Changes in Supply

Worksheet 6.4: Supply Summary Study Guide

Worksheet 6.5: Veterinary Shortages

Exit Slip: Module 6

Module 7

Module 7 Sample Lecture

Worksheet 7.1: Simple Supply and Demand

Worksheet 7.2: Equilibrium Questions

Worksheet 7.3: Changes to Markets

Worksheet 7.4: Shifting Supply and Demand

Worksheet 7.5: Simultaneous Shifts

Worksheet 7.6: Graphing Equilibrium

Worksheet 7.7: Supply and Demand

Exit Slip: Module 7

Module 8

Module 8 Sample Lecture

Worksheet 8.1: Analyzing Figures 8.1 and 8.2

Worksheet 8.2: Price Ceilings

Worksheet 8.3: Analyzing Figures 8.3 and 8.4

Worksheet 8.4: Price Floors

Worksheet 8.5: Price Floors and Ceilings

Exit Slip: Module 8

Module 9

Module 9: Sample Lecture

Worksheet 9.1: Graphing Quotas

Worksheet 9.2: Graphing Quotas—Peanuts!

Exit Slip: Module 9

Section 2 Review Video (for students)

St. Louis Federal Reserve Bank Resources

Many of the Federal Reserve Banks have educational departments that offer helpful resources for studying economics. Members of the Educators Advisory Board of the St. Louis Federal Reserve Bank have handpicked some of their best resources for use with your AP® Economics students. References to these resources are included in the margin notes. A complete list of the St. Louis Fed resources for each section with the corresponding URL (as of fall 2014) can be found in the TRM.

NOTE We have included a number of links to useful videos and articles in the margin notes in this section. Although all are active at the time of publication, we know that some may expire over the next few years. If a link is no longer active, you may wish to search for a similar article or video to illustrate the point. We may also periodically refresh resources on the book's companion website.

PD Section 2 Overview

Watch the video overview of Section 2 (for teachers), which is accessible through the Teacher's e-Book, the TR-flash drive, or the book's website bcs.worthpublishers.com/krugmanap2e (teacher log-in required).

FOCUS Active Learning

Have students read Chapter 3 of *Economics by Example* to gain further insights into supply and demand.

SECTION 2

Supply and Demand

SAM PANTHAKY/AFP/Getty Images

Blue Jean Blues

If you bought a pair of blue jeans in 2012, you may have been shocked at the price. Or maybe not: fashions change, and maybe you thought you were paying the price for being fashionable. But you weren't—you were paying for cotton. Jeans are made of denim, a particular weave of cotton. In 2011, when jeans manufacturers were buying supplies for the coming year, the price of cotton climbed to more than triple its level just two years earlier. In March 2011, the price of a pound of cotton hit a 141-year high, the highest cotton price since record keeping began in 1870.

Why were cotton prices so high? On one side, demand for clothing of all kinds was surging. In 2008–2009, as the world struggled with the effects of a financial crisis, nervous consumers cut back on clothing purchases. But by 2011, with the worst apparently over, buyers were back in force. On the supply side, severe weather events hit world cotton production. Most notably, Pakistan, the world's fourth-largest cotton producer, was hit by devastating floods that put one-fifth of the country underwater and virtually destroyed its cotton crop.

Fearing that consumers had limited tolerance for large increases in the price of cotton clothing, apparel makers began scrambling to find ways to reduce costs without offending consumers' fashion sense. They adopted changes like smaller buttons, cheaper linings, and—yes—polyester, doubting that consumers would be willing to pay more for cotton goods. In fact, some experts on the cotton market warned that the sky-high prices of cotton in 2011 might lead to a permanent shift in tastes, with consumers becoming more willing to wear synthetics even when cotton prices came down.

At the same time, it was not all bad news for everyone connected with the cotton trade. In the United States, cotton producers had not been hit by bad weather and were relishing the higher prices. American farmers responded to the sky-high cotton prices by sharply increasing the acreage they devoted to the crop. None of these measures were enough, however, to produce immediate price relief.

Wait a minute: how, exactly, does flooding in Pakistan translate into higher jeans prices and more polyester in your T-shirts? It's a matter of supply and demand—but what does that mean? Many people use "supply and demand" as a catchphrase to mean "the laws of the marketplace at work." To economists, however, the concept of supply and demand has a precise meaning: it is a *model* of market behavior that is extremely useful for understanding many—but not all—markets.

In this section, we lay out the pieces that make up the *supply and demand model*, put them together, and show how this model can be used to understand how most markets behave.

St. Louis Federal Reserve Bank Resources

Supply and Demand Online Course for Teachers and Students

The supply and demand model is one of the fundamental models in economics. The St. Louis Fed online course includes three interactive lessons that introduce this model using a fictitious chocolate market.

48 Section 2 Supply and Demand

Getty Images/Somos RF

MODULE 5 Supply and Demand: Introduction and Demand

In this Module, you will learn to:

- Explain what a competitive market is and how it is described by the supply and demand model
- Draw a demand curve and interpret its meaning
- Discuss the difference between movements along the demand curve and changes in demand
- List the factors that shift the demand curve

Supply and Demand: A Model of a Competitive Market

Cotton sellers and cotton buyers constitute a *market*—a group of producers and consumers who exchange a good or service for payment. In this section, we'll focus on a particular type of market known as a *competitive market*. Roughly, a **competitive market** is one in which there are many buyers and sellers of the same good or service. More precisely, the key feature of a competitive market is that no individual's actions have a noticeable effect on the price at which the good or service is sold. It's important to understand, however, that this is not an accurate description of every market. For example, it's not an accurate description of the market for cola beverages. That's because in the market for cola beverages, Coca-Cola and Pepsi account for such a large proportion of total sales that they are able to influence the price at which cola beverages are bought and sold. But it *is* an accurate description of the market for cotton. The global marketplace for cotton is so huge that even a jeans retailer as large as Levi Strauss & Co. accounts for only a tiny fraction of transactions, making it unable to influence the price at which cotton is bought and sold.

It's a little hard to explain why competitive markets are different from other markets until we've seen how a competitive market works. For now, let's just say that it's easier to model competitive markets than other markets. When taking an exam, it's always a good strategy to begin by answering the easier questions. In this book, we're going to do the same thing. So we will start with competitive markets.

AP® Exam Tip

Supply and demand graphs are some of the most important graphs to master for success on the AP® exam. You must be able to draw, label, and interpret the graphs for the exam. They are the basis of future graphs you will learn in the course, too.

A **competitive market** is a market in which there are many buyers and sellers of the same good or service, none of whom can influence the price at which the good or service is sold.

PD To prepare for teaching this lesson, you may want to consult the **Module 5 Sample Lecture** in the TRM.

OPEN & CLOSE Start Here

To introduce Module 5, hold up an item that many students will want (like a candy bar). Ask each student how much he or she would pay for the item, and then write the prices given on the board. Based on the recorded prices, ask which student is likely to get the candy bar if it is sold in a classroom auction and what the auction price is likely to be. Explain whether you would be willing to sell the candy for that price and why (e.g., how much it cost you and whether you could get a replacement). With your class, discuss why some will pay a higher price for the item. Ask students how they think the price of the candy bar might change if 10, 20, or even 30 bars were being auctioned instead of just one. What if all students at the school were allowed to bid in the auction, not just students in the class? Use this discussion to introduce the supply and demand model as a way of understanding how prices are determined in a market and how changes in the market affect the market price.

TEACH Connect It

In Section 1, students studied the production possibilities curve. Ask them what variables were measured on the axes of a *PPC* and what the *PPC* model is used to explain *(goods are shown on the axes and the model represents the possible production of the two goods in an economy)*. Now ask students what else it would be useful to know about a good, besides the economy's ability to produce it. For example, help students to understand that it would be useful to know how much people want a good (i.e., the demand for it) and the price of a good.

FOCUS Active Learning

Divide your class into small groups to discuss the following questions:

- Who might be interested in knowing the price of a good or service and how it might change in the future? *For example, buyers, sellers, speculators*
- Who might be interested in knowing the quantity of a good or service that will be sold in a market and how that quantity might change in the future? *For example, buyers, sellers, speculators*
- How could you benefit from knowledge of an upcoming price change? *Buy low and sell high!*

The supply and demand model is used to explain and predict how changes in the economy lead to changes in price and quantity in individual markets. Buyers and sellers benefit from knowing when and how much to buy or produce to minimize their cost or maximize their profit. Speculators earn a profit from buying low and selling high.

TEACH Teach It

A competitive market is one with many buyers and sellers. Ask students what they would call a market with only one seller. Chances are they will know the term *monopoly*. Explain that competitive markets and monopoly markets, along with a couple of other types of markets, are studied in depth later in microeconomics courses. Making this connection will help students better understand the idea of a competitive market and can also be used to foreshadow later micro topics.

TEACH Teach It

Demand represents the inverse relationship between price and quantity demanded. Make sure students understand that this relationship can be shown using a demand schedule (a table of prices with their corresponding quantities demanded) or a demand curve (a curve, or line, that plots the values in the demand schedule). At higher levels, economists also represent the demand relationship using equations.

FOCUS Active Learning

Organize students into groups of five or six. Each team will survey the quantity demanded for a specific product. Assign each team only one product to survey. Some possibilities:

- A private parking space on campus
- A new Dell laptop computer
- A three-ring notebook
- Visits to a tanning salon
- Downloadable songs on iTunes
- A new Xbox game system

Then establish tasks for the teams:

- Teams should brainstorm five possible prices for their product, from high to low.
- Teams should agree on how all members will conduct the survey. For example, they can ask: "If the price is ____, how many will you buy (in a week, a month, or a year)?" or, "If the price is____, will you buy it?" (A "yes" is counted as 1, and a "no" is counted as 0.)
- Each team member should interview two students in the class regarding their demand for the team's product.
- Students should return to the team and add the quantity demanded at each price for all team member surveys.
- Teams should draw the demand curve for their product and post it on the board.

The **supply and demand model** is a model of how a competitive market works.

When a market is competitive, its behavior is well described by the **supply and demand model**. Because many markets *are* competitive, the supply and demand model is a very useful one indeed.

There are five key elements in this model:

- The *demand curve*
- The *supply curve*
- The set of factors that cause the demand curve to shift and the set of factors that cause the supply curve to shift
- The *market equilibrium*, which includes the *equilibrium price* and *equilibrium quantity*
- The way the market equilibrium changes when the supply curve or demand curve shifts

To explain the supply and demand model, we will examine each of these elements in turn. In this module we begin with demand.

The Demand Curve

How many pounds of cotton, packaged in the form of blue jeans, do consumers around the world want to buy in a given year? You might at first think that we can answer this question by multiplying the number of pairs of blue jeans purchased around the world each day by the amount of cotton it takes to make a pair of jeans, and then multiplying by 365. But that's not enough to answer the question because how many pairs of jeans—in other words, how many pounds of cotton—consumers want to buy depends on the price of cotton. When the price of cotton rises, as it did in 2011, some people will respond to the higher price of cotton clothing by buying fewer cotton garments or, perhaps, by switching completely to garments made from other materials, such as synthetics or linen. In general, the quantity of cotton clothing, or of any good or service that people want to buy (taking "want" to mean they are willing and able to buy it), depends on the price. The higher the price, the less of the good or service people want to purchase; alternatively, the lower the price, the more they want to purchase.

So the answer to the question "How many pounds of cotton do consumers want to buy?" depends on the price of a pound of cotton. If you don't yet know what the price will be, you can start by making a table of how many pounds of cotton people would want to buy at a number of different prices. Such a table is known as a *demand schedule*. This, in turn, can be used to draw a *demand curve*, which is one of the key elements of the supply and demand model.

The Demand Schedule and the Demand Curve

A **demand schedule** shows how much of a good or service consumers will be willing and able to buy at different prices.

A **demand schedule** is a table that shows how much of a good or service consumers will want to buy at different prices. On the right side of **Figure 5.1**, we show a hypothetical demand schedule for cotton. It's hypothetical in that it doesn't use actual data on the world demand for cotton, and it assumes that all cotton is of equal quality.

According to the table, if cotton costs $1 a pound, consumers around the world will want to purchase 10 billion pounds of cotton over the course of a year. If the price is $1.25 a pound, they will want to buy only 8.9 billion pounds; if the price is only $0.75 a pound, they will want to buy 11.5 billion pounds; and so on. So the higher the price, the fewer pounds of cotton consumers will want to purchase. In other words, as the price rises, the **quantity demanded** of cotton—the actual amount consumers are willing and able to buy at some specific price—falls.

The **quantity demanded** is the actual amount of a good or service consumers are willing and able to buy at some specific price.

The graph in Figure 5.1 is a visual representation of the information in the table. The vertical axis shows the price of a pound of cotton and the horizontal axis shows the quantity of cotton in pounds. Each point on the graph corresponds to one of the

St. Louis Federal Reserve Bank Resources

"Demand," *The Economic Lowdown Podcast Series*, Volume 1, Episode 6

The sixth podcast in this series examines the law of demand. Those who love candy bars will find this lesson especially easy to digest (7 minutes).

Figure 5.1 The Demand Schedule and the Demand Curve

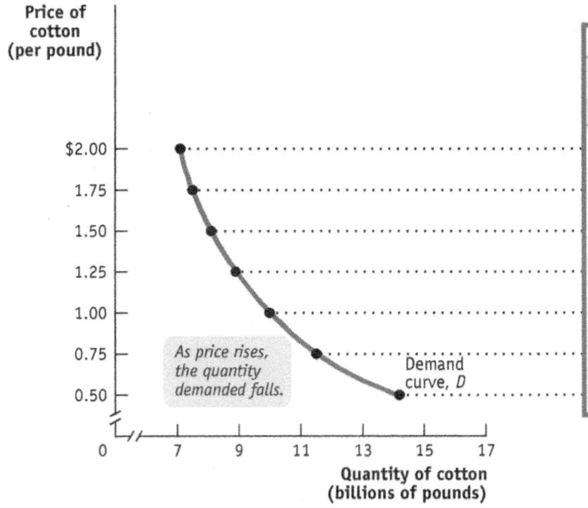

Demand Schedule for Cotton

Price of cotton (per pound)	Quantity of cotton demanded (billions of pounds)
$2.00	7.1
1.75	7.5
1.50	8.1
1.25	8.9
1.00	10.0
0.75	11.5
0.50	14.2

The demand schedule for cotton yields the corresponding demand curve, which shows how much of a good or service consumers want to buy at any given price. The demand curve and the demand schedule reflect the law of demand: As price rises, the quantity demanded falls. Similarly, a decrease in price raises the quantity demanded. As a result, the demand curve is downward-sloping.

entries in the table. The curve that connects these points is a **demand curve**, a graphical representation of the demand schedule, which is another way of showing the relationship between the quantity demanded and the price.

Note that the demand curve shown in Figure 5.1 slopes downward. This reflects the general proposition that a higher price reduces the quantity demanded. For example, jeans-makers know they will sell fewer pairs of jeans when the price of jeans is higher, reflecting a $2 price per pound of cotton, compared to the number they will sell when the price of jeans is lower, reflecting a price of only $1 per pound of cotton. When the price of jeans is relatively high, some people buy pants less often, and some people buy pants made of wool, linen, or synthetics instead of cotton. In the real world, demand curves almost always slope downward. It is so likely that, all other things being equal, a higher price for a good will lead people to demand a smaller quantity of it, that economists are willing to call it a "law"—the **law of demand**.

A **demand curve** is a graphical representation of the demand schedule. It shows the relationship between quantity demanded and price.

The **law of demand** says that a higher price for a good or service, all other things being equal, leads people to demand a smaller quantity of that good or service.

Shifts of the Demand Curve

Even though cotton prices were higher in 2013 than they had been in 2012, total world consumption of cotton was higher in 2013. How can we reconcile this fact with the law of demand, which says that a higher price reduces the quantity demanded, all other things being equal?

The answer lies in the crucial phrase *all other things being equal*. In this case, all other things weren't equal: there were changes between 2012 and 2013 that increased the quantity of cotton demanded at any given price. For one thing, the world's population

AP® Exam Tip

In several common economics graphs including the graph of supply and demand, the dependent variable is on the vertical axis and the independent variable is on the horizontal axis. You learned the opposite convention in math and science classes, so graphing in economics may be a little difficult at first.

TEACH Teach It

It is important that students understand the difference between a change in quantity demanded and a change in demand. When the price of a good changes, the quantity demanded will change as well. This concept is illustrated in Figure 5.1 by the movement to a new row of the demand schedule or a new point on the demand curve. The demand schedule and demand curve have not changed—we just moved to a different place on the same table/curve. We refer to this as a change in quantity demanded, and changes in quantity demanded are caused *only* by a change in price (remember, price is the variable on the vertical axis).

When the entire table/curve changes, this is called a change in demand. Changes in demand result from changes in factors *other than price* and cause each and every row in the table/point on the curve to change.

TEACH Teach It

Point out to students that they probably already understood the "law of demand" before they took AP® economics. People buy more when the price is lower and less when the price goes up. This is common sense, and students probably didn't need an economist to explain this concept to them. Emphasize their familiarity with the law of demand because it so often holds true in the real world. Caution students not to break the law (or they might have to deal with the econ police!).

FOCUS Active Learning

TRM Watch Jacob Clifford's video "Demand and Supply Explained (1 of 2)" as a class activity (see econextras video list with hyperlinks on the bcs and TRFD). The video explains the law of demand, the substitution effect, the income effect, the law of diminishing marginal utility, and the shifters of demand. See **Worksheet 5.1 (Demand and Supply Explained: 1 of 2)** from the TRM; it includes teaching notes for the video.

St. Louis Federal Reserve Bank Resources

"Demand," *The Economic Lowdown Video Series*, Episode 2

In the second episode of the *Economic Lowdown Video Series*, economic education specialist Scott Wolla explains the concept of demand. Viewers will learn how a change in the price of a good affects the quantity of the good consumers will buy and how changes in market conditions affect the demand for a good.

FOCUS Graph It

Looking at Figure 5.2, ask:

- At the price of $1.25, what is the quantity demanded in 2012 and 2013? *9, 11*
- What are some of the factors that might have brought about greater demand for cotton in 2013 than in 2012? *Increased income, people's tastes and preferences, prices of other goods*
- If students in 2014 started to wear only moisture-wicking gym clothes and stopped purchasing cotton athletic clothes, how would you expect the demand curve for cotton to react in 2014? *Shift to the left*

TEACH Teach It

Stress that as demand changes, so does the quantity demanded at each and every price. Students can see this by looking at the demand curves in Figure 5.2 (D_1 and D_2) and associating them with the demand schedules given for cotton for 2012 and 2013.

TEACH Connect It

Note that Figure 5.1 shows the demand for cotton in 2012 in a demand schedule and with the corresponding demand curve. Figure 5.2 shows the demand for cotton in both 2012 and 2013. The demand schedules illustrate that at each price, the quantity of cotton demanded has increased between 2012 and 2013. It gives the corresponding demand curve for 2012 (D_1) and 2013 (D_2). The higher values in the demand schedule and the shift of the demand curve to the right represent the increase in demand caused by several changes in the economy discussed in the text.

Figure 5.2 An Increase in Demand

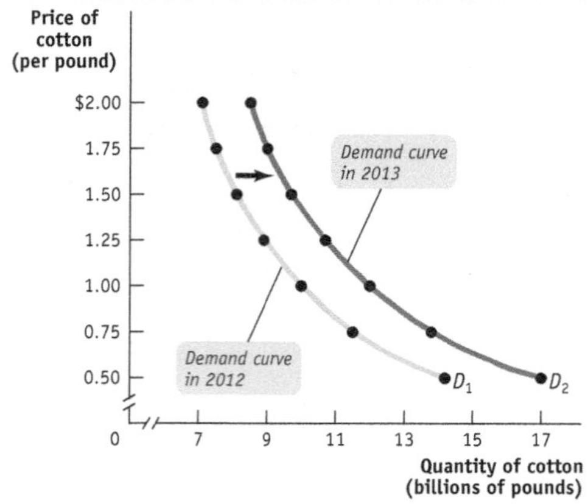

Demand Schedules for Cotton

Price of cotton (per pound)	Quantity of cotton demanded (billions of pounds)	
	in 2012	in 2013
$2.00	7.1	8.5
1.75	7.5	9.0
1.50	8.1	9.7
1.25	8.9	10.7
1.00	10.0	12.0
0.75	11.5	13.8
0.50	14.2	17.0

Increases in population and income, among other changes, generate an increase in demand—a rise in the quantity demanded at any given price. This is represented by the two demand schedules—one showing demand in 2012, before the rise in population and income, the other showing demand in 2013, after the rise in population and income—and their corresponding demand curves. The increase in demand shifts the demand curve to the right.

AP® Exam Tip

A price change causes a change in the quantity demanded, shown by a movement along the demand curve. When a nonprice factor of demand changes, this changes demand, and therefore shifts the demand curve. It would be correct to say that an increase in the price of apples decreases the quantity of apples demanded; it would be incorrect to say that an increase in the price of apples decreases the demand for apples.

increased by 77 million, and therefore the number of potential wearers of cotton clothing increased. In addition, higher incomes in countries like China allowed people to buy more clothing than before. These changes led to an increase in the quantity of cotton demanded at any given price. **Figure 5.2** illustrates this phenomenon using the demand schedule and demand curve for cotton. (As before, the numbers in Figure 5.2 are hypothetical.)

The table in Figure 5.2 shows two demand schedules. The first is a demand schedule for 2012, the same one shown in Figure 5.1. The second is a demand schedule for 2013. It differs from the 2012 demand schedule due to factors such as a larger population and higher incomes, factors that led to an increase in the quantity of cotton demanded at any given price. So at each price, the 2013 schedule shows a larger quantity demanded than the 2012 schedule. For example, the quantity of cotton consumers wanted to buy at a price of $1 per pound increased from 10 billion to 12 billion pounds per year, the quantity demanded at $1.25 per pound went from 8.9 billion to 10.7 billion pounds, and so on.

A **change in demand** is a shift of the demand curve, which changes the quantity demanded at any given price.

A **movement along the demand curve** is a change in the quantity demanded of a good that is the result of a change in that good's price.

What is clear from this example is that the changes that occurred between 2012 and 2013 generated a *new* demand schedule, one in which the quantity demanded was greater at any given price than in the original demand schedule. The two curves in Figure 5.2 show the same information graphically. As you can see, the demand schedule for 2013 corresponds to a new demand curve, D_2, that is to the right of the demand curve for 2012, D_1. This **change in demand** shows the increase in the quantity demanded at any given price, represented by the shift in position of the original demand curve, D_1, to its new location at D_2.

It's crucial to make the distinction between such changes in demand and **movements along the demand curve**, changes in the quantity demanded of a good that result from a change in that good's price. **Figure 5.3** illustrates the difference.

FOCUS Flip It

Students can view Jacob Clifford's video "Change in Demand vs. Change in Quantity Demanded—Key Concept" (see econextras video list with hyperlinks on the bcs and TRFD) for a quick review of this concept. Use **Worksheet 5.2 (Change in Demand vs. Change in Quantity Demanded)** found in the TRM.

Figure 5.3 A Movement Along the Demand Curve Versus a Shift of the Demand Curve

The rise in the quantity demanded when going from point *A* to point *B* reflects a movement along the demand curve: it is the result of a fall in the price of the good. The rise in the quantity demanded when going from point *A* to point *C* reflects a change in demand: this shift to the right is the result of a rise in the quantity demanded at any given price.

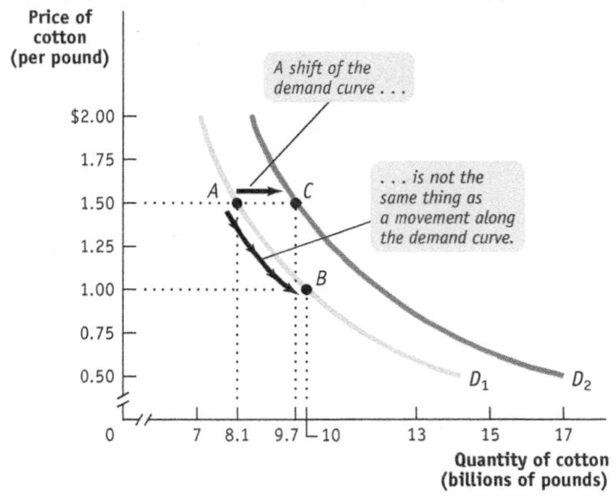

FOCUS Graph It

Have students consider the points shown in Figure 5.3. Ask them to identify what caused the movement from point *A* to point *B* (*a decrease in price*) and how they would describe what happened as a result of the change in price (*a change/increase in **quantity demanded***). Next ask them what caused the movement from point *A* to point *C* (*a shift of the demand curve from D_1 to D_2*) and how they would describe what occurred when the demand curve shifted (*a change/increase in **demand***). Tell your class that a variety of factors can lead to a change in demand (i.e., a shift of the demand curve)—and that is what the rest of the module is about!

The movement from point *A* to point *B* is a movement along the demand curve: the quantity demanded rises due to a fall in price as you move down D_1. Here, a fall in the price of cotton from $1.50 to $1 per pound generates a rise in the quantity demanded from 8.1 billion to 10 billion pounds per year. But the quantity demanded can also rise when the price is unchanged if there is an *increase in demand*—a rightward shift of the demand curve. This is illustrated in Figure 5.3 by the shift of the demand curve from D_1 to D_2. Holding the price constant at $1.50 a pound, the quantity demanded rises from 8.1 billion pounds at point *A* on D_1 to 9.7 billion pounds at point *C* on D_2.

When economists talk about a "change in demand," saying "the demand for *X* increased" or "the demand for *Y* decreased," they mean that the demand curve for *X* or *Y* shifted—*not* that the quantity demanded rose or fell because of a change in the price.

AP® Exam Tip

When shifting curves, *left is less and right is more.*

Understanding Shifts of the Demand Curve

Figure 5.4 on the next page illustrates the two basic ways in which demand curves can shift. When economists talk about an "increase in demand," they mean a *rightward* shift of the demand curve: at any given price, consumers demand a larger quantity of the good or service than before. This is shown by the rightward shift of the original demand curve D_1 to D_2. And when economists talk about a "decrease in demand," they mean a *leftward* shift of the demand curve: at any given price, consumers demand a smaller quantity of the good or service than before. This is shown by the leftward shift of the original demand curve D_1 to D_3.

What caused the demand curve for cotton to shift? We have already mentioned two reasons: changes in population and income. If you think about it, you can come up with other things that would be likely to shift the demand curve for cotton. For example, suppose that the price of polyester rises. This will induce some people who previously bought polyester clothing to buy cotton clothing instead, increasing the demand for cotton.

FOCUS In the News

TRM This section introduces the supply and demand model using the example of blue jeans. You can find other examples of changes in supply and demand in the news every day. For example, Starbucks, a business familiar to most students, is planning to open teahouses throughout the world. Have students read CBC's "From Starbucks to Davids Tea: Why Big Business Is Betting on Tea" at www.cbc.ca/thecurrent/episode/2013/11/12/from-starbucks-to-davidstea-why-big-business-is-betting-on-tea/ and make note of the question, "What's behind the steep demand?" While reading, have students refer to **Worksheet 5.3 (Starbucks Tea)** in the TRM.

FOCUS Graph It

Have students consider Figure 5.4. Ask them what happens to quantity as you move along the *x*-axis to the right (*it increases*). What happens to quantity as you move along the *x*-axis to the left? (*It decreases.*) Help students make the link between the changes in quantity as you move along the horizontal axis and the increase and decrease in demand shown in Figure 5.4. Such an exercise may seem remedial at this stage, but the link becomes even more important with the supply curve, so emphasizing this point here can be helpful later. Students should think left and right when they consider increases and decreases.

TEACH Teach It

This is a good point to reemphasize—that price is measured on the vertical axis and therefore a change in price changes quantity demanded (a movement to a different point on the same demand curve). Demand refers to the demand relationship (the entire curve) that does not change when price changes. However, a variety of factors *will* cause the entire curve to shift (i.e., lead to a change in demand). These things cause the quantity demanded to be different at each and every price. For example, at every price on D_2, the quantity demanded is higher than it was on D_1.

TEACH Teach It

Students need to understand, define, and recognize examples of substitutes and complements.

- Substitute goods can be interchanged. You use one *instead* of the other—for example, hamburgers may be substituted for pizza for lunch. When the price of a substitute good (like pizza) increases, you buy less of it (that's just the law of demand—you buy less when things cost more!). The demand for the good (hamburgers) increases when you buy it instead of the now higher-priced substitute good (pizza).
- Complements are goods that are consumed at the same time. You use one *along with* the other—for example, cars and gasoline. When the price of a complement (like cars) increases, you buy less of it (that's just the law of demand—you buy less when things cost more!). The demand for the good (gasoline) decreases when you don't need as much of it because there are fewer cars.

Figure 5.4 Shifts of the Demand Curve

Any event that increases demand shifts the demand curve to the right, reflecting a rise in the quantity demanded at any given price. Any event that decreases demand shifts the demand curve to the left, reflecting a fall in the quantity demanded at any given price.

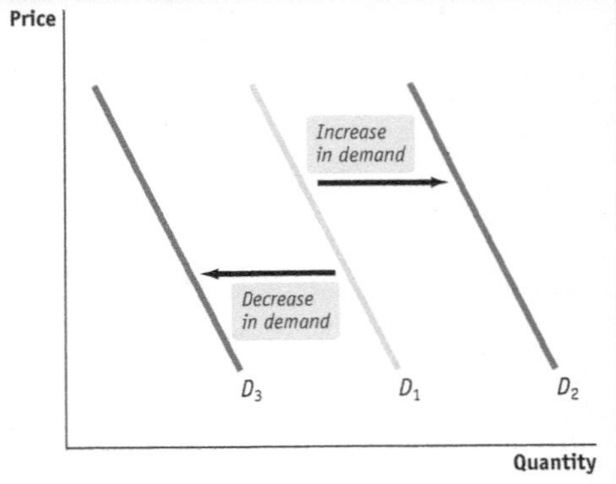

There are five principal factors that shift the demand curve for a good or service:

- Changes in the prices of related goods or services
- Changes in income
- Changes in tastes
- Changes in expectations
- Changes in the number of consumers

Although this is not an exhaustive list, it contains the five most important factors that can shift demand curves. So when we say that the quantity of a good or service demanded falls as its price rises, all other things being equal, we are in fact stating that the factors that shift demand are remaining unchanged. Let's now explore, in more detail, how those factors shift the demand curve.

Two goods are **substitutes** if a rise in the price of one of the goods leads to an increase in the demand for the other good.

Two goods are **complements** if a rise in the price of one of the goods leads to a decrease in the demand for the other good.

Changes in the Prices of Related Goods or Services While there's nothing quite like a comfortable pair of all-cotton blue jeans, for some purposes khakis—typically made from polyester blends—aren't a bad alternative. Khakis are what economists call a *substitute* for jeans. A pair of goods are **substitutes** if a rise in the price of one good (jeans) makes consumers more willing to buy the other good (polyester-blend khakis). Substitutes are usually goods that in some way serve a similar function: coffee and tea, muffins and doughnuts, train rides and airplane rides. A rise in the price of the alternative good induces some consumers to purchase the original good *instead* of it, shifting demand for the original good to the right.

But sometimes a fall in the price of one good makes consumers *more* willing to buy another good. Such pairs of goods are known as **complements**. Complements are usually goods that in some sense are consumed together: computers and software, cookies and milk, cars and gasoline. Because consumers like to consume a good and its complement together, a change in the price of one of the goods will affect the demand for its complement. In particular, when the price of one good rises, the demand for its complement decreases, shifting the demand curve for the complement to the left. So a rise in the price of cookies is likely to precipitate a leftward shift in the demand curve for milk, as people consume fewer snacks of cookies and milk. Likewise, when the price of one good falls, the quantity demanded of its complement rises, shifting the demand curve for the complement to the right.

FOCUS Active Learning

Have students make a list of five pairs of goods that are substitutes for each other and five pairs of goods that are complements for each other. Discuss the students' lists and explain that what we consider substitutes or complements depends on our tastes and preferences. As an example, you can discuss the fact that although some people will substitute tea for coffee, some people will only drink coffee, and others will never drink coffee.

FOCUS Active Learning

TRM Have students do **Worksheet 5.4 (Market Changes in Demand)** from the TRM for exercises that involve graphing changes in demand and supply. Students will graph situations where a change in demand or supply, or a change in quantity demanded or quantity supplied, occurs.

This means that if, for some reason, the price of cookies falls, we should see a rightward shift in the demand curve for milk, as people consume more cookies *and* more milk.

Changes in Income When individuals have more income, they are normally more likely to purchase a good at any given price. For example, if a family's income rises, it is more likely to take that summer trip to Disney World—and therefore also more likely to buy plane tickets. So a rise in consumer incomes will cause the demand curves for most goods to shift to the right.

Why do we say "most goods," rather than "all goods"? Most goods are **normal goods**—the demand for them increases when consumer income rises. However, the demand for some products falls when income rises. Goods for which demand decreases when income rises are known as **inferior goods**. Usually an inferior good is one that is considered less desirable than more expensive alternatives—such as a bus ride versus a taxi ride. When they can afford to, people stop buying an inferior good and switch their consumption to the preferred, more expensive alternative. So when a good is inferior, a rise in income shifts the demand curve to the left. And, not surprisingly, a fall in income shifts the demand curve to the right.

When a rise in income increases the demand for a good—the normal case—it is a **normal good**.

When a rise in income decreases the demand for a good, it is an **inferior good**.

One example of the distinction between normal and inferior goods that has drawn considerable attention in the business press is the difference between so-called casual-dining restaurants such as Applebee's and Olive Garden and fast-food chains such as McDonald's and KFC. When their incomes rise, Americans tend to eat out more at casual-dining restaurants. However, some of this increased dining out comes at the expense of fast-food venues—to some extent, people visit McDonald's less once they can afford to move upscale. So casual dining is a normal good, while fast-food appears to be an inferior good.

Changes in Tastes Why do people want what they want? Fortunately, we don't need to answer that question—we just need to acknowledge that people have certain preferences, or tastes, that determine what they choose to consume and that these tastes can change. Economists usually lump together changes in demand due to fads, beliefs, cultural shifts, and so on under the heading of changes in *tastes,* or *preferences.*

Chimpinski/Shutterstock

For example, once upon a time men wore hats. Up until around World War II, a respectable man wasn't fully dressed unless he wore a dignified hat along with his suit. But the returning soldiers adopted a more informal style, perhaps due to the rigors of the war. And President Eisenhower, who had been supreme commander of Allied Forces before becoming president, often went hatless. After World War II, it was clear that the demand curve for hats had shifted leftward, reflecting a decrease in the demand for hats.

Economists have little to say about the forces that influence consumers' tastes. (Marketers and advertisers, however, have plenty to say about them!) However, a *change* in tastes has a predictable impact on demand. When tastes change in favor of a good, more people want to buy it at any given price, so the demand curve shifts to the right. When tastes change against a good, fewer people want to buy it at any given price, so the demand curve shifts to the left.

Changes in Expectations When consumers have some choice about when to make a purchase, current demand for a good is often affected by expectations about its future price. For example, savvy shoppers often wait for seasonal sales—say, buying next year's holiday gifts during the post-holiday markdowns. In this case, expectations of a future drop in price lead to a decrease in demand today. Alternatively, expectations of a future rise in price are likely to cause an increase in demand today. For example, if you heard that the price of jeans would increase next year, you might go out and buy an extra pair now.

Changes in expectations about future income can also lead to changes in demand. If you learned today that you would inherit a large sum of money sometime in the future, you might borrow some money today and increase your demand for certain goods. On the other hand, if you learned that you would earn less in the future than you thought, you might reduce your demand for some goods and save more money today.

TEACH Teach It

Students need to understand the difference between normal goods and inferior goods. The effect of income on demand depends on what type of good you are considering (normal or inferior). The demand for normal goods varies directly with income (you buy more when your income goes up and you buy less when your income goes down). Most things we can think of are normal goods. The demand for inferior goods varies inversely with income (you buy less when your income goes up and more when your income goes down).

FOCUS Active Learning

Have students list five goods they would no longer buy if they won millions of dollars from the lottery. Discuss the students' lists and explain that whether a good is normal or inferior depends on a person's tastes and preferences. For example, one student might buy less macaroni and cheese if he or she won the lottery, while another might be happy because he or she could now buy more!

FOCUS Test It

Use the following questions to assess and reinforce your students' understanding of related goods (substitutes and complements):

1 If two goods are substitutes, a decrease in the price of one will lead to a(n) ________________ in the demand for the other. If two goods are complements, a decrease in the price of one will lead to a(n) ____________in the demand for the other.

   a. increase, decrease
   b. decrease, increase
   c. increase, increase
   d. decrease, decrease
   e. It cannot be determined.

   (b)

2. A(n) __________________ in consumer income will lead to a decrease in the demand for an inferior good, while an increase in consumer income will lead to a(n) __________________ in the demand for a normal good.

   a. increase, decrease
   b. decrease, increase
   c. increase, increase
   d. decrease, decrease
   e. It cannot be determined.

   (c)

St. Louis Federal Reserve Bank Resources

"Higher Gasoline Prices: Temporary or Time to Buy a Hybrid?," *PAGE ONE ECONOMICS*, (September 2012)

How long will an increase in gasoline prices last? Will prices eventually decrease, or do price increases signal a need to change driving habits or buy a hybrid fuel vehicle? This article discusses factors that might influence drivers' decisions.

FOCUS Graph It

Refer to Figure 5.5 to compare individual and market demand curves. The market demand curve is a summation of the individual demand curves.

Figure 5.5 Individual Demand Curves and the Market Demand Curve

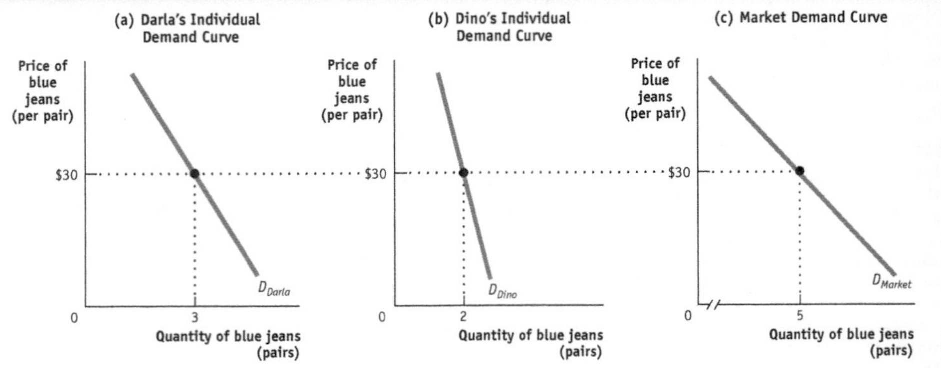

Darla and Dino are the only two consumers of blue jeans in the market. Panel (a) shows Darla's individual demand curve: the number of pairs of jeans she will buy per year at any given price. Panel (b) shows Dino's individual demand curve. Given that Darla and Dino are the only two consumers, the *market demand* curve, which shows the quantity of blue jeans demanded by all consumers at any given price, is shown in panel (c). The market demand curve is the *horizontal sum* of the individual demand curves of all consumers. In this case, at any given price, the quantity demanded by the market is the sum of the quantities demanded by Darla and Dino.

An **individual demand curve** illustrates the relationship between quantity demanded and price for an individual consumer.

AP® Exam Tip

A mnemonic to help you remember the factors that shift demand is TRIBE. Demand is shifted by changes in . . .
Tastes and preferences,
prices of **R**elated goods
Income,
the number of **B**uyers, and
Expectations.

Changes in the Number of Consumers As we've already noted, one of the reasons for rising cotton demand between 2012 and 2013 was a growing world population. Because of population growth, overall demand for cotton would have risen even if the demand of each individual wearer of cotton clothing had remained unchanged.

Let's introduce a new concept: the **individual demand curve**, which shows the relationship between quantity demanded and price for an individual consumer. For example, suppose that Darla is a consumer of cotton blue jeans; also suppose that all blue jeans are the same, so they sell for the same price. Panel (a) of **Figure 5.5** shows how many pairs of jeans she will buy per year at any given price per pound. Then D_{Darla} is Darla's individual demand curve.

The *market demand curve* shows how the combined quantity demanded by all consumers depends on the market price of that good. (Most of the time, when economists refer to the demand curve, they mean the market demand curve.) The market demand curve is the *horizontal sum* of the individual demand curves of all consumers in that market. To see what we mean by the term *horizontal sum*, assume for a moment that there are only two consumers of blue jeans, Darla and Dino. Dino's individual demand curve, D_{Dino}, is shown in panel (b). Panel (c) shows the market demand curve. At any given price, the quantity demanded by the market is the sum of the quantities demanded by Darla and Dino. For example, at a price of $30 per pair, Darla demands 3 pairs of jeans per year and Dino demands 2 pairs per year. So the quantity demanded by the market is 5 pairs per year.

Clearly, the quantity demanded by the market at any given price is larger with Dino present than it would be if Darla were the only consumer. The quantity demanded at any given price would be even larger if we added a third consumer, then a fourth, and so on. So an increase in the number of consumers leads to an increase in demand.

For an overview of the factors that shift demand, see **Table 5.1**.

56 Section 2 Supply and Demand

Table 5.1 Factors That Shift Demand

When this happens . . .		. . . demand increases	But when this happens . . .		. . . demand decreases
When the price of a substitute rises . . .	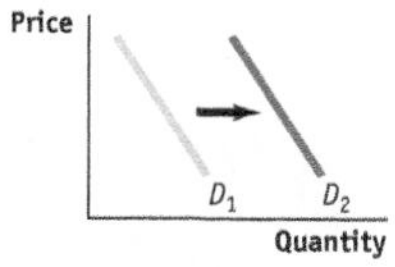	. . . demand for the original good increases.	When the price of a substitute falls . . .	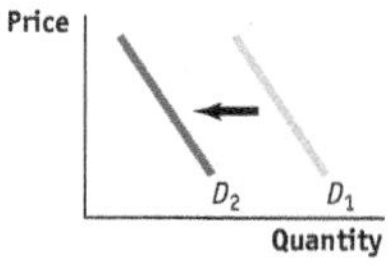	. . . demand for the original good decreases.
When the price of a complement falls . . .	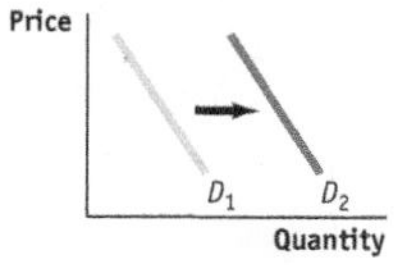	. . . demand for the original good increases.	When the price of a complement rises . . .	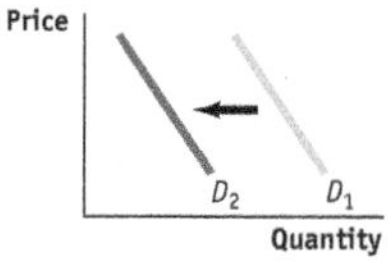	. . . demand for the original good decreases.
When income rises . . .	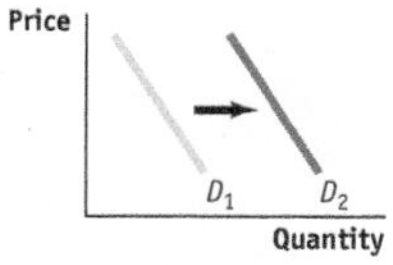	. . . demand for a normal good increases.	When income falls . . .	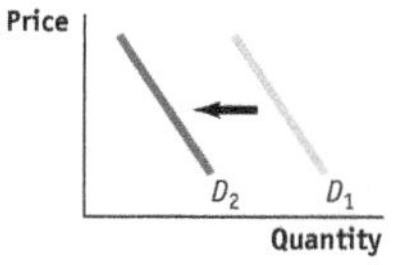	. . . demand for a normal good decreases.
When income falls . . .	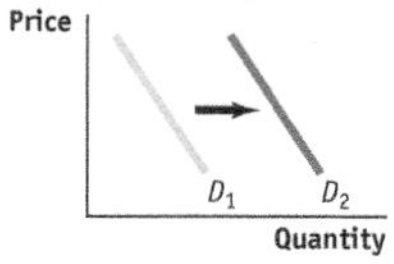	. . . demand for an inferior good increases.	When income rises . . .	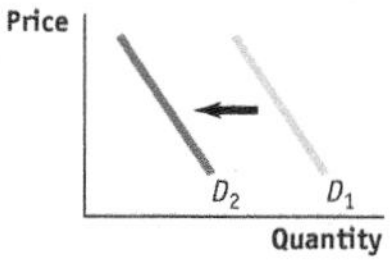	. . . demand for an inferior good decreases.
When tastes change in favor of a good . . .	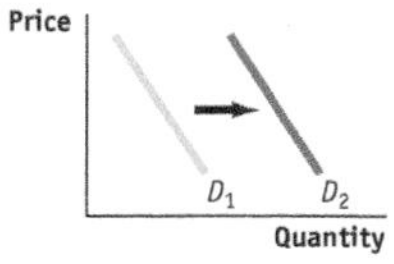	. . . demand for the good increases.	When tastes change against a good . . .	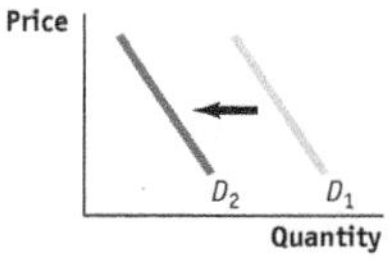	. . . demand for the good decreases.
When the price is expected to rise in the future . . .	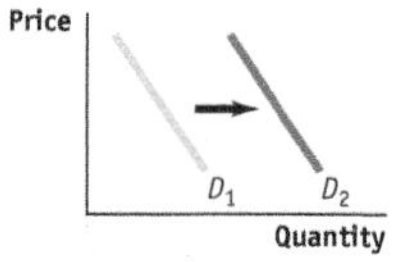	. . . demand for the good increases today.	When the price is expected to fall in the future . . .	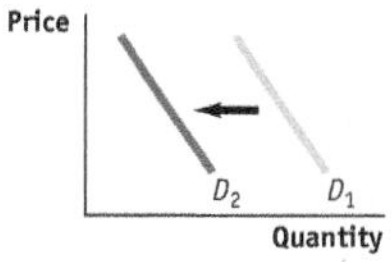	. . . demand for the good decreases today.
When the number of consumers rises . . .	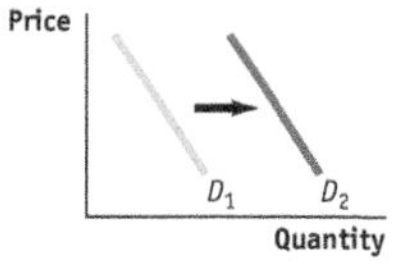	. . . market demand for the good increases.	When the number of consumers falls . . .	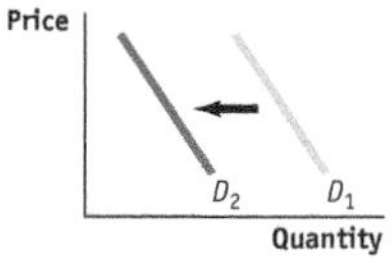	. . . market demand for the good decreases.

FOCUS Graph It

Table 5.1 summarizes the factors that shift demand and how they affect demand. Call out changes listed in the "When this happens. . ." and "But when this happens" columns in random order. After you call out each change, have students draw the change in demand on their individual whiteboards and hold them up. Tell your class the correct direction of the change. Quickly check each student's graph to make sure it has correct labels on the axes and demand curves, that the demand curve slopes downward, and that demand has shifted in the correct direction (as shown in Table 5.1). Alert students to any errors or omissions on their graphs. As you go through the table of changes, the corrections needed should decrease, and the graphing should go more quickly. You can make this a team or group activity and perhaps use competition to generate interest and excitement!

FOCUS Active Learning

TRM To build a study guide for the topics covered in this module, use **Worksheet 5.5 (Demand Summary Study Guide)** from the TRM.

Module 5 Supply and Demand: Introduction and Demand 57

FOCUS Active Learning

Here is a way to motivate students to generate examples rather than to simply listen to the instructor lecture with prepared examples. You might liken it to Improv Theatre rather than a scripted play.

- Once you have explained demand shifters, have the students generate a list of about six to eight goods and/or services. Write them on the board.
- Use these, and the demand shifters, to practice.

Example: Suppose the first good is pizza. Ask the class to consider how the price of a substitute (hamburgers?) or complement (breadsticks?) to pizza might affect the demand for it. Once your students have correctly analyzed such a shift, move to the next good and ask how income would affect demand for this good. Is it normal or inferior? If it's normal, can they think of something that is an inferior good?

OPEN & CLOSE Exit Slip

TRM *Please see* ***Exit Slip: Module 5*** *in the TRM for formative multiple-choice questions to ask before finishing your lesson. These questions will help you quickly assess whether your students have mastered the module's concepts before moving on.*

Answers to the Exit Slip Questions

1. C
2. C
3. A

Answers to Module 5 Review Questions

Check Your Understanding

1. a. The quantity of umbrellas demanded is higher at any given price on a rainy day than on a dry day. This is a rightward *shift* of the demand curve.

b. The quantity of weekend calls demanded rises in response to a price reduction. This is a *movement along* the demand curve for weekend calls.

c. The demand for roses increases the week of Valentine's Day. This is a rightward *shift* of the demand curve.

d. The quantity of gasoline demanded falls in response to a rise in price. This is a *movement along* the demand curve.

FYI Beating the Traffic

All big cities have traffic problems, and many local authorities try to discourage driving in the crowded city center. If we think of an auto trip to the city center as a good that people consume, we can use the economics of demand to analyze anti-traffic policies.

One common strategy of local governments is to reduce the demand for auto trips by lowering the prices of substitutes. Many metropolitan areas subsidize bus and rail service, hoping to lure commuters out of their cars.

An alternative strategy is to raise the price of complements: several major U.S. cities impose high taxes on commercial parking garages, both to raise revenue and to discourage people from driving into the city. High tolls for bridges and tunnels going into cities such as New York serve the same purposes.

However, few cities have been willing to adopt the politically controversial direct approach: reducing congestion by raising the price of simply driving in the city. So it was a shock when, in 2003, London imposed a "congestion charge" on all cars entering the city center during business hours—currently £10 (about $16) for drivers who pay on the same day they travel.

Compliance is monitored with automatic cameras that photograph license plates. People can either pay the charge in advance or pay it by midnight of the day they have driven. If they pay on the day after they have driven, the charge increases to £12 (about $20). And if they don't pay and are caught, a fine of £130 (about $212) is imposed for each transgression. (A full description of the rules can be found at www.cclondon.com.)

Not surprisingly, the result of the new policy confirms the law of demand: three years after the charge was put in place, traffic in central London was about 10 percent lower than before the charge. In February 2007, the British government doubled the area of London covered by the congestion charge, and it suggested that it might institute congestion charging across the country by 2015. Several American and European municipalities, having seen the success of London's congestion charge, have said that they are seriously considering adopting a congestion charge as well.

London's bold policy to charge cars a fee to enter the city center proved effective in reducing traffic congestion.

MODULE 5 Review

Check Your Understanding

1. Explain whether each of the following events represents (i) a *change in demand* (a *shift* of the demand curve) or (ii) a *movement along* the demand curve (a *change in the quantity demanded*).
   - **a.** A store owner finds that customers are willing to pay more for umbrellas on rainy days.
   - **b.** When XYZ Telecom, a long-distance telephone service provider, offered reduced rates on weekends, its volume of weekend calling increased sharply.
   - **c.** People buy more long-stem roses the week of Valentine's Day, even though the prices are higher than at other times during the year.
   - **d.** A sharp rise in the price of gasoline leads many commuters to join carpools in order to reduce their gasoline purchases.

Tackle the Test: Multiple-Choice Questions

1. Which of the following would increase demand for a normal good? A decrease in
   - a. price
   - b. income
   - c. the price of a substitute
   - d. consumer taste for a good
   - e. the price of a complement
2. A decrease in the price of butter would most likely decrease the demand for
   - a. margarine.
   - b. bagels.
   - c. jelly.
   - d. milk.
   - e. syrup.
3. If an increase in income leads to a decrease in demand, the good is
   - a. a complement.
   - b. a substitute.
   - c. inferior.
   - d. abnormal.
   - e. normal.
4. Which of the following will occur if consumers expect the price of a good to fall in the coming months?
   - a. The quantity demanded will rise today.
   - b. The quantity demanded will remain the same today.
   - c. Demand will increase today.
   - d. Demand will decrease today.
   - e. No change will occur today.
5. Which of the following will increase the demand for disposable diapers?
   - a. a new "baby boom"
   - b. concern over the environmental effect of landfills
   - c. a decrease in the price of cloth diapers
   - d. a move toward earlier potty training of children
   - e. a decrease in the price of disposable diapers

Tackle the Test: Free-Response Questions

1. Create a table with two hypothetical prices for a good and two corresponding quantities demanded. Choose the prices and quantities so that they illustrate the law of demand. Using your data, draw a correctly labeled graph showing the demand curve for the good. Using the same graph, illustrate an increase in demand for the good.

Rubric for FRQ 1 (6 points)

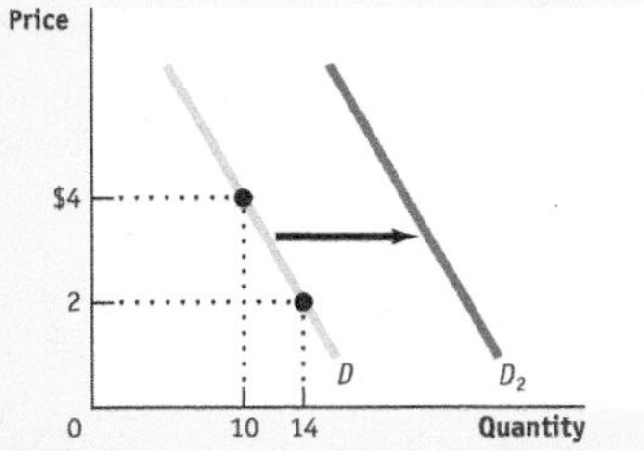

Price	Quantity
$4	10
2	14

1 point: Table with data labeled "Price" (or "*P*") and "Quantity" (or "*Q*")

1 point: Values in the table show a negative relationship between *P* and *Q*

1 point: Graph with "Price" on the vertical axis and "Quantity" on the horizontal axis

1 point: Negatively sloped curve labeled "Demand" or "*D*"

1 point: Demand curve correctly plots the data from the table

1 point: A second demand curve (with a label such as D_2) shown to the right of the original demand curve

2. Draw a correctly labeled graph showing the demand for apples. On your graph, illustrate what happens to the demand for apples if a new report from the Surgeon General finds that an apple a day really *does* keep the doctor away.
(3 points)

Tackle the Test: Multiple-Choice Questions

1. e
2. a
3. c
4. d
5. a

Tackle the Test: Free-Response Question

Rubric for FRQ 2 (3 points)

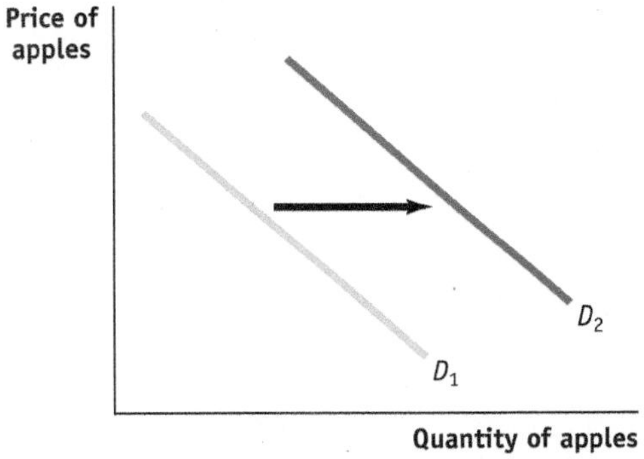

1 point: The vertical axis is labeled "Price" and the horizontal axis is labeled "Quantity."

1 point: The original demand curve is downward-sloping and labeled.

1 point: The new demand curve is labeled, downward-sloping, and to the right of the original demand curve.

Module 5 Supply and Demand: Introduction and Demand **59**

PD To prepare for teaching this lesson, you may want to consult the **Module 6 Sample Lecture** in the TRM.

OPEN & CLOSE Start Here

To introduce Module 6, remind students that the purpose of the supply and demand model is to understand how price and quantity sold are determined in a market. Also remind them how a change in the number of items auctioned affected price in the auction example that opened Module 5. Ask students to suggest ways that supply is similar to and different from demand (*both part of the market for a good or service, demand is the buyers versus sellers on the supply side, list of determinates will be different*). In this module, the supply side of the market is developed so that later, in Module 7, the two can be put together to find equilibrium market price and quantity sold.

TEACH Connect It

Studying the supply side of the market requires students to adopt the perspective of the producer. This can be more difficult for students than adopting the perspective of a consumer because they are much more familiar with consuming than producing. However, working with the demand side of the model has given students practice that can help them more easily develop the supply side of the model. For example, the distinction between a change in supply and a change in quantity supplied is the same idea as the distinction between a change in demand and a change in quantity demanded. You should also point out the similarity between the list of factors that shift demand and the factors that shift supply. For example, highlight the parallel between the number of consumers and the number of producers, and consumer and producer expectations.

TEACH Connect It

Supply schedules and supply curves are constructed in the same way as demand schedules and demand curves were constructed in Module 5. Help students see this commonality when they start their study of supply. Of course, they should realize that supply curves slope upward and demand curves slope downward (and why).

Bonnie Taylor Barry/Shutterstock

MODULE 6 Supply and Demand: Supply

In this Module, you will learn to:

- Draw a supply curve and interpret its meaning
- Discuss the difference between movements along the supply curve and changes in supply
- List the factors that shift the supply curve

The Supply Curve

Some parts of the world are especially well suited to growing cotton, and the United States is one of those. But even in the United States, some land is better suited to growing cotton than other land. Whether American farmers restrict their cotton-growing to only the most ideal locations or expand it to less suitable land depends on the price they expect to get for their cotton. Moreover, there are many other areas in the world where cotton could be grown—such as Pakistan, Brazil, Turkey, and China. Whether farmers there actually grow cotton depends, again, on the price.

So just as the quantity of cotton that consumers want to buy depends on the price they have to pay, the quantity that producers are willing to produce and sell—the **quantity supplied**—depends on the price they are offered.

AP® Exam Tip

A change in demand does not affect the supply schedule, and it does not affect the supply curve, which represents the supply schedule on a graph. A change in demand does cause a change in the price, so it will affect the quantity supplied by causing a movement along the supply curve.

The Supply Schedule and the Supply Curve

The table in **Figure 6.1** shows how the quantity of cotton made available varies with the price—that is, it shows a hypothetical **supply schedule** for cotton.

A supply schedule works the same way as the demand schedule shown in Figure 5.1: in this case, the table shows the number of pounds of cotton farmers are willing to sell at different prices. At a price of $0.50 per pound, farmers are willing to sell only 8 billion pounds of cotton per year. At $0.75 per pound, they're willing to sell 9.1 billion pounds. At $1, they're willing to sell 10 billion pounds, and so on.

In the same way that a demand schedule can be represented graphically by a demand curve, a supply schedule can be represented by a **supply curve**, as shown in Figure 6.1. Each point on the curve represents an entry from the table.

Suppose that the price of cotton rises from $1 to $1.25; we can see that the quantity of cotton farmers are willing to sell rises from 10 billion to 10.7 billion pounds. This is

The **quantity supplied** is the actual amount of a good or service people are willing to sell at some specific price.

A **supply schedule** shows how much of a good or service producers would supply at different prices.

A **supply curve** shows the relationship between the quantity supplied and the price.

St. Louis Federal Reserve Bank Resources

"Supply," *The Economic Lowdown Podcast Series*, Volume 1, Episode 7

The seventh episode of our podcast series discusses the supply side of the market: the law of supply, the slope of the curve, and the difference between a change in supply and a change in quantity supplied.

Figure 6.1 The Supply Schedule and the Supply Curve

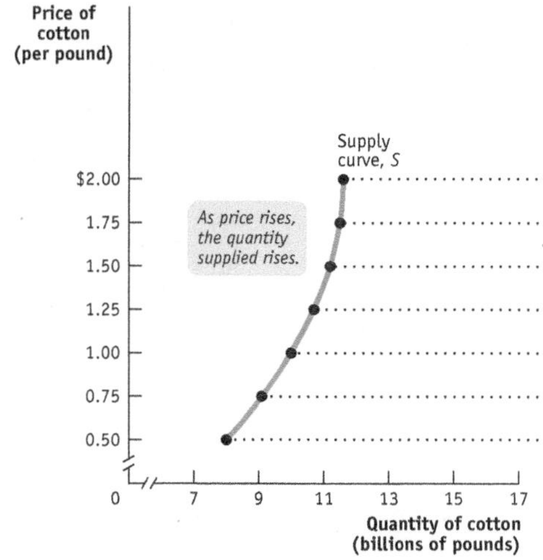

Supply Schedule for Cotton

Price of cotton (per pound)	Quantity of cotton supplied (billions of pounds)
$2.00	11.6
1.75	11.5
1.50	11.2
1.25	10.7
1.00	10.0
0.75	9.1
0.50	8.0

The supply schedule for cotton is plotted to yield the corresponding supply curve, which shows how much of a good producers are willing to sell at any given price. The supply curve and the supply schedule reflect the fact that supply curves are usually upward sloping: the quantity supplied rises when the price rises.

the normal situation for a supply curve, that a higher price leads to a higher quantity supplied. Some economists refer to this positive relationship as the **law of supply**. So just as demand curves normally slope downward, supply curves normally slope upward: the higher the price being offered, the more of any good or service producers will be willing to sell.

The **law of supply** says that, other things being equal, the price and quantity supplied of a good are positively related.

Shifts of the Supply Curve

Until recently, cotton remained relatively cheap over the past several decades. One reason is that the amount of land cultivated for cotton expanded over 35% from 1945 to 2007. However, the major factor accounting for cotton's relative cheapness was advances in the production technology, with output per acre more than quadrupling from 1945 to 2007. **Figure 6.2** on the next page illustrates these events in terms of the supply schedule and the supply curve for cotton.

The table in Figure 6.2 shows two supply schedules. The schedule before improved cotton-growing technology was adopted is the same one as in Figure 6.1. The second schedule shows the supply of cotton *after* the improved technology was adopted. Just as a change in demand schedules leads to a shift of the demand curve, a change in supply schedules leads to a shift of the supply curve—a **change in supply**. This is shown in Figure 6.2 by the shift of the supply curve before the adoption of new cotton-growing technology, S_1, to its new position after the adoption of new cotton-growing technology, S_2. Notice that S_2 lies to the right of S_1, a reflection of the fact that the quantity supplied rises at any given price.

AP® Exam Tip

The supply curve itself shows the relationship between the price and the quantity supplied, so you should not shift the supply curve to show the effect of a change in the price. When there is a change in a nonprice determinant of supply, such as production costs or the number of firms, supply changes and the supply curve shifts.

A **change in supply** is a shift of the supply curve, which changes the quantity supplied at any given price.

FOCUS Active Learning

TRM Watch Jacob Clifford's video "Demand and Supply Explained (2 of 2)" with the class (see econextras video list with hyperlinks on the bcs and TRFD) as an introduction to the module. **Worksheet 6.1 (Demand and Supply Explained: 2 of 2)** in the TRM includes teacher notes to aid in understanding.

FOCUS Graph It

Have students look at the graph in Figure 6.1.

- Notice that when the price of cotton increased from $1.00 to $1.50, the corresponding quantity supplied goes up from 10 billions of pounds to 11.2 billions of pounds. Remind students that producers want to sell *more* of a product at a *higher* price.
- This situation is different from that depicted in Figure 5.1. As the price of cotton increased, the quantity demanded decreased. Consumers want to buy *fewer* products at a *higher* price.

TEACH Teach It

As with demand, a change in supply versus a change in quantity supplied can be confusing.

Reviewing that only a change in price will cause a change in quantity supplied will help the students recognize that any other change (determinants of supply) will cause a change in supply, thus shifting the supply curve.

Key points:

- Only a change in price causes a change in quantity supplied.
- A change in quantity supplied causes a movement along an existing supply curve.
- A change in one or more of the determinants of supply causes a change in supply.
- A change in supply leads to a shift in the supply curve.

St. Louis Federal Reserve Bank Resources

"Supply," *The Economic Lowdown Video Series*, Episode 1

Education Specialist Scott Wolla explains the concept of supply in the first episode of the Economic Lowdown Video Series.

FOCUS Active Learning

TRM Refer to **Worksheet 6.2 (Market Changes in Supply)** from the TRM to practice graphing changes in supply and quantity supplied.

Students will start with a market in equilibrium and, given certain changes, decide whether demand or quantity demand changes.

FOCUS Active Learning

Although it is very easy for people to imagine themselves as consumers (demanders), it's difficult for most people to imagine themselves as producers (suppliers), so the supply curve is less intuitive.

- Ask your students if they have ever had a job. Tell those who respond "yes" that they have been a supplier of labor.
- Pick a job that involves a high degree of manual labor (e.g., raking leaves). Ask students to write down how many hours they are willing to rake leaves at each of the following hourly rates: $16.00, $12.00, $10.00, $8.00, $6.00.
- Repeat this exercise for a job that involves very little manual labor (e.g., a cashier). Again, ask students to write down how many hours they are willing to work at the cash register at each of the following hourly wages: $16.00, $12.00, $10.00, $8.00, $6.00.
- Then for each job, ask three students to report their responses. Add up the hours at each wage and draw the upward-sloping supply curve. *Note* A few students may choose to work fewer hours as the wage rises, but generally the overall response produces an upward-sloping supply curve.

Figure 6.2 An Increase in Supply

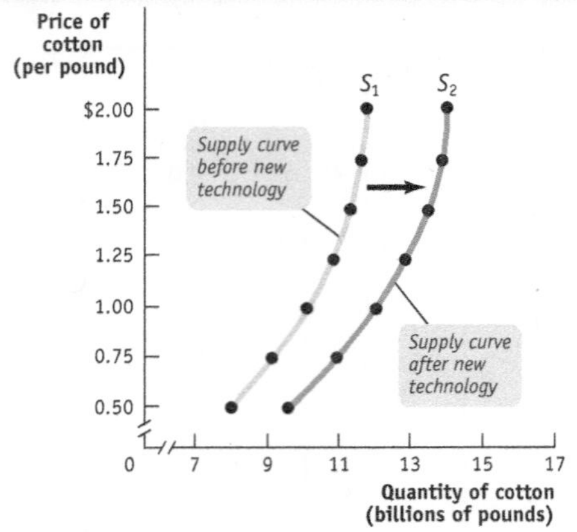

Supply Schedules for Cotton		
Price of cotton (per pound)	Quantity of cotton supplied (billions of pounds)	
	Before new technology	After new technology
$2.00	11.6	13.9
1.75	11.5	13.8
1.50	11.2	13.4
1.25	10.7	12.8
1.00	10.0	12.0
0.75	9.1	10.9
0.50	8.0	9.6

The adoption of improved cotton-growing technology generated an increase in supply—a rise in the quantity supplied at any given price. This event is represented by the two supply schedules—one showing supply before the new technology was adopted, the other showing supply after the new technology was adopted—and their corresponding supply curves. The increase in supply shifts the supply curve to the right.

A **movement along the supply curve** is a change in the quantity supplied of a good arising from a change in the good's price.

As in the analysis of demand, it's crucial to draw a distinction between such changes in supply and **movements along the supply curve**—changes in the quantity supplied arising from a change in price. We can see this difference in **Figure 6.3**. The movement from point *A* to point *B* is a movement along the supply curve: the quantity supplied rises along S_1 due to a rise in price. Here, a rise in price from $1 to $1.50 leads to a rise in the quantity supplied from 10 billion to 11.2 billion pounds of cotton. But the quantity supplied can also rise when the price is unchanged if there is an increase in supply—a rightward shift of the supply curve. This is shown by the rightward shift of the supply curve from S_1 to S_2. Holding the price constant at $1, the quantity supplied rises from 10 billion pounds at point *A* on S_1 to 12 billion pounds at point *C* on S_2.

Understanding Shifts of the Supply Curve

AP® Exam Tip

Looks can be deceiving. An increase in supply is not a shift down; it is a shift to the right, indicating an increase in the quantity supplied at every price. A decrease in supply is not a shift up, but a shift to the left, indicating a decrease in the quantity supplied at every price.

Figure 6.4 illustrates the two basic ways in which supply curves can shift. When economists talk about an "increase in supply," they mean a *rightward* shift of the supply curve: at any given price, producers supply a larger quantity of the good than before. This is shown in Figure 6.4 by the rightward shift of the original supply curve S_1 to S_2. And when economists talk about a "decrease in supply," they mean a *leftward* shift of the supply curve: at any given price, producers supply a smaller quantity of the good than before. This is represented by the leftward shift of S_1 to S_3.

Shifts of the supply curve for a good or service are mainly the result of five factors (though, as in the case of demand, there are other possible causes):

- Changes in input prices
- Changes in the prices of related goods or services

Figure 6.3 A Movement Along the Supply Curve Versus a Shift of the Supply Curve

The increase in quantity supplied when going from point *A* to point *B* reflects a movement along the supply curve: it is the result of a rise in the price of the good. The increase in quantity supplied when going from point *A* to point *C* reflects a shift of the supply curve: it is the result of an increase in the quantity supplied at any given price.

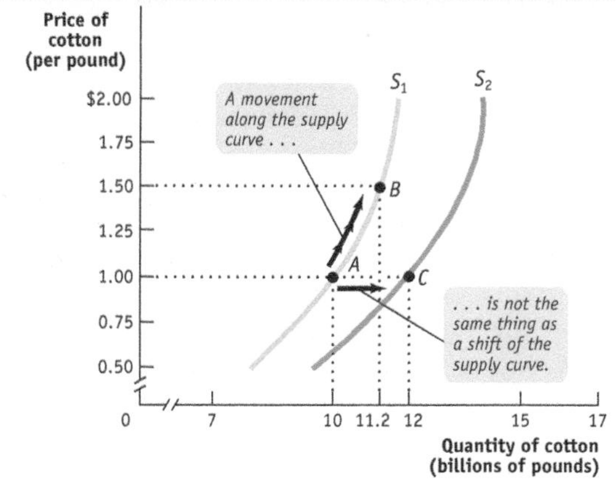

- Changes in technology
- Changes in expectations
- Changes in the number of producers

Changes in Input Prices To produce output, you need *inputs*. For example, to make vanilla ice cream, you need vanilla beans, cream, sugar, and so on. An **input** is any good or service that is used to produce another good or service. Inputs, like outputs, have prices. And an increase in the price of an input makes the production of the final

An **input** is a good or service that is used to produce another good or service.

Figure 6.4 Shifts of the Supply Curve

Any event that increases supply shifts the supply curve to the right, reflecting a rise in the quantity supplied at any given price. Any event that decreases supply shifts the supply curve to the left, reflecting a fall in the quantity supplied at any given price.

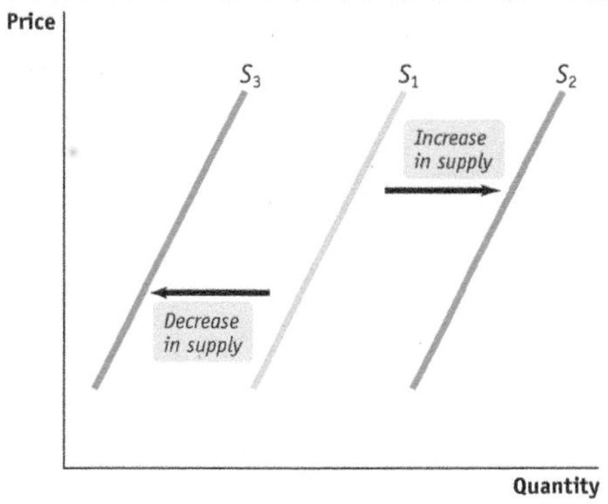

FOCUS Graph It

Have students consider the points shown in Figure 6.3. Ask them to identify what caused the movement from point *A* to point *B* (*an increase in price*) and how they would describe what happened as a result of the change in price (*a change/increase in quantity supplied*). Next ask them what caused the movement from point *A* to point *C* (*a shift of the supply curve from S_1 to S_2*) and how they would describe what occurred when the supply curve shifted (*a change/increase in supply*). Point out that a variety of factors can lead to a change in supply (i.e., a shift of the supply curve)—and that is what the rest of the module is about!

FOCUS Graph It

Have students consider Figure 6.4. Again (as in Module 5), ask them what happens to quantity as you move along the *x*-axis to the right (*it increases*). What happens to quantity as you move along the *x*-axis to the left? (*It decreases.*) Help students make the link between the changes in quantity as you move along the horizontal axis and the increase and decrease in demand shown in Figure 6.4. This may seem redundant, but the link becomes even more important with the supply curve, since a supply curve shifted to the right appears higher and a supply curve shifted to the left appears lower. Make sure your students think right and left!

FOCUS Active Learning

For each of the following changes, have students identify if there is a movement along the supply curve for pizza or a shift of the supply curve for pizza. If the supply curve shifts, in which direction does it move?

- The cost of pizza sauce increases. *Shift of the supply curve (left)*
- A new and improved pizza oven is developed to cook pizzas in half the time. *Shift of the supply curve (right)*
- Local pizza parlors start to offer a "buy one, get one free" special. *Movement along the curve (price falls)*
- The wages of pizza workers increase. *Shift of the supply curve (left)*

TEACH Teach It

This is a good point at which to again emphasize that price is measured on the vertical axis and therefore a change in price changes quantity demanded (a movement to a different point on the same demand curve). Demand refers to the demand relationship (the entire curve) that does not change when price changes. However, a variety of things will cause the entire curve to shift (i.e., cause a change in demand). These factors cause the quantity demanded to be different at each and every price. For example, at every price on D_2, the quantity demanded is higher than it was on D_1.

TEACH Teach It

Remind students that the following will change supply and shift the supply curve:

- Changes in input prices
- Changes in prices of related goods or services
- Changes in technology
- Changes in expectations
- Changes in the number of producers

TEACH Test It

Ask students whether the following pairs of goods are related in production and, if so, if they are complements in production or substitutes in production. Remind them that complements in production are goods produced at the same time, while firms can switch back and forth easily between producing substitutes in production.

- Lumber and sawdust *Yes, complements in production*
- Beef and leather *Yes, complements in production*
- Red shirts and green shirts *Yes, substitutes in production*
- Bagels and cream cheese *No, unrelated in production (maybe complements in consumption)*
- Tomatoes and steel *No, unrelated*
- Corn and wheat *Yes, substitutes in production*

TEACH Teach It

It is probably useful to remind students that technology refers to the way that resources are combined to produce output. For example, you can write a manuscript by hand or on a computer. You can dig a ditch with a shovel or a bulldozer. Each approach uses a different technology to produce the output. An advance in technology means there is a new and better way to produce, which allows firms to produce more at any given price (i.e., shifts the supply curve). Students may think of technology from the point of view of consumers (e.g., their new phone or computer gadget). Make sure they understand that technology affects the supply side of the model.

good more costly for those who produce and sell it. So producers are less willing to supply the final good at any given price, and the supply curve shifts to the left. For example, fuel is a major cost for airlines. When oil prices surged in 2007–2008, airlines began cutting back on their flight schedules and some went out of business. Similarly, a fall in the price of an input makes the production of the final good less costly for sellers. They are more willing to supply the good at any given price, and the supply curve shifts to the right.

Changes in the Prices of Related Goods or Services A single producer often produces a mix of goods rather than a single product. For example, an oil refinery produces gasoline from crude oil, but it also produces heating oil and other products from the same raw material. When a producer sells several products, the quantity of any one good it is willing to supply at any given price depends on the prices of its other co-produced goods.

This effect can run in either direction. An oil refiner will supply less gasoline at any given price when the price of heating oil rises, shifting the supply curve for gasoline to the left. But it will supply more gasoline at any given price when the price of heating oil falls, shifting the supply curve for gasoline to the right. This means that gasoline and other co-produced oil products are *substitutes in production* for refiners.

In contrast, due to the nature of the production process, other goods can be *complements in production*. For example, producers of crude oil—oil-well drillers—often find that oil wells also produce natural gas as a by-product of oil extraction. The higher the price at which a driller can sell its natural gas, the more oil wells it will drill and the more oil it will supply at any given price for oil. As a result, natural gas is a complement in production for crude oil.

Changes in Technology When economists talk about "technology," they don't necessarily mean high technology—they mean all the methods people can use to turn inputs into useful goods and services. In that sense, the whole complex sequence of activities that turn cotton from Pakistan into the pair of jeans hanging in your closet is technology.

Improvements in technology enable producers to spend less on inputs yet still produce the same output. When a better technology becomes available, reducing the cost of production, supply increases, and the supply curve shifts to the right. As we have already mentioned, improved technology enabled farmers to more than quadruple cotton output per acre planted over the past several decades. Improved technology is the main reason that, until recently, cotton remained relatively cheap even as worldwide demand grew.

Changes in Expectations Just as changes in expectations can shift the demand curve, they can also shift the supply curve. When suppliers have some choice about when they put their good up for sale, changes in the expected future price of the good can lead a supplier to supply less or more of the good today.

For example, consider the fact that gasoline and other oil products are often stored for significant periods of time at oil refineries before being sold to consumers. In fact, storage is normally part of producers' business strategy. Knowing that the demand for gasoline peaks in the summer, oil refiners normally store some of their gasoline produced during the spring for summer sale. Similarly, knowing that the demand for heating oil peaks in the winter, they normally store some of their heating oil produced during the fall for winter sale. In each case, there's a decision to be made between selling the product now versus storing it for later sale. Which choice a producer makes depends on a comparison of the current price versus the expected future price. This example illustrates how changes in expectations can alter supply: an increase in the anticipated future price of a good or service reduces supply today, a leftward shift of the supply curve. But a fall in the anticipated future price increases supply today, a rightward shift of the supply curve.

St. Louis Federal Reserve Bank Resources

"Why Do Gasoline Prices React to Things That Have Not Happened?," *Inside the Vault* (Fall, 2007)

This resource discusses how determinants of supply (e.g,. producer expectations) affect the supply of gasoline.

Changes in the Number of Producers Just as changes in the number of consumers affect the demand curve, changes in the number of producers affect the supply curve. Let's examine the **individual supply curve**, by looking at panel (a) in **Figure 6.5**. The individual supply curve shows the relationship between quantity supplied and price for an individual producer. For example, suppose that Mr. Silva is a Brazilian cotton farmer and that panel (a) of Figure 6.5 shows how many pounds of cotton he will supply per year at any given price. Then S_{Silva} is his individual supply curve.

The *market supply curve* shows how the combined total quantity supplied by all individual producers in the market depends on the market price of that good. Just as the market demand curve is the horizontal sum of the individual demand curves of all consumers, the market supply curve is the horizontal sum of the individual supply curves of all producers. Assume for a moment that there are only two producers of cotton, Mr. Silva and Mr. Liu, a Chinese cotton farmer. Mr. Liu's individual supply curve is shown in panel (b). Panel (c) shows the market supply curve. At any given price, the quantity supplied to the market is the sum of the quantities supplied by Mr. Silva and Mr. Liu. For example, at a price of $2 per pound, Mr. Silva supplies 3,000 pounds of cotton per year and Mr. Liu supplies 2,000 pounds per year, making the quantity supplied to the market 5,000 pounds.

Clearly, the quantity supplied to the market at any given price is larger with Mr. Liu present than it would be if Mr. Silva were the only supplier. The quantity supplied at a given price would be even larger if we added a third producer, then a fourth, and so on. So an increase in the number of producers leads to an increase in supply and a rightward shift of the supply curve.

For an overview of the factors that shift supply, see **Table 6.1** on the next page.

An **individual supply curve** illustrates the relationship between quantity supplied and price for an individual producer.

AP® Exam Tip

A mnemonic to help you remember the factors that shift supply is *I-RENT*. Supply is shifted by changes in . . .
Input (resource) prices,
prices of **R**elated goods and services,
Expectations,
the **N**umber of producers, and
Technology.

Figure 6.5 Individual Supply Curves and the Market Supply Curve

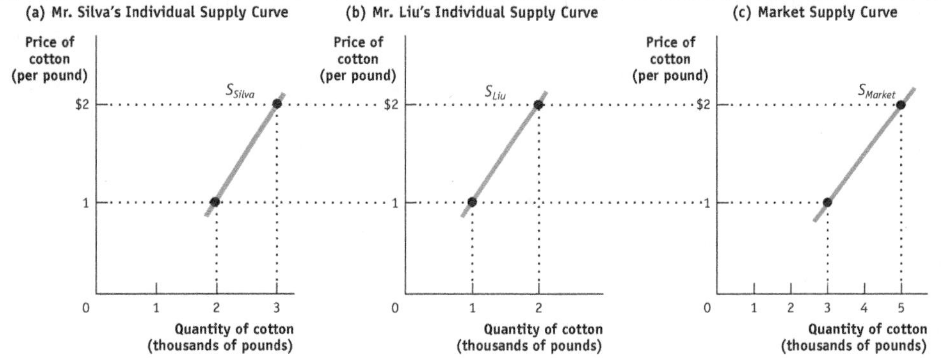

Panel (a) shows the individual supply curve for Mr. Silva, S_{Silva}, the quantity of cotton he will sell at any given price. Panel (b) shows the individual supply curve for Mr. Liu, S_{Liu}. The market supply curve, which shows the quantity of cotton supplied by all producers at any given price, is shown in panel (c). The market supply curve is the horizontal sum of the individual supply curves of all producers.

FOCUS Graph It

Figure 6.5 shows the individual and market supply curves of Mr. Silva and Mr. Liu. The quantity supplied of each individual cotton producer is represented by an individual supply curve. When we add together all of the quantities supplied by all of the individual cotton producers, they result in a market supply curve. Be sure you understand the difference between the individual supply curve and the market supply curve. The market supply curve is the horizontal sum of Mr. Silva's and Mr. Liu's individual supply curves.

Module 6 Supply and Demand: Supply 65

FOCUS Graph It

Table 6.1 summarizes the factors that shift supply and how they affect supply. Call out changes listed in the "When this happens. . ." and "But when this happens" columns in random order. After you call out each change, have students draw the change in supply on their individual whiteboards and hold them up. Tell your class the correct direction of the change. Quickly check each student's graph to make sure it has the correct labels on the axes and supply curves, that their supply curve slopes upward, and that supply has shifted in the correct direction (as shown in Table 6.1). Alert students to any errors or omissions on their graphs. As you go through the table of changes, the corrections needed should decrease and the graphing should go more quickly. You can make this a team or group activity and perhaps use competition to generate interest and excitement!

FOCUS Active Learning

TRM For a review of change in supply or change in quantity supplied, assign the video "Changes in Supply and Shifts of the Supply Curve" by Jodie Biggs (see econextras video list with hyperlinks on the bcs and TRFD). Use **Worksheet 6.3 (Changes in Supply)** from the TRM for questions on this video.

FOCUS Active Learning

TRM Use **Worksheet 6.4 (Supply Summary Study Guide)** in the TRM to prepare a study guide for the topics covered in this module.

OPEN & CLOSE Exit Slip

*TRM Please see **Exit Slip: Module 6** in the TRM for formative multiple-choice questions to ask before finishing your lesson. These questions will help you quickly assess whether your students have mastered the module's concepts before moving on.*

Answers to the Exit Slip Questions

1. D
2. C

Table 6.1 Factors That Shift Supply

When this happens . . .		. . . supply increases	But when this happens . . .		. . . supply decreases
When the price of an input falls . . .	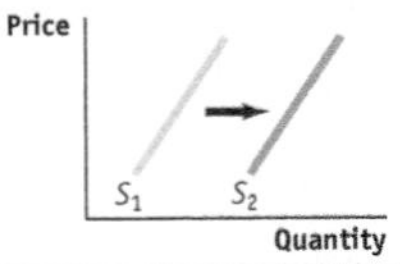	. . . supply of the good increases.	When the price of an input rises . . .	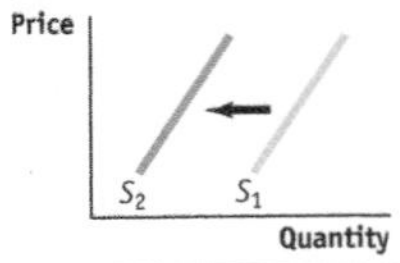	. . . supply of the good decreases.
When the price of a substitute in production falls . . .	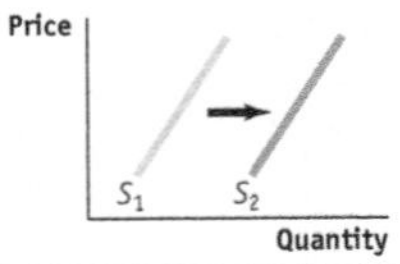	. . . supply of the original good increases.	When the price of a substitute in production rises . . .	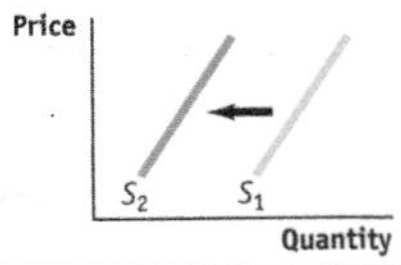	. . . supply of the original good decreases.
When the price of a complement in production rises . . .	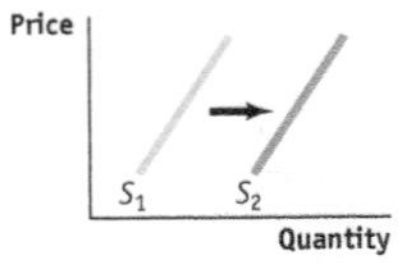	. . . supply of the original good increases.	When the price of a complement in production falls . . .	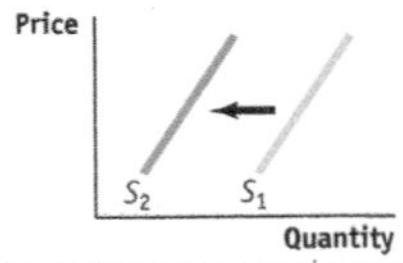	. . . supply of the original good decreases.
When the technology used to produce the good improves . . .	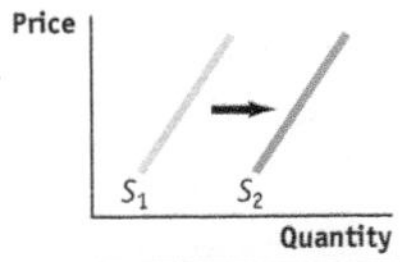	. . . supply of the good increases.	When the best technology used to produce the good is no longer available . . .	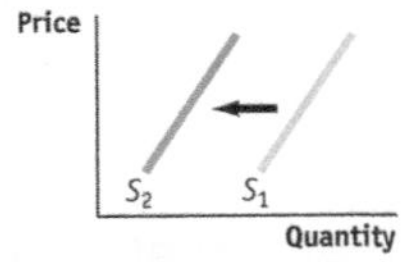	. . . supply of the good decreases.
When the price is expected to fall in the future . . .	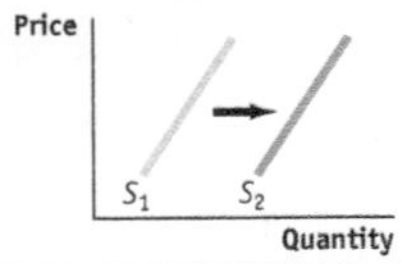	. . . supply of the good increases today.	When the price is expected to rise in the future . . .	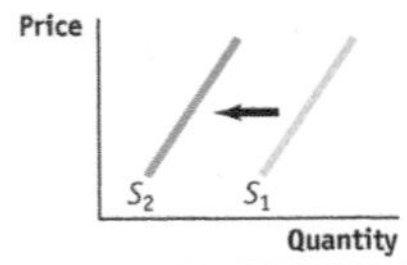	. . . supply of the good decreases today.
When the number of producers rises . . .	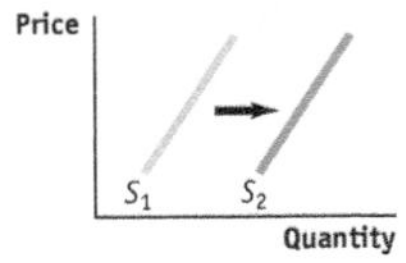	. . . market supply of the good increases.	When the number of producers falls . . .	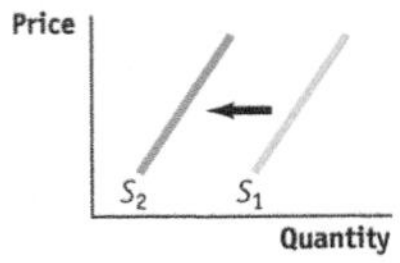	. . . market supply of the good decreases.

3.

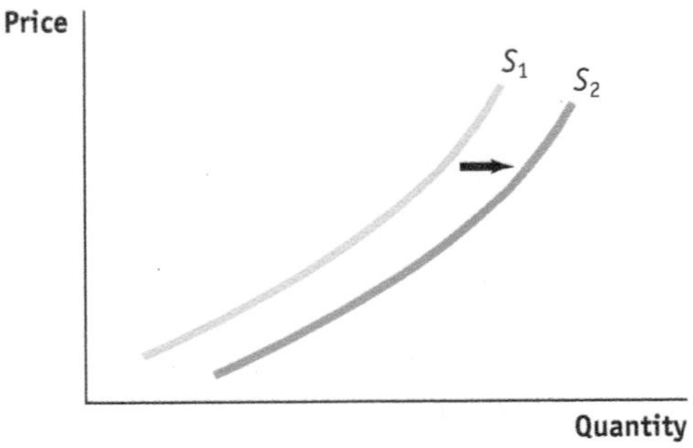

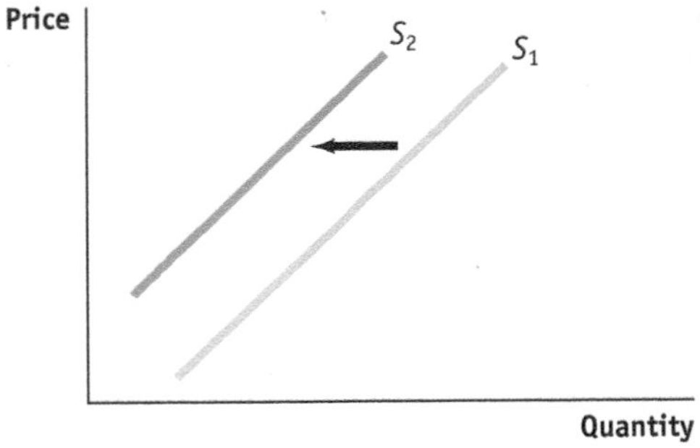

FYI Only Creatures Small and Pampered

During the 1970s, British television featured a popular show titled *All Creatures Great and Small*. It chronicled the real life of James Herriot, a country veterinarian who tended to cows, pigs, sheep, horses, and the occasional house pet, often under arduous conditions, in rural England during the 1930s. The show made it clear that, in those days, the local vet was a critical member of farming communities, saving valuable farm animals and helping farmers survive financially. And it was also clear that Mr. Herriot considered his life's work well spent.

But that was then and this is now. According to a recent article in the *New York Times*, the United States has experienced a severe decline in the number of farm veterinarians over the past two decades. The source of the problem is competition. As the number of household pets has increased and the incomes of pet owners have grown, the demand for pet veterinarians has increased sharply. As a result, vets are being drawn away from the business of caring for farm animals into the more lucrative business of caring for pets. As one vet stated, she began her career caring for farm animals but changed her mind after "doing a C-section on a cow and it's 50 bucks. Do a C-section on a Chihuahua and you get $300. It's the money. I hate to say that."

How can we translate this into supply and demand curves? Farm veterinary services and pet veterinary services are like gasoline and fuel oil: they're related goods that are substitutes in production. A veterinarian typically specializes in one type of practice or the other, and that decision often depends on the going price for the service. America's growing pet population, combined with the increased willingness of doting owners to spend on their companions' care, has driven up the price of pet veterinary services. As a result, fewer and fewer veterinarians have gone into farm animal practice. So the supply curve of farm veterinarians has shifted leftward—fewer farm veterinarians are offering their services at any given price.

In the end, farmers understand that it is all a matter of dollars and cents: they get fewer veterinarians because they are unwilling to pay more. As one farmer, who had recently lost an expensive cow due to the unavailability of a veterinarian, stated, "The fact that there's nothing you can do, you accept it as a business expense now. You didn't used to. If you have livestock, sooner or later you're going to have deadstock." (Although we should note that this farmer could have chosen to pay more for a vet who would then have saved his cow.)

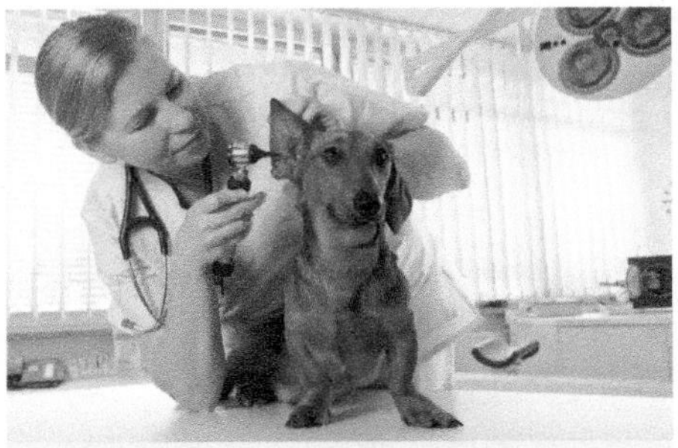

Stockphoto/Thinkstock

Higher spending on pets means fewer veterinarians are available to tend to farm animals.

MODULE 6 Review

Check Your Understanding

1. Explain whether each of the following events represents (i) a *change in* supply or (ii) a *movement along* the supply curve.
   a. During a real estate boom that causes house prices to rise, more homeowners put their houses up for sale.
   b. Many strawberry farmers open temporary roadside stands during harvest season, even though prices are usually low at that time.
   c. Immediately after the school year begins, fewer young people are available to work. Fast-food chains must raise wages, which represent the price of labor, to attract workers.
   d. Many construction workers temporarily move to areas that have suffered hurricane damage, lured by higher wages.
   e. Since new technologies have made it possible to build larger cruise ships (which are cheaper to run per passenger), Caribbean cruise lines have offered more cabins, at lower prices, than before.
2. After each of the following events, will the supply curve for the good that is mentioned shift to the left, shift to the right, or remain unchanged?
   a. The coffee berry borer beetle destroys large quantities of coffee berries.
   b. Consumers demand more bike helmets than ever.
   c. The number of tea producers increases.
   d. The price of leather, an input in wallet production, increases.

FOCUS Active Learning

TRM Have students read the August 2012 *Star Tribune* article "Rural Veterinarians: Too Few, Far Between," as it provides a more current view of farm veterinarians. Use **Worksheet 6.5 (Veterinary Shortages)** from the TRM for questions on this article.

Answers to Module 6 Review Questions

Check Your Understanding

1. a. The quantity of houses supplied rises as a result of an increase in prices. This is a *movement along* the supply curve.
   b. The quantity of strawberries supplied is higher at any given price. This is an *increase in* supply, which shifts the supply curve to the right.
   c. The quantity of labor supplied is lower at any given wage when school is in session. This is a *decrease in* supply, which shifts the supply curve to the left.
   d. The quantity of labor supplied rises in response to a rise in wages. This is a *movement along* the supply curve.
   e. The quantity of cabins supplied is higher at any given price. This is an *increase in* supply, which shifts the supply curve to the right.
2. a. The supply curve shifts to the left.
   b. The supply curve remains unchanged.
   c. The supply curve shifts to the right.
   d. The supply curve shifts to the left.

St. Louis Federal Reserve Bank Resources

Supply and Demand.notebook

This series of slides aids students in reviewing the determinants of supply and demand, provides an exercise for them to choose which of the curves shift and why, and allows them to determine which curve will shift given a market event.

Tackle the Test: Multiple-Choice Questions

1. d
2. d
3. c
4. c
5. d

Tackle the Test: Free-Response Question

Rubric for FRQ 2 (3 points)

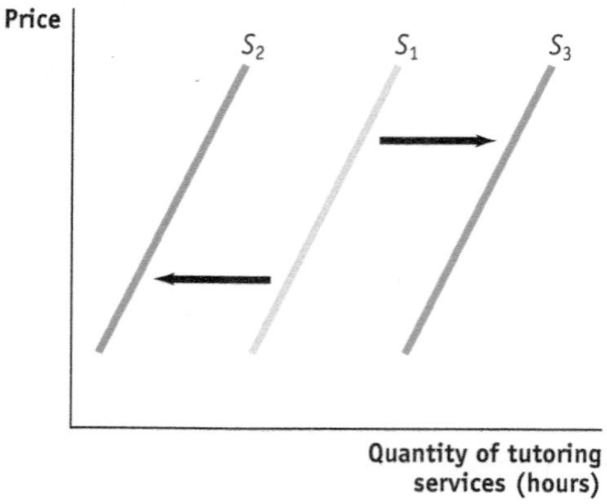

1 point: A graph with the vertical axis labeled "Price" or *P*, the horizontal axis labeled "Quantity" or *Q*, and an upward-sloping supply curve labeled S_1.

1 point: A supply curve labeled S_2 is shown to the left of S_1.

1 point: A supply curve labeled S_3 is shown to the right of S_1.

Tackle the Test: Multiple-Choice Questions

1. Which of the following will decrease the supply of rice?
   a. There is a technological advance that affects the production of *all* goods.
   b. The price of rice falls.
   c. The price of corn (which consumers regard as a substitute for rice) decreases.
   d. The wages of workers producing rice increase.
   e. The demand for rice decreases.
2. An increase in the demand for steak, which increases the price of steak, will lead to an increase in which of the following?
   a. the supply of steak
   b. the supply of hamburger (a substitute in production)
   c. the supply of chicken (a substitute in consumption)
   d. the supply of leather (a complement in production)
   e. the demand for leather
3. A technological advance in textbook production will lead to which of the following?
   a. a decrease in textbook supply
   b. an increase in textbook demand
   c. an increase in textbook supply
   d. a movement along the supply curve for textbooks
   e. an increase in textbook prices
4. Expectations among hiking boot makers that boot prices will rise significantly in the future will lead to which of the following now?
   a. an increase in boot supply
   b. no change in boot supply
   c. a decrease in boot supply
   d. a movement to the left along the boot supply curve
   e. a movement to the right along the boot supply curve
5. Starch from the stalks of potato plants is used to make packing peanuts, a complement in production. A decrease in potato demand that lowers potato prices will cause which of the following in the packing-peanut market?
   a. an increase in supply and no change in demand
   b. an increase in supply and a decrease in demand
   c. a decrease in both demand and supply
   d. a decrease in supply and no change in demand
   e. a decrease in supply and an increase in demand

Tackle the Test: Free-Response Questions

1. Tesla Motors makes sports cars powered by lithium batteries.
   a. Draw a correctly labeled graph showing a hypothetical supply curve for Tesla sports cars.
   b. On the same graph, show the effect of a major new discovery of lithium that lowers the price of lithium.
   c. Suppose Tesla Motors expects to be able to sell its cars for a higher price next month. Explain the effect that will have on the supply of Tesla cars this month.

Rubric for FRQ 1 (4 points)

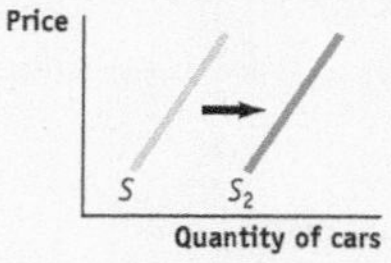

1 point: Graph with "Price" or "*P*" on the vertical axis and "Quantity" or "*Q*" on the horizontal axis

1 point: Positively-sloped curve labeled "Supply" or "*S*"

1 point: A second supply curve shown to the right of the original supply curve with a label such as S_2 indicating that it is the new supply curve

1 point: Correct explanation that the expectation of higher prices next month would lead to a decrease in the supply of Tesla cars this month because the company will want to sell more of its cars when the price is higher

2. Suppose AP® Economics students at your school offer tutoring services to students in regular economics courses.
   a. Draw a correctly labeled graph showing the supply curve for tutoring services measured in hours. Label the supply curve "S_1".
   b. Suppose the wage paid for babysitting, an alternative activity for AP® Economics students, increases. Show the effect of this wage increase on the graph you drew for part a. Label the new supply curve "S_2".
   c. Suppose instead that the number of AP® Economics students increases. Show the effect of this increase in AP® Economics students on the same graph you drew for parts a and b. Label the new supply curve "S_3".

   (3 points)

STR/AFP/Getty Images

MODULE 7 Supply and Demand: Equilibrium

In this Module, you will learn to:

- Explain how supply and demand curves determine a market's equilibrium price and equilibrium quantity
- Describe how price moves the market back to equilibrium in the case of a shortage or surplus
- Explain how equilibrium price and quantity are affected when there is a change in either supply or demand
- Explain how equilibrium price and quantity are affected when there is a simultaneous change in both supply and demand

Supply, Demand, and Equilibrium

We have now covered the first three key elements in the supply and demand model: the demand curve, the supply curve, and the set of factors that shift each curve. The next step is to put these elements together to show how they can be used to predict the actual price at which the good is bought and sold, as well as the actual quantity transacted.

In competitive markets this interaction of supply and demand tends to move toward what economists call *equilibrium*. Imagine a busy afternoon at your local supermarket; there are long lines at the checkout counters. Then one of the previously closed registers opens. The first thing that happens is a rush to the newly opened register. But soon enough things settle down and shoppers have rearranged themselves so that the line at the newly opened register is about as long as all the others. This situation—all the checkout lines are now the same length, and none of the shoppers can be better off by doing something different—is what economists call **equilibrium**.

The concept of equilibrium helps us understand the price at which a good or service is bought and sold as well as the quantity transacted of the good or service. A competitive market is in equilibrium when the price has moved to a level at which the quantity of a good demanded equals the quantity of that good supplied. At that price, no individual seller could make herself better off by offering to sell either more or less of the good and no individual buyer could make himself better off by offering to buy more or less of the good. Recall the shoppers at the supermarket who cannot make themselves better off (cannot save time) by changing lines. Similarly, at the market equilibrium, the price has moved to a level that exactly matches the quantity demanded by consumers to the quantity supplied by sellers.

An economic situation is in **equilibrium** when no individual would be better off doing something different.

AP® Exam Tip

Equilibrium is a term you will hear often throughout the course. When a market is in equilibrium, the quantity supplied equals the quantity demanded. There are no shortages or surpluses pushing the price up or down, and therefore there is no tendency for the price or the quantity to change.

PD To prepare for teaching this lesson, you may want to consult the **Module 7 Sample Lecture** in the TRM.

OPEN & CLOSE Start Here

This module brings together supply and demand and introduces equilibrium in the supply and demand model. Students should understand that when markets are allowed to operate freely, the price and quantity sold will always move toward the market equilibrium. With supply and demand together at last, we can use the model to analyze how a change in a factor that affects demand or supply (discussed in Modules 5 and 6) will affect the market price and quantity of a good or service.

Ask students for examples of a recent price change for something they have purchased. Have the class discuss what demand or supply factor might have led to the price change. Help students start to look for applications of the supply and demand model in the world around them.

St. Louis Federal Reserve Bank Resources

"Market Equilibrium," *The Economic Lowdown Podcast Series*, Episode 8

This podcast discusses how market equilibrium and the price we pay is determined in a market.

TEACH Connect It

Help students remember that the term *equilibrium* is used outside economics. Ask them where else they might have heard the term used (*e.g., in other subjects like physics or in everyday use*). Ask them what it means if you lose your equilibrium when walking (*you fall down*). And then you lay there in equilibrium until you get back up! In general, equilibrium means balance or no tendency for change. If students understand the general concept of equilibrium, they will better understand it in the supply and demand model and in other models later in the course.

FOCUS Graph It

The equilibrium point is found at the intersection of the supply and demand curves, as shown in Figure 7.1. However, make sure your students understand that the equilibrium price is shown on the vertical axis and the equilibrium quantity on the horizontal axis. It is important that students learn to draw the lines over and down to find the price and quantity on the axes—they will not receive points on the AP® exam for internally labeled points that do not show *P* and *Q* on the axes.

A competitive market is in equilibrium when the price has moved to a level at which the quantity demanded of a good equals the quantity supplied of that good. The price at which this takes place is the **equilibrium price**, also referred to as the **market-clearing price**. The quantity of the good bought and sold at that price is the **equilibrium quantity**.

The price that matches the quantity supplied and the quantity demanded is the **equilibrium price**; the quantity bought and sold at that price is the **equilibrium quantity**. The equilibrium price is also known as the **market-clearing price**: it is the price that "clears the market" by ensuring that every buyer willing to pay that price finds a seller willing to sell at that price, and vice versa. So how do we find the equilibrium price and quantity?

Finding the Equilibrium Price and Quantity

The easiest way to determine the equilibrium price and quantity in a market is by putting the supply curve and the demand curve on the same diagram. Since the supply curve shows the quantity supplied at any given price and the demand curve shows the quantity demanded at any given price, the price at which the two curves cross is the equilibrium price: the price at which quantity supplied equals quantity demanded.

Figure 7.1 combines the demand curve from Figure 5.1 and the supply curve from Figure 6.1. They *intersect* at point *E*, which is the equilibrium of this market; $1 is the equilibrium price and 10 billion pounds is the equilibrium quantity.

Let's confirm that point *E* fits our definition of equilibrium. At a price of $1 per pound, cotton farmers are willing to sell 10 billion pounds a year and cotton consumers want to buy 10 billion pounds a year. So at the price of $1 a pound, the quantity of cotton supplied equals the quantity demanded. Notice that at any other price the market would not clear: every willing buyer would not be able to find a willing seller, or vice versa. More specifically, if the price were more than $1, the quantity supplied would exceed the quantity demanded; if the price were less than $1, the quantity demanded would exceed the quantity supplied.

The model of supply and demand, then, predicts that given the demand and supply curves shown in Figure 7.1, 10 billion pounds of cotton would change

Figure 7.1 Market Equilibrium

Market equilibrium occurs at point *E*, where the supply curve and the demand curve intersect. In equilibrium, the quantity demanded is equal to the quantity supplied. In this market, the equilibrium price is $1 per pound and the equilibrium quantity is 10 billion pounds per year.

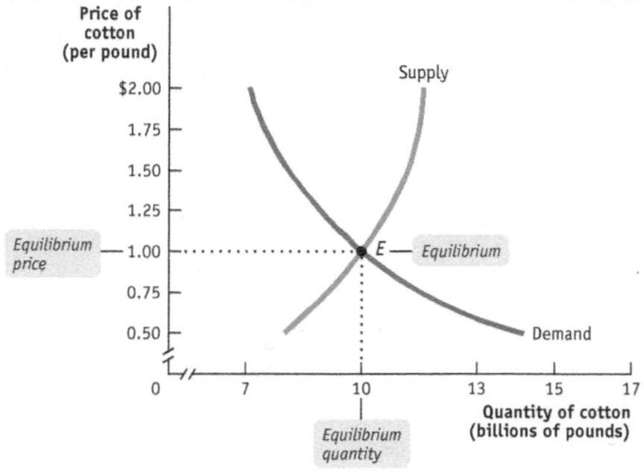

hands at a price of $1 per pound. But how can we be sure that the market will arrive at the equilibrium price? We begin by answering three simple questions:

1. Why do all sales and purchases in a market take place at the same price?
2. Why does the market price fall if it is above the equilibrium price?
3. Why does the market price rise if it is below the equilibrium price?

Why Do All Sales and Purchases in a Market Take Place at the Same Price?

There are some markets where the same good can sell for many different prices, depending on who is selling or who is buying. For example, have you ever bought a souvenir in a "tourist trap" and then seen the same item on sale somewhere else (perhaps even in the shop next door) for a lower price? Because tourists don't know which shops offer the best deals and don't have time for comparison shopping, sellers in tourist areas can charge different prices for the same good.

But in any market in which the buyers and sellers have both been around for some time, sales and purchases tend to converge at a generally uniform price, so we can safely talk about *the* market price. It's easy to see why. Suppose a seller offered a potential buyer a price noticeably above what the buyer knew other people were paying. The buyer would clearly be better off shopping elsewhere—unless the seller were prepared to offer a better deal. Conversely, a seller would not be willing to sell for significantly less than the amount he knew most buyers were paying; he would be better off waiting to get a more reasonable customer. So in any well-established, ongoing market, all sellers receive and all buyers pay approximately the same price. This is what we call the *market price.*

Why Does the Market Price Fall If It Is Above the Equilibrium Price?

Suppose the supply and demand curves are as shown in Figure 7.1 but the market price is above the equilibrium level of $1—say, $1.50. This situation is illustrated in **Figure 7.2** on the next page. Why can't the price stay there?

As the figure shows, at a price of $1.50 there would be more pounds of cotton available than consumers wanted to buy: 11.2 billion pounds versus 8.1 billion pounds. The difference of 3.1 billion pounds is the **surplus**—also known as the *excess supply*—of cotton at $1.50.

This surplus means that some cotton farmers are frustrated: at the current price, they cannot find consumers who want to buy their cotton. The surplus offers an incentive for those frustrated would-be sellers to offer a lower price in order to poach business from other producers and entice more consumers to buy. The result of this price cutting will be to push the prevailing price down until it reaches the equilibrium price. So the price of a good will fall whenever there is a surplus—that is, whenever the market price is above its equilibrium level.

There is a **surplus** of a good or service when the quantity supplied exceeds the quantity demanded. Surpluses occur when the price is above its equilibrium level.

There is a **shortage** of a good or service when the quantity demanded exceeds the quantity supplied. Shortages occur when the price is below its equilibrium level.

Why Does the Market Price Rise If It Is Below the Equilibrium Price?

Now suppose the price is below its equilibrium level—say, at $0.75 per pound, as shown in **Figure 7.3** on the next page. In this case, the quantity demanded, 11.5 billion pounds, exceeds the quantity supplied, 9.1 billion pounds, implying that there are would-be buyers who cannot find cotton: there is a **shortage**, also known as an *excess demand,* of 2.4 billion pounds.

TEACH Teach It

In the supply and demand model, price is the independent variable and quantity is the dependent variable. This means that price changes on its own (i.e., independently) and quantity responds to the change (i.e., quantity depends on price). Producers adjust their price, and the quantity produced and sold depends on that price. Price adjustments are what move markets toward equilibrium.

FOCUS Active Learning

TRM Have students watch Jeremy Goad's "Simple Supply and Demand" video (see econextras video list with hyperlinks on the bcs and TRFD). **Worksheet 7.1 (Simple Supply and Demand)** from the TRM offers related questions on surpluses and shortages.

TEACH Teach It

The best way to help students understand why equilibrium occurs at the intersection of the supply and demand curves is to have them think through what will happen at prices above and below the equilibrium price.

At a price above equilibrium, the quantity that consumers demand is lower (consumers don't like high prices!) and the quantity supplied is higher (producers like high prices!) compared to equilibrium. When quantity supplied exceeds quantity demanded, as in Figure 7.2, there is a surplus of the good. When producers see a surplus (their shelves filling up with unpurchased goods), what do they do? *Lower the price, so more will sell (e.g., put the items "on sale").*

At a price below equilibrium, the quantity that consumers demand is higher (consumers love low prices!) and the quantity supplied is lower (producers don't like to sell at low prices) compared to equilibrium. When the quantity demanded is greater than the quantity supplied, as shown in Figure 7.3, there is a shortage of the good. When producers see a shortage (consumers lined up to buy the good and there is not enough for everyone), what do they do? *Raise the price and sell to those willing to pay the most!*

FOCUS Active Learning

TRM If you want to give students more practice, assign **Worksheet 7.2 (Equilibrium Questions)** from the TRM.

FOCUS Active Learning

TRM Assign **Worksheet 7.3 (Changes to Markets)** from the TRM for practice identifying surpluses and shortages.

Figure 7.2 Price Above Its Equilibrium Level Creates a Surplus

The market price of $1.50 is above the equilibrium price of $1. This creates a surplus: at a price of $1.50, producers would like to sell 11.2 billion pounds but consumers want to buy only 8.1 billion pounds, so there is a surplus of 3.1 billion pounds. This surplus will push the price down until it reaches the equilibrium price of $1.

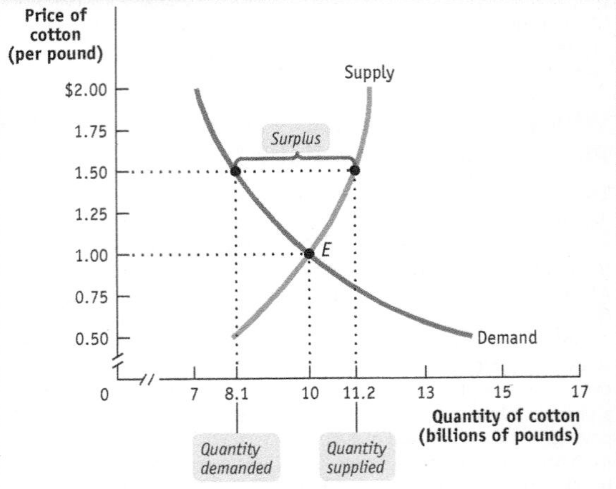

Figure 7.3 Price Below Its Equilibrium Level Creates a Shortage

The market price of $0.75 is below the equilibrium price of $1. This creates a shortage: consumers want to buy 11.5 billion pounds, but only 9.1 billion pounds are for sale, so there is a shortage of 2.4 billion pounds. This shortage will push the price up until it reaches the equilibrium price of $1.

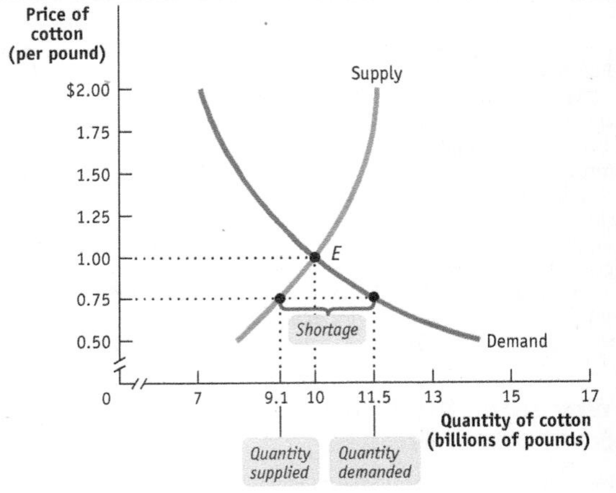

72 Section 2 Supply and Demand

FYI The Price of Admission

The market equilibrium, so the theory goes, is pretty egalitarian because the equilibrium price applies to everyone. That is, all buyers pay the same price—the equilibrium price—and all sellers receive that same price. But is this realistic?

The market for concert tickets is an example that seems to contradict the theory—there's one price at the box office, and there's another price (typically much higher) for the same event on Internet sites where people who already have tickets resell them, such as StubHub.com or eBay. For example, compare the box office price for a recent Drake concert in Miami, Florida, to the StubHub.com price for seats in the same location: $88.50 versus $155.

Puzzling as this may seem, there is no contradiction once we take opportunity costs and tastes into account. For major events, buying tickets from the box office means waiting in very long lines. Ticket buyers who use Internet resellers have decided that the opportunity cost of their time is too high to spend waiting in line. And tickets for major events being sold at face value by online box offices often sell out within minutes. In this case, some people who want to go to the concert badly but have missed out on the opportunity to buy cheaper tickets from the online box office are willing to pay the higher Internet reseller price.

Not only that—perusing the StubHub.com website, you can see that markets really do move to equilibrium. You'll notice that the prices quoted by different sellers for seats close to one another are also very close: $184.99 versus $185 for seats on the main floor of the Drake concert. As the competitive market model predicts, units of the same good end up selling for the same price. And prices move in response to demand and supply. According to an article in the *New York Times*, tickets on StubHub.com can sell for less than the face value for events with little appeal, but prices can skyrocket for events that are in high demand. (The article quotes a price of $3,530 for a Madonna concert.) Even StubHub.com's chief executive says his site is "the embodiment of supply-and-demand economics."

So the theory of competitive markets isn't just speculation. If you want to experience it for yourself, try buying tickets to a concert.

Claire R. Greenway/Getty Images

The competitive market model determines the price you pay for concert tickets.

When there is a shortage, there are frustrated would-be buyers—people who want to purchase cotton but cannot find willing sellers at the current price. In this situation, either buyers will offer more than the prevailing price or sellers will realize that they can charge higher prices. Either way, the result is to drive up the prevailing price. This bidding up of prices happens whenever there are shortages—and there will be shortages whenever the price is below its equilibrium level. So the market price will always rise if it is below the equilibrium level.

Using Equilibrium to Describe Markets

We have now seen that a market tends to have a single price, the equilibrium price. If the market price is above the equilibrium level, the ensuing surplus leads buyers and sellers to take actions that lower the price. And if the market price is below the equilibrium level, the ensuing shortage leads buyers and sellers to take actions that raise the price. So the market price always *moves toward* the equilibrium price, the price at which there is neither surplus nor shortage.

Changes in Supply and Demand

The 2010 floods in Pakistan came as a surprise, but the subsequent increase in the price of cotton was no surprise at all. Suddenly there was a fall in supply: the quantity of cotton available at any given price fell. Predictably, a fall in supply raises the equilibrium price.

FOCUS Active Learning

Discuss with the class the effect that ticket scalping and businesses like StubHub have on the market.

- Why do ticket scalpers tend to profit more at small venues and with a smaller supply of tickets? *Larger demand for tickets by people who really want to see the show and will pay more to do so.*
- Why do some artists sell their tickets at a price far below what they could get in the marketplace? *Many truly want their fans to be able to afford the tickets; they also know they will make high profits on the other goods for sale at the concert.*
- Can students think of any other markets that might work similarly? *Sporting events*

FOCUS Active Learning

Have students work in pairs. To begin, ask each student to fill in the blanks of the following supply and demand question, listing the market for a good or service and an example of a change in demand factor within that market, so he or she has written a supply and demand model question:

> Graph the effect on equilibrium price and quantity in the market for ____________ if there is a change in ____________.

For example, *oranges* and *a decrease in the price of tangerines* (a substitute for oranges). *The demand for oranges would decrease, causing price and quantity to decrease.*

When the partners have finished writing their questions, have each one draw the graph that answers his or her partner's question. The two students should then check each other's graph.

Module 7 Supply and Demand: Equilibrium **73**

TEACH Teach It

Make sure students notice that an increase in demand will lead to an increase in both price and quantity, whereas a decrease in demand will decrease both price and quantity. But it is much more useful to be able to draw a graph to figure this out than to try to memorize a "rule."

FOCUS Graph It

Ask your students to refer to Figure 7.4 and answer the following questions:

- Has there been a change in demand? Why or why not? *Yes, because the price of a substitute changed.*
- Has there been a change in quantity demanded? Why or why not? *Yes, all quantities demanded (including the equilibrium quantity demanded) increased when the demand curve shifted.*
- Has there been a change in supply? Why or why not? *No, none of the factors that change supply have changed. The supply curve stayed the same.*
- Has there been a change in quantity supplied? Why or why not? *Yes, when the demand curve shifted, the new equilibrium quantity is at a higher quantity supplied.*

The flooding in Pakistan is an example of an event that shifted the supply curve for a good without having much effect on the demand curve. There are many such events. There are also events that shift the demand curve without shifting the supply curve. For example, a medical report that chocolate is good for you increases the demand for chocolate but does not affect the supply. Events often shift either the supply curve or the demand curve, but not both; it is therefore useful to ask what happens in each case.

We have seen that when a curve shifts, the equilibrium price and quantity change. We will now concentrate on exactly how the shift of a curve alters the equilibrium price and quantity.

What Happens When the Demand Curve Shifts

AP® Exam Tip

A shift of the demand curve changes the price, which changes the quantity supplied. A shift of the supply curve also changes the price, which changes the quantity demanded. Note that these price changes cause movements *along* the curve that didn't shift. A shift of the demand curve never causes a shift of the supply curve, and a shift of the supply curve never causes a shift of the demand curve.

Cotton and polyester are substitutes: if the price of polyester rises, the demand for cotton will increase, and if the price of polyester falls, the demand for cotton will decrease. But how does the price of polyester affect the *market equilibrium* for cotton?

Figure 7.4 shows the effect of a rise in the price of polyester on the market for cotton. The rise in the price of polyester increases the demand for cotton. Point E_1 shows the equilibrium corresponding to the original demand curve, with P_1 the equilibrium price and Q_1 the equilibrium quantity bought and sold.

An increase in demand is indicated by a *rightward* shift of the demand curve from D_1 to D_2. At the original market price P_1, this market is no longer in equilibrium: a shortage occurs because the quantity demanded exceeds the quantity supplied. So the price of cotton rises and generates an increase in the quantity supplied, an upward *movement along the supply curve.* A new equilibrium is established at point E_2, with a higher equilibrium price, P_2, and higher equilibrium quantity, Q_2. This sequence of events reflects a general principle: *When demand for a good or service increases, the equilibrium price and the equilibrium quantity of the good or service both rise.*

What would happen in the reverse case, a fall in the price of polyester? A fall in the price of polyester reduces the demand for cotton, shifting the demand curve to the *left.* At the original price, a surplus occurs as quantity supplied exceeds quantity demanded. The price falls and leads to a decrease in the quantity supplied, resulting in a lower

Figure 7.4 Equilibrium and Shifts of the Demand Curve

The original equilibrium in the market for cotton is at E_1, at the intersection of the supply curve and the original demand curve, D_1. A rise in the price of polyester, a substitute, shifts the demand curve rightward to D_2. A shortage exists at the original price, P_1, causing both the price and quantity supplied to rise, a movement along the supply curve. A new equilibrium is reached at E_2, with a higher equilibrium price, P_2, and a higher equilibrium quantity, Q_2. When demand for a good or service increases, the equilibrium price and the equilibrium quantity of the good or service both rise.

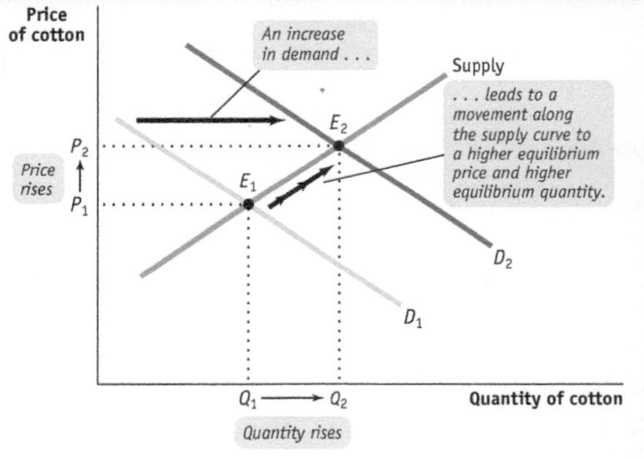

equilibrium price and a lower equilibrium quantity. This illustrates another general principle: *When demand for a good or service decreases, the equilibrium price and the equilibrium quantity of the good or service both fall.*

To summarize how a market responds to a change in demand: *An increase in demand leads to a rise in both the equilibrium price and the equilibrium quantity. A decrease in demand leads to a fall in both the equilibrium price and the equilibrium quantity.*

What Happens When the Supply Curve Shifts

In the real world, it is a bit easier to predict changes in supply than changes in demand. Physical factors that affect supply, like weather or the availability of inputs, are easier to get a handle on than the fickle tastes that affect demand. Still, with supply as with demand, what we can best predict are the *effects* of shifts of the supply curve.

As we mentioned earlier, devastating floods in Pakistan sharply reduced the supply of cotton in 2010. **Figure 7.5** shows how this shift affected the market equilibrium. The original equilibrium is at E_1, the point of intersection of the original supply curve, S_1, and the demand curve, with an equilibrium price P_1 and equilibrium quantity Q_1. As a result of the bad weather, supply falls and S_1 shifts *leftward* to S_2. At the original price P_1, a shortage of cotton now exists and the market is no longer in equilibrium. The shortage causes a rise in price and a fall in quantity demanded, an upward movement along the demand curve. The new equilibrium is at E_2, with an equilibrium price P_2 and an equilibrium quantity Q_2. In the new equilibrium, E_2, the price is higher and the equilibrium quantity lower than before. This can be stated as a general principle: *When supply of a good or service decreases, the equilibrium price of the good or service rises and the equilibrium quantity of the good or service falls.*

What happens to the market when supply increases? An increase in supply leads to a *rightward* shift of the supply curve. At the original price, a surplus now exists; as a result, the equilibrium price falls and the quantity demanded rises. This describes what happened to the market for cotton as new technology increased cotton yields. We can formulate a general principle: *When supply of a good or service increases, the equilibrium price of the good or service falls and the equilibrium quantity of the good or service rises.*

AP® Exam Tip

The graph never lies! If asked to determine what happens to price and quantity when supply or demand shifts, draw the graph first and then look where the old equilibrium was and compare it to the new equilibrium. Draw quick graphs whenever you can to help you answer multiple choice questions about changes in quantity and price.

Figure 7.5 Equilibrium and Shifts of the Supply Curve

The original equilibrium in the market for cotton is at E_1. Bad weather in cotton-growing areas causes a fall in the supply of cotton and shifts the supply curve leftward from S_1 to S_2. A new equilibrium is established at E_2, with a higher equilibrium price, P_2, and a lower equilibrium quantity, Q_2.

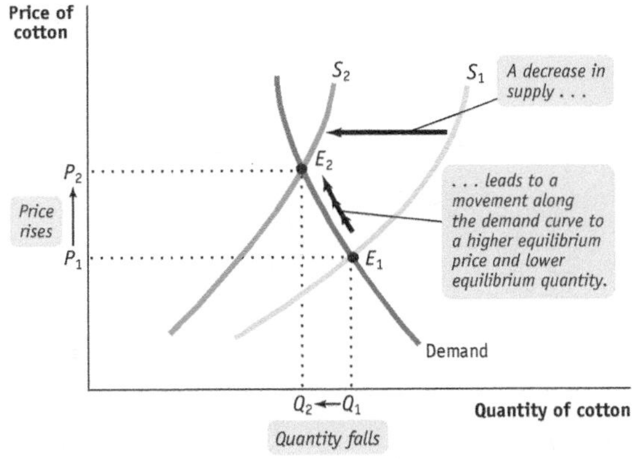

TEACH Teach It

Make sure students notice that an increase in supply will lead to an increase in quantity and a decrease in price, whereas a decrease in supply will lead to an increase in price and a decrease in quantity. But it is much more useful to be able to draw a graph to figure this out than to try to memorize a "rule."

FOCUS Graph It

Have students refer to Figure 7.5 and answer the following questions:

- Which of the following changed in the graph? *Demand, quantity demanded, supply, quantity supplied*
- How is the effect on price and quantity in this figure the same as, or different from, the one in Figure 7.4? *Price increases in both examples, but quantity goes up in Figure 7.4 and down in Figure 7.5*

TEACH Teach It

If students have trouble using the supply and demand model to analyze changes in the market, suggesting "steps" for them to follow may help. You can provide the following steps for use while they learn how to apply the supply and demand model:

Step 1: Draw a "starting point" graph. This should have *P* and *Q* labeled on the axes, downward-sloping and labeled demand curve, upward-sloping and labeled supply curve, equilibrium price shown on the vertical axis, and equilibrium quantity labeled on the horizontal axis where supply and demand cross. Students should be able to draw this same starting point for any supply and demand question.

Step 2: Think about the change being considered. Does the change represent a change in demand (an item on the list of factors that affect demand) or a change in supply (an item on the list of factors that affect supply)? Any given change will affect *supply OR demand*—not both.

Step 3: Does the supply or demand (whichever was selected in Step 2) increase or decrease as a result of the change being considered? Does supply or demand *increase or decrease*?

Step 4: Draw the new curve on the graph to the *left or right*, and label the new equilibrium *P* and *Q* on the axes. Remember, increases are to the right and decreases are to the left.

St. Louis Federal Reserve Bank Resources

Oil Prices: Demand and Supply

This lesson reviews the factors that shift demand and supply curves and how changes in supply and demand affect equilibrium price and quantity, using the article "What is Driving Oil Prices?"

TEACH Teach It

It is possible to use the supply and demand model to analyze a case of two different factors changing at the same time—that is, a simultaneous shift in supply and demand. When both curves change at the same time, students should understand that the supply and demand model will be able to determine what happens to one of the variables (either price or quantity) but not the other.

FOCUS Flip It

TRM The following 2 videos from Jacob Clifford's ACDC Leadership site can be assigned for help understanding the shifting of supply or demand and the shifting of supply and demand together. When supply and demand shift at the same time, often the results in equilibrium can be indeterminate.

- "Shifting Demand and Supply"
- "Micro 2.4, Double Shifts in Supply and Demand"

(See econextras video list with hyperlinks on the bcs and TRFD.) Use **Worksheet 7.4 (Shifting Supply and Demand)** from the TRM for questions on these videos and practice graphing unequal shifts in supply and demand.

FOCUS Graph It

Refer to Figure 7.6 to explain to students why one of the variables (either price or quantity) can't be determined when both curves shift simultaneously. Point out that in both graphs, supply decreases (shifts left) and demand increases (shifts right). However, the size of the shifts is different in the two graphs. One graph shows a large demand shift and a small supply shift, while the other shows a large supply shift and a small demand shift. Since we don't know how big the shifts are (we just know their direction), we get a different answer for the equilibrium quantity in the two graphs. But we know price will go up no matter how large the shifts are.

FOCUS Active Learning

TRM Assign **Worksheet 7.5 (Simultaneous Shifts)** from the TRM for students to get practice graphing situations with simultaneous changes in demand and supply and to determine the effects on price and quantity.

AP® Exam Tip

You can do supply and demand analysis in three easy steps. First, draw the graph before the change. Be sure to label the equilibrium price and quantity on the appropriate axes. Second, identify which line shifts and add the shift to your graph. Third, label the new equilibrium price and quantity on the appropriate axes and note how each value changed.

To summarize how a market responds to a change in supply: *An increase in supply leads to a fall in the equilibrium price and a rise in the equilibrium quantity. A decrease in supply leads to a rise in the equilibrium price and a fall in the equilibrium quantity.*

Simultaneous Shifts of Supply and Demand Curves

Finally, it sometimes happens that events shift *both* the demand and supply curves at the same time. This is not unusual; in real life, supply curves and demand curves for many goods and services shift quite often because the economic environment continually changes. **Figure 7.6** illustrates two examples of simultaneous shifts. In both panels there is an increase in demand—that is, a rightward shift of the demand curve, from D_1 to D_2—say, for example, representing an increase in the demand for cotton due to changing tastes. Notice that the rightward shift in panel (a) is larger than the one in panel (b): we can suppose that panel (a) represents a year in which many more people than usual choose to buy jeans and cotton T-shirts and panel (b) represents a normal year. Both panels also show a decrease in supply—that is, a leftward shift of the supply curve from S_1 to S_2. Also notice that the leftward shift in panel (b) is relatively larger than the one in panel (a): we can suppose that panel (b) represents the effect of particularly bad weather in Pakistan and panel (a) represents the effect of a much less severe weather event.

In both cases, the equilibrium price rises from P_1 to P_2, as the equilibrium moves from E_1 to E_2. But what happens to the equilibrium quantity, the quantity of cotton

Figure 7.6 Simultaneous Shifts of the Demand and Supply Curves

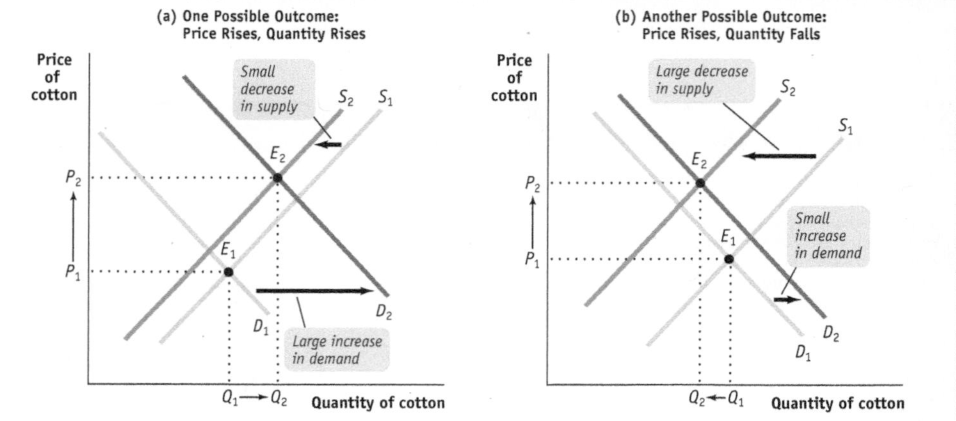

In panel (a) there is a simultaneous rightward shift of the demand curve and leftward shift of the supply curve. Here the increase in demand is relatively larger than the decrease in supply, so the equilibrium price and equilibrium quantity both rise. In panel (b) there is also a simultaneous rightward shift of the demand curve and leftward shift of the supply curve. Here the decrease in supply is relatively larger than the increase in demand, so the equilibrium price rises and the equilibrium quantity falls.

76 Section 2 Supply and Demand

bought and sold? In panel (a) the increase in demand is large relative to the decrease in supply, and the equilibrium quantity rises as a result. In panel (b), the decrease in supply is large relative to the increase in demand, and the equilibrium quantity falls as a result. That is, when demand increases and supply decreases, the actual quantity bought and sold can go either way, depending on *how much* the demand and supply curves have shifted.

In general, when supply and demand shift in opposite directions, we can't predict what the ultimate effect will be on the quantity bought and sold. What we can say is that a curve that shifts a disproportionately greater distance than the other curve will have a disproportionately greater effect on the quantity bought and sold. That said, we can make the following prediction about the outcome when the supply and demand curves shift in opposite directions:

- When demand increases and supply decreases, the equilibrium price rises but the change in the equilibrium quantity is ambiguous.
- When demand decreases and supply increases, the equilibrium price falls but the change in the equilibrium quantity is ambiguous.

But suppose that the demand and supply curves shift in the same direction. Before 2010, this was the case in the global market for cotton, where both supply and demand had increased over the past decade. Can we safely make any predictions about the changes in price and quantity? In this situation, the change in quantity bought and sold can be predicted, but the change in price is ambiguous. The two possible outcomes when the supply and demand curves shift in the same direction (which you should check for yourself) are as follows:

- When both demand and supply increase, the equilibrium quantity rises but the change in the equilibrium price is ambiguous.
- When both demand and supply decrease, the equilibrium quantity falls but the change in the equilibrium price is ambiguous.

FYI Makin' Bacon?

"Pork plight looming: Worldwide bacon shortage 'unavoidable' after drought, pig farmers warn." So read a recent headline in Canada's *National Post*. Behind the gloom and doom were droughts in 2012 that reduced the supply of corn. Why was the supply of bacon threatened? Because of what happens to the equilibrium price of corn, a key ingredient in a pig's dinner, when its supply decreases. High corn prices make it more expensive to raise the pigs whose bellies become bacon. This added expense reduced the supply of bacon. And with that, the price of bacon rose by 26 percent between mid-2012 and mid-2013.

Was there a shortage? No. There would have been a shortage if something prevented the price from rising to the equilibrium level. But as we have seen in our models, rising prices close the gap between the quantity supplied and the quantity demanded. Or, as explained by Andrew Dickson, general manager of the Manitoba Pork Council, "Is there less pork in the world? Probably, but I wouldn't call it a shortage. You give me the right price, and I will produce as much bacon as you want."

Lisovskaya Natalia/Shutterstock

A decrease in the supply of bacon may cause consumers to squeal, but it won't cause a lasting shortage, because higher bacon prices will decrease the quantity demanded and increase the quantity supplied.

FOCUS Test It

How will each of the following changes affect the equilibrium price and quantity in the market for ham? Use a graph to determine your answer.

- An increase in the price of eggs (if people eat ham and eggs together). *Demand for ham decreases, equilibrium price and quantity of ham decrease.*
- An increase in the price of pig feed. *Supply of ham decreases, equilibrium price increases, quantity decreases.*
- A simultaneous increase in the price of pig feed and eggs. *Equilibrium quantity decreases (note that it decreased in both examples above), equilibrium price is indeterminate (note that price went up in one example above and down in the other—we don't know which change was larger).*

FOCUS Active Learning

TRM Assign **Worksheet 7.6 (Graphing Equilibrium)** from the TRM for additional practice determining whether changes in the market bring about a change in demand or quantity demanded, or supply or quantity supplied.

FOCUS Flip It

TRM Have students watch Jacob Clifford's video "Micro 2.2 Supply and Demand" (see econextras video list with hyperlinks on the bcs and TRFD). This video will assist in cementing the concepts of supply, demand, equilibrium, and disequilibrium; it also explains surpluses and shortages.

Assign **Worksheet 7.7 (Supply and Demand)** from the TRM for related questions.

OPEN & CLOSE Exit Slip

TRM *Please see **Exit Slip: Module 7** in the TRM for formative multiple-choice questions to ask before finishing your lesson. These questions will help you quickly assess whether your students have mastered the module's concepts before moving on.*

Answers to the Exit Slip Questions

1. C
2. D
3. B

Answers to Module 7 Review Questions

Check Your Understanding

1. a. This is an increase in supply, so the supply curve shifts rightward. At the original equilibrium price of the year before, the quantity of grapes supplied exceeds the quantity demanded, and the result is a surplus. The price of grapes will fall.

b. This is a decrease in demand, so the demand curve shifts leftward. At the original equilibrium price, the quantity of hotel rooms supplied exceeds the quantity demanded. The result is a surplus. The rates for hotel rooms will fall.

c. The snowfall increases the demand for snow blowers, so the demand curve shifts rightward. At the original equilibrium price, the quantity of snow blowers demanded exceeds the quantity supplied. The result is a shortage. The price of snow blowers will rise.

2. a. The decrease in the price of gasoline caused a rightward shift in the demand for large cars. As a result of the shift, the equilibrium price of large cars rose and the equilibrium quantity of large cars bought and sold also rose.

b. The technological innovation causes a rightward shift in the supply of fresh paper made from recycled stock. As a result of this shift, the equilibrium price of fresh paper made from recycled stock falls and the equilibrium quantity bought and sold rises.

c. The fall in the price of pay-per-view movies causes a leftward shift in the demand for movies at local movie theaters. As a result of this shift, the equilibrium price of movie tickets falls and the equilibrium number of people who go to the movies also falls.

3. Upon announcement of the new chip, the demand curve for computers using the earlier chip shifts leftward (demand decreases), and the supply curve for these computers shifts rightward (supply increases).

a. If demand decreases relatively more than supply increases, then the equilibrium quantity falls, as shown in graph a.

b. If supply increases relatively more than demand decreases, then the equilibrium quantity rises, as shown in graph b.

In both cases, the equilibrium price falls.

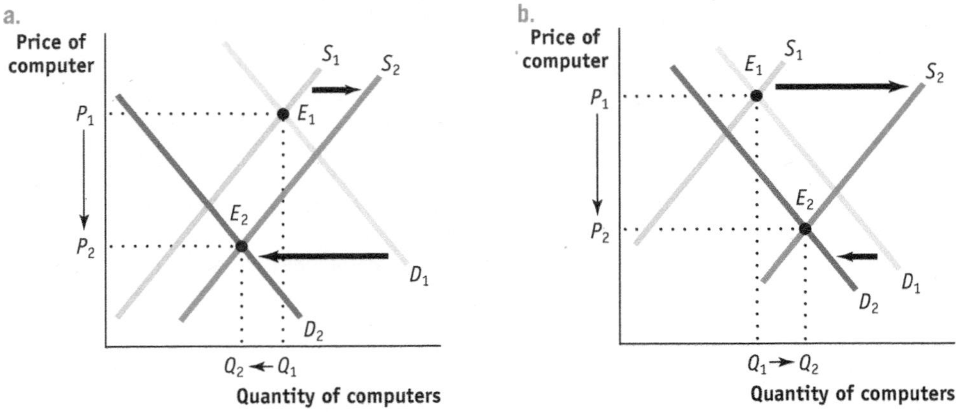

MODULE 7 Review

Check Your Understanding

1. In the following three situations, the market is initially in equilibrium. After each event described below, does a surplus or shortage exist at the original equilibrium price? What will happen to the equilibrium price as a result?
   a. In 2014 there was a bumper crop of wine grapes.
   b. After a hurricane, Florida hoteliers often find that many people cancel their upcoming vacations, leaving them with empty hotel rooms.
   c. After a heavy snowfall, many people want to buy second-hand snowblowers at the local tool shop.
2. For each of the following examples, explain how the indicated change affects supply or demand for the good in question and how the shift you describe affects the equilibrium price and quantity.
   a. As the price of gasoline fell in the United States during the 1990s, more people bought large cars.
   b. Technological innovation in the use of recycled paper has lowered the cost of paper production.
   c. When a local cable company offers cheaper pay-per-view films, local movie theaters have more unfilled seats.
3. Periodically, a computer chip maker like Intel introduces a new chip that is faster than the previous one. In response, demand for computers using the earlier chip decreases as customers put off purchases in anticipation of machines containing the new chip. Simultaneously, computer makers increase their production of computers containing the earlier chip in order to clear out their stocks of those chips.

   Draw two diagrams of the market for computers containing the earlier chip: (a) one in which the equilibrium quantity falls in response to these events and (b) one in which the equilibrium quantity rises. What happens to the equilibrium price in each diagram?

Tackle the Test: Multiple-Choice Questions

1. Which of the following describes what will happen in the market for tomatoes if a salmonella outbreak is attributed to tainted tomatoes?
   a. Supply will decrease and price will increase.
   b. Supply will decrease and price will decrease.
   c. Demand will decrease and price will increase.
   d. Demand will decrease and price will decrease.
   e. Supply and demand will both decrease.
2. Which of the following will lead to an increase in the equilibrium price of product "X"? A(n)
   a. increase in consumer incomes if product "X" is an inferior good
   b. increase in the price of machinery used to produce product "X"
   c. technological advance in the production of good "X"
   d. decrease in the price of good "Y" (a substitute for good "X")
   e. expectation by consumers that the price of good "X" is going to fall
3. The equilibrium price will rise, but the equilibrium quantity may increase, decrease, or stay the same if
   a. demand increases and supply decreases.
   b. demand increases and supply increases.
   c. demand decreases and supply increases.
   d. demand decreases and supply decreases.
   e. demand increases and supply does not change.
4. An increase in the number of buyers and a technological advance will cause
   a. demand to increase and supply to increase.
   b. demand to increase and supply to decrease.
   c. demand to decrease and supply to increase.
   d. demand to decrease and supply to decrease.
   e. no change in demand and an increase in supply.
5. Which of the following is certainly true if demand and supply increase at the same time?
   a. The equilibrium price will increase.
   b. The equilibrium price will decrease.
   c. The equilibrium quantity will increase.
   d. The equilibrium quantity will decrease.
   e. The equilibrium quantity may increase, decrease, or stay the same.

78 Section 2 Supply and Demand

Tackle the Test: Free-Response Questions

1. Draw a correctly labeled graph showing the market for tomatoes in equilibrium. Label the equilibrium price "P_E" and the equilibrium quantity "Q_E." On your graph, draw a horizontal line indicating a price, labeled "P_C", that would lead to a shortage of tomatoes. Label the size of the shortage on your graph.

2. Draw a correctly labeled graph showing the market for cups of coffee in equilibrium. On your graph, show the effect of a decrease in the price of coffee beans on the equilibrium price and the equilibrium quantity in the market for cups of coffee.
(5 points)

Rubric for FRQ 1 (6 points)

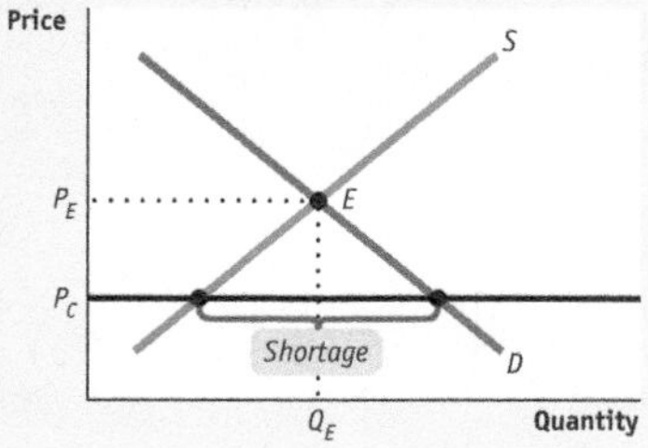

1 point: Graph with the vertical axis labeled "Price" or "P" and the horizontal axis labeled "Quantity" or "Q"

1 point: Downward-sloping demand curve labeled "Demand" or "D"

1 point: Upward-sloping supply curve labeled "Supply" or "S"

1 point: Equilibrium price "P_E" labeled on the vertical axis and quantity "Q_E" labeled on the horizontal axis at the intersection of the supply and demand curves

1 point: Price line at a price "P_C" below the equilibrium price

1 point: Correct indication of the shortage, which is the horizontal distance between the quantity demanded and the quantity supplied at the height of P_C

Tackle the Test: Free-Response Question

Rubric for FRQ 2 (5 points)

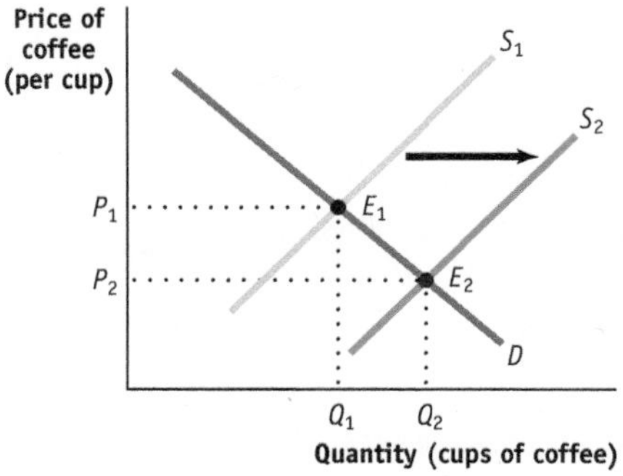

1 point: The vertical axis is labeled "Price" and the horizontal axis is labeled "Quantity."

1 point: Upward-sloping and labeled "Supply curve" and downward-sloping and labeled "Demand curve."

1 point: Equilibrium price and quantity are shown on the axes.

1 point: An upward-sloping and labeled supply curve is shown to the right of the original supply curve.

1 point: The new equilibrium price and quantity are shown on the axes.

Tackle the Test: Multiple-Choice Questions

1. d
2. b
3. a
4. a
5. c

Module 7 Supply and Demand: Equilibrium 79

PD To prepare for teaching this lesson, you may want to consult the **Module 8 Sample Lecture** in the TRM.

OPEN & CLOSE Start Here

In the previous modules, students learned about demand, supply, and equilibrium. They learned that the price mechanism in markets works to lower the price when there is a surplus and raise the price when there is a shortage. However, sometimes governments intervene in markets to regulate the price, preventing the market from moving toward equilibrium. Ask students if they can think of an example of a law passed by the government that regulates the price in a market. (*Rent controls, gasoline or water restrictions, minimum wage*) Ask them to explain why the minimum wage is an example of a price control in the labor market. (*When a wage is set that is binding on an employer, it takes away the employer's ability to hire labor at a lower wage.*) Have your students discuss why the government passed a minimum wage law and if they think it is a good idea or not (and why).

TEACH Connect It

This module uses the supply and demand model developed in previous modules to investigate price controls. The government sometimes intervenes in markets by setting price ceilings and floors that prevent the market from moving toward equilibrium. This module shows the effects of price controls on markets using the supply and demand model.

istockphoto

MODULE 8

Supply and Demand: Price Controls (Ceilings and Floors)

In this Module, you will learn to:

- Explain the workings of price controls, one way government intervenes in markets
- Describe how price controls can create problems and make a market inefficient
- Explain why economists are often deeply skeptical of attempts to intervene in markets
- Identify who benefits and who loses from price controls

Why Governments Control Prices

In Module 7, you learned that a market moves to equilibrium—that is, the market price moves to the level at which the quantity supplied equals the quantity demanded. But this equilibrium price does not necessarily please either buyers or sellers.

After all, buyers would always like to pay less if they could, and sometimes they can make a strong moral or political case that they should pay lower prices. For example, what if the equilibrium between supply and demand for apartments in a major city leads to rental rates that an average working person can't afford? In that case, a government might well be under pressure to impose limits on the rents landlords can charge.

Sellers, however, would always like to get more money for what they sell, and sometimes they can make a strong moral or political case that they should receive higher prices. For example, consider the labor market: the price for an hour of a worker's time is the wage rate. What if the equilibrium between supply and demand for less skilled workers leads to wage rates that yield an income below the poverty level? In that case, a government might well be pressured to require employers to pay a rate no lower than some specified minimum wage.

In other words, there is often a strong political demand for governments to intervene in markets. And powerful interests can make a compelling case that a market intervention favoring them is "fair." When a government intervenes to regulate prices, we say that it imposes **price controls**. These controls typically take the form of either an upper limit, a **price ceiling**, or a lower limit, a **price floor**.

Unfortunately, it's not that easy to tell a market what to do. As we will now see, when a government tries to legislate prices—whether it legislates them *down* by imposing a

Price controls are legal restrictions on how high or low a market price may go. They can take two forms: a **price ceiling**, a maximum price sellers are allowed to charge for a good or service, or a **price floor**, a minimum price buyers are required to pay for a good or service.

St. Louis Federal Reserve Bank Resources

"Price Signals," *The Economic Lowdown Podcast Series,* Episode 12

This podcast discusses how price signals in the gasoline market influence both consumer and producer decision making.

price ceiling or *up* by imposing a price floor—there are certain predictable and unpleasant side effects.

We make an important assumption in this module: the markets in question are efficient before price controls are imposed. Markets can sometimes be inefficient—for example, a market dominated by a monopolist, a single seller who has the power to influence the market price. When markets are inefficient, price controls don't necessarily cause problems and can potentially move the market closer to efficiency. In practice, however, price controls often *are* imposed on efficient markets—like the New York City apartment market. And so the analysis in this module applies to many important real-world situations.

Price Ceilings

Aside from rent control, there are not many price ceilings in the United States today. But at times they have been widespread. Price ceilings are typically imposed during crises—wars, harvest failures, natural disasters—because these events often lead to sudden price increases that hurt many people but produce big gains for a lucky few. The U.S. government imposed ceilings on many prices during World War II: the war sharply increased demand for raw materials, such as aluminum and steel, and price controls prevented those with access to these raw materials from earning huge profits. Price controls on oil were imposed in 1973, when an embargo by Arab oil-exporting countries seemed likely to generate huge profits for U.S. oil companies. Price controls were imposed on California's wholesale electricity market in 2001, when a shortage created big profits for a few power-generating companies but led to higher electricity bills for consumers.

Believe it or not, rent control in New York is a legacy of World War II: it was imposed because wartime production created an economic boom, which increased demand for apartments at a time when the labor and raw materials that might have been used to build them were being used to win the war instead. Although most price controls were removed soon after the war ended, New York's rent limits were retained and gradually extended to buildings not previously covered, leading to some very strange situations.

You can rent a one-bedroom apartment in Manhattan on fairly short notice—if you are able and willing to pay several thousand dollars a month and live in a less-than-desirable area. Yet some people pay only a small fraction of this amount for comparable apartments, and others pay hardly more for bigger apartments in better locations.

Aside from producing great deals for some renters, however, what are the broader consequences of New York's rent control system? To answer this question, we turn to the supply and demand model.

Modeling a Price Ceiling

To see what can go wrong when a government imposes a price ceiling on an efficient market, consider **Figure 8.1** on the next page, which shows a simplified model of the market for apartments in New York. For the sake of simplicity, we imagine that all apartments are exactly the same and so would rent for the same price in an unregulated market. The table in the figure shows the demand and supply schedules; the demand and supply curves are shown on the left. We show the quantity of apartments on the horizontal axis and the monthly rent per apartment on the vertical axis. You can see that in an unregulated market the equilibrium would be at point *E:* 2 million apartments would be rented for $1,000 each per month.

Now suppose that the government imposes a price ceiling, limiting rents to a price below the equilibrium price—say, no more than $800. **Figure 8.2** on the next page shows the effect of the price ceiling, represented by the line at $800. At the enforced rental rate of $800, landlords have less incentive to offer apartments, so they won't be willing to supply as many as they would at the equilibrium rate of $1,000. They will choose point *A* on the supply curve, offering only 1.8 million apartments for rent, 200,000 fewer than in the unregulated market. At the same time, more people will want to rent apartments at a price of $800 than at the equilibrium price of $1,000; as shown at point *B* on the demand curve,

Module 8 Supply and Demand: Price Controls (Ceilings and Floors) **81**

Figure 8.1 The Market for Apartments in the Absence of Government Controls

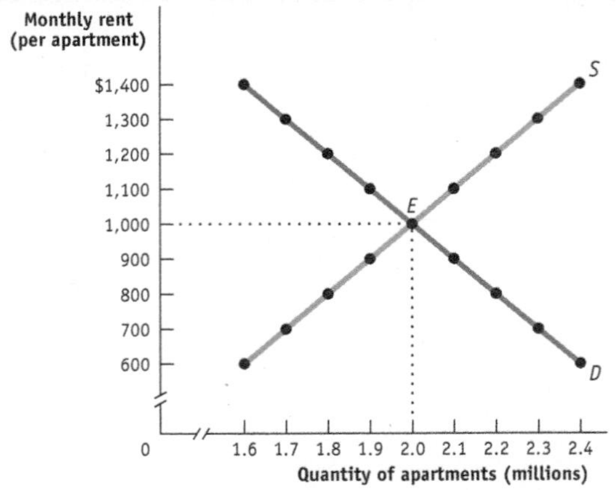

Monthly rent (per apartment)	Quantity of apartments (millions)	
	Quantity demanded	Quantity supplied
$1,400	1.6	2.4
1,300	1.7	2.3
1,200	1.8	2.2
1,100	1.9	2.1
1,000	2.0	2.0
900	2.1	1.9
800	2.2	1.8
700	2.3	1.7
600	2.4	1.6

Without government intervention, the market for apartments reaches equilibrium at point *E* with a market rent of $1,000 per month and 2 million apartments rented.

Figure 8.2 The Effects of a Price Ceiling

The black horizontal line represents the government-imposed price ceiling on rents of $800 per month. This price ceiling reduces the quantity of apartments supplied to 1.8 million, point *A*, and increases the quantity demanded to 2.2 million, point *B*. This creates a persistent shortage of 400,000 units: 400,000 of the people who want apartments at the legal rent of $800 cannot get them.

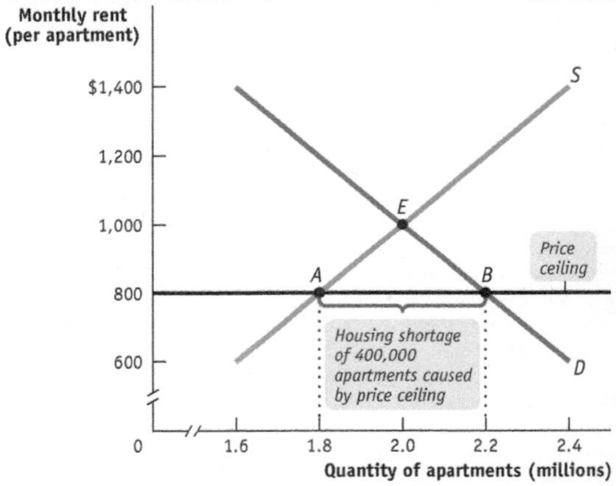

FOCUS Active Learning

TRM Use **Worksheet 8.1 (Analyzing Figures 8.1 and 8.2)** in the TRM for practice with graphical analysis.

TEACH Teach It

Ask students to pretend that they are a seller in the market for apartments shown in Figure 8.1, and then ask what price they would charge for their apartment. Help them to understand that they would still charge $1,000—the equilibrium price (because they would want to get the highest price at which their apartment could be rented). Now ask them what would happen if the government intervened and indicated they were *not* allowed to charge more than $1,200 for their apartment. Help them to understand that they could respond by simply telling the government they aren't overcharging—they are charging $1,000 (so the government should go away and leave them alone!). Use this discussion to help your students see that a binding price ceiling must fall below equilibrium.

FOCUS Active Learning

TRM You may want to assign **Worksheet 8.2 (Price Ceilings)** from the TRM for practice on price ceilings.

at a monthly rent of $800 the quantity of apartments demanded rises to 2.2 million, 200,000 more than in the unregulated market and 400,000 more than are actually available at the price of $800. So there is now a persistent shortage of rental housing: at that price, there are 400,000 more people who want to rent than are able to find apartments.

Do price ceilings always cause shortages? No. If a price ceiling is set above the equilibrium price, it won't have any effect. Suppose that the equilibrium rental rate on apartments is $1,000 per month and the city government sets a ceiling of $1,200. Who cares? In this case, the price ceiling won't be binding—it won't actually constrain market behavior—and it will have no effect.

Inefficient Allocation to Consumers Rent control doesn't just lead to too few apartments being available. It can also lead to misallocation of the apartments that are available: people who badly need a place to live may not be able to find an apartment, while some apartments may be occupied by people with much less urgent needs.

In the case shown in Figure 8.2, 2.2 million people would like to rent an apartment at $800 per month, but only 1.8 million apartments are available. Of those 2.2 million who are seeking an apartment, some want an apartment badly and are willing to pay a high price to get one. Others have a less urgent need and are only willing to pay a low price, perhaps because they have alternative housing. An efficient allocation of apartments would reflect these differences: people who really want an apartment will get one and people who aren't all that eager to find an apartment won't. In an inefficient distribution of apartments, the opposite will happen: some people who are not especially eager to find an apartment will get one and others who are very eager to find an apartment won't. Because people usually get apartments through luck or personal connections under rent control, it generally results in an **inefficient allocation to consumers** of the few apartments available.

To see the inefficiency involved, consider the plight of the Lees, a family with young children who have no alternative housing and would be willing to pay up to $1,500 for an apartment—but are unable to find one. Also consider George, a retiree who lives most of the year in Florida but still has a lease on the New York apartment he moved into 40 years ago. George pays $800 per month for this apartment, but if the rent were even slightly more—say, $850—he would give it up and stay with his children when he is in New York.

This allocation of apartments—George has one and the Lees do not—is a missed opportunity: there is a way to make the Lees and George both better off at no additional cost. The Lees would be happy to pay George, say, $1,200 a month to sublease his apartment, which he would happily accept since the apartment is worth no more than $849 a month to him. George would prefer the money he gets from the Lees to keeping his apartment; the Lees would prefer to have the apartment rather than the money. So both would be made better off by this transaction—and nobody else would be made worse off.

Generally, if people who really want apartments could sublease them from people who are less eager to live there, both those who gain apartments and those who trade their occupancy for money would be better off. However, subletting is illegal under rent control because it would occur at prices above the price ceiling. The fact that subletting is illegal doesn't mean it never happens. In fact, chasing down illegal subletting is a major business for New York private investigators. A 2007 report in the *New York Times* described how private investigators use hidden cameras and other tricks to prove that the legal tenants in rent-controlled apartments actually live in the suburbs, or even in other states, and have sublet their apartments at two or three times the controlled rent. This subletting is a kind of illegal activity, which we will discuss shortly. For now, just notice that the aggressive pursuit of illegal subletting surely discourages the practice, so there isn't enough subletting to eliminate the inefficient allocation of apartments.

Price ceilings often lead to inefficiency in the form of **inefficient allocation to consumers**: people who want the good badly and are willing to pay a high price don't get it, and those who care relatively little about the good and are only willing to pay a relatively low price do get it.

Wasted Resources Another reason a price ceiling causes inefficiency is that it leads to **wasted resources**: people expend money, effort, and time to cope with the shortages caused by the price ceiling. Back in 1979, U.S. price controls on gasoline led to shortages that forced millions of Americans to spend hours each week waiting in lines at gas stations. The opportunity cost of the time spent in gas lines—the wages not earned, the leisure time not enjoyed—constituted wasted resources from the point of

Price ceilings typically lead to inefficiency in the form of **wasted resources**: people expend money, effort, and time to cope with the shortages caused by the price ceiling.

TEACH Teach It

Use the distinction between positive and normative from Section 1 to help students understand that the effect of price controls shown with the supply and demand model is positive (i.e., can be tested) and the reasons for enacting price controls are normative (i.e., involve opinions and value judgments). So, although our economic model can be used to identify the effects of price controls placed on markets, the decision to enact them isn't always made solely (or even partially) based on those effects.

FOCUS Test It

Ask students the following questions:

- Where must a price ceiling be set to have an effect on the market (above or below equilibrium)? *Below*
- What are three common problems resulting from price ceilings? *Persistent shortages; inefficiency (low quantity, low quality, wasted resources); black markets*
- Why do governments impose price ceilings? *Fairness, politics, history, misunderstanding of supply and demand*

Signs advertising apartments to rent or sublet are common in New York City.

view of consumers and of the economy as a whole. Because of rent control, the Lees will spend all their spare time for several months searching for an apartment, time they would rather have spent working or engaged in family activities. That is, there is an opportunity cost to the Lees' prolonged search for an apartment—the leisure or income they had to forgo. If the market for apartments worked freely, the Lees would quickly find an apartment at the equilibrium rent of $1,000, leaving them time to earn more or to enjoy themselves—an outcome that would make them better off without making anyone else worse off. Again, rent control creates missed opportunities.

Inefficiently Low Quality Yet another way a price ceiling causes inefficiency is by causing goods to be of inefficiently low quality. **Inefficiently low quality** means that sellers offer low-quality goods at a low price even though buyers would rather have higher quality and are willing to pay a higher price for it.

Again, consider rent control. Landlords have no incentive to provide better conditions because they cannot raise rents to cover their repair costs but are able to find tenants easily. In many cases, tenants would be willing to pay much more for improved conditions than it would cost for the landlord to provide them—for example, the upgrade of an antiquated electrical system that cannot safely run air conditioners or computers. But any additional payment for such improvements would be legally considered a rent increase, which is prohibited. Indeed, rent-controlled apartments are notoriously badly maintained, rarely painted, subject to frequent electrical and plumbing problems, sometimes even hazardous to inhabit. As one former manager of Manhattan buildings explained, "At unregulated apartments we'd do most things that the tenants requested. But on the rent-regulated units, we did absolutely only what the law required. . . . We had a perverse incentive to make those tenants unhappy. With regulated apartments, the ultimate objective is to get people out of the building [because rents can be raised for new tenants]."

This whole situation is a missed opportunity—some tenants would be happy to pay for better conditions, and landlords would be happy to provide them for payment. But such an exchange would occur only if the market were allowed to operate freely.

Price ceilings often lead to inefficiency in that the goods being offered are of **inefficiently low quality**: sellers offer low quality goods at a low price even though buyers would prefer a higher quality at a higher price.

A **black market** is a market in which goods or services are bought and sold illegally—either because it is illegal to sell them at all or because the prices charged are legally prohibited by a price ceiling.

Black Markets And that leads us to a last aspect of price ceilings: the incentive they provide for illegal activities, specifically the emergence of **black markets**. We have already described one kind of black market activity—illegal subletting by tenants. But it does not stop there. Clearly, there is a temptation for a landlord to say to a potential tenant, "Look, you can have the place if you slip me an extra few hundred in cash each month"—and for the tenant to agree, if he or she is one of those people who would be willing to pay much more than the maximum legal rent.

What's wrong with black markets? In general, it's a bad thing if people break *any* law because it encourages disrespect for the law in general. Worse yet, in this case illegal activity worsens the position of those who try to be honest. If the Lees are scrupulous about upholding the rent control law but other people—who may need an apartment less than the Lees—are willing to bribe landlords, the Lees may *never* find an apartment.

So Why Are There Price Ceilings?

We have seen three common results of price ceilings:

- a persistent shortage of the good
- inefficiency arising from this persistent shortage in the form of inefficiently low quantity, inefficient allocation of the good to consumers, resources wasted in searching for the good, and the inefficiently low quality of the good offered for sale
- the emergence of illegal, black market activity

Given these unpleasant consequences, why do governments still sometimes impose price ceilings? Why does rent control, in particular, persist in New York?

One answer is that although price ceilings may have adverse effects, they do benefit some people. In practice, New York's rent control rules—which are more complex than our simple model—hurt most residents but give a small minority of renters much cheaper housing than they would get in an unregulated market. And those who benefit from the controls may be better organized and more vocal than those who are harmed by them.

Also, when price ceilings have been in effect for a long time, buyers may not have a realistic idea of what would happen without the price ceilings. In our previous example, the rental rate in an unregulated market (Figure 8.1) would be only 25% higher than in the regulated market (Figure 8.2): $1,000 instead of $800. But how would renters know that? Indeed, they might have heard about black market transactions at much higher prices—the Lees or some other family paying George $1,200 or more—and would not realize that these black market prices are much higher than the price that would prevail in a fully unregulated market.

A last answer is that government officials often do not understand supply and demand analysis! It is a great mistake to suppose that economic policies in the real world are always sensible or well informed.

Price Floors

Sometimes governments intervene to push market prices up instead of down. *Price floors* have been widely legislated for agricultural products, such as wheat and milk, as a way to support the incomes of farmers. Historically, there were also price floors on such services as trucking and air travel, although these were phased out by the U.S. government in the 1970s. If you have ever worked in a fast-food restaurant, you are likely to have encountered a price floor: governments in the United States and many other countries maintain a lower limit on the hourly wage rate paid for a worker's labor—that is, a floor on the price of labor—called the **minimum wage**.

Just like price ceilings, price floors are intended to help some people but generate predictable and undesirable side effects. **Figure 8.3** shows hypothetical supply and demand

AP® Exam Tip

When it comes to price controls, the ceiling is down low and the floor is up high. That is, to have any effect, a price ceiling must be below the equilibrium price, and a price floor must be above the equilibrium price.

The **minimum wage** is a legal floor on the hourly wage rate paid for a worker's labor.

Figure 8.3 The Market for Butter in the Absence of Government Controls

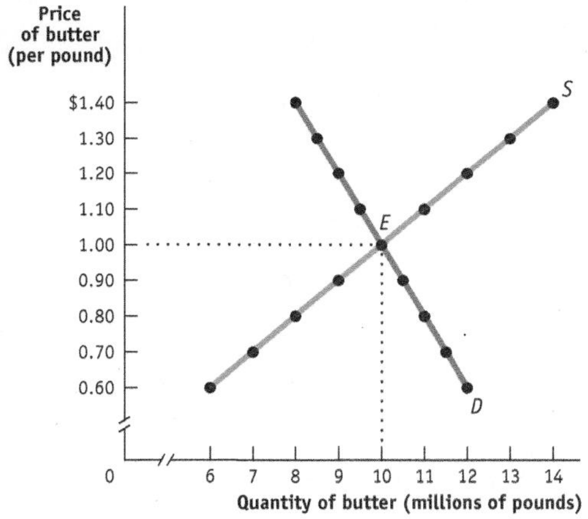

Price of butter (per pound)	Quantity of butter (millions of pounds) Quantity demanded	Quantity supplied
$1.40	8.0	14.0
1.30	8.5	13.0
1.20	9.0	12.0
1.10	9.5	11.0
1.00	10.0	10.0
0.90	10.5	9.0
0.80	11.0	8.0
0.70	11.5	7.0
0.60	12.0	6.0

Without government intervention, the market for butter reaches equilibrium at a price of $1 per pound with 10 million pounds of butter bought and sold.

TEACH Teach It

Ask students to pretend that they are a seller in the market for butter shown in Figure 8.3, and then ask what price they would charge for their butter. Help them to understand that they would still sell their butter for $1.00 per pound—the equilibrium price (because they would want to get the highest price they could while selling all their butter). Now ask them what would happen if the government intervened and indicated they were *not* allowed to sell their butter for more than $0.80. Help them to understand that they could respond by simply telling the government they aren't overcharging—they are selling for $1.00 (so the government should go away and leave them alone!). Use this discussion to help your students see that a binding price floor must fall above equilibrium.

FOCUS Graph It

Have students compare Figure 8.4 to Figure 8.2. Discuss their comparison and use this opportunity to emphasize where a price ceiling or floor must be set to have any effect in the market (i.e., to be binding).

FOCUS Active Learning

TRM Use **Worksheet 8.3 (Analyzing Figures 8.3 and 8.4)** in the TRM for practice with graphical analysis.

FOCUS Active Learning

TRM Go to **Worksheet 8.4 (Price Floors)** in the TRM for additional questions on price floors.

curves for butter. Left to itself, the market would move to equilibrium at point *E*, with 10 million pounds of butter bought and sold at a price of $1 per pound.

Now suppose that the government, in order to help dairy farmers, imposes a price floor on butter of $1.20 per pound. Its effects are shown in **Figure 8.4**, where the line at $1.20 represents the price floor. At a price of $1.20 per pound, producers would want to supply 12 million pounds (point *B* on the supply curve) but consumers would want to buy only 9 million pounds (point *A* on the demand curve). So the price floor leads to a persistent surplus of 3 million pounds of butter.

Does a price floor always lead to an unwanted surplus? No. Just as in the case of a price ceiling, the floor may not be binding—that is, it may be irrelevant. If the equilibrium price of butter is $1 per pound but the floor is set at only $0.80, the floor has no effect.

But suppose that a price floor *is* binding: what happens to the unwanted surplus? The answer depends on government policy. In the case of agricultural price floors, governments buy up unwanted surplus. As a result, the U.S. government has at times found itself warehousing thousands of tons of butter, cheese, and other farm products. (The European Commission, which administers price floors for a number of European countries, once found itself the owner of a so-called butter mountain, equal in weight to the entire population of Austria.) The government then has to find a way to dispose of these unwanted goods.

Some countries pay exporters to sell products at a loss overseas; this is standard procedure for the European Union. The United States gives surplus food away to schools, which use the products in school lunches. In some cases, governments have actually destroyed the surplus production. To avoid the problem of dealing with the unwanted surplus, the U.S. government typically pays farmers not to produce the products at all.

When the government is not prepared to purchase the unwanted surplus, a price floor means that would-be sellers cannot find buyers. This is what happens when there is a price floor on the wage rate paid for an hour of labor, the *minimum wage:* when the minimum wage is above the equilibrium wage rate, some people who are willing to work—that is, sell labor—cannot find buyers—that is, employers—willing to give them jobs.

Figure 8.4 The Effects of a Price Floor

The dark horizontal line represents the government-imposed price floor of $1.20 per pound of butter. The quantity of butter demanded falls to 9 million pounds, and the quantity supplied rises to 12 million pounds, generating a persistent surplus of 3 million pounds of butter.

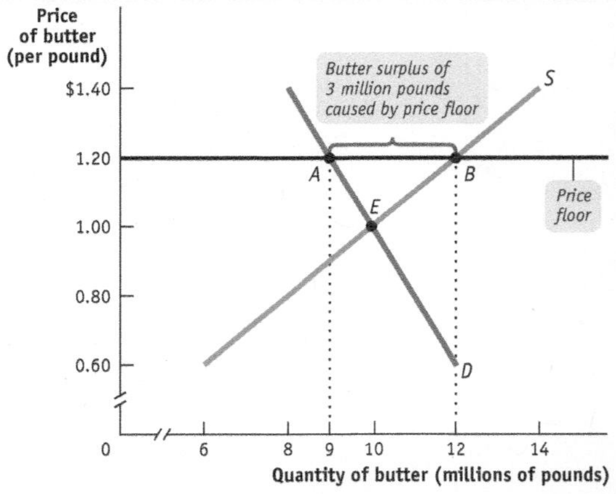

86 Section 2 Supply and Demand

FYI Price Floors and School Lunches

When you were in grade school, did your school offer free or very cheap lunches? If so, you were probably a beneficiary of price floors.

Where did all the cheap food come from? During the 1930s, when the U.S. economy was going through the Great Depression, a prolonged economic slump, prices were low and farmers were suffering severely. In an effort to help rural Americans, the U.S. government imposed price floors on a number of agricultural products. The system of agricultural price floors—officially called price support programs—continues to this day. Among the products subject to price support are sugar and various dairy products; at times grains, beef, and pork have also had a minimum price.

The big problem with any attempt to impose a price floor is that it creates a surplus. To some extent the U.S. Department of Agriculture has tried to head off surpluses by taking steps to reduce supply; for example, by paying farmers *not* to grow crops. As a last resort, however, the U.S. government has been willing to buy up the surplus, taking the excess supply off the market.

But then what? The government has to find a way to get rid of the agricultural products it has bought. It can't just sell them: that would depress market prices, forcing the government to buy the stuff right back. So it has to give it away in ways that don't depress market prices. One of the ways it does this is by giving surplus food, free, to school lunch programs. These gifts are known as "bonus foods." Along with financial aid, bonus foods are what allow many school districts to provide free or very cheap lunches to their students. Is this a story with a happy ending?

Mike Flippo/Shutterstock

Not really. Nutritionists, concerned about growing child obesity in the United States, place part of the blame on those bonus foods. Schools get whatever the government has too much of—and that has tended to include a lot of dairy products, beef, and corn, and not much in the way of fresh vegetables or fruit. As a result, school lunches that make extensive use of bonus foods tend to be very high in fat and calories. So this is a case in which there is such a thing as a free lunch—but this lunch may be bad for your health.

How a Price Floor Causes Inefficiency

The persistent surplus that results from a price floor creates missed opportunities—inefficiencies—that resemble those created by the shortage that results from a price ceiling.

Inefficiently Low Quantity Because a price floor raises the price of a good to consumers, it reduces the quantity of that good demanded; because sellers can't sell more units of a good than buyers are willing to buy, a price floor reduces the quantity of a good bought and sold below the market equilibrium quantity. Notice that this is the *same* effect as a price ceiling. You might be tempted to think that a price floor and a price ceiling have opposite effects, but both have the effect of reducing the quantity of a good bought and sold.

Inefficient Allocation of Sales Among Sellers Like a price ceiling, a price floor can lead to *inefficient allocation*—but in this case **inefficient allocation of sales among sellers** rather than inefficient allocation to consumers.

Price floors lead to **inefficient allocation of sales among sellers**: those who would be willing to sell the good at the lowest price are not always those who manage to sell it.

Suppose you would be willing to sell your English tutoring services for $5 per hour, but the minimum wage is $9 per hour. The job might go to someone else who would tutor for $9 per hour but not for less. In this case, the price floor on wages prevents the worker who would sell tutoring services for the lowest amount from being able to do so.

Wasted Resources Also like a price ceiling, a price floor generates inefficiency by *wasting resources*. The most graphic examples involve government purchases of the unwanted surpluses of agricultural products caused by price floors. When the surplus production is simply destroyed, and when the stored produce goes, as officials euphemistically put it, "out of condition" and must be thrown away, it is pure waste.

FOCUS In the News

Students will find the March 2013 *Washington Times* article "Bloomberg Sets Sights on Smokers: $10.50 Price Floor for Cigarettes" at www.washingtontimes.com/news/2013/mar/28/bloomberg-sets-sights-smokers-1050-price-floor-cig/ of interest. It describes former New York City Mayor Mike Bloomberg's attempt to set a minimum price on cigarettes in a push to develop a potentially healthier population.

Module 8 Supply and Demand: Price Controls (Ceilings and Floors) 87

FOCUS Test It

Ask students the following questions:

- Where must a price floor be set to have an effect on the market (above or below equilibrium)? *Above*
- What are common problems resulting from price floors? *Persistent surpluses; inefficiency (low quantity, high quality, wasted resources); illegal activities*
- Why do governments impose price ceilings? *Fairness, politics, history, misunderstanding of supply and demand*

FOCUS Flip It

TRM Have students watch Jacob Clifford's video "Econ 2.5 Price Ceilings and Floors" (see econextras video list with hyperlinks on the bcs and TRFD) to briefly and efficiently explain, and graphically show, the differences between price floors and ceilings. Assign **Worksheet 8.5 (Price Floors and Ceilings)** from the TRM for questions on this video.

OPEN & CLOSE Exit Slip

TRM *Please see **Exit Slip: Module 8** in the TRM for formative questions to ask before finishing your lesson. These questions will help you quickly assess whether your students have mastered the module's concepts before moving on.*

Answers to the Exit Slip Questions

1. price floor
2. D
3. surpluses; shortages

Price floors also lead to wasted time and effort. Consider the minimum wage. Would-be workers who spend many hours searching for jobs, or waiting in line in the hope of getting jobs, play the same role in the case of price floors as hapless families searching for apartments in the case of price ceilings.

Inefficiently High Quality Again like price ceilings, price floors lead to inefficiency in the quality of goods produced.

We've seen that when there is a price ceiling, suppliers produce goods that are of inefficiently low quality: buyers prefer higher-quality products and are willing to pay for them, but sellers refuse to improve the quality of their products because the price ceiling prevents their being compensated for doing so. This same logic applies to price floors, but in reverse: suppliers offer goods of **inefficiently high quality**.

Price floors often lead to inefficiency in that goods of **inefficiently high quality** are offered: sellers offer high-quality goods at a high price, even though buyers would prefer a lower quality at a lower price.

How can this be? Isn't high quality a good thing? Yes, but only if it is worth the cost. Suppose that suppliers spend a lot to make goods of very high quality but that this quality isn't worth much to consumers, who would rather receive the money spent on that quality in the form of a lower price. This represents a missed opportunity: suppliers and buyers could make a mutually beneficial deal in which buyers got goods of lower quality for a much lower price.

A good example of the inefficiency of excessive quality comes from the days when transatlantic airfares were set artificially high by international treaty. Forbidden to compete for customers by offering lower ticket prices, airlines instead offered expensive services, like lavish in-flight meals that went largely uneaten. At one point the regulators tried to restrict this practice by defining maximum service standards—for example, that snack service should consist of no more than a sandwich. One airline then introduced what it called a "Scandinavian Sandwich," a towering affair that forced the convening of another conference to define *sandwich*. All of this was wasteful, especially considering that what passengers really wanted was less food and lower airfares.

Since the deregulation of U.S. airlines in the 1970s, American passengers have experienced a large decrease in ticket prices accompanied by a decrease in the quality of in-flight service—smaller seats, lower-quality food, and so on. Everyone complains about the service—but thanks to lower fares, the number of people flying on U.S. carriers has grown several hundred percent since airline deregulation.

Illegal Activity Finally, like price ceilings, price floors provide incentives for illegal activity. For example, in countries where the minimum wage is far above the equilibrium wage rate, workers desperate for jobs sometimes agree to work off the books for employers who conceal their employment from the government—or bribe the government inspectors. This practice, known in Europe as "black labor," is especially common in southern European countries such as Italy and Spain.

So Why Are There Price Floors?

To sum up, a price floor creates various negative side effects:

- a persistent surplus of the good
- inefficiency arising from the persistent surplus in the form of inefficiently low quantity, inefficient allocation of sales among sellers, wasted resources, and an inefficiently high level of quality offered by suppliers
- the temptation to engage in illegal activity, particularly bribery and corruption of government officials

So why do governments impose price floors when they have so many negative side effects? The reasons are similar to those for imposing price ceilings. Government officials often disregard warnings about the consequences of price floors either because they believe that the relevant market is poorly described by the supply and demand model or, more often, because they do not understand the model. Above all, just as price ceilings are often imposed because they benefit some influential buyers of a good, price floors are often imposed because they benefit some influential sellers.

Answers to Module 8 Review Questions

Check Your Understanding

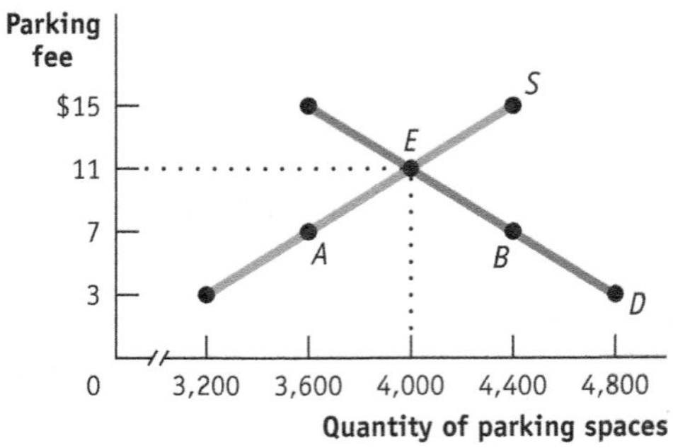

1. a. Fewer homeowners are willing to rent out their driveways because the price ceiling has reduced the payment they receive. This is an example of a fall in price leading to a fall in the quantity supplied. It is shown in the accompanying diagram by the movement from point *E* to point *A* along the supply curve, a reduction in quantity of 400 parking spaces.

b. The quantity demanded increases by 400 spaces as the price decreases. At a lower price, more fans are willing to drive and rent a parking space. It is shown in the diagram by the movement from point *E* to point *B* along the demand curve.

c. Under a price ceiling, the quantity demanded exceeds the quantity supplied; as a result, shortages arise. In this case, there will be a shortage of 800 parking spaces. It is shown by the horizontal distance between points *A* and *B*.

MODULE 8 Review

Check Your Understanding

1. On game days, homeowners near Middletown University's stadium used to rent parking spaces in their driveways to fans at a going rate of \$11. A new town ordinance now sets a maximum parking fee of \$7. Use the accompanying supply and demand diagram to show how each of the following can result from the price ceiling.

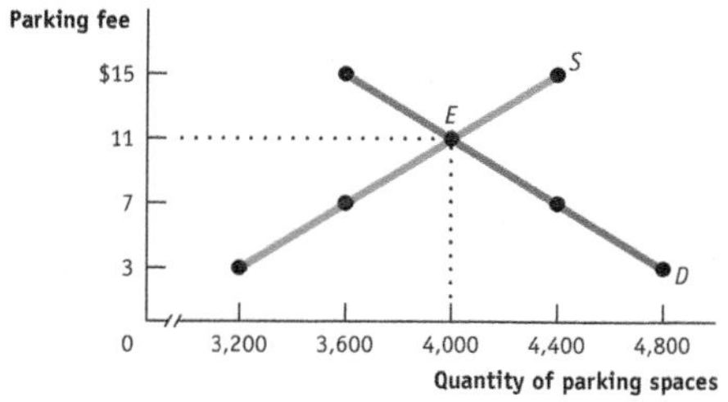

a. Some homeowners now think it's not worth the hassle to rent out spaces.
b. Some fans who used to carpool to the game now drive alone.
c. Some fans can't find parking and leave without seeing the game.

Explain how each of the following adverse effects arises from the price ceiling.

d. Some fans now arrive several hours early to find parking.
e. Friends of homeowners near the stadium regularly attend games, even if they aren't big fans. But some serious fans have given up because of the parking situation.
f. Some homeowners rent spaces for more than \$7 but pretend that the buyers are nonpaying friends or family.

2. True or false? Explain your answer. A price ceiling below the equilibrium price in an otherwise efficient market does the following:
a. increases quantity supplied
b. makes some people who want to consume the good worse off
c. makes all producers worse off

3. The state legislature mandates a price floor for gasoline of P_F per gallon. Assess the following statements and illustrate your answer using the figure provided.

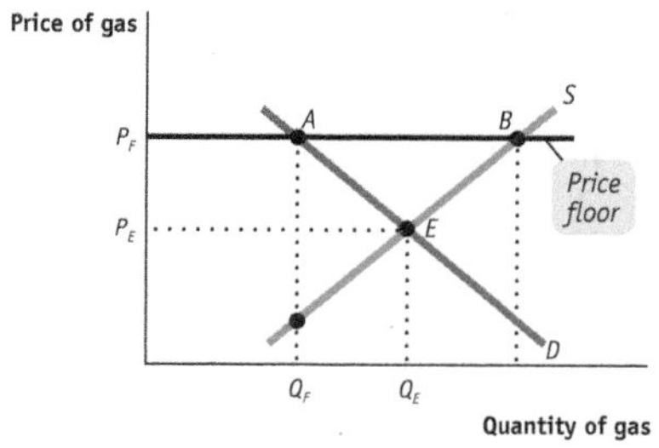

a. Proponents of the law claim it will increase the income of gas station owners. Opponents claim it will hurt gas station owners because they will lose customers.
b. Proponents claim consumers will be better off because gas stations will provide better service. Opponents claim consumers will be generally worse off because they prefer to buy gas at cheaper prices.
c. Proponents claim that they are helping gas station owners without hurting anyone else. Opponents claim that consumers are hurt and will end up doing things like buying gas in a nearby state or on the black market.

d. Price ceilings result in wasted resources. The additional time fans spend to guarantee a parking space is wasted time.

e. Price ceilings lead to the inefficient allocation of goods— here, the parking spaces—to consumers. If less serious fans with connections end up with the parking spaces, diehard fans will have no place to park.

f. Price ceilings lead to black markets.

2. a. False. By lowering the price that producers receive, a price ceiling leads to a decrease in the quantity supplied.

b. True. A price ceiling leads to a lower quantity supplied than in an efficient, unregulated market. As a result, some people who would have been willing to pay the market price, and so would have gotten the good in an unregulated market, are unable to obtain it when a price ceiling is imposed.

c. True. Those producers who still sell the product now receive less for it and are therefore worse off. Other producers will no longer find it worthwhile to sell the product at all and so will also be made worse off.

3.

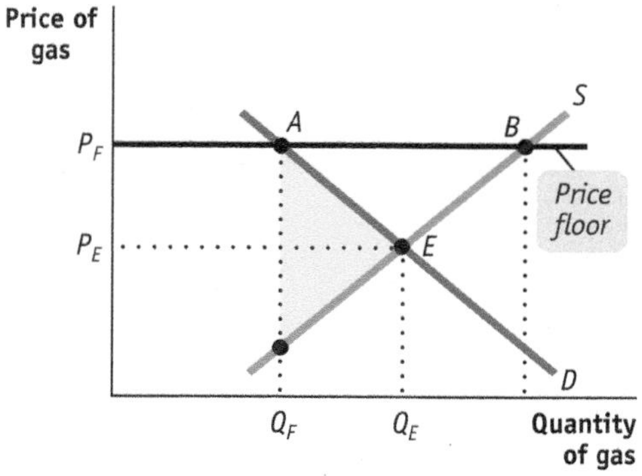

a. Some gas station owners will benefit from getting a higher price. Q_F indicates the sales made by these owners. But some will lose; there are those who make sales at the market equilibrium price of P_E but do not make sales at the regulated price of P_F. These missed sales are indicated on the graph by the fall in the quantity demanded along the demand curve, from point *E* to point *A*.

b. Those who buy gas at the higher price of P_F will probably receive better service; this is an example of inefficiently high quality caused by a price floor as gas station owners compete on quality rather than price. But opponents are correct to claim that consumers are generally worse off—those who buy at P_F would have been happy to buy at P_E, and many who were willing to buy at a price between P_E and P_F are now unwilling to buy. This is indicated on the graph by the fall in the quantity demanded along the demand curve, from point *E* to point *A*.

c. Proponents are wrong because consumers and some gas station owners are hurt by the price floor, which creates "missed opportunities"—desirable transactions between consumers and station owners that never take place. The deadweight loss, the net gains forgone because of missed opportunities, is indicated by the shaded area in the accompanying figure. Moreover, the inefficiency of wasted resources arises as consumers spend time and money driving to other states. The price floor also tempts people to engage in black market activity. With the price floor, only Q_F units are sold. But at prices between P_E and P_F, there are drivers who together want to buy more than Q_F and owners who are willing to sell to them, a situation likely to lead to illegal activity.

Tackle the Test: Multiple-Choice Questions

1. e
2. b
3. e
4. b
5. c

Tackle the Test: Multiple-Choice Questions

1. To be effective, a price ceiling must be set
  I. above the equilibrium price.
  II. in the housing market.
  III. to achieve the equilibrium market quantity.

a. I
b. II
c. III
d. I, II, and III
e. None of the above

2. Refer to the graph provided. A price floor set at $5 will result in

a. a shortage of 100 units.
b. a surplus of 100 units.
c. a shortage of 200 units.
d. a surplus of 200 units.
e. a surplus of 50 units.

3. Effective price ceilings are inefficient because they
a. create shortages.
b. lead to wasted resources.
c. decrease quality.
d. create black markets.
e. do all of the above.

4. Refer to the graph provided. If the government establishes a minimum wage at $10, how many workers will benefit from the higher wage?

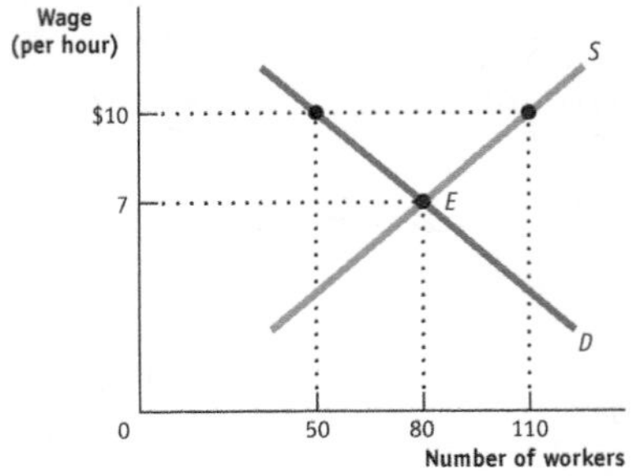

a. 30
b. 50
c. 60
d. 80
e. 110

5. Refer to the graph for Question 4. With a minimum wage of $10, how many workers are unemployed (would like to work, but are unable to find a job)?
a. 30
b. 50
c. 60
d. 80
e. 110

90 Section 2 Supply and Demand

Tackle the Test: Free-Response Questions

1. Refer to the graph provided to answer the following questions.

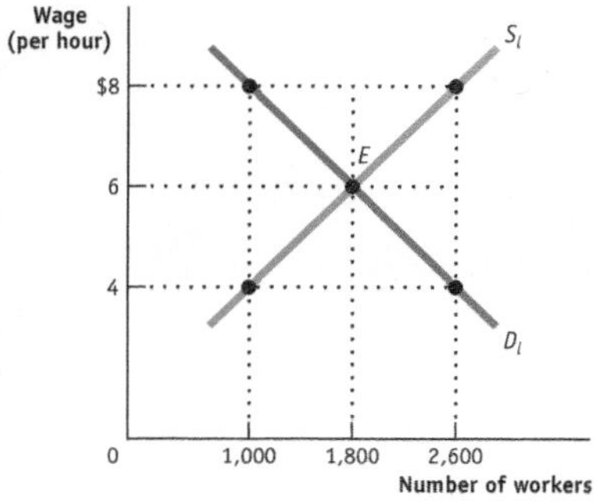

a. What are the equilibrium wage and quantity of workers in this market?

b. For it to have an effect, where would the government have to set a minimum wage?

c. If the government set a minimum wage at $8,

i. how many workers would supply their labor?

ii. how many workers would be hired?

iii. how many workers would want to work that did *not* want to work for the equilibrium wage?

iv. how many previously employed workers would no longer have a job?

Rubric for FRQ 1 (6 points)

1 point: equilibrium wage = $6, quantity of labor = 1,800

1 point: The minimum wage will have an effect if it is set anywhere above $6.

1 point: 2,600 workers would supply their labor

1 point: 1,000 workers would be hired

1 point: 800 (the number of workers who would want to work for $8 but did not supply labor for $6)

1 point: 800 (at the equilibrium wage of $6, 1,800 workers were hired; at a wage of $8, 1,000 workers would be hired. 1,800 – 1,000 = 800)

2. Draw a correctly labeled graph of a housing market in equilibrium. On your graph, illustrate an effective legal limit (ceiling) on rent. Identify the quantity of housing demanded, the quantity of housing supplied, and the size of the resulting surplus or shortage.
(6 points)

Tackle the Test: Free-Response Question

Rubric for FRQ 2 (6 points)

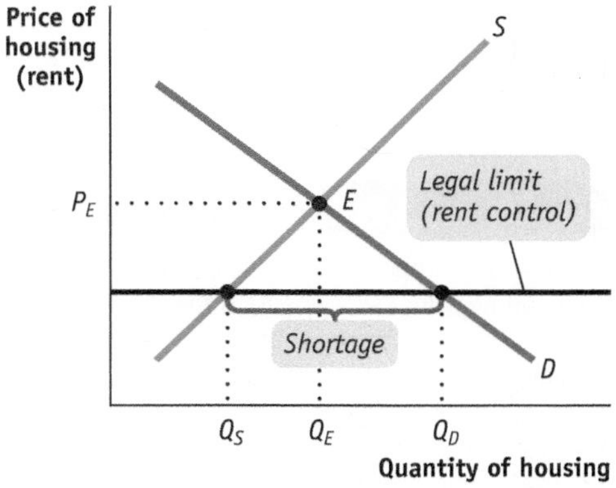

1 point: Vertical axis is labeled "Price," horizontal axis is labeled "Quantity," demand curve is downward-sloping and labeled, supply curve is upward-sloping and labeled.

1 point: Equilibrium price and quantity are shown on the axes.

1 point: Price ceiling is shown as a horizontal line below equilibrium.

1 point: Showing Q_D at the price ceiling on the demand curve

1 point: Showing Q_S at the price ceiling on the supply curve

1 point: Showing a shortage equal to the distance between Q_D and Q_S

PD To prepare for teaching this lesson, you may want to consult the **Module 9 Sample Lecture** in the TRM.

OPEN & CLOSE **Start Here**

A quota is an upper limit on the quantity of a good that can be sold. Ask students if they know what a quota is and if they can think of an example of a quota. Students may be familiar with quotas on imports or fishing or hunting quotas. Distinguish these from quotas in a nonmarket context (like sales quotas for people working in sales) that can actually be **minimum** quantities (i.e., lower limits). Discuss quantity controls (quotas) and possible reasons why governments establish them. Tell students that the purpose of this module is to use the supply and demand model to see how quotas affect market price, quantity, and efficiency.

TEACH **Connect It**

The previous module introduced government attempts to control prices in a market. This module looks at how governments can intervene in a market to control the other variable in our model—quantity. Just as price controls have predictable effects on markets, quantity controls have certain predictable economic consequences. This module uses the supply and demand model to determine those effects.

iStockphoto

MODULE 9 Supply and Demand: Quantity Controls

In this Module, you will learn to:

- Explain the workings of quantity controls, another way government intervenes in markets
- Describe how quantity controls create problems and can make a market inefficient
- Explain who benefits and who loses from quantity controls

Controlling Quantities

In the 1930s, New York City instituted a system of licensing for taxicabs: only taxis with a "medallion" were allowed to pick up passengers. Because this system was intended to ensure quality, medallion owners were supposed to maintain certain standards, including safety and cleanliness. A total of 11,787 medallions were issued, with taxi owners paying $10 for each medallion.

In 1995, there were still only 11,787 licensed taxicabs in New York, even though the city had meanwhile become the financial capital of the world, a place where hundreds of thousands of people in a hurry tried to hail a cab every day. (An additional 400 medallions were issued in 1995; after several rounds of sales of additional medallions, today there are 13,257 medallions.) The result of this restriction on the number of taxis was that a New York City taxi medallion became very valuable: if you wanted to operate a taxi in New York, you had to lease a medallion from someone else or buy one for a going price of several hundred thousand dollars.

It turns out that this story is not unique; other cities introduced similar medallion systems in the 1930s and, like New York, have issued few new medallions since. In San Francisco and Boston, as in New York, taxi medallions trade for six-figure prices.

A taxi medallion system is a form of **quantity control**, or **quota**, by which the government regulates the quantity of a good that can be bought and sold rather than regulating the price. Typically, the government limits quantity in a market by issuing **licenses**; only people with a license can legally supply the good. A taxi medallion is just such a license. The government of New York City limits the number of taxi rides that can be sold by limiting the number of taxis to only those who hold medallions. There are many other cases of quantity controls, ranging from limits on how much foreign currency (for instance, British pounds or Mexican pesos) people are allowed to buy to the quantity of clams New Jersey fishing boats are allowed to catch. Section 8 discusses quotas on goods imported from other countries.

AP® Exam Tip

Quantity controls and price controls are graphed differently. Graph a quota as a vertical line at the quantity limit. Graph a price ceiling or floor as a horizontal line at the price limit.

A **quantity control**, or **quota**, is an upper limit on the quantity of some good that can be bought or sold.

A **license** gives its owner the right to supply a good or service.

St. Louis Federal Reserve Bank Resources

Unintended Consequences

Students determine the costs, benefits, and unintended consequences of policies, beginning with analysis of a policy that would allow them to take 2 years off from school between grades 10 and 11. They then analyze the costs, benefits, and unintended consequences of various government policies, including rent controls and import quotas.

Some attempts to control quantities are undertaken for good economic reasons, some for bad ones. In many cases, as we will see, quantity controls introduced to address a temporary problem become politically hard to remove later because the beneficiaries don't want them abolished, even after the original reason for their existence is long gone. But whatever the reasons for such controls, they have certain predictable—and usually undesirable—economic consequences.

The Anatomy of Quantity Controls

To understand why a New York taxi medallion is worth so much money, we consider a simplified version of the market for taxi rides, shown in **Figure 9.1**. Just as we assumed in the analysis of rent control that all apartments were the same, we now suppose that all taxi rides are the same—ignoring the real-world complication that some taxi rides are longer, and therefore more expensive, than others. The table in the figure shows supply and demand schedules. The equilibrium—indicated by point *E* in the figure and by the shaded entries in the table—is a fare of $5 per ride, with 10 million rides taken per year. (You'll see in a minute why we present the equilibrium this way.)

© Ed Rooney/Alamy

The New York medallion system limits the number of taxis, but each taxi driver can offer as many rides as he or she can manage. (Now you know why New York taxi drivers are so aggressive!) To simplify our analysis, however, we will assume that a medallion system limits the number of taxi rides that can legally be given to 8 million per year.

Until now, we have derived the demand curve by answering questions of the form: "How many taxi rides will passengers want to take if the price is $5 per ride?" But it is possible to reverse the question and ask instead: "At what price will consumers want to buy 10 million rides per year?" The price at which consumers want to buy a given quantity—in this case, 10 million rides at $5 per ride—is the **demand price** of that quantity. You can see from the demand schedule in Figure 9.1 that the demand price of 6 million rides is $7 per ride, the demand price of 7 million rides is $6.50 per ride, and so on.

The **demand price** of a given quantity is the price at which consumers will demand that quantity.

Figure 9.1 The Market for Taxi Rides in the Absence of Government Controls

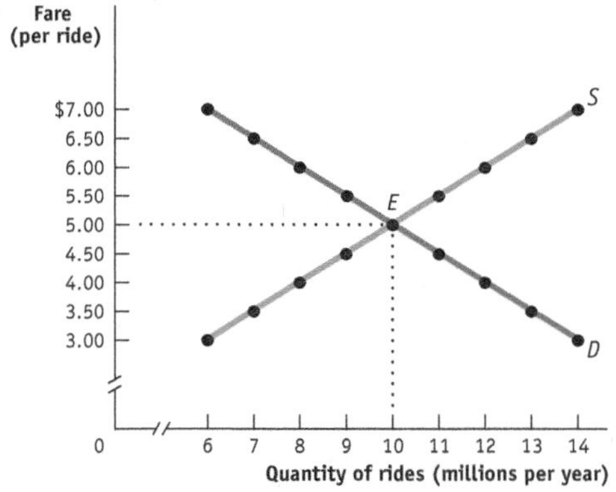

Fare (per ride)	Quantity of rides (millions per year): Quantity demanded	Quantity supplied
$7.00	6	14
6.50	7	13
6.00	8	12
5.50	9	11
5.00	10	10
4.50	11	9
4.00	12	8
3.50	13	7
3.00	14	6

Without government intervention, the market reaches equilibrium with 10 million rides taken per year at a fare of $5 per ride.

TEACH Teach It

- The demand price of a given quantity is the price at which consumers will demand that quantity of a good or service.
- The supply price of a given quantity is the price at which producers will supply that quantity.
- A limit (or quota placed on the quantity of a good or service) is shown by drawing a vertical line at the number of the quantity deemed to be a quota on our supply and demand graph.
- Point out that a quota is also a price control instituted by government.
- A license grants rights to supply a good or service and is often issued by government as a way to control the quantity of a good or service supplied to the market.

TEACH Teach It

Use the distinction between positive and normative from Section 1 to help students understand that the effect of quantity controls shown with the supply and demand model is positive (i.e., can be tested) and the reasons for enacting quantity controls are normative (i.e., involve opinions and value judgments). So, although our economic model can be used to identify the effects of price controls placed on markets, the decision to enact them isn't always made solely (or even partially) based on those effects. And it can be difficult to remove existing quantity controls because the beneficiaries don't want to lose their benefits from them.

FOCUS Graph It

Refer students to Figure 9.1 where there is no government quantity control. Ask:

- What are the equilibrium price and quantity of taxi rides per year? *$5, 10 million*
- What would happen if the price per taxi ride rose to $6.50? *$Q_d$ would be 7 rides, Q_s would be 13 rides—there would be a surplus.*
- What would happen if the price per taxi ride decreased to $3.50? *$Q_s$ would be 7 rides, Q_d would be 13 rides—there would be a shortage.*

FOCUS Active Learning

Have students draw a graph of a market in equilibrium and label the equilibrium price and quantity as P_e and Q_e. Tell them that they are the firm producing in this market. They should have *P* and *Q* labeled on the axes, downward-sloping and labeled demand, upward-sloping and labeled supply, and equilibrium P_e and Q_e shown on the axes where supply and demand cross. Check the students' graphs to make sure they are correct. Ask students if a quota set at a quantity higher than the equilibrium quantity would affect them (e.g., how they would react if the government said, "You can't sell more than 15" and they are only selling 10). They should assert that they *aren't* selling more than 15, so the government should leave them alone. Now ask students how they would respond if a quota were set at a quantity below what they were producing (e.g., how they would react if the government said, "You can't sell more than 5" and they are indeed selling 10). They should indicate that they will reduce the number they sell to comply with the law.

Finally, ask students to illustrate the binding quota (the one with a quantity below equilibrium) on their graphs by drawing a vertical line at the quota amount. Have your class use the line to find the price consumers will pay and the price producers will accept at that quantity and to identify the "wedge" between them.

TEACH Connect It

Note that a quantity control (quota) is drawn as a vertical line on our graph, while a price floor or ceiling (price control) is drawn as a horizontal line.

FOCUS Graph It

Have students refer to Figure 9.2; ask them:

- What are the equilibrium price and quantity in the market? *$5 million and $10 million*
- What is the quota set in this market? *8 million*
- What are the demand price and the supply price with the quota? *$4 and $6*
- How large is the wedge (the "quota rent per ride") from the quota? *$6 – $4 = $2*

The **supply price** of a given quantity is the price at which producers will supply that quantity.

Similarly, the supply curve represents the answer to questions of the form: "How many taxi rides would taxi drivers supply at a price of $5 each?" But we can also reverse this question to ask: "At what price will producers be willing to supply 10 million rides per year?" The price at which producers will supply a given quantity—in this case, 10 million rides at $5 per ride—is the **supply price** of that quantity. We can see from the supply schedule in Figure 9.1 that the supply price of 6 million rides is $3 per ride, the supply price of 7 million rides is $3.50 per ride, and so on.

Now we are ready to analyze a quota. We have assumed that the city government limits the quantity of taxi rides to 8 million per year. Medallions, each of which carries the right to provide a certain number of taxi rides per year, are made available to selected people in such a way that a total of 8 million rides will be provided. Medallion holders may then either drive their own taxis or rent their medallions to others for a fee.

Figure 9.2 shows the resulting market for taxi rides, with the black vertical line at 8 million rides per year representing the quota. Because the quantity of rides is limited to 8 million, consumers must be at point *A* on the demand curve, corresponding to the shaded entry in the demand schedule: the demand price of 8 million rides is $6 per ride. Meanwhile, taxi drivers must be at point *B* on the supply curve, corresponding to the shaded entry in the supply schedule: the supply price of 8 million rides is $4 per ride.

But how can the price received by taxi drivers be $4 when the price paid by taxi riders is $6? The answer is that in addition to the market in taxi rides, there is also a market in medallions. Medallion-holders may not always want to drive their taxis: they may be ill or on vacation. Those who do not want to drive their own taxis will sell the right to use the medallion to someone else. So we need to consider two sets of transactions here, and so two prices: (1) the transactions in taxi rides and the price at which these will occur

Figure 9.2 Effect of a Quota on the Market for Taxi Rides

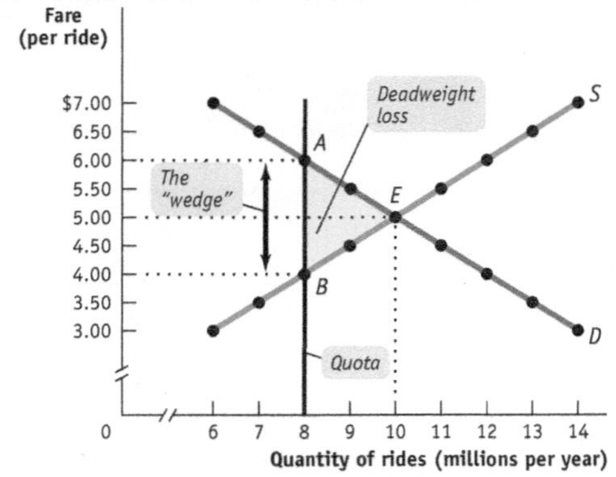

Fare (per ride)	Quantity of rides (millions per year) Quantity demanded	Quantity supplied
$7.00	6	14
6.50	7	13
6.00	8	12
5.50	9	11
5.00	10	10
4.50	11	9
4.00	12	8
3.50	13	7
3.00	14	6

The table shows the demand price and the supply price corresponding to each quantity: the price at which that quantity would be demanded and supplied, respectively. The city government imposes a quota of 8 million rides by selling enough medallions for only 8 million rides, represented by the black vertical line. The price paid by consumers rises to $6 per ride, the demand price of 8 million rides, shown by point *A*. The supply price of 8 million rides is only $4 per ride, shown by point *B*. The difference between these two prices is the quota rent per ride, the earnings that accrue to the owner of a medallion. The quota rent drives a wedge between the demand price and the supply price. Because the quota discourages mutually beneficial transactions, it creates a deadweight loss equal to the shaded triangle.

and (2) the transactions in medallions and the price at which these will occur. It turns out that since we are looking at two markets, the $4 and $6 prices will both be right.

To see how all of this works, consider two imaginary New York taxi drivers, Sunil and Harriet. Sunil has a medallion but can't use it because he's recovering from a severely sprained wrist. So he's looking to rent his medallion out to someone else. Harriet doesn't have a medallion but would like to rent one. Furthermore, at any point in time there are many other people like Harriet who would like to rent a medallion. Suppose Sunil agrees to rent his medallion to Harriet. To make things simple, assume that any driver can give only one ride per day and that Sunil is renting his medallion to Harriet for one day. What rental price will they agree on?

To answer this question, we need to look at the transactions from the viewpoints of both drivers. Once she has the medallion, Harriet knows she can make $6 per day—the demand price of a ride under the quota. And she is willing to rent the medallion only if she makes at least $4 per day—the supply price of a ride under the quota. So Sunil cannot demand a rent of more than $2—the difference between $6 and $4. And if Harriet offered Sunil less than $2—say, $1.50—there would be other eager drivers willing to offer him more, up to $2. So, in order to get the medallion, Harriet must offer Sunil at least $2. Since the rent can be no more than $2 and no less than $2, it must be exactly $2.

It is no coincidence that $2 is exactly the difference between $6, the demand price of 8 million rides, and $4, the supply price of 8 million rides. In every case in which the supply of a good is legally restricted, there is a **wedge** between the demand price of the quantity transacted and the supply price of the quantity transacted. This wedge, illustrated by the double-headed arrow in Figure 9.2, has a special name: the **quota rent**. It is the earnings that accrue to the medallion holder from ownership of a valuable commodity, the medallion. In the case of Sunil and Harriet, the quota rent of $2 goes to Sunil because he owns the medallion, and the remaining $4 from the total fare of $6 goes to Harriet.

So Figure 9.2 also illustrates the quota rent in the market for New York taxi rides. The quota limits the quantity of rides to 8 million per year, a quantity at which the demand price of $6 exceeds the supply price of $4. The wedge between these two prices, $2, is the quota rent that results from the restrictions placed on the quantity of taxi rides in this market.

But wait a second. What if Sunil doesn't rent out his medallion? What if he uses it himself? Doesn't this mean that he gets a price of $6? No, not really. Even if Sunil doesn't rent out his medallion, he could have rented it out, which means that the medallion has an *opportunity cost* of $2: if Sunil decides to use his own medallion and drive his own taxi rather than renting his medallion to Harriet, the $2 represents his opportunity cost of not renting out his medallion. That is, the $2 quota rent is now the rental income he forgoes by driving his own taxi. In effect, Sunil is in two businesses—the taxi-driving business and the medallion-renting business. He makes $4 per ride from driving his taxi and $2 per ride from renting out his medallion. It doesn't make any difference that in this particular case he has rented his medallion to himself! So regardless of whether the medallion owner uses the medallion himself or herself, or rents it to others, it is a valuable asset. And this is represented in the going price for a New York City taxi medallion. Notice, by the way, that quotas—like price ceilings and price floors—don't always have a real effect. If the quota were set at 12 million rides—that is, above the equilibrium quantity in an unregulated market—it would have no effect because it would not be binding.

New York City: An empty cab is hard to find.

A quantity control, or quota, drives a **wedge** between the demand price and the supply price of a good; that is, the price paid by buyers ends up being higher than that received by sellers.

The difference between the demand and supply price at the quota amount is the **quota rent**, the earnings that accrue to the license-holder from ownership of the right to sell the good. It is equal to the market price of the license when the licenses are traded.

AP® Exam Tip

Drawing a quick graph using the data given will aid you in answering questions on quotas. For example, quota rent is simply the difference between the height of the demand curve and the height of the supply curve at the quota amount.

The Costs of Quantity Controls

Like price controls, quantity controls can have some predictable and undesirable side effects. The first is the by-now-familiar problem of inefficiency due to missed opportunities: quantity controls prevent mutually beneficial transactions from occurring, transactions that would benefit both buyers and sellers. Looking back at Figure 9.2, you can see that starting at the quota of 8 million rides, New Yorkers would be willing to pay at least $5.50 per ride for an additional 1 million rides and that taxi drivers would be willing to provide those rides as long as they got at least $4.50 per ride. These are rides that would have taken place if there had been no quota. The same is true for the next 1 million rides: New Yorkers

FOCUS Test It

- What happens if a quota is set at a quantity above the equilibrium quantity? *It has no effect.*
- Explain why a binding quota results in a "deadweight loss." *Because it prevents mutually beneficial trades—the quantity of the good sold is kept below the equilibrium quantity.*

FOCUS Active Learning

TRM Assign **Worksheet 9.1 (Graphing Quotas)** from the TRM for students to practice drawing a graph with a quantity control given.

would be willing to pay at least $5 per ride when the quantity of rides is increased from 9 to 10 million, and taxi drivers would be willing to provide those rides as long as they got at least $5 per ride. Again, these rides would have occurred without the quota. Only when the market has reached the unregulated market equilibrium quantity of 10 million rides are there no "missed-opportunity rides"—the quota of 8 million rides has caused 2 million "missed-opportunity rides." A buyer would be willing to buy the good at a price that the seller would be willing to accept, but such a transaction does not occur because it is forbidden by the quota. Economists have a special term for the lost gains from missed opportunities such as these: **deadweight loss**. Generally, when the demand price exceeds the supply price, there is a deadweight loss. Figure 9.2 illustrates the deadweight loss with a shaded triangle between the demand and supply curves. This triangle represents the missed gains from taxi rides prevented by the quota, a loss that is experienced by both disappointed would-be riders and frustrated would-be drivers.

Deadweight loss is the value of foregone mutually beneficial transactions.

Because there are transactions that people would like to make but are not allowed to, quantity controls generate an incentive to evade them or even to break the law. New York's taxi industry again provides clear examples. Taxi regulation applies only to those drivers who are hailed by passengers on the street. A car service that makes prearranged pickups does not need a medallion. As a result, such hired cars provide much of the service that might otherwise be provided by taxis, as in other cities. In addition, there are substantial numbers of unlicensed cabs that simply defy the law by picking up passengers without a medallion. Because these cabs are illegal, their drivers are completely unregulated, and they generate a disproportionately large share of traffic accidents in New York City.

In fact, in 2004 the hardships caused by the limited number of New York taxis led city leaders to authorize an increase in the number of licensed taxis. In a series of sales, the city sold more than 1,000 new medallions, to bring the total number up to the current 13,257 medallions—a move that certainly cheered New York riders. But those who already owned medallions were less happy with the increase; they understood that the nearly 1,000 new taxis would reduce or eliminate the shortage of taxis. As a result, taxi drivers anticipated a decline in their revenues as they would no longer always be assured of finding willing customers. And, in turn, the value of a medallion would fall. So to placate the medallion owners, city officials also raised taxi fares: by 25% in 2004, and again—by a smaller percentage—in 2006 and 2012. Although taxis are now easier to find, a ride now costs more—and that price increase slightly diminished the newfound cheer of New York taxi riders.

FYI The Clams of New Jersey

Forget the refineries along the Jersey Turnpike; one industry that New Jersey *really* dominates is clam fishing. In 2012 the Garden State supplied 50% of the country's surf clams, whose tongues are used in fried-clam dinners, and 53% of the quahogs, which are used to make clam chowder.

In the 1980s, however, excessive fishing threatened to wipe out New Jersey's clam beds. To save the resource, the U.S. government introduced a clam quota, which sets an overall limit on the number of bushels of clams that may be caught and allocates licenses to owners of fishing boats based on their historical catches.

Laura Stone/Shutterstock

A fried clam feast is a favorite on the Jersey shore.

Notice, by the way, that this is an example of a quota that is probably justified by broader economic and environmental considerations—unlike the New York taxicab quota, which has long since lost any economic rationale. Still, whatever its rationale, the New Jersey clam quota works the same way as any other quota.

Once the quota system was established, many boat owners stopped fishing for clams. They realized that rather than operate a boat part time, it was more profitable to sell or rent their licenses to someone else, who could then assemble enough licenses to operate a boat full time. Today, there are approximately 50 New Jersey boats fishing for clams; the license required to operate one is worth more than the boat itself.

Source: NOAA

FOCUS Active Learning

TRM Assign **Worksheet 9.2 (Graphing Quotas—Peanuts!)** from the TRM, so students can continue to practice drawing graphs related to quotas.

OPEN & CLOSE Exit Slip

TRM *Please see **Exit Slip: Module 9** in the TRM for formative multiple-choice questions to ask before finishing your lesson. These questions will help you quickly assess whether your students have mastered the module's concepts before moving on.*

Answers to the Exit Slip Questions

1. E
2. D
3. D

MODULE 9 Review

Check Your Understanding

1. Suppose that the supply and demand for taxi rides is given by Figure 9.1 and a quota is set at 6 million rides. Replicate the graph from Figure 9.1, and identify each of the following on your graph:
   a. the price of a ride
   b. the quota rent
   c. the deadweight loss resulting from the quota.
   Suppose the quota on taxi rides is increased to 9 million.
   d. What happens to the quota rent and the deadweight loss?
2. Again replicate the graph from Figure 9.1. Suppose that the quota is 8 million rides and that demand decreases due to a decline in tourism. Show on your graph the smallest parallel leftward shift in demand that would result in the quota no longer having an effect on the market.

Tackle the Test: Multiple-Choice Questions

Refer to the graph provided for Questions 1–3.

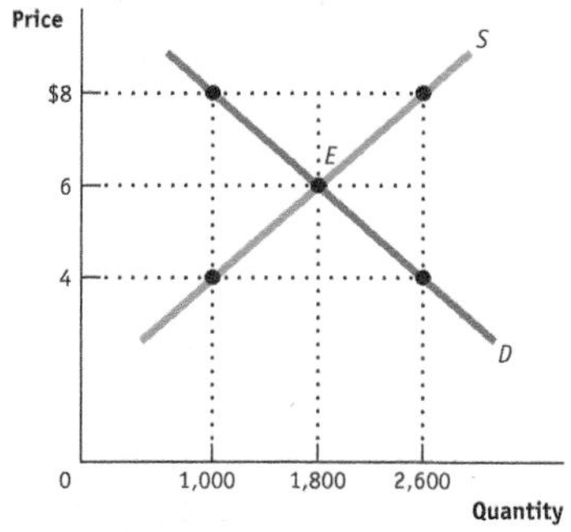

1. If the government established a quota of 1,000 in this market, the demand price would be
   a. less than $4.
   b. $4.
   c. $6.
   d. $8.
   e. more than $8.
2. If the government established a quota of 1,000 in this market, the supply price would be
   a. less than $4.
   b. $4.
   c. $6.
   d. $8.
   e. more than $8.
3. If the government established a quota of 1,000 in this market, the quota rent would be
   a. $2.
   b. $4.
   c. $6.
   d. $8.
   e. more than $8.
4. Quotas lead to which of the following?
   I. inefficiency due to missed opportunities
   II. incentives to evade or break the law
   III. a surplus in the market
   a. I
   b. II
   c. III
   d. I and II
   e. I, II, and III
5. Which of the following would decrease the effect a quota has on the quantity sold in a market?
   a. decrease in demand
   b. increase in supply
   c. increase in demand
   d. price ceiling above the equilibrium price
   e. none of the above

Answers to Module 9 Review Questions

Check Your Understanding

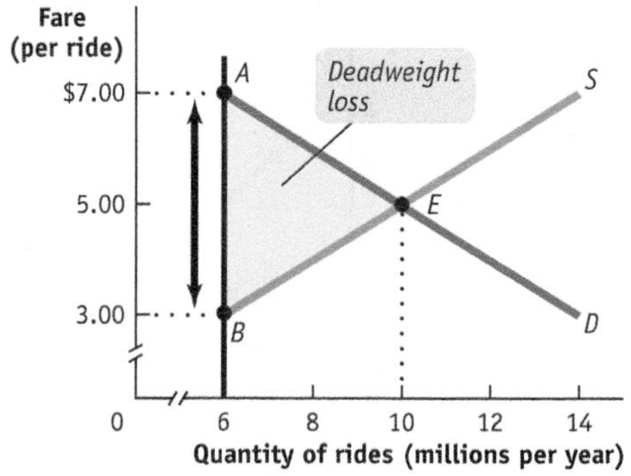

1. a. The price of a ride is $7 since the quantity demanded at this price is 6 million: $7 is the *demand price* of 6 million rides. This is represented by point *A* in the accompanying figure.

b. At 6 million rides, the supply price is $3 per ride, represented by point *B* in the figure. The wedge between the demand price of $7 per ride and the supply price of $3 per ride is the quota rent per ride, $4. This is represented in the figure above by the vertical distance between points *A* and *B*.

c. The quota discourages 4 million mutually beneficial transactions. The shaded triangle in the figure represents the deadweight loss.

d. At 9 million rides, the demand price is $5.50 per ride, indicated by point *C* in the figure below, and the supply price is $4.50 per ride, indicated by point *D*. The quota rent is the difference between the demand price and the supply price: $1. The deadweight loss is represented by the shaded triangle in the figure. As you can see, the deadweight loss is smaller when the quota is set at 9 million rides than when it is set at 6 million rides.

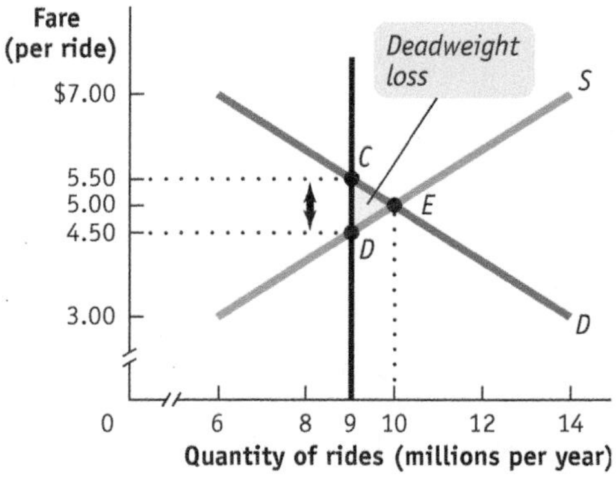

2. The accompanying figure shows a decrease in demand by 4 million rides, represented by a leftward shift of the demand curve from D_1 to D_2: at any given price, the quantity demanded falls by 4 million rides. (For example, at a price of $5, the quantity demanded falls from 10 million to 6 million rides per year.) This eliminates the effect of a quota limit of 8 million rides. At point E_2, the new market equilibrium, the equilibrium quantity is equal to the quota limit; as a result, the quota has no effect on the market.

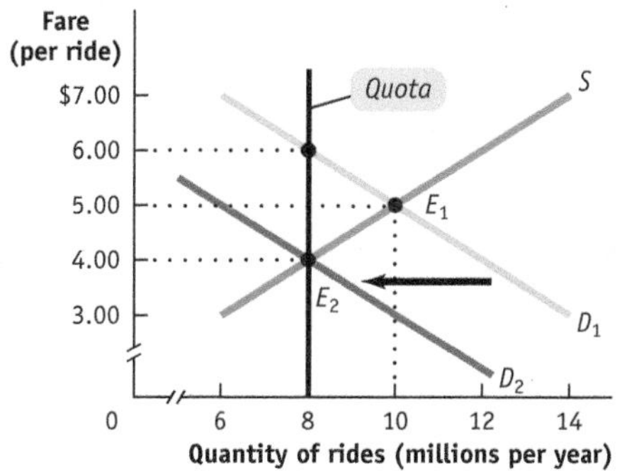

Tackle the Test: Multiple-Choice Questions

1. d 2. b 3. b 4. d 5. a

Tackle the Test: Free-Response Question

Rubric for FRQ 2 (6 points)

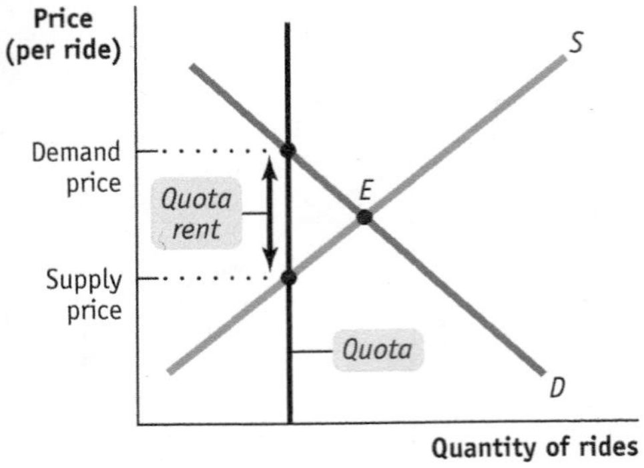

1 point: Correctly labeled supply and demand diagram (vertical axis labeled "Price" or "P," horizontal axis labeled "Quantity" or "Q," upward-sloping supply curve with label, downward-sloping demand curve with label)

1 point: Equilibrium price and quantity are shown on the axes.

1 point: Quota is shown as a vertical line to the left of equilibrium.

1 point: Showing demand price on the vertical axis at the level where the quota intersects the demand curve

1 point: Showing supply price on the vertical axis at the level where the quota intersects the supply curve

1 point: Showing the quota rent as the difference between demand price and supply price

FOCUS **Flip It**

TRM Encourage your students to watch the **Section 2 Review Video** which was created as a special student review tool and is linked into the e-Book or may be found on the book's companion website.

Tackle the Test: Free-Response Questions

1. Draw a correctly labeled graph illustrating hypothetical supply and demand curves for the U.S. automobile market. Label the equilibrium price and quantity. Suppose the government institutes a quota to limit automobile production. Draw a vertical line labeled "$Q_{ineffective}$" to show the level of a quota that would have no effect on the market. Draw a vertical line labeled "$Q_{effective}$" to show the level of a quota that would have an effect on the market. Shade in and label the deadweight loss resulting from the effective quota.

Rubric for FRQ 1 (5 points)

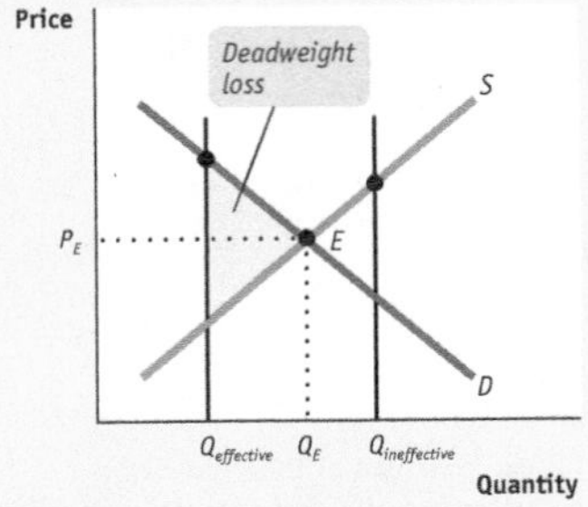

1 point: Correctly labeled supply and demand diagram (vertical axis labeled "Price" or "P," horizontal axis labeled "Quantity" or "Q," upward-sloping supply curve with label, downward-sloping demand curve with label)

1 point: Equilibrium at the intersection of supply and demand with the equilibrium price labeled on the vertical axis and the equilibrium quantity labeled on the horizontal axis

1 point: Vertical line to the right of equilibrium quantity labeled $Q_{ineffective}$

1 point: Vertical line to the left of equilibrium quantity labeled $Q_{effective}$

1 point: The triangle to the right of the effective quota line and to the left of supply and demand shaded in and labeled as the deadweight loss

2. Draw a correctly labeled graph of the market for taxicab rides. On the graph, draw and label a vertical line showing the level of an effective quota. Label the demand price, the supply price, and the quota rent. **(6 points)**

SECTION 2 Review

Section 2 Review Video

Module 5

1. The **supply and demand model** illustrates how a **competitive market**, one with many buyers and sellers of the same product, works.
2. The **demand schedule** shows the **quantity demanded** at each price and is represented graphically by a **demand curve**. The **law of demand** says that demand curves slope downward, meaning that as price decreases, the quantity demanded increases.
3. A **movement along the demand curve** occurs when the price changes and causes a change in the quantity demanded. When economists talk of **changes in demand**, they mean shifts of the demand curve—a change in the quantity demanded at any given price. An increase in demand causes a rightward shift of the demand curve. A decrease in demand causes a leftward shift.
4. There are five main factors that shift the demand curve:
   - A change in the prices of related goods, such as substitutes or complements
   - A change in income: when income rises, the demand for **normal goods** increases and the demand for **inferior goods** decreases
   - A change in tastes
   - A change in expectations
   - A change in the number of consumers

Module 6

5. The **supply schedule** shows the **quantity supplied** at each price and is represented graphically by a **supply curve**. According to the **law of supply**, supply curves slope upward, meaning that as price increases, the quantity demanded increases.

6. A **movement along the supply curve** occurs when the price changes and causes a change in the quantity supplied. When economists talk of **changes in supply**, they mean shifts of the supply curve—a change in the quantity supplied at any given price. An increase in supply causes a rightward shift of the supply curve. A decrease in supply causes a leftward shift.

7. There are five main factors that shift the supply curve:

- A change in **input** prices
- A change in the prices of related goods and services
- A change in technology
- A change in expectations
- A change in the number of producers

Module 7

8. An economic situation is in **equilibrium** when no individual would be better off doing something different. The supply and demand model is based on the principle that the price in a market moves to its **equilibrium price**, or **market-clearing price**, the price at which the quantity demanded is equal to the quantity supplied. This quantity is the **equilibrium quantity**. When the price is above its market-clearing level, there is a **surplus** that pushes the price down. When the price is below its market-clearing level, there is a **shortage** that pushes the price up.

9. An increase in demand increases both the equilibrium price and the equilibrium quantity; a decrease in demand has the opposite effect. An increase in supply reduces the equilibrium price and increases the equilibrium quantity; a decrease in supply has the opposite effect.

10. Shifts of the demand curve and the supply curve can happen simultaneously. When they shift in opposite directions, the change in price is predictable but the change in quantity is not. When they shift in the same direction, the change in quantity is predictable but the change in price is not. In general, the curve that shifts the greater distance has a greater effect on the changes in price and quantity.

Module 8

11. Even when a market is efficient, governments often intervene to pursue greater fairness or to please a powerful interest group. Interventions can take the form of **price controls** or quantity controls, both of which generate predictable and undesirable side effects, consisting of various forms of inefficiency and illegal activity.

12. A **price ceiling**, a maximum market price below the equilibrium price, benefits successful buyers but creates persistent shortages. Because the price is maintained below the equilibrium price, the quantity demanded is increased and the quantity supplied is decreased compared to the equilibrium quantity. This leads to predictable problems including **inefficient allocation to consumers**, **wasted resources**, and **inefficiently low quality**. It also encourages illegal activity as people turn to **black markets** to get the good. Because of these problems, price ceilings have generally lost favor as an economic policy tool. But some governments continue to impose them either because they don't understand the effects or because the price ceilings benefit some influential group.

13. A **price floor**, a minimum market price above the equilibrium price, benefits successful sellers but creates a persistent surplus: because the price is maintained above the equilibrium price, the quantity demanded is decreased and the quantity supplied is increased compared to the equilibrium quantity. This leads to predictable problems: inefficiencies in the form of **inefficient allocation of sales among sellers**, wasted resources, and **inefficiently high quality**. It also encourages illegal activity and black markets. The most well-known kind of price floor is the **minimum wage**, but price floors are also commonly applied to agricultural products.

Section 2 Review 99

Module 9

14. **Quantity controls**, or **quotas**, limit the quantity of a good that can be bought or sold. The government issues **licenses** to individuals, the right to sell a given quantity of the good. The owner of a license earns a **quota rent**, earnings that accrue from ownership of the right to sell the good. It is equal to the difference between the **demand price** at the quota amount, what consumers are willing to pay for that amount, and the **supply price** at the quota amount, what suppliers are willing to accept for that amount. Economists say that a quota drives a **wedge** between the demand price and the supply price; this wedge is equal to the quota rent. By limiting mutually beneficial transactions, quantity controls generate inefficiency. Like price controls, quantity controls lead to **deadweight loss** and encourage illegal activity.

Key Terms

Competitive market, p. 49
Supply and demand model, p. 50
Demand schedule, p. 50
Quantity demanded, p. 50
Demand curve, p. 51
Law of demand, p. 51
Change in demand, p. 52
Movement along the demand curve, p. 52
Substitutes, p. 54
Complements, p. 54
Normal good, p. 55
Inferior good, p. 55
Individual demand curve, p. 56
Quantity supplied, p. 60
Supply schedule, p. 60
Supply curve, p. 60
Law of supply, p. 61
Change in supply, p. 61
Movement along the supply curve, p. 62
Input, p. 63
Individual supply curve, p. 65
Equilibrium, p. 69
Equilibrium price, p. 70
Market-clearing price, p. 70
Equilibrium quantity, p. 70
Surplus, p. 71
Shortage, p. 71
Price controls, p. 80
Price ceiling, p. 80
Price floor, p. 80
Inefficient allocation to consumers, p. 83
Wasted resources, p. 83
Inefficiently low quality, p. 84
Black market, p. 84
Minimum wage, p. 85
Inefficient allocation of sales among sellers, p. 87
Inefficiently high quality, p. 88
Quantity control or quota, p. 92
License, p. 92
Demand price, p. 93
Supply price, p. 94
Wedge, p. 95
Quota rent, p. 95
Deadweight loss, p. 96

Answers to Section 2 AP® Exam Practice Questions

Multiple-Choice Questions

1. e
2. e
3. a

AP® Exam Practice Questions

Multiple-Choice Questions

1. Which of the following changes will most likely result in an increase in the demand for hamburgers in your hometown?
   a. The price of hotdogs decreases.
   b. The price of drinks sold at hamburger restaurants increases.
   c. Income in your town decreases and hamburgers are a normal good.
   d. The local newspaper publishes a story on health problems caused by red meat.
   e. The number of vegetarians in your town decreases and the population size remains the same.
2. Which of the following changes will most likely result in a decrease in the supply of guitars?
   a. The popularity of guitar music increases.
   b. Consumer incomes decrease.
   c. A new firm enters the guitar industry.
   d. The guitar-making process is reengineered to be more efficient.
   e. The wages of guitar makers increase.
3. Which of the following will most likely result in a decrease in the quantity of lemons demanded?
   a. an increase in the price of lemons
   b. an increase in the price of limes
   c. an increase in the price of lemonade
   d. an increase in the number of lemonade stands
   e. a decrease in consumer income

4. Which of the following will occur if consumer incomes increase?
- **a.** The demand for inferior goods will increase.
- **b.** The demand for normal goods will increase.
- **c.** The demand for all goods will increase.
- **d.** The demand for normal goods will decrease.
- **e.** The demand for all goods will decrease.

5. If two goods are complements, an increase in the price of one good will cause which of the following?
- **a.** a decrease in the demand for the other
- **b.** a decrease in the quantity demanded of the other
- **c.** an increase in the demand for the other
- **d.** an increase in the quantity demanded of the other
- **e.** no change in the demand for the other

6. An increase in the wages of workers producing a good will most likely lead to which of the following?
- **a.** a decrease in the quantity of the good supplied
- **b.** a decrease in the supply of the good
- **c.** an increase in the quantity of the good supplied
- **d.** an increase in the supply of the good
- **e.** no change in the supply of the good

7. Which of the following is true at the equilibrium price in a market?
- **a.** Consumers who purchase the good may be better off buying something else instead.
- **b.** The market has not yet cleared.
- **c.** There is a tendency for the price to decrease over time.
- **d.** There may be either a surplus or a shortage of the good.
- **e.** The quantity demanded of the good equals the quantity supplied.

8. A survey indicated that chocolate is America's favorite ice cream flavor. Which of the following will lead to a decrease in the price of chocolate ice cream?
- **a.** A drought in the Midwest causes farmers to reduce the number of dairy cows they raise.
- **b.** A new report from the American Medical Association concludes that chocolate has significant health benefits.
- **c.** The price of vanilla ice cream increases.
- **d.** New freezer technology lowers the cost of producing ice cream.
- **e.** The price of ice cream toppings decreases.

9. Which of the following events will increase both the price and the quantity of pizza?
- **a.** The price of mozzarella cheese increases.
- **b.** New health hazards of eating pizza are widely publicized.
- **c.** The price of pizza ovens rises.
- **d.** Consumers expect the price of pizza to fall next week.
- **e.** Consumer income falls and pizza is an inferior good.

Use the following situation and diagram to answer Questions 10–15.

For the last 70 years, the U.S. government has used price supports to provide income assistance to U.S. farmers. At times, the government has used price floors, which it maintains by buying up the surplus farm products. At other times, it has used target prices, giving the farmer an amount equal to the difference between the market price and the target price for each unit sold.

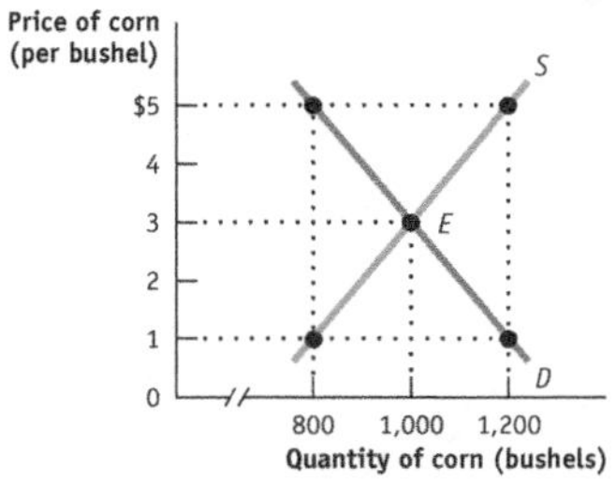

10. What are the equilibrium price and quantity in the market for corn?

	Price	*Quantity*
a.	$1	800
b.	$1	1,200
c.	$3	1,000
d.	$5	800
e.	$5	1,200

11. If the government sets a price floor of $5 per bushel, how many bushels of corn are produced?
- **a.** 0
- **b.** 400
- **c.** 800
- **d.** 1,000
- **e.** 1,200

12. If the government sets a price floor of $5 per bushel, how many bushels of corn are purchased by consumers?
- **a.** 0
- **b.** 400
- **c.** 800
- **d.** 1,000
- **e.** 1,200

13. How many bushels of corn are purchased by the government if it maintains a price floor of $5 by buying all surplus corn?
- **a.** 0
- **b.** 400
- **c.** 800
- **d.** 1,000
- **e.** 1,200

4. b
5. a
6. b
7. e
8. d
9. e
10. c
11. e
12. c
13. b

Section 2 Review 101

14. b
15. e
16. e
17. e
18. c
19. d
20. c

14. How much does a price floor of $5 cost the government if it maintains the price floor by buying any surplus corn?
a. $0
b. $2,000
c. $4,000
d. $5,000
e. $6,000

15. How much revenue do corn farmers receive if there is a price floor at $5?
a. $0
b. $1,200
c. $3,000
d. $4,000
e. $6,000

Use the following diagram to answer Questions 16–20.

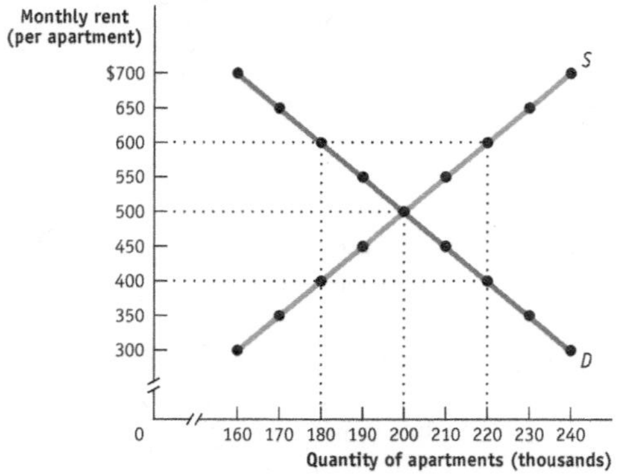

16. Where must an effective price ceiling in this market be set?
a. at $500
b. above $400
c. above $500
d. below $600
e. below $500

17. If the government sets a price ceiling at $400, how many apartments will be demanded by consumers?
a. 0
b. 40,000
c. 180,000
d. 200,000
e. 220,000

18. How many apartments will be offered for rent if the government sets a price ceiling at $400?
a. 0
b. 40,000
c. 180,000
d. 200,000
e. 220,000

19. A price ceiling set at $400 will result in which of the following in the market for apartments?
a. a surplus of 40,000 apartments
b. a surplus of 220,000 apartments
c. no surplus or shortage
d. a shortage of 40,000 apartments
e. a shortage of 220,000 apartments

20. A price ceiling set at $600 will result in which of the following in the market for apartments?
a. a surplus of 40,000 apartments
b. a surplus of 220,000 apartments
c. no surplus or shortage
d. a shortage of 40,000 apartments
e. a shortage of 220,000 apartments

Refer to the following table and information to answer Questions 21–24.

Only fishing boats licensed by the U.S. government are allowed to catch swordfish in the waters off the North Atlantic coast. The following table shows hypothetical demand and supply schedules for swordfish caught in the United States each year.

	Quantity of swordfish (millions of pounds per year)	
Price of swordfish (per pound)	**Quantity demanded**	**Quantity supplied**
$20	6	15
18	7	13
16	8	11
14	9	9
12	10	7

102 **Section 2** Supply and Demand

21. If the government establishes a quota of 7 million pounds in the market, what will the demand price of swordfish be (per pound)?
a. $20
b. $18
c. $16
d. $14
e. $12

22. If the government establishes a quota of 7 million pounds in the market, what will the supply price of swordfish be (per pound)?
a. $20
b. $18
c. $16
d. $14
e. $12

23. What is the quota rent per pound of swordfish received by licensed fishing boats when the government sets a quota of 7 million pounds?
a. $0
b. $6
c. $12
d. $18
e. $30

24. If there is a quota of 7 million pounds and swordfish fishing licenses are traded in a market, how much will the price of a fishing license be per pound?
a. $0
b. $6
c. $12
d. $18
e. $30

25. When transactions do not occur due to price or quantity controls, what is the term for the lost gains?
a. wasted resources
b. inefficient quality
c. price wedge
d. black market losses
e. deadweight loss

Free-Response Question

1. Pablo Picasso died having painted only 1,000 paintings during his "Blue Period."
a. Draw a correctly labeled graph of the market for Picasso "Blue Period" paintings showing each of the following:
i. the supply and demand curves for paintings
ii. the equilibrium price and quantity of paintings
b. List the five principal factors that will lead to a change in the price of paintings in this market.
c. Show the effect on price in your market for paintings if wealthy art collectors decide that it is essential to acquire Picasso "Blue Period" paintings for their collections.
(5 points)

21. b
22. e
23. b
24. b
25. e

Rubric for Free-Response Question

1 point: A graph with "Price" on the vertical axis, "Quantity" on the horizontal axis, and a labeled, downward-sloping demand curve

1 point: A vertical supply curve at a quantity of 1,000 and an equilibrium price labeled on the vertical axis at the height of the intersection of the supply and demand curves

1 point: A list of the five principal factors that shift the demand curve: a change in the price of related goods, income, tastes, consumer expectations, and the number of consumers

1 point: A new, labeled, and downward-sloping demand curve to the right of the original demand curve

1 point: An increased price labeled on the vertical axis at the height of the intersection of the new demand curve and the initial supply curve

Please see page SG-1 for sample student graphs for this Free-Response Question.

SECTION 3

Measurement of Economic Performance

PD Section 3 Overview:

Watch the video overview of Section 3 (for teachers), which is accessible through the Teacher's e-Book, the TR-flash drive, or the book's website, bcs.worthpublishers.com/krugmanap2e *(teacher log-in required).*

Section 3 addresses the foundational measures of economic performance. These measures of gross domestic product, unemployment, and inflation will be incorporated into the models that are covered in later lessons. Students may recognize these measures from news reports. Stress the idea that we must determine the size of the macroeconomy in order to efficiently implement stabilization and growth policies.

Topics that your students will study in Section 3 are:

- the circular-flow model.
- defining gross domestic product using the expenditure and income approaches.
- distinguishing between nominal GDP and real GDP.
- explaining the limitations of GDP measures.
- distinguishing between actual and potential GDP.
- calculating price indices—CPI and PPI.
- how to utilize price indices to calculate real wages and real interest rates.
- how the effects of inflation affect various groups of consumers and others.
- how to define and categorize the types of unemployment.
- how to calculate the unemployment rate.
- how to define the labor force participation rate.
- how to identify the full employment level of GDP.

Alignment to AP® Macroeconomics Course Description

Macroeconomics II. Measurement of Economic Performance: 12–16%

AP® Outline	Module
A. National income accounts	10: The Circular-Flow and Gross Domestic Product 11: Interpreting Real Gross Domestic Product
B. Inflation measurement and adjustment	14: Inflation: An Overview 15: The Measurement and Calculation of Inflation
C. Unemployment	12: The Meaning and Calculation of Unemployment 13: The Causes and Categories of Unemployment

Pacing Guide

Module	Standard Teaching Days	Block Teaching Days
10	1½	1
11	1	½
12	1	½
13	1	½
14	1	½
15	1	½
Section 3 Assessment	1	½
Total	**7½**	**4**

TRM Section Resources

All section resources may be accessed through the Teacher's e-Book, the TR-flash drive, or the book's website, bcs.worthpublishers.com/krugmanap2e *(teacher log-in required).*

Section 3 PD Video (for teachers)

Module 10

Module 10 Sample Lecture
Worksheet 10.1: Circular-Flow Video
Worksheet 10.2: Three Approaches to GDP
Worksheet 10.3: Gross Domestic Product
Exit Slip: Module 10

Module 11

Module 11 Sample Lecture
Activity 11.1: Calculating GDP Notes
Worksheet 11.2: GDP and Economic Growth Video
Activity 11.3: GDP in the Economy
Exit Slip: Module 11

Module 12

Module 12 Sample Lecture
Worksheet 12.1: Unemployment Rates
Worksheet 12.2: Unemployment
Exit Slip: Module 12

Module 13

Module 13 Sample Lecture
Worksheet 13.1: Classifying Unemployment
Worksheet 13.2: Structural or Cyclical
Worksheet 13.3: Unemployment and Natural Rate of Unemployment
Exit Slip: Module 13

Module 14

Module 14 Sample Lecture
Activity 14.1: Level or Rate?
Worksheet 14.2: Bitcoin
Worksheet 14.3: Helped or Hurt?
Exit Slip: Module 14

Module 15

Module 15 Sample Lecture
Activity 15.1: Inflation Auction
Worksheet 15.2: Inflation & Price Indices
Worksheet 15.3: Consumer Price Index
Exit Slip: Module 15

Section 3 Review Video (for students)

St. Louis Federal Reserve Bank Resources

Many of the Federal Reserve Banks have educational departments that offer helpful resources for studying economics. Members of the Educators Advisory Board of the St. Louis Federal Reserve Bank have handpicked some of their best resources for use with your AP® Economics students. References to these resources are included in the margin notes. A complete list of the St. Louis Fed resources for each section with the corresponding URL (as of fall 2014) can be found in the TRM.

NOTE We have included a number of links to useful videos and articles in the margin notes in this section. Although all are active at the time of publication, we know that some may expire over the next few years. If a link is no longer active, you may wish to search for a similar article or video to illustrate the point. We may also periodically refresh resources on the book's companion website.

PD Section 3 Overview

Watch the video overview of Section 3 (for teachers), which is accessible through the Teacher's e-Book, the TR-flash drive, or the book's companion website bcs.worthpublishers.com/krugmanap2e (teacher log-in required).

TEACH Teach It

Students find it easy to derail the lesson by asking the infinite number of "what if?" questions. For example, "What if the final product is assembled in China, but the components came from Canada and the corporation is headquartered in Germany?" Keep it simple and move forward before this line of discussion bogs down an entire class period. In the above question, the final product was produced in China and therefore is counted toward China's GDP.

FOCUS Active Learning

Encourage students to read Chapter 21 of *Economics by Example* to learn more about the divergence of gross domestic product and measures of well-being.

SECTION 3

Measurement of Economic Performance

ALY SONG/Reuters/Landov

The New #2

"China Passes Japan as Second-Largest Economy." That was the headline in the *New York Times* on August 15, 2010. Citing evidence that Japan's economy was weakening while China's was roaring ahead, the article predicted—correctly, as it turned out—that 2010 would mark the first year in which the surging Chinese economy finally overtook Japan's, taking second place to the United States on the world economic stage. "The milestone," wrote the *Times*, "though anticipated for some time, is the most striking evidence yet that China's ascendance is for real and that the rest of the world will have to reckon with a new economic superpower."

But wait a minute—what does it mean to say that China's economy is larger than Japan's? After all, the two economies are producing very different mixes of goods. Despite its rapid advance, China is still a fairly poor country whose greatest strength is in relatively low-tech production. Japan, by contrast, is very much a high-tech nation, and it dominates world output of some sophisticated goods, like electronic sensors for automobiles. That's why the 2011 earthquake in northeastern Japan, which put many factories out of action, temporarily caused major production disruptions for auto factories around the world.

How can you compare the sizes of two economies when they aren't producing the same things? The answer is that comparisons of national economies are based on the *value* of their production. When news reports declared that China's economy had overtaken Japan's, they meant that China's *gross domestic product*, or *GDP*—a measure of the overall value of goods and services produced—had surpassed Japan's GDP.

GDP is one of the most important measures used to track the macroeconomy—that is, to quantify movements in the overall level of output and prices. Measures like GDP and *price indexes* play a central role in the formulation of economic policy, because policy makers need to know what's going on, and anecdotes are no substitute for hard data. These measures are also important for business decisions—to such an extent that corporations and other players are willing to pay consulting firms such as Macroeconomic Advisors for early estimates of what official economic measurements will find.

In this section we explain three of the most useful macroeconomic measures: gross domestic product, unemployment, and inflation.

104 Section 3 Measurement of Economic Performance

Spencer Platt/Getty Images

MODULE 10 The Circular Flow and Gross Domestic Product

In this Module, you will learn to:

- Explain how economists use aggregate measures to track the performance of the economy
- Interpret the circular-flow diagram of the economy
- Define and calculate gross domestic product, or GDP

The National Accounts

Almost all countries calculate a set of numbers known as the *national income and product accounts.* In fact, the accuracy of a country's accounts is a remarkably reliable indicator of its state of economic development—in general, the more reliable the accounts, the more economically advanced the country. When international economic agencies seek to help a less developed country, typically the first order of business is to send a team of experts to audit and improve the country's accounts.

In the United States, these numbers are calculated by the Bureau of Economic Analysis, a division of the U.S. government's Department of Commerce. The **national income and product accounts,** often referred to simply as the **national accounts,** keep track of the spending of consumers, sales of producers, business investment spending, government purchases, and a variety of other flows of money among different sectors of the economy. Let's see how they work.

National income and product accounts, or **national accounts,** keep track of the flows of money among different sectors of the economy.

The Circular-Flow Diagram

To understand the principles behind the national accounts, it helps to look at a graphic called a *circular-flow diagram.* This diagram is a simplified representation of the macroeconomy. It shows the flows of money, goods and services, and factors of production through the economy. It allows us to visualize the key concepts behind the national accounts. The underlying principle is that the flow of money into each market or sector is equal to the flow of money coming out of that market or sector.

The Simple Circular-Flow Diagram The U.S. economy is a vastly complex entity, with more than a hundred million workers employed by millions of companies, producing millions of different goods and services. Yet you can learn some very important

AP® Exam Tip

Be prepared to draw the simple circular-flow diagram with two markets and three sectors on the AP® exam. Make sure you use the proper terms between markets, firms, and households.

PD To prepare for teaching this lesson, you may want to consult the **Module 10 Sample Lecture** in the TRM.

OPEN & CLOSE Start Here

Post these questions on the board and have students answer them on their personal whiteboards or in their notebooks.

- What is profit? *Profit is the difference between the revenue a firm receives and the firm's costs.*
- Who earns profit? *Entrepreneurs earn profit as part of household income.*

Point out that firms earn profits and those profits are distributed to the entrepreneurs who own or invest in the business. Ultimately, profits become income for households because entrepreneurs are part of the household. Profits flow through the business to the household via the factor market.

TEACH Teach It

National income accounting is a method for measuring the flows of income and expenditures in the economy over a period of time. It is similar to an income statement that is used by businesses. Only its basics will be covered in this course.

FOCUS Active Learning

TRM Have students watch Jason Welker's video "The Circular-Flow of a Market Economy" (see econextras video list with hyperlinks on the bcs and TRFD). Assign **Worksheet 10.1 (Circular-Flow Video)** from the TRM for questions on this video.

FOCUS Active Learning

If you have time after watching the video (1 class period), use the circular-flow simulation lesson plan at http://welkerswikinomics.com/blog/2010/09/08/circular-flow/ to help students understand how money and goods and services flow through the economy.

TEACH AP® Exam Tip

In the past, students have been asked to draw the circular-flow diagram as part of an AP® exam FRQ. Have your students draw a simple circular-flow diagram on their whiteboards or paper and then label all the lines correctly. Direct them to hold up their diagrams when they are done so you can see who needs more help understanding the model.

Figure 10.1 The Circular-Flow Diagram

This diagram represents the flows of money, factors of production, and goods and services in the economy. In the markets for goods and services, households purchase goods and services from firms, generating a flow of money to the firms and a flow of goods and services to the households. The money flows back to households as firms purchase factors of production from the households in factor markets.

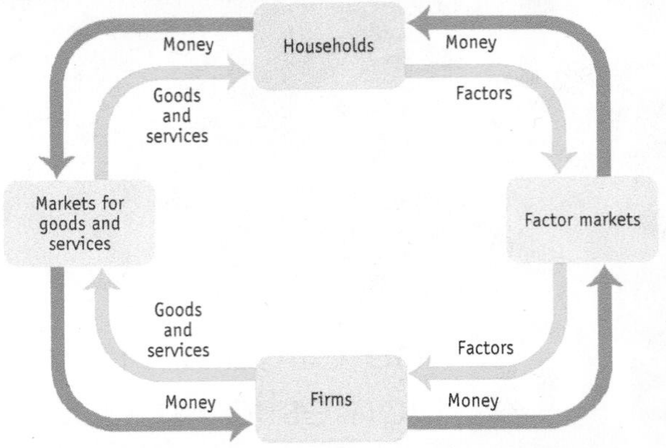

things about the economy by considering a simple diagram, shown in **Figure 10.1**. This simple model of the macroeconomy represents the transactions that take place by two kinds of flows around a circle: flows of physical things such as goods, services, labor, or raw materials in one direction, and flows of money that pay for these things in the opposite direction. In this case, the physical flows are shown in yellow and the money flows are shown in green.

The simplest circular-flow diagram illustrates an economy that contains only two kinds of "inhabitants": households and firms. A **household** consists of either an individual or a group of people who share their income. A **firm** is an organization that produces goods and services for sale—and that employs members of households.

As you can see in Figure 10.1, there are two kinds of markets in this simple economy. On one side (here the left side) there are markets for goods and services (also known as **product markets**) in which households buy the goods and services they want from firms. This produces a flow of goods and services to the households and a return flow of money to the firms.

On the other side, there are **factor markets** in which firms buy the resources they need to produce goods and services. The best known factor market is the *labor market*, in which workers are paid for their time. Besides labor, we can think of households as owning the other factors of production and selling them to firms.

This simple circular-flow diagram omits a number of real-world complications in the interest of simplicity. However, the diagram is a useful aid to thinking about the economy—and we can use it as the starting point for developing a more realistic (and therefore more complicated) circular-flow diagram.

The Expanded Circular-Flow Diagram **Figure 10.2** is a revised and expanded circular-flow diagram. This diagram shows only the flows of money in the economy, but is expanded to include extra elements that were ignored in the interest of simplicity in Figure 10.1. The underlying principle that the inflow of money into each market or sector must equal the outflow of money coming from that market or sector still applies in this model.

In Figure 10.2, the circular flow of money between households and firms illustrated in Figure 10.1 remains. In the product markets, households engage in **consumer spending**,

A **household** is a person or group of people who share income.

A **firm** is an organization that produces goods and services for sale.

Product markets are where goods and services are bought and sold.

Factor markets are where resources, especially capital and labor, are bought and sold.

Consumer spending is household spending on goods and services.

St. Louis Federal Reserve Bank Resources

"Circular-Flow," *The Economic Lowdown Video Series*, Episode 6

In this episode, viewers learn how households and businesses interact in the market for resources and in the market for goods and services, and they see how money keeps the whole process moving.

Figure 10.2 An Expanded Circular-Flow Diagram: How Money Flows Through the Economy

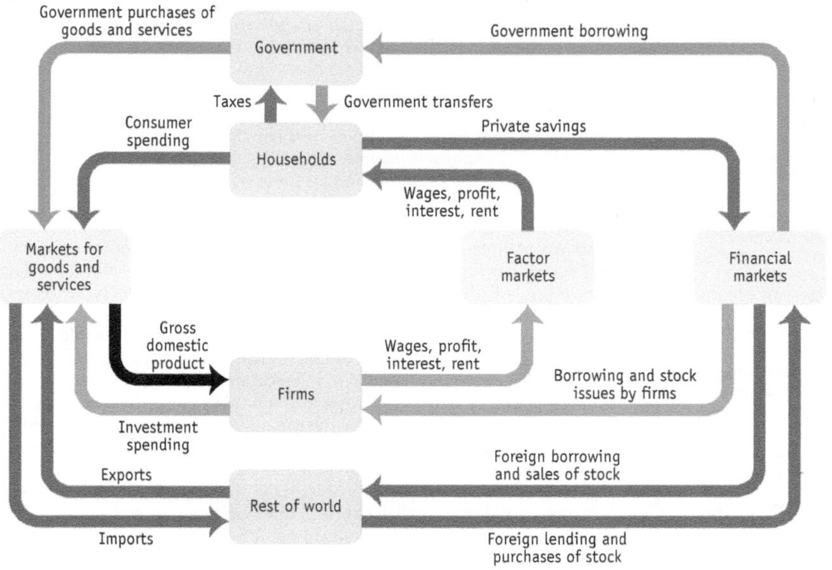

A circular flow of funds connects the four sectors of the economy—households, firms, government, and the rest of the world—via three types of markets: the factor markets, the markets for goods and services, and the *financial markets*. Funds flow from firms to households in the form of wages, profit, interest, and rent through the factor markets. After paying taxes to the government and receiving *government transfers*, households allocate the remaining income—*disposable income*—to private savings and consumer spending. Via the financial markets, *private savings* and funds from the rest of the world are channeled into investment spending by firms, government borrowing, foreign borrowing and lending, and foreign transactions of stocks. In turn, funds flow from the government and households to firms to pay for purchases of goods and services. Finally, exports to the rest of the world generate a flow of funds into the economy and imports lead to a flow of funds out of the economy. We can determine the total flow of funds by adding all spending—consumer spending on goods and services, investment spending by firms, government purchases of goods and services, and exports—and then subtracting the value of imports. This is the value of all the final goods and services produced in the United States—that is, the *gross domestic product* of the economy.

buying goods and services from both domestic firms and firms in the rest of the world. Households receive money as owners of the factors of production—land, labor, and capital. They sell the use of these factors of production to firms, receiving rent, wages, and interest payments in return. Firms buy, and pay households for, the use of those factors of production in factor markets, represented to the right of center in the diagram. Most households derive the bulk of their income from wages earned by selling labor. Some households derive additional income from their indirect ownership of the physical capital used by firms, mainly in the form of **stocks**—shares in the ownership of a company—and **bonds**—loans to firms in the form of an IOU that pays interest. In other words, the income households receive from the factor markets includes profit distributed to

A **stock** is a share in the ownership of a company held by a shareholder.

A **bond** is a loan in the form of an IOU that pays interest.

FOCUS Active Learning

Project a copy of the expanded circular-flow diagram (Figure 10.2). Ask students how the addition of the "Rest of world" and "Financial markets" has affected the flow.

St. Louis Federal Reserve Bank Resources

"Get Into Stocks," *No-Frills Money Skills*, Video 3

Through the story of a local ice-cream cart owner trying to expand her business, students learn about the process by which companies become publicly owned and traded by issuing stock. Students learn key terms, such as *capital gains* and *dividends*, and they discover how the prices of stocks are affected by how successful a company is in its respective industry.

"Understanding Bonds," *No-Frills Money Skills*, Video 4

This video's host employs high-tech tools to foil Miss Information in her attempts to misguide investors. The video provides viewers with information about government bonds, corporate bonds, coupon and noncoupon bonds, and the potential risk and return of investments.

FOCUS Active Learning

If students need more practice, create labels from the circular-flow diagram using poster board paper and hand pieces to students as they enter the classroom door. You can have students create a living circular-flow diagram by arranging themselves around the room in the shape of the expanded circular-flow diagram. Alternatively, you can create a blank circular-flow diagram on the board similar to the one in Figure 10.2. Randomly select students to fill in one blank on the board until the diagram is completely labeled.

FOCUS Test It

The circular-flow diagram illustrates how households ____________ goods and services and ____________ factors of production.

A. buy; sell
B. buy; buy
C. own; buy
D. own; sell
E. sell; buy

Answer: A

Provide your students with this helpful tip: Quickly sketch the diagram next to the question to ensure the answer selected is correct. It is often a good idea to sketch a diagram or graph to help answer the question.

In the circular-flow model, businesses:

A. sell resources in the factor market.
B. earn profit from the factor market.
C. sell products in the market for goods and services.
D. pay taxes to the government in the market for goods and services.
E. issue stock in the market for goods and services.

Answer: C

Government transfers are payments that the government makes to individuals without expecting a good or service in return.

Disposable income, equal to income plus government transfers minus taxes, is the total amount of household income available to spend on consumption and to save.

Private savings, equal to disposable income minus consumer spending, is disposable income that is not spent on consumption.

The banking, stock, and bond markets, which channel private savings and foreign lending into investment spending, government borrowing, and foreign borrowing, are known as the **financial markets**.

Government borrowing is the amount of funds borrowed by the government in the financial markets.

Government purchases of goods and services are total expenditures on goods and services by federal, state, and local governments.

Goods and services sold to other countries are **exports**. Goods and services purchased from other countries are **imports**.

company shareholders and the interest payments on any bonds that they hold. Finally, households receive rent from firms in exchange for the use of land or structures that the households own. So in factor markets, households receive income in the form of wages, profit, interest, and rent.

Some households receive **government transfers**—payments that the government makes to individuals without expecting a good or service in return. Unemployment insurance payments are one example of a government transfer. Households spend most of their income on goods and services. However, in Figure 10.2 we see two reasons why the markets for goods and services don't in fact absorb *all* of a household's income. First, households don't get to keep all the income they receive. They must pay part of their income to the government in the form of taxes, such as income taxes and sales taxes. The total income households have left after receiving government transfers and paying taxes is **disposable income**.

The second reason that the markets for goods and services do not absorb all household income is that many households set aside a portion of their income for **private savings**. These private savings go into **financial markets** where individuals, banks, and other institutions buy and sell stocks and bonds as well as make loans. As Figure 10.2 shows, the financial markets (on the far right of the circular-flow diagram) also receive funds from the rest of the world and provide funds to the government, to firms, and to the rest of the world.

Before going further, we can use the box representing households to illustrate an important general characteristic of the circular-flow diagram: the total sum of flows of money out of a given box is equal to the total sum of flows of money into that box. It's simply a matter of accounting: what goes in must come out. So, for example, the total flow of money out of households—the sum of taxes paid, consumer spending, and private savings—must equal the total flow of money into households—the sum of wages, profit, interest, rent, and government transfers.

Now let's look at the other inhabitants in the circular-flow diagram, including the government and the rest of the world. The government returns a portion of the money it collects from taxes to households in the form of government transfers. However, it uses much of its tax revenue, plus additional funds borrowed in the financial markets through **government borrowing**, to buy goods and services. **Government purchases of goods and services**, the total of purchases made by federal, state, and local governments, includes everything from military spending on ammunition to your local public school's spending on chalk, erasers, and teacher salaries.

The rest of the world participates in the U.S. economy in three ways. First, some of the goods and services produced in the United States are sold to residents of other countries. For example, more than half of America's annual wheat and cotton crops are sold abroad. Goods and services sold to other countries are known as **exports**. Export sales lead to a flow of funds from the rest of the world into the United States to pay for them. Second, some of the goods and services purchased by residents of the United States are produced abroad. For example, many consumer goods are now made in China. Goods and services purchased from other countries are known as **imports**. Import purchases lead to a flow of funds out of the United States to pay for them. Third, foreigners can participate in U.S. financial markets. Foreign lending—lending by foreigners to borrowers in the United States and purchases by foreigners of shares of stock in American companies—generates a flow of funds into the United States from the rest of the world. Conversely, foreign borrowing—borrowing by foreigners from U.S. lenders and purchases by Americans of stock in foreign companies—leads to a flow of funds out of the United States to the rest of the world.

Thinkstock/Comstock/Getty Images

Supplies used in public schools, such as the chalk shown here, are among the goods and services purchased by the government.

Notice that, like households, firms also buy goods and services in our economy. For example, an automobile company that is building a new factory will buy investment goods—machinery like stamping presses and welding robots—from companies that manufacture these items. It will also accumulate an *inventory* of finished cars in preparation for shipment to dealers. **Inventories**, then, are goods and raw materials that firms hold to facilitate their operations. The national accounts count this **investment spending**—spending on new productive physical capital, such as machinery and buildings, and on changes in inventories—as part of total spending on goods and services.

You might ask why changes in inventories are included in investment spending—after all, finished cars aren't used to produce more cars. Changes in inventories of finished goods are counted as investment spending because, like machinery, they change the ability of a firm to make future sales. So spending on additions to inventories is a form of investment spending by a firm. Conversely, a drawing-down of inventories is counted as a fall in investment spending because it leads to lower future sales. It's also important to understand that investment spending includes spending on the construction of any structure, regardless of whether it is an assembly plant or a new house. Why include the construction of homes? Because, like a plant, a new house produces a future stream of output—housing services for its occupants.

Suppose we add up consumer spending on goods and services, investment spending, government purchases of goods and services, and the value of exports, then subtract the value of imports. This gives us a measure of the overall market value of the goods and services the economy produces. That measure has a name: it's a country's *gross domestic product.* But before we can formally define gross domestic product, or GDP, we have to examine an important distinction between classes of goods and services: the difference between *final goods and services* versus *intermediate goods and services*.

Gross Domestic Product

A consumer's purchase of a new car from a dealer is one example of a sale of **final goods and services**: goods and services sold to the final, or end, user. But an automobile manufacturer's purchase of steel from a steel foundry or glass from a glassmaker is an example of a sale of **intermediate goods and services**: goods and services that are inputs into the production of final goods and services. In the case of intermediate goods and services, the purchaser—another firm—is *not* the final user.

Gross domestic product, or **GDP**, is the total value of all *final goods and services* produced in an economy during a given period, usually a year. In 2013 the GDP of the United States was $16,803 billion, or about $53,086 per person.

There are three approaches to the calculation of GDP. The **value-added approach** is to survey firms and add up their contributions to the value of final goods and services. The **expenditure approach** is to add up **aggregate spending** on domestically produced final goods and services in the economy—the sum of consumer spending, investment spending, government purchases of goods and services, and exports minus imports. The **income approach** is to add up the total factor income earned by households from firms in the economy, including rent, wages, interest, and profit.

Government statisticians use all three methods. To illustrate how they work, we will consider a hypothetical economy, shown in **Figure 10.3** on the next page. This economy consists of three firms—American Motors, Inc., which produces one car per year; American Steel, Inc., which produces the steel that goes into the car; and American Ore, Inc., which mines the iron ore that goes into the steel. GDP in this economy is $21,500, the value of the one car per year the economy produces. Let's look at how the three different methods of calculating GDP yield the same result.

The Value-Added Approach The first method for calculating GDP is to add up the value of all the final goods and services produced in the economy—a calculation that excludes the value of intermediate goods and services. Why are intermediate goods and services excluded? After all, don't they represent a very large and valuable portion of the economy?

Inventories are stocks of goods and raw materials held to facilitate business operations.

Investment spending is spending on new productive physical capital, such as machinery and structures, and on changes in inventories.

Final goods and services are goods and services sold to the final, or end, user.

Intermediate goods and services are goods and services bought from one firm by another firm to be used as inputs into the production of final goods and services.

Gross domestic product, or **GDP**, is the total value of all final goods and services produced in the economy during a given year.

The **value-added approach** to calculating GDP is to survey firms and add up their contributions to the value of final goods and services.

The **expenditure approach** to calculating GDP is to add up *aggregate spending* on domestically produced final goods and services in the economy—the sum of consumer spending, investment spending, government purchases of goods and services, and exports minus imports.

Aggregate spending—the total spending on domestically produced final goods and services in the economy—is the sum of consumer spending, investment spending, government purchases of goods and services, and exports minus imports.

The **income approach** to calculating GDP is to add up the total factor income earned by households from firms in the economy, including rent, wages, interest, and profit.

TEACH Teach It

Ensure that students understand that GDP is the total market value of all final goods and services produced within a nation in 1 year. It doesn't matter if the firm is foreign owned or if the good is consumed in another nation: if it is produced in the nation, it is counted in the nation's GDP. Students often confuse GDP with GNP (gross national product). GNP is the total market value of all final goods and services produced by a nation's citizens (no matter where they live) in 1 year.

TEACH AP® Exam Tip

There are three ways to calculate GDP: the value-added approach, the income approach, and the expenditure approach. In the past, the first two have rarely been tested. Thoroughly teach the expenditure approach as that is what students will most likely see on the AP® exam. They should be aware of the components of the other approaches as well.

FOCUS Active Learning

Use Jacob Clifford's video "Expenditures Approach and Income Approach" to begin the lesson on counting GDP (see econextras video list with hyperlinks on the bcs and TRFD). After the video, ask students to list the elements of each of the approaches. (*Expenditure—consumption, investment, government spending, and net exports. Income—rent, wages, interest, and profit*)
Now, discuss the value-added approach, and ask students why we do not count intermediate goods. (*This would be double counting, as shown in Figure 10.3.*)

TEACH Teach It

Use Figure 10.3 to explain the value-added approach. Remember, students should recognize the approach and be able to explain the basics of how to attain GDP using it.

FOCUS In the News

To find the current GDP, go to the Bureau of Economic Analysis page at www.bea.gov. Under National, select GDP, then news release: Gross Domestic Product, and finally Release Highlights from the sidebar. This report with graphs provides students with a visual comparison of GDP for several years. Place students in groups to determine which GDP components (C, I, G, $X - M$) are a part of the trend over time. Once each group has decided on its answer, have groups share their assessments orally. As homework, have them find an article demonstrating how the data are reflected in daily living. They should write a brief summary explaining their answer. Hold a discussion regarding the trends students uncovered and how they support or refute the trend in GDP reported by the government.

Figure 10.3 Calculating GDP

In this hypothetical economy consisting of three firms, GDP can be calculated in three different ways: measuring GDP as the value of production of final goods and services by summing each firm's value added; measuring GDP as aggregate spending on domestically produced final goods and services; and measuring GDP as factor income earned by households from firms in the economy.

Aggregate spending on domestically produced final goods and services = $21,500

	American Ore, Inc.	American Steel, Inc.	American Motors, Inc.	Total factor income
Value of sales	$4,200 (ore)	$9,000 (steel)	$21,500 (car)	
Intermediate goods	0	4,200 (iron ore)	9,000 (steel)	
Wages	2,000	3,700	10,000	$15,700
Interest payments	1,000	600	1,000	2,600
Rent	200	300	500	1,000
Profit	1,000	200	1,000	2,200
Total expenditure by firm	4,200	9,000	21,500	
Value added per firm = Value of sales – cost of intermediate goods	4,200	4,800	12,500	

Total payments to factors = $21,500

Sum of value added = $21,500

AP® Exam Tip

The trick to measuring GDP is to avoid double-counting. Each approach to calculating GDP includes a way to avoid counting the value of inputs twice—once at the production stage and again in the value of the final product. Likewise, the value of used goods should not be counted because their value was part of GDP when the goods were new.

The **value added** of a producer is the value of its sales minus the value of its purchases of inputs.

To understand why only final goods and services are included in GDP, look at the simplified economy described in Figure 10.3. Should we measure the GDP of this economy by adding up the total sales of the iron ore producer, the steel producer, and the auto producer? If we did, we would in effect be counting the value of the steel twice—once when it is sold by the steel plant to the auto plant and again when the steel auto body is sold to a consumer as a finished car. And we would be counting the value of the iron ore *three* times—once when it is mined and sold to the steel company, a second time when it is made into steel and sold to the auto producer, and a third time when the steel is made into a car and sold to the consumer. So counting the full value of each producer's sales would cause us to count the same items several times and artificially inflate the calculation of GDP.

In Figure 10.3, the total value of all sales, intermediate and final, is $34,700: $21,500 from the sale of the car, plus $9,000 from the sale of the steel, plus $4,200 from the sale of the iron ore. Yet we know that GDP—the total value of all final goods and services in a given year—is only $21,500. To avoid double-counting, we count only each producer's **value added** in the calculation of GDP: the difference between the value of its sales and the value of the inputs it purchases from other businesses. That is, at each stage of the production process we subtract the cost of inputs—the intermediate goods—at that stage. In this case, the value added of the auto producer is the dollar value of the cars it manufactures *minus* the cost of the steel it buys, or $12,500. The value added of the steel producer is the dollar value of the steel it produces *minus* the cost of the ore it buys, or $4,800. Only the ore producer, who we have assumed doesn't buy any inputs, has value added equal to its total sales, $4,200. The sum of the three producers' value added is $12,500 + $4,800 + $4,200 = $21,500, equal to GDP.

The Expenditure Approach Another way to calculate GDP is by adding up aggregate spending on domestically produced final goods and services. That is, GDP can be measured by the flow of funds into firms. Like the method that estimates GDP as the value of domestic production of final goods and services, this measurement must be carried out in a way that avoids double-counting. In terms of our steel and auto example, we don't want to count both consumer spending on a car (represented in Figure 10.3 by the sales price of the car) and the auto producer's spending on steel (represented in Figure 10.3 by the price of a car's worth of steel). If we counted both, we would be counting the steel embodied in the car twice. We solve this problem by counting only the value of sales to *final buyers*, such as consumers, firms that purchase investment goods, the government, or foreign buyers. In other words, in order to avoid the double-counting of spending, we omit sales of inputs from one business to another when estimating GDP using spending data. You can see from Figure 10.3 that aggregate spending on final goods and services—the finished car—is $21,500.

Steel is an intermediate good because it is sold to other product manufacturers like automakers or refrigerator makers, and rarely to the final consumer.

As we've already pointed out, the national accounts *do* include investment spending by firms as a part of final spending. That is, an auto company's purchase of steel to make a car isn't considered a part of final spending, but the company's purchase of new machinery for its factory *is* considered a part of final spending. What's the difference? Steel is an input that is used up in production; machinery will last for a number of years. Since purchases of capital goods that will last for a considerable time aren't closely tied to current production, the national accounts consider such purchases a form of final sales.

What types of spending make up GDP? Look again at the markets for goods and services in Figure 10.2, and you will see that one source of sales revenue for firms is consumer spending. Let's denote consumer spending with the symbol *C*. Figure 10.2 shows three other components of sales: sales of investment goods to other businesses, or investment spending, which we will denote by *I*; government purchases of goods and services, which we will denote by *G*; and sales to foreigners—that is, exports—which we will denote by *X*.

In reality, not all of this final spending goes toward domestically produced goods and services. We must take account of spending on imports, which we will denote by *IM*. Income spent on imports is income not spent on domestic goods and services—it is income that has "leaked" across national borders. So to calculate domestic production using spending data, we must subtract spending on imports. Putting this all together gives us the following equation, which breaks GDP down by the four sources of aggregate spending:

$$\textbf{(10-1)} \quad GDP = C + I + G + X - IM$$

Note that the value of $X - IM$—the difference between the value of exports and the value of imports—is known as **net exports**. We'll be seeing a lot of Equation 10-1 in later modules!

Net exports are the difference between the value of exports and the value of imports ($X - IM$).

The Income Approach A final way to calculate GDP is to add up all the income earned by factors of production in the economy—the wages earned by labor; the interest earned by those who lend their savings to firms and the government; the rent earned by those who lease their land or structures to firms; and the profit earned by the shareholders, the owners of the firms' physical capital. This is a valid measure because the money firms earn by selling goods and services must go somewhere; whatever isn't paid as wages, interest, or rent is profit. And part of profit is paid out to shareholders as *dividends*.

Figure 10.3 shows how this calculation works for our simplified economy. The shaded column at the far right shows the total wages, interest, and rent paid by all these firms, as well as their total profit. Adding up all of these yields a total factor income of $21,500—again, equal to GDP.

We won't emphasize the income approach as much as the other two approaches to calculating GDP. It's important to keep in mind, however, that all the money spent

TEACH Teach It

Understanding what is counted as spending using the expenditure approach can be difficult for students, especially where investment spending is concerned. Investment spending is not spending on stocks and bonds as many students surmise. It involves investment in purchases of machinery, equipment and tools, changes in business inventories, and construction (including both commercial and residential construction). It does not include spending on inputs because they are not final goods.

TEACH Teach It

Net exports (exports minus imports) may be abbreviated a number of ways. The AP® exam is generally explicit about what abbreviations mean, but since students encounter information from many sources in their studies, make sure they are familiar with these:

$(X - IM)$ (which is seen in Equation 10-1)

$(X - M)$

N_x

X_n

St. Louis Federal Reserve Bank Resources

"GDP: Does It Measure Up?," *Page One Economics*

The brief essay discusses GDP components and how GDP is calculated. It also describes what GDP does—and does not—measure. Student questions are included.

TEACH Teach It

The income method is used when all the income earned in the economy is totaled. The income approach to calculating GDP is to sum all of the income earned in the economy. Here is a quick formula for remembering what to count: Wages + Interest + Rents + Profits (WIRP). Figure 10.3 (page 110) offers students a concrete example.

TEACH Connect It

The portion of the circular-flow diagram from factor market to households to product market matches the expenditures in an economy, while the other half of the model matches the incomes earned in an economy.

FOCUS Active Learning

TRM Assign **Worksheet 10.2 (Three Approaches to GDP)** from the TRM to give students practice on calculating GDP using the expenditure approach, the income approach, and the value-added approach.

FOCUS Flip It

Students can review the components of GDP by viewing the Jacob Clifford video entitled "Macro Unit 2.1—GDP and Economic Growth" (see econextras video list with hyperlinks on the bcs and TRFD).

on domestically produced goods and services generates factor income to households—that is, there really is a circular flow.

The Components of GDP Now that we know how GDP is calculated in principle, let's see what it looks like in practice.

Figure 10.4 shows the first two methods of calculating GDP side by side. The height of each bar above the horizontal axis represents the GDP of the U.S. economy in 2013: $16,803 billion. Each bar is divided to show the breakdown of that total in terms of where the value was added and how the money was spent.

In the left bar in Figure 10.4, we see the breakdown of GDP by value added according to sector, the first method of calculating GDP. Of the $16,803 billion, $12,688 billion consisted of value added by businesses. Another $1,830 billion of value added was contributed by households and institutions. Finally, $2,036 billion consisted of value added by government, in the form of military, education, and other government services.

The right bar in Figure 10.4 corresponds to the second method of calculating GDP, showing the breakdown by the four types of aggregate spending. The total height of the right bar is greater than the total height of the left bar, a difference of $494 billion (which, as you can see, extends below the horizontal axis). That's because the total height of the right bar represents total spending in the economy, spending on both domestically produced and foreign-produced—imported—final goods and services. Within the bar, consumer spending (*C*), which is 66.5% of GDP, dominates the picture. But some of that spending was absorbed by foreign-produced goods and services. In 2013, the value of net exports, the difference between the value of exports and the value of imports ($X - IM$ in Equation 10-1), was negative—the United States was a net importer of foreign goods and services. The 2013 value of $X - IM$ was −$494 billion, or −2.9% of GDP. Thus, a portion of the right bar extends below the horizontal axis by $494 billion to represent

Figure 10.4 U.S. GDP in 2013: Two Methods of Calculating GDP

The two bars show two equivalent ways of calculating GDP. The height of each bar above the horizontal axis represents $16,803 billion, U.S. GDP in 2013. The left bar shows the breakdown of GDP according to the value added of each sector of the economy. The right bar shows the breakdown of GDP according to the four types of aggregate spending: $C + I + G + X - IM$. The right bar has a total height of $16,803 billion + $494 billion = $17,297 billion. The $494 billion, shown as the area extending below the horizontal axis, is the amount of total spending absorbed by net imports (negative net exports) in 2013.
Source: Bureau of Economic Analysis.

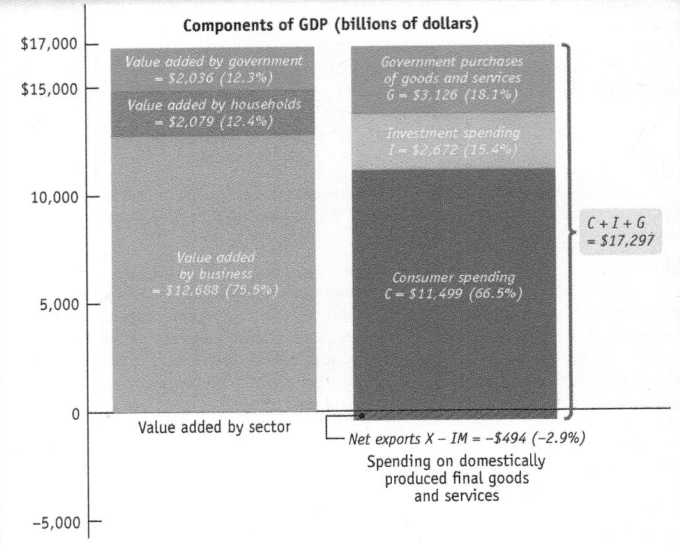

112 Section 3 Measurement of Economic Performance

the amount of total spending that was absorbed by net imports and so did not lead to higher U.S. GDP. Investment spending (I) constituted 15.4% of GDP; government purchases of goods and services (G) constituted 18.1% of GDP.

GDP: What's In and What's Out? It's easy to confuse what is included and what isn't included in GDP. So let's stop here and make sure the distinction is clear. Don't confuse investment spending with spending on inputs. Investment spending—spending on productive physical capital, the construction of structures (residential as well as commercial), and changes to inventories—is included in GDP. But spending on inputs is not. Why the difference? Recall the distinction between resources that are *used up* and those that are *not used up* in production. An input, like steel, is used up in production. A metal-stamping machine, an investment good, is not. It will last for many years and will be used repeatedly to make many cars. Since spending on productive physical capital—investment goods—and the construction of structures is not directly tied to current output, economists consider such spending to be spending on final goods. Spending on changes to inventories is considered a part of investment spending so it is also included in GDP. Why? Because, like a machine, additional inventory is an investment in future sales. And when a good is released for sale from inventories, its value is subtracted from the value of inventories and so from GDP. Used goods are not included in GDP because, as with inputs, to include them would be to double-count: counting them once when sold as new and again when sold as used.

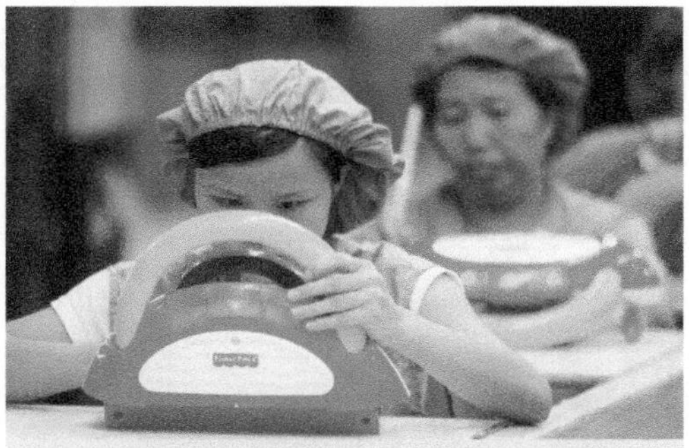

Photo by Feng Li/Getty Images

The United States is a net importer of goods and services, such as these toys made on a production line in China.

Also, financial assets such as stocks and bonds are not included in GDP because they don't represent either the production or the sale of final goods and services. Rather, a bond represents a promise to repay with interest, and a stock represents a proof of ownership. And for obvious reasons, foreign-produced goods and services are not included in calculations of gross *domestic* product.

Here is a summary of what's included and not included in GDP:

Included

- Domestically produced final goods and services, including capital goods, new construction of structures, and changes to inventories

Not Included

- Intermediate goods and services
- Inputs
- Used goods
- Financial assets such as stocks and bonds
- Foreign-produced goods and services

AP® Exam Tip

Use this mnemonic to help you remember what isn't counted in GDP: **IF IF U**
Intermediate goods and services
Financial assets and transfer payments
Inputs used up in production
Foreign-produced goods and services
Used goods

FOCUS Active Learning

TRM Assign **Worksheet 10.3 (Gross Domestic Product)** from the TRM in class or as homework. Students are given examples of transactions and must determine if each would be counted in GDP or not, and why.

FOCUS Test It

Indicate whether each of the following is counted in the U.S. gross domestic product for the current year. Explain your answers.

A. The value of radios used in the production of new automobiles built in the current year *Not counted: intermediate good*

B. Commissions earned by a realtor in the current year for selling a home built 4 years ago *Counted: new income for a service provided in the current year*

C. The value of a used cell phone purchased on e-Bay *Not counted: used good*

D. The value of headsets produced entirely in the United States by a Chinese company *Counted: final good made entirely in the United States*

E. The value of stock purchased on the New York Stock Exchange *Not counted: financial transaction*

Tip: On an FRQ, 1 point may be awarded for the assertion and 1 point for the explanation. Alternatively, 1 point may be awarded for both the assertion and the explanation to eliminate guessing to earn points in the first part of the question.

OPEN & CLOSE Exit Slip

TRM *Please see **Exit Slip: Module 10** in the TRM for formative multiple-choice questions to ask before finishing your lesson. These questions will help you quickly assess whether your students have mastered the module's concepts before moving on.*

Answers to the Exit Slip Questions

1. C
2. C
3. A

TEACH AP® Exam Tip

Make sure students memorize the items that are not counted in GDP. Suggest they develop a mnemonic like IFIFU (**I**ntermediate goods and services, **F**inancial assets and transfer payments, **I**nputs, **F**oreign-produced goods and services, **U**sed goods) to help them remember the material. This concept has been tested on the AP® exam as part of an FRQ in the past.

FOCUS Active Learning

Students sometimes ask how illegal activities are counted in GDP. If you have time, play the Freakonomics Radio podcast "How Deep Is the Shadow Economy?" (20 minutes)—see econextras video list with hyperlinks on the bcs and TRFD. Alternatively, assign this podcast for homework and have students write a paragraph that answers the following question: What is the shadow economy and how does it impact GDP? Give examples from the podcast to support your assertion. *Answers will vary, but they should identify the shadow economy as those activities not reported to the government, so GDP is undercounted as a result.*

Answers to Module 10 Review Questions

Check Your Understanding

1. Let's start by considering the relationship between the total value added of all domestically produced final goods and services, and aggregate spending on domestically produced final goods and services. These two quantities are equal because every final good and service produced in the economy is either purchased by someone or added to inventories, and additions to inventories are counted as spending by firms. Next, consider the relationship between aggregate spending on domestically produced final goods and services, and total factor income. These two quantities are equal because all spending that is channeled to firms to pay for purchases of domestically produced final goods and services is revenue for firms. Those revenues must be paid out by firms to their factors of production in the form of wages, profit, interest, and rent. Taken together, this means that all three methods of calculating GDP are equivalent.

2. Firms make sales to other firms, households, the government, and the rest of the world. Households are linked to firms through the sale of factors of production to firms, through purchases from firms of final goods and services, and through lending funds to firms in the financial markets. Households are linked to the government through their payment of taxes, their receipt of transfers, and their lending of funds to the government to finance government borrowing via the financial markets. Finally, households are linked to the rest of the world through their purchases of imports and transactions with foreigners in financial markets.

3. You would be counting the value of the steel twice—once as it was sold by American Steel to American Motors and once as part of the car sold by American Motors.

Tackle the Test: Multiple-Choice Questions

1. c 2. e 3. a 4. b 5. a

Tackle the Test: Free-Response Question

Rubric for FRQ 2 (5 points)

1 point: Correctly showing the markets for goods and services, factor markets, households, and firms on the diagram

1 point: Correctly illustrating the flows of goods and services, factors, and money

1 point: Showing the government linked to households through taxes flowing from households to the government (*Note:* Taxes can also flow from firms to the government.)

1 point: Showing the government linked to households through transfers flowing from the government to households (*Note:* Transfers can also flow to firms.)

1 point: Showing the government linked to the market for goods and services through government purchases of goods and services

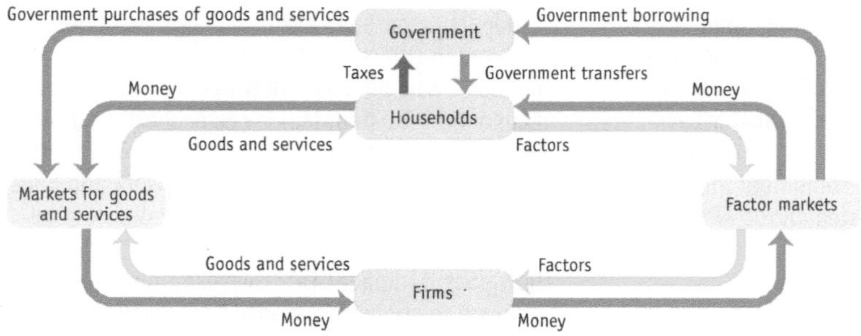

MODULE 10 Review

Check Your Understanding

1. Explain why the three methods of calculating GDP produce the same estimate of GDP.
2. Identify each of the sectors to which firms make sales. What are the various ways in which households are linked with other sectors of the economy?
3. Consider Figure 10.3. Explain why it would be incorrect to calculate total value added as $30,500, the sum of the sales price of a car and a car's worth of steel.

Tackle the Test: Multiple-Choice Questions

1. The circular-flow diagram is a simple model of the macroeconomy in which
   a. the flow of money into each market or sector exceeds the flow of money coming out of that market or sector.
   b. the value of stocks equals the value of bonds.
   c. households own the factors of production.
   d. there is only one household and one firm.
   e. goods and services are sold in factor markets.
2. GDP is equal to
   a. the total value of all goods and services produced in an economy during a given period.
   b. $C + I + G + IM$.
   c. the total value of intermediate goods plus final goods.
   d. the total income received by producers of final goods and services.
   e. none of the above.
3. Which of the following is included in GDP?
   a. changes to inventories
   b. intermediate goods
   c. used goods
   d. financial assets (stocks and bonds)
   e. foreign-produced goods
4. Which of the following is *not* included in GDP?
   a. capital goods such as machinery
   b. imports
   c. the value of domestically produced services
   d. government purchases of goods and services
   e. the construction of structures
5. Which of the following components makes up the largest percentage of GDP measured by aggregate spending?
   a. consumer spending
   b. investment spending
   c. government purchases of goods and services
   d. exports
   e. imports

Tackle the Test: Free-Response Questions

1. Will each of the following transactions be included in GDP for the United States? Explain why or why not.
   a. Coca-Cola builds a new bottling plant in the United States.
   b. Delta sells one of its existing airplanes to Korean Air.
   c. Ms. Moneybags buys an existing share of Disney stock.
   d. A California winery produces a bottle of Chardonnay and sells it to a customer in Montreal, Canada.
   e. An American buys a bottle of French perfume in Tulsa.
   f. A book publisher produces too many copies of a new book; the books don't sell this year, so the publisher adds the surplus books to inventories.

Rubric for FRQ 1 (6 points)

1 point: Yes. New structures built in the United States are included in U.S. GDP.

1 point: No. The airplane is used, and sales of used goods are not included in GDP.

1 point: No. This is a transfer of ownership—not new production.

1 point: Yes. This is an export.

1 point: No. This is an import—it was not produced in the United States.

1 point: Yes. Additions to inventories are considered investments.

2. Draw a correctly labeled circular-flow diagram showing the flows of funds between the markets for goods and services and the factor markets. Add the government to your diagram, and show how money leaks out of the economy to the government and how money is injected back into the economy by the government. **(5 points)**

Michael Hitoshi/Getty Images

MODULE 11 Interpreting Real Gross Domestic Product

In this Module, you will learn to:

- Differentiate between real GDP and nominal GDP
- Explain why real GDP is the appropriate measure of real economic activity

What GDP Tells Us

Now we've seen the various ways that gross domestic product is calculated. But what does the measurement of GDP tell us?

The most important use of GDP is as a measure of the size of the economy, providing us a scale against which to compare the economic performance of other years or other countries. For example, in 2013, as we've seen, U.S. GDP was $16,803 billion. By comparison, Japan's GDP was $4,902 billion, and the combined GDP of the 28 countries that make up the European Union was $17,371 billion. This comparison tells us that Japan, although it has the world's third-largest national economy, carries considerably less economic weight than does the United States. When taken in aggregate, Europe's economy is larger than the U.S. economy.

Lim Yong Hian/Shutterstock

Still, one must be careful when using GDP numbers, especially when making comparisons over time. That's because part of the increase in the value of GDP over time represents increases in the *prices* of goods and services rather than an increase in output. For example, U.S. GDP was $7,751 billion in 1996 and had more than doubled to $16,803 billion by 2013. But U.S. production didn't actually double over that period. To measure actual changes in aggregate output, we need a modified version of GDP that is adjusted for price changes, known as *real GDP*. We'll see how real GDP is calculated next.

Real GDP: A Measure of Aggregate Output

At the beginning of this section we described how China passed Japan as the world's second-largest economy in 2010. At the time, Japan's economy was weakening: during the second quarter of 2010, output declined by an annual rate of 6.3%. Oddly, however,

PD To prepare for teaching this lesson, you may want to consult the **Module 11 Sample Lecture** in the TRM.

OPEN & CLOSE Start Here

Show the clip of a speech by Robert F. Kennedy talking about GDP (see econextras video list with hyperlinks on the bcs and TRFD). Ask students to write down categories of items that are counted and not counted in GDP. *Possible answers include: Counted—air pollution, cigarette advertising, ambulances, special locks, jails, destruction of redwoods, nuclear warheads. Not counted—health, quality of education, integrity of public officials, learning, and devotion to country.* Ask why all items are not counted in GDP. *Answers will vary, but what students should note is that there is no final good in the list of things not counted.*

TEACH Teach It

When we listen to a media report on the latest GDP, we are hearing the value of current production in the nation at current prices (current-dollar GDP). This figure allows us to compare our economy to that of other nations. If the GDP in the U.S. is twice the size of the GDP of another nation, we often say that our economy is twice as big. As we will see, this statement can be misleading.

FOCUS Active Learning

Show your students the world GDP chart at www.indexq.org/economy/gdp.php and ask them to compare and contrast the GDPs listed. (*Note:* Final data are slow to be reported, so the table will normally lag by 1 or 2 years.) Assign students to a country and have them write down the most current year data for its GDP and growth rate on a piece of paper.

- Let students cluster together based on the size of their assigned country's GDP—large, medium, and small. Can they identify the haves and have-nots based on GDP?
- Now cluster based on growth rates. Have the groups changed?

St. Louis Federal Reserve Bank Resources

"Economics for Life," *GDP and Pizza Online Course*

GDP and Pizza: Economics for Life is a 90-minute course that defines GDP and explains the components of GDP, per capita GDP, real vs. nominal GDP, levels vs. percent change, growth rates and trends, and automatic stabilizers. The course provides interaction and pre- and post-testing.

Module 11 Interpreting Real Gross Domestic Product 115

FOCUS Active Learning

Show students the interesting map at http://bigthink.com/strange-maps/131-us-states-renamed-for-countries-with-similar-gdps. It compares states with nations having similar GDPs and is a great graphical representation of the size of the U.S. economy. Ask students to discuss anything that surprises them. For example, Singapore is a very small nation, yet its economy is the size of South Carolina's. Hong Kong is a single city, but its economy is the size of Maryland's.

TEACH Teach It

GDP is really a $P \times Q$ measure. You take the quantity of output (Q) and multiply by the price of the output (P). If prices rise and Q stays the same, GDP will increase. This is misleading because the size of the economy hasn't truly increased; goods and services have just become more expensive. To adjust for changing prices, we calculate real GDP, a measure of the value of production that is based on prices from a fixed point in time. This fixed point in time is called the base year.

FOCUS Active Learning

TRM The calculation of GDP is daunting for some students. To easily explain GDP calculation, use **Activity 11.1 (Calculating GDP Notes)** from the TRM. This activity allows you to explain the process step by step, which will build student understanding.

FYI Creating the National Accounts

The national accounts, like modern macroeconomics, owe their creation to the Great Depression. As the economy plunged into depression, government officials found their ability to respond crippled not only by the lack of adequate economic theories but also by the lack of adequate information. All they had were scattered statistics: railroad freight car loadings, stock prices, and incomplete indexes of industrial production. They could only guess at what was happening to the economy as a whole.

In response to this perceived lack of information, the Department of Commerce commissioned Simon Kuznets, a young Russian-born economist, to develop a set of national income accounts. (Kuznets later won the Nobel Prize in economics for his work.) The first version of these accounts was presented to Congress in 1937 and in a research report titled *National Income, 1929–35*.

Kuznets's initial estimates fell short of the full modern set of accounts because they focused on income rather than production. The push to complete the national accounts came during World War II, when policy makers were in even more need of comprehensive measures of the economy's performance. The federal government began issuing estimates of gross domestic product and gross national product in 1942.

In January 2000, in its publication *Survey of Current Business*, the Department of Commerce ran an article titled "GDP: One of the Great Inventions of the 20th Century." This may seem a bit over the top, but national income accounting, invented in the United States, has since become a tool of economic analysis and policy making around the world.

GDP was up. In fact, Japan's GDP measured in yen, its national currency, rose by an annual rate of 4.8% during the quarter. How was that possible? The answer is that Japan was experiencing inflation at the time. As a result, the yen value of Japan's GDP rose although output actually fell.

The moral of this story is that the commonly cited GDP number is an interesting and useful statistic, one that provides a good way to compare the size of different economies, but it's not a good measure of the economy's growth over time. GDP can grow because the economy grows, but it can also grow simply because of inflation. Even if an economy's output doesn't change, GDP will go up if the prices of the goods and services the economy produces increase. Likewise, GDP can fall either because the economy is producing less or because prices have fallen.

Aggregate output is the total quantity of final goods and services produced within an economy.

To measure the economy's growth with accuracy, we need a measure of **aggregate output**: the total quantity of final goods and services the economy produces. As we noted above, the measure that is used for this purpose is known as real GDP. By tracking real GDP over time, we avoid the problem of changes in prices distorting the value of changes in production over time. Let's look first at how real GDP is calculated and then at what it means.

AP® Exam Tip

Aggregate output is another name for GDP. You may see (or hear) it referred to as output, economic output, or aggregate output.

Calculating Real GDP

To understand how real GDP is calculated, imagine an economy in which only two goods, apples and oranges, are produced and in which both goods are sold only to final consumers. The outputs and prices of the two fruits for two consecutive years are shown in **Table 11.1**.

The first thing we can say about these data is that the value of sales increased from year 1 to year 2. In the first year, the total value of sales was (2,000 billion × \$0.25) + (1,000 billion × \$0.50) = \$1,000 billion; in the second, it was (2,200 billion × \$0.30) + (1,200 billion × \$0.70) = \$1,500 billion, which is 50% larger. But it is also clear from the table that this increase in the dollar value of GDP overstates the real growth in the economy. Although the quantities of both apples and oranges increased, the prices of both apples and oranges also rose. So part of the 50% increase in the dollar value of GDP simply reflects higher prices, not increased production.

St. Louis Federal Reserve Bank Resources

"Gross Domestic Product," *The Economic Lowdown Podcast Series*, Episode 13

This podcast explains what GDP measures, how it is calculated, how it is useful in determining whether and how quickly the economy is growing, and how GDP can be used as an indicator of the standard of living.

"Gross Domestic Product," *Economic Lowdown Video Companion Series*, Episode 7

An 8-minute video developed from the podcast is also available.

Table 11.1 Calculating GDP and Real GDP in a Simple Economy

	Year 1	Year 2
Quantity of apples (billions)	2,000	2,200
Price of an apple	$0.25	$0.30
Quantity of oranges (billions)	1,000	1,200
Price of an orange	$0.50	$0.70
GDP (billions of dollars)	$1,000	$1,500
Real GDP (billions of year 1 dollars)	$1,000	$1,150

To estimate the true increase in aggregate output produced, we have to ask the following question: How much would GDP have gone up if prices had *not* changed? To answer this question, we need to find the value of output in year 2 expressed in year 1 prices. In year 1, the price of apples was $0.25 each and the price of oranges $0.50 each. So year 2 output *at year 1 prices* is (2,200 billion × $0.25) + (1,200 billion × $0.50) = $1,150 billion. Since output in year 1 at year 1 prices was $1,000 billion, GDP measured in year 1 prices rose 15%—from $1,000 billion to $1,150 billion.

Now we can define **real GDP**: it is the total value of all final goods and services produced in the economy during a year, calculated as if prices had stayed constant at the level of some given base year in order to remove the effects of price changes. A real GDP number always comes with information about what the base year is. A GDP number that has not been adjusted for changes in prices is calculated using the prices in the year in which the output is produced. Economists call this measure **nominal GDP**, or GDP at current prices. If we had used nominal GDP to measure the change in output from year 1 to year 2 in our apples and oranges example, we would have overstated the true growth in output: we would have claimed it to be 50%, when in fact it was only 15%. By comparing output in the two years using a common set of prices—the year 1 prices in this example—we are able to focus solely on changes in the quantity of output by eliminating the influence of changes in prices.

Table 11.2 shows a real-life version of our apples and oranges example. The second column shows nominal GDP in 2000, 2005, and 2013. The third column shows real GDP for each year in 2005 dollars (that is, using the value of the dollar in the year 2005). For 2005 the nominal GDP and the real GDP are the same. But real GDP in 2000 expressed in 2005 dollars was higher than nominal GDP in 2000, reflecting the fact that prices were in general higher in 2005 than in 2000. Real GDP in 2013 expressed in 2005 dollars, however, was less than nominal GDP in 2013 because prices in 2005 were lower than in 2013.

Real GDP is the total value of all final goods and services produced in the economy during a given year, calculated using the prices of a selected base year in order to remove the effects of price changes.

Nominal GDP is the total value of all final goods and services produced in the economy during a given year, calculated with the prices current in the year in which the output is produced.

Table 11.2 Nominal versus Real GDP in 2000, 2005, and 2013

	Nominal GDP (billions of current dollars)	Real GDP (billions of 2005 dollars)
2000	$9,951.5	$11,286
2005	12,683	12,638
2013	16,803	14,504

Source: Bureau of Economic Analysis.

FOCUS Flip It

TRM To reinforce the difference between nominal and real GDP, have students watch Jacob Clifford's short explanation, "Macro Unit 2.2—Nominal and Real GDP" (see econextras video list with hyperlinks on the bcs and TRFD). Assign **Worksheet 11.2 (GDP and Economic Growth Video)** from the TRM for questions on this video.

FOCUS Test It

	Year 1 Quantity	Year 1 Price (base year)	Year 2 Quantity	Year 2 Price
Apples	20	$1	25	$2
Peaches	30	$3	20	$6
Pears	10	$4	25	$4

Bigtown uses its resources to produce apples, peaches, and pears as shown in the table above. Assuming that year 1 is the base year, calculate each of the following:

A. The nominal GDP in year 1 *(20 × $1) + (30 × $3) + (10 × $4) = $150*

B. The nominal GDP in year 2 *(25 × $2) + (20 × $6) + (25 × $4) = $270*

C. The real GDP in year 2 *(25 × $1) + (20 × $3) + (25 × $4) = $185*

D. The percentage change in real GDP from year 1 to year 2 *(185 – 150)/150 = .23 or 23%*

Tip: Calculate means "show your work." For some past problems on the AP® exam, if students correctly set up the equation but the math was not correct, they were awarded the points since calculators are not allowed. That is why it is essential they show their work. For this problem, students would receive 1 point for each correct calculation.

FOCUS Active Learning

TRM Use **Activity 11.3 (GDP in the Economy)** from the TRM for extra practice in calculating real and nominal GDP.

TEACH Teach It

GDP per capita is a good indicator of how an economy is doing compared to that of other nations because it is based on population. For example, if two nations both have a GDP of $1 billion, students might assume that both nations have a high standard of living. But what if one of the nations is China and the other is Haiti? With a population of over 1.3 billion people, the GDP per capita in China would be less than $1 per person, while Haiti's 6.8 million people would earn more than $1,470 per person. In reality, China's per capita GDP is almost twice that of Haiti.

FOCUS Active Learning

Stress to your students that GDP and real GDP are just statistical measures. They are positive, not normative. They should not be used to measure a nation's self-esteem, well-being, or sense of overall happiness. Ask students to come up with examples of things not counted in GDP that make people happy and things counted in GDP that don't make people happy. Some things that do not contribute to GDP make us happier:

- *Volunteering at a summer camp rather than getting a summer job. Volunteerism detracts from GDP.*
- *Many forms of leisure do not contribute to GDP. Read a book, take a walk, play catch with your friend, and you are lowering the level of GDP.*
- *Work around the house. If you rake your own leaves rather than hire a company to do it, you detract from GDP.*

Some things that contribute to GDP don't make us happier:

- *Spending money to put bars in your windows because your neighborhood is unsafe will add to GDP, but such spending increases in the unhappy event that crime increases.*
- *Paying to clean up a polluted river or lake will add to GDP, but more spending on cleanups is necessary when pollution problems increase.*
- *Spending money to fight a war will add to GDP.*

You might have noticed that there is an alternative way to calculate real GDP using the data in Table 11.1. Why not measure it using the prices of year 2 rather than year 1 as the base-year prices? This procedure seems equally valid. According to that calculation, real GDP in year 1 at year 2 prices is (2,000 billion × $0.30) + (1,000 billion × $0.70) = $1,300 billion; real GDP in year 2 at year 2 prices is $1,500 billion, the same as nominal GDP in year 2. So using year 2 prices as the base year, the growth rate of real GDP is equal to ($1,500 billion − $1,300 billion)/$1,300 billion = 0.154, or 15.4%. This is slightly higher than the figure we got from the previous calculation, in which year 1 prices were the base-year prices. In that calculation, we found that real GDP increased by 15.0%. Neither answer, 15.4% versus 15.0%, is more "correct" than the other. In reality, the government economists who put together the U.S. national accounts have adopted a method to measure the change in real GDP known as **chain-linking**, which uses the average between the GDP growth rate calculated using an early base year and the GDP growth rate calculated using a late base year. As a result, U.S. statistics on real GDP are always expressed in *chained dollars*, which splits the difference between using early and late base years.

Chain-linking is the method of calculating changes in real GDP using the average between the growth rate calculated using an early base year and the growth rate calculated using a late base year.

What Real GDP Doesn't Measure

GDP is a measure of a country's aggregate output. Other things equal, a country with a larger population will have higher GDP simply because there are more people working. So if we want to compare GDP across countries but want to eliminate the effect of differences in population size, we use the measure **GDP per capita**—GDP divided by the size of the population, equivalent to the average GDP per person. Correspondingly, real GDP per capita is the average real GDP per person.

GDP per capita is GDP divided by the size of the population; it is equivalent to the average GDP per person.

Real GDP per capita can be a useful measure in some circumstances, such as in a comparison of labor productivity between two countries. However, despite the fact that it is a rough measure of the average real output per person, real GDP per capita has well-known limitations as a measure of a country's living standards. Every once in a while, economists are accused of believing that growth in real GDP per capita is the only thing that matters—that is, thinking that increasing real GDP per capita is a goal in itself. In fact, economists rarely make that mistake; the idea that economists care only about real GDP per capita is a sort of urban legend. Let's take a moment to be clear about why a country's real GDP per capita is not a sufficient measure of human welfare in that country and why growth in real GDP per capita is not an appropriate policy goal in itself.

istockphoto

Real GDP does not include many of the things that contribute to happiness, such as leisure time, volunteerism, housework, and natural beauty. And real GDP increases with expenditures on some things that make people unhappy, including disease, divorce, crime, and natural disasters.

Real GDP per capita is a measure of an economy's average aggregate output per person—an indication of the economy's potential for certain achievements. Having studied the income approach to calculating GDP, you know that the value of output corresponds to the value of income. A country with a relatively high GDP per capita can afford relatively high expenditures on health, education, and other goods and services that contribute to a high quality of life. But how output is actually used is another matter. To put it differently, your income might be higher this year than last year, but whether you use that higher income to actually improve your quality of life is up to you. There is not a one-to-one match between real GDP and the quality of life. The real GDP per capita measure does not indicate how income is distributed. It doesn't include some sources of well-being, and it does include some things that are detriments to well-being.

118 Section 3 Measurement of Economic Performance

St. Louis Federal Reserve Bank Resources

"The Output Gap: A 'Potentially' Unreliable Measure of Economic Health?,"
Page One Economics

The output gap is one economic indicator (out of many) that is used by economists to measure the strength of the economy. What exactly is the output gap, and how accurately does it predict the state of the economy? This essay provides both an explanation of the output gap and answers to these questions. Student questions are included.

FYI Miracle in Venezuela?

The South American nation of Venezuela has a distinction that may surprise you: in recent years, it has had one of the world's fastest-growing nominal GDPs. Between 2000 and 2012, Venezuelan nominal GDP grew by an average of 27% each year—much faster than nominal GDP in the United States or even in booming economies like China.

So is Venezuela experiencing an economic miracle? No, it's just suffering from unusually high inflation. The figure shows Venezuela's nominal and real GDP from 2000 to 2012, with real GDP measured in 2000 prices. Real GDP did grow over the period, but at an annual rate of only 2.0%. That's about the same as the U.S. growth rate over the same period and far short of China's 10% growth.

Source: World Bank.

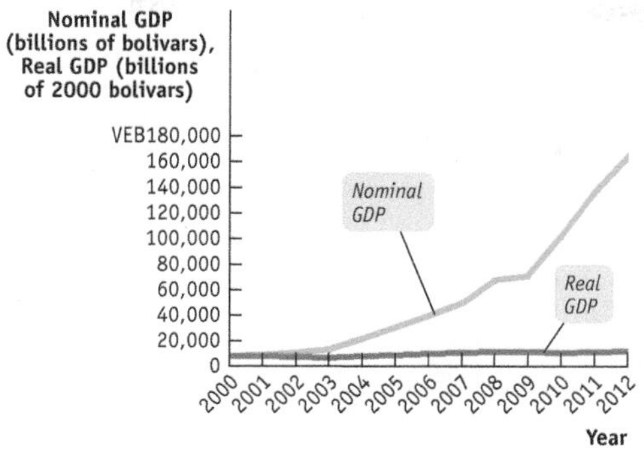

MODULE 11 Review

Check Your Understanding

1. Assume there are only two goods in the economy, french fries and onion rings. In 2013, 1,000,000 servings of french fries were sold for \$0.40 each and 800,000 servings of onion rings were sold for \$0.60 each. From 2013 to 2014, the price of french fries rose to \$0.50 and the servings sold fell to 900,000; the price of onion rings fell to \$0.51 and the servings sold rose to 840,000.
   - **a.** Calculate nominal GDP in 2013 and 2014. Calculate real GDP in 2014 using 2013 prices.
   - **b.** Why would an assessment of growth using nominal GDP be misguided?
2. Indicate the effect of each of the following on real GDP:
   - **a.** Chevrolet increases its production of Corvettes.
   - **b.** Consumer expenditures increase as a result of inflation.
   - **c.** \$50 billion is spent on hurricane cleanup.
   - **d.** Citizens spend 10,000 hours as neighborhood watch volunteers.

Tackle the Test: Multiple-Choice Questions

1. Which of the following is true of real GDP?
   - **I.** It is adjusted for changes in prices.
   - **II.** It is always equal to nominal GDP.
   - **III.** It increases whenever aggregate output increases.
   - **a.** I only
   - **b.** II only
   - **c.** III only
   - **d.** I and III
   - **e.** I, II, and III
2. The best measure for comparing a country's aggregate output over time is
   - **a.** nominal GDP.
   - **b.** real GDP.
   - **c.** nominal GDP per capita.
   - **d.** real GDP per capita.
   - **e.** average GDP per capita.

Answers to Module 11 Review Questions

Check Your Understanding

1. a. In 2013 nominal GDP was (1,000,000 × \$0.40) + (800,000 × \$0.60) = \$400,000 + \$480,000 = \$880,000. The total value of sales of french fries in 2014 was 900,000 × \$0.50 = \$450,000. The total value of sales of onion rings in 2014 was 840,000 × \$0.51 = \$428,400. Nominal GDP in 2014 was \$450,000 + \$428,400 = \$878,400. To find real GDP in 2014, we must calculate the value of sales in 2014 using 2013 prices: (900,000 × \$0.40) + (840,000 × \$0.60) = \$360,000 + \$504,000 = \$864,000.

b. A comparison of nominal GDP in 2013 to nominal GDP in 2014 shows a decline of ((\$880,000 − \$878,400)/\$880,000) × 100 = 0.18%. But a comparison using real GDP shows a decline of ((\$880,000 − \$864,000)/\$880,000) × 100 = 1.8%. That is, a calculation based on real GDP shows a drop 10 times larger (1.8%) than a calculation based on nominal GDP (0.18%): in this case, the calculation based on nominal GDP underestimates the true magnitude of the change because it incorporates both quantity changes and price changes.

2. a. Real GDP increases as the result of increased output.

b. There is no change in real GDP; inflation only affects nominal GDP.

c. Real GDP increases as a result of the new spending.

d. There is no change in real GDP, which does not capture volunteer work.

Tackle the Test: Multiple-Choice Questions

1. d
2. b

OPEN & CLOSE Exit Slip

TRM *Please see **Exit Slip: Module 11** in the TRM for formative multiple-choice questions to ask before finishing your lesson. These questions will help you quickly assess whether your students have mastered the module's concepts before moving on.*

Answers to the Exit Slip Questions

1. B
2. E
3. B *((10 × \$4,000) + (9 × \$1,000) + (6 × \$1,000) + (7 × \$2,000) = \$69,000)*

Module 11 Interpreting Real Gross Domestic Product **119**

3. c
4. c
5. c

3. Use the information provided in the table below for an economy that produces only apples and oranges. Assume year 1 is the base year.

	Year 1	Year 2
Quantity of apples	3,000	4,000
Price of an apple	$0.20	$0.30
Quantity of oranges	2,000	3,000
Price of an orange	$0.40	$0.50

What was the value of real GDP in each year?

	Year 1	*Year 2*
a.	$1,400	$2,700
b.	1,900	2,700
c.	1,400	2,000
d.	1,900	2,000
e.	1,400	1,900

4. Real GDP per capita is an imperfect measure of the quality of life in part because it
   a. includes the value of leisure time.
   b. excludes expenditures on education.
   c. includes expenditures on natural disasters.
   d. excludes expenditures on entertainment.
   e. includes the value of housework.

5. Refer to the 2013 data in the table below.

	Nominal GDP in billions of dollars
United States	$16,803
Japan	4,902
European Union	17,371

Which of the following can be determined with the information in the table?
   I. Residents of Japan were worse off than residents of the United States or the European Union.
   II. The European Union had a higher nominal GDP per capita than the United States.
   III. The European Union had a larger economy than the United States.
   a. I only
   b. II only
   c. III only
   d. II and III
   e. I, II, and III

Tackle the Test: Free-Response Questions

1. The economy of Britannica produces three goods: computers, DVDs, and pizza. The accompanying table shows the prices and output of the three goods for the years 2012 and 2014.

	Computers		DVDs		Pizza	
Year	Price	Quantity	Price	Quantity	Price	Quantity
2012	$900	10	$10	100	$15	2
2014	1,050	12	14	110	17	3

   a. Calculate the nominal GDP in Britannica for 2012.
   b. Calculate the real GDP in Britannica for 2012 using 2012 as the base year.
   c. Calculate the real GDP in Britannica for 2014 using 2012 as the base year.

Rubric for FRQ 1 (3 points)

1 point: ($900 × 10) + ($10 × 100) + ($15 × 2) = $9,000 + $1,000 + $30 = $10,030

1 point: Real GDP equals nominal GDP in the base year, so this answer is the same as in part a.

1 point: ($900 × 12) + ($10 × 110) + ($15 × 3) = $10,800 + $1,100 + $45 = $11,945

2. The country of Hungry produces only pizzas and the country of Thirsty produces only smoothies. Use the information in the table below to answer the following questions:
   a. Calculate the number of pizzas made in Hungry and the number of smoothies made in Thirsty in each year.
   b. Calculate the real GDP in each country in year 2 using year 1 prices.
   c. In which country did real GDP increase the most between year 1 and year 2?
   d. In which country did real GDP per capita decrease the most between year 1 and year 2? Show your work.

	Nominal GDP	Price	Population
Hungry			
Year 1	$10,000	$10	5
Year 2	20,000	10	16
Thirsty			
Year 1	$10,000	$10	5
Year 2	30,000	20	10

(6 points)

Tackle the Test: Free-Response Question

Rubric for FRQ 2 (6 points)

1 point: Hungry—1,000, 2,000 (In Year 1, Hungry made $10,000/$10 = 1,000 pizzas. In Year 2, Hungry made $20,000/$10 = 2,000 pizzas.)

1 point: Thirsty—1,000, 1,500 (In Year 1, Thirsty made $10,000/$10 = 1,000 smoothies. In Year 2, Thirsty made $30,000/$20 = 1,500 smoothies.)

1 point: Hungry—The real GDP in Hungry in Year 2 is $10 × 2,000 = $20,000.

1 point: Thirsty—The real GDP in Thirsty in Year 2 is $10 × 1,500 = $15,000.

1 point: Hungry—The increase of $10,000 or 100% in Hungry exceeded the increase of $5,000 or 50% in Thirsty.

1 point: Hungry—In Year 1, the real GDP per capita was $10,000/5 = $2,000 in each country. In Year 2, the real GDP per capita in Hungry was $20,000/16 = $1,250 and the real GDP per capita in Thirsty was $15,000/10 = $1,500. Thus, the decrease of $750 in Hungry exceeded the decrease of $500 in Thirsty.

120 Section 3 Measurement of Economic Performance

AP Photo/Rick Bowme

MODULE 12

The Meaning and Calculation of Unemployment

In this Module, you will learn to:

- Explain how unemployment is measured
- Calculate the unemployment rate
- Summarize the significance of the unemployment rate for the economy
- Explain the relationship between the unemployment rate and economic growth

The Unemployment Rate

The economy—and unemployment in particular—topped the list of issues important to voters in the 2012 presidential election. **Figure 12.1** on the next page shows the U.S. unemployment rate from 1948 to the early part of 2013. As you can see, the labor market hit a difficult patch starting in mid-2008, with the unemployment rate rising from 4.8% in February 2008 to 10.1% in October 2009. What did the rise in the unemployment rate mean, and why was it still a major concern for U.S. citizens in 2012 and beyond? To make sense of the attention paid to employment and unemployment, we need to understand how they are both defined and measured.

Defining and Measuring Unemployment

It's easy to define employment: you're **employed** if and only if you have a job.

Unemployment, however, is a more subtle concept. Just because a person isn't working doesn't mean that we consider that person *unemployed*. For example, in April 2014 there were 38 million retired workers in the United States receiving Social Security checks. Most of them were probably happy that they were no longer working, so we wouldn't consider someone who has settled into a comfortable, well-earned retirement to be unemployed. There were also 8 million disabled U.S. workers receiving benefits because they were unable to work. Again, although they weren't working, we wouldn't normally consider them to be unemployed.

The U.S. Census Bureau, the federal agency that collects data on unemployment, considers the unemployed to be those who are "jobless, looking for jobs, and available for work." Retired people don't count because they aren't looking for jobs; the disabled don't count because they aren't available for work. More specifically, an individual is

Employed people are currently holding a job in the economy, either full time or part time.

PD To prepare for teaching this lesson, you may want to consult the **Module 12 Sample Lecture** in the TRM.

OPEN & CLOSE Start Here

Show students *The Short Answer* video clip from the *Wall Street Journal* article "Ignore the Unemployment Rate" (see econextras video list with hyperlinks on the bcs and TRFD). Ask students to pay attention to the percentage of working-age Americans in the workforce. *63%.* Why is the labor force participation rate falling? *Retirement, workers who have lost their jobs due to technology or geographic relocation, less educated workers find the jobs less appealing, some can't find jobs so they have quit looking, some have gone back to school, and many are on disability.*

St. Louis Federal Reserve Bank Resources

***The Story of Unemployment Online Course,* Lesson 1**

This lesson focuses on how unemployment data are collected and how unemployment is measured. How do we know how many people are unemployed? Why are they unemployed? What can be done to get people back to work? Students get the answers to these and other questions in *The Story of Unemployment,* including why education might be the best way to avoid unemployment in their futures.

"Unemployment," *Economic Lowdown Podcast*, Episode 5

The 9-minute podcast on unemployment covers the basics of unemployment—how it is defined, how it is measured, and how it is categorized into three types. A "game show" quiz winds up the lesson.

Module 12 The Meaning and Calculation of Unemployment 121

FOCUS Active Learning

Using Figure 12.1, ask students to identify periods of high unemployment and offer a reason for the high rate. *Answers will vary, but may include: 2007–2009, the financial crisis; 2010, the housing bubble; 2001, 9/11; 1990, the Gulf War.*

Visit www.bls.gov/web/laus/lauhsthl.htm and take a look at the BLS Current Unemployment Rates for States and Historical Highs/Lows chart. Show students the unemployment rate for your state compared to that of the nation. Ask students to consider how the state and the nation overall are similar and how they are different. What do they think accounts for the differences in unemployment rates? *Answers will vary, but students should talk about the types of industries in the state that affect unemployment and economic events that impact the national unemployment figures.*

TEACH Teach It

When crunching numbers for labor statistics, the BLS narrows the population by categorizing only those citizens above the age of 16 who are not institutionalized (not incarcerated, serving in the armed forces, etc.). The population is then divided into three groups:

- those who are working at least 1 hour per week (the employed)
- those not working at least 1 hour, but who are seeking work (the unemployed)
- those "not in the labor force"

Labor Force = Employed + Unemployed

TEACH Teach It

Students can easily forget that jobless workers who are not seeking work are not counted as unemployed; they are "out of the labor force." Remind them throughout the lesson that in order to be counted as unemployed, a jobless individual must be willing and able to work and actively seeking work.

Figure 12.1 The U.S. Unemployment Rate, 1948-2013

The unemployment rate has fluctuated widely over time. It always rises during recessions, which are shown by the shaded bars. It usually, but not always, falls during periods of economic expansion.

Source: Bureau of Labor Statistics; National Bureau of Economic Research.

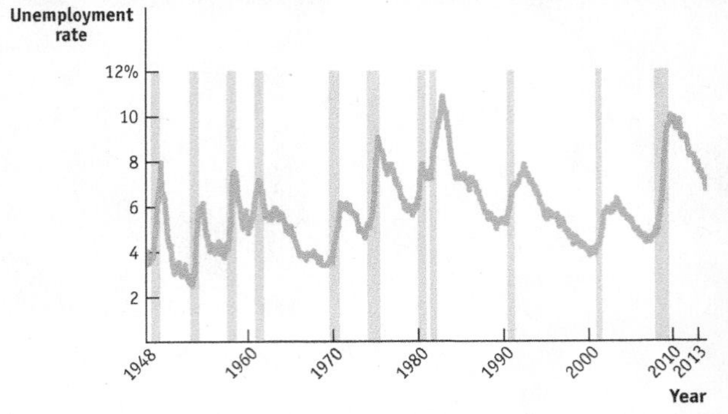

considered unemployed if he or she doesn't currently have a job and has been actively seeking a job during the past four weeks. So the **unemployed** are people who are actively looking for work but aren't currently employed.

A country's **labor force** is the sum of the employed and the unemployed—that is, the people who are currently working and the people who are currently looking for work. The **labor force participation rate**, defined as the share of the working-age population that is in the labor force, is calculated as follows:

AP® Exam Tip

A formula sheet is not provided during the AP® exam. You will need to remember these formulas to calculate the size of the labor force and the unemployment rate.

$$\textbf{(12-1)}\quad \text{Labor force participation rate} = \frac{\text{Labor force}}{\text{Population age 16 and older}} \times 100$$

The **unemployment rate**, defined as the percentage of the total number of people in the labor force who are unemployed, is calculated as follows:

$$\textbf{(12-2)}\quad \text{Unemployment rate} = \frac{\text{Number of unemployed workers}}{\text{Labor force}} \times 100$$

To estimate the numbers that go into calculating the unemployment rate, the U.S. Census Bureau carries out a monthly survey called the Current Population Survey, which involves interviewing a random sample of 60,000 American families. People are asked whether they are currently employed. If they are not employed, they are asked whether they have been looking for a job during the past four weeks. The results are then scaled up, using estimates of the total population, to estimate the total number of employed and unemployed Americans.

Unemployed people are actively looking for work but aren't currently employed.

The **labor force** is equal to the sum of the employed and the unemployed.

The **labor force participation rate** is the percentage of the population aged 16 or older that is in the labor force.

The **unemployment rate** is the percentage of the total number of people in the labor force who are unemployed.

The Significance of the Unemployment Rate

In general, the unemployment rate is a good indicator of how easy or difficult it is to find a job given the current state of the economy. When the unemployment rate is low, nearly everyone who wants a job can find one. In 2000, when the unemployment rate averaged 4%, jobs were so abundant that employers spoke of a "mirror test" for getting a job: if you were breathing (therefore, your breath would fog a

FOCUS Active Learning

TRM To provide practice in calculating unemployment rates, assign **Worksheet 12.1 (Unemployment Rates)** from the TRM in class or as homework.

FOCUS Active Learning

TRM For a quick review, have students watch "Episode 18: Unemployment" (see econextras video list with hyperlinks on the bcs and TRFD). Assign **Worksheet 12.2 (Unemployment)** from the TRM for questions on this video.

mirror), you could find work. By contrast, in 2009, the unemployment rate in 17 states rose to over 10% (over 15% in Michigan), with many highly qualified workers having lost their jobs and having a hard time finding new ones. Although the unemployment rate is a good indicator of current labor market conditions, it is not a perfect measure.

© Inspirestock Inc./Alamy

How the Unemployment Rate Can Overstate the True Level of Unemployment If you are searching for work, it's normal to take at least a few weeks to find a suitable job. Yet a worker who is quite confident of finding a job, but has not yet accepted a position, is counted as unemployed. As a consequence, the unemployment rate never falls to zero, even in boom times when jobs are plentiful. Even in the buoyant labor market of 2000, when it was easy to find work, the unemployment rate was still 4%. Later, we'll discuss in greater depth the reasons that measured unemployment persists even when jobs are abundant.

How the Unemployment Rate Can Understate the True Level of Unemployment Frequently, some of the people who would like to work but aren't working still don't get counted as unemployed. In particular, an individual who has given up looking for a job for the time being because there are no jobs available isn't counted as unemployed because he or she has not been searching for a job during the previous four weeks. Individuals who want to work but aren't currently searching because they see little prospect of finding a job given the state of the job market are known as **discouraged workers**. Because it does not count discouraged workers, the measured unemployment rate may understate the percentage of people who want to work but are unable to find jobs.

Discouraged workers are part of a larger group known as **marginally attached workers**. These are people who say they would like to have a job and have looked for work in the recent past but are not currently looking for work. The difference between discouraged workers and other marginally attached workers is that the other marginally attached workers ended their job search for a reason other than a belief that no job was available for them. For example, they may have gone back to school or become disabled. Marginally attached workers are also not included when calculating the unemployment rate.

Finally, another category of workers who are frustrated in their ability to find work but aren't counted as unemployed are the **underemployed**: workers who would like to work more hours or who are overqualified for their jobs. For example, some part-time workers would like to work full time, and some college graduates work as fast-food clerks. Again, they aren't counted in the unemployment rate.

The Bureau of Labor Statistics is the federal agency that calculates the official unemployment rate. It also calculates broader "measures of labor underutilization" that include the three categories of frustrated workers. **Figure 12.2** on the next page shows what happens to the measured unemployment rate once marginally attached workers (including discouraged workers) and the underemployed are counted. The broadest measure of unemployment and underemployment, known as *U6*, is the sum of these three measures plus the unemployed; it is substantially higher than the rate usually quoted by the news media. But U6 and the unemployment rate move very much in parallel, so changes in the unemployment rate remain a good guide to what's happening in the overall labor market.

Finally, it's important to realize that the unemployment rate varies greatly among demographic groups. Other things equal, jobs are generally easier to find for more experienced workers and for workers during their "prime" working years, from ages 25 to 54. For younger workers, as well as workers nearing retirement age, jobs are typically harder to find. **Figure 12.3** on the next page shows unemployment rates for different

Discouraged workers are nonworking people who are capable of working but have given up looking for a job due to the state of the job market.

Marginally attached workers would like to be employed and have looked for a job in the recent past but are not currently looking for work.

The **underemployed** are workers who would like to work more hours or who are overqualified for their jobs.

TEACH Connect It

Remind your students of the business cycle that illustrates the ebb and flow of the macroeconomy. Show Jacob Clifford's video "Macro 2.6—Business Cycle Unit Summary" in class, so they can make the connections (see econextras video list with hyperlinks on the bcs and TRFD). Discuss what happens when the economy is weakening. This is also a good opportunity to review the circular-flow model.

FOCUS Active Learning

The unemployment rate is not a perfect measure of the true strength or weakness of the labor market and economy. Ask students to go to "The Unemployment Game Show" (see econextras video list with hyperlinks on the bcs and TRFD). Talk about the following additional examples to further their understanding:

- The economy is weak and Jerome has had his hours cut from 40 to 10 per week. Jerome is still employed, but his weekly income has decreased.
- Terri has a master's degree, but can only find work as a barista in a coffee shop. She is employed, though not in a job that matches her skills. Terri is considered underemployed.
- Jim has been unsuccessfully seeking work for nearly a year and finally decides to give up. People like Jim are classified as discouraged workers and not counted as unemployed; they are out of the labor force.

The presence of underemployed workers and discouraged workers causes the official unemployment rate to appear lower (better) than the actual labor market conditions.

FOCUS Active Learning

So they might get a real feel for unemployment, show your students all the levels of unemployment (U1 through U6). Have them take a look at Table A-15: Alternative Measures of Labor Underutilization at www.bls.gov/news.release/empsit.t15.htm. Ask why the government would only report U3 as opposed to reporting the actual U6 unemployment rate. *Answers will vary, but students should talk about how people and businesses would react if the larger numbers of unemployed were reported.*

FOCUS Active Learning

Civilian Population	236,832
Employed	138,333
Unemployed	14,837
Discouraged workers*	1,065

*A subset of those not in the labor force.

Ask students to answer the following questions on their personal whiteboards or in their notebooks:

1. What is the size of the labor force? *Employed + Unemployed = 138,333 + 14,837 = 153,170*
2. What is the labor force participation rate? *Labor Force/Civilian Population = 153,170/236,832 = 64.7%*
3. What is the unemployment rate? *Unemployed/Labor Force = 14,837/153,170 = 9.7%*
4. What is the unemployment rate, including discouraged workers? *(Unemployed + Discouraged Workers)/(Labor Force + Discouraged Workers) = (14,837 + 1,065)/(153,170 + 1,065) = 10.3%*

Figure 12.2 Alternative Measures of Unemployment, 1994–2013

The unemployment number usually quoted in the news media counts someone as unemployed only if he or she has been looking for work during the past four weeks. Broader measures also count discouraged workers, other marginally attached workers, and the underemployed. These broader measures show a higher unemployment rate—but they move closely in parallel with the standard rate.
Source: Bureau of Labor Statistics.

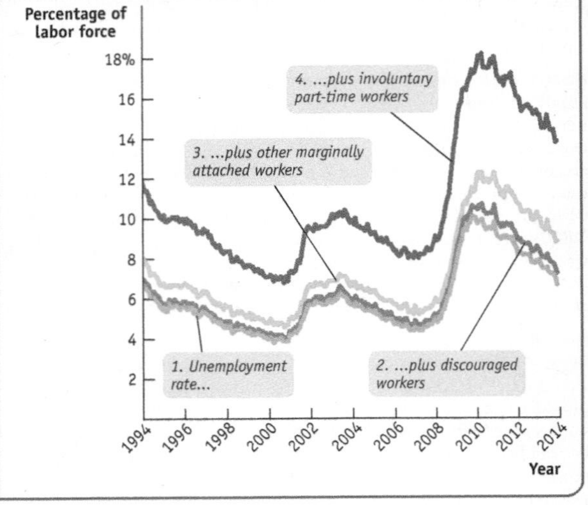

groups in December 2013, when the overall unemployment rate of 6.7% was low by historical standards. As you can see, in December 2013 the unemployment rate for African-American workers was much higher than the national average; the unemployment rate for White teenagers (ages 16–19) was almost three times the national average; and the unemployment rate for African-American teenagers, at more than 35%, was over five times the national average. (Bear in mind that a teenager isn't considered unemployed, even if he or she isn't working, unless that teenager is looking for work but can't find it.) So even at a time when the overall unemployment rate was relatively low, jobs were hard to find for some groups.

Figure 12.3 Unemployment Rates of Different Groups, 2013

Unemployment rates vary greatly among different demographic groups. For example, although the overall unemployment rate in December 2013 was 6.7%, the unemployment rate among African-American teenagers was 35.5%. As a result, even during periods of low overall unemployment, unemployment remains a serious problem for some groups.
Source: Bureau of Labor Statistics.

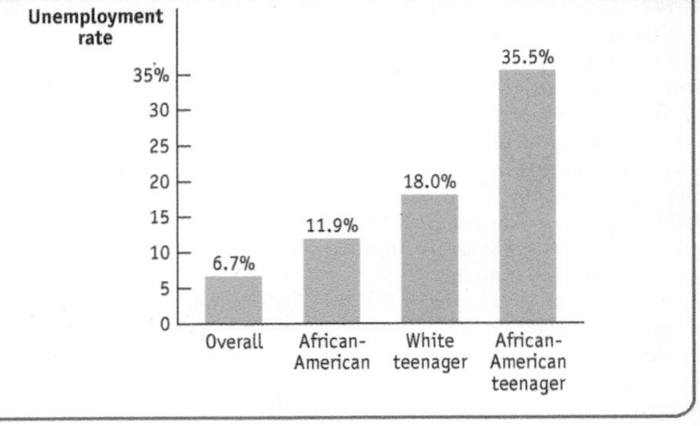

Although the unemployment rate is not an exact, literal measure of the percentage of people unable to find jobs, it is a good indicator of overall labor market conditions. The ups and downs of the unemployment rate closely reflect economic changes that have a significant impact on people's lives. Let's turn now to the causes of these fluctuations.

Growth and Unemployment

Compared to Figure 12.1, **Figure 12.4** shows the U.S. unemployment rate over a somewhat shorter period, the 33 years from 1980 to 2013. The shaded bars represent periods of recession. As you can see, during every recession, without exception, the unemployment rate rose. The recession of 1981–1982, the most severe one shown, pushed the unemployment rate into double digits: unemployment peaked in November 1982 at 10.8%. And during the most recent recession shown, in late 2009 the unemployment rate rose to above 10%.

Correspondingly, during periods of economic expansion the unemployment rate usually falls. The long economic expansion of the 1990s eventually brought the unemployment rate below 4%. However, it's important to recognize that *economic expansions aren't always periods of falling unemployment.* Look at the periods immediately following two recent recessions, those of 1990–1991 and 2001. In each case the unemployment rate continued to rise for more than a year after the recession was officially over. The explanation in both cases is that, although the economy was growing, it was not growing fast enough to reduce the unemployment rate.

Figure 12.5 on the next page is a scatter diagram showing U.S. data for the period from 1949 to 2013.The horizontal axis measures the annual rate of growth in real GDP—the percent by which each year's real GDP changed compared to the previous year's real GDP. (Notice that there were nine years in which growth was negative—that is, real GDP shrank.) The vertical axis measures the *change* in the unemployment rate over the previous year in percentage points. Each dot represents the observed growth rate of real GDP and change in the unemployment rate for a given year. For example, in 2000 the average unemployment rate fell to 4.0% from 4.2% in 1999; this is shown as a value of −0.2 along the vertical axis for the year 2000. Over the same period, real GDP grew by 4.1%; this is the value shown along the horizontal axis for the year 2000.

AP® Exam Tip

Unemployment always rises during recessions and usually falls during expansions. If a question indicates that real GDP is falling and asks about the effect on unemployment, you can conclude that it is rising.

Figure 12.4 Unemployment and Recessions, 1980–2013

This figure shows a close-up of the unemployment rate since the 1980s, with the shaded bars indicating recessions. It's clear that unemployment always rises during recessions and *usually* falls during expansions. But in both the early 1990s and the early 2000s, unemployment continued to rise for some time after the recession was officially declared over.
Source: Bureau of Labor Statistics; National Bureau of Economic Research.

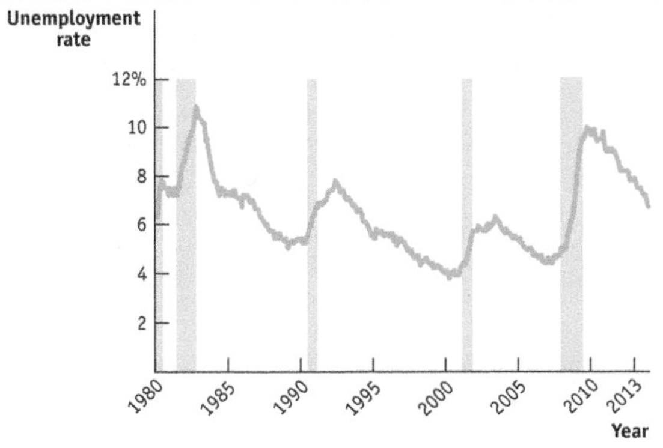

FOCUS Active Learning

When the economy is growing, unemployment is low. Now is a great time to discuss Chapter 19, "Will Technology Put Us All Out of Work?," from *Economics by Example* that students read for homework. Use Questions 1–3 of the discussion starters to explore unemployment and economic growth in more depth. *Note:* Question 4 can be used in Micro after students study the product market.

Module 12 The Meaning and Calculation of Unemployment 125

TEACH Teach It

Ask students to look at the scatterplot in Figure 12.5. Have them describe the relationship between unemployment and the GDP growth rate. *There is an inverse relationship between growth and unemployment.* Take time to discuss this relationship. In later modules, we discuss unemployment as it relates to the aggregate supply and demand model, which measures real GDP on the horizontal axis. Students will need to automatically relate falling (or rising) real GDP with rising (or falling) unemployment in that model. We will also explore the relationship again as we discuss the Phillips curve.

Figure 12.5 Growth and Changes in Unemployment, 1949–2013

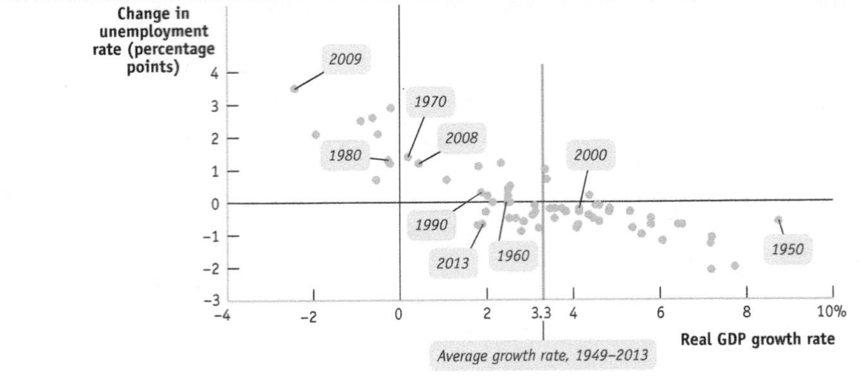

Each dot shows the growth rate of the economy and the change in the unemployment rate for a specific year between 1949 and 2013. For example, in 2000 the economy grew 4.1% and the unemployment rate fell 0.2 percentage points, from 4.2% to 4.0%. In general, the unemployment rate fell when growth was above its average rate of 3.3% a year and rose when growth was below average. Unemployment always rose when real GDP fell.

Source: Bureau of Labor Statistics; Bureau of Economic Analysis.

The downward trend of the scatter points in Figure 12.5 shows that there is a generally strong negative relationship between growth in the economy and the rate of unemployment. Years of high growth in real GDP were also years in which the unemployment rate fell, and years of low or negative growth in real GDP were years in which the unemployment rate rose. The green vertical line in Figure 12.5 at the value of 3.3% indicates the average growth rate of real GDP over the period from 1949 to 2013. Points lying to the right of the vertical line are years of above-average growth. In these years, the value on the vertical axis is usually negative, meaning that the unemployment rate fell. That is, years of above-average growth were usually years in which the unemployment rate was falling. Conversely, points lying to the left of the vertical line were years of below-average growth. In these years, the value on the vertical axis is usually positive, meaning that the unemployment rate rose. That is, years of below-average growth were usually years in which the unemployment rate was rising. There are periods in which GDP is growing, but at a below-average rate; these are periods in which the economy isn't in a recession but unemployment is still rising—sometimes called a "growth recession." But true recessions, periods when real GDP falls, are especially painful for workers. As illustrated by the points to the left of the vertical axis in Figure 12.5, falling real GDP is always associated with a rising rate of unemployment, causing a great deal of hardship to families.

126 Section 3 Measurement of Economic Performance

FYI Failure to Launch

In March 2010, when the U.S. job situation was near its worst, the *Harvard Law Record* published a brief note titled "Unemployed law student will work for $160K plus benefits." In a self-mocking tone, the author admitted to having graduated from Harvard Law School the previous year but not landing a job offer. "What mark on our résumé is so bad that it outweighs the crimson H?" the note asked.

The answer, of course, is that it wasn't about the résumé—it was about the economy. Times of high unemployment are especially hard on new graduates, who often find it hard to get any kind of full-time job. How bad was it in March 2010, around the time that note was written? Researchers at the San Francisco Fed analyzed the employment experience of college graduates, ages 21–23, and their findings are in the figure to the right.

Although the overall unemployment rate for college graduates 25 and older, even at its peak, was only about 5%, unemployment among recent graduates aged 21–23 peaked in 2010 at 10.7%. And many of those who *were* employed had been able to get only part-time jobs. In December 2007, at the beginning of the 2007–2009 recession, 83% of college graduates under the age of 24 who weren't still in school were employed full time. By December 2009, that number was down to just 72%. Quite simply, many college graduates were having a hard time getting their working lives started.

A year later, the situation was starting to improve, but slowly: in December 2010, 74% of recent graduates had full-time jobs. The U.S. labor market had a long way to go before being able to offer college graduates—and young people in general—the kinds of opportunities they deserved.

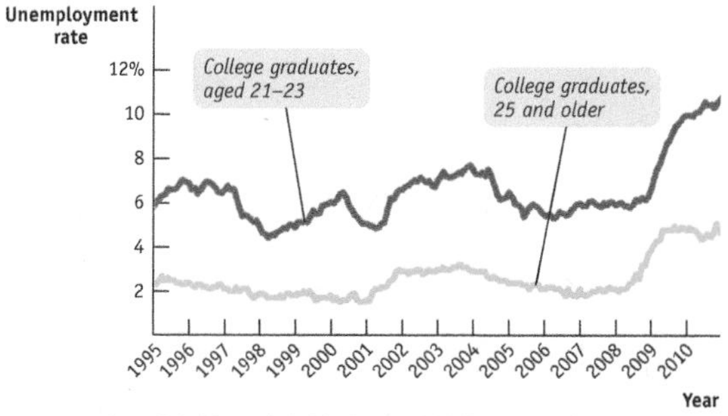

Source: Federal Reserve Bank of San Francisco, 2010; Bureau of Labor Statistics.

MODULE 12 Review

Check Your Understanding

1. Suppose that employment websites enable job-seekers to find suitable jobs more quickly. What effect will this have on the unemployment rate over time? Also suppose that these websites encourage job-seekers who had given up their searches to begin looking again. What effect will this have on the unemployment rate?
2. In which of the following cases would the worker be counted as unemployed? Explain.
   a. Rosa, an older worker, has been laid off and gave up looking for work months ago.
   b. Anthony, a schoolteacher, has chosen not to work during his three-month summer break.
   c. Grace, an investment banker, has been laid off and is currently searching for another position.
   d. Sergio, a classically trained musician, can only find work playing for local parties.
   e. Natasha, a graduate student, went back to school because jobs were scarce.
3. Which of the following are consistent with the observed relationship between growth in real GDP and changes in the unemployment rate? Which are not?
   a. A rise in the unemployment rate accompanies a fall in real GDP.
   b. An exceptionally strong business recovery is associated with a greater percentage of the labor force being employed.
   c. Negative real GDP growth is associated with a fall in the unemployment rate.

OPEN & CLOSE Exit Slip

*Please see **Exit Slip: Module 12** in the TRM for formative multiple-choice questions to ask your students before finishing your lesson. These questions will help you quickly assess whether your students have mastered the module's concepts before moving on.*

Answers to the Exit Slip Questions

1. D
2. C
3. B

Answers to Module 12 Review Questions

Check Your Understanding

1. The advent of websites that enable job-seekers to find jobs more quickly will reduce the unemployment rate over time. However, websites that induce discouraged workers to begin actively looking for work again will lead to an increase in the unemployment rate over time.

2. a. Not counted as unemployed because not actively looking for work, but counted in broader measures of labor underutilization as a discouraged worker

b. Not counted as unemployed—considered employed because the teacher has a job

c. Unemployed: not working, actively looking for work

d. Not unemployed, but underemployed: working part time for economic reasons. Counted in broader measures of labor underutilization.

e. Not unemployed, but considered "marginally attached." Counted in broader measures of labor underutilization.

3. Items (a) and (b) are consistent with the observed relationship between growth in GDP and changes in the unemployment rate. Item (c) is not.

Module 12 The Meaning and Calculation of Unemployment 127

Tackle the Test: Multiple-Choice Questions

1. To be considered unemployed, a person must
   I. not be working.
   II. be actively seeking a job.
   III. be available for work.
   a. I only
   b. II only
   c. III only
   d. II and III
   e. I, II, and III

Use the information for a hypothetical economy presented in the following table to answer questions 2, 3, and 4.

Population age 16 and older = 200,000
Labor force = 100,000
Number of people working part time = 20,000
Number of people working full time = 70,000

2. What is the labor force participation rate?
   a. 70%
   b. 50%
   c. 20%
   d. 10%
   e. 5%
3. How many people are unemployed?
   a. 10,000
   b. 20,000
   c. 30,000
   d. 100,000
   e. 110,000
4. What is the unemployment rate?
   a. 70%
   b. 50%
   c. 20%
   d. 10%
   e. 5%
5. The unemployment problem in an economy may be understated by the unemployment rate due to
   a. people lying about seeking a job.
   b. discouraged workers.
   c. job candidates with one offer but waiting for more.
   d. overemployed workers.
   e. none of the above.

Tackle the Test: Free-Response Questions

1. Use the data provided below to calculate each of the following. Show how you calculate each.
   a. the size of the labor force
   b. the labor force participation rate
   c. the unemployment rate

   Population age 16 and older = 12 million
   Employment = 5 million
   Unemployment = 1 million

Rubric for FRQ 1 (6 points)

1 point: 6 million

1 point: employment + unemployment = 5 million + 1 million = 6 million

1 point: 50%

1 point: (labor force/population) × 100 = ((5 million + 1 million)/12 million) × 100 = (6 million/12 million) × 100 = 50%

1 point: 17%

1 point: (unemployment/labor force) × 100 = (1 million/(5 million + 1 million)) × 100 = (1 million/6 million) × 100 = 17%

2. What is the labor market classification of each of the following individuals? Be as specific as possible, and explain your answer.
   a. Julie has a graduate degree in mechanical engineering. She works full-time mowing lawns.
   b. Jeff was laid off from his previous job. He would very much like to work at any job, but, after looking for work for a year, he has stopped looking for work.
   c. Ian is working 25 hours per week at a bookstore and has no desire to work full time.
   d. Raj has decided to take a year off from work to stay home with his daughter.
   (4 points)

Tackle the Test: Multiple-Choice Questions

1. e
2. b
3. a
4. d
5. b

Tackle the Test: Free-Response Question

Rubric for FRQ 2 (4 points)

1 point: Employed (underemployed); she is working, but not working up to her full potential.

1 point: Not in the labor force (discouraged); once a worker stops actively seeking work, he or she falls out of the labor force.

1 point: Employed; individuals are classified as employed if they work full or part time.

1 point: Not in the labor force; he is not actively seeking employment.

128 Section 3 Measurement of Economic Performance

Adam Gault/Photodisc/Getty Images

MODULE 13

The Causes and Categories of Unemployment

In this Module, you will learn to:

- Explain the three different types of unemployment and their causes
- Identify the factors that determine the natural rate of unemployment

The Natural Rate of Unemployment

Fast economic growth tends to reduce the unemployment rate. So how low can the unemployment rate go? You might be tempted to say zero, but that isn't feasible. Over the past half century, the national unemployment rate has never dropped below 2.9%.

Can there be unemployment even when many businesses are having a hard time finding workers? To answer this question, we need to examine the nature of labor markets and why they normally lead to substantial measured unemployment even when jobs are plentiful. Our starting point is the observation that, even in the best of times, jobs are constantly being created and destroyed.

Job Creation and Job Destruction

In early 2010 the unemployment rate hovered close to 10%. Even during good times, most Americans know someone who has lost his or her job. The U.S. unemployment rate in July 2007 was only 4.7%, relatively low by historical standards, yet in that month there were 4.5 million "job separations"—terminations of employment that occurred because a worker was either fired or quit voluntarily.

There are many reasons for such job loss. One is structural change in the economy: industries rise and fall as new technologies emerge and consumers' tastes change. For example, employment in high-tech industries such as telecommunications surged in the late 1990s but slumped severely after 2000. However, structural change also brings the creation of new jobs: since 2000, the number of jobs in the American health care sector has surged as new medical technologies have emerged and the aging of the population has increased the demand for medical care. Poor management performance or bad luck at individual companies also leads to job loss for their employees. For example, in 2013, smartphone maker BlackBerry announced plans to eliminate about 4,500 jobs after years of lagging sales, even as companies such as Apple and Samsung faced growing demand for their phones.

AP® Exam Tip

Be prepared to identify the type of unemployment given a specific scenario in both the multiple-choice and free-response questions on the AP® exam.

PD To prepare for teaching this lesson, you may want to consult the **Module 13 Sample Lecture** in the TRM.

OPEN & CLOSE Start Here

Play the song "Blue Collar Man" by Styx. After students listen to the lyrics, ask them the following questions:

- What do you think the artist meant by "long nights" and "impossible odds"? *Answers will vary.*
- Does high cyclical unemployment affect the wages that prospective employees are willing to accept? *Yes, because workers unable to find a job are more willing to accept lower wages to pay their bills.*

TEACH Connect It

Show students a diagram of the business cycle, like the one below. Ask how much unemployment they believe exists at the peak of the business cycle. *Something greater than zero.* There is always some unemployment even when jobs are plentiful. Ask students to think of a new business that has opened or one that has shut down recently. *When businesses start up during an expansion or close down during a contraction and as technology changes, jobs are created and destroyed, impacting the unemployment rate.*

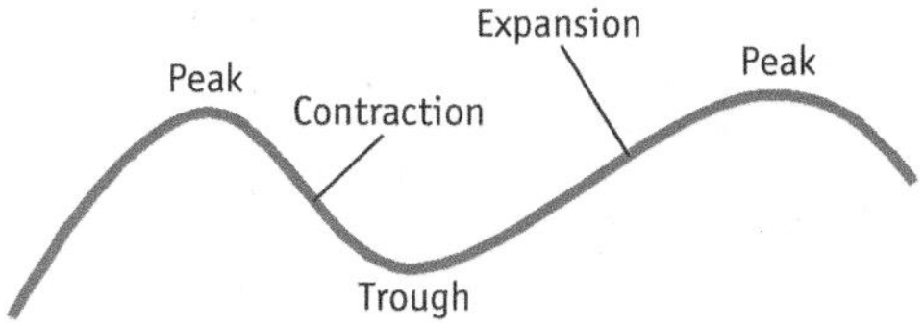

St. Louis Federal Reserve Bank Resources

***The Story of Unemployment Online Course*, Lesson 2**

This lesson focuses on the three types of unemployment, efforts by the government and the Federal Reserve to reduce unemployment, and the role of education in limiting the incidence of unemployment.

TEACH Teach It

Explain that frictional unemployment includes workers entering the labor market for the first time and those who are between jobs. A college student who graduates but doesn't find a job for a month and a truck driver who has decided to quit her job with one company because she believes there is a better driving route with a competitor are examples of frictionally unemployed workers. Ask students to think of other examples of frictional unemployment.

TEACH Teach It

A certain amount of frictional unemployment is regarded as somewhat desirable because it indicates there is mobility as people change or seek jobs. If workers are seeking new jobs that better fit their skills or lifestyle, this increases productivity and efficiency in the labor markets. It is part of the natural rate of unemployment because it always exists in the economy.

FOCUS Active Learning

Hold a debate on the benefits and drawbacks of offering unemployment benefits to laid off workers. The drawback to offering benefits is that it may reduce the incentive to quickly find a new job. That means more people will stay unemployed because they have an income to fall back on. The alternative to providing unemployment benefits is to provide nothing and let workers, and their families, fend for themselves. This may cause strain on other social service programs available through the state. Unemployment benefits can give job-seekers the ability both to provide for their families while searching for a job and also to take the time to find better jobs.

FOCUS Active Learning

Students can watch the short video by Jacob Clifford entitled "Unemployment" (see econextras video list with hyperlinks on the bcs and TRFD) to review the three types of unemployment. Ask students to define each of the types after the video.

During the housing slump of 2009 when unemployment was running very high, many construction workers resorted to more traditional methods of finding work.

This constant churning of the workforce is an inevitable feature of the modern economy. And this churning, in turn, is one source of *frictional unemployment*—one main reason that there is a considerable amount of unemployment even when jobs are abundant.

Frictional Unemployment

Workers who lose a job involuntarily due to job destruction often choose not to take the first new job offered. For example, suppose a skilled programmer, laid off because her software company's product line was unsuccessful, sees a help-wanted ad for clerical work in the local newspaper. She might respond to the ad and get the job—but that would be foolish. Instead, she should take the time to look for a job that takes advantage of her skills and pays accordingly. In addition, individual workers are constantly leaving jobs voluntarily, typically for personal reasons—family moves, dissatisfaction, and better job prospects elsewhere.

Economists say that workers who spend time looking for employment are engaged in **job search**. If all workers and all jobs were alike, job search wouldn't be necessary; if information about jobs and workers were perfect, job search would be very quick. In practice, however, it's normal for a worker who loses a job, or a young worker seeking a first job, to spend at least a few weeks searching.

Frictional unemployment is unemployment due to the time workers spend in job search. A certain amount of frictional unemployment is inevitable, for two reasons. One is the constant process of job creation and job destruction. The other is the fact that new workers are always entering the labor market. For example, in January 2014, out of 10.2 million workers counted as unemployed, 1.2 million were new entrants to the workforce and another 2.9 million were "re-entrants"—people who had come back after being out of the workforce for a time.

A limited amount of frictional unemployment is relatively harmless and may even be a good thing. The economy is more productive if workers take the time to find jobs that are well matched to their skills, and workers who are unemployed for a brief period while searching for the right job don't experience great hardship. In fact, when there is a low unemployment rate, periods of unemployment tend to be quite short, suggesting that much of the unemployment is frictional. **Figure 13.1** shows the composition of unemployment in 2000, when the unemployment rate was only 4%. Forty-five percent of the unemployed had been unemployed for less than 5 weeks and only 23% had been unemployed for 15 or more weeks. Just 11% were considered to be "long-term unemployed"—unemployed for 27 or more weeks. The picture looked very different in January 2010, after unemployment had been high for an extended period of time.

Workers who spend time looking for employment are engaged in **job search**.

Frictional unemployment is unemployment due to the time workers spend in job search.

AP® Exam Tip

Frictional unemployment always exists in an economy. There are always people looking for better jobs or even their first job.

Figure 13.1 Distribution of the Unemployed by Duration of Unemployment, 2000 and 2010

In years when the unemployment rate is low, most unemployed workers are unemployed for only a short period. In 2000, a year of low unemployment, 45% of the unemployed had been unemployed for less than 5 weeks and 77% for less than 15 weeks. The short duration of unemployment for most workers suggests that most unemployment in 2000 was frictional. In early 2010, by contrast, only 20% of the unemployed had been unemployed for less than 5 weeks, but 41% had been unemployed for 27 or more weeks, indicating that during periods of high unemployment, a smaller share of unemployment is frictional.
Source: Bureau of Labor Statistics.

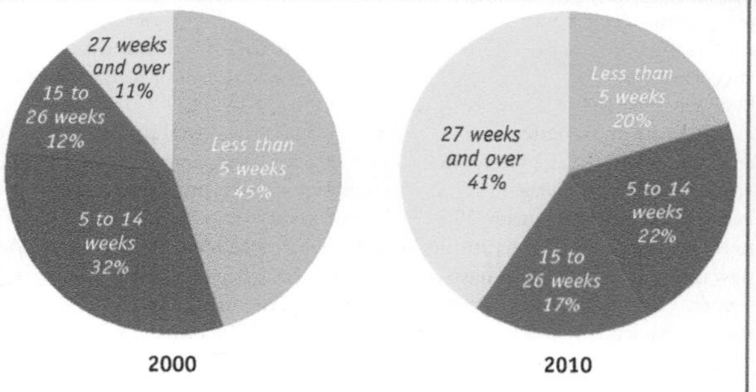

St. Louis Federal Reserve Bank Resources

"What Is Unemployment, How Is It Measured, and Why Does the Fed Care?"

In this lesson, students read and interpret choropleth maps, which contain unemployment data. They compare verbal descriptions of the labor market from the Federal Reserve's *Beige Book* with the mapped data. In addition, students compare unemployment data for different years. Students access or observe how to access this data online, using GeoFRED®.

"Why Scarce Resources Are Sometimes Unemployed," ***Page One Economics***

The unemployment rate always seems to be in the news, but did you know there are different kinds of unemployment? There is the natural rate of unemployment; cyclical, frictional, and structural unemployment; plus underemployment. Student questions are included.

In periods of higher unemployment, workers tend to be jobless for longer periods of time, suggesting that a smaller share of unemployment is frictional. By early 2010, when unemployment had been high for several months, for instance, the fraction of unemployed workers considered "long-term unemployed" had jumped to 41%.

Public policy designed to help workers who lose their jobs can lead to frictional unemployment as an unintended side effect. Most economically advanced countries provide benefits to laid-off workers as a way to tide them over until they find a new job. In the United States, these benefits typically replace only a small fraction of a worker's income and expire after 26 weeks. In other countries, particularly in Europe, benefits are more generous and last longer. The drawback to this generosity is that it reduces the incentive to quickly find a new job. By keeping more people searching for longer, the benefits increase frictional unemployment. Generous unemployment benefits in some European countries are widely believed to be one of the main causes of "Eurosclerosis," the persistent high unemployment that afflicts a number of European economies.

Structural Unemployment

Frictional unemployment exists even when the number of people seeking jobs is equal to the number of jobs being offered—that is, the existence of frictional unemployment doesn't mean that there is a surplus of labor. Sometimes, however, there is a *persistent surplus* of job-seekers in a particular labor market. For example, there may be more workers with a particular skill than there are jobs available using that skill, or there may be more workers in a particular geographic region than there are jobs available in that region. **Structural unemployment** is unemployment that results when workers lack the skills required for the available jobs, or there are more people seeking jobs in a labor market than there are jobs available at the current wage rate.

The supply and demand model tells us that the price of a good, service, or factor of production tends to move toward an equilibrium level that matches the quantity supplied with the quantity demanded. This is equally true, in general, of labor markets. **Figure 13.2** shows a typical market for labor. The labor demand curve indicates that when the price of labor—the wage rate—increases, employers demand less labor. The labor supply curve indicates that when the price of labor increases, more workers are willing to supply labor at the prevailing wage rate. These two forces coincide to lead to

Structural unemployment is unemployment that results when workers lack the skills required for the available jobs, or there are more people seeking jobs in a labor market than there are jobs available at the current wage rate.

AP® Exam Tip

Structural unemployment is common in an economy. Its causes include lack of skills, automation, geographic migration, minimum wages, and insufficient product demand.

Figure 13.2 The Effect of a Minimum Wage on the Labor Market

When the government sets a minimum wage, W_F, that exceeds the market equilibrium wage rate, W_E, the number of workers, Q_S, who would like to work at that minimum wage is greater than the number of workers, Q_D, demanded at that wage rate. This surplus of labor is considered structural unemployment.

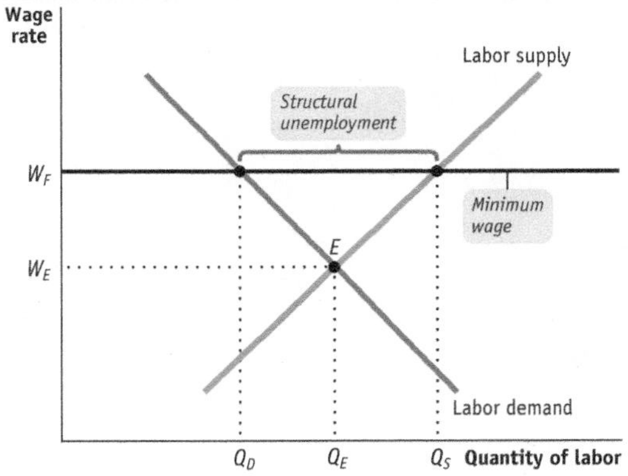

FOCUS Graph It

Ask students to use their personal whiteboards or notebook paper to draw a labor market that is experiencing a minimum wage. Once all the students have shown you that they can draw a price floor, ask them what they believe will happen to the quantity of labor supplied and demanded as a result of the minimum wage. *Quantity supplied increases (higher wage so workers want to work more), while quantity demanded decreases (higher wage so firms cut back on hiring).* Then use Figure 13.2 to discuss the impact of a minimum wage on the labor market. Ask, "Why is this considered structural unemployment?" *More people want to work than can find jobs at the minimum wage.*

TEACH Teach It

A labor union will negotiate with employers on behalf of its workers. The goal is usually to raise wages above market equilibrium. Ask students to explain why a union action is similar to a minimum wage causing structural unemployment. *The union negotiates a wage that is the lowest wage an employer can pay. This is similar to a price floor. At the higher wage, more people are willing to work than employers are willing to hire.* On their personal whiteboards or notebook paper, have students draw a labor market graph showing a wage labeled W_{union} negotiated by a union. *The graph will look like Figure 13.2 with the wage labeled* W_{union} *somewhere above equilibrium.*

TEACH Teach It

Structural unemployment exists when either workers lack the skills required for the available jobs or there are more people seeking jobs in a labor market than there are jobs available at the current wage rate. This may be due to changes in the structural demand for labor—for example, when certain skills become obsolete or the geographic distribution of jobs changes. Robots replacing workers on an assembly line or an automobile manufacturer moving its assembly plant to another state are both causes of structural unemployment.

FOCUS Active Learning

Show a clip from Seinfeld: Season 2's "Revenge" episode on unemployment (see econextras video list with hyperlinks on the bcs and TRFD). Based on their readings, ask students to identify the types of employment George Costanza is facing:

A. cyclical unemployment *(real estate jobs are unavailable due to a weak economy)*

B. structural unemployment *(George doesn't have the skills required to be a projectionist or a college professor)*

C. frictional unemployment *(George quit his job voluntarily to seek a better job)*

TEACH Connect It

The minimum wage is a price floor, so in some industries, there may always be structural unemployment because a surplus of labor may always exist. Can you give an example of an industry where that might occur? *Answers will vary. Examples include fast-food restaurants and any commercial retailers.*

FOCUS Flip It

For reinforcement and review of a price floor, have students watch Jacob Clifford's "Minimum Wage" video (see econextras video list with hyperlinks on the bcs and TRFD).

an equilibrium wage rate for any given type of labor in a particular location. That equilibrium wage rate is shown as W_E.

Even at the equilibrium wage rate, W_E, there will still be some frictional unemployment. That's because there will always be some workers engaged in job search even when the number of jobs available is equal to the number of workers seeking jobs. But there wouldn't be any structural unemployment caused by a surplus of labor, as there is when the wage rate, for some reason, is persistently above W_E. Several factors can lead to a wage rate in excess of W_E, the most important being minimum wages, labor unions, *efficiency wages,* and the side effects of government policies.

Minimum Wages As explained in Module 8, a minimum wage is a government-mandated floor on the price of labor. In the United States, the national minimum wage in mid-2014 was \$7.25 an hour. For many American workers, the minimum wage is irrelevant; the market equilibrium wage for these workers is well above this price floor. But for less skilled workers, the minimum wage may be binding—it affects the wages that people are actually paid and can lead to structural unemployment. In countries that have higher minimum wages, the range of workers for whom the minimum wage is binding is larger.

Figure 13.2 shows the effect of a binding minimum wage. In this market, there is a legal floor on wages, W_F, which is above the equilibrium wage rate, W_E. This leads to a persistent surplus in the labor market: the quantity of labor supplied, Q_S, is larger than the quantity demanded, Q_D. In other words, more people want to work than can find jobs at the minimum wage, leading to structural unemployment.

Given that minimum wages—that is, binding minimum wages—generally lead to structural unemployment, you might wonder why governments impose them. The rationale is to help ensure that people who work can earn enough income to afford at least a minimally comfortable lifestyle. However, this may come at a cost, because it may eliminate employment opportunities for some workers who would have willingly worked for lower wages. As illustrated in Figure 13.2, not only are there more sellers of labor than there are buyers, but there are also fewer people working at a minimum wage (Q_D) than there would have been with no minimum wage at all (Q_E).

Although economists broadly agree that a high minimum wage has the employment-reducing effects shown in Figure 13.2, there is some question about whether this is a good description of how the minimum wage actually works in the United States. The minimum wage in the United States is quite low compared with that in other wealthy countries. For three decades, from the 1970s to the mid-2000s, the U.S. minimum wage was so low that it was not binding for the vast majority of workers—employers paid most workers more than the minimum wage. In addition, some researchers have produced evidence that increases in the minimum wage actually lead to higher employment when, as was the case in the United States at one time, the minimum wage is low compared to average wages. They argue that firms that employ low-skilled workers sometimes restrict their hiring in order to keep wages low and that, as a result, the minimum wage can sometimes be increased without any loss of jobs. Most economists, however, agree that a sufficiently high minimum wage *does* lead to structural unemployment.

Bill Pugliano/Stringer/Getty Images

Members of the United Auto Workers (UAW) union march on a picket line during a strike to protest unfair labor practices.

Labor Unions The actions of *labor unions* can have effects similar to those of minimum wages, leading to structural unemployment. By bargaining collectively for all of a firm's workers, unions can often win higher wages from employers than workers would have obtained by bargaining individually. This process, known as *collective bargaining,* is intended to tip the scales of bargaining power more toward workers and away from employers. Labor unions exercise bargaining power by threatening firms with a *labor strike,* a collective refusal to work. The threat of a strike can have very serious consequences for firms that have difficulty replacing striking workers.

In such cases, workers acting collectively can exercise more power than they could if they acted individually.

When workers have greater bargaining power, they tend to demand and receive higher wages. Unions also bargain over benefits, such as health care and pensions, which we can think of as additional wages. Indeed, economists who study the effects of unions on wages find that unionized workers earn higher wages and more generous benefits than non-union workers with similar skills. The result of these increased wages can be the same as the result of a minimum wage: labor unions push the wage that workers receive above the equilibrium wage. Consequently, there are more people willing to work at the wage being paid than there are jobs available. Like a binding minimum wage, this leads to structural unemployment.

Efficiency Wages Actions by firms may also contribute to structural unemployment. Firms may choose to pay **efficiency wages**—wages that employers set above the equilibrium wage rate as an incentive for their workers to deliver better performance.

Employers may feel the need for such incentives for several reasons. For example, employers often have difficulty directly observing how hard an employee works. They can, however, elicit more work effort by paying above-market wages: employees receiving these higher wages are more likely to work harder to ensure that they aren't fired, which would cause them to lose their higher wages.

When many firms pay efficiency wages, the result is a pool of workers who want jobs but can't find them. So the use of efficiency wages by firms leads to structural unemployment.

Efficiency wages are wages that employers set above the equilibrium wage rate as an incentive for better employee performance.

The **natural rate of unemployment** is the unemployment rate that arises from the effects of frictional plus structural unemployment.

Cyclical unemployment is the deviation of the actual rate of unemployment from the natural rate.

The Natural Rate of Unemployment

Because some frictional unemployment is inevitable and because many economies also suffer from structural unemployment, a certain amount of unemployment is normal, or "natural." Actual unemployment fluctuates around this normal level. The **natural rate of unemployment** is the rate of unemployment that arises from the effects of frictional plus structural unemployment. It is the normal unemployment rate around which the actual unemployment rate fluctuates. **Figure 13.3** on the next page provides estimates of the natural rates of unemployment in the 34 relatively wealthy countries that belong to the Organization for Economic Cooperation and Development (OECD). **Cyclical unemployment** is the deviation of the actual rate of unemployment from the natural rate; that is, it is the difference between the actual and natural rates of unemployment. As the name suggests, cyclical unemployment is the share of unemployment that arises from the business cycle. We'll see later that public policy cannot keep the unemployment rate persistently below the natural rate without leading to accelerating inflation.

We can summarize the relationships between the various types of unemployment as follows:

(13-1) Natural unemployment =
Frictional unemployment + Structural unemployment

(13-2) Actual unemployment =
Natural unemployment + Cyclical unemployment

Perhaps because of its name, people often imagine that the natural rate of unemployment is a constant that doesn't change over time and can't be affected by policy. Neither proposition is true. Let's take a moment to stress two facts: the natural rate of unemployment changes over time, and it can be affected by economic policies.

AP® Exam Tip

The natural rate of unemployment is never zero because frictional employment always exists in an economy.

Changes in the Natural Rate of Unemployment

Private-sector economists and government agencies need estimates of the natural rate of unemployment both to make forecasts and to conduct policy analyses. Almost all these estimates show that the U.S. natural rate rises and falls over time. For example,

FOCUS In the News

TRM Listen to NPR's 2013 podcast "Structural or Cyclical? The Type of Unemployment Matters" (see econextras video list with hyperlinks on the bcs and TRFD). Use **Worksheet 13.2 (Structural or Cyclical)** from the TRM for questions on this podcast.

FOCUS Flip It

TRM Have students watch Jacob Clifford's video "NRU" (see econextras video list with hyperlinks on the bcs and TRFD). Assign **Worksheet 13.3 (Unemployment and Natural Rate of Unemployment)** from the TRM for questions on this video.

TEACH Teach It

Firms may choose to pay efficiency wages—wages that employers set above the equilibrium wage rate as an incentive for their workers to deliver better performance. If the efficiency wage results in a surplus of workers, it has created structural unemployment.

FOCUS Active Learning

TRM To give students practice with classifying different types of unemployment using scenarios, assign **Worksheet 13.1 (Classifying Unemployment)** from the TRM.

TEACH Teach It

Make sure students understand the difference between the actual rate and the natural rate of unemployment. They will see this again when you study the Phillips curve.

FOCUS Active Learning

Ask your students to provide examples of changes in the natural rate of unemployment in the local area based on changes in labor force characteristics, market institutions, or government policies. *Answers will vary based on the geographic region, but may include aging population, a recently unionized facility, a new high-tech employer that moved to the area, or extensions to unemployment benefits.*

Figure 13.3 Natural Unemployment in OECD Countries

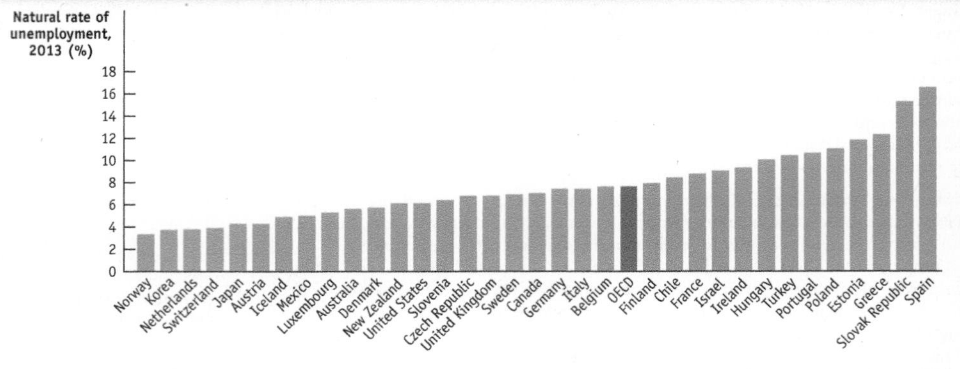

Among members of the OECD, estimates of the natural rates of unemployment in 2013 ranged from 3.3% in Norway to 16.5% in Spain. The blue bar shows the average across all the OECD countries, 7.6%. The U.S. natural rate of unemployment, 6.1%, is low relative to both the average rate and the rates in the major European economies of the United Kingdom, Germany, Italy, France, and Spain. As mentioned earlier, the rates in Europe may be elevated by frictional unemployment caused by generous unemployment benefits. In addition, high minimum wages in Europe can discourage employers from offering jobs and lead to higher rates of structural unemployment.

Source: OECD.

the Congressional Budget Office, the independent agency that conducts budget and economic analyses for Congress, believes that the U.S. natural rate of unemployment was 5.3% in 1950, rose to 6.3% by the end of the 1970s, and fell back to 5.0% from late 1999 until early 2008. In 2013, the estimated rate was back up to 6%. European countries have experienced even larger swings in their natural rates of unemployment.

What causes the natural rate of unemployment to change? The most important factors are changes in the characteristics of the labor force, changes in labor market institutions, and changes in government policies. Let's look briefly at each factor.

Changes in Labor Force Characteristics In January 2014 the overall rate of unemployment in the United States was 6.6%. Young workers, however, had much higher unemployment rates: 20.7% for teenagers and 12.9% for workers aged 20 to 24. Workers aged 25 to 54 had an unemployment rate of only 6.1%.

In general, unemployment rates tend to be lower for experienced than for inexperienced workers. Because experienced workers tend to stay in a given job longer than do inexperienced ones, they have lower frictional unemployment. Also, because older workers are more likely than young workers to be family breadwinners, they have a stronger incentive to find and keep jobs.

One reason the natural rate of unemployment rose during the 1970s was a large rise in the number of new workers—children of the post–World War II baby boom entered the labor force, as did a rising percentage of married women. As **Figure 13.4** shows, both the percentage of the labor force less than 25 years old and the percentage of women in the labor force surged in the 1970s. By the end of the 1990s, however, the share of women in the labor force had leveled off and the percentage of workers under 25 had fallen sharply. As a result, the labor force as a whole is more experienced today than it was in the 1970s, one likely reason that the natural rate of unemployment is lower today than in the 1970s.

134 Section 3 Measurement of Economic Performance

Figure 13.4 The Changing Makeup of the U.S. Labor Force, 1948–2013

In the 1970s the percentage of the labor force consisting of women rose rapidly, as did the percentage under age 25. These changes reflected the entry of large numbers of women into the paid labor force for the first time and the fact that baby boomers were reaching working age. The natural rate of unemployment may have risen because many of these workers were relatively inexperienced. Today, the labor force is much more experienced, which is one possible reason the natural rate has fallen since the 1970s.
Source: Bureau of Labor Statistics.

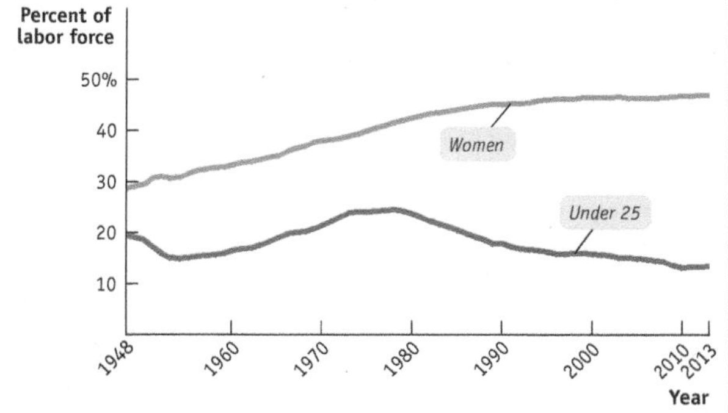

Changes in Labor Market Institutions As we pointed out earlier, unions that negotiate wages above the equilibrium level can be a source of structural unemployment. Some economists believe that strong labor unions are one of the reasons for the high natural rate of unemployment in Europe. In the United States, a sharp fall in union membership after 1980 may have been one reason the natural rate of unemployment fell between the 1970s and the 1990s.

Other institutional changes may also have been at work. For example, some labor economists believe that temporary employment agencies, which have proliferated in recent years, have reduced frictional unemployment by matching workers to jobs. Furthermore, Internet websites such as monster.com may have reduced frictional unemployment by making information about job openings and job-seekers more widely available, thereby helping workers avoid a prolonged job search.

Technological change, coupled with labor market institutions, can also affect the natural rate of unemployment. Technological change probably leads to an increase in the demand for skilled workers who are familiar with the relevant technology and a reduction in the demand for unskilled workers. Economic theory predicts that wages should increase for skilled workers and decrease for unskilled workers. But if wages for unskilled workers cannot go down—say, due to a binding minimum wage—increased structural unemployment, and therefore a higher natural rate of unemployment, will result.

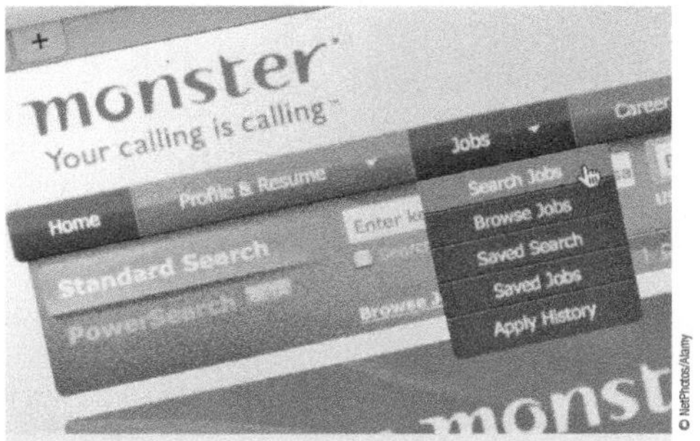

Websites such as monster.com may have reduced frictional unemployment by helping to match employers with job-seekers.

Changes in Government Policies A high minimum wage can cause structural unemployment. Generous unemployment benefits can increase frictional unemployment. So government policies intended to help workers can have the undesirable side effect of raising the natural rate of unemployment.

Some government policies, however, may reduce the natural rate. Two examples are job training and employment subsidies. Job -training programs are supposed to provide unemployed workers with skills that widen the range of jobs they can perform. Employment subsidies are payments either to workers or to employers that provide a financial incentive to accept or offer jobs.

FOCUS Active Learning

In considering Figure 13.4, ask your students the following questions: What are the long-run trends for women and workers under the age of 25? *More women are working and fewer people under the age of 25 are working.* What do you think accounts for the rise in the number of women? *Possible answers include more single-family households, higher costs of living, and more opportunities for women in the workplace.* What do you think accounts for the decrease in the number of workers under the age of 25? *Possible answers include more young people staying in college or entering the military, smaller families, and higher household incomes that allow more students to stay at home.*

St. Louis Federal Reserve Bank Resources

"Would Increasing the Minimum Wage Reduce Poverty?," *Page One Economics*

This essay highlights the trade-off presented by increasing the minimum wage, based on a nonpartisan Congressional Budget Office analysis. The essay explains the debate and discusses whether other approaches may be more effective in helping alleviate poverty.

FYI Structural Unemployment in Eastern Germany

In one of the most dramatic events in world history, a spontaneous popular uprising in 1989 overthrew the communist dictatorship in East Germany. Citizens quickly tore down the wall that had divided Berlin, and in short order East and West Germany became a united, democratic nation.

Then the trouble started.

After reunification, employment in East Germany plunged and the unemployment rate soared. This high unemployment rate has persisted: despite receiving massive aid from the federal German government, the economy of the former East Germany has remained persistently depressed, with an unemployment rate of 10.1% in December 2013, compared to West Germany's unemployment rate of 6%. Other parts of formerly communist Eastern Europe have done much better. For example, the Czech Republic, which was often cited along with East Germany as a relatively successful communist economy, had a comparatively lower unemployment rate of only 7.7% in December 2013. What went wrong in East Germany?

The answer is that, through nobody's fault, East Germany found itself suffering from severe structural unemployment. When Germany was reunified, it became clear that workers in East Germany were much less productive than their cousins in the west. Yet unions initially demanded wage rates equal to those in West Germany, and these wage rates have been slow to come down because East German workers don't want to be treated as inferior to their West German counterparts. Meanwhile, productivity in the former East Germany has remained well below West German levels, in part because of decades of misguided investment. The result has been a persistently large mismatch between the number of workers demanded and the number of those seeking jobs.

After reunification in 1989, East Germany found itself suffering from severe structural unemployment that continues to this day.

MODULE 13 Review

Check Your Understanding

1. Explain the following.
   a. Frictional unemployment always exists.
   b. Frictional unemployment accounts for a larger share of total unemployment when the unemployment rate is low.
2. Why does collective bargaining have the same general effect on unemployment as a minimum wage? Illustrate your answer with a diagram.
3. Suppose the United States dramatically increases benefits for unemployed workers. Explain what will happen to the natural rate of unemployment.

OPEN & CLOSE Exit Slip

*TRM Please see **Exit Slip: Module 13** in the TRM for formative multiple-choice questions to ask your students before finishing your lesson. These questions will help you quickly assess whether your students have mastered the module's concepts before moving on.*

Answers to the Exit Slip Questions

1. B
2. A
3. B

Answers to Module 13 Review Questions

Check Your Understanding

1. a. Frictional unemployment is unemployment due to the time workers spend searching for jobs. It is inevitable because workers may leave one job in search of another for a variety of reasons. Furthermore, there will always be new entrants in the labor force who are seeking a first job. During the search process, these individuals will be counted as part of the frictionally unemployed.

b. When the unemployment rate is low, frictional unemployment will account for a larger share of total unemployment because other sources of unemployment will be diminished. Thus, the share of total unemployment composed of the frictionally unemployed will rise.

2. A binding minimum wage represents a price floor below which wages cannot fall. As a result, actual wages cannot move toward equilibrium. A minimum wage therefore causes the quantity of labor supplied to exceed the quantity of labor demanded. Because this surplus of labor reflects unemployed workers, it affects the unemployment rate. Collective bargaining has a similar effect—unions are able to raise the wage above the equilibrium level. This will act like a minimum wage by causing the number of job-seekers to be larger than the number of workers firms are willing to hire. Collective bargaining causes the unemployment rate to be higher than it otherwise would be, as shown in the accompanying figure.

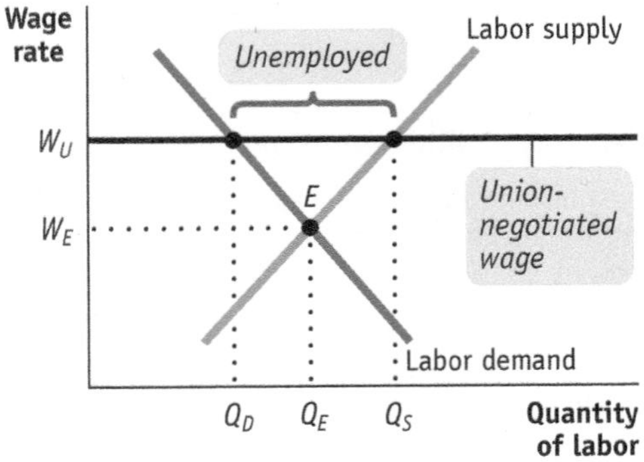

3. An increase in unemployment benefits reduces the cost to individuals of being unemployed, causing them to spend more time searching for a new job. Thus, the natural rate of unemployment would increase.

Tackle the Test: Multiple-Choice Questions

1. A person who moved to a new state and took two months to find a new job experienced which type of unemployment?
   a. frictional
   b. structural
   c. cyclical
   d. natural
   e. none of the above
2. What type of unemployment is created by a recession?
   a. frictional
   b. structural
   c. cyclical
   d. natural
   e. none of the above
3. A person who is unemployed because of a mismatch between the quantity of labor supplied and the quantity of labor demanded is experiencing what type of unemployment?
   a. frictional
   b. structural
   c. cyclical
   d. natural
   e. none of the above
4. Which of the following is true of the natural rate of unemployment?
   I. It includes frictional unemployment.
   II. It includes structural unemployment.
   III. It is equal to 0%.
   a. I only
   b. II only
   c. III only
   d. I and II
   e. I, II, and III
5. Which of the following can affect the natural rate of unemployment in an economy over time?
   a. labor force characteristics such as age and work experience
   b. the existence of labor unions
   c. advances in technologies that help workers find jobs
   d. government job-training programs
   e. all of the above

Tackle the Test: Free-Response Questions

1. a. The natural rate of unemployment is made up of which of the types of unemployment?
   b. Explain how cyclical unemployment relates to the natural rate of unemployment.
   c. List three factors that can lead to a change in the natural rate of unemployment.

Rubric for FRQ 1 (6 points)

1 point: The natural rate of unemployment is made up of frictional unemployment . . .

1 point: . . . plus structural unemployment.

1 point: Cyclical unemployment is the deviation of the actual rate of unemployment from the natural rate. *Or*, cyclical unemployment is the difference between the actual and natural rates of unemployment.

1 point: Changes in labor force characteristics

1 point: Changes in labor market institutions such as unions

1 point: Changes in government policies

2. In each of the following situations, what type of unemployment is Melanie facing? Explain.
   a. After completing a complex programming project, Melanie is laid off. Her prospects for a new job requiring similar skills are good, and she has signed up with a programmer placement service. She has passed up offers for low-paying jobs.
   b. Melanie loses her programming job because the development of new packaged software programs means employers no longer need to hire as many programmers.
   c. Due to the current slump in investment spending, Melanie has been laid off from her programming job. Her employer promises to rehire her when business picks up.
   (6 points)

Tackle the Test: Multiple-Choice Questions

1. a
2. c
3. b
4. d
5. e

Tackle the Test: Free-Response Question

Rubric for FRQ 2 (6 points)

1 point: Frictional

1 point: Melanie is between jobs.

1 point: Structural

1 point: Melanie is unemployed because the demand for her skills has decreased.

1 point: Cyclical

1 point: Melanie is unemployed due to an economic slowdown (recession).

PD To prepare for teaching this lesson, you may want to consult the **Module 14 Sample Lecture** in the TRM.

OPEN & CLOSE **Start Here**

TRM Conduct **Activity 14.1 (Level or Rate?)** found in the TRM. This activity will help your students see how inflation impacts their purchasing power.

AP PHOTO/PAUL SAKUMA

MODULE 14 Inflation: An Overview

In this Module, you will learn to:

- Calculate the rate of inflation
- Specify the economic costs of inflation
- Identify who is helped and who is hurt by inflation
- Explain why policy makers try to maintain a stable rate of inflation
- Differentiate between real and nominal values of income, wages, and interest rates
- Discuss the problems of deflation and disinflation

Inflation and Deflation

In 1980 Americans were dismayed about the state of the economy for two reasons: the unemployment rate was high, and so was inflation. In fact, the high rate of inflation, not the high rate of unemployment, was the principal concern of policy makers at the time—so much so that Paul Volcker, the chairman of the Federal Reserve Board (which controls monetary policy), more or less deliberately created a deep recession in order to bring inflation under control. Only in 1982, after inflation had dropped sharply and the unemployment rate had risen to more than 10%, did fighting unemployment become the chief priority.

Why is inflation something to worry about? Why do policy makers even now get anxious when they see the inflation rate moving upward? The answer is that inflation can impose costs on the economy—but not in the way most people think.

The Level of Prices Doesn't Matter . . .

The most common complaint about inflation, an increase in the price level, is that it makes everyone poorer—after all, a given amount of money buys less. But inflation does *not* make everyone poorer. To see why, it's helpful to imagine what would happen if the United States did something other countries have done from time to time—replaced the dollar with a new currency.

An example of this kind of currency conversion happened in 2002, when France, like a number of other European countries, replaced its national currency, the franc, with the new Pan-European currency, the euro. People turned in their franc coins and notes, and received euro coins and notes in exchange, at a rate of precisely 6.55957 francs per euro. At the same time, all contracts were restated in euros at the same rate of exchange.

St. Louis Federal Reserve Bank Resources

"Inflation," *The Economic Lowdown Podcast Series*, Episode 4

This podcast on inflation discusses three aspects of inflation: what it is, what causes it, and how it is measured. The episode also addresses deflation, disinflation, and the role of the Federal Reserve in monitoring inflation.

138 **Section 3** Measurement of Economic Performance

For example, if a French citizen had a home mortgage debt of 500,000 francs, this became a debt of 500,000/6.55957 = 76,224.51 euros. If a worker's contract specified that he or she should be paid 100 francs per hour, it became a contract specifying a wage of 100/6.55957 = 15.2449 euros per hour, and so on.

You could imagine doing the same thing here, replacing the dollar with a "new dollar" at a rate of exchange of, say, 7 to 1. If you owed $140,000 on your home, that would become a debt of 20,000 new dollars. If you had a wage rate of $14 an hour, it would become 2 new dollars an hour, and so on. This would bring the overall U.S. price level back to about what it was when John F. Kennedy was president.

So would everyone be richer as a result because prices would be only one-seventh as high? Of course not. Prices would be lower, but so would wages and incomes in general. If you cut a worker's wage to one-seventh of its previous value, but also cut all prices to one-seventh of their previous level, the worker's **real wage**—the wage rate divided by the price level to adjust for the effects of inflation or deflation—doesn't change. In fact, bringing the overall price level back to what it was during the Kennedy administration would have no effect on overall purchasing power, because doing so would reduce income exactly as much as it reduced prices. Conversely, the rise in prices that has actually taken place since the early 1960s hasn't made America poorer, because it has also raised incomes by the same amount: **real income**—income divided by the price level to adjust for the effects of inflation or deflation—hasn't been affected by the rise in overall prices.

The moral of this story is that the *level* of prices doesn't matter: the United States would be no richer than it is now if the overall level of prices was still as low as it was in 1961; conversely, the rise in prices over the past 45 years hasn't made us poorer.

The **real wage** is the wage rate divided by the price level to adjust for the effects of inflation or deflation.

Real income is income divided by the price level to adjust for the effects of inflation or deflation.

AP® Exam Tip

Inflation is an increase in the general price level that causes the real value of money to decrease. That means your dollar will buy less today than it could buy in previous years.

. . . But the Rate of Change of Prices Does

The conclusion that the level of prices doesn't matter might seem to imply that the inflation rate doesn't matter either. But that's not true.

To see why, it's crucial to distinguish between the *level of prices* and the *inflation rate*. In the next module, we will discuss precisely how the level of prices in the economy is measured using price indexes such as the consumer price index. For now, let's look at the **inflation rate**, the percentage increase in the overall level of prices per year. The inflation rate is calculated as follows:

$$\text{Inflation rate} = \frac{\text{Price level in year 2} - \text{Price level in year 1}}{\text{Price level in year 1}} \times 100$$

The **inflation rate** is the percentage increase in the overall level of prices per year.

Figure 14.1 on the next page highlights the difference between the price level and the inflation rate in the United States since 1969, with the price level measured along the left vertical axis and the inflation rate measured along the right vertical axis. In the 2000s, the overall level of prices in the United States was much higher than it was in 1969—but that, as we've learned, didn't matter. The inflation rate in the 2000s, however, was much lower than in the 1970s—and that almost certainly made the economy richer than it would have been if high inflation had continued.

Economists believe that high rates of inflation impose significant economic costs. The most important of these costs are *shoe-leather costs*, *menu costs*, and *unit-of-account costs*. We'll discuss each in turn.

Shoe-Leather Costs People hold money—cash in their wallets and bank deposits on which they can write checks—for convenience in making transactions. A high inflation rate, however, discourages people from holding money, because the purchasing power of the cash in their wallets and the funds in their bank accounts steadily erodes as the overall level of prices rises. This leads people to search for ways to reduce the amount of money they hold, often at considerable economic cost.

During the most famous of all inflations, the German *hyperinflation* of 1921–1923, merchants employed runners to take their cash to the bank many times a day to convert

FOCUS Active Learning

Print out a listing of movies equal to the number of students in your class (http://boxofficemojo.com/alltime/domestic.htm). Also print a copy of the GDP Deflator by Year, using 2009 as the base year (http://www.multpl.com/gdp-deflator/table for each student). Ask students to write down their prediction of the five top grossing movies of all time on a piece of paper and set it aside. Tell them they will be checking the real (2009) values to see if their guesses are correct. Pass around the handouts and assign each student a movie to determine the real GDP for it. Have students line up in order of real value and then ask the first five to state the movie they represent. See if their individual responses match what they guessed. *Example: Mary Poppins (1964) is number 554 on the list. ($102/18.49) × 100 = $552 (rounded to the nearest million).* Ask them how inflation impacts the price of goods and services. *It makes the nominal price increase relative to the real price.* As you progress through this section, refer to this exercise to remind students to think in terms of real values.

TEACH AP® Exam Tip

Make sure your students learn the formula for calculating the rate of inflation. They may be asked to use it on the AP® exam.

TEACH Teach It

When inflation is high, people don't want to hold onto cash because it loses its purchasing power. Shoe-leather cost is an allusion to the wear and tear caused by the extra running around that takes place when people are trying to change their money into something that will retain its value.

St. Louis Federal Reserve Bank Resources

The Great Inflation Online Course

In *The Great Inflation* online course, Jack of All Trades and his sidekick Andy time travel to the period known as The Great Inflation to discover the truth about inflation. Dr. Equilibrium helps them understand what exactly inflation is and how the Federal Reserve System plays a key role in maintaining stable prices.

Inflation Online Course

Inflation is a short, interactive online course that explains what inflation is and its impact on saving and spending decisions.

FOCUS In the News

TRM With your class, watch the *PBS NewsHour Extra* video "Digital Currency Bitcoin Attracts New Mainstream Appeal" (see econextras video list with hyperlinks on the bcs and TRFD). Use **Worksheet 14.2 (Bitcoin)** from the TRM for questions on this video.

FOCUS Active Learning

Menu costs are costs incurred by the sellers just to update the posted prices. The business owner must decide if the gains from increasing prices justify the cost of reprinting menus. Ask students to give examples of menu costs. *Answers will vary but might include the costs of changing signs at gas stations, restaurant menus, and price tags at stores.* Ask students if there are ways a business owner can avoid most menu costs. *Answers will vary, but might include not posting prices on the menu or printing the menu on a board where people can see it.* Do Internet retailers experience menu costs? *They may have more costs. It takes effort and time to update prices on sites like Macys.com, Overstock.com, and those of other retailers. This is true especially in times of higher inflation.* Do the costs of changing the prices mean that prices do not rise as fast as they would if there were no menu costs? *Answers will vary, but the costs are likely to inhibit some price changes, and as technology lowers those costs, prices may increase more often.*

Figure 14.1 The Price Level Versus the Inflation Rate, 1969–2013

Over the past 44 years, the price level has continuously gone up. But the *inflation rate*—the rate at which consumer prices are rising—has had both ups and downs.
Source: Bureau of Labor Statistics.

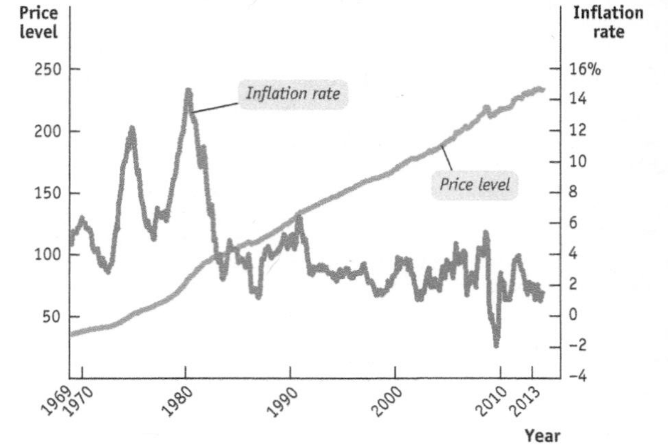

During the German hyperinflation of the early 1920s, people burned worthless paper money in their stoves.

Shoe-leather costs are the increased costs of transactions caused by inflation.

Menu costs are the real costs of changing listed prices.

it into something that would hold its value, such as a stable foreign currency. In an effort to avoid having the purchasing power of their money eroded, people used up valuable resources—the time and labor of the runners—that could have been used productively elsewhere. During the German hyperinflation, so many banking transactions were taking place that the number of employees at German banks nearly quadrupled—from around 100,000 in 1913 to 375,000 in 1923. More recently, Brazil experienced hyperinflation during the early 1990s; during that episode, the Brazilian banking sector grew so large that it accounted for 15% of GDP, more than twice the size of the financial sector in the United States measured as a share of GDP. The large increase in the Brazilian banking sector that was needed to cope with the consequences of inflation represented a loss of real resources to its society.

Increased costs of transactions caused by inflation are known as **shoe-leather costs**, an allusion to the wear and tear caused by the extra running around that takes place when people are trying to avoid holding money. Shoe-leather costs are substantial in economies with very high inflation rates, as anyone who has lived in such an economy—say, one suffering inflation of 100% or more per year—can attest. Most estimates suggest, however, that the shoe-leather costs of inflation at the rates seen in the United States—which in peacetime has never had inflation above 15%—are quite small.

Menu Costs In a modern economy, most of the things we buy have a listed price. There's a price listed under each item on a supermarket shelf, a price printed on the front page of your newspaper, a price listed for each dish on a restaurant's menu. Changing a listed price has a real cost, called a **menu cost**. For example, to change a price in a supermarket may require a clerk to change the price listed under the item on the shelf and an office worker to change the price associated with the item's UPC code in the store's computer. In the face of inflation, of course, firms are forced to change prices more often than they would if the price level was more or less stable. This means higher costs for the economy as a whole.

In times of very high inflation rates, menu costs can be substantial. During the Brazilian inflation of the early 1990s, for instance, supermarket workers reportedly spent half of their time replacing old price stickers with new ones. When the inflation

St. Louis Federal Reserve Bank Resources

"Making Sense of the Ups and Downs of Prices," *Page One Economics*

This essay makes the distinction between real and nominal prices, addresses the costs of inflation and deflation, and explains the importance of price stability. Student questions are included.

140 Section 3 Measurement of Economic Performance

FYI Israel's Experience with Inflation

It's hard to see the costs of inflation clearly because serious inflation is often associated with other problems that disrupt the economy and life in general, notably war or political instability (or both). In the mid-1980s, however, Israel experienced a "clean" inflation: there was no war, the government was stable, and there was order in the streets. Yet a series of policy errors led to very high inflation, with prices often rising more than 10% a month.

As it happens, one of the authors spent a month visiting Tel Aviv University at the height of the inflation, so we can give a first-hand account of the effects.

First, the shoe-leather costs of inflation were substantial. At the time, Israelis spent a lot of time in lines at the bank, moving money in and out of accounts that provided high enough interest rates to offset inflation. People walked around with very little cash in their wallets; they had to go to the bank whenever they needed to make even a moderately large cash payment. Banks responded by opening a lot of branches, a costly business expense.

Ricki Rosen/Corbis Saba

The shoe-leather costs of inflation in Israel: when the inflation rate hit 500% in 1985, people spent a lot of time in line at banks.

Second, although menu costs weren't that visible to a visitor, what you could see were the efforts businesses made to minimize them. For example, restaurant menus often didn't list prices. Instead, they listed numbers that you had to multiply by another number, written on a chalkboard and changed every day, to figure out the price of a dish.

Finally, it was hard to make decisions because prices changed so much and so often. It was a common experience to walk out of a store because prices were 25% higher than at one's usual shopping destination, only to discover that prices had just been increased 25% there, too.

rate is high, merchants may decide to stop listing prices in terms of the local currency and use either an artificial unit—in effect, measuring prices relative to one another—or a more stable currency, such as the U.S. dollar. This is exactly what the Israeli real estate market began doing in the mid-1980s: prices were quoted in U.S. dollars, even though payment was made in Israeli shekels. And this is also what happened in Zimbabwe when, in May 2008, official estimates of the inflation rate reached 1,694,000%.

Menu costs are also present in low-inflation economies, but they are not severe. In low-inflation economies, businesses might update their prices only sporadically—not daily or even more frequently, as is the case in high-inflation or hyperinflation economies. Also, with technological advances, menu costs are becoming less and less important, since prices can be changed electronically and fewer merchants attach price stickers to merchandise.

© Graham Oliver/Alamy

To fight menu costs, some restaurants list their prices with chalk.

Unit-of-Account Costs In the Middle Ages, contracts were often specified "in kind": for example, a tenant might be obliged to provide his landlord with a certain number of cattle each year (the phrase *in kind* actually comes from an ancient word for *cattle*). This may have made sense at the time, but it would be an awkward way to conduct modern business. Instead, we state contracts in monetary terms: a renter owes a certain number of dollars per month, a company that issues a bond promises to pay the bondholder the dollar value of the bond when it comes due, and so on. We also tend to make our economic calculations in dollars: a family planning its budget, or a small business owner trying to figure out how well the business is doing, makes estimates of the amount of money coming in and going out.

This role of the dollar as a basis for contracts and calculation is called the *unit-of-account* role of money. It's an important aspect of the modern economy. Yet it's a role that can be degraded by inflation, which causes the purchasing power of a dollar to change over time—a dollar next year is worth less than a dollar this year. The effect,

FOCUS Active Learning

Use this short video, "Interest Rates: Real vs Nominal Practice" from Jacob Clifford (see econ-extras video list with hyperlinks on the bcs and TRFD). Pause the video (1:42) and let the students calculate the effect of inflation on interest rates.

TEACH Teach It

Unit-of-account costs are the costs arising from the way inflation makes money a less reliable unit of measurement. Review the tax system example with students to ensure they understand the problems associated with unit-of-account costs.

Module 14 Inflation: An Overview 141

TEACH AP® Exam Tip

Because lenders understand that they may be hurt by inflation, they charge enough interest to compensate for the expected inflation rate. The lenders try to anticipate what the real interest rate will be over the life of the loan and offer loans based on that amount. The relationship between real and nominal interest rates should be memorized for the AP® exam:

Real Interest Rate = Nominal Interest Rate − Expected Inflation

Nominal Interest Rate = Real Interest Rate + Expected Inflation

FOCUS Active Learning

TRM Understanding that borrowers are helped and lenders are hurt by unanticipated inflation is a key concept for students to grasp. Use **Worksheet 14.3 (Helped or Hurt?)** from the TRM to assess their understanding. Students will determine if individuals are helped, hurt, or not impacted by unanticipated inflation in a variety of scenarios.

FOCUS Test It

Your friend asks for a $100 loan. Suppose you and your friend agree that inflation next year will be 5% and that your lending services are worth another 3%. In each of the following situations, explain what happened to your purchasing power:

A. You expected 5% inflation and you experienced exactly 8% inflation. *The purchasing power of the $100 you loaned was unchanged when your friend paid you back exactly enough to compensate for the inflation.*

B. You expected 5% inflation and you experienced only 1% inflation. *Your purchasing power has actually increased because your friend paid you back more than enough to compensate for the inflation. (The borrower loses.)*

C. You expected 5% inflation and you experienced 9% inflation. *Your purchasing power has actually decreased because your friend paid you back less than enough to compensate for the inflation. (The lender loses.)*

many economists argue, is to reduce the quality of economic decisions: the economy as a whole makes less efficient use of its resources because of the uncertainty caused by changes in the unit of account, the dollar. The **unit-of-account costs** of inflation are the costs arising from the way inflation makes money a less reliable unit of measurement.

Unit-of-account costs arise from the way inflation makes money a less reliable unit of measurement.

Unit-of-account costs may be particularly important in the tax system, because inflation can distort the measures of income on which taxes are collected. Here's an example: assume that the inflation rate is 10%, so that the overall level of prices rises 10% each year. Suppose that a business buys an asset, such as a piece of land, for $100,000 and then resells it a year later at a price of $110,000. In a fundamental sense, the business didn't make a profit on the deal: in real terms, it got no more for the land than it paid for it, because the $110,000 would purchase no more goods than the $100,000 would have a year earlier. But U.S. tax law would say that the business made a capital gain of $10,000, and it would have to pay taxes on that phantom gain.

During the 1970s, when the United States had a relatively high inflation rate, the distorting effects of inflation on the tax system were a serious problem. Some businesses were discouraged from productive investment spending because they found themselves paying taxes on phantom gains. Meanwhile, some unproductive investments became attractive because they led to phantom losses that reduced tax bills. When the inflation rate fell in the 1980s—and tax rates were reduced—these problems became much less important.

Winners and Losers from Inflation

AP® Exam Tip

In general, borrowers are helped by inflation because it decreases the real value of what they must repay. Lenders, savers, and people with fixed incomes are hurt by inflation because it decreases the real value of the money available to them in the future.

As we've just learned, a high inflation rate imposes overall costs on the economy. In addition, inflation can produce winners and losers within the economy. The main reason inflation sometimes helps some people while hurting others is that economic transactions, such as loans, often involve contracts that extend over a period of time and these contracts are normally specified in nominal—that is, in dollar—terms. In the case of a loan, the borrower receives a certain amount of funds at the beginning, and the loan contract specifies how much he or she must repay at some future date. But what that dollar repayment is worth in real terms—that is, in terms of purchasing power—depends greatly on the rate of inflation over the intervening years of the loan.

The *interest rate* on a loan is the percentage of the loan amount that the borrower must pay to the lender, typically on an annual basis, in addition to the repayment of the loan amount itself. Economists summarize the effect of inflation on borrowers and lenders by distinguishing between *nominal* interest rates and *real* interest rates. The **nominal interest rate** is the interest rate that is actually paid for a loan, unadjusted for the effects of inflation. For example, the interest rates advertised on student loans and every interest rate you see listed by a bank is a nominal rate. The **real interest rate** is the nominal interest rate adjusted for inflation. This adjustment is achieved by simply subtracting the inflation rate from the nominal interest rate. For example, if a loan carries a nominal interest rate of 8%, but the inflation rate is 5%, the real interest rate is 8% − 5% = 3%.

The **nominal interest rate** is the interest rate actually paid for a loan.

The **real interest rate** is the nominal interest rate minus the rate of inflation.

When a borrower and a lender enter into a loan contract, the contract normally specifies a nominal interest rate. But each party has an expectation about the future rate of inflation and therefore an expectation about the real interest rate on the loan. If the actual inflation rate is *higher* than expected, borrowers gain at the expense of lenders: borrowers will repay their loans with funds that have a lower real value than had been expected—they can purchase fewer goods and services than expected due to the surprisingly high inflation rate. Conversely, if the inflation rate is *lower* than expected, lenders will gain at the expense of borrowers: borrowers must repay their loans with funds that have a higher real value than had been expected.

Historically, the fact that inflation creates winners and losers has sometimes been a major source of political controversy. In 1896 William Jennings Bryan electrified the Democratic presidential convention with a speech in which he declared, "You shall not crucify mankind on a cross of gold." What he was actually demanding was an inflationary policy. At the time, the U.S. dollar had a fixed value in terms of gold. Bryan wanted the U.S. government

St. Louis Federal Reserve Bank Resources

"Getting Real About Interest Rates," ***The Economic Lowdown Podcast Series*****, Episode 14**

This episode covers the difference between nominal and real interest rates, how inflation influences the real return on your deposits, how it impacts borrowers and lenders differently, and why price stability—a responsibility of the Federal Reserve System—is important.

to abandon the gold standard and print more money, which would have raised the level of prices and, he believed, helped the nation's farmers who were deeply in debt.

In modern America, home mortgages (loans for the purchase of homes) are the most important source of gains and losses from inflation. Americans who took out mortgages in the early 1970s quickly found their real payments reduced by higher-than-expected inflation: by 1983, the purchasing power of a dollar was only 45% of what it had been in 1973. Those who took out mortgages in the early 1990s were not so lucky, because the inflation rate fell to lower-than-expected levels in the following years: in 2003 the purchasing power of a dollar was 78% of what it had been in 1993.

Because gains for some and losses for others result from inflation that is either higher or lower than expected, yet another problem arises: uncertainty about the future inflation rate discourages people from entering into any form of long-term contract. This is an additional cost of high inflation, because high rates of inflation are usually unpredictable, too. In countries with high and uncertain inflation, long-term loans are rare. This, in turn, makes it difficult for people to commit to long-term investments.

One last point: unexpected deflation—a surprise fall in the price level—creates winners and losers, too. Between 1929 and 1933, as the U.S. economy plunged into the Great Depression, the price level fell by 35%. This meant that debtors, including many farmers and homeowners, saw a sharp rise in the real value of their debts, which led to widespread bankruptcy and helped create a banking crisis, as lenders found their customers unable to pay back their loans.

Inflation Is Easy; Disinflation Is Hard

There is not much evidence that a rise in the inflation rate from, say, 2% to 5% would do a great deal of harm to the economy. Still, policy makers generally move forcefully to bring inflation back down when it creeps above 2% or 3%. Why? Because experience shows that bringing the inflation rate down—a process called **disinflation**—is very difficult and costly once a higher rate of inflation has become well established in the economy.

Disinflation is the process of bringing the inflation rate down.

Figure 14.2 shows the inflation rate and the unemployment rate in the United States over a crucial decade, from 1978 to 1988. The decade began with an alarming rise in the

Figure 14.2 The Cost of Disinflation

The U.S. inflation rate peaked in 1980 and then fell sharply. Progress against inflation, however, was accompanied by a temporary but very large increase in the unemployment rate, demonstrating the high cost of disinflation.
Source: Bureau of Labor Statistics.

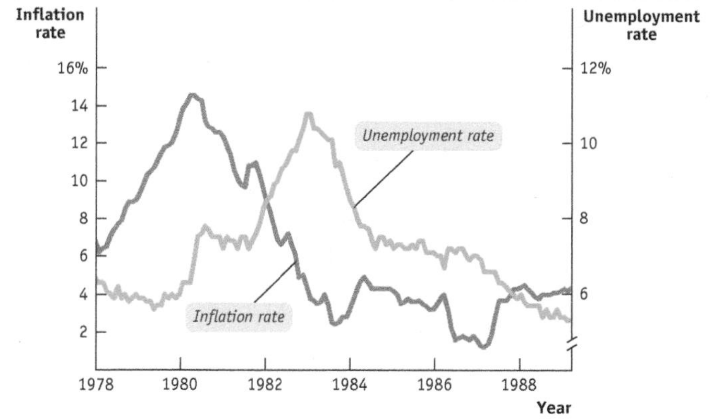

TEACH Teach It

Often, a high rate of inflation is caused by "too much" money being circulated and spent in the economy. The obvious way to reduce the inflation rate is to reduce the amount of money being circulated and spent. This can be painful because it typically reduces the demand for goods and services and puts some workers out of work. Since the 1980s, policy makers in the United States have tried to maintain a very low and stable amount of inflation so that painful corrections like this are unnecessary.

St. Louis Federal Reserve Bank Resources

"Deflation: Who Let the Air Out?," ***Page One Economics***

This article covers the effects of inflation, deflation, and disinflation. Student questions are included.

OPEN & CLOSE Exit Slip

TRM *Please see **Exit Slip: Module 14** in the TRM for formative multiple-choice questions to ask your students before finishing your lesson. These questions will help you quickly assess whether your students have mastered the module's concepts before moving on.*

Answers to the Exit Slip Questions

1. B
2. B
3. B

Answers to Module 14 Review Questions

Check Your Understanding

1. Shoe-leather costs as a result of inflation will be lower because it is now less costly for individuals to manage their assets in order to economize on their money holdings. ATM machines, for example, give customers 24-hour access to cash in thousands of locations. This reduction in the cost of obtaining money translates into lower shoe-leather costs.

2. If inflation came to a complete stop for several years, the inflation rate of zero would be less than the expected inflation rate of 2–3%. Because the real interest rate is the nominal interest rate minus the inflation rate, the real interest rates on loans would be higher than expected, and lenders would gain at the expense of borrowers. Borrowers would have to repay their loans with funds that had a higher real value than was expected.

Tackle the Test: Multiple-Choice Questions

1. e
2. c
3. b
4. d
5. c

inflation rate, but by the end of the period inflation averaged only about 4%. This was considered a major economic achievement—but it came at a high cost. Much of the fall in inflation probably resulted from the very severe recession of 1981–1982, which drove the unemployment rate to 10.8%—its highest level since the Great Depression.

Many economists believe that this period of high unemployment was necessary, because they believe that the only way to reduce inflation that has become deeply embedded in the economy is through policies that temporarily depress the economy. The best way to avoid having to put the economy through a wringer to reduce inflation, however, is to avoid having a serious inflation problem in the first place. So, policy makers respond forcefully to signs that inflation may be accelerating as a form of preventive medicine for the economy.

MODULE 14 Review

Check Your Understanding

1. The widespread use of technology has revolutionized the banking industry, making it much easier for customers to access and manage their money. Does this mean that the shoe-leather costs of inflation are higher or lower than they used to be? Explain.

2. Most people in the United States have grown accustomed to a modest inflation rate of around 2–3%. Who would gain and who would lose if inflation came to a complete stop for several years? Explain.

Tackle the Test: Multiple-Choice Questions

1. Which of the following is true regarding prices in an economy?
   I. An increase in the price level is called inflation.
   II. The level of prices doesn't matter.
   III. The rate of change in prices matters.
   a. I only
   b. II only
   c. III only
   d. II and III only
   e. I, II, and III

2. If your nominal wage doubles at the same time as prices double, your real wage will
   a. increase.
   b. decrease
   c. not change.
   d. double.
   e. be impossible to determine.

3. If inflation causes people to frequently convert their dollars into other assets, the economy experiences what type of cost?
   a. price level
   b. shoe-leather
   c. menu
   d. unit-of-account
   e. none of the above

4. Because dollars are used as the basis for contracts, inflation leads to which type of cost?
   a. price level
   b. shoe-leather
   c. menu
   d. unit-of-account
   e. none of the above

5. Changing the listed price when inflation leads to a price increase is an example of which type of cost?
   a. price level
   b. shoe-leather
   c. menu
   d. unit-of-account
   e. none of the above

144 Section 3 Measurement of Economic Performance

Tackle the Test: Free-Response Questions

1. In the following examples: (i) indicate whether inflation imposes a net cost on the economy; (ii) explain your answer; and (iii) identify the type of net cost involved if there is one.
   a. When inflation is expected to be high, workers get paid more frequently and make more trips to the bank.
   b. Lanwei is reimbursed by her company for her work-related travel expenses. Sometimes, however, the company takes a long time to reimburse her. So when inflation is high, she is less willing to travel for her job.
   c. Hector Homeowner has a mortgage loan that he took out five years ago with a fixed 6% nominal interest rate. Over the years, the inflation rate has crept up unexpectedly to its present level of 7%.
   d. In response to unexpectedly high inflation, the manager of Cozy Cottages of Cape Cod must reprint and resend expensive color brochures correcting the price of rentals this season.

Rubric for FRQ 1 (11 points)

1 point: There is a net cost to the economy.
1 point: There is an increase in the cost of financial transactions imposed by inflation.
1 point: This type of cost is called a shoe-leather cost.
1 point: There is a net cost to the economy.
1 point: Lanwei's forgone output is a cost to the economy.
1 point: This type of cost is called a unit-of-account cost.
1 point: There is no net cost to the economy.
1 point: Hector gains and the bank loses because the money Hector pays back is worth less than expected.
1 point: There is a net cost to the economy.
1 point: Cozy Cottages must reprint and resend the expensive brochure when inflation causes rental prices to rise.
1 point: This type of cost is called a menu cost.

2. You borrow $1,000 for one year at 5% interest to buy a couch. Although you did not anticipate any inflation, there is unexpected inflation of 5% over the life of your loan.
   a. What was the real interest rate on your loan?
   b. Explain how you gained from the inflation.
   c. Who lost as a result of the situation described? Explain.
   (4 points)

Tackle the Test: Free-Response Question

Rubric for FRQ 2 (4 points)

1 point: 0%

1 point: You borrowed enough money to buy a couch and paid back just enough to buy the same couch (after inflation). Therefore, you gained the benefit of the loan (having the couch for 1 year) without paying any real interest for it.

1 point: The lender lost.

1 point: The loan was paid back after prices unexpectedly increased, so the lender received a real interest rate of 0% for allowing you to use the money for a year.

PD To prepare for teaching this lesson, you may want to consult the **Module 15 Sample Lecture** in the TRM.

OPEN & CLOSE Start Here

TRM Conduct **Activity 15.1 (Inflation Auction)** from the TRM. This activity will help your students learn how inflation impacts their purchasing power by participating in an auction in which items go to the highest bidder.

FOCUS Active Learning

Ask students if they think inflation is a problem today and count how many believe this to be the case. Before discussing their answers, show students the BLS chart "Consumer Prices up 1.2% over the Year Ended September 2013" at www.bls.gov/opub/ted/2013/ted_20131031.htm. (*Note:* You can find the most current chart by searching the Bureau of Labor Statistics website.) After they review the chart, query your students again to see who thinks inflation is a problem today. If the new count is different from the initial count, ask the class why their vote changed. What number would constitute high inflation? Let students know that over the past 100 years, the average inflation rate in the United States was 3.3%.

TEACH Teach It

Students struggle with the idea of the market basket. Let them know that a market basket is just an imaginary shopping basket filled with the goods an average consumer buys. As practice throughout the module, you will use partial market baskets to simulate the larger basket used to determine the change in prices.

Getty Images/GlowImages

MODULE 15 The Measurement and Calculation of Inflation

In this Module, you will learn to:

- Explain what a price index is and how it is calculated
- Calculate the inflation rate using the values of a price index
- Describe the importance of the consumer price index and other price indexes

Price Indexes and the Aggregate Price Level

In the summer of 2008, Americans were facing sticker shock at the gas pump: the price of a gallon of regular gasoline had risen from about $3 in late 2007 to more than $4 in most places. Many other prices were also up. Some prices, though, were heading down: the prices of some foods, like eggs, were coming down from a run-up earlier in the year, and virtually anything involving electronics was also getting cheaper. Yet practically everyone felt that the overall cost of living seemed to be rising. But how fast?

Clearly there was a need for a single number that would summarize what was happening to consumer prices. Just as macroeconomists find it useful to have a single number to represent the overall level of output, they also find it useful to have a single number to represent the overall level of prices: the **aggregate price level**. Yet a huge variety of goods and services are produced and consumed in the economy. How can we summarize the prices of all these goods and services with a single number? The answer lies in the concept of a *price index*—a concept best introduced with an example.

The **aggregate price level** is a measure of the overall level of prices in the economy.

Market Baskets and Price Indexes

Suppose that a frost in Florida destroys most of the citrus harvest. As a result, the price of oranges rises from $0.20 each to $0.40 each, the price of grapefruit rises from $0.60 to $1.00, and the price of lemons rises from $0.25 to $0.45. How much has the price of citrus fruit increased?

One way to answer that question is to state three numbers—the changes in prices for oranges, grapefruit, and lemons. But this is a very cumbersome method. Rather

St. Louis Federal Reserve Bank Resources

The Market Basket

In this lesson, students compare the price of goods from one time period to another and interpret the effects of inflation on consumers. Students get to categorize goods and services according to the eight major groups of the CPI and are able to determine the difference between the CPI and core CPI. This lesson includes interactive whiteboard slides.

than having to recite three numbers in an effort to track changes in the prices of citrus fruit, we would prefer to have some kind of overall measure of the *average* price change.

To measure average price changes for consumer goods and services, economists track changes in the cost of a typical consumer's *consumption bundle*—the typical basket of goods and services purchased before the price changes. A hypothetical consumption bundle, used to measure changes in the overall price level, is known as a **market basket**. For our market basket in this example we will suppose that, before the frost, a typical consumer bought 200 oranges, 50 grapefruit, and 100 lemons over the course of a year.

A **market basket** is a hypothetical set of consumer purchases of goods and services.

Table 15.1 shows the pre-frost and post-frost costs of this market basket. Before the frost, it cost \$95; after the frost, the same basket of goods cost \$175. Since \$175/\$95 = 1.842, the post-frost basket costs 1.842 times the cost of the pre-frost basket, a cost increase of 84.2%. In this example, the average price of citrus fruit has increased 84.2% since the base year as a result of the frost, where the base year is the initial year used in the measurement of the price change.

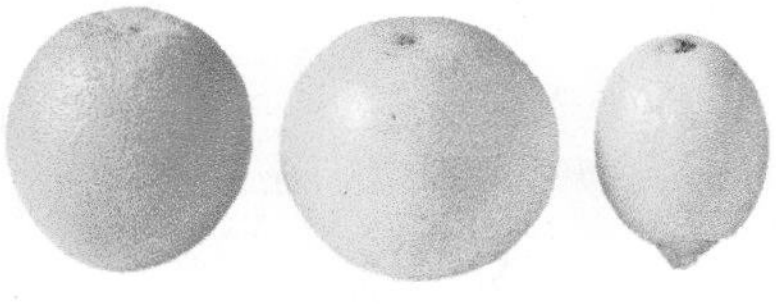

© PhotoAlto/Alamy

Table 15.1 Calculating the Cost of a Market Basket

	Pre-frost	Post-frost
Price of orange	\$0.20	\$0.40
Price of grapefruit	0.60	1.00
Price of lemon	0.25	0.45
Cost of market basket (200 oranges, 50 grapefruit, 100 lemons)	(200 × \$0.20) + (50 × \$0.60) + (100 × \$0.25) = \$95.00	(200 × \$0.40) + (50 × \$1.00) + (100 × \$0.45) = \$175.00

AP® Exam Tip

Don't let the term *market basket* confuse you. It simply means a group of goods and services that represents what consumers buy. On the AP® exam, market baskets usually consist of three or four goods, a simplification of the real market basket used to compute a price index.

Economists use the same method to measure changes in the overall price level: they track changes in the cost of buying a given market basket. Working with a market basket and a base year, we obtain what is known as a **price index**, a measure of the overall price level. It is always cited along with the year for which the aggregate price level is being measured and the base year. A price index can be calculated using the following formula:

A **price index** measures the cost of purchasing a given market basket in a given year. The index value is normalized so that it is equal to 100 in the selected base year.

$$\textbf{(15-1)}\quad \text{Price index in a given year} = \frac{\text{Cost of market basket in a given year}}{\text{Cost of market basket in base year}} \times 100$$

In our example, the citrus fruit market basket cost \$95 in the base year, the year before the frost. So by applying Equation 15-1, we define the price index for citrus fruit as (cost of market basket in the current year/\$95) × 100, yielding an index of 100 for the period before the frost and 184.2 after the frost. You should note that applying Equation 15-1 to calculate the price index for the base year always results in a price index of (cost of market basket in base year/cost of market basket in base year) × 100 = 100. Choosing a price index formula that always normalizes the index value to 100 in the base year avoids the need to keep track of the cost of the market basket, for example, \$95, in such and such a year.

The price index makes it clear that the average price of citrus has risen 84.2% as a consequence of the frost. Because of its simplicity and intuitive appeal, the method we've just described is used to calculate a variety of price indexes to track average price changes among a variety of different groups of goods and services. Examples include the *consumer price index* and the *producer price index*, which we'll discuss shortly. Price indexes are also the basis for measuring inflation. The price level mentioned in the inflation rate formula in Module 14 is simply a price index value, and the inflation rate is determined as the annual percentage change in an official price index. The inflation

TEACH Teach It

Walk students through the steps in calculating a market basket using Table 15.1. First multiply price times quantity for each column to get the total cost of each good. Then total the goods in the market basket for each column. Make sure your students understand that the steps are the same regardless of the size of the basket.

FOCUS Active Learning

TRM Have students watch "Episode 16: Inflation & Price Indexes" (see econextras video list with hyperlinks on the bcs and TRFD). Use **Worksheet 15.2 (Inflation & Price Indices)** from the TRM for questions on this video.

FOCUS Flip It

Review price indices by assigning Jacob Clifford's video "Macro Unit 2.4—CPI Practice" (see econ-extras video list with hyperlinks on the bcs and TRFD). Ask your class to solve the problem at the end of the session in the bonus material. *Tell students to stop the video at 3:45 to give them time to solve the problem posed by Mr. Clifford.*

FOCUS Active Learning

TRM Assign **Worksheet 15.3 (Consumer Price Index)** from the TRM in class or as homework. Students will practice calculating both market baskets and inflation.

TEACH Teach It

Project the link found at http://www.bls.gov/dolfaq/bls_ques3.htm. Use this link to help students recognize what is in the market basket. They will be able to see the general categories, but you can also assign groups to make lists of specific products that would be included in their assigned category. You can then ask groups to report on their category and make lists on the board.

rate from year 1 to year 2 is thus calculated using the following formula, with year 1 and year 2 being consecutive years.

The **consumer price index**, or **CPI**, measures the cost of the market basket of a typical urban American family.

$$\text{(15-2)}\quad \text{Inflation rate} = \frac{\text{Price index in year 2} - \text{Price index in year 1}}{\text{Price index in year 1}} \times 100$$

Typically, a news report that cites "the inflation rate" is referring to the annual percentage change in the consumer price index.

© Daniel Koebe/Corbis

The Consumer Price Index

The most widely used measure of the overall price level in the United States is the **consumer price index** (often referred to simply as the **CPI**), which is intended to show how the cost of all purchases by a typical urban family has changed over time. It is calculated by surveying market prices for a market basket that is constructed to represent the consumption of a typical family of four living in a typical American city. Rather than having a single base year, the CPI currently has a base period of 1982–1984.

The market basket used to calculate the CPI is far more complex than the three-fruit market basket we described above. In fact, to calculate the CPI, the Bureau of Labor Statistics sends its employees out to survey supermarkets, gas stations, hardware stores, and so on—some 23,000 retail outlets in 87 cities. Every month it tabulates about 80,000 prices, on everything from romaine lettuce to a medical checkup. **Figure 15.1** shows the weight of major categories in the consumer price index as of December 2012. For example, motor fuel, mainly gasoline, accounted for 5% of the CPI in December 2012.

Figure 15.2 shows how the CPI has changed since measurement began in 1913. Since 1940, the CPI has risen steadily, although its annual percentage increases in recent years have been much smaller than those of the 1970s and early 1980s. A logarithmic scale is used so that equal percentage changes in the CPI appear the same.

AP® Exam Tip

The CPI is the most commonly used price index on the AP® exam. Make sure you learn how to calculate both the index value in a given year and the inflation rate using the index value.

Figure 15.1 The Makeup of the Consumer Price Index in 2012

This chart shows the percentage shares of major types of spending in the CPI as of December 2012. Housing, food, transportation, and motor fuel made up about 73% of the CPI market basket.
Source: Bureau of Labor Statistics.

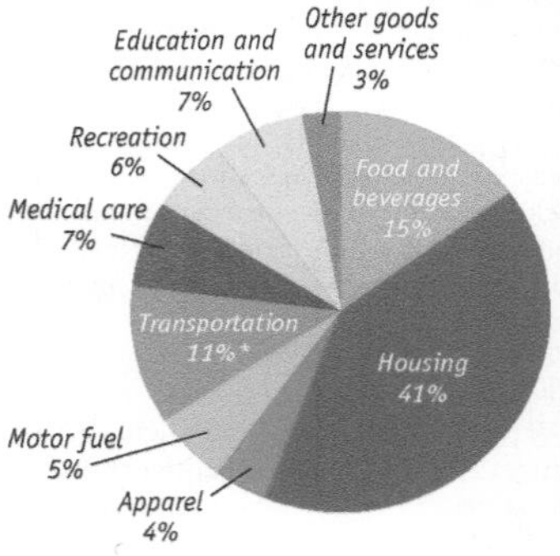

*Excludes motor fuel.

Figure 15.2 The CPI, 1913–2013

Since 1940, the CPI has risen steadily. But the annual percentage increases in recent years have been much smaller than those of the 1970s and early 1980s. (The vertical axis is measured on a logarithmic scale so that equal percentage changes in the CPI appear the same.)
Source: Bureau of Labor Statistics.

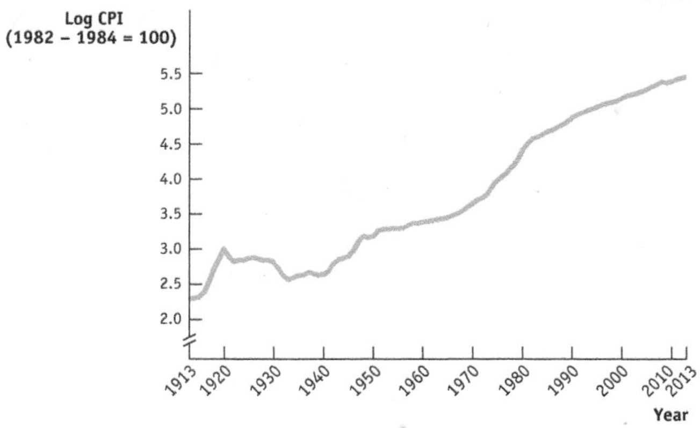

Some economists believe that the consumer price index systematically overstates the actual rate of inflation. Why? Suppose the price of everything in the market basket used to calculate the CPI increased by 10% over the past year. The typical consumer might not need to spend 10% more this year to be as well off as last year, for three reasons.

First, each item remains in the studied market basket for four years. Yet consumers frequently alter the mix of goods and services they buy, reducing purchases of products that have become relatively more expensive and increasing purchases of products that have become relatively cheaper. For example, suppose that the price of hamburgers suddenly doubled. Americans currently eat a lot of hamburgers, but in the face of such a price rise many of them would switch to chicken sandwiches, pizza, or other substitutes whose prices hadn't increased as much. As a result, a price index based on a market basket with a lot of hamburgers in it would overstate the true rise in the cost of living.

The second reason arises from product improvements. It's likely that over the years your favorite toothpaste, laundry detergent, and snack foods have both increased in price and come out in "new and improved" versions. If what you're getting is really better than before, you aren't paying more for the same product. Rather, you're paying more and getting more. The Bureau of Labor Statistics does its best to make adjustments for changes in product quality, but it is hard to measure the extent to which consumers are getting more as opposed to simply paying more.

The third reason that inflation rate estimates may be misleading is innovation. Every new year brings new items, such as new electronic gadgets, new smartphone apps, new health care solutions, and new clothing options. By widening the range of consumer choice, innovation makes a given amount of money worth more. That is, innovation creates benefits similar to those of a fall in consumer prices. For all of these reasons, changes in the CPI may overstate changes in the cost of maintaining a particular standard of living. However, with more frequent updates of the market basket, among other tweaks in its methods, the Bureau of Labor Statistics has improved the accuracy of the CPI in recent years. And, despite some remaining controversy, the CPI remains the basis for most estimates of inflation.

The United States is not the only country that calculates a consumer price index. In fact, nearly every country calculates one. As you might expect, the market baskets that make up these indexes differ quite a lot from country to country. In poor countries,

TEACH Teach It

The Consumer Price Index (CPI) is the most widely used measure of price inflation. The Producer Price Index (PPI) measures the cost of a typical basket of goods and services—containing raw commodities such as steel, electricity, coal, and so on—purchased by producers.

FOCUS Active Learning

Have students read the BLS article at http://www.bls.gov/ppi/ppifaq.htm#4. Ask them to explain how the PPI is different from the CPI. *The CPI and PPI differ based on the composition of the set of goods and services, the types of prices collected for the included goods and services, and coverage of the services sector.* Give an example of an item that would be counted in the PPI but not the CPI. *Possible answers include exports, medical services, inputs of production and capital investment.*

Module 15 The Measurement and Calculation of Inflation 149

TEACH Teach It

The GDP deflator is technically not a price index, but it is used in the same way as the CPI and PPI to determine inflation. You can display a graph showing the GDP deflator using the data at http://research.stlouisfed.org/fred2/graph/?s[1][id]=GDPDEF. You can manipulate the data for time periods and other features that students and teachers might find of interest. The formula to find the deflator is

GDP Deflator = Nominal GDP/Real GDP × 100

where people must spend a high proportion of their income just to feed themselves, food makes up a large share of the price index. Among high-income countries, differences in consumption patterns lead to differences in the price indexes: the Japanese price index puts a larger weight on raw fish and a smaller weight on beef than ours does, and the French price index puts a larger weight on wine.

Other Price Measures

The **producer price index**, or **PPI**, measures the prices of goods and services purchased by producers.

There are two other price measures that are also widely used to track economy-wide price changes. One is the **producer price index** (or **PPI**, which used to be known as the *wholesale price index*). As its name suggests, the producer price index measures the cost of a typical basket of goods and services—containing raw commodities such as steel, electricity, coal, and so on—purchased by producers. Because commodity producers are relatively quick to raise prices when they perceive a change in overall demand for their goods, the PPI often responds to inflationary or deflationary pressures more quickly than the CPI. As a result, the PPI is often regarded as an "early warning signal" of changes in the inflation rate.

The **GDP deflator** for a given year is 100 times the ratio of nominal GDP to real GDP in that year.

The other widely used price measure is the *GDP deflator;* it isn't exactly a price index, although it serves the same purpose. Recall how we distinguished between nominal GDP (GDP in current prices) and real GDP (GDP calculated using the prices of a base year). The **GDP deflator** for a given year is 100 times the ratio of nominal GDP to real GDP in that year. Since the Bureau of Economic Analysis—the source of the GDP deflator—calculates real GDP using a base year of 2005, the nominal GDP and the real GDP for 2005 are the same. This makes the GDP deflator for 2005 equal to 100. For this reason, later in this book you will see measures of the aggregate price level with the designation "GDP Deflator, 2005 = 100." And in many cases you will see real GDP measured in 2005 dollars. Inflation raises nominal GDP but not real GDP, causing the GDP deflator to rise. If nominal GDP doubles but real GDP does not change, the GDP deflator indicates that the aggregate price level has doubled.

Perhaps the most important point about the different inflation rates generated by these three measures of prices is that they usually move closely together (although the producer price index tends to fluctuate more than either of the other two measures). **Figure 15.3** shows the annual percentage changes in the three indexes since 1930. By all three measures, the U.S. economy experienced deflation during the early years of

Figure 15.3 The CPI, the PPI, and the GDP Deflator

As the figure shows, these three different measures of inflation usually move closely together. Each reveals a drastic acceleration of inflation during the 1970s and a return to relative price stability in the 1990s.
Source: Bureau of Labor Statistics; Bureau of Economic Analysis.

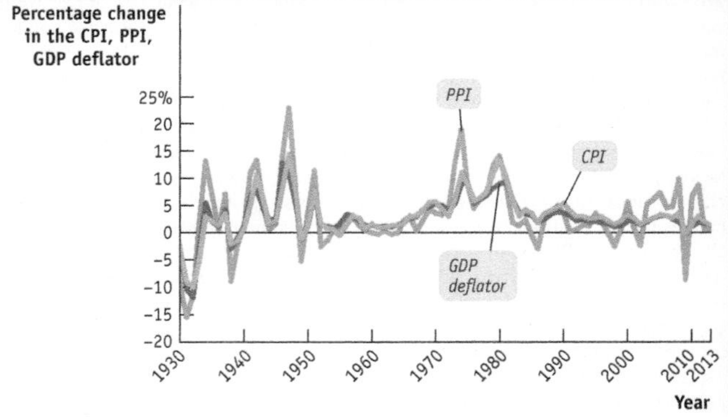

the Great Depression, inflation during World War II, accelerating inflation during the 1970s, and a return to relative price stability in the 1990s. Notice, by the way, the dramatic ups and downs in producer prices from 2000 to 2012. This reflects large swings in energy and food prices, which play a much bigger role in the PPI than they do in either the CPI or the GDP deflator.

FYI Indexing to the CPI

Although GDP is a very important number for shaping economic policy, official statistics on GDP don't have a direct effect on people's lives. The CPI, by contrast, has a direct and immediate impact on millions of Americans. The reason is that many payments are tied, or "indexed," to the CPI—the amount paid rises or falls when the CPI rises or falls.

The practice of indexing payments to consumer prices goes back to the dawn of the United States as a nation. In 1780 the Massachusetts State Legislature recognized that the pay of its soldiers fighting the British needed to be increased because of inflation that occurred during the Revolutionary War. The legislature adopted a formula that made a soldier's pay proportional to the cost of a market basket consisting of 5 bushels of corn, 68 4/7 pounds of beef, 10 pounds of sheep's wool, and 16 pounds of sole leather.

Today, 58 million people, most of them old or disabled, receive checks from Social Security, a national retirement program that accounts for almost a quarter of current total federal spending—more than the defense budget. The amount of an individual's check is determined by a formula that reflects his or her previous payments into the system as well as other factors. In addition, all Social Security payments are adjusted each year to offset any increase in consumer prices over the previous year. The CPI is used to calculate the official estimate of the inflation rate used to adjust these payments annually. So every percentage point added to the official estimate of the rate of inflation adds 1% to the checks received by tens of millions of individuals.

Other government payments are also indexed to the CPI. In addition, income tax brackets, the bands of income levels that determine a taxpayer's income tax rate, are indexed to the CPI. (An individual in a higher income bracket pays a higher income tax rate in a progressive tax system like ours.) Indexing also extends to the private sector, where many private contracts, including some wage settlements, contain cost-of-living allowances (called COLAs) that adjust payments in proportion to changes in the CPI.

Because the CPI plays such an important and direct role in people's lives, it's a politically sensitive number. The Bureau of Labor Statistics, which calculates the CPI, takes great care in collecting and interpreting price and consumption data. It uses a complex method in which households are surveyed to determine what they buy and where they shop, and a carefully selected sample of stores are surveyed to get representative prices. As explained in the preceding section, however, there is still controversy about whether the CPI accurately measures inflation.

Superstock

A small change in the CPI has large consequences for those who depend on Social Security payments.

OPEN & CLOSE Exit Slip

TRM *Please see* ***Exit Slip: Module 15*** *in the TRM for formative multiple-choice questions to ask before finishing your lesson. These questions will help you quickly assess whether your students have mastered the module's concepts before moving on.*

Answers to the Exit Slip Questions

1. A
2. E
3. A

MODULE 15 Review

Check Your Understanding

1. Consider Table 15.1 but suppose that the market basket is composed of 100 oranges, 50 grapefruit, and 200 lemons. How does this change the pre-frost and post-frost consumer price indexes? Explain. Generalize your answer to explain how the construction of the market basket affects the CPI.
2. For each of the following events, explain how the use of a 10-year-old market basket would bias measurements of price changes over the past decade.
   a. A typical family owns more cars than it would have a decade ago. Over that time, the average price of a car has increased more than the average prices of other goods.
   b. Virtually no households had tablet PCs a decade ago. Now many households have them, and their prices have been falling.
3. The consumer price index in the United States (base period 1982–1984) was 214.537 in 2009 and 218.056 in 2010. Calculate the inflation rate from 2009 to 2010.

Tackle the Test: Multiple-Choice Questions

1. If the cost of a market basket of goods increases from \$100 in year 1 to \$108 in year 2, the consumer price index in year 2 equals ___ if year 1 is the base year.
   a. 8
   b. 10
   c. 100
   d. 108
   e. 110
2. If the consumer price index increases from 80 to 120 from one year to the next, the inflation rate over that time period was
   a. 20%
   b. 40%
   c. 50%
   d. 80%
   e. 120%
3. Which of the following is true of the CPI?
   I. It is the most common measure of the price level.
   II. It measures the price of a typical market basket of goods.
   III. It currently uses a base period of 1982–1984.
   a. I only
   b. II only
   c. III only
   d. I and II only
   e. I, II, and III
4. The value of a price index in the base year is
   a. 0.
   b. 100.
   c. 200.
   d. the inflation rate.
   e. the average cost of a market basket of goods.
5. If your wage doubles at the same time as the consumer price index goes from 100 to 300, your real wage
   a. doubles.
   b. falls.
   c. increases.
   d. stays the same.
   e. cannot be determined.

Tackle the Test: Free-Response Questions

1. Suppose the year 2000 is the base year for a price index. Between 2000 and 2020 prices double and at the same time your nominal income increases from \$40,000 to \$80,000.
   a. What is the value of the price index in 2000?
   b. What is the value of the price index in 2020?
   c. What is the percentage increase in your nominal income between 2000 and 2020?
   d. What has happened to your real income between 2000 and 2020? Explain.

Rubric for FRQ 1 (5 points)

1 point: 100

1 point: 200

1 point: 100%

1 point: It stayed the same.

1 point: Real income is a measure of the purchasing power of my income, and because my income and the price level both doubled, the purchasing power of my income has not been affected: \$40,000/100 = \$80,000/200.

2. The accompanying table contains the values of the CPI for 2012 and 2013.
   a. What does the CPI measure?
   b. Calculate the inflation rate from 2012 to 2013.

Year	CPI
2012	229.6
2013	233.0

(2 points)

152 Section 3 Measurement of Economic Performance

Answers to Module 15 Review Questions

Check Your Understanding

1. Pre-frost, this market basket costs (100 × \$0.20) + (50 × \$0.60) + (200 × \$0.25) = \$20 + \$30 + \$50 = \$100. The same market basket, post-frost, costs (100 × \$0.40) + (50 × \$1.00) + (200 × \$0.45) = \$40 + \$50 + \$90 = \$180. Thus, the price index is (\$100/\$100) × 100 = 100 before the frost and (\$180/\$100) × 100 = 180 after the frost, implying a rise in the price index of 80%. This increase in the price index is less than the 84.2% increase calculated in the text. The reason for this difference is that the new market basket of 100 oranges, 50 grapefruit, and 200 lemons contains proportionately more of an item that has experienced a relatively small price increase (the lemons, the price of which has increased by 80%) and proportionately fewer of an item that has experienced a relatively large price increase (the oranges, the price of which has increased by 100%). This shows that the price index can be very sensitive to the composition of the market basket. If the market basket contains a large proportion of goods whose prices have risen faster than the prices of other goods, it will lead to a higher estimate of the increase in the price level. If it contains a large proportion of goods whose prices have risen more slowly than the prices of other goods, it will lead to a lower estimate of the increase in the price level.

2. a. A market basket determined 10 years ago will contain fewer cars than at present. Given that the average price of a car has grown faster than the average prices of other goods, this basket will underestimate the true increase in the price level because it contains relatively too few cars.

b. A market basket determined 10 years ago will not contain tablet PCs, so it cannot track the fall in prices of tablet PCs over the past few years. As a result, it will overestimate the true increase in the price level.

3. Using Equation 15-2, we determine that the inflation rate from 2009 to 2010 is (218.056 − 214.537)/214.537 × 100 = 1.640%.

Tackle the Test: Multiple-Choice Questions

1. d
2. c
3. e
4. b
5. b

Tackle the Test: Free-Response Question

Rubric for FRQ 2 (2 points)

1 point: The CPI measures the cost of the market basket of a typical urban family in the United States.

1 point: (233.0 − 229.6)/229.6 × 100 = 1.5%

SECTION 3 Review

Section 3 Review Video

Module 10

1. Economists keep track of the flows of money between sectors with the **national income and product accounts**, or **national accounts. Households** earn income via the **factor markets** from wages, interest on **bonds**, profit accruing to owners of **stocks**, and rent on land. In addition, they receive **government transfers. Disposable income**, total household income minus taxes plus government transfers, is allocated to **consumer spending** (*C*) in the **product markets** and **private savings**. Via the **financial markets**, private savings and foreign lending are channeled to **investment spending** (*I*), government borrowing, and foreign borrowing. **Government purchases of goods and services** (*G*) are paid for by tax revenues and **government borrowing**. **Exports** (*X*) generate an inflow of funds into the country from the rest of the world, but **imports** (*IM*) lead to an outflow of funds to the rest of the world. Foreigners can also buy stocks and bonds in the U.S. financial markets.

2. **Gross domestic product**, or **GDP**, measures the value of all **final goods and services** produced in the economy. It does not include the value of **intermediate goods and services**, but it does include **inventories** and **net exports** ($X - IM$). There are three approaches to calculating GDP: the **value-added approach** of adding up the **value added** by all producers; the **expenditure approach** of adding up all spending on domestically produced final goods and services, leading to the equation $GDP = C + I + G + X - IM$, also known as **aggregate spending**; and the **income approach** of adding up all the income paid by domestic **firms** to factors of production. These three methods are equivalent because in the economy as a whole, total income paid by domestic firms to factors of production must equal total spending on domestically produced final goods and services.

Module 11

3. **Real GDP** is the value of the final goods and services produced, calculated using the prices of a selected base year. Except in the base year, real GDP is not the same as **nominal GDP**, the value of **aggregate output** calculated using current prices. Analysis of the growth rate of aggregate output must use real GDP because doing so eliminates any change in the value of aggregate output due solely to price changes. Real **GDP per capita** is a measure of average aggregate output per person but is not in itself an appropriate policy goal. U.S. statistics on real GDP are always expressed in "chained dollars," which means they are calculated with the **chain-linking** method of averaging the GDP growth rate found using an early base year and the GDP growth rate found using a late base year.

Module 12

4. **Employed** people currently hold a part-time or full-time job; **unemployed** people do not hold a job but are actively looking for work. Their sum is equal to the **labor force**; the **labor force participation rate** is the percentage of the population age 16 or older that is in the labor force.

5. The **unemployment rate**, the percentage of the labor force that is unemployed and actively looking for work, can overstate or understate the true level of unemployment. It can overstate because it counts as unemployed those who are continuing to search for a job despite having been offered one (that is, workers who are frictionally unemployed). It can understate because it ignores frustrated workers, such as **discouraged workers**, **marginally attached workers**, and the **underemployed**. In addition, the unemployment rate varies greatly among different groups in the population; it is typically higher for younger workers and for workers near retirement age than for workers in their prime working years.

6. The unemployment rate is affected by the business cycle. The unemployment rate generally falls when the growth rate of real GDP is above average and generally rises when the growth rate of real GDP is below average.

Module 13

7. Job creation and destruction, as well as voluntary job separations, lead to **job search** and **frictional unemployment**. In addition, a variety of factors, such as minimum wages, unions, and **efficiency wages**, result in a situation in which there is a surplus of labor at the market wage rate, creating **structural unemployment**. As a result, the **natural rate of unemployment**, the sum of frictional and structural unemployment, is well above zero, even when jobs are plentiful.

FOCUS Flip It

Encourage your students to watch the **Section 3 Review Video**, which was created as a special student review tool and is linked into the e-Book or may be found on the book's companion website.

8. The actual unemployment rate is equal to the natural rate of unemployment, the share of unemployment that is independent of the business cycle, plus **cyclical unemployment**, the share of unemployment that depends on fluctuations in the business cycle.

9. The natural rate of unemployment changes over time, largely in response to changes in labor force characteristics, labor market institutions, and government policies.

Module 14

10. Inflation does not, as many assume, make everyone poorer by raising the level of prices. That's because if wages and incomes are adjusted to take into account a rising price level, **real wages** and **real income** remain unchanged. However, a high **inflation rate** imposes overall costs on the economy: **shoe-leather costs**, **menu costs**, and **unit-of-account costs**.

11. Inflation can produce winners and losers within the economy, because long-term contracts are generally written in dollar terms. Loans typically specify a **nominal interest rate**, which differs from the **real interest rate** due to inflation. A higher-than-expected inflation rate is good for borrowers and bad for lenders. A lower-than-expected inflation rate is good for lenders and bad for borrowers.

12. **Disinflation**, the process of bringing the inflation rate down, usually comes at the cost of a higher unemployment rate. So policy makers try to prevent inflation from becoming excessive in the first place.

Module 15

13. To measure the **aggregate price level**, economists calculate the cost of purchasing a **market basket**. A **price index** is the ratio of the current cost of that market basket to the cost in a selected base year, multiplied by 100.

14. The inflation rate is calculated as the annual percentage change in a price index, typically based on the **consumer price index**, or **CPI**, the most common measure of the aggregate price level. A similar index for goods and services purchased by firms is the **producer price index**, or **PPI**. Finally, economists also use the **GDP deflator**, which measures the price level by calculating the ratio of nominal to real GDP times 100.

Key Terms

National income and product accounts, p. 105
National accounts, p. 105
Household, p. 106
Firm, p. 106
Product markets, p. 106
Factor markets, p. 106
Consumer spending, p. 106
Stock, p. 107
Bond, p. 107
Government transfers, p. 108
Disposable income, p. 108
Private savings, p. 108
Financial markets, p. 108
Government borrowing, p. 108
Government purchases of goods and services, p. 108
Exports, p. 108
Imports, p. 108
Inventories, p. 109
Investment spending, p. 109
Final goods and services, p. 109
Intermediate goods and services, p. 109
Gross domestic product (GDP), p. 109
Value-added approach, p. 109
Expenditure approach, p. 109
Aggregate spending, p. 109
Income approach, p. 109
Value added, p. 110
Net exports, p. 111
Aggregate output, p. 116
Real GDP, p. 117
Nominal GDP, p. 117
Chain-linking, p. 118
GDP per capita, p. 118
Employed, p. 121
Unemployed, p. 122
Labor force, p. 122
Labor force participation rate, p. 122
Unemployment rate, p. 122
Discouraged workers, p. 123
Marginally attached workers, p. 123
Underemployed, p. 123
Job search, p. 130
Frictional unemployment, p. 130
Structural unemployment, p. 131
Efficiency wages, p. 133
Natural rate of unemployment, p. 133
Cyclical unemployment, p. 133
Real wage, p. 139
Real income, p. 139
Inflation rate, p. 139
Shoe-leather costs, p. 140
Menu costs, p. 140
Unit-of-account costs, p. 142
Nominal interest rate, p. 142
Real interest rate, p. 142
Disinflation, p. 143
Aggregate price level, p. 146
Market basket, p. 147
Price index, p. 147
Consumer price index (CPI), p. 148
Producer price index (PPI), p. 150
GDP deflator, p. 150

154 Section 3 Measurement of Economic Performance

AP® Exam Practice Questions

Multiple-Choice Questions

Refer to the following diagram for Questions 1–3.

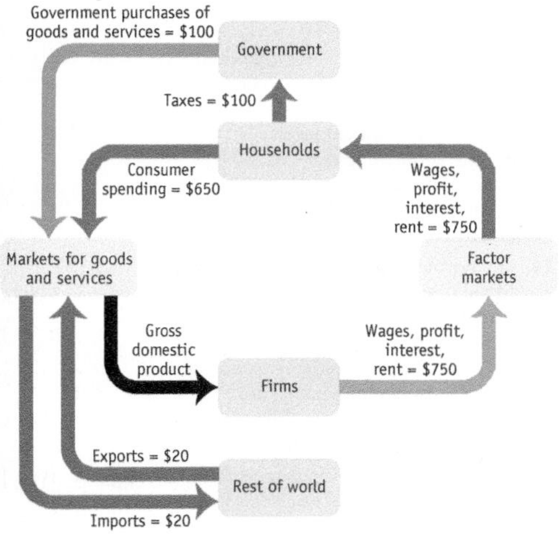

1. What is the value of GDP?
a. $550
b. $650
c. $750
d. $770
e. $790

2. What is the value of disposable income?
a. $750
b. $650
c. $550
d. $530
e. $510

3. The $750 of wages, profit, interest, and rent shown by the red arrow pointing into the factor markets box illustrates the calculation of GDP using which approach?
a. value-added
b. aggregate spending
c. expenditure
d. income
e. resource

Refer to the following table for Questions 4–6.

Category	Components of GDP (billions of dollars)
Consumer spending	
Durable goods	$1,000
Nondurable goods	2,000
Services	7,000
Private Investment Spending	
Fixed investment spending	1,700
Nonresidential	1,400
Structures	500
Equipment and software	900
Residential	300
Change in private inventories	−100
Net exports	
Exports	1,500
Imports	2,000
Government purchases of goods and services and investment spending	
Federal	1,400
State and local	1,600

4. What is the value of GDP?
a. $10,000
b. $11,600
c. $14,100
d. $15,100
e. $18,100

5. What is the value of net exports?
a. $3,500
b. $2,000
c. $1,500
d. $500
e. −$500

6. Which of the following refers to a loan in the form of an IOU that pays interest?
a. stock
b. bond
c. disposable income
d. government transfer
e. investment

Answers to Section 3 AP® Exam Practice Questions

Multiple-Choice Questions

1. c
2. b
3. d
4. c
5. e
6. b

Section 3 Review 155

7. b
8. e
9. a
10. c
11. e
12. c
13. b
14. a
15. b
16. d
17. b
18. c
19. a
20. d

7. Investment spending includes spending on which of the following?
a. stocks
b. physical capital
c. inputs
d. services
e. reductions in inventories

8. Which of the following is included in the calculation of GDP?
a. intermediate goods and services
b. used goods
c. stocks and bonds
d. foreign-produced goods and services
e. domestically produced capital goods

9. Which of the following is true for this year if real GDP is greater than nominal GDP?
a. The price level has decreased since the base year.
b. The consumer price index has increased since the base year.
c. The economy is experiencing inflation.
d. There has been economic growth.
e. Net exports are positive.

10. A country's labor force is equal to which of the following?
a. the number of people aged 16 and above
b. the number of people employed plus the number retired
c. the number of people employed plus the number unemployed
d. the number of people working for pay
e. the number of people employed for pay plus the number who have given up looking for work

11. The number of people who are considered unemployed is equal to the number of people who are not working and
a. are receiving unemployment compensation.
b. have given up seeking work.
c. plan to look for work in the future.
d. have looked for work in the recent past.
e. are actively seeking work.

12. The unemployment rate is the number of people unemployed divided by the number
a. employed.
b. employed plus the number discouraged.
c. in the labor force.
d. in the population aged 16 and above.
e. in the population.

13. The number of people counted as unemployed includes which of the following types of workers?
a. discouraged workers
b. aspiring workers seeking their first job
c. underemployed workers
d. retired workers
e. part-time workers

14. A worker who is not working while engaged in a job search after moving to a new city is considered which of the following?
a. frictionally unemployed
b. structurally unemployed
c. cyclically unemployed
d. underemployed
e. a discouraged worker

15. A worker who is not working because his or her skills are no longer demanded in the labor market is considered which of the following?
a. frictionally unemployed
b. structurally unemployed
c. cyclically unemployed
d. underemployed
e. a discouraged worker

16. The normal unemployment rate around which the actual unemployment rate fluctuates is known as which of the following?
a. frictional unemployment rate
b. structural unemployment rate
c. cyclical unemployment rate
d. natural rate of unemployment
e. maximum unemployment rate

17. Which of the following is true if the real wage rate is equal to the nominal wage rate?
a. Real income is constant.
b. The price level for the current year is the same as the price level in the base year.
c. The CPI is increasing.
d. The demand for labor is increasing.
e. The economy is experiencing deflation.

18. A worker who is unemployed due to fluctuations in the business cycle is considered which of the following?
a. frictionally unemployed
b. structurally unemployed
c. cyclically unemployed
d. underemployed
e. a discouraged worker

19. When inflation makes money a less reliable unit of measurement, the economy is experiencing which of the following costs of inflation?
a. unit-of-account
b. shoe-leather
c. menu
d. measurement
e. monetary

20. Bringing down the inflation rate is known as
a. negative inflation.
b. deflation.
c. bubble popping.
d. disinflation.
e. contraction.

21. The real interest rate is equal to the nominal interest rate
  a. minus the inflation rate.
  b. plus the inflation rate.
  c. divided by the inflation rate.
  d. times the inflation rate.
  e. plus the real interest rate divided by the inflation rate.

22. Who loses from unanticipated inflation?
  a. borrowers
  b. the government
  c. investors
  d. mortgage owners
  e. people on fixed incomes

23. Assume a country has a population of 1,000. If 400 people are employed and 100 people are unemployed, what is the country's unemployment rate?
  a. 50%
  b. 40%
  c. 25%
  d. 20%
  e. 10%

24. Which of the following changes will result in an increase in the natural rate of unemployment?
  a. More teenagers focus on their studies and do not look for jobs until after college.
  b. The government increases the time during which an unemployed worker can receive benefits.
  c. Greater access to the Internet makes it easier for job-seekers to find a job.
  d. Union membership declines.
  e. Opportunities for job training improve.

25. If the consumer price index rises from 120 to 132, what is the inflation rate?
  a. 8%
  b. 10%
  c. 12%
  d. 20%
  e. 32%

Free-Response Question

1. Assume the country of Technologia invests in an online system that efficiently matches job-seekers with employers and significantly reduces the time required for job searches.
  a. Which type of unemployment will Technologia's investment affect?
  b. Will unemployment increase or decrease?
  c. Given the change in unemployment from part b. what will happen to the natural rate of unemployment in Technologia? Explain.
  d. Given your answer to part b. what will happen to real GDP in Technologia? Explain.
  (6 points)

21. a
22. e
23. d
24. b
25. b

Rubric for Free-Response Question

1 point: Frictional unemployment

1 point: Unemployment will decrease.

1 point: The natural rate of unemployment will decrease.

1 point: Because it is made up of frictional and structural unemployment, and because frictional unemployment has decreased, the natural state of unemployment will decrease.

1 point: Real GDP in Technologia will increase.

1 point: Because frictional unemployment will decrease, and more people will be working, real GDP will increase; there is an inverse relationship between unemployment and real GDP.

SECTION 4

National Income and Price Determination

PD Section 4 Overview:

Watch the video overview of Section 4 (for teachers), which is accessible through the Teacher's e-Book, the TR-flash drive, or the book's website, bcs.worthpublishers.com/krugmanap2e *(teacher log-in required).*

Section 4 introduces national income and price determination and presents the aggregate demand–aggregate supply model. New terms and relationships in the macroeconomy are introduced in this section. Just as supply/demand models are useful in demonstrating many microeconomic concepts, this model of aggregate demand and aggregate supply will form the foundation for later lessons in macroeconomics.

Topics that your students will study in Section 4 are:

- how the consumption function relates to disposable income.
- how the determinants of investment spending affect GDP.
- determining the size of the spending multiplier and assessing its impact on aggregate demand spending.
- listing the determinants of aggregate demand and distinguishing between a change in *AD* and a change in the price level that causes a movement along the *AD* curve.
- explaining why the aggregate demand curve is downward-sloping.
- listing the determinants of aggregate supply and distinguishing between a change in *AS* and a change in the price level that causes a movement along the *AS* curve.
- how the shape of the aggregate supply curve differs between the short run and the long run.
- determining the potential or full-employment level of output.
- how the shape of the *AS* curve has an effect on changes in the price level and real GDP caused by changes in the *AD* curve.
- how equilibrium is defined using an aggregate demand–aggregate supply graph.
- how the price level and real GDP change when equilibrium changes in both the short run and the long run.
- how expansionary fiscal policy affects the price level, aggregate demand, and real GDP.
- how contractionary fiscal policy affects the price level, aggregate demand, and real GDP.
- determining the size of the tax multiplier and assessing its impact on aggregate demand.
- understanding the differences between discretionary fiscal policy and automatic stabilizers.

Alignment to AP® Macroeconomics Course Description

Macroeconomics III. National Income and Price Determination: 10–15%

AP® Outline	Module
A. Aggregate demand	16: Income and Expenditure 17: Aggregate Demand: Introduction and Determinants
B. Aggregate supply	18: Aggregate Supply: Introduction and Determinants
C. Macroeconomic equilibrium	19: Equilibrium in the Aggregate Demand–Aggregate Supply Model 20: Economic Policy and the Aggregate Demand–Aggregate Supply Model 21: Fiscal Policy and Multiplier Effects

Pacing Guide

Module	Standard Teaching Days	Block Teaching Days
16	1	½
17	1	½
18	1	½
19	1	½
20	1	½
21	1	½
Section 4 Assessment	1	½
Total	**7**	**3½**

TRM Section Resources

All section resources may be accessed through the Teacher's e-Book, the TR-flash drive, or the book's website, bcs.worthpublishers.com/krugmanap2e *(teacher log-in required).*

Section 4 PD Video (for teachers)

Module 16

Module 16 Sample Lecture
Worksheet 16.1: Multiplier Effect, *MPC*, and *MPS*
Worksheet 16.2: Multiplier Practice
Worksheet 16.3: Investment Cliff
Exit Slip: Module 16

Module 17

Module 17 Sample Lecture
Worksheet 17.1: Intro to *AD*
Worksheet 17.2: Aggregate Demand
Exit Slip: Module 17

Module 18

Module 18 Sample Lecture
Worksheet 18.1: Why Are Wages Still So Low?
Worksheet 18.2: Restraining Labor Costs
Worksheet 18.3: Long-Run Economic Growth
Worksheet 18.4: Aggregate Supply
Exit Slip: Module 18

Module 19

Module 19 Sample Lecture
Worksheet 19.1: *AD–AS*
Worksheet 19.2: Equilibrium
Exit Slip: Module 19

Module 20

Module 20 Sample Lecture
Worksheet 20.1: Output Gaps
Handout 20.2: Circular-Flow Diagram
Handout 20.3: Taxes
Worksheet 20.4: Stimulus
Worksheet 20.5: Intro to Fiscal Policy
Worksheet 20.6: Fiscal Policy
Exit Slip: Module 20

Module 21

Module 21 Sample Lecture
Worksheet 21.1: Tax and Transfer Multiplier
Worksheet 21.2: Fiscal Policy and the Multiplier
Worksheet 21.3: Discretionary or Not?
Worksheet 21.4: *AD–AS* Review
Exit Slip: Module 21
Section 4 Review Video (for students)

St. Louis Federal Reserve Bank Resources

Many of the Federal Reserve Banks have educational departments that offer helpful resources for studying economics. Members of the Educators Advisory Board of the St. Louis Federal Reserve Bank have handpicked some of their best resources for use with your AP® Economics students. References to these resources are included in the margin notes. A complete list of the St. Louis Fed resources for each section with the corresponding URL (as of fall 2014) can be found in the TRM.

NOTE We have included a number of links to useful videos and articles in the margin notes in this section. Although all are active at the time of publication, we know that some may expire over the next few years. If a link is no longer active, you may wish to search for a similar article or video to illustrate the point. We may also periodically refresh resources on the book's companion website.

PD Section 4 Overview

Watch the video overview of Section 4 (for teachers), which is accessible through the Teacher's e-Book, the TR-flash drive, or the book's companion website, bcs.worthpublishers.com/krugmanap2e (teacher log-in required).

FOCUS Active Learning

Refer students to Chapter 25 of *Economics by Example* for a discussion of fiscal policy as it relates to debt, crowding out, and consumption smoothing.

SECTION 4

National Income and Price Determination

Ethan Miller/Getty Images

From Boom to Bust

Ft. Myers, Florida, was a boom town in 2005. Jobs were plentiful: the unemployment rate was less than 3%. The shopping malls were humming, and new stores were opening everywhere.

But then the boom went bust. Jobs became scarce, and by 2010, the unemployment rate was above 13%. Stores had few customers, and many were closing. One new business was flourishing, however. Marc Joseph, a real estate agent, began offering "foreclosure tours": visits to homes that had been seized by banks after the owners were unable to make mortgage payments.

What happened? Ft. Myers boomed because of a surge in home construction, fueled in part by speculators who bought houses not to live in, but because they believed they could resell those houses at much higher prices. Home construction gave jobs to construction workers, electricians, real estate agents, and others. And these workers, in turn, spent money locally, creating jobs for sales workers, waiters, gardeners, pool cleaners, and more. These workers also spent money locally, creating further expansion, and so on.

The boom turned into a bust when home construction came to a virtual halt. It turned out that speculation had been feeding on itself: people were buying houses as investments, then selling them to other people who were also buying houses as investments, and the prices had risen to levels far beyond what people who actually wanted to live in houses were willing to pay.

The abrupt collapse of the housing market pulled the local economy down with it, as the process that had created the earlier boom operated in reverse.

The boom and bust in Ft. Myers illustrates, on a small scale, the way booms and busts often happen for the economy as a whole. The business cycle is often driven by ups or downs in investment spending—either residential investment spending (spending on home construction) or nonresidential investment spending (such as spending on construction of office buildings, factories, and shopping malls). Changes in investment spending, in turn, indirectly lead to changes in consumer spending, which magnify—or *multiply*—the effect of the investment spending changes on the economy as a whole.

In this section we'll study how this process works on a grand scale. As a first step, we introduce *multiplier* analysis and show how it helps us understand the business cycle. We then explore how *aggregate supply* and *aggregate demand* determine the levels of prices and real output in an economy. Finally, we use the aggregate demand–aggregate supply model to visualize the state of the economy and examine the effects of economic policy.

St. Louis Federal Reserve Bank Resources

"The Legacy of the Olympics: Economic Burden or Boom?," *Page One Economics Classroom Edition* (August 2012)

Competition, sportsmanship, and national pride are the foundations of the Olympics, but how much do the Olympics cost the host city and country? What are some of the economic benefits? Is the investment in the Olympics worth it in the end? This issue discusses previous host experiences in terms of the economic side of the Olympics.

Maria Teijeiro/Digital Vision/Getty Images

MODULE 16

Income and Expenditure

In this Module, you will learn to:

- Describe the multiplier process by which initial changes in spending lead to further changes in spending
- Use the consumption function to show how current disposable income affects consumer spending
- Explain how expected future income and aggregate wealth affect consumer spending
- Identify the determinants of investment spending
- Explain why investment spending is considered a leading indicator of the future state of the economy

The Spending Multiplier: An Informal Introduction

The story of the boom and bust in Ft. Myers involves a sort of chain reaction in which an initial rise or fall in spending leads to changes in income, which lead to further changes in spending, and so on. Let's examine that chain reaction more closely, this time thinking through the effects of changes in spending on the economy as a whole.

For the sake of this analysis, we'll make the following four simplifying assumptions that we will have to reconsider in later modules:

1. We assume that *producers are willing to supply additional output at a fixed price.* That is, if consumers or businesses buying investment goods decide to spend an additional $1 billion, that will translate into the production of $1 billion worth of additional goods and services without driving up the overall level of prices. As a result, *changes in overall spending translate into changes in aggregate output,* as measured by real GDP. This assumption isn't too unrealistic in the short run, but in this section we'll learn that it needs to be changed when we think about the long-run effects of changes in demand.
2. We take the interest rate as given.
3. We assume that there is no government spending and no taxes.
4. We assume that exports and imports are zero.

Given these simplifying assumptions, consider what happens if there is a change in investment spending. Specifically, imagine that for some reason home builders decide to spend an extra $100 billion on home construction over the next year.

PD To prepare for teaching this lesson, you may want to consult the **Module 16 Sample Lecture** in the TRM.

OPEN & CLOSE Start Here

Before class, create a series of eight product cards with even number prices indicated on them, ranging from $18 to $2 ($18, $16, $14, etc.). Give one student twenty $2 bills in play money and pass out the cards to different members of the class. Tell the student that the goal is to buy the most expensive product possible with the money, insofar as he or she will only get one opportunity to buy something. Ask the student to make the purchase. Have the student write the amount he or she spent on the board and then take a seat. Next ask the student who made the sale to buy a product, write the amount of his or her purchase on the board, and have a seat. Continue this process until no cards are left to buy. Total up the amount spent on all the purchases. Ask students how this much money could be spent with only $20 in income to start with? *They should explain something similar to the multiplier effect because each purchase except the first was made using money from a previous sale.*

TEACH Connect It

Remind the students that the circular-flow diagram showed that money spent by one person is received as income by another person. Thinking back to this diagram will help them understand the spending multiplier.

St. Louis Federal Reserve Bank Resources

Econ Lowdown Glossary Flash Cards

Vocabulary, vocabulary, vocabulary is the first step in learning a new discipline like economics or personal finance. We can help with that! Create and print flash cards, or have your students create and print their own from more than 300 economics and personal-finance terms. Create flash cards for each new section or module. It's as easy as 1, 2, 3.

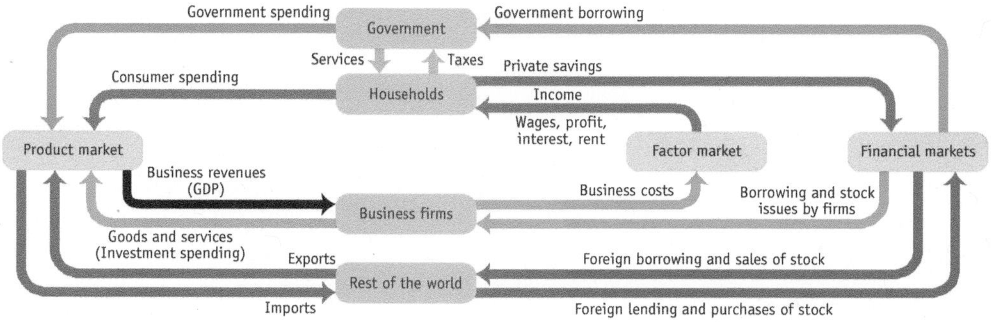

Module 16 Income and Expenditure 159

TEACH Teach It

Students don't need to know all the math behind the spending multiplier. Tell them that a portion of the initial amount is spent multiple times, adding to GDP each time. The following example should help students understand the multiplier.

Assume $MPC = 0.8$ and Δ Investment = \$1,000.

The initial increase in investment spending = \$1,000, which adds \$1,000 to GDP.

The next round of spending = 0.8 × \$1,000, which adds \$800 to the increase in GDP.

The next round of spending = 0.8 × \$800, which adds \$640 to the increase in GDP.

The next round of spending = 0.8 × \$640, which adds \$512 to the increase in GDP.

This continues until the 80% of the last amount spent is such a small amount that it can't be spent.

FOCUS Active Learning

Ask students what two courses of action they could take if they had \$1. *Save it or spend it.*

TEACH AP® Exam Tip

The marginal propensity to consume is how much of an additional dollar an individual would spend, while the marginal propensity to save is how much of the additional dollar that same person would save. Students will need to memorize the formula for the *MPC* along with the other formulas in the course. They will not have a formula sheet on the AP® exam or a calculator, so they should become familiar with solving these formulas through mental math.

Juice Images/Alamy

Many businesses, such as those that support home improvement and interior design, benefit during housing booms.

AP® Exam Tip

You will need to be able to calculate the multiplier. Learn the *MPC* formula: $\frac{\Delta \text{ Consumer spending}}{\Delta \text{ Disposable income}}$, as well as the multiplier formula itself: $\frac{1}{(1 - MPC)}$. For the *MPS*, substitute the change in savings for the change in consumer spending.

The **marginal propensity to consume**, or ***MPC***, is the increase in consumer spending when disposable income rises by \$1.

The **marginal propensity to save**, or ***MPS***, is the increase in household savings when disposable income rises by \$1.

The direct effect of this increase in investment spending will be to increase income and the value of aggregate output by the same amount. That's because each dollar spent on home construction translates into a dollar's worth of income for construction workers, suppliers of building materials, electricians, and so on. If the process stopped there, the increase in residential investment spending would raise overall income by exactly \$100 billion.

But the process doesn't stop there. The increase in aggregate output leads to an increase in disposable income that flows to households in the form of profits and wages. The increase in households' disposable income leads to a rise in consumer spending, which, in turn, induces firms to increase output yet again. This generates another rise in disposable income, which leads to another round of consumer spending increases, and so on. So there are multiple rounds of increases in aggregate output.

How large is the total effect on aggregate output if we sum the effect from all these rounds of spending increases? To answer this question, we need to introduce the concept of the **marginal propensity to consume**, or ***MPC***: the increase in consumer spending when disposable income rises by \$1. When consumer spending changes because of a rise or fall in disposable income, *MPC* is the change in consumer spending divided by the change in disposable income:

$$\textbf{(16-1)} \quad MPC = \frac{\Delta \text{ Consumer spending}}{\Delta \text{ Disposable income}}$$

where the symbol Δ (delta) means "change in." For example, if consumer spending goes up by \$6 billion when disposable income goes up by \$10 billion, *MPC* is \$6 billion/\$10 billion = 0.6.

Because consumers normally spend part but not all of an additional dollar of disposable income, *MPC* is a number between 0 and 1. The additional disposable income that consumers don't spend is saved; the **marginal propensity to save**, or ***MPS***, is the fraction of an additional \$1 of disposable income that is saved. *MPS* is equal to $1 - MPC$.

With the assumption of no taxes and no international trade, each \$1 increase in spending raises both real GDP and disposable income by \$1. So the \$100 billion increase in investment spending initially raises real GDP by \$100 billion. The corresponding \$100 billion increase in disposable income leads to a second-round increase in consumer spending, which raises real GDP by a further $MPC \times \$100$ billion. It is followed by a third-round increase in consumer spending of $MPC \times MPC \times \$100$ billion, and so on. After an infinite number of rounds, the total effect on real GDP is:

Increase in investment spending	=	\$100 billion
+ Second-round increase in consumer spending	=	$MPC \times \$100$ billion
+ Third-round increase in consumer spending	=	$MPC^2 \times \$100$ billion
+ Fourth-round increase in consumer spending	=	$MPC^3 \times \$100$ billion
⋮		⋮
Total increase in real GDP = $(1 + MPC + MPC^2 + MPC^3 + \ldots) \times \$100$ billion		

So the \$100 billion increase in investment spending sets off a chain reaction in the economy. The net result of this chain reaction is that a \$100 billion increase in investment spending leads to a change in real GDP that is a *multiple* of the size of that initial change in spending.

How large is this multiple? It's a mathematical fact that an infinite series of the form $1 + x + x^2 + x^3 + \ldots$, where x is between 0 and 1, is equal to $1/(1 - x)$. So the total effect of a \$100 billion increase in investment spending, *I*, taking into account all the subsequent

160 Section 4 National Income and Price Determination

increases in consumer spending (and assuming no taxes and no international trade), is given by:

(16-2) Total increase in real GDP from \$100 billion rise in

$$I = \frac{1}{(1 - MPC)} \times \$100 \text{ billion}$$

Let's consider a numerical example in which $MPC = 0.6$: each \$1 in additional disposable income causes a \$0.60 rise in consumer spending. In that case, a \$100 billion increase in investment spending raises real GDP by \$100 billion in the first round. The second-round increase in consumer spending raises real GDP by another $0.6 \times \$100$ billion, or \$60 billion. The third-round increase in consumer spending raises real GDP by another $0.6 \times \$60$ billion, or \$36 billion. This process goes on and on until the amount of spending in another round would be virtually zero. In the end, real GDP rises by \$250 billion as a consequence of the initial \$100 billion rise in investment spending:

$$\frac{1}{(1 - 0.6)} \times \$100 \text{ billion} = 2.5 \times \$100 \text{ billion} = \$250 \text{ billion}$$

Notice that even though there can be a nearly endless number of rounds of expansion of real GDP, the total rise in real GDP is limited to \$250 billion. The reason is that at each stage some of the rise in disposable income "leaks out" because it is saved, leaving less and less to be spent in the next round. How much of an additional dollar of disposable income is saved depends on *MPS,* the marginal propensity to save.

We've described the effects of a change in investment spending, but the same analysis can be applied to any other change in spending. The important thing is to distinguish between the initial change in aggregate spending, before real GDP rises, and the additional change in aggregate spending caused by the change in real GDP as the chain reaction unfolds. For example, suppose that a boom in housing prices makes consumers feel richer and that, as a result, they become willing to spend more at any given level of disposable income. This will lead to an initial rise in consumer spending, before real GDP rises. But it will also lead to second and later rounds of higher consumer spending as real GDP and disposable income rise.

An initial rise or fall in aggregate spending at a given level of real GDP is called an **autonomous change in aggregate spending**. It's autonomous–which means "self-governing"–because it's the cause, not the result, of the chain reaction we've just described. Formally, the **spending multiplier** is the ratio of the total change in real GDP caused by an autonomous change in aggregate spending to the size of that autonomous change. If we let ΔAAS stand for the autonomous change in aggregate spending and ΔY stand for the total change in real GDP, then the spending multiplier is equal to $\Delta Y/\Delta AAS$. We've already seen how to find the value of the spending multiplier. Assuming no taxes and no trade, the total change in real GDP caused by an autonomous change in aggregate spending is:

$$\textbf{(16-3)}\quad \Delta Y = \frac{1}{(1 - MPC)} \times \Delta AAS$$

So the spending multiplier is:

$$\textbf{(16-4)}\quad \frac{\Delta Y}{\Delta AAS} = \frac{1}{(1 - MPC)}$$

Notice that the size of the spending multiplier depends on *MPC.* If the marginal propensity to consume is high, so is the spending multiplier. This is true because the size of *MPC* determines how large each round of expansion is compared with the previous round. To put it another way, the higher *MPC* is, the less disposable income "leaks out" into savings at each round of expansion.

An **autonomous change in aggregate spending** is an initial rise or fall in aggregate spending that is the cause, not the result, of a series of income and spending changes.

The **spending multiplier** is the ratio of the total change in real GDP caused by an autonomous change in aggregate spending to the size of that autonomous change. It indicates the total rise in real GDP that results from each \$1 of an initial rise in spending.

TEACH Teach It

The spending multiplier indicates the total increase in real GDP that results from each \$1 of initial spending. The multiplier is generally larger than 1, so real GDP increases by more than the amount of the initial spending. The spending multiplier formula is $M = \frac{1}{(1 - MPC)}$, or, since $1 - MPC = MPS$, we can also say that $M = \frac{1}{MPS}$. Make sure students know both formulas as sometimes they are given *MPS* and sometimes they are given *MPC* in an exam question.

FOCUS Flip It

TRM To help students understand how one person's spending becomes another person's income, have students watch Jacob Clifford's video "Macro 3.8—Multiplier Effect, *MPC,* and *MPS*" (see econextras video list with hyperlinks on the bcs and TRFD). Assign **Worksheet 16.1 (Multiplier Effect, *MPC*, and *MPS*)** from the TRM for questions on this video.

FOCUS Active Learning

Use the short video, "Macro 3.9—Calculating the Multiplier" from Jacob Clifford (see econextras video list with hyperlinks on the bcs and TRFD). Pause the video (at 0:24), and let the students calculate the multiplier given the data shown.

FOCUS Active Learning

TRM For more practice with multipliers, you may choose to assign **Worksheet 16.2 (Multiplier Practice)** from the TRM in class or as homework.

TEACH Teach It

The largest portion of GDP is consumer spending. At about two-thirds of total spending in the United States, consumer spending is a critical driver of the macroeconomy. When consumer spending falls, we experience it more in terms of reduced real GDP. A rise in the unemployment rate is likely to cause a decrease in spending; it is called a demand shock.

FYI The Spending Multiplier and the Great Depression

The concept of the spending multiplier was originally devised by economists trying to understand the greatest economic disaster in history, the collapse of output and employment from 1929 to 1933, which began the Great Depression. Most economists believe that the slump from 1929 to 1933 was driven by a collapse in investment spending. But as the economy shrank, consumer spending also fell sharply, multiplying the effect on real GDP.

The table below shows what happened to investment spending, consumer spending, and GDP during those four terrible years. All data are in 2005 dollars for consistency with most of the other data in this section that are adjusted for inflation to 2005, the base year for the GDP deflator. What we see is that investment spending imploded, falling by more than 80%. But consumer spending also fell drastically and actually accounted for more of the fall in real GDP. (The total fall in real GDP was larger than the combined fall in consumer and investment spending, mainly because of technical accounting issues.)

The numbers in the table suggest that at the time of the Great Depression, the spending multiplier was around 3. Most current estimates put the size of the spending multiplier considerably lower—but there's a reason for that change. In 1929, the government of the United States was very small by modern standards: taxes were low and major government programs like Social Security and Medicare had not yet come into being. In the modern U.S. economy, taxes are much higher, and so is government spending. Why does this matter? Because taxes and some government programs act as *automatic stabilizers*, reducing the size of the spending multiplier. For example, when incomes are relatively high, tax payments are relatively high as well, thus moderating increases in expenditures. And when incomes are relatively low, the unemployment insurance program pays more money out to individuals, thus boosting expenditures higher than they would otherwise be.

Investment Spending, Consumer Spending, and Real GDP in the Great Depression (billions of 2005 dollars)

	1929	1933	Change
Investment spending	$101.7	$18.9	−$82.8
Consumer spending	736.6	601.1	−135.5
Real GDP	977.0	716.4	−260.6

Source: Bureau of Economic Analysis.

In later modules we'll use the concept of the spending multiplier to analyze the effects of fiscal and monetary policies. We'll also see that the spending multiplier changes when we introduce various complications, including taxes and foreign trade. First, however, we need to look more deeply at what determines consumer spending.

Consumer Spending

Should you splurge on a restaurant meal or save money by eating at home? Should you buy a new car and, if so, how expensive a model? Should you redo that bathroom or live with it for another year? In the real world, households are constantly confronted with such choices—not just about the consumption mix but also about how much to spend in total. These choices, in turn, have a powerful effect on the economy: consumer spending normally accounts for two-thirds of total spending on final goods and services. But what determines how much consumers spend?

Current Disposable Income and Consumer Spending

The most important factor affecting a family's consumer spending is its current disposable income—income after taxes are paid and government transfers are received. It's obvious from daily life that people with high disposable incomes on average drive more expensive cars, live in more expensive houses, and spend more on meals and clothing than people with lower disposable incomes. And the relationship between current disposable income and spending is clear in the data.

St. Louis Federal Reserve Bank Resources

Great Depression Online Course for Teachers and Students

History holds many economic lessons. The Great Depression, in particular, is an event that provides the opportunity to teach and learn a great deal about economics—whether you're studying the economic reasons that the Depression took place, the factors that helped it come to an end, or the impact on Americans who lived through it. This curriculum is designed to provide teachers with economic lessons that they can share with their students to help them understand this significant experience in U.S. history.

The Bureau of Labor Statistics (BLS) collects annual data on family income and spending. Families are grouped by levels of before-tax income; after-tax income for each group is also reported. Since the income figures include transfers from the government, what the BLS calls a household's after-tax income is equivalent to its current disposable income.

Figure 16.1 is a scatter diagram that illustrates the relationship between household current disposable income and household consumer spending for U.S. households by income group in 2012. For example, point *A* shows that in 2012 the middle fifth of the population had an average current disposable income of $46,777 and average spending of $43,004. The pattern of the dots slopes upward from left to right, making it clear that households with higher current disposable income had higher consumer spending.

A **consumption function** uses an equation or a graph to show how a household's consumer spending varies with the household's current disposable income.

Figure 16.2 on the next page provides the graph of a consumption function. The vertical intercept is the household's **autonomous consumer spending**: the amount the household would spend if its current disposable income were zero. Autonomous consumer spending is greater than zero because a household with no disposable income can buy some things by borrowing or using its savings.

Recall that the marginal propensity to consume, or *MPC*, is the amount the household spends out of each additional $1 of current disposable income. The slope of any line is "rise over run"; for the consumption function, the rise is the increase in consumer spending and the run is the increase in current disposable income. For each $1 "run" in income, the "rise" is the *MPC*, so the slope of the consumption function is $MPC/1 = MPC$.

According to the data on U.S. households in Figure 16.1, the best estimate of autonomous consumption for that population in 2012 was $18,478 and the best estimate of *MPC* was $0.52. This implies that the marginal propensity to save (*MPS*)—the amount of an additional $1 of disposable income that is saved—is approximately $1 - 0.52 = 0.48$ and the spending multiplier is $1/(1 - MPC) = 1/MPS =$ approximately $1/0.48 = 2.08$.

An individual household's consumption function shows a microeconomic relationship between the household's current disposable income and its spending on goods

A **consumption function** shows how a household's consumer spending varies with the household's current disposable income.

Autonomous consumer spending is the amount of money a household would spend if it had no disposable income.

Figure 16.1 Current Disposable Income and Consumer Spending for U.S. Households in 2012

For each income group of households, average current disposable income in 2012 is plotted versus average consumer spending in 2012. For example, the middle income group, with an annual income of $36,134 to $59,514, is represented by point *A*, indicating a household average current disposable income of $46,777 and average household consumer spending of $43,004. The data clearly show a positive relationship between current disposable income and consumer spending: families with higher current disposable income have higher consumer spending.
Source: Bureau of Labor Statistics.

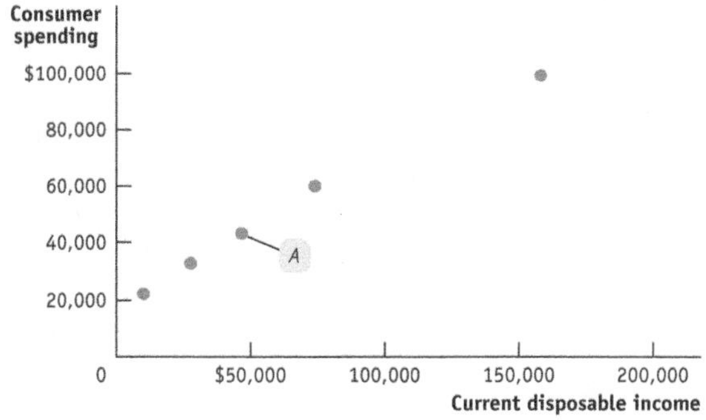

TEACH Connect It

Remind your students of the demand "shifters" from earlier in the course. Factors that change the aggregate consumption function are similar because they increase or decrease consumption at all levels of current disposable income.

Module 16 Income and Expenditure 163

Figure 16.2 The Consumption Function

The consumption function relates a household's current disposable income to its consumer spending. The vertical intercept is the household's autonomous consumer spending: the amount the household would spend if its current disposable income were zero. The slope of the consumption function is the marginal propensity to consume, or *MPC*: the amount the household spends out of each additional $1 of current disposable income.

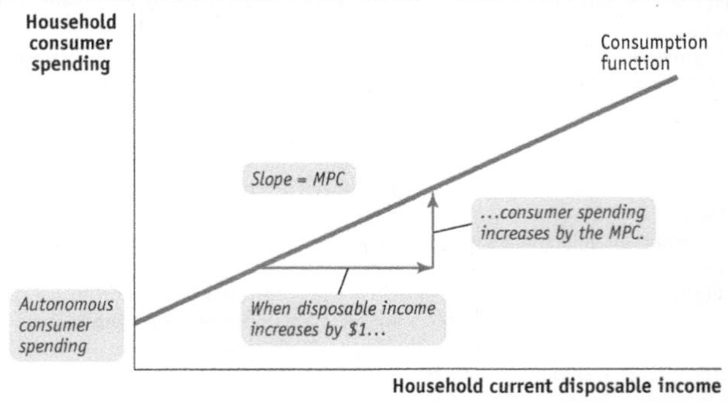

The **aggregate consumption function** is the relationship for the economy as a whole between aggregate current disposable income and aggregate consumer spending.

and services. Macroeconomists study the **aggregate consumption function**, which shows the relationship between current disposable income and consumer spending for the economy as a whole. We can represent this relationship with the following equation:

$$\textbf{(16-5)}\quad C = A + MPC \times Y_D$$

Here, C is aggregate consumer spending, Y_D is aggregate current disposable income, and A is aggregate autonomous consumer spending, the amount of consumer spending when disposable income is zero. **Figure 16.3** shows two aggregate consumption functions as graphs, analogous to the graph of the household consumption function in Figure 16.2.

Shifts of the Aggregate Consumption Function

The aggregate consumption function shows the relationship between current disposable income and consumer spending for the economy as a whole, other things equal. When things other than current disposable income change, the aggregate consumption function shifts. There are two principal causes of shifts of the aggregate consumption function: changes in expected future disposable income and changes in aggregate wealth.

Changes in Expected Future Disposable Income Milton Friedman argued that consumer spending ultimately depends primarily on the income people expect to have over the long term rather than on their current income. This argument is known as the *permanent income hypothesis*. Suppose you land a really good, well-paying job on graduating from college—but the job, and the paychecks, won't start for several months. So your disposable income hasn't risen yet. Even so, it's likely that you will start spending more on final goods and services right away—maybe buying nicer work clothes than you originally planned—because you know that higher income is coming.

Conversely, suppose you have a good job but learn that the company is planning to downsize your division, raising the possibility that you may lose your job and have to take a lower-paying one somewhere else. Even though your disposable income hasn't gone down yet, you might well cut back on spending even while still employed, to save for a rainy day.

FOCUS Active Learning

Ask students to give examples of changes in expected future disposable income. *Answers will vary. For example: Suppose a college senior lines up a job that will pay more than she expected to earn after graduation. Or perhaps your mom decides to pursue an advanced degree that will allow her to earn more than expected in a few years. These increases in expected future income will shift the consumption functions of the recipients upward as consumption smoothing leads them to spend some of their higher expected income before it is actually received.*

164 Section 4 National Income and Price Determination

Figure 16.3 Shifts of the Aggregate Consumption Function

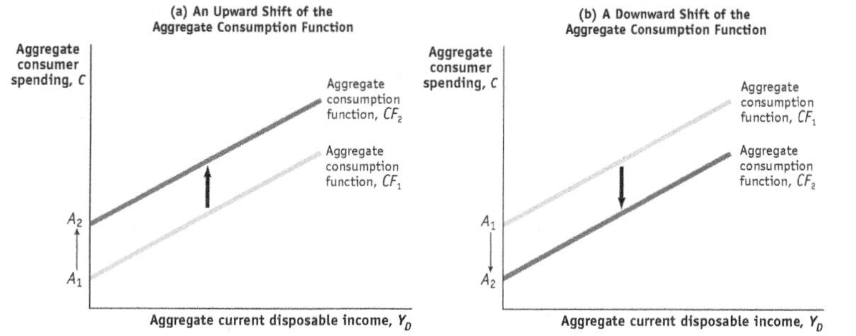

Panel (a) illustrates the effect of an increase in expected aggregate future disposable income. Consumers will spend more at every given level of aggregate current disposable income, Y_D. As a result, the initial aggregate consumption function CF_1, with aggregate autonomous consumer spending A_1, shifts up to a new position at CF_2 with aggregate autonomous consumer spending A_2. An increase in aggregate wealth will also shift the aggregate consumption function up. Panel (b), by contrast, illustrates the effect of a reduction in expected aggregate future disposable income. Consumers will spend less at every given level of aggregate current disposable income, Y_D. Consequently, the initial aggregate consumption function CF_1, with aggregate autonomous consumer spending A_1, shifts down to a new position at CF_2 with aggregate autonomous consumer spending A_2. A reduction in aggregate wealth will have the same effect.

Both of these examples show how expectations about future disposable income can affect consumer spending. The two panels of Figure 16.3, which plot aggregate current disposable income against aggregate consumer spending, show how changes in expected future disposable income affect the aggregate consumption function. In both panels, CF_1 is the initial aggregate consumption function. Panel (a) shows the effect of good news: information that leads consumers to expect higher disposable income in the future than they had expected before. Consumers will now spend more at any given level of aggregate current disposable income Y_D, corresponding to an increase in A, aggregate autonomous consumer spending, from A_1 to A_2. The effect is to shift the aggregate consumption function up, from CF_1 to CF_2. Panel (b) shows the effect of bad news: information that leads consumers to expect lower disposable income in the future than they had expected before. Consumers will now spend less at any given level of aggregate current disposable income, Y_D, corresponding to a fall in A from A_1 to A_2. The effect is to shift the aggregate consumption function down, from CF_1 to CF_2.

Changes in Aggregate Wealth Imagine two individuals, Maria and Mark, both of whom expect to earn $30,000 this year. Suppose, however, that they have different histories. Maria has been working steadily for the past 10 years, owns her own home, and has $200,000 in the bank. Mark is the same age as Maria, but he has been in and out of work, hasn't managed to buy a house, and has very little in savings. In this case, Maria has something that Mark doesn't have: wealth. Even though they have the same disposable income, other things equal, you'd expect Maria to spend more on consumption than Mark. That is, *wealth* has an effect on consumer spending.

The effect of wealth on spending is emphasized by an influential economic model of how consumers make choices about spending versus saving called the *life-cycle hypothesis.* According to this hypothesis, consumers plan their spending over their lifetime, not just in response to their current disposable income. As a result, people try to *smooth* their

Mike Kemp/Rubberball/Getty Images

FOCUS Active Learning

Ask students to give examples of changes in aggregate wealth. *Answers will vary. For example: Suppose that the stock market has a bad year and the value of many people's wealth substantially declines. This lost wealth, even if it is only on paper, usually causes people to reduce their consumption. The consumption function shifts downward.*

TEACH Connect It

Remind students that they already discussed investment spending in Module 10. Ask them to give examples. *Answers will vary but may include constructing factories, increasing inventories, or building a new home.*

TEACH Teach It

When a firm considers investment spending, it is really doing a little cost-benefit analysis on the dollars it is about to spend. For example, if a firm is considering building a new factory, planners assume that this will increase sales, but it may also require borrowing to fund the investment. The market interest rate is the cost of investment. The expected return on the investment, which is the expected economic profit from the factory, is equal to $\frac{\textit{(Total revenue} - \textit{Total cost)}}{\textit{Investment cost}}$. Businesses will make decisions to buy new equipment or build new factories when the rate of expected return is greater than the rate of interest on the borrowed funds.

consumption over their lifetimes—they save some of their current disposable income during their years of peak earnings (typically occurring during a worker's 40s and 50s) and live off the wealth they accumulated while working during their retirement. We won't go into the details of this hypothesis but will simply point out that it implies an important role for wealth in determining consumer spending. For example, a middle-aged couple who have accumulated a lot of wealth—who have paid off the mortgage on their house and already own plenty of stocks and bonds—will, other things equal, spend more on goods and services than a couple who have the same current disposable income but still need to save for their retirement.

Because wealth affects household consumer spending, changes in wealth across the economy can shift the aggregate consumption function. A rise in aggregate wealth—say, because of a booming stock market—increases the vertical intercept *A*, aggregate autonomous consumer spending. This, in turn, shifts the aggregate consumption function up in the same way as does an expected increase in future disposable income. A decline in aggregate wealth—say, because of a fall in housing prices as occurred in 2008—reduces *A* and shifts the aggregate consumption function down.

Investment Spending

Although consumer spending is much greater than investment spending, booms and busts in investment spending tend to drive the business cycle. In fact, most recessions originate as a fall in investment spending. **Figure 16.4** illustrates this point; it shows the annual percentage change of investment spending and consumer spending in the United States, both measured in 2005 dollars, during six recessions from 1973 to 2009. As you can see, swings in investment spending are much more dramatic than those in consumer spending. In addition, economists believe that declines in consumer spending are usually the result of slumps in investment spending that trigger the spending multiplier process. Soon we'll examine in more detail how investment spending affects consumer spending.

Planned investment spending is the investment spending that businesses intend to undertake during a given period.

Before we do that, however, let's analyze the factors that determine investment spending, which are somewhat different from those that determine consumer spending. **Planned investment spending** is the investment spending that firms *intend* to undertake during a given period. For reasons explained shortly, the level of investment spending

Figure 16.4 Fluctuations in Investment Spending and Consumer Spending

The bars illustrate the annual percent change in investment spending and consumer spending during six recent recessions. As the heights of the bars show, swings in investment spending were much larger in percentage terms than those in consumer spending. The pattern has led economists to believe that recessions typically originate as a slump in investment spending.

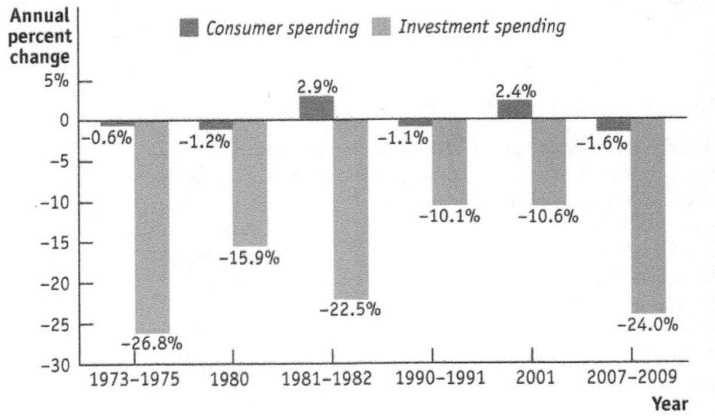

166 Section 4 National Income and Price Determination

that businesses *actually* carry out is sometimes not the same level as was planned. Planned investment spending depends on three principal factors: the interest rate, the expected future level of real GDP, and the current level of production capacity. First, we'll analyze the effect of the interest rate.

The Interest Rate and Investment Spending

Interest rates have their clearest effect on one particular form of investment spending: spending on residential construction—that is, on the construction of homes. The reason is straightforward: home builders only build houses they think they can sell, and houses are more affordable—and so more likely to sell—when the interest rate is low. Consider a potential home-buying family that needs to borrow $150,000 to buy a house. At an interest rate of 7.5%, a 30-year home mortgage will mean payments of $1,048 per month. At an interest rate of 5.5%, those payments would be only $851 per month, making houses significantly more affordable. Interest rates actually did drop from roughly 7.5% to 5.5% between the late 1990s and 2003, helping set off a housing boom.

Interest rates also affect other forms of investment spending. Firms with investment spending projects will go ahead with a project only if they expect a rate of return higher than the cost of the funds they would have to borrow to finance that project. If the interest rate rises, fewer projects will pass that test, and, as a result, investment spending will be lower.

You might think that the trade-off a firm faces is different if it can fund its investment project with its past profits rather than through borrowing. Past profits used to finance investment spending are called *retained earnings*. But even if a firm pays for investment spending out of retained earnings, the trade-off it must make in deciding whether or not to fund a project remains the same because it must take into account the opportunity cost of its funds. For example, instead of purchasing new equipment, the firm could lend out the funds and earn interest. The forgone interest earned is the opportunity cost of using retained earnings to fund an investment project. So the trade-off the firm faces when comparing a project's rate of return to the market interest rate has not changed when it uses retained earnings rather than borrowed funds. Either way, a rise in the market interest rate makes any given investment project less profitable. Conversely, a fall in the interest rate makes some investment projects that were unprofitable before profitable at the new lower interest rate. As a result, some projects that had been unfunded before will be funded now.

Dmitry Kalinovsky/Shutterstock

Interest rates have a direct impact on whether or not construction companies decide to invest in the construction of new homes.

So planned investment spending—spending on investment projects that firms voluntarily decide whether or not to undertake—is negatively related to the interest rate. Other things equal, a higher interest rate leads to a lower level of planned investment spending.

Expected Future Real GDP, Production Capacity, and Investment Spending

Suppose a firm has enough capacity to continue to produce the amount it is currently selling but doesn't expect its sales to grow in the future. Then it will engage in investment spending only to replace existing equipment and structures that wear out or are rendered obsolete by new technologies. But if, instead, the firm expects its sales to grow rapidly in the future, it will find its existing production capacity insufficient for its future production needs. So the firm will undertake investment spending to meet those needs. This implies that, other things equal, firms will undertake more investment spending when they expect their sales to grow.

Now suppose that the firm currently has considerably more capacity than necessary to meet current production needs. Even if it expects sales to grow, it won't

FOCUS In the News

TRM Find a recent article about interest rates and the automobile industry. Alternatively, you may use the *Wall Street Journal* article "Investment Falls Off a Cliff" at http://tinyurl.com/m4d6bph. **Worksheet 16.3 (Investment Cliff)** includes questions on this reading.

TEACH Teach It

Students should understand the conditions under which a business will invest even with high interest rates.

- **Expected Future Real GDP**: Suppose a firm believed that the economy was really going to take off next year. This firm might increase investment spending in anticipation of increased sales. After all, you can't build a factory overnight; the firm must begin the factory now to take advantage of more customers in the coming year.
- **Production Capacity**: Suppose a firm can produce 100,000 units if the factory is producing 24/7. The firm's full capacity is 100,000 units. Right now, the firm has enough customers to produce only 50%, or 50,000 units, of full capacity. A firm in this situation would not be looking to increase investment. After all, if orders from customers were to increase, it would be easy to satisfy those orders without increasing the size of the factory. The best conditions for new investment spending consist of firms that are near production capacity with expectations of strong real GDP in the future.

St. Louis Federal Reserve Bank Resources

"Gross Domestic Product," *The Economic Lowdown Video Series*, Episode 7

GDP data are among the most important economic data available for measuring economic growth, but measuring the output of a large, dynamic economy is a complex task. In the seventh episode of the *Economic Lowdown Video Series*, economic education specialist Scott Wolla explains what GDP measures, how it is calculated, how it is useful in determining whether and how quickly the economy is growing, and how GDP can be used as an indicator of the standard of living.

TEACH Teach It

Remind students that planned investment spending would have an inverse relationship to interest rates.

TEACH Connect It

Use the business cycle to show and explain that during a business contraction, unplanned inventories increase, while during an expansion, they decrease.

have to undertake investment spending for a while—not until the growth in sales catches up with its excess capacity. This illustrates the fact that, other things equal, the current level of productive capacity has a negative effect on investment spending: other things equal, the higher the current capacity, the lower the investment spending.

If we put together the effects on investment spending of (1) growth in expected future sales and (2) the size of current production capacity, we can see one situation in which firms will most likely undertake high levels of investment spending: when they expect sales to grow rapidly. In that case, even excess production capacity will soon be used up, leading firms to resume investment spending.

What is an indicator of high expected growth in future sales? It's a high expected future growth rate of real GDP. A higher expected future growth rate of real GDP results in a higher level of planned investment spending, but a lower expected future growth rate of real GDP leads to lower planned investment spending.

AP® Exam Tip

An increase in unplanned inventories is preceded by a decrease in consumer spending. A decrease in unplanned inventories is preceded by an increase in consumer spending.

Inventory investment is the value of the change in total inventories held in the economy during a given period.

Positive **unplanned inventory investment** occurs when actual sales are lower than businesses expected, leading to unplanned increases in inventories. Sales in excess of expectations result in negative unplanned inventory investment.

Actual investment spending is the sum of planned investment spending and unplanned inventory investment.

Getty Images

Inventories and Unplanned Investment Spending

Most firms maintain inventories, stocks of goods held to satisfy future sales. Firms hold inventories so they can quickly satisfy buyers—a consumer can purchase an item off the shelf rather than waiting for it to be manufactured. In addition, businesses often hold inventories of their inputs to be sure they have a steady supply of necessary materials and spare parts. At the end of 2013, the overall value of inventories in the U.S. economy was estimated at \$2.5 trillion, more than 14% of GDP.

A firm that increases its inventories is engaging in a form of investment spending. Suppose, for example, that the U.S. auto industry produces 800,000 cars per month but sells only 700,000. The remaining 100,000 cars are added to the inventory at auto company warehouses or car dealerships, ready to be sold in the future.

Inventory investment is the value of the change in total inventories held in the economy during a given period. Unlike other forms of investment spending, inventory investment can actually be negative. If, for example, the auto industry reduces its inventory over the course of a month, we say that it has engaged in negative inventory investment.

To understand inventory investment, think about a manager stocking the canned goods section of a supermarket. The manager tries to keep the store fully stocked so that shoppers can almost always find what they're looking for. But the manager does not want the shelves too heavily stocked because shelf space is limited and products can spoil. Similar considerations apply to many firms and typically lead them to manage their inventories carefully. However, sales fluctuate. And because firms cannot always accurately predict sales, they often find themselves holding larger or smaller inventories than they had intended. When a firm's inventories are higher than intended due to an unforeseen decrease in sales, the result is **unplanned inventory investment.** An unexpected increase in sales depletes inventories and causes the value of unplanned inventory investment to be negative.

So in any given period, **actual investment spending** is equal to planned investment spending plus unplanned inventory investment. If we let $I_{Unplanned}$ represent unplanned inventory investment, $I_{Planned}$ represent planned investment spending, and I represent actual investment spending, then the relationship among all three can be represented as:

$$\textbf{(16-6)}\quad I = I_{Unplanned} + I_{Planned}$$

To see how unplanned inventory investment can occur, let's continue to focus on the auto industry and make the following assumptions. First, let's assume that the industry must determine each month's production volume in advance, before it knows the volume of actual sales. Second, let's assume that it anticipates selling 800,000 cars next month and that it plans neither to add to nor subtract from existing inventories. In that case, it will produce 800,000 cars to match anticipated sales.

168 Section 4 National Income and Price Determination

FYI Interest Rates and the U.S. Housing Boom

Interest rates in the United States dropped from roughly 7.5% to 5.5% between the late 1990s and 2003, helping set off a nationwide housing boom. There is little question that this housing boom was caused, in the first instance, by low interest rates.

The figure below shows the interest rate on 30-year home mortgages—the traditional way to borrow money for a home purchase—and the number of housing starts—the number of homes for which construction is started per month—from 1995 to the end of 2013 in the United States. Panel (a), which shows the mortgage rate, gives you an idea of how much interest rates fell. In the second half of the 1990s, mortgage rates generally fluctuated between 7% and 8%; by 2003, they were down to between 5% and 6%. These lower rates were largely the result of Federal Reserve policy: the Fed cut rates in response to the 2001 recession and continued cutting them into 2003 out of concern that the economy's recovery was too weak to generate sustained job growth.

The low interest rates led to a large increase in residential investment spending, reflected in a surge of housing starts, shown in panel (b). This rise in investment spending drove an overall economic expansion, both through its direct effects and through the spending multiplier process.

Unfortunately, the housing boom eventually turned into too much of a good thing. By 2006, it was clear that the U.S. housing market was experiencing a bubble: people were buying housing based on unrealistic expectations about future price increases. When the bubble burst, housing—and the U.S. economy—took a fall. The fall was so severe that, even when the Fed cut interest rates to near zero and mortgage rates consequently dropped to below 5% beginning in 2009, housing starts merely stabilized. As of early 2014, housing starts had not yet fully recovered.

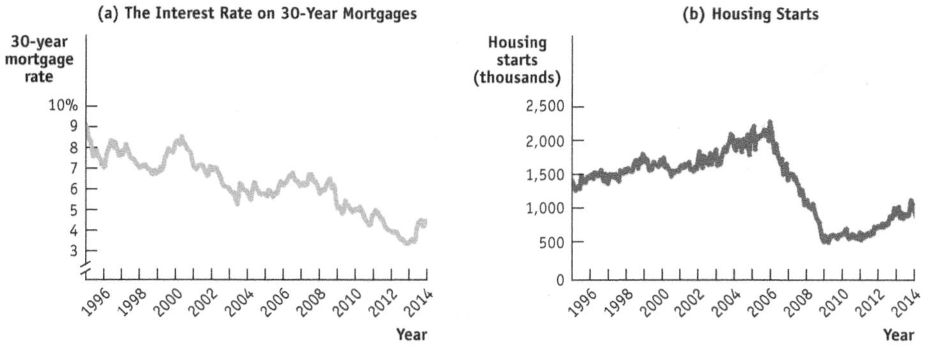

Source: Federal Reserve Bank of St. Louis.

Now imagine that next month's actual sales are less than expected, only 700,000 cars. As a result, the value of 100,000 cars will be added to investment spending as unplanned inventory investment.

The auto industry will, of course, eventually adjust to this slowdown in sales and the resulting unplanned inventory investment. It is likely that it will cut next month's production volume in order to reduce inventories. In fact, economists who study macroeconomic variables in an attempt to determine the future path of the economy pay careful attention to changes in inventory levels. Rising inventories typically indicate positive unplanned inventory investment and a slowing economy, as sales are less than had been forecast. Falling inventories typically indicate negative unplanned inventory investment and a growing economy, as sales are greater than forecast. In the next section, we will see how production adjustments in response to fluctuations in sales and inventories ensure that the value of final goods and services actually produced is equal to desired purchases of those final goods and services.

FOCUS In the News

After students read the FYI box, have them read the *Wall Street Journal* Market Watch December 2013 article "Mortgage Rates Won't Derail 2014 Housing Market" at http://www.marketwatch.com/story/mortgage-rates-wont-derail-2014-housing-market-2013-12-27. Ask students to explain why sales were expected to rise even with higher interest rates. *Hiring in 2014 was expected to be strong enough to unleash a chunk of the pent-up demand that accumulated during the recession, and there was evidence that purchasers were becoming accustomed to the pricier sales environment.*

OPEN & CLOSE Exit Slip

TRM *Please see **Exit Slip: Module 16** in the TRM for formative multiple-choice questions to ask your students before finishing your lesson. These questions will help you quickly assess whether your students have mastered the module's concepts before moving on.*

Answers to the Exit Slip Questions

1. C
2. B
3. C

MODULE 16 Review

Check Your Understanding

1. Explain why a decline in investment spending caused by a change in business expectations leads to a fall in consumer spending.
2. What is the spending multiplier if the marginal propensity to consume is 0.5? What is it if *MPC* is 0.8?
3. Suppose a crisis in the capital markets makes consumers unable to borrow and unable to save money. What implication does this have for the effects of expected future disposable income on consumer spending?
4. For each event, explain whether the initial effect is a change in planned investment spending or a change in unplanned inventory investment, and indicate the direction of the change.
   a. an unexpected increase in consumer spending
   b. a sharp rise in the interest rate
   c. a sharp increase in the economy's growth rate of real GDP
   d. an unanticipated fall in sales

Tackle the Test: Multiple-Choice Questions

1. Changes in which of the following leads to a shift of the aggregate consumption function?
   I. expected future disposable income
   II. aggregate wealth
   III. current disposable income
   a. I only
   b. II only
   c. III only
   d. I and II only
   e. I, II, and III
2. The slope of a household's consumption function is equal to
   a. the real interest rate.
   b. the inflation rate.
   c. the marginal propensity to consume.
   d. the rate of increase in household current disposable income.
   e. the tax rate.
3. Given the aggregate consumption function $C = \$1.6$ trillion $+ 0.5Y_D$, if aggregate current disposable income is \$2.0 trillion, aggregate consumption spending will equal
   a. \$3.6 trillion.
   b. \$2.6 trillion.
   c. \$2.0 trillion.
   d. \$1.6 trillion.
   e. \$0.6 trillion.
4. The level of planned investment spending is negatively related to
   a. the rate of return on investment.
   b. the level of consumer spending.
   c. the level of actual investment spending.
   d. the interest rate.
   e. all of the above.
5. Actual investment spending in any period is equal to
   a. planned investment spending + unplanned inventory investment.
   b. planned investment spending − unplanned inventory investment.
   c. planned investment spending + inventory decreases.
   d. unplanned inventory investment + inventory increases.
   e. unplanned inventory investment − inventory increases.

Tackle the Test: Free-Response Questions

1. Use the aggregate consumption function provided to answer the following questions:

$$C = \$1.5 \text{ trillion} + 0.8Y_D$$

   a. What is the value of the marginal propensity to consume?
   b. Suppose aggregate current disposable income is \$4.0 trillion. Calculate the amount of aggregate consumer spending.
   c. Draw a correctly labeled graph showing this aggregate consumption function.
   d. What is the slope of this aggregate consumption function?
   e. On your graph from part c, show what would happen if expected future income decreases.

Answers to Module 16 Review Questions

Check Your Understanding

1. A decline in investment spending has a multiplier effect on real GDP. The fall in actual investment spending, *I*, leads to an initial fall in real GDP, which leads to a fall in disposable income (because less production means a decrease in payments to workers), which leads to lower consumer spending, which leads to another fall in real GDP, and so on. Thus, consumer spending falls as an indirect result of the fall in investment spending.

2. When *MPC* is 0.5, the spending multiplier is equal to $1/(1 - 0.5) = 1/0.5 = 2$. When *MPC* is 0.8, the spending multiplier is equal to $1/(1 - 0.8) = 1/0.2 = 5$.

3. If you expect your future disposable income to fall, you would like to save some of today's disposable income to tide you over in the future. But you cannot do this if you cannot save. If you expect your future disposable income to rise, you would like to spend some of tomorrow's higher income today. But you cannot do this if you cannot borrow. If you cannot save or borrow, your expected future disposable income will have no effect on your consumer spending today. In fact, your *MPC* must always equal 1: you must consume all your current disposable income today, and you will be unable to smooth your consumption over time.

4. a. An unexpected increase in consumer spending will result in a reduction in inventories as producers sell items from their inventories to satisfy this short-term increase in demand. This is negative unplanned inventory investment: it reduces the value of producers' inventories.

b. A rise in the interest rate means that fewer investment spending projects are now profitable to producers, whether they are financed through borrowing or retained earnings. As a result, producers will reduce the amount of planned investment spending.

c. A sharp increase in the rate of real GDP growth leads to a higher level of planned investment spending by producers as they increase production capacity to meet higher demand.

d. As sales fall, producers sell less, and their inventories grow. This leads to positive unplanned inventory investment.

Tackle the Test: Multiple-Choice Questions

1. d
2. c
3. b
4. d
5. a

Rubric for FRQ 1 (7 points)

1 point: 0.8

1 point: $4.7 trillion

1 point: Vertical axis labeled "Aggregate consumer spending" and horizontal axis labeled "Aggregate current disposable income"

1 point: Vertical intercept of $1.5 trillion

1 point: Upward-sloping aggregate consumption function

1 point: 0.8

1 point: Aggregate consumption function shifts downward

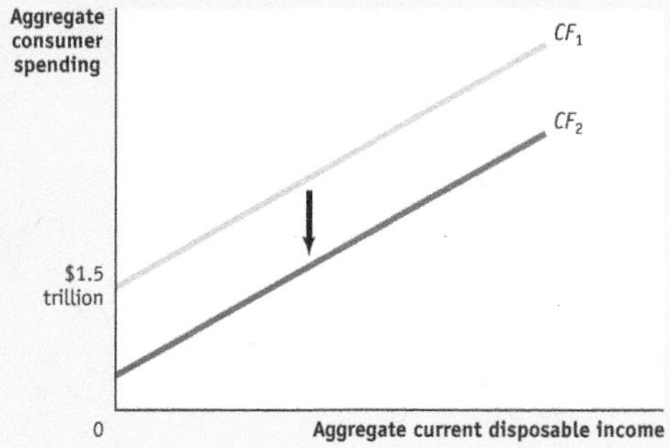

2. List the three most important factors affecting planned investment spending. Explain how each is related to actual investment spending.
(6 points)

Tackle the Test: Free-Response Question

Rubric for FRQ 2 (6 points)

1 point: The interest rate

1 point: The interest rate is the opportunity cost of investing. As the interest rate increases, investment spending decreases; as the interest rate decreases, investment spending increases.

1 point: Expected future real GDP

1 point: If a firm expects its sales to grow in the future, it will invest in expanded production capacity.

1 point: Production capacity

1 point: If a firm finds its existing production capacity insufficient for its future production needs, it will undertake investment spending to meet those needs; if it has more capacity than it needs, there is no need for investment spending.

Module 16 Income and Expenditure 171

PD To prepare for teaching this lesson, you may want to consult the **Module 17 Sample Lecture** in the TRM.

OPEN & CLOSE **Start Here**

Play the Beatles' song "Taxman." Then ask students the following questions:

- What does this song imply about the level of tax rates? *They are high.*
- How do you think an increase in tax rates will impact consumer spending in an economy? *Consumer spending should go down because people have less disposable income.*

Introduce aggregate demand by stating that some changes have an effect on large portions of the spending in an economy. For example, overall consumer spending goes down due to substantial increases in income tax rates and this impacts the spending on all goods and services in the economy.

Toogs/Getty Images

MODULE 17

Aggregate Demand: Introduction and Determinants

In this Module, you will learn to:

- Use the aggregate demand curve to illustrate the relationship between the aggregate price level and the quantity of aggregate output demanded in the economy
- Explain how the wealth effect and the interest rate effect give the aggregate demand curve a negative slope
- Identify the factors that can shift the aggregate demand curve

Aggregate Demand

AP® Exam Tip

Aggregate demand is the demand for all goods and services in all markets rather than the demand for one good or service in one market.

The **aggregate demand curve** shows the relationship between the aggregate price level and the quantity of aggregate output demanded by households, businesses, the government, and the rest of the world.

The Great Depression, the great majority of economists agree, was the result of a massive negative demand shock. What does that mean? When economists talk about a fall in the demand for a particular good or service, they're referring to a leftward shift of the demand curve. Similarly, when economists talk about a negative demand shock to the economy as a whole, they're referring to a leftward shift of the **aggregate demand curve**, a curve that shows the relationship between the aggregate price level and the quantity of aggregate output demanded by households, firms, the government, and the rest of the world.

Figure 17.1 shows what the aggregate demand curve may have looked like in 1933, at the end of the 1929–1933 recession. The horizontal axis shows the total quantity of domestic goods and services demanded, measured in 2005 dollars. We use real GDP to measure aggregate output and will use the two terms interchangeably. The vertical axis shows the aggregate price level, measured by the GDP deflator. With these variables on the axes, we can draw a curve, *AD*, that shows how much aggregate output would have been demanded at any given aggregate price level. Since *AD* is meant to illustrate aggregate demand in 1933, one point on the curve corresponds to actual data for 1933, when the aggregate price level was 7.9 and the total quantity of domestic final goods and services purchased was $716 billion in 2005 dollars.

As drawn in Figure 17.1, the aggregate demand curve is downward sloping, indicating a negative relationship between the aggregate price level and the quantity of aggregate output demanded. A higher aggregate price level, other things equal, reduces the quantity of aggregate output demanded; a lower aggregate price level, other things equal,

St. Louis Federal Reserve Bank Resources

"Demand," *The Economic Lowdown Podcast Series,* Volume 1, Episode 6

The sixth podcast in this series examines the law of demand. Those who love candy bars will find this lesson especially easy to digest. A demand curve is simply defined, as are the sorts of changes that might affect that curve—all in less than seven minutes.

Figure 17.1 The Aggregate Demand Curve

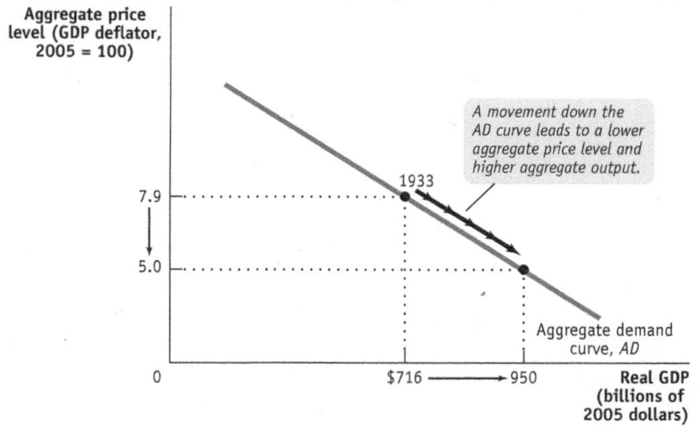

The aggregate demand curve shows the relationship between the aggregate price level and the quantity of aggregate output demanded. The curve is downward sloping due to the wealth effect of a change in the aggregate price level and the interest rate effect of a change in the aggregate price level. Corresponding to the actual 1933 data, here the total quantity of goods and services demanded at an aggregate price level of 7.9 is $716 billion in 2005 dollars. According to our hypothetical curve, however, if the aggregate price level had been only 5.0, the quantity of aggregate output demanded would have risen to $950 billion.

increases the quantity of aggregate output demanded. According to Figure 17.1, if the price level in 1933 had been 5.0 instead of 7.9, the total quantity of domestic final goods and services demanded would have been $950 billion in 2005 dollars instead of $716 billion.

The first key question about the aggregate demand curve involves its negative slope.

AP® Exam Tip

Notice the axis labels in Figure 17.1. These will be important when you create *AD–AS* graphs. Points are awarded for correctly drawn and labeled graphs on the AP® exam.

Why Is the Aggregate Demand Curve Downward Sloping?

In Figure 17.1, the curve *AD* slopes downward. Why? Recall the basic equation of national income accounting:

$$\textbf{(17-1)}\quad GDP = C + I + G + X - IM$$

where *C* is consumer spending, *I* is investment spending, *G* is government purchases of goods and services, *X* is exports to other countries, and *IM* is imports. If we measure these variables in constant dollars—that is, in prices of a base year—then $C + I + G + X - IM$ represents the quantity of domestically produced final goods and services demanded during a given period. *G* is decided by the government, but the other variables are private-sector decisions. To understand why the aggregate demand curve slopes downward, we need to understand why a rise in the aggregate price level reduces *C*, *I*, and $X - IM$.

You might think that the downward slope of the aggregate demand curve is a natural consequence of the *law of demand*. That is, since the demand curve for any one good

FOCUS Graph It

Use Figure 17.1 to show students the *AD* curve. Make sure to note that the labels on the graph are the only thing that makes *AD* look different from individual demand graphs. Have them draw a demand curve with correct labels on their personal whiteboards or notebook paper and then draw an *AD* curve next to the demand curve with correct labels, so they can see the difference. Let students know they can use *PL* for aggregate price level and *RGDP* or *Y* for real GDP.

FOCUS Active Learning

Use the video "Aggregate Demand Practice" from Jacob Clifford (see econextras video list with hyperlinks on the bcs and TRFD). Ask students to list the four factors that shift the aggregate demand curve (*spending changes from consumption, investment, government, imports*). Pause the video (at 2:25), and let the students discuss the four questions Mr. Clifford presents before revealing the answers.

St. Louis Federal Reserve Bank Resources

Supply and Demand.notebook

This series of slides aids students in reviewing the determinants of supply and demand, provides an exercise for them to choose which of the curves shift and why, and allows them to determine which curve will shift given a market event.

TEACH Teach It

Students should understand the reason *AD* is downward-sloping.

- **The wealth effect**: If the aggregate price level changes, the purchasing power of existing consumer wealth changes. For example, if the price level decreases, then consumers can purchase more with their existing wealth, causing a movement downward and to the right along the *AD* curve.
- **The interest rate effect**: As interest rates change, the opportunity cost of holding money changes. A lower price level increases the purchasing power of money in your pocket, so you need to hold less money to buy your goods and services. This drives down interest rates. Lower interest rates will increase consumer and investment spending, thus increasing real GDP along the *AD* curve.

FOCUS Active Learning

TRM Have your students watch Jason Welker's "An Introduction to Aggregate Demand" video (see econextras video list with hyperlinks on the bcs and TRFD). Suggested questions for use with the video may be found in **Worksheet 17.1 (Intro to *AD*)**.

is downward-sloping, isn't it natural that the demand curve for aggregate output is also downward-sloping? This turns out, however, to be a misleading parallel. The demand curve for any individual good shows how the quantity demanded depends on the price of that good, *holding the prices of other goods and services constant.* The main reason the quantity of a good demanded falls when the price of that good rises—that is, the quantity of a good demanded falls as we move up the demand curve—is that people switch their consumption to other goods and services that have become relatively less expensive.

But when we consider movements up or down the aggregate demand curve, we're considering *a simultaneous change in the prices of all final goods and services.* Furthermore, changes in the composition of goods and services in consumer spending aren't relevant to the aggregate demand curve: if consumers decide to buy fewer clothes but more cars, this doesn't necessarily change the total quantity of final goods and services they demand.

Why, then, does a rise in the aggregate price level lead to a fall in the quantity of all domestically produced final goods and services demanded? There are two main reasons: the *wealth effect* and the *interest rate effect* of a change in the aggregate price level.

Tasos Katopodis/Getty Images

When the aggregate price level falls, the purchasing power of consumers' assets rises, leading shoppers to place more items in their carts.

The Wealth Effect An increase in the aggregate price level, other things equal, reduces the purchasing power of many assets. Consider, for example, someone who has \$5,000 in a bank account. If the aggregate price level were to rise by 25%, that \$5,000 would buy only as much as \$4,000 would have bought previously. With the loss in purchasing power, the owner of that bank account would probably scale back his or her consumption plans. Millions of other people would respond the same way, leading to a fall in spending on final goods and services, because a rise in the aggregate price level reduces the purchasing power of everyone's bank account.

Correspondingly, a fall in the aggregate price level increases the purchasing power of consumers' assets and leads to more consumer demand. The **wealth effect of a change in the aggregate price level** is the change in consumer spending caused by the altered purchasing power of consumers' assets. Because of the wealth effect, consumer spending, *C*, falls when the aggregate price level rises, leading to a downward-sloping aggregate demand curve.

AP® Exam Tip

You may see a question about the wealth or interest rate effects on the AP® exam. They will help you explain why *AD* is downward-sloping.

The **wealth effect of a change in the aggregate price level** is the change in consumer spending caused by the altered purchasing power of consumers' assets.

The **interest rate effect of a change in the aggregate price level** is the change in investment and consumer spending caused by altered interest rates that result from changes in the demand for money.

The Interest Rate Effect Economists use the term *money* in its narrowest sense to refer to cash and bank deposits on which people can write checks. People and firms hold money because it reduces the cost and inconvenience of making transactions. An increase in the aggregate price level, other things equal, reduces the purchasing power of a given amount of money holdings. To purchase the same basket of goods and services as before, people and firms now need to hold more money. So, in response to an increase in the aggregate price level, the public tries to increase its money holdings, either by borrowing more or by selling assets such as bonds. This reduces the funds available for lending to other borrowers and drives interest rates up. A rise in the interest rate reduces investment spending because it makes the cost of borrowing higher. It also reduces consumer spending because households save more of their disposable income. So a rise in the aggregate price level depresses investment spending, *I*, and consumer spending, *C*, through its effect on the purchasing power of money holdings, an effect known as the **interest rate effect of a change in the aggregate price level**. This also leads to a downward-sloping aggregate demand curve.

Shifts of the Aggregate Demand Curve

When we introduced the analysis of supply and demand in the market for an individual good, we stressed the importance of the distinction between *movements along* the demand curve and *shifts of* the demand curve. The same distinction applies to the aggregate demand curve. Figure 17.1 shows a *movement along* the aggregate demand

174 Section 4 National Income and Price Determination

Figure 17.2 Shifts of the Aggregate Demand Curve

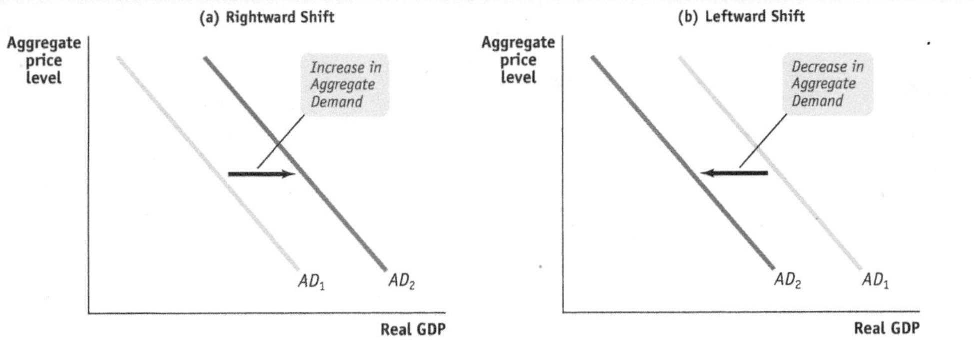

Panel (a) shows the effect of events that increase the quantity of aggregate output demanded at any given aggregate price level, such as a rise in consumer optimism about future income or a rise in government spending. Such changes shift the aggregate demand curve to the right, from AD_1 to AD_2. Panel (b) shows the effect of events that decrease the quantity of aggregate output demanded at any given aggregate price level, such as a fall in wealth caused by a stock market decline. This shifts the aggregate demand curve leftward from AD_1 to AD_2.

curve, a change in the aggregate quantity of goods and services demanded as the aggregate price level changes. But there can also be *shifts of* the aggregate demand curve, changes in the quantity of goods and services demanded at any given price level, as shown in **Figure 17.2**. When we talk about an increase in aggregate demand, we mean a shift of the aggregate demand curve to the right, as shown in panel (a) by the shift from AD_1 to AD_2. A rightward shift occurs when the quantity of aggregate output demanded increases at any given aggregate price level. A decrease in aggregate demand means that the *AD* curve shifts to the left, as in panel (b). A leftward shift implies that the quantity of aggregate output demanded falls at any given aggregate price level.

A number of factors can shift the aggregate demand curve. Among the most important factors are changes in expectations, changes in wealth, and the size of the existing stock of physical capital. In addition, both fiscal and monetary policy can shift the aggregate demand curve. All five factors set the spending multiplier process in motion. By causing an initial rise or fall in real GDP, they change disposable income, which leads to additional changes in aggregate spending, which lead to further changes in real GDP, and so on. For an overview of factors that shift the aggregate demand curve, see **Table 17.1** on the next page.

Changes in Expectations Both consumer spending and planned investment spending depend in part on people's expectations about the future. Consumers base their spending not only on the income they have now but also on the income they expect to have in the future. Firms base their planned investment spending not only on current conditions but also on the sales they expect to make in the future. As a result, changes in expectations can push consumer spending and planned investment spending up or down. If consumers and firms become more optimistic, aggregate spending rises; if they become more pessimistic, aggregate spending falls. In fact, short-run economic forecasters pay careful attention to surveys of consumer and business sentiment. In particular, forecasters watch the Consumer Confidence Index, a monthly measure calculated by the Conference Board, and the Michigan Consumer Sentiment Index, a similar measure calculated by the University of Michigan.

FOCUS In the News

Have your students read the *CNN Money* article "Target Credit Card Hack: The Latest" at http://money.cnn.com/2013/12/24/news/companies/target-credit-card-hack-latest/. Ask them the following questions:

- How will this incident impact aggregate demand? *Answers will vary. If consumers think the problem is industrywide, AD will decrease. If consumers think the problem only exists with Target, they will shift their spending to other stores.*
- Which component of *AD* will be impacted? *The consumer spending portion of aggregate demand will be affected.*

Module 17 Aggregate Demand: Introduction and Determinants 175

Table 17.1 Factors that Shift the Aggregate Demand Curve

When this happens, . . .	. . . aggregate demand increases:		But when this happens, . . .	. . . aggregate demand decreases:	
Changes in expectations:					
When consumers and firms become more optimistic, . . .	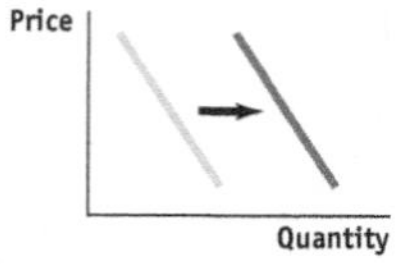	. . . aggregate demand increases.	When consumers and firms become more pessimistic, . . .	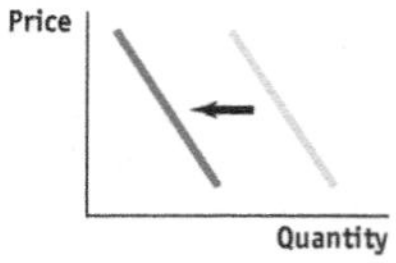	. . . aggregate demand decreases.
Changes in wealth:					
When the real value of household assets rises, . . .	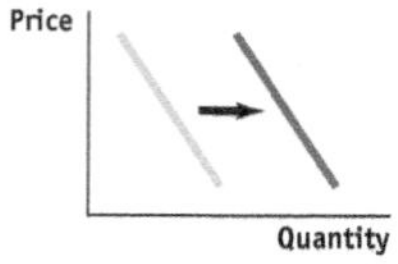	. . . aggregate demand increases.	When the real value of household assets falls, . . .	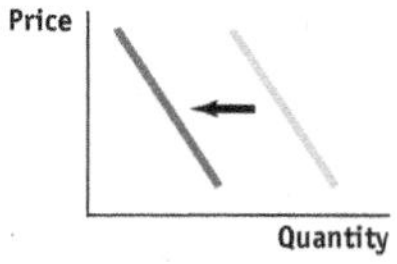	. . . aggregate demand decreases.
Size of the existing stock of physical capital:					
When the existing stock of physical capital is relatively small, . . .	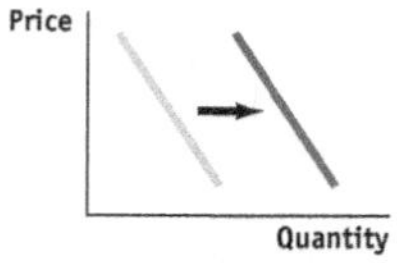	. . . aggregate demand increases.	When the existing stock of physical capital is relatively large, . . .	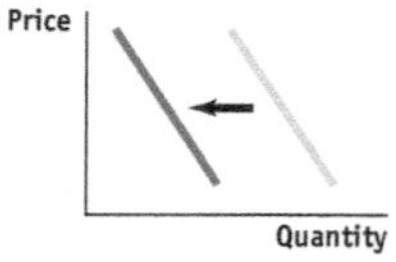	. . . aggregate demand decreases.
Fiscal policy:					
When the government increases spending or cuts taxes, . . .	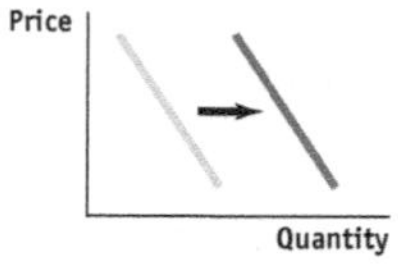	. . . aggregate demand increases.	When the government reduces spending or raises taxes, . . .	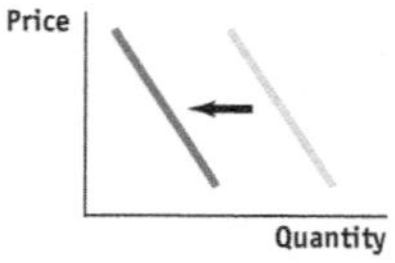	. . . aggregate demand decreases.
Monetary policy:					
When the central bank increases the quantity of money, . . .	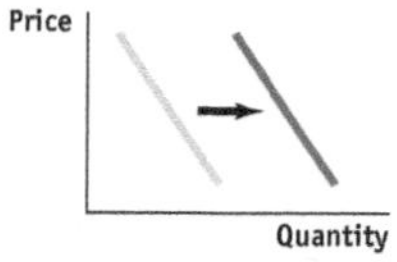	. . . aggregate demand increases.	When the central bank reduces the quantity of money, . . .	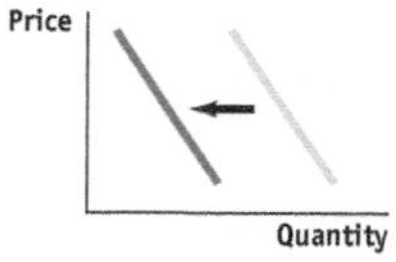	. . . aggregate demand decreases.

Changes in Wealth Consumer spending depends in part on the value of household assets. When the real value of these assets rises, the purchasing power they embody also rises, leading to an increase in aggregate spending. For example, in the 1990s, there was a significant rise in the stock market that increased aggregate demand. And when the real value of household assets falls—for example, because of a stock market crash—the purchasing power they embody is reduced and aggregate demand also falls. The stock market crash of 1929 was a significant factor leading to the Great Depression. Similarly, a sharp decline in real estate values was a major factor depressing consumer spending in 2008.

TEACH Teach It

Fiscal policy is the use of either government spending—government purchases of final goods and services and government transfers—or tax policy to stabilize the economy. An increase in government spending or a decrease in income taxes (which increases disposable income and therefore spending) will increase *AD*. The opposite action by the government will decrease *AD*. An increase in government spending will have a greater impact on *AD* because the multiplier effect for a change in spending is greater than that of a change in taxes due to people's saving habits.

St. Louis Federal Reserve Bank Resources

Fiscal Policy Online Course for Teachers and Students

Inflation, unemployment, recession, economic growth—these economic concepts affect people in very real ways. In two thought-provoking, interactive lessons, this course teaches students about fiscal policy, the avenue by which Congress and the president attempt to influence the economy.

Size of the Existing Stock of Physical Capital Firms engage in planned investment spending to add to their stock of physical capital. Their incentive to spend depends in part on how much physical capital they already have: the more they have, the less they will feel a need to add more, other things equal. The same applies to other types of investment spending—for example, if a large number of houses have been built in recent years, this will depress the demand for new houses and, as a result, will also tend to reduce residential investment spending. In fact, that's part of the reason for the deep slump in residential investment spending that began in 2006. The housing boom of the previous few years had created an oversupply of houses: by spring 2008, the inventory of unsold houses on the market was equal to more than 11 months of sales, and prices had fallen more than 20% from their peak. This gave the construction industry little incentive to build even more homes.

BROOKLYN DAILY EAGLE

WALL ST. IN PANIC AS STOCKS CRASH

Attempt Made to Kill Italy's Crown Prince

Hollywood Fire Destroys Films Worth Millions

High Duty Group Gave $700,000 to Coolidge Drive

FPG/Getty Images

The loss of wealth resulting from the stock market crash of 1929 was a significant factor leading to the Great Depression.

Government Policies and Aggregate Demand One of the key insights of macroeconomics is that the government can have a powerful influence on aggregate demand and that, in some circumstances, this influence can be used to improve economic performance.

The two main ways the government can influence the aggregate demand curve are through *fiscal policy* and *monetary policy*. We'll briefly discuss their influence on aggregate demand, leaving a full-length discussion for later.

Fiscal Policy **Fiscal policy** is the use of either government spending—government purchases of final goods and services and government transfers—or tax policy to stabilize the economy. In practice, governments often respond to recessions by increasing spending, cutting taxes, or both. They often respond to inflation by reducing spending or increasing taxes.

Fiscal policy is the use of government purchases of goods and services, government transfers, or tax policy to stabilize the economy.

The effect of government purchases of final goods and services, *G*, on the aggregate demand curve is *direct* because government purchases are themselves a component of aggregate demand. So an increase in government purchases shifts the aggregate demand curve to the right and a decrease shifts it to the left. History's most dramatic example of how increased government purchases affect aggregate demand was the effect of wartime government spending during World War II. Because of the war, purchases by the U.S. federal government surged 400%. This increase in purchases is usually credited with ending the Great Depression. In the 1990s, Japan used large public works projects—such as government-financed construction of roads, bridges, and dams—in an effort to increase aggregate demand in the face of a slumping economy.

In contrast, changes in either tax rates or government transfers influence the economy *indirectly* through their effect on disposable income. A lower tax rate means that consumers get to keep more of what they earn, increasing their disposable income. An increase in government transfers also increases consumers' disposable income. In either case, this increases consumer spending and shifts the aggregate demand curve to the right. A higher tax rate or a reduction in transfers reduces the amount of disposable income received by consumers. This reduces consumer spending and shifts the aggregate demand curve to the left.

Monetary Policy In the next section, we will study the Federal Reserve System and monetary policy in detail. At this point, we just need to note that the Federal Reserve controls **monetary policy**—the use of changes in the quantity of money or the interest rate to stabilize the economy. We've just discussed how a rise in the aggregate price level, by reducing the purchasing power of money holdings, causes a rise in the interest rate. That, in turn, reduces both investment spending and consumer spending.

Monetary policy is the central bank's use of changes in the quantity of money or the interest rate to stabilize the economy.

But what happens if the quantity of money in the hands of households and firms changes? In modern economies, the quantity of money in circulation is largely determined by the decisions of a *central bank* created by the government. As we'll learn in

TEACH AP® Exam Tip

Fiscal and monetary policy will be explored in depth in later modules. Government policy is heavily tested on the AP® exam.

TEACH Teach It

The Federal Reserve manages monetary policy—changes in the quantity of money that affect the interest rate, or other monetary tools to stabilize the economy. When the Fed increases the quantity of money in circulation, households and firms have more money, some of which is saved and lent out. This drives down the interest rate at any given aggregate price level, leading to higher investment spending and higher consumer spending. Thus, increasing the quantity of money shifts the aggregate demand curve to the right, while decreasing the quantity of money has the opposite effect.

FOCUS Graph It

TRM Understanding shifts in *AD* is one of the key skills required to do well on the AP® exam. Assign **Worksheet 17.2 (Aggregate Demand)** from the TRM, where students will graph changes on paper or on their personal whiteboards. Discuss the direction and cause of the shift for each scenario.

St. Louis Federal Reserve Bank Resources

Monetary Policy Online Course for Teachers and Students

Inflation, unemployment, recession, economic growth—these economic concepts affect people in very real ways. In this course containing three interactive, thought-provoking lessons, students will learn about monetary policy, the avenue by which the Federal Reserve System attempts to influence the economy

St. Louis Federal Reserve Bank Resources

"Fiscal and Monetary Policy in Times of Crisis," *Page One Economics Classroom Edition* (March 2011)

This issue provides more information about fiscal policy and monetary policy—who conducts them, how they work, and their roles during economic downturns.

OPEN & CLOSE Exit Slip

TRM *Please see* ***Exit Slip: Module 17*** *in the TRM for formative questions to ask your students before finishing your lesson. These questions will help you quickly assess whether your students have mastered the module's concepts before moving on.*

Answers to the Exit Slip Questions

1. C
2.

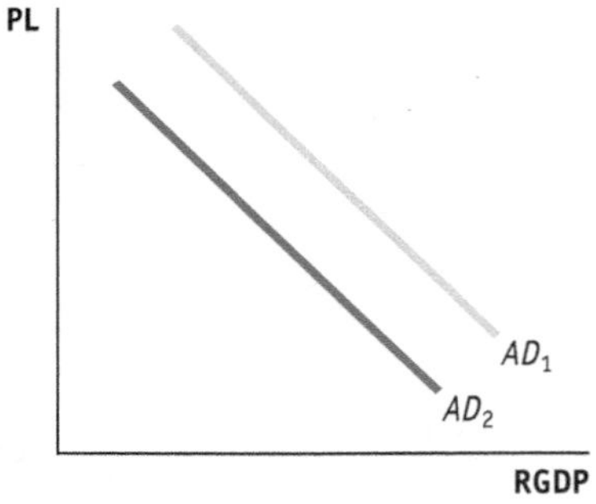

3. C

more detail later, the Federal Reserve, the U.S. central bank, is a special institution that is neither exactly part of the government nor exactly a private institution. When the central bank increases the quantity of money in circulation, households and firms have more money, which they are willing to lend out. The effect is to drive the interest rate down at any given aggregate price level, leading to higher investment spending and higher consumer spending. That is, increasing the quantity of money shifts the aggregate demand curve to the right. Reducing the quantity of money has the opposite effect: households and firms have less money holdings than before, leading them to borrow more and lend less. This raises the interest rate, reduces investment spending and consumer spending, and shifts the aggregate demand curve to the left.

MODULE 17 Review

Check Your Understanding

1. Determine the effect on aggregate demand of each of the following events. Explain whether it represents a movement along the aggregate demand curve (up or down) or a shift of the curve (leftward or rightward).
   a. a rise in the interest rate caused by a change in monetary policy
   b. a fall in the real value of money in the economy due to a higher aggregate price level
   c. news of a worse-than-expected job market next year
   d. a fall in tax rates
   e. a rise in the real value of assets in the economy due to a lower aggregate price level
   f. a rise in the real value of assets in the economy due to a surge in real estate values

Tackle the Test: Multiple-Choice Questions

1. Which of the following explains the slope of the aggregate demand curve?
   I. the wealth effect of a change in the aggregate price level
   II. the interest rate effect of a change in the aggregate price level
   III. the product-substitution effect of a change in the aggregate price level
   a. I only
   b. II only
   c. III only
   d. I and II only
   e. I, II, and III
2. Which of the following will shift the aggregate demand curve to the right?
   a. a decrease in wealth
   b. pessimistic consumer expectations
   c. a decrease in the existing stock of capital
   d. contractionary fiscal policy
   e. a decrease in the quantity of money
3. The Consumer Confidence Index is used to measure which of the following?
   a. the level of consumer spending
   b. the rate of return on investments
   c. consumer expectations
   d. planned investment spending
   e. the level of current disposable income
4. Decreases in the stock market decrease aggregate demand by decreasing which of the following?
   a. consumer wealth
   b. the price level
   c. the stock of existing physical capital
   d. interest rates
   e. tax revenues
5. Which of the following government policies will shift the aggregate demand curve to the left?
   a. a decrease in the quantity of money
   b. an increase in government purchases of goods and services
   c. a decrease in taxes
   d. a decrease in interest rates
   e. an increase in government transfers

Answers to Module 17 Review Questions

Check Your Understanding

1. a. This is a shift of the aggregate demand curve. A decrease in the quantity of money raises the interest rate, since people now want to borrow more and lend less. A higher interest rate reduces investment and consumer spending at any given aggregate price level, so the aggregate demand curve shifts to the left.

b. This is a movement up along the aggregate demand curve. As the aggregate price level rises, the real value of money holdings falls. This is the interest rate effect of a change in the aggregate price level: as the value of money falls, people want to hold more money. They do so by borrowing more and lending less. This leads to a rise in the interest rate and a reduction in consumer and investment spending. Thus, it is a movement along the aggregate demand curve.

c. This is a shift of the aggregate demand curve. Expectations of a poor job market, and so lower average disposable incomes, will reduce people's consumer spending today at any given aggregate price level. Thus, the aggregate demand curve shifts to the left.

d. This is a shift of the aggregate demand curve. A fall in tax rates raises people's disposable income. At any given aggregate price level, consumer spending is now higher. Thus, the aggregate demand curve shifts to the right.

e. This is a movement down along the aggregate demand curve. As the aggregate price level falls, the real value of assets rises. This is the wealth effect of a change in the aggregate price level: as the value of assets rises, people will increase their consumption plans. This leads to higher consumer spending. Thus, it is a movement along the aggregate demand curve.

f. This is a shift of the aggregate demand curve. A rise in the real value of assets in the economy due to a surge in real estate values raises consumer spending at any given aggregate price level. Thus, the aggregate demand curve shifts to the right.

Tackle the Test: Multiple-Choice Questions

1. d
2. c
3. c
4. a
5. a

Tackle the Test: Free-Response Questions

1. a. Draw a correctly labeled graph showing aggregate demand.
   b. On your graph from part a, illustrate an increase in aggregate demand.
   c. List the four factors that shift aggregate demand.
   d. Describe a change in each determinant of aggregate demand that would lead to the shift you illustrated in part b.

2. Identify the two effects that cause the aggregate demand curve to have a downward slope. Explain each. **(4 points)**

Rubric for FRQ 1 (12 points)

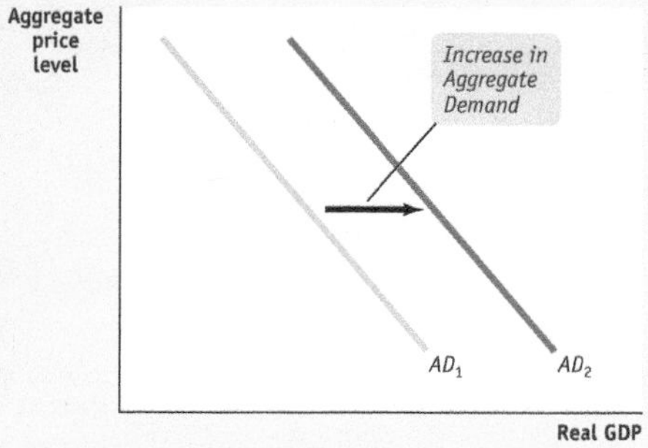

1 point: Vertical axis labeled "Aggregate price level" (or "Price level")

1 point: Horizontal axis labeled "Real GDP"

1 point: Downward-sloping curve labeled "*AD*" (or "AD_1")

1 point: *AD* curve shifted to the right

1 point: Expectations

1 point: Wealth

1 point: Size of existing stock of physical capital

1 point: Government policies

1 point: Consumers/Producers more confident

1 point: Increase in wealth

1 point: Lower existing stock of physical capital

1 point: An increase in government spending or in the money supply

Tackle the Test: Free-Response Question

Rubric for FRQ 2 (4 points)

1 point: The wealth effect

1 point: The interest rate effect

1 point: The wealth effect: When the price level increases, the purchasing power of money decreases, causing consumers to scale back on spending. Because consumer spending is a component of aggregate demand, increases in the aggregate price level lead to decreases in the quantity of aggregate output demanded. The opposite is true for decreases in the price level. This negative relationship between the price level and the quantity of aggregate output demanded results in a downward-sloping aggregate demand curve.

1 point: The interest rate effect: Increases in the aggregate price level cause people to want to hold more money, which increases the demand for money and drives up interest rates. Higher interest rates reduce investment spending because it costs more to borrow money. Thus, a rise in the price level leads to less investment spending, which is a component of aggregate demand, and causes the quantity of aggregate output demanded to decrease (and vice versa). The result is a downward-sloping aggregate demand curve.

Module 17 Aggregate Demand: Introduction and Determinants 179

PD To prepare for teaching this lesson, you may want to consult the **Module 18 Sample Lecture** in the TRM.

OPEN & CLOSE Start Here

Show the first 20 seconds of the 2013 video "Oil Prices Headed for $200 a Barrel" (see econ-extras video list with hyperlinks on the bcs and TRFD). Ask students how the reporting of this news will impact the economy. *Answers will vary, but they should come to the conclusion that suppliers will be most impacted as the cost of an input will go up.*

Steer students away from changes in *AD* if they head that way.

TEACH Teach It

The idea of two aggregate supply curves often confuses students. The difference between them is that prices and wages are slow to change in the short run, while prices and wages are flexible in the long run. Explain that the difference is the time needed to make the prices of all inputs flexible. Wage flexibility will alter the long-run relationship between the price level and the short-run aggregate supply. Discuss each of the curves separately, beginning with the short-run curve.

Digital Vision

MODULE 18 Aggregate Supply: Introduction and Determinants

In this Module, you will learn to:

- Use the aggregate supply curve to illustrate the relationship between the aggregate price level and the quantity of aggregate output supplied in the economy
- Identify the factors that can shift the aggregate supply curve
- Explain why the aggregate supply curve is different in the short run from in the long run

Aggregate Supply

Between 1929 and 1933, there was a sharp fall in aggregate demand—a reduction in the quantity of goods and services demanded at any given price level. One consequence of the economy-wide decline in demand was a fall in the prices of most goods and services. By 1933, the GDP deflator (one of the price indexes) was 26% below its 1929 level, and other indexes were down by similar amounts. A second consequence was a decline in the output of most goods and services: by 1933, real GDP was 27% below its 1929 level. A third consequence, closely tied to the fall in real GDP, was a surge in the unemployment rate from 3% to 25%.

The **aggregate supply curve** shows the relationship between the aggregate price level and the quantity of aggregate output supplied in the economy.

The association between the plunge in real GDP and the plunge in prices wasn't an accident. Between 1929 and 1933, the U.S. economy was moving down its **aggregate supply curve**, which shows the relationship between the economy's aggregate price level (the overall price level of final goods and services in the economy) and the total quantity of final goods and services, or aggregate output, producers are willing to supply. (As you will recall, we use real GDP to measure aggregate output, and we'll often use the two terms interchangeably.) More specifically, between 1929 and 1933, the U.S. economy moved down its *short-run aggregate supply curve.*

The Short-Run Aggregate Supply Curve

The period from 1929 to 1933 demonstrated that there is a positive relationship in the short run between the aggregate price level and the quantity of aggregate output supplied. That is, a rise in the aggregate price level is associated with a rise in the quantity of aggregate output supplied, other things equal; a fall in the aggregate price level is

180 Section 4 National Income and Price Determination

associated with a fall in the quantity of aggregate output supplied, other things equal. To understand why this positive relationship exists, consider the most basic question facing a producer: is producing a unit of output profitable or not? Let's define profit per unit:

(18-1) Profit per unit of output =
Price per unit of output − Production cost per unit of output

Thus, the answer to the question depends on whether the price the producer receives for a unit of output is greater or less than the cost of producing that unit of output. At any given point in time, many of the costs producers face are fixed per unit of output and can't be changed for an extended period of time. Typically, the largest source of inflexible production cost is the wages paid to workers. *Wages* here refers to all forms of worker compensation, including employer-paid health care and retirement benefits in addition to earnings.

Wages are typically an inflexible production cost because the dollar amount of any given wage paid, called the **nominal wage**, is often determined by contracts that were signed some time ago. And even when there are no formal contracts, there are often informal agreements between management and workers, making companies reluctant to change wages in response to economic conditions. For example, companies usually will not reduce wages during poor economic times—unless the downturn has been particularly long and severe—for fear of generating worker resentment. Correspondingly, they typically won't raise wages during better economic times—until they are at risk of losing workers to competitors—because they don't want to encourage workers to routinely demand higher wages. As a result of both formal and informal agreements, then, the economy is characterized by **sticky wages**: nominal wages that are slow to fall even in the face of high unemployment and slow to rise even in the face of labor shortages. It's important to note, however, that nominal wages cannot be sticky forever: ultimately, formal contracts and informal agreements will be renegotiated to take into account changed economic circumstances. How long it takes for nominal wages to become flexible is an integral component of what distinguishes the short run from the long run.

To understand how the fact that many costs are fixed in nominal terms gives rise to an upward-sloping short-run aggregate supply curve, it's helpful to know that prices are set somewhat differently in different kinds of markets. In *perfectly competitive markets,* producers take prices as given; in *imperfectly competitive markets,* producers have some ability to choose the prices they charge. In both kinds of markets, there is a positive relationship between prices and output in the short run, but for slightly different reasons.

Let's start with the behavior of producers in perfectly competitive markets; remember, they take the price as given. Imagine that, for some reason, the aggregate price level falls, which means that the price received by the typical producer of a final good or service falls. Because many production costs are fixed in the short run, the production cost per unit of output doesn't fall in proportion to the price of output. So the profit per unit of output declines, leading perfectly competitive producers to reduce the quantity supplied in the short run.

On the other hand, suppose that for some reason the aggregate price level rises. As a result, the typical producer receives a higher price for its final good or service. Again, many production costs are fixed in the short run, so the production cost per unit of output doesn't rise in proportion to the rise in the price of a unit. And since the typical perfectly competitive producer takes the price as given, profit per unit of output rises and output increases.

Now consider an imperfectly competitive producer that is able to set its own price. If there is a rise in the demand for this producer's product, it will be able to sell more at any given price. Given stronger demand for its products, it will probably choose to increase its prices as well as its output, as a way of increasing profit per unit of output.

AP® Exam Tip

Because wages are "sticky," they fall very slowly even when the unemployment rate is high. This is important to know when you look at how the economy reacts with no government involvement.

The **nominal wage** is the dollar amount of the wage paid.

Sticky wages are nominal wages that are slow to fall even in the face of high unemployment and slow to rise even in the face of labor shortages.

TEACH Connect It

Ask students what the difference is between nominal and real GDP. *Real GDP is adjusted for inflation.* Let them know that nominal wages are not adjusted for the change in the price level. It is the wage received for work. If the price level is rising, the wage received cannot buy the same set of goods and services. Any time your students see nominal, they should remember "not adjusted for inflation," while real means the value is adjusted for inflation.

TEACH Teach It

Producers want to make a profit. If the price of goods is rising faster than the cost of producing them, firms will be willing to supply more units of those goods. Because some input prices like wages are "sticky," they don't rise or fall very quickly in response to a change in demand for them. This causes the *SRAS* curve to be upward-sloping.

Module 18 Aggregate Supply: Introduction and Determinants 181

TEACH Teach It

The students need to equate an "increase in *SRAS*" to a "rightward shift" in the *SRAS* curve. Let them know that ↑ *SRAS* indicates an increase in *SRAS* and a rightward shift of the curve.

FOCUS Graph It

Discuss the short-run aggregate supply curve using Figure 18.1. Drill students on the concept that a change in the price level will mean a change in the level of real GDP. Have them draw and label the curve on their personal whiteboards or on paper. Check that each of the axes is labeled correctly. The rubric for the AP® exam typically allows the short-run aggregate supply curve to be labeled *SRAS*, AS_{sr}, or *AS*.

In fact, industry analysts often talk about variations in an industry's "pricing power": when demand is strong, firms with pricing power are able to raise prices—and they do.

Conversely, if there is a fall in demand, firms will normally try to limit the fall in their sales by cutting prices.

Both the responses of firms in perfectly competitive industries and those of firms in imperfectly competitive industries lead to an upward-sloping relationship between aggregate output and the aggregate price level. The positive relationship between the aggregate price level and the quantity of aggregate output producers are willing to supply during the time period when many production costs, particularly nominal wages, can be taken as fixed is illustrated by the **short-run aggregate supply curve**. The positive relationship between the aggregate price level and aggregate output in the short run gives the short-run aggregate supply curve its upward slope. **Figure 18.1** shows a hypothetical short-run aggregate supply curve, *SRAS*, that matches actual U.S. data for 1929 and 1933. On the horizontal axis is aggregate output (or, equivalently, real GDP)—the total quantity of final goods and services supplied in the economy—measured in 2005 dollars. On the vertical axis is the aggregate price level as measured by the GDP deflator, with the value for the year 2005 equal to 100. In 1929, the aggregate price level was 10.6 and real GDP was $977 billion. In 1933, the aggregate price level was 7.9 and real GDP was only $716 billion. The movement down the *SRAS* curve corresponds to the deflation and fall in aggregate output experienced over those years.

The **short-run aggregate supply curve** shows the relationship between the aggregate price level and the quantity of aggregate output supplied that exists in the short run, the time period when many production costs can be taken as fixed.

Shifts of the Short-Run Aggregate Supply Curve

Figure 18.1 shows a *movement along* the short-run aggregate supply curve, as the aggregate price level and aggregate output fell from 1929 to 1933. But there can also be *shifts of* the short-run aggregate supply curve, as shown in **Figure 18.2**. Panel (a) shows

Figure 18.1 The Short-Run Aggregate Supply Curve

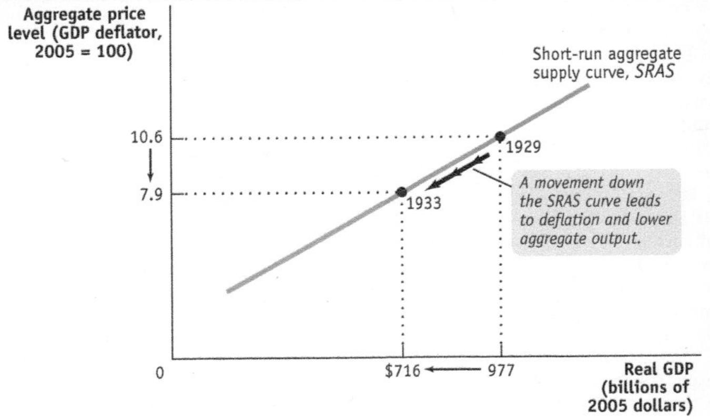

The short-run aggregate supply curve shows the relationship between the aggregate price level and the quantity of aggregate output supplied in the short run, the period in which many production costs such as nominal wages are fixed. It is upward sloping because a higher aggregate price level leads to higher profit per unit of output and higher aggregate output given fixed nominal wages. Here we show numbers corresponding to the Great Depression, from 1929 to 1933: when deflation occurred and the aggregate price level fell from 10.6 (in 1929) to 7.9 (in 1933), firms responded by reducing the quantity of aggregate output supplied from $977 billion to $716 billion measured in 2005 dollars.

182 Section 4 National Income and Price Determination

Figure 18.2 Shifts of the Short-Run Aggregate Supply Curve

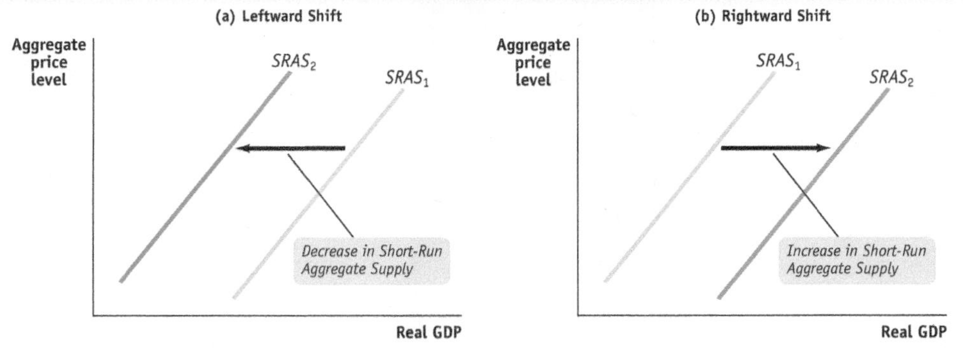

Panel (a) shows a decrease in short-run aggregate supply: the short-run aggregate supply curve shifts leftward from $SRAS_1$ to $SRAS_2$, and the quantity of aggregate output supplied at any given aggregate price level falls. Panel (b) shows an increase in short-run aggregate supply: the short-run aggregate supply curve shifts rightward from $SRAS_1$ to $SRAS_2$, and the quantity of aggregate output supplied at any given aggregate price level rises.

a *decrease in short-run aggregate supply*—a leftward shift of the short-run aggregate supply curve. Aggregate supply decreases when producers reduce the quantity of aggregate output they are willing to supply at any given aggregate price level. Panel (b) shows an *increase in short-run aggregate supply*—a rightward shift of the short-run aggregate supply curve. Aggregate supply increases when producers increase the quantity of aggregate output they are willing to supply at any given aggregate price level.

To understand why the short-run aggregate supply curve can shift, it's important to recall that producers make output decisions based on their profit per unit of output. The short-run aggregate supply curve illustrates the relationship between the aggregate price level and aggregate output: because some production costs are fixed in the short run, a change in the aggregate price level leads to a change in producers' profit per unit of output and, in turn, leads to a change in aggregate output. But other factors besides the aggregate price level can affect profit per unit and, in turn, aggregate output. It is changes in these other factors that will shift the short-run aggregate supply curve.

To develop some intuition, suppose something happens that raises production costs—say, an increase in the price of oil. At any given price of output, a producer now earns a smaller profit per unit of output. As a result, producers reduce the quantity supplied at any given aggregate price level, and the short-run aggregate supply curve shifts to the left. If, by contrast, something happens that lowers production costs—say, a fall in the nominal wage—a producer now earns a higher profit per unit of output at any given price of output. This leads producers to increase the quantity of aggregate output supplied at any given aggregate price level, and the short-run aggregate supply curve shifts to the right.

Now we'll look more closely at the link between important factors that affect producers' profit per unit and shifts in the short-run aggregate supply curve.

Changes in Commodity Prices A surge in the price of oil caused problems for the U.S. economy in the 1970s and in early 2008. Oil is a *commodity,* a standardized input bought and sold in bulk quantities. An increase in the price of a commodity—in

AP® Exam Tip

Remember, left is less and right is more. Shifting *SRAS* can be confusing because it appears as if left would be more because the line is higher on the graph. Look at the horizontal axis to see the resulting change in quantity to help you get this right.

TEACH Connect It

Have students look at Figure 18.2. Make sure they understand that a rightward shift is an increase in *SRAS* and a leftward shift is a decrease in *SRAS*. Based on their knowledge of supply and demand, ask them to predict what will happen to the price level when *SRAS* increases (*the price level decreases*) or decreases (*the price level increases*).

FOCUS Active Learning

Use the video "Aggregate Supply Practice" from Jacob Clifford (see econextras video list with hyperlinks on the bcs and TRFD). Ask students to list the three factors that shift the aggregate supply curve (*resources costs, productivity changes, government action on taxes and subsidies*). Pause the video (at 1:13), and let the students discuss the four questions Mr. Clifford presents before revealing the answers.

FOCUS In the News

Have students read a recent article in which commodity prices are increasing the costs of production for producers. You may use the *Business First* article "Food Commodity Prices to Increase for Several Years" at www.bizjournals.com/louisville/news/2012/12/03/food-commodity-prices-to-increase-for.html if you can't find a more recent one in your local newspaper. Challenge students to determine what would happen to aggregate supply when commodity prices increase. Ask for an explanation as this is often required on the free-response section of the AP® exams. *Students should respond that AS will decrease because the costs of inputs have increased.*

FOCUS In the News

TRM Have students read the *Mother Jones* article "If the Economy Is Back, Why Are Wages Still So Low?" at http://www.motherjones.com/kevin-drum/2013/06/permanent-wage-decline-great-recession. Suggested questions about the article may be found in **Worksheet 18.1 (Why Are Wages Still So Low?)** from the TRM.

FOCUS In the News

TRM Have students read the Bloomberg article "Increase in U.S. Productivity Helps to Restrain Labor Costs" at http://www.bloomberg.com/news/2014-02-06/productivity-rises-more-than-forecast-u-s-labor-costs-decline.html. You may also find a local article about productivity to use. Review questions about the article are in **Worksheet 18.2 (Restraining Labor Costs)** from the TRM.

Signs of the times: high oil prices caused high gasoline prices in 2008.

this case, oil—raised production costs across the economy and reduced the quantity of aggregate output supplied at any given aggregate price level, shifting the short-run aggregate supply curve to the left. Conversely, a decline in commodity prices reduces production costs, leading to an increase in the quantity supplied at any given aggregate price level and a rightward shift of the short-run aggregate supply curve.

Why isn't the influence of commodity prices already captured by the short-run aggregate supply curve? Because commodities—unlike, say, soft drinks—are not a final good, their prices are not included in the calculation of the aggregate price level. Furthermore, commodities represent a significant cost of production to most suppliers, just like nominal wages do. So changes in commodity prices have large impacts on production costs. And in contrast to noncommodities, the prices of commodities can sometimes change drastically due to industry-specific shocks to supply—such as wars in the Middle East or rising Chinese demand that leaves less oil for the United States.

AP® Exam Tip

Think of a PEAR to remember the factors that shift *SRAS*:
Productivity
Expectations about inflation
Actions by the government (business taxes and subsidies)
Resource (input) prices like wages and commodities

Changes in Nominal Wages At any given point in time, the dollar wages of many workers are fixed because they are set by contracts or informal agreements made in the past. Nominal wages can change, however, once enough time has passed for contracts and informal agreements to be renegotiated. Suppose, for example, that there is an economy-wide rise in the cost of health care insurance premiums paid by employers as part of employees' wages. From the employers' perspective, this is equivalent to a rise in nominal wages because it is an increase in employer-paid compensation. So this rise in nominal wages increases production costs and shifts the short-run aggregate supply curve to the left. Conversely, suppose there is an economy-wide fall in the cost of such premiums. This is equivalent to a fall in nominal wages from the point of view of employers; it reduces production costs and shifts the short-run aggregate supply curve to the right.

An important historical fact is that during the 1970s, the surge in the price of oil had the indirect effect of also raising nominal wages. This "knock-on" effect occurred because many wage contracts included *cost-of-living allowances* that automatically raised the nominal wage when consumer prices increased. Through this channel, the surge in the price of oil—which led to an increase in overall consumer prices—ultimately caused a rise in nominal wages. So the economy, in the end, experienced two leftward shifts of the aggregate supply curve: the first generated by the initial surge in the price of oil and the second generated by the induced increase in nominal wages. The negative effect on the economy of rising oil prices was greatly magnified through the cost-of-living allowances in wage contracts. Today, cost-of-living allowances in wage contracts are rare.

Shutterstock

Almost every good purchased today has a UPC bar code on it, which allows stores to scan and track merchandise with great speed.

Changes in Productivity An increase in productivity means that a worker can produce more units of output with the same quantity of inputs. For example, the introduction of bar-code scanners in retail stores greatly increased the ability of a single worker to stock, inventory, and resupply store shelves. As a result, the cost to a store of "producing" a dollar of sales fell and profit rose. And, correspondingly, the quantity supplied increased. (Think of Walmart and the increase in the number of its stores as an increase in aggregate supply.) So a rise in productivity, whatever the source, increases producers' profits and shifts the short-run aggregate supply curve to the right.

St. Louis Federal Reserve Bank Resources

"The Labor Market," ***The Economic Lowdown Podcast Series*****, Volume 1, Episode 10**

In this episode (run time 7:55), students can learn about the basics of the labor market in this country. A brief explanation is given of the roles played by education, supply, demand, productivity, and government regulation.

Conversely, a fall in productivity—say, due to new regulations that require workers to spend more time filling out forms—reduces the number of units of output a worker can produce with the same quantity of inputs. Consequently, the cost per unit of output rises, profit falls, and quantity supplied falls. This shifts the short-run aggregate supply curve to the left.

Changes in Expectations about Inflation If inflation is expected to be higher than previously thought, workers will seek higher nominal wages to keep pace with the higher prices. Suppose you saw prices rising more rapidly than in the recent past. You might expect a particularly high inflation rate over the coming year. To prevent the expected inflation from eroding your real wages, you and other workers would pressure employers to raise nominal wages. As we've discussed, nominal wages are temporarily inflexible due to wage contracts, but when contracts are renewed and nominal wages rise, the short-run aggregate supply curve shifts to the left. Likewise, if inflation is expected to be lower than previously thought, workers will accept lower nominal wages and the short-run aggregate supply curve will shift to the right.

For a summary of the factors that shift the short-run aggregate supply curve, see **Table 18.1**.

Table 18.1 Factors that Shift the Short-Run Aggregate Supply Curve

When this happens, . . .		. . . short-run aggregate supply increases:	But when this happens, . . .		. . . short-run aggregate supply decreases:
Changes in commodity prices:					
When commodity prices fall, . . .	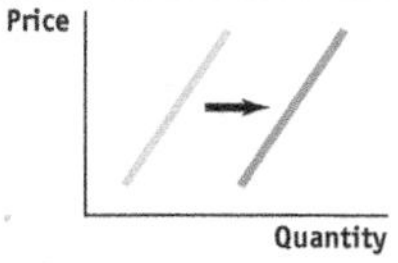	. . . short-run aggregate supply increases.	When commodity prices rise, . . .	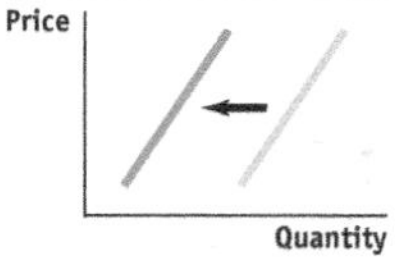	. . . short-run aggregate supply decreases.
Changes in nominal wages:					
When nominal wages fall, . . .	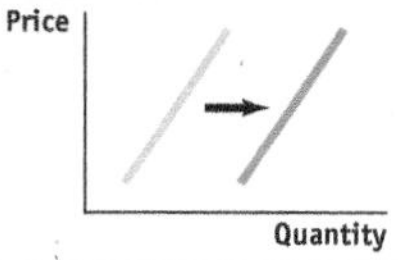	. . . short-run aggregate supply increases.	When nominal wages rise, . . .	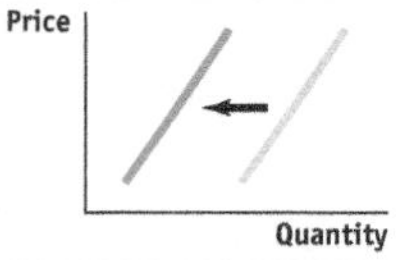	. . . short-run aggregate supply decreases.
Changes in productivity:					
When workers become more productive, . . .	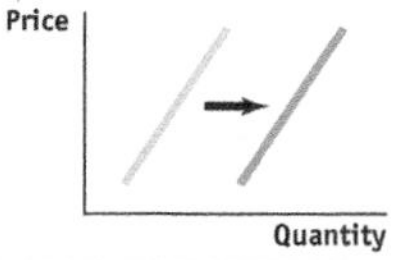	. . . short-run aggregate supply increases.	When workers become less productive, . . .	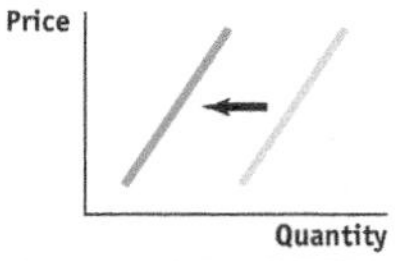	. . . short-run aggregate supply decreases.
Changes in expectations about inflation:					
If inflation is expected to be lower, . . .	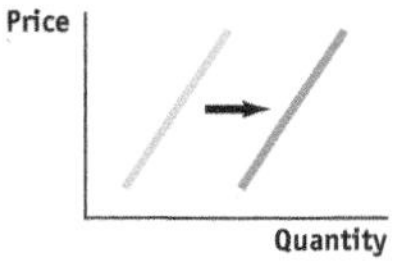	. . . short-run aggregate supply increases.	If inflation is expected to be higher, . . .	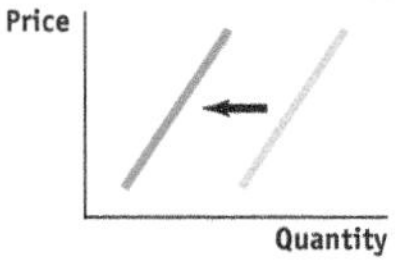	. . . short-run aggregate supply decreases.

TEACH Teach It

Aggregate supply changes when the costs of production change. An easy way for students to remember the factors that shift *AS* is to think about PEAR:

- **P**roductivity
- **E**xpectations about inflation
- **A**ctions by the government (business taxes and subsidies)
- **R**esource (input) prices like wages and commodity prices

Module 18 Aggregate Supply: Introduction and Determinants 185

TEACH **Teach It**

LRAS is difficult for students to understand. The difference is that in the long run, all input prices are variable, including wages. This eliminates the sticky prices that caused the *SRAS* curve to be upward-sloping, and it causes the *LRAS* curve to be vertical at the economy's potential output.

TEACH **Teach It**

Many economists believe that, given enough time, the economy will adjust back to potential output. *Note:* Point out to the students that *LRAS* has been gradually shifting to the right over time. Our economy's potential output has increased thanks in large part to better technology and a larger and more educated workforce.

TEACH **Teach It**

Project Figure 18.3 on the board. Explain that *LRAS* is the potential or full-employment output in an economy. Ask students what happens if a change occurs in the aggregate price level. *There is a movement along LRAS.* Show them the change on the graph. Explain that there are no changes in *LRAS* in the short run because prices and wages are not fully flexible. Ask what would happen to *LRAS* if potential output increased. *LRAS would shift right.* Show an increase in *LRAS* on the whiteboard and then show a decrease in *LRAS*.

The Long-Run Aggregate Supply Curve

We've just seen that in the short run, a fall in the aggregate price level leads to a decline in the quantity of aggregate output supplied. This is the result of nominal wages that are sticky in the short run. But as we mentioned earlier, contracts and informal agreements are renegotiated in the long run. So in the long run, nominal wages—like the aggregate price level—are flexible, not sticky. Wage flexibility greatly alters the long-run relationship between the aggregate price level and aggregate supply. In fact, in the long run the aggregate price level has *no* effect on the quantity of aggregate output supplied.

To see why, let's conduct a thought experiment. Imagine that you could wave a magic wand—or maybe a magic bar-code scanner—and cut *all prices* in the economy in half at the same time. By "all prices" we mean the prices of all inputs, including nominal wages, as well as the prices of final goods and services. What would happen to aggregate output, given that the aggregate price level has been halved and all input prices, including nominal wages, have been halved?

The answer is: nothing. Consider Equation 18-1 again: each producer would receive a lower price for its product, but costs would fall by the same proportion. As a result, every unit of output that was profitable to produce before the change in prices would still be profitable to produce after the change in prices. So a halving of *all* prices in the economy has no effect on the economy's aggregate output. In other words, changes in the aggregate price level now have no effect on the quantity of aggregate output supplied.

In reality, of course, no one can change all prices by the same proportion at the same time. But now, we'll consider the *long run*, the period of time over which all prices are fully flexible. In the long run, inflation or deflation has the same effect as someone changing all prices by the same proportion. As a result, changes in the aggregate price level do not change the quantity of aggregate output supplied in the long run. That's because changes in the aggregate price level, in the long run, will be accompanied by equal proportional changes in *all* input prices, including nominal wages.

The **long-run aggregate supply curve** shows the relationship between the aggregate price level and the quantity of aggregate output supplied that would exist if all prices, including nominal wages, were fully flexible.

The **long-run aggregate supply curve**, illustrated in **Figure 18.3** by the curve *LRAS*, shows the relationship between the aggregate price level and the quantity of aggregate output supplied that would exist if all prices, including nominal wages, were fully flexible. The long-run aggregate supply curve is vertical because changes in the

Figure 18.3 The Long -Run Aggregate Supply Curve

The long-run aggregate supply curve shows the quantity of aggregate output supplied when all prices, including nominal wages, are flexible. It is vertical at potential output, Y_P, because in the long run a change in the aggregate price level has no effect on the quantity of aggregate output supplied.

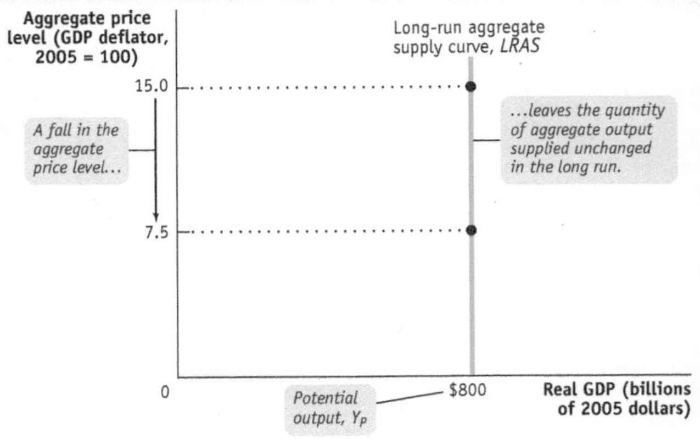

aggregate price level have *no* effect on aggregate output in the long run. At an aggregate price level of 15.0, the quantity of aggregate output supplied is $800 billion in 2005 dollars. If the aggregate price level falls by 50% to 7.5, the quantity of aggregate output supplied is unchanged in the long run at $800 billion in 2005 dollars.

It's important to understand not only that the *LRAS* curve is vertical but also that its position along the horizontal axis marks an important benchmark for output. The horizontal intercept in Figure 18.3, where *LRAS* touches the horizontal axis ($800 billion in 2005 dollars), is the economy's **potential output**, Y_P: the level of real GDP the economy would produce if all prices, including nominal wages, were fully flexible.

Potential output is the level of real GDP the economy would produce if all prices, including nominal wages, were fully flexible.

In reality, the actual level of real GDP is almost always either above or below potential output. We'll see why later, when we discuss the *AD–AS* model. Still, an economy's potential output is an important number because it defines the trend around which actual aggregate output fluctuates from year to year.

In the United States, the Congressional Budget Office (CBO) estimates annual potential output for the purpose of federal budget analysis. In **Figure 18.4**, the CBO's estimates of U.S. potential output from 1989 to 2013 are represented by the orange line and the actual values of U.S. real GDP over the same period are represented by the blue line. Years shaded purple on the horizontal axis correspond to periods in which actual aggregate output fell short of potential output, while years shaded green correspond to periods in which actual aggregate output exceeded potential output.

Figure 18.4 Actual and Potential Output from 1989 to 2013

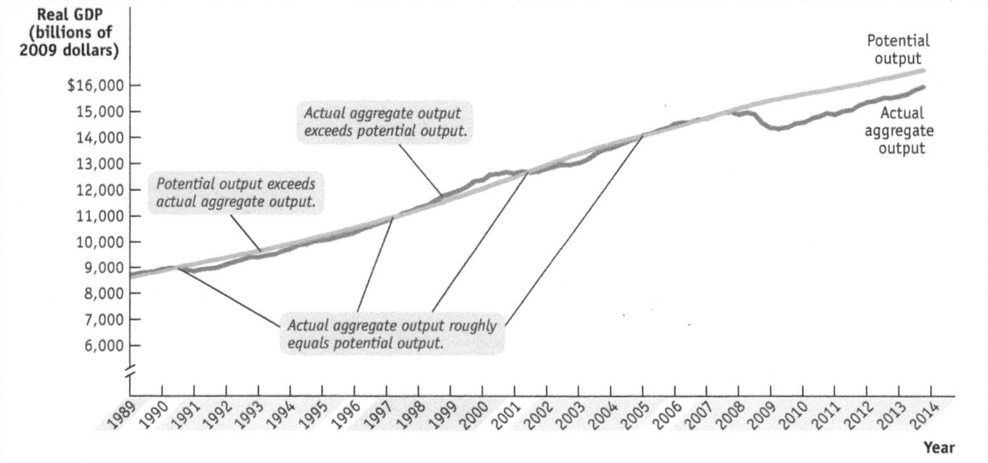

This figure shows the performance of actual and potential output in the United States from 1989 to 2013. The orange line shows estimates, produced by the Congressional Budget Office, of U.S. potential output, and the blue line shows actual aggregate output. The purple-shaded years are periods in which actual aggregate output fell below potential output, while the green-shaded years are periods in which actual aggregate output exceeded potential output. As shown, significant shortfalls occurred in the recessions of the early 1990s and after 2000—particularly during the recession that began in 2007. Actual aggregate output was significantly above potential output in the boom of the late 1990s.

Source: Congressional Budget Office; Bureau of Economic Analysis.

TEACH Teach It

The economy fluctuates around the level of potential output from year to year. Some years the economy is weak and real GDP lies below potential output. Other years the economy is extremely strong and real GDP lies above output.

FOCUS In the News

TRM Have students read the article "The Remarkable Consistency of Long-Run U.S. Economic Growth" at http://conversableeconomist.blogspot.com/2012/02/remarkable-consistency-of-long-run-us.html. Suggested questions for review and discussion are found in **Worksheet 18.3 (Long-Run Economic Growth)** from the TRM.

Module 18 Aggregate Supply: Introduction and Determinants 187

As you can see, U.S. potential output has risen steadily over time—implying a series of rightward shifts of the *LRAS* curve. What has caused these rightward shifts? The answer lies in the factors related to long-run growth:

- increases in the quantity of resources, including land, labor, capital, and entrepreneurship
- increases in the quality of resources, such as a better-educated workforce
- technological progress

Over the long run, as the size of the labor force and the productivity of labor both rise, for example, the level of real GDP that the economy is capable of producing also rises. Indeed, one way to think about economic growth is that it is the growth in the economy's potential output. We generally think of the long-run aggregate supply curve as shifting to the right over time as an economy experiences long-run growth.

From the Short Run to the Long Run

As you can see in Figure 18.4, the economy normally produces more or less than potential output: actual aggregate output was below potential output in the early 1990s, above potential output in the late 1990s, and below potential output for most of the 2000s. So the economy is normally operating at a point on its short-run aggregate supply curve—but not at a point on its long-run aggregate supply curve. Why, then, is the long-run curve relevant? Does the economy ever move from the short run to the long run? And if so, how?

The first step to answering these questions is to understand that the economy is always in one of only two states with respect to the short-run and long-run aggregate supply curves. It can be on both curves simultaneously by being at a point where the curves cross (as in the few years in Figure 18.4 in which actual aggregate output and potential output roughly coincided). Or it can be on the short-run aggregate supply curve but not the long-run aggregate supply curve (as in the years in which actual aggregate output and potential output *did not* coincide). But that is not the end of the story. If the economy is on the short-run but not the long-run aggregate supply curve, the short-run aggregate supply curve will shift over time until the economy is at a point where both curves cross—a point where actual aggregate output is equal to potential output.

Figure 18.5 illustrates how this process works. In both panels *LRAS* is the long-run aggregate supply curve, $SRAS_1$ is the initial short-run aggregate supply curve, and the aggregate price level is at P_1. In panel (a) the economy starts at the initial production point, A_1, which corresponds to a quantity of aggregate output supplied, Y_1, that is higher than potential output, Y_P. Producing an aggregate output level (such as Y_1) that is higher than potential output (Y_P) is possible only because nominal wages have not yet fully adjusted upward. Until this upward adjustment in nominal wages occurs, producers are earning high profits and producing a high level of output. But a level of aggregate output higher than potential output means a low level of unemployment. Because jobs are abundant and workers are scarce, nominal wages will rise over time, gradually shifting the short-run aggregate supply curve leftward. Eventually, it will be in a new position, such as $SRAS_2$. (Later, we'll show where the short-run aggregate supply curve ends up. As we'll see, that depends on the aggregate demand curve as well.)

In panel (b), the initial production point, A_1, corresponds to an aggregate output level, Y_1, that is lower than potential output, Y_P. Producing an aggregate output level (such as Y_1) that is lower than potential output (Y_P) is possible only because nominal wages have not yet fully adjusted downward. Until this downward adjustment occurs, producers are earning low (or negative) profits and producing a low level of output. An aggregate output level lower than potential output means high unemployment. Because workers are abundant and jobs are scarce, nominal wages will fall over time, shifting the short-run aggregate supply curve gradually to the right. Eventually, it will be in a new position, such as $SRAS_2$.

We'll see shortly that these shifts of the short-run aggregate supply curve will return the economy to potential output in the long run.

FOCUS Active Learning

Use the video "Macro 3.3—Long-run Aggregate Supply" from Jacob Clifford (see econextras video list with hyperlinks on the bcs and TRFD) to aid in understanding how the long-run *AS* is determined and influenced by changes to the short-run *AD* and *AS*. Figure 18.5 presents the same concept.

FOCUS Graph It

TRM Understanding shifts in *SRAS* is another of the key skills that is required to do well on the AP® exam. Assign **Worksheet 18.4 (Aggregate Supply)** from the TRM for students to graph each scenario on paper or on their personal whiteboards. Discuss the direction and cause of the shift for each scenario.

St. Louis Federal Reserve Bank Resources

"What Are the 'Ingredients' for Economic Growth?," *Page One Economics Classroom Edition* (September 2013)

Is there a recipe for economic growth? Perhaps some Miracle-Gro for the economy? If only it were that easy. While the exact recipe is a mystery, economists have identified some of the key ingredients. This issue discusses the role that economic institutions play in fostering long-term economic growth.

Figure 18.5 From the Short Run to the Long Run

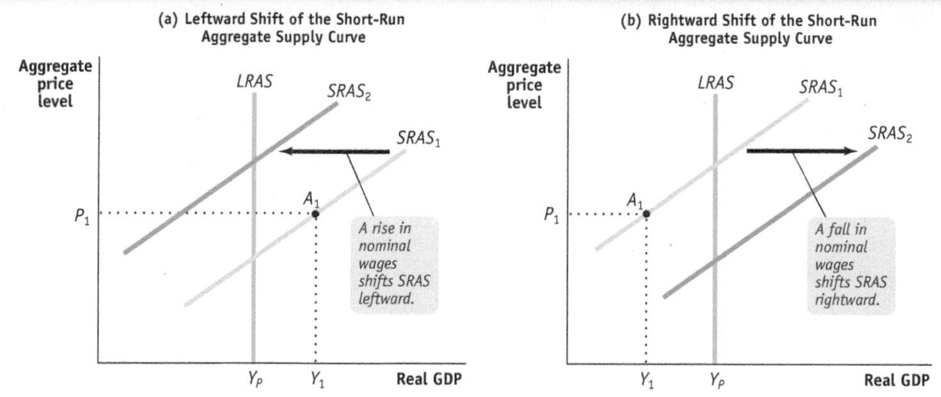

In panel (a), the initial short-run aggregate supply curve is $SRAS_1$. At the aggregate price level, P_1, the quantity of aggregate output supplied, Y_1, exceeds potential output, Y_P. Eventually, low unemployment will cause nominal wages to rise, leading to a leftward shift of the short-run aggregate supply curve from $SRAS_1$ to $SRAS_2$.

In panel (b), the reverse happens: at the aggregate price level, P_1, the quantity of aggregate output supplied is less than potential output. High unemployment eventually leads to a fall in nominal wages over time and a rightward shift of the short-run aggregate supply curve.

FYI Prices and Output During the Great Depression

The figure shows the actual track of the aggregate price level, as measured by the GDP deflator, and real GDP, from 1929 to 1942. As you can see, aggregate output and the aggregate price level fell together from 1929 to 1933 and rose together from 1933 to 1937. This is what we'd expect to see if the economy were moving down the short-run aggregate supply curve from 1929 to 1933 and moving up it (with a brief reversal in 1937–1938) thereafter.

But even in 1942 the aggregate price level was still lower than it was in 1929; yet real GDP was much higher. What happened?

The answer is that the short-run aggregate supply curve shifted to the right over time. This shift partly reflected rising productivity—a rightward shift of the underlying long-run aggregate supply curve. But since the U.S. economy was producing below potential output and had high unemployment during this period, the rightward shift of the short-run aggregate supply curve also reflected the adjustment process shown in panel (b) of Figure 18.5. So the movement of aggregate output from 1929 to 1942 reflected both movements along and shifts of the short-run aggregate supply curve.

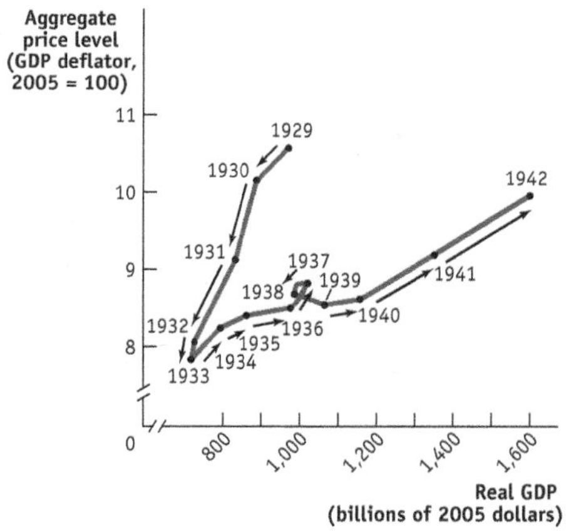

TEACH Teach It

Some economists believe the economy will self-adjust to full employment. When the economy is weak, prices and wages decrease, thereby decreasing the costs of production and shifting *SRAS* to the right. When the economy is strong, prices and wages increase, thereby increasing the costs of production and shifting *SRAS* to the left. Project Figure 18.5, if possible, to illustrate how this process works graphically.

TEACH Connect It

Direct student's attention to the FYI box, which provides a real-world example of how the economy adjusts through shifts of and movements along the short-run *AS* curve, as seen in Figure 18.5. From 1929 to 1933, a movement occurred downward along the *SRAS*. With the exception of a brief downward movement from 1937 to 1938, there was a movement up the *SRAS* curve from 1933 to 1942. In 1942, the *SRAS* shifted rightward, causing output to increase while the price level decreased.

OPEN & CLOSE Exit Slip

TRM *Please see **Exit Slip: Module 18** in the TRM for formative questions to ask before finishing your lesson. These questions will help you quickly assess whether your students have mastered the module's concepts before moving on.*

Answers to the Exit Slip Questions

1.

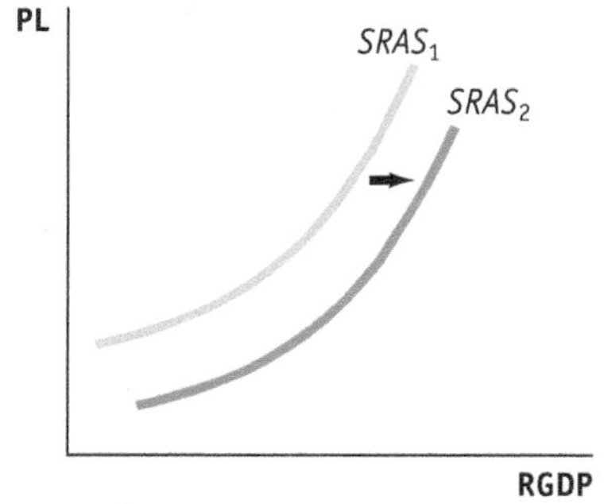

2. C
3. A

MODULE 18 Review

Check Your Understanding

1. Determine the effect on short-run aggregate supply of each of the following events. Explain whether it represents a movement along the *SRAS* curve or a shift of the *SRAS* curve.
   a. A rise in the consumer price index (CPI) leads producers to increase output.
   b. A fall in the price of oil leads producers to increase output.
   c. A rise in legally mandated retirement benefits paid to workers leads producers to reduce output.
2. Suppose the economy is initially at potential output and the quantity of aggregate output supplied increases. What information would you need to determine whether this was due to a movement along the *SRAS* curve or a shift of the LRAS curve?

Tackle the Test: Multiple-Choice Questions

1. Which of the following will shift the short-run aggregate supply curve? A change in
   a. profit per unit at any given price level
   b. commodity prices
   c. nominal wages
   d. productivity
   e. all of the above
2. Because changes in the aggregate price level have no effect on aggregate output in the long run, the long-run aggregate supply curve is
   a. vertical.
   b. horizontal.
   c. fixed.
   d. negatively sloped.
   e. positively sloped.
3. The horizontal intercept of the long-run aggregate supply curve is
   a. at the origin.
   b. negative.
   c. at potential output.
   d. equal to the vertical intercept.
   e. always the same as the horizontal intercept of the short-run aggregate supply curve.
4. A decrease in which of the following will cause the short-run aggregate supply curve to shift to the left?
   a. commodity prices
   b. the cost of health care insurance premiums paid by employers
   c. nominal wages
   d. productivity
   e. the use of cost-of-living allowances in labor contracts
5. That employers are reluctant to decrease nominal wages during economic downturns and raise nominal wages during economic expansions is one reason nominal wages are described as
   a. long-run.
   b. unyielding.
   c. flexible.
   d. real.
   e. sticky.

Answers to Module 18 Review Questions

Check Your Understanding

1. a. This represents a movement along the *SRAS* curve because the CPI—like the GDP deflator—is a measure of the aggregate price level, the overall price level of final goods and services in the economy.

b. This represents a shift of the *SRAS* curve because oil is a commodity. The *SRAS* curve will shift to the right because production costs are now lower, leading to a higher quantity of aggregate output supplied at any given aggregate price level.

c. This represents a shift of the *SRAS* curve because it involves a change in nominal wages. An increase in legally mandated benefits to workers is equivalent to an increase in nominal wages. As a result, the *SRAS* curve will shift leftward because production costs are now higher, leading to a lower quantity of aggregate output supplied at any given aggregate price level.

2. You would need to know what happened to the aggregate price level. If the increase in the quantity of aggregate output supplied was due to a movement along the *SRAS* curve, the aggregate price level would have increased at the same time as the quantity of aggregate output supplied increased. If the increase in the quantity of aggregate output supplied was due to a rightward shift of the *LRAS* curve, the aggregate price level might not rise. Alternatively, you could make the determination by observing what happened to aggregate output in the long run. If it fell back to its initial level in the long run, then the temporary increase in aggregate output was due to a movement along the *SRAS* curve. If it stayed at the higher level in the long run, the increase in aggregate output was due to a rightward shift of the *LRAS* curve.

Tackle the Test: Multiple-Choice Questions

1. e
2. a
3. c
4. d
5. e

Tackle the Test: Free-Response Questions

1. **a.** Draw a correctly labeled graph illustrating a long-run aggregate supply curve.
   b On your graph from part a, label potential output.
   c. On your graph from part a, illustrate an increase in long-run aggregate supply.
   d. What could have caused the change you illustrated in part c? List three possible causes.

Rubric for FRQ 1 (8 points)

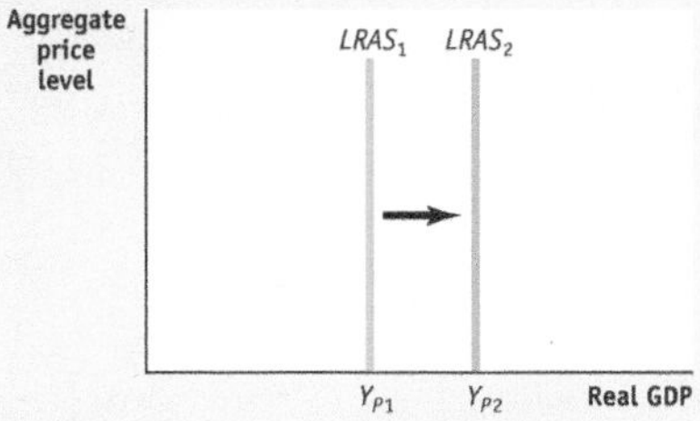

1 point: Vertical axis labeled "Aggregate price level" (or "Price level")
1 point: Horizontal axis labeled "Real GDP"
1 point: Vertical curve labeled "*LRAS*" (or "$LRAS_1$")
1 point: Potential output labeled Y_P (or Y_{P1}) on the horizontal axis at the intercept of the long-run aggregate supply curve
1 point: Long-run aggregate supply curve shifted to the right
1 point: An increase in the quantity of resources (land, labor, capital, or entrepreneurship)
1 point: An increase in the quality of resources
1 point: Technological progress

2. **a.** Draw a correctly labeled short-run aggregate supply curve.
   b. On your graph from part a, illustrate a decrease in short-run aggregate supply.
   c. List three types of changes, including the factor that changes and the direction of the change, that could lead to a decrease in short-run aggregate supply.
   (6 points)

Tackle the Test: Free-Response Question Rubric for FRQ 2 (6 points)

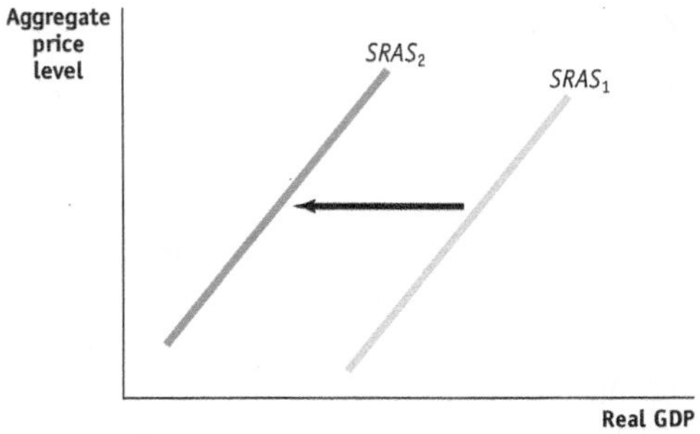

1 point: The vertical axis is labeled "Aggregate price level" or "Price level" and the horizontal axis is labeled "Real GDP."

1 point: The short-run aggregate supply curve is upward-sloping and labeled.

1 point: A new short-run aggregate supply curve is upward-sloping, labeled, and shown to the left of the original *SRAS* curve.

1 point each for up to three of the following four answers:

An increase in commodity prices

An increase in nominal wages

A decrease in productivity

An increase in the expected inflation rate

Module 18 Aggregate Supply: Introduction and Determinants 191

PD To prepare for teaching this lesson, you may want to consult the **Module 19 Sample Lecture** in the TRM.

OPEN & CLOSE **Start Here**

As a review, show students Jacob Clifford's video "Long-Run Aggregate Supply, Recession, and Inflation (*LRAS*)" (see econextras video list with hyperlinks on the bcs and TRFD). Ask students to recall the factors that shift *AD*, *SRAS*, and *LRAS*. Record those factors on the whiteboard as they list them. Tell your students they are now going to put together all that they have learned in the last two modules.

TEACH **AP® Exam Tip**

The *AD–AS* graph shows up in the FRQ section of almost every AP® exam. It is one of the most important graphs students will learn to draw. Tell them they must be able to graph and label it correctly to earn as many points as possible.

TEACH **Teach It**

Sometimes students wonder if the economy is currently in the short run or the long run. Stress that we are always currently in the short run. Sometimes our short-run level of output happens to be below, or above, the economy's potential level of output. With new resources employed, productivity improvements and technology changes drive long-run aggregate supply changes.

Kurt Brady/Alamy

MODULE 19 Equilibrium in the Aggregate Demand–Aggregate Supply Model

In this Module, you will learn to:

- Explain the difference between short-run and long-run macroeconomic equilibrium
- Describe the causes and effects of demand shocks and supply shocks
- Determine if an economy is experiencing a recessionary gap or an inflationary gap and explain how to calculate the size of an output gap

AP® Exam Tip

The *AD–AS* model is one of the most important models you will study. Make sure you can correctly draw, label, and interpret the model, and practice using it to show the effects of policies.

The *AD–AS* Model

From 1929 to 1933, the U.S. economy moved down the short-run aggregate supply curve as the aggregate price level fell. In contrast, from 1979 to 1980, the U.S. economy moved up the aggregate demand curve as the aggregate price level rose. In each case, the cause of the movement along the curve was a shift of the other curve. In 1929–1933, it was a leftward shift of the aggregate demand curve—a major fall in consumer spending. In 1979–1980, it was a leftward shift of the short-run aggregate supply curve—a dramatic fall in short-run aggregate supply caused by the oil *price shock*.

So to understand the behavior of the economy, we must put the aggregate supply curve and the aggregate demand curve together. The result is the ***AD–AS* model**, the basic model we use to understand economic fluctuations.

In the ***AD–AS* model**, the aggregate supply curve and the aggregate demand curve are used together to analyze economic fluctuations.

The economy is in **short-run macroeconomic equilibrium** when the quantity of aggregate output supplied is equal to the quantity demanded.

Short-Run Macroeconomic Equilibrium

We'll begin our analysis by focusing on the short run. **Figure 19.1** shows the aggregate demand curve and the short-run aggregate supply curve on the same diagram. The point at which the *AD* and *SRAS* curves intersect, E_{SR}, is the **short-run macroeconomic equilibrium**: the point at which the quantity of aggregate output supplied is equal to the quantity demanded by domestic households, businesses, the government, and the rest of the world. The aggregate price level at E_{SR}, P_E, is the

St. Louis Federal Reserve Bank Resources

"Market Equilibrium," *The Economic Lowdown Podcast Series*, Volume 1, Episode 8

This episode (run time 8:08) answers a crucial economic question: Where do prices come from? Listeners discover that supply and demand work together like the two blades of a pair of scissors to determine the market equilibrium and the prices of the things you buy.

Figure 19.1 The *AD-AS* Model

The *AD–AS* model combines the aggregate demand curve and the short-run aggregate supply curve. Their point of intersection, E_{SR}, is the point of short-run macroeconomic equilibrium where the quantity of aggregate output demanded is equal to the quantity of aggregate output supplied. P_E is the short-run equilibrium aggregate price level, and Y_E is the short-run equilibrium level of aggregate output.

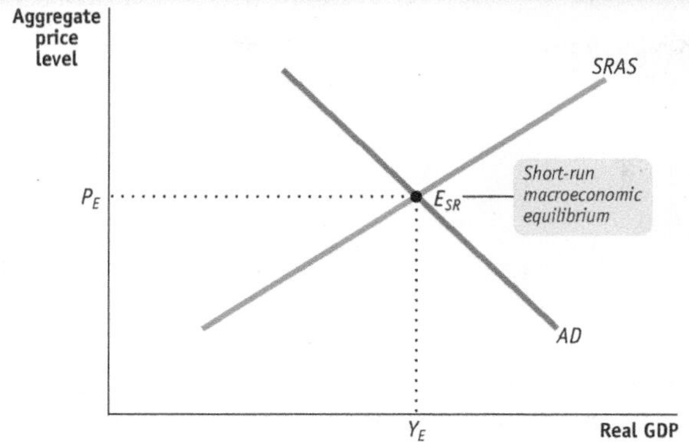

short-run equilibrium aggregate price level. The level of aggregate output at E_{SR}, Y_E, is the **short-run equilibrium aggregate output**.

We have seen that a shortage of any individual good causes its market price to rise and a surplus of the good causes its market price to fall. These forces ensure that the market reaches equilibrium. The same logic applies to short-run macroeconomic equilibrium. If the aggregate price level is above its equilibrium level, the quantity of aggregate output supplied exceeds the quantity of aggregate output demanded. This leads to a fall in the aggregate price level and pushes it toward its equilibrium level. If the aggregate price level is below its equilibrium level, the quantity of aggregate output supplied is less than the quantity of aggregate output demanded. This leads to a rise in the aggregate price level, again pushing it toward its equilibrium level. In the discussion that follows, we'll assume that the economy is always in short-run macroeconomic equilibrium.

We'll also make another important simplification based on the observation that, in reality, there is a long-term upward trend in both aggregate output and the aggregate price level. We'll assume that a fall in either variable really means a fall compared to the long-run trend. For example, if the aggregate price level normally rises 4% per year, a year in which the aggregate price level rises only 3% would count, for our purposes, as a 1% decline. In fact, since the Great Depression there have been very few years in which the aggregate price level of any major nation actually declined—Japan's period of deflation from 1995 to 2005 is one of the few exceptions (which we will explain later). However, there have been many cases in which the aggregate price level fell relative to the long-run trend.

The short-run equilibrium aggregate output and the short-run equilibrium aggregate price level can change because of shifts of either the *AD* curve or the *SRAS* curve. Let's look at each case in turn.

The **short-run equilibrium aggregate price level** is the aggregate price level in the short-run macroeconomic equilibrium.

Short-run equilibrium aggregate output is the quantity of aggregate output produced in the short-run macroeconomic equilibrium.

AP® Exam Tip

When asked to graph the effect of a change, graph the first thing that happens in the short-run unless the question tells you to look at the long-run.

Shifts of Aggregate Demand: Short-Run Effects

An event that shifts the aggregate demand curve, such as a change in expectations or wealth, the effect of the size of the existing stock of physical capital, or the use of fiscal or monetary policy, is known as a **demand shock**. The Great Depression was caused by a negative demand shock, the collapse of wealth and of business and consumer confidence that followed the stock market crash of 1929 and the banking

An event that shifts the aggregate demand curve is a **demand shock**.

TEACH AP® Exam Tip

Point out that the level of employment is tied to output in the economy. If output (real GDP) decreases, employment decreases and unemployment increases. If output (real GDP) increases, employment increases and unemployment decreases. This relationship is often tested on the AP® exam.

TEACH Connect It

Remind students that as unemployment rises, so do transfer payments like unemployment insurance payments made by the government. When unemployment falls, transfer payments decrease. Workers go back to work and earn an income. This action helps to provide balance in the economy and is the result of automatic stabilizers, which make these funds available to the unemployed without specific government action.

FOCUS Graph It

Ask students to draw the short-run aggregate supply curve on their personal whiteboards or in their notebooks. Check to see that each has correctly labeled the axes and that the *AD* and *SRAS* are correct. Students should also show the equilibrium price level and output. This model is often called the "set-up" or starting point for questions posed on the AP® exam.

St. Louis Federal Reserve Bank Resources

"Equilibrium," *The Economic Lowdown Video Series*, Episode 3

In this episode, economic education specialist Scott Wolla explains the concept of equilibrium. Students will get a refresher on the laws of supply and demand before they learn about market equilibrium—the point at which there is no shortage or surplus of a good or service.

FOCUS Active Learning

Use Figure 19.2 to talk about demand shocks. If possible, project the figure on the board. Show students a positive demand shock. Have them determine what happens to output and price level. *Both increase.* Explain that output drives employment, so they can determine what happens to employment as well. *It increases.* Let them know that output, price level, and employment are often tested on the AP® exam. Next show them a negative demand shock. Ask them to identify the change in output, price level, and employment in this situation. *All three decrease.* Finally, direct students to draw the *AD–AS* graph on paper or on their personal whiteboards. Ask them to use the graph to show what happens when consumers become more pessimistic about the direction of the economy.

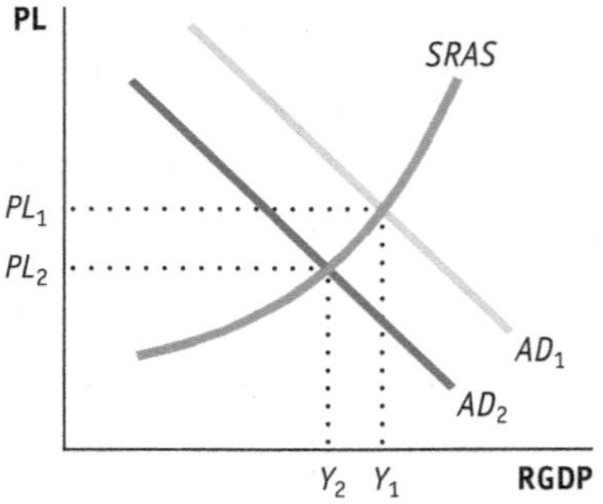

crises of 1930–1931. The Depression was ended by a positive demand shock—the huge increase in government purchases during World War II. In 2008, the U.S. economy experienced another significant negative demand shock as the housing market turned from boom to bust, leading consumers and firms to scale back their spending.

Figure 19.2 shows the short-run effects of negative and positive demand shocks. A negative demand shock shifts the aggregate demand curve, *AD*, to the left, from AD_1 to AD_2, as shown in panel (a). The economy moves down along the *SRAS* curve from E_1 to E_2, leading to lower short-run equilibrium aggregate output and a lower short-run equilibrium aggregate price level. A positive demand shock shifts the aggregate demand curve, *AD*, to the right, as shown in panel (b). Here, the economy moves up along the *SRAS* curve, from E_1 to E_2. This leads to higher short-run equilibrium aggregate output and a higher short-run equilibrium aggregate price level. Demand shocks cause aggregate output and the aggregate price level to move in the same direction.

Figure 19.2 Demand Shocks

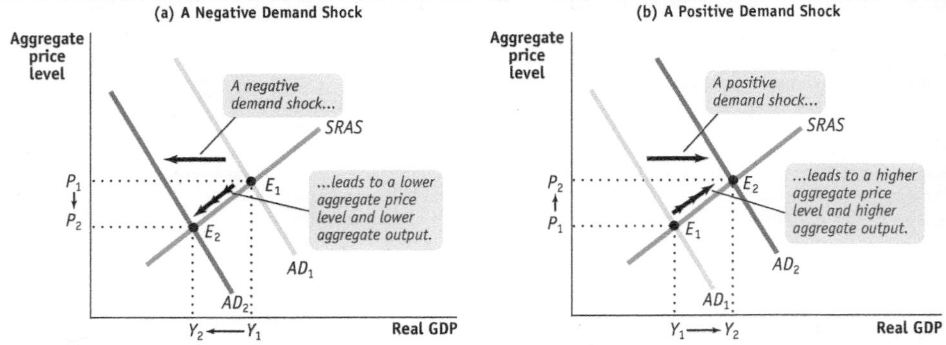

A demand shock shifts the aggregate demand curve, moving the aggregate price level and aggregate output in the same direction. In panel (a), a negative demand shock shifts the aggregate demand curve leftward from AD_1 to AD_2, reducing the aggregate price level from P_1 to P_2 and aggregate output from Y_1 to Y_2. In panel (b), a positive demand shock shifts the aggregate demand curve rightward, increasing the aggregate price level from P_1 to P_2 and aggregate output from Y_1 to Y_2.

Shifts of the *SRAS* Curve

An event that shifts the short-run aggregate supply curve, such as a change in commodity prices, nominal wages, or productivity, is known as a **supply shock**. A *negative* supply shock raises production costs and reduces the quantity producers are willing to supply at any given aggregate price level, leading to a leftward shift of the short-run aggregate supply curve. The U.S. economy experienced severe negative supply shocks following disruptions to world oil supplies in 1973 and 1979. In contrast, a *positive* supply shock reduces production costs and increases the quantity supplied at any given aggregate price level, leading to a rightward shift of the short-run aggregate supply curve. The United States experienced a positive supply shock between 1995 and 2000, when the increasing use of the Internet and other information technologies caused productivity growth to surge.

An event that shifts the short-run aggregate supply curve is a **supply shock**.

The effects of a negative supply shock are shown in panel (a) of **Figure 19.3**. The initial equilibrium is at E_1, with aggregate price level P_1 and aggregate output Y_1. The disruption in the oil supply causes the short-run aggregate supply curve to shift to the left, from $SRAS_1$ to $SRAS_2$. As a consequence, aggregate output falls and the aggregate price level rises, an upward movement along the *AD* curve. At the new equilibrium, E_2, the short-run equilibrium aggregate price level, P_2, is higher, and the short-run equilibrium aggregate output level, Y_2, is lower than before.

Producers are vulnerable to dramatic changes in the price of oil, a cause of supply shocks.

The combination of inflation and falling aggregate output shown in panel (a) has a special name: **stagflation**, for "stagnation plus inflation." When an economy experiences stagflation, it's very unpleasant: falling aggregate output leads to rising unemployment, and people feel that their purchasing power is squeezed by rising prices. Stagflation in the 1970s led to a mood of national pessimism. As we'll see shortly, it also poses a dilemma for policy makers.

A positive supply shock, shown in panel (b), has exactly the opposite effects. A rightward shift of the *SRAS* curve, from $SRAS_1$ to $SRAS_2$ results in a rise in aggregate output and a fall in the aggregate price level, a downward movement along the *AD* curve. The favorable supply shocks of the late 1990s led to a combination of full employment and declining inflation. That is, the aggregate price level fell compared with the long-run trend. For a few years, this combination produced a great wave of national optimism.

Stagflation is the combination of inflation and stagnating (or falling) aggregate output.

The distinctive feature of supply shocks, both negative and positive, is that, unlike demand shocks, they cause the aggregate price level and aggregate output to move in *opposite* directions.

Figure 19.3 Supply Shocks

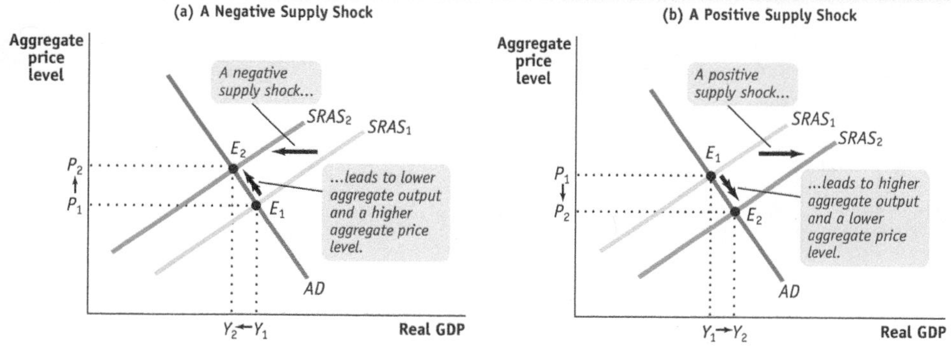

A supply shock shifts the short-run aggregate supply curve, moving the aggregate price level and aggregate output in opposite directions. Panel (a) shows a negative supply shock, which shifts the short-run aggregate supply curve leftward and causes stagflation—lower aggregate output and a higher aggregate price level. Here, the short-run aggregate supply curve shifts from $SRAS_1$ to $SRAS_2$, and the economy moves from E_1 to E_2. The aggregate price level rises from P_1 to P_2, and aggregate output falls from Y_1 to Y_2. Panel (b) shows a positive supply shock, which shifts the short-run aggregate supply curve rightward, generating higher aggregate output and a lower aggregate price level. The short-run aggregate supply curve shifts from $SRAS_1$ to $SRAS_2$, and the economy moves from E_1 to E_2. The aggregate price level falls from P_1 to P_2, and aggregate output rises from Y_1 to Y_2.

FOCUS Active Learning

Use Figure 19.3 to talk about supply shocks. If possible, project the figure on the board. Show students a positive supply shock. Have them determine what happens to output, price level, and employment. *Price level decreases; output and employment increase.* Next show students a negative supply shock. Ask them to identify the change in output, price level, and employment in this situation. *Price level increases; output and employment decrease.* Finally, direct students to draw the *AD–AS* graph on paper or on their personal whiteboards. Ask them to use the graph to show what happens when input prices decrease.

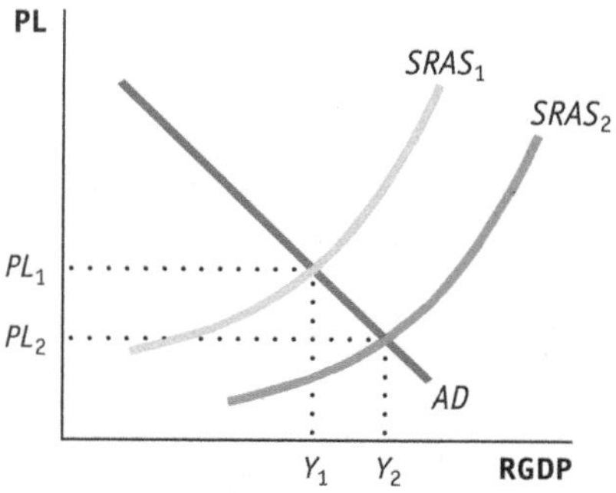

FOCUS Active Learning

TRM For extra practice identifying changes in *AD* and *AS*, assign **Worksheet 19.1 (*AD–AS*)** from the TRM in class or as homework. Students will identify the curve that shifts, the cause of the shift, its direction, and what happens to the price level and real GDP.

Module 19 Equilibrium in the Aggregate Demand-Aggregate Supply Model 195

FOCUS Graph It

The goal of every economy is to reach potential output. Show students what long-run equilibrium looks like. Tell them there are two problems in the economy that the government worries about: inflation, when real GDP is greater than potential output, and unemployment (recession), when real GDP is less than potential output. The goal is to move the economy to full employment output where unemployment and inflation are at the most acceptable levels. Have students draw an *AD–AS* graph of long-run equilibrium on paper or on their personal whiteboards. Make sure they correctly label potential output.

FOCUS Test It

Assign Question 3 from the released 2012 AP® Macroeconomics exam (http://apcentral.collegeboard.com/apc/public/repository/ap12_frq_macroeconomics.pdf). This question will provide a thorough review of all *AD–AS* content. It is recommended that students take $12\frac{1}{2}$ minutes to answer this question to match the time suggested for the AP® exam. The rubric for this question may be viewed at http://tinyurl.com/2012RubricMacro.

There's another important contrast between supply shocks and demand shocks. As we've seen, monetary policy and fiscal policy enable the government to shift the *AD* curve, meaning that governments are in a position to create the kinds of shocks shown in Figure 19.2. It's much harder for governments to shift the *AS* curve. Are there good policy reasons to shift the *AD* curve? We'll turn to that question soon. First, however, let's look at the difference between short-run macroeconomic equilibrium and long-run macroeconomic equilibrium.

Long-Run Macroeconomic Equilibrium

Figure 19.4 combines the aggregate demand curve with both the short-run and long-run aggregate supply curves. The aggregate demand curve, *AD*, crosses the short-run aggregate supply curve, *SRAS*, at E_{LR}. Here we assume that enough time has elapsed that the economy is also on the long-run aggregate supply curve, *LRAS*. As a result, E_{LR} is at the intersection of all three curves—*SRAS*, *LRAS*, and *AD*. So short-run equilibrium aggregate output is equal to potential output, Y_P. Such a situation, in which the point of short-run macroeconomic equilibrium is on the long-run aggregate supply curve, is known as **long-run macroeconomic equilibrium**.

The economy is in **long-run macroeconomic equilibrium** when the point of short-run macroeconomic equilibrium is on the long-run aggregate supply curve.

To see the significance of long-run macroeconomic equilibrium, let's consider what happens if a demand shock moves the economy away from long-run macroeconomic equilibrium. In **Figure 19.5**, we assume that the initial aggregate demand curve is AD_1 and the initial short-run aggregate supply curve is $SRAS_1$. So the initial macroeconomic equilibrium is at E_1, which lies on the long-run aggregate supply curve, *LRAS*. The economy, then, starts from a point of short-run and long-run macroeconomic equilibrium, and short-run equilibrium aggregate output equals potential output at Y_1.

Now suppose that for some reason—such as a sudden worsening of business and consumer expectations—aggregate demand falls and the aggregate demand curve shifts leftward to AD_2. This results in a lower equilibrium aggregate price level at P_2 and a lower equilibrium aggregate output level at Y_2 as the economy settles in the

Figure 19.4 Long-Run Macroeconomic Equilibrium

Here the point of short-run macroeconomic equilibrium also lies on the long-run aggregate supply curve, *LRAS*. As a result, short-run equilibrium aggregate output is equal to potential output, Y_P. The economy is in long-run macroeconomic equilibrium at E_{LR}.

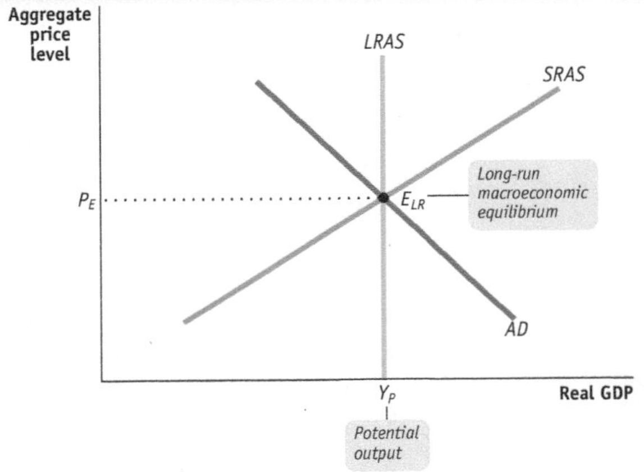

Figure 19.5 Short-Run Versus Long-Run Effects of a Negative Demand Shock

In the long run the economy is self-correcting: demand shocks have only a short-run effect on aggregate output. Starting at E_1, a negative demand shock shifts AD_1 leftward to AD_2. In the short run the economy moves to E_2 and a recessionary gap arises: the aggregate price level declines from P_1 to P_2, aggregate output declines from Y_1 to Y_2, and unemployment rises. But in the long run nominal wages fall in response to high unemployment at Y_2, and $SRAS_1$ shifts rightward to $SRAS_2$. Aggregate output rises from Y_2 to Y_1, and the aggregate price level declines again, from P_2 to P_3. Long-run macroeconomic equilibrium is eventually restored at E_3.

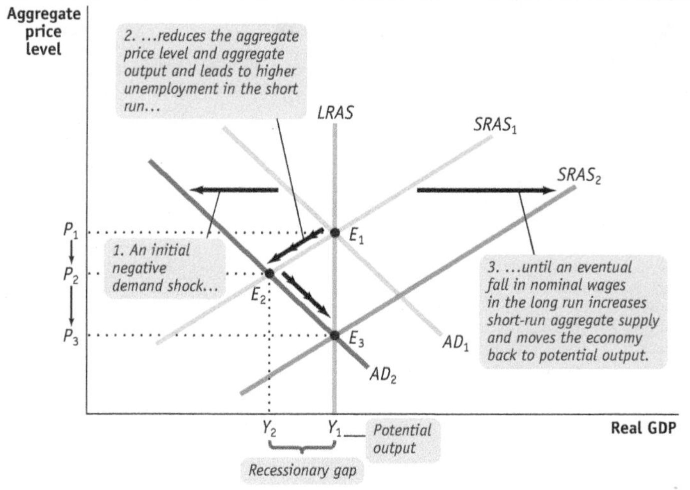

short run at E_2. The short-run effect of such a fall in aggregate demand is what the U.S. economy experienced in 1929–1933: a falling aggregate price level and falling aggregate output.

Aggregate output in this new short-run equilibrium, E_2, is below potential output. When this happens, the economy faces a **recessionary gap**. A recessionary gap inflicts a great deal of pain because it corresponds to high unemployment. The large recessionary gap that had opened up in the United States by 1933 caused intense social and political turmoil. And the devastating recessionary gap that opened up in Germany at the same time played an important role in Hitler's rise to power.

But this isn't the end of the story. In the face of high unemployment, nominal wages eventually fall, as do any other sticky prices, ultimately leading producers to increase output. As a result, a recessionary gap causes the short-run aggregate supply curve to gradually shift to the right. This process continues until $SRAS_1$ reaches its new position at $SRAS_2$, bringing the economy to equilibrium at E_3, where AD_2, $SRAS_2$, and *LRAS* all intersect. At E_3, the economy is back in long-run macroeconomic equilibrium; it is back at potential output Y_1 but at a lower aggregate price level, P_3, reflecting a long-run fall in the aggregate price level. The economy is *self-correcting* in the long run.

What if, instead, there was an increase in aggregate demand? The results are shown in **Figure 19.6** on the next page, where we again assume that the initial aggregate demand curve is AD_1 and the initial short-run aggregate supply curve is $SRAS_1$. The initial macroeconomic equilibrium, at E_1, lies on the long-run aggregate supply curve, *LRAS*. Initially, then, the economy is in long-run macroeconomic equilibrium.

Now suppose that aggregate demand rises, and the *AD* curve shifts rightward to AD_2. This results in a higher aggregate price level, at P_2, and a higher aggregate output level,

There is a **recessionary gap** when aggregate output is below potential output.

AP® Exam Tip

If you have drawn a recessionary gap correctly, the intersection of *AD* and *SRAS* will be to the left of *LRAS* and potential output.

FOCUS Active Learning

Have students draw an *AD–AS* graph of long-run equilibrium on their personal whiteboards or notebook paper. Once each student has correctly done so, tell your class that the real value of household assets has decreased. Have students show you what that would look like on the graph. *AD decreases.* Pose the following questions:

- What problem would exist in the economy based on the graph? *Unemployment because real output is less than potential output.* This is called a recessionary gap.
- What will happen in the long run to eliminate this gap? *Sticky prices and wages will fall, and AS will shift to the right as the costs of production decrease.*

Ask students to show the change on their graphs and ensure that each has correctly drawn and labeled the graph. Project Figure 19.5 on the board or direct students to look at the figure to see what their graphs should look like.

FOCUS Active Learning

Have students draw long-run equilibrium on their personal whiteboards or notebook paper. Once each student has correctly done so, tell your class that personal income taxes have been decreased. Have students show you how that would affect the graph. *AD increases.* Pose the following questions:

- What problem would exist in the economy based on the graph? *Inflation because real output is greater than potential output.* This is called an inflationary gap.
- What will happen in the long run to eliminate this gap? *Prices and wages will rise, and AS will shift to the left as the costs of production increase.*

Ask students to show the change on their graphs and ensure that each has correctly drawn and labeled the graph. Project Figure 19.6 on the board or direct students to look at the figure to see what their graphs should look like.

TEACH AP® Exam Tip

On the AP® exam, students will be asked to graph a problem in the economy using a correctly drawn aggregate demand and aggregate supply graph. They should draw the *AD–AS* graph showing the problem without including the initial shift that caused it. Later in the question, they will be asked to show the correction in the economy *on the same graph.* They should not draw two graphs. Their graphs should be large as there is enough room on the answer sheet to use as much as half a page for the graph. They also need to graph in the answer area and not in the planning area as no graphs in the planning area can be scored.

FOCUS Active Learning

TRM You may wish to assign **Worksheet 19.2 (Equilibrium)** from the TRM in class or as homework. It will provide additional practice drawing the *AD–AS* graph in the short and long run.

Figure 19.6 Short-Run Versus Long-Run Effects of a Positive Demand Shock

Starting at E_1, a positive demand shock shifts AD_1 rightward to AD_2, and the economy moves to E_2 in the short run. This results in an inflationary gap as aggregate output rises from Y_1 to Y_2, the aggregate price level rises from P_1 to P_2, and unemployment falls to a low level. In the long run, $SRAS_1$ shifts leftward to $SRAS_2$ as nominal wages rise in response to low unemployment at Y_2. Aggregate output falls back to Y_1, the aggregate price level rises again to P_3, and the economy self-corrects as it returns to long-run macroeconomic equilibrium at E_3.

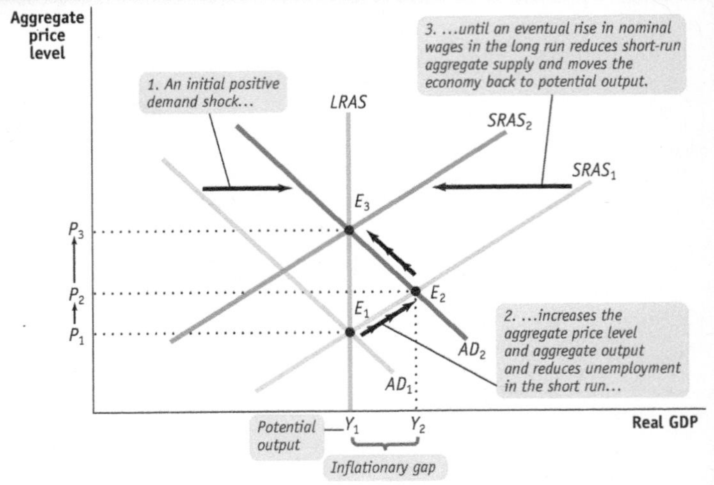

There is an **inflationary gap** when aggregate output is above potential output.

The **output gap** is the percentage difference between actual aggregate output and potential output.

at Y_2, as the economy settles in the short run at E_2. Aggregate output in this new short-run equilibrium is above potential output, and unemployment is low in order to produce this higher level of aggregate output. When this happens, the economy experiences an **inflationary gap**. As in the case of a recessionary gap, this isn't the end of the story. In the face of low unemployment, nominal wages will rise, as will other sticky prices. An inflationary gap causes the short-run aggregate supply curve to shift gradually to the left as producers reduce output in the face of rising nominal wages. This process continues until $SRAS_1$ reaches its new position at $SRAS_2$, bringing the economy into equilibrium at E_3, where AD_2, $SRAS_2$, and *LRAS* all intersect. At E_3, the economy is back in long-run macroeconomic equilibrium. It is back at potential output, but at a higher price level, P_3, reflecting a long-run rise in the aggregate price level. Again, the economy is self-correcting in the long run.

To summarize the analysis of how the economy responds to recessionary and inflationary gaps, we can focus on the **output gap**, the percentage difference between actual aggregate output and potential output. The output gap is calculated as follows:

AP® Exam Tip

If you have drawn an inflationary gap correctly, the intersection of *AD* and *SRAS* will be to the right of *LRAS* and potential output.

$$\textbf{(19-1)}\quad \text{Output gap} = \frac{\text{Actual aggregate output} - \text{Potential output}}{\text{Potential output}} \times 100$$

Our analysis says that the output gap always tends toward zero.

If there is a recessionary gap, so that the output gap is negative, nominal wages eventually fall, moving the economy back to potential output and bringing the output gap back to zero. If there is an inflationary gap, so that the output gap is positive, nominal wages eventually rise, also moving the economy back to potential output and again bringing the output gap back to zero. So in the long run the economy is **self-correcting**: shocks to aggregate demand affect aggregate output in the short run but not in the long run.

The economy is **self-correcting** when shocks to aggregate demand affect aggregate output in the short run, but not the long run.

198 Section 4 National Income and Price Determination

St. Louis Federal Reserve Bank Resources

"The Output Gap: A 'Potentially' Unreliable Measure of Economic Health?," *Page One Economics Classroom Edition* (November 2012)

This issue explains the output gap, one of many economic indicators used by economists to measure the strength of the economy. It also answers the following questions: What exactly is the output gap, and how accurately does it predict the state of the economy?

FYI Supply Shocks Versus Demand Shocks in Practice

How often do supply shocks and demand shocks, respectively, cause recessions? The verdict of most, though not all, macroeconomists is that recessions are mainly caused by demand shocks. But when a negative supply shock does happen, the resulting recession tends to be particularly severe.

Let's get specific. Officially there have been twelve recessions in the United States since World War II. However, two of these, in 1979–1980 and 1981–1982, are often treated as a single "double-dip" recession, bringing the total number down to 11. Of these 11 recessions, only two—the recession of 1973–1975 and the double-dip recession of 1979–1982—showed the distinctive combination of falling aggregate output and a surge in the price level that we call stagflation. In each case, the cause of the supply shock was political turmoil in the Middle East—the Arab-Israeli war of 1973 and the Iranian revolution of 1979—that disrupted world oil supplies and sent oil prices skyrocketing. In fact, economists sometimes refer to the two slumps as "OPEC I" and "OPEC II," after the Organization of Petroleum Exporting Countries, the world oil cartel. A third recession that began in December 2007and ended in June 2009 was at least partially caused by a spike in oil prices.

So 8 of 11 postwar recessions were purely the result of demand shocks, not supply shocks. The few supply-shock recessions, however, were the worst as measured by the unemployment rate. The figure shows the U.S. unemployment rate since 1948, with the dates of the 1973 Arab-Israeli war, the 1979 Iranian revolution, and the 2007 oil price shock marked on the graph. As you can see, the three highest unemployment rates since World War II came after these big negative supply shocks.

There's a reason the aftermath of a supply shock tends to be particularly severe for the economy: macroeconomic policy has a much harder time dealing with supply shocks than with demand shocks, as explained in the next module.

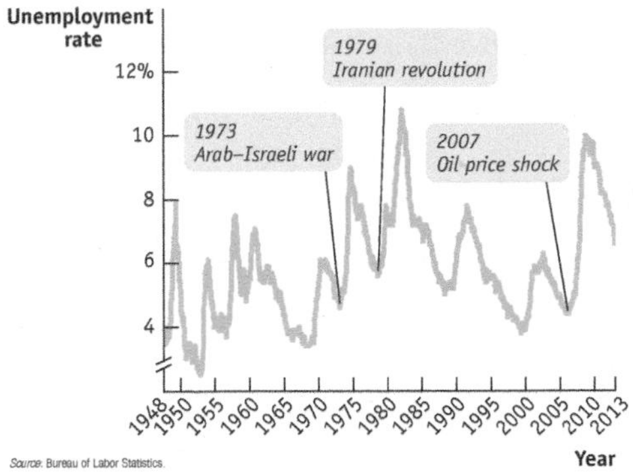

Source: Bureau of Labor Statistics.

MODULE 19 Review

Check Your Understanding

1. Describe the short-run effects of each of the following shocks on the aggregate price level and on aggregate output:
   a. The government sharply increases the minimum wage, raising the wages of many workers.
   b. Solar energy firms launch a major program of investment spending.
   c. Congress raises taxes and cuts spending.
   d. Severe weather destroys crops around the world.
2. Suppose a rise in productivity increases potential output and creates a recessionary gap. Explain how the economy can self-correct in the long run.

OPEN & CLOSE Exit Slip

TRM Please see ***Exit Slip: Module 19*** *in the TRM for formative multiple-choice questions to ask your students before finishing your lesson. These questions will help you quickly assess whether your students have mastered the module's concepts before moving on.*

Answers to the Exit Slip Questions

1. D

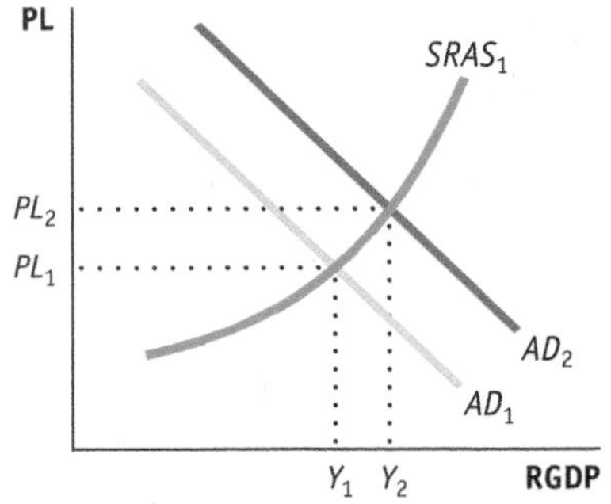

2. C

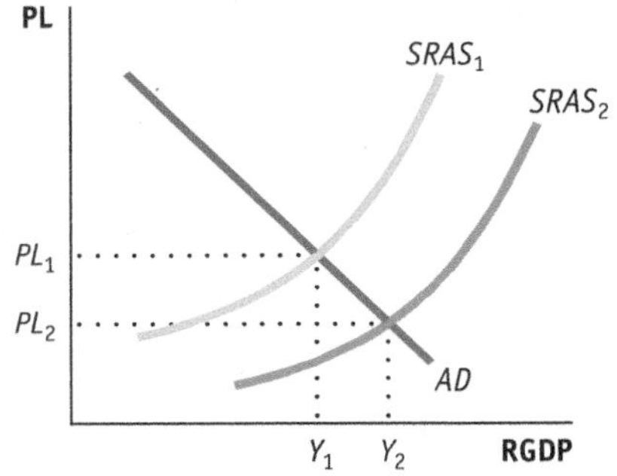

3. A

Answers to Module 19 Review Questions

Check Your Understanding

1. a. An increase in the minimum wage raises the nominal wage and, as a result, shifts the short-run aggregate supply curve to the left. As a result of this negative supply shock, the aggregate price level rises and aggregate output falls.

b. Increased investment spending shifts the aggregate demand curve to the right. As a result of this positive demand shock, both the aggregate price level and aggregate output rise.

c. An increase in taxes and a reduction in government spending both result in negative demand shocks, shifting the aggregate demand curve to the left. As a result, both the aggregate price level and aggregate output fall.

d. This is a negative supply shock, shifting the short-run aggregate supply curve to the left. As a result, the aggregate price level rises and aggregate output falls.

2. As economic growth increases potential output, the long-run aggregate supply curve shifts to the right. If, in the short run, a recessionary gap (aggregate output is less than potential output) now exists, nominal wages will fall, shifting the short-run aggregate supply curve to the right. This results in a fall in the aggregate price level and a rise in aggregate output. As prices fall, we move along the aggregate demand curve due to the wealth and interest rate effects of a change in the aggregate price level. Eventually, as long-run macroeconomic equilibrium is reestablished, aggregate output will rise to become equal to potential output, and the aggregate price level will fall to the level that equates the quantity of aggregate output demanded with potential output.

Tackle the Test: Multiple-Choice Questions

1. c
2. a
3. d
4. b
5. b

Tackle the Test: Free-Response Question

Rubric for FRQ 2 (5 points)

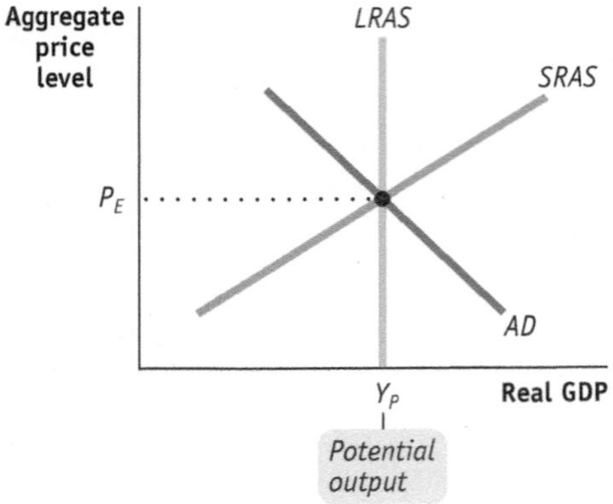

1 point: The vertical axis is labeled "Aggregate price level" or "Price level" and the horizontal axis "Real GDP."

1 point: The short-run aggregate supply curve is upward-sloping and labeled.

1 point: The aggregate demand curve is downward-sloping and labeled.

1 point: The long-run aggregate supply curve is vertical at potential output.

1 point: The equilibrium price level is shown on the vertical axis where *SRAS* and *AD* intersect.

Tackle the Test: Multiple-Choice Questions

1. Which of the following causes a negative supply shock?
  - **I.** a technological advance
  - **II.** increasing productivity
  - **III.** an increase in oil prices

  a. I only
  b. II only
  c. III only
  d. I and III only
  e. I, II, and III

2. Which of the following causes a positive demand shock?
  a. an increase in wealth
  b. pessimistic consumer expectations
  c. a decrease in government spending
  d. an increase in taxes
  e. a relatively high existing stock of capital

3. During stagflation, what happens to the aggregate price level and real GDP?

	Aggregate price level	*Real GDP*
a.	decreases	increases
b.	decreases	decreases
c.	increases	increases
d.	increases	decreases
e.	stays the same	stays the same

Refer to the graph for Questions 4 and 5.

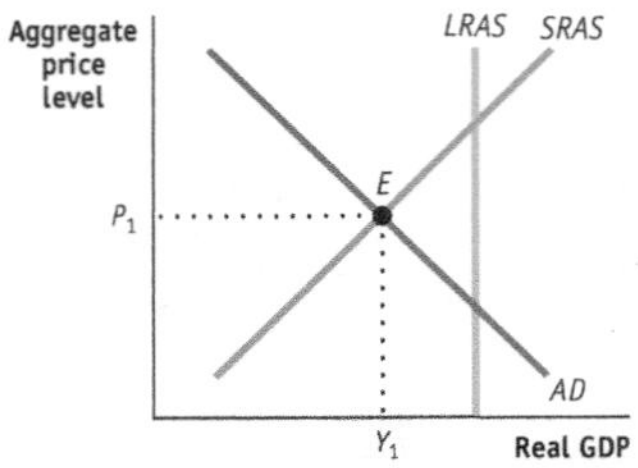

4. Which of the following statements is true if this economy is operating at P_1 and Y_1?
  - **I.** The level of aggregate output equals potential output.
  - **II.** It is in short-run macroeconomic equilibrium.
  - **III.** It is in long-run macroeconomic equilibrium.

  a. I only
  b. II only
  c. III only
  d. II and III
  e. I and III

5. The economy depicted in the graph is experiencing a(n)
  a. contractionary gap.
  b. recessionary gap.
  c. inflationary gap.
  d. demand gap.
  e. supply gap.

Tackle the Test: Free-Response Questions

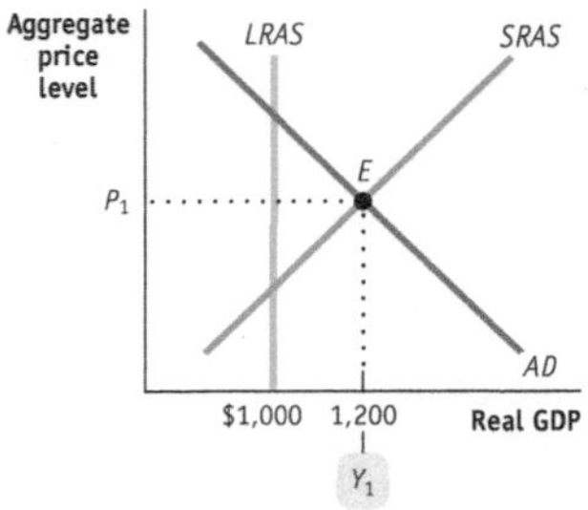

1. Refer to the graph above, with the economy operating at P_1 and Y_1.
  a. Is the economy in short-run macroeconomic equilibrium? Explain.
  b. Is the economy in long-run macroeconomic equilibrium? Explain.
  c. What type of gap exists in this economy?
  d. Calculate the size of the output gap.
  e. What will happen to the size of the output gap in the long run?

Rubric for FRQ 1 (7 points)

1 point: Yes
1 point: The economy is in short-run equilibrium because it operates at the point where short-run aggregate supply and aggregate demand intersect.
1 point: No
1 point: Short-run equilibrium occurs at a level of aggregate output that is not equal to potential output
1 point: Inflationary gap
1 point: $[(\$1,200 - \$1,000)/\$1,000] \times 100 = 20\%$
1 point: It will decrease (or approach zero).

2. Draw a correctly labeled aggregate demand and aggregate supply graph illustrating an economy in long-run macroeconomic equilibrium.
(5 points)

Mark Wilson/Getty Images

MODULE 20 Economic Policy and the Aggregate Demand–Aggregate Supply Model

In this Module, you will learn to:

- Discuss how the *AD–AS* model is used to formulate macroeconomic policy
- Explain the rationale for stabilization policy
- Describe the importance of fiscal policy as a tool for managing economic fluctuations
- Identify the policies that constitute expansionary fiscal policy and those that constitute contractionary fiscal policy

Macroeconomic Policy

Tim Gidal/Picture Post/Getty Images

Some people use *Keynesian economics* as a synonym for *left-wing economics*—but the truth is that the ideas of John Maynard Keynes have been accepted across a broad range of the political spectrum.

We've just seen that the economy is self-correcting in the long run: it will eventually trend back to potential output. Most macroeconomists believe, however, that the process of self-correction typically takes a decade or more. In particular, if aggregate output is below potential output, the economy can suffer an extended period of depressed aggregate output and high unemployment before it returns to normal.

This belief is the background to one of the most famous quotations in economics: John Maynard Keynes's declaration, "In the long run we are all dead." Economists usually interpret Keynes as having recommended that governments not wait for the economy to correct itself. Instead, it is argued by many economists, but not all, that the government should use fiscal policy to get the economy back to potential output in the aftermath of a shift of the aggregate demand curve. This is the rationale for active **stabilization policy**, which is the use of government policy to reduce the severity of recessions and rein in excessively strong expansions.

Stabilization policy is the use of government policy to reduce the severity of recessions and rein in excessively strong expansions.

PD To prepare for teaching this lesson, you may want to consult the **Module 20 Sample Lecture** in the TRM.

OPEN & CLOSE Start Here

As an introduction to fiscal policy, play "Keynes vs. Hayek: Late Economists' Hip-Hop Legacy" (see econextras video list with hyperlinks on the bcs and TRFD) as an introduction to fiscal policy. Ask the questions created for this song (http://www.pbs.org/newshour/extra/daily_videos/economists-rap-about-keynes/).

TEACH Teach It

The long-run adjustment back to full employment may take a long time, so most economists believe that the government can help expedite the return to full employment and stable prices. Most governments adopt a stabilization policy—the use of government policy to reduce the severity of recessions and rein in excessively strong inflationary expansions.

Module 20 Economic Policy and the Aggregate Demand–Aggregate Supply Model 201

TEACH Teach It

If an economy is in long-run equilibrium, negative demand shocks cause a recessionary gap. The price level falls and so does real GDP. Unemployment becomes a problem. Expansionary fiscal and monetary policy is designed to reverse this decline in *AD*. When successful, this shortens the duration of a recession.

TEACH Teach It

If an economy is in long-run equilibrium, positive demand shocks cause an inflationary gap. The price level rises and so does real GDP. Unemployment falls, but inflation is the real problem. Contractionary fiscal and monetary policy is geared toward reversing the increase in *AD*. When successful, this shortens the duration of an inflationary period.

TEACH Teach It

When the government changes spending (*G*), the change affects *AD* in the same direction. Students easily understand this. However, a change in taxes affects *AD* in the opposite direction. A tax decrease causes *AD* to increase. A tax increase causes *AD* to decrease.

Can stabilization policy improve the economy's performance? As we saw in Figure 18.4, the answer certainly appears to be yes. Under active stabilization policy, the U.S. economy returned to potential output in 1996 after an approximately five-year recessionary gap. Likewise, in 2001, it also returned to potential output after an approximately four-year inflationary gap. These periods are much shorter than the decade or more that economists believe it would take for the economy to self-correct in the absence of active stabilization policy. However, as we'll see shortly, the ability to improve the economy's performance is not always guaranteed. It depends on the kinds of shocks the economy faces.

Policy in the Face of Demand Shocks

Imagine that the economy experiences a negative demand shock, like the one shown by the shift from AD_1 to AD_2 in Figure 19.5. Monetary and fiscal policy shift the aggregate demand curve. If policy makers react quickly to the fall in aggregate demand, they can use monetary or fiscal policy to shift the aggregate demand curve back to the right. And if policy were able to perfectly anticipate shifts of the aggregate demand curve and counteract them, it could short-circuit the whole process shown in Figure 19.5. Instead of going through a period of low aggregate output and falling prices, the government could manage the economy so that it would stay at E_1.

Why might a policy that short-circuits the adjustment shown in Figure 19.5 and maintains the economy at its original equilibrium be desirable? For two reasons: First, the temporary fall in aggregate output that would happen without policy intervention is a bad thing, particularly because such a decline is associated with high unemployment. Second, *price stability* is generally regarded as a desirable goal. So preventing deflation—a fall in the aggregate price level—is a good thing.

Does this mean that policy makers should always act to offset declines in aggregate demand? Not necessarily. As we'll see, some policy measures to increase aggregate demand, especially those that increase budget deficits, may have long-term costs in terms of lower long-run growth. Furthermore, in the real world policy makers aren't perfectly informed, and the effects of their policies aren't perfectly predictable. This creates the danger that stabilization policy will do more harm than good; that is, attempts to stabilize the economy may end up creating more instability. We'll describe the long-running debate over macroeconomic policy in later modules. Despite these qualifications, most economists believe that a good case can be made for using macroeconomic policy to offset major negative shocks to the *AD* curve.

Should policy makers also try to offset positive shocks to aggregate demand? It may not seem obvious that they should. After all, even though inflation may be a bad thing, isn't more output and lower unemployment a good thing? Again, not necessarily. Most economists now believe that any short-run gains from an inflationary gap must be paid back later. So policy makers today usually try to offset positive as well as negative demand shocks. For reasons we'll explain later, attempts to eliminate recessionary gaps and inflationary gaps usually rely on monetary rather than fiscal policy. For now, let's explore how macroeconomic policy can respond to supply shocks.

Responding to Supply Shocks

In panel (a) of Figure 19.3, we showed the effects of a negative supply shock: in the short run such a shock leads to lower aggregate output but a higher aggregate price level. As we've noted, policy makers can respond to a negative *demand* shock by using monetary and fiscal policy to return aggregate demand to its original level. But what can or should they do about a negative *supply* shock?

In contrast to the case of a demand shock, there are no easy remedies for a supply shock. That is, there are no government policies that can easily counteract the changes in production costs that shift the short-run aggregate supply curve. So the policy response to a negative supply shock cannot aim to simply push the curve that shifted back to its original position.

In addition, if you consider using monetary or fiscal policy to shift the aggregate demand curve in response to a supply shock, the right response isn't obvious. Two bad things are

202 Section 4 National Income and Price Determination

FYI Is Stabilization Policy Stabilizing?

We've described the theoretical rationale for stabilization policy as a way of responding to demand shocks. But does stabilization policy actually stabilize the economy? One way we might try to answer this question is to look at the long-term historical record. Before World War II, the U.S. government didn't really have a stabilization policy, largely because macroeconomics as we know it didn't exist, and there was no consensus about what to do. Since World War II, and especially since 1960, active stabilization policy has become standard practice.

So here's the question: has the economy actually become more stable since the government began trying to stabilize it? The answer is a qualified yes. It's qualified because data from the pre-World War II era are less reliable than more modern data. But there still seems to be a clear reduction in the size of economic fluctuations.

The figure on the right shows the number of unemployed as a percentage of the nonfarm labor force since 1890. (We focus on nonfarm workers because farmers, though they often suffer economic hardship, are rarely reported as unemployed.) Even ignoring the huge spike in unemployment during the Great Depression, unemployment seems to have varied a lot more before World War II than after. It's also worth noticing that the peaks in postwar unemployment in 1975 and 1982 corresponded to major supply shocks—the kind of shock for which stabilization policy has no good answer.

It's possible that the greater stability of the economy reflects good luck rather than policy. But on the face of it, the evidence suggests that stabilization policy is indeed stabilizing.

Source: C. Romer, "Spurious Volatility in Historical Unemployment Data," *Journal of Political Economy* 94, no. 1 (1986): 1–37 (years 1890–1928); Bureau of Labor Statistics (years 1929–2013).

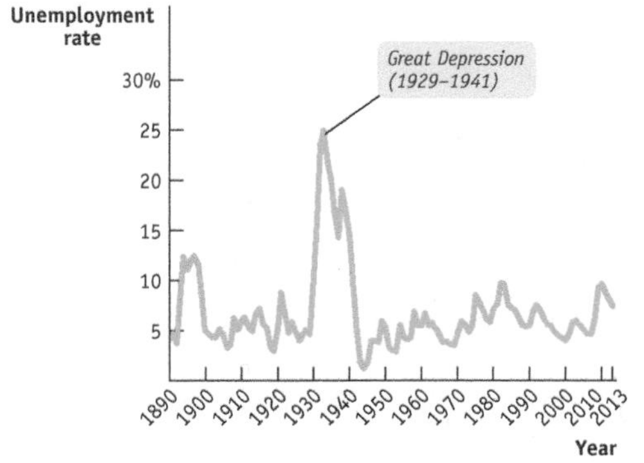

happening simultaneously: a fall in aggregate output, leading to a rise in unemployment, *and* a rise in the aggregate price level. Any policy that shifts the aggregate demand curve alleviates one problem only by making the other problem worse. If the government acts to increase aggregate demand and limit the rise in unemployment, it reduces the decline in output but causes even more inflation. If it acts to reduce aggregate demand, it curbs inflation but causes a further rise in unemployment.

It's a trade-off with no good answer. In the end, the United States and other economically advanced nations suffering from the supply shocks of the 1970s eventually chose to stabilize prices even at the cost of higher unemployment. But being an economic policy maker in the 1970s, or in early 2008, meant facing even harder choices than usual.

Negative supply shocks cause inflation and unemployment. This makes for difficult policy choices for Federal Reserve Chairman Janet Yellen because any policy that alleviates one problem worsens the other.

Fiscal Policy: The Basics

Let's begin with the obvious: modern governments spend a great deal of money and collect a lot in taxes. **Figure 20.1** on the next page shows government spending and tax revenue as percentages of GDP for a selection of high-income countries in 2012. As you can see, the French government sector is relatively large, accounting for more than half of the French economy. The government of the United States plays a smaller role in the economy than do the governments of Canada or most European countries. But that role is still sizable. As a result, changes in the

TEACH Teach It

There is very little that fiscal policy makers can do to reverse a supply shock. It is much easier to affect spending (through *AD*) than it is to affect production (through *AS*). When *AS* decreases, both unemployment and inflation increase. Shifting *AD* will decrease one or the other, but not both. Illustrate this on the board for students, so they can see the changes in output and price level as you shift *AD*.

FOCUS Flip It

TRM Have students watch Jacob Clifford's video "Macro 3.2—Inflationary and Recessionary Gaps with Fiscal and Monetary Policy" (see econextras video list with hyperlinks on the bcs and TRFD). Let students know they should pause it at 0:49, so they can draw the two graphs Clifford refers to. They can also stop the video at 3:20 before monetary policy is explained. Follow up in class with **Worksheet 20.1 (Output Gaps)** from the TRM for questions on this video.

Module 20 Economic Policy and the Aggregate Demand–Aggregate Supply Model 203

TEACH Connect It

TRM This is the perfect time to review the extended circular-flow diagram with students. As you talk about the diagram, explain the flow of money into and out of the government block. Ask students to look at **Figure 10.2 (Expanded Circular-Flow Diagram)** on page 107 to follow along. A completed circular-flow diagram may also be found in **Handout 20.2 (Circular-Flow Diagram)** from the TRM.

FOCUS Active Learning

TRM Any governmental action that reduces people's real income can be considered a tax. Such action can also reduce the profit of businesses. Taxes act as a leakage from the GDP–income stream and will reduce both income and GDP over time. Use **Handout 20.3 (Taxes)** from the TRM to conduct a discussion of taxes. *Answers:*
1. Yes. 2. To pay for public goods that help us in some ways and that give us satisfaction.
3. Infrastructure projects, fire and police protection, national defense, national and local parks, social welfare programs such as Social Security and Medicare, and so on.

Figure 20.1 Government Spending and Tax Revenue for Some High-Income Countries in 2012

Government spending and tax revenue are represented as a percentage of GDP. France has a particularly large government sector, representing nearly 60% of its GDP. The U.S. government sector, although sizable, is smaller than the government sectors of Canada and most European countries.
Source: OECD (data for Japan is for year 2011).

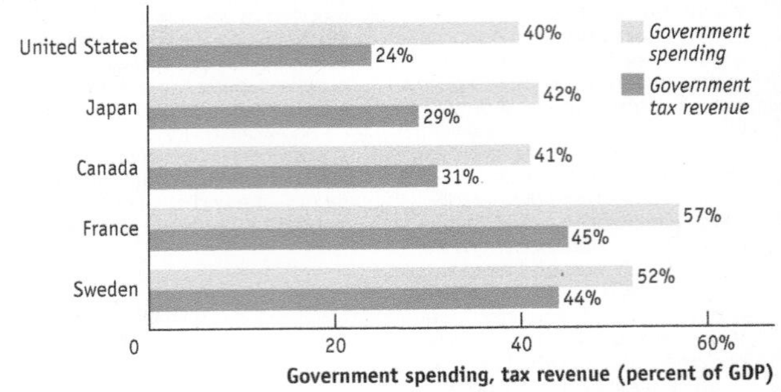

federal budget—changes in government spending or in taxation—can have large effects on the U.S. economy.

To analyze these effects, we begin by showing how taxes and government spending affect the economy's flow of income. Then we can see how changes in spending and tax policy affect aggregate demand.

AP® Exam Tip

When the government increases spending or transfer payments or decreases taxes (to give consumers more income), the economy expands. When the government decreases spending or transfer payments or increases taxes, the economy contracts.

Taxes, Government Purchases of Goods and Services, Transfers, and Borrowing

In the circular-flow diagram discussed in Module 10, we showed the circular flow of income and spending in the economy as a whole. One of the sectors represented in that figure was the government. Funds flow *into* the government in the form of taxes and government borrowing; funds flow *out* in the form of government purchases of goods and services and government transfers to households.

What kinds of taxes do Americans pay, and where does the money go? **Figure 20.2** shows the composition of U.S. tax revenue in 2013. Taxes, of course, are required

Figure 20.2 Sources of Tax Revenue in the United States, 2013

Personal income taxes, taxes on corporate profits, and social insurance taxes account for most government tax revenue. The rest is a mix of property taxes, sales taxes, and other sources of revenue.
Source: Bureau of Economic Analysis.

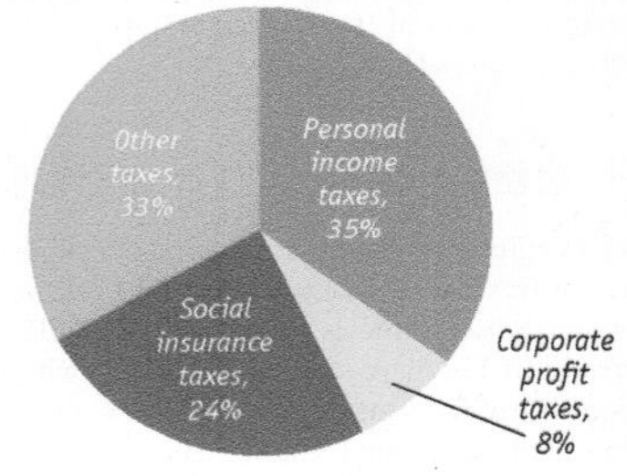

St. Louis Federal Reserve Bank Resources

Government Spending and Taxes

Students engage in an activity that matches programs for low-income people with the type of economic inequity the program addresses and observe an activity simulating tax payments and transfers.

Figure 20.3 Government Spending in the United States, 2013

The two types of government spending are purchases of goods and services and government transfers. The big items in government purchases are national defense and education. The big items in government transfers are Social Security and the Medicare and Medicaid health care programs.

Source: Bureau of Economic Analysis.

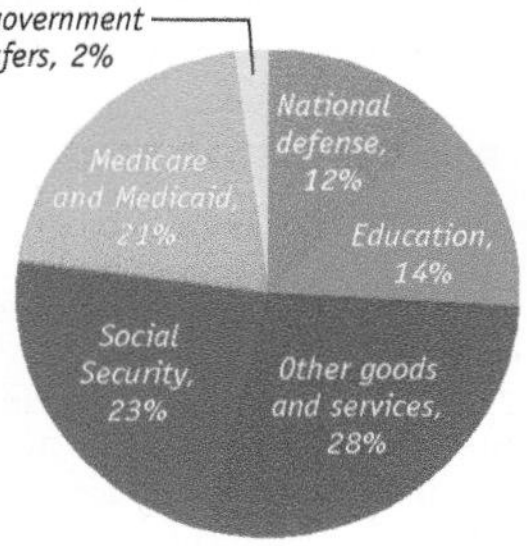

payments to the government. In the United States, taxes are collected at the national level by the federal government; at the state level by each state government; and at local levels by counties, cities, and towns. At the federal level, the main taxes are income taxes on both personal income and corporate profits as well as *social insurance* taxes, which we'll explain shortly. At the state and local levels, the picture is more complex: these governments rely on a mix of sales taxes, property taxes, income taxes, and fees of various kinds. Overall, taxes on personal income and corporate profits accounted for 43% of total government revenue in 2013; social insurance taxes accounted for 24%; and a variety of other taxes, collected mainly at the state and local levels, accounted for the rest.

Figure 20.3 shows the composition of total U.S. government spending in 2013, which takes two forms. One form is purchases of goods and services. This includes everything from ammunition for the military to the salaries of public schoolteachers (who are treated in the national accounts as providers of a service—education). The big items here are national defense and education. The large category labeled "Other goods and services" consists mainly of state and local spending on a variety of services, from police and firefighters to highway construction and maintenance.

Social insurance programs are government programs intended to protect families against economic hardship.

The other form of government spending is government transfers, which are payments by the government to households for which no good or service is provided in return. In the modern United States, as well as in Canada and Europe, government transfers represent a very large proportion of the budget. Most U.S. government spending on transfer payments is accounted for by three big programs:

- Social Security, which provides guaranteed income to older Americans, disabled Americans, and the surviving spouses and dependent children of deceased beneficiaries
- Medicare, which covers much of the cost of health care for Americans over age 65
- Medicaid, which covers much of the cost of health care for Americans with low incomes

The term **social insurance** is used to describe government programs that are intended to protect families

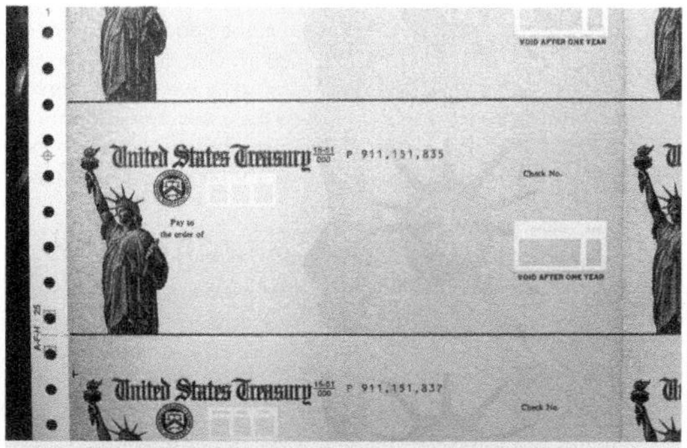

William Thomas Cain/Getty Images

Government transfers on their way: Social Security checks are run through a printer at the U.S. Treasury printing facility in Philadelphia, Pennsylvania.

TEACH Teach It

The government also provides transfer payments to some households. Students have trouble with the concept of transfer payments. Explain that they are payments of money the government provides to certain individuals who qualify for support. Stress that these individuals must meet entitlement criteria to receive such benefits. Ask students for examples. *Social Security, unemployment insurance, student aid, Medicare, Medicaid, VA benefits, food stamps, and the like.*

FOCUS In the News

TRM To better understand how the stimulus package worked, have students read the *Washington Times* article "Obama's Stimulus Package, 5 Years Later: Dems Defend, Republicans Ridicule" at http://tinyurl.com/m6tr7fo. Suggested questions for this reading may be found in **Worksheet 20.4 (Stimulus)** in the TRM.

FOCUS Active Learning

TRM Show Jason Welker's video "Introduction to Fiscal Policy—Expansionary vs. Contractionary Policies" (see econextras video list with hyperlinks on the bcs and TRFD). Assign **Worksheet 20.5 (Intro to Fiscal Policy)** from the TRM for questions on this video.

against economic hardship. These include Social Security, Medicare, and Medicaid, as well as smaller programs such as unemployment insurance and food stamps. In the United States, social insurance programs are largely paid for with special, dedicated taxes on wages—the social insurance taxes we mentioned earlier.

But how do tax policy and government spending affect the economy? The answer is that taxation and government spending have a strong effect on aggregate spending.

The Government Budget and Total Spending

Let's recall the basic equation of national income accounting:

$$\textbf{(20-1)} \quad GDP = C + I + G + X - IM$$

The left-hand side of this equation is GDP, the value of all final goods and services produced in the economy. The right-hand side is aggregate spending, the total spending on final goods and services produced in the economy. It is the sum of consumer spending (C), investment spending (I), government purchases of goods and services (G), and the value of exports (X) minus the value of imports (IM). It includes all the sources of aggregate demand.

The government directly controls one of the variables on the right-hand side of Equation 20-1: government purchases of goods and services (G). But that's not the only effect fiscal policy has on aggregate spending in the economy. Through changes in taxes and transfers, it also influences consumer spending (C) and, in some cases, investment spending (I).

To see why the budget affects consumer spending, recall that *disposable income,* the total income households have available to spend, is equal to the total income they receive from wages, dividends, interest, and rent, *minus* taxes, *plus* government transfers. So either an increase in taxes or a decrease in government transfers *reduces* disposable income. And a fall in disposable income, other things equal, leads to a fall in consumer spending. Conversely, either a decrease in taxes or an increase in government transfers *increases* disposable income. And a rise in disposable income, other things equal, leads to a rise in consumer spending.

The government's ability to affect investment spending is a more complex story, which we won't discuss in detail. The important point is that the government taxes profits, and changes in the rules that determine how much a business owes can increase or decrease the incentive to spend on investment goods.

Because the government itself is one source of spending in the economy, and because taxes and transfers can affect spending by consumers and firms, the government can use changes in taxes or government spending to *shift the aggregate demand curve,* and there can be good reasons for doing so. In early 2008, for example, there was bipartisan agreement that the U.S. government should act to prevent a fall in aggregate demand—that is, to move the aggregate demand curve to the right of where it would otherwise be. The resulting Economic Stimulus Act of 2008 was a classic example of fiscal policy: the use of taxes, government transfers, or government purchases of goods and services to stabilize the economy by shifting the aggregate demand curve.

Expansionary and Contractionary Fiscal Policy

Why would the government want to shift the aggregate demand curve? Because it wants to close either a recessionary gap, created when aggregate output falls below potential output, or an inflationary gap, created when aggregate output exceeds potential output.

Figure 20.4 shows the case of an economy facing a recessionary gap. *SRAS* is the short-run aggregate supply curve, *LRAS* is the long-run aggregate supply curve, and AD_1 is the initial aggregate demand curve. At the initial short-run macroeconomic equilibrium, E_1, aggregate output is Y_1, below potential output, Y_P. What the government would like to do is increase aggregate demand, shifting the aggregate demand curve rightward to AD_2. This would increase aggregate output, making it equal to potential

206 Section 4 National Income and Price Determination

Figure 20.4 Expansionary Fiscal Policy Can Close a Recessionary Gap

At E_1 the economy is in short-run macroeconomic equilibrium where the aggregate demand curve, AD_1, intersects the *SRAS* curve. At E_1, there is a recessionary gap of $Y_P - Y_1$. An expansionary fiscal policy—an increase in government purchases of goods and services, a reduction in taxes, or an increase in government transfers—shifts the aggregate demand curve rightward. It can close the recessionary gap by shifting AD_1 to AD_2, moving the economy to a new short-run macroeconomic equilibrium, E_2, which is also a long-run macroeconomic equilibrium.

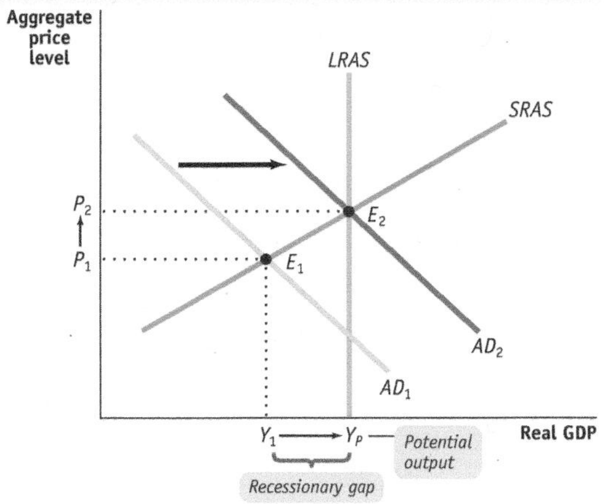

output. Fiscal policy that increases aggregate demand, called **expansionary fiscal policy**, normally takes one of three forms:

- an increase in government purchases of goods and services
- a cut in taxes
- an increase in government transfers

Expansionary fiscal policy increases aggregate demand.

Figure 20.5 on the next page shows the opposite case—an economy facing an inflationary gap. At the initial equilibrium, E_1, aggregate output is Y_1, above potential output, Y_P. Policy makers often try to head off inflation by eliminating inflationary gaps. To eliminate the inflationary gap shown in Figure 20.5, fiscal policy must reduce aggregate demand and shift the aggregate demand curve leftward to AD_2. This reduces aggregate output and makes it equal to potential output. Fiscal policy that reduces aggregate demand, called **contractionary fiscal policy**, is implemented by:

- a reduction in government purchases of goods and services
- an increase in taxes
- a reduction in government transfers

AP® Exam Tip

If a question on the AP® exam asks you to identify a policy that would be appropriate to close a recessionary gap or an inflationary gap, don't simply say "expansionary" or "contractionary." Your answer should specify a policy (a change in spending, transfer payments, or taxes) that would close the gap described in the question.

A classic example of contractionary fiscal policy occurred in 1968, when U.S. policy makers grew worried about rising inflation. President Lyndon Johnson imposed a temporary 10% surcharge on income taxes—everyone's income taxes were increased by 10%. He also tried to scale back government purchases of goods and services, which had risen dramatically because of the cost of the Vietnam War.

Contractionary fiscal policy reduces aggregate demand.

A Cautionary Note: Lags in Fiscal Policy

Looking at Figures 20.4 and 20.5, it may seem obvious that the government should actively use fiscal policy—always adopting an expansionary fiscal policy when the economy faces a recessionary gap and always adopting a contractionary fiscal policy when the economy faces an inflationary gap. But many economists caution against an extremely active stabilization policy, arguing that a government that tries too hard to stabilize

FOCUS Graph It

Ask students to draw an *AD–AS* graph showing a recessionary gap on paper or on their personal whiteboards. Have students identify the gap on their graphs. Use Figure 20.4 to point out the gap and see if it matches the area they identified. Ask what type of fiscal policy would close the gap. *Increase government spending or decrease taxes.* Have them use their graphs to show how fiscal policy action would affect *AD*. Call on individual students to explain how the increase in spending or the decrease in taxes will impact *AD*.

FOCUS Active Learning

TRM So your students can practice fiscal policy, assign **Worksheet 20.6 (Fiscal Policy)** from the TRM in class or as homework.

St. Louis Federal Reserve Bank Resources

Crowding Out

Students learn that the loanable funds market is a virtual clearing house matching borrowers and savers. They participate in an activity to demonstrate crowding out in the loanable funds market. They use demand and supply analysis to graphically represent the results of crowding out.

FOCUS Graph It

Ask students to draw an *AD–AS* graph showing an inflationary gap on paper or on their personal whiteboards. Have students identify the gap on their graphs. Use Figure 20.5 to point out the gap and see if it matches the area they identified. Ask what type of fiscal policy would close the gap. *Decrease government spending or increase taxes.* Have them use their graphs to show how fiscal policy action would affect *AD*. Call on individual students to explain how the decrease in spending or the increase in taxes will impact *AD*.

TEACH Teach It

Fiscal policy looks easy on the chalkboard. In reality, it is more difficult because there are important time lags in its use. This may delay economic recovery or allow time for the economy to self-correct.

- **Recognition lag**: The government has to realize that the recessionary gap exists because economic data take time to collect and analyze, and recessions are often recognized only months after they have begun.
- **Decision lag**: The government has to develop a spending plan, which can itself drag on for months, particularly if politicians take time debating how the money should be spent and passing legislation.
- **Implementation lag**: It takes time to spend money. For example, a road construction project begins with activities such as surveying that don't involve spending large sums.

Figure 20.5 Contractionary Fiscal Policy Can Close an Inflationary Gap

At E_1 the economy is in short-run macroeconomic equilibrium where the aggregate demand curve, AD_1, intersects the *SRAS* curve. At E_1, there is an inflationary gap of $Y_1 - Y_P$. A contractionary fiscal policy—such as reduced government purchases of goods and services, an increase in taxes, or a reduction in government transfers—shifts the aggregate demand curve leftward. It closes the inflationary gap by shifting AD_1 to AD_2, moving the economy to a new short-run macroeconomic equilibrium, E_2, which is also a long-run macroeconomic equilibrium.

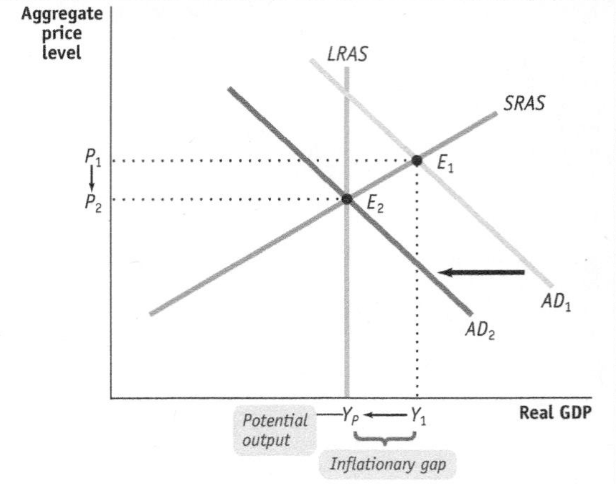

the economy through fiscal policy, or a central bank that does the same with monetary policy, can end up making the economy less stable.

We'll leave discussion of the warnings associated with monetary policy to later modules. In the case of fiscal policy, one key reason for caution is that there are important *time lags* in its use. To understand the nature of these lags, think about what has to happen before the government increases spending to fight a recessionary gap. First, the government has to realize that the recessionary gap exists: economic data take time to collect and analyze, and recessions are often recognized only months after they have begun. Second, the government has to develop a spending plan, which can itself take months, particularly if politicians take time debating how the money should be spent and passing legislation. Finally, it takes time to spend money. For example, a road construction project begins with activities such as surveying that don't involve spending large sums. It may be quite some time before the big spending begins.

Because of these lags, an attempt to increase spending to fight a recessionary gap may take so long to get going that the economy has already recovered on its own. In fact, the recessionary gap may have turned into an inflationary gap by the time the fiscal policy takes effect. In that case, the fiscal policy will make things worse instead of better.

This doesn't mean that fiscal policy should never be actively used. In early 2008, for example, there was good reason to believe that the U.S. economy had begun a lengthy slowdown caused by turmoil in the financial markets, so a fiscal stimulus designed to arrive within a few months would almost surely push aggregate demand in the right direction. But the problem of lags makes the actual use of both fiscal and monetary policy harder than you might think from a simple analysis like the one we have just given.

AP Photo/Ron Edmonds

Will the stimulus come in time to be worthwhile? President Barack Obama listens to a question during a news conference in the East Room of the White House in Washington, D.C.

208 Section 4 National Income and Price Determination

MODULE 20 Review

Check Your Understanding

1. In each of the following cases, determine whether the policy is an expansionary or contractionary fiscal policy:
   a. Several military bases around the country, which together employ tens of thousands of people, are closed.
   b. The number of weeks an unemployed person is eligible for unemployment benefits is increased.
   c. The federal tax on gasoline is increased.
2. Explain why federal disaster relief, which quickly disburses funds to victims of natural disasters such as hurricanes, floods, and large-scale crop failures, will stabilize the economy more effectively after a disaster than relief that must be legislated.
3. Suppose someone says, "Using monetary or fiscal policy to pump up the economy is counterproductive—you get a brief high, but then you have the pain of inflation."
   a. Explain what this means in terms of the *AD–AS* model.
   b. Is this a valid argument against stabilization policy? Why or why not?

Tackle the Test: Multiple-Choice Questions

1. Which of the following contributes to the lag in implementing fiscal policy?
   I. It takes time for Congress and the president to pass spending and tax changes.
   II. Current economic data take time to collect and analyze.
   III. It takes time to realize an output gap exists.
   a. I only
   b. II only
   c. III only
   d. I and III only
   e. I, II, and III
2. Which of the following is a government transfer program?
   a. Social Security
   b. Medicare/Medicaid
   c. unemployment insurance
   d. food stamps
   e. all of the above
3. Which of the following is an example of expansionary fiscal policy?
   a. increasing taxes
   b. increasing government spending
   c. decreasing government transfers
   d. decreasing interest rates
   e. increasing the money supply
4. Which of the following is a fiscal policy that is appropriate to combat inflation?
   a. decreasing taxes
   b. decreasing government spending
   c. increasing government transfers
   d. increasing interest rates
   e. expansionary fiscal policy
5. A cut in income taxes is an example of
   a. an expansionary fiscal policy.
   b. a contractionary fiscal policy.
   c. an expansionary monetary policy.
   d. a contractionary monetary policy.
   e. none of the above.

OPEN & CLOSE Exit Slip

*TRM Please see **Exit Slip: Module 20** in the TRM for formative multiple-choice questions to ask your students before finishing your lesson. These questions will help you quickly assess whether your students have mastered the module's concepts before moving on.*

Answers to the Exit Slip Questions

1. D

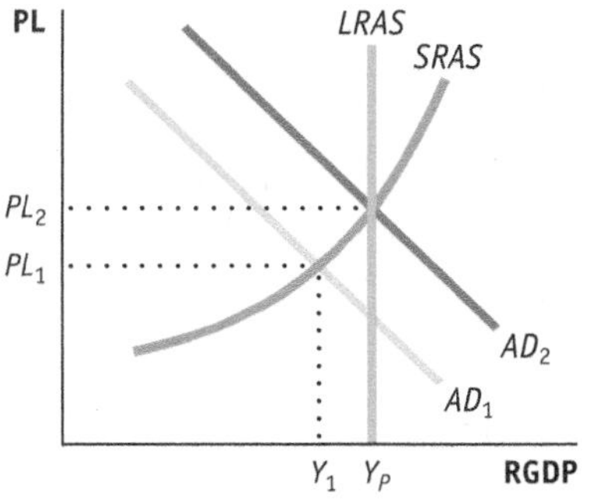

2. C
3. A

Answers to Module 20 Review Questions

Check Your Understanding

1. a. This is a contractionary fiscal policy because it is a reduction in government purchases of goods and services.

b. This is an expansionary fiscal policy because it is an increase in government transfers that will increase disposable income.

c. This is a contractionary fiscal policy because it is an increase in taxes, which will reduce disposable income.

2. Federal disaster relief that is quickly disbursed is more effective at stabilizing the economy than legislated aid because there is very little time lag between the time of the disaster and the time when relief is received by victims. In contrast, the process of creating new legislation is relatively slow, so legislated aid is likely to entail a time lag in its disbursement, potentially destabilizing the economy.

3. a. An economy is overstimulated when an inflationary gap is present. This will arise if an expansionary monetary or fiscal policy is implemented when the economy is currently in long-run macroeconomic equilibrium. This shifts the aggregate demand curve to the right, in the short run raising the aggregate price level and aggregate output and creating an inflationary gap. Eventually, nominal wages will rise and shift the short-run aggregate supply curve to the left, and aggregate output will fall back to potential output. This is the scenario predicted by the speaker.

b. No, this is not a valid argument. When the economy is not currently in long-run macroeconomic equilibrium, an expansionary monetary or fiscal policy does not lead to the outcome described above. Suppose a negative demand shock has shifted the aggregate demand curve to the left, resulting in a recessionary gap. An expansionary monetary or fiscal policy can shift the aggregate demand curve back to its original position in long-run macroeconomic equilibrium. In this way, the short-run fall in aggregate output and deflation caused by the original negative demand shock can be avoided. So, if used in response to demand shocks, fiscal or monetary policy is an effective policy tool.

Tackle the Test: Multiple-Choice Questions

1. e **2.** e **3.** b **4.** b **5.** a

Tackle the Test: Free-Response Question Rubric for FRQ 2 (6 points)

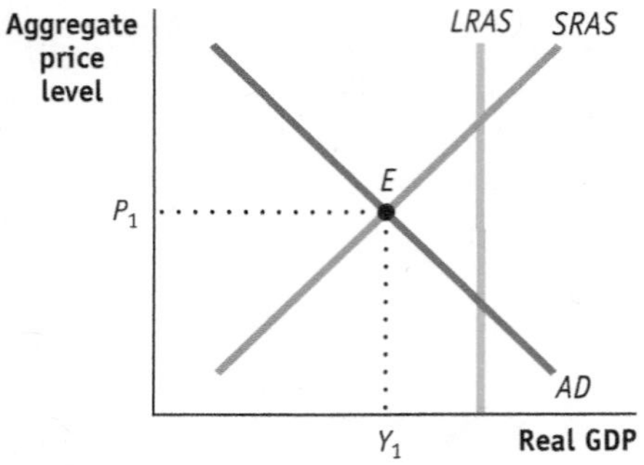

1 point: The vertical axis is labeled "Aggregate price level" or "Price level" and the horizontal axis "Real GDP."

1 point: *SRAS* is upward-sloping and labeled; *AD* is downward-sloping and labeled.

1 point: Equilibrium price level is labeled on the vertical axis and equilibrium real GDP is labeled on the horizontal axis, both where *SRAS* and *AD* intersect.

1 point: *LRAS* is vertical above Y_P and to the right of equilibrium real GDP.

1 point: Expansionary fiscal policy

1 point: Citing either decreased taxes, increased government purchases of goods and services, or increased government transfers as an example of a type of expansionary fiscal policy

Tackle the Test: Free-Response Questions

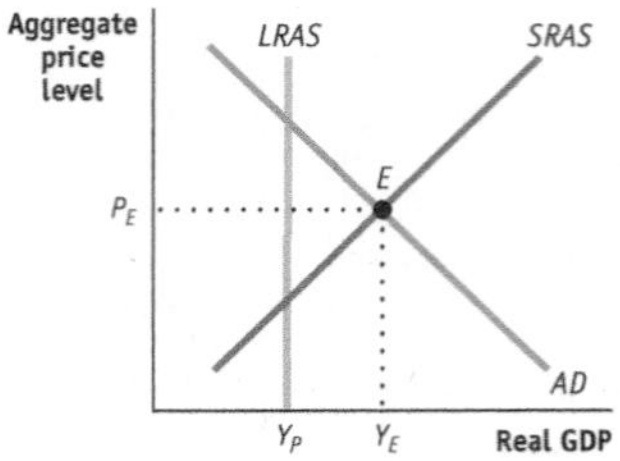

1. Refer to the graph above.
   a. What type of gap exists in this economy?
   b. What type of fiscal policy is appropriate in this situation?
   c. List the three variables the government can change to implement fiscal policy.
   d. How would the government change each of the three variables to implement the policy you listed in part b?

Rubric for FRQ 1 (8 points)

1 point: Inflationary
1 point: Contractionary
1 point: Taxes
1 point: Government transfers
1 point: Government purchases of goods and services
1 point: Increase taxes
1 point: Decrease government transfers
1 point: Decrease government purchases of goods and services

2. a. Draw a correctly labeled graph showing an economy experiencing a recessionary gap.
   b. What type of fiscal policy is appropriate in this situation?
   c. Give an example of what the government could do to implement the type of policy you listed in part b.
   (6 points)

© Axel Koester/Corbis

MODULE 21 Fiscal Policy and Multiplier Effects

In this Module, you will learn to:

- Explain why fiscal policy has a multiplier effect
- Describe how automatic stabilizers influence the multiplier effect

The Spending Multiplier and Estimates of the Influence of Government Policy

An expansionary fiscal policy, like the American Recovery and Reinvestment Act, pushes the aggregate demand curve to the right. A contractionary fiscal policy, like Lyndon Johnson's tax surcharge, pushes the aggregate demand curve to the left. For policy makers, however, knowing the direction of the shift isn't enough: they need estimates of *how much* the aggregate demand curve will be shifted by a given policy. To get these estimates, they use the concept of the multiplier.

Multiplier Effects of Changes in Government Purchases

Suppose that a government decides to spend $50 billion to build bridges and roads. The government's purchases of goods and services will directly increase total spending on final goods and services by $50 billion. But there will also be an indirect effect because the government's purchases will start a chain reaction throughout the economy. The firms producing the goods and services purchased by the government will earn revenues that flow to households in the form of wages, profit, interest, and rent. This increase in disposable income will lead to a rise in consumer spending. The rise in consumer spending, in turn, will induce firms to increase output, leading to a further rise in disposable income, which will lead to another round of consumer spending increases, and so on.

In Module 16 we learned about the *spending multiplier*: the factor by which we multiply the amount of an autonomous change in aggregate spending to find the resulting change in real GDP. An increase in government purchases of goods and services is

PD To prepare for teaching this lesson, you may want to consult the **Module 21 Sample Lecture** in the TRM.

OPEN & CLOSE Start Here

Ask students to explain why an increase in government spending of $100 billion will have a greater impact on real GDP than simply $100 billion. Take a minute to challenge them to define the spending multiplier and explain how it works. In this lesson, the multiplier will be applied to fiscal policy. Let students know that they will be applying the spending multiplier to a change in government spending.

FOCUS Active Learning

Show Jacob Clifford's video "Macro 3.10—Multiplier and Spending Practice" (see econextras video list with hyperlinks on the bcs and TRFD). Stop the video at 0:40 when the practice problem is assigned and ask students to work the problem. Have them show you the answer on their personal whiteboards or in their notebooks. Start the video again. After the video has ended, assign the same question with an *MPC* of 0.75 and see how many students come up with the right answer.

Answer: $\frac{1}{(1-0.75)} = 4; \frac{\$40}{4} = \$10$ *billion increase in spending.*

NASA/Tony Gray; Tom Farrar

When the government hires Boeing to build spacecraft, Boeing employees spend their earnings on things like cars, and the automakers spend their earnings on things like education, and so on, creating a multiplier effect.

an example of an autonomous increase in aggregate spending. Any increase in government purchases of goods and services will lead to a series of additional purchases, resulting in an even larger final increase in real GDP. The initial change in spending, multiplied by the spending multiplier gives us the final change in real GDP.

Let's consider a simple case that does not involve taxes or international trade. In this case, any change in GDP accrues entirely to households. Assume that the aggregate price level is fixed, so that any increase in nominal GDP is also a rise in real GDP, and that the interest rate is fixed. In that case, the spending multiplier is $1/(1 - MPC)$. Recall that *MPC* is the ***marginal propensity to consume,*** the fraction of an additional \$1 in disposable income that is spent. For example, if the marginal propensity to consume is 0.5, the spending multiplier is $1/(1 - 0.5) = 1/0.5 = 2$. Given a spending multiplier of 2, a \$50 billion increase in government purchases of goods and services would increase real GDP by \$100 billion. Of that \$100 billion, \$50 billion is the initial effect from the increase in *G*, and the remaining \$50 billion is the subsequent effect of more production leading to more income which leads to more consumer spending, which leads to more production, and so on.

What happens if government purchases of goods and services are reduced instead? The math is exactly the same, except that there's a minus sign in front: if government purchases of goods and services fall by \$50 billion and the marginal propensity to consume is 0.5, real GDP falls by \$100 billion. This is the result of less production leading to less income, which leads to less consumption, which leads to less production, and so on.

Multiplier Effects of Changes in Government Transfers and Taxes

Expansionary or contractionary fiscal policy need not take the form of changes in government purchases of goods and services. Governments can also change transfer payments or taxes. In general, however, a change in government transfers or taxes shifts the aggregate demand curve by *less* than an equal-sized change in government purchases, resulting in a smaller effect on real GDP.

To see why, imagine that instead of spending \$50 billion on building bridges, the government simply hands out \$50 billion in the form of government transfers. In this case, there is no direct effect on aggregate demand as there was with government purchases of goods and services. Real GDP and income grow only because households spend some of that \$50 billion—and they probably won't spend it all. In fact, they will spend additional income according to the *MPC*. If the *MPC* is 0.5, households will spend only 50 cents of every additional dollar they receive in transfers.

Table 21.1 shows a hypothetical comparison of two expansionary fiscal policies assuming an *MPC* equal to 0.5 and a multiplier equal to 2: one in which the government directly purchases \$50 billion in goods and services and one in which the government makes transfer payments instead, sending out \$50 billion in checks to consumers. In each case, there is a first-round effect on real GDP, either from purchases by the government or from purchases by the consumers who received the checks. This first round is followed by a series of additional rounds as rising real GDP raises income (all of which is disposable under our assumption of no taxes), which in turn raises consumption.

However, the first-round effect of the transfer program is smaller; because we have assumed that the *MPC* is 0.5, only \$25 billion of the \$50 billion is spent, with the other \$25 billion saved. As a result, all the further rounds are smaller, too. In the end, the transfer payment increases real GDP by only \$50 billion. In comparison, a \$50 billion increase in government purchases produces a \$100 billion increase in real GDP.

TEACH Connect It

Remind students that in Module 10, they learned that transfer payments occur when the government transfers money to individuals and receives no good or service in return. Ask them to give you some examples of transfer payments. *Pell grants, unemployment insurance, and welfare benefits.* Explain that like a change in taxes, individuals will not spend all of every dollar they receive in transfer payments. They will save some of those dollars.

TEACH Connect It

Remind students that in Module 16, they learned how the spending multiplier works. Ask them to calculate the change in GDP based on an *MPC* of 0.5 and a change in spending of \$50 billion.

$$\text{Multiplier} = \frac{1}{(1 - MPC)} = \frac{1}{(1 - 0.5)} = \frac{1}{0.5} = 2$$

2 × \$50 billion = \$100 billion change in GDP

There is a multiplier process for a change in taxes and transfer payments as well. But because people save part of their income, the multiplier is not the same as the tax and transfer multiplier. Use Table 21.1 to walk students through the effects of fiscal policy with a multiplier of 2 when *MPC* is equal to 0.5. In each round, make sure they realize that people only spend half of the government transfer payments, so GDP changes by half as much.

212 Section 4 National Income and Price Determination

Table 21.1 Hypothetical Effects of a Fiscal Policy with a Multiplier of 2

Effect on real GDP	$50 billion rise in government purchases of goods and services	$50 billion rise in government transfer payments
First round	$50 billion	$25 billion
Second round	$25 billion	$12.5 billion
Third round	$12.5 billion	$6.25 billion
•	•	•
•	•	•
•	•	•
Eventual effect	$100 billion	$50 billion

A tax cut has an effect similar to the effect of a transfer. It increases disposable income, leading to a series of increases in consumer spending. But the overall effect is smaller than that of an equal-sized increase in government purchases of goods and services: the autonomous increase in aggregate spending is smaller because households save part of the amount of the tax cut. They save a fraction of the tax cut equal to their *MPS* (which equals 1−*MPC*). So, for each $1 decrease in taxes, spending increases only by the portion of the dollar that is not saved: the *MPC*. A tax increase has the opposite effect. For each $1 of additional taxes collected, savings decrease by the *MPS* and spending decreases by the *MPC*.

The **tax multiplier** is the factor by which we multiply a change in tax collections to find the total change in real GDP. Recall that the spending multiplier is 1/(1−*MPC*). The tax multiplier has "*MPC*" in place of "1" in the numerator to reflect the initial spending decrease of *MPC* for each $1 of taxes collected. And the tax multiplier is negative because spending decreases when taxes increase, and spending increases when taxes decrease. This makes the tax multiplier:

The **tax multiplier** is the factor by which a change in tax collections changes real GDP.

$$-MPC/(1-MPC)$$

For example, if the *MPC* is 0.80, then the tax multiplier is −0.80/(1−0.80) = −4. So a $10 billion increase in taxes would cause a change in spending of −4 × $10 billion = −$40 billion.

The multiplier for a change in transfers is the same as the tax multiplier, except the multiplier is positive, because when transfers increase, spending increases, and when transfers decrease, spending decreases. In our example above, the *MPC* was 0.5, so the multiplier was 0.5/(1−0.5) = 1. This explains why the $50 billion increase in transfers led to a $50 billion total increase in real GDP. If the *MPC* had been 0.75, the multiplier would have been 0.75/(1−0.75) = 3, and the $50 billion increase in transfers would have led to a 3 × $50 billion = $150 billion total increase in real GDP.

When a government collects taxes to cover its expenditures, it activates both the spending multiplier and the tax multiplier. The spending multiplier applies to the government spending and the tax multiplier applies to the equivalent taxes. By combining these multipliers, the **balanced budget multiplier** is the factor by which we multiply a change in both spending and taxes to find the total change in real GDP. We can find the balanced budget multiplier by adding the spending and tax multipliers together: 1/(1−*MPC*) + (−*MPC*)/(1−*MPC*) = (1−*MPC*)/(1−*MPC*) = 1. So each $1 of government spending funded with new tax collections increases aggregate spending by $1.

While a balanced budget simplifies the multiplier story, the existence of taxes that depend on real GDP complicate it. In the real world, governments rarely impose **lump-sum taxes**, for which the amount owed is independent of the taxpayer's income. Instead, the great majority of tax revenue is raised with taxes that depend positively on

The **balanced budget multiplier** is the factor by which a change in both spending and taxes changes real GDP.

Lump-sum taxes are taxes that don't depend on the taxpayer's income.

TEACH Teach It

The tax multiplier is equal to $\frac{-MPC}{(1-MPC)}$. It is also equal to $\frac{-MPC}{MPS}$. Work through a problem with the students. Assume *MPC* is 0.8 and there is a $60 billion recessionary gap. *MPS* would equal $1 - MPC = 1 - 0.8 = 0.2$. The tax multiplier is $-\frac{0.8}{0.2} = -4$. A $\frac{\$60}{-4} = -\$15$ billion change in taxes (a $15 billion decrease) will close the gap.

FOCUS Active Learning

Show Jacob Clifford's video "Macro 3.11—Multiplier and Taxes Practice" (see econextras video list with hyperlinks on the bcs and TRFD). Stop the video at 2:15 when the practice problem is assigned, and ask students to work the problem. Have them show you the answer on their personal whiteboards or notebook paper. Start the video again to allow students to watch the solution explanation.

TEACH Teach It

Students sometimes have difficulty with the concept of a tax multiplier. Since people save part of their income, changes in tax policy or transfer payments have a smaller impact on real GDP.

TEACH Teach It

Make sure students understand that lump-sum taxes don't depend upon an individual's income. Examples of a lump-sum tax would be a license tag fee, property tax, or poll tax.

FOCUS Active Learning

TRM To confirm your students' understanding of how a change in taxes or transfer payments impacts GDP, assign **Worksheet 21.1 (Tax and Transfer Multiplier)** from the TRM in class or as homework.

FOCUS Active Learning

TRM So your students can practice calculating the multiplier when using fiscal policy, assign **Worksheet 21.2 (Fiscal Policy and the Multiplier)** from the TRM in class or as homework.

TEACH AP® Exam Tip

Make sure students understand automatic stabilizers and discretionary fiscal policy as both have shown up in the multiple-choice section of the AP® exam in past years.

FOCUS Flip It

TRM Have students watch Jacob Clifford's video "Long-Run Aggregate Supply, Recession, and Inflation (*LRAS*)." Have them watch the video again if you showed it at the beginning of Module 19 (see econextras video list with hyperlinks on the bcs and TRFD). In class the next day, assign **Worksheet 21.3 (Discretionary or Not?)** from the TRM, so they can work through questions on the video.

the level of real GDP. As we'll discuss shortly, these taxes make the spending and tax multipliers smaller.

In practice, economists often argue that *who* among the population gets tax cuts or increases in government transfers also matters. For example, compare the effects of an increase in unemployment benefits with a cut in taxes on profits distributed to shareholders as dividends. Consumer surveys suggest that the average unemployed worker will spend a higher share of any increase in his or her disposable income than would the average recipient of dividend income. That is, people who are unemployed tend to have a higher *MPC* than people who own a lot of stocks, because the latter tend to be wealthier and tend to save more of any increase in disposable income. If that's true, a dollar spent on unemployment benefits increases aggregate demand more than a dollar's worth of dividend tax cuts. Such arguments played an important role in the final provisions of the 2008 stimulus package.

AP® Exam Tip

Simplify your calculations! The tax multiplier is always 1 less than the spending multiplier, and the opposite sign. When taxes and government spending both increase or decrease by the same amount, the net change in real GDP is simply the change in government spending. That is, the *balanced budget multiplier* is simply 1.

How Taxes Affect the Multiplier

Government taxes capture some part of the increase in real GDP that occurs in each round of the multiplier process, since most government taxes depend positively on real GDP. As a result, disposable income increases by considerably less than $1 for each $1 spent once we include taxes in the model.

The increase in government tax revenue when real GDP rises isn't the result of a deliberate decision or action by the government. It's a consequence of the way the tax laws are written, which causes most sources of government revenue to increase *automatically* when real GDP goes up. For example, income tax receipts increase when real GDP rises because the amount each individual owes in taxes depends positively on his or her income, and households' taxable income rises when real GDP rises. Sales tax receipts increase when real GDP rises because people with more income spend more on goods and services. And corporate profit tax receipts increase when real GDP rises because profits increase when the economy expands.

The effect of these automatic increases in tax revenue is to reduce the size of the spending and tax multipliers. Remember, the multipliers are the result of a chain reaction in which higher real GDP leads to higher disposable income, which leads to higher consumer spending, which leads to further increases in real GDP. The fact that the government siphons off some of any increase in real GDP means that at each stage of this process, the increase in consumer spending is smaller than it would be if taxes weren't part of the picture. As a result, these multipliers become smaller.

Many macroeconomists believe it's a good thing that taxes reduce the multipliers in real life. Most, though not all, recessions are the result of negative demand shocks. The same mechanism that causes tax revenue to increase when the economy expands causes it to decrease when the economy contracts. Since tax receipts decrease when real GDP falls, the effects of these negative demand shocks are smaller than they would be if there were no taxes. The decrease in tax revenue reduces the adverse effect of the initial fall in aggregate demand. The automatic decrease in government tax revenue generated by a fall in real GDP—caused by a decrease in the amount of taxes households pay—acts like an automatic expansionary fiscal policy implemented in the face of a recession. Similarly, when the economy expands, the government finds itself automatically pursuing a contractionary fiscal policy—a tax increase. Government spending and taxation rules that cause fiscal policy

An historical example of discretionary fiscal policy was the Works Progress Administration (WPA), a relief measure established during the Great Depression that put the unemployed to work building bridges, roads, buildings, and parks.

214 Section 4 National Income and Price Determination

to be automatically expansionary when the economy contracts and automatically contractionary when the economy expands, without requiring any deliberate action by policy makers, are called **automatic stabilizers.**

The rules that govern tax collection aren't the only automatic stabilizers, although they are the most important ones. Some types of government transfers also play a stabilizing role. For example, more people receive unemployment insurance when the economy is depressed than when it is booming. The same is true of Medicaid and food stamps. So transfer payments tend to rise when the economy is contracting and fall when the economy is expanding. Like changes in tax revenue, these automatic changes in transfers tend to reduce the size of the multipliers because the total change in disposable income that results from a given rise or fall in real GDP is smaller.

As in the case of government tax revenue, many macroeconomists believe that it's a good thing that government transfers reduce the spending and tax multipliers. Expansionary and contractionary fiscal policies that are the result of automatic stabilizers are widely considered helpful to macroeconomic stabilization, because they blunt the extremes of the business cycle. But what about fiscal policy that *isn't* the result of automatic stabilizers? **Discretionary fiscal policy** is fiscal policy that is the direct result of deliberate actions by policy makers rather than automatic adjustment. For example, during a recession, the government may pass legislation that cuts taxes and increases government spending in order to stimulate the economy. In general, mainly due to problems with time lags as discussed in Module 10, economists tend to support the use of discretionary fiscal policy only in special circumstances, such as during an especially severe recession.

Automatic stabilizers are government spending and taxation rules that cause fiscal policy to be automatically expansionary when the economy contracts and automatically contractionary when the economy expands.

Discretionary fiscal policy is fiscal policy that is the result of deliberate actions by policy makers rather than rules.

FYI About That Stimulus Package . . .

In early 2008, there was broad bipartisan agreement that the U.S. economy needed a fiscal stimulus. However, there was sharp partisan disagreement about what form that stimulus should take. The eventual bill was a compromise that left both sides unhappy and arguably made the stimulus less effective than it could have been.

Initially, there was little support for an increase in government purchases of goods and services—that is, neither party wanted to build bridges and roads to stimulate the economy. Both parties believed that the economy needed a quick boost, and ramping up spending would take too long. But there was a fierce debate over whether the stimulus should take the form of a tax cut, which would deliver its biggest benefits to those who paid the most taxes, or an increase in transfer payments targeted at those Americans who were most in economic distress.

The eventual compromise gave most taxpayers a flat $600 rebate, $1,200 for married couples. Very high-income taxpayers were not entitled to a rebate; low earners who didn't make enough to pay income taxes, but did pay other taxes, received $300. In effect, the plan was a combination of tax cuts for most Americans and transfer payments to Americans with low incomes.

How well designed was the stimulus plan? Many economists believed that only a fraction of the rebate checks would actually be spent, so that the eventual multiplier would be fairly low. White House economists appeared to agree: they estimated that the stimulus would raise employment by half a million jobs above what it would have been otherwise, the same number offered by independent economists who believed that the multiplier on the plan would be around 0.75. Some economists were critical, arguing that Congress should have insisted on a plan that yielded more "bang for the buck."

Both Democratic and Republican economists working for Congress defended the plan, arguing that the perfect is the enemy of the good—that it was the best that could be negotiated on short notice and was likely to be of real help in fighting the economy's weakness. But by late summer 2008, with the U.S. economy still in the doldrums, there was widespread agreement that the plan's results had been disappointing. And by late 2008, with the economy shrinking further, policy makers were working on a new, much larger stimulus plan that relied more heavily on government purchases. The American Recovery and Reinvestment Act was passed in February 2009. The bill called for $787 billion in expenditures on stimulus in three areas: help for the unemployed and those receiving Medicaid and food stamps; investments in infrastructure, energy, and health care; and tax cuts for families and small businesses.

Despite controversies over specifics, the general consensus about active stabilization policy is apparent: when at first you don't succeed, try, try again.

FOCUS In the News

Have students read NPR's "U.S. Budget Deficit Falls under $1 Trillion; Lowest Since 2008" at http://www.npr.org/blogs/thetwo-way/2013/10/30/241929386/u-s-budget-deficit-falls-under-1-trillion-lowest-since-2008. Ask them to identify at least one example of automatic stabilizers in the economy and two examples of discretionary fiscal policy. *Automatic: Higher wages and salaries made collections of individual and payroll taxes strong throughout the year. Transfer payments dropped. Discretionary: Tax changes agreed to as part of the fiscal cliff deal. The savings come from the automatic across-the-board government spending cuts known as the sequester.*

FOCUS Active Learning

TRM To review these concepts prior to the section exam, assign **Activity 21.4 (*AD–AS* Review)** from the TRM.

OPEN & CLOSE Exit Slip

TRM *Please see **Exit Slip: Module 21** in the TRM for formative multiple-choice questions to ask before finishing your lesson. These questions will help you quickly assess whether your students have mastered the module's concepts before moving on.*

Answers to the Exit Slip Questions

1. D
2. C
3. C

Answers to Module 21 Review Questions

Check Your Understanding

1. A $500 million increase in government purchases of goods and services directly increases aggregate spending by $500 million, which then starts the spending multiplier in motion. It will increase real GDP by $500 million × 1/(1 − *MPC*). A $500 million increase in government transfers increases aggregate spending only to the extent that it leads to an increase in consumer spending. Consumer spending rises by *MPC* × $1 for every $1 increase in disposable income, where *MPC* is less than 1. Thus, a $500 million increase in government transfers will cause a rise in real GDP only *MPC* times as much as a $500 million increase in government purchases of goods and services. It will increase real GDP by $500 million × *MPC*/(1 − *MPC*).

2. The tax multiplier is relatively small because the initial change in spending is relatively small. For each $1 increase in taxes, the initial decrease in spending is only the *MPC*, whereas a $1 decrease in government purchases decreases spending by a full $1.

3. Boldovia will experience greater variation in its real GDP than Moldovia because Moldovia has automatic stabilizers while Boldovia does not. In Moldovia, the effects of slumps will be lessened by unemployment insurance benefits, which will support residents' incomes, while the effects of booms will be diminished because tax revenues will go up. In contrast, incomes will not be supported in Boldovia during slumps because there is no unemployment insurance. In addition, because Boldovia has lump-sum taxes, its booms will not be diminished by increases in tax revenue.

Tackle the Test: Multiple-Choice Questions

1. c
2. b
3. b
4. c
5. e

MODULE 21 Review

Check Your Understanding

1. Explain why a $500 million increase in government purchases of goods and services will generate a larger rise in real GDP than a $500 million increase in government transfers.
2. Explain why the tax multiplier is smaller than the spending multiplier for a decrease in government purchases.
3. The country of Boldovia has no unemployment insurance benefits and a tax system that uses only lump-sum taxes. The neighboring country of Moldovia has generous unemployment benefits and a tax system in which residents must pay a percentage of their income. Which country will experience greater variation in real GDP in response to demand shocks, positive and negative? Explain.

Tackle the Test: Multiple-Choice Questions

1. The marginal propensity to consume
   - I. has a negative relationship to the spending multiplier.
   - II. is equal to 1.
   - III. represents the proportion of consumers' disposable income that is spent.
   - a. I only
   - b. II only
   - c. III only
   - d. I and III only
   - e. I, II, and III
2. Assume that taxes and interest rates remain unchanged when government spending increases, and that both savings and consumer spending increase when income increases. The ultimate effect on real GDP of a $100 million increase in government purchases of goods and services will be
   - a. an increase of $100 million.
   - b. an increase of more than $100 million.
   - c. an increase of less than $100 million.
   - d. an increase of either more than or less than $100 million, depending on the *MPC*.
   - e. a decrease of $100 million.
3. The presence of income taxes has what effect on the spending multiplier? They
   - a. increase it.
   - b. decrease it.
   - c. destabilize it.
   - d. negate it.
   - e. have no effect on it.
4. A lump-sum tax is
   - a. higher as income increases.
   - b. lower as income increases.
   - c. independent of income.
   - d. the most common form of tax.
   - e. a type of business tax.
5. Which of the following is NOT an automatic stabilizer?
   - a. income taxes
   - b. unemployment insurance
   - c. Medicaid
   - d. food stamps
   - e. monetary policy

Tackle the Test: Free-Response Questions

1. Assume the *MPC* in an economy is 0.8 and the government increases government purchases of goods and services by $60 million. Also assume the absence of taxes, international trade, and changes in the aggregate price level.
   - a. What is the value of the spending multiplier?
   - b. By how much will real GDP change as a result of the increase in government purchases?
   - c. What would happen to the size of the effect on real GDP if the *MPC* fell? Explain.
   - d. If we relax the assumption of no taxes, automatic changes in tax revenue as income changes will have what effect on the size of the spending multiplier?
   - e. Suppose the government collects $60 million in taxes to balance its $60 million in expenditures. By how much would real GDP change as a result of this increase in both government spending and taxes?

Rubric for FRQ 1 (6 points)

1 point: Spending multiplier = 1/(1 − *MPC*) = 1/(1 − 0.8) = 1/0.2 = 5

1 point: $60 million × 5 = $300 million

1 point: It would decrease.

1 point: The spending multiplier is 1/(1 − *MPC*). A fall in *MPC* increases the denominator, (1 − *MPC*), and therefore decreases the spending multiplier.

1 point: Decrease it

1 point: $60 million × 1 = $60 million

216 Section 4 National Income and Price Determination

2. A change in government purchases of goods and services results in a change in real GDP equal to $200 million. Assume the absence of taxes, international trade, and changes in the aggregate price level.
   a. Suppose that the *MPC* is equal to 0.75. What was the size of the change in government purchases of goods and services that resulted in the increase in real GDP of $200 million?
   b. Now suppose that the change in government purchases of goods and services was $20 million. What value of the spending multiplier would result in an increase in real GDP of $200 million?
   c. Given the value of the spending multiplier you calculated in part b, what marginal propensity to save would have led to that value of the spending multiplier?

   (3 points)

Tackle the Test: Free-Response Question Rubric for FRQ 2 (3 points)

1 point: $50 million

(spending multiplier = $1/(1 - MPC) = 1/(1 - 0.75) = 1/0.25 = 4$; change in $G \times 4 =$ $200 million; change in $G =$ $50 million)

1 point: 10

($20 × spending multiplier = $200 million; spending multiplier = 200/20 = 10)

1 point: 0.1

($1/(1 - MPC) = 1/MPS = 10$; $MPS = 0.1$)

FOCUS Flip It

Encourage your students to watch the **Section 4 Review Video,** which was created as a special student review tool and is linked into the e-Book or can be found on the book's companion website.

SECTION 4 Review

Section 4 Review Video

MODULE 16

1. An **autonomous change in aggregate spending** leads to a chain reaction in which the total change in real GDP is equal to the spending multiplier times the initial change in aggregate spending. The size of the **spending multiplier**, 1/(1 – *MPC*), depends on the **marginal propensity to consume, *MPC***, the fraction of an additional dollar of disposable income spent on consumption. The larger the *MPC*, the larger the multiplier and the larger the change in real GDP for any given autonomous change in aggregate spending. The fraction of an additional dollar of disposable income that is saved is called the **marginal propensity to save, *MPS***.
2. The **consumption function** shows how an individual household's consumer spending is determined by its current disposable income. Autonomous consumer spending is the amount a household would spend if it had no disposable income. The **aggregate consumption function** shows the relationship for the entire economy. According to the life-cycle hypothesis, households try to smooth their consumption over their lifetimes. As a result, the aggregate consumption function shifts in response to changes in expected future disposable income and changes in aggregate wealth.
3. **Planned investment spending** depends negatively on the interest rate and on existing production capacity; it depends positively on expected future real GDP.
4. Firms hold inventories of goods so that they can satisfy consumer demand quickly. **Inventory investment** is positive when firms add to their inventories, negative when they reduce them. Often, however, changes in inventories are not a deliberate decision but the result of mistakes in forecasts about sales. The result is **unplanned inventory investment**, which can be either positive or negative. **Actual investment spending** is the sum of planned investment spending and unplanned inventory investment.

MODULE 17

5. The **aggregate demand curve** shows the relationship between the aggregate price level and the quantity of aggregate output demanded.
6. The aggregate demand curve is downward sloping for two reasons. The first is the **wealth effect of a change in the aggregate price level**—a higher aggregate price level reduces the purchasing power of households' wealth and reduces consumer spending. The second is the **interest rate effect of a change in the aggregate price level**—a higher aggregate price level reduces the purchasing power of households' and firms' money holdings, leading to a rise in interest rates and a fall in investment spending and consumer spending.
7. The aggregate demand curve shifts because of changes in expectations, changes in wealth not due to changes in the aggregate price level, and the effect of the size of the existing stock of physical capital. Policy makers can also influence aggregate demand. **Fiscal policy** is the use of taxes, government transfers, or government purchases of goods and services to shift the aggregate demand curve. **Monetary policy** is the Fed's use of changes in the quantity of money or the interest rate to stabilize the economy, which involves shifting the aggregate demand curve.

MODULE 18

8. The **aggregate supply curve** shows the relationship between the aggregate price level and the quantity of aggregate output supplied.
9. The **short-run aggregate supply curve** is upward sloping because **nominal wages** are **sticky** in the short run: a higher aggregate price level leads to higher profit per unit of output and increased aggregate output in the short run.
10. Changes in commodity prices, nominal wages, and productivity lead to changes in producers' profits and shift the short-run aggregate supply curve.
11. In the long run, all prices, including nominal wages, are flexible and the economy produces at its **potential output**. If actual aggregate output exceeds potential output, nominal wages will eventually rise in response to low unemployment and aggregate output will fall. If potential output exceeds actual aggregate output, nominal wages will eventually fall in response to high unemployment and aggregate output will rise. So the **long-run aggregate supply curve** is vertical at potential output.

MODULE 19

12. In the ***AD-AS* model**, the intersection of the short-run aggregate supply curve and the aggregate demand curve is the point of **short-run macroeconomic equilibrium**. It determines the **short-run equilibrium aggregate price level** and the level of **short-run equilibrium aggregate output**.
13. Economic fluctuations occur because of a shift of the aggregate demand curve (a *demand shock*) or the short-run aggregate supply curve (a *supply shock*). A **demand shock** causes the aggregate price level and aggregate output to move in the same direction as the economy moves along the short-run aggregate supply curve. A **supply shock** causes them to move in opposite directions as the economy moves along the aggregate demand curve. A particularly nasty occurrence is **stagflation**—inflation and falling aggregate output—which is caused by a negative supply shock.
14. Demand shocks have only short-run effects on aggregate output because the economy is **self-correcting** in the long run. In a **recessionary gap**, an eventual fall in nominal wages moves the economy to **long-run macroeconomic equilibrium**, in which aggregate output is equal to potential output. In an **inflationary gap**, an eventual rise in nominal wages moves the economy to long-run macroeconomic equilibrium. We can use the **output gap**, the percentage difference between actual aggregate output and potential output, to summarize how the economy responds to recessionary and inflationary gaps. Because the economy tends to be self-correcting in the long run, the output gap always tends toward zero.

MODULE 20

15. The high cost—in terms of unemployment—of a recessionary gap and the future adverse consequences of an inflationary gap lead many economists to advocate active **stabilization policy**: using fiscal or monetary policy to offset demand shocks. There can be drawbacks, however, because such policies may contribute to a long-term rise in the budget deficit, leading to lower long-run growth. Also, poorly timed policies can increase economic instability.
16. Negative supply shocks pose a policy dilemma: a policy that counteracts the fall in aggregate output by increasing aggregate demand will lead to higher inflation, but a policy that counteracts inflation by reducing aggregate demand will deepen the output slump.
17. The government plays a large role in the economy, collecting a large share of GDP in taxes and spending a large share both to purchase goods and services and to make transfer payments, largely for **social insurance**. Fiscal policy is the government's tool for stabilizing the economy, although many economists caution that a very active fiscal policy may in fact make the economy less stable due to time lags in policy formulation and implementation.
18. Government purchases of goods and services directly affect aggregate demand, and changes in taxes and government transfers affect aggregate demand indirectly by changing households' disposable income. **Expansionary fiscal policy** shifts the aggregate demand curve rightward; **contractionary fiscal policy** shifts the aggregate demand curve leftward.

218 Section 4 National Income and Price Determination

MODULE 21

19. Fiscal policy has a multiplier effect on the economy, the size of which depends upon the fiscal policy. Except in the case of lump-sum taxes, taxes reduce the size of the spending and tax multipliers. Expansionary fiscal policy leads to an increase in real GDP, while contractionary fiscal policy leads to a decrease in real GDP. Because part of any change in taxes or transfers is absorbed by savings in the first round of spending, changes in government purchases of goods and services have a more powerful effect on the economy than equal-size changes in taxes or transfers.

20. The **tax multiplier** indicates the total change in aggregate spending that results from each $1 increase in tax collections. It is smaller than the spending multiplier because some of the tax collections would have been saved, not spent. Smaller still, with a value of 1, is the **balanced budget multiplier**, which indicates the total increase in aggregate spending that results from each $1 increase in both government spending and taxes.

21. Rules governing taxes—with the exception of **lump-sum taxes**—and some transfers act as **automatic stabilizers**, reducing the size of the spending multiplier and automatically reducing the size of fluctuations in the business cycle. In contrast, **discretionary fiscal policy** arises from deliberate actions by policy makers rather than from the business cycle.

Key Terms

Marginal propensity to consume (*MPC*), p. 160
Marginal propensity to save (*MPS*), p. 160
Autonomous change in aggregate spending, p. 161
Spending multiplier, p. 161
Consumption function, p. 163
Autonomous consumer spending, p. 163
Aggregate consumption function, p. 164
Planned investment spending, p. 166
Inventory investment, p. 168
Unplanned inventory investment, p. 168
Actual investment spending, p. 168
Aggregate demand curve, p. 172
Wealth effect of a change in the aggregate price level, p. 174
Interest rate effect of a change in the aggregate price level, p. 174
Fiscal policy, p. 177
Monetary policy, p. 177
Aggregate supply curve, p. 180
Nominal wage, p. 181
Sticky wages, p. 181
Short-run aggregate supply curve, p. 182
Long-run aggregate supply curve, p. 186
Potential output, p. 187
AD–AS model, p. 192
Short-run macroeconomic equilibrium, p. 192
Short-run equilibrium aggregate price level, p. 193
Short-run equilibrium aggregate output, p. 193
Demand shock, p. 193
Supply shock, p. 194
Stagflation, p. 195
Long-run macroeconomic equilibrium, p. 196
Recessionary gap, p. 197
Inflationary gap, p. 198
Output gap, p. 198
Self-correcting, p. 198
Stabilization policy, p. 201
Social insurance, p. 205
Expansionary fiscal policy, p. 207
Contractionary fiscal policy, p. 207
Tax multiplier, p. 213
Balanced budget multiplier, p. 213
Lump-sum taxes, p. 213
Automatic stabilizers, p. 215
Discretionary fiscal policy, p. 215

AP® Exam Practice Questions

Multiple-Choice Questions

1. Which of the following will occur if the federal government reduces defense spending?
a. Aggregate demand will increase.
b. Aggregate demand will decrease.
c. There will be no change in aggregate demand or supply.
d. Aggregate supply will increase.
e. Aggregate supply will decrease.

2. Which of the following will occur if an increase in interest rates leads to a decrease in investment spending?
a. Aggregate demand will increase.
b. Aggregate demand will decrease.
c. There will be no change in aggregate demand or supply.
d. Aggregate supply will increase.
e. Aggregate supply will decrease.

Answers to Section 4 Review AP® Exam Practice Questions

Multiple-Choice Questions

1. b
2. b

Section 4 Review 219

3. c
4. d
5. c
6. a
7. b
8. a
9. c
10. d
11. b
12. b
13. c
14. a
15. d
16. e

3. Which of the following will occur as a result of an increase in the aggregate price level?
   a. Aggregate demand will increase.
   b. Aggregate demand will decrease.
   c. There will be no change in aggregate demand or supply.
   d. Aggregate supply will increase.
   e. Aggregate supply will decrease.
4. Which of the following will occur if the price of steel decreases as a result of the discovery of new deposits of iron ore used to make steel?
   a. Aggregate demand will increase.
   b. Aggregate demand will decrease.
   c. There will be no change in aggregate demand or supply.
   d. Aggregate supply will increase.
   e. Aggregate supply will decrease.
5. Sticky nominal wages in the short run cause the short-run aggregate supply curve to
   a. shift to the right.
   b. shift to the left.
   c. slope upward.
   d. slope downward.
   e. be vertical.
6. As a result of the wealth effect, a higher aggregate price level will reduce which of the following?
   a. households' purchasing power
   b. interest rates
   c. investment spending
   d. nominal wages
   e. aggregate demand
7. The interest rate effect of a decrease in the aggregate price level will increase which of the following?
   a. the purchasing power of money holdings
   b. investment spending
   c. interest rates
   d. aggregate supply
   e. aggregate demand
8. Which of the following types of shocks poses a policy dilemma due to the inability to use stabilization policy to address inflation and unemployment at the same time?
   a. negative supply shock
   b. positive supply shock
   c. negative demand shock
   d. positive demand shock
   e. negative budget shock
9. A higher aggregate price level leads to higher profit per unit of output and increased output in the short run because of which of the following?
   a. the wealth effect
   b. the interest rate effect
   c. sticky nominal wages
   d. productivity gains
   e. stabilization policy
10. If potential output is equal to actual aggregate output, which of the following is true?
   a. The economy is experiencing inflation.
   b. The economy is experiencing cyclical unemployment.
   c. Nominal wages are sticky.
   d. The economy is in long-run equilibrium.
   e. The aggregate price level is rising.
11. Which of the following is true about the long-run aggregate supply curve?
   a. It is horizontal.
   b. It is the result of nominal wages being fully flexible.
   c. It is the result of sticky prices.
   d. It is upward sloping.
   e. It intersects the horizontal axis at the actual level of real GDP.
12. Short-run equilibrium aggregate output is the quantity of aggregate output produced when
   a. the aggregate demand curve and the short-run aggregate supply curve are identical.
   b. the quantity of aggregate output supplied is equal to the quantity demanded.
   c. the economy reaches its potential output.
   d. the short-run aggregate supply curve is vertical.
   e. all prices, including nominal wages, are fully flexible.
13. The collapse of wealth and business and consumer confidence that caused the Great Depression is an example of which type of shock?
   a. negative supply shock
   b. positive supply shock
   c. negative demand shock
   d. positive demand shock
   e. negative recessionary shock
14. Which of the following is an example of a positive demand shock?
   a. a large increase in defense spending
   b. the stock market crash of 1929
   c. the discovery of a large, previously unknown oil field
   d. a reduction in the aggregate price level
   e. an increase in nominal wages
15. A positive supply shock will lead to which of the following?
   a. stagflation
   b. an increase in the aggregate price level
   c. a recession
   d. a rightward shift of the short-run aggregate supply curve
   e. an increase in aggregate output along with inflation
16. Which of the following is an example of a negative supply shock?
   a. Production costs decrease.
   b. Information technologies lead to productivity growth.
   c. The stock market collapses.
   d. The government runs a budget deficit.
   e. World oil supplies are disrupted.

220 Section 4 National Income and Price Determination

17. Which of the following is true when the economy is experiencing a recessionary gap?
 a. Potential output is below aggregate output.
 b. Aggregate demand is below aggregate supply.
 c. There is high unemployment.
 d. The aggregate price level is rising.
 e. The economy has self-corrected.

18. When the economy is experiencing an inflationary gap, the output gap is
 a. positive.
 b. negative.
 c. zero.
 d. decreasing.
 e. increasing.

19. Which of the following leads to self-correction when the economy is experiencing a recessionary gap?
 a. Nominal wages and prices rise.
 b. The short-run aggregate supply curve decreases.
 c. The long-run aggregate supply curve decreases.
 d. The short-run aggregate supply curve shifts to the right.
 e. Unemployment leads to an increase in aggregate demand.

20. Which type of policy can be used to address a decrease in aggregate output to below potential output?
 a. expansionary
 b. contractionary
 c. indiscretionary
 d. recessionary
 e. inflationary

21. If the marginal propensity to consume is equal to 0.80, the spending multiplier is
 a. 0.80
 b. 1.25
 c. 4.00
 d. −4.00
 e. 5.00

22. If the marginal propensity to consume is 0.75, an initial increase in aggregate spending of $1,000 will lead to a total change in real GDP equal to
 a. $750
 b. $1,000
 c. $1,333
 d. $4,000
 e. $7,500

23. If the marginal propensity to consume is 0.9, every $10 billion increase in taxes will cause a change in spending equal to
 a. $100 billion.
 b. $90 billion.
 c. $9 billion.
 d. −$10 billion.
 e. −$90 billion.

24. Compared to an increase in taxes, an equal-sized increase in government spending will have what effect on real GDP?
 a. a larger, negative effect
 b. a smaller, negative effect
 c. a larger, positive effect
 d. a smaller, positive effect
 e. an equal, offsetting effect

25. Which of the following is an example of an automatic stabilizer?
 a. the Works Progress Administration established during the Great Depression
 b. lump-sum taxes
 c. a balanced budget requirement for the government
 d. sales taxes
 e. economic stimulus checks from the government

Free-Response Questions

1. Consider an economy operating at full employment.
 a. Draw a correctly labeled aggregate supply and aggregate demand graph for the economy. On your graph, show each of the following:
  i. equilibrium price level, labeled P_1
  ii. equilibrium output level, labeled Y_1
 b. Assume the government increases transfer payments to families with dependent children.
  i. Show the effect of the increase in transfer payments on your graph.
  ii. Label the new short-run equilibrium price level P_2 and the new short-run equilibrium output level Y_2.
 c. Refer to the new short-run equilibrium shown on your graph in response to part b.
  i. The new short-run equilibrium illustrates what type of output gap?
  ii. What type of fiscal policy would be appropriate for an economy facing a persistent gap of the type you identified in part i?

 (7 points)

17. c
18. a
19. d
20. a
21. e
22. d
23. e
24. c
25. d

Rubric for Free-Response Question

1 point: A graph with "Aggregate price level" or "Price level" and "Real GDP" on the vertical and horizontal axes; a labeled, downward-sloping *AD* curve; and a labeled, upward-sloping *SRAS* curve

1 point: A vertical *LRAS* curve that passes through the intersection of the *AD* and *SRAS* curves

1 point: Showing P_1 on the vertical axis and Y_1 on the horizontal axis, both at the intersection of the *AD* and *SRAS* curves

1 point: Showing a labeled, downward-sloping *AD* curve to the right of the original *AD* curve

1 point: Showing P_2 on the vertical axis and Y_2 on the horizontal axis, both at the intersection of the new *AD* and original *SRAS* curves

1 point: Inflationary gap

1 point: Contractionary policy

Please see page SG-2 for sample student graphs for this Free-Response Question.

SECTION 5

The Financial Sector

PD Section 5 Overview:

Watch the video overview of Section 5 (for teachers), which is accessible through the Teacher's e-Book, the TR-flash drive, or the book's website bcs.worthpublishers.com/krugmanap2e *(teacher log-in required).*

In Section 5, we add the topics of money, banking, and the Federal Reserve System to our model of the macroeconomy. The study of the banking system and the Fed leads to the concept of monetary policy, the second tool of macroeconomic stabilization. Students often have difficulty understanding the banking system's process of money creation, so teachers are advised to employ the T-account approach in Module 25. The distinction between the money market and the loanable funds market should also be stressed as it relates to nominal and real interest rates.

Topics that your students will study in Section 5 are:

- how the savings–investment spending identity explains that savings and investment spending are always equal.
- how the three tasks of a financial system bring forth efficiency in the financial markets.
- how the four types of financial assets differ in purpose.
- how financial intermediaries help investors achieve diversification.
- defining and listing the functions of money.
- how the money supply is measured.
- how time is an issue in economic decision making.
- how the concept of present value can help one make decisions when costs or benefits materialize in the future.
- how a bank creates money and increases the money supply.
- how the monetary base defines the money multiplier.
- how the Federal Reserve System acts as a central bank for the United States.
- how the Fed responded to banking crises in the 1980s and in 2008.
- how the tools of the Fed serve its functions.
- defining money demand and listing factors that shift the money demand curve.
- how the equilibrium interest rate is determined in the liquidity preference model (money market).
- how the loanable funds market matches savers and investors.
- how the determinants of supply and demand in the loanable funds market change the equilibrium interest rate.
- how crowding out leads to a decrease in investment spending.
- how the two models of interest rates are reconciled.
- how the Fischer effect explains the distinction between nominal and real interest rates.

Alignment to AP® Macroeconomics Course Description

Macroeconomics IV. Financial Sector: 15–20%

AP® Outline	Module
A. Money, banking, and financial markets	22: Saving, Investment, and the Financial System 23: The Definition and Measurement of Money 24: The Time Value of Money 25: Banking and Money Creation 28: The Money Market
B. Loanable funds market	29: The Market for Loanable Funds
C. Central bank and control of the money supply	26: The Federal Reserve System: History and Structure 27: The Federal Reserve System: Monetary Policy

Pacing Guide

Module	Standard Teaching Days	Block Teaching Days
22	½	¼
23	½	¼
24	1	½
25	1	½
26	1	½
27	1	½
28	1	½
29	1	½
Section 5 Assessment	1	½
Total	**8**	**4**

TRM Section Resources

All section resources may be accessed through the Teacher's e-Book, the TR-flash drive, or the book's website bcs.worthpublishers.com/krugmanap2e *(teacher log-in required).*

Section 5 PD Video (for teachers)

Module 22

Module 22 Sample Lecture
Worksheet 22.1: Budget Cliff
Exit Slip: Module 22

Module 23

Module 23 Sample Lecture
Worksheet 23.1: Bitcoin
Worksheet 23.2: The Functions of Money
Worksheet 23.3: What Is Money?
Worksheet 23.4: Why Is It Money?
Worksheet 23.5: All About Money
Exit Slip: Module 23

Module 24

Module 24 Sample Lecture
Worksheet 24.1: Time Value of Money
Worksheet 24.2: Using Present Value
Exit Slip: Module 24

Module 25

Module 25 Sample Lecture
Worksheet 25.1: Big Banks
Worksheet 25.2: Bank Expansion of Deposits
Worksheet 25.3: T-Accounts
Worksheet 25.4: Reserve Requirement and the Multiplier
Exit Slip: Module 25

Module 26

Module 26 Sample Lecture
Exit Slip: Module 26

Module 27

Module 27 Sample Lecture
Worksheet 27.1: Monetary Policy Cause and Effect
Worksheet 27.2: Bank Requirements
Worksheet 27.3: Tools of Monetary Policy
Exit Slip: Module 27

Module 28

Module 28 Sample Lecture
Activity 28.1: A Budgetary Exercise
Exit Slip: Module 28

Module 29

Module 29 Sample Lecture
Worksheet 29.1: Loanable Funds and Crowding Out
Worksheet 29.2: The Market for Loanable Funds
Exit Slip: Module 29
Section 5 Review Video (for students)

St. Louis Federal Reserve Bank Resources

Many of the Federal Reserve Banks have educational departments that offer helpful resources for studying economics. Members of the Educators Advisory Board of the St. Louis Federal Reserve Bank have handpicked some of their best resources for use with your AP® Economics students. References to these resources are included in the margin notes. A complete list of the St. Louis Fed resources for each section with the corresponding URL (as of fall 2014) can be found in the TRM.

NOTE We have included a number of links to useful videos and articles in the margin notes in this section. Although all are active at the time of publication, we know that some may expire over the next few years. If a link is no longer active, you may wish to search for a similar article or video to illustrate the point. We may also periodically refresh resources on the book's companion website.

PD Section 5 Overview

Watch the video overview of Section 5 (for teachers), which is accessible through the Teacher's e-Book, the TR-flash drive, or the book's companion website bcs.worthpublishers.com/krugmanap2e (teacher log-in required).

FOCUS Active Learning

Have students read Chapter 22 of *Economics by Example* to learn more about money, the Fed, and monetary policy.

SECTION 5

The Financial Sector

Pixtal/SuperStock

Funny Money

On October 2, 2004, FBI and Secret Service agents seized a shipping container that had just arrived in Newark, New Jersey, on a ship from China. Inside the container, under cardboard boxes containing plastic toys, they found what they were looking for: more than $300,000 in counterfeit $100 bills. Two months later, another shipment with $3 million in counterfeit bills was intercepted. Government and law enforcement officials began alleging publicly that these bills—which were high-quality fakes, very hard to tell from the real thing—were being produced by the government of North Korea.

The funny thing is that elaborately decorated pieces of paper have little or no intrinsic value. Indeed, a $100 bill printed with blue or orange ink literally wouldn't be worth the paper it was printed on. But if the ink on that decorated piece of paper is just the right shade of green, people will think that it's *money* and will accept it as payment for very real goods and services. Why? Because they believe, correctly, that they can do the same thing: exchange that piece of green paper for real goods and services.

In fact, here's a riddle: If a fake $100 bill from North Korea enters the United States, and nobody ever realizes it's fake, who gets hurt? Accepting a fake $100 bill isn't like buying a car that turns out to be a lemon or a meal that turns out to be inedible; as long as the bill's counterfeit nature remains undiscovered, it will pass from hand to hand just like a real $100 bill. The answer to the riddle is that the real victims of North Korean counterfeiting are U.S. taxpayers because counterfeit dollars reduce the revenues available to pay for the operations of the U.S. government. Accordingly, the Secret Service diligently monitors the integrity of U.S. currency, promptly investigating any reports of counterfeit dollars.

The efforts of the Secret Service attest to the fact that money isn't like ordinary goods and services. In this section we'll look at the role money plays, the workings of a modern monetary system, and the institutions that sustain and regulate it. We'll then see how models of the money and loanable funds markets help us understand *monetary policy* as carried out by our central bank—the *Federal Reserve*.

Michael Belardo/Alamy

MODULE

22 Saving, Investment, and the Financial System

In this Module, you will learn to:

- Describe the relationship between savings and investment spending
- Explain how financial intermediaries help investors achieve diversification
- Identify the purposes of the four principal types of financial assets: stocks, bonds, loans, and bank deposits

Matching Up Savings and Investment Spending

Two instrumental sources of economic growth are increases in the skills and knowledge of the workforce, known as *human capital*, and increases in capital—goods used to make other goods—which can also be called *physical capital* to distinguish it from human capital. Human capital is largely provided by the government through public education. (In countries with a large private education sector, like the United States, private post-secondary education is also an important source of human capital.) But physical capital, with the exception of infrastructure such as roads and bridges, is mainly created through private investment spending—that is, spending by firms rather than by the government.

Who pays for private investment spending? In some cases it's the people or corporations who actually do the spending—for example, a family that owns a business might use its own savings to buy new equipment or a new building, or a corporation might reinvest some of its own profits to build a new factory. In the modern economy, however, individuals and firms who create physical capital often do it with other people's money—money that they borrow or raise by selling stock. If they borrow money to create physical capital, they are charged an *interest rate*. The **interest rate** is the price, calculated as a percentage of the amount borrowed, charged by lenders to borrowers for the use of their savings for one year.

To understand how investment spending is financed, we need to look first at how savings and investment spending are related for the economy as a whole.

AP® Exam Tip

The amount of savings is equal to the amount of investment.

The **interest rate** is the price, calculated as a percentage of the amount borrowed, charged by lenders to borrowers for the use of their savings for one year.

PD To prepare for teaching this lesson, you may want to consult the **Module 22 Sample Lecture** in the TRM.

OPEN & CLOSE Start Here

Ask students what it means when someone says, "Pay yourself first." *Students should come to the conclusion that they should get into the habit of saving some of their income so they will have money remaining for retirement or other goals.*

Use the Rule of 72 to determine how long it will take for a $5,000 deposit to double if the interest rate was 2%, 5%, and 10%. *It will take 36 years at 2%, 14.4 years at 5%, and 7.2 years at 10%.* Imagine what could happen if you put away a little money each month!

TEACH Teach It

Much of this material will aid students in understanding monetary policy. It is unlikely, however, that the content will be heavily tested.

TEACH Teach It

Remind students of the following:

- Economists view investment spending as spending on real capital. The investment discussed in this module is financial investment.
- The amount of savings is always equal to the amount of investment in an economy.

TEACH Connect It

Remind students that one way businesses grow is by investing in technology and inventories. To do that, they borrow money that comes from household savings. Draw the circular-flow diagram and show students how businesses are connected to the financial market.

TEACH Teach It

Let students know that Savings = Investment, which is known as the *savings–investment spending identity*. Talk about budget surpluses and deficits, and relate them to the level of government spending in the economy.

FOCUS Test It

Refer students to http://www.cram.com/flashcards/savings-investment-spending-identity-600850, where they can test themselves on the key terms associated with the Savings–Investment Spending Identity.

FOCUS In the News

TRM Have students read the article "U.S. Budget Deficit Narrows Sharply in March" at http://tinyurl.com/n6rp5nl. Suggested questions for this article can be found in the TRM on **Worksheet 22.1 (Budget Cliff)**.

TEACH Teach It

Tell students that to an economist, investment spending means spending on physical capital, whereas making a financial investment means buying stocks, bonds, or some other type of financial asset.

The Savings–Investment Spending Identity

According to the **savings-investment spending identity**, savings and investment spending are always equal for the economy as a whole.

The most basic point to understand about savings and investment spending is that they are always equal. This is not a theory; it's a fact of accounting called the **savings-investment spending identity**.

To see why the savings-investment spending identity must be true, first imagine a highly simplified economy in which there is no government and no interaction with other countries. The overall income of this simplified economy, by definition, would be equal to total spending in the economy. Why? Because the only way people could earn income would be by selling something to someone else, and every dollar spent in the economy would create income for somebody. So, in this simplified economy,

(22-1) Total income = Total spending

Now, what can people do with income? They can either spend it on consumption or save it. So it must be true that

(22-2) Total income = Consumer spending + Savings

Meanwhile, spending consists of either consumer spending or investment spending:

(22-3) Total spending = Consumer spending + Investment spending

Putting these together, we get:

(22-4) Consumer spending + Savings = Consumer spending + Investment spending

Subtract consumer spending from both sides, and we get:

(22-5) Savings = Investment spending

As we said, then, it's a basic accounting fact that savings equals investment spending for the economy as a whole.

So far, however, we've looked only at a simplified economy in which there is no government and no economic interaction with the rest of the world. Bringing these realistic complications back into the story changes things in two ways.

The **budget surplus** is the difference between tax revenue and government spending when tax revenue exceeds government spending.

The **budget deficit** is the difference between tax revenue and government spending when government spending exceeds tax revenue.

The **budget balance** is the difference between tax revenue and government spending.

National savings, the sum of private savings and the budget balance, is the total amount of savings generated within the economy.

First, households are not the only parties that can save in an economy. In any given year, the government can save, too, if it collects more tax revenue than it spends. When this occurs, the difference is called a **budget surplus** and is equivalent to savings by the government. If, alternatively, government spending exceeds tax revenue, there is a **budget deficit**—a negative budget surplus. In this case, we often say that the government is "dissaving": by spending more than its tax revenues, the government is engaged in the opposite of saving. We'll define the term **budget balance** to refer to both cases, with the understanding that the budget balance can be positive (a budget surplus) or negative (a budget deficit). **National savings** is equal to the sum of private savings and the budget balance, whereas private savings is disposable income (income after taxes) minus consumption.

Second, the fact that any one country is part of a wider world economy means that savings need not be spent on physical capital located in the same country in which the savings are generated. That's because the savings of people who live in any one country can be used to finance investment spending that takes place in other countries. So any given country can receive *inflows* of funds—foreign savings that finance investment spending in the country. Any given country can also generate *outflows* of funds—domestic savings that finance investment spending in another country.

The net effect of international inflows and outflows of funds on the total savings available for investment spending in any given country is known as the **capital inflow** into that country, equal to the total inflow of foreign funds minus the total outflow of domestic funds to other countries. Like the budget balance, a capital inflow can be negative—that is, more capital can flow out of a country than flows into it. In recent years, the United States has experienced a consistent net inflow of capital from foreigners, who view our economy as an attractive place to put their savings. In 2012, for example, capital inflows into the United States were $446 billion.

Capital inflow is equal to the total inflow of foreign funds minus the total outflow of domestic funds to other countries.

It's important to note that, from a national perspective, a dollar generated by national savings and a dollar generated by capital inflow are not equivalent. Yes, they can both finance the same dollar's worth of investment spending, but any dollar borrowed from a saver must eventually be repaid with interest. A dollar that comes from national savings is repaid with interest to someone domestically—either a private party or the government. But a dollar that comes as capital inflow must be repaid with interest to a foreigner. So a dollar of investment spending financed by a capital inflow comes at a higher *national* cost—the interest that must eventually be paid to a foreigner—than a dollar of investment spending financed by national savings.

So the application of the savings-investment spending identity to an economy that is open to inflows or outflows of capital means that investment spending is equal to savings, where savings is equal to national savings *plus* capital inflow. That is, in an economy with a positive capital inflow, some investment spending is funded by the savings of foreigners. And, in an economy with a negative capital inflow (a net outflow), some portion of national savings is funding investment spending in other countries. In the United States in 2012, investment spending totaled $2,475.2 billion. Private savings were $1,491.7 billion, offset by a budget deficit of $1,109.7 billion and supplemented by capital inflows of $446 billion. Notice that these numbers don't quite add up; because data collection isn't perfect, there is a "statistical discrepancy" of $17 billion. But we know that this is an error in the data, not in the theory, because the savings-investment spending identity must hold in reality.

The corner of Wall and Broad Streets is at the center of New York City's financial district.

The Financial System

Financial markets are where households invest their current savings and their accumulated savings, or **wealth**, by purchasing *financial assets*.

A **financial asset** is a paper claim that entitles the buyer to future income from the seller. For example, when a saver lends funds to a company, the loan is a financial asset sold by the company that entitles the lender (the buyer) to future income from the company. A household can also invest its current savings or wealth by purchasing a **physical asset**, a claim on a tangible object, such as a preexisting house or a preexisting piece of equipment. It gives the owner the right to dispose of the object as he or she wishes (for example, rent it or sell it).

If you were to go to your local bank and get a loan—say, to buy a new car—you and the bank would be creating a financial asset: your loan. A *loan* is one important kind of financial asset in the real world, one that is owned by the lender—in this case, your local bank. In creating that loan, you and the bank would also be creating a **liability**, a requirement to pay money in the future. So, although your loan is a financial asset from the bank's point of view, it is a liability from your point of view: a requirement that you repay the loan, including any interest. In addition to loans, there are three other important kinds of financial assets: stocks, bonds, and *bank deposits*. Because a financial asset is a claim to future income that someone has to pay, it is also someone else's liability. Shortly, we'll explain in detail who bears the liability for each type of financial asset.

AP® Exam Tip

When other nations buy financial assets from the United States, there is a capital inflow. When Americans buy financial assets in other countries, there is a capital outflow.

A household's **wealth** is the value of its accumulated savings.

A **financial asset** is a paper claim that entitles the buyer to future income from the seller.

A **physical asset** is a claim on a tangible object that gives the owner the right to dispose of the object as he or she wishes.

A **liability** is a requirement to pay money in the future.

FOCUS Flip It

Students can view the Jacob Clifford video "The Financial Sector" (see econextras video list with hyperlinks on the bcs and TRFD) to learn a set of terms that will be useful in this section. Students can create a set of notecards for later study as they view the video.

TEACH Teach It

Financial markets are where households invest their current savings and their accumulated savings, or wealth, by purchasing financial assets. Businesses, governments, and the foreign sector can invest in financial markets as well. Distinguish between income and wealth. Income is a stream and wealth is a stock. Ask students to compare financial assets and physical assets.

FOCUS Active Learning

TRM The financial system is an integral part of the economy. Find the song "Tu'ppence" from the movie *Mary Poppins* online, and play it for your students. Have them listen to the lyrics and ask what the line "As your influence expands" means. *It means the money will provide funding for other investment.* Using the circular-flow diagram, show how household savings provide funding for business investment and government borrowing. (A copy of the circular-flow diagram may be found in Module 10 of the TRM.)

TEACH Teach It

Make sure students understand the role the financial system plays in exchanging assets from the seller to the buyer.

1. **Reducing transaction costs.** Banks and other financial services companies are able to make it easier and less costly for firms to engage in financial transactions, like borrowing, to make investments.
2. **Reducing financial risk.** Investing in several assets with unrelated, or independent, risks allows a business owner to lower his or her risk of total loss.
3. **Providing liquidity.** The financial system can provide liquidity in a variety of ways, so assets can be converted to cash without loss of much value.

These four types of financial assets exist because the economy has developed a set of specialized markets, such as the stock market and the bond market, and specialized institutions, such as banks, that facilitate the flow of funds from lenders to borrowers. A well-functioning financial system is a critical ingredient in achieving long-run growth because it encourages greater savings and investment spending. It also ensures that savings and investment spending are undertaken efficiently. To understand how this occurs, we first need to know what tasks the financial system needs to accomplish. Then we can see how the job gets done.

Three Tasks of a Financial System

There are three important problems facing borrowers and lenders: *transaction costs,* financial risk, and the desire for *liquidity.* The three tasks of a financial system are to reduce these problems in a cost-effective way. Doing so enhances the efficiency of financial markets: it makes it more likely that lenders and borrowers will make mutually beneficial trades—trades that make society as a whole richer.

Transaction costs are the expenses of negotiating and executing a deal.

Reducing Transaction Costs **Transaction costs** are the expenses of actually putting together and executing a deal. For example, arranging a loan requires spending time and money negotiating the terms of the deal, verifying the borrower's ability to pay, drawing up and executing legal documents, and so on. Suppose a large business decided that it wanted to raise $1 billion for investment spending. No individual would be willing to lend that much. And negotiating individual loans from thousands of different people, each willing to lend a modest amount, would impose very large total costs because each individual transaction would incur a cost. Total costs would be so large that the entire deal would probably be unprofitable for the business.

Fortunately, that's not necessary: when large businesses want to borrow money, they either get a loan from a bank or sell bonds in the bond market. Obtaining a loan from a bank avoids large transaction costs because it involves only a single borrower and a single lender. We'll explain more about how bonds work in the next section. For now, it is enough to know that the principal reason there is a bond market is that it allows companies to borrow large sums of money without incurring large transaction costs.

Financial risk is uncertainty about future outcomes that involve financial losses and gains.

Reducing Risk A second problem that real-world borrowers and lenders face is **financial risk**, uncertainty about future outcomes that involve financial losses or gains. Financial risk (which from now on we'll simply call "risk") is a problem because the future is uncertain; it holds the potential for losses as well as gains.

Most people are risk-averse, although to differing degrees. A well-functioning financial system helps people reduce their exposure to risk. Suppose the owner of a business expects to make a greater profit if she buys additional capital equipment but isn't completely sure of this result. She could pay for the equipment by using her savings or selling her house. But if the profit is significantly less than expected, she will have lost her savings, or her house, or both. That is, she would be exposing herself to a lot of risk due to uncertainty about how well or poorly the business performs. So, being risk-averse, this business owner wants to share the risk of purchasing new capital equipment with someone, even if that requires sharing some of the profit if all goes well. How can she do this? By selling shares of her company to other people and using the money she receives from selling shares, rather than money from the sale of her other assets, to finance the equipment purchase. By selling shares in her company, she reduces her personal losses if the profit is less than expected: she won't have lost her other assets. But if things go well, the shareholders earn a share of the profit as a return on their investment.

An individual can engage in **diversification** by investing in several different assets with unrelated risks.

By selling a share of her business, the owner has been able to invest in several things in a way that lowers her total risk. She has maintained her investment in her bank account, a financial asset; in ownership of her house, a physical asset; and in ownership of the unsold portion of her business, also a physical asset. By engaging in **diversification**—investing in several assets with unrelated, or independent, risks—our business owner has

St. Louis Federal Reserve Bank Resources

Time Value of Money Online Course for Teachers and Students

This course is designed to help students in economics, math, and personal finance classes through what is often dry, mathematical content by featuring student-oriented language, program interactions, checks for understanding, and video. It will enhance students' in-class study of present and future value and also serve as a tutorial for those students who struggle with the concepts.

lowered her total risk of loss. The desire of individuals to reduce their total risk by engaging in diversification is why we have stocks and a stock market.

Providing Liquidity The third and final task of the financial system is to provide investors with *liquidity*, which—like risk—becomes relevant because the future is uncertain. Suppose that you want to start a new business at some point. Even if you have no concerns about the risk of the business failing, you probably won't want to invest all of your savings into the business. This is because you might suddenly find yourself in need of cash—say, to pay for a medical emergency. Money invested in a business is not easily converted into cash in the event that it is needed for other purposes. For this reason, savvy investors like you are reluctant to lock up too much money in businesses among other large purchases.

An asset is **liquid** if, as with money deposited in a bank, it can be quickly converted into cash without much loss of value. An asset is **illiquid** if, as with a business, car, or home, it cannot. The reluctance to invest heavily in illiquid assets would deter business growth and many major purchases if financial systems offered no remedy. As we'll see, however, the initial sale of stocks and bonds can resolve some liquidity problems by raising money for new and expanding projects. And, by taking deposits and lending them out, banks allow individuals to own liquid assets (their deposits) while financing investments in illiquid assets such as businesses and homes.

An asset is **liquid** if it can be quickly converted into cash without much loss of value.

An asset is **illiquid** if it cannot be quickly converted into cash without much loss of value.

To help lenders and borrowers make mutually beneficial deals, then, the economy needs ways to reduce transaction costs, to reduce and manage risk through diversification, and to provide liquidity. How does it achieve these tasks? With a variety of financial assets.

Types of Financial Assets

In the modern economy there are four main types of financial assets: *loans*, bonds, stocks, and *bank deposits*. In addition, financial innovation has allowed the creation of a wide range of *loan-backed securities*. Each type of asset serves a somewhat different purpose. We'll explain loans, bonds, stocks, and loan-backed securities first. Then we'll turn to bank deposits when we explain the role banks play as financial intermediaries.

A **loan** is a lending agreement between an individual lender and an individual borrower.

Loans A **loan** is a lending agreement between an individual lender and an individual borrower. Most people encounter loans in the form of bank loans to finance the purchase of a car or a house. And small businesses usually use bank loans to buy new equipment.

The good aspect of loans is that a given loan is usually tailored to the needs of the borrower. Before a small business can get a loan, it usually has to discuss its business plans, its profits, and so on with the lender. This results in a loan that meets the borrower's needs and ability to repay.

The bad aspect of loans is that making a loan to an individual person or a business typically involves a lot of transaction costs, such as the cost of negotiating the terms of the loan, investigating the borrower's credit history and ability to repay, and so on. To minimize these costs, large borrowers such as major corporations and governments often take a more streamlined approach: they sell (or issue) bonds.

Bonds A bond is an IOU issued by the borrower. Normally, the seller of the bond promises to pay a fixed sum of interest each year and to repay the principal—the value stated on the face of the bond—to the owner

FOCUS Active Learning

In order to save time for other topics that are more likely to be covered on the AP® exam, you may not want to present the remaining topics in this module in class. However, students should still be familiar with these assets and intermediaries.

St. Louis Federal Reserve Bank Resources

"Understanding Bonds," *No-Frills Money Skills*, Episode 4

In this episode, the video host employs high-tech tools to foil Miss Information in her attempts to misguide investors. The video provides viewers with information about government bonds, corporate bonds, coupon and noncoupon bonds, and the potential risk and return of investments.

Module 22 Saving, Investment, and the Financial System 227

of the bond on a particular date. So a bond is a financial asset from its owner's point of view and a liability from its issuer's point of view. A bond issuer sells a number of bonds with a given interest rate and maturity date to whoever is willing to buy them, a process that avoids costly negotiation of the terms of a loan with many individual lenders.

Bond purchasers can acquire information free of charge on the quality of the bond issuer, such as the bond issuer's credit history, from *bond-rating agencies* rather than having to incur the expense of investigating it themselves. A particular concern for investors is the possibility of **default**, the risk that the bond issuer might fail to make payments as specified by the bond contract. Once a bond's risk of default has been rated, it can be sold on the bond market as a more or less standardized product—a product with clearly defined terms and quality. In general, bonds with a higher default risk must pay a higher interest rate to attract investors.

A **default** occurs when a borrower fails to make payments as specified by the loan or bond contract.

Another important advantage of bonds is that they are easy to resell. This provides liquidity to bond purchasers. Indeed, a bond will often pass through many hands before it finally comes due. Loans, in contrast, are much more difficult to resell because, unlike bonds, they are not standardized: they differ in size, quality, terms, and so on. This makes them a lot less liquid than bonds.

Loan-backed Securities **Loan-backed securities**, assets created by pooling individual loans and selling shares in that pool (a process called *securitization*), have become extremely popular over the past two decades. Mortgage-backed securities, created by pooling thousands of individual home mortgage loans and selling shares to investors, are the best known example. Securitization has also been widely applied to student loans, credit card loans, and auto loans. These loan-backed securities trade on financial markets like bonds. They are appealing to investors because they provide more diversification and liquidity than individual loans. However, with so many loans packaged together, it can be difficult to assess the true quality of the asset. That difficulty came to haunt investors during the financial crisis of 2007–2008, when the bursting of the housing bubble led to widespread defaults on mortgages and large losses for holders of "supposedly safe" mortgage-backed securities, causing pain that spread throughout the entire financial system.

A **loan-backed security** is an asset created by pooling individual loans and selling shares in that pool.

AP® Exam Tip

It is worthwhile to understand the categories of assets so you can understand their use in different macroeconomic models.

Stocks A stock is a share in the ownership of a company. A share of stock is a financial asset from its owner's point of view and a liability from the company's point of view.

Not all companies sell shares of their stock; "privately held" companies are owned by an individual or a few partners, who get to keep all of the company's profit. Most large companies, however, do sell stock. For example, as this book goes to press, Microsoft has more than 8 billion shares outstanding; if you buy one of those shares, you are entitled to about one-eight billionth of the company's profit, as well as 1 of 8 billion votes on company decisions.

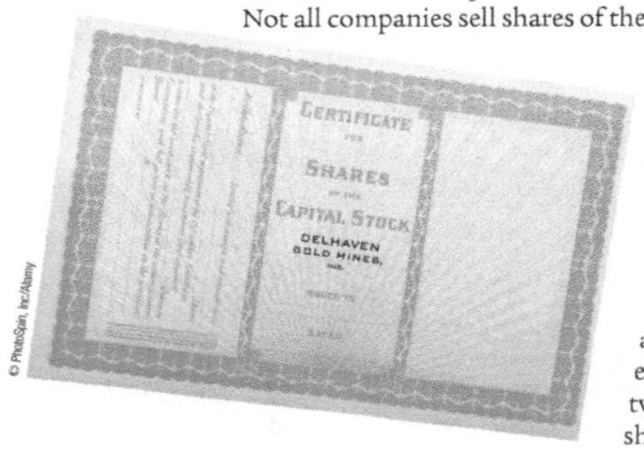

© PhotoSpin, Inc/Alamy

Why does Microsoft, historically a very profitable company, allow you to buy a share in its ownership? Why don't Bill Gates and Paul Allen, the two founders of Microsoft, keep complete ownership for themselves and just sell bonds for their investment spending needs? The reason, as we have just learned, is risk: few individuals are risk-tolerant enough to face the risk involved in being the sole owner of a large company.

Reducing the risk that business owners face, however, is not the only way in which the existence of stocks improves society's welfare: it also improves the welfare of investors who buy stocks (that is, shareowners, or shareholders). Shareowners are able to enjoy the higher returns over time that stocks generally offer in comparison to bonds. Over the past century, the average annual return on U.S. stocks has been about 7% after adjusting for inflation; for U.S. bonds the average annual return during the same time

St. Louis Federal Reserve Bank Resources

"Get into Stocks," *No-Frills Money Skills*, Episode 3

Through the story of a local ice-cream cart owner trying to expand her business, students learn about the process by which companies become publicly owned and traded by issuing stock. Students learn key terms, such as *capital gains* and *dividends*, and they discover how the prices of stocks are affected by how successful a company is in its industry.

228 Section 5 The Financial Sector

period has been only about 2%. But as investment companies warn you, "Past performance is no guarantee of future performance." And there is a downside: owning the stock of a given company is riskier than owning a bond issued by the same company. Why? Loosely speaking, a bond is a promise while a stock is a hope: by law, a company must pay what it owes its lenders (bondholders) before it distributes any profit to its shareholders. And if the company should fail (that is, be unable to pay its interest obligations and declare bankruptcy), its physical and financial assets go to its bondholders—its lenders—while its shareholders typically receive nothing. So, although a stock generally provides a higher return to an investor than a bond, it also carries higher risk.

The financial system has devised ways to help investors as well as business owners simultaneously manage risk and enjoy somewhat higher returns. It does that through the services of institutions known as *financial intermediaries*.

Financial Intermediaries

A **financial intermediary** is an institution that transforms funds gathered from many individuals into financial assets. The most important types of financial intermediaries are *mutual funds*, *pension funds*, *life insurance companies*, and *banks*. About three-quarters of the financial assets Americans own are held through these intermediaries rather than directly.

A **financial intermediary** is an institution that transforms the funds it gathers from many individuals into financial assets.

Mutual Funds As we've explained, owning shares of a company entails risk in return for a higher potential reward. But it should come as no surprise that stock investors can lower their total risk by engaging in diversification. By owning a *diversified portfolio* of stocks—a group of stocks in which risks are unrelated to, or offset, one another—rather than concentrating investment in the shares of a single company or a group of related companies, investors can reduce their risk. In addition, financial advisers, aware that most people are risk-averse, almost always advise their clients to diversify not only their stock portfolio but also their entire wealth by holding other assets in addition to stock—assets such as bonds, real estate, and cash. (And, for good measure, to have plenty of insurance in case of accidental losses!)

Jay Brousseau/Getty Images

The daily performance of hundreds of different mutual funds is listed in the business section of most large city newspapers.

However, for individuals who don't have a large amount of money to invest—say $1 million or more—building a diversified stock portfolio can incur high transaction costs (particularly fees paid to stockbrokers) because they are buying a few shares of a lot of companies. Fortunately for such investors, mutual funds help solve the problem of achieving diversification without high transaction costs. A **mutual fund** is a financial intermediary that creates a stock portfolio by buying and holding shares in companies and then selling *shares of the stock portfolio* to individual investors. By buying these shares, investors with a relatively small amount of money to invest can indirectly hold a diversified portfolio, achieving a better return for any given level of risk than they could otherwise achieve.

A **mutual fund** is a financial intermediary that creates a stock portfolio and then resells shares of this portfolio to individual investors.

The mutual fund industry represents a huge portion of the modern U.S. economy, not just of the U.S. financial system. In total, U.S. mutual funds had assets of $13 trillion at the end of 2012. The largest mutual fund company at the end of 2013 was Vanguard Group, Inc., which managed almost $2.4 trillion in funds.

We should mention, by the way, that mutual funds do charge fees for their services. These fees are quite small for mutual funds that simply hold a diversified portfolio of stocks, without trying to pick winners. But the fees charged by mutual funds that claim to have special expertise in investing your money can be quite high.

Pension Funds and Life Insurance Companies In addition to mutual funds, many Americans have holdings in **pension funds**, nonprofit institutions that collect the savings of their members and invest those funds in a wide variety of assets, providing their members with income when they retire. Although pension funds are subject to

A **pension fund** is a nonprofit institution that invests the savings of members and provides them with income when they retire.

TEACH Teach It

Financial intermediaries serve as middlemen between buyers and sellers of financial assets. If you have a bank account, you are using a financial intermediary.

OPEN & CLOSE Exit Slip

TRM *Please see* ***Exit Slip: Module 22*** *in the TRM for formative multiple-choice questions to ask your students before finishing your lesson. These questions will help you quickly assess whether your students have mastered the module's concepts before moving on.*

Answers to the Exit Slip Questions

1. C
2. A
3. C

some special rules and receive special treatment for tax purposes, they function much like mutual funds. They invest in a diverse array of financial assets, allowing their members to achieve more cost-effective diversification and conduct more market research than they would be able to individually. At the end of 2013, pension funds in the United States held more than $18.9 trillion in assets.

> A **life insurance company** sells policies that guarantee a payment to a policyholder's beneficiaries when the policyholder dies.

Americans also have substantial holdings in the policies of **life insurance companies**, which guarantee a payment to the policyholder's beneficiaries (typically, the family) when the policyholder dies. By enabling policyholders to cushion their beneficiaries from financial hardship arising from their death, life insurance companies also improve welfare by reducing risk.

Banks Recall the problem of liquidity: other things equal, people want assets that can be readily converted into cash. Bonds and stocks are much more liquid than physical assets or loans, yet the transaction cost of selling bonds or stocks to meet a sudden expense can be large. Furthermore, for many small and moderate-sized companies, the cost of issuing bonds and stocks is too large, given the modest amount of money they seek to raise. A *bank* is an institution that helps resolve the conflict between lenders' needs for liquidity and the financing needs of borrowers who don't want to use the stock or bond markets.

> A **bank deposit** is a claim on a bank that obliges the bank to give the depositor his or her cash when demanded.

A bank works by first accepting funds from *depositors*: when you put your money in a bank, you are essentially becoming a lender by lending the bank your money. In return, you receive credit for a **bank deposit**—a claim on the bank, which is obliged to give you your cash if and when you demand it. So a bank deposit is a financial asset owned by the depositor and a liability of the bank that holds it.

> A **bank** is a financial intermediary that provides liquid assets in the form of bank deposits to lenders and uses those funds to finance borrowers' investment spending on illiquid assets.

A bank, however, keeps only a fraction of its customers' deposits in the form of ready cash. Most of its deposits are lent out to businesses, buyers of new homes, and other borrowers. These loans come with a long-term commitment by the bank to the borrower: as long as the borrower makes his or her payments on time, the loan cannot be recalled by the bank and converted into cash. So a bank enables those who wish to borrow for long lengths of time to use the funds of those who wish to lend but simultaneously want to maintain the ability to get their cash back on demand. More formally, a **bank** is a financial intermediary that provides liquid financial assets in the form of deposits to lenders and uses their funds to finance borrowers' investment spending on illiquid assets.

In essence, a bank is engaging in a kind of mismatch: lending for long periods of time but also subject to the condition that its depositors could demand their funds back at any time. How can it manage that?

The bank counts on the fact that, on average, only a small fraction of its depositors will want their cash at the same time. On any given day, some people will make withdrawals and others will make new deposits; these will roughly cancel each other out. So the bank needs to keep only a limited amount of cash on hand to satisfy its depositors. In addition, if a bank becomes financially incapable of paying its depositors, individual bank deposits are currently guaranteed to depositors up to $250,000 by the Federal Deposit Insurance Corporation, or FDIC, a federal agency. This reduces the risk to a depositor of holding a bank deposit, in turn reducing the incentive to withdraw funds if concerns about the financial state of the bank should arise. So, under normal conditions, banks need hold only a fraction of their depositors' cash.

By reconciling the needs of savers for liquid assets with the needs of borrowers for long-term financing, banks play a key economic role.

St. Louis Federal Reserve Bank Resources

"Traditional Versus Shadow Banking," *Page One Economics Classroom Edition* (February 2012)

Modern economies rely heavily on financial intermediaries to channel funds between borrowers and lenders. In this issue, the role of traditional banking is outlined, and a parallel system—shadow banking—is explored.

St. Louis Federal Reserve Bank Resources

Paying and Receiving Interest Online Course for Teachers and Students

You've probably heard this quote from Shakespeare—"Neither a borrower nor a lender be." What did Shakespeare have against borrowing and lending?

Perhaps he was concerned that the lender might not be repaid in a timely way. Or maybe he was fearful that friendships and family relations might be strained by people's disagreements over loans and repayments. However, Shakespeare might not have considered the role of interest. Interest payments can allow both borrowers and lenders to benefit from their transactions. This course is designed to help you better understand paying and receiving interest.

MODULE 22 Review

Check Your Understanding

1. Rank the following assets from the lowest level to the highest level of (i) transaction costs, (ii) risk, and (iii) liquidity. Ties are acceptable for items that have indistinguishable rankings.
   a. a bank deposit with a guaranteed interest rate
   b. a share of a highly diversified mutual fund, which can be quickly sold
   c. a share of the family business, which can be sold only if you find a buyer and all other family members agree to the sale
2. What relationship would you expect to find between the level of development of a country's financial system and the country's level of economic development? Explain in terms of the country's levels of savings and investment spending.

Tackle the Test: Multiple-Choice Questions

1. Decreasing which of the following is a task of the financial system?
   I. transaction costs
   II. risk
   III. liquidity
   a. I only
   b. II only
   c. III only
   d. I and II only
   e. I, II, and III
2. Which of the following is NOT a type of financial asset?
   a. bonds
   b. stocks
   c. bank deposits
   d. loans
   e. houses
3. The federal government is said to be "dissaving" when
   a. there is a budget deficit.
   b. there is a budget surplus.
   c. there is no budget surplus or deficit.
   d. savings does not equal investment spending.
   e. national savings equals private savings.
4. A nonprofit institution collects the savings of its members and invests those funds in a wide variety of assets in order to provide its members with income after retirement. This describes a
   a. mutual fund.
   b. bank.
   c. savings and loan.
   d. pension fund.
   e. life insurance company.
5. A financial intermediary that provides liquid financial assets in the form of deposits to lenders and uses their funds to finance borrowers' investment spending on illiquid assets is called a
   a. mutual fund.
   b. bank.
   c. corporation.
   d. pension fund.
   e. life insurance company.

Tackle the Test: Free-Response Questions

1. Identify and describe the three tasks of a well-functioning financial system.

Rubric for FRQ 1 (6 points)

1 point: Decrease transaction costs

1 point: A well-functioning financial system facilitates investment spending by allowing companies to borrow large sums of money without incurring large transaction costs.

1 point: Decrease risk

1 point: A well-functioning financial system helps people reduce their exposure to risk, so that they are more willing to engage in investment spending in the face of uncertainty in the economy.

1 point: Provide liquidity

1 point: A well-functioning financial system allows the fast, low-cost conversion of assets into cash.

2. List and describe the four most important types of financial intermediaries.
(4 points)

Answers to Module 22 Review Questions

Check Your Understanding

1. The transaction costs for (a) a bank deposit and (b) a share of a mutual fund are approximately equivalent because each can typically be accomplished by making a phone call, going online, or visiting a branch office. Transaction costs are highest for (c) a share of a family business since finding a buyer for the share consumes time and resources. The level of risk is lowest for (a) a bank deposit since these deposits are insured by the Federal Deposit Insurance Corporation (FDIC) up to $250,000; somewhat higher for (b) a share of a mutual fund since despite diversification, there is still risk associated with holding stocks; and highest for (c) a share of a family business since this investment is not diversified. The level of liquidity is the lowest for (c) a share of a family business since it can be sold only with the unanimous agreement of other members and it will take some time to find a buyer; higher for (b) a share of a mutual fund since it will take only a few days between selling your shares and the payment being processed; and highest for (a) a bank deposit since withdrawals can usually be made immediately.

2. Economic development and growth are the result of, among other factors, investment spending on physical capital. Since investment spending is equal to savings, the greater the amount saved, the higher investment spending will be, and so the higher growth and economic development will be. Thus, the existence of institutions that facilitate savings will help a country's growth and economic development. As a result, a country with a financial system that provides low transaction costs, opportunities for diversification of risk, and high liquidity to its savers will experience faster growth and economic development than a country that doesn't.

Tackle the Test: Multiple-Choice Questions

1. d
2. e
3. a
4. d
5. b

Tackle the Test: Free-Response Question

Rubric for FRQ 2 (4 points)

1 point: A **mutual fund** is a financial intermediary that creates a stock portfolio by buying and holding shares in companies and then selling *shares of the stock portfolio* to individual investors.

1 point: A **life insurance company** is a firm that guarantees a payment to the policyholder's beneficiaries (typically, the family) when the policyholder dies.

1 point: A **bank** is an institution that helps resolve the conflict between lenders' needs for liquidity and the illiquid financing needs of borrowers who don't want to use the stock or bond markets.

1 point: A **pension fund** is a nonprofit institution that collects the savings of its members and invests those funds in a variety of assets, providing its members with income when they retire.

Module 22 Saving, Investment, and the Financial System 231

PD To prepare for teaching this lesson, you may want to consult the **Module 23 Sample Lecture** in the TRM.

OPEN & CLOSE Start Here

TRM Ask students what money is. *Answers will vary, but they will probably talk about U.S. bills and coins.* Then ask students to read an article about bitcoin. (You can use *The Verge* December 2013 article "Why Don't Economists Like Bitcoin?" at http://www.theverge.com/2013/12/31/5260534/krugman-bitcoin-evil-economists.) See **Worksheet 23.1 (Bitcoin)** from the TRM for questions on this article.

FOCUS Active Learning

To help students understand the concepts in this module, conduct the econedlink activity "Why Do We Need Money? Think about eBay!" at http://www.econedlink.org/lessons/index.php?lid=629&type=educator. Use the questions provided to guide students through a discussion of the activity.

TEACH Teach It

Define money as essentially anything that is easily exchangeable for goods and services. Let students know that money eliminates the need for barter.

Shutterstock

MODULE 23

The Definition and Measurement of Money

In this Module, you will learn to:

- Identify the functions of money
- Explain the various roles money plays and the many forms it takes in the economy
- Describe how the amount of money in the economy is measured

AP® Exam Tip

You'll need to know the functions and characteristics of money for the AP® exam.

The Meaning of Money

In everyday conversation, people often use the word *money* to mean "wealth." If you ask, "How much money does Bill Gates have?" the answer will be something like, "Oh, $50 billion or so, but who's counting?" That is, the number will include the value of the stocks, bonds, real estate, and other assets he owns.

But the economist's definition of money doesn't include all forms of wealth. The dollar bills in your wallet are money; other forms of wealth—such as cars, houses, and stocks—aren't money. Let's examine what, according to economists, distinguishes money from other forms of wealth.

What Is Money?

Money is any asset that can easily be used to purchase goods and services.

Money is defined in terms of what it does: **money** is any asset that can easily be used to purchase goods and services. For ease of use, money must be widely accepted by sellers. It is also desirable for money to be durable, portable, uniform, in limited supply, and divisible into smaller units, as with dollars and cents. In Module 22 we defined an asset as *liquid* if it can easily be converted into cash. Money consists of cash itself, which is liquid by definition, as well as other assets that are highly liquid.

You can see the distinction between money and other assets by asking yourself how you pay for groceries. The person at the cash register will accept dollar bills in return for milk and frozen pizza—but he or she won't accept stock certificates or a collection of vintage baseball cards. If you want to convert stock certificates or vintage baseball cards into groceries, you have to sell them—trade them for money—and then use the money to buy groceries.

St. Louis Federal Reserve Bank Resources

The Free Silver Movement and Inflation

Students learn that money is a medium of exchange that facilitates economic activity. Next, students learn the relationship between the money supply and inflation by participating in an inflation auction using gold and silver notes to better understand the historic debate of the Free Silver Movement. Students then read William Jennings Bryan's "Cross of Gold" speech to relate the historical context. The students use historical data to calculate the income, fixed expenses, and variable expenses of a farmer to further understand the historical argument presented by the Free Silver Movement. Finally, students analyze two political cartoons that criticize the Free Silver Movement. This lesson includes primary source documents obtained from FRASER®.

Of course, many stores allow you to write a check on your bank account in payment for goods (or to pay with a debit card that is linked to your bank account). Does that make your bank account money, even if you haven't converted it into cash? Yes. **Currency in circulation**—actual cash in the hands of the public—is considered money. So are **checkable bank deposits**—bank accounts on which people can write checks.

Are currency and checkable bank deposits the only assets that are considered money? It depends. As we'll see later, there are two widely used definitions of the **money supply**, the total value of financial assets in the economy that are considered money. The narrower definition considers only the most liquid assets to be money: currency in circulation, traveler's checks, and checkable bank deposits. The broader definition includes these three categories plus other assets that are "almost" checkable, such as savings account deposits that can be transferred into a checking account online with a few mouse clicks. Both definitions of the money supply, however, make a distinction between those assets that can easily be used to purchase goods and services, and those that can't.

Currency in circulation is cash held by the public.

Checkable bank deposits are bank accounts on which people can write checks.

The **money supply** is the total value of financial assets in the economy that are considered money.

Money plays a crucial role in generating *gains from trade* because it makes indirect exchange possible. Think of what happens when a cardiac surgeon buys a new refrigerator. The surgeon has valuable services to offer—namely, performing heart operations. The owner of the store has valuable goods to offer: refrigerators and other appliances. It would be extremely difficult for both parties if, instead of using money, they had to directly barter the goods and services they sell. In a barter system, a cardiac surgeon and an appliance store owner could trade only if the store owner happened to want a heart operation *and* the surgeon happened to want a new refrigerator. This is known as the problem of finding a "double coincidence of wants": in a barter system, two parties can trade only when each wants what the other has to offer. Money solves this problem: individuals can trade what they have to offer for money and trade money for what they want.

Because the ability to make transactions with money rather than relying on bartering makes it easier to achieve gains from trade, the existence of money increases welfare, even though money does not directly produce anything. As Adam Smith put it, money "may very properly be compared to a highway, which, while it circulates and carries to market all the grass and corn of the country, produces itself not a single pile of either."

Let's take a closer look at the roles money plays in the economy.

Roles of Money

Money plays three main roles in any modern economy: it is a *medium of exchange*, a *store of value*, and a *unit of account*.

A **medium of exchange** is an asset that individuals acquire for the purpose of trading for goods and services rather than for their own consumption.

Medium of Exchange Our cardiac surgeon/appliance store owner example illustrates the role of money as a **medium of exchange**—an asset that individuals use to trade for goods and services rather than for consumption. People can't eat dollar bills; rather, they use dollar bills to trade for food among other goods and services.

In normal times, the official money of a given country—the dollar in the United States, the peso in Mexico, and so on—is also the medium of exchange in virtually all transactions in that country. During troubled economic times, however, other goods or assets often play that role instead. For example, during economic turmoil people often turn to other countries' moneys as the medium of exchange: U.S. dollars have played this role in troubled Latin American countries, as have euros in troubled Eastern European countries. In a famous example, cigarettes functioned as the medium of exchange in World War II prisoner-of-war camps. Even nonsmokers traded goods and services for cigarettes because the cigarettes could in turn be easily traded for other items. During the extreme German inflation of 1923, goods such as eggs and lumps of coal briefly became mediums of exchange.

With permission of the New Zealand Ministry for Culture and Heritage

Gambling at the Stalag 383 prisoner of war camp during World War II was carried out using cigarettes as currency.

FOCUS Flip It

Have students view the Jacob Clifford video "Macro Unit 4, Question 1—Function of Money" (see econextras video list with hyperlinks on the bcs and TRFD) to begin their work on the role and types of money. To avoid confusion, assure students that there is no question from this text that relates to this video; therefore, disregard his references to "question/answers." Use the Active Learning set below to continue the lesson.

FOCUS Active Learning

Make sure students understand the three functions of money and ask them to give personal examples of each function.

Role of Money	Definition
Medium of exchange	Pay for a good or service.
Store of value	Save your money to spend at a later time.
Unit of account	Set the price or measure the value of a good or service.

FOCUS Active Learning

TRM For practice identifying the functions of money, assign **Worksheet 23.2 (The Functions of Money)** from the TRM in class or as homework.

St. Louis Federal Reserve Bank Resources

Ben Franklin: Highlighting the Printer

Students will learn that money is an invention. They will read and analyze an essay focusing primarily on one aspect of Ben Franklin's life—his work as a printer—and how he was an inventor and entrepreneur who also promoted the use of currency in the United States. Students will cite specific textual evidence regarding problems and solutions and will answer questions and complete a time line. By using evidence and information gleaned from the text, students will write a fictitious social media post defending the selection of Ben Franklin's portrait for the $100 note.

FOCUS Active Learning

TRM Have students watch "Episode 29: What Is Money?" (see econextras video list with hyperlinks on the bcs and TRFD). Assign **Worksheet 23.3 (What Is Money?)** from the TRM for questions on this video. Use this to transition to the next part of the lesson.

TEACH Teach It

Students sometimes struggle with how to classify credit cards. Remind them that credit cards are not money; they are short-term loans made to the holder by a bank.

A **store of value** is a means of holding purchasing power over time.

Store of Value In order to act as a medium of exchange, money must also be a **store of value**—a means of holding purchasing power over time. To see why this is necessary, imagine trying to operate an economy in which ice cream cones were the medium of exchange. Such an economy would quickly suffer from, well, monetary meltdown: your medium of exchange would often turn into a sticky puddle before you could use it to buy something else. Of course, money is by no means the only store of value. Any asset that holds its purchasing power over time is a store of value. Examples include farmland and classic cars. So the store-of-value role is a necessary but not a distinctive feature of money.

A **unit of account** is a measure used to set prices and make economic calculations.

Unit of Account Finally, money normally serves as the **unit of account**—the commonly accepted measure individuals use to set prices and make economic calculations. To understand the importance of this role, consider a historical fact: during the Middle Ages, peasants typically were required to provide landowners with goods and labor rather than money in exchange for a place to live. For example, a peasant might be required to work on the landowner's land one day a week and also hand over one-fifth of his harvest. Today, rents, like other prices, are almost always specified in money terms. That makes things much clearer: imagine how hard it would be to decide which apartment to rent if modern landowners followed medieval practice. Suppose, for example, that Mr. Smith says he'll let you have a place if you clean his house twice a week and bring him a pound of steak every day, whereas Ms. Jones wants you to clean her house just once a week but wants four pounds of chicken every day. Who's offering the better deal? It's hard to say. If, on the other hand, Mr. Smith wants $600 a month and Ms. Jones wants $700, the comparison is easy. In other words, without a commonly accepted measure, the terms of a transaction are harder to determine, making it more difficult to make transactions and achieve gains from trade.

Types of Money

Commodity money is a good used as a medium of exchange that has intrinsic value in other uses.

In some form or another, money has been in use for thousands of years. For most of that period, people used **commodity money**: the medium of exchange was a good, normally gold or silver, that had intrinsic value in other uses. These alternative uses gave commodity money value independent of its role as a medium of exchange. For example, the cigarettes that served as money in World War II POW camps were valuable because many prisoners smoked. Gold was valuable because it was used for jewelry and ornamentation, aside from the fact that it was minted into coins.

By 1776, the year in which the United States declared its independence and Adam Smith published *The Wealth of Nations*, there was widespread use of paper money in addition to gold and silver coins. Unlike modern dollar bills, however, this paper money consisted of notes issued by private banks, which promised to exchange their notes for gold or silver coins on demand. So the paper currency that initially replaced commodity money was **commodity-backed money**, a medium of exchange with no intrinsic value whose ultimate value was guaranteed by a promise that it could always be converted into valuable goods on demand.

Commodity-backed money is a medium of exchange with no intrinsic value whose ultimate value is guaranteed by a promise that it can be converted into valuable goods.

The big advantage of commodity-backed money over simple commodity money, like gold and silver coins, was that it tied up fewer valuable resources. Although a note-issuing bank still had to keep some gold and silver on hand, it had to keep only enough to satisfy demands for redemption of its notes. And it could rely on the fact that only a fraction of its paper notes would be redeemed on a normal day. So the bank needed to keep only a portion of the total value of its notes in circulation in the form of gold and silver in its vaults. It could lend out the remaining gold and silver to those who wished to use it. This allowed society to use the remaining gold and silver for other purposes, all with no loss in the ability to achieve gains from trade.

In a famous passage in *The Wealth of Nations*, Adam Smith described paper money as a "waggon-way through the air." Smith was making an analogy between money and an

St. Louis Federal Reserve Bank Resources

"Functions of Money," *The Economic Lowdown Podcast Series*

Money has taken many forms through the ages: shells, wheels, beads, and even cows. All forms, though, have always had three things in common. Students will find out what they are in this eight-minute podcast. They will also learn how commodity money differs from representative money and how both differ from today's fiat money.

FYI The History of the Dollar

U.S. dollar bills are pure fiat money: they have no intrinsic value, and they are not backed by anything that does. But American money wasn't always like that. In the early days of European settlement, the colonies that would become the United States used commodity money, partly consisting of gold and silver coins minted in Europe. But such coins were scarce on this side of the Atlantic, so the colonists relied on a variety of other forms of commodity money. For example, settlers in Virginia used tobacco as money and settlers in the Northeast used "wampum," a type of clamshell.

Later in American history, commodity-backed paper money came into widespread use. But this wasn't paper money as we now know it, issued by the U.S. government and bearing the signature of the Secretary of the Treasury. Before the Civil War, the U.S. government didn't issue any paper money. Instead, dollar bills were issued by private banks, which promised that their bills could be redeemed for silver coins on demand. These promises weren't always credible because banks sometimes failed, leaving holders of their bills with worthless pieces of paper. Understandably, people were reluctant to accept currency from any bank rumored to be in financial trouble. In other words, in this private money system, some dollars were less valuable than others.

A curious legacy of that time was notes issued by the Citizens' Bank of Louisiana, based in New Orleans. They became among the most widely used bank notes in the southern states. These notes were printed in English on one side and French on the other. (At the time, many people in New Orleans, originally a colony of France, spoke French.) Thus, the $10 bill read *Ten* on one side and *Dix*, the French word for "ten," on the other. These $10 bills became known as "dixies," probably the source of the nickname of the U.S. South.

The U.S. government began issuing official paper money, called "greenbacks," during the Civil War, as a way to help pay for the war. At first greenbacks had no fixed value in terms of commodities. After 1873, however, the U.S. government guaranteed the value of a dollar in terms of gold, effectively turning dollars into commodity-backed money.

In 1933, when President Franklin D. Roosevelt broke the link between dollars and gold, his own federal budget director—who feared that the public would lose confidence in the dollar if it wasn't ultimately backed by gold—declared ominously, "This will be the end of Western civilization." It wasn't. The link between the dollar and gold was restored a few years later, and then dropped again—seemingly for good—in August 1971. Despite the warnings of doom, the U.S. dollar is still the world's most widely used currency.

imaginary highway that did not absorb the valuable land beneath it. An actual highway provides a useful service but at a cost: land that could be used to grow crops is instead paved over. If the highway could be built through the air, it wouldn't destroy useful land. As Smith understood, when banks replaced gold and silver money with paper notes, they accomplished a similar feat: they reduced the amount of real resources used by society to provide the functions of money.

At this point you may ask, why make any use at all of gold and silver in the monetary system, even to back paper money? In fact, today's monetary system goes even further than the system Smith admired, having eliminated any role for gold and silver. A U.S. dollar bill isn't commodity money, and it isn't even commodity-backed. Rather, its value arises entirely from the fact that it is generally accepted as a means of payment, a role that is ultimately decreed by the U.S. government. Money whose value derives entirely from its official status as a means of exchange is known as **fiat money** because it exists by government *fiat*, a historical term for a policy declared by a ruler.

Fiat money is a medium of exchange whose value derives entirely from its official status as a means of payment.

Fiat money has two major advantages over commodity-backed money. First, it is even more of a "waggon-way through the air"—it doesn't tie up any real resources, except for the paper it's printed on. Second, the money supply can be managed based on the needs of the economy, instead of being determined by the amount of gold and silver prospectors happen to discover.

On the other hand, fiat money poses some risks. One such risk is counterfeiting. Counterfeiters usurp a privilege of the U.S. government, which has the sole legal right to print dollar bills. And the benefit that counterfeiters get by exchanging fake bills for real goods and services comes at the expense of the U.S. federal government, which covers a small but nontrivial part of its own expenses by issuing new currency to meet a growing demand for money.

The image of a valid U.S. five-dollar bill shows a pattern in the background of the Lincoln Memorial image as seen through a Document Security Systems, Inc. document verifier.

FOCUS Active Learning

TRM Have students read through and answer the questions in **Worksheet 23.4 (Why Is It Money?)** from the TRM. If you have a $5 bill, hold it up as you ask the first question. *Answers: 1. No, it is paper and not a commodity. 2. No, it is fiat money. 3. Yes, because the government says it is legal tender. 4. Because it is legal tender and can be spent elsewhere without problems. 5. No, because I can't use it everywhere. 6. I can take it somewhere and buy something I really want. It has general acceptance in exchange for goods and services. 7. People would not be able to buy the goods and services they want or need.*

Now show your class the small print on the front, bottom left, corner of the bill. It reads, "This note is legal tender for all debts, public and private." This is a declaration from the U.S. government that you can use this money to pay your taxes (a public debt) or buy a soda (a private debt). It is our money because the government has decreed it to be. Everyone accepts the bill as payment for nearly anything, so it serves the purpose of money.

TEACH Teach It

Commodity money is backed by some commodity such as silver or gold, while fiat money is only backed by the government's word that it is legal for all trade in a nation.

St. Louis Federal Reserve Bank Resources

Currency and the Fed

In this lesson, students consider who is pictured on the different denominations of U.S. currency and why. They participate in an activity to identify functions of everyday items and then identify and explain the functions of another everyday item—money. Students learn some facts about money as well as some basics about the Federal Reserve System. In addition, they describe the Federal Reserve's role in the distribution of money by identifying features of the $5 note.

TEACH Teach It

There are two measures of money students need to know, M1 and M2.

- M1 = Currency and coin in circulation + Checking deposits + Traveler's checks. This is the most liquid form of money.
- M2 is made up of M1 plus near-moneys such as savings that pay interest. M2 is less liquid than M1.
- M2 = M1 + Savings accounts + Short-term CDs + Money market accounts.

TEACH Teach It

Tell students that M1 is the most liquid form of money; it is what you can spend right away. M2 is broader and includes savings accounts and other assets that can be quickly converted to money. Assets that cannot be quickly converted to cash, like stocks and bonds, are not counted as either M1 or M2.

FOCUS Active Learning

TRM Ask students to complete **Worksheet 23.5 (All About Money)** from the TRM in class or as homework.

OPEN & CLOSE Exit Slip

TRM *Please see **Exit Slip: Module 23** in the TRM for formative multiple-choice questions to ask your students before finishing your lesson. These questions will help you quickly assess whether your students have mastered the module's concepts before moving on.*

Answers to the Exit Slip Questions

1. E
2. A
3. E

The larger risk is that government officials who have the authority to print money will be tempted to abuse the privilege by printing so much money that they create inflation.

Measuring the Money Supply

AP® Exam Tip

When you see "money supply" on the AP® exam, that usually refers to the M1 measure of the money supply.

A **monetary aggregate** is an overall measure of the money supply.

Near-moneys are financial assets that can't be directly used as a medium of exchange but can be readily converted into cash or checkable bank deposits.

The Federal Reserve (an institution we'll talk more about shortly) calculates the size of two **monetary aggregates**, overall measures of the money supply, which differ in how strictly money is defined. The two aggregates are known, rather cryptically, as M1 and M2. (There used to be a third aggregate named—you guessed it—M3, but in 2006 the Federal Reserve concluded that measuring it was no longer useful.) M1, the narrowest definition, contains only currency in circulation (also known as cash), traveler's checks, and checkable bank deposits. M2 starts with M1 and adds several other kinds of assets, often referred to as **near-moneys**—financial assets that aren't directly usable as a medium of exchange but can be readily converted into cash or checkable bank deposits. Examples include savings accounts and time deposits such as small-denomination certificates of deposit (CDs), which aren't checkable but can be withdrawn at any time before their maturity date by paying a penalty. Other types of assets in M2 include money market funds, which are mutual funds that invest only in liquid assets and bear a close resemblance to bank deposits. These near-moneys pay interest while cash (currency in circulation) does not; in addition, they typically pay higher interest rates than any offered on checkable bank deposits. Because currency and checkable deposits are directly usable as a medium of exchange, however, M1 is the most liquid measure of money.

In January 2014, M1 was valued at $2,698.2 billion, with approximately 43% accounted for by currency in circulation, approximately 57% accounted for by checkable bank deposits, and a tiny slice accounted for by traveler's checks. In turn, M1 made up 24% of M2, valued at $11,039.1 billion.

FYI What's with All the Currency?

Alert readers may be a bit startled at one of the numbers in the money supply: $1,159 billion of currency in circulation in January 2014. That's $3,652 in cash for every man, woman, and child in the United States. How many people do you know who carry $3,652 in their wallets? Not many. So where is all that cash?

Part of the answer is that it isn't in individuals' wallets: it's in cash registers. Businesses as well as individuals need to hold cash.

Economists also believe that cash plays an important role in transactions that people want to keep hidden. Small businesses and the self-employed sometimes prefer to be paid in cash so they can avoid paying taxes by hiding income from the Internal Revenue Service. Also, drug dealers and other criminals obviously don't want bank records of their dealings. In fact, some analysts have tried to infer the amount of illegal activity in the economy from the total amount of cash held by the public. The most important reason for those huge currency holdings, however, is foreign use of dollars. The Federal Reserve estimates that 60% of U.S. currency is actually held outside the United States—largely in countries in which residents are so distrustful of their national currencies that the U.S. dollar has become a widely accepted medium of exchange.

Steven Puetzer/Getty Images

236 Section 5 The Financial Sector

MODULE 23 Review

Check Your Understanding

1. Suppose you hold a gift certificate, good for certain products at participating stores. Is this gift certificate money? Why or why not?
2. Although most bank accounts pay some interest, depositors can get a higher interest rate by buying a certificate of deposit, or CD. The difference between a CD and a checking account is that the depositor pays a penalty for withdrawing the money before the CD comes due—a period of months or even years. Small CDs are counted in M2, but not in M1. Explain why they are not part of M1.
3. Explain why a system of commodity-backed money uses resources more efficiently than a system of commodity money.

Tackle the Test: Multiple-Choice Questions

1. When you use money to purchase the $6 lunch special, money is serving which role(s)?
   - I. medium of exchange
   - II. store of value
   - III. unit of account
   - a. I only
   - b. II only
   - c. III only
   - d. I and III only
   - e. I, II, and III
2. When you decide you want "$10 worth" of a product, money is serving which role(s)?
   - I. medium of exchange
   - II. store of value
   - III. unit of account
   - a. I only
   - b. II only
   - c. III only
   - d. I and II only
   - e. I, II, and III
3. In the United States, the dollar is
   - a. backed by silver.
   - b. backed by gold and silver.
   - c. commodity-backed money.
   - d. commodity money.
   - e. fiat money.
4. Which of the following is the most liquid monetary aggregate?
   - a. M1
   - b. M2
   - c. M3
   - d. near-moneys
   - e. dollar bills
5. Which of the following is the best example of using money as a store of value?
   - a. A customer pays in advance for $10 worth of gasoline at a gas station.
   - b. A babysitter puts her earnings in a dresser drawer while she saves to buy a bicycle.
   - c. Travelers buy meals on board an airline flight.
   - d. Foreign visitors to the United States convert their currency to dollars at the airport.
   - e. You use $1 bills to purchase soda from a vending machine.

Tackle the Test: Free-Response Questions

1. a. What does it mean for an asset to be "liquid"?
   b. Which of the assets listed below is the most liquid? Explain.
   A Federal Reserve note (dollar bill)
   A savings account deposit
   A house
   c. Which of the assets listed above is the least liquid? Explain.
   d. In which monetary aggregate(s) calculated by the Federal Reserve are checkable deposits included?

Rubric for FRQ 1 (6 points)

1 point: It can easily be converted into cash.

1 point: A Federal Reserve note

1 point: It is already cash.

1 point: A house

1 point: It takes time and resources to sell a house.

1 point: M1 and M2 (They were part of M3 as well, but the Fed no longer uses this measure.)

2. a. The U.S. dollar derives its value from what? That is, what "backs" U.S. currency?
   b. What is the term used to describe the type of money used in the United States today?
   c. What two other types of money have been used in the past? Define each.
   (5 points)

Answers to Module 23 Review Questions

Check Your Understanding

1. The defining characteristic of money is its liquidity: how easily it can be used to purchase goods and services. Although a gift certificate can easily be used to purchase a very defined set of goods or services (the goods or services available at the store issuing the gift certificate), it cannot be used to purchase any other goods or services. A gift certificate is therefore not money since it cannot easily be used to purchase all goods or services.

2. Again, the important characteristic of money is its liquidity: how easily it can be used to purchase goods and services. M1, the narrowest definition of the money supply, consists only of currency in circulation, traveler's checks, and checkable bank deposits. CDs aren't checkable—and they can't be made checkable without incurring a cost because there's a penalty for early withdrawal. This makes them less liquid than the assets counted in M1.

3. Commodity-backed money uses resources more efficiently than simple commodity money, like gold and silver coins, because commodity-backed money ties up fewer valuable resources. Although a bank must keep some of the commodity—generally gold and silver—on hand, it has to keep only enough to satisfy demand for redemptions. It can then lend out the remaining gold and silver, which allows society to use these resources for other purposes, with no loss in the ability to achieve gains from trade.

Tackle the Test: Multiple-Choice Questions

1. d
2. c
3. e
4. a
5. b

Tackle the Test: Free-Response Question

Rubric for FRQ 2 (5 points)

1 point: U.S. currency is backed by its official status granted by the U.S. government.

1 point: Fiat money

1 point: Commodity money and commodity-backed money

1 point: Commodity money is money that has intrinsic value in other uses.

1 point: Commodity-backed money is money that has no intrinsic value but can be converted into valuable goods on demand.

PD To prepare for teaching this lesson, you may want to consult the **Module 24 Sample Lecture** in the TRM.

OPEN & CLOSE Start Here

Ask students whether they would take a reduced amount now or the full amount paid out at $20,000 a year if they won $100,000 playing the lottery. Why? *Many may say they would want the money now. They might come to the conclusion that more can be done with the money now than in the future if they remember the lessons on inflation.*

FOCUS Active Learning

TRM Have students watch the video "Time Value of Money" (see econextras video list with hyperlinks on the bcs and TRFD). Suggested questions for this video can be found in the TRM on **Worksheet 24.1 (Time Value of Money)**. Always remember that a dollar today is worth more than a dollar in the future because increasing inflation decreases the purchasing power of each dollar. Also, a dollar received now can be invested to earn more than a dollar in the future, and impatience leads to a general preference to have a given amount of money now rather than later.

Oli Scarff/Getty Images

MODULE 24 The Time Value of Money

In this Module, you will learn to:

- Explain why a dollar today is worth more than a dollar a year from now
- Use the concept of present value to make better decisions about costs and benefits that come in the future

The Concept of Present Value

Individuals often face financial decisions that will have consequences long into the future. For example, when you decide to attend college, you are committing yourself to years of study, which you expect will pay off for the rest of your life. So the decision to attend college is a decision to embark on a long-term project.

The basic rule in deciding whether or not to undertake a project is that you should compare the benefits of that project with its costs, implicit as well as explicit. But making these comparisons can sometimes be difficult because the benefits and costs of a project may not arrive at the same time. Sometimes the costs of a project come at an earlier date than the benefits. For example, going to college involves large immediate costs: tuition, income forgone because you are in school, and so on. The benefits, such as a higher salary in your future career, come later, often much later. In other cases, the benefits of a project come at an earlier date than the costs. If you take out a loan to pay for a vacation cruise, the satisfaction of the vacation will come immediately, but the burden of making payments will come later.

How, specifically, is time an issue in economic decision making?

Borrowing, Lending, and Interest

In general, having a dollar today is worth more than having a dollar a year from now. To see why, let's consider two examples.

First, suppose that you get a new job that comes with a $1,000 bonus, which will be paid at the end of the first year. But you would like to spend the extra money now—say, on new clothes for work. Can you do that? The answer is yes—you can borrow money today and use the bonus to repay the debt a year from now. But if that is your plan, you cannot borrow the full $1,000 today. You must borrow *less* than that because a year from now you will have to repay the amount borrowed *plus interest*.

238 Section 5 The Financial Sector

Now consider a different scenario. Suppose that you are paid a bonus of $1,000 today, and you decide that you don't want to spend the money until a year from now. What do you do with it? You put it in the bank; in effect, you are lending the $1,000 to the bank, which in turn lends it out to its customers who wish to borrow. At the end of a year, you will get *more* than $1,000 back—you will receive the $1,000 plus the interest earned.

All of this means that having $1,000 today is worth more than having $1,000 a year from now. As any borrower and lender know, this is what allows a lender to charge a borrower interest on a loan: borrowers are willing to pay interest in order to have money today rather than waiting until they acquire that money later on. Most interest rates are stated as the percentage of the borrowed amount that must be paid to the lender for each year of the loan. Whether money is actually borrowed for 1 month or 10 years, and regardless of the amount, the same principle applies: money in your pocket today is worth more than money in your pocket tomorrow. To keep things simple in the discussions that follow, we'll restrict ourselves to examples of loans of $1.

Because the value of money depends on when it is paid or received, you can't evaluate a project by simply adding up the costs and benefits when those costs and benefits arrive at different times. You must take time into account when evaluating the project because $1 that is paid to you today is worth more than $1 that is paid to you a year from now. Similarly, $1 that you must pay today is more burdensome than $1 that you must pay next year. Fortunately, there is a simple way to adjust for these complications so that we can correctly compare the value of dollars received and paid out at different times.

Next we'll see how the interest rate can be used to convert future benefits and costs into what economists call *present values.* By using present values when evaluating a project, you can evaluate a project *as if* all relevant costs and benefits were occurring today rather than at different times. This allows people to "factor out" the complications created by time. We'll start by defining the concept of present value.

Defining Present Value

The key to the concept of present value is to understand that you can use the interest rate to compare the value of a dollar realized (paid or received) today with the value of a dollar realized later. Why the interest rate? Because the interest rate correctly measures the cost to you of delaying the receipt of a dollar of benefit and, correspondingly, the benefit to you of delaying the payment of a dollar of cost. Let's illustrate this with some examples.

Suppose that you are evaluating whether or not to take a job in which your employer promises to pay you a bonus at the end of the first year. What is the value to you today of $1 of bonus money to be paid one year in the future? Or, to put the question somewhat differently, what amount would you be willing to accept today as a substitute for receiving $1 one year from now?

To answer this question, begin by observing that you need *less* than $1 today in order to be assured of having $1 one year from now. Why? Because any money that you have today can be lent out at interest—say, by depositing it in a bank account so that the bank can then lend it out to its borrowers. The accumulation of interest turns any amount you have today into a greater sum, called the **future value** of today's amount, at the end of the loan period.

Let's work this out mathematically. We'll use the symbol r to represent the interest rate, expressed in decimal terms—that is, if the interest rate is 10%, then $r = 0.10$. If you lend out $X for one year, at the end of that year you will receive your $X back, plus the interest on your $X, which is $\$X \times r$. Thus, at the end of the year you will receive:

(24-1) Future value of $X in one year $= \$X + \$X \times r = \$X \times (1 + r)$

The **future value** of some current amount of money is the amount to which it will grow as interest accumulates over a specified period of time.

TEACH Teach It

Make sure students know the following key points about the time value of money:

- Money today is more valuable than the same amount of money in the future.
- With an interest rate of r, the present value of $1 received one year from now is $\frac{\$1}{1 + r}$.
- The future value of $1 invested today is $\$1 \times (1 + r)$.
- Interest paid on savings and interest charged on borrowing is designed to equate the value of dollars today with the value of future dollars.

TEACH Teach It

When you borrow money to buy a good or service, lenders charge you interest. Lenders anticipate the inflation rate and add that amount to the price of your loan. The interest rate is what a borrower is willing to pay to spend money today rather than in a year.

St. Louis Federal Reserve Bank Resources

Present Value Online Course

Suppose that you want to have a certain amount of money in the future—say $25,000 to make a down payment on a home. How much do you have to put away today to achieve that goal? Or what if you win the lottery—do you take a lump sum payment today or equal payments over the next 26 years? Present value is a tool to help your students make choices like these.

Module 24 The Time Value of Money 239

FOCUS Test It

By adding an N to represent the number of years, we obtain formulas for present value and future value that apply to any period of time:

The present value of $X received in N years $= \frac{\$X}{(1+r)^N}$.

The future value in N years of today's $X = $X × $(1 + r)^N$.

Test your students' understanding of these formulas with this problem:

Your younger brother is a freshman in high school. He deposited $1,000 in a certificate of deposit this year and will earn an annual interest rate of 6%. You have a certificate of deposit earning an annual interest rate of 5% that will be worth $2,500 next year and are considering cashing it out to buy a car for college.

1. What will your brother's certificate of deposit be worth in 4 years? *$1,000 × (1 + .06)⁴ ≈ $1,262.48*
2. What is the present value of your certificate of deposit? $\frac{\$2{,}500}{(1+0.05)^1} = \$2{,}380.95$

The next step is to find out how much you would have to lend out today to have $1 a year from now. To do that, we just need to set the future value in Equation 24-1 equal to $1 and solve for $X. That is, we solve the following equation for $X:

$$\textbf{(24-2)}\quad \$X \times (1 + r) = \$1$$

When we rearrange Equation 24-2 to solve for $X, we find the amount you need to lend out today in order to receive $1 one year from now. Economists have a special name for $X—it's called the **present value** of $1:

The **present value** of $1 realized one year from now is $1/(1 + r): the amount of money you must lend out today in order to have $1 in one year. It is the value to you today of $1 realized one year from now.

$$\textbf{(24-3)}\quad \text{Present value of \$1 realized in one year} = \$X = \$1/(1 + r)$$

This means that you would be willing to accept $X today in place of each $1 to be paid to you one year in the future. The reason is that, if you were to lend out $X today, you would be assured of receiving $1 one year from now.

Now let's find the value of $X. To do this we simply need to plug the actual value of r (a value determined by the financial markets) into Equation 24-3. Let's assume that the interest rate is 10%, which means that $r = 0.10$. In that case:

$$\textbf{(24-4)}\quad \$X = \$1/(1 + 0.10) = \$1/1.10 = \$0.91$$

So you would be willing to accept $0.91 today in exchange for every $1 to be paid to you one year in the future. That is, the present value of $1 realized in one year is $0.91. Note that the present value of any given amount will change as the interest rate changes.

Baerbel Schmidt/Getty Images

Having it someday isn't the same as having it now.

To see that this technique works for evaluating future costs as well as evaluating future benefits, consider the following example. Suppose you enter into an agreement that obliges you to pay $1 one year from now—say, to pay off a car loan from your parents when you graduate in a year. How much money would you need today to ensure that you have $1 in a year? The answer is $X, the present value of $1, which in our example is $0.91. The reason $0.91 is the right answer is that if you lend it out for one year at an interest rate of 10%, you will receive $1 in return at the end. So if, for example, you must pay back $5,000 one year from now, then you need to deposit $5,000 × 0.91 = $4,550 into a bank account today earning an interest rate of 10% in order to have $5,000 one year from now. (There is a slight discrepancy due to rounding.) In other words, today you need to have the present value of $5,000, which equals $4,550, in order to be assured of paying off your debt in a year.

These examples show us that the present value concept provides a way to calculate the value today of $1 that is realized in a year—regardless of whether that $1 is realized as a benefit (the bonus) or a cost (the car loan payback). To evaluate a project today that has benefits, costs, or both to be realized in a year, we just use the relevant interest rate to convert those future dollars into their present values. In that way we have "factored out" the complication that time creates for decision making.

Below we will use the present value concept to evaluate a project. But before we do that, it is worthwhile to note that the present value method can be used for projects in which the $1 is realized more than a year later—say, two, three, or even more years. Suppose you are considering a project that will pay you $1 *two* years from today. What is the value to you today of $1 received two years into the future? We can find the answer with extensions of the formulas we've already seen.

Let's call $V the amount of money you need to lend today at an interest rate of r in order to have $1 in two years. So if you lend $V today, in one year you will receive:

$$\textbf{(24-5)}\quad \text{Future value of \$}V\text{ in one year} = \$V \times (1 + r)$$

240 Section 5 The Financial Sector

And if you re-lend that sum for another year, at the end of the second year you will receive:

(24-6) Future value of $\$V$ in two years $= \$V \times (1 + r) \times (1 + r) = \$V \times (1 + r)^2$

For example, if $r = 0.10$, then $\$V \times (1.10)^2 = \$V \times 1.21$.

Now we are ready to find the present value of $1 realized in two years. First we set the future value in Equation 24-6 equal to $1:

(24-7) Condition satisfied when $1 is received two years from now as a result of lending $V today: $\$V \times (1 + r)^2 = \$1$

Rearranging Equation 24-7, we can solve for $V:

(24-8) $\$V = \$1/(1 + r)^2$

Given $r = 0.10$ and using Equation 24-8, we arrive at $\$V = \$1/1.21 = \$0.83$.

(24-9) $\$V = \$1/(1.10)^2 = \$1/1.21 = \$0.83$

So, when the interest rate is 10%, $1 realized two years from today is worth $0.83 today because by lending out $0.83 today you can be assured of having $1 in two years. And that means that the present value of $1 realized two years into the future is $0.83.

Equation 24-9 points the way toward a general expression for present value, where $1 is paid after *N* years:

(24-10) Present value of $1 received in *N* years $= \$1/(1 + r)^N$

Likewise, each $1 lent today for *N* years has a future value of:

(24-11) Future value of today's $1 in *N* years $= \$1(1 + r)^N$

For example, $1 lent for 5 years at an interest rate of 6% has a future value of $\$1(1 + 0.06)^5 = \$1.34$.

Using Present Value

Suppose you have three choices for a project to undertake. Project A costs nothing and has an immediate payoff to you of $100. Project B requires that you pay $10 today in order to receive $115 a year from now. Project C gives you an immediate payoff of $119 but requires that you pay $20 a year from now. Let's assume that the annual interest rate is 10%—that is, $r = 0.10$.

The problem in evaluating these three projects is that their costs and benefits are realized at different times. That is, of course, where the concept of present value becomes extremely helpful: by using present value to convert any dollars realized in the future into today's value, you factor out the issue of time. Appropriate comparisons can be made using the **net present value** of a project—the present value of current and future benefits minus the present value of current and future costs. The best project to undertake is the one with the highest net present value.

Table 24.1 on the next page shows how to calculate net present value for each of the three projects. The second and third columns show how many dollars are realized and when they are realized; costs are indicated by a minus sign. The fourth column shows the equations used to convert the flows of dollars into their present

The **net present value** of a project is the present value of current and future benefits minus the present value of current and future costs.

FOCUS Active Learning

TRM The most prevalent difficulty when learning present value is simply the math. Several simple examples can help students overcome this difficulty. Assign **Worksheet 24.2 (Using Present Value)** from the TRM to provide them with the practice they need to do well with this content.

OPEN & CLOSE Exit Slip

TRM *Please see **Exit Slip: Module 24** in the TRM for formative multiple-choice questions to ask your students before finishing your lesson. These questions will help you quickly assess whether your students have mastered the module's concepts before moving on.*

Answers to the Exit Slip Questions

1. A: $\frac{\$1{,}000}{(1 + 0.04)^2} = \$924.56$
2. B: $\frac{\$100}{(1 + 0.02)} = \$98.04$
3. C: $\frac{\$1.00}{(1 + 0.03)} = \$0.97$

Table 24.1 The Net Present Value of Three Hypothetical Projects

Project	Dollars realized today	Dollars realized one year from today	Present value formula	Net present value given $r = 0.10$
A	\$100	—	\$100	\$100.00
B	–\$10	\$115	$-\$10 + \$115/(1 + r)$	\$94.55
C	\$119	–\$20	$\$119 - \$20/(1 + r)$	\$100.82

value, and the fifth column shows the actual amounts of the total net present value for each of the three projects.

For instance, to calculate the net present value of project B, we need to calculate the present value of \$115 received in one year. The present value of \$1 received in one year would be $\$1/(1 + r)$. So the present value of \$115 is equal to $115 \times \$1/(1 + r)$; that is, $\$115/(1 + r)$. The net present value of project B is the present value of today's and future benefits minus the present value of today's and future costs: $-\$10 + \$115/(1 + r)$.

From the fifth column, we can immediately see which is the preferred project—it is project C. That's because it has the highest net present value, \$100.82, which is higher than the net present value of project A (\$100) and much higher than the net present value of project B (\$94.55).

This example shows how important the concept of present value is. If we had failed to use the present value calculations and instead simply added up the dollars generated by each of the three projects, we could easily have been misled into believing that project B was the best project and project C was the worst when the reverse is actually the case.

FYI How Big Is That Jackpot, Anyway?

For a clear example of present value at work, consider the case of lottery jackpots.

On March 30, 2012, Mega Millions set the record for the largest jackpot ever in North America, with a payout of \$656 million. Well, sort of. That \$656 million was available only if you chose to take your winnings in the form of an "annuity," consisting of an annual payment for the next 26 years. If you wanted cash up front, the jackpot was only \$471 million and change.

Why was Mega Millions so stingy about quick payoffs? It was all a matter of present value. If the winner had been willing to take the annuity, the lottery would have invested the jackpot money, buying U.S. government bonds (in effect lending the money to the federal government). The money would have been invested in such a way that the investments would pay just enough to cover the annuity. This worked, of course, because at the interest rates prevailing at the time, the present value of a \$656 million annuity spread over 26 years was just about \$471 million. To put it another way, the opportunity cost to the lottery of that annuity in present value terms was \$471 million.

So why didn't they just call it a \$471 million jackpot? Well, \$656 million sounds more impressive! But receiving \$656 million over 26 years is essentially the same as receiving \$471 million today.

David Gould/Photographer's Choice RF/Getty Images

242 Section 5 The Financial Sector

MODULE 24 Review

Check Your Understanding

1. Consider the three hypothetical projects shown in Table 24.1. This time, however, suppose that the interest rate is only 2%.
   a. Calculate the net present values of the three projects. Which one is now preferred?
   b. Explain why the preferred choice is different with a 2% interest rate than with a 10% interest rate.

Tackle the Test: Multiple-Choice Questions

1. Suppose, for simplicity, that a bank uses a single interest rate for loans and deposits, there is no inflation, and all unspent money is deposited in the bank. The interest rate measures which of the following?
   I. the cost of using a dollar today rather than a year from now
   II. the benefit of delaying the use of a dollar from today until a year from now
   III. the price of borrowing money calculated as a percentage of the amount borrowed
   a. I only
   b. II only
   c. III only
   d. I and II only
   e. I, II, and III
2. If the interest rate is zero, then the present value of a dollar received at the end of the year is
   a. more than $1.
   b. equal to $1.
   c. less than $1.
   d. zero.
   e. infinite.
3. If the interest rate is 10%, the present value of $1 paid to you one year from now is
   a. $0.
   b. $0.89.
   c. $0.91.
   d. $1.
   e. more than $1.
4. If the interest rate is 5%, the future value of $100 lent today is
   a. $90.
   b. $95.
   c. $100.
   d. $105.
   e. $110.
5. What is the present value of $100 realized two years from now if the interest rate is 10%?
   a. $80
   b. $83
   c. $90
   d. $100
   e. $110

Tackle the Test: Free-Response Questions

1. **a.** Calculate the net present value of each of the three hypothetical projects described below. Assume the interest rate is 5%.
   Project A: You receive an immediate payoff of $1,000.
   Project B: You pay $100 today in order to receive $1,200 a year from now.
   Project C: You receive $1,200 today but must pay $200 one year from now.
   b. Which of the three projects would you choose to undertake based on your net present value calculations? Explain.

Rubric for FRQ 1 (5 points)

1 point: Project A net present value: $1,000

1 point: Project B net present value: –$100 + ($1,200/1.05) = $1,042.86

1 point: Project C net present value: $1,200 – ($200/1.05) = $1,009.52

1 point: Choose project B.

1 point: It has the highest net present value.

2. **a.** What is the future value of a 3-year loan of $1,000 at 5% interest? Show your work.
   b. What is the present value of $1,000 received in three years if the interest rate is 5%? Show your work.
   (4 points)

Answers to Module 24 Review Questions

Check Your Understanding

1. a. The net present value of project A is unaffected by the interest rate since it is money received today; its present value is still $100. The net present value of project B is now –$10 + $115/1.02 = $102.75. The net present value of project C is now $119 – $20/1.02 = $99.39. Project B is preferred.

b. When the interest rate is lower, the cost of waiting for money that arrives in the future is lower. For example, at a 10% interest rate, $1 arriving one year from today is worth only $1/1.10 = $0.91. But when the interest rate is 2%, $1 arriving one year from today is worth $1/1.02 = $0.98, a sizable increase. As a result, project B, which has a benefit one year from today, becomes more attractive. And project C, which has a cost one year from today, becomes less attractive.

Tackle the Test: Multiple-Choice Questions

1. e
2. b
3. c
4. d
5. b

Tackle the Test: Free-Response Question

Rubric for FRQ 2 (4 points)

1 point: $1,157.63

1 point: $\$1{,}000 \times (1.05)^3 = \$1{,}000 \times 1.16 = \$1{,}157.63$

1 point: $863.84

1 point: $\$1{,}000/(1.05)^3 = \$863.84$

PD To prepare for teaching this lesson, you may want to consult the **Module 25 Sample Lecture** in the TRM.

OPEN & CLOSE Start Here

Ask students where money comes from. Most will say the government (which is true). This opens the door for you to talk about the U.S. Treasury and banking. Let students know that you will be discussing how banks create money but don't actually print it. See if anyone can explain the difference between the two. Assure them that at the end of the lesson, they will understand this important distinction.

FOCUS Active Learning

If time allows, conduct the "Show Me the Money" activity at http://www.fte.org/teacher-resources/lesson-plans/efiahlessons/show-me-the-money-activity. Handouts may be found at http://fte.org/wp-content/uploads/Fractional-Reserve-Banking-Simulation-2010.docx. Use the debriefing questions associated with the activity. This 45-minute lesson will introduce students to money creation and fractional reserves at the same time.

Spencer Platt/Getty Images

MODULE 25 Banking and Money Creation

In this Module, you will learn to:

- Describe the role of banks in the economy
- Identify the reasons for and types of banking regulation
- Explain how banks create money

The Monetary Role of Banks

More than half of M1, the narrowest definition of the money supply, consists of currency in circulation—those bills and coins held by the public. It's obvious where currency comes from: it's printed or minted by the U.S. Treasury. But the rest of M1 consists of bank deposits, and deposits account for the great bulk of M2, the broader definition of the money supply. By either measure, then, bank deposits are a major component of the money supply. And this fact brings us to our next topic: the monetary role of banks.

What Banks Do

A bank is a *financial intermediary* that uses bank deposits, which you will recall are liquid assets, to finance borrowers' investments in illiquid assets such as businesses and homes. Banks can lend depositors' money to investors and thereby create liquidity because it isn't necessary for a bank to keep all of its deposits on hand. Except in the case of a *bank run*—which we'll discuss shortly—all of a bank's depositors won't want to withdraw their funds at the same time.

However, banks can't lend out *all* the funds placed in their hands by depositors because they have to satisfy any depositor who wants to withdraw his or her funds. In order to meet these demands, a bank must keep substantial quantities of liquid assets on hand. In the modern U.S. banking system, these assets take the form of either currency in the bank's vault or deposits held in the bank's own account at the Federal Reserve. As we'll see shortly, the latter can be converted into currency more or less instantly. Currency in bank vaults and bank deposits held at the Federal Reserve are called **bank reserves**. Because bank reserves are in bank vaults and at the Federal Reserve, not held by the public, they are not part of currency in circulation.

Bank reserves are the currency that banks hold in their vaults plus their deposits at the Federal Reserve.

Figure 25.1 A T-Account for Samantha's Smoothies

A T-account summarizes a business's financial position. Its assets, in this case consisting of a building and some smoothie-making machinery, are on the left side. Its liabilities, consisting of the money it owes to a local bank, are on the right side.

Assets		Liabilities	
Building	$30,000	Loan from bank	$20,000
Smoothie-making machines	$15,000		

To understand the role of banks in determining the money supply, we start by introducing a simple tool for analyzing a bank's financial position: a **T-account**. A business's T-account summarizes its financial position by showing, in a single table, the business's assets and liabilities, with assets on the left and liabilities on the right. **Figure 25.1** shows the T-account for a hypothetical business that *isn't* a bank—Samantha's Smoothies. According to Figure 25.1, Samantha's Smoothies owns a building worth $30,000 and has $15,000 worth of smoothie-making equipment. These are assets, so they're on the left side of the table. To finance its opening, the business borrowed $20,000 from a local bank. That's a liability, so the loan is on the right side of the table. By looking at the T-account, you can immediately see what Samantha's Smoothies owns and what it owes. This type of table is called a T-account because the lines in the table make a T-shape.

Samantha's Smoothies is an ordinary, nonbank business. Now let's look at the T-account for a hypothetical bank, First Street Bank, which is the repository of $1 million in bank deposits.

Figure 25.2 shows First Street's financial position. The loans First Street has made are on the left side because they're assets: they represent funds that those who have borrowed from the bank are expected to repay. The bank's only other assets, in this simplified example, are its reserves, which, as we've learned, can take the form of either cash in the bank's vault or deposits at the Federal Reserve. On the right side we show the bank's liabilities, which in this example consist entirely of deposits made by customers at First Street. These are liabilities because they represent funds that must ultimately be repaid to depositors. Notice, by the way, that in this example First Street's assets are larger than its liabilities. That's the way it's supposed to be! In fact, as we'll see shortly, banks are required by law to maintain assets larger than their liabilities by a specific percentage.

In this example, First Street Bank holds reserves equal to 10% of its customers' bank deposits. The fraction of bank deposits that a bank holds as reserves is its **reserve ratio**.

In the modern American system, the Federal Reserve—which, among other things, regulates banks operating in the United States—sets a **required reserve ratio**, which is the smallest fraction of bank deposits that a bank must hold. To understand why banks are regulated, let's consider a problem banks can face: *bank runs.*

A **T-account** is a tool for analyzing a business's financial position by showing, in a single table, the business's assets (on the left) and liabilities (on the right).

AP® Exam Tip

Make sure you understand T-accounts as they do show up on the AP® exam.

The **reserve ratio** is the fraction of bank deposits that a bank holds as reserves.

The **required reserve ratio** is the smallest fraction of deposits that the Federal Reserve allows banks to hold.

Figure 25.2 Assets and Liabilities of First Street Bank

First Street Bank's assets consist of $1,000,000 in loans and $100,000 in reserves. Its liabilities consist of $1,000,000 in deposits—money owed to people who have placed funds in First Street's hands.

Assets		Liabilities	
Loans	$1,000,000	Deposits	$1,000,000
Reserves	$100,000		

TEACH Teach It

Use Figure 25.1 to walk students through the parts of a T-account. Show what happens when deposits to and withdrawals from the bank occur. Let students know they may see liabilities to depositors described as checkable deposits, demand deposits, or deposits. They should take note of these deposits as they are subject to reserve requirements in the banking system.

TEACH Teach It

Students struggle to understand T-accounts. Stress that what is on the left (assets) is what the bank owns, and what is on the right (liabilities) is what the bank owes. The statement is sometimes called a balance sheet because assets should always equal liabilities. Remember that in a T-account, assets will always equal liabilities.

TEACH Teach It

Banks use the money deposited into accounts to make loans to other clients. They are required to keep a certain amount of that money on hold as required reserves to make sure patrons can obtain cash from their accounts at any time.

The Problem of Bank Runs

A bank can lend out most of the funds deposited in its care because in normal times only a small fraction of its depositors want to withdraw their funds on any given day. But what would happen if, for some reason, all or at least a large fraction of its depositors *did* try to withdraw their funds during a short period of time, such as a couple of days?

The answer is that the bank wouldn't be able to raise enough cash to meet those demands. The reason is that banks convert most of their depositors' funds into loans made to borrowers; that's how banks earn revenue—by charging interest on loans. Bank loans, however, are illiquid: they can't easily be converted into cash on short notice. To see why, imagine that First Street Bank has lent $100,000 to Drive-a-Peach Used Cars, a local dealership. To raise cash to meet demands for withdrawals, First Street can sell its loan to Drive-a-Peach to someone else—another bank or an individual investor. But if First Street tries to sell the loan quickly, potential buyers will be wary: they will suspect that First Street wants to sell the loan because there is something wrong and the loan might not be repaid. As a result, First Street Bank can sell the loan quickly only by offering it for sale at a deep discount—say, a discount of 50%, or $50,000.

The upshot is that, if a significant number of First Street's depositors suddenly decided to withdraw their funds, the bank's efforts to raise the necessary cash quickly would force it to sell off its assets very cheaply. Inevitably, this would lead to a *bank failure*: the bank would be unable to pay off its depositors in full.

What might start this whole process? That is, what might lead First Street's depositors to rush to pull their money out? A plausible answer is a spreading rumor that the bank is in financial trouble. Even if depositors aren't sure the rumor is true, they are likely to play it safe and get their money out while they still can. And it gets worse: a depositor who simply thinks that *other* depositors are going to panic and try to get their money out will realize that this could "break the bank." So he or she joins the rush. In other words, fear about a bank's financial condition can be a self-fulfilling prophecy:

FYI It's a Wonderful Banking System

Next Christmastime, it's a sure thing that at least one TV channel will show the 1946 film *It's a Wonderful Life*, featuring Jimmy Stewart as George Bailey, a small-town banker whose life is saved by an angel. The movie's climactic scene is a run on Bailey's bank, as fearful depositors rush to take their funds out.

When the movie was made, such scenes were still fresh in Americans' memories. There was a wave of bank runs in late 1930, a second wave in the spring of 1931, and a third wave in early 1933. By the end, more than a third of the nation's banks had failed. To bring the panic to an end, on March 6, 1933, the newly inaugurated president, Franklin Delano Roosevelt, closed all banks for a week to give bank regulators time to shut down unhealthy banks and certify healthy ones.

Since then, regulation has protected the United States and other wealthy countries against most bank runs. In fact, the scene in *It's a Wonderful Life* was already out of date when the movie was made. But the last decade has seen several waves of bank runs in developing countries. For example, bank runs played a role in an economic crisis that swept Southeast Asia in 1997–1998 and in the severe economic crisis in Argentina, which began in late 2001.

In July 2008, panicky IndyMac depositors lined up to pull their money out of the troubled California bank.

Notice that we said "most bank runs." There are some limits on deposit insurance; in particular, currently only the first $250,000 of any bank account is insured. As a result, there can still be a rush to pull money out of a bank perceived as troubled. In fact, that's exactly what happened to IndyMac, a Pasadena-based lender that had made a large number of questionable home loans, in July 2008. As questions about IndyMac's financial soundness were raised, depositors began pulling out funds, forcing federal regulators to step in and close the bank. Unlike in the bank runs of the 1930s, however, most depositors got all their funds back—and the panic at IndyMac did not spread to other institutions.

FOCUS Flip It

For review, students can view the Jacob Clifford video "How Banks Create Money and the Money Multiplier" (see econextras video list with hyperlinks on the bcs and TRFD).

FOCUS Active Learning

To show students what a bank run looks like, show the related clip from *It's a Wonderful Life* with Jimmy Stewart. Either play the actual movie or search YouTube.com for the clip. Ask the following:

- Why doesn't the bank have all of its money on hand? *The bank loaned most of it out to other people.*
- Bank runs seldom happen today. What stops people from making runs on banks? *Safety measures such as deposit insurance, reserve and capital requirements, other banking regulations, and the ability to borrow money from the Federal Reserve help prevent bank runs.*

St. Louis Federal Reserve Bank Resources

"What Really Caused the Great Depression?," *The Great Depression Curriculum Unit, Lesson 3*

Through participation in two simulations, students determine that bank panics and a shrinking money supply were the primary causes of the Great Depression. Through an additional activity, they see how the many other factors they have discussed, such as problems in the agricultural sector and the stock market crash, exacerbated the situation.

depositors who believe that other depositors will rush to the exit will rush to the exit themselves.

A **bank run** is a phenomenon in which many of a bank's depositors try to withdraw their funds due to fears of a bank failure. Moreover, bank runs aren't bad only for the bank in question and its depositors. Historically, they have often proved contagious, with a run on one bank leading to a loss of faith in other banks, causing additional bank runs. The FYI "It's a Wonderful Banking System" describes an actual case of just such a contagion, the wave of bank runs that swept across the United States in the early 1930s. In response to that experience and similar experiences in other countries, the United States and most other modern governments have established a system of bank regulations that protects depositors and prevents most bank runs.

A **bank run** is a phenomenon in which many of a bank's depositors try to withdraw their funds due to fears of a bank failure.

Bank Regulation

Should you worry about losing money in the United States due to a bank run? No. After the banking crises of the 1930s, the United States and most other countries put into place a system designed to protect depositors and the economy as a whole against bank runs. This system has three main features: *deposit insurance, capital requirements,* and *reserve requirements.* In addition, banks have access to the *discount window,* a source of loans from the Federal Reserve when they're needed.

Deposit Insurance Almost all banks in the United States advertise themselves as a "member of the FDIC"—the Federal Deposit Insurance Corporation. The FDIC provides **deposit insurance**, a guarantee that depositors will be paid even if the bank can't come up with the funds, up to a maximum amount per account. As this book was going to press, the FDIC guaranteed the first $250,000 of each account.

It's important to realize that deposit insurance doesn't just protect depositors if a bank actually fails. The insurance also eliminates the main reason for bank runs: since depositors know their funds are safe even if a bank fails, they have no incentive to rush to pull them out because of a rumor that the bank is in trouble.

Deposit insurance guarantees that a bank's depositors will be paid even if the bank can't come up with the funds, up to a maximum amount per account.

Capital Requirements Deposit insurance, although it protects the banking system against bank runs, creates a well-known incentive problem. Because depositors are protected from loss, they have no incentive to monitor their bank's financial health, allowing risky behavior by the bank to go undetected. At the same time, the owners of banks have an incentive to engage in overly risky investment behavior, such as making questionable loans at high interest rates. That's because if all goes well, the owners profit; and if things go badly, the government covers the losses through federal deposit insurance.

To reduce the incentive for excessive risk-taking, regulators require that the owners of banks hold substantially more assets than the value of bank deposits. That way, the bank will have assets larger than its deposits even if some of its loans go bad, and losses will accrue against the bank owners' assets, rather than against the government. The excess of a bank's assets over its bank deposits and other liabilities is called the *bank's capital.* For example, First Street Bank has capital of $100,000, equal to 9% of the total value of its assets. In practice, banks' capital is required to equal at least 7% of the value of their assets.

Reserve Requirements Another regulation used to reduce the risk of bank runs is **reserve requirements**, rules set by the Federal Reserve that establish the required reserve ratio for banks. For example, in the United States, the required reserve ratio for checkable bank deposits is currently between zero and 10%, depending on the amount deposited at the bank.

The Discount Window One final protection against bank runs is the fact that the Federal Reserve stands ready to lend money to banks through a channel known as the **discount window**. The ability to borrow money means a bank can avoid being forced

Reserve requirements are rules set by the Federal Reserve that determine the required reserve ratio for banks.

The **discount window** is the channel through which the Federal Reserve lends money to banks.

TEACH Teach It

Stress that there are measures in place to protect banks and depositors. Make sure to discuss the fractional reserves and discount window with students. If banks can't meet their reserve requirement, they can acquire short-term loans from the central bank or from other banks. You will discuss this further in Module 27.

TEACH Teach It

Let students know that anyone can start a bank if he or she has enough money. They should only put their money in a bank that is FDIC insured. This insurance is designed to prevent bank runs like the one depicted in the opening film clip. Capital requirements also help protect deposits by requiring banks to keep a specific capital-to-asset ratio.

FOCUS In the News

TRM Have students read the Reuters article "Big U.S. Banks Must Boost Capital by $68 Billion under New Rules" at http://tinyurl.com/mbsmw3c. See **Worksheet 25.1 (Big Banks)** from the TRM for questions on this article.

St. Louis Federal Reserve Bank Resources

The Fed's Toolbox

In this lesson, students learn that the Federal Reserve System uses its monetary policy tools to influence the level of reserves in the banking system. Students participate in a simulation to demonstrate how the Fed uses open market operations to achieve its dual mandate of price stability and maximum employment. Students also learn about other monetary tools: the discount rate, reserve requirements, and interest on reserves—a relatively new monetary policy tool. Finally, students apply their knowledge of monetary policy to suggest possible Federal Reserve policy responses to proposed economic conditions.

FOCUS Active Learning

Show the video "Episode 30: Creating Money" which explains how money is created (see econextras video list with hyperlinks on the bcs and TRFD). Conduct a think-pair-share and have students explain the money creation process to a partner. What happens when money is withdrawn from the banking system? *The money that was "created" by the banking system is now destroyed.* Explain that the bank doesn't actually shred the money because it was only created in accounting records. All the bank does is reduce its loans, so the money that was created in the accounts isn't there anymore.

TEACH Teach It

Walk students through the money creation process using Figure 25.3 and Table 25.1. This is a frequently tested topic, so students need to be comfortable with the concept.

FOCUS Active Learning

TRM For practice working with T-accounts, assign **Worksheet 25.2 (Bank Expansion of Deposits)** from the TRM. Students can complete this as homework or in-class group work.

to sell its assets at fire-sale prices in order to satisfy the demands of a sudden rush of depositors demanding cash. Instead, it can turn to the Federal Reserve and borrow the funds it needs to pay off depositors.

Determining the Money Supply

Without banks, there would be no checkable deposits, and so the quantity of currency in circulation would equal the money supply. In that case, the money supply would be determined solely by whoever controls government minting and printing presses. But banks do exist, and through their creation of checkable bank deposits, they affect the money supply in two ways. First, banks remove some currency from circulation: dollar bills that are sitting in bank vaults, as opposed to sitting in people's wallets, aren't part of the money supply. Second, and much more importantly, banks create money by accepting deposits and making loans—that is, they make the money supply larger than just the value of currency in circulation. Our next topic is how banks create money and what determines the amount of money they create.

AP® Exam Tip

The money that banks create is recorded in accounts. Banks do not print money—only the Treasury can do that.

How Banks Create Money

To see how banks create money, let's examine what happens when someone decides to deposit currency in a bank. Consider the example of Silas, a miser, who keeps a shoebox full of cash under his bed. Suppose Silas realizes that it would be safer, as well as more convenient, to deposit that cash in the bank and to use his debit card when shopping. Assume that he deposits $1,000 into a checkable account at First Street Bank. What effect will Silas's actions have on the money supply?

Jonathan Kitchen/Photographer's Choice RF/Getty Images

Panel (a) of **Figure 25.3** shows the initial effect of his deposit. First Street Bank credits Silas with $1,000 in his account, so the economy's checkable bank deposits rise by $1,000. Meanwhile, Silas's cash goes into the vault, raising First Street's reserves by $1,000 as well.

This initial transaction has no effect on the money supply. Currency in circulation, part of the money supply, falls by $1,000; checkable bank deposits, also part of the money supply, rise by the same amount.

Figure 25.3 Effect on the Money Supply of Turning Cash into a Checkable Deposit at First Street Bank

(a) Initial Effect Before Bank Makes a New Loan

Assets		Liabilities	
Loans	No change	Checkable deposits	+$1,000
Reserves	+$1,000		

(b) Effect When Bank Makes a New Loan

Assets		Liabilities
Loans	+$900	No change
Reserves	−$900	

When Silas deposits $1,000 (which had been stashed under his bed) into a checkable bank account, there is initially no effect on the money supply: currency in circulation falls by $1,000, but checkable bank deposits rise by $1,000. The corresponding entries on the bank's T-account, depicted in panel (a), show deposits initially rising by $1,000 and the bank's reserves initially rising by $1,000. In the second stage, depicted in panel (b), the bank holds 10% of Silas's deposit ($100) as reserves and lends out the rest ($900) to Mary. As a result, its reserves fall by $900 and its loans increase by $900. Its liabilities, including Silas's $1,000 deposit, are unchanged. The money supply, the sum of checkable bank deposits and currency in circulation, has now increased by $900—the $900 now held by Mary.

But this is not the end of the story because First Street Bank can now lend out part of Silas's deposit. Assume that it holds 10% of Silas's deposit—$100—in reserves and lends the rest out in cash to Silas's neighbor, Mary. The effect of this second stage is shown in panel (b) of Figure 25.3. First Street's deposits remain unchanged, and so does the value of its assets. But the composition of its assets changes: by making the loan, it reduces its reserves by $900, so that they are only $100 larger than they were before Silas made his deposit. In the place of the $900 reduction in reserves, the bank has acquired an IOU, its $900 cash loan to Mary. So by putting $900 of Silas's cash back into circulation by lending it to Mary, First Street Bank has, in fact, increased the money supply. That is, the sum of currency in circulation and checkable bank deposits has risen by $900 compared to what it had been when Silas's cash was still under his bed. Although Silas is still the owner of $1,000, now in the form of a checkable deposit, Mary has the use of $900 in cash from her borrowings.

This may not be the end of the story either. Suppose that Mary uses her cash to buy a television and a Blu-ray player from Acme Merchandise. What does Anne Acme, the store's owner, do with the cash? If she holds on to it, the money supply doesn't increase any further. But suppose she deposits the $900 into a checkable bank deposit—say, at Second Street Bank. Second Street Bank, in turn, will keep only part of that deposit in reserves, lending out the rest, creating still more money.

Assume that Second Street Bank, like First Street Bank, keeps 10% of any bank deposit in reserves and lends out the rest. Then it will keep $90 in reserves and lend out $810 of Anne's deposit to another borrower, further increasing the money supply.

Table 25.1 shows the process of money creation we have described so far. At first the money supply consists only of Silas's $1,000. After he deposits the cash into a checkable bank deposit and the bank makes a loan, the money supply rises to $1,900. After the second deposit and the second loan, the money supply rises to $2,710. And the process will, of course, continue from there. (Although we have considered the case in which Silas places his cash in a checkable bank deposit, the results would be the same if he put it into any type of near-money.)

Table 25.1 How Banks Create Money

	Currency in circulation	Checkable bank deposits	Money supply
First stage: Silas keeps his cash under his bed.	$1,000	$0	$1,000
Second stage: Silas deposits cash in First Street Bank, which lends out $900 to Mary, who then pays it to Anne Acme.	900	1,000	1,900
Third stage: Anne Acme deposits $900 in Second Street Bank, which lends out $810 to another borrower.	810	1,900	2,710

This process of money creation may sound familiar. Recall the *spending multiplier process* that we described in Module 16: an initial increase in spending leads to a rise in real GDP, which leads to a further rise in spending, which leads to a further rise in real GDP, and so on. What we have here is another kind of multiplier—the *money multiplier.* Next, we'll learn what determines the size of this multiplier.

Reserves, Bank Deposits, and the Money Multiplier

In tracing out the effect of Silas's deposit in Table 25.1, we assumed that the funds a bank lends out always end up being deposited either in the same bank or in another bank—so funds disbursed as loans come back to the banking system, even if not to the lending

FOCUS In the News

Listen to the March 24, 2013, NPR podcast "Where's George?: The Trail of $1 Bills Across the U.S." (http://www.npr.org/2013/03/24/174966382/wheres-george-the-trail-of-1-bills-across-the-u-s). Ask students to explain how this project might help them understand the way in which the money multiplier works. *It allows them to see how a dollar can be spent more than once during the same year and how it travels around the nation and possibly the world.*

FOCUS Active Learning

TRM For practice working with T-accounts, assign **Worksheet 25.3 (T-Accounts)** from the TRM. Students can complete this as homework or in-class group work.

FOCUS Active Learning

TRM Remind students that banks can only loan out what is in excess reserves. For practice working with the money multiplier, assign **Worksheet 25.4 (Reserve Requirement and the Multiplier)** from the TRM. Students can complete this as homework or in-class group work.

FOCUS Flip It

For review, students can view the Jacob Clifford video "Macro 4.4—Money Multiplier and the Reserve Requirement" (see econextras video list with hyperlinks on the bcs and TRFD).

bank itself. In reality, some of these loaned funds may be held by borrowers in their wallets and not deposited in a bank, meaning that some of the loaned amount "leaks" out of the banking system. Such leaks reduce the size of the money multiplier, just as leaks of real income into savings reduce the size of the real GDP multiplier. (Bear in mind, however, that the "leak" here comes from the fact that borrowers keep some of their funds in currency, rather than the fact that consumers save some of their income.) But let's set that complication aside for a moment and consider how the money supply is determined in a "checkable-deposits-only" monetary system, in which funds are always deposited in bank accounts and none are held in wallets as currency. That is, in our checkable-deposits-only monetary system, any and all funds borrowed from a bank are immediately deposited into a checkable bank account. We'll assume that banks are required to satisfy a minimum reserve ratio of 10% and that every bank lends out all of its **excess reserves**, reserves over and above the amount needed to satisfy the minimum reserve ratio.

Excess reserves are a bank's reserves over and above its required reserves.

AP® Exam Tip

Excess reserves are important because these reserves are what banks can loan out to borrowers.

Now suppose that for some reason a bank suddenly finds itself with $1,000 in excess reserves. What happens? The answer is that the bank will lend out that $1,000, which will end up as a checkable bank deposit somewhere in the banking system, launching a money multiplier process very similar to the process shown in Table 25.1. In the first stage, the bank lends out its excess reserves of $1,000, which becomes a checkable bank deposit somewhere. The bank that receives the $1,000 deposit keeps 10%, or $100, as reserves and lends out the remaining 90%, or $900, which again becomes a checkable bank deposit somewhere. The bank receiving this $900 deposit again keeps 10%, which is $90, as reserves and lends out the remaining $810. The bank receiving this $810 keeps $81 in reserves and lends out the remaining $729, and so on. As a result of this process, the total increase in checkable bank deposits is equal to a sum that looks like:

$$\$1{,}000 + \$900 + \$810 + \$729 + \ldots$$

We'll use the symbol rr for the reserve ratio. More generally, the total increase in checkable bank deposits that is generated when a bank lends out $1,000 in excess reserves is:

$$\textbf{(25-1)}\quad \$1{,}000 + \$1{,}000 \times (1 - rr) + \$1{,}000 \times (1 - rr)^2 + \$1{,}000 \times (1 - rr)^3 + \ldots$$

As we have seen, an infinite series of this form can be simplified to $\$1{,}000/rr$. We must introduce another term before formally defining the money multiplier, but we can now see its usefulness: it is the factor by which we multiply an initial increase in excess reserves to find the total resulting increase in checkable bank deposits:

$$\textbf{(25-2)}\quad \text{Money multiplier} = \frac{1}{rr}$$

AP® Exam Tip

The money multiplier is $\frac{1}{rr}$ where rr is the reserve ratio. Be sure to know this frequently tested formula.

Given a reserve ratio of 10%, or 0.1, a $1,000 increase in excess reserves will increase the total value of checkable bank deposits by $\$1{,}000 \times 1/rr = \$1{,}000/0.1 = \$10{,}000$. In fact, in a checkable-deposits-only monetary system, the total value of checkable bank deposits will be equal to the value of bank reserves divided by the reserve ratio. Or to put it a different way, if the reserve ratio is 10%, each $1 of reserves held by a bank supports $\$1/rr = \$1/0.1 = \$10$ of checkable bank deposits.

The Money Multiplier in Reality

In reality, the determination of the money supply is more complicated than our simple model suggests because it depends not only on the ratio of reserves to bank deposits but also on the fraction of the money supply that individuals choose to hold in the form of currency. In fact, we already saw this in our example of Silas depositing the cash instead of holding it under his bed: when he chose to hold a checkable bank deposit instead of currency, he set in motion an increase in the money supply.

250 Section 5 The Financial Sector

To define the money multiplier in practice, we need to understand that the Federal Reserve controls the **monetary base**, the sum of currency in circulation and the reserves held by banks. The Federal Reserve does not determine how that sum is allocated between bank reserves and currency in circulation. Consider Silas and his deposit one more time: by taking the cash from under his bed and depositing it in a bank, he reduced the quantity of currency in circulation but increased bank reserves by an equal amount. So while the allocation of the monetary base changes—the amount in reserves grows and the amount in circulation shrinks—the total of these two, the monetary base, remains unchanged.

The monetary base is different from the money supply in two ways. First, bank reserves, which are part of the monetary base, aren't considered part of the money supply. A $1 bill in someone's wallet is considered money because it's available for an individual to spend, but a $1 bill held as bank reserves in a bank vault or deposited at the Federal Reserve isn't considered part of the money supply because it's not available for spending. Second, checkable bank deposits, which are part of the money supply because they are available for spending, aren't part of the monetary base.

Figure 25.4 shows the two concepts schematically. The circle on the left represents the monetary base, consisting of bank reserves plus currency in circulation. The circle on the right represents the money supply, consisting mainly of currency in circulation plus checkable or near-checkable bank deposits. As the figure indicates, currency in circulation is part of both the monetary base and the money supply. But bank reserves aren't part of the money supply, and checkable or near-checkable bank deposits aren't part of the monetary base. In normal times, most of the monetary base actually consists of currency in circulation, which also makes up about half of the money supply.

Now we can formally define the **money multiplier**: it's the ratio of the money supply to the monetary base. Most importantly, this tells us the total number of dollars created in the banking system by each $1 addition to the monetary base. We have seen that in a simple situation in which banks hold no excess reserves and all cash is deposited in banks, the money multiplier is $1/rr$. So if the reserve requirement is 0.1 (the minimum required ratio for most checkable deposits in the United States), the money multiplier is $1/0.1 = 10$; if the Federal Reserve adds $100 to the monetary base, the money supply will increase by $10 \times \$100 = \$1{,}000$. During normal times, the actual money multiplier in the United States, using M1 as our measure of money, is about 1.9. That's a lot smaller than 10. Normally, the reason the actual money multiplier is so small arises from the fact that people hold significant amounts of cash, and a dollar of currency in circulation, unlike a dollar in reserves, doesn't support multiple dollars of the money supply. In fact, currency in circulation normally accounts for more than 90% of the monetary base.

Currency held as bank reserves isn't part of the money supply, but it is part of the monetary base.

The **monetary base** is the sum of currency in circulation and bank reserves.

The **money multiplier** is the ratio of the money supply to the monetary base. It indicates the total number of dollars created in the banking system by each $1 addition to the monetary base.

Figure 25.4 The Monetary Base and the Money Supply

The monetary base is equal to bank reserves plus currency in circulation. It is different from the money supply, consisting mainly of checkable or near-checkable bank deposits plus currency in circulation. Each dollar of bank reserves backs several dollars of bank deposits, making the money supply larger than the monetary base.

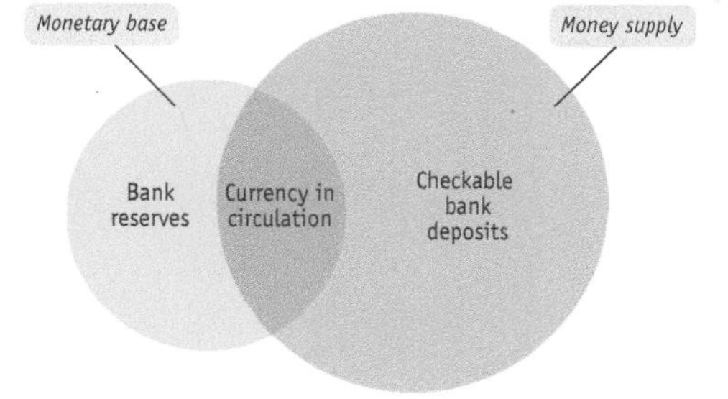

FOCUS Test It

Assign Question 2 from the 2012 released AP® exam at http://tinyurl.com/k8flhc5. It is recommended that students take $12\frac{1}{2}$ minutes to answer this question to match the time suggested for the AP® exam. The rubric may be found at http://tinyurl.com/lta6pdq.

TEACH Teach It

The money supply is M1, the value of financial assets in the economy. Bank reserves include vault cash plus the money that banks have on deposit with the Federal Reserve. The monetary base is currency in circulation plus the bank reserves; it is thus smaller than the money supply (M1).

OPEN & CLOSE Exit Slip

TRM *Please see **Exit Slip: Module 25** in the TRM for formative multiple-choice questions to ask before finishing your lesson. These questions will help you quickly assess whether your students have mastered the module's concepts before moving on.*

Answers to the Exit Slip Questions

1. C
2. C
3. C

MODULE 25 Review

Check Your Understanding

1. Suppose you are a depositor at First Street Bank. You hear a rumor that the bank has suffered serious losses on its loans. Every depositor knows that the rumor isn't true, but each thinks that most other depositors believe the rumor. Why, in the absence of deposit insurance, could this lead to a bank run? How does deposit insurance change the situation?

2. A con artist has a great idea: he'll open a bank without investing any capital and lend all the deposits at high interest rates to real estate developers. If the real estate market booms, the loans will be repaid and he'll make high profits. If the real estate market goes bust, the loans won't be repaid and the bank will fail—but he will not lose any of his own wealth. How would modern bank regulation frustrate his scheme?

3. Assume that total reserves are equal to $200 and total checkable bank deposits are equal to $1,000. Also assume that the public does not hold any currency and banks hold no excess reserves. Now suppose that the required reserve ratio falls from 20% to 10%. Trace out how this leads to an expansion in bank deposits.

4. Take the example of Silas depositing his $1,000 in cash into First Street Bank and assume that the required reserve ratio is 10%. But now assume that each recipient of a bank loan keeps half the loan in cash and deposits the rest. Trace out the resulting expansion in the money supply through at least three rounds of deposits.

Tackle the Test: Multiple-Choice Questions

1. Bank reserves include which of the following?
   - I. currency in bank vaults
   - II. bank deposits held in accounts at the Federal Reserve
   - III. customer deposits in bank checking accounts
   - a. I only
   - b. II only
   - c. III only
   - d. I and II only
   - e. I, II, and III

2. The fraction of bank deposits actually held as reserves is the
   - a. reserve ratio.
   - b. required reserve ratio.
   - c. excess reserve ratio.
   - d. reserve requirement.
   - e. monetary base.

3. Bank regulation includes which of the following?
   - I. deposit insurance
   - II. capital requirements
   - III. reserve requirements
   - a. I only
   - b. II only
   - c. III only
   - d. I and II
   - e. I, II, and III

4. Which of the following changes would be the most likely to reduce the size of the money multiplier?
   - a. a decrease in the required reserve ratio
   - b. a decrease in excess reserves
   - c. an increase in cash holding by consumers
   - d. a decrease in bank runs
   - e. an increase in deposit insurance

5. The monetary base equals
   - a. currency in circulation.
   - b. bank reserves.
   - c. currency in circulation − bank reserves.
   - d. currency in circulation + bank reserves.
   - e. currency in circulation/bank reserves.

Answers to Module 25 Review Questions

Check Your Understanding

1. Even though you know that the rumor about the bank is not true, you are concerned about other depositors pulling their money out of the bank. And you know that if enough other depositors pull out their money, the bank will fail. In that case, it is rational for you to withdraw your money before the bank fails. All depositors will think like this, so even if they all know that the rumor is false, they may still rationally pull out their money, leading to a bank run. Deposit insurance leads depositors to worry less about the possibility of a bank run. Even if a bank fails, the FDIC will currently pay each depositor up to $250,000 per account. This will make you much less likely to withdraw your money in response to a rumor. Since other depositors will think the same, there will be no bank run.

2. The aspects of modern bank regulation that would frustrate this scheme are capital requirements and reserve requirements. Capital requirements mean that a bank has to have a certain amount of capital—the difference between its assets (loans plus reserves) and its liabilities (deposits). Thus, the con artist could not open a bank without putting in any of his own wealth because his bank would need the required amount of capital—that is, it would need to hold more assets (loans plus reserves) than deposits. So the con artist would be at risk of losing his own wealth if his loans turned out badly. Also, the reserve requirement would prevent the con artist from lending out all of the deposits.

3. Since they have to hold only $100 in reserves, instead of $200, banks now lend out $100 of their reserves. Whoever borrows the $100 will deposit it in a bank (or spend it, and the recipient will deposit it in a bank), which will lend out $100 × (1 − *rr*) = $100 × 0.9 = $90. The borrowed $90 will likewise find its way into a bank, which will lend out $90 × 0.9 = $81, and so on. Overall, deposits will increase by $100/0.1 = $1,000.

4. Silas puts $1,000 in the bank, of which the bank lends out $1,000 × (1 − *rr*) = $1,000 × 0.9 = $900. Whoever borrows the $900 will keep $450 in cash and deposit $450 in the bank. The bank will lend out $450 × 0.9 = $405. Whoever borrows the $405 will keep $202.50 in cash and deposit $202.50 in the bank. The bank will lend out $202.50 × 0.9 = $182.25, and so on. Overall, this leads to an increase in deposits of $1,000 + $450 + $202.50 + ... Unlike the case in which loan recipients deposit their entire loans, this story involves loans partially held as cash. That cash is part of the money supply, so the calculation of the change in the money supply must account for both the reduction in cash holdings by Silas and the additional amounts held in cash by borrowers. That is, the amount of currency in circulation changes by −$1,000 + $450 + $202.50 + ... The money supply therefore increases by the sum of the increase in deposits and the change in currency in circulation, which is $1,000 − $1,000 + $450 + $450 + $202.50 + $202.50 + . . . and so on.

Tackle the Test: Multiple-Choice Questions

1. d
2. a
3. e
4. c
5. d

Tackle the Test: Free-Response Questions

1. How will each of the following affect the money supply through the money multiplier process? Explain.
   a. People hold more cash.
   b. Banks hold more excess reserves.
   c. The Fed increases the required reserve ratio.

Rubric for FRQ 1 (6 points)

1 point: It will decrease.

1 point: Money held as cash does not support multiple dollars in the money supply.

1 point: It will decrease.

1 point: Excess reserves are not loaned out and therefore do not expand the money supply.

1 point: It will decrease.

1 point: Banks will have to hold more as reserves and therefore loan out less.

2. Suppose the required reserve ratio is 5%.
   a. If a bank has deposits of $100,000 and holds $10,000 as reserves, how much are its excess reserves? Explain.
   b. If a bank holds no excess reserves and it receives a new deposit of $1,000, how much of that $1,000 can the bank lend out and how much is the bank required to add to its reserves? Explain.
   c. By how much can an increase in excess reserves of $2,000 change the money supply in a checkable-deposits-only system? Explain.
   (4 points)

Tackle the Test: Free-Response Question

Rubric for FRQ 2 (4 points)

1 point: The bank must hold $5,000 as required reserves (5% of $100,000). It is holding $10,000, so $5,000 must be excess reserves.

1 point: The bank must hold an additional $50 as reserves because that is the reserve requirement multiplied by the deposit: 5% of $1,000. The bank can lend out $950.

1 point: $40,000

1 point: The money multiplier is $1/0.05 = 20$. An increase of $2,000 in excess reserves can increase the money supply by $\$2,000 \times 20 = \$40,000$.

PD To prepare for teaching this lesson, you may want to consult the **Module 26 Sample Lecture** in the TRM.

OPEN & CLOSE Start Here

Show the video "Episode 31: The Fed" (see econextras video list with hyperlinks on the bcs and TRFD). Do you think the 14-year terms for governors effectively insulate them from political pressure, as was intended by legislation establishing the Federal Reserve System? *Not really. Congressional legislation is needed to regulate the financial system, so the governors must have the support of Congress and the president in order for favorable legislation to pass.*

Corbis Premium RF/Alamy

MODULE 26 The Federal Reserve System: History and Structure

In this Module, you will learn to:

- Discuss the history of the Federal Reserve System
- Describe the structure of the Federal Reserve System
- Explain how the Federal Reserve has responded to major financial crises

AP® Exam Tip

The Federal Reserve is responsible for conducting monetary policy for the United States. Other nations have central banks with different names, and the AP® exam may simply refer to the "central bank" rather than identifying a particular central bank.

A **central bank** is an institution that oversees and regulates the banking system and controls the monetary base.

The Federal Reserve System

Who's in charge of ensuring that banks maintain enough reserves? Who decides how large the monetary base will be? The answer, in the United States, is an institution known as the Federal Reserve (or, informally, as "the Fed"). The Federal Reserve is a **central bank**—an institution that oversees and regulates the banking system and controls the monetary base. Other central banks include the Bank of England, the Bank of Japan, and the European Central Bank, or ECB.

An Overview of the Twenty-first Century American Banking System

Under normal circumstances, banking is a rather staid and unexciting business. Fortunately, bankers and their customers like it that way. However, there have been repeated episodes in which "sheer panic" would be the best description of banking conditions—the panic induced by a bank run and the specter of the collapse of a bank or multiple banks, leaving depositors penniless, bank shareholders wiped out, and borrowers unable to get credit. In this section, we'll give an overview of the behavior and regulation of the American banking system over the last century.

The creation of the Federal Reserve System in 1913 was largely a response to lessons learned in the Panic of 1907. In 2008, the United States found itself in the midst of a financial crisis that in many ways mirrored the Panic of 1907, which occurred almost exactly 100 years earlier.

St. Louis Federal Reserve Bank Resources

"Financial Crises, Reform, and Central Banking: Establishing the Federal Reserve," ***Page One Economics Classroom Edition*** **(January 2011)**

Financial crises and recessions have often led to significant financial reform. Perhaps the most noteworthy financial reform of the past century was the formation of the Federal Reserve System in 1913. This issue provides historical details of events leading up to the founding of the Federal Reserve.

254 Section 5 The Financial Sector

Crisis in American Banking at the Turn of the Twentieth Century

The creation of the Federal Reserve System in 1913 marked the beginning of the modern era of American banking. From 1864 until 1913, American banking was dominated by a federally regulated system of national banks. They alone were allowed to issue currency, and the currency notes they issued were printed by the federal government with uniform size and design. How much currency a national bank could issue depended on its capital. Although this system was an improvement on the earlier period in which banks issued their own notes with no uniformity and virtually no regulation, the national banking regime still suffered numerous bank failures and major financial crises—at least one and often two per decade.

The main problem afflicting the system was that the money supply was not sufficiently responsive: it was difficult to shift currency around the country to respond quickly to local economic changes. In particular, there was often a tug-of-war between New York City banks and rural banks for adequate amounts of currency. Rumors that a bank had insufficient currency to satisfy demands for withdrawals would quickly lead to a bank run. A bank run would then spark a contagion, setting off runs at other nearby banks, sowing widespread panic and devastation in the local economy. In response, bankers in some locations pooled their resources to create local clearinghouses that would jointly guarantee a member's liabilities in the event of a panic, and some state governments began offering deposit insurance on their banks' deposits.

The Pierpont Morgan Library/Art Resource, NY

In both the Panic of 1907 and the financial crisis of 2008, large losses from risky speculation destabilized the banking system.

However, the cause of the Panic of 1907 was different from those of previous crises; in fact, its cause was eerily similar to the roots of the 2008 crisis. Ground zero of the 1907 panic was New York City, but the consequences devastated the entire country, leading to a deep four-year recession. The crisis originated in institutions in New York known as trusts, bank-like institutions that accepted deposits but that were originally intended to manage only inheritances and estates for wealthy clients. Because these trusts were supposed to engage only in low-risk activities, they were less regulated, had lower reserve requirements, and had lower cash reserves than national banks. However, as the American economy boomed during the first decade of the twentieth century, trusts began speculating in real estate and the stock market, areas of speculation forbidden to national banks.

Being less regulated than national banks, trusts were able to pay their depositors higher returns. Yet trusts took a free ride on national banks' reputation for soundness, with depositors considering them equally safe. As a result, trusts grew rapidly: by 1907, the total assets of trusts in New York City were as large as those of national banks. Meanwhile, the trusts declined to join the New York Clearinghouse, a consortium of New York City national banks that guaranteed one another's soundness; that would have required the trusts to hold higher cash reserves, reducing their profits.

The Panic of 1907 began with the failure of the Knickerbocker Trust, a large New York City trust that failed when it suffered massive losses in unsuccessful stock market speculation. Quickly, other New York trusts came under pressure, and frightened depositors began queuing in long lines to withdraw their funds. The New York Clearinghouse declined to step in and lend to the trusts, and even healthy trusts came under serious assault. Within two days, a dozen major trusts had gone under. Credit markets froze, and the stock market fell dramatically as stock traders were unable to get credit to finance their trades and business confidence evaporated.

TEACH Teach It

Like many developments in government and business, our current Federal Reserve is a product of our history. When our banks and economies experienced periods of crisis, government created various laws and agencies to oversee the system and protect borrowers and lenders.

TEACH AP® Exam Tip

Alert students to the fact that they may see the term "central bank" rather than "Federal Reserve" on the AP® exam. The AP® exam is administered worldwide, and this terminology allows testing in other nations that have central banks that are not named as federal reserves. However, the central bank in the United States is indeed the Federal Reserve.

FOCUS Flip It

For review, students can view the Jacob Clifford video "Federal Reserve System—Quick Review" (see econextras video list with hyperlinks on the bcs and TRFD). Students should link this video to a discussion on the need for the creation of the Federal Reserve System in the first decades of the 20th century and the current role of the Fed in our economy.

Module 26 The Federal Reserve System: History and Structure 255

Fortunately, one of New York City's wealthiest men, the banker J. P. Morgan, quickly stepped in to stop the panic. Understanding that the crisis was spreading and would soon engulf healthy institutions, trusts and banks alike, he worked with other bankers, wealthy men such as John D. Rockefeller, and the U.S. Secretary of the Treasury to shore up the reserves of banks and trusts so they could withstand the onslaught of withdrawals. Once people were assured that they could withdraw their money, the panic ceased. Although the panic itself lasted little more than a week, it and the stock market collapse decimated the economy. A four-year recession ensued, with production falling 11% and unemployment rising from 3% to 8%.

Responding to Banking Crises: The Creation of the Federal Reserve

Concerns over the frequency of banking crises and the unprecedented role of J. P. Morgan in saving the financial system prompted the federal government to initiate banking reform. In 1913 the national banking system was eliminated and the Federal Reserve System was created as a way to compel all deposit-taking institutions to hold adequate reserves and to open their accounts to inspection by regulators. The Panic of 1907 convinced many that the time for centralized control of bank reserves had come. The Federal Reserve was given the sole right to issue currency in order to make the money supply sufficiently responsive to satisfy economic conditions around the country.

The Structure of the Fed

The legal status of the Fed is unusual: it is not exactly part of the U.S. government, but it is not really a private institution either. Strictly speaking, the Federal Reserve System consists of two parts: the Board of Governors and the 12 regional Federal Reserve Banks.

The Board of Governors, which oversees the entire system from its offices in Washington, D.C., is constituted like a government agency: its seven members are appointed by the president and must be approved by the Senate. However, they are appointed for 14-year terms, to insulate them from political pressure in their conduct of monetary policy. Although the chair is appointed more frequently—every four years—it is traditional for the chair to be reappointed and serve much longer terms. For example, William McChesney Martin was chair of the Fed from 1951 until 1970. Alan Greenspan, appointed in 1987, served as the Fed's chair until 2006.

The 12 Federal Reserve Banks each serve a region of the country, known as a *Federal Reserve district,* providing various banking and supervisory services. One of their jobs, for example, is to audit the books of private-sector banks to ensure their financial health. Each regional bank is run by a board of directors chosen from the local banking and business community. The Federal Reserve Bank of New York plays a special role: it carries out *open-market operations,* usually the main tool of monetary policy. **Figure 26.1** shows the 12 Federal Reserve districts and the city in which each regional Federal Reserve Bank is located.

Decisions about monetary policy are made by the Federal Open Market Committee, which consists of the Board of Governors plus five of the regional bank presidents. The president of the Federal Reserve Bank of New York is always on the committee, and the other four seats rotate among the 11 other regional bank presidents. The chair of the Board of Governors normally also serves as the chair of the Federal Open Market Committee.

The effect of this complex structure is to create an institution that is ultimately accountable to the voting public because the Board of Governors is chosen by the president and confirmed by the Senate, all of whom are themselves elected officials. But the long terms served by board members, as well as the indirectness of their appointment process, largely insulate them from short-term political pressures.

TEACH Teach It

Make sure students understand the structure of the Federal Reserve system, but don't spend a lot of time on this material as it is not heavily tested on the AP® exam. Ask these clarifying questions:

- Who appoints governors to serve on the Fed board? *The president, and then they are confirmed by the Senate.*
- How long do governors serve on the Fed board? *14-year terms*
- Why do they serve such long terms? *To insulate them from political pressure in their conduct of monetary policy*
- What is the Fed's most important function? *To conduct monetary policy*

The 7-member Board of Governors oversees the Federal Reserve System. The chair's term lasts 4 years, and reappointment for multiple terms is common.

TEACH Teach It

The 12-member Federal Open Market Committee (FOMC) is the most important committee of the Federal Reserve as it makes decisions about monetary policy for the nation.

St. Louis Federal Reserve Bank Resources

In Plain English Online Course for Consumers

Want your students to learn about the Federal Reserve? Have no fear! *In Plain English* describes the structure and functions of the Federal Reserve System in an easy-to-understand interactive format.

Additional St. Louis Fed resources on these topics are provided in the St. Louis Fed resource list in the TRM.

Figure 26.1 The Federal Reserve System

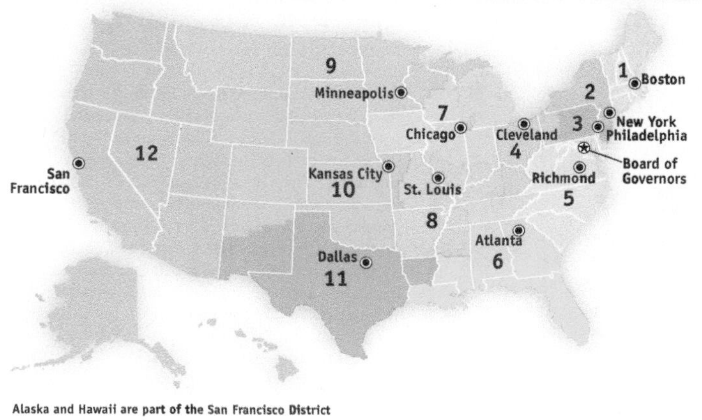

The Federal Reserve System consists of the Board of Governors in Washington, D.C., plus 12 regional Federal Reserve Banks. This map shows each of the 12 Federal Reserve districts.
Source: Board of Governors of the Federal Reserve System.

The Effectiveness of the Federal Reserve System

Although the Federal Reserve System standardized and centralized the holding of bank reserves, it did not eliminate the potential for bank runs because banks' reserves were still less than the total value of their deposits. The potential for more bank runs became a reality during the Great Depression. Plunging commodity prices hit American farmers particularly hard, precipitating a series of bank runs in 1930, 1931, and 1933, each of which started at midwestern banks and then spread throughout the country. After the failure of a particularly large bank in 1930, federal officials realized that the economy-wide effects compelled them to take a less hands-off approach and to intervene more vigorously. In 1932, the Reconstruction Finance Corporation (RFC) was established and given the authority to make loans to banks in order to stabilize the banking sector. In addition, the Glass-Steagall Act of 1933, which increased the ability of banks to borrow from the Federal Reserve System, was passed. A loan to a leading Chicago bank from the Federal Reserve appears to have stopped a major banking crisis in 1932. However, the beast had not yet been tamed. Banks became fearful of borrowing from the RFC because doing so signaled weakness to the public.

In the midst of the catastrophic bank run of 1933, the new U.S. president, Franklin Delano Roosevelt, was inaugurated. He immediately declared a "bank holiday," closing all banks until regulators could get a handle on the problem. In March 1933, emergency measures were adopted that gave the RFC extraordinary powers to stabilize and restructure the banking industry by providing capital to banks either by loans or by outright purchases of bank shares. With the new regulations, regulators closed nonviable banks and recapitalized viable ones by allowing the RFC to buy preferred shares in banks (shares that gave the U.S. government more rights than regular shareholders) and by greatly expanding banks' ability to borrow from the Federal Reserve. By 1933,

St. Louis Federal Reserve Bank Resources

Constitutionality of a Central Bank

Students learn about *McCulloch v. Maryland*, a case decided in 1819 over (1) whether the state of Maryland had the right to tax the Second Bank of the United States and (2) whether Congress had violated the Constitution in establishing the Bank. Students also review the expressed powers of Congress identified in the Constitution and analyze how Congress implements the necessary and proper (elastic) clause to enact its expressed powers. Finally, students use their knowledge of *McCulloch v. Maryland* and the necessary and proper clause to consider the constitutionality of the Federal Reserve System.

Module 26 The Federal Reserve System: History and Structure 257

Official White House Photo by Pete Souza

Like Franklin Delano Roosevelt, President Obama, shown here meeting with economic advisers, was faced with a major financial crisis upon taking office.

the RFC had invested over $17 billion (2013 dollars) in bank capital—one-third of the total capital of all banks in the United States at that time—and purchased shares in almost one-half of all banks. The RFC loaned more than $34 billion (2013 dollars) to banks during this period. Economic historians uniformly agree that the banking crises of the early 1930s greatly exacerbated the severity of the Great Depression, rendering monetary policy ineffective as the banking sector broke down and currency, withdrawn from banks and stashed under beds, reduced the money supply.

Although the powerful actions of the RFC stabilized the banking industry, new legislation was needed to prevent future banking crises. The Glass-Steagall Act of 1933 separated banks into two categories, **commercial banks**, depository banks that accepted deposits and were covered by deposit insurance, and **investment banks**, which engaged in creating and trading financial assets such as stocks and corporate bonds but were not covered by deposit insurance because their activities were considered more risky. Regulation Q prevented commercial banks from paying interest on checking accounts, in the belief that this would promote unhealthy competition between banks. In addition, investment banks were much more lightly regulated than commercial banks. The most important measure for the prevention of bank runs, however, was the adoption of federal deposit insurance (with an original limit of $2,500 per deposit).

These measures were clearly successful, and the United States enjoyed a long period of financial and banking stability. As memories of the bad old days dimmed, Depression-era bank regulations were lifted. Regulation Q was eliminated in 1980 and by 1999, the Glass-Steagall Act had been so weakened that commercial banks could deal in stocks and bonds among other financial assets.

A **commercial bank** accepts deposits and is covered by deposit insurance.

An **investment bank** trades in financial assets and is not covered by deposit insurance.

A **savings and loan (thrift)** is another type of deposit-taking bank, usually specialized in issuing home loans.

The Savings and Loan Crisis of the 1980s

Along with banks, the banking industry also included **savings and loans** (also called S&Ls or **thrifts**), institutions established to accept savings and turn them into long-term mortgages for home-buyers. S&Ls were covered by federal deposit insurance and were tightly regulated for safety. However, trouble hit in the 1970s, as high inflation led savers to withdraw their funds from low-interest-paying S&L accounts and put them into higher-paying money market accounts. In addition, the high inflation rate severely eroded the value of the S&Ls' assets, the long-term mortgages they held on their books.

In order to improve S&Ls' competitive position versus banks, Congress eased regulations to allow S&Ls to undertake much more risky investments in addition to long-term home mortgages. However, the new freedom did not bring with it increased oversight, leaving S&Ls with less oversight than banks.

Not surprisingly, during the real estate boom of the 1970s and 1980s, S&Ls engaged in overly risky real estate lending. Also, corruption occurred as some S&L executives used their institutions as private piggy banks. By the early 1980s, a large number of S&Ls had failed. Because accounts were covered by federal deposit insurance, the liabilities of a failed S&L were now liabilities of the federal government. From 1986 through 1995, the federal government closed over 1,000 failed S&Ls, costing U.S. taxpayers over $124 billion.

In a classic case of shutting the barn door after the horse has escaped, in 1989 Congress put in place comprehensive oversight of S&L activities. It also empowered Fannie Mae and Freddie Mac to take over much of the home mortgage lending previously done by S&Ls. Fannie Mae and Freddie Mac are quasi-governmental agencies created during the Great Depression to make homeownership more affordable for low- and moderate-income households. There is evidence that the S&L crisis helped cause a steep slowdown in the finance and real estate industries, leading to the recession of the early 1990s.

FOCUS Active Learning

Direct students to read the FAQ on how the Federal Reserve helps decrease the likelihood of another financial crisis, as answered by former Chairman Ben Bernanke (http://www.federalreserve.gov/faqs/banking_12777.htm). Ask students what the Fed is currently doing to prevent future financial crises like those of the 1980s and 2008. *The Fed is implementing Dodd–Frank Wall Street reform and the Consumer Protection Act, which will:*

- *Enhance regulators' ability to monitor and address threats to financial stability,*
- *Strengthen both the oversight of and ability to safely wind down systemically important financial institutions, and*
- *Improve the capacity of financial markets and infrastructures to absorb shocks.*

In addition, financial regulators are overseeing the system as a whole to identify risks in the system through the Office of Financial Stability Policy and Research.

258 Section 5 The Financial Sector

Back to the Future: The Financial Crisis of 2008

The financial crisis of 2008 shared features of previous crises. Like the Panic of 1907 and the S&L crisis, it involved institutions that were not as strictly regulated as deposit-taking banks, as well as excessive speculation. And like the crises of the early 1930s, it involved a U.S. government that was reluctant to take aggressive action until the scale of the devastation became clear. Enrichment Module A: Financial Markets and Crises provides a detailed account of the financial crisis of 2008. To summarize the situation briefly, historically low interest rates helped cause a boom in housing between 2003 and 2006. With home prices rising steadily, loans to home buyers with questionable finances seemed deceptively safe, and the number of such loans exploded. But then housing prices started falling in 2006, leaving many borrowers with homes that were worth less than the mortgage loans used to buy them. The resulting losses for lenders caused a collapse of trust in the financial system. Lending institutions were reluctant to make loans, and firms had difficulty obtaining enough money to continue their operations.

Beginning in mid-2007, the Federal Reserve took ambitious steps to make more cash available in the economy. It provided liquidity to the troubled financial system through discount window lending, and bought large quantities of other assets, mainly long-term government debt and the debt of Fannie Mae and Freddie Mac. The Fed and the Treasury Department also rescued several firms whose collapse could have been catastrophic for the economy, including the investment bank Bear Stearns and the insurance company AIG.

By the fall of 2010, the financial system was relatively stable, and major institutions had repaid much of the money the federal government had injected during the crisis. It was generally expected that taxpayers would end up losing little if any money. However, the recovery of the banks was not matched by a successful turnaround for the overall economy: although the recession that began in December 2007 officially ended in June 2009, unemployment remained stubbornly high.

Like earlier crises, the crisis of 2008 led to changes in banking regulation, most notably the Dodd-Frank financial regulatory reform bill enacted in 2010. We describe that bill briefly in the FYI box that follows.

FYI Regulation After the 2008 Crisis

In July 2010, President Obama signed the Wall Street Reform and Consumer Protection Act—generally known as Dodd-Frank, after its sponsors in the Senate and House, respectively—into law. It was the biggest financial reform enacted since the 1930s—not surprising given that the nation had just gone through the worst financial crisis since the 1930s. How did it change regulation?

For the most part, it left regulation of traditional deposit-taking banks more or less as it was. The main change these banks would face was the creation of a new agency, the Consumer Financial Protection Bureau, whose mission was to protect borrowers from being exploited through seemingly attractive financial deals they didn't understand.

The major changes came in the regulation of financial institutions other than banks—institutions that, as the fall of Lehman Brothers showed, could trigger banking crises. The new law gave a special government committee, the Financial Stability Oversight Council, the right to designate certain institutions as "systemically important" even if they weren't ordinary deposit-taking banks. These systemically important institutions would be subjected to bank-style regulation, including relatively high capital requirements and limits on the kinds of risks they could take. In addition, the federal government would acquire "resolution authority," meaning the right to seize troubled financial institutions in much the same way that it routinely takes over troubled banks.

Beyond this, the law established new rules on the trading of derivatives, those complex financial instruments that played an important role in the 2008 crisis: most derivatives would henceforth have to be bought and sold on exchanges, where everyone could observe their prices and the volume of transactions. The idea was to make the risks taken by financial institutions more transparent.

Overall, Dodd-Frank is probably best seen as an attempt to extend the spirit of old-fashioned bank regulation to the more complex financial system of the twenty-first century. Will it succeed in heading off future banking crises? Stay tuned.

Oli Scarff/Getty Images

St. Louis Federal Reserve Bank Resources

"Financial Regulation: A Primer on the Dodd-Frank Act," *Page One Economics Classroom Edition (May 2011)*

In July 2010, the Dodd-Frank Wall Street Reform and Consumer Protection Act of 2010 brought the most sweeping financial regulatory reform since the Great Depression. This issue outlines key provisions of the Act intended to prevent or reduce the impact of future financial crises and enhance consumer protection.

TEACH Teach It

This section deals with the history of the 2008 financial crisis, which will probably not be tested on the AP® exam. However, it will allow your students to understand how the crisis evolved and how the Federal Reserve sought to ease the crisis and increase stability in the economy.

FOCUS In the News

Have students read the article "The Federal Reserve's Response to the Financial Crisis and Actions to Foster Maximum Employment and Price Stability" at http://www.federalreserve.gov/monetarypolicy/bst_crisisresponse.htm.

Ask students to describe the three sets of tools used by the Fed in response to the financial crisis.

- *"The first set of tools, which are closely tied to the central bank's traditional role as the lender of last resort, involve the provision of short-term liquidity to banks and other depositories and financial institutions."*
- *"A second set of tools involve the provision of liquidity directly to borrowers and investors in key credit markets."*
- *"As a third set of instruments, the Federal Reserve expanded its traditional tool of open market operations to support the functioning of credit markets, put downward pressure on longer-term interest rates, and help to make broader financial conditions more accommodating through the purchase of longer-term securities for the Federal Reserve's portfolio."*

OPEN & CLOSE Exit Slip

TRM *Please see **Exit Slip: Module 26** in the TRM for formative multiple-choice questions to ask before finishing your lesson. These questions will help you quickly assess whether your students have mastered the module's concepts before moving on.*

Answers to the Exit Slip Questions

1. E
2. D
3. B

Answers to Module 26 Review Questions

Check Your Understanding

1. The Panic of 1907, the S&L crisis, and the crisis of 2008 all involved losses by financial institutions that were less regulated than banks. In the crises of 1907 and 2008, there was a widespread loss of confidence in the financial sector and collapse of credit markets. Like the crisis of 1907 and the S&L crisis, the crisis of 2008 exerted a powerful negative effect on the economy.

2. The creation of the Federal Reserve failed to prevent bank runs because it did not eradicate the fears of depositors that a bank collapse would cause them to lose their money. The bank run eventually stopped after federal deposit insurance was instituted and the public came to understand that their deposits were protected.

Tackle the Test: Multiple-Choice Questions

1. a
2. a
3. b
4. d
5. e

Tackle the Test: Free-Response Question

Rubric for FRQ 2 (6 points)

1 point: Oversees the Federal Reserve System and serves on the Federal Open Market Committee.

1 point: 7

1 point: The president of the United States

1 point: 14-year terms

1 point: To insulate appointees from political pressure

1 point: 4 years; may be reappointed

MODULE 26 Review

Check Your Understanding

1. What are the similarities between the Panic of 1907, the S&L crisis, and the crisis of 2008?
2. Why did the creation of the Federal Reserve fail to prevent the bank runs of the Great Depression? What measures did stop the bank runs?

Tackle the Test: Multiple-Choice Questions

1. Which of the following contributed to the creation of the Federal Reserve System?
   - I. the bank panic of 1907
   - II. the Great Depression
   - III. the savings and loan crisis of the 1980s
   - a. I only
   - b. II only
   - c. III only
   - d. I and II only
   - e. I, II, and III
2. Which of the following controls the monetary base?
   - a. the central bank
   - b. the Treasury
   - c. Congress
   - d. commercial banks
   - e. investment banks
3. Which of the following is NOT a role of the Federal Reserve System?
   - a. controlling bank reserves
   - b. printing currency (Federal Reserve notes)
   - c. carrying out monetary policy
   - d. supervising and regulating banks
   - e. holding reserves for commercial banks
4. Who oversees the Federal Reserve System?
   - a. Congress
   - b. the president of the United States
   - c. the Federal Open Market Committee
   - d. the Board of Governors of the Federal Reserve System
   - e. the Reconstruction Finance Corporation
5. Which of the following contributed to the financial crisis of 2008?
   - a. excessive speculation
   - b. inadequate regulation
   - c. delays in aggressive action by the government
   - d. low interest rates leading to a housing boom
   - e. all of the above

Tackle the Test: Free-Response Questions

1. a. What group determines monetary policy?
   b. How many members serve in this group?
   c. Who always serves in this group?
   d. Who sometimes serves in this group? Explain.

Rubric for FRQ 1 (5 points)

1 point: The Federal Open Market Committee (FOMC)

1 point: 12

1 point: Members of the Board of Governors and the New York Federal Reserve Bank president

1 point: 4 of the other 11 Federal Reserve Bank presidents

1 point: The 11 other Federal Reserve Bank presidents rotate their service on the FOMC.

2. a. What does the Board of Governors of the Federal Reserve System do?
   b. How many members serve on the group?
   c. Who appoints members?
   d. How long do members serve?
   e. Why do they serve a term of this length?
   f. How long does the chair serve?
   (6 points)

Drew Angerer/Getty Images

MODULE 27

The Federal Reserve System: Monetary Policy

In this Module, you will learn to:

- Describe the functions of the Federal Reserve System
- Explain the primary tools the Federal Reserve uses to influence the economy

The Federal Reserve System

In the previous module, you learned that the Federal Reserve System serves as the central bank of the United States. It has two parts: the Board of Governors, which is part of the U.S. government, and the 12 regional Federal Reserve Banks, which are privately owned. But what are the functions of the Federal Reserve System, and how does it serve them?

The Functions of the Federal Reserve System

Today, the Federal Reserve's functions fall into four basic categories: providing financial services to depository institutions, supervising and regulating banks and other financial institutions, maintaining the stability of the financial system, and conducting monetary policy. Let's look at each in turn.

AP® Exam Tip

Among the most important functions of the Federal Reserve is the conduct of monetary policy.

Provide Financial Services The 12 regional Federal Reserve Banks provide financial services to depository institutions such as banks and other large institutions, including the U.S. government. The Federal Reserve is sometimes referred to as the "banker's bank" because it holds reserves, clears checks, provides cash, and transfers funds for commercial banks—all services that banks provide for their customers. The Federal Reserve also acts as the banker and fiscal agent for the federal government. The U.S. Treasury has its checking account with the Federal Reserve, so when the federal government writes a check, it is written on an account at the Fed.

Supervise and Regulate Banking Institutions The Federal Reserve System is charged with ensuring the safety and soundness of the nation's banking and financial system. Each regional Federal Reserve Bank examines and regulates commercial banks

PD To prepare for teaching this lesson, you may want to consult the **Module 27 Sample Lecture** in the TRM.

OPEN & CLOSE Start Here

Go to http://www.econedlink.org/lessons/index.php?lid=1209&type=educator for the *EconEdLink* FOCUS ON ECONOMIC DATA lesson entitled "The Federal Reserve and Monetary Policy, October 29, 2014,".which discusses the state of the economy and the role of the Fed in achieving its twin goals of price stability and full employment. Use the student version, and work with the students to explore the ideas that will introduce this section.

TEACH AP® Exam Tip

There are four basic functions performed by a central bank: providing financial services to depository institutions, supervising and regulating banks and other financial institutions, maintaining the stability of the financial system, and conducting monetary policy. The AP® Macro exam will stress monetary policy over all other functions.

St. Louis Federal Reserve Bank Resources

Fedcation Video Series (Episodes 1 through 4)

The four episodes of this video series are designed to provide a brief overview of timely economics and personal finance topics, such as Fed monetary policy tools, credit scores, and more.

St. Louis Federal Reserve Bank Resources

"Could It Happen Again?," *The Great Depression Curriculum Unit, Lesson 6*

Students learn about the roles and functions of the Federal Reserve System. Through a simulation, they learn how the Fed manages the money supply through open market operations. They identify what central bankers have learned about implementing monetary policy as a result of the Great Depression. Furthermore, they recognize the steps the central bank has taken to respond effectively to financial crises since that time.

FOCUS Active Learning

TRM To help them better understand the tools of the Fed, have students watch "Episode 32: Monetary Policy" (see econextras video list with hyperlinks on the bcs and TRFD). They will need to understand and explain the effects of monetary policy for the AP® exam. To help students remember the linkages created through monetary policy, have them complete **Worksheet 27.1 (Monetary Policy Cause and Effect)** from the TRM. You can assign this as homework or in-class group work.

TEACH AP® Exam Tip

The Federal Reserve has three main policy tools at its disposal: reserve requirements, the discount rate, and, perhaps most importantly, open-market operations. Discuss each independently and ensure that your students know how to use them to correct problems in the economy like unemployment and inflation. Questions about the meaning and use of these tools have appeared in recent AP® Macro exams.

TEACH Connect It

Remind students that the reserve requirement (or required reserve ratio) is the fraction of deposits that banks must hold in their required reserves. The Fed can change the reserve requirement to manage the money supply, but it rarely does so because it is difficult for banks to change the amount of cash they hold in a short period of time.

TEACH Teach It

If banks don't have enough money to meet the reserve requirement, they can do one of two things: they can borrow from the Federal Reserve at the discount window or they can borrow from other banks in the federal funds market.

The federal funds rate often confuses students. They see it as borrowing from the Fed, so make sure you stress that the rate is determined by a market. Suppliers are banks that have excess funds to loan and demanders are banks that need short-term loans.

in its district. The Board of Governors also engages in regulation and supervision of financial institutions.

Maintain the Stability of the Financial System As we have seen, one of the major reasons the Federal Reserve System was created was to provide the nation with a safe and stable monetary and financial system. The Fed is charged with maintaining the integrity of the financial system. As part of this function, Federal Reserve Banks provide liquidity to financial institutions to ensure their safety and soundness.

Conduct Monetary Policy One of the Federal Reserve's most important functions is the conduct of monetary policy. As we will see, the Federal Reserve uses the tools of monetary policy to prevent or address extreme macroeconomic fluctuations in the U.S. economy.

What the Fed Does

How does the Fed perform its functions? The Federal Reserve has three main policy tools at its disposal: *reserve requirements,* the *discount rate,* and, perhaps most importantly, *open-market operations.* These tools play a part in how the Fed performs each of its functions as outlined below.

The **federal funds market** allows banks that fall short of the reserve requirement to borrow funds from banks with excess reserves.

The **federal funds rate** is the interest rate that banks charge other banks for loans, as determined in the federal funds market.

The **discount rate** is the interest rate the Fed charges on loans to banks.

The Reserve Requirement

In our discussion of bank runs, we noted that the Fed sets a minimum required reserve ratio, currently between zero and 10% for checkable bank deposits. Banks that fail to maintain at least the required reserve ratio on average over a two-week period face penalties.

What does a bank do if it has insufficient reserves to meet the Fed's reserve requirement? Normally, it borrows additional reserves from other banks via the **federal funds market**, a financial market that allows banks that fall short of the reserve requirement to borrow reserves (usually just overnight) from banks that are holding excess reserves. The interest rate in this market is determined by supply and demand, but the supply and demand for bank reserves are both strongly affected by Federal Reserve actions. Later we will see how the **federal funds rate**, the interest rate at which funds are borrowed and lent among banks in the federal funds market, plays a key role in modern monetary policy.

In order to alter the money supply, the Fed can change reserve requirements. If the Fed reduces the required reserve ratio, banks will lend a larger percentage of their deposits, leading to more loans and an increase in the money supply via the money multiplier. Alternatively, if the Fed increases the required reserve ratio, banks are forced to reduce their lending, leading to a fall in the money supply via the money multiplier. Under current practice, however, the Fed doesn't use changes in reserve requirements to actively manage the money supply. The last significant change in reserve requirements was in 1992.

Spencer Platt/Getty Images

A trader works on the floor of the New York Stock Exchange as the Federal Reserve announces that it will be keeping its key interest rate near zero.

The Discount Rate

Banks in need of reserves can also borrow from the Fed itself via the *discount window.* The **discount rate** is the interest rate the Fed charges on those loans. Normally, the discount rate is set 1 percentage point above the federal funds rate in order to discourage banks from turning to the Fed when they are in need of reserves.

In order to alter the money supply, the Fed can change the discount rate. Beginning in the fall of 2007, the Fed reduced the spread between the federal funds rate and the discount rate as part of its response to the ongoing financial crisis. As a result, by the spring of 2008 the discount rate was only 0.25 percentage points above the federal funds rate.

TEACH Teach It

To alter the money supply, the Fed can change the spread between the discount rate and the federal funds rate. How?

- If the Fed reduces the spread between the discount rate and the federal funds rate, the cost to banks of being short of reserves falls; banks respond by increasing their lending, and the money supply increases via the money multiplier.
- If the Fed increases the spread between the discount rate and the federal funds rate, bank lending falls—and so will the money supply via the money multiplier.

If the Fed reduces the spread between the discount rate and the federal funds rate, the cost to banks of being short of reserves falls. Banks respond by increasing their lending, and the money supply increases via the money multiplier. If the Fed increases the spread between the discount rate and the federal funds rate, bank lending falls—and so will the money supply via the money multiplier.

The Fed normally doesn't use the discount rate to actively manage the money supply. As we mentioned earlier, however, there was a temporary surge in lending through the discount window in 2007 in response to the financial crisis. Today, normal monetary policy is conducted almost exclusively using the Fed's third policy tool: open-market operations.

Open-Market Operations

Like the banks it oversees, the Federal Reserve has assets and liabilities. The Fed's assets consist of its holdings of debt issued by the U.S. government, mainly short-term U.S. government bonds with a maturity of less than one year, known as U.S. Treasury bills. Remember, the Fed and the U.S. government are not one entity; U.S. Treasury bills held by the Fed are a liability of the government but an asset of the Fed. The Fed's liabilities consist of currency in circulation and bank reserves. **Figure 27.1** summarizes the normal assets and liabilities of the Fed in the form of a T-account.

Figure 27.1 The Federal Reserve's Assets and Liabilities

The Federal Reserve holds its assets mostly in short-term government bonds called U.S. Treasury bills. Its liabilities are the monetary base—currency in circulation plus bank reserves.

Assets	Liabilities
Government debt (Treasury bills)	Monetary base (Currency in circulation + bank reserves)

In an **open-market operation**, the Federal Reserve buys or sells U.S. Treasury bills, normally through a transaction with *commercial banks*—banks that mainly make business loans, as opposed to home loans. The Fed never buys U.S. Treasury bills directly from the federal government. There's a good reason for this: when a central bank buys government debt directly from the government, it is lending directly to the government—in effect, the central bank is issuing "printing money" to finance the government's budget deficit. As we'll see later in the book, this has historically been a formula for disastrous levels of inflation.

An **open-market operation** is a purchase or sale of government debt by the Fed.

The two panels of **Figure 27.2** on the next page show the changes in the financial position of both the Fed and commercial banks that result from open-market operations. When the Fed buys U.S. Treasury bills from a commercial bank, it pays by crediting the bank's reserve account by an amount equal to the value of the Treasury bills. This is illustrated in panel (a): the Fed buys $100 million of U.S. Treasury bills from commercial banks, which increases the monetary base by $100 million because it increases bank reserves by $100 million. When the Fed sells U.S. Treasury bills to commercial banks, it debits the banks' accounts, reducing their reserves. This is shown in panel (b), where the Fed sells $100 million of U.S. Treasury bills. Here, bank reserves and the monetary base decrease.

You might wonder where the Fed gets the funds to purchase U.S. Treasury bills from banks. The answer is that it simply creates them with a stroke of the pen—or, these days, a click of the mouse—that credits the banks' accounts with extra reserves. The Fed issues currency to pay for Treasury bills only when banks want the additional reserves

TEACH Teach It

To alter the money supply, the Fed can buy or sell U.S. Treasury bills. How?

- When the Fed buys U.S. Treasury bills from a commercial bank, it pays by crediting the bank's reserve account by an amount equal to the value of the Treasury bills. For example, if the Fed buys $100 million of U.S. Treasury bills from commercial banks, this increases the monetary base by $100 million because it increases bank reserves by $100 million.
- When the Fed sells U.S. Treasury bills to commercial banks, it debits the banks' accounts, reducing their reserves. For example, when the Fed sells $100 million of U.S. Treasury bills, bank reserves and the monetary base decrease.

FOCUS Test It

To ______________ the money supply, the Fed could ______________.

A. decrease; lower the reserve requirements
B. increase; lower the discount rate
C. increase; conduct open-market sales
D. decrease; lower the federal funds rate
E. decrease; raise income taxes

Answer: B

If the Federal Reserve wants to increase the money supply, it will:

A. sell U.S. Treasury bills.
B. cut taxes across the board.
C. raise the reserve requirement.
D. buy U.S. Treasury bills.
E. increase the discount rate.

Answer: D

FOCUS In the News

TRM Ask students to read the October 2013 *Huffington Post* article "Federal Reserve Toughens Requirements for Biggest Banks" on liquidity coverage ratios (http://www.huffingtonpost.com/2013/10/24/federal-reserve-liquidity_n_4158388.html). See **Worksheet 27.2 (Bank Requirements)** from the TRM for questions on this article.

TEACH AP® Exam Tip

Open-market operations are the most important and frequently used tool the Fed utilizes to manage the money supply. These operations are frequently tested on the AP® exam, so it is essential that students have a good understanding of how they work.

TEACH Teach It

Remind students that the change in bank reserves caused by an open-market operation doesn't directly affect the money supply. Instead, it starts the money multiplier in motion. These funds are not subject to the reserve requirement, so the money multiplier acts on the entire amount.

FOCUS Active Learning

TRM Assign **Worksheet 27.3 (Tools of Monetary Policy)** from the TRM in class or as homework.

FOCUS Flip It

For review, students can view the Jacob Clifford video "Money Supply Macro Review" (see econ-extras video list with hyperlinks on the bcs and TRFD) and think about the three tools of the Fed and how they work.

Figure 27.2 Open-Market Operations by the Federal Reserve

(a) An Open-Market Purchase of $100 Million

	Assets		Liabilities	
Federal Reserve	Treasury bills	+$100 million	Monetary base	+$100 million
Commercial banks	Treasury bills	−$100 million	No change	
	Reserves	+$100 million		

(b) An Open-Market Sale of $100 Million

	Assets		Liabilities	
Federal Reserve	Treasury bills	−$100 million	Monetary base	−$100 million
Commercial banks	Treasury bills	+$100 million	No change	
	Reserves	−$100 million		

In panel (a), the Federal Reserve increases the monetary base by purchasing U.S. Treasury bills from private commercial banks in an open-market operation. Here, a $100 million purchase of U.S. Treasury bills by the Federal Reserve is paid for by a $100 million increase in the monetary base. This will ultimately lead to an increase in the money supply via the money multiplier as banks lend out some of these new reserves. In panel (b), the Federal Reserve reduces the monetary base by selling U.S. Treasury bills to private commercial banks in an open-market operation. Here, a $100 million sale of U.S. Treasury bills leads to a $100 million reduction in commercial bank reserves, resulting in a $100 million decrease in the monetary base. This will ultimately lead to a fall in the money supply via the money multiplier as banks reduce their loans in response to a fall in their reserves.

in the form of currency. Remember, the modern dollar is fiat money, which isn't backed by anything. So the Fed can add to the monetary base at its own discretion.

The change in bank reserves caused by an open-market operation doesn't directly affect the money supply. Instead, it starts the money multiplier in motion. After the $100 million increase in reserves shown in panel (a), commercial banks would lend out their additional reserves, immediately increasing the money supply by $100 million. Some of those loans would be deposited back into the banking system, increasing reserves again and permitting a further round of loans, and so on, leading to a rise in the money supply. An open-market sale has the reverse effect: bank reserves fall, requiring banks to reduce their loans, leading to a fall in the money supply.

Economists often say, loosely, that the Fed controls the money supply—checkable deposits plus currency in circulation. In fact, it controls only the monetary base—bank reserves plus currency in circulation. But by increasing or decreasing the monetary base, the Fed can exert a powerful influence on both the money supply and interest rates. This influence is the basis of monetary policy, discussed in detail in Modules 28 and 29.

The European Central Bank

As we noted earlier, the Fed is only one of a number of central banks around the world, and it's much younger than Sweden's Sveriges Riksbank and Britain's Bank of England. In general, other central banks operate in much the same way as the Fed. That's especially true of the only other central bank that rivals the Fed in terms of importance to the world economy: the European Central Bank.

The European Central Bank, known as the ECB, was created in January 1999 when 11 European nations abandoned their national currencies, adopted the euro as their

St. Louis Federal Reserve Bank Resources

Monetary Policy Online Course for Teachers and Students

Inflation, unemployment, recession, economic growth—these economic concepts affect people in very real ways. In this course containing three interactive, thought-provoking lessons, you will learn about monetary policy, the avenue by which the Federal Reserve System attempts to influence the economy.

St. Louis Federal Reserve Bank Resources

"Monetary and Fiscal Policy in Times of Crisis," ***Page One Economics Classroom Edition (March 2011)***

Have your students read this issue to find out more about fiscal and monetary policies—who conducts them, how they work, and what their roles are during economic downturns.

FYI Who Gets the Interest on the Fed's Assets?

As we've just learned, the Fed owns a lot of assets—Treasury bills—which it bought from commercial banks in exchange for the monetary base in the form of credits to banks' reserve accounts. These assets pay interest. Yet the Fed's liabilities consist mainly of the monetary base, liabilities on which the Fed *doesn't* pay interest. So the Fed, in effect, is an institution that has the privilege of borrowing funds at a zero interest rate and lending them out at a positive interest rate. That sounds like a pretty profitable business. Who gets the profits?

You do—or rather, U.S. taxpayers do. The Fed keeps some of the interest it receives to finance its operations but turns most of it over to the U.S. Treasury. For example, in 2013 the Federal Reserve System received $79.5 billion in income—largely in interest on its holdings of Treasury bills, of which $77.7 billion was returned to the Treasury.

We can now finish the story of the impact of those forged $100 bills allegedly printed in North Korea. When a fake $100 bill enters circulation, it has the same economic effect as a real $100 bill printed by the U.S. government. That is, as long as nobody catches the forgery, the fake bill, for all practical purposes, serves as part of the monetary base. Meanwhile, the Fed decides on the size of the monetary base based on economic considerations—in particular, the Fed doesn't let the monetary base get too large because that can cause inflation. So every fake $100 bill that enters circulation basically means that the Fed issues one less real $100 bill. When the Fed issues a $100 bill legally, however, it gets Treasury bills in return—and the interest on those bills helps pay for the U.S. government's expenses. So a counterfeit $100 bill reduces the amount of Treasury bills the Fed can acquire and thereby reduces the interest payments going to the Fed and the U.S. Treasury. So taxpayers bear the real cost of counterfeiting.

common currency, and placed their joint monetary policy in the ECB's hands. (Six more countries have joined since 1999.) The ECB instantly became an extremely important institution: although no single European nation has an economy anywhere near as large as that of the United States, the combined economies of the eurozone, the group of countries that have adopted the euro as their currency, are roughly as big as the U.S. economy. As a result, the ECB and the Fed are the two giants of the monetary world.

Like the Fed, the ECB has a special status: it's not a private institution, but it's not exactly a government agency either. In fact, it can't be a government agency because there is no pan-European government! Luckily for puzzled Americans, there are strong analogies between European central banking and the Federal Reserve System.

First of all, the ECB, which is located in the German city of Frankfurt, isn't really the counterpart of the whole Federal Reserve System: it's the equivalent of the Board of Governors in Washington. The European counterparts of the regional Federal Reserve Banks are Europe's national central banks: the Bank of France, the Bank of Italy, and so on. Until 1999, each of these national banks was its country's equivalent to the Fed. For example, the Bank of France controlled the French monetary base.

Today these national banks, like regional Feds, provide various financial services to local banks and businesses and conduct open-market operations, but the making of monetary policy has moved upstream to the ECB. Still, the various European national central banks aren't small institutions: in total, they employ more than 50,000 people; in December 2012, the ECB employed only 1,638.

In the eurozone, each country chooses who runs its own national central bank. The ECB's Executive Board is the counterpart of the Fed's Board of Governors; its members are chosen by unanimous consent of the eurozone national governments. The counterpart of the Federal Open Market Committee is the ECB's Governing Council. Just as the Fed's Open Market Committee consists of the Board of Governors plus a rotating group of regional Fed presidents, the ECB's Governing Council consists of the Executive Board plus the heads of the national central banks.

Like the Fed, the ECB is ultimately answerable to voters. Given the fragmentation of political forces across national boundaries, however, it appears to be even more insulated than the Fed from short-term political pressures.

OPEN & CLOSE Exit Slip

TRM *Please see **Exit Slip: Module 27** in the TRM for formative multiple-choice questions to ask your students before finishing your lesson. These questions will help you quickly assess whether your students have mastered the module's concepts before moving on.*

Answers to the Exit Slip Questions

1. D
2. D
3. B

MODULE 27 Review

Check Your Understanding

1. Assume that any money lent by a bank is deposited back into the banking system as a checkable deposit and that the reserve ratio is 10%. Trace out the effects of a $100 million open-market purchase of U.S. Treasury bills by the Fed on the value of checkable bank deposits. What is the size of the money multiplier?

Tackle the Test: Multiple-Choice Questions

1. Which of the following is a function of the Federal Reserve System?
   - I. examine commercial banks
   - II. conduct fiscal policy
   - III. conduct monetary policy

   a. I only
   b. II only
   c. III only
   d. I and III only
   e. I, II, and III
2. Which of the following financial services does the Federal Reserve provide for commercial banks?
   - I. clearing checks
   - II. holding reserves
   - III. making loans

   a. I only
   b. II only
   c. III only
   d. I and II
   e. I, II, and III
3. When the Fed makes a loan to a commercial bank, it charges
   a. no interest.
   b. the prime rate.
   c. the federal funds rate.
   d. the discount rate.
   e. the market interest rate.
4. If the Fed purchases U.S. Treasury bills from a commercial bank, what happens to bank reserves and the money supply?

	Bank reserves	*Money supply*
a.	increase	decrease
b.	increase	increase
c.	decrease	decrease
d.	decrease	increase
e.	increase	no change

5. When banks make loans to each other, they charge the
   a. prime rate.
   b. discount rate.
   c. federal funds rate.
   d. CD rate.
   e. mortgage rate.

Tackle the Test: Free-Response Questions

1. a. What are the three major tools of the Federal Reserve System?
   b. What would the Fed do with each tool to increase the money supply? Explain for each.

Rubric for FRQ 1 (9 points)

1 point: The discount rate
1 point: The reserve requirement
1 point: Open-market operations
1 point: Decrease the discount rate
1 point: A lower discount rate makes it cheaper to borrow from the Fed so the money supply increases.
1 point: Decrease the reserve requirement
1 point: A lower reserve requirement allows banks to loan more, increasing the money supply.
1 point: Buy U.S. Treasury bills
1 point: When the Fed buys U.S. Treasury bills, banks' excess reserves increase. When lent out, these excess reserves increase the money supply with the assistance of the money multiplier.

2. What are the four basic functions of the Federal Reserve System and what part of the system is responsible for each?
(8 points)

Answers to Module 27 Review Questions

Check Your Understanding

1. An open-market purchase of $100 million by the Fed increases banks' reserves by $100 million as the Fed credits their accounts with additional reserves. In other words, this open-market purchase increases the monetary base (currency in circulation plus bank reserves) by $100 million. Banks lend out the additional $100 million. Whoever borrows the money puts it back into the banking system in the form of deposits. Of these deposits, banks lend out $100 million × (1 − *rr*) = $100 million × 0.9 = $90 million. Whoever borrows the money deposits it back into the banking system. And banks lend out $90 million × 0.9 = $81 million, and so on. As a result, bank deposits increased by $100 million + $90 million + $81 million + . . . = $100 million/*rr* = $100 million/0.1 = $1,000 million = $1 billion. Since in this simplified example all money lent out is deposited back into the banking system, there is no increase of currency in circulation, so the increase in bank deposits is equal to the increase in the money supply. In other words, the money supply increases by $1 billion. This is greater than the increase in the monetary base by a factor of 10: in this simplified model in which deposits are the only component of the money supply and in which banks hold no excess reserves, the money multiplier is 1/*rr* = 10.

Tackle the Test: Multiple-Choice Questions

1. d
2. e
3. d
4. b
5. c

Tackle the Test: Free-Response Question

Rubric for FRQ 2 (8 points)

1 point: Provide financial services to depository institutions.
1 point: Regional Federal Reserve Banks are responsible.
1 point: Supervise and regulate banking institutions.
1 point: Regional Federal Reserve Banks and the Board of Governors are responsible.
1 point: Maintain the stability of the financial system.
1 point: The Board of Governors is responsible.
1 point: Conduct monetary policy.
1 point: The Federal Open Market Committee is responsible.

istockphoto

MODULE 28 The Money Market

In this Module, you will learn to:

- Illustrate the relationship between the demand for money and the interest rate with a graph
- Explain why the liquidity preference model determines the interest rate in the short run

The Demand for Money

Remember that M1, the most commonly used definition of the money supply, consists of currency in circulation (cash), plus checkable bank deposits, plus traveler's checks. M2, a broader definition of the money supply, consists of M1 plus deposits that can easily be transferred into checkable deposits. You also learned why people hold money—to make it easier to purchase goods and services. Now we'll go deeper, examining what determines *how much* money individuals and firms want to hold at any given time.

The Opportunity Cost of Holding Money

Most economic decisions involve trade-offs at the margin. That is, individuals decide how much of a good to consume by determining whether the benefit they'd gain from consuming a bit more of that good is worth the cost. The same decision process is used when deciding how much money to hold.

Individuals and firms find it useful to hold some of their assets in the form of money because of the convenience money provides: money can be used to make purchases directly, while other assets can't. But there is a price to be paid—an opportunity cost—for that convenience: money held in your wallet earns no interest.

As an example of how convenience makes it worth incurring some opportunity costs, consider the fact that even today—with the prevalence of credit cards, debit cards, and ATMs—people continue to keep cash in their wallets rather than leave the funds in an interest-bearing account. They do this because they don't want to have to go to an ATM to withdraw money every time they want to make a small purchase. In other words, the convenience of keeping some cash in your wallet is more valuable than the interest you would earn by keeping that money in the bank.

PD To prepare for teaching this lesson, you may want to consult the **Module 28 Sample Lecture** in the TRM.

OPEN & CLOSE Start Here

Ask students to decide which policy is best used in different situations by going to "So You Want to Be in Charge of Monetary Policy" at http://sffed-education.org/chairman. To access the simulation, have students click on the screen and then select "Play Game." Students will adjust the interest rates based on 16 newspaper headlines. They will see the impact of their decisions on unemployment and inflation. While it takes less than a minute to decide what to do, to play all 16 as a group will take about 30 minutes if you discuss each scenario individually. To give them the feel, only do the first 4 or 5 headlines. If students don't have individual computers, you can show this simulation on the overhead and ask them to write their choices on their personal whiteboards or notebook paper and gather a consensus on what to do.

FOCUS Active Learning

Ask students the following questions:

- Why do you want to have money in your pocket? *Students should say that they need money to buy things.*
- Why might you choose to hold more money in your pocket today than you had yesterday? *Good answers include needing to buy more today than yesterday, facing higher prices than yesterday, having a lower opportunity cost of holding money due to a lower interest rate, or some change in institutions or technology that makes it desirable to hold more money.*
- You have money in your pocket so that you can spend it. What else can you do with your money? *They can save it!*
- And what would make you interested in saving more of it? *They should say a higher interest rate.*

This prepares the way to discuss the opportunity cost of holding money.

Module 28 The Money Market 267

TEACH Teach It

Students often think that the desirable quantity of money demanded is an infinite amount! Stress that even the wealthiest of persons doesn't walk around with all of his or her money in a pocket or checking account. There is an opportunity cost of holding money and most students don't understand that.

FOCUS Active Learning

TRM To help students intuitively understand the relationship between interest rates and the quantity demanded of money, assign **Activity 28.1 (A Budgetary Exercise)** from the TRM.

Table 28.1 Selected Interest Rates, June 2007

One-month CDs	5.30%
Interest-bearing demand deposits	2.30
Currency	0

Source: Federal Reserve Bank of St. Louis.

Even holding money in a checking account involves a trade-off between convenience and interest payments. That's because you can earn a higher interest rate by putting your money in assets other than a checking account. For example, many banks offer certificates of deposit, or CDs, which pay a higher interest rate than ordinary bank accounts. But CDs also carry a penalty if you withdraw the funds before a certain amount of time—say, six months—has elapsed. An individual who keeps funds in a checking account is forgoing the higher interest rate those funds would have earned if placed in a CD in return for the convenience of having cash readily available when needed.

Table 28.1 illustrates the opportunity cost of holding money in a specific month. Because interest rates are currently at abnormally low levels, we refer back to June 2007. The first row shows the interest rate on one-month certificates of deposit—that is, the interest rate individuals could get if they were willing to tie their funds up for one month. In June 2007, one-month CDs yielded 5.30%. The second row shows the interest rate on interest-bearing bank accounts (specifically, those included in M1). Funds in these accounts were more accessible than those in CDs, but the price of that convenience was a much lower interest rate, only 2.30%. Finally, the last row shows the interest rate on currency—cash in your wallet—which, of course, was zero.

Table 28.1 shows the opportunity cost of holding money at one point in time, but the opportunity cost of holding money changes when the overall level of interest rates changes. Specifically, when the overall level of interest rates falls, the opportunity cost of holding money falls, too.

Table 28.2 illustrates this point by showing how selected interest rates changed between June 2007 and June 2008, a period when the Federal Reserve was slashing rates in an effort to fight off recession. Between June 2007 and June 2008, the federal funds rate, which is the rate the Fed controls most directly, fell by 3.25 percentage points. The interest rate on one-month CDs fell almost as much, 2.8 percentage points. That's not an accident: all **short-term interest rates**—rates on financial assets that come due, or mature, within a year—tend to move together, with rare exceptions. The reason short-term interest rates tend to move together is that CDs and other short-term assets (like one-month and three-month U.S. Treasury bills) are in effect competing for the same business. Any short-term asset that offers a lower-than-average interest rate will be sold by investors, who will move their wealth into a higher-yielding short-term asset. The selling of the asset, in turn, forces its interest rate up because investors must be rewarded with a higher rate in order to induce them to buy it. Conversely, investors will move their wealth into any short-term financial asset that offers an above-average interest rate. The purchase of the asset drives its interest rate down when sellers find they can lower the rate of return on the asset and still find willing buyers. So interest rates on short-term financial assets tend to be roughly the same because no asset will consistently offer a higher-than-average or a lower-than-average interest rate.

Short-term interest rates are the interest rates on financial assets that mature within a year.

Table 28.2 Interest Rates and the Opportunity Cost of Holding Money

	June 2007	June 2008
Federal funds rate	5.25%	2.00%
One-month certificates of deposit (CD)	5.30	2.50
Interest-bearing demand deposits	2.30	1.24
Currency	0	0
CDs minus interest-bearing demand deposits	3.00	1.26
CDs minus currency	5.30	2.50

Source: Federal Reserve Bank of St. Louis.

FYI Long-Term Interest Rates

Long-term interest rates—rates on bonds or loans that mature in several years—don't necessarily move with short-term interest rates. How is that possible?

Consider the case of Millie, who has already decided to place $1,000 in CDs for the next two years. However, she hasn't decided whether to put the money in a one-year CD, at a 4% rate of interest, or a two-year CD, at a 5% rate of interest.

You might think that the two-year CD is a clearly better deal—but it may not be. Suppose that Millie expects the rate of interest on one-year CDs to rise sharply next year. If she puts her funds in a one-year CD this year, she will be able to reinvest the money at a much higher rate next year. And this could give her a two-year rate of return that is higher than if she put her funds into the two-year CD. For example, if the rate of interest on one-year CDs rises from 4% this year to 8% next year, putting her funds in a one-year CD will give her an annual rate of return over the next two years of about 6%, better than the 5% rate on two-year CDs.

The same considerations apply to investors deciding between short-term and long-term bonds. If they expect short-term interest rates to rise, investors may buy short-term bonds even if long-term bonds offer a higher interest rate. If they expect short-term interest rates to fall, investors may buy long-term bonds even if short-term bonds offer a higher interest rate.

In practice, long-term interest rates reflect the average expectation in the market about what's going to happen to short-term rates in the future. When long-term rates are higher than short-term rates, as they were in 2014, the market is signaling that it expects short-term rates to rise in the future.

But as short-term interest rates fell between June 2007 and June 2008, the interest rates on money didn't fall by the same amount. The interest rate on currency, of course, remained at zero. The interest rate paid on demand deposits did fall, but by much less than short-term interest rates. As a result, the opportunity cost of holding money fell. The last two rows of Table 28.2 show the differences between the interest rates on demand deposits and currency and the interest rate on CDs. These differences declined sharply between June 2007 and June 2008. This reflects a general result: the higher the short-term interest rate, the higher the opportunity cost of holding money; the lower the short-term interest rate, the lower the opportunity cost of holding money.

Table 28.2 contains only short-term interest rates. At any given moment, **long-term interest rates**—interest rates on financial assets that mature, or come due, a number of years in the future—may be different from short-term interest rates. The difference between short-term and long-term interest rates is sometimes important as a practical matter. Moreover, it's short-term rates rather than long-term rates that affect money demand, because the decision to hold money involves trading off the convenience of holding cash versus the payoff from holding assets that mature in the short-term—a year or less. For our current purposes, however, it's useful to ignore the distinction between short-term and long-term rates and assume that there is only one interest rate.

Long-term interest rates are interest rates on financial assets that mature a number of years in the future.

The Money Demand Curve

Because the overall level of interest rates affects the opportunity cost of holding money, the quantity of money individuals and firms want to hold, other things equal, is negatively related to the interest rate. In **Figure 28.1** on the next page, the horizontal axis shows the quantity of money demanded and the vertical axis shows the nominal interest rate, *r*, which you can think of as a representative short-term interest rate such as the rate on one-month CDs. Why do we place the nominal interest rate and not the real interest rate on the vertical axis? Because the opportunity cost of holding money includes both the real return that could be earned on a bank deposit and the erosion in purchasing power caused by inflation. The nominal interest rate includes both the forgone real return and the expected loss due to inflation. Hence, *r* in Figure 28.1 and all subsequent figures is the nominal interest rate.

FOCUS Graph It

As you draw the money market graph, have students draw it on their personal whiteboards or notebook paper for practice. Confirm that they have drawn and labeled it correctly.

TEACH Teach It

The higher the short-term interest rate, the higher the opportunity cost of holding money; the lower the short-term interest rate, the lower the opportunity cost of holding money.

TEACH Teach It

It is time to introduce the money market graph. As you draw the axes, explain to students that we use the nominal interest rate on the vertical axis because that is the opportunity cost of holding money, including both the forgone real return the money could earn elsewhere and the erosion of its purchasing power caused by inflation. Acceptable labels for the vertical axis include spelling out the words, using a lowercase cursive *i*, or *r*. Students may lose points on the AP® exam if they incorrectly label the vertical axis.

TEACH Connect It

Ask the following questions:

- What will the money demand curve look like? *Students should indicate that it is downsloping just like other demand curves they have seen.*
- Why? *There is less demand for money at higher interest rates.*
- What will happen if the nominal interest rate increases? *An increase in the nominal interest rate will cause a movement upward along the money demand curve.*

Using Figure 28.1, explain that the money demand curve behaves like other demand curves students have already studied.

TEACH Teach It

Demand for money will shift just as other demand curves shift. If an external change makes holding money in their pockets more desirable at any interest rate, the demand curve for money will shift rightward. The most important factors causing the money demand curve to shift are changes in the aggregate price level, changes in real GDP, changes in banking technology, and changes in banking institutions. Take time to discuss each of these factors.

Figure 28.1 The Money Demand Curve

The money demand curve illustrates the relationship between the interest rate and the quantity of money demanded. It slopes downward: a higher interest rate leads to a higher opportunity cost of holding money and reduces the quantity of money demanded.

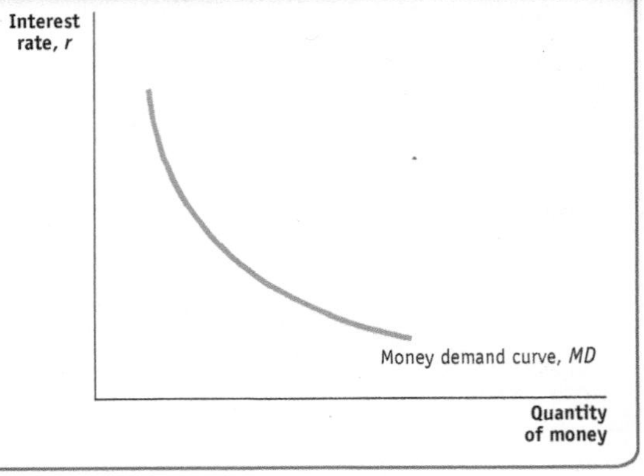

The **money demand curve** shows the relationship between the quantity of money demanded and the interest rate.

AP® Exam Tip

The money market graph is one of the essential graphs you must be able to correctly draw, label, and interpret for the AP® exam. The interest rate measured along the vertical axis is the nominal interest rate.

The relationship between the interest rate and the quantity of money demanded by the public is illustrated by the **money demand curve**, *MD*, in Figure 28.1. The money demand curve slopes downward because, other things equal, a higher interest rate increases the opportunity cost of holding money, leading the public to reduce the quantity of money it demands. For example, if the interest rate is very low—say, 0.15%, a common rate for one-month CDs in 2014—the interest forgone by holding money is relatively small. As a result, individuals and firms will tend to hold relatively large amounts of money to avoid the cost and nuisance of converting other assets into money when making purchases. By contrast, if the interest rate is relatively high—say, 15%, a level it reached in the United States in the early 1980s—the opportunity cost of holding money is high. People will respond by keeping only small amounts in cash and deposits, converting assets into money only when needed.

You might ask why we draw the money demand curve with the interest rate—as opposed to rates of return on other assets, such as stocks or real estate—on the vertical axis. The answer is that, for most people, the relevant question in deciding how much money to hold is whether to put the funds in the form of other assets that can be turned fairly quickly and easily into money. Stocks don't fit that definition because there are significant broker's fees when you sell stock (which is why stock market investors are advised not to buy and sell too often); selling real estate involves even larger fees and can take a long time as well. So the relevant comparison is with assets that are "close to" money—fairly liquid assets like CDs. And, as we've already seen, the interest rates on all these assets normally move closely together.

Shifts of the Money Demand Curve

Like the demand curve for an ordinary good, the money demand curve can be shifted by a number of factors. **Figure 28.2** shows shifts of the money demand curve: an increase in the demand for money corresponds to a rightward shift of the *MD* curve, raising the quantity of money demanded at any given interest rate; a fall in the demand for money corresponds to a leftward shift of the *MD* curve, reducing the quantity of money demanded at any given interest rate. The most important factors causing the money demand curve to shift are changes in the aggregate price level, changes in real GDP, changes in banking technology, and changes in banking institutions.

Figure 28.2 Increases and Decreases in the Demand for Money

A rise in money demand shifts the money demand curve to the right, from MD_1 to MD_2, and the quantity of money demanded rises at any given interest rate. A fall in money demand shifts the money demand curve to the left, from MD_1 to MD_3, and the quantity of money demanded falls at any given interest rate.

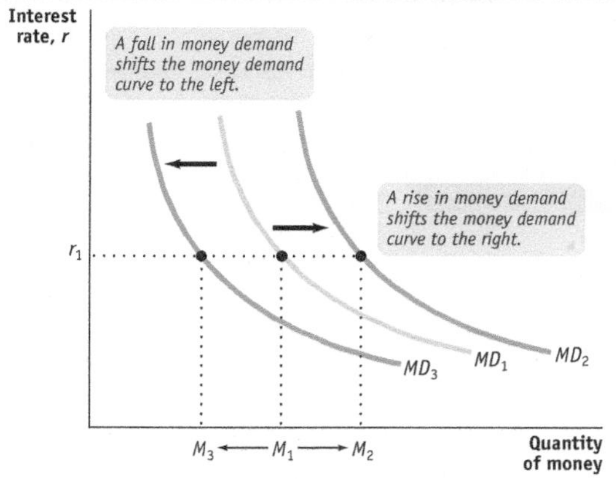

Changes in the Aggregate Price Level Americans keep a lot more cash in their wallets and funds in their checking accounts today than they did in the 1950s. One reason is that they have to if they want to be able to buy anything: almost everything costs more now than it did when you could get a burger, fries, and a drink at McDonald's for 45 cents and a gallon of gasoline for 29 cents. So higher prices increase the demand for money (a rightward shift of the *MD* curve), and lower prices decrease the demand for money (a leftward shift of the *MD* curve).

We can actually be more specific than this: other things equal, the demand for money is *proportional* to the price level. That is, if the aggregate price level rises by 20%, the quantity of money demanded at any given interest rate, such as r_1 in Figure 28.2, also rises by 20%—the movement from M_1 to M_2. Why? Because if the price of everything rises by 20%, it takes 20% more money to buy the same basket of goods and services. And if the aggregate price level falls by 20%, at any given interest rate the quantity of money demanded falls by 20%—shown by the movement from M_1 to M_3 at the interest rate r_1. As we'll see later, the fact that money demand is proportional to the price level has important implications for the long-run effects of monetary policy.

© tom carter/Alamy

A re-creation of a McDonald's in the 1950s at the Ford Museum in Detroit, Michigan.

Changes in Real GDP Households and firms hold money as a way to facilitate purchases of goods and services. The larger the quantity of goods and services they buy, the larger the quantity of money they will want to hold at any given interest rate. So an increase in real GDP—the total quantity of goods and services produced and sold in the economy—shifts the money demand curve rightward. A fall in real GDP shifts the money demand curve leftward.

Changes in Technology There was a time, not so long ago, when withdrawing cash from a bank account required a visit during the bank's hours of operation. Since most people tried to do their banking during lunch hour, they often found themselves standing in line. So people limited the number of times they needed to withdraw funds by keeping substantial amounts of cash on hand. Not surprisingly, this tendency diminished greatly with the advent of ATMs in the 1970s. As a result, the demand for money fell and the money demand curve shifted leftward.

These events illustrate how changes in technology can affect the demand for money. In general, advances in information technology have tended to reduce the demand

AP® Exam Tip

Changes in the aggregate price level, real GDP, technology, and banking institutions shift the money demand curve. On the AP® exam you may be given scenarios in which you must determine the direction of a shift in this curve.

FOCUS Active Learning

Use the Jacob Clifford video "Money Market—Macro Review" (see econextras video list with hyperlinks on the bcs and TRFD) to help students gain an understanding of the demand for money. Pay close attention to the concept of the money demand curve. What are the two reasons behind the downward-sloping money demand? *(People have transaction demand for money when they need cash for goods and services. They have asset demand for money when the interest rates go up higher. When interest rates are high, the opportunity cost of using money to spend is too high and people wish to save. When the interest rate shifts to a lower rate, then the opportunity cost of spending your money is lower.)* What moves the money demand curve? *(Change in the price level will mean more or less money needed for transaction demand purposes. Changes in income and a change of technology in the banking system can also mean a shift of the money demand.)*

Module 28 The Money Market 271

for money by making it easier for the public to make purchases without holding significant sums of money. ATMs are only one example of how changes in technology have altered the demand for money. The ability of stores to process credit card and debit card transactions via the Internet has widened their acceptance and similarly reduced the demand for cash.

Changes in Institutions Changes in institutions can increase or decrease the demand for money. For example, until Regulation Q was eliminated in 1980, U.S. banks weren't allowed to offer interest on checking accounts. So the interest you would forgo by holding funds in a checking account instead of an interest-bearing asset made the opportunity cost of holding funds in checking accounts very high. When banking regulations changed, allowing banks to pay interest on checking account funds, the demand for money rose and shifted the money demand curve to the right.

Money and Interest Rates

The Federal Open Market Committee decided today to lower its target for the federal funds rate 75 basis points to 2¼ percent.

Recent information indicates that the outlook for economic activity has weakened further. Growth in consumer spending has slowed and labor markets have softened. Financial markets remain under considerable stress, and the tightening of credit conditions and the deepening of the housing contraction are likely to weigh on economic growth over the next few quarters.

So read the beginning of a press release from the Federal Reserve issued on March 18, 2008. (A basis point is equal to 0.01 percentage point. So the statement implies that the Fed lowered the target from 3% to 2.25%.) Remember that the federal funds rate is the rate at which banks lend reserves to each other to meet the required reserve ratio. As the statement implies, at each of its eight-times-a-year meetings, the Federal Open Market Committee sets a target value for the federal funds rate. It's then up to Fed officials to achieve that target. This is done by the Open Market Desk at the Federal Reserve Bank of New York, which buys and sells short-term U.S. government debt, known as Treasury bills, to achieve that target.

As we've already seen, other short-term interest rates, such as the rates on CDs, move with the federal funds rate. So when the Fed reduced its target for the federal funds rate from 3% to 2.25% in March 2008, many other short-term interest rates also fell by about three-quarters of a percentage point.

How does the Fed go about achieving a *target federal funds rate*? And more to the point, how is the Fed able to affect interest rates at all?

The Equilibrium Interest Rate

According to the **liquidity preference model of the interest rate**, the interest rate is determined by the supply and demand for money.

The **money supply curve** shows the relationship between the quantity of money supplied and the interest rate.

Recall that, for simplicity, we've assumed that there is only one interest rate paid on nonmonetary financial assets, both in the short run and in the long run. To understand how the interest rate is determined, consider **Figure 28.3**, which illustrates the **liquidity preference model of the interest rate**; this model says that the interest rate is determined by the supply and demand for money in the market for money. Figure 28.3 combines the money demand curve, *MD,* with the **money supply curve**, *MS,* which shows the relationship between the quantity of money supplied by the Federal Reserve and the interest rate.

The Federal Reserve can increase or decrease the money supply: it usually does this through *open-market operations*, buying or selling Treasury bills, but it can also lend via the *discount window* or change *reserve requirements*. Let's assume for simplicity that the Fed, using one or more of these methods, simply chooses the level of the money supply that it believes will achieve its interest rate target. Then the money supply curve is a vertical line, *MS* in Figure 28.3, with a horizontal intercept corresponding to the money supply chosen by the Fed, $\overline{M}$. The money market equilibrium is at *E,* where *MS*

TEACH Teach It

The money supply curve (*MS*) is vertical because there is a fixed amount of money in the money supply that is controlled by the Fed. The Fed cannot directly change the federal funds rate. Instead, the Fed uses the three major tools of monetary policy to achieve a target level for the federal funds rate. Since most interest rates will move closely with the federal funds rate, you can use the money market to show how these policies work.

Figure 28.3 Equilibrium in the Money Market

The money supply curve, *MS*, is vertical at the money supply chosen by the Federal Reserve, $\overline{M}$. The money market is in equilibrium at the interest rate r_E: the quantity of money demanded by the public is equal to $\overline{M}$, the quantity of money supplied. At a point such as *L*, the interest rate, r_L, is below r_E and the corresponding quantity of money demanded, M_L, exceeds the money supply, $\overline{M}$. In an attempt to shift their wealth out of nonmoney interest-bearing financial assets and raise their money holdings, investors drive the interest rate up to r_E. At a point such as *H*, the interest rate r_H is above r_E and the corresponding quantity of money demanded, M_H, is less than the money supply, $\overline{M}$. In an attempt to shift out of money holdings into nonmoney interest-bearing financial assets, investors drive the interest rate down to r_E.

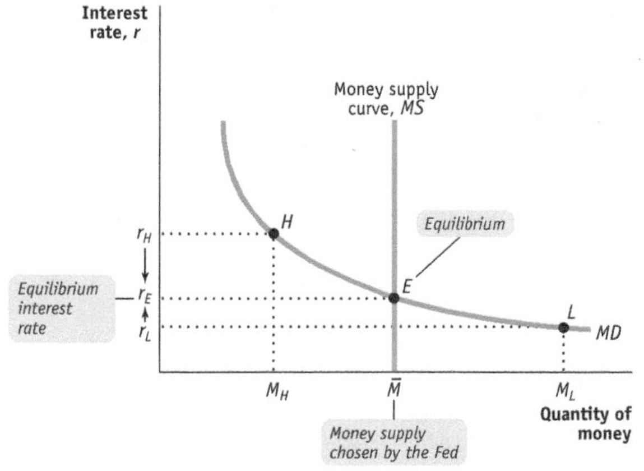

and *MD* cross. At this point the quantity of money demanded equals the money supply, $\overline{M}$, leading to an equilibrium interest rate of r_E.

To understand why r_E is the equilibrium interest rate, consider what happens if the money market is at a point like *L*, where the interest rate, r_L, is below r_E. At r_L the public wants to hold the quantity of money M_L, an amount larger than the actual money supply, $\overline{M}$. This means that at point *L*, the public wants to shift some of its wealth out of interest-bearing assets such as high-denomination CDs (which aren't money) into money. This has two implications. One is that the quantity of money demanded is *more* than the quantity of money supplied. The other is that the quantity of interest-bearing nonmoney assets demanded is *less* than the quantity supplied. So those trying to sell nonmoney assets will find that they have to offer a higher interest rate to attract buyers. As a result, the interest rate will be driven up from r_L until the public wants to hold the quantity of money that is actually available, *M*. That is, the interest rate will rise until it is equal to r_E.

Now consider what happens if the money market is at a point such as *H* in Figure 28.3, where the interest rate r_H is above r_E. In that case the quantity of money demanded, M_H, is less than the quantity of money supplied, $\overline{M}$. Correspondingly, the quantity of interest-bearing nonmoney assets demanded is greater than the quantity supplied. Those trying to sell interest-bearing nonmoney assets will find that they can offer a lower interest rate and still find willing buyers. This leads to a fall in the interest rate from r_H. It falls until the public wants to hold the quantity of money that is actually available, $\overline{M}$. Again, the interest rate will end up at r_E.

Two Models of the Interest Rate

Here we have developed the liquidity preference model of the interest rate. In this model, the equilibrium interest rate is the rate at which the quantity of money demanded equals the quantity of money supplied in the money market. This model is different from, but consistent with, another model known as the loanable funds model of the interest rate, which is developed in the next module. In the loanable funds model, we will see that the interest rate matches the quantity of loanable funds supplied by savers with the quantity of loanable funds demanded for investment spending.

TEACH Teach It

Use Figure 28.3 to explain equilibrium in the money market. It will be helpful for students to think of only two places to put their money. They can put money in CDs that provide interest, or they can hold cash that earns no interest.

FOCUS Flip It

For a quick review of the tools of monetary policy and how each tool impacts the money market graph, have students watch Jacob Clifford's video "Macro 4.1—Money Market and FED Tools (Monetary Policy)" (see econextras video list with hyperlinks on the bcs and TRFD). After they have watched the video, put students in groups of three, and ask them to explain and diagram easy money policy using one of the three tools. Each student in every group should explain a different tool.

FOCUS Graph It

Ask students to use paper or their personal whiteboards to graph a correctly labeled money market graph showing the equilibrium interest rate. Make sure that the vertical axis is labeled interest rate.

OPEN & CLOSE Exit Slip

TRM *Please see **Exit Slip: Module 28** in the TRM for formative multiple-choice questions to ask before finishing your lesson. These questions will help you quickly assess whether your students have mastered the module's concepts before moving on.*

Answers to the Exit Slip Questions

1. E
2. A
3. D

MODULE 28 Review

Check Your Understanding

1. Explain how each of the following would affect the quantity of money demanded, and indicate whether each change would cause a movement along the money demand curve or a shift of the money demand curve.
   a. The short-term interest rate rises from 5% to 30%.
   b. All prices fall by 10%.
   c. New wireless technology automatically charges supermarket purchases to credit cards, eliminating the need to stop at the cash register.
   d. In order to avoid paying taxes, a vast underground economy develops in which workers are paid their wages in cash rather than with checks.
2. How will each of the following affect the opportunity cost or benefit of holding cash? Explain.
   a. Merchants charge a 1% fee on debit/credit card transactions for purchases of less than $50.
   b. To attract more deposits, banks raise the interest paid on six-month CDs.
   c. The cost of food rises significantly.

Tackle the Test: Multiple-Choice Questions

1. A change in which of the following will shift the money demand curve?
   I. the aggregate price level
   II. real GDP
   III. the interest rate
   a. I only
   b. II only
   c. III only
   d. I and II only
   e. I, II, and III
2. Which of the following will decrease the demand for money?
   a. an increase in the interest rate
   b. inflation
   c. an increase in real GDP
   d. an increase in the availability of ATMs
   e. the adoption of Regulation Q
3. What will happen to the money supply and the equilibrium interest rate if the Federal Reserve sells Treasury securities?

	Money supply	*Equilibrium interest rate*
a.	increase	increase
b.	decrease	increase
c.	increase	decrease
d.	decrease	decrease
e.	decrease	no change

4. Which of the following is true regarding short-term and long-term interest rates?
   a. Short-term interest rates are always above long-term interest rates.
   b. Short-term interest rates are always below long-term interest rates.
   c. Short-term interest rates are always equal to long-term interest rates.
   d. Short-term interest rates are more important for determining the demand for money.
   e. Long-term interest rates are more important for determining the demand for money.
5. The quantity of money demanded rises (that is, there is a movement along the money demand curve) when
   a. the aggregate price level increases.
   b. the aggregate price level falls.
   c. real GDP increases.
   d. new technology makes banking easier.
   e. short-term interest rates fall.

Answers to Module 28 Review Questions

Check Your Understanding

1. a. By increasing the opportunity cost of holding money, a high interest rate reduces the quantity of money demanded. This is a movement up and to the left along the money demand curve.

b. A 10% fall in prices reduces the quantity of money demanded at any given interest rate, shifting the money demand curve leftward.

c. This technological change reduces the quantity of money demanded at any given interest rate, so it shifts the money demand curve leftward.

d. Payments in cash require employers to hold more money, increasing the quantity of money demanded at any given interest rate. Thus, it shifts the money demand curve rightward.

2. a. A 1% purchase fee on debit/credit card transactions for purchases less than $50 increases the benefit of holding cash because consumers will save money by paying with cash.

b. An increase in the interest paid on six-month CDs raises the opportunity cost of holding cash because holding cash requires forgoing the higher interest paid.

c. Because many purchases of food are made in cash, a significant increase in the cost of food increases the benefit of holding cash.

Tackle the Test: Multiple-Choice Questions

1. d
2. d
3. b
4. d
5. e

Tackle the Test: Free-Response Questions

1. Draw three correctly labeled graphs of the money market. Show the effect of each of the following three changes on a separate graph.
   a. The aggregate price level increases.
   b. Real GDP falls.
   c. There is a dramatic increase in online banking.

Rubric for FRQ 1 (6 points)

1 point: The vertical axis is labeled "Interest rate" or "*r*" and the horizontal axis is labeled "Quantity of money."

1 point: The money supply curve is vertical and labeled.

1 point: The money demand curve is negatively sloped and labeled.

1 point: The money demand curve shifts right.

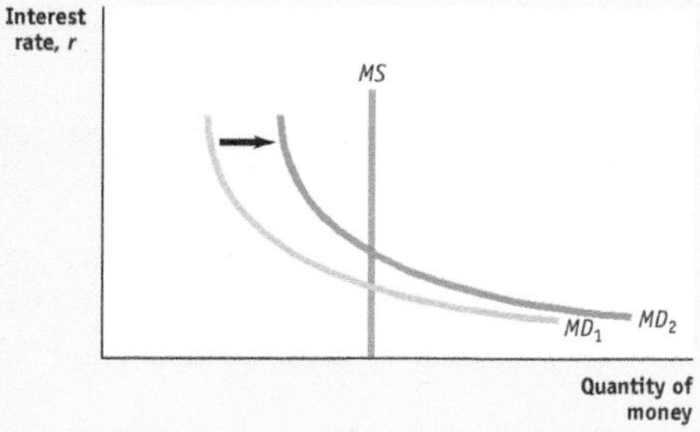

1 point: The money demand curve shifts left.

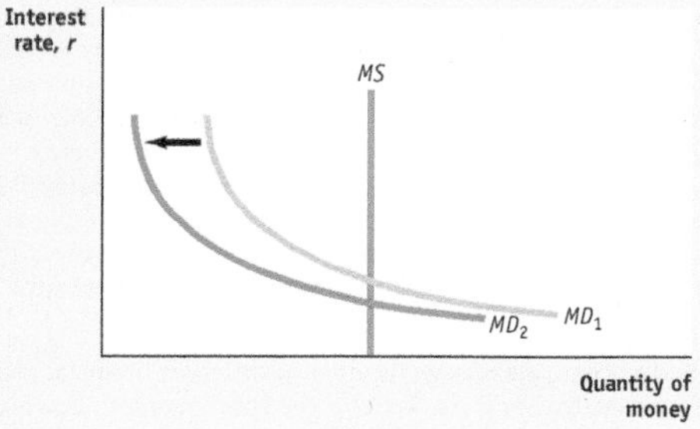

1 point: The money demand curve shifts left.

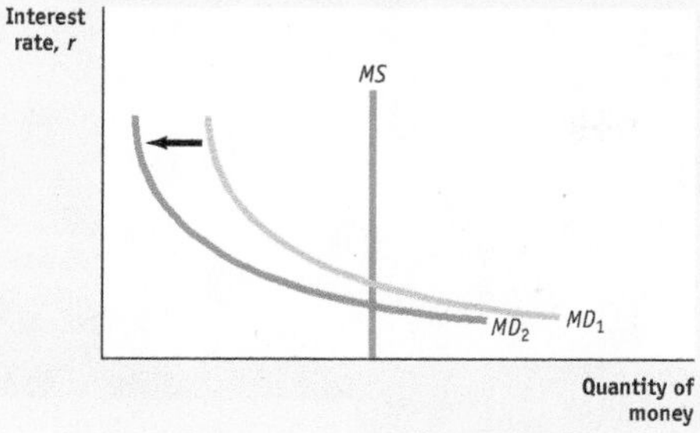

2. Draw a correctly labeled graph showing equilibrium in the money market. Label the equilibrium interest rate r_E and label an interest rate below the equilibrium interest rate r_L. Explain what occurs in the market when the interest rate is r_L and how the market will eventually return to equilibrium.
(7 points)

Tackle the Test: Free-Response Question Rubric for FRQ 2 (7 points)

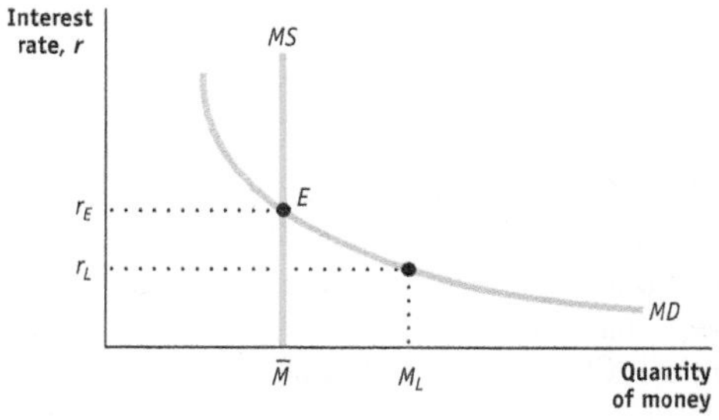

1 point: The vertical axis is labeled "Interest rate" or "*r*" and the horizontal axis is labeled "Quantity of money."

1 point: Money supply curve is vertical and labeled.

1 point: Money demand curve is negatively sloped and labeled.

1 point: The equilibrium interest rate is labeled *on the vertical axis* and a rate below the equilibrium rate is also labeled.

1 point: At an interest rate below equilibrium, the quantity of money demanded exceeds the quantity of money supplied.

1 point: People want to shift more of their wealth out of interest-bearing assets such as CDs and hold it as money instead. Because the quantity of interest-bearing nonmoney assets demanded is less than the quantity supplied, those trying to sell such assets will have to offer a higher interest rate to attract buyers.

1 point: As the interest rate rises, the quantity of money demanded decreases. This process continues until the market returns to equilibrium.

Module 28 The Money Market 275

PD To prepare for teaching this lesson, you may want to consult the **Module 29 Sample Lecture** in the TRM.

OPEN & CLOSE Start Here

Ask students to read a recent article on consumer debt. You may use the January 2014 *Dallas News* article "Consumer, Student Debt on an Upward Spiral" at http://tinyurl.com/lec9nc7. Ask students where people get the money to fund their debt. *Answers will vary. Use this as an opportunity to introduce them to the loanable funds market.*

TEACH AP® Exam Tip

Stress that the loanable funds market plays a significant role in AP® exams; it tells us some very useful things about how interest rates are determined. Emphasize, too, that the loanable funds market is graphed as just another supply and demand graph with labels specific to a new situation. Recent scoring of the AP® Macro free-response questions required an accurate labeling of the vertical axis of the loanable funds graph, which should show a small *r* or a spelled out label for the interest rate.

TEACH Teach It

Students may wonder why we need two graphs that show interest rates. The answer is simple. The money market graph indicates the fixed amount of money in the economy and the demand for holding money. The loanable funds market indicates the variable amount of money savers are willing to lend out and the amount that borrowers would demand at each interest rate.

Brad Schloss/Icon SMI/Corbis

MODULE 29

The Market for Loanable Funds

In this Module, you will learn to:

- Describe how the loanable funds market matches savers and investors
- Identify the determinants of supply and demand in the loanable funds market
- Explain how the two models of interest rates can be reconciled

The Market for Loanable Funds

Recall that, for the economy as a whole, savings always equals investment spending. In a closed economy, savings is equal to national savings. In an open economy, savings is equal to national savings plus capital inflow. At any given time, however, savers, the people with funds to lend, are usually not the same as borrowers, the people who want to borrow to finance their investment spending. How are savers and borrowers brought together?

Savers and borrowers are matched up with one another in much the same way producers and consumers are matched up: through markets governed by supply and demand. In the circular-flow diagram, we noted that the *financial markets* channel the savings of households to businesses that want to borrow in order to purchase capital equipment. It's now time to take a look at how those financial markets work.

The Equilibrium Interest Rate There are a large number of different financial markets in the financial system, such as the bond market and the stock market. However, economists often work with a simplified model in which they assume that there is just one market that brings together those who want to lend money (savers) and those who want to borrow money (firms with investment spending projects). This hypothetical market is known as the **loanable funds market**. The price that is determined in the loanable funds market is the interest rate, denoted by *r*. It is the return a lender receives for allowing borrowers the use of a dollar for one year, calculated as a percentage of the amount borrowed.

The **loanable funds market** is a hypothetical market that brings together those who want to lend money and those who want to borrow money.

Recall that in the money market, the *nominal* interest rate is of central importance and always serves as the "price" measured on the vertical axis. The interest rate in the loanable funds market can be measured in either real or nominal terms—with or without the inclusion of expected inflation that makes nominal rates differ from real rates. Investors and savers care about the *real* interest rate, which tells them the price paid for the use of

St. Louis Federal Reserve Bank Resources

"Getting Real about Interest Rates," *The Economic Lowdown Podcast Series*

Do your students know the difference between nominal and real interest rates? If you're not sure, then it's time to "get real" about interest rates. In this episode of *The Economic Lowdown*, students will learn how inflation influences the real return on your deposits, how it impacts borrowers and lenders differently, and why price stability—a responsibility of the Federal Reserve System—is important.

276 Section 5 The Financial Sector

money aside from the amount paid to keep up with inflation. However, in the real world neither borrowers nor lenders know what the future inflation rate will be when they make a deal, so actual loan contracts specify a nominal interest rate rather than a real interest rate. For this reason, and because it facilitates comparisons between the money market and the loanable funds market, the figures in this section are drawn with the vertical axis measuring the *nominal interest rate for a given expected future inflation rate.* As long as the expected inflation rate is unchanged, changes in the nominal interest rate also lead to changes in the real interest rate. We take up the influence of inflation later in this module.

We should also note at this point that, in reality, there are many different kinds of nominal interest rates because there are many different kinds of loans—short-term loans, long-term loans, loans made to corporate borrowers, loans made to governments, and so on. In the interest of simplicity, we'll ignore those differences and assume that there is only one type of loan. **Figure 29.1** illustrates the hypothetical demand for loanable funds. On the horizontal axis we show the quantity of loanable funds demanded. On the vertical axis we show the interest rate, which is the "price" of borrowing. To see why the demand curve for loanable funds, *D*, slopes downward, imagine that there are many businesses, each of which has one potential investment project. How does a given business decide whether or not to borrow money to finance its project? The decision depends on the interest rate the business faces and the **rate of return** on its project—the profit earned on the project expressed as a percentage of its cost. This can be expressed in a formula as:

$$\textbf{(29-1)}\quad \text{Rate of return} = \frac{\text{Revenue from project} - \text{Cost of project}}{\text{Cost of project}} \times 100$$

For example, a project that costs \$300,000 and produces revenue of \$315,000 provides a rate of return of [(\$315,000 − \$300,000)/\$300,000] × 100 = 5%.

A business will want a loan when the rate of return on its project is greater than or equal to the interest rate. So, for example, at an interest rate of 12%, only businesses with projects that yield a rate of return greater than or equal to 12% will want a loan. A business will not pay 12% interest to fund a project with a 5% rate of return. The demand curve in Figure 29.1 shows that if the interest rate is 12%, businesses will want to borrow \$150 billion (point *A*); if the interest rate is only 4%, businesses will want to borrow a

The **rate of return** on a project is the profit earned on the project expressed as a percentage of its cost.

AP® Exam Tip

When expectations about the future inflation rate remain unchanged, the real interest rate and the nominal interest rate rise and fall together, and either rate can appear on the vertical axis of the loanable funds graph. We use the nominal interest rate here for comparability with the money market graph. If a question asks you to draw conclusions about the real interest rate on the basis of the loanable funds graph, simply label the vertical axis "real interest rate."

Figure 29.1 The Demand for Loanable Funds

The demand curve for loanable funds slopes downward: the lower the interest rate, the greater the quantity of loanable funds demanded. Here, reducing the interest rate from 12% to 4% increases the quantity of loanable funds demanded from \$150 billion to \$450 billion.

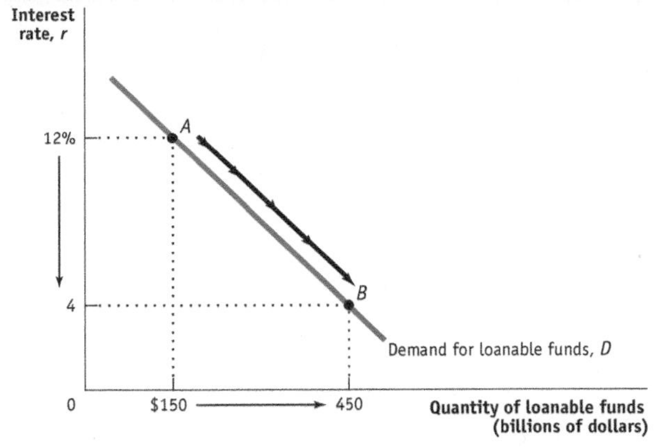

TEACH Teach It

The demand for loans is downward-sloping because borrowers demand more loans at lower interest rates. Firms borrow to pay for capital investment projects. If the project has an expected rate of return that exceeds the interest rate, the investment will be profitable, and the funds will be demanded. As the interest rate falls, more projects become profitable, so the quantity of funds demanded will increase.

Module 29 The Market for Loanable Funds 277

TEACH Teach It

The supply of loanable funds is upward-sloping. It comes from savers who lend their money to borrowers. In order to compensate them, savers must receive interest income. As the interest rate rises, the opportunity to earn more income rises, so more dollars will be saved.

Figure 29.2 The Supply of Loanable Funds

The supply curve for loanable funds slopes upward: the higher the interest rate, the greater the quantity of loanable funds supplied. Here, increasing the interest rate from 4% to 12% increases the quantity of loanable funds supplied from $150 billion to $450 billion.

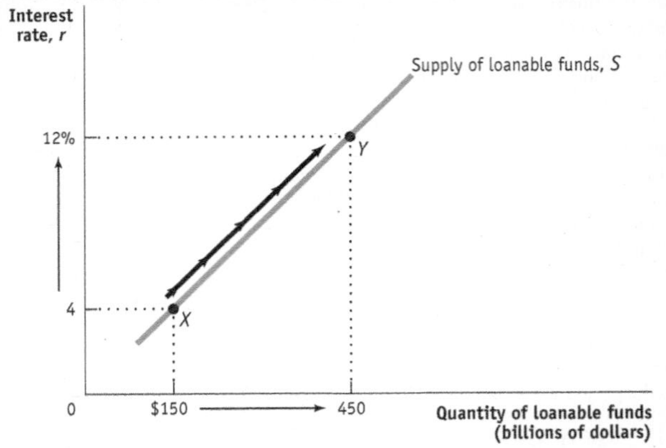

larger amount, $450 billion (point *B*). That's a consequence of our assumption that the demand curve slopes downward: the lower the interest rate, the larger the total quantity of loanable funds demanded. Why do we make that assumption? Because, in reality, the number of potential investment projects that yield at least 4% is always greater than the number that yield at least 12%.

Figure 29.2 shows the hypothetical supply of loanable funds. Again, the interest rate plays the same role that the price plays in ordinary supply and demand analysis. Savers incur an opportunity cost when they lend to a business; the funds could instead be spent on consumption—say, a nice vacation. Whether a given individual becomes a lender by making funds available to borrowers depends on the interest rate received in return. By saving your money today and earning interest on it, you are rewarded with higher consumption in the future when your loan is repaid with interest. So it is a good assumption that more people are willing to forgo current consumption and make a loan when the interest rate is higher. As a result, our hypothetical supply curve of loanable funds slopes upward. In Figure 29.2, lenders will supply $150 billion to the loanable funds market at an interest rate of 4% (point *X*); if the interest rate rises to 12%, the quantity of loanable funds supplied will rise to $450 billion (point *Y*).

AP® Exam Tip

The loanable funds graph is another essential graph for the AP® exam. The incentive to lend money is higher when the interest rate is higher, so the supply curve for loanable funds has an upward slope.

The equilibrium interest rate is the interest rate at which the quantity of loanable funds supplied equals the quantity of loanable funds demanded. As you can see in **Figure 29.3**, the equilibrium interest rate, r_E, and the total quantity of lending, Q_E, are determined by the intersection of the supply and demand curves, at point *E*. Here, the equilibrium interest rate is 8%, at which $300 billion is lent and borrowed. Investment spending projects with a rate of return of 8% or more are funded; projects with a rate of return of less than 8% are not. Correspondingly, only lenders who are willing to accept an interest rate of 8% or less will have their offers to lend funds accepted.

Figure 29.3 shows how the market for loanable funds matches up desired savings with desired investment spending: in equilibrium, the quantity of funds that savers want to lend is equal to the quantity of funds that firms want to borrow. The figure also shows that this match-up is efficient in two senses. First, the right investments get made: the investment spending projects that are actually financed have higher rates of return than those that do not get financed. Second, the right people do the saving: the potential savers who actually lend funds are willing to lend for lower interest rates than

St. Louis Federal Reserve Bank Resources

"Traditional Versus Shadow Banking," ***Page One Economics Classroom Edition*** **(February 2012)**

Modern economies rely heavily on financial intermediaries to channel funds between borrowers and lenders. In this issue, the role of traditional banking is outlined, and a parallel system—shadow banking—is explored.

Figure 29.3 Equilibrium in the Loanable Funds Market

At the equilibrium interest rate, the quantity of loanable funds supplied equals the quantity of loanable funds demanded. Here, the equilibrium interest rate is 8%, with $300 billion of funds lent and borrowed. Investment spending projects with a rate of return of 8% or higher receive funding; those with a lower rate of return do not. Lenders who demand an interest rate of 8% or lower have their offers of loans accepted; those who demand a higher interest rate do not.

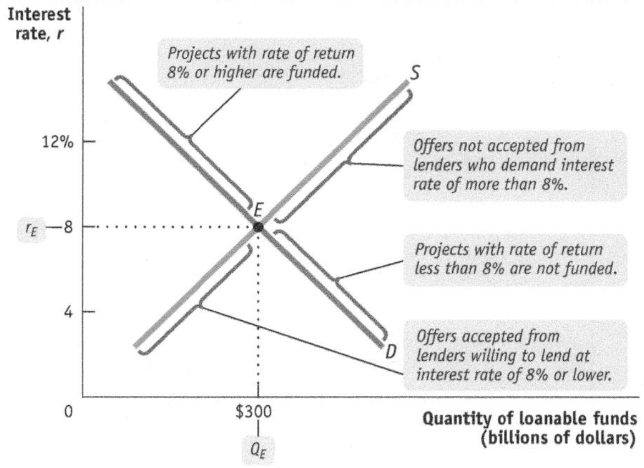

those who do not. The insight that the loanable funds market leads to an efficient use of savings, although drawn from a highly simplified model, has important implications for real life. As we'll see shortly, it is the reason that a well-functioning financial system increases an economy's long-run economic growth rate.

Before we get to that, however, let's look at how the market for loanable funds responds to shifts of demand and supply.

Shifts of the Demand for Loanable Funds The equilibrium interest rate changes when there are shifts of the demand curve for loanable funds, the supply curve for loanable funds, or both. Let's start by looking at the causes and effects of changes in demand.

The factors that can cause the demand curve for loanable funds to shift include the following:

- *Changes in perceived business opportunities.* A change in beliefs about the rate of return on investment spending can increase or reduce the amount of desired spending at any given interest rate. For example, during the 1990s there was great excitement over the business possibilities created by the Internet, which had just begun to be widely used. As a result, businesses rushed to buy computer equipment, put fiber-optic cables in the ground, and so on. This shifted the demand for loanable funds to the right. By 2001, the failure of many dot-com businesses led to disillusionment with technology-related investment; this shifted the demand for loanable funds back to the left.
- *Changes in the government's borrowing.* Governments that run budget deficits are major sources of the demand for loanable funds. As a result, changes in the budget deficit can shift the demand curve for loanable funds. For example, between 2000 and 2003, as the U.S. federal government went from a budget surplus to a budget deficit, net federal borrowing went from *minus* $189 billion—that is, in 2000 the federal government was actually providing loanable funds to the market because it was paying off some of its debt—to *plus* $416 billion because in 2003 the government had to borrow large sums to pay its bills. This change in the federal budget position had the effect, other things equal, of shifting the demand curve for loanable funds to the right.

FOCUS Graph It

Have students draw a correctly labeled loanable funds graph on their personal whiteboards or notebook paper. Ensure that the vertical and horizontal axes are labeled correctly. AP® exam readers typically look for a horizontal axis label that distinguishes the loanable funds market from the money market, so to be safe, have students write out "quantity of loanable funds." They should *not* use a label such as "Money" or "$," which would signal confusion between the two markets. Ask students what would happen if a shortage of loanable funds occurred in the market. *Interest rates would rise to attract savings.* You can use Figure 29.3 to discuss what happens with shortages and surpluses in the market.

TEACH Teach It

Make sure students know the factors that shift the demand for loanable funds. There are only two, but they are important:

- Changes in perceived business opportunities (investment demand)
- Changes in the government's borrowing

Students may be asked to determine if the curve shifts left or right and then draw the graph as part of a free-response question.

Module 29 The Market for Loanable Funds 279

FOCUS Graph It

Have students look at Figure 29.4. What happens to interest rates when the demand for loanable funds increases? *Interest rates increase.* What will cause a decrease in the demand for loanable funds? *A decrease in investment demand or government borrowing.* Ask your students to draw a loanable funds graph showing a decrease in demand for loanable funds. Verify that they have drawn and labeled it correctly. What happens to interest rates when demand for loanable funds decreases? *Interest rates decrease.*

FOCUS Active Learning

Ask students:

- What happens to interest rates if the government is deficit spending? *Demand for loanable funds increases, increasing interest rates.*
- How will the increase in interest rates impact investment spending? *It will decrease.*

Explain that this is called crowding out and it makes fiscal policy less effective because with a decrease in investment spending, *AD* will not shift as far right as anticipated.

FOCUS Flip It

TRM To help them better understand the loanable funds graph, have students watch Jacob Clifford's video "Macro 4.7—Loanable Funds & Crowding Out" (see econextras video list with hyperlinks on the bcs and TRFD). Assign **Worksheet 29.1 (Loanable Funds and Crowding Out)** from the TRM for questions on this video.

TEACH Teach It

Introduce the factors that shift the supply of loanable funds. Again, there are only two that students should remember:

- Changes in private savings
- Changes in capital inflows

Figure 29.4 An Increase in the Demand for Loanable Funds

If the quantity of funds demanded by borrowers rises at any given interest rate, the demand for loanable funds shifts rightward from D_1 to D_2. As a result, the equilibrium interest rate rises from r_1 to r_2.

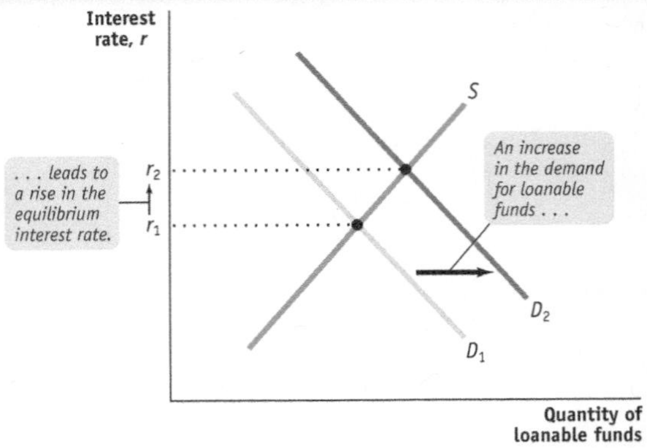

Figure 29.4 shows the effects of an increase in the demand for loanable funds. *S* is the supply of loanable funds, and D_1 is the initial demand curve. The initial equilibrium interest rate is r_1. An increase in the demand for loanable funds means that the quantity of funds demanded rises at any given interest rate, so the demand curve shifts rightward to D_2. As a result, the equilibrium interest rate rises to r_2.

The fact that, other things equal, an increase in the demand for loanable funds leads to a rise in the interest rate has one especially important implication: beyond concern about repayment, there are other reasons to be wary of government budget deficits. As we've already seen, an increase in the government's deficit shifts the demand curve for loanable funds to the right, which leads to a higher interest rate. If the interest rate rises, businesses will cut back on their investment spending. So a rise in the government budget deficit tends to reduce overall investment spending. Economists call the negative effect of government budget deficits on investment spending **crowding out**. The threat of crowding out is a key source of concern about persistent budget deficits.

Crowding out occurs when a government deficit drives up the interest rate and leads to reduced investment spending.

Shifts of the Supply of Loanable Funds Like the demand for loanable funds, the supply of loanable funds can shift. Among the factors that can cause the supply of loanable funds to shift are the following:

- *Changes in private saving behavior.* A number of factors can cause the level of private savings to change at any given rate of interest. For example, between 2000 and 2006 rising home prices in the United States made many homeowners feel richer, making them willing to spend more and save less. This had the effect of shifting the supply of loanable funds to the left. The drop in home prices between 2006 and 2009 had the opposite effect, shifting the supply of loanable funds to the right.
- *Changes in capital inflows.* Capital flows into a country can change as investors' perceptions of that country change. For example, Brazil experienced large capital inflows during much of the last decade because international investors believed that years of economic reforms made it a safe place to put their funds. As we've already seen, the United States has received large capital inflows in recent years, with much of the money coming from China and the Middle East. Those inflows helped fuel a big increase in residential investment spending—newly constructed homes—from 2003 to 2006. As a result of the worldwide slump, those inflows trailed off in 2008 and remained relatively low through early 2014.

Photodisc

St. Louis Federal Reserve Bank Resources

Crowding Out

Students learn that the loanable funds market is a virtual clearinghouse that matches borrowers and savers. Students will participate in an activity to demonstrate crowding out in the loanable funds market. They use demand and supply analysis to graphically represent the results of crowding out.

Figure 29.5 An Increase in the Supply of Loanable Funds

If the quantity of funds supplied by lenders rises at any given interest rate, the supply of loanable funds shifts rightward from S_1 to S_2. As a result, the equilibrium interest rate falls from r_1 to r_2.

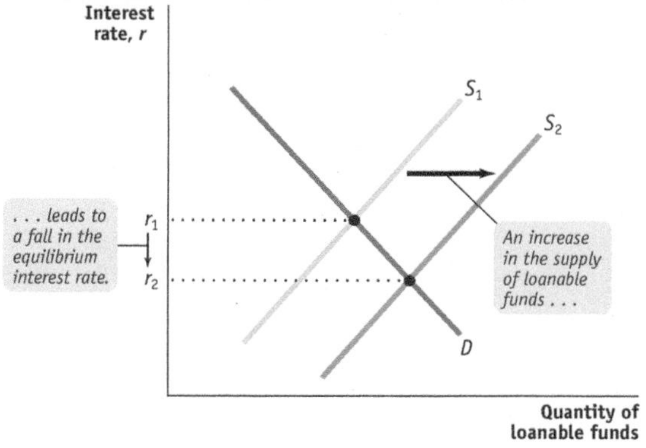

Figure 29.5 shows the effects of an increase in the supply of loanable funds. *D* is the demand for loanable funds, and S_1 is the initial supply curve. The initial equilibrium interest rate is r_1. An increase in the supply of loanable funds means that the quantity of funds supplied rises at any given interest rate, so the supply curve shifts rightward to S_2. As a result, the equilibrium interest rate falls to r_2.

Inflation and Interest Rates Anything that shifts either the supply of loanable funds curve or the demand for loanable funds curve changes the interest rate. Historically, major changes in interest rates have been driven by many factors, including changes in government policy and technological innovations that created new investment opportunities. However, arguably the most important factor affecting interest rates over time—the reason, for example, why interest rates today are much lower than they were in the late 1970s and early 1980s—is changing expectations about future inflation, which shift both the supply of and the demand for loanable funds.

To understand the effect of expected inflation on interest rates, recall our discussion in Module 14 of the way inflation creates winners and losers—for example, the way that high U.S. inflation in the 1970s and 1980s reduced the real value of homeowners' mortgages, which was good for the homeowners but bad for the banks. We know that economists capture the effect of inflation on borrowers and lenders by distinguishing between the *nominal interest rate* and the *real interest rate*, where the distinction is as follows:

$$\text{Real interest rate} = \text{Nominal interest rate} - \text{Inflation rate}$$

The true cost of borrowing is the real interest rate, not the nominal interest rate. To see why, suppose a firm borrows $10,000 for one year at a 10% nominal interest rate. At the end of the year, it must repay $11,000—the amount borrowed plus the interest. But suppose that over the course of the year the average level of prices increases by 10%, so that the real interest rate is zero. Then the $11,000 repayment has the same purchasing power as the original $10,000 loan. In effect, the borrower has received a zero-interest loan.

Similarly, the true payoff to lending is the real interest rate, not the nominal rate. The bank that makes the one-year $10,000 loan at a 10% nominal interest rate receives an $11,000 repayment at the end of the year. But the 10% increase in the average level

FOCUS Graph It

Have students look at Figure 29.5. What happens to interest rates when the supply of loanable funds increases? *Interest rates decrease.* What will cause a decrease in the supply of loanable funds? *A decrease in savings or capital inflows.* Ask your students to draw a loanable funds graph showing a decrease in the supply of loanable funds. Verify that they have drawn and labeled it correctly. What happens to interest rates when the supply of loanable funds decreases? *Interest rates increase.*

TEACH Connect It

We have seen in previous modules that unexpected inflation creates winners and losers, particularly among borrowers and lenders. The real interest rate helps economists identify winners and losers. Recall that Real interest rate = Nominal interest rate − Inflation. For borrowers, the true cost of borrowing is the real interest rate, not the nominal interest rate. For lenders, the true payoff to lending is the real interest rate, not the nominal interest rate.

FOCUS Active Learning

TRM Assign **Worksheet 29.2 (The Market for Loanable Funds)** from the TRM in class or as homework. Students will graph four scenarios to determine if the supply or demand of loanable funds will change.

St. Louis Federal Reserve Bank Resources

"Inflation," *The Economic Lowdown Podcast Series*, Episode 4

The fourth episode of this series discusses three aspects of inflation: what it is, what causes it, and how it is measured. The episode also addresses related topics such as deflation, disinflation, and the role of the Federal Reserve in monitoring inflation.

St. Louis Federal Reserve Bank Resources

Inflation Online Course for Teachers and Students

What impact does inflation have on saving? Would you prefer that your friend repay you the $50 he owes you today or a year from today? To make an informed decision, your students need an understanding of inflation.

of prices means that the purchasing power of the money the bank gets back is no more than that of the money it lent out. In effect, the bank has made a zero-interest loan.

The expectations of borrowers and lenders about future inflation rates are normally based on recent experience. In the late 1970s, after a decade of high inflation, borrowers and lenders expected future inflation to be high. By the late 1990s, after a decade of fairly low inflation, borrowers and lenders expected future inflation to be low. And these changing expectations about future inflation had a strong effect on the nominal interest rate, largely explaining why interest rates were much lower in the early years of the twenty-first century than they were in the early 1980s.

Let's look at how changes in the expected future rate of inflation are reflected in the loanable funds model. In **Figure 29.6**, the curves S_0 and D_0 show the supply of and demand for loanable funds given that the expected future rate of inflation is 0%. In that case, equilibrium is at E_0 and the equilibrium nominal interest rate is 4%. Because expected future inflation is 0%, the equilibrium expected real interest rate over the life of the loan, the real interest rate expected by borrowers and lenders when the loan is contracted, is also 4%.

Now suppose that the expected future inflation rate rises to 10%. The demand curve for funds shifts upward to D_{10}: borrowers are now willing to borrow as much at a nominal interest rate of 14% as they were previously willing to borrow at 4%. That's because with a 10% inflation rate, a borrower who pays a 14% nominal interest rate pays a 4% real interest rate. Similarly, the supply curve of funds shifts upward to S_{10}: lenders require a nominal interest rate of 14% to persuade them to lend as much as they would previously have lent at 4%. That's because with a 10% inflation rate, a lender who receives a 14% nominal interest rate receives a 4% real interest rate. The new equilibrium is at E_{10}: the result of an increase in the expected future inflation rate from 0% to 10% is that the equilibrium nominal interest rate rises from 4% to 14%.

According to the **Fisher effect**, an increase in expected future inflation drives up the nominal interest rate by the same number of percentage points, leaving the expected real interest rate unchanged.

This situation can be summarized as a general principle, named the **Fisher effect** after the American economist Irving Fisher, who proposed it in 1930: an increase in expected inflation drives up the nominal interest rate by the same number of percentage points, leaving the expected real interest rate unchanged. The central point is that both lenders and borrowers base their decisions on the expected real interest rate. As a result, a change in the expected rate of inflation does not affect the equilibrium quantity of loanable funds or the expected real interest rate; all it affects is the equilibrium nominal interest rate.

Figure 29.6 The Fisher Effect

D_0 and S_0 are the demand and supply curves for loanable funds when the expected future inflation rate is 0%. At an expected inflation rate of 0%, the equilibrium nominal interest rate is 4%. An increase in expected future inflation pushes both the demand and supply curves upward by 1 percentage point for every percentage point increase in expected future inflation. D_{10} and S_{10} are the demand and supply curves for loanable funds when the expected future inflation rate is 10%. The 10 percentage point increase in expected future inflation raises the equilibrium nominal interest rate to 14%. The expected real interest rate remains at 4%, and the equilibrium quantity of loanable funds also remains unchanged.

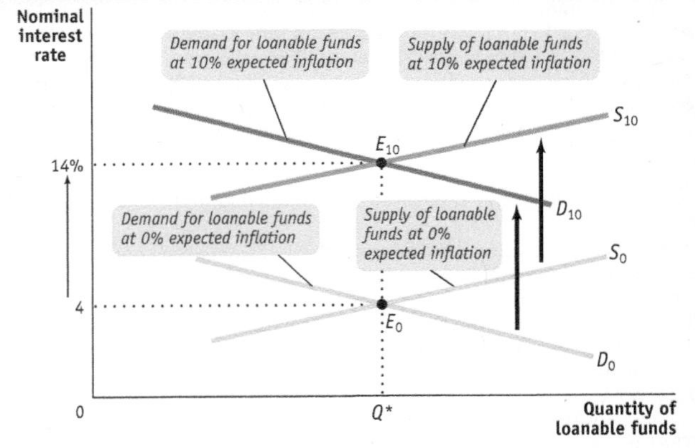

TEACH Teach It

Use Figure 29.6 to help students understand the Fisher effect. The Fisher effect states that the expected real interest rate is unaffected by the change in expected future inflation. The central point is that both lenders and borrowers base their decisions on the *expected* real interest rate. As long as the level of inflation is expected, it does not affect the equilibrium quantity of loanable funds or the expected real interest rate; all it affects is the equilibrium nominal interest rate. If expected future interest rates rise from 6% to 10%, while the expected real interest rates remain unchanged, what will happen to the quantity of loans demanded? *They will remain unchanged because the expected real interest rate did not change.*

FOCUS Flip It

As a review of real and nominal interest rates, have students watch Jacob Clifford's video "Macro 4.6—Interest Rates: Real vs Nominal Practice" (see econextras video list with hyperlinks on the bcs and TRFD). Tell students to pause the video at 1:40 to allow them time to calculate the real and nominal interest rates and rate of inflation in the practice questions.

St. Louis Federal Reserve Bank Resources

"Making Sense of the Ups and Downs of Prices," *Page One Economics Classroom Edition (August 2013)*

Have you ever heard someone say, "Back in my day, a gallon of gas cost a quarter!"? Comparing today's prices with prices "back in the day" can be misleading. Both inflation and deflation between then and now have to be taken into account. Have your students read this issue to learn more about the effects of inflation on prices.

Additional St. Louis Fed resources on these topics are provided in the St. Louis Fed resource list in the TRM.

St. Louis Federal Reserve Bank Resources

"Money and Inflation: A Functional Relationship," *Page One Economics Classroom Edition* (March 2013)

They say that "money makes the world go round." Just imagine a world without money as our method of payment for everyday transactions. Without money, we would all need to barter for necessary goods and services. For example, suppose an accountant needs to have her car fixed. Under a barter system, she would have to find someone who needed some tax advice in exchange for car repairs. The search to find a barter partner is time-consuming and wasteful. Money solves this problem and many others. Read more about the three main functions of money and the damaging effects of too much inflation on these functions in this issue.

Reconciling the Two Interest Rate Models

In Module 28 we developed what is known as the liquidity preference model of the interest rate. In that model, the equilibrium interest rate is the rate at which the quantity of money demanded equals the quantity of money supplied in the money market. In the loanable funds model, we see that the interest rate matches the quantity of loanable funds supplied by savers with the quantity of loanable funds demanded for investment spending. How do the two models compare?

The Interest Rate in the Short Run

As we explained using the liquidity preference model, a fall in the interest rate leads to a rise in investment spending, I, which then leads to a rise in both real GDP and consumer spending, C. The rise in real GDP doesn't lead only to a rise in consumer spending, however. It also leads to a rise in savings: at each stage of the multiplier process, part of the increase in disposable income is saved. How much do savings rise? According to the *savings–investment spending identity*, total savings in the economy is always equal to investment spending. This tells us that when a fall in the interest rate leads to higher investment spending, the resulting increase in real GDP generates exactly enough additional savings to match the rise in investment spending. To put it another way, after a fall in the interest rate, the quantity of savings supplied rises exactly enough to match the quantity of savings demanded.

Figure 29.7 shows how our two models of the interest rate are reconciled in the short run by the links among changes in the interest rate, changes in real GDP, and changes in savings. Panel (a) represents the liquidity preference model of the interest rate. MS_1 and MD_1 are the initial supply and demand curves for money. According to the liquidity preference model, the equilibrium interest rate in the economy is the rate at which the quantity of money supplied is equal to the quantity of money demanded

Figure 29.7 The Short-Run Determination of the Interest Rate

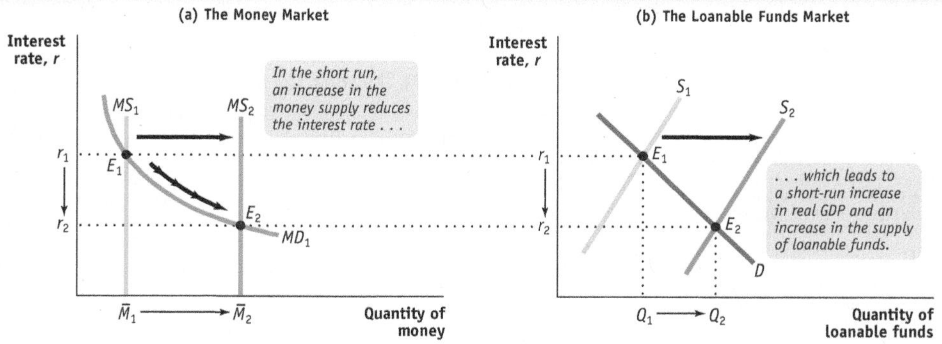

Panel (a) shows the liquidity preference model of the interest rate: the equilibrium interest rate matches the money supply to the quantity of money demanded. In the short run, the interest rate is determined in the money market, where an increase in the money supply, from $\overline{M}_1$ to $\overline{M}_2$, pushes the equilibrium interest rate down, from r_1 to r_2. Panel (b) shows the loanable funds model of the interest rate. The fall in the interest rate in the money market leads, through the multiplier effect, to an increase in real GDP and savings; to a rightward shift of the supply curve of loanable funds, from S_1 to S_2; and to a fall in the interest rate, from r_1 to r_2. As a result, the new equilibrium interest rate in the loanable funds market matches the new equilibrium interest rate in the money market at r_2.

TEACH **Teach It**

Make sure students understand that total savings in the economy is always equal to investment spending. Use Figure 29.7 to explain the interest rates in the two models in the short run. When the Fed increases the money supply, interest rates drop. However, the supply of loanable funds will increase in the short run to match the increase in the quantity demanded at a new lower interest rate.

in the money market. Panel (b) represents the loanable funds model of the interest rate. S_1 is the initial supply curve and D is the demand curve for loanable funds. According to the loanable funds model, the equilibrium interest rate in the economy is the rate at which the quantity of loanable funds supplied is equal to the quantity of loanable funds demanded in the market for loanable funds.

In Figure 29.7 both the money market and the market for loanable funds are initially in equilibrium at E_1 with the same interest rate, r_1. You might think that this would happen only by accident, but in fact it will always be true. To see why, let's look at what happens when the Fed increases the money supply from $\overline{M}_1$ to $\overline{M}_2$. This pushes the money supply curve rightward to MS_2, causing the equilibrium interest rate in the market for money to fall to r_2, and the economy moves to a short-run equilibrium at E_2. What happens in panel (b), in the market for loanable funds? In the short run, the fall in the interest rate due to the increase in the money supply leads to a rise in real GDP, which generates a rise in savings through the multiplier process. This rise in savings shifts the supply curve for loanable funds rightward, from S_1 to S_2, moving the equilibrium in the loanable funds market from E_1 to E_2 and also reducing the equilibrium interest rate in the loanable funds market. And we know that savings rise by exactly enough to match the rise in investment spending. This tells us that the equilibrium rate in the loanable funds market falls to r_2, the same as the new equilibrium interest rate in the money market.

In the short run, then, the supply and demand for money determine the interest rate, and the loanable funds market follows the lead of the money market. When a change in the supply of money leads to a change in the interest rate, the resulting change in real GDP causes the supply of loanable funds to change as well. As a result, the equilibrium interest rate in the loanable funds market is the same as the equilibrium interest rate in the money market.

Notice our use of the phrase "in the short run." Changes in aggregate demand affect aggregate output only in the short run. In the long run, aggregate output is equal to potential output. So our story about how a fall in the interest rate leads to a rise in aggregate output, which leads to a rise in savings, applies only to the short run. In the long run, as we'll see next, the determination of the interest rate is quite different because the roles of the two markets are reversed. In the long run, the loanable funds market determines the equilibrium interest rate, and it is the market for money that follows the lead of the loanable funds market.

The Interest Rate in the Long Run

In the short run an increase in the money supply leads to a fall in the interest rate, and a decrease in the money supply leads to a rise in the interest rate. In the long run, however, changes in the money supply don't affect the interest rate.

Figure 29.8 shows why. As in Figure 29.7, panel (a) shows the liquidity preference model of the interest rate and panel (b) shows the supply and demand for loanable funds. We assume that in both panels the economy is initially at E_1, in long-run macroeconomic equilibrium at potential output with the money supply equal to $\overline{M}_1$. The demand curve for loanable funds is D, and the initial supply curve for loanable funds is S_1. The initial equilibrium interest rate in both markets is r_1.

Now suppose the money supply rises from $\overline{M}_1$ to $\overline{M}_2$. As we saw in Figure 29.7, this initially reduces the interest rate to r_2. However, in the long run the aggregate price level will rise by the same proportion as the increase in the money supply (due to the *neutrality of money*, a topic presented in detail in the next section). A rise in the aggregate price level increases money demand by the same proportion. So in the long run the money demand curve shifts out to MD_2, and the equilibrium interest rate rises back to its original level, r_1.

Panel (b) of Figure 29.8 shows what happens in the market for loanable funds. We saw earlier that an increase in the money supply leads to a short-run rise in real GDP and that this rise shifts the supply of loanable funds rightward from S_1 to S_2. In the long run, however, real GDP falls back to its original level as wages and other nominal prices rise. As a result, the supply of loanable funds, S, which initially shifted from S_1 to S_2, shifts back to S_1.

AP® Exam Tip

To determine which graph to draw for an AP® exam question, watch for mentions of the money market, which indicate that you should draw a *money market* graph with a vertical supply curve, or mentions of loanable funds, which suggest that you should draw a *loanable funds* market graph with an upward-sloping supply curve.

TEACH Teach It

In the long run, changes in the money supply don't affect the interest rate. Use Figure 29.8 to help students understand long-run changes. In the long run, an increase in the money supply increases real GDP and the price level, prompting increases in wages and other nominal prices. This then shifts the money demand curve up until the equilibrium interest rate equals the original interest rate. In the loanable funds market, supply increases, only to decrease when real GDP falls back to its original level as wages and other nominal prices rise.

OPEN & CLOSE Exit Slip

TRM *Please see **Exit Slip: Module 29** in the TRM for formative multiple-choice questions to ask before finishing your lesson. These questions will help you quickly assess whether your students have mastered the module's concepts before moving on.*

Answers to the Exit Slip Questions

1. D
2. B
3. D

284 Section 5 The Financial Sector

Figure 29.8 The Long-Run Determination of the Interest Rate

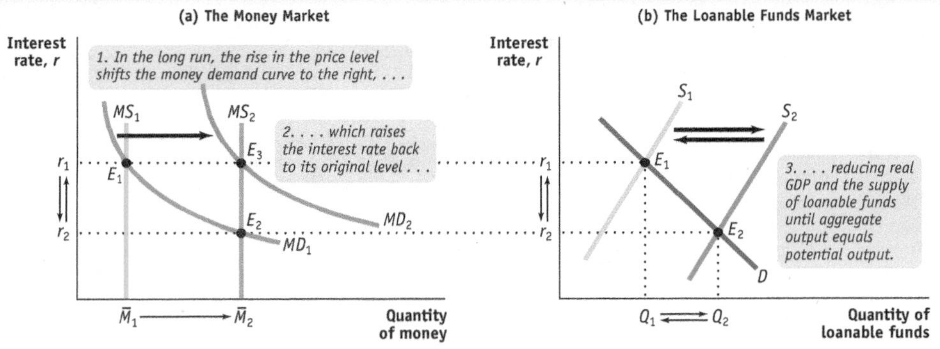

Panel (a) shows the liquidity preference model long-run adjustment to an increase in the money supply from $\bar{M}_1$ to $\bar{M}_2$; panel (b) shows the corresponding long-run adjustment in the loanable funds market. As we discussed in Figure 29.7, the increase in the money supply reduces the interest rate from r_1 to r_2, increases real GDP, and increases savings in the short run. This is shown in panel (a) and panel (b) as the movement from E_1 to E_2. In the long run, however, the increase in the money supply raises wages and other nominal prices; this shifts the money demand curve in panel (a) from MD_1 to MD_2, leading to an increase in the interest rate from r_2 to r_1 as the economy moves from E_2 to E_3. The rise in the interest rate causes a fall in real GDP and a fall in savings, shifting the loanable funds supply curve back to S_1 from S_2 and moving the loanable funds market from E_2 back to E_1. In the long run, the equilibrium interest rate is the rate that matches the supply and demand for loanable funds when real GDP equals potential output.

In the long run, then, changes in the money supply do not affect the interest rate. So what determines the interest rate in the long run—that is, what determines r_1 in Figure 29.8? The answer is the supply and demand for loanable funds. More specifically, in the long run the equilibrium interest rate is the rate that matches the supply of loanable funds with the demand for loanable funds when real GDP equals potential output.

MODULE 29 Review

Check Your Understanding

1. Use a diagram of the loanable funds market to illustrate the effect of the following events on the equilibrium interest rate and quantity of loanable funds.
   a. An economy is opened to international movements of capital, and a capital inflow occurs.
   b. Retired people generally save less than working people at any interest rate. The proportion of retired people in the population goes up.
2. Explain what is wrong with the following statement: "Savings and investment spending may not be equal in the economy as a whole in equilibrium because when the interest rate rises, households will want to save more money than businesses will want to invest."
3. Suppose that expected inflation rises from 3% to 6%.
   a. How will the real interest rate be affected by this change?
   b. How will the nominal interest rate be affected by this change?
   c. What will happen to the equilibrium quantity of loanable funds?

Answers to Module 29 Review Questions

Check Your Understanding

1. a. As capital flows into the economy, the supply of loanable funds increases. This is illustrated by the shift of the supply curve from S_1 to S_2 in the accompanying diagram. As the equilibrium moves from E_1 to E_2, the equilibrium interest rate falls from r_1 to r_2, and the equilibrium quantity of loanable funds increases from Q_1 to Q_2.

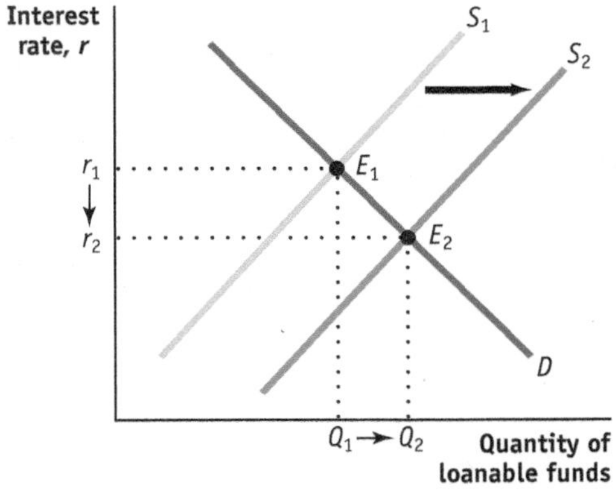

b. Savings fall due to the higher proportion of retired people, and the supply of loanable funds decreases. This is illustrated by the leftward shift of the supply curve from S_1 to S_2 in the accompanying diagram. The equilibrium moves from E_1 to E_2, the equilibrium interest rate rises from r_1 to r_2, and the equilibrium quantity of loanable funds falls from Q_1 to Q_2.

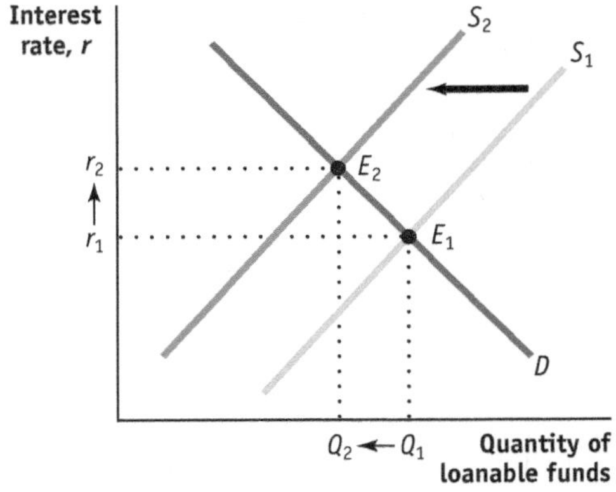

2. We know from the loanable funds market that as the interest rate rises, households want to save more and consume less. But at the same time, an increase in the interest rate lowers the number of investment spending projects with returns at least as high as the interest rate. The statement "Households will want to save more money than businesses will want to invest" cannot represent an equilibrium in the loanable funds market because it says that the quantity of loanable funds offered exceeds the quantity of loanable funds demanded. If that were to occur, the interest rate would fall to make the quantity of loanable funds offered equal to the quantity of loanable funds demanded.

3. a. The real interest rate will not change. According to the Fisher effect, an increase in expected inflation drives up the nominal interest rate, leaving the real interest rate unchanged.
b. The nominal interest rate will rise by 3%. Each additional percentage point of expected inflation drives up the nominal interest rate by 1 percentage point.
c. As long as inflation is expected, it does not affect the equilibrium quantity of loanable funds. Both the supply and demand curves for loanable funds are pushed upward, leaving the equilibrium quantity of loanable funds unchanged.

Tackle the Test: Multiple-Choice Questions

1. c
2. b
3. b
4. c
5. a

Tackle the Test: Free-Response Question

Rubric for FRQ 2 (4 points)

1 point: This causes an increase (rightward shift) in the supply of loanable funds.

1 point: This causes a decrease (leftward shift) in the demand for loanable funds.

1 point: This causes an increase (rightward shift) in the demand for loanable funds.

1 point: This causes a decrease (leftward shift) in the supply of loanable funds.

Tackle the Test: Multiple-Choice Questions

1. A business will decide whether or not to borrow money to finance a project based on a comparison of the interest rate with the ______ from its project.
   a. expected revenue
   b. profit
   c. rate of return
   d. cost generated
   e. demand generated
2. The real interest rate equals the
   a. nominal interest rate plus the inflation rate.
   b. nominal interest rate minus the inflation rate.
   c. nominal interest rate divided by the inflation rate.
   d. nominal interest rate times the inflation rate.
   e. federal funds rate.
3. Which of the following will increase the demand for loanable funds?
   a. a federal government budget surplus
   b. an increase in perceived business opportunities
   c. a decrease in the interest rate
   d. positive capital inflows
   e. decreased private saving rates
4. Which of the following will increase the supply of loanable funds?
   a. an increase in perceived business opportunities
   b. decreased government borrowing
   c. an increased private saving rate
   d. an increase in the expected inflation rate
   e. a decrease in capital inflows
5. Both lenders and borrowers base their decisions on
   a. expected real interest rates.
   b. expected nominal interest rates.
   c. real interest rates.
   d. nominal interest rates.
   e. nominal interest rates minus real interest rates.

Tackle the Test: Free-Response Questions

1. Draw a correctly labeled graph showing equilibrium in the loanable funds market.

Rubric for FRQ 1 (6 points)

1 point: Vertical axis labeled "Interest rate" or "r"

1 point: Horizontal axis labeled "Quantity of loanable funds"

1 point: Downward-sloping demand curve for loanable funds (labeled)

1 point: Upward-sloping supply curve for loanable funds (labeled)

1 point: Equilibrium quantity of loanable funds shown on horizontal axis below where curves intersect

1 point: Equilibrium interest rate shown on vertical axis across from where curves intersect

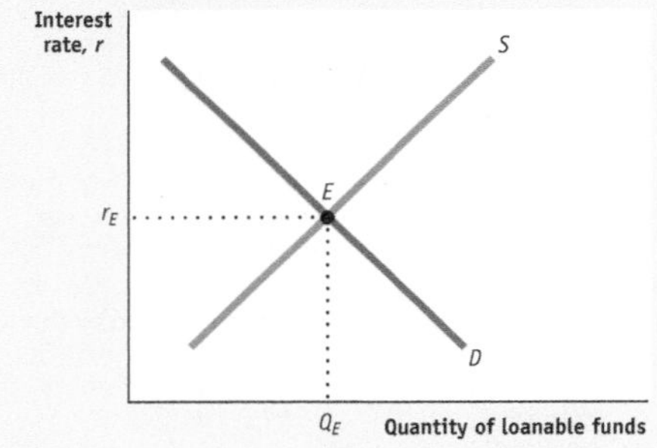

2. Does each of the following affect either the supply or the demand for loanable funds, and if so, does the affected curve increase (shift to the right) or decrease (shift to the left)?
   a. There is an increase in capital inflows into the economy.
   b. Businesses are pessimistic about future business conditions.
   c. The government increases borrowing.
   d. The private saving rate decreases.
   (4 points)

286 Section 5 The Financial Sector

SECTION 5 Review

Section 5 Review Video

Module 22

1. Investment in physical capital is necessary for long-run economic growth. So in order for an economy to grow, it must channel savings into investment spending. The price charged per year by lenders to investors and other borrowers for the use of their savings is the **interest rate**, which is calculated as a percentage of the amount borrowed.
2. According to the **savings-investment spending identity**, savings and investment spending are always equal for the economy as a whole. The government is a source of savings when it runs a positive **budget balance**, also known as a **budget surplus**; it is a source of dissavings when it runs a negative budget balance, also known as a **budget deficit**. In a closed economy, savings is equal to **national savings**, the sum of private savings plus the budget balance. In an open economy, savings is equal to national savings plus **capital inflow** of foreign savings. When a capital outflow, or negative capital inflow, occurs, some portion of national savings is funding investment spending in other countries.
3. Households invest their current savings or **wealth**—their accumulated savings—by purchasing assets. Assets come in the form of either a **financial asset**, a paper claim that entitles the buyer to future income from the seller, or a **physical asset**, a claim on a tangible object that gives the owner the right to dispose of it as desired. A financial asset is also a **liability** from the point of view of its seller. There are four main types of financial assets: loans, bonds, stocks, and **bank deposits**. Each of them serves a different purpose in addressing the three fundamental tasks of a financial system: reducing **transaction costs**—the cost of making a deal; reducing **financial risk**—uncertainty about future outcomes that involves financial gains and losses; and providing **liquid** assets—assets that can be quickly converted into cash without much loss of value (in contrast to **illiquid** assets, which are not easily converted).
4. Although many small and moderate-size borrowers use bank **loans** to fund investment spending, larger companies typically issue bonds. Bonds with a higher risk of **default** must typically pay a higher interest rate. Business owners reduce their risk by selling stock. Although stocks usually generate a higher return than bonds, investors typically wish to reduce their risk by engaging in **diversification**, owning a wide range of assets whose returns are based on unrelated, or independent, events. Most people are risk-averse, viewing the loss of a given amount of money as a significant hardship but viewing the gain of an equal amount of money as a much less significant benefit. **Loan-backed securities**, a recent innovation, are assets created by pooling individual loans and selling shares of that pool to investors. Because they are more diversified and more liquid than individual loans, trading on financial markets like bonds, they are preferred by investors. It can be difficult, however, to assess their quality.
5. **Financial intermediaries**—institutions such as **mutual funds**, **pension funds**, **life insurance companies**, and **banks**—are critical components of the financial system. Mutual funds and pension funds allow small investors to diversify and life insurance companies allow families to reduce risk.
6. A bank allows individuals to hold liquid bank deposits that are then used to finance investments in illiquid assets. Banks can perform this mismatch because on average only a small fraction of depositors withdraw their savings at any one time. Banks are a key ingredient in long-run economic growth.

Module 23

7. **Money** is any asset that can easily be used to purchase goods and services. **Currency in circulation** and **checkable bank deposits** are both considered part of the **money supply**. Money plays three roles: it is a **medium of exchange** used for transactions, a **store of value** that holds purchasing power over time, and a **unit of account** in which prices are stated.
8. Over time, **commodity money**, which consists of goods possessing value aside from their role as money, such as gold and silver coins, was replaced by **commodity-backed money**, such as paper currency backed by gold. Today the dollar is pure **fiat money**, whose value derives solely from its official role.
9. The Federal Reserve calculates two measures of the money supply. M1 is the narrowest **monetary aggregate**; it contains only currency in circulation, traveler's checks, and checkable bank deposits. M2 includes a wider range of assets called **near-moneys**, mainly other forms of bank deposits, that can easily be converted into checkable bank deposits.

FOCUS Flip It

Encourage your students to watch the **Section 5 Review Video**, which was created as a special student review tool and is linked into the e-Book or can be found on the book's companion website.

Module 24

10. The accumulation of interest causes any amount of money loaned today to grow into a larger amount, called the **future value**, over the loan period.
11. In order to evaluate a project in which costs or benefits are realized in the future, you must first transform them into their **present values** using the interest rate, *r*. The present value of $1 realized one year from now is $\$1/(1 + r)$, the amount of money you must lend out today to have $1 one year from now. Once this transformation is done, you should choose the project with the highest **net present value**.

Module 25

12. Banks allow depositors immediate access to their funds, but they also lend out most of the funds deposited in their care. To meet demands for cash, they maintain **bank reserves** composed of both currency held in vaults and deposits at the Federal Reserve. The **reserve ratio** is the ratio of bank reserves to bank deposits. A **T-account** summarizes a bank's financial position, with loans and reserves counted as assets, and deposits counted as liabilities.
13. Banks have sometimes been subject to **bank runs**, most notably in the early 1930s. To avert this danger, depositors are now protected by **deposit insurance**, bank owners face capital requirements that reduce the incentive to make overly risky loans with depositors' funds, banks must satisfy **reserve requirements**—a legally mandated **required reserve ratio**, and the Federal Reserve stands ready to lend money to banks through the **discount window**.
14. When currency is deposited in a bank, it starts a multiplier process in which banks lend out **excess reserves**, leading to an increase in the money supply—so banks create money. If the entire money supply consisted of checkable bank deposits, the money supply would be equal to the value of reserves divided by the reserve ratio. In reality, much of the **monetary base** consists of currency in circulation, and the **money multiplier** is the ratio of the money supply to the monetary base.

Module 26

15. The Federal Reserve or "the Fed" is the **central bank** of the United States. In response to the Panic of 1907, the Fed was created to centralize holding of reserves, inspect banks' books, and make the money supply sufficiently responsive to varying economic conditions.
16. The Great Depression sparked widespread bank runs in the early 1930s, which greatly worsened and lengthened the depth of the Depression. Federal deposit insurance was created, and the government recapitalized banks by lending to them and by buying shares of banks. By 1933, banks had been separated into two categories: **commercial** (covered by deposit insurance) and **investment** (not covered). Public acceptance of deposit insurance finally stopped the bank runs of the Great Depression.
17. The **savings and loan (thrift)** crisis of the 1980s arose because insufficiently regulated S&Ls engaged in overly risky speculation and incurred huge losses. Depositors in failed S&Ls were compensated with taxpayer funds because they were covered by deposit insurance. However, the crisis caused steep losses in the financial and real estate sectors, resulting in a recession in the early 1990s.
18. As housing prices rose between 2003 and 2006, lenders made large quantities of questionable mortgage loans. When housing prices tumbled, massive losses by banks and nonbank financial institutions led to widespread collapse in the financial system. To prevent another Great Depression, the Fed and the U.S. Treasury expanded lending to bank and nonbank institutions, provided capital through the purchase of bank shares, and purchased private debt. Because much of the crisis originated in nontraditional bank institutions, the crisis of 2008 raised the question of whether a wider safety net and broader regulation were needed in the financial sector.

Module 27

19. The Fed regulates banks and sets reserve requirements. To meet those requirements, banks borrow and lend reserves in the **federal funds market** at the **federal funds rate**. Banks can also borrow from the Fed at the **discount rate**.
20. **Open-market operations** by the Fed are the principal tool of monetary policy: the Fed can increase or reduce the monetary base by buying U.S. Treasury bills from banks or selling U.S. Treasury bills to banks.

288 Section 5 The Financial Sector

Module 28

21. The **money demand curve** arises from a trade-off between the opportunity cost of holding money and the liquidity that money provides. The opportunity cost of holding money depends on **short-term interest rates**, not **long-term interest rates**. Changes in the aggregate price level, real GDP, technology, and institutions shift the money demand curve.

22. According to the **liquidity preference model of the interest rate**, the interest rate is determined in the money market by the money demand curve and the **money supply curve**. The Federal Reserve can change the interest rate in the short run by shifting the money supply curve. In practice, the Fed uses open-market operations to achieve a target federal funds rate, which other short-term interest rates generally follow.

Module 29

23. The hypothetical **loanable funds market** shows how loans from savers are allocated among borrowers with investment spending projects. In equilibrium, only those projects with a **rate of return** greater than or equal to the equilibrium interest rate will be funded. By showing how gains from trade between lenders and borrowers are maximized, the loanable funds market shows why a well-functioning financial system leads to greater long-run economic growth. Government budget deficits can raise the interest rate and can lead to **crowding out** of investment spending. Changes in perceived business opportunities and in government borrowing shift the demand curve for loanable funds; changes in private savings and capital inflows shift the supply curve.

24. Because neither borrowers nor lenders can know the future inflation rate, loans specify a nominal interest rate rather than a real interest rate. For a given expected future inflation rate, shifts of the demand and supply curves of loanable funds result in changes in the underlying real interest rate, leading to changes in the nominal interest rate. According to the **Fisher effect**, an increase in expected future inflation raises the nominal interest rate by the same number of percentage points, so that the expected real interest rate remains unchanged.

Key Terms

Interest rate, p. 223
Savings–investment spending identity, p. 224
Budget surplus, p. 224
Budget deficit, p. 224
Budget balance, p. 224
National savings, p. 224
Capital inflow, p. 225
Wealth, p. 225
Financial asset, p. 225
Physical asset, p. 225
Liability, p. 225
Transaction costs, p. 226
Financial risk, p. 226
Diversification, p. 226
Liquid, p. 227
Illiquid, p. 227
Loan, p. 227
Default, p. 228
Loan-backed securities, p. 228
Financial intermediary, p. 229
Mutual fund, p. 229
Pension fund, p. 229
Life insurance company, p. 230
Bank deposit, p. 230
Bank, p. 230
Money, p. 232
Currency in circulation, p. 233
Checkable bank deposits, p. 233
Money supply, p. 233
Medium of exchange, p. 233
Store of value, p. 234
Unit of account, p. 234
Commodity money, p. 234
Commodity-backed money, p. 234
Fiat money, p. 235
Monetary aggregate, p. 236
Near-moneys, p. 236
Future value, p. 239
Present value, p. 240
Net present value, p. 241
Bank reserves, p. 244
T-account, p. 245
Reserve ratio, p. 245
Required reserve ratio, p. 245
Bank run, p. 247
Deposit insurance, p. 247
Reserve requirements, p. 247
Discount window, p. 247
Excess reserves, p. 250
Monetary base, p. 251
Money multiplier, p. 251
Central bank, p. 254
Commercial bank, p. 258
Investment bank, p. 258
Savings and loan (thrift), p. 258
Federal funds market, p. 262
Federal funds rate, p. 262
Discount rate, p. 262
Open-market operation, p. 263
Short-term interest rates, p. 268
Long-term interest rates, p. 269
Money demand curve, p. 270
Liquidity preference model of the interest rate, p. 272
Money supply curve, p. 272
Loanable funds market, p. 276
Rate of return, p. 277
Crowding out, p. 280
Fisher effect, p. 282

Section 5 Review 289

Answers to Section 5 AP® Exam Practice Questions

Multiple-Choice Questions

1. b	6. e	11. b
2. e	7. c	12. c
3. a	8. b	13. c
4. e	9. d	14. c
5. a	10. a	

AP® Exam Practice Questions

Multiple-Choice Questions

1. The interest rate is
   a. the opportunity cost of lending money.
   b. the price borrowers pay for the use of lenders' savings.
   c. a percentage of the amount saved by borrowers.
   d. the rate charged by banks to hold savings for one year.
   e. the amount earned by using profits to build a new factory.
2. Which of the following identities is true in a simplified economy with no government and no interaction with other countries?
   a. consumer spending = investment spending
   b. total income = consumer spending − investment spending
   c. total spending = investment spending + savings
   d. investment spending = total spending − savings
   e. savings = investment spending
3. A budget surplus exists when the government does which of the following?
   a. saves
   b. collects less tax revenue than it spends
   c. has a negative budget balance
   d. increases the national debt
   e. uses expansionary fiscal policy
4. Which of the following is a task of an economy's financial system?
   a. maximizing risk
   b. increasing transactions costs
   c. decreasing diversification
   d. eliminating liquidity
   e. enhancing the efficiency of financial markets
5. A financial intermediary that resells shares of a stock portfolio is a
   a. mutual fund.
   b. pension fund.
   c. loan-backed security.
   d. bond broker.
   e. depository institution.
6. Which of the following assets is most liquid?
   a. stock
   b. bond
   c. loan
   d. mutual fund
   e. cash
7. When money acts as a means of holding purchasing power over time, it is serving which function?
   a. medium of exchange
   b. source of liquidity
   c. store of value
   d. unit of account
   e. source of wealth
8. Which of the following is an example of using money as a unit of account?
   a. buying a new T-shirt
   b. purchasing $10 worth of candy
   c. keeping the dollar you receive each year for your birthday for 10 years
   d. putting money into your savings account
   e. paying for lunch with your debit card
9. Which of the following is a desirable characteristic of money?
   a. fixed supply
   b. large denominations
   c. made of precious metal
   d. widely accepted
   e. backed by commodities
10. Fiat money derives its value from which of the following?
    a. its official status
    b. the good being used as a medium of exchange
    c. a promise it can be converted into something valuable
    d. gold or silver
    e. exchange rates
11. The M1 money supply includes which of the following?
    a. near-moneys
    b. checkable deposits
    c. savings accounts
    d. time deposits
    e. mutual funds
12. The present value of $1 you receive one year from now is equal to
    a. $\$1(1 + r)$.
    b. $\$1/(1 - r)$.
    c. $\$1/(1 + r)$.
    d. $\$1(1 + r^2)$.
    e. $\$1(1 + r)^2$.
13. If the interest rate is 2%, the amount received 1 year from now as a result of lending $1,000 today is
    a. $980.
    b. $1,000.
    c. $1,020.
    d. $1,200.
    e. $2,000.
14. The liquid assets banks keep in their vaults are known as bank
    a. deposits.
    b. savings.
    c. reserves.
    d. money.
    e. returns.

15. The required reserve ratio is
a. the most cash that banks are allowed to hold in their vault.
b. set by the Federal Reserve.
c. responsible for most bank runs.
d. equal to 5% of bank deposits.
e. the fraction of bank loans held as reserves.

16. If rr is the reserve requirement, the money multiplier is equal to
a. rr.
b. $1-rr$.
c. $1/rr$.
d. rr^2.
e. $1/rr^2$.

17. Which of the following is part of the money supply but not part of the monetary base?
a. checkable bank deposits
b. bank reserves
c. currency in circulation
d. deposits at the Fed
e. savings accounts

18. The Federal Reserve is a(n)
a. single central bank located in New York.
b. government agency overseen by the Secretary of the Treasury.
c. system of 10 regional banks.
d. institution that oversees the banking system.
e. depository institution that lends to large corporations.

19. The Federal Reserve is charged with doing all of the following EXCEPT
a. providing financial services to commercial banks.
b. supervising and regulating banks.
c. maintaining the stability of the financial system.
d. conducting monetary policy.
e. insuring bank deposits.

20. Which of the following will increase the demand for money?
a. a fall in the aggregate price level
b. an increase in real GDP
c. technological advances
d. open-market operations by the Fed
e. a decrease in the interest rate

21. The money supply curve is
a. upward sloping.
b. vertical.
c. horizontal.
d. downward sloping.
e. U-shaped.

22. When banking regulations were changed so that banks could pay interest on checking accounts, what was the effect on interest rates and the equilibrium quantity of money?

	Interest rate	*Quantity of money*
a.	increase	decrease
b.	decrease	increase
c.	increase	increase
d.	decrease	decrease
e.	increase	no change

23. Which of the following will shift the supply curve for loanable funds to the right?
a. an increase in the rate of return on investment spending
b. an increase in the government budget deficit
c. a decrease in the national saving rate
d. an increase in expected inflation
e. capital inflows from abroad

24. Crowding out is illustrated by which of the following changes in the loanable funds market?
a. a decreasing equilibrium interest rate
b. an increase in the demand for loanable funds
c. a decrease in the demand for loanable funds
d. an increase in the supply of loanable funds
e. a decrease in the supply of loanable funds

25. The supply curve for loanable funds is
a. upward sloping.
b. vertical.
c. horizontal.
d. downward sloping.
e. U-shaped.

Free-Response Question

1. a. Draw a correctly labeled graph of the market for loanable funds. On your graph, indicate each of the following:
i. the equilibrium interest rate, labeled r_1
ii. the equilibrium quantity of loanable funds, labeled Q_1
b. Use your graph from (a) to show how an increase in government spending affects the loanable funds market. On the graph, indicate each of the following:
i. the new equilibrium interest rate, labeled r_2
ii. the new equilibrium quantity of loanable funds, labeled Q_2
c. Explain how the new interest rate (r_2) affects the level of real GDP.
(5 points)

15. b	19. e	23. e
16. c	20. b	24. b
17. a	21. b	25. a
18. d	22. e	

Rubric for Free-Response Question

1 point: The vertical axis is labeled "Interest rate (r)," the horizontal axis is labeled "Quantity of loanable funds (Q_{LF})," the demand for loanable funds curve is labeled and downward-sloping, and the supply of loanable funds curve is labeled and upward-sloping.

1 point: Showing the equilibrium interest rate on the vertical axis to the left of where the supply and demand curves intersect, and showing the equilibrium quantity of loanable funds on the horizontal axis below where the supply and demand curves intersect

1 point: Showing a shift of the demand for loanable funds to the right

1 point: Showing the new equilibrium interest rate and quantity of loanable funds using the old supply curve and the new demand curve

1 point: The higher interest rate decreases investment spending (and interest-sensitive consumption spending) and therefore reduces real GDP.

Please see page SG-2 for sample student graphs for this Free-Response Question.

Section 5 Review 291

SECTION 6

Inflation, Unemployment, and Stabilization Policies

PD Section 6 Overview:

Watch the video overview of Section 6 (for teachers), which is accessible through the Teacher's e-Book, the TR-flash drive, or the book's website bcs.worthpublishers.com/krugmanap2e *(teacher log-in required).*

Section 6 continues the coverage of monetary and fiscal policies. Macroeconomic thought moves from theory to monetary policy and its implications. This section shows students the effects of policy decisions in clear terms—how deficits and changing interest rates change the price level and real GDP. The Phillips curve is introduced in this section. The opening story reveals to students how the previous lessons fit together and are fully integrated in these new module lessons.

Topics that your students will study in Section 6 are:

- how the government calculates the cyclically adjusted budget.
- how the size and burden of the national debt affect further budget planning.
- how the long-run implications of government deficit budgets and crowding out create concern.
- how implicit liabilities—Social Security and Medicare—pose problems for budget planners.
- how the Fed targets the federal funds rate to change interest rates.
- how expansionary and contractionary monetary policy affects interest rates, investment, *AD*, price level, and real GDP in the short and long run.
- how monetary neutrality means that money is neutral in the long run.
- how the classic model of the price level explains that the real quantity of money is always at its long-run equilibrium.
- how an inflation tax on money holders is imposed when government prints money to pay for spending.
- how cost–push inflation differs from demand-pull inflation.
- how the unemployment rate and the output gap are related.
- how the short-run Phillips curve shows the inverse relationship between unemployment and inflation.
- how no trade-off exists between unemployment and inflation in the long run.
- how expansionary policies are limited due to the effect of expected inflation.
- how disinflation can be difficult to bear.
- how deflation is a problem for policy makers and leads to a low but positive inflation rate.
- differentiation between the classical view and the Keynesian view.
- how the monetarist view explains the monetary policy rule.
- how the term *political business cycle* explains the action of politicians using macroeconomic policy to serve political ends.
- how challenges led to revisions of a Keynesian and classical view of the macroeconomy.

Alignment to AP® Macroeconomics Course Description

Macroeconomics V. Stabilization Policies: 20–30%

AP® Outline	Module
A. Fiscal and monetary policies	30: Long-Run Implications of Fiscal Policy: Deficits and the Public Debt
	31: Monetary Policy and the Interest Rate
	32: Money, Output, and Prices in the Long Run
B. The Phillips curve	33: Types of Inflation, Disinflation, and Deflation
	34: Inflation and Unemployment: The Phillips Curve
	35: History and Alternative Views of Macroeconomics
	36: Consensus and Conflict in Modern Macroeconomics

Pacing Guide

Module	Standard Teaching Days	Block Teaching Days
30	1½	1
31	1	½
32	1	½
33	1	½
34	1	½
35	½	¼
36	½	¼
Section 6 Assessment	1	½
Total	**7½**	**4**

TRM Section Resources

All section resources may be accessed through the Teacher's e-Book, the TR-flash drive, or the book's website bcs.worthpublishers.com/krugmanap2e *(teacher log-in required).*

Section 6 PD Video (for teachers)

Module 30

Module 30 Sample Lecture
Activity 30.1: Debt & Deficit Interview
Worksheet 30.2: Debt Ceiling
Worksheet 30.3: 2014 Is Looking Good
Worksheet 30.4: Debt & Deficit
Exit Slip: Module 30

Module 31

Module 31 Sample Lecture
Worksheet 31.1: Issues Facing Fed Chairman Yellen
Worksheet 31.2: Monetary Policy
Exit Slip: Module 31

Module 32

Module 32 Sample Lecture
Worksheet 32.1: Effects of Expansionary Monetary Policy
Worksheet 32.2: Interest Rates in the Long Run
Worksheet 32.3: Monetary Policy in the Short and Long Run
Exit Slip: Module 32

Module 33

Module 33 Sample Lecture
Worksheet 33.1: The Inflation Tax
Worksheet 33.2: Venezuela's Biggest Enemy
Exit Slip: Module 33

Module 34

Module 34 Sample Lecture
Worksheet 34.1: The Phillips Curve (Short and Long Run)
Worksheet 34.2: The Phillips Curve
Worksheet 34.3: The Long-Run Phillips Curve
Exit Slip: Module 34

Module 35

Module 35 Sample Lecture
Worksheet 35.1: Quantity Theory of Money
Worksheet 35.2: Alternate Theories
Exit Slip: Module 35

Module 36

Module 36 Sample Lecture
Worksheet 36.1: Supply-Side Economics
Exit Slip: Module 36
Section 6 Review Video (for students)

St. Louis Federal Reserve Bank Resources

Many of the Federal Reserve Banks have educational departments that offer helpful resources for studying economics. Members of the Educators Advisory Board of the St. Louis Federal Reserve Bank have handpicked some of their best resources for use with your AP® Economics students. References to these resources are included in the margin notes. A complete list of the St. Louis Fed resources for each section with the corresponding URL (as of fall 2014) can be found in the TRM.

NOTE We have included a number of links to useful videos and articles in the margin notes in this section. Although all are active at the time of publication, we know that some may expire over the next few years. If a link is no longer active, you may wish to search for a similar article or video to illustrate the point. We may also periodically refresh resources on the book's companion website.

Section 6 Overview

Watch the video overview of Section 6 (for teachers), which is accessible through the Teacher's e-Book, the TR-flash drive, or the book's companion website bcs.worthpublishers.com/krugmanap2e (teacher log-in required).

FOCUS Active Learning

For relevant discussions of unemployment, creative destruction, and the quality of life, refer students to Chapter 19 of *Economics by Example*.

SECTION 6

Inflation, Unemployment, and Stabilization Policies

The Fed as First Responder

Jim Cramer's *Mad Money* is one of the most popular shows on CNBC, a cable TV network that specializes in business and financial news. In January of 2014, Cramer touted the "invisible positives" in the economy, such as companies with enough financial strength to pay billions of dollars to acquire other companies. It was a different story on August 3, 2007, when Cramer was so alarmed about negatives he felt were invisible to the Federal Reserve that he screamed about Fed leaders:

"Bernanke is being an academic! It is no time to be an academic. . . . **He has no idea how bad it is out there. He has no idea! He has no idea!** . . . and Bill Poole? Has no idea what it's like out there! . . . They're nuts! **They know nothing!** . . . The Fed is asleep! Bill Poole is a shame! He's shameful!!"

G. Paul Burnett/The New York Times/Redux

Who are Bernanke and Bill Poole? In the previous chapter, we described the role of the Federal Reserve System, the U.S. central bank. At the time of Cramer's tirade, Ben Bernanke, a former Princeton professor of economics, was the chair of the Fed's Board of Governors, and William Poole, a former Brown professor of economics, was the president of the Federal Reserve Bank of St. Louis. Both men, because of their positions, are members of the Federal Open Market Committee, which meets eight times a year to set monetary policy. In 2007, Cramer was crying out for the Fed to change monetary policy in order to address what he perceived to be a growing financial crisis.

Why was Cramer screaming at the Federal Reserve rather than, say, the U.S. Treasury—or, for that matter, the president? The answer is that the Fed's control of monetary policy makes it the first line of response to macroeconomic difficulties—very much including the financial crisis that had Cramer so upset. Indeed, within a few weeks, the Fed swung into action with a dramatic reversal of its previous policies.

In Section 4, we developed the aggregate demand and supply model and introduced the use of fiscal policy to stabilize the economy. In Section 5, we introduced money, banking, and the Federal Reserve System, and began to look at how monetary policy is used to stabilize the economy. In this section, we use the models introduced in Sections 4 and 5 to further develop our understanding of stabilization policies (both fiscal and monetary), including their long-run effects on the economy. In addition, we introduce the Phillips curve—a short-run tradeoff between unexpected inflation and unemployment—and investigate the role of expectations in the economy. We end the section with a brief summary of the history of macroeconomic thought and how the modern consensus view of stabilization policy has developed.

292 Section 6 Inflation, Unemployment, and Stabilization Policies

Marmaduke St. John/Alamy

MODULE 30 Long-Run Implications of Fiscal Policy: Deficits and the Public Debt

In this Module, you will learn to:

- Explain why governments calculate the cyclically adjusted budget balance
- Identify problems posed by a large public debt
- Discuss why implicit liabilities of the government are also a cause for concern

In Module 20 we discussed how discretionary fiscal policy can be used to stabilize the economy in the short run. During a recession, an expansionary fiscal policy—raising government spending, lowering taxes, or both—can be used to shift the aggregate demand curve to the right. And when there are inflationary pressures in the economy, a contractionary fiscal policy—lowering government spending, raising taxes, or both—can be used to shift the aggregate demand curve to the left. But how do these policies affect the economy over a longer period of time? In this module we will look at some of the long-term effects of fiscal policy, including budget balance, debt, and liabilities.

The Budget Balance

Headlines about the government's budget tend to focus on just one point: whether the government is running a budget surplus or a budget deficit and, in either case, how big. People usually think of surpluses as good: when the federal government ran a record surplus in 2000, many people regarded it as a cause for celebration. Conversely, people usually think of deficits as bad: when the Congressional Budget Office projected a $675 billion federal deficit in 2014, many people regarded it as a cause for concern.

How do surpluses and deficits fit into the analysis of fiscal policy? Are deficits ever a good thing and surpluses ever a bad thing? To answer those questions, let's look at the causes and consequences of surpluses and deficits.

AP® Exam Tip

The budget balance is the difference between the government's tax revenue and its spending, both on goods and services and on government transfers, in a given year.

The Budget Balance as a Measure of Fiscal Policy

What do we mean by surpluses and deficits? The budget balance, which we have previously defined, is the difference between the government's tax revenue and its spending, both on goods and services and on government transfers, in a

PD To prepare for teaching this lesson, you may want to consult the **Module 30 Sample Lecture** in the TRM.

OPEN & CLOSE Start Here

Show students the May 28, 2012, *U.S. News* political cartoon at http://tinyurl.com/o863nza. Ask students:

- Who do the two animals and the man with the microphone represent? *The two animals represent Congress, and the man represents a reporter or the American public.*
- This cartoon came out at a time when the national debt was rising. Where does each party place the blame based on the cartoonist? *Each side believes that the other party's plan will hurt the nation.*
- According to the cartoonist, why will the debt get larger? Students shou*ld determine that Congress is not willing to cut spending or raise taxes.*
- Why do you think the cartoonist included the news reporter? *The reporter is there to let the reader know that neither party is willing to work together to fix budget issues.*

TEACH Teach It

Throughout this unit, don't let the discussion of the national debt turn into a political debate. Budget deficits and surpluses both have ramifications for the economy.

TEACH Teach It

The budget balance is the difference between the government's tax revenue and its spending, both on goods and services and on government transfers, in a given year. When the government spends more than it takes in, a deficit adds to the national debt. If the government spends less than it takes in, a surplus can be used to lower the national debt.

Module 30 Long-Run Implications of Fiscal Policy: Deficits and the Public Debt **293**

TEACH Connect It

Fiscal policy was discussed in previous modules. Now, connect that to this topic by asking students:

- If a recessionary gap exists, what can Congress do to correct it? *Cut taxes, increase spending, or increase transfer payments.*
- How do these policies impact national output? *AD will increase.* What do you think will happen to the deficit? *The deficit will increase in the short run due to lower government revenues and higher government expenditures. If the expansionary policies successfully revive the economy, the deficit will decrease in the long run as rising incomes and profits lead to growth in tax collections and as spending on programs such as unemployment insurance decreases.*
- What if an inflationary gap exists? What can Congress do to correct it? *Increase taxes, decrease spending, or decrease transfer payments.*
- What do you think will happen to the deficit in this case? *The deficit will decrease in the short run due to higher government revenues and lower government spending. If the contractionary policies slow the economy considerably, the deficit may increase in the long run as falling incomes and profits lead to decreased tax collections and as spending on unemployment insurance and related programs increases.*

TEACH Connect It

Which has greater impact on the economy, government spending or a change in taxes and transfers, and why? *The change in government spending because the tax multiplier is less than the spending multiplier*

FOCUS Active Learning

This is a good time for a practice problem to remind students how multipliers work. Tell them the *MPC* is 0.75 and there is a $100 billion increase in both government spending and personal income taxes. Ask them to find the overall effect of these changes on real GDP.

Spending multiplier

$$= \frac{1}{(1 - MPC)} = \frac{1}{1 - 0.75} = \frac{1}{0.25} = 4$$

Tax multiplier

$$= \frac{-MPC}{(1 - MPC)} = \frac{-0.75}{1 - 0.75} = \frac{-0.75}{0.25} = -3$$

$4 \times \$100 = \$400$ *billion change in spending*

$-3 \times \$100 = -\$300$ *billion change in spending*

The decrease in spending due to the increase in taxes ($300 billion) is less than the increase in spending due to the increase in government spending ($400 billion). In fact, the difference between the two is the same as the initial change in government spending. This is a good reminder of the fact that the balanced budget multiplier is 1.

AP® Exam Tip

The budget deficit almost always rises when the unemployment rate rises and falls when the unemployment rate falls.

given year. That is, the budget balance—savings by government—is defined by Equation 30-1:

$$\textbf{(30-1)} \quad S_{Government} = T - G - TR$$

where *T* is the value of tax revenues, *G* is government purchases of goods and services, and *TR* is the value of government transfers. A budget surplus is a positive budget balance, and a budget deficit is a negative budget balance.

Other things equal, expansionary fiscal policies—increased government purchases of goods and services, higher government transfers, or lower taxes—reduce the budget balance for that year. That is, expansionary fiscal policies make a budget surplus smaller or a budget deficit bigger. Conversely, contractionary fiscal policies—reduced government purchases of goods and services, lower government transfers, or higher taxes—increase the budget balance for that year, making a budget surplus bigger or a budget deficit smaller.

You might think this means that changes in the budget balance can be used to measure fiscal policy. In fact, economists often do just that: they use changes in the budget balance as a "quick-and-dirty" way to assess whether current fiscal policy is expansionary or contractionary. But they always keep in mind two reasons this quick-and-dirty approach is sometimes misleading:

- Two different changes in fiscal policy that have equal-sized effects on the budget balance may have quite unequal effects on the economy. As we have already seen, changes in government purchases of goods and services have a larger effect on real GDP than equal-sized changes in taxes and government transfers.
- Often, changes in the budget balance are themselves the result, not the cause, of fluctuations in the economy.

To understand the second point, we need to examine the effects of the business cycle on the budget.

The Business Cycle and the Cyclically Adjusted Budget Balance

Historically, there has been a strong relationship between the federal government's budget balance and the business cycle. The budget tends to move into deficit when the economy experiences a recession, but deficits tend to get smaller or even turn into surpluses when the economy is expanding. **Figure 30.1** shows the federal budget deficit as a percentage of GDP from 1970 to 2013. Shaded areas indicate recessions; unshaded areas indicate expansions. As you can see, the federal budget deficit increased around the time of each recession and usually declined during expansions. In fact, in the late stages of the long expansion from 1991 to 2000, the deficit actually became negative—the budget deficit became a budget surplus.

The relationship between the business cycle and the budget balance is even more clear if we compare the budget deficit as a percentage of GDP with the unemployment rate, as we do in **Figure 30.2**. The budget deficit almost always rises when the unemployment rate rises and falls when the unemployment rate falls.

Is this relationship between the business cycle and the budget balance evidence that policy makers engage in discretionary fiscal policy? Not necessarily. It is largely automatic stabilizers that drive the relationship shown in Figure 30.2. As we learned in the discussion of automatic stabilizers in Module 21, government tax revenue tends to rise and some government transfers, like unemployment insurance payments, tend to fall when the economy expands. Conversely, government tax revenue tends to fall and some government transfers tend to rise when the economy contracts. So the budget tends to move toward surplus during expansions and toward deficit during recessions even without any deliberate action on the part of policy makers.

In assessing budget policy, it's often useful to separate movements in the budget balance due to the business cycle from movements due to discretionary fiscal policy changes.

Figure 30.1 The U.S. Federal Budget Deficit and the Business Cycle

The budget deficit as a percentage of GDP tends to rise during recessions (indicated by shaded areas) and fall during expansions.
Source: Bureau of Economic Analysis; National Bureau of Economic Research.

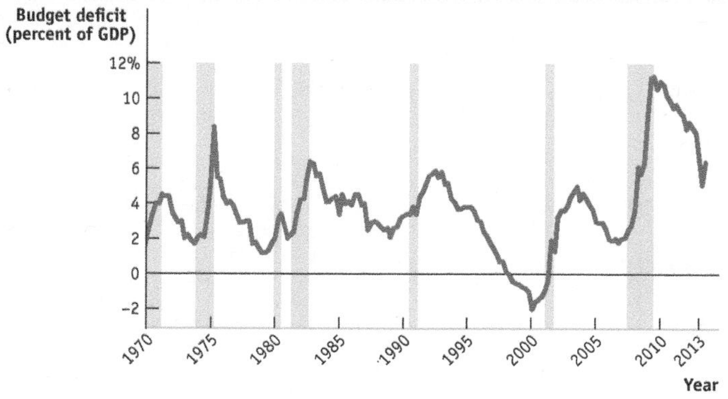

Figure 30.2 The U.S. Federal Budget Deficit and the Unemployment Rate

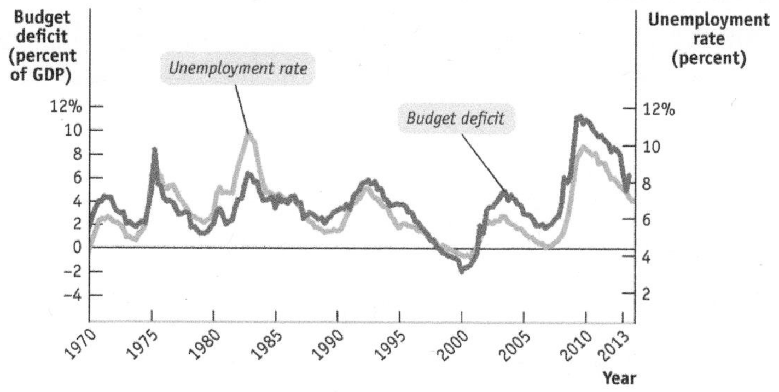

There is a close relationship between the budget balance and the business cycle: a recession moves the budget balance toward deficit, but an expansion moves it toward surplus. Here, the unemployment rate serves as an indicator of the business cycle, and we should expect to see a higher unemployment rate associated with a higher budget deficit. This is confirmed by the figure: the budget deficit as a percentage of GDP moves closely in tandem with the unemployment rate.
Source: Bureau of Economic Analysis; Bureau of Labor Statistics.

TEACH Connect It

Ask students to define automatic stabilizers. *These are programs built into our tax and transfer system that work to reduce the swings of the business cycle.*

TEACH Teach It

The budget deficit almost always rises when the unemployment rate rises, and falls when the unemployment rate falls. This happens even if there are no new fiscal policies because when the economy heads into a recession, two events take place:

- Tax revenues decline because incomes and profits are declining.
- Transfer payments, like those for welfare assistance and unemployment insurance, begin to rise as more people find themselves unemployed and struggling.

During an expansion, the opposite happens:

- Tax revenues rise because incomes and profits are rising.
- Transfer payments, like those for welfare assistance and unemployment insurance, begin to fall as fewer people find themselves unemployed and struggling.

These changes transpire without any deliberate fiscal policy changes and the budget balance declines.

TEACH Teach It

Most economists believe that the government should only balance its budget on average—that is, it should be allowed to run deficits in bad years, offset by surpluses in good years. Political pressures for added tax cuts and government spending during good years make this difficult. Ask students how the automatic stabilizer role of taxes and transfers would be affected by a balanced budget approach. *Students may answer that taxes and transfers cushion the effects of recessionary and inflationary gaps. Because they increase tax revenue and decrease government spending in good years, automatic stabilizers can be consistent with a balanced budget approach.*

FOCUS Active Learning

To help your students learn more about the budget process, show Paul Solmon's video "'Red Ink' in the Federal Budget: Understanding Why the U.S. Has So Much Debt" (see econextras video list with hyperlinks on the bcs and TRFD). Print out the questions found on the site for students to answer as they watch. Discuss their answers.

The former are affected by automatic stabilizers and the latter by deliberate changes in government purchases, government transfers, or taxes. It's important to realize that business-cycle effects on the budget balance are temporary: both recessionary gaps (in which real GDP is below potential output) and inflationary gaps (in which real GDP is above potential output) tend to be eliminated in the long run. Removing their effects on the budget balance sheds light on whether the government's taxing and spending policies are sustainable in the long run. In other words, do the government's tax policies yield enough revenue to fund its spending in the long run? As we'll learn shortly, this is a fundamentally more important question than whether the government runs a budget surplus or deficit in the current year.

To separate the effect of the business cycle from the effects of other factors, many governments produce an estimate of what the budget balance would be if there were neither a recessionary nor an inflationary gap. The **cyclically adjusted budget balance** is an estimate of what the budget balance would be if real GDP were exactly equal to potential output. It takes into account the extra tax revenue the government would collect and the transfers it would save if a recessionary gap were eliminated—or the revenue the government would lose and the extra transfers it would make if an inflationary gap were eliminated.

The **cyclically adjusted budget balance** is an estimate of what the budget balance would be if real GDP were exactly equal to potential output.

Figure 30.3 shows the actual budget deficit and the Congressional Budget Office estimate of the cyclically adjusted budget deficit, both as a percentage of GDP, since 1970. As you can see, the cyclically adjusted budget deficit doesn't fluctuate as much as the actual budget deficit. In particular, large actual deficits, such as those of 1975 and 1983, are usually caused in part by a depressed economy.

Should the Budget Be Balanced?

Persistent budget deficits can cause problems for both the government and the economy. Yet politicians are always tempted to run deficits because this allows them to cater to voters by cutting taxes without cutting spending or by increasing

Figure 30.3 The Actual Budget Deficit Versus the Cyclically Adjusted Budget Deficit

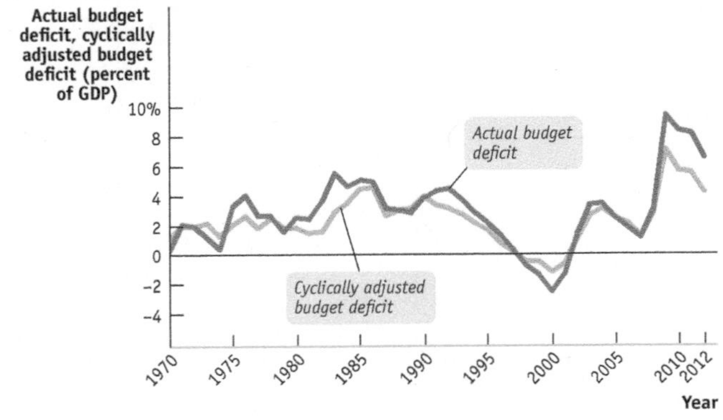

The cyclically adjusted budget deficit is an estimate of what the budget deficit would be if the economy were at potential output. It fluctuates less than the actual budget deficit, because years of large budget deficits also tend to be years when the economy has a large recessionary gap. *Source:* Congressional Budget Office.

296 Section 6 Inflation, Unemployment, and Stabilization Policies

spending without increasing taxes. As a result, there are occasional attempts by policy makers to force fiscal discipline by introducing legislation—even a constitutional amendment—forbidding the government from running budget deficits. This is usually stated as a requirement that the budget be "balanced"—that revenues at least equal spending each fiscal year. Would it be a good idea to require a balanced budget annually?

Most economists don't think so. They believe that the government should only balance its budget on average—that it should be allowed to run deficits in bad years, offset by surpluses in good years. They don't believe the government should be forced to run a balanced budget *every year* because this would undermine the role of taxes and transfers as automatic stabilizers. As we learned earlier, the tendency of tax revenue to fall and transfers to rise when the economy contracts helps to limit the size of recessions. But falling tax revenue and rising transfer payments push the budget toward deficit. If constrained by a balanced-budget rule, the government would have to respond to this deficit with contractionary fiscal policies that would tend to deepen a recession.

Nonetheless, policy makers concerned about excessive deficits sometimes feel that rigid rules prohibiting—or at least setting an upper limit on—deficits are necessary.

Colin Anderson/Brand X Pictures/Getty Images

Long-Run Implications of Fiscal Policy

During the 1990s, the Japanese government engaged in massive deficit spending in an effort to increase aggregate demand. That policy was partly successful: although Japan's economy was sluggish during the 1990s, it avoided a severe slump comparable to what happened to many countries in the 1930s. Yet the fact that Japan was running large budget deficits year after year made many observers uneasy, as Japan's **government debt**—the accumulation of past budget deficits, minus past budget surpluses—climbed to alarming levels. Now that we understand how budget deficits and surpluses arise, let's take a closer look at their long-run effects on the economy.

Government debt is the accumulation of past budget deficits, minus past budget surpluses.

Deficits, Surpluses, and Debt

When a family spends more than it earns over the course of a year, it has to raise the extra funds either by selling assets or by borrowing. And if a family borrows year after year, it will eventually end up with a lot of debt.

The same is true for governments. With a few exceptions, governments don't raise large sums by selling assets such as national parkland. Instead, when a government spends more than the tax revenue it receives—when it runs a budget deficit—it almost always borrows the extra funds. And governments that run persistent budget deficits end up with substantial debts.

To interpret the numbers that follow, you need to know a slightly peculiar feature of federal government accounting. For historical reasons, the U.S. government does not keep the books by calendar years. Instead, budget totals are kept by **fiscal years**, which run from October 1 to September 30 and are labeled by the calendar year in which they end. For example, fiscal 2013 began on October 1, 2012, and ended on September 30, 2013.

At the end of fiscal 2013, the total debt of the U.S. federal government was $16.7 trillion, or about 100% of gross domestic product. However, part of that debt represented special accounting rules specifying that the federal government as a whole owes funds to certain government programs, especially Social Security. We'll explain those rules shortly. For now, however, let's focus on **public debt**: government debt held by individuals and institutions outside the government. At the end of fiscal 2013, the federal government's public debt was "only" $12.0 trillion, or about 72% of GDP. If we include the debts of state and local governments, total government public debt was approximately 88% of GDP.

AP® Exam Tip

A budget deficit occurs when the government's revenue is less than its spending in a given year.

A **fiscal year** runs from October 1 to September 30 and is labeled according to the calendar year in which it ends.

Public debt is government debt held by individuals and institutions outside the government.

FOCUS Active Learning

TRM It is important to understand economics in order to understand political issues. Assign students the task of interviewing a family member or neighbor who voted in the last election out of concern about the national debt. Suggested questions for this interview may be found in **Activity 30.1 (Debt & Deficit Interview)** from the TRM. Students may have to explain the difference between government debt and a budget deficit to the individual they interview. After the interview, poll students to see how many interviewees were unaware of the difference between these terms. Discuss the results of the interviews and students' reactions to them.

TEACH Teach It

When a government spends more than the tax revenue it receives—when it runs a budget deficit—it almost always borrows the extra funds. Governments that run persistent budget deficits end up with substantial debts. The national debt is the accumulation of all past deficits, minus all past surpluses. Many Americans do not understand the difference between the two.

- What is the difference between government debt and an annual budget deficit? *A budget deficit arises when less money comes in than goes out in one year. Government debt is the accumulation of past budget deficits minus past budget surpluses.*

FOCUS Active Learning

Compare the current public debt to the debt that existed the year most of your students were born (http://www.treasurydirect.gov/NP/debt/current). Ask students to speculate on why the debt has increased or decreased. *Answers will vary. Talk about significant events in the United States that may have caused the changes (e.g., 9/11, the Great Recession, the sequester, the wars in Iraq and Afghanistan).*

FOCUS Active Learning

Show students *The Economist* video "KAL Draws: A Distinction (Debt and Deficit)" (see econextras video list with hyperlinks on the bcs and TRFD). Ask the following:

- What is a benefit of debt? *Debt allows economic growth. It allows governments to make investments they would not otherwise be able to afford.*
- What is a danger of debt? *Debt may become a liability for other generations, especially if money is not invested wisely.*

Module 30 Long-Run Implications of Fiscal Policy: Deficits and the Public Debt **297**

FOCUS Active Learning

TRM Tell students that Congress has established a debt ceiling, which forces a debate about spending each time the debt nears the ceiling. Show the music video "Remy: Raise The Debt Ceiling Rap" (see econextras video list with hyperlinks on the bcs and TRFD). Suggested questions for this video can be found in **Worksheet 30.2 (Debt Ceiling)** from the TRM.

TEACH Teach It

There are two reasons to be concerned when a government runs persistent budget deficits:

1. When the government borrows funds in the financial markets, it is competing with firms that plan to borrow funds for investment spending. As a result, the government's borrowing may "crowd out" private investment spending, increasing interest rates and reducing the economy's long-run rate of growth.
2. By increasing the government's debt, today's deficits place financial pressure on future budgets. Interest must be paid in the future, and this can take away dollars from other future obligations like education, the military, disease control, and so on.

TEACH Teach It

How can a government pay off its debt?

- Borrowing to pay off debt is not a good option. That's like getting a new credit card to pay off an old credit card: it eventually leads to bankruptcy. Some nations have essentially declared bankruptcy in the past. It's not a pretty picture.
- Increasing taxes or cutting spending is probably the best solution. This solution is neither very popular politically nor easily implemented, especially when a nation has become accustomed to low taxes.
- Printing money means the Fed "creates" new money through its tools to pay the debts of the Treasury. This proves to be a fast track to serious inflation.

U.S. federal government public debt at the end of fiscal 2013 was larger than it was at the end of fiscal 2012 because the federal government ran a budget deficit during fiscal 2013. A government that runs persistent budget deficits will experience a rising level of debt. Why is this a problem?

Problems Posed by Rising Government Debt

There are two reasons to be concerned when a government runs persistent budget deficits. We described one reason previously: when the economy is at potential output and the government borrows funds in the financial markets, it is competing with firms that plan to borrow funds for investment spending. As a result, the government's borrowing may crowd out private investment spending, thereby increasing interest rates and reducing the economy's long-run rate of growth.

The second reason: today's deficits, by increasing the government's debt, place financial pressure on future budgets. The impact of current deficits on future budgets is straightforward. Like individuals, governments must pay their bills, including interest payments on their accumulated debt. When a government is deeply in debt, those interest payments can be substantial. In fiscal 2013, the U.S. federal government paid 2.4% of GDP—$415.7 billion—in interest on its debt. And although this is a relatively large fraction of GDP, other countries pay even greater fractions of their GDP to service their debt. For example, in 2013, Greece paid interest of about 3.6% of GDP.

Other things equal, a government paying large sums in interest must raise more revenue from taxes or spend less than it would otherwise be able to afford—or it must borrow even more to cover the gap. And a government that borrows to pay interest on its outstanding debt pushes itself even deeper into debt. This process can eventually push a government to the point at which lenders question its ability to repay. Like consumers who have maxed out their credit cards, the government will find that lenders are unwilling to lend any more funds. The result can be that the government defaults on its debt—it stops paying what it owes. Default is often followed by deep financial and economic turmoil.

Lautario Palacios, 7, holds a sign that calls for politicians to stop robbing, during a January 9, 2002 demonstration in Buenos Aires, Argentina.

The idea of a government defaulting sounds far-fetched, but it is not impossible. In the 1990s, Argentina, a relatively high-income developing country, was widely praised for its economic policies—and it was able to borrow large sums from foreign lenders. By 2001, however, Argentina's interest payments were spiraling out of control, and the country stopped paying the sums that were due. In the end, Argentina reached a settlement with most of its lenders under which it paid less than a third of the amount originally due. Similarly, the government of Greece faced default in 2012, and bond holders agreed to trade their bonds for new ones worth less than half as much. In the same year, concerns about economic frailty forced the governments of Ireland, Portugal, Italy, and Spain to pay high interest rates on their debt to compensate for the risk of default.

Default creates havoc in a country's financial markets and badly shakes public confidence in both the government and the economy. For example, Argentina's debt default was accompanied by a crisis in the country's banking system and a very severe recession. And even if a highly indebted government avoids default, a heavy debt burden typically forces it to slash spending or raise taxes, politically unpopular measures that can also damage the economy.

One question some people ask is: can't a government that has trouble borrowing just print money to pay its bills? Yes, it can, but this leads to another problem: inflation. In fact, budget problems are the main cause of very severe inflation, as we'll see later. The point for now is that governments do not want to find themselves in a position where the choice is between defaulting on their debts and inflating those debts away.

FOCUS In the News

TRM Have students read the January 2014 *U.S. News* article "5 Reasons 2014 Is Looking Good for the U.S. Economy" at http://www.usnews.com/opinion/articles/2014/01/15/5-reasons-2014-is-looking-good-for-the-us-economy. Suggested questions for this article can be found in the TRM on **Worksheet 30.3 (2014 Is Looking Good)**.

St. Louis Federal Reserve Bank Resources

Crowding Out

In this lesson, students learn that the loanable funds market is a virtual clearinghouse matching borrowers and savers. They participate in an activity to demonstrate crowding out in the loanable funds market. They use demand and supply analysis to graphically represent the results of crowding out.

Concerns about the long-run effects of deficits need not rule out the use of fiscal policy to stimulate the economy when it is depressed. However, these concerns do mean that governments should try to offset budget deficits in bad years with budget surpluses in good years. In other words, governments should run a budget that is approximately balanced over time. Have they actually done so?

Deficits and Debt in Practice

Figure 30.4 shows how the U.S. federal government's budget deficit and its debt have evolved since 1940. Panel (a) shows the federal deficit as a percentage of GDP. As you can see, the federal government ran huge deficits during World War II. It briefly ran surpluses after the war, but it has normally run deficits ever since, especially after 1980. This seems inconsistent with the advice that governments should offset deficits in bad times with surpluses in good times.

However, panel (b) of Figure 30.4 shows that these deficits have not led to runaway debt. To assess the ability of governments to pay their debt, we often use the **debt-GDP ratio**, the government's debt as a percentage of GDP. We use this measure, rather than simply looking at the size of the debt because GDP, which measures the size of the economy as a whole, is a good indicator of the potential taxes the government can collect. If the government's debt grows more slowly than GDP, the burden of paying that debt is actually falling compared with the government's potential tax revenue.

The **debt-GDP ratio** is the government's debt as a percentage of GDP.

What we see from panel (b) is that, although the federal debt has grown in almost every year, the debt-GDP ratio fell for 30 years after the end of World War II. This shows that the debt-GDP ratio can fall, even when debt is rising, as long as GDP grows faster than debt. Growth and inflation sometimes allow a government that runs persistent budget deficits to have a declining debt-GDP ratio nevertheless.

Figure 30.4 U.S. Federal Deficits and Debt

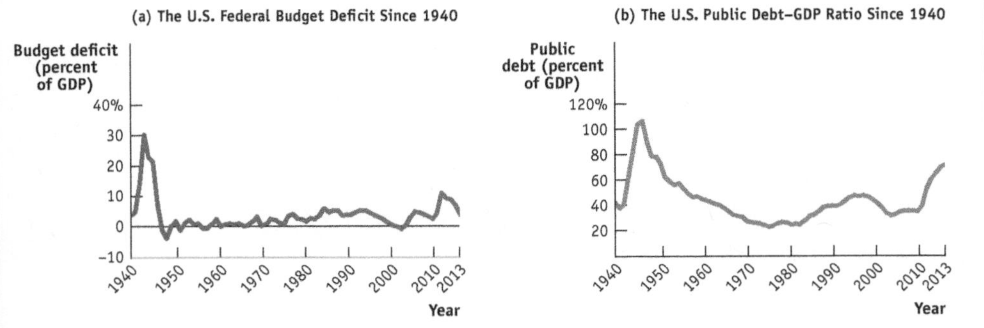

Panel (a) shows the U.S. federal budget deficit as a percentage of GDP since 1940. The U.S. government ran huge deficits during World War II and has usually run smaller deficits ever since. Panel (b) shows the U.S. debt-GDP ratio. Comparing panels (a) and (b), you can see that in many years the debt-GDP ratio has declined in spite of government deficits. This seeming paradox reflects the fact that the debt-GDP ratio can fall, even when debt is rising, as long as GDP grows faster than debt.
Source: Office of Management and Budget.

TEACH Teach It

The debt–GDP ratio is used because it is a good indicator of the potential taxes the government can collect (versus just looking at the size of the debt). If the government's debt grows more slowly than GDP, the burden of paying that debt actually falls compared with the government's potential tax revenue.

Module 30 Long-Run Implications of Fiscal Policy: Deficits and the Public Debt **299**

Figure 30.5 Japanese Deficits and Debt

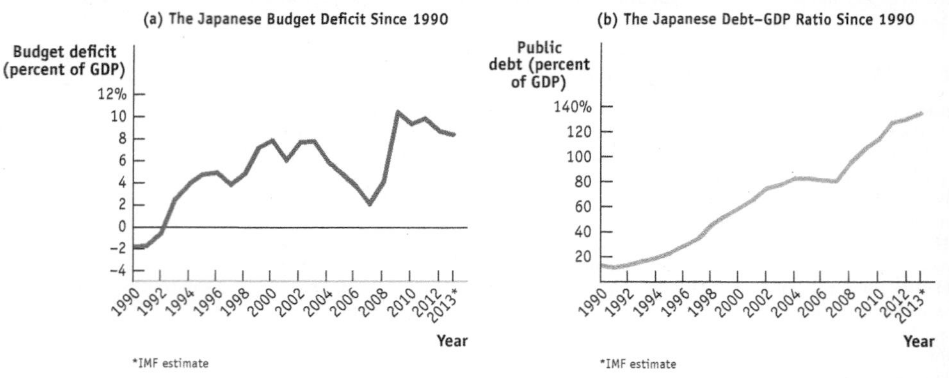

Panel (a) shows the budget deficit of Japan as a percentage of GDP since 1990 and panel (b) shows its debt–GDP ratio. The large deficits that the Japanese government began running in the early 1990s have led to a rapid rise in its debt–GDP ratio as debt has grown more quickly than GDP. This has led some analysts to express concern about the long-run fiscal health of the Japanese economy.
Source: International Monetary Fund.

Still, a government that runs persistent *large* deficits will have a rising debt–GDP ratio when debt grows faster than GDP. Panel (a) of **Figure 30.5** shows Japan's budget deficit as a percentage of GDP, and panel (b) shows Japan's debt–GDP ratio, both since 1990. As we have already mentioned, Japan began running large deficits in the early 1990s, a by-product of its effort to prop up aggregate demand with government spending. This has led to a rapid rise in the debt–GDP ratio. For this reason, some economic analysts are concerned about the long-run fiscal health of the Japanese economy.

Implicit Liabilities

Looking at Figure 30.4, you might be tempted to conclude that, until the 2008 economic crisis struck, the U.S. federal budget was in fairly decent shape: the return to budget deficits after 2001 caused the debt–GDP ratio to rise a bit, but that ratio was

FYI What Happened to the Debt from World War II?

As you can see from Figure 30.4, the government paid for World War II by borrowing on a huge scale. By the war's end, the public debt was more than 100% of GDP, and many people worried about how it could ever be paid off.

The truth is that it never was paid off. In 1946, the public debt was $242 billion; that number dipped slightly in the next few years, as the United States ran postwar budget surpluses, but the government budget went back into deficit in 1950 with the start of the Korean War. By 1962, the public debt was back up to $248 billion.

But by that time nobody was worried about the fiscal health of the U.S. government because the debt-GDP ratio had fallen by more than half. The reason? Vigorous economic growth, plus mild inflation, had led to a rapid rise in GDP. The experience was a clear lesson in the peculiar fact that modern governments can run deficits forever, as long as they aren't too large.

TEACH Teach It

Implicit liabilities are spending promises made by governments that are effectively a debt, yet they are not included in the usual debt statistics. In the United States, promises to honor Social Security, Medicare, and Medicaid entitlements amount to 40% of federal spending. Is this a big deal? Maybe, because the American population is aging and these commitments will only grow larger.

TEACH AP® Exam Tip

You can expand this discussion with current event articles or charts from the text. However, for the AP® exam, it is enough for students to know that these implicit liabilities will add to the U.S. debt as American demographics shift to an older population.

still low compared with both historical experience and some other wealthy countries. However, experts on long-run budget issues view the situation of the United States (and other countries with high public debt, such as Japan and Greece) with alarm. The reason is the problem of *implicit liabilities*. **Implicit liabilities** are spending promises made by governments that are effectively a debt despite the fact that they are not included in the usual debt statistics.

The largest implicit liabilities of the U.S. government arise from two transfer programs that principally benefit older Americans: Social Security and Medicare. The third-largest implicit liability, Medicaid, benefits low-income families. In each of these cases, the government has promised to provide transfer payments to future as well as current beneficiaries. So these programs represent a future debt that must be honored, even though the debt does not currently show up in the usual statistics. Together, these three programs currently account for almost 40% of federal spending.

The implicit liabilities created by these transfer programs worry fiscal experts. **Figure 30.6** shows why. It shows actual spending on Social Security and on Medicare and Medicaid as percentages of GDP from 1980 to 2013, with Congressional Budget Office projections of spending through 2085. According to these projections, spending on Social Security will rise substantially over the next few decades and spending on the two health care programs will soar. Why?

In the case of Social Security, the answer is demography. Social Security is a "pay-as-you-go" system: current workers pay payroll taxes that fund the benefits of current retirees. So the ratio of the number of retirees drawing benefits to the number of workers paying into Social Security has a major impact on the system's finances. There was a huge surge in the U.S. birth rate between 1946 and 1964, the years of the baby boom. Baby boomers are currently of working age—which means they are paying taxes, not collecting benefits. But some are starting to retire, and as more and more of them do so, they will stop earning income that is taxed and start collecting benefits. As a result, the ratio of retirees receiving benefits to workers paying into the Social Security system

Implicit liabilities are spending promises made by governments that are effectively a debt despite the fact that they are not included in the usual debt statistics.

Figure 30.6 Future Demands on the Federal Budget

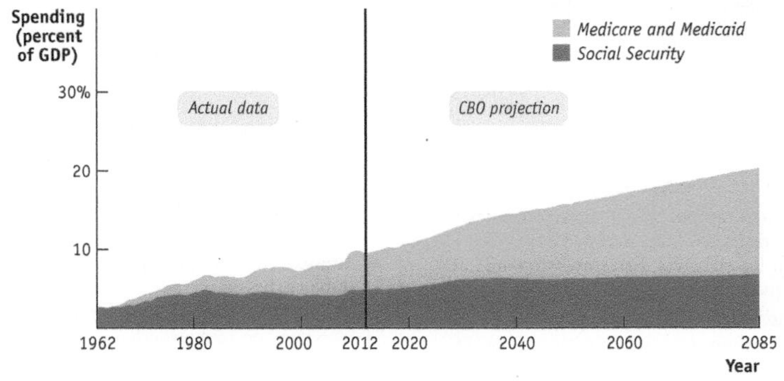

This figure shows actual and projected spending on social insurance programs as a share of GDP. Partly as a result of an aging population, but mainly because of rising health care costs, these programs are expected to become much more expensive over time, posing problems for the federal budget.
Source: Congressional Budget Office.

FOCUS Active Learning

The budget challenge activity at http://www.federalbudgetchallenge.org/pages/overview provides students with another opportunity to balance the budget. Assign students to groups of 4–5 to work through the decisions and then report on their success. The results will reveal who did best, arriving at the lowest figure for deficit spending.

FOCUS Active Learning

TRM To provide students with a review of debt and deficit, assign **Worksheet 30.4 (Debt & Deficit)** from the TRM in class or as homework.

Module 30 Long-Run Implications of Fiscal Policy: Deficits and the Public Debt **301**

will rise. In 2010, there were 34 retirees for every 100 workers paying into the system. By 2030, according to the Social Security Administration, that number will rise to 46; by 2050, it will rise to 48; and by 2080 that number will be 51. This will raise benefit payments relative to the size of the economy.

The aging of the baby boomers, by itself, poses a problem, but the projected rise in Medicare and Medicaid spending is a much more serious concern. The main story behind projections of higher Medicare and Medicaid spending is the long-run tendency of health care spending to rise faster than overall spending, both for government-funded and for private-funded health care.

To some extent, the implicit liabilities of the U.S. government are already reflected in debt statistics. We mentioned earlier that the government had a total debt of $16.7 trillion at the end of fiscal 2013, but that only $12.0 trillion of that total was owed to the public. The main explanation for that discrepancy is that both Social Security and part of Medicare (the hospital insurance program) are supported by *dedicated taxes*: their expenses are paid out of special taxes on wages. At times, these dedicated taxes yield more revenue than is needed to pay current benefits. In particular, since the mid-1980s the Social Security system has been taking in more revenue than it currently needs in order to prepare for the retirement of the baby boomers. This surplus in the Social Security system has been used to accumulate a *Social Security trust fund*, which was $2.8 trillion at the end of fiscal 2013.

The money in the trust fund is held in the form of U.S. government bonds, which are included in the $16.7 trillion in total debt. You could say that there's something funny about counting bonds in the Social Security trust fund as part of government debt. After all, these bonds are owed by one part of the government (the government outside the Social Security system) to another part of the government (the Social Security system itself). But the debt corresponds to a real, if implicit, liability: promises by the government to pay future retirement benefits. So, many economists argue that the gross debt of $16.7 trillion, the sum of public debt and government debt held by Social Security and other trust funds, is a more accurate indication of the government's fiscal health than the smaller amount owed to the public alone.

MODULE 30 Review

Check Your Understanding

1. Why is the cyclically adjusted budget balance a better measure of the long-run sustainability of government policies than the actual budget balance?
2. Explain why states required by their constitutions to balance their budgets are likely to experience more severe economic fluctuations than states that are not held to that requirement.
3. Explain how each of the following events would affect the public debt or implicit liabilities of the U.S. government, other things equal. Would the public debt or implicit liabilities be larger or smaller if they occurred?
   a. The growth rate of real GDP increases.
   b. Retirees live longer.
   c. Tax revenue decreases.
   d. The government borrows to pay interest on its current public debt.
4. Suppose the economy is in a slump and the current public debt is quite large. Explain the trade-off of short-run versus long-run objectives that policy makers face when deciding whether or not to engage in deficit spending.

OPEN & CLOSE Exit Slip

TRM *Please see **Exit Slip: Module 30** in the TRM for formative multiple-choice questions to ask your students before finishing your lesson. These questions will help you quickly assess whether your students have mastered the module's concepts before moving on.*

Answers to the Exit Slip Questions

1. D
2. B
3. A

Answers to Module 30 Review Questions

Check Your Understanding

1. The actual budget balance takes into account the effects of the business cycle on the budget deficit. During recessionary gaps, it incorporates the effect of lower tax revenues and higher transfers on the budget balance; during inflationary gaps, it incorporates the effect of higher tax revenues and reduced transfers. In contrast, the cyclically adjusted budget balance factors out the effects of the business cycle and assumes that real GDP is at potential output. Since, in the long run, real GDP tends to potential output, the cyclically adjusted budget balance is a better measure of the long-run sustainability of government policies.

2. In recessions, real GDP falls. This implies that consumers' incomes, consumer spending, and producers' profits also fall. So in recessions, states' tax revenue (which depends in large part on consumers' income, consumer spending, and producers' profits) falls. In order to balance the state budget, states have to cut spending or raise taxes, but that deepens the recession. States without a balanced-budget requirement don't have to take steps that would make things worse during a recession, and they can use expansionary fiscal policy to lessen the fall in real GDP.

3. a. A higher growth rate of real GDP implies that tax revenue will increase. If government spending remains constant and the government runs a budget surplus, the size of the public debt will be less than it would otherwise have been.

b. If retirees live longer, the average age of the population increases. As a result, the implicit liabilities of the government increase because spending on programs for older Americans, such as Social Security and Medicare, will rise.

c. A decrease in tax revenue without offsetting reductions in government spending will cause the public debt to increase.

d. Public debt will increase as a result of government borrowing to pay interest on its current public debt.

4. In order to stimulate the economy in the short run, the government can use fiscal policy to increase real GDP. This entails borrowing, increasing the size of public debt further and leading to undesirable consequences: in extreme cases, governments can be forced to default on their debts. Even in less extreme cases, a large public debt is undesirable because government borrowing "crowds out" borrowing for private investment spending. This reduces the amount of investment spending, reducing the long-run growth of the economy.

Tackle the Test: Multiple-Choice Questions

1. If government spending exceeds tax revenues, which of the following is necessarily true? There is a
- **I.** positive budget balance.
- **II.** budget deficit.
- **III.** recession.

a. I only
b. II only
c. III only
d. I and II only
e. I, II, and III

2. Which of the following fiscal policies is expansionary?

	Taxes	*Government spending*
a.	increase by \$100 million	increases by \$100 million
b.	decrease by \$100 million	decreases by \$100 million
c.	increase by \$100 million	decreases by \$100 million
d.	decrease by \$100 million	increases by \$100 million

e. both (a) and (d)

3. The cyclically adjusted budget deficit is an estimate of what the budget balance would be if real GDP were
a. greater than potential output.
b. equal to nominal GDP.
c. equal to potential output.
d. falling.
e. calculated during a recession.

4. During a recession in the United States, what happens automatically to tax revenues and government spending?

	Tax revenues	*Government spending*
a.	increase	increases
b.	decrease	decreases
c.	increase	decreases
d.	decrease	increases
e.	decrease	does not change

5. Which of the following is a reason to be concerned about persistent budget deficits?
a. crowding out
b. government default
c. the opportunity cost of future interest payments
d. higher interest rates leading to decreased long-run growth
e. all of the above

Tackle the Test: Free-Response Questions

1. Consider the information provided below for the hypothetical country of Zeta.

Tax revenues = \$2,000
Government purchases of goods and services = \$1,500
Government transfers = \$1,000
Real GDP = \$20,000
Potential output = \$18,000

a. Is the budget balance in Zeta positive or negative? What is the amount of the budget balance?
b. Zeta is currently in what phase of the business cycle? Explain.
c. Is Zeta implementing the appropriate fiscal policy given the current state of the economy? Explain.
d. How does Zeta's cyclically adjusted budget deficit compare with its actual budget deficit? Explain.

Rubric for FRQ 1 (8 points)

1 point: Negative
1 point: –\$500
1 point: Expansion
1 point: Real GDP > potential output
1 point: No
1 point: Zeta is running a budget deficit during an expansion.
1 point: It is larger.
1 point: Because if real GDP equaled potential output, tax revenues would be lower and government transfers would be higher.

2. In Module 29 you learned about the market for loanable funds, which is intimately related to our current topic of budget deficits. Use a correctly labeled graph of the market for loanable funds to illustrate the effect of a persistent budget deficit. Identify and explain the effect persistent budget deficits can have on private investment.
(6 points)

Tackle the Test: Multiple-Choice Questions

1. b
2. d
3. c
4. d
5. e

Tackle the Test: Free-Response Question

Rubric for FRQ 2 (6 points)

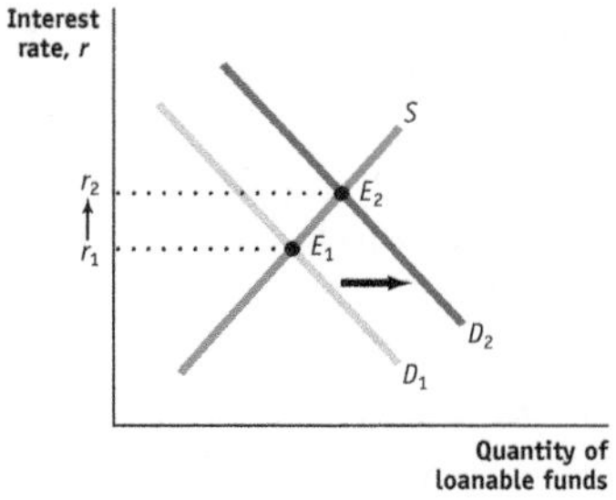

1 point: Graph labeled "Interest rate" on the vertical axis, "Quantity of loanable funds" on the horizontal axis, and a downward-sloping demand curve
1 point: Upward-sloping supply curve
1 point: Rightward shift of demand curve
1 point: Increase in the equilibrium interest rate shown on graph
1 point: This effect is called "crowding out."
1 point: Persistent budget deficits increase the demand for loanable funds, thereby increasing interest rates and decreasing private investment.

Module 30 Long-Run Implications of Fiscal Policy: Deficits and the Public Debt 303

PD To prepare for teaching this lesson, you may want to consult the **Module 31 Sample Lecture** in the TRM.

OPEN & CLOSE Start Here

To help students review what they have already learned, ask them to answer the following question on their personal whiteboards or notebook paper:

> Using a correctly labeled *AD–AS* graph, show an economy facing a recessionary gap. Name three tools the Federal Reserve could use to fix the recessionary gap.

Answer: The Fed could make an open market purchase, decrease the discount rate, or decrease the reserve requirement.

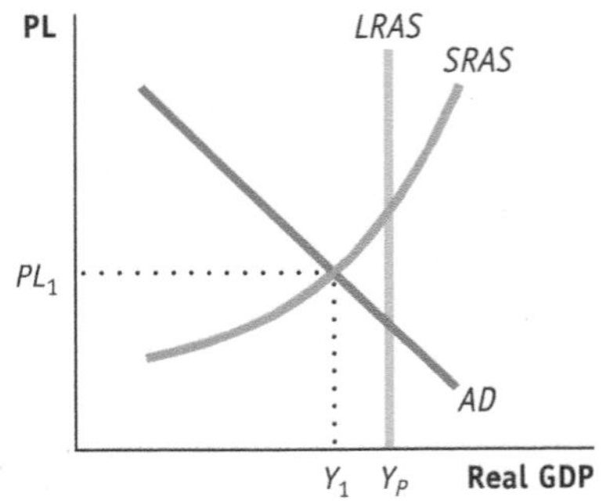

TEACH Teach It

Usually, the Fed adjusts the money supply to target a specific federal funds rate. Remember, the Fed cannot set this rate since it is set through the interaction of supply and demand in the financial market.

- If the current federal funds rate is higher than the target, the Fed will increase the money supply so that the rate falls to the target. Ask how the Fed would do that. *The Fed would buy bonds in the open market.*
- If the current federal funds rate is lower than the target, the Fed will decrease the money supply so that the rate rises to the target. Ask how the Fed would do that. *The Fed would sell bonds in the open market.*

© Nader Khouri/MCT/ZUMAPRESS.com

MODULE 31 Monetary Policy and the Interest Rate

In this Module, you will learn to:

- Describe how the Federal Reserve implements monetary policy, moving the interest rate to affect aggregate output
- Explain why monetary policy is the main tool for stabilizing the economy

In Modules 28 and 29 we developed models of the money market and the loanable funds market. We also saw how these two markets are consistent and related. In the short run, the interest rate is determined in the money market and the loanable funds market adjusts in response to changes in the money market. However, in the long run, the interest rate is determined by matching the supply and demand of loanable funds that arise when real GDP equals potential output. Now we are ready to use these models to explain how the Federal Reserve can use monetary policy to stabilize the economy in the short run.

AP® Exam Tip

Don't confuse the federal funds rate with the discount rate. The Fed can only target the federal funds rate because it is set through the interaction of supply and demand.

The Federal Reserve can move the interest rate through open-market operations that shift the money supply curve. In practice, the Fed sets a **target federal funds rate** and uses open-market operations to achieve that target.

Monetary Policy and the Interest Rate

Let's examine how the Federal Reserve can use changes in the money supply to change the interest rate. **Figure 31.1** shows what happens when the Fed increases the money supply from $\overline{M}_1$ to $\overline{M}_2$. The economy is originally in equilibrium at E_1, with the equilibrium interest rate r_1 and the money supply $\overline{M}_1$. When the Fed increases the money supply to $\overline{M}_2$, the money supply curve shifts to the right, from MS_1 to MS_2, and the equilibrium interest rate falls to r_2. Why? Because r_2 is the only interest rate at which the public is willing to hold the quantity of money actually supplied, $\overline{M}_2$. So an increase in the money supply drives the interest rate down. Similarly, a reduction in the money supply drives the interest rate up. By adjusting the money supply up or down, the Fed can set the interest rate.

In practice, at each meeting the Federal Open Market Committee decides on the interest rate to prevail for the next six weeks, until its next meeting. The Fed sets a **target federal funds rate**, a desired level for the federal funds rate. This target is then enforced by the Open Market Desk of the Federal Reserve Bank of New York, which adjusts the money supply through *open-market operations*—the purchase or sale of Treasury bills—until the actual federal funds rate equals the target rate. The other tools of

St. Louis Federal Reserve Bank Resources

Monetary Policy Online Course

In this *Monetary Policy* online interactive program, students learn about the tools of monetary policy that are used by the Federal Reserve in response to periods of recession and inflation.

St. Louis Federal Reserve Bank Resources

In Plain English Online Course

This online interactive course describes the structure and functions of the Federal Reserve System.

In Plain English Video

This video introduces students to the Federal Reserve System, its makeup, and its mission.

Figure 31.1 The Effect of an Increase in the Money Supply on the Interest Rate

The Federal Reserve can lower the interest rate by increasing the money supply. Here, the equilibrium interest rate falls from r_1 to r_2 in response to an increase in the money supply from $\overline{M}_1$ to $\overline{M}_2$. In order to induce people to hold the larger quantity of money, the interest rate must fall from r_1 to r_2.

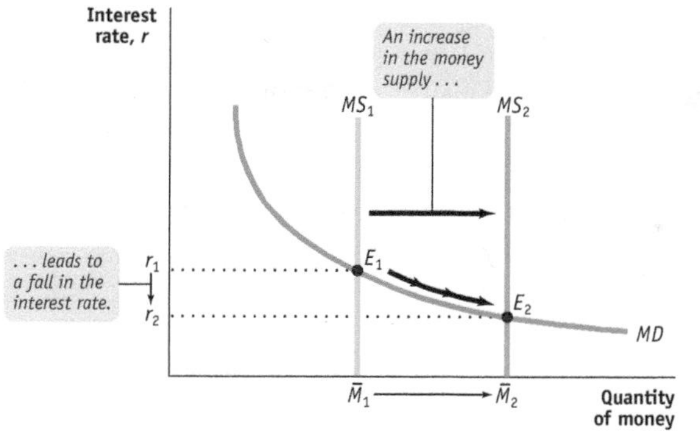

monetary policy, lending through the discount window and changes in reserve requirements, aren't used on a regular basis (although the Fed used discount window lending in its efforts to address the 2008 financial crisis).

Figure 31.2 shows how interest rate targeting works. In both panels, r_T is the target federal funds rate. In panel (a), the initial money supply curve is MS_1 with money supply

Figure 31.2 Setting the Federal Funds Rate

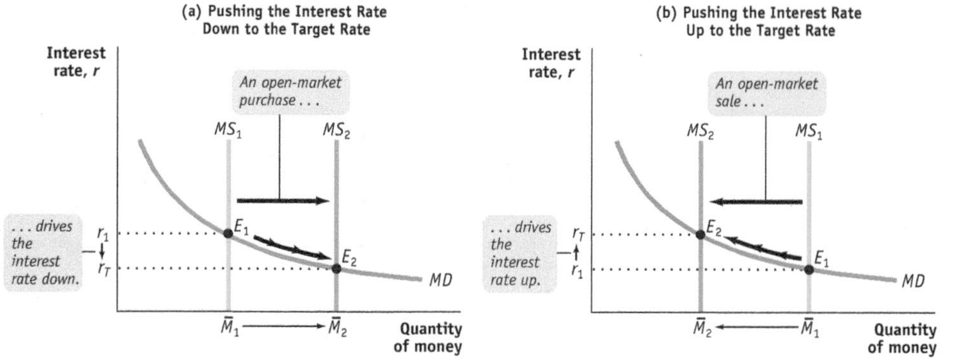

The Federal Reserve sets a target for the federal funds rate and uses open-market operations to achieve that target. In both panels the target rate is r_T. In panel (a) the initial equilibrium interest rate, r_1, is above the target rate. The Fed increases the money supply by making an open-market purchase of Treasury bills, pushing the money supply curve rightward, from MS_1 to MS_2, and driving the interest rate down to r_T. In panel (b) the initial equilibrium interest rate, r_1, is below the target rate. The Fed reduces the money supply by making an open-market sale of Treasury bills, pushing the money supply curve leftward, from MS_1 to MS_2, and driving the interest rate up to r_T.

TEACH AP® Exam Tip

Monetary policy is consistently tested in the free-response section of the AP® exam. The more students practice, the better they will do.

FOCUS Graph It

Use Figures 31.1 and 31.2 to teach the effects of an increase or decrease in the money supply on interest rates. On their whiteboards or notebook paper, have students graph an increase in the money supply and share the results with a partner. *Interest rates should decrease and the quantity of money increases.* Now ask them to graph a decrease in the money supply and share that with a partner. *Interest rates should increase and the quantity of money decreases.* Make sure partners check for correct labels.

TEACH Teach It

Remind students that the interest rate is the cost of borrowing money.

FOCUS Flip It

Students can view the Jacob Clifford video "Macro Unit 4, Question 11—Federal Funds Rate" (see econextras video list with hyperlinks on the bcs and TRFD) to reinforce an understanding of the Fed's ability to change the money supply and affect the macroeconomy.

St. Louis Federal Reserve Bank Resources

The Fed's Toolbox

In The Fed's Toolbox, students learn that the Federal Reserve System uses its monetary policy tools to influence the level of reserves in the banking system. Students participate in a simulation to demonstrate how the Fed uses open market operations to achieve its dual mandate of price stability and maximum employment. Students also learn about other monetary tools: the discount rate, reserve requirements, and interest on reserves—a recent monetary policy tool. Finally, students apply their knowledge of monetary policy to suggest possible Federal Reserve policy responses to proposed economic conditions.

FOCUS In the News

TRM Find a recent article on Fed policy or use *Businessweek*'s January 2014 "The Big Issues Facing Fed Chair Janet Yellen" at http://www.businessweek.com/articles/2014-01-09/janet-yellen-at-federal-reserve-interest-rates-bubbles-transparency. It identifies the issues facing Janet Yellen, the new Fed chair. Suggested questions for this article can be found in **Worksheet 31.1 (Issues Facing Fed Chairman Yellen)** from the TRM.

TEACH Teach It

Monetary policy changes interest rates. Investment spending and interest-sensitive consumer spending will vary when interest rates change. Tell students to remember that the aggregate demand curve shifts in the same direction as the money supply curve. This will help them avoid making mistakes on the AP® exam.

FYI The Fed Reverses Course

During the summer of 2007, many called for a change in Federal Reserve policy. At first the Fed remained unmoved. On August 7, 2007, the Federal Open Market Committee decided to make no change in its interest rate policy. The official statement, however, did concede that "financial markets have been volatile in recent weeks" and that "credit conditions have become tighter for some households and businesses."

Just three days later, the Fed issued a special statement basically assuring market players that it was paying attention; on August 17 it issued another statement declaring that it was "monitoring the situation," which is Fed-speak for "we're getting nervous." And on September 18, the Fed did what CNBC analyst Jim Cramer wanted: it cut the target federal funds rate "to help forestall some of the adverse effects on the broader economy that might otherwise arise from the disruptions in financial markets." In effect, it conceded that Cramer's worries were at least partly right.

It was the beginning of a major change in monetary policy. The figure on the right shows two interest rates from the beginning of 2004 to 2013: the target federal funds rate decided by the Federal Open Market Committee, which dropped in a series of steps starting in September 2007, and the average effective rate that prevailed in the market each day. The figure shows that the interest rate cut six weeks after Cramer's diatribe was only the first of several cuts. As you can see, this was a reversal of previous policy: previously the Fed had generally been raising rates, not reducing them, out of concern that inflation might become a problem. But starting in September 2007, fighting the financial crisis took priority. By the way, notice how beginning late in 2008, it looks as if there are two target federal funds rates. What happened? The Federal Open Market Committee set a target *range* for the federal funds rate, between 0% and 0.25%. That target range was still in effect at the time of writing in 2014.

The figure also shows that the Fed doesn't always hit its target. There were a number of days, especially in 2008, when the actual federal funds rate was significantly above or below the target rate. But these episodes didn't last long, and overall the Fed got what it wanted, at least as far as short-term interest rates were concerned.

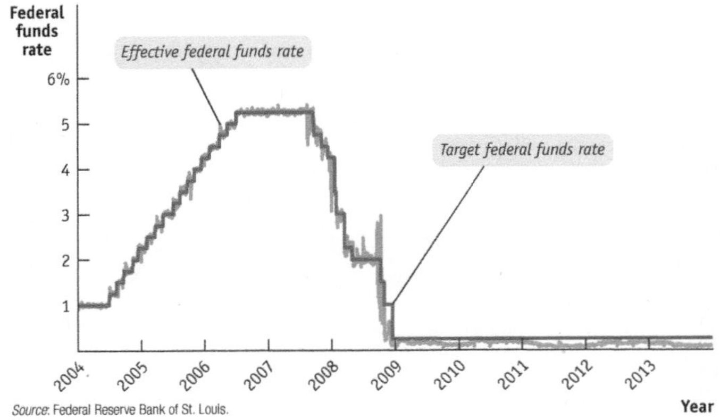

Source: Federal Reserve Bank of St. Louis.

$\overline{M}_1$, and the equilibrium interest rate, r_1, is above the target rate. To lower the interest rate to r_T, the Fed makes an open-market purchase of Treasury bills, which leads to an increase in the money supply via the money multiplier. This is illustrated in panel (a) by the rightward shift of the money supply curve from MS_1 to MS_2 and an increase in the money supply to $\overline{M}_2$. This drives the equilibrium interest rate *down* to the target rate, r_T.

Panel (b) shows the opposite case. Again, the initial money supply curve is MS_1 with money supply $\overline{M}_1$. But this time the equilibrium interest rate, r_1, is below the target federal funds rate, r_T. In this case, the Fed will make an open-market sale of Treasury bills, leading to a fall in the money supply to $\overline{M}_2$ via the money multiplier. The money supply curve shifts leftward from MS_1 to MS_2, driving the equilibrium interest rate *up* to the target federal funds rate, r_T.

AP® Exam Tip

Remember that the aggregate demand curve shifts in the same direction as the money supply curve when the Fed conducts monetary policy.

Monetary Policy and Aggregate Demand

We have seen how fiscal policy can be used to stabilize the economy. Now we will see how monetary policy—changes in the money supply or the interest rate, or both—can play the same role.

St. Louis Federal Reserve Bank Resources

"Then and Now: Fed Policy Actions During the Great Depression and the Great Recession," *Page One Economics Classroom Edition* (November 2011)

Although the recent Great Recession was severe, its financial impact never paralleled that of the Great Depression. This issue of *Page One Economics* compares these two economic downturns and shows how lessons learned in the Great Depression helped current Federal Reserve policy makers stabilize the economy during the recent economic crisis.

Expansionary and Contractionary Monetary Policy

Previously we said that monetary policy shifts the aggregate demand curve. We can now explain how that works: through the effect of monetary policy on the interest rate.

Figure 31.3 illustrates the process. Suppose that the Federal Reserve wants to reduce interest rates, so it expands the money supply. As we've seen, this leads to a lower interest rate. A lower interest rate, in turn, will lead to more investment spending, which will lead to higher real GDP, which will lead to higher consumer spending, and so on through the multiplier process. So the total quantity of goods and services demanded at any given aggregate price level rises when the quantity of money increases, and the *AD* curve shifts to the right. Monetary policy that shifts the *AD* curve to the right, as illustrated in the top portion of Figure 31.3, is known as **expansionary monetary policy**.

Expansionary monetary policy is monetary policy that increases aggregate demand.

Figure 31.3 Expansionary and Contractionary Monetary Policy

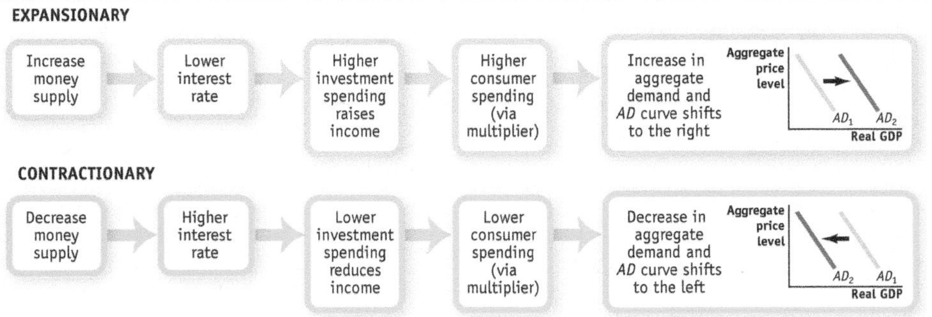

The top portion shows what happens when the Fed adopts an expansionary monetary policy and increases the money supply. Interest rates fall, leading to higher investment spending, which raises income, which, in turn, raises consumer spending and shifts the *AD* curve to the right.

The bottom portion shows what happens when the Fed adopts a contractionary monetary policy and reduces the money supply. Interest rates rise, leading to lower investment spending and a reduction in income. This lowers consumer spending and shifts the *AD* curve to the left.

Suppose, alternatively, that the Federal Reserve contracts the money supply. This leads to a higher interest rate. The higher interest rate leads to lower investment spending, which leads to lower real GDP, which leads to lower consumer spending, and so on. So the total quantity of goods and services demanded falls when the money supply is reduced, and the *AD* curve shifts to the left. Monetary policy that shifts the *AD* curve to the left, as illustrated in the lower portion of Figure 31.3, is called **contractionary monetary policy**.

Contractionary monetary policy is monetary policy that reduces aggregate demand.

Monetary Policy in Practice

We have learned that policy makers try to fight recessions. They also try to ensure *price stability*: low (though usually not zero) inflation. Actual monetary policy reflects a combination of these goals.

In general, the Federal Reserve and other central banks tend to engage in expansionary monetary policy when actual real GDP is below potential output. Panel (a) of **Figure 31.4** on the next page shows the U.S. output gap, which we defined as the

AP® Exam Tip

On the AP® exam, if you are asked what policy the central bank could use to correct a particular problem in the economy, don't just say "expansionary policy" or "contractionary policy." Identify a specific policy tool (open-market operations, the reserve ratio, or the discount rate) and indicate how that tool would be applied to remedy the situation.

FOCUS Active Learning

Students need to understand the cause-and-effect chain created by monetary policy. Ask this series of spiral questions to guide students through the process. They can make the thumbs up sign for an increase and thumbs down for a decrease to make the process easier.

- When the Fed sells bonds, what happens to the money supply? *Decreases*
- When the money supply decreases, what happens to interest rates? *Increase*
- When interest rates increase, what happens to investment and consumer spending? *Decrease*
- When investment and consumer spending decrease, what happens to aggregate demand? *Decreases*
- When aggregate demand decreases, what happens to output and price level? *Decrease*
- When output decreases, what happens to employment? *Decreases*

TEACH Teach It

The Taylor rule is a rule for setting the federal funds rate using both the inflation rate and the output gap. Students should already be familiar with the Taylor rule, so do not spend a great deal of time on it. Working with monetary policy questions from previous exams will benefit students more.

Figure 31.4 Tracking Monetary Policy Using the Output Gap, Inflation, and the Taylor Rule

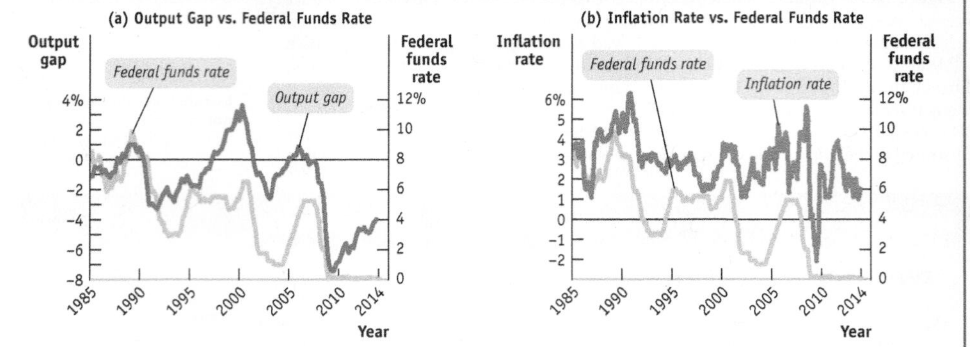

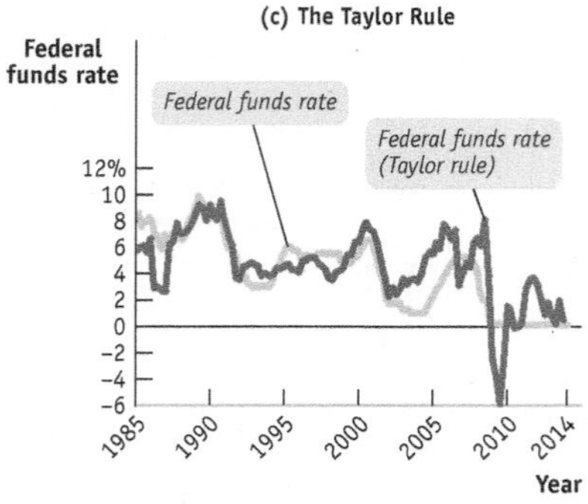

Panel (a) shows that the federal funds rate usually rises when the output gap is positive—that is, when actual real GDP is above potential output—and falls when the output gap is negative. Panel (b) illustrates that the federal funds rate tends to be high when inflation is high and low when inflation is low. Panel (c) shows the Taylor rule in action. The green line shows the actual federal funds rate from 1985 to 2010. The purple line shows the interest rate the Fed *should* have set according to the Taylor rule. The fit isn't perfect—in fact, for a period after 2009 the Taylor rule suggests a negative interest rate, an impossibility—but the Taylor rule does a better job of tracking U.S. monetary policy than either the output gap or the inflation rate alone.

Sources: Federal Reserve Bank of St. Louis; Bureau of Economic Analysis; Bureau of Labor Statistics.

percentage difference between actual real GDP and potential output, versus the federal funds rate since 1985. (Recall that the output gap is positive when actual real GDP exceeds potential output.) As you can see, the Fed has tended to raise interest rates when the output gap is rising—that is, when the economy is developing an inflationary gap—and cut rates when the output gap is falling. The big exception was the late 1990s, when the Fed left rates steady for several years even as the economy developed a positive output gap (which went along with a low unemployment rate).

One reason the Fed was willing to keep interest rates low in the late 1990s was that inflation was low. Panel (b) of Figure 31.4 compares the inflation rate, measured as the rate of change in consumer prices excluding food and energy, with the federal funds rate. You can see how low inflation during the mid-1990s and early 2000s helped encourage loose monetary policy both in the late 1990s and in 2002–2003.

The **Taylor rule for monetary policy** is a rule for setting the federal funds rate that takes into account both the inflation rate and the output gap.

In 1993, Stanford economist John Taylor suggested that monetary policy should follow a simple rule that takes into account concerns about both the business cycle and inflation. The **Taylor rule for monetary policy** is a rule for setting the federal funds rate that takes into account both the inflation rate and the output gap. He also

308 Section 6 Inflation, Unemployment, and Stabilization Policies

suggested that actual monetary policy often looks as if the Federal Reserve was, in fact, more or less following the proposed rule. The rule Taylor originally suggested was as follows:

$$\text{Federal funds rate} = 1 + (1.5 \times \text{inflation rate}) + (0.5 \times \text{output gap})$$

Panel (c) of Figure 31.4 compares the federal funds rate specified by the Taylor rule with the actual federal funds rate from 1985 to 2010. With the exception of a period beginning in 2009, the Taylor rule does a pretty good job of predicting the Fed's actual behavior—better than looking at either the output gap alone or the inflation rate alone. Furthermore, the direction of changes in interest rates predicted by an application of the Taylor rule to monetary policy and the direction of changes in actual interest rates have always been the same—further evidence that the Fed is using some form of the Taylor rule to set monetary policy. But, what happened in 2009? A combination of low inflation and a large and negative output gap put the Taylor's rule of prediction of the federal funds into negative territory. But, of course, a negative federal funds rate is impossible. So the Fed did the best it could—it cut rates aggressively and the federal funds rate fell to almost zero.

Monetary policy, rather than fiscal policy, is the main tool of stabilization policy. Like fiscal policy, it is subject to lags: it takes time for the Fed to recognize economic problems and time for monetary policy to affect the economy. However, since the Fed moves much more quickly than Congress, monetary policy is typically the preferred tool.

Stanford economist John Taylor suggested a simple rule for monetary policy.

Inflation Targeting

Until 2012, the Fed did not explicitly commit itself to achieving a particular inflation rate. However, in January 2012, Ben Bernanke, the chair of the Federal Reserve at the time, announced that the Fed would set its policy to maintain an approximately 2% inflation rate per year. With that statement, the Fed joined a number of other central banks that have explicit *inflation targets.* So rather than using the Taylor rule to set monetary policy, they instead announce the inflation rate that they want to achieve—the inflation target—and set policy in an attempt to hit that target. This method of setting monetary policy is called **inflation targeting**. The central bank of New Zealand, which was the first country to adopt inflation targeting, specified a range for that target of 1% to 3%. Other central banks commit themselves to achieving a specific number. For example, the Bank of England is supposed to keep inflation at 2%. In practice, there doesn't seem to be much difference between these versions: central banks with a target range for inflation seem to aim for the middle of that range, and central banks with a fixed target tend to give themselves considerable wiggle room.

Inflation targeting occurs when the central bank sets an explicit target for the inflation rate and sets monetary policy in order to hit that target.

One major difference between inflation targeting and the Taylor rule is that inflation targeting is forward-looking rather than backward-looking. That is, the Taylor rule adjusts monetary policy in response to *past* inflation, but inflation targeting is based on a forecast of *future* inflation.

Advocates of inflation targeting argue that it has two key advantages, *transparency* and *accountability.* First, economic uncertainty is reduced because the public knows the objective of an inflation-targeting central bank. Second, the central bank's success can be judged by seeing how closely actual inflation rates have matched the inflation target, making central bankers accountable.

Critics of inflation targeting argue that it's too restrictive because there are times when other concerns—like the stability of the financial system—should take priority over achieving any particular inflation rate. Indeed, in late 2007 and early 2008 the Fed cut interest rates much more than either the Taylor rule or inflation targeting would have dictated because it feared that turmoil in the financial markets would lead to a major recession (which it did).

TEACH Teach It

One major difference between inflation targeting and the Taylor rule is that inflation targeting is forward-looking rather than backward-looking. That is, the Taylor rule adjusts monetary policy in response to past inflation, but inflation targeting is based on a forecast of future inflation.

The advantages of inflation targeting are:

- **Transparency**: Economic uncertainty is reduced because the public knows the objective of an inflation-targeting central bank.
- **Accountability**: The central bank's success can be judged by observing how closely actual inflation rates have matched the inflation target, making central bankers accountable.

FOCUS Active Learning

TRM Ask students to complete **Worksheet 31.2 (Monetary Policy)** from the TRM in class or as homework. This worksheet gives students practice in applying monetary policy to different problems in the economy and drawing the associated graphs.

FOCUS Test It

For a great review of monetary policy, assign Question 2 from the released 2010 AP® Macroeconomics exam at http://apcentral.collegeboard.com/apc/public/repository/ap10_frq_macroecon.pdf. It is recommended that students take $12\frac{1}{2}$ minutes to answer this question to match the time suggested for the AP® exam. The rubric may be viewed at http://apcentral.collegeboard.com/apc/public/repository/ap10_macroeconomics_scoring_guidelines.pdf.

OPEN & CLOSE Exit Slip

TRM *Please see **Exit Slip: Module 31** in the TRM for formative multiple-choice questions to ask your students before finishing your lesson. These questions will help you quickly assess whether your students have mastered the module's concepts before moving on.*

Answers to the Exit Slip Questions

1. E
2. B
3. A

Answers to Module 31 Review Questions

Check Your Understanding

1. In the accompanying diagram, the increase in the demand for money is shown as a rightward shift of the money demand curve, from MD_1 to MD_2. This raises the equilibrium interest rate from r_1 to r_2.

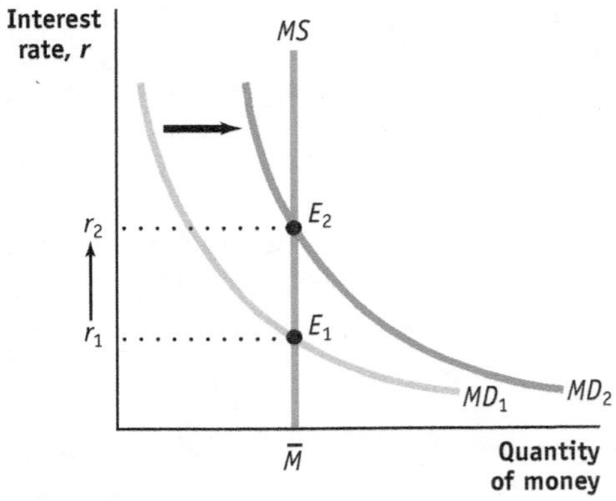

2. In order to prevent the interest rate from rising, the Federal Reserve must make an open-market purchase of Treasury bills, shifting the money supply curve rightward. This is shown in the accompanying diagram as the move from MS_1 to MS_2.

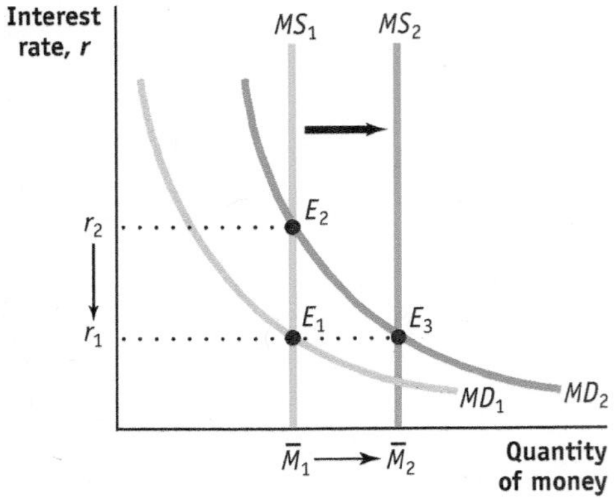

3. a. The money supply curve shifts to the right.

b. The equilibrium interest rate falls.

c. Investment spending rises due to the fall in the interest rate.

d. Consumer spending rises due to the multiplier process.

e. Aggregate output rises because of the rightward shift of the aggregate demand curve that results from the increase in investment and consumer spending.

FYI What the Fed Wants, the Fed Gets

What's the evidence that the Fed can actually cause an economic contraction or expansion? You might think that finding such evidence is just a matter of looking at what happens to the economy when interest rates go up or down. But it turns out that there's a big problem with that approach: the Fed usually changes interest rates in an attempt to tame the business cycle, raising rates if the economy is expanding and reducing rates if the economy is slumping. So, in the actual data, it often looks as if low interest rates go along with a weak economy and high rates go along with a strong economy.

In a famous 1994 paper titled "Monetary Policy Matters," the macroeconomists Christina Romer and David Romer solved this problem by focusing on episodes in which monetary policy *wasn't* a reaction to the business cycle. Specifically, they used minutes from the Federal Open Market Committee and other sources to identify episodes "in which the Federal Reserve in effect decided to attempt to create a recession to reduce inflation." Contractionary monetary policy is sometimes used to eliminate inflation that has become *embedded* in the economy, rather than just as a tool of macroeconomic stabilization. In this case, the Fed needs to create a recessionary gap—not just eliminate an inflationary gap—to wring embedded inflation out of the economy.

The figure shows the unemployment rate between 1952 and 1984 (orange) and identifies five dates on which, according to Romer and Romer, the Fed decided that it wanted a recession (vertical red lines). In four out of the five cases, the decision to contract the economy was followed, after a modest lag, by a rise in the unemployment rate. On average, Romer and Romer found, the unemployment rate rises by 2 percentage points after the Fed decides that unemployment needs to go up.

So yes, the Fed gets what it wants.

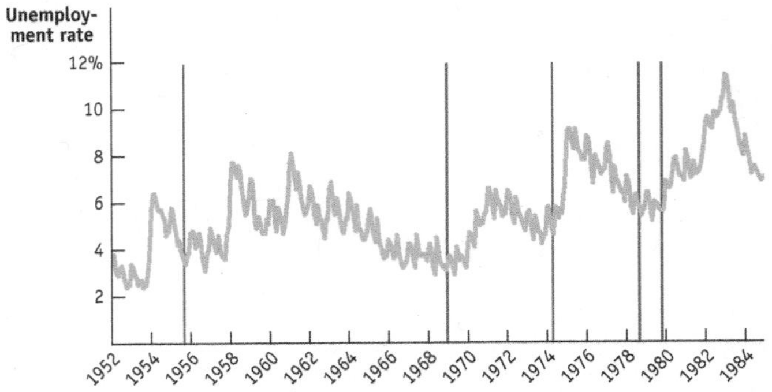

Sources: Bureau of Labor Statistics; Christina D. Romer and David H. Romer, "Monetary Policy Matters," *Journal of Monetary Economics* 34 (August 1994): 75–88.

MODULE 31 Review

Check Your Understanding

1. Assume that there is an increase in the demand for money at every interest rate. Using a diagram, show what effect this will have on the equilibrium interest rate for a given money supply.
2. Now assume that the Fed is following a policy of targeting the federal funds rate. What will the Fed do in the situation described in Question 1 to keep the federal funds rate unchanged? Illustrate with a diagram.
3. Suppose the economy is currently suffering from a recessionary gap and the Federal Reserve uses an expansionary monetary policy to close that gap. Describe the short-run effect of this policy on the following.
   a. the money supply curve
   b. the equilibrium interest rate
   c. investment spending
   d. consumer spending
   e. aggregate output

Tackle the Test: Multiple-Choice Questions

1. At each meeting of the Federal Open Market Committee, the Federal Reserve sets a target for which of the following?
   I. the federal funds rate
   II. the prime interest rate
   III. the market interest rate
   a. I only
   b. II only
   c. III only
   d. I and III only
   e. I, II, and III
2. Which of the following actions can the Fed take to decrease the equilibrium interest rate?
   a. increase the money supply
   b. increase money demand
   c. decrease the money supply
   d. decrease money demand
   e. both (a) and (d)
3. Contractionary monetary policy attempts to ________ aggregate demand by ________ interest rates.
   a. decrease increasing
   b. increase decreasing
   c. decrease decreasing
   d. increase increasing
   e. increase maintaining
4. Which of the following is a goal of monetary policy?
   a. zero inflation
   b. deflation
   c. price stability
   d. increased potential output
   e. decreased actual real GDP
5. When implementing monetary policy, the Federal Reserve attempts to achieve
   a. an explicit target real GDP growth rate.
   b. zero inflation.
   c. a low rate of deflation.
   d. an explicit target inflation rate.
   e. 4–5% inflation.

Tackle the Test: Free-Response Questions

1. a. Give the equation for the Taylor rule.
   b. How well does the Taylor rule fit the Fed's actual behavior? Explain.
   c. Suppose the inflation rate is 1% and the output gap is 3%. What federal funds rate does the Taylor rule predict?
   d. Suppose the inflation rate increases by 2 percentage points. If the Fed follows the Taylor rule, what specific change in the target federal funds rate will the Fed seek? Identify the general type of policy the Fed uses to achieve that sort of change.

Rubric for FRQ 1 (6 points)

1 point: Federal funds rate = 1 + (1.5 × inflation rate) + (0.5 × output gap)

1 point: It's not a perfect fit but it is usually a close approximation.

1 point: It does better than any one measure alone, and it has always correctly predicted the direction of change of interest rates.

1 point: 1 + (1.5 × 1) + (0.5 × 3) = 4%

1 point: An increase of 3 (1.5 × 2) percentage points

1 point: Contractionary monetary policy

2. a. What can the Fed do with each of its three primary tools to implement expansionary monetary policy during a recession?
   b. Use a correctly labeled graph of the money market to explain how the Fed's use of expansionary monetary policy affects interest rates in the short run.
   c. Explain how the interest rate change you graphed in part b affects aggregate supply and demand in the short run.
   d. Use a correctly labeled aggregate demand and supply graph to show how expansionary monetary policy affects aggregate output in the short run.
   (11 points)

Tackle the Test: Multiple-Choice Questions

1. a
2. a
3. a
4. c
5. d

Tackle the Test: Free-Response Question

Rubric for FRQ 2 (11 points)

1 point: Decrease the discount rate.

1 point: Decrease the reserve requirement.

1 point: Buy Treasury bills.

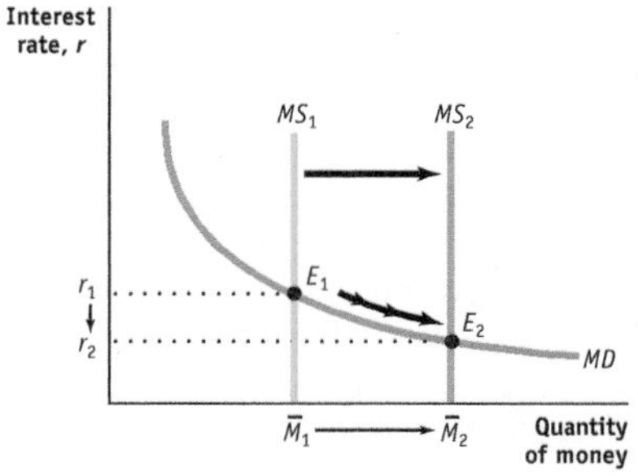

1 point: Graph labeled "Interest rate" on the vertical axis, "Quantity of money" on the horizontal axis, and a downward-sloping money demand curve

1 point: Vertical money supply curve

1 point: Rightward shift of money supply curve and corresponding decrease in the equilibrium interest rate

1 point: The interest rate change does not affect aggregate supply in the short run.

1 point: Aggregate demand increases because the lower interest rate leads to more investment spending, and investment is a component of aggregate demand.

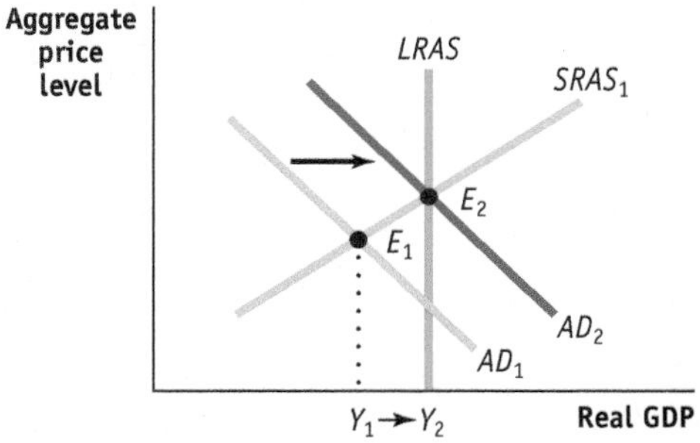

1 point: Graph labeled "Aggregate price level" or "*PL*" on the vertical axis and "Real GDP" on the horizontal axis with downward-sloping *AD*, upward-sloping *SRAS*, and an initial equilibrium to the left of the vertical *LRAS*

1 point: Rightward shift of aggregate demand

1 point: Indication that real GDP increases on the figure, as from Y_1 to Y_2

Module 31 Monetary Policy and the Interest Rate 311

PD To prepare for teaching this lesson, you may want to consult the **Module 32 Sample Lecture** in the TRM.

OPEN & CLOSE Start Here

Show students the video "The Neutrality of Money" (see econextras video list with hyperlinks on the bcs and TRFD). Afterwards, ask students if they think this concept decreases the importance of the Federal Reserve.

TEACH Teach It

After learning about the short-run impact of monetary policy in Module 31, students may find the notion of money neutrality rather off-putting. After all, if monetary policy is believed to have no long-run impact on interest rates or real GDP, what is the point? Stress that monetary policy in the short run can be effective at shortening the duration of a recession or an inflationary period, and that's certainly a positive economic outcome.

iStockphoto

MODULE 32 Money, Output, and Prices in the Long Run

In this Module, you will learn to:

- Identify the effects of an inappropriate monetary policy
- Explain the concept of monetary neutrality and its relationship to the long-term economic effects of monetary policy

In the previous module we discussed how expansionary and contractionary monetary policy can be used to stabilize the economy. The Federal Reserve can use its monetary policy tools to change the money supply and cause the equilibrium interest rate in the money market to increase or decrease. But what if a central bank pursues a monetary policy that is not appropriate? That is, what if a central bank pursues expansionary policy during an expansion or contractionary policy during a recession? In this module we consider how a counterproductive action by a central bank can actually destabilize the economy in the short run. We also introduce the long-run effects of monetary policy. As we learned in the last section, the money market (where monetary policy has its effect on the money supply) determines the interest rate only in the short run. In the long run, the interest rate is determined in the market for loanable funds. Here we look at long-run adjustments and consider the long-run effects of monetary policy.

Money, Output, and Prices

Because of its expansionary and contractionary effects, monetary policy is generally the policy tool of choice to help stabilize the economy. However, not all actions by central banks are productive. In particular, as we'll see later, central banks sometimes print money not to fight a recessionary gap but to help the government pay its bills, an action that typically destabilizes the economy.

What happens when a change in the money supply pushes the economy away from, rather than toward, long-run equilibrium? The economy is self-correcting in the long run: a demand shock has only a temporary effect on aggregate output. If the demand shock is the result of a change in the money supply, we can make a stronger statement: in the long run, changes in the quantity of money affect the

312 Section 6 Inflation, Unemployment, and Stabilization Policies

aggregate price level, but they do not change real aggregate output or the interest rate. To see why, let's look at what happens if the central bank permanently increases the money supply.

Short-Run and Long-Run Effects of an Increase in the Money Supply

To analyze the long-run effects of monetary policy, it's helpful to think of the central bank as choosing a target for the money supply rather than for the interest rate. In assessing the effects of an increase in the money supply, we return to the analysis of the long-run effects of an increase in aggregate demand.

Figure 32.1 shows the short-run and long-run effects of an increase in the money supply when the economy begins at potential output, Y_1. The initial short-run aggregate supply curve is $SRAS_1$, the long-run aggregate supply curve is *LRAS*, and the initial aggregate demand curve is AD_1. The economy's initial equilibrium is at E_1, a point of both short-run and long-run macroeconomic equilibrium because it is on both the short-run and the long-run aggregate supply curves. Real GDP is at potential output, Y_1.

Now suppose there is an increase in the money supply. Other things equal, an increase in the money supply reduces the interest rate, which increases investment spending, which leads to a further rise in consumer spending, and so on. So an increase in the money supply increases the demand for goods and services, shifting the *AD* curve rightward to AD_2. In the short run, the economy moves to a new short-run macroeconomic equilibrium at E_2. The price level rises from P_1 to P_2, and real GDP rises from Y_1 to Y_2. That is, both the aggregate price level and aggregate output increase in the short run.

But the aggregate output level, Y_2, is above potential output. Production at a level above potential output leads to low unemployment, which brings about a rise in nominal wages over time, causing the short-run aggregate supply curve to shift leftward. This process stops only when the *SRAS* curve ends up at $SRAS_2$ and the economy ends up at

Figure 32.1 The Short-Run and Long-Run Effects of an Increase in the Money Supply

An increase in the money supply generates a positive short-run effect, but no long-run effect, on real GDP. Here, the economy begins at E_1, a point of short-run and long-run macroeconomic equilibrium. An increase in the money supply shifts the *AD* curve rightward, and the economy moves to a new short-run equilibrium at E_2 and a new real GDP of Y_2. But E_2 is not a long-run equilibrium: Y_2 exceeds potential output, Y_1, leading to an increase in nominal wages over time. In the long run, the increase in nominal wages shifts the short-run aggregate supply curve leftward, to a new position at $SRAS_2$. The economy reaches a new short-run and long-run macroeconomic equilibrium at E_3 on the *LRAS* curve, and output falls back to potential output, Y_1. The only long-run effect of an increase in the money supply is an increase in the aggregate price level from P_1 to P_3.

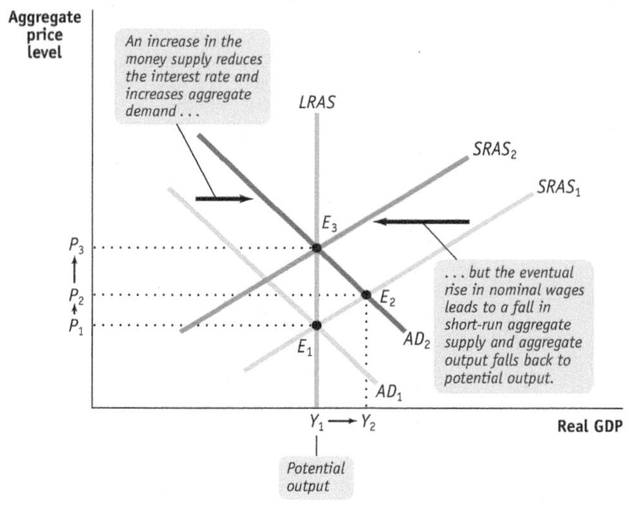

TEACH Teach It

Remind students that in the long run, prices and wages are fully flexible, while in the short run, at least one input is fixed.

FOCUS Active Learning

Show the two Jacob Clifford videos "Macro 4.2—Monetary Policy and Aggregate Demand" and "Macro 4.3—Graphing Monetary Policy Practice" (see econextras video list with hyperlinks on the bcs and TRFD). Pause the videos at the appropriate times, and challenge students to draw the graphs in their notebooks or on their whiteboards. Then continue the video and show the answers. This is great practice for the AP® Exam.

TEACH Teach It

There are times when the central bank can engage in monetary policy that is actually counterproductive. In other words, the policy might move the economy away from potential GDP rather than closer to it.

FOCUS Graph It

TRM Use Figure 32.1 and **Worksheet 32.1 (Effects of Expansionary Monetary Policy)** from the TRM to explain the short- and long-run effects of an increase in the money supply. Once students work through the series of questions, explain that long-run equilibrium would be established back at potential GDP and a higher price level. So in the long run, expansionary monetary policy doesn't increase real GDP; it only causes inflation.

point E_3, a point of both short-run and long-run macroeconomic equilibrium. The long-run effect of an increase in the money supply, then, is that the aggregate price level has increased from P_1 to P_3, but aggregate output is back at potential output, Y_1. In the long run, a monetary expansion raises the aggregate price level but has no effect on real GDP.

If the money supply decreases, the story we have just told plays out in reverse. Other things equal, a decrease in the money supply raises the interest rate, which decreases investment spending, which leads to a further decrease in consumer spending, and so on. So a decrease in the money supply decreases the demand for goods and services at any given aggregate price level, shifting the aggregate demand curve to the left. In the short run, the economy moves to a new short-run macroeconomic equilibrium at a level of real GDP below potential output and a lower aggregate price level. That is, both the aggregate price level and aggregate output decrease in the short run. But what happens over time? When the aggregate output level is below potential output, nominal wages fall. When this happens, the short-run aggregate supply curve shifts rightward. This process stops only when the *SRAS* curve ends up at a point of both short-run and long-run macroeconomic equilibrium. The long-run effect of a decrease in the money supply, then, is that the aggregate price level decreases, but aggregate output is back at potential output. In the long run, a monetary contraction decreases the aggregate price level but has no effect on real GDP.

Monetary Neutrality

How much does a change in the money supply change the aggregate price level in the long run? The answer is that a change in the money supply leads to a proportional change in the aggregate price level in the long run. For example, if the money supply falls 25%, the aggregate price level falls 25% in the long run; if the money supply rises 50%, the aggregate price level rises 50% in the long run.

How do we know this? Consider the following thought experiment: suppose all prices in the economy—prices of final goods and services and also factor prices, such as nominal wage rates—double. And suppose the money supply doubles at the same time. What difference does this make to the economy in real terms? None. All real variables in the economy—such as real GDP and the real value of the money supply (the amount of goods and services it can buy)—are unchanged. So there is no reason for anyone to behave any differently.

We can state this argument in reverse: if the economy starts out in long-run macroeconomic equilibrium and the money supply changes, restoring long-run macroeconomic equilibrium requires restoring all real values to their original values. This includes restoring the real value of the money supply to its original level. So if the money supply falls 25%, the aggregate price level must fall 25%; if the money supply rises 50%, the price level must rise 50%; and so on.

According to the concept of **monetary neutrality**, changes in the money supply have no real effects on the economy.

This analysis demonstrates the concept known as **monetary neutrality**, in which changes in the money supply have no real effects on the economy. In the long run, the only effect of an increase in the money supply is to raise the aggregate price level by an equal percentage. Economists argue that *money is neutral in the long run.*

However, this is a good time to recall the dictum of John Maynard Keynes: "In the long run we are all dead." In the long run, changes in the money supply don't have any effect on real GDP, interest rates, or anything else except the price level. But it would be foolish to conclude from this that the Fed is irrelevant. Monetary policy does have powerful real effects on the economy in the short run, often making the difference between recession and expansion. And that matters a lot for society's welfare.

Changes in the Money Supply and the Interest Rate in the Long Run

In the short run, an increase in the money supply leads to a fall in the interest rate, and a decrease in the money supply leads to a rise in the interest rate. Module 29 explained that in the long run it's a different story: changes in the money supply don't affect the interest rate at all. Here we'll review that story and discuss the reasons behind it in greater detail.

TEACH Teach It

How does money neutrality work? Suppose all prices in the economy—prices of final goods and services and also factor prices, such as nominal wage rates—double. Then suppose the money supply doubles at the same time. What difference does this make to the economy in real terms? The answer is none. All real variables in the economy, such as real GDP and the real value of the money supply (the amount of goods and services it can buy), are unchanged. So, there is no reason for anyone to behave any differently. Ask students to explain this statement: Money is neutral in the long run. *In the long run, changes in the money supply have no real effects on real GDP, interest rates, or anything else except the price level.*

314 Section 6 Inflation, Unemployment, and Stabilization Policies

Figure 32.2 The Long-Run Determination of the Interest Rate

In the short run, an increase in the money supply from $\overline{M}_1$ to $\overline{M}_2$ pushes the interest rate down from r_1 to r_2 and the economy moves to E_2, a short-run equilibrium. In the long run, however, the aggregate price level rises in proportion to the increase in the money supply, leading to an increase in money demand at any given interest rate in proportion to the increase in the aggregate price level, as shown by the shift from MD_1 to MD_2. The result is that the quantity of money demanded at any given interest rate rises by the same amount as the quantity of money supplied. The economy moves to long-run equilibrium at E_3 and the interest rate returns to r_1.

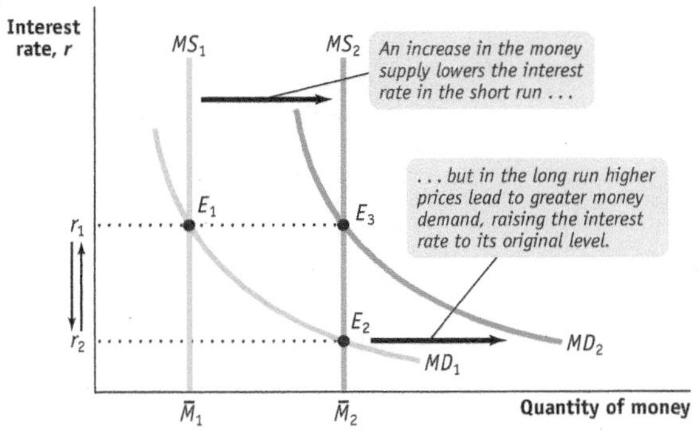

Figure 32.2 shows the money supply curve and the money demand curve before and after the Fed increases the money supply. We assume that the economy is initially at E_1, in long-run macroeconomic equilibrium at potential output, and with money supply $\overline{M}_1$. The initial equilibrium interest rate, determined by the intersection of the money demand curve MD_1 and the money supply curve MS_1, is r_1.

FYI International Evidence of Monetary Neutrality

These days monetary policy is quite similar among wealthy countries. Each major nation (or, in the case of the euro, the eurozone) has a central bank that is insulated from political pressure. All of these central banks try to keep the aggregate price level roughly stable, which usually means inflation of at most 2% to 3% per year.

But if we look at a longer period and a wider group of countries, we see large differences in the growth of the money supply. Between 1970 and the present, the money supply rose only a few percentage points per year in countries such as Switzerland and the United States, but rose much more rapidly in some poorer countries, such as South Africa. These differences allow us to see whether it is really true that increases in the money supply, in the long run, lead to equal percentage increases in the aggregate price level.

The figure shows the annual percentage increases in the money supply and average annual increases in the aggregate price level—that is, the average rate of inflation—for a sample of countries during the period 1970–2012, with each point representing a country. If the relationship between increases in the money supply and changes in the aggregate price level were exact, the points would lie precisely on a 45-degree line. In fact, the relationship isn't exact because other factors besides money affect the aggregate price level. But the scatter of points clearly lies close to a 45-degree line, showing a more or less proportional relationship between money and the aggregate price level. That is, the data support the concept of monetary neutrality in the long run.

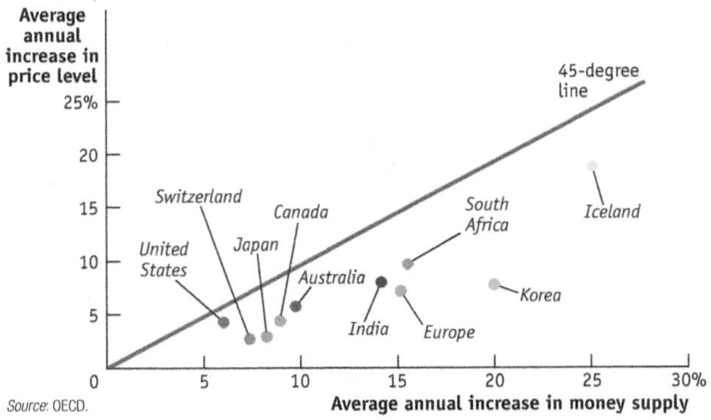

Source: OECD.

FOCUS Graph It

TRM In the short run, an increase in the money supply causes short-term interest rates to fall. But what happens in the long run? Use Figure 32.2 and **Worksheet 32.2 (Interest Rates in the Long Run)** from the TRM to explain the cause-and-effect chain in the long run. Explain that in the long run, monetary neutrality ensures that the interest rate won't change after a change in the money supply.

FOCUS Active Learning

Explain to students that research has shown evidence of monetary neutrality. If possible, project the graph from the FYI box on the board. Ask students to explain the relationship using the graph to explain why the concept is valid. *The graph shows the average annual increase in the money supply compared to the price level. Over time, the money supply and the price level increase at close to the same rate.*

Module 32 Money, Output, and Prices in the Long Run 315

FOCUS Active Learning

TRM To practice the concepts in this module, have students complete **Worksheet 32.3 (Monetary Policy in the Short and Long Run)** from the TRM in class or as homework. Students will practice graphing the impact of monetary policy in the short and long run to help them prepare for the AP® exam.

OPEN & CLOSE Exit Slip

TRM *Please see **Exit Slip: Module 32** in the TRM for formative multiple-choice questions to ask your students before finishing your lesson. These questions will help you quickly assess whether your students have mastered the module's concepts before moving on.*

Answers to the Exit Slip Questions

1. A
2. B
3. C

Now suppose that the money supply increases from $\overline{M}_1$ to $\overline{M}_2$. In the short run, the economy moves from E_1 to E_2 and the interest rate falls from r_1 to r_2. Over time, however, the aggregate price level rises, and this raises money demand, shifting the money demand curve rightward from MD_1 to MD_2. The economy moves to a new long-run equilibrium at E_3, and the interest rate rises to its original level of r_1.

How do we know that the long-run equilibrium interest rate is the original interest rate, r_1? Because the eventual increase in money demand is proportional to the increase in money supply, thus counteracting the initial downward effect on interest rates. Let's follow the chain of events to see why. With monetary neutrality, an increase in the money supply is matched by a proportional increase in the price level in the long run. If the money supply rises by, say, 50%, the price level will also rise by 50%. Changes in the price level, in turn, cause proportional changes in the demand for money. So a 50% increase in the money supply raises the aggregate price level by 50%, which increases the quantity of money demanded at any given interest rate by 50%. Thus, at the initial interest rate of r_1, the quantity of money demanded rises exactly as much as the money supply, and r_1 is again the equilibrium interest rate. In the long run, then, changes in the money supply do not affect the interest rate.

MODULE 32 Review

Check Your Understanding

1. Suppose the economy begins in long-run macroeconomic equilibrium. What is the long-run effect on the aggregate price level of a 5% increase in the money supply? Explain.
2. Suppose the economy begins in long-run macroeconomic equilibrium. What is the long-run effect on the interest rate of a 5% increase in the money supply? Explain.

Tackle the Test: Multiple-Choice Questions

1. In the long run, changes in the quantity of money affect which of the following?
   - I. real aggregate output
   - II. interest rates
   - III. the aggregate price level
   - a. I only
   - b. II only
   - c. III only
   - d. I and II only
   - e. I, II, and III
2. An increase in the money supply will lead to which of the following in the short run?
   - a. higher interest rates
   - b. decreased investment spending
   - c. decreased consumer spending
   - d. increased aggregate demand
   - e. lower real GDP
3. A 10% decrease in the money supply will change the aggregate price level in the long run by
   - a. zero.
   - b. less than 10%.
   - c. 10%.
   - d. 20%.
   - e. more than 20%.
4. Monetary neutrality means that, in the long run, changes in the money supply
   - a. cannot happen.
   - b. have no effect on the economy.
   - c. have no real effect on the economy.
   - d. increase real GDP.
   - e. change real interest rates.
5. A graph of percentage increases in the money supply and average annual increases in the price level for various countries provides evidence that
   - a. changes in the two variables are exactly equal.
   - b. the money supply and aggregate price level are unrelated.
   - c. money neutrality holds only in wealthy countries.
   - d. monetary policy is ineffective.
   - e. money is neutral in the long run.

Answers to Module 32 Review Questions

Check Your Understanding

1. A 5% increase in the money supply will cause a 5% increase in the aggregate price level in the long run. The process begins in the short run, when the larger money supply decreases the interest rate and promotes investment spending. Investment spending is a component of aggregate demand, so the increase in investment spending leads to an increase in aggregate demand, which causes real GDP to increase beyond potential output. The resulting upward pressure on nominal wages and other input prices shifts aggregate supply to the left until a new long-run equilibrium is reached. Although real GDP returns to its original level, both the increase in aggregate demand and the decrease in aggregate supply cause the aggregate price level to increase. The end result is 5% more money being spent on the same quantity of goods and services, which could only mean a 5% increase in the aggregate price level.

2. A 5% increase in the money supply will have no effect on the interest rate in the long run. As explained in the previous answer, a 5% increase in the money supply is matched by a 5% increase in the aggregate price level in the long run. Changes in the aggregate price level, in turn, cause proportional changes in the demand for money. Thus, a 5% increase in the aggregate price level increases the quantity of money demanded at any given interest rate by 5%. This means that at the initial interest rate, the quantity of money demanded rises exactly as much as the money supply, and the new, long-run interest rate is therefore no different from the initial interest rate.

Tackle the Test: Multiple-Choice Questions

1. c
2. d
3. c
4. c
5. e

Tackle the Test: Free-Response Questions

1. Assume the central bank increases the quantity of money by 25%, even though the economy is initially in both short-run and long-run macroeconomic equilibrium. Describe the effects, in the short run and in the long run (giving numbers where possible), on the following:
   a. aggregate output
   b. the aggregate price level
   c. the real value of the money supply (its purchasing power for goods and services)
   d. the interest rate

Rubric for FRQ 1 (8 points)

1 point: Aggregate output rises in the short run.

1 point: Aggregate output falls back to potential output in the long run.

1 point: The aggregate price level rises in the short run (by less than 25%).

1 point: The aggregate price level rises by 25% in the long run.

1 point: The real value of the money supply increases in the short run.

1 point: The real value of the money supply does not change (relative to its original value) in the long run.

1 point: The interest rate falls in the short run.

1 point: The interest rate rises back to its original level in the long run.

2. a. Draw a correctly labeled graph of aggregate demand and aggregate supply showing an economy in long-run macroeconomic equilibrium.
   b. On your graph, show what happens in the short run if the central bank increases the money supply to pay off a government deficit. Explain.
   c. On your graph, show what will happen in the long run. Explain.
   (6 points)

Tackle the Test: Free-Response Question Rubric for FRQ 2 (6 points)

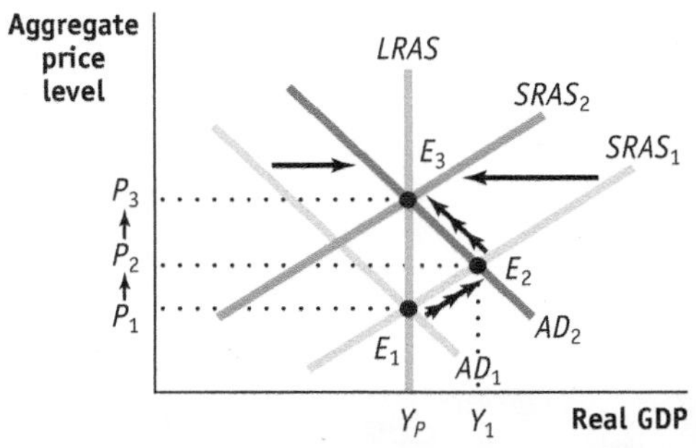

1 point: Graph with "Price level" or "Aggregate price level" on the vertical axis, "Real GDP" on the horizontal axis, a downward-sloping aggregate demand curve, and an upward-sloping aggregate supply curve

1 point: A vertical long-run aggregate supply curve and equilibrium of aggregate demand and short-run aggregate supply at a point on the long-run aggregate supply curve

1 point: Rightward shift of the aggregate demand curve

1 point: The higher money supply leads to a lower interest rate, which increases investment spending (and consumer spending) and, in turn, aggregate demand. Thus, the aggregate demand curve shifts to the right, creating a new equilibrium price level and real GDP.

1 point: Leftward shift of the short-run aggregate supply curve

1 point: The higher price level and production beyond potential output cause wages to rise over time, shifting short-run aggregate supply to the left. This brings the equilibrium level of real GDP back to potential output, but at a higher price level than before.

Module 32 Money, Output, and Prices in the Long Run 317

PD To prepare for teaching this lesson, you may want to consult the **Module 33 Sample Lecture** in the TRM.

OPEN & CLOSE Start Here

Ask students to name some products that have shrunk in size over the last few years. *Answers will vary but might include toilet paper, orange juice, cheese, or ice cream.* Ask them to then read the *Today* article "That Shrinking Feeling—10 Downsized Products" at http://www.today.com/id/40915489/ns/today-money/t/shrinking-feeling-downsized-products. What is the main reason that producers give for changes in size? *Increasing costs of production.*

When prices increase as a result of increases in the costs of production, this is called cost-push inflation. To avoid passing along the increased costs to customers, manufacturers try to decrease the size of the product. If producers increase prices, this may alienate their customer base and create even more inflation.

TEACH Connect It

Remind students of inflation's winners and losers from Module 14. Ask them to explain how lenders, borrowers, savers, and debtors are affected when inflation is higher than expected. *Savers and lenders are generally hurt, while borrowers and debtors are helped by higher than expected inflation.*

DESMOND KWANDE/AFP/Getty Images

MODULE 33 Types of Inflation, Disinflation, and Deflation

In this Module, you will learn to:

- Use the classical model of the price level
- Explain why efforts to collect an inflation tax by printing money can lead to high rates of inflation and even hyperinflation
- Define the types of inflation: cost-push and demand-pull

We have seen that monetary policy affects economic welfare in the short-run. Let's take a closer look at two phenomena that involve monetary policy: inflation and deflation.

Money and Inflation

In the summer of 2008, the African nation of Zimbabwe achieved the unenviable distinction of having the world's highest inflation rate: 11 million percent a year. Although the United States has not experienced the inflation levels that some countries have seen, in the late 1970s and early 1980s, consumer prices were rising at an annual rate as high as 13%. The policies that the Federal Reserve instituted to reduce this high level led to the deepest recession since the Great Depression. As we'll see later, moderate levels of inflation such as those experienced in the United States—even the double-digit inflation of the late 1970s—can have complex causes. Very high inflation, the type suffered by Zimbabwe, is associated with rapid increases in the money supply, but the causes of moderate inflation, the type experienced in the United States, are quite different.

To understand what causes inflation, we need to revisit the effect of changes in the money supply on the overall price level. Then we'll turn to the reasons why governments sometimes increase the money supply very rapidly.

St. Louis Federal Reserve Bank Resources

"Money and Inflation: a Functional Relationship," ***Page One Economics Classroom Edition*** **(March 2013)**

They say that money makes the world go 'round. Just imagine a world without money as our method of payment for everyday transactions. Without money, we would all need to barter for necessary goods and services. Students learn about the three main functions of money and the damaging effects of too much inflation on these functions in this issue.

The Classical Model of Money and Prices

The Turkish currency is the *lira*. When Turkey made 1,000,000 "old" lira equivalent to 1 "new" lira, real GDP was unaffected because of the neutrality of money.

We learned that in the short run an increase in the money supply increases real GDP by lowering the interest rate and stimulating investment spending and consumer spending. However, in the long run, as nominal wages and other sticky prices rise, real GDP falls back to its original level. So in the long run, an increase in the money supply does not change real GDP. Instead, other things equal, it leads to an equal percentage rise in the overall price level; that is, the prices of all goods and services in the economy, including nominal wages and the prices of intermediate goods, rise by the same percentage as the money supply. And when the overall price level rises, the aggregate price level—the prices of all final goods and services—rises as well. As a result, in the long run, a change in the *nominal* money supply, *M*, leads to a change in the aggregate price level, *P*, that leaves the *real* quantity of money, *M/P*, at its original level. As a result, there is no long-run effect on aggregate demand or real GDP. For example, when Turkey dropped six zeros from its currency, the Turkish lira, in January 2005, Turkish real GDP did not change. The only thing that changed was the number of zeros in prices: instead of something costing 2,000,000 lira, it cost 2 lira.

To repeat, this is what happens in the long run. When analyzing large changes in the aggregate price level, however, macroeconomists often find it useful to ignore the distinction between the short run and the long run. Instead, they work with a simplified model in which the effect of a change in the money supply on the aggregate price level takes place instantaneously rather than over a long period of time. You might be concerned about this assumption given the emphasis we've placed on the difference between the short run and the long run. However, for reasons we'll explain shortly, this is a reasonable assumption to make in the case of high inflation.

According to the **classical model of the price level**, the real quantity of money is always at its long-run equilibrium level.

The simplified model in which the real quantity of money, *M/P*, is always at its long-run equilibrium level is known as the **classical model of the price level** because it was commonly used by "classical" economists prior to the influence of John Maynard Keynes. To understand the classical model and why it is useful in the context of high inflation, let's revisit the *AD–AS* model and what it says about the effects of an increase in the money supply. (Unless otherwise noted, we will always be referring to changes in the *nominal* supply of money.)

AP® Exam Tip

In the Keynesian model, sticky prices and wages slow the economy's process of self correction. Classical economists believe that prices and wages are flexible enough to allow the economy to correct itself quickly.

Figure 33.1 reviews the effects of an increase in the money supply according to the *AD–AS* model. The economy starts at E_1, a point of short-run and long-run

Figure 33.1 The Classical Model of the Price Level

Starting at E_1, an increase in the money supply shifts the aggregate demand curve rightward, as shown by the movement from AD_1 to AD_2. There is a new short-run macroeconomic equilibrium at E_2 and a higher price level at P_2. In the long run, nominal wages adjust upward and push the *SRAS* curve leftward to $SRAS_2$. The total percent increase in the price level from P_1 to P_3 is equal to the percent increase in the money supply. In the *classical model of the price level*, we ignore the transition period and think of the price level as rising to P_3 immediately. This is a good approximation under conditions of high inflation.

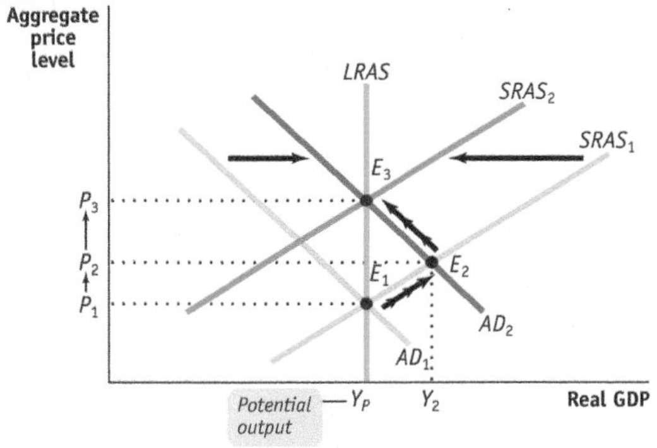

FOCUS Graph It

This is a good time to review long-run equilibrium. Ask students to use their personal whiteboards or notebook paper to:

- draw long-run equilibrium in the *AD–AS* model,
- show the short-run impact of expansionary monetary policy, and
- show the long-run self-correction and explain how it happens.

See Figure 33.1 for the correct graph. A change in the nominal money supply leads to a change in the aggregate price level in the long run and that leaves the real quantity of money at its original level. As a result, there is no long-run effect on aggregate demand or real GDP.

TEACH Teach It

The classical model presumes that the adjustment from the first long-run equilibrium point to the second is automatic and instantaneous. In reality, this is a poor assumption during periods of low inflation. With a low inflation rate, it may take a while for workers and firms to react to a monetary expansion by raising wages and prices. Thus, some nominal wages and the prices of some goods are sticky in the short run. As a result, under low inflation there is an upward-sloping *SRAS* curve, and changes in the money supply can indeed change real GDP in the short run.

St. Louis Federal Reserve Bank Resources

The Great Inflation Online Course

In this course, Jack of All Trades and his sidekick Andy time-travel to the period known as The Great Inflation to discover the truth about inflation. Dr. Equilibirum helps them understand what exactly inflation is and how the Federal Reserve System plays a key role in maintaining stable prices.

TEACH Teach It

The classical model more closely reflects reality in periods of high inflation. Why?

Under high inflation, there is a quicker adjustment of wages and prices of intermediate goods than occurs in the case of low inflation—the stickiness vanishes. The short-run aggregate supply curve shifts leftward more quickly, and a more rapid return to long-run equilibrium occurs under high inflation. As a result, in countries with persistently high inflation, changes in the money supply are quickly translated into changes in the inflation rate.

TEACH Teach It

Show students Khan Academy's "Hyperinflation" video (see econextras video list with hyperlinks on the bcs and TRFD) as an introduction to hyperinflation. Ask the following:

- What is hyperinflation? *It is inflation gone wild caused by a nation printing money, which causes prices to go up, which causes the government to print more money.*
- How do people react to the increase in prices? *People begin hoarding goods, which leads to even higher prices.*

TEACH Teach It

The inflation tax can be difficult for students to understand. Simplify the concept by telling them that the government needs to pay the bills, so rather than increasing your taxes to do so, it increases the money supply. When the price level rises, we all end up paying since inflation erodes purchasing power.

macroeconomic equilibrium. It lies at the intersection of the aggregate demand curve, AD_1, and the short-run aggregate supply curve, $SRAS_1$. It also lies on the long-run aggregate supply curve, *LRAS*. At E_1, the equilibrium aggregate price level is P_1.

Now suppose there is an increase in the money supply. This is an expansionary monetary policy, which shifts the aggregate demand curve to the right, to AD_2, and moves the economy to a new short-run macroeconomic equilibrium at E_2. Over time, however, nominal wages adjust upward in response to low unemployment and the rise in the aggregate price level, and the *SRAS* curve shifts to the left, to $SRAS_2$. The new long-run macroeconomic equilibrium is at E_3, and real GDP returns to its initial level. The long-run increase in the aggregate price level from P_1 to P_3 is proportional to the increase in the money supply. As a result, in the long run, changes in the money supply have no effect on the real quantity of money, M/P, or on real GDP. In the long run, money—as we learned—is *neutral*.

The classical model of the price level ignores the short-run movement from E_1 to E_2, assuming that the economy moves directly from one long-run equilibrium to another long-run equilibrium. In other words, it assumes that the economy moves directly from E_1 to E_3 and that real GDP never changes in response to a change in the money supply. In effect, in the classical model the effects of money supply changes are analyzed as if the short-run as well as the long-run aggregate supply curves were vertical.

With a low inflation rate, it may take a while for workers and firms to react to a monetary expansion by raising wages and prices.

In reality, this is a poor assumption during periods of low inflation. With a low inflation rate, it may take a while for workers and firms to react to a monetary expansion by raising wages and prices. In this scenario, some nominal wages and the prices of some goods are sticky in the short run. As a result, under low inflation there is an upward-sloping *SRAS* curve, and changes in the money supply can indeed change real GDP in the short run.

But what about periods of high inflation? In the face of high inflation, economists have observed that the short-run stickiness of nominal wages and prices tends to vanish. Workers and businesses, sensitized to inflation, are quick to raise their wages and prices in response to changes in the money supply. This implies that under high inflation there is a quicker adjustment of wages and prices of intermediate goods than occurs in the case of low inflation. So the short-run aggregate supply curve shifts leftward more quickly and there is a more rapid return to long-run equilibrium under high inflation. As a result, the classical model of the price level is much more likely to be a good approximation of reality for economies experiencing persistently high inflation.

The consequence of this rapid adjustment of all prices in the economy is that in countries with persistently high inflation, changes in the money supply are quickly translated into changes in the inflation rate. Let's look at Zimbabwe. **Figure 33.2** shows the annual rate of growth in the money supply and the annual rate of change of consumer prices from 2003 through January 2008. As you can see, the surge in the growth rate of the money supply coincided closely with a roughly equal surge in the inflation rate. Note that to fit these very large percentage increases—exceeding 100,000%—onto the figure, we have drawn the vertical axis using a logarithmic scale.

In late 2008, Zimbabwe's inflation rate reached 231 million percent. What leads a country to increase its money supply so much that the result is an inflation rate in the millions of percent?

The Inflation Tax

Modern economies use fiat money—pieces of paper that have no intrinsic value but are accepted as a medium of exchange. In the United States and most other wealthy countries, the decision about how many pieces of paper to issue is placed in the hands of a central bank that is somewhat independent of the political process. However, this

320 Section 6 Inflation, Unemployment, and Stabilization Policies

Figure 33.2 Money Supply Growth and Inflation in Zimbabwe

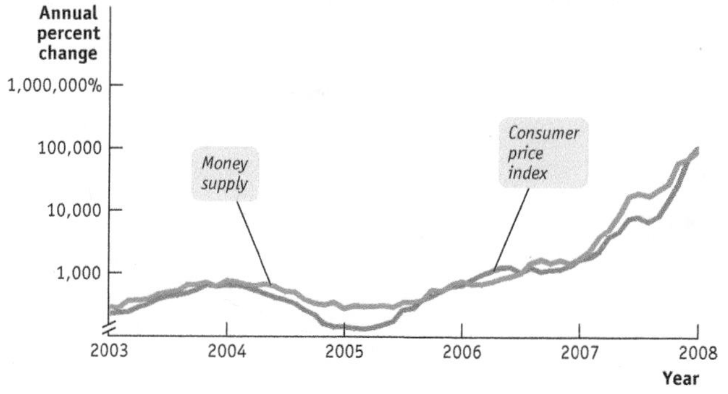

This figure, drawn on a logarithmic scale, shows the annual rates of change of the money supply and the price level in Zimbabwe from 2003 through January 2008. The surges in the money supply were quickly reflected in a roughly equal surge in the price level.
Source: International Monetary Fund.

independence can always be taken away if politicians decide to seize control of monetary policy.

So what is to prevent a government from paying for some of its expenses not by raising taxes or borrowing but simply by printing money? Nothing. In fact, governments, including the U.S. government, do it all the time. How can the U.S. government do this, given that the Federal Reserve, not the U.S. Treasury, issues money? The answer is that the Treasury and the Federal Reserve work in concert. The Treasury issues debt to finance the government's purchases of goods and services, and the Fed *monetizes* the debt by creating money and buying the debt back from the public through open-market purchases of Treasury bills. In effect, the U.S. government can and does raise revenue by printing money.

For example, in February 2010, the U.S. monetary base—bank reserves plus currency in circulation—was $559 billion larger than it had been a year earlier. This occurred because, over the course of that year, the Federal Reserve had issued $559 billion in money or its electronic equivalent and put it into circulation mainly through open-market operations. To put it another way, the Fed created money out of thin air and used it to buy valuable government securities from the private sector. It's true that the U.S. government pays interest on debt owned by the Federal Reserve—but the Fed, by law, hands the interest payments it receives on government debt back to the Treasury, keeping only enough to fund its own operations. In effect, then, the Federal Reserve's actions enabled the government to pay off $559 billion in outstanding government debt by printing money.

An alternative way to look at this is to say that the right to print money is itself a source of revenue. Economists refer to the revenue generated by the government's right to print money as *seignorage,* an archaic term that goes back to the Middle Ages. It refers to the right to stamp gold and silver into coins, and charge a fee for doing so, that medieval lords—seigneurs, in France—reserved for themselves.

Seignorage accounts for only a tiny fraction (less than 1%) of the U.S. government's budget. Furthermore, concerns about seignorage don't have any influence on the Federal Reserve's decisions about how much money to print; the Fed is worried about inflation and unemployment, not revenue. But this hasn't always been true, even in the United States: both sides relied on seignorage to help cover budget deficits during the Civil War. And there have been many occasions in history when governments turned to their printing presses as a crucial source of revenue. According to the usual scenario, a government finds itself running a large budget deficit—and lacks either the competence

FOCUS In the News

TRM Find an article on quantitative easing and the inflation tax, or use the October 2012 *Deseret News* article "When the U.S. Creates Lots of Money, It's Just Like Taxation" at http://www.deseretnews.com/article/765611836/Creating-lots-of-money-is-just-like-taxation.html?pg=all. Suggested questions for this article can be found in the TRM on **Worksheet 33.1 (The Inflation Tax)**.

Module 33 Types of Inflation, Disinflation, and Deflation **321**

FOCUS In the News

TRM Have students read the February 2014 *Miami Herald* article "Andres Oppenheimer: Venezuela's Biggest Enemy—Hyperinflation" at http://interamericansecuritywatch.com/andres-oppenheimer-venezuelas-biggest-enemy-hyperinflation/. Suggested questions for this article can be found in **Worksheet 33.2 (Venezuela's Biggest Enemy)** from the TRM.

TEACH Teach It

Show students *The Economist*'s "KAL Draws: Hyperinflation" (see econextras video list with hyperlinks on the bcs and TRFD). Ask students:

- What causes hyperinflation? *When governments allow the money supply to grow too fast*
- How is currency impacted by hyperinflation? *As the currency loses value, people lose confidence in it.*
- How do a nation's citizens protect their wealth? *They try to accumulate gold and other commodities.*

or the political will to eliminate this deficit by raising taxes or cutting spending. Furthermore, the government can't borrow to cover the gap because potential lenders won't extend loans, given the fear that the government's weakness will continue and leave it unable to repay its debts.

In such a situation, governments end up printing money to cover the budget deficit. But by printing money to pay its bills, a government increases the quantity of money in circulation. And as we've just seen, increases in the money supply translate into equally large increases in the aggregate price level. So printing money to cover a budget deficit leads to inflation.

Who ends up paying for the goods and services the government purchases with newly printed money? The people who currently hold money pay. They pay because inflation erodes the purchasing power of their money holdings. In other words, a government imposes an **inflation tax**, a reduction in the value of the money held by the public, by printing money to cover its budget deficit and creating inflation.

An **inflation tax** is a reduction in the value of money held by the public caused by inflation.

It's helpful to think about what this tax represents. If the inflation rate is 5%, then a year from now $1 will buy goods and services worth only about $0.95 today. So a 5% inflation rate in effect imposes a tax rate of 5% on the value of all money held by the public.

But why would any government push the inflation tax to rates of hundreds or thousands of percent? We turn next to the process by which high inflation turns into explosive hyperinflation.

The Logic of Hyperinflation

Keystone/Getty Images

In the 1920s, hyperinflation made German currency worth so little that children made kites from banknotes.

Inflation imposes a tax on individuals who hold money. And, like most taxes, it will lead people to change their behavior. In particular, when inflation is high, people have a strong incentive to either spend money quickly or acquire interest-bearing assets. The goal is to avoid holding money and thereby reduce the burden of the inflation tax. During the German hyperinflation, people began using eggs or lumps of coal as a medium of exchange. They did this because lumps of coal maintained their real value over time but money did not. Indeed, during the peak of German hyperinflation, people often burned paper money, which was less valuable than wood.

We are now prepared to understand how countries can get themselves into situations of extreme inflation. Suppose the government prints enough money to pay for a given quantity of goods and services each month. The increase in the money supply causes the inflation rate to rise, which means the government must print more money each month to buy the same quantity of goods and services. If the desire to reduce money holdings causes people to spend money faster than the government prints money, prices increase faster than the money supply. As a result, the government must accelerate the rate of growth of the money supply, which leads to an even higher rate of inflation. As this process becomes self-reinforcing, it can easily spiral out of control.

Here's an analogy: imagine a city government that tries to raise a lot of money with a special fee on taxi rides. The fee will raise the cost of taxi rides, and this will cause people to turn to substitutes, such as walking or taking the bus. As taxi use declines, the government finds that its tax revenue declines and it must impose a higher fee to raise the same amount of revenue as before. You can imagine the ensuing vicious circle: the government imposes fees on taxi rides, which leads to less taxi use, which causes the government to raise the fee on taxi rides, which leads to even less taxi use, and so on.

Shutterstock

Substitute the real money supply for taxi rides and the inflation rate for the increase in the fee on taxi rides, and you have the story of hyperinflation. A race develops between the government printing presses and the public: the presses churn out money at a faster and faster rate to try to compensate for the fact that the

322 Section 6 Inflation, Unemployment, and Stabilization Policies

FYI Zimbabwe's Inflation

Zimbabwe offers a recent example of a country experiencing very high inflation. Figure 33.2 showed that surges in Zimbabwe's money supply growth were matched by almost simultaneous surges in its inflation rate. But looking at rates of change doesn't give a true feel for just how much prices went up.

The figure here shows Zimbabwe's consumer price index from 1999 to June 2008, with the 2000 level set equal to 100. As in Figure 33.2, we use a logarithmic scale, which lets us draw equal-sized percentage changes as the same size. Over the course of about nine years, consumer prices rose by approximately 4.5 trillion percent.

Why did Zimbabwe's government pursue policies that led to runaway inflation? The reason boils down to political instability, which in turn had its roots in Zimbabwe's history. Until the 1970s, Zimbabwe had been ruled by its small white minority; even after the shift to majority rule, many of the country's farms remained in the hands of whites. Eventually Robert Mugabe, Zimbabwe's president, tried to solidify his position by seizing these farms and turning them over to his political supporters. But because this seizure disrupted production, the result was to undermine the country's economy and its tax base. It became impossible for the country's government to balance its budget either by raising taxes or by cutting spending. At the same time, the regime's instability left Zimbabwe unable to borrow money in world markets. Like many others before it, Zimbabwe's government turned to the printing press to cover the gap—leading to massive inflation.

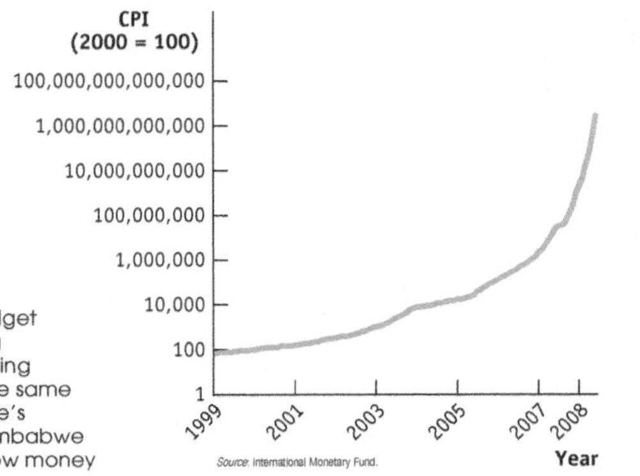

public is reducing its real money holdings. At some point the inflation rate explodes into hyperinflation, and people are unwilling to hold any money at all (and resort to trading in eggs and lumps of coal). The government is then forced to abandon its use of the inflation tax and shut down the printing presses.

Moderate Inflation and Disinflation

The governments of wealthy, politically stable countries like the United States and Britain don't find themselves forced to print money to pay their bills. Yet over the past 40 years, both countries, along with a number of other nations, have experienced uncomfortable episodes of inflation. In the United States, the inflation rate peaked at 13% in 1980. In Britain, the inflation rate reached 26% in 1975. Why did policy makers allow this to happen?

Using the aggregate demand and supply model, we can see that there are two possible changes that can lead to an increase in the aggregate price level: a decrease in aggregate supply or an increase in aggregate demand. Inflation that is caused by a significant increase in the price of an input with economy-wide importance is called **cost-push inflation**. For example, it is argued that the oil crisis in the 1970s led to an increase in energy prices in the United States, causing a leftward shift of the aggregate supply curve, increasing the aggregate price level. However, aside from crude oil, it is difficult to think of examples of inputs with economy-wide importance that experience significant price increases.

Inflation that is caused by an increase in aggregate demand is known as **demand-pull inflation**. When a rightward shift of the aggregate demand curve leads to an increase in the aggregate price level, the economy experiences demand-pull inflation. This is

Cost-push inflation is inflation that is caused by a significant increase in the price of an input with economy-wide importance.

Demand-pull inflation is inflation that is caused by an increase in aggregate demand.

TEACH Teach It

Here is a simple way of explaining how an inflationary spiral works:

- As people hold smaller amounts of real money due to a high rate of inflation, the government has to respond by accelerating the rate of growth of the money supply.
- This will lead to an even higher rate of inflation.
- People will respond to this new higher rate of inflation by reducing their real money holdings yet again.
- The government is forced to increase the money supply more rapidly, leading to an even higher rate of inflation, and so on.

FOCUS Active Learning

Show the Jacob Clifford video "Cost-push and Demand-pull Inflation" that shows the two causes of inflation graphically (see econextras video list with hyperlinks on the bcs and TRFD). Challenge students to draw two types of inflation on correctly labeled *AD–AS* graphs and share with another student an explanation of the concept.

FOCUS In the News

Have students read the November 2013 *International Business Times* article "Inflation, Shortages and Economic Turmoil: Venezuela on the Brink" at http://www.ibtimes.com/inflation-shortages-economic-turmoil-venezuela-brink-1470274. Ask them to explain three economic concepts described in the article.

FOCUS Active Learning

Have students participate in the Inflation Island simulation at https://www.ecb.europa.eu/ecb/educational/inflationisland/html/index.en.html. Assign students to groups of 4 and assign each group a different area of the island to explore for approximately 15 minutes. Have them report what they learned to the entire class. You can also project the simulation on the board and take them through it as a whole-group activity if time allows.

TEACH AP® Exam Tip

Two causes of inflation are tested on the AP® exam: cost-push inflation and demand-pull inflation. Students should understand what causes each and how to graph them.

FOCUS Active Learning

Cost-push inflation is caused by increases in costs of production throughout the economy, while demand-pull inflation is caused by increased aggregate demand for goods and services. Have students watch "Causes of Inflation: Cost-Push and Demand-Pull" (see econextras video list with hyperlinks on the bcs and TRFD). Ask them:

- What are the two main types of inflation? *Cost-push inflation and demand-pull inflation*
- How do economists illustrate cost-push inflation? *It is illustrated as a decrease, or a leftward shift, in the short-run aggregate supply curve caused by an increase in the costs of production.*
- How do economists illustrate demand-pull inflation? *It is illustrated as an increase, or a rightward shift, in the aggregate demand curve caused by an increase in aggregate demand for goods and services.*

TEACH Teach It

Demand-pull inflation is likely to be caused by economic growth often coupled with either expansionary fiscal or monetary policy that causes *AD* to shift right. In the case of fiscal policy, politicians can sometimes boost their election possibilities by cutting taxes even if the economy is near full employment. This creates inflation, but usually long after the polls close.

FOCUS Graph It

Have students draw a correctly labeled *AD–AS* graph on their personal whiteboards or notebook paper, and have them show demand-pull inflation (*AD shifts right*) and then cost-push inflation (*SRAS shifts left*). In each case, ask students what the effect of inflation is on the price level and real GDP. *Demand-pull inflation will cause the price level and real GDP to rise. Cost-push inflation will raise the price level but lower real GDP.*

AP® Exam Tip

Make sure you can graph and explain cost-push inflation and demand-pull inflation, as these are both tested frequently on the AP® exam. Remember that cost-push inflation is a leftward shift of *AS* and demand-pull inflation is a rightward shift of *AD*.

sometimes described by the phrase "too much money chasing too few goods," which means that the aggregate demand for goods and services is outpacing the aggregate supply and driving up the prices of goods.

In the short run, policies that produce a booming economy also tend to lead to higher inflation, and policies that reduce inflation tend to depress the economy. This creates both temptations and dilemmas for governments.

Imagine yourself as a politician facing an election in a year, and suppose that inflation is fairly low at the moment. You might well be tempted to pursue expansionary policies that will push the unemployment rate down, as a way to please voters, even if your economic advisers warn that this will eventually lead to higher inflation. You might also be tempted to find different economic advisers, who will tell you not to worry: in politics, as in ordinary life, wishful thinking often prevails over realistic analysis.

Conversely, imagine yourself as a politician in an economy suffering from inflation. Your economic advisers will probably tell you that the only way to bring inflation down is to push the economy into a recession, which will lead to temporarily higher unemployment. Are you willing to pay that price? Maybe not.

This political asymmetry—inflationary policies often produce short-term political gains, but policies to bring inflation down carry short-term political costs—explains how countries with no need to impose an inflation tax sometimes end up with serious inflation problems. For example, that 26% rate of inflation in Britain was largely the result of the British government's decision in 1971 to pursue highly expansionary monetary and fiscal policies. Politicians disregarded warnings that these policies would be inflationary and were extremely reluctant to reverse course even when it became clear that the warnings had been correct.

But why do expansionary policies lead to inflation? To answer that question, we need to look first at the relationship between output and unemployment. Then we'll add inflation to the story in Module 34.

The Output Gap and the Unemployment Rate

Earlier we introduced the concept of *potential output*, the level of real GDP that the economy would produce once all prices had fully adjusted. Potential output typically grows steadily over time, reflecting long-run growth. However, as we learned from the aggregate demand–aggregate supply model, actual aggregate output fluctuates around potential output in the short run: a recessionary gap arises when actual aggregate output falls short of potential output; an inflationary gap arises when actual aggregate output exceeds potential output. Recall that the percentage difference between the actual level of real GDP and potential output is called the *output gap*. A positive or negative output gap occurs when an economy is producing more or less than what would be "expected" because all prices have not yet adjusted. And, as we've learned, wages are the prices in the labor market.

Meanwhile, we learned that the unemployment rate is composed of cyclical unemployment and natural unemployment, the portion of the unemployment rate unaffected by the business cycle. So there is a relationship between the unemployment rate and the output gap. This relationship is defined by two rules:

- When actual aggregate output is equal to potential output, the actual unemployment rate is equal to the natural rate of unemployment.
- When the output gap is positive (an inflationary gap), the unemployment rate is *below* the natural rate. When the output gap is negative (a recessionary gap), the unemployment rate is *above* the natural rate.

In other words, fluctuations of aggregate output around the long-run trend of potential output correspond to fluctuations of the unemployment rate around the natural rate.

This makes sense. When the economy is producing less than potential output—when the output gap is negative—it is not making full use of its productive resources.

St. Louis Federal Reserve Bank Resources

"The Output Gap: A 'Potentially' Unreliable Measure of Economic Health?," *Page One Economics Classroom Edition* (November 2012)

This issue describes the output gap as one of the many economic indicators used by economists to measure the strength of the economy. What exactly is the output gap, and how accurately does it predict the state of the economy?

Among the resources that are not fully used is labor, the economy's most important resource. So we would expect a negative output gap to be associated with unusually high unemployment. Conversely, when the economy is producing more than potential output, it is temporarily using resources at higher-than-normal rates. With this positive output gap, we would expect to see lower-than-normal unemployment.

Figure 33.3 confirms this rule. Panel (a) shows the actual and natural rates of unemployment, as estimated by the Congressional Budget Office (CBO). Panel (b) shows two series. One is cyclical unemployment: the difference between the actual unemployment rate and the CBO estimate of the natural rate of unemployment, measured on the left. The other is the CBO estimate of the output gap, measured on the right. To make the relationship clearer, the output gap series is inverted—shown upside down—so that the line goes down if actual output rises above potential output and up if actual output falls below potential output. As you can see, the two series move together quite closely, showing the strong relationship between the output gap and cyclical unemployment. Years of high cyclical unemployment, like 1982 or 2009, were also years of a strongly negative output gap. Years of low cyclical unemployment, like the late 1960s or 2000, were years of a strongly positive output gap.

Figure 33.3 Cyclical Unemployment and the Output Gap

Panel (a) shows the actual U.S. unemployment rate from 1949 to 2013, together with the Congressional Budget Office (CBO) estimate of the natural rate of unemployment. The actual rate fluctuates around the natural rate, often for extended periods. Panel (b) shows cyclical unemployment—the difference between the actual unemployment rate and the natural rate of unemployment—and the output gap, also estimated by the CBO. The unemployment rate is measured on the left vertical axis, and the output gap is measured with an inverted scale on the right vertical axis. With an inverted scale, it moves in the same direction as the unemployment rate: when the output gap is positive, the actual unemployment rate is below its natural rate; when the output gap is negative, the actual unemployment rate is above its natural rate. The two series track one another closely, showing the strong relationship between the output gap and cyclical unemployment.

Sources: Congressional Budget Office; Bureau of Labor Statistics; Bureau of Economic Analysis.

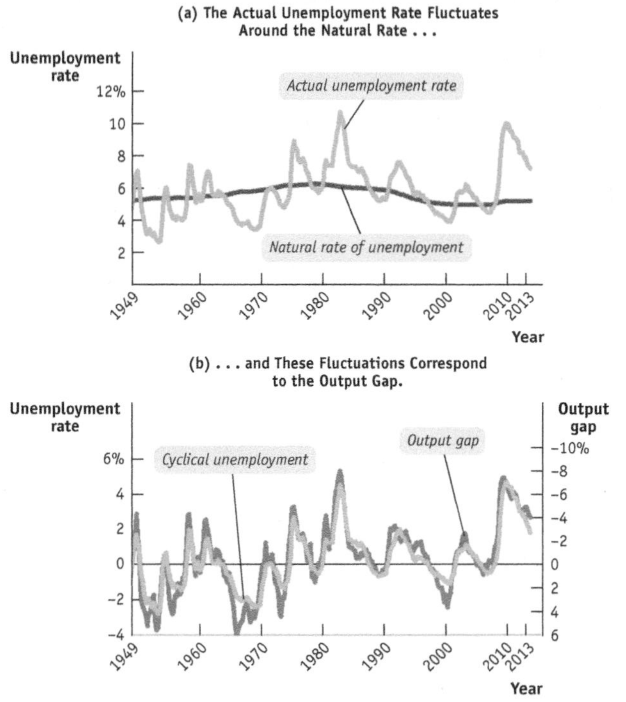

TEACH Connect It

Remind students that the percentage difference between the actual level of real GDP and potential output is called the output gap. Ask students to reflect on why an output gap arises. *When resources like labor are not fully employed, output falls below potential output, and a recessionary gap is created. When resources are extended beyond their normal capacity, as with overtime work or machines running longer than recommended, output rises above potential output, and an inflationary gap is obtained.* If the output gap is positive, unemployment should be low. If the output gap is negative, unemployment should be high. Have students draw the graph for each type of gap, including labels of the gaps, as a refresher on what they look like.

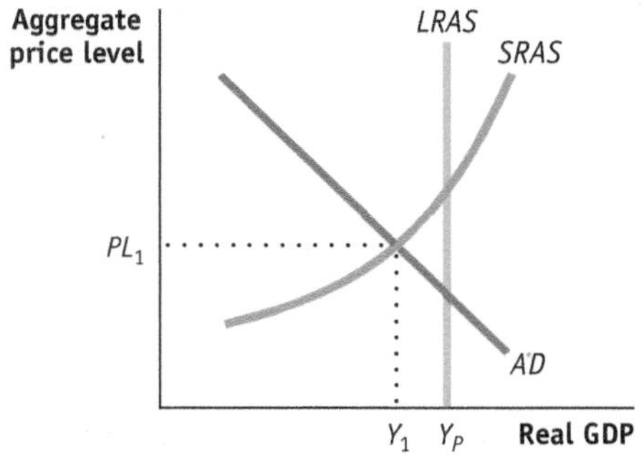

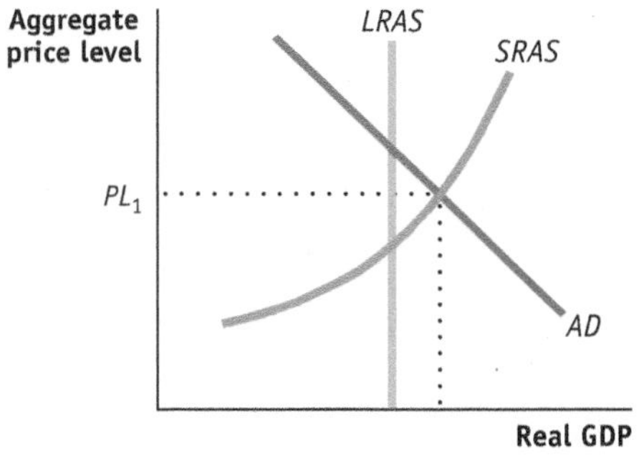

FOCUS Graph It

Use Figure 33.3 to teach the relationship between output and unemployment. Begin by asking what the natural rate of unemployment is. *It is the sum of the rates of frictional and structural unemployment that are always present in the economy.* On paper or their personal whiteboards, have students graph a recessionary gap. Remind them that the unemployment rate equals the natural rate of unemployment when real GDP equals potential output (Y_p). What happens to the unemployment rate when output falls below potential output? *The unemployment rate rises above the natural rate of unemployment due to cyclical unemployment.* What happens to unemployment as output increases? *It decreases.* Tell students that the level of output determines the level of unemployment. This has been tested on past AP® exams.

TEACH Teach It

On the board, draw a correctly labeled *AD–AS* graph in equilibrium. Ask students if there is unemployment in the economy. *They may say no, but some level of unemployment always exists in the economy even when the economy is at potential output.* Ask them to define frictional and structural unemployment. *Frictional and structural unemployment are two conditions we live with as people are in job-searching mode or their skills do not match the needs of the market anymore. These types of unemployment always exist in the economy.* Together, they are called the natural rate of unemployment. We will revisit this concept in Module 34.

MODULE 33 Review

Check Your Understanding

1. Explain why a large increase in the money supply causes a larger short-run increase in real GDP in an economy that previously had low inflation than in an economy that previously had high inflation. What does this say about situations in which the classical model of the price level applies?
2. Suppose that all wages and prices in an economy are indexed to inflation, meaning that they increase at the same rate as the price level. Can there still be an inflation tax?

Tackle the Test: Multiple-Choice Questions

1. The real quantity of money is
   - **I.** equal to M/P.
   - **II.** the money supply adjusted for inflation.
   - **III.** higher in the long run when the Fed buys government securities.

   a. I only
   b. II only
   c. III only
   d. I and II only
   e. I, II, and III
2. In the classical model of the price level
   a. only the short-run aggregate supply curve is vertical.
   b. both the short-run and long-run aggregate supply curves are vertical.
   c. only the long-run aggregate supply curve is vertical.
   d. both the short-run aggregate demand and supply curves are vertical.
   e. both the long-run aggregate demand and supply curves are vertical.
3. The classical model of the price level is most applicable in
   a. the United States.
   b. periods of high inflation.
   c. periods of low inflation.
   d. recessions.
   e. depressions.
4. An inflation tax is
   a. imposed by governments to offset price increases.
   b. paid directly as a percentage of the sale price on purchases.
   c. the result of a decrease in the value of money held by the public.
   d. generally levied by states rather than the federal government.
   e. higher during periods of low inflation.
5. Revenue generated by the government's right to print money is known as
   a. seignorage.
   b. an inflation tax.
   c. hyperinflation.
   d. fiat money.
   e. monetary funds.

OPEN & CLOSE Exit Slip

*TRM Please see **Exit Slip: Module 33** in the TRM for formative multiple-choice questions to ask your students before finishing your lesson. These questions will help you quickly assess whether your students have mastered the module's concepts before moving on.*

Answers to the Exit Slip Questions

1. B
2. B
3. C

Answers to Module 33 Review Questions

Check Your Understanding

1. The inflation rate is more likely to quickly reflect changes in the money supply when the economy has had an extended period of high inflation. That's because an extended period of high inflation sensitizes workers and firms to raise nominal wages and prices of intermediate goods when the aggregate price level rises. As a result, there will be little or no increase in real output in the short run after an increase in the money supply, and the increase in the money supply will simply be reflected in a proportional increase in prices. In an economy in which people are not sensitized to high inflation because of low inflation in the past, an increase in the money supply will lead to an increase in real output in the short run. This illustrates the fact that the classical model of the price level best applies to economies with persistently high inflation, not those with little or no history of high inflation even though they may currently have high inflation.
2. Yes, there can still be an inflation tax because the tax is levied on people who hold money. As long as people hold money, regardless of whether prices are indexed or not, the government is able to use seignorage to capture real resources from the public.

Tackle the Test: Multiple-Choice Questions

1. d
2. b
3. b
4. c
5. a

326 **Section 6** Inflation, Unemployment, and Stabilization Policies

Tackle the Test: Free-Response Questions

1. Use a correctly labeled aggregate demand and aggregate supply graph to illustrate cost-push inflation. Give an example of what might cause cost-push inflation in the economy.

Rubric for FRQ 1 (9 points)

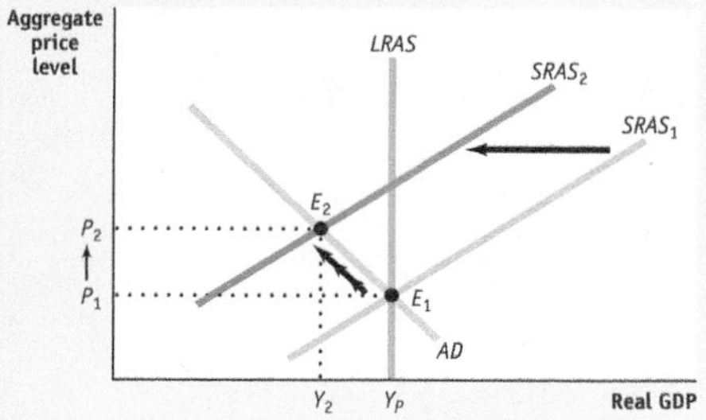

1 point: Graph labeled "Aggregate price level" or "*PL*" on the vertical axis and "Real GDP" on the horizontal axis

1 point: *AD* downward-sloping and labeled

1 point: *SRAS* upward-sloping and labeled

1 point: *LRAS* vertical and labeled

1 point: Potential output labeled at horizontal intercept of *LRAS*

1 point: Long-run macroeconomic equilibrium aggregate price level labeled on vertical axis at intersection of *SRAS, LRAS*, and *AD*

1 point: Leftward shift of the SRAS curve

1 point: Higher equilibrium aggregate price level at new intersection of *SRAS* and *AD*

1 point: This could be caused by anything that would shift the short-run aggregate supply curve to the left, such as an increase in the price of energy, labor, or another input with economy-wide importance.

2. Draw a correctly labeled aggregate demand and aggregate supply graph showing an economy in long-run macroeconomic equilibrium. On your graph, show the effect of an increase in the money supply, according to the classical model of the price level.
(4 points)

Tackle the Test: Free-Response Question Rubric for FRQ 2 (4 points)

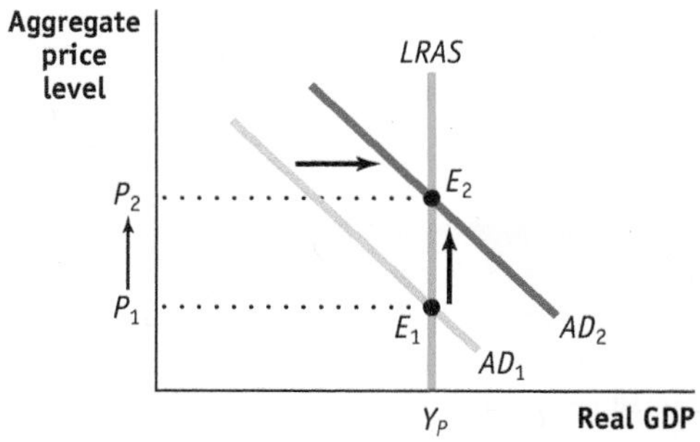

1 point: Graph labeled "Aggregate price level" or "*PL*" on the vertical axis and "Real GDP" on the horizontal axis with a downward-sloping *AD*

1 point: Vertical *LRAS*. If there is also an *SRAS* curve, it must intersect the *AD* curve at the same point where the *AD* curve intersects the *LRAS* curve.

1 point: Rightward shift of aggregate demand

1 point: Indication that the price level increases, but there is no increase in real GDP

Module 33 Types of Inflation, Disinflation, and Deflation **327**

PD To prepare for teaching this lesson, you may want to consult the **Module 34 Sample Lecture** in the TRM.

Tom Bonaventure/ Photographer's Choice RF/Getty Images

MODULE 34 Inflation and Unemployment: The Phillips Curve

In this Module, you will learn to:

- Use the Phillips curve to show the nature of the short-run trade-off between inflation and unemployment
- Explain why there is no long-run trade-off between inflation and unemployment
- Discuss why expansionary policies are limited due to the effects of expected inflation
- Explain why even moderate levels of inflation can be hard to end
- Identify the problems with deflation that lead policy makers to prefer a low but positive inflation rate

OPEN & CLOSE Start Here

Draw a table on the board like this one without the answers and have students copy it on paper or their personal whiteboards:

	Unemployment	**Inflation**
AD ↑	*Decrease*	*Increase*
AD ↓	*Increase*	*Decrease*
AS ↑	*Decrease*	*Decrease*
AS ↓	*Increase*	*Increase*

Have students fill in the columns for unemployment and inflation by stating if there is an increase or decrease in each as *AD* and *AS* change. Ask the following:

- Describe the relationship between unemployment and inflation when *AD* shifts. *An inverse relationship exists.*
- Why? *As output increases, more workers are needed and unemployment decreases, while the price level is increasing due to the increase in AD.*
- What is the relationship between unemployment and inflation when *AS* shifts? *There is a direct relationship.*
- Why? *As output increases, unemployment still decreases due to the need for more workers, but with an increase in output, inflation (price level) will decrease.*

This will serve as an introduction to the short-run Phillips curve, which shows the relationship between unemployment and inflation.

The Short-Run Phillips Curve

We've just seen that expansionary policies lead to a lower unemployment rate. Our next step in understanding the temptations and dilemmas facing governments is to show that there is a short-run trade-off between unemployment and inflation—lower unemployment tends to lead to higher inflation, and vice versa. The key concept is that of the *Phillips curve.*

The origins of this concept lie in a famous 1958 paper by the New Zealand-born economist Alban W. H. Phillips. Looking at historical data for Britain, he found that when the unemployment rate was high, the wage rate tended to fall, and when the unemployment rate was low, the wage rate tended to rise. Using data from Britain, the United States, and elsewhere, other economists soon found a similar apparent relationship between the unemployment rate and the rate of inflation—that is, the rate of change in the aggregate price level. For example, **Figure 34.1** shows the U.S. unemployment rate and the rate of consumer price inflation over each subsequent year from 1955 to 1968, with each dot representing one year's data.

The **short-run Phillips curve** represents the negative short-run relationship between the unemployment rate and the inflation rate.

Looking at evidence like Figure 34.1, many economists concluded that there is a negative short-run relationship between the unemployment rate and the inflation rate, represented by the **short-run Phillips curve**, or *SRPC.* (We'll explain the difference between the short-run and the long-run Phillips curve soon.) **Figure 34.2** shows a hypothetical short-run Phillips curve.

TEACH AP® Exam Tip

Both the short-run and long-run Phillips curve have shown up in recent years on the free-response section of the AP® exam. Students must be able to draw the curve correctly for the short and long run. The axis labels cannot be switched, and it is better not to abbreviate inflation and unemployment.

Figure 34.1 Unemployment and Inflation, 1955–1968

Each dot shows the average U.S. unemployment rate for one year and the percentage increase in the consumer price index over the subsequent year. Data like this lay behind the initial concept of the Phillips curve.
Source: Bureau of Labor Statistics.

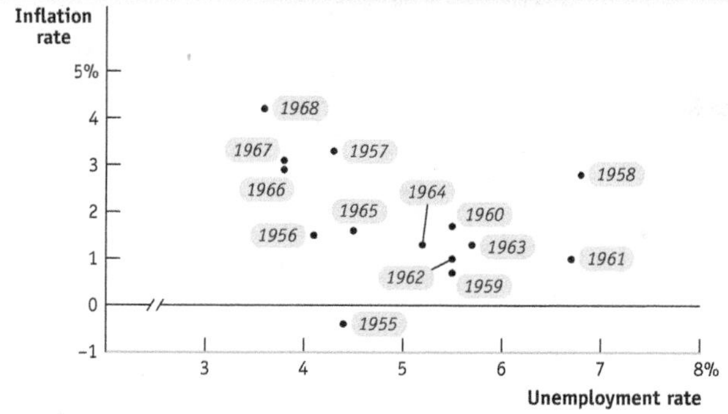

We can better understand the shape of the Phillips curve by examining its ties to the *AD–AS* model. Panel (a) of **Figure 34.3** on the next page shows how changes in the aggregate price level and the output gap depend on changes in aggregate demand. Assume that in year 1 the aggregate demand curve is AD_1, the long-run aggregate supply curve is *LRAS*, and the short-run aggregate supply curve is *SRAS*. The initial macroeconomic equilibrium is at E_1, where the price level is 100 and real GDP is \$10 trillion. Notice that at E_1 real GDP is equal to potential output, so the output gap is zero.

Now consider what happens if aggregate demand shifts rightward to AD_2 and the economy moves to E_2. At E_2, Real GDP is \$10.4 trillion, \$0.4 trillion more than potential output—forming a 4% output gap. Meanwhile, at E_2 the aggregate price level has risen to 102—a 2% increase. So panel (a) indicates that in this example a zero output gap is associated with zero inflation and a 4% output gap is associated with 2% inflation.

Panel (b) shows what this implies for the relationship between unemployment and inflation: an increase in aggregate demand leads to a fall in the unemployment rate and

Figure 34.2 The Short-Run Phillips Curve

The short-run Phillips curve, *SRPC*, slopes downward because the relationship between the unemployment rate and the inflation rate is negative.

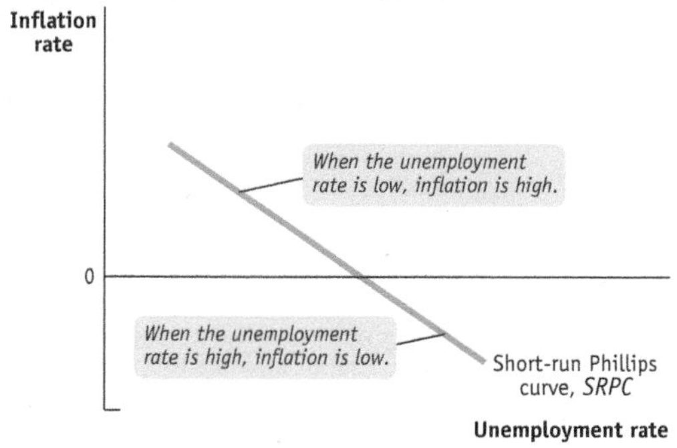

TEACH Teach It

Draw the axes of a Phillips curve on the board, and label the axes with inflation and unemployment. Remind students that the labels on each axis matter as they will affect how you illustrate the long-run Phillips curve. Draw the short-run Phillips curve and ask students to describe the relationship between unemployment and inflation in the short run that they observed during the opener. *It is an inverse relationship.*

Module 34 Inflation and Unemployment: The Phillips Curve 329

Teach It

Project Figure 34.3 on the board if possible, or draw an *AD–AS* graph and shift *AD* to the right, causing inflation to increase and unemployment to decrease. Show students that there would be a movement up the Phillips curve toward inflation and away from unemployment to match the changes caused by the increase in *AD*. Explain that when *AD* shifts, movement occurs along the short-run Phillips curve.

Figure 34.3 The *AD–AS* Model and the Short-Run Phillips Curve

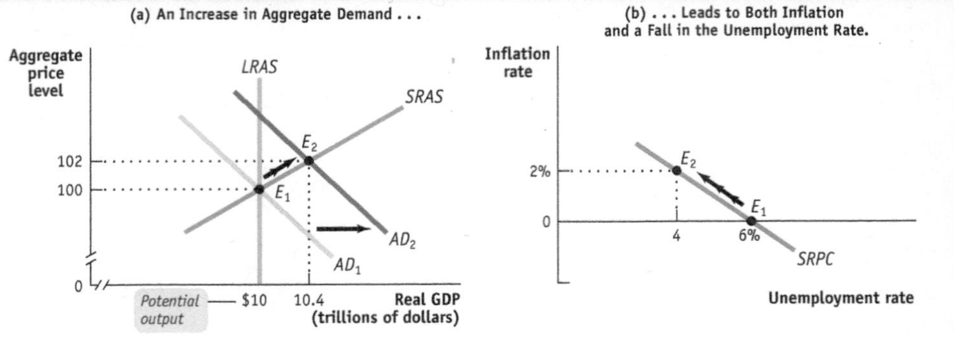

Shifts in aggregate demand lead to movements along the Phillips curve. In panel (a), the economy is initially in equilibrium at E_1, with the aggregate price level at 100 and aggregate output at $10 trillion, which we assume is potential output. Now consider two possibilities. If the aggregate demand curve remains at AD_1, there is an output gap of zero and 0% inflation. If the aggregate demand curve shifts out to AD_2, the positive output gap reduces unemployment to 4%, and inflation rises to 2%. Assuming that the natural rate of unemployment is 6%, the implications for unemployment and inflation are shown in panel (b): with aggregate demand at AD_1, 6% unemployment and 0% inflation will result; if aggregate demand increases to AD_2, 4% unemployment and 2% inflation will result.

an increase in the inflation rate. Assume that the natural rate of unemployment is 6% and that a rise of 1 percentage point in the output gap causes a fall of ½ percentage point in the unemployment rate (this is a predicted relationship between the output gap and the unemployment rate known as *Okun's law*). Then E_1 and E_2 in panel (a) correspond to E_1 and E_2 in panel (b). At E_1, the unemployment rate is 6% and the inflation rate is 0%. At E_2, the unemployment rate is 4%, because an output gap of 4% reduces the unemployment rate by $4\% \times 0.5 = 2\%$ below its natural rate of 6%—and the inflation rate is 2%. This is an example of the negative relationship between unemployment and inflation.

Going in the other direction, a decrease in aggregate demand leads to a rise in the unemployment rate and a fall in the inflation rate. This corresponds to a movement downward and to the right along the short-run Phillips curve. So, other things equal, increases and decreases in aggregate demand result in movements to the left and right along the short-run Phillips curve.

Changes in aggregate supply also affect the Phillips curve. Previously, we discussed the effect of *supply shocks,* such as sudden changes in the price of oil, that shift the short-run aggregate supply curve. Such shocks shift the short-run Phillips curve: surging oil prices were an important factor in the inflation of the 1970s and also played an important role in the acceleration of inflation in 2007–2008. In general, a negative supply shock shifts *SRPC* up, as the inflation rate increases for every level of the unemployment rate, and a positive supply shock shifts it down as the inflation rate falls for every level of the unemployment rate. Both outcomes are shown in **Figure 34.4**.

But supply shocks are not the only factors that can shift the Phillips curve. In the early 1960s, Americans had little experience with inflation, as inflation rates had been low for decades. But by the late 1960s, after inflation had been steadily increasing for a number of years, Americans had come to expect future inflation. In 1968 two economists—Milton Friedman of the University of Chicago and Edmund Phelps of Columbia University—independently set forth a crucial hypothesis: that expectations about future inflation

Figure 34.4 The Short-Run Phillips Curve and Supply Shocks

A negative supply shock shifts the *SRPC* up, and a positive supply shock shifts the *SRPC* down.

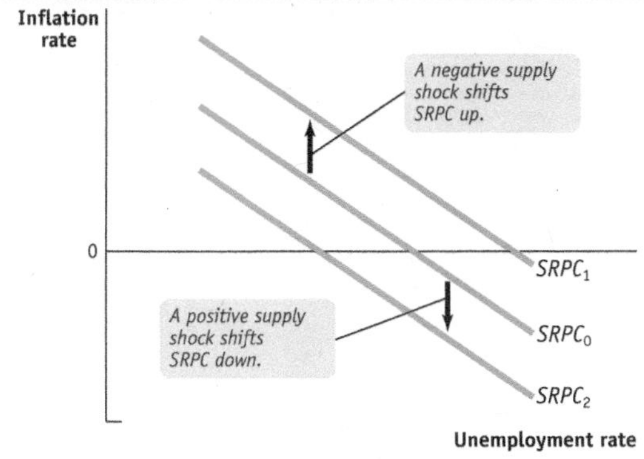

directly affect the present inflation rate. Today most economists accept that the *expected inflation rate*—the rate of inflation that employers and workers expect in the near future—is the most important factor, other than the unemployment rate, affecting inflation.

Inflation Expectations and the Short-Run Phillips Curve

The expected rate of inflation is the rate that employers and workers expect in the near future. One of the crucial discoveries of modern macroeconomics is that changes in the expected rate of inflation affect the short-run trade-off between unemployment and inflation and shift the short-run Phillips curve.

Why do changes in expected inflation affect the short-run Phillips curve? Put yourself in the position of a worker or employer about to sign a contract setting the worker's wages over the next year. For a number of reasons, the wage rate they agree to will be higher if everyone expects high inflation (including rising wages) than if everyone expects prices to be stable. The worker will want a wage rate that takes into account future declines in the purchasing power of earnings. He or she will also want a wage rate that won't fall behind the wages of other workers. And the employer will be more willing to agree to a wage increase now if hiring workers later will be even more expensive. Also, rising prices will make paying a higher wage rate more affordable for the employer because the employer's output will sell for more.

For these reasons, an increase in expected inflation shifts the short-run Phillips curve upward: the actual rate of inflation at any given unemployment rate is higher when the expected inflation rate is higher. In fact, macroeconomists believe that the relationship between changes in expected inflation and changes in actual inflation is one-to-one. That is, when the expected inflation rate increases, the actual inflation rate at any given unemployment rate will increase by the same amount. When the expected inflation rate falls, the actual inflation rate at any given level of unemployment will fall by the same amount.

Figure 34.5 on the next page shows how the expected rate of inflation affects the short-run Phillips curve. First, suppose that the expected rate of inflation is 0%. $SRPC_0$ is the short-run Phillips curve when the public expects 0% inflation. According to $SRPC_0$, the actual inflation rate will be 0% if the unemployment rate is 6%; it will be 2% if the unemployment rate is 4%.

Alternatively, suppose the expected rate of inflation is 2%. In that case, employers and workers will build this expectation into wages and prices: at any given unemployment

AP® Exam Tip

Inflationary expectations shift the short-run *AS* curve as well as the short-run Phillips curve.

TEACH Teach It

Draw an *AD–AS* graph and this time shift *SRAS* to the *right*, causing inflation and unemployment to decrease. Show students that there would be a shift of the Phillips curve to the *left* so that inflation and unemployment decrease to match the changes caused by the increase in *SRAS*. Explain that when *SRAS* shifts, a shift of the short-run Phillips curve occurs in the opposite direction from the shift in *SRAS*.

TEACH Teach It

To simplify: Shifts in *AD* reflect a movement along the short-run Phillips curve in the opposite direction from the *AD* shift. Shifts in *SRAS* result in a shift of the short-run Phillips curve in the opposite direction from the *SRAS* shift.

Module 34 Inflation and Unemployment: The Phillips Curve **331**

TEACH Teach It

Inflationary expectations are difficult for students to understand. Have them imagine they are working at their dream job and are given the opportunity to negotiate their new wage or salary for the next year. Tell them to suppose they expect inflation to be 5% next year. Ask them to identify the minimum raise they would request so that they can buy as much next year as they can this year. *5% because that will just cover inflation.* If everyone were able to make such a request, actual inflation would approach 5% because of the raises workers across the nation received. This would drive up the costs of production, causing *SRAS* to shift to the left and the Phillips curve to shift upward and to the right. It works in the reverse as well.

Figure 34.5 Expected Inflation and the Short-Run Phillips Curve

An increase in expected inflation shifts the short-run Phillips curve up. $SRPC_0$ is the initial short-run Phillips curve with an expected inflation rate of 0%; $SRPC_2$ is the short-run Phillips curve with an expected inflation rate of 2%. Each additional percentage point of expected inflation raises the actual inflation rate at any given unemployment rate by 1 percentage point.

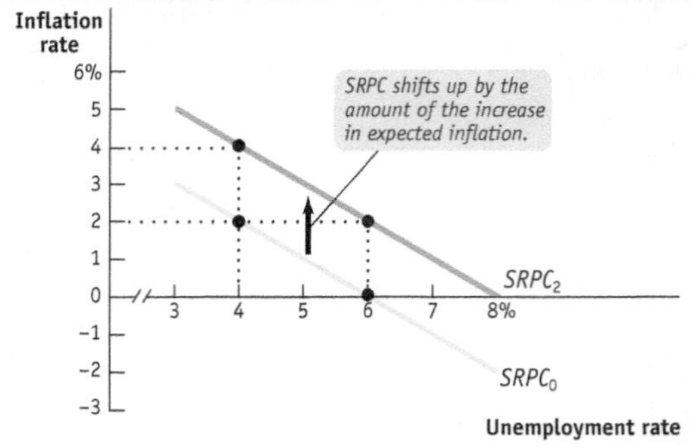

FYI From the Scary Seventies to the Nifty Nineties

Figure 34.1 showed that the American experience during the 1950s and 1960s supported the belief in the existence of a short-run Phillips curve for the U.S. economy, with a short-run trade-off between unemployment and inflation.

After 1969, however, that relationship appeared to fall apart according to the data. The figure here plots the course of U.S. unemployment and inflation rates from 1961 to 1990. As you can see, the course looks more like a tangled piece of yarn than like a smooth curve.

Through much of the 1970s and early 1980s, the economy suffered from a combination of above-average unemployment rates coupled with inflation rates unprecedented in modern American history. This condition came to be known as *stagflation*—for stagnation combined with high inflation. In the late 1990s, by contrast, the economy was experiencing a blissful combination of low unemployment and low inflation. What explains these developments?

Part of the answer can be attributed to a series of negative supply shocks that the U.S. economy suffered during the 1970s. The price of oil, in particular, soared as wars and revolutions in the Middle East led to a reduction in oil supplies and as oil-exporting countries deliberately curbed production to drive up prices. Compounding the oil price shocks, there was also a slowdown in labor productivity growth. Both of these factors shifted the short-run Phillips curve upward. During the 1990s, by contrast, supply shocks were positive. Prices of oil and other raw materials were generally falling, and productivity growth accelerated. As a result, the short-run Phillips curve shifted downward.

Equally important, however, was the role of expected inflation. As mentioned earlier, inflation accelerated during the 1960s. During the 1970s, the public came to expect high inflation, and this also shifted the short-run Phillips curve up. It took a sustained and costly effort during the 1980s to get inflation back down. The result, however, was that expected inflation was very low by the late 1990s, allowing actual inflation to be low even with low rates of unemployment.

Source: Bureau of Labor Statistics.

332 **Section 6** Inflation, Unemployment, and Stabilization Policies

rate, the actual inflation rate will be 2 percentage points higher than it would be if people expected 0% inflation. $SRPC_2$, which shows the Phillips curve when the expected inflation rate is 2%, is $SRPC_0$ shifted upward by 2 percentage points at every level of unemployment. According to $SRPC_2$, the actual inflation rate will be 2% if the unemployment rate is 6%; it will be 4% if the unemployment rate is 4%.

What determines the expected rate of inflation? In general, people base their expectations about inflation on experience. If the inflation rate has hovered around 0% in the last few years, people will expect it to be around 0% in the near future. But if the inflation rate has averaged around 5% lately, people will expect inflation to be around 5% in the near future.

Since expected inflation is an important part of the modern discussion about the short-run Phillips curve, you might wonder why it was not in the original formulation of the Phillips curve. The answer lies in history. Think back to what we said about the early 1960s: at that time, people were accustomed to low inflation rates and reasonably expected that future inflation rates would also be low. It was only after 1965 that persistent inflation became a fact of life. So only then did it become clear that expected inflation would play an important role in price-setting.

Inflation and Unemployment in the Long Run

The short-run Phillips curve says that at any given point in time there is a trade-off between unemployment and inflation. According to this view, policy makers have a choice: they can choose to accept the price of high inflation in order to achieve low unemployment, or they can reject high inflation and pay the price of high unemployment. In fact, during the 1960s many economists believed that this trade-off represented a real choice.

However, this view was greatly altered by the later recognition that expected inflation affects the short-run Phillips curve. In the short run, expectations often diverge from reality. In the long run, however, any consistent rate of inflation will be reflected in expectations. If inflation is consistently high, as it was in the 1970s, people will come to expect more of the same; if inflation is consistently low, as it has been in recent years, that, too, will become part of expectations. So what does the trade-off between inflation and unemployment look like in the long run, when actual inflation is incorporated into expectations? Most macroeconomists believe that, in fact, there is no long-run trade-off. That is, it is not possible to achieve lower unemployment in the long run by accepting higher inflation. To see why, we need to introduce another concept: the *long-run Phillips curve*.

The Long-Run Phillips Curve

Figure 34.6 on the next page reproduces the two short-run Phillips curves from Figure 34.5, $SRPC_0$ and $SRPC_2$. It also adds an additional short-run Phillips curve, $SRPC_4$, representing a 4% expected rate of inflation. In a moment, we'll explain the significance of the vertical long-run Phillips curve, *LRPC*.

Suppose that the economy has had a 0% inflation rate in the past. In that case, the current short-run Phillips curve will be $SRPC_0$, reflecting a 0% expected inflation rate. If the unemployment rate is 6%, the actual inflation rate will be 0%.

Also suppose that policy makers decide to trade off lower unemployment for a higher rate of inflation. They use monetary policy, fiscal policy, or both to drive the unemployment rate down to 4%. This puts the economy at point *A* on $SRPC_0$, leading to an actual inflation rate of 2%.

Over time, the public will come to expect a 2% inflation rate. *This increase in inflationary expectations will shift the short-run Phillips curve upward* to $SRPC_2$. Now, when the unemployment rate is 6%, the actual inflation rate will be 2%. Given this new short-run Phillips curve, policies adopted to keep the unemployment rate at 4% will lead to a 4% actual inflation rate—point *B* on $SRPC_2$—rather than point *A* with a 2% actual inflation rate.

FOCUS **Active Learning**

TRM Have students complete **Worksheet 34.2 (The Phillips Curve)** from the TRM in class or as homework. Students will practice graphing situations that involve a movement along or a shift in the short-run Phillips curve.

FOCUS **Test It**

Ask students to complete Question 3 from the 2013 AP® Macroeconomics exam, which can be found at http://media.collegeboard.com/digitalServices/pdf/ap/apcentral/ap13_frq_macroeconomics.pdf. This is a short free-response question and they should be able to complete it in less than $12\frac{1}{2}$ minutes, as recommended by the College Board®. The rubric can be found at http://tinyurl.com/kr3osws.

FOCUS **Flip It**

TRM To help them better understand the short- and long-run Phillips curve, have students watch Jacob Clifford's video "The Phillips Curve" (see econextras video list with hyperlinks on the bcs and TRFD). Suggested questions for this video can be found in **Worksheet 34.1 [The Phillips Curve (Short and Long Run)]** from the TRM.

TEACH **Connect It**

Tell students that the long-run Phillips curve works similarly to the long-run aggregate supply curve. As you increase *AD*, you move to a new point on the short-run Phillips curve. Once that happens, flexible wages increase, which decreases *SRAS*. The change in *SRAS* is reflected in a shift of the short-run Phillips curve, bringing back the economy to the natural rate of unemployment on the *LRPC*.

TEACH Teach It

The long-run Phillips curve is a vertical line that illustrates the NAIRU (nonaccelerating inflation rate of unemployment). NAIRU is just another name for the natural rate of unemployment—the frictional and structural unemployment that always exists in an economy. The level of unemployment the economy "needs" in order to avoid accelerating inflation is equal to the natural rate of unemployment. Project Figure 34.6 on the board if possible and explain the long-run Phillips curve to students. Ask the following:

- Using point *C* as a starting point, if *AD* decreased enough to bring the unemployment rate up to 5%, what would happen on the graph in the short run? *There would be a movement down curve $SRPC_4$ to the point at which the rates of unemployment and inflation are both 5%.*
- In the long run, how would *SRAS* be affected? *Prices and wages would decrease, causing SRAS to shift to the right.*
- How does the change in *SRAS* affect the Phillips curve? *SRPC shifts left to reflect the lower inflation and unemployment, and it creates a new equilibrium on the LRPC.*

FOCUS Active Learning

TRM Have students watch Jason Welker's "The Long-Run Phillips Curve" (see econextras video list with hyperlinks on the bcs and TRFD) to help them better understand this topic. Assign **Worksheet 34.3 (The Long-Run Phillips Curve)** from the TRM for questions on this video.

Figure 34.6 The NAIRU and the Long-Run Phillips Curve

$SRPC_0$ is the short-run Phillips curve when the expected inflation rate is 0%. At a 4% unemployment rate, the economy is at point *A* with an actual inflation rate of 2%. The higher inflation rate will be incorporated into expectations, and the *SRPC* will shift upward to $SRPC_2$. If policy makers act to keep the unemployment rate at 4%, the economy will be at *B* and the actual inflation rate will rise to 4%. Inflationary expectations will be revised upward again, and *SRPC* will shift to $SRPC_4$. At a 4% unemployment rate, the economy will be at *C* and the actual inflation rate will rise to 6%. Here, an unemployment rate of 6% is the NAIRU, or nonaccelerating inflation rate of unemployment. As long as unemployment is at the NAIRU, the actual inflation rate will match expectations and remain constant. An unemployment rate below 6% requires ever-accelerating inflation. The long-run Phillips curve, *LRPC*, which passes through E_0, E_2, and E_4, is vertical: no long-run trade-off between unemployment and inflation exists.

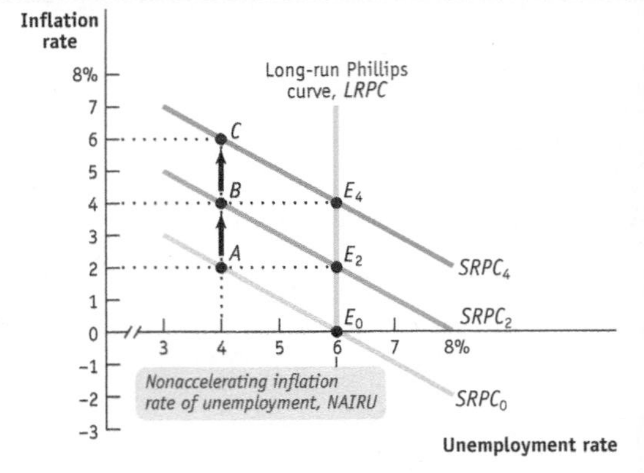

The **nonaccelerating inflation rate of unemployment**, or **NAIRU**, is the unemployment rate at which inflation does not change over time.

The **long-run Phillips curve** shows the relationship between unemployment and inflation after expectations of inflation have had time to adjust to experience.

Eventually, the 4% actual inflation rate gets built into expectations about the future inflation rate, and the short-run Phillips curve shifts upward yet again to $SRPC_4$. To keep the unemployment rate at 4% would now require accepting a 6% actual inflation rate, point *C* on $SRPC_4$, and so on. In short, a persistent attempt to trade off lower unemployment for higher inflation leads to *accelerating* inflation over time.

To avoid accelerating inflation over time, the unemployment rate must be high enough that the actual rate of inflation matches the expected rate of inflation. This is the situation at E_0 on $SRPC_0$: when the expected inflation rate is 0% and the unemployment rate is 6%, the actual inflation rate is 0%. It is also the situation at E_2 on $SRPC_2$: when the expected inflation rate is 2% and the unemployment rate is 6%, the actual inflation rate is 2%. And it is the situation at E_4 on $SRPC_4$: when the expected inflation rate is 4% and the unemployment rate is 6%, the actual inflation rate is 4%. As we'll learn shortly, this relationship between accelerating inflation and the unemployment rate is known as the *natural rate hypothesis.*

Andy Sacks/Stone/Getty Images

The nonaccelerating inflation rate of unemployment, or NAIRU, is the unemployment rate at which inflation does not change over time.

The unemployment rate at which inflation does not change over time—6% in Figure 34.6—is known as the **nonaccelerating inflation rate of unemployment**, or **NAIRU** for short. Keeping the unemployment rate below the NAIRU leads to ever-accelerating inflation and cannot be maintained. Most macroeconomists believe that there is a NAIRU and that there is no long-run trade-off between unemployment and inflation.

We can now explain the significance of the vertical line *LRPC*. It is the **long-run Phillips curve**, which shows the relationship between unemployment and inflation in the long run, after expectations of inflation have had time to adjust to experience. It is vertical because any unemployment rate below the NAIRU leads to ever-accelerating inflation. In other words, the long-run Phillips curve shows that there are limits to expansionary policies because an unemployment rate below the NAIRU cannot be maintained in the long run. Moreover, there is a corresponding point we have not yet emphasized: any unemployment rate above the NAIRU leads to decelerating inflation.

The Natural Rate of Unemployment, Revisited

Recall the concept of the natural rate of unemployment, the portion of the unemployment rate unaffected by the swings of the business cycle. Now we have introduced the concept of the NAIRU. How do these two concepts relate to each other?

The answer is that the NAIRU is another name for the natural rate. The level of unemployment the economy "needs" in order to avoid accelerating inflation is equal to the natural rate of unemployment.

In fact, economists estimate the natural rate of unemployment by looking for evidence about the NAIRU from the behavior of the inflation rate and the unemployment rate over the course of the business cycle. For example, the way major European countries learned, to their dismay, that their natural rates of unemployment were 9% or more was through unpleasant experience. In the late 1980s, and again in the late 1990s, European inflation began to accelerate as European unemployment rates, which had been above 9%, began to fall, approaching 8%.

In Figure 33.3 we cited Congressional Budget Office estimates of the U.S. natural rate of unemployment. The CBO has a model that predicts changes in the inflation

FYI The Great Disinflation of the 1980s

As we've mentioned, the United States ended the 1970s with a high rate of inflation, at least by its own peacetime historical standards—13% in 1980. Part of this inflation was the result of one-time events, especially a world oil crisis. But expectations of future inflation at 10% or more per year appeared to be firmly embedded in the economy.

By the mid-1980s, however, inflation was running at about 4% per year. Panel (a) of the figure shows the annual rate of change in the "core" consumer price index (CPI)—also called the *core inflation rate*. This index, which excludes volatile energy and food prices, is widely regarded as a better indicator of underlying inflation trends than the overall CPI. By this measure, inflation fell from about 12% at the end of the 1970s to about 4% by the mid-1980s.

How was this disinflation achieved? At great cost. Beginning in late 1979, the Federal Reserve imposed strongly contractionary monetary policies, which pushed the economy into its worst recession since the Great Depression. Panel (b) shows the Congressional Budget Office estimate of the U.S. output gap from 1979 to 1989: by 1982, actual output was 7% below potential output, corresponding to an unemployment rate of more than 9%. Aggregate output didn't get back to potential output until 1987.

Our analysis of the Phillips curve tells us that a temporary rise in unemployment, like that of the 1980s, is needed to break the cycle of inflationary expectations. Once expectations of inflation are reduced, the economy can return to the natural rate of unemployment at a lower inflation rate. And that's just what happened.

At what cost? If you add up the output gaps over 1980–1987, you find that the economy sacrificed approximately 18% of an average year's output over the period. If we had to do the same thing today, that would mean giving up roughly $2.6 trillion worth of goods and services.

(a) The Core Inflation Rate in the United States Came Down in the 1980s . . .

(b) . . . but Only at the Expense of a Huge Sacrifice of Output and High Unemployment.

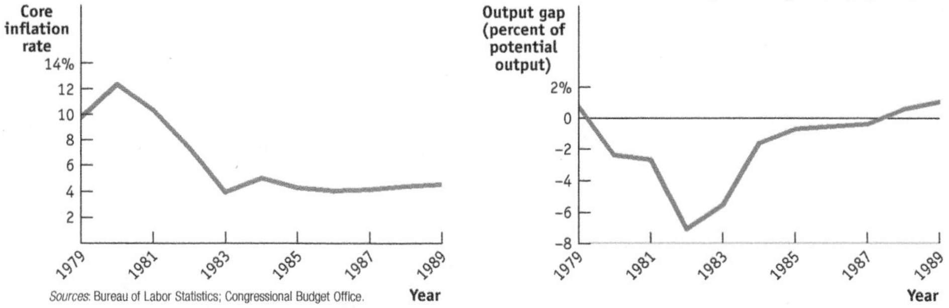

Sources: Bureau of Labor Statistics; Congressional Budget Office.

TEACH Teach It

Ask students to read the February 2011 *St. Louis Fed* Liber8 article "Deflation: Who Let the Air Out?" at http://research.stlouisfed.org/pageone-economics/uploads/newsletter/2011/201102_ClassroomEdition.pdf. Print out the article and the discussion questions for students. Also print out the answer key for your records.

TEACH Connect It

Let students know that periods of disinflation are difficult for the population because high unemployment is present throughout the period. Use the FYI box to show them the output gap created by disinflation in the 1980s. How might disinflation affect the national debt? *Deficit spending will increase, causing the debt to increase.*

FOCUS Active Learning

Show the Jacob Clifford video "Macro 3.5—Graphing Practice" (see econextras video list with hyperlinks on the bcs and TRFD), in which he connects four graphs: the *AD–AS* model, Phillips curve, Business cycle, and Production Possibilities curve. He uses long-run equilibrium, a recessionary gap, and an inflationary gap to show the relationships among the four graphs. Pause the video before each solution for students to think about the connection.

rate based on the deviation of the actual unemployment rate from the natural rate. Given data on actual unemployment and inflation, this model can be used to deduce estimates of the natural rate—and that's where the CBO numbers come from.

The Costs of Disinflation

Through experience, policy makers have found that bringing inflation down is a much harder task than increasing it. The reason is that once the public has come to expect continuing inflation, bringing inflation down is painful.

A persistent attempt to keep unemployment below the natural rate leads to accelerating inflation that becomes incorporated into expectations. To reduce inflationary expectations, policy makers need to run the process in reverse, adopting contractionary policies that keep the unemployment rate above the natural rate for an extended period of time. The process of bringing down inflation that has become embedded in expectations is known as *disinflation*.

Disinflation can be very expensive. The U.S. retreat from high inflation at the beginning of the 1980s appears to have cost the equivalent of about 18% of a year's real GDP, the equivalent of roughly $2.6 trillion today. The justification for paying these costs is that they lead to a permanent gain. Although the economy does not recover the short-term production losses caused by disinflation, it no longer suffers from the costs associated with persistently high inflation. In fact, the United States, Britain, and other wealthy countries that experienced inflation in the 1970s eventually decided that the benefit of bringing inflation down was worth the required suffering—the large reduction in real GDP in the short term.

Some economists argue that the costs of disinflation can be reduced if policy makers explicitly state their determination to reduce inflation. A clearly announced, credible policy of disinflation, they contend, can reduce expectations of future inflation and so shift the short-run Phillips curve downward. Some economists believe that the clear determination of the Federal Reserve to combat the inflation of the 1970s was credible enough that the costs of disinflation, huge though they were, were lower than they might otherwise have been.

Deflation

Before World War II, *deflation*—a falling aggregate price level—was almost as common as inflation. In fact, the U.S. consumer price index on the eve of World War II was 30% lower than it had been in 1920. After World War II, inflation became the norm in all countries. But in the 1990s, deflation reappeared in Japan and proved difficult to reverse. Concerns about potential deflation played a crucial role in U.S. monetary policy in the early 2000s and again in late 2008. In fact, in late 2008, the U.S. experienced a brief period of deflation.

Why is deflation a problem? And why is it hard to end?

Debt Deflation

Deflation, like inflation, produces both winners and losers—but in the opposite direction. Due to the falling price level, a dollar in the future has a higher real value than a dollar today. So lenders, who are owed money, gain under deflation because the real value of borrowers' payments increases. Borrowers lose because the real burden of their debt rises.

In a famous analysis at the beginning of the Great Depression, Irving Fisher claimed that the effects of deflation on borrowers and lenders can worsen an economic slump. In effect, deflation takes real resources away from borrowers and redistributes them to lenders. Fisher argued that borrowers, who lose from deflation, are typically short of cash and will be forced to cut their spending sharply when their debt burden rises. However, lenders are less likely to increase spending sharply when the values of the

FOCUS Active Learning

If inflation is bad for the economy, is deflation good for the economy? Not necessarily. Deflation causes a dollar to be worth more in the future than it is today. Ask:

- How does deflation affect borrowers and lenders? *Lenders over time are helped because they are paid back with dollars that are worth more than the dollars they lent out. Borrowers are hurt since they are paying back dollars that are worth more than the dollars they borrowed.*
- What actions do you expect consumers to take during a deflationary period? *Consumers will cut back on spending now in anticipation of lower prices in the future, and spending financed by loans will decrease for the added reason that deflation makes loan repayments more costly in real terms.*
- Given your last answer, discuss the effects of deflation on real GDP. *Reduced spending by consumers reduces AD, making an economic slump deeper.*

Thus, weak spending causes deflation, which causes less spending, which causes even more deflation. It is difficult to break the cycle.

loans they own rise. The overall effect, said Fisher, is that deflation reduces aggregate demand, deepening an economic slump, which, in a vicious circle, may lead to further deflation. The effect of deflation in reducing aggregate demand, known as **debt deflation**, probably played a significant role in the Great Depression.

Debt deflation is the reduction in aggregate demand arising from the increase in the real burden of outstanding debt caused by deflation.

Effects of Expected Deflation

Like expected inflation, expected deflation affects the nominal interest rate. Consider Figure 29.6 from Section 5 (repeated here as **Figure 34.7**), which demonstrates how expected inflation affects the equilibrium interest rate. As shown, the equilibrium nominal interest rate is 4% if the expected inflation rate is 0%. Clearly, if the expected inflation rate is −3%—meaning that the public expects deflation at 3% per year—the equilibrium nominal interest rate will be 4% − 3% = 1%.

But what would happen if the expected rate of inflation were −5%? Would the nominal interest rate fall to −1%, meaning that lenders are paying borrowers 1% on their debt? No. Nobody would lend money at a negative nominal rate of interest because they could do better by simply holding cash. This illustrates what economists call the **zero bound** on the nominal interest rate: it cannot go below zero.

There is a **zero bound** on the nominal interest rate: it cannot go below zero.

This zero bound can limit the effectiveness of monetary policy. Suppose the economy is depressed, with output below potential output and the unemployment rate above the natural rate. Normally, the central bank can respond by cutting interest rates so as to increase aggregate demand. If the nominal interest rate is already zero, however, the central bank cannot push it down any further. Banks refuse to lend and consumers and firms refuse to spend because, with a negative inflation rate and a 0% nominal interest rate, holding cash yields a positive real rate of return. Any further increases in the monetary base will either be held in bank vaults or held as cash by individuals and firms, without being spent.

A situation in which conventional monetary policy to fight a slump—cutting interest rates—can't be used because nominal interest rates are up against the zero bound is known as a **liquidity trap**. A liquidity trap can occur whenever there is a sharp reduction

A **liquidity trap** is a situation in which conventional monetary policy is ineffective because nominal interest rates are up against the zero bound.

Figure 34.7 The Fisher Effect

D_0 and S_0 are the demand and supply curves for loanable funds when the expected future inflation rate is 0%. At an expected inflation rate of 0%, the equilibrium nominal interest rate is 4%. An increase in expected future inflation pushes both the demand and supply curves upward by 1 percentage point for every percentage point increase in expected future inflation. D_{10} and S_{10} are the demand and supply curves for loanable funds when the expected future inflation rate is 10%. The 10 percentage point increase in expected future inflation raises the equilibrium nominal interest rate to 14%. The expected real interest rate remains at 4%, and the equilibrium quantity of loanable funds also remains unchanged.

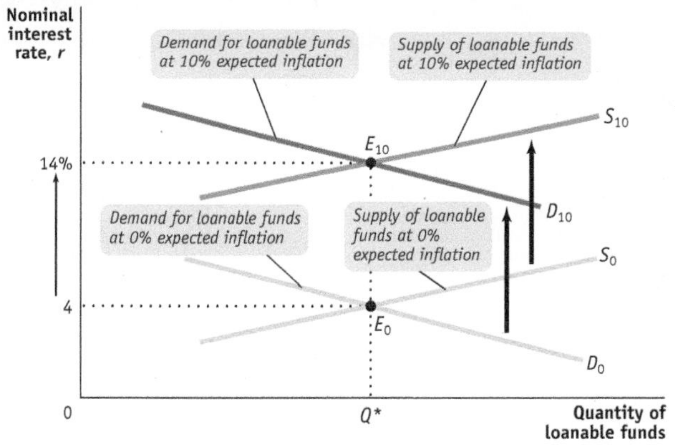

TEACH Teach It

When interest rates reach 0%, lenders quit lending. Because the Fed can't lower interest rates any lower than 0%, monetary policy becomes ineffective. This is called the liquidity trap.

FOCUS In the News

Find a recent article on the liquidity trap or use *The Economist*'s October 2013 article "Why Is the Liquidity Trap?" at http://www.economist.com/blogs/freeexchange/2013/10/monetary-policy-2. What does the article say the Fed needs to do to end policy ineffectiveness at the zero bound? *Raise inflation expectations. (This could be achieved by embracing a higher inflation rate target or a price level target.)* Why do expectations of higher inflation encourage spending and borrowing? *Spending is encouraged because people want to make purchases before the price level rises. Borrowing is encouraged when, after subtracting the expected inflation rate from the nominal interest rate, potential borrowers see an attractively low real interest rate.*

Follow the discussion of this article with *USA Today*'s September 2013 article "What Exactly Is Quantitative Easing?" at http://www.usatoday.com/story/money/business/2013/09/18/federal-reserve-quantitative-easing/2831097. Ask students if they believe monetary policy worked based on what they read. *Answers will vary but students should justify their positions either way.*

OPEN & CLOSE Exit Slip

TRM *Please see* ***Exit Slip: Module 34*** *in the TRM for formative questions to ask your students before finishing your lesson. These questions will help you quickly assess whether your students have mastered the module's concepts before moving on.*

Answers to the Exit Slip Questions

1. C

2. D

3. If business taxes are increased, *SRAS* shifts left, increasing the price level and decreasing real GDP. The resulting rise in inflation and unemployment causes the short-run Phillips curve to shift upward and to the right.

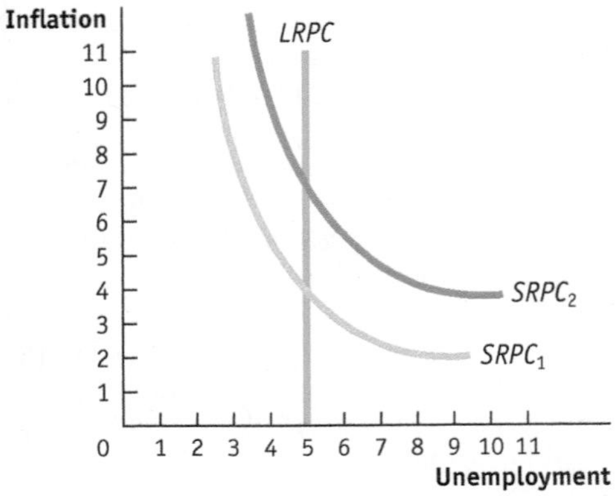

Figure 34.8 The Zero Bound in U.S. History

This figure shows U.S. short-term interest rates, specifically the interest rate on three-month Treasury bills, since 1920. As shown by the shaded area on the left, for much of the 1930s, interest rates were very close to zero, leaving little room for expansionary monetary policy. After World War II, persistent inflation generally kept rates well above zero. However, starting in late 2008, in the wake of the housing bubble bursting and the financial crisis, the interest rate on three-month Treasury bills was again virtually zero.

Source: Federal Reserve Bank of St. Louis.

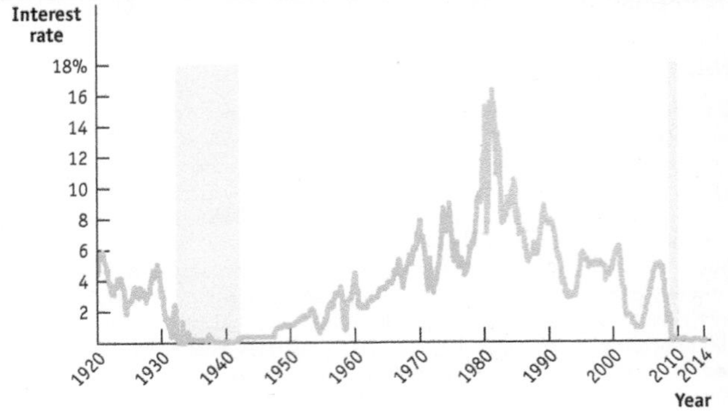

in demand for loanable funds—which is exactly what happened during the Great Depression. **Figure 34.8** shows the interest rate on short-term U.S. government debt from 1920 to February 2014. As you can see, starting in 1933 and ending when World War II brought a full economic recovery, the U.S. economy was either close to or up against the zero bound. After World War II, when inflation became the norm around the world, the zero bound problem largely vanished as the public came to expect inflation rather than deflation.

However, the recent history of the Japanese economy, shown in **Figure 34.9**, provides a modern illustration of the problem of deflation and the liquidity trap. Japan experienced a huge boom in the prices of both stocks and real estate in the late 1980s, and then saw both bubbles burst. The result was a prolonged period of economic

Figure 34.9 Japan's Lost Decade

A prolonged economic slump in Japan led to deflation from the late 1990s on. The Bank of Japan responded by cutting interest rates—but eventually ran up against the zero bound.

Sources: Japanese Ministry of Internal Affairs and Communications, Statistics Bureau; Bank of Japan.

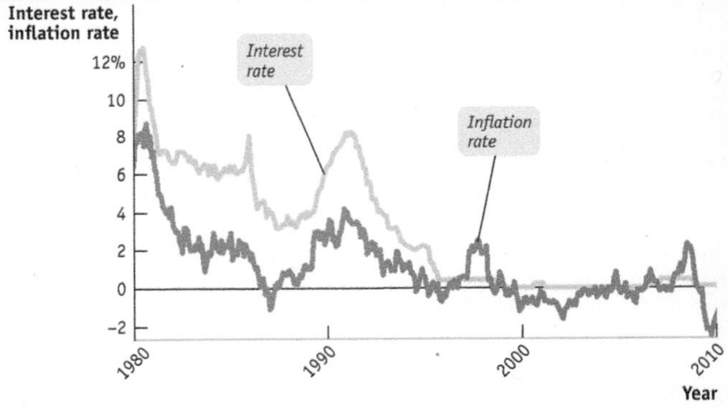

338 Section 6 Inflation, Unemployment, and Stabilization Policies

stagnation, the so-called Lost Decade, which gradually reduced the inflation rate and eventually led to persistent deflation. In an effort to fight the weakness of the economy, the Bank of Japan—the equivalent of the Federal Reserve—repeatedly cut interest rates. Eventually, it arrived at the "ZIRP": the zero interest rate policy. The "call money rate," the equivalent of the U.S. federal funds rate, was literally set equal to zero. Because the economy was still depressed, it would have been desirable to cut interest rates even further. But that wasn't possible: Japan was up against the zero bound.

From 2008 until at least 2014, the Federal Reserve also found itself up against the zero bound. In the aftermath of the bursting of the housing bubble and the ensuing financial crisis, the interest on short-term U.S. government debt fell to virtually zero.

MODULE 34 Review

Check Your Understanding

1. Explain why a decrease in aggregate demand causes a movement along the short-run Phillips curve.
2. Why is there no long-run trade-off between unemployment and inflation?
3. Why is disinflation so costly for an economy? Are there ways to reduce these costs?
4. Why won't anyone lend money at a negative nominal rate of interest? How can this pose problems for monetary policy?

Tackle the Test: Multiple-Choice Questions

1. The long-run Phillips curve is
   I. the same as the short-run Phillips curve.
   II. vertical.
   III. the short-run Phillips curve plus expected inflation.
   a. I only
   b. II only
   c. III only
   d. I and II only
   e. I, II, and III
2. The short-run Phillips curve shows a __________ relationship between __________.
   a. negative — the aggregate price level and aggregate output
   b. positive — the aggregate price level and aggregate output
   c. negative — unemployment and inflation
   d. positive — unemployment and aggregate output
   e. positive — unemployment and the aggregate price level
3. An increase in expected inflation will shift
   a. the short-run Phillips curve downward.
   b. the short-run Phillips curve upward.
   c. the long-run Phillips curve upward.
   d. the long-run Phillips curve downward.
   e. neither the short-run nor the long-run Phillips curve.
4. Bringing down inflation that has become embedded in expectations is called
   a. deflation.
   b. negative inflation.
   c. anti-inflation.
   d. unexpected inflation.
   e. disinflation.
5. Debt deflation is
   a. the effect of deflation in decreasing aggregate demand.
   b. an idea proposed by Irving Fisher.
   c. a contributing factor in causing the Great Depression.
   d. due to differences in how borrowers/lenders respond to inflation losses/gains.
   e. all of the above.

Answers to Module 34 Review Questions

Check Your Understanding

1. A decrease in aggregate demand leads to a new short-run equilibrium at a lower level of output and a lower price level. It takes fewer workers to produce less output, so the unemployment rate increases. And the lower price level corresponds with a decrease in inflation (or with deflation). So, with a higher unemployment rate and a lower inflation rate, there is a movement downward and to the right along the short-run Phillips curve.

2. There is no long-run trade-off between unemployment and inflation because, after expectations of inflation change, wages will adjust to the change, returning the employment and unemployment rates to their equilibrium (natural) levels. This implies that once expectations of inflation fully adjust to any change in actual inflation, the unemployment rate will return to the natural rate of unemployment, or NAIRU. This also implies that the long-run Phillips curve is vertical.

3. Disinflation is costly because, in order to reduce the inflation rate, aggregate output in the short run must typically fall below potential output. This, in turn, results in an increase in the unemployment rate above the natural rate. In general, we would observe a reduction in real GDP. The costs of disinflation can be reduced by not allowing inflation to increase in the first place. The costs of any disinflation will also be lower if the central bank is credible and it announces its policy to reduce inflation in advance. In this situation, the adjustment to the disinflationary policy will be more rapid, resulting in a smaller loss of aggregate output.

4. If the nominal interest rate is negative, an individual is better off simply holding cash, which has a 0% nominal rate of return. If the options facing an individual are to lend and receive a negative nominal interest rate or to hold cash and receive a 0% nominal rate of return, the individual will hold cash. Such a scenario creates the possibility of a liquidity trap, in which monetary policy is ineffective because the nominal interest rate cannot fall below zero. Once the nominal interest rate falls to zero, further increases in the money supply will lead firms and individuals to simply hold the additional cash.

Tackle the Test: Multiple-Choice Questions

1. b
2. c
3. b
4. e
5. e

Tackle the Test: Free-Response Question Rubric for FRQ 2 (6 points).

1 point: 4%

1 point: In this scenario, the nominal interest rate is 4% plus the expected inflation rate, which makes it: 2% because 4% − 2% = 2%

1 point: 0% because although 4% − 6% = −2%, nominal interest rates can't go below zero

1 point: Lenders would effectively have to pay people to borrow their money because what the lenders received back would be less than what they lent out. No lending would take place. It is better to hold cash and get 0% interest than to pay people to borrow money.

1 point: Conventional monetary policy (decreasing interest rates) can't happen if the nominal interest rate is already zero.

1 point: This is called the zero bound OR a liquidity trap.

Tackle the Test: Free-Response Questions

1. a. Draw a correctly labeled graph showing a short-run Phillips curve with an expected inflation rate of 0% and the corresponding long-run Phillips curve.

b. On your graph, label the nonaccelerating inflation rate of unemployment.

c. On your graph, show what happens in the long run if the government decides to decrease the unemployment rate below the nonaccelerating inflation rate of unemployment. Explain.

Rubric for FRQ 1 (8 points)

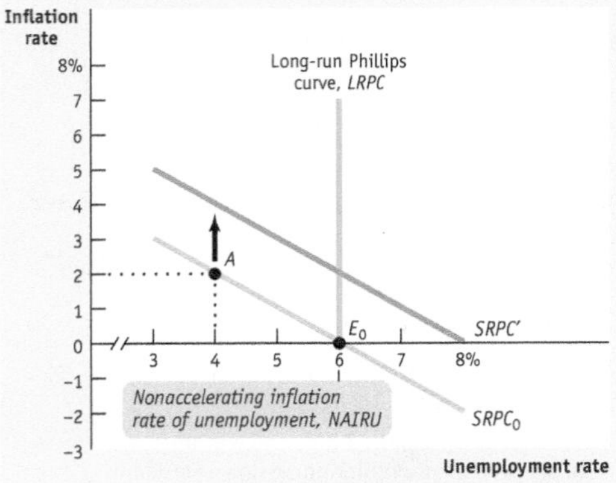

1 point: Vertical axis labeled "Inflation rate"

1 point: Horizontal axis labeled "Unemployment rate"

1 point: Downward-sloping curve labeled "$SRPC_0$"

1 point: Vertical curve labeled "*LRPC*"

1 point: $SRPC_0$ crosses horizontal axis where it crosses *LRPC*

1 point: NAIRU is labeled where $SRPC_0$ crosses *LRPC* and horizontal axis

1 point: New *SRPC* is labeled, for example as "*SRPC′*," and shown above the original $SRPC_0$

1 point: When the unemployment rate moves below the NAIRU, it creates inflation and moves the economy to a point such as *A*. This leads to positive inflationary expectations, which shift the *SRPC* up as shown by *SRPC′*.

2. Consider the accompanying figure.

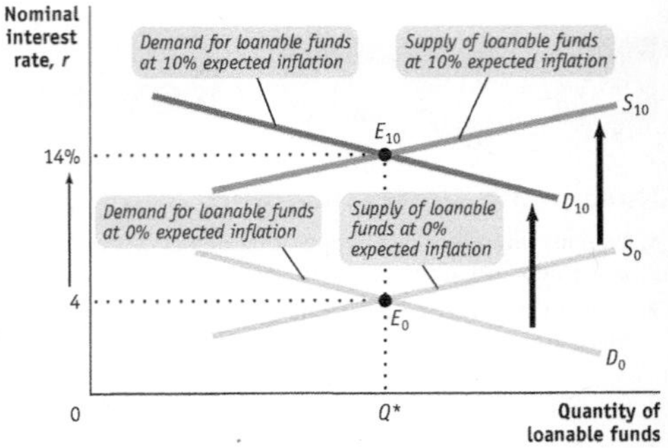

a. What is the nominal interest rate if expected inflation is 0%?

b. What would the nominal interest rate be if the expected inflation rate were −2%? Explain.

c. What would the nominal interest rate be if the expected inflation rate were −6%? Explain.

d. What would a negative nominal interest rate mean for lenders? How much lending would take place at a negative nominal interest rate? Explain.

e. What effect does a nominal interest rate of zero have on monetary policy? What is this situation called?

(6 points)

340 Section 6 Inflation, Unemployment, and Stabilization Policies

AP Photo

MODULE 35

History and Alternative Views of Macroeconomics

In this Module, you will learn to:

- Explain why classical macroeconomics wasn't adequate for the problems posed by the Great Depression
- Discuss how Keynes and the experience of the Great Depression legitimized macroeconomic policy activism
- Define monetarism and identify monetarist views on the limits of discretionary monetary policy
- Describe how challenges led to a revision of Keynesian ideas and the emergence of the new classical macroeconomics

Classical Macroeconomics

The term *macroeconomics* appears to have been coined in 1933 by the Norwegian economist Ragnar Frisch. The timing, during the worst year of the Great Depression, was no accident. Still, there were economists analyzing what we now consider macroeconomic issues—the behavior of the aggregate price level and aggregate output—before then.

Money and the Price Level

Previously, we described the *classical model of the price level.* According to the classical model, prices are flexible, making the aggregate supply curve vertical even in the short run. In this model, other things equal, an increase in the money supply leads to a proportional rise in the aggregate price level, with no effect on aggregate output. As a result, increases in the money supply lead to inflation, and that's all. Before the 1930s, the classical model of the price level dominated economic thinking about the effects of monetary policy.

Did classical economists really believe that changes in the money supply affected only aggregate prices, without any effect on aggregate output? Probably not. Historians of economic thought argue that before 1930 most economists were aware that changes in the money supply affected aggregate output as well as aggregate prices in the short run—or, to use modern terms, they were aware that the short-run aggregate supply curve sloped upward. But they regarded such short-run effects as unimportant,

PD To prepare for teaching this lesson, you may want to consult the **Module 35 Sample Lecture** in the TRM.

OPEN & CLOSE Start Here

Have students watch Keynes and Hayek argue (see econextras video list with hyperlinks on the bcs and TRFD). Stop the video at 8:45. These men provide two opposing viewpoints on how to fix problems in the economy. As students listen, ask them to write down the basics of what each economist believes.

TEACH Teach It

It is a good idea to teach Modules 35 and 36 at the same time. If you do that, select any three questions from either module to use for your exit slip.

TEACH AP® Exam Tip

Stress that one of the frustrating things about economics is that models aren't perfect representations of the real world (which is also what keeps economics interesting). As the world around us changes, so must our economic models. If the economic models do not evolve with the world, our policies can become outdated and disastrously ineffective. Students will need to be able to answer questions about all the different models on the AP® exam.

TEACH Connect It

Remind students about the earlier discussion of positive and normative economics. At that time, we talked about sources of differences between economists: differing political opinions, individual values, and economic assumptions.

TEACH Teach It

According to the classical model:

- Prices and wages are flexible.
- The aggregate supply curve is vertical even in the short run.
- An increase in the money supply, other things being equal, leads to a proportional rise in the aggregate price level.
- An increase in the money supply does not increase aggregate output.
- The key result is that increases in the money supply lead to inflation, and that's all.

stressing the long run instead. It was this attitude that led John Maynard Keynes to scoff at the focus on the long run, in which, as he said, "we are all dead."

The Business Cycle

Of course, classical economists were also aware that the economy did not grow smoothly. The American economist Wesley Mitchell pioneered the quantitative study of business cycles. In 1920, he founded the National Bureau of Economic Research, an independent, nonprofit organization that to this day has the official role of declaring the beginnings of recessions and expansions. Thanks to Mitchell's work, the *measurement* of business cycles was well advanced by 1930. But there was no widely accepted *theory* of business cycles.

In the absence of any clear theory, views about how policy makers should respond to a recession were conflicting. Some economists favored expansionary monetary and fiscal policies to fight a recession. Others believed that such policies would worsen the slump or merely postpone the inevitable. For example, in 1934 Harvard's Joseph Schumpeter, now famous for his early recognition of the importance of technological change, warned that any attempt to alleviate the Great Depression with expansionary monetary policy "would, in the end, lead to a collapse worse than the one it was called in to remedy." When the Great Depression hit, the policy-making process was paralyzed by this lack of consensus. In many cases, economists now believe, policy makers took steps in the wrong direction.

Necessity, however, was the mother of invention. As we'll explain next, the Great Depression provided a strong incentive for economists to develop theories that could serve as a guide to policy—and economists responded.

The Great Depression and the Keynesian Revolution

Alfred Eisenstaedt/Time & Life Pictures/Getty Images

The work of John Maynard Keynes (right), seen here with U.S. Treasury Secretary Henry Morgenthau, Jr., legitimized the use of monetary and fiscal policy to smooth out the business cycle.

The Great Depression demonstrated, once and for all, that economists cannot safely ignore the short run. Not only was the economic pain severe, it threatened to destabilize societies and political systems. In particular, the economic plunge helped Adolf Hitler rise to power in Germany.

The whole world wanted to know how this economic disaster could be happening and what should be done about it. But because there was no widely accepted theory of the business cycle, economists gave conflicting and, we now believe, often harmful advice. Some believed that only a huge change in the economic system—such as having the government take over much of private industry and replace markets with a command economy—could end the slump. Others argued that slumps were natural—even beneficial—and that nothing should be done.

Some economists, however, argued that the slump both could have and should have been cured—without giving up on the basic idea of a market economy. In 1930, the British economist John Maynard Keynes compared the problems of the U.S. and British economies to those of a car with a defective alternator. Getting the economy running, he argued, would require only a modest repair, not a complete overhaul.

Nice metaphor. But what was the nature of the trouble?

Keynes's Theory

In 1936, Keynes presented his analysis of the Great Depression—his explanation of what was wrong with the economy's alternator—in a book titled *The General Theory of Employment, Interest, and Money*. In 1946, the great American economist Paul Samuelson wrote that "it is a badly written book, poorly organized. . . . Flashes of insight and intuition intersperse tedious algebra. . . . We find its analysis to be obvious and at the same time new. In short, it is a work of genius." *The General Theory* isn't easy reading, but it stands with Adam Smith's *The Wealth of Nations* as one of the most influential books on economics ever written.

St. Louis Federal Reserve Bank Resources

"Dealing with the Great Depression," ***The Great Depression Curriculum Unit*****, Lesson 4**

In this lesson, students learn about programs initiated through the New Deal. By comparing and categorizing New Deal programs, they recognize that the value of most of these programs was their effects on the confidence that U.S. citizens had in the economy. Students also identify the impact that these programs had on the role of the U.S. government in the economy.

As Samuelson's description suggests, Keynes's book is a vast stew of ideas. **Keynesian economics** mainly reflected two innovations. First, Keynes emphasized the short-run effects of shifts in aggregate demand on aggregate output, rather than the long-run determination of the aggregate price level. As Keynes's famous remark about being dead in the long run suggests, until his book appeared, most economists had treated short-run macroeconomics as a minor issue. Keynes focused the attention of economists on situations in which the short-run aggregate supply curve slopes upward and shifts in the aggregate demand curve affect aggregate output and employment as well as aggregate prices.

Keynesian economics focuses on the ability of shifts in aggregate demand to influence aggregate output in the short run.

Figure 35.1 illustrates the difference between Keynesian and classical macroeconomics. Both panels of the figure show the short-run aggregate supply curve, *SRAS*; in both it is assumed that for some reason the aggregate demand curve shifts leftward from AD_1 to AD_2—let's say in response to a fall in stock market prices that leads households to reduce consumer spending.

Figure 35.1 Classical Versus Keynesian Macroeconomics

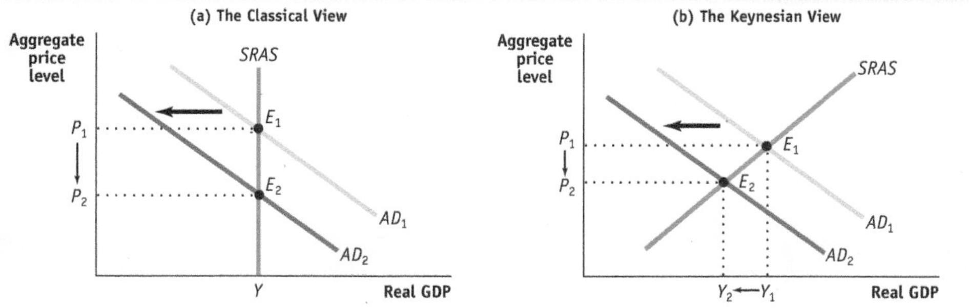

One important difference between classical and Keynesian economics involves the short-run aggregate supply curve. Panel (a) shows the classical view: the *SRAS* curve is vertical, so shifts in aggregate demand affect the aggregate price level but not aggregate output. Panel (b) shows the Keynesian view: in the short run the *SRAS* curve slopes upward, so shifts in aggregate demand affect aggregate output as well as aggregate prices.

Panel (a) shows the classical view: the short-run aggregate supply curve is vertical. The decline in aggregate demand leads to a fall in the aggregate price level, from P_1 to P_2, but no change in aggregate output. Panel (b) shows the Keynesian view: the short-run aggregate supply curve slopes upward, so the decline in aggregate demand leads to both a fall in the aggregate price level, from P_1 to P_2, and a fall in aggregate output, from Y_1 to Y_2. As we've already explained, many classical macroeconomists would have agreed that panel (b) was an accurate story in the short run—but they regarded the short run as unimportant. Keynes disagreed. (Just to be clear, there isn't any diagram that looks like panel (b) of Figure 35.1 in Keynes's *The General Theory*. But Keynes's discussion of aggregate supply, translated into modern terminology, clearly implies an upward-sloping *SRAS* curve.)

Second, classical economists emphasized the role of changes in the money supply in shifting the aggregate demand curve, paying little attention to other factors. Keynes, however, argued that other factors, especially changes in "animal spirits"—these days usually referred to with the bland term *business confidence*—are mainly responsible for business cycles. Before Keynes, economists often argued that a decline in business

TEACH Teach It

According to the Keynesian model:

- Prices are downwardly inflexible and wages are sticky.
- Short-run shifts in aggregate demand do affect aggregate output and the price level because there is an upward-sloping aggregate supply curve and these short-run shifts are important.
- The government should use fiscal and monetary policy to help smooth out changes in the business cycle.

TEACH Teach It

Use Figure 35.1 to show students the difference between the classical and Keynesian theories.

- Why is *SRAS* vertical in the classical view and upsloping in the Keynesian view? *Classical economists believe prices and wages are fully flexible, so a decrease in the price level is accompanied by a decrease in input prices that eliminates incentives to produce less despite the lower prices. Keynesians believe prices and wages are sticky, so a decrease in the price level is not matched by a decrease in input prices in the short run, and the resulting lower profits provide incentives to produce less in response to the lower prices.*
- How does the decrease in *AD* in each panel change the price level and real GDP? *Only the price level will fall in the classical model, while output remains unchanged. Both the price level and output fall with a decrease in AD according to the Keynesian model.*

FOCUS Flip It

Students can view the Jacob Clifford video "Macro 3.6—Classical vs. Keynesian Aggregate Supply" (see econextras video list with hyperlinks on the bcs and TRFD) to review the discussion of the classical and Keynesian views of the macroeconomy.

TEACH Teach It

Explain to students that Keynesian theories did not take hold in the United States until the Great Depression and World War II. Some of FDR's advisors did not agree with Keynesian theories. Other economists tied the decrease in unemployment to the massive outlays of spending during World War II. Project the chart from the FYI on the board if possible, or direct students to look at the chart. Ask them to explain the relationship between unemployment and deficit spending in their own words. *Unemployment remained high, while government spending was low. When spending increased significantly, unemployment decreased significantly.*

confidence would have no effect on either the aggregate price level or aggregate output, as long as the money supply stayed constant. Keynes offered a very different picture.

Keynes's ideas have penetrated deeply into the public consciousness, to the extent that many people who have never heard of Keynes, or have heard of him but think they disagree with his theory, use Keynesian ideas all the time. For example, suppose that a business commentator says something like this: "Because of a decline in business confidence, investment spending slumped, causing a recession." Whether the commentator knows it or not, that statement is pure Keynesian economics.

Keynes himself more or less predicted that his ideas would become part of what "everyone knows." In another famous passage, this from the end of *The General Theory*, he wrote: "Practical men, who believe themselves to be quite exempt from any intellectual influences, are usually the slaves of some defunct economist."

Policy to Fight Recessions

Macroeconomic policy activism is the use of monetary and fiscal policy to smooth out the business cycle.

The main practical consequence of Keynes's work was that it legitimized **macroeconomic policy activism**—the use of monetary and fiscal policy to smooth out the business cycle.

Macroeconomic policy activism wasn't something completely new. Before Keynes, many economists had argued for using monetary expansion to fight economic downturns—though others were fiercely opposed. Some economists had even argued that temporary budget deficits were a good thing in times of recession—though others disagreed strongly. In practice, during the 1930s many governments followed policies that we would now call Keynesian. In the United States, the administration of Franklin Roosevelt engaged in modest deficit spending in an effort to create jobs.

But these efforts were half-hearted. Roosevelt's advisers were deeply divided over the appropriate policies to adopt. In fact, in 1937 Roosevelt gave in to advice from

FYI The End of the Great Depression

It would make a good story if Keynes's ideas had led to a change in economic policy that brought the Great Depression to an end. Unfortunately, that's not what happened. Still, the way the Depression ended did a lot to convince economists that Keynes was right.

The basic message many of the young economists who adopted Keynes's ideas in the 1930s took from his work was that economic recovery requires aggressive fiscal expansion—deficit spending on a large scale to create jobs. And that is what they eventually got, but it wasn't because politicians were persuaded. Instead, what happened was a very large and expensive war, World War II.

The figure here shows the U.S. unemployment rate and the federal budget deficit as a share of GDP from 1930 to 1947. As you can see, deficit spending during the 1930s was on a modest scale. In 1940, as the risk of war grew larger, the United States began a large military buildup, and the budget moved deep into deficit. After the attack on Pearl Harbor on December 7, 1941, the country began deficit spending on an enormous scale: in fiscal 1943, which began in July 1942, the deficit was 30% of GDP. Today that would be a deficit of $4.3 trillion.

And the economy recovered. World War II wasn't intended as a Keynesian fiscal policy, but it demonstrated that expansionary fiscal policy can, in fact, create jobs in the short run.

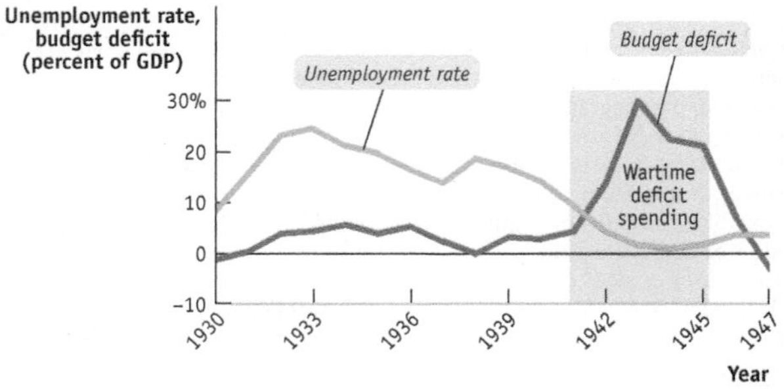

Source: U.S. Census Bureau.

344 Section 6 Inflation, Unemployment, and Stabilization Policies

non-Keynesian economists who urged him to balance the budget and raise interest rates, even though the economy was still depressed. The result was a renewed slump.

Today, by contrast, there is broad consensus about the useful role monetary and fiscal policy can play in fighting recessions. The 2004 Economic Report of the President was issued by a conservative Republican administration that was generally opposed to government intervention in the economy. Yet its view on economic policy in the face of recession was far more like that of Keynes than like that of most economists before 1936.

It would be wrong, however, to suggest that Keynes's ideas have been fully accepted by modern macroeconomists. In the decades that followed the publication of *The General Theory*, Keynesian economics faced a series of challenges, some of which succeeded in modifying the macroeconomic consensus in important ways.

Challenges to Keynesian Economics

Keynes's ideas fundamentally changed the way economists think about business cycles. However, they did not go unquestioned. In the decades that followed the publication of *The General Theory*, Keynesian economics faced a series of challenges. As a result, the consensus of macroeconomists retreated somewhat from the strong version of Keynesianism that prevailed in the 1950s. In particular, economists became much more aware of the limits to macroeconomic policy activism.

The Revival of Monetary Policy

Keynes's *The General Theory* suggested that monetary policy wouldn't be very effective in depression conditions. Many modern macroeconomists agree: earlier we introduced the concept of a *liquidity trap*, a situation in which monetary policy is ineffective because the interest rate is down against the zero bound. In the 1930s, when Keynes wrote, interest rates, in fact, were very close to 0%. (The term *liquidity trap* was first introduced by the British economist John Hicks in a 1937 paper, "Mr. Keynes and the Classics: A Suggested Interpretation," that summarized Keynes's ideas.)

But even when the era of near-0% interest rates came to an end after World War II, many economists continued to emphasize fiscal policy and downplay the usefulness of monetary policy. Eventually, however, macroeconomists reassessed the importance of monetary policy. A key milestone in this reassessment was the 1963 publication of *A Monetary History of the United States, 1867–1960* by Milton Friedman, of the University of Chicago, and Anna Schwartz, of the National Bureau of Economic Research. Friedman and Schwartz showed that business cycles had historically been associated with fluctuations in the money supply. In particular, the money supply fell sharply during the onset of the Great Depression. Friedman and Schwartz persuaded many, though not all, economists that the Great Depression could have been avoided if the Federal Reserve had acted to prevent that monetary contraction. They persuaded most economists that monetary policy should play a key role in economic management.

Roger Ressmeyer/Corbis; Teresa Zabala/The New York Times

Milton Friedman and his co-author Anna Schwartz played a key role in convincing macroeconomists of the importance of monetary policy.

The revival of interest in monetary policy was significant because it suggested that the burden of managing the economy could be shifted away from fiscal policy—meaning that economic management could largely be taken out of the hands of politicians. Fiscal policy, which must involve changing tax rates or government spending, necessitates political choices. If the government tries

TEACH Teach It

Tell students that as politicians from both political parties are swayed by lobbyists, fiscal policy decisions may be made that are not in the best interest of society. This is one of the reasons some people are skeptical of Keynesian policies. Friedman and Schwartz are among that group. They claimed that business cycles had historically been associated with fluctuations in the money supply and showed that the money supply fell sharply during the onset of the Great Depression. They persuaded most economists that monetary policy should play a key role in economic management, which gave rise to a new theory called **monetarism**.

Module 35 History and Alternative Views of Macroeconomics 345

TEACH Teach It

According to the monetarist model:

- GDP will grow steadily if the money supply grows steadily.
- The Fed should target a constant rate of growth of the money supply and maintain that target regardless of any fluctuations in the economy.
- Crowding out does not occur as it would with fiscal policy.

FOCUS Graph It

As a review of crowding out and fiscal policy, have students graph the following on their personal whiteboards or a piece of paper. Ask them to explain the entire process. Suppose government spending increases.

- What happens in the *AD–AS* model? *AD shifts to the right.*
- What happens to output and price level? *They both increase.*
- What happens in the money market? *There is an increase in money demand.*
- What happens to the interest rate? *The interest rate begins to rise.*
- What happens to private investment? *The higher interest rate reduces private investment, which decreases AD.*

Thus, the final effect of expansionary fiscal policy is weakened because private investment is crowded out.

to stimulate the economy by cutting taxes, it must decide whose taxes will be cut. If it tries to stimulate the economy with government spending, it must decide what to spend the money on.

Monetary policy, by contrast, does not involve such choices: when the central bank cuts interest rates to fight a recession, it cuts everyone's interest rate at the same time. So a shift from relying on fiscal policy to relying on monetary policy makes macroeconomics a more technical, less political issue. In fact, monetary policy in most major economies is set by an independent central bank that is insulated from the political process.

Monetarism

Monetarism asserts that GDP will grow steadily if the money supply grows steadily.

After the publication of *A Monetary History*, Milton Friedman led a movement, called *monetarism*, that sought to eliminate macroeconomic policy activism while maintaining the importance of monetary policy. **Monetarism** asserted that GDP will grow steadily if the money supply grows steadily. The monetarist policy prescription was to have the central bank target a constant rate of growth of the money supply, such as 3% per year, and maintain that target regardless of any fluctuations in the economy.

It's important to realize that monetarism retained many Keynesian ideas. Like Keynes, Friedman asserted that the short run is important and that short-run changes in aggregate demand affect aggregate output as well as aggregate prices. Like Keynes, he argued that policy should have been much more expansionary during the Great Depression.

However, monetarists argued that most of the efforts of policy makers to smooth out the business cycle actually make things worse. We have already discussed concerns over the usefulness of *discretionary fiscal policy*—changes in taxes or government spending, or both—in response to the state of the economy. As we explained, government perceptions about the economy often lag behind reality, and there are further lags in changing fiscal policy and in its effects on the economy. As a result, discretionary fiscal policies intended to fight a recession often end up feeding a boom, and vice versa. According to monetarists, **discretionary monetary policy**, changes in the interest rate or the money supply by the central bank in order to stabilize the economy, faces the same problem of lags as fiscal policy, but to a lesser extent.

Discretionary monetary policy is the use of changes in the interest rate or the money supply by the central bank to stabilize the economy.

Friedman also argued that if the central bank followed his advice and refused to change the money supply in response to fluctuations in the economy, fiscal policy would be much less effective than Keynesians believed. Earlier we analyzed the phenomenon of *crowding out*, in which government deficits drive up interest rates and lead to reduced investment spending. Friedman and others pointed out that if the money supply is held fixed while the government pursues an expansionary fiscal policy, crowding out will limit the effect of the fiscal expansion on aggregate demand.

Figure 35.2 illustrates this argument. Panel (a) shows aggregate output and the aggregate price level. AD_1 is the initial aggregate demand curve and *SRAS* is the short-run aggregate supply curve. At the initial equilibrium, E_1, the level of aggregate output is Y_1 and the aggregate price level is P_1. Panel (b) shows the money market. *MS* is the money supply curve and MD_1 is the initial money demand curve, so the initial interest rate is r_1.

Now suppose the government increases purchases of goods and services. We know that this will shift the *AD* curve rightward, as illustrated by the shift from AD_1 to AD_2; that aggregate output will rise, from Y_1 to Y_2, and that the aggregate price level will rise, from P_1 to P_2. Both the rise in aggregate output and the rise in the aggregate price level, however, will increase the demand for money, shifting the money demand curve rightward from MD_1 to MD_2. This drives up the equilibrium interest rate to r_2. Friedman's point was that this rise in the interest rate reduces investment spending, partially offsetting the initial rise in government spending. As a result, the rightward shift of the *AD* curve is smaller than multiplier analysis indicates. And Friedman argued that with a constant money supply, the multiplier is so small that there's not much point in using fiscal policy.

But Friedman didn't favor activist monetary policy either. He argued that the problem of time lags that limit the ability of discretionary fiscal policy to stabilize the economy also apply to discretionary monetary policy. Friedman's solution was

346 Section 6 Inflation, Unemployment, and Stabilization Policies

Figure 35.2 Fiscal Policy with a Fixed Money Supply

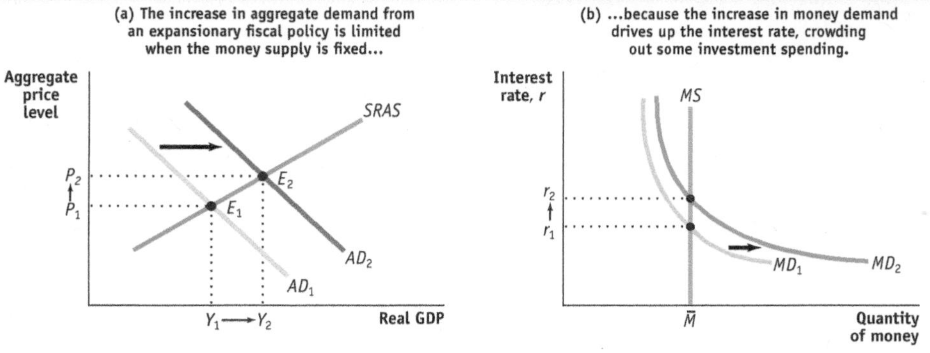

In panel (a) an expansionary fiscal policy shifts the *AD* curve rightward, driving up both the aggregate price level and aggregate output. However, this leads to an increase in the demand for money. If the money supply is held fixed, as in panel (b), the increase in money demand drives up the interest rate, reducing investment spending and offsetting part of the fiscal expansion. So the shift of the *AD* curve is less than it would otherwise be: fiscal policy becomes less effective when the money supply is held fixed.

to put monetary policy on "autopilot." The central bank, he argued, should follow a **monetary policy rule**, a formula that determines its actions and leaves it relatively little discretion. During the 1960s and 1970s, most monetarists favored a monetary policy rule of slow, steady growth in the money supply. Underlying this view was the **Quantity Theory of Money**, which relies on the concept of the **velocity of money**, the ratio of nominal GDP to the money supply. Velocity is a measure of the number of times the average dollar bill in the economy turns over per year between buyers and sellers (e.g., I tip the Starbucks barista a dollar, she uses it to buy lunch, and so on). This concept gives rise to the *velocity equation*:

$$M \times V = P \times Y \quad \textbf{(35-1)}$$

Where M is the money supply, V is velocity, P is the aggregate price level, and Y is real GDP.

Monetarists believed, with considerable historical justification, that the velocity of money was stable in the short run and changed only slowly in the long run. As a result, they claimed, steady growth in the money supply by the central bank would ensure steady growth in spending, and therefore in GDP.

Monetarism strongly influenced actual monetary policy in the late 1970s and early 1980s. It quickly became clear, however, that steady growth in the money supply didn't ensure steady growth in the economy: the velocity of money wasn't stable enough for such a simple policy rule to work. **Figure 35.3** on the next page shows how events eventually undermined the monetarists' view. The figure shows the velocity of money, as measured by the ratio of nominal GDP to M1, from 1960 to the middle of 2013. As you can see, until 1980, velocity followed a fairly smooth, seemingly predictable trend. After the Fed began to adopt monetarist ideas in the late 1970s and early 1980s, however, the velocity of money began moving erratically—probably due to financial market innovations.

A **monetary policy rule** is a formula that determines the central bank's actions.

The **Quantity Theory of Money** emphasizes the positive relationship between the price level and the money supply. It relies on the velocity equation ($M \times V = P \times Y$).

The **velocity of money** is the ratio of nominal GDP to the money supply. It is a measure of the number of times the average dollar bill is spent per year.

St. Louis Federal Reserve Bank Resources

"Money and Inflation," ***Feducation Video Series*****, Episode 1**

How are the money supply and inflation related? And what does the Federal Reserve have to do with this relationship? This video reviews the functions of money, features an interactive auction that demonstrates the relationship between the money supply and inflation, then utilizes a simple equation to show how changes in the money supply affect the economy. The video also describes how the Fed uses monetary policy to achieve its dual mandate of maximum employment and price stability.

TEACH AP® Exam Tip

Make sure students have been exposed to the velocity equation and know what each part is. This equation is sometimes called the equation of exchange. It states that the money supply multiplied by the number of times the average dollar is spent per year equals the total value of goods and services sold. The formula is $MV = PY$, where M is the M1 money supply and V is the velocity of money. P is the aggregate price level and Y is real GDP. (On older AP® exams, Q was used rather than Y.) Together, PY is nominal GDP. This formula sometimes shows up in the multiple-choice section of the AP® exam.

FOCUS Flip It

As review, have students watch Jacob Clifford's video "Quantity Theory of Money" (see econextras video list with hyperlinks on the bcs and TRFD). Ask students to explain the relationship between the money supply and the price level according to the Quantity Theory of Money. *There is a direct relationship between the money supply and the price level. If one goes up, the other goes up proportionately.*

FOCUS Active Learning

TRM To provide students with practice using the equation of exchange, assign **Worksheet 35.1 (Quantity Theory of Money)** from the TRM in class or as homework.

Figure 35.3 The Velocity of Money

From 1960 to 1980, the velocity of money was stable, leading monetarists to believe that steady growth in the money supply would lead to a stable economy. After 1980, however, velocity began moving erratically, undermining the case for traditional monetarism. As a result, traditional monetarism fell out of favor.

Sources: Bureau of Economic Analysis; Federal Reserve Bank of St. Louis.

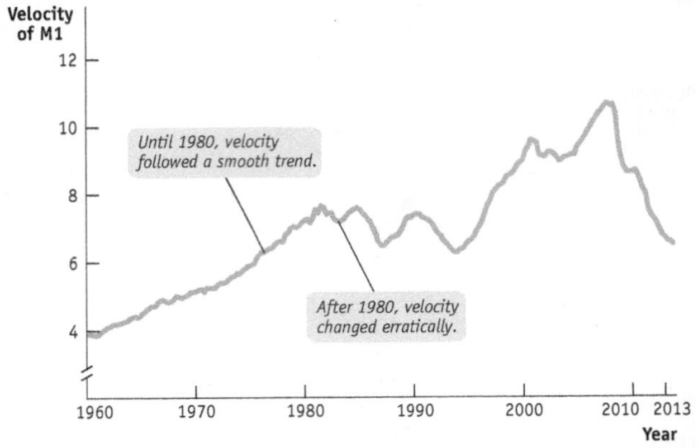

Traditional monetarists are hard to find among today's macroeconomists. As we'll see later, however, the concern that originally motivated the monetarists—that too much discretionary monetary policy can actually destabilize the economy—has become widely accepted.

Inflation and the Natural Rate of Unemployment

At the same time that monetarists were challenging Keynesian views about how macroeconomic policy should be conducted, a somewhat broader group of economists was emphasizing the limits to what activist macroeconomic policy could achieve.

In the 1940s and 1950s, many Keynesian economists believed that expansionary fiscal policy could be used to achieve full employment on a permanent basis. In the 1960s, however, many economists realized that expansionary policies could cause problems with inflation, but they still believed policy makers could choose to trade off low unemployment for higher inflation even in the long run.

In 1968, however, Edmund Phelps of Columbia University and Milton Friedman, working independently, proposed the concept of the natural rate of unemployment. In Module 34 we saw that the natural rate of unemployment is also the nonaccelerating inflation rate of unemployment, or NAIRU. According to the **natural rate hypothesis**, because inflation is eventually embedded in expectations, to avoid accelerating inflation over time, the unemployment rate must be high enough that the actual inflation rate equals the expected rate of inflation. Attempts to keep the unemployment rate below the natural rate will lead to an ever-rising inflation rate.

According to the **natural rate hypothesis**, to avoid accelerating inflation over time, the unemployment rate must be high enough that the actual inflation rate equals the expected inflation rate.

The natural rate hypothesis limits the role of activist macroeconomic policy compared to earlier theories. Because the government can't keep unemployment below the natural rate, its task is not to keep unemployment low but to keep it *stable*—to prevent large fluctuations in unemployment in either direction.

The Friedman-Phelps hypothesis made a strong prediction: that the apparent tradeoff between unemployment and inflation would not survive an extended period of rising prices. Once inflation was embedded in the public's expectations, inflation would continue even in the face of high unemployment. Sure enough, that's exactly what happened in the 1970s. This accurate prediction was one of the triumphs of macroeconomic

TEACH Connect It

This is a good opportunity to use the Phillips curve to review how higher inflation becomes embedded in expectations. In order to avoid accelerating inflation over time, the unemployment rate must be high enough so that actual inflation equals the expected inflation rate.

348 Section 6 Inflation, Unemployment, and Stabilization Policies analysis, and it convinced the great majority of economists that the natural rate hypothesis was correct. In contrast to traditional monetarism, which declined in influence as more evidence accumulated, the natural rate hypothesis has become almost universally accepted among macroeconomists, with a few qualifications. (Some macroeconomists believe that at very low or negative rates of inflation the hypothesis doesn't work.)

The Political Business Cycle

One final challenge to Keynesian economics focused not on the validity of the economic analysis but on its political consequences. A number of economists and political scientists pointed out that activist macroeconomic policy lends itself to political manipulation.

Statistical evidence suggests that election results tend to be determined by the state of the economy in the months just before the election. In the United States, if the economy is growing rapidly and the unemployment rate is falling in the six months or so before Election Day, the incumbent party tends to be re-elected even if the economy performed poorly in the preceding three years.

This creates an obvious temptation to abuse activist macroeconomic policy: pump up the economy in an election year, and pay the price in higher inflation and/or higher unemployment later. The result can be unnecessary instability in the economy, a **political business cycle** caused by the use of macroeconomic policy to serve political ends.

A **political business cycle** results when politicians use macroeconomic policy to serve political ends.

An often-cited example is the combination of expansionary fiscal and monetary policy that led to rapid growth in the U.S. economy just before the 1972 election and a sharp acceleration in inflation after the election. Kenneth Rogoff, a respected macroeconomist who served as chief economist at the International Monetary Fund, proclaimed Richard Nixon, the president at the time, "the all-time hero of political business cycles."

One way to avoid a political business cycle is to place monetary policy in the hands of an independent central bank, insulated from political pressure. The political business cycle is also a reason to limit the use of discretionary fiscal policy to extreme circumstances.

Win McNamee/Getty Images

Election results tend to be determined by the state of the economy in the months just before the election.

Rational Expectations, Real Business Cycles, and New Classical Macroeconomics

As we have seen, one key difference between classical economics and Keynesian economics is that classical economists believed that the short-run aggregate supply curve is vertical, but Keynes emphasized the idea that the aggregate supply curve slopes upward in the short run. As a result, Keynes argued that demand shocks—shifts in the aggregate demand curve—can cause fluctuations in aggregate output.

The challenges to Keynesian economics that arose in the 1950s and 1960s—the renewed emphasis on monetary policy and the natural rate hypothesis—didn't question the view that an increase in aggregate demand leads to a rise in aggregate output in the short run nor that a decrease in aggregate demand leads to a fall in aggregate output in the short run. In the 1970s and 1980s, however, some economists developed an approach to the business cycle known as **new classical macroeconomics**, which returned to the classical view that shifts in the aggregate demand curve affect only the aggregate price level, not aggregate output. The new approach evolved in two steps. First, some economists challenged traditional arguments about the slope of the short-run aggregate supply curve based on the concept of *rational expectations*. Second, some

New classical macroeconomics is an approach to the business cycle that returns to the classical view that shifts in the aggregate demand curve affect only the aggregate price level, not aggregate output.

TEACH Connect It

Ask students if they can figure out how fiscal policy might be used around election time. *Often, prior to an election, the government either cuts taxes or announces new spending programs. These policies put more money in the pockets of voters and also tend to lower the unemployment rate. The eventual cost is inflation, but by then the election is over and inflation can be addressed at a later date.* This is an argument that monetarists use to justify using only monetary policy.

Module 35 History and Alternative Views of Macroeconomics **349**

TEACH Teach It

According to the rational expectations model:

- Instability in the economy is caused by unanticipated *AD* and *AS* shocks in the short run.
- Monetary or fiscal policy will have no effect on output because rational consumers will build changes into their expectations.

TEACH Teach It

According to the real business cycle model:

- Aggregate supply curve is vertical, so *AS* shocks change the business cycle.
- A recession occurs when a slowdown in productivity growth shifts the aggregate supply curve leftward.
- A recovery occurs when a pickup in productivity growth shifts the aggregate supply curve rightward.

economists suggested that changes in productivity caused economic fluctuations, a view known as *real business cycle theory*.

Rational Expectations

Rational expectations is the view that individuals and firms make decisions optimally, using all available information.

In the 1970s, a concept known as *rational expectations* had a powerful impact on macroeconomics. **Rational expectations**, a theory originally introduced by John Muth in 1961, is the view that individuals and firms make decisions optimally, using all available information.

For example, workers and employers bargaining over long-term wage contracts need to estimate the inflation rate they expect over the life of that contract. Rational expectations says that in making estimates of future inflation, they won't just look at past rates of inflation; they will also take into account available information about monetary and fiscal policy. Suppose that prices didn't rise last year, but that the monetary and fiscal policies announced by policy makers made it clear to economic analysts that there would be substantial inflation over the next few years. According to rational expectations, long-term wage contracts will be adjusted today to reflect this future inflation, even though prices didn't rise in the past.

Rational expectations can make a major difference to the effects of government policy. According to the original version of the natural rate hypothesis, a government attempt to trade off higher inflation for lower unemployment would work in the short run but would eventually fail because higher inflation would get built into expectations. According to rational expectations, we should remove the word *eventually*: if it's clear that the government intends to trade off higher inflation for lower unemployment, the public will understand this, and expected inflation will immediately rise.

In the 1970s, Robert Lucas of the University of Chicago, in a series of highly influential papers, used this logic to argue that monetary policy can change the level of unemployment only if it comes as a surprise to the public. If his analysis was right, monetary policy isn't useful in stabilizing the economy after all. In 1995 Lucas won the Nobel Prize in economics for this work, which remains widely admired. However, many—perhaps most—macroeconomists, especially those advising policy makers, now believe that his conclusions were overstated. The Federal Reserve certainly thinks that it can play a useful role in economic stabilization.

According to **new Keynesian economics**, market imperfections can lead to price stickiness for the economy as a whole.

Why, in the view of many macroeconomists, doesn't the rational expectations hypothesis accurately describe how the economy behaves? **New Keynesian economics**, a set of ideas that became influential in the 1990s, provides an explanation. It argues that market imperfections interact to make many prices in the economy temporarily sticky. For example, one new Keynesian argument points out that monopolists don't have to be too careful about setting prices exactly "right": if they set a price a bit too high, they'll lose some sales but make more profit on each sale; if they set the price too low, they'll reduce the profit per sale but sell more. As a result, even small costs to changing prices can lead to substantial price stickiness and make the economy as a whole behave in a Keynesian fashion.

Over time, new Keynesian ideas combined with actual experience have reduced the practical influence of the rational expectations concept. Nonetheless, the idea of rational expectations served as a useful caution for macroeconomists who had become excessively optimistic about their ability to manage the economy.

Real Business Cycles

Real business cycle theory claims that fluctuations in the rate of growth of total factor productivity cause the business cycle.

Earlier we introduced the concept of *total factor productivity*, the amount of output that can be generated with a given level of factor inputs. Total factor productivity grows over time, but that growth isn't smooth. In the 1980s, a number of economists argued that slowdowns in productivity growth, which they attributed to pauses in technological progress, are the main cause of recessions. **Real business cycle theory** claims that fluctuations in the rate of growth of total factor productivity cause the business cycle.

FOCUS Active Learning

TRM This unit can be completed as a jigsaw activity using **Worksheet 35.2 (Alternate Theories)** from the TRM. Place students in groups and have them become experts on one economic view, and then have them teach each of the other groups the material related to their view. Alternately, Worksheet 35.2 can be filled out in class or as homework.

OPEN & CLOSE Exit Slip

TRM *Please see* ***Exit Slip: Module 35*** *in the TRM for formative multiple-choice questions to ask your students before finishing your lesson. These questions will help you quickly assess whether your students have mastered the module's concepts before moving on.*

Answers to the Exit Slip Questions

1. C
2. D
3. A

Believing that the aggregate supply curve is vertical, real business cycle theorists attribute the source of business cycles to shifts of the aggregate supply curve: a recession occurs when a slowdown in productivity growth shifts the aggregate supply curve leftward, and a recovery occurs when a pickup in productivity growth shifts the aggregate supply curve rightward. In the early days of real business cycle theory, the theory's proponents denied that changes in aggregate demand had any effect on aggregate output.

This theory was strongly influential, as shown by the fact that two of the founders of real business cycle theory, Finn Kydland of Carnegie Mellon University and Edward Prescott of the Federal Reserve Bank of Minneapolis, won the 2004 Nobel Prize in economics. The current status of real business cycle theory, however, is somewhat similar to that of rational expectations. The theory is widely recognized as having made valuable contributions to our understanding of the economy, and it serves as a useful caution against too much emphasis on aggregate demand. But many of the real business cycle theorists themselves now acknowledge that their models need an upward-sloping aggregate supply curve to fit the economic data—and that this gives aggregate demand a potential role in determining aggregate output. And as we have seen, policy makers strongly believe that aggregate demand policy has an important role to play in fighting recessions.

MODULE 35 Review

Check Your Understanding

1. The figure below shows the behavior of M1 before, during, and after the 2001 recession. What would a classical economist have said about the Fed's policy?

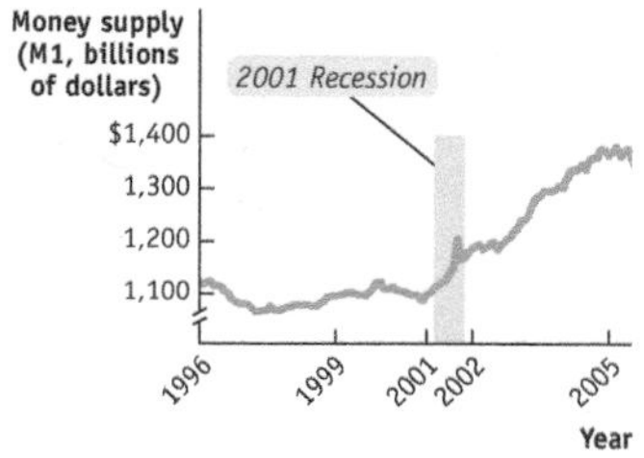

2. What would the figure in Question 1 have looked like if the Fed had been following a monetarist policy since 1996?
3. Now look at Figure 35.3, which shows the path of the velocity of money. What problems do you think the United States would have had since 1996 if the Fed had followed a monetarist policy?
4. In addition to praising aggressive monetary policy, the 2004 Economic Report of the President says that "tax cuts can boost economic activity by raising after-tax income and enhancing incentives to work, save, and invest." Which part of the report is a Keynesian statement and which part is not? Explain your answer.
5. In early 2001, as it became clear that the United States was experiencing a recession, the Fed stated that it would fight the recession with an aggressive monetary policy. By 2004, most observers concluded that this aggressive monetary expansion should be given credit for ending the recession.
   a. What would rational expectations theorists say about this conclusion?
   b. What would real business cycle theorists say?

Tackle the Test: Multiple-Choice Questions

1. Which of the following was a point made in Keynes's influential work?
   I. In the short run, shifts in aggregate demand affect aggregate output.
   II. Animal spirits are an important determinant of business cycles.
   III. In the long run we're all dead.

   a. I only
   b. II only
   c. III only
   d. I and II only
   e. I, II, and III

Tackle the Test: Multiple-Choice Questions

1. e

Answers to Module 35 Review Questions

Check Your Understanding

1. A classical economist would have said that the aggressive monetary expansion would have had no short-run effect on aggregate output and would simply have resulted in a proportionate increase in the aggregate price level.

2. Monetarists argue that central banks should implement policy so that the money supply grows at some constant rate. Had the Fed pursued a monetarist policy during this period, we would have observed movements in M1 that would have shown a fixed rate of growth. Therefore, we would not have observed any of the reductions in M1 that are observed in the figure, nor would we have observed the acceleration in the rate of growth of M1 that occurred in 2001.

3. As in Problem 2, a monetarist policy would have resulted in a constant rate of growth in M1. Between 1996 and 2000, the velocity of M1 rose steadily. After 2000, the velocity leveled off a bit and then rose again. Given a constant rate of money growth, these increases in the velocity of M1 would have been expansionary, causing increases in aggregate demand and the aggregate price level, other things being equal.

4. The advocacy of fiscal policy (here in the form of tax cuts) to boost economic activity is Keynesian because Keynes promoted fiscal policy as a useful tool to dampen fluctuations in the business cycle. The praise of aggressive monetary policy is not Keynesian because Keynes worried that a liquidity trap would thwart the ability of monetary policy to change interest rates and influence investment spending.

5. a. Rational expectations theorists would argue that only unexpected changes in money supply would have any short-run effect on economic activity. They would also argue that expected changes in the money supply would affect only the aggregate price level, with no short-run effect of aggregate output. Thus, such theorists would give credit to the Fed for limiting the severity of the 2001 recession only if the Fed's monetary policy had been more aggressive than individuals expected during this period.

b. Real business cycle theorists would argue that the Fed's policy had no effect on ending the 2001 recession because they believe that fluctuations in aggregate output are caused largely by changes in total factor productivity.

2. d
3. b
4. a
5. d

Tackle the Test: Free-Response Question

Rubric for FRQ 2 (6 points)

1 point: The aggregate supply curve is vertical, so changes in the money supply affect only the aggregate price level.

1 point: Changes in aggregate demand will affect aggregate output.

1 point: Business cycles are associated with fluctuations in the money supply.

1 point: To avoid inflation, the unemployment rate must be set so that actual inflation equals expected inflation.

1 point: Individuals and firms make optimal decisions using all available information.

1 point: Fluctuations in total factor productivity growth cause business cycles.

2. Which of the following is a central point of monetarism?
- **a.** Business cycles are associated with fluctuations in money demand.
- **b.** Activist monetary policy is the best way to address business cycles.
- **c.** Discretionary monetary policy is effective while discretionary fiscal policy is not.
- **d.** The Fed should follow a monetary policy rule.
- **e.** All of the above.

3. The natural rate hypothesis says that the unemployment rate should be
- **a.** below the NAIRU.
- **b.** high enough that the actual rate of inflation equals the expected rate.
- **c.** as close to zero as possible.
- **d.** 5%.
- **e.** left wherever the economy sets it.

4. The main difference between the classical model of the price level and Keynesian economics is that
- **a.** the classical model assumes a vertical short-run aggregate supply curve.
- **b.** Keynesian economics assumes a vertical short-run aggregate supply curve.
- **c.** the classical model assumes an upward-sloping long-run aggregate supply curve.
- **d.** Keynesian economics assumes a vertical long-run aggregate supply curve.
- **e.** the classical model assumes that aggregate demand cannot change in the long run.

5. That fluctuations in total factor productivity growth cause the business cycle is the main tenet of which theory?
- **a.** Keynesian
- **b.** classical
- **c.** rational expectations
- **d.** real business cycle
- **e.** natural rate

Tackle the Test: Free-Response Questions

1. a. According to monetarism, business cycles are associated with fluctuations in what?
- **b.** Does monetarism advocate discretionary fiscal policy? Discretionary monetary policy?
- **c.** What monetary policy does monetarism suggest?
- **d.** What is the velocity equation? Indicate what each letter in the equation stands for.
- **e.** Use the velocity equation to explain the major conclusion of monetarism.

Rubric for FRQ 1 (10 points)

1 point: The money supply
1 point: No
1 point: No
1 point: A monetary policy rule
1 point: $M \times V = P \times Y$
1 point: M is the money supply.
1 point: V is the velocity of money.
1 point: P is the aggregate price level.
1 point: Y is real GDP.
1 point: Since V is stable, a steady growth of M will lead to a steady growth in GDP.

2. For each of the following economic theories, identify its fundamental conclusion.
- **a.** the classical model of the price level
- **b.** Keynesian economics
- **c.** monetarism
- **d.** the natural rate hypothesis
- **e.** rational expectations
- **f.** real business cycle theory

(6 points)

352 **Section 6** Inflation, Unemployment, and Stabilization Policies

Pete Souza/The White House via Getty Images

MODULE 36 Consensus and Conflict in Modern Macroeconomics

In this Module, you will learn to:

- List and describe the elements of the modern macroeconomic consensus
- Explain the main remaining disputes

The Modern Consensus

The 1970s and the first half of the 1980s were a stormy period for the U.S. economy (and for other major economies, too). There was a severe recession in 1974–1975, then two back-to-back recessions in 1979–1982 that sent the unemployment rate to almost 11%. At the same time, the inflation rate soared into double digits—and then plunged. As we have seen, these events left a strong mark on macroeconomic thought.

After about 1985, however, the economy settled down. The recession of 1990–1991 was much milder than the 1974–1975 recession or the double-dip slump from 1979 to 1982, and the inflation rate generally stayed below 4%. The period of relative calm in the economy from 1985 to 2007 came to be known as the *Great Moderation*. To a large extent, the calmness of the economy was marked by a similar calm in macroeconomic policy discussion. In fact, it seemed that a broad consensus had emerged about several key macroeconomic issues.

Unfortunately, the Great Moderation was followed by the *Great Recession*, the severe and persistent slump that followed the 2008 financial crisis. We'll talk shortly about the policy disputes caused by the Great Recession. First, however, let's examine the apparent consensus that emerged during the Great Moderation. It combines a belief in monetary policy as the main tool of stabilization, with skepticism toward the use of fiscal policy, and an acknowledgement of the policy constraints imposed by the natural rate of unemployment and the political business cycle.

To understand the modern consensus, where it came from, and what still remains in dispute, we'll look at how macroeconomists have changed their answers to five key questions about macroeconomic policy. The five questions, and the answers given by macroeconomists over the past 70 years, are summarized in **Table 36.1** on the next page. (In the table, new classical economics is subsumed under classical economics, and new Keynesian economics is subsumed under the modern consensus.) Notice that

PD To prepare for teaching this lesson, you may want to consult the **Module 36 Sample Lecture** in the TRM.

OPEN & CLOSE Start Here

Hold a panel discussion with the four economists who were studied in the last module. Select four students to play the roles of Smith, Keynes, Friedman, and a modern-day economist. Have each student in the audience submit three questions to ask the economists. Pick two or three questions and ask each of the panel members to answer in the persona of the economist he or she represents.

TEACH Teach It

The material in this module is rarely included on the AP® Exam. Make sure students understand the modern consensus, but if time is an issue, this content can be compacted and taught in tandem with the previous module.

TEACH Teach It

Use Table 36.1 to discuss and review the effectiveness of discretionary monetary and fiscal policy in correcting recessionary gaps.

TEACH Teach It

Let students know that although there are varying degrees of consensus among economists, areas of disagreement still exist. The source of disagreements normally arises from normative questions that involve value judgments or political beliefs. In fact, students' own values and political beliefs will impact their responses to normative questions.

Table 36.1 Five Key Questions About Macroeconomic Policy

	Classical macroeconomics	Keynesian macroeconomics	Monetarism	Modern consensus
Is expansionary monetary policy helpful in fighting recessions?	No	Not very	Yes	Yes, except in special circumstances
Is expansionary fiscal policy effective in fighting recessions?	No	Yes	No	Yes
Can monetary and/or fiscal policy reduce unemployment in the long run?	No	Yes	No	No
Should fiscal policy be used in a discretionary way?	No	Yes	No	No, except in special circumstances
Should monetary policy be used in a discretionary way?	No	Yes	No	Still in dispute

classical macroeconomics said no to each question; basically, classical macroeconomists didn't think macroeconomic policy could accomplish very much. But let's go through the questions one by one.

Is Expansionary Monetary Policy Helpful in Fighting Recessions?

As we've seen, classical macroeconomists generally believed that expansionary monetary policy was ineffective or even harmful in fighting recessions. In the early years of Keynesian economics, macroeconomists weren't against monetary expansion during recessions, but they tended to believe that it was of doubtful effectiveness. Milton Friedman and his followers convinced economists that monetary policy was effective after all.

Nearly all macroeconomists now agree that monetary policy can be used to shift the aggregate demand curve and to reduce economic instability. The classical view that changes in the money supply affect only aggregate prices, not aggregate output, has few supporters today. The view once held by some Keynesian economists—that changes in the money supply have little effect—has equally few supporters. Now, it is generally agreed that monetary policy is ineffective only in the case of a liquidity trap.

Is Expansionary Fiscal Policy Effective in Fighting Recessions?

Classical macroeconomists were, if anything, even more opposed to fiscal expansion than to monetary expansion. Keynesian economists, on the other hand, gave fiscal policy a central role in fighting recessions. Monetarists argued that fiscal policy was ineffective as long as the money supply was held constant. But that strong view has become relatively rare.

Most macroeconomists now agree that fiscal policy, like monetary policy, can shift the aggregate demand curve. Most macroeconomists also agree that the government should not seek to balance the budget regardless of the state of the economy: they agree that the role of the budget as an automatic stabilizer helps keep the economy on an even keel.

Can Monetary and/or Fiscal Policy Reduce Unemployment in the Long Run?

Classical macroeconomists didn't believe the government could do anything about unemployment. Some Keynesian economists moved to the opposite extreme, arguing that expansionary policies could be used to achieve a permanently low unemployment rate, perhaps at the cost of some inflation. Monetarists believed that unemployment could not be kept below the natural rate.

Almost all macroeconomists now accept the natural rate hypothesis and agree on the limitations of monetary and fiscal policy. They believe that effective monetary and fiscal policy can limit the size of fluctuations of the actual unemployment rate around the natural rate but can't keep unemployment below the natural rate.

354 Section 6 Inflation, Unemployment, and Stabilization Policies

Should Fiscal Policy Be Used in a Discretionary Way?

As we've already seen, views about the effectiveness of fiscal policy have gone back and forth, from rejection by classical macroeconomists, to a positive view by Keynesian economists, to a negative view once again by monetarists. Today, most macroeconomists believe that tax cuts and spending increases are at least somewhat effective in increasing aggregate demand. However, *discretionary fiscal policy* is subject to the various types of lags discussed in Module 20. All too often, policies intended to fight a slump affect aggregate demand after the economy has turned around, and end up intensifying a boom.

As a result, the macroeconomic consensus gives monetary policy the lead role in economic stabilization. Discretionary fiscal policy plays the leading role only in special circumstances when monetary policy is ineffective and fiscal policy is likely to take effect before the economy has recovered. For example, many macroeconomists favored the use of discretionary fiscal policy in 2008–2010, when interest rates were near the zero bound and the economy was likely to remain depressed for an extended period.

Should Monetary Policy Be Used in a Discretionary Way?

Classical macroeconomists didn't think that monetary policy should be used to fight recessions; Keynesian economists didn't oppose discretionary monetary policy, but they were skeptical about its effectiveness. Monetarists argued that discretionary monetary policy was doing more harm than good. Where are we today? This remains an area of dispute. Today there is a broad consensus among macroeconomists on these points:

- Monetary policy should play the main role in stabilization policy.
- The central bank should be independent, insulated from political pressures, in order to avoid a political business cycle.
- Discretionary fiscal policy should be used sparingly, both because of policy lags and because of the risks of a political business cycle.

However, the Great Moderation was upended by events that posed very difficult questions—questions that rage on to this day. We'll now examine what happened and why the ongoing debate is so fierce.

Crisis and Aftermath

The Great Recession shattered any sense among macroeconomists that they had entered a permanent era of agreement over key policy questions. Given the nature of the slump, however, this should have come as no surprise. Why? Because the severity of the slump arguably made the policies that seemed to work during the Great Moderation inadequate.

During the Great Moderation, there had been broad agreement that the job of stabilizing the economy was best carried out by having the Federal Reserve and its counterparts abroad raise or lower interest rates as the economic situation warranted. But what should be done if the economy is deeply depressed, while the interest rates the Fed normally controls are already close to zero and can go no lower (that is, when the economy is in a liquidity trap)? Some economists called for aggressive discretionary fiscal policy and/or unconventional monetary policies that might achieve results despite the zero lower bound. Others strongly opposed these measures, arguing either that they would be ineffective or that they would produce undesirable side effects.

Brendan Smialowski/Bloomberg via Getty Images

In 2008, the Fed took a series of unconventional monetary policy actions in response to the deepening recession and financial crisis.

The Debate over Fiscal Policy In 2009, a number of governments, including that of the United States, responded with expansionary fiscal policy, or "stimulus," generally taking the form of a mix of temporary spending measures and temporary tax cuts. From the start, however, these efforts were highly controversial.

FOCUS Active Learning

Show the Jacob Clifford video "Fiscal and Monetary Policy" to review the two policy approaches to recessionary and inflationary gaps. Set up groups of students, and allow them to challenge each other to solve the recessionary and inflationary gaps scenarios. Drawing the graphs and explaining the options to stabilize the economy provides a good drill for the AP® Exam.

St. Louis Federal Reserve Bank Resources

"Fiscal and Monetary Policy in Times of Crisis," *Page One Economics Classroom Edition* (March 2011)

To find out more about fiscal and monetary policies—who conducts them, how they work, and their roles during economic downturns—have your students read this issue.

St. Louis Federal Reserve Bank Resources

"Quantitative Easing Explained," *Page One Economics Classroom Edition* (April 2011)

"Quantitative easing" was in the headlines a lot from 2009 to 2011. First, there was QE and then QE2. What exactly is quantitative easing, who does it, and how does it affect the economy? This issue provides the answers.

Module 36 Consensus and Conflict in Modern Macroeconomics **355**

TEACH AP® Exam Tip

Some students become strong advocates of supply-side policy. Advise them not to let their preferences distract them from careful study of the other types of economic policy that often appear on the AP® exam.

FOCUS Active Learning

TRM To provide practice using supply-side policy, have students complete **Worksheet 36.1 (Supply-Side Economics)** from the TRM in class or as homework.

FYI Supply-Side Economics

During the 1970s, a group of economic writers began propounding a view of economic policy that came to be known as "supply-side economics." The core of this view was the belief that reducing tax rates, and so increasing the incentives to work and invest, would have a powerful positive effect on the growth rate of potential output. The supply-siders urged the government to cut taxes without worrying about matching spending cuts: economic growth, they argued, would offset any negative effects from budget deficits. Some supply-siders even argued that a cut in tax *rates* would have such an effect on economic growth that tax *revenues*—the total amount taxpayers pay to the government—would actually rise. That is, some supply-siders argued that the United States was on the wrong side of the *Laffer curve*, a hypothetical relationship between tax rates and total tax revenue that slopes upward (meaning higher taxes bring higher tax revenues) at low tax rates but turns downward (meaning higher taxes bring lower tax revenues) when tax rates are very high, as shown in the figure.

In the 1970s, supply-side economics was enthusiastically supported by the editors of the *Wall Street Journal* and other figures in the media, and it became popular with politicians. In 1980, Ronald Reagan made supply-side economics the basis of his presidential campaign.

Because supply-side economics emphasizes supply rather than demand, and because the supply-siders themselves are harshly critical of Keynesian economics, it might seem as if supply-side theory belongs in our discussion of new classical macroeconomics. But unlike rational expectations and real business cycle theory, supply-side economics is generally dismissed by economic researchers.

The main reason for this dismissal is lack of evidence. Almost all economists agree that tax cuts increase incentives to work and invest, but attempts to estimate these incentive effects indicate that at current U.S. tax levels they aren't nearly strong enough to support the strong claims made by supply-siders. In particular, the supply-side doctrine implies that large tax cuts, such as those implemented by Ronald Reagan in the early 1980s, should sharply raise potential output. Yet estimates of potential output by the Congressional Budget Office and others show no sign of an acceleration in growth after the Reagan tax cuts.

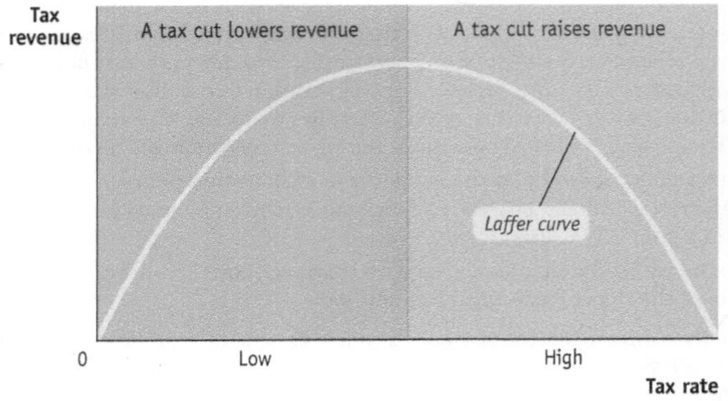

© The New Yorker Collection 2010/Gahan Wilson from cartoonbank.com

"I'll pause for a moment so you can let this information sink in."

Supporters of fiscal stimulus offered three main arguments for breaking with the normal presumption against discretionary fiscal policy:

1. They argued that discretionary fiscal expansion was needed because the usual tool for stabilizing the economy, monetary policy, could no longer be used now that interest rates were near zero.
2. They argued that one normal concern about expansionary fiscal policy—that deficit spending would drive up interest rates, crowding out private investment spending—was unlikely to be a problem in a depressed economy. Again, this was because interest rates were close to zero and likely to stay there as long as the economy was depressed.
3. Finally, they argued that another concern about discretionary fiscal policy—that it might take a long time to get going—was less of a concern than usual given the likelihood that the economy would be depressed for an extended period. These arguments generally won the day in early 2009.

However, opponents of fiscal stimulus raised two main objections:

1. They argued that households and firms would see any rise in government spending as a sign that tax burdens were likely to rise in the future, leading to a fall in

St. Louis Federal Reserve Bank Resources

"Traditional and Non-Traditional Monetary Policy Tools," ***Feducation Video Series*****, Episode 2**

What monetary policy tools did the Federal Reserve use prior to the Great Recession? What did it do differently during and after the Great Recession? This episode includes a simple demonstration of open market operations and a discussion of non-traditional monetary policy tools.

356 **Section 6** Inflation, Unemployment, and Stabilization Policies

private spending that would undo any positive effect. This is known as the *Ricardian equivalence* argument.

2. They also warned that spending programs might undermine investors' faith in the government's ability to repay its debts, leading to an increase in long-term interest rates despite increases in the money supply.

In fact, by 2010 a number of economists were arguing that the best way to boost the economy was actually to cut government spending, which they argued would increase private-sector confidence and lead to a rise in output and employment. This notion, often referred to as the doctrine of "expansionary austerity," was especially popular in Europe, where it was supported by officials at the European Central Bank and became the official policy of the Cameron government in Britain, which took office in the spring of 2010.

Critics of fiscal stimulus pointed out that the U.S. stimulus had failed to deliver a convincing fall in unemployment; stimulus advocates, however, had warned from the start that this was likely to happen because the stimulus was too small compared with the depth of the slump. Meanwhile, austerity programs in Britain and elsewhere had also failed to deliver an economic turnaround and, in fact, had seemed to deepen the slump. Supporters of these programs, however, argued that they were nonetheless necessary to head off a potential collapse of confidence.

One thing that was clear, however, was that those who had predicted a sharp rise in U.S. interest rates due to budget deficits, leading to conventional crowding out, had been wrong: by the fall of 2011, U.S. long-term rates were hitting record lows despite continuing large deficits.

MODULE 36 Review

Check Your Understanding

1. What debates has the modern consensus resolved? What debates has it not resolved?

Tackle the Test: Multiple-Choice Questions

1. Which of the following is an example of an opinion on which economists have reached a broad consensus?
   - I. The natural rate hypothesis holds true.
   - II. Discretionary fiscal policy is usually counterproductive.
   - III. Monetary policy is effective, especially in a liquidity trap.

   a. I only
   b. II only
   c. III only
   d. I and II only
   e. I, II, and III

2. In the FYI box in this module, you learned about supply-side economics. Which of the following is stressed by supply-siders?
   a. Taxes should be increased.
   b. Lower taxes will lead to lower tax revenues.
   c. It is important to increase incentives to work, save, and invest.
   d. The economy operates on the upward-sloping section of the Laffer curve.
   e. Supply-side views are widely supported by empirical evidence.

3. Which of the following was one of the main arguments against using fiscal stimulus during the Great Recession?
   a. Monetary policy could no longer be used because interest rates were so low.
   b. The crowding out of private investment was no longer a problem in the depressed economy.
   c. Implementation lags were less of a concern than usual because the economy was likely to be depressed for an extended period.

OPEN & CLOSE Exit Slip

TRM *Please see **Exit Slip: Module 36** in the TRM for formative multiple-choice questions to ask your students before finishing your lesson. These questions will help you quickly assess whether your students have mastered the module's concepts before moving on.*

Answers to the Exit Slip Questions

1. B
2. B
3. C

Answers to Module 36 Review Questions

Check Your Understanding

1. The modern consensus has resolved the debate over the effectiveness of both expansionary fiscal and monetary policy. Expansionary fiscal policy is considered effective, although it is limited by the problem of time lags, making monetary policy the stabilization tool of choice except in special circumstances. Expansionary monetary policy is considered effective except in the case of a liquidity trap. However, the modern consensus has not resolved the advisability of the Fed's inflation target, and what, if any, kind of unconventional monetary policy it should use in the situation of a liquidity trap.

Tackle the Test: Multiple-Choice Questions

1. d
2. c
3. e

Module 36 Consensus and Conflict in Modern Macroeconomics 357

4. a
5. c

Tackle the Test: Free-Response Question

Rubric for FRQ 2 (3 points)

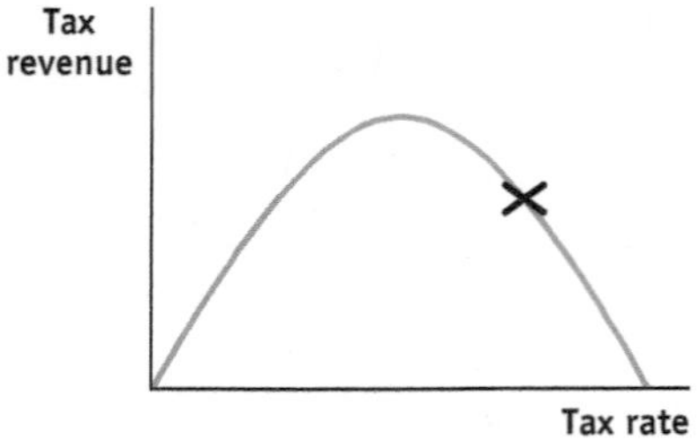

1 point: The vertical axis is labeled "Tax revenue" and the horizontal axis is labeled "Tax rate." (It is also acceptable to have these axes reversed, in which case the Laffer curve begins and ends on the vertical axis and the "X" is on the upper half of the curve.)

1 point: The Laffer curve begins at the origin, rises, and then falls back to the horizontal axis.

1 point: The "X" is to the right of the peak of the Laffer curve.

FOCUS Flip It

Encourage your students to watch the **Section 6 Review Video**, which was created as a special student review tool and is linked into the e-Book or can be found on the book's companion website.

d. Consumers would see an increase in government spending as a signal that the tax burden would decrease in the future, and therefore they would spend more.
e. Spending programs might undermine investors' faith in the government's ability to repay its debts, leading to an increase in long-term interest rates.

4. Which of the following is a major source of disagreement among macroeconomists?
a. The Fed conducted the appropriate amount of quantitative easing during the Great Recession.
b. The central bank should be independent, insulated from political pressures.
c. Discretionary fiscal policy should be used sparingly.
d. Monetary policy should play the main role in stabilization policy.
e. Budget deficits caused high rates of inflation shortly after the Great Recession.

5. Which of the following best describes the 23 years prior to the Great Recession?
a. a period of growing disagreement among macroeconomists
b. a period of high inflation
c. a period of consensus building among economists
d. a period of consistently high unemployment
e. the Great Depression

Tackle the Test: Free-Response Questions

1. What is the consensus view of macroeconomists on each of the following?
a. monetary policy and aggregate demand
b. when monetary policy is ineffective
c. fiscal policy and aggregate demand
d. a balanced budget mandate
e. the effectiveness of discretionary fiscal policy

Rubric for FRQ 1 (5 points)

1 point: Monetary policy can shift aggregate demand in the short run.

1 point: Monetary policy is ineffective when in a liquidity trap.

1 point: Fiscal policy can shift aggregate demand.

1 point: This is not a good idea. Fluctuations in the budget act as an automatic stabilizer for the economy.

1 point: It is usually counterproductive (for example, due to lags in implementation).

2. Draw a correctly labeled graph of the Laffer curve. Use an "x" to identify a point on the curve at which a reduction in tax rates would lead to increased tax revenue. **(3 points)**

SECTION 6 Review

Section 6 Review Video

Module 30

1. Some of the fluctuations in the budget balance are due to the effects of the business cycle. In order to separate the effects of the business cycle from the effects of discretionary fiscal policy, governments estimate the **cyclically adjusted budget balance**, an estimate of the budget balance if the economy were at potential output.

2. U.S. government budget accounting is calculated on the basis of **fiscal years** that run from October 1 to September 30. Annual budget deficits, minus budget surpluses, accumulate into **government debt**. Persistent budget deficits have long-run consequences because they lead to an increase in **public debt**—government debt held by the individuals and institutions outside the government. This can be a problem for two reasons. Public debt may crowd out investment spending, which reduces long-run economic growth. And in extreme cases, rising debt may lead to government default, resulting in economic and financial turmoil.

358 Section 6 Inflation, Unemployment, and Stabilization Policies

3. A widely used measure of fiscal health is the **debt–GDP ratio**. This number can remain stable or fall even in the face of moderate budget deficits if GDP rises over time. However, a stable debt–GDP ratio may give a misleading impression that all is well because modern governments often have large **implicit liabilities**. The largest implicit liabilities of the U.S. government come from Social Security, Medicare, and Medicaid, the costs of which are increasing due to the aging of the population and rising medical costs.

Module 31

4. The Federal Reserve can use monetary policy to change the interest rate. In practice, this involves setting a **target federal funds rate**. **Expansionary monetary policy** reduces the interest rate by increasing the money supply. This increases investment spending and consumer spending, which in turn increases aggregate demand and real GDP in the short run. **Contractionary monetary policy** raises the interest rate by reducing the money supply. This reduces investment spending and consumer spending, which in turn reduces aggregate demand and real GDP in the short run.
5. The Federal Reserve and other central banks try to stabilize their economies, limiting fluctuations of actual output to around potential output, while also keeping inflation low but positive. Under the **Taylor rule for monetary policy**, the target interest rate rises when there is inflation, or a positive output gap, or both; the target interest rate falls when inflation is low or negative, or when the output gap is negative, or both. Some central banks engage in **inflation targeting**, which is a forward-looking policy rule, whereas the Taylor rule is a backward-looking policy rule. In practice, the Fed appears to operate on a loosely defined version of the Taylor rule. In 2012, the Fed adopted an explicit inflation target as well. Because monetary policy is subject to fewer implementation lags than fiscal policy, monetary policy is the preferred policy tool for stabilizing the economy.

Module 32

6. In the long run, changes in the money supply affect the aggregate price level but not real GDP or the interest rate. Data show that the concept of **monetary neutrality** holds: changes in the money supply have no real effect on the economy in the long run.

Module 33

7. In analyzing high inflation, economists use the **classical model of the price level**, which says that changes in the money supply lead to proportional changes in the aggregate price level even in the short run.
8. Governments sometimes print money in order to finance budget deficits. When they do, they impose an **inflation tax**, generating tax revenue equal to the inflation rate times the money supply, on those who hold money. Revenue from the real inflation tax, the inflation rate times the real money supply, is the real value of resources captured by the government. In order to avoid paying the inflation tax, people reduce their real money holdings and force the government to increase inflation to capture the same amount of real inflation tax revenue. In some cases, this leads to a vicious circle of a shrinking real money supply and a rising rate of inflation, leading to hyperinflation and a fiscal crisis.
9. Countries that don't need to print money to cover government deficits can still stumble into moderate inflation. When an increase in the price of a key input such as oil decreases aggregate supply, the result is **cost-push inflation**. Inflation caused by an increase in aggregate demand is called **demand-pull inflation**.
10. A positive output gap is associated with lower-than-normal unemployment; a negative output gap is associated with higher-than-normal unemployment.

Section 6 Review 359

Module 34

11. At a given point in time, there is a downward-sloping relationship between unemployment and inflation known as the **short-run Phillips curve**. This curve is shifted by changes in the expected rate of inflation. The **long-run Phillips curve**, which shows the relationship between unemployment and inflation once expectations have had time to adjust, is vertical. It defines the **nonaccelerating inflation rate of unemployment**, or **NAIRU**, which is equal to the natural rate of unemployment.
12. Once inflation has become embedded in expectations, getting inflation back down can be difficult because disinflation can be very costly, requiring the sacrifice of large amounts of aggregate output and imposing high levels of unemployment. However, policy makers in the United States and other wealthy countries were willing to pay that price of bringing down the high inflation of the 1970s.
13. Deflation poses several problems. It can lead to **debt deflation**, in which a rising real burden of outstanding debt intensifies an economic downturn. Also, interest rates are more likely to run up against the **zero bound** in an economy experiencing deflation. When this happens, the economy enters a **liquidity trap**, rendering conventional monetary policy ineffective.

Module 35

14. Classical macroeconomics asserted that monetary policy affected only the aggregate price level, not aggregate output, and that the short run was unimportant. By the 1930s, measurement of business cycles was a well-established subject, but there was no widely accepted theory of business cycles.
15. **Keynesian economics** attributed the business cycle to shifts of the aggregate demand curve, often the result of changes in business confidence. Keynesian economics also offered a rationale for **macroeconomic policy activism**.
16. In the decades that followed Keynes's work, economists came to agree that monetary policy as well as fiscal policy is effective under certain conditions. **Monetarism** is a doctrine that called for a **monetary policy rule** as opposed to **discretionary monetary policy**. On the basis of the **Quantity Theory of Money** and a belief that the **velocity of money** was stable, monetarists argued that GDP would grow steadily if the money supply grew steadily. This idea was influential for a time but was eventually rejected by many macroeconomists.
17. The **natural rate hypothesis** became almost universally accepted, limiting the role of macroeconomic policy to stabilizing the economy rather than seeking a permanently low unemployment rate. Fears of a **political business cycle** concocted to advance the careers of the politicians in power led to a consensus that monetary policy should be insulated from politics.
18. **Rational expectations** suggests that even in the short run there might not be a trade-off between inflation and unemployment because expected inflation would change immediately in the face of expected changes in policy. **Real business cycle theory** claims that changes in the rate of growth of total factor productivity are the main cause of business cycles. Both of these versions of **new classical macroeconomics** received wide attention and respect, but policy makers and many economists haven't accepted the conclusion that monetary and fiscal policy are ineffective in changing aggregate output.
19. **New Keynesian economics** argues that market imperfections can lead to price stickiness, so that changes in aggregate demand have effects on aggregate output after all.

Module 36

20. The modern consensus is that monetary and fiscal policy are both effective in the short run but that neither can reduce the unemployment rate in the long run. Discretionary fiscal policy is considered generally unadvisable, except in special circumstances.
21. There are continuing debates about the appropriate role of monetary policy. Some economists advocate the explicit use of an inflation target, but others oppose it. There's also a debate about what kind of unconventional monetary policy, if any, should be adopted to address a liquidity trap.

360 **Section 6** Inflation, Unemployment, and Stabilization Policies

Key Terms

AP® Exam Practice Questions

Multiple-Choice Questions

1. The budget balance is equal to
   a. total spending by the government.
   b. taxes minus transfer payments.
   c. taxes minus government spending and transfer payments.
   d. the sum of deficits and surpluses over time.
   e. total tax revenues collected.
2. The cyclically adjusted budget deficit adjusts the actual budget deficit for the effect of
   a. discretionary fiscal policy.
   b. discretionary monetary policy.
   c. inflation.
   d. transfer payments.
   e. the business cycle.
3. The public debt increases when
   a. the government collects more in taxes than it spends.
   b. the government runs a budget deficit.
   c. taxes exceed transfer payments.
   d. the budget balance is positive.
   e. individuals borrow for goods like houses and cars.
4. Which of the following is a potential problem with persistent increases in government debt?
   a. Government borrowing may crowd out private investment.
   b. Government debt is caused by budget deficits, which are always bad for the economy.
   c. It will always lead the government to default.
   d. It creates inflation because the government has to print money to pay it off.
   e. It causes automatic stabilizers to raise taxes in the future.
5. The Federal Open Market Committee sets a target for which of the following?
   a. the income tax rate
   b. the federal funds rate
   c. the money supply
   d. the prime interest rate
   e. the unemployment rate
6. Which of the following will occur if the Federal Reserve buys Treasury bills?
   a. The money supply will increase.
   b. The money supply curve will shift to the left.
   c. The money demand curve will shift to the right.
   d. Interest rates will rise.
   e. Aggregate demand will decrease.
7. Which of the following actions would the Federal Reserve use to address inflation?
   a. make an open-market sale of Treasury bills
   b. increase the money supply
   c. lower the discount rate
   d. decrease money demand
   e. raise taxes

Answers to Section 6 AP® Exam Practice Questions

Multiple-Choice Questions

1. c
2. e
3. b
4. a
5. b
6. a
7. a

8. e
9. e
10. b
11. d
12. d
13. d
14. b
15. c
16. b
17. c
18. a
19. d
20. a

8. The Taylor rule sets the target federal funds rate based on which of the following?
a. the inflation rate only
b. the unemployment rate only
c. the output gap only
d. both the inflation rate and the unemployment rate
e. both the output gap and the inflation rate

9. An increase in the money supply will generate which of the following?
a. a negative short-run effect on real GDP
b. an increase in real GDP in the long run
c. a decrease in real GDP in the long run
d. a decrease in the aggregate price level in the long run
e. an increase in the aggregate price level in the short run and the long run

10. According to the concept of money neutrality, changes in the money supply will affect which of the following in the long run?
a. only real values
b. the aggregate price level
c. employment
d. aggregate output
e. aggregate demand

11. An inflation tax is the result of
a. the federal government running a budget surplus.
b. the Federal Reserve raising the federal funds rate.
c. an increase in the demand for money.
d. printing money to cover a budget deficit.
e. contractionary fiscal policy.

12. An increase in the aggregate price level caused by a significant increase in the price of an input with economy-wide importance is called
a. demand-pull inflation.
b. seignorage inflation.
c. supply-push inflation.
d. cost-push inflation.
e. input-pull inflation.

13. Which of the following is true when the output gap is negative?
a. Aggregate output is above potential output.
b. The unemployment rate is below the natural rate.
c. The economy is experiencing inflation.
d. Potential output is above aggregate output.
e. The natural rate of unemployment is decreasing.

14. The short-run Phillips curve shows the relationship between the inflation rate and the
a. GDP growth rate.
b. unemployment rate.
c. employment rate.
d. real interest rate.
e. nominal interest rate.

15. An increase in expected inflation has what effect on the short-run Phillips curve?
a. a movement up and to the left along the curve
b. a movement down and to the right along the curve
c. an upward shift of the curve
d. a downward shift of the curve
e. an increase in the slope of the curve

16. The long-run Phillips curve is
a. horizontal.
b. vertical.
c. upward sloping.
d. downward sloping.
e. U-shaped.

17. The long-run Phillips curve illustrates which of the following?
a. a positive relationship between unemployment and inflation
b. a negative relationship between unemployment and inflation
c. that unemployment will always return to the NAIRU
d. that unemployment will adjust so that the economy experiences 2% inflation
e. that output will adjust so that there is no unemployment or inflation in the long run

18. The process of bringing down the rate of inflation that has become embedded in expectations is known as
a. disinflation.
b. deflation.
c. negative inflation.
d. debt deflation.
e. monetary policy.

19. A liquidity trap occurs when conventional monetary policy is ineffective because
a. the short-run Phillips curve is negatively sloped.
b. the public will not buy or sell Treasury bills.
c. the unemployment rate can't go below 5%.
d. the nominal interest rate can't be negative.
e. the real interest rate can't be negative.

20. According to the Quantity Theory of Money,
a. the money supply times velocity is equal to nominal GDP.
b. velocity varies significantly with the business cycle.
c. changes in the money supply have no long-run effect on the economy.
d. activist monetary policy is necessary to promote economic growth.
e. monetary policy rules promote business-cycle fluctuations.

362 Section 6 Inflation, Unemployment, and Stabilization Policies

Free-Response Question

1. Draw a correctly labeled graph showing a short-run Phillips curve.
   a. On your graph, show a long-run Phillips curve and label
      i. the NAIRU
      ii. the equilibrium inflation rate
   b. On your graph, show the effect of an increase in the expected inflation rate.
   (6 points)

Rubric for Free-Response Question

1 point: Axes labeled with "Unemployment rate" and "Inflation rate"

1 point: Downward-sloping, labeled, short-run Phillips curve

1 point: Vertical, labeled, long-run Phillips curve

1 point: NAIRU is labeled where the long-run Phillips curve intersects the horizontal axis.

1 point: The equilibrium inflation rate is shown on the vertical axis at the point where the short-run and long-run Phillips curves intersect.

1 point: A new, labeled short-run Phillips curve is shown above the original short-run Phillips curve.

Please see page SG-2 for sample student graphs for this Free-Response Question.

SECTION 7

Economic Growth and Productivity

PD Section 7 Overview:

Watch the video overview of Section 7 (for teachers), which is accessible through the Teacher's e-Book, the TR-flash drive, or the book's website bcs.worthpublishers.com/krugmanap2e *(teacher log-in required).*

Section 7 addresses the goal of economic growth. Productivity is a major factor in generating growth in the economy, while differences in human and physical capital, research and development, and technology lead to variations in long-run economic growth rates. Module 40 clearly shows the role of economic growth in the macroeconomic models presented in earlier sections.

Topics that your students will study in Section 7 are:

- how we measure long-run economic growth.
- defining the factors that stimulate long-run economic growth.
- how productivity is driven by physical and human capital, and technological progress.
- how changes in productivity are shown using an aggregate production function.
- how economic growth has varied among regions of the world and why the convergence hypothesis applies to economically advanced countries.
- defining factors to explain why long-run economic growth rates differ among countries.
- how the scarcity of natural resources, environmental degradation, and efforts to make growth sustainable pose challenges to growth.
- how long-run economic growth is represented in macroeconomic models and how to model growth effects in these models.

Alignment to AP® Macroeconomics Course Description

Macroeonomics VI. Economic Growth: 5–10%

AP® Outline	Module
A. Definition of economic growth	37: Long-Run Economic Growth
B. Determinants of economic growth	38: Productivity and Growth
C. Growth policy	39: Growth Policy: Why Economic Growth Rates Differ 40: Economic Growth in Macroeconomic Models

Pacing Guide

Module	Standard Teaching Days	Block Teaching Days
37	1	½
38	1	½
39	1	½
40	1	½
Section 7 Assessment	1	½
Total	**5**	**2½**

TRM Section Resources

All section resources may be accessed through the Teacher's e-Book, the TR-flash drive, or the book's website bcs.worthpublishers.com/krugmanap2e *(teacher log-in required).*

Section 7 PD Video (for teachers)

Module 37

Module 37 Sample Lecture

Worksheet 37.1: Beat the Clock

Worksheet 37.2: Productivity

Exit Slip: Module 37

Module 38

Module 38 Sample Lecture

Worksheet 38.1: China and Growth

Exit Slip: Module 38

Module 39

Module 39 Sample Lecture

Worksheet 39.1: Emerging Markets

Worksheet 39.2: Sustainability

Exit Slip: Module 39

Module 40

Module 40 Sample Lecture

Worksheet 40.1: Economic Growth

Exit Slip: Module 40

Section 7 Review Video (for students)

St. Louis Federal Reserve Bank Resources

Many of the Federal Reserve Banks have educational departments that offer helpful resources for studying economics. Members of the Educators Advisory Board of the St. Louis Federal Reserve Bank have handpicked some of their best resources for use with your AP® Economics students. References to these resources are included in the margin notes. A complete list of the St. Louis Fed resources for each section with the corresponding URL (as of fall 2014) can be found in the TRM.

NOTE We have included a number of links to useful videos and articles in the margin notes in this section. Although all are active at the time of publication, we know that some may expire over the next few years. If a link is no longer active, you may wish to search for a similar article or video to illustrate the point. We may also periodically refresh resources on the book's companion website.

PD Section 7 Overview

Watch the video overview of Section 7 (for teachers), which is accessible through the Teacher's e-Book, the TR-flash drive, or the book's companion website bcs.worthpublishers.com/krugmanap2e (teacher log-in required).

FOCUS Active Learning

Have students read Chapter 28 of *Economics by Example* to delve further into growth models and the process of economic development.

SECTION 7

Economic Growth and Productivity

Grown in China

China is growing—and so are the Chinese. According to official statistics, children in China are almost 2½ inches taller now than they were 30 years ago. The average Chinese citizen is still a lot shorter than the average American, but at the current rate of growth the difference may be largely gone in a couple of generations.

If that does happen, China will be following in Japan's footsteps. Older Americans tend to think of the Japanese as short, but today young Japanese men are more than 5 inches taller on average than they were in 1900, which makes them almost as tall as their American counterparts.

There's no mystery about why the Japanese grew taller—it's because they grew richer. In the early twentieth century, Japan was a relatively poor country in which many families couldn't afford to give their children adequate nutrition. As a result, their children grew up to be short adults. However, since World War II, Japan has become an economic powerhouse in which food is ample and young adults are much taller than before.

The same phenomenon is now happening in China. Although it continues to be a relatively poor country, China has made great economic strides over the past 30 years. Its recent history is probably the world's most dramatic example of economic growth—a sustained increase in the productive capacity of an economy. Yet despite its impressive performance, China is currently playing catch-up with economically advanced countries like the United States and Japan. It's still relatively poor because these other nations began their own processes of economic growth many decades ago—and in the case of the United States and European countries, more than a century ago.

Unlike a short-run increase in real GDP caused by an increase in aggregate demand or short-run aggregate supply, we'll see that economic growth pushes the production possibilities curve outward and shifts the long-run aggregate supply curve to the right. Because economic growth is a long-run concept, we often refer to it as *long-run economic growth* for clarity. Many economists have argued that long-run economic growth—why it happens and how to achieve it—is the single most important issue in macroeconomics. In this section, we present some facts about long-run growth, look at the factors that economists believe determine its pace, examine how government policies can help or hinder growth, and address questions about the environmental sustainability of growth.

AP Photo/EyePress

364 Section 7 Economic Growth and Productivity

Stockbyte/Getty Images

MODULE 37 Long-Run Economic Growth

In this Module, you will learn to:

- Interpret measures of long-run economic growth
- Describe how real GDP has changed over time
- Explain how real GDP varies across countries
- Identify the sources of long-run economic growth
- Explain how productivity is driven by physical capital, human capital, and technological progress

Comparing Economies Across Time and Space

Before we analyze the sources of long-run economic growth, it's useful to have a sense of just how much the U.S. economy has grown over time and how large the gaps are between wealthy countries like the United States and countries that have yet to achieve a comparable standard of living. So let's take a look at the numbers.

Real GDP per Capita

The key statistic used to track economic growth is *real GDP per capita*—real GDP divided by the population size. We focus on GDP because, as we have learned, GDP measures the total value of an economy's production of final goods and services as well as the income earned in that economy in a given year. We use *real* GDP because we want to separate changes in the quantity of goods and services from the effects of a rising price level. We focus on real GDP *per capita* because we want to isolate the effect of changes in the population. For example, other things equal, an increase in the population lowers the standard of living for the average person—there are now more people to share a given amount of real GDP. An increase in real GDP that only matches an increase in population leaves the real GDP per capita unchanged.

Although we learned that growth in real GDP per capita should not be a policy goal in and of itself, it does serve as a very useful summary measure of a country's economic progress over time. **Figure 37.1** on the next page shows real GDP per capita for the United States, India, and China, measured in 2005 dollars, from 1910 to 2010. (We'll talk about India and China in a moment.) The vertical axis is drawn on a logarithmic scale so that

PD To prepare for teaching this lesson, you may want to consult the **Module 37 Sample Lecture** in the TRM.

OPEN & CLOSE **Start Here**

Show students the video "World's Top 10 Largest Economies" (see econextras video list with hyperlinks on the bcs and TRFD). Ask if nominal GDP is the best way to measure the world's largest economies. Then show the "Top 10: Countries with the Highest GDP per Capita" (see econextras video list with hyperlinks on the bcs and TRFD). Discuss why this list is different from the first. Is it better to use real GDP per capita? Why? Explain that in this module, students will compare economies and look at economic growth.

TEACH **Teach It**

Real GDP per capita is real GDP divided by the population. Other things being equal, an increase in the population lowers the standard of living for the average person, as there are now more people to share a given amount of real GDP. An increase in real GDP that only matches an increase in population leaves the average standard of living unchanged.

St. Louis Federal Reserve Bank Resources

"Gross Domestic Product," *The Economic Lowdown Podcast Series* (Volume 1, Episode 13); "Gross Domestic Product," *The Economic Lowdown Video Series*, Episode 7

GDP data are among the most important economic data available for measuring economic growth, but measuring the output of a large, dynamic economy is a complex task. In this episode of the podcast or video series (running time 9:35), students hear what GDP measures, how it is calculated, how it is useful in determining whether and how quickly the economy is growing, and how GDP can be used as an indicator of standard of living.

St. Louis Federal Reserve Bank Resources

"Investing in Yourself: An Economic Approach to Education Decisions," *Page One Economics Classroom Edition* (February 2013)

Human capital may not be the first thing that comes to mind when we think about investments, but investments in education and training require important economic decisions. Students can learn about human capital and the return on such an investment in this issue.

FOCUS Active Learning

Refer students to Figure 37.1, illustrating economic growth in the United States, India, and China over the past century. Ask the following:

- How would you characterize the growth of the 3 economies depicted? *All 3 are growing, but China appears to be growing at a faster rate than the other 2. The United States seems to have the slowest growth rate.*
- What factors may have caused the growth? *Changes in productivity (physical capital, education, or technology)*
- Why did India experience no gain in the WWII era? *Prior to 1946, India was part of the British Empire. Britain controlled its resources and development. With independence, India was free to explore other trade relationships.*
- Why does no record exist for China before 1950? *Prior to 1950, China functioned as an agricultural economy barely able to meet the basic needs of its population.*

Figure 37.1 Economic Growth in the United States, India, and China over the Past Century

Real GDP per capita from 1910 to 2010, measured in 2005 dollars, is shown for the United States, India, and China. Equal percentage changes in real GDP per capita are drawn the same size. India and China currently have a much higher growth rate than the United States. However, China has only recently attained the standard of living achieved in the United States in 1910, while India is still poorer than the United States was in 1910.

Sources: Angus Maddison, January 2003; J. Bolt and J. L. van Zanden, "The First Update of the Maddison Project; Re-Estimating Growth Before 1820," Maddison Project Working Paper 4, January 2003, http://www.ggdc.net/maddison/maddison-project/home.htm.

equal percentage changes in real GDP per capita across countries are the same size in the graph.

To give a sense of how much the U.S. economy grew during the last century, **Table 37.1** shows real GDP per capita at 20-year intervals, expressed two ways: as a percentage of the 1910 level and as a percentage of the 2010 level. In 1930, the U.S. economy already produced 125% as much per person as it did in 1910. In 2010, it produced 614% as much per person as it did in 1910. Alternatively, in 1910, the U.S. economy produced only 16% as much per person as it did in 2010.

The income of the typical family normally grows more or less in proportion to per capita income. For example, a 1% increase in real GDP per capita corresponds, roughly, to a 1% increase in the income of the median or typical family—a family at the center of the income distribution. In 2010, the median American household had an income of about $45,600. Since Table 37.1 tells us that real GDP per capita in 1910 was only 16% of its 2010 level, a typical family in 1910 probably had purchasing power only 16% as large as the purchasing power of a typical family in 2010. That's around $7,400 in

Table 37.1 U.S. Real GDP per Capita

Year	Percentage of 1910 real GDP per capita	Percentage of 2010 real GDP per capita
1910	100%	16%
1930	125	20
1950	192	31
1970	302	49
1990	467	76
2010	614	100

Sources: Angus Maddison, January 2003; J. Bolt and J. L. van Zanden, "The First Update of the Maddison Project; Re-Estimating Growth Before 1820," Maddison Project Working Paper 4, January 2003, http://www.ggdc.net/maddison/maddison-project/home.htm.

366 Section 7 Economic Growth and Productivity

Figure 37.2 Incomes Around the World, 2013

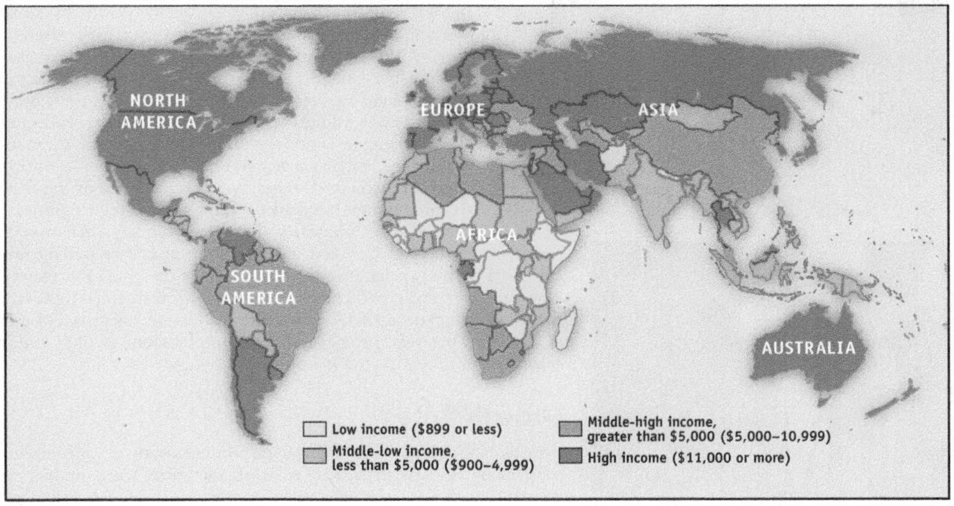

Although the countries of Europe and North America—along with a few in East Asia—have high incomes, much of the world is still very poor. Today, more than 50% of the world's population lives in countries with a lower standard of living than the United States had a century ago.

Source: International Monetary Fund.

today's dollars, representing a standard of living that we would now consider severe poverty. Today's typical American family, if transported back to the United States of 1910, would feel quite deprived.

Yet many people in the world have a standard of living equal to or lower than that of the United States a century ago. That's the message about China and India in Figure 37.1: despite dramatic economic growth in China over the last three decades and the less dramatic acceleration of economic growth in India, China has only recently attained the standard of living that the United States enjoyed in 1910, while India is still poorer than the United States was in 1910. And much of the world today is poorer than China or India.

You can get a sense of how poor much of the world remains by looking at **Figure 37.2**, a map of the world in which countries are classified according to their 2013 levels of GDP per capita, in U.S. dollars. As you can see, large parts of the world have very low incomes. Generally speaking, the countries of Europe and North America, as well as a few in the Pacific, have high incomes. The rest of the world, containing most of its population, is dominated by countries with GDP less than $7,000 per capita—and often much less. In fact, today more than 50% of the world's people live in countries with a lower standard of living than the United States had a century ago.

When Did Long-Run Growth Begin?

In 2013, the United States was much richer than it was in 1953; in 1953, it was much richer than it had been in 1903. But how did 1853 compare with 1803? Or 1753? How far back does long-run economic growth go?

FOCUS Active Learning

Refer students to Figure 37.2 that illustrates incomes around the world. Ask them the following:

- What do you notice about income levels in the developed nations? *They are middle-high to high.*
- Why would their incomes be higher than those of less developed nations? *Less developed nations generally lack physical capital, human capital, and technology. They don't have the financial resources and infrastructure to encourage economic growth.*
- How might this map be different today than it was in the first half of the twentieth century? *Some nations in the Middle East, Asia, and South America might have had lower incomes because the world wasn't oil dependent, outsourcing wasn't prevalent, and colonialism was still active.*
- How might you expect this map to change over the next 25 years? *More nations in Southeast Asia and Asia might move into the higher income categories.*

TEACH Connect It

Growth rates are like compounded interest. If the annual interest rate is 10% at the bank and you save $100, after Year 1, you will have $110, an increase of $10. After Year 2, you will have $121, an additional increase of $11. If the economy grows by 2% one year, another 2% the following year, and yet another 2% the year after that, these annual growth rates are compounded into larger and larger increases in per capital real GDP.

© Corbis

Thinkstock

The answer is that long-run growth is a relatively modern phenomenon. The U.S. economy was already growing steadily by the mid-nineteenth century—think railroads. But if you go back to the period before 1800, you find a world economy that grew extremely slowly by today's standards. Furthermore, the population grew almost as fast as the economy, so there was very little increase in output per person. According to the economic historian Angus Maddison, from 1000 to 1800, real aggregate output around the world grew less than 0.2% per year, with population rising at about the same rate. Economic stagnation meant unchanging living standards. For example, information on prices and wages from sources such as monastery records shows that workers in England weren't significantly better off in the early eighteenth century than they had been five centuries earlier. And it's a good bet that they weren't much better off than Egyptian peasants in the age of the pharaohs. However, long-run economic growth has increased significantly since 1800. In the last 50 years or so, real GDP per capita worldwide has grown at a rate of about 2% per year. Let's examine the implications of high and low growth rates.

Growth Rates

How did the United States manage to produce nearly seven times more per person in 2010 than in 1910? A little bit at a time. Long-run economic growth is normally a gradual process in which real GDP per capita grows at most a few percent per year. From 1910 to 2010, real GDP per capita in the United States increased an average of 2.1% each year.

FYI India Takes Off

India achieved independence from Great Britain in 1947, becoming the world's most populous democracy—a status it has maintained to this day. For more than three decades after independence, however, this happy political story was partly overshadowed by economic disappointment. Despite ambitious economic development plans, India's performance was consistently sluggish. In 1980, India's real GDP per capita was only about 50% higher than it had been in 1947; the gap between Indian living standards and those in wealthy countries like the United States had been growing rather than shrinking.

Since then, however, India has done much better. As Figure 37.3 shows, real GDP per capita has grown at an average rate of 3% a year, tripling between 1980 and 2013. India now has a large and rapidly growing middle class. And yes, the well-fed children of that middle class are much taller than their parents.

What went right in India after 1980? Many economists point to policy reforms. For decades after independence, India had a tightly controlled, highly regulated economy. Today, things are very different: a series of reforms opened the economy to international trade and freed up domestic competition. Some economists, however, argue that this can't be the main story because the big policy reforms weren't adopted until 1991, yet growth accelerated around 1980.

Regardless of the explanation, India's economic rise has transformed it into a major new economic power—and allowed hundreds of millions of people to have a much better life, better than their grandparents could have imagined.

Verity Steel/Alamy

India's high rate of economic growth since 1980 has raised living standards and led to the emergence of a rapidly growing middle class.

368 Section 7 Economic Growth and Productivity

To have a sense of the relationship between the annual growth rate of real GDP per capita and the long-run change in real GDP per capita, it's helpful to keep in mind the **Rule of 70**, a mathematical formula that tells us how long it takes real GDP per capita, or any other variable that grows gradually over time, to double. The approximate answer is:

$$\text{(37-1)} \quad \text{Number of years for variable to double} = \frac{70}{\text{Annual growth rate of variable}}$$

The **Rule of 70** tells us that the time it takes a variable that grows gradually over time to double is approximately 70 divided by that variable's annual growth rate.

(Note that the Rule of 70 can only be applied to a positive growth rate.) So if real GDP per capita grows at 1% per year, it will take 70 years to double. If it grows at 2% per year, it will take only 35 years to double. Applying the Rule of 70 to the 2.1% average growth rate in the United States implies that it should have taken 33.3 years for real GDP per capita to double; it would have taken 100 years—three periods of 33.3 years each—for U.S. real GDP per capita to double three times. That is, the Rule of 70 implies that over the course of 100 years, U.S. real GDP per capita should have increased by a factor of $2 \times 2 \times 2 = 8$. And this does turn out to be a pretty good approximation of reality. Between 1910 and 2013—a period of 103 years—real GDP per capita rose just about eightfold.

Figure 37.3 shows the average annual rate of growth of real GDP per capita for selected countries from 1980 to 2012. Some countries were notable success stories: we've already mentioned China, which has made spectacular progress. India, although not matching China's performance, has also achieved impressive growth.

Figure 37.3 Comparing Recent Growth Rates

Here the average annual rate of growth of real GDP per capita from 1980 to 2012 is shown for selected countries. China and, to a lesser extent, India and Ireland have achieved impressive growth. The United States, Argentina, and France have had moderate growth. Still others, such as Zimbabwe, have slid backward.

Source: International Monetary Fund and World Bank.

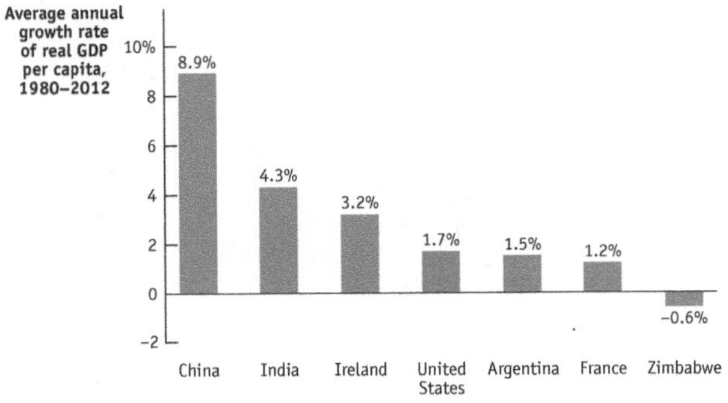

Some countries, though, have had very disappointing growth. This includes many of the countries in Africa and South America, where growth rates below 1% are common. A few countries, such as Zimbabwe, have actually slid backward.

What explains these differences in growth rates? To answer that question, we need to examine the sources of long-run growth.

The Sources of Long-Run Growth

Long-run economic growth depends almost entirely on one ingredient: rising *productivity*. However, a number of factors affect the growth of productivity. Let's look first at why productivity is the key ingredient. After that, we'll examine what affects it.

TEACH AP® Exam Tip

The Rule of 70 *approximates* how many years it will take for the economy to double at a given rate of economic growth. Questions about the Rule of 70 have appeared in the multiple-choice section on past AP® exams, so students should study this formula.

TEACH Teach It

When real GDP "grows," that means the level of real GDP is increasing or decreasing (from, say, $100 to $200 billion). When the rate of growth changes, that means the amount of change is increasing or decreasing (from, say, 2% to 4%, or 4% to 4.5%).

FOCUS Active Learning

Refer students to Figure 37.3 on comparing recent growth rates. Ask the following:

- How are nations with the highest growth rates per capita similar? *They are developing nations.*
- At their present rates of growth, how long will it take for the economies of China, the United States, and France to double in size? *China: 7.9 years; the United States: 41.2 years; France: 58.3 years.*

FOCUS Active Learning

TRM To help students better understand productivity, have them do the activity found in **Worksheet 37.1 (Beat the Clock)** from the TRM.

FOCUS In the News

TRM Find an article about productivity in the United States or use the Hoover Institution's February 2014 article "U.S. Productivity Growth Has Taken a Dive" at http://www.hoover.org/news/daily-report/167541. Suggested discussion questions and answers for this article may be found in the TRM under **Worksheet 37.2 (Productivity)**.

TEACH AP® Exam Tip

Productivity is transformed in three ways: through changes in physical or real capital, changes in human capital (through education), and changes in technology. On the AP® exam, the correct answer to most questions about what increases economic growth is not simply "an increase in productivity." Students should go further into the cause of the change in productivity. For example, a decrease in the interest rate leads to increased investments in capital. The additional capital will increase productivity and lead to economic growth. Tell students to be sure to specify each of these steps, and to be clear that the increased investment is in *capital*, so that exam readers know that the students aren't thinking of another type of investment.

FYI The Walmart Effect

After 20 years of being sluggish, U.S. productivity growth accelerated sharply in the late 1990s. What caused that acceleration? Was it the rise of the Internet?

Not according to analysts at McKinsey and Co., a famous business consulting firm. They found that a major source of productivity improvement after 1995 was a surge in output per worker in retailing—stores were selling much more merchandise per worker. And why did productivity surge in retailing in the United States? "The reason can be explained in just two syllables: Walmart," wrote McKinsey.

Walmart has been a pioneer in using modern technology to improve productivity. For example, it was one of the first companies to use computers to track inventory, to use bar-code scanners, to establish direct electronic links with suppliers, and so on. It continued to set the pace in the 1990s, but, increasingly, other companies have imitated Walmart's business practices.

There are two lessons from the "Walmart effect," as McKinsey calls it. One is that how you apply a technology makes all the difference: everyone in the retail business knew about computers, but Walmart figured out what to do with them. The other is that a lot of economic growth comes from everyday improvements rather than glamorous new technologies.

PAUL J. RICHARDS/AFP/Getty Images

AP® Exam Tip

Productivity is the most important factor that changes economic growth. Productivity is impacted by improvements in human capital (worker education) and technology.

Labor productivity, often referred to simply as **productivity**, is output per worker.

The Crucial Importance of Productivity

Sustained growth in real GDP per capita occurs only when the amount of output produced by the average worker increases steadily. The term **labor productivity**, or **productivity** for short, is used to refer either to output per worker or, in some cases, to output per hour (the number of hours worked by an average worker differs to some extent across countries, although this isn't an important factor in the difference between living standards in, say, India and the United States). In this book we'll focus on output per worker. For the economy as a whole, productivity—output per worker—is simply real GDP divided by the number of people working.

You might wonder why we say that higher productivity is the only source of long-run growth in real GDP per capita. Can't an economy also increase its real GDP per capita by putting more of the population to work? The answer is, yes, but . . . . For short periods of time, an economy can experience a burst of growth in output per capita by putting a higher percentage of the population to work. That happened in the United States during World War II, when millions of women who previously worked only in the home entered the paid workforce. The percentage of adult civilians employed outside the home rose from 50% in 1941 to 58% in 1944, and you can see the resulting bump in real GDP per capita during those years in Figure 37.1.

Over the longer run, however, the rate of employment growth is never very different from the rate of population growth. Over the course of the twentieth century, for example, the population of the United States rose at an average rate of 1.3% per year and employment rose 1.5% per year. Real GDP per capita rose 1.9% per year; of that, 1.7%—that is, almost 90% of the total—was the result of rising productivity. In general, overall real GDP can grow because of population growth, but any large increase in real GDP *per capita* must be the result of increased output *per worker*. That is, it must be due to higher productivity.

We have just seen that increased productivity is the key to long-run economic growth. But what leads to higher productivity?

AP® Exam Tip

If you're asked to identify a source of economic growth, "increased investment in physical capital" is a good answer. Don't just say "increased investment," because the meaning of that is more ambiguous.

Explaining Growth in Productivity

There are three main reasons why the average U.S. worker today produces far more than his or her counterpart a century ago. First, the modern worker has far more *physical capital*, such as tools and office space, to work with. Second, the modern worker is much better educated and so possesses much more *human capital*. Finally, modern firms have

FOCUS Active Learning

Ask your students to go home and make a list of the types of production that occur in their homes or communities—for example, cooking meals, washing clothes, bathing children, washing dishes, coaching teams, and the like. Have the students observe household members engaged in these activities on a typical night. For example, one student's dad might be cooking dinner while her mom is coaching soccer and her brother is doing laundry.

Ask the students to make a second list of the physical capital and technology that allows their households to be more productive. For instance, a microwave allows the father to cook more quickly, which gives him time to check on his children's homework. A washer and dryer allow the brother to get the family laundry done while still having time to study for economics class the next day. A cell phone allows the mother to coach soccer and check in on the family during breaks.

If the students can see that the physical capital and technology in their households increase each member's productivity, it will be clear that the same is true of increased productivity in the workplace and nation.

the advantage of a century's accumulation of technical advancements reflecting a great deal of *technological progress.*

Let's look at each of these factors in turn.

Physical Capital Module 22 explained that capital—manufactured goods used to produce other goods and services—is often described as **physical capital** to distinguish it from human capital and other types of capital. Physical capital such as buildings and machinery makes workers more productive. For example, a worker operating a backhoe can dig a lot more feet of trench per day than one equipped with only a shovel.

The average U.S. private-sector worker today makes use of approximately $130,000 worth of physical capital—far more than a U.S. worker had 100 years ago and far more than the average worker in most other countries has today.

Human Capital It's not enough for a worker to have good equipment—he or she must also know what to do with it. **Human capital** refers to the improvement in labor created by the education and knowledge embodied in the workforce.

The human capital of the United States has increased dramatically over the past century. A century ago, although most Americans were able to read and write, very few had an extensive education. In 1910, only 13.5% of Americans over 25 had graduated from high school and only 3% had four-year college degrees. By 2013, the percentages were 88% and 31%, respectively. It would be impossible to run today's economy with a population as poorly educated as that of a century ago.

Analyses based on *growth accounting,* described later in this section, suggest that education—and its effect on productivity—is an even more important determinant of growth than increases in physical capital.

Technology Probably the most important driver of productivity growth is progress in **technology**, which is broadly defined as the technical means for the production of goods and services. We'll see shortly how economists measure the impact of technology on growth.

Workers today are able to produce more than those in the past, even with the same amount of physical and human capital, because technology has advanced over time. It's important to realize that economically important technological progress need not be flashy or rely on cutting-edge science. Historians have noted that past economic growth has been driven not only by major inventions, such as the railroad or the semiconductor chip, but also by thousands of modest innovations, such as the flat-bottomed paper bag, patented in 1870, which made packing groceries and many other goods much easier, and the Post-it note, introduced in 1981, which has had surprisingly large benefits for office productivity. Experts attribute much of the productivity surge that took place in the United States late in the twentieth century to new technology adopted by retail companies like Walmart rather than to high-technology companies.

Physical capital consists of human-made goods such as buildings and machines used to produce other goods and services.

Human capital is the improvement in labor created by the education and knowledge of members of the workforce.

Technology is the technical means for the production of goods and services.

If you've ever had doubts about attending college, consider this: factory workers with only high school degrees will make much less than college grads. The present discounted value of the difference in lifetime earnings is as much as $300,000.

MODULE 37 Review

Check Your Understanding

1. Why do economists focus on real GDP per capita as a measure of economic progress rather than on some other measure, such as nominal GDP per capita or real GDP?
2. Apply the Rule of 70 to the data in Figure 37.3 to determine how long it will take each of the countries listed there to double its real GDP per capita. Will India's real GDP per capita exceed that of the United States in the future if growth rates remain the same? Why or why not?
3. Although China and India currently have growth rates much higher than the U.S. growth rate, the typical Chinese or Indian household is far poorer than the typical American household. Explain why.

FOCUS Test It

Have students answer the 2010 free-response question (1) found at http://apcentral.collegeboard.com/apc/public/repository/ap10_frq_macroecon.pdf. The question will provide a comprehensive review of *AD–AS*, fiscal policy, and economic growth. It is recommended that students take no more than 25 minutes to answer this question. The rubric for the question may be viewed at http://tinyurl.com/lfxvlll.

OPEN & CLOSE Exit Slip

*TRM Please see **Exit Slip: Module 37** in the TRM for formative multiple-choice questions to ask your students before finishing your lesson. These questions will help you quickly assess whether your students have mastered the module's concepts before moving on.*

Answers to the Exit Slip Questions

1. B
2. A
3. B

Answers to Module 37 Review Questions

Check Your Understanding

1. Economists want a measure of economic progress that rises with increases in the living standard of the average resident of a country. An increase in overall real GDP does not accurately reflect an increase in an average resident's living standard because it does not account for growth in the number of residents. For example, if real GDP rises by 10% but population grows by 20%, the living standard of the average resident falls: after the change, the average resident has only $(110/120) \times 100 = 91.6\%$ as much real income as before the change. Similarly, an increase in nominal GDP per capita does not accurately reflect an increase in living standards because it does not account for any change in prices. For example, a 5% increase in nominal GDP per capita generated by a 5% increase in prices results in no change in living standards. Real GDP per capita is the only measure that accounts for both changes in the population and changes in prices.

2. Using the Rule of 70, the amount of time it will take China to double its real GDP per capita is $(70/8.9) = 7.9$ years; India, $(70/4.3) = 16.3$ years; Ireland, $(70/3.2) = 21.9$ years; the United States, $(70/1.7) = 41.2$ years; Argentina, $(70/1.5) = 46.7$ years; and France, $(70/1.2) = 58.3$ years. Since the Rule of 70 can be applied to only a positive growth rate, we cannot apply it to the case of Zimbabwe, which experienced negative growth. If India continues to experience a higher growth rate of real GDP per capita than the United States, then India's real GDP per capita will eventually surpass that of the United States.

3. The United States began growing rapidly over a century ago, but China and India have begun growing rapidly only recently. As a result, the living standard of the typical Chinese or Indian household has not yet caught up with that of the typical American household.

Tackle the Test: Multiple-Choice Questions

1. d
2. c
3. c
4. b
5. b

Tackle the Test: Free-Response Question

Rubric for FRQ 2 (4 points)

1 point: Increases in real GDP per capita result primarily from changes in productivity (or labor productivity).

1 point: Productivity is defined as output per worker or output per hour.

1 point: Increased labor force participation could also lead to higher real GDP per capita.

1 point: The rate of employment growth is rarely very different from the rate of population growth, meaning that the corresponding increase in output does not lead to an increase in output per capita.

Tackle the Test: Multiple-Choice Questions

1. Which of the following is true regarding growth rates for countries around the world compared to the United States?

- **I.** More than fifty percent of the world's people live in countries with a lower standard of living than the U.S. had a century ago.
- **II.** The U.S. growth rate is six times the growth rate in the rest of the world.
- **III.** China has only recently attained the same standard of living the U.S. had a century ago.

a. I only
b. II only
c. III only
d. I and III only
e. I, II, and III

2. Which of the following is the key statistic used to track economic growth?
a. GDP
b. real GDP
c. real GDP per capita
d. median real GDP
e. median real GDP per capita

3. According to the "Rule of 70," if a country's real GDP per capita grows at a rate of 2% per year, it will take how many years for real GDP per capita to double?
a. 3.5
b. 20
c. 35
d. 70
e. It will never double at that rate.

4. If a country's real GDP per capita doubles in 10 years, what was its average annual rate of growth of real GDP per capita?
a. 3.5%
b. 7%
c. 10%
d. 70%
e. 700%

5. Long-run economic growth depends almost entirely on
a. technological change.
b. rising productivity.
c. increased labor force participation.
d. rising real GDP per capita.
e. population growth.

Tackle the Test: Free-Response Questions

1. Refer to Figure 37.3, reproduced below, to answer each of the questions that follow.

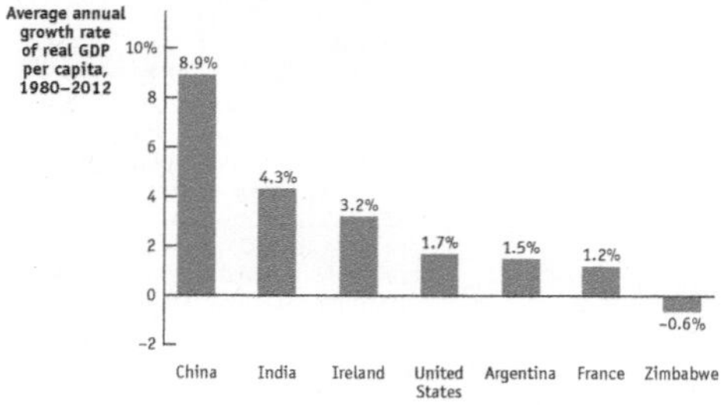

a. If growth continued at the rates shown in the figure, which of the seven countries would have had a lower real GDP per capita in 2014 than in 2013? Explain.
b. If growth continued at the rates shown in the figure, which of the seven countries would have had the highest real GDP per capita in 2014? Explain.
c. If growth continues at the rates shown in the figure, real GDP per capita for which of the seven countries will at least double over the next 10 years? Explain.

Rubric for FRQ 1 (6 points)

1 point: Zimbabwe

1 point: It has a negative average annual growth rate of real GDP per capita.

1 point: It cannot be determined.

1 point: The figure provides data for growth rates, but not for the level of real GDP per capita. Higher growth rates do not indicate higher levels.

1 point: China

1 point: A country has to have an average annual growth rate of 7% or higher for real GDP to at least double in 10 years. China has a growth rate of 8.9%.

2. Increases in real GDP per capita result primarily from changes in what variable? (Hint: This is a general source of long-run growth and not a particular input such as capital.) Define that variable. Increases in what other variable could also lead to increased real GDP per capita? Why is this other factor less significant? **(4 points)**

372 Section 7 Economic Growth and Productivity

AP Photo/Jacques Brinon

MODULE 38 Productivity and Growth

In this Module, you will learn to:

- Illustrate changes in productivity using an aggregate production function
- Discuss how growth has varied among several important regions of the world and explain why the convergence hypothesis applies to economically advanced countries

Accounting for Growth: The Aggregate Production Function

Productivity is higher, other things equal, when workers are equipped with more physical capital, more human capital, better technology, or any combination of the three. But can we put numbers to these effects? To do this, economists make use of estimates of the **aggregate production function**, which shows how productivity depends on the quantities of physical capital per worker and human capital per worker as well as the state of technology. In general, all three factors tend to rise over time, as workers are equipped with more machinery, receive more education, and benefit from technological advances. What the aggregate production function does is allow economists to disentangle the effects of these three factors on overall productivity.

The **aggregate production function** is a hypothetical function that shows how productivity (output per worker) depends on the quantities of physical capital per worker and human capital per worker as well as the state of technology.

An example of an aggregate production function applied to real data comes from a comparative study of Chinese and Indian economic growth conducted by the economists Barry Bosworth and Susan Collins of the Brookings Institution. They used the following aggregate production function:

$$\text{GDP per worker} = T \times (\text{physical capital per worker})^{0.4} \times (\text{human capital per worker})^{0.6}$$

where T represented an estimate of the level of technology and they assumed that each year of education raised workers' human capital by 7%. Using this function, they tried to explain why China grew faster than India between 1978 and 2004. They found that

PD To prepare for teaching this lesson, you may want to consult the **Module 38 Sample Lecture** in the TRM.

OPEN & CLOSE Start Here

If students have not taken microeconomics, the concept of diminishing returns may be foreign to them. To get an understanding of diminishing marginal productivity, have them complete the activity "Widget Production in the Classroom" at http://www.marietta.edu/~delemeeg/expernom/s93.html#neral1. Run the experiment 6 or 7 times. Ask what happened to the marginal product of labor as additional labor was added to the production line? *The marginal product of labor increased and then decreased. (This is not always the case—learning, distractions, and changes in strategy can cause a variety of outcomes).* Why does this happen? *Specialization among the workers can allow the marginal product to increase initially, but eventually, redundancy, congestion, and the fixed quantity of capital cause the marginal product of labor to fall.*

TEACH Teach It

The aggregate production function shows how physical capital per worker, human capital per worker, and technology are combined to produce real GDP per worker.

TEACH Teach It

While diminishing returns is an important microeconomic concept, it also applies to the aggregate production function. All else being equal, as the physical capital per worker increases, the real GDP per worker increases by a smaller and smaller amount.

Module 38 Productivity and Growth 373

FOCUS Graph It

Have students look at Table 38.1. Ask them whether the productivity gain increases, decreases, or stays the same as more investments in $15,000 worth of physical capital per worker are made. *Although productivity increases with each investment in $15,000 worth of capital per worker, the real GDP per worker increases at a decreasing rate, meaning that the productivity gain decreases as the physical capital per worker increases.* As you talk about diminishing returns to physical capital, have the students plot the 4 points from Table 38.1 in a graph that illustrates the production function increasing at a decreasing rate. The graph shows the diminishing returns as a flattening of the upward-sloping curve. Then refer your students to Figure 38.1 to see if their graphs match the one in the figure.

TEACH Teach It

It is very important for you to stress the "all else equal" (*ceteris paribus*) assumption when looking at the aggregate production function. If the typists also were given training to increase their average words per minute, then a doubling of the physical capital per worker may indeed provide a doubling of the real output per worker. We have to hold technology and human capital constant to see the impact of a change in physical capital on aggregate output.

Table 38.1 A Hypothetical Example: How Physical Capital per Worker Affects Productivity, Holding Human Capital and Technology Fixed

Physical capital investment per worker	Real GDP per worker
$0	$0
15,000	30,000
30,000	45,000
45,000	55,000

about half the difference was due to China's higher levels of investment spending, which raised its level of physical capital per worker faster than India's. The other half was due to faster Chinese technological progress.

An aggregate production function exhibits **diminishing returns to physical capital** when, holding the amount of human capital per worker and the state of technology fixed, each successive increase in the amount of physical capital per worker leads to a smaller increase in productivity.

In analyzing historical economic growth, economists have discovered a crucial fact about the estimated aggregate production function: it exhibits **diminishing returns to physical capital**. That is, when the amount of human capital per worker and the state of technology are held fixed, each successive increase in the amount of physical capital per worker leads to a smaller increase in productivity. **Table 38.1** gives a hypothetical example of how the level of physical capital per worker might affect the level of real GDP per worker, holding human capital per worker and the state of technology fixed. In this example, we measure the quantity of physical capital in terms of the dollars worth of investment.

As you can see from the table, there is a big payoff from the first $15,000 invested in physical capital: real GDP per worker rises by $30,000. The second $15,000 worth of physical capital also raises productivity, but not by as much: real GDP per worker goes up by only $15,000. The third $15,000 worth of physical capital raises real GDP per worker by only $10,000.

AP® Exam Tip

Recognize that diminishing returns to physical capital can only be measured accurately if other factors like technology and human capital per worker are held constant.

To see why the relationship between physical capital per worker and productivity exhibits diminishing returns, think about how having farm equipment affects the productivity of farm workers. A little bit of equipment makes a big difference: a worker equipped with a tractor can do much more than a worker without one. And, other things equal, a worker using more expensive equipment will be more productive: a worker with a $30,000 tractor will normally be able to cultivate more farmland in a given amount of time than a worker with a $15,000 tractor because the more expensive machine will be more powerful, perform more tasks, or both.

But will a worker with a $30,000 tractor, holding human capital and technology constant, be twice as productive as a worker with a $15,000 tractor? Probably not: there's a huge difference between not having a tractor at all and having even an inexpensive tractor; there's much less difference between having an inexpensive tractor and having a better tractor. And we can be sure that a worker with a $150,000 tractor won't be 10 times as productive: a tractor can be improved only so much. Because the same is true of other kinds of equipment, the aggregate production function shows diminishing returns to physical capital.

Figure 38.1 is a graphical representation of the aggregate production function with diminishing returns to physical capital. As the *productivity curve* illustrates, more physical capital per worker leads to more output per worker. But each $30,000 increment in physical capital per worker adds less to productivity. By comparing points *A*, *B*, and *C*, you can also see that, as physical capital per worker rises, output per worker also rises—but at a diminishing rate. Going from point *A* to point *B*, representing a $30,000 increase in physical capital per worker, leads to an increase of $20,000 in real GDP per worker. Going from point *B* to point *C*, a second $30,000 increase in physical capital per worker, leads to an increase of only $10,000 in real GDP per worker.

It's important to realize that diminishing returns to physical capital is an "other things equal" phenomenon: additional amounts of physical capital are less productive

Figure 38.1 Physical Capital and Productivity

Other things equal, a greater quantity of physical capital per worker leads to higher real GDP per worker but is subject to diminishing returns: each successive addition to physical capital per worker produces a smaller increase in productivity. Starting at point *A*, with $20,000 in physical capital per worker, a $30,000 increase in physical capital per worker leads to an increase of $20,000 in real GDP per worker. At point *B*, with $50,000 in physical capital per worker, a $30,000 increase in physical capital per worker leads to an increase of only $10,000 in real GDP per worker.

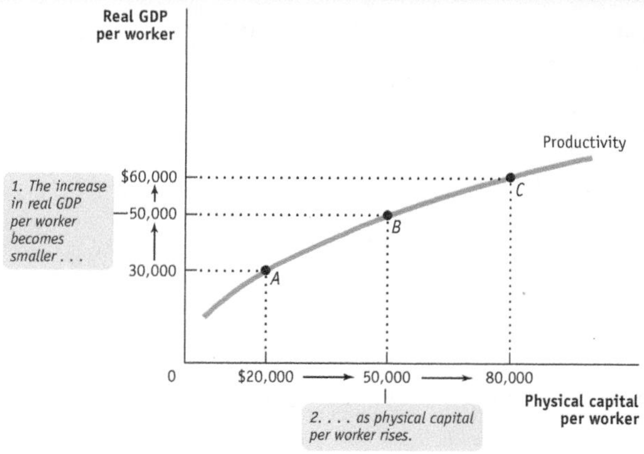

when the amount of human capital per worker and the technology are held fixed. Diminishing returns may disappear if we increase the amount of human capital per worker, or improve the technology, or both when the amount of physical capital per worker is increased. For example, a worker with a $30,000 tractor who has also been trained in the most advanced cultivation techniques may in fact be more than twice as productive as a worker with only a $15,000 tractor and no additional human capital. But diminishing returns to any one input—regardless of whether it is physical capital, human capital, or labor—is a pervasive characteristic of production. Typical estimates suggest that, in practice, a 1% increase in the quantity of physical capital per worker increases output per worker by only one-third of 1%, or 0.33%.

In practice, all the factors contributing to higher productivity rise during the course of economic growth: both physical capital and human capital per worker increase, and technology advances as well. To disentangle the effects of these factors, economists use **growth accounting** to estimate the contribution of each major factor in the aggregate production function to economic growth. For example, suppose the following are true:

- The amount of physical capital per worker grows 3% a year.
- According to estimates of the aggregate production function, each 1% rise in physical capital per worker, holding human capital and technology constant, raises output per worker by one-third of 1%, or 0.33%.

Economists use **growth accounting** to estimate the contribution of each major factor in the aggregate production function to economic growth.

In that case, we would estimate that growing physical capital per worker is responsible for 1 percentage point (3% × 0.33) of productivity growth per year. A similar but more complex procedure is used to estimate the effects of growing human capital. The procedure is more complex because there aren't simple dollar measures of the quantity of human capital.

Growth accounting allows us to calculate the effects of greater amounts of physical and human capital on economic growth. But how can we estimate the effects of technological progress? We can do so by estimating what is left over after the effects of physical and human capital have been taken into account. For example, let's imagine that there was no increase in human capital per worker so that we can focus on changes in physical capital

TEACH AP® Exam Tip

The AP® Macroeconomics exam will not cover the specific growth rates of Asia, South America, and Africa. The ideas presented in the growth section can be useful for understanding the testable material, however. Once the AP® exam is over, the material in this section would provide the basis for some outstanding research reports on economics.

Module 38 Productivity and Growth 375

TEACH AP® Exam Tip

Economic growth has been a heavily tested area on recent AP® exams. Make sure students understand and can explain the factors that cause or hinder economic growth.

Figure 38.2 Technological Progress and Productivity Growth

Technological progress shifts the productivity curve upward. Here we hold human capital per worker fixed. We assume that the lower curve (the same curve as in Figure 38.1) reflects technology in 1940 and the upper curve reflects technology in 2010. Holding technology and human capital fixed, quadrupling physical capital per worker from \$20,000 to \$80,000 leads to a doubling of real GDP per worker, from \$30,000 to \$60,000. This is shown by the movement from point *A* to point *C*, reflecting an approximately 1% per year rise in real GDP per worker. In reality, technological progress shifted the productivity curve upward and the actual rise in real GDP per worker is shown by the movement from point *A* to point *D*. Real GDP per worker grew 2% per year, leading to a quadrupling during the period. The extra 1% in growth of real GDP per worker is due to higher total factor productivity.

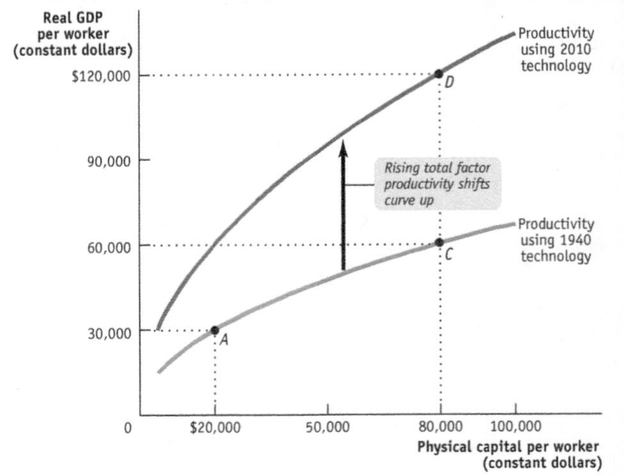

Total factor productivity is the amount of output that can be achieved with a given amount of factor inputs.

and in technology. In **Figure 38.2**, the lower curve shows the same hypothetical relationship between physical capital per worker and output per worker shown in Figure 38.1. Let's assume that this was the relationship given the technology available in 1940. The upper curve also shows a relationship between physical capital per worker and productivity, but this time given the technology available in 2010. (We've chosen a 70-year stretch to allow us to use the Rule of 70.) The 2010 curve is shifted up compared to the 1940 curve because technologies developed over the previous 70 years make it possible to produce more output for a given amount of physical capital per worker than was possible with the technology available in 1940. (Note that the two curves are measured in constant dollars.)

Let's assume that between 1940 and 2010 the amount of physical capital per worker rose from \$20,000 to \$80,000. If this increase in physical capital per worker had taken place without any technological progress, the economy would have moved from *A* to *C*: output per worker would have risen, but only from \$30,000 to \$60,000, or 1% per year (using the Rule of 70 tells us that a 1% growth rate over 70 years doubles output). In fact, however, the economy moved from *A* to *D*: output rose from \$30,000 to \$120,000, or 2% per year. There was an increase in both physical capital per worker and technological progress, which shifted the aggregate production function.

In this case, 50% of the annual 2% increase in productivity—that is, 1% in annual productivity growth—is due to higher **total factor productivity**, the amount of output that can be produced with a given amount of factor inputs. So when total factor productivity increases, the economy can produce more output with the same quantity of physical capital, human capital, and labor.

"Productivity is up nine per cent since I made everyone a vice-president."

376 Section 7 Economic Growth and Productivity

Most estimates find that increases in total factor productivity are central to a country's economic growth. We believe that observed increases in total factor productivity in fact measure the economic effects of technological progress. All of this implies that technological change is crucial to economic growth. The Bureau of Labor Statistics estimates the growth rate of both labor productivity and total factor productivity for nonfarm business in the United States. According to the Bureau's estimates, over the period from 1948 to 2010, American labor productivity rose 2.3% per year. Only 49% of that rise is explained by increases in physical and human capital per worker; the rest is explained by rising total factor productivity—that is, by technological progress.

What About Natural Resources?

In our discussion so far, we haven't mentioned natural resources, which certainly have an effect on productivity. Other things equal, countries that are abundant in valuable natural resources, such as highly fertile land or rich mineral deposits, have higher real GDP per capita than less fortunate countries. The most obvious modern example is the Middle East, where enormous oil deposits have made a few sparsely populated countries very rich. For instance, Kuwait has about the same level of real GDP per capita as South Korea, but Kuwait's wealth is based on oil, not manufacturing, the source of South Korea's high output per worker.

But other things are often not equal. In the modern world, natural resources are a much less important determinant of productivity than human or physical capital for the great majority of countries. For example, some nations with very high real GDP per capita, such as Japan, have very few natural resources. Some resource-rich nations, such as Nigeria (which has sizable oil deposits), are very poor.

Historically, natural resources played a much more prominent role in determining productivity. In the nineteenth century, the countries with the highest real GDP per capita were those abundant in rich farmland and mineral deposits: the United States, Canada, Argentina, and Australia. As a consequence, natural resources figured prominently in the development of economic thought. In a famous book published in 1798, *An Essay on the Principle of Population*, the English economist Thomas Malthus made the fixed quantity of land in the world the basis of a pessimistic prediction about future productivity. As population grew, he pointed out, the amount of land per worker would decline. And, other things equal, this would cause productivity to fall. In fact, his view was that improvements in technology or increases in physical capital would lead only to temporary improvements in productivity because they would always be offset by the pressure of rising population and more workers on the supply of land. In the long run, he concluded, the great majority of people were condemned to living on the edge of starvation. Only then would death rates be high enough and birth rates low enough to prevent rapid population growth from outstripping productivity growth.

© Frans Lemmens/Alamy

The offerings at markets such as this one in Lagos, Nigeria, are shaped by the available natural resources, human and physical capital, and technology.

It hasn't turned out that way, although many historians believe that Malthus's prediction of falling or stagnant productivity was valid for much of human history. Population pressure probably did prevent large productivity increases until the eighteenth century. But in the time since Malthus wrote his book, any negative effects on productivity from population growth have been far outweighed by other, positive factors—advances in technology, increases in human and physical capital, and the opening up of enormous amounts of cultivatable land in the New World.

It remains true, however, that we live on a finite planet, with limited supplies of resources such as oil and limited ability to absorb environmental damage. We address the concerns these limitations pose for economic growth later in this section.

TEACH Teach It

You should mention that natural resources do affect economic growth. Clearly, a nation that overexploits or pollutes its natural resources cannot enjoy much long-run growth, but the actual possession of many natural resources has become less important to productivity because nations that lack natural resources can often trade what they do have for what they need.

St. Louis Federal Reserve Bank Resources

"What Are the 'Ingredients' for Economic Growth?," *Page One Economics Classroom Edition* (September 2013)

Is there a recipe for economic growth? Perhaps some Miracle-Gro for the economy? If only it were that easy. While the exact recipe is a mystery, economists have identified some of the key ingredients. This issue discusses the role that economic institutions play in fostering long-term economic growth.

Module 38 Productivity and Growth 377

FYI The Information Technology Paradox

From the early 1970s through the mid-1990s, the United States went through a slump in total factor productivity growth. The figure shows Bureau of Labor Statistics estimates of annual total factor productivity growth since 1949. As you can see, there was a large fall in the productivity growth rate beginning in the early 1970s. Because higher total factor productivity plays such a key role in long-run growth, the economy's overall growth was also disappointing, leading to a widespread sense that economic progress had ground to a halt.

Many economists were puzzled by the slowdown in total factor productivity growth after 1973, since in other ways the era seemed to be one of rapid technological progress. Modern information technology really began with the development of the first microprocessor—a computer on a chip—in 1971. In the 25 years that followed, a series of inventions that seemed revolutionary became standard equipment in the business world: fax machines, desktop computers, cell phones, and e-mail. Yet the rate of growth of productivity remained stagnant. In a famous remark, MIT economics professor and Nobel laureate Robert Solow, a pioneer in the analysis of economic growth, declared that the information technology revolution could be seen everywhere except in the economic statistics.

Why didn't information technology show large rewards? Paul David, a Stanford University economic historian, offered a theory and a prediction. He pointed out that 100 years earlier another miracle technology—electric power—had spread through the economy, again with surprisingly little impact on productivity growth at first. The reason, he suggested, was that a new technology doesn't yield its full potential if you use it in old ways.

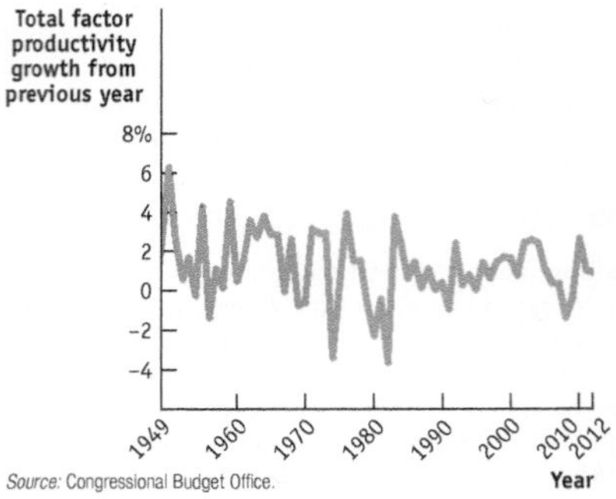

Source: Congressional Budget Office.

For example, a traditional factory around 1900 was a multistory building, with the machinery tightly crowded together and designed to be powered by a steam engine in the basement. This design had problems: it was very difficult to move people and materials around. Yet owners who electrified their factories initially maintained the multistory, tightly packed layout. Only with the switch to spread-out, one-story factories that took advantage of the flexibility of electric power—most famously Henry Ford's auto assembly line—did productivity take off.

David suggested that the same phenomenon was happening with information technology. Productivity, he predicted, would take off when people really changed their way of doing business to take advantage of the new technology—such as replacing letters and phone calls with e-mail. Sure enough, productivity growth accelerated dramatically in the second half of the 1990s. And, a lot of that may have been due to the discovery by companies like Walmart of how to effectively use information technology.

Success, Disappointment, and Failure

Rates of long-run economic growth differ markedly around the world. Let's look at three regions that have had quite different experiences with economic growth over the last few decades.

Figure 38.3 shows trends since 1960 in real GDP per capita in 2005 dollars for three countries: Argentina, Nigeria, and South Korea. (As in Figure 37.1, the vertical axis is drawn in logarithmic scale.) We have chosen these countries because each is a particularly striking example of what has happened in its region. South Korea's amazing rise is part of a larger success story in East Asia. Argentina's slow progress, interrupted by repeated setbacks, is more or less typical of the disappointment that has characterized Latin America. And Nigeria's unhappy story—real GDP per capita is barely higher now than it was in 1960—is, unfortunately, an experience shared by many African countries.

East Asia's Miracle

In 1960, South Korea was a very poor country. In fact, in 1960 its real GDP per capita was lower than that of India today. But, as you can see from Figure 38.3, beginning in the early 1960s, South Korea began an extremely rapid economic ascent: real GDP per

378 Section 7 Economic Growth and Productivity

Figure 38.3 Success and Disappointment

Real GDP per capita from 1960 to 2012, measured in 2005 dollars, is shown for Argentina, South Korea, and Nigeria, using a logarithmic scale. South Korea and some other East Asian countries have been highly successful at achieving economic growth. Argentina, like much of Latin America, has had several setbacks, slowing its growth. Nigeria's standard of living in 2012 was only barely higher than it had been in 1960, an experience shared by many African countries.

Source: World Bank.

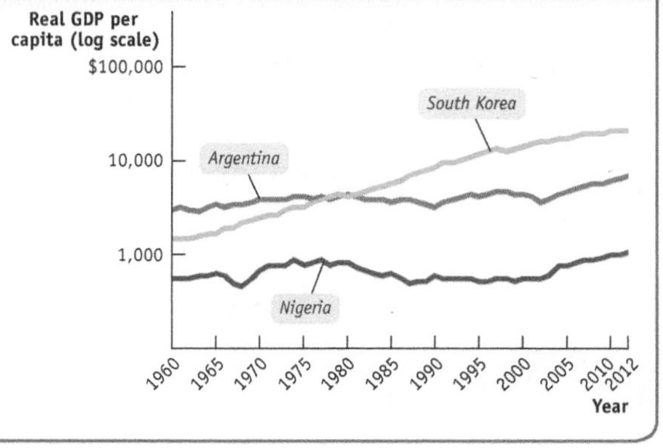

capita grew about 7% per year for more than 30 years. Today South Korea, though still somewhat poorer than Europe or the United States, looks very much like an economically advanced country.

South Korea's economic growth is unprecedented in history: it took the country only 35 years to achieve growth that required centuries elsewhere. Yet South Korea is only part of a broader phenomenon, often referred to as the East Asian economic miracle. High growth rates first appeared in South Korea, Taiwan, Hong Kong, and Singapore but then spread across the region, most notably to China. Since 1975, the whole region has increased real GDP per capita by 6% per year, three times America's historical rate of growth.

How have the Asian countries achieved such high growth rates? The answer is that all of the sources of productivity growth have been firing on all cylinders. Very high savings rates, the percentage of GDP that is saved nationally in any given year, have allowed the countries to significantly increase the amount of physical capital per worker. Very good basic education has permitted a rapid improvement in human capital. And these countries have experienced substantial technological progress.

Countries in East Asia have enjoyed unprecedented growth since the 1970s, thanks largely to the adoption of modern technology and the accumulation of human capital.

Why hasn't any economy achieved this kind of growth in the past? Most economic analysts think that East Asia's growth spurt was possible because of its *relative* backwardness. That is, by the time that East Asian economies began to move into the modern world, they could benefit from adopting the technological advances that had been generated in technologically advanced countries such as the United States. In 1900, the United States could not have moved quickly to a modern level of productivity because much of the technology that powers the modern economy, from jet planes to computers, hadn't been invented yet. In 1970, South Korea probably still had lower labor productivity than the United States had in 1900, but it could rapidly upgrade its productivity by adopting technology that had been developed in the United States, Europe, and Japan over the previous century. This was aided by a huge investment in human capital through widespread schooling.

The East Asian experience demonstrates that economic growth can be especially fast in countries that are playing catch-up to other countries with higher GDP per capita.

FOCUS Active Learning

TRM Have students watch any *PBS Newshour* story on economic growth or use the program's April 2011 news segment "China Weighs Environmental Concerns Against Economic Growth" (see econextras video list with hyperlinks on the bcs and TRFD). Suggested discussion questions and answers for this news segment can be found in the TRM under **Worksheet 38.1 (China and Growth)**.

St. Louis Federal Reserve Bank Resources

"Which Came First–Democracy or Growth?," *Inside the Vault*

In this article, students will compute real GDP and GDP per capita for three fictional countries. The Index of Economic Freedom will be used to compare and contrast the relationship between the degree of a country's economic freedom and the total output of that country and its standard of living.

Module 38 Productivity and Growth 379

According to the **convergence hypothesis**, international differences in real GDP per capita tend to narrow over time.

On this basis, many economists have suggested a general principle known as the **convergence hypothesis**. It says that differences in real GDP per capita among countries tend to narrow over time because countries that start with lower real GDP per capita tend to have higher growth rates. We'll look at the evidence for the convergence hypothesis later in this section.

Even before we get to that evidence, however, we can say right away that starting with a relatively low level of real GDP per capita is no guarantee of rapid growth, as the examples of Latin America and Africa both demonstrate.

Latin America's Disappointment

In 1900, Latin America was not regarded as an economically backward region. Natural resources, including both minerals and cultivatable land, were abundant. Some countries, notably Argentina, attracted millions of immigrants from Europe in search of a better life. Measures of real GDP per capita in Argentina, Uruguay, and southern Brazil were comparable to those in economically advanced countries.

David R. Frazier Photolibrary, Inc./Alamy

Relatively low rates of savings, investment spending, and education, along with political instability, have hampered economic growth in Latin America.

Since about 1920, however, growth in Latin America has been disappointing. As Figure 38.3 shows in the case of Argentina, it has remained disappointing to this day. The fact that South Korea is now much richer than Argentina would have seemed inconceivable a few generations ago.

Why has Latin America stagnated? Comparisons with East Asian success stories suggest several factors. The rates of savings and investment spending in Latin America have been much lower than in East Asia, partly as a result of irresponsible government policy that has eroded savings through high inflation, bank failures, and other disruptions. Education—especially broad basic education—has been underemphasized: even Latin American nations rich in natural resources often failed to channel that wealth into their educational systems. And political instability, leading to irresponsible economic policies, has taken a toll.

In the 1980s, many economists came to believe that Latin America was suffering from excessive government intervention in markets. They recommended opening the economies to imports, selling off government-owned companies, and, in general, freeing up individual initiative. The hope was that this would produce an East Asian–type economic surge. So far, however, only one Latin American nation, Chile, has achieved rapid growth. It now seems that pulling off an economic miracle is harder than it looks.

Africa's Troubles

Africa south of the Sahara is home to about 930 million people, nearly three times the population of the United States. On average, they are very poor, nowhere close to U.S. living standards 100 or even 200 years ago. And economic progress has been both slow and uneven, as the example of Nigeria, the most populous nation in the region, suggests. In fact, real GDP per capita in sub-Saharan Africa actually fell 13 percent from 1980 to 1994, although it has recovered since then. The consequence of this poor growth performance has been intense and continuing poverty.

This is a very disheartening picture. What explains it?

Perhaps first and foremost is the problem of political instability. In the years since 1975, large parts of Africa have experienced savage civil wars (often with outside powers backing rival sides) that have killed millions of people and made productive investment spending impossible. The threat of war and general anarchy has also inhibited other important preconditions for growth, such as education and provision of necessary infrastructure.

380 Section 7 Economic Growth and Productivity

FYI Are Economies Converging?

In the 1950s, much of Europe seemed quaint and backward to American visitors, and Japan seemed very poor. Today, a visitor to Paris or Tokyo sees a city that looks about as rich as New York. Although real GDP per capita is still somewhat higher in the United States, the differences in the standards of living among the United States, Europe, and Japan are relatively small.

Many economists have argued that this convergence in living standards is normal; the convergence hypothesis says that relatively poor countries should have higher rates of growth of real GDP per capita than relatively rich countries. And if we look at today's relatively well-off countries, the convergence hypothesis seems to be true. Panel (a) of the figure shows data for a number of today's wealthy economies measured in 2005 dollars. On the horizontal axis is real GDP per capita in 1955; on the vertical axis is the average annual growth rate of real GDP per capita from 1955 to 2010. There is a clear negative relationship. The United States was the richest country in this group in 1955 and had the slowest rate of growth. Japan and Spain were the poorest countries in 1955 and had the fastest rates of growth. These data suggest that the convergence hypothesis is true.

But economists who looked at similar data realized that these results depended on the countries selected. If you look at successful economies that have a high standard of living today, you find that real GDP per capita has converged. But looking across the world as a whole, including countries that remain poor, there is little evidence of convergence. Panel (b) of the figure illustrates this point using data for regions rather than individual countries (other than the United States). In 1955, East Asia and Africa were both very poor regions. Over the next 55 years, the East Asian regional economy grew quickly, as the convergence hypothesis would have predicted, but the African regional economy grew very slowly. In 1955, Western Europe had substantially higher real GDP per capita than Latin America. But, contrary to the convergence hypothesis, the Western European regional economy grew more quickly over the next 55 years, widening the gap between the regions.

So is the convergence hypothesis all wrong? No: economists still believe that countries with relatively low real GDP per capita tend to have higher rates of growth than countries with relatively high real GDP per capita, *other things equal*. But other things—education, infrastructure, rule of law, and so on—are often not equal. Statistical studies find that when you adjust for differences in these other factors, poorer countries do tend to have higher growth rates. This result is known as *conditional convergence*.

Because other factors differ, however, there is no clear tendency toward convergence in the world economy as a whole. Western Europe, North America, and parts of Asia are becoming more similar in real GDP per capita, but the gap between these regions and the rest of the world is growing.

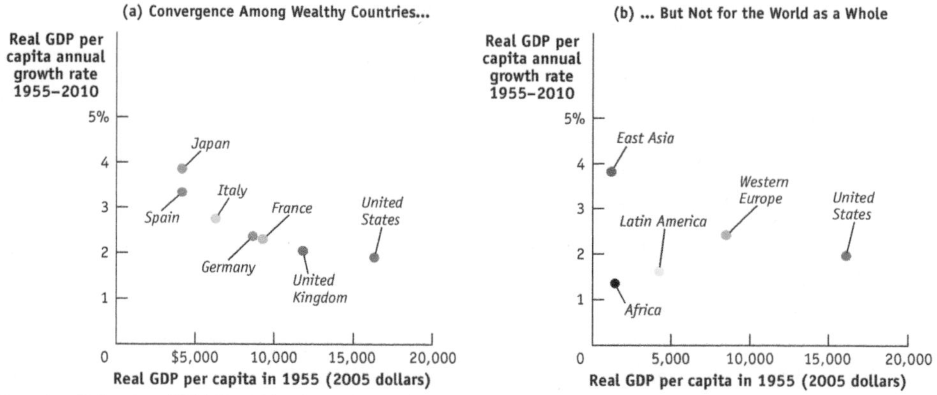

Sources: Angus Maddison, January 2003; J. Bolt and J. L. van Zanden, "The First Update of the Maddison Project; Re-Estimating Growth Before 1820," Maddison Project Working Paper 4, January 2003, http://www.ggdc.net/ maddison/maddison-project/home.htm.

Property rights are also a problem. The lack of legal safeguards means that property owners are often subject to extortion because of government corruption, making them averse to owning property or improving it. This is especially damaging in a country that is very poor.

While many economists see political instability and government corruption as the leading causes of underdevelopment in Africa, some—most notably Jeffrey Sachs of

Module 38 Productivity and Growth 381

OPEN & CLOSE Exit Slip

TRM *Please see **Exit Slip: Module 38** in the TRM for formative multiple-choice questions to ask your students before finishing your lesson. These questions will help you quickly assess whether your students have mastered the module's concepts before moving on.*

Answers to the Exit Slip Questions

1. C
2. E
3. A

Answers to Module 38 Review Questions

Check Your Understanding

1. a. Significant technological progress will allow an increase in productivity (real GDP per worker) at any given level of physical capital per worker. The result is an upward shift of the productivity curve.

b. An increase in the amount of physical capital per worker causes a movement upward and to the right along the productivity curve. Due to diminishing marginal returns, each successive increase in physical capital per worker results in a smaller increase in productivity than the one before it.

2. a. The amount of physical capital has increased by 4% per year and the size of the labor force hasn't changed, so the amount of physical capital per worker has increased by 4% per year. Given that each 1% increase in physical capital per worker raises productivity by 0.3%, the productivity growth attributable to growth in physical capital per worker is $4\% \times 0.3 = 1.2\%$ per year. Output has increased by 5% per year and the number of workers hasn't changed, so productivity (output per worker) has increased by 5% per year. The growth in physical capital per worker contributed $1.2\%/5\% \times 100\% = 24\%$ of this productivity growth.

b. If the labor force had grown by 4% per year, the 4% increase in physical capital per year would have been just enough to keep the physical capital per worker unchanged. Thus, none of the increase in productivity would have been attributable to growth in physical capital per worker.

3. It will take time for workers to learn how to use the new computer system and to adjust their routines. And because there are often setbacks in learning a new system, such as accidentally erasing your computer files, productivity at Multinomics may decrease for a period of time.

Columbia University and the United Nations—believe the opposite. They argue that Africa is politically unstable because Africa is poor. And Africa's poverty, they go on to claim, stems from its extremely unfavorable geographic conditions—much of the continent is landlocked, hot, infested with tropical diseases, and cursed with poor soil.

Sachs, along with economists from the World Health Organization, has highlighted the importance of health problems in Africa. In poor countries, worker productivity is often severely hampered by malnutrition and disease. In particular, tropical diseases such as malaria can be controlled only with an effective public health infrastructure, something that is lacking in much of Africa. At the time of this writing, economists are studying certain regions of Africa to determine whether modest amounts of aid given directly to residents for the purposes of increasing crop yields, reducing malaria, and increasing school attendance can produce self-sustaining gains in living standards.

Although the example of African countries represents a warning that long-run economic growth cannot be taken for granted, there are some signs of hope. Mauritius has developed a successful textile industry. Several African countries that are dependent on exporting commodities such as coffee and oil have benefited from the higher prices of those commodities. And Africa's economic performance since the mid-1990s has been generally much better than it was in preceding decades.

MODULE 38 Review

Check Your Understanding

1. Describe the shift in, or movement along, the productivity curve caused by each of the following:
   a. The amounts of physical and human capital per worker are unchanged, but there is significant technological progress.
   b. The amount of physical capital per worker grows, but the level of human capital per worker and technology are unchanged.
2. The real GDP of Erehwon has grown 5% per year over the past 30 years. The amount of physical capital has grown 4% per year. The size of the labor force hasn't changed. Estimates by economists say that each 1% increase in the amount of physical capital per worker, other things equal, raises productivity by 0.3%.
   a. How much has growing physical capital per worker contributed to productivity growth? What percentage of total productivity growth is that?
   b. How would your answer to part a change if the labor force had grown by 4% per year?
3. Multinomics, Inc., is a large company with many offices around the country. It has just adopted a new computer system that will affect virtually every function performed within the company. Why might a period of time pass before employees' productivity is improved by the new computer system? Why might there be a temporary decrease in employees' productivity?

Tackle the Test: Multiple-Choice Questions

1. Which of the following is a source of productivity growth?
   I. increased physical capital
   II. increased human capital
   III. technological progress
   a. I only
   b. II only
   c. III only
   d. I and II only
   e. I, II, and III
2. Which of the following is an example of physical capital?
   a. machinery
   b. health care
   c. education
   d. money
   e. all of the above

Tackle the Test: Multiple-Choice Questions

1. e
2. a

382 Section 7 Economic Growth and Productivity

3. The following statement describes which area of the world? "This area has experienced growth rates unprecedented in history and now looks like an economically advanced country."
   a. North America
   b. Latin America
   c. Europe
   d. East Asia
   e. Africa
4. Which of the following is cited as an important factor preventing long-run economic growth in Africa?
   a. political instability
   b. lack of property rights
   c. unfavorable geographic conditions
   d. poor health
   e. all of the above
5. The "convergence hypothesis"
   a. states that differences in real GDP per capita among countries widen over time.
   b. states that low levels of real GDP per capita are associated with higher growth rates.
   c. states that low levels of real GDP per capita are associated with lower growth rates.
   d. contradicts the "Rule of 70."
   e. has been proven by evidence from all parts of the world.

3. d
4. e
5. b

Tackle the Test: Free-Response Questions

1. A productivity curve is a graphical representation of an aggregate production function.
   a. Draw a correctly labeled graph of a productivity curve that illustrates diminishing returns to physical capital.
   b. Explain what it is about your productivity curve that indicates that there are diminishing returns to physical capital.
   c. On your graph, illustrate the effect of technological progress.
   d. How is the level of human capital per worker addressed on your graph?

Rubric for FRQ 1 (7 points)

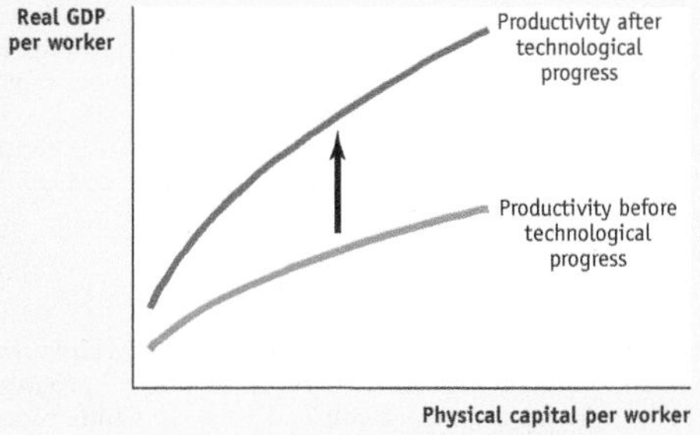

1 point: Vertical axis is labeled "Real GDP per worker."

1 point: Horizontal axis is labeled "Physical capital per worker."

1 point: Upward-sloping curve is labeled "Aggregate production function" or "Productivity."

1 point: Curve increases at a decreasing rate (the slope is positive and decreasing).

1 point: Equal increases in physical capital per worker lead to smaller increases in real GDP per worker.

1 point: Upward shift of production function is labeled to indicate technological progress.

1 point: Human capital per worker is held constant.

2. Croatia is a small country in Eastern Europe.
   a. Suppose that in Croatia each successive increase in the amount of physical capital per worker leads to the same increase in productivity. Use a correctly labeled graph to show what Croatia's productivity curve would look like.
   b. Suppose instead that each successive increase in the amount of physical capital per worker leads to a larger increase in productivity. Use a correctly labeled graph to show what Croatia's productivity curve would look like.
   c. Between 1991 and 1995, Croatia fought a war for independence from Yugoslavia. This war destroyed a significant portion of the physical capital in Croatia. Supposing all other things remained unchanged, explain how the effect of this change would be illustrated on your graph from part a.
   d. After the war, Croatia invested in education that increased each worker's ability to make productive use of any given amount of capital. Explain how this affected Croatia's productivity curve.

   (5 points)

Tackle the Test: Free-Response Question

Rubric for FRQ 2 (5 points)

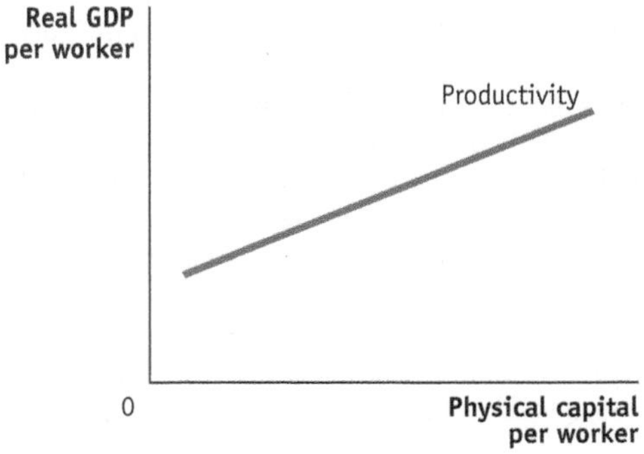

1 point: Graph with "Real GDP per worker" on the vertical axis and "Physical capital per worker" on the horizontal axis

1 point: Straight, upward-sloping productivity curve shown on graph

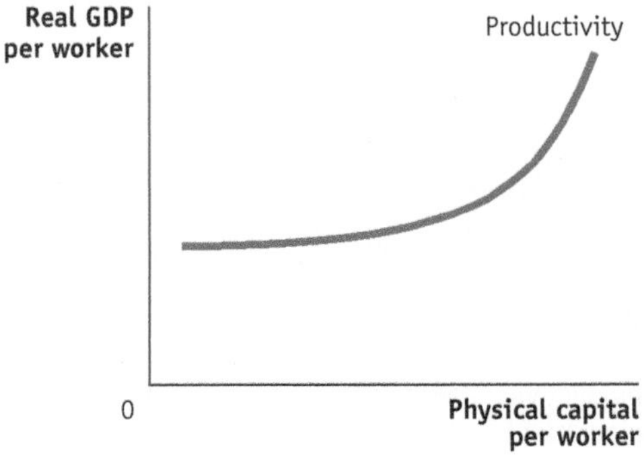

1 point: Graph with curve that increases at an increasing rate

1 point: Movement would occur to the left along the same productivity curve to indicate a decrease in the amount of physical capital per worker.

1 point: It shifted the productivity curve upward, because the real GDP per capita increased for any given amount of capital.

Module 38 Productivity and Growth 383

PD To prepare for teaching this lesson, you may want to consult the **Module 39 Sample Lecture** in the TRM.

OPEN & CLOSE Start Here

Show students the Real GDP Growth Rate chart at www.indexmundi.com/g/r.aspx?t=0&v=66&l=en. Ask them to identify any patterns in nations with high economic growth. Where does the United States rank in the listing? Why? *Answers will vary depending on when the table is used as data are dynamic. Students should talk about changes in productivity and natural resource availability as reasons for the rankings.* Students might believe that some nations just happen to be poor or rich and that how each nation got there was just some sort of random coincidence. It is important to stress that nations can make decisions today that have long-term consequences, both good and bad, on economic growth.

TEACH Teach It

If you are running short of time, skip this module if you have discussed the factors that cause a change in economic growth and productivity in previous chapters.

TEACH Connect It

Now is a great time to review how productivity affects the *AD–AS* model. Ask half your students, using their personal whiteboards or a piece of paper, to draw and explain how an increase in productivity affects the *AD–AS* model, while the other half graphs how a decrease in productivity affects the *AD–AS* model. *An increase in productivity decreases costs of production, shifting AS to the right, while a decrease in productivity increases the costs of production, shifting AS to the left.* This module explores the factors that change productivity a little more in depth.

FocusJapan/Alamy

MODULE 39 Growth Policy: Why Economic Growth Rates Differ

In this Module, you will learn to:

- Discuss the factors that explain why long-run growth rates differ so much among countries
- Explain the challenges to growth posed by the scarcity of natural resources, environmental degradation, and efforts to make growth sustainable

Why Growth Rates Differ

In 1820, according to estimates by the economic historian Angus Maddison, Mexico had somewhat higher real GDP per capita than Japan. Today, Japan has higher real GDP per capita than most European nations and Mexico is a poor country, though by no means among the poorest. The difference? Over the long run, real GDP per capita grew at 1.9% per year in Japan but at only 1.2% per year in Mexico.

As this example illustrates, even small differences in growth rates have large consequences over the long run. So why do growth rates differ across countries and across periods of time?

Explaining Differences in Growth Rates

As one might expect, economies with rapid growth tend to be economies that add physical capital, increase their human capital, or experience rapid technological progress. Striking economic success stories, like Japan in the 1950s and 1960s or China today, tend to be countries that do all three: rapidly add to their physical capital, upgrade their educational level, and make fast technological progress.

Adding to Physical Capital One reason for differences in growth rates among countries is that some countries are increasing their stock of physical capital much more rapidly than others, through high rates of investment spending. In the 1960s, Japan was the fastest-growing major economy; it also spent a much higher share of its GDP on investment goods than other major economies. Today, China is the fastest-growing major economy, and it similarly spends a very large share of its GDP on investment goods. In 2013, investment spending was 54.4% of China's GDP, compared with only 19% in the United States.

384 Section 7 Economic Growth and Productivity

Where does the money for high investment spending come from? We have already analyzed how financial markets channel savings into investment spending. The key point is that investment spending must be paid for either out of savings from domestic households or by an inflow of foreign capital—that is, savings from foreign households. Foreign capital has played an important role in the long-run economic growth of some countries, including the United States, which relied heavily on foreign funds during its early industrialization. For the most part, however, countries that invest a large share of their GDP are able to do so because they have high domestic savings. One reason for differences in growth rates, then, is that countries have different rates of savings and investment spending.

Adding to Human Capital Just as countries differ substantially in the rate at which they add to their physical capital, there have been large differences in the rate at which countries add to their human capital through education.

A case in point is the comparison between Argentina and China. In both countries, the average educational level has risen steadily over time, but it has risen much faster in China. **Figure 39.1** shows the average years of education of adults in China, which we have highlighted as a spectacular example of long-run growth, and in Argentina, a country whose growth has been disappointing. Compared to China, 60 years ago, Argentina had a much more educated population, while many Chinese were still illiterate. Today, the average educational level in China is still slightly below that in Argentina—but that's mainly because there are still many elderly adults who never received basic education. In terms of high school and college education, China has outstripped once-rich Argentina.

AP® Exam Tip

Growth rates between nations differ due to differing levels of physical capital, human capital, and technology. Past AP® exams have tested economic growth concepts but not actual growth rates.

Research and development, or **R&D**, is spending to create and implement new technologies.

Figure 39.1 China's Students Are Catching Up

In both China and Argentina, the average educational level—measured by the number of years the average adult aged 25 or older has spent in school—has risen over time. Although China is still lagging behind Argentina, it is catching up—and China's success at adding human capital is one key to its spectacular long-run growth.

Source: Robert Barro and Jong-Wha Lee, "A New Data Set of Educational Attainment in the World, 1950–2010," NBER Working Paper No. 15902 (April 2010).

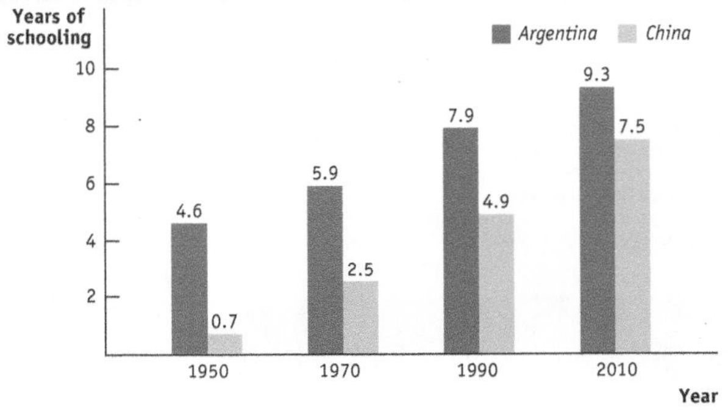

Technological Progress The advance of technology is a key force behind economic growth. What drives technology?

Scientific advances make new technologies possible. To take the most spectacular example in today's world, the semiconductor chip—which is the basis for all modern information technology—could not have been developed without the theory of quantum mechanics in physics.

But science alone is not enough: scientific knowledge must be translated into useful products and processes. And that often requires devoting a lot of resources to **research and development**, or **R&D**, spending to create new technologies and prepare them for practical use.

TEACH Teach It

Nations that have invested in physical capital such as factories and machinery grow faster than those that do not make the investment in growth strategies. Some of this investment comes from foreigners who are looking for a higher rate of return on their investments than they can earn in their own nations.

FOCUS In the News

TRM Ask students to read the February 2014 *Forbes* article "Why Panic-Prone Emerging Markets Are Breaking Down in 2014" on foreign capital investment at http://www.forbes.com/sites/steveschaefer/2014/02/03/why-panic-prone-emerging-markets-are-breaking-down-in-2014/. Suggested discussion questions and answers for this article can be found in the TRM under **Worksheet 39.1 (Emerging Markets).** You will encounter this article again in Section 8 when discussing foreign exchange markets.

TEACH Teach It

Higher educational levels increase economic growth. A more educated populace means a more productive worker. Use Figure 39.1 to point out the strides China is making in education, which is one key reason for its long-run economic growth.

TEACH Teach It

Nations that invest in R&D should experience more economic growth than nations that do not. New technology often allows businesses to do more with the same resources.

FYI Inventing R&D

Thomas Edison is best known as the inventor of the lightbulb and the phonograph. But his biggest invention may surprise you: he invented research and development.

Before Edison's time, of course, there had been many inventors. Some of them worked in teams. But in 1875 Edison created something new: his Menlo Park, New Jersey, laboratory. It employed 25 men full-time to generate new products and processes for business. In other words, he did not set out to pursue a particular idea and then cash in. He created an organization whose purpose was to create new ideas year after year.

Edison's Menlo Park lab is now a museum. "To name a few of the products that were developed in Menlo Park," says the museum's website, "we can list the following: the carbon button mouthpiece for the telephone, the phonograph, the incandescent lightbulb and the electrical distribution system, the electric train, ore separation, the Edison effect bulb, early experiments in wireless, the grasshopper telegraph, and improvements in telegraphic transmission."

You could say that before Edison's lab, technology just sort of happened: people came up with ideas, but businesses didn't plan to make continuous technological progress.

Now R&D operations, often much bigger than Edison's original team, are standard practice throughout the business world.

© Bettmann/CORBIS

Thomas Alva Edison in his laboratory in East Orange, New Jersey, in 1901.

Roads, power lines, ports, information networks, and other underpinnings for economic activity are known as **infrastructure**.

AP® Exam Tip

Don't automatically assume that government spending will have an impact on economic growth. Some government spending is on things that are not sources of economic growth.

Although some research and development is conducted by governments, much R&D is paid for by the private sector, as discussed in the FYI box. The United States became the world's leading economy in large part because American businesses were among the first to make systematic research and development a part of their operations.

Developing new technology is one thing; applying it is another. There have often been notable differences in the pace at which different countries take advantage of new technologies. America's surge in productivity growth after 1995, as firms learned to make use of information technology, was at least initially not matched in Europe.

The Role of Government in Promoting Economic Growth

Governments can play an important role in promoting—or blocking—all three sources of long-term economic growth: physical capital, human capital, and technological progress.

TEACH Teach It

The government can aid (or stifle) economic growth. By building infrastructure, governments open the way for private companies to invest in building factories, office space, and housing projects. Nations without infrastructure suffer from a lack of development. Ask students to give examples of how infrastructure has helped their local economy develop.

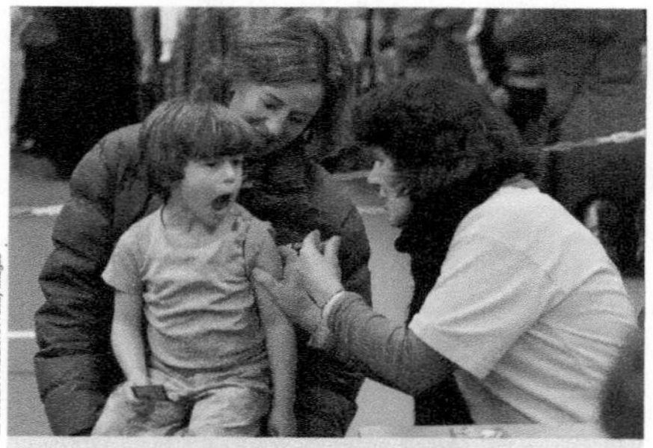
ED OUDENAARDEN/AFP/Getty Images

Governments play a vital role in health maintenance. A child is vaccinated against the influenza A (H1N1) virus during a mass vaccination in Schiedam, Netherlands.

Governments and Physical Capital Governments play an important direct role in building **infrastructure**: roads, power lines, ports, information networks, and other parts of an economy's physical capital that provide an underpinning, or foundation, for economic activity. Although some infrastructure is provided by private companies, much of it is either provided by the government or requires a great deal of government regulation and support. Ireland, whose economy really took off in the 1990s, is often cited as an example of the importance of government-provided infrastructure: the government invested in an excellent telecommunications infrastructure in the 1980s, and this helped make Ireland a favored location for high-technology companies.

Poor infrastructure—for example, a power grid that often fails, cutting off electricity to homes and businesses—is a major obstacle to economic growth in some countries. To provide good infrastructure, an economy must be able to afford it, but it must also have the political discipline to maintain it and provide for the future.

386 Section 7 Economic Growth and Productivity

Perhaps the most crucial infrastructure is something we rarely think about: basic public health measures in the form of a clean water supply and disease control. As we'll see in the next section, poor health infrastructure is a major obstacle to economic growth in poor countries, especially those in Africa.

Governments also play an important indirect role in making high rates of private investment spending possible. Both the amount of savings and the ability of an economy to direct savings into productive investment spending depend on the economy's institutions, notably its financial system. In particular, a well-functioning banking system is very important for economic growth because, in most countries, it is the principal way in which savings are channeled into business investment spending. If a country's citizens trust their banks, they will place their savings in bank deposits, which the banks will then lend to their business customers. But if people don't trust their banks, they will hoard gold or foreign currency, keeping their savings in safe deposit boxes or under their mattresses, where it cannot be turned into productive investment spending. A well-functioning financial system requires appropriate government regulation that assures depositors that their funds are protected.

Governments and Human Capital An economy's physical capital is created mainly through investment spending by individuals and private companies. Much of an economy's human capital, by contrast, is the result of government spending on education. Governments pay for the great bulk of primary and secondary education, although individuals pay a significant share of the costs of higher education.

As a result, differences in the rate at which countries add to their human capital largely reflect government policy. For example, East Asia now has a more educated population than Latin America. This isn't because East Asia is richer than Latin America and so can afford to spend more on education. Until very recently, East Asia, on average, was poorer than Latin America. Instead, it reflects the fact that Asian governments made broad education of the population a higher priority.

Governments and Technology Technological progress is largely the result of private initiative. But much important R&D is done by government agencies. For example, Brazil's agricultural boom was made possible by government researchers who discovered that adding crucial nutrients to the soil would allow crops to be grown on previously unusable land. They also developed new varieties of soybeans and breeds of cattle that flourish in Brazil's tropical climate.

Political Stability, Property Rights, and Excessive Government Intervention There's not much point in investing in a business if rioting mobs are likely to destroy it. And why save your money if someone with political connections can steal it? Political stability and protection of property rights are crucial ingredients in long-run economic growth.

Long-run economic growth in successful economies, like that of the United States, has been possible because there are good laws, institutions that enforce those laws, and a stable political system that maintains those institutions. The law must say that your property is really yours so that someone else can't take it away. The courts and the police must be honest so that they can't be bribed to ignore the law. And the political system must be stable so that the law doesn't change capriciously.

Americans take these preconditions for granted, but they are by no means guaranteed. Aside from the disruption caused by war or revolution, many countries find that their economic growth suffers due to corruption among the government officials who should be enforcing the law. For example, until 1991 the Indian government imposed many bureaucratic restrictions on businesses, which often had to bribe government officials to get approval for even routine activities—a tax on business, in effect. Economists have argued that a reduction in this burden of corruption is one reason Indian growth has been much faster in recent years than it was in the first 40 years after India gained independence in 1947.

TEACH Teach It

A country's government can do a lot to ensure economic growth. Governments subsidize education, particularly at the primary and secondary levels. Grants and scholarships may also be available to help students who wish to earn a higher education. This is just one way government can contribute to human capital. Governments may also contribute to research and development in the technology arena that filters down to private companies. What a government doesn't do itself may be subsidized with research grants for private corporations. Finally, providing a stable political system assists in the process of creating financial investments that will prove safe for foreign and domestic investors.

FYI The Brazilian Breadbasket

A wry Brazilian joke says that "Brazil is the country of the future—and always will be." The world's fifth most populous country has often been considered a possible major economic power, yet has never fulfilled that promise.

In recent years, however, Brazil's economy has made a better showing, especially in agriculture. This success depends on exploiting a natural resource, the tropical savanna land known as the *cerrado*. Until a quarter century ago, the land was considered unsuitable for farming. A combination of three factors changed that: technological progress due to research and development, improved economic policies, and greater physical capital.

The Brazilian Enterprise for Agricultural and Livestock Research, a government-run agency, developed the crucial technologies. It showed that adding lime and phosphorus made *cerrado* land productive, and it developed breeds of cattle and varieties of soybeans suited for the climate. (Now they're working on wheat.) Also, until the 1980s, Brazilian international trade policies discouraged exports, as did an overvalued exchange rate that made the country's goods more expensive to foreigners. After economic reform, investing in Brazilian agriculture became much more profitable and companies began putting in place the farm machinery, buildings, and other forms of physical capital needed to exploit the land.

What still limits Brazil's growth? Infrastructure. According to a report in the *New York Times*, Brazilian farmers are "concerned about the lack of reliable highways, railways and barge routes, which adds to the cost of doing business." Recognizing this, the Brazilian government is investing in infrastructure, and Brazilian agriculture is continuing to expand. The country has already overtaken the United States as the world's largest beef exporter and may not be far behind in soybeans.

Even when governments aren't corrupt, excessive government intervention can be a brake on economic growth. If large parts of the economy are supported by government subsidies, protected from imports, or otherwise insulated from competition, productivity tends to suffer because of a lack of incentives. As we saw in Module 38, excessive government intervention is one often-cited explanation for slow growth in Latin America.

Is World Growth Sustainable?

AP® Exam Tip

Understanding sustainability may be useful in answering free-response questions on the AP® exam.

Earlier, we described the views of Thomas Malthus, the nineteenth-century economist who warned that the pressure of population growth would tend to limit the standard of living. Malthus was right—about the past: for around 58 centuries, from the origins of civilization until his own time, limited land supplies effectively prevented any large rise in real incomes per capita. Since then, however, technological progress and rapid accumulation of physical and human capital have allowed the world to defy Malthusian pessimism.

But will this always be the case? Some skeptics have expressed doubt about whether long-run economic growth is **sustainable**—whether it can continue in the face of the limited supply of natural resources and the impact of growth on the environment.

Long-run economic growth is **sustainable** if it can continue in the face of the limited supply of natural resources and the impact of growth on the environment.

Natural Resources and Growth, Revisited

In 1972, a group of scientists called the Club of Rome made a big splash with a book titled *The Limits to Growth*, which argued that long-run economic growth wasn't sustainable due to limited supplies of nonrenewable resources such as oil and natural gas. These "neo-Malthusian" concerns at first seemed to be validated by a sharp rise in resource prices in the 1970s, then came to seem foolish when resource prices fell sharply in the 1980s. After 2005, however, resource prices rose sharply again, leading to renewed concern about resource limitations to growth. **Figure 39.2** shows the real price of oil—the price of oil adjusted for inflation in the rest of the economy. The rise and fall of concerns about resource-based limits to growth have more or less followed the rise and fall of oil prices shown in the figure.

Differing views about the impact of limited natural resources on long-run economic growth turn on the answers to three questions:

- How large are the supplies of key natural resources?
- How effective will technology be at providing alternatives to natural resources?
- Can long-run economic growth continue in the face of resource scarcity?

FOCUS Active Learning

TRM Have students read the February 2014 article "Public Capital in Countries with Abundant Natural Resources: Is There a Curse?" at http://journalistsresource.org/studies/international/development/public-capital-natural-resource-curse. Assign **Worksheet 39.2 (Sustainability)** from the TRM for suggested discussion questions and answers on this article. Hold a discussion with students to determine if they think that there really is a resource curse.

TEACH Teach It

Differing views about the impact of limited natural resources on long-run economic growth revolve around the answers to three key questions:

- How large are the supplies of key natural resources? *We need to ask geologists or officials in the oil, gas, and mining industries. Some believe that there are vast untapped resources "out there" and others believe that we are close to a plateau of oil and mineral extraction.*
- How effective will technology be at providing alternatives to natural resources? *Engineers will determine the answer to this question. Scientists around the world are already developing renewable ways to generate electricity on a large scale.*
- Can long-run economic growth continue in the face of resource scarcity? *This is a question for economists, and most economists are optimistic because they believe in human nature to respond to incentives. When prices are high, people consume less and put more effort into finding better (cheaper) alternatives. As oil becomes more scarce, oil prices will rise. The higher prices will provide a profit incentive for entrepreneurs to offer products that use less oil. Economists also theorize that we will never run completely out of oil, because the price of oil will eventually rise so high that consumers will find it less appealing than the alternatives.*

Figure 39.2 The Real Price of Oil, 1949–2013

The real price of natural resources, like oil, rose dramatically in the 1970s and then fell just as dramatically in the 1980s. Since 2005, however, the real prices of natural resources have soared.

Sources: Energy Information Administration, Bureau of Labor Statistics.

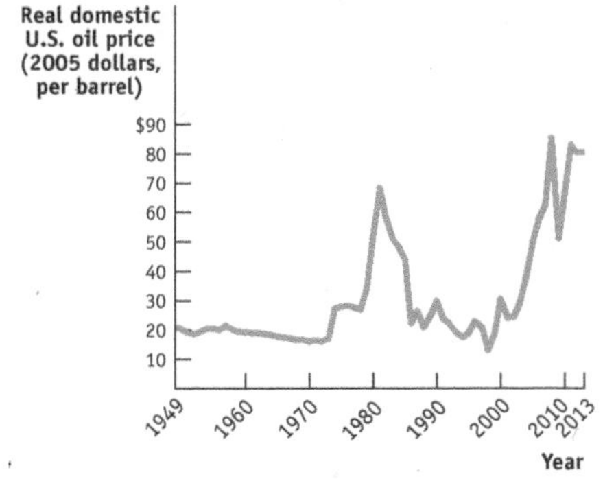

FOCUS Active Learning

Have students take a look at Figure 39.2. Ask the following questions:

- How has oil consumption changed over time? *Through conservation efforts, oil consumption has decreased.*
- Why do you think real GDP has continued to increase even though oil consumption has decreased? *Technology has allowed for more efficient use of oil. Also, the service sector, which places less reliance on oil, has grown relative to the manufacturing sector of the economy.*

It's mainly up to geologists to answer the first question. Unfortunately, there's wide disagreement among the experts, especially about the prospects for future oil production. Some analysts believe that there is so much untapped oil in the ground that world oil production can continue to rise for several decades. Others—including a number of oil company executives—believe that the growing difficulty of finding new oil fields will cause oil production to plateau—that is, stop growing and eventually begin a gradual decline—in the fairly near future. Some analysts believe that we have already reached that plateau.

The answer to the second question, whether there are alternatives to certain natural resources, will come from engineers. There's no question that there are many alternatives to the natural resources currently being depleted, some of which are already being exploited. For example, "unconventional" oil extracted from Canadian tar sands is already making a significant contribution to world oil supplies, and electricity generated by wind turbines is rapidly becoming big business in the United States—a development highlighted by the fact that in 2009 the United States surpassed Germany to become the world's largest producer of wind energy.

The third question, whether economies can continue to grow in the face of resource scarcity, is mainly a question for economists. And most, though not all, economists are optimistic: they believe that modern economies can find ways to work around limits on the supply of natural resources. One reason for this optimism is the fact that resource scarcity leads to high resource prices. These high prices in turn provide strong incentives to conserve the scarce resource and to find alternatives.

For example, after the sharp increases in oil prices during the 1970s, American consumers turned to smaller, more fuel-efficient cars, and U.S. industry also greatly intensified its efforts to reduce energy bills. The result is shown in **Figure 39.3** on the next page, which compares the growth rates of real GDP per capita and oil consumption before and after the 1970s energy crisis. Before 1973, there seemed to be a more or less one-to-one relationship between economic growth and oil consumption, but after 1973 the U.S. economy continued to deliver growth in real GDP per capita even as it substantially reduced its use of oil. This move toward conservation paused after 1990, as low real oil prices

The Tehachapi Wind Farm, in Tehachapi, California, is the second largest collection of wind generators in the world. The turbines are operated by several private companies and collectively produce enough electricity to meet the needs of 350,000 people every year.

St. Louis Federal Reserve Bank Resources

"Higher Gasoline Prices: Temporary or Time to Buy a Hybrid?" ***Page One Economics Classroom Edition*** **(September 2012)**

When gasoline prices spike, drivers may wonder whether the high prices are temporary or permanent. Will prices eventually return to the lower levels of the past? Or is it time for drivers to alter their driving habits, maybe by buying a hybrid car? Students should be sure to read this issue for a discussion of factors that might influence that decision.

Module 39 Growth Policy: Why Economic Growth Rates Differ 389

FOCUS In the News

Have students read the following two articles from October 2013: "Report: Climate change may pose threat to economic growth" at http://www.cnn.com/2013/10/29/world/climate-change-vulnerability-index/ and "Germany's Renewable Energy Subsidies Could Threaten Economic Growth" at http://www.forbes.com/sites/williampentland/2013/10/11/germanys-renewable-energy-subsidies-could-threaten-economic-growth/.

After reading the articles, ask students to use their understanding of the concept of economic growth and the information found in the 2 articles to support or refute the following statement: It is more important for a nation to protect the environment than to enhance economic growth.

Figure 39.3 U.S. Oil Consumption and Growth over Time

Until 1973, the real price of oil was relatively low and there was a more or less one-to-one relationship between economic growth and oil consumption. Conservation efforts increased sharply after the spike in the real price of oil in the mid-1970s. Yet the U.S. economy was still able to grow despite cutting back on oil consumption.

Sources: Energy Information Administration; Bureau of Economic Analysis.

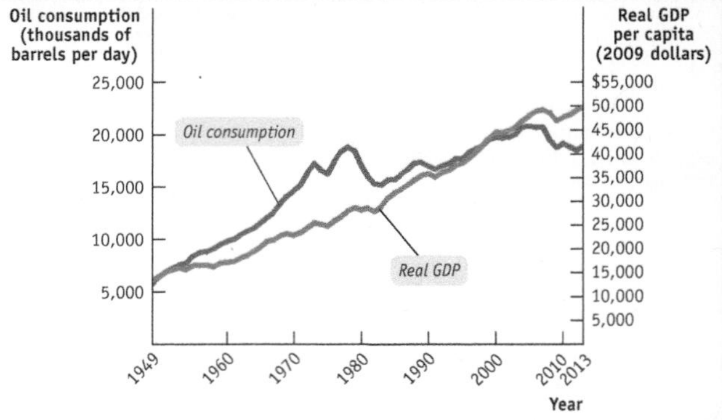

encouraged consumers to shift back to gas-greedy larger cars and SUVs. A sharp rise in oil prices from 2005 to 2008 encouraged renewed shifts toward oil conservation, although these shifts lost some steam as prices started falling again in late 2008.

Given such responses to prices, economists generally tend to see resource scarcity as a problem that modern economies handle fairly well, rather than a fundamental limit to long-run economic growth. Environmental issues, however, pose a more difficult problem because dealing with them requires effective political action.

Economic Growth and the Environment

Economic growth, other things equal, tends to increase the human impact on the environment. For example, China's spectacular economic growth has also brought a spectacular increase in air pollution in that nation's cities. It's important to realize, however, that other things aren't necessarily equal: countries can and do take action to protect their environments. In fact, air and water quality in today's advanced countries is generally much better than it was a few decades ago. London's famous "fog"—actually a form of air pollution, which killed 4,000 people during a two-week episode in 1952—is gone, thanks to regulations that virtually eliminated the use of coal heat. The equally famous smog of Los Angeles, although not extinguished, is far less severe than it was in the 1960s and early 1970s, again thanks to pollution regulations.

Despite these past environmental success stories, there is widespread concern today about the environmental impacts of continuing economic growth, reflecting a change in the scale of the problem. Environmental success stories have mainly involved dealing with *local* impacts of economic growth, such as the effect of widespread car ownership on air quality in the Los Angeles basin. Today, however, we are faced with *global* environmental issues—the adverse impacts on the environment of the Earth as a whole by worldwide economic growth. The biggest of these issues involves the impact of fossil-fuel consumption on the world's climate.

Burning coal and oil releases carbon dioxide into the atmosphere. There is broad scientific consensus that rising levels of carbon dioxide and other gases are causing a greenhouse effect on the Earth, trapping more of the sun's energy and raising the planet's overall temperature. And rising temperatures may impose high human and

St. Louis Federal Reserve Bank Resources

"Economics and the Environment," *Page One Economics Classroom Edition* (September 2014)

How are economics and the environment related? The quick answer is that environmental quality is a worthy goal, but there is an economic trade-off—a clean environment does not come without costs. This article provides some economic strategies for protecting the environment.

FYI Coal Comfort on Resources

Those who worry that exhaustion of natural resources will bring an end to economic growth can take some comfort from the story of William Stanley Jevons, a nineteenth-century British economist best known today for his role in the development of marginal analysis. In addition to his work in economic theory, Jevons worked on the real-world economic problems of the day, and in 1865 he published an influential book, *The Coal Question*, that foreshadowed many modern concerns about resources and growth. But his pessimism was proved wrong.

The Industrial Revolution was launched in Britain, and in 1865 Britain still had the world's richest major economy. But Jevons argued that Britain's economic success had depended on the availability of cheap coal and that the gradual exhaustion of Britain's coal resources, as miners were forced to dig ever deeper, would threaten the nation's long-run prosperity.

He was right about the exhaustion of Britain's coal: production peaked in 1913, and today the British coal industry is a shadow of its former self. But Britain was able to turn to alternative sources of energy, including imported coal and oil. And economic growth did not collapse: real GDP per capita in Britain today is about seven times its level in 1865.

economic costs: rising sea levels may flood coastal areas; changing climate may disrupt agriculture, especially in poor countries; and so on.

The problem of climate change is clearly linked to economic growth. **Figure 39.4** shows carbon dioxide emissions from the United States, Europe, and China since 1980. Historically, the wealthy nations have been responsible for the bulk of these emissions because they have consumed far more energy per person than poorer countries. As China and other emerging economies have grown, however, they have begun to consume much more energy and emit much more carbon dioxide.

Is it possible to continue long-run economic growth while curbing the emissions of greenhouse gases? The answer, according to most economists who have studied the issue, is yes. It should be possible to reduce greenhouse gas emissions in a wide variety of ways, ranging from the use of non-fossil-fuel energy sources such as wind, solar, and nuclear power; to preventive measures such as carbon sequestration (capturing carbon dioxide and storing it); to simpler things like designing buildings so that they're easier to keep warm in winter and cool in summer. Such measures would impose costs on the economy, but the best available estimates suggest that even a large reduction in greenhouse gas emissions over the next few decades would only modestly dent the long-term rise in real GDP per capita.

Figure 39.4 Climate Change and Growth

Greenhouse gas emissions are positively related to growth. As shown here by the United States and Europe, wealthy countries have historically been responsible for the great bulk of greenhouse gas emissions because of their richer and faster-growing economies. As China and other emerging economies have grown, they have begun to emit much more carbon dioxide.

Source: Energy Information Administration.

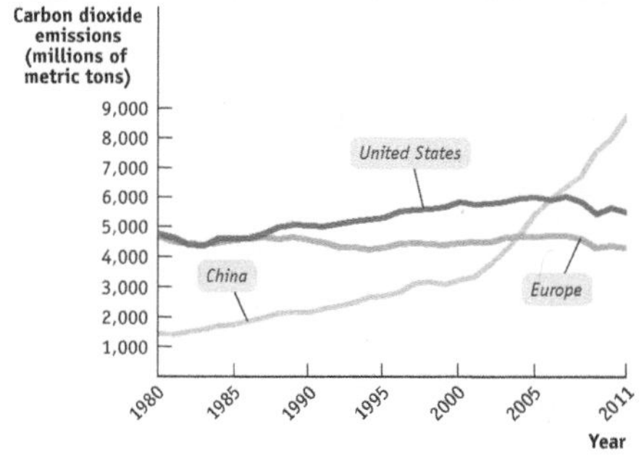

Module 39 Growth Policy: Why Economic Growth Rates Differ 391

OPEN & CLOSE Exit Slip

TRM *Please see **Exit Slip: Module 39** in the TRM for formative multiple-choice questions to ask your students before finishing your lesson. These questions will help you quickly assess whether your students have mastered the module's concepts before moving on.*

Answers to the Exit Slip Questions

1. C
2. E
3. D

The problem is how to make all of this happen. Unlike resource scarcity, environmental problems don't automatically provide incentives for changed behavior. Pollution is an example of a *negative externality*, a cost that individuals or firms impose on others without having to offer compensation. In the absence of government intervention, individuals and firms have no incentive to reduce negative externalities, which is why it took regulation to reduce air pollution in America's cities. And as Nicholas Stern, the author of an influential report on climate change, put it, greenhouse gas emissions are "the mother of all externalities."

So there is a broad consensus among economists—although there are some dissenters—that government action is needed to deal with climate change. There is also broad consensus that this action should take the form of market-based incentives, either in the form of a carbon tax—a tax per unit of carbon emitted—or a cap and trade system in which the total amount of emissions is capped, and producers must buy licenses to emit greenhouse gases. However, there is considerable dispute about how much action is appropriate, reflecting both uncertainty about the costs and benefits and scientific uncertainty about the pace and extent of climate change.

There are also several aspects of the climate change problem that make it much more difficult to deal with than, say, smog in Los Angeles. One is the problem of taking the long view. The impact of greenhouse gas emissions on the climate is very gradual: carbon dioxide put into the atmosphere today won't have its full effect on the climate for several generations. As a result, there is the political problem of persuading voters to accept pain today in return for gains that will benefit their children, grandchildren, or even great-grandchildren.

The added problem of international burden sharing presents a stumbling block for consensus, as it did at the United Nations Climate Change Conference in 2013. As Figure 39.4 shows, today's rich countries have historically been responsible for most greenhouse gas emissions, but newly emerging economies like China are responsible for most of the recent growth. Inevitably, rich countries are reluctant to pay the price of reducing emissions only to have their efforts frustrated by rapidly growing emissions from new players. On the other hand, countries like China, which are still relatively poor, consider it unfair that they should be expected to bear the burden of protecting an environment threatened by the past actions of rich nations.

Despite political issues and the need for compromise, the general moral of this story is that it is possible to reconcile long-run economic growth with environmental protection. The main question is one of getting political consensus around the necessary policies.

FYI The Cost of Climate Protection

In recent years, members of Congress have introduced a number of bills, some of them with bipartisan sponsorship, calling for ambitious, long-term efforts to reduce U.S. emissions of greenhouse gases. For example, a bill sponsored by Senators Joseph Lieberman and John McCain would use a cap and trade system to gradually reduce emissions over time, eventually—by 2050—reducing them to 60% below their 1990 level. Another bill, sponsored by Senators Barbara Boxer and Bernie Sanders, called for an 80% reduction by 2050.

Would implementing these bills put a stop to long-run economic growth? Not according to a comprehensive study by a team at MIT, which found that reducing emissions would impose significant but not overwhelming costs. Using an elaborate model of the interaction between environmental policy and the economy, the MIT group estimated that the Lieberman-McCain proposal would reduce real GDP per capita in 2050 by 1.11% and the more stringent Sanders-Boxer proposal would reduce real GDP per capita by 1.79%.

These may sound like big numbers—they would amount to between $200 billion and $250 billion today—but they would hardly make a dent in the economy's long-run growth rate. Remember that over the long run the U.S. economy has on average seen real GDP per capita rise by almost 2% a year. If the MIT group's estimates are correct, even a strong policy to avert climate change would, in effect, require that we give up less than one year's growth over the next four decades.

St. Louis Federal Reserve Bank Resources

"Externalities," *The Economic Lowdown Podcast Series* (Volume 1, Episode 11)

Ever feel as if you are paying the price for someone else's "deal"? Perhaps you are choking on the pollution from a foundry where cheap widgets are made. That spillover effect is called an externality. There are positive ones, too. The running time of this podcast is 8:09.

St. Louis Federal Reserve Bank Resources

"Externalities," *The Economic Lowdown Video Series*, Episode 5

In this episode, Scott Wolla, economic education specialist, explains externalities. Students will learn how costs and benefits sometimes affect bystanders and discover how taxes and subsidies can be used to "internalize" externalities.

MODULE 39 Review

Check Your Understanding

1. Explain the link between a country's growth rate, its investment spending as a percent of GDP, and its domestic savings.
2. Which of the following is the better predictor of a future high long-run growth rate: a high standard of living today or high levels of savings and investment spending? Explain your answer.
3. Some economists think the best way to help African countries is for wealthier countries to provide more funds for basic infrastructure. Others think this policy will have no long-run effect unless African countries have the financial and political means to maintain this infrastructure. What policies would you suggest?
4. What is the link between greenhouse gas emissions and growth? What is the expected effect on growth from emissions reduction? Why is international burden sharing of greenhouse gas emissions reduction a contentious problem?

Tackle the Test: Multiple-Choice Questions

1. Economies experience more rapid economic growth when they do which of the following?
   - I. add physical capital
   - II. promote technological progress
   - III. limit human capital

   a. I only
   b. II only
   c. III only
   d. I and II only
   e. I, II, and III
2. Which of the following can lead to increases in physical capital in an economy?
   a. increased investment spending
   b. increased savings by domestic households
   c. increased savings from foreign households
   d. an inflow of foreign capital
   e. all of the above
3. Which of the following is true of sustainable long-run economic growth?
   a. Long-run growth can continue in the face of the limited supply of natural resources.
   b. It was predicted by Thomas Malthus.
   c. Modern economies handle resource scarcity problems poorly.
   d. It is less likely when we find alternatives to natural resources.
   e. All of the above are true.
4. Which of the following statements is true of environmental quality?
   a. It is typically not affected by government policy.
   b. Other things equal, it tends to improve with economic growth.
   c. There is broad scientific consensus that rising levels of carbon dioxide and other gases are raising the planet's overall temperature.
   d. Most economists believe it is not possible to reduce greenhouse gas emissions while economic growth continues.
   e. Most environmental success stories involve dealing with global, rather than local impacts.
5. According to the MIT study discussed in the module, a cap and trade system to reduce greenhouse gas emissions in the United States would lead to
   a. no significant costs.
   b. significant but not overwhelming costs.
   c. a loss of roughly three year's real GDP over the next 40 years.
   d. a reduction in real GDP per capita of over 10%.
   e. a loss of 5 years' worth of economic growth over the next 40 years.

Answers to Module 39 Review Questions

Check Your Understanding

1. A country that has high domestic savings is able to achieve a high rate of investment spending as a percent of GDP. This, in turn, allows the country to achieve a high growth rate.

2. As you can see from panel (b) of the figure in the FYI box on page 381, although it is important in determining the growth rate for some countries (such as those of Western Europe), the initial level of GDP per capita isn't a particularly good predictor of high future growth rates. High rates of savings and investment appear to be better predictors of future growth than today's standard of living.

3. The evidence suggests that both sets of factors matter: better infrastructure is important for growth, but so is political and financial stability. Policies should try to address both areas.

4. Growth increases a country's greenhouse gas emissions. The current best estimates are that a large reduction in emissions will result in only a modest reduction in growth. The international burden sharing of greenhouse gas emissions reduction is contentious because rich countries are reluctant to pay the costs of reducing their emissions only to see newly emerging countries like China rapidly increase their emissions. Poorer countries like China are equally reluctant to limit their growth to protect an environment threatened by the past actions of rich countries.

Tackle the Test: Multiple-Choice Questions

1. d	3. a	5. b
2. e	4. c	

Module 39 Growth Policy: Why Economic Growth Rates Differ 393

Tackle the Test: Free-Response Question Rubric for FRQ 2 (4 points)

1 point: Countries that have increased their stock of physical capital more rapidly than others have experienced higher rates of economic growth.

1 point: Countries that have made relatively large investments in education to add to their human capital have experienced higher rates of economic growth.

1 point: Countries that have devoted a lot of resources to R&D have enjoyed technological progress, which is a key driver of economic growth.

1 point: Historically, natural resources played a prominent role in determining productivity, while today they play a less important role in increasing productivity than do increases in human or physical capital in most countries.

Tackle the Test: Free-Response Questions

1. List and explain five different actions the government can take to promote long-run economic growth.

Rubric for FRQ 1 (10 points)

A maximum of 10 points can be earned for any 5 of the 6 possible actions/descriptions.

1 point: Build infrastructure

1 point: The government can provide roads, power lines, ports, rail lines, and related systems to support economic activity.

1 point: Invest in human capital

1 point: The government can improve access to quality education.

1 point: Invest in research and development

1 point: The government can promote technological progress by having government agencies support and participate in R&D.

1 point: Provide political stability

1 point: The government can create and maintain institutions that make and enforce laws that promote stability.

1 point: Establish and protect property rights

1 point: Growth is promoted by laws that define what property belongs to whom and by institutions that defend those property rights.

1 point: Minimize government intervention

1 point: The government can limit its intervention in the economy and promote competition.

2. What roles do physical capital, human capital, technology, and natural resources play in influencing the differences in long-run economic growth rates among countries? **(4 points)**

394 Section 7 Economic Growth and Productivity

Jetta Productions/Getty Images

MODULE 40 Economic Growth in Macroeconomic Models

In this Module, you will learn to:

- Explain how long-run economic growth is represented in macroeconomic models
- Model the effects of economic growth policies

Long-run economic growth is fundamental to solving many of today's most pressing economic problems. It is even more critical in poorer, less developed countries. But the policies we have studied in earlier sections to address short-run fluctuations and the business cycle may not encourage long-run economic growth. For example, an increase in household consumption can help an economy to recover from a recession. However, when households increase consumption, they decrease their savings, which leads to decreased investment spending and slows long-run economic growth.

In addition to understanding short-run stabilization policies, we need to understand the factors that influence economic growth and how choices by governments and individuals can promote or retard that growth in the long-run.

Long-run economic growth is the sustained rise in the quantity of goods and services the economy produces, as opposed to the short-run ups and downs of the business cycle. In Module 18, we looked at actual and potential output in the United States from 1989 to 2013. As shown in **Figure 40.1** on the next page, increases in potential output during that time represent long-run economic growth in the economy. The fluctuations of actual output compared to potential output are the result of the business cycle.

As we have seen throughout this section, long-run economic growth depends almost entirely on rising productivity. Good macroeconomic policy strives to foster increases in productivity, which in turn leads to long-run economic growth. In this module, we will learn how to evaluate the effects of long-run growth policies using the production possibilities curve and the aggregate demand and supply model.

PD To prepare for teaching this lesson, you may want to consult the **Module 40 Sample Lecture** in the TRM.

OPEN & CLOSE Start Here

This module is about graphing economic growth. Ask your students to use their personal whiteboards or a piece of paper to draw a *PPC* for a nation producing clothing and food. Next to that graph, have them draw an *AD–AS* model for a nation in long-run equilibrium. As a review, ask students to identify the following on the *PPC*:

- a point that is unattainable (labeled *A*) *Anywhere outside the curve*
- a point that could indicate that there is unemployment in the economy (labeled *B*) *Anywhere inside the curve*
- a point that corresponds with productive efficiency (labeled *C*) *Anywhere on the curve*

Draw the two graphs correctly on the board so that students can check their own graphs.

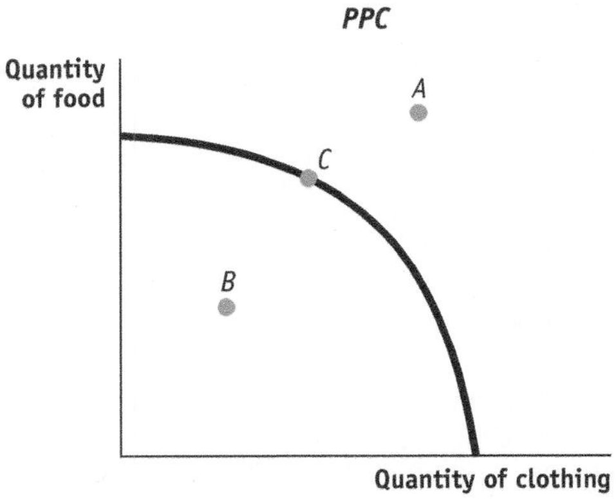

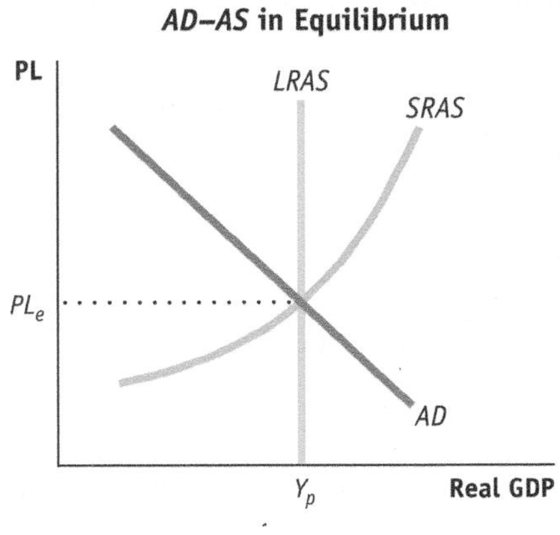

Module 40 Economic Growth in Macroeconomic Models 395

FOCUS Active Learning

Point to the *A* on the production possibilities curve you drew on the board. How can the economy ever hope to reach point *A*? If your students say "through trade," how would the economy reach point *A* if the nation had no trading partners? *Through economic growth attained by increasing productivity in the nation, more training for human capital, and new resource availability*

TEACH Connect It

Have students refer to your drawing of *AD–AS* in long-run equilibrium. Using Figure 40.1, point out that any time actual and potential outputs are the same, the *AD–AS* graph will take this form.

Next, have students draw the *AD–AS* graph that would represent the relationship between actual and potential output in 2000. In this case, actual aggregate output exceeds potential output and the *AD–AS* graph would exhibit an inflationary gap.

***AD–AS* in 2000**

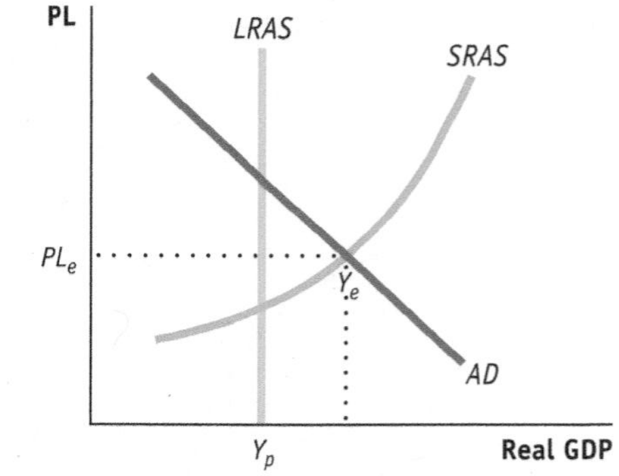

Finally, have students draw the *AD–AS* graph that would represent the relationship between actual and potential output in 2010. In this case, potential aggregate output exceeds actual output and the *AD–AS* graph would exhibit a recessionary gap.

***AD–AS* in 2010**

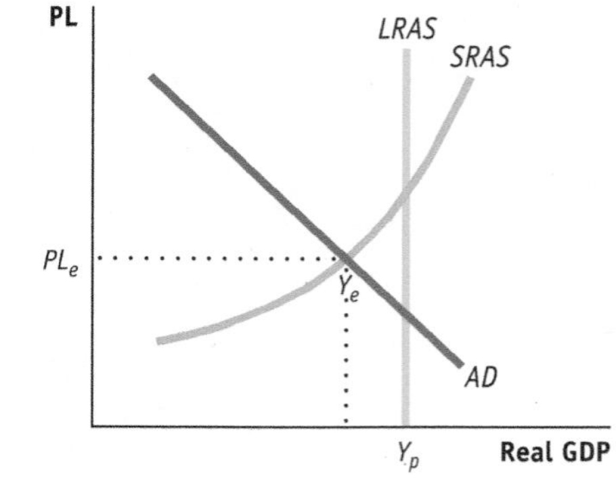

Figure 40.1 Actual and Potential Output from 1989 to 2013

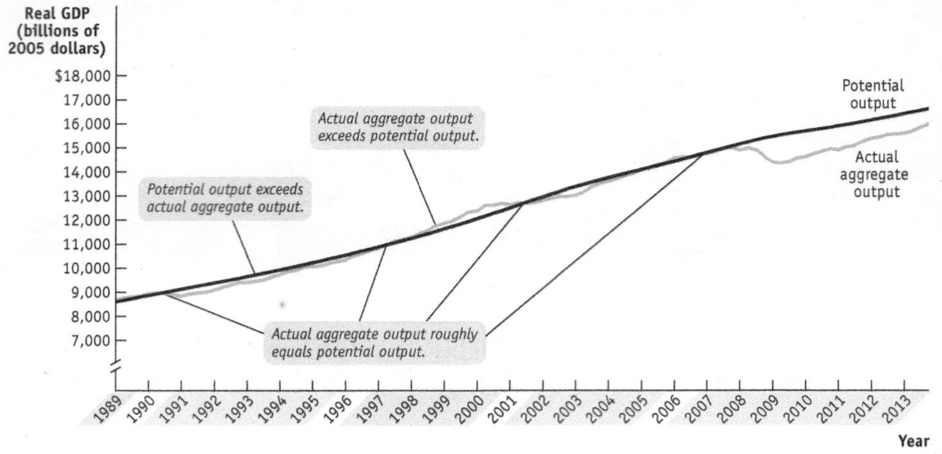

This figure shows the performance of actual and potential output in the United States from 1989 to 2013. The black line shows estimates, produced by the Congressional Budget Office, of U.S. potential output. The blue line shows actual aggregate output. The purple-shaded years are periods in which actual aggregate output fell below potential output, and the green-shaded years are periods in which actual aggregate output exceeded potential output. As shown, significant shortfalls occurred in the recessions of the early 1990s and after 2000. Actual aggregate output was significantly above potential output in the boom of the late 1990s.

Sources: Congressional Budget Office, Bureau of Economic Analysis.

AP® Exam Tip

The AP® exam has included questions on how to show economic growth on a graph. You should be able to draw a correctly labeled *PPC* and show economic growth with an outward shift.

Long-Run Economic Growth and the Production Possibilities Curve

Recall from Section 1 that we defined the production possibilities curve as a graph that illustrates the trade-offs facing an economy that produces only two goods. In our example, we developed the production possibilities curve for Tom, a castaway facing a trade-off between producing fish and coconuts. Looking at **Figure 40.2**, we see that economic growth is shown as an outward shift of the production possibilities curve. Now let's return to the production possibilities curve model and use a different example to illustrate how economic growth policies can lead to long-run economic growth.

Figure 40.3 shows a hypothetical production possibilities curve for a fictional country we'll call Kyland. In our previous production possibilities examples, the trade-off was between producing quantities of two different goods. In this example, our production possibilities curve illustrates Kyland's trade-off between two different *categories* of goods. The production possibilities curve shows the alternative combinations of investment goods and consumer goods that Kyland can produce. The consumer goods category includes everything purchased for consumption by households, such as food, clothing, and sporting goods. Investment goods include all forms of physical capital, that is, goods that are used to produce other goods. Kyland's production possibilities curve shows the trade-off between the production of consumer goods and

St. Louis Federal Reserve Bank Resources

Production Possibilities

Students develop the production possibilities frontier model while discussing the value of models in general in explaining complex ideas. They see what movement along the production possibilities curve entails—on both the constant-cost curve and a bowed curve indicating increasing costs. They discuss ways a society can consume beyond the limits of its production possibilities through specialization and trade, as well as through an increase in resources, capital investment, and technological advance.

Figure 40.2 Economic Growth

Economic growth results in an *outward shift* of the production possibilities curve because production possibilities are expanded. The economy can now produce more of everything. For example, if production is initially at point *A* (20 fish and 25 coconuts), it could move to point *E* (25 fish and 30 coconuts).

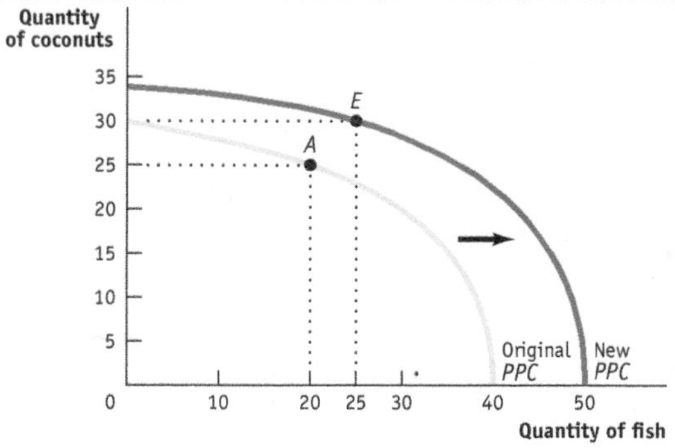

the production of investment goods. Recall that the bowed-out shape of the production possibilities curve reflects increasing opportunity cost.

Kyland's production possibilities curve shows all possible combinations of consumer and investment goods that can be produced with full and efficient use of all of Kyland's resources. However, the production possibilities curve model does not tell us which of the possible points Kyland *should* select.

Figure 40.3 illustrates four points on Kyland's production possibilities curve. At point *A*, Kyland is producing all investment goods and no consumer goods. Investment in physical capital, one of the economy's factors of production, causes the production possibilities curve to shift outward. Choosing to produce at a point on the production possibilities curve that creates more capital for the economy will result in greater

Figure 40.3 The Trade-off Between Investment and Consumer Goods

This production possibilities curve illustrates Kyland's trade-off between the production of investment goods and consumer goods. At point *A*, Kyland produces all investment goods and no consumer goods. At point *D*, Kyland produces all consumer goods and no investment goods. Points *B* and *C* represent two of the many possible combinations of investment goods and consumer goods.

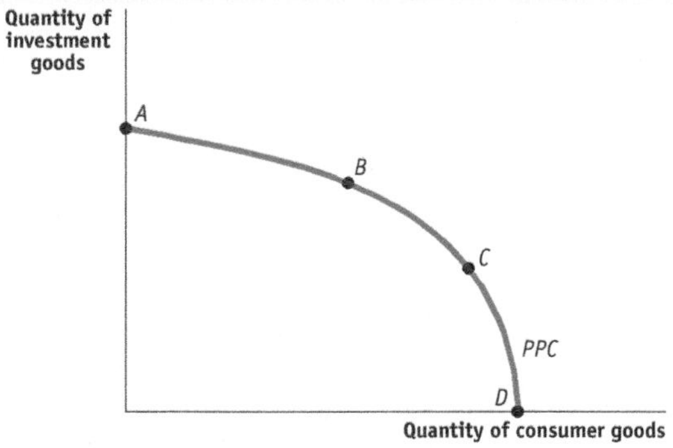

TEACH Teach It

Using Figure 40.2, discuss how economic growth occurs and what it looks like on the *PPC*. *Economic growth causes an outward shift of the PPC as shown in graph (1).* Explore several different options on your graph as well. Show students what the graph would look like if productivity only increased in the clothing industry. *The intercept with the food axis doesn't change and the outward shift is smaller where the quantity of food is larger as shown in graph (2).* Then show them what the graph would look like if productivity only increased in the food industry. *The intercept with the clothing axis doesn't change and the outward shift is smaller where the quantity of clothing is larger as shown in graph (3).* Finally, talk about what would happen if there was no capital investment while the production of goods continued. *Machinery used to produce other goods would eventually wear out and become useless. That means the production possibilities curve would shift inward over time as shown in graph (4) and there would be negative economic growth.*

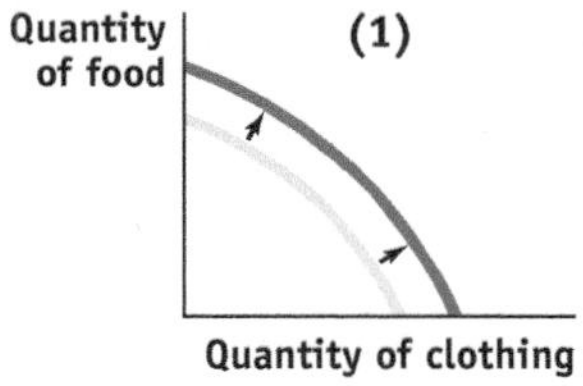

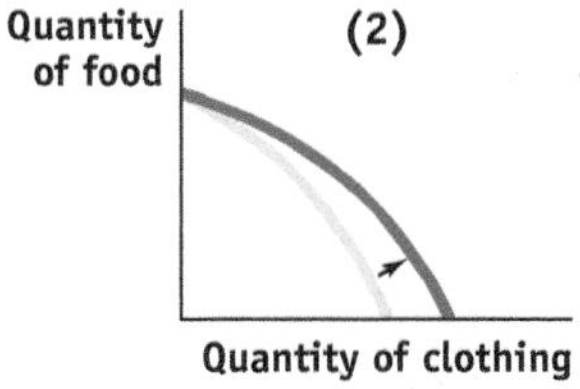

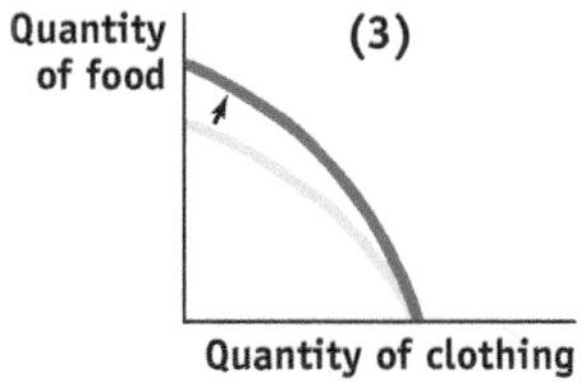

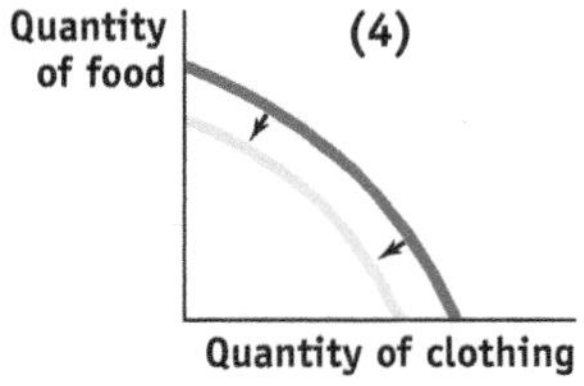

TEACH Connect It

Students sometimes struggle with the concept of trade-offs. Have them look at the lower *PPC* in Figure 40.2 and ask them:

- What is the largest number of coconuts the nation could produce if it also produced 20 fish? *25 coconuts*
- Starting at point *A*, approximately how many coconuts would the nation have to give up if it decided to produce 30 fish? *It would have to give up 5 coconuts.*
- Again starting at point *A*, how many fish would the nation have to give up if it wanted to produce 30 coconuts? *The opportunity cost would then be 20 fish because it would use all of its resources to produce coconuts.*

Show students the movement along the curve in Figure 40.2 from 25 to 30 coconuts and from 20 to 0 fish, so they can visually see the change.

production possibilities in the future. Note that at point *A*, there are no consumer goods being produced, a situation which the economy cannot survive.

At point *D*, Kyland is producing all consumer goods and no investment goods. While this point provides goods and services for consumers in Kyland, it does not include the production of any physical capital. Over time, as an economy produces more goods and services, some of its capital is used up in that production. A loss in the value of physical capital due to wear, age, or obsolescence is called **depreciation**. If Kyland were to produce at point *D* year after year, it would soon find its stock of physical capital depreciating and its production possibilities curve would shift inward over time, indicating a decrease in production possibilities. Points *B* and *C* represent a mix of consumer and investment goods for the economy. While we can see that points *A* and *D* would not be acceptable choices over a long period of time, the choice between points *B* and *C* would depend on the values, politics, and other details related to the economy and people of Kyland. What we do know is that the choice made by Kyland each year will affect the position of the production possibilities curve in the future. An emphasis on the production of consumer goods will make consumers better off in the short run but will prevent the production possibilities curve from moving farther out in the future. An emphasis on investment goods will lead the production possibilities curve to shift out farther in the future but will decrease the quantity of consumer goods available in the short run.

So what does the production possibilities curve tell us about economic growth? Since long-run economic growth depends almost entirely on rising productivity, a country's decision regarding investment in physical capital, human capital, and technology affects its long-run economic growth. Governments can promote long-run economic growth, shifting the country's production possibilities curve outward over time, by investing in physical capital such as infrastructure. They can also encourage high rates of private investment in physical capital by promoting a well-functioning financial system, property rights, and political stability.

Investments in capital help the economy reach new heights of productivity.

Depreciation occurs when the value of an asset is reduced by wear, age, or obsolescence.

AP® Exam Tip

Shifting *LRAS* is another way to show a change in economic growth because *LRAS* shows the potential output in an economy.

Long-Run Economic Growth and the Aggregate Demand–Aggregate Supply Model

The aggregate demand and supply model we developed in Section 4 is another useful tool for understanding long-run economic growth. Recall that in the aggregate demand–aggregate supply model, the long-run aggregate supply curve shows the relationship between the aggregate price level and the quantity of aggregate output supplied when all prices, including nominal wages, are flexible. As shown in **Figure 40.4**, the long-run aggregate supply curve is vertical at the level of potential output. While actual real GDP is almost always above or below potential output, reflecting the current phase of the business cycle, potential output is the level of output around which actual aggregate output fluctuates. Potential output in the United States has risen steadily over time. This corresponds to a rightward shift of the long-run aggregate supply curve, as shown in **Figure 40.5**. Thus, the same government policies that promote an outward shift of the production possibilities curve promote a rightward shift of the long-run aggregate supply curve.

Distinguishing Between Long-Run Growth and Short-Run Fluctuations

When considering changes in real GDP, it is important to distinguish long-run growth from short-run fluctuations due to the business cycle. Both the production possibilities curve model and the aggregate demand–aggregate supply model can help us do this.

The points along a production possibilities curve are achievable if there is efficient use of the economy's resources. If the economy experiences a macroeconomic fluctuation

398 Section 7 Economic Growth and Productivity

Figure 40.4 The Long-Run Aggregate Supply Curve

The long-run aggregate supply curve shows the quantity of aggregate output supplied when all prices, including nominal wages, are flexible. It is vertical at potential output, Y_P, because in the long run a change in the aggregate price level has no effect on the quantity of aggregate supplied.

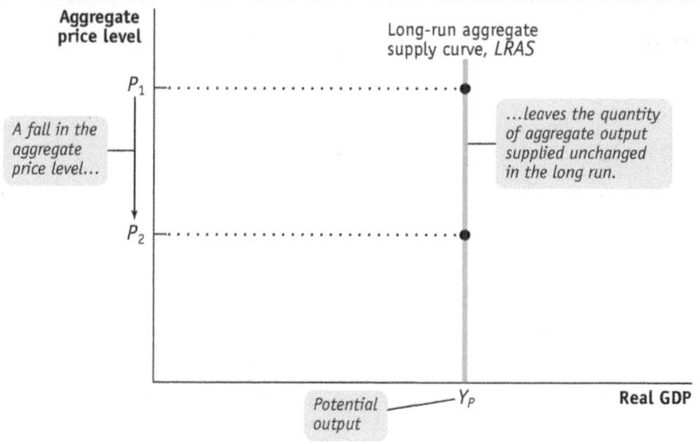

due to the business cycle, such as unemployment due to a recession, production falls to a point inside the production possibilities curve. On the other hand, long-run growth will appear as an outward shift of the production possibilities curve.

In the aggregate demand–aggregate supply model, fluctuations of actual aggregate output around potential output are illustrated by shifts of aggregate demand or short-run aggregate supply that result in a short-run macroeconomic equilibrium above or below potential output. In both panels of **Figure 40.6** on the next page, E_1 indicates a short-run equilibrium that differs from long-run equilibrium due to the business cycle. In the case of short-run fluctuations like these, adjustments in nominal wages will eventually bring the equilibrium level of real GDP back to the potential level. By contrast, we saw in Figure 40.5 that long-run economic growth is represented by a rightward shift of the long-run aggregate supply curve and corresponds to an increase in the economy's level of potential output.

Figure 40.5 Long-Run Growth and the *LRAS* Curve

The growth in potential output over time can be shown as a rightward shift of the long-run aggregate supply curve.

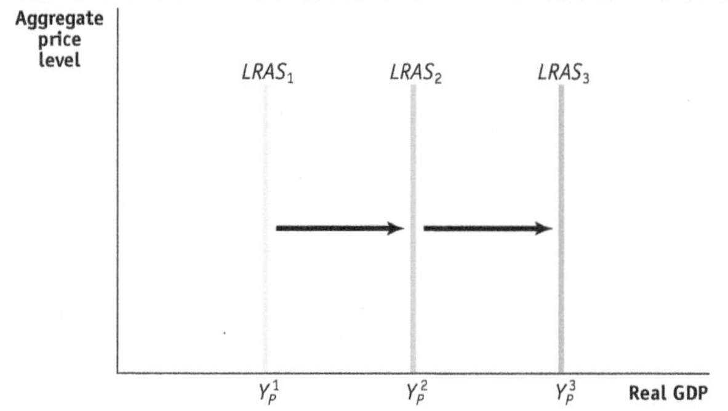

TEACH Connect It

Like the *PPC*, the long-run aggregate supply curve can be used to show economic growth in the economy. When economic growth occurs in the economy, the *LRAS* shifts right because there is a new potential output as a result of the growth. Teach students that *Growth means PPC out and LRAS right* to help them associate changes in economic growth, the *PPC*, and *LRAS*.

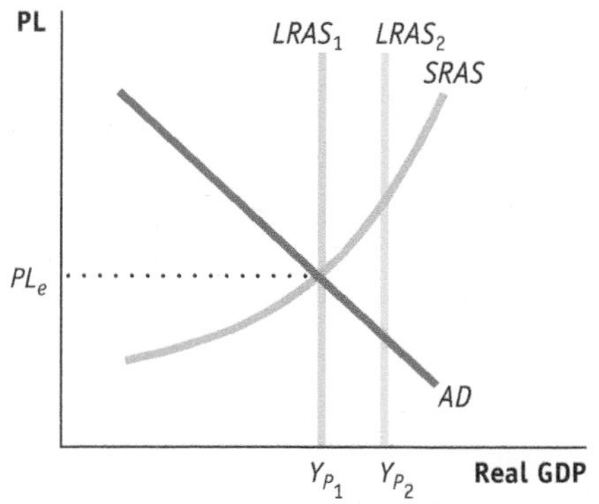

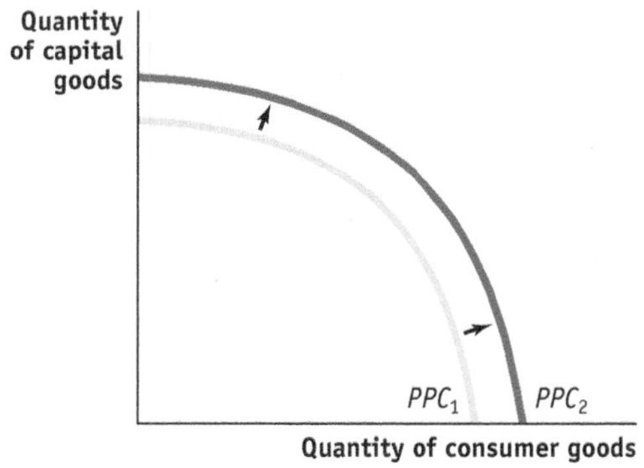

FOCUS Flip it

TRM Have students watch Jacob Clifford's "Macro 3.13 Economic Growth" video (see econextras video list with hyperlinks on the bcs and TRFD). Tell them to do the practice work as directed in the video. Assign **Worksheet 40.1 (Economic Growth)** from the TRM for questions on this topic. Students will see the connection between the *LRAS* and the *PPC* after viewing this tutorial.

TEACH Teach It

Students need to be able to tell the difference between short- and long-run changes in the economy. In the production possibilities model, an increase in the production of both goods can be achieved in the short run with a movement from a point inside the *PPC* to a point upward and to the right, closer to or on the original *PPC*. In the long run, economic growth can shift the whole *PPC* outward. In the *AD–AS* model, *AD* and *SRAS* can shift in the short run. For example, a recessionary gap is the result of a decrease in *AD* or a decrease in *SRAS*. In the long run, *LRAS* can shift along with *AD* and *SRAS*.

FOCUS Test It

Have students answer short FRQ Question 2 from the 2005 AP® exam at http://apcentral.collegeboard.com/apc/public/repository/_ap05_frq_macro_b_45732.pdf. The question will serve as a good review for this section. It is recommended that students take 12½ minutes to answer this question, as suggested in the exam. The rubric for the question may be viewed at http://apcentral.collegeboard.com/apc/public/repository/_ap05_sg_macro_46576.pdf.

TEACH Teach It

Without government involvement, any gap between potential output and equilibrium output will cause changes in nominal wages in the long run, shifting *SRAS* and closing the gap.

OPEN & CLOSE Exit Slip

TRM *Please see **Exit Slip: Module 40** in the TRM for formative multiple-choice questions to ask your students before finishing your lesson. These questions will help you quickly assess whether your students have mastered the module's concepts before moving on.*

Answers to the Exit Slip Questions

1. D
2. C
3. A

Figure 40.6 From the Short Run to the Long Run

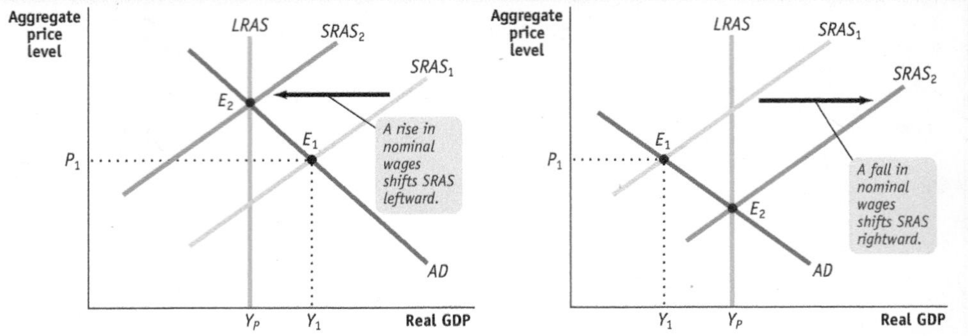

In panel (a), the initial equilibrium is E_1. At the aggregate price level, P_1, the quantity of aggregate output supplied, Y_1, exceeds potential output, Y_P. Eventually, low unemployment will cause nominal wages to rise, leading to a leftward shift of the short-run aggregate supply curve from $SRAS_1$ to $SRAS_2$ and a long-run equilibrium at E_2. In panel (b), the reverse happens: at the short-run equilibrium, E_1, the quantity of aggregate output supplied is less than potential output. High unemployment eventually leads to a fall in nominal wages over time and a rightward shift of the short-run aggregate supply curve. The end result is long-run equilibrium at E_2.

MODULE 40 Review

Check Your Understanding

1. How are long-run economic growth and short-run fluctuations during a business cycle represented using the production possibilities curve model?
2. How are long-run economic growth and short-run fluctuations during a business cycle represented using the aggregate demand–aggregate supply model?

Tackle the Test: Multiple-Choice Questions

1. Which of the following will shift the production possibilities curve outward?
   I. an increase in the production of investment goods
   II. an increase in the production of consumer goods
   III. technological progress
   a. I only
   b. II only
   c. III only
   d. I and III only
   e. I, II, and III
2. In the production possibilities curve model, long-run economic growth is shown by a(n)
   a. outward shift of the *PPC*.
   b. inward shift of the *PPC*.
   c. movement from a point below the *PPC* to a point on the *PPC*.
   d. movement from a point on the *PPC* to a point below the *PPC*.
   e. movement from a point on the *PPC* to a point beyond the *PPC*.

Answers to Module 40 Review Questions

Check Your Understanding

1. Long-run economic growth is represented by an outward shift of the production possibilities curve. Short-run fluctuations are represented by a movement from a point below the production possibilities curve toward a point on the production possibilities curve (this shows an economic recovery/expansion) or by a movement to a point farther below the production possibilities curve (this shows a recession/contraction).

2. Long-run economic growth is represented by a rightward shift of the long-run aggregate supply curve. Short-run fluctuations are represented by shifts in aggregate demand or short-run aggregate supply that cause movements of short-run equilibrium output (the level of real GDP at the intersection of short-run aggregate supply and aggregate demand) above or below potential output.

Tackle the Test: Multiple-Choice Questions

1. d
2. a

400 Section 7 Economic Growth and Productivity

3. The reduction in the value of an asset due to wear and tear is known as
   a. depreciation.
   b. negative investment.
   c. economic decline.
   d. disinvestment.
   e. net investment.
4. In the aggregate demand–aggregate supply model, long-run economic growth is shown by a
   a. leftward shift of the aggregate demand curve.
   b. rightward shift of the aggregate demand curve.
   c. rightward shift of the long-run aggregate supply curve.
   d. rightward shift of the short-run aggregate supply curve.
   e. leftward shift of the short-run aggregate supply curve.
5. Which of the following is listed among the key sources of growth in potential output?
   a. expansionary fiscal policy
   b. expansionary monetary policy
   c. a rightward shift of the short-run aggregate supply curve
   d. investment in human capital
   e. both a and b

Tackle the Test: Free-Response Questions

1. Refer to the graph provided.

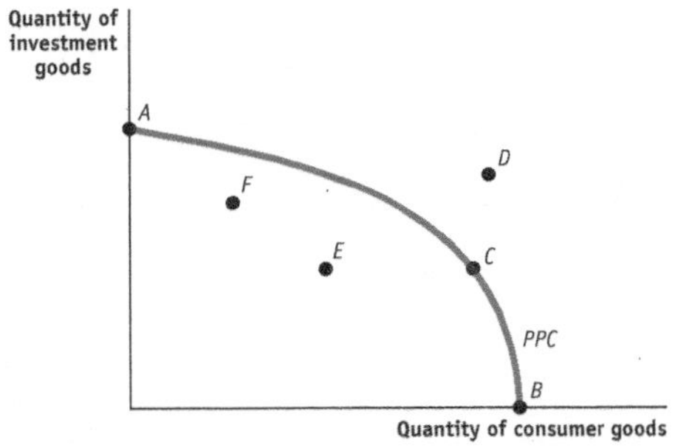

   a. Which point(s) could represent a downturn in the business cycle?
   b. Which point(s) represent efficient production?
   c. Which point(s) are attainable only after long-run economic growth?
   d. How would long-run economic growth be represented on this graph?
   e. Policy that results in an increase in the production of consumer goods without reducing the production of investment goods is represented by a movement from point _____ to point _____.
   f. Producing at which efficient point this year would lead to the most economic growth next year?

Rubric for FRQ 1 (9 points)

2 points: A downturn could be represented by points *E* or *F*.

3 points: Points *A*, *B*, and *C* represent efficient production.

1 point: Point *D* is attainable only after long-run economic growth.

1 point: Long-run economic growth would be represented by an outward shift of the curve.

1 point: Consumer goods increase and investment goods remain unchanged when moving from point *E* to point *C*.

1 point: Producing at point *A* would lead to the most economic growth.

2. Draw a separate, correctly labeled aggregate demand and supply graph to illustrate each of the following situations. On each of your graphs, include the relevant short-run aggregate supply curve(s), long-run aggregate supply curve(s), and aggregate demand curve(s).
   a. Expansionary fiscal policy moves the economy out of a recession.
   b. Investment in infrastructure by the government leads to long-run economic growth.
   (6 points)

3. a
4. c
5. d

Tackle the Test: Free-Response Question

Rubric for FRQ 2 (6 points)

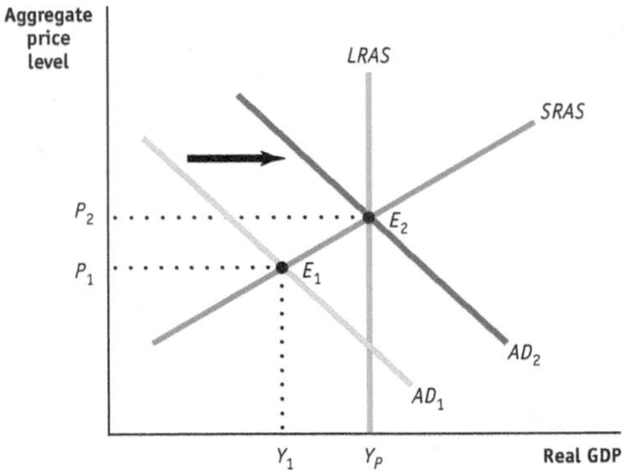

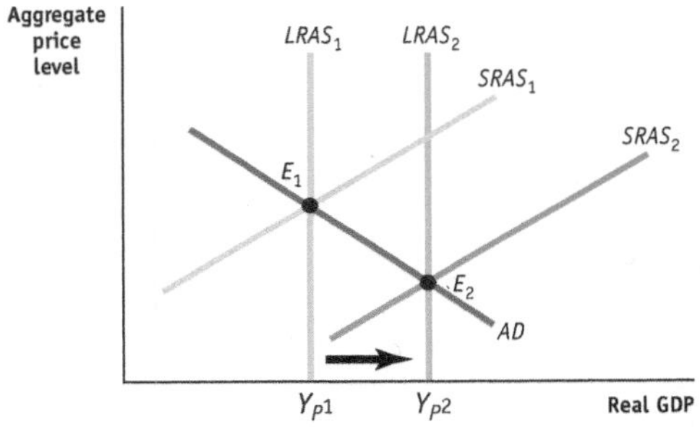

1 point: Vertical axis labeled "Aggregate price level" or "*PL*" and horizontal axis labeled "Real GDP"

1 point: Downward-sloping *AD* and upward-sloping *SRAS*

1 point: Vertical *LRAS* to the right of the initial equilibrium of *AD* and *SRAS*

1 point: *AD* shifts rightward.

1 point: 2nd graph with correctly labeled initial equilibrium of *AD*, *SRAS*, and *LRAS*

1 point: Shift of *LRAS* and *SRAS* to the right (but it is not necessary to show a new long-run equilibrium of *SRAS* and *AD*)

SECTION 7 Review

FOCUS **Flip It**

Encourage your students to watch the **Section 7 Review Video**, which was created as a special student review tool and is linked into the e-Book or can be found on the book's companion website.

Section 7 Review Video

Module 37

1. Economic growth is a sustained increase in the productive capacity of an economy and can be measured as changes in real GDP per capita. This measurement eliminates the effects of changes in both the price level and population size. Levels of real GDP per capita vary greatly around the world: more than half of the world's population lives in countries that are still poorer than the United States was in 1910.
2. Growth rates of real GDP per capita also vary widely. According to the **Rule of 70**, the number of years it takes for real GDP per capita to double is equal to 70 divided by the annual growth rate of real GDP per capita.
3. The key to long-run economic growth is rising **labor productivity**, or just **productivity**, which is output per worker. Increases in productivity arise from increases in **physical capital** per worker and **human capital** per worker as well as advances in **technology**.

Module 38

4. The **aggregate production function** shows how real GDP per worker depends on physical capital per worker, human capital per worker, and technology. Other things equal, there are **diminishing returns to physical capital**: holding human capital per worker and technology fixed, each successive addition to physical capital per worker yields a smaller increase in productivity than the one before. Similarly, there are diminishing returns to human capital among other inputs. With **growth accounting**, which involves estimates of each factor's contribution to economic growth, economists have shown that rising **total factor productivity**, the amount of output produced from a given amount of factor inputs, is key to long-run growth. Rising total factor productivity is usually interpreted as the effect of technological progress. In most countries, natural resources are a less significant source of productivity growth today than in earlier times.
5. The world economy contains examples of success and failure in the effort to achieve long-run economic growth. East Asian economies have done many things right and achieved very high growth rates. In Latin America, where some important conditions are lacking, growth has generally been disappointing. In Africa, real GDP per capita declined for several decades, although there are recent signs of progress. The growth rates of economically advanced countries have converged, but the growth rates of countries across the world have not. This has led economists to believe that the **convergence hypothesis** fits the data only when factors that affect growth, such as education, infrastructure, and favorable policies and institutions, are held equal across countries.

Module 39

6. The large differences in countries' growth rates are largely due to differences in their rates of accumulation of physical and human capital, as well as differences in technological progress. A prime factor is differences in savings and investment rates, since most countries that have high investment in physical capital finance it by high domestic savings. Technological progress is largely a result of **research and development**, or **R&D**.
7. Government actions that contribute to growth include the building of **infrastructure**, particularly for transportation and public health; the creation and regulation of a well-functioning banking system that channels savings into investment spending; and the financing of both education and R&D. Government actions that slow growth are corruption, political instability, excessive government intervention, and the neglect or violation of property rights.
8. In regard to making economic growth **sustainable**, economists generally believe that environmental degradation poses a greater problem than natural resource scarcity does. Addressing environmental degradation requires effective governmental intervention, but the problem of natural resource scarcity is often well handled by the incentives created by market prices.
9. The emission of greenhouse gases is clearly linked to growth, and limiting emissions will require some reduction in growth. However, the best available estimates suggest that a large reduction in emissions would require only a modest reduction in the growth rate.
10. There is broad consensus that government action to address climate change and greenhouse gases should be in the form of market-based incentives, like a carbon tax or a cap and trade system. It will also require rich and poor countries to come to some agreement on how the cost of emissions reductions will be shared.

Module 40

11. Long-run economic growth can be analyzed using the production possibilities curve and the aggregate demand–aggregate supply model. In these models, long-run economic growth is represented by an outward shift of the production possibilities curve and a rightward shift of the long-run aggregate supply curve.

12. Physical capital **depreciates** with use. Therefore, over time, the production possibilities curve will shift inward and the long-run aggregate supply curve will shift to the left if the stock of capital is not replaced.

Key Terms

Rule of 70, p. 369
Labor productivity (productivity), p. 370
Physical capital, p. 371
Human capital, p. 371
Technology, p. 371
Aggregate production function, p. 373
Diminishing returns to physical capital, p. 374
Growth accounting, p. 375
Total factor productivity, p. 376
Convergence hypothesis, p. 380
Research and development (R&D), p. 385
Infrastructure, p. 386
Sustainable, p. 388
Depreciation, p. 398

AP® Exam Practice Questions

Multiple-Choice Questions

1. If real GDP grows by 5% per year, approximately how many years will it take for it to double?
   a. 150
   b. 75
   c. 35
   d. 15
   e. 5

2. What is the most important ingredient in long-run economic growth?
   a. increased labor productivity
   b. increased population
   c. low price level
   d. expansionary monetary and fiscal policies
   e. deficit spending

3. The technical means for the production of goods and services is known as
   a. physical capital.
   b. technology.
   c. human capital.
   d. productivity.
   e. machinery and equipment.

4. Which of the following is a major reason for productivity growth?
   a. financial investment
   b. an increase in the amount of capital available per worker
   c. a decrease in the amount of capital available per worker
   d. an increase in the price of capital
   e. technological progress

Refer to the following figure for Questions 5–6.

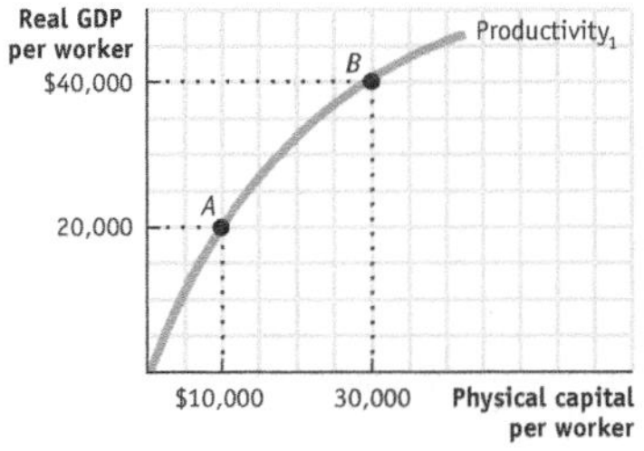

5. Assuming diminishing returns to physical capital, if physical capital per worker is 50,000, real GDP per worker will most likely equal which of the following?
   a. more than 60,000
   b. 60,000
   c. less than 60,000 but greater than 40,000
   d. 40,000
   e. 0

6. An upward shift of the curve shown could be caused by which of the following?
   a. an increase in real GDP per worker
   b. investment in physical capital
   c. diminishing returns to physical capital
   d. increases in population
   e. rising total factor productivity

Answers to Section 7 AP® Exam Practice Questions

Multiple-Choice Questions

1. d
2. a
3. b
4. e
5. c
6. e

Section 7 Review 403

7. e
8. c
9. d
10. a
11. d
12. b
13. a
14. d
15. a
16. c

Rubric for Free-Response Question

1 point: A production possibilities curve graph with "Quantity of capital goods" and "Quantity of consumer goods" labels on the axes

1 point: The *PPC* is downward-sloping.

1 point: Economic growth is indicated by a rightward shift of the *PPC.*

1 point: An *AS-AD* graph with "Aggregate price level" or "*PL*" on the vertical axis, "Real GDP" on the horizontal axis, a downward-sloping *AD* curve, and an upward-sloping *SRAS* curve

1 point: *LRAS* is vertical and crosses *SRAS* and *AD*, where they intersect.

1 point: Economic growth is indicated by a rightward shift of the *LRAS* curve.

Please see page SG-3 for sample student graphs for this Free-Response Question.

7. Which of the following is true about the role of natural resources in productivity growth?
- **a.** They are a more important determinant of productivity than human or physical capital.
- **b.** They have played an increasingly prominent role in productivity growth in recent years.
- **c.** They play no role in determining productivity growth.
- **d.** They played a less important role in productivity growth in the 1800s.
- **e.** They result in higher productivity, other things equal.

8. According to the convergence hypothesis, over time, international differences in real GDP per capita will
- **a.** increase exponentially.
- **b.** increase slightly.
- **c.** decrease.
- **d.** remain the same.
- **e.** disappear.

9. When the government spends money to create and implement new technologies, it has invested in
- **a.** human capital.
- **b.** physical capital.
- **c.** infrastructure.
- **d.** research and development.
- **e.** political stability.

10. Which of the following is part of an economy's infrastructure?
- **a.** highways
- **b.** factories
- **c.** banks
- **d.** automobiles
- **e.** workers

11. If long-run economic growth can continue into the future despite limited natural resources, it is considered
- **a.** acceptable.
- **b.** equitable.
- **c.** economical.
- **d.** sustainable.
- **e.** expandable.

12. An outward shift of the production possibilities curve indicates which of the following?
- **a.** a decrease in cyclical unemployment
- **b.** long-run economic growth
- **c.** a reduction in productive resources
- **d.** a decrease in opportunity cost
- **e.** a decrease in potential output and the natural rate of unemployment

13. In the aggregate supply and demand model, a rightward shift of the *LRAS* curve indicates which of the following?
- **a.** long-run economic growth
- **b.** an increase in unemployment
- **c.** a decrease in real GDP
- **d.** an increase in the aggregate price level
- **e.** an economic recovery

14. Which of the following will lead to long-run economic growth?
- **a.** a decrease in nominal wages
- **b.** a decrease in the aggregate price level
- **c.** an increase in the production of consumer goods
- **d.** an increase in total factor productivity
- **e.** actual output that exceeds potential output

15. If an economy experiences long-run economic growth, which of the following is true of its potential output?
- **a.** It has increased.
- **b.** It has decreased.
- **c.** It is greater than actual output.
- **d.** It is less than actual output.
- **e.** It is no longer equal to *LRAS*.

16. Depreciation leads to
- **a.** a reduction in human capital.
- **b.** an increase in human capital.
- **c.** a reduction in physical capital.
- **d.** an advance in technology.
- **e.** an outward shift of the production possibilities curve.

Free-Response Question

1. Economic growth can be illustrated using macroeconomic models.
- **a.** Draw a correctly labeled production possibilities curve for an economy producing capital goods and consumer goods. Use your graph to illustrate economic growth.
- **b.** Draw a correctly labeled aggregate supply and demand graph showing an economy in long-run equilibrium. On your graph, illustrate economic growth.

(6 points)

NOTES

SECTION 8

The Open Economy: International Trade and Finance

PD Section 8 Overview

Watch the video overview of Section 8 (for teachers), which is accessible through the Teacher's e-Book, the TR-flash drive, or the book's website bcs.worthpublishers.com/krugmanap2e *(teacher log-in required).*

Section 8 adds the international sector to the macroeconomic models presented in earlier sections. The role of international trade and finance in U.S. markets expands the reach of our products, services, and technology. It has allowed for a huge increase in the quantity and quality of goods and services we enjoy. Furthermore, the expansion of financial markets worldwide has increased the flow of capital to projects where a profit can be earned. Any macroeconomics course must include a study of these topics in order to complete the picture of national and global economies.

Topics that your students will study in Section 8 are:

- how the balance of payments accounts are recorded and analyzed.
- how the loanable funds market graph can be used to model international capital flows.
- how market forces and public policy affect currency demand and currency supply.
- how the equilibrium exchange rate can be modeled using supply/demand analysis.
- how changes in capital flows affect the balance of payments accounts.
- how the current account responds only to changes in real exchange rates.
- how a fixed exchange rate system differs from a floating exchange rate system.
- how specific considerations affect a country's choice of an exchange rate system.
- how currency appreciation and depreciation relate to macroeconomic policy decisions.
- how to determine the effectiveness of a protectionist trade policy.
- how to illustrate the effects of a tariff and an import quota.
- how to approach AP® Macroeconomics free-response questions.

Alignment to AP® Macroeconomics Course Description

Macroeconomics VII. Open Economy: International Trade and Finance: 10–15%

AP® Outline	Module
A. Balance of payments accounts	41: Capital Flows and the Balance of Payments
B. Foreign exchange market	42: The Foreign Exchange Market 43: Exchange Rate Policy and Macroeconomic Policy
C. Imports, exports, and financial capital flows	41: Capital Flows and the Balance of Payments 44: Barriers to Trade
D. Relationships between international and domestic financial and goods markets	45: Putting It All Together

Pacing Guide

Module	Standard Teaching Days	Block Teaching Days
41	1	½
42	2	1
43	1	½
44	1	½
45	1	½
Section 8 Assessment	1	½
Total	**7**	**3½**

TRM Section Resources

All section resources may be accessed through the Teacher's e-Book, the TR-flash drive, or the book's website bcs.worthpublishers.com/krugmanap2e *(teacher log-in required).*

Section 8 PD Video (for teachers)

Module 41

Module 41 Sample Lecture

Worksheet 41.1: Balance of Payments Transactions

Worksheet 41.2: Balance of Payments

Activity 41.3: Financial Flows

Exit Slip: Module 41

Module 42

Module 42 Sample Lecture

Worksheet 42.1: Understanding Exchange Rates

Worksheet 42.2: Exchange Rates

Worksheet 42.3: Big Mac Index

Worksheet 42.4: Graphing Exchange Rates

Exit Slip: Module 42

Module 43

Module 43 Sample Lecture

Worksheet 43.1: Currency Tango

Worksheet 43.2: Exchange Rate Policy

Worksheet 43.3: The Euro

Worksheet 43.4: Exchange Rates and Macroeconomic Policy

Exit Slip: Module 43

Module 44

Module 44 Sample Lecture

Worksheet 44.1: Comparative Advantage

Worksheet 44.2: Trade Barriers

Exit Slip: Module 44

Module 45

Module 45 Sample Lecture

Activity 45.1: The Macro Analysis Framework

Section 8 Review Video (for students)

St. Louis Federal Reserve Bank Resources

Many of the Federal Reserve Banks have educational departments that offer helpful resources for studying economics. Members of the Educators Advisory Board of the St. Louis Federal Reserve Bank have handpicked some of their best resources for use with your AP® Economics students. References to these resources are included in the margin notes. A complete list of the St. Louis Fed resources for each section with the corresponding URL (as of fall 2014) can be found in the TRM.

NOTE We have included a number of links to useful videos and articles in the margin notes in this section. Although all are active at the time of publication, we know that some may expire over the next few years. If a link is no longer active, you may wish to search for a similar article or video to illustrate the point. We may also periodically refresh resources on the book's companion website.

NOTES

SECTION 8

The Open Economy: International Trade and Finance

A Roller Coaster Ride for the Exchange Rate

Bloomberg via Getty Images

"You should see, when they come in the door, the shopping bags they hand off to the coat check. I mean, they're just spending. It's Monopoly money to them." So declared a New York restaurant manager, describing the European tourists who, in the summer of 2008, accounted for a large share of her business. Meanwhile, American tourists in Europe were suffering sticker shock. One American, whose family of four was visiting Paris, explained his changing vacation plans: "We might not stay as long. We might eat cheese sandwiches."

It was quite a change from 2000, when an article in the *New York Times* bore the headline: "Dollar makes the good life a tourist bargain in Europe." What happened? The answer is that there was a large shift in the relative values of the euro, the currency used by much of Europe, and the U.S. dollar. At its low point in 2000, a euro was worth only about 85 cents. By mid-2008 it was worth more than $1.50; in early 2010 its value had fallen again, to less than $1.25. In early 2014, a euro was worth $1.36.

What causes the ups and downs of the relative value of the dollar and the euro? What are the effects of such changes? These are among the questions addressed by *open-economy macroeconomics*, the branch of macroeconomics that deals with the relationships between national economies. In this section we'll learn about some of the key issues in open-economy macroeconomics: the determinants of a country's *balance of payments*, the factors affecting *exchange rates*, the different forms of *exchange rate policy* adopted by various countries, and the relationship between exchange rates and macroeconomic policy. In the final module we will apply what we have learned about macroeconomic modeling to conduct policy analysis.

PD Section 8 Overview

Watch the video overview of Section 8 (for teachers), which is accessible through the Teacher's e-Book, the TR-flash drive, or the book's companion website bcs.worthpublishers.com/krugmanap2e (teacher log-in required).

FOCUS Active Learning

Students can read Chapter 27 of *Economics by Example* to advance their understanding of global markets and the gains from trade.

PD To prepare for teaching this lesson, you may want to consult the **Module 41 Sample Lecture** in the TRM.

OPEN & CLOSE Start Here

Ask students if they think everyone should "buy American." You might take a vote and record yes and no answer totals. Have students do the "Tag Check" activity at http://www.fte.org/wp-content/uploads/TagCheckActivity1.doc. It will make students aware of international trade in their daily lives and includes debriefing questions.

TEACH Connect It

Have students explain what physical capital is. *Physical capital is human-made goods such as tools, machines, and equipment that are used in the production process.*

Stress that when we talk about the balance of payments on the financial account, we count financial capital such as stocks, bonds, or certificates of deposit and not physical capital such as hammers. When discussing the flow of financial capital, students must understand that relative differences in real interest rates drive the flow of financial capital, not physical capital.

Stockbyte/Thinkstock

MODULE 41

Capital Flows and the Balance of Payments

In this Module, you will learn to:

- Explain the meaning of the balance of payments accounts
- Identify the determinants of international capital flows

Capital Flows and the Balance of Payments

In 2012, people living in the United States sold about $3.5 trillion worth of stuff to people living in other countries and bought about $3.2 trillion worth of stuff in return. What kind of stuff? All kinds. Residents of the United States (including employees of firms operating in the United States) sold airplanes, bonds, wheat, and many other items to residents of other countries. Residents of the United States bought cars, stocks, oil, and many other items from residents of other countries.

How can we keep track of these transactions? Earlier we learned that economists keep track of the domestic economy using the national income and product accounts. Economists keep track of international transactions using a different but related set of numbers, the *balance of payments accounts*.

A country's **balance of payments accounts** are a summary of the country's transactions with other countries.

Balance of Payments Accounts

A country's **balance of payments accounts** are a summary of the country's transactions with other countries.

To understand the basic idea behind the balance of payments accounts, let's consider a small-scale example: not a country, but a family farm. Let's say that we know the following about how last year went financially for the Costas, who own a small artichoke farm in California:

Rob MacDougall/Getty Images

- They made $100,000 by selling artichokes.
- They spent $70,000 on running the farm, including purchases of new farm machinery, and another $40,000 buying food, paying utility bills for their home, replacing their worn-out car, and so on.

Table 41.1 The Costas' Financial Year

	Sources of cash	Uses of cash	Net
Purchases or sales of goods and services	Artichoke sales: $100,000	Farm operation and living expenses: $110,000	−$10,000
Interest payments	Interest received on bank account: $500	Interest paid on mortgage: $10,000	−$9,500
Loans and deposits	Funds received from new loan: $25,000	Funds deposited in bank: $5,500	+$19,500
Total	**$125,500**	**$125,500**	**$0**

- They received $500 in interest on their bank account but paid $10,000 in interest on their mortgage.
- They took out a new $25,000 loan to help pay for farm improvements but didn't use all the money immediately. So they put the extra in the bank.

How could we summarize the Costas' year? One way would be with a table like **Table 41.1**, which shows sources of cash coming in and money going out, characterized under a few broad headings. The first row of Table 41.1 shows sales and purchases of goods and services: sales of artichokes; purchases of farm machinery, groceries, heating oil, that new car, and so on. The second row shows interest payments: the interest the Costas received from their bank account and the interest they paid on their mortgage. The third row shows cash coming in from new borrowing versus money deposited in the bank.

In each row we show the net inflow of cash from that type of transaction. So the net in the first row is −$10,000 because the Costas spent $10,000 more than they earned. The net in the second row is −$9,500, the difference between the interest the Costas received on their bank account and the interest they paid on the mortgage. The net in the third row is $19,500: the Costas brought in $25,000 with their new loan but put only $5,500 of that sum in the bank.

The last row shows the sum of cash coming in from all sources and the sum of all cash used. These sums are equal, by definition: every dollar has a source, and every dollar received gets used somewhere. (What if the Costas hid money under the mattress? Then that would be counted as another "use" of cash.)

A country's balance of payments accounts summarize its transactions with the world using a table similar to the one we just used to summarize the Costas' financial year.

"This is how our new no risk pension scheme works."

TEACH Teach It

Use Table 41.1 to walk students through an example of *The Costas' Financial Year.* Understanding this example will help prepare them for international transactions found in the balance of payments accounts.

TEACH Teach It

Explain that the balance of payments has two accounts—the financial and current accounts—that balance the inflow and outflow of money between nations. Students will be expected to identify if transactions should be placed in the current account or the financial account and how policies might affect their balances. Until a few years ago, economists often referred to the financial account as the capital account. We'll use the modern term, but point out to students that they may run across the older term on their practice AP® Macro exams.

St. Louis Federal Reserve Bank Resources

GeoFRED®

Use GeoFRED® to examine current account balances of countries over time and to make country comparisons.

TEACH Teach It

Let students know that goods and services, factor income (interest and dividends on foreign financial assets), and transfers (foreign aid and private cash transfers) are counted in the current account. Financial assets such as stocks, bonds, and real estate (buildings and land) are counted in the financial account.

TEACH Teach It

A great way to help the students see how the information in Table 41.2 is separated is to point out that the balance of payments accounts distinguish between transactions that do not create liabilities (like when an American buys a jacket produced in Honduras) and those that do (like when a Honduran banker buys a U.S. Treasury bond).

TEACH Teach It

If imports are greater than exports, a trade deficit occurs in the current account. If exports are greater than imports, the nation has a trade surplus in the current account.

FOCUS Active Learning

TRM To ensure that students understand balance of payments transactions, have them complete **Worksheet 41.1 (Balance of Payments Transactions)** from the TRM in class or as homework.

AP® Exam Tip

Remember that the current account includes goods and services and cash transfers such as foreign aid, gifts, and grants. You may be asked to identify these transactions on the AP® exam.

Table 41.2 The U.S. Balance of Payments in 2012 (billions of dollars)

	Payments from foreigners	Payments to foreigners	Net
1 Sales and purchases of goods and services	$2,211	$2,745	−$534
2 Factor income	776	552	224
3 Transfers	—	—	−130
Current account (1 + 2 + 3)			−440
4 Official asset sales and purchases	394	−81	475
5 Private sales and purchases of assets	150	178	−28
Financial account (4 + 5)			447
Total	—	—	7

Source: Bureau of Economic Analysis.

Table 41.2 shows a simplified version of the U.S. balance of payments accounts for 2012. Where the Costa family's accounts show sources and uses of cash, the balance of payments accounts show payments from foreigners—in effect, sources of cash for the United States as a whole—and payments to foreigners.

Row 1 of Table 41.2 shows payments that arise from sales and purchases of goods and services. For example, the value of U.S. wheat exports and the fees foreigners pay to U.S. consulting companies appear in the second column of row 1; the value of U.S. oil imports and the fees American companies pay to Indian call centers—the people who often answer your 1-800 calls—appear in the third column of row 1.

Row 2 shows *factor income*—payments for the use of factors of production owned by residents of other countries. Mostly this means investment income: interest paid on loans from overseas, the profits of foreign-owned corporations, and so on. For example, the profits earned by Disneyland Paris, which is owned by the U.S.-based Walt Disney Company, appear in the second column of row 2; the profits earned by the U.S. operations of Japanese auto companies appear in the third column. Factor income also includes labor income. For example, the wages of an American engineer who works temporarily on a construction site in Dubai are counted in the second column of row 2.

Row 3 shows *international transfers*—funds sent by residents of one country to residents of another. The main element here is the remittances that immigrants, such as the millions of Mexican-born workers employed in the United States, send to their families in their country of origin. Notice that Table 41.2 shows only the net value of transfers. That's because the U.S. government provides only an estimate of the net, not a breakdown between payments to foreigners and payments from foreigners.

The next two rows of Table 41.2 show payments resulting from sales and purchases of assets, broken down by who is doing the buying and selling. Row 4 shows transactions that involve governments or government agencies, mainly central banks. As we'll learn later, in 2012, most of the U.S. sales in this category involved the accumulation of *foreign exchange reserves* by the central banks of China and oil-exporting countries. Row 5 shows private sales and purchases of assets. For example, the 2012 purchase of the AMC cinema chain by the Chinese corporation Dalian Wanda showed up in the second column of row 5; purchases of European stocks by U.S. investors show up as positive values in the third column. However, because U.S. residents sold more foreign assets than they purchased in 2012, the value for this category is negative.

In laying out Table 41.2, we have separated rows 1, 2, and 3 into one group and rows 4 and 5 into another. This reflects a fundamental difference in how these two groups of transactions affect the future.

When a U.S. resident sells a good, such as wheat, to a foreigner, that's the end of the transaction. But a financial asset, such as a bond, is different. Remember, a bond is a

408 Section 8 The Open Economy: International Trade and Finance

promise to pay interest and principal in the future. So when a U.S. resident sells a bond to a foreigner, that sale creates a liability: the U.S. resident will have to pay interest and repay principal in the future. The balance of payments accounts distinguish between transactions that don't create liabilities and those that do.

Transactions that don't create liabilities are considered part of the **balance of payments on the current account**, often referred to simply as the **current account**: the balance of payments on goods and services plus factor income and net international transfer payments. The balance of row 1 of Table 41.2, -$534 billion, corresponds to the most important part of the current account: **the balance of payments on goods and services**, the difference between the value of exports and the value of imports during a given period.

By the way, if you read news reports on the economy, you may well see references to another measure, the **merchandise trade balance**, sometimes referred to as the **trade balance** for short. This is the difference between a country's exports and imports of goods alone—not including services. Economists sometimes focus on the merchandise trade balance, even though it's an incomplete measure, because data on international trade in services aren't as accurate as data on trade in physical goods, and they are also slower to arrive.

The current account, as we've just learned, consists of international transactions that don't create liabilities. Transactions that involve the sale or purchase of assets, and therefore do create future liabilities, are considered part of the **balance of payments on the financial account**, or the **financial account** for short. (Until a few years ago, economists often referred to the financial account as the *capital account*. We'll use the modern term, but you may run across the older term.)

So how does it all add up? The shaded rows of Table 41.2 show the bottom lines: the overall U.S. current account and financial account for 2012. As you can see, in 2012, the United States ran a current account deficit: the amount it paid to foreigners for goods, services, factors, and transfers was greater than the amount it received. Simultaneously, it ran a financial account surplus: the value of the assets it sold to foreigners was greater than the value of the assets it bought from foreigners.

In the official data, the U.S. current account deficit and financial account surplus almost, but not quite, offset each other: the financial account surplus was $7 billion larger than the current account deficit. But that's just a statistical error, reflecting the imperfection of official data. (And a $7 billion error when you're measuring inflows and outflows of $3.5 trillion isn't bad!) In fact, it's a basic rule of balance of payments accounting that the current account and the financial account must sum to zero:

$$\textbf{(41-1)} \quad \text{Current account } (CA) + \text{Financial account } (FA) = 0$$

or

$$CA = -FA$$

Why must Equation 41-1 be true? We already saw the fundamental explanation in Table 41.1, which showed the accounts of the Costa family: in total, the sources of cash must equal the uses of cash. The same applies to balance of payments accounts. **Figure 41.1** on the next page, a variant on the circular-flow diagram we have found useful in discussing domestic macroeconomics, may help you visualize how this adding up works.

Instead of showing the flow of money *within* a national economy, Figure 41.1 shows the flow of money *between* national economies. Money flows into the United States from the rest of the world as payment for U.S. exports of goods and services, as payment for the use of U.S.-owned factors of production, and as transfer payments. These flows (indicated by the lower green arrow) are the positive components of the U.S. current account. Money also flows into the United States from foreigners who purchase U.S. assets (as shown by the lower red arrow)—the positive component of the U.S. financial account.

At the same time, money flows from the United States to the rest of the world as payment for U.S. imports of goods and services, as

A country's **balance of payments on the current account**, or the **current account**, is its balance of payments on goods and services plus net international transfer payments and factor income.

A country's **balance of payments on goods and services** is the difference between the value of its exports and the value of its imports during a given period.

The **merchandise trade balance**, or **trade balance**, is the difference between a country's exports and imports of goods.

A country's **balance of payments on the financial account**, or simply the **financial account**, is the difference between its sales of assets to foreigners and its purchases of assets from foreigners during a given period.

AP® Exam Tip

Remember that the financial account tracks assets such as real estate, stocks, and bonds. Dividends and interest paid are not assets, so they are counted in the current account. You may be asked to identify these transactions on the AP® exam.

FOCUS Active Learning

Conduct the "Balance of Trade Among States" activity at http://www.fte.org/wp-content/uploads/Lesson6BalanceActivity1.doc. This lesson gives students practice tracking the balance of payments. The activity includes debriefing questions.

TEACH Teach It

When the current and financial accounts are added together, they will always equal 0 because the sources of cash must equal the uses of cash. If there is a surplus in one account, there must be a deficit in the other. Point out that in Table 41.2 the total balance is not 0; it is $44 billion. This is just a statistical error, reflecting the imperfection of official data. (And a $44 billion error when you're measuring inflows and outflows of $4.5 trillion isn't bad!)

Figure 41.1 The Balance of Payments

The green arrows represent payments that are counted in the current account. The red arrows represent payments that are counted in the financial account. Because the total flow into the United States must equal the total flow out of the United States, the sum of the current account plus the financial account is zero.

payment for the use of foreign-owned factors of production, and as transfer payments. These flows, indicated by the upper green arrow, are the negative components of the U.S. current account. Money also flows from the United States to purchase foreign assets, as shown by the upper red arrow—the negative component of the U.S. financial account. As in all circular-flow diagrams, the flow into a box and the flow out of a box are equal. This means that the sum of the red and green arrows going

FYI GDP, GNP, and the Current Account

When we discussed national income accounting, we derived the basic equation relating GDP to the components of spending:

$$Y = C + I + G + X - IM$$

where X and IM are exports and imports, respectively, of goods and services. But as we've learned, the balance of payments on goods and services is only one component of the current account balance. Why doesn't the national income equation use the current account as a whole?

The answer is that gross domestic product, which is the value of goods and services produced in a country, doesn't include two sources of income that are included in calculating the current account balance: international factor income and international transfers. The profits of Ford Motors U.K. aren't included in America's GDP, and the funds Latin American immigrants send home to their families aren't subtracted from GDP.

Shouldn't we have a broader measure that does include these sources of income? Actually, gross national product—GNP—does include international factor income. Estimates of U.S. GNP differ slightly from estimates of GDP because GNP adds in items such as the earnings of U.S. companies abroad and subtracts items such as the interest payments on bonds owned by residents of China and Japan. However, there isn't any regularly calculated measure that includes transfer payments.

Why do economists use GDP rather than a broader measure? Two reasons. First, the original purpose of the national accounts was to track production rather than income. Second, data on international factor income and transfer payments are generally considered somewhat unreliable. So if you're trying to keep track of movements in the economy, it makes sense to focus on GDP, which doesn't rely on these unreliable data.

Shutterstock

The funds Latin American immigrants send home through Western Union wires, as advertised on this billboard, aren't subtracted from GDP.

410 Section 8 The Open Economy: International Trade and Finance

into the United States is equal to the sum of the red and green arrows going out of the United States. That is,

(41-2) Positive entries on the current account (lower green arrow) + Positive entries on the financial account (lower red arrow) = Negative entries on the current account (upper green arrow) + Negative entries on the financial account (upper red arrow)

Equation 41-2 can be rearranged as follows:

(41-3) Positive entries on the current account − Negative entries on the current account + Positive entries on the financial account − Negative entries on the financial account = 0

Equation 41-3 is equivalent to Equation 41-1: the current account plus the financial account—both equal to positive entries minus negative entries—is equal to zero.

But what determines the current account and the financial account?

AP® Exam Tip

The current and financial accounts balance each other out. If there is a surplus in one account, there is a deficit in the other.

Modeling the Financial Account

A country's financial account measures its net sales of assets, such as currencies, securities, and factories, to foreigners. Those assets are exchanged for a type of capital called *financial capital*, which is funds from savings that are available for investment spending. So we can think of the financial account as a measure of *capital inflows* in the form of foreign savings that become available to finance domestic investment spending.

What determines these capital inflows?

Part of our explanation will have to wait for a little while because some international capital flows are created by governments and central banks, which sometimes act very differently from private investors. But we can gain insight into the motivations for capital flows that are the result of private decisions by using the *loanable funds model* we developed previously. In using this model, we make two important simplifications:

- We simplify the reality of international capital flows by assuming that all flows are in the form of loans. In reality, capital flows take many forms, including purchases of shares of stock in foreign companies and foreign real estate as well as *foreign direct investment*, in which companies build factories or acquire other productive assets abroad.
- We also ignore the effects of expected changes in *exchange rates*, the relative values of different national currencies. We'll analyze the determination of exchange rates later.

Figure 41.2 on the next page recaps the loanable funds model for a closed economy. Equilibrium corresponds to point *E*, at an interest rate of 4%, at which the supply curve for loanable funds (*S*) intersects the demand curve for loanable funds (*D*). If international capital flows are possible, this diagram changes and *E* may no longer be the equilibrium. We can analyze the causes and effects of international capital flows using **Figure 41.3** on the next page, which places the loanable funds market diagrams for two countries side by side.

Figure 41.3 illustrates a world consisting of only two countries, the United States and Britain. Panel (a) shows the loanable funds market in the United States, where the equilibrium in the absence of international capital flows is at point E_{US} with an interest rate of 6%. Panel (b) shows the loanable funds market in Britain, where the equilibrium in the absence of international capital flows is at point E_B with an interest rate of 2%.

Will the actual interest rate in the United States remain at 6% and that in Britain at 2%? Not if it is easy for British residents to make loans to Americans. In that case, British lenders, attracted by high U.S. interest rates, will send some of their loanable funds to the United States. This capital inflow will increase the quantity of loanable funds supplied to American borrowers, pushing the U.S. interest rate down. At the same time, it will reduce the quantity of loanable funds supplied to British borrowers, pushing the British interest rate up. So international capital flows will narrow the gap between U.S. and British interest rates.

AP® Exam Tip

The financial account will have capital inflows and capital outflows based on changes in interest rates. This is financial capital and not capital in the form of machinery and equipment used in the production process.

TEACH **Connect It**

Now is a good time to review the circular-flow diagram. Explain the relationship between the rest of the world and the United States using Figure 41.1. Then ask students to draw the circular-flow diagram on their personal whiteboards or on paper. Make sure they add in the rest of the world as shown in the diagram at the bottom of the page. How do participants in the U.S. product market interact with the rest of the world? *U.S. consumers buy goods and services from foreign sellers as imports and sell goods and services to foreign buyers as exports.* What account would these transactions be registered in? *The current account.* Which transactions would be registered in the financial account? *Transactions in financial markets and other transactions that create a liability. This would not include transfer payments, dividends, or interest that would be counted in the current account.*

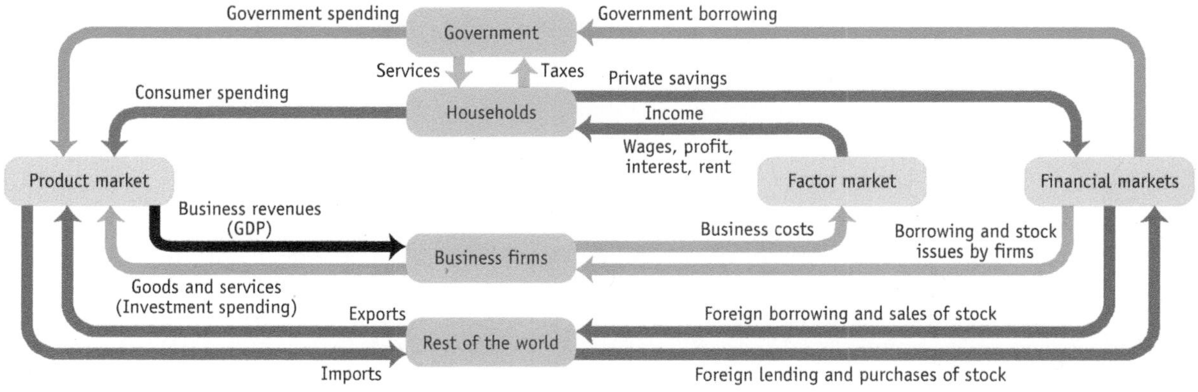

Module 41 Capital Flows and the Balance of Payments 411

FOCUS Flip It

TRM For a review of the balance of payments, have students watch Jacob Clifford's "Macro 5.1—Balance of Payments" video (see econextras video list with hyperlinks on the bcs and TRFD). Questions for this video may be found in **Worksheet 41.2 (Balance of Payments)** from the TRM.

TEACH Connect It

Review the loanable funds market. Have students draw the loanable funds graph they studied in Module 29 on their personal whiteboards or on paper. Review the axis labels and factors that shift the supply and demand curves for loanable funds. *The demand curve for loanable funds is shifted by changes in perceived business opportunities and government borrowing. The supply curve for loanable funds is shifted by changes in private savings behavior and capital inflows.*

FOCUS Graph It

Draw the loanable funds graph for two different nations on the board, with the different equilibrium interest rates on each similar to the graphs in Figure 41.3. Ask students where they would want to put their money if they had $1,000 to invest. *The answer should be the nation with the highest interest rate.* Stress that recent AP® Macro exams have been very strict on this point. Students struggle with this concept as they often confuse financial capital and physical capital. Remind them:

- When they are borrowing to invest in physical capital, low interest rates are better because the investors pay back the interest.
- When they invest in financial capital, high interest rates are better because the investors will be paid the interest.

Figure 41.2 The Loanable Funds Model Revisited

According to the loanable funds model of the interest rate, the equilibrium interest rate is determined by the intersection of the supply curve for loanable funds, *S*, and the demand curve for loanable funds, *D*. At point *E*, the equilibrium interest rate is 4%.

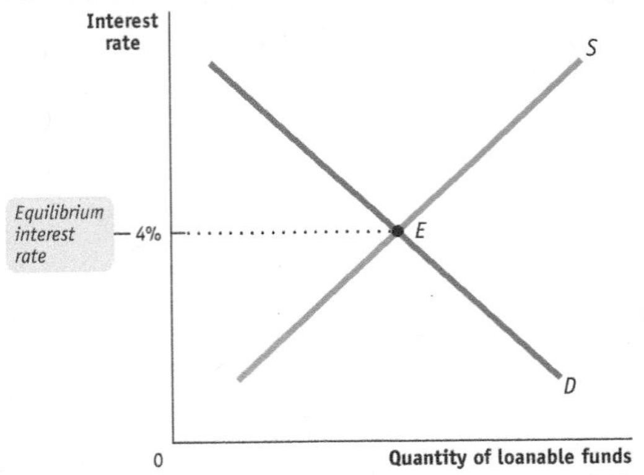

Let's further suppose that British lenders regard a loan to an American as being just as good as a loan to one of their own compatriots, and American borrowers regard a debt to a British lender as no more costly than a debt to an American lender. In that case, the flow of funds from Britain to the United States will continue until the gap between their interest rates is eliminated. In other words, international capital flows will equalize the interest rates in the two countries. **Figure 41.4** shows an international equilibrium in the loanable funds markets where the equilibrium interest rate is 4% in both the United States and Britain. At this interest rate, the quantity of loanable

Figure 41.3 Loanable Funds Markets in Two Countries

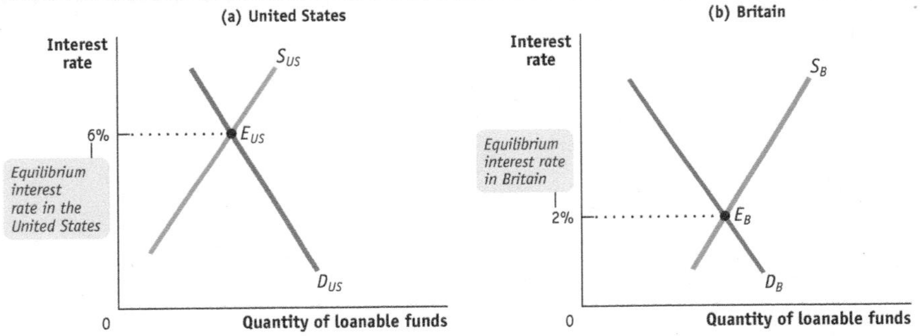

Here we show two countries, the United States and Britain, each with its own loanable funds market. The equilibrium interest rate is 6% in the U.S. market but only 2% in the British market. This creates an incentive for capital to flow from Britain to the United States.

Figure 41.4 International Capital Flows

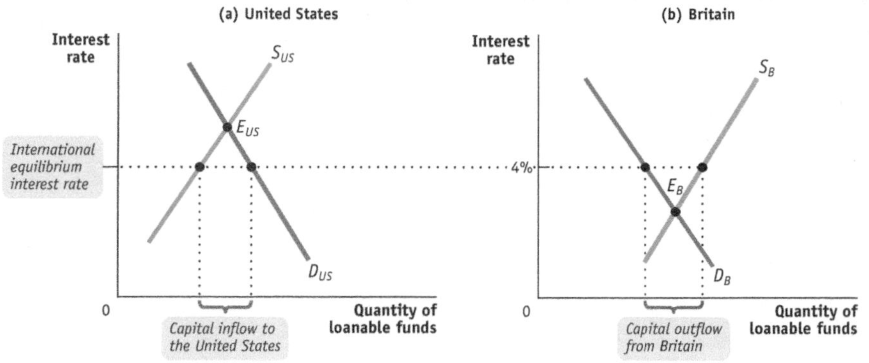

British lenders lend to borrowers in the United States, leading to equalization of interest rates at 4% in both countries. At that rate, American borrowing exceeds American lending; the difference is made up by capital inflows to the United States. Meanwhile, British lending exceeds British borrowing; the excess is a capital outflow from Britain.

funds demanded by American borrowers exceeds the quantity of loanable funds supplied by American lenders. This gap is filled by "imported" funds—a capital inflow from Britain. At the same time, the quantity of loanable funds supplied by British lenders is greater than the quantity of loanable funds demanded by British borrowers. This excess is "exported" in the form of a capital outflow to the United States. And the two markets are in equilibrium at a common interest rate of 4%. At that interest rate, the total quantity of loans demanded by borrowers across the two markets is equal to the total quantity of loans supplied by lenders across the two markets.

In short, international flows of capital are like international flows of goods and services. Capital moves from places where it would be cheap in the absence of international capital flows to places where it would be expensive in the absence of such flows.

Underlying Determinants of International Capital Flows

The open-economy version of the loanable funds model helps us understand international capital flows in terms of the supply and demand for funds. But what underlies differences across countries in the supply and demand for funds? And why, in the absence of international capital flows, would interest rates differ internationally, creating an incentive for international capital flows?

International differences in the demand for funds reflect underlying differences in investment opportunities. In particular, a country with a rapidly growing economy, other things equal, tends to offer more investment opportunities than a country with a slowly growing economy. So a rapidly growing economy typically—though not always—has a higher demand for capital and offers higher returns to investors than a slowly growing economy in the absence of capital flows. As a result, capital tends to flow from slowly growing to rapidly growing economies.

FOCUS Graph It

Have students draw the loanable funds graph for two different nations on their personal whiteboards or on paper. The interest rate in one nation is 6% and the interest rate in the other nation is 4%. (Refer students to Figure 41.3 if they need help.) In which direction will capital flow? *Toward the nation with the higher interest rate.* Ask them to show how each loanable funds graph will change as a result of the change in capital flows. Remind them that capital flows affect the supply of loanable funds. Notice that capital will flow until the equilibrium interest rate is the same in each nation, as shown in Figure 41.4.

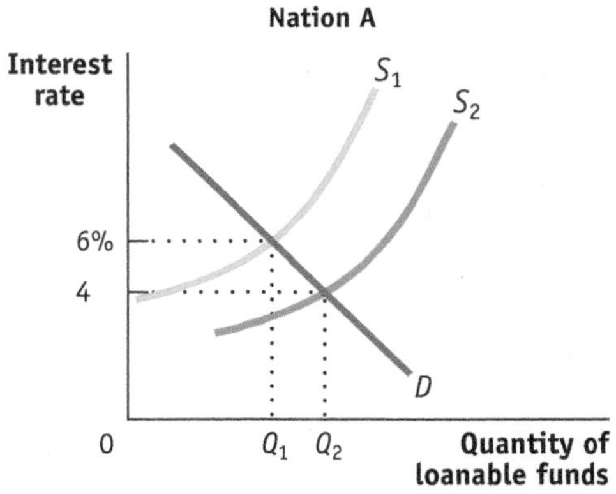

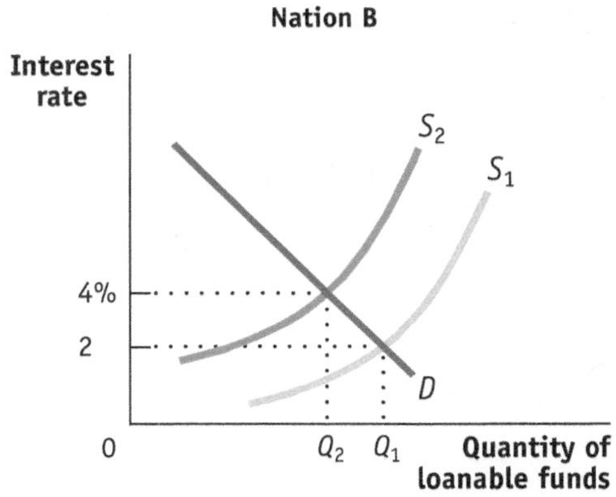

TEACH Teach It

Students should learn the factors that affect the flow of financial capital in an economy:

- Rapidly increasing real GDP or economic growth often means higher returns on financial investment. As a result, capital tends to flow from slowly growing economies to rapidly growing economies.
- Differences in private savings rates vary widely among countries. Higher rates attract capital inflows.
- The loanable funds graph may also reflect differences in savings by governments. In particular, government budget deficits, which reduce overall national savings, can lead to capital inflows.

Module 41 Capital Flows and the Balance of Payments 413

FYI A Global Savings Glut?

In the early years of the twenty-first century, the United States entered into a massive current account deficit, which meant that it became the recipient of huge capital inflows from the rest of the world, especially China, other Asian countries, and the Middle East. Why did that happen?

In an influential speech early in 2005, Ben Bernanke—who was at that time a governor of the Federal Reserve and who would soon become the Fed's chair—offered a hypothesis: the United States wasn't responsible. The "principal causes of the U.S. current account deficit," he declared, lie "outside the country's borders." Specifically, he argued that special factors had created a "global savings glut" that had pushed down interest rates worldwide and thereby led to an excess of investment spending over savings in the United States.

What caused this global savings glut? According to Bernanke, the main cause was the series of financial crises that began in Thailand in 1997, ricocheted across much of Asia, and then hit Russia in 1998, Brazil in 1999, and Argentina in 2002. The ensuing fear and economic devastation led to a fall in investment spending and a rise in savings in many relatively poor countries. As a result, a number of these countries, which had previously been the recipients of capital inflows from developed countries like the United States, began experiencing large capital outflows. For the most part, the capital flowed to the United States, perhaps because "the depth and sophistication of the country's financial markets" made it an attractive destination.

When Bernanke gave his speech, it was viewed as reassuring: basically, he argued that the United States was responding in a sensible way to the availability of cheap money in world financial markets. Later, however, it would become clear that the cheap money from abroad helped fuel a housing bubble, which caused widespread financial and economic damage when it burst.

The classic example is the flow of capital from Britain to the United States, among other countries, between 1870 and 1914. During that era, the U.S. economy was growing rapidly as the population increased and spread westward, and as the nation industrialized. This created a demand for investment spending on railroads, factories, and so on. Meanwhile, Britain had a much more slowly growing population, was already industrialized, and already had a railroad network covering the country. This left Britain with savings to spare, much of which were lent to the United States and other New World economies.

International differences in the supply of funds reflect differences in savings across countries. These may be the result of differences in private savings rates, which vary widely among countries. For example, in 2013, private savings were 27.1% of Japan's GDP but only 15.9% of U.S. GDP. They may also reflect differences in savings by governments. In particular, government budget deficits, which reduce overall national savings, can lead to capital inflows.

Nike, like many other companies, has opened plants in China to take advantage of low labor costs and to gain better access to the large Chinese market. Here, two Chinese employees assemble running shoes in a Nike factory in China.

Two-Way Capital Flows

The loanable funds model helps us understand the direction of *net* capital flows—the excess of inflows into a country over outflows, or vice versa. As we saw in Table 41.2, however, *gross* flows take place in both directions: for example, the United States both sells assets to foreigners and buys assets from foreigners. Why does capital move in both directions?

The answer to this question is that in the real world, as opposed to the simple model we've just constructed, there are other motives for international capital flows besides seeking a higher rate of interest. Individual investors often seek to diversify against risk by buying stocks in a number of countries. Stocks in Europe may do well when stocks in the United States do badly, or vice versa, so investors in Europe try to reduce their risk by buying some U.S. stocks, even as investors in the United States try to reduce their risk by buying some European stocks. The result is capital flows in both directions. Meanwhile, corporations often engage in international investment as part of their business strategy—for example, auto companies may

TEACH Teach It

Students need to understand that investors should diversify their portfolios. Holding financial assets in other nations affords them one opportunity to diversify. As a result, some financial capital will flow out of a nation because interest rates might be higher overseas, providing a higher return on investment. Alternately, capital inflow from foreign investors may occur because they believe a foreign economy has a brighter future and better opportunity for return on investments.

FOCUS Active Learning

TRM Complete **Activity 41.3 (Financial Flows)** from the TRM in class or assign as homework. In this activity, students will draw a correctly labeled loanable funds graph. After completing the activity, students will understand the impact of interest rates on financial capital investments between nations.

414 Section 8 The Open Economy: International Trade and Finance

find that they can compete better in a national market if they assemble some of their cars locally. Such business investments can also lead to two-way capital flows, as, say, European carmakers build plants in the United States even as U.S. computer companies open facilities in Europe.

Finally, some countries, including the United States, are international banking centers: people from all over the world put money in U.S. financial institutions, which then invest many of those funds overseas.

The result of these two-way flows is that modern economies are typically both debtors (countries that owe money to the rest of the world) and creditors (countries to which the rest of the world owes money). Due to years of both capital inflows and outflows, at the end of 2013, the United States had accumulated foreign assets worth $22 trillion and foreigners had accumulated assets in the United States worth $26.5 trillion.

MODULE 41 Review

Check Your Understanding

1. Which of the balance of payments accounts do the following events affect?
   a. Boeing, a U.S.-based company, sells a newly built airplane to China.
   b. Chinese investors buy stock in Boeing from Americans.
   c. A Chinese company buys a used airplane from American Airlines and ships it to China.
   d. A Chinese investor who owns property in the United States buys a corporate jet, which he will keep in the United States so he can travel around America.

Tackle the Test: Multiple-Choice Questions

1. The current account includes which of the following?
   I. payments for goods and services
   II. transfer payments
   III. factor income
   a. I only
   b. II only
   c. III only
   d. I and II only
   e. I, II, and III
2. The balance of payments on the current account plus the balance of payments on the financial account is equal to
   a. zero.
   b. one.
   c. the trade balance.
   d. net capital flows.
   e. the size of the trade deficit.
3. The financial account was previously known as the
   a. gross national product.
   b. capital account.
   c. trade deficit.
   d. investment account.
   e. trade balance.
4. The trade balance includes which of the following?
   I. imports and exports of goods
   II. imports and exports of services
   III. net capital flows
   a. I only
   b. II only
   c. III only
   d. I and II only
   e. I, II, and III
5. Which of the following will increase the demand for loanable funds in a country?
   a. economic growth
   b. decreased investment opportunities
   c. a recession
   d. decreased private savings rates
   e. government budget surpluses

OPEN & CLOSE Exit Slip

TRM *Please see **Exit Slip: Module 41** in the TRM for formative multiple-choice questions to ask your students before finishing your lesson. These questions will help you quickly assess whether your students have mastered the module's concepts before moving on.*

Answers to the Exit Slip Questions

1. C
2. D
3. B

Answers to Module 41 Review Questions

Check Your Understanding

1. a. The sale of the new airplane to China represents an export of a good to China and so enters the current account.

b. The sale of Boeing stock to Chinese investors is a sale of a U.S. asset and so enters the financial account.

c. Even though the plane already exists, when it is shipped to China, it is an export of a good from the United States. Thus, the sale of the plane enters the current account.

d. Because the plane stays in the United States, the Chinese investor is buying a U.S. asset. The sale of the jet enters the financial account.

Tackle the Test: Multiple-Choice Questions

1. e
2. a
3. b
4. a
5. a

Tackle the Test: Free-Response Questions

1. **a.** How would a decrease in real income in the United States affect the U.S. current account balance? Explain.
   b. Suppose China financed a huge program of infrastructure spending by borrowing. How would this borrowing affect the U.S. balance of payments? Explain.

Rubric for FRQ 1 (4 points)

1 point: The current account balance would increase (or move toward a surplus).

1 point: The decrease in income would cause imports to decrease.

1 point: The increase in infrastructure spending in China would reduce the surplus in the U.S. financial account and reduce the deficit in the U.S. current account.

1 point: Because China is financing the program by borrowing, the demand for loanable funds in China would increase, causing an increase in the interest rate. It is likely that other countries would increase their lending to China, decreasing their lending to the United States. These capital outflows from the United States would reduce the U.S. surplus in the financial account and reduce the deficit in the current account.

2. Use two correctly labeled side-by-side graphs of the loanable funds market in the United States and China to show how a higher interest rate in the United States will lead to capital flows between the two countries. On your graphs, be sure to label the equilibrium interest rate in each country in the absence of international capital flows, the international equilibrium interest rate, and the size of the capital inflows and outflows. **(6 points)**

Tackle the Test: Free-Response Question

Rubric for FRQ 2 (6 points)

1 point: Two graphs with "Interest rate" on the vertical axes and "Quantity of loanable funds" on the horizontal axes

1 point: An upward-sloping supply curve and a downward-sloping demand curve on each graph

1 point: Starting equilibrium interest rates labeled on each graph, with the rate in the United States higher than that in China

1 point: The same ending or "International equilibrium" interest rate labeled on both graphs

1 point: Indication of the correct capital inflow to the United States, as shown on the graph

1 point: Indication of the correct capital outflow from China, as shown on the graph

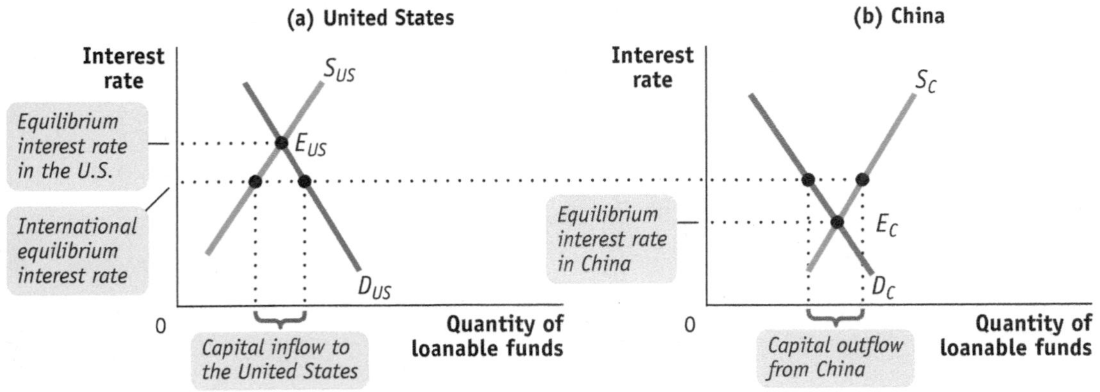

Udo Weitz/Bloomberg via Getty Images

MODULE 42

The Foreign Exchange Market

In this Module, you will learn to:

- Explain the role of the foreign exchange market and the exchange rate
- Discuss the importance of real exchange rates and their role in the current account

The Role of the Exchange Rate

We've just seen how differences in the supply of loanable funds from savings and the demand for loanable funds for investment spending lead to international capital flows. We've also learned that a country's balance of payments on the current account plus its balance of payments on the financial account add up to zero: a country that receives net capital inflows must run a matching current account deficit, and a country that generates net capital outflows must run a matching current account surplus.

The behavior of the financial account—reflecting inflows or outflows of capital—is best described as equilibrium in the international loanable funds market. At the same time, the balance of payments on goods and services, the main component of the current account, is determined by decisions in the international markets for goods and services. So given that the financial account reflects the movement of capital and the current account reflects the movement of goods and services, what ensures that the balance of payments really does balance? That is, what ensures that the two accounts actually offset each other?

The answer lies in the role of the *exchange rate*, which is determined in the *foreign exchange market*.

AP® Exam Tip

The foreign exchange market appears frequently on the AP® exam. You may be expected to graph and explain this market in the free-response section.

Understanding Exchange Rates

In general, goods, services, and assets produced in a country must be paid for in that country's currency. U.S. products must be paid for in dollars; most European products must be paid for in euros; Japanese products must be paid for in yen. Occasionally, sellers will accept payment in foreign currency, but they will then exchange that currency for domestic money.

International transactions, then, require a market—the **foreign exchange market**—in which currencies can be exchanged for each other. This market determines **exchange rates**, the prices at which currencies trade. (The foreign exchange market, in fact, is not

Currencies are traded in the **foreign exchange market**.

The prices at which currencies trade are known as **exchange rates**.

PD To prepare for teaching this lesson, you may want to consult the **Module 42 Sample Lecture** in the TRM.

OPEN & CLOSE **Start Here**

It is often difficult for students to understand the foreign exchange market. To introduce this concept, show the short *Investopedia* video "Forex Market Basics" (see econextras video list with hyperlinks on the bcs and TRFD). Ask students to explain in their own words how the foreign exchange market works. *If a U.S. company wants to buy a good from a foreign nation, the company exchanges U.S. dollars for foreign dollars to pay for the good.* What are some factors that contribute to changes in the exchange rate? *Changes in monetary policy, political stability, interest rates, and imports and exports*

FOCUS **Active Learning**

Assign the foreign exchange activity "Foreign Currency and Foreign Exchange" at http://tinyurl.com/kvertx3. Students will participate in a simulated foreign exchange market. They will need to exchange currencies to purchase foreign goods and gain a better understanding of how supply and demand work to set the international exchange rate. If time is short, conduct 1 or 2 rounds rather than the recommended 4. Use the questions in the lesson to debrief your students.

TEACH **AP® Exam Tip**

Foreign exchange rate graphs have been heavily tested on the AP® exam. As you move through this section, stress how important it is to correctly draw and label such graphs.

St. Louis Federal Reserve Bank Resources

"Currency Crusaders of Justice," ***Currency Crusaders Online Course***

In this episode, Jack of All Trades and his best bud, Andy, are traveling the world by cape, having a coffee at each stop. Andy learns that purchasing those coffees using the currencies of their host countries presents a minor complication—the relative value of currencies around the world can change and make those coffees more expensive or less expensive. How does that happen? Students can stay tuned to learn how economic conditions affect exchange rates. . .and the price of coffee everywhere.

TEACH Teach It

The exchange rate is just a price. It is the price of one unit of currency in terms of another currency. Students who have traveled abroad tend to have an easier time understanding the foreign exchange market.

TEACH Teach It

To help students better understand foreign exchange, refer to a local establishment that uses tokens for playing games (e.g., Chuck-E-Cheese, Dave & Buster's, and amusement parks). In order to play the games, you must have the right tokens. Dollars and coins do not work in the machines. If you have a dollar, you must exchange it for tokens in order to play. Countries also require tokens; they just call them yen, euros, pounds, etc. Now the question is, why do people want Chuck-E-Cheese tokens? *To play their games.* Why do people want foreign currency? *To buy foreign goods and services, or to invest in foreign markets.* Using this analogy should help students grasp the concept of exchange rates.

TEACH Teach It

Tell your students that the current exchange rate is $1 = 4 tokens. What would happen if the token machine changed such that $1 = 10 tokens? Would the demand for games increase? Absolutely! The dollar has appreciated in value and more of these foreign "games" will be purchased. This is what happens when the dollar appreciates: imports rise, so net exports fall. What would happen if the token machine changed such that $1 = 2 tokens? *Fewer dollars would be converted (supplied) and the demand for games would decrease.* This is what happens when the dollar depreciates: imports fall, so net exports rise.

TEACH Teach It

When you hear the terms *appreciate* or *depreciate*, you should think of changes in the value of one nation's currency relative to the value of another nation's currency, not changes in what a nation's currency will buy domestically. When one nation's currency appreciates, the other nation's currency depreciates.

Table 42.1 Exchange Rates, April 3, 2014, 12:50 A.M.

	U.S. dollars	Yen	Euros
One U.S. dollar exchanged for	1	103.97	0.7269
One yen exchanged for	0.0096	1	0.007
One euro exchanged for	1.3757	143.04	1

located in any one geographic spot. Rather, it is a global electronic market that traders around the world use to buy and sell currencies.)

Table 42.1 shows exchange rates among the world's three most important currencies as of 12:50 A.M., EST, on April 3, 2014. Each entry shows the price of the "row" currency in terms of the "column" currency. For example, at that time US$1 exchanged for €0.7269, so it took €0.7269 to buy US$1. Similarly, it took US$1.3757 to buy €1. These two numbers reflect the same rate of exchange between the euro and the U.S. dollar: 1/1.3757 = €0.7269.

There are two ways to write any given exchange rate. In this case, there were €0.7269 to US$1 and US$1.3757 to €1. Which is the correct way to write it? The answer is that there is no fixed rule. In most countries, people tend to express the exchange rate as the price of a dollar in domestic currency. However, this rule isn't universal, and the U.S. dollar–euro rate is commonly quoted both ways. The important thing is to be sure you know which one you are using!

When a currency becomes more valuable in terms of other currencies, it **appreciates**.

When a currency becomes less valuable in terms of other currencies, it **depreciates**.

When discussing movements in exchange rates, economists use specialized terms to avoid confusion. When a currency becomes more valuable in terms of other currencies, economists say that the currency **appreciates**. When a currency becomes less valuable in terms of other currencies, it **depreciates**. Suppose, for example, that the value of €1 went from $1 to $1.25, which means that the value of US$1 went from €1 to €0.80 (because 1/1.25 = 0.80). In this case, we would say that the euro appreciated and the U.S. dollar depreciated.

Movements in exchange rates, other things equal, affect the relative prices of goods, services, and assets in different countries. Suppose, for example, that the price of an American hotel room is US$100 and the price of a French hotel room is €100. If the exchange rate is €1 = US$1, these hotel rooms have the same price. If the exchange rate is €1.25 = US$1, however, the French hotel room is 20% cheaper than the American hotel room. If the exchange rate is €0.80 = US$1, the French hotel room is 25% more expensive than the American hotel room.

But what determines exchange rates? Supply and demand in the foreign exchange market.

The Equilibrium Exchange Rate

For the sake of simplicity, imagine that there are only two currencies in the world: U.S. dollars and euros. Europeans who want to purchase American goods, services, and assets come to the foreign exchange market to exchange euros for U.S. dollars. That is, Europeans demand U.S. dollars from the foreign exchange market and, correspondingly, supply euros to that market. Americans who want to buy European goods, services, and assets come to the foreign exchange market to exchange U.S. dollars for euros. That is, Americans supply U.S. dollars to the foreign exchange market and, correspondingly, demand euros from that market. International transfers and payments of factor income also enter into the foreign exchange market, but to make things simple, we'll ignore these.

Figure 42.1 shows how the foreign exchange market works. The quantity of dollars demanded and supplied at any given euro–U.S. dollar exchange rate is shown on the horizontal axis, and the euro–U.S. dollar exchange rate is shown on the vertical axis. The exchange rate plays the same role as the price of a good or service in an ordinary supply and demand diagram.

The figure shows two curves, the demand curve for U.S. dollars and the supply curve for U.S. dollars. The key to understanding the slopes of these curves is that the level of the exchange rate affects exports and imports. When a country's currency appreciates (becomes more valuable), exports fall and imports rise. When a country's currency depreciates (becomes less valuable), exports rise and imports fall. To understand why the demand curve for U.S. dollars slopes downward, recall that the exchange rate, other things equal, determines the prices of American goods, services, and assets relative to

418 Section 8 The Open Economy: International Trade and Finance

Figure 42.1 The Foreign Exchange Market

The foreign exchange market matches up the demand for a currency from foreigners who want to buy domestic goods, services, and assets with the supply of a currency from domestic residents who want to buy foreign goods, services, and assets. Here the equilibrium in the market for dollars is at point *E*, corresponding to an equilibrium exchange rate of €0.95 per US$1.

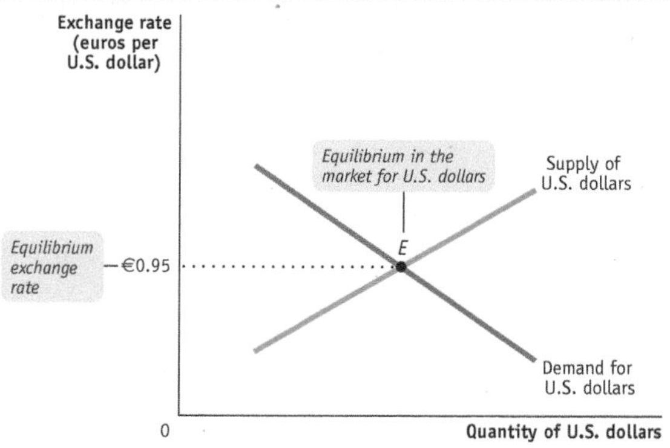

those of European goods, services, and assets. If the U.S. dollar rises against the euro (the dollar appreciates), American products will become more expensive to Europeans relative to European products. So Europeans will buy less from the United States and will acquire fewer dollars in the foreign exchange market: the quantity of U.S. dollars demanded falls as the number of euros needed to buy a U.S. dollar rises. If the U.S. dollar falls against the euro (the dollar depreciates), American products will become relatively cheaper for Europeans. Europeans will respond by buying more from the United States and acquiring more dollars in the foreign exchange market: the quantity of U.S. dollars demanded rises as the number of euros needed to buy a U.S. dollar falls.

A similar argument explains why the supply curve of U.S. dollars in Figure 42.1 slopes upward: the more euros required to buy a U.S. dollar, the more dollars Americans will supply. Again, the reason is the effect of the exchange rate on relative prices. If the U.S. dollar rises against the euro, European products look cheaper to Americans—who will demand more of them. This will require Americans to convert more dollars into euros.

The **equilibrium exchange rate** is the exchange rate at which the quantity of U.S. dollars demanded in the foreign exchange market is equal to the quantity of U.S. dollars supplied. In Figure 42.1, the equilibrium is at point *E*, and the equilibrium exchange rate is 0.95. That is, at an exchange rate of €0.95 per US$1, the quantity of U.S. dollars supplied to the foreign exchange market is equal to the quantity of U.S. dollars demanded.

The **equilibrium exchange rate** is the exchange rate at which the quantity of a currency demanded in the foreign exchange market is equal to the quantity supplied.

To understand the significance of the equilibrium exchange rate, it's helpful to consider a numerical example of what equilibrium in the foreign exchange market looks like. Such an example is shown in **Table 42.2** on the next page. (This is a hypothetical table that isn't intended to match real numbers.) The first row shows European purchases of U.S. dollars, either to buy U.S. goods and services or to buy U.S. assets such as real estate or shares of stock in U.S. companies. The second row shows U.S. sales of U.S. dollars, either to buy European goods and services or to buy European assets. At the equilibrium exchange rate, the total quantity of U.S. dollars Europeans want to buy is equal to the total quantity of U.S. dollars Americans want to sell.

Remember that the balance of payments accounts divide international transactions into two types. Purchases and sales of goods and services are counted in the current account. (Again, we're leaving out transfers and factor income to keep things simple.) Purchases and sales of assets are counted in the financial account. At the equilibrium exchange rate, then, we have the situation shown in Table 42.2: the sum of the balance of payments on the current account plus the balance of payments on the financial account is zero.

FOCUS Active Learning

TRM Use **Worksheet 42.1 (Understanding Exchange Rates)** from the TRM to guide students through an example of how to calculate exchange rates.

TEACH Connect It

Ask students to draw a standard supply and demand graph on their personal whiteboards or on paper as you draw one on the board. Begin with the generic labels of "Price" on the vertical axis and "Quantity" on the horizontal axis. Tell the students that you can easily convert this graph into a foreign exchange market graph, which is essentially a supply and demand graph with modified labels. Change the horizontal axis to read "Quantity of U.S. dollars" and tell them that this supply and demand graph is going to represent the U.S. dollar market. Explain that the price of the dollar in terms of the other currency is the exchange rate. Change the label on the vertical axis from "Price" to "$\frac{\text{Foreign Currency}}{\text{U.S. dollar}}$" to represent the exchange rate. Stress the correct way to label the axes: the horizontal axis measures the quantity of the currency for which you're examining the supply and demand; the name of that currency also appears below the line (in the place of the denominator) in the label of the vertical axis. The name of the currency being exchanged for the first currency appears above the line (in the place of the numerator) in the label on the vertical axis.

FOCUS Active Learning

Refer students to Table 42.2. Recall that if a deficit exists in the current account, there must be a surplus in the financial account. Ask the following questions:

- Why do Europeans want U.S. dollars? *To buy U.S. goods and services and financial assets*
- Why do Americans want euros? *To buy European goods and services and financial assets*
- What affect do these needs have on the balance of payments on the current and financial accounts? *All purchases of foreign goods, services, and assets are recorded in the current account or the financial account, and each transaction recorded in one of the accounts has an offsetting transaction that keeps the sum of the two accounts at zero.*

Point out that, in Table 42.2, the sum of the balance of payments on the current account and the balance of payments on the financial account is zero. Also, the total purchases of U.S. dollars equals the total sales of U.S. dollars, even though the dollars aren't allocated the same way between purchases of goods/services and assets as the euros for which they were exchanged.

FOCUS Graph It

Have students draw two supply and demand graphs on their personal whiteboards or paper. Tell them to leave the axes blank for the time being. Explain that when two nations participate in trade, each nation will have a different supply and demand graph representing the foreign exchange market. Remind them that the horizontal axis label always indicates which nation's foreign exchange market the graph represents. On the left graph, ask students to label the horizontal axis "Quantity of U.S. dollars" and the vertical axis "euros per U.S. dollar" or "$\frac{\text{euros}}{\text{USD}}$". Tell students that whenever they draw this type of graph, the currency name on the horizontal axis should match the currency named after the "per" (or in the bottom, denominator spot) in the vertical axis label. Have them label the graph on the right so that it represents the foreign exchange market for euros. Then draw the correct graph and help them check their work.

Table 42.2 Equilibrium in the Foreign Exchange Market: A Hypothetical Example

European purchases of U.S. dollars (trillions of U.S. dollars)	To buy U.S. goods and services: 1.0	To buy U.S. assets: 1.0	Total purchases of U.S. dollars: 2.0
U.S. sales of U.S. dollars (trillions of U.S. dollars)	To buy European goods and services: 1.5	To buy European assets: 0.5	Total sales of U.S. dollars: 2.0
	U.S. balance of payments on the current account: –0.5	U.S. balance of payments on the financial account: +0.5	

Now let's briefly consider how a shift in the demand for U.S. dollars affects equilibrium in the foreign exchange market. Suppose that for some reason capital flows from Europe to the United States increase—say, due to a change in the preferences of European investors. The effects are shown in **Figure 42.2**. The demand for U.S. dollars in the foreign exchange market increases as European investors convert euros into dollars to fund their new investments in the United States. This is shown by the shift of the demand curve from D_1 to D_2. As a result, the U.S. dollar appreciates: the number of euros per U.S. dollar at the equilibrium exchange rate rises from XR_1 to XR_2.

What are the consequences of this increased capital inflow for the balance of payments? The total quantity of U.S. dollars supplied to the foreign exchange market still must equal the total quantity of U.S. dollars demanded. So the increased capital inflow to the United States—an increase in the balance of payments on the financial account—must be matched by a decline in the balance of payments on the current account. What causes the balance of payments on the current account to decline? The appreciation of the U.S. dollar. A rise in the number of euros per U.S. dollar leads Americans to buy more European goods and services and Europeans to buy fewer American goods and services.

Table 42.3 shows how this might work. Europeans are buying more U.S. assets, increasing the balance of payments on the financial account from 0.5 to 1.0. This is offset by a reduction in European purchases of U.S. goods and services and a rise in U.S. purchases of European goods and services, both the result of the dollar's appreciation. *So any change in the U.S. balance of payments on the financial account generates an equal*

Figure 42.2 An Increase in the Demand for U.S. Dollars

An increase in the demand for U.S. dollars might result from a change in the preferences of European investors. The demand curve for U.S. dollars shifts from D_1 to D_2. So the equilibrium number of euros per U.S. dollar rises—the dollar *appreciates*. As a result, the balance of payments on the current account falls as the balance of payments on the financial account rises.

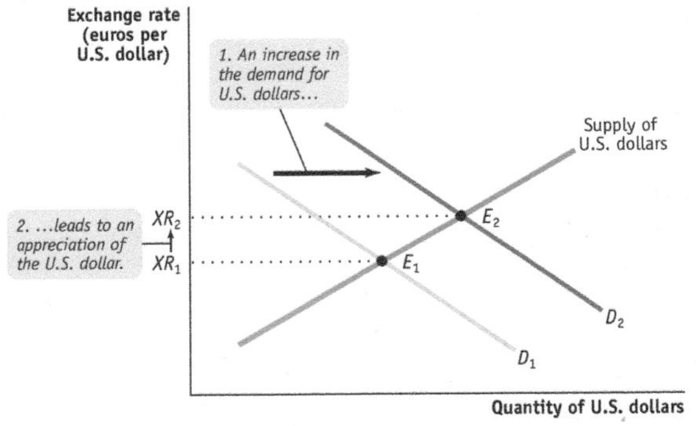

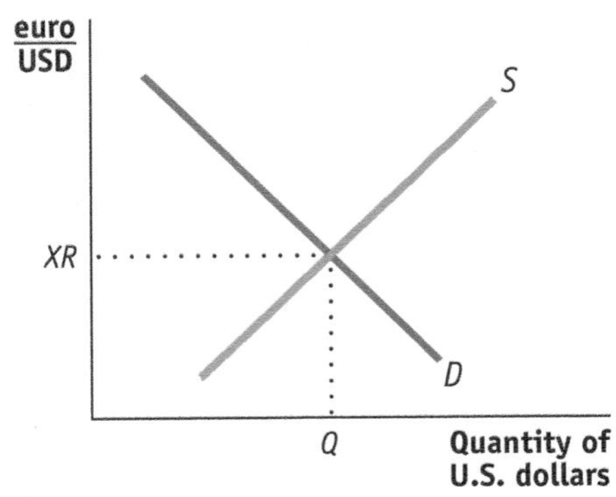

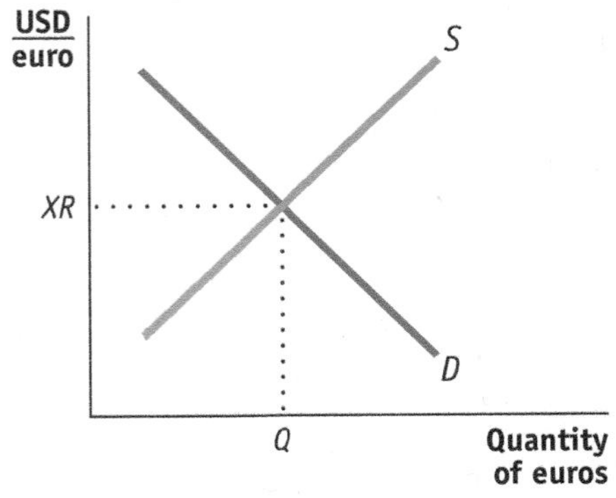

420 Section 8 The Open Economy: International Trade and Finance

Table 42.3 Effects of Increased Capital Inflows

European purchases of U.S. dollars (trillions of U.S. dollars)	To buy U.S. goods and services: 0.75 (down 0.25)	To buy U.S. assets: 1.5 (up 0.5)	Total purchases of U.S. dollars: 2.25
U.S. sales of U.S. dollars (trillions of U.S. dollars)	To buy European goods and services: 1.75 (up 0.25)	To buy European assets: 0.5 (no change)	Total sales of U.S. dollars: 2.25
	U.S. balance of payments on the current account: −1.0 (down 0.5)	U.S. balance of payments on the financial account: +1.0 (up 0.5)	

and opposite reaction in the balance of payments on the current account. Movements in the exchange rate ensure that changes in the financial account and in the current account offset each other.

Let's briefly run this process in reverse. Suppose there is a reduction in capital flows from Europe to the United States—again due to a change in the preferences of European investors. The demand for U.S. dollars in the foreign exchange market falls, and the dollar depreciates: the number of euros per U.S. dollar at the equilibrium exchange rate falls. This leads Americans to buy fewer European products and Europeans to buy more American products. Ultimately, this generates an increase in the U.S. balance of payments on the current account. So a fall in capital flows into the United States leads to a weaker dollar, which in turn generates an increase in U.S. net exports.

Inflation and Real Exchange Rates

In 1994, on average, one U.S. dollar exchanged for 3.4 Mexican pesos. By 2014, the peso had fallen against the dollar by almost 75%, with an average exchange rate in early 2014 of 13.3 pesos per dollar. Did Mexican products also become much cheaper relative to U.S. products over that 20-year period? Did the price of Mexican products expressed in terms of U.S. dollars also fall by almost 75%? The answer is no, because Mexico had much higher inflation than the United States over that period. In fact, the relative price of U.S. and Mexican products changed little between 1994 and 2014, although the exchange rate changed a lot.

To take account of the effects of differences in inflation rates, economists calculate **real exchange rates**, exchange rates adjusted for international differences in aggregate price levels. Suppose that the exchange rate we are looking at is the number of Mexican pesos per U.S. dollar. Let P_{US} and P_{Mex} be indexes of the aggregate price levels in the United States and Mexico, respectively. Then the real exchange rate between the Mexican peso and the U.S. dollar is defined as:

The exchange rates listed at currency exchange booths are nominal exchange rates. The current account responds only to changes in real exchange rates, which have been adjusted for differing levels of inflation.

(42-1) $$\text{Real exchange rate} = \text{Mexican pesos per U.S. dollar} \times \frac{P_{US}}{P_{Mex}}$$

Real exchange rates are exchange rates adjusted for international differences in aggregate price levels.

To distinguish it from the real exchange rate, the exchange rate unadjusted for aggregate price levels is sometimes called the *nominal* exchange rate.

To understand the significance of the difference between the real and nominal exchange rates, let's consider the following example. Suppose that the Mexican peso depreciates against the U.S. dollar, with the exchange rate going from 10 pesos per U.S. dollar to 15 pesos per U.S. dollar, a 50% change. But suppose that at the same time the price of everything in Mexico, measured in pesos, increases by 50%, so that the Mexican price index rises from 100 to 150. We'll assume that there is no change in U.S. prices, so that the U.S. price index remains at 100. The initial real exchange rate is:

$$\text{Pesos per dollar} \times \frac{P_{US}}{P_{Mex}} = 10 \times \frac{100}{100} = 10$$

FOCUS Active Learning

Refer students to Table 42.3 and ask the following:

- What effect do increased capital flows into the United States have on the exchange rate for the U.S. dollar? *Increased capital inflows cause the U.S. dollar to appreciate.*
- Why do Europeans need U.S. dollars to purchase U.S. financial capital? *American financial institutions only accept U.S. dollars for transactions.*
- What effect do these needs and the resulting appreciation of the U.S. dollar have on the balance of payments on the current and financial accounts? *This appreciation increases imports and decreases exports, which causes a decrease in the balance of payments on the current account to balance the increase in the balance of payments on the financial account brought about by the capital inflow.*

TEACH Connect It

Foreign exchange impacts GDP through net exports. Have students show and explain how a stronger dollar will affect GDP using their personal whiteboards or paper. *A stronger dollar means imports will increase and exports will decrease, so net exports will decrease, which causes GDP to decrease.*

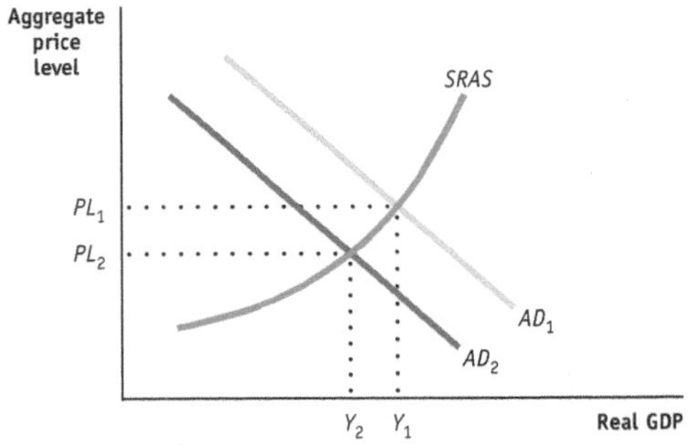

FOCUS Graph It

When you buy goods from another nation, you supply your currency to the foreign exchange market and demand the foreign currency. In the foreign exchange graphs, one nation's supply and one nation's demand will shift in the same direction. Using their personal whiteboards or paper, ask students to show what will happen to the two graphs if the demand for U.S. goods increases among nations that use the euro. Make sure they can explain that more euros are supplied to the foreign exchange market to buy U.S. dollars with which to buy the goods. As a result, the demand curve for U.S. dollars and the supply curve for euros both shift to the right.

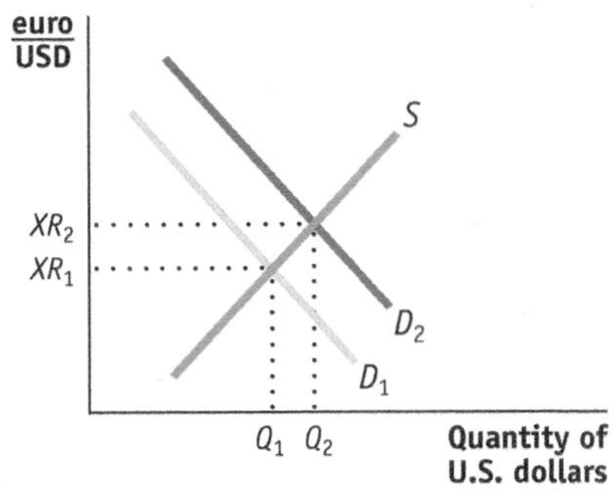

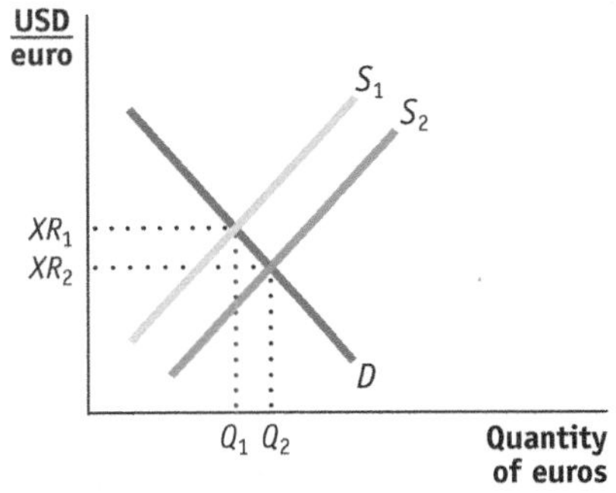

After the peso depreciates and the Mexican price level increases, the real exchange rate is:

$$\text{Pesos per dollar} \times \frac{P_{US}}{P_{Mex}} = 15 \times \frac{100}{150} = 10$$

In this example, the peso has depreciated substantially in terms of the U.S. dollar, but the *real* exchange rate between the peso and the U.S. dollar hasn't changed at all. And because the real peso–U.S. dollar exchange rate hasn't changed, the nominal depreciation of the peso against the U.S. dollar will have no effect either on the quantity of goods and services exported by Mexico to the United States or on the quantity of goods and services imported by Mexico from the United States. To see why, consider again the example of a hotel room. Suppose that this room initially costs 1,000 pesos per night, which is $100 at an exchange rate of 10 pesos per dollar. After both Mexican prices and the number of pesos per dollar rise by 50%, the hotel room costs 1,500 pesos per night—but 1,500 pesos divided by 15 pesos per dollar is $100, so the Mexican hotel room still costs $100. As a result, a U.S. tourist considering a trip to Mexico will have no reason to change plans.

PhotoSpin, Inc/Alamy

The same is true for all goods and services that enter into trade: *the current account responds only to changes in the real exchange rate, not the nominal exchange rate.* A country's products become cheaper to foreigners only when that country's currency depreciates in real terms, and those products become more expensive to foreigners only when the currency appreciates in real terms. As a consequence, economists who analyze movements in exports and imports of goods and services focus on the real exchange rate, not the nominal exchange rate.

Figure 42.3 illustrates just how important it can be to distinguish between nominal and real exchange rates. The line labeled "Nominal exchange rate" shows the number of pesos exchanged for a U.S. dollar from 1990 to 2013. As you can see, the peso depreciated massively over that period. But the line labeled "Real exchange rate" indicates the cost of Mexican products to U.S. consumers: it was calculated using Equation 42.1, with price indexes for both Mexico and the United States set so that the value in 1990 was 100. In real terms, the peso depreciated between 1994 and 1995, and again in 2008, but not by nearly as much as the nominal depreciation. By 2013, the real peso–U.S. dollar exchange rate was just about back where it started.

Figure 42.3 Real Versus Nominal Exchange Rates, 1990-2013

Between 1990 and 2013, the price of a dollar in Mexican pesos increased dramatically. But because Mexico had higher inflation than the United States, the real exchange rate, which accounts for the relative price of Mexican goods and services, ended up roughly where it started.
Source: OECD.

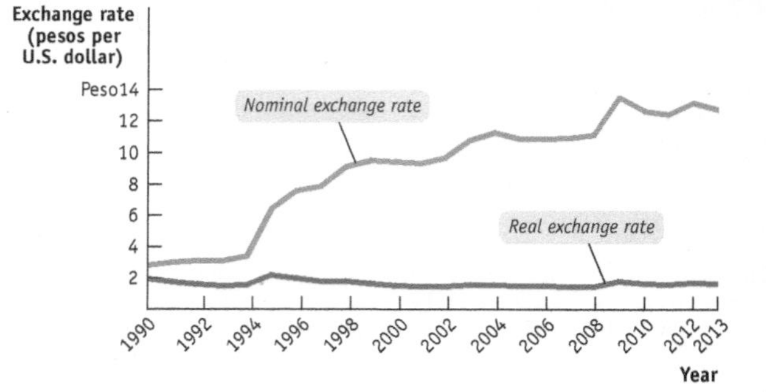

FOCUS Active Learning

TRM Have students watch the "Episode 33: Exchange Rates" video (see econextras video list with hyperlinks on the bcs and TRFD). Suggested discussion questions and answers for this video may be found in **Worksheet 42.2 (Exchange Rates)** from the TRM.

TEACH Teach It

The factors that cause a change in demand for a nation's currency can be remembered using the mnemonic TRYPS:

- **T**—Taste and preferences for imports and exports
- **R**—Relative interest rate (a high rate attracts financial investment)
- **Y**—Relative national income, GDP, or economic growth (high levels boost imports)
- **P**—Relative price level (a low level attracts foreign consumers)
- **S**—Speculation (buy low and sell high)

FOCUS Graph It

Ask your students to use their personal whiteboards or paper to draw and label foreign exchange market graphs for the United States and Canada, which exchange the U.S. dollar for the Canadian dollar. Then have them show the effect on these markets of a significant increase in Canada's GDP.

United States

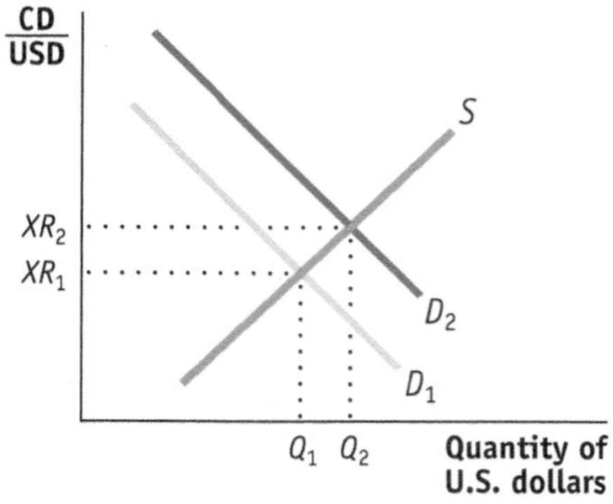

Canada

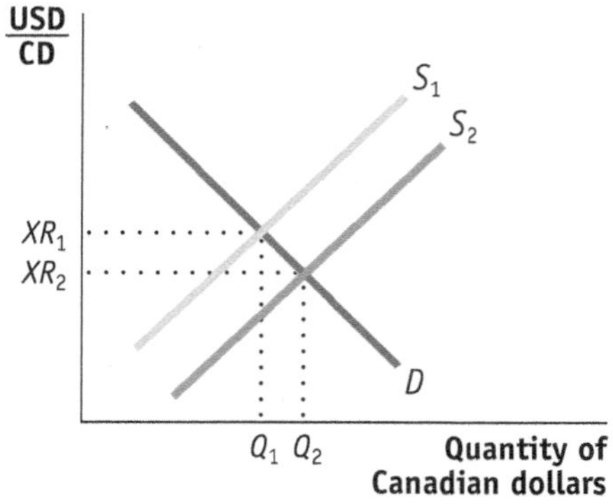

Canadians will supply more money to the U.S. foreign exchange market because part of their increase in income will go towards an increase in imports. This will increase demand for the U.S. dollar and cause it to appreciate. The increased supply of the Canadian dollar will cause it to depreciate.

Purchasing Power Parity

A useful tool for analyzing exchange rates, closely connected to the concept of the real exchange rate, is known as *purchasing power parity*. The **purchasing power parity** between two countries' currencies is the nominal exchange rate at which a given basket of goods and services would cost the same amount in each country. For example, suppose that a basket of goods and services that costs $100 in the United States costs 1,000 pesos in Mexico. Then the purchasing power parity is 10 pesos per U.S. dollar: at that exchange rate, 1,000 pesos = $100, so the market basket costs the same amount in both countries.

The **purchasing power parity** between two countries' currencies is the nominal exchange rate at which a given basket of goods and services would cost the same amount in each country.

Calculations of purchasing power parities are usually made by estimating the cost of buying broad market baskets containing many goods and services—everything from automobiles and groceries to housing and telephone calls. But once a year the magazine *The Economist* publishes a list of purchasing power parities based on the cost of buying a market basket that contains only one item—a McDonald's Big Mac.

Nominal exchange rates almost always differ from purchasing power parities. Some of these differences are systematic: in general, aggregate price levels are lower in poor countries than in rich countries because services tend to be cheaper in poor countries. But even among countries at roughly the same level of economic development, nominal exchange rates vary quite a lot from purchasing power parity. **Figure 42.4** on the next page shows the nominal exchange rate between the Canadian dollar and the U.S. dollar, measured as the number of Canadian dollars per U.S. dollar, from 1990 to 2013, together with an estimate of the purchasing power parity exchange rate between the United States and Canada over the same period. The purchasing power parity didn't change much over the whole period because the United States and Canada had about the same rate of inflation. But at the beginning of the period the nominal exchange rate was below purchasing power parity, so a given market basket was more expensive in Canada than in the United States. By 2002, the nominal exchange rate was far above the purchasing power parity, so a market basket was much cheaper in Canada than in the United States.

Over the long run, however, purchasing power parities are pretty good at predicting actual changes in nominal exchange rates. In particular, nominal exchange rates

FYI Burgernomics

For a number of years the British magazine *The Economist* has produced an annual comparison of the cost in different countries of one particular consumption item that is found around the world—a McDonald's Big Mac. The magazine finds the price of a Big Mac in local currency, then computes two numbers: the price of a Big Mac in U.S. dollars using the prevailing exchange rate, and the exchange rate at which the price of a Big Mac would equal the U.S. price. If purchasing power parity held for Big Macs, the dollar price of a Big Mac would be the same everywhere. If purchasing power parity is a good theory for the long run, the exchange rate at which a Big Mac's price matches the U.S. price should offer some guidance about where the exchange rate will eventually end up.

Aleks Kend/Shutterstock

In the January 2014 version of the Big Mac index, there were some wide variations in the dollar price of a Big Mac. In the U.S., the price was $4.62. In China, converting at the official exchange rate, a Big Mac cost only $2.74. In Switzerland, though, the price was $7.14.

The Big Mac index suggested that the euro would eventually fall against the dollar: a Big Mac on average cost €3.66, so that the purchasing power parity was $1.26 per €1 versus an actual market exchange rate of $1.38.

Serious economic studies of purchasing power parity require data on the prices of many goods and services. However, it turns out that estimates of purchasing power parity based on the Big Mac index usually aren't that different from more elaborate measures. Fast food seems to make for pretty good fast research.

FOCUS In the News

TRM Show students the Big Mac index from *The Economist* (http://www.economist.com/content/big-mac-index). This is an interactive tool that allows you to compare different currencies. Explore the index with students and then have them read *The Week's* January 2014 article "What Does the Big Mac Index Really Measure?" at http://theweek.com/article/index/255775/what-does-the-big-mac-index-really-measure. Assign **Worksheet 42.3 (Big Mac Index)** from the TRM for discussion questions on this article.

FOCUS Active Learning

Show the Jacob Clifford video "Macro 5.3—Foreign Exchange Practice" (see econextras video list with hyperlinks on the bcs and TRFD). Stop the video at 2:09, and challenge students to explain the shifts described and how exports and imports will be affected. Then continue the video for the answers.

FOCUS Active Learning

TRM Use **Worksheet 42.4 (Graphing Exchange Rates)** from the TRM to test your students' understanding of exchange rate graphs.

FOCUS Test It

Have your students complete Question 1 from the 2013 AP® Macroeconomics exam at http://media.collegeboard.com/digitalServices/pdf/ap/apcentral/ap13_frq_macroeconomics.pdf. This question will provide a comprehensive review of all the relevant topics: *AD–AS,* loanable funds, economic growth, foreign exchange, and the balance of payments. It is recommended that students take 25 minutes to answer this question to match the time suggested for the AP® exam. The rubric for the question may be viewed at http://tinyurl.com/kr3osws.

Module 42 The Foreign Exchange Market 423

OPEN & CLOSE Exit Slip

TRM *Please see **Exit Slip: Module 42** in the TRM for formative multiple-choice questions to ask your students before finishing your lesson. These questions will help you quickly assess whether your students have mastered the module's concepts before moving on.*

Answers to the Exit Slip Questions

1. C
2. B
3. D

Figure 42.4 Purchasing Power Parity Versus the Nominal Exchange Rate, 1990–2013

The purchasing power parity between the United States and Canada—the exchange rate at which a basket of goods and services would have cost the same amount in both countries—changed very little over the period shown, staying near C$1.20 per US$1. But the nominal exchange rate fluctuated widely.
Source: OECD.

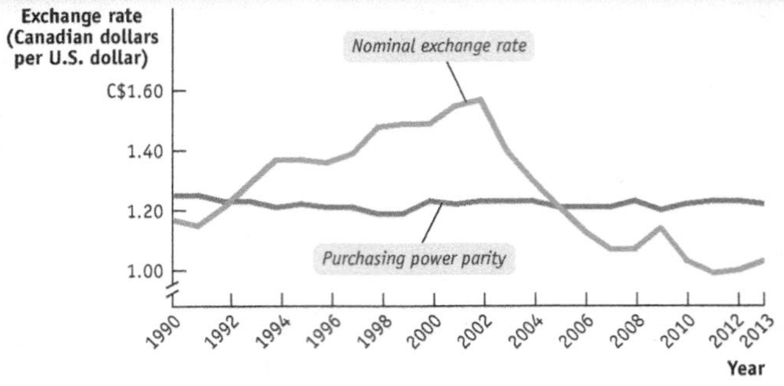

between countries at similar levels of economic development tend to fluctuate around levels that lead to similar costs for a given market basket. In fact, by July 2005, the nominal exchange rate between the United States and Canada was C$1.22 per US$1—just about the purchasing power parity. And by 2006, the cost of living was once again higher in Canada than in the United States.

FYI Low-Cost America

Does the exchange rate matter for business decisions? And how. Consider what European auto manufacturers were doing in 2008. One report from the University of Iowa summarized the situation as follows:

"While luxury German carmakers BMW and Mercedes have maintained plants in the American South since the 1990s, BMW aims to expand U.S. manufacturing in South Carolina by 50% during the next five years. Volvo of Sweden is in negotiations to build a plant in New Mexico. Analysts at Italian carmaker Fiat determined that it needs to build a North American factory to profit from the upcoming re-launch of its Alfa Romeo model. Tennessee recently closed a deal with Volkswagen to build a $1 billion factory by offering $577 million in incentives."

Why were European automakers flocking to America? To some extent because they were being offered special incentives, as the case of Volkswagen in Tennessee illustrates. But the big factor was the exchange rate. In the early 2000s, on average, one euro was worth less than a dollar; by the summer of 2008 the exchange rate was around €1 = $1.50. This change in the exchange rate made it substantially cheaper for European car manufacturers to produce in the United States than at home—especially if the cars were intended for the U.S. market.

Automobile manufacturing wasn't the only U.S. industry benefiting from the weak dollar; across the board, U.S. exports surged after 2006 while import growth fell off. The figure shows one measure of U.S. trade performance, real net exports of goods and services: exports minus imports, both measured in 2005 dollars. As you can see, this balance, after a long slide, turned sharply upward in 2006.

There was a modest reversal in 2009–2010, as the recovery from the 2007–2009 recession pulled in more imports, but a major narrowing of the trade gap remained in place.

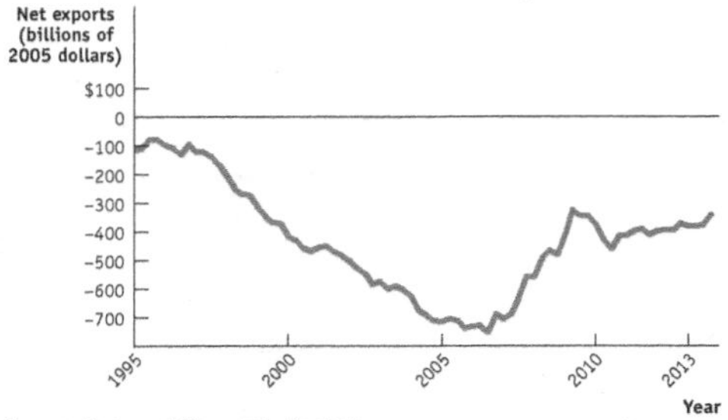

Source: Bureau of Economic Analysis.

424 Section 8 The Open Economy: International Trade and Finance

MODULE 42 Review

Check Your Understanding

1. Suppose Mexico discovers huge reserves of oil and starts exporting oil to the United States. Describe how this would affect the following:
   a. the nominal peso–U.S. dollar exchange rate
   b. Mexican exports of other goods and services
   c. Mexican imports of goods and services
2. Suppose a basket of goods and services that costs \$100 in the United States costs 800 pesos in Mexico and the current nominal exchange rate is 10 pesos per U.S. dollar. Over the next five years, the cost of that market basket rises to \$120 in the United States and to 1,200 pesos in Mexico, although the nominal exchange rate remains at 10 pesos per U.S. dollar. Calculate the following:
   a. the real exchange rate now and five years from now, if today's price index in both countries is 100. [Reminder: Equation 15-1 provides the price index formula: (Cost of market basket in a given year/Cost of market basket in base year) × 100. For this problem, use the current year as the base year.]
   b. purchasing power parity today and five years from now

Tackle the Test: Multiple-Choice Questions

1. When the U.S. dollar buys more Japanese yen, the U.S. dollar has
   I. become more valuable in terms of the yen.
   II. appreciated.
   III. depreciated.
   a. I only
   b. II only
   c. III only
   d. I and II only
   e. I and III only
2. The nominal exchange rate at which a given basket of goods and services would cost the same in each country describes
   a. the international consumer price index.
   b. appreciation.
   c. depreciation.
   d. purchasing power parity.
   e. the balance of payments on the current account.
3. What happens to the real exchange rate between the euro and the U.S. dollar (expressed as euros per dollar) if the aggregate price levels in Europe and the United States both fall? It
   a. is unaffected.
   b. increases.
   c. decreases.
   d. may increase, decrease, or stay the same.
   e. cannot be calculated.
4. Which of the following would cause the real exchange rate between pesos and U.S. dollars (in terms of pesos per dollar) to decrease?
   a. an increase in net capital flows from Mexico to the United States
   b. an increase in the real interest rate in Mexico relative to the United States
   c. a doubling of prices in both Mexico and the United States
   d. a decrease in oil exports from Mexico to the United States
   e. an increase in the balance of payments on the current account in the United States
5. Which of the following will decrease the supply of U.S. dollars in the foreign exchange market?
   a. U.S. residents increase their travel abroad.
   b. U.S. consumers demand fewer imports.
   c. Foreigners increase their demand for U.S. goods.
   d. Foreigners increase their travel to the United States.
   e. Foreign investors see increased investment opportunities in the United States.

Answers to Module 42 Review Questions

Check Your Understanding

1. a. The increased purchase of Mexican oil would cause U.S. individuals (and firms) to increase their demand for the peso. To purchase pesos, individuals would increase their supply of U.S. dollars to the foreign exchange market, causing a rightward shift in the supply curve of U.S. dollars. This would cause the nominal peso-U.S. dollar exchange rate to fall (the number of pesos per dollar would fall). The peso would appreciate and the U.S. dollar would depreciate as a result.

b. With the appreciation of the peso, it would take more U.S. dollars to obtain the same quantity of Mexican pesos. If we assume that the price level (measured in Mexican pesos) of other Mexican goods and services would not change, other Mexican goods and services would become more expensive for U.S. households and firms. The dollar cost of other Mexican goods and services would rise as the peso appreciated. Thus, Mexican exports of goods and services other than oil would fall.

c. U.S. goods and services would become cheaper in terms of pesos, so Mexican imports of goods and services would rise.

2. a. The real exchange rate equals pesos per U.S. dollar × aggregate price level in the U.S./aggregate price level in Mexico. Today, the aggregate price level in both countries, as measured by the price index, is 100. The real exchange rate today is $10 \times (100/100) = 10$. The aggregate price level in 5 years in the United States will be $(120/100) \times 100 = 120$, and in Mexico it will be $(1{,}200/800) \times 100 = 150$. Thus, the real exchange rate in 5 years, assuming the nominal exchange rate does not change, will be $10 \times (120/150) = 8$.

b. Today, a basket of goods and services that costs \$100 costs 800 pesos, so the purchasing power parity is 8 pesos per U.S. dollar. In 5 years, a basket that costs \$120 will cost 1,200 pesos, so the purchasing power parity will be 10 pesos per U.S. dollar.

Tackle the Test: Multiple-Choice Questions

1. d
2. d
3. d
4. b
5. b

Tackle the Test: Free-Response Question

Rubric for FRQ 2 (6 points)

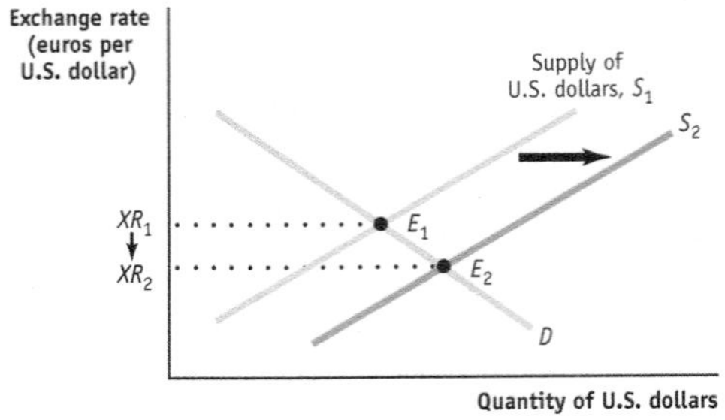

1 point: The vertical axis is labeled "Exchange rate (euros per U.S. dollar)" and the horizontal axis is labeled "Quantity of U.S. dollars."

1 point: The supply curve is labeled and slopes upward, and the demand curve is labeled and slopes downward.

1 point: The initial equilibrium exchange rate is found at the intersection of the initial supply and demand curves and is labeled on the vertical axis.

1 point: The new supply curve for U.S. dollars occurs to the right of the initial supply curve.

1 point: The new equilibrium exchange rate is found where the initial demand curve and new supply curve intersect and is shown on the vertical axis.

1 point: In order to purchase more imports from Europe, U.S. consumers must supply more dollars in exchange for euros. The increase in the supply of dollars shifts the dollar supply curve to the right and decreases the exchange rate from XR_1 to XR_2.

Tackle the Test: Free-Response Questions

1. Draw a correctly labeled graph of the foreign exchange market showing the effect on the equilibrium exchange rate between the U.S. and Japan (the number of yen per U.S. dollar) if capital flows from Japan to the United States decrease due to a change in the preferences of Japanese investors. Has the U.S. dollar appreciated or depreciated?

Rubric for FRQ 1 (7 points)

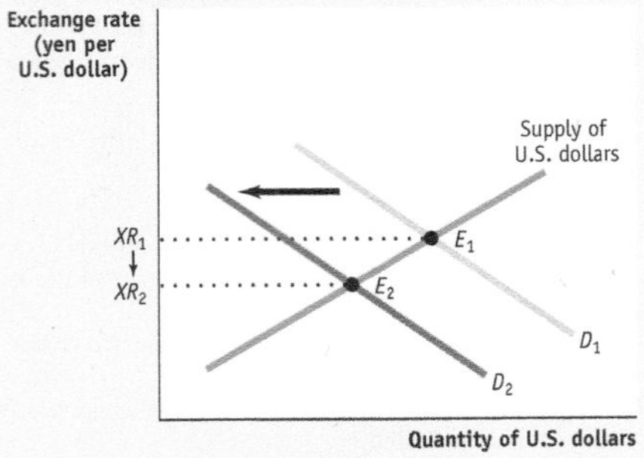

1 point: The vertical axis is labeled "Exchange rate (yen per U.S. dollar)" and the horizontal axis is labeled "Quantity of U.S. dollars."

1 point: The supply of U.S. dollars is labeled and slopes upward.

1 point: The demand for U.S. dollars is labeled and slopes downward.

1 point: The initial equilibrium exchange rate is found at the intersection of the initial supply and demand curves and is labeled on the vertical axis.

1 point: The new demand for U.S. dollars is to the left of the initial demand.

1 point: The new equilibrium exchange rate is found where the initial supply curve and new demand curve intersect and is labeled on the vertical axis.

1 point: The U.S. dollar has depreciated.

2. Use a correctly labeled graph of the foreign exchange market between the United States and Europe to illustrate what would happen to the value of the U.S. dollar if there were an increase in the U.S. demand for imports from Europe. Explain your answer.
(6 points)

Udo Weitz/Bloomberg via Getty Images

MODULE 43

Exchange Rate Policy and Macroeconomic Policy

In this Module, you will learn to:

- Explain the difference between fixed exchange rates and floating exchange rates
- Discuss the considerations that lead countries to choose different exchange rate regimes
- Describe the effects of currency devaluation and revaluation under a fixed exchange rate regime
- Explain how macroeconomic policy affects exchange rates under a floating exchange rate regime

Exchange Rate Policy

The nominal exchange rate, like other prices, is determined by supply and demand. Unlike the price of wheat or oil, however, the exchange rate is the price of a country's money (in terms of another country's money). Money isn't a good or service produced by the private sector; it's an asset whose quantity is determined by government policy. As a result, governments have much more power to influence nominal exchange rates than they have to influence ordinary prices.

The nominal exchange rate is a very important price: the exchange rate determines the price of imports; it determines the price of exports; in economies where exports and imports are large relative to GDP, movements in the exchange rate can have major effects on aggregate output and the aggregate price level. What do governments do with their power to influence this important price?

The answer is, it depends. At different times and in different places, governments have adopted a variety of *exchange rate regimes*. Let's examine these regimes, how they are enforced, and how governments choose a regime. (From now on, we'll adopt the convention that we mean the nominal exchange rate when we refer to the exchange rate.)

Exchange Rate Regimes

An **exchange rate regime** is a rule governing policy toward the exchange rate. There are two main kinds of exchange rate regimes. A country has a **fixed exchange rate** when the government keeps the exchange rate against some other currency at or near a particular target. For example, Hong Kong has an official policy of setting an exchange rate of HK$7.80 per US$1. A country has a **floating exchange rate** when the government lets the exchange rate go wherever the market takes it. This is the policy followed by Britain, Canada, and the United States.

An **exchange rate regime** is a rule governing policy toward the exchange rate.

A country has a **fixed exchange rate** when the government keeps the exchange rate against some other currency at or near a particular target.

A country has a **floating exchange rate** when the government lets the exchange rate go wherever the market takes it.

PD To prepare for teaching this lesson, you may want to consult the **Module 43 Sample Lecture** in the TRM.

OPEN & CLOSE Start Here

TRM Have students read Investopedia's February 2014 article "Why China's Currency Tangos with the USD" at http://www.investopedia.com/articles/forex/09/chinas-peg-to-the-dollar.asp. Suggested discussion questions may be found in **Worksheet 43.1 (Currency Tango)** from the TRM.

TEACH Teach It

Sometimes a nation will deliberately manipulate the exchange rate of its own currency to achieve certain economic goals because the exchange rate has a great deal of influence on net exports. If your nation's currency is inexpensive, foreigners will find your goods to be inexpensive and your net exports will rise, adding to the nation's GDP. When a nation sets the exchange rate of its own currency at a particular target in relation to another currency, it is using a fixed exchange rate system rather than allowing the forces of supply and demand to work in the market.

Module 43 Exchange Rate Policy and Macroeconomic Policy 427

TEACH Connect It

Have students draw a supply and demand graph on their personal whiteboards or on paper while you draw one on the board. Ask them to mark the equilibrium price and quantity. Now is a good time to review price ceilings and floors because having a fixed exchange rate is very much like having a price ceiling or floor. Direct students to draw a price floor and label the horizontal distance that represents the surplus of the item with the price floor. Next, have them draw a price ceiling and label the horizontal distance that represents the shortage of the item with the price ceiling. Compare their graphs to those in Figure 43.1. Fixed exchange rates are simply ceilings and floors in the foreign exchange markets.

FOCUS Graph It

Ask students to draw a foreign exchange market graph for 2 nations on their personal whiteboards or on paper while you do the same on the board. The text uses the hypothetical nation of Genovia as an example. It might be interesting if you modified the example by creating a nation that sounds suspiciously similar to a local town or high school. Draw the equilibrium exchange rate at 1 on the first graph and 3 on the second graph. Tell students that the target exchange rate for one of the nations is $2. Have them identify the $2 level on each graph and determine if a surplus or a shortage exists at that level. *There will be a surplus for one nation and a shortage for the other.* Ask how this target will impact each nation's balance of trade. *The nation with the exchange rate below equilibrium will see greater exports because its goods appear cheaper, while the other will see greater imports because it will buy the cheaper goods.*

Fixed exchange rates and floating exchange rates aren't the only possibilities. At various times, countries have adopted compromise policies that lie somewhere between fixed and floating exchange rates. These include exchange rates that are fixed at any given time but are adjusted frequently, exchange rates that aren't fixed but are "managed" by the government to avoid wide swings, and exchange rates that float within a "target zone" but are prevented from leaving that zone. In this book, however, we'll focus on the two main exchange rate regimes.

The immediate question about a fixed exchange rate is how it is possible for governments to fix the exchange rate when the exchange rate is determined by supply and demand.

How Can an Exchange Rate Be Held Fixed?

To understand how it is possible for a country to fix its exchange rate, let's consider a hypothetical country, Genovia, which for some reason has decided to fix the value of its currency, the geno, at US$1.50.

The obvious problem is that $1.50 may not be the equilibrium exchange rate in the foreign exchange market: the equilibrium rate may be either higher or lower than the target exchange rate. **Figure 43.1** shows the foreign exchange market for genos, with the quantities of genos supplied and demanded on the horizontal axis and the exchange rate of the geno, measured in U.S. dollars per geno, on the vertical axis. Panel (a) shows the case in which the equilibrium value of the geno is *below* the target exchange rate. Panel (b) shows the case in which the equilibrium value of the geno is *above* the target exchange rate.

AP® Exam Tip

Think of a fixed exchange rate as a price ceiling or a price floor. That will help you understand if there is a shortage (ceiling) or surplus (floor) of a nation's currency.

Consider first the case in which the equilibrium value of the geno is below the target exchange rate. As panel (a) shows, at the target exchange rate there is a surplus of genos in the foreign exchange market, which would normally push the value of the geno down. How can the Genovian government support the value of the geno to keep the rate where it wants? There are three possible answers, all of which have been used by governments at some point.

Figure 43.1 Exchange Market Intervention

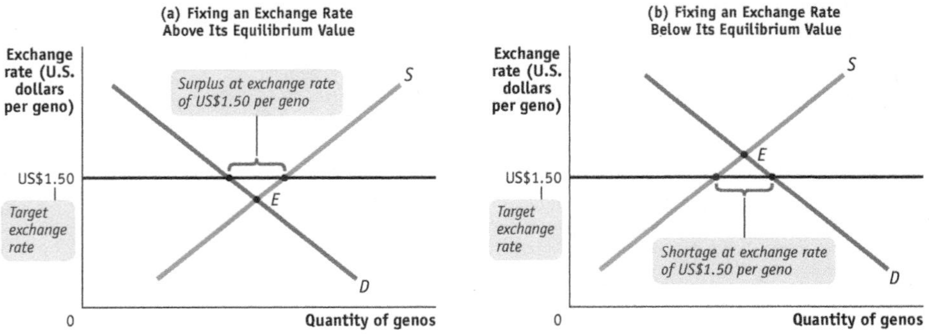

In both panels, the imaginary country of Genovia is trying to keep the value of its currency, the geno, fixed at US$1.50. In panel (a), there is a surplus of genos on the foreign exchange market. To keep the geno from falling, the Genovian government can buy genos and sell U.S. dollars. In panel (b), there is a shortage of genos. To keep the geno from rising, the Genovian government can sell genos and buy U.S. dollars.

428 Section 8 The Open Economy: International Trade and Finance

One way the Genovian government can support the geno is to "soak up" the surplus of genos by buying its own currency in the foreign exchange market. Government purchases or sales of currency in the foreign exchange market are called **exchange market intervention**. To buy genos in the foreign exchange market, of course, the Genovian government must have U.S. dollars to exchange for genos. In fact, most countries maintain **foreign exchange reserves**, stocks of foreign currency (usually U.S. dollars or euros) that they can use to buy their own currency to support its price.

We mentioned earlier that an important part of international capital flows is the result of purchases and sales of foreign assets by governments and central banks. Now we can see why governments sell foreign assets: they are supporting their currency through exchange market intervention. As we'll see in a moment, governments that keep the value of their currency *down* through exchange market intervention must *buy* foreign assets. First, however, let's talk about the other ways governments fix exchange rates.

A second way for the Genovian government to support the geno is to try to shift the supply and demand curves for the geno in the foreign exchange market. Governments usually do this by changing monetary policy. For example, to support the geno, the Genovian central bank can raise the Genovian interest rate. This will increase capital flows into Genovia, increasing the demand for genos, at the same time that it reduces capital flows out of Genovia, reducing the supply of genos. So, other things equal, an increase in a country's interest rate will increase the value of its currency.

Third, the Genovian government can support the geno by reducing the supply of genos to the foreign exchange market. It can do this by requiring domestic residents who want to buy foreign currency to get a license and giving these licenses only to people engaging in approved transactions (such as the purchase of imported goods the Genovian government thinks are essential). Licensing systems that limit the right of individuals to buy foreign currency are called **foreign exchange controls**. Other things equal, foreign exchange controls increase the value of a country's currency.

So far we've been discussing a situation in which the government is trying to prevent a depreciation of the geno. Suppose, instead, that the situation is as shown in panel (b) of Figure 43.1, where the equilibrium value of the geno is *above* the target exchange rate and there is a shortage of genos. To maintain the target exchange rate, the Genovian government can apply the same three basic options in the reverse direction. It can intervene in the foreign exchange market, in this case *selling* genos and acquiring U.S. dollars, which it can add to its foreign exchange reserves. It can *reduce* interest rates to increase the supply of genos and reduce the demand. Or it can impose foreign exchange controls that limit the ability of foreigners to buy genos. All of these actions, other things equal, will reduce the value of the geno.

As we said, all three techniques have been used to manage fixed exchange rates. But we haven't said whether fixing the exchange rate is a good idea. In fact, the choice of exchange rate regime poses a dilemma for policy makers because fixed and floating exchange rates each have both advantages and disadvantages.

Government purchases or sales of currency in the foreign exchange market constitute **exchange market intervention**.

Foreign exchange reserves are stocks of foreign currency that governments maintain to buy their own currency on the foreign exchange market.

Foreign exchange controls are licensing systems that limit the right of individuals to buy foreign currency.

The Exchange Rate Regime Dilemma

Few questions in macroeconomics produce as many arguments as that of whether a country should adopt a fixed or a floating exchange rate. The reason there are so many arguments is that both sides have a case.

To understand the case for a fixed exchange rate, consider for a moment how easy it is to conduct business across state lines in the United States. There are a number of things that make interstate commerce trouble-free, but one of them is the absence of any uncertainty about the value of money: a dollar is a dollar, in both New York City and Los Angeles.

By contrast, a dollar isn't a dollar in transactions between New York City and Toronto. The exchange rate between the Canadian dollar and the U.S. dollar fluctuates, sometimes widely. If a U.S. firm promises to pay a Canadian firm a given number of U.S. dollars a year from now, the value of that promise in Canadian currency can vary by 10%

Robert Nickelsberg/Getty Images

Once you cross the border into Canada, a dollar is no longer worth a dollar.

FOCUS Flip It

Students can watch the Jacob Clifford video "Macro 5.4—Floating vs. Fixed Exchange Rates" (see econextras video list with hyperlinks on the bcs and TRFD) to gain a greater understanding of the two types of foreign exchange regimes.

TEACH Teach It

One of the factors that affects the demand for loanable funds is speculation about foreign currency. Point out that foreign exchange controls allow a nation to control investment in funds based on speculation by limiting how much currency a speculator can buy.

TEACH Teach It

A fixed exchange rate provides stability in foreign transactions in much the same way we experience transactions across state lines. If you take your dollars from Indiana to Kentucky, you know that the value of your dollars is unchanged. But if you take your dollars from Indiana to Europe, the value of those dollars can change daily. A fixed exchange rate avoids this uncertainty. The fixed exchange rate also commits the central bank to monetary policies that would not upset the exchange rate. For example, if the central bank adhered to the exchange rate regime, it could not dramatically increase the money supply. A sudden increase in the money supply would cause inflation and reduce the value of the currency.

Module 43 Exchange Rate Policy and Macroeconomic Policy 429

TEACH Teach It

A fixed exchange rate also has disadvantages. To stabilize an exchange rate through intervention, a country must keep large quantities of foreign currency on hand, and that currency is usually a low-return investment. Even large reserves can be quickly exhausted when there are large capital flows out of a country. If a country chooses to stabilize an exchange rate by adjusting monetary policy rather than through intervention, it must divert monetary policy from other goals, notably stabilizing the economy and managing the inflation rate. Finally, foreign exchange controls, such as import quotas and tariffs, distort incentives for importing and exporting goods and services. They can also create substantial costs in terms of red tape and corruption.

FOCUS Test It

TRM Have students complete **Worksheet 43.2 (Exchange Rate Policy)** from the TRM in class or as homework. This practice free-response question will allow them to practice graphing foreign exchange rates with government intervention.

or more. This uncertainty has the effect of deterring trade between the two countries. So one benefit of a fixed exchange rate is certainty about the future value of a currency.

In some cases, there is an additional benefit to adopting a fixed exchange rate: by committing itself to a fixed rate, a country is also committing itself not to engage in inflationary policies because such policies would destabilize the exchange rate. For example, in 1991, Argentina, which has a long history of irresponsible policies leading to severe inflation, adopted a fixed exchange rate of US$1 per Argentine peso in an attempt to commit itself to non-inflationary policies in the future. (Argentina's fixed exchange rate regime collapsed disastrously in late 2001. But that's another story.)

The point is that there is some economic value in having a stable exchange rate. Indeed, the presumed benefits of stable exchange rates motivated the international system of fixed exchange rates created after World War II. It was also a major reason for the creation of the euro.

However, there are also costs to fixing the exchange rate. To stabilize an exchange rate through intervention, a country must keep large quantities of foreign currency on hand, and that currency is usually a low-return investment. Furthermore, even large reserves can be quickly exhausted when there are large capital flows out of a country. If a country chooses to stabilize an exchange rate by adjusting monetary policy rather than through intervention, it must divert monetary policy from other goals, notably stabilizing the economy and managing the inflation rate. Finally, foreign exchange controls, like import quotas and tariffs, distort incentives for importing and exporting goods and services. They can also create substantial costs in terms of red tape and corruption.

So there's a dilemma. Should a country let its currency float, which leaves monetary policy available for macroeconomic stabilization but creates uncertainty for everyone affected by trade? Or should it fix the exchange rate, which eliminates the uncertainty but means giving up monetary policy, adopting exchange controls, or both? Different countries reach different conclusions at different times. Most European countries, except for Britain, have long believed that exchange rates among major European economies, which do most of their international trade with each other, should be fixed. But

FYI China Pegs the Yuan

In the early years of the twenty-first century, China provided a striking example of the lengths to which countries sometimes go to maintain a fixed exchange rate. Here's the background: China's spectacular success as an exporter led to a rising surplus on the current account. At the same time, non-Chinese private investors became increasingly eager to shift funds into China, to take advantage of its growing domestic economy. These capital flows were somewhat limited by foreign exchange controls—but kept coming in anyway. As a result of the current account surplus and private capital inflows, China found itself in the position described by panel (b) of Figure 43.1: at the target exchange rate, the demand for yuan exceeded the supply. Yet the Chinese government was determined to keep the exchange rate fixed (although it began allowing gradual appreciation in 2005).

To keep the rate fixed, China had to engage in large-scale exchange market intervention, selling yuan, buying up other countries' currencies (mainly U.S. dollars) on the foreign exchange market, and adding them to its reserves. During 2013, China added $510 billion to its foreign exchange reserves, bringing the year-end total to $3.8 trillion.

To get a sense of how big these totals are, you have to know that in 2013 China's nominal GDP, converted into U.S. dollars at the prevailing exchange rate, was $9.4 trillion. So in 2013, China bought U.S. dollars and other currencies equal to about 5.4% of its GDP. That's as if the U.S. government had bought $900 billion worth of yen and euros in just a single year—and was continuing to buy yen and euros even though it was already sitting on a $6.8 trillion pile of foreign currencies.

China has a history of intervention in the foreign exchange market that kept its currency, and therefore its exports, relatively cheap for foreign consumers to buy.

430 Section 8 The Open Economy: International Trade and Finance

Canada seems happy with a floating exchange rate with the United States, even though the United States accounts for most of Canada's trade.

Next we'll consider macroeconomic policy under each type of exchange rate regime.

Exchange Rates and Macroeconomic Policy

When the euro was created in 1999, there were celebrations across the nations of Europe—with a few notable exceptions. You see, some countries chose not to adopt the new currency. The most important of these was Britain, but other European countries, such as Switzerland and Sweden, also decided that the euro was not for them.

Why did Britain say no? Part of the answer was national pride: for example, if Britain gave up the pound, it would also have to give up currency that bears the portrait of the queen. But there were also serious economic concerns about giving up the pound in favor of the euro. British economists who favored adoption of the euro argued that if Britain used the same currency as its neighbors, the country's international trade would expand and its economy would become more productive. But other economists pointed out that adopting the euro would take away Britain's ability to have an independent monetary policy and might lead to macroeconomic problems.

As this discussion suggests, the fact that modern economies are open to international trade and capital flows adds a new level of complication to our analysis of macroeconomic policy. Let's look at three policy issues raised by open-economy macroeconomics.

Devaluation and Revaluation of Fixed Exchange Rates

Historically, fixed exchange rates haven't been permanent commitments. Sometimes countries with a fixed exchange rate switch to a floating rate. In other cases, they retain a fixed exchange rate regime but change the target exchange rate. Such adjustments in the target were common during the Bretton Woods era, discussed in the next FYI box. For example, in 1967, Britain changed the exchange rate of the pound against the U.S. dollar from US$2.80 per £1 to US$2.40 per £1. A modern example is Argentina, which maintained a fixed exchange rate against the dollar from 1991 to 2001, but switched to a floating exchange rate at the end of 2001.

A reduction in the value of a currency that is set under a fixed exchange rate regime is called a **devaluation**. As we've already learned, a *depreciation* is a downward move in a currency. A devaluation is a depreciation that is due to a revision in a fixed exchange rate target. An increase in the value of a currency that is set under a fixed exchange rate regime is called a **revaluation**.

A devaluation, like any depreciation, makes domestic goods cheaper in terms of foreign currency, which leads to higher exports. At the same time, it makes foreign goods more expensive in terms of domestic currency, which reduces imports. The effect is to increase the balance of payments on the current account. Similarly, a revaluation makes domestic goods more expensive in terms of foreign currency, which reduces exports, and makes foreign goods cheaper in domestic currency, which increases imports. So a revaluation reduces the balance of payments on the current account.

Devaluations and revaluations serve two purposes under a fixed exchange rate regime. First, they can be used to eliminate shortages or surpluses in the foreign exchange market. For example, in 2010, some economists urged China to revalue the yuan so that it would not have to buy up so many U.S. dollars on the foreign exchange market.

Second, devaluation and revaluation can be used as tools of macroeconomic policy. A devaluation, by increasing exports and reducing imports, increases aggregate demand. So a devaluation can be used to reduce or eliminate a recessionary gap. A revaluation has the opposite effect, reducing aggregate demand. So a revaluation can be used to reduce or eliminate an inflationary gap.

A **devaluation** is a reduction in the value of a currency that is set under a fixed exchange rate regime.

A **revaluation** is an increase in the value of a currency that is set under a fixed exchange rate regime.

AP® Exam Tip

A devaluation of a currency makes exports increase because they appear cheaper to foreign buyers, and a revaluation of a currency makes exports decrease because they appear more expensive to foreign buyers.

FOCUS In the News

TRM Have students read the European Commission's article "The Euro" at http://ec.europa.eu/economy_finance/euro/index_en.htm. Suggested discussion questions for this article may be found in **Worksheet 43.3 (The Euro)** from the TRM.

TEACH AP® Exam Tip

Increasingly, the AP® Macro exams have stressed connections between, for example, monetary policy and the value of a nation's currency. This is a good opportunity for you to review past models and emphasize the connections to foreign exchange with which students often struggle. You can touch on how changes in net exports affect the *AD–AS* model and how changes in interest rates affect the flows of financial capital and the exchange rate.

TEACH Teach It

Nations devalue and revalue their money to reduce shortages and surpluses in the foreign exchange market and to influence the balance of trade between nations through macroeconomic policy. Ask your students to explain when a depreciation is not a devaluation. *A devaluation is a depreciation that results from a decision by the government to lower the target exchange rate. A depreciation is not a devaluation when the depreciation is caused by market forces, rather than by policy actions designed to change the exchange rate.*

FOCUS In the News

Recall an article students read in Section 7: "Why Panic-Prone Emerging Markets Are Breaking Down in 2014" (http://www.forbes.com/sites/steveschaefer/2014/02/03/why-panic-prone-emerging-markets-are-breaking-down-in-2014/). Ask students how the Fed's decrease in quantitative easing has impacted economic growth in emerging markets. *Because there is less "cheap" money, it is more expensive to operate in emerging markets, so their growth is slowing down.*

FYI From Bretton Woods to the Euro

In 1944, while World War II was still raging, representatives of the Allied nations met in Bretton Woods, New Hampshire, to establish a postwar international monetary system of fixed exchange rates among major currencies. The system was highly successful at first, but it broke down in 1971. After a confusing interval during which policy makers tried unsuccessfully to establish a new fixed exchange rate system, by 1973 most economically advanced countries had moved to floating exchange rates.

In Europe, however, many policy makers were unhappy with floating exchange rates, which they believed created too much uncertainty for business. From the late 1970s onward they tried several times to create a system of more or less fixed exchange rates in Europe, culminating in an arrangement known as the Exchange Rate Mechanism. (The Exchange Rate Mechanism, strictly speaking, was a "target zone" system—exchange rates were free to move within a narrow band, but not outside it.) And in 1991 they agreed to move to the ultimate in fixed exchange rates: a common European currency, the euro. To the surprise of many analysts, they pulled it off: today most of Europe has abandoned national currencies for euros.

The accompanying figure illustrates the history of European exchange rate arrangements. It shows the exchange rate between the French franc and the German mark, measured as francs per mark, since 1971.

The exchange rate fluctuated widely at first. The "plateaus" you can see in the data—eras when the exchange rate fluctuated only modestly—are periods when attempts to restore fixed exchange rates were in process. The Exchange Rate Mechanism, after a couple of false starts, became effective in 1987, stabilizing the exchange rate at about 3.4 francs per mark. (The wobbles in the early 1990s reflect two currency crises—episodes in which widespread expectations of imminent devaluations led to large but temporary capital flows.)

In 1999 the exchange rate was "locked"—no further fluctuations were allowed as the countries prepared to switch from francs and marks to euros. At the end of 2001, the franc and the mark ceased to exist.

The transition to the euro has not been without costs. With most of Europe sharing the same currency, it must also share the same monetary policy. Yet economic conditions in the different countries aren't always the same.

For example, there were serious stresses within the eurozone between 2008 and 2012, when the global financial crisis hit some countries, such as Greece, Portugal, Spain, and Ireland, much more severely than it hit others, notably Germany.

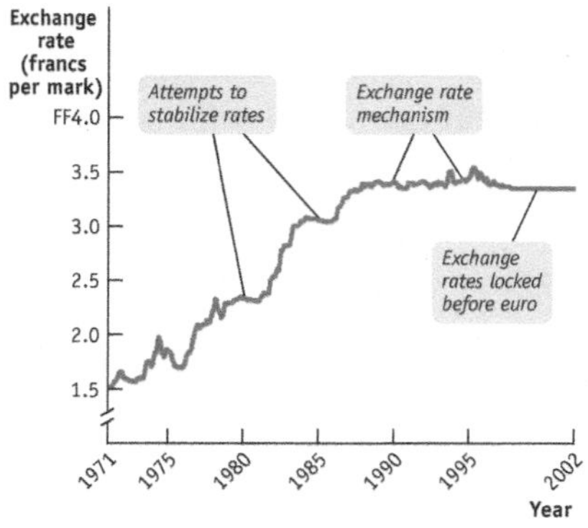

Source: Federal Reserve Bank of St. Louis.

Monetary Policy Under a Floating Exchange Rate Regime

Under a floating exchange rate regime, a country's central bank retains its ability to pursue independent monetary policy: it can increase aggregate demand by cutting the interest rate or decrease aggregate demand by raising the interest rate. But the exchange rate adds another dimension to the effects of monetary policy. To see why, let's return to the hypothetical country of Genovia and ask what happens if the central bank cuts the interest rate.

Just as in a closed economy, a lower interest rate leads to higher investment spending and higher consumer spending. But the decline in the interest rate also affects the foreign exchange market. Foreigners have less incentive to move funds into Genovia because they will receive a lower rate of return on their loans. As a result, they have less need to exchange U.S. dollars for genos, so the demand for genos falls. At the same time, Genovians have *more* incentive to move funds abroad because the rate of return

432 Section 8 The Open Economy: International Trade and Finance

on loans at home has fallen, making investments outside the country more attractive. Thus, they need to exchange more genos for U.S. dollars and the supply of genos rises.

Figure 43.2 shows the effect of an interest rate reduction on the foreign exchange market. The demand curve for genos shifts leftward, from D_1 to D_2, and the supply curve shifts rightward, from S_1 to S_2. The equilibrium exchange rate, as measured in U.S. dollars per geno, falls from XR_1 to XR_2. That is, a reduction in the Genovian interest rate causes the geno to *depreciate.*

The depreciation of the geno, in turn, affects aggregate demand. We've already seen that a devaluation—a depreciation that is the result of a change in a fixed exchange rate—increases exports and reduces imports, thereby increasing aggregate demand. A depreciation that results from an interest rate cut has the same effect: it increases exports and reduces imports, increasing aggregate demand.

In other words, monetary policy under floating rates has effects beyond those we've described in looking at closed economies. In a closed economy, a reduction in the interest rate leads to a rise in aggregate demand because it leads to more investment spending and consumer spending. In an open economy with a floating exchange rate, the interest rate reduction leads to increased investment spending and consumer spending, but it also increases aggregate demand in another way: it leads to a currency depreciation, which increases exports and reduces imports, further increasing aggregate demand.

International Business Cycles

Up to this point, we have discussed macroeconomics, even in an open economy, as if all demand changes or *shocks* originated from the domestic economy. In reality, however, economies sometimes face shocks coming from abroad. For example, recessions in the United States have historically led to recessions in Mexico.

Figure 43.2 Monetary Policy and the Exchange Rate

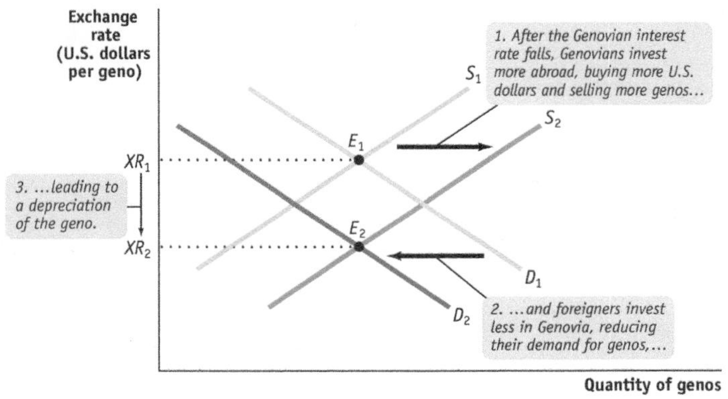

Here we show what happens in the foreign exchange market if Genovia cuts its interest rate. Residents of Genovia have a reduced incentive to keep their funds at home, so they invest more abroad. As a result, the supply of genos shifts rightward, from S_1 to S_2. Meanwhile, foreigners have less incentive to put funds into Genovia, so the demand for genos shifts leftward, from D_1 to D_2. The geno depreciates: the equilibrium exchange rate falls from XR_1 to XR_2.

TEACH Connect It

The central bank can influence exchange rates by conducting open market operations to influence interest rates. Remember, high interest rates attract foreign financial investors who seek higher rates of return. Ask students the following series of questions to make the connection between monetary policy and foreign exchange rates.

- If the Fed buys bonds, what happens to interest rates? *Interest rates decrease.*
- When interest rates decrease, what happens to domestic investment spending? *Domestic investment spending increases.*
- When domestic investment spending increases, what happens to aggregate demand? *Aggregate demand increases.*
- When interest rates decrease, what happens to demand for U.S. financial assets? *It decreases as investors look for higher rates of return on their financial investment dollars in other places.*
- What influence does an outflow of capital have on the international value of the U.S. dollar? *It causes the U.S. dollar to depreciate.*
- What happens to U.S. net exports as a result of the changing value of the dollar? *Exports will increase as our goods and services are less expensive to foreigners, but imports will decrease as they are more expensive to foreigners. Net exports increase as a result.*
- What happens to *AD*? *A larger increase*

Module 43 Exchange Rate Policy and Macroeconomic Policy 433

TEACH Teach It

Floating exchange rates provide some insulation from recessions that begin in other nations. To help students understand why, walk them through this example:

- Imagine that a recession hits the Canadian economy.
- Canadians lower their demand for goods made in the United States, decreasing *AD*.
- This leads to a decrease in the demand for the U.S. dollar, causing it to depreciate.
- A depreciating U.S. dollar means that goods made in the United States now appear cheaper to Canadian consumers.
- Exports to Canada increase, shifting *AD* back to the right.

This partial insulation from recessions in other nations does not exist when the nations share the same currency, or when the exchange rate is fixed.

FOCUS Active Learning

Have students watch Jason Welker's video "The Determinants of Exchange Rates and Managed Exchange Rate Systems" (see econextras video list with hyperlinks on the bcs and TRFD) as homework. Discussion questions to accompany this video may be found at http://welkerswikinomics.com/blog/wp-content/uploads/2011/10/Exchange-Rate-Practice.pdf.

FOCUS Active Learning

TRM Ask students to complete **Worksheet 43.4 (Exchange Rates and Macroeconomic Policy)** from the TRM. This worksheet will help them make the necessary connections between exchange rates and macro policy.

FOCUS Test It

Assign Question 1 from the released 2012 AP® Macroeconomics exam at http://apcentral.collegeboard.com/apc/public/repository/ap12_frq_macroeconomics.pdf. This question will provide an excellent review of the *PPC*, monetary policy, the money market, and foreign exchange. It is recommended that students take 25 minutes to answer this question to match the time suggested for the AP® exam. The rubric for the question may be viewed at http://apcentral.collegeboard.com/apc/public/repository/ap12_macroeconomics_scoring_guidelines.pdf.

Sipa via AP Images

For better or worse, trading partners tend to import each other's business cycles in addition to each other's goods.

The key point is that changes in aggregate demand affect the demand for goods and services produced abroad as well as at home: other things equal, a recession leads to a fall in imports and an expansion leads to a rise in imports. And one country's imports are another country's exports. This link between aggregate demand in different national economies is one reason business cycles in different countries sometimes—but not always—seem to be synchronized. The prime example is the Great Depression, which affected countries around the world.

However, the extent of this link depends on the exchange rate regime. To see why, think about what happens if a recession abroad reduces the demand for Genovia's exports. A reduction in foreign demand for Genovian goods and services is also a reduction in demand for genos on the foreign exchange market. If Genovia has a fixed exchange rate, it responds to this decline with exchange market intervention. But if Genovia has a floating exchange rate, the geno depreciates. Because Genovian goods and services become cheaper to foreigners when the demand for exports falls, the quantity of goods and services exported doesn't fall by as much as it would under a fixed rate. At the same time, the fall in the geno makes imports more expensive to Genovians, leading to a fall in imports. Both effects limit the decline in Genovia's aggregate demand compared to what it would have been under a fixed exchange rate regime.

One of the virtues of floating exchange rates, according to their advocates, is that they help insulate countries from recessions originating abroad. This theory looked pretty good in the early 2000s: Britain, with a floating exchange rate, managed to stay

FYI The Joy of a Devalued Pound

The Exchange Rate Mechanism is the system of European fixed exchange rates that paved the way for the creation of the euro in 1999. Britain joined that system in 1990 but dropped out in 1992. The story of Britain's exit from the Exchange Rate Mechanism is a classic example of open-economy macroeconomic policy.

Britain originally fixed its exchange rate for both of the reasons we described earlier: British leaders believed that a fixed exchange rate would help promote international trade, and they also hoped that it would help fight inflation. But by 1992 Britain was suffering from high unemployment: the unemployment rate in September 1992 was over 10%. And as long as the country had a fixed exchange rate, there wasn't much the government could do. In particular, the government wasn't able to cut interest rates because it was using high interest rates to help support the value of the pound.

In the summer of 1992, investors began speculating against the pound—selling pounds in the expectation that the currency would drop in value. As its foreign reserves dwindled, this speculation forced the British government's hand. On September 16, 1992, Britain abandoned its fixed exchange rate. The pound promptly dropped 20% against the German mark, the most important European currency at the time.

At first, the devaluation of the pound greatly damaged the prestige of the British government. But the Chancellor of the Exchequer—the equivalent of the U.S. Treasury Secretary—claimed to be happy about it. "My wife has never before heard me singing in the bath," he told reporters. There were several reasons for his joy. One was that the British government would no longer have to engage in large-scale exchange market intervention to support the pound's value. Another was that devaluation increases aggregate demand, so the pound's fall would help reduce British unemployment. Finally, because Britain no longer had a fixed exchange rate, it was free to pursue an expansionary monetary policy to fight its slump.

Photodisc

Indeed, events made it clear that the chancellor's joy was well founded. British unemployment fell over the next two years, even as the unemployment rate rose in France and Germany. One person who did not share in the improving employment picture, however, was the chancellor himself. Soon after his remark about singing in the bath, he was fired.

OPEN & CLOSE Exit Slip

TRM *Please see **Exit Slip: Module 43** in the TRM for formative multiple-choice questions to ask your students before finishing your lesson. These questions will help you quickly assess whether your students have mastered the module's concepts before moving on.*

Answers to the Exit Slip Questions

1. C
2. D
3. B

out of a recession that affected the rest of Europe, and Canada, which also has a floating rate, suffered a less severe recession than the United States.

In 2008, however, a financial crisis that began in the United States produced a recession in virtually every country. In this case, it appears that the international linkages between financial markets were much stronger than any insulation from overseas disturbances provided by floating exchange rates.

MODULE 43 Review

Check Your Understanding

1. Draw a diagram, similar to Figure 43.1, representing the foreign exchange situation of China when it kept the exchange rate fixed at a target rate of $0.121 per yuan and the market equilibrium rate was higher than the target rate. Then show with a diagram how each of the following policy changes might eliminate the disequilibrium in the market.
   a. allowing the exchange rate to float more freely
   b. placing restrictions on foreigners who want to invest in China
   c. removing restrictions on Chinese who want to invest abroad
   d. imposing taxes on Chinese exports, such as clothing
2. In the late 1980s, Canadian economists argued that the high interest rate policies of the Bank of Canada weren't just causing high unemployment—they were also making it hard for Canadian manufacturers to compete with U.S. manufacturers. Explain this complaint, using our analysis of how monetary policy works under floating exchange rates.

Tackle the Test: Multiple-Choice Questions

1. Which of the following methods can be used to fix a country's exchange rate at a predetermined level?
   I. using foreign exchange reserves to buy its own currency
   II. using monetary policy to change interest rates
   III. implementing foreign exchange controls
   a. I only
   b. II only
   c. III only
   d. I and II only
   e. I, II, and III
2. The United States has which of the following exchange rate regimes?
   a. fixed
   b. floating
   c. fixed, but adjusted frequently
   d. fixed, but managed
   e. floating within a target zone
3. Devaluation of a currency occurs when which of the following happens?
   I. The supply of a currency with a floating exchange rate increases.
   II. The demand for a currency with a floating exchange rate decreases.
   III. The government decreases the fixed exchange rate.
   a. I only
   b. II only
   c. III only
   d. I and II only
   e. I, II, and III
4. Devaluation of a currency is used to achieve which of the following?
   a. an elimination of a surplus in the foreign exchange market
   b. an elimination of a shortage in the foreign exchange market
   c. a reduction in aggregate demand
   d. a lower inflation rate
   e. a floating exchange rate
5. Monetary policy that reduces the interest rate will do which of the following?
   a. appreciate the domestic currency
   b. decrease exports
   c. increase imports
   d. depreciate the domestic currency
   e. prevent inflation

Answers to Module 43 Review Questions

Check Your Understanding

1. The accompanying diagram shows the supply of and demand for the yuan, with the U.S. dollar price of the yuan on the vertical axis. In 2005, prior to the revaluation, the exchange rate was pegged at 8.28 yuan per U.S. dollar or, equivalently, 0.121 U.S. dollars per yuan ($0.121). At the target exchange rate of $0.121, the quantity of yuan demanded exceeded the quantity of yuan supplied, creating the shortage depicted in the diagram. Without any intervention by the Chinese government, the U.S. dollar price of the yuan would be bid up, causing an appreciation of the yuan. The Chinese government, however, intervened to prevent this appreciation.

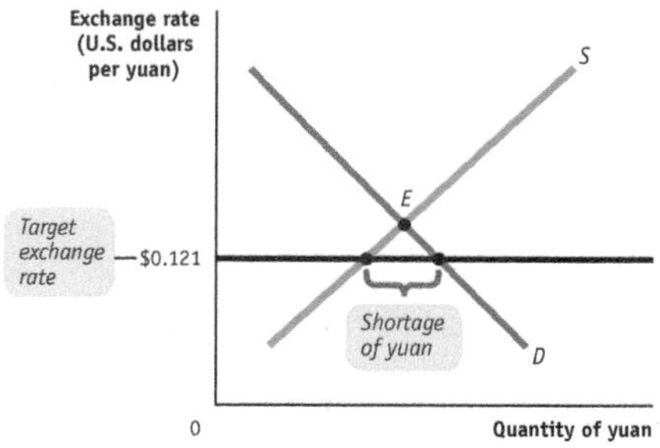

a. If the exchange rate were allowed to float more freely, the U.S. dollar price of the exchange rate would move toward the equilibrium exchange rate (labeled *XR** in the diagram below). This would occur as a result of the shortage, when buyers of the yuan would bid up its U.S. dollar price. As the exchange rate increased, the quantity of yuan demanded would fall and the quantity of yuan supplied would increase. If the exchange rate were allowed to increase to *XR**, the disequilibrium would be entirely eliminated.

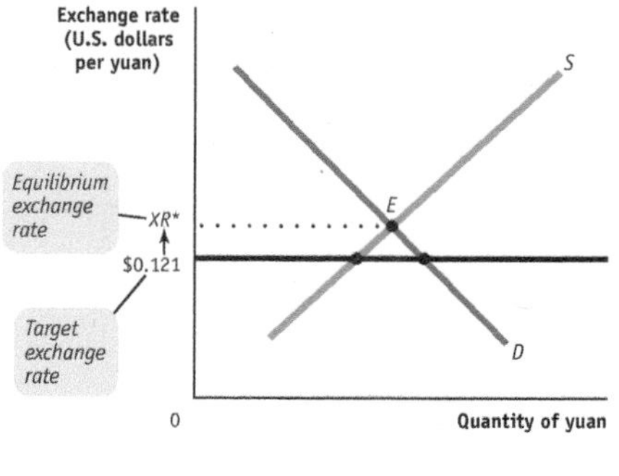

b. Placing restrictions on foreigners who want to invest in China would reduce the demand for the yuan, causing the demand curve to shift in the accompanying diagram from D_1 to something like D_2. This would cause a reduction in the shortage of the yuan. If demand fell to D_3, the disequilibrium would be completely eliminated.

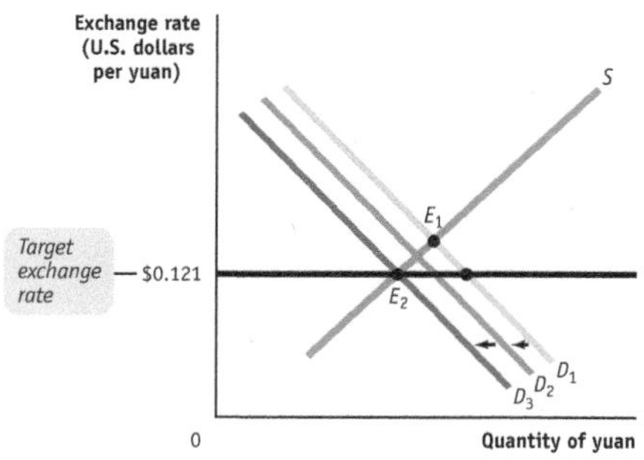

Module 43 Exchange Rate Policy and Macroeconomic Policy 435

c. Removing restrictions on Chinese who wish to invest abroad would cause an increase in the supply of the yuan and a rightward shift of the supply curve. This increase in supply would reduce the size of the shortage. If, for example, supply increased from S_1 to S_2, the disequilibrium would be eliminated completely, as shown in the accompanying diagram.

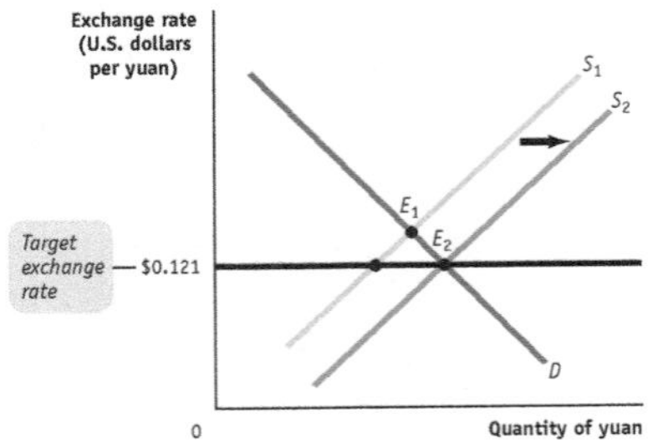

d. Imposing a tax on exports (Chinese goods sold to foreigners) would raise the price of these goods and decrease the amount of Chinese goods purchased. This would also decrease the demand for yuan with which to purchase those goods. The graphical analysis here is the same as that found in the figure accompanying part b.

2. The high Canadian interest rates caused an increase in capital inflows to Canada. To obtain assets that yielded a relatively high interest rate in Canada, investors first had to obtain Canadian dollars. The increase in the demand for the Canadian dollar caused the Canadian dollar to appreciate. This appreciation of the Canadian currency raised the price of Canadian goods to foreigners (measured in terms of the foreign currency). This made it more difficult for Canadian firms to compete in other markets.

Tackle the Test: Multiple-Choice Questions

1. e
2. b
3. c
4. a
5. d

Tackle the Test: Free-Response Questions

Rubric for FRQ 2 (10 points)

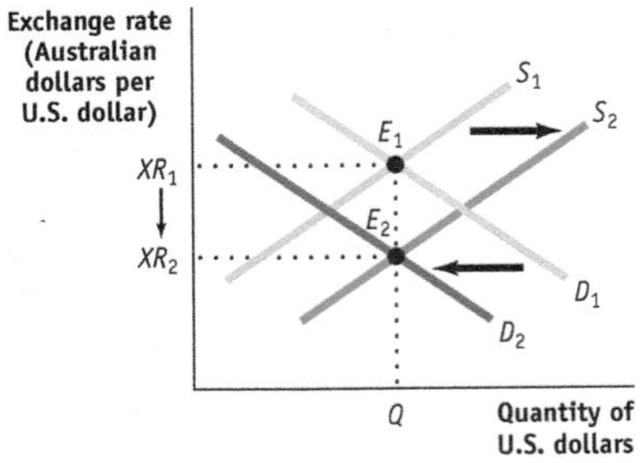

1 point: The vertical axis is labeled "Exchange rate (Australian dollars per U.S. dollar)" and the horizontal axis is labeled "Quantity of U.S. dollars."

1 point: Demand is downward-sloping and labeled; supply is upward-sloping and labeled.

1 point: The equilibrium exchange rate and equilibrium quantity of dollars are labeled on the axes at the point where the supply and demand curves intersect.

1 point: The U.S. interest rate falls.

1 point: There are an increase in the capital flow into Australia and an increase in the capital flow out of the United States.

1 point: The lower interest rate in the United States reduces the incentive to invest in the United States and increases the incentive to invest in Australia.

1 point: The supply of U.S. dollars increases.

1 point: The demand for U.S. dollars decreases.

1 point: The exchange rate falls (the U.S. dollar depreciates).

1 point: The lower exchange rate leads to more exports from the United States to Australia (they are cheaper now) and fewer imports into the United States from Australia (they are more expensive now). When exports increase and imports decrease, U.S. aggregate demand increases.

Tackle the Test: Free-Response Questions

1. Suppose the United States and India were the only two countries in the world.
   a. Draw a correctly labeled graph of the foreign exchange market for U.S. dollars showing the equilibrium in the market.
   b. On your graph, indicate a fixed exchange rate set above the equilibrium exchange rate. Does the fixed exchange rate lead to a surplus or shortage of U.S. dollars? Explain and show the amount of the surplus/shortage on your graph.
   c. To bring the foreign exchange market back to an equilibrium at the fixed exchange rate, would the U.S. government need to buy or sell dollars? On your graph, illustrate how the government's buying or selling of dollars would bring the equilibrium exchange rate back to the desired fixed rate.

Rubric for FRQ 1 (9 points)

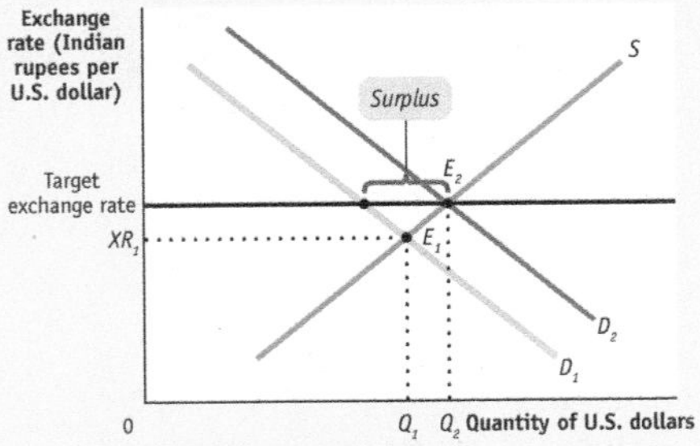

1 point: The vertical axis is labeled "Exchange rate (Indian rupees per U.S. dollar)" and the horizontal axis is labeled "Quantity of U.S. dollars."

1 point: Demand is downward-sloping and labeled, supply is upward-sloping and labeled.

1 point: The equilibrium exchange rate and the equilibrium quantity of dollars are labeled on the axes at the point where the supply and demand curves intersect.

1 point: The fixed exchange rate level is depicted above the equilibrium exchange rate.

1 point: Surplus

1 point: The quantity supplied exceeds the quantity demanded at the higher fixed exchange rate.

1 point: The surplus is labeled as the horizontal distance between the supply and demand curves at the fixed exchange rate.

1 point: Buy

1 point: The new demand curve is shown to the right of the old demand curve, crossing the supply curve at the fixed exchange rate.

2. Suppose the United States and Australia were the only two countries in the world, and that both countries pursued a floating exchange rate regime. Note that the currency in Australia is the Australian dollar.
   a. Draw a correctly labeled graph showing equilibrium in the foreign exchange market for U.S. dollars.
   b. If the Federal Reserve pursues expansionary monetary policy, what will happen to the U.S. interest rate and international capital flows? Explain.
   c. On your graph of the foreign exchange market, illustrate the effect of the Fed's policy on the supply of U.S. dollars, the demand for U.S. dollars, and the equilibrium exchange rate.
   d. How does the Fed's monetary policy affect U.S. aggregate demand? Explain.

   (10 points)

436 Section 8 The Open Economy: International Trade and Finance

Shutterstock

MODULE 44 Barriers to Trade

In this Module, you will learn to:

- Explain the pros and cons of protectionism
- Illustrate the effects of a tariff and an import quota

Trade Restrictions

It's natural for the citizens of a country to say, "We can make food, clothing, and almost everything we need. Why should we buy these goods from other countries and send our money overseas?" Module 4 explained the answer to this question: because specialization and trade make larger quantities of goods and services available to consumers. Yet the gains from trade are often overlooked, and many countries have experimented with a closed economy. Examples from the last century include Germany from 1933–1945, Spain from 1939–1959, Cambodia from 1975–1979, and Afghanistan from 1996–2001. The outcomes of these experiments were disappointing. By trying to make too many different products, these countries failed to specialize in what they were best at making; as a result, they ended up with less of most goods than trade would have provided.

Every country now has an open economy, although some economies are more open than others. **Figure 44.1** on the next page shows expenditures on imports as a percentage of GDP for select countries, which ranged from 14% in Brazil to 178% in Singapore. Several factors affect a country's approach to trade. Beyond the natural tendency for each country to want to make everything, special circumstances can limit the options for trade. For example, high transportation costs hinder trade for countries with primitive transportation systems as well as for countries that specialize in heavy, low-priced commodities such as bricks, drinking water, watermelons, or sand. Countries are wary of specialization that would make them overly reliant on other countries, because relationships with those countries could sour. And, as a matter of national pride, countries may prefer to make certain products on their own despite comparative disadvantages, such as food, art, weapons, and products that showcase technical know-how.

International trade can also have its casualties. As production shifts toward a country's comparative advantage, many workers in declining industries will lose their jobs, and will remain structurally unemployed until or unless they can obtain the skills required in other industries. For example, as the United States imported more clothing

PD To prepare for teaching this lesson, you may want to consult the **Module 44 Sample Lecture** in the TRM.

OPEN & CLOSE Start Here

Before the lesson, make sure you have a large world map open for students to see. Ask students to take small Post-it notes, then write their initials and the name of something they are wearing or have in their backpack on the note. Next, ask each student to approach the map and stick his or her Post-it on the nation where that good was made. Ask your students to describe how their lives have been changed by trade. Once they do, announce that the government has passed a law that prohibits trade with one of the nations with lots of Post-it notes on it, and remove this country from the map. Ask students to explain how this trade barrier might impact their lives.

FOCUS Flip It

TRM Have students watch Jacob Clifford's "Econ 1.4—Comparative Advantage" video (see econextras video list with hyperlinks on the bcs and TRFD). It will serve as a good review of comparative advantage. Assign **Worksheet 44.1 (Comparative Advantage)** from the TRM for suggested questions on this video.

TEACH Teach It

Spend some time talking about the reasons why some nations are wary of specialization and why trade based on comparative advantage makes good economic sense. You can show the ABC video "Made in America: US Spends Millions on Foreign-Made Sneakers for the Military" (see econextras video list with hyperlinks on the bcs and TRFD). Discuss the pros and cons of buying American.

TEACH Connect It

This is a great time to remind students about comparative advantage. Have them determine, using their personal whiteboards or paper, who has the comparative advantage in the production of each good: Nation A producing 5 violins and 10 tubas, or Nation B producing 10 violins and 10 tubas utilizing the same resources. *Nation B has the comparative advantage in violin production and Nation A has the comparative advantage in tuba production.* If terms of trade were set such that 1 violin could be traded for 1.5 tubas, would each nation benefit? And if so, how? *Yes. It costs Nation A 2 tubas to make 1 violin. Through trade, that cost is only 1.5 tubas. Nation B receives 1.5 tubas for each 1 violin it trades, rather than the 1 tuba it could produce on its own instead of 1 violin.*

FOCUS Active Learning

Have students read Global Envision's case study "Sanchez Electronic Devices—A Case Study" at http://www.globalenvision.org/forteachers/17/825#hand2. Discuss Question 6 from the case study questions provided.

TEACH Teach It

TRM Trade barriers raise the price of goods and services for consumers and decrease the quantity available for purchase. This may lead to a lower standard of living for the consumer. Assign **Worksheet 44.2 (Trade Barriers)** from the TRM for practice with the workings of barriers to trade

Figure 44.1 Imports of Goods and Services as a Percentage of GDP

International trade is an important part of every country's economy, but some economies are more open than others. In 2012, imports as a percentage of GDP ranged from 14% in Brazil to 178% in Singapore.

Source: The World Bank.

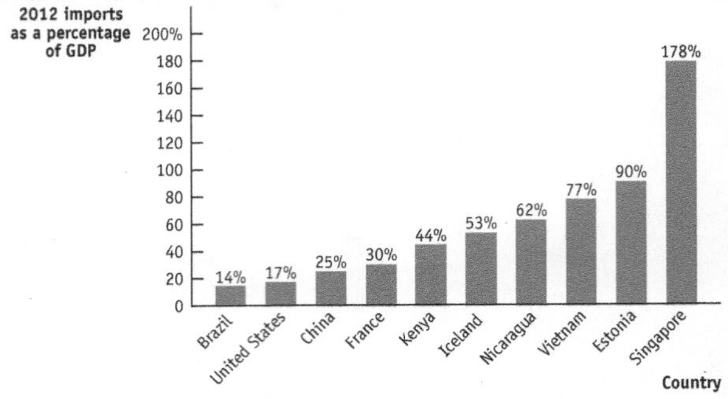

from countries with a comparative advantage in textiles, workers in the Fruit of the Loom factory in Campbellsville, Kentucky, were among many who lost their jobs. Fortunately, the unemployment rates in Campbellsville and in the United States as a whole rose only temporarily. Many of these workers were able to adapt to the requirements of growing industries such as construction, automotive parts, health care, and software design, and were able to secure new jobs as a result.

Protectionism is the practice of limiting trade to protect domestic industries.

Tariffs are taxes on imports.

Some industries may not initially be competitive at the international level, but they could attain a comparative advantage after a period of protection from lower-priced imports. This is the motivation for **protectionism**, the practice of limiting trade to protect domestic industries. *Tariffs* and *import quotas* are the primary tools of protectionism.

Tariffs

Shutterstock

The imposition of **tariffs**, which are taxes on imports, helps domestic industries and provides revenue for the government. The bad news is that tariffs make prices higher for domestic consumers and can spark trade wars. Early in American history, tariffs provided a majority of the revenue for the U.S. government, reaching a high of 97.9% in 1825. As the benefits of free trade came to light, and income and payroll taxes were adopted in the early 1900s, the use of tariffs diminished. By 1944, tariff revenue amounted to only about 1% of federal government revenue, which is still the case today.

Consider the U.S. market for ceramic plates, a hypothetical version of which is shown in **Figure 44.2**. The upward-sloping supply curve shows the supply from U.S. firms. The demand curve is for U.S. consumers only. If the United States had a closed economy, 5 million plates would sell for the no-trade equilibrium price of $15 each. However, suppose that an unlimited quantity of plates could be imported for the equilibrium price in the world market, $9. In the absence of trade restrictions, domestic firms would be unable to charge more than the world price. At the $9 world price, domestic firms would be willing to supply 3 million plates, but domestic consumers would demand 7 million. Four million imported plates would make up the difference between the 7 million plates demanded and the 3 million supplied in the domestic market.

AP® Exam Tip

The effects of tariffs and quotas can be shown on supply and demand graphs. You may need to illustrate or interpret a graph that involves trade barriers for the AP® exam.

Now suppose that the U.S. imposes a tariff of $3 per imported ceramic plate. As shown in **Figure 44.3**, that would effectively raise the curve that represents the supply from the rest of the world by $3. For every imported plate, the required payment would

St. Louis Federal Reserve Bank Resources

"The Great Trade Collapse and Rebound: A State-by-State View, Trade Margins"

In this video presentation, Cletus Coughlin, senior vice president and policy advisor to the president of the St. Louis Fed, provides an overview of how exports and imports were impacted by the Great Recession and the subsequent recovery.

438 Section 8 The Open Economy: International Trade and Finance

Figure 44.2 The U.S. Ceramic Plate Market with Imports

Without trade, 5 million plates would be sold at the no-trade equilibrium price of $15. An unlimited quantity of plates can be imported at the equilibrium world price of $9. With unrestricted trade, domestic firms will be unable to charge more than the world price, for which they are willing to supply 3 million plates. Domestic consumers will demand 7 million plates at a price of $9 each. The difference between the domestic demand and the domestic supply, 4 million plates, will be imported.

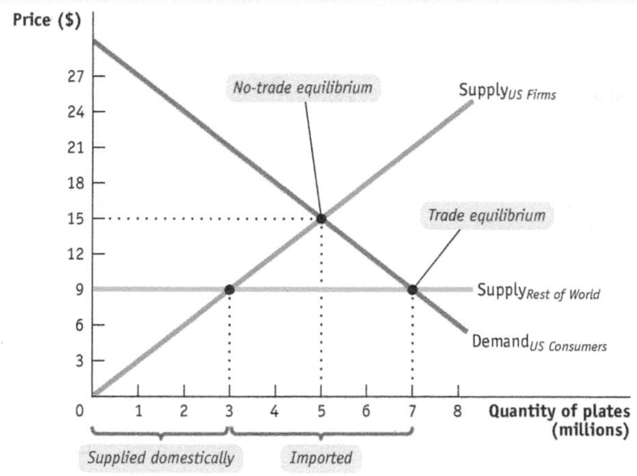

be $9 to the foreign suppliers plus $3 for the tariff, for a total of $12. Domestic firms would now be able to charge up to $12, for which they would be willing to supply 4 million plates, an increase of 1 million compared to the no-tariff situation. Domestic consumers would demand 6 million plates for $12, a decrease of 1 million from the no-tariff situation. Two million plates would be imported to make up the difference between the

Figure 44.3 A Tariff on Ceramic Plates

A tariff of $3 per imported ceramic plate effectively raises the curve that represents the supply from the rest of the world by $3. To receive an imported plate, one must pay $9 to the foreign suppliers plus $3 for the tariff, for a total of $12. Domestic firms can then charge up to $12, for which they are willing to supply 4 million plates. Domestic consumers demand 6 million plates for $12 each. Two million plates will be imported to make up the difference between the domestic supply and the domestic demand. This is 2 million less than the 4 million plates imported without the tariff.

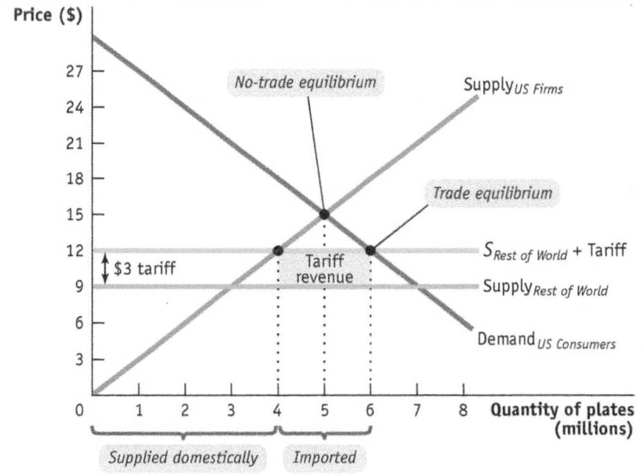

FOCUS Test It

Assign Question 3 from the released 2012 AP® Microeconomics exam (available at http://apcentral.collegeboard.com/apc/public/repository/ap12_frq_microeconomics.pdf). Although this appeared on the AP® Microeconomics exam, international trade is on the topic outline for AP® Macroeconomics, so this type of question could appear on the AP® Macroeconomics exam. This question requires students to understand the effects of a tariff on a market that faces a world price below the domestic equilibrium. Students should take $12\frac{1}{2}$ minutes to answer this question to match the time suggested for the AP® exam. The rubric for the question may be viewed at http://apcentral.collegeboard.com/apc/public/repository/ap12_microeconomics_scoring_guidelines.pdf.

Module 44 Barriers to Trade 439

FOCUS Graph It

Ask students to use their personal whiteboards or paper to draw two identical graphs of a market with free trade at a world price that is below the domestic equilibrium price. Have them show the effect of a tariff on the first graph and the effect of an import quota on the second graph. We know that starting from a free-trade equilibrium, a tariff increases the price and reduces the quantity purchased. How does a quota affect a market that formerly had free trade? *A quota also raises the price and decreases the quantity.* The changes in price and quantity depend on the sizes of the tariff and the quota, but as shown in Figures 44.3 and 44.4, a quota that results in the same quantity of imports as a given tariff will have the same effect on the equilibrium price and quantity.

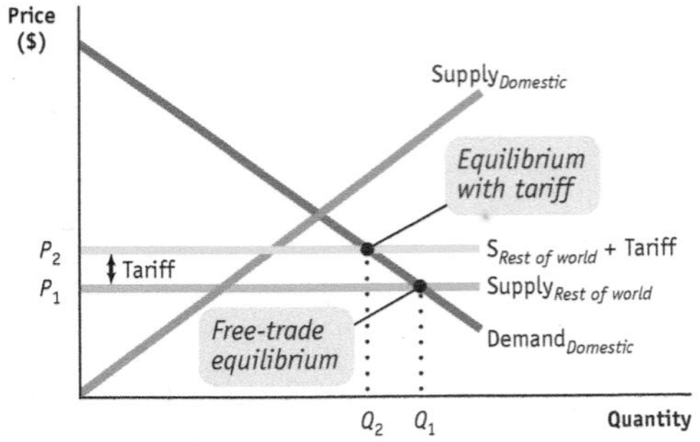

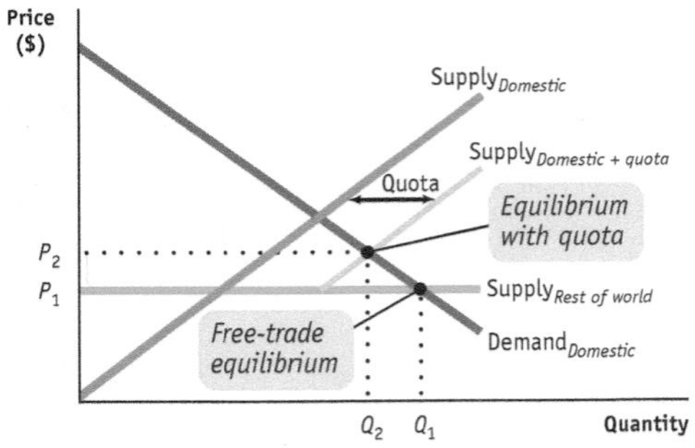

domestic supply of 4 million and the domestic demand of 6 million plates. Note that this is a drop of 2 million from the 4 million plates imported without the tariff. The tariff revenue would be 2 million × \$3 = \$6 million, as represented by the shaded rectangle in the figure.

Import Quotas

An **import quota** is a limit on the quantity of a good that can be imported within a given period.

AP® Exam Tip

Tariffs provide governments with revenues and quotas do not.

An **import quota** is a limit on the quantity of a good that can be imported within a given period. By restricting the supply of imports, import quotas reduce the equilibrium quantity and increase the equilibrium price. Like tariffs, quotas help domestic firms compete with foreign suppliers, but they also cause prices to be higher for domestic consumers. Consider sugar, which Americans consume at a rate of about 11 million tons per year. To protect domestic sugar cane and sugar beet farmers, the U.S. Department of Agriculture (USDA) sets a quota for the amount of sugar that can be imported—1.2 million tons in 2014—before a substantial tariff is applied.

Suppose that the United States imposes an import quota of 2 million ceramic plates. That quota would prevent a trade equilibrium at the intersection of U.S. consumers' demand and the supply from the rest of the world because, as we saw in Figure 44.2, that equilibrium would require imports of 4 million plates. Instead, consumers would face the pink supply curve in **Figure 44.4**, which represents the U.S. supply plus the 2 million plates that could be imported with the quota. Imports would not be available for less than \$9, so the pink U.S.-plus-quota supply curve does not extend below a price of \$9. The equilibrium price with the quota is \$12. Six million plates would be sold at that price, 4 million of which would be made domestically. Notice that the quota of 2 million plates would have the same effect on the price, imports, and domestic supply as the \$3 tariff. One difference is that with the quota, no tariff revenue would be collected.

The use of tariffs and import quotas is seldom one-sided. When one country erects a trade barrier against another, retaliation is common. For instance, after the

Figure 44.4 A Ceramic Plates Quota

With an import quota of 2 million ceramic plates, consumers face the pink supply curve made up of the U.S. supply plus the 2 million plates that can be imported. Imports are not available for less than \$9, so the pink U.S.-plus-quota supply curve does not extend below \$9. At the \$12 equilibrium price with the quota, a quantity of 6 million plates are purchased, 4 million of which are supplied domestically.

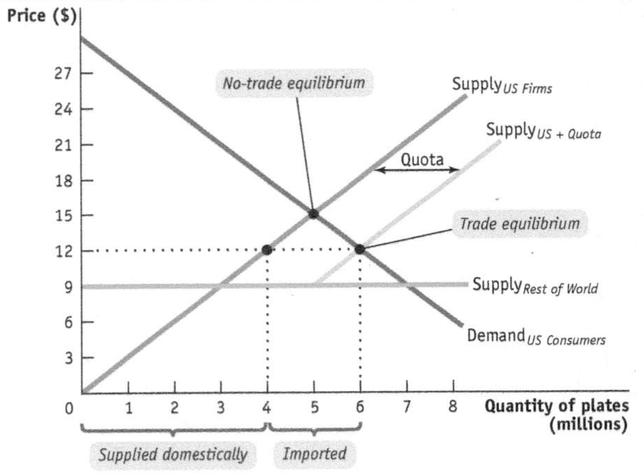

FOCUS Flip It

For more on the graphs for tariffs and quotas, have your students watch Jacob Clifford's "Micro 2.8—Tariffs and Quotas" video (see econextras video list with hyperlinks on the bcs and TRFD).

FOCUS Active Learning

Break students into groups of three or four. Assign each group one of the following arguments against free trade to evaluate. The group should explain what type of barrier might be instituted and develop one pro and one con regarding the argument. After the small group discussions, a speaker from each group should present the group's position.

- Barriers help protect domestic jobs.
- Barriers help protect military secrets.
- Barriers help protect the environment.
- Barriers help prevent dependency on another nation.
- Barriers help protect industries in their infancy.

FOCUS Test It

Assign Question 2 from the released 2008 Form B AP® Macroeconomics exam at http://apcentral.collegeboard.com/apc/public/repository/ap08_macro_form_b_frq.pdf. It provides a comprehensive review of trade barriers and the balance of payments. Students should take $12\frac{1}{2}$ minutes to answer this question to match the time suggested for the AP® exam. The rubric for the question may be viewed at http://apcentral.collegeboard.com/apc/public/repository/ap08_macroecon_form_b_sgs.pdf.

Obama administration imposed a tariff on tires imported from China, China threatened to cut off imports of chickens from the United States. Escalating trade wars can obliterate the gains from trade, which motivates many countries to move in the opposite direction and negotiate the elimination of trade barriers. Trade agreements such as the North American Free Trade Agreement and the Dominican Republic-Central America Free Trade Agreement limit the use of tariffs, quotas, regulations, and other impediments to trade among the economies involved. As discussed in the FYI that follows, these agreements can provide substantial benefits to citizens in the participating countries.

FYI Bringing Down the Walls

The United States and the European Union have the two largest economies in the world, and these economies trade more with each other than with any other economy. Yet trade barriers prevent this relationship from reaching its full potential. The average tariff between these two economies is 4%. Regulations and bureaucratic red tape add to the barriers that restrict transatlantic trade. For example, the United States and the European Union have differing regulations on food products and automobile safety that make it difficult to trade the affected products between the two economies. However, the Transatlantic Trade and Investment Partnership (TTIP) may bring these barriers down.

In March of 2014, representatives of the United States and the European Union completed their fourth round of talks on the details of the TTIP. Although it is relatively straightforward to eliminate tariffs as part of trade negotiations, differing regulations pose larger challenges. For example, regulations on genetically modified crops are stricter in the European Union than in the United States. And the European Union requires different safety tests for automobiles than the United States. Sometimes, mutually accepted revisions can close the gap between regulations. In the case of auto safety, the parties involved may determine that their differing approaches have the same effect of providing an acceptable level of consumer safety. And when the effect is the same, the trading partners can agree to accept each other's goods despite differences in the specific tests and guidelines imposed.

Analysts estimate that the TTIP could be a win-win for citizens of the United States and the European Union, adding between $545 and $900 to the disposable annual income of a typical family of four in each economy. Eighty percent of the gains are expected to come from cutting the costs imposed by regulations and bureaucracy.

The reduction of trade barriers also has its victims. For example, workers in industries protected by trade barriers may lose their jobs. To lessen this burden, the governments of the United States and European countries provide assistance to unemployed workers as they transition from industries that are contracting to industries that are growing.

Overall, the growing popularity of free-trade agreements reflects the demonstrated benefits of specialization and trade and the success of past experiments with free trade.

TEACH Teach It

After students complete the activity on free trade on the preceding page, talk about the advantages and disadvantages of free trade agreements such as NAFTA and CAFTA with them. Information on the two agreements is available at http://www.ustr.gov/trade-agreements/free-trade-agreements/north-american-free-trade-agreement-nafta. Information on other free trade agreements can be found at http://www.trade.gov/fta/.

OPEN & CLOSE Exit Slip

TRM *Please see **Exit Slip: Module 44** in the TRM for formative multiple-choice questions to ask your students before finishing your lesson. These questions will help you quickly assess whether your students have mastered the module's concepts before moving on.*

Answers to the Exit Slip Questions

1. C
2. D
3. B

Answers to Module 44 Review Questions

Check Your Understanding

1. $6. A tariff of $5.99 or less would make the price of imported plates (including the tariff) $9.00 + $5.99 = $14.99 or less, and at these prices, the demand exceeds the domestic supply.

2. 4 million plates. A quota of 4 million plates or more would not affect international trade because consumers only want to import 4 million plates, which this quota would allow. However, a quota of fewer than 4 million plates would affect international trade because consumers could not obtain all of the plates that they want for $9, and the restriction on total supply would cause the price to rise above $9.

Tackle the Test: Multiple-Choice Questions

1. e
2. c
3. b
4. c
5. d

MODULE 44 Review

Check Your Understanding

Use the information provided in Figure 44.2 to answer the following questions:

1. What is the smallest tariff that would cause all plates to be supplied by U.S. firms?

2. What is the smallest import quota that would have no effect on international trade? Hint: You can think of the question this way: Every import quota smaller than what level would have an effect on international trade?

Tackle the Test: Multiple-Choice Questions

1. Which of the following is put forth as a reason for trade restrictions?
   a. National pride can take precedence over the gains from trade.
   b. Domestic industries need protection from foreign competition while they develop a comparative advantage.
   c. Citizens don't want to send their money overseas.
   d. Countries don't want to become overly reliant on other countries.
   e. All of the above.

2. The purpose of protectionism is to protect domestic
   a. resources.
   b. consumption levels.
   c. industries.
   d. exporters.
   e. all of the above.

3. Which of the following would result from a U.S. tariff on imported cars?
   a. The profit of U.S. car manufacturers would decrease.
   b. The price paid for cars in the U.S. would increase.
   c. More cars would be imported.
   d. Fewer domestically made cars would be sold in the United States.
   e. More cars from all sources would be sold in the United States.

4. An import quota is a
   a. minimum quantity of a good that may be imported.
   b. minimum quantity of a good that a factory must produce and sell overseas.
   c. maximum quantity of a good that may be imported.
   d. maximum quantity of a good that a factory may produce and sell overseas.
   e. maximum price that a company can charge for imports.

5. Which of the following would result if China imposed an import quota on telephones that influenced the amount of trade?
   a. The price of telephones in China would decrease.
   b. The Chinese government would collect more taxes on imported telephones.
   c. More telephones made outside of China would be sold in China.
   d. More telephones made in China would be sold in China.
   e. More telephones from all sources would be sold in China.

442 Section 8 The Open Economy: International Trade and Finance

Tackle the Test: Free-Response Questions

1. Suppose that rice is traded in the world market at a price of $1 per pound, and that in the absence of trade, the equilibrium price of rice in Mexico is $1.25 per pound.
   a. Draw a correctly labeled graph that shows the domestic supply and demand for rice in Mexico.
   b. Label the no-trade equilibrium and the trade equilibrium.
   c. Use labeled brackets to indicate the portions of the horizontal axis that represent
      i. the quantity of rice imported at the world price.
      ii. the quantity of rice supplied domestically at the world price.
   d. Suppose that Mexico imposes a $0.15 tariff per pound of imported rice.
      i. Label the new trade equilibrium.
      ii. Shade the area that represents the total tariff revenue.

Rubric for FRQ 1 (6 points)

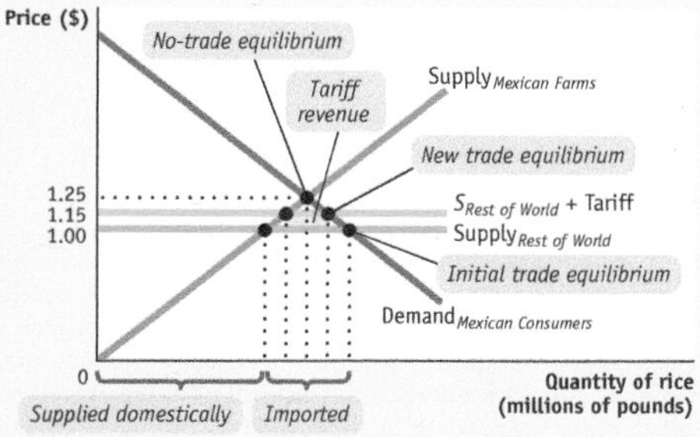

1 point: Graph with "Price" on the vertical axis, "Quantity of Rice" on the horizontal axis, downward-sloping demand, upward-sloping supply, and the no-trade equilibrium

1 point: Horizontal rest-of-world supply curve and trade equilibrium as shown in the figure

1 point: Correct indication of imported quantity

1 point: Correct indication of domestically supplied quantity

1 point: Horizontal rest-of-world supply + tariff curve and new trade equilibrium as in the figure

1 point: Shaded area that represents tariff revenue as in the figure

2. Suppose that cheese is traded in the world market at a price of €3 per pound. Assume that France has no trade barriers and has supply and demand curves for cheese as shown in the graph.

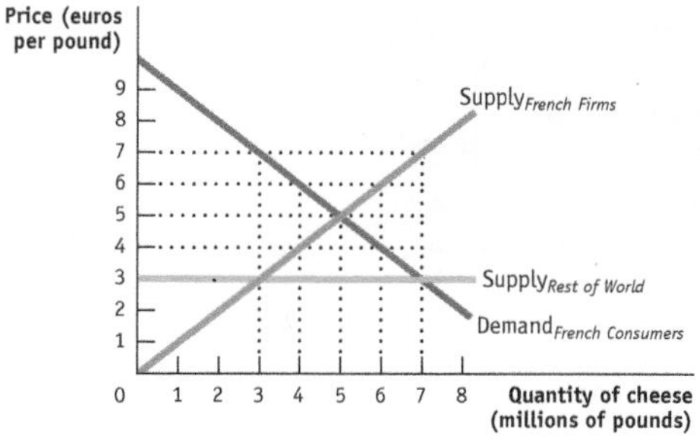

   a. How much cheese does France import?
   b. Suppose that France adopts an import quota of 2 million pounds of cheese.
      i. What will the price be at the new trade equilibrium?
      ii. How much cheese will French suppliers provide domestically with the quota in place?
      iii. If France imposed a tariff instead of a quota to restrict cheese imports, a tariff of what amount per pound would result in imports of 2 million pounds of cheese?
   c. Suppose that instead of any other trade restriction, France imposed a tariff of €4 per pound of cheese. How much cheese would France import? Explain.
   (6 points)

Tackle the Test: Free-Response Question
Rubric for FRQ 2 (6 points)

1 point: France imports 4 million pounds of cheese.

1 point: The price will be 4 euros per pound.

1 point: French suppliers will provide 4 million pounds of cheese domestically.

1 point: A tariff of 1 euro per pound would result in imports of 2 million pounds of cheese.

1 point: None

1 point: A tariff of 4 euros per pound of cheese would raise the import price up to 7 euros per pound. However, the domestic supply equals the domestic demand at a price of 5 euros per pound. As a result, there would be an excess supply of domestic cheese at prices above 5 euros per pound.

Module 44 Barriers to Trade 443

PD To prepare for teaching this lesson, you may want to consult the **Module 45 Sample Lecture** in the TRM.

OPEN & CLOSE **Start Here**

Assign Question 1 from the released 2011 AP® Macroeconomics exam at http://apcentral.collegeboard.com/apc/public/repository/ap11_frq_macroeconomics_formb.pdf. It is recommended that students take 25 minutes to answer this question to match the time suggested for the AP® exam. The rubric for the question may be viewed at http://apcentral.collegeboard.com/apc/public/repository/ap11_macroeconomics_form_b_scoring_guidelines.pdf.

TEACH **AP® Exam Tip**

Teach students the four-step process for analyzing a free-response question. This framework will greatly assist students in their preparation for the AP® exam. If time allows, provide more practice with free-response questions and multiple-choice questions as a basis for review of the content prior to the AP® exam testing date. To find essential course resources including past free-response questions, visit AP® Central at http://apcentral.collegeboard.com/apc/public/courses/teachers_corner/2120.html.

iStockphoto

MODULE 45 Putting It All Together

In this Module, you will learn to:

- Use macroeconomic models to conduct policy analysis
- Improve your approach to free-response macroeconomics questions

Having completed our study of the basic macroeconomic models, we can use them to analyze scenarios and evaluate policy recommendations. In this module we develop a step-by-step approach to macroeconomic analysis. You can adapt this approach to problems involving any macroeconomic model, including models of aggregate demand and supply, production possibilities, money markets, and the Phillips curve. By the end of this module you will be able to combine mastery of the principles of macroeconomics with problem solving skills to analyze a new scenario on your own.

A Structure for Macroeconomic Analysis

In our study of macroeconomics we have seen questions about the macroeconomy take many different forms. No matter what the specific question, most macroeconomic problems have the following components:

1. *A starting point.* To analyze any situation, you have to know where to start.
2. *A pivotal event.* This might be a change in the economy or a policy response to the initial situation.
3. *Initial effects of the event.* An event will generally have some initial, short-run effects.
4. *Secondary and long-run effects of the event.* After the short-run effects run their course, there are typically secondary effects and the economy will move toward its long-run equilibrium.

© ZUMA Press, Inc./Alamy

How will the Fed's monetary policy change nominal interest rates?

For example, you might be asked to consider the following scenario and answer the associated questions.

Assume the U.S. economy is currently operating at an aggregate output level above potential output. Draw a correctly labeled graph showing aggregate demand, short-run aggregate supply, long-run aggregate supply, equilibrium output, and the aggregate price level.

444 Section 8 The Open Economy: International Trade and Finance

Now assume that the Federal Reserve conducts contractionary monetary policy. Identify the open-market operation the Fed would conduct, and draw a correctly labeled graph of the money market to show the effect of the monetary policy on the nominal interest rate.

Show and explain how the Fed's actions will affect equilibrium in the aggregate demand and supply graph you drew previously. Indicate the new aggregate price level on your graph.

Assume Canada is the largest trading partner of the United States. Draw a correctly labeled graph of the foreign exchange market for the U.S. dollar showing how the change in the aggregate price level you indicate on your graph above will affect the foreign exchange market. What will happen to the value of the U.S. dollar relative to the Canadian dollar?

How will the Federal Reserve's contractionary monetary policy affect the real interest rate in the United States in the long run? Explain.

Taken as a whole, this scenario and the associated questions can seem overwhelming. Let's start by breaking down our analysis into four components.

1. **The starting point**
   Assume the U.S. economy is currently operating at an aggregate output level above potential output.
2. **The pivotal event**
   Now assume that the Federal Reserve conducts contractionary monetary policy.
3. **Initial effects of the event**
   Show and explain how the Fed's actions will affect equilibrium.
4. **Secondary and long-run effects of the event**
   Assume Canada is the largest trading partner of the United States. What will happen to the value of the U.S. dollar relative to the Canadian dollar?
   How will the Federal Reserve's contractionary monetary policy affect the real interest rate in the United States in the long run? Explain.

Now we are ready to look at each of the steps and untangle this scenario.

The Starting Point

Assume the U.S. economy is currently operating at an aggregate output level above potential output. Draw a correctly labeled graph showing aggregate demand, short-run aggregate supply, long-run aggregate supply, equilibrium output, and the aggregate price level.

To analyze a situation, you have to know where to start. You will most often use the aggregate demand–aggregate supply model to evaluate macroeconomic scenarios. In this model, there are three possible starting points: long-run macroeconomic equilibrium, a recessionary gap, and an inflationary gap. This means that there are three possible "starting-point" graphs, as shown in **Figure 45.1** on the next page. The economy can be in long-run macroeconomic equilibrium with production at potential output as in panel (a); it can be in short-run macroeconomic equilibrium at an aggregate output level below potential output (creating a recessionary gap) as in panel (b); or it can be in short-run macroeconomic equilibrium at an aggregate output level above potential output (creating an inflationary gap) as in panel (c) and in our scenario.

The Pivotal Event

Now assume that the Federal Reserve conducts contractionary monetary policy.

It is the events in a scenario that make it interesting. Perhaps a country goes into or recovers from a recession, inflation catches consumers off guard or becomes expected, consumers or businesses become more or less confident, holdings of money or wealth change, trading partners prosper or falter, or oil prices plummet or spike. The event can also be expansionary or contractionary monetary or fiscal policy. With the infinite number of possible changes in policy, politics, the economy, and markets around the world, don't expect to analyze a familiar scenario on the exam.

While it's impossible to foresee all of the scenarios you might encounter, we can group the determinants of change into a reasonably small set of major factors that

FOCUS Active Learning

TRM Use **Activity 45.1 (The Macro Analysis Framework)** from the TRM to walk students through the framework as you teach them each step to approaching a free-response question.

St. Louis Federal Reserve Bank Resources

The Fed's Toolbox

In this lesson, students learn that the Federal Reserve System uses its monetary policy tools to influence the level of reserves in the banking system. Students participate in a simulation to demonstrate how the Fed uses open market operations to achieve its dual mandate of price stability and maximum employment. Students also learn about other monetary tools: the discount rate, reserve requirements, and interest on reserves—a recent monetary policy tool. Finally, students apply their knowledge of monetary policy to suggest possible Federal Reserve policy responses to proposed economic conditions.

Figure 45.1 Analysis Starting Points

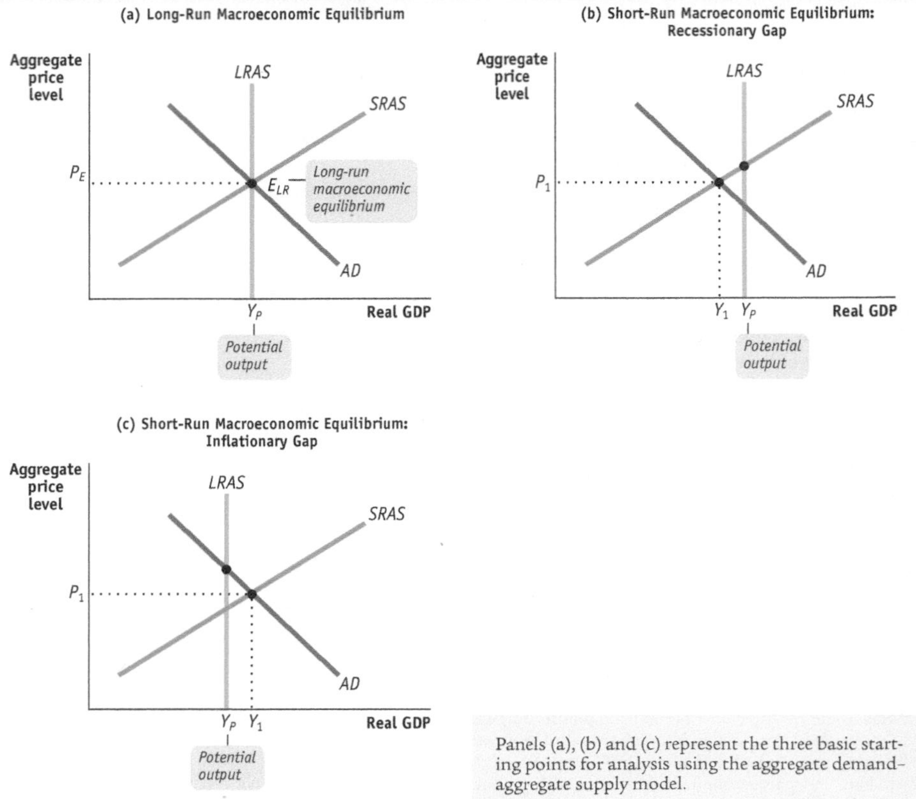

Panels (a), (b) and (c) represent the three basic starting points for analysis using the aggregate demand–aggregate supply model.

AP Photo/Gus Ruelas

You've seen the speech, now, how would you analyze the proposed policy?

influence macroeconomic models. **Table 45.1** matches major factors with the curves they affect. With these influences in mind, it is relatively easy to proceed through a problem by identifying how the given events affect these factors. Most hypothetical scenarios involve changes in just one or two major factors. Although the real world is more complex, it is largely the same factors that change—there are just more of them changing at once.

As shown in Table 45.1, many curves are shifted by changes in only two or three major factors. Even for the aggregate demand curve, which has the largest number of associated factors, you can simplify the task further by asking yourself, "Does the event influence consumer spending, investment spending, government spending, or net exports?" If so, aggregate demand shifts. A shift

St. Louis Federal Reserve Bank Resources

Monetary Policy Online Course for Teachers and Students

Inflation, unemployment, recession, economic growth—these economic concepts affect people in very real ways. In this course containing three interactive, thought-provoking lessons, students will learn about monetary policy, the avenue by which the Federal Reserve System attempts to influence the economy.

Table 45.1 Major Factors that Shift Curves in Each Model

Aggregate Demand and Aggregate Supply		
Aggregate Demand Curve	**Short-Run Aggregate Supply Curve**	**Long-Run Aggregate Supply Curve**
Expectations Wealth Size of existing capital stock Fiscal and monetary policy Net exports Interest rates Investment spending	Commodity prices Nominal wages Productivity Business taxes	Productivity Physical capital Human capital Technology Quantity of resources

Supply and Demand	
Demand Curve	**Supply Curve**
Income Prices of substitutes and complements Tastes Consumer expectations Number of consumers	Input prices Prices of substitutes and complements in production Technology Producer expectations Number of producers

Loanable Funds Market	
Demand Curve	**Supply Curve**
Investment opportunities Government borrowing	Private saving behavior Capital inflows

Money Market	
Demand Curve	**Supply Curve**
Aggregate price level Real GDP Technology (related to money market) Institutions (related to money market)	Set by the Federal Reserve

Foreign Exchange Market	
Demand	**Supply**
Foreigners' purchases of domestic Goods Services Assets	Domestic residents' purchases of foreign Goods Services Assets

Note: It is the *real* exchange rate (adjusted for international differences in aggregate price levels) that affects imports and exports.

of the long-run aggregate supply curve is caused only by events that affect labor productivity or the number of workers.

In the supply and demand model there are five major factors that shift the demand curve and five major factors that shift the supply curve. Most examples using this model will represent a change in one of these ten factors. The loanable funds market, money market, and foreign exchange market have their own clearly identified factors that affect supply or demand. With this information you can link specific events to relevant factors in the models to see what changes will occur. Remember that having correctly labeled axes on your graphs is crucial to a correct analysis.

Often, as in our scenario, the event is a policy response to an undesirable starting point such as a recessionary or inflationary gap. Expansionary policy is used to combat a recession, and contractionary policy is used to combat inflationary pressures. To begin analyzing a policy response, you need to fully understand how the Federal Reserve can implement each type of monetary policy (e.g., increase or decrease the money supply)

TEACH Teach It

Use Table 45.1 to review some of the major content in the course.

FOCUS Flip It

Students can view the Jacob Clifford video "Macro 5.6—Key Graphs of AP® Macroeconomics" (see econextras video list with hyperlinks on the bcs and TRFD) to review the key graphs and gain knowledge about answering the Free-Response Questions on the AP® Macro exam.

FOCUS Flip It

Students can view the Jacob Clifford video "Macro 2009 FRQ #1" (see econextras video list with hyperlinks on the bcs and TRFD) to see an explanation of the correct response to a past AP® Macro FRQ. Students can pause the video at various places and try to determine the answer before Mr. Clifford explains it.

and how that policy eventually affects the economy. You also need to understand how the government can implement expansionary or contractionary fiscal policy by raising or lowering taxes or government spending.

The Initial Effect of the Event

Show and explain how the Fed's actions will affect equilibrium.

We have seen that events will create short-run effects in our models. In the short-run, fiscal and monetary policy both affect the economy by shifting the aggregate demand curve. As shown in panel (a) of **Figure 45.2**, expansionary policy shifts aggregate demand to the right, and as shown in panel (b), contractionary policy shifts aggregate demand to the left. To illustrate the effect of a policy response, shift the aggregate demand curve on your starting point graph and indicate the effects of the shift on the aggregate price level and aggregate output.

Secondary and Long-Run Effects of the Event

Assume Canada is the largest trading partner of the United States. What will happen to the value of the U.S. dollar relative to the Canadian dollar?

How will the Federal Reserve's contractionary monetary policy affect the real interest rate in the United States in the long run? Explain.

Secondary Effects In addition to the initial, short-run effects of any event, there will be secondary effects and the economy will move to its long-run equilibrium after the short-run effects run their course.

We have seen that negative or positive demand shocks (including those created by inappropriate monetary or fiscal policy) move the economy away from long-run macroeconomic equilibrium. As explained in Module 18, in the absence of policy responses,

Figure 45.2 Monetary and Fiscal Policy Close Output Gaps

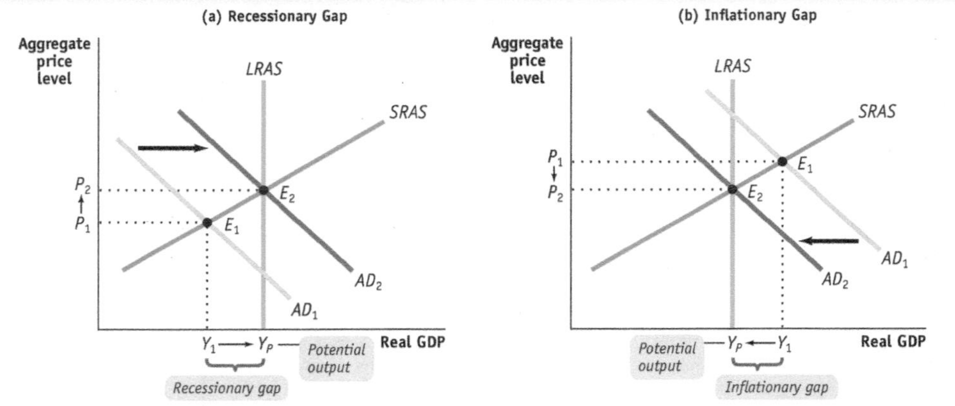

By shifting the aggregate demand curve, monetary and fiscal policy can close output gaps in the economy as shown in panel (a) for a recessionary gap and panel (b) for an inflationary gap.

448 Section 8 The Open Economy: International Trade and Finance

such events will eventually be offset through changes in short-run aggregate supply resulting from changes in nominal wage rates. This will move the economy back to long-run macroeconomic equilibrium.

If the short-run effects of an action result in changes in the aggregate price level or real interest rate, there will also be secondary effects throughout the open economy. International capital flows and international trade will be affected as a result of the initial effects experienced in the economy. A price level decrease, as in our scenario, will encourage exports and discourage imports, causing an appreciation in the domestic currency on the foreign exchange market. A change in the interest rate affects aggregate demand through changes in investment spending and consumer spending. Interest rate changes also affect aggregate demand through changes in imports or exports caused by currency appreciation and depreciation. These secondary effects act to reinforce the effects of monetary policy.

Long-Run Effects While deviations from potential output are ironed out in the long run, other effects remain. For example, in the long run the use of fiscal policy affects the federal budget. Changes in taxes or government spending that lead to budget deficits (and increased federal debt) can "crowd out" private investment spending in the long run. The government's increased demand for loanable funds drives up the interest rate, decreases investment spending, and partially offsets the initial increase in aggregate demand. Of course, the deficit could be addressed by printing money, but that would lead to problems with inflation in the long run.

We know that in the long run, monetary policy affects only the aggregate price level, not real GDP. Because money is neutral, changes in the money supply have no effect on the real economy. The aggregate price level and nominal values will be affected by the same proportion, leaving real values (including the real interest rate as mentioned in our scenario) unchanged.

Analyzing Our Scenario

Now let's address the specific demands of our problem.

- *Draw a correctly labeled graph showing aggregate demand, short-run aggregate supply, long-run aggregate supply, equilibrium output, and the aggregate price level.*

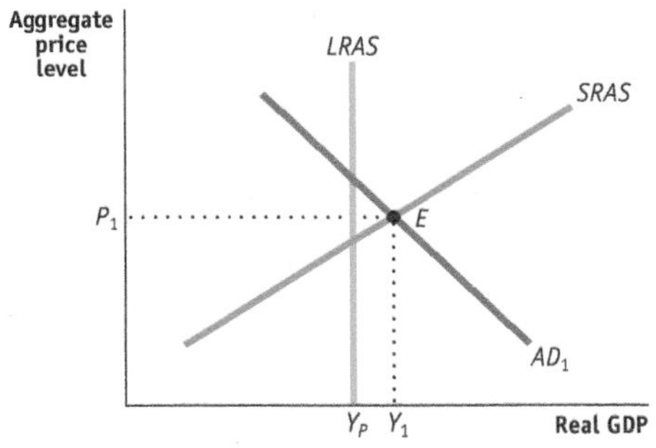

- *Identify the open-market operation the Fed would conduct.*

The Fed would sell U.S. Treasury securities (bonds, bills, or notes).

- *Draw a correctly labeled graph of the money market to show the effect of the monetary policy on the nominal interest rate.*

FOCUS Flip It

Students can view the Jacob Clifford video "Macro 2011 FRQ #1" (see econextras video list with hyperlinks on the bcs and TRFD) to see an explanation of the correct response for a past AP® Macro FRQ. Students can pause the video at various places and try to determine the answer before Mr. Clifford explains it.

FOCUS Flip It

Students can view the Jacob Clifford video "Macro 2012 FRQ #3" (see econextras video list with hyperlinks on the bcs and TRFD) to see an explanation of the correct response for a past AP® Macro FRQ. Students can pause the video at various places and try to determine the answer before Mr. Clifford explains it.

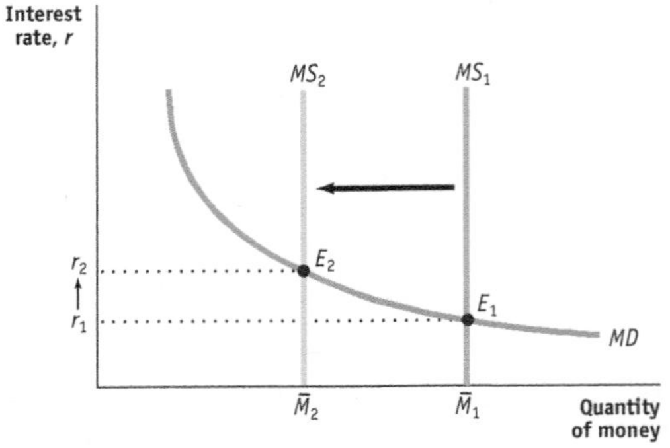

- *Show and explain how the Fed's actions will affect equilibrium in the aggregate demand and supply graph you drew previously. Indicate the new aggregate price level on your graph.*

A higher interest rate will lead to decreased investment and consumer spending, decreasing aggregate demand. The equilibrium price level and real GDP will fall.

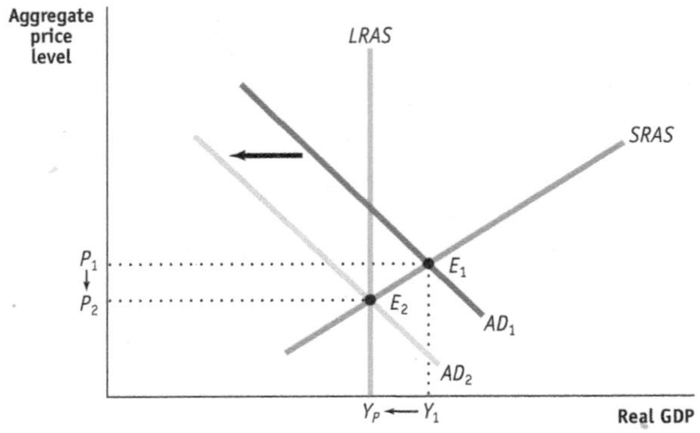

- *Draw a correctly labeled graph of the foreign exchange market for the U.S. dollar showing how the change in the aggregate price level you indicate on your graph above will affect the foreign exchange market.*

The decrease in the U.S. price level will make U.S. exports relatively inexpensive for Canadians to purchase and lead to an increase in demand for U.S. dollars with which to purchase those exports.

450 Section 8 The Open Economy: International Trade and Finance

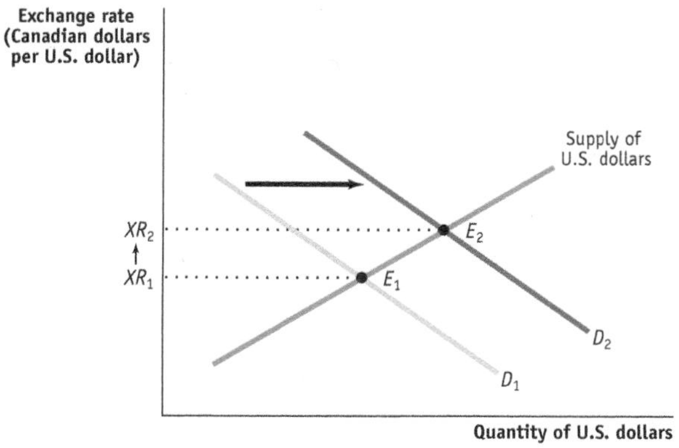

- *What will happen to the U.S. dollar relative to the Canadian dollar?*

The U.S. dollar will appreciate.

- *How will the Federal Reserve's contractionary monetary policy affect the real interest rate in the United States in the long run? Explain.*

There will be no effect on the real interest rate in the long run because, due to the neutrality of money, changes in the money supply do not affect real values in the long run.

MODULE 45 Review

Check Your Understanding

1. The economy is operating in long-run macroeconomic equilibrium.
   a. Illustrate this situation using a correctly labeled aggregate demand–aggregate supply graph.
   b. Use your graph to show the short-run effect on real GDP and the aggregate price level if there is a decrease in government spending.
   c. What will happen to the aggregate price level and real GDP in the long run? Explain.
   d. Suppose the government is experiencing a persistent budget deficit. How will the decrease in government spending affect that deficit? Use a correctly labeled graph of the loanable funds market to show the effect of a decrease in government spending on the interest rate.

Answers to Module 45 Review Questions

Check Your Understanding

1. a.

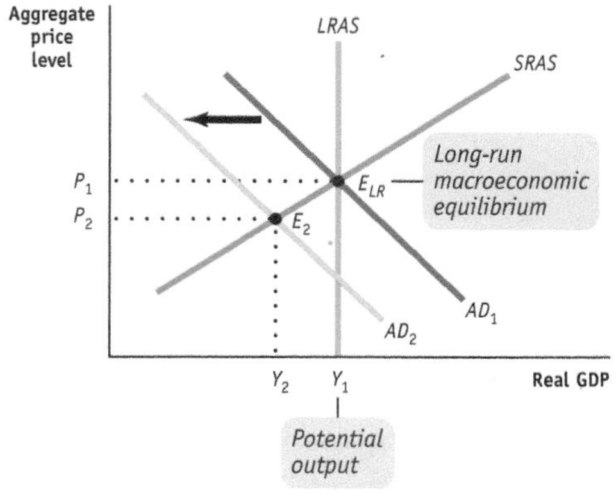

b. Aggregate demand shifts left; real GDP and the aggregate price level fall.

c. Nominal wages will decrease as a result of the recessionary gap and the decrease in the aggregate price level, leading to an increase in short-run aggregate supply. The rightward shift in the short-run aggregate supply curve moves the economy back to long-run equilibrium at potential output and a lower aggregate price level.

d. Lower government spending will decrease the government budget deficit. With less borrowing by the government, the demand for loanable funds will decrease, shifting the demand curve from D_1 to D_2 and decreasing the interest rate from r_1 to r_2 in the accompanying figure.

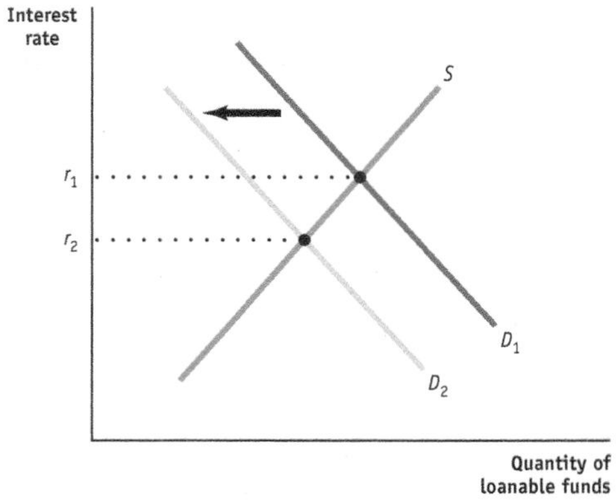

Tackle the Test: Multiple-Choice Questions

1. e
2. b
3. e
4. a
5. e

Tackle the Test: Free-Response Question

Rubric for FRQ 2 (12 points)

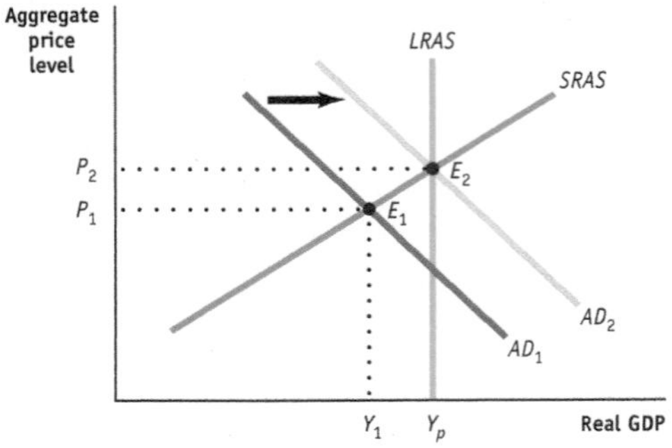

1 point: The vertical axis is labeled "Aggregate price level" or "Price level" and the horizontal axis is labeled "Real GDP."

1 point: The *AD* curve is labeled and slopes downward, the *SRAS* curve is labeled and slopes upward, and the *LRAS* curve is labeled and vertical at Y_p. The equilibrium aggregate price level and aggregate output are shown on the axes where the *AD* curve and *SRAS* curve intersect, which is to the left of the *LRAS* curve.

1 point: A new, labeled *AD* curve is shown to the right of the original *AD* curve. The new equilibrium price level and aggregate output are shown on the axes at the new equilibrium point. The new equilibrium does not need to be at potential output.

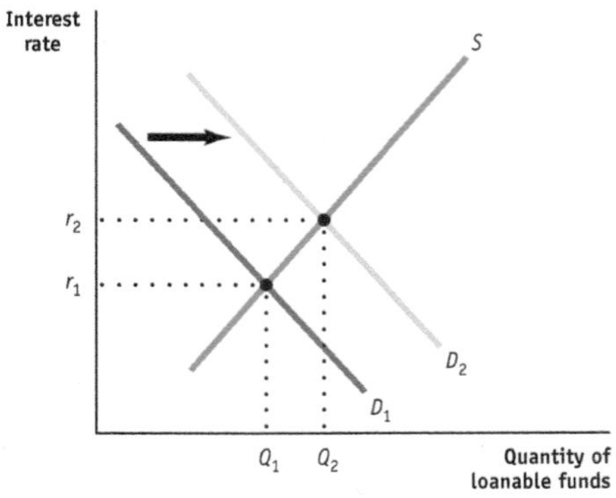

1 point: The vertical axis is labeled "Interest rate" and the horizontal axis is labeled "Quantity of loanable funds."

1 point: The demand curve is labeled and slopes downward; the supply curve is labeled and slopes upward. The equilibrium interest rate and quantity are shown on the axes at the point where the curves intersect.

1 point: The demand for loanable funds shifts to the right and the new equilibrium values are shown on the axes. The interest rate is higher.

(continued at the top of page 453)

Tackle the Test: Multiple-Choice Questions

Questions 1–5 refer to the following scenario:

The United States and Mexico are trading partners. Suppose a flu outbreak significantly decreases U.S. tourism in Mexico and causes the Mexican economy to enter a recession. Assume that the money that would have been spent by U.S. tourists in Mexico is, instead, not spent at all.

1. Which of the following occurs as a result of the recession in Mexico?
   I. Output in Mexico decreases.
   II. Aggregate demand in the United States decreases.
   III. Output in the United States decreases.
   a. I only
   b. II only
   c. III only
   d. I and II only
   e. I, II, and III

2. What is the effect of Mexico's falling income on the demand for money and the nominal interest rate in Mexico?

	Demand for money	*Nominal interest rate*
a.	increases	decreases
b.	decreases	decreases
c.	increases	increases
d.	decreases	increases
e.	increases	unchanged

3. Given what happens to the nominal interest rate, if the aggregate price level in Mexico decreases, what will happen to the real interest rate?
   a. It will increase.
   b. It will decrease.
   c. It will be unchanged.
   d. It will stabilize.
   e. It cannot be determined.

4. Suppose the aggregate price level in Mexico decreases relative to that in the United States. What is the effect of this price level change on the demand, and on the exchange rate, for Mexican pesos?

	Demand for pesos	*Exchange rate*
a.	increases	appreciates
b.	increases	depreciates
c.	decreases	appreciates
d.	decreases	depreciates
e.	decreases	is unchanged

5. If the Mexican government pursues expansionary fiscal policy in response to the recession, what will happen to aggregate demand and aggregate supply in Mexico in the short run?

	Aggregate demand	*Short-run aggregate supply*
a.	increases	increases
b.	increases	decreases
c.	decreases	increases
d.	decreases	decreases
e.	increases	is unchanged

Tackle the Test: Free-Response Questions

1. Suppose the U.S. economy is experiencing a recession.
   a. Draw a correctly labeled aggregate demand–aggregate supply graph showing the aggregate demand, short-run aggregate supply, long-run aggregate supply, equilibrium output, and aggregate price level.
   b. Assume that energy prices increase in the United States. Show the effects of this increase on the equilibrium in your graph from part a.
   c. According to your graph, how does the increase in energy prices affect unemployment and inflation in the economy?
   d. Assume the United States and Canada are the only two countries in an open economy and that energy prices have remained unchanged in Canada. Draw a correctly labeled graph of the foreign exchange market for U.S. dollars, and use it to show the effect of increased U.S. energy prices on the demand for U.S. dollars. Explain.

Rubric for FRQ 1 (12 points)

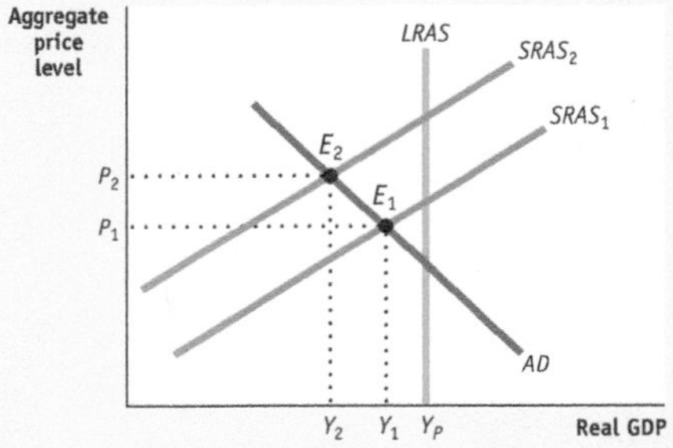

1 point: The vertical axis is labeled "Aggregate price level" and the horizontal axis is labeled "Aggregate output" or "Real GDP."

1 point: The *AD* curve slopes downward, the *SRAS* curve slopes upward, and the *LRAS* curve is vertical.

1 point: The equilibrium is found where the *SRAS* curve crosses the *AD* curve, and the equilibrium aggregate price level and aggregate output are shown on the axes at this point.

1 point: The equilibrium is to the left of the *LRAS* curve.

1 point: The *SRAS* curve shifts to the left.

1 point: The equilibrium aggregate price level and output are shown on the axes at the new equilibrium (increased aggregate price level, decreased aggregate output).

1 point: It increases unemployment.

1 point: It increases the aggregate price level (inflation).

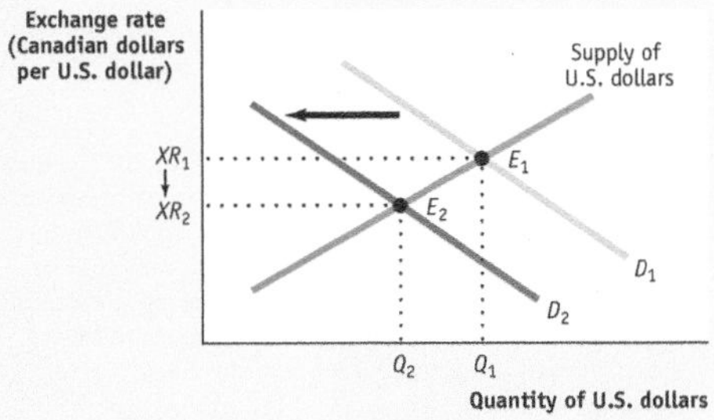

1 point: The vertical axis is labeled "Exchange rate (Canadian dollars per U.S. dollar)," and the horizontal axis is labeled "Quantity of U.S. dollars." Demand for U.S. dollars slopes downward and is labeled; supply of U.S. dollars slopes upward and is labeled.

1 point: The equilibrium exchange rate and quantity of U.S. dollars are shown on the axes at the intersection of the demand and supply curves.

1 point: The demand for U.S. dollars will decrease.

1 point: The inflation in the United States will lead to a decrease in the demand for U.S. exports (which must be purchased with U.S. dollars).

2. Assume the United States is operating below potential output.
- **a.** Draw a correctly labeled aggregate demand–aggregate supply graph showing equilibrium in the economy.
- **b.** Suppose the government decreases taxes. On your graph, show how the decrease in taxes will affect *AD, SRAS, LRAS*, equilibrium aggregate price level, and output.
- **c.** Assume the decrease in taxes led to an increased budget deficit and that the deficit spending was funded through government borrowing from the public. Use a correctly labeled graph of the market for loanable funds to show the effect of increased borrowing on the interest rate.
- **d.** Given the effect on the interest rate from part c, draw a correctly labeled graph of the foreign exchange market showing the effect of the change in the interest rate on the supply of U.S. dollars. Explain how the interest rate affects the supply of U.S. dollars.
- **e.** According to your graph from part d, what has happened to the value of the U.S. dollar? How will this affect U.S. exports and aggregate demand?

(12 points)

SECTION 8 Review

Section 8 Review Video

Module 41

1. A country's **balance of payments accounts** summarize its transactions with the rest of the world. The **balance of payments on the current account**, or the **current account**, includes the **balance of payments on goods and services** together with balances on factor income and transfers. The **merchandise trade balance**, or **trade balance**, is a frequently cited component of the balance of payments on goods and services. The **balance of payments on the financial account**, or the **financial account**, measures capital flows. By definition, the balance of payments on the current account plus the balance of payments on the financial account is zero.

2. Capital flows respond to international differences in interest rates and other rates of return; they can be usefully analyzed using an international version of the loanable funds model, which shows how a country where the interest rate would be low in the absence of capital flows sends funds to a country where the interest rate would be high in the absence of capital flows. The underlying determinants of capital flows are international differences in savings and opportunities for investment spending.

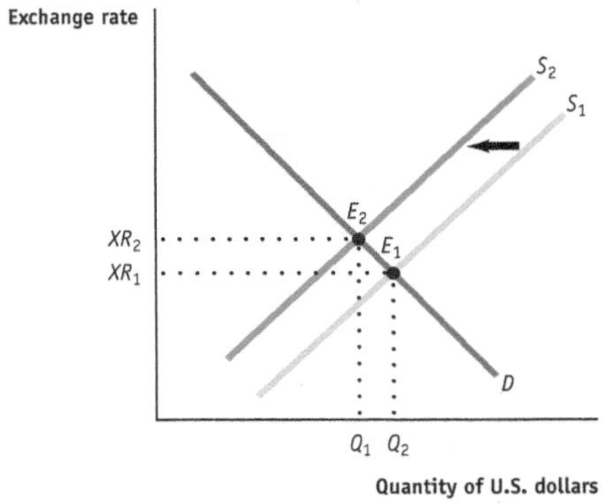

1 point: On the foreign exchange market graph, the vertical axis is labeled "Exchange rate" and the horizontal axis is labeled "Quantity of U.S. dollars."

1 point: The demand curve slopes downward, the supply curve slopes upward, and the curves are labeled. The equilibrium exchange rate and quantity are shown on the axes at the point where the two curves intersect.

1 point: The supply of U.S dollars decreases, shifting the supply curve to the left.

1 point: This occurs because the higher interest rate in the United States decreases the outflow of capital to countries with a relatively low interest rate.

1 point: The value of the U.S. dollar has increased (it has appreciated).

1 point: Both U.S. exports and aggregate demand will decline.

FOCUS **Flip It**

Encourage your students to watch the **Section 8 Review Video**, which was created as a special student review tool and is linked into the e-Book or can be found on the book's companion website.

Section 8 Review 453

Module 42

3. Currencies are traded in the **foreign exchange market**; the prices at which they are traded are **exchange rates**. When a currency rises against another currency, it **appreciates**; when it falls, it **depreciates**. The **equilibrium exchange rate** matches the quantity of that currency supplied to the foreign exchange market to the quantity demanded.
4. To correct for international differences in inflation rates, economists calculate **real exchange rates**, which multiply the exchange rate between two countries' respective currencies by the ratio of the countries' price levels. The current account responds only to changes in the real exchange rate, not the nominal exchange rate. **Purchasing power parity** is the exchange rate that makes the cost of a basket of goods and services equal in two countries. While purchasing power parity and the nominal exchange rate almost always differ, purchasing power parity is a good predictor of actual changes in the nominal exchange rate.

Module 43

5. Countries adopt different **exchange rate regimes**, rules governing exchange rate policy. The main types are **fixed exchange rates**, where the government takes action to keep the exchange rate at a target level, and **floating exchange rates**, where the exchange rate is free to fluctuate. Countries can fix exchange rates using **exchange market intervention**, which requires them to hold **foreign exchange reserves** that they use to buy any surplus of their currency. Alternatively, they can change domestic policies, especially monetary policy, to shift the demand and supply curves in the foreign exchange market. Finally, they can use **foreign exchange controls**.
6. Exchange rate policy poses a dilemma: there are economic payoffs to stable exchange rates, but the policies used to fix the exchange rate have costs. Exchange market intervention requires large reserves, and exchange controls distort incentives. If monetary policy is used to help fix the exchange rate, it isn't available to use for domestic policy.
7. Fixed exchange rates aren't always permanent commitments: countries with a fixed exchange rate sometimes engage in **devaluations** or **revaluations**. In addition to helping eliminate a surplus of domestic currency on the foreign exchange market, a devaluation increases aggregate demand. Similarly, a revaluation reduces shortages of domestic currency and reduces aggregate demand.
8. Under floating exchange rates, expansionary monetary policy works in part through the exchange rate: cutting domestic interest rates leads to a depreciation, and through that to higher exports and lower imports, which increases aggregate demand. Contractionary monetary policy has the reverse effect.
9. The fact that one country's imports are another country's exports creates a link between the business cycles in different countries. Floating exchange rates, however, may reduce the strength of that link.

Module 44

10. **Protectionism** is the practice of limiting trade to protect domestic industries. The idea is to allow domestic producers to gain enough strength to compete in global markets. Taxes on imports, known as **tariffs**, and limits of the quantities of goods that can be imported, known as **import quotas**, are the primary tools of protectionism.

Module 45

11. Most macroeconomic problems have a starting point, a pivotal event, initial effects of the event, and secondary and long-run effects of the event. A good approach is to consider these components sequentially: (1) if possible, draw a graph that illustrates the starting point; (2) show how the graph changes due to the pivotal event—often a curve shifts; (3) indicate the initial effects of the change; (4) analyze the secondary and long-run effects, as appropriate.

454 Section 8 The Open Economy: International Trade and Finance

Key Terms

Balance of payments accounts, p. 406
Balance of payments on the current account (the current account), p. 408
Balance of payments on goods and services, p. 408
Merchandise trade balance (trade balance), p. 408
Balance of payments on the financial account (the financial account), p. 409
Foreign exchange market, p. 417
Exchange rates, p. 417
Appreciates, p. 418
Depreciates, p. 418
Equilibrium exchange rate, p. 419
Real exchange rate, p. 421
Purchasing power parity, p. 423
Exchange rate regime, p. 427
Fixed exchange rate, p. 427
Floating exchange rate, p. 427
Exchange market intervention, p. 429
Foreign exchange reserves, p. 429
Foreign exchange controls, p. 429
Devaluation, p. 431
Revaluation, p. 431
Protectionism, p. 438
Tariffs, p. 438
Import quota, p. 440

AP® Exam Practice Questions

Multiple-Choice Questions

1. Which of the following transactions is counted in the U.S. current account?
   a. A French importer buys a case of California wine.
   b. An American working for a Brazilian company deposits her paycheck.
   c. An American buys a bond from a Japanese company.
   d. An American charity sends money to an African aid agency.
   e. A Chinese national buys stock in a U.S. company.
2. The difference between a country's exports and imports of goods is that country's
   a. balance of payments on its current account.
   b. balance of payments on its financial account.
   c. balance of payments on its capital account.
   d. merchandise trade balance.
   e. balance of payments on goods and services.
3. Which of the following relationships between the current account (CA) and the financial account (FA) must be true?
   a. $CA - FA = 0$
   b. $CA + FA = 0$
   c. $CA = FA$
   d. $CA = 1/FA$
   e. $(CA)(FA) = 1$
4. Which of the following is a reason for capital to flow into a country?
   a. a rapidly growing economy
   b. government budget surpluses
   c. higher savings rates
   d. lower interest rates
   e. a relatively high supply of loanable funds

Refer to the following graphs and information for Questions 5–7.

Suppose that Northlandia and Southlandia are the only two trading countries in the world, that each nation runs a balance of payments on both the current account and the financial account equal to zero, and that each nation sees the other's assets as identical to its own.

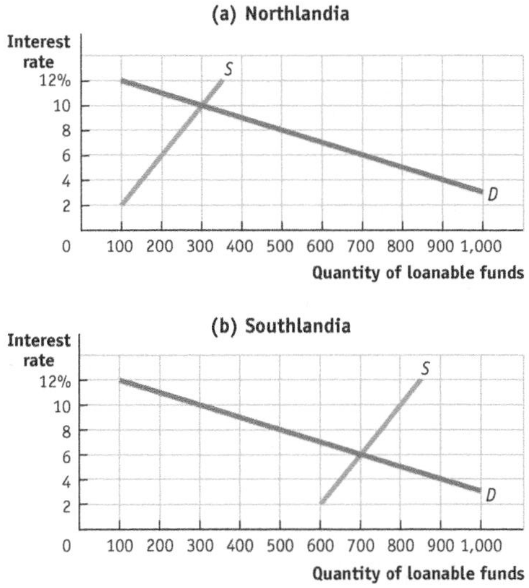

Answers to Section 8 AP® Exam Practice Questions

Multiple-Choice Questions

1. a
2. d
3. b
4. a

5. c
6. d
7. a
8. e
9. d
10. a
11. b
12. b
13. d
14. c
15. c
16. a

5. Given the situation depicted in the graphs, which of the following will happen?
a. The interest rate in Northlandia will rise.
b. The interest rate in Southlandia will fall.
c. Capital will flow into Northlandia.
d. Capital will flow into Southlandia.
e. Southlandia will experience a balance of trade deficit.

6. Which of the following will happen in Southlandia?
a. The quantity of loanable funds supplied will decrease.
b. The supply of loanable funds will increase.
c. The demand for loanable funds will decrease.
d. The supply of loanable funds will decrease.
e. The interest rate will decrease.

7. If the international equilibrium interest rate is 8%, which of the following will be true?
a. Southlandia will experience a capital outflow of 250.
b. Southlandia will experience a capital outflow of 700.
c. Northlandia will experience a capital outflow of 250.
d. Northlandia will experience a capital outflow of 300.
e. The international equilibrium quantity of loanable funds will be 1,200.

8. Which of the following is traded in a foreign exchange market?
a. imported goods only
b. exported goods only
c. both imported and exported goods
d. international stocks and bonds
e. currency

9. The price in a foreign exchange market is a(n)
a. real interest rate.
b. nominal interest rate.
c. tariff.
d. exchange rate.
e. discount rate.

Refer to the following graph and information for Questions 10–11.

The graph shows the foreign exchange market for the bern, the currency used in the country of Albernia.

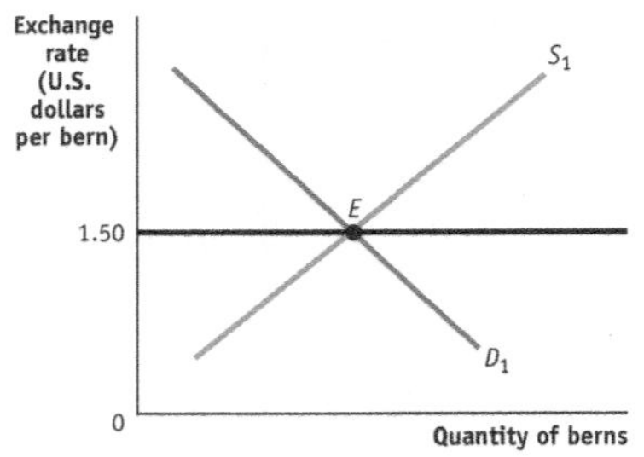

10. Given the equilibrium exchange rate on the graph, which of the following is true regarding the bern?
a. It takes $1.50 to buy a bern.
b. It takes $.75 to buy a bern.
c. It takes $.67 to buy a bern.
d. It takes 1.50 bern to buy a dollar.
e. It takes .75 bern to buy a dollar.

11. How could depreciation of the bern be shown on the graph?
a. a movement of the equilibrium exchange rate to 2
b. a movement of the equilibrium exchange rate to 1
c. a decrease in the equilibrium quantity of berns
d. a rightward shift of the demand for berns
e. a leftward shift of the supply of berns

12. Real exchange rates are adjusted for international differences in
a. exchange rates.
b. aggregate price levels.
c. GDP per capita.
d. capital flows.
e. income.

13. Which of the following will occur in the foreign exchange market as a result of capital inflow to the United States?
a. a decrease in the demand for dollars
b. a decrease in the dollar exchange rate
c. an increase in the supply of dollars
d. appreciation of the dollar
e. a decrease in the quantity of dollars exchanged

14. Which of the following is true if two countries have purchasing power parity?
a. The two countries' real GDP per capita is the same.
b. The two countries' imports equal their exports.
c. The nominal exchange rate assures that goods cost the same amount in each country.
d. There are no capital inflows or outflows between the two countries.
e. The countries' exchange rates do not appreciate or depreciate.

15. When a government lets exchange rates be determined by foreign exchange markets, it is called
a. an exchange rate regime.
b. a fixed exchange rate.
c. a floating exchange rate.
d. a market exchange rate.
e. a foreign exchange control.

16. Governments intervene to keep the value of their currency down in order to
a. make domestic goods cheaper in the world market.
b. decrease the price of imported goods.
c. promote capital inflows.
d. decrease exports.
e. reduce aggregate demand.

456 Section 8 The Open Economy: International Trade and Finance

17. A decrease in domestic interest rates will necessarily have which of the following effects in the foreign exchange market?
 a. The supply of the domestic currency will decrease.
 b. The demand for the domestic currency will decrease.
 c. The exchange rate will increase.
 d. The quantity of the domestic currency exchanged will rise.
 e. The quantity of the domestic currency exchanged will fall.

18. An import quota on a good will do which of the following?
 a. It will raise revenue for the government.
 b. It will reduce the domestic price of the good.
 c. It will raise the international price of the good.
 d. It will reduce the quantity of the good sold domestically.
 e. It will decrease domestic production of the good.

19. Which of the following is true of tariffs?
 a. They are limits on the quantity of a good that can be imported.
 b. They account for over 10% of federal government revenue in the United States.
 c. They can result in trade wars between countries.
 d. They do not protect domestic industries from competition.
 e. They decrease the price of goods.

20. The goal of protectionism is to
 a. generate revenue for the federal government.
 b. lower the price of goods for domestic consumers.
 c. increase world output through specialization and comparative advantage.
 d. decrease competition for domestic industries.
 e. raise the price of imported goods.

Free-Response Question

1. Draw a correctly labeled graph showing equilibrium in the U.S. foreign exchange market for Chinese yuan.
 a. Assume the real interest rate in China falls relative to the real interest rate in the United States. Show the impact of the change in the real interest rate on each of the following.
  i. The demand for Chinese yuan. Explain.
  ii. The value of Chinese yuan relative to the U.S. dollar.
 b. Assume that the U.S. current account balance is zero. Based on the change in the value of the yuan, will the U.S. current account balance move to a surplus, move to a deficit, or stay the same? Explain.

 (6 points)

17. b
18. d
19. c
20. d

Rubric for Free-Response Question

1 point: A foreign exchange market graph labeled "Dollar/yuan" on the vertical axis and "Quantity of yuan" on the horizontal axis, with a downward-sloping demand curve and an upward-sloping supply curve.

1 point: The equilibrium exchange rate is labeled on the vertical axis and the equilibrium quantity of yuan is labeled on the horizontal axis, and both values correspond with the intersection of the supply and demand curves.

1 point: The demand curve shifts to the left and a new, lower value of the Chinese yuan is labeled on the vertical axis to the left of the new equilibrium point.

1 point: The demand for Chinese yuan decreases because the lower real interest rate in China leads to lower returns on financial investments, which decreases capital inflow from the United States.

1 point: The U.S. current account balance will move to a deficit.

1 point: The decrease in the value of the Chinese yuan will decrease U.S. exports to China and increase U.S. imports from China, because U.S. exports become more expensive and imports from China become less expensive. These changes result in a current account deficit in the United States.

Please see page SG-3 for sample student graphs for this Free-Response Question.

SECTION 9

Behind the Demand Curve: Consumer Choice

PD Section 9 Overview

Watch the video overview of Section 9 (for teachers), which is accessible through the Teacher's e-Book, the TR-flash drive, or the book's website bcs.worthpublishers.com/krugmanap2e *(teacher log-in required).*

Section 9 looks more closely at topics related to the demand curve. The section begins with a more in-depth explanation of the law of demand. Earlier, students learned that the demand curve slopes downward. In this section, they learn WHY: the income and substitution effects. Previously, students learned that a negative relationship exists between price and quantity demanded—that is, when the price rises, people buy less, and when the price falls, people buy more. The question of HOW MUCH less or more people buy when the price changes (i.e., the concept of elasticity) is introduced in this section. Finally, the meaning and calculation of consumer surplus are covered in this section along with producer surplus and deadweight loss. These concepts are used throughout the course to evaluate efficiency in market and market structure models.

Topics that your students will study in Section 9 are:

- how the income effect and substitution effect explain the downward-sloping demand curve.
- elasticity as a measure of responsiveness to changes in price or income.
- price elasticity of demand as buyer responsiveness to a price change.
- how to calculate price elasticity of demand.
- interpreting price elasticity of demand (e.g., elastic vs. inelastic demand).
- the relationship between elasticity and total revenue.
- the determinants of price elasticity of demand.
- the calculation and interpretation of cross-price elasticity (e.g., substitutes and complements).
- the calculation and interpretation of income elasticity of demand (e.g., normal vs. inferior goods).
- price elasticity of supply as the seller responsiveness to a price change.
- how to calculate price elasticity of supply.
- the determinants of price elasticity of supply.
- the calculation and meaning of consumer and producer surplus.
- the use of total surplus to evaluate efficiency in markets.
- the difference between efficiency and equity.
- how taxes can affect total surplus and create deadweight loss.
- the relationship between price elasticities and tax incidence.
- total and marginal utility and utility maximization.
- the principle of diminishing marginal utility.
- how marginal analysis is used to determine optimal consumption.

Alignment to AP® Microeconomics Course Description

Microeconomics II. The Nature and Function of Product Markets: 55–70%

AP® Outline	Module
A. Supply and demand	46: Income Effects, Substitution Effects, and Elasticity 47: Interpreting Price Elasticity of Demand 48: Other Important Elasticities 49: Consumer and Producer Surplus 50: Efficiency and Deadweight Loss
B. Theory of consumer choice	51: Utility Maximization

Pacing Guide

Module	Standard Teaching Days	Block Teaching Days
46	1	1
47	2	1
48	1	1
49	2	1
50	2	1
51	2	1
Section 9 Assessment	1	½
Total	**11**	**6½**

TRM Section Resources

All section resources may be accessed through the Teacher's e-Book, the TR-flash drive, or the book's website bcs.worthpublishers.com/krugmanap2e *(teacher log-in required)*

Section 9 PD Video (for Teachers)

Module 46

Module 46 Sample Lecture
Worksheet 46.1: Income and Substitution Effects
Worksheet 46.2: Normal and Inferior Goods
Worksheet 46.3: Elasticity Analogy
Worksheet 46.4: Elasticity of Demand Calculation
Worksheet 46.5: Elasticity of Demand
Worksheet 46.6: Practice for Elasticity of Demand
Exit Slip: Module 46

Module 47

Module 47 Sample Lecture
Worksheet 47.1: Total Revenue and Elasticity
Worksheet 47.2: Elasticity Practice
Worksheet 47.3: Higher or Lower Elasticity?
Worksheet 47.4: College Tuition and Elasticity
Exit Slip: Module 47

Module 48

Module 48 Sample Lecture
Worksheet 48.1: Drawing Perfect Elasticity and Inelasticity
Worksheet 48.2: Elasticities
Worksheet 48.3: Elasticity and Oil
Exit Slip: Module 48

Module 49

Module 49 Sample Lecture
Worksheet 49.1: Practicing Consumer Surplus
Worksheet 49.2: Consumer Surplus Questions
Worksheet 49.3: Starbucks and Producer Surplus
Worksheet 49.4: Producer Surplus
Worksheet 49.5: You and the Surplus
Worksheet 49.6: Consumer and Producer Surplus Review
Exit Slip: Module 49

Module 50

Module 50 Sample Lecture
Worksheet 50.1: Efficiency of Markets with Surpluses
Worksheet 50.2: Consumer and Producer Surplus
Worksheet 50.3: Tax Systems
Worksheet 50.4: Excise Taxes and Surplus
Worksheet 50.5: Deadweight Loss
Worksheet 50.6: Calculating Deadweight Loss
Worksheet 50.7: Costs and Benefits of Taxation
Exit Slip: Module 50

Module 51

Module 51 Sample Lecture
Worksheet 51.1: Utility
Worksheet 51.2: Marginal Utility per Dollar
Worksheet 51.3: Utility Maximization
Exit Slip: Module 51
Section 9 Review Video (for students)

St. Louis Federal Reserve Bank Resources

Many of the Federal Reserve Banks have educational departments that offer helpful resources for studying economics. Members of the Educators Advisory Board of the St. Louis Federal Reserve Bank have handpicked some of their best resources for use with your AP® Economics students. References to these resources are included in the marginal notes. A complete list of the St. Louis Fed resources for each section with the corresponding URL (as of fall 2014) can be found in the TRM.

NOTE We have included a number of links to useful videos and articles in the marginal notes in this section. Although all are active at the time of publication, we know that some may expire over the next few years. If a link is no longer active, you may wish to search for a similar article or video to illustrate the same point. We may also periodically refresh resources on the book's companion website.

PD Section 9 Overview

Watch the video overview of Section 9 (for teachers), which is accessible through the Teacher's e-Book, the TR-flash drive, or the book's companion website bcs.worthpublishers.com/krugmanap2e (teacher log-in required).

FOCUS Active Learning

Have students read Chapter 4 of *Economics by Example* to explore more real-world examples of diminishing marginal utility and the price elasticity of demand.

SECTION 9

Behind the Demand Curve: Consumer Choice

Paying Whatever It Takes for Health

Panic was the only word to describe the situation at hospitals, clinics, and nursing homes across the United States in October 2004. Early that month, Chiron Corporation, one of only two suppliers of flu vaccine for the entire U.S. market, announced that contamination problems would force the closure of its manufacturing plant. With that closure, the U.S. supply of vaccine for the 2004–2005 flu season was suddenly cut in half, from 100 million to 50 million doses. Because making flu vaccine is a costly and time-consuming process, no more doses could be made to replace Chiron's lost output. And since every country jealously guards its supply of flu vaccine for its own citizens, none could be obtained from other countries.

Every year the flu kills approximately 36,000 Americans and sends another 200,000 to the hospital. But the flu vaccine shortfall of 2004 threatened to make matters worse. As news of it spread, there was a rush to get the shots. People lined up in the middle of the night at the few locations that had somehow obtained the vaccine and were offering it at a reasonable price. Meanwhile, some pharmaceutical distributors—the companies that obtain vaccine from manufacturers and then distribute it to hospitals and pharmacies—detected a profit-making opportunity in the frenzy. One company, Med-Stat, which normally charged $8.50 for a dose, began charging $90, more than 10 times the normal price. A survey of pharmacists found that price-gouging was fairly widespread.

Med-Stat judged, correctly, that consumers of the vaccine were relatively *unresponsive* to price; that is, the large increase in the price of the vaccine left the quantity demanded by consumers relatively unchanged.

Clearly, the demand for flu vaccine is unusual in this respect. For many, getting vaccinated meant the difference between life and death. Let's consider a very different and less urgent scenario. Suppose, for example, that the supply of a particular type of breakfast cereal was halved due to manufacturing problems. It would be extremely unlikely, if not impossible, to find a consumer willing to pay 10 times the original price for a box of this particular cereal. In other words, consumers of breakfast cereal are much more responsive to price than

AP Photo/Pat Wellenbach

consumers of flu vaccine. But how do we define *responsiveness?* Economists measure consumers' responsiveness to price with a particular number, called the *price elasticity of demand.*

In this section we take a closer look at the supply and demand model developed in Section 2 and present several economic concepts used to evaluate market results. We will see how the price elasticity of demand is calculated and why it is the best measure of how the quantity demanded responds to changes in price. We will then discover a family of related concepts, including the *income elasticity of demand* and the *price elasticity of supply.* We will look at how the price and the quantity bought and sold in a market affect consumer, producer, and overall welfare. And we will consider how consumers make choices to maximize their individual *utility,* the term economists use to describe "satisfaction."

458 Section 9 Behind the Demand Curve: Consumer Choice

© Joe Belanger/Alamy

MODULE 46 Income Effects, Substitution Effects, and Elasticity

In this Module, you will learn to:

- Explain the law of demand on the basis of income and substitution effects
- Calculate the price elasticity of demand, a measure of consumer responsiveness to price changes

Explaining the Law of Demand

In Section 2 we introduced the demand curve and the law of demand. To this point, we have accepted that the demand curve has a negative slope. And we have drawn demand curves that are somewhere in the middle between flat and steep (with a negative slope). In this module, we present more detail about why demand curves slope downward and what the slope of the demand curve tells us. We begin with the *income* and *substitution effects*, which explain why the demand curve has a negative slope.

The Substitution Effect

When the price of a good increases, an individual will normally consume less of that good and more of other goods. Correspondingly, when the price of a good decreases, an individual will normally consume more of that good and less of other goods. This explains why the individual demand curve, which relates an individual's consumption of a good to the price of that good, normally slopes downward—that is, it obeys the law of demand.

An alternative way to think about why demand curves slope downward is to focus on opportunity costs. For simplicity, let's suppose there are only two goods between which to choose. When the price of one good decreases, an individual doesn't have to give up as many units of the other good in order to buy one more unit of the first good. That makes it attractive to buy more of the good whose price has gone down. Conversely, when the price of one good increases, one must give up more units of the other good to buy one more unit of the first good, so consuming that good becomes less attractive and the consumer buys fewer. The change in the quantity demanded as the good that has become relatively cheaper is substituted for the good that has become relatively more expensive is known as the **substitution effect**. When a good absorbs only a

The **substitution effect** of a change in the price of a good is the change in the quantity of that good demanded as the consumer substitutes the good that has become relatively cheaper for the good that has become relatively more expensive.

PD To prepare for teaching this lesson, you may want to consult the **Module 46 Sample Lecture** in the TRM.

OPEN & CLOSE Start Here

Give students the following scenario: Imagine you have $5 to spend each day and every morning you buy a cup of coffee from your favorite coffee shop for $2. One morning you arrive to discover that the price of a cup of coffee has been raised to $4. What would you do? *Some students will answer that they would still buy a cup of coffee, but many will say otherwise.* Ask them, "WHY?" *Help students get at the idea that they will buy something else—something cheaper—instead (the substitution effect) AND that they won't have much left to spend on other things if they spend $4 on coffee (the income effect).*

TEACH Connect It

In Section 2, students first learned about the law of demand. The idea was presented as intuitively obvious. We all "know" that we buy more when the price is lower and less when the price is higher. In this module, we get more specific about WHY people buy less or more when a price changes. When the price of a good changes, two things are affected: the opportunity cost (what we give up) and our purchasing power. These two changes lead to the substitution and income effects. For students who have studied macroeconomics, connecting the income effect to what they learned about nominal versus real values can be helpful.

FOCUS Active Learning

TRM For a review exercise on the demand curve, refer students to **Worksheet 46.1 (Income and Substitution Effects)** from the TRM.

TEACH Teach It

Remind your students of the definition of normal and inferior goods from Section 2 (*income and demand move in the same direction for normal goods and in opposite directions for inferior goods*). Make sure students understand that the substitution effect works the same way for all goods because opportunity cost always increases when price increases (and decreases when the price decreases). However, make sure students understand that the income effect is different for normal and inferior goods.

- A price increase will decrease purchasing power (in effect, it decreases available income). And we know a decrease in income causes us to decrease purchases of normal goods and increase purchases of inferior goods.
- A price decrease will increase purchasing power (in effect, it increases available income). And we know an increase in income causes us to increase purchases of normal goods and decrease purchases of inferior goods.

Thus, for normal goods, the income and substitution effects move in the same direction. For inferior goods, the income and substitution effects move in the opposite direction (i.e., the income effect partially offsets the substitution effect).

small share of the typical consumer's income, as with pillowcases and swim goggles, the substitution effect is essentially the sole explanation of why the market demand curve slopes downward. However, there are some goods, like food and housing, that account for a substantial share of many consumers' incomes. In such cases, another effect, called the *income effect,* also comes into play.

AP® Exam Tip

The substitution effect comes from a change in the price of one good relative to the price of another good. The income effect comes from a change in purchasing power, which can result from a change in one or more prices or from a change in the actual income received.

The Income Effect

Consider the case of a family that spends half of its income on rental housing. Now suppose that the price of housing increases everywhere. This will have a substitution effect on the family's demand: other things equal, the family will have an incentive to consume less housing—say, by moving to a smaller apartment—and more of other goods. But, in a real sense, the family will also be made poorer by that higher housing price—its income will buy less housing than before. When income is adjusted to reflect its true purchasing power, it is called *real income,* in contrast to *money income* or *nominal income,* which has not been adjusted. And this reduction in a consumer's real income will have an additional effect, beyond the substitution effect, on the family's consumption choices, including its consumption of housing. The **income effect** of a change in the price of a good is the change in the quantity of that good demanded that results from a change in the overall purchasing power of the consumer's income when the price of the good changes.

The **income effect** of a change in the price of a good is the change in the quantity of that good demanded that results from a change in the consumer's purchasing power when the price of the good changes.

It's possible to give more precise definitions of the substitution effect and the income effect of a price change, but for most purposes, there are only two things you need to know about the distinction between these two effects.

First, for the majority of goods and services, the income effect is not important and has no significant effect on individual consumption. Thus, most market demand curves slope downward solely because of the substitution effect—end of story.

Second, when it matters at all, the income effect usually reinforces the substitution effect. That is, when the price of a good that absorbs a substantial share of income rises, consumers of that good become a bit poorer because their purchasing power falls. And the vast majority of goods are *normal* goods, goods for which demand decreases when income falls. So this effective reduction in income leads to a reduction in the quantity demanded and reinforces the substitution effect.

FYI Giffen Goods

In the mid-nineteenth century, when Ireland was a desperately poor country, it was claimed that the Irish would eat *more* potatoes when the price of potatoes went up. That is, some observers claimed that Ireland's demand curve for potatoes sloped upward rather than downward.

Can this happen? In theory, yes. If Irish demand for potatoes actually sloped upward, it would have been a real-life case of a "Giffen good," named after a nineteenth-century statistician who thought (probably wrongly) that he saw an upward-sloping demand curve in some data he was studying.

Here's the story. Suppose that there is some good that absorbs a large share of consumers' budgets and that this good is also *inferior*—people demand less of it when their income rises. The classic supposed example, as you might guess, was potatoes in Ireland, back when potatoes were an inferior good—they were what poor people ate—and when the Irish were very poor.

Now suppose that the price of potatoes increases. *Other things equal,* this would cause people to substitute other goods for potatoes. But other things are not equal: given the higher price of potatoes, people are poorer. And this *increases* the demand for potatoes, because potatoes are an inferior good.

If this income effect outweighs the substitution effect, a rise in the price of potatoes would increase the quantity demanded; the law of demand would not hold.

In a way the point of this story—which has never been validated in any real situation, nineteenth-century Ireland included—is how unlikely such an event is. The law of demand really is a law, with few exceptions.

FOCUS Active Learning

TRM Ask students to complete **Worksheet 46.2 (Normal and Inferior Goods)** from the TRM for practice with normal and inferior goods.

However, in the case of an *inferior* good, a good for which demand increases when income falls, the income and substitution effects work in opposite directions. Although the substitution effect decreases the quantity of any good demanded as its price increases, the income effect of a price increase for an inferior good is an *increase* in the quantity demanded. This makes sense because the price increase lowers the real income of the consumer, and as real income falls, the demand for an inferior good increases.

If a good were so inferior that the income effect exceeded the substitution effect, a price increase would lead to an increase in the quantity demanded. There is controversy over whether such goods, known as "Giffen goods," exist at all. If they do, they are very rare. You can generally assume that the income effect for an inferior good is smaller than the substitution effect, and so a price increase will lead to a decrease in the quantity demanded.

Defining and Measuring Elasticity

As we saw in Section 1, *dependent variables* respond to changes in *independent variables*. For example, if two variables are negatively related and the independent variable increases, the dependent variable will respond by decreasing. But often the important question is not whether the variables are negatively or positively related, but how responsive the dependent variable is to changes in the independent variable (that is, *by how much* will the dependent variable change?). If price increases, we know that quantity demanded will decrease (that is the *law of demand*). The question in this context is *by how much* will quantity demanded decrease if price goes up?

Economists use the concept of *elasticity* to measure the responsiveness of one variable to changes in another. For example, *price elasticity of demand* measures the responsiveness of quantity demanded to changes in price—something a firm considering changing its price would certainly want to know! Elasticity can be used to measure responsiveness using any two related variables. We will start by looking at the price elasticity of demand and then move on to other types of elasticities commonly used by economists.

Think back to the opening example of the flu shot panic. In order for Flunomics, a hypothetical flu vaccine distributor, to know whether it could raise its revenue by significantly raising the price of its flu vaccine, it would have to know whether the price increase would decrease the quantity demanded by a lot or a little. That is, it would have to know the price elasticity of demand for flu vaccinations.

AP® Exam Tip

Elasticity often appears on the AP® exam. Make sure you are able to calculate and interpret elasticity information.

Calculating the Price Elasticity of Demand

Figure 46.1 on the next page shows a hypothetical demand curve for flu vaccinations. At a price of $20 per vaccination, consumers would demand 10 million vaccinations per year (point *A*); at a price of $21, the quantity demanded would fall to 9.9 million vaccinations per year (point *B*).

Figure 46.1, then, tells us the change in the quantity demanded for a particular change in the price. But how can we turn this into a measure of price responsiveness? The answer is to calculate the price elasticity of demand. The **price elasticity of demand** compares the *percent change in quantity demanded* to the *percent change in price* as we move along the demand curve. As we'll see later, economists use percent changes to get a measure that doesn't depend on the units involved (say, a child-sized dose versus an adult-sized dose of vaccine). But before we get to that, let's look at how elasticity is calculated.

To calculate the price elasticity of demand, we first calculate the *percent change in the quantity demanded* and the corresponding *percent change in the price* as we move along the demand curve. These are defined as follows:

The **price elasticity of demand** is the ratio of the percent change in the quantity demanded to the percent change in the price as we move along the demand curve (dropping the minus sign).

(46-1) $$\%\text{ change in quantity demanded} = \frac{\text{Change in quantity demanded}}{\text{Initial quantity demanded}} \times 100$$

and

(46-2) $$\%\text{ change in price} = \frac{\text{Change in price}}{\text{Initial price}} \times 100$$

TEACH Teach It

Elasticity refers to the responsiveness of one variable to changes in another. It can be used to measure the responsiveness of any dependent variable to changes in an independent variable. It is helpful to introduce elasticity as a general concept. If students understand the concept, they are less likely to think they need to memorize four formulae or learn four different things (recall that the AP course includes four elasticities: price elasticity of demand, price elasticity of supply, income elasticity, and cross-price elasticity).

Before starting with price elasticity of demand, discuss a "noneconomic" elasticity with students—for example, the "temperature elasticity of ice cream." Students will understand that the quantity of ice cream consumed is related to the temperature outside. We know that when it is hot, people buy more ice cream, and when it is cold, people buy less ice cream. The question that elasticity answers is HOW MUCH more or less ice cream will people buy when the temperature changes. The temperature elasticity of demand for ice cream measures the specific responsiveness of ice cream consumption to changes in the temperature.

FOCUS Active Learning

TRM Refer your class to **Worksheet 46.3 (Elasticity Analogy)** from the TRM for a group exercise on elasticity. For this activity, you will need a large supply of different-sized rubber bands.

St. Louis Federal Reserve Bank Resources

"Higher Gasoline Prices: Temporary or Time to Buy a Hybrid?," ***Page One Economics*** **(September 2012)**

When gasoline prices spike, drivers may wonder whether the high prices are temporary or permanent. Will prices eventually return to the lower levels of the past? Or is it time for drivers to alter their driving habits, maybe by buying a hybrid car? Students can read this issue for a discussion of factors that might influence such a decision.

TEACH Teach It

Students learn to calculate price elasticity of demand in this module, although the interpretation of the calculation is not introduced until the next module. Before moving on to interpreting elasticity values, make sure students understand the general formula for calculating elasticity.

Elasticity is always the percentage change in the dependent variable divided by the percentage change in the independent variable:

$$E = \frac{\text{\% Change dependent}}{\text{\% Change independent}}$$

For price elasticity of demand, $E_d = \dfrac{\text{\% change } Q_d}{\text{\% change in } P}$

TEACH Connect It

Price elasticity of demand connects back to the law of demand introduced in Section 2. Point out that the law of demand identifies an inverse relationship between price and quantity demanded. This familiar relationship is why the value of price elasticity of demand is often referred to without a negative sign (even though we know, based on the law of demand, that the value will be negative because price and quantity demanded are inversely related). However, for simplicity and because we all KNOW it must be negative, economists often use the absolute value (i.e., drop the negative) FOR PRICE ELASTICITY OF DEMAND ONLY. For later elasticities, whether elasticity is positive or negative is very important!

TEACH Connect It

Note that Figure 46.1 shows a change in quantity demanded as a movement along an existing demand curve, caused by a change in price (and NOT a change in demand), as students learned in Section 2. Make sure students remember that price and quantity demanded are the two related variables measured by price elasticity of demand. "Demand" is not a variable (it is a relationship).

Figure 46.1 The Demand for Vaccinations

At a price of $20 per vaccination, the quantity of vaccinations demanded is 10 million per year (point *A*). When price rises to $21 per vaccination, the quantity demanded falls to 9.9 million vaccinations per year (point *B*). With the price elasticity of demand, one can measure this sort of influence of price changes on the quantity demanded.

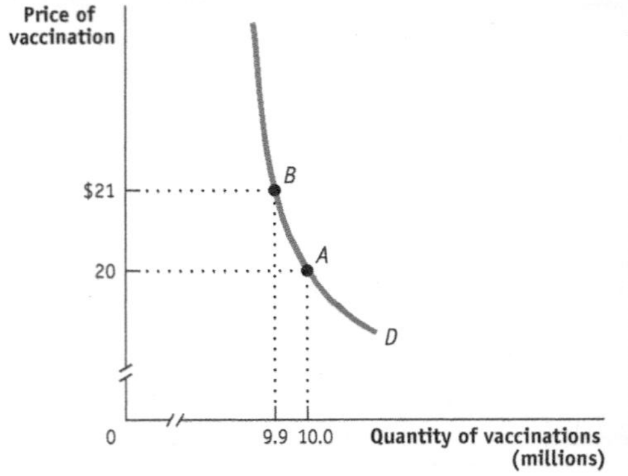

In Figure 46.1, we see that when the price rises from $20 to $21, the quantity demanded falls from 10 million to 9.9 million vaccinations, yielding a change in the quantity demanded of 0.1 million vaccinations. So the percent change in the quantity demanded is

$$\text{\% change in quantity demanded} = \frac{-0.1 \text{ million vaccinations}}{10 \text{ million vaccinations}} \times 100 = -1\%$$

The initial price is $20 and the change in the price is $1, so the percent change in the price is

$$\text{\% change in price} = \frac{\$1}{\$20} \times 100 = 5\%$$

To calculate the price elasticity of demand, we find the ratio of the percent change in the quantity demanded to the percent change in the price:

$$\textbf{(46-3)} \quad \text{Price elasticity of demand} = \frac{\text{\% change in quantity demanded}}{\text{\% change in price}}$$

In Figure 46.1, the price elasticity of demand is therefore

$$\text{Price elasticity of demand} = \frac{1\%}{5\%} = 0.2$$

The *law of demand* says that demand curves slope downward, so price and quantity demanded always move in opposite directions. In other words, a positive percent change in price (a rise in price) leads to a negative percent change in the quantity demanded; a negative percent change in price (a fall in price) leads to a positive percent change in the quantity demanded. This means that the price elasticity of demand, in strictly mathematical terms, is a negative number. However, it is inconvenient to repeatedly write a minus sign. So when economists talk about the price elasticity of demand, they usually drop the minus sign and report the absolute value of the price elasticity of demand. In this case, for example, economists would usually say "the price elasticity of demand is 0.2," taking it for granted that you understand they mean *minus* 0.2. We follow this convention here.

The larger the price elasticity of demand, the more responsive the quantity demanded is to the price. When the price elasticity of demand is large—when consumers change

AP® Exam Tip

Be sure to use *absolute values* when computing the price elasticity of demand.

FOCUS Graph It

Figure 46.1 shows the change in quantity demanded (from 10.0 to 9.9) when price increases from $20 to $21. Price elasticity of demand is the percentage change in quantity demanded divided by the percentage change in price. Some students may not recall how to compute a percentage change between two numbers. Have them think about the "new" price and the "old" price and maybe this mnemonic will be helpful: N-OOO!

"New – Old Over Old" = N-OOO! (*Note:* The "!" is added to reflect enthusiasm for fractions.)

$$\text{Percentage change in price} = \frac{\text{(New price} - \text{Old price)}}{\text{Old price}}$$

$$\frac{(21-20)}{20} = \frac{1}{20} = 0.5$$

$$\text{Percentage change in quantity} = \frac{\text{(New quantity} - \text{Old quantity)}}{\text{Old quantity}}$$

$$\frac{(9.9-10)}{10} = \frac{-.1}{10} = -.01$$

$$\text{Price elasticity of demand} = \frac{-1\%}{5\%} = 0.2$$

462 Section 9 Behind the Demand Curve: Consumer Choice

their quantity demanded by a large percentage compared with the percent change in the price—economists say that demand is highly elastic.

As we'll see shortly, a price elasticity of 0.2 indicates a small response of quantity demanded to price. That is, the quantity demanded will fall by a relatively small amount when price rises. This is what economists call *inelastic* demand. And in the next module we'll see why inelastic demand was exactly what Flunomics needed for its strategy to increase revenue by raising the price of its flu vaccines.

An Alternative Way to Calculate Elasticities: The Midpoint Method

We've seen that price elasticity of demand compares the *percent change in quantity demanded* with the *percent change in price.* When we look at some other elasticities, which we will do shortly, we'll see why it is important to focus on percent changes. But at this point we need to discuss a technical issue that arises when you calculate percent changes in variables and how economists deal with it.

The best way to understand the issue is with a real example. Suppose you were trying to estimate the price elasticity of demand for gasoline by comparing gasoline prices and consumption in different countries. Because of high taxes, gasoline usually costs about three times as much per gallon in Europe as it does in the United States. So what is the percent difference between U.S. and European gas prices?

Well, it depends on which way you measure it. Because the price of gasoline in Europe is approximately three times higher than in the United States, it is 200 percent higher. Because the price of gasoline in the United States is one-third as high as in Europe, it is 66.7 percent lower.

In our previous example, we found an elasticity of demand for vaccinations of 0.200 when considering a movement from point *A* to point *B*. However, when going from point *B* to point *A*, the same elasticity formula would indicate an elasticity of 0.212. This is a nuisance: we'd like to have an elasticity measure that doesn't depend on the direction of change. A good way to avoid computing different elasticities for rising and falling prices is to use the *midpoint method* (sometimes called the *arc method*).

The **midpoint method** replaces the usual definition of the percent change in a variable, *X*, with a slightly different definition:

$$\textbf{(46-4)}\quad \%\text{ change in } X = \frac{\text{Change in } X}{\text{Average value of } X} \times 100$$

where the average value of *X* is defined as

$$\text{Average value of } X = \frac{\text{Starting value of } X + \text{Final value of } X}{2}$$

When calculating the price elasticity of demand using the midpoint method, both the percent change in the price and the percent change in the quantity demanded are found using average values in this way. To see how this method works, suppose you have the following data for chocolate bars:

	Price	Quantity demanded
Situation A	$0.90	1,100
Situation B	$1.10	900

To calculate the percent change in quantity going from situation A to situation B, we compare the change in the quantity demanded—a fall of 200 units—with the *average* of the quantity demanded in the two situations. So we calculate

$$\%\text{ change in quantity demanded} = \frac{-200}{(1{,}100 + 900)/2} \times 100 = \frac{-200}{1{,}000} \times 100 = -20\%$$

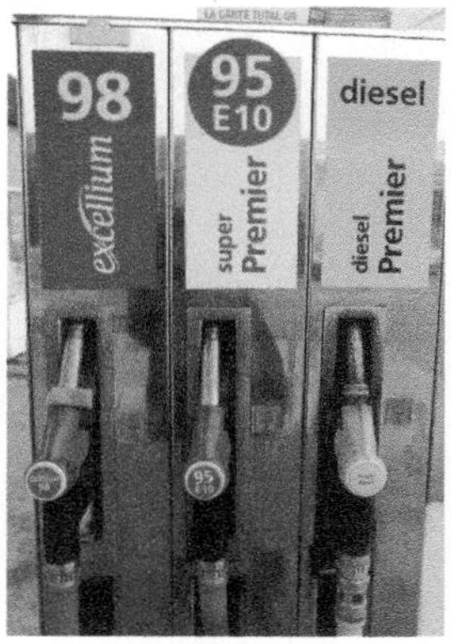

CHARLES PLATIAU/Reuters/Corbis

AP® Exam Tip

The midpoint formula yields the same elasticity for a specified range regardless of the direction of the change in price.

The **midpoint method** is a technique for calculating the percent change by dividing the change in a variable by the average, or midpoint, of the initial and final values of that variable.

FOCUS Active Learning

TRM Refer students to **Worksheet 46.4 (Elasticity of Demand Calculation)** from the TRM for an exercise on elasticity calculation.

TEACH Teach It

The funny thing about elasticity computations is that they can change if the new and old prices (or quantities) are reversed.

Example: If a variable goes from a value of 100 to a value of 110, this represents a 10% increase. But if the variable were to go from a value of 110 to a value of 100, it is a 9.1% decrease.

Because of this, the value of price elasticity changes along a demand curve, depending on whether the price is rising or falling. To account for this, economists sometimes use the average price and average quantity between two points on a demand curve. This method is called the *midpoint method.*

$$\text{Percentage change in price} = \frac{(\text{New price} - \text{Old price})}{\text{Average price}}$$

$$\text{Percentage change in quantity} = \frac{(\text{New quantity} - \text{Old quantity})}{\text{Average quantity}}$$

Example: The price of a college's tuition increases from $20,000 to $22,000 per year. The college discovers that the entering class of first-year students declined from 500 to 450.

$$\%\Delta P = \frac{(\text{New price} - \text{Old price})}{\text{Average price}} = \frac{(\$2{,}000)}{\$21{,}000} = 9.5\%$$

$$\%\Delta Q_d = \frac{(\text{New quantity} - \text{Old quantity})}{\text{Average quantity}} = \frac{(-50)}{475} = -10.5\%$$

$$E_d = \frac{9.5\%}{10.5\%} = 0.90$$

TEACH AP® Exam Tip

Which elasticity formula should students use on the AP® exam? Finding a solution to a particular problem might only be possible (or might be much easier) using one approach or the other. For example, the available information in a problem or the multiple-choice answers might require one of the two approaches. Students should be comfortable using either. But if a question does not specify which formula to use, students will receive credit for a correct answer using either approach.

TEACH AP® Exam Tip

The use of calculators is not permitted on the AP® Economics exams, but recent exams have asked students to make very simple calculations. So it will likely pay dividends for students to practice some elasticity computations. Make sure they realize that since elasticity is calculated as a percentage change divided by a percentage change, the percentage changes cancel each other out and the resulting value for elasticity is NOT a percentage.

FOCUS Test It

1. Why do economists often ignore the negative sign when discussing elasticity of demand? *Because we all know there is an inverse relationship between price and quantity demanded (the law of demand), it is easier to discuss price elasticity of demand values without referencing the negative sign.*

2. Why might someone prefer to use the midpoint formula for calculating elasticity of demand? *Because it gets the same value for a given price change along a demand curve whether price increases or decreases.*

TEACH Teach It

TRM Dr. Mary J. McGlasson's video "Episode 16: Elasticity of Demand" discusses price elasticity of demand (see econextras video list with hyperlinks on the bcs and TRFD). Refer students to **Worksheet 46.5 (Elasticity of Demand)** from the TRM for questions related to this video.

FOCUS Test It

1. Pesto Pizza raises the price of a pizza from \$10 to \$14. Within a week, sales of pizza go from 200 to 100. Use the midpoint formula to calculate the price elasticity of demand. In the next section, you will learn what your answer means!

$$\frac{\frac{(200-100)}{(300/2)}}{\frac{(14-10)}{24/2}} = \frac{100/150}{4/12} = \frac{0.66}{0.33} = 2$$

2. The ice cream store on the boardwalk sells ice cream cones for \$2.50. At that price, it sells 100 ice cream cones a day. When it raises the price to \$3.50, the store sells 75 ice cream cones. Calculate the elasticity of demand for ice cream cones.

$$E_d = \frac{\frac{(100-75)}{(100+75)/2}}{\frac{(3.50-2.50)}{(2.50+3.50)/2}} = \frac{25/87.5}{0.33} = .29/.33 = 0.88$$

In the same way, we calculate the percent change in price as

$$\%\text{ change in price} = \frac{\$0.20}{(\$0.90 + \$1.10)/2} \times 100 = \frac{\$0.20}{\$1.00} \times 100 = 20\%$$

So in this case we would calculate the price elasticity of demand to be

$$\text{Price elasticity of demand} = \frac{\%\text{ change in quantity demanded}}{\%\text{ change in price}} = \frac{20\%}{20\%} = 1$$

again dropping the minus sign.

The important point is that we would get the same result, a price elasticity of demand of 1, whether we went up the demand curve from situation A to situation B or down from situation B to situation A.

To arrive at a more general formula for price elasticity of demand, suppose that we have data for two points on a demand curve. At point 1 the quantity demanded and the price are (Q_1, P_1); at point 2 they are (Q_2, P_2). Then the formula for calculating the price elasticity of demand is:

$$\text{(46-5)}\quad \text{Price elasticity of demand} = \frac{\dfrac{Q_2 - Q_1}{(Q_1 + Q_2)/2}}{\dfrac{P_2 - P_1}{(P_1 + P_2)/2}}$$

As before, when reporting a price elasticity of demand calculated by the midpoint method, we drop the minus sign and report the absolute value.

FYI Estimating Elasticities

You might think it's easy to estimate price elasticities of demand from real-world data: just compare percent changes in prices with percent changes in quantities demanded. Unfortunately, it's rarely that simple because changes in price aren't the only thing affecting changes in the quantity demanded: other factors—such as changes in income, changes in population, and changes in the prices of other goods—shift the demand curve, thereby changing the quantity demanded at any given price. To estimate price elasticities of demand, economists must use careful statistical analysis to separate the influence of these different factors, holding other things equal.

The most comprehensive effort to estimate price elasticities of demand was a mammoth study by the economists Hendrik S. Houthakker and Lester D. Taylor. Some of their results are summarized in **Table 46.1**. These estimates show a wide range of price elasticities. There are some goods, like eggs, for which demand hardly responds at all to changes in the price; there are other goods, most notably foreign travel, for which the quantity demanded is very sensitive to the price.

Notice that Table 46.1 is divided into two parts: inelastic and elastic demand. We'll explain the significance of that division in the next section.

Table 46.1 Some Estimated Price Elasticities of Demand

Good	Price elasticity of demand
Inelastic demand	
Eggs	0.1
Beef	0.4
Stationery	0.5
Gasoline	0.5
Elastic demand	
Housing	1.2
Restaurant meals	2.3
Airline travel	2.4
Foreign travel	4.1

Source: Hendrick S. Houthakker and Lester D. Taylor, *Consumer Demand in the United States, 1929–1970* (Cambridge: Harvard University Press, 1970).

FOCUS Active Learning

TRM Have students watch the Khan Academy video "Price Elasticity of Demand" (see econextras video list with hyperlinks on the bcs and TRFD). Although lengthy, it thoroughly explains elasticity of demand and will help students see the connections between the demand schedule and the demand curve to the elasticity concept. This video can also be used for a comprehensive review, with the entire class viewing it together. In addition, this video will provide a useful connection later on, when you can point out to students that no connection exists between elasticity and slope. **Worksheet 46.6 (Practice for Elasticity of Demand)** from the TRM offers questions related to this video.

MODULE 46 Review

Check Your Understanding

1. In each of the following cases, state whether the income effect, the substitution effect, or both are significant. In which cases do they move in the same direction? In opposite directions? Why?
   a. Orange juice represents a small share of Clare's spending. She buys more lemonade and less orange juice when the price of orange juice goes up. She does not change her spending on other goods.
   b. Apartment rents have risen dramatically this year. Since rent absorbs a major part of her income, Delia moves to a smaller apartment. Assume that rental housing is a normal good.
   c. The cost of a semester-long meal ticket at the student cafeteria rises, representing a significant increase in living costs. As a result, many students have less money to spend on weekend meals at restaurants and eat in the cafeteria instead. Assume that cafeteria meals are an inferior good.
2. The price of strawberries falls from \$1.50 to \$1.00 per carton, and the quantity demanded goes from 100,000 to 200,000 cartons. Use the midpoint method to find the price elasticity of demand.
3. At the present level of consumption, 4,000 movie tickets, and at the current price, \$5 per ticket, the price elasticity of demand for movie tickets is 1. Using the midpoint method, calculate the percentage by which the owners of movie theaters must reduce the price in order to sell 5,000 tickets.
4. The price elasticity of demand for ice cream sandwiches is 1.2 at the current price of \$0.50 per sandwich and the current consumption level of 100,000 sandwiches. Calculate the change in the quantity demanded when price rises by \$0.05. Use Equations 46-1 and 46-2 to calculate percent changes and Equation 46-3 to relate price elasticity of demand to the percent changes.

Tackle the Test: Multiple-Choice Questions

1. Which of the following statements is true?
   I. When a good absorbs only a small share of the typical consumer's income, the income effect explains the demand curve's negative slope.
   II. A change in consumption brought about by a change in purchasing power describes the income effect.
   III. In the case of an inferior good, the income and substitution effects work in opposite directions.
   a. I only
   b. II only
   c. III only
   d. II and III only
   e. I, II, and III
2. If there is an increase in the price of an inferior good on which consumers spend a large share of their income, which of the following will decrease the quantity of that good demanded?
   a. the Giffen effect
   b. the income effect only
   c. the substitution effect only
   d. the income effect and the substitution effect
   e. neither the income effect nor the substitution effect
3. If a decrease in price from \$2 to \$1 causes an increase in quantity demanded from 100 to 120, using the midpoint method, price elasticity of demand equals
   a. 0.17.
   b. 0.27.
   c. 0.40.
   d. 2.5.
   e. 3.72.
4. Which of the following is likely to have the highest price elasticity of demand?
   a. eggs
   b. beef
   c. housing
   d. gasoline
   e. foreign travel
5. If a 2% change in the price of a good leads to a 10% change in the quantity demanded of a good, what is the price elasticity of demand?
   a. 0.02
   b. 0.2
   c. 5
   d. 10
   e. 20

OPEN & CLOSE Exit Slip

TRM *Please see **Exit Slip: Module 46** in the TRM for formative multiple-choice questions to ask your students before finishing your lesson. These questions will help you quickly assess whether your students have mastered the module's concepts before moving on.*

Answers to the Exit Slip Questions

1. C *People would be less likely to buy this compared to the other goods if its price increased.*
2. D
3. C

Answers to Module 46 Review Questions

Check Your Understanding

1. a. Since spending on orange juice is a small share of Clare's spending, the income effect from a rise in the price of orange juice is insignificant. Only the substitution effect, represented by the substitution of lemonade for orange juice, is significant.

b. Since rent is a large share of Delia's expenditures, the increase in rent generates an income effect, making Delia feel poorer. Since housing is a normal good for Delia, the income and substitution effects move in the same direction, leading her to reduce her consumption of housing by moving to a smaller apartment.

c. Since a meal ticket is a significant share of the students' living costs, an increase in its price will generate an income effect. Students respond to the price increase by eating more often in the cafeteria. So, the substitution effect (which would induce them to eat in the cafeteria less often as they substitute restaurant meals in place of meals at the cafeteria) and the income effect (which would induce them to eat in the cafeteria more often because they are poorer) move in opposite directions. This happens because cafeteria meals are an inferior good. In fact, since the income effect outweighs the substitution effect (students eat in the cafeteria more as the price of meal tickets increases), cafeteria meals are a Giffen good.

2. By the midpoint method, the percent change in the price of strawberries is

$$\frac{\$1.00 - \$1.50}{(\$1.50 + \$1.00)/2} \times 100 = \frac{-\$0.50}{\$1.25} \times 100$$

$= -40\%$. Similarly, the percent change in the quantity of strawberries demanded is

$$\frac{200{,}000 - 100{,}000}{(100{,}000 + 200{,}000)/2} \times 100 = \frac{100{,}000}{150{,}000} \times 100$$

$= 67\%$. Dropping the minus sign, the price elasticity of demand using the midpoint method is $67\%/40\% = 1.7$.

3. By the midpoint method, the percent change in the quantity of movie tickets demanded in going from 4,000 tickets to 5,000 tickets is

$$\frac{5{,}000 - 4{,}000}{(4{,}000 + 5{,}000)/2} \times 100 = \frac{1{,}000}{4{,}500} \times 100 = 22\%$$

Since the price elasticity of demand is 1 at the current consumption level, it will take a 22% reduction in the price of movie tickets to generate a 22% increase in quantity demanded.

4. Since price rises, we know that quantity demanded must fall. Given the current price of \$0.50, a \$0.05 increase in price represents a 10% change, using the method in Equation 46-2.

Thus, the price elasticity of demand is

$$\frac{\%\text{ change in quantity demanded}}{10\%} = 1.2$$

so that the percent change in quantity demanded is 12%. A 12% decrease in quantity demanded represents $100{,}000 \times 0.12$, or 12,000 sandwiches.

Tackle the Test: Multiple-Choice Questions

1. d
2. c
3. b
4. e
5. c

Tackle the Test: Free-Response Question Rubric for FRQ 2 (6 points)

1 point: The substitution effect will decrease the quantity demanded.

1 point: As the price increases, consumers will buy other goods instead.

1 point: The income effect will increase the quantity demanded.

1 point: As the price increases, real income decreases, so consumers will purchase more of the inferior good.

1 point: The substitution effect is larger than the income effect.

1 point: If the income effect were larger than the substitution effect, more of the good would be purchased as the price increased, and the demand curve would be upward-sloping.

Tackle the Test: Free-Response Questions

1. **a.** Define the price elasticity of demand and provide the formula for calculating the price elasticity of demand using the midpoint method.
   b. Refer to the table provided. Using the midpoint method, calculate the price elasticity of demand for good *X*.
   c. Based on your calculation of the price elasticity of demand in part b, if the price increases by 10%, in what direction and by what percentage will the quantity demanded change?

Good X

Price	*Quantity demanded*
$2	800
$4	500

Rubric for FRQ 1 (5 points)

1 point: The price elasticity of demand measures the responsiveness of the quantity demanded to price changes.

1 point: (Change in quantity demanded/average quantity demanded)/(change in price/average price)

1 point: 0.69

1 point: Decrease

1 point: 6.9%

2. Assume the price of an inferior good increases.
   a. In what direction will the substitution effect change the quantity demanded? Explain.
   b. In what direction will the income effect change the quantity demanded? Explain.
   c. Given that the demand curve for the good slopes downward, what is true of the relative sizes of the income and substitution effects for the inferior good? Explain.
   (6 points)

466 Section 9 Behind the Demand Curve: Consumer Choice

iStockphoto

MODULE 47

Interpreting Price Elasticity of Demand

In this Module, you will learn to:

- Explain the difference between elastic and inelastic demand
- Describe the relationship between elasticity and total revenue
- Illustrate how the price elasticity changes along a demand curve
- Identify the factors that determine price elasticity of demand

What the Price Elasticity of Demand Tells Us

Med-Stat and other pharmaceutical distributors believed they could sharply drive up flu vaccine prices in the face of a shortage because the price elasticity of vaccine demand was low. But what does that mean? How low does a price elasticity have to be for us to classify it as low? How high does it have to be for us to consider it high? And what determines whether the price elasticity of demand is high or low, anyway? To answer these questions, we need to look more deeply at the price elasticity of demand.

How Elastic Is Elastic?

As a first step toward classifying price elasticities of demand, let's look at the extreme cases.

First, consider the demand for a good when people pay no attention to its price. Suppose, for example, that consumers would buy 1 billion pairs of shoelaces per year regardless of the price. If that were true, the demand curve for shoelaces would look like the curve shown in panel (a) of **Figure 47.1** on the next page: it would be a vertical line at 1 billion pairs of shoelaces. Since the percent change in the quantity demanded is zero for *any* change in the price, the price elasticity of demand in this case is zero. The case of a zero price elasticity of demand is known as **perfectly inelastic** demand.

The opposite extreme occurs when even a tiny rise in the price will cause the quantity demanded to drop to zero or even a tiny fall in the price will cause the quantity demanded to get extremely large. Panel (b) of Figure 47.1 shows the case of pink tennis balls; we suppose that tennis players really don't care what color their balls are and that other colors, such as neon green and vivid yellow, are available at $5 per dozen balls.

Demand is **perfectly inelastic** when the quantity demanded does not respond at all to changes in the price. When demand is perfectly inelastic, the demand curve is a vertical line.

PD To prepare for teaching this lesson, you may want to consult the **Module 47 Sample Lecture** in the TRM.

OPEN & CLOSE Start Here

Remind students that they have been studying price elasticity of demand as a way to measure the responsiveness of quantity demanded to a change in price. Ask students how responsive they would be if the price of the good were to increase in each scenario given below. Refer back to these extreme cases as examples throughout your discussion of elasticity.

1. You have a medical condition that requires you to take 1 pill each day to stay healthy. How does the number of pills you take each day change if the price of the pill decreases or increases? *The quantity demanded of pills would not change—you only need 1 and you must have 1.*

2. You buy a hamburger for lunch every day at a food court that has 8 hamburger restaurants. You think they are all the same. You always eat at the same restaurant, which you selected randomly the first day you went to lunch. How does the number of hamburgers you buy from your usual restaurant change if the price increases but the other restaurant's hamburger prices don't change? *The quantity demanded would fall to zero because you would buy equally good but cheaper hamburgers from some other restaurant in the mall.*

TEACH AP® Exam Tip

The math involved in learning about elasticity can make it difficult for many students (and easier for others). Make sure students realize that the AP® exam is an economics test and not a math test. Any calculations will be simple and questions focus on interpreting the economic meaning of elasticity. Help them see the pattern for calculating all elasticities and give your class plenty of practice crunching numbers through the formula. But, emphasize that understanding of the concept and its connection to real-world examples is most important.

TEACH Teach It

Now that students understand how to calculate the price elasticity of demand, they need to interpret elasticity values. Price elasticity of demand measures the degree of responsiveness of quantity demanded to a change in price. If consumers are relatively responsive to price changes (in, for instance, the hamburger example above), demand is said to be elastic, and if consumers are relatively unresponsive to price changes (the pill example above), demand is said to be inelastic. In both cases, consumers respond according to the law of demand. The term *elastic* or *inelastic* describes the degree of responsiveness. A precise definition of what we mean by "responsive" or "unresponsive" follows.

Module 47 Interpreting Price Elasticity of Demand 467

TEACH Teach It

- The value of price elasticity is interpreted relative to 1. If the percentage change in quantity demanded (the numerator) is exactly equal to the percentage change in price (the denominator),price elasticity will equal 1 (e.g., $\frac{5\%}{5\%} = 1$). This is called unitary elastic.
- If the percentage change in quantity demanded (the numerator) is greater than the percentage change in price (the denominator), the value of price elasticity is greater than 1 (e.g., $\frac{15\%}{5\%} = 3$). In this case, the quantity was very responsive (15% compared to 5%). Price elasticity would be described as ELASTIC.
- If the percentage change in quantity demanded (the numerator) is less than the percentage change in price (the denominator), the value of price elasticity is less than 1 (e.g., $\frac{5\%}{15\%} = \frac{1}{3}$). In this case, the quantity was NOT very responsive (5% compared to 15%). Price elasticity would be described as INELASTIC.

TEACH Teach It

Now that students understand a price elasticity of demand is interpreted by comparing it to 1, help them understand the "perfect" cases.

- A value below 1 is considered inelastic. Ask students how far below 1 the value can go. Remind them that we drop the negative sign on price elasticity of demand values (but NOT on other elasticities). Zero is the farthest below 1 the value can go without becoming negative. A price elasticity of demand equal to 0 means there is NO response to a change in price. This is known as perfectly inelastic demand (as, for instance, in the pill example above).
- How much higher than 1 can price elasticity go? Positive values can reach infinity! A value equal to infinity means that any increase in price will cause quantity demanded to fall to 0—quantity has an infinite response to a price change (it goes away completely). This is known as perfectly elastic demand (the hamburger example above).

Figure 47.1 Two Extreme Cases of Price Elasticity of Demand

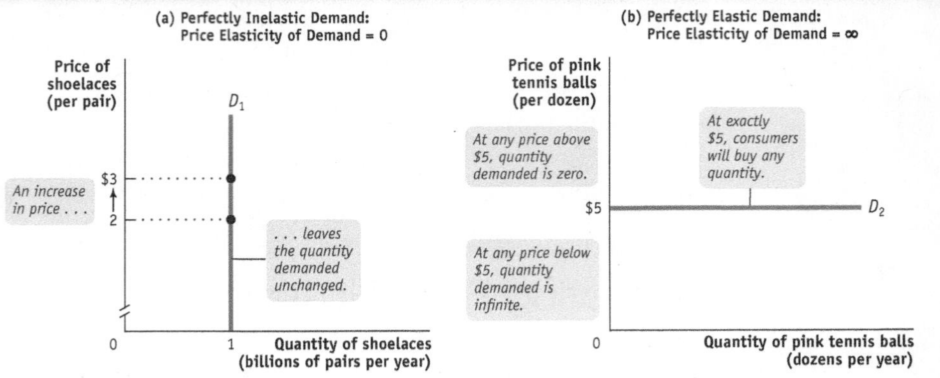

Panel (a) shows a perfectly inelastic demand curve, which is a vertical line. The quantity of shoelaces demanded is always 1 billion pairs, regardless of price. As a result, the price elasticity of demand is zero—the quantity demanded is unaffected by the price. Panel (b) shows a perfectly elastic demand curve, which is a horizontal line. At a price of $5, consumers will buy any quantity of pink tennis balls, but will buy none at a price above $5. If the price falls below $5, they will buy an extremely large number of pink tennis balls and none of any other color.

In this case, consumers will buy no pink balls if they cost more than $5 per dozen but will buy only pink balls if they cost less than $5. The demand curve will therefore be a horizontal line at a price of $5 per dozen balls. As you move back and forth along this line, there is a change in the quantity demanded but no change in the price. When you divide a number by zero, you get infinity, denoted by the symbol ∞. So a horizontal demand curve implies an infinite price elasticity of demand. When the price elasticity of demand is infinite, economists say that demand is **perfectly elastic**.

Demand is **perfectly elastic** when any price increase will cause the quantity demanded to drop to zero. When demand is perfectly elastic, the demand curve is a horizontal line.

Demand is **elastic** if the price elasticity of demand is greater than 1, **inelastic** if the price elasticity of demand is less than 1, and **unit-elastic** if the price elasticity of demand is exactly 1.

Photodisc

When the Bay Area Toll Authority deliberated a toll increase from $4 to $6 for San Francisco's Bay Bridge in 2010, at issue was the price elasticity of demand, which would determine the resulting drop in use.

The price elasticity of demand for the vast majority of goods is somewhere between these two extreme cases. Economists use one main criterion for classifying these intermediate cases: they ask whether the price elasticity of demand is greater or less than 1. When the price elasticity of demand is greater than 1, economists say that demand is **elastic**. When the price elasticity of demand is less than 1, they say that demand is **inelastic**. The borderline case is **unit-elastic** demand, where the price elasticity of demand is—surprise—exactly 1.

To see why a price elasticity of demand equal to 1 is a useful dividing line, let's consider a hypothetical example: a toll bridge operated by the state highway department. Other things equal, the number of drivers who use the bridge depends on the toll, the price the highway department charges for crossing the bridge: the higher the toll, the fewer the drivers who use the bridge.

FOCUS Graph It

Have students refer to Figure 47.1. Remind them that price elasticity of demand is

$$\frac{\%\ \text{Change in } Q_d}{\%\ \text{Change in } P}$$

- Ask students how much quantity can change in panel (a). *It doesn't ever change.* Have students use zero for percentage change in quantity and solve. *0/% change in price = 0.*
- Ask students how much price can change in panel (b). *It doesn't ever change.* Have students put in zero for percentage change in price and solve. $\frac{\%\ \text{Change in } Q_d}{0} =$ *undefined or infinite.*
- Show students this visual to help them relate elasticity to the slope of the demand curve:

Elastic Inelastic

Figure 47.2 Unit-Elastic Demand, Inelastic Demand, and Elastic Demand

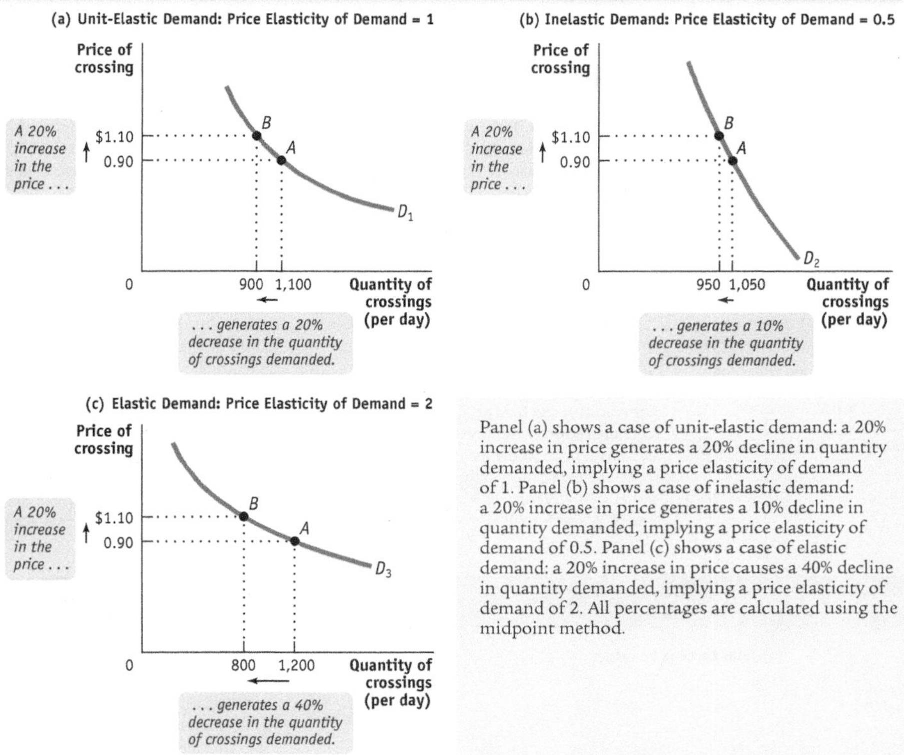

Panel (a) shows a case of unit-elastic demand: a 20% increase in price generates a 20% decline in quantity demanded, implying a price elasticity of demand of 1. Panel (b) shows a case of inelastic demand: a 20% increase in price generates a 10% decline in quantity demanded, implying a price elasticity of demand of 0.5. Panel (c) shows a case of elastic demand: a 20% increase in price causes a 40% decline in quantity demanded, implying a price elasticity of demand of 2. All percentages are calculated using the midpoint method.

Figure 47.2 shows three hypothetical demand curves that exhibit unit-elastic demand, inelastic demand, and elastic demand, respectively. In each case, point *A* shows the quantity demanded if the toll is $0.90 and point *B* shows the quantity demanded if the toll is $1.10. An increase in the toll from $0.90 to $1.10 is an increase of 20% if we use the midpoint method to calculate percent changes.

Panel (a) shows what happens when the toll is raised from $0.90 to $1.10 and the demand curve is unit-elastic. Here the 20% increase in price leads to a fall in the quantity of cars using the bridge each day from 1,100 to 900, a 20% decline (again using the midpoint method). So the price elasticity of demand is 20%/20% = 1.

Panel (b) shows a case of inelastic demand when the toll is raised from $0.90 to $1.10. The same 20% increase in price reduces the quantity demanded from 1,050 to 950. That's only a 10% decline, so in this case the price elasticity of demand is 10%/20% = 0.5.

Panel (c) shows a case of elastic demand when the toll is raised from $0.90 to $1.10. The 20% price increase causes the quantity demanded to fall from 1,200 to 800, a 40% decline, so the price elasticity of demand is 40%/20% = 2.

AP® Exam Tip

When thinking of perfectly inelastic demand, think *I* = *Inelastic*, with the I representing the vertical perfectly inelastic demand curve. When thinking of perfectly elastic demand, think *E* = *Elastic*, with the horizontal middle line of the E representing the horizontal perfectly elastic demand curve.

FOCUS Graph It

Figure 47.2 shows the graphs of unit elasticity of demand, inelastic demand, and elastic demand. Emphasize that the price change in each case is the same (*20% increase*). Have students compare the resulting changes in quantity demanded (*20%, 10%, 40%*).

TEACH Teach It

Make sure students understand that although slope and price elasticity of demand are related, they are NOT the same. The slope (rise/run) of a straight-line demand curve is the change in price divided by the change in quantity (no percentages), and it is the same no matter which two points you use to calculate it. But because the value of elasticity is the *percentage change in quantity divided by percentage change in price*, it will vary depending on where along the demand curve you calculate it. To help students see that elasticity will vary along a demand curve mathematically, remind them that when they calculated the percentage changes needed to find elasticity, they divided the change by either the starting point (for point elasticity) or the average (for midpoint formula). In either case, the value is different at different points on a demand curve.

To help your students understand that elasticity varies along a demand curve intuitively, ask them when they are more responsive to a price change—when the price is high or when it is low? For example, will they respond more to a change in price from $1 to $2 or from $1,000 to $2,000? *Demand is more responsive (elastic) at higher prices and less responsive (inelastic) at lower prices.*

TEACH Connect It

It may seem contradictory to talk about steeper demand curves being more inelastic (and flatter demand curves being more elastic) and to also say that elasticity varies along any downward-sloping demand curve. Connect these two ideas and help students realize both that a relatively steep demand curve has all three ranges of elasticity but that the inelastic portion is larger, whereas a relatively flat demand curve has all three ranges of elasticity but the elastic portion is larger. The elasticity of a particular demand curve and elasticity varying along a demand curve will be important when discussing market structures and the marginal revenue curve in later modules.

TEACH Teach It

Remind students that they have been studying elasticity as a way to measure the responsiveness of quantity demanded to changes in price. We know that when price increases, quantity demanded falls (the law of demand). Elasticity tells us HOW MUCH quantity demanded will fall when price increases. Ask students who might be interested in knowing about elasticity and why? That is, help them see who might want to know how consumers will respond if price is increased. Producers will want to know because elasticity tells them that changing their price will change how much money they receive for selling their product! A *firm's total revenue* is equal to the number sold (*Q*) times the price they are sold for (*P*).

Have students think of a price change in terms of good news and bad news. For example, when a firm increases the price of its product, there is good news and bad news. The good news is that the firm sells each unit for a higher price (YAY!); the bad news is that, at a higher price, the firm will not sell as many units (BOO!). Whether the firm's total revenue increases or decreases depends on whether the good news or bad news is larger.

FOCUS Active Learning

Use Figure 47.3 to extend the "good news," "bad news" approach described above. When price increases from .90 to 1.10 (YAY!), quantity demanded decreases from 1,100 to 900 (BOO!). The area labeled *C* represents the good news (the price effect) and area *A* represents the bad news (the quantity effect). The overall effect on total revenue depends on which area (good news or bad news) is larger. Elasticity determines the size of the good news and bad news areas. Have students shade the areas using first a steep curve and then a flat demand curve to see the difference. Note that this works in the opposite direction for a price decrease.

Total revenue is the total value of sales of a good or service. It is equal to the price multiplied by the quantity sold.

Why does it matter whether demand is unit-elastic, inelastic, or elastic? Because this classification indicates how changes in the price of a good will affect the *total revenue* earned by producers from the sale of that good. In many real-life situations, such as the one faced by Med-Stat, it is crucial to know how price changes affect total revenue. **Total revenue** is defined as the total value of sales of a good or service: the price multiplied by the quantity sold.

(47-1) Total revenue = Price × Quantity sold

Total revenue has a useful graphical representation that can help us understand why knowing the price elasticity of demand is crucial when we ask whether an increase in price will increase or reduce total revenue. Panel (a) of **Figure 47.3** shows the same demand curve as panel (a) of Figure 47.2. We see that 1,100 drivers will use the bridge if the toll is \$0.90. So the total revenue at a price of \$0.90 is \$0.90 × 1,100 = \$990. This value is equal to the area of the green rectangle, which is drawn with the bottom left corner at the point (0, 0) and the top right corner at (1,100, 0.90). In general, the total revenue at any given price is equal to the area of a rectangle whose height is the price and whose width is the quantity demanded at that price.

AP® Exam Tip

Don't confuse revenue with profit. Revenue is what the firm receives; profit is what the firm receives minus the firm's costs.

To get an idea of why total revenue is important, consider the following scenario. Suppose that the toll on the bridge is currently \$0.90 but that the highway department must raise extra money for road repairs. One way to do this is to raise the toll on the bridge. But this plan might backfire, since a higher toll will reduce the number of drivers who use the bridge. And if traffic on the bridge dropped a lot, a higher toll would actually reduce total revenue instead of increasing it. So it's important for the highway department to know how drivers will respond to a toll increase.

We can see graphically how the toll increase affects total bridge revenue by examining panel (b) of Figure 47.3. At a toll of \$0.90, total revenue is given by the sum of areas *A* and *B*. After the toll is raised to \$1.10, total revenue is given by the sum of areas *B* and *C*.

Figure 47.3 Total Revenue

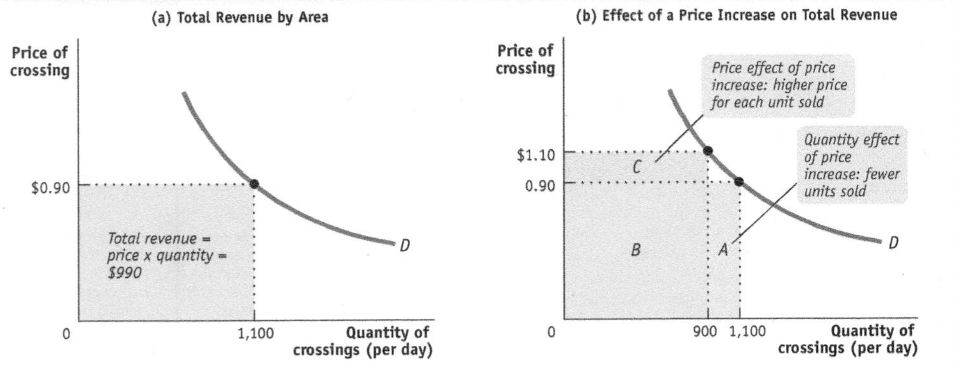

The green rectangle in panel (a) represents the total revenue generated from 1,100 drivers who each pay a toll of \$0.90. Panel (b) shows how total revenue is affected when the price increases from \$0.90 to \$1.10. Due to the quantity effect, total revenue falls by area *A*. Due to the price effect, total revenue increases by area *C*. In general, the overall effect can go either way, depending on the price elasticity of demand.

So when the toll is raised, revenue represented by area *A* is lost but revenue represented by area *C* is gained. These two areas have important interpretations. Area *C* represents the revenue gain that comes from the additional $0.20 paid by drivers who continue to use the bridge. That is, the 900 who continue to use the bridge contribute an additional $\$0.20 \times 900 = \$180$ per day to total revenue, represented by area *C*. But 200 drivers who would have used the bridge at a price of $0.90 no longer do so, generating a loss to total revenue of $\$0.90 \times 200 = \$180$ per day, represented by area *A*. (In this particular example, because demand is unit-elastic—the same as in panel (a) of Figure 47.2—the rise in the toll has no effect on total revenue; areas *A* and *C* are the same size.)

Except in the rare case of a good with perfectly elastic or perfectly inelastic demand, when a seller raises the price of a good, two countervailing effects are present:

- *A price effect.* After a price increase, each unit sold sells at a higher price, which tends to raise revenue.
- *A quantity effect.* After a price increase, fewer units are sold, which tends to lower revenue.

But what is the net ultimate effect on total revenue: does it go up or down? The answer is that, in general, total revenue can go either way—an increase in price may either increase total revenue or decrease it. If the price effect, which tends to raise total revenue, is the stronger of the two effects, then total revenue goes up. If the quantity effect, which tends to reduce total revenue, is the stronger, then total revenue goes down. And if the strengths of the two effects are exactly equal—as in our toll bridge example, where a $180 gain offsets a $180 loss—total revenue is unchanged by the price increase.

The price elasticity of demand tells us what happens to total revenue when price changes: its size determines which effect—the price effect or the quantity effect—is stronger. Specifically:

- If demand for a good is *unit-elastic* (the price elasticity of demand is 1), an increase in price does not change total revenue. In this case, the quantity effect and the price effect exactly offset each other.
- If demand for a good is *inelastic* (the price elasticity of demand is less than 1), a higher price increases total revenue. In this case, the price effect is stronger than the quantity effect.
- If demand for a good is *elastic* (the price elasticity of demand is greater than 1), an increase in price reduces total revenue. In this case, the quantity effect is stronger than the price effect.

Table 47.1 shows how the effect of a price increase on total revenue depends on the price elasticity of demand, using the same data as in Figure 47.2. An increase in the

AP® Exam Tip

If total revenue and price move in the same direction, the good is inelastic. If total revenue and price move in opposite directions, the good is elastic. If total revenue does not change when price changes, the good is unit-elastic.

Table 47.1 Price Elasticity of Demand and Total Revenue

	Price of crossing = $0.90	Price of crossing = $1.10
Unit-elastic demand (price elasticity of demand = 1)		
Quantity demanded	1,100	900
Total revenue	$990	$990
Inelastic demand (price elasticity of demand = 0.5)		
Quantity demanded	1,050	950
Total revenue	$945	$1,045
Elastic demand (price elasticity of demand = 2)		
Quantity demanded	1,200	800
Total revenue	$1,080	$880

TEACH Teach It

Help students understand the relationship between price elasticity of demand and changes in total revenue:

- If E_d is unit-elastic ($E_d = 1$), an increase (decrease) in price does not change TR. The good news and bad news are equal.
- If E_d is inelastic ($E_d < 1$), an increase (decrease) in price increases (decreases) TR. Quantity is not very responsive, so the price effect is larger (the good news when price increases, the bad news when price decreases).
- If E_d is elastic ($E_d > 1$), an increase (decrease) in price reduces (increases) TR. Quantity is very responsive, so the quantity effect is larger (the bad news when price increases, the good news when price decreases).

FOCUS Test It

Have students calculate the total revenue for the following prices. Then use the TR test to state where the good has elastic demand or inelastic demand at the various prices.

Price	Quantity	TR	E
$100	1	(100)	
80	4	(320)	elastic
60	11	(666)	elastic
40	18	(720)	elastic
20	21	(440)	inelastic

FOCUS Flip It

TRM Ask students to watch Jacob Clifford's video "Micro 2.9 Elasticity and the Total Revenue Test" (see econextras video list with hyperlinks on the bcs and TRFD). Then have them answer the questions on the accompanying **Worksheet 47.1 (Total Revenue and Elasticity)** from the TRM.

price from \$0.90 to \$1.10 leaves total revenue unchanged at \$990 when demand is unit-elastic. When demand is inelastic, the price effect dominates the quantity effect; the same price increase leads to an increase in total revenue from \$945 to \$1,045. And when demand is elastic, the quantity effect dominates the price effect; the price increase leads to a decline in total revenue from \$1,080 to \$880.

The price elasticity of demand also predicts the effect of a *fall* in price on total revenue. When the price falls, the same two countervailing effects are present, but they work in the opposite directions as compared to the case of an increase in price. There is the price effect of a lower price per unit sold, which tends to lower revenue. This is countered by the quantity effect of more units sold, which tends to raise revenue. Which effect dominates depends on the price elasticity. Here is a quick summary:

- When demand is *unit-elastic*, the two effects exactly balance each other out; so a fall in price has no effect on total revenue.
- When demand is *inelastic*, the price effect dominates the quantity effect; so a fall in price reduces total revenue.
- When demand is *elastic*, the quantity effect dominates the price effect; so a fall in price increases total revenue.

Price Elasticity Along the Demand Curve

Suppose an economist says that "the price elasticity of demand for coffee is 0.25." What he or she means is that *at the current price* the elasticity is 0.25. In the previous discussion of the toll bridge, what we were really describing was the elasticity *at the price* of \$0.90. Why this qualification? Because for the vast majority of demand curves, the price elasticity of demand at one point along the curve is different from the price elasticity of demand at other points along the same curve.

To see this, consider the table in **Figure 47.4**, which shows a hypothetical demand schedule. It also shows in the last column the total revenue generated at each price. The upper panel of the graph in Figure 47.4 shows the corresponding demand curve. The lower panel illustrates the same data on total revenue: the height of a bar at each quantity demanded—which corresponds to a particular price—measures the total revenue generated at that price.

In Figure 47.4, you can see that when the price is low, raising the price increases total revenue: starting at a price of \$1, raising the price to \$2 increases total revenue from \$9 to \$16. This means that when the price is low, demand is inelastic. Moreover, you can see that demand is inelastic on the entire section of the demand curve from a price of \$0 to a price of \$5.

When the price is high, however, raising it further reduces total revenue: starting at a price of \$8, for example, raising the price to \$9 reduces total revenue, from \$16 to \$9. This means that when the price is high, demand is elastic. Furthermore, you can see that demand is elastic over the section of the demand curve from a price of \$5 to \$10.

For the vast majority of goods, the price elasticity of demand changes along the demand curve. So whenever you measure a good's elasticity, you are really measuring it at a particular point or section of the good's demand curve.

AP® Exam Tip

For a straight, downward-sloping demand curve, the upper left segment of the demand curve is elastic and the bottom right segment is inelastic.

What Factors Determine the Price Elasticity of Demand?

The flu vaccine shortfall of 2004–2005 allowed vaccine distributors to significantly raise their prices for two important reasons: there were no substitutes, and for many people the vaccine was a medical necessity. People responded in various ways. Some paid the high prices, and some traveled to Canada and other countries to get vaccinated. Some simply did without (and over time often changed their habits to avoid catching the flu, such as eating out less often and avoiding mass transit). This experience illustrates

472 Section 9 Behind the Demand Curve: Consumer Choice

Figure 47.4 The Price Elasticity of Demand Changes Along the Demand Curve

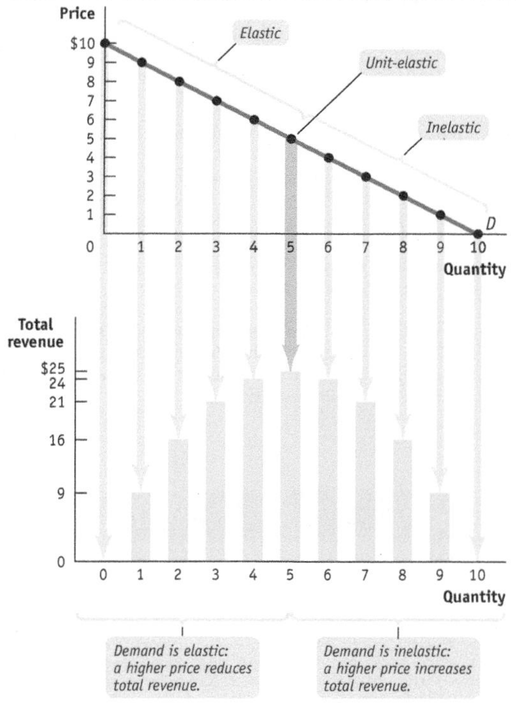

Demand Schedule and Total Revenue for a Linear Demand Curve

Price	Quantity demanded	Total revenue
$0	10	$0
1	9	9
2	8	16
3	7	21
4	6	24
5	5	25
6	4	24
7	3	21
8	2	16
9	1	9
10	0	0

The upper panel shows a demand curve corresponding to the demand schedule in the table. The lower panel shows how total revenue changes along that demand curve: at each price and quantity combination, the height of the bar represents the total revenue generated. You can see that at a low price, raising the price increases total revenue. So demand is inelastic at low prices. At a high price, however, a rise in price reduces total revenue. So demand is elastic at high prices.

the four main factors that determine elasticity: whether close substitutes are available, whether the good is a necessity or a luxury, the share of income a consumer spends on the good, and how much time has elapsed since the price change. We'll briefly examine each of these factors.

Whether Close Substitutes Are Available The price elasticity of demand tends to be high if there are other goods that consumers regard as similar and would be willing to consume instead. The price elasticity of demand tends to be low if there are no close substitutes.

Whether the Good Is a Necessity or a Luxury The price elasticity of demand tends to be low if a good is something you must have, like a life-saving medicine. The price elasticity of demand tends to be high if the good is a luxury—something you can easily live without.

Share of Income Spent on the Good The price elasticity of demand tends to be low when spending on a good accounts for a small

FOCUS Graph It

Figure 47.4 shows the graphic relationship between the demand curve and total revenue curve. Have students plot the points of total revenue and quantity demanded. Direct them to connect the points. Then have them graph the demand curve and indicate the sections of the demand curve that correspond to increasing, decreasing, and maximum total revenue.

- Note that the peak of the curve aligns with the middle of the demand curve identifying unit elasticity.
- The upper left of the demand curve and the increasing portion of the TR curve are the elastic region.
- The lower right quadrant of the demand curve and the downward-sloping portion of the TR curve represent the inelastic regions of the curves.

FOCUS Active Learning

Request that a student volunteer copy the demand and total revenue curves from Figure 47.4 on the board. It will be reinforcing for the class to see the shapes of the curves, especially the inverted U shape of the TR curve. Have another student go to the board and mark the elastic, unit-elastic, and inelastic regions of both curves.

FOCUS Test It

Instruct your students to complete the following statements:

If TR and *P* move in opposite directions, elasticity is __________. *elastic*

If TR and *P* move in the same direction, elasticity is __________. *inelastic*

FOCUS Active Learning

TRM For practice with the price and quantity effects, assign **Worksheet 47.2 (Elasticity Practice)** from the TRM.

TEACH Connect It

Students learned about substitute goods in Section 2. Remind students what they learned about substitute goods to introduce them as a determinant of price elasticity of demand. Also use the discussion of substitutes as an opportunity to foreshadow the study of cross-price elasticity in the next module. The quantity demanded of a good is affected by not only a change in its own price, but also a change in the price of a related good (substitute or complement).

FOCUS Test It

Have students answer True or False:

The slope of a straight-line demand curve is constant. *T*

Price elasticity of demand along a straight-line demand curve is constant. *F*

TEACH Teach It

There are three important determinants of elasticity of demand:

- **Substitutability**: Elasticity of demand is greater the more substitutes there are in the market.
- **Necessity or luxury good**: Elasticity of demand is greater when the good is a luxury good. The more necessary the good, the lower its elasticity of demand.
- **Percentage of income**: The greater the percentage of your income the cost of the good is, the greater its elasticity of demand.

FOCUS Active Learning

TRM You may wish to have students complete **Worksheet 47.3 (Higher or Lower Elasticity?)** from the TRM for practice with factors that determine elasticity of demand.

FOCUS In the News

TRM Have students discuss how increases in college tuition might affect their demand for college classes. Ask them about their price elasticity of demand for their favorite college (e.g., is it elastic or inelastic)? Discuss what factors might determine a high school student's elasticity of demand for a particular college.

Have students read Kayla Webley's *Time US* article "College Costs: Would Tuition Discounts Get More Students to Major in Science?" at http://nation.time.com/2013/01/03/college-costs-will-tuition-discounts-get-more-students-to-major-in-science/. It will reinforce much of what students have learned.

Refer your class to **Worksheet 47.4 (College Tuition and Elasticity)** from the TRM for questions about this article.

OPEN & CLOSE Exit Slip

TRM Please see ***Exit Slip: Module 47*** *in the TRM for formative questions to ask your students before finishing your lesson. These questions will help you quickly assess whether your students have mastered the module's concepts before moving on.*

Mick Stevens/The New Yorker Collection

"It runs on its conventional gasoline-powered engine until it senses guilt, at which point it switches over to battery power."

share of a consumer's income. In that case, a significant change in the price of the good has little impact on how much the consumer spends. In contrast, when a good accounts for a significant share of a consumer's spending, the consumer is likely to be very responsive to a change in price. In this case, the price elasticity of demand is high.

Time In general, the price elasticity of demand tends to increase as consumers have more time to adjust to a price change. This means that the long-run price elasticity of demand is often higher than the short-run elasticity.

A good illustration of the effect of time on the elasticity of demand is drawn from the 1970s, the first time gasoline prices increased dramatically in the United States. Initially, consumption fell very little because there were no close substitutes for gasoline and because driving their cars was necessary for people to carry out the ordinary tasks of life. Over time, however, Americans changed their habits in ways that enabled them to gradually reduce their gasoline consumption. The result was a steady decline in gasoline consumption over the next decade, even though the price of gasoline did not continue to rise, confirming that the long-run price elasticity of demand for gasoline was indeed much larger than the short-run elasticity.

AP® Exam Tip

The determinants of price elasticity of demand are:

S - Substitutes
P - Proportion of income
L - Luxury or necessity
A - Addictive or habit forming
T - Time

FYI Responding to Your Tuition Bill

College costs more than ever—and not just because of overall inflation. Tuition has been rising faster than the overall cost of living for years. But does rising tuition keep people from going to college? Two studies found that the answer depends on the type of college. Both studies assessed how responsive the decision to go to college is to a change in tuition.

A 1988 study found that a 3% increase in tuition led to an approximately 2% fall in the number of students enrolled at four-year institutions, giving a price elasticity of demand of 0.67 (2%/3%). In the case of two-year institutions, the study found a significantly higher response: a 3% increase in tuition led to a 2.7% fall in enrollments, giving a price elasticity of demand of 0.9. In other words, the enrollment decision for students at two-year colleges was significantly more responsive to price than for students at four-year colleges. The result: students at two-year colleges are more likely to forgo getting a degree because of tuition costs than students at four-year colleges.

A 1999 study confirmed this pattern. In comparison to four-year colleges, it found that two-year college enrollment rates were significantly more responsive to changes in state financial aid (a decline in aid leading to a decline in enrollments), a predictable effect given these students' greater sensitivity to the cost of tuition. Another piece of evidence suggests that students at two-year colleges are more likely to be paying their own way and making a trade-off between attending college and working: the study found that enrollments at two-year colleges are much more responsive to changes in the unemployment rate (an increase in the unemployment rate leading to an increase in enrollments) than enrollments at four-year colleges. So is the cost of tuition a barrier to getting a college degree in the United States? Yes, but more so at two-year colleges than at four-year colleges.

Interestingly, the 1999 study found that for both two-year and four-year colleges, price sensitivity of demand had fallen somewhat since the 1988 study. One possible explanation is that because the value of a college education has risen considerably over time, fewer people forgo college, even if tuition goes up. And the price elasticity of demand for education has remained low. A 2008 study estimates that the price elasticity of demand for education at four-year institutions may be as low as 0.11.

Sources: Leslie, L. L., & Brinkman, P. T. (1988). The Economic Value of Higher Education. Washington, DC: American Council on Education: Heller, D. E. (1999). The Effects of Tuition and State Financial Aid on Public College Enrollment. The Review of Higher Education, 23(1), 65–89; Hemelt, S. W., and Marcotte, D. E. (2008). "Rising Tuition and Enrollment in Public Higher Education," IZA Discussion Paper No. 3827.

Answers to the Exit Slip Questions

1. $$E_d = \frac{\frac{(100-150)}{(100+150)/2}}{\frac{15-12}{(12+15)/2}} = \frac{\frac{50}{125}}{\frac{3}{13.5}} = \frac{0.4}{.22} = 1.8$$

Very elastic!

2. B
3. D

MODULE 47 Review

Check Your Understanding

1. For each case, choose the condition that characterizes demand: elastic demand, inelastic demand, or unit-elastic demand.
   a. Total revenue decreases when price increases.
   b. When price falls, the additional revenue generated by the increase in the quantity sold is exactly offset by the revenue lost from the fall in the price received per unit.
   c. Total revenue falls when output increases.
   d. Producers in an industry find they can increase their total revenues by working together to reduce industry output.
2. For the following goods, is demand elastic, inelastic, or unit-elastic? Explain. What is the shape of the demand curve?
   a. demand by a snake-bite victim for an antidote
   b. demand by students for blue pencils

Tackle the Test: Multiple-Choice Questions

1. A perfectly elastic demand curve is
   a. upward-sloping.
   b. vertical.
   c. not a straight line.
   d. horizontal.
   e. downward-sloping.
2. Which of the following would cause the demand for a good to be relatively inelastic?
   a. The good has a large number of close substitutes.
   b. Expenditures on the good represent a large share of consumer income.
   c. There is ample time to adjust to price changes.
   d. The good is a necessity.
   e. The price of the good is in the upper left section of a linear demand curve.
3. Which of the following is true if the price elasticity of demand for a good is zero?
   a. The slope of the demand curve is zero.
   b. The slope of the demand curve is one.
   c. The demand curve is vertical.
   d. The demand curve is horizontal.
   e. The price of the good is high.
4. Which of the following is correct for a price increase? When demand is ______, total revenue will ______.

	Demand	*Total Revenue*
a.	inelastic	decrease
b.	elastic	decrease
c.	unit-elastic	increase
d.	unit-elastic	decrease
e.	elastic	increase

5. Total revenue is maximized when demand is
   a. elastic.
   b. inelastic.
   c. unit-elastic.
   d. zero.
   e. infinite.

Answers to Module 47 Review Questions

Check Your Understanding

1. a. Demand is elastic. Consumers are highly responsive to changes in price. For a rise in price, the quantity effect (which reduces total revenue) outweighs the price effect (which increases total revenue). Overall, this leads to a fall in total revenue.

b. Demand is unit-elastic. Here, the revenue lost to the fall in price is exactly equal to the revenue gained from higher sales. The quantity effect exactly offsets the price effect.

c. Demand is inelastic. Consumers are relatively unresponsive to changes in price. For consumers to purchase a given percent more, the price must fall by an even greater percent. The price effect of a fall in price (which reduces total revenue) outweighs the quantity effect (which increases total revenue). As a result, total revenue decreases.

d. Demand is inelastic. Consumers are relatively unresponsive to price, so a given percent fall in output is accompanied by an even greater percent rise in price. The price effect of a rise in price (which increases total revenue) outweighs the quantity effect (which reduces total revenue). As a result, total revenue increases.

2. a. Once bitten by a venomous snake, the victim's demand for an antidote is very likely to be perfectly inelastic because there is no substitute and it is necessary for survival. The demand curve will be vertical at a quantity equal to the needed dose.

b. Students' demand for blue pencils is likely to be perfectly elastic because there are readily available substitutes, such as yellow pencils. The demand curve will be horizontal at a price equal to that of nonblue pencils.

Tackle the Test: Multiple-Choice Questions

1. d
2. d
3. c
4. b
5. c

Module 47 Interpreting Price Elasticity of Demand **475**

Tackle the Test: Free-Response Question Rubric for FRQ 2 (4 points)

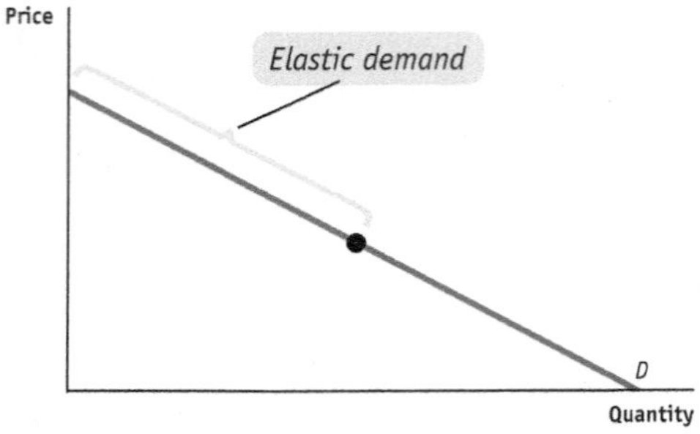

1 point: A graph with "Price" (or "*P*") on the vertical axis, "Quantity" (or "*Q*") on the horizontal axis, and a downward-sloping, straight line labeled "Demand" (or "*D*")

1 point: The top half of the demand curve is labeled "elastic."

1 point: An increase in price will decrease total revenue.

1 point: Because the negative quantity effect of the price increase is greater than the positive price effect of the price increase

Tackle the Test: Free-Response Questions

1. Draw a correctly labeled graph of a perfectly inelastic demand curve.
   a. What is the price elasticity of demand for this good?
   b. What is the slope of the demand curve for this good?
   c. Is this good more likely to be a luxury or a necessity? Explain.

Rubric for FRQ 1 (5 points)

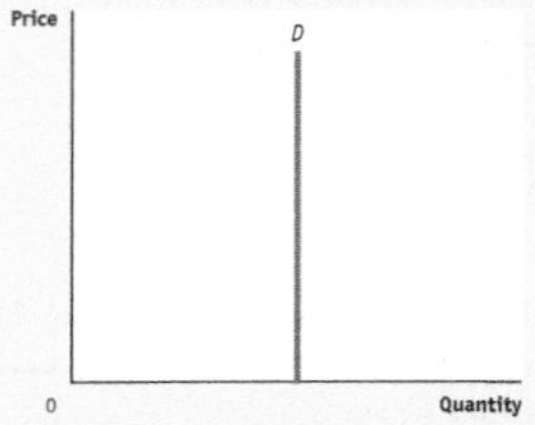

1 point: A graph with "Price" (or "*P*") on the vertical axis, "Quantity" (or "*Q*") on the horizontal axis, and a vertical line labeled "Demand" (or "*D*")

1 point: Zero

1 point: Infinite or undefined

1 point: Necessity

1 point: Since you have to have a necessity (such as a life-saving medicine), you do not change the quantity you purchase when the price changes.

2. Draw a correctly labeled graph illustrating a demand curve that is a straight line and is neither perfectly elastic nor perfectly inelastic.
   a. On your graph, indicate the half of the demand curve along which demand is elastic.
   b. In the elastic range, how will an increase in price affect total revenue? Explain.
   (4 points)

476 **Section 9** Behind the Demand Curve: Consumer Choice

iStockphoto

MODULE

48 Other Important Elasticities

In this Module, you will learn to:

- Measure the responsiveness of demand for one good to changes in the price of another good using the cross-price elasticity of demand
- Measure the responsiveness of demand to changes in income using the income elasticity of demand
- Explain the significance of the price elasticity of supply, which measures the responsiveness of the quantity supplied to changes in price
- Identify and describe the factors that influence the size of these various elasticities

Measuring Responses to Other Changes

We stated earlier that economists use the concept of *elasticity* to measure the responsiveness of one variable to changes in another. However, up to this point we have focused on the price elasticity of demand. Now that we have used elasticity to measure the responsiveness of quantity demanded to changes in price, we can go on to look at how elasticity is used to understand the relationship between other important variables in economics.

The quantity of a good demanded depends not only on the price of that good but also on other variables. In particular, demand curves shift because of changes in the prices of related goods and changes in consumers' incomes. It is often important to have a measure of these other effects, and the best measures are—you guessed it—elasticities. Specifically, we can best measure how the demand for a good is affected by prices of other goods using a measure called the *cross-price elasticity of demand,* and we can best measure how demand is affected by changes in income using the *income elasticity of demand.*

Finally, we can also use elasticity to measure supply responses. The *price elasticity of supply* measures the responsiveness of the quantity supplied to changes in price.

AP® Exam Tip

A negative cross-price elasticity identifies a complement (one you buy less of when the price of the other goes up). A positive cross-price elasticity identifies a substitute (one you buy more of when the price of the other goes up).

The Cross-Price Elasticity of Demand

The demand for a good is often affected by the prices of other, related goods—goods that are substitutes or complements. A change in the price of a related good shifts the demand curve of the original good, reflecting a change in the quantity demanded at

St. Louis Federal Reserve Bank Resources

"The Economics of Immigration: A Story of Substitutes and Complements," ***Page One Economics***

America is a nation of immigrants, who currently make up about 13 percent of the overall population. This issue shows how immigration affects the average American. The essay weighs the costs and benefits of immigration and discusses the concept of immigrant workers as substitutes for and complements to native-born workers.

PD To prepare for teaching this lesson, you may want to consult the **Module 48 Sample Lecture** in the TRM.

OPEN & CLOSE Start Here

Ask students to answer the following Section 2 review questions. Students should be able to answer the questions and explain "why," but will not be able to answer the question of "how much." Hopefully, they will realize after studying price elasticity of demand over the past two modules that they do need to understand the concept of elasticity to determine "by how much."

1. Will the quantity of ketchup demanded increase or decrease if the price of hot dogs increases? Why? By how much? *Decrease. People buy fewer hot dogs, and hot dogs and ketchup are complements.*

2. Will the quantity of chocolate chip cookies demanded increase or decrease if the price of oatmeal cookies decreases? Why? By how much? *Decrease. People buy more oatmeal cookies, and chocolate chip cookies and oatmeal cookies are substitutes.*

3. Will the quantity of good X demanded increase or decrease if consumer incomes increase? Why? By how much? *It depends on whether good X is normal or inferior.*

TEACH Connect It

Remind students of the discussion of the price of related goods as a determinant of demand. Have them work through the relationship between the price of a complement and the quantity of the good demanded (e.g., using the hot dog/ketchup and cookie examples in the opener) and determine whether the relationship is positive (substitutes) or negative (complements). Use students' understanding of the complement/substitute relationships to introduce the formula for cross-price elasticity.

FOCUS Test It

Ask students to give examples of pairs of goods that have a positive cross-price elasticity and pairs of goods that have a negative cross-price elasticity. Have them define the goods as complements or substitutes until they are comfortable with the connections. *Examples may be peanut butter and jelly, film and cameras, tennis racquet and tennis balls for negative/complements and green shirts and blue shirts, hot dogs and hamburgers, pens and pencils for positive/substitutes.*

TEACH Connect It

Remind students that income is a determinant of demand. Ask them how a change in income will affect quantity demanded for a good. By now students should be quick to respond "it depends!" when asked about the effect of any change in income. The effect of income depends on the type of good (normal or inferior). Income elasticity of demand measures responsiveness of quantity demanded to changes in consumer income and therefore its sign (positive or negative) identifies the good as normal or inferior.

$$E_i = \frac{\text{\% Change in quantity demanded}}{\text{\% Change in income}}$$

- If E_i is positive, it tells us that the good is a normal good; as income rises, so does the quantity demanded for the good.
- If E_i is negative, it tells us that the good is an inferior good; as income rises, the quantity demanded for the good decreases.

The **cross-price elasticity of demand** between two goods measures the effect of the change in one good's price on the quantity demanded of the other good. It is equal to the percent change in the quantity demanded of one good divided by the percent change in the other good's price.

any given price. The strength of such a "cross" effect on demand can be measured by the **cross-price elasticity of demand**, defined as the ratio of the percent change in the quantity demanded of one good to the percent change in the price of another.

(48-1) Cross-price elasticity of demand between goods A and B

$$= \frac{\text{\% change in quantity of A demanded}}{\text{\% change in price of B}}$$

When two goods are substitutes, like hot dogs and hamburgers, the cross-price elasticity of demand is positive: a rise in the price of hot dogs increases the demand for hamburgers—that is, it causes a rightward shift of the demand curve for hamburgers. If the goods are close substitutes, the cross-price elasticity will be positive and large; if they are not close substitutes, the cross-price elasticity will be positive and small. So when the cross-price elasticity of demand is positive, its size is a measure of how closely substitutable the two goods are.

When two goods are complements, like hot dogs and hot dog buns, the cross-price elasticity is negative: a rise in the price of hot dogs decreases the demand for hot dog buns—that is, it causes a leftward shift of the demand curve for hot dog buns. As with substitutes, the size of the cross-price elasticity of demand between two complements tells us how strongly complementary they are: if the cross-price elasticity is only slightly below zero, they are weak complements; if it is very negative, they are strong complements.

Note that in the case of the cross-price elasticity of demand, the sign (plus or minus) is very important: it tells us whether the two goods are complements or substitutes. So we cannot drop the minus sign as we did for the price elasticity of demand.

Our discussion of the cross-price elasticity of demand is a useful place to return to a point we made earlier: elasticity is a *unit-free* measure—that is, it doesn't depend on the units in which goods are measured.

To see the potential problem, suppose someone told you that "if the price of hot dog buns rises by $0.30, Americans will buy 10 million fewer hot dogs this year." If you've ever bought hot dog buns, you'll immediately wonder: is that a $0.30 increase in the price *per bun,* or is it a $0.30 increase in the price *per package* of buns? It makes a big difference what units we are talking about! However, if someone says that the cross-price elasticity of demand between buns and hot dogs is −0.3, you'll know that a 1% increase in the price of buns causes a 0.3% decrease in the quantity of hot dogs demanded, regardless of whether buns are sold individually or by the package. So elasticity is defined as a ratio of percent changes, which avoids confusion over units.

AP® Exam Tip

A negative income elasticity identifies an inferior good (one you buy less of when your income goes up). A positive income elasticity identifies a normal good (one you buy more of when your income goes up).

The Income Elasticity of Demand

The **income elasticity of demand** measures how changes in income affect the demand for a good. It indicates whether a good is normal or inferior and specifies how responsive demand for the good is to changes in income. Having learned the price and cross-price elasticity formulas, the income elasticity formula will look familiar:

(48-2) $$\text{Income elasticity of demand} = \frac{\text{\% change in quantity demanded}}{\text{\% change in income}}$$

The **income elasticity of demand** is the percent change in the quantity of a good demanded when a consumer's income changes divided by the percent change in the consumer's income.

Just as the cross-price elasticity of demand between two goods can be either positive or negative, depending on whether the goods are substitutes or complements, the income elasticity of demand for a good can also be either positive or negative. Recall that goods can be either *normal goods,* for which demand increases when income rises, or *inferior goods,* for which demand decreases when income rises. These definitions relate directly to the sign of the income elasticity of demand:

- When the income elasticity of demand is positive, the good is a normal good.
- When the income elasticity of demand is negative, the good is an inferior good.

478 Section 9 Behind the Demand Curve: Consumer Choice

FYI Where Have All the Farmers Gone?

What percentage of Americans live on farms? Sad to say, the U.S. government no longer publishes that number. In 1991, the official percentage was 1.9, but in that year the government decided it was no longer a meaningful indicator of the size of the agricultural sector because a large proportion of those who live on farms actually make their living doing something else. In the days of the Founding Fathers, the great majority of Americans lived on farms. As recently as the 1940s, one American in six—or approximately 17%—still did.

Why do so few people now live and work on farms in the United States? There are two main reasons, both involving elasticities.

First, the income elasticity of demand for food is much less than 1—food demand is income-inelastic. As consumers grow richer, other things equal, spending on food rises less than in proportion to income. As a result, as the U.S. economy has grown, the share of income spent on food—and therefore the share of total U.S. income earned by farmers—has fallen.

Second, agriculture has been a technologically progressive sector for approximately 150 years in the United States, with steadily increasing yields over time. You might think that technological progress would be good for farmers. But competition among farmers means that technological progress leads to lower food prices. Meanwhile, the demand for food is price-inelastic, so falling prices of agricultural goods, other things equal, reduce the total revenue of farmers. That's right: progress in farming is good for consumers but bad for farmers.

Photodisc

The combination of these effects explains the relative decline of farming. Even if farming weren't such a technologically progressive sector, the low income elasticity of demand for food would ensure that the income of farmers grows more slowly than the economy as a whole. The combination of rapid technological progress in farming with price-inelastic demand for farm products reinforces this effect, further reducing the growth of farm income. In short, the U.S. farm sector has been a victim of success—the U.S. economy's success as a whole (which reduces the importance of spending on food) and its own success in increasing yields.

Economists often use estimates of the income elasticity of demand to predict which industries will grow most rapidly as the incomes of consumers grow over time. In doing this, they often find it useful to make a further distinction among normal goods, identifying which are *income-elastic* and which are *income-inelastic.*

The demand for a good is **income-elastic** if the income elasticity of demand for that good is greater than 1. When income rises, the demand for income-elastic goods rises *faster* than income. Luxury goods, such as second homes and international travel, tend to be income-elastic. The demand for a good is **income-inelastic** if the income elasticity of demand for that good is positive but less than 1. When income rises, the demand for income-inelastic goods rises as well, but more slowly than income. Necessities such as food and clothing tend to be income-inelastic.

The demand for a good is **income-elastic** if the income elasticity of demand for that good is greater than 1.

The demand for a good is **income-inelastic** if the income elasticity of demand for that good is positive but less than 1.

The Price Elasticity of Supply

In the wake of the flu vaccine shortfall of 2004, attempts by vaccine distributors to drive up the price of vaccines would have been much less effective if a higher price had induced a large increase in the output of flu vaccines by flu vaccine manufacturers other than Chiron. In fact, if the rise in price had precipitated a significant increase in flu vaccine production, the price would have been pushed back down. But that didn't happen because, as we mentioned earlier, it would have been far too costly and technically difficult to produce more vaccine for the 2004–2005 flu season. (In reality, the production of flu vaccine is begun a year before it is to be distributed.) This was another critical element in the ability of some flu vaccine distributors, like Med-Stat, to get

TEACH Connect It

Now that students have learned about several elasticities as well as price elasticity of demand, making the connection to price elasticity of supply should be straightforward. Elasticity of supply looks at the responsiveness of quantity supplied to the price of that good:

$$E_s = \frac{\%\text{ Change in } Q_s}{\%\text{ Change in } P}$$

- When $E_s = 0$ (vertical supply curve), E_s is perfectly inelastic and P has no effect on Q_s (Q_s remains constant).
- When $E_s =$ infinity (horizontal supply curve), E_s is perfectly elastic when Q_s has no effect on P (P is constant).

TEACH Teach It

The major determinants of elasticity of supply are the availability of inputs (more available allows more response to price change and thus more elastic) and time (longer time allows more response to price change and thus more elastic).

TEACH Teach It

Make sure students note that price elasticity of demand (and supply) are evaluated relative to 1, but other elasticities are evaluated relative to 0. That is, we talk about elastic and inelastic demand and supply, depending on whether the value is greater than or less than 1. But with cross-price elasticity and income elasticity of demand, we are interested in whether they are greater than or less than 0 (whether they are positive or negative).

Module 48 Other Important Elasticities 479

TEACH Graph It

Have students refer to Figure 48.1. Remind them that price elasticity of supply is

$$\frac{\%\text{ Change in } Q_s}{\%\text{ Change in } P}$$

- Ask students how much quantity can change in panel (a). *It doesn't ever change.* Have students enter 0 for percentage change in quantity and solve. *0/% change in price = 0.*
- Ask students how much price can change in panel (b). *It doesn't ever change.* Have students put in 0 for percentage change in price and solve. *% change in Q_d/0 = undefined or infinite.*
- Show students this visual to help them relate elasticity to the slope of the demand curve:

Elastic Inelastic

TEACH Teach It

Reminders:

- Perfectly inelastic supply has $E_s = 0$ and is shown by a vertical line. A change in price leaves quantity supplied unchanged.
- Perfectly elastic supply has E_s = infinity and is shown by a horizontal line. A price above the vertical line price will have a quantity supplied being infinite and a price below the vertical line price will have a quantity supplied of zero.

FOCUS Active Learning

TRM Assign **Worksheet 48.1 (Drawing Perfect Elasticity and Inelasticity)** from the TRM for an exercise and practice in the elasticity of supply.

significantly higher prices for their product: a low responsiveness in the quantity of output supplied to the higher price of flu vaccine by flu vaccine producers. To measure the response of producers to price changes, we need a measure parallel to the price elasticity of demand—the *price elasticity of supply*.

Measuring the Price Elasticity of Supply

The **price elasticity of supply** is a measure of the responsiveness of the quantity of a good supplied to the price of that good. It is the ratio of the percent change in the quantity supplied to the percent change in the price as we move along the supply curve.

The **price elasticity of supply** is defined the same way as the price elasticity of demand (although there is no minus sign to be eliminated here):

$$\textbf{(48-3)}\quad \text{Price elasticity of supply} = \frac{\%\text{ change in quantity supplied}}{\%\text{ change in price}}$$

The only difference is that here we consider movements along the supply curve rather than movements along the demand curve.

Suppose that the price of tomatoes rises by 10%. If the quantity of tomatoes supplied also increases by 10% in response, the price elasticity of supply of tomatoes is 1 (10%/10%) and supply is unit-elastic. If the quantity supplied increases by 5%, the price elasticity of supply is 0.5 and supply is inelastic; if the quantity increases by 20%, the price elasticity of supply is 2 and supply is elastic.

As in the case of demand, the extreme values of the price elasticity of supply have a simple graphical representation. Panel (a) of **Figure 48.1** shows the supply of cell phone frequencies, the portion of the radio spectrum that is suitable for sending and receiving cell phone signals. Governments own the right to sell the use of this part of the radio spectrum to cell phone operators inside their borders. But governments can't increase or decrease the number of cell phone frequencies they have to offer—for technical reasons, the quantity of frequencies suitable for cell phone operation is fixed. So the supply curve for cell phone frequencies is a vertical line, which we have assumed is set at

Figure 48.1 Two Extreme Cases of Price Elasticity of Supply

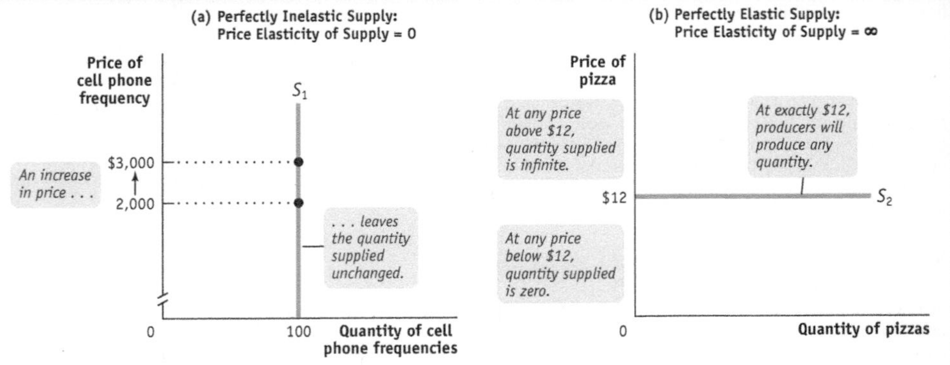

Panel (a) shows a perfectly inelastic supply curve, which is a vertical line. The price elasticity of supply is zero: the quantity supplied is always the same, regardless of price. Panel (b) shows a perfectly elastic supply curve, which is a horizontal line. At a price of $12, producers will supply any quantity, but they will supply none at a price below $12. If the price rises above $12, they will supply an extremely large quantity.

480 **Section 9** Behind the Demand Curve: Consumer Choice the quantity of 100 frequencies. As you move up and down that curve, the change in the quantity supplied by the government is zero, whatever the change in price. So panel (a) illustrates a case of **perfectly inelastic supply**, meaning that the price elasticity of supply is zero.

Panel (b) shows the supply curve for pizza. We suppose that it costs $12 to produce a pizza, including all opportunity costs. At any price below $12, it would be unprofitable to produce pizza and all the pizza parlors would go out of business. At a price of $12 or more, there are many producers who could operate pizza parlors. The ingredients—flour, tomatoes, cheese—are plentiful. And if necessary, more tomatoes could be grown, more milk could be produced to make mozzarella cheese, and so on. So by allowing profits, any price above $12 would elicit the supply of an extremely large quantity of pizzas. The implied supply curve is therefore a horizontal line at $12. Since even a tiny increase in the price would lead to an enormous increase in the quantity supplied, the price elasticity of supply would be virtually infinite. A horizontal supply curve such as this represents a case of **perfectly elastic supply**.

As our cell phone frequencies and pizza examples suggest, real-world instances of both perfectly inelastic and perfectly elastic supply are easier to find than their counterparts in demand.

There is **perfectly inelastic supply** when the price elasticity of supply is zero, so that changes in the price of the good have no effect on the quantity supplied. A perfectly inelastic supply curve is a vertical line.

There is **perfectly elastic supply** if the quantity supplied is zero below some price and infinite above that price. A perfectly elastic supply curve is a horizontal line.

What Factors Determine the Price Elasticity of Supply?

Our examples tell us the main determinant of the price elasticity of supply: the availability of inputs. In addition, as with the price elasticity of demand, time may also play a role in the price elasticity of supply. Here we briefly summarize the two factors.

The Availability of Inputs The price elasticity of supply tends to be large when inputs are readily available and can be shifted into and out of production at a relatively low cost. It tends to be small when inputs are available only in a more-or-less fixed quantity or can be shifted into and out of production only at a relatively high cost.

Time The price elasticity of supply tends to grow larger as producers have more time to respond to a price change. This means that the long-run price elasticity of supply is typically higher than the short-run elasticity. In the case of the flu vaccine shortfall, time was the crucial element because flu vaccine must be grown in cultures over many months.

The price elasticity of pizza supply is very high because the inputs needed to make more pizza are readily available. The price elasticity of cell phone frequencies is zero because an essential input—the radio spectrum—cannot be increased at all.

Many industries are like pizza and have large price elasticities of supply: they can be readily expanded because they don't require any special or unique resources. On the other hand, the price elasticity of supply is usually substantially less than perfectly elastic for goods that involve limited natural resources: minerals like gold or copper, agricultural products like coffee that flourish only on certain types of land, and renewable resources like ocean fish that can be exploited only up to a point without destroying the resource.

Given enough time, producers are often able to significantly change the amount they produce in response to a price change, even when production involves a limited natural resource. For example, consider again the effects of a surge in flu vaccine prices, but this time focus on the supply response. If the price were to rise to $90 per vaccination

AP® Exam Tip

Time gives firms a chance to adjust their size and find new sources of inputs. So the more time, the more ability to respond to price changes and the greater the elasticity of supply.

FOCUS Flip It

TRM Show Jacob Clifford's video "Micro 2.9A Elasticity of Demand Coefficients" (see econextras video list with hyperlinks on the bcs and TRFD). It explains elasticity of demand and supply, cross-price elasticity, and income elasticity and will be a good review of what students have already studied; it will also provide an introduction to this module. Refer your class to **Worksheet 48.2 (Elasticities)** from the TRM for questions to accompany this video.

Module 48 Other Important Elasticities **481**

FOCUS Active Learning

TRM Have students find information on the oil markets since 2008 in Tom Konrad's article "The End of Elastic Oil" at http://www.forbes.com/sites/tomkonrad/2012/01/26/the-end-of-elastic-oil/. Direct students to **Worksheet 48.3 (Elasticity and Oil)** from the TRM for information on this comparison.

OPEN & CLOSE Exit Slip

TRM *Please see* ***Exit Slip: Module 48*** *in the TRM for formative multiple-choice questions to ask your students before finishing your lesson. These questions will help you quickly assess whether your students have mastered the module's concepts before moving on.*

Answers to the Exit Slip Questions

1. D
2. E
3. C

and stay there for a number of years, there would almost certainly be a substantial increase in flu vaccine production. Producers such as Chiron would eventually respond by increasing the size of their manufacturing plants, hiring more lab technicians, and so on. But significantly enlarging the capacity of a biotech manufacturing lab takes several years, not weeks or months or even a single year.

For this reason, economists often make a distinction between the short-run elasticity of supply, usually referring to a few weeks or months, and the long-run elasticity of supply, usually referring to several years. In most industries, the long-run elasticity of supply is larger than the short-run elasticity.

An Elasticity Menagerie

We've just run through quite a few different types of elasticity. Keeping them all straight can be a challenge, but all of these elasticities are important. So we provide a summary of all the types of elasticity we have discussed and their implications in **Table 48.1**.

Table 48.1 An Elasticity Menagerie

Name	Elasticity values	Significance
Price elasticity of demand = $\frac{\text{\% change in quantity demanded}}{\text{\% change in price}}$ (dropping the minus sign)		
Perfectly inelastic demand	0	Price has no effect on quantity demanded (vertical demand curve).
Inelastic demand	Between 0 and 1	A rise in price increases total revenue.
Unit-elastic demand	Exactly 1	Changes in price have no effect on total revenue.
Elastic demand	Greater than 1, less than ∞	A rise in price reduces total revenue.
Perfectly elastic demand	∞	A rise in price causes quantity demanded to fall to 0. A fall in price leads to an infinite quantity demanded (horizontal demand curve).
Cross-price elasticity of demand = $\frac{\text{\% change in quantity } \textit{of one good} \text{ demanded}}{\text{\% change in price } \textit{of another good}}$		
Complements	Negative	Quantity demanded of one good falls when the price of another rises.
Substitutes	Positive	Quantity demanded of one good rises when the price of another rises.
Income elasticity of demand = $\frac{\text{\% change in quantity demanded}}{\text{\% change in income}}$		
Inferior good	Negative	Quantity demanded falls when income rises.
Normal good, income-inelastic	Positive, less than 1	Quantity demanded rises when income rises, but not as rapidly as income.
Normal good, income-elastic	Greater than 1	Quantity demanded rises when income rises, and more rapidly than income.
Price elasticity of supply = $\frac{\text{\% change in quantity supplied}}{\text{\% change in price}}$		
Perfectly inelastic supply	0	Price has no effect on quantity supplied (vertical supply curve).
Inelastic supply	Between 0 and 1	Upward-sloping supply curve
Unit-elastic supply	Exactly 1	Upward-sloping supply curve
Elastic supply	Greater than 1, less than ∞	Upward-sloping supply curve
Perfectly elastic supply	∞	Any fall in price causes quantity supplied to fall to 0. Any rise in price elicits an infinite quantity supplied (horizontal supply curve).

482 Section 9 Behind the Demand Curve: Consumer Choice

MODULE 48 Review

Check Your Understanding

1. After Chelsea's income increased from $12,000 to $18,000 a year, her purchases of music downloads increased from 10 to 40 music downloads a year. Calculate Chelsea's income elasticity of demand for music downloads using the midpoint method.
2. As the price of margarine rises by 20%, a manufacturer of baked goods increases its quantity of butter demanded by 5%. Calculate the cross-price elasticity of demand between butter and margarine. Are butter and margarine substitutes or complements for this manufacturer?
3. Using the midpoint method, calculate the price elasticity of supply for web-design services when the price per hour rises from $100 to $150 and the number of hours supplied increases from 300,000 hours to 500,000. Is supply elastic, inelastic, or unit-elastic?

Tackle the Test: Multiple-Choice Questions

1. If the cross-price elasticity between two goods is negative, this means that the two goods are
   - a. substitutes.
   - b. complements.
   - c. normal.
   - d. inferior.
   - e. luxuries.
2. If Kylie buys 200 units of good X when her income is $20,000 and 300 units of good X when her income increases to $25,000, her income elasticity of demand, using the midpoint method, is
   - a. 0.06.
   - b. 0.5.
   - c. 1.65.
   - d. 1.8.
   - e. 2.00.
3. The income elasticity of demand for a normal good is
   - a. zero.
   - b. 1.
   - c. infinite.
   - d. positive.
   - e. negative.
4. A perfectly elastic supply curve is
   - a. positively sloped.
   - b. negatively sloped.
   - c. vertical.
   - d. horizontal.
   - e. U-shaped
5. Which of the following leads to a more inelastic price elasticity of supply?
   - I. the use of inputs that are easily obtained
   - II. a high degree of substitutability between inputs
   - III. a shorter time period in which to supply the good
   - a. I only
   - b. II only
   - c. III only
   - d. I and II only
   - e. I, II, and III

Answers to Module 48 Review Questions

Check Your Understanding

1. By the midpoint method, the percent increase in Chelsea's income is $\frac{\$18{,}000 - \$12{,}000}{(\$12{,}000 + \$18{,}000)/2} \times 100 = \frac{\$6{,}000}{\$15{,}000} \times 100 = 40\%$. Similarly, the percent increase in her consumption of music downloads is $\frac{40 - 10}{(10 + 40)/2} \times 100 = \frac{30}{25} \times 100 =$ 120%. Chelsea's income elasticity of demand for music downloads is therefore $\frac{120\%}{40\%} = 3$.

2. The cross-price elasticity of demand is $\frac{5\%}{20\%} = 0.25$. Since the cross-price elasticity of demand is positive, the two goods are substitutes.

3. By the midpoint method, the percent change in the number of hours of web-design services supplied is $\frac{500{,}000 - 300{,}000}{(300{,}000 + 500{,}000)/2} \times 100 = \frac{200{,}000}{400{,}000} \times 100 = 50\%$. Similarly, the percent change in the price of web-design services is $\frac{\$150 - \$100}{(\$100 + \$150)/2} \times 100 = \frac{\$50}{\$125} \times 100 = 40\%$. The price elasticity of supply is $\frac{50\%}{40\%} = 1.25$. Since elasticity is greater than 1, supply is elastic.

Tackle the Test: Multiple-Choice Questions

1. b
2. d
3. d
4. d
5. c

Tackle the Test: Free-Response Question Rubric for FRQ 2 (5 points)

1 point: 40%/20% = 2

1 point: Elastic

1 point: Horizontal supply curve on correctly labeled graph, as shown in the figure.

1 point: Inputs are readily available.

1 point: When inputs are available to be shifted into or out of production at a low cost, firms can easily expand the quantity of output supplied.

Tackle the Test: Free-Response Questions

1. Refer to the table below to answer the following questions.

Price of Good A	Quantity of Good A Demanded	Quantity of Good B Demanded
$10	100	5
8	110	10

a. Using the midpoint method, calculate the price elasticity of demand for good A.

b. Give the formula for calculating the cross-price elasticity of demand between good B and good A.

c. Using the midpoint method, calculate the cross-price elasticity of demand between good A and good B.

d. What does your answer for part c tell you about the relationship between the two goods? Explain.

Rubric for FRQ 1 (5 points)

1 point: 0.43

1 point: % change in quantity of good B/% change in price of good A or (change in Q_B/average Q_B)/(change in P_A/average P_A)

1 point: −3

1 point: They are complements.

1 point: Cross-price elasticity is negative—when the price of good A goes down, in addition to buying more of good A, people buy more of good B to go along with it.

2. Assume the price of corn rises by 20% and this causes suppliers to increase the quantity of corn supplied by 40%.

a. Calculate the price elasticity of supply.

b. In this case, is supply elastic or inelastic?

c. Draw a correctly labeled graph of a supply curve illustrating the most extreme case of the category of elasticity you found in part b (either perfectly elastic or perfectly inelastic supply).

d. What would likely be true of the availability of inputs for a firm with the supply curve you drew in part c? Explain.

(5 points)

484 **Section 9** Behind the Demand Curve: Consumer Choice

Glenn Asakawa/The Denver Post via Getty Images

MODULE 49 Consumer and Producer Surplus

In this Module, you will learn to:

- Explain the meaning of consumer surplus and its relationship to the demand curve
- Explain the meaning of producer surplus and its relationship to the supply curve

There is a lively market in second-hand college textbooks. At the end of each term, some students who took a course decide that the money they can make by selling their used books is worth more to them than keeping the books. And some students who are taking the course next term prefer to buy a somewhat battered but less expensive used textbook rather than pay full price for a new one.

Textbook publishers and authors are not happy about these transactions because they cut into sales of new books. But both the students who sell used books and those who buy them clearly benefit from the existence of the market. That is why many college bookstores facilitate their trade, buying used textbooks and selling them alongside the new books.

Can we put a number on what used textbook buyers and sellers gain from these transactions? Can we answer the question "*How much* do the buyers and sellers of textbooks gain from the existence of the used-book market?"

Yes, we can. In this module we will see how to measure benefits, such as those to buyers of used textbooks, from being able to purchase a good—known as *consumer surplus*. And we will see that there is a corresponding measure, *producer surplus*, of the benefits sellers receive from being able to sell a good.

The concepts of consumer surplus and producer surplus are useful for analyzing a wide variety of economic issues. They let us calculate how much benefit producers and consumers receive from the existence of a market. They also allow us to calculate how the welfare of consumers and producers is affected by changes in market prices. Such calculations play a crucial role in evaluating many economic policies.

What information do we need to calculate consumer and producer surplus? Surprisingly, all we need are the demand and supply curves for a good. That is, the supply and demand model isn't just a model of how a competitive market works—it's also a model of how much consumers and producers gain from participating in that market. So our

AP® Exam Tip

On the AP® exam you may be asked to draw a graph and shade the areas that represent consumer and producer surplus.

PD To prepare for teaching this lesson, you may want to consult the **Module 49 Sample Lecture** in the TRM.

OPEN & CLOSE Start Here

Show your students a good that many of them would probably like to have (e.g., a mini candy bar), and direct them to write down how much they would be willing and able to pay for it. Indicate how much you paid for the good, and ask your class how that price was determined (supply and demand!). Ask those students willing and able to pay more than the price of the candy bar to calculate the difference between what they said they would pay and the market price, and identify the student(s) with the largest difference. You might want to offer the item to a student and ask her to state the difference between what she would pay for the candy bar and the price of zero. Ask the student(s) how they feel about not having to pay as much as they were willing to pay. Use this discussion to introduce consumer surplus.

St. Louis Federal Reserve Bank Resources

The Illustrated Consumer and Producer Surplus

This series of slides aids students in defining and calculating consumer surplus, producer surplus, and total economic surplus.

FOCUS Graph It

Use the data from the opening discussion to have students plot a demand curve. For each student who was willing to spend more than you did for the good, record his or her willingness to pay on the blackboard. Place the values in descending order and have students plot the quantity demanded at the various willingness-to-pay amounts (remind students that any student willing to spend a particular amount is also willing to pay any lower amount). Note that the resulting willingness-to-pay curve is the demand curve.

first step will be to learn how consumer and producer surplus can be derived from the demand and supply curves. We will then see how these concepts can be applied to actual economic issues.

Consumer Surplus and the Demand Curve

First-year college students are often surprised by the prices of the textbooks required for their classes. The College Board estimates that in 2013–2014 students at public four-year schools, on average, spent $1,207 for books and supplies. But at the end of the semester, students might again be surprised to find out that they can sell back at least some of the textbooks they used for the semester for a percentage of the purchase price (offsetting some of the cost of textbooks). The ability to purchase used textbooks at the start of the semester and to sell back used textbooks at the end of the semester is beneficial to students on a budget. In fact, the market for used textbooks is a big business in terms of dollars and cents—approximately $1.5 billion in 2011–2012. This market provides a convenient starting point for us to develop the concepts of consumer and producer surplus. We'll use the concepts of consumer and producer surplus to understand exactly how buyers and sellers benefit from a competitive market and how big those benefits are. In addition, these concepts assist in the analysis of what happens when competitive markets don't work well or there is interference in the market.

Let's begin by looking at the market for used textbooks, starting with the buyers. The key point, as we'll see in a minute, is that the demand curve is derived from their tastes or preferences—and that those same preferences also determine how much they gain from the opportunity to buy used books.

Willingness to Pay and the Demand Curve

A consumer's **willingness to pay** for a good is the maximum price at which he or she would buy that good.

A used book is not as good as a new book—it will be battered and coffee-stained, may include someone else's highlighting, and may not be completely up to date. How much this bothers you depends on your preferences. Some potential buyers would prefer to buy the used book even if it is only slightly cheaper than a new one, while others would buy the used book only if it is considerably cheaper. Let's define a potential buyer's **willingness to pay** as the maximum price at which he or she would buy a good, in this case a used textbook. An individual won't buy the good if it costs more than this amount but is eager to do so if it costs less. If the price is just equal to an individual's willingness to pay, he or she is indifferent between buying and not buying. For the sake of simplicity, we'll assume that the individual buys the good in this case.

The table in **Figure 49.1** shows five potential buyers of a used book that costs $100 new, listed in order of their willingness to pay. At one extreme is Aleisha, who will buy a second-hand book even if the price is as high as $59. Brad is less willing to have a used book and will buy one only if the price is $45 or less. Claudia is willing to pay only $35 and Darren, only $25. Edwina, who really doesn't like the idea of a used book, will buy one only if it costs no more than $10.

How many of these five students will actually buy a used book? It depends on the price. If the price of a used book is $55, only Aleisha buys one; if the price is $40, Aleisha and Brad both buy used books, and so on. So the information in the table can be used to construct the *demand schedule* for used textbooks.

We can use this demand schedule to derive the market demand curve shown in Figure 49.1. Because we are considering only a small number of consumers, this curve doesn't look like the smooth demand curves we have seen previously, for markets that contained hundreds or thousands of consumers. This demand curve is step-shaped, with alternating horizontal and vertical segments. Each horizontal segment—each step—corresponds to one potential buyer's willingness to pay. However, we'll see shortly

Figure 49.1 The Demand Curve for Used Textbooks

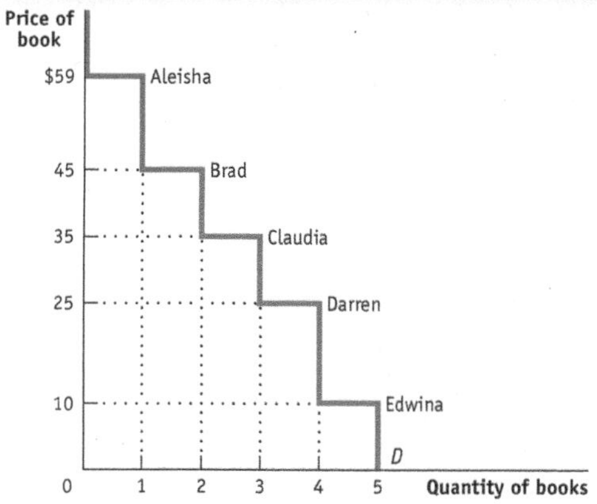

Potential buyers	Willingness to pay
Aleisha	$59
Brad	45
Claudia	35
Darren	25
Edwina	10

With only five potential consumers in this market, the demand curve is step-shaped. Each step represents one consumer, and its height indicates that consumer's willingness to pay—the maximum price at which each will buy a used textbook—as indicated in the table. Aleisha has the highest willingness to pay at $59, Brad has the next highest at $45, and so on down to Edwina with the lowest willingness to pay at $10. At a price of $59, the quantity demanded is one (by Aleisha); at a price of $45, the quantity demanded is two (by Aleisha and Brad); and so on until you reach a price of $10, at which all five students are willing to purchase a book.

that for the analysis of consumer surplus it doesn't matter whether the demand curve is step-shaped, as in this figure, or whether there are many consumers, making the curve smooth.

Willingness to Pay and Consumer Surplus

Suppose that the campus bookstore makes used textbooks available at a price of $30. In that case Aleisha, Brad, and Claudia will buy books. Do they gain from their purchases, and if so, how much?

The answer, shown in **Table 49.1** on the next page, is that each student who purchases a book does achieve a net gain, but that the amount of the gain differs among students. Aleisha would have been willing to pay $59, so her net gain is $59 – $30 = $29. Brad would have been willing to pay $45, so his net gain is $45 – $30 = $15. Claudia would have been willing to pay $35, so her net gain is $35 – $30 = $5. Darren and Edwina, however, won't be willing to buy a used book at a price of $30, so they neither gain nor lose.

The net gain that a buyer achieves from the purchase of a good is called that buyer's **individual consumer surplus**. What we learn from this example is that whenever a buyer pays a price less than his or her willingness to pay, the buyer achieves some individual consumer surplus.

The sum of the individual consumer surpluses achieved by all the buyers of a good is known as the **total consumer surplus** achieved in the market. In Table 49.1, the total consumer surplus is the sum of the individual consumer surpluses achieved by Aleisha, Brad, and Claudia: $29 + $15 + $5 = $49.

Individual consumer surplus is the net gain to an individual buyer from the purchase of a good. It is equal to the difference between the buyer's willingness to pay and the price paid.

Total consumer surplus is the sum of the individual consumer surpluses of all the buyers of a good in a market.

TEACH Connect It

Examples of consumer surplus can be for an individual (e.g., MY demand for 1, 2, 3, 4, or 5 units of a good) OR for a market (e.g., 1 unit of the good demanded by 1, 2, 3, 4, or 5 individuals). In either case, the demand curve shows that price and quantity demanded are inversely related, as students learned in Section 2 when we introduced the concept of demand. For an individual to be willing and able to purchase more of a good (or for more individuals to be willing to do so), the price must be lower (and vice versa). *Willingness to pay is found on the demand curve* in either example. So that students are not confused by the "step-shaped" demand curve in Figure 49.1, explain the difference between a discrete demand function (one that only shows quantity at whole units of quantity) and a continuous demand function (one that allows for whole units AND fractions of units). Up to this point, we have shown discrete values in demand schedules and continuous units when we connect the points for straight-line demand functions. The discrete unit demand schedules and step demand functions are used to introduce the concept of consumer surplus.

FOCUS Test It

TRM For practice problems, refer students to **Worksheet 49.1 (Practicing Consumer Surplus)** from the TRM.

Module 49 Consumer and Producer Surplus 487

Table 49.1 Consumer Surplus When the Price of a Used Textbook Is $30			
Potential buyer	Willingness to pay	Price paid	Individual consumer surplus = Willingness to pay − Price paid
Aleisha	$59	$30	$29
Brad	45	30	15
Claudia	35	30	5
Darren	25	—	—
Edwina	10	—	—
All buyers			Total consumer surplus = $49

The term **consumer surplus** is often used to refer to both individual and total consumer surplus.

Economists often use the term **consumer surplus** to refer to both individual and total consumer surplus. We will follow this practice; it will always be clear in context whether we are referring to the consumer surplus achieved by an individual or by all buyers.

Total consumer surplus can be represented graphically. **Figure 49.2** reproduces the demand curve from Figure 49.1. Each step in that demand curve is one book wide and represents one consumer. For example, the height of Aleisha's step is $59, her willingness to pay. This step forms the top of a rectangle, with $30—the price she actually pays for a book—forming the bottom. The area of Aleisha's rectangle, ($59 − $30) × 1 = $29, is her consumer surplus from purchasing one book at $30. So the individual consumer surplus Aleisha gains is the *area of the dark blue rectangle* shown in Figure 49.2.

In addition to Aleisha, Brad and Claudia will also each buy a book when the price is $30. Like Aleisha, they benefit from their purchases, though not as much, because they each have a lower willingness to pay. Figure 49.2 also shows the consumer surplus gained by Brad and Claudia; again, this can be measured by the areas of the appropriate rectangles. Darren and Edwina, because they do not buy books at a price of $30, receive no consumer surplus.

Figure 49.2 Consumer Surplus in the Used-Textbook Market

At a price of $30, Aleisha, Brad, and Claudia each buy a book but Darren and Edwina do not. Aleisha, Brad, and Claudia get individual consumer surpluses equal to the difference between their willingness to pay and the price, illustrated by the areas of the shaded rectangles. Both Darren and Edwina have a willingness to pay less than $30, so they are unwilling to buy a book in this market; they receive zero consumer surplus. The total consumer surplus is given by the entire shaded area—the sum of the individual consumer surpluses of Aleisha, Brad, and Claudia—equal to $29 + $15 + $5 = $49.

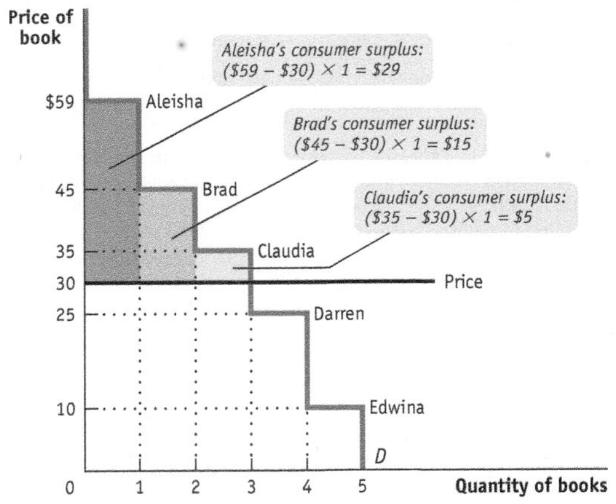

FOCUS Active Learning

Have students use the data from the opening discussion to calculate the difference between students' willingness to pay and the price you paid (for students willing to pay at least the price of the good). Explain that the resulting amount is each student's individual consumer surplus (IF he or she purchased the good). Have students add up these amounts to get the total consumer surplus for the class. Ask them to compare their calculation of total consumer surplus to the calculation of consumer surplus in Figure 49.2.

TEACH Teach It

Now show students the process of summing individual consumer surpluses to calculate total consumer surplus using a continuous (straight-line) demand curve. Label the axes *P* and *Q* and draw a downward-sloping straight-line demand curve. Add a horizontal line labeled "Price." Emphasize that the market price is determined by supply and demand, but the supply curve isn't shown because we want to focus on demand and keep the graph from becoming too cluttered.

Start with a quantity of 1 and ask students how much consumers have to pay for 1 unit. You want them to learn that the market price is always the answer to what consumers have to pay. Next ask how much consumers are willing to pay. You want students to learn that the point on the demand curve is always the answer to what consumers are willing to pay. Draw a line from the market price up to the demand curve. Do the same thing for a quantity of 2, 3, 4, etc. out to where the market price crosses the demand curve. Ask students about the difference between what consumers have to pay and what they are willing to pay at the market price. Students should see that there is no difference—therefore, no consumer surplus for that unit. Ask your class what happens at higher quantities (consumers aren't willing to pay the market price for any units beyond the market quantity).

Now tell students you plan to repeat the same process for 1.5, 2.5, 3.5, 4.5, 1.25, 2.25, 3.25, 4.25, etc. units. Keep drawing lines between the market price and the demand curve until the area starts to fill in. Ask students what will happen if you continue doing this for all possible fractions of units of output (*the triangle area will be filled in*). Use the discussion to move to the calculation of total consumer surplus as the area of the triangle above price and below the demand curve.

488 Section 9 Behind the Demand Curve: Consumer Choice

The total consumer surplus achieved in this market is just the sum of the individual consumer surpluses received by Aleisha, Brad, and Claudia. So total consumer surplus is equal to the combined area of the three rectangles—the entire shaded area in Figure 49.2. Another way to say this is that total consumer surplus is equal to the area below the demand curve but above the price.

This is worth repeating as a general principle: *The total consumer surplus generated by purchases of a good at a given price is equal to the area below the demand curve but above that price.* The same principle applies regardless of the number of consumers.

When we consider large markets, this graphical representation becomes particularly helpful. Consider, for example, the sales of personal computers to millions of potential buyers. Each potential buyer has a maximum price that he or she is willing to pay. With so many potential buyers, the demand curve will be smooth, like the one shown in **Figure 49.3**.

Suppose that at a price of $1,500, a total of 1 million computers are purchased. How much do consumers gain from being able to buy those 1 million computers? We could answer that question by calculating the individual consumer surplus of each buyer and then adding these numbers up to arrive at a total. But it is much easier just to look at Figure 49.3 and use the fact that total consumer surplus is equal to the shaded area below the demand curve but above the price. Recall that the area of a triangle is ½ × the base of the triangle × the height of the triangle. So the total consumer surplus in this case is ½ × 1 million × $3,500 = $1.75 billion.

How Changing Prices Affect Consumer Surplus

It is often important to know how price *changes* affect consumer surplus. For example, we may want to know the harm to consumers from a frost in Florida that drives up the prices of oranges, or consumers' gain from the introduction of fish farming that makes salmon steaks less expensive. The same approach we have used to derive consumer surplus can be used to answer questions about how changes in prices affect consumers.

Let's return to the example of the market for used textbooks. Suppose that the bookstore decided to sell used textbooks for $20 instead of $30. By how much would this fall in price increase consumer surplus?

AP® Exam Tip

You may be asked to calculate the size of the area that represents consumer surplus, which is bounded by the demand curve, the price line, and the vertical axis. Remember: the area of a triangle is ½ the base times the height.

iStockphoto

Figure 49.3 Consumer Surplus

The demand curve for computers is smooth because there are many potential buyers. At a price of $1,500, 1 million computers are demanded. The consumer surplus at this price is equal to the shaded area: the area below the demand curve but above the price. The area of a triangle is ½ × the base of the triangle × the height of the triangle. So the total consumer surplus in this case is ½ × 1 million × $3,500 = $1.75 billion. This is the total net gain to consumers generated from buying and consuming computers when the price is $1,500.

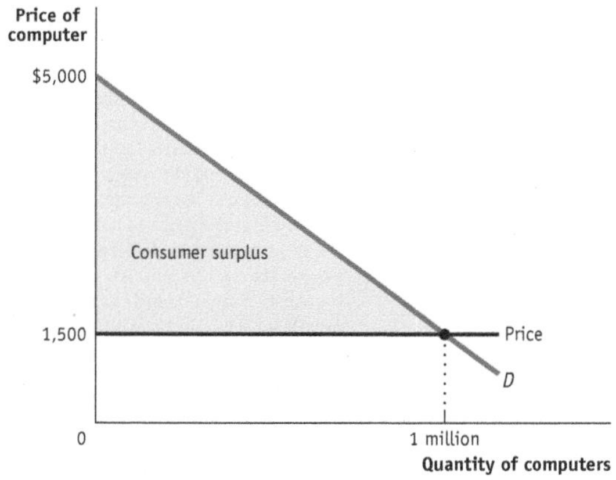

FOCUS Graph It

Have students draw a correctly labeled, straight-line demand curve and label the consumer surplus triangle on their graph. Ask them to write an explanation of what that area represents. Make sure they realize that the value of consumer surplus is in dollars and represents the difference between what consumers would have paid (from the demand curve) and what they actually paid (the market price). Therefore, it represents benefits consumers received but did not have to pay for.

Module 49 Consumer and Producer Surplus 489

FOCUS Test It

TRM To answer questions relating to consumer surplus, refer students to **Worksheet 49.2 (Consumer Surplus Questions)** from the TRM.

FOCUS Active Learning

Have students use their straight-line demand curve labeled with the consumer surplus triangle (or create a new consumer surplus graph) to show a decrease in price and identify the new total consumer surplus area. Ask them whether consumer surplus has increased or decreased (*increased*), and have them shade the area of change in consumer surplus. Have them explain WHY consumer surplus increases when the price falls.

Figure 49.4 Consumer Surplus and a Fall in the Price of Used Textbooks

There are two parts to the increase in consumer surplus generated by a fall in price from \$30 to \$20. The first is given by the dark blue rectangle: each person who would have bought at the original price of \$30—Aleisha, Brad, and Claudia—receives an increase in consumer surplus equal to the total reduction in price, \$10. So the area of the dark blue rectangle corresponds to an amount equal to $3 \times \$10 = \$30$. The second part is given by the light blue area: the increase in consumer surplus for those who would *not* have bought at the original price of \$30 but who buy at the new price of \$20—namely, Darren. Darren's willingness to pay is \$25, so he now receives consumer surplus of \$5. The total increase in consumer surplus is $3 \times \$10 + \$5 = \$35$, represented by the sum of the shaded areas. Likewise, a rise in price from \$20 to \$30 would decrease consumer surplus by an amount equal to the sum of the shaded areas.

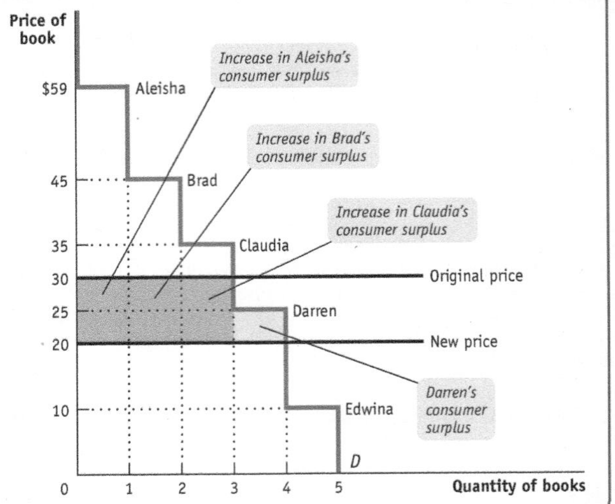

The answer is illustrated in **Figure 49.4**. As shown in the figure, there are two parts to the increase in consumer surplus. The first part, shaded dark blue, is the gain of those who would have bought books even at the higher price of \$30. Each of the students who would have bought books at \$30—Aleisha, Brad, and Claudia—now pays \$10 less, and therefore each gains \$10 in consumer surplus from the fall in price to \$20. So the dark blue area represents the $\$10 \times 3 = \$30$ increase in consumer surplus to those three buyers. The second part, shaded light blue, is the gain to those who would not have bought a book at \$30 but are willing to pay more than \$20. In this case that gain goes to Darren, who would not have bought a book at \$30 but does buy one at \$20. He gains \$5—the difference between his willingness to pay of \$25 and the new price of \$20. So the light blue area represents a further \$5 gain in consumer surplus. The total increase in consumer surplus is the sum of the shaded areas, \$35. Likewise, a rise in price from \$20 to \$30 would decrease consumer surplus by an amount equal to the sum of the shaded areas.

Figure 49.4 illustrates that when the price of a good falls, the area under the demand curve but above the price—the total consumer surplus—increases. **Figure 49.5** shows the same result for the case of a smooth demand curve for personal computers. Here we assume that the price of computers falls from \$4,300 to \$1,500, leading to an increase in the quantity demanded from 200,000 to 1 million units. As in the used-textbook example, we divide the gain in consumer surplus into two parts. The dark blue rectangle in Figure 49.5 corresponds to the dark blue area in Figure 49.4: it is the gain to the 200,000 people who would have bought computers even at the higher price of \$4,300. As a result of the price reduction, each receives additional surplus of \$2,800, so the area of the dark blue rectangle is $200{,}000 \times \$2{,}800 = \$560$ million. The light blue triangle in Figure 49.5 corresponds to the light blue area in Figure 49.4: it is the gain to people who would not have bought the good at the higher price but are willing to do so at a price of \$1,500. For example, the light blue triangle includes the gain to someone who would have been willing to pay \$2,000 for a computer and therefore gains \$500 in consumer surplus when

490 Section 9 Behind the Demand Curve: Consumer Choice

Figure 49.5 A Fall in the Price Increases Consumer Surplus

A fall in the price of a computer from \$4,300 to \$1,500 leads to an increase in the quantity demanded and an increase in consumer surplus. The change in total consumer surplus is given by the sum of the shaded areas: the total area below the demand curve and between the old and new prices. Here, the dark blue area represents the increase in consumer surplus for the 200,000 consumers who would have bought a computer at the original price of \$4,300; they each receive an increase in consumer surplus of \$2,800. The light blue area represents the increase in consumer surplus for those willing to buy at a price equal to or greater than \$1,500 but less than \$4,300. Similarly, a rise in the price of a computer from \$1,500 to \$4,300 generates a decrease in consumer surplus equal to the sum of the two shaded areas.

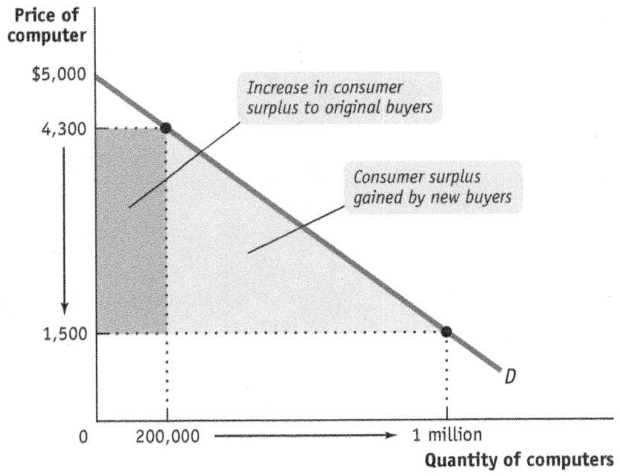

FOCUS Graph It

Have students refer to Figure 49.5 and use the formula for the area of a triangle to calculate consumer surplus if the price is \$1,500. Note that consumer surplus is the entire area under the demand curve, so the base of the triangle is 1 million (from zero to 1 million) and the height is \$3,500 (from \$1,500 to \$5,000). Make sure students go from the market price up to the intercept.

FYI A Matter of Life and Death

Each year about 4,000 people in the United States die while waiting for a kidney transplant. In 2014, some 99,200 were on the waiting list. Since the number of those in need of a kidney far exceeds availability, what is the best way to allocate available organs? A market isn't feasible. For understandable reasons, the sale of human body parts is illegal in this country. So the task of establishing a protocol for these situations has fallen to the nonprofit group United Network for Organ Sharing (UNOS).

Under current UNOS guidelines, a donated kidney goes to the person who has been waiting the longest. According to this system, an available kidney would go to a 75-year-old who has been waiting for 2 years instead of to a 25-year-old who has been waiting 6 months, even though the 25-year-old will likely live longer and benefit from the transplanted organ for a longer period of time.

To address this issue, the UNOS Kidney Transplantation Committee has proposed a new set of guidelines based on a concept it calls "net benefit." According to these new guidelines, kidneys would be allocated on the basis of who will receive the greatest net benefit, where net benefit is measured as the expected increase in lifespan from the transplant. And age is by far the biggest predictor of how long someone will live after a transplant. For example, a typical 25-year-old diabetic will gain an extra 8.7 years of life from a transplant, but a typical 55-year-old diabetic will gain only 3.6 extra years.

Under the current system, based on waiting times, transplants lead to about 44,000 extra years of life for recipients; under the proposed system, that number would jump to 55,000 extra years. The share of kidneys going to those in their 20s would triple; the share going to those 60 and older would be halved.

What does this have to do with consumer surplus? As you may have guessed, the UNOS concept of "net benefit" is a lot like individual consumer surplus—the individual consumer surplus generated from getting a new kidney. In essence, the proposed system would allocate donated kidneys according to who gets the greatest individual consumer surplus. In terms of results, then, its proposed "net benefit" system would operate a lot like a competitive market.

TEACH AP® Exam Tip

Consumer and producer surplus are represented by the area below the demand curve and above the supply curve. Students must be able to show the consumer/producer surplus triangle on a graph, identify the consumer/producer surplus on a graph they are shown, and calculate the area of the consumer/producer surplus triangle. Many students will thus need to review how to calculate the area of a triangle:

$\frac{1}{2}$ (base)(height) OR $\frac{\text{(base)(height)}}{2}$. Students who don't remember this formula may remember that the area of a rectangle is length times width. A triangle is a rectangle cut in half, so the formula is just $\frac{1}{2}$ (length)(width).

Module 49 Consumer and Producer Surplus 491

TEACH Connect It

Since students have already learned about consumer surplus, they can draw upon their understanding of consumer surplus as they study producer surplus. As you develop the concept and calculation of producer surplus, refer back to your presentation of consumer surplus.

FOCUS In the News

TRM Have your class read Victoria Duff's article "What Is a Good Example of a Producer Surplus?" at http://smallbusiness.chron.com/good-example-producer-surplus-36378.html. It is written from a business perspective and thus gives students the viewpoint of a producer. Refer them to **Worksheet 49.3 (Starbucks and Producer Surplus)** from the TRM for questions related to this article.

FOCUS Graph It

Remind students that the supply curve shows that price and quantity supplied are directly related, as they observed in Section 2. For a firm to be willing and able to sell more of a good, the price must be higher. Willingness to sell is based on seller cost (the seller's cost is the lowest price the seller will accept) and is found on the supply curve. So that students are not confused by the "step-shaped" supply curve in Figure 49.6, remind them of the difference between a discrete supply function (one that only shows quantity at whole units of quantity) and a continuous supply function (one that allows for whole units AND fractions of units). Up to this point, we have shown discrete values in supply schedules and continuous units when we connect the points for straight-line supply curves. The discrete unit supply schedules and step supply functions are used to introduce the concept of consumer surplus.

it is possible to buy a computer for only $1,500. The area of the light blue triangle is ½ × 800,000 × $2,800 = $1.12 billion. As before, the total gain in consumer surplus is the sum of the shaded areas, the increase in the area under the demand curve but above the price: $560 million + $1.12 billion = $1.68 billion.

What would happen if the price of a good were to rise instead of fall? We would do the same analysis in reverse. Suppose, for example, that for some reason the price of computers rises from $1,500 to $4,300. This would lead to a fall in consumer surplus equal to the sum of the shaded areas in Figure 49.5. This loss consists of two parts. The dark blue rectangle represents the loss to consumers who would still buy a computer, even at a price of $4,300. The light blue triangle represents the loss to consumers who decide not to buy a computer at the higher price.

Producer Surplus and the Supply Curve

Just as some buyers of a good would have been willing to pay more for their purchase than the price they actually pay, some sellers of a good would have been willing to sell it for less than the price they actually receive. We can therefore carry out an analysis of producer surplus and the supply curve that is almost exactly parallel to that of consumer surplus and the demand curve.

Cost and Producer Surplus

Consider a group of students who are potential sellers of used textbooks. Because they have different preferences, the various potential sellers differ in regard to the lowest price they would accept for their books. The table in **Figure 49.6** shows the prices at

Figure 49.6 The Supply Curve for Used Textbooks

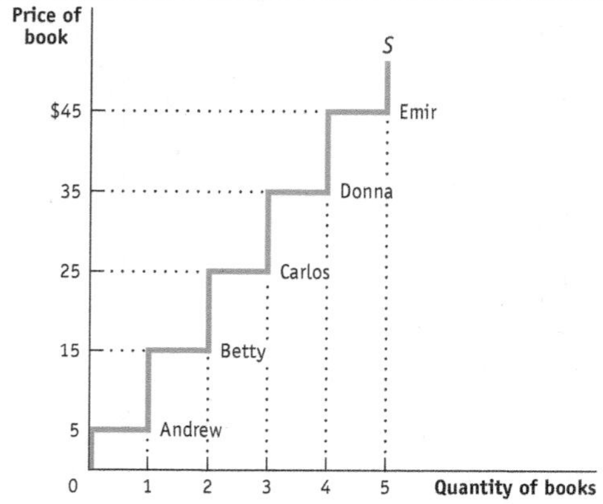

Potential sellers	Cost
Andrew	$5
Betty	15
Carlos	25
Donna	35
Emir	45

The supply curve illustrates sellers' cost, the lowest price at which a potential seller is willing to sell the good, and the quantity supplied at that price. Each of the five students has one book to sell and each has a different cost, as indicated in the accompanying table. At a price of $5 the quantity supplied is one (Andrew), at $15 it is two (Andrew and Betty), and so on until you reach $45, the price at which all five students are willing to sell.

which several different students would be willing to sell. Andrew is willing to sell the book as long as he can get at least $5; Betty won't sell unless she can get at least $15; Carlos requires $25; Donna requires $35; Emir $45.

The lowest price at which a potential seller is willing to sell is called the seller's **cost**. So Andrew's cost is $5, Betty's is $15, and so on.

A seller's **cost** is the lowest price at which he or she is willing to sell a good.

Using the term *cost*, which people normally associate with the monetary cost of producing a good, may sound a little strange when applied to sellers of used textbooks. The students don't have to manufacture the books, so it doesn't cost the student who sells a book anything to make that book available for sale, does it?

Yes, it does. A student who sells a book won't have it later, as part of his or her personal collection. So there is an *opportunity cost* to selling a textbook, even if the owner has completed the course for which it was required. And remember that one of the basic principles of economics is that the true measure of the cost of doing something is always its opportunity cost. That is, the real cost of something is what you must give up to get it.

So it is good economics to talk of the minimum price at which someone will sell a good as the "cost" of selling that good, even if he or she doesn't spend any money to make the good available for sale. Of course, in most real-world markets the sellers are also those who produce the good and therefore *do* spend money to make the good available for sale. In this case the cost of making the good available for sale *includes* monetary costs, but it may also include other opportunity costs.

Getting back to the example, suppose that Andrew sells his book for $30. Clearly he has gained from the transaction: he would have been willing to sell for only $5, so he has gained $25. This net gain, the difference between the price he actually gets and his cost—the minimum price at which he would have been willing to sell—is known as his **individual producer surplus**.

Individual producer surplus is the net gain to an individual seller from selling a good. It is equal to the difference between the price received and the seller's cost.

Total producer surplus in a market is the sum of the individual producer surpluses of all the sellers of a good in a market. Economists use the term **producer surplus** to refer both to individual and to total producer surplus.

Just as we derived the demand curve from the willingness to pay of different consumers, we can derive the supply curve from the cost of different producers. The step-shaped curve in Figure 49.6 shows the supply curve implied by the costs shown in the accompanying table. At a price less than $5, none of the students are willing to sell; at a price between $5 and $15, only Andrew is willing to sell, and so on.

As in the case of consumer surplus, we can add the individual producer surpluses of sellers to calculate the **total producer surplus**, the total net gain to all sellers in the market. Economists use the term **producer surplus** to refer to either total or individual producer surplus. **Table 49.2** shows the net gain to each of the students who would sell a used book at a price of $30: $25 for Andrew, $15 for Betty, and $5 for Carlos. The total producer surplus is $25 + $15 + $5 = $45.

As with consumer surplus, the producer surplus gained by those who sell books can be represented graphically. **Figure 49.7** on the next page reproduces the supply curve from Figure 49.6. Each step in that supply curve has a width that represents one book from one seller. The height of Andrew's step is $5, his cost. This forms the bottom of a rectangle, with $30, the price he actually receives for his book, forming the top. The area of this rectangle, ($30 − $5) × 1 = $25, is his producer surplus. So the producer surplus

Table 49.2 Producer Surplus When the Price of a Used Textbook Is $30

Potential seller	Cost	Price received	Individual producer surplus = Price received − Cost
Andrew	$5	$30	$25
Betty	15	30	15
Carlos	25	30	5
Donna	35	—	—
Emir	45	—	—
All sellers			Total producer surplus = $45

TEACH Teach It

Now show students the process of summing individual consumer surpluses to calculate total consumer surplus using a continuous (straight-line) demand curve. Label the axes *P* and *Q*, and draw an upward-sloping straight-line supply curve. Add a horizontal line labeled "Price." Emphasize that the market price is determined by supply and demand, but the demand curve isn't shown.

Start with a quantity of 1 and ask students how much producers receive for 1 unit. You want them to learn that the market price is always the answer to what producers receive. Next ask students the seller's cost for that same quantity. You want students to learn that the point on the supply curve gives the sellers a price and a quantity. Draw a line from the market price down to the supply curve. Do the same thing for a quantity of 2, 3, 4, etc. out to where the market price crosses the supply curve. Ask students about the difference between what sellers receive and the seller's cost at the market price. Students should see that there is no difference—therefore, no producer surplus for that unit. Ask your class what happens at higher quantities (producers aren't willing to sell at the market price for any units beyond the market quantity).

Now tell students you plan to repeat the same process for 1.5, 2.5, 3.5, 4.5, 1.25, 2.25, 3.25, 4.25, etc. units. Keep drawing lines between the market price and the supply curve until the area starts to fill in. Ask students what will happen if you continue doing this for all possible fractions of units of output *(the triangle area will be filled in)*. Use the discussion to move to the calculation of total producer surplus as the area of the triangle below price and above the supply curve.

FOCUS Active Learning

TRM Refer students to **Worksheet 49.4 (Producer Surplus)** from the TRM for an exercise on producer surplus.

Figure 49.7 Producer Surplus in the Used-Textbook Market

At a price of $30, Andrew, Betty, and Carlos each sell a book but Donna and Emir do not. Andrew, Betty, and Carlos get individual producer surpluses equal to the difference between the price and their cost, illustrated here by the shaded rectangles. Donna and Emir each have a cost that is greater than the price of $30, so they are unwilling to sell a book and so receive zero producer surplus. The total producer surplus is given by the entire shaded area, the sum of the individual producer surpluses of Andrew, Betty, and Carlos, equal to $25 + $15 + $5 = $45.

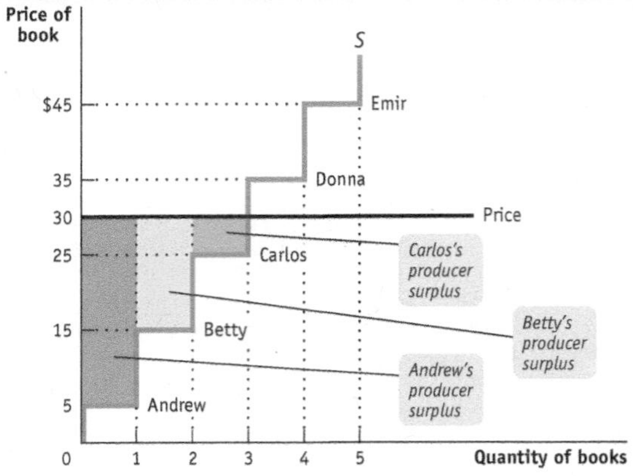

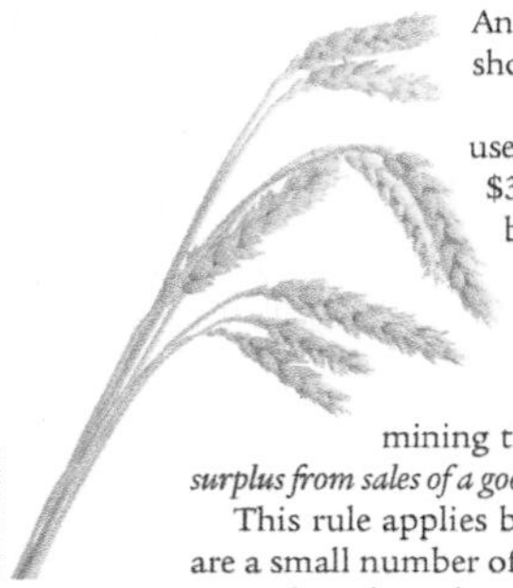

Andrew gains from selling his book is the *area of the dark red rectangle* shown in the figure.

Let's assume that the campus bookstore is willing to buy all the used copies of this book that students are willing to sell at a price of $30. Then, in addition to Andrew, Betty and Carlos will also sell their books. They will also benefit from their sales, though not as much as Andrew, because they have higher costs. Andrew, as we have seen, gains $25. Betty gains a smaller amount: since her cost is $15, she gains only $15. Carlos gains even less, only $5.

Again, as with consumer surplus, we have a general rule for determining the total producer surplus from sales of a good: *The total producer surplus from sales of a good at a given price is the area above the supply curve but below that price.*

This rule applies both to examples like the one shown in Figure 49.7, where there are a small number of producers and a step-shaped supply curve, and to more realistic examples, where there are many producers and the supply curve is more or less smooth.

Consider, for example, the supply of wheat. **Figure 49.8** shows how producer surplus depends on the price per bushel. Suppose that, as shown in the figure, the price is $5 per bushel and farmers supply 1 million bushels. What is the benefit to the farmers from selling their wheat at a price of $5? Their producer surplus is equal to the shaded area above the supply curve but below the price of $5 per bushel: ½ × 1 million × $4 = $2 million.

How Changing Prices Affect Producer Surplus

As in the case of consumer surplus, a change in price alters producer surplus. However, although a fall in price increases consumer surplus, it reduces producer surplus. Similarly, a rise in price reduces consumer surplus but increases producer surplus.

To see this, let's first consider a rise in the price of the good. Producers of the good will experience an increase in producer surplus, though not all producers gain the same amount. Some producers would have produced the good even at the original price; they will gain the entire price increase on every unit they produce. Other producers will enter the market because of the higher price; they will gain only the difference between the new price and their cost.

Figure 49.9 is the supply counterpart of Figure 49.5. It shows the effect on producer surplus of a rise in the price of wheat from $5 to $7 per bushel. The increase in

AP® Exam Tip

The area on a graph that represents producer surplus is bounded by the supply curve, the price line, and the vertical axis.

Figure 49.8 Producer Surplus

Here is the supply curve for wheat. At a price of $5 per bushel, farmers supply 1 million bushels. The producer surplus at this price is equal to the shaded area above the supply curve but below the price: ½ × 1 million × $4 = $2 million. This is the total gain to producers—farmers in this case—from supplying their product when the price is $5.

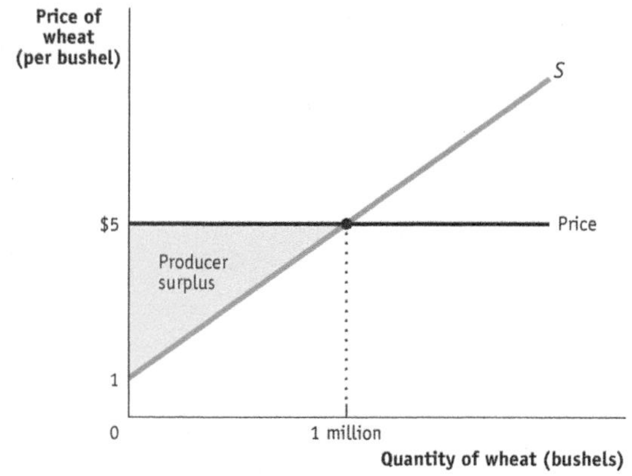

producer surplus is the sum of the shaded areas, which consists of two parts. First, there is a dark red rectangle corresponding to the gains to those farmers who would have supplied wheat even at the original $5 price. The area of the dark red triangle is 1 million × $2 = $2 million. Second, there is an additional light red triangle that corresponds to the gains to those farmers who would not have supplied wheat at the original price but are drawn into the market by the higher price. The area of the light red triangle is ½ × 0.5 million × $2 = $500,000. So the total gain in producer surplus is $2 million + $500,000 = $2.5 million.

Figure 49.9 A Rise in the Price Increases Producer Surplus

A rise in the price of wheat from $5 to $7 leads to an increase in the quantity supplied and an increase in producer surplus. The change in total producer surplus is given by the sum of the shaded areas: the total area above the supply curve but between the old and new prices. The dark red area represents the gain to the farmers who would have supplied 1 million bushels at the original price of $5; they each receive an increase in producer surplus of $2 for each of those bushels. The triangular light red area represents the increase in producer surplus achieved by the farmers who supply the additional 500,000 bushels because of the higher price. Similarly, a fall in the price of wheat generates a reduction in producer surplus equal to the sum of the shaded areas.

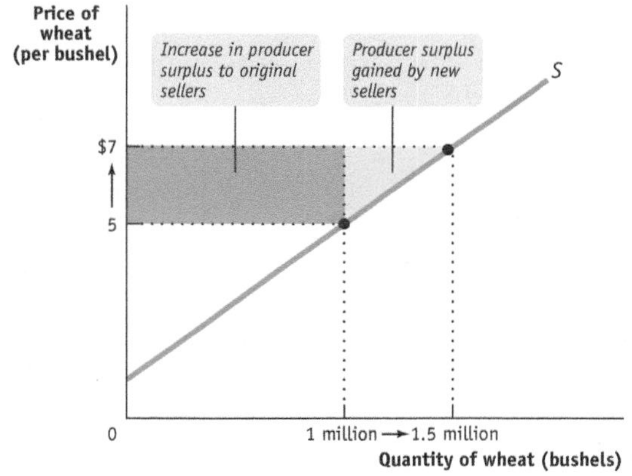

FOCUS Graph It

Refer students to Figure 49.8. Have them draw a correctly labeled, straight-line supply curve and label the producer surplus triangle on their graph. Ask them to write an explanation of what that area represents. Make sure they realize that the value of producer surplus is in dollars and represents the difference between what producers would have accepted (i.e., the cost of production from the supply curve) and what they were actually paid (the market price). Therefore, it represents the difference between price received and seller cost.

FOCUS Graph It

Refer students to Figure 49.8 and have them calculate producer surplus if the market price is $5. The base is 1 million (0 to 1 million) and the height is $4 ($1 to $5). The area of producer surplus is $\frac{1}{2}$ (1 million)($4) or $\frac{1}{2}$ ($4 million), which equals $2 million.

FOCUS Test It

TRM For questions on producer surplus, refer students to **Worksheet 49.5 (You and the Surplus)** from the TRM. Either discuss in class, or assign as written homework.

FOCUS Graph It

Have students use their correctly labeled, straight-line supply curve labeled with the producer surplus triangle (or create a new producer surplus graph) to show a decrease in price and identify the new total producer surplus area. Ask them whether producer surplus has increased or decreased (*decreased*) and have them shade the area of change in producer surplus. Direct them to explain WHY producer surplus decreases when the price falls.

FOCUS Flip It

TRM Have students watch Jacob Clifford's "Micro 2.7 Consumer and Producer Surplus and Dead Weight Loss" (see econextras video list with hyperlinks on the bcs and TRFD). The first part of the video nicely reviews consumer and product surplus; the second part goes further in explaining deadweight loss. This will serve as an introduction to Module 50. Assign **Worksheet 49.6 (Consumer and Producer Surplus Review)** from the TRM for accompanying questions to the video.

If the price were to fall from $7 to $5 per bushel, the story would run in reverse. The sum of the shaded areas would now be the decline in producer surplus, the decrease in the area above the supply curve but below the price. The loss would consist of two parts, the loss to farmers who would still grow wheat at a price of $5 (the dark red rectangle) and the loss to farmers who decide to no longer grow wheat because of the lower price (the light red triangle).

MODULE 49 Review

Check Your Understanding

1. Consider the market for cheese-stuffed jalapeño peppers. There are two consumers, Casey and Josey, and their willingness to pay for each pepper is given in the accompanying table. (Neither is willing to consume more than 4 peppers at any price.) Use the table (i) to construct the demand schedule for peppers for prices of $0.00, $0.10, and so on, up to $0.90, and (ii) to calculate the total consumer surplus when the price of a pepper is $0.40.

Quantity of peppers	*Casey's willingness to pay*	*Josey's willingness to pay*
1st pepper	$0.90	$0.80
2nd pepper	0.70	0.60
3rd pepper	0.50	0.40
4th pepper	0.30	0.30

2. Again consider the market for cheese-stuffed jalapeño peppers. There are two producers, Cara and Jamie, and their costs of producing each pepper are given in the accompanying table. (Neither is willing to produce more than 4 peppers at any price.) Use the table (i) to construct the supply schedule for peppers for prices of $0.00, $0.10, and so on, up to $0.90, and (ii) to calculate the total producer surplus when the price of a pepper is $0.70.

Quantity of peppers	*Cara's cost*	*Jamie's cost*
1st pepper	$0.10	$0.30
2nd pepper	0.10	0.50
3rd pepper	0.40	0.70
4th pepper	0.60	0.90

Tackle the Test: Multiple-Choice Questions

1. Refer to the graph below. What is the value of consumer surplus when the market price is $40?

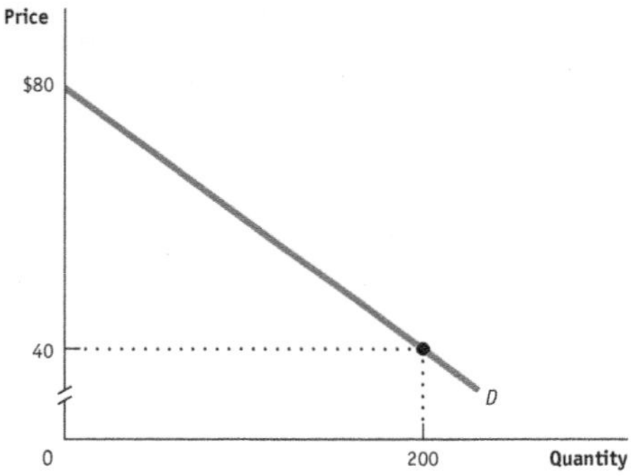

a. $400
b. $800
c. $4,000
d. $8,000
e. $16,000

2. Refer to the graph below. What is the value of producer surplus when the market price is $60?

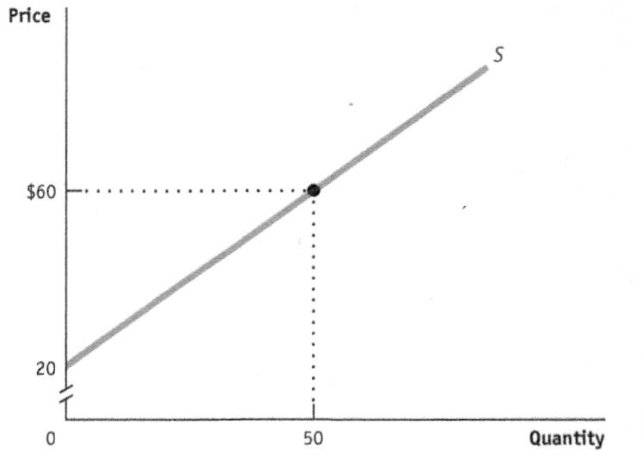

a. $100
b. $150
c. $1,000
d. $1,500
e. $3,000

OPEN & CLOSE Exit Slip

TRM *Please see **Exit Slip: Module 49** in the TRM for formative questions to ask your students before finishing your lesson. These questions will help you quickly assess whether your students have mastered the module's concepts before moving on.*

Answers to the Exit Slip Questions

1. B
2. below
3. D

Answers to Module 49 Review Questions

Check Your Understanding

1. A consumer buys each pepper if the price is less than (or equal to) the consumer's willingness to pay for that pepper. The demand schedule is constructed by asking how many peppers will be demanded at any given price. The accompanying table illustrates the demand schedule:

Price of pepper	Quantity of peppers demanded	Quantity of peppers demanded by Casey	Quantity of peppers demanded by Josey
$0.90	1	1	0
0.80	2	1	1
0.70	3	2	1
0.60	4	2	2
0.50	5	3	2
0.40	6	3	3
0.30	8	4	4
0.20	8	4	4
0.10	8	4	4
0.00	8	4	4

When the price is $0.40, Casey's consumer surplus is $0.50 from the first pepper, $0.30 from his second pepper, and $0.10 from his third pepper. He does not buy any more peppers. Casey's individual consumer surplus is therefore $0.90. Josey's consumer surplus is $0.40 from her first pepper, $0.20 from her second pepper, and $0.00 from her third pepper (since the price is exactly equal to her willingness to pay, she buys the third pepper but receives no consumer surplus from it). She does not buy any more peppers. Josey's individual consumer surplus is thus $0.60. Therefore, total consumer surplus at a price of $0.40 is $0.90 + $0.60 = $1.50.

2. A producer supplies each pepper if the price is greater than (or equal to) the producer's cost of producing that pepper. The supply schedule is constructed by asking how many peppers will be supplied at any price. The accompanying table illustrates the supply schedule:

3. Other things equal, a rise in price will result in which of the following?
   a. Producer surplus will rise; consumer surplus will rise.
   b. Producer surplus will fall; consumer surplus will fall.
   c. Producer surplus will rise; consumer surplus will fall.
   d. Producer surplus will fall; consumer surplus will rise.
   e. Producer surplus will not change; consumer surplus will rise.
4. Consumer surplus is found as the area
   a. above the supply curve but below the price.
   b. below the demand curve but above the price.
   c. above the demand curve but below the price.
   d. below the supply curve but above the price.
   e. below the supply curve but above the demand curve.
5. Allocating kidneys to those with the highest net benefit (where net benefit is measured as the expected increase in life span from a transplant) is an attempt to maximize
   a. consumer surplus.
   b. producer surplus.
   c. profit.
   d. equity.
   e. respect for elders.

Tackle the Test: Free-Response Questions

1. Refer to the graph provided.

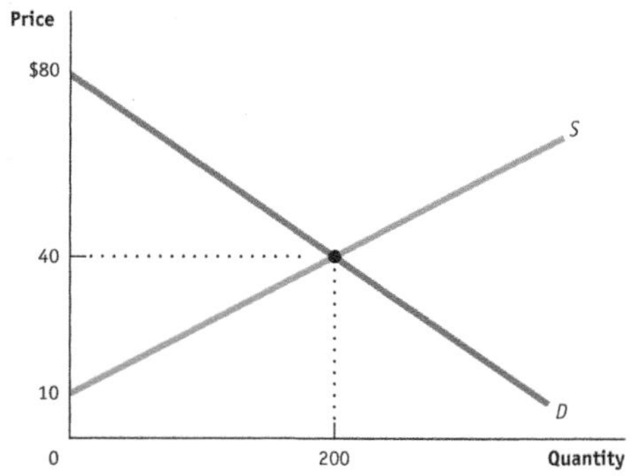

   a. Calculate consumer surplus.
   b. Calculate producer surplus.
   c. If supply increases, what will happen to consumer surplus? Explain.
   d. If demand decreases, what will happen to producer surplus? Explain.

Rubric for FRQ 1 (6 points)

1 point: $4,000

1 point: $3,000

1 point: Consumer surplus will increase.

1 point: An increase in supply lowers the equilibrium price, which causes consumer surplus to increase.

1 point: Producer surplus will decrease.

1 point: A decrease in demand decreases the equilibrium price, which causes producer surplus to decrease.

2. Draw a correctly labeled graph showing a competitive market in equilibrium. On your graph, clearly indicate and label the area of consumer surplus and the area of producer surplus. **(3 points)**

Price of pepper	Quantity of peppers supplied	Quantity of peppers supplied by Cara	Quantity of peppers supplied by Jamie
$0.90	8	4	4
0.80	7	4	3
0.70	7	4	3
0.60	6	4	2
0.50	5	3	2
0.40	4	3	1
0.30	3	2	1
0.20	2	2	0
0.10	2	2	0
0.00	0	0	0

When the price is $0.70, Cara's producer surplus is $0.60 from the first pepper, $0.60 from her second pepper, $0.30 from her third pepper, and $0.10 from her fourth pepper. She does not supply any more peppers. Cara's individual producer surplus is therefore $1.60. Jamie's producer surplus is $0.40 from his first pepper, $0.20 from his second pepper, and $0.00 from his third pepper (since the price is exactly equal to his cost, he sells the third pepper but receives no producer surplus from it). He does not supply any more peppers. Jamie's individual producer surplus is therefore $0.60. Total producer surplus at a price of $0.70 is thus $1.60 + $0.60 = $2.20.

Tackle the Test: Multiple-Choice Questions

1. c
2. c
3. c
4. b
5. a

Tackle the Test: Free-Response Questions

Rubric for FRQ 2 (3 points)

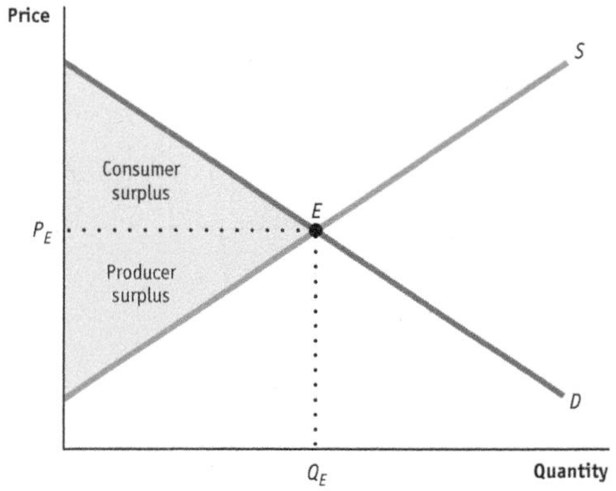

1 point: Graph with vertical axis labeled "Price," horizontal axis labeled "Quantity," an upward-sloping supply curve, and a downward-sloping demand curve

1 point: Consumer surplus correctly identified below the demand curve but above the equilibrium price

1 point: Producer surplus correctly identified above the supply curve but below the equilibrium price

PD To prepare for teaching this lesson, you may want to consult the **Module 50 Sample Lecture** in the TRM.

OPEN & CLOSE Start Here

Have students consider the statement "A market allocation is efficient if there is no way to make someone better off without making someone else worse off." Use the following example to help them understand this idea.

Example: Tell students you have a bag with a number of cookies equal to the number of students in the class. Ask them for an efficient way to allocate the cookies. Various student responses are likely: Hand out 1 cookie per student; or the person distributing the cookies will keep all of them; or the cookies will be awarded based on which student is the most hungry or has the best grades or behavior. Write each suggested method of allocation on the board. Evaluate each one by looking at what would have to happen in order to make someone better off (i.e., give them another cookie). In most suggestions offered by students, all cookies are allocated to someone. So, in order to make someone better off, you must make someone else worse off (take away a cookie), and the suggested way to allocate cookies is efficient. The two possibilities—one student having all the cookies or each student having only one cookie—are equally efficient.

Students will very likely bring up fairness. Which allocation is FAIR? That is an entirely different question!

What allocation would NOT be efficient in this example? If, for instance, you passed out half the cookies and threw away the other half. That would not be efficient because you could make someone better off (give them a cookie) without making someone else worse off (taking away a cookie). When no one gets the cookie, waste occurs. Efficiency means no waste.

© Chloe Johnson/Alamy

MODULE 50 Efficiency and Deadweight Loss

In this Module, you will learn to:

- Define total surplus and discuss its relevance to market efficiency
- Explain how taxes affect total surplus and can create deadweight loss

Consumer Surplus, Producer Surplus, and Efficiency

Markets are a remarkably effective way to organize economic activity: under the right conditions, they can make society as well off as possible given the available resources. The concepts of consumer and producer surplus can help us deepen our understanding of why this is so.

The Gains from Trade

Let's return to the market for used textbooks, but now consider a much bigger market—say, one at a large state university. There are many potential buyers and sellers, so the market is competitive. Let's line up incoming students who are potential buyers of a book in order of their willingness to pay, so that the entering student with the highest willingness to pay is potential buyer number 1, the student with the next highest willingness to pay is number 2, and so on. Then we can use their willingness to pay to derive a demand curve like the one in **Figure 50.1**. Similarly, we can line up outgoing students, the potential sellers of the book, in order of their cost, starting with the student with the lowest cost, followed by the student with the next lowest cost, and so on, to derive a supply curve like the one shown in the same figure.

As we have drawn the curves, the market reaches equilibrium at a price of $30 per book, and 1,000 books are bought and sold at that price. The two shaded triangles show the consumer surplus (blue) and the producer surplus (pink) generated by this market. The sum of consumer and producer surplus, the total net gain to consumers and producers from trading in a market, is known as **total surplus**.

Total surplus is the total net gain to consumers and producers from trading in a market. It is the sum of producer and consumer surplus.

TEACH Teach It

The text mentions "gains from trade." Make your students aware that this module refers to trade as the exchange of goods and services in markets rather than trade between countries.

TEACH Teach It

Total surplus is the total gain to consumers and producers from exchange in a market. Total surplus equals consumer surplus plus producer surplus.

498 Section 9 Behind the Demand Curve: Consumer Choice

Figure 50.1 Total Surplus

In the market for used textbooks, the equilibrium price is $30 and the equilibrium quantity is 1,000 books. Consumer surplus is given by the blue area, the area below the demand curve but above the price. Producer surplus is given by the pink area, the area above the supply curve but below the price. The sum of the blue and the pink areas is total surplus, the total benefit to society from the production and consumption of the good.

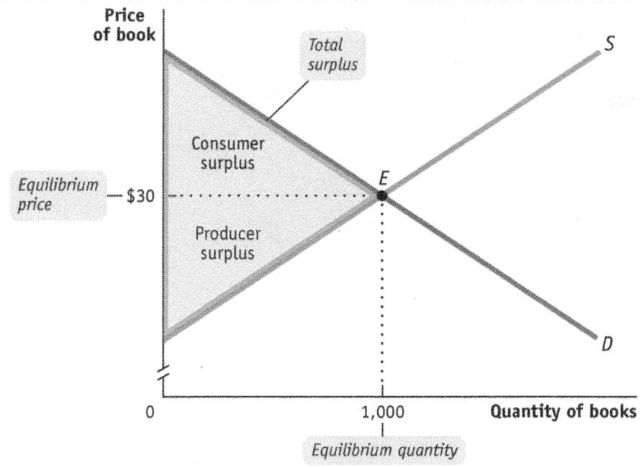

The striking thing about this picture is that both consumers and producers gain—that is, both consumers and producers are better off because there is a market in this good. But this should come as no surprise—it illustrates another core principle of economics: *There are gains from trade*. These gains from trade are the reason everyone is better off participating in a market economy than they would be if each individual tried to be self-sufficient.

But are we as well off as we could be? This brings us to the question of the efficiency of markets.

The Efficiency of Markets

A market is *efficient* if, once the market has produced its gains from trade, there is no way to make some people better off without making other people worse off. Note that market equilibrium is just *one* way of deciding who consumes a good and who sells a good. To better understand how markets promote efficiency, let's examine some alternatives. Consider the example of kidney transplants discussed earlier in an FYI box. There is no market for kidneys, and available kidneys currently go to whoever has been on the waiting list the longest. Of course, those who have been waiting the longest aren't necessarily those who would benefit the most from a new kidney.

Similarly, imagine a committee charged with improving on the market equilibrium by deciding who gets and who gives up a used textbook. The committee's ultimate goal would be to bypass the market outcome and come up with another arrangement that would increase total surplus.

Let's consider three approaches the committee could take:

1. It could reallocate consumption among consumers.
2. It could reallocate sales among sellers.
3. It could change the quantity traded.

The Reallocation of Consumption Among Consumers The committee might try to increase total surplus by selling the used books to different consumers.

FOCUS Graph It

Refer students to Figure 50.1. Have them calculate total surplus by calculating and adding consumer and producer surplus if the demand curve intersects the vertical axis at $50 and the supply curve intersects the vertical axis at $15.

Consumer surplus $= \frac{1}{2}(1{,}000 \times \$20)$
$= \frac{1}{2} \times \$20{,}000 = \$10{,}000$

Producer surplus $= \frac{1}{2}(1{,}000 \times \$15)$
$= \frac{1}{2} \times \$15{,}000 = \$7{,}500$

Total surplus $= \$10{,}000 + \$7{,}500$
$= \$17{,}500$

FOCUS Active Learning

TRM Refer students to **Worksheet 50.1 (Efficiency of Markets with Surpluses)** from the TRM for a review of the efficiency of markets with surpluses.

St. Louis Federal Reserve Bank Resources

"Equilibrium," *The Economic Lowdown Video Series*, Episode 3

Host Scott Wolla explains the concept of equilibrium and viewers get a refresher on the laws of supply and demand before they learn about market equilibrium—the point at which there is no shortage or surplus of a good or service.

FOCUS Graph It

Figures 50.2, 50.3, and 50.4 illustrate how the market allocation of books maximizes consumer and producer surplus.

Figure 50.2 Reallocating Consumption Lowers Consumer Surplus

Ana (point *A*) has a willingness to pay of $35. Bob (point *B*) has a willingness to pay of only $25. At the market equilibrium price of $30, Ana purchases a book but Bob does not. If we rearrange consumption by taking a book from Ana and giving it to Bob, consumer surplus declines by $10 and, as a result, total surplus declines by $10. The market equilibrium generates the highest possible consumer surplus by ensuring that those who consume the good are those who most value it.

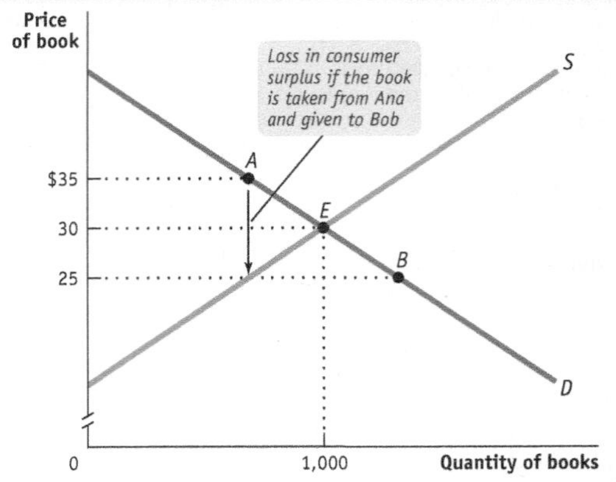

Figure 50.2 shows why this will result in lower surplus compared to the market equilibrium outcome. Points *A* and *B* show the positions on the demand curve of two potential buyers of used books, Ana and Bob. As we can see from the figure, Ana is willing to pay $35 for a book, but Bob is willing to pay only $25. Since the market equilibrium price is $30, under the market outcome Ana gets a book and Bob does not.

Now suppose the committee reallocates consumption. This would mean taking the book away from Ana and giving it to Bob. Since the book is worth $35 to Ana but only $25 to Bob, this change *reduces total consumer surplus* by $35 – $25 = $10. Moreover, this result doesn't depend on which two students we pick. Every student who buys a book at the market equilibrium price has a willingness to pay of $30 or more, and every student who doesn't buy a book has a willingness to pay of less than $30. So reallocating the good among consumers always means taking a book away from a student who values it more and giving it to one who values it less. This necessarily reduces total consumer surplus.

AP® Exam Tip

Anything that prevents the sale of a unit that would have occurred in market equilibrium reduces total surplus.

The Reallocation of Sales Among Sellers The committee might try to increase total surplus by altering who sells their books, taking sales away from sellers who would have sold their books in the market equilibrium and instead compelling those who would not have sold their books in the market equilibrium to sell them. **Figure 50.3** shows why this will result in lower surplus. Here points *X* and *Y* show the positions on the supply curve of Xavier, who has a cost of $25, and Yvonne, who has a cost of $35. At the equilibrium market price of $30, Xavier would sell his book but Yvonne would not sell hers. If the committee reallocated sales, forcing Xavier to keep his book and Yvonne to sell hers, total producer surplus would be reduced by $35 – $25 = $10. Again, it doesn't matter which two students we choose. Any student who sells a book at the market equilibrium price has a lower cost than any student who keeps a book. So reallocating sales among sellers necessarily increases total cost and reduces total producer surplus.

Changes in the Quantity Traded The committee might try to increase total surplus by compelling students to trade either more books or fewer books than the market equilibrium quantity. **Figure 50.4** shows why this will result in lower surplus. It shows all four students: potential buyers Ana and Bob, and potential sellers Xavier and Yvonne. To reduce sales, the committee will have to prevent a transaction that

St. Louis Federal Reserve Bank Resources

"Price Signals," *The Economic Lowdown Podcast Series*, Episode 12

Prices send signals and provide incentives for buyers and sellers in ways students possibly never thought about. In a market economy, price signals prevent massive shortages and ensure that consumer wants are largely satisfied. In this podcast, students will hear how price signals from gas prices influence the decision making of both a father of three and a production supervisor for an oil refinery.

Figure 50.3 Reallocating Sales Lowers Producer Surplus

Yvonne (point *Y*) has a cost of $35, $10 more than Xavier (point *X*), who has a cost of $25. At the market equilibrium price of $30, Xavier sells a book but Yvonne does not. If we rearrange sales by preventing Xavier from selling his book and compelling Yvonne to sell hers, producer surplus declines by $10 and, as a result, total surplus declines by $10. The market equilibrium generates the highest possible producer surplus by assuring that those who sell the good are those who most value the right to sell it.

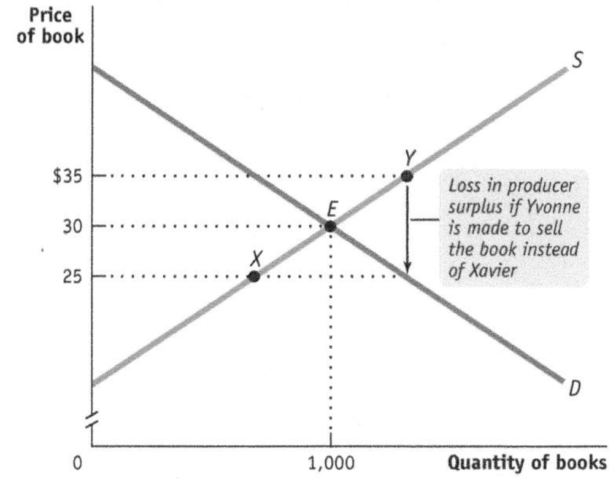

would have occurred in the market equilibrium—that is, prevent Xavier from selling to Ana. Since Ana is willing to pay $35 and Xavier's cost is $25, preventing this transaction reduces total surplus by $35 − $25 = $10. Once again, this result doesn't depend on which two students we pick: any student who would have sold the book in the market equilibrium has a cost of $30 or less, and any student who would have purchased the book in the market equilibrium has a willingness to pay of $30 or more. So preventing any sale that would have occurred in the market equilibrium necessarily reduces total surplus.

Figure 50.4 Changing the Quantity Lowers Total Surplus

If Xavier (point *X*) were prevented from selling his book to someone like Ana (point *A*), total surplus would fall by $10, the difference between Ana's willingness to pay ($35) and Xavier's cost ($25). This means that total surplus falls whenever fewer than 1,000 books—the equilibrium quantity—are transacted. Likewise, if Yvonne (point *Y*) were compelled to sell her book to someone like Bob (point *B*), total surplus would also fall by $10, the difference between Yvonne's cost ($35) and Bob's willingness to pay ($25). This means that total surplus falls whenever more than 1,000 books are transacted. These two examples show that at market equilibrium, all mutually beneficial transactions—and only mutually beneficial transactions—occur.

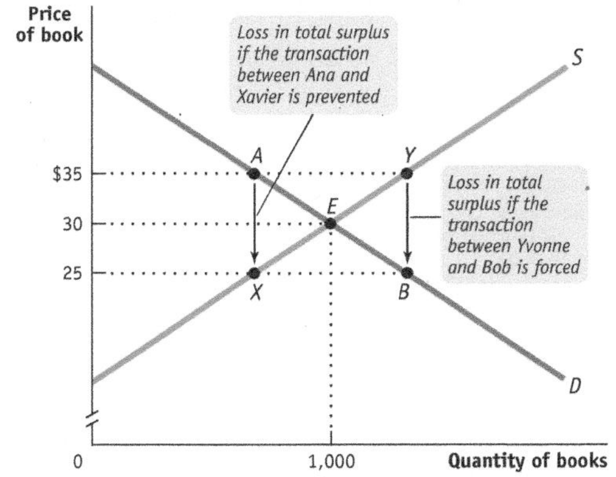

FOCUS Active Learning

TRM Refer students to **Worksheet 50.2 (Consumer and Producer Surplus)** from the TRM for a practice exercise with consumer and producer surplus.

FOCUS Graph It

Have students refer to Figure 50.4 and draw a correctly labeled supply and demand graph of a market in equilibrium (no need for numbers on the graph). Ask them to put points on their graph and use the points to label consumer, producer, and total surplus.

Now have students draw a vertical line at a quantity below the equilibrium quantity and then shade the loss in total surplus that would occur if the market only sold the lower quantity.

FOCUS Test It

Ask students to answer the following questions in their own words:

- How does reallocating consumption reduce the total surplus? *Consumer surplus is reduced by taking a good from one buyer who has a higher willingness to pay (or has a higher value for the good) and reallocating that good to another buyer who has a lower willingness to pay. When consumer surplus is decreased, total surplus decreases.*
- How does reallocating sales among sellers reduce total surplus? *Producer surplus is reduced by preventing a sale by a seller with a lower cost and forcing the sale of the good by a seller with a higher cost. When producer surplus is decreased, total surplus decreases.*
- How does a change in the quantity reduce total surplus? *When a market transaction is prevented but would have occurred in the market equilibrium, the total surplus decreases as the consumer and producer surpluses decrease.*

Module 50 Efficiency and Deadweight Loss 501

FOCUS Active Learning

Have students define and discuss the terms "fair," "equal," and "efficient" and then use the following demonstration to help students understand the terms. Tell students you have $300 to split among the class and you have decided to give each student an equal share. Ask if that seems fair, equal, or efficient. You might even want to hand out play money to students. Then explain that since none of the students have rent or mortgage payments, or must pay for their own food or utility bills and you do, you should get $1 more per month and each class member $1 less. If you handed out play money, take back $1 from each student. Ask if that seems fair, equal, or efficient. Go on to say that some students you identify have worked extra hard and deserve more money, so you believe they should also get $1 extra per month and everyone else an additional $1 less. Ask again if that seems fair, equal, and efficient.

TEACH Connect It

Students should be familiar with the following three types of tax systems:

- **Progressive**: The tax rate percentage rises as the tax base increases. High-income taxpayers pay a larger percentage of their income than low-income taxpayers.
- **Proportional**: The tax rate percentage stays the same as the tax base changes. All taxpayers pay the same proportion of their income.
- **Regressive**: The tax rate percentage rises as the tax base decreases. High-income taxpayers pay a lower percentage of their income than low-income taxpayers.

Have students discuss these tax systems in terms of fairness. Make sure they see that there is no answer as to which is fair—fairness is normative. Connect the discussion of equity and efficiency of taxes back to the discussion of positive and normative in Section 1.

FOCUS Active Learning

TRM Assign **Worksheet 50.3 (Tax Systems)** from the TRM for practice with tax systems.

Finally, the committee might try to increase sales by forcing Yvonne, who would not have sold her book in the market equilibrium, to sell it to someone like Bob, who would not have bought a book in the market equilibrium. Because Yvonne's cost is $35, but Bob is only willing to pay $25, this transaction reduces total surplus by $10. And once again it doesn't matter which two students we pick—anyone who wouldn't have bought the book has a willingness to pay of less than $30, and anyone who wouldn't have sold the book has a cost of more than $30.

The key point is that once this market is in equilibrium, there is no way to increase the gains from trade. Any other outcome reduces total surplus. We can summarize our results by stating that an efficient market performs four important functions:

1. It allocates consumption of the good to the potential buyers who most value it, as indicated by the fact that they have the highest willingness to pay.
2. It allocates sales to the potential sellers who most value the right to sell the good, as indicated by the fact that they have the lowest cost.
3. It ensures that every consumer who makes a purchase values the good more than every seller who makes a sale, so that all transactions are mutually beneficial.
4. It ensures that every potential buyer who doesn't make a purchase values the good less than every potential seller who doesn't make a sale, so that no mutually beneficial transactions are missed.

Shutterstock

There are three caveats, however. First, although a market may be efficient, it isn't necessarily *fair*. In fact, fairness, or *equity*, is often in conflict with efficiency. We'll discuss this next.

The second caveat is that markets sometimes *fail*. Under some well-defined conditions, markets can fail to deliver efficiency. When this occurs, markets no longer maximize total surplus. We'll take a closer look at market failures in later modules.

Third, even when the market equilibrium maximizes total surplus, this does not mean that it results in the best outcome for every *individual* consumer and producer. Other things equal, each buyer would like to pay a lower price and each seller would like to receive a higher price. So if the government were to intervene in the market—say, by lowering the price below the equilibrium price to make consumers happy or by raising the price above the equilibrium price to make producers happy—the outcome would no longer be efficient. Although some people would be happier, society as a whole would be worse off because total surplus would be lower.

Equity and Efficiency

It's easy to get carried away with the idea that markets are always good and that economic policies that interfere with efficiency are bad. But that would be misguided because there is another factor to consider: society cares about equity, or what's "fair." There is often a trade-off between equity and efficiency: policies that promote equity often come at the cost of decreased efficiency, and policies that promote efficiency often result in decreased equity. So it's important to realize that a society's choice to sacrifice some efficiency for the sake of equity, however it defines equity, may well be a valid one. And it's important to understand that fairness, unlike efficiency, can be very hard to define. Fairness is a concept about which well-intentioned people often disagree.

In fact, the debate about equity and efficiency is at the core of most debates about taxation. Proponents of taxes that redistribute income from the rich to the poor often argue for the fairness of such redistributive taxes. Opponents of taxation often argue that phasing out certain taxes would make the economy more efficient.

Because taxes are ultimately paid out of income, economists classify taxes according to how they vary with the income of individuals. A tax that rises more than in proportion to income, so that high-income taxpayers pay a larger percentage of their income than low-income taxpayers, is a **progressive tax**. A tax that rises less than in proportion

AP® Exam Tip

Be prepared to identify and provide examples of various taxes for the AP® exam. You may also be asked to determine how a change in taxes affects consumer and producer surplus.

A **progressive tax** rises more than in proportion to income.

to income, so that high-income taxpayers pay a smaller percentage of their income than low-income taxpayers, is a **regressive tax**. A tax that rises in proportion to income, so that all taxpayers pay the same percentage of their income, is a **proportional tax**. The U.S. tax system contains a mixture of progressive and regressive taxes, though it is somewhat progressive overall.

A **regressive tax** rises less than in proportion to income.

A **proportional tax** rises in proportion to income.

The Effects of Taxes on Total Surplus

To understand the economics of taxes, it's helpful to look at a simple type of tax known as an **excise tax**—a tax charged on each unit of a particular good or service that is sold. Most tax revenue in the United States comes from other kinds of taxes, but excise taxes are common. For example, there are excise taxes on gasoline, cigarettes, and foreign-made trucks, and many local governments impose excise taxes on services such as hotel room rentals. The lessons we'll learn from studying excise taxes apply to other, more complex taxes as well.

An **excise tax** is a tax on sales of a particular good or service.

The Effect of an Excise Tax on Quantities and Prices

Suppose that the supply and demand for hotel rooms in the city of Potterville are as shown in **Figure 50.5**. We'll make the simplifying assumption that all hotel rooms are the same. In the absence of taxes, the equilibrium price of a room is $80 per night and the equilibrium quantity of hotel rooms rented is 10,000 per night.

Now suppose that Potterville's government imposes an excise tax of $40 per night on hotel rooms—that is, every time a room is rented for the night, the owner of the hotel must pay the city $40. For example, if a customer pays $80, $40 is collected as a tax, leaving the hotel owner with only $40. As a result, hotel owners are less willing to supply rooms at any given price.

Figure 50.5 The Supply and Demand for Hotel Rooms in Potterville

In the absence of taxes, the equilibrium price of hotel rooms is $80 per night, and the equilibrium number of rooms rented is 10,000 per night, as shown by point *E*. The supply curve, *S*, shows the quantity supplied at any given price, pre-tax. At a price of $60 per night, hotel owners are willing to supply 5,000 rooms, as shown by point *B*. But post-tax, hotel owners are willing to supply the same quantity only at a price of $100 per night: $60 for themselves plus $40 paid to the city as tax.

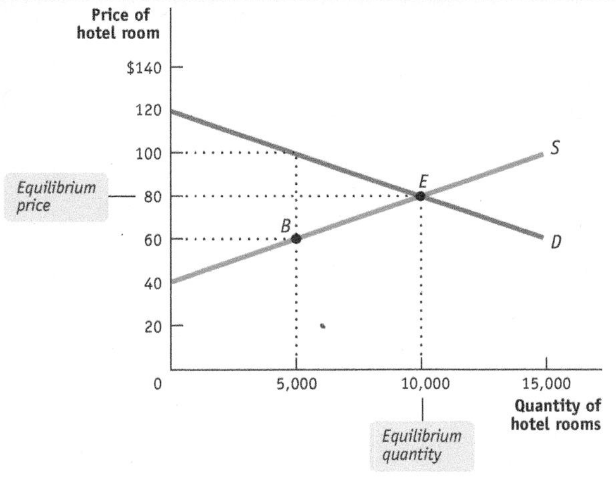

TEACH Connect It

Remind students that they learned about quotas in Module 9—its effect of driving a wedge or deadweight loss between what was supplied and demanded at a certain quantity of a good (refer to the text on page 94). Explain that an excise tax (on a good or service) operates in a similar fashion. Excise taxes drive a wedge between the price paid by consumers and the price received by producers.

St. Louis Federal Reserve Bank Resources

Tax Incidence

Use these slides to demonstrate the shifting tax burden and changes in tax revenue and deadweight loss when taxes are applied. Students have the opportunity to identify tax burden, revenue, and deadweight loss when the slopes of supply and demand change.

St. Louis Federal Reserve Bank Resources

Government Spending and Taxes

Students engage in an activity that matches programs for low-income people with the type of economic inequity the program addresses and observe an activity simulating tax payments and transfers.

FOCUS Active Learning

Show the Jacob Clifford video "Micro 2.10 Taxes on Producers" (see econextras video list with hyperlinks on the bcs and TRFD). Pause the video at 3:14, and challenge students to answer the questions posed. Continue the video, and then pause again at 5:34. Let students explain each of the graphs referring to elasticity of demand and the imposition of the tax. Challenge students to draw a set of graphs that change the elasticity of supply while holding the demand constant.

FOCUS Graph It

Figure 50.6 shows the consequence of an excise tax imposed on producers. The effect on the market is as if the supply curve shifted upward by the amount of the tax. The excise tax drives a wedge between the price paid by consumers and the price received by producers so that consumers pay more and producers receive less.

What does this imply about the supply curve for hotel rooms in Potterville? To answer this question, we must compare the incentives of hotel owners *pre-tax* (before the tax is levied) to their incentives *post-tax* (after the tax is levied). From Figure 50.5 we know that pre-tax, hotel owners are willing to supply 5,000 rooms per night at a price of $60 per room. But after the $40 tax per room is levied, they are willing to supply the same amount, 5,000 rooms, only if they receive $100 per room—$60 for themselves plus $40 paid to the city as tax. In other words, in order for hotel owners to be willing to supply the same quantity post-tax as they would have pre-tax, they must receive an additional $40 per room, the amount of the tax. This implies that the post-tax supply curve shifts up by the amount of the tax compared to the pre-tax supply curve. At every quantity supplied, the supply price—the price that producers must receive to produce a given quantity—has increased by $40.

The upward shift of the supply curve caused by the tax is shown in **Figure 50.6**, where S_1 is the pre-tax supply curve and S_2 is the post-tax supply curve. As you can see, the market equilibrium moves from *E*, at the equilibrium price of $80 per room and 10,000 rooms rented each night, to *A*, at a market price of $100 per room and only 5,000 rooms rented each night. Of course, *A* is on both the demand curve *D* and the new supply curve S_2. In this case, $100 is the demand price of 5,000 rooms—but in effect hotel owners receive only $60, when you account for the fact that they have to pay the $40 tax. From the point of view of hotel owners, it is as if they were on their original supply curve at point *B*.

Let's check this again. How do we know that 5,000 rooms will be supplied at a price of $100? Because the price *net of tax* is $60, and according to the original supply curve, 5,000 rooms will be supplied at a price of $60, as shown by point *B* in Figure 50.6.

An excise tax *drives a wedge* between the price paid by consumers and the price received by producers. As a result of this wedge, consumers pay more and producers receive less. In our example, consumers—people who rent hotel rooms—end up paying $100 per night, $20 more than the pre-tax price of $80. At the same time, producers—the hotel owners—receive a price net of tax of $60 per room, $20 less than the pre-tax price. In addition, the tax creates missed opportunities: 5,000 potential consumers who would have rented hotel rooms—those willing to pay $80 but not $100 per night—are

AP® Exam Tip

A tax of a certain amount or percent per unit of a good, such as a $1 per unit excise tax or a 5% sales tax, generally increases the equilibrium price and decreases the equilibrium quantity.

Figure 50.6 An Excise Tax Imposed on Hotel Owners

A $40 per room tax imposed on hotel owners shifts the supply curve from S_1 to S_2, an upward shift of $40. The equilibrium price of hotel rooms rises from $80 to $100 per night, and the equilibrium quantity of rooms rented falls from 10,000 to 5,000. Although hotel owners pay the tax, they actually bear only half the burden: the price they receive net of tax falls only $20, from $80 to $60. Guests who rent rooms bear the other half of the burden because the price they pay rises by $20, from $80 to $100.

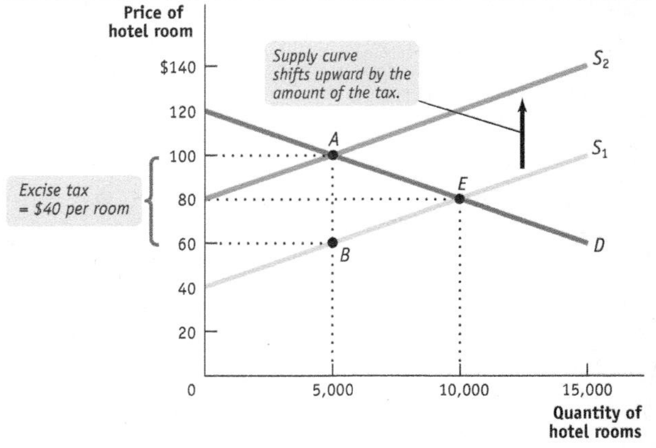

discouraged from renting rooms. Correspondingly, 5,000 rooms that would have been made available by hotel owners for $80 are not offered when they receive only $60. Like a quota on sales as discussed in Module 9, this tax leads to inefficiency by distorting incentives and creating missed opportunities for mutually beneficial transactions.

It's important to recognize that as we've described it, Potterville's hotel tax is a tax on the hotel owners, not their guests—it's a tax on the producers, not the consumers. Yet the price received by producers, net of tax, is down by only $20, half the amount of the tax, and the price paid by consumers is up by $20. In effect, half the tax is being paid by consumers.

What would happen if the city levied a tax on consumers instead of producers? That is, suppose that instead of requiring hotel owners to pay $40 per night for each room they rent, the city required hotel *guests* to pay $40 for each night they stayed in a hotel. The answer is shown in **Figure 50.7**. If a hotel guest must pay a tax of $40 per night, then the price for a room paid by that guest must be reduced by $40 in order for the quantity of hotel rooms demanded post-tax to be the same as that demanded pre-tax. So the demand curve shifts *downward*, from D_1 to D_2, by the amount of the tax. At every quantity demanded, the demand price—the price that consumers must be offered to demand a given quantity—has fallen by $40. This shifts the equilibrium from *E* to *B*, where the market price of hotel rooms is $60 and 5,000 hotel rooms are bought and sold. In effect, hotel guests pay $100 when you include the tax. So from the point of view of guests, it is as if they were on their original demand curve at point *A*.

Figure 50.7 An Excise Tax Imposed on Hotel Guests

A $40 per room tax imposed on hotel guests shifts the demand curve from D_1 to D_2, a downward shift of $40. The equilibrium price of hotel rooms falls from $80 to $60 per night, and the quantity of rooms rented falls from 10,000 to 5,000. Although in this case the tax is officially paid by consumers, while in Figure 50.6 the tax was paid by producers, the outcome is the same: after taxes, hotel owners receive $60 per room but guests pay $100. This illustrates a general principle: *The incidence of an excise tax doesn't depend on whether consumers or producers officially pay the tax.*

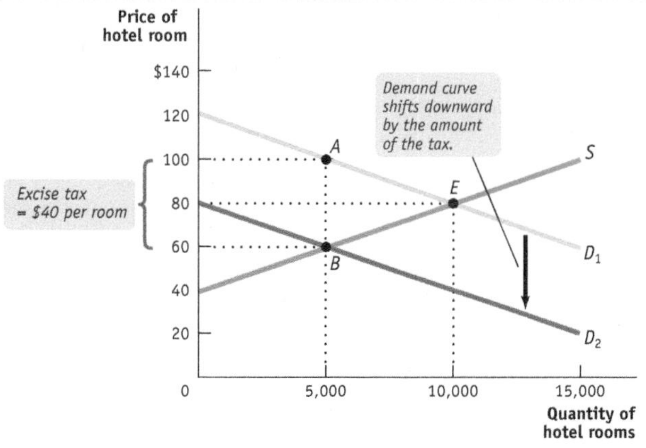

If you compare Figures 50.6 and 50.7, you will notice that the effects of the tax are the same even though different curves are shifted. In each case, consumers pay $100 per unit (including the tax, if it is their responsibility), producers receive $60 per unit (after paying the tax, if it is their responsibility), and 5,000 hotel rooms are bought and sold. *In fact, it doesn't matter who officially pays the tax—the equilibrium outcome is the same.*

This example illustrates a general principle of **tax incidence**, a measure of who really pays a tax: the burden of a tax cannot be determined by looking at who writes the check to the government. In this particular case, a $40 tax on hotel rooms brings about a $20 increase in the price paid by consumers and a $20 decrease in the price received

Tax incidence is the distribution of the tax burden.

FOCUS Graph It

Point out that Figure 50.7 shows the effect of an excise tax when imposed on consumers. The result in the market is the same as a decrease in demand by the amount of the tax. The consumer pays more and the producer receives less due to the tax.

TEACH Teach It

Students should understand the difference between the imposition of a tax and the incidence of a tax. The imposition of the tax determines who must turn the amount of the tax over to the government. But the group that must make the payment to the government rarely bears the entire burden of the tax. Buyers and sellers usually share the burden of a tax. For example, part of the burden of a tax imposed on sellers will likely be passed on to buyers in the form of higher prices. The *tax incidence* refers to the distribution of the burden of the tax between buyers and sellers.

FOCUS Active Learning

TRM Refer to **Worksheet 50.4 (Excise Taxes and Surplus)** from the TRM for a review of excise taxes and surpluses.

TEACH Teach It

This module presents examples of excise taxes. Excise taxes are per unit taxes. That is, the tax is placed on the sale of each unit of the good. Lump sum taxes are different from excise taxes. A lump sum tax is charged as a total amount, regardless of the number of units of the good sold. Lump sum taxes do not affect the market in the same way and will be discussed in later modules.

TEACH Connect It

Have students consider Figures 50.8 and 50.9. For each figure, ask students to identify the relative elasticity of the demand and supply curves. *In Figure 50.8, demand is relatively inelastic (steep) and supply is relatively elastic (flat). Figure 50.9 shows the opposite.* Help students draw the following conclusions from the graphs:

- When demand is relatively inelastic and supply is relatively elastic, the burden of an excise tax falls primarily on consumers. Why? *The quantity is not very responsive to the higher price as few substitutes are available.*
- When supply is relatively inelastic and demand is relatively elastic, the burden of an excise tax falls primarily on producers. Why? *The quantity is not very responsive to changes in price due to a lack of resource availability and time to produce.*

by producers. Regardless of whether the tax is levied on consumers or producers, the incidence of the tax is the same. As we will see next, the burden of a tax depends on the price elasticities of supply and demand.

Price Elasticities and Tax Incidence

We've just learned that the incidence of an excise tax doesn't depend on who officially pays it. In the example shown in Figures 50.5 through 50.7, a tax on hotel rooms falls equally on consumers and producers, no matter on whom the tax is levied. But it's important to note that this 50–50 split between consumers and producers is a result of our assumptions in this example. In the real world, the incidence of an excise tax usually falls unevenly between consumers and producers: one group bears more of the burden than the other.

What determines how the burden of an excise tax is allocated between consumers and producers? The answer depends on the shapes of the supply and the demand curves. *More specifically, the incidence of an excise tax depends on the price elasticity of supply and the price elasticity of demand.* We can see this by looking first at a case in which consumers pay most of an excise tax, and then at a case in which producers pay most of the tax.

When an Excise Tax Is Paid Mainly by Consumers **Figure 50.8** shows an excise tax that falls mainly on consumers: an excise tax on gasoline, which we set at $1 per gallon. (There really is a federal excise tax on gasoline, though it is actually only about $0.18 per gallon in the United States. In addition, states impose excise taxes between $0.04 and $0.37 per gallon.) According to Figure 50.8, in the absence of the tax, gasoline would sell for $2 per gallon.

Two key assumptions are reflected in the shapes of the supply and demand curves in Figure 50.8. First, the price elasticity of demand for gasoline is assumed to be very low, so the demand curve is relatively steep. Recall that a low price elasticity of demand means that the quantity demanded changes little in response to a change in price. Second, the price elasticity of supply of gasoline is assumed to be very high, so the supply curve is relatively flat. A high price elasticity of supply means that the quantity supplied changes a lot in response to a change in price.

We have just learned that an excise tax drives a wedge, equal to the size of the tax, between the price paid by consumers and the price received by producers. This wedge

Figure 50.8 An Excise Tax Paid Mainly by Consumers

The relatively steep demand curve here reflects a low price elasticity of demand for gasoline. The relatively flat supply curve reflects a high price elasticity of supply. The pre-tax price of a gallon of gasoline is $2.00, and a tax of $1.00 per gallon is imposed. The price paid by consumers rises by $0.95 to $2.95, reflecting the fact that most of the burden of the tax falls on consumers. Only a small portion of the tax is borne by producers: the price they receive falls by only $0.05 to $1.95.

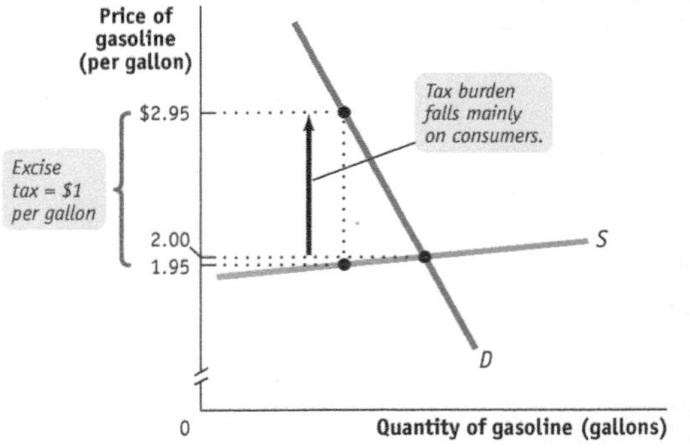

506 Section 9 Behind the Demand Curve: Consumer Choice

drives the price paid by consumers up and the price received by producers down. But as we can see from Figure 50.8, in this case those two effects are very unequal in size. The price received by producers falls only slightly, from $2.00 to $1.95, but the price paid by consumers rises by a lot, from $2.00 to $2.95. This means that consumers bear the greater share of the tax burden.

This example illustrates another general principle of taxation: *When the price elasticity of demand is low and the price elasticity of supply is high, the burden of an excise tax falls mainly on consumers.* Why? A low price elasticity of demand means that consumers have few substitutes and, therefore, little alternative to buying higher-priced gasoline. In contrast, a high price elasticity of supply results from the fact that producers have many production substitutes for their gasoline (that is, the crude oil from which gasoline is refined can be made into other things, such as plastic). This gives producers much greater flexibility in refusing to accept lower prices for their gasoline. And, not surprisingly, the party with the least flexibility—in this case, consumers—gets stuck paying most of the tax. This is a good description of how the burden of the main excise taxes actually collected in the United States today, such as those on cigarettes and alcoholic beverages, is allocated between consumers and producers.

When an Excise Tax Is Paid Mainly by Producers **Figure 50.9** shows an example of an excise tax paid mainly by producers: a $5.00 per day tax on downtown parking in a small city. In the absence of the tax, the market equilibrium price of parking is $6.00 per day.

We've assumed in this case that the price elasticity of supply is very low because the lots used for parking have very few alternative uses. This makes the supply curve for parking spaces relatively steep. The price elasticity of demand, however, is assumed to be high: consumers can easily switch from the downtown spaces to other parking spaces a few minutes' walk from downtown, spaces that are not subject to the tax. This makes the demand curve relatively flat.

The tax drives a wedge between the price paid by consumers and the price received by producers. In this example, however, the tax causes the price paid by consumers to rise only slightly, from $6.00 to $6.50, but the price received by producers falls a lot, from $6.00 to $1.50. In the end, a consumer bears only $0.50 of the $5 tax burden, with a producer bearing the remaining $4.50.

Again, this example illustrates a general principle: *When the price elasticity of demand is high and the price elasticity of supply is low, the burden of an excise tax falls mainly on*

Figure 50.9 An Excise Tax Paid Mainly by Producers

The relatively flat demand curve here reflects a high price elasticity of demand for downtown parking, and the relatively steep supply curve results from a low price elasticity of supply. The pre-tax price of a daily parking space is $6.00 and a tax of $5.00 is imposed. The price received by producers falls a lot, to $1.50, reflecting the fact that they bear most of the tax burden. The price paid by consumers rises a small amount, $0.50, to $6.50, so they bear very little of the burden.

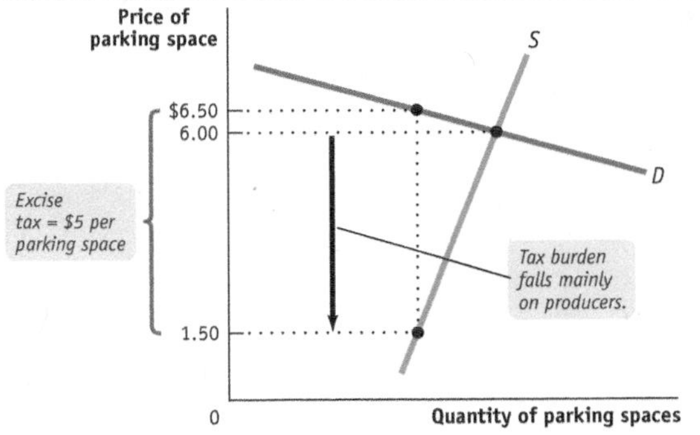

TEACH Connect It

Students will recall from page 469 in this section that a good with low elasticity of demand has a steep demand curve, while one with high elasticity of demand has a more flat demand curve. Ask students to list the factors that contribute to a highly elastic good. *A highly elastic good has more substitutes, is not a necessity, and costs a larger portion of income.*

A good with low elasticity of supply has a steep supply curve, while one with high elasticity of supply has a more flat supply curve, as discussed on page 480. Ask students what factors influence the elasticity of supply. *Availability of inputs and time needed for production.*

FOCUS Test It

Have students refer again to Figures 50.8 and 50.9, and calculate the tax revenue from the excise tax and how much of the burden falls on consumers and producers if the quantity sold with the tax is 100.

Figure number	Tax revenue	Consumers pay	Producers pay
50.8	$5 × 100 = $500	$.50 × 100 = $50	$4.50 × 100 = $450
50.9	$1 × 100 = $100	$.05 × 100 = $5	$0.95 × 100 = $95

producers. A real-world example is a tax on purchases of existing houses. In many American towns, house prices in desirable locations have risen as well-off outsiders have moved in and purchased homes from the less well-off original occupants, a phenomenon called gentrification. Some of these towns have imposed taxes on house sales intended to extract money from the new arrivals. But this ignores the fact that the price elasticity of demand for houses in a particular town is often high because potential buyers can choose to move to other towns. Furthermore, the price elasticity of supply is often low because most sellers must sell their houses due to job transfers or to provide funds for their retirement. So taxes on home purchases are actually paid mainly by the less well-off sellers—not, as town officials imagine, by wealthy buyers.

Karin Hildebrand Lau/Shutterstock

The Benefits and Costs of Taxation

When a government is considering whether to impose a tax or how to design a tax system, it has to weigh the benefits of a tax against its costs. We may not think of a tax as something that provides benefits, but governments need money to provide things people want, such as streets, schools, national defense, and health care for those unable to afford it. The benefit of a tax is the revenue it raises for the government to pay for these services. Unfortunately, this benefit comes at a cost—a cost that is normally larger than the amount consumers and producers pay. Let's look first at what determines how much money a tax raises and then at the costs a tax imposes.

AP® Exam Tip

Be prepared to calculate the revenue earned from a tax. On a graph, this is the area of the rectangle that represents tax revenue. Remember: the area of a rectangle is the width times the height.

The Revenue from an Excise Tax

How much revenue does the government collect from an excise tax? In our hotel tax example, the revenue is equal to the area of the shaded rectangle in **Figure 50.10**.

To see why this area represents the revenue collected by a $40 tax on hotel rooms, notice that the *height* of the rectangle is $40, equal to the tax per room. As we've seen, it is also the size of the wedge that the tax drives between the supply price (the price received by producers) and the demand price (the price paid by consumers). Meanwhile, the *width* of the rectangle is 5,000 rooms, equal to the equilibrium

Figure 50.10 The Revenue from an Excise Tax

The revenue from a $40 excise tax on hotel rooms is $200,000, equal to the tax rate, $40—the size of the wedge that the tax drives between the supply price and the demand price—multiplied by the number of rooms rented, 5,000. This is equal to the area of the shaded rectangle.

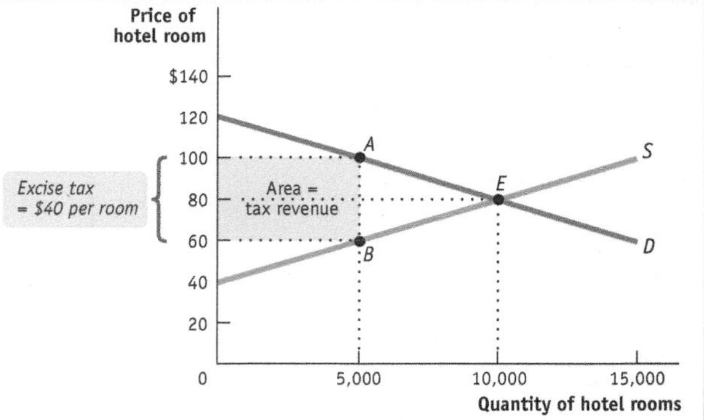

FOCUS Graph It

Students should look at Figure 50.10 and answer the following questions about the revenue obtained from an excise tax:

- What would the formula to determine the revenue be? *The revenue formula is the excise tax times the quantity.* Now calculate the amount of the revenue. *The excise tax of the difference between point A and B on the price axis—$40. With the excise tax of $40, 5,000 rooms are rented. Total revenue is $200,000.*
- What is the effect of this statement: "An excise tax drives a wedge between the price paid by consumers and the price received by producers"? *Consumers pay more and producers get less.*
- How much of this tax does the seller pay? *Sellers had received $80 per room before the tax and now they get $60 per room. They are paying $20 of the $40 tax out of their own profit.*
- How much of this tax does the buyer pay? *Consumers had paid $80 per room before the tax and now they pay $100 per room. They are paying $20 of the $40 tax out of their own pocket.*

508 Section 9 Behind the Demand Curve: Consumer Choice

quantity of rooms given the $40 tax. With that information, we can make the following calculations.

The tax revenue collected is:

Tax revenue = $40 per room × 5,000 rooms = $200,000

The area of the shaded rectangle is:

Area = Height × Width = $40 per room × 5,000 rooms = $200,000,

or

Tax revenue = Area of shaded rectangle

This is a general principle: *The revenue collected by an excise tax is equal to the area of a rectangle with the height of the tax wedge between the supply price and the demand price and the width of the quantity sold under the tax.*

The Costs of Taxation

What is the cost of a tax? You might be inclined to answer that it is the amount of money taxpayers pay to the government—the tax revenue collected. But suppose the government uses the tax revenue to provide services that taxpayers want. Or suppose that the government simply hands the tax revenue back to taxpayers. Would we say in those cases that the tax didn't actually cost anything?

No—because a tax, like a quota, prevents mutually beneficial transactions from occurring. Consider Figure 50.10 once more. Here, with a $40 tax on hotel rooms, guests pay $100 per room but hotel owners receive only $60 per room. Because of the wedge created by the tax, we know that some transactions didn't occur that would have occurred without the tax. More specifically, we know from the supply and demand curves that there are some potential guests who would be willing to pay up to $90 per night and some hotel owners who would be willing to supply rooms if they received at least $70 per night. If these two sets of people were allowed to trade with each other without the tax, they would engage in mutually beneficial transactions—hotel rooms would be rented. But such deals would be illegal because the $40 tax would not be paid. In our example, 5,000 potential hotel room rentals that would have occurred in the absence of the tax, to the mutual benefit of guests and hotel owners, do not take place because of the tax.

So an excise tax imposes costs over and above the tax revenue collected in the form of inefficiency, which occurs because the tax discourages mutually beneficial transactions. You may recall from Module 9 that the cost to society of this kind of inefficiency—the value of the forgone mutually beneficial transactions—is called the **deadweight loss**. While most real-world taxes impose some deadweight loss, a badly designed tax imposes a larger deadweight loss than a well-designed one.

To measure the deadweight loss from a tax, we turn to the concepts of producer and consumer surplus. **Figure 50.11** on the next page shows the effects of an excise tax on consumer and producer surplus. In the absence of the tax, the equilibrium is at *E* and the equilibrium price and quantity are P_E and Q_E, respectively. An excise tax drives a wedge equal to the amount of the tax between the price received by producers and the price paid by consumers, reducing the quantity sold. In this case, with a tax of *T* dollars per unit, the quantity sold falls to Q_T. The price paid by consumers rises to P_C, the demand price of the reduced quantity, Q_T, and the price received by producers falls to P_P, the supply price of that quantity. The difference between these prices, $P_C - P_P$, is equal to the excise tax, *T*.

Using the concepts of producer and consumer surplus, we can show exactly how much surplus producers and consumers lose as a result of the tax. We learned previously that a fall in the price of a good generates a gain in consumer surplus that is equal to the

AP® Exam Tip

It is useful to practice some problems in which letters represent numbers, because you may need to solve problems like that on the AP® exam.

The **deadweight loss** (from a tax) is the decrease in total surplus resulting from the tax, minus the tax revenues generated.

TEACH Connect It

Remind students that in Module 9 they learned that the cost to society of inefficiency—the value of a forgone mutually beneficial transaction—is called a deadweight loss. Remind students that a tax drives a wedge equal to the amount of the tax between the price received by producers and the price paid by consumers. The outcome is a decreased quantity sold, which we saw previously will create deadweight loss. The deadweight loss from a tax is the decrease in total surplus resulting from the tax minus the tax revenues generated.

FOCUS Flip It

TRM Have students watch Jacob Clifford's video "Micro 4.13 Deadweight Loss—Key Graphs in Microeconomics" (see econextras video list with hyperlinks on the bcs and TRFD). It does address deadweight loss in monopoly (which we have not yet studied); however, it also shows the tax effect, a concept covered in this module. Questions for this assignment may be found on **Worksheet 50.5 (Deadweight Loss)** from the TRM.

The video "How to Calculate Deadweight Loss" (see econextras video list with hyperlinks on the bcs and TRFD) provides an alternative explanation and visual of deadweight loss. Refer your students to **Worksheet 50.6 (Calculating Deadweight Loss)** from the TRM for questions on this video.

FOCUS Graph It

Have students draw a correctly labeled supply and demand graph showing equilibrium price and quantity. Ask them to show the effect on quantity and the price paid by consumers and producers if an excise tax is imposed on sellers. Then have students add points to their graph and use them to identify the following:

- Consumer surplus before and after the tax
- Producer surplus before and after the tax
- Tax revenue
- Deadweight loss

FOCUS Active Learning

TRM For a review of the costs and benefits of taxation, assign **Worksheet 50.7 (Costs and Benefits of Taxation)** from the TRM.

Figure 50.11 A Tax Reduces Consumer and Producer Surplus

Before the tax, the equilibrium price and quantity are P_E and Q_E, respectively. After an excise tax of T per unit is imposed, the price to consumers rises to P_C and consumer surplus falls by the sum of the dark blue rectangle, labeled A, and the light blue triangle, labeled B. The tax also causes the price to producers to fall to P_P; producer surplus falls by the sum of the red rectangle, labeled C, and the pink triangle, labeled F. The government receives revenue from the tax, $Q_T \times T$, which is given by the sum of the areas A and C. Areas B and F represent the losses to consumer and producer surplus that are not collected by the government as revenue; they are the deadweight loss to society of the tax.

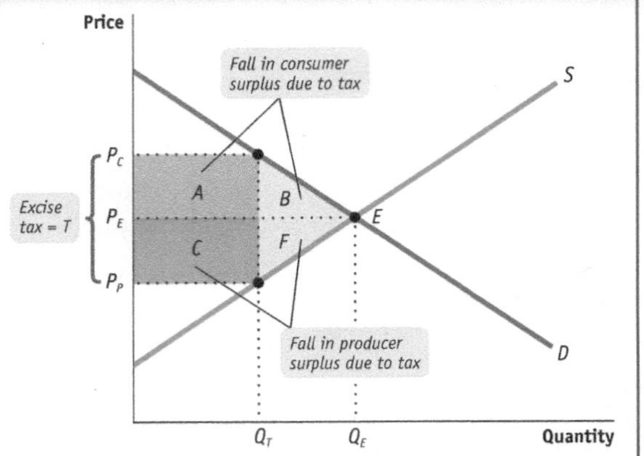

sum of the areas of a rectangle and a triangle. Similarly, a price increase causes a loss to consumers that is represented by the sum of the areas of a rectangle and a triangle. So it's not surprising that in the case of an excise tax, the rise in the price paid by consumers causes a loss equal to the sum of the areas of a rectangle and a triangle: the dark blue rectangle labeled A and the area of the light blue triangle labeled B in Figure 50.11.

Meanwhile, the fall in the price received by producers leads to a fall in producer surplus. This, too, is equal to the sum of the areas of a rectangle and a triangle. The loss in producer surplus is the sum of the areas of the red rectangle labeled C and the pink triangle labeled F in Figure 50.11.

Of course, although consumers and producers are hurt by the tax, the government gains revenue. The revenue the government collects is equal to the tax per unit sold, T, multiplied by the quantity sold, Q_T. This revenue is equal to the area of a rectangle Q_T wide and T high. And we already have that rectangle in the figure: it is the sum of rectangles A and C. So the government gains part of what consumers and producers lose from an excise tax.

But a portion of the loss to producers and consumers from the tax is not offset by a gain to the government—specifically, the two triangles B and F. The deadweight loss caused by the tax is equal to the combined area of these two triangles. It represents the total surplus lost to society because of the tax—that is, the amount of surplus that would have been generated by transactions that now do not take place because of the tax.

Figure 50.12 is a version of Figure 50.11 that leaves out rectangles A (the surplus shifted from consumers to the government) and C (the surplus shifted from producers to the government) and shows only the deadweight loss, drawn here as a triangle shaded yellow. The base of that triangle is equal to the tax wedge, T; the height of the triangle is equal to the reduction in the quantity transacted due to the tax, $Q_E - Q_T$. Clearly, the larger the tax wedge and the larger the reduction in the quantity transacted, the greater the inefficiency from the tax. But also note an important, contrasting point: if the excise tax somehow *didn't* reduce the quantity bought and sold in this market—if Q_T remained equal to Q_E after the tax was levied—the yellow triangle would disappear and the deadweight loss from the tax would be zero. So if a tax does *not* discourage transactions, it causes no deadweight loss. In this case, the tax simply shifts surplus straight from consumers and producers to the government.

AP® Exam Tip

Be prepared to calculate the deadweight loss created by a tax. On a graph, deadweight loss is represented by a triangle that points in the direction of the efficient quantity.

Figure 50.12 The Deadweight Loss of a Tax

A tax leads to a deadweight loss because it creates inefficiency: some mutually beneficial transactions never take place because of the tax, namely the transactions $Q_E - Q_T$. The yellow area here represents the value of the deadweight loss: it is the total surplus that would have been gained from the $Q_E - Q_T$ transactions. If the tax had not discouraged transactions—had the number of transactions remained at Q_E—no deadweight loss would have been incurred.

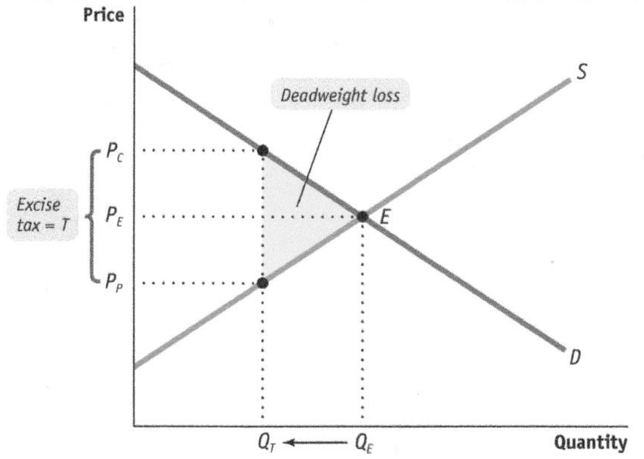

Using a triangle to measure deadweight loss is a technique used in many economic applications. For example, triangles are used to measure the deadweight loss produced by types of taxes other than excise taxes. They are also used to measure the deadweight loss produced by monopoly, another kind of market distortion. And deadweight-loss triangles are often used to evaluate the benefits and costs of public policies besides taxation—such as whether to impose stricter safety standards on a product.

In considering the total amount of inefficiency caused by a tax, we must also take into account something not shown in Figure 50.12: the resources actually used by the government to collect the tax, and by taxpayers to pay it, over and above the amount of the tax. These lost resources are called the **administrative costs** of the tax. The most familiar administrative cost of the U.S. tax system is the time individuals spend filling out their income tax forms or the money they spend on accountants to prepare their tax forms for them. (The latter is considered an inefficiency from the point of view of society because accountants could instead be performing other, non-tax-related services.) Included in the administrative costs that taxpayers incur are resources used to evade the tax, both legally and illegally. The costs of operating the Internal Revenue Service, the arm of the federal government tasked with collecting the federal income tax, are actually quite small in comparison to the administrative costs paid by taxpayers. The total inefficiency caused by a tax can be measured by the sum of its deadweight loss and its administrative costs.

Some extreme forms of taxation, such as the *poll tax* instituted by the government of British Prime Minister Margaret Thatcher in 1989, are notably unfair but very efficient. A poll tax is an example of a **lump-sum tax**, a tax that is the same for everyone regardless of any actions people take. The poll tax in Britain was widely perceived as much less fair than the tax structure it replaced, in which local taxes were proportional to property values.

Under the old system, the highest local taxes were paid by the people with the most expensive houses. Because these people tended to be wealthy, they were also best able to bear the burden. But the old system definitely distorted incentives to engage in mutually beneficial transactions and created deadweight loss. People who were considering home improvements knew that such improvements, by making their property more valuable, would increase their tax bills. The result, surely, was that some home improvements

The **administrative costs** of a tax are the resources used by the government to collect the tax, and by taxpayers to pay (or to evade) it, over and above the amount collected.

A **lump-sum tax** is a tax of a fixed amount paid by all taxpayers.

AP® Exam Tip

Unless they cause a firm to shut down, lump-sum taxes do not affect price or quantity, so they do not create deadweight loss.

TEACH Teach It

Taxes have administrative costs as well. These are the costs of the resources used by the government to collect taxes and the costs borne by consumers to pay such taxes. They fall above the cost of the tax itself.

TEACH AP® Exam Tip

Explain and emphasize that lump sum taxes do not distort incentives and are therefore better at promoting economic efficiency. This idea is revisited and becomes important in later modules and on the AP® exam.

OPEN & CLOSE Exit Slip

TRM *Please see* ***Exit Slip: Module 50*** *in the TRM for formative multiple-choice questions to ask your students before finishing your lesson. These questions will help you quickly assess whether your students have mastered the module's concepts before moving on.*

Answers to the Exit Slip Questions

1. D
2. E
3. C

that would have taken place without the tax did not take place because of it. In contrast, a lump-sum tax does not distort incentives. Because under a lump-sum tax people have to pay the same amount of tax regardless of their actions, it does not cause them to substitute untaxed goods for a good whose price has been artificially inflated by a tax, as occurs with an excise tax. So lump-sum taxes, although unfair, are better than other taxes at promoting economic efficiency.

MODULE 50 Review

Check Your Understanding

1. Using the tables in Check Your Understanding Questions 1 and 2 in Module 49, find the equilibrium price and quantity in the market for cheese-stuffed jalapeño peppers. What is the total surplus in the equilibrium in this market, and how much of it does each consumer and producer receive?
2. Consider the market for butter, shown in the accompanying figure. The government imposes an excise tax of \$0.30 per pound of butter. What is the price paid by consumers post-tax? What is the price received by producers post-tax? What is the quantity of butter sold? How is the incidence of the tax allocated between consumers and producers? Show this on the figure.

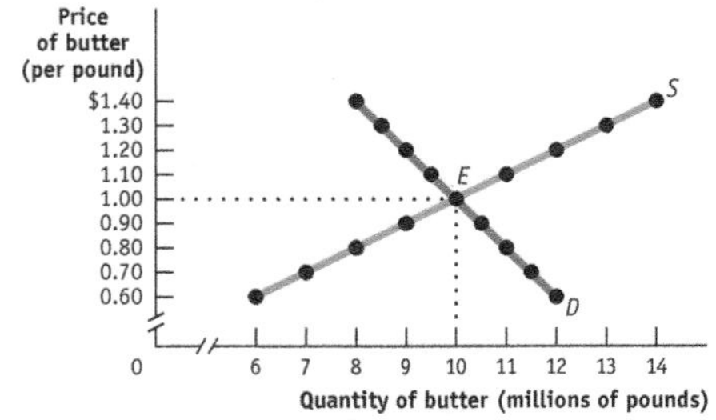

3. The accompanying table shows five consumers' willingness to pay for one can of diet soda each as well as five producers' costs of selling one can of diet soda each. Each consumer buys at most one can of soda; each producer sells at most one can of soda. The government asks your advice about the effects of an excise tax of \$0.40 per can of diet soda. Assume that there are no administrative costs from the tax.

	Consumer Willingness to Pay		*Producer Cost*
Ana	\$0.70	Zhang	\$0.10
Bernice	0.60	Yves	0.20
Chizuko	0.50	Xavier	0.30
Dagmar	0.40	Walter	0.40
Ella	0.30	Vern	0.50

a. Without the excise tax, what is the equilibrium price and the equilibrium quantity of soda?
b. The excise tax raises the price paid by consumers post-tax to \$0.60 and lowers the price received by producers post-tax to \$0.20. With the excise tax, what is the quantity of soda sold?
c. Without the excise tax, how much individual consumer surplus does each of the consumers gain? How much individual consumer surplus does each consumer gain with the tax? How much total consumer surplus is lost as a result of the tax?
d. Without the excise tax, how much individual producer surplus does each of the producers gain? How much individual producer surplus does each producer gain with the tax? How much total producer surplus is lost as a result of the tax?
e. How much government revenue does the excise tax create?
f. What is the deadweight loss from the imposition of this excise tax?

Tackle the Test: Multiple-Choice Questions

1. At market equilibrium in a competitive market, which of the following is necessarily true?
   I. Consumer surplus is maximized.
   II. Producer surplus is maximized.
   III. Total surplus is maximized.

   a. I only
   b. II only
   c. III only
   d. I and II only
   e. I, II, and III

Answers to Module 50 Review Questions

Check Your Understanding

1. The quantity demanded equals the quantity supplied at a price of \$0.50, the equilibrium price. At that price, a total quantity of 5 peppers will be bought and sold. Casey will buy 3 peppers and receive a consumer surplus of \$0.40 on his first, \$0.20 on his second, and \$0.00 on his third pepper. Josey will buy 2 peppers and receive a consumer surplus of \$0.30 on her first and \$0.10 on her second pepper. Total consumer surplus is therefore \$1.00. Cara will supply 3 peppers and receive a producer surplus of \$0.40 on her first, \$0.40 on her second, and \$0.10 on her third pepper. Jamie will supply 2 peppers and receive a producer surplus of \$0.20 on his first and \$0.00 on his second pepper. Total producer surplus is therefore \$1.10. Total surplus in this market is thus \$1.00 + \$1.10 = \$2.10.

2. The following figure shows that, after the introduction of the excise tax, the price paid by consumers rises to \$1.20; the price received by producers falls to \$0.90. Consumers bear \$0.20 of the \$0.30 tax per pound of butter; producers bear \$0.10 of the tax. The tax drives a wedge of \$0.30 between the price paid by consumers and the price received by producers. As a result, the quantity of butter sold is now 9 million pounds.

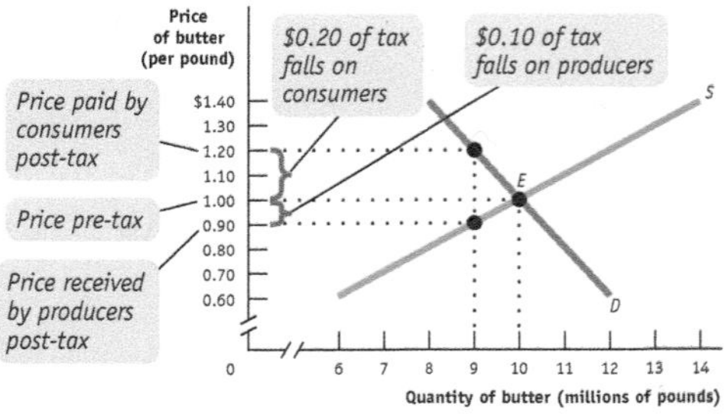

3. a. Without the excise tax, Zhang, Yves, Xavier, and Walter sell, and Ana, Bernice, Chizuko, and Dagmar buy 1 can of soda each, at \$0.40 per can. Thus, the quantity bought and sold is 4.

b. With the excise tax, Zhang and Yves sell, and Ana and Bernice buy 1 can of soda each. So, the quantity sold is 2.

c. Without the excise tax, Ana's individual consumer surplus is \$0.70 − \$0.40 = \$0.30, Bernice's is \$0.60 − \$0.40 = \$0.20, Chizuko's is \$0.50 − \$0.40 = \$0.10, and Dagmar's is \$0.40 − \$0.40 = \$0.00. Total consumer surplus is \$0.30 + \$0.20 + \$0.10 + \$0.00 = \$0.60. With the tax, Ana's individual consumer surplus is \$0.70 − \$0.60 = \$0.10 and Bernice's is \$0.60 − \$0.60 = \$0.00. Total consumer surplus post-tax is \$0.10 + \$0.00 = \$0.10. Thus, the total consumer surplus lost because of the tax is \$0.60 − \$0.10 = \$0.50.

d. Without the excise tax, Zhang's individual producer surplus is \$0.40 − \$0.10 = \$0.30, Yves's is \$0.40 − \$0.20 = \$0.20, Xavier's is \$0.40 − \$0.30 = \$0.10, and Walter's is \$0.40 − \$0.40 = \$0.00. Total producer surplus is \$0.30 + \$0.20 + \$0.10 + \$0.00 = \$0.60. With the tax, Zhang's individual producer surplus is \$0.20 − \$0.10 = \$0.10 and Yves's is \$0.20 − \$0.20 = \$0.00. Total producer surplus post-tax is \$0.10 + \$0.00 = \$0.10. Thus, the total producer surplus lost because of the tax is \$0.60 − \$0.10 = \$0.50.

e. With the tax, 2 cans of soda are sold, so the government tax revenue from this excise tax is 2 × \$0.40 = \$0.80.

f. Total surplus is the sum of producer surplus and consumer surplus. Total surplus without the tax is \$0.60 + \$0.60 = \$1.20. With the tax, total surplus is \$0.10 + \$0.10 = \$0.20. Government tax revenue is \$0.80. Deadweight loss from this excise tax is therefore \$1.20 − (\$0.20 + \$0.80) = \$0.20.

2. Which of the following is true regarding equity and efficiency in competitive markets?
   a. Competitive markets ensure equity and efficiency.
   b. There is often a trade-off between equity and efficiency.
   c. Competitive markets lead to neither equity nor efficiency.
   d. There is generally agreement about the level of equity and efficiency in a market.
   e. None of the above
3. An excise tax imposed on sellers in a market will result in which of the following?
   I. an upward shift of the supply curve
   II. a downward shift of the demand curve
   III. deadweight loss
   a. I only
   b. II only
   c. III only
   d. I and III only
   e. I, II, and III
4. An excise tax will be paid mainly by producers when
   a. it is imposed on producers.
   b. it is imposed on consumers.
   c. the price elasticity of supply is low and the price elasticity of demand is high.
   d. the price elasticity of supply is high and the price elasticity of demand is low.
   e. the price elasticity of supply is perfectly elastic.
5. When a competitive market is in equilibrium, total surplus can be increased by
   I. reallocating consumption among consumers.
   II. reallocating sales among sellers.
   III. changing the quantity traded.
   a. I only
   b. II only
   c. III only
   d. I, II, and III
   e. None of the above

Tackle the Test: Free-Response Questions

1. Refer to the graph provided. Assume the government has imposed an excise tax of $60 on producers in this market.

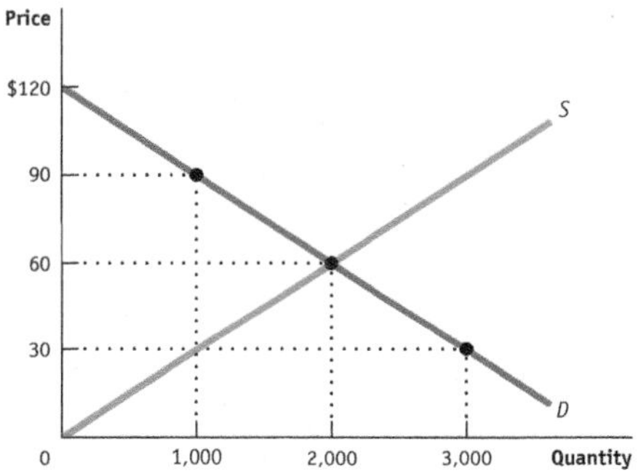

   a. What quantity will be sold in the market?
   b. What price will consumers pay in the market?
   c. By how much will consumer surplus change as a result of the tax?
   d. By how much will producer surplus change as a result of the tax?
   e. How much revenue will the government collect from this excise tax?
   f. Calculate the deadweight loss created by the tax.

Rubric for FRQ 1 (6 points)

1 point: 1,000

1 point: $90

1 point: Consumer surplus will decrease by $45,000, from ½ ($2,000 × 60) = $60,000 before the tax to ½ ($1,000 × 30) = $15,000 after the tax.

1 point: Producer surplus will decrease by $45,000, from ½ ($2,000 × 60) = $60,000 before the tax to ½ ($1,000 × 30) = $15,000 after the tax.

1 point: $60 × 1,000 = $60,000

1 point: ½ × $60 × 1,000 = $30,000

2. Draw a correctly labeled graph of a competitive market in equilibrium. Use your graph to illustrate the effect of an excise tax imposed on consumers. Indicate each of the following on your graph:
   a. the equilibrium price and quantity without the tax, labeled P_E and Q_E
   b. the quantity sold in the market post-tax, labeled Q_T
   c. the price paid by consumers post-tax, labeled P_C
   d. the price received by producers post-tax, labeled P_P
   e. the tax revenue generated by the tax, labeled "Tax revenue"
   f. the deadweight loss resulting from the tax, labeled "DWL"
   (7 points)

Tackle the Test: Multiple-Choice Questions

1. c
2. b
3. d
4. c
5. e

Tackle the Test: Free-Response Question

Rubric for FRQ 2 (7 points)

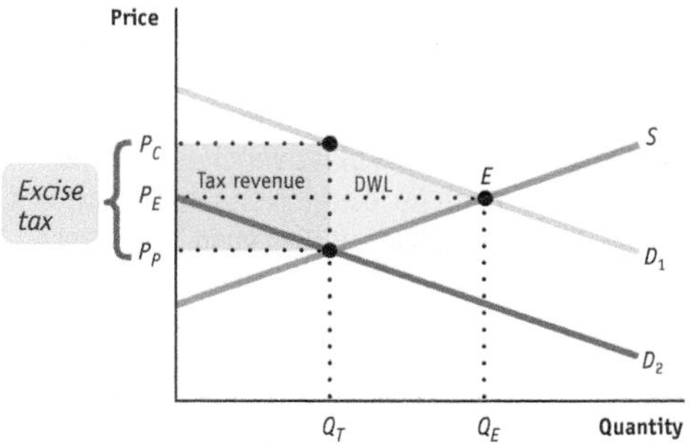

1 point: A graph with "Price" (or *P*) on the vertical axis, "Quantity" (or *Q*) on the horizontal axis, a downward-sloping demand curve, and an upward-sloping supply curve

1 point: P_E and Q_E labeled along the appropriate axes at the equilibrium levels

1 point: Post-tax quantity labeled Q_T

1 point: Post-tax consumer price labeled P_c

1 point: Post-tax producer price labeled P_p

1 point: Tax revenue area labeled "Tax revenue"

1 point: Deadweight loss area labeled "DWL"

PD To prepare for teaching this lesson, you may want to consult the **Module 51 Sample Lecture** in the TRM.

OPEN & CLOSE Start Here

Bring a snack to class that is easily divided into small bites (e.g., donut holes or "fun size" candy bars), and select a student volunteer who likes the snack for a demonstration. Have the student eat the snack while the class watches. Ask the student how much he liked the snack. The student will say something like, "It was good," but press him to tell you *how much* he liked it by choosing a rating or number. The student will find answering the question difficult, but stress that the class demonstration depends on his selecting a number. Remind the student that he is the only one who knows how much he liked it. Once you get a number, write it on the board, and give the student a second number: say, 5,678 (or some other made up number). Continue coaxing the student to eat more of the snack and recording on the board each subsequent number he gives you. Eventually, the student will refuse to eat more of the snack, assigning zero to indicate how much he liked it. Use the demonstration to discuss the definition and measurement of utility and the difficulties of measuring and comparing utilities. Use the numbers generated to discuss marginal utility and diminishing marginal utility and to calculate total utility.

craftvision/Getty Images

MODULE 51 Utility Maximization

In this Module, you will learn to:

- Describe how consumers make choices about the purchase of goods and services
- Explain why consumers' general goal is to maximize utility
- Explain why the principle of diminishing marginal utility applies to the consumption of most goods and services
- Use marginal analysis to find the optimal consumption bundle

We have used the demand curve to study consumer responsiveness to changes in prices and discovered its usefulness in predicting how consumers will gain from the availability of goods and services in a market. But where does the demand curve come from? In other words, what lies behind the demand curve? The demand curve represents the tastes, preferences, and resulting choices of individual consumers. Its shape reflects the additional satisfaction, or *utility*, people receive from consuming more and more of a good or service.

Utility: It's All About Getting Satisfaction

Utility is a measure of personal satisfaction.

When analyzing consumer behavior, we're looking into how people pursue their needs and wants and the subjective feelings that motivate purchases. Yet there is no simple way to measure subjective feelings. How much satisfaction do I get from my third cookie? Is it less or more than the satisfaction you receive from your third cookie? Does it even make sense to ask that question?

© Drive Images/Alamy

Luckily, we don't need to make comparisons between your feelings and mine. The analysis of consumer behavior that follows requires only the assumption that individuals try to maximize some personal measure of the satisfaction gained from consumption. That measure of satisfaction is known as **utility**, a concept we use to understand behavior but don't expect to measure in practice.

Utility and Consumption

We can think of consumers as using consumption to "produce" utility, much in the same way that producers use inputs to produce output. As consumers, we do not make explicit calculations of the utility generated by consumption choices. However, we must

St. Louis Federal Reserve Bank Resources

"Demand," *The Economic Lowdown Podcast Series*, Episode 6

This podcast examines the law of demand. Those who love candy bars will find this lesson especially easy to digest. A demand curve is simply defined, as are the sorts of changes that might affect that curve—all in less than 7 minutes.

"Demand," *The Economic Lowdown Video Series*, Episode 2

In this episode, economic education specialist Scott Wolla explains the concept of demand. Viewers will learn how a change in the price of a good affects the quantity of the good consumers will buy and how changes in market conditions affect the demand for a good.

514 Section 9 Behind the Demand Curve: Consumer Choice

make choices, and we usually base them on at least a rough attempt to achieve greater satisfaction. You can have either soup or salad with your dinner. Which would you enjoy more? You can go to Disney World this year or put the money toward buying a new car. Which would make you happier? These are the types of questions that go into utility maximization.

The concept of utility offers a way to study choices that are made in a more or less rational way.

How do we measure utility? For the sake of simplicity, it is useful to suppose that we can measure utility in hypothetical units called—what else?—**utils**. A *utility function* shows the relationship between a consumer's utility and the combination of goods and services—the *consumption bundle*—he or she consumes.

A **util** is a unit of utility.

Figure 51.1 illustrates a utility function. It shows the total utility that Cassie, who likes fried clams, gets from an all-you-can-eat clam dinner. We suppose that her consumption bundle consists of a side of coleslaw, which comes with the meal, plus a

Figure 51.1 Cassie's Total Utility and Marginal Utility

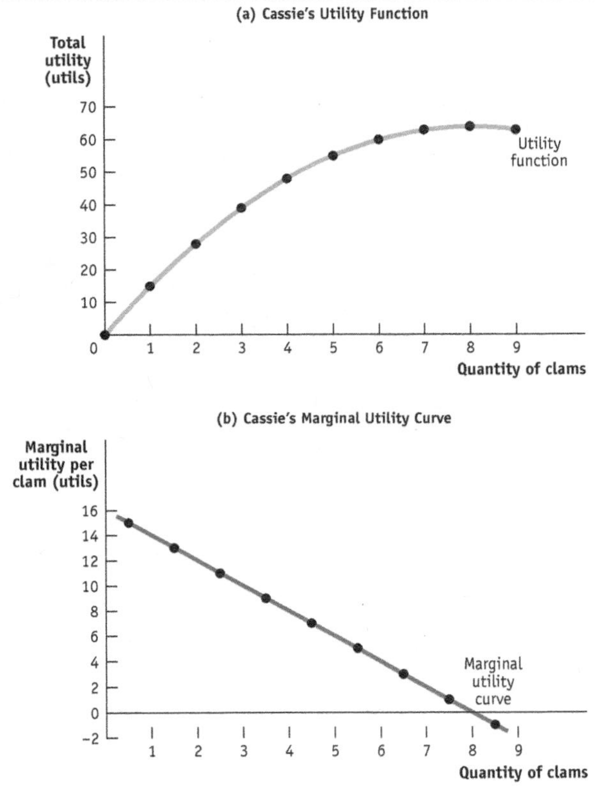

Quantity of clams	Total utility (utils)	Marginal utility per clam (utils)
0	0	
		15
1	15	
		13
2	28	
		11
3	39	
		9
4	48	
		7
5	55	
		5
6	60	
		3
7	63	
		1
8	64	
		−1
9	63	

Panel (a) shows how Cassie's total utility depends on her consumption of fried clams. It increases until it reaches its maximum utility level of 64 utils at 8 clams consumed and decreases after that. Marginal utility is calculated in the table. Panel (b) shows the marginal utility curve, which slopes downward due to diminishing marginal utility. That is, each additional clam gives Cassie less utility than the previous clam.

FOCUS Graph It

Graph the numbers for marginal utility and total utility in your opening demonstration and compare the results to the graphs in Figure 51.1.

TEACH Connect It

Marginal analysis was presented in the first module. Remind students that *marginal* always refers to a change—doing a little bit more or less of something. Marginal utility is the change in total utility from consuming one more. Marginal values are very important in future modules, so emphasize the meaning of marginal!

FOCUS Graph It

Reinforce the idea that marginal values refer to changes. Have students look at Figure 51.1, specifically panel (a). Remind students that marginal utility is the change in total utility when you consume one more. Where is a change in total utility measured? *On the vertical axis (change in Total Utility—TU).* Where is a change in the quantity consumed measured? *On the horizontal axis (change in Quantity—Q).* Marginal utility is the change in *TU* divided by the change in *Q*.

Have students compare marginal utility (*MU*) to the slope of the utility function (rise/run). Since the rise is the change in *TU* and the run is the change in *Q*, they are the same! As you move along the *TU* curve, it gets flatter (the slope decreases), indicating that *MU* is decreasing, as shown in panel (b). *Note:* The slope of *any* total curve is the marginal.

TEACH Teach It

Ask students if they think marginal utility can ever be negative. What would it mean if *MU* were negative? *It would mean that you were less happy after consuming the last unit than you were before consuming it.* Ask students if they have ever experienced negative marginal utility. Chances are that they have—and they realized that consuming the last unit was a bad choice!

FOCUS Active Learning

TRM Refer students to **Worksheet 51.1 (Utility)** from the TRM for activities about utility.

TEACH Connect It

Remind students they have learned that the demand curve shows the quantity consumers are *willing* and *able* to purchase at various prices. Utility measures a consumer's willingness to purchase a good. But we also need to consider income (a determinant of demand) to determine a consumer's ability to purchase a good. A budget line shows the consumption bundles a consumer can purchase if all income is spent.

number of clams to be determined. The table that accompanies the figure shows how Cassie's total utility depends on the number of clams; the curve in panel (a) of the figure shows that same information graphically.

Cassie's utility function slopes upward over most of the range shown, but it gets flatter as the number of clams consumed increases. And in this example it eventually turns downward. According to the information in the table in Figure 51.1, nine clams is a clam too far. Adding that additional clam actually makes Cassie worse off: it would lower her total utility. If she's rational, of course, Cassie will realize that and not consume the ninth clam.

So when Cassie chooses how many clams to consume, she will make this decision by considering the *change* in her total utility from consuming one more clam. This illustrates the general point: to maximize *total* utility, consumers must focus on *marginal* utility.

The Principle of Diminishing Marginal Utility

The **marginal utility** of a good or service is the change in total utility generated by consuming one additional unit of that good or service. The **marginal utility curve** shows how marginal utility depends on the quantity of a good or service consumed.

In addition to showing how Cassie's total utility depends on the number of clams she consumes, the table in Figure 51.1 also shows the **marginal utility** generated by consuming each additional clam—that is, the *change* in total utility from consuming one additional clam. The **marginal utility curve** shows how marginal utility depends on the quantity of clams consumed. The curve is constructed by plotting points at the midpoint between the numbered quantities since marginal utility is found as consumption levels change. For example, when consumption rises from 1 to 2 clams, marginal utility is 13. Therefore, we place the point corresponding to the marginal utility of 13 halfway between 1 and 2 clams.

The marginal utility curve slopes downward because each successive clam adds less to total utility than the previous clam. This is reflected in the table: marginal utility falls from a high of 15 utils for the first clam consumed to −1 for the ninth clam consumed. The fact that the ninth clam has negative marginal utility means that consuming

FYI Is Marginal Utility Really Diminishing?

Are all goods really subject to diminishing marginal utility? Of course not; there are a number of goods for which, at least over some range, marginal utility is surely *increasing*.

For example, there are goods that require some experience to enjoy. The first time you do it, downhill skiing involves a lot more fear than enjoyment—or so they say: two of the authors have never tried it! It only becomes a pleasurable activity if you do it enough to become reasonably competent. And even some less strenuous forms of consumption take practice; people who are not accustomed to drinking coffee say it has a bitter taste and can't understand its appeal. (The authors, on the other hand, regard coffee as one of the basic food groups.)

Another example would be goods that only deliver positive utility if you buy enough. The great Victorian economist Alfred Marshall, who more or less invented the supply and demand model, gave the example of wallpaper: buying only enough to do half a room is worse than useless. If you need two rolls of wallpaper to finish a room, the marginal utility of the second roll is larger than the marginal utility of the first roll.

So why does it make sense to assume diminishing marginal utility? For one thing, most goods don't suffer

Johnny Adolphson/Shutterstock

from these qualifications: nobody needs to learn to like ice cream. Also, although most people don't ski and some people don't drink coffee, those who do ski or drink coffee do enough of it that the marginal utility of one more ski run or one more cup is less than that of the last. So *in the relevant range* of consumption, marginal utility is still diminishing.

St. Louis Federal Reserve Bank Resources

Supply and Demand Online Course for Teachers and Students

Supply and demand are among the most fundamental concepts in economics. An understanding of these topics helps students better understand the economic world in which they live. This course includes three interactive lessons that introduce supply, demand, and market equilibrium. It uses a fictitious chocolate market to help explain the concept.

516 Section 9 Behind the Demand Curve: Consumer Choice

it actually reduces total utility. (Restaurants that offer all-you-can-eat meals depend on the proposition that you can have too much of a good thing.) Not all marginal utility curves eventually become negative. But it is generally accepted that marginal utility curves do slope downward—that consumption of most goods and services is subject to *diminishing marginal utility*.

The basic idea behind the **principle of diminishing marginal utility** is that the additional satisfaction a consumer gets from one more unit of a good or service declines as the amount of that good or service consumed rises. Or, to put it slightly differently, the more of a good or service you consume, the closer you are to being satiated—reaching a point at which an additional unit of the good adds nothing to your satisfaction. For someone who almost never gets to eat a banana, the occasional banana is a marvelous treat (as it was in Eastern Europe before the fall of communism, when bananas were very hard to find). For someone who eats them all the time, a banana is just, well, a banana.

The principle of diminishing marginal utility doesn't always apply, but it does apply in the great majority of cases, enough to serve as a foundation for our analysis of consumer behavior.

According to the **principle of diminishing marginal utility**, each successive unit of a good or service consumed adds less to total utility than does the previous unit.

Budgets and Optimal Consumption

The principle of diminishing marginal utility explains why most people eventually reach a limit, even at an all-you-can-eat buffet where the cost of another clam is measured only in future indigestion. Under ordinary circumstances, however, it costs some additional resources to consume more of a good, and consumers must take that cost into account when making choices.

What do we mean by cost? As always, the fundamental measure of cost is *opportunity cost*. Because the amount of money a consumer can spend is limited, a decision to consume more of one good is also a decision to consume less of some other good.

Budget Constraints and Budget Lines

Consider Sammy, whose appetite is exclusively for clams and potatoes. (There's no accounting for tastes.) He has a weekly income of $20 and since, given his appetite, more of either good is better than less, he spends all of it on clams and potatoes. We will assume that clams cost $4 per pound and potatoes cost $2 per pound. What are his possible choices?

Whatever Sammy chooses, we know that the cost of his consumption bundle cannot exceed the amount of money he has to spend. That is,

(51-1) Expenditure on clams + Expenditure on potatoes $\leq$ Total income

Consumers always have limited income, which constrains how much they can consume. So the requirement illustrated by Equation 51-1—that a consumer must choose a consumption bundle that costs no more than his or her income—is known as the consumer's **budget constraint**. It's a simple way of saying that a consumer can't spend more than the total amount of income available to him or her. In other words, consumption bundles are affordable when they obey the budget constraint. We call the set of all of Sammy's affordable consumption bundles his **consumption possibilities**. In general, whether or not a particular consumption bundle is included in a consumer's consumption possibilities depends on the consumer's income and the prices of goods and services.

Figure 51.2 on the next page shows Sammy's consumption possibilities. The quantity of clams in his consumption bundle is measured on the horizontal axis and the quantity of potatoes on the vertical axis. The downward-sloping line connecting

A **budget constraint** limits the cost of a consumer's consumption bundle to no more than the consumer's income.

A consumer's **consumption possibilities** is the set of all consumption bundles that are affordable, given the consumer's income and prevailing prices.

FOCUS Active Learning

Use a simple example to have students derive a budget line, individually or in pairs. Give students a budget of $100 in play money.

- Tell them there are two goods they can buy (if you want, you can identify actual goods, like pieces of candy, and even allow your students to purchase them with their budget!).
- The price of good 1 is $10 and the price of good 2 is $20.
- Have students draw a graph with good 1 on the vertical axis and good 2 on the horizontal axis.
- Ask them to determine the maximum amount of good 1 they can buy and plot that on their graph.
- They should realize that they can't buy good 2 if they spend all their money on good 1, so the point is the vertical intercept.
- Now do the same for good 2, which should give students the horizontal intercept.
- Finally, ask students to spend all their money buying some of both goods and plot that point on their graph. Have them connect the points to get the budget line.

St. Louis Federal Reserve Bank Resources

"What Is Driving Oil Prices?," ***Oil Prices: Demand and Supply***

Upon completing this lesson, students will be able to list the determinants of supply and demand, recognize which factors will cause demand curves or supply curves to shift, determine equilibrium using a demand/supply graph, and show the effects on price and quantity when equilibrium changes.

Module 51 Utility Maximization 517

TEACH Connect It

Refer students to Figure 51.2 and compare this graph to the production possibilities curve they studied previously. Review the meaning of points on the line, below the line, and beyond the line and their similarity when looking at the *PPC* and the budget line.

- Any point on the budget line shows an affordable consumption bundle for the consumer.
- Any point beneath the budget line shows affordable consumption bundles, but the consumer chooses not to spend all her income.
- Any point beyond the budget line shows unaffordable consumption bundles that exceed the consumer's income.

TEACH Teach It

The optimal consumption bundle is the combined amount of two goods that maximizes a consumer's total utility, given the budget constraint. A consumer is purchasing the optimal consumption bundle if all income is spent and no change in consumption can increase total utility.

Figure 51.2 The Budget Line

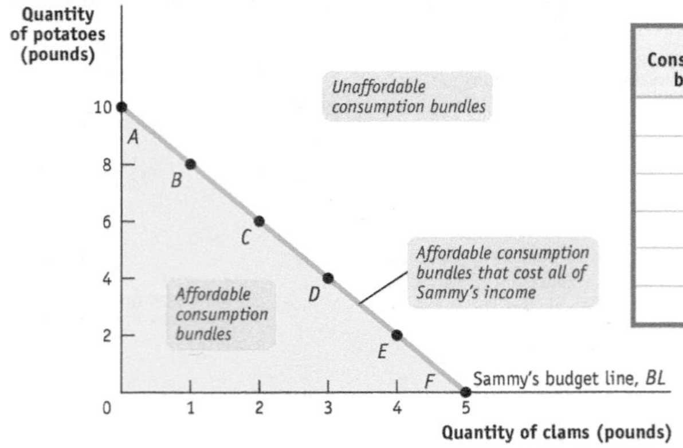

Consumption bundle	Quantity of clams (pounds)	Quantity of potatoes (pounds)
A	0	10
B	1	8
C	2	6
D	3	4
E	4	2
F	5	0

The *budget line* represents all the possible combinations of quantities of potatoes and clams that Sammy can purchase if he spends all of his income. Also, it is the boundary between the set of affordable consumption bundles (the *consumption possibilities*) and the unaffordable ones. Given that clams cost $4 per pound and potatoes cost $2 per pound, if Sammy spends all of his income on clams (bundle *F*), he can purchase 5 pounds of clams; if he spends all of his income on potatoes (bundle *A*), he can purchase 10 pounds of potatoes.

A consumer's **budget line** shows the consumption bundles available to a consumer who spends all of his or her income.

points *A* through *F* shows which consumption bundles are affordable and which are not. Every bundle on or inside this line (the shaded area) is affordable; every bundle outside this line is unaffordable. As an example of one of the points, let's look at point *C*, representing 2 pounds of clams and 6 pounds of potatoes, and check whether it satisfies Sammy's budget constraint. The cost of bundle *C* is 6 pounds of potatoes × $2 per pound + 2 pounds of clams × $4 per pound = $12 + $8 = $20. So bundle *C* does indeed satisfy Sammy's budget constraint: it costs no more than his weekly income of $20. In fact, bundle *C* costs exactly as much as Sammy's income. By doing the arithmetic, you can check that all the other points lying on the downward-sloping line are also bundles at which Sammy spends all of his income.

The downward-sloping line has a special name, the **budget line**. It shows all the consumption bundles available to Sammy when he spends all of his income. It's downward-sloping because when Sammy is spending all of his income, say by consuming at point *A* on the budget line, then in order to consume more clams he must consume fewer potatoes—that is, he must move to a point like *B*. In other words, when Sammy is on his budget line, the opportunity cost of consuming more clams is consuming fewer potatoes, and vice versa. As Figure 51.2 indicates, any consumption bundle that lies above the budget line is unaffordable.

Do we need to consider the other bundles in Sammy's consumption possibilities—the ones that lie *within* the shaded region in Figure 51.2 bounded by the budget line? The answer, for all practical situations, is no: as long as Sammy doesn't get satiated—that is, as long as his marginal utility from consuming either good is always positive—and he doesn't get any utility from saving income rather than spending it, then he will always choose to consume a bundle that lies on his budget line.

Given that $20 per week budget, next we can consider the culinary dilemma of what point on his budget line Sammy will choose.

St. Louis Federal Reserve Bank Resources

Supply and Demand.notebook

This series of slides aids students in reviewing the determinants of supply and demand, provides an exercise in which they choose which of the curves shift and why, and allows them to determine which curve will shift given a market event.

518 Section 9 Behind the Demand Curve: Consumer Choice

The Optimal Consumption Bundle

Because Sammy's budget constrains him to a consumption bundle somewhere along the budget line, a choice to consume a given quantity of clams also determines his potato consumption, and vice versa. We want to find the consumption bundle—represented by a point on the budget line—that maximizes Sammy's total utility. This bundle is Sammy's **optimal consumption bundle**.

A consumer's **optimal consumption bundle** is the consumption bundle that maximizes the consumer's total utility given his or her budget constraint.

Table 51.1 shows hypothetical levels of utility Sammy gets from consuming various quantities of clams and potatoes, respectively. According to the table, Sammy has a healthy appetite; the more of either good he consumes, the higher his utility. But because he has a limited budget, he must make a trade-off: the more pounds of clams he consumes, the fewer pounds of potatoes, and vice versa. That is, he must choose a point on his budget line.

Table 51.1 Sammy's Utility from Clam and Potato Consumption

Utility from clam consumption		Utility from potato consumption	
Quantity of clams (pounds)	**Utility from clams (utils)**	**Quantity of potatoes (pounds)**	**Utility from potatoes (utils)**
0	0	0	0
1	15	1	11.5
2	25	2	21.4
3	31	3	29.8
4	34	4	36.8
5	36	5	42.5
		6	47.0
		7	50.5
		8	53.2
		9	55.2
		10	56.7

Table 51.2 shows how his total utility varies for the different consumption bundles along his budget line. Each of six possible consumption bundles, *A* through *F* from Figure 51.2, is given in the first column. The second column shows the level of clam consumption corresponding to each choice. The third column shows the utility Sammy gets from consuming those clams. The fourth column shows the quantity of potatoes Sammy can afford *given* the level of clam consumption; this quantity goes down as his clam consumption goes up because he is sliding down the budget line. The fifth column shows the utility he gets from consuming those potatoes. And the final column shows his *total utility*. In this example, Sammy's total utility is the sum of the utility he gets from clams and the utility he gets from potatoes.

Table 51.2 Sammy's Budget and Total Utility

Consumption bundle	Quantity of clams (pounds)	Utility from clams (utils)	Quantity of potatoes (pounds)	Utility from potatoes (utils)	Total utility (utils)
A	0	0	10	56.7	56.7
B	1	15	8	53.2	68.2
C	2	25	6	47.0	72.0
D	3	31	4	36.8	67.8
E	4	34	2	21.4	55.4
F	5	36	0	0	36.0

Module 51 Utility Maximization 519

FOCUS Graph It

The horizontal axis of Figure 51.3, panel (b), may be confusing for students. Explain that since the consumer has a limited budget, buying more clams means the consumer can't afford as many potatoes, and vice versa. Measuring clams from left to right, the axis shows that 5 is the maximum number of pounds of clams the consumer can afford. As more clams are purchased, the consumer can afford fewer potatoes, so increasing clams reduces potatoes from left to right. And reducing clams from right to left increases potatoes (up to the maximum of 10 pounds of potatoes the consumer can afford).

TEACH AP® Exam Tip

AP® FRQs often ask students to "use marginal analysis" to answer a question. When students are asked to use marginal analysis, they will only receive points if they can show their answer has been determined using marginal values. For example, if students are asked to find the optimal consumption bundle using marginal analysis and they find the correct bundle by calculating total utility from each bundle, they will not receive points. They must use a marginal approach (as illustrated in Figure 51.3).

Figure 51.3 gives a visual representation of the data shown in Table 51.2. Panel (a) shows Sammy's budget line, to remind us that when he decides to consume more clams he is also deciding to consume fewer potatoes. Panel (b) then shows how his total utility depends on that choice. The horizontal axis in panel (b) has two sets of labels: it shows both the quantity of clams, increasing from left to right, and the quantity of potatoes, increasing from right to left. The reason we can use the same axis to represent consumption of both goods is, of course, that he is constrained by the budget line: the more pounds of clams Sammy consumes, the fewer pounds of potatoes he can afford, and vice versa.

Clearly, the consumption bundle that makes the best of the trade-off between clam consumption and potato consumption, the optimal consumption bundle, is the one that maximizes Sammy's total utility. That is, Sammy's optimal consumption bundle puts him at the top of the total utility curve.

As always, we can find the top of the curve by direct observation. We can see from Figure 51.3 that Sammy's total utility is maximized at point C—that his optimal

Figure 51.3 Optimal Consumption Bundle

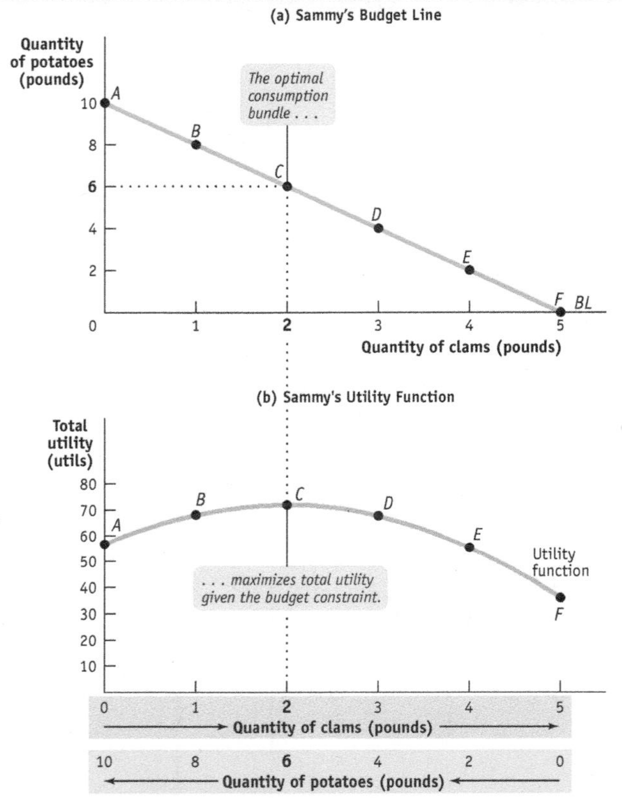

Panel (a) shows Sammy's budget line and his six possible consumption bundles. Panel (b) shows how his total utility is affected by his consumption bundle, which must lie on his budget line. The quantity of clams is measured from left to right on the horizontal axis, and the quantity of potatoes is measured from right to left. As he consumes more clams, due to his fixed budget, he must consume fewer potatoes. As a result, the quantity of potatoes decreases as the quantity of clams increases. His total utility is maximized at bundle C, where he consumes 2 pounds of clams and 6 pounds of potatoes. This is Sammy's *optimal consumption bundle.*

520 Section 9 Behind the Demand Curve: Consumer Choice

consumption bundle contains 2 pounds of clams and 6 pounds of potatoes. But we know that we usually gain more insight into "how much" problems when we use marginal analysis. So in the next section we turn to representing and solving the optimal consumption choice problem with marginal analysis.

Spending the Marginal Dollar

As we've just seen, we can find Sammy's optimal consumption choice by finding the total utility he receives from each consumption bundle on his budget line and then choosing the bundle at which total utility is maximized. But we can use marginal analysis instead, turning Sammy's problem of finding his optimal consumption choice into a "how much" problem. How do we do this? By thinking about choosing an optimal consumption bundle as a problem of *how much to spend on each good*. That is, to find the optimal consumption bundle with marginal analysis we ask the question of whether Sammy can make himself better off by spending a little bit more of his income on clams and less on potatoes, or by doing the opposite—spending a little bit more on potatoes and less on clams. In other words, the marginal decision is a question of how to *spend the marginal dollar*—how to allocate an additional dollar between clams and potatoes in a way that maximizes utility.

Our first step in applying marginal analysis is to ask if Sammy is made better off by spending an additional dollar on either good; and if so, by how much is he better off. To answer this question we must calculate the **marginal utility per dollar** spent on either clams or potatoes—how much additional utility Sammy gets from spending an additional dollar on either good.

Marginal Utility per Dollar

We've already introduced the concept of marginal utility, the additional utility a consumer gets from consuming one more unit of a good or service; now let's see how this concept can be used to derive the related measure of marginal utility per dollar.

Table 51.3 shows how to calculate the marginal utility per dollar spent on clams and potatoes, respectively.

The **marginal utility per dollar** spent on a good or service is the additional utility from spending one more dollar on that good or service.

AP® Exam Tip

To determine whether a consumer should buy more of one good or another, compare the marginal utility *per dollar* received from each good, not just the marginal utility received from each good.

AP® Exam Tip

You may need to construct and interpret a marginal utility table like Table 51.3 for the AP® exam. You may also be asked to determine how a change in price affects the quantity demanded for each good.

Table 51.3 Sammy's Marginal Utility per Dollar

(a) Clams (price of clams = $4 per pound)				(b) Potatoes (price of potatoes = $2 per pound)			
Quantity of clams (pounds)	Utility from clams (utils)	Marginal utility per pound of clams (utils)	Marginal utility per dollar (utils)	Quantity of potatoes (pounds)	Utility from potatoes (utils)	Marginal utility per pound of potatoes (utils)	Marginal utility per dollar (utils)
0	0			0	0		
		15	3.75			11.5	5.75
1	15			1	11.5		
		10	2.50			9.9	4.95
2	25			2	21.4		
		6	1.50			8.4	4.20
3	31			3	29.8		
		3	0.75			7.0	3.50
4	34			4	36.8		
		2	0.50			5.7	2.85
5	36			5	42.5		
						4.5	2.25
				6	47.0		
						3.5	1.75
				7	50.5		
						2.7	1.35
				8	53.2		
						2.0	1.00
				9	55.2		
						1.5	0.75
				10	56.7		

TEACH Teach It

The optimal consumption bundle maximizes the consumer's total utility, given the budget constraint. To determine the optimal consumption bundle, we use marginal analysis. Marginal analysis involves calculating how much an additional unit of each good increases total utility and choosing the next purchase based on which increases total utility the most. However, in most cases, the goods will have different prices, so the additional utility received from the higher-priced good costs more than the additional utility received from the lower-priced good. To take price differences into account, we compare the marginal utility obtained from each dollar spent purchasing an additional unit of each good. We make the decision about which good to purchase next based on the marginal utility *per dollar.*

FOCUS Active Learning

Walking through Table 51.3 will help students learn to find the optimal consumption bundle from a table of data. Assume Sammy has $26 to spend on clams and potatoes. Write $26 at the top of the board and keep a running tally of how much Sammy spends. Have students decide which item to purchase based on which gives the highest $\frac{MU}{\$}$. The first pound of potatoes has the highest $\frac{MU}{\$}$ (5.75 vs. 3.75), so Sammy selects that first. Cross off the first unit of potatoes since he purchased it and subtract $2 from his income. Now compare the second pound of potatoes to the first pound of clams. The second pound of potatoes is higher, so Sammy buys that next (cross off the second pound of potatoes and subtract 2 more dollars from his income). Now compare the third pound of potatoes to the first pound of clams and continue this process until all of Sammy's income is gone (after purchasing 7 pounds of potatoes and 3 pounds of clams).

FOCUS Active Learning

TRM Refer students to **Worksheet 51.2 (Marginal Utility per Dollar)** from the TRM for questions on marginal utility per dollar.

TEACH Teach It

The optimal consumption rule says that utility maximization occurs when all income is spent and the marginal utility per dollar is equal for all goods: $\left(\frac{MU}{\$}\right)_A = \left(\frac{MU}{\$}\right)_B$. A good way to help students understand the optimal consumption rule is to look at what happens when $\frac{MU}{P}$ is not equal. Assume a consumer spends all her income on apples and oranges. If $\left(\frac{MU}{P}\right)_a > \left(\frac{MU}{P}\right)_o$, what should she do? Buy more apples—they will give her more utility for her money! That means she has to buy fewer oranges to afford more apples. And when she does, the *MU* of apples falls (the law of diminishing returns states that *MU* falls when she buys more) and the *MU* of oranges increases (the same law says that *MU* is higher when she buys less). $\left(\frac{MU}{P}\right)_a$ falls and $\left(\frac{MU}{P}\right)_o$ rises, and she stops buying more apples when $\frac{MU}{P}$ is equal.

The opposite happens if $\left(\frac{MU}{P}\right)_a < \left(\frac{MU}{P}\right)_o$. A consumer would buy more oranges and fewer apples, decreasing the *MU* of oranges and increasing the *MU* of apples until $\frac{MU}{P}$ is equal.

TEACH Teach It

On occasion, it is not possible to adjust purchases so that $\frac{MU}{P}$ is exactly equal for all goods. For example, making $\frac{MU}{P}$ exactly equal may require buying $\frac{1}{2}$ apple. Very often examples use values that make the solution come out exactly equal. But sometimes students must understand and apply the rule so that $\frac{MU}{P}$ is as close to equal as possible, but it is not exactly equal. Make sure students understand how to apply marginal analysis even if an exact solution does not exist.

FOCUS Test It

Assume Peggy spends all her income on good *X* and good *Y*. Peggy is consuming 3 units of good *X*, and the third unit of good *X* gives her marginal utility of 100. She is also consuming 5 units of good *Y*, and the fifth unit of good *Y* gives her marginal utility of 200. If the price of good *X* is $5 and that of good *Y* is $20, is Peggy maximizing her utility if she buys 3 *X* and 5 *Y*? *No.* $\left(\frac{MU}{P}\right) X = \frac{100}{5} = 20$. $\left(\frac{MU}{P}\right) Y = \frac{200}{20} = 10$. *Since* $\frac{MU}{P}$ *for good X is higher (20 vs. 10), she should buy more X and less Y to maximize utility.*

FOCUS Flip It

TRM Assign Jacob Clifford's video "Micro 2.11 Utility Maximization" (see econextras video list with hyperlinks on the bcs and TRFD). Use **Worksheet 51.3 (Utility Maximization)** from the TRM for questions related to the video.

In panel (a) of the table, the first column shows different possible amounts of clam consumption. The second column shows the utility Sammy derives from each amount of clam consumption; the third column then shows the marginal utility, the increase in utility Sammy gets from consuming an additional pound of clams. Panel (b) provides the same information for potatoes. The next step is to derive marginal utility *per dollar* for each good. To do this, we just divide the marginal utility of the good by its price in dollars.

To see why we divide by the price, compare the third and fourth columns of panel (a). Consider what happens if Sammy increases his clam consumption from 2 pounds to 3 pounds. This raises his total utility by 6 utils. But he must spend $4 for that additional pound, so the increase in his utility per additional dollar spent on clams is 6 utils/$4 = 1.5 utils per dollar. Similarly, if he increases his clam consumption from 3 pounds to 4 pounds, his marginal utility is 3 utils but his marginal utility per dollar is 3 utils/$4 = 0.75 utils per dollar. Notice that because of diminishing marginal utility, Sammy's marginal utility per pound of clams falls as the quantity of clams he consumes rises. As a result, his marginal utility per dollar spent on clams also falls as the quantity of clams he consumes rises.

So the last column of panel (a) shows how Sammy's marginal utility per dollar spent on clams depends on the quantity of clams he consumes. Similarly, the last column of panel (b) shows how his marginal utility per dollar spent on potatoes depends on the quantity of potatoes he consumes. Again, marginal utility per dollar spent on each good declines as the quantity of that good consumed rises because of diminishing marginal utility.

We will use the symbols MU_C and MU_P to represent the marginal utility per pound of clams and potatoes, respectively. And we will use the symbols P_C and P_P to represent the price of clams (per pound) and the price of potatoes (per pound), respectively. Then the marginal utility per dollar spent on clams is MU_C/P_C and the marginal utility per dollar spent on potatoes is MU_P/P_P. In general, the additional utility generated from an additional dollar spent on a good is equal to:

(51-2) Marginal utility per dollar spent on a good
= Marginal utility of one unit of the good/Price of one unit of the good
$= MU_{good}/P_{good}$

Next we'll see how this concept helps us determine a consumer's optimal consumption bundle using marginal analysis.

Optimal Consumption

Let's consider **Figure 51.4**. As in Figure 51.3, we can measure both the quantity of clams and the quantity of potatoes on the horizontal axis due to the budget constraint. Along the horizontal axis of Figure 51.4—also as in Figure 51.3—the quantity of clams increases as you move from left to right, and the quantity of potatoes increases as you move from right to left. The curve labeled MU_C/P_C in Figure 51.4 shows Sammy's marginal utility per dollar spent on clams as derived in Table 51.3. Likewise, the curve labeled MU_P/P_P shows his marginal utility per dollar spent on potatoes. Notice that the two curves, MU_C/P_C and MU_P/P_P, cross at the optimal consumption bundle, point *C*, consisting of 2 pounds of clams and 6 pounds of potatoes. Moreover, Figure 51.4 illustrates an important feature of Sammy's optimal consumption bundle: when Sammy consumes 2 pounds of clams and 6 pounds of potatoes, his marginal utility per dollar spent is the same, 2, for both goods. That is, at the optimal consumption bundle, $MU_C/P_C = MU_P/P_P = 2$.

This isn't an accident. Consider another one of Sammy's possible consumption bundles—say, *B* in Figure 51.3, at which he consumes 1 pound of clams and 8 pounds of potatoes. The marginal utility per dollar spent on each good is shown by points B_C and B_P in Figure 51.4. At that consumption bundle, Sammy's marginal utility per dollar spent on clams would be approximately 3, but his marginal utility per dollar spent on potatoes would be only approximately 1. This shows that he has made a mistake: he is consuming too many potatoes and not enough clams.

Figure 51.4 Marginal Utility per Dollar

Sammy's optimal consumption bundle is at point C, where his marginal utility per dollar spent on clams, MU_C/P_C, is equal to his marginal utility per dollar spent on potatoes, MU_P/P_P. This illustrates the optimal consumption rule: *at the optimal consumption bundle, the marginal utility per dollar spent on each good and service is the same.* At any other consumption bundle on Sammy's budget line, such as bundle *B* in Figure 51.3, represented here by points B_C and B_P, consumption is not optimal: Sammy can increase his utility at no additional cost by reallocating his spending.

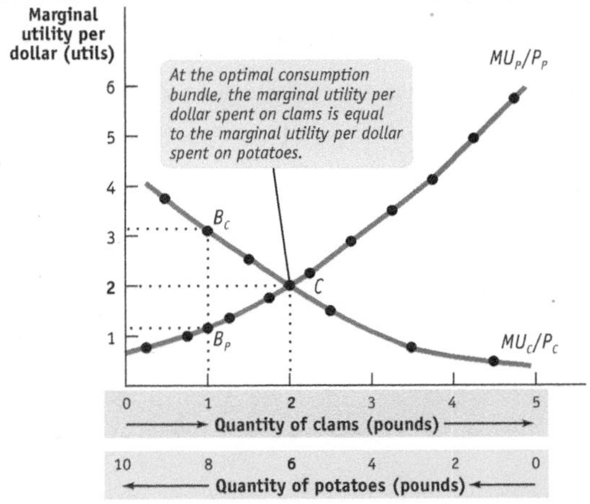

How do we know this? If Sammy's marginal utility per dollar spent on clams is higher than his marginal utility per dollar spent on potatoes, he has a simple way to make himself better off while staying within his budget: spend \$1 less on potatoes and \$1 more on clams. By spending an additional dollar on clams, he adds about 3 utils to his total utility; meanwhile, by spending \$1 less on potatoes, he subtracts only about 1 util from his total utility. Because his marginal utility per dollar spent is higher for clams than for potatoes, reallocating his spending toward clams and away from potatoes would increase his total utility. On the other hand, if his marginal utility per dollar spent on potatoes is higher, he can increase his utility by spending less on clams and more on potatoes. So if Sammy has in fact chosen his optimal consumption bundle, his marginal utility per dollar spent on clams and potatoes must be equal.

This is a general principle, known as the **optimal consumption rule**: *when a consumer maximizes utility in the face of a budget constraint, the marginal utility per dollar spent on each good or service in the consumption bundle is the same.* That is, for any two goods C and P, the optimal consumption rule says that at the optimal consumption bundle

$$\frac{MU_C}{P_C} = \frac{MU_P}{P_P} \qquad (51\text{-}3)$$

It's easiest to understand this rule using examples in which the consumption bundle contains only two goods, but it applies no matter how many goods or services a consumer buys: the marginal utilities per dollar spent for each and every good or service in the optimal consumption bundle are equal.

The main reason for studying consumer behavior is to look behind the market demand curve. In Module 46 we explained how the *substitution effect* leads consumers to buy less of a good when its price increases. We used the substitution effect to explain, in general, why the individual demand curve obeys the law of demand. Marginal analysis adds clarity to the utility-maximizing behavior of individuals and explains more precisely how an increase in price leads to less marginal utility per dollar and therefore a decrease in the quantity demanded.

AP® Exam Tip

When the price of a good changes, the marginal utility per dollar spent on the good changes and so does the optimal consumption bundle.

The **optimal consumption rule** says that in order to maximize utility, a consumer must equate the marginal utility per dollar spent on each good and service in the consumption bundle.

OPEN & CLOSE Exit Slip

TRM *Please see **Exit Slip: Module 51** in the TRM for formative multiple-choice questions to ask your students before finishing your lesson. These questions will help you quickly assess whether your students have mastered the module's concepts before moving on.*

Answers to the Exit Slip Questions

1. C
2. D
3. A

Module 51 Utility Maximization 523

MODULE 51 Review

Check Your Understanding

1. Explain why a rational consumer who has diminishing marginal utility for a good would not consume an additional unit when it generates negative marginal utility, even when that unit is free.
2. In the following two examples, find all the consumption bundles that lie on the consumer's budget line. Illustrate these consumption possibilities in a diagram, and draw the budget line through them.
   a. The consumption bundle consists of movie tickets and buckets of popcorn. The price of each ticket is $10.00, the price of each bucket of popcorn is $5.00, and the consumer's income is $20.00. In your diagram, put movie tickets on the vertical axis and buckets of popcorn on the horizontal axis.
   b. The consumption bundle consists of underwear and socks. The price of each pair of underwear is $4.00, the price of each pair of socks is $2.00, and the consumer's income is $12.00. In your diagram, put pairs of socks on the vertical axis and pairs of underwear on the horizontal axis.
3. In Table 51.3 you can see that the marginal utility per dollar spent on clams and the marginal utility per dollar spent on potatoes are equal when Sammy increases his consumption of clams from 3 pounds to 4 pounds and his consumption of potatoes from 9 pounds to 10 pounds. Explain why this is not Sammy's optimal consumption bundle. Illustrate your answer using a budget line like the one in Figure 51.3.

Tackle the Test: Multiple-Choice Questions

1. Generally, each successive unit of a good consumed will cause marginal utility to
   a. increase at an increasing rate.
   b. increase at a decreasing rate.
   c. increase at a constant rate.
   d. decrease.
   e. either increase or decrease.
2. Assume there are two goods, good X and good Y. Good X costs $5 and good Y costs $10. If your income is $200, which of the following combinations of good X and good Y is on your budget line?
   a. 0 units of good X and 18 units of good Y
   b. 0 units of good X and 20 units of good Y
   c. 20 units of good X and 0 units of good Y
   d. 10 units of good X and 12 units of good Y
   e. all of the above
3. The optimal consumption rule states that total utility is maximized when all income is spent and
   a. *MU/P* is equal for all goods.
   b. *MU* is equal for all goods.
   c. *P/MU* is equal for all goods.
   d. *MU* is as high as possible for all goods.
   e. the amount spent on each good is equal.
4. A consumer is spending all of her income and receiving 100 utils from the last unit of good A and 80 utils from the last unit of good B. If the price of good A is $2 and the price of good B is $1, to maximize total utility the consumer should buy
   a. more of good A.
   b. more of good B.
   c. less of good B.
   d. more of both goods.
   e. less of both goods.
5. The optimal consumption bundle is always represented by a point
   a. inside the consumer's budget line.
   b. outside the consumer's budget line.
   c. at the highest point on the consumer's budget line.
   d. on the consumer's budget line.
   e. at the horizontal intercept of the consumer's budget line.

Answers to Module 51 Review Questions

Check Your Understanding

1. Consuming a unit that generates negative marginal utility leaves the consumer with lower total utility than not consuming that unit at all. A rational consumer, a consumer who maximizes utility, would not make such a choice. For example, Figure 51.1 shows that Cassie receives 64 utils if she consumes 8 clams, but if she consumes a ninth clam, she loses a util, decreasing her total utility to only 63 utils. Whenever consuming a unit generates negative marginal utility, the consumer is better off not consuming that unit, even when it is free.

2. a. The accompanying table shows the consumer's consumption possibilities, bundles *A* through *C*. These consumption possibilities are plotted in the accompanying diagram, along with the consumer's budget line.

Consumption bundle	Quantity of popcorn (buckets)	Quantity of movie tickets
A	0	2
B	2	1
C	4	0

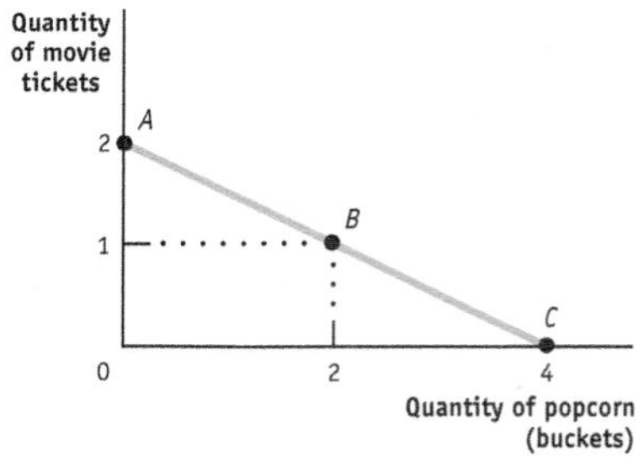

b. The accompanying table shows the consumer's consumption possibilities, *A* through *D*. These consumption possibilities are plotted in the accompanying diagram, along with the consumer's budget line.

Consumption bundle	Quantity of underwear (pairs)	Quantity of socks (pairs)
A	0	6
B	1	4
C	2	2
D	3	0

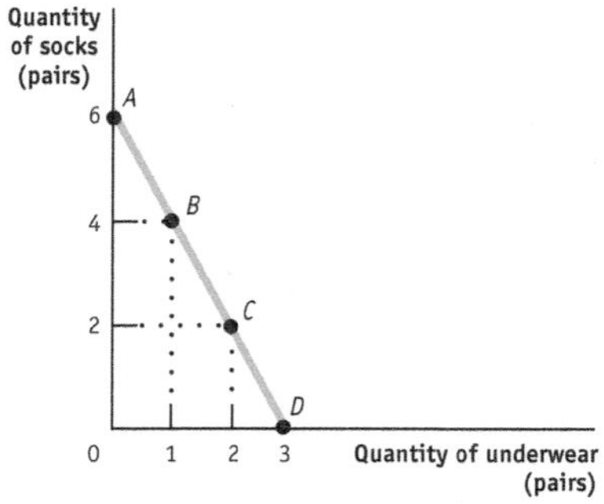

3. From Table 51.3, you can see that Sammy's marginal utility per dollar from increasing his consumption of clams from 3 to 4 pounds and his marginal utility per dollar from increasing his consumption of potatoes from 9 to 10 pounds are the same, 0.75 utils. But a consumption bundle consisting of 4 pounds of clams and 10 pounds of potatoes is not Sammy's optimal consumption bundle because it is not affordable given his income of $20; a bundle of 4 pounds of clams and 10 pounds of potatoes costs $4 × 4 + $2 × 10 = $36, $16 more than Sammy's income. This can be illustrated with Sammy's budget line from

524 Section 9 Behind the Demand Curve: Consumer Choice

Tackle the Test: Free-Response Questions

1. Refer to the table provided. Assume you have $20 to spend.

Snacks (price = $4)		Drinks (price = $2)	
Quantity	Total Utility (utils)	Quantity	Total Utility (utils)
1	15	1	12
2	25	2	21
3	31	3	29
4	34	4	36
5	36	5	42
		6	47
		7	50
		8	52

a. Draw a correctly labeled budget line.
b. Determine the marginal utility and the marginal utility per dollar spent on the fourth drink.
c. What is the optimal consumption rule?
d. How many drinks and snacks should you purchase to maximize your total utility?

Rubric for FRQ 1 (6 points)

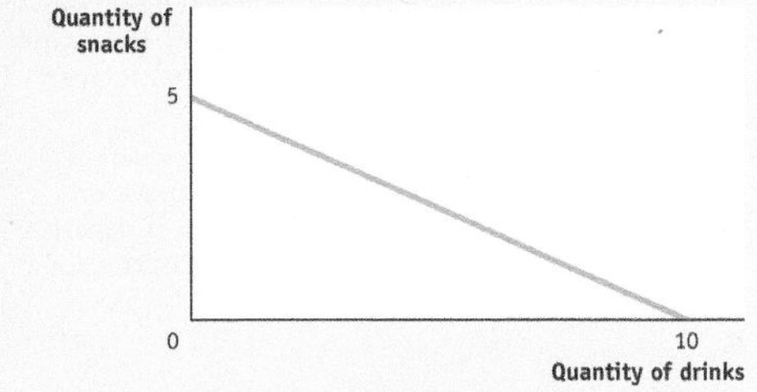

1 point: Graph with "Quantity of snacks" and "Quantity of drinks" as axis labels

1 point: Straight budget line with intercepts at 5 snacks and 0 drinks and at 0 snacks and 10 drinks

1 point: $MU = 7$ utils

1 point: $MU/P = 3.5$ utils per dollar

1 point: Total utility is maximized when the marginal utility per dollar is equal for all goods.

1 point: 6 drinks, 2 snacks

2. Assume you have an income of $100. The price of good X is $5, and the price of good Y is $20.
a. Draw a correctly labeled budget line with "Quantity of good X" on the horizontal axis and "Quantity of good Y" on the vertical axis. Be sure to correctly label the horizontal and vertical intercepts.
b. With your current consumption bundle, you spend all of your income and receive 100 utils from consuming your last unit of good X and 400 utils from consuming your last unit of good Y. Are you maximizing your total utility? Explain.
c. What will happen to the total and marginal utility you receive from consuming good X if you decide to consume another unit of good X? Explain.
(**4 points**)

Figure 51.3: a bundle of 4 pounds of clams and 10 pounds of potatoes is represented by point *X* in the accompanying diagram, a point that lies outside Sammy's budget line. If you look at the horizontal axis of Figure 51.4, it is quite clear that there is no such thing in Sammy's consumption possibilities as a bundle consisting of 4 pounds of clams and 10 pounds of potatoes.

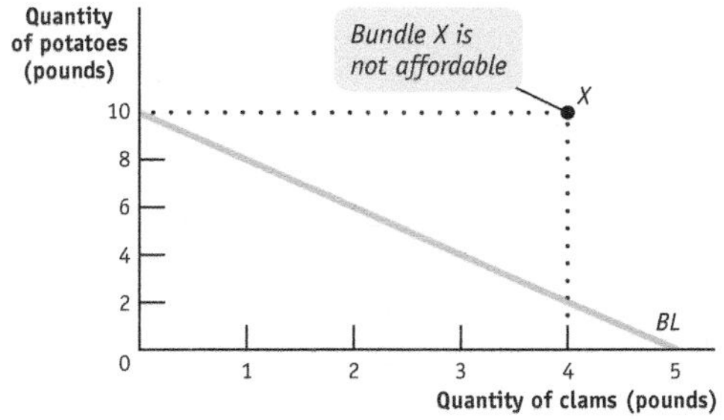

Tackle the Test: Multiple-Choice Questions

1. d
2. b
3. a
4. b
5. d

Tackle the Test: Free-Response Question Rubric for FRQ 2 (4 points)

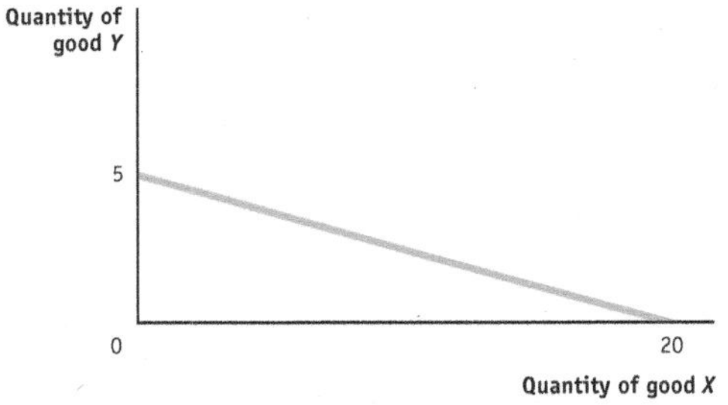

1 point: Graph with "Quantity of good *X*" on the horizontal axis, "Quantity of good *Y*" on the vertical axis, and a straight budget line

1 point: Intercepts correctly labeled at 5 units of good *Y* and 0 units of good *X* and at 0 units of good *Y* and 20 units of good *X*

1 point: Yes, because this consumption bundle satisfies the optimal consumption rule: 100/$5 = 400/$20

1 point: Total utility will increase because marginal utility is positive, while marginal utility will decrease due to the principle of diminishing marginal utility.

Module 51 Utility Maximization 525

SECTION 9 Review

FOCUS Flip It

Encourage your students to watch the **Section 9 Review Video**, which was created as a special student review tool and is linked to the e-Book or may be found on the book's companion website.

Section 9 Review Video

Module 46

1. Changes in the price of a good affect the quantity consumed as a result of the **substitution effect**, and in some cases the **income effect**. Most goods absorb only a small share of a consumer's spending; for these goods, only the substitution effect—buying less of the good that has become relatively more expensive and more of the good that has become relatively cheaper—is significant. The income effect becomes substantial when there is a change in the price of a good that absorbs a large share of a consumer's spending, thereby changing the purchasing power of the consumer's income.
2. Many economic questions depend on the size of consumer or producer responses to changes in prices or other variables. *Elasticity* is a general measure of responsiveness that can be used to answer such questions.
3. The **price elasticity of demand**—the percent change in the quantity demanded divided by the percent change in the price (dropping the minus sign)—is a measure of the responsiveness of the quantity demanded to changes in the price. In practical calculations, it is usually best to use the **midpoint method**, which calculates percent changes in prices and quantities based on the average of the initial and final values.

Module 47

4. Demand can fall anywhere in the range from **perfectly inelastic**, meaning the quantity demanded is unaffected by the price, to **perfectly elastic**, meaning there is a unique price at which consumers will buy as much or as little as they are offered. When demand is perfectly inelastic, the demand curve is a vertical line; when it is perfectly elastic, the demand curve is a horizontal line.
5. The price elasticity of demand is classified according to whether it is more or less than 1. If it is greater than 1, demand is **elastic**; if it is less than 1, demand is **inelastic**; if it is exactly 1, demand is **unit-elastic**. This classification determines how **total revenue**, the total value of sales, changes when the price changes. If demand is elastic, total revenue falls when the price increases and rises when the price decreases. If demand is inelastic, total revenue rises when the price increases and falls when the price decreases.
6. The price elasticity of demand depends on whether there are close substitutes for the good in question, whether the good is a necessity or a luxury, the share of income spent on the good, and the length of time that has elapsed since the price change.

Module 48

7. The **cross-price elasticity of demand** measures the effect of a change in one good's price on the quantity of another good demanded. The cross-price elasticity of demand can be positive, in which case the goods are substitutes, or negative, in which case they are complements.
8. The **income elasticity of demand** is the percent change in the quantity of a good demanded when a consumer's income changes divided by the percent change in income. The income elasticity of demand indicates how intensely the demand for a good responds to changes in income. It can be negative; in that case the good is an inferior good. Goods with positive income elasticities of demand are normal goods. If the income elasticity is greater than 1, a good is **income-elastic**; if it is positive and less than 1, the good is **income-inelastic**.
9. The **price elasticity of supply** is the percent change in the quantity of a good supplied divided by the percent change in the price. If the quantity supplied does not change at all, we have an instance of **perfectly inelastic supply**; the supply curve is a vertical line. If the quantity supplied is zero below some price but infinite above that price, we have an instance of **perfectly elastic supply**; the supply curve is a horizontal line.
10. The price elasticity of supply depends on the availability of resources to expand production and on time. It is higher when inputs are available at relatively low cost and when more time has elapsed since the price change.

Module 49

11. The **willingness to pay** of each individual consumer determines the shape of the demand curve. When price is less than or equal to the willingness to pay, the potential consumer purchases the good. The difference between willingness to pay and price is the net gain to the consumer, the **individual consumer surplus**.
12. **Total consumer surplus** in a market, which is the sum of all individual consumer surpluses in a market, is equal to the area below the market demand curve but above the price. A rise in the price of a good reduces consumer surplus; a fall in the price increases consumer surplus. The term **consumer surplus** is often used to refer to both individual and total consumer surplus.
13. The **cost** of each potential producer of a good, the lowest price at which he or she is willing to supply a unit of that good, determines the supply curve. If the price of a good is above a producer's cost, a sale generates a net gain to the producer, known as the **individual producer surplus**.
14. **Total producer surplus** in a market, the sum of the individual producer surpluses in a market, is equal to the area above the market supply curve but below the price. A rise in the price of a good increases producer surplus; a fall in the price reduces producer surplus. The term **producer surplus** is often used to refer to both individual and total producer surplus.

Module 50

15. **Total surplus**, the total gain to society from the production and consumption of a good, is the sum of consumer and producer surplus.
16. Usually, markets are efficient and achieve the maximum total surplus. Any possible reallocation of consumption or sales, or change in the quantity bought and sold, reduces total surplus. However, society also cares about equity. So government intervention in a market that reduces efficiency but increases equity can be a valid choice by society.
17. A tax that rises more than in proportion to income is a **progressive tax**. A tax that rises less than in proportion to income is a **regressive tax**. A tax that rises in proportion to income is, you guessed it, a **proportional tax**.
18. An **excise tax**—a tax on the purchase or sale of a good—raises the price paid by consumers and reduces the price received by producers, driving a wedge between the two. **Tax incidence**—how the burden of the tax is divided between consumers and producers—does not depend on who officially pays the tax.
19. The incidence of an excise tax depends on the price elasticities of supply and demand. If the price elasticity of demand is higher than the price elasticity of supply, the tax falls mainly on producers; if the price elasticity of supply is higher than the price elasticity of demand, the tax falls mainly on consumers.
20. The tax revenue generated by a tax depends on the tax rate and on the number of units sold with the tax. Excise taxes cause inefficiency in the form of **deadweight loss** because they discourage some mutually beneficial transactions. Taxes also impose **administrative costs**: resources used to collect the tax, to pay it (over and above the amount of the tax), and to evade it.
21. An excise tax generates revenue for the government but lowers total surplus. The loss in total surplus exceeds the tax revenue, resulting in a deadweight loss to society. This deadweight loss is represented by a triangle, the area of which equals the value of the transactions discouraged by the tax. The greater the elasticity of demand or supply, or both, the larger the deadweight loss from a tax. If either demand or supply is perfectly inelastic, there is no deadweight loss from a tax.
22. A **lump-sum tax** is a tax of a fixed amount paid by all taxpayers. Because a lump-sum tax does not depend on the behavior of taxpayers, it does not discourage mutually beneficial transactions and therefore causes no deadweight loss.

Module 51

23. Consumers maximize a measure of satisfaction called **utility**. We measure utility in hypothetical units called **utils**.
24. A good's or service's **marginal utility** is the additional utility generated by consuming one more unit of the good or service. We usually assume that the **principle of diminishing marginal utility** holds: consumption of another unit of a good or service yields less additional utility than the previous unit. As a result, the **marginal utility curve** slopes downward.
25. A **budget constraint** limits a consumer's spending to no more than his or her income. It defines the

Section 9 Review 527

consumer's **consumption possibilities**, the set of all affordable consumption bundles. A consumer who spends all of his or her income will choose a consumption bundle on the **budget line**. An individual chooses the consumption bundle that maximizes total utility, the **optimal consumption bundle**.

26. We use marginal analysis to find the optimal consumption bundle by analyzing how to allocate the marginal dollar. According to the **optimal consumption rule**, with the optimal consumption bundle, the **marginal utility per dollar** spent on each good and service—the marginal utility of a good divided by its price—is the same.

Key Terms

Substitution effect, p. 459
Income effect, p. 460
Price elasticity of demand, p. 461
Midpoint method, p. 463
Perfectly inelastic, p. 467
Perfectly elastic, p. 468
Elastic, p. 468
Inelastic, p. 468
Unit-elastic, p. 468
Total revenue, p. 470
Cross-price elasticity of demand, p. 478
Income elasticity of demand, p. 478
Income-elastic, p. 479
Income-inelastic, p. 479
Price elasticity of supply, p. 480
Perfectly inelastic supply, p. 481
Perfectly elastic supply, p. 481
Willingness to pay, p. 486
Individual consumer surplus, p. 487
Total consumer surplus, p. 487
Consumer surplus, p. 488
Cost, p. 493
Individual producer surplus, p. 493
Total producer surplus, p. 493
Producer surplus, p. 493
Total surplus, p. 498
Progressive tax, p. 502
Regressive tax, p. 503
Proportional tax, p. 503
Excise tax, p. 503
Tax incidence, p. 505
Deadweight loss, p. 509
Administrative costs, p. 511
Lump-sum tax, p. 511
Utility, p. 514
Util, p. 515
Marginal utility, p. 516
Marginal utility curve, p. 516
Principle of diminishing marginal utility, p. 517
Budget constraint, p. 517
Consumption possibilities, p. 517
Budget line, p. 518
Optimal consumption bundle, p. 519
Marginal utility per dollar, p. 521
Optimal consumption rule, p. 523

Answers to Section 9 AP® Exam Practice Questions

Multiple-Choice Questions

1. e
2. d
3. b
4. c

AP® Exam Practice Questions

Multiple-Choice Questions

1. When the price of a normal good falls, consumers will ______ the quantity they want, in part because they now have more money to spend on these units, which economists call ______

a.	increase	the substitution effect
b.	decrease	the unit effect
c.	increase	the price effect
d.	decrease	the quantity effect
e.	increase	the income effect

2. Suppose market prices for potatoes were to increase by 10%, and potato farmers wanted to know whether or not their overall total revenues would rise or fall as a consequence. The farmers could figure this out by calculating which of the following economic concepts?

a. deadweight loss
b. producer surplus
c. diminishing marginal utility
d. price elasticity of demand
e. administrative costs

3. Suppose Jolene buys apples weekly. If the price of apples were to drop, Jolene would experience ______ in ______.

a.	a decrease	total revenue
b.	an increase	consumer surplus
c.	a decrease	her budget constraint
d.	an increase	marginal utility
e.	a decrease	willingness to pay

4. Pizza and soda are often consumed together at Joe's Diner. Suppose that the price of pizza rises from $0.75 a slice to $1.25 a slice, and consequently April sales of pizza drop from 1,050 to 950 slices. Using the midpoint method and this information, an economist could conclude the following:

a. The cross price elasticity of demand is 0.2.
b. The price elasticity of supply is 0.1.
c. The price elasticity of demand is 0.2.
d. The income elasticity of demand is 0.5.
e. The unit elasticity of demand is 0.1.

528 Section 9 Behind the Demand Curve: Consumer Choice

Use the following information to answer Questions 5–8.

Suppose the government levies a tax of $0.50 per pack on the buyers of cigarettes. Suppose also that the price elasticity of demand for cigarettes is 1.2 and the price elasticity of supply is 0.7.

5. Because this tax is levied on the sale of a specific good, it is
- **a.** an excise tax.
- **b.** a progressive tax.
- **c.** a regressive tax.
- **d.** a proportional tax.
- **e.** a lump-sum tax.

6. After this tax is levied, total surplus will ______, and the price received by producers (not including the tax) will ______.

a.	increase	increase by exactly $0.50
b.	decrease	fall by exactly $0.50
c.	increase	fall by less than $0.50
d.	decrease	fall by less than $0.50
e.	increase	increase by more than $0.50

7. If economists were to study the tax incidence in this cigarette market, they would conclude which of the following?
- **a.** The burden of this tax falls entirely on consumers.
- **b.** The burden of this tax falls entirely on producers.
- **c.** The burden of this tax falls equally on consumers and producers.
- **d.** The burden of this tax falls more on consumers than on producers.
- **e.** The burden of this tax falls more on producers than on consumers.

8. In this example, cigarettes have
- **a.** perfectly inelastic demand.
- **b.** perfectly elastic demand.
- **c.** unit-inelastic demand.
- **d.** inelastic demand.
- **e.** elastic demand.

9. Jill is willing to sell her used calculator for $20. Her friend Jack is willing to pay $90 for a used calculator. They agree and trade at a price of $50. Which of the following is correct?
- **a.** Jill's cost is $50.
- **b.** Jack's individual consumer surplus is $30.
- **c.** Jill's individual producer surplus is $30.
- **d.** Jack's budget line is $90.
- **e.** Jill's deadweight loss is $70.

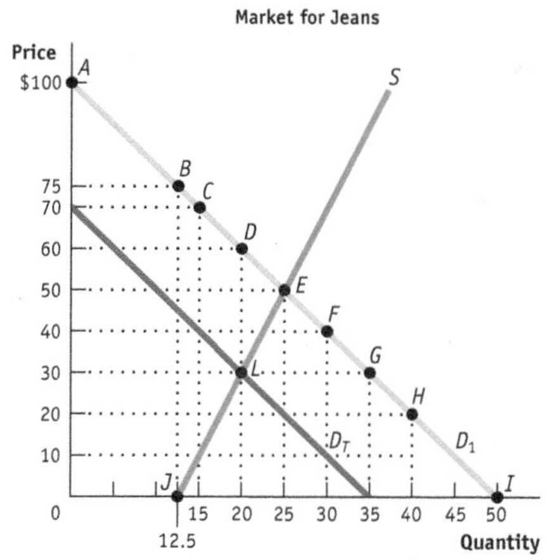

Refer to the figure for Questions 10–17.

10. Using the midpoint method, the price elasticity of demand between points *C* and *E* is ______ and economists would classify it as ______.

a.	0.67	inelastic
b.	1.5	elastic
c.	1	unit-elastic
d.	0.67	elastic
e.	1.5	inelastic

11. Using the midpoint method, the price elasticity of supply between points *J* and *E* is ______ and economists would classify it as ______.

a.	2.67	inelastic
b.	0.375	elastic
c.	0	perfectly inelastic
d.	2.67	elastic
e.	0.33	inelastic

12. Suppose the government levies a tax on the buyers of jeans that shifts the demand curve from D_1 to D_T. Using the diagram, determine the amount of the tax per pair of jeans sold.
- **a.** 50
- **b.** 40
- **c.** 30
- **d.** 20
- **e.** The exact amount of the tax cannot be determined.

5. a
6. d
7. e
8. e
9. c
10. b
11. e
12. c

Section 9 Review 529

13. d 15. a 17. e
14. d 16. b 18. a

13. Which of the following statements about the tax on jeans is true?
   a. Buyers bear the entire burden of the tax, since the tax was levied on them.
   b. Buyers bear most of the burden of the tax, since the tax was levied on them.
   c. Buyers bear most of the burden of the tax, since demand is more *inelastic* than supply.
   d. Buyers bear a smaller tax burden than sellers, since demand is more *elastic* than supply.
   e. Buyers and sellers share the tax burden equally.

14. How much revenue would the government collect from the tax on jeans?
   a. $1,250
   b. $1,200
   c. $750
   d. $600
   e. $300

15. Buyers in the jeans market gain ______ in consumer surplus before the imposition of the tax, and they gain ______ in consumer surplus after the imposition of the tax.
   a. $625 $400
   b. $400 $225
   c. $400 $625
   d. $625 $225
   e. $225 $400

16. Jeans and product X (not shown) have a cross price elasticity of 3.7. After the imposition of the tax on jeans, buyers' consumption of product X would ______ because jeans and product X are ______
   a. decrease normal goods
   b. increase substitutes
   c. decrease complements
   d. increase complements
   e. decrease substitutes

17. The deadweight loss caused by the tax on jeans is
   a. $5.
   b. $30.
   c. $50.
   d. $60.
   e. $75.

Quantity of ball toss games	Total utility (utils)
0	0
1	70
2	130
3	180
4	220
5	250
6	270
7	280

Quantity of video games	Total utility (utils)
0	0
1	30
2	55
3	75
4	90
5	100
6	105
7	109
8	112
9	114

Use the information from the tables above to complete Questions 18–20.

18. If Jill purchased 5 video games and 1 ball toss game, she would receive ______ and ______
   a. a marginal utility of 10 from her last video game — a marginal utility of 70 from her last ball toss game
   b. a marginal utility of 105 from her last video game — a marginal utility of 130 from her last ball toss game
   c. her highest possible marginal utility from video games — 170 total utils from both products
   d. less than her highest possible marginal utility from ball toss games — 90 utils of marginal utility from both products
   e. 100 utils in total utility from video games — a marginal utility of zero from ball toss games

530 Section 9 Behind the Demand Curve: Consumer Choice

19. At the arcade, Jill likes the video games, which cost $0.50 to play, and the ball toss, which costs $2 to play. She has $6 to spend at the arcade. If Jill maximizes her utility, she will
   a. spend all of her $6 on the ball toss because she likes it the best.
   b. achieve a total utility of 220.
   c. spend all of her $6 on video games because they are the cheapest.
   d. play 9 video games and 7 games of ball toss.
   e. find where the marginal utility of playing video games equals the marginal utility of playing ball toss.

20. Suppose that video games still cost $0.50 and the ball toss still costs $2, but Jill now has $10.50 to spend at the arcade. If Jill chooses her optimal consumption bundle,
   a. she will purchase 9 video games and 3 games of ball toss.
   b. her marginal utility per dollar spent on video games will be 10.
   c. her marginal utility from her last game of ball toss will be 40.
   d. her total utility will be 280.
   e. she will spend less than $10.50.

Free-Response Question

On the island of Rockville, the equilibrium quantity of acres of land sold is currently 1,000, and the equilibrium price per acre is $500. Landowners have an elasticity of supply equal to 0. Consumers have an elasticity of demand greater than 1.

   a. Using a correctly labeled graph of supply and demand for acres of land, show the equilibrium price ($500) and equilibrium quantity (1,000).

Now suppose that the government of Rockville imposes an excise tax of $20 per acre on the buyers of land.

   b. Show the effects of the tax on your graph from part a, and indicate the new equilibrium price and equilibrium quantity.
   c. Calculate the amount of tax revenue that is collected.
   d. Calculate the amount of deadweight loss.
   e. Who bears the burden of this tax? Explain.
   (9 points)

19. b
20. c

Rubric for Free-Response Question

1 point: $P = \$500$ and $Q = 1,000$ shown on graph with correctly labeled axes and title

1 point: The demand curve is downward-sloping.

1 point: The supply curve is drawn as a vertical line.

1 point: A new demand curve is drawn and labeled below the original demand curve.

1 point: The new equilibrium price is $480 and the equilibrium quantity remains the same.

1 point: Tax revenue = $20 × 1,000 = $20,000

1 point: Deadweight loss = $0

1 point: Sellers bear the entire burden of the tax.

1 point: Because the supply curve is perfectly inelastic

Please see page SG-4 for sample student graphs for this Free-Response Question.

SECTION 10

Behind the Supply Curve: Profit, Production, and Costs

PD Section 10 Overview

Watch the video overview of Section 10 (for teachers), which is accessible through the Teacher's e-Book, the TR-flash drive, or the book's website bcs.worthpublishers.com/krugmanap2e *(teacher log-in required).*

Section 10 presents the production and cost concepts underlying the supply curve. The presentation is similar to that in Section 9, which introduced utility maximization and examined the demand curve. This section addresses profit maximization and looks more closely at the production and costs of the supply curve. In this section, students develop an understanding of the cost curves necessary for them to understand the market structure models introduced in this section and developed in later sections.

Topics that your students will study in Section 10 are:

- implicit and explicit costs and how they differ.
- economic profit and accounting profit and how they differ.
- calculating accounting profit, economic profit, and normal profit.
- using marginal analysis to determine the profit-maximizing level of output.
- the relationship between the quantity of inputs and the quantity of outputs as shown by a production function.
- the effect of diminishing returns to inputs.
- short-run costs including fixed and variable costs.
- the definition and calculation of marginal and average costs.
- graphing short-run costs (*TC*, *FC*, *VC*, *ATC*, *AVC*, *AFC*, *MC*).
- the shapes of the total, marginal, and average cost curves.
- the short run versus the long run.
- economies of scale and the shape of the long-run average cost curve.
- the optimal input mix and the cost-minimization rule.
- the characteristics of perfect competition, monopoly, monopolistic competition, and oligopoly.

Alignment to AP® Microeconomics Course Description

Microeconomics II. The Nature and Function of Product Markets: 55–70%

AP® Outline	Module
C. Production and costs	54: The Production Function 55: Firm Costs 56: Long-Run Costs and Economies of Scale
D. Firm behavior and market structure	52: Defining Profit 53: Profit Maximization 57: Introduction to Market Structure

Pacing Guide

Module	Standard Teaching Days	Block Teaching Days
52	½	¼
53	1	½
54	1	1
55	1	1
56	1	½
57	1	1
Section 10 Assessment	1	½
Total	**6½**	**4¾**

TRM Section Resources

All section resources may be accessed through the Teacher's e-Book, the TR-flash drive, or the book's website bcs.worthpublishers.com/krugmanap2e *(teacher log-in required).*

Section 10 PD Video (for Teachers)

Module 52

Module 52 Sample Lecture

Worksheet 52.1: Economic Profit and Cost Review

Worksheet 52.2: Determining Profit

Worksheet 52.3: The Signal of Economic Profits

Exit Slip: Module 52

Module 53

Module 53 Sample Lecture

Worksheet 53.1: $MR = MC$ Practice Video

Worksheet 53.2: Maximizing Profit

Exit Slip: Module 53

Module 54

Module 54 Sample Lecture

Worksheet 54.1: The Lego® Factory Is Open!

Worksheet 54.2: Production Terms to Know

Worksheet 54.3: Law of Diminishing Returns

Exit Slip: Module 54

Module 55

Module 55 Sample Lecture

Worksheet 55.1: Costs of Production and Cost Curves

Worksheet 55.2: Firm Costs

Worksheet 55.3: Practice with Cost Curves

Worksheet 55.4: Marginal Cost and *ATC*: Why Do Cost Curves Do That?

Exit Slip: Module 55

Module 56

Module 56 Sample Lecture

Worksheet 56.1: Economies and Diseconomies of Scale

Worksheet 56.2: Returns to Scale

Exit Slip: Module 56

Module 57

Module 57 Sample Lecture

Worksheet 57.1: Types of Market Structures

Worksheet 57.2: Questions about Market Structures

Exit Slip: Module 57

Section 10 Review Video (for students)

St. Louis Federal Reserve Bank Resources

Many of the Federal Reserve Banks have educational departments that offer helpful resources for studying economics. Members of the Educators Advisory Board of the St. Louis Federal Reserve Bank have handpicked some of their best resources for use with your AP® Economics students. References to these resources are included in the marginal notes. A complete list of the St. Louis Fed resources for each section with the corresponding URL (as of fall 2014) can be found in the TRM.

NOTE We have included a number of links to useful videos and articles in the margin notes in this section. Although all are active at the time of publication, we know that some may expire over the next few years. If a link is no longer active, you may wish to search for a similar article or video to illustrate the same point. We may also periodically refresh resources on the book's companion website.

PD Section 10 Overview

Watch the video overview of Section 10 (for teachers), which is accessible through the Teacher's e-Book, the TR-flash drive, or the book's companion website bcs.worthpublishers.com/krugmanap2e (teacher log-in required).

FOCUS Active Learning

Students can read Chapter 8 of *Economics by Example* to learn about production costs in the context of energy production.

SECTION 10

Behind the Supply Curve: Profit, Production, and Costs

The Cost of Power

In Section 9 we examined the factors that affect consumer choice—the demand side of the supply and demand model. In this section we focus on the factors that affect producer choice and the supply side of the supply and demand model. Producers seek profit, which is the difference between total revenue and total cost. We turn to graphs to illustrate the story of what happens to various measures of revenue, cost, and profit as output changes. Different situations lead to different stories.

Consider the Spinning Spur Wind Project in Texas, which cost an estimated $322 million to build in 2012. The wind farm's 70 turbines have the capacity to produce 161 megawatts of electricity at a negligible additional cost per kilowatt-hour, because the primary input—wind—is free.

The Current Creek natural gas-fired power plant in Utah cost an estimated $350 million to build in 2006, and has a capacity of 550 megawatts. The cost story at Current Creek differs from that at Spinning Spur because each kilowatt-hour of electricity produced at Current Creek requires the use of additional natural gas, which isn't free. But the larger capacity at Current Creek allows the cost of constructing the plant to be spread across more units of output.

Given the complexity of cost and revenue stories, the need to visualize them with graphs is clear. In 2014, Google liked what it saw in the graphs for the Spinning Spur Wind Project enough to invest $200 million in the operation. In this section you will learn several analytical tools used to inform such decisions.

After a discussion of profit maximization, we will investigate the production function, which shows the relationship between the inputs used for production and the output that is produced. Then we'll consider the costs that influence firms' decisions about supply. The final module in this section introduces the models of market structure used to understand how the supply side of the economy works.

Brand X Pictures

532 Section 10 Behind the Supply Curve: Profit, Production, and Costs

Rosemarie Gearhart/Getty Images

MODULE 52 Defining Profit

In this Module, you will learn to:

- Explain the difference between explicit and implicit costs and their importance in decision making
- Describe the different types of profit, including accounting profit, economic profit, and normal profit
- Calculate profit

Understanding Profit

The primary goal of most firms is to maximize profit. Other goals, such as maximizing market share or protecting the environment, may also figure into a firm's mission. But economic models generally start with the assumption that firms attempt to maximize profit. So we will begin with an explanation of how economists define and calculate profit. In the next module we will look at how firms go about maximizing their profit.

In general, a firm's profit equals its *total revenue*—which is equal to the price of the output times the quantity sold, or $P \times Q$—minus the cost of all the inputs used to produce its output, its *total cost*. That is,

$$\text{Profit} = \text{Total Revenue} - \text{Total Cost}$$

However, there are different types of costs that may be used to calculate different types of profit. To start the discussion of how to calculate profit, we'll look at two different types of costs, *explicit costs* and *implicit costs*.

Explicit Versus Implicit Costs

Suppose that, after graduating from high school, you have two options: to go to college or to take a job immediately. You would like to continue your education but are concerned about the cost.

What exactly is the cost of attending college? Here it is important to remember the concept of opportunity cost, because the cost of getting a degree includes what you forgo by not taking a job for the years you go to college. The opportunity cost of additional education, like any cost, can be broken into two parts: the *explicit cost* and the *implicit cost*.

PD To prepare for teaching this lesson, you may want to consult the **Module 52 Sample Lecture** in the TRM.

OPEN & CLOSE Start Here

Explain to students that this module starts by defining explicit and implicit costs. As an example, ask students to list and estimate the costs of going to college. They will likely list tuition, books, fees, room and board, and maybe interest charges (if they have to borrow) or opportunity cost. Discuss their lists and use them to create a master list on the board. Then discuss an estimate for each cost on the list, starting with the explicit costs:

- Tuition will depend on the type of school attended: public or private, in-state or out-of-state, and how much financial aid it offers.
- Books can be much more expensive than you might think!
- Fees may include a parking fee, a student activity fee, lab fees.
- Interest charges apply if students must borrow to pay their college expenses.

Note: Room and board is not really a college cost since students must eat whether they attend school or not! You can find estimates of college costs at http://cgi.money.cnn.com/tools/collegecost/collegecost.jsp.

After discussing and estimating these explicit costs, discuss the idea of implicit (opportunity) costs: What was given up to attend college for four or more years? The largest implicit cost of attending college, and perhaps the largest cost of all, is the salary a student could earn with a high school degree. Estimates may be found at the Bureau of Labor Statistics website (http://bls.gov/bls/wages.htm). For example, in September 2010, 18-year-olds might expect weekly earnings of about $450 per week.

TEACH Connect It

Earlier, in Module 1, students were introduced to the economic concept of opportunity cost. Remind students what they have already learned about opportunity costs and connect those ideas to implicit costs.

TEACH Teach It

Establish that economists assume the goal of a firm is to maximize profits. Firms will sometimes have other goals, but introductory models assume profit maximization. Ask students to tell you how a firm figures out its profits. They often already understand that profits are equal to what the firm brings in minus what it has to pay out. Use their understanding to present the more precise definition of profit as total revenue (the amount of sales the firm brings in) minus total cost (what the firm has to pay out for its inputs). Remind students that TR is equal to P times Q, as they learned in Section 9. And explain that the total cost is equal to the cost per unit (average cost) times the number of units. Introducing AC at this point foreshadows firm costs, and it introduces the complete framework for calculating profit that students will need throughout later sections.

Make sure that students don't confuse profit with total revenue. Emphasize that firms must subtract their costs of production to find their profit. Show students the profit equation displayed below frequently through this and the following sections!

$$\text{Profit} = \underset{(P \times Q)}{TR} - \underset{(AC \times Q)}{TC}$$

Module 52 Defining Profit 533

TEACH Teach It

Distinguish the two types of costs for students. They will be most familiar with *explicit costs*. These are the financial costs of a good or service. These costs will involve invoices, receipts, emails, or other "paper trail" items that show cost. They are also referred to as accounting costs. The term *implicit cost* relates to opportunity cost and measures the cost of a forgone benefit in financial terms. Firms do not make a payment or receive a receipt for implicit costs.

- For a firm, explicit costs include the payments made for labor, materials, services, fuel, transportation services, and power.
- For a firm, implicit costs include the value of the owner's labor or the use of firm-owned equipment that could have been rented to someone else.

FOCUS Flip It

TRM For an explanation and example of accounting versus economic costs, students can watch Jacob Clifford's video "Micro 3.7 Economic Profit and Costs" (see econextras video list with hyperlinks on the bcs and TRFD). Refer to **Worksheet 52.1 (Economic Profit and Cost Review)** from the TRM for questions on this video.

An **explicit cost** is a cost that involves actually laying out money. An **implicit cost** does not require an outlay of money; it is measured by the value, in dollar terms, of benefits that are forgone.

An **explicit cost** is a cost that requires an outlay of money. For example, the explicit cost of a year of college includes tuition. An **implicit cost**, though, does not involve an outlay of money; instead, it is measured by the value, in dollar terms, of the benefits that are forgone. For example, the implicit cost of a year spent in college includes the income you would have earned if you had taken a job instead.

A common mistake, both in economic analysis and in real business situations, is to ignore implicit costs and focus exclusively on explicit costs. But often the implicit cost of an activity is quite substantial—indeed, sometimes it is much larger than the explicit cost.

Table 52.1 gives a breakdown of hypothetical explicit and implicit costs associated with spending a year in college instead of taking a job. The explicit cost consists of tuition, books, supplies, and a computer for doing assignments—all of which require you to spend money. The implicit cost is the salary you would have earned if you had taken a job instead. As you can see, the forgone salary is $35,000 and the explicit cost is $19,500, making the implicit cost more than the explicit cost in this example. So ignoring the implicit cost of an action can lead to a seriously misguided decision.

Table 52.1 Opportunity Cost of a Year of College

Explicit cost		Implicit cost	
Tuition	$17,000	Forgone salary	$35,000
Books and supplies	1,000		
Computer	1,500		
Total explicit cost	19,500	Total implicit cost	35,000
Total opportunity cost = Total explicit cost + Total implicit cost = $54,500			

AP® Exam Tip

Accounting profit, often discussed by the media and business community, is calculated without subtracting a full measure of the costs of production.

A slightly different way of looking at the implicit cost in this example can deepen our understanding of opportunity cost. The forgone salary is the cost of using your own resources—your time—in going to college rather than working. The use of your *time* for more education, despite the fact that you don't have to spend any money, is still costly to you. This illustrates an important aspect of opportunity cost: in considering the cost of an activity, you should include the cost of using any of your own resources for that activity. You can calculate the cost of using your own resources by determining what they would have earned in their next best alternative use.

The **accounting profit** of a business is the business's total revenue minus the explicit cost and depreciation.

Accounting Profit Versus Economic Profit

As the example of going to college suggests, taking account of implicit as well as explicit costs can be very important when making decisions. This is true whether the decisions affect individuals, groups, governments, or businesses.

Consider the case of Babette's Cajun Café, a small restaurant in New Orleans. This year Babette brought in $100,000 in revenue. Out of that revenue, she paid her expenses: the cost of food ingredients and other supplies, the cost of wages for her employees, and the rent for her restaurant space. This year her expenses were $60,000. We assume that Babette owns her restaurant equipment—items such as appliances and furnishings. The question is: Is Babette's restaurant profitable?

At first it might seem that the answer is obviously yes: she receives $100,000 from her customers and has expenses of only $60,000. Doesn't this mean that she has a profit of $40,000? Not according to her accountant, who reduces the number by $5,000 for the yearly *depreciation* (reduction in value) of the restaurant equipment. Depreciation occurs because equipment wears out over time. As a consequence, every few years Babette must replace her appliances and furnishings. The yearly depreciation amount reflects what an accountant estimates to be the reduction in the value of the machines due to wear and tear that year. This leaves $35,000, which is the business's **accounting profit**. That is, the accounting profit of a business is its total revenue minus its *explicit* cost and depreciation.

534 Section 10 Behind the Supply Curve: Profit, Production, and Costs

The accounting profit is the number that Babette has to report on her income tax forms and that she would be obliged to report to anyone thinking of investing in her business.

Accounting profit is a very useful number, but suppose that Babette wants to decide whether to keep her restaurant open or to do something else. To make this decision, she will need to calculate her **economic profit**—the total revenue she receives minus her *opportunity* cost, which includes implicit as well as explicit costs. In general, when economists use the simple term *profit*, they are referring to economic profit. (We adopt this simplification in this book.)

Why does Babette's economic profit differ from her accounting profit? Because she may have an implicit cost over and above the explicit cost her accountant has calculated. Businesses can face an implicit cost for two reasons. First, a business's capital—its equipment, buildings, tools, inventory, and financial assets—could have been put to use in some other way. If the business owns its capital, it does not pay any money for its use, but it pays an implicit cost because it does not use the capital in some other way. Second, the owner devotes time and energy to the business that could have been used elsewhere—a particularly important factor in small businesses, whose owners tend to put in many long hours.

If Babette had rented her appliances and furnishings instead of owning them, her rent would have been an explicit cost. But because Babette owns her own equipment, she does not pay rent on it and her accountant deducts an estimate of its depreciation in the profit statement. However, this does not account for the opportunity cost of the equipment—what Babette forgoes by owning it. Suppose that instead of using the equipment in her own restaurant, the best alternative Babette has is to sell the equipment for $50,000 and put the money into a bank account where it would earn yearly interest of $3,000. This $3,000 is an implicit cost of running the business. The **implicit cost of capital** is the opportunity cost of the capital used by a business; it reflects the income that could have been earned if the capital had been used in its next best alternative way. It is just as much a true cost as if Babette had rented her equipment instead of owning it.

Finally, Babette should take into account the opportunity cost of her own time. Suppose that instead of running her own restaurant, she could earn $34,000 as a chef in someone else's restaurant. That $34,000 is also an implicit cost of her business.

Table 52.2, in the column titled Case 1, summarizes the accounting for Babette's Cajun Café, taking both explicit and implicit costs into account. It turns out, unfortunately, that although the business makes an accounting profit of $35,000, its economic profit is actually negative. This means that Babette would be better off financially if she closed the restaurant and devoted her time and capital to something else. If, however, some of Babette's cost should fall sufficiently, she could earn a positive economic profit. In that case, she would be better off financially if she continued to operate the restaurant. For instance, consider the column titled Case 2: here we assume that what Babette could earn as a chef employed by someone else has dropped to $30,000

Table 52.2 **Profit at Babette's Cajun Café**

	Case 1	Case 2
Revenue	$100,000	$100,000
Explicit cost	−60,000	−60,000
Depreciation	−5,000	−5,000
Accounting profit	**35,000**	**35,000**
Implicit cost of business		
Income Babette could have earned on capital used in the next best way	−3,000	−3,000
Income Babette could have earned as a chef in someone else's restaurant	−34,000	−30,000
Economic profit	**−2,000**	**+2,000**

The **economic profit** of a business is the business's total revenue minus the opportunity cost of its resources. It is usually less than the accounting profit.

AP® Exam Tip

Economic profit can be negative. You would be correct in saying that a firm is incurring a loss when economic profit is negative.

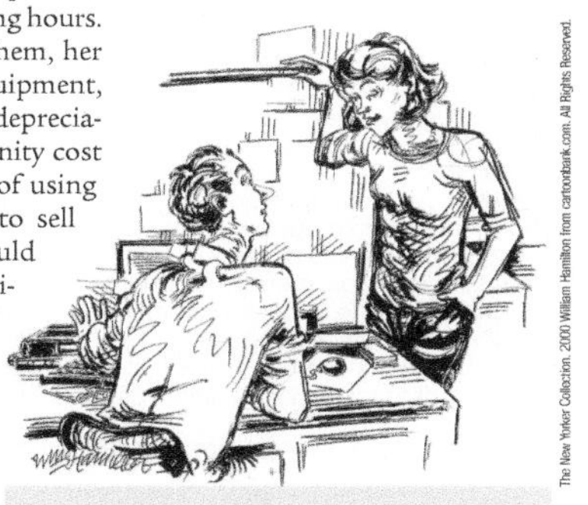

"I've done the numbers, and I will marry you."

The **implicit cost of capital** is the opportunity cost of the capital used by a business—the income the owner could have realized from that capital if it had been used in its next best alternative way.

TEACH Connect It

You can now connect implicit and explicit costs with accounting and economic profit:

- Accounting profit only takes into account explicit costs (Accounting profit = *TR* − Explicit costs).
- Economic profit takes into account both implicit and explicit costs (Economic profit = *TR* − (Implicit + Explicit costs)).

TEACH Teach It

Students often have a hard time understanding the difference between economic profit and accounting profit. As it is commonly used, the term *profit* most often refers to accounting profit. Remind students that economists are concerned with evaluating choices. Therefore, they include opportunity cost when they calculate profit because, in order to determine if the current choice is best, they must consider what was given up. That is why an economic profit of zero is not so bad (the firm has covered the value of the next best alternative!), whereas an accounting profit of zero is a big problem (there is no money left to pay self-employed resources).

FOCUS Active Learning

TRM Have students complete **Worksheet 52.2 (Determining Profit)** from the TRM for practice calculating accounting and economic profit.

FOCUS Test It

Betsy operates a retail clothing store from a building she owns (but could rent to someone else for $1,000 per month). When she opened her clothing store, she left a job at Macy's, from which she earned $45,000 per year. Calculate accounting profit and economic profit if Betsy earns $250,000 in total revenue from her retail clothing store and incurs the following explicit costs:

$1,200 in debt repayment every month × 12 = $14,400
Wages to employees = $35,000
Insurance and utilities = $40,000
Inventory = $150,000

Accounting profit = Total revenue − Total explicit costs
= $250,000 − $14,400 − $35,000 − $40,000 − $150,000 = $10,600

Economic profit = Total revenue − Total explicit costs − Total implicit costs
= $250,000 − $14,400 − $35,000 − $40,000 − $150,000 − $12,000 − $45,000
= −$46,400

TEACH Teach It

Normal profit occurs when a firm earns just enough to keep using its resources in its current activity. Normal profit corresponds to an economic profit of zero and means that a firm could not be doing any better using its resources in another activity. A positive economic profit means the firm's current use of resources is the best use and a negative economic profit means the firm's current use of resources is not the best use.

FOCUS Active Learning

TRM For further practice with and understanding of economic, accounting, and normal profit, ask your students to complete **Worksheet 52.3 (The Signal of Economic Profits)** from the TRM.

OPEN & CLOSE Exit Slip

TRM *Please see **Exit Slip: Module 52** in the TRM for formative questions to ask your students before finishing your lesson. These questions will help you quickly assess whether your students have mastered the module's concepts before moving on.*

Answers to the Exit Slip Questions

1. D
2. C
3. Economic profit = Total revenue − Explicit costs − Implicit costs

   Accounting profit = Total revenue − Explicit costs

FYI Farming in the Shadow of Suburbia

Beyond the sprawling suburbs, most of New England is covered by dense forest. This is not the forest primeval: if you hike through the woods, you encounter many stone walls, relics of the region's agricultural past when stone walls enclosed fields and pastures. In 1880, more than half of New England's land was farmed; by 2014, the amount was down to 10%.

The remaining farms of New England are mainly located close to large metropolitan areas. There farmers get high prices for their produce from city dwellers who are willing to pay a premium for locally grown, extremely fresh fruits and vegetables.

But now even these farms are under economic pressure caused by a rise in the implicit cost of farming close to a metropolitan area. As metropolitan areas have expanded during the last two decades, farmers increasingly ask themselves whether they could do better by selling their land to property developers.

In 2013, the average value of an acre of farmland in the United States as a whole was $2,900; in Rhode Island, the most densely populated of the New England states, the average was $11,800. The Federal Reserve Bank of Boston has noted that "high land prices put intense pressure on the region's farms to generate incomes that are substantial enough to justify keeping the land in agriculture." The important point is that the pressure is intense even if the farmer owns the land because the land is a form of capital used to run the business. Maintaining the land as a farm instead of selling it to a developer constitutes a large implicit cost of capital. A fact provided by the U.S. Department of Agriculture (USDA) helps us put a dollar figure on the portion of the implicit cost of capital due to development pressure for some Rhode Island farms. In 2004, a USDA program designed to prevent development of Rhode Island farmland paid owners an average of $4,949 per acre for the "development rights" to their land. By 2012, the amount had risen to $31,585.

Michael S. Lewis/National Geographic/Getty Images

About two-thirds of the New England farms that remain in business earn very little money. They are maintained as "rural residences" by people with other sources of income—not so much because they are commercially viable, but more out of a personal commitment and the satisfaction these people derive from farm life. Although many businesses have important implicit costs, they can also have important benefits to their owners that go beyond the revenue earned.

Source: United States Department of Agriculture.

(say, due to a soft labor market). In this case, her economic profit is positive: she is earning more than her explicit and implicit costs and she should keep her restaurant open.

In real life, discrepancies between accounting profit and economic profit are extremely common. As the FYI above explains, this is a message that has found a receptive audience among real-world businesses.

Normal Profit

In the example above, when Babette is earning an economic profit, her total revenue is higher than the sum of her implicit and explicit costs. This means that operating her restaurant makes Babette better off financially than she would be using her resources in any other activity. When Babette earns a negative economic profit (which can also be described as a *loss*), it means that Babette would be better off financially if she devoted her resources to her next best alternative. As this example illustrates, economic profits signal the best use of resources. A positive economic profit indicates that the current use is the best use of resources. A negative economic profit indicates that there is a better alternative use for resources.

But what about an economic profit *equal to* zero? Most of us would generally think earning zero profit was a bad thing. After all, a firm's goal is to maximize profit—profit is what firms are after! However, an economic profit equal to zero is not bad at all. An economic profit of zero means that the firm could not do any better using its resources in any alternative activity. Another name for an economic profit of zero is a **normal profit**. A firm earning a normal profit is earning just enough to keep it using its resources in its current activity. After all, it can't do any better in any other activity! In Module 59 we'll see that firms earning negative economic profit can sometimes minimize their losses by staying open for a while, but all such firms will close in the long run unless conditions change.

AP® Exam Tip

Remember that a firm with zero economic profit earns just enough to cover its implicit and explicit costs. The firm may have zero economic profit and a positive accounting profit.

An economic profit equal to zero is also known as a **normal profit**. It is an economic profit just high enough to keep a firm engaged in its current activity.

536 Section 10 Behind the Supply Curve: Profit, Production, and Costs

MODULE 52 Review

Check Your Understanding

1. Karma and Don run a furniture-refinishing business from their home. Which of the following represent an explicit cost of the business and which represent an implicit cost?
   a. supplies such as paint stripper, varnish, polish, sandpaper, and so on
   b. basement space that has been converted into a workroom
   c. wages paid to a part-time helper
   d. a van that they inherited and use only for transporting furniture
   e. the job at a larger furniture restorer that Karma gave up in order to run the business

2. a. Suppose you are in business earning an accounting profit of $25,000. What is your economic profit if the implicit cost of your capital is $2,000 and the opportunity cost of your time is $23,000? Explain your answer.
   b. What does your answer to part a tell you about the advisability of devoting your time and capital to this business?

Tackle the Test: Multiple-Choice Questions

1. Which of the following is an example of an *implicit* cost of going out for lunch?
   a. the amount of the tip you leave the waiter
   b. the total bill you charge to your credit card
   c. the cost of gas to drive to the restaurant
   d. the value of the time you spent eating lunch
   e. all of the above
2. Which of the following is an *implicit* cost of attending college?
   a. tuition
   b. books
   c. laptop computer
   d. lab fees
   e. forgone salary
3. Which of the following is the best definition of accounting profit? Accounting profit equals total revenue minus depreciation and total
   a. explicit cost only.
   b. implicit cost only.
   c. explicit cost plus implicit cost.
   d. opportunity cost.
   e. explicit cost plus opportunity cost.
4. Which of the following is considered when calculating economic profit but not accounting profit?
   a. implicit cost
   b. explicit cost
   c. total revenue
   d. marginal cost
   e. All of the above are considered when calculating accounting profit.
5. You sell T-shirts at your school's football games. Each shirt costs $5 to make and sells for $10. Each game lasts two hours and you sell 100 shirts per game. You could always be earning $8 per hour at your other job. Which of the following is correct? Your accounting profit from selling shirts at a game is
   a. $1,000 and your economic profit is $500.
   b. $500 and your economic profit is $1,000.
   c. $500 and your economic profit is $484.
   d. $484 and your economic profit is $500.
   e. $500 and your economic profit is also $500.

Answers to Module 52 Review Questions

Check Your Understanding

1. a. Supplies are an explicit cost because they require an outlay of money.

b. The inability to use the basement for other purposes is an implicit cost.

c. Wages are an explicit cost.

d. By using the van for their business, Karma and Don forgo the money they could have gained by selling it. So, the use of the van is an implicit cost.

e. Karma's forgone wages from her job are an implicit cost.

2. a. Economic profit is zero:

$$\text{Implicit cost} = \$2{,}000 + \$23{,}000 = \$25{,}000$$

$$\text{Accounting profit} = \text{Total revenue} - \text{Explicit cost} - \text{Depreciation} = \$25{,}000$$

$$\text{Economic profit} = \text{Total revenue} - \text{Explicit cost} - \text{Depreciation} - \text{Implicit cost}$$

$$= \text{Accounting profit} - \text{Implicit cost}$$

$$= \$25{,}000 - \$25{,}000 = \$0$$

b. An economic profit of zero is considered a "normal profit." The resources devoted to this business could not earn more if used in the next best activity. This is just enough profit to keep you in this business with no regrets.

Tackle the Test: Multiple-Choice Questions

1. d
2. e
3. a
4. a
5. c

Tackle the Test: Free-Response Question Rubric for FRQ 2 (4 points)

1 point: Total revenue = 2,000 Sno Cones sold × $2 per Sno Cone = $4,000

1 point: Accounting profit = $4,000 – $400 – $100 = $3,500

1 point: Sunny needs to know the opportunity cost of her time.

1 point: In general, a firm should continue to operate in the long run if it can earn at least normal profit (meaning zero economic profit). In Sunny's case, she earns $3,500 in accounting profit minus the $200 implicit cost of capital and the opportunity cost of her time. Because $3,500 – $200 = $3,300, she will make at least a normal profit if the opportunity cost of her time is less than or equal to $3,300.

Tackle the Test: Free-Response Questions

1. Your firm is selling 10,000 units of output at a price of $10 per unit. Your firm's total explicit cost is $70,000. Your firm's implicit cost of capital is $10,000, and your opportunity cost is $20,000.

a. Calculate total revenue.
b. Calculate total implicit cost.
c. Calculate your accounting profit.
d. Calculate your economic profit.
e. What does the value of your economic profit calculated in part d tell you?

Rubric for FRQ 1 (5 points)

1 point: Total revenue = $100,000

1 point: Total implicit cost = $30,000

1 point: Accounting profit = $30,000

1 point: Economic profit = $0

1 point: Because your firm earns normal profit, there is no better alternative use for your resources.

2. Sunny owns and operates Sunny's Sno Cone Stand. Use the data in the table provided to answer the questions below.

Sunny's Sno Cone Stand: January

Price of Sno Cone	$2
Sno Cones sold	2,000
Explicit cost	$400
Depreciation	$100
Implicit cost of capital	$200

a. Calculate Sunny's Sno Cone Stand's total revenue for January.
b. Calculate Sunny's Sno Cone Stand's accounting profit for January.
c. What additional information does Sunny need in order to determine whether or not to continue operating the Sno Cone Stand?
d. Suppose these numbers remain unchanged in the long run. Explain how Sunny will determine whether or not to continue operating the business in the long run on the basis of these numbers.
(4 points)

538 Section 10 Behind the Supply Curve: Profit, Production, and Costs

Michael Melford/National Geographic/Getty Images

MODULE 53 Profit Maximization

In this Module, you will learn to:

- Perform marginal analysis
- Determine the profit-maximizing level of output using the optimal output rule

Maximizing Profit

In the previous module we learned about different types of profit, how to calculate profit, and how firms can use profit calculations to make decisions—for instance to determine whether to continue using resources for the same activity or not. In this module we ask the question: what quantity of output would maximize the producer's profit? First we will find the profit-maximizing quantity by calculating the total profit at each quantity for comparison. Then we will use marginal analysis to determine the *optimal output rule*, which turns out to be simple: as our discussion of marginal analysis in Module 1 suggested, a producer should produce up until marginal benefit equals marginal cost.

Consider Jennifer and Jason, who run an organic tomato farm. Suppose that the market price of organic tomatoes is \$18 per bushel and that Jennifer and Jason can sell as many as they would like at that price. Then we can use the data in **Table 53.1** on the next page to find their profit-maximizing level of output.

The first column shows the quantity of output in bushels, and the second column shows Jennifer and Jason's total revenue from their output: the market value of their output. Total revenue, *TR*, is equal to the market price multiplied by the quantity of output:

$$\textbf{(53-1)} \quad TR = P \times Q$$

In this example, total revenue is equal to \$18 per bushel times the quantity of output in bushels.

The third column of Table 53.1 shows Jennifer and Jason's total cost, *TC*. Even if they don't grow any tomatoes, Jennifer and Jason must pay \$14 to rent the land

PD To prepare for teaching this lesson, you may want to consult the **Module 53 Sample Lecture** in the TRM.

OPEN & CLOSE Start Here

Now that students have learned the definition of profit and that the goal of firms is to maximize profit, it is time to introduce the profit maximization rule, $MC = MR$. This rule applies to any firm, in any market structure, in any part of this course. When students don't know what else to do to solve a problem, they should start with $MC = MR$. The concept will come up over and over again for the duration of the class, and it is relevant for answering questions throughout the AP® exam. If students only learn one thing from this course, this should be it!

If they don't have an answer, write $MC = MR$ on the board. Explain its importance (and also that you will describe the how and why shortly), and discuss creative ways for students to remember the rule. Teachers have had their students chant it, wear it on a T-shirt or hat, hang up posters illustrating it, sing or rap it. Some students have even taught their parrot to say it out loud.

It is okay to go over the top in emphasizing the importance of $MC = MR$. Be silly, fun, and creative, and encourage your students to do the same. Give an extra-credit assignment or hold a competition. Make the profit-maximization rule more memorable than anything else!

TEACH AP® Exam Tip

The AP® test will often ask students to "use marginal analysis" as part of the FRQs. Profit maximization is another area where this might happen. Although students may be able to calculate profit and identify the highest level, if the question asks them to use marginal analysis, they will have to utilize the profit-maximization rule and set *MC* equal to *MR* in order to receive points.

TEACH Connect It

In the last module, students learned about accounting and economic profit. Make sure they understand that unless accounting profit is specified, the term *profit* always refers to economic profit (this IS an economics course, after all!).

TEACH Teach It

In marginal analysis, we study things "at the margin" or the point of adding one additional unit. Marginal revenue is the additional revenue from selling one more. Marginal cost is the additional cost of producing one more.

- Marginal revenue = Change in *TR*/Change in *Q*
- Marginal cost = Change in *TC*/Change in *Q*

TEACH AP® Exam Tip

Marginal values are often calculated for a 1-unit change in quantity. Because dividing by 1 is so easy, it is easy to become lazy and forget to divide by the denominator (the change in *Q*). Students may encounter questions on the AP® exam in which the change in quantity is more than 1. Make sure they know to divide by the change in quantity in these cases!

TEACH Teach It

Students need to know the profit-maximization rule. But more importantly, they need to understand WHY profit is maximized where $MC = MR$. To help them understand, discuss what happens when *MC* does not equal *MR*. As more is produced, *MC* increases (due to increasing costs):

$MC = MR$
(stop here)

↗ *MC* increases ↖ *MC* decreases

$MC < MR$
(profit on this unit, so produce more)

$MC > MR$
(loss on this unit, so produce less)

Table 53.1 Profit for Jennifer and Jason's Farm When Market Price Is $18

Quantity of tomatoes *Q* (bushels)	Total revenue *TR*	Total cost *TC*	Profit *TR* − *TC*
0	$0	$14	−$14
1	18	30	−12
2	36	36	0
3	54	44	10
4	72	56	16
5	90	72	18
6	108	92	16
7	126	116	10

for their farm. As the quantity of tomatoes increases, so does the total cost of seeds, fertilizer, labor, and other inputs. You will learn more about firm costs in Module 55.

The fourth column shows their profit, equal to total revenue minus total cost:

$$\textbf{(53-2)} \quad \text{Profit} = TR - TC$$

As indicated by the numbers in the table, profit is maximized at an output of five bushels, where profit is equal to $18. But we can gain more insight into the profit-maximizing choice of output by viewing it as a problem of marginal analysis, a task we'll dive into next.

Using Marginal Analysis to Choose the Profit-Maximizing Quantity of Output

AP® Exam Tip

The quantity of output at which $MR = MC$ is the focus of firms and wise AP® exam takers because it is that quantity that maximizes profit for firms in every type of market structure.

According to the **principle of marginal analysis**, every activity should continue until marginal benefit equals marginal cost.

Marginal revenue is the change in total revenue generated by an additional unit of output.

The **optimal output rule** says that profit is maximized by producing the quantity of output at which the marginal revenue of the last unit produced is equal to its marginal cost.

The **principle of marginal analysis** provides a clear message about when to stop doing anything: proceed until *marginal benefit* equals *marginal cost*. To apply this principle, consider the effect on a producer's profit of increasing output by one unit. The marginal benefit of that unit is the additional revenue generated by selling it; this measure has a name—it is called the **marginal revenue** of that output. The general formula for marginal revenue is:

$$\textbf{(53-3)} \quad \text{Marginal revenue} = \begin{matrix}\text{Change in total} \\ \text{revenue generated} \\ \text{by one additional} \\ \text{unit of output}\end{matrix} = \frac{\text{Change in total revenue}}{\text{Change in quantity of output}}$$

or

$$MR = \Delta TR/\Delta Q$$

In this equation, the Greek uppercase delta (the triangular symbol) represents the change in a variable.

The application of the principle of marginal analysis to the producer's decision of how much to produce is called the **optimal output rule**, which states that profit is maximized by producing the quantity at which the marginal revenue of the last unit produced is equal to its marginal cost. As this rule suggests, we will see that Jennifer and Jason maximize their profit by equating marginal revenue and marginal cost.

Note that there may not be any particular quantity at which marginal revenue exactly equals marginal cost. In this case the producer should produce until one more unit would cause marginal benefit to fall below marginal cost. As a common simplification, we can think of marginal cost as rising steadily, rather than jumping from one level at

540 Section 10 Behind the Supply Curve: Profit, Production, and Costs

Table 53.2 Short-Run Costs for Jennifer and Jason's Farm

Quantity of tomatoes *Q* (bushels)	Total cost *TC*	Marginal cost of bushel $MC = \Delta TC/\Delta Q$	Marginal revenue of bushel *MR*	Net gain of bushel = *MR* – *MC*
0	$14			
		$16	$18	$2
1	30			
		6	18	12
2	36			
		8	18	10
3	44			
		12	18	6
4	56			
		16	18	2
5	72			
		20	18	−2
6	92			
		24	18	−6
7	116			

one quantity to a different level at the next quantity. This ensures that marginal cost will equal marginal revenue at some quantity. We employ this simplified approach in what follows.

Consider **Table 53.2**, which provides cost and revenue data for Jennifer and Jason's farm. The second column contains the farm's total cost of output. The third column shows their marginal cost. Notice that, in this example, marginal cost initially falls as output rises but then begins to increase, so that the marginal cost curve has a "swoosh" shape. Later it will become clear that this shape has important implications for short-run production decisions.

The fourth column contains the farm's marginal revenue, which has an important feature: Jennifer and Jason's marginal revenue is assumed to be constant at $18 for every output level. The assumption holds true for a particular type of market—perfectly competitive markets—which we will study in Modules 58–60, but for now it is just to make the calculations easier. The fifth and final column shows the calculation of the net gain per bushel of tomatoes, which is equal to marginal revenue minus marginal cost. As you can see, it is positive for the first through fifth bushels: producing each of these bushels raises Jennifer and Jason's profit. For the sixth and seventh bushels, however, net gain is negative: producing them would decrease, not increase, profit. (You can verify this by reexamining Table 53.1.) So five bushels are Jennifer and Jason's profit-maximizing output; it is the level of output at which marginal cost is equal to the market price, $18.

Figure 53.1 on the next page shows that Jennifer and Jason's profit-maximizing quantity of output is, indeed, the number of bushels at which the marginal cost of production is equal to marginal revenue (which is equivalent to price in perfectly competitive markets). The figure illustrates the **marginal cost curve**, *MC*, which shows the relationship between marginal cost and output. We plot the marginal cost of increasing output from one to two bushels halfway between one and two, and so on. The horizontal line at $18 is Jennifer and Jason's **marginal revenue curve**, which shows the relationship between marginal revenue and output. Note that marginal revenue stays the same regardless of how much Jennifer and Jason sell because we have assumed marginal revenue is constant.

Does this mean that the firm's production decision can be entirely summed up as "produce up to the point where the marginal cost of production is equal to the price"? No, not quite. Before applying the principle of marginal analysis to determine how much to produce, a potential producer must, as a first step, answer an

The **marginal cost curve** shows how the cost of producing one more unit depends on the quantity that has already been produced.

The **marginal revenue curve** shows how marginal revenue varies as output varies.

FOCUS Test It

Ask your class to study Table 53.1 in the text. Remind students of the meaning of marginal (change). Have them do the following:

1. Redraw the table and create a new column next to the total revenue column and label it marginal revenue. Create a new column next to total cost and label it marginal cost.

2. Calculate the change in total revenue (*MR*) for each row for the quantity 1 – 7. *18, 18, 18, 18, 18, 18, 18*

3. Calculate the change in total cost (*MC*) for each row for the quantity 1 – 7. *16, 6, 8, 12, 16, 20, 24*

Table 53.1 points out that 5 units is the profit-maximizing quantity. What do students notice when they look at the values for the 5th unit in their newly created columns? *The MR is greater than the MC. The additional revenue from selling the 5th unit is greater than the additional cost (therefore, selling the 5th unit adds to profit). Note that for the 6th unit, MC becomes greater than MR.*

FOCUS Graph It

Table 53.2 walks the student through finding *MC* and *MR*:

- Point out that the *MR* column here is the difference (or change) in *TR* from Table 53.1.
- The final column in Table 53.2 shows values for *MR* – *MC*. The optimum profit rule directs us to produce where these are equal, or at the last unit before this calculation becomes negative.

TEACH Connect It

We teach students that profit maximization occurs where *MR* = *MC*. But there are examples when *MR* does not exactly equal *MC*. In those cases, profit maximization occurs at the output level before *MC* becomes greater than *MR*. That is, firms will produce all units where *MR* > *MC* and stop producing before *MR* < *MC*. This is similar to using the utility-maximization rule—the solution is not always where the values are exactly equal. Be sure to explain this caveat because such a situation frequently comes up on the AP® exam.

FOCUS Flip It

TRM Assign Jacob Clifford's video "Micro 3.7 *MR* = *MC* Practice" (see econextras video list with hyperlinks on the bcs and TRFD), and refer to **Worksheet 53.1 (*MR* = *MC* Practice Video)** from the TRM for questions regarding this video and the underlying concept.

FOCUS Flip It

TRM Assign another Jacob Clifford video "Micro Unit 3, Question 9—Maximizing Profit" (see econextras video list with hyperlinks on the bcs and TRFD). **Worksheet 53.2 (Maximizing Profit)** from the TRM gives questions to answer based on this video.

TEACH Connect It

Figure 53.1 shows the *MR* and *MC* curves from the data in Table 53.2. Explain what the horizontal marginal revenue curve means. *The firm can sell as many units as it wants and will always receive the market price.* Remind students that this is a *perfectly elastic* demand curve. This discussion will set up the introduction of the perfect competition market structure model presented later on.

FOCUS Graph It

Point out in Figure 53.1 that *MR* > *MC* below the profit-maximizing quantity, so firms sell for more than their cost and add to profit. Therefore, they want to produce these units. But above the profit-maximizing quantity, *MC* > *MR*, so firms do not want to produce because these units of output cost more than they can sell them for. Firms maximize profit when they produce up to the profit-maximizing output level.

OPEN & CLOSE Exit Slip

TRM *Please see **Exit Slip: Module 53** in the TRM for formative multiple-choice questions to ask your students before finishing your lesson. These questions will help you quickly assess whether your students have mastered the module's concepts before moving on.*

Answers to the Exit Slip Questions

1. C
2. A
3. D

Figure 53.1 The Firm's Profit-Maximizing Quantity of Output

At the profit-maximizing quantity of output, marginal revenue is equal to marginal cost. It is located at the point where the marginal cost curve crosses the marginal revenue curve, which is a horizontal line at the market price. Here, the profit-maximizing point is at an output of 5 bushels of tomatoes, the output quantity at point *E*.

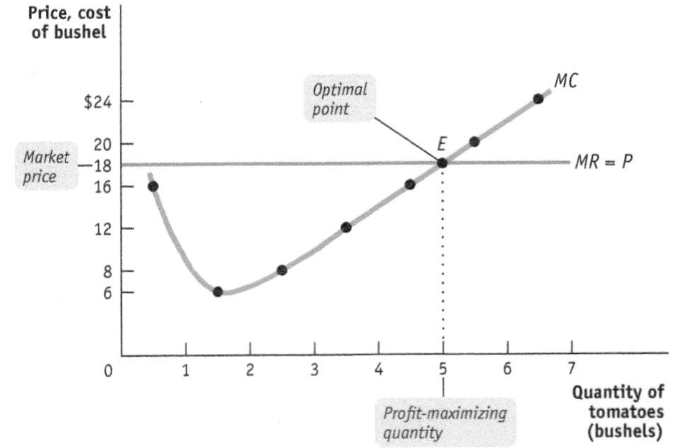

"either–or" question: Should I produce at all? If the answer to that question is yes, the producer then proceeds to the second step—a "how much" decision: maximizing profit by choosing the quantity of output at which marginal cost is equal to price.

To understand why the first step in the production decision involves an "either–or" question, we need to ask how we determine whether it is profitable or unprofitable to produce at all.

AP® Exam Tip

If there is no output level at which *MR* = *MC*, the firm should produce the largest quantity at which *MR* is greater than *MC*.

When Is Production Profitable?

Recall that a firm's decision whether or not to stay in a given business in the long run depends on its *economic profit*—a measure based on the opportunity cost of resources used in the business. To put it a slightly different way: in the calculation of economic profit, a firm's total cost incorporates the implicit cost—the benefits forgone in the next best use of the firm's resources—as well as the explicit cost in the form of actual cash outlays. In contrast, *accounting profit* is profit calculated using only the explicit costs incurred by the firm. This means that economic profit incorporates the opportunity cost of resources owned by the firm and used in the production of output, while accounting profit does not. As in the example of Babette's Cajun Café, a firm may make positive accounting profit while making zero or even negative economic profit. It's important to understand clearly that a firm's long-run decision to produce or not, to stay in business or to close down permanently, should be based on economic profit, not accounting profit.

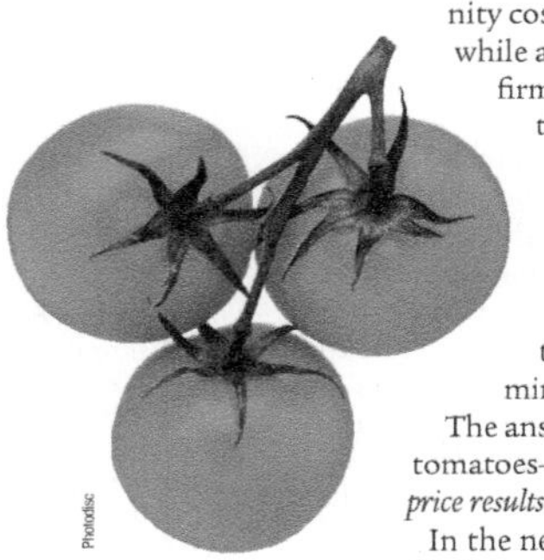

Photodisc

So we will assume, as we always do, that the cost numbers given in Tables 53.1 and 53.2 include all costs, implicit as well as explicit, and that the profit numbers in Table 53.1 are economic profit. What determines whether Jennifer and Jason's farm earns a profit or generates a loss? The answer is that whether or not it is profitable depends on the market price of tomatoes—specifically, *whether selling the firm's optimal quantity of output at the market price results in at least a normal profit.*

In the next modules, we look in detail at the two components used to calculate profit: firm revenue (which is determined by the level of production) and firm cost.

542 Section 10 Behind the Supply Curve: Profit, Production, and Costs

MODULE 53 Review

Check Your Understanding

1. Suppose a firm can sell as many units of output as it wants for a price of $15 per unit and faces total costs as indicated in the table below. Use the optimal output rule to determine the profit-maximizing level of output for the firm.

Quantity	*Total cost*
0	$2
1	10
2	20
3	33
4	50
5	71

2. Use the data from Question 1 to graph the firm's marginal cost and marginal revenue curves and show the profit-maximizing level of output.

Tackle the Test: Multiple-Choice Questions

Use the data in the table provided to answer Questions 1–3.

Quantity	*Total revenue*	*Total cost*
0	$0	$14
1	18	30
2	36	36
3	54	44
4	72	56
5	90	72
6	108	92
7	126	116

1. What is the marginal revenue of the third unit of output?
   a. $8
   b. $14
   c. $18
   d. $44
   e. $54
2. What is the marginal cost of the first unit of output?
   a. $0
   b. $14
   c. $16
   d. $18
   e. $30
3. At what level of output is profit maximized?
   a. 0
   b. 1
   c. 3
   d. 5
   e. 7
4. A firm should continue to produce in the long run if its
   a. total revenue is less than its total costs.
   b. total revenue is greater than its total explicit costs.
   c. accounting profit is greater than its economic profit.
   d. accounting profit is not negative.
   e. economic profit is at least zero.
5. A firm earns a normal profit when its
   a. accounting profit equals 0.
   b. economic profit is positive.
   c. total revenue equals its total costs.
   d. accounting profit equals its economic profit.
   e. economic profit equals its total explicit and implicit costs.

Answers to Module 53 Review Questions

Check Your Understanding

1. The profit-maximizing level of output is 3 units because marginal cost goes from being below marginal revenue at a quantity of 3 to being above marginal revenue at a quantity of 4, thus passing through marginal revenue at the 3rd unit.

2.

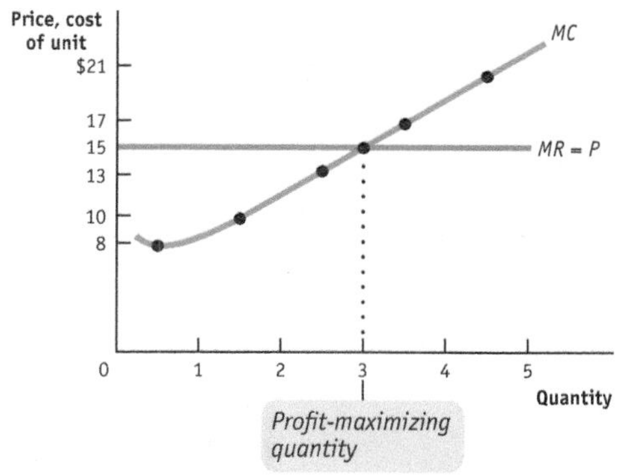

Tackle the Test: Multiple-Choice Questions

1. c
2. c
3. d
4. e
5. c

Module 53 Profit Maximization 543

Tackle the Test: Free-Response Questions

1. Use the data in the table provided.

Quantity	*Total revenue*	*Total cost*
0	$0	$7
1	18	23
2	36	29
3	54	37
4	72	49
5	90	65
6	108	87
7	126	112

a. What is the marginal revenue of the fourth unit?
b. Calculate profit at a quantity of two. Explain how you calculated the profit.
c. What is the profit-maximizing level of output? Explain how to use the optimal output rule to determine the profit-maximizing level of output.

Rubric for FRQ 1 (5 points)

1 point: $18

1 point: $7

1 point: $36 – $29 or *TR* – *TC*

1 point: 5 units

1 point: The optimal output rule states that profit is maximized when *MC* = *MR*. Here, *MC* never exactly equals *MR*. When this occurs, the firm should produce the largest quantity at which *MR* exceeds *MC*. At a quantity of 5, *MC* = $16 and *MR* = $18. For the sixth unit, *MC* = $22 and *MR* = $18, and because *MC* > *MR*, the sixth unit would add more to total cost than it would to total revenue, and it therefore should not be produced.

2. Use a graph to illustrate the typical shape of the two curves used to find a firm's profit-maximizing level of output on the basis of the optimal output rule. Assume all units of output can be sold for $5. Indicate the profit-maximizing level of output with a "*Q**" on the appropriate axis. (You don't have enough information to provide a specific numerical answer.)
(3 points)

Tackle the Test: Free-Response Question

Rubric for FRQ 2 (3 points)

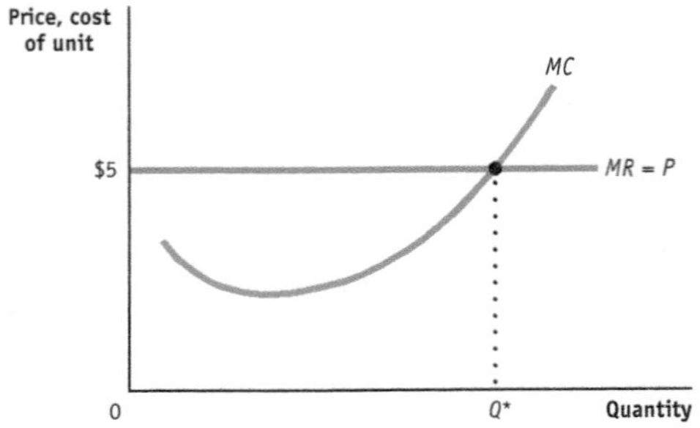

1 point: A graph with a horizontal marginal revenue curve at a height of $5

1 point: A marginal cost curve with a slope that starts out negative and then becomes positive as the quantity increases

1 point: *Q** labeled on the horizontal axis below where *MR* = *MC*

Felipe DuPouy/Lifesize/Getty Images

MODULE 54 The Production Function

In this Module, you will learn to:

- Discuss the importance of the firm's production function, the relationship between the quantity of inputs and the quantity of output
- Explain why production is often subject to diminishing returns to inputs

The Production Function

A *firm* produces goods or services for sale. To do this, it must transform inputs into output. The quantity of output a firm produces depends on the quantity of inputs; this relationship is known as the firm's **production function**. As we'll see, a firm's production function underlies its *cost curves*. As a first step, let's look at the characteristics of a hypothetical production function.

A **production function** is the relationship between the quantity of inputs a firm uses and the quantity of output it produces.

Inputs and Output

To understand the concept of a production function, let's consider a farm that we assume, for the sake of simplicity, produces only one output, wheat, and uses only two inputs, land and labor. This particular farm is owned by a couple named George and Martha. They hire workers to do the actual physical labor on the farm. Moreover, we will assume that all potential workers are of the same quality—they are all equally knowledgeable and capable of performing farmwork.

George and Martha's farm sits on 10 acres of land; no more acres are available to them, and they are currently unable to either increase or decrease the size of their farm by selling, buying, or leasing acreage. Land here is what economists call a **fixed input**—an input whose quantity is fixed for a period of time and cannot be varied. George and Martha,

A **fixed input** is an input whose quantity is fixed for a period of time and cannot be varied.

PD To prepare for teaching this lesson, you may want to consult the **Module 54 Sample Lecture** in the TRM.

OPEN & CLOSE Start Here

TRM Use **Worksheet 54.1 (The Lego® Factory Is Open!)** from the TRM to introduce this module. The worksheet gives instructions on how to play a game with Legos® that demonstrates the law of diminishing returns.

TEACH Connect It

This module looks at the relationship between inputs and outputs. Remind students that they studied resources in Module 1 (land, labor, capital, entrepreneurship). And point out that inputs, factors of production (Section 7), and resources all refer to these same four categories.

TEACH Teach It

Make sure that students understand the difference between the short run and the long run, and also that the definitions are not based on a specific length of time. The length of the short run or long run depends on what is being produced. The time periods are very different for a tomato stand and a nuclear power plant (tomatoes go bad in a matter of days, whereas a new nuclear power plant takes decades to get up and running). To make the point, compare this to the different perspective of the short run between a fruit fly (which might live 40 days) and a tortoise (which can live 177 years). Forty days may seem like no time to the tortoise and 1 year will be an eternity for a fruit fly!

FOCUS Active Learning

Show Kris Reed's video "Law of Diminishing Returns" (see econextras video list with hyperlinks on the bcs and TRFD). If time permits, carry out the experiment together!

FOCUS Graph It

Figure 54.1 illustrates a production function (total product curve), which shows the relationship between output and inputs. The curve slopes upward because more inputs result in more output. But point out to students that the rate at which output increases slows down as inputs continue to increase (the curve flattens out).

Highlight for students that a production function has output on the vertical axis (wheat) and the variable input on the horizontal axis (labor). In our simple model, labor is usually the one variable input and other inputs (e.g., land and capital) are fixed. It is certainly possible for examples to have different fixed or variable inputs. But if students understand that the variable input goes on the horizontal axis and all other inputs are fixed, they should be able to graph any production function.

FOCUS Active Learning

TRM To give students extra practice in adding economics words to their vocabulary, assign **Worksheet 54.2 (Production Terms to Know)** from the TRM.

A **variable input** is an input whose quantity the firm can vary at any time.

The **long run** is the time period in which all inputs can be varied.

The **short run** is the time period in which at least one input is fixed.

AP® Exam Tip

Questions about the short run and the long run can cause confusion. Just remember that in the long run, all inputs are variable, and in the short run, at least one of them is fixed.

however, are free to decide how many workers to hire. The labor provided by these workers is called a **variable input**—an input whose quantity the firm can vary at any time.

In reality, whether or not the quantity of an input is really fixed depends on the time horizon. Given a long enough period of time, firms can adjust the quantity of any input. Economists define the **long run** as the time period in which all inputs can be varied. So there are no fixed inputs in the long run. In contrast, the **short run** is defined as the time period in which at least one input is fixed. Later, we'll look more carefully at the distinction between the short run and the long run. For now, we will restrict our attention to the short run and assume that at least one input (land) is fixed.

George and Martha know that the quantity of wheat they produce depends on the number of workers they hire. Using modern farming techniques, one worker can cultivate the 10-acre farm, albeit not very intensively. When an additional worker is added, the land is divided equally among all the workers: each worker has 5 acres to cultivate when 2 workers are employed, each cultivates 3⅓ acres when 3 are employed, and so on. So, as additional workers are employed, the 10 acres of land are cultivated more intensively and more bushels of wheat are produced. The relationship between the quantity of labor and the quantity of output, for a given amount of the fixed input, constitutes the farm's production function. The production function for George and Martha's farm, where land is the fixed input and labor is the variable input, is shown in the first two columns of the table in **Figure 54.1**; the diagram there shows the same information graphically. The curve in Figure 54.1 shows how the quantity of output depends on the quantity of the variable input for a given quantity of the fixed input; it is called the

Figure 54.1 The Production Function and the Total Product Curve for George and Martha's Farm

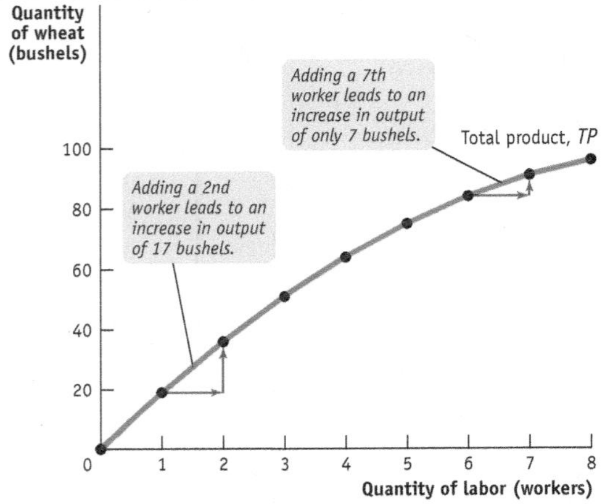

Quantity of labor L (workers)	Quantity of wheat Q (bushels)	Marginal product of labor $MPL = \Delta Q/\Delta L$ (bushels per worker)
0	0	
		19
1	19	
		17
2	36	
		15
3	51	
		13
4	64	
		11
5	75	
		9
6	84	
		7
7	91	
		5
8	96	

The table shows the production function, the relationship between the quantity of the variable input (labor, measured in number of workers) and the quantity of output (wheat, measured in bushels) for a given quantity of the fixed input. It also shows the marginal product of labor on George and Martha's farm. The total product curve shows the production function graphically. It slopes upward because more wheat is produced as more workers are employed. It also becomes flatter because the marginal product of labor declines as more and more workers are employed.

546 Section 10 Behind the Supply Curve: Profit, Production, and Costs

farm's **total product curve**. The physical quantity of output, bushels of wheat, is measured on the vertical axis; the quantity of the variable input, labor (that is, the number of workers employed), is measured on the horizontal axis. The total product curve here slopes upward, reflecting the fact that more bushels of wheat are produced as more workers are employed.

Although the total product curve in Figure 54.1 slopes upward along its entire length, the slope isn't constant: as you move up the curve to the right, it flattens out. To understand this changing slope, look at the third column of the table in Figure 54.1, which shows the *change in the quantity of output* generated by adding one more worker. That is, it shows the **marginal product** of labor, or *MPL*: the additional quantity of output from using one more unit of labor (one more worker).

In this example, we have data at intervals of 1 worker—that is, we have information on the quantity of output when there are 3 workers, 4 workers, and so on. Sometimes data aren't available in increments of 1 unit—for example, you might have information on the quantity of output only when there are 40 workers and when there are 50 workers. In this case, you can use the following equation to calculate the marginal product of labor:

$$\text{(54-1)}\quad \begin{array}{l}\text{Marginal}\\ \text{product of}\\ \text{labor}\end{array} = \begin{array}{l}\text{Change in quantity of}\\ \text{output produced by one}\\ \text{additional unit of labor}\end{array} = \frac{\text{Change in quantity of output}}{\text{Change in quantity of labor}}$$

or

$$MPL = \frac{\Delta Q}{\Delta L}$$

Recall that Δ, the Greek uppercase delta, represents the change in a variable. Now we can explain the significance of the slope of the total product curve: it is equal to the marginal product of labor. The slope of a line is equal to "rise" over "run." This implies that the slope of the total product curve is the change in the quantity of output (the "rise") divided by the change in the quantity of labor (the "run"). And, as we can see from Equation 54-1,

The **total product curve** shows how the quantity of output depends on the quantity of the variable input, for a given quantity of the fixed input.

The **marginal product** of an input is the additional quantity of output produced by using one more unit of that input.

AP® Exam Tip

Whatever units you choose to use in marginal analysis, always be careful that you use the same units throughout the problem.

FYI Was Malthus Right?

In 1798, Thomas Malthus, an English pastor, introduced the principle of diminishing returns to an input. Malthus's writings were influential in his own time and continue to provoke heated argument to this day.

Malthus argued that as a country's population grew but its land area remained fixed, it would become increasingly difficult to grow enough food. Though more intensive cultivation of the land could increase yields, as the marginal product of labor declined, each successive farmer would add less to the total than the last.

From this argument, Malthus drew a powerful conclusion—that misery was the normal condition of humankind. In a country with a small population and abundant land (a description of the United States at the time), he argued, families would be large and the population would grow rapidly. Ultimately, the pressure of population on the land would reduce the condition of most people to a level at which starvation and disease held the population in check. (Arguments like this led the historian Thomas Carlyle to dub economics the "dismal science.")

Happily, over the long term, Malthus's predictions have turned out to be wrong. World population has increased from about 1 billion when Malthus wrote to more than 7.2 billion in 2014, but in most of the world people eat better now than ever before. So was Malthus completely wrong? And do his incorrect predictions refute the idea of diminishing returns? No, on both counts.

First, the Malthusian story is a pretty accurate description of 57 of the last 59 centuries: peasants in eighteenth-century France probably did not live much better than Egyptian peasants in the age of the pyramids. Yet diminishing returns does not mean that using more labor to grow food on a given amount of land will lead to a decline in the marginal product of labor—*if* there is also a radical improvement in farming technology. Fortunately, since the eighteenth century, technological progress has been so rapid that it has alleviated much of the limits imposed by diminishing returns. Diminishing returns implies that the marginal product declines when *all* other things—including technology—remain the same. So the happy fact that Malthus's predictions were wrong does not invalidate the concept of diminishing returns.

TEACH Connect It

The law of diminishing returns explains why the production function becomes flatter (i.e., the *MP* of the variable input decreases as more is added with a fixed input). Since the cost curves in later modules are based on the production function, it will also explain why cost curves have the shapes they do. Make sure students understand that the basic idea behind diminishing returns is that the more you do something, the harder and harder it is to keep doing it. This was also why the *PPC* was bowed out!

FOCUS Active Learning

Ask a student to pass out one sheet of paper to each of his or her classmates. Then ask another student to hand out paper to the class. Continue to add a student to assist in passing out paper to the class. (If you have a very large class, add 2 students at a time.) Eventually, more students will be handing out paper then receiving it. At that point, discuss diminishing returns.

TEACH Teach It

The marginal product of labor is equal to the change in quantity of output divided by the change in quantity of labor. In previous modules, students calculated *MC* and *MR* as the change in *TR* divided by the change in output and the change in total cost divided by the change in output. The change in output was in the denominator before; now it is in the numerator. Make sure students understand and remember this difference when they move from calculating marginal revenue and cost to calculating marginal product!

- *MPL* = Change in *Q*/Change in *L*
- *MPL* = Change in *Q* of output produced by one additional unit of labor

FOCUS Graph It

Figure 54.2 illustrates the marginal product of the labor curve, with the *Q* of labor on the horizontal axis and the *MP* of labor on the vertical axis. Point out that this is downward-sloping, which shows us the diminishing returns to labor (as more cooks enter the kitchen, it gets too crowded and output is diminished).

FOCUS Flip It

TRM Assign Jacob Clifford's video "Micro 3.1 Law of Diminishing Marginal Returns," which explains production and diminishing returns (see econextras video list with hyperlinks on the bcs and TRFD). Refer students to **Worksheet 54.3 (Law of Diminishing Returns)** from the TRM for questions about this video.

this is simply the marginal product of labor. So in Figure 54.1, the fact that the marginal product of the first worker is 19 also means that the slope of the total product curve in going from 0 to 1 worker is 19. Similarly, the slope of the total product curve in going from 1 to 2 workers is the same as the marginal product of the second worker, 17, and so on.

In this example, the marginal product of labor steadily declines as more workers are hired—that is, each successive worker adds less to output than the previous worker. So as employment increases, the total product curve gets flatter.

Figure 54.2 shows how the marginal product of labor depends on the number of workers employed on the farm. The marginal product of labor, *MPL*, is measured on the vertical axis in units of physical output—bushels of wheat—produced per additional worker, and the number of workers employed is measured on the horizontal axis. You can see from the table in Figure 54.1 that if 5 workers are employed instead of 4, output rises from 64 to 75 bushels; in this case the marginal product of labor is 11 bushels—the same number found in Figure 54.2. To indicate that 11 bushels is the marginal product when employment rises from 4 to 5, we place the point corresponding to that information halfway between 4 and 5 workers.

There are **diminishing returns to an input** when an increase in the quantity of that input, holding the levels of all other inputs fixed, leads to a decline in the marginal product of that input.

In this example the marginal product of labor falls as the number of workers increases. That is, there are *diminishing returns to labor* on George and Martha's farm. In general, there are **diminishing returns to an input** when an increase in the quantity of that input, holding the quantity of all other inputs fixed, reduces that input's marginal product. Due to diminishing returns to labor, the *MPL* curve is negatively sloped.

To grasp why diminishing returns can occur, think about what happens as George and Martha add more and more workers without increasing the number of acres. As the number of workers increases, the land is farmed more intensively and the number of bushels increases. But each additional worker is working with a smaller share of the 10 acres—the fixed input—than the previous worker. As a result, the additional worker cannot produce as much output as the previous worker. So it's not surprising that the marginal product of the additional worker falls.

The next module explains that opportunities for specialization among workers can allow the marginal product of labor to increase for the first few workers, but eventually diminishing returns set in as the result of redundancy and congestion. The crucial

Figure 54.2 The Marginal Product of Labor Curve for George and Martha's Farm

The marginal product of labor curve plots each worker's marginal product, the increase in the quantity of output generated by each additional worker. The change in the quantity of output is measured on the vertical axis and the number of workers employed on the horizontal axis. The first worker employed generates an increase in output of 19 bushels, the second worker generates an increase of 17 bushels, and so on. The curve slopes downward due to diminishing returns to labor.

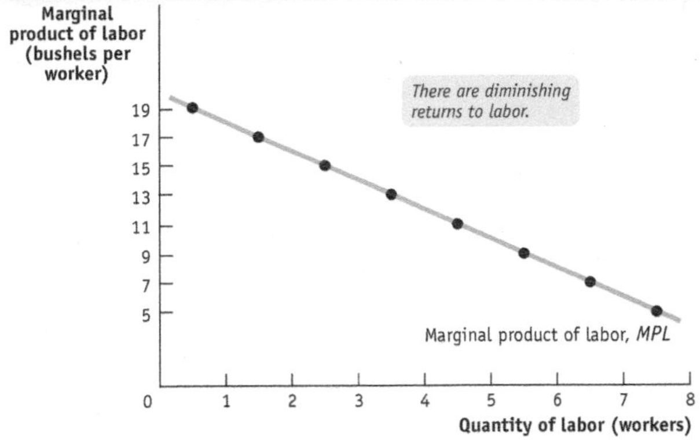

548 Section 10 Behind the Supply Curve: Profit, Production, and Costs

point to emphasize about diminishing returns is that, like many propositions in economics, it is an "other things equal" proposition: each successive unit of an input will raise production by less than the last *if the quantity of all other inputs is held fixed.*

What would happen if the levels of other inputs were allowed to change? You can see the answer illustrated in **Figure 54.3**. Panel (a) shows two total product curves, TP_{10} and TP_{20}. TP_{10} is the farm's total product curve when its total area is 10 acres (the same curve as in Figure 54.1). TP_{20} is the total product curve when the farm's area has increased to 20 acres. Except when 0 workers are employed, TP_{20} lies everywhere above TP_{10} because with more acres available, any given number of workers produces more output. Panel (b) shows the corresponding marginal product of labor curves. MPL_{10} is the marginal product of labor curve given 10 acres to cultivate (the same curve as in Figure 54.2), and MPL_{20} is the marginal product of labor curve given 20 acres. Both curves slope downward because, in each case, the amount of land is fixed, albeit at different levels. But MPL_{20} lies everywhere above MPL_{10}, reflecting the fact that the marginal product of the same worker is higher when he or she has more of the fixed input to work with.

Figure 54.3 demonstrates a general result: the position of the total product curve depends on the quantities of other inputs. If you change the quantities of the other inputs, both the total product curve and the marginal product curve of the remaining input will shift. The importance of the "other things equal" assumption in discussing diminishing returns is illustrated in the FYI on page 547.

With diminishing returns to labor, as more and more workers are added to a fixed amount of land, each worker adds less to total output than the previous worker.

AP® Exam Tip

The *MPL* typically falls as more workers are hired because increases in production are limited by a fixed amount of capital that must be shared among the growing number of workers. Also, it may be necessary to hire less qualified workers.

Figure 54.3 Total Product, Marginal Product, and the Fixed Input

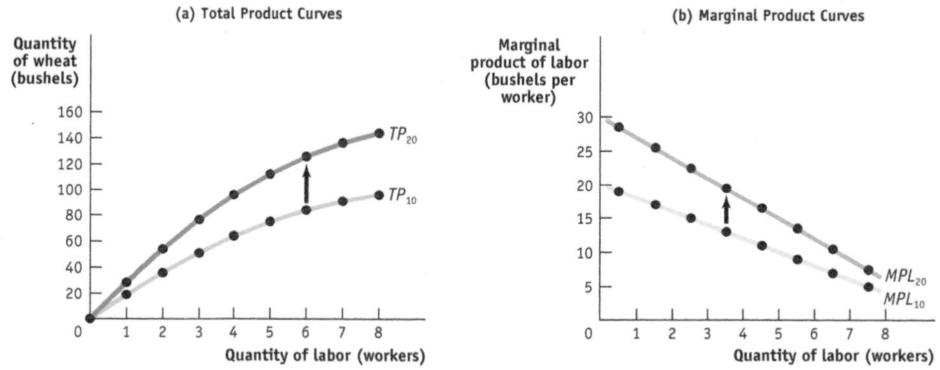

This figure shows how the quantity of output—illustrated by the total product curve—and marginal product depend on the level of the fixed input. Panel (a) shows two total product curves for George and Martha's farm, TP_{10} when their farm is 10 acres and TP_{20} when it is 20 acres. With more land, each worker can produce more wheat. So an increase in the fixed input shifts the total product curve up from TP_{10} to TP_{20}. This also implies that the marginal product of each worker is higher when the farm is 20 acres than when it is 10 acres. As a result, an increase in acreage also shifts the marginal product of labor curve up from MPL_{10} to MPL_{20}. Panel (b) shows the marginal product of labor curves. Note that both marginal product of labor curves still slope downward due to diminishing returns to labor.

TEACH Connect It

Figure 54.3 presents total product and marginal product curves for different levels of a fixed input. For a given production function, the amount of fixed inputs is, well, fixed! When the amount of a fixed input is higher, more output can be produced with any given level of variable inputs. This is shown by an upward shift in the production function and a corresponding increase in *MP* of the variable input. For example, with a larger kitchen, any given number of cooks can produce more and increase their marginal productivity!

FOCUS Test It

Does a production function illustrate a short-run situation or a long-run situation? Explain. *It must be the short run because there is a fixed input!*

FOCUS Graph It

Direct student attention to Figure 54.3, showing that when we change the fixed inputs, we can increase the total and marginal product curves. Ask students to comment on why this is true. *With new resources, each worker can produce more. With more training, each worker can produce more.* Ask students why both *TP* and *MP* still slope downward. *Because of the law of diminishing returns*

OPEN & CLOSE Exit Slip

TRM *Please see **Exit Slip: Module 54** in the TRM for formative questions to ask your students before finishing your lesson. These questions will help you quickly assess whether your students have mastered the module's concepts before moving on.*

Answers to the Exit Slip Questions

1. C
2. D
3. In the short run at least one input is fixed, while in the long run all inputs can be variable.

Module 54 The Production Function 549

MODULE 54 Review

Check Your Understanding

1. Bernie's ice-making company produces ice cubes using a 10-ton machine and electricity (along with water, which we will ignore as an input for simplicity). The quantity of output, measured in pounds of ice, is given in the table below.

Quantity of electricity (kilowatts)	*Quantity of ice (pounds)*
0	0
1	1,000
2	1,800
3	2,400
4	2,800

   a. What is the fixed input? What is the variable input?
   b. Construct a table showing the marginal product of the variable input. Does it show diminishing returns?
   c. Suppose a 50% increase in the size of the fixed input increases output by 100% for any given amount of the variable input. Construct a table showing the quantity of output and the marginal product in this case.

Tackle the Test: Multiple-Choice Questions

1. A production function shows the relationship between inputs and
   a. fixed costs.
   b. variable costs.
   c. total revenue.
   d. output.
   e. profit.
2. Which of the following defines the short run?
   a. less than a year
   b. when all inputs are fixed
   c. when no inputs are variable
   d. when only one input is variable
   e. when at least one input is fixed
3. The slope of the total product curve is also known as the
   a. marginal product.
   b. marginal cost.
   c. average product.
   d. average revenue.
   e. profit.
4. When the returns to an input are diminishing and a profit-maximizing firm chooses to hire more of the input, the total product curve has what kind of slope?
   a. negative decreasing
   b. positive decreasing
   c. negative increasing
   d. positive increasing
   e. positive constant
5. Historically, the limits imposed by diminishing returns have been alleviated primarily by
   a. investment in capital.
   b. increases in the population.
   c. discovery of more land.
   d. Thomas Malthus.
   e. economic models.

Answers to Module 54 Review Questions

Check Your Understanding

1. a. The fixed input is the 10-ton machine and the variable input is electricity.

b. As you can see from the declining numbers in the third column of the accompanying table, electricity does indeed exhibit diminishing returns: the marginal product of each additional kilowatt of electricity is less than that of the previous kilowatt:

Quantity of electricity (kilowatts)	Quantity of ice (pounds)	Marginal product of electricity (pounds per kilowatt)
0	0	
		1,000
1	1,000	
		800
2	1,800	
		600
3	2,400	
		400
4	2,800	

c. A 50% increase in the size of the fixed input means that Bernie now has a 15-ton machine. Since it generates a 100% increase in output for any given amount of electricity, the quantity of output and the marginal product are now as shown in the accompanying table:

Quantity of electricity (kilowatts)	Quantity of ice (pounds)	Marginal product of electricity (pounds per kilowatt)
0	0	
		2,000
1	2,000	
		1,600
2	3,600	
		1,200
3	4,800	
		800
4	5,600	

Tackle the Test: Multiple-Choice Questions

1. d
2. e
3. a
4. b
5. a

Tackle the Test: Free-Response Questions

1. Draw a correctly labeled graph of a production function that exhibits diminishing returns to labor. Assume labor is the variable input and capital is the fixed input. Explain how your graph illustrates diminishing returns to labor.

Rubric for FRQ 1 (4 points)

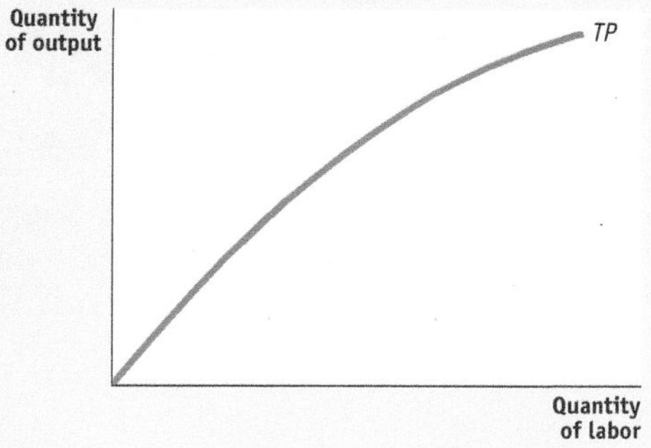

1 point: Graph with vertical axis labeled "Quantity of output" or "*Q*" and horizontal axis labeled "Quantity of labor" or "*L*"

1 point: Upward-sloping curve labeled "Total product" or "*TP*"

1 point: The slope of the total product curve is positive and decreasing.

1 point: Explanation that a positive and decreasing slope illustrates diminishing returns to labor because each additional unit of labor increases total product by less than the previous unit of labor

2. Use the data in the table below to graph the production function and the marginal product of labor. Do the data illustrate diminishing returns to labor? Explain.

Quantity of labor	*Quantity of output*
0	0
1	25
2	47
3	66
4	82
5	95
6	105
7	112
8	116

(5 points)

Tackle the Test: Free-Response Question

Rubric for FRQ 2 (5 points)

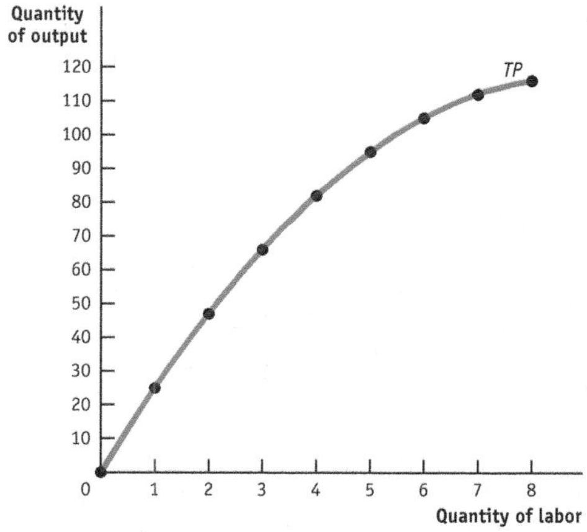

1 point: A graph with the vertical axis labeled "Quantity of output" or "*Q*" and the horizontal axis labeled "Quantity of labor" or "*L*"

1 point: An upward-sloping curve labeled "Total product" or "*TP*," with the points as shown in the graph that accompanies this answer

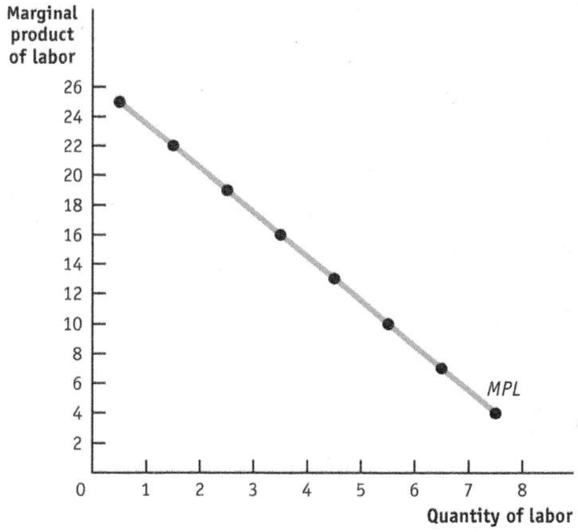

1 point: A second graph with the vertical axis labeled "Marginal product of labor" or "*MPL*" and the horizontal axis labeled "Quantity of labor" or "*L*"

1 point: A downward-sloping curve labeled "Marginal product" or "*MPL*," as shown in the graph that accompanies this answer

1 point: An explanation that the data illustrate diminishing returns to labor because each additional unit of labor increases total product by less than the previous unit of labor, resulting in a downward-sloping marginal product curve

Module 54 The Production Function 551

PD To prepare for teaching this lesson, you may want to consult the **Module 55 Sample Lecture** in the TRM.

OPEN & CLOSE Start Here

We have just completed studying a firm's production function—the relationship between inputs and outputs. Next, we use the production function to study the firm costs. Firm costs are used throughout Sections 11 and 12, where we develop market structure models, so make sure students understand that they need to learn the cost curves we study here to be able to understand the two sections that follow!

At this point, you can repeat the Lego® production demonstration from the last module, and add the price of capital at $100 and the wage per worker of $10. Have students again calculate the *TP* and *MP*, and now add the *MC*, *FC*, *VC*, *ATC*, *AVC*, and *AFC*. Ask them to plot their data and to compare the graphs of these curves in this module.

TEACH Connect It

Remind students that the goal of the firm is to maximize profit. At this point, they should know that profit equals total revenue minus total costs. In this module, we will learn to determine the firm's costs so that we can identify and calculate its maximum profit! Because both fixed and variable inputs exist in the short run, we will also have fixed and variable costs.

MODULE 55 Firm Costs

In this Module, you will learn to:

- Describe the various types of cost a firm faces, including fixed cost, variable cost, and total cost
- Explain how a firm's costs generate marginal cost curves and average cost curves

AP® Exam Tip

Understanding cost curves is crucial to understanding the market structure models in the coming sections. Create note cards with definitions and formulas from this module to aid you in your studies.

From the Production Function to Cost Curves

Now that we have learned about the firm's production function, we can use that knowledge to develop its cost curves. To see how a firm's production function is related to its cost curves, let's turn once again to George and Martha's farm. Once George and Martha know their production function, they know the relationship between inputs of labor and land and output of wheat. But if they want to maximize their profits, they need to translate this knowledge into information about the relationship between the quantity of output and cost. Let's see how they can do this.

To translate information about a firm's production function into information about its cost, we need to know how much the firm must pay for its inputs. We will assume that George and Martha face either an explicit or an implicit cost of $400 for the use of the land. As we learned previously, it is irrelevant whether George and Martha must rent the land for $400 from someone else or whether they own the land themselves and forgo earning $400 from renting it to someone else. Either way, they pay an opportunity cost of $400 by using the land to grow wheat. Moreover, since the land is a fixed input for which George and Martha pay $400 whether they grow one bushel of wheat or one hundred, its cost is a **fixed cost**, denoted by *FC*—a cost that does not depend on the quantity of output produced. In business, a fixed cost is often referred to as an "overhead cost."

A **fixed cost** is a cost that does not depend on the quantity of output produced. It is the cost of the fixed input.

TEACH Teach It

Students will need to know an "alphabet soup" of costs from this module:

- Fixed cost (*FC*) = Cost of fixed input. It does not depend on quantity of output.
- Variable cost (*VC*) = Cost of variable input. It depends on quantity of output produced.
- Total cost (*TC*) = (*FC* + *VC*).
- Marginal cost (*MC*) = Additional cost of doing something one more time. It is the change in *TC* generated by producing one more unit of output. *MC* = Change in *TC*/Change in *Q* output.
- Average total cost (*ATC*) = *TC*/*Q* Output. The total cost *per unit.*
- Average fixed cost (*AFC*) = *FC*/*Q* Output. The fixed cost *per unit.*
- Average variable cost (*AVC*) = *VC*/*Q* Output. The variable cost *per unit.*

We also assume that George and Martha must pay each worker $200. Using their production function, George and Martha know that the number of workers they must hire depends on the amount of wheat they intend to produce. So the cost of labor, which is equal to the number of workers multiplied by $200, is a **variable cost**, denoted by *VC*—a cost that depends on the quantity of output produced. Adding the fixed cost and the variable cost of a given quantity of output gives the **total cost**, or *TC*, of that quantity of output. We can express the relationship among fixed cost, variable cost, and total cost as an equation:

$$\text{(55-1)} \quad \text{Total cost} = \text{Fixed cost} + \text{Variable cost}$$

or

$$TC = FC + VC$$

The table in **Figure 55.1** shows how total cost is calculated for George and Martha's farm. The second column shows the number of workers employed, *L*. The third column shows the corresponding level of output, *Q*, taken from the table in Figure 54.1.

A **variable cost** is a cost that depends on the quantity of output produced. It is the cost of the variable input.

The **total cost** of producing a given quantity of output is the sum of the fixed cost and the variable cost of producing that quantity of output.

Figure 55.1 The Total Cost Curve for George and Martha's Farm

The table shows the variable cost, fixed cost, and total cost for various output quantities on George and Martha's 10-acre farm. The total cost curve shows how total cost (measured on the vertical axis) depends on the quantity of output (measured on the horizontal axis). The labeled points on the curve correspond to the rows of the table. The total cost curve slopes upward because the number of workers employed, and hence total cost, increases as the quantity of output increases. The curve gets steeper as output increases due to diminishing returns to labor.

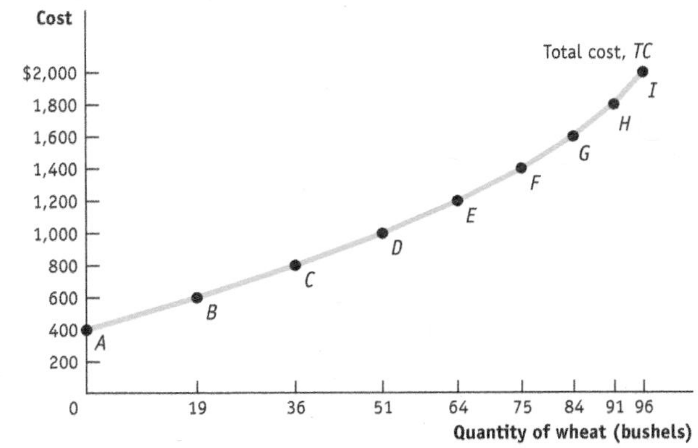

Point on graph	Quantity of labor *L* (workers)	Quantity of wheat *Q* (bushels)	Variable cost *VC*	Fixed cost *FC*	Total cost *TC* = *FC* + *VC*
A	0	0	$0	$400	$400
B	1	19	200	400	600
C	2	36	400	400	800
D	3	51	600	400	1,000
E	4	64	800	400	1,200
F	5	75	1,000	400	1,400
G	6	84	1,200	400	1,600
H	7	91	1,400	400	1,800
I	8	96	1,600	400	2,000

FOCUS Test It

Ask students which of the following are fixed costs and which are variable costs:

Rent (*F*)
Electricity (*V*)
Loan payment (*F*)
Phone bill (*V*)
Wages (*V*)
Food (*V*)

TEACH Connect It

Note that unlike the *TP* (total product) curve that becomes flatter as employment rises, the *TC* (total cost) curve gets steeper as output increases, both due to diminishing returns.

TEACH AP® Exam Tip

The total cost curves are important since they connect cost curves to the production function. However, average and marginal costs are used more frequently in later models and on the AP® test. Students should have a solid enough understanding, so they know that marginal refers to a change and average is per unit!

St. Louis Federal Reserve Bank Resources

Perfect Competition

This collection of cost curve slides is available in SMART or PowerPoint presentations. The slides illustrate firms' short-run decisions.

FOCUS Flip It

TRM Have your students watch Jacob Clifford's video "Micro 3.2 Cost of Production and Cost Curves (1 of 2)" (see econextras video list with hyperlinks on the bcs and TRFD). **Worksheet 55.1 (Costs of Production and Cost Curves)** from the TRM will give them the information needed to complete the data as requested from the video.

The fourth column shows the variable cost, *VC*, equal to the number of workers multiplied by $200. The fifth column shows the fixed cost, *FC*, which is $400 regardless of the quantity of wheat produced. The sixth column shows the total cost of output, *TC*, which is the variable cost plus the fixed cost.

The first column labels each row of the table with a letter, from *A* to *I*. These labels will be helpful in understanding our next step: drawing the **total cost curve**, a curve that shows how total cost depends on the quantity of output.

The **total cost curve** shows how total cost depends on the quantity of output.

George and Martha's total cost curve is shown in the diagram in Figure 55.1, where the horizontal axis measures the quantity of output in bushels of wheat and the vertical axis measures total cost in dollars. Each point on the curve corresponds to one row of the table in Figure 55.1. For example, point *A* shows the situation when 0 workers are employed: output is 0, and total cost is equal to fixed cost, $400. Similarly, point *B* shows the situation when 1 worker is employed: output is 19 bushels, and total cost is $600, equal to the sum of $400 in fixed cost and $200 in variable cost.

Like the total product curve, the total cost curve slopes upward: due to the increasing variable cost, the more output produced, the higher the farm's total cost. But unlike the total product curve, which gets flatter as employment rises, the total cost curve gets *steeper*. That is, the slope of the total cost curve is greater as the amount of output produced increases. As we will soon see, the steepening of the total cost curve is also due to diminishing returns to the variable input. Before we can see why, we must first look at the relationships among several useful measures of cost.

Two Key Concepts: Marginal Cost and Average Cost

We've just learned how to derive a firm's total cost curve from its production function. Our next step is to take a deeper look at total cost by deriving two extremely useful measures: *marginal cost* and *average cost*. As we'll see, these two measures of the cost of production have a somewhat surprising relationship to each other. Moreover, they will prove to be vitally important in later modules, where we will use them to analyze the firm's output decision and the market supply curve.

Marginal Cost

In Module 53, you learned that marginal cost is the added cost of doing something one more time. In the context of production, marginal cost is the change in total cost generated by producing one more unit of output. We've already seen that marginal product is easiest to calculate if data on output are available in increments of one unit of input. Similarly, marginal cost is easiest to calculate if data on total cost are available in increments of one unit of output because the increase in total cost for each unit is clear. When the data come in less convenient increments, it's still possible to calculate marginal cost over each interval. But for the sake of simplicity, let's work with an example in which the data come in convenient one-unit increments.

Selena's Gourmet Salsas produces bottled salsa; **Table 55.1** shows how its costs per day depend on the number of cases of salsa it produces per day. The firm has a fixed cost of $108 per day, shown in the second column, which is the daily rental cost of its food-preparation equipment. The third column shows the variable cost, and the fourth column shows the total cost. Panel (a) of **Figure 55.2** plots the total cost curve. Like the total cost curve for George and Martha's farm in Figure 55.1, this curve slopes upward, getting steeper as quantity increases.

Table 55.1 Costs at Selena's Gourmet Salsas

Quantity of salsa Q (cases)	Fixed cost FC	Variable cost VC	Total cost TC = FC + VC	Marginal cost of case MC = ΔTC/ΔQ
0	$108	$0	$108	
1	108	12	120	$12
2	108	48	156	36
3	108	108	216	60
4	108	192	300	84
5	108	300	408	108
6	108	432	540	132
7	108	588	696	156
8	108	768	876	180
9	108	972	1,080	204
10	108	1,200	1,308	228

The significance of the slope of the total cost curve is shown by the fifth column of Table 55.1, which indicates marginal cost—the additional cost of each additional unit. The general formula for marginal cost is:

$$\text{(55-2)}\quad \text{Marginal cost} = \begin{array}{l}\text{Change in total}\\ \text{cost generated by}\\ \text{one additional unit}\\ \text{of output}\end{array} = \frac{\text{Change in total cost}}{\text{Change in quantity of output}}$$

or

$$MC = \frac{\Delta TC}{\Delta Q}$$

AP® Exam Tip

Marginal cost is equal to the slope of the total cost curve.

Figure 55.2 The Total and Marginal Cost Curves for Selena's Gourmet Salsas

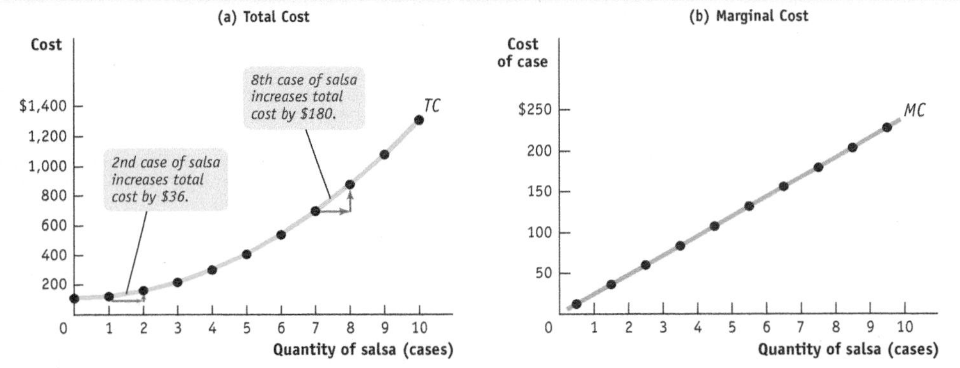

Panel (a) shows the total cost curve from Table 55.1. Like the total cost curve in Figure 55.1, it slopes upward and gets steeper as we move up it to the right. Panel (b) shows the marginal cost curve. It also slopes upward, reflecting diminishing returns to the variable input.

FOCUS Graph It

The *TC* curve and corresponding *MC* curve can be seen in contrast and explained in Figure 55.2. Ask students the following questions:

1. Why is the *TC* rising faster at higher outputs? *As output increases, cost increases at an increasing rate because inputs are most costly due to the scarcity of resources.*
2. How is the shape of the *MC* curve related to diminishing returns? *MC slopes upward, reflecting the diminishing returns to variable inputs.*

Note: Remind students that *MC* is directly caused by changes in variable costs in the short run. In the long run, all costs are variable.

TEACH Teach It

The marginal and average cost curves can be found using the total cost curves.

- Marginal cost is indicated by the slope of the total cost curve, since marginal cost is the change in total cost (rise) divided by the change in quantity (run).

  MC = Change in TC/Change in Q output

- Average cost is the cost per unit of output and is equal to the total cost divided by the quantity (NOT changes). The average cost is the slope of a line drawn from the origin to the point of the total cost curve (which has a rise equal to TC and a run equal to Q).

Shutterstock

As in the case of marginal product, marginal cost is equal to "rise" (the increase in total cost) divided by "run" (the increase in the quantity of output). So just as marginal product is equal to the slope of the total product curve, marginal cost is equal to the slope of the total cost curve.

Now we can understand why the total cost curve gets steeper as it increases from left to right: as you can see in Table 55.1, marginal cost at Selena's Gourmet Salsas rises as output increases. And because marginal cost equals the slope of the total cost curve, a higher marginal cost means a steeper slope. Panel (b) of Figure 55.2 shows the marginal cost curve corresponding to the data in Table 55.1. Notice that, as in Figure 53.1, we plot the marginal cost for increasing output from 0 to 1 case of salsa halfway between 0 and 1, the marginal cost for increasing output from 1 to 2 cases of salsa halfway between 1 and 2, and so on.

Why does the marginal cost curve slope upward? Because there are diminishing returns to inputs in this example. As output increases, the marginal product of the variable input declines. This implies that more and more of the variable input must be used to produce each additional unit of output as the amount of output already produced rises. And since each unit of the variable input must be paid for, the additional cost per additional unit of output also rises.

Recall that the flattening of the total product curve is also due to diminishing returns: if the quantities of other inputs are fixed, the marginal product of an input falls as more of that input is used. The flattening of the total product curve as output increases and the steepening of the total cost curve as output increases are just flip-sides of the same phenomenon. That is, as output increases, the marginal cost of output also increases because the marginal product of the variable input decreases. Our next step is to introduce another measure of cost: *average cost.*

Average Cost

Average total cost, often referred to simply as **average cost**, is total cost divided by quantity of output produced.

In addition to total cost and marginal cost, it's useful to calculate **average total cost**, often simply called **average cost**. The average total cost is total cost divided by the quantity of output produced; that is, it is equal to total cost per unit of output. If we let ATC denote average total cost, the equation looks like this:

$$\text{(55-3)} \quad ATC = \frac{\text{Total cost}}{\text{Quantity of output}} = \frac{TC}{Q}$$

Average total cost is important because it tells the producer how much the *average* or *typical* unit of output costs to produce. Marginal cost, meanwhile, tells the producer how much *one more* unit of output costs to produce. Although they may look very similar, these two measures of cost typically differ. And confusion between them is a major source of error in economics, both in the classroom and in real life. **Table 55.2** uses data from Selena's Gourmet Salsas to calculate average total cost. For example, the total cost of producing 4 cases of salsa is \$300, consisting of \$108 in fixed cost and \$192 in variable cost (from Table 55.1). So the average total cost of producing 4 cases of salsa is \$300/4 = \$75. You can see from Table 55.2 that as the quantity of output increases, average total cost first falls, then rises.

AP® Exam Tip

Be prepared to calculate total, fixed, variable, marginal, and average costs on the AP® Exam.

Figure 55.3 plots that data to yield the *average total cost curve*, which shows how average total cost depends on output. As before, cost in dollars is measured on the vertical axis and quantity of output is measured on the horizontal axis. The average total cost curve has a distinctive U shape that corresponds to how average total cost first falls and then rises as output increases. Economists believe that such **U-shaped average total cost curves** are the norm for firms in many industries.

A **U-shaped average total cost curve** falls at low levels of output and then rises at higher levels.

Average fixed cost is the fixed cost per unit of output.

To help our understanding of why the average total cost curve is U-shaped, Table 55.2 breaks average total cost into its two underlying components, *average fixed cost* and *average variable cost.* **Average fixed cost**, or AFC, is fixed cost divided by the quantity of output, also known as the fixed cost per unit of output. For example, if Selena's Gourmet

556 Section 10 Behind the Supply Curve: Profit, Production, and Costs

Table 55.2 Average Costs for Selena's Gourmet Salsas

Quantity of salsa Q (cases)	Total cost TC	Average total cost of case $ATC = TC/Q$	Average fixed cost of case $AFC = FC/Q$	Average variable cost of case $AVC = VC/Q$
1	$120	$120.00	$108.00	$12.00
2	156	78.00	54.00	24.00
3	216	72.00	36.00	36.00
4	300	75.00	27.00	48.00
5	408	81.60	21.60	60.00
6	540	90.00	18.00	72.00
7	696	99.43	15.43	84.00
8	876	109.50	13.50	96.00
9	1,080	120.00	12.00	108.00
10	1,308	130.80	10.80	120.00

Salsas produces 4 cases of salsa, average fixed cost is $108/4 = $27 per case. **Average variable cost**, or *AVC*, is variable cost divided by the quantity of output, also known as variable cost per unit of output. At an output of 4 cases, average variable cost is $192/4 = $48 per case. Writing these in the form of equations:

Average variable cost is the variable cost per unit of output.

$$(55\text{-}4) \quad AFC = \frac{\text{Fixed cost}}{\text{Quantity of output}} = \frac{FC}{Q}$$

$$AVC = \frac{\text{Variable cost}}{\text{Quantity of output}} = \frac{VC}{Q}$$

Average total cost is the sum of average fixed cost and average variable cost; it has a U shape because these components move in opposite directions as output rises.

Figure 55.3 The Average Total Cost Curve for Selena's Gourmet Salsas

The average total cost curve at Selena's Gourmet Salsas is U-shaped. At low levels of output, average total cost falls because the "spreading effect" of falling average fixed cost dominates the "diminishing returns effect" of rising average variable cost. At higher levels of output, the opposite is true and average total cost rises. At point *M*, corresponding to an output of three cases of salsa per day, average total cost is at its minimum level, the minimum average total cost.

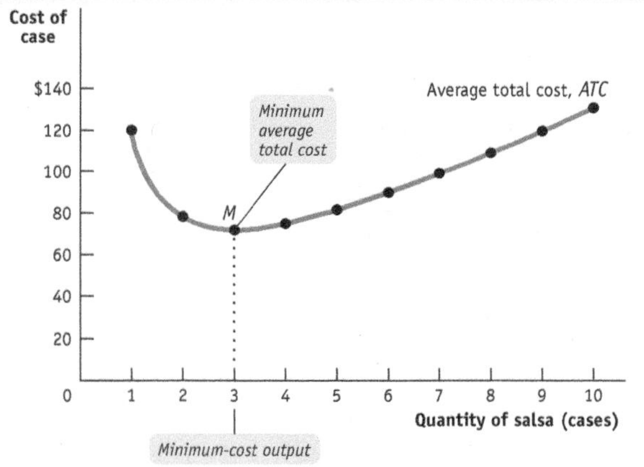

FOCUS Test It

- Calculate *MC* from Table 55.2.
  MC = 36, 60, 84, 108, 132, 156, 180, 204, 228
- Explain the differences between *FC*, *VC*, and *TC* in Table 55.1 and *AFC*, *AVC*, and *ATC* in Table 55.2 to verify understanding.
  AFC = FC/Q output, AVC = VC/Q output, ATC = TC/Q output

FOCUS Graph It

The *ATC* curve in Figure 55.3 shows that it is U-shaped.

- At low levels of output, *ATC* falls. What is the *ATC* for cases of salsa when output is 2? *$78*
- At higher levels of output, *ATC* rises. What is the *ATC* for cases of salsa when output is 8? *$109.50*
- What is the minimum *ATC*? *Point M, $72*

FOCUS Flip It

TRM As a first drill with cost curves, have students watch Jacob Clifford's video "Cost of Production and Cost Curves (2 of 2)" (see econextras video list with hyperlinks on the bcs and TRFD). Assign **Worksheet 55.2 (Firm Costs)** from the TRM for accompanying questions.

TEACH Teach It

Most students are familiar with calculating their average grades. Use this knowledge to help your class understand the mathematical relationship between average and marginal. Ask students what happens to their average grade when their marginal (i.e., next) grade is below their average in a class. Many will probably realize that a lower grade pulls their average down. Next ask them what will happen when their marginal (i.e., next) grade is higher than their average. They should see that a higher grade will pull their grade average up. Use this same reasoning while presenting a graph with average and marginal cost. Draw arrows showing the *AC* falling when *MC* is below it and showing *AC* rising when *MC* is above it. Make sure students see that *MC* must cross the *AC* at the *AC* minimum. This is important in later modules and is tested in many FRQs.

Module 55 Firm Costs 557

TEACH Teach It

Average cost means the cost, on average, or the cost *per unit.* An average cost is always the total cost divided by the number of units. For example, if your cost to make T-shirts was \$100 and you made 10 T-shirts, your cost per shirt (average cost) was $\frac{\$100}{10} = \$10$. Each shirt cost an average of \$10!

FOCUS Graph It

Figure 55.4 shows students the *MC, ATC, AVC,* and *AFC* curves. Explain why the *AFC* curve is always decreasing but will never equal zero. Illustrate with a fixed cost of \$100. Since $AFC = \frac{TFC}{Q}$, $AFC = \frac{100}{Q}$. Divide the total cost by larger and larger numbers to show that *AFC* continues to fall. $\frac{100}{1} = 100, \frac{100}{2} = 50, \frac{100}{4} = 25, \frac{100}{5} = 20,$ $\frac{100}{10} = 10$, etc. (skip the *Q*'s that are harder to divide by!). If *Q* were infinity, $\frac{100}{Q}$ would still be greater than zero (though really close to it).

Since the difference between total cost and total variable cost is total fixed cost, the difference between *ATC* and *AVC* is the *AFC*. $TC = TVC + TFC$, so $\frac{TC}{Q} = \frac{TVC}{Q} + \frac{TFC}{Q}$ and $ATC = AVC + AFC$. The difference between the *ATC* and *AVC* curves is *AFC*. Since *AFC* gets smaller as *Q* increases, the distance between *ATC* and *AVC* grows smaller on the graph.

AP® Exam Tip

You may be required to draw these cost curves from memory on the AP® Exam. Questions about the relationship between the curves are common.

Average fixed cost falls as more output is produced because the numerator (the fixed cost) is a fixed number but the denominator (the quantity of output) increases as more is produced. Another way to think about this relationship is that, as more output is produced, the fixed cost is spread over more units of output; the end result is that the fixed cost *per unit of output*—the average fixed cost—falls. You can see this effect in the fourth column of Table 55.2: average fixed cost drops continuously as output increases. Average variable cost, however, rises as output increases. As we've seen, this reflects diminishing returns to the variable input: each additional unit of output adds more to variable cost than the previous unit because increasing amounts of the variable input are required to make another unit.

So increasing output has two opposing effects on average total cost—the "spreading effect" and the "diminishing returns effect":

- *The spreading effect.* The larger the output, the greater the quantity of output over which fixed cost is spread, leading to lower average fixed cost.
- *The diminishing returns effect.* The larger the output, the greater the amount of variable input required to produce additional units, leading to higher average variable cost.

At low levels of output, the spreading effect is very powerful because even small increases in output cause large reductions in average fixed cost. So at low levels of output, the spreading effect dominates the diminishing returns effect and causes the average total cost curve to slope downward. But when output is large, average fixed cost is already quite small, so increasing output further has only a very small spreading effect. Diminishing returns, however, usually grow increasingly important as output rises. As a result, when output is large, the diminishing returns effect dominates the spreading effect, causing the average total cost curve to slope upward. At the bottom of the U-shaped average total cost curve, point *M* in Figure 55.3, the two effects exactly balance each other. At this point average total cost is at its minimum level, the minimum average total cost.

Figure 55.4 brings together in a single picture the four other cost curves that we have derived from the total cost curve for Selena's Gourmet Salsas: the marginal cost curve (*MC*), the average total cost curve (*ATC*), the average variable cost curve (*AVC*), and the average fixed cost curve (*AFC*). All are based on the information in Tables 55.1

Figure 55.4 The Marginal and Average Cost Curves for Selena's Gourmet Salsas

Here we have the family of cost curves for Selena's Gourmet Salsas: the marginal cost curve (*MC*), the average total cost curve (*ATC*), the average variable cost curve (*AVC*), and the average fixed cost curve (*AFC*). Note that the average total cost curve is U-shaped and the marginal cost curve crosses the average total cost curve at the bottom of the U, point *M*, corresponding to the minimum average total cost from Table 55.2 and Figure 55.3.

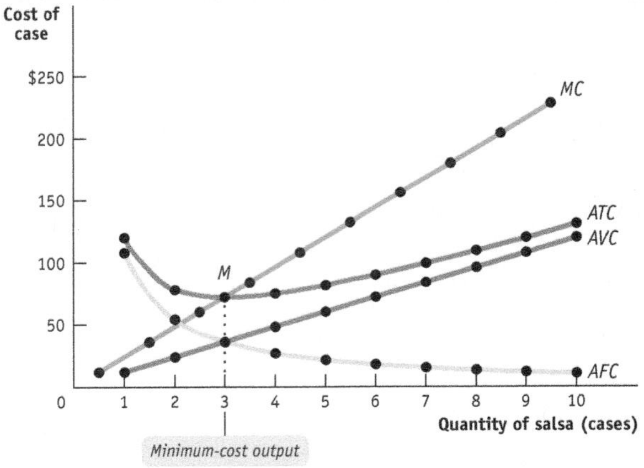

FOCUS Active Learning

TRM Assign **Worksheet 55.3 (Practice with Cost Curves)** from the TRM for practice on cost curves.

FOCUS Flip It

TRM To visually familiarize themselves with cost curves, have students watch Jacob Clifford's video "Micro 3.4 Marginal Cost and *ATC*—Why Do Cost Curves Do That?" (see econextras video list with hyperlinks on the bcs and TRFD). Assign **Worksheet 55.4 (Marginal Cost and *ATC*: Why Do Cost Curves Do That?)** from the TRM for accompanying questions.

558 Section 10 Behind the Supply Curve: Profit, Production, and Costs

and 55.2. As before, cost is measured on the vertical axis and the quantity of output is measured on the horizontal axis.

Let's take a moment to note some features of the various cost curves. First of all, marginal cost slopes upward—the result of diminishing returns that make an additional unit of output more costly to produce than the one before. Average variable cost also slopes upward—again, due to diminishing returns—but is flatter than the marginal cost curve. This is because the higher cost of an additional unit of output is averaged across all units, not just the additional unit, in the average variable cost measure. Meanwhile, average fixed cost slopes downward because of the spreading effect.

Finally, notice that the marginal cost curve intersects the average total cost curve from below, crossing it at its lowest point, point M in Figure 55.4. This last feature is our next subject of study.

Minimum Average Total Cost

For a U-shaped average total cost curve, average total cost is at its minimum level at the bottom of the U. Economists call the quantity of output that corresponds to the minimum average total cost the **minimum-cost output**. In the case of Selena's Gourmet Salsas, the minimum-cost output is three cases of salsa per day.

In Figure 55.4, the bottom of the U is at the level of output at which the marginal cost curve crosses the average total cost curve from below. Is this an accident? No—it reflects general principles that are always true about a firm's marginal cost and average total cost curves:

- At the minimum-cost output, average total cost *is equal to* marginal cost.
- At output less than the minimum-cost output, marginal cost *is less than* average total cost and average total cost is falling.
- And at output greater than the minimum-cost output, marginal cost *is greater than* average total cost and average total cost is rising.

To understand these principles, think about how your grade in one course—say, a 3.0 in physics—affects your overall grade point average. If your GPA before receiving that grade was more than 3.0, the new grade lowers your average.

Similarly, if marginal cost—the cost of producing one more unit—is less than average total cost, producing that extra unit lowers average total cost. This is shown in **Figure 55.5** on the next page by the movement from A_1 to A_2. In this case, the marginal cost of producing an additional unit of output is low, as indicated by the point MC_L on the marginal cost curve. When the cost of producing the next unit of output is less than average total cost, increasing production reduces average total cost. So any quantity of output at which marginal cost is less than average total cost must be on the downward-sloping segment of the U.

But if your grade in physics is more than the average of your previous grades, this new grade raises your GPA. Similarly, if marginal cost is greater than average total cost, producing that extra unit raises average total cost. This is illustrated by the movement from B_1 to B_2 in Figure 55.5, where the marginal cost, MC_H, is higher than average total cost. So any quantity of output at which marginal cost is greater than average total cost must be on the upward-sloping segment of the U.

Finally, if a new grade is exactly equal to your previous GPA, the additional grade neither raises nor lowers that average—it stays the same. This corresponds to point M in Figure 55.5: when marginal cost equals average total cost, we must be at the bottom of the U because only at that point is average total cost neither falling nor rising.

Does the Marginal Cost Curve Always Slope Upward?

Up to this point, we have emphasized the importance of diminishing returns, which lead to a marginal product curve that always slopes downward and a marginal cost curve that always slopes upward. In practice, however, economists believe that marginal

The **minimum-cost output** is the quantity of output at which average total cost is lowest—it corresponds to the bottom of the U-shaped average total cost curve.

AP® Exam Tip

When drawing cost curves, be sure to have the marginal cost curve intersect the average total cost curve at the lowest point on the average total cost curve.

FOCUS Test It

Ask students the following questions:

1. Why does the *AFC* curve always lie below the *AVC* and *ATC* curves? *FC are constant and always apparent. VC are added to FC to equal TC.*

2. Why does *MC* often fall as a firm increases output from a low level? *With specialization that occurs as more workers are hired, diminishing returns set in and MC will rise, forming a U-shaped curve.*

TEACH Teach It

Minimum cost output is the quantity of output at which we find average total cost to be the lowest. The minimum cost output occurs at the bottom (lowest point) of the U-shaped *ATC* curve.

FOCUS Graph It

In Figure 55.5, we can see the minimum cost output at *M*. Point out that *MC* will intersect *ATC* at this point.

- At minimum cost output, $ATC = MC$.
- At output below minimum cost output, what is the relationship between *MC* and *ATC*? *$MC < ATC$ and ATC is falling.*
- At output above minimum cost output, what is the relationship between *MC* and *ATC*? *$MC > ATC$ and ATC is rising.*

Figure 55.5 The Relationship Between the Average Total Cost Curve and the Marginal Cost Curve

To see why the marginal cost curve (*MC*) must cut through the average total cost curve at the minimum average total cost (point *M*), corresponding to the minimum-cost output, we look at what happens if marginal cost is different from average total cost. If marginal cost is *less* than average total cost, an increase in output must reduce average total cost, as in the movement from A_1 to A_2. If marginal cost is *greater* than average total cost, an increase in output must increase average total cost, as in the movement from B_1 to B_2.

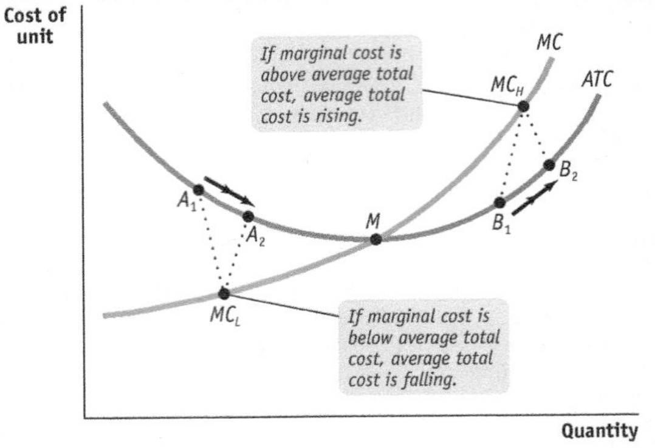

cost curves often slope *downward* as a firm increases its production from zero up to some low level, sloping upward only at higher levels of production: marginal cost curves look like the curve labeled *MC* in **Figure 55.6**.

This initial downward slope occurs because a firm often finds that, when it starts with only a very small number of workers, employing more workers and expanding output allows its workers to specialize in various tasks. This, in turn, lowers the firm's marginal cost as it expands output. For example, one individual producing salsa would have to perform all the tasks involved: selecting and preparing the ingredients, mixing the salsa, bottling and labeling it, packing it into cases, and so on. As more workers are employed, they can divide the tasks, with each worker specializing in one aspect or a

AP® Exam Tip

As is true for the average total cost curve, the marginal cost curve intersects the average variable cost curve at the lowest point on the average variable cost curve.

Figure 55.6 More Realistic Cost Curves

A realistic marginal cost curve has a "swoosh" shape. Starting from a very low output level, marginal cost often falls as the firm increases output. That's because hiring additional workers allows greater specialization of their tasks and leads to increasing returns. Once specialization is achieved, however, diminishing returns to additional workers set in and marginal cost rises. The corresponding average variable cost curve is now U-shaped, like the average total cost curve.

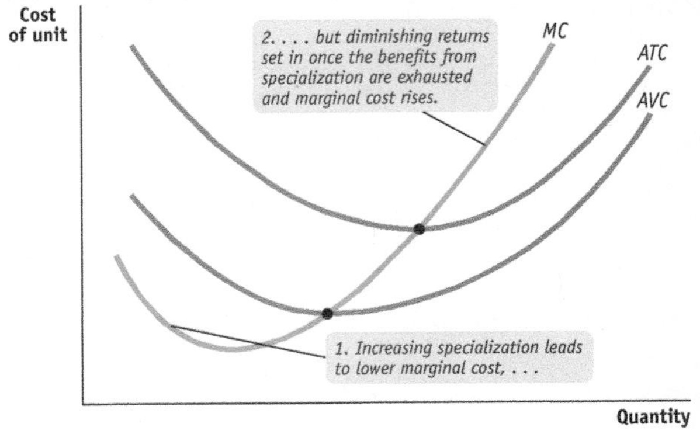

560 Section 10 Behind the Supply Curve: Profit, Production, and Costs

few aspects of salsa-making. This specialization leads to *increasing returns* to the hiring of additional workers and results in a marginal product of labor curve that initially slopes upward and a marginal cost curve that initially slopes downward. Once there are enough workers to have completely exhausted the benefits of further specialization, diminishing returns to labor set in and the marginal cost curve changes direction and slopes upward. So typical marginal cost curves actually have the "swoosh" shape shown by *MC* in Figure 55.6. For the same reason, average variable cost curves typically look like *AVC* in Figure 55.6: they are U-shaped rather than strictly upward sloping.

However, as Figure 55.6 also shows, the key features we saw from the example of Selena's Gourmet Salsas remain true: the average total cost curve is U-shaped, and the marginal cost curve passes through the point of minimum average total cost.

Figure 55.7 shows the relationship between the marginal product of labor curve and the marginal cost curve under the assumptions that labor is the only variable input and the wage rate remains unchanged. The horizontal axis on the top graph measures the quantity of labor; the horizontal axis on the bottom graph measures the quantity of output produced by the quantity of labor shown in the top graph. As marginal product rises to its peak at the dotted line, marginal cost falls, because less and less additional labor is needed to make each additional unit of output. To the right of the dotted line, marginal cost rises as marginal product falls, because more and more additional labor is needed to make each additional unit of output. So marginal product and marginal cost go in opposite directions.

Figure 55.7 Links Between Productivity and Cost

If labor is the only variable input and the wage rate remains unchanged, marginal cost falls as marginal product rises and marginal cost rises as marginal product falls. Similarly, average variable cost rises as average product falls and average variable cost falls as average product rises.

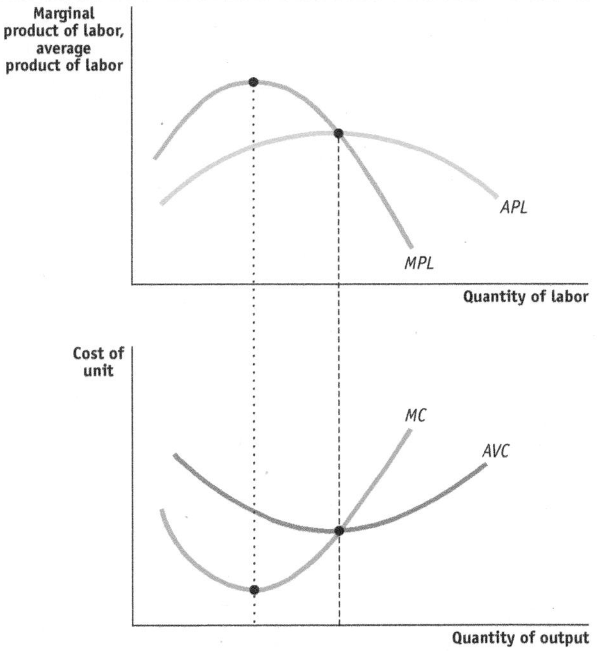

FOCUS Test It

Ask students to explain why *MC* decreases as the *MP* of labor increases until *MP* reaches its peak. *As MP rises until it reaches its peak, less and less additional labor is needed to make each additional unit of output.*

Ask students to explain why *MC* increases as *MP* decreases after *MP* leaves its peak. *After it reaches its peak, as MP declines, MC increases because more and more additional labor is needed to make each additional amount of output.*

Module 55 Firm Costs 561

The **average product** of an input is the total product divided by the quantity of the input.

The **average product curve** for an input shows the relationship between the average product and the quantity of the input.

The **average product** of an input is the total product divided by the quantity of the input. For example, if 5 workers produce 75 bushels of wheat, the average product of labor is 75/5 = 15 bushels. The **average product curve** for labor, labeled *APL* in Figure 55.7, shows the relationship between the average product of labor and the quantity of labor. With labor as the only variable input and a fixed wage rate, average product and average variable cost go in opposite directions, just like marginal product and marginal cost. To the left of the dashed line in Figure 55.7, the average product is rising and the average variable cost is falling, while to the right of the dashed line, average product is falling and average variable cost is rising.

MODULE 55 Review

Check Your Understanding

1. Alicia's Apple Pies is a roadside business. Alicia must pay $9.00 in rent each day. In addition, it costs her $1.00 to produce the first pie of the day. The additional cost of each subsequent pie is 50% more than the one before. For example, the second pie costs $1.00 × 1.5 = $1.50 to produce, and so on.
   a. Calculate Alicia's marginal cost, variable cost, average fixed cost, average variable cost, and average total cost as her daily pie output rises from 0 to 6. (*Hint:* The variable cost of two pies is just the marginal cost of the first pie, plus the marginal cost of the second, and so on.)
   b. Indicate the range of pies for which the spreading effect dominates and the range for which the diminishing returns effect dominates.
   c. What is Alicia's minimum-cost output? Explain why making one more pie lowers Alicia's average total cost when output is lower than the minimum-cost output. Similarly, explain why making one more pie raises Alicia's average total cost when output is greater than the minimum-cost output.

Tackle the Test: Multiple-Choice Questions

1. When a firm is producing zero output, total cost equals
   a. zero.
   b. variable cost.
   c. fixed cost.
   d. average total cost.
   e. marginal cost.
2. Which of the following statements is true?
   I. Marginal cost is the change in total cost generated by one additional unit of output.
   II. Marginal cost is the change in variable cost generated by one additional unit of output.
   III. The marginal cost curve must cross the minimum of the average total cost curve.
   a. I only
   b. II only
   c. III only
   d. I and II only
   e. I, II, and III
3. Which of the following is correct?
   a. *AVC* is the change in total cost generated by one additional unit of output.
   b. $MC = TC/Q$
   c. The average cost curve crosses at the minimum of the marginal cost curve.
   d. The *AFC* curve slopes upward.
   e. $AVC = ATC - AFC$
4. The slope of the total cost curve equals
   a. variable cost.
   b. average variable cost.
   c. average total cost.
   d. average fixed cost.
   e. marginal cost.
5.

Quantity	*Variable cost*	*Total cost*
0	$0	$40
1	20	60
2	50	90
3	90	130
4	140	180
5	200	240

   On the basis of the data in the table above, what is the marginal cost of the third unit of output?
   a. 40
   b. 50
   c. 60
   d. 90
   e. 130

FOCUS Test It

Ask students what relationship the *AP* of labor curve exhibits. *AP of labor and Q of input.* If 12 workers produce 72 computers, what is the *AP* of labor? $\frac{72}{12} = 6$

OPEN & CLOSE Exit Slip

TRM *Please see **Exit Slip: Module 55** in the TRM for formative questions to ask your students before finishing your lesson. These questions will help you quickly assess whether your students have mastered the module's concepts before moving on.*

Answers to the Exit Slip Questions

1. B
2. a. *MC* (10, 20, 30, 40, 50); b. *ATC* (30, 25, 26.67, 30, 34); c. *FC* (20)
3. A

Answers to Module 55 Review Questions

Check Your Understanding

1. a. As shown in the table below, the marginal cost for each pie is found by multiplying the marginal cost of the previous pie by 1.5. The variable cost for each output level is found by summing the marginal cost for all the pies produced to reach that output level. So, for example, the variable cost of 3 pies is $1.00 + $1.50 + $2.25 = $4.75. Average fixed cost for *Q* pies is calculated as $9.00/*Q* since the fixed cost is $9.00. Average variable cost for *Q* pies is equal to the variable cost for the *Q* pies divided by *Q*; for example, the average variable cost of 5 pies is $13.19/5, or approximately $2.64. Finally, average total cost can be calculated in two equivalent ways: as $\frac{TC}{Q}$ or as $AVC + AFC$.

Quantity of pies	Marginal cost of pie	Variable cost	Average fixed cost of pie	Average variable cost of pie	Average total cost of pie
0		$0.00	—	—	—
	$1.00				
1		1.00	$9.00	$1.00	$10.00
	1.50				
2		2.50	4.50	1.25	5.75
	2.25				
3		4.75	3.00	1.58	4.58
	3.38				
4		8.13	2.25	2.03	4.28
	5.06				
5		13.19	1.80	2.64	4.44
	7.59				
6		20.78	1.50	3.46	4.96

562 Section 10 Behind the Supply Curve: Profit, Production, and Costs

Tackle the Test: Free-Response Questions

1. Use the information in the table below to answer the following questions.

Quantity	*Variable cost*	*Total cost*
0	$0	$40
1	20	60
2	50	90
3	90	130
4	140	180
5	200	240

a. What is the firm's level of fixed cost? Explain how you know.

b. Draw one correctly labeled graph showing the firm's marginal and average total cost curves.

Rubric for FRQ 1 (6 points)

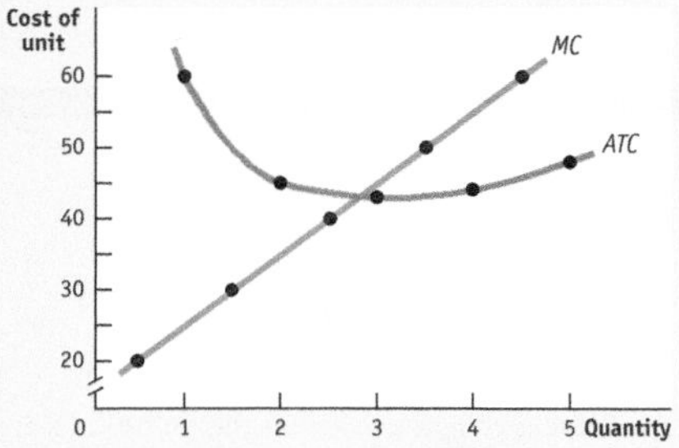

1 point: $FC = \$40$

1 point: We can identify the fixed cost as $40 because when the firm is not producing, it still incurs a cost of $40. This could only be the result of a fixed cost because variable cost is zero when output is zero.

1 point: Graph with correct labels ("Cost of unit" on vertical axis; "Quantity" on horizontal axis)

1 point Upward-sloping *MC* curve plotted according to data, labeled "*MC*"

1 point: U-shaped *ATC* curve plotted according to the provided data, labeled "*ATC*"

1 point: *MC* curve crossing at minimum of *ATC* curve (Note: We have simplified this graph by drawing smooth lines between discrete points. If we had drawn the *MC* curve as a step function instead, the *MC* curve would have crossed the *ATC* curve exactly at its minimum point.)

2. Draw a correctly labeled graph showing a firm with a realistic "swoosh-shaped" *MC* curve and *ATC*, *AVC*, and *AFC* curves with their usual shapes. **(6 points)**

b. The spreading effect dominates the diminishing returns effect when average total cost is falling: the fall in *AFC* dominates the rise in *AVC* for pies 1 to 4. The diminishing returns effect dominates when average total cost is rising: the rise in *AVC* dominates the fall in *AFC* for pies 5 and 6.

c. Alicia's minimum-cost output is 4 pies; this generates the lowest average total cost, $4.28. When output is less than 4, the marginal cost of a pie is less than the average total cost of the pies already produced. So, making an additional pie lowers average total cost. For example, the marginal cost of pie 3 is $2.25, whereas the average total cost of pies 1 and 2 is $5.75. Thus, making pie 3 lowers the average total cost to $4.58, equal to $[(2 \times \$5.75) + \$2.25]/3$. When output is more than 4, the marginal cost of a pie is greater than the average total cost of the pies already produced. Consequently, making an additional pie raises average total cost. So, although the marginal cost of pie 6 is $7.59, the average total cost of pies 1 through 5 is $4.44. Making pie 6 raises average total cost to $4.96, equal to $\frac{[(5 \times \$4.44) + \$7.59]}{6}$.

Tackle the Test: Multiple-Choice Questions

1. c
2. e
3. e
4. e
5. a

Tackle the Test: Free-Response Question Rubric for FRQ 2 (6 points)

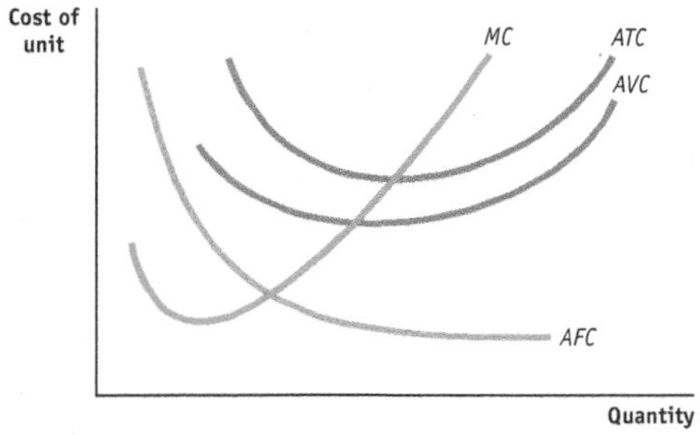

1 point: Graph labeled "Cost of unit" or "Dollars per unit" on the vertical axis and "Quantity" or "*Q*" on the horizontal axis

1 point: Swoosh-shaped *MC* curve labeled "*MC*"

1 point: U-shaped *ATC* curve labeled "*ATC*"

1 point: U-shaped *AVC* curve that is below the *ATC* curve and is labeled "*AVC*"

1 point: Downward-sloping *AFC* curve that is below the *ATC* curve and is labeled "*AFC*"

1 point: The *MC* curve intersects the minimum points of the *ATC* curve and the *AVC* curve.

PD To prepare for teaching this lesson, you may want to consult the **Module 56 Sample Lecture** in the TRM.

OPEN & CLOSE Start Here

This module focuses on costs in the long run. Make sure that students understand the difference between the short run and the long run, and also that they can switch to a long-run perspective before you start your discussion of long-run costs. Ask students if 5 years is considered the long run. Hopefully, they will respond, "It depends." If not, review the definitions of long run and short run. Review the concept of diminishing returns with students (*as more of a variable factor is added to a fixed factor, MP declines*) and that it is a short-run concept (*because there is a fixed factor*). Ask students how a firm might avoid diminishing returns, and help them see that in the LONG RUN, a firm can increase its fixed input to delay diminishing returns. Link this idea to any production activities you have done in class through a discussion of how a larger table (or whatever the fixed factor was in your activity) would have allowed students to produce more.

Martin Barraud/Getty Images

MODULE 56 Long-Run Costs and Economies of Scale

In this Module, you will learn to:

- Explain why a firm's costs may differ between the short run and the long run
- Describe how a firm can enjoy economies of scale

Up to this point, we have treated fixed cost as completely outside the control of a firm because we have focused on the short run. But all inputs are variable in the long run: this means that in the long run, even "fixed cost" may change. *In the long run, in other words, a firm's fixed cost becomes a variable it can choose.* For example, given time, Selena's Gourmet Salsas can acquire additional food-preparation equipment or dispose of some of its existing equipment. In this module, we will examine how a firm's costs behave in the short run and in the long run. We will also see that the firm will choose its fixed cost in the long run based on the level of output it expects to produce.

Short-Run Versus Long-Run Costs

AP® Exam Tip

Remember that the long run and the short run don't refer to predetermined periods of time. They are defined by the degree to which inputs are variable.

Let's begin by supposing that Selena's Gourmet Salsas is considering whether to acquire additional food-preparation equipment. Acquiring additional machinery will affect its total cost in two ways. First, the firm will have to either rent or buy the additional equipment; either way, that will mean a higher fixed cost in the short run. Second, if the workers have more equipment, they will be more productive: fewer workers will be needed to produce any given output, so the variable cost for any given output level will be reduced.

The table in **Figure 56.1** shows how acquiring an additional machine affects costs. In our original example, we assumed that Selena's Gourmet Salsas had a fixed cost of $108. The left half of the table shows variable cost as well as total cost and average total cost assuming a fixed cost of $108. The average total cost curve for this level of fixed cost is given by ATC_1 in Figure 56.1. Let's compare that to a situation in which the firm buys additional food-preparation equipment, doubling its fixed cost to $216 but reducing its variable cost at any given level of output. The right half of the table shows the firm's variable cost, total cost, and average total cost with this higher level of fixed cost. The average total cost curve corresponding to $216 in fixed cost is given by ATC_2 in Figure 56.1.

Figure 56.1 Choosing the Level of Fixed Cost for Selena's Gourmet Salsas

There is a trade-off between higher fixed cost and lower variable cost for any given output level, and vice versa. ATC_1 is the average total cost curve corresponding to a fixed cost of $108; it leads to lower fixed cost and higher variable cost. ATC_2 is the average total cost curve corresponding to a higher fixed cost of $216 but lower variable cost. At low output levels, at 4 or fewer cases of salsa per day, ATC_1 lies below ATC_2: average total cost is lower with only $108 in fixed cost. But as output goes up, average total cost is lower with the higher amount of fixed cost, $216: at more than 4 cases of salsa per day, ATC_2 lies below ATC_1.

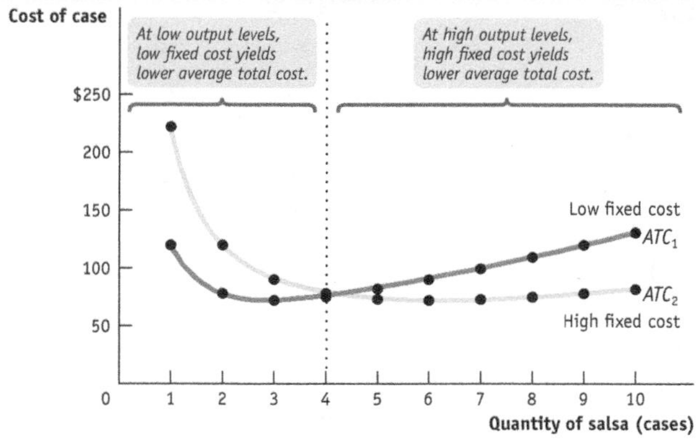

	Low fixed cost (FC = $108)			High fixed cost (FC = $216)		
Quantity of salsa (cases)	High variable cost	Total cost	Average total cost of case ATC_1	Low variable cost	Total cost	Average total cost of case ATC_2
1	$12	$120	$120.00	$6	$222	$222.00
2	48	156	78.00	24	240	120.00
3	108	216	72.00	54	270	90.00
4	192	300	75.00	96	312	78.00
5	300	408	81.60	150	366	73.20
6	432	540	90.00	216	432	72.00
7	588	696	99.43	294	510	72.86
8	768	876	109.50	384	600	75.00
9	972	1,080	120.00	486	702	78.00
10	1,200	1,308	130.80	600	816	81.60

From the figure you can see that when output is small, 4 cases of salsa per day or fewer, average total cost is smaller when Selena forgoes the additional equipment and maintains the lower fixed cost of $108: ATC_1 lies below ATC_2. For example, at 3 cases per day, average total cost is $72 without the additional machinery and $90 with the additional machinery. But as output increases beyond 4 cases per day, the firm's average total cost is lower if it acquires the additional equipment, raising its fixed cost to $216. For example, at 9 cases of salsa per day, average total cost is $120 when fixed cost is $108 but only $78 when fixed cost is $216.

Why does average total cost change like this when fixed cost increases? When output is low, the increase in fixed cost from the additional equipment outweighs the reduction in variable cost from higher worker productivity—that is, there are too few units of output over which to spread the additional fixed cost. So if Selena plans to produce 4 or fewer cases per day, she would be better off choosing the lower level of fixed cost, $108, to achieve a lower average total cost of production. When planned output is high, however, she should acquire the additional machinery.

TEACH Teach It

Help students see intuitively what is happening in Figure 56.1 before presenting the numbers in the example. Ask students when it makes more sense to use more of a fixed input (capital, e.g., equipment and machinery): When producing a low output or a high output? They should see that it makes sense to have more capital when you are producing a larger quantity. The benefit of adding more capital is that it increases the productivity of the variable input (i.e., labor productivity). Explain that with low levels of output, there are fewer workers to make more productive with the added capital. But at high levels of output, adding more capital affects a larger number of workers, so adding it has a higher benefit. You can relate this idea to producing by hand versus producing with an assembly line. It doesn't make sense to invest in an assembly line when you are only making a few units. Think of paying for an expensive assembly line and then only using it to make 3 units of output. It makes sense, though, to use an assembly line when you are producing many units. Think how difficult it would be to produce a huge quantity by hand!

FOCUS Graph It

Figure 56.1 gives numerical examples of low fixed cost and high fixed cost, low output levels and high output levels. Link the numbers in the figure to the intuitive discussion of adding capital (fixed costs) above. Ask students to find the corresponding points for 3 and 9 units of output plotted on the graphs of ATC_1 and ATC_2. Producing 3 units of output costs more ($90 vs. $72) when produced with more capital (and therefore fixed costs) because there are few workers using the added capital. Producing 9 units of output costs more ($120 vs. $78) because there are many workers using the added capital.

- When output is low, there are fewer units of output over which to spread additional fixed costs. How does the increase in fixed cost from additional equipment relate to variable cost from higher worker productivity? *The increase in FC outweighs the reduction in VC from higher worker productivity.*
- When output is high, what happens to additional costs that the firm bears? *There are more units over which to spread the additional costs, so the average costs decrease.*

In general, for each output level there is some choice of fixed cost that minimizes the firm's average total cost for that output level. So when the firm has a desired output level that it expects to maintain over time, it should choose the optimal fixed cost for that level—that is, the level of fixed cost that minimizes its average total cost.

Now that we are studying a situation in which fixed cost can change, we need to take *time* into account when discussing average total cost. All of the average total cost curves we have considered until now are defined for a given level of fixed cost—that is, they are defined for the short run, the period of time over which fixed cost doesn't vary. To reinforce that distinction, for the rest of this module we will refer to these average total cost curves as "short-run average total cost curves."

For most firms, it is realistic to assume that there are many possible choices of fixed cost, not just two. The implication: for such a firm, many possible short-run average total cost curves will exist, each corresponding to a different choice of fixed cost and so giving rise to what is called a firm's "family" of short-run average total cost curves.

At any given time, a firm will find itself on one of its short-run cost curves, the one corresponding to its current level of fixed cost; a change in output will cause it to move along that curve. If the firm expects that change in output level to be long-standing, then it is likely that the firm's current level of fixed cost is no longer optimal. Given sufficient time, it will want to adjust its fixed cost to a new level that minimizes average total cost for its new output level. For example, if Selena had been producing 2 cases of salsa per day with a fixed cost of $108 but found herself increasing her output to 8 cases per day for the foreseeable future, then in the long run she should purchase more equipment and increase her fixed cost to a level that minimizes average total cost at the 8-cases-per-day output level.

The **long-run average total cost curve** shows the relationship between output and average total cost when fixed cost has been chosen to minimize average total cost for each level of output.

Suppose we do a thought experiment and calculate the lowest possible average total cost that can be achieved for each output level if the firm were to choose its fixed cost for each output level. Economists have given this thought experiment a name: the *long-run average total cost curve.* Specifically, the **long-run average total cost curve**, or *LRATC*, is the relationship between output and average total cost when fixed cost has been chosen to minimize average total cost *for each level of output.* If there are many possible choices of fixed cost, the long-run average total cost curve will have the familiar, smooth U shape, as shown by *LRATC* in **Figure 56.2**.

Figure 56.2 Short-Run and Long-Run Average Total Cost Curves

Short-run and long-run average total cost curves differ because a firm can choose its fixed cost in the long run. If Selena has chosen the level of fixed cost that minimizes short-run average total cost at an output of 6 cases, and actually produces 6 cases, then she will be at point *C* on *LRATC* and ATC_6. But if she produces only 3 cases, she will move to point *B*. If she expects to produce only 3 cases for a long time, in the long run she will reduce her fixed cost and move to point *A* on ATC_3. Likewise, if she produces 9 cases (putting her at point *Y*) and expects to continue this for a long time, she will increase her fixed cost in the long run and move to point *X*.

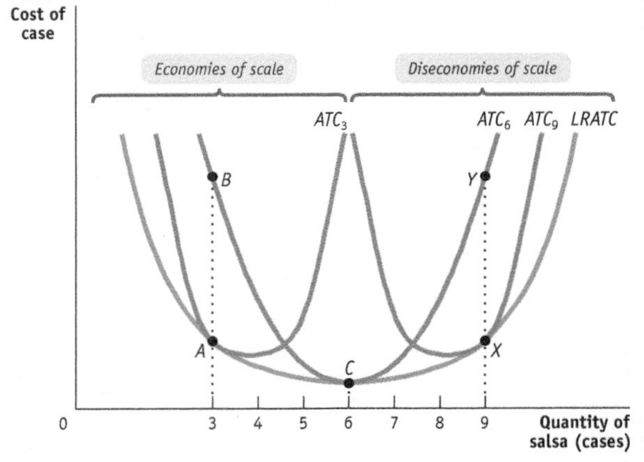

FOCUS Graph It

Figure 56.2 shows the relationship between short-run and long-run average total cost curves. In the long run, all inputs can vary, so firms must choose the level of all inputs (e.g., both capital and labor). ATC_3, ATC_6, and ATC_9 each corresponds to a different level of fixed costs (e.g., capital). In the long run, the firm will choose the level of fixed costs (capital) that minimizes the average total cost for the output level produced. That is, the firm will select ATC_3 if it produces 3 or 4 units of output, ATC_6 if it produces 5 to 7 units of output, and ATC_9 if it produces 8 or 9 units of output. The *LRATC* represents the minimum *AC* for producing each level of output, assuming the firm is using the optimal level of the input that was fixed in the short run (capital).

TEACH Teach It

Economies of scale exist when it is cheaper per unit to produce more (i.e., *AC* falls as output increases). Diseconomies of scale occur when it is more expensive per unit to produce more (i.e., *AC* rises as output increases). Economies of scale explain the "U" shape of the long-run total cost curve. Returns to scale is a long-run concept because all inputs are variable. Distinguish this from diminishing returns, the explanation for the "U"-shaped, short-run cost curves (which required a fixed input).

TEACH Teach It

Make sure students understand the explanation behind returns to scale. At first when a firm grows, there are benefits. For example, the firm can specialize, it can spread fixed costs over more output, and it can buy its inputs in bulk. However, eventually there are drawbacks to further growth. The firm becomes difficult to manage, and communication and coordination become more difficult when the firm gets very large.

FOCUS Flip It

TRM To reinforce the concepts illustrated in Figure 56.2, have students watch Jacob Clifford's video "Micro Unit 3, Question 6—Economies of Scale" (see econextras video list with hyperlinks on the bcs and TRFD). Assign **Worksheet 56.1 (Economies and Diseconomies of Scale)** from the TRM for questions relating to the video and topic.

We can now draw the distinction between the short run and the long run more fully. In the long run, when a producer has had time to choose the fixed cost appropriate for its desired level of output, that producer will be at some point on the long-run average total cost curve. But if the output level is altered, the firm will no longer be on its long-run average total cost curve and will instead be moving along its current short-run average total cost curve. It will not be on its long-run average total cost curve again until it readjusts its fixed cost for its new output level.

Figure 56.2 illustrates this point. The curve ATC_3 shows short-run average total cost if Selena has chosen the level of fixed cost that minimizes average total cost at an output of 3 cases of salsa per day. This is confirmed by the fact that at 3 cases per day, ATC_3 touches *LRATC*, the long-run average total cost curve. Similarly, ATC_6 shows short-run average total cost if Selena has chosen the level of fixed cost that minimizes average total cost if her output is 6 cases per day. It touches *LRATC* at 6 cases per day. And ATC_9 shows short-run average total cost if Selena has chosen the level of fixed cost that minimizes average total cost if her output is 9 cases per day. It touches *LRATC* at 9 cases per day.

Suppose that Selena initially chose to be on ATC_6. If she actually produces 6 cases of salsa per day, her firm will be at point *C* on both its short-run and long-run average total cost curves. Suppose, however, that Selena ends up producing only 3 cases of salsa per day. In the short run, her average total cost is indicated by point *B* on ATC_6; it is no longer on *LRATC*. If Selena had known that she would be producing only 3 cases per day, she would have been better off choosing a lower level of fixed cost, the one corresponding to ATC_3, thereby achieving a lower average total cost. Then her firm would have found itself at point *A* on the long-run average total cost curve, which lies below point *B*.

Photodisc

Suppose, conversely, that Selena ends up producing 9 cases per day even though she initially chose to be on ATC_6. In the short run her average total cost is indicated by point *Y* on ATC_6. But she would be better off purchasing more equipment and incurring a higher fixed cost in order to reduce her variable cost and move to ATC_9. This would allow her to reach point *X* on the long-run average total cost curve, which lies below *Y*. The distinction between short-run and long-run average total costs is extremely important in making sense of how real firms operate over time. A company that has to increase output suddenly to meet a surge in demand will typically find that in the short run its average total cost rises sharply because it is hard to get extra production out of existing facilities. But given time to build new factories or add machinery, short-run average total cost falls.

Returns to Scale

What determines the shape of the long-run average total cost curve? It is the influence of *scale*, the size of a firm's operations, on its long-run average total cost of production. Firms that experience *scale effects* in production find that their long-run average total cost changes substantially depending on the quantity of output they produce. There are **economies of scale** when long-run average total cost declines as output increases. As you can see in Figure 56.2, Selena's Gourmet Salsas experiences economies of scale over output levels ranging from 0 up to 6 cases of salsa per day—the output levels over which the long-run average total cost curve is declining. Economies of scale can result from **increasing returns to scale**, which exist when output increases more than in proportion to an increase in all inputs. For example, if Selena could double all of her inputs and make more than twice as much salsa, she would be experiencing increasing returns to scale. With twice the inputs (and costs) and more than twice the salsa, she would be enjoying decreasing long-run average total costs, and thus economies of scale. Increasing returns to scale therefore imply economies of scale, although economies of scale exist whenever long-run average total cost is falling, whether or not all inputs are increasing by the same proportion.

In contrast, there are **diseconomies of scale** when long-run average total cost increases as output increases. For Selena's Gourmet Salsas, decreasing returns to scale occur at output levels greater than 6 cases, the output levels over which its long-run

AP® Exam Tip

Don't mix up the concepts of diminishing returns and returns to scale. Diminishing returns is a short-run concept because at least one input is being held constant. Returns to scale is a long-run concept because all inputs are variable.

There are **economies of scale** when long-run average total cost declines as output increases.

There are **increasing returns to scale** when output increases more than in proportion to an increase in all inputs. For example, with increasing returns to scale, doubling all inputs would cause output to more than double.

There are **diseconomies of scale** when long-run average total cost increases as output increases.

FOCUS Active Learning

TRM Refer students to **Worksheet 56.2 (Returns to Scale)** from the TRM for practice with *LRATC* and economies of scale.

TEACH Teach It

Make sure students understand "returns to scale," in general, before you begin discussing the concept with them. Returns to scale refer to the change in benefits (returns) from a firm getting larger (its scale). Increasing, decreasing, and constant returns to scale are terms that identify what happens to a firm's *output* when it becomes larger (i.e., when its inputs increase by some proportion). Economies of scale identify what happens to a firm's *costs per unit* when it becomes larger. The terms *increasing returns to scale* and *economies of scale* are related—but increasing returns to scale look at output, while economies of scale look at costs.

TEACH Teach It

Increasing, decreasing, and constant returns to scale look at what happens to a firm's output when inputs increase proportionally. For example, a firm is experiencing constant returns to scale when doubling inputs doubles the firm's output. Increasing returns to scale occur when doubling inputs *more than* doubles output, and decreasing returns to scale occur when doubling inputs *less than* doubles output.

Module 56 Long-Run Costs and Economies of Scale 567

TEACH Teach It

A sunk cost has been paid and cannot be recovered. For example, buying an exercise bicycle is a fixed cost, but you can recover at least part of that cost if you resell the bicycle. A gym membership is a sunk cost because you can't recover it (e.g., resell it). In decision making, the rule is that *sunk costs don't matter.* The money you paid for the gym membership is gone and will never come back! Therefore, the membership fee shouldn't matter when you decide whether to go to the gym each day (you will have paid for the membership either way). It is sometimes difficult to apply this rule. For example, some people decide to go to the gym because, after all, they already paid for the membership. But they should make the decision to go to the gym only if $MB > MC$. They are worse off from going to the gym if they go when $MC > MB$, regardless of the membership fee. Psychology and economics are sometimes in conflict when it comes to sunk costs!

TEACH Test It

Give students the following scenario:

Last week you purchased a $50 ticket for a concert featuring your favorite band. The day of the concert, you realize that you have lost your ticket. You can purchase another ticket to the concert at the door for $50. Should you go to the concert? Explain your answer. *Students should realize that the $50 spent for the first ticket is a sunk cost and therefore doesn't matter when determining whether to go to the concert. They should go as long as $MB > MC$ for the concert, assuming nothing has changed since they bought the first ticket.*

There are **decreasing returns to scale** when output increases less than in proportion to an increase in all inputs.

There are **constant returns to scale** when output increases directly in proportion to an increase in all inputs.

AP® Exam Tip

Firms with increasing returns to scale benefit from their larger size as long-run average total cost decreases with increased output, while firms with decreasing returns to scale are hurt by their size as long-run average total cost rises with increased output.

average total cost curve is rising. Diseconomies of scale can result from **decreasing returns to scale**, which exist when output increases less than in proportion to an increase in all inputs—doubling the inputs results in less than double the output. When output increases directly in proportion to an increase in all inputs—doubling the inputs results in double the output—the firm is experiencing **constant returns to scale**.

What explains these scale effects in production? The answer ultimately lies in the firm's technology of production. Economies of scale often arise from the increased *specialization* that larger output levels allow—a larger scale of operation means that individual workers can limit themselves to more specialized tasks, becoming more skilled and efficient at doing them. Another source of economies of scale is a very large initial setup cost; in some industries—such as auto manufacturing, electricity generating, and petroleum refining—it is necessary to pay a high fixed cost in the form of plant and equipment before producing any output. A third source of economies of scale, found in certain high-tech industries such as software development, is *network externalities*, a topic covered in a later module. As we'll see when we study monopoly, increasing returns have very important implications for how firms and industries behave and interact.

Diseconomies of scale—the opposite scenario—typically arise in large firms due to problems of coordination and communication: as a firm grows in size, it becomes ever more difficult and therefore costly to communicate and to organize activities. Although economies of scale induce firms to grow larger, diseconomies of scale tend to limit their size.

Sunk Costs

To complete our discussion of costs, we need to include the concept of sunk costs. When making decisions, knowing what to ignore is important. Although we have devoted much attention to costs that should be taken into account when making a decision, some costs should be ignored when doing so. This section presents the kind of costs that people should ignore when making decisions—what economists call *sunk costs*—and explains why they should be ignored.

To gain some intuition, consider the following scenario. You own a car that is a few years old, and you have just replaced the brake pads at a cost of $250. But then you find out that the entire brake system is defective and also must be replaced. This will cost you an additional $1,500. Alternatively, you could sell the car and buy another of comparable quality, but with no brake defects, by spending an additional $1,600. What should you do: fix your old car, or sell it and buy another?

© Greatstock Photographic Library / Alamy

Some might say that you should take the latter option. After all, this line of reasoning goes, if you repair your car, you will end up having spent $1,750: $1,500 for the brake system and $250 for the brake pads. If you were instead to sell your old car and buy another, you would spend only $1,600.

However, this reasoning, although it sounds plausible, is wrong. It ignores the fact that you have *already* spent $250 on brake pads, and that $250 is *nonrecoverable*. That is, having already been spent, the $250 cannot be recouped. Therefore, it should be ignored and should have no effect on your decision whether to repair your car and keep it or not. From a rational viewpoint, the real cost at this time of repairing and keeping your car is $1,500, not $1,750. So the correct decision is to repair your car and keep it rather than spend $1,600 on a new car.

A **sunk cost** is a cost that has already been incurred and is nonrecoverable. A sunk cost should be ignored in a decision about future actions.

In this example, the $250 that has already been spent and cannot be recovered is what economists call a **sunk cost**. Sunk costs should be ignored in making decisions because they have no influence on future costs and benefits. It's like the old saying, "There's no use crying over spilled milk": once something can't be recovered, it is irrelevant in making decisions about what to do in the future. This applies equally to individuals, firms, and governments—regardless of how much has been spent on a project in the past, if the future costs exceed the future benefits, the project should not continue.

It is often psychologically hard to ignore sunk costs. And if, in fact, you haven't yet incurred the costs, then you should take them into consideration. That is, if you had

568 Section 10 Behind the Supply Curve: Profit, Production, and Costs

FYI There's No Business Like Snow Business

Anyone who has lived both in a snowy city, like Chicago, and in a city that only occasionally experiences significant snowfall, like Washington, D.C., is aware of the differences in total cost that arise from making different choices about fixed cost.

In Washington, even a minor snowfall—say, an inch or two overnight—is enough to create chaos during the next morning's commute. The same snowfall in Chicago has hardly any effect at all. The reason is not that Washingtonians are wimps and Chicagoans are made of sterner stuff; it is that Washington, where it rarely snows, has only a fraction as many snowplows and other snow-clearing equipment as cities where heavy snow is a fact of life.

In this sense Washington and Chicago are like two producers who expect to produce different levels of output, where the "output" is snow removal. Washington, which rarely has significant snow, has chosen a low level of fixed cost in the form of snow-clearing equipment. This makes sense under normal circumstances but leaves the city unprepared when major snow does fall. Chicago, which knows that it will face lots of snow, chooses to accept the higher fixed cost that leaves it in a position to respond effectively.

Thinkstock

A lesson in returns to scale: cities with higher average annual snowfall maintain larger snowplow fleets.

known at the beginning that it would cost $1,750 to repair your car, then the right choice *at that time* would have been to buy a new car for $1,600. But once you have already paid the $250 for brake pads, you should no longer include it in your decision making about your next actions. It may be hard to "let bygones be bygones," but it is the right way to make a decision.

Summing Up Costs: The Short and Long of It

If a firm is to make the best decisions about how much to produce, it has to understand how its costs relate to the quantity of output it chooses to produce. **Table 56.1** provides a quick summary of the concepts and measures of cost you have learned about.

Table 56.1 Concepts and Measures of Cost

	Measurement	Definition	Mathematical term
Short run	Fixed cost	Cost that does not depend on the quantity of output produced	*FC*
	Average fixed cost	Fixed cost per unit of output	$AFC = FC/Q$
Short run and long run	Variable cost	Cost that depends on the quantity of output produced	*VC*
	Average variable cost	Variable cost per unit of output	$AVC = VC/Q$
	Total cost	The sum of fixed cost (short run) and variable cost	$TC = FC$ (short run) $+ VC$
	Average total cost (average cost)	Total cost per unit of output	$ATC = TC/Q$
	Marginal cost	The change in total cost generated by producing one more unit of output	$MC = \Delta TC/\Delta Q$
Long run	Long-run average total cost	Average total cost when fixed cost has been chosen to minimize average total cost for each level of output	*LRATC*

TEACH Teach It

Note that Table 56.1 summarizes cost concepts and provides the definitions for short- and long-run costs.

OPEN & CLOSE Exit Slip

TRM *Please see **Exit Slip: Module 56** in the TRM for formative multiple-choice questions to ask your students before finishing your lesson. These questions will help you quickly assess whether your students have mastered the module's concepts before moving on.*

Answers to the Exit Slip Questions

1. A
2. D
3. B

Module 56 Long-Run Costs and Economies of Scale 569

MODULE 56 Review

Check Your Understanding

1. The accompanying table shows three possible combinations of fixed cost and average variable cost. For each choice, average variable cost is constant (it does not vary with the quantity of output produced).

Choice	*Fixed cost*	*Average variable cost*
1	$8,000	$1.00
2	12,000	0.75
3	24,000	0.25

   a. For each of the three choices, calculate the average total cost of producing 12,000, 22,000, and 30,000 units. For each of these quantities, which choice results in the lowest average total cost?

   b. Suppose that the firm, which has historically produced 12,000 units, experiences a sharp, permanent increase in demand that leads it to produce 22,000 units. Explain how its average total cost will change in the short run and in the long run.

   c. Explain what the firm should do instead if it believes the change in demand is temporary.

2. In each of the following cases, explain whether the firm is likely to experience economies of scale or diseconomies of scale and why.
   a. an interior design firm in which design projects are based on the expertise of the firm's owner
   b. a diamond-mining company

Tackle the Test: Multiple-Choice Questions

1. In the long run,
   a. all inputs are variable.
   b. all inputs are fixed.
   c. some inputs are variable and others are fixed.
   d. a firm will go out of business.
   e. firms increase in size.

2. Which of the following is always considered the long run?
   a. 1 month
   b. 1 year
   c. 5 years
   d. 10 years
   e. none of the above

3. Which of the following statements is generally correct?
   I. The long-run average total cost curve is U-shaped.
   II. The short-run average total cost curve is U-shaped.
   III. Firms tend to experience economies of scale at low levels of production and diseconomies of scale at high levels of production.
   a. I only
   b. II only
   c. III only
   d. I and II only
   e. I, II, and III

4. When making decisions, which of the following costs should be ignored?
   a. average costs
   b. total costs
   c. marginal costs
   d. sunk costs
   e. None of the above—no costs should be ignored.

5. Economies of scale will allow which of the following types of cities to lower their average total cost of clearing snow by investing in larger snow plow fleets? Cities with
   a. more people
   b. more existing snow plows
   c. less snowfall
   d. larger budgets
   e. more snowfall

Answers to Module 56 Review Questions

Check Your Understanding

1. a. The accompanying table shows the average total cost of producing 12,000, 22,000, and 30,000 units for each of the three choices of fixed cost. For example, if the firm makes Choice 1, the total cost of producing 12,000 units of output is $8,000 + 12,000 × $1.00 = $20,000. The average total cost of producing 12,000 units of output is therefore $20,000/12,000 = $1.67. The other average total costs are calculated similarly.

	12,000 units	22,000 units	30,000 units
Average total cost from Choice 1	$1.67	$1.36	$1.27
Average total cost from Choice 2	1.75	1.30	1.15
Average total cost from Choice 3	2.25	1.34	1.05

Thus, if the firm wanted to produce 12,000 units, it would make Choice 1 because this gives the firm the lowest average total cost. If it wanted to produce 22,000 units, it would make Choice 2. If it wanted to produce 30,000 units, it would make Choice 3.

b. Having historically produced 12,000 units, the firm would have adopted Choice 1. When producing 12,000 units, the firm would have had an average total cost of $1.67. When output jumps to 22,000 units, the firm cannot alter its choice of fixed cost in the short run, so its average total cost in the short run will be $1.36. In the long run, however, it will adopt Choice 2, making its average total cost fall to $1.30.

c. If the firm believes that the increase in demand is temporary, it should not alter its fixed cost from Choice 1 because Choice 2 generates higher average total cost as soon as output falls back to its original quantity of 12,000 units: $1.75 versus $1.67.

2. a. This firm is likely to experience diseconomies of scale. As the firm takes on more projects, the costs of communication and coordination required to implement the expertise of the firm's owner are likely to increase.

b. This firm is likely to experience economies of scale. Because diamond mining requires a large initial setup cost for excavation equipment, long-run average total cost will fall as output increases.

Tackle the Test: Multiple-Choice Questions

1. a
2. e
3. e
4. d
5. e

Tackle the Test: Free-Response Questions

1. Refer to the graph provided to answer the following questions.

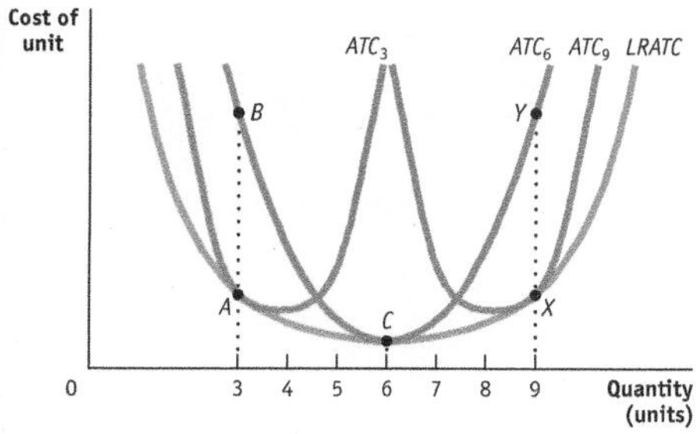

a. The same level of fixed cost that puts the firm at point *B* when the quantity is 3 minimizes short-run average total cost for what output level?

b. At an output level of 3, is the firm experiencing economies or diseconomies of scale? Explain.

c. In the long run, if the firm expects to produce an output of 9, the firm will produce on which short-run average total cost curve and at which point on the graph?

Rubric for FRQ 1 (5 points)

1 point: 6
1 point: economies of scale
1 point: Because at an output of 3, the *LRATC* is decreasing.
1 point: In the long run the firm will produce on ATC_9.
1 point: In the long run the firm will produce at point *X*.

2. Draw a correctly labeled graph showing a short-run average total cost curve and the corresponding long-run average total cost curve. On your graph, identify the areas of economies and diseconomies of scale. **(5 points)**

Tackle the Test: Free-Response Question
Rubric for FRQ 2 (5 points)

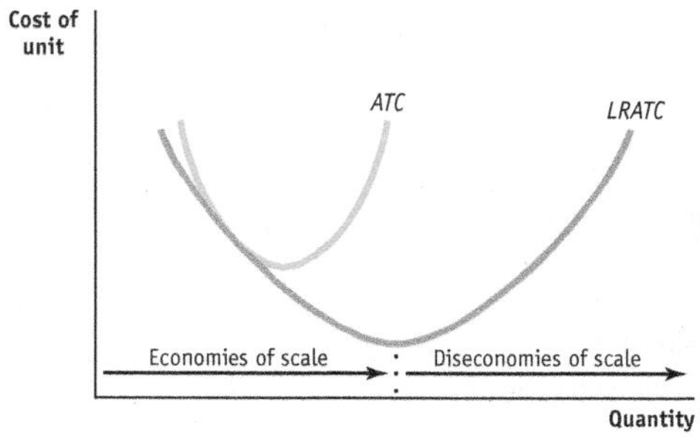

1 point: Graph with "Cost of unit" or "Dollars per unit" on the vertical axis and "Quantity" or "*Q*" on the horizontal axis

1 point: U-shaped *ATC* curve labeled "*ATC*"

1 point: U-shaped *LRATC* curve labeled "*LRATC*" that is below the *ATC* curve everywhere except at one point, at which the *LRATC* curve is tangent to the *ATC* curve

1 point: The area to the left of the minimum point of the long-run average total cost curve is labeled "economies of scale."

1 point: The area to the right of the minimum point of the long-run average total cost curve is labeled "diseconomies of scale."

Module 56 Long-Run Costs and Economies of Scale **571**

PD To prepare for teaching this lesson, you may want to consult the **Module 57 Sample Lecture** in the TRM.

OPEN & CLOSE **Start Here**

Ask students which firm(s) produce(s) each of the following:

1. the soda they drink
2. the cereal they eat
3. the music they listen to
4. the clothes they wear
5. the corn they eat
6. the cable television they watch

Students will likely list only a few soda and cereal companies (Coke/Pepsi, General Mills/Kelloggs/Post) but a large number of differentiated products (e.g., diet, caffeine-free, Sprite or Fruit Loops, Special K, Cheerios). There will be LOTS of different types of music and clothes sold by lots of different stores and bands. But students aren't likely to know (or care) who grew the corn they eat. There is only one cable company operating in most locations. Help students see that some markets have many firms and others only a few. In some markets the product is always the same, while in other markets it differs significantly between firms. The next section will develop the models economists use to study these different types of markets.

© Chris A. Crumley/Alamy

MODULE 57 Introduction to Market Structure

In this Module, you will learn to:

- Explain the meaning and dimensions of market structure
- Describe the four principal types of market structure--perfect competition, monopoly, oligopoly, and monopolistic competition

You may have noticed that this section is titled "Behind the Supply Curve," but we have yet to mention any supply curve. The reason is that we need to identify the type of market we are looking at before we can discuss the supply curve in a market. In this module we will learn about the basic characteristics of the four major types of markets in the economy.

Types of Market Structure

AP® Exam Tip

Create a chart showing the differences between the four types of market structures found in this module. These comparisons show up frequently on the AP® exam.

The real world holds a mind-boggling array of different markets. Patterns of firm behavior vary as widely as the markets themselves: in some markets firms are extremely competitive; in others, they seem to coordinate their actions to limit competition; and some markets are monopolies in which there is no competition at all. In order to develop principles and make predictions about markets and firm behavior, economists have developed four primary models of market structure: *perfect competition*, *monopoly*, *oligopoly*, and *monopolistic competition*.

This system of market structure is based on two dimensions:

- the number of firms in the market (one, few, or many)
- whether the goods offered are identical or *differentiated*

Differentiated goods are goods that are different but considered at least somewhat substitutable by consumers (think Coke versus Pepsi).

Figure 57.1 provides a simple visual summary of the types of market structure classified according to the two dimensions. A more detailed summary appears at the end of the module. In *perfect competition* many firms each sell an identical product. In *monopoly*, a single firm sells a single, undifferentiated product. In *oligopoly*, a few firms—more than one but not a large number—sell products that may be either identical or differentiated.

572 Section 10 Behind the Supply Curve: Profit, Production, and Costs

Figure 57.1 Types of Market Structure

The behavior of any given firm and the market it occupies are analyzed using one of four models of market structure—monopoly, oligopoly, perfect competition, or monopolistic competition. This system for categorizing market structure is based on two dimensions: (1) whether products are differentiated or identical and (2) the number of firms in the industry—one, a few, or many.

How many firms are there?	Are products differentiated? No	Are products differentiated? Yes
One	Monopoly	Not applicable
Few	Oligopoly	Oligopoly
Many	Perfect competition	Monopolistic competition

And in *monopolistic competition*, many firms each sell a differentiated product (think of producers of economics textbooks).

Perfect Competition

Suppose that Yves and Zoe are neighboring farmers, both of whom grow organic tomatoes. Both sell their output to the same grocery store chains that carry organic foods; so, in a real sense, Yves and Zoe compete with each other.

Does this mean that Yves should try to stop Zoe from growing tomatoes or that Yves and Zoe should form an agreement to grow fewer tomatoes? Almost certainly not: there are hundreds or thousands of organic tomato farmers (let's not forget Jennifer and Jason from Module 53!), and Yves and Zoe are competing with all those other growers as well as with each other. Because so many farmers sell organic tomatoes, if any one of them produced more or fewer, there would be no measurable effect on market prices.

When people talk about business competition, they often imagine a situation in which two or three rival firms are struggling for advantage. But economists know that when a business focuses on a few main competitors, it's actually a sign that competition is fairly limited. As the example of organic tomatoes suggests, when the number of competitors is large, it doesn't even make sense to identify rivals and engage in aggressive competition because each firm is too small within the scope of the market to make a significant difference.

We can put it another way: Yves and Zoe are *price-takers*. A **price-taking firm** is one whose actions cannot affect the market price of the good or service it sells. As a result, a price-taking firm takes the market price as given. When there is enough competition—when competition is what economists call "perfect"—then every firm is a price-taker. There is a similar definition for consumers: a **price-taking consumer** is a consumer who cannot influence the market price of the good or service by his or her actions. That is, the market price is unaffected by how much or how little of the good the consumer buys.

A **price-taking firm** is a firm whose actions have no effect on the market price of the good or service it sells.

A **price-taking consumer** is a consumer whose actions have no effect on the market price of the good or service he or she buys.

A **perfectly competitive market** is a market in which all market participants are price-takers.

Defining Perfect Competition

In a **perfectly competitive market**, all market participants, both consumers and producers, are price-takers. That is, neither consumption decisions by individual consumers nor production decisions by individual producers affect the market price of the good.

FOCUS Test It

Market structures have different characteristics based on the number of firms in the market and whether the goods are different or identical. Figure 57.1 shows the types of market structure based on these two characteristics. Review this figure with your students and then have them identify a market that represents each of the market structures:

1. Perfectly competitive *While very few markets are perfectly competitive, agricultural markets and online auction markets are good examples.*
2. Monopoly *There are also few pure monopoly markets, but regulated monopolies such as electricity and cable television are good examples.*
3. Oligopoly *There are many examples, including the markets for soft drinks, pickup trucks, or cereal.*
4. Monopolistic competition *Most retail stores your students shop at will fall into this category.*

TEACH Teach It

The difference between price taker and price maker is another characteristic of market structures. A price taker is either a firm or consumer whose actions have no effect on the market price of the good it purchases or sells. Perfectly competitive firms are price takers and a price maker is a firm that can set the price in the market.

FOCUS Active Learning

TRM To give students more practice identifying the characteristics of different market structures, assign **Worksheet 57.1 (Types of Market Structures)** from the TRM.

St. Louis Federal Reserve Bank Resources

Perfect Competition

These slides, in SMART and PowerPoint formats, present graphs related to perfect competition, the market structure in which there are many buyers and sellers of an identical product and no barriers to enter or exit the market exist. The slides illustrate firms' short-run decisions.

FOCUS Test It

Have students list the characteristics of perfect competition. *Many small buyers and sellers, price takers, standardized product, free entry and exit*

The supply and demand model is a model of a perfectly competitive market. It depends fundamentally on the assumption that no individual buyer or seller of a good, such as coffee beans or organic tomatoes, believes that it is possible to individually affect the price at which he or she can buy or sell the good. For a firm, being a price-taker means that the demand curve is a horizontal line at the market price. If the firm charged more than the market price, buyers would go to any of the many alternative sellers of the same product. And it is unnecessary to charge a lower price because, as an insignificantly small part of the perfectly competitive market, the firm can sell all that it wants at the market price.

As a general rule, consumers are indeed price-takers. Instances in which consumers are able to affect the prices they pay are rare. However, it is quite common for producers to have a significant ability to affect the prices they receive, a phenomenon we'll address later. So the model of perfect competition is appropriate for some but not all markets. An industry in which firms are price-takers is called a **perfectly competitive industry**. Clearly, some industries aren't perfectly competitive; in later modules we'll focus on industries that don't fit the perfectly competitive model.

A **perfectly competitive industry** is an industry in which firms are price-takers.

Under what circumstances will all firms be price-takers? As we'll discover next, there are two necessary conditions for a perfectly competitive industry and a third condition is often present as well.

Two Necessary Conditions for Perfect Competition

Scott Bauer/ARS/USDA

The markets for major grains, such as wheat and corn, are perfectly competitive: individual wheat and corn farmers, as well as individual buyers of wheat and corn, take market prices as given. In contrast, the markets for some of the food items made from these grains—in particular, breakfast cereals—are by no means perfectly competitive. There is intense competition among cereal brands, but not *perfect* competition. To understand the difference between the market for wheat and the market for shredded wheat cereal is to understand the two necessary conditions for perfect competition.

First, for an industry to be perfectly competitive, it must contain many firms, none of whom have a large **market share**. A firm's market share is the fraction of the total industry output accounted for by that firm's output. The distribution of market share constitutes a major difference between the grain industry and the breakfast cereal industry. There are thousands of wheat farmers, none of whom account for more than a tiny fraction of total wheat sales. The breakfast cereal industry, however, is dominated by four firms: Kellogg's, General Mills, Post, and Quaker Foods. Kellogg's alone accounts for about one-third of all cereal sales. Kellogg's executives know that if they try to sell more corn flakes, they are likely to drive down the market price of corn flakes. That is, they know that their actions influence market prices—due to their tremendous size, changes in their production will significantly affect the overall quantity supplied. It makes sense to assume that firms are price-takers only when they are numerous and relatively small.

A firm's **market share** is the fraction of the total industry output accounted for by that firm's output.

Second, an industry can be perfectly competitive only if consumers regard the products of all firms as equivalent. This clearly isn't true in the breakfast cereal market: consumers don't consider Cap'n Crunch to be a good substitute for Wheaties. As a result, the maker of Wheaties has some ability to increase its price without fear that it will lose all its customers to the maker of Cap'n Crunch. Contrast this with the case of a **standardized product**, sometimes known as a **commodity**, which is a product that consumers regard as the same good even when it comes from different firms. Because wheat is a standardized product, consumers regard the output of one wheat producer as a perfect substitute for that of another producer. This means that one farmer cannot increase the price for his or her wheat without losing all sales to other wheat farmers. So the second necessary condition for a perfectly competitive industry is that the industry output is a standardized product. (See the FYI that follows.)

A good is a **standardized product**, also known as a **commodity**, when consumers regard the products of different firms as the same good.

574 Section 10 Behind the Supply Curve: Profit, Production, and Costs

FYI What's a Standardized Product?

A perfectly competitive industry must produce a standardized product. Is it enough for the products of different firms to actually be the same? No: people must also *think* that they are the same. Many producers go to great lengths to convince consumers that they have a distinctive, or *differentiated*, product, even when they don't.

For example, consider champagne—not the super-expensive premium champagnes, but the more ordinary stuff. Most people cannot tell the difference between champagne actually produced in the Champagne region of France, where the product originated, and similar products from Spain or California. But the French government has sought and obtained legal protection for the winemakers of Champagne, ensuring that around the world only bubbly wine from that region can be called champagne. If it's from someplace else, all the seller can do is say that it was produced using the *méthode Champenoise*. This creates a differentiation in the minds of consumers and lets the champagne producers of Champagne charge higher prices.

Similarly, Korean producers of *kimchi*, the spicy fermented cabbage that is the Korean national side dish, are doing their best to convince consumers that the same product packaged by Japanese firms is just not the real thing. The purpose, of course, is to ensure higher prices for Korean *kimchi*.

So is an industry perfectly competitive if it sells products that are indistinguishable except in name but that consumers, for whatever reason, don't think are standardized? No. When it comes to defining the nature of competition, the consumer is always right.

Free Entry and Exit

All perfectly competitive industries have many firms with small market shares, producing a standardized product. Most perfectly competitive industries are also characterized by one more feature: it is easy for new firms to enter the industry or for firms that are currently in the industry to leave. That is, no obstacles in the form of government regulations or limited access to key resources prevent new firms from entering the market. And no additional costs are associated with shutting down a company and leaving the industry. Economists refer to the arrival of new firms into an industry as *entry;* they refer to the departure of firms from an industry as *exit.* When there are no obstacles to entry into or exit from an industry, we say that the industry has **free entry and exit**.

Free entry and exit is not strictly necessary for perfect competition. However, it ensures that the number of firms in an industry can adjust to changing market conditions. And, in particular, it ensures that firms in an industry cannot act to keep other firms out.

To sum up, then, perfect competition depends on two necessary conditions. First, the industry must contain many firms, each having a small market share. Second, the industry must produce a standardized product. In addition, perfectly competitive industries are normally characterized by free entry and exit.

An industry has **free entry and exit** when new firms can easily enter into the industry and existing firms can easily leave the industry.

AP® Exam Tip

A perfectly competitive firm has a very small market share because it is easy for competing firms to enter into the industry.

Monopoly

The De Beers monopoly of South Africa was created in the 1880s by Cecil Rhodes, a British businessman. By 1880, mines in South Africa already dominated the world's supply of diamonds. However, there were many mining companies, all competing with each other. During the 1880s Rhodes bought the great majority of those mines and consolidated them into a single company, De Beers. By 1889, De Beers controlled almost all of the world's diamond production.

In other words, De Beers became a *monopolist.* But what does it mean to be a monopolist? And what do monopolists do?

Paul Katz/Digital Vision/Getty Images

Defining Monopoly

As we mentioned earlier, the supply and demand model of a market is not universally valid. Instead, it's a model of perfect competition, which is only one of several types of market structure. A market will be perfectly competitive only if there are many firms, all

FOCUS Test It

Have students identify the characteristics of monopoly markets. *One producer, the good has no close substitutes, there are barriers to entry*

TEACH Connect It

A "natural" monopoly exists when economies of scale, discussed in the previous module, provide a large cost advantage to a single firm that produces all of an industry's output. Remind students what they already know about economies of scale, and discuss what they learned about the meaning of economies of scale in terms of the optimal size of the firm (*one large monopoly has lower per unit costs*). Foreshadow the discussion of government policy toward natural monopoly in later modules.

St. Louis Federal Reserve Bank Resources

Monopoly

These slides, in SMART, PowerPoint, and pdf formats, present graphs related to monopoly, the market structure in which there is only one producer of a good or service and high barriers to entry exist. The slides illustrate firms' short-run decisions.

TEACH Teach It

Ask students to provide examples of each type of barrier to entry; then discuss them. DeBeers diamonds are an example of a monopoly due to control of a scarce resource or input (it owns the diamonds). Electric companies are examples of monopolies due to economies of scale (it is cheaper per unit to produce electricity with large power plants than with lots of little hamsters on wheels). High-tech firms often have monopolies (at least for a short time) due to technological superiority. Apple's iPhone might have been an example of this. A patent gives a drug company a monopoly on a pharmaceutical drug, as it once gave Xerox a monopoly on copy machines.

of which produce the same good. Monopoly is the most extreme departure from perfect competition.

A **monopolist** is a firm that is the only producer of a good that has no close substitutes. An industry controlled by a monopolist is known as a **monopoly**.

> A **monopolist** is the only producer of a good that has no close substitutes. An industry controlled by a monopolist is known as a **monopoly**.

In practice, true monopolies are hard to find in the modern American economy, partly because of legal obstacles. A contemporary entrepreneur who tried to consolidate all the firms in an industry the way Rhodes did would soon find himself in court, accused of breaking *antitrust* laws, which are intended to prevent monopolies from emerging. However, monopolies do play an important role in some sectors of the economy.

Why Do Monopolies Exist?

> **AP® Exam Tip**
>
> Barriers to entry allow a monopoly to persist. Be prepared to identify the types of barriers that create a lasting monopoly.

A monopolist making profits will not go unnoticed by others. (Recall that this is "economic profit," revenue over and above the opportunity costs of the firm's resources.) But won't other firms crash the party, grab a piece of the action, and drive down prices and profits in the long run? If possible, yes, they will. For a profitable monopoly to persist, something must keep others from going into the same business; that "something" is known as a **barrier to entry**. There are four principal types of barriers to entry: control of a scarce resource or input, economies of scale, technological superiority, and government-created barriers.

> To earn economic profits, a monopolist must be protected by a **barrier to entry**—something that prevents other firms from entering the industry.

Control of a Scarce Resource or Input A monopolist that controls a resource or input crucial to an industry can prevent other firms from entering its market. Cecil Rhodes made De Beers into a monopolist by establishing control over the mines that produced the great bulk of the world's diamonds.

Economies of Scale Many Americans have natural gas piped into their homes for cooking and heating. Invariably, the local gas company is a monopolist. But why don't rival companies compete to provide gas?

In the early nineteenth century, when the gas industry was just starting up, companies did compete for local customers. But this competition didn't last long; soon local gas companies became monopolists in almost every town because of the large fixed cost of providing a town with gas lines. The cost of laying gas lines didn't depend on how much gas a company sold, so a firm with a larger volume of sales had a cost advantage: because it was able to spread the fixed cost over a larger volume, it had a lower average total cost than smaller firms.

The natural gas industry is one in which average total cost falls as output increases, resulting in economies of scale and encouraging firms to grow larger. In an industry characterized by economies of scale, larger firms are more profitable and drive out smaller ones. For the same reason, established firms have a cost advantage over any potential entrant—a potent barrier to entry. So economies of scale can both give rise to and sustain a monopoly.

A monopoly created and sustained by economies of scale is called a **natural monopoly**. The defining characteristic of a natural monopoly is that it possesses economies of scale over the range of output that is relevant for the industry. The source of this condition is large fixed costs: when large fixed costs are required to operate, a given quantity of output is produced at lower average total cost by one large firm than by two or more smaller firms.

> A **natural monopoly** exists when economies of scale provide a large cost advantage to a single firm that produces all of an industry's output.

The most visible natural monopolies in the modern economy are local utilities—water, gas, electricity, local landline phone service, and, in most locations, cable television. As we'll see later, natural monopolies pose a special challenge to public policy.

Technological Superiority A firm that maintains a consistent technological advantage over potential competitors can establish itself as a monopolist. For example, from the 1970s through the 1990s, the chip manufacturer Intel was able to maintain a consistent advantage over potential competitors in both the design and production of microprocessors, the chips that run computers. But technological superiority is typically

576 Section 10 Behind the Supply Curve: Profit, Production, and Costs

not a barrier to entry over the longer term: over time competitors will invest in upgrading their technology to match that of the technology leader. In fact, in the last few years Intel found its technological superiority eroded by a competitor, Advanced Micro Devices (also known as AMD), which now produces chips approximately as fast and as powerful as Intel chips.

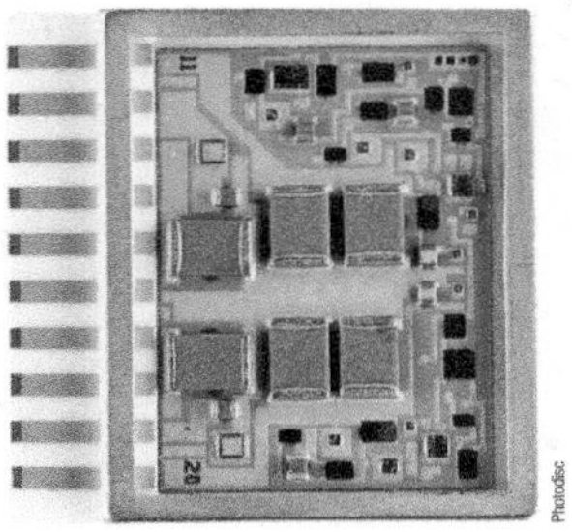

We should note, however, that in certain high-tech industries, technological superiority is not a guarantee of success against competitors. Some high-tech industries are characterized by *network externalities*, a condition that arises when the value of a good to a consumer rises as the number of other people who also use the good rises. In these industries, the firm possessing the largest network—the largest number of consumers currently using its product—has an advantage over its competitors in attracting new customers, an advantage that may allow it to become a monopolist. Microsoft is often cited as an example of a company with a technologically inferior product—its computer operating system—that grew into a monopolist through the phenomenon of network externalities.

Government-Created Barriers In 1998 the pharmaceutical company Merck introduced Propecia, a drug effective against baldness. Despite the fact that Propecia was very profitable and other drug companies had the know-how to produce it, no other firms challenged Merck's monopoly. That's because the U.S. government had given Merck the sole legal right to produce the drug in the United States. Propecia is an example of a monopoly protected by government-created barriers.

The most important legally created monopolies today arise from *patents* and *copyrights*. A **patent** gives an inventor the sole right to make, use, or sell that invention for a period that in most countries lasts between 16 and 20 years. Patents are given to the creators of new products, such as drugs or mechanical devices. Similarly, a **copyright** gives the creator of a literary or artistic work the sole right to profit from that work, usually for a period equal to the creator's lifetime plus 70 years.

A **patent** gives an inventor a temporary monopoly in the use or sale of an invention.

A **copyright** gives the creator of a literary or artistic work the sole right to profit from that work for a specified period of time.

The justification for patents and copyrights is a matter of incentives. If inventors were not protected by patents, they would gain little reward from their efforts: as soon as a valuable invention was made public, others would copy it and sell products based on it. And if inventors could not expect to profit from their inventions, then there would be no incentive to incur the costs of invention in the first place. Likewise for the creators of literary or artistic works. So the law allows a monopoly to exist temporarily by granting property rights that encourage invention and creation. Patents and copyrights are temporary because the law strikes a compromise. The higher price for the good that holds while the legal protection is in effect compensates inventors for the cost of invention; conversely, the lower price that results once the legal protection lapses benefits consumers.

Because the lifetime of the temporary monopoly cannot be tailored to specific cases, this system is imperfect and leads to some missed opportunities. In some cases there can be significant welfare issues. For example, the violation of American drug patents by pharmaceutical companies in poor countries has been a major source of controversy, pitting the needs of poor patients who cannot afford to pay retail drug prices against the interests of drug manufacturers who have incurred high research costs to discover these drugs. To solve this problem, some American drug companies and poor countries have negotiated deals in which the patents are honored but the American companies sell their drugs at deeply discounted prices. (This is an example of *price discrimination*, which we'll learn more about later.)

Oligopoly

An industry with only a few firms is known as an **oligopoly**; a producer in such an industry is known as an **oligopolist**.

An **oligopoly** is an industry with only a small number of firms. A producer in such an industry is known as an **oligopolist**.

Oligopolists compete with each other for sales. But oligopolists aren't like producers in a perfectly competitive industry, who take the market as given. Oligopolists know

Module 57 Introduction to Market Structure 577

TEACH **Teach It**

Imperfect competition describes markets that fall between perfect competition and monopoly. They are oligopoly and monopolistic competition.

When no one firm has a monopoly, but producers nonetheless realize that they can affect market prices, an industry is characterized by **imperfect competition**.

their decisions about how much to produce will affect the market price. That is, like monopolists, oligopolists have some *market power*. Economists refer to a situation in which firms compete but also possess market power—which enables them to affect market prices—as **imperfect competition**. There are two important forms of imperfect competition: oligopoly and *monopolistic competition*. Of these, oligopoly is probably the more important in practice.

Many familiar goods and services are supplied by only a few competing sellers, which means the industries in question are oligopolies. For example, most air routes are served by only two or three airlines: in recent years, regularly scheduled shuttle service between New York and either Boston or Washington, D.C., has been provided only by Delta and US Airways. Three firms—Chiquita, Dole, and Del Monte, which own huge banana plantations in Central America—control 63% of world banana exports. Most cola beverages are sold by Coca-Cola and Pepsi. This list could go on for many pages.

Photodisc

It's important to realize that an oligopoly isn't necessarily made up of large firms. What matters isn't size per se; the question is how many competitors there are. When a small town has only two grocery stores, grocery service there is just as much an oligopoly as air shuttle service between New York and Washington.

Why are oligopolies so prevalent? Essentially, an oligopoly is the result of the same factors that sometimes produce a monopoly, but in somewhat weaker form. Probably the most important source of oligopolies is the existence of economies of scale, which give bigger firms a cost advantage over smaller ones. When these effects are very strong, as we have seen, they lead to a monopoly; when they are not that strong, they lead to an industry with a small number of firms. For example, larger grocery stores typically have lower costs than smaller stores. But the advantages of large scale taper off once grocery stores are reasonably large, which is why two or three stores often survive in small towns.

Is It an Oligopoly or Not?

In practice, it is not always easy to determine an industry's market structure just by looking at the number of sellers. Many oligopolistic industries contain a number of small "niche" firms, which don't really compete with the major players. For example, the U.S. airline industry includes a number of regional airlines such as New Mexico Airlines, which flies propeller planes between Albuquerque and Carlsbad, New Mexico; if you count these carriers, the U.S. airline industry contains nearly one hundred firms, which doesn't sound like competition among a small group. But there are only a handful of national competitors like Delta and United, and on many routes, as we've seen, there are only two or three competitors.

Concentration ratios measure the percentage of industry sales accounted for by the "X" largest firms, for example the four-firm concentration ratio or the eight-firm concentration ratio.

To get a better picture of market structure, economists often use two measures of market power: **concentration ratios** and the *Herfindahl–Hirschman Index*. Concentration ratios measure the percentage of industry sales accounted for by the "X" largest firms, where "X" can equal any number of firms. For example, the four-firm concentration ratio is the percentage of sales accounted for by the four largest firms and the eight-firm concentration ratio is the percentage of industry sales accounted for by the eight largest firms. If the largest four firms accounted for 25%, 20%, 15%, and10% of industry sales, then the four-firm concentration ratio would equal 70 (25+20+15+10). And if the next largest four firms in that industry accounted for 9%, 8%, 6%, and 2% of sales, the eight-firm concentration ratio would equal 95 (70+9+8+6+2). The four- and eight-firm concentration ratios are the most commonly used. A higher concentration ratio signals that a market is more concentrated and therefore is more likely to be an oligopoly.

Herfindahl-Hirschman Index, or HHI, is the square of each firm's share of market sales summed over the industry. It gives a picture of the industry market structure.

Another measure of market concentration is the **Herfindahl-Hirschman index**, or HHI. The HHI for an industry is the square of each firm's share of market sales summed over the firms in the industry. Unlike concentration ratios, the HHI takes into account the distribution of market sales among the top firms by squaring each firm's market share, thereby giving more weight to larger firms. For example, if an industry contains only 3 firms and their market shares are 60%, 25%, and 15%, then the HHI for the industry is:

$$HHI = 60^2 + 25^2 + 15^2 = 4{,}450$$

By squaring each market share, the HHI calculation produces numbers that are much larger when a larger share of an industry output is dominated by fewer firms. This is confirmed by the data in **Table 57.1**. Here, the indices for industries dominated by a small number of firms, like the personal computer operating systems industry or the wide-body aircraft industry, are many times larger than the index for the retail grocery industry, which has numerous firms of approximately equal size.

AP® Exam Tip

You may need to interpret Herfindahl-Hirschman Index numbers on the AP® exam.

Table 57.1 The HHI for Some Oligopolistic Industries

Industry	HHI	Largest firms
PC operating systems	9,182	Microsoft, Linux
Wide-body aircraft	5,098	Boeing, Airbus
Diamond mining	2,338	De Beers, Alrosa, Rio Tinto
Automobiles	1,432	GM, Ford, Chrysler, Toyota, Honda, Nissan, VW
Movie distributors	1,096	Buena Vista, Sony Pictures, 20th Century Fox, Warner Bros., Universal, Paramount, Lionsgate
Internet service providers	750	SBC, Comcast, AOL, Verizon, Road Runner, Earthlink, Charter, Qwest
Retail grocers	321	Walmart, Kroger, Sears, Target, Costco, Walgreens, Ahold, Albertsons

Sources: Canadian Government; Diamond Facts 2006; www.w3counter.com; Planet retail; Autodata; Reuters; ISP Planet; Swivel. Data cover 2006–2007.

Monopolistic Competition

Leo manages the Wonderful Wok stand in the food court of a big shopping mall. He offers the only Chinese food there, but there are more than a dozen alternatives, from Bodacious Burgers to Pizza Paradise. When deciding what to charge for a meal, Leo knows that he must take those alternatives into account: even people who normally prefer stir-fry won't order a $15 lunch from Leo when they can get a burger, fries, and drink for $4.

But Leo also knows that he won't lose all his business even if his lunches cost a bit more than the alternatives. Chinese food isn't the same thing as burgers or pizza. Some people will really be in the mood for Chinese that day, and they will buy from Leo even if they could have dined more cheaply on burgers. Of course, the reverse is also true: even if Chinese is a bit cheaper, some people will choose burgers instead. In other words, Leo does have some market power: he has *some* ability to set his own price.

So how would you describe Leo's situation? He definitely isn't a price-taker, so he isn't in a situation of perfect competition. But you wouldn't exactly call him a monopolist, either. Although he's the only seller of Chinese food in that food court, he does face competition from other food vendors.

Nick Fraser/Alamy

A restaurant in a food court is not a perfect competitor, a monopolist, or even an oligopolist. The many firms serving differentiated products in an industry with free entry satisfy the recipe for monopolistic competition.

FOCUS In the News

Students will relate to this article about cloud computing (http://www.forbes.com/sites/joemckendrick/2013/07/11/cloud-computing-market-may-become-an-oligopoly-of-high-volume-vendors/). You will like the way it immediately defines oligopoly and then explores how cloud computing may become a market for oligopolists.

Ask your class the following questions:

1. What does the author suggest the firms will do to avoid the high start-up costs? *Developers will not build and run their own data centers. Instead, they will lease capacity from the big vendors. This action reduces one of the barriers to entry.*

2. How will the pricing model for cloud computing relate to supply and demand? *High capacity in data centers will increase prices, while idle capacity will lead to lower prices.*

TEACH Teach It

Have students provide an example of a firm and explain how it exhibits each of the characteristics of monopolistic competition:

- There are a large number of competing firms.
- Products are differentiated on the basis of styles, locations, or level of quality.
- No barriers to entry exist.

Module 57 Introduction to Market Structure 579

FOCUS Active Learning

Have students watch Dr. Mary McGlasson's video "Episode 25: Market Structures" (see econextras video list with hyperlinks on the bcs and TRFD).

1. Which is the most complicated market structure to operate in and what is one reason why? *Oligopoly, relies on mutual interdependence*

2. Which market structure has no ability to drive price and which has complete ability to set price? *Perfectly competitive, monopoly*

FOCUS Active Learning

As an alternative, you may want to watch the Jacob Clifford video "Micro 3.12 Four Market Structures Simulation for AP® Economics" (see econextras video list with hyperlinks on the bcs and TRFD) for a clever simulation on market structures. The game divides the class into four groups that act as the four market structures. Each group is asked to determine a price, and the discussion follows. It is a visual look at how to play a game in class and debrief the class at its conclusion.

FOCUS Active Learning

TRM Assign **Worksheet 57.2 (Questions about Market Structures)** from the TRM, so students can practice their knowledge on the introduction to market structures.

Monopolistic competition is a market structure in which there are many competing firms in an industry, each firm sells a differentiated product, and there is free entry into and exit from the industry in the long run.

AP® Exam Tip

Don't confuse monopolistic competition and monopoly or perfect competition. Monopolistic competition has low barriers to entry, unlike a monopoly, and a differentiated product, unlike a perfectly competitive firm.

Yet it would also be wrong to call him an oligopolist. Oligopoly, remember, involves competition among a small number of interdependent firms in an industry protected by some—albeit limited—barriers to entry and whose profits are highly interdependent. Because of this interdependence, oligopolists have an incentive to collude, tacitly or explicitly. But in Leo's case there are *lots* of vendors in the shopping mall, too many to make tacit collusion feasible.

Economists describe Leo's situation as one of **monopolistic competition**. Monopolistic competition is particularly common in service industries such as the restaurant and gas station industries, but it also exists in some manufacturing industries. It involves three conditions:

- a large number of competing firms,
- differentiated products, and
- free entry into and exit from the industry in the long run.

In a monopolistically competitive industry, each producer has some ability to set the price of her differentiated product. But exactly how high she can set it is limited by the competition she faces from other existing and potential firms that produce close, but not identical, products.

Defining Monopolistic Competition

Large Numbers In a monopolistically competitive industry there are many firms. Such an industry does not look either like a monopoly, where the firm faces no competition, or like an oligopoly, where each firm has only a few rivals. Instead, each seller has many competitors. For example, there are many vendors in a big food court, many gas stations along a major highway, and many hotels at a popular beach resort.

Differentiated Products In a monopolistically competitive industry, each firm has a product that consumers view as somewhat distinct from the products of competing firms. Such product differentiation can come in the form of different styles or types, different locations, or different levels of quality. At the same time, though, consumers see these competing products as close substitutes. If Leo's food court contained 15 vendors selling exactly the same kind and quality of food, there would be perfect competition: any seller who tried to charge a higher price would have no customers. But suppose that Wonderful Wok is the only Chinese food vendor, Bodacious Burgers is the only hamburger stand, and so on. The result of this differentiation is that each vendor has some ability to set his or her own price: each firm has some—albeit limited—market power.

Free Entry and Exit in the Long Run In monopolistically competitive industries, new firms, with their own distinct products, can enter the industry freely in the long run. For example, other food vendors would open outlets in the food court if they thought it would be profitable to do so. In addition, firms will exit the industry if they find they are not covering their costs in the long run.

Monopolistic competition, then, differs from the three market structures we have examined so far. It's not the same as perfect competition: firms have some power to set prices. It's not pure monopoly: firms face some competition. And it's not the same as oligopoly: there are many firms and free entry, which eliminates the potential for collusion that is so important in oligopoly. As we'll see in Modules 66 and 67, competition among the sellers of differentiated products is the key to understanding how monopolistic competition works.

Table 57.2 summarizes the characteristics of each market structure.

Now that we have introduced the idea of market structure and presented the four principal models of market structure, we can proceed in the next two sections to use the cost curves we have developed to build each of the four market structure models. These models will allow us to explain and predict firm behavior (e.g., price and quantity determination) and analyze individual markets.

580 Section 10 Behind the Supply Curve: Profit, Production, and Costs

St. Louis Federal Reserve Bank Resources

Monopolistic Competition

These slides, in SMART and PowerPoint formats, present graphs related to monopolistic competition, the market structure in which there are many firms that produce similar, but not identical, products and few barriers to entry exist. The slides illustrate firms' short-run decisions.

Table 57.2 Market Structure

Characteristic	Perfect Competition	Monopolistic Competition	Oligopoly	Monopoly
Number of firms	Many	Many	Few	One
Product differentiation	No	Yes	Yes or No	No
Control over price	None	Within narrow limits	Varies, depending on the degree of mutual interdependence and collusion	Considerable, limited by consumers' willingness to pay
Barriers to entry	None	Few if any	Considerable	Prohibitive
Example	Agriculture	Restaurants	Airlines	Utilities

MODULE 57 Review

Check Your Understanding

1. In each of the following situations, what type of market structure do you think the industry represents?
   a. There are three producers of aluminum in the world, a good sold in many places.
   b. There are thousands of farms that produce indistinguishable soybeans, a commodity sold to thousands of buyers.
   c. Many designers sell high-fashion clothes. Each designer has a distinctive style and a somewhat loyal clientele.
   d. A small town in the middle of Alaska has one bicycle shop.

Tackle the Test: Multiple-Choice Questions

1. Which of the following is true for a perfectly competitive industry?
   a. There are many firms, each with a large market share.
   b. The firms in the industry produce a standardized product.
   c. There are barriers to entry.
   d. There are barriers to exit.
   e. There are a few firms, each with a small market share.
2. Which of the following is true for a monopoly?
   I. There is only one firm.
   II. The firm produces a product with many close substitutes.
   III. The industry has free entry and exit.
   a. I only
   b. II only
   c. III only
   d. I and II only
   e. I, II, and III
3. Which of the following is true for an oligopoly?
   I. There are a few firms, each with a large market share.
   II. The firms in the industry are interdependent.
   III. The industry experiences diseconomies of scale.
   a. I only
   b. II only
   c. III only
   d. I and II only
   e. I, II, and III
4. Which of the following is true for a monopolistically competitive industry?
   I. There are many firms, each with a small market share.
   II. The firms in the industry produce a standardized product.
   III. Firms are price-takers.
   a. I only
   b. II only
   c. III only
   d. I and II only
   e. I, II, and III
5. Which of the following is an example of differentiated products?
   a. Coke and Pepsi
   b. automobiles and bicycles
   c. trucks and gasoline
   d. stocks and bonds
   e. gold and silver

OPEN & CLOSE Exit Slip

TRM *Please see* ***Exit Slip: Module 57*** *in the TRM for formative multiple-choice questions to ask your students before finishing your lesson. These questions will help you quickly assess whether your students have mastered the module's concepts before moving on.*

Answers to the Exit Slip Questions

1. D
2. B
3. E

Answers to Module 57 Review Questions

Check Your Understanding

1. a. oligopoly
   b. perfect competition
   c. monopolistic competition
   d. monopoly

Tackle the Test: Multiple-Choice Questions

1. b
2. a
3. d
4. a
5. a

Tackle the Test: Free-Response Question Rubric for FRQ 2 (3 points)

1 point: A graph with "Price," "*P*," or "Dollars per unit" on the vertical axis and "Quantity" or "*Q*" on the horizontal axis

1 point: A horizontal demand curve at a height of $10

1 point: $10

FOCUS Flip It

Encourage your students to watch the **Section 10 Review Video**, which was created as a special student review tool and is linked into the e-Book or can be found on the book's companion website.

Tackle the Test: Free-Response Questions

1. For each of the following characteristics, indicate which market structure(s) exhibit that characteristic.
   a. many sellers
   b. price-takers
   c. barriers to entry
   d. differentiated product

Rubric for FRQ 1 (7 points)

a. **1 point:** perfect competition
   1 point: monopolistic competition
b. **1 point:** perfect competition
c. **1 point:** monopoly
   1 point: oligopoly
d. **1 point:** oligopoly
   1 point: monopolistic competition

2. a. Draw a correctly labeled graph of a perfectly competitive firm's demand curve if the market price is $10.
   b. What does the firm's marginal revenue equal any time it sells one more unit of its output?
   (3 points)

SECTION 10 Review

Section 10 Review Video

Module 52

1. The cost of using a resource for a particular activity is the opportunity cost of that resource. Some opportunity costs are **explicit costs**; they involve a direct payment of cash. Other opportunity costs, however, are **implicit costs**; they involve no outlay of money but represent the inflows of cash that are forgone. Both explicit and implicit costs should be taken into account when making decisions. Firms use capital and their owners' time, so firms should base decisions on **economic profit**, which takes into account implicit costs such as the opportunity cost of the owners' time and the **implicit cost of capital**. **Accounting profit**, which firms calculate for the purposes of taxes and public reporting, is often considerably larger than economic profit because it includes only explicit costs and depreciation, not implicit costs. Finally, **normal profit** is a term used to describe an economic profit equal to zero—a profit just high enough to justify the use of resources in an activity.

Module 53

2. A producer chooses output according to the **optimal output rule**: produce the quantity at which marginal revenue equals marginal cost. The **marginal revenue curve** shows the **marginal revenue** for each unit; the **marginal cost curve** shows the marginal cost for each unit. More generally, the **principle of marginal analysis** suggests that every activity should continue until marginal benefit equals marginal cost.

Module 54

3. The relationship between inputs and output is represented by a firm's **production function**. In the **short run**, the quantity of a **fixed input** cannot be varied but the quantity of a **variable input**, by definition, can. In the **long run**, the quantities of all inputs can be varied. For a given amount of the fixed input, the **total product curve** shows how the quantity of output changes as the quantity of the variable input changes. The **marginal product** of an input is the increase in output that results from using one more unit of that input.
4. There are **diminishing returns to an input** when its marginal product declines as more of the input is used, holding the quantity of all other inputs fixed.

582 Section 10 Behind the Supply Curve: Profit, Production, and Costs

Module 55

5. **Total cost**, represented by the **total cost curve**, is equal to the sum of **fixed cost**, which does not depend on output, and **variable cost**, which does depend on output. Due to diminishing returns, marginal cost, the increase in total cost generated by producing one more unit of output, normally increases as output increases.
6. **Average total cost** (also known as **average cost**) is the total cost divided by the quantity of output. Economists believe that **U-shaped average total cost curves** are typical because average total cost consists of two parts: **average fixed cost**, which falls when output increases (the spreading effect), and **average variable cost**, which rises with output (the diminishing returns effect).
7. When average total cost is U-shaped, the bottom of the U is the level of output at which average total cost is minimized, the point of **minimum-cost output**. This is also the point at which the marginal cost curve crosses the average total cost curve from below. Due to gains from specialization, the marginal cost curve may slope downward initially before sloping upward, giving it a "swoosh" shape.
8. The **average product** of an input is the total product divided by the quantity of the input, and the **average product curve** shows the relationship between the average product and the quantity of the input. When labor is the only variable input and the wage is constant, average variable cost falls when average product rises, and average variable cost rises when average product falls. Likewise, marginal cost rises when marginal product falls and vice versa.

Module 56

9. In the long run, a firm can change its fixed input and its level of fixed cost. By accepting higher fixed cost, a firm can lower its variable cost for any given output level, and vice versa. The **long-run average total cost curve** shows the relationship between output and average total cost when fixed cost has been chosen to minimize average total cost at each level of output. A firm moves along its short-run average total cost curve as it changes the quantity of output, and it returns to a point on both its short-run and long-run average total cost curves once it has adjusted fixed cost to its new output level.
10. As output increases, there are **economies of scale** if long-run average total cost decreases and **diseconomies of scale** if long-run average total cost increases. As all inputs are increased by the same proportion, there are **increasing returns to scale** if output increases by a larger proportion than the inputs; **decreasing returns to scale** if output increases by a smaller proportion; and **constant returns to scale** if output increases by the same proportion.
11. **Sunk costs** are expenditures that have already been made and cannot be recovered. Sunk costs should be ignored in making decisions about future actions because what is important is a comparison of future costs and future benefits.

Module 57

12. There are four main types of market structure based on the number of firms in the industry and product differentiation: perfect competition, monopoly, oligopoly, and monopolistic competition.
13. A **monopolist** is a producer who is the sole supplier of a good without close substitutes. An industry controlled by a monopolist is a **monopoly**.
14. To persist, a monopoly must be protected by a **barrier to entry**. This can take the form of control of a natural resource or input, increasing returns to scale that give rise to a **natural monopoly**, technological superiority, or government rules that prevent entry by other firms, such as **patents** or **copyrights**.
15. In a **perfectly competitive market** all firms are **price-taking firms** and all consumers are **price-taking consumers**—no one's actions can influence the market price. Consumers are normally price-takers, but firms often are not. In a **perfectly competitive industry**, every firm in the industry is a price-taker.
16. There are two necessary conditions for a perfectly competitive industry: there are many firms, none of which has a large **market share**, and the industry produces a **standardized product** or **commodity**—goods that consumers regard as equivalent. A third condition is often satisfied as well: **free entry and exit** into and from the industry.

17. Many industries are **oligopolies**, in which there are only a few sellers, known as **oligopolists**. Oligopolies exist for more or less the same reasons that monopolies exist, but in weaker form. They are characterized by **imperfect competition**: firms compete but possess some market power.

18. **Monopolistic competition** is a market structure in which there are many competing firms, each producing a differentiated product, and there is free entry and exit in the long run. Product differentiation takes three main forms: by style or type, by location, and by quality. The extent of imperfect competition can be measured by the **concentration ratio**, or the **Herfindahl–Hirschman Index**.

Key Terms

Explicit cost, p. 534
Implicit cost, p. 534
Accounting profit, p. 534
Economic profit, p. 535
Implicit cost of capital, p. 535
Normal profit, p. 536
Principle of marginal analysis, p. 540
Marginal revenue, p. 540
Optimal output rule, p. 540
Marginal cost curve, p. 541
Marginal revenue curve, p. 541
Production function, p. 545
Fixed input, p. 545
Variable input, p. 546
Long run, p. 546
Short run, p. 546
Total product curve, p. 547
Marginal product, p. 547
Diminishing returns to an input, p. 548
Fixed cost, p. 552
Variable cost, p. 553
Total cost, p. 553
Total cost curve, p. 554
Average total cost, p. 556
Average cost, p. 556
U-shaped average total cost curve, p. 556
Average fixed cost, p. 556
Average variable cost, p. 557
Minimum-cost output, p. 559
Average product, p. 562
Average product curve, p. 562
Long-run average total cost curve, p. 566
Economies of scale, p. 567
Increasing returns to scale, p. 567
Diseconomies of scale, p. 567
Decreasing returns to scale, p. 568
Constant returns to scale, p. 568
Sunk cost, p. 568
Price-taking firm, p. 573
Price-taking consumer, p. 573
Perfectly competitive market, p. 573
Perfectly competitive industry, p. 574
Market share, p. 574
Standardized product, p. 574
Commodity, p. 574
Free entry and exit, p. 575
Monopolist, p. 576
Monopoly, p. 576
Barrier to entry, p. 576
Natural monopoly, p. 576
Patent, p. 577
Copyright, p. 577
Oligopoly, p. 577
Oligopolist, p. 577
Imperfect competition, p. 578
Concentration ratios, p. 578
Herfindahl–Hirschman Index, p. 578
Monopolistic competition, p. 580

Answers to Section 10 AP® Exam Practice Questions

Multiple-Choice Questions

1. d
2. c
3. a

AP® Exam Practice Questions

Multiple-Choice Questions

1. Consider the data about the cost of each year of college in the table below:

Opportunity Cost of a Year of College

Explicit cost		Implicit cost	
Tuition	$17,000	Forgone salary	$35,000
Books and supplies	1,000		
Computer	1,500		
Total explicit cost	19,500	Total implicit cost	35,000

Total opportunity cost = Total explicit cost + Total implicit cost = $54,500

A rational person would attend another year of college if the additional income expected plus the value of improved quality of life were worth at least

a. $17,000.
b. $19,500.
c. $35,000.
d. $54,500.
e. $89,500.

2. Comparing accounting profit to economic profit, accounting profit can
a. only be greater than economic profit.
b. only be less than economic profit.
c. be equal to or more than economic profit.
d. be equal to or less than economic profit.
e. only be equal to economic profit.

3. Which kind of profit is just enough to keep a firm operating in the long run?
a. normal
b. economic
c. accounting
d. implicit
e. explicit

Refer to the cost data in the table below to answer Question 4.

Quantity of tomatoes Q (bushels)	Total cost TC	Marginal cost of bushel $MC = \Delta TC/\Delta Q$
0	$14	
1	30	$16
2	36	6
3	44	8
4	56	12
5	72	16
6	92	20
7	116	24

4. If this business can sell all it can produce at a market price of $16, the firm should produce how many units in order to maximize profits?
a. 1
b. 3
c. 5
d. 6
e. 7

5. Assume a perfectly competitive firm is producing at a level of output where marginal revenue is greater than marginal cost. To maximize profits, the firm should
a. continue to produce at that level.
b. increase output.
c. decrease output.
d. raise prices.
e. lower prices.

6. When a firm is producing where marginal cost is equal to marginal revenue, the firm
a. may be making profits or losses.
b. will definitely be maximizing profits.
c. should produce more to maximize profits.
d. should produce less to maximize profits.
e. will definitely be minimizing losses.

7. A fixed input
a. never changes.
b. is a long-run phenomenon.
c. does not change with the output level in the short run.
d. causes marginal cost to fall as it is increased.
e. causes marginal cost to rise as it is increased.

8. If marginal product is positive and declining as more workers are hired, then total product is
a. decreasing at an increasing rate.
b. decreasing at a decreasing rate.
c. increasing at an increasing rate.
d. increasing at a decreasing rate.
e. increasing at a constant rate.

9. Diminishing marginal returns always involve
a. too much plant capacity.
b. a rapid expansion of plant size.
c. a slow expansion of plant size.
d. a fixed input.
e. inputs that are all variable.

10. If marginal cost is positive and rising as more output is produced, then total cost is
a. decreasing at an increasing rate.
b. decreasing at a decreasing rate.
c. increasing at an increasing rate.
d. increasing at a decreasing rate.
e. increasing at a constant rate.

11. Marginal cost rises due to
a. diminishing marginal returns.
b. increasing marginal returns.
c. constant returns to scale.
d. increasing returns to scale.
e. increasing average returns.

12. The relationship between the marginal cost curve and the average cost curve is that when marginal cost is
a. rising, average cost must be rising.
b. falling, average cost must be falling.
c. above average cost, average cost must be rising.
d. below average cost, average cost must be rising.
e. above average cost, average cost must be falling.

13. In the short-run, as output increases, average fixed cost
a. remains constant.
b. falls and then rises after a certain output level.
c. rises initially, and then falls continuously.
d. falls continuously.
e. rises continuously.

14. If at the current level of output of 200 units, average variable cost is $10 per unit and average total cost is $15 per unit, then
a. total fixed cost is equal to $1,000.
b. total fixed cost is equal to $2,000.
c. total fixed cost is equal to $3,000.
d. marginal cost is equal to $5.
e. marginal cost is equal to $25.

15. If labor is the only variable input and the wage rate is constant, marginal cost reaches its minimum when
a. marginal product reaches its maximum.
b. average product reaches its maximum.
c. marginal product reaches its minimum.
d. average product reaches its minimum.
e. average cost reaches its minimum.

16. The spreading effect causes the average total cost curve to
a. rise, while the diminishing returns effect causes it to fall.
b. rise, as does the diminishing returns effect.
c. fall, while the diminishing returns effect causes it to rise.
d. fall, as does the diminishing returns effect.
e. remain constant until the beginning of the diminishing marginal returns effect.

4. c
5. b
6. a
7. c
8. d
9. d
10. c
11. a
12. c
13. d
14. a
15. a
16. c

17. a
18. c
19. c
20. e
21. c
22. a
23. e
24. e

Rubric for Free-Response Question

1 point: The axes on the left graph are labeled "Quantity of computers" and "Quantity of cell phones," and the axes on the right graph are labeled "Quantity of corn" and "Quantity of grapes."

1 point: The left *PPC* is a straight, downward-sloping line.

1 point: The right *PPC* is bowed out from the origin.

1 point: Resources are equally suitable for the production of computers and cell phones, but resources are not equally suitable for the production of corn and grapes.

1 point: The marginal cost curve for the production of cell phones would be horizontal.

1 point: The marginal cost curve for the production of corn would be upward-sloping.

1 point: Each additional bushel of corn would cost more than the previous bushel due to the increasing opportunity cost of production or due to having to use progressively less suitable resources that were better suited for grape production.

1 point: The total cost curve rises at an increasing rate.

1 point: The average fixed cost curve (as always) is downward-sloping.

Please see page SG-4 for sample student graphs for this Free-Response Question.

17. If marginal cost is rising and lies above average variable cost, then average total cost
- **a.** may be rising or falling.
- **b.** will definitely be rising.
- **c.** will definitely be falling.
- **d.** will definitely be constant.
- **e.** None of the above are correct.

18. If the average product of labor is rising as more workers are hired, then
- **a.** the marginal product of labor must be rising.
- **b.** the marginal product of labor must be falling.
- **c.** the marginal product of labor must be higher than the average product of labor.
- **d.** the average total cost must be rising.
- **e.** the marginal cost must be falling.

19. The long-run average cost curve eventually slopes up due to
- **a.** economies of scale.
- **b.** economies of scope.
- **c.** diseconomies of scale.
- **d.** overcrowding of the fixed factors of production.
- **e.** diminishing marginal returns.

20. When a firm makes production decisions, the sunk cost should be
- **a.** set equal to the variable cost.
- **b.** set equal to the marginal cost.
- **c.** set equal to the total cost.
- **d.** subtracted from the fixed cost to determine profit.
- **e.** ignored.

21. Monopolistically competitive industries are characterized by
- **a.** standardized products, many firms, and easy entry and exit.
- **b.** standardized products, few firms, and easy entry and exit.
- **c.** differentiated products, many firms, and easy entry and exit.
- **d.** subtracted from the fixed cost to determine profit.
- **e.** ignored

22. Compared to a monopolistically competitive industry, an oligopoly has
- **a.** a higher Herfindahl-Hirschman Index, fewer firms, and more barriers to entry.
- **b.** a higher Herfindahl-Hirschman Index, more firms, and more barriers to entry.
- **c.** a higher Herfindahl-Hirschman Index, fewer firms, and fewer barriers to entry.
- **d.** a lower Herfindahl-Hirschman Index, fewer firms, and more barriers to entry.
- **e.** a lower Herfindahl-Hirschman Index, more firms, and more barriers to entry.

23. Compared to a monopoly, an oligopoly has
- **a.** a higher Herfindahl-Hirschman Index, fewer firms, and more barriers to entry.
- **b.** a higher Herfindahl-Hirschman Index, more firms, and more barriers to entry.
- **c.** a lower Herfindahl-Hirschman Index, fewer firms, and fewer barriers to entry.
- **d.** a lower Herfindahl-Hirschman Index, more firms, and more barriers to entry.
- **e.** a lower Herfindahl-Hirschman Index, more firms, and fewer barriers to entry.

24. Diseconomies of scale can be caused by
- **a.** increasing returns to scale.
- **b.** overcrowding of the fixed factors of production.
- **c.** increasing average fixed cost.
- **d.** decreasing average fixed cost.
- **e.** communication problems.

Free-Response Question

One way to examine the marginal cost of a good is by looking at the opportunity cost using the production possibilities curve (PPC) model. Draw a correctly labeled *PPC* graph for computers and cell phones which exhibits constant opportunity cost. To the right of this *PPC* graph, draw another *PPC* graph for corn and grapes which exhibits increasing opportunity cost.
- **a.** Explain what the shape of each PPC implies about the resources used to make the goods.
- **b.** Indicate whether the marginal cost curve for the production of cell phones would be upward-sloping, downward-sloping, horizontal, vertical, or swoosh-shaped.
- **c.** Indicate whether the marginal cost curve for the production of corn would be upward-sloping, downward-sloping, horizontal, vertical, or swoosh-shaped. Explain.
- **d.** Given your answer to part c, indicate whether the total cost curve for corn production rises or falls as more corn is produced, and whether it does so at an increasing, decreasing, or constant rate.
- **e.** Assuming there is also a fixed cost of corn production, indicate whether the average fixed cost curve for corn production is upward-sloping, downward-sloping, horizontal, or vertical.

(9 points)

586 Section 10 Behind the Supply Curve: Profit, Production, and Costs

NOTES

SECTION 11

Market Structures: Perfect Competition and Monopoly

PD Section 11 Overview

Watch the video overview of Section 11 (for teachers), which is accessible through the Teacher's e-Book, the TR-flash drive, or the book's website, bcs.worthpublishers.com/krugmanap2e *(teacher log-in required).*

Section 11 looks at the opposite sides of the spectrum of market power—perfect competition and monopoly. Students are introduced to the perfect competition and monopoly models and how to use them for short-run and long-run analysis of markets and firms. Price discrimination and public policies toward monopoly are also covered. This section develops an essential skill set for the AP® Microeconomics exam.

Topics that your students will study in Section 11 are:

- price-taking behavior in perfect competition.
- profit maximization in perfect competition.
- graphing the perfect competition model.
- determining profit, loss, and shut-down conditions and representing them on a perfect competition graph.
- long-run equilibrium and the adjustment process leading to long-run equilibrium in perfect competition.
- the firm's short-run supply curve in perfect competition.
- the effect of changes in the market on perfectly competitive firms.
- price-making behavior in a monopoly market.
- profit maximization for a monopoly.
- graphing the monopoly model.
- determining profit, loss, and shutdown conditions and representing them on a monopoly graph.
- comparing price and output in a monopoly and in perfect competition.
- comparing efficiency in competitive and monopoly markets.
- understanding and graphing deadweight loss resulting from monopoly.
- natural monopoly and its regulation by the government.
- defining and graphing price discrimination and evaluating its effect on efficiency (including perfect price discrimination).
- the relationship between elasticity and price discrimination.

Alignment to AP® Microeconomics Course Description

Microeconomics II. The Nature and Function of Product Markets: 55–70%

AP® Outline	Module
D. Firm behavior and market structure	58: Introduction to Perfect Competition
	59: Graphing Perfect Competition
	60: Long-Run Outcomes in Perfect Competition
	61: Introduction to Monopoly
	62: Monopoly and Public Policy
	63: Price Discrimination

Pacing Guide

Module	Standard Teaching Days	Block Teaching Days
58	1	½
59	2	1
60	2	1½
61	2	1
62	1	½
63	2	1
Section 11 Assessment	1	½
Total	**11**	**6**

TRM Section Resources

All section resources may be accessed through the Teacher's e-Book, the TR-flash drive, or the book's website bcs.worthpublishers.com/krugmanap2e *(teacher log-in required).*

Section 11 PD Video (for teachers)

Module 58

Module 58 Sample Lecture
Worksheet 58.1: Perfect Competition Basics
Worksheet 58.2: Graphing Perfect Competition
Exit Slip: Module 58

Module 59

Module 59 Sample Lecture
Worksheet 59.1: Perfect Competition in the Short Run
Worksheet 59.2: The Shut-Down Rule
Worksheet 59.3: Summary of Profit and Production
Exit Slip: Module 59

Module 60

Module 60 Sample Lecture
Worksheet 60.1: Profit-Maximization and Loss-Minimization Practice
Worksheet 60.2: Perfect Competition in the Long Run
Worksheet 60.3: Long-Run Equilibrium Teaching Aid
Worksheet 60.4: Market and Firm Relationships
Worksheet 60.5: Constant-Cost Industry
Worksheet 60.6: Increasing-Cost Industry
Worksheet 60.7: Perfectly Competitive Markets Review
Worksheet 60.8: Long-Run Equilibrium and Efficiency
Exit Slip: Module 60

Module 61

Module 61 Sample Lecture
Worksheet 61.1: Monopoly *D* and *MR*
Worksheet 61.2: Monopoly Profit
Worksheet 61.3: Drawing a Monopoly Graph Test It
Worksheet 61.4: Monopoly Graph Review
Exit Slip: Module 61

Module 62

Module 62 Sample Lecture
Worksheet 62.1: Deadweight Loss
Worksheet 62.2: Monopoly and Inefficiency
Worksheet 62.3: Monopoly and Perfectly Competitive Market Comparisons
Exit Slip: Module 62

Module 63

Module 63 Sample Lecture
Worksheet 63.1: Spot It
Worksheet 63.2: Price Discriminating Monopoly
Worksheet 63.3: Price Discrimination Practice
Exit Slip: Module 63

Section 11 Review Video (for students)

St. Louis Federal Reserve Bank Resources

Many of the Federal Reserve Banks have educational departments that offer helpful resources for studying economics. Members of the Educators Advisory Board of the St. Louis Federal Reserve Bank have handpicked some of their best resources for use with your AP® Economics students. References to these resources are included in the marginal notes. A complete list of the St. Louis Fed resources for each section with the corresponding URL (as of fall 2014) can be found in the TRM.

NOTE We have included a number of links to useful videos and articles in the margin notes in this section. Although all are active at the time of publication, we know that some may expire over the next few years. If a link is no longer active, you may wish to search for a similar article or video to illustrate the same point. We may also periodically refresh resources on the book's companion website.

NOTES

SECTION 11

Market Structures: Perfect Competition and Monopoly

Some Carrots Are More Expensive Than Others

Section 10 explained how factors including the number of firms in the industry, the type of product sold, and the existence of barriers to entry determine the market power of firms. We can think about the four basic market structures as falling along a spectrum from perfect competition at one end to monopoly at the other, with monopolistic competition and oligopoly lying in between. To shed more light on the market structure spectrum, consider two very different markets introduced in previous sections: the market for organic tomatoes and the market for diamonds.

In the United States, a growing interest in healthy living has steadily increased the demand for products such as organically grown fruits and vegetables. Over the past decade, the markets for these products have been healthy as well, with an average growth rate of 20% per year. It costs a bit more to grow crops without chemical fertilizers and pesticides, but consumers are willing to pay higher prices for the benefits of fruits and vegetables grown the natural way. The farmers in each area who pioneered organic farming techniques had little competition and many prospered thanks to these higher prices.

But with profit as a lure for expanded production, the high prices were unlikely to persist. Over time, farmers already producing organically would increase their capacity, and conventional farmers would enter the organic food fray, increasing supply and driving down price. With a large and growing number of buyers and sellers, undifferentiated products, and few barriers to entry, the organic food market increasingly resembles a *perfectly competitive* market.

In contrast, the market for diamonds is dominated by one supplier, De Beers.

© Mexo69/ Dreamstime.com

For generations, diamonds have been valued not just for their attractive appearance, but also for their rarity. But geologists will tell you that diamonds aren't all that rare. In fact, they are fairly common and only seem rare compared to other gem-quality stones. This is because De Beers *makes* them rare: the company controls most of the world's diamond mines and limits the quantity supplied to the market. This makes De Beers resemble a *monopolist*, the sole producer of a good. Because De Beers controls so much of the world's diamond supply, other firms have considerable difficulty trying to enter the diamond market and increase the quantity of the gems available.

In this section we will study how markets like those for organic tomatoes and diamonds differ, and how these markets respond to market conditions. We will see how firms positioned at opposite ends of the spectrum of market power—from perfect competition to monopoly—make key decisions about output and prices. Then, in Section 12, we will complete our exploration of market structure with a closer look at oligopoly and monopolistic competition.

PD Section 11 Overview

Watch the video overview of Section 11 (for teachers), which is accessible through the Teacher's e-Book, the TR-flash drive, or the book's companion website bcs.worthpublishers.com/krugmanap2e (teacher log-in required).

FOCUS Active Learning

Have students read Chapter 6 of *Economics by Example* for historical perspectives on perfect competition and efficiency.

PD To prepare for teaching this lesson, you may want to consult the **Module 58 Sample Lecture** in the TRM.

OPEN & CLOSE Start Here

Models are simplified representations of reality. Market structure models are simplified representations of types of markets with the same general characteristics. In reality, markets don't always fit neatly into one of the four market structure categories. Introduce market structure models as part of a spectrum. Draw a line and put perfect competition at one end (many small firms that are price-takers). Ask students what would go on the other end of the spectrum; help them see that it would be monopoly (one firm that is a price-maker). Monopolistic competition would go in the middle (a mix of perfect competition and monopoly; many small firms like perfect competition, price-makers like monopoly), and oligopoly would exist between monopolistic competition and monopoly (few firms with control over price). Use the idea of a spectrum when students ask you to define the market structure for a specific industry in the real world—sometimes it is difficult to know for certain because an industry can fall between the models on our spectrum!

Explain that it is difficult to think of a true example of perfect competition or an unregulated monopoly in the real world. Students will likely then ask WHY we study perfect competition and monopoly. Make sure that they understand the reason: to define the ends of the spectrum. Later we will see that perfect competition represents an "ideal" (in terms of efficiency) and that makes it important to understand the perfect competition outcome. Monopoly is the farthest from such an ideal and therefore illustrates the extreme of inefficiency (DWL).

© UpperCut Images/Alamy

MODULE 58 Introduction to Perfect Competition

In this Module, you will learn to:

- Determine the profit-maximizing quantity of output for a price-taking firm
- Assess whether or not a competitive firm is profitable

Recall the example of the market for organic tomatoes from our discussions in Section 10. Jennifer and Jason run an organic tomato farm, but many other organic tomato farmers, such as Yves and Zoe, sell their output to the same grocery store chains. Since organic tomatoes are a standardized product, consumers don't care which farmer produces the organic tomatoes they buy. And because so many farmers sell organic tomatoes, no individual farmer has a large market share, which means that no individual farmer can have a measurable effect on market prices. These farmers are price-taking producers and their customers are price-taking consumers. The market for organic tomatoes meets the two necessary conditions for perfect competition: there are many producers each with a small market share, and the firms produce a standardized product. In this module, we build the model of perfect competition and use it to look at a representative firm in the market.

AP® Exam Tip

One of the most important concepts to learn in microeconomics is that firms maximize total profit by choosing the quantity of output that equates marginal revenue and marginal cost.

Production and Profit

Jennifer and Jason's tomato farm will maximize its profit by producing bushels of tomatoes up to the point at which marginal revenue equals marginal cost. We know this from the producer's *optimal output rule* introduced in Module 53—profit is maximized by producing the quantity at which the marginal revenue of the last unit produced is equal to its marginal cost. Always remember, $MR = MC$ at the optimal quantity of output. This will be true for any profit-maximizing firm in any market structure.

We can review how to apply the optimal output rule with the help of **Table 58.1**, which provides various short-run cost measures for Jennifer and Jason's farm. The second column contains the farm's variable cost, and the third column shows its total cost based on the assumption that the farm incurs a fixed cost of $14. The fourth column

TEACH Connect It

TRM Have students refer back to **Worksheet 57.1 (Types of Market Structures)** from the TRM for a review of the characteristics of perfect competition.

TEACH Connect It

Remind students what they learned about profit maximization in Module 53. Firms maximize profit when $MC = MR$ (or at the highest quantity where MR exceeds MC). This rule for profit maximization holds in any situation in any market structure!

Table 58.1 Short-Run Costs for Jennifer and Jason's Farm

Quantity of tomatoes Q (bushels)	Variable cost VC	Total cost TC	Marginal cost of bushel $MC = \Delta TC/\Delta Q$	Marginal revenue of bushel MR	Net gain of bushel $= MR - MC$
0	$0	$14			
			$16	$18	$2
1	16	30			
			6	18	12
2	22	36			
			8	18	10
3	30	44			
			12	18	6
4	42	56			
			16	18	2
5	58	72			
			20	18	−2
6	78	92			
			24	18	−6
7	102	116			

shows the farm's marginal cost. Notice that, in this example, the marginal cost initially falls as output rises but then begins to increase, so that the marginal cost curve has the familiar "swoosh" shape.

The fifth column contains the farm's marginal revenue, which has an important feature: Jennifer and Jason's marginal revenue is constant at $18 for every output level. The sixth and final column shows the calculation of the net gain per bushel of tomatoes, which is equal to the marginal revenue minus the marginal cost—or, equivalently in this case, the market price minus the marginal cost. As you can see, it is positive for the 1st through 5th bushels; producing each of these bushels raises Jennifer and Jason's profit. For the 6th bushel, however, net gain is negative: producing it would decrease, not increase, profit. So 5 bushels are Jennifer and Jason's profit-maximizing output; it is the level of output at which the marginal cost rises from a level below the market price to a level above the market price, passing through the market price of $18 along the way.

Anthony-Masterson/Digital Vision/Getty Images

This example illustrates an application of the optimal output rule to the particular case of a price-taking firm—the **price-taking firm's optimal output rule**: *price equals marginal cost at the price-taking firm's optimal quantity of output.* That is, a price-taking firm's profit is maximized by producing the quantity of output at which the market price is equal to the marginal cost of the last unit produced. Why? Because *in the case of a price-taking firm, the marginal revenue is equal to the market price*. A price-taking firm cannot influence the market price by its actions. It always takes the market price as given because it cannot lower the market price by selling more or raise the market price by selling less. So, for a price-taking firm, the additional revenue generated by producing one more unit is always the market price. We will need to keep this fact in mind in future modules, in which we will learn that in the three other market structures, firms are *not* price-takers. Therefore, the marginal revenue is *not* equal to the market price.

The **price-taking firm's optimal output rule** says that a price-taking firm's profit is maximized by producing the quantity of output at which the market price is equal to the marginal cost of the last unit produced.

Figure 58.1 on the next page shows Jennifer and Jason's profit-maximizing quantity of output. The figure shows the marginal cost curve, MC, drawn from the data in the fourth column of Table 58.1. We plot the marginal cost of increasing output from 1 to 2 bushels halfway between 1 and 2, and likewise for each incremental change. The horizontal line at $18 is Jennifer and Jason's marginal revenue curve. Remember from Module 53 that whenever a firm is a price-taker, its marginal revenue curve is a horizontal line at the market price: it can sell as much as it likes at the market price. Regardless of whether it sells more or less, the market price is unaffected. In effect, the individual

TEACH Connect It

In Module 53, students found the profit-maximizing level of output on a graph with a horizontal *MR* curve. At that point, students didn't know that a horizontal *MR* curve meant that the firm was a price-taker. The *MR* curve was horizontal at the market price because a price-taking firm cannot influence the market and takes the market price as given, so the additional revenue generated by producing one more unit is always the market price. Firms can't raise their price because buyers would buy elsewhere and firms will never lower their price because they can already sell all they want at the market price. Thus, the *MR* and *D* curves for a perfectly competitive firm are equal to the price. The firm's demand curve is perfectly elastic.

FOCUS Test It

Indicate whether the following statements are True or False:

1. If *P* is greater than *MC*, firms should stop production. *F*

2. If *MR* is less than *MC*, firms should increase output. *F*

3. Firms in perfectly competitive markets have some market power to influence the price. *F*

4. A firm in a perfectly competitive market maximizes profit when $MR = MC$. *T*

5. A firm in a perfectly competitive market will increase production when *MR* is greater than *MC*. *T, unless the next unit causes $MC > MR$.*

6. The price for a firm in a perfectly competitive market is also *MR*. *T*

7. *MR* for a firm in a perfectly competitive market is the additional revenue gain by the same of an additional unit of output. *T*

8. Demand in a perfectly competitive market is perfectly elastic *F, the FIRM demand is perfectly elastic.*

Module 58 Introduction to Perfect Competition 589

TEACH Teach It

For the perfectly competitive firm, $MR = D = AR = P$, and demand for the firm is perfectly elastic. Students can remember this by thinking of Mr. Darp (Mr = D = ar = p).

Note: Average revenue is the revenue "per unit," which equals $\frac{TR}{Q}$. Since $TR = P \times Q$, then $AR = \frac{(P \times Q)}{Q} = P$. Another name for the demand curve is the average revenue curve.

TEACH Connect It

Figure 58.1 shows the perfectly competitive $D = MR = P$ curve. Students should note that profit maximization for this firm occurs where the *MC* curve intersects the *MR* curve. Figure 53.1 in Section 10 was the same.

FOCUS Test It

Ask students, "What is the goal of a firm?" *(to maximize profit).* Then ask them where firms maximize their profit *(where MC = MR).* How is profit calculated? *(The profit equation is TR − TC; TR = P × Q; = ATC × Q.)* Repeat these questions frequently, for example, any time you draw a *perfectly competitive firm* graph.

Figure 58.1 The Price-Taking Firm's Profit-Maximizing Quantity of Output

At the profit-maximizing quantity of output, the market price is equal to the marginal cost. It is located at the point where the marginal cost curve crosses the marginal revenue curve, which is a horizontal line at the market price and represents the firm's demand curve. Here, the profit-maximizing point is at an output of 5 bushels of tomatoes, the output quantity at point *E*.

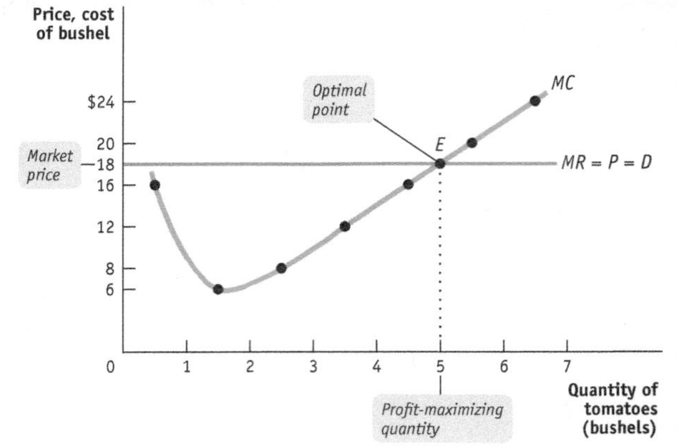

AP® Exam Tip

Notice that for a perfectly competitive firm, the horizontal line at the market price also represents the marginal revenue curve and the demand curve. Be prepared to draw and label this line for the AP® exam.

firm faces a horizontal, perfectly elastic demand curve for its output—a demand curve that is equivalent to its marginal revenue curve. In fact, the horizontal line with the height of the market price represents the perfectly competitive firm's demand, marginal revenue, and *average revenue*—the average amount of revenue taken in per unit—because price equals average revenue whenever every unit is sold for the same price. The marginal cost curve crosses the marginal revenue curve at point *E*. Sure enough, the quantity of output at *E* is 5 bushels.

Does this mean that the price-taking firm's production decision can be entirely summed up as "produce up to the point where the marginal cost of production is equal to the price"? No, not quite. Before applying the principle of marginal analysis to determine how much to produce, a potential producer must as a first step answer an "either–or" question: should it produce at all? If the answer to that question is yes, it then proceeds to the second step—a "how much" decision: maximizing profit by choosing the quantity of output at which the marginal cost is equal to the price.

To understand why the first step in the production decision involves an "either–or" question, we need to ask how we determine whether it is profitable or unprofitable to produce at all. In the next module we'll see that unprofitable firms shut down in the long run, but tolerate losses in the short run up to a certain point.

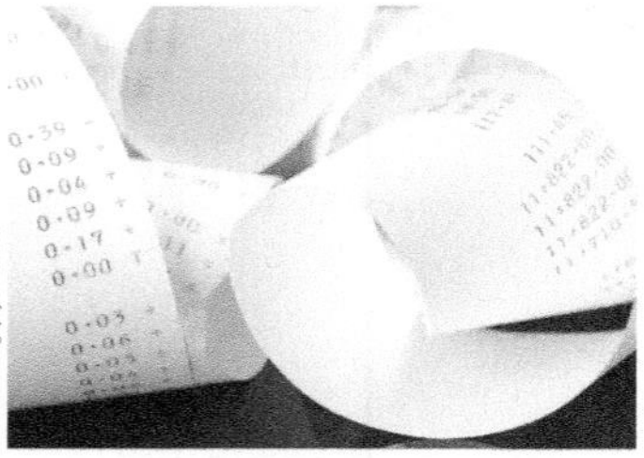
South12th Photography/Shutterstock

When Is Production Profitable?

Remember from Module 52 that firms make their production decisions with the goal of maximizing *economic profit*—a measure based on the opportunity cost of resources used by the firm. In the calculation of economic profit, a firm's total cost incorporates the implicit cost—the benefits forgone in the next best use of the firm's resources—as well as the explicit cost in the form of actual cash outlays. In contrast, *accounting profit* is profit calculated using only the explicit costs incurred by the firm. This means that economic profit incorporates all of the opportunity cost of resources owned by the firm and used in the production of output, while accounting profit does not. A firm may make

590 Section 11 Market Structures: Perfect Competition and Monopoly

Table 58.2 Short-Run Average Costs for Jennifer and Jason's Farm

Quantity of tomatoes Q (bushels)	Variable cost VC	Total cost TC	Short-run average variable cost of bushel $AVC = VC/Q$	Short-run average total cost of bushel $ATC = TC/Q$
1	$16.00	$30.00	$16.00	$30.00
2	22.00	36.00	11.00	18.00
3	30.00	44.00	10.00	14.67
4	42.00	56.00	10.50	14.00
5	58.00	72.00	11.60	14.40
6	78.00	92.00	13.00	15.33
7	102.00	116.00	14.57	16.57

positive accounting profit while making zero or even negative economic profit. It's important to understand that a firm's decisions of how much to produce and whether or not to stay in business should be based on economic profit, not accounting profit.

So we will assume, as usual, that the cost numbers given in Table 58.1 include all costs, implicit as well as explicit. What determines whether Jennifer and Jason's farm earns a profit or generates a loss? This depends on the market price of tomatoes—specifically, *whether the market price is more or less than the farm's minimum average total cost.*

In **Table 58.2** we calculate the short-run average variable cost and the short-run average total cost for Jennifer and Jason's farm. These are short-run values because we take the fixed cost as given. (We'll turn to the effects of changing fixed cost shortly.) The short-run average total cost curve, *ATC*, is shown in **Figure 58.2**, along with the marginal cost curve, *MC*, from Figure 58.1. As you can see, average total cost is minimized at point *C*, corresponding to an output of 4 bushels—the *minimum-cost output*—and an average total cost of $14 per bushel.

Figure 58.2 Costs and Production in the Short Run

This figure shows the marginal cost curve, *MC*, and the short-run average total cost curve, *ATC*. When the market price is $14, output will be 4 bushels of tomatoes (the minimum-cost output), represented by point *C*. The price of $14 is equal to the firm's minimum average total cost, so at this price the firm breaks even.

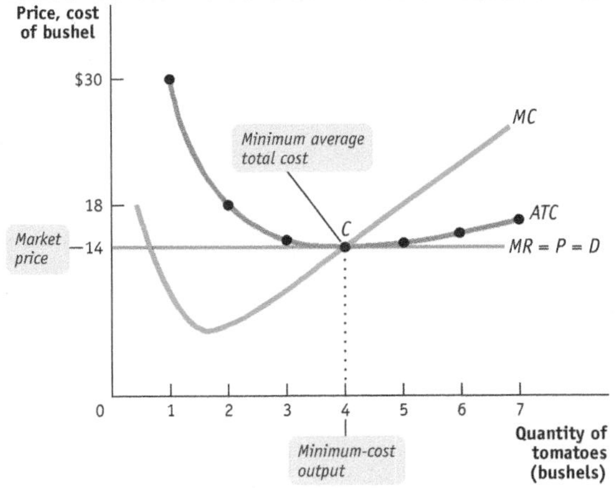

FOCUS Graph It

Figure 58.2 adds an *ATC* curve to the model. The graph represents the information provided in Table 58.2. Ask students to state the goal of the firm and the profit-maximization rule, and how to calculate profit (the questions from the Test It on page 590). Then direct them to look at Figure 58.2, identify the profit-maximizing output (*4*), and calculate the firm's profit (*$0 because TR is $14 × 4 and TC is $14 × 4*). In this case, what is true of the *ATC* at the profit-maximizing point? (*ATC is at its minimum.*)

TEACH Teach It

(Total) Profit = *TR* − *TC*, so if *TR* is larger than *TC*, the firm earns a positive profit. If *TC* is greater than *TR*, the firm earns a negative profit (aka a loss). If *TR* = *TC*, the firm earns zero profit. Make sure students also understand how to look at profit per unit. A firm's Profit per unit = Revenue per unit − Cost per unit. That is,

$$\text{Profit per unit} = \left(\frac{TR}{Q}\right) - \left(\frac{TC}{Q}\right) = P - ATC$$

If $P > ATC$, the firm earns a profit; if $P < ATC$, the firm earns a negative profit (aka a loss), and if $P = ATC$, the firm earns zero profit.

FOCUS Flip It

TRM Have students watch Jacob Clifford's video "Micro Unit 3, Question 11—Perfect Competition" (see econextras video list with hyperlinks on the bcs and TRFD), which will introduce them to the perfectly competitive firm's basic graphs and concepts. Assign **Worksheet 58.1 (Perfect Competition Basics)** from the TRM for questions about this video.

FOCUS Active Learning

TRM For practice graphing this market structure, refer students to **Worksheet 58.2 (Graphing Perfect Competition)** from the TRM.

OPEN & CLOSE Exit Slip

TRM *Please see **Exit Slip: Module 58** in the TRM for formative multiple-choice questions to ask your students before finishing your lesson. These questions will help you quickly assess whether your students have mastered the module's concepts before moving on.*

Answers to the Exit Slip Questions

1. C
2. B
3. E

Answers to Module 58 Review Questions

Check Your Understanding

1. a. The firm maximizes profit at a quantity of 4, because at that quantity, *MC* = *MR*.

b. At a quantity of 4, the firm just breaks even. This is because at a quantity of 4, *P* = *ATC*, so the amount the firm takes in for each unit—the price—exactly equals the average total cost per unit.

2. The lowest price that would allow the firm to break even is \$10, for the minimum average total cost is \$500/50 = \$10, and price must equal minimum average total cost in order for the firm to break even.

To see how these curves can be used to decide whether production is profitable or unprofitable, recall that profit is equal to total revenue minus total cost, $TR - TC$. This means:

- If the firm produces a quantity at which $TR > TC$, the firm is profitable.
- If the firm produces a quantity at which $TR = TC$, the firm breaks even.
- If the firm produces a quantity at which $TR < TC$, the firm incurs a loss.

We can also express this idea in terms of revenue and cost per unit of output. If we divide profit by the number of units of output, Q, we obtain the following expression for profit per unit of output:

$$\text{(58-1)}\quad \text{Profit}/Q = TR/Q - TC/Q$$

TR/Q is average revenue, which is the market price. TC/Q is average total cost. So a firm is profitable if the market price for its product is more than the average total cost of the quantity the firm produces; a firm experiences losses if the market price is less than the average total cost of the quantity the firm produces. This means:

- If the firm produces a quantity at which $P > ATC$, the firm is profitable.
- If the firm produces a quantity at which $P = ATC$, the firm breaks even.
- If the firm produces a quantity at which $P < ATC$, the firm incurs a loss.

In summary, in the short run a firm will maximize profit by producing the quantity of output at which $MC = MR$. A perfectly competitive firm is a price-taker, so it can sell as many units of output as it would like at the market price. This means that for a perfectly competitive firm it is always true that $MR = P$. The firm is profitable, or breaks even, as long as the market price is greater than, or equal to, the average total cost. In the next module, we develop the perfect competition model using graphs to analyze the firm's level of profit.

MODULE 58 Review

Check Your Understanding

1. Refer to the graph provided.

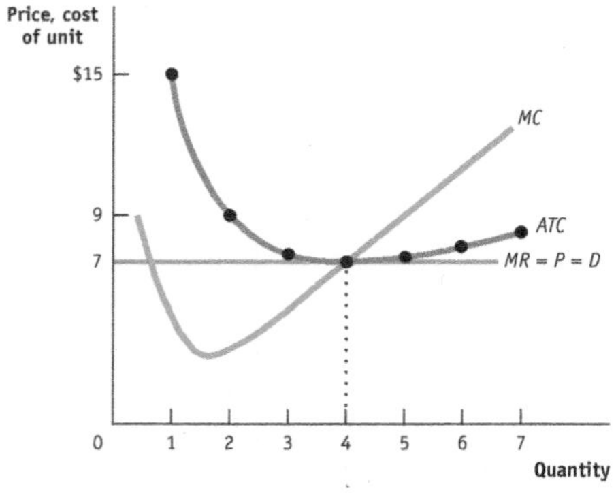

a. At what level of output does the firm maximize profit? Explain how you know.

b. At the profit-maximizing quantity of output, is the firm profitable, does it just break even, or does it incur a loss? Explain.

2. If a firm has a total cost of \$500 at a quantity of 50 units, and it is at that quantity that average total cost is minimized for the firm, what is the lowest price that would allow the firm to break even (that is, earn a normal profit)? Explain.

592 Section 11 Market Structures: Perfect Competition and Monopoly

Tackle the Test: Multiple-Choice Questions

1. A perfectly competitive firm will maximize profit at the quantity at which the firm's marginal revenue equals
   - a. price.
   - b. average revenue.
   - c. total cost.
   - d. marginal cost.
   - e. demand.
2. Which of the following is correct for a perfectly competitive firm?
   - I. The marginal revenue curve is the demand curve.
   - II. The firm maximizes profit when price equals marginal cost.
   - III. The market demand curve is horizontal.
   - a. I only
   - b. II only
   - c. III only
   - d. I and II only
   - e. I, II, and III
3. A firm is profitable if
   - a. $TR < TC$.
   - b. $AR < ATC$.
   - c. $MC < ATC$.
   - d. $ATC < P$.
   - e. $ATC > MC$.
4. If a firm has a total cost of $200, its profit-maximizing level of output is 10 units, and it is breaking even (that is, earning a normal profit), what is the market price?
   - a. $200
   - b. $100
   - c. $20
   - d. $10
   - e. $2
5. What is the firm's profit if the price of its product is $5 and it produces 500 units of output at a total cost of $1,000?
   - a. $5,000
   - b. $2,500
   - c. $1,500
   - d. −$1,500
   - e. −$2,500

Tackle the Test: Free-Response Questions

1. Draw a correctly labeled graph showing a profit-maximizing perfectly competitive firm producing at its minimum average total cost.

Rubric for FRQ 1 (6 points)

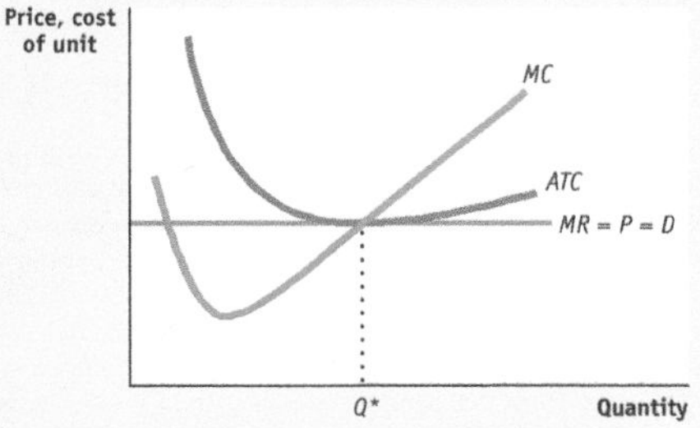

1 point: Vertical axis and horizontal axis labels are correct ("Price, cost of unit" on vertical axis; "Quantity" on horizontal axis).

1 point: The line representing demand, marginal revenue, and price is horizontal and correctly labeled.

1 point: Marginal cost is "swoosh" shaped or upward-sloping and correctly labeled.

1 point: Average total cost is U-shaped and correctly labeled.

1 point: Quantity is found where $MC = MR$.

1 point: Average total cost reaches its minimum point at the profit-maximizing level of output.

2. Refer to the table provided. Price is equal to $14.
   - a. Calculate the firm's marginal cost at each quantity.
   - b. Determine the firm's profit-maximizing level of output.
   - c. Calculate the firm's profit at the profit-maximizing level of output.

Short-Run Costs for Jennifer and Jason's Farm

Quantity of tomatoes (bushels)	*Variable cost*	*Total cost*
0	$0	$14
1	16	30
2	22	36
3	30	44
4	42	56
5	58	72
6	78	92
7	102	116

(3 points)

Tackle the Test: Multiple-Choice Questions

1. d
2. d
3. d
4. c
5. c

Tackle the Test: Free-Response Question

Rubric for FRQ 2 (3 points)

Q	*MC*
0	
	16
1	
	6
2	
	8
3	
	12
4	
	16
5	
	20
6	
	24
7	

1 point: Correct marginal cost values as shown in the table above.

1 point: The profit-maximizing quantity is 4.

1 point: The firm's maximum profit is $TR - TC = (4 \times \$14) - \$56 = \$56 - \$56 = \$0$.

Module 58 Introduction to Perfect Competition 593

PD To prepare for teaching this lesson, you may want to consult the **Module 59 Sample Lecture** in the TRM.

OPEN & CLOSE Start Here

Have students draw a correctly labeled graph of a perfectly competitive firm showing the firm's price, demand, and *MC* and *MR* curves, and the profit-maximizing level of output. Ask them to check each other's graphs. The vertical axis should be labeled *P*/cost and the horizontal axis should be labeled *Q*. Emphasize the importance of correctly labeled axes on any graph and that these are the correct labels for a market structure graph. Their graphs should have a horizontal line labeled $MR = P = D$, because perfectly competitive firms are price-takers (they take the price from the market). Therefore, the additional revenue from selling one more is always equal to *P*, and that gives their demand curve. The *MC* curve should be mostly upward-sloping (a checkmark shape) due to diminishing returns. The profit-maximizing output should be labeled on the horizontal axis below where $MC = MR$ (as with the profit-maximization rule). Refer to Figure 59.1 as an example.

TEACH AP® Exam Tip

Students should understand that the price used in their perfectly competitive firm graph is determined in the market. That is, the perfectly competitive firm's price is the equilibrium price they found where the supply and demand curves cross in Section 2. Drawing the market graph and showing that the perfectly competitive firm takes its price from the market will set up the presentation of side-by-side graphs in the next module. Students are frequently asked to draw side-by-side graphs on the AP® exam.

TEACH Teach It

The graph that students draw in the Open & Close above is the "starting point" for any perfectly competitive firm graph. The difference between a firm with a profit and a firm with a loss is the location of the *ATC* curve relative to the price. Remember from the last module that if $P > ATC$, the firm earns a profit, and if $P < ATC$, the firm incurs a loss. To draw a perfectly competitive firm earning a profit, the *ATC* should be low—below price. To show a loss, the *ATC* should be high—above price. To show a profit of zero, *ATC* must equal price.

Brand New Images/Getty Images

MODULE 59

Graphing Perfect Competition

In this Module, you will learn to:

- Evaluate a perfectly competitive firm's situation using a graph
- Determine a perfectly competitive firm's profit or loss
- Explain how a firm decides whether to produce or shut down in the short run

We have just learned that for a perfectly competitive firm, a comparison of the market price to the firm's average total cost determines whether the firm is earning a profit, taking a loss, or breaking even with a normal profit of zero. Now we can evaluate the profitability of perfectly competitive firms in a variety of situations.

Interpreting Perfect Competition Graphs

Figure 59.1 illustrates how the market price determines whether a firm is profitable. It also shows how profit is depicted graphically. Each panel shows the marginal cost curve, *MC*, and the short-run average total cost curve, *ATC*. Average total cost is minimized at point *C*. Panel (a) shows the case in which the market price of tomatoes is \$18 per bushel. Panel (b) shows the case in which the market price of tomatoes is lower, \$10 per bushel.

In panel (a), we see that at a price of \$18 per bushel the profit-maximizing quantity of output is 5 bushels, indicated by point *E*, where the marginal cost curve, *MC*, intersects the marginal revenue curve, *MR*—which for a price-taking firm is a horizontal line at the market price. At that quantity of output, average total cost is \$14.40 per bushel, indicated by point *Z*. Since the price per bushel exceeds the average total cost per bushel, Jennifer and Jason's farm is profitable.

Jennifer and Jason's total profit when the market price is \$18 is represented by the area of the shaded rectangle in panel (a). To see why, notice that total profit can be expressed in terms of profit per unit:

AP® Exam Tip

Memorize the formula for profit because you won't be given a formula sheet for the AP® exam.

$$\text{(59-1)} \quad \text{Profit} = TR - TC = (TR/Q - TC/Q) \times Q$$

or, equivalently, because *P* is equal to *TR*/*Q* and *ATC* is equal to *TC*/*Q*,

$$\text{Profit} = (P - ATC) \times Q$$

TEACH AP® Exam Tip

When students draw market structure graphs, they should always include all the curves required to answer the questions, even if a curve is not specifically requested. For example, if they are asked to find the profit-maximizing quantity, they will need to draw the *MC* and *MR* curves, regardless of whether the question specifically asks for those curves. If a question asks about loss minimizing or shutting down, students will need the *AVC* curve. Students must know what curves are required to indicate what they are asked to show.

St. Louis Federal Reserve Bank Resources

Perfect Competition

Teaching market structures in a microeconomics class? These slides present graphs related to perfect competition, the market structure in which there are many buyers and sellers of an identical product and no barriers to enter or exit the market exist. The slides illustrate firms' short-run decisions.

594 Section 11 Market Structures: Perfect Competition and Monopoly

Figure 59.1 Profitability and the Market Price

In panel (a) the market price is $18. The farm is profitable because price exceeds minimum average total cost, the break-even price, $14. The farm's optimal output choice is indicated by point *E*, corresponding to an output of 5 bushels. The average total cost of producing 5 bushels is indicated by point *Z* on the *ATC* curve, corresponding to an amount of $14.40. The vertical distance between *E* and *Z* corresponds to the farm's per-unit profit, $18.00 – $14.40 = $3.60. Total profit is given by the area of the shaded rectangle, 5 × $3.60 = $18.00. In panel (b) the market price is $10; the farm is unprofitable because the price falls below the minimum average total cost, $14. If it continues to produce, the farm's optimal output choice is indicated by point *A*, corresponding to an output of 3 bushels. The farm's per-unit loss, $14.67 – $10.00 = $4.67, is represented by the vertical distance between *A* and *Y*. The farm's total loss is represented by the shaded rectangle, 3 × $4.67 = $14.00 (adjusted for rounding error).

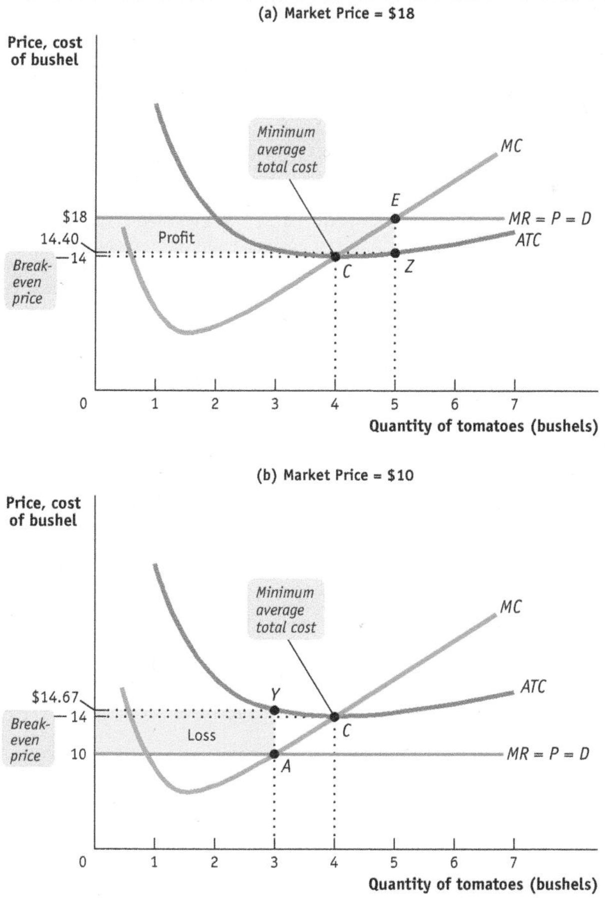

The height of the shaded rectangle in panel (a) corresponds to the vertical distance between points *E* and *Z*. It is equal to *P* – *ATC* = $18.00 – $14.40 = $3.60 per bushel. The shaded rectangle has a width equal to the output: *Q* = 5 bushels. So the area of that rectangle is equal to Jennifer and Jason's profit: 5 bushels × $3.60 profit per bushel = $18.

What about the situation illustrated in panel (b)? Here the market price of tomatoes is $10 per bushel. Producing until price equals marginal cost leads to a profit-maximizing output of 3 bushels, indicated by point *A*. At this output, Jennifer and Jason have an average total cost of $14.67 per bushel, indicated by point *Y*. At their profit-maximizing output quantity—3 bushels—the average total cost exceeds the market price. This means that Jennifer and Jason's farm generates a loss, not a profit.

AP® Exam Tip

AP® exam questions may give you a scenario about profit, cost, or revenue at a specific output. Drawing the firm's graph may help you visualize the answer more easily.

TEACH AP® Exam Tip

On the AP® exam, students are frequently asked to identify profit or loss on the graph of a perfectly competitive firm, either by shading the corresponding rectangle or using numbers that are provided to calculate it. Observe examples of shading and calculating profit and loss in Figure 59.1.

FOCUS Flip It

TRM Have students watch Jacob Clifford's video "Micro 3.8 Perfect Competition in the Short Run" (see econextras video list with hyperlinks on the bcs and TRFD). Refer to **Worksheet 59.1 (Perfect Competition in the Short Run)** from the TRM for questions about the video.

FOCUS Test It

Ask students to draw a graph of a perfectly competitive firm earning a profit, a loss, and zero profit. Remind them that the only difference between these graphs is the location of the *ATC* curve relative to the price!

TEACH Connect It

Remind students that they learned the *MC* curve must cross the *ATC* curve at the minimum point of *ATC*. Point out that this means the firm will be at minimum *ATC* any time it earns zero economic profit because $MR = MC = ATC$ at its minimum.

TEACH Teach It

To help students draw their graphs, suggest they create their *AC* curves in two parts, starting at the *MC* curve. If they begin at a point on the *MC* curve and then draw the two sides of the U-shaped curve separately, the *MC* will always cross *AC* at its minimum. They should select a point on the *MC* curve below *P* to show a profit and above *P* to show a loss.

TEACH Connect It

Remind students of the definition of the short run and long run from Module 54. In the short run, at least one factor of production is fixed; therefore, firms incur a fixed cost. Fixed costs must be paid in the short run, whether or not the firm produces and no matter how much it produces. That is why fixed costs are not used to determine whether or not a firm should shut down.

How much do they lose by producing when the market price is \$10? On each bushel they lose $ATC - P = \$14.67 - \$10.00 = \$4.67$, an amount corresponding to the vertical distance between points *A* and *Y*. And they produce 3 bushels, which corresponds to the width of the shaded rectangle. So the total value of the losses is $\$4.67 \times 3 = \$14.00$ (adjusted for rounding error), an amount that corresponds to the area of the shaded rectangle in panel (b).

But how does a producer know, in general, whether or not its business will be profitable? It turns out that the crucial test lies in a comparison of the market price to the firm's *minimum average total cost*. On Jennifer and Jason's farm, average total cost reaches its minimum, \$14, at an output of 4 bushels, indicated by point C. Whenever the market price exceeds the minimum average total cost, there are output levels for which the average total cost is less than the market price. In other words, the producer can find a level of output at which the firm makes a profit. So Jennifer and Jason's farm will be profitable whenever the market price exceeds \$14. And they will achieve the highest possible profit by producing the quantity at which marginal cost equals price.

Conversely, if the market price is less than the minimum average total cost, there is no output level at which price exceeds average total cost. As a result, the firm will be unprofitable at any quantity of output. As we saw, at a price of \$10—an amount less than the minimum average total cost—Jennifer and Jason did indeed lose money. By producing the quantity at which marginal cost equaled price, Jennifer and Jason did the best they could, but the best they could do was a loss of \$14. Any other quantity would have increased the size of their loss.

The **break-even price** of a price-taking firm is the market price at which it earns zero profit.

The minimum average total cost of a price-taking firm is called its **break-even price**, the price at which it earns zero economic profit (which we now know as a *normal profit*). A firm will earn positive profit when the market price is above the break-even price, and it will suffer losses when the market price is below the break-even price. Jennifer and Jason's break-even price of \$14 is the price at point C in Figure 59.1.

So the rule for determining whether a firm is profitable depends on a comparison of the market price of the good to the firm's break-even price—its minimum average total cost:

- Whenever the market price exceeds the minimum average total cost, the producer is profitable.
- Whenever the market price equals the minimum average total cost, the producer breaks even.
- Whenever the market price is less than the minimum average total cost, the producer is unprofitable.

The Short-Run Production Decision

You might be tempted to say that if a firm is unprofitable because the market price is below its minimum average total cost, it shouldn't produce any output. In the short run, however, this conclusion isn't right. In the short run, sometimes the firm should produce even if price falls below minimum average total cost. The reason is that total cost includes *fixed cost*—cost that does not depend on the amount of output produced and can be altered only in the long run. In the short run, fixed cost must still be paid, regardless of whether or not a firm produces. For example, if Jennifer and Jason have rented a tractor for the year, they have to pay the rent on the tractor regardless of whether they produce any tomatoes. *Since it cannot be changed in the short run, their fixed cost is irrelevant to their decision about whether to produce or shut down in the short run.* Although fixed cost should play no role in the decision about whether to produce in the short run, another type of cost—variable cost—does matter. Part of the variable cost for Jennifer and Jason is the wage cost of workers who must be hired to help with planting and harvesting. Variable cost can be eliminated by *not* producing, which makes it a critical consideration when determining whether or not to produce in the short run.

596 Section 11 Market Structures: Perfect Competition and Monopoly

Figure 59.2 The Short-Run Individual Supply Curve

When the market price equals or exceeds Jennifer and Jason's *shut-down price* of $10, the minimum average variable cost indicated by point *A*, they will produce the output quantity at which marginal cost is equal to price. So at any price equal to or above the minimum average *variable* cost, the short-run individual supply curve is the firm's marginal cost curve; this corresponds to the upward-sloping segment of the individual supply curve. When market price falls below minimum average variable cost, the firm ceases operation in the short run. This corresponds to the vertical segment of the individual supply curve along the vertical axis.

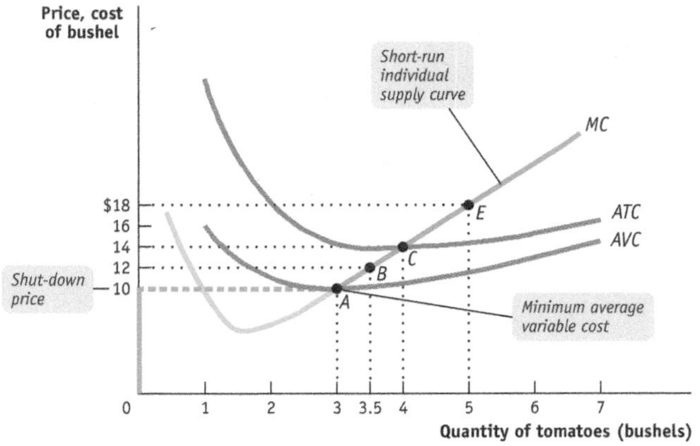

Let's turn to **Figure 59.2**: it shows both the short-run average total cost curve, *ATC*, and the short-run average variable cost curve, *AVC*, drawn from the information in Table 59.1. Recall that the difference between the two curves—the vertical distance between them—represents average fixed cost, the fixed cost per unit of output, *FC/Q*. Because the marginal cost curve has a "swoosh" shape—falling at first before rising—the short-run average variable cost curve is U-shaped: the initial fall in marginal cost causes average variable cost to fall as well, and then the rise in marginal cost eventually pulls average variable cost up again. The short-run average variable cost curve reaches its minimum value of $10 at point *A*, at an output of 3 bushels.

The Shut-Down Price

We are now prepared to analyze the optimal production decision in the short run. We have two cases to consider:

- When the market price is below the minimum average *variable* cost
- When the market price is greater than or equal to the minimum average *variable* cost

When the market price is below the minimum average variable cost, the price the firm receives per unit is not covering its variable cost per unit. A firm in this situation should cease production immediately. Why? Because there is no level of output at which the firm's total revenue covers its variable cost—the cost it can avoid by not operating. In this case the firm maximizes its profit by not producing at all—by, in effect, minimizing its loss. It will still incur a fixed cost in the short run, but it will no longer incur any variable cost. This means that the minimum average variable cost determines the **shut-down price**, the price at which the firm ceases production in the short run.

When price is greater than minimum average variable cost, however, the firm should produce in the short run. In this case, the firm maximizes profit—or minimizes loss—by choosing the output level at which its marginal cost is equal to the market price. For example, if the market price of tomatoes is $18 per bushel, Jennifer and Jason should

A firm will cease production in the short run if the market price falls below the **shut-down price**, which is equal to minimum average variable cost.

TEACH Teach It

Variable costs increase as more output is produced and decrease as less output is produced. Therefore, variable costs are eliminated in the short run if the firm shuts down (no output produced). So, variable costs are the key to determining if a firm should produce in the short run. If $P < AVC$, the firm's revenue can't even cover the variable costs of producing. That means that for every additional unit produced, the firm's losses increase. Minimum losses occur when zero is produced, so the firm shuts down and loses only its fixed costs. But if $P > AVC$, the firm covers the variable costs of producing. Even if it is losing in the short run, it should continue to produce because it will be able to cover its variable costs and at least a portion of its fixed costs (which is better than covering none of them!). Of course in the long run, all costs become variable and this no longer applies! The shut-down rule is that a firm should *shut down if* $P < AVC$.

FOCUS Flip It

TRM After viewing Jacob Clifford's video "Micro 3.6 The Shut-Down Rule" (see econextras video list with hyperlinks on the bcs and TRFD), assign **Worksheet 59.2 (The Shut-Down Rule)** from the TRM so students gain practice with a shut-down case for a perfectly competitive firm.

FOCUS Graph It

Figure 59.2 shows the firm's cost curves. Remind students what they learned about cost curves in the last section. The *ATC* and *AVC* curves are U-shaped and the *MC* curve is upward-sloping and crosses their minimum points. The difference between the *ATC* and *AVC* curves—the vertical distance between them—represents average fixed cost. According to the shut-down rule, firms shut down if $P < AVC$. Therefore, the lowest possible price at which firms will produce is the minimum *AVC*, which may be found where the *MC* curve crosses the *AVC* curve. In this graph, $10 is the shut-down price. Below $10, firms do not produce, so quantity supplied is zero. Above $10, the quantity supplied is found where *P* and *MR* equal *MC*. *So, the supply curve for a perfectly competitive firm is the MC curve from the AVC upward.*

FOCUS Test It

Ask students the following questions:

1. A firm is producing 100 units of output and the market price is $10. If the firm's total cost of production is $1,200, what is the firm's profit and should the firm continue producing? Explain. *–$200; it cannot be determined because VC is not known.*
2. If the firm's total fixed cost is $300, should the firm produce? *Yes. If it shuts down, the firm loses its fixed costs of $300. If it produces, it only loses $200.*

produce at point *E* in Figure 59.2, corresponding to an output of 5 bushels. Note that point *C* in Figure 59.2 corresponds to the farm's break-even price of $14 per bushel. Since *E* lies above *C*, Jennifer and Jason's farm will be profitable; they will generate a per-bushel profit of $18.00 – $14.40 = $3.60 when the market price is $18.

But what if the market price lies between the shut-down price and the break-even price—that is, between the minimum average *variable* cost and the minimum average *total* cost? In the case of Jennifer and Jason's farm, this corresponds to prices anywhere between $10 and $14—say, a market price of $12. At $12, Jennifer and Jason's farm is not profitable; since the market price is below the minimum average total cost, the farm is losing (on average) the difference between price and average total cost on every unit produced. Yet even though the market price isn't covering Jennifer and Jason's average total cost, it is covering their average variable cost and some—but not all—of the average fixed cost. If a firm in this situation shuts down, it will incur no variable cost but it will incur the *full* fixed cost. As a result, shutting down will generate an even greater loss than continuing to operate.

This means that whenever price falls between minimum average total cost and minimum average variable cost, the firm is better off producing some output in the short run. The reason is that by producing, it can cover its variable cost and at least some of its fixed cost, even though it is incurring a loss. In this case, the firm maximizes profit—that is, minimizes loss—by choosing the quantity of output at which its marginal cost is equal to the market price. So if Jennifer and Jason face a market price of $12 per bushel, their profit-maximizing output is given by point *B* in Figure 59.2, corresponding to an output of 3.5 bushels.

It's worth noting that the decision to produce when the firm is covering its variable cost but not all of its fixed cost is similar to the decision to ignore a *sunk cost*, a concept we studied previously. You may recall that a sunk cost is a cost that has already been incurred and cannot be recouped; and because it cannot be changed, it should have no effect on any current decision. In the short-run production decision, fixed cost, in effect, is like a sunk cost—it has been spent, and it can't be recovered in the short run. This comparison also illustrates why variable cost does indeed matter in the short run: it can be avoided by not producing.

And what happens if the market price is exactly equal to the shut-down price, the minimum average variable cost? In this instance, the firm is indifferent between producing 3 units or 0 units. As we'll see shortly, this is an important point when looking at the behavior of an industry as a whole. For the sake of clarity, we'll assume that the firm, although indifferent, does indeed produce output when the market price is equal to the shut-down price.

The **short-run individual supply curve** shows how an individual firm's profit-maximizing level of output depends on the market price, taking the fixed cost as given.

Putting everything together, we can now draw the **short-run individual supply curve** of Jennifer and Jason's farm, the red line in Figure 59.2; it shows how the profit-maximizing quantity of output in the short run depends on the price. As you can see, the curve is in two segments. The upward-sloping red segment starting at point *A* shows the short-run profit-maximizing output when market price is equal to or above the shut-down price of $10 per bushel. As long as the market price is equal to or above the shut-down price, Jennifer and Jason will produce the quantity of output at which marginal cost is equal to the market price. So at market prices equal to or above the shut-down price, the firm's short-run supply curve corresponds to its marginal cost curve. But at any market price below the minimum average variable cost, in this case, $10 per bushel—the firm shuts down and output drops to zero in the short run. This corresponds to the vertical segment of the curve that lies on top of the vertical axis.

Munz/Stone/Getty Images

Do firms sometimes shut down temporarily without going out of business? Yes. In fact, in some industries temporary shut-downs are routine. The most common examples are industries in which demand is highly seasonal, like outdoor amusement parks in climates with cold winters. Such parks would have to offer very low prices to entice customers during the colder months—prices so low that the owners would not cover their variable cost (principally wages and electricity). The wiser choice economically is to shut down until warm weather brings enough customers who are willing to pay a higher price.

598 Section 11 Market Structures: Perfect Competition and Monopoly

Changing Fixed Cost

Although fixed cost cannot be altered in the short run, in the long run firms can acquire or get rid of machines, buildings, and so on. In the long run the level of fixed cost is a matter of choice, and a firm will choose the level of fixed cost that minimizes the average total cost for its desired output level. Now we will focus on an even bigger question facing a firm when choosing its fixed cost: whether to incur *any* fixed cost at all by continuing to operate.

In the long run, a firm can always eliminate fixed cost by selling off its plant and equipment. If it does so, of course, it can't produce any output—it has exited the industry. In contrast, a new firm can take on some fixed cost by acquiring machines and other resources, which puts it in a position to produce—it can enter the industry. In most perfectly competitive industries the set of firms, although fixed in the short run, changes in the long run as some firms enter or exit the industry.

Consider Jennifer and Jason's farm once again. In order to simplify our analysis, we will sidestep the issue of choosing among several possible levels of fixed cost. Instead, we will assume that if they operate at all, Jennifer and Jason have only one possible choice of fixed cost: $14. Alternatively, they can choose a fixed cost of zero if they exit the industry. It is changes in fixed cost that cause short-run average total cost curves to differ from long-run total cost curves, so with this assumption, Jennifer and Jason's short-run and long-run average total cost curves are one and the same.

Suppose that the market price of organic tomatoes is consistently less than the break-even price of $14 over an extended period of time. In that case, Jennifer and Jason never fully cover their total cost: their business runs at a persistent loss. In the long run, then, they can do better by closing their business and leaving the industry. In other words, *in the long run* firms will exit an industry if the market price is consistently less than their break-even price—their minimum average total cost.

Conversely, suppose that the price of organic tomatoes is consistently above the break-even price, $14, for an extended period of time. Because their farm is profitable, Jennifer and Jason will remain in the industry and continue producing. But things won't stop there. The organic tomato industry meets the criterion of *free entry*: there are many potential organic tomato producers because the necessary inputs are easy to obtain. And the cost curves of those potential producers are likely to be similar to those of Jennifer and Jason, since the technology used by other producers is likely to be very similar to that used by Jennifer and Jason. If the price is high enough to generate profit for existing producers, it will also attract some of these potential producers into the industry. So *in the long run* a price in excess of $14 should lead to entry: new producers will come into the organic tomato industry.

As we will see shortly, exit and entry lead to an important distinction between the *short-run industry supply curve* and the *long-run industry supply curve*.

Summing Up: The Perfectly Competitive Firm's Profitability and Production Conditions

In this module we've studied what's behind the supply curve for a perfectly competitive, price-taking firm. A perfectly competitive firm maximizes profit, or minimizes loss, by producing the quantity that equates price and marginal cost. The exception is if price is below minimum average variable cost in the short run, or below minimum average total cost in the long run, in which case the firm is better off shutting down. **Table 59.1** on the next page summarizes the perfectly competitive firm's profitability and production conditions. It also relates them to entry into and exit from the industry in the long run. Now that we understand how a perfectly competitive *firm* makes its decisions, we can go on to look at the supply curve for a perfectly competitive *market* and the long-run equilibrium in perfect competition.

TEACH Teach It

In the long run, the level of fixed cost becomes a choice, as decision makers choose whether to increase or decrease capital (or other previously fixed inputs). The next module moves the model into the long run.

FOCUS Active Learning

TRM Assign **Worksheet 59.3 (Summary of Profit and Production)** in the TRM. This will be a useful summary study sheet for students.

OPEN & CLOSE Exit Slip

*TRM Please see **Exit Slip: Module 59** in the TRM for formative questions to ask your students before finishing your lesson. These questions will help you quickly assess whether your students have mastered the module's concepts before moving on.*

Answers to the Exit Slip Questions

1. D

2. See chart below.

3. 5 units will be produced.

Bushels of Corn	Total Cost (*TC*)	Total Revenue (*TR*)	Marginal Cost (*MC*)	Marginal Revenue (*MR*)
0	10	0	-	-
1	10	5	0	5
2	14	10	4	5
3	17	15	3	5
4	19	20	2	5
5*	24	25	5*	5*
6	31	30	7	5
7	37	35	6	5

Table 59.1 Summary of the Perfectly Competitive Firm's Profitability and Production Conditions

Profitability condition (minimum *ATC* = break-even price)	Result
$P >$ minimum *ATC*	Firm profitable. Entry into industry in the long run.
$P =$ minimum *ATC*	Firm breaks even. No entry into or exit from industry in the long run.
$P <$ minimum *ATC*	Firm unprofitable. Exit from industry in the long run.
Production condition (minimum *AVC* = shut-down price)	**Result**
$P >$ minimum *AVC*	Firm produces in the short run. If $P <$ minimum *ATC*, firm covers variable cost and some but not all of fixed cost. If $P >$ minimum *ATC*, firm covers all variable cost and fixed cost.
$P =$ minimum *AVC*	Firm indifferent between producing in the short run or not. Just covers variable cost.
$P <$ minimum *AVC*	Firm shuts down in the short run. Does not cover variable cost.

FYI Prices Are Up . . . but So Are Costs

In 2005 Congress passed the Energy Policy Act, mandating that by the year 2012, 7.5 billion gallons of alternative fuel—mostly corn-based ethanol—be added to the American fuel supply with the goal of reducing gasoline consumption. The unsurprising result of this mandate: the demand for corn skyrocketed, along with its price. In spring 2007, the price of corn was 50% higher than it had been a year earlier.

This development caught the eye of American farmers like Ronnie Gerik of Aquilla, Texas, who, in response to surging corn prices, reduced the size of his cotton crop and increased his corn acreage by 40%. He was not alone; within a year, the amount of U.S. acreage planted in corn increased by 15%.

Although this sounds like a sure way to make a profit, Gerik was actually taking a big gamble: even though the price of corn increased, so did the cost of the raw materials needed to grow it—by 20%. Consider the cost of just two inputs: fertilizer and fuel. Corn requires more fertilizer than other crops and, with more farmers planting corn, the increased demand for fertilizer led to a price increase. Corn also has to be transported farther away from the farm than cotton. At the same time that Gerik began shifting to greater corn production, diesel fuel became very expensive. And corn is much more sensitive to the amount of rainfall than a crop like cotton. So farmers who plant corn in drought-prone places like Texas are increasing their risk of loss. Gerik had to incorporate his best guess of what a dry spell would cost him into his calculations.

Despite all of this, what Gerik did made complete economic sense. By planting more corn, he was moving up his individual short-run supply curve for corn production. And because his individual supply curve is his marginal cost curve, his costs also went up because he had to use more inputs—inputs that had become more expensive to obtain.

So the moral of this story is that farmers will increase their corn acreage until the marginal cost of producing corn is approximately equal to the market price of corn—which shouldn't come as a surprise because corn production satisfies all the requirements of a perfectly competitive industry.

Courtesy of Ronnie Gerik

Although Gerik was taking a big gamble when he cut the size of his cotton crop to plant more corn, his decision made good economic sense.

600 Section 11 Market Structures: Perfect Competition and Monopoly

MODULE 59 Review

Check Your Understanding

1. Draw a short-run diagram showing a U-shaped average total cost curve, a U-shaped average variable cost curve, and a "swoosh"-shaped marginal cost curve. On it, indicate the range of prices for which the following actions are optimal.
   a. The firm shuts down immediately.
   b. The firm operates in the short run despite sustaining a loss.
   c. The firm operates while making a profit.

2. The state of Maine has a very active lobster industry, which harvests lobsters during the summer months. During the rest of the year, lobsters can be obtained by restaurants from producers in other parts of the world, but at a much higher price. Maine is also full of "lobster shacks," roadside restaurants serving lobster dishes that are open only during the summer. Supposing that the market demand for lobster dishes remains the same throughout the year, explain why it is optimal for lobster shacks to operate only during the summer.

Tackle the Test: Multiple-Choice Questions

For Questions 1–3, refer to the graph provided, and assume that the firm produces the profit-maximizing quantity.

Market Price = $20

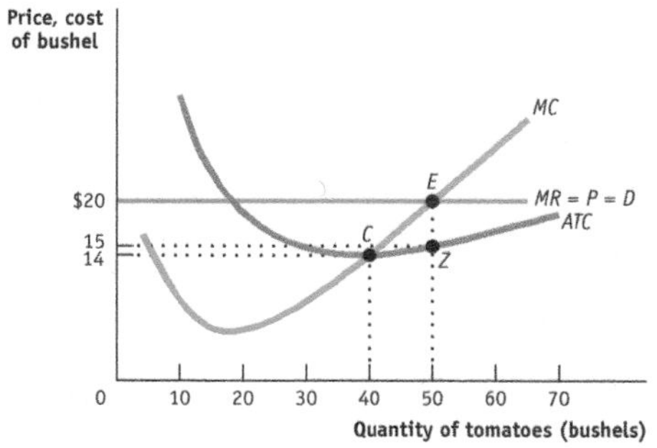

1. The firm's total revenue is equal to
   a. $14.
   b. $20.
   c. $560.
   d. $750.
   e. $1,000.

2. The firm's total cost is equal to
   a. $14.
   b. $15.
   c. $560.
   d. $750.
   e. $1,000.

3. The firm is earning a
   a. profit equal to $5.
   b. profit equal to $250.
   c. loss equal to $15.
   d. loss equal to $750.
   e. loss equal to $250.

4. A firm should continue to produce in the short run as long as price is at least equal to
   a. *MR*.
   b. *MC*.
   c. minimum *ATC*.
   d. minimum *AVC*.
   e. *AFC*.

5. At prices that motivate the firm to produce at all, the short-run supply curve for a perfect competitor corresponds to which curve?
   a. the *ATC* curve
   b. the *AVC* curve
   c. the *MC* curve
   d. the *AFC* curve
   e. the *MR* curve

Tackle the Test: Multiple-Choice Questions

1. e
2. d
3. b
4. d
5. c

Answers to Module 59 Review Questions

Check Your Understanding

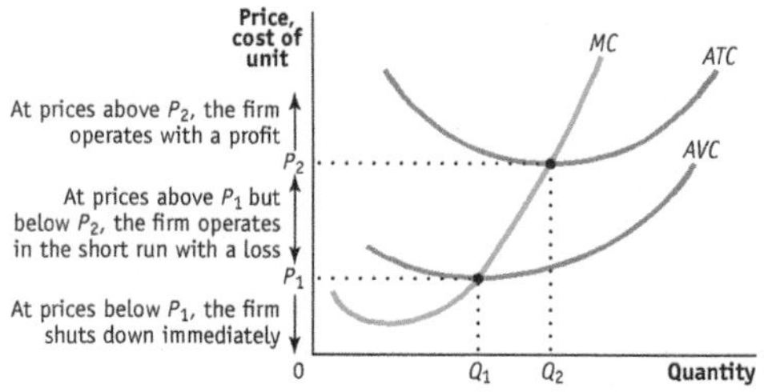

1. a. The firm should shut down immediately when price is less than minimum average variable cost, the shut-down price. In the accompanying diagram, this is optimal for prices in the range from 0 to P_1.

b. When the price is greater than the minimum average variable cost (the shut-down price) but less than the minimum average total cost (the break-even price), the firm should continue to operate in the short run even though it is incurring a loss. This is optimal for prices in the range from P_1 to P_2.

c. When the price exceeds the minimum average total cost (the break-even price), the firm makes a profit. This happens for prices in excess of P_2.

2. This is an example of a temporary shut-down by a firm when the market price lies below the shut-down price, the minimum average variable cost. The market price is the price of a lobster meal and the variable cost is the cost of the lobster, employee wages, and other expenses that increase as more meals are served. In this example, however, it is the average variable cost curve rather than the market price that shifts over time, due to seasonal changes in the cost of lobsters. Maine lobster shacks have relatively low average variable cost during the summer, when cheap Maine lobsters are available; during the rest of the year, their average variable cost is relatively high due to the high cost of imported lobsters. Thus, the lobster shacks are open for business during the summer, when the market price is above their minimum average variable cost; but they close during the rest of the year, when the price lies below their minimum average variable cost.

Module 59 Graphing Perfect Competition 601

Tackle the Test: Free-Response Question

Rubric for FRQ 2 (5 points)

1 point: 6, where $MR = MC$

1 point: $\$20 \times 6 = \$120$

1 point: $\$29.50 \times 6 = \$177$

1 point: $\$120 - \$177 = -\$57$ (or a loss of \$57)

1 point: No, because $P < AVC$

Tackle the Test: Free-Response Questions

Draw a correctly labeled graph showing a perfectly competitive firm producing and incurring a loss in the short run.

Rubric for FRQ 1 (10 points)

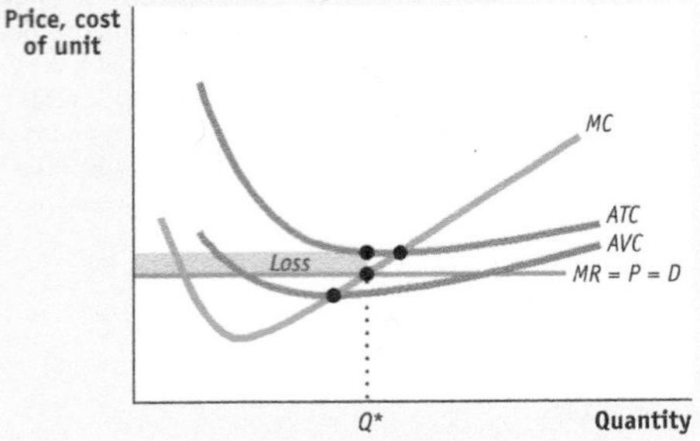

1 point: Vertical axis is labeled "Price, cost of unit" or "Dollars per unit"; horizontal axis is labeled "Quantity" or "Q."

1 point: Demand curve is horizontal and labeled with some combination of "P," "MR," or "D."

1 point: *MC* is labeled and slopes upward in the shape of a swoosh.

1 point: Profit-maximizing quantity is labeled (for example, as "Q*") on the horizontal axis where *MC* = *MR*.

1 point: *ATC* is labeled and U-shaped.

1 point: *ATC* is above price at the profit-maximizing output.

1 point: *MC* crosses *ATC* at the lowest point on *ATC*.

1 point: *AVC* is labeled and U-shaped.

1 point: *AVC* is below price at the profit-maximizing output.

1 point: Loss rectangle is correctly located and identified.

2. Refer to the graph provided.

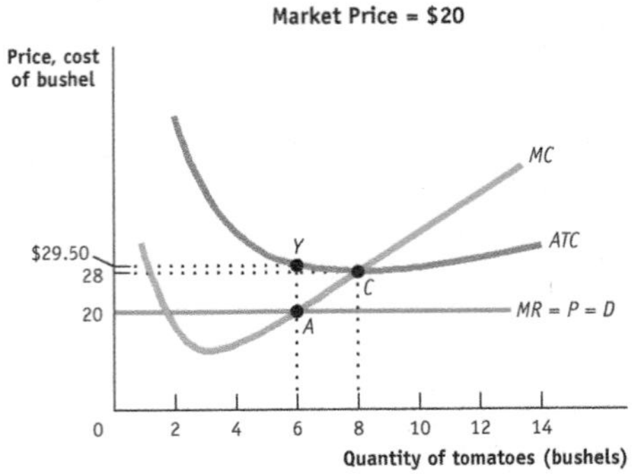

a. Assuming it is appropriate for the firm to produce in the short run, what is the firm's profit-maximizing level of output?

b. Calculate the firm's total revenue.

c. Calculate the firm's total cost.

d. Calculate the firm's profit or loss.

e. If *AVC* were \$22 at the profit-maximizing level of output, would the firm produce in the short run? Explain why or why not.

(5 points)

602 Section 11 Market Structures: Perfect Competition and Monopoly

Getty Images

MODULE 60

Long-Run Outcomes in Perfect Competition

In this Module, you will learn to:

- Explain why industry behavior differs between the short run and the long run
- Discuss what determines the industry supply curve in both the short run and the long run

Up to this point we have been discussing the perfectly competitive firm's short-run situation—whether to produce or not, and if so, whether the firm earns a positive profit, breaks even with a normal profit, or takes a loss. In this module, we look at the long-run situation in a perfectly competitive market. We will see that perfect competition leads to some interesting and desirable market outcomes. Later, we will contrast these outcomes with the outcomes in monopolistic and imperfectly competitive markets.

The Industry Supply Curve

Why will an increase in the demand for organic tomatoes lead to a large price increase at first but a much smaller increase in the long run? The answer lies in the behavior of the **industry supply curve**, which represents the relationship between the price of a good and the total output of the industry as a whole. The industry supply curve is what we referred to in earlier modules as the supply curve or the market supply curve. But here we take some extra care to distinguish between the *individual supply curve* of a single firm and the supply curve of the industry as a whole.

As you might guess from the previous module, the industry supply curve must be analyzed in somewhat different ways for the short run and the long run. Let's start with the short run.

The **industry supply curve** shows the relationship between the price of a good and the total output of the industry as a whole.

The Short-Run Industry Supply Curve

Recall that in the short run the number of firms in an industry is fixed. You may also remember that the industry supply curve is the horizontal sum of the individual supply curves of all firms—you find it by summing the total output across all suppliers at every given price. We will do that exercise here under the assumption that all the

PD To prepare for teaching this lesson, you may want to consult the **Module 60 Sample Lecture** in the TRM.

OPEN & CLOSE Start Here

Have students draw a correctly labeled graph of a perfectly competitive MARKET showing equilibrium price and quantity. Tell your class that, at this equilibrium price, firms are earning an economic profit. Ask the students what they would do if they encountered a market in which firms were earning huge economic profit. Students will eventually respond that they would want to get into the market to make lots of money. Have them draw the effect on equilibrium price in the market if aspiring entrepreneurs entered this market in search of profit. On their graphs, they should show an increase in supply, which causes the equilibrium price to fall. Ask them what will happen to profit if price falls. Help students understand that a lower price will decrease profit. Repeat this exercise with the example of firms earning a loss. These examples will set up the discussion of long-run equilibrium in this module.

TEACH Connect It

Remind students about the short run for a perfectly competitive firm. The supply curve is the *MC* curve above minimum average variable cost; the firm maximizes profit where $MC = MR$; and the number of firms in an industry is fixed because entry and exit only occur in the long run.

TEACH Teach It

The short-run industry supply curve is the sum of existing firms' individual supply curves. In the long run, the industry supply curve is the sum of all existing and potential firms' individual supply curves after all entry and exit have taken place.

TEACH Connect It

Figure 59.2 reviews the individual firm's short-run supply curve and Figure 60.1 shows the short-run market equilibrium. Point out that Figure 60.1 is the same supply and demand graph presented in Section 2.

Figure 59.2 The Short-Run Individual Supply Curve

When the market price equals or exceeds Jennifer and Jason's *shut-down price* of $10, the minimum average variable cost indicated by point *A*, they will produce the output quantity at which marginal cost is equal to price. So at any price equal to or above the minimum average *variable* cost, the short-run individual supply curve is the firm's marginal cost curve; this corresponds to the upward-sloping segment of the individual supply curve. When market price falls below minimum average variable cost, the firm ceases operation in the short run. This corresponds to the vertical segment of the individual supply curve along the vertical axis.

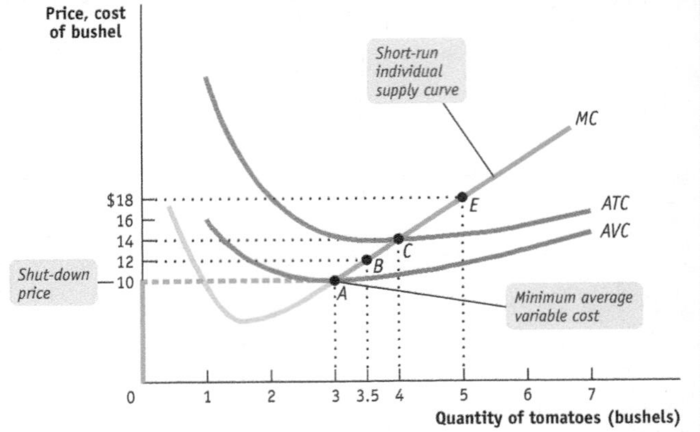

firms are alike—an assumption that makes the derivation particularly simple. So let's assume that there are 100 organic tomato farms, each with the same costs as Jennifer and Jason's farm. Each of these 100 farms will have an individual short-run supply curve like the one in Figure 59.2 from the previous module, which is reprinted above for your convenience.

At a price below $10, no farms will produce. At a price of more than $10, each farm will produce the quantity of output at which its marginal cost is equal to the market price. As you can see from Figure 59.2, this will lead each farm to produce 4 bushels if the price is $14 per bushel, 5 bushels if the price is $18, and so on. So if there are 100 organic tomato farms and the price of organic tomatoes is $18 per bushel, the industry as a whole will produce 500 bushels, corresponding to 100 farms × 5 bushels per farm. The result is the **short-run industry supply curve**, shown as *S* in **Figure 60.1**. This curve shows the quantity that producers in an industry will supply at each price, *taking the number of farms as given*.

The **short-run industry supply curve** shows how the quantity supplied by an industry depends on the market price, given a fixed number of firms.

There is a **short-run market equilibrium** when the quantity supplied equals the quantity demanded, taking the number of producers as given.

The demand curve, labeled *D* in Figure 60.1, crosses the short-run industry supply curve at E_{MKT}, corresponding to a price of $18 and a quantity of 500 bushels. Point E_{MKT} is a **short-run market equilibrium**: the quantity supplied equals the quantity demanded, taking the number of farms as given. But the long run may look quite different because in the long run farms may enter or exit the industry.

The Long-Run Industry Supply Curve

Suppose that in addition to the 100 farms currently in the organic tomato business, there are many other potential organic tomato farms. Suppose also that each of these potential farms would have the same cost curves as existing farms, like the one owned by Jennifer and Jason, upon entering the industry.

When will additional farms enter the industry? Whenever existing farms are making a profit—that is, whenever the market price is above the break-even price of $14 per bushel, the minimum average total cost of production. For example, at a price of $18 per bushel, new farms will enter the industry.

604 Section 11 Market Structures: Perfect Competition and Monopoly

Figure 60.1 The Short-Run Market Equilibrium

The short-run industry supply curve, S, is the industry supply curve taking the number of producers—here, 100—as given. It is generated by adding together the individual supply curves of the 100 producers. Below the shut-down price of $10, no producer wants to produce in the short run. Above $10, the short-run industry supply curve slopes upward, as each producer increases output as price increases. It intersects the demand curve, D, at point E_{MKT}, the point of short-run market equilibrium, corresponding to a market price of $18 and a quantity of 500 bushels.

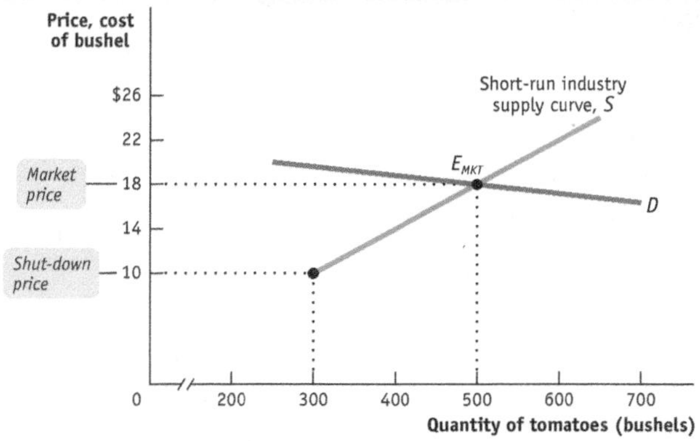

What will happen as additional farms enter the industry? Clearly, the quantity supplied at any given price will increase. The short-run industry supply curve will shift to the right. This will alter the market equilibrium in turn and result in a lower market price. Existing farms will respond to the lower market price by reducing their output, but the total industry output will increase because of the larger number of farms in the industry.

Figure 60.2 on the next page illustrates the effects of this chain of events on an existing farm and on the market; panel (a) shows how the market responds to entry, and panel (b) shows how an individual existing farm responds to entry. (Note that these two graphs have been rescaled in comparison to Figures 59.2 and 60.1 to better illustrate how profit changes in response to price.) In panel (a), S_1 is the initial short-run industry supply curve, based on the existence of 100 producers. The initial short-run market equilibrium is at E_{MKT}, with an equilibrium market price of $18 and a quantity of 500 bushels. At this price existing farms are profitable, which is reflected in panel (b): an existing farm makes a total profit represented by the green shaded rectangle labeled A when the market price is $18.

This profit will induce new producers to enter the industry, shifting the short-run industry supply curve to the right. For example, the short-run industry supply curve when the number of farms has increased to 167 is S_2. Corresponding to this supply curve is a new short-run market equilibrium labeled D_{MKT}, with a market price of $16 and a quantity of 750 bushels. At $16, each farm produces 4.5 bushels, so that industry output is $167 \times 4.5 = 750$ bushels (rounded). From panel (b) you can see the effect of the entry of 67 new farms on an existing farm: the fall in price causes it to reduce its output, and its profit falls to the area represented by the striped rectangle labeled B.

Although diminished, the profit of existing farms at D_{MKT} means that entry will continue and the number of farms will continue to rise. If the number of farms rises to 250, the short-run industry supply curve shifts out again to S_3, and the market equilibrium is at C_{MKT}, with a quantity supplied and demanded of 1,000 bushels and a market price of $14 per bushel.

Like E_{MKT} and D_{MKT}, C_{MKT} is a short-run equilibrium. But it is also something more. Because the price of $14 is each farm's break-even price, an existing producer makes zero economic profit—neither a profit nor a loss, earning only the opportunity cost

TEACH Teach It

As described in the opening example, profit creates an incentive for firms to enter an industry and losses lead firms to exit an industry. Entry and exit lead to changes in market supply (remember that the number of firms was a factor that affected supply). Entry causes an increase in supply, so supply shifts to the right, causing price and profit to decrease. Exit causes a decrease in supply, so supply shifts to the left, causing price to increase and losses to decrease. Show students these visuals:

Profit → Entry → ↑ S → ↓ P → ↓ Profit (until Profit = 0)

Losses → Exit → ↓ S → ↑ P → ↓ Losses (until Profit = 0)

FOCUS Active Learning

TRM Students can practice ideas about profit maximization and loss minimization by completing **Worksheet 60.1 (Profit-Maximization and Loss-Minimization Practice)** from the TRM.

Module 60 Long-Run Outcomes in Perfect Competition 605

FOCUS Graph It

Figure 60.2 illustrates the long-run equilibrating process using side-by-side graphs of the market and the firm. Since price is measured on the vertical axis of both graphs, horizontal lines are used to compare the same price for the market and the firm. At a price of $18, the firm earns a profit of $18. *TR* is 5 units times the price of $18 ($90), and *TC* is 5 units times the cost of $14.40 ($72). Entry leads to a rightward shift of supply to S_2, causing price to fall to $16 and profit to decrease to striped area *B*. Entry continues until supply shifts to S_3, where price equals $14 and there is zero profit. With zero profit, no incentive exists for entry or exit and the firm is in long-run equilibrium.

FOCUS Flip It

TRM Have your class watch Jacob Clifford's video "Micro 3.10 Perfect Competition in the Long Run" (see econextras video list with hyperlinks on the bcs and TRFD), and then assign **Worksheet 60.2 (Perfect Competition in the Long Run)** from the TRM.

FOCUS Active Learning

TRM You can use **Worksheet 60.3 (Long-Run Equilibrium Teaching Aid)** from the TRM to assist students in understanding the elements of long-run equilibrium.

Figure 60.2 The Long-Run Market Equilibrium

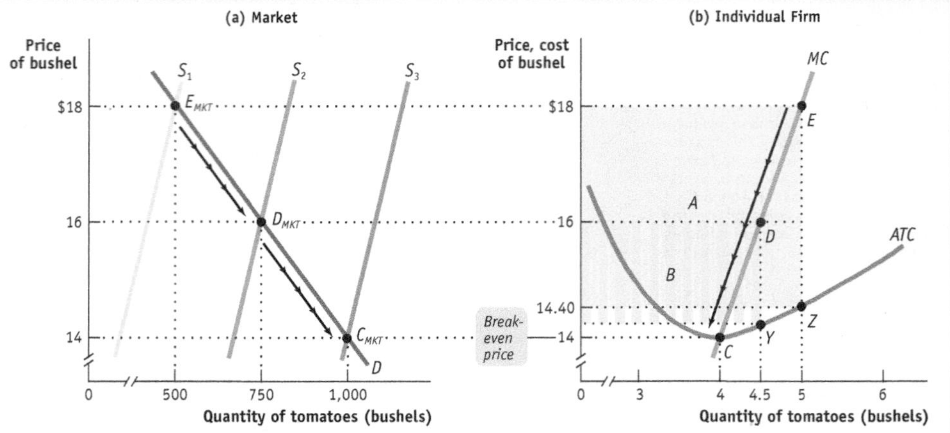

Point E_{MKT} of panel (a) shows the initial short-run market equilibrium. Each of the 100 existing producers makes an economic profit, illustrated in panel (b) by the green rectangle labeled *A*, the profit of an existing firm. Profit induces entry by additional producers, shifting the short-run industry supply curve outward from S_1 to S_2 in panel (a), resulting in a new short-run equilibrium at point D_{MKT}, at a lower market price of $16 and higher industry output. Existing firms reduce output and profit falls to the area given by the striped rectangle labeled *B* in panel (b). Entry continues to shift out the short-run industry supply curve, as price falls and industry output increases yet again. Entry ceases at point C_{MKT} on supply curve S_3 in panel (a). Here market price is equal to the break-even price; existing producers make zero economic profit and there is no incentive for entry or exit. Therefore C_{MKT} is also a long-run market equilibrium.

AP® Exam Tip

Draw dotted lines taking the equilibrium price from the market graph over to the firm graph to show your understanding that the firm is a price-taker.

A market is in **long-run market equilibrium** when the quantity supplied equals the quantity demanded, given that sufficient time has elapsed for entry into and exit from the industry to occur.

of the resources used in production—when producing its profit-maximizing output of 4 bushels. At this price there is no incentive either for potential producers to enter or for existing producers to exit the industry. So C_{MKT} corresponds to a **long-run market equilibrium**—a situation in which the quantity supplied equals the quantity demanded, given that sufficient time has elapsed for producers to either enter or exit the industry. In a long-run market equilibrium, all existing and potential producers have fully adjusted to their optimal long-run choices; as a result, no producer has an incentive to either enter or exit the industry.

To explore further the difference between short-run and long-run equilibrium, consider the effect of an increase in demand on an industry with free entry that is initially in long-run equilibrium. Panel (b) in **Figure 60.3** shows the market adjustment; panels (a) and (c) show how an existing individual firm behaves during the process.

In panel (b) of Figure 60.3, D_1 is the initial demand curve and S_1 is the initial short-run industry supply curve. Their intersection at point X_{MKT} is both a short-run and a long-run market equilibrium because the equilibrium price of $14 leads to zero economic profit—and therefore neither entry nor exit. It corresponds to point *X* in panel (a), where an individual existing firm is operating at the minimum of its average total cost curve.

Now suppose that the demand curve shifts out for some reason to D_2. As shown in panel (b), in the short run, industry output moves along the short-run industry supply curve, S_1, to the new short-run market equilibrium at Y_{MKT}, the intersection of S_1 and D_2. The market price rises to $18 per bushel, and industry output increases from Q_X to Q_Y.

606 Section 11 Market Structures: Perfect Competition and Monopoly

Figure 60.3 The Effect of an Increase in Demand in the Short Run and the Long Run for a Constant-Cost Industry

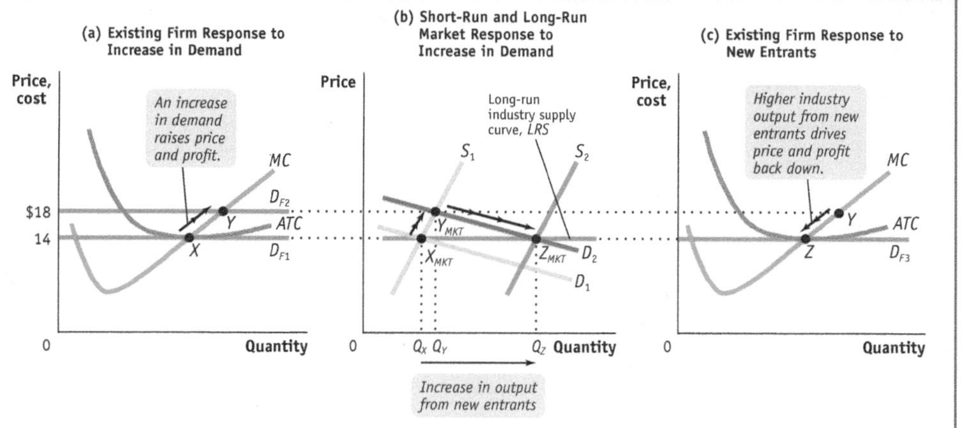

Panel (b) shows how an industry adjusts in the short and long run to an increase in demand; panels (a) and (c) show the corresponding adjustments by an existing firm. Initially the market is at point X_{MKT} in panel (b), a short-run and long-run equilibrium at a price of $14 and industry output of Q_X. An existing firm makes zero economic profit, operating at point *X* in panel (a) at minimum average total cost. Demand increases as D_1 shifts rightward to D_2, in panel (b), raising the market price to $18. Existing firms increase their output, and industry output moves along the short-run industry supply curve S_1 to a short-run equilibrium at Y_{MKT}. Correspondingly, the existing firm in panel (a) moves from point *X* to point *Y* as its demand rises from D_{F1} to D_{F2}. But at a price of $18 existing firms are profitable. As shown in panel (b), in the long run new entrants arrive and the short-run industry supply curve shifts rightward, from S_1 to S_2. There is a new equilibrium at point Z_{MKT}, at a lower price of $14 and higher industry output of Q_Z. An existing firm responds to the decrease in its demand to D_{F3} by moving from *Y* to *Z* in panel (c), returning to its initial output level and zero economic profit. Production by new entrants accounts for the total increase in industry output, $Q_Z - Q_X$. Like X_{MKT}, Z_{MKT} is also a short-run and long-run equilibrium: with existing firms earning zero economic profit, there is no incentive for any firms to enter or exit the industry. The horizontal line passing through X_{MKT} and Z_{MKT}, *LRS*, is the *long-run industry supply curve:* at the break-even price of $14, producers will produce any amount that consumers demand in the long run.

This corresponds to an existing firm's movement from *X* to *Y* in panel (a) as the firm increases its output in response to the rise in its demand curve (which also represents price and marginal revenue) from D_{F1} to D_{F2}.

But we know that Y_{MKT} is not a long-run equilibrium because $18 is higher than minimum average total cost, so existing firms are making economic profit. This will lead additional firms to enter the industry. Over time entry will cause the short-run industry supply curve to shift to the right. In the long run, the short-run industry supply curve will have shifted out to S_2, and the equilibrium will be at Z_{MKT}—with the price falling back to $14 per bushel and industry output increasing yet again, from Q_Y to Q_Z. Like X_{MKT} before the increase in demand, Z_{MKT} is both a short-run and a long-run market equilibrium.

The effect of entry on an existing firm is illustrated in panel (c), in the movement from *Y* to *Z* along the firm's individual supply curve. The firm reduces its output in response to the fall in the market price, which lowers the firm's demand curve from D_{F2} to D_{F3}. The firm ultimately arrives back at its original output quantity, corresponding to the minimum of its average total cost curve. In fact, every firm that is now in the

AP® Exam Tip

Approach changes that have long-run repercussions one small step at a time. First show the initial change on your graph. Then analyze the short-run effects of that change. Finally, focus on the adjustments that lead to long-run equilibrium.

TEACH AP® Exam Tip

On the AP® exam, students are asked to draw side-by-side graphs of the market and the firm to show the adjustment process that leads to long-run equilibrium. Students are asked to draw side-by-side graphs again in Section 13 when they create factor market graphs.

TEACH Teach It

Figure 60.3 provides an example of the use of side-by-side graphs for the firm and the market. This figure traces the effect of an increase in demand for a firm [shown in panel (a) as an increase from $14 to $18] that leads to a movement from *X* to *Y* (where the firm earns a profit) to the market [shown as a shift in demand from D_1 to D_2 in panel (b)].

The profit resulting from the increase in demand leads to entry, which increases supply from S_1 to S_2 [as shown in panel (b)]. The effect of the increase in supply is traced back to the firm [shown in panel (c) as a shift from point *Y* to point *Z*], illustrating that profit is eliminated.

FOCUS Active Learning

TRM Use **Worksheet 60.4 (Market and Firm Relationships)** from the TRM to practice drawing side-by-side graphs showing how changes in the market affect the fortunes of a firm.

FOCUS Graph It

Have students draw side-by-side graphs of the market and firm in long-run equilibrium. They should create a correctly labeled market supply and demand graph showing equilibrium price and quantity. The market equilibrium price ought to be traced over to their firm graph (which should look like the graph in the answer to the Tackle the Test FRQ for this module).

TEACH Teach It

A perfectly competitive industry is a constant-cost industry if the firm's cost curves and price are unaffected by changes in the size of the industry. Figure 60.3 shows a constant-cost industry. The perfectly elastic long-run supply curve is a characteristic of a constant-cost industry. It is the gray line in panel (b) of Figure 60.3. If an increase in industry size leads to higher costs, the long-run supply curve is upward-sloping (an increasing-cost industry), and if an increase in industry size leads to lower costs, the long-run industry supply curve slopes downward (a decreasing-cost industry).

FOCUS Active Learning

TRM Direct students to watch Austin Boyle's video "Creating Long-Run Supply Curve in Perfectly Competitive Constant-Cost Industry" (see econextras video list with hyperlinks on the bcs and TRFD) for a walk through constant cost and long-run supply. Assign **Worksheet 60.5 (Constant-Cost Industry)** from the TRM.

TEACH Teach It

In some industries, a limited supply of resources exists, and as the industry expands, the price of the inputs increases, causing costs to increase. This type of industry is known as an increasing-cost industry.

FOCUS Active Learning

TRM Have your class watch Austin Boyle's video "Creating Long-Run Supply Curve in Perfectly Competitive Increasing-Cost Industry" (see econextras video list with hyperlinks on the bcs and TRFD) and assign **Worksheet 60.6 (Increasing-Cost Industry)** from the TRM for questions about it.

FOCUS Test It

TRM Use **Worksheet 60.7 (Perfectly Competitive Markets Review)** from the TRM as an assessment lesson on perfectly competitive markets.

The **long-run industry supply curve** shows how the quantity supplied responds to the price once producers have had time to enter or exit the industry.

A **constant-cost industry** is one with a horizontal (perfectly elastic) long-run supply curve.

An **increasing-cost industry** is one with an upward-sloping long-run supply curve.

industry—the initial set of firms and the new entrants—will operate at the minimum of its average total cost curve, at point *Z*. This means that the entire increase in industry output, from Q_X to Q_Z, comes from production by new entrants.

The line *LRS* that passes through X_{MKT} and Z_{MKT} in panel (b) is the **long-run industry supply curve**. It shows how the quantity supplied by an industry responds to the price, given that firms have had time to enter or exit the industry.

In this particular case, the long-run industry supply curve is horizontal at $14. In other words, in this industry supply is *perfectly elastic* in the long run: given time to enter or exit, firms will supply any quantity that consumers demand at a price of $14. Perfectly elastic long-run supply is characteristic of a **constant-cost industry**. In a constant-cost industry, the firms' cost curves are unaffected by changes in the size of the industry, either because there is a perfectly elastic supply of inputs, or because the industry's input demand is too small relative to the overall input market to influence the input price. For example, the wooden pencil industry can expand without causing a significant increase in the price of wood.

In an **increasing-cost industry**, even the long-run industry supply curve slopes upward. The usual reason for this is that producers must use a significant amount of an input that is in limited supply (that is, their supply is at least somewhat inelastic). As the industry expands, the price of that input is driven up. Consequently, the cost structure for firms becomes higher than it was when the industry was smaller. An example is the cotton clothing industry, an expansion in which could drive up the price of cotton. **Figure 60.4** illustrates the short-run and long-run effects of an increase in demand in an increasing-cost industry. In panel (b), D_1 is the initial demand curve for cotton pants

Figure 60.4 The Effect of an Increase in Demand in the Short Run and the Long Run in an Increasing-Cost Industry

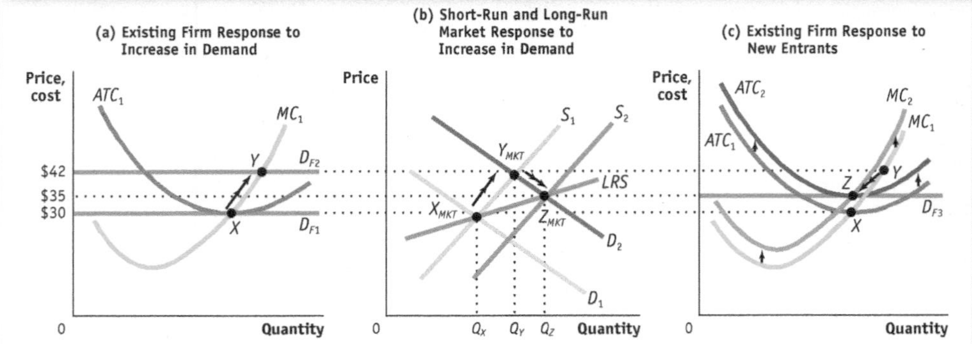

In an increasing-cost industry, an increase in demand leads to a higher price both in the short run *and* in the long run. Suppose demand increases from D_1 to D_2 as shown in panel (b). This raises the market price to $42. Existing firms increase their output, and industry output expands along the short-run industry supply curve, S_1, to a short-run equilibrium at Y_{MKT}. The increase in output from Q_X to Q_Y is the result of existing firms increasing their output as shown for a representative firm by the move from point *X* to point *Y* in panel (a). Because the new price is above the minimum of average total cost, economic profit attracts new entrants in the long run, shifting the short-run industry supply curve rightward and lowering the market price. Meanwhile, industry expansion drives up the cost of inputs and shifts the firms' cost curves upward as shown in panel (c). This continues until the falling equilibrium price meets the rising minimum of average total cost. As shown in panel (b), that occurs at equilibrium point Z_{MKT} with a price of $35 and an industry output of Q_Z. Assuming that the higher input prices raise the cost of making each unit by the same amount, the firms' cost curves shift straight up. In the long run, an existing firm moves from *Y* to *Z* in panel (c), returning to its initial output level and earning zero economic profit. The upward-sloping line passing through X_{MKT} and Z_{MKT}, labeled *LRS*, is the long-run industry supply curve.

608 Section 11 Market Structures: Perfect Competition and Monopoly

and S_1 is the initial short-run industry supply curve. The market equilibrium at point X_{MKT} corresponds to point X in panel (a), where an individual firm is operating at the minimum of its average total cost curve.

Now suppose that the demand curve shifts out to D_2. As shown in panel (b), in the short run, industry output expands along the short-run industry supply curve, S_1, to the new short-run market equilibrium at Y_{MKT}, the intersection of S_1 and D_2. The market price rises from $30 to $42 per pair, and industry output increases from Q_X to Q_Y. This corresponds to an existing firm's movement from X to Y in panel (a), as it increases its output in response to the increase in its demand curve from D_{F1} to D_{F2}.

At the new market price, existing firms earn economic profit, so additional firms enter the industry. Entry shifts the short-run industry supply curve to the right and lowers the price of pants. At the same time, increasing demand for cotton drives up the cost of this input. The resulting rise in input costs shifts the marginal and average total cost curves upward for firms. This process continues until the falling market price and the rising minimum average total cost meet somewhere in between the initial price of $30 and the short-run price of $42. In Figure 60.4, that occurs at a price of $35, after the short-run supply curve has shifted out to S_2 and the cost of making each pair of pants has risen by $5.

An expansion in the cotton clothing industry drives up the price of cotton.

When the market reaches long-run equilibrium at Z_{MKT}, each firm faces a demand curve of D_{F3} as shown in panel (c). Firms earn zero economic profit and there is no incentive for additional entry. Assuming that the cost increase is the same for each unit of output, each firm (that is not new) ends up making the same quantity of output as it did before the increase in demand. If the cost increase is not the same for each unit of output, the cost curves will not shift straight up as they did here, so the new profit-maximizing quantity of output could be more or less than before. The upward-sloping line *LRS* that passes through X_{MKT} and Z_{MKT} in panel (b) is the long-run industry supply curve for this increasing-cost industry.

A decrease in demand triggers the same process in reverse: the lower market price causes losses and the exit of firms, which lowers the cost of inputs and shifts the cost curves down until the falling minimum of average total cost meets the rising market price.

Finally, it is possible for the long-run industry supply curve to slope downward, a condition that occurs when the cost structure for firms becomes lower as the industry expands. This is the case in industries such as the electric car industry, in which increased output allows for economies of scale in the production of lithium batteries and other specialized inputs, and thus lower input prices.

A downward-sloping industry supply curve indicates a **decreasing-cost industry**. **Figure 60.5** on the next page illustrates the short-run and long-run effects of an increase in demand in a decreasing-cost industry. In panel (b), D_1 is the initial demand curve for electric cars and S_1 is the initial short-run industry supply curve. If the demand curve shifts out to D_2, the new short-run market equilibrium is Y_{MKT}. The market price rises from $40,000 to $49,000 per electric car, and industry output increases from Q_X to Q_Y. This corresponds to an existing firm's movement from X to Y in panel (a), caused by the increase in its demand curve from D_{F1} to D_{F2}.

A **decreasing-cost industry** is one with a downward-sloping long-run supply curve.

At the new market price, economic profit attracts additional firms. Entry shifts the short-run industry supply curve to the right and lowers the price of electric cars. At the same time, increasing demand for lithium batteries allows for economies of scale in battery production, and lowers the cost of this input. The resulting decrease in input costs shifts the marginal and average total cost curves downward for firms. This process continues until the falling market price catches up to the falling minimum average total cost somewhere below the initial price of $40,000. In Figure 60.5, that occurs at a price of $36,000, after the short-run supply curve has shifted out to S_2 in panel (b).

At the long-run equilibrium of Z_{MKT}, each firm faces a demand curve of D_{F3} as shown in panel (c). Firms earn zero economic profit and there is no incentive for additional entry. Assuming that the cost decrease is the same for each car produced, each firm

TEACH Teach It

In some industries, firms experience economies of scale and therefore costs decrease as the industry expands. These industries are known as decreasing-cost industries.

Module 60 Long-Run Outcomes in Perfect Competition 609

FOCUS Graph It

Figure 60.5 shows short-run and long-run supply curves for a decreasing-cost industry. Have a student redraw Figure 60.5 on the board for the class to see and ask the following questions:

- Which supply curve is flatter and which is steeper: the long-run or the short-run supply curve and why? *The long-run supply curve is flatter due to the entry and exit of firms to and from the industry.*
- Which supply curve is more elastic: the short- or long-run supply curve? *Long-run*
- What effect does an increase in price have on the industry? *A higher price attracts new entrants in the long run, which results in an increase in industry output and a decrease in price.*
- What effect does a lower price have on the industry? *A lower price causes existing producers to exit the industry in the long run, leading to a decrease in industry output and an increase in price.*

Figure 60.5 The Effect of an Increase in Demand in the Short Run and the Long Run in a Decreasing-Cost Industry

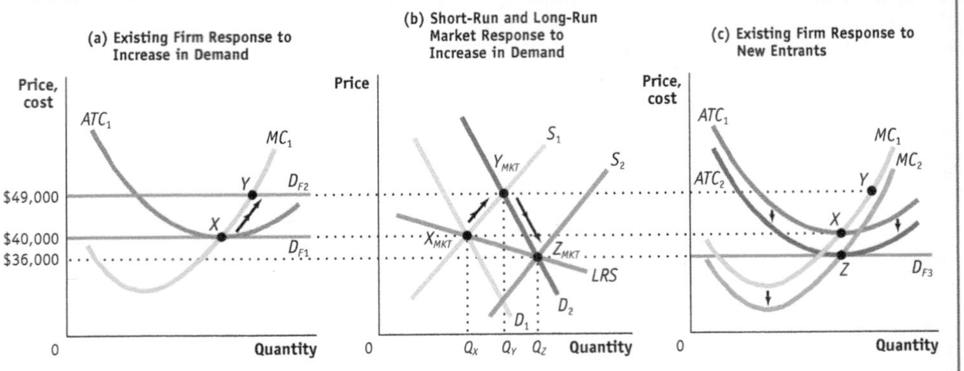

In a decreasing-cost industry, an increase in demand leads to a higher price in the short run and a lower price in the long run. Suppose demand increases from D_1 to D_2 as shown in panel (b). This raises the market price from $40,000 to $49,000. Existing firms increase their output, and industry output expands along the short-run industry supply curve, S_1, to a short-run equilibrium at Y_{MKT}. Economic profit attracts new entrants in the long run, shifting the short-run industry supply curve rightward and lowering the market price. Meanwhile, industry expansion lowers the cost of inputs and shifts the firms' cost curves downward as shown in panel (c). This continues until the falling equilibrium price catches up to the falling minimum of average total cost. As shown in panel (b), that occurs at equilibrium point Z_{MKT} with a price of $36,000 and an industry output of Q_Z. Assuming that the lower input cost decreases the cost of making each unit by the same amount, the firms' cost curves shift straight down. In the long run, an existing firm moves from *Y* to *Z* in panel (c), returning to its initial output level and earning zero economic profit. The downward-sloping line passing through X_{MKT} and Z_{MKT}, labeled *LRS*, is the long-run industry supply curve.

ends up making the same quantity of cars as it did before the increase in demand. The downward-sloping line *LRS* that passes through X_{MKT} and Z_{MKT} in panel (b) is the long-run industry supply curve for this decreasing-cost industry.

Regardless of whether the long-run industry supply curve is horizontal, upward-sloping, or downward-sloping, the long-run price elasticity of supply is *higher* than the short-run price elasticity whenever there is free entry and exit. As shown in **Figure 60.6**, the long-run industry supply curve is always flatter than the short-run industry supply curve. The reason is entry and exit: a high price caused by an increase in demand attracts entry by new firms, resulting in a rise in industry output and an eventual fall in price; a low price caused by a decrease in demand induces existing firms to exit, leading to a fall in industry output and an eventual increase in price.

The distinction between the short-run industry supply curve and the long-run industry supply curve is very important in practice. We often see a sequence of events like those shown in Figures 60.3, 60.4, and 60.5: an increase in demand initially leads to a large price increase, but prices return to a more moderate level once new firms have entered the industry. Or we see the sequence in reverse: a fall in demand reduces prices considerably in the short run, but they return to a more moderate level as producers exit the industry.

610 Section 11 Market Structures: Perfect Competition and Monopoly

Figure 60.6 Comparing the Short-Run and Long-Run Industry Supply Curves

The long-run industry supply curve may slope upward, but it is always flatter—more elastic—than the short-run industry supply curve. This is because of entry and exit: a higher price attracts new entrants in the long run, resulting in a rise in industry output and a fall in price; a lower price induces existing producers to exit in the long run, generating a fall in industry output and a rise in price.

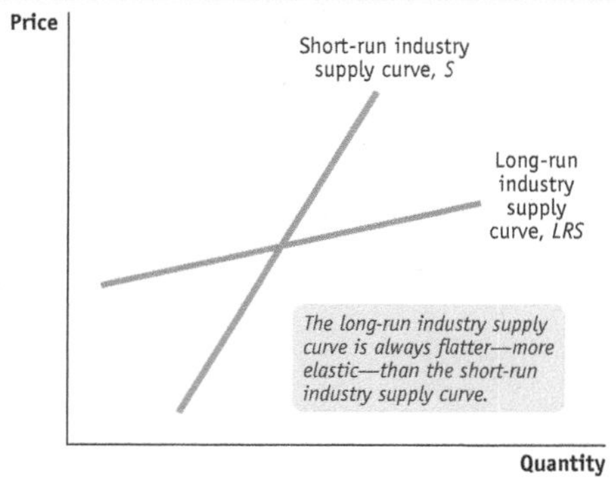

The Cost of Production and Efficiency in Long-Run Equilibrium

Our analysis leads us to three conclusions about the cost of production and efficiency in the long-run equilibrium of a perfectly competitive industry. These results will be important in our upcoming discussion of how monopoly gives rise to inefficiency.

First, in a perfectly competitive industry in equilibrium, all firms produce the quantity of output at which the marginal cost equals the market price. This $P = MC$ outcome leads to allocative efficiency, meaning that it yields the mix of goods and services that society most values, as discussed in Module 3. This efficiency comes from the production of more of the good until the price consumers are willing to pay—an indication of the marginal benefit received from the good—equals the marginal cost of making it. After that point, the marginal cost exceeds the marginal benefit, so additional units should not be made.

Second, in a perfectly competitive industry with free entry and exit, each firm will have zero economic profit in the long-run equilibrium. Each firm produces the quantity of output that minimizes its average total cost—corresponding to point Z in panel (c) of Figures 60.3, 60.4, and 60.5. Because the total cost of producing the industry's output is minimized, a perfectly competitive industry achieves productive efficiency.

Third, in the long-run market equilibrium of a perfectly competitive industry, the consumers who are willing to pay an amount greater than or equal to the sellers' marginal cost actually get the good. No mutually beneficial transactions go unexploited because the market price matches the consumers who are willing to pay the most for the good with the sellers who have a cost of production that is less than or equal to the market price.

So the long-run equilibrium of a perfectly competitive industry delivers efficiency. There is allocative efficiency because $P = MC$; there is productive efficiency because costs are minimized and no resources are wasted; and the goods are distributed to those who are willing to pay the most for them. Moreover, these conditions tend to persist over time as the environment changes: the force of competition makes producers responsive to changes in consumers' desires and to changes in technology.

TEACH Connect It

Review the concept of efficiency, which was first discussed in Module 3. In general, efficiency means "no waste." An important outcome of long-run equilibrium in perfect competition is that it results in efficiency, both allocative and productive.

TEACH Teach It

Allocative efficiency occurs when $P = MC$. When it does, every consumer willing to pay the cost of production gets the good. For firms in a perfectly competitive industry in equilibrium, MC is the same for all firms because all firms are price-takers and they produce the quantity of output where $MC = MR = P$.

TEACH Teach It

Productive efficiency occurs when the average total cost of production is minimized. A firm in a perfectly competitive industry achieves productive efficiency ($P =$ Minimum ATC) in the long run because firms maximize profit when $MC = MR = P$ and firms earn a normal profit ($P = ATC$), so $MC = ATC$. We know from Section 10 that MC crosses the ATC curve at the minimum point on the ATC curve.

FOCUS Test It

TRM Use **Worksheet 60.8 (Long-Run Equilibrium and Efficiency)** from the TRM to test students on the concepts discussed here.

OPEN & CLOSE Exit Slip

TRM *Please see* ***Exit Slip: Module 60*** *in the TRM for formative multiple-choice questions to ask your students before finishing your lesson. These questions will help you quickly assess whether your students have mastered the module's concepts before moving on.*

Answers to the Exit Slip Questions

1. E
2. D
3. E

Module 60 Long-Run Outcomes in Perfect Competition 611

Answers to Module 60 Review Questions

Check Your Understanding

1. a. When fixed costs fall, *ATC* decreases and each firm's profit at the current output level increases. In the long run, new firms will enter the industry. This increase in supply drives down price and profits. Once profits are driven back to zero, entry will cease.

b. An increase in wages means that *AVC* and *ATC* increase. In the short run, some firms incur losses. As a result, in the long run, some firms will exit the industry. As firms exit, supply decreases, price rises, and losses are reduced. Exit will cease once losses return to zero.

c. Price increases as demand increases, leading to short-run profits. In the long run, firms will enter the industry, generating an increase in supply, a fall in price, and a fall in profits. Once profits are driven back to zero, entry will cease.

d. The shortage of inputs causes resource price to increase, increasing *AVC* and *ATC*. Firms incur losses in the short run, and some firms will exit the industry in the long run. The fall in supply means an increase in price and a reduction in losses. Exit will cease once losses return to zero.

2. In the accompanying diagram, point X_{MKT} in panel (b), the intersection of S_1 and D_1, represents the long-run industry equilibrium before the change in consumer tastes. When tastes change, demand falls and the industry moves in the short run to point Y_{MKT} in panel (b), at the intersection of the new demand curve D_2 and S_1, the short-run supply curve representing the same number of egg producers as in the original equilibrium at point X_{MKT}. As the market price falls, each individual firm reacts by producing less—shown in panel (a) as the movement from point *X* to point *Y*—so long as the market price remains above the minimum average variable cost. If market price falls below minimum average variable cost, the firm would shut down immediately. At point Y_{MKT}, the price of eggs is below minimum average total cost, creating losses for producers. This leads some firms to exit, which shifts the short-run industry supply curve leftward to S_2. A new long-run equilibrium is established at point Z_{MKT}. As this occurs, the market price rises again, and as shown in panel (c), each remaining producer reacts by increasing output (here, from point *Y* to point *Z*). All remaining producers again make zero profit. The decrease in the quantity of eggs supplied in the industry comes entirely from the exit of some producers from the industry. The long-run industry supply curve is the curve labeled *LRS* in panel (b).

FYI: A Crushing Reversal

For some reason, starting in the mid-1990s, Americans began drinking a lot more wine. Part of this increase in demand may have reflected a booming economy, but the surge in wine consumption continued through two recessions. By 2012, Americans were consuming 57% more wine than they did in 1993—a total of 2.7 gallons of wine per year per U.S. resident.

At first, the increase in wine demand led to sharply higher prices; between 1993 and 2000, the price of red wine grapes rose approximately 50%, and California grape growers earned high profits. Then, as the discussions of long-run supply foretell, there was a rapid expansion of the industry, both because existing grape growers expanded their capacity and because new growers entered the industry. Between 1994 and 2002, production of red wine grapes almost doubled. The result was predictable: the price of grapes fell as the supply curve shifted out. As demand growth slowed in 2002, grape prices plunged by 17%. The effect was to end the California grape industry's expansion. In fact, some grape producers began to exit the industry. By 2004, U.S. grape production had fallen by 20% compared to 2002. Over the past decade this process has repeated itself, with new highs in wine demand raising grape prices, but only until record-crushing levels of grape crushing brought them back down.

MODULE 60 Review

Check Your Understanding

1. Which of the following events will induce firms to enter an industry? Which will induce firms to exit? When will entry or exit cease? Explain your answers.
   a. A technological advance lowers the fixed cost of production of every firm in the industry.
   b. The wages paid to workers in the industry go up for an extended period of time.
   c. A permanent change in consumer tastes increases demand for the good.
   d. The price of a key input rises due to a long-term shortage of that input.
2. Assume that the egg industry is perfectly competitive and is in long-run equilibrium with a perfectly elastic long-run industry supply curve. Health concerns about cholesterol then lead to a decrease in demand. Construct a figure similar to Figure 60.3, showing the short-run behavior of the industry and how long-run equilibrium is reestablished.

Tackle the Test: Multiple-Choice Questions

1. In the long run, a perfectly competitive firm will earn
   a. a negative market return.
   b. a positive profit.
   c. a loss.
   d. a normal profit.
   e. excess profit.
2. With perfect competition, efficiency is generally attained in
   a. the short run but not the long run.
   b. the long run but not the short run.
   c. both the short run and the long run.
   d. neither the short run nor the long run.
   e. specific firms only.
3. Compared to the short-run industry supply curve, the long-run industry supply curve will be more
   a. elastic.
   b. inelastic.
   c. steeply sloped.
   d. profitable.
   e. accurate.

612 Section 11 Market Structures: Perfect Competition and Monopoly

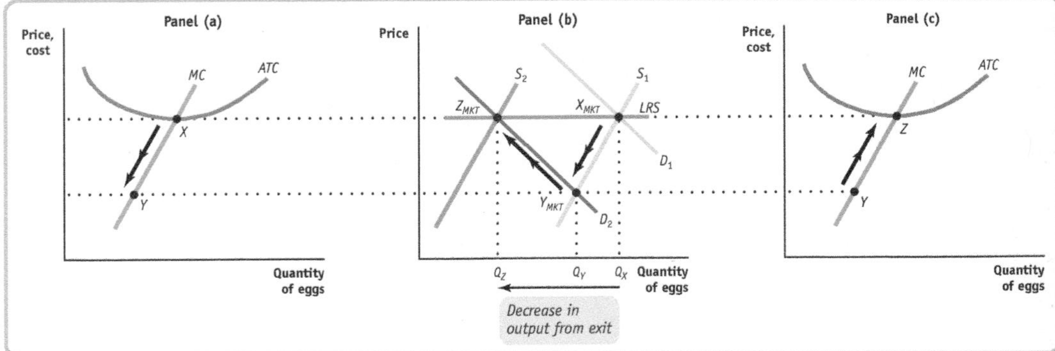

4. Which of the following is generally true for perfect competition?
   I. There is free entry and exit.
   II. Long-run market equilibrium is efficient.
   III. Firms maximize profit at the output level where $P = MC$.
   a. I only
   b. II only
   c. III only
   d. I and II only
   e. I, II, and III

5. Which of the following will happen in response if perfectly competitive firms are earning positive economic profit?
   a. Firms will exit the industry.
   b. The short-run industry supply curve will shift right.
   c. The short-run industry supply curve will shift left.
   d. Firm output will increase.
   e. Market price will increase.

Tackle the Test: Free-Response Questions

1. Draw a correctly labeled graph showing a perfectly competitive firm in long-run equilibrium.

Rubric for FRQ 1 (7 points)

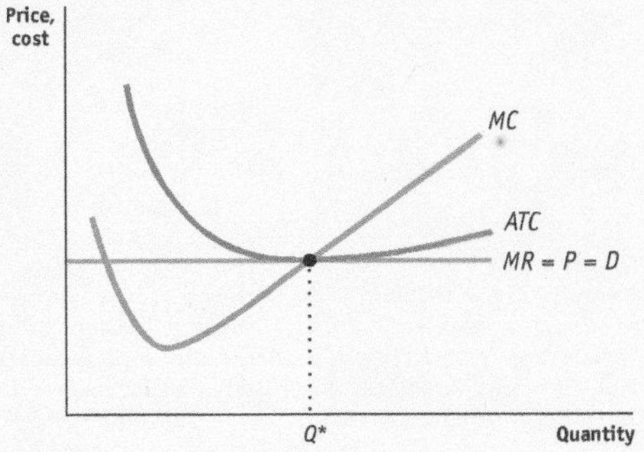

1 point: Axes are correctly labeled.

1 point: Demand curve is horizontal and labeled with some combination of "P," "MR," or "D."

1 point: Marginal cost curve is labeled and slopes upward.

1 point: Profit-maximizing quantity is labeled on horizontal axis where $MC = MR$.

1 point: Average total cost curve is labeled and U-shaped.

1 point: Average total cost is equal to price at the profit-maximizing output.

1 point: Marginal cost curve crosses the average total cost curve at the lowest point on the average total cost curve.

2. Suppose that paper is produced in a perfectly competitive, increasing-cost industry.
   a. Draw correctly labeled side-by-side graphs for a representative firm and for the paper market in long-run equilibrium.
      i. Label the market equilibrium price "P_{M1}" and the equilibrium quantity "Q_{M1}."
      ii. Label the firm's marginal cost "MC_1," its average total cost "ATC_1," its demand curve "D_{F1}," and its profit-maximizing price and quantity "Q_{F1}" and "P_{F1}," respectively.
   b. Now suppose that increased reliance on digital communications causes a decrease in the demand for paper. Show the following on the graphs you drew for part (a):
      i. The new short-run market equilibrium price and quantity, labeled "P_{M2}" and "Q_{M2}."
      ii. The new short-run profit-maximizing price and quantity for the representative firm, labeled "P_{F2}" and "Q_{F2}."
   c. Now suppose the market and the representative firm have adjusted to a new long-run equilibrium.
      i. Label the new equilibrium market price and quantity "P_{M3}" and "Q_{M3}."
      ii. Explain how and why the representative firm's new average total cost curve differs from ATC_1.
      iii. Draw the long-run supply curve for the market and label it "*LRS*."

   (8 points)

Tackle the Test: Multiple-Choice Questions

1. d
2. b
3. a
4. e
5. b

Tackle the Test: Free-Response Question

Rubric for FRQ 2 (8 points)

1 point: Correctly labeled graph of the market with an upward-sloping supply curve, a downward-sloping demand curve, and the equilibrium price and quantity, P_{M1} and Q_{M1}

1 point: The firm's profit-maximizing quantity, Q_{F1}, is shown on the quantity axis below the intersection of M_{C1} and D_{F1}, which is horizontal at P_{F1}.

1 point: The firm's average total cost curve, ATC_1, is tangent to D_{F1} above Q_{F1}.

1 point: The market demand curve shifts leftward and the new short-run equilibrium price and quantity are labeled P_{M2} and Q_{M2}.

1 point: The firm's demand curve shifts downward and the profit-maximizing price and quantity for the firm are labeled P_{F2} and Q_{F2}.

1 point: The market supply curve shifts leftward and the new equilibrium price and quantity are labeled P_{M3} and Q_{M3}.

1 point: The firm's average total cost curve shifted down below ATC_1 because, when the size of an increasing-cost industry decreases, the resulting decrease in the demand for inputs leads to a decrease in the cost of those inputs.

1 point: The long-run supply curve slopes upward and goes through the points (Q_{M3}, P_{M3}) and (Q_{M1}, P_{M1}).

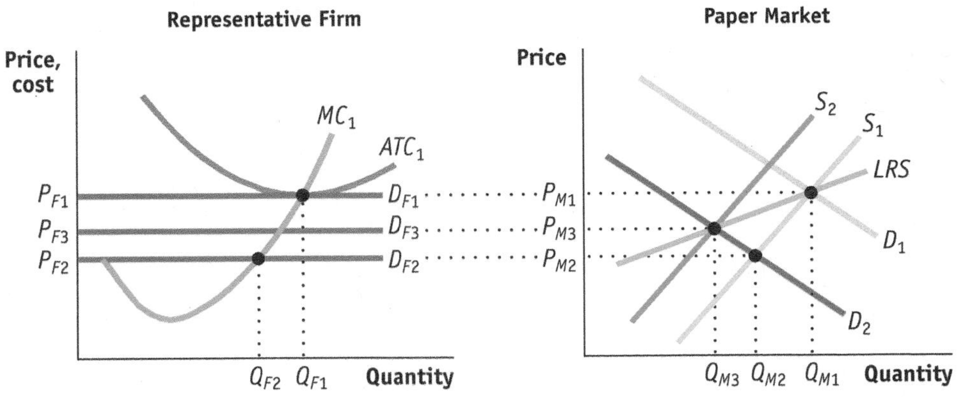

Module 60 Long-Run Outcomes in Perfect Competition 613

PD To prepare for teaching this lesson, you may want to consult the **Module 61 Sample Lecture** in the TRM.

OPEN & CLOSE Start Here

Ask students if they have ever played the board game Monopoly. Ask those who have played it what strategy they employ. When students mention acquiring all the property of a certain color, ask them why it is good to have a *monopoly* for (be the only owner of) that color. When someone owns all the properties of one color, the rent on the property doubles and the owner gains the right to improve the property (invest in houses and hotels to earn even more rent). Explain that the game contains some of the same elements as the market structure model. For example, monopolies reduce quantity and raise price, so just having a monopoly in the game raises the rent!

TEACH Connect It

TRM Again refer students to **Worksheet 57.1 (Types of Market Structures)** from the TRM, so that they can compare what they have just learned about the characteristics of perfectly competitive firms in Module 60 with those of monopoly firms in Module 61.

TEACH Teach It

Draw a downward-sloping demand curve and title the graph "monopoly." Ask students if this is a market demand curve or a firm demand curve. Allow them to call out "market" or "firm" until they realize that there is only one firm in a monopoly, so the firm IS the market and the market demand curve IS the demand curve for a monopoly—thus, the demand curve you have drawn is BOTH.

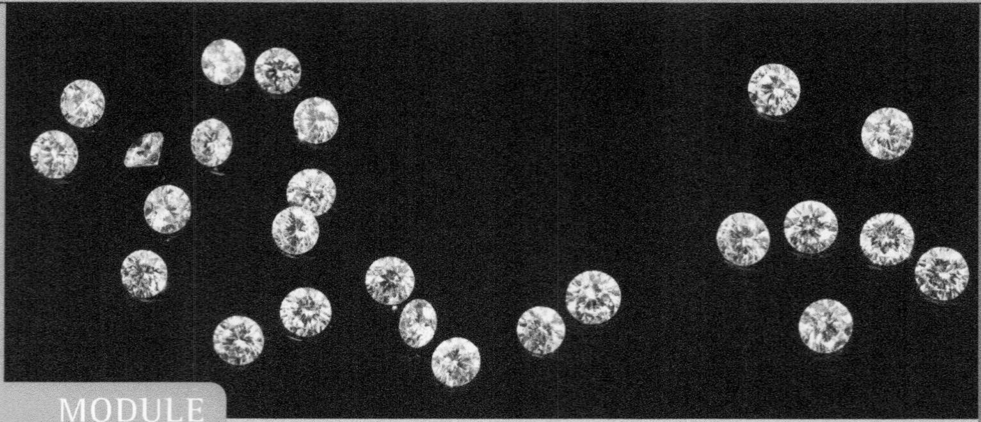

© Jewellery specialist/Alamy

MODULE 61 Introduction to Monopoly

In this Module, you will learn to:

- Identify the profit-maximizing price and quantity for a monopolist
- Determine whether a monopoly is earning a profit or a loss

In this module we turn to monopoly, the market structure at the opposite end of the spectrum from perfect competition. A monopolist's profit-maximizing decision is subtly different from that of a price-taking producer, but it has large implications for the output produced and the welfare created. We will see the crucial role that market demand plays in leading a monopolist to behave differently from a firm in a perfectly competitive industry.

The Monopolist's Demand Curve and Marginal Revenue

Recall the firm's optimal output rule: a profit-maximizing firm produces the quantity of output at which the marginal cost of producing the last unit of output equals marginal revenue—the change in total revenue generated by the last unit of output. That is, $MR = MC$ at the profit-maximizing quantity of output. Although the optimal output rule holds for *all* firms, decisions about price and the quantity of output differ between monopolies and perfectly competitive industries due to differences in the demand curves faced by monopolists and perfectly competitive firms.

We have learned that even though the *market* demand curve always slopes downward, each of the firms that make up a perfectly competitive industry faces a horizontal, *perfectly elastic* demand curve, like D_C in panel (a) of **Figure 61.1**. Any attempt by an individual firm in a perfectly competitive industry to charge more than the going market price will cause the firm to lose all its sales. However, it can sell as much as it likes at the market price. We saw that the marginal revenue of a perfectly competitive firm is simply the market price. As a result, the price-taking firm's optimal output rule is to produce the output level at which the marginal cost of the last unit produced is equal to the market price.

Figure 61.1 Comparing the Demand Curves of a Perfectly Competitive Producer and a Monopolist

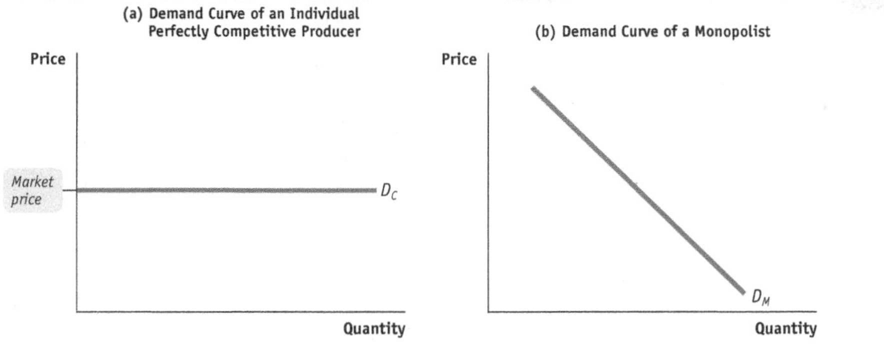

Because an individual perfectly competitive producer cannot affect the market price of the good, it faces a horizontal demand curve D_C, as shown in panel (a). A monopolist, on the other hand, can affect the price. Because it is the sole supplier in the industry, its demand curve is the market demand curve D_M, as shown in panel (b). To sell more output, it must lower the price; by reducing output, it raises the price.

By contrast, a monopolist is the sole supplier of its good. So its demand curve is simply the market demand curve, which slopes downward, like D_M in panel (b) of Figure 61.1. This downward slope creates a "wedge" between the price of the good and the marginal revenue of the good. **Table 61.1** on the next page shows how this wedge develops. The first two columns of Table 61.1 show a hypothetical demand schedule for De Beers diamonds. For the sake of simplicity, we assume that all diamonds are exactly alike. And to make the arithmetic easy, we suppose that the number of diamonds sold is far smaller than is actually the case. For instance, at a price of $500 per diamond, we assume that only 10 diamonds are sold. The demand curve implied by this schedule is shown in panel (a) of **Figure 61.2** on page 617.

The third column of Table 61.1 shows De Beers's total revenue from selling each quantity of diamonds—the price per diamond multiplied by the number of diamonds sold. The last column shows marginal revenue, the change in total revenue from producing and selling another diamond.

Clearly, after the 1st diamond, the marginal revenue a monopolist receives from selling one more unit is less than the price at which that unit is sold. For example, if De Beers sells 10 diamonds, the price at which the 10th diamond is sold is $500. But the marginal revenue—the change in total revenue in going from 9 to 10 diamonds—is only $50.

Why is the marginal revenue from that 10th diamond less than the price? Because an increase in production by a monopolist has two opposing effects on revenue:

- *A quantity effect.* One more unit is sold, increasing total revenue by the price at which the unit is sold (in this case, +$500).
- *A price effect.* In order to sell that last unit, the monopolist must cut the market price on *all* units sold. This decreases total revenue (in this case, by 9 × −$50 = −$450).

The quantity effect and the price effect are illustrated by the two shaded areas in panel (a) of Figure 61.2. Increasing diamond sales from 9 to 10 means moving down the demand curve from *A* to *B*, reducing the price per diamond from $550 to $500.

FOCUS Test It

Where is the marginal revenue curve relative to the demand curve and why? *MR is below D, because to sell one more unit, the firm has to lower price on all units.*

FOCUS Graph It

Figure 61.1 compares the demand curve for a perfect competitor to that for a monopolist. Ask students why the demand curve for the perfect competitor is horizontal (*because the firm is a price-taker*). The horizontal demand curve means that a price-taker can always sell more for the market price. Ask students what the monopoly has to do in order to sell more (*it has to lower price because its demand curve sloped downward*).

FOCUS Test It

Ask students whether it is TRUE or FALSE that a monopoly can charge any price it wants. *FALSE. Although the monopolist is a price-maker, which means it is able to charge any price along its demand curve, its choice is limited by the demand curve. For example, the monopolist in Figure 61.2 on page 617 can't charge a price above $1,000 because people won't buy any of the product at that price.*

TEACH Teach It

Remind students that the demand curve for a perfectly competitive firm was its demand curve (which was also equal to price). $MR = D = P$ for a perfect competitor because it could sell all it wanted at the market price and the additional revenue from selling one more unit (*MR*) was always the market price. The marginal revenue curve for a monopolist doesn't equal price (demand). The marginal revenue curve lies below the demand curve because the demand curve is downward-sloping, and in order to sell one more, the monopolist has to lower its price. When it lowers its price, there is good news and bad news for the monopolist. The bad news is that price is lower (the price effect). The good news is that it sells more (the quantity effect). Marginal revenue is equal to the good news (*P*) minus the bad news (the lower *P* on previous units). Thus, $MR = P -$ (bad news), which means $MR < P$. For example, if the monopoly lowers its price from $22 to $21 in order to raise output from 15 to 16, the good news is +$21 and the bad news is (−$1 × 15). $MR =$ $21 − $15 = $6. $6 < $21, marginal revenue is less than price (demand), so the marginal revenue curve lies below the demand curve.

TEACH Connect It

Refer back to Figure 47.4 in Section 9, which shows the relationship between elasticity along a demand curve and total revenue using stacked graphs. Have students redraw this figure and add the *MR* curve to see how elasticity relates to the *MR* curve.

TEACH Teach It

Ask students the following with regard to Table 61.1:

- At what quantity of diamonds is *TR* the largest? *9*
- After the first diamond, what do you notice about the price and *MR*? *(MR < P)* Why is this so? *Because increasing quantity requires the firm to lower price on all units*
- What are the quantity and price effects of selling 12 rather than 11 diamonds? *Quantity effect—one more unit is sold, which increases TR by the P ($400). Price effect—to sell the 12th unit, the monopolist must decrease price from $450 to $400 on 11 units ($50 × 11 = $550).*
- What is the difference between a monopolist's *MR* curve and a perfect competitor's *MR* curve? *(For a monopolist, the MR curve lies below D; for a perfect competitor, MR = D.)* Which "effect" causes the monopolist's *MR* curve to lie below the *D* curve? *The price effect*

Table 61.1 Demand, Total Revenue, and Marginal Revenue for the De Beers Diamond Monopoly

Price of diamond *P*	Quantity of diamonds demanded *Q*	Total revenue $TR = P \times Q$	Marginal Revenue $MC = \Delta TC / \Delta Q$
$1,000	0	$0	
950	1	950	$950
900	2	1,800	850
850	3	2,550	750
800	4	3,200	650
750	5	3,750	550
700	6	4,200	450
650	7	4,550	350
600	8	4,800	250
550	9	4,950	150
500	10	5,000	50
450	11	4,950	−50
400	12	4,800	−150
350	13	4,550	−250
300	14	4,200	−350
250	15	3,750	−450
200	16	3,200	−550
150	17	2,550	−650
100	18	1,800	−750
50	19	950	−850
0	20	0	−950

The green-shaded area represents the quantity effect: De Beers sells the 10th diamond at a price of $500. This is offset, however, by the price effect, represented by the orange-shaded area. In order to sell that 10th diamond, De Beers must reduce the price on all its diamonds from $550 to $500. So it loses 9 × $50 = $450 in revenue, the orange-shaded area. So, as point *C* indicates, the total effect on revenue of selling one more diamond—the marginal revenue—derived from an increase in diamond sales from 9 to 10 is only $50.

Point *C* lies on the monopolist's marginal revenue curve, labeled *MR* in panel (a) of Figure 61.2 and taken from the last column of Table 61.1. The crucial point about the monopolist's marginal revenue curve is that it is always *below* the demand curve. That's because of the price effect, which means that a monopolist's marginal revenue from selling an additional unit is always less than the price the monopolist receives for that unit. It is the price effect that creates the wedge between the monopolist's marginal revenue curve and the demand curve: in order to sell an additional diamond, De Beers must cut the market price on all units sold.

In fact, this wedge exists for any firm that possesses market power, such as an oligopolist, except in the case of price discrimination as explained in Module 63. Having market power means that the firm faces a downward-sloping demand curve. As a result, there will always be a price effect from an increase in output for a firm with market power that charges every customer the same price. So for such a firm, the marginal revenue curve always lies below the demand curve.

Take a moment to compare the monopolist's marginal revenue curve with the marginal revenue curve for a perfectly competitive firm, which has no market power.

616 Section 11 Market Structures: Perfect Competition and Monopoly

Figure 61.2 A Monopolist's Demand, Total Revenue, and Marginal Revenue Curves

Panel (a) shows the monopolist's demand and marginal revenue curves for diamonds from Table 61.1. The marginal revenue curve lies below the demand curve. To see why, consider point *A* on the demand curve, where 9 diamonds are sold at $550 each, generating total revenue of $4,950. To sell a 10th diamond, the price on all 10 diamonds must be cut to $500, as shown by point *B*. As a result, total revenue increases by the green area (the quantity effect: +$500) but decreases by the orange area (the price effect: −$450). So the marginal revenue from the 10th diamond is $50 (the difference between the green and orange areas), which is much lower than its price, $500. Panel (b) shows the monopolist's total revenue curve for diamonds. As output goes from 0 to 10 diamonds, total revenue increases. It reaches its maximum at 10 diamonds—the level at which marginal revenue is equal to 0—and declines thereafter. The quantity effect dominates the price effect when total revenue is rising; the price effect dominates the quantity effect when total revenue is falling.

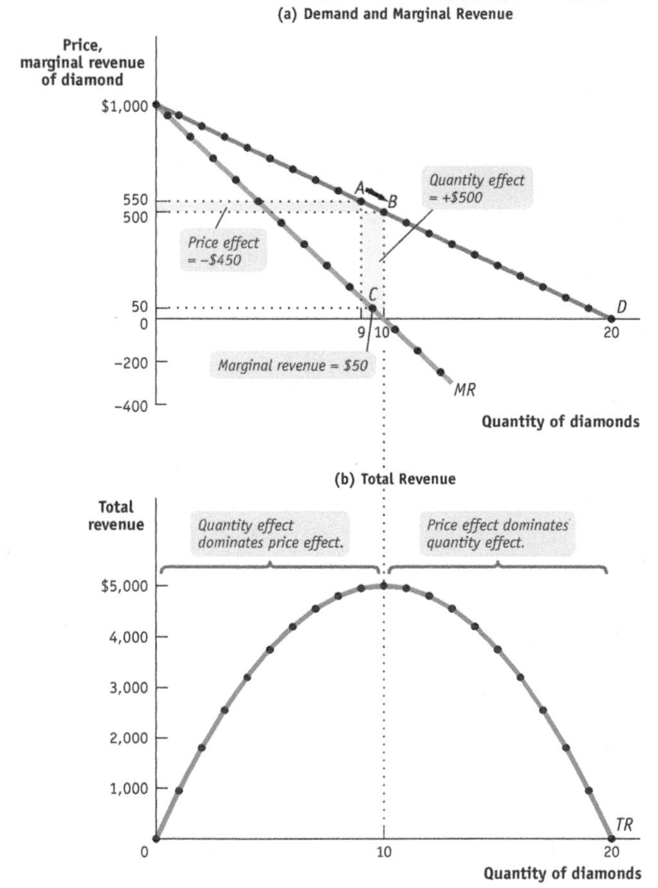

For such a firm there is no price effect from an increase in output: its marginal revenue curve is simply its horizontal demand curve. So for a perfectly competitive firm, market price and marginal revenue are always equal.

To emphasize how the quantity and price effects offset each other for a firm with market power, De Beers's total revenue curve is shown in panel (b) of Figure 61.2. Notice that it is hill-shaped: as output rises from 0 to 10 diamonds, total revenue increases. This reflects the fact that *at low levels of output, the quantity effect is stronger than the price effect:* as the monopolist sells more, it has to lower the price on only very few units, so the price effect is small. As output rises beyond 10 diamonds, total revenue actually falls. This reflects the fact that *at high levels of output, the price effect is stronger than the*

AP® Exam Tip

Past AP® exams have asked questions about why a monopoly's marginal revenue is below its price. Be prepared to explain that the firm must lower its price on all units sold in order to sell more units.

FOCUS Test It

Figure 61.2 describes the calculation of the price and quantity effect between 9 and 10 units. Calculate these effects between 2 and 3 units and determine *MR*. *P at 2 units = $900 and TR = $1,800. To sell a third unit, they must reduce price to $850, making TR $2,550. The change in price is $50 and therefore the price effect is that $50 times the first 2 diamonds or $100. The quantity effect is 1 more unit at $850. The difference between the two is ($850 − $750= $100), the MR of $750.*

FOCUS Active Learning

TRM Show Jacob Clifford's video "Micro Unit 4, Question 1—Monopoly Demand and *MR*" (see econextras video list with hyperlinks on the bcs and TRFD) and assign **Worksheet 61.1 (Monopoly *D* and *MR*)** from the TRM as a class activity.

TEACH Connect It

Remind students of the rule for profit maximization, *MC* = *MR*. This same rule always works!

TEACH Teach It

A monopoly can't charge any price it wants, but it WILL charge the highest price that it can for any given quantity (which is given by its demand curve). Make sure students know how to find the monopoly price: by going up to the demand curve at any given quantity.

FOCUS Active Learning

Show Jacob Clifford's video "Micro 4.1 Monopoly Demand and *MR* Monopoly Graph" (see econextras video list with hyperlinks on the bcs and TRFD), which will further explain the separation of *MR* and *D* for the monopolist. As instructed in the video, pause it and have students complete the table of *P*, *Q*, *TR*, and *MR* for 5, 4, 3, and 2 units, so they can practice the process together.

P	*Q*	*TR*	*MR*
5	6	30	0
4	7	28	−2
3	8	24	−4
2	9	18	−6

St. Louis Federal Reserve Bank Resources

Monopoly

Teaching market structures in a microeconomics class? These slides present graphs related to monopoly, the market structure in which there is only one producer of a good or service and high barriers to entry exist. The slides illustrate firms' short-run decisions.

TEACH Teach It

- At low levels of output, the quantity effect is stronger than the price effect. As the monopolist sells more output, it has to lower the price on very few units, so the price effect remains small.
- As output increases to higher levels, the monopolist has to lower the price on more units, making the price effect larger than the quantity effect.

FOCUS Graph It

Figure 61.3 compares the price and output in monopoly to price and output in perfect competition. This graph puts perfect competition and monopoly on the same graph, so we can compare their *P* and *Q*. Emphasize to students that this is the graph of the *market*. It is not the perfectly competitive firm. Of course, the market and firm graphs are the same for the monopoly because the firm IS the market. The *MC* curve is a horizontal line just to make things easier since it means that $MC = ATC$. The perfectly competitive price and quantity are found where *S* and *D* cross (remember that the *MC* curve is the *S* curve for perfect competition). Make sure students see that the demand curve is the purple line and the supply curve is the red line, so the competitive outcome is located where *S* and *D* cross (point *C*)—like it has been since Section 2! The monopolist maximizes profit where $MC = MR$ (point *A*) and sets its price on the demand curve (point *B*). The graph shows that a monopolist will sell less and charge a higher price than the perfectly competitive market.

Challenge students to explain:

1. How the monopolist determines output and price. *The monopolist sets MC = MR to determine the profit-maximizing quantity (8) and finds P on the demand curve at that quantity ($600).*
2. The monopoly's profit at the profit-maximizing level of output. *$400 × 8 = $3,200*
3. The perfectly competitive price and quantity. *$200 and 16 units*
4. The profit for the purely competitive firm at this output. *Zero economic profit since P = ATC*

AP® Exam Tip

Like a perfect competitor, a monopolist chooses the quantity at which $MR = MC$. The monopolist's price is found by going up from where $MR = MC$ to the demand curve, and then straight over to the price axis.

quantity effect: as the monopolist sells more, it now has to lower the price on many units of output, making the price effect very large. Correspondingly, the marginal revenue curve lies below zero at output levels above 10 diamonds. For example, an increase in diamond production from 11 to 12 yields only $400 for the 12th diamond, simultaneously reducing the revenue from diamonds 1 through 11 by $550. As a result, the marginal revenue of the 12th diamond is −$150.

The Monopolist's Profit-Maximizing Output and Price

To complete the story of how a monopolist maximizes profit, we now bring in the monopolist's marginal cost. Let's assume that there is no fixed cost of production; we'll also assume that the marginal cost of producing an additional diamond is constant at $200, no matter how many diamonds De Beers produces. Then marginal cost will always equal average total cost, and the marginal cost curve (and the average total cost curve) is a horizontal line at $200, as shown in **Figure 61.3**.

To maximize profit, the monopolist compares marginal cost with marginal revenue. If marginal revenue exceeds marginal cost, De Beers increases profit by producing more; if marginal revenue is less than marginal cost, De Beers increases profit by producing less. So the monopolist maximizes its profit by using the optimal output rule:

(61-1) $MR = MC$ at the monopolist's profit-maximizing quantity of output

Figure 61.3 The Monopolist's Profit-Maximizing Output and Price

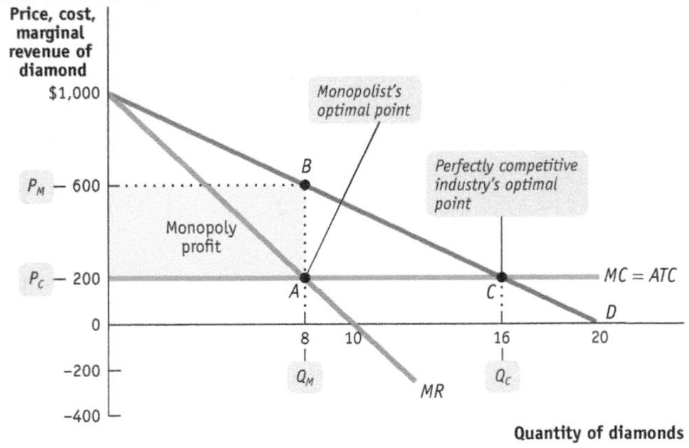

This figure shows the demand, marginal revenue, and marginal cost curves. Marginal cost per diamond is constant at $200, so the marginal cost curve is horizontal at $200. According to the optimal output rule, the profit-maximizing quantity of output for the monopolist is at $MR = MC$, shown by point *A*, where the marginal cost and marginal revenue curves cross at an output of 8 diamonds. The price De Beers can charge per diamond is found by going to the point on the demand curve directly above point *A*, which is point *B* here—a price of $600 per diamond. It makes a profit of $400 × 8 = $3,200. A perfectly competitive industry produces the output level at which $P = MC$, given by point *C*, where the demand curve and marginal cost curves cross. So a competitive industry produces 16 diamonds, sells at a price of $200, and makes zero profit.

The monopolist's optimal point is shown in Figure 61.3. At *A*, the marginal cost curve, *MC*, crosses the marginal revenue curve, *MR*. The corresponding output level, 8 diamonds, is the monopolist's profit-maximizing quantity of output, Q_M. The price at which consumers demand 8 diamonds is \$600, so the monopolist's price, P_M, is \$600—corresponding to point *B*. The average total cost of producing each diamond is \$200, so the monopolist earns a profit of \$600 – \$200 = \$400 per diamond, and total profit is 8 × \$400 = \$3,200, as indicated by the shaded area.

Monopoly Versus Perfect Competition

When Cecil Rhodes consolidated many independent diamond producers into De Beers, he converted a perfectly competitive industry into a monopoly. We can now use our analysis to see the effects of such a consolidation.

Let's look again at Figure 61.3 and ask how this same market would work if, instead of being a monopoly, the industry were perfectly competitive. We will continue to assume that there is no fixed cost and that marginal cost is constant, so average total cost and marginal cost are equal.

If the diamond industry consists of many perfectly competitive firms, each of those producers takes the market price as given. That is, each producer acts as if its marginal revenue is equal to the market price. So each firm within the industry uses the price-taking firm's optimal output rule:

(61-2) $P = MC$ at the perfectly competitive firm's profit-maximizing quantity of output

In Figure 61.3, this would correspond to producing at *C*, where the price per diamond, P_C, is \$200, equal to the marginal cost of production. So the profit-maximizing output of an industry under perfect competition, Q_C, is 16 diamonds.

Recall that the perfectly competitive outcome of $P = MC$ is allocatively efficient: by producing up to point *C*, the firm provides every unit for which consumers are willing to pay at least the marginal cost. But does the perfectly competitive industry earn any profit at *C*? No: the price of \$200 is equal to the average total cost per diamond. So there is no economic profit for this industry when it produces at the perfectly competitive output level.

We've already seen that once the industry is consolidated into a monopoly, the result is very different. The monopolist's marginal revenue is influenced by the price effect, so that marginal revenue is less than the price. That is,

(61-3) $P > MR = MC$ at the monopolist's profit-maximizing quantity of output

So the monopolist does not meet the $P = MC$ condition for allocative efficiency. As we've already seen, the monopolist produces less than the competitive industry—8 diamonds rather than 16. The price under monopoly is \$600, compared with only \$200 under perfect competition. The monopolist earns a positive profit, but the competitive industry does not.

We can see that compared with a competitive industry, a monopolist does the following:

- produces a smaller quantity: $Q_M < Q_C$
- charges a higher price: $P_M > P_C$
- earns a profit

TEACH Teach It

The monopolist will also maximize profit by using the optimal output rule: $MR = MC$ at the profit-maximizing quantity of output. Make sure students understand that the optimal output rule is used to determine the profit-maximizing output level—not the price. The PRICE for the monopolist is determined by going from the profit-maximizing output level UP to the monopolist's *D* curve and finding the corresponding price. Emphasize this by using a different color to go from the $MC = MR$ point to the demand curve when you draw the graph!

TEACH Teach It

If $MR > MC$, the monopolist increases profit by producing more. If $MR < MC$, the monopolist increases profit by producing less. Remember that the monopolist also follows the optimal output rule of operating at the profit-maximizing quantity of OUTPUT where $MR = MC$ and then moves directly up to the corresponding point on the demand curve to set its price.

FOCUS Active Learning

TRM For practice determining output and profit for the monopoly, assign **Worksheet 61.2 (Monopoly Profit)** from the TRM.

TEACH Connect It

Review the shape of the *ATC* curve and its relationship to the *MC* curve from Section 10. The *ATC* should be U-shaped and *MC* should cross it at its minimum.

TEACH AP® Exam Tip

Points may be lost on the FRQs for not showing an *ATC* with the correct shape or not having *MC* cross *ATC* at the minimum point of *ATC*.

FOCUS Test It

TRM **Worksheet 61.3 (Drawing a Monopoly Graph Test It)** in the TRM will test the ability of students to draw the monopoly graph and to understand profit-maximizing quantity and price determination.

FOCUS Flip It

TRM Have your class watch Jacob Clifford's video "Micro 4.2 Monopoly Graph Review and Practice" (see econextras video list with hyperlinks on the bcs and TRFD). Assign **Worksheet 61.4 (Monopoly Graph Review)** from the TRM for questions about and practice with monopoly graphs.

FOCUS Test It

If a monopolist has to decrease price to sell more units, what can you say about the product's elasticity in order for the monopolist to increase its *TR*? *(E_d would have to be positive; the higher the elasticity, the greater the TR.)* If E_d is negative, what will happen to *TR* and *MR* when the monopolist decreases its price? *(TR goes down and MR becomes negative.)*

FOCUS Graph It

Figure 61.4 shows a profit-maximizing monopoly. This is similar to Figure 61.3, but with an upward-sloping *MC* curve and U-shaped *ATC* curve rather than a horizontal *MC/AC* curve. Have students draw this graph and then re-create it with an *ATC* curve that shows a loss instead of a profit.

TEACH Teach It

We know that perfectly competitive firms can earn a profit in the short run but earn no economic profit in the long run as competitive firms enter the industry. Monopoly firms can earn profit in both the short and long run as there are barriers to entry that prevent firms from entering the industry.

OPEN & CLOSE Exit Slip

TRM *Please see* ***Exit Slip: Module 61*** *in the TRM for formative multiple-choice questions to ask your students before finishing your lesson. These questions will help you quickly assess whether your students have mastered the module's concepts before moving on.*

Answers to the Exit Slip Questions

1. E
2. D
3. E

FYI Monopoly Behavior and the Price Elasticity of Demand

A monopolist faces marginal revenue that is lower than the market price. But how much lower? The answer depends on the *price elasticity of demand.*

Remember that the price elasticity of demand determines how total revenue from sales changes when the price changes. If the price elasticity is greater than 1 (demand is elastic), a fall in the price increases total revenue because the rise in the quantity demanded outweighs the lower price of each unit sold. If the price elasticity is less than 1 (demand is inelastic), a lower price reduces total revenue.

When a monopolist increases output by one unit, it must reduce the market price in order to sell that unit. If the price elasticity of demand is less than 1, this will actually reduce revenue—that is, marginal revenue will be negative. The monopolist can increase revenue by producing more only if the price elasticity of demand is greater than 1; the higher the elasticity, the closer the additional revenue is to the initial market price.

What this tells us is that the difference between monopoly behavior and perfectly competitive behavior depends on the price elasticity of demand. A monopolist that faces highly elastic demand will behave almost like a firm in a perfectly competitive industry.

For example, Amtrak has a monopoly on intercity passenger service in the Northeast Corridor, but it has very little ability to raise prices: potential train travelers will switch to cars and planes. In contrast, a monopolist that faces less elastic demand—like most cable TV companies—will behave very differently from a perfect competitor: it will charge much higher prices and restrict output more.

KAREN BLEIER/AFP/Getty Images

AP® Exam Tip

Be prepared to draw and analyze the monopoly graph for the AP® exam. Remember, the monopolist's profit per unit is the difference between the price the firm charges and its *ATC*.

Monopoly: The General Picture

Figure 61.3 involved specific numbers and assumed that marginal cost was constant, there was no fixed cost, and therefore, that the average total cost curve was a horizontal line. **Figure 61.4** shows a more general picture of monopoly in action: *D* is the market demand curve; *MR*, the marginal revenue curve; *MC*, the marginal cost curve; and *ATC*, the average total cost curve. Here we return to the usual assumption that the marginal cost curve has a "swoosh" shape and the average total cost curve is U-shaped.

Figure 61.4 The Monopolist's Profit

In this case, the marginal cost curve has a "swoosh" shape and the average total cost curve is U-shaped. The monopolist maximizes profit by producing the level of output at which $MR = MC$, given by point *A*, generating quantity Q_M. It finds its monopoly price, P_M, from the point on the demand curve directly above point *A*, point *B* here. The average total cost of Q_M is shown by point *C*. Profit is given by the area of the shaded rectangle.

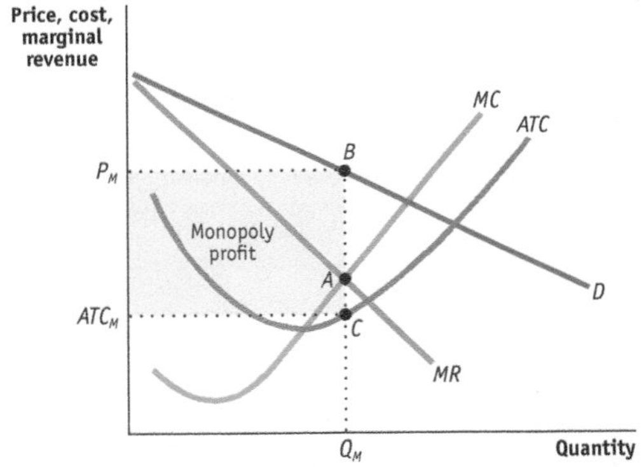

Answers to Module 61 Review Questions

Check Your Understanding

1. a. The demand schedule is found by determining the price at which each quantity would be demanded. This price is the average revenue, found at each output level by dividing the total revenue by the number of emeralds produced. For example, the price when 3 emeralds are

Applying the optimal output rule, we see that the profit-maximizing level of output, identified as the quantity at which marginal revenue and marginal cost intersect (see point *A*), is Q_M. The monopolist charges the highest price possible for this quantity, P_M, found at the height of the demand curve at Q_M (see point *B*). At the profit-maximizing level of output, the monopolist's average total cost is ATC_M (see point *C*).

Recalling how we calculated profit in Equation 59-1, profit is equal to the difference between total revenue and total cost. So we have

$$\text{(61-4)}\quad \text{Profit} = TR - TC$$
$$= (P_M \times Q_M) - (ATC_M \times Q_M)$$
$$= (P_M - ATC_M) \times Q_M$$

Profit is equal to the area of the shaded rectangle in Figure 61.4, with a height of $P_M - ATC_M$ and a width of Q_M.

We learned that a perfectly competitive industry can have profit *in the short run but not in the long run*. In the short run, price can exceed average total cost, allowing a perfectly competitive firm to make a profit. But we also know that this cannot persist. In the long run, any profit in a perfectly competitive industry will be competed away as new firms enter the market. In contrast, while a monopoly can earn a profit or a loss in the short run, barriers to entry make it possible for a monopolist to make positive profit in the long run.

MODULE 61 Review

Check Your Understanding

1. Use the accompanying total revenue schedule of Emerald, Inc., a monopoly producer of 10-carat emeralds, to calculate the items listed in parts a–d. Then answer part e.

Quantity of emeralds demanded	*Total revenue*
1	$100
2	186
3	252
4	280
5	250

   a. the demand schedule (Hint: the average revenue at each quantity indicates the price at which that quantity would be demanded.)
   b. the marginal revenue schedule
   c. the quantity effect component of marginal revenue at each output level
   d. the price effect component of marginal revenue at each output level
   e. What additional information is needed to determine Emerald, Inc.'s profit-maximizing output?

2. Replicate Figure 61.3 and use your graph to show what happens to the following when the marginal cost of diamond production rises from $200 to $400. Use the information in Table 61.1 to identify specific numbers for prices and quantities on your graph.
   a. the marginal cost curve
   b. the profit-maximizing price and quantity
   c. the profit of the monopolist
   d. the quantity that would be produced if the diamond industry were perfectly competitive, and the associated profit

produced is $252/3 = $84. The price at the various output levels is then used to construct the demand schedule in the table at the bottom of the page.

b. The marginal revenue schedule is found by calculating the change in total revenue as output increases by 1 unit. For example, the marginal revenue generated by increasing output from 2 to 3 emeralds is ($252 − $186) = $66.

c. The quantity effect component of marginal revenue is the additional revenue generated by selling one more unit of the good at the market price. For example, as shown in the table below, at 3 emeralds, the market price is $84; thus, when going from 2 to 3 emeralds, the quantity effect is equal to $84.

d. The price effect component of marginal revenue is the decline in total revenue caused by the fall in price when one more unit is sold. For example, as shown in the table below, when only 2 emeralds are sold, each emerald sells at a price of $93. However, when Emerald, Inc. sells an additional emerald, the price must fall by $9 to $84. Thus, the price effect component in going from 2 to 3 emeralds is (−$9) × 2 = −$18. That's because 2 emeralds can only be sold at a price of $84 when 3 emeralds in total are sold, although they could have been sold at a price of $93 when only a total of 2 were sold.

e. In order to determine Emerald, Inc.'s profit-maximizing output level, you must know its marginal cost at each output level. Its profit-maximizing output level is the one at which marginal revenue is equal to marginal cost.

2. As the diagram on the bottom left shows, the marginal cost curve shifts upward to $400. The profit-maximizing price rises from $600 to $700 and quantity falls from 8 to 6. Profit falls from $400 × 8 = $3,200 to $300 × 6 = $1,800. The quantity that a perfectly competitive industry would produce decreases from 16 to 12, and profit remains unchanged at zero.

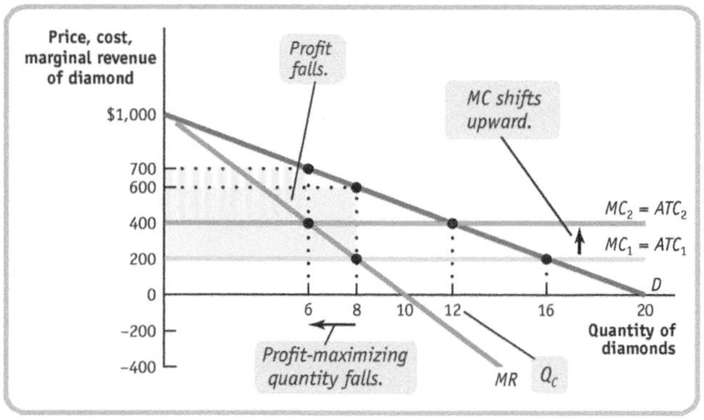

Quantity of emeralds demanded	Price of emerald	Total revenue	Marginal revenue	Quantity effect component	Price effect component
1	$100	$100			
			$86	$93	−$7
2	93	186			
			66	84	−18
3	84	252			
			28	70	−42
4	70	280			
			−30	50	−80
5	50	250			

Tackle the Test: Multiple-Choice Questions

1. b
2. c
3. b
4. d
5. d

Tackle the Test: Free-Response Question

Rubric for FRQ 2 (9 points)

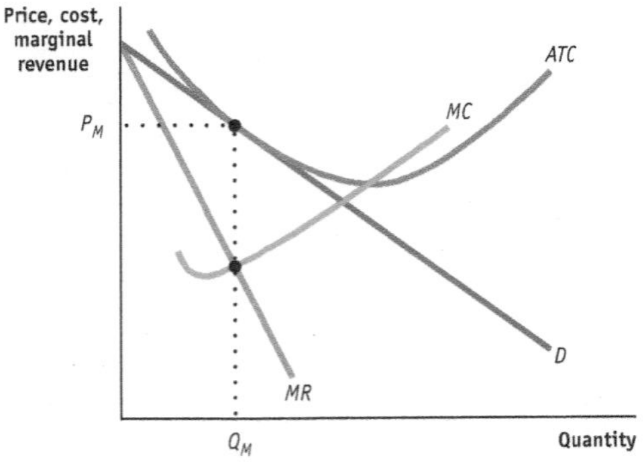

1 point: Axes are correctly labeled as "$ per unit" or "Price, cost, marginal revenue" and "Quantity."

1 point: The demand curve is labeled and downward-sloping.

1 point: The marginal revenue curve is labeled, downward-sloping, and below the demand curve.

1 point: The profit-maximizing quantity is labeled on the horizontal axis where $MC = MR$.

1 point: Price is determined on the demand curve above the point where $MC = MR$.

1 point: The average total cost curve is labeled and U–shaped.

1 point: Average total cost equals price at the profit-maximizing output.

1 point: The marginal cost curve crosses the average total cost curve at the lowest point on the average total cost curve.

1 point: Yes, a monopoly can earn a positive profit in the long run with the help of barriers to entry that keep out competitors.

Tackle the Test: Multiple-Choice Questions

Refer to the graph provided for Questions 1–4.

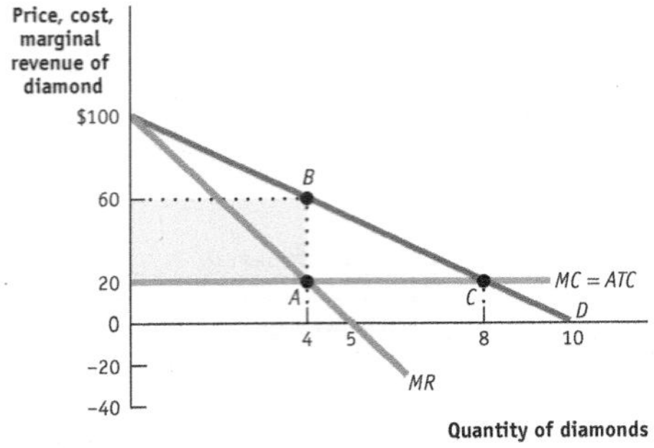

1. The monopolist's profit-maximizing output is
   a. 0.
   b. 4.
   c. 5.
   d. 8.
   e. 10.
2. The monopolist's total revenue equals
   a. \$80.
   b. \$160.
   c. \$240.
   d. \$300.
   e. \$480.
3. The monopolist's total cost equals
   a. \$20.
   b. \$80.
   c. \$160.
   d. \$240.
   e. \$480.
4. The monopolist is earning a profit equal to
   a. \$0.
   b. \$40.
   c. \$80.
   d. \$160.
   e. \$240.
5. How does a monopoly differ from a perfectly competitive industry with the same costs?
   I. It produces a smaller quantity.
   II. It charges a higher price.
   III. It earns normal profit in the long run.
   a. I only
   b. II only
   c. III only
   d. I and II only
   e. I, II, and III

Tackle the Test: Free-Response Questions

1. a. Draw a correctly labeled graph showing a monopoly incurring a loss in the short run. Assume that the marginal cost curve is swoosh-shaped.
   b. How can the monopolist determine whether to shut down or produce at a loss in the short run?

Rubric for FRQ1 (9 points)

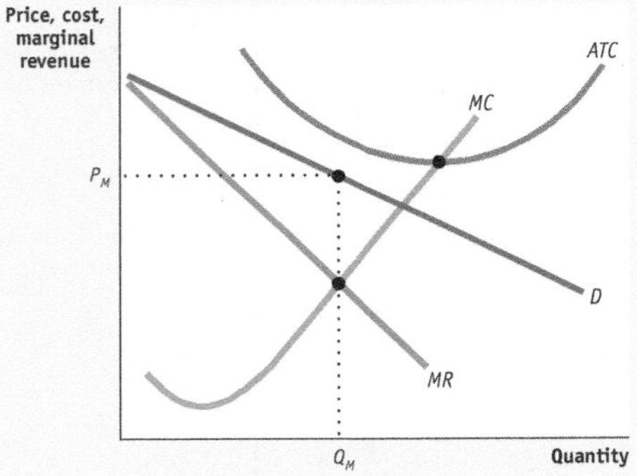

1 point: Axes are correctly labeled.

1 point: The demand curve is labeled and negatively sloped.

1 point: The marginal revenue curve is labeled, negatively sloped, and below the demand curve.

1 point: The profit-maximizing quantity is labeled on the horizontal axis where $MC = MR$.

1 point: Price is determined on the demand curve above the point where $MC = MR$.

1 point: The average total cost curve is labeled and U-shaped.

1 point: Average total cost is above price at the profit-maximizing output.

1 point: The marginal cost curve crosses the average total cost curve at the lowest point on the average total cost curve.

1 point: The firm will produce despite a loss in the short run if $P \geq AVC$.

2. a. Draw a graph showing a monopoly earning a normal profit in the short run. Assume that the marginal cost curve is swoosh-shaped.
   b. Can a monopoly earn a positive profit in the long run? Explain.
   (9 points)

MODULE 62

Monopoly and Public Policy

In this Module, you will learn to:

- Compare the effects of monopoly and perfect competition on society's welfare
- Explain how policy makers address the problems posed by monopoly

If you've ever played Hasbro's Monopoly game, you know that it's good to be a monopolist, but it's not so good to be a monopolist's customer. Players of the Monopoly game pay higher rents when they land on a monopoly. In real life, customers generally pay higher prices when the seller is a monopolist. But buyers and sellers always have conflicting interests when it comes to prices. Is the conflict of interest under monopoly any different from what it is under perfect competition?

The answer is yes, because monopoly is a source of inefficiency: the losses to consumers from monopoly behavior are larger than the gains to the monopolist. Because monopoly leads to net losses for the economy, governments often try either to prevent the emergence of monopolies or to limit their effects. In this module, we will see why monopoly leads to inefficiency and examine the policies governments adopt in an attempt to prevent this inefficiency.

Welfare Effects of Monopoly

By holding output below the level at which marginal cost is equal to the market price, a monopolist increases its profit but hurts consumers. To assess whether this is a net benefit or loss to society, we must compare the monopolist's gain in profit to the consumers' loss. What we learn is that the consumers' loss is larger than the monopolist's gain. Monopoly causes a net loss for society.

To see why, let's return to the case in which the marginal cost curve is horizontal, as shown in the two panels of **Figure 62.1** on the next page. Here the marginal cost curve is *MC*, the demand curve is *D*, and, in panel (b), the marginal revenue curve is *MR*.

Panel (a) shows what happens if this industry is perfectly competitive. Equilibrium output is Q_C; the price of the good, P_C, is equal to marginal cost, and marginal cost is also equal to average total cost because there is no fixed cost and marginal cost is constant. Each firm is earning exactly its average total cost per unit of output, so there is no producer surplus in this equilibrium. The consumer surplus generated by the market

PD To prepare for teaching this lesson, you may want to consult the **Module 62 Sample Lecture** in the TRM.

OPEN & CLOSE Start Here

Ask students if they know anything about antitrust law. Often economics students have already studied U.S. history and some will know about such laws. Discuss the creation of antitrust laws to prevent monopolization. Ask students what problems monopolies caused, which then led the United States to enact antitrust laws. There are many possible problems that can be cited, but emphasize the problem most economists associate with a monopoly: It is *inefficient.*

Next ask students to name a monopoly. In addition to the De Beers example in the book, students are likely to name a regulated monopoly like a cable TV company or an electric company. These are examples of a monopoly that the government has *created.* Ask students to consider why antitrust laws work to prevent monopolies, while local governments actually grant monopolies. This apparent contradiction is explained by the main topic of this module—natural monopolies.

TEACH AP® Exam Tip

This module focuses on the deadweight loss created by a monopoly. Deadweight loss is the loss associated with producing an output less than the efficient level. It was discussed earlier in the modules that addressed quotas and taxes, and the concept is applied throughout this section and later sections. Identifying the efficient level of output and/or DWL is an important skill tested on the AP® exam.

TEACH Teach It

Have students draw a graph of a monopoly earning a profit. The graph should look something like Figure 61.4. Ask students to look at their graph and determine if the monopoly they drew is allocatively efficient and if it is productively efficient. (*Allocative efficiency is $P = MC$, so the monopoly is not allocatively efficient since $P > MC$; productive efficiency is the minimum ATC, so the monopoly is not productively efficient since $P > ATC$*). *Note:* It is possible to have a monopoly that is productively efficient if the profit-maximizing quantity occurs where $MC = MR$ and just happens to cross exactly at the minimum of the *ATC* curve.

FOCUS Flip It

TRM Have your class watch Jacob Clifford's video "Micro 4.13 Dead Weight Loss" (see econextras video list with hyperlinks on the bcs and TRFD). This video explains deadweight loss as it applies to monopoly, tax, and price ceiling. Then assign **Worksheet 62.1 (Deadweight Loss)** from the TRM for questions about the video.

TEACH Teach It

Figure 62.1 compares total surplus with perfect competition to total surplus with a monopoly. Note that the *MC* curve is horizontal in these graphs. The constant *MC* is used because it simplifies the comparison of total surplus. With a horizontal *MC* curve, the perfect competitor has no producer surplus, so the comparison can focus on only consumer surplus. When the monopoly reduces quantity and raises price to maximize its profit, the consumer surplus (blue triangle) is smaller. Part of that triangle goes to the monopoly as additional revenues (producer surplus), but the rest is lost—it is the *DWL*.

FOCUS Graph It

Ask students to look at the graphs in Figure 62.1 and determine whether each market is allocatively efficient. *Perfect competition is allocatively efficient ($P = MC$), but a monopoly is not ($P > MC$).*

FOCUS Active Learning

TRM For practice identifying the consumer and producer surplus and deadweight loss in the monopoly, assign **Worksheet 62.2 (Monopoly and Inefficiency)** from the TRM.

TEACH AP® Exam Tip

Students may be asked to calculate the area of consumer surplus, producer surplus, or deadweight loss on the AP® exam. Make sure they know the formula for calculating the area of a triangle ($\frac{1}{2}$ base × height) and are comfortable applying it to find these values.

Figure 62.1 Monopoly Causes Inefficiency

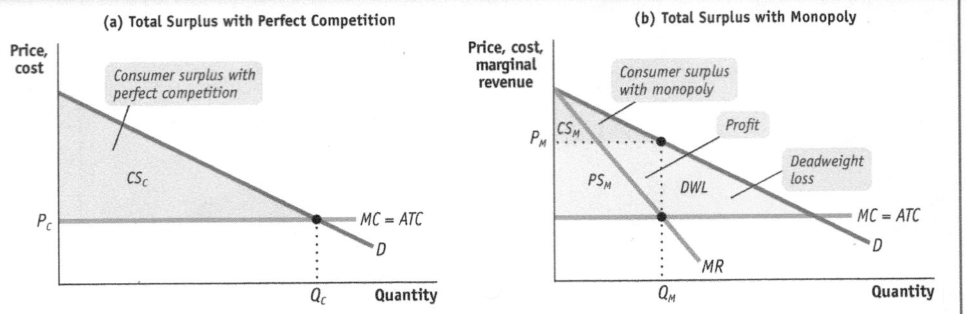

Panel (a) depicts a perfectly competitive industry: output is Q_C, and market price, P_C, is equal to *MC*. Since price is exactly equal to each producer's average total cost of production per unit, there is no producer surplus. So total surplus is equal to consumer surplus, the entire shaded area. Panel (b) depicts the industry under monopoly: the monopolist decreases output to Q_M and charges P_M. Consumer surplus (blue area) has shrunk: a portion of it has been captured as profit (green area), and a portion of it has been lost to deadweight loss (yellow area), the value of mutually beneficial transactions that do not occur because of monopoly behavior. As a result, total surplus falls.

is equal to the area of the blue-shaded triangle CS_C shown in panel (a). Since there is no producer surplus when the industry is perfectly competitive, CS_C also represents the total surplus.

Panel (b) shows the results for the same market, but this time assuming that the industry is a monopoly. The monopolist produces the level of output, Q_M, at which marginal cost is equal to marginal revenue, and it charges the price, P_M. The industry now earns profit—which is also the producer surplus in this case—equal to the area of the green rectangle, PS_M. Note that this profit is part of what was consumer surplus in the perfectly competitive market, and consumer surplus with the monopoly shrinks to the area of the blue triangle, CS_M.

AP® Exam Tip

Be prepared to identify and calculate the areas of consumer surplus, producer surplus, and deadweight loss for a monopoly on the AP® exam.

By comparing panels (a) and (b), we see that in addition to the redistribution of surplus from consumers to the monopolist, another important change has occurred: the sum of profit and consumer surplus—total surplus—is *smaller* under monopoly than under perfect competition. That is, the sum of CS_M and PS_M in panel (b) is less than the area CS_C in panel (a). Previously, we analyzed how taxes could cause *deadweight loss* for society. Here we show that a monopoly creates deadweight loss equal to the area of the yellow triangle, *DWL*. So monopoly produces a net loss for society.

This net loss arises because some mutually beneficial transactions do not occur. There are people for whom an additional unit of the good is worth more than the marginal cost of producing it but who don't consume it because they are not willing to pay the monopoly price, P_M. Indeed, by driving a wedge between price and marginal cost, a monopoly acts much like a tax on consumers and produces the same kind of inefficiency.

When an excise tax is imposed on a good produced by a monopoly, even less of the good is sold, and the deadweight loss grows. However, a lump-sum tax—one that does not depend on the quantity sold—does not contribute to the deadweight loss unless it is so high that it causes the monopoly to close down. The reason is that a lump-sum tax does not affect the marginal cost or the marginal revenue, so the monopoly goes on producing the same profit-maximizing quantity.

624 Section 11 Market Structures: Perfect Competition and Monopoly

We have seen that monopoly power detracts from the welfare of society as a whole and is a source of market failure. Is there anything government policy can do about it?

Preventing Monopoly Power

Policy toward monopolies depends crucially on whether or not the industry in question is a natural monopoly, one in which increasing returns to scale ensure that a bigger producer has lower average total cost. If the industry is *not* a natural monopoly, the best policy is to prevent a monopoly from arising or to break it up if it already exists. Government policy used to prevent or eliminate monopolies is known as *antitrust policy*, which we will discuss in Module 77. For now, let's focus on the more difficult problem of dealing with a natural monopoly.

Dealing with a Natural Monopoly

Breaking up a monopoly that isn't natural is clearly a good idea: the gains to consumers outweigh the loss to the producer. But it's not so clear whether a natural monopoly, one in which large producers have lower average total costs than small producers, should be broken up, because this would raise average total cost. For example, a town government that tried to prevent a single company from dominating local gas supply—which, as we've discussed, is almost surely a natural monopoly—would raise the cost of providing gas to its residents.

Yet even in the case of a natural monopoly, a profit-maximizing monopolist acts in a way that causes inefficiency—it charges consumers a price that is higher than marginal cost and, by doing so, prevents some potentially beneficial transactions. Also, it can seem unfair that a firm that has managed to establish a monopoly position earns a large profit at the expense of consumers.

What can public policy do about this? There are two common answers.

Public Ownership

In many countries, the preferred answer to the problem of natural monopoly has been **public ownership**. Instead of allowing a private monopolist to control an industry, the government establishes a public agency to provide the good and protect consumers' interests.

The advantage of public ownership, in principle, is that a publicly owned natural monopoly can set prices based on the criterion of efficiency rather than profit maximization. In a perfectly competitive industry, profit-maximizing behavior *is* efficient because producers set price equal to marginal cost; that is why there is no economic argument for public ownership of, say, wheat farms.

Experience suggests, however, that public ownership as a solution to the problem of natural monopoly often works badly in practice. One reason is that publicly owned firms are often less eager than private companies to keep costs down or offer high-quality products. Another is that publicly owned companies all too often end up serving political interests—providing contracts or jobs to people with the right connections.

David Livingston/Getty Images

With **public ownership** of a monopoly, the good is supplied by the government or by a firm owned by the government.

Price regulation limits the price that a monopolist is allowed to charge.

Regulation

In the United States, the more common answer has been to leave the industry in private hands but subject it to regulation. In particular, most local utilities, like electricity, telephone service, natural gas, and so on, are covered by **price regulation** that limits the prices they can charge.

TEACH Connect It

Natural monopoly was introduced in Section 4. A natural monopoly occurs when cost advantages make it cheaper per unit to produce larger quantities. That is, *AC* is lower at higher levels of output (the *AC* curve is downward-sloping). Natural monopolies are generally associated with economies of scale. With a natural monopoly, a monopoly market is productively efficient (i.e., the lowest *ATC* occurs with one firm), while more firms lead to inefficiency. But we have already shown that monopoly leads to allocative inefficiency (i.e., *DWL*). So, a natural monopoly creates a conflict between the two efficiency goals. This conflict can be addressed by government regulation (public ownership or price regulation). A monopoly is allowed to create productive efficiency, but regulated to prevent allocative inefficiency.

TEACH Connect It

Remind students of the relationship between marginal and average from Section 4. *MC* crosses the *AC* curve at the *AC* curve's lowest point. With economies of scale, *AC* is falling. Therefore, *MC* must be below *AC* when economies of scale exist, as shown in the graphs in this module.

FOCUS Test It

Ask students to list the advantages and disadvantages of public ownership when dealing with natural monopolies. *Advantage: price set due to efficiency not profit; disadvantage: publicly owned firms are often less inclined to keep costs down; they frequently don't have the incentive to create high-quality products; they all too commonly serve political interests.*

Module 62 Monopoly and Public Policy 625

FOCUS Active Learning

Have students watch Jacob Clifford's video "Micro 4.6 Socially Optimal and Fair Return for Monopolies" (see econextras video list with hyperlinks on the bcs and TRFD) as you work with Figure 62.2. Ask students why government policy makers will generally go with the Fair Return method of regulation of natural monopolies. *(Fair Return pricing provides a normal profit since P is equal to AC.)*

FOCUS Graph It

- Have students refer to Figure 62.2 showing both a regulated and an unregulated natural monopoly. Ask students: How can you tell the graph shows a natural monopoly? *ATC slopes downward.*
- Panel (a) shows a natural monopoly without regulation. Why does the monopolist produce Q_M and charge P_M? *Because the monopoly maximizes profit by producing the quantity where MC = MR and charging the price on the demand curve for that quantity*
- Panel (b) shows a natural monopoly with government regulation. The monopoly must charge P_R^*, so what happens to the monopoly profit and consumer surplus, compared to an unregulated monopoly? *Profit goes to zero because P = ATC and CS decreases because price is lower.*
- Is the regulated price P_R^* above, below, or equal to the allocatively efficient price? *$P_R^* > MC$, so it is NOT allocatively efficient.*
- What would happen to the regulated monopoly's profit if the regulated price were set to be allocatively efficient? *The monopoly would incur a loss because P = MC is below ATC.*

FOCUS Active Learning

TRM For an activity to aid understanding of the differences between perfectly competitive and monopoly firms, use **Worksheet 62.3 (Monopoly and Perfectly Competitive Market Comparisons)** from the TRM.

Figure 62.2 Unregulated and Regulated Natural Monopoly

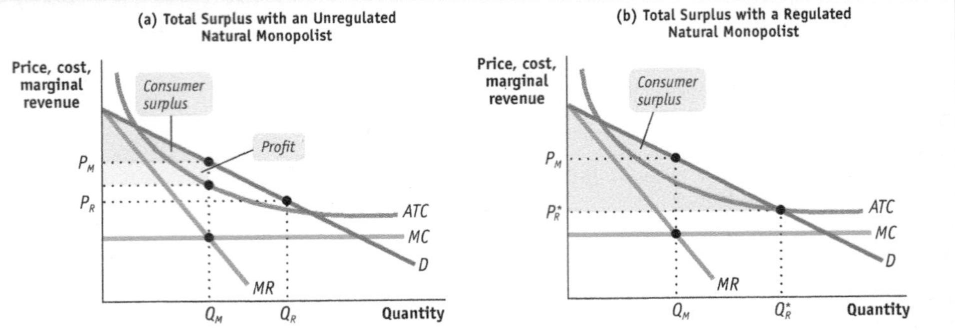

This figure shows the case of a natural monopolist. In panel (a), if the monopolist is allowed to charge P_M, it makes a profit, shown by the green area; consumer surplus is shown by the blue area. If it is regulated and must charge the lower price, P_R, output increases from Q_M to Q_R and consumer surplus increases. Panel (b) shows what happens when the monopolist must charge a price equal to average total cost, the price P_R^*. Output expands to Q_R^*, and consumer surplus is now the entire blue area. The monopolist makes zero profit. This is the greatest total surplus possible without the monopoly incurring losses.

Figure 62.2 shows an example of price regulation of a natural monopoly—a highly simplified version of a local gas company. The company faces a demand curve, *D*, with an associated marginal revenue curve, *MR*. For simplicity, we assume that the firm's total cost consists of two parts: a fixed cost and a variable cost that is the same for every unit. So marginal cost is constant in this case, and the marginal cost curve (which here is also the average variable cost curve) is the horizontal line *MC*. The average total cost curve is the downward-sloping curve *ATC*; it slopes downward because the higher the output, the lower the average fixed cost (the fixed cost per unit of output). Because average total cost slopes downward over the range of output relevant for market demand, this is a natural monopoly.

Panel (a) illustrates a case of natural monopoly without regulation. The unregulated natural monopolist chooses the monopoly output Q_M and charges the price P_M. Since the monopolist receives a price greater than average total cost, she or he earns a profit, represented by the green-shaded rectangle in panel (a). Consumer surplus is given by the blue-shaded triangle.

Now suppose that regulators impose a price ceiling on local gas deliveries—one that falls below the monopoly price P_M but above average total cost, say, at P_R in panel (a). At that price the quantity demanded is Q_R.

Does the company have an incentive to produce that quantity? Yes. If the price the monopolist can charge is fixed at P_R by regulators, the firm can sell any quantity between zero and Q_R for the same price, P_R. Because it doesn't have to lower its price to sell more (up to Q_R), there is no price effect to bring marginal revenue below price, so the regulated price becomes the marginal revenue for the monopoly just like the market price is the marginal revenue for a perfectly competitive firm. With marginal revenue being above marginal cost and price exceeding average cost, the firm expands output to meet the quantity demanded, Q_R. This policy has appeal because at the regulated price, the monopolist produces more at a lower price.

AP® Exam Tip

You may be asked to explain what happens to consumer surplus, producer surplus, and deadweight loss when a monopoly is regulated. Remember that a regulated price equal to the average total cost is the lowest price that would not cause the firm to take losses and eventually close.

626 Section 11 Market Structures: Perfect Competition and Monopoly

If regulators pursued allocative efficiency by setting a price ceiling equal to marginal cost, the monopolist would not be willing to produce at all in the long run, because it would be producing at a loss. That is, the price ceiling has to be set high enough to allow the firm to cover its average total cost. Panel (b) shows a situation in which regulators have pushed the price down as far as possible, at the level where the average total cost curve crosses the demand curve. At any lower price the firm loses money. The price here, P^*_R, is the best regulated price: the monopolist is just willing to operate and produces Q^*_R, the quantity demanded at that price. Consumers and society gain as a result.

The welfare effects of this regulation can be seen by comparing the shaded areas in the two panels of Figure 62.2. Consumer surplus is increased by the regulation, with the gains coming from two sources. First, profit is eliminated and added instead to consumer surplus. Second, the larger output and lower price leads to an overall welfare gain—an increase in total surplus. In fact, panel (b) illustrates the largest total surplus possible.

Must Monopoly Be Controlled?

Sometimes the cure is worse than the disease. Some economists have argued that the best solution, even in the case of a natural monopoly, may be to live with it. The case for doing nothing is that attempts to control monopoly, one way or another, will do more harm than good.

The following FYI describes the case of cable television, a natural monopoly that has been alternately regulated and deregulated as politicians change their minds about the appropriate policy.

FYI Cable Dilemmas

Most price regulation in the United States goes back a long way: electricity, local phone service, water, and gas have been regulated in most places for generations. But cable television is a relatively new industry. Until the late 1970s, only rural areas too remote to support local broadcast stations were served by cable. After 1972, new technology and looser rules made it profitable to offer cable service to major metropolitan areas; new networks like HBO and CNN emerged to take advantage of the possibilities.

Until recently, local cable TV was a natural monopoly: running cable through a town entails large fixed costs that don't depend on how many people actually subscribe. Having more than one cable company would involve a lot of wasteful duplication. But if the local cable company is a monopoly, should its prices be regulated?

At first, most local governments thought so, and cable TV was subject to price regulation. In 1984, however, Congress passed a law prohibiting most local governments from regulating cable prices. (The law was the result both of widespread skepticism about whether price regulation was actually a good idea and of intensive lobbying by the cable companies.)

After the law went into effect, however, cable television rates increased sharply. The resulting consumer backlash led to a new law, in 1992, which once again allowed local governments to set limits on cable prices.

Was the second round of regulation a success? As measured by the prices of "basic" cable service, it was: after rising rapidly during the period of deregulation, the cost of basic service leveled off.

However, price regulation in cable applies only to "basic" service. Cable operators can try to evade the restrictions by charging more for premium channels like HBO or by offering fewer channels in the "basic" package. So some skeptics have questioned whether current regulation has actually been effective.

Yet technological change has begun providing relief to consumers in some areas. Although cable TV is a natural monopoly, there is now another means of delivering video programs to homes: over a high-speed fiber-optic Internet connection. In some locations, fiber-optic Internet providers have begun competing aggressively with traditional cable TV companies. Studies have shown that when a second provider enters a market, prices can drop significantly, as much as 30%. In fact, the United States is currently behind on this front: today more than 60% of households in Hong Kong watch TV programs delivered over the Internet. What will these changes mean for the cable TV monopolies? Stay tuned.

Stringer/Getty Images

OPEN & CLOSE Exit Slip

TRM *Please see **Exit Slip: Module 62** in the TRM for formative multiple-choice questions to ask your students before finishing your lesson. These questions will help you quickly assess whether your students have mastered the module's concepts before moving on.*

Answers to the Exit Slip Questions

1. D
2. C
3. B

MODULE 62 Review

Check Your Understanding

1. What policy should the government adopt in the following cases? Explain.
   a. Internet service in Anytown, OH, is provided by cable. Customers feel they are being overcharged, but the cable company claims it must charge prices that let it recover the costs of laying cable.
   b. The only two airlines that currently fly to Alaska need government approval to merge. Other airlines wish to fly to Alaska but need government-allocated landing slots to do so.
2. True or false? Explain your answer.
   a. Society's welfare is lower under monopoly because some consumer surplus is transformed into profit for the monopolist.
   b. A monopolist causes inefficiency because there are consumers who are willing to pay a price greater than or equal to marginal cost but less than the monopoly price.
3. Suppose a monopolist mistakenly believes that his or her marginal revenue is always equal to the market price. Assuming constant marginal cost and no fixed cost, draw a diagram comparing the level of profit, consumer surplus, total surplus, and deadweight loss for this misguided monopolist compared to a smart monopolist.

Tackle the Test: Multiple-Choice Questions

1. Which of the following statements is true of a monopoly as compared to a perfectly competitive market with the same costs?
   I. Consumer surplus is smaller.
   II. Profit is smaller.
   III. Deadweight loss is smaller.
   a. I only
   b. II only
   c. III only
   d. I and II only
   e. I, II, and III
2. Which of the following is true of a natural monopoly?
   a. It experiences diseconomies of scale.
   b. *ATC* is lower if there is a single firm in the market.
   c. It occurs in a market that relies on natural resources for its production.
   d. There are decreasing returns to scale in the industry.
   e. The government must provide the good or service to achieve efficiency.
3. Which of the following government actions is the most common for a natural monopoly in the United States?
   a. prevent its formation
   b. break it up using antitrust laws
   c. use price regulation
   d. public ownership
   e. elimination of the market
4. Which of the following markets is an example of a regulated natural monopoly?
   a. local cable TV
   b. gasoline
   c. cell phone service
   d. organic tomatoes
   e. diamonds
5. Which of the following is most likely to be higher for a regulated natural monopoly than for an unregulated natural monopoly?
   a. product variety
   b. quantity
   c. price
   d. profit
   e. deadweight loss

Answers to Module 62 Review Questions

Check Your Understanding

1. a. Cable Internet service is a natural monopoly, so the government should intervene if it believes that the current price exceeds average total cost, which includes the cost of laying the cable. In this case, it should impose a price ceiling equal to average total cost. If the price does not exceed average total cost, the government should do nothing.

b. The government should approve the merger only if it fosters competition by transferring some of the company's landing slots to another, competing airline.

2. a. False. Although some consumer surplus is indeed transformed into monopoly profit, this is not the source of inefficiency. As can be seen from Figure 62.1, panel (b), the inefficiency arises from the fact that some of the consumer surplus is transformed into deadweight loss (the yellow area), which is a complete loss not captured by consumers, producers, or anyone else.

b. True. If a monopolist sold to all customers willing to pay an amount greater than or equal to marginal cost, all mutually beneficial transactions would occur and there would be no deadweight loss.

3. As shown in the accompanying diagram, a "smart" profit-maximizing monopolist produces Q_M, the output level at which $MR = MC$. A monopolist that mistakenly believes that $P = MR$ produces the output level at which $P = MC$ (when, in fact, $P > MR$, and at the true profit-maximizing level of output, $P > MR = MC$). This misguided monopolist will produce the output level Q_C, where the demand curve crosses the marginal cost curve—the same output level that would be produced if the industry were perfectly competitive. It will charge the price P_C, which is equal to marginal cost, and make zero profit. The entire shaded area is equal to consumer surplus, which is also equal to total surplus in this case (since the monopolist receives zero producer surplus). There is no deadweight loss because every consumer who is willing to pay as much as or more than marginal cost gets the good. A smart monopolist, however, will produce the output level Q_M and charge the price P_M. Profit for the smart monopolist is represented by the green area, consumer surplus corresponds to the blue area, and total surplus is equal to the sum of the green and blue areas. The yellow area is the deadweight loss generated by the monopolist.

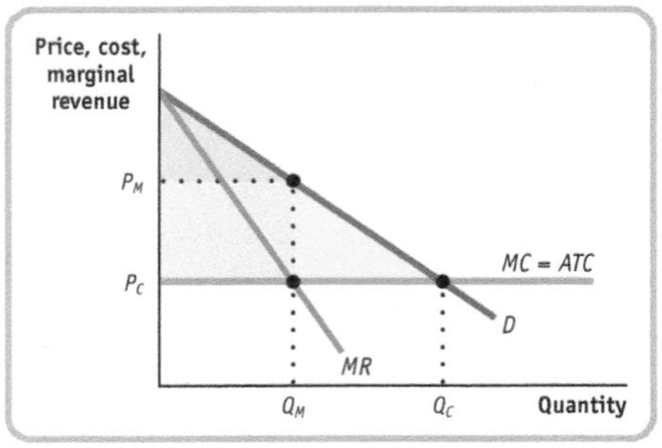

Tackle the Test: Multiple-Choice Questions

1. a
2. b
3. c
4. a
5. b

Tackle the Test: Free-Response Questions

1. Draw a correctly labeled graph showing a profit-making natural monopoly. On your graph, indicate each of the following:
   a. the monopoly's profit-maximizing output (Q_M)
   b. the monopoly's price (P_M)
   c. the monopoly's profit
   d. the regulated price that would maximize consumer surplus without creating losses for the firm (P_R)

Rubric for FRQ 1 (9 points)

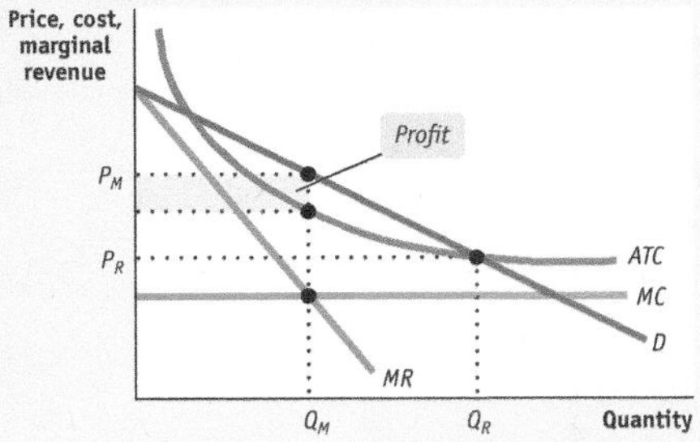

1 point: The axes are correctly labeled.

1 point: The demand curve is labeled and sloped downward.

1 point: The marginal revenue curve is labeled, sloped downward, and below the demand curve.

1 point: The average total cost curve is labeled and downward-sloping (not U-shaped!).

1 point: The marginal cost curve is labeled and below the average total cost curve (it does not need to be flat).

1 point: The profit-maximizing output, Q_M, is shown on the horizontal axis where $MC = MR$.

1 point: The profit-maximizing price is found on the demand curve above the point where $MC = MR$.

1 point: The monopoly profit area is correctly shaded and labeled.

1 point: The regulated price is labeled on the vertical axis to the left of the point where the demand curve crosses the average total cost curve.

2. Draw a correctly labeled graph of a natural monopoly. Use your graph to identify each of the following:
   a. consumer surplus if the market were somehow able to operate as a perfectly competitive market
   b. consumer surplus with the monopoly
   c. monopoly profit
   d. deadweight loss with the monopoly

   (8 points)

Tackle the Test: Free-Response Question

Rubric for FRQ 2 (8 points)

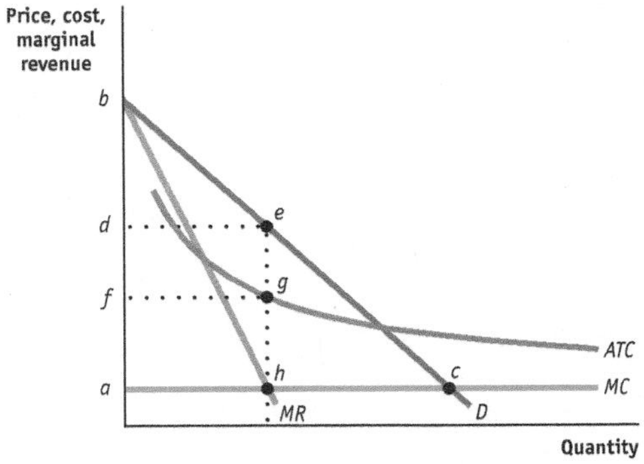

1 point: Axes are correctly labeled as "\$ per unit" or "Price, cost, marginal revenue" and "Quantity."

1 point: The demand curve is labeled and downward-sloping, and the marginal revenue curve is labeled, downward-sloping, and below the demand curve.

1 point: The average total cost curve is labeled and downward-sloping.

1 point: The marginal cost curve is labeled and below the average total cost curve (but not necessarily flat).

1 point: An area analogous to triangle *bca* in the graph above is identified with shading or letters as the consumer surplus with a perfectly competitive market.

1 point: An area analogous to triangle *bed* is identified with shading or letters as the consumer surplus with the monopoly.

1 point: An area analogous to rectangle *degf* is identified with shading or letters as the monopoly profit.

1 point: An area analogous to triangle *ech* is identified with shading or letters as the deadweight loss with the monopoly.

Module 62 Monopoly and Public Policy 629

PD To prepare for teaching this lesson, you may want to consult the **Module 63 Sample Lecture** in the TRM.

OPEN & CLOSE Start Here

Up to this point, we have always discussed single-price monopolists—monopolists that maximize profit by producing the output where $MC = MR$ and charging the price on the demand curve at that quantity. But since monopolists have market power and are price-makers, they can sometimes earn *even more* profit by charging different prices to different consumers for the same good. That is price discrimination. Ask students for examples of markets in which different consumers may pay different prices for the same good. Students may mention airline tickets, movie tickets, new cars, or many other examples.

TEACH Connect It

Remind students that consumers receive consumer surplus with a single-price monopolist. Consumer surplus is the area above price and below the demand curve. The goal of price discrimination is to increase profits even further by taking away consumer surplus. With price discrimination, monopolists charge each consumer, or group of consumers, their maximum willingness to pay (i.e., the price on the demand curve).

redbrickstock.com/Alamy

MODULE 63 Price Discrimination

In this Module, you will learn to:

- Explain the meaning of price discrimination
- Discuss why price discrimination is common when producers have market power

Up to this point, we have considered only the case of a monopolist who charges all consumers the same price. However, monopolists want to maximize their profit and often they do so by charging different prices for the same product. In this module we look at how monopolists increase their profit by engaging in *price discrimination*.

Price Discrimination Defined

AP® Exam Tip

Price discrimination allows firms that are able to charge more than one price to make profit out of what would otherwise be consumer surplus.

A **single-price monopolist** charges all consumers the same price.

Sellers engage in **price discrimination** when they charge different prices to different consumers for the same good.

A monopolist who charges everyone the same price is known as a **single-price monopolist**. As the term suggests, not all monopolists do this. In fact, many monopolists find that they can increase their profit by selling the same good to different customers for different prices: they practice **price discrimination**.

An example of price discrimination that travelers encounter regularly involves airline tickets. Although there are a number of airlines, most routes in the United States are serviced by only one or two carriers, which, as a result, have market power and can influence prices. So any regular airline passenger quickly becomes aware that the simple question "How much will it cost me to fly there?" rarely has a simple answer. If you are willing to buy a nonrefundable ticket a month in advance and stay over a Saturday night, the round trip may cost only $150—or less if you are a senior citizen or a student. But if you have to go on a business trip tomorrow, which happens to be Tuesday, and want to come back on Wednesday, the same round trip might cost $550. Yet the business traveler and the visiting grandparent receive the same product.

You might object that airlines are not usually monopolies—that in most flight markets the airline industry is an oligopoly. In fact, price discrimination takes place under oligopoly and monopolistic competition as well as monopoly. But it doesn't happen under perfect competition. And once we've seen why monopolists sometimes price-discriminate, we'll be in a good position to understand why it happens in other cases, too.

The Logic of Price Discrimination

To get a preliminary view of why price discrimination might be more profitable than charging all consumers the same price, imagine that Air Sunshine offers the only non-stop flights between Bismarck, North Dakota, and Ft. Lauderdale, Florida. Assume that there are no capacity problems—the airline can fly as many planes as the number of passengers warrants. Also assume that there is no fixed cost. The marginal cost to the airline of providing a seat is $125 however many passengers it carries.

Further assume that the airline knows there are two kinds of potential passengers. First, there are business travelers, 2,000 of whom want to travel between the destinations each week. Second, there are high school students, 2,000 of whom also want to travel each week.

Will potential passengers take the flight? It depends on the price. The business travelers, it turns out, really need to fly; they will take the plane as long as the price is no more than $550. Since they are flying purely for business, we assume that cutting the price below $550 will not lead to any increase in business travel. The students, however, have less money and more time; if the price goes above $150, they will take the bus. The implied demand curve is shown in **Figure 63.1**.

So what should the airline do? If it has to charge everyone the same price, its options are limited. It could charge $550; that way it would get as much as possible out of the business travelers but lose the student market. Or it could charge only $150; that way it would get both types of travelers but would make significantly less money from sales to business travelers.

We can quickly calculate the profit from each of these alternatives. If the airline charged $550, it would sell 2,000 tickets to the business travelers, earning a total revenue of 2,000 × $550 = $1.1 million and incurring costs of 2,000 × $125 = $250,000; so its profit would be $850,000, illustrated by the shaded area *B* in Figure 63.1. If the airline charged only $150, it would sell 4,000 tickets, receiving revenue of 4,000 × $150 = $600,000 and incurring costs of 4,000 × $125 = $500,000; so its profit would be $100,000. If the airline must charge everyone the same price, charging the higher price and forgoing sales to students is clearly more profitable.

What the airline would really like to do, however, is charge the business travelers the full $550 but offer $150 tickets to the students. That's a lot less than the price paid by

Figure 63.1 Two Types of Airline Customers

Air Sunshine has two types of customers, business travelers willing to pay at most $550 per ticket and students willing to pay at most $150 per ticket. There are 2,000 of each kind of customer. Air Sunshine has a constant marginal cost of $125 per seat. If Air Sunshine could charge these two types of customers different prices, it would maximize its profit by charging business travelers $550 and students $150 per ticket. This price discrimination would allow Air Sunshine to capture all of the consumer surplus as profit.

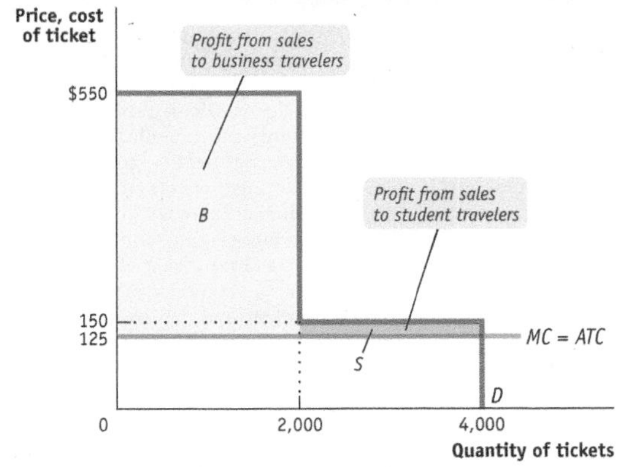

TEACH Teach It

In order to price-discriminate, (1) a firm must have some control over price; (2) there must be different consumers, or groups of consumers, with a different willingness to pay (i.e., demand); and (3) the firm must be able to identify the consumers or groups with different demand. Also, (4) price discrimination will not increase profits if consumers are able to resell the good (i.e., arbitrage) from the lower-priced and higher-priced consumers.

FOCUS Graph It

Figure 63.1 shows how price discrimination captures consumer surplus and increases profit. Have students calculate consumer surplus with a single price of $150 ($400 × 2,000) and $550 ($0 × 2,000), and with price discrimination at $150 and $550 ($0 × 4,000).

FOCUS Test It

Why do firms price-discriminate? *To increase their profit* Can a perfectly competitive firm price-discriminate? Explain. *No, it is a price taker.*

TEACH Connect It

Remind students that price elasticity of demand measures the relative responsiveness of quantity demanded against changes in price. An inelastic demand is not very responsive to price changes, while an elastic demand is very responsive. Price discrimination is based on price elasticity of demand. Use what students learned about elasticity and *TR* in Section 3 to help them understand price discrimination. Firms want to raise the price for consumers with a relatively inelastic demand, because they will not be very responsive to such a price change (they will still buy about the same quantity). With a higher price and about the same quantity, *TR* increases. But firms do not want to raise price when a consumer's demand is relatively elastic, because the consumer will respond by buying a lot less. Even though price is higher, *TR* decreases, because consumers buy so much less.

FOCUS Active Learning

TRM Assign the video "Spotting the Price Discrimination" by OpenLectures sg (see econextras video list with hyperlinks on the bcs and TRFD) and **Worksheet 63.1 (Spot It)** from the TRM.

business travelers, but it's still above the marginal cost; so if the airline could sell those extra 2,000 tickets to students, it would make an additional $50,000 in profit. That is, it would make a profit equal to the areas *B* plus *S* in Figure 63.1.

It would be more realistic to suppose that there is some "give" in the demand of each group: at a price below $550, there would be some increase in business travel; and at a price above $150, some students would still purchase tickets. But, it turns out, this does not do away with the argument for price discrimination. The important point is that the two groups of consumers differ in their *sensitivity to price*—that a high price has a larger effect in discouraging purchases by students than by business travelers. As long as different groups of customers respond differently to the price, a monopolist will find that it can capture more consumer surplus and increase its profit by charging them different prices.

Price Discrimination and Elasticity

A more realistic description of the demand that airlines face would not specify particular prices at which different types of travelers would choose to fly. Instead, it would distinguish between the groups on the basis of their sensitivity to the price—their price elasticity of demand.

Suppose that a company sells its product to two easily identifiable groups of people—business travelers and students. It just so happens that business travelers are very insensitive to the price: there is a certain amount of the product they just have to have whatever the price, but they cannot be persuaded to buy much more than that no matter how cheap it is. Students, though, are more flexible: offer a good enough price and they will buy quite a lot, but raise the price too high and they will switch to something else. Which approach is best for the company in this case?

William Thomas Cain/Getty Images

On many airline routes, the fare you pay depends on the type of traveler you are.

The answer is the one already suggested by our simplified example: the company should charge business travelers, with their low price elasticity of demand, a higher price than it charges students, with their high price elasticity of demand.

The actual situation of the airlines is very much like this hypothetical example. Business travelers typically place a high priority on being in the right place at the right time and are not very sensitive to the price. But leisure travelers are fairly sensitive to the price: faced with a high price, they might take the bus, drive to another airport to get a lower fare, or skip the trip altogether.

So why doesn't an airline simply announce different prices for business and leisure customers? First, this would probably be illegal. (U.S. law places some limits on the ability of companies to practice blatant price discrimination.) Second, even if it were legal, it would be a hard policy to enforce: business travelers might be willing to wear casual clothing and claim they were visiting family in Ft. Lauderdale in order to save $400.

So what the airlines do—quite successfully—is impose rules that indirectly have the effect of charging business and leisure travelers different fares. Business travelers usually travel during the week and want to be home on the weekend, so the round-trip fare is much higher if you don't stay over a Saturday night. The requirement of a weekend stay for a cheap ticket effectively separates business travelers from leisure travelers. Similarly, business travelers often visit several cities in succession rather than make a simple round trip; so round-trip fares are much lower than twice the one-way fare. Many business trips are scheduled on short notice, so fares are much lower if you book far in advance. Fares are also lower if you travel standby, taking your chances on whether you actually get a seat—business travelers have to make it to that meeting; people visiting their relatives don't. And because customers must show their ID at check-in, airlines make sure there are no resales of tickets between the two groups that would undermine their ability to price-discriminate—students can't buy cheap tickets

St. Louis Federal Reserve Bank Resources

"The Rising Cost of College: Tuition, Financial Aid, and Price Discrimination," ***Page One Economics Classroom Edition***

The cost of a college education seems to be skyrocketing—but is it really? Learn about the concept of price discrimination and how it affects college costs.

632 Section 11 Market Structures: Perfect Competition and Monopoly

and resell them to business travelers. Look at the rules that govern ticket pricing, and you will see an ingenious implementation of profit-maximizing price discrimination.

Perfect Price Discrimination

Let's return to the example of business travelers and students traveling between Bismarck and Ft. Lauderdale, illustrated in Figure 63.1, and ask what would happen if the airline could distinguish between the two groups of customers in order to charge each a different price.

Clearly, the airline would charge each group its *willingness to pay*—that is, the maximum that each group is willing to pay. For business travelers, the willingness to pay is $550; for students, it is $150. As we have assumed, the marginal cost is $125 and does not depend on output, making the marginal cost curve a horizontal line. And as we noted earlier, we can easily determine the airline's profit: it is the sum of the areas of rectangle *B* and rectangle *S*.

In this case, the consumers do not get any consumer surplus! The entire surplus is captured by the monopolist in the form of profit. When a monopolist is able to capture the entire surplus in this way, we say that the monopolist achieves **perfect price discrimination**.

In general, the greater the number of different prices charged, the closer the monopolist is to perfect price discrimination. **Figure 63.2** on the next page shows a monopolist facing a downward-sloping demand curve, a monopolist who we assume is able to charge different prices to different groups of consumers, with the consumers who are willing to pay the most being charged the most. In panel (a) the monopolist charges two different prices; in panel (b) the monopolist charges three different prices. Two things are apparent:

- The greater the number of prices the monopolist charges, the lower the lowest price—that is, some consumers will pay prices that approach marginal cost.
- The greater the number of prices the monopolist charges, the more money is extracted from consumers.

With a very large number of different prices, the picture would look like panel (c), a case of perfect price discrimination. Here, every consumer pays the most he or she is willing to pay, and the entire consumer surplus is extracted as profit.

Both our airline example and the example in Figure 63.2 can be used to make another point: a monopolist who can engage in perfect price discrimination doesn't cause any allocative inefficiency! The reason is that the source of allocative inefficiency is eliminated: all potential consumers who are willing to purchase the good at a price equal to or above marginal cost are able to do so. The perfectly price-discriminating monopolist manages to "scoop up" these consumers by offering some of them lower prices than others.

Perfect price discrimination is almost never possible in practice. At a fundamental level, the inability to achieve perfect price discrimination is a problem of prices as economic signals. When prices work as economic signals, they convey the information needed to ensure that all mutually beneficial transactions will indeed occur: the market price signals the seller's cost, and a consumer signals willingness to pay by purchasing the good whenever that willingness to pay is at least as high as the market price. The problem in reality, however, is that prices are often not perfect signals: a consumer's true willingness to pay can be disguised, as by a business traveler who claims to be a student when buying a ticket in order to obtain a lower fare. When such disguises work, a monopolist cannot achieve perfect price discrimination. However, monopolists do try to move in the direction of perfect price discrimination through a variety of pricing strategies. Common techniques for price discrimination include the following:

- *Advance purchase restrictions.* Prices are lower for those who purchase well in advance (or in some cases for those who purchase at the last minute). This separates those who are likely to shop for better prices from those who won't.
- *Volume discounts.* Often the price is lower if you buy a large quantity. For a consumer who plans to consume a lot of a good, the cost of the last unit—the marginal cost to

Perfect price discrimination takes place when a monopolist charges each consumer his or her willingness to pay—the maximum that the consumer is willing to pay.

AP® Exam Tip

A perfectly price-discriminating monopolist produces the efficient quantity, as there is no deadweight loss.

TEACH Teach It

Perfect price discrimination occurs when a firm charges consumers their maximum willingness to pay for each unit of output. With perfect price discrimination, there is no consumer surplus because no difference exists between what consumers pay (the market price) and what they are willing to pay (demand).

FOCUS Graph It

Figure 63.2 (on the next page) illustrates consumer surplus with 2 price, 3 price, and perfect price discrimination. For each graph, ask students if the outcome is allocatively efficient? (i.e., is there a *DWL*)? *In graphs (a) and (b), the firm is* ***allocatively inefficient*** *since P > MC and the firm does not capture all the lost consumer surplus; in graph (c), P = MC means the firm is* ***allocatively efficient*** *as it captures all the lost consumer surplus.*

FOCUS Flip It

TRM Assign Jacob Clifford's video "Micro 4.14 Price Discriminating Monopoly" (see econextras video list with hyperlinks on the bcs and TRFD) and **Worksheet 63.2 (Price Discriminating Monopoly)** from the TRM.

FOCUS Active Learning

TRM For a review of perfect price discrimination, assign **Worksheet 63.3 (Price Discrimination Practice)** from the TRM.

OPEN & CLOSE Exit Slip

TRM *Please see **Exit Slip: Module 63** in the TRM for formative multiple-choice questions to ask your students before finishing your lesson. These questions will help you quickly assess whether your students have mastered the module's concepts before moving on.*

Answers to the Exit Slip Questions

1. D
2. C
3. D

Figure 63.2 Price Discrimination

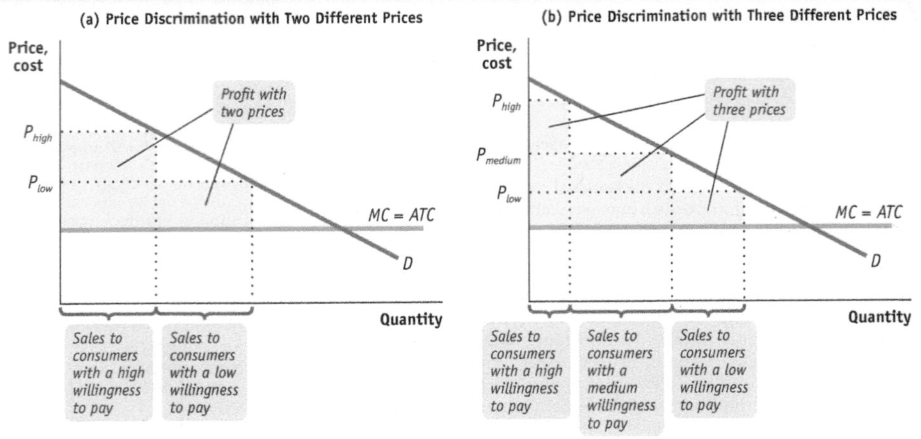

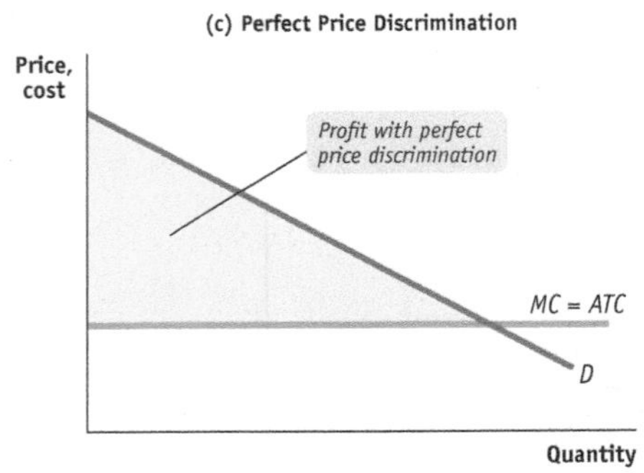

Panel (a) shows a monopolist that charges two different prices; its profit is shown by the shaded area. Panel (b) shows a monopolist that charges three different prices; its profit, too, is shown by the shaded area. It is able to capture more of the consumer surplus and to increase its profit. That is, by increasing the number of different prices charged, the monopolist captures more of the consumer surplus and makes a larger profit. Panel (c) shows the case of perfect price discrimination, where a monopolist charges each consumer his or her willingness to pay; the monopolist's profit is given by the shaded triangle.

© Mark Marcus/Alamy

the consumer—is considerably less than the average price. This separates those who plan to buy a lot, and so are likely to be more sensitive to price, from those who don't.

- *Two-part tariffs.* In a discount club like Costco or Sam's Club (which are not monopolists but monopolistic competitors), you pay an annual fee (the first part of the tariff) in addition to the price of the item(s) you purchase (the second part of the tariff). So the full price of the first item you buy is in effect much higher than that of subsequent items, making the two-part tariff behave like a volume discount.

Our discussion also helps explain why government policies on monopoly typically focus on preventing deadweight loss, not preventing price discrimination—unless it causes serious issues of equity. Compared to a single-price monopolist, price discrimination—even when it is not perfect—can increase the efficiency of the market. When a single, medium-level price is replaced by a high price and a low price, some consumers who were formerly priced out of the market will be able to purchase the good. The price discrimination increases efficiency because more of the units for which the willingness to pay (as indicated by the height of the demand curve) exceeds the marginal cost are produced and sold. Consider a drug that is disproportionately prescribed to senior citizens, who are often on fixed incomes and so are very sensitive to price. A policy that allows a drug company to charge senior citizens a low price and everyone else a high price will serve more consumers and create more total surplus than a situation in which everyone is charged the same price. But price discrimination that creates serious concerns about equity is likely to be prohibited—for example, an ambulance service that charges patients based on the severity of their emergency.

MODULE 63 Review

Check Your Understanding

1. True or false? Explain your answer.
   a. A single-price monopolist sells to some customers that would not find the product affordable if purchasing from a price-discriminating monopolist.
   b. A price-discriminating monopolist creates more inefficiency than a single-price monopolist because it captures more of the consumer surplus.
   c. Under price discrimination, a customer with highly elastic demand will pay a lower price than a customer with inelastic demand.
2. Which of the following are cases of price discrimination and which are not? In the cases of price discrimination, identify the consumers with high price elasticity of demand and those with low price elasticity of demand.
   a. Damaged merchandise is marked down.
   b. Restaurants have senior citizen discounts.
   c. Food manufacturers place discount coupons for their merchandise in newspapers.
   d. Airline tickets cost more during the summer peak flying season.

Tackle the Test: Multiple-Choice Questions

1. Which of the following characteristics is necessary in order for a firm to price-discriminate?
   a. free entry and exit
   b. differentiated product
   c. many sellers
   d. some control over price
   e. horizontal demand curve
2. Price discrimination
   a. is the opposite of volume discounts.
   b. is a practice limited to movie theaters and the airline industry.
   c. can lead to increased efficiency in the market.
   d. rarely occurs in the real world.
   e. helps to increase the profit of perfect competitors.
3. With perfect price discrimination, consumer surplus
   a. is maximized.
   b. equals zero.
   c. is increased.
   d. cannot be determined.
   e. is the area below the demand curve and above the marginal cost curve.
4. Which of the following is a technique used by price-discriminating monopolists?
   I. advance purchase restrictions
   II. two-part tariffs
   III. volume discounts
   a. I only
   b. II only
   c. III only
   d. I and II only
   e. I, II, and III
5. A price-discriminating monopolist will charge a higher price to consumers with
   a. a more inelastic demand.
   b. a less inelastic demand.
   c. higher income.
   d. lower willingness to pay.
   e. less experience in the market.

Answers to Module 63 Review Questions

Check Your Understanding

1. a. False. The opposite is true. A price-discriminating monopolist will sell to some customers that would not find the product affordable if purchasing from a single-price monopolist—namely, customers with a high price elasticity of demand who are willing to pay only a relatively low price for the good.

b. False. Although a price-discriminating monopolist does indeed capture more of the consumer surplus, less inefficiency is created: more mutually beneficial transactions occur because the monopolist makes more sales to customers with a low willingness to pay for the good.

c. True. Under price discrimination, consumers are charged prices that depend on their price elasticity of demand. A consumer with highly elastic demand will pay a lower price than a consumer with inelastic demand.

2. a. This is not a case of price discrimination because the product itself is different and all consumers, regardless of their price elasticities of demand, value the damaged merchandise less than undamaged merchandise. So, the price must be lowered to sell the merchandise.

b. This is a case of price discrimination. Senior citizens have a higher price elasticity of demand for restaurant meals (their demand for restaurant meals is more responsive to price changes) than other patrons. Restaurants lower the price to high-elasticity consumers (senior citizens). Consumers with low price elasticity of demand will pay the full price.

c. This is a case of price discrimination. Consumers with a high price elasticity of demand will pay a lower price by collecting and using discount coupons. Consumers with a low price elasticity of demand will not use coupons.

d. This is not a case of price discrimination; it is simply a case of supply and demand.

Tackle the Test: Multiple-Choice Questions

1. d
2. c
3. b
4. e
5. a

Tackle the Test: Free-Response Question Rubric for FRQ 2 (6 points)

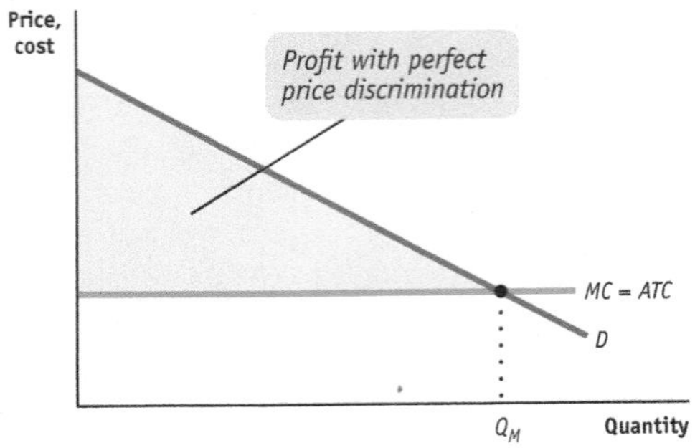

1 point: Axes are correctly labeled as "$ per unit" or "Price, cost" and "Quantity."

1 point: The demand curve is labeled and downward-sloping.

1 point: The profit-maximizing quantity is labeled on the horizontal axis where $MC = D$.

1 point: The monopoly's profit is identified as the area above average total cost and below the demand curve.

1 point: Consumer surplus is zero.

1 point: Because each consumer is charged the maximum he or she is willing to pay for each unit.

FOCUS Flip It

Encourage your students to watch the **Section 11 Review Video**, which was created as a special student review tool and is linked into the e-Book or can be found on the book's companion website.

Tackle the Test: Free-Response Questions

1. **a.** Define price discrimination.
   b. Why do firms price-discriminate?
   c. In which market structures can firms price-discriminate? Explain why.
   d. Give an example of price discrimination.

Rubric for FRQ 1 (5 points)

1 point: Price discrimination is the practice of charging different prices to different customers for the same product.

1 point: Firms price-discriminate to increase their profit.

1 point: In order to price-discriminate, firms must be in the monopoly, oligopoly, or monopolistic competition market structure.

1 point: Because rather than being price-takers, firms in these market structures have some degree of market power, which gives them the ability to charge more than one price.

1 point: An example is different prices for movie tickets charged for people of different ages.

2. Draw a correctly labeled graph showing a monopoly with a horizontal average total cost curve practicing perfect price discrimination. On your graph, identify the monopoly's profit. What does consumer surplus equal in this case? Explain.
(6 points)

SECTION 11 Review

Section 11 Review Video

Module 58

1. A producer chooses output according to the **price-taking firm's optimal output rule**: produce the quantity at which price equals marginal cost. However, a firm that produces the optimal quantity may not be profitable.

Module 59

2. A firm is profitable if total revenue exceeds total cost or, equivalently, if the market price exceeds its **break-even price**—minimum average total cost. If market price exceeds the break-even price, the firm is profitable. If market price is less than minimum average total cost, the firm is unprofitable. If market price is equal to minimum average total cost, the firm breaks even. When profitable, the firm's per-unit profit is $P - ATC$; when unprofitable, its per-unit loss is $ATC - P$.
3. Fixed cost is irrelevant to the firm's optimal short-run production decision. The short-run production decision depends on the firm's **shut-down price**—its minimum average variable cost—and the market price. When the market price is equal to or exceeds the shut-down price, the firm produces the output quantity at which marginal cost equals the market price. When the market price falls below the shut-down price, the firm ceases production in the short run. This generates the firm's **short-run individual supply curve**.
4. Fixed cost matters over time. If the market price is below minimum average total cost for an extended period of time, firms will exit the industry in the long run. If market price is above minimum average total cost, existing firms are profitable and new firms will enter the industry in the long run.

Module 60

5. The **industry supply curve** depends on the time period (short run or long run). When the number of firms is fixed, the **short-run industry supply curve** applies. The **short-run market equilibrium** occurs where the short-run industry supply curve and the demand curve intersect.
6. With sufficient time for entry into and exit from an industry, the **long-run industry supply curve** applies. The **long-run market equilibrium** occurs at the intersection of the long-run industry supply curve and the demand curve. At this point, no producer has an incentive to enter or exit. The long-run industry supply curve is horizontal for a **constant-cost industry**. It may slope upward if the industry's demand represents a significant portion of the overall demand for an input, resulting in an **increasing-cost industry**. It may even slope downward, as in the case of a **decreasing-cost industry**. But the long-run industry supply curve is always more elastic than the short-run industry supply curve.
7. In the long-run market equilibrium of a competitive industry, profit maximization leads each firm to produce at the same marginal cost, which is equal to the market price. Free entry and exit means that each firm earns zero economic profit—producing the output corresponding to its minimum average total cost. So the total cost of production of an industry's output is minimized and productive efficiency is achieved. The outcome is also allocatively efficient because price equals marginal cost, and every consumer with willingness to pay greater than or equal to marginal cost gets the good.

Module 61

8. The key difference between a monopoly and a perfectly competitive industry is that a single, perfectly competitive firm faces a horizontal demand curve but a monopolist faces a downward-sloping demand curve. This gives the monopolist market power, the ability to raise the market price by reducing output.
9. The marginal revenue of a monopolist is composed of a quantity effect (the price received from the additional unit) and a price effect (the reduction in the price at which all units are sold). Because of the price effect, a monopolist's marginal revenue is always less than the market price, and the marginal revenue curve lies below the demand curve.
10. At the monopolist's profit-maximizing output level, marginal cost equals marginal revenue, which is less than market price. At the perfectly competitive firm's profit-maximizing output level, marginal cost equals the market price. So in comparison to perfectly competitive industries, monopolies produce less, charge higher prices, and can earn profit in both the short run and the long run.

Module 62

11. A monopoly creates deadweight losses by charging a price above marginal cost: the loss in consumer surplus exceeds the monopolist's profit. This makes monopolies a source of market failure and governments often make policies to prevent or end them.
12. Natural monopolies also cause deadweight losses. To limit these losses, governments sometimes impose **public ownership** and at other times impose **price regulation**. A price ceiling on a monopolist, as opposed to a perfectly competitive industry, need not cause shortages and can increase total surplus.

Module 63

13. Not all monopolists are **single-price monopolists**. Monopolists, as well as oligopolists and monopolistic competitors, often engage in **price discrimination** to make higher profit, using various techniques to differentiate consumers based on their sensitivity to price and charging those with less elastic demand higher prices. A monopolist that achieves **perfect price discrimination** charges each consumer a price equal to his or her willingness to pay and captures the total surplus in the market. Although perfect price discrimination creates no allocative inefficiency, it is practically impossible to implement.

Section 11 Review 637

Answers to Section 11 AP® Exam Practice Questions

Multiple-Choice Questions

1. e
2. d
3. a
4. d
5. b
6. b
7. d

Key Terms

Price-taking firm's optimal output rule, p. 589
Break-even price, p. 596
Shut-down price, p. 597
Short-run individual supply curve, p. 598
Industry supply curve, p. 603
Short-run industry supply curve, p. 604
Short-run market equilibrium, p. 604
Long-run market equilibrium, p. 606
Long-run industry supply curve, p. 608
Constant-cost industry, p. 608
Increasing-cost industry, p. 608
Decreasing-cost industry, p. 609
Public ownership, p. 625
Price regulation, p. 625
Single-price monopolist, p. 630
Price discrimination, p. 630
Perfect price discrimination, p. 633

AP® Exam Practice Questions

Multiple-Choice Questions

1. According to the price-taking firm's optimal output rule, a perfectly competitive firm should produce the quantity at which marginal cost is equal to
a. total cost.
b. average variable cost.
c. average fixed cost.
d. marginal revenue but not price.
e. marginal revenue and price.

2. A perfectly competitive firm is a price-taker because
a. the government sets its price.
b. it produces a differentiated product.
c. a larger firm sets the price for the industry.
d. intense competition prevents it from influencing the market price.
e. a powerful consumer group establishes the market price.

3. Because a perfectly competitive firm is a price-taker, its short-run demand curve is
a. perfectly elastic.
b. perfectly inelastic.
c. equal to its average total cost curve.
d. downward-sloping.
e. upward-sloping.

4. A perfectly competitive firm is guaranteed to be profitable when it produces a level of output where
a. marginal revenue is equal to price.
b. price is equal to average fixed cost.
c. price is greater than average fixed cost.
d. price is greater than average total cost.
e. price is greater than average variable cost.

5. Average total cost is minimized by producing the level of output where the marginal cost
a. is minimized.
b. curve intersects the average total cost curve.
c. curve intersects the average fixed cost curve.
d. curve intersects the average variable cost curve.
e. curve intersects the marginal revenue curve.

Consider the data below for Questions 6, 7, and 8 for a perfectly competitive firm.

Quantity of tomatoes Q (bushels)	Variable cost VC	Total cost TC	Marginal cost of bushel $MC = \Delta TC/\Delta Q$	Marginal revenue of bushel MR	*Net gain of bushel = MR − MC*
0	$0	$14			
			$16	$18	$2
1	16	30			
			6	18	12
2	22	36			
			8	18	10
3	30	44			
			12	18	6
4	42	56			
			16	18	2
5	58	72			
			20	18	−2
6	78	92			
			24	18	−6
7	102	116			

6. Suppose an increase in the demand for tomatoes brings the market price up to $22. How many tomatoes should be produced in order to maximize profit?
a. 7
b. 6
c. 5
d. 4
e. 3

7. Now suppose a decrease in the demand for tomatoes brings the market price down to $15. How many tomatoes should be produced in order to maximize profit?
a. 7
b. 6
c. 5
d. 4
e. 3

638 Section 11 Market Structures: Perfect Competition and Monopoly

8. What price represents the shut-down price in the short run?
a. $8
b. $10
c. $16
d. $18
e. $20

9. Oscar sells bicycles in a perfectly competitive market. In the short run, at the quantity that equates marginal revenue and marginal cost, the market price is above Oscar's average variable cost and below his average total cost. Oscar should
a. shut down his business.
b. raise his price.
c. produce at a loss because he is covering his fixed costs.
d. produce at a loss because he is covering his variable costs.
e. produce at a profit because he is covering his variable costs.

10. The short-run supply curve for a perfectly competitive firm is its
a. marginal cost curve above the average variable cost curve.
b. marginal cost curve above the average fixed cost curve.
c. average variable cost curve above the marginal cost curve.
d. average variable cost curve above the average total cost curve.
e. average variable cost curve above the average fixed cost curve.

11. For a perfectly competitive industry, the short-run industry supply curve is determined by
a. horizontally summing all the firm's profit-maximizing output levels.
b. horizontally summing all the firm's supply curves.
c. vertically summing all the firm's profit-maximizing output levels.
d. vertically summing all the firm's marginal cost curves.
e. vertically summing all the firm's supply curves.

12. Tia sells hats in a perfectly competitive market. If, in the long run, the market price exceeds the minimum of Tia's average variable cost but is below the minimum of her average total cost, Tia should
a. shut down her business if the situation continues for another year.
b. shut down her business at that time.
c. produce at a loss since she is covering her variable cost.
d. produce at a loss since she is covering her fixed cost.
e. produce at a loss since she is covering her marginal cost.

13. In the long run for a perfectly competitive constant-cost industry, if existing firms are producing where price is greater than average total cost, firms will enter the industry, price will
a. fall, and existing firms will increase production.
b. fall, and existing firms will decrease production.
c. rise, and existing firms will increase production.
d. rise, and existing firms will decrease production.
e. remain constant, and existing firms will increase production.

14. For a perfectly competitive increasing-cost industry, an increase in demand will cause the price to
a. rise and the cost of inputs to fall.
b. rise and the cost of inputs to rise.
c. fall and the cost of inputs to fall.
d. fall and the cost of inputs to rise.
e. remain constant and the cost of inputs to rise.

15. The long-run industry supply curve for a perfectly competitive firm is
a. flatter and more elastic than the short-run supply curve.
b. flatter and more inelastic than the short-run supply curve.
c. steeper and more elastic than the short-run supply curve.
d. steeper and more inelastic than the short-run supply curve.
e. more horizontal and more inelastic than the short-run supply curve.

16. The demand curve for a monopolist producing a normal good is downward-sloping because of
a. the substitution effect being larger than the income effect.
b. the income effect being larger than the substitution effect.
c. diminishing marginal returns.
d. price discrimination.
e. diminishing marginal utility.

17. The marginal revenue curve for a monopolist lies below the demand curve because of
a. the income effect.
b. the quantity effect.
c. price discrimination.
d. the price effect.
e. the substitution effect.

18. If a monopolist is charging a price such that marginal revenue is greater than marginal cost, then the monopolist
a. will be earning profit.
b. will be earning losses.
c. will be breaking even.
d. can improve its profit by reducing its price.
e. can improve its profit by raising its price.

8. b
9. d
10. a
11. b
12. b
13. b
14. b
15. a
16. e
17. d
18. d

Section 11 Review 639

19. a
20. c
21. a
22. b
23. d
24. a
25. b

Rubric for Free-Response Question

1 point: Correctly labeled market graph with an upward-sloping supply curve and a downward-sloping demand curve

1 point: Correctly labeled firm graph with a horizontal $MR = D$ curve and a U-shaped ATC curve

1 point: Initial output level labeled directly below where $MR = MC$

1 point: Rightward shift in industry supply curve

1 point: The price of knives decreases.

1 point: Holly's Cutlery produces less.

1 point: Holly's Cutlery's initial economic profit is shaded as shown on the sample graph.

1 point: Explanation that in the long run new firms will enter the market until the economic profit for each firm is zero

1 point: Correctly labeled monopoly graph with a downward-sloping D curve and a MR curve below the D curve

1 point: Output level labeled directly below where $MR = MC$ and price labeled at the height of the D curve above the output level

1 point: The ATC curve is U-shaped and lies below the price at the indicated level of output. A student can earn this point even if the wrong quantity was indicated for the previous point.

1 point: Holly's Cutlery does not produce at the allocatively efficient level.

1 point: Explanation that monopolies are not allocatively efficient because their price exceeds marginal cost

1 point: The correct deadweight loss area is shaded.

Please see page SG-5 for sample student graphs for this Free-Response Question.

19. For a monopolist, when marginal revenue is positive
- **a.** the quantity effect outweighs the price effect.
- **b.** the price effect outweighs the quantity effect.
- **c.** total revenue is rising at an increasing rate.
- **d.** total revenue is declining at an increasing rate.
- **e.** total revenue is declining at a declining rate.

20. Relative to a competitive industry with the same costs, a monopolist charges
- **a.** a higher price and produces more output.
- **b.** a lower price and produces more output.
- **c.** a higher price and produces less output.
- **d.** a lower price and produces less output.
- **e.** a higher price and produces the same level of output.

21. If a monopolist finds that demand is elastic at the level of output where marginal revenue is equal to marginal cost, the monopolist will
- **a.** maintain that level of output.
- **b.** increase output.
- **c.** decrease output.
- **d.** raise the price.
- **e.** lower the price.

22. A perfectly competitive industry will likely have
- **a.** more consumer surplus, more producer surplus, and more deadweight loss than a monopoly.
- **b.** more consumer surplus, less producer surplus, and less deadweight loss than a monopoly.
- **c.** less consumer surplus, more producer surplus, and more deadweight loss than a monopoly.
- **d.** more consumer surplus, less producer surplus, and more deadweight loss than a monopoly.
- **e.** less consumer surplus, more producer surplus, and less deadweight loss than a monopoly.

23. If a regulatory commission wants to ensure that a monopolist produces the largest quantity of output that is consistent with earning a normal profit, it will require the monopolist to charge a price equal to its
- **a.** marginal cost.
- **b.** average fixed cost.
- **c.** average variable cost.
- **d.** average total cost.
- **e.** total cost.

24. In order to practice price discrimination, a firm must have
- **a.** market power.
- **b.** customers of different ages.
- **c.** customers with the same price elasticity of demand.
- **d.** customers with different income levels.
- **e.** customers in different locations.

25. Perfect price discrimination will result in
- **a.** more output and more consumer surplus.
- **b.** more output and less consumer surplus.
- **c.** less output and more producer surplus.
- **d.** less output and less consumer surplus.
- **e.** less output and more consumer surplus.

Free-Response Question

1. Holly's Cutlery is one of many producers of knives in a perfectly competitive market. Holly's Cutlery is earning a greater than normal profit. Draw correctly labeled side-by-side graphs showing the market for knives and the marginal cost, average total cost, demand, and marginal revenue curves for Holly's Cutlery.
- **a.** Show what will happen to each of the following in the long run:
  - **i.** the industry supply curve for knives
  - **ii.** the price of knives
  - **iii.** Holly's Cutlery's output compared to the initial level
- **b.** On your graph for part a, shade the area that represents Holly's Cutlery's initial economic profit and explain what will happen to it in the long run.
- **c.** Now assume that in order to ensure overall public safety, the local government grants Holly's Cutlery the exclusive right to produce knives. Draw a correctly labeled graph showing Holly's Cutlery's output level and price, assuming Holly's Cutlery makes a greater than normal economic profit. Does Holly's Cutlery produce the allocatively efficient level of output? Explain.
- **d.** Shade in the area of deadweight loss, if any, in the graph for part c.

(14 points)

NOTES

SECTION 12

Market Structures: Imperfect Competition

PD Section 12 Overview

Watch the video overview of Section 12 (for teachers), which is accessible through the Teacher's e-Book, the TR-flash drive, or the book's website, bcs.worthpublishers.com/krugmanap2e *(teacher log-in required).*

Section 12 introduces the more complicated and realistic imperfectly competitive market structures—oligopoly and monopolistic competition. Because interdependence is the key characteristic of oligopoly, this section introduces game theory. Game theory is a way to model strategic decision making when the outcome of a decision depends on the actions of others. Product differentiation and advertising are key characteristics of monopolistic competition that results in a market structure model that combines the characteristics of perfect competition and monopoly.

Topics that your students will study in Section 12 are:

- the role of interdependence in oligopoly.
- collusive versus noncooperative behavior by firms.
- the use of collusion and cartels to raise joint profits for oligopoly firms.
- the effect of incentives to cheat on the success of collusive agreements.
- price competition versus quantity competition.
- the use of game theory to analyze firm behavior in a duopoly.
- understanding and applying payoff matrices.
- the prisoners' dilemma game, dominant strategies, and Nash equilibrium in game theory.
- the use of strategic behavior to influence the future behavior of other firms.
- how repeated interactions among oligopolists can result in collusion, including tacit collusion.
- the use of antitrust policies to prevent collusive actions by oligopolists.
- the factors that limit tacit collusion to raise prices.
- how oligopolists are affected by price wars, product differentiation, price leadership, and nonprice competition in oligopoly markets.
- the determination of profit-maximizing price and quantity in monopolistic competition in the short and long run.
- comparison of monopolistic competition to perfect competition and monopoly.
- inefficiency and excess capacity in monopolistic competition.
- product differentiation by monopolistically competitive firms.
- advertising and branding in monopolistic competition.

Alignment to AP® Microeconomics Course Description

Microeconomics II. The Nature and Function of Product Markets: 55–70%

AP® Outline	Module
D. Firm behavior and market structure	64: Introduction to Oligopoly 65: Game Theory 66: Oligopoly in Practice 67: Introduction to Monopolistic Competition 68: Product Differentiation and Advertising

Pacing Guide

Module	Standard Teaching Days	Block Teaching Days
64	2	1
65	3	2
66	1	1
67	2	1
68	1	1
Section 12 Assessment	1	½
Total	**10**	**6½**

TRM Section Resources

All section resources may be accessed through the Teacher's e-Book, the TR-flash drive, or the book's website bcs.worthpublishers.com/krugmanap2e *(teacher log-in required).*

Section 12 PD Video (for teachers)

Module 64

Module 64 Sample Lecture
Worksheet 64.1: Oligopoly And Collusion
Exit Slip: Module 64

Module 65

Module 65 Sample Lecture
Worksheet 65.1: Game Theory
Worksheet 65.2: Games of Avoidance
Worksheet 65.3: Dominant Strategy
Exit Slip: Module 65

Module 66

Module 66 Sample Lecture
Worksheet 66.1: Oligopoly Terms
Exit Slip: Module 66

Module 67

Module 67 Sample Lecture
Worksheet 67.1: Monopolistic Competition
Worksheet 67.2: Entry and Exit Effects for Monopolistic Competition
Worksheet 67.3: Long-Run Monopolistic Competition
Exit Slip: Module 67

Module 68

Module 68 Sample Lecture
Worksheet 68.1: Imperfect Competition in the News
Worksheet 68.2: Hershey
Exit Slip: Module 68
Section 12 Review Video (for students)

St. Louis Federal Reserve Bank Resources

Many of the Federal Reserve Banks have educational departments that offer helpful resources for studying economics. Members of the Educators Advisory Board of the St. Louis Federal Reserve Bank have handpicked some of their best resources for use with your AP® Economics students. References to these resources are included in the marginal notes. A complete list of the St. Louis Fed resources for each section with the corresponding URL (as of fall 2014) can be found in the TRM.

NOTE We have included a number of links to useful videos and articles in the margin notes in this section. Although all are active at the time of publication, we know that some may expire over the next few years. If a link is no longer active, you may wish to search for a similar article or video to illustrate the same point. We may also periodically refresh resources on the book's companion website.

NOTES

SECTION 12

Market Structures: Imperfect Competition

Corporate Misdeeds and the Differentiation Dance

© Prisma Bildagentur AG/Alamy

The agricultural products company Archer Daniels Midland (also known as ADM) has often described itself as "supermarket to the world." In 1993, executives from ADM and its Japanese competitor Ajinomoto met to discuss the market for lysine, an additive used in animal feed. In this and subsequent meetings, the two companies joined with several other producers to set targets for the price of lysine, behavior known as *price-fixing.* Each company agreed to limit its production to achieve the price targets, with the goal of raising industry profits. But what the companies were doing was illegal, and the FBI had bugged the meeting room with microphones and cameras hidden in table lamps. Over the past few years, there have been numerous investigations and some convictions for price-fixing in a variety of industries, from insurance to college education to computer chips. Despite its illegality, some firms continue to attempt to fix the prices of their products.

In the fast-food market, it is the legal practice of *product differentiation* that occupies the minds of marketing executives. Fast-food producers go to great lengths to convince you they have something special to offer beyond the ordinary burger: it's flame broiled or 100% beef or superthick or lathered with special sauce. Or maybe they offer chicken or fish or roast beef. The differentiation dance goes on in the pizza industry as well. Pizza Hut offers cheese in the crust. Papa John's claims "better ingredients." Dominoes has a "new recipe," and if you don't want thin crust, the alternative isn't "regular," it's "hand tossed"! The slogans and logos for fast-food restaurants often seem to differ more than the food itself.

To understand why ADM engaged in illegal price-fixing and why fast-food joints go to great lengths to differentiate their patties and pizzas, we need to understand the two market structures in between perfect competition and monopoly in the spectrum of market power—oligopoly and monopolistic competition. The models of these two market structures are at the same time more complicated and more realistic than those we studied in the previous section. Indeed, they describe the behavior of most of the firms in the real world.

PD Section 12 Overview

Watch the video overview of Section 12 (for teachers), which is accessible through the Teacher's e-Book, the TR-flash drive, or the book's companion website bcs.worthpublishers.com/krugmanap2e (teacher log-in required).

FOCUS Active Learning

For a discussion of market power in the music industry, encourage students to read Chapter 13 of *Economics by Example.*

St. Louis Federal Reserve Bank Resources

"Prices: The Marketplace's Communication System," *Page One Economics Classroom Edition* (April 2013)

Ask your students if they remember when airlines started charging for checked bags. What happened to the number of checked bags after this added charge? And what happened to the availability of in-cabin storage space on planes? This issue of *Page One Economics* answers these questions and discusses the pivotal role price plays in a market economy.

PD To prepare for teaching this lesson, you may want to consult the **Module 64 Sample Lecture** in the TRM.

OPEN & CLOSE Start Here

The key characteristic of oligopoly is interdependence. The outcome for each firm depends on the decision of other firms in the market. Game theory for a duopoly uses a 2 by 2 payoff matrix to show the players, strategies, and outcomes for two interdependent players (e.g., firms). To help students learn how to use a payoff matrix and let them experience interdependence, tell them that you are going to give them an easy assignment. All they have to do is to decide what grade they would like to receive, either an A or a C. Explain that the grade they will actually receive on the assignment depends on the grade selected by a randomly assigned classmate, as shown in this payoff matrix. Have them write their name and their choice (A or C) on a slip of paper. Collect the slips and place them in a container. Draw out two names and announce the grade for each student, based on the payoff matrix. Separate the slips into piles for each grade received. Students will have a variety of reactions and comments to experiencing this interdependence!

		Your choice	
		A	**C**
Your partner's choice	**A**	You: F Partner: F	You: F Partner: A
	C	You: A Partner: F	You: C Partner: C

Ianni Dimitrov/age fotostock

MODULE 64 Introduction to Oligopoly

In this Module, you will learn to:

- Explain why oligopolists have an incentive to act in ways that reduce their combined profit
- Explain why oligopolies can benefit from collusion

AP® Exam Tip

When you see the term "mutual interdependence" or "price leadership" on the AP® exam, be prepared to answer a question on oligopoly, because this market structure is characterized by interdependence among firms.

In Module 57 we learned that an oligopoly is an industry with only a few sellers. But what number constitutes a "few"? There is no universal answer, and it is not always easy to determine an industry's market structure just by looking at the number of sellers. Economists use various measures to gain a better picture of market structure, including concentration ratios and the Herfindahl–Hirschman Index, as explained in Module 57.

In addition to having a small number of sellers in the industry, an oligopoly is characterized by **interdependence**, a relationship in which the outcome (profit) of each firm depends on the actions of the other firms in the market. This is not true for monopolies because, by definition, they have no other firms to consider. On the other hand, competitive markets contain so many firms that no one firm has a significant effect on the outcome of the others. However, in an oligopoly, an industry with few sellers, the outcome for each seller depends on the behavior of the others. Interdependence makes studying a market much more interesting because firms must observe and predict the behavior of other firms. But it is also more complicated. To understand the strategies of oligopolists, we must do more than find the point where the *MC* and *MR* curves intersect!

Firms are **interdependent** when the outcome (profit) of each firm depends on the actions of the other firms in the market.

Understanding Oligopoly

How much will a firm produce? Up to this point, we have always answered: the quantity that maximizes its profit. When a firm is a perfect competitor or a monopolist, we can assume that the firm will use its cost curves to determine its profit-maximizing output. When it comes to oligopoly, however, we run into some difficulties.

A Duopoly Example

An oligopoly consisting of only two firms is a **duopoly**. Each firm is known as a **duopolist**.

Let's begin looking at the puzzle of oligopoly with the simplest version, an industry in which there are only two firms—a **duopoly**—and each is known as a **duopolist**.

TEACH Connect It

TRM Have students refer back to **Worksheet 57.1 (Types of Market Structures)** from the TRM for a review of the following characteristics of the oligopoly structure:

- few major sellers
- interdependence
- differentiated or same product
- some market power
- some barriers to entry

TEACH Teach It

Interdependence, the key characteristic of oligopoly, exists in a market when the outcome of each firm depends on the actions of other firms in the market.

642 Section 12 Market Structures: Imperfect Competition

Table 64.1 Demand Schedule for Lysine

Price of lysine (per pound)	Quantity of lysine demanded (millions of pounds)	Total revenue (millions)
$12	0	$ 0
11	10	110
10	20	200
9	30	270
8	40	320
7	50	350
6	60	360
5	70	350
4	80	320
3	90	270
2	100	200
1	110	110
0	120	0

Imagine that there are only two producers of lysine (the animal feed additive mentioned in the section opener). To make things even simpler, suppose that once a company has incurred the fixed cost needed to produce lysine, the marginal cost of producing another pound is zero. So the companies are concerned only with the revenue they receive from sales.

Table 64.1 shows a hypothetical demand schedule for lysine and the total revenue of the industry at each price-quantity combination.

If this were a perfectly competitive industry, each firm would have an incentive to produce more as long as the market price was above marginal cost. Since the marginal cost is assumed to be zero, this would mean that at equilibrium, lysine would be provided for free. Firms would produce until price equals zero, yielding a total output of 120 million pounds and zero revenue for both firms.

However, with only two firms in the industry, it would seem foolish to allow price and revenue to plummet to zero. Each would realize that with more production comes a lower market price. So, like a monopolist, each firm would see that profits would be higher if it and its rival limited their production.

So how much will the two firms produce?

One possibility is that the two companies will engage in **collusion**—they will cooperate to raise their joint profits. The strongest form of collusion is a **cartel**, a group of producers with an agreement to work together to limit output and increase price, and therefore profit. The world's most famous cartel is the Organization of Petroleum Exporting Countries (OPEC).

As its name indicates, OPEC is actually a cartel made up of governments rather than firms. There's a reason for this: cartels among firms are illegal in the United States and many other jurisdictions. But let's ignore the law for a moment. Suppose the firms producing lysine were to form a cartel and that this cartel decided to act as if it were a monopolist, maximizing total industry profits. It's obvious from Table 64.1 that in order to maximize the combined profits of the firms, this cartel should set total industry output at 60 million pounds of lysine, which would sell at a price of $6 per pound, leading to revenue of $360 million, the maximum possible. Then the only question

AP® Exam Tip

Collusion is illegal in the United States but legal in some parts of the world.

Sellers engage in **collusion** when they cooperate to raise their joint profits. A **cartel** is a group of producers that agree to restrict output in order to increase prices and their joint profits.

OPEC representatives discuss the cartel's policies of cooperation.

AP Photo/Hans Punz

FOCUS Test It

Ask students why interdependence is not a characteristic of perfect competition or monopoly. *Perfect competition has so many small firms that none is important enough to affect the others and monopoly has no other firms to be interdependent with!*

TEACH Teach It

A duopoly is an oligopoly that consists of two firms. Each firm is called a duopolist. Help students learn this vocabulary by explaining that *mono* means "one" (monopoly), *duo* means "two" (duopoly), and *oli* means "few" (oligopoly).

TEACH Teach It

Collusion occurs when firms cooperate with each other to raise their joint profit. When firms ignore each other, they are engaging in noncooperative behavior.

FOCUS Test It

How many firms can exist in an oligopoly market? *"A few"—but there is no set number; the key to oligopoly is interdependence.*

If firms in an oligopoly collude to maximize joint profit, where do they find the profit-maximizing level of output? *Where MC = MR, as usual!*

FOCUS Active Learning

TRM Have students watch Dr. Mary Jane McGlasson's video "Episode 30A: Collusion" (see econextras video list with hyperlinks on the bcs and TRFD) and assign **Worksheet 64.1 (Oligopoly and Collusion)** from the TRM for questions about oligopoly collusion.

TEACH Connect It

Point out that, with collusion, in order to maximize joint profit, oligopolists behave like monopolists and set $MC = MR$. Remind students that the monopolist's *MR* curve lies below demand because it must lower price to sell more. Like a monopolist, colluding duopoly firms experience quantity and price effects when they produce an additional unit of a good, as described in Section 11 on page 671.

TEACH Teach It

In a duopoly that colludes to maximize joint profit, each firm only experiences the negative price effect from selling more units on the units it sells, not on the units the other firm sells. Therefore, each duopolist only experiences part of the price effect from increasing output. This makes the duopolist believe that increasing production will increase its own profit, which it will, if only one firm increases production. But if the other firm thinks the same thing and both firms increase production, profit will fall. This is an example of how the incentive to cheat on an agreement (increase production to raise one firm's profit) causes collusive agreements to fall apart.

TEACH Teach It

Noncooperative behavior exists when firms in an oligopoly act in their own self-interest and ignore the effects of their actions on each other's profit. Ask students to contemplate the opening activity for this module (or perhaps repeat the activity). What was the class GPA for the activity? *(Note: It must be below 2.0 unless every student picked "C," because any Fs, even those offset by an A, will fall below 2.0.)* Have them think about how the joint GPA of the class could be maximized. *(It would be maximized by every student choosing "C," so the class GPA is 2.0.)* Why didn't the class collude to all pick Cs so that the class GPA was 2.0? *(Because some students try for an A and reduce the joint GPA!)*

would be how much of that 60 million pounds each firm gets to produce. A "fair" solution might be for each firm to produce 30 million pounds and receive revenues of $180 million.

But even if the two firms agreed on such a deal, they might have a problem: each of the firms would have an incentive to break its word and produce more than the agreed-upon quantity.

Collusion and Competition

Suppose that the presidents of the two lysine producers were to agree that each would produce 30 million pounds of lysine over the next year. Both would understand that this plan maximizes their combined profits. And both would have an incentive to cheat.

To see why, consider what would happen if one firm honored its agreement, producing only 30 million pounds, but the other ignored its promise and produced 40 million pounds. This increase in total output would drive the price down from $6 to $5 per pound, the price at which 70 million pounds are demanded. The industry's total revenue would fall from $360 million ($\$6 \times 60$ million pounds) to $350 million ($\$5 \times 70$ million pounds). However, the cheating firm's revenue would *rise,* from $180 million to $200 million. Since we are assuming a marginal cost of zero, this would mean a $20 million increase in profits.

But both firms' presidents might make exactly the same calculation. And if *both* firms were to produce 40 million pounds of lysine, the price would drop to $4 per pound. So each firm's profits would fall, from $180 million to $160 million.

The incentive to cheat motivates the firms to produce more than the quantity that maximizes their joint profits rather than limiting output as a true monopolist would. We know that a profit-maximizing monopolist sets marginal cost (which in this case is zero) equal to marginal revenue. But what is marginal revenue? Recall that producing an additional unit of a good has two effects:

1. A positive *quantity effect*: one more unit is sold, increasing total revenue by the price at which that unit is sold.
2. A negative *price effect*: in order to sell one more unit, the monopolist must cut the market price on *all* units sold.

The negative price effect is the reason marginal revenue for a monopolist is less than the market price. But when considering the effect of increasing production, a firm is concerned only with the price effect on its *own* units of output, not on those of its fellow oligopolists. In the lysine example, both duopolists suffer a negative price effect if one firm decides to produce extra lysine and so drives down the price. But each firm cares only about the portion of the negative price effect that falls on the lysine it produces.

This tells us that an individual firm in an oligopolistic industry faces a smaller price effect from an additional unit of output than a monopolist; therefore, the marginal revenue that such a firm calculates is higher. So it will seem to be profitable for any one firm in an oligopoly to increase production, even if that increase reduces the profits of the industry as a whole. But if everyone thinks that way, the result is that everyone earns a lower profit!

Until now, we have been able to analyze producer behavior by asking what a producer should do to maximize profits. But even if the duopolists are both trying to maximize profits, what does this predict about their behavior? Will they engage in collusion, reaching and holding to an agreement that maximizes their combined profits? Or will they engage in **noncooperative behavior**, with each firm acting in its own self-interest, even though this has the effect of driving down everyone's profits? Both strategies can be carried out with a goal of profit maximization. Which will actually describe their behavior?

When firms act in their own self-interest, ignoring the effects of their actions on each other's profits, they engage in **noncooperative behavior**.

Now you see why oligopoly presents a puzzle: there are only a small number of players, making collusion a real possibility. If there were dozens or hundreds of firms, it would be safe to assume they would behave noncooperatively. Yet, when there are only a handful of firms in an industry, it's hard to determine whether collusion will actually occur.

Since collusion is ultimately more profitable than noncooperative behavior, firms have an incentive to collude if they can. One way to do so is to formalize it—sign an agreement (maybe even make a legal contract) or establish some financial incentives for the companies to set their prices high. But in the United States and many other nations, firms can't do that—at least not legally. A contract among firms to keep prices high would be unenforceable, and it could be a one-way ticket to jail. The same goes for an informal agreement. In fact, executives from rival firms rarely meet without lawyers present, who make sure that the conversation does not stray into inappropriate territory. Even hinting at how nice it would be if prices were higher can bring an unwelcome interview with the Justice Department or the Federal Trade Commission. For example, in 2003 the Justice Department launched a price-fixing case against Monsanto and other large producers of genetically modified seed. The Justice Department was alerted by a series of meetings held between Monsanto and Pioneer Hi-Bred International, two companies that account for 60% of the U.S. market in maize and soybean seed. These companies, parties to a licensing agreement involving genetically modified seed, claimed that no illegal discussions of price-fixing occurred in those meetings. But the fact that the two firms discussed prices as part of the licensing agreement was enough to trigger action by the Justice Department.

Bryan Smith/Zuma Press

A contract among firms to keep prices high would be unenforceable, and could be a one-way ticket to jail.

Sometimes, as we've seen, oligopolistic firms just ignore the rules. But more often they develop strategies for making the best of the situation depending on what they know, or assume, about the other firms' behavior. In some cases, oligopolists repeatedly undercut each others' prices—charging a bit less than the others to steal their customers—until price reaches the level of marginal cost, as under perfect competition.

Understandably, oligopolists would prefer to avoid direct price competition that leaves them earning zero economic profit. One strategy for limiting competition is to produce products that are not perfect substitutes but are instead differentiated. We'll examine this strategy in more detail in Module 68. For now, we note that producing differentiated products allows oligopolists to cultivate a loyal set of customers and to charge prices higher than marginal cost.

Collusion is another approach to dodging the profit-suppressing effects of competition. In the next module, we'll see why informal collusion often works but sometimes fails.

GREG WOOD/AFP/Getty Images

In the absence of collusion, price competition among oligopolists can be intense, as with the airfare war between Jetstar and Virgin Blue that has led to $300 fares to Bali.

TEACH Teach It

In order to steal competitors' customers, at times oligopolists may undercut each other's prices until their price reaches the level of marginal cost. Ask students what this practice is called (*a price war*) and what the result of this action usually is (*losses for all firms*). Generally, oligopolists prefer to produce a differentiated product (not identical), so they can create their own loyal clientele and increase their price above marginal cost.

OPEN & CLOSE Exit Slip

*TRM Please see **Exit Slip: Module 64** in the TRM for formative multiple-choice questions to ask your students before finishing your lesson. These questions will help you quickly assess whether your students have mastered the module's concepts before moving on.*

Answers to the Exit Slip Questions

1. C
2. A
3. D

Answers to Module 64 Review Questions

Check Your Understanding

1. a. This will decrease the likelihood that the firm will collude to restrict output. By increasing output, the firm will generate a negative price effect. But because the firm's current market share is small, the price effect will fall mostly on its rivals' revenues rather than on its own. At the same time, the firm will benefit from a positive quantity effect.

b. This will decrease the likelihood that the firm will collude to restrict output. By acting noncooperatively and raising output, the firm will cause the price to fall. Because its rivals have higher costs, they will lose money at the lower price while the firm continues to make profits. So the firm may be able to drive its rivals out of business by increasing its output.

c. This will increase the likelihood that the firm will collude. Because it is costly for consumers to switch products, the firm would have to lower its price substantially (with a commensurate increase in quantity) to induce consumers to switch to its product. So increasing output is likely to be unprofitable, given the large negative price effect.

d. This will increase the likelihood that the firm will collude. It cannot increase sales because it is currently at maximum production capacity, making attempts to undercut rivals' prices as under the Bertrand model fruitless due to the inability to produce the output needed to steal the rivals' customers. This makes the option to cooperate in restricting output relatively attractive.

FYI The Great Vitamin Conspiracy

It was a bitter pill to swallow. In the late 1990s, some of the world's largest drug companies (mainly European and Japanese) agreed to pay billions of dollars in damages to customers after being convicted of a huge conspiracy to rig the world vitamin market.

The conspiracy began in 1989 when the Swiss company Roche and the German company BASF began secret talks about raising prices for vitamins. Soon a French company, Rhone-Poulenc, joined in, followed by several Japanese companies and other companies around the world. The members of the group, which referred to itself as "Vitamins, Inc.," met regularly—sometimes at hotels, sometimes at the private homes of executives—to set prices and divide up markets for "bulk" vitamins (like vitamin A, vitamin C, and so on). These bulk vitamins are sold mainly to other companies, such as animal feed makers, food producers, and so on, which include them in their products. Indeed, it was the animal feed companies that grew suspicious about the prices they were being charged, which led to a series of investigations. The case eventually broke open when Rhone-Poulenc made a deal with U.S. officials to provide evidence of the conspiracy. The French company was concerned that rumors about price-fixing would lead U.S. officials to block its planned merger with another company.

How could it have happened?

The main answer probably lies in different national traditions about how to treat oligopolists. The United States has a long tradition of taking tough legal action against price-fixing. European governments, however, have historically been much less stringent. Indeed, in the past some European governments have actually encouraged major companies to form cartels. But European antitrust law has changed recently to become more like U.S. antitrust law. Despite this change, however, the cultural tradition of forming cartels as normal business practice lingers within the boardrooms of some European companies.

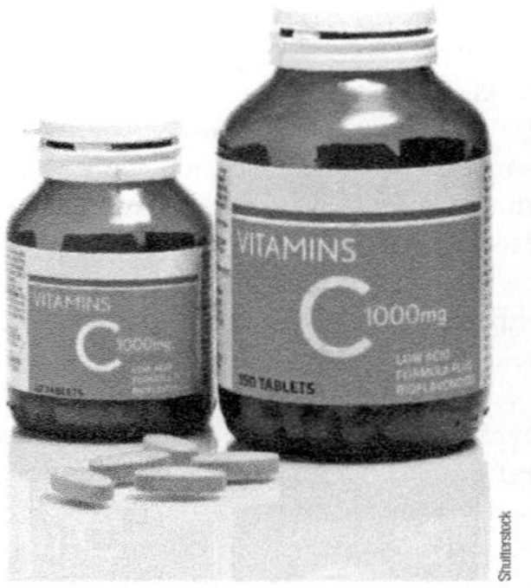

Shutterstock

MODULE 64 Review

Check Your Understanding

1. Explain whether each of the following characteristics will increase or decrease the likelihood that a firm will collude with other firms in an oligopoly to restrict output.
   a. The firm's initial market share is small. (Hint: Think about the price effect.)
   b. The firm has a cost advantage over its rivals.
   c. The firm's customers face additional costs when they switch from one firm's product to another firm's product.
   d. The firm and its rivals are currently operating at maximum production capacity, which cannot be altered in the short run.

Tackle the Test: Multiple-Choice Questions

1. When firms cooperate to raise their joint profits, they are necessarily
   a. colluding.
   b. in a cartel.
   c. a monopoly.
   d. in a duopoly.
   e. in a competitive industry.

Tackle the Test: Multiple-Choice Questions

1. a

646 Section 12 Market Structures: Imperfect Competition

2. Use the information in the table below on market shares in the search engine industry and measures of market power (defined in Section 10) to determine which of the following statements are correct.

Search Engine	*Market share*
Google	44%
Yahoo	29
MSN	13
AOL	6
Ask	5
Other	3

I. The 4-firm concentration ratio is 92.
II. The Herfindahl–Hirschman index is 3,016.
III. The industry is likely to be an oligopoly.

a. I only
b. II only
c. III only
d. I and II only
e. I, II, and III

3. An agreement among several producers to restrict output and increase profit is necessary for
a. cooperation.
b. collusion.
c. monopolization.
d. a cartel.
e. competition.

4. Oligopolists are tempted to produce more than the quantity that would maximize industry profits because when they increase output,
a. the price effect is zero.
b. the quantity effect is zero.
c. the price effect equals the quantity effect.
d. the price effect is larger than the quantity effect.
e. the price effect is spread across multiple firms.

5. Which of the following will make it easier for firms in an industry to maintain positive economic profit?
a. a ban on cartels
b. a small number of firms in the industry
c. a lack of product differentiation
d. low start-up costs for new firms
e. the assumption by firms that other firms have variable output levels

2. e
3. d
4. e
5. b

Tackle the Test: Free-Response Questions

1. Refer to the table provided to answer the following questions. Assume that marginal cost is zero.

Demand Schedule

Price	*Quantity*
$24	0
22	1
20	2
18	3
16	4
14	5
12	6
10	7
8	8
6	9
4	10
2	11
0	12

a. If the market is perfectly competitive, what will the market equilibrium price and quantity be in the long run? Explain.
b. If the market is a duopoly and the firms collude to maximize joint profits, what will market price and quantity be? Explain.
c. If the market is a duopoly and the firms collude to maximize joint profits, what is each firm's total revenue if the firms split the market equally?

Rubric for FRQ 1 (7 points)

1 point: If the market is perfectly competitive, price will be zero.
1 point: If the market is perfectly competitive, quantity will be 12.
1 point: Price equals marginal cost in the long-run equilibrium of a perfectly competitive market, so price will be zero, at which price the quantity is 12.
1 point: If the market is a duopoly, price will be $12.
1 point: If the market is a duopoly, quantity will be 6.
1 point: In order to maximize joint profits, the two firms would act as a monopoly, setting marginal revenue equal to marginal cost and finding price on the demand curve above the profit-maximizing quantity. Marginal revenue passes through zero (going from 2 to −2) after the 6th unit, making 6 the profit-maximizing quantity. The most consumers would pay for 6 units is $12, so that is the profit-maximizing price.
1 point: Total revenue is $\$12 \times 6 = \$72$. By dividing this equally, each firm receives $36.

2. **a.** What are the two major reasons we don't see cartels among oligopolistic industries in the United States?
b. Explain why firms in an oligopoly are interdependent, but firms in a perfectly competitive market or a monopoly are not.
(4 points)

Tackle the Test: Free-Response Question

Rubric for FRQ 2 (4 points)

1 point: The first major reason is that cartels are illegal in the United States.

1 point: The second major reason is that cartels set prices above marginal cost, which creates an incentive for each firm to cheat on the cartel agreement in order to make more profit. This incentive to cheat tends to cause cartels to fall apart.

1 point: Firms in an oligopoly are interdependent because in an industry with only a small number of firms, the outcome for each firm depends on the behavior of other firms.

1 point: In a perfectly competitive market, there are so many firms that no one firm has a significant influence on the outcome of other firms. A monopoly has only one firm, so interdependence is not an issue.

PD To prepare for teaching this lesson, you may want to consult the **Module 65 Sample Lecture** in the TRM.

OPEN & CLOSE Start Here

Game theory is appropriate for analyzing decision making in strategic situations. Strategic decision making occurs when the results of a decision depend on the choices made by others. For example, chess is a strategic situation. Good chess players are able to anticipate an opponent's next move and make their best decision accordingly. Game theory was developed by economists and mathematicians, including one winner of the Nobel Prize in Economics, John Nash. Students may have seen the Oscar-winning movie *A Beautiful Mind* about Nash's life. Watching the movie can be a great post-AP® exam or extracurricular class activity. The movie highlights how game theory has far-reaching applications, including military strategy and—more recently—fighting terrorism.

Richard Levine/Alamy

MODULE 65 Game Theory

In this Module, you will learn to:

- Use game theory to enhance your understanding of oligopoly
- Analyze a prisoners' dilemma using a payoff matrix
- Determine dominant strategies and Nash equilibria in a variety of games

AP® Exam Tip

Game theory questions show up frequently on the AP® exam. To improve your performance on these questions, learn how to find dominant strategies, Nash equilibria, and the payoff for each firm.

Games Oligopolists Play

In our duopoly example and in real life, each oligopolistic firm realizes both that its profit depends on what its competitor does and that its competitor's profit depends on what it does. That is, the two firms are in a situation of interdependence, whereby each firm's decision significantly affects the profit of the other firm (or firms, in the case of more than two).

In effect, the two firms are playing a "game" in which the profit of each player depends not only on its own actions but on those of the other player (or players). In order to understand more fully how oligopolists behave, economists, along with mathematicians, developed the area of study of such games, known as **game theory**. It has many applications, not just to economics but also to military strategy, politics, and other social sciences.

Let's see how game theory helps us understand oligopoly.

The study of behavior in situations of interdependence is known as **game theory**.

The reward received by a player in a game, such as the profit earned by an oligopolist, is that player's **payoff**.

A **payoff matrix** shows how the payoff to each of the participants in a two-player game depends on the actions of both. Such a matrix helps us analyze situations of interdependence.

The Prisoners' Dilemma

Game theory deals with any situation in which the reward to any one player—the **payoff**—depends not only on his or her own actions but also on those of other players in the game. In the case of oligopolistic firms, the payoff is simply the firm's profit.

When there are only two players, as in a lysine duopoly, the interdependence between the players can be represented with a **payoff matrix** like that shown in **Figure 65.1**. Each row corresponds to an action by one player; each column corresponds to an action by the other. For simplicity, let's assume that each firm can pick only one of two alternatives: produce 30 million pounds of lysine or produce 40 million pounds.

648 Section 12 Market Structures: Imperfect Competition

Figure 65.1 A Payoff Matrix

Two firms must decide how much lysine to produce. The profits of the two firms are *interdependent*: each firm's profit depends not only on its own decision but also on the other's decision. Each row represents an action by Firm 1, each column one by Firm 2. Both firms will be better off if they both choose the lower output; but it is in each firm's individual interest to choose the higher output.

Firm 1 \ Firm 2	Produce 30 million pounds	Produce 40 million pounds
Produce 30 million pounds	Firm 2 makes $180 million profit. / Firm 1 makes $180 million profit.	Firm 2 makes $200 million profit. / Firm 1 makes $150 million profit.
Produce 40 million pounds	Firm 2 makes $150 million profit. / Firm 1 makes $200 million profit.	Firm 2 makes $160 million profit. / Firm 1 makes $160 million profit.

The matrix contains four boxes, each divided by a diagonal line. Each box shows the payoff to the two firms that results from a pair of choices; the number below the diagonal shows Firm 1's profits, the number above the diagonal shows Firm 2's profits.

These payoffs show what we concluded from our earlier analysis: the combined profit of the two firms is maximized if they each produce 30 million pounds. However, either firm can increase its own profits by producing 40 million pounds if the other produces only 30 million pounds. But if both produce the larger quantity, both will have lower profits than if they had both held their output down.

The particular situation shown here is a version of a famous—and seemingly paradoxical—case of interdependence that appears in many contexts. Known as the **prisoners' dilemma**, it is a type of game in which the payoff matrix implies the following:

- Each player has an incentive, regardless of what the other player does, to cheat—to take an action that benefits it at the other's expense.
- When both players cheat, both are worse off than they would have been if neither had cheated.

The original illustration of the prisoners' dilemma occurred in a fictional story about two accomplices in crime—let's call them Richard and Justin—who have been caught by the police. The police have enough evidence to put them behind bars for 5 years. They also know that the pair have committed a more serious crime, one that carries a 20-year sentence; unfortunately, they don't have

Warner Bros./Photofest

In the 2002 movie *Murder by Numbers*, the police know that high schoolers Richard and Justin were involved in a crime, but they lack the information needed to impose a serious punishment, so they offer a lighter sentence in exchange for a confession from either one of them.

AP® Exam Tip

Learn how to interpret a payoff matrix. These matrices won't be color-coded on the AP® exam.

The prisoners' dilemma is a game based on two premises: (1) Each player has an incentive to choose an action that benefits itself at the other player's expense; and (2) When both players act in this way, both are worse off than if they had acted cooperatively.

FOCUS Graph It

In a duopoly, interdependence can be illustrated and analyzed using a payoff matrix that has rows and columns representing the alternative actions of each firm and entries in the matrix showing the outcome of each possible combination of actions. Figure 65.1 depicts a game theory situation with a duopoly made up of Firm 1 and Firm 2 with two possible actions—produce 30 or 40 million pounds—and 4 possible payoffs—$150, $160, $180, or $200 million in profit.

TEACH Teach It

In a prisoners' dilemma game, each player has an incentive to cheat. However, when both cheat, the two players are worse off than if they had cooperated. The opening activity for Module 64 was an example of a prisoners' dilemma.

FOCUS Graph It

Figure 65.2 shows a payoff matrix based on the prisoners' dilemma. Ask students the following questions:

- What is the lowest possible punishment; what is necessary for each to receive the lowest punishment? *2 years; that ONLY ONE of them confesses while the other does not*
- Why does each prisoner have an incentive to confess to the crime he or she is accused of? *Each will receive a lower punishment if he or she confesses: 2 versus 5 years and 15 versus 20 years.*
- What is the best joint outcome for Richard and Justin (i.e., the lowest combined years in prison)? *For both not to confess, 10 years*
- What is the dominant strategy for both? *To confess*

TEACH Teach It

A dominant strategy exists when a player takes the most beneficial action regardless of the action taken by the other player. To help students determine whether a player has a dominant strategy, ask them to start by assuming the other player chooses one of the possible actions and then to cover up the other player's unselected action with a piece of paper or their hands. Looking only at the exposed row (or column), have them circle the best of the two payoffs for the player. Next, tell them to assume the other player chooses the other possible action and have them again conceal the unchosen row (or column). Looking only at the exposed row (or column), have them circle the best of the two payoffs for the player. If the circled payoff is in the same column (or row), the player has a dominant strategy.

FOCUS Active Learning

Show "**Game Theory 101: The Prisoner's Dilemma**" by William Spaniel for an in-class reinforcement of the prisoners' dilemma (see econextras video list with hyperlinks on the bcs and TRFD). Students can also use Figure 65.2 to reinforce the explanation in the video.

Figure 65.2 The Prisoners' Dilemma

Each of two prisoners, held in separate cells, is offered a deal by the police—a light sentence if he confesses and implicates his accomplice but his accomplice does not do the same, a heavy sentence if he does not confess but his accomplice does, and so on. It is in the joint interest of both prisoners not to confess; it is in each one's individual interest to confess.

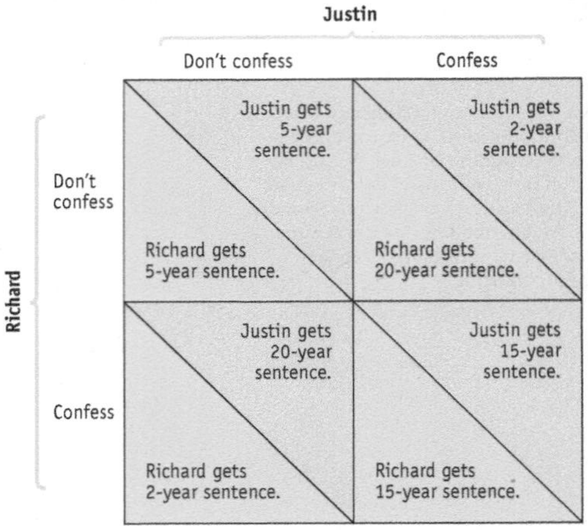

enough evidence to convict the young men on that charge. To do so, they would need each of the prisoners to implicate the other in the second crime.

So the police put the miscreants in separate cells and say the following to each: "Here's the deal: if neither of you confesses, you know that we'll send you to jail for 5 years. If you confess and implicate your partner, and he doesn't do the same, we reduce your sentence from 5 years to 2. But if your partner confesses and you don't, you'll get the maximum of 20 years. And if both of you confess, we'll give you both 15 years."

Figure 65.2 shows the payoffs that face the prisoners, depending on the decision of each to remain silent or to confess. (Usually the payoff matrix reflects the players' payoffs, and higher payoffs are better than lower payoffs. This case is an exception: a higher number of years in prison is bad, not good!) Let's assume that the prisoners have no way to communicate and that they have not sworn an oath not to harm each other or anything of that sort. So each acts in his own self-interest. What will they do?

The answer is clear: both will confess. Look at it first from Richard's point of view: he is better off confessing, regardless of what Justin does. If Justin doesn't confess, Richard's confession reduces his own sentence from 5 years to 2. If Justin *does* confess, Richard's confession reduces his sentence from 20 to 15 years. Either way, it's clearly in Richard's interest to confess. And because he faces the same incentives, it's clearly in Justin's interest to confess, too. To confess in this situation is a type of action that economists call a *dominant strategy*. An action is a **dominant strategy** when it is the player's best action regardless of the action taken by the other player. It's important to note that not all games have a dominant strategy—it depends on the structure of payoffs in the game. But in the case of Richard and Justin, it is clearly in the interest of the police to structure the payoffs so that confessing is a dominant strategy for each person. As long as the two prisoners have no way to make an enforceable agreement that neither will confess (something they can't do if they can't communicate, and the police certainly won't allow them to do so because the police want to compel each one to confess), the dominant strategy exists as the best alternative.

An action is a **dominant strategy** when it is a player's best action regardless of the action taken by the other player.

So if each prisoner acts rationally in his own interest, both will confess. Yet if neither of them had confessed, both would have received a much lighter sentence! In a

TEACH Teach It

A Nash (aka noncooperative) equilibrium exists when each player in a game chooses the action that maximizes his or her payoff given the actions of the other player.

TEACH Connect It

The term *equilibrium* refers to a situation in which no tendency for change exists. In the supply and demand model, there was no tendency for firms to raise or lower price; in the perfectly competitive long-run equilibrium, there was no tendency for firms to enter or exit. With Nash equilibrium, no tendency exists for players to change their actions.

FYI Prisoners of the Arms Race

Between World War II and the late 1980s, the United States and the Soviet Union were locked in a seemingly endless struggle that never broke out into open war. During this Cold War, both countries spent huge sums on arms, sums that were a significant drain on the U.S. economy and eventually proved a crippling burden for the Soviet Union, whose underlying economic base was much weaker. Yet neither country was ever able to achieve a decisive military advantage.

As many people pointed out, both nations would have been better off if they had both spent less on arms. Yet the arms race continued for 40 years.

Why? As political scientists were quick to notice, one way to explain the arms race was to suppose that the two countries were locked in a classic prisoners' dilemma. Each government would have liked to achieve decisive military superiority, and each feared military inferiority. But both would have preferred a stalemate with low military spending to one with high spending. However, each government rationally chose to engage in high spending. If its rival did not spend heavily, this would lead to military superiority; not spending heavily would lead to inferiority if the other government continued its arms buildup. So the countries were trapped.

The answer to this trap could have been an agreement not to spend as much; indeed, the two sides tried repeatedly to negotiate limits on some kinds of weapons. But these agreements weren't very effective. In the end the issue was resolved as heavy military spending hastened the collapse of the Soviet Union in 1991.

Unfortunately, the logic of an arms race has not disappeared. A nuclear arms race has developed between Pakistan and India, neighboring countries with a history of mutual antagonism. In 1998 the two countries confirmed the unrelenting logic of the prisoners' dilemma: both publicly tested their nuclear weapons, each seeking to prove to the other that it could inflict just as much damage as its rival.

TASS/Sovfoto

prisoners' dilemma, each player has a clear incentive to act in a way that hurts the other player—but when both make that choice, it leaves both of them worse off.

When Richard and Justin both confess, they reach an *equilibrium* of the game. We have used the concept of equilibrium many times in this book; it is an outcome in which no individual or firm has any incentive to change his or her action. In game theory, this kind of equilibrium, in which each player takes the action that is best for him or her, given the actions taken by other players, is known as a **Nash equilibrium**, after the mathematician and Nobel Laureate John Nash. (Nash's life was chronicled in the best-selling biography *A Beautiful Mind,* which was made into a movie.) Because the players in a Nash equilibrium do not take into account the effect of their actions on others, this is also known as a **noncooperative equilibrium**.

Now look back at Figure 65.1: the two firms face a prisoners' dilemma just like Richard and Justin did after the crimes. Each firm is better off producing the higher output, regardless of what the other firm does. Yet if both produce 40 million pounds, both are worse off than if they had followed their agreement and produced only 30 million pounds. In both cases, then, the pursuit of individual self-interest—the effort to maximize profit or to minimize jail time—has the perverse effect of hurting both players.

Prisoners' dilemmas appear in many situations. The FYI above describes an example from the days of the Cold War.

More Games

We can use payoff matrices to analyze any number of games played by individuals and firms. The equilibria of many of these games differ from what we've seen in the prisoners' dilemma. For example, in the prisoners' dilemma, the Nash equilibrium happens to be an equilibrium of two dominant strategies—a *dominant strategy equilibrium*—but Nash equilibria can exist when there is no dominant strategy at all. Also, a game can have multiple Nash equilibria.

A **Nash equilibrium**, also known as a **noncooperative equilibrium**, is the result when each player in a game chooses the action that maximizes his or her payoff, given the actions of other players.

Associated Press/PLINIO LEPRI

Mathematician and Nobel Laureate John Forbes Nash proposed one of the key ideas in game theory.

TEACH Teach It

When there are two dominant strategies in a duopoly game, a Nash equilibrium will be present. However, Nash equilibria can exist when there is no dominant strategy if each player chooses the action that maximizes his or her payoff given the action of the other player.

FOCUS Active Learning

Direct student attention to the FYI box, Prisoners of the Arms Race. Ask your class to explain how this is a classic prisoners' dilemma situation. *Each government would have liked to achieve military superiority, but each feared military inferiority. Both would have preferred the stalemate with low military spending, but each government irrationally chose high military spending. They could have agreed to place limits on armaments, but collusion is generally not effective.*

Module 65 Game Theory 651

FOCUS Flip It

TRM Have students watch Jacob Clifford's video "Micro 4.9 Oligopolies and Game Theory" (see econextras video list with hyperlinks on the bcs and TRFD) and assign **Worksheet 65.1 (Game Theory)** with accompanying questions from the TRM.

FOCUS Graph It

TRM Refer students to Figure 65.3. Use **Worksheet 65.2 (Games of Avoidance)** from the TRM as they work through the lesson. Have students talk among themselves and circle the best outcomes for Richard and Justin. Remind the class that a dominant strategy exists if there are 2 circles in the SAME column or row, and a Nash equilibrium is present if a BOX contains 2 circles.

Consider Richard and Justin, who are disheartened by the mutual distrust that led them to confess to their crime. After serving their jail time, each wants nothing more than to avoid seeing the other. On a Saturday night, they might each have to choose between going to the nightclub and going to the movie theater. Neither has a dominant strategy because the best strategy for each depends on what the other is doing. However, Richard going to the nightclub and Justin going to the movie theater is a Nash equilibrium because each player takes the action that is best given the action of the other. Richard going to the movie theater and Justin going to the nightclub is also a Nash equilibrium, because again, neither wants to change his behavior given what the other is doing. This game resembles those played by two firms that do not want to locate in the same area, or to advertise on the same website.

The following section explains tricks to identify dominant strategies and Nash equilibria using a payoff matrix. We'll use these methods to analyze several games with varying outcomes.

Approaches and Applications **Figure 65.3** provides a payoff matrix for the game of Richard and Justin trying to avoid each other. The numbers in the matrix represent the players' levels of happiness, measured in utils. In each case, the utility levels are influenced by both the location and the presence or absence of the other player. For example, the upper-left set of numbers indicates that if both young men go to the nightclub, Richard will receive 2 utils and Justin will receive 4 utils. By comparing the utility levels, we can see that Richard gets less enjoyment out of the nightclub than Justin, and that both players would be happier if they were not in the same place. If, instead, just Richard goes to the nightclub and Justin goes to the movie theater, Richard will receive 4 utils while Justin receives 6, as indicated by the upper-right set of numbers.

AP® Exam Tip

Whenever there are two circles in the same box, a Nash equilibrium exists.

Here's a trick for finding dominant strategies and Nash equilibria. Begin by supposing that Justin goes to the nightclub. In the "Nightclub" column for Justin, we see that Richard receives 2 utils by going to the nightclub and 5 utils by going to the movie theater. Circle the best outcome for Richard, which is the 5 utils received by going to the movie theater. Then suppose that Justin goes to the movie theater.

Figure 65.3 A Game of Avoidance

The game of Richard and Justin trying not to be in the same place has no dominant strategies and two Nash equilibria. The same is true for the game of two firms trying not to locate in the same town.

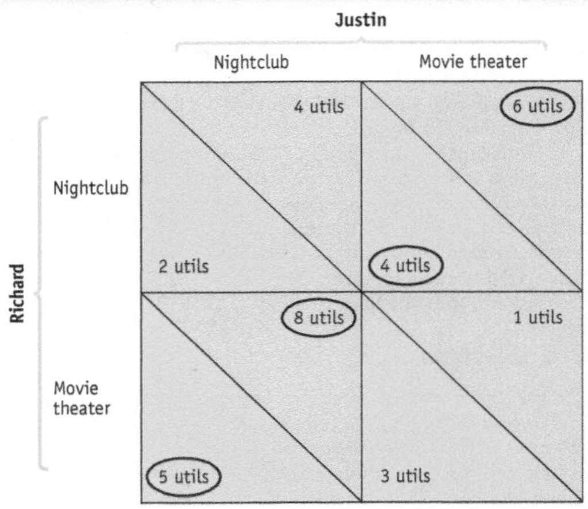

652 Section 12 Market Structures: Imperfect Competition

Circle the best outcome for Richard, which is to receive 4 utils by going to the nightclub.

Now look at things from Justin's point of view. If Richard goes to the nightclub, the options for Justin are to receive 4 utils by going to the nightclub or 6 utils by going to the movie theater. Circle the best outcome for Justin: 6 utils. Finally, suppose that Richard goes to the movie theater. Circle the best outcome for Justin in that case, which is to receive 8 utils by going to the nightclub.

Justin has a dominant strategy if there are two circles around his outcomes in the same column. In this game Justin does not have a dominant strategy, because he has one circle in the "Movie theater" column and one circle in the "Nightclub" column. Richard has a dominant strategy if there are two circles around his outcomes in the same row. Here Richard does not have a dominant strategy, because he has only one circle in each row.

A combination of strategies is a Nash equilibrium if the box representing that combination contains two circles. In this game, there are two circles in the box representing Richard going to the movie theater and Justin going to the nightclub, so that is a Nash equilibrium. The two circles in the box representing Richard going to the nightclub and Justin going to the movie theater indicate a second Nash equilibrium.

The same outcome of two Nash equilibria and no dominant strategy occurs when two grocery store chains consider opening a store in a town that can only support one grocery store. Just like Richard and Justin, if one is there, the other doesn't want to be there. So if the two chains are Chain 1 and Chain 2, the two Nash equilibria are: Chain 1 there and Chain 2 not there, and Chain 2 there and Chain 1 not there. Whichever chain can commit to being in that town first has the *first-mover advantage* of being able to ward off the other chain.

Sometimes firms face differing choices. For example, suppose that Juice Tree is deciding whether to raise its price on orange juice, while competitor Juice Max is deciding whether to spend more on advertising. **Figure 65.4** shows hypothetical profits for each firm, depending on the chosen strategies. For example, if Juice Tree raises its price and Juice Max doesn't advertise more, some of Juice Tree's customers will switch to

AP® Exam Tip

Whenever there are two circles in a column (or row) for a player, a dominant strategy exists.

Figure 65.4 Differing Choices

Players don't always face the same choices. In this game, Juice Tree is deciding whether to raise its price on orange juice, while competitor Juice Max is deciding whether to spend more on advertising. Juice Max has a dominant strategy of spending more on advertising, while Juice Tree has no dominant strategy. There is one Nash equilibrium of Juice Tree keeping the same price and Juice Max spending more on advertising.

Juice Tree \ Juice Max	More advertising	Same advertising
Higher price	Juice Max: $7 million (circled); Juice Tree: $2 million	Juice Max: $6 million; Juice Tree: $6 million (circled)
Same price	Juice Max: $5 million (circled); Juice Tree: $3 million (circled)	Juice Max: $4 million; Juice Tree: $5 million

FOCUS Graph It

Point out that we can use the payoff matrix even when firms have different choices, so long as the firms are interdependent. Figure 65.4 shows us this case where one firm must face a price decision and another an advertising decision. Again work with your students as they sort through this example and have them circle the best outcomes for both firms given different decisions for the other firm. Ask students the following:

- Is there a dominant strategy for Juice Max? Explain. *Yes, two circles appear in the same column.*
- Is there a dominant strategy for Juice Tree? Explain. *No, two circles do not appear in the same column or row.*
- Is there a Nash equilibrium? *Yes, Juice Tree keeps the price the same, while Juice Max advertises more.*

Module 65 Game Theory 653

Juice Max, increasing Juice Max's profit from $4 million to $6 million. In this case, Juice Tree's profit increases from $5 million to $6 million, indicating that the price effect of receiving more per unit is larger than the quantity effect of losing customers. The story changes if Juice Max advertises more: Juice Tree's profit decreases from $3 million to $2 million if it raises its price, because Juice Max is better able to draw attention to Juice Tree's higher prices and attract its customers.

Using the circle trick, we find one Nash equilibrium where Juice Tree keeps its price the same and Juice Max advertises more. The two circles around Juice Max's payoffs in the left column indicate that Juice Max has a dominant strategy of advertising more. Juice Tree does not have a dominant strategy because its best strategy depends on the strategy of Juice Max—Juice Tree is better off raising its price if Juice Max doesn't advertise more, and better off not raising its price if Juice Max does advertise more.

Spending more on advertising was a wise strategy for Juice Max, but the cost of more advertising can exceed the benefit. Suppose Ally and Barto offer competing painting services, and each must decide whether to rent a billboard to attract customers. **Figure 65.5** shows each painter's annual profits depending on the chosen strategies. Remember that oligopolists are not identical, so differing characteristics can result in differing payoffs for two firms in analogous situations. In this case, Barto is relatively unknown among the potential customers, and receives a net gain from billboard advertising regardless of Ally's decision. If Barto does not rent a billboard, Ally receives a net gain of $5,000 from a billboard. But if Barto does rent a billboard, he attracts so many new customers that Ally cannot gain enough to cover the cost of a billboard, and Ally loses $4,000 by renting one.

Applying the circle trick, the two circles around Barto's payoffs in the left column indicate that Barto has a dominant strategy of advertising. There are not two circles around Ally's payoffs in any one row, so she does not have a dominant strategy. The two circles in the box for Ally not getting a billboard and Barto getting a billboard indicate that neither side would want to take a different action given what the other is doing, so that combination is a Nash equilibrium.

Figure 65.5 Differing Payoffs

Even when facing the same choices, differences among oligopolists can cause them to receive different payoffs in analogous situations. In this example of painters Ally and Barto, Ally is well known in the area but Barto is a newcomer. This makes it a dominant strategy for Barto to rent a billboard to make customers aware of his services, whereas Ally is better off not renting a billboard if Barto rents one. The one Nash equilibrium in this case is for Barto to rent a billboard and for Ally not to.

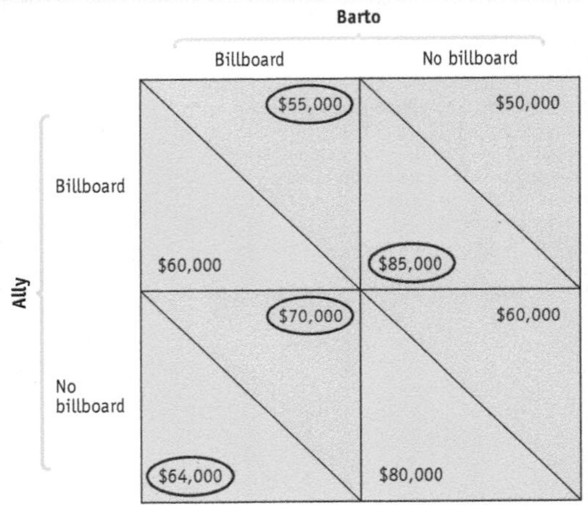

FOCUS Graph It

Figure 65.5 shows a payoff matrix involving the decision of whether or not to spend more on advertising. Work through this scenario with your students, having them circle the best choices for each individual based on the choices of his or her competitor.

FOCUS Test It

Ask students the following questions regarding Figure 65.5:

- Does Barto have a dominant strategy to advertise? Explain. *Yes, there are two circles in the same column showing a dominant strategy to advertise.*
- Does Ally have a dominant strategy? Explain. *No, no row contains two circles; therefore, no dominant strategy exists for Ally.*
- Is there a Nash equilibrium? Explain. *Yes, Nash equilibrium is where Ally will not advertise and Barto will. There are two circles in the same column to determine a Nash equilibrium.*
- What does the Nash equilibrium tell you about Ally and Barto wanting to select a different action? *The Nash equilibrium is the point where neither party would want to select a different action given what the other is doing.*

654 Section 12 Market Structures: Imperfect Competition

We can explore more possible outcomes by supposing that the annual cost of renting a billboard decreases by $4,000. As shown with green numbers in **Figure 65.6**, this increases each profit level associated with renting a billboard by $4,000. Notice that if Barto rents a billboard, Ally receives a profit of $64,000 with or without a billboard. Which number do we circle when applying the circle trick to two identical choices? Both! This indicates that Ally is indifferent between the two strategies if Barto has a billboard. If Barto doesn't have a billboard, Ally earns more profit with a billboard. Because Ally is sometimes indifferent about having a billboard and sometimes she is better off with one, we describe having a billboard as a *weakly dominant strategy* for Ally. Having a billboard is again a dominant strategy for Barto. And now there are two Nash equilibria: both having a billboard, and Ally having no billboard while Barto does have a billboard. If Ally and Barto had to decide whether to rent billboards year after year, this would be considered a *repeated game*. The next module explains how repeated games create new options for strategy and cooperation.

Figure 65.6 Adjusting for Changes

Changes in prices, taxes, or related policies can change the payoffs of a game. If the change only affects one strategy, as with a $4,000 decrease in the cost of renting a billboard, be careful to adjust only the payoffs for that strategy. The changes in this figure relative to Figure 65.5 are shown in green. The lower cost makes renting a billboard a weakly dominant strategy for Ally, meaning that the payoffs from that strategy are at least as good, and in some cases better, than the payoffs from the alternative strategy. The lower rental cost also creates an additional Nash equilibrium of both players renting a billboard.

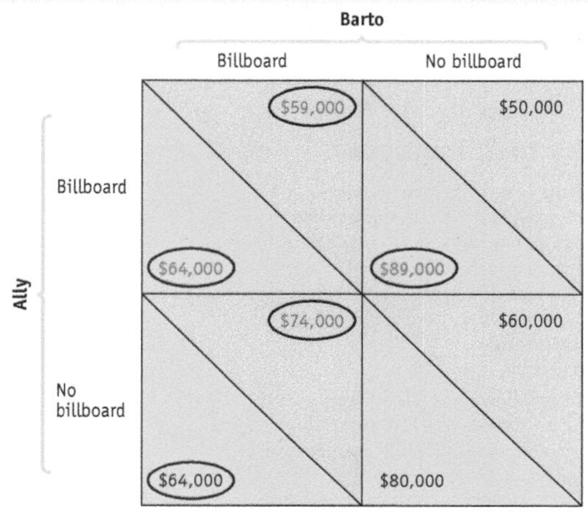

TEACH Teach It

If prices, taxes, or policies change, profits and therefore payoffs can change in a payoff matrix.

FOCUS Test It

The payoffs in a matrix can change, for example, if prices, taxes, or policies change. The case of a change affecting payoffs is illustrated in Figure 65.6. Ask students the following questions about the figure:

- Is there a dominant strategy for Barto? Explain. *Two circles occur twice in the same column, showing a dominant strategy exists for Barto (having a billboard).*
- Is there a dominant strategy for Ally? Explain. *A weakly dominant strategy exists—she is indifferent about having a billboard—the payoffs are at least as good and sometimes better than an alternative strategy.*
- Are there Nash equilibria? Explain. *Yes, two Nash equilibria exist: two circles occurring in two separate boxes. (1) Barto has a billboard/Ally has a billboard and (2) Barto has a billboard/Ally does not have a billboard.*

FOCUS Flip It

TRM Have students watch Jacob Clifford's video "Micro 4.10 Game Theory Dominant Strategy Practice" (see econextras video list with hyperlinks on the bcs and TRFD) and assign **Worksheet 65.3 (Dominant Strategy)** from the TRM.

FOCUS Active Learning

You may choose to watch the video "Economics Tube—Game Theory on a British Game Show" with the class. It depicts a game show in England that presents a real game theory lesson. (See econextras video list with hyperlinks on the bcs and TRFD.)

Have students describe the dominant strategies and the final decision made.

Module 65 Game Theory 655

OPEN & CLOSE Exit Slip

*TRM Please see **Exit Slip: Module 65** in the TRM for formative multiple-choice questions to ask your students before finishing your lesson. These questions will help you quickly assess whether your students have mastered the module's concepts before moving on.*

Answers to the Exit Slip Questions

1. A
2. B
3. B

Answers to Module 65 Review Questions

Check Your Understanding

1. a. A Nash equilibrium is a set of actions from which neither side wants to deviate (change actions), given what the other is doing. Both sides building a missile is a Nash equilibrium because neither player wants to deviate from the decision to build a missile. To switch from building to not building a missile, given that the other player is building a missile, would result in a change from −10 to −20 utils. There is no other Nash equilibrium in this game because for any other set of actions, at least one side is not building a missile, and would be better off switching to building a missile.

b. The total payoff is greatest for Margaret and Nikita when neither side builds a missile, in which case their total payoff is 0 + 0 = 0.

c. This outcome would require cooperation because each side sees itself as better off by building a missile. If Margaret builds a missile but Nikita does not, Margaret gets a payoff of +8, rather than the 0 she obtains if she doesn't build a missile. Similarly, Nikita is better off if he builds a missile but Margaret doesn't: he gets a payoff of +8, rather than the 0 he obtains if he doesn't build a missile. Indeed, both players have an incentive to build a missile regardless of what the other side does. So unless Nikita and Margaret are able to communicate in some way to enforce cooperation, they will act in their own individual interests and each will pursue its dominant strategy of building a missile.

2. Refer students to page 652. There are no dominant strategies in this game because each player's best outcome depends on the strategy of the other player. Two Nash equilibria exist: both players going to the nightclub and both players going to the movie theater.

Tackle the Test: Multiple-Choice Questions

1. b
2. b
3. c
4. a

MODULE 65 Review

Check Your Understanding

1. Suppose world leaders Nikita and Margaret are engaged in an arms race and face the decision of whether to build a missile. Answer the following questions using the information in the payoff matrix below, which shows how each set of actions will affect the utility of the players (the numbers represent utils gained or lost).

Margaret \ Nikita	Build missile	Don't build missile
Build missile	Nikita: −10; Margaret: −10	Nikita: −20; Margaret: 8
Don't build missile	Nikita: 8; Margaret: −20	Nikita: 0; Margaret: 0

a. Identify any Nash equilibria that exist in this game, and explain why they do or do not exist.

b. Which set of actions maximizes the total payoff for Nikita and Margaret?

c. Why is it unlikely that they will choose the payoff-maximizing set of actions without some communication?

2. Consider a new version of the game in which Richard and Justin must decide whether to go to the nightclub or the movie theater (see page 652). In this version, rather than being disheartened, the two young men bond in jail and want nothing more than to be in the same place after their release. Describe any dominant strategies and Nash equilibria in this game.

Tackle the Test: Multiple-Choice Questions

1. Each player has an incentive to choose an action that, when both players choose it, makes them both worse off than if neither had chosen it. This situation describes

a. a dominant strategy.
b. the prisoners' dilemma.
c. interdependence.
d. Nash equilibrium.
e. game theory.

2. Which of the following is true of every Nash equilibrium?

a. It is the only Nash equilibrium in the game.
b. Neither player wants to independently change his or her strategy.
c. It is also a dominant strategy equilibrium.
d. Each player receives the same payoff.
e. There is no better outcome in the payoff matrix for either player.

3. A situation in which each player in a game chooses the action that maximizes his or her payoff, given the actions of the other players, ignoring the effects of his or her action on the payoffs received by others, is known as a

a. dominant strategy.
b. cooperative equilibrium.
c. Nash equilibrium.
d. strategic situation.
e. prisoners' dilemma.

4. In the context of the Richard and Justin story in the module, suppose that Justin discovers Richard's action (confess or don't confess) before choosing his own action.

Richard \ Justin	Don't confess	Confess
Don't confess	Justin gets 5-year sentence. Richard gets 5-year sentence.	Justin gets 2-year sentence. Richard gets 20-year sentence.
Confess	Justin gets 20-year sentence. Richard gets 2-year sentence.	Justin gets 15-year sentence. Richard gets 15-year sentence.

Based on the payoff matrix provided, Justin will

a. confess whether or not Richard confessed.
b. not confess only if Richard confessed.
c. not confess only if Richard didn't confess.
d. not confess regardless of whether or not Richard confessed.
e. confess only if Richard did not confess.

656 Section 12 Market Structures: Imperfect Competition

5. Which of the following is true on the basis of the payoff matrix provided in Question 4?
   a. Justin has no dominant strategy, but Richard does.
   b. Richard has no dominant strategy, but Justin does.
   c. Both Richard and Justin have a dominant strategy.
   d. Neither Richard nor Justin has a dominant strategy.
   e. Justin has a dominant strategy only if Richard confesses.

Tackle the Test: Free-Response Questions

1. Refer to the payoff matrix provided. You and your competitor must decide whether or not to market a new product.

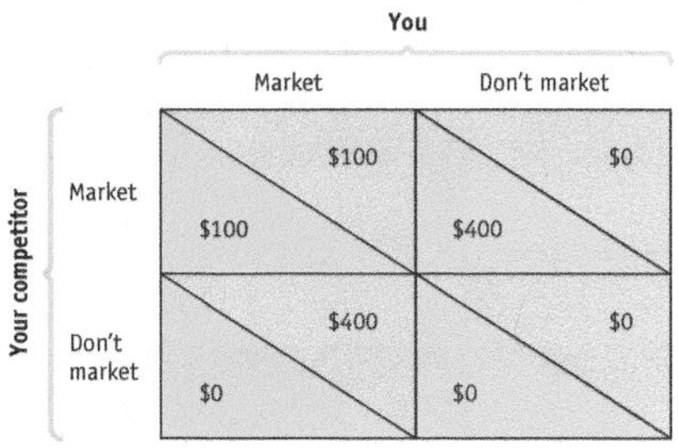

   a. If you market the new product and your competitor does not, how much profit will you earn?
   b. If you market the new product, what should your competitor do?
   c. Do you have a dominant strategy? Explain.
   d. Does this situation have a Nash equilibrium? Explain.

Rubric for FRQ 1 (6 points)

1 point: $400

1 point: Market the new product

1 point: Yes

1 point: Profits are greater (either $100 or $400 versus $0) if I market the new product, regardless of what my competitor does.

1 point: Yes

1 point: Both players marketing the product is a Nash equilibrium because neither side wants to change to not marketing, given what the other side is doing. (In fact, in this case both sides want to market the product regardless of what the other side is doing, so it is a dominant strategy equilibrium as well as a Nash equilibrium.)

2. Suppose there are two firms in an oligopoly, Firm A and Firm B. If both firms charge a low price, each earns $2 million in profit. If both firms charge a high price, each earns $3 million in profit. If one firm charges a high price and one charges a low price, customers flock to the firm with the low price, and that firm earns $4 million in profit while the firm with the high price earns $1 million in profit.
   a. Draw a clearly labeled payoff matrix for this game and fill in each of the payoffs. Arrange the matrix so that Firm A is on the left, and make the upper-left set of strategies both firms choosing low prices.
   b. Identify the dominant strategy for each player, if one exists.
   c. Identify the Nash equilibria in this game, if any exist.
   d. Now suppose a tax on high-priced goods causes a $500,000 decrease in the payoffs received from charging a high price. Redraw the payoff matrix with adjustments for this change.
   (5 points)

5. c

Tackle the Test: Free-Response Question Rubric for FRQ 2 (5 points)

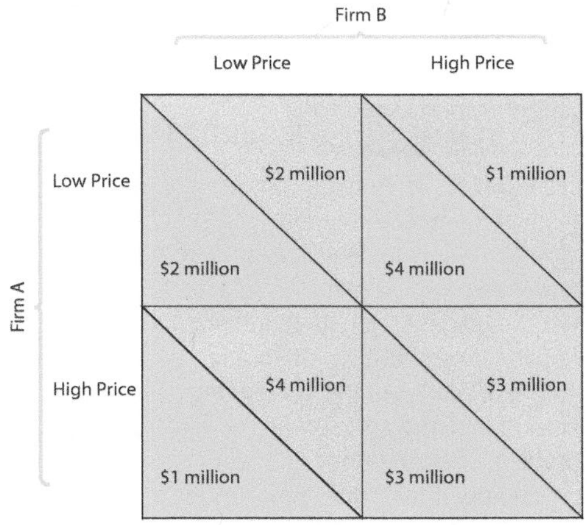

1 point: The firm and strategy labels are correctly placed as shown above.

1 point: The payoffs are listed correctly in the payoff matrix for part a as shown above.

1 point: Each firm has a dominant strategy of choosing a low price.

1 point: There is a Nash equilibrium of each firm choosing a low price.

1 point: The payoffs are listed correctly in the payoff matrix for part d as shown below.

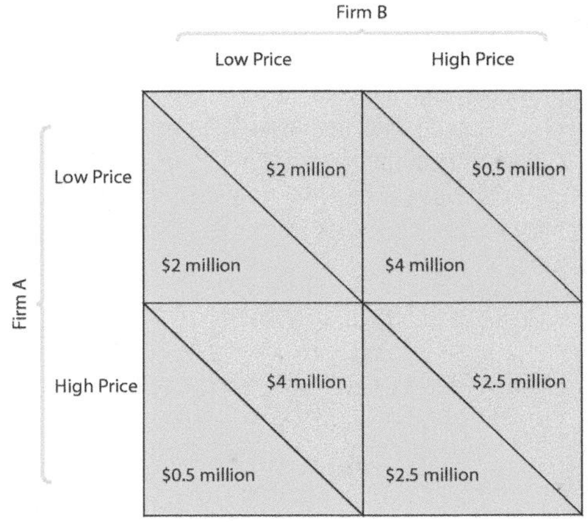

Module 65 Game Theory 657

PD To prepare for teaching this lesson, you may want to consult the **Module 66 Sample Lecture** in the TRM.

OPEN & CLOSE Start Here

Tell students to imagine that each of them is going to become the manager of a firm, in charge of making decisions about production and marketing. Ask which market structure would make their job more interesting and why. In perfect competition, the manager would set $MC = MR$ and sell the same thing as everyone else. In monopoly, the manager would set the profit-maximizing price and quantity, and consumers would have to buy from the monopoly if they wanted the good. But in oligopoly, firms engage in product differentiation, collusion, price wars, and strategic decision making! Later, students will see that monopolistic competitors also engage in product differentiation, advertising, and branding. Imperfect competition allows for much more interesting firm behavior and is much more common in the real world!

TEACH Teach It

Firms in an oligopoly can behave like perfect competitors when they engage in noncooperative behavior and like monopolies when they collude or form cartels or trusts. Most oligopoly behavior results in outcomes somewhere between monopoly and perfect competition. Tacit collusion assures that price rises above marginal cost, but antitrust policy keeps oligopolies from raising prices to monopoly levels.

Richard Levine/Alamy

MODULE

66 Oligopoly in Practice

In this Module, you will learn to:

- Discuss the legal constraints of antitrust policy
- Explain how repeated interactions among oligopolists can result in collusion in the absence of any formal agreement
- Explain the cause and effect of price wars, product differentiation, price leadership, and nonprice competition
- Describe the importance of oligopoly in the real world

Previously, we described the cartel known as "Vitamins, Inc.," which effectively sustained collusion for many years. Fortunately, the conspiratorial dealings of the vitamin makers were not the norm. But how do oligopolies usually work in practice? The answer depends both on the legal framework that limits what firms can do and on the underlying ability of firms in a given industry to cooperate without formal agreements. In this module we will explore a variety of oligopoly behaviors and how antitrust laws limit oligopolists' attempts to maximize their profits.

The Legal Framework

To understand oligopoly pricing in practice, we must be familiar with the legal constraints under which oligopolistic firms operate. In the United States, oligopoly first became an issue during the second half of the nineteenth century, when the growth of railroads—themselves an oligopolistic industry—created a national market for many goods. Large firms producing oil, steel, and many other products soon emerged. The industrialists quickly realized that profits would be higher if they could limit price competition. So many industries formed cartels—that is, they signed formal agreements to limit production and raise prices. Until 1890, when the first federal legislation against such cartels was passed, this was perfectly legal.

However, although these cartels were legal, their agreements weren't legally *enforceable*—members of a cartel couldn't ask the courts to force a firm that was violating its agreement to reduce its production. And firms often did violate their agreements, for the

658 Section 12 Market Structures: Imperfect Competition

reason already suggested by our duopoly example in Module 64: there is always a temptation for each firm in a cartel to produce more than it is supposed to.

In 1881, clever lawyers at John D. Rockefeller's Standard Oil Company came up with a solution—the so-called *trust*. In a trust, shareholders of all the major companies in an industry placed their shares in the hands of a board of trustees who controlled the companies. This, in effect, merged the companies into a single firm that could then engage in monopoly pricing. In this way, the Standard Oil Trust established what was essentially a monopoly of the oil industry, and it was soon followed by trusts in sugar, whiskey, lead, cottonseed oil, and linseed oil.

Eventually, there was a public backlash, driven partly by concern about the economic effects of the trust movement and partly by fear that the owners of the trusts were simply becoming too powerful. The result was the Sherman Antitrust Act of 1890, which was intended both to prevent the creation of more monopolies and to break up existing ones. At first this law went largely unenforced. But over the decades that followed, the federal government became increasingly committed to making it difficult for oligopolistic industries either to become monopolies or to behave like them. Such efforts are known to this day as **antitrust policy**.

Antitrust policy involves efforts by the government to prevent oligopolistic industries from becoming or behaving like monopolies.

One of the most striking early actions of antitrust policy was the breakup of Standard Oil in 1911. Its components formed the nuclei of many of today's large oil companies—Standard Oil of New Jersey became Exxon, Standard Oil of New York became Mobil, and so on. In the 1980s a long-running case led to the breakup of Bell Telephone, which once had a monopoly on both local and long-distance phone service in the United States. As we mentioned earlier, the Justice Department reviews proposed mergers between companies in the same industry and will bar mergers that it believes will reduce competition.

Among advanced countries, the United States is unique in its long tradition of antitrust policy. Until recently, other advanced countries did not have policies against price-fixing, and some even supported the creation of cartels, believing that it would help their own firms compete against foreign rivals. But the situation has changed radically over the past 25 years, as the European Union (EU)—an international body with the duty of enforcing antitrust policy for its member countries—has converged toward U.S. practices. Today, EU and U.S. regulators often target the same firms because price-fixing has "gone global" as international trade has expanded. During the early 1990s, the United States instituted an amnesty program in which a price-fixer receives a much-reduced penalty if it provides information on its co-conspirators. (Remember that the Great Vitamin Conspiracy was busted when a French company, Rhone-Poulenc, revealed the cartel in order to get favorable treatment from U.S. regulators.) In addition, Congress substantially increased maximum fines levied upon conviction. These two new policies clearly made informing on cartel partners a dominant strategy, and it has paid off: in recent years, executives from Belgium, Britain, Canada, France, Germany, Italy, Mexico, the Netherlands, South Korea, and Switzerland, as well as from the United States, have been convicted in U.S. courts of cartel crimes. As one lawyer commented, "You get a race to the courthouse" as each conspirator seeks to be the first to come clean.

Life has gotten much tougher over the past few years if you want to operate a cartel. So what's an oligopolist to do?

In 1911, Standard Oil was broken up into 34 separate companies, 3 of which later became Chevron, Conoco, and Exxon.

Tacit Collusion

Clearly, the players in any prisoners' dilemma would be better off if they had some way of enforcing cooperative behavior. In terms of the examples from the previous module, criminals Richard and Justin would benefit from successfully swearing to a code of silence, and the lysine producers would benefit from signing an enforceable agreement not to produce more than 30 million pounds of lysine. But we know that in the United States and many other countries, an agreement setting the output levels of two oligopolists isn't just unenforceable, it's illegal. So it seems that a noncooperative equilibrium is the only possible outcome. Or is it?

TEACH Teach It

In 1890, the United States passed antitrust laws to prevent monopolization. Many other advanced countries allowed cartels to exist up until recent decades. At the same time, countries in the European Union moved to stricter antitrust policies, and the United States enacted policies to increase the incentive for firms to provide information about illegal activities and made informing on cartel partners a dominant strategy!

TEACH Connect It

The word *tacit* means "understood without being stated." Tacit collusion occurs when there is cooperation among producers without anyone meeting, saying a word, or creating a formal agreement. For example, it may be obvious to all firms that profit will be higher if everyone reduces output. If all firms believe that everyone understands this, they will reduce their output without needing a meeting or discussion or having a formal agreement.

Module 66 Oligopoly in Practice 659

Overcoming the Prisoners' Dilemma: Repeated Interaction and Tacit Collusion

Richard and Justin are playing what is known as a *one-shot* game—they play the game with each other only once. They get to choose once and for all whether to confess or deny, and that's it. However, most of the games that oligopolists play aren't one-shot games; instead, the players expect to play the game repeatedly with the same rivals.

A firm engages in **strategic behavior** when it attempts to influence the future behavior of other firms.

An oligopolist usually expects to be in business for many years, and knows that a decision today about whether to cheat is likely to affect the decisions of other firms in the future. So a smart oligopolist doesn't just decide what to do based on the effect on profit in the short run. Instead, it engages in **strategic behavior**, taking into account the effects of its action on the future actions of other players. And under some conditions oligopolists that behave strategically can manage to behave as if they had a formal agreement to collude.

Suppose that our two firms expect to be in the lysine business for many years and therefore expect to play the game of cheat versus collude many times. Would they really betray each other time and again? Probably not. Suppose that each firm considers two strategies. In one strategy, it always cheats, producing 40 million pounds of lysine each year, regardless of what the other firm does. In the other strategy, it starts with good behavior, producing only 30 million pounds in the first year, and watches to see what its rival does. If the other firm also keeps its production down, each firm will stay cooperative, producing 30 million pounds again for the next year. But if one firm produces 40 million pounds, the other firm will take the gloves off and also produce 40 million pounds the following year. This latter strategy—start by behaving cooperatively, but thereafter do whatever the other player did in the previous period—is generally known as **tit for tat**.

A strategy of **tit for tat** involves playing cooperatively at first, then doing whatever the other player did in the previous period.

Playing "tit for tat" is a form of strategic behavior because it is intended to influence the future actions of other players. The "tit for tat" strategy offers a reward to the other player for cooperative behavior—if you behave cooperatively, so will I. It also provides a punishment for cheating—if you cheat, don't expect me to be nice in the future.

The payoff to each firm of each of these strategies would depend on which strategy the other chooses. Consider the four possibilities, shown in **Figure 66.1**:

1. If one firm plays "tit for tat" and so does the other, both firms will make a profit of $180 million each year.
2. If one firm plays "always cheat" but the other plays "tit for tat," one makes a profit of $200 million the first year but only $160 million per year thereafter.
3. If one firm plays "tit for tat" but the other plays "always cheat," one makes a profit of only $150 million in the first year but $160 million per year thereafter.
4. If one firm plays "always cheat" and the other does the same, both firms will make a profit of $160 million each year.

Which strategy is better? In the first year, one firm does better playing "always cheat," whatever its rival's strategy: it assures itself that it will get either $200 million or $160 million. (Which of the two payoffs it actually receives depends on whether the other plays "tit for tat" or "always cheat.") This is better than what it would get in the first year if it played "tit for tat": either $180 million or $150 million. But by the second year, a strategy of "always cheat" gains the firm only $160 million per year for the second and all subsequent years, regardless of the other firm's actions. Over time, the total amount gained by playing "always cheat" is less than the amount gained by playing "tit for tat": for the second and all subsequent years, it would never get any less than $160 million and would get as much as $180 million if the other firm played "tit for tat" as well. Which strategy, "always cheat" or "tit for tat," is more profitable depends on two things: how many years each firm expects to play the game and what strategy its rival follows.

If the firm expects the lysine business to end in the near future, it is in effect playing a one-shot game. So it might as well cheat and grab what it can. Even if the firm expects to remain in the lysine business for many years (therefore to find itself repeatedly playing this game) and, for some reason, expects the other firm will always cheat, it should

660 Section 12 Market Structures: Imperfect Competition

Figure 66.1 How Repeated Interaction Can Support Collusion

A strategy of "tit for tat" involves playing cooperatively at first, then following the other player's move. This rewards good behavior and punishes bad behavior. If the other player cheats, playing "tit for tat" will lead to only a short-term loss in comparison to playing "always cheat." But if the other player plays "tit for tat," also playing "tit for tat" leads to a long-term gain. So a firm that expects other firms to play "tit for tat" may well choose to do the same, leading to successful tacit collusion.

Firm 1 \ Firm 2	Tit for tat	Always cheat
Tit for tat	Firm 2 makes $180 million profit each year. / Firm 1 makes $180 million profit each year.	Firm 2 makes $200 million profit 1st year, $160 million profit each later year. / Firm 1 makes $150 million profit 1st year, $160 million profit each later year.
Always cheat	Firm 2 makes $150 million profit 1st year, $160 million profit each later year. / Firm 1 makes $200 million profit 1st year, $160 million profit each later year.	Firm 2 makes $160 million profit each year. / Firm 1 makes $160 million profit each year.

also always cheat. That is, the firm should follow the old rule, "Do unto others before they do unto you."

But if the firm expects to be in the business for a long time and thinks the other firm is likely to play "tit for tat," it will make more profits over the long run by playing "tit for tat," too. It could have made some extra short-term profit by cheating at the beginning, but this would provoke the other firm into cheating, too, and, in the end, would mean less profit.

The lesson of this story is that when oligopolists expect to compete with each other over an extended period of time, each individual firm will often conclude that it is in its own best interest to be helpful to the other firms in the industry. So it will restrict its output in a way that raises the profit of the other firms, expecting them to return the favor. Despite the fact that firms have no way of making an enforceable agreement to limit output and raise prices (and are in legal jeopardy if they even discuss prices), they manage to act "as if" they had such an agreement. When this type of unspoken agreement comes about, we say that the firms are engaging in **tacit collusion**.

When firms limit production and raise prices in a way that raises each other's profits, even though they have not made any formal agreement, they are engaged in **tacit collusion.**

Business decisions in real life are nowhere near as simple as those in our lysine story; nonetheless, in most oligopolistic industries, most of the time, the sellers do appear to succeed in keeping prices above their noncooperative level. Tacit collusion, in other words, is the normal state of oligopoly.

Constraints on Collusion

Although tacit collusion is common, it rarely allows an industry to push prices all the way up to their monopoly level; collusion is usually far from perfect. A variety of factors make it hard for an industry to coordinate on high prices.

Large Numbers

Suppose that there were three instead of two firms in the lysine industry and that each was currently producing only 20 million pounds. In that case any one firm that decided to produce an extra 10 million pounds would gain more in short-term profits—and

FOCUS Graph It

Figure 66.1 uses game theory to illustrate an example of tit for tat behavior. In a long-term relationship, tit for tat behavior rewards cooperation and can lead firms to increase their profit through tacit collusion.

FOCUS Test It

What factors limit firms' ability to collude (either formally or tacitly)? *Laws, a large number of firms, complex products or pricing schemes, different firm goals, and buyer power*

Module 66 Oligopoly in Practice 661

TEACH Teach It

A price war can break out when tacit collusion ends. If the tacit collusion that has kept prices above the noncooperative level ends—for example, because one firm begins cheating on the agreement—prices fall quickly. Prices may fall rapidly to the noncooperative level or even lower, if firms seek to punish cheaters.

lose less once another firm responded in kind—than in our original example because it has fewer units on which to feel the price effect. The general point is that the more firms there are in an oligopoly, the less is the incentive of any one firm to behave cooperatively, taking into account the impact of its actions on the profits of the other firms. Large numbers of firms in an industry also make the monitoring of price and output levels more difficult, and typically indicate low barriers to entry.

Complex Products and Pricing Schemes

In our simplified lysine example the two firms produce only one product. In reality, however, oligopolists often sell thousands or even tens of thousands of different products. A Walmart Supercenter sells over 100,000 items! Under these circumstances, as when there are a large number of firms, keeping track of what other firms are producing and what prices they are charging is difficult. This makes it hard to determine whether a firm is cheating on the tacit agreement.

Differences in Interests

In the lysine example, a tacit agreement for the firms to split the market equally is a natural outcome, probably acceptable to both firms. In other situations, however, firms often differ both in their perceptions about what is fair and in their real interests.

For example, suppose that one firm in a duopoly was a long-established producer and the other a more recent entrant into the industry. The long-established firm might feel that it deserved to continue producing more than the newer firm, but the newer firm might feel that it was entitled to 50% of the business.

Alternatively, suppose that the newer firm's marginal costs were lower than the long-established firm's. Even if they could agree on market shares, they would then disagree about the profit-maximizing level of output.

Bargaining Power of Buyers

Often oligopolists sell not to individual consumers but to large buyers—other industrial enterprises, nationwide chains of stores, and so on. These large buyers are in a position to bargain for lower prices from the oligopolists: they can ask for a discount from an oligopolist, and warn that they will go to a competitor if they don't get it. An important reason large retailers like Target are able to offer lower prices to customers than small retailers is precisely their ability to use their size to extract lower prices from their suppliers.

These difficulties in enforcing tacit collusion have sometimes led companies to defy the law and create illegal cartels. We've already examined the cases of the lysine industry and the bulk vitamin industry. An older, classic example was the U.S. electrical equipment conspiracy of the 1950s, which led to the indictment of and jail sentences for some executives. The industry was one in which tacit collusion was especially difficult because of all the reasons just mentioned. There were many firms—40 companies were indicted. They produced a very complex array of products, often more or less custom-built for particular clients. They differed greatly in size, from giants like General Electric to family firms with only a few dozen employees. And the customers in many cases were large buyers like electrical utilities, which would normally try to force suppliers to compete for their business. Tacit collusion just didn't seem practical—so executives met secretly and illegally to decide who would bid what price for which contract.

The FYI describes yet another price-fixing conspiracy: the one between the very posh auction houses Sotheby's and Christie's.

Because tacit collusion is often hard to achieve, most oligopolies charge prices that are well below what the same industry would charge if it were controlled by a monopolist—or what they would charge if they were able to collude explicitly. In addition, sometimes

662 Section 12 Market Structures: Imperfect Competition

FYI The Art of Conspiracy

If you want to sell a valuable work of art, there are really only two places to go: Christie's, the London-based auction house, or Sotheby's, its New York counterpart and competitor. Both are classy operations—literally: many of the employees of Christie's come from Britain's aristocracy, and many of Sotheby's come from blue-blooded American families that might as well have titles. They're not the sort of people you would expect to be seeking plea bargains from prosecutors.

But on October 6, 2000, Diana D. Brooks, the very upper-class former president of Sotheby's, pleaded guilty to a conspiracy. With her counterpart at Christie's, she had engaged in the illegal practice of price-fixing—agreeing on the fees they would charge people who sold artwork through either house. As part of her guilty plea, and in an effort to avoid going to jail, she agreed to help in the investigation of her boss, the former chairman of Sotheby's.

Why would such upper-crust types engage in illegal practices? For the same reasons that respectable electrical equipment industry executives did. By definition, no two works of art are alike; it wasn't easy for the two houses to collude tacitly because it was too hard to determine what commissions they were charging on any given transaction. To increase profits, then, the companies felt that they needed to reach a detailed agreement. They did, and they got caught.

AFP/Getty Images

tacit collusion breaks down and aggressive price competition amounts to a **price war**. A price war sometimes precipitates a collapse of prices to their noncooperative level, or even lower, as sellers try to put each other out of business or at least punish what they regard as cheating.

A **price war** occurs when tacit collusion breaks down and aggressive price competition causes prices to collapse.

Product Differentiation and Price Leadership

In many oligopolies, however, firms produce products that consumers regard as similar but not identical. A $10 difference in the price won't make many customers switch from a Ford to a Chrysler, or vice versa. Sometimes the differences between products are real, like differences between Froot Loops and Wheaties; sometimes, they exist mainly in the minds of consumers, like differences between brands of vodka (which is *supposed* to be tasteless). Either way, the effect is to reduce the intensity of competition among the firms: consumers will not all rush to buy whichever product is cheapest.

As you might imagine, oligopolists welcome the extra market power that comes when consumers think that their product is different from that of competitors. So in many oligopolistic industries, firms make considerable efforts to create the perception that their product is different—that is, they engage in **product differentiation**.

A firm that tries to differentiate its product may do so by altering what it actually produces, adding "extras," or choosing a different design. It may also use advertising and marketing campaigns to create a differentiation in the minds of consumers, even though its product is more or less identical to the products of rivals.

A classic case of how products may be perceived as different even when they are really pretty much the same is over-the-counter medication. For many years there were only three widely sold pain relievers—aspirin, ibuprofen, and acetaminophen. Yet each of these generic pain relievers were marketed under a number of brand names. And each brand used a marketing campaign implying some special superiority.

Whatever the nature of product differentiation, oligopolists producing differentiated products often reach a tacit understanding not to compete on price. For example,

AP® Exam Tip

Advertising is a form of product differentiation used by oligopolists.

Product differentiation is an attempt by a firm to convince buyers that its product is different from the products of other firms in the industry.

FOCUS Active Learning

Ask students which candy is their favorite (or which breakfast cereal, car, phone, etc. is). Then ask them why. Use their responses to provoke a discussion of product differentiation. They will mention a variety of characteristics that differ between brands. The differences may be real or merely perceived. For example, a candy may have nuts or not (a real difference), or one may be exactly the same as another, except for an "M" appearing on its chocolate covering.

TEACH Teach It

Product differentiation occurs when a firm attempts to convince consumers that its product is different from that of other firms in the industry. Ask students to think of ways in which toothpaste manufacturers differentiate their product (*gel vs. paste, whitener, plaque fighting, mouthwash added, pump dispenser, cartoon characters on the tube, etc.*). Then have them give examples of other industries in which firms differentiate their products (*autos, cereal, clothing lines, gaming, athletic wear, etc.*).

FOCUS Test It

Why does product differentiation occur in oligopoly markets but not in monopoly or perfectly competitive markets? *Oligopolies use product differentiation to create market power. They have the ability and incentive to try to convince consumers that their product is better. Monopoly is the only seller, so there is no one to differentiate their product from—though a monopoly may use differentiation to increase demand. Perfect competitors sell a homogeneous product, so it can't be differentiated, and they don't have the resources available to differentiate their product anyway.*

TEACH Teach It

Price leadership is a tacit agreement to let one firm lead in setting the market price. Other firms follow the price set by the leader. In these cases, firms compete for customers in areas other than price. Nonprice competition includes product differentiation, advertising, and branding.

Module 66 Oligopoly in Practice 663

FOCUS Active Learning

TRM For practice with the terms and ideas of oligopolies, assign **Worksheet 66.1 (Oligopoly Terms)** from the TRM.

OPEN & CLOSE Exit Slip

TRM *Please see **Exit Slip: Module 66** in the TRM for formative multiple-choice questions to ask your students before finishing your lesson. These questions will help you quickly assess whether your students have mastered the module's concepts before moving on.*

Answers to the Exit Slip Questions

1. E
2. C
3. B

during the years when the great majority of cars sold in the United States were produced by the Big Three auto companies (General Motors, Ford, and Chrysler), there was an unwritten rule that none of the three companies would try to gain market share by making its cars noticeably cheaper than those of the other two.

But then who would decide on the overall price of cars? The answer was normally General Motors: as the biggest of the three, it would announce its prices for the year first; and the other companies would adopt similar prices. This pattern of behavior, in which one company tacitly sets prices for the industry as a whole, is known as **price leadership**.

In **price leadership**, one firm sets its price first, and other firms then follow.

Firms that have a tacit understanding not to compete on price often engage in intense **nonprice competition**, using advertising and other means to try to increase their sales.

Interestingly, firms that have a tacit agreement not to compete on price often engage in vigorous **nonprice competition**—adding new features to their products, spending large sums on ads that proclaim the inferiority of their rivals' offerings, and so on.

Perhaps the best way to understand the mix of cooperation and competition in such industries is with a political analogy. During the long Cold War between the United States and the Soviet Union, the two countries engaged in intense rivalry for global influence. They not only provided financial and military aid to their allies; they sometimes supported forces trying to overthrow governments allied with their rival (as the Soviet Union did in Vietnam in the 1960s and early 1970s, and as the United States did in Afghanistan from 1979 until the collapse of the Soviet Union in 1991). They even sent their own soldiers to support allied governments against rebels (as the United States did in Vietnam and the Soviet Union did in Afghanistan). But they did not get into direct military confrontations with each other; open warfare between the two superpowers was regarded by both as too dangerous—and tacitly avoided.

Price wars aren't as serious as shooting wars, but the principle is the same.

How Important Is Oligopoly?

AP® Exam Tip

You should understand how oligopolists respond to their competitors. However, oligopoly *graphs* have not appeared on the AP® exam for many years.

We have seen that, across industries, oligopoly is far more common than either perfect competition or monopoly. When we try to analyze oligopoly, the economist's usual way of thinking—asking how self-interested individuals would behave, then analyzing their interaction—does not work as well as we might hope because we do not know whether rival firms will engage in noncooperative behavior or manage to engage in some kind of collusion. Given the prevalence of oligopoly, then, is the analysis we developed in earlier modules, which was based on perfect competition, still useful?

The conclusion of the great majority of economists is yes. For one thing, important parts of the economy are fairly well described by perfect competition. And even though many industries are oligopolistic, in many cases the limits to collusion keep prices relatively close to marginal costs—in other words, the industry behaves "almost" as if it were perfectly competitive.

AP Photo

Cars line up for gasoline in 1973 after the U.S. government imposed price controls.

It is also true that predictions from supply and demand analysis are often valid for oligopolies. For example, we saw that price controls will produce shortages. Strictly speaking, this conclusion is certain only for perfectly competitive industries. But in the 1970s, when the U.S. government imposed price controls on the definitely oligopolistic oil industry, the result was indeed to produce shortages and lines at the gas pumps.

So how important is it to take account of oligopoly? Most economists adopt a pragmatic approach. As we have seen here, the analysis of oligopoly is far more difficult and messy than that of perfect competition; so in situations where they do not expect the complications associated with oligopoly to be crucial, economists prefer to adopt the working assumption of perfectly competitive markets. They always keep in mind the possibility that oligopoly might be important; they recognize that there are important issues, from antitrust policies to price wars, that make trying to understand oligopolistic behavior crucial.

664 Section 12 Market Structures: Imperfect Competition

MODULE 66 Review

Check Your Understanding

1. For each of the following industry practices, explain whether the practice supports the conclusion that there is tacit collusion in this industry.
   a. For many years the price in the industry has changed infrequently, and all the firms in the industry charge the same price. The largest firm publishes a catalog containing a "suggested" retail price. Changes in price coincide with changes in the catalog.
   b. There has been considerable variation in the market shares of the firms in the industry over time.
   c. Firms in the industry build into their products unnecessary features that make it hard for consumers to switch from one company's products to another's.
   d. Firms meet yearly to discuss their annual sales forecasts.
   e. Firms tend to adjust their prices upward at the same times.

Tackle the Test: Multiple-Choice Questions

1. Having which of the following makes it easier for oligopolies to coordinate on raising prices?
   a. a large number of firms
   b. differentiated products
   c. buyers with bargaining power
   d. identical perceptions of fairness
   e. complex pricing schemes
2. Which of the following led to the passage of the first antitrust laws?
   I. growth of the railroad industry
   II. the emergence of the Standard Oil Company
   III. increased competition in agricultural industries
   a. I only
   b. II only
   c. III only
   d. I and II only
   e. I, II, and III
3. When was the first federal legislation against cartels passed?
   a. 1776
   b. 1800
   c. 1890
   d. 1900
   e. 1980
4. Which of the following industries has been prosecuted for creating an illegal cartel?
   a. the lysine industry
   b. the art auction house industry
   c. the U.S. electrical equipment industry
   d. the bulk vitamin industry
   e. all of the above
5. Oligopolists engage in tacit collusion in order to
   a. raise prices.
   b. increase output.
   c. share profits.
   d. increase market share.
   e. all of the above.

Tackle the Test: Free-Response Questions

1. Like other firms, universities face temptations to collude in order to limit the effects of competition and avoid price wars. (In fact, the U.S. Department of Justice formally accused a group of universities of price-fixing in 1991.) Answer the following questions about behavior in the market for higher education.
   a. Describe one factor of the market for higher education that invites tacit collusion.
   b. Describe one factor of the market for higher education that works against tacit collusion.
   c. Explain one way in which universities could engage in illegal collusion.
   d. What are three ways in which universities engage in product differentiation?
   e. Explain how price leadership might work in the university setting.
   f. What forms of nonprice competition do you see universities engaged in?

Answers to Module 66 Review Questions

Check Your Understanding

1. a. This is evidence of tacit collusion. Firms in the industry are able to tacitly collude by setting their prices according to the published "suggested" price of the largest firm in the industry. This is a form of price leadership.

b. This is no evidence of tacit collusion. Considerable variation in market shares indicates that firms have been competing to capture each other's business.

c. This is no evidence of tacit collusion. These features make it less likely that consumers will switch products in response to lower prices. So this is a way for firms to avoid any temptation to gain market share by lowering price. This is a form of product differentiation used to avoid direct competition.

d. This is evidence of tacit collusion. Under the guise of discussing sales targets, firms can create a cartel by designating quantities to be produced by each firm.

e. This is evidence of tacit collusion. By raising prices together, each firm in the industry is refusing to undercut its rivals by leaving its price unchanged or lowering it. Because it could gain market share by doing so, refusing to do so supports the conclusion that there is tacit collusion.

Tackle the Test: Multiple-Choice Questions

1. d
2. d
3. c
4. e
5. a

Tackle the Test: Free-Response Question

Rubric for FRQ 2 (6 points)

1 point: Difficulty detecting each other's output makes it more likely that the firms will behave noncooperatively.

1 point: When it is very difficult for a firm to detect if another firm has raised output, it is also very hard to enforce cooperation by playing "tit for tat."

1 point: Long-term coexistence with high prices makes it more likely that the firms will engage in tacit collusion.

1 point: When firms have maintained high prices for a long time, a pattern of cooperation has been established. And because this is a long-term repeated game, the value of behaving cooperatively is high.

1 point: This makes each oligopolist more likely to behave noncooperatively.

1 point: Future entry by several new firms will increase competition and drive down industry profits. As a result, there is less future profit to protect by behaving cooperatively now.

Rubric for FRQ 1 (6 points)

1 point: The fact that universities offer a small number of products—enrollment into a small number of programs—invites tacit collusion. They may also have similar perceptions of fairness.

1 point: Factors that work against tacit collusion in the market for higher education include the large number of universities and the bargaining power of the better applicants.

1 point: Universities could engage in illegal collusion by holding meetings to establish uniform tuition rates, divvying up applicants so that each is accepted by a limited number of schools (to avoid competition), or sharing information on scholarship offerings so that applicants will receive similar offers from the competing schools.

1 point: Universities seek product differentiation in regard to athletic programs, facilities, academic standards, location, overseas programs, faculty, graduation requirements, and class size, among other areas.

1 point: Price leadership could be achieved in the university setting if one school, perhaps a large or prestigious university, announced its tuition early and then other schools based their tuition on that announcement.

1 point: Universities can engage in nonprice competition by offering better food, bigger dorm rooms, more accomplished faculty members, plush student centers, and similar amenities.

2. Indicate whether each of the following circumstances makes it more likely that oligopolists will behave noncooperatively or engage in tacit collusion. Explain your answers.
   a. It is difficult for a firm to detect whether another firm has raised output.
   b. The firms have coexisted while maintaining high prices for a long time.
   c. Each oligopolist expects several new firms to enter the market in the future.

   (6 points)

666 Section 12 Market Structures: Imperfect Competition

AP Photo/Kiichiro Sato

MODULE 67 Introduction to Monopolistic Competition

In this Module, you will learn to:

- Determine prices and profit in monopolistic competition, both in the short run and in the long run
- Explain how monopolistic competition can lead to inefficiency and excess capacity

Understanding Monopolistic Competition

Suppose an industry is monopolistically competitive: it consists of many producers, all competing for the same consumers but offering differentiated products. How does such an industry behave?

As the term *monopolistic competition* suggests, this market structure combines some features typical of monopoly with others typical of perfect competition. Because each firm is offering a distinct product, it is in a way like a monopolist: it faces a downward-sloping demand curve and has some market power—the ability within limits to determine the price of its product. However, unlike a pure monopolist, a monopolistically competitive firm does face competition: the amount of its product it can sell depends on the prices and products offered by other firms in the industry.

The same, of course, is true of an oligopoly. In a monopolistically competitive industry, however, there are *many* producers, as opposed to the small number that defines an oligopoly. This means that the "puzzle" of oligopoly—whether firms will collude or behave noncooperatively—does not arise in the case of monopolistically competitive industries. True, if all the gas stations or all the restaurants in a town could agree—explicitly or tacitly—to raise prices, it would be in their mutual interest to do so. But such collusion is virtually impossible when the number of firms is large and, by implication, there are no barriers to entry. So in situations of monopolistic competition, we can safely assume that firms behave noncooperatively and ignore the potential for collusion.

AP® Exam Tip

In a monopolistically competitive industry there are many firms and low barriers to entry, as in a perfectly competitive industry. However, the sale of differentiated products gives the monopolistically competitive firms some monopoly power.

Monopolistic Competition in the Short Run

We introduced the distinction between short-run and long-run equilibrium when we studied perfect competition. The short-run equilibrium of an industry takes the

St. Louis Federal Reserve Bank Resources

Monopolistic Competition

Teaching market structures in a microeconomics class? These slides present graphs related to monopolistic competition, the market structure in which there are many firms that produce similar, but not identical, products, and few barriers to entry exist. The slides illustrate firms' short-run decisions.

St. Louis Federal Reserve Bank Resources

Perfect Competition

Teaching market structures in a microeconomics class? These slides present graphs related to perfect competition, the market structure in which there are many buyers and sellers of an identical product, and no barriers to enter or exit the market exist. The slides illustrate firms' short-run decisions.

PD To prepare for teaching this lesson, you may want to consult the **Module 67 Sample Lecture** in the TRM.

OPEN & CLOSE Start Here

Now that students have studied three of the four market structures in depth, draw the market structure spectrum again and review where each model goes on the spectrum. Perfect competition (the ideal for efficiency) is on one end and monopoly (which creates deadweight loss) is on the other. Duopoly is next to monopoly and oligopoly is near duopoly. Emphasize that monopolistic competition is between monopoly and perfect competition, and shares important characteristics of each. In the short run, monopolistic competition will be like a monopoly, but in the long run it has much in common with perfect competition. Note that perfect competition is the ONLY market structure that guarantees efficiency.

TEACH Connect It

TRM Have students review the characteristics of perfect competition, monopoly, and monopolistic competition in **Worksheet 57.1 (Types of Market Structures)** from the TRM.

TEACH Connect It

Monopolistic competition combines some of the features of monopolies and perfectly competitive firms. Like a monopoly, monopolistically competitive firms face a downward-sloping demand curve and have some market power. However, many other firms sell similar products, so the monopolistic competitor's demand curve is fairly elastic. Students can think of monopolistic competition as sort of a "mini monopoly." For example, Burger King is the only firm selling the Whopper, so in that sense it has a monopoly in the Whopper market. However, since many other firms sell similar hamburgers, Burger King is really not a monopolist in the *Whopper market* but a monopolistic competitor in the *hamburger market*. Like a perfectly competitive market, a monopolistically competitive market has many firms and free entry and exit. Free entry and exit means that profits and losses provide an incentive for firms to enter and exit the industry.

TEACH Teach It

In the short run, the monopolistic competition model is the same as the monopoly model. To maximize profit, the monopolistically competitive firm operates at the quantity where $MR = MC$ and charges the price on the demand curve above that quantity. The graphs for monopolistic competition in the short run look the same as those for a monopoly.

FOCUS Graph It

Figure 67.1 shows a monopolistically competitive firm in the short run. Have students compare the graphs to those for a monopoly in Section 11.

FOCUS Test It

Ask students the following questions regarding Figure 67.1:

- Given the situation depicted in panel (a), what will happen in the market in the long run? *Profit will cause firms to enter the market; D and MR shift left (decrease), and therefore quantity decreases.*
- Given the situation depicted in panel (b), what will happen in the market in the long run? *Losses will cause firms to exit the market; D and MR will shift right (increase), and therefore quantity will increase.*

FOCUS Active Learning

TRM For practice graphing this market structure, assign **Worksheet 67.1 (Monopolistic Competition)** from the TRM.

---

number of firms as given. The long-run equilibrium, by contrast, is reached only after enough time has elapsed for firms to enter or exit the industry. To analyze monopolistic competition, we focus first on the short run and then on how an industry moves from the short run to the long run.

Panels (a) and (b) of **Figure 67.1** show two possible situations that a typical firm in a monopolistically competitive industry might face in the short run. In each case, the firm looks like any monopolist: it faces a downward-sloping demand curve, which implies a downward-sloping marginal revenue curve.

We assume that every firm has an upward-sloping marginal cost curve but that it also faces some fixed costs, so that its average total cost curve is U-shaped. This assumption doesn't matter in the short run; but, as we'll see shortly, it is crucial to understanding the long-run equilibrium.

AP® Exam Tip

Like a monopolist, a monopolistically competitive firm faces a downward-sloping demand curve and a marginal revenue curve that is below the demand curve. Unlike a monopolist, a monopolistically competitive firm will necessarily earn zero economic profit in the long run.

In each case the firm, in order to maximize profit, sets marginal revenue equal to marginal cost. So how do these two figures differ? In panel (a) the firm is profitable; in panel (b) it is unprofitable. (Recall that we are referring always to economic profit and not accounting profit—that is, a profit given that all factors of production are earning their opportunity costs.)

In panel (a) the firm faces the demand curve D_P and the marginal revenue curve MR_P. It produces the profit-maximizing output Q_P, the quantity at which marginal revenue is equal to marginal cost, and sells it at the price P_P. This price is above the average total cost at this output, ATC_P. The firm's profit is indicated by the area of the shaded rectangle.

Figure 67.1 The Monopolistically Competitive Firm in the Short Run

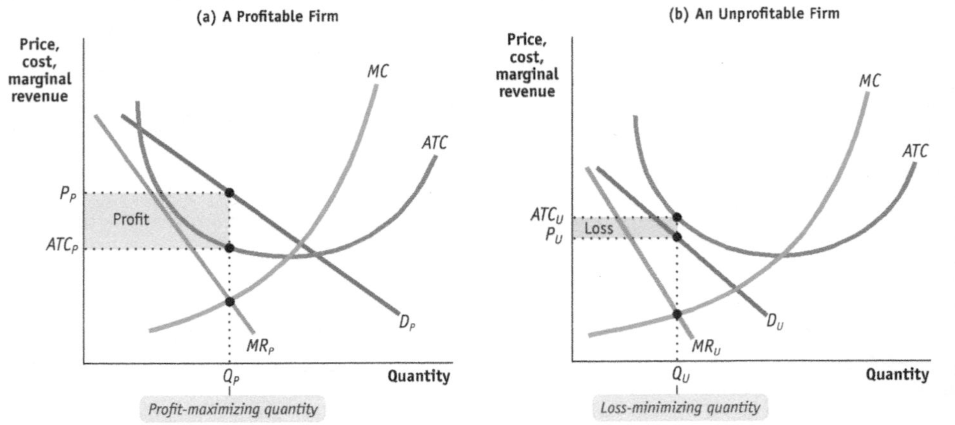

The firm in panel (a) can be profitable for some output quantities: the quantities for which its average total cost curve, *ATC*, lies below its demand curve, D_P. The profit-maximizing output quantity is Q_P, the output at which marginal revenue, MR_P, is equal to marginal cost, *MC*. The firm charges price P_P and earns a profit, represented by the area of the green shaded rectangle. The firm in panel (b), however, can never be profitable because its average total cost curve lies above its demand curve, D_U, for every output quantity. The best that it can do if it produces at all is to produce quantity Q_U and charge price P_U. This generates a loss, indicated by the area of the orange shaded rectangle. Any other output quantity results in a greater loss.

In panel (b) the firm faces the demand curve D_U and the marginal revenue curve MR_U. It chooses the quantity Q_U at which marginal revenue is equal to marginal cost. However, in this case the price P_U is *below* the average total cost ATC_U; so at this quantity the firm loses money. Its loss is equal to the area of the shaded rectangle. Since Q_U is the profit-maximizing quantity—which means, in this case, the loss-minimizing quantity—there is no way for a firm in this situation to make a profit. We can confirm this by noting that at any quantity of output, the average total cost curve in panel (b) lies above the demand curve D_U. Because $ATC > P$ at all quantities of output, this firm always suffers a loss.

As this comparison suggests, the key to whether a firm with market power is profitable or unprofitable in the short run lies in the relationship between its demand curve and its average total cost curve. In panel (a) the demand curve D_P crosses the average total cost curve, meaning that some of the demand curve lies above the average total cost curve. So there are some price-quantity combinations available at which price is higher than average total cost, indicating that the firm can choose a quantity at which it makes positive profit.

In panel (b), by contrast, the demand curve D_U does not cross the average total cost curve—it always lies below it. So the price corresponding to each quantity demanded is always less than the average total cost of producing that quantity. There is no quantity at which the firm can avoid losing money.

These figures, showing firms facing downward-sloping demand curves and their associated marginal revenue curves, look just like ordinary monopoly graphs. The "competition" aspect of monopolistic competition comes into play, however, when we move from the short run to the long run.

Monopolistic Competition in the Long Run

Obviously, an industry in which existing firms are losing money, like the one in panel (b) of Figure 67.1, is not in long-run equilibrium. When existing firms are losing money, some firms will *exit* the industry. The industry will not be in long-run equilibrium until the persistent losses have been eliminated by the exit of some firms.

It may be less obvious that an industry in which existing firms are earning profits, like the one in panel (a) of Figure 67.1, is also not in long-run equilibrium. Given there is *free entry* into the industry, persistent profits earned by the existing firms will lead to the entry of additional producers. The industry will not be in long-run equilibrium until the persistent profits have been eliminated by the entry of new producers.

In the long-run, profit lures new firms to enter an industry.

Anton Foltin/Shutterstock

How will entry or exit by other firms affect the profit of a typical existing firm? Because the differentiated products offered by firms in a monopolistically competitive industry are available to the same set of customers, entry or exit by other firms will affect the demand curve facing every existing producer. If new gas stations open along a highway, each of the existing gas stations will no longer be able to sell as much gas as before at any given price. So, as illustrated in panel (a) of **Figure 67.2** on the next page, entry of additional producers into a monopolistically competitive industry will lead to a *leftward* shift of the demand curve and the marginal revenue curve facing a typical existing producer.

Conversely, suppose that some of the gas stations along the highway close. Then each of the remaining stations will be able to sell more gasoline at any given price. So as illustrated in panel (b), exit of firms from an industry leads to a *rightward* shift of the demand curve and marginal revenue curve facing a typical remaining producer.

The industry will be in long-run equilibrium when there is neither entry nor exit. This will occur only when every firm earns zero profit. So in the long run, a monopolistically

TEACH Connect It

The adjustment process for achieving long-run equilibrium is the same for monopolistic competition as it was for perfect competition. In the long run, a monopolistically competitive firm will earn equilibrium at zero profit due to entry and exit. Firms will continue entering the market as long as they are earning a profit. As new firms enter, the demand curve for existing firms shifts left (with new firms, each firm gets a smaller share of the market demand). The demand curve shifts left until it is just tangent to the *ATC* curve. At that point, $P = ATC$, so the firm is earning zero economic profit and entry stops. With losses, firms exit. As firms exit, existing firms get a larger share of the market demand. Their demand curve shifts to the right until it is just tangent to the *ATC* curve. At that point, $P = ATC$, so the firm is earning zero economic profit and exit stops. In the long run, firms earn zero economic profit and the demand curve is tangent to the *ATC* curve.

FOCUS Active Learning

TRM Watch Dr. Mary J. McGlasson's video "Episode 29: Monopolistic Competition" (see econextras video list with hyperlinks on the bcs and TRFD) and assign **Worksheet 67.2 (Entry and Exit Effects for Monopolistic Competition)** from the TRM for questions regarding the video.

Module 67 Introduction to Monopolistic Competition 669

FOCUS Graph It

Figure 67.2 illustrates the shifting of *D* and *MR* curves with entry and exit.

- Entry to the industry when firms are profitable causes *D* and *MR* to shift left.
- Exit from the industry occurs when existing firms are unprofitable and causes *D* and *MR* to shift right.
- Entry and exit will stop when remaining firms in the industry make zero profit.

Figure 67.2 Entry and Exit Shift Existing Firms' Demand Curves and Marginal Revenue Curves

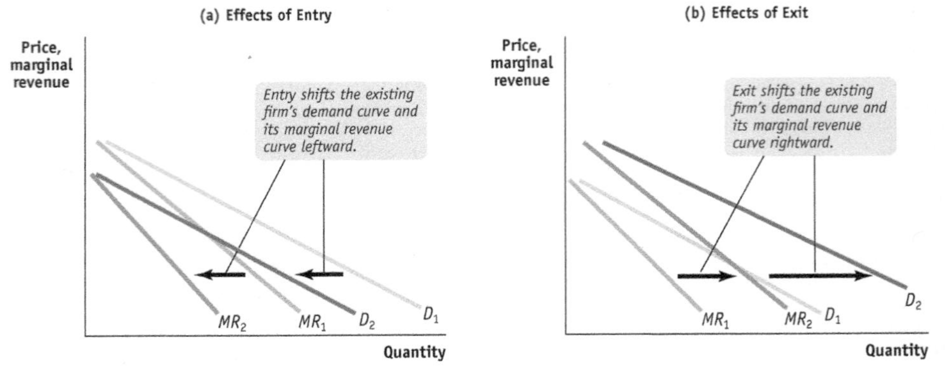

Entry will occur in the long run when existing firms are profitable. In panel (a), entry causes each existing firm's demand curve and marginal revenue curve to shift to the left. The firm receives a lower price for every unit it sells, and its profit falls. Entry will cease when firms make zero profit. Exit will occur in the long run when existing firms are unprofitable. In panel (b), exit from the industry shifts each remaining firm's demand curve and marginal revenue curve to the right. The firm receives a higher price for every unit it sells, and profit rises. Exit will cease when the remaining firms make zero profit.

In the long run, a monopolistically competitive industry ends up in **zero-profit equilibrium**: each firm makes zero profit at its profit-maximizing quantity.

competitive industry will end up in **zero-profit equilibrium**, in which firms just manage to cover their costs at their profit-maximizing output quantities.

We have seen that a firm facing a downward-sloping demand curve will earn positive profit if any part of that demand curve lies above its average total cost curve; it will incur a loss if its entire demand curve lies below its average total cost curve. So in zero-profit equilibrium, the firm must be in a borderline position between these two cases; its demand curve must just touch its average total cost curve. That is, the demand curve must be just *tangent* to the average total cost curve at the firm's profit-maximizing output quantity—the output quantity at which marginal revenue equals marginal cost.

If this is not the case, the firm operating at its profit-maximizing quantity will find itself making either a profit or loss, as illustrated in the panels of Figure 67.1. But we also know that free entry and exit means that this cannot be a long-run equilibrium. Why? In the case of a profit, new firms will enter the industry, shifting the demand curve of every existing firm leftward until all profit is eliminated. In the case of a loss, some existing firms exit and so shift the demand curve of every remaining firm to the right until all losses are eliminated. All entry and exit ceases only when every existing firm makes zero profit at its profit-maximizing quantity of output.

Figure 67.3 shows a typical monopolistically competitive firm in such a zero-profit equilibrium. The firm produces Q_{MC}, the output at which $MR_{MC} = MC$, and charges price P_{MC}. At this price and quantity, represented by point *Z*, the demand curve is just tangent to its average total cost curve. The firm earns zero profit because price, P_{MC}, is equal to average total cost, ATC_{MC}.

Figure 67.3 The Long-Run Zero-Profit Equilibrium

If existing firms are profitable, entry will occur and shift each existing firm's demand curve leftward. If existing firms are unprofitable, each remaining firm's demand curve shifts rightward as some firms exit the industry. Entry and exit will cease when every existing firm makes zero profit at its profit-maximizing quantity. So, in long-run zero-profit equilibrium, the demand curve of each firm is tangent to its average total cost curve at its profit-maximizing quantity: at the profit-maximizing quantity, Q_{MC}, price, P_{MC}, equals average total cost, ATC_{MC}. A monopolistically competitive firm is like a monopolist without monopoly profits.

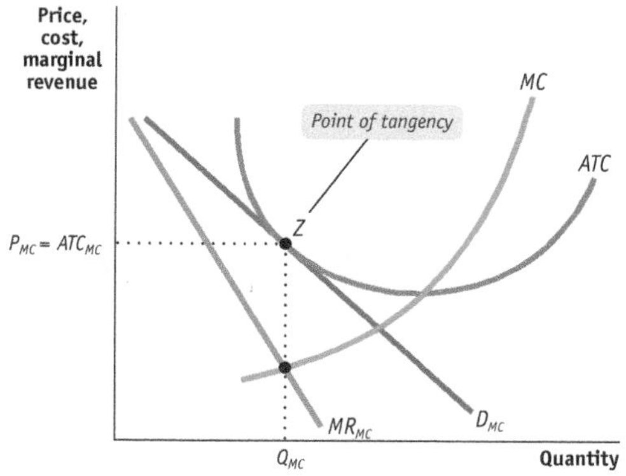

The normal long-run condition of a monopolistically competitive industry, then, is that each producer is in the situation shown in Figure 67.3. Each producer acts like a monopolist, facing a downward-sloping demand curve and setting marginal cost equal to marginal revenue so as to maximize profit. But this is just enough to achieve zero economic profit. The producers in the industry are like monopolists without monopoly profit.

FYI Hits and Flops

On the face of it, the movie business seems to meet the criteria for monopolistic competition. Movies compete for the same consumers; each movie is different from the others; new companies can and do enter the business. But where's the zero-profit equilibrium? After all, some movies are enormously profitable.

The key is to realize that for every successful blockbuster, there are several flops—and that the movie studios don't know in advance which will be which. (One observer of Hollywood summed up his conclusions as follows: "Nobody knows anything.") By the time it becomes clear that a movie will be a flop, it's too late to cancel it.

The difference between movie-making and the type of monopolistic competition we model in this section is that the fixed costs of making a movie are also *sunk costs*—once they've been incurred, they can't be recovered.

Yet there is still, in a way, a zero-profit equilibrium. If movies on average were highly profitable, more studios would enter the industry and more movies would be made. If movies on average lost money, fewer movies would be made. In fact, as you might expect, the movie industry on average earns just about enough to cover the cost of production—that is, it earns roughly zero economic profit.

This kind of situation—in which firms earn zero profit on average but have a mixture of highly profitable hits and money-losing flops—can be found in other industries characterized by high up-front sunk costs. A notable example is the pharmaceutical industry, in which many research projects lead nowhere but a few lead to highly profitable drugs.

AP Photo/Nick Ut

FOCUS Graph It

Figure 67.3 illustrates a monopolistically competitive firm in long-run equilibrium. Because $P = ATC$ (the demand curve is tangent to the *ATC* curve), the firm is earning zero economic profit.

FOCUS Test It

Have students graph a monopolistic competitor in long-run equilibrium. Their graph should look like Figure 67.3. Learning how to show all the required points correctly can be difficult. Provide your class with these two graphing tips: (1) After drawing *D*, *MR*, and *MC* as with the monopoly graph, place a point on the demand curve and a point to the right of and below that point on the *MC* curve. Draw upward to the left from the *MC* curve point, hitting the *D* curve point, and then upward from the *MC* point to the right. (2) Drawing a large point can help the demand curve be tangent to the *ATC* curve!

Module 67 Introduction to Monopolistic Competition 671

Monopolistic Competition Versus Perfect Competition

In a way, long-run equilibrium in a monopolistically competitive industry looks a lot like long-run equilibrium in a perfectly competitive industry. In both cases, there are many firms; in both cases, profits have been competed away; in both cases, the price received by every firm is equal to the average total cost of production.

However, the two versions of long-run equilibrium are different—in ways that are economically significant.

Price, Marginal Cost, and Average Total Cost

Figure 67.4 compares the long-run equilibrium of a typical firm in a perfectly competitive industry with that of a typical firm in a monopolistically competitive industry. Panel (a) shows a perfectly competitive firm facing a market price equal to its minimum average total cost; panel (b) reproduces Figure 67.3. Comparing the panels, we see two important differences.

First, in the case of the perfectly competitive firm shown in panel (a), the price, P_{PC}, received by the firm at the profit-maximizing quantity, Q_{PC}, is equal to the firm's marginal cost of production, MC_{PC}, at that quantity of output. By contrast, at the profit-maximizing quantity chosen by the monopolistically competitive firm in panel (b), Q_{MC}, the price, P_{MC}, is *higher* than the marginal cost of production, MC_{MC}.

FOCUS Graph It

Figure 67.4 compares long-run equilibrium for perfect competition and monopolistic competition. Ask students the following questions about it:

- Is the perfect competitor allocatively efficient? Explain. Yes, $P = MC$.
- Is the perfect competitor productively efficient? Explain. Yes, $P =$ minimum ATC.
- Is the monopolistic competitor allocatively efficient? Explain. No, $P > MC$.
- Is the monopolistic competitor productively efficient? Explain. No, $P \neq$ minimum ATC.

Figure 67.4 Comparing Long-Run Equilibrium in Perfect Competition and Monopolistic Competition

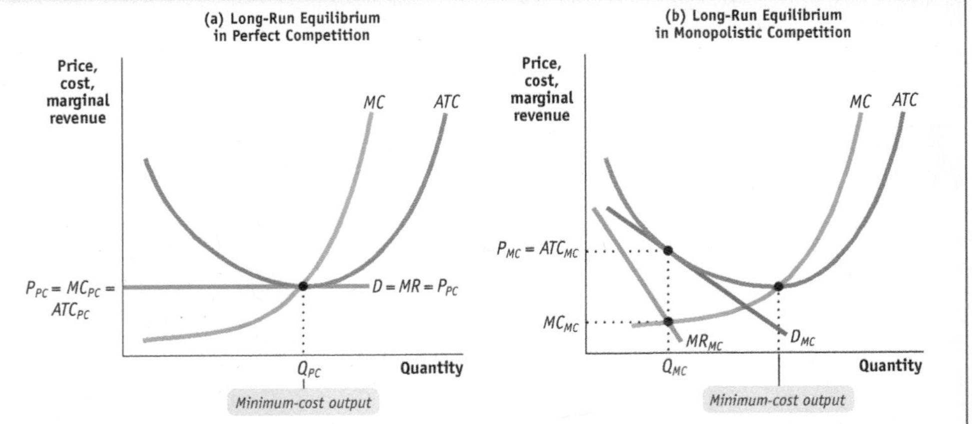

Panel (a) shows the situation of the typical firm in long-run equilibrium in a perfectly competitive industry. The firm operates at the minimum-cost output Q_{PC}, sells at the competitive market price P_{PC}, and makes zero profit. It is indifferent to selling another unit of output because P_{PC} is equal to its marginal cost, MC_{PC}. Panel (b) shows the situation of the typical firm in long-run equilibrium in a monopolistically competitive industry. At Q_{MC} it makes zero profit because its price P_{MC} just equals average total cost, ATC_{MC}. At Q_{MC} the firm would like to sell another unit at price P_{MC} since P_{MC} exceeds marginal cost, MC_{MC}. But it is unwilling to lower the price to make more sales. It therefore operates to the left of the minimum-cost output level and has excess capacity.

672 Section 12 Market Structures: Imperfect Competition

This difference translates into a difference in the attitude of firms toward consumers. A wheat farmer who can sell as much wheat as he likes at the going market price would not get particularly excited if you offered to buy some more wheat at the market price. Since he has no desire to produce more at that price and can sell the wheat to someone else, you are not doing him a favor.

But if you decide to fill up your tank at Jamil's gas station rather than at Katy's, you are doing Jamil a favor. He is not willing to cut his price to get more customers—he's already made the best of that trade-off. If he gets a few more customers than he expected at the posted price, that's good news: an additional sale at the *posted* price increases his revenue more than it increases his cost because the posted price exceeds marginal cost.

The fact that monopolistic competitors, unlike perfect competitors, want to sell more at the going price is crucial to understanding why they engage in activities like advertising that help increase sales.

The other difference between monopolistic competition and perfect competition that is visible in Figure 67.4 involves the position of each firm on its average total cost curve. In panel (a), the perfectly competitive firm produces at point Q_{PC}, at the bottom of the U-shaped *ATC* curve. That is, each firm produces the quantity at which average total cost is minimized—the *minimum-cost output*. As a consequence, the total cost of industry output is also minimized.

Under monopolistic competition, in panel (b), the firm produces at Q_{MC}, on the *downward-sloping* part of the U-shaped *ATC* curve: it produces less than the quantity that would minimize average total cost. This failure to produce enough to minimize average total cost is sometimes described as the **excess capacity** issue. The typical vendor in a food court or a gas station along a road is not big enough to take maximum advantage of available cost savings. So the total cost of industry output is not minimized in the case of a monopolistically competitive industry.

Firms in a monopolistically competitive industry have **excess capacity**: they produce less than the output at which average total cost is minimized.

Some people have argued that, because every monopolistic competitor has excess capacity, monopolistically competitive industries are inefficient. But the issue of efficiency under monopolistic competition turns out to be a subtle one that does not have a clear answer.

Is Monopolistic Competition Inefficient?

A monopolistic competitor, like a monopolist, charges a price that is above marginal cost. As a result, some people who are willing to pay at least as much for an egg roll at Wonderful Wok as it costs to produce it are deterred from doing so. In monopolistic competition, some mutually beneficial transactions go unexploited.

Furthermore, it is often argued that monopolistic competition is subject to a further kind of inefficiency: that the excess capacity of every monopolistic competitor implies *wasteful duplication* because monopolistically competitive industries offer too many varieties. According to this argument, it would be better if there were only two or three vendors in the food court, not six or seven. If there were fewer vendors, they would each have lower average total costs and so could offer food more cheaply.

Is this argument against monopolistic competition right—that it lowers total surplus by causing inefficiency? Not necessarily. It's true that if there were fewer gas stations along a highway, each gas station would sell more gasoline and so would have a lower cost per gallon. But there is a drawback: motorists would be inconvenienced because gas stations would be farther apart. The point is that the diversity of products offered in a monopolistically competitive industry is beneficial to consumers. So the higher price consumers pay because of excess capacity is offset to some extent by the value they receive from greater diversity.

In other words, there is a trade-off: more producers mean higher average total costs but also greater product diversity. Does a monopolistically competitive industry arrive at the socially optimal point in this trade-off? Probably not—but it is hard to say whether there are too many firms or too few! Most economists now believe that duplication of effort and excess capacity in monopolistically competitive industries are not large problems in practice.

AP® Exam Tip

Like monopolists and oligopolists, monopolistically competitive firms are allocatively inefficient both in the short run and in the long run because they charge a price that exceeds the marginal cost.

FOCUS Flip It

TRM Have students watch Jacob Clifford's video "Micro 4.12 Monopolistic Competition—Short Run and Long Run" (see econextras video list with hyperlinks on the bcs and TRFD) and assign **Worksheet 67.3 (Long-Run Monopolistic Competition)** from the TRM for questions about the video.

TEACH Teach It

Monopolistically competitive firms are not allocatively or productively efficient. A term used to describe inefficiency in monopolistic competition is *excess capacity*. The profit-maximizing output for a monopolistically competitive firm is below the output level that minimizes *ATC*. So firms do not produce enough to achieve the maximum cost savings a larger firm would achieve.

FOCUS Test It

The 2004 AP® Microeconomics exam free-response question on monopolistically competitive firms (Question 3) can be found at http://apcentral.collegeboard.com/apc/public/repository/ap04_frq_micro_36233.pdf. Ask students to work individually or in groups. The rubric may be viewed at http://apcentral.collegeboard.com/apc/public/repository/ap04_sg_micro_37001.pdf.

TEACH Teach It

Monopolistic competition is not allocatively or productively inefficient—it results in prices above *MC* and creates excess capacity. But monopolistic competition also provides a benefit to consumers through diversity of products and product differentiation. By providing product variety and alternative locations, monopolistic competitors offset allocative and productive inefficiency.

St. Louis Federal Reserve Bank Resources

The Illustrated Consumer and Producer Surplus

This series of slides aids students in defining and calculating consumer surplus, producer surplus, and total economic surplus.

MODULE 67 Review

Check Your Understanding

1. Suppose a monopolistically competitive industry composed of firms with U-shaped average total cost curves is in long-run equilibrium. For each of the following changes, explain how the industry is affected in the short run and how it adjusts to a new long-run equilibrium.
   a. a technological change that increases fixed cost for every firm in the industry
   b. a technological change that decreases marginal cost for every firm in the industry
2. Why is it impossible for firms in a monopolistically competitive industry to join together to form a monopoly that is capable of maintaining positive economic profit in the long run?
3. Indicate whether the following statements are true or false, and explain your answers.
   a. Like a firm in a perfectly competitive industry, a firm in a monopolistically competitive industry is willing to sell a good at any price that equals or exceeds marginal cost.
   b. Suppose there is a monopolistically competitive industry in long-run equilibrium that possesses excess capacity. All the firms in the industry would be better off if they merged into a single firm and produced a single product, but whether consumers would be made better off by this is ambiguous.
   c. Fads and fashions are more likely to arise in industries characterized by monopolistic competition or oligopoly than in those characterized by perfect competition or monopoly.

Tackle the Test: Multiple-Choice Questions

1. Which of the following is a characteristic of monopolistic competition?
   a. a standardized product
   b. many sellers
   c. substantial barriers to entry
   d. positive long-run profits
   e. a perfectly elastic demand curve
2. Which of the following results is possible for a monopolistic competitor in the short run?
   I. positive economic profit
   II. normal profit
   III. loss
   a. I only
   b. II only
   c. III only
   d. I and II only
   e. I, II, and III
3. Which of the following results is possible for a monopolistic competitor in the long run?
   I. positive economic profit
   II. normal profit
   III. loss
   a. I only
   b. II only
   c. III only
   d. I and II only
   e. I, II, and III
4. Which of the following best describes a monopolistic competitor's demand curve?
   a. upward-sloping
   b. downward-sloping
   c. U-shaped
   d. horizontal
   e. vertical
5. The long-run outcome in a monopolistically competitive industry results in
   a. inefficiency because firms earn positive economic profits.
   b. efficiency due to excess capacity.
   c. inefficiency due to product diversity.
   d. efficiency because price exceeds marginal cost.
   e. a trade-off between higher average total cost and more product diversity.

OPEN & CLOSE Exit Slip

TRM *Please see **Exit Slip: Module 67** in the TRM for formative multiple-choice questions to ask your students before finishing your lesson. These questions will help you quickly assess whether your students have mastered the module's concepts before moving on.*

Answers to the Exit Slip Questions

1. C
2. D
3. B

Answers to Module 67 Review Questions

Check Your Understanding

1. a. An increase in fixed cost shifts the average total cost curve upward. In the short run, firms incur losses because price is below average total cost. In the long run, some firms will exit the industry, resulting in a rightward shift of the demand curves for those firms that remain, since each firm now serves a larger share of the market. Long-run equilibrium is reestablished when the demand curve for each remaining firm has shifted rightward to the point where it is tangent to the firm's new, higher average total cost curve. At this point, each firm's price just equals its average total cost, and each firm makes zero profit.

b. A decrease in marginal cost shifts the average total cost curve and the marginal cost curve downward. In the short run, firms earn positive economic profit. In the long run, new entrants are attracted to the industry by the profit. This results in a leftward shift of each existing firm's demand curve because each firm now has a smaller share of the market. Long-run equilibrium is reestablished when each firm's demand curve has shifted leftward to the point where it is tangent to the new, lower average total cost curve. At this point, each firm's price just equals average total cost, and each firm makes zero profit.

2. If all the existing firms in the industry joined together to create a monopoly, they could achieve positive economic profit in the short run. But this would induce new firms to create new, differentiated products and then enter the industry and capture some of the profit. So, in the long run, thanks to the lack of barriers to entry, it would be impossible to maintain such a monopoly.

3. a. False. As illustrated in panel (b) of Figure 67.4, a monopolistically competitive firm sells its output at a price that exceeds marginal cost—unlike a perfectly competitive firm, which sells at a price equal to marginal cost. Not only does a monopolistically competitive firm maximize profit by charging more than marginal cost, but in long-run equilibrium, a price equal to marginal cost would be below average total cost and cause the firm to incur a loss.

b. True. Firms in a monopolistically competitive industry could achieve higher profit (monopoly profit) if they all joined together as a single firm with a single product. Because each of the smaller firms possesses excess capacity, a single firm producing a larger quantity would have a lower average total cost. The effect on consumers, however, is ambiguous. They would experience less choice. But if consolidation substantially reduced industrywide average total cost and increased industrywide output, consumers could experience lower prices with the monopoly.

c. True. Fads and fashions are promulgated by advertising and a desire for product differentiation, which are common in oligopolies and monopolistically competitive industries, but not in monopolies or perfectly competitive industries.

Tackle the Test: Multiple-Choice Questions

1. b 2. e 3. b 4. b 5. e

Tackle the Test: Free-Response Questions

1. Draw a correctly labeled graph for a monopolistically competitive firm that is taking a loss in the short run. Shade the area that represents the firm's loss.

Rubric for FRQ 1 (7 points)

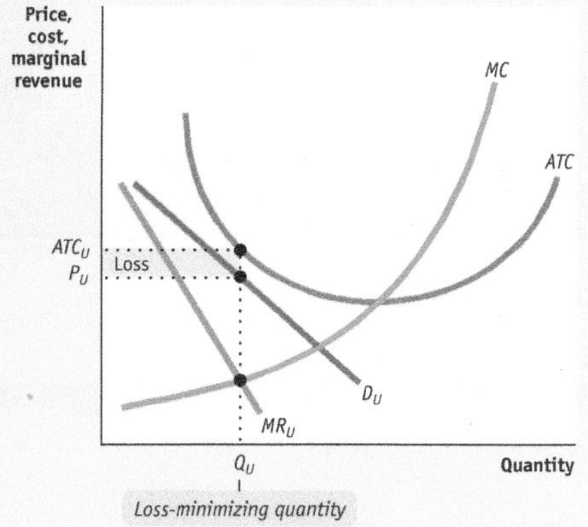

1 point: Correctly labeled axes

1 point: Downward-sloping demand curve

1 point: Marginal revenue curve below the demand curve

1 point: Loss-minimizing quantity below where $MC = MR$

1 point: Loss-minimizing price on demand curve above where $MC = MR$

1 point: U-shaped average total cost curve above the demand curve at every quantity

1 point: Correct loss area shaded

2. Draw a correctly labeled graph for a monopolistically competitive firm in long-run equilibrium. Label the distance along the quantity axis that represents excess capacity.
(6 points)

Tackle the Test: Free-Response Question Rubric for FRQ 2 (6 points)

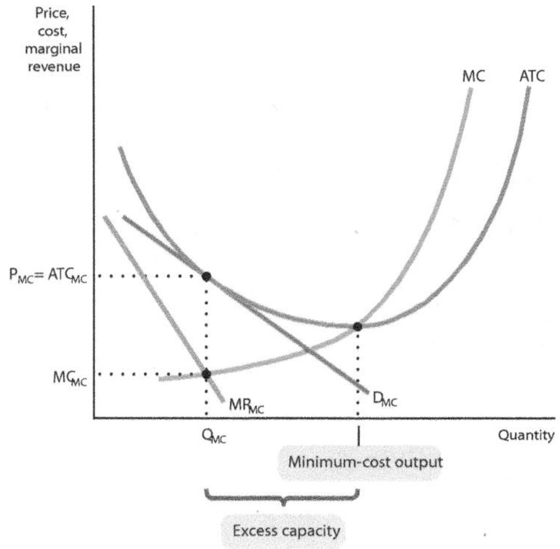

1 point: Correctly labeled axes

1 point: Downward-sloping demand curve and marginal revenue curve below the demand curve

1 point: Quantity below where $MC = MR$

1 point: Price on demand curve above where $MC = MR$

1 point: U-shaped average total cost curve tangent to the demand curve at the firm's price level

1 point: Correct excess capacity distance labeled

PD To prepare for teaching this lesson, you may want to consult the **Module 68 Sample Lecture** in the TRM.

OPEN & CLOSE Start Here

Give students 60 seconds to see how many different fast-food restaurants they can list. Compare and discuss their lists.

TEACH AP® Exam Tip

AP® exam questions do not address advertising to the depth in which it is presented in this module.

TEACH Connect It

Product differentiation is a characteristic of both oligopoly and monopolistic competition.

TEACH Teach It

Since tacit collusion is virtually impossible for monopolistically competitive firms due to the number of producers, product differentiation is the only way firms can acquire market power.

© Robert Landau / Alamy

MODULE 68 Product Differentiation and Advertising

In this Module, you will learn to:

- Explain why oligopolists and monopolistic competitors differentiate their products
- Discuss the economic significance of advertising and brand names

AP® Exam Tip

Product differentiation allows oligopolists and monopolistic competitors to decrease competition, increase market power, and ultimately increase sales.

In Module 66 we saw that product differentiation often plays an important role in oligopolistic industries. In such industries, product differentiation reduces the intensity of competition between firms when tacit collusion cannot be achieved. Product differentiation plays an even more crucial role in monopolistically competitive industries. Because tacit collusion is virtually impossible when there are many producers, product differentiation is the only way monopolistically competitive firms can acquire some market power. In this module, we look at how oligopolists and monopolistic competitors differentiate their products in order to maximize profits.

How Firms Differentiate Their Products

How do firms in the same industry—such as fast-food vendors, gas stations, or chocolate makers—differentiate their products? Sometimes the difference is mainly in the minds of consumers rather than in the products themselves. We'll discuss the role of advertising and the importance of brand names in achieving this kind of product differentiation later. But, in general, firms differentiate their products by—surprise!—actually making them different.

The key to product differentiation is that consumers have different preferences and are willing to pay somewhat more to satisfy those preferences. Each producer can carve out a market niche by producing something that caters to the particular preferences of some group of consumers better than the products of other firms. There are three important forms of product differentiation: differentiation by style or type, differentiation by location, and differentiation by quality.

676 Section 12 Market Structures: Imperfect Competition

Differentiation by Style or Type

The sellers in Leo's food court offer different types of fast food: hamburgers, pizza, Chinese food, Mexican food, and so on. Each consumer arrives at the food court with some preference for one or another of these offerings. This preference may depend on the consumer's mood, her diet, or what she has already eaten that day. These preferences will not make consumers indifferent to price: if Wonderful Wok were to charge $15 for an egg roll, everybody would go to Bodacious Burgers or Pizza Paradise instead. But some people will choose a more expensive meal if that type of food is closer to their preference. So the products of the different vendors are substitutes, but they aren't *perfect* substitutes—they are *imperfect substitutes.*

Vendors in a food court aren't the only sellers who differentiate their offerings by type. Clothing stores concentrate on women's or men's clothes, on business attire or sportswear, on trendy or classic styles, and so on. Auto manufacturers offer sedans, minivans, sport-utility vehicles, and sports cars, each type aimed at drivers with different needs and tastes.

Books offer yet another example of differentiation by type and style. Mysteries are differentiated from romances; among mysteries, we can differentiate among hard-boiled detective stories, whodunits, and police procedurals. And no two writers of hard-boiled detective stories are exactly alike: Raymond Chandler and Sue Grafton each have their devoted fans, for example.

In fact, product differentiation is characteristic of most consumer goods. As long as people differ in their tastes, producers find it possible and profitable to offer variety.

Differentiation by Location

Gas stations along a road offer differentiated products. True, the gas may be exactly the same. But the location of the stations is different, and location matters to consumers: it's more convenient to stop for gas near your home, near your workplace, or near wherever you are when the gas gauge gets low.

In fact, many monopolistically competitive industries supply goods differentiated by location. This is especially true in service industries, from dry cleaners to hairdressers, where customers often choose the seller who is closest rather than cheapest.

Differentiation by Quality

Do you have a craving for chocolate? How much are you willing to spend on it? You see, there's chocolate and then there's chocolate: although ordinary chocolate may not be very expensive, gourmet chocolate can cost several dollars per bite.

Shutterstock

With chocolate, as with many goods, there is a range of possible qualities. You can get a usable bicycle for less than $100; you can get a much fancier bicycle for 10 times as much. It all depends on how much the additional quality matters to you and how much you will miss the other things you could have purchased with that money.

Because consumers vary in what they are willing to pay for higher quality, producers can differentiate their products by quality—some offering lower-quality, inexpensive products and others offering higher-quality products at a higher price.

Product differentiation, then, can take several forms. Whatever form it takes, however, there are two important features of industries with differentiated products: *competition among sellers* and *value in diversity.*

Competition among sellers means that even though sellers of differentiated products are not offering identical goods, they are to some extent competing for a limited market. If more businesses enter the market, each will find that it sells a lower quantity at any given price. For example, if a new gas station opens along a road, each of the existing gas stations will sell a bit less.

TEACH Teach It

There are three key types of product differentiation: style, location, and quality.

FOCUS Active Learning

TRM Ask students to find an article in the media that illustrates market structures using these forms of nonprice competition. Then ask students to answer the questions in **Worksheet 68.1 (Imperfect Competition in the News)** from the TRM.

FOCUS In the News

TRM Assign Nikhil Raheja's article "Hershey: Strong Product Differentiation and Good Key Ratios" at http://seekingalpha.com/article/1448301-hershey-strong-product-differentiation-and-good-key-ratios. Have students read just the first two sections and answer the questions in **Worksheet 68.2 (Hershey)** from the TRM.

FYI Any Color, So Long As It's Black

The early history of the auto industry offers a classic illustration of the power of product differentiation.

The modern automobile industry was created by Henry Ford, who first introduced assembly-line production. This technique made it possible for him to offer the famous Model T at a far lower price than anyone else was charging for a car; by 1920, Ford dominated the automobile business.

Ford's strategy was to offer just one style of car, which maximized his economies of scale in production but made no concessions to differences in consumers' tastes. He supposedly declared that customers could get the Model T in "any color, so long as it's black."

This strategy was challenged by Alfred P. Sloan, who had merged a number of smaller automobile companies into General Motors. Sloan's strategy was to offer a range of car types, differentiated by quality and price. Chevrolets were basic cars that directly challenged the Model T, Buicks were bigger and more expensive, and so on up to Cadillacs. And you could get each model in several different colors.

By the 1930s the verdict was clear: customers preferred a range of styles, and General Motors, not Ford, became the dominant auto manufacturer for the rest of the twentieth century.

Peter Mah/Getty Images

Value in diversity refers to the gain to consumers from the proliferation of differentiated products. A food court with eight vendors makes consumers happier than one with only six vendors, even if the prices are the same, because some customers will get a meal that is closer to what they had in mind. A road on which there is a gas station every two miles is more convenient for motorists than a road where gas stations are five miles apart. When a product is available in many different qualities, fewer people are forced to pay for more quality than they need or to settle for lower quality than they want. In other words, there are benefits to consumers from a greater diversity of available products.

As we'll see next, competition among the sellers of differentiated products is the key to understanding how monopolistic competition works.

Controversies About Product Differentiation

Up to this point, we have assumed that products are differentiated in a way that corresponds to some real desire of consumers. There is real convenience in having a gas station in your neighborhood; Chinese food and Mexican food are really different from each other.

In the real world, however, some instances of product differentiation can seem puzzling if you think about them. What is the real difference between Crest and Colgate toothpaste? Between Energizer and Duracell batteries? Or a Marriott and a Hilton hotel room? Most people would be hard-pressed to answer any of these questions. Yet the producers of these goods make considerable efforts to convince consumers that their products are different from and better than those of their competitors.

No discussion of product differentiation is complete without spending at least a bit of time on the two related issues—and puzzles—of *advertising* and *brand names.*

The Role of Advertising

Wheat farmers don't advertise their wares on TV, but car dealers do. That's not because farmers are shy and car dealers are outgoing; it's because advertising is worthwhile only in industries in which firms have at least some market power. The purpose of advertisements is to persuade people to buy more of a seller's product at the going

678 Section 12 Market Structures: Imperfect Competition

price. A perfectly competitive firm, which can sell as much as it likes at the going market price, has no incentive to spend money persuading consumers to buy more. Only a firm that has some market power, and which therefore charges a price that is above marginal cost, can gain from advertising. (Industries that are more or less perfectly competitive, like the milk industry, do advertise—but these ads are sponsored by an association on behalf of the industry as a whole, not on behalf of a particular farm.)

Given that advertising "works," it's not hard to see why firms with market power would spend money on it. But the big question about advertising is, *why* does it work? A related question is whether advertising, from society's point of view, is a waste of resources.

Not all advertising poses a puzzle. Much of it is straightforward: it's a way for sellers to inform potential buyers about what they have to offer (or, occasionally, for buyers to inform potential sellers about what they want). Nor is there much controversy about the economic usefulness of ads that provide information: the real estate ad that declares "sunny, charming, 2 bedrooms, 1 bath, a/c" tells you things you need to know (even if a few euphemisms are involved—"charming," of course, means "small").

But what information is being conveyed when a TV actress proclaims the virtues of one or another toothpaste or a sports hero declares that some company's batteries are better than those inside that pink mechanical rabbit? Surely nobody believes that the sports star is an expert on batteries—or that he chose the company that he personally believes makes the best batteries, as opposed to the company that offered to pay him the most. Yet companies believe, with good reason, that money spent on such promotions increases their sales—and that they would be in big trouble if they stopped advertising but their competitors continued to do so.

Jim Borgman © Reprinted with special permission of Universal Press/Uclick

Why are consumers influenced by ads that do not really provide any information about the product? One answer is that consumers are not as rational as economists typically assume. Perhaps consumers' judgments, or even their tastes, can be influenced by things that economists think ought to be irrelevant, such as which company has hired the most charismatic celebrity to endorse its product. And there is surely some truth to this. Consumer rationality is a useful working assumption; it is not an absolute truth.

However, another answer is that consumer response to advertising is not entirely irrational because ads can serve as indirect "signals" in a world in which consumers don't have good information about products. To take a common example, suppose that you need to avail yourself of some local service that you don't use regularly—body work on your car, say, or furniture moving. You turn to the Yellow Pages, where you see a number of small listings and several large display ads. You know that those display ads are large because the firms paid extra for them; still, it may be quite rational to call one of the firms with a big display ad. After all, the big ad probably means that it's a relatively large, successful company—otherwise, the company wouldn't have found it worth spending the money for the larger ad.

The same principle may partly explain why ads feature celebrities. You don't really believe that the supermodel prefers that watch; but the fact that the watch manufacturer is willing and able to pay her fee tells you that it is a major company that is likely to stand behind its product. According to this reasoning, an expensive advertisement serves to establish the quality of a firm's products in the eyes of consumers.

The possibility that it is rational for consumers to respond to advertising also has some bearing on the question of whether advertising is a waste of resources. If ads work by manipulating only the weak-minded, the $177 billion U.S. businesses spent on advertising in 2013 would have been an economic waste—except to the extent that ads sometimes provide entertainment. To the extent that advertising conveys important information, however, it is an economically productive activity after all.

AP® Exam Tip

Advertising and brand name development are forms of non-price competition that competitors use to modify consumers' perceptions about their products in order to gain more sales.

TEACH Teach It

Advertising is only possible for firms that have some market power. Perfect competitors have neither the incentive nor the resources to advertise.

Module 68 Product Differentiation and Advertising 679

OPEN & CLOSE Exit Slip

TRM *Please see **Exit Slip: Module 68** in the TRM for formative multiple-choice questions to ask your students before finishing your lesson. These questions will help you quickly assess whether your students have mastered the module's concepts before moving on.*

Answers to the Exit Slip Questions

1. D
2. E
3. C

Answers to Module 68 Review Questions

Check Your Understanding

1. **a.** This type of advertising is likely to be useful because it provides new information on an important product.

b. This type of advertising is likely to be wasteful because it is focused on promoting Bayer aspirin over a rival's aspirin despite the two products being medically indistinguishable.

c. This is useful because the longevity of a business gives a potential customer information about its quality.

2. A successful brand name indicates a desirable attribute, such as quality, to a potential buyer. So, other things equal—such as price—a firm with a successful brand name will achieve higher sales than a rival with a comparable product but without a successful brand name. This is likely to deter new firms from entering an industry in which an existing firm has a successful brand name.

Brand Names

You've been driving all day, and you decide that it's time to find a place to sleep. On your right, you see a sign for the Bates Motel; on your left, you see a sign for a Motel 6, or a Best Western, or some other national chain. Which one do you choose?

Unless they were familiar with the area, most people would head for the chain. In fact, most motels in the United States are members of major chains; the same is true of most fast-food restaurants and many, if not most, stores in shopping malls.

Motel chains and fast-food restaurants are only one aspect of a broader phenomenon: the role of **brand names**, names owned by particular companies that differentiate their products in the minds of consumers. In many cases, a company's brand name is the most important asset it possesses: clearly, McDonald's is worth far more than the sum of the deep-fat fryers and hamburger grills the company owns.

A **brand name** is a name owned by a particular firm that distinguishes its products from those of other firms.

© Jonathan Larsen/Diadem Images/Alamy

In fact, companies often go to considerable lengths to defend their brand names, suing anyone else who uses them without permission. You may talk about blowing your nose on a kleenex or xeroxing a term paper, but unless the product in question comes from Kleenex or Xerox, legally the seller must describe it as a facial tissue or a photocopier.

As with advertising, with which they are closely linked, the social usefulness of brand names is a source of dispute. Does the preference of consumers for known brands reflect consumer irrationality? Or do brand names convey real information? That is, do brand names create unnecessary market power, or do they serve a real purpose?

As in the case of advertising, the answer is probably some of both. On the one hand, brand names often do create unjustified market power. Consumers often pay more for brand-name goods in the supermarket even though consumer experts assure us that the cheaper store brands are equally good. Similarly, many common medicines, like aspirin, are cheaper—with no loss of quality—in their generic form.

On the other hand, for many products the brand name does convey information. A traveler arriving in a strange town can be sure of what awaits in a Holiday Inn or a McDonald's; a tired and hungry traveler may find this preferable to trying an independent hotel or restaurant that might be better—but might be worse.

In addition, brand names offer some assurance that the seller is engaged in repeated interaction with its customers and so has a reputation to protect. If a traveler eats a bad meal at a restaurant in a tourist trap and vows never to eat there again, the restaurant owner may not care, since the chance is small that the traveler will be in the same area again in the future. But if that traveler eats a bad meal at McDonald's and vows never to eat at a McDonald's again, that matters to the company. This gives McDonald's an incentive to provide consistent quality, thereby assuring travelers that quality controls are in place.

MODULE 68 Review

Check Your Understanding

1. For each of the following types of advertising, explain whether it is likely to be useful or wasteful from the standpoint of consumers.
   a. advertisements explaining the benefits of aspirin
   b. advertisements for Bayer aspirin
   c. advertisements that state how long a plumber or an electrician has been in business

2. Some industry analysts have stated that a successful brand name is like a barrier to entry. Explain why this might be true.

680 Section 12 Market Structures: Imperfect Competition

Tackle the Test: Multiple-Choice Questions

1. Which of the following is a form of product differentiation?
   - I. style or type
   - II. location
   - III. quality
   - a. I only
   - b. II only
   - c. III only
   - d. I and II only
   - e. I, II, and III
2. In which of the following market structures will individual firms advertise?
   - I. perfect competition
   - II. oligopoly
   - III. monopolistic competition
   - a. I only
   - b. II only
   - c. III only
   - d. II and III only
   - e. I, II, and III
3. Advertising is an attempt to affect which of the following?
   - a. consumer tastes and preferences
   - b. consumer income
   - c. the price of complements
   - d. the price of substitutes
   - e. input prices
4. Brand names generally serve to
   - a. waste resources.
   - b. decrease firm profits.
   - c. confuse consumers.
   - d. decrease information.
   - e. signal quality.
5. Which of the following is true of advertising expenditures in monopolistic competition? Monopolistic competitors
   - a. will not advertise.
   - b. use only informational advertising.
   - c. always waste resources on advertising.
   - d. attempt to create popular brand names.
   - e. earn long-run profits through advertising.

Tackle the Test: Free-Response Questions

1. Refer to the table below showing the effects of running television commercials on a firm's total revenue. Assume that each commercial costs $1,000 to run.

Number of commercials	*Total revenue*
0	$20,000
1	30,000
2	38,000
3	44,000
4	48,000
5	50,000
6	50,500

   - a. What is the marginal revenue from running the second commercial?
   - b. Should the firm run a third commercial? Explain.
   - c. If the firm has no variable costs aside from the cost of commercials, how many commercials should the firm run to maximize profits? Explain.

Rubric for FRQ 1 (5 points)

1 point: $8,000

1 point: Yes

1 point: Because the marginal revenue of $6,000 exceeds the marginal cost of $1,000

1 point: 5

1 point: Marginal revenue exceeds marginal cost for the first 5 commercials. Marginal revenue is less than marginal cost for the 6th commercial.

2. Explain two ways in which product differentiation can be useful to consumers and two ways in which it can be detrimental to consumers. **(4 points)**

Tackle the Test: Multiple-Choice Questions

1. e
2. d
3. a
4. e
5. d

Tackle the Test: Free-Response Question

Rubric for FRQ 2 (4 points)

1 point: Any one of the following: Product differentiation can provide variety, information through advertising, predictability through branding, and incentives for good quality because firms want to protect their brand image.

1 point: A second item from the list above

1 point: Any one of the following: Product differentiation can involve misleading advertising, brand images that lead customers to pay too much for goods, and an increase in market power (and therefore prices).

1 point: A second item from the list above

Module 68 Product Differentiation and Advertising **681**

FOCUS Flip It

Encourage your students to watch the **Section 12 Review Video**, which was created as a special student review tool and is linked into the e-Book or can be found on the book's companion website.

SECTION 12 Review

Section 12 Review Video

Module 64

1. Many industries are oligopolies, characterized by a small number of **interdependent** sellers. The smallest type of oligopoly, a **duopoly**, has only two sellers, known as **duopolists**. Oligopolies exist for more or less the same reasons that monopolies exist, but in weaker form. They are characterized by imperfect competition: firms compete but possess market power.
2. Predicting the behavior of oligopolists poses something of a puzzle. The firms in an oligopoly could maximize their combined profits by acting as a **cartel**, setting output levels for each firm as if they were a single monopolist; to the extent that firms manage to do this, they engage in **collusion**. But each individual firm has an incentive to produce more than the agreed upon quantity of output—to engage in **noncooperative behavior**. Informal collusion is likely to be easier to achieve in industries in which firms face capacity constraints.

Module 65

3. The situation of interdependence, in which each firm's profit depends noticeably on what other firms do, is the subject of **game theory**. In the case of a game with two players, the **payoff** of each player depends on both its own actions and on the actions of the other; this interdependence can be shown in a **payoff matrix**. Depending on the structure of payoffs in the payoff matrix, a player may have a **dominant strategy**—an action that is always the best regardless of the other player's actions.
4. Some duopolists face a particular type of game known as a **prisoners' dilemma**; if each acts independently on its own interest, the resulting **Nash equilibrium** or **noncooperative equilibrium** will be bad for both.

Module 66

5. Firms that expect to play a game repeatedly tend to engage in **strategic behavior**, trying to influence each other's future actions. A particular strategy that seems to work well in such situations is **tit for tat**, which often leads to **tacit collusion**. In order to limit the ability of oligopolists to collude and act like monopolists, most governments pursue **antitrust policy** designed to make collusion more difficult. In practice, however, tacit collusion is widespread.
6. A variety of factors make tacit collusion difficult: a large number of firms, complex products and pricing, differences in interests, and buyers with bargaining power. When tacit collusion breaks down, there can be a **price war**. Oligopolists try to avoid price wars in various ways, such as through **product differentiation** and through **price leadership**, in which one firm sets prices for the industry. Another approach is **nonprice competition**, such as advertising.

Module 67

7. Monopolistic competition is a market structure in which there are many competing producers, each producing a differentiated product, and there is free entry and exit in the long run.
8. Short-run profits will attract the entry of new firms in the long run. This reduces the quantity each existing producer sells at any given price and shifts its demand curve to the left. Short-run losses will induce exit by some firms in the long run. This shifts the demand curve of each remaining firm to the right.
9. In the long run, a monopolistically competitive industry is in **zero-profit equilibrium**: at its profit-maximizing quantity, the demand curve for each existing firm is tangent to its average total cost curve. There are zero profits in the industry and no entry or exit.
10. In long-run equilibrium, firms in a monopolistically competitive industry sell at a price greater than marginal cost. They also have **excess capacity** because they produce less than the minimum-cost output; as a result, they have higher costs than firms in a perfectly competitive industry. Whether or not monopolistic competition is inefficient is ambiguous because consumers value the product diversity that it creates.

Module 68

11. Product differentiation takes three main forms: style or type, location, or quality. Firms will engage in advertising to increase demand for their products and enhance their market power. Advertising and **brand names** that provide useful information to consumers are valuable to society. Advertisements can be wasteful from a societal standpoint when their only purpose is to create market power.

Key Terms

Interdependence, p. 642	Payoff matrix, p. 648	Tacit collusion, p. 661
Duopoly, p. 642	Prisoners' dilemma, p. 649	Price war, p. 663
Duopolist, p. 642	Dominant strategy, p. 650	Product differentiation, p. 663
Collusion, p. 643	Nash equilibrium, p. 651	Price leadership, p. 664
Cartel, p. 643	Noncooperative equilibrium, p. 651	Nonprice competition, p. 664
Noncooperative behavior, p. 644	Antitrust policy, p. 659	Zero-profit equilibrium, p. 670
Game theory, p. 648	Strategic behavior, p. 660	Excess capacity, p. 673
Payoff, p. 648	Tit for tat, p. 660	Brand name, p. 680

AP® Exam Practice Questions

Multiple-Choice Questions

1. A difference between oligopolists and monopolistic competitors is that only
   a. monopolistic competitors collude.
   b. oligopolists engage in product differentiation.
   c. monopolistic competitors can form a cartel.
   d. oligopolists can earn economic profit in the long run.
   e. monopolistic competitors can incur losses.

2. In studying market structures, economists have observed that when an industry has a relatively large number of firms, the firms are more likely to engage in ________________ and prices are likely be relatively ________________.

a.	collusion	high
b.	noncooperative behavior	low
c.	a dominant strategy	high
d.	strategic behavior	low
e.	tit for tat	high

3 The government would attempt to enforce antitrust policy under which of the following circumstances?
   a. to prevent cartels from agreeing to limit quantities and set prices
   b. to prevent firms' strategic behavior that leads to tacit collusion
   c. to prevent firms' interdependence that leads to tit for tat behavior
   d. to prevent duopolists from engaging in product differentiation that leads to higher prices
   e. to prevent excess capacity because of the unnecessary waste that it creates

4. Government regulators should be concerned with ________________ if firms in an industry have ________________.

a.	designing a prisoners' dilemma	found a Nash equilibrium
b.	encouraging competition	started a price war
c.	instituting a zero-profit equilibrium	low barriers to entry
d.	enforcing antitrust policy	acted as a cartel and not just in tacit collusion
e.	increasing nonprice competition	differentiated their products

5. Brand names can lead to higher prices because
   a. they are a sign that firms have formed a cartel and engaged in collusion.
   b. maximizing profits requires firms to follow a dominant strategy.
   c. a zero-profit equilibrium can be avoided by raising prices to equal the marginal cost.
   d. price leadership occurs when one firm sets a high price and others follow.
   e. they create additional market power for firms even if they provide information.

Answers to Section 12 AP® Exam Practice Questions

Multiple-Choice Questions

1. d
2. b
3. a
4. d
5. e

6. c
7. d
8. c
9. c
10. e
11. e

TEACH Teach It

In the second printing of the student textbook, we modified Question 11 for clarity. Here is the revised question:

11. Suppose the same payoff matrix applies every month. For the current month, Firm X has set low prices and Firm Y has set high prices. If each firm follows a tit for tat strategy, then
   a. Firm X would set high prices next time, earn $500 for one month, and then $200 thereafter.
   b. Firm X would set low prices next time, earn $600 for one month, and then $200 thereafter.
   c. Firm X would set high prices next time, earn $100 for one month, and then $500 the following month.
   d. Firm X would set low prices next time, earn $200 for one month, and then $200 the following month.
   e. Firm X would set high prices next time, earn $100 for one month, and then $600 the following month.

6. Which of the following is the most likely to lead to lower prices in an oligopoly?
   a. the formation of a cartel
   b. tacit collusion
   c. low barriers to entry
   d. price leadership
   e. product differentiation

Use the information and table below to answer Questions 7 and 8.

Suppose that Firm A and Firm B are the only companies that make a common food preservative. The marginal cost of production is zero and the industry demand schedule for the preservative in a typical month is as follows:

Price (per pound)	Quantity demanded (millions of pounds)
$6	0
$5	10
$4	20
$3	30
$2	40
$1	50
$0	60

7. If the two companies agree to each produce half of the quantity that maximizes their combined profits and to share the revenue equally, what is the dollar amount (in millions) of revenue that each firm collects?
   a. $100
   b. $90
   c. $50
   d. $45
   e. $40

8. Suppose Firm A continues to honor the production agreement from Question 7 while Firm B breaks it and produces more. Now what is the maximum dollar amount (in millions) that Firm B would collect?
   a. $100
   b. $90
   c. $50
   d. $45
   e. $40

Suppose a breakfast cereal market consists of only two firms, Firm X and Firm Y. Each firm sets either high prices or low prices for one month at a time. Use the information on each firm's monthly profit in the payoff matrix below to answer Questions 9–12.

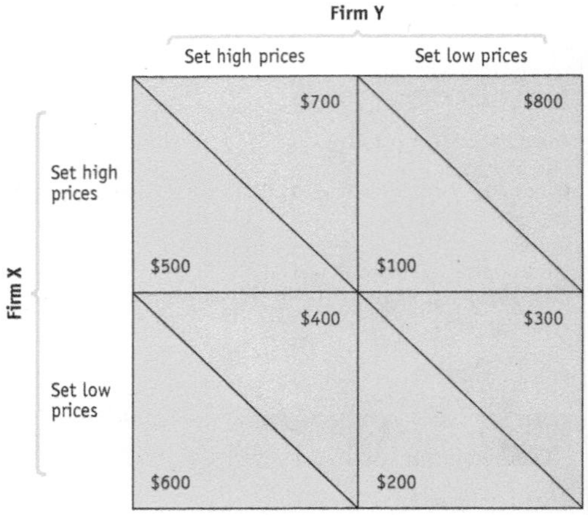

9. Which of the following statements is true?
   a. Firm X and Firm Y are engaged in a prisoners' dilemma.
   b. At the noncooperative equilibrium, the total profits for both firms combined are equal to $1,200.
   c. At the Nash equilibrium, the total profits for both firms combined are equal to $1,000.
   d. At the noncooperative equilibrium, the total profits for both firms combined are equal to $900.
   e. At the Nash equilibrium, the total profits for both firms combined are equal to $500.

10. Which of the following accurately describes the dominant strategies of Firm X and Firm Y?

	Dominant strategy for Firm X	*Dominant strategy for Firm Y*
a.	high prices	high prices
b.	high prices	low prices
c.	low prices	high prices
d.	low prices	low prices
e.	low prices	no dominant strategy

11. Suppose the same payoff matrix applies every month. For the current month, Firm X has set low prices and Firm Y has set high prices. If each firm follows a tit for tat strategy, then
   a. Firm X would set high prices next time, earn $500 for one month, and then $200 thereafter.
   b. Firm X would set low prices next time, earn $600 for one month, and then $200 thereafter.

c. Firm X would set high prices next time, earn $100 for one month, and then $500 the following month.
d. Firm X would set low prices next time, earn $200 for one month, and then $200 the following month.
e. Firm X would set high prices next time, earn $100 for one month, and then $600 the following month.

12. Suppose all the profit payoffs for Firm X double, but they remain the same for Firm Y. Which of the following is a true statement?
a. The noncooperative equilibrium would remain the same.
b. The dominant strategy would change for Firm X but remain the same for Firm Y.
c. The Nash equilibrium would also double.
d. Firm Y would be more likely to engage in a tit for tat strategy.
e. Both firms would be more likely to engage in tacit collusion.

13. Which of the following works in favor of tacit collusion in an oligopolistic industry?
a. The bargaining power of large buyers can keep prices low.
b. Over time, firms realize it is in their best interest to collectively restrict output.
c. Selling thousands of products makes it hard to keep track of competitors' output and prices.
d. With a larger number of sellers, there is less incentive for any one firm to cooperate.
e. The threat of enforcement of antitrust policy is always present.

14. Which of the following business tactics are ways that firms in an oligopolistic industry attempt to legally collude?
I. engaging in nonprice competition
II. utilizing price leadership for signaling
III. following the actions of others in a price war
a. I & II
b. II only
c. II & III
d. III only
e. I, II, & III

15. In a monopolistically competitive soda industry, assume the following facts: a typical firm produces 10,000 beverage cans in a month; the price per can is $1.00; average total cost is $0.50 at the current production level, and marginal cost is $0.25 at the current production level. What will happen to the equilibrium quantity and profits for a typical firm in the soda industry in the long run?

	Equilibrium quantity for a typical firm	*Profits for a typical firm*
a.	increase	decrease
b.	decrease	remain the same
c.	remain the same	increase
d.	decrease	decrease
e.	decrease	increase

16. Economists have argued that there may be inefficiencies in industries that are monopolistically competitive. Which of the following are some of the reasons cited for this inefficiency?
I. Prices are set above marginal cost.
II. There is excess capacity at current production levels.
III. There are zero profits in the long run.
a. I & II
b. II only
c. II & III
d. III only
e. I, II, & III

Use the following graph of a typical firm in a monopolistically competitive industry for Questions 17–19.

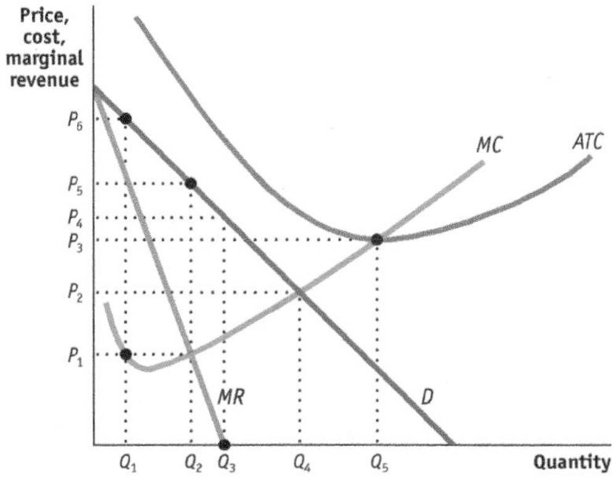

17. What price and quantity combination would we expect from a profit-maximizing firm in this monopolistically competitive industry?
a. P_6, Q_1
b. P_5, Q_2
c. P_4, Q_3
d. P_3, Q_5
e. P_2, Q_4

18. Firms in this industry are earning ____________ and over time we would expect these profits or losses to ____________.

a.	economic losses	remain the same
b.	economic profits	increase
c.	economic losses	decrease
d.	economic profits	decrease
e.	economic losses	increase

12. a
13. b
14. b
15. d
16. a
17. b
18. c

Section 12 Review 685

19. a

20. e

Rubric for Free-Response Question 1

1 point: Graph with "Price, cost, marginal revenue" or "$ per unit" on the vertical axis and "Quantity of hot dogs" on the horizontal axis. The average total cost curve is U-shaped and the marginal cost curve is swoosh-shaped.

1 point: Downward-sloping demand curve with the marginal revenue curve below it

1 point: The quantity below the intersection of marginal cost and marginal revenue is labeled 10,000 and the price at the height of the demand curve at the equilibrium quantity is labeled $3.00.

1 point: Profit $= (P - ATC) \times Q = (\$3 - \$1) \times 10{,}000 = \$20{,}000$

1 point: The rectangle $(P - ATC) \times Q$ is shaded, as shown in the graph.

1 point: Price and quantity remain the same.

1 point: The license fee is a lump-sum tax and therefore a fixed and sunk cost that does not affect marginal cost, marginal revenue, or demand—the two determinants of price and quantity. The exception would be if the license fee caused a firm to close, but that does not occur in this case because the firm earns a normal profit after paying the tax.

1 point: The average total cost curve shifts up to the point of tangency with the demand curve (while the other curves remain the same).

1 point: The number of hot dog stands will remain the same.

1 point: A typical stand earns zero economic profit with the license fee and thus is in long-run equilibrium—there is no incentive for exit or entry.

Please see page SG-5 for a sample student graph for this Free-Response Question.

19. Over time, what will happen to the number of firms in this industry and the output per firm?

	Number of firms in the industry	*Output per firm*
a.	decrease	increase
b.	increase	decrease
c.	decrease	decrease
d.	increase	increase
e.	decrease	remain the same

20. Which of the following is NOT an example of product differentiation?

a. a clothing store that advertises jean jackets that will make anyone cool
b. a grocery store that chooses to locate closer to customers than a competing grocer
c. a chef who chooses to put arugula and spinach on his hamburgers
d. a coffee house that offers drinks made from Fair Trade coffee beans
e. a farmer who doesn't advertise his watermelons because consumers already know that watermelon tastes better than other produce

Free-Response Questions

1. The hot dog stand industry in Frankland is monopolistically competitive. A typical stand produces and sells 10,000 hot dogs during the summer season. For that stand, the price per hot dog is $3.00, the average total cost is $1.00 at the current production level, and the marginal cost is $0.50 at the current production level.

a. Draw a correctly labeled graph of this typical hot dog stand under current market conditions, labeling the equilibrium quantity and the equilibrium price with the numbers provided.
b. Calculate the economic profit or loss for the typical hot dog stand.
c. On your graph from part a, shade in the area of the profit or loss.

Now assume that the government imposes a $20,000 lump sum license fee for the summer season.

d. What happens to the price and quantity for the typical hot dog stand as a result of the license fee? Explain.
e. Show the impact of the license fee on the graph from part a and provide a clear label for anything that changed.
f. What will happen to the number of hot dog stands over the course of the season? Explain.
(10 points)

2. The following diagram shows the pricing strategies and payoffs for the two bubble gum firms in town.

		Long Lasting Flavor Co.	
		Set high prices	Set low prices
Big Bubble Co.	Set high prices	$250 / $400	$350 / $200
	Set low prices	$100 / $500	$50 / $150

a. Does Big Bubble Co. have a dominant strategy? Explain.
b. Does Long Lasting Flavor Co. have a dominant strategy? Explain.
c. Does this situation have any Nash equilibria? Explain.
(6 points)

Rubric for Free-Response Question 2

1 point: There is no dominant strategy for Big Bubble Co.

1 point: The best strategy for Big Bubble Co. depends on the strategy chosen by Long Lasting Flavor Co.

1 point: There is no dominant strategy for Long Lasting Flavor Co.

1 point: The best strategy for Long Lasting Flavor Co. depends on the strategy chosen by Big Bubble Co.

1 point: There are 2 Nash equilibria: (1) Big Bubble Co. sets high prices and Long Lasting Flavor Co. sets low prices; and (2) Big Bubble Co. sets low prices and Long Lasting Flavor Co. sets high prices.

1 point: These combinations of strategies are Nash equilibria because in each case, neither firm has an incentive to change its pricing decision given what its competitor is doing.

686 Section 12 Market Structures: Imperfect Competition

NOTES

SECTION 13

Factor Markets

PD Section 13 Overview

Watch the video overview of Section 13 (for teachers), which is accessible through the Teacher's e-Book, the TR-flash drive, or the book's website, bcs.worthpublishers.com/krugmanap2e *(teacher log-in required).*

Section 13 introduces the markets for the factors of production (land, labor, and capital). The basic framework of supply and demand studied in Section 2 is applied to the market for inputs. The discussion of input markets also includes the cost-minimizing input combination, analogous to the optimal consumption rule discussed in Section 9. Finally, the section discusses alternative theories of income distribution.

Topics that your students will study in Section 13 are:

- the definition of physical and human capital.
- the derived demand for factors of production.
- the factor distribution of income between land, labor, capital, and entrepreneurship.
- marginal productivity and the *MP* curve.
- the *MRP* and factor demand curves.
- shifts in the factor demand curve.
- supply and demand in the markets for land and capital.
- marginal productivity theory.
- the labor supply curve, individual and market.
- equilibrium in the labor market.
- perfectly competitive and imperfectly competitive labor markets.
- the cost-minimizing input combination and the optimal input mix.
- theories of income distribution.

Alignment to AP® Microeconomics Course Description

Microeconomics III. Factor Markets: 10–18%

AP® Outline	Module
A. Derived factor demand	69: Introduction and Factor Demand
B. Marginal revenue product	69: Introduction and Factor Demand
C. Hiring decisions in the markets for labor and capital	70: The Markets for Land and Capital 71: The Market for Labor 72: The Cost-Minimizing Input Combination
D. Market distribution of income	73: Theories of Income Distribution

Pacing Guide

Module	Standard Teaching Days	Block Teaching Days
69	1	½
70	½	½
71	2	1
72	1	½
73	1	½
Section 13 Assessment	1	½
Total	**6½**	**3½**

TRM Section Resources

All section resources may be accessed through the Teacher's e-Book, the TR-flash drive, or the book's website bcs.worthpublishers.com/krugmanap2e *(teacher log-in required).*

Section 13 PD Video (for teachers)

Module 69

Module 69 Sample Lecture

Worksheet 69.1: Resources

Worksheet 69.2: Hiring Workers

Worksheet 69.3: Value of the Marginal Product

Worksheet 69.4: Changes in Factor Demand

Exit Slip: Module 69

Module 70

Module 70 Sample Lecture

Worksheet 70.1: Fixed Factors

Worksheet 70.2: Compensation

Exit Slip: Module 70

Module 71

Module 71 Sample Lecture

Worksheet 71.1: Thinking About the Supply of Labor

Worksheet 71.2: Perfectly Competitive Labor Markets

Worksheet 71.3: Resource Markets, *MRP*, and *MRC*

Worksheet 71.4: How Many Workers to Hire?

Worksheet 71.5: Graphing Perfectly Competitive Labor Markets

Worksheet 71.6: Imperfectly Competitive Labor Markets

Exit Slip: Module 71

Module 72

Module 72 Sample Lecture

Worksheet 72.1: Cost Minimization

Exit Slip: Module 72

Module 73

Module 73 Sample Lecture

Worksheet 73.1: Efficiency Wages

Exit Slip: Module 73

Section 13 Review Video (for students)

St. Louis Federal Reserve Bank Resources

Many of the Federal Reserve Banks have educational departments that offer helpful resources for studying economics. Members of the Educators Advisory Board of the St. Louis Federal Reserve Bank have handpicked some of their best resources for use with your AP® Economics students. References to these resources are included in the marginal notes. A complete list of the St. Louis Fed resources for each section with the corresponding URL (as of fall 2014) can be found in the TRM.

NOTE We have included a number of links to useful videos and articles in the margin notes in this section. Although all are active at the time of publication, we know that some may expire over the next few years. If a link is no longer active, you may wish to search for a similar article or video to illustrate the point. We may also periodically refresh resources on the book's companion website.

NOTES

SECTION 13

Factor Markets

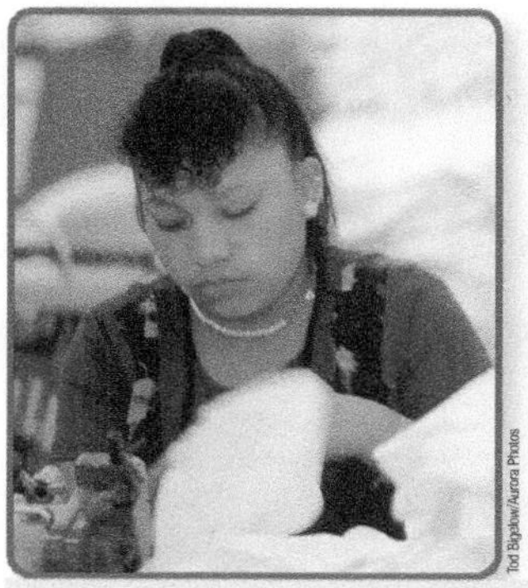

If you've ever had doubts about attending college, consider this: factory workers with only high school degrees will make much less than college grads. The present discounted value of the difference in lifetime earnings is as much as $1 million.

From Whence Wages Arise

Does higher education pay? Yes, it does: In the modern economy, employers are willing to pay a premium for workers with more education. And the size of that premium has increased a lot over the last few decades. Back in 1973 workers with advanced degrees, such as law degrees or MBAs, earned only 76% more than those who had only graduated from high school. By 2013, the premium for an advanced degree had risen to over 113%.

Who decided that the wages of workers with advanced degrees would rise so much compared with those of high school grads? The answer, of course, is that nobody decided it. Wage rates are prices, the prices of different kinds of labor; and they are decided, like other prices, by supply and demand.

Still, there is a qualitative difference between the wage rate of high school grads and the price of used textbooks: the wage rate isn't the price of a *good*; it's the price of a *factor of production*. And although markets for factors of production are in many ways similar to those for goods, there are also some important differences.

In this section, we examine *factor markets*, the markets in which the factors of production such as labor, land, and capital are traded. Factor markets, like goods markets, play a crucial role in the economy: they allocate productive resources to firms and help ensure that those resources are used efficiently.

Shakespeare wrote that "all friends shall taste the wages of their virtue." This section concludes with a module focused on the *marginal productivity theory of income distribution*, which qualifies Shakespeare's prediction with insights about the wages workers "taste." How do they compare with the lowest wages that workers would accept? How do they compare with the workers' contributions to revenue? And what controversies surround the markets for labor among other factors of production? Read on, or as Shakespeare said, "O, see, see!"

PD Section 13 Overview

Watch the video overview of Section 13 (for teachers), which is accessible through the Teacher's e-Book, the TR-flash drive, or the book's companion website bcs.worthpublishers.com/krugmanap2e (teacher log-in required).

FOCUS Active Learning

Students can read Chapter 30 of *Economics by Example* to learn about the costs and benefits of immigration.

PD To prepare for teaching this lesson, you may want to consult the **Module 69 Sample Lecture** in the TRM.

OPEN & CLOSE Start Here

To kick off the study of factor markets, have your students consider the following question: "What do you think is the most important price you will encounter throughout your life?" *Answers may vary, but the one answer you want to guide them to is "the price of my labor."*

TEACH Connect It

This is a good place to review the definition of the factors of production from Section 1:

- Labor—work done by human beings
- Land—resources provided by nature
- Capital—physical: equipment, machines, buildings, and tools; human: improved labor through education and training
- Entrepreneurship—innovation and risk-taking activities by a person who brings together ideas leading to production

TEACH AP® Exam Tip

In different models, land, labor, capital, and entrepreneurship are called inputs, resources, or factors of production. Students may see these alternative descriptors on the AP® exam when referring to land, labor, capital, and entrepreneurship.

Digital Vision

MODULE 69

Introduction and Factor Demand

In this Module, you will learn to:

- Describe features that make markets for factors of production—resources like labor, land, and capital—different from goods markets
- Explain how factor markets determine the factor distribution of income
- Discuss how the demand for a factor of production is determined

AP® Exam Tip

The factors of production are sometimes referred to as inputs on the AP® exam.

The Economy's Factors of Production

You may recall that we have already defined a factor of production in the context of the circular-flow diagram: it is any resource that is used by firms to produce goods and services. To help distinguish factors of production from goods and services, remember that goods and services are consumed by households, but factors of production are not. The markets in which factors of production are bought and sold are called *factor markets*, and the prices in factor markets are known as *factor prices*.

What are these factors of production, and why do factor prices matter?

The Factors of Production

Physical capital—often referred to simply as "capital"—consists of manufactured productive resources such as equipment, buildings, tools, and machines.

Human capital is the improvement in labor created by education and knowledge that is embodied in the workforce.

Economists divide factors of production into four principal classes. The first is *labor*, the work done by human beings. The second is *land*, which encompasses resources provided by nature. The third is capital, which can be divided into two categories: **physical capital**—often referred to simply as "capital"—consists of manufactured productive resources such as equipment, buildings, tools, and machines. In the modern economy, **human capital**, the improvement in labor created by education and knowledge, and embodied in the workforce, is at least equally significant. Technological progress has boosted the importance of human capital and made technical sophistication essential to many jobs, thus helping to create the premium for workers with advanced degrees. The final factor of production, *entrepreneurship*, is a unique resource that is not purchased in an easily identifiable factor market like the other three. It refers to innovation and risk-taking activities that bring together resources for production.

688 Section 13 Factor Markets

Why Factor Prices Matter: The Allocation of Resources

The factor prices determined in factor markets play a vital role in the important process of allocating resources among firms.

Consider the example of Mississippi and Louisiana in the aftermath of Hurricane Katrina, the costliest hurricane ever to hit the U.S. mainland. The states had an urgent need for workers in the building trades—everything from excavation to roofing—to repair or replace damaged structures. What ensured that those needed workers actually came? The factor market: the high demand for workers drove up wages. During 2005, the average U.S. wage grew at a rate of around 6%. But in areas heavily affected by Katrina, the average wage during the fall of 2005 grew by 30% more than the national rate, and some areas saw twice that rate of increase. Over time, these higher wages led large numbers of workers with the right skills to move temporarily to these states to do the work.

In other words, the market for a factor of production—construction workers—allocated that factor of production to where it was needed.

In the months after Hurricane Katrina, home repair signs like these were abundant throughout New Orleans.

In this sense factor markets are similar to goods markets, which allocate goods among consumers. But there are two features that make factor markets special. Unlike in a goods market, demand in a factor market is what we call **derived demand**. That is, demand for the factor is derived from demand for the firm's output. The second feature is that factor markets are where most of us get the largest shares of our income (government transfers being the next largest source of income in the economy).

The demand for a factor is a **derived demand**. It results from (that is, it is derived from) the demand for the output being produced.

Factor Incomes and the Distribution of Income

Most American families get the majority of their income in the form of wages and salaries—that is, they get their income by selling labor. Some people, however, get most of their income from physical capital: when you own stock in a company, what you really own is a share of that company's physical capital. Some people get much of their income from rents earned on land they own. And successful entrepreneurs earn income in the form of profit.

Obviously, then, the prices of factors of production have a major impact on how the economic "pie" is sliced among different groups. For example, a higher wage rate, other things equal, means that a larger proportion of the total income in the economy goes to people who derive their income from labor and less goes to those who derive their income from capital, land, or entrepreneurship. Economists refer to how the economic pie is sliced as the "distribution of income." Specifically, factor prices determine the **factor distribution of income**—how the total income of the economy is divided among labor, land, capital, and entrepreneurship.

The factor distribution of income in the United States has been quite stable over the past few decades. In other times and places, however, large changes have taken place in the factor distribution. One notable example: during the Industrial Revolution, the share of total income earned by landowners fell sharply, while the share earned by capital owners rose.

The **factor distribution of income** is the division of total income among land, labor, capital, and entrepreneurship.

TEACH Connect It

In macroeconomics, the circular-flow model included both product and factor markets. The factors of production, land, labor, and capital are traded in factor markets. As we first saw in the production possibilities model, the factors of production are labor, land, capital, and entrepreneurship. They are used by firms to produce goods and services. The payments for the factors of production are wages, rent, interest, and profit.

FOCUS Active Learning

TRM You may want to assign Dr. Mary J. McGlasson's video "Episode 3: Resources" (see econextras video list with hyperlinks on the bcs and TRFD) and then have your students answer the questions in **Worksheet 69.1 (Resources)** from the TRM.

TEACH Teach It

Students need to understand that the demand in factor markets is a *derived* demand—that is, the demand for factors of production is derived from (comes from) the demand for the output they produce. For example, firms do not demand labor because they like to have workers around the factory. They demand labor because there is a demand for what the workers produce. Firms demand labor so that they can produce output and sell it to earn a profit.

St. Louis Federal Reserve Bank Resources

"Factors of Production," *The Economic Lowdown Podcast Series*, Episode 2

The second episode of the podcast series, *The Economic Lowdown*, discusses the building blocks of the economy, the factors of production.

"Factors of Production," *Economic Short Takes*

The *Economic Short Takes* features showcase the winning submissions on factors of production to the 2010 National Economic Education Video Contest. First Place: What Are the Four Factors of Production?; Second Place: Four Factors of Economic Production; Third Place: Factors of Production.

St. Louis Federal Reserve Bank Resources

"Invest in Yourself," *It's Your Paycheck! Curriculum Unit*, Lesson 1

In this lesson, students are divided into groups to produce name tents. Each of four groups in the classroom produce name tents in a different way to highlight different levels of human capital.

FOCUS Graph It

Factor distribution of income shows us how the total income of the economy is divided among labor, land, capital, and entrepreneurship. Figure 69.1 illustrates the factor distribution of income in the United States in 2013. Ask students which factor receives the greatest portion of income. *Labor*

TEACH Teach It

When labor is the only variable factor (and other inputs are fixed), the additional output produced by hiring additional labor is called the marginal product of labor:

$$MPL = \frac{\Delta \text{Output}}{\Delta \text{Labor}}$$

The Factor Distribution of Income in the United States

When we talk about the factor distribution of income, what are we talking about in practice?

In the United States, as in all advanced economies, payments to labor account for most of the economy's total income. **Figure 69.1** shows the factor distribution of income in the United States in 2013: in that year, 69.2% of total income in the economy took the form of "compensation of employees"—a number that includes both

Figure 69.1 Factor Distribution of Income in the United States in 2013

In 2013, compensation of employees accounted for most income earned in the United States—69.2% of the total. Most of the remainder—consisting of earnings paid in the form of interest, corporate profits, and rent—went to owners of physical capital. Finally, proprietors' income—10.5% of the total—went to individual owners of businesses as compensation for their labor, entrepreneurship, and capital expended in their businesses.

Source: Bureau of Economic Analysis.

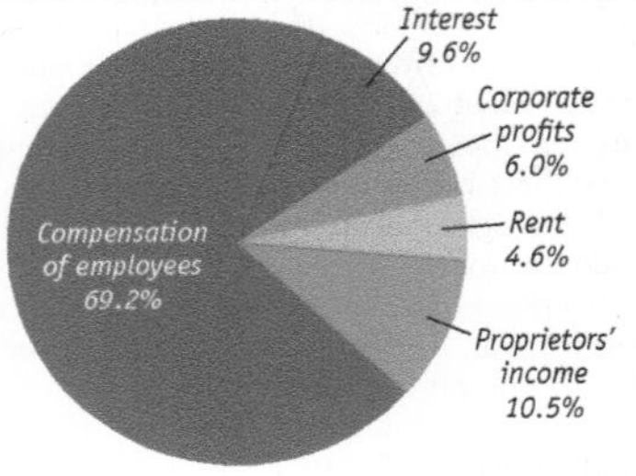

wages and benefits such as health insurance. This number has been quite stable over the long run; 41 years earlier, in 1972, compensation of employees was very similar, at 72.2% of total income.

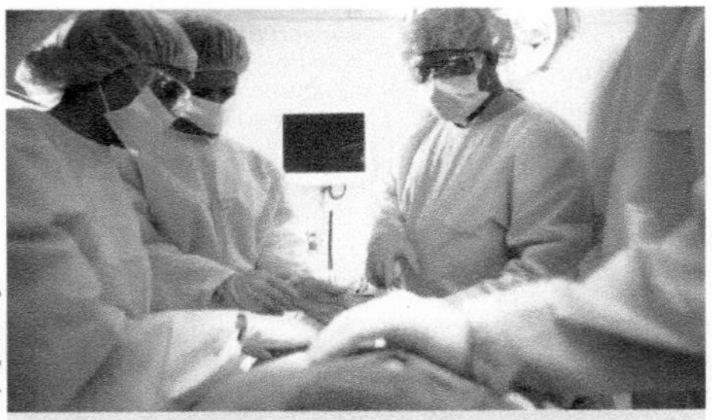
The income of surgeons is largely a return on human capital.

Much of what we call compensation of employees is really a return on human capital. A surgeon isn't just supplying the services of a pair of ordinary hands (at least the patient hopes not!): that individual is also supplying the result of many years and hundreds of thousands of dollars invested in training and experience. We can't directly measure what fraction of wages is really a payment for education and training, but many economists believe that labor resources created through additional human capital have become *the* most important factor of production in modern economies.

Marginal Productivity and Factor Demand

All economic decisions are about comparing costs and benefits—and usually about comparing marginal costs and marginal benefits. This goes both for a consumer, deciding whether to buy more goods or services, and for a firm, deciding whether to hire an additional worker.

AP® Exam Tip

In factor markets, firms are the buyers of inputs and households are the sellers of inputs. The principles that guide the factor and product markets are similar, making the factor market easier to understand.

Although there are some important exceptions, most factor markets in the modern American economy are perfectly competitive. This means that most buyers and sellers of factors are price-takers because they are too small relative to the market to do anything but accept the market price. And in a competitive labor market, it's clear how to define the marginal cost an employer pays for a worker: it is simply the worker's wage rate. But what is the marginal benefit of that worker? To answer that question, we

690 Section 13 Factor Markets

return to the production function, which relates inputs to output. We begin by examining a firm that is a price-taker in the output market—that is, it operates in a perfectly competitive industry.

Marginal Revenue Product

Figure 69.2 shows the production function for wheat on George and Martha's farm, as introduced in Module 54. Panel (a) uses the total product curve to show how total wheat production depends on the number of workers employed on the farm; panel (b) shows how the *marginal product of labor*, the increase in output from employing one more worker, depends on the number of workers employed. **Table 69.1** on the next page shows the numbers behind the figure. Note: sometimes the marginal product (*MP*) is called the *marginal physical product* or *MPP*. These two terms are the same; the extra "P" just emphasizes that the term refers to the quantity of physical output being produced, not the monetary value of that output.

Figure 69.2 The Production Function for George and Martha's Farm

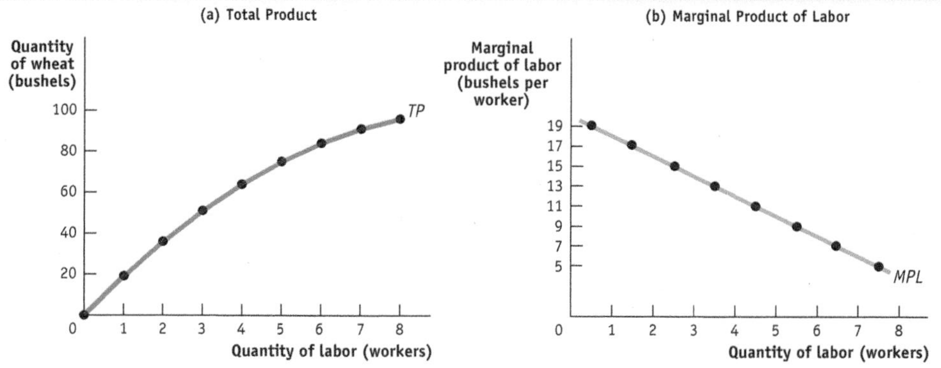

Panel (a) shows how the quantity of output of wheat on George and Martha's farm depends on the number of workers employed. Panel (b) shows how the marginal product of labor depends on the number of workers employed.

If workers are paid $200 each and George and Martha can sell an unlimited amount of wheat for $20 per bushel, how many workers should George and Martha employ to maximize profit?

Earlier we showed how to answer this question in several steps. First, we used information from the production function to derive the firm's total cost and its marginal cost. Then we used the *price-taking firm's optimal output rule*: a price-taking firm's profit is maximized by producing the quantity of output at which the marginal cost is equal to the market price. Having determined the optimal quantity of output, we went back to the production function to find the optimal number of workers—which was simply the number of workers needed to produce the optimal quantity of output.

As you might have guessed, marginal analysis provides a more direct way to find the number of workers that maximizes a firm's profit. This alternative approach is just a different way of looking at the same thing. But it gives us more insight into the demand for factors as opposed to the supply of goods.

FOCUS Graph It

Figure 69.2 illustrates a total product curve and a marginal product curve.

- Panel (a) in Figure 69.2, reproduced from Module 54, shows a total product curve.
- Panel (b) shows the marginal product curve associated with the total product curve in panel (a).
- The *MP* curve shows the additional output produced as a result of hiring additional workers.

Module 69 Introduction and Factor Demand **691**

FOCUS Graph It

Students can see how the value of the marginal product of labor is determined in Table 69.1. Make sure they note that the *MP* curve in Figure 69.2 plots values shown in Table 69.1.

FOCUS Test It

Ask students:

- What is the term for the additional output that results from hiring additional workers and how is it determined? *Marginal product; by finding the change in total product and dividing by the change in the number of workers*
- What is the term for the additional revenue generated by employing one more unit of labor and how is it calculated? *Marginal revenue product of labor = MPL × MR*
- How does the firm decide whether to continue to hire more workers? *It will hire workers as long as the marginal benefit from hiring another worker (MRPL) is greater than the cost of hiring another worker (W).*
- At what point will the firm stop hiring additional workers? *The firm will continue to hire workers up to the point where MRPL = W.*

Table 69.1 Employment and Output for George and Martha's Farm

Quantity of labor L (workers)	Quantity of wheat Q (bushels)	Marginal product of labor $MPL = \frac{\Delta Q}{\Delta L}$ (bushels per worker)
0	0	
		19
1	19	
		17
2	36	
		15
3	51	
		13
4	64	
		11
5	75	
		9
6	84	
		7
7	91	
		5
8	96	

To see how this alternative approach works, suppose that George and Martha are deciding whether to employ another worker. The increase in *cost* from employing another worker is the wage rate, W, at which the firm can hire any number of workers in a perfectly competitive labor market. The *benefit* to George and Martha from employing another worker is the additional revenue gained from the hire. To determine the change in revenue, we can multiply the marginal product of labor, MPL, by the marginal revenue received from selling the additional output, MR. This amount—the additional revenue generated by employing one more unit of labor—is known as the **marginal revenue product** of labor, or $MRPL$:

The **marginal revenue product** of a factor is the additional revenue generated by employing one more unit of that factor.

$$\textbf{(69-1)} \quad \text{Marginal revenue product of labor} = MRPL = MPL \times MR$$

So should George and Martha hire another worker? Yes, if the resulting increase in revenue exceeds the cost of the additional worker—that is, if $MRPL > W$. Otherwise, they should not.

The hiring decision is made using marginal analysis, by comparing the marginal benefit from hiring another worker ($MRPL$) with the marginal cost (W). And as with any decision that is made on the margin, the optimal choice is made by equating marginal benefit with marginal cost (or if they're never equal, by continuing to hire until the marginal cost of one more unit would exceed the marginal benefit). So to maximize profit, George and Martha will employ workers up to the point at which, for the last worker employed,

$$\textbf{(69-2)} \quad MRPL = W.$$

This rule isn't limited to labor; it applies to any factor of production. The marginal revenue product of any factor is its marginal product times the marginal revenue received from the good it produces. And as a general rule, profit-maximizing, price-taking firms will keep adding more units of each factor of production until the marginal revenue product of the last unit employed is equal to the factor's price.

This rule is consistent with our previous analysis. We saw that a profit-maximizing firm chooses the level of output at which the marginal revenue of the good it produces equals the marginal cost of producing that good. It turns out that if the level of output is chosen so that marginal revenue equals marginal cost, then it is also true that with the amount of labor required to produce that output level, the marginal revenue product of labor will equal the wage rate.

Now let's look more closely at why firms should choose the level of employment that equates *MRPL* and *W*, and at how that decision helps us understand factor demand.

Table 69.2 Marginal Revenue Product of Labor for George and Martha's Farm

Quantity of labor *L* (workers)	Marginal product of labor *MPL* (bushels per worker)	Marginal revenue product of labor *MRPL* = *MPL* × *MR*
0		
	19	$380
1		
	17	340
2		
	15	300
3		
	13	260
4		
	11	220
5		
	9	180
6		
	7	140
7		
	5	100
8		

Marginal Revenue Product and Factor Demand

Table 69.2 shows the marginal revenue product of labor on George and Martha's farm when the price of wheat (and thus the marginal revenue for this price-taking firm) is $20 per bushel. In **Figure 69.3**, the horizontal axis shows the number of workers

Figure 69.3 The Marginal Revenue Product Curve

This curve shows how the marginal revenue product of labor depends on the number of workers employed. It slopes downward because of diminishing returns to labor in production. To maximize profit, George and Martha choose the level of employment at which the marginal revenue product of labor is equal to the market wage rate. For example, at a wage rate of $200 the profit-maximizing level of employment is 5 workers, shown by point *A*. The marginal revenue product curve of a factor is the firm's individual demand curve for that factor.

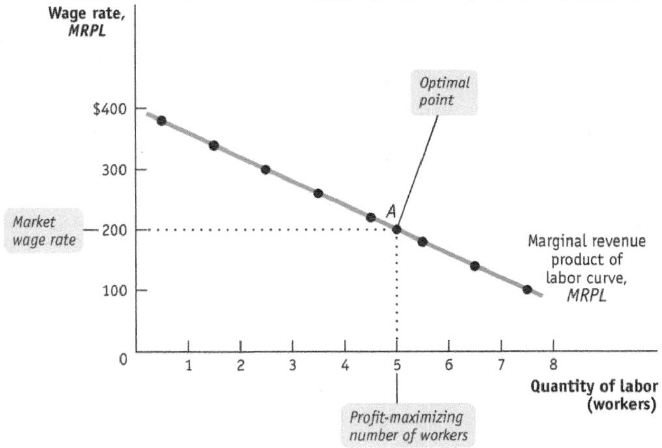

TEACH Connect It

Remind students that a profit-maximizing firm produces the level of output where *MC* = *MR*. In factor markets, a firm hires the quantity of the factor (land, labor, capital, entrepreneurship) where *MRP* = *MRC*. *MRP* = *MRC* is the same idea as *MR* = *MC*, but it uses the terms specific to factor markets. For review and reinforcement, you can show Jacob Clifford's video "Micro 5.3 Comparing Product and Resource Markets" (see econextras video list with hyperlinks on the bcs and TRFD).

FOCUS Graph It

Table 69.2 and Figure 69.3 show the marginal product of labor (*MPL*) and the marginal revenue product of labor (*MRPL*). Make sure students understand the following:

- The *MRPL* curve slopes downward due to diminishing returns to labor in production.
- The level of employment is chosen where *MRPL* = Wage rate.
- The *MRPL* curve of a factor is the producer's individual demand curve for that factor.
- Challenge students to determine the number of workers to be hired by George and Martha to maximize their profit if the wage rate is $200 and the price of wheat increases to $40 per bushel. *8 workers*

Q of L	TP	MP	MRPL
0	0		(*MP* × *P*)
1	19	19	$760
2	36	17	680
3	51	15	600
4	64	13	520
5	75	11	440
6	84	9	360
7	91	7	280
→ 8	96	5	200

FOCUS Flip It

TRM Assign Jacob Clifford's video "Micro Unit 5, Question 8—Hiring Workers" (see econextras video list with hyperlinks on the bcs and TRFD) and **Worksheet 69.2 (Hiring Workers)** from the TRM that provides questions about the video.

FOCUS Active Learning

TRM Assign **Worksheet 69.3 (Value of the Marginal Product)** from the TRM for practice determining the value of the marginal product.

TEACH Teach It

A firm can increase (decrease) profit by employing one more (less) unit of a factor of production as long as the value of the marginal product produced by that unit exceeds (is less than) the factor price. To maximize profit, producers should employ workers up to but not beyond the point at which the value of the marginal product of the last worker employed is equal to the wage rate. Recall in Table 69.2 that the 6th worker was not hired since the value of the marginal product had fallen below the wage rate.

TEACH AP® Exam Tip

The profit-maximizing hiring decision is frequently asked about on the AP® Micro exam. Make sure students understand that firms continue hiring as long as *MRP* > *MRC* and stop hiring when *MRP* < *MRC*. It is not enough to say that firms will hire the last worker because *MRP* > *MRC*; to receive a point, the student must also indicate that the firm will not hire the next worker because *MRP* is no longer ≥ *MRC* (or *MRP* < MRC).

The **marginal revenue product curve** of a factor shows how the marginal revenue product of that factor depends on the quantity of the factor employed.

employed; the vertical axis measures the marginal revenue product of labor *and* the wage rate. The curve shown is the **marginal revenue product curve** of labor. This curve, like the marginal revenue product of labor curve, slopes downward because of diminishing returns to labor in production. That is, the marginal revenue product of each worker is less than that of the preceding worker because the marginal product of each worker is less than that of the preceding worker. For a firm that is not a price-taker, the curve also slopes downward because marginal revenue decreases as more units are sold.

We have just seen that to maximize profit, George and Martha hire workers until the wage rate is equal to the marginal revenue product of the last worker employed. Let's use the example to see how this principle really works.

Assume that George and Martha currently employ 3 workers and that these workers must be paid the market wage rate of $200. Should they employ an additional worker?

Looking at Table 69.2, we see that if George and Martha currently employ 3 workers, the marginal revenue product of an additional worker is $260. So if they employ an additional worker, they will increase their revenue by $260 but increase their cost by only $200, yielding a $60 increase in profit. In fact, a firm can always increase profit by employing one more unit of a factor of production as long as the marginal revenue product of that unit exceeds the factor price.

Alternatively, suppose that George and Martha employ 8 workers. By reducing the number of workers to 7, they can save $200 in wages. In addition, the marginal revenue product of the 8th worker is only $100. So, by reducing employment by one worker, they can increase profit by $200 − $100 = $100. In other words, a firm can always increase profit by employing one less unit of a factor of production as long as the marginal revenue product of that unit is less than the factor price.

Koki Iino/Getty Images

Firms keep hiring more workers until the marginal revenue product of labor equals the wage rate.

Using this method, we can see from Table 69.2 that the profit-maximizing employment level is 5 workers, given a wage rate of $200. The marginal revenue product of the 5th worker is $220, so adding the 5th worker results in $220 of additional revenue ($20 of additional profit). But George and Martha should not hire more than 5 workers: the marginal revenue product of the 6th worker is only $180, $20 less than the cost of that worker. So, to maximize profit, George and Martha should employ workers up to but not beyond the point at which the marginal revenue product of the last worker employed is equal to the wage rate.

Look again at the marginal revenue product curve in Figure 69.3. To determine the profit-maximizing level of employment, we set the marginal revenue product of labor equal to the price of labor—a wage rate of $200 per worker. This means that the profit-maximizing level of employment is at point *A*, corresponding to an employment level of 5 workers. If the wage rate were higher than $200, we would simply move up the curve and decrease the number of workers employed: if the wage rate were lower than $200, we would move down the curve and increase the number of workers employed.

In this example, George and Martha have a small farm in which the potential employment level varies from 0 to 8 workers, and they hire workers up to the point at which the marginal revenue product of another worker would fall below the wage rate. For a larger farm with many employees, the marginal revenue product of labor falls only slightly when an additional worker is employed. As a result, there will be some worker whose marginal revenue product almost exactly equals the wage rate. (In keeping with the George and Martha example, this means that some worker generates a marginal revenue product of approximately $200.) In this case, the firm maximizes profit by choosing a level of employment at which the marginal revenue product of the last worker hired *equals* (to a very good approximation) the wage rate.

AP® Exam Tip

Given the total product and product price, you may be expected to calculate the marginal product, marginal revenue product, and total revenue for the AP® exam.

In the interest of simplicity, we will assume from now on that firms use this rule to determine the profit-maximizing level of employment. *This means that the marginal*

694 Section 13 Factor Markets

revenue product of labor curve is the individual firm's labor demand curve. And in general, a firm's marginal revenue product curve for any factor of production is that firm's individual demand curve for that factor of production.

Because many firms are not price-takers, let's now consider the marginal revenue product for a firm in an imperfectly competitive market. Suppose John and Abigail own the only pizzeria in their town, and like all monopolists, they must lower their price in order to sell more pizzas. In this case, due to the price effect, the marginal revenue gained from each pizza is less than its price. **Table 69.3** shows the calculation of the marginal revenue product for each of John and Abigail's workers. For example, by hiring the 3rd worker, they are able to produce 18 additional pizzas. The marginal revenue received from these pizzas is \$9.69, so the marginal revenue product of the 3rd worker is 18 × \$9.69 = \$169.74.

Table 69.3 Marginal Revenue Product of Labor with Imperfect Competition in the Product Market

Quantity of Labor *L*	Quantity of Output *Q*	Marginal Product of labor *MPL*	Product Price *P*	Total Revenue *TR = P × Q*	Marginal Revenue *MR = ΔTR/ΔQ*	Marginal Revenue Product of labor *MRPL = MPL × MR*
0	0			\$0.00		
		20			\$10.00	\$200.00
1	20		\$10.00	200.00		
		19			9.61	182.59
2	39		9.81	382.59		
		18			9.43	169.74
3	57		9.69	552.33		
		16			8.96	143.36
4	73		9.53	695.69		
		13			8.67	112.71
5	86		9.40	806.40		

Shifts of the Factor Demand Curve

As in the case of ordinary demand curves, it is important to distinguish between movements along the factor demand curve and shifts of the factor demand curve. What causes factor demand curves to shift? There are three main causes:

- Changes in the prices of goods
- Changes in the supply of other factors
- Changes in technology

Changes in the Prices of Goods Remember that factor demand is derived demand: if the price of the good that is produced with a factor changes, so will the marginal revenue received from the good and thus the marginal revenue product of the factor. That is, in the case of labor demand, if *P* changes, *MR* changes, and *MRPL* = *MPL* × *MR* will change at any given level of employment.

Figure 69.4 on the next page illustrates the effects of changes in the price of wheat on George and Martha's demand for labor, assuming that \$200 is the current wage rate. Panel (a) shows the effect of an *increase* in the price of wheat. Note that the price increase is the same as the marginal revenue increase here because *P* = *MR* in a perfectly competitive market. This increase shifts the marginal revenue product of labor curve upward because *MRPL* rises at any given level of employment. If the wage rate remains unchanged at \$200, then the optimal point moves from point *A* to point *B*: the profit-maximizing level of employment rises from 5 to 8 workers.

Panel (b) shows the effect of a *decrease* in the price of wheat. This shifts the marginal revenue product of labor curve downward. If the wage rate remains unchanged at \$200, then the optimal point moves from point *A* to point *C*: the profit-maximizing level of employment falls from 5 to 2 workers.

AP® Exam Tip

Note that the factor demand curve looks and acts like other demand curves you have studied but the causes of a shift in demand are different.

TEACH Teach It

The marginal revenue product of labor curve is the individual firm's labor demand curve. In general, a firm's marginal revenue product curve for any factor of production is the firm's individual demand curve for that factor of production.

TEACH Teach It

Firms in imperfectly competitive product markets (e.g., monopolies) must lower their price to sell more output. For these firms, the marginal revenue gained by selling one more unit is less than the price, due to the price effect. Therefore, their *MR* curve is below their demand curve. Since *MR* ≠ *P*, the marginal revenue product for a firm in an imperfectly competitive product market is different than *MRP* in a perfectly competitive product market.

FOCUS Graph It

Table 69.3 shows the calculation of the marginal revenue product in imperfect competition. Multiplying the *MPL* by the *MR* of the product determines the *MRPL* for that quantity. Have students give you the calculation for *MRPL* at 4 units of labor. *MPL at 4 units = 16, MR at 4 units = \$8.96; therefore, the MRPL at 4 units = 16 × \$8.96 = \$143.36*

Module 69 Introduction and Factor Demand **695**

TEACH Connect It

Recall that a change in the price of a good will be shown as movement along the demand curve and not a shift of the demand curve. Here, the same idea applies. A wage change is shown as a movement along the same *MRPL* curve and not a shift of the *MRPL* curve.

FOCUS Graph It

Figure 69.4 shows shifts of the *MRPL* curve. As with the supply and demand curve in product markets, increases are to the right and decreases are to the left. Ask students to explain what will cause the *MRPL* curve to shift. *Changes in the price of the good produced, the supply of other factors, or technology*

FOCUS Active Learning

TRM Assign **Worksheet 69.4 (Changes in Factor Demand)** from the TRM for an exercise to consider how changes in product demand influence the labor market.

OPEN & CLOSE Exit Slip

TRM *Please see* ***Exit Slip: Module 69*** *in the TRM for formative multiple-choice questions to ask your students before finishing your lesson. These questions will help you quickly assess whether your students have mastered the module's concepts before moving on.*

Answers to the Exit Slip Questions

1. B
2. D
3. D

Figure 69.4 Shifts of the Marginal Revenue Product Curve

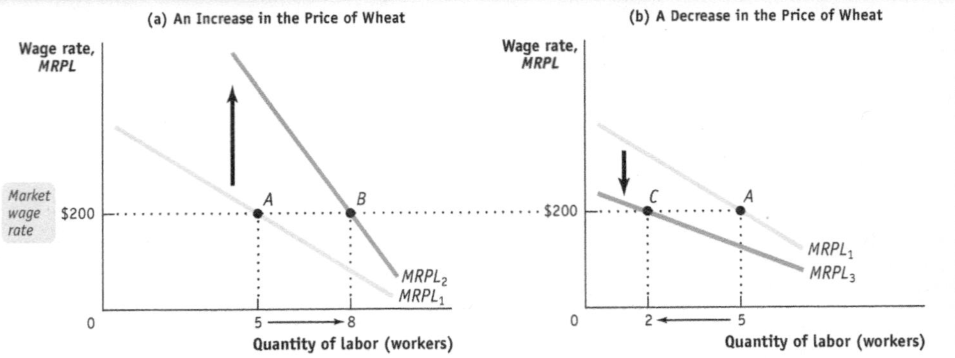

Panel (a) shows the effect of an increase in the price of wheat on George and Martha's demand for labor. The increase in price (and thus marginal revenue) shifts the marginal revenue product of labor curve upward from $MRPL_1$ to $MRPL_2$. If the market wage rate remains at $200, the profit-maximizing quantity of labor rises from 5 workers to 8 workers, shown by the movement from point *A* to point *B*. Panel (b) shows the effect of a decrease in the price of wheat. The marginal revenue product of labor curve shifts downward, from $MRPL_1$ to $MRPL_3$. At the market wage rate of $200, the profit-maximizing quantity of labor falls from 5 workers to 2 workers, shown by the movement from point *A* to point *C*.

Changes in the Supply of Other Factors Suppose that George and Martha acquire more land to cultivate—say, by clearing a woodland on their property. Each worker now produces more wheat because each one has more land to work with. As a result, the marginal product of labor on the farm rises at any given level of employment. This has the same effect as an increase in the price of wheat, which is illustrated in panel (a) of Figure 69.4: the marginal revenue product of labor curve shifts upward, and at any given wage rate the profit-maximizing level of employment rises. Similarly, suppose George and Martha cultivate less land. This leads to a fall in the marginal product of labor at any given employment level. Each worker produces less wheat because each has less land to work with. As a result, the marginal revenue product of labor curve shifts downward—as in panel (b) of Figure 69.4—and the profit-maximizing level of employment falls.

Changes in Technology In general, the effect of technological progress on the demand for any given factor can go either way: improved technology can either increase or decrease the demand for a given factor of production.

How can technological progress decrease factor demand? Consider horses, which were once an important factor of production. The development of substitutes for horse power, such as automobiles and tractors, greatly reduced the demand for horses.

The usual effect of technological progress, however, is to increase the demand for a given factor, often because it raises the marginal product of the factor. In particular, although there have been persistent fears that machinery would reduce the demand for labor, over the long run the U.S. economy has seen both large wage increases and large increases in employment, suggesting that technological progress has greatly increased labor demand.

696 Section 13 Factor Markets

MODULE 69 Review

Check Your Understanding

1. Suppose that the government places price controls on the market for college professors, imposing a wage that is lower than the market wage. Describe the effect of this policy on the production of college degrees. What sectors of the economy do you think would be adversely affected by this policy? What sectors of the economy might benefit?

2. **a.** Suppose service industries, such as retailing and banking, experience an increase in demand. These industries use relatively more labor than nonservice industries. Does the demand curve for labor shift to the right, shift to the left, or remain unchanged?
   b. Suppose diminishing fish populations off the coast of Maine lead to policies restricting the use of the most productive types of nets in that area. The result is a decrease in the number of fish caught per day by commercial fishers in Maine. The price of fish is unaffected. Does the demand curve for fishers in Maine shift to the right, shift to the left, or remain unchanged?

Tackle the Test: Multiple-Choice Questions

1. Which of the following is an example of *physical* capital?
   a. manual labor
   b. welding equipment
   c. farm land
   d. lumber
   e. education

2. Which of the following can shift the factor demand curve to the right?
   I. an increase in the price of the good being produced
   II. an increase in the factor's marginal productivity
   III. a technological advance
   a. I only
   b. II only
   c. III only
   d. I and II only
   e. I, II, and III

3. Factor market demand is called a *derived* demand because it
   a. derives its name from the Latin *factorus*.
   b. is derived from the market wage received by workers.
   c. is derived from the productivity of workers.
   d. is derived from the product market.
   e. derives its shape from the price of the factor.

4. Which factor of production receives the largest portion of income in the United States?
   a. land
   b. labor
   c. physical capital
   d. entrepreneurship
   e. interest

5. The individual firm's demand curve for labor is
   a. the *MRPL* curve.
   b. upward-sloping.
   c. horizontal at the level of the product price.
   d. vertical.
   e. equal to the *MPL* curve.

Tackle the Test: Free-Response Questions

1. Refer to the table below. Assume the firm can sell all of the output it produces at a price of $15.

Quantity of labor (workers)	*Quantity of output*
0	0
1	300
2	550
3	700
4	800
5	850
6	890

   a. What is the marginal revenue product of labor of the 3rd worker?
   b. Draw a correctly labeled graph showing the firm's demand curve for labor.
   c. What happens to the demand curve for labor if the price of the product increases to $20? Show the result on your graph from part b.
   d. Assume that a technological advance doubles the productivity of workers. Calculate the total quantity that will now be produced with each quantity of workers.

Answers to Module 69 Review Questions

Check Your Understanding

1. Many college professors will depart for other lines of work if the government imposes a wage that is lower than the market wage. Fewer professors will result in fewer courses taught and therefore fewer college degrees produced. It will adversely affect sectors of the economy that depend directly on colleges, such as the local shopkeepers who sell goods and services to students and faculty, college textbook publishers, and so on. It will also adversely affect firms that use the "output" produced by colleges: new college graduates. Firms that need to hire new employees with college degrees will be hurt as a smaller supply results in a higher market wage for college graduates. Ultimately, the reduced supply of college-educated workers will result in a lower level of human capital in the entire economy relative to what it would have been without the policy. And this will hurt all sectors of the economy that depend on human capital. The sectors of the economy that might benefit are firms that compete with colleges in the hiring of would-be college professors. For example, accounting firms will find it easier to hire people who would otherwise have been professors of accounting, and publishers will find it easier to hire people who would otherwise have been professors of English (easier in the sense that the firms can recruit would-be professors with a lower wage than before). In addition, workers who already have college degrees will benefit; they will command higher wages as the supply of college-educated workers falls.

2. **a.** The demand curve for labor shifts to the right.
   b. The demand curve for fishers shifts to the left.

Tackle the Test: Multiple-Choice Questions

1. b
2. e
3. d
4. b
5. a

Tackle the Test: Free-Response Question
Rubric for FRQ 2 (5 points)

a.

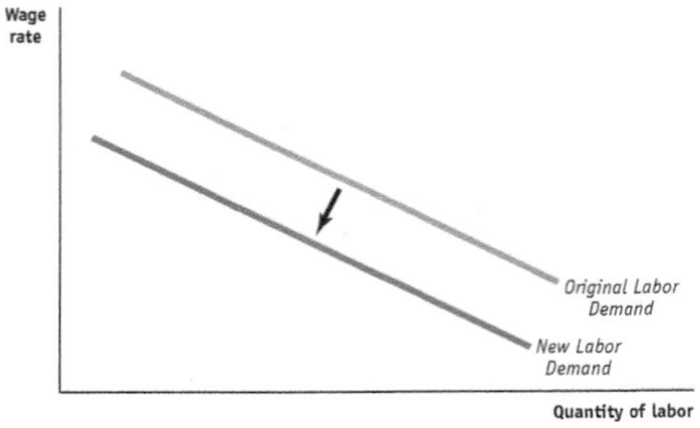

b.

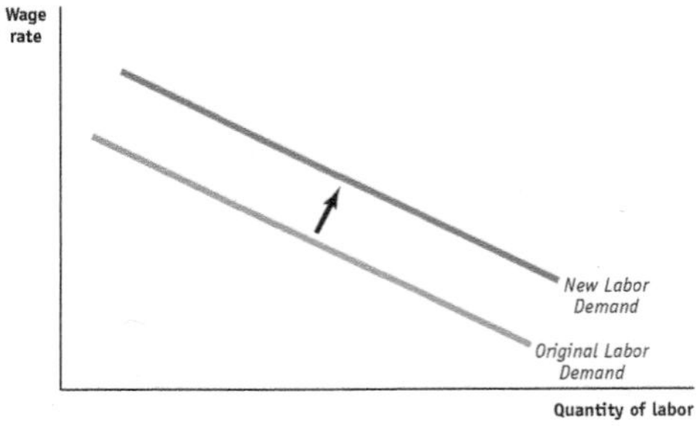

c.

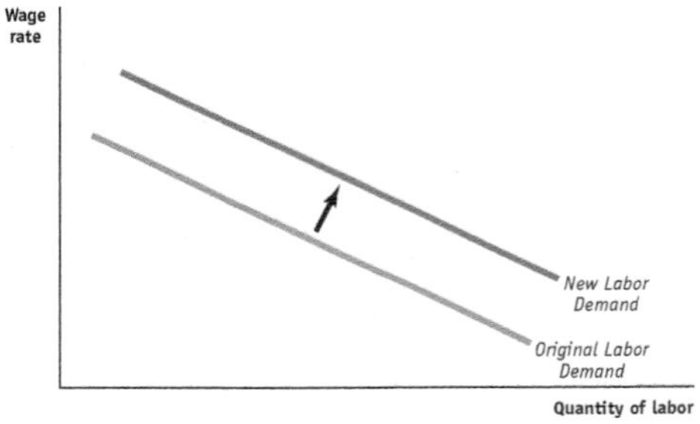

1 point: The vertical axis on each graph is labeled "*MRPL*" and/or "Wage rate"; the horizontal axis on each graph is labeled "Quantity of labor."

1 point: The labor demand curve on each graph is downward-sloping and labeled.

1 point: The graph for part a illustrates a shift downward/leftward.

1 point: The graph for part b illustrates a shift upward/rightward.

1 point: The graph for part c illustrates a shift upward/rightward.

Rubric for FRQ 1 (7 points)

1 point: *MRPL* = 150 × \$15 = \$2,250

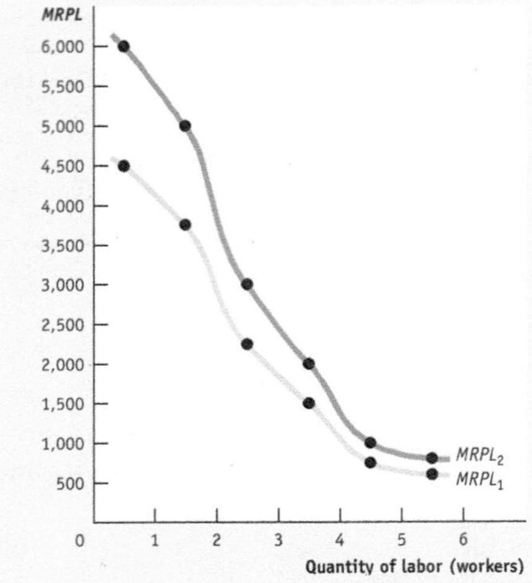

1 point: The vertical axis is labeled "*MRPL*" and/or "Wage rate"; the horizontal axis is labeled "Quantity of labor."

1 point: *MRPL* is downward-sloping and labeled.

1 point: *MRPL* is plotted using correct numbers (see graph).

1 point: The demand curve for labor shifts to the right.

1 point: *MRPL* curve is shown shifted to the right.

1 point: The new quantities produced are 600; 1,100; 1,400; 1,600; 1,700; and 1,780.

2. Draw a separate, correctly labeled graph illustrating the effect of each of the following changes on the demand for labor. Adopt the usual *ceteris paribus* assumption that all else remains unchanged in each case.

a. The price of the product being produced decreases.

b. Worker productivity increases.

c. Firms invest in more capital to be used by workers.

(5 points)

698 Section 13 Factor Markets

Stacey Newman/E+/Getty Images

MODULE **70**

The Markets for Land and Capital

In this Module, you will learn to:

- Determine supply and demand in the markets for land and capital
- Find equilibrium in the land and capital markets
- Explain how the demand for factors leads to the marginal productivity theory of income distribution

In Figure 69.1 we saw the factor distribution of income and found that approximately 69% of total income in the economy took the form of compensation for employees. Because labor is such an important resource, it is often used as the example in discussions of factor markets. But land and capital are critical resources as well, and their markets have unique characteristics worthy of examination. In this module we look more closely at the markets for land and capital before moving on to discuss the labor market further in Module 71.

Land and Capital

In the previous module we used a labor market example to explain why a firm's individual demand curve for a factor is its marginal revenue product curve. Now we look at the distinguishing characteristics of demand and supply in land and capital markets, and how the equilibrium price and quantity of these factors are determined.

Demand in the Markets for Land and Capital

The result that we derived for demand in the labor market also applies to other factors of production. For example, suppose that a farmer is considering whether to rent an additional acre of land for the next year. He or she will compare the cost of renting that acre with the additional revenue generated by employing an additional acre—the marginal revenue product of an acre of land. To maximize profit, the farmer will rent more land up until the marginal revenue product of an acre of land is equal to the rental cost per acre. The same is true for capital: the decision of whether to rent an additional piece

PD To prepare for teaching this lesson, you may want to consult the **Module 70 Sample Lecture** in the TRM.

OPEN & CLOSE Start Here

Because the majority of factor income goes to labor (approximately 70%), we often focus on the labor market. But it is important to also apply the supply and demand model to the markets for other factors (land and capital). The markets for land and capital work much the same as the market for labor. Have students identify differences between labor and land/capital. *Answers will vary but may include: land/capital are not human, capital is more homogeneous than labor, land is more fixed than labor (e.g., supply is more inelastic), capital has a special role in macroeconomic models.*

TEACH Connect It

Remind students that *land* refers to resources that come from nature. So, land is not only the ground, but also minerals, timber, lakes, and other natural resources. *Capital* refers to goods like tools and machines that are used to produce other goods.

TEACH Teach It

Students generally understand that the price of labor is the wage. The prices of capital and land are more difficult for them to grasp. The payment for land is rent, which often makes sense to students if you present the example of paying for the use of an apartment. The payment for capital can be explained as the cost of using a machine for a given period of time (e.g., the direct cost of renting a machine if the firm does not own it or the opportunity cost of using the machine instead of renting it if the firm does own one).

FOCUS Test It

Ask students why they think economists often use labor as examples to explain factor markets. *Because the greatest percentage of total income in the economy takes the form of wages and compensation*

TEACH AP® Exam Tip

Recent AP® Micro exams have included questions on factor markets other than labor. It is important for students to have practice answering such questions.

TEACH Teach It

A profit-maximizing firm will employ additional units of land and capital until the cost of the last unit employed is equal to the value of the marginal revenue product of that unit, much the same as labor. For example, to maximize profit, owners of land will rent more land up to the point where MRP_{Land} = Rental cost. The same is true for capital. A firm will hire additional capital up to the point where MRP_c = Interest rate.

TEACH Connect It

The individual demand curve (the marginal revenue product curve) for land and capital slopes downward because of diminishing returns. This is the same as we saw in product markets.

FOCUS Graph It

Figure 70.1 shows us the equilibrium in the land and capital markets. Point out the difference in elasticities of the supply curves in the markets for land versus capital. The supply curve for land is steeper (more inelastic) because the supply of land is relatively fixed. The market will be relatively responsive to changes in the price of capital (investment in capital will increase or decrease as the rental rate changes), but can't be very responsive to changes in the price of land because there is a fixed amount of land available.

of equipment comes down to a comparison of the additional cost of the equipment with the additional revenue it generates.

What if the farmer already owns the land or the firm already owns the equipment? As discussed in Module 52 in the context of Babette's Cajun Café, even if you own land or capital, there is an implicit cost—the opportunity cost—of using it for a given activity because it could be used for something else, such as renting it out to other firms at the market rental rate. So a profit-maximizing firm employs additional units of land and capital until the cost of the last unit employed, explicit or implicit, is equal to the marginal revenue product of that unit. We call the explicit or implicit cost of using a unit of land or capital for a set period of time its **rental rate**.

As with labor, due to diminishing returns, the marginal revenue product curve and therefore the individual firm's demand curves for land and capital slope downward.

The **rental rate** of either land or capital is the cost, explicit or implicit, of using a unit of that asset for a given period of time.

AP® Exam Tip

The factor market graph is a supply and demand graph with different labels. For the AP® exam, you should be able to draw, label, and analyze changes just as you do for other supply and demand graphs.

Supply in the Markets for Land and Capital

Figure 70.1 illustrates the markets for land and capital. The red curve in panel (a) is the supply curve for land. As we have drawn it, the supply curve for land is relatively steep and therefore relatively inelastic. This reflects the fact that finding new supplies of land for production is typically difficult and expensive—for example, creating new farmland through expensive irrigation.

The red curve in panel (b) is the supply curve for capital. In contrast to the supply curve for land, the supply curve for capital is relatively flat and therefore relatively elastic. That's because the supply of capital is relatively responsive to price: capital is typically paid for with the savings of investors, and the amount of savings that investors make available is relatively responsive to the rental rate for capital.

Figure 70.1 Equilibria in the Land and Capital Markets

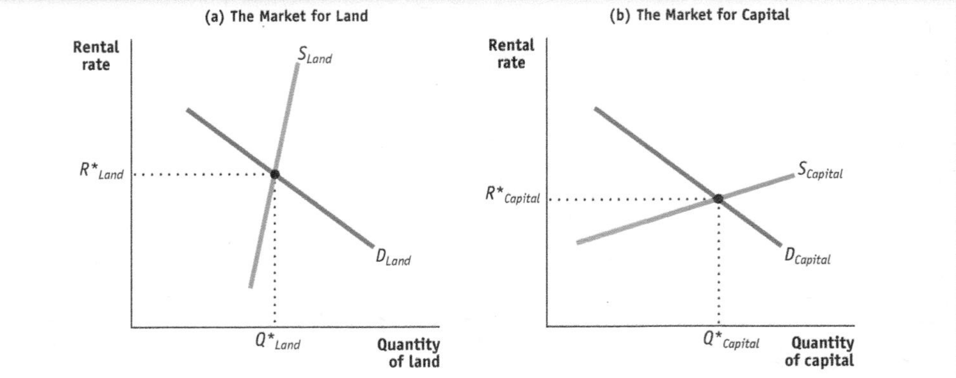

Panel (a) illustrates equilibrium in the market for land; panel (b) illustrates equilibrium in the market for capital. The supply curve for land is relatively steep, reflecting the high cost of increasing the quantity of productive land. The supply curve for capital, by contrast, is relatively flat, due to the relatively high responsiveness of savings to changes in the rental rate for capital. The equilibrium rental rates for land and capital, as well as the equilibrium quantities transacted, are given by the intersections of the demand and supply curves. In a competitive land market, each unit of land will be paid the equilibrium marginal revenue product of land, R^*_{Land}. Likewise, in a competitive capital market, each unit of capital will be paid the equilibrium marginal revenue product of capital, $R^*_{Capital}$.

FOCUS In the News

We learned that the economic rent of land increases as the demand for it increases. Have students read the following advertisement by LunarLand.com at http://www.lunarland.com/?aff_id=5&gclid=CKaUuczFyMECFSZo7AodHwgAKQ, where they will see the market for purchasing land on the moon. You can discuss how the price may have been set and if students believe the demand and price for land on the moon will increase over time.

- Discuss with students the fixed supply of land (is the supply of land on the moon fixed?) and ask them what determines the rental rate *(demand for the land).*
- Students can debate whether land should be publicly owned or bought and sold in the marketplace. Ask them to discuss the pros and cons. *(Being owned means benefits are shared broadly; however, resources may not be efficiently allocated. In the marketplace, markets can provide incentives for resources to be allocated to their most productive uses.)*

As in the case of supply curves for goods and services, the supply curve for a factor of production will shift as the factor becomes more or less available. For example, the supply of farmland could decrease as a result of a drought or the supply of capital could increase as a result of a government policy to promote investment. Because of diminishing returns, when the supply of land or capital changes, its marginal product will change. When the supply of land or capital decreases, the marginal product and rental rate increase. For example, if the number of available delivery trucks decreased, the additional benefit from the last truck used would be higher than before—it would serve more critical delivery needs—and firms would pay more for it. Likewise, when the supply of land or capital increases, the marginal product and rental rate decrease.

Equilibrium in Land and Capital Markets

The equilibrium rental rate and quantity in the land and capital markets are found at the intersection of the supply and demand curves in Figure 70.1. Panel (a) shows the equilibrium in the market for land. Summing all of the firm demand curves for land gives us the market demand curve for land. The equilibrium rental rate for land is R^*_{Land}, and the equilibrium quantity of land employed in production is Q^*_{Land}. In a competitive land market, each unit of land will be paid the *equilibrium marginal revenue product* of land. The **equilibrium marginal revenue product** of a factor is the additional revenue generated by the last unit of that factor employed in the entire market for that factor.

Panel (b) shows the equilibrium in the market for capital. The equilibrium rental rate for capital is $R^*_{Capital}$, and the equilibrium quantity of capital employed in production is $Q^*_{Capital}$. In a competitive capital market, each unit of capital will be paid the equilibrium marginal revenue product of capital.

AP® Exam Tip

When studying competitive factor markets remember that all inputs are paid the equilibrium marginal revenue product *in that market*.

The **equilibrium marginal revenue product** of a factor is the additional revenue generated by the last unit of that factor employed in the factor market as a whole.

Economic Rent

When the payment for a factor of production is higher than it would need to be to employ that factor, the factor is earning **economic rent**. Consider the 512 acres of flat land in Ouray, Colorado, which is ringed by mountains too steep to build or farm on. Because the land is in fixed supply, the supply curve is vertical as shown in **Figure 70.2** on the next page, and the monthly rental rate is determined by the level of demand. The land would be there even if the rental rate were zero, as it would be if the demand curve were D_1. Since no payment is needed to make the land available, the entire payment for the land is economic rent. If the demand curve were D_2, the rental rate would be \$1,000 an acre, and the economic rent would be $\$1,000 \times 512 = \$512,000$. If the demand curve were D_3, the rental rate would be \$4,000 per acre, and the economic rent would be $\$4,000 \times 512 = \$2,480,000$.

The appropriate distribution of the economic rent from land is a source of debate. Socialists argue that land should be publicly owned so that its benefits can be shared broadly. Critics argue that markets provide incentives for resources to be allocated to their most productive uses, whereas publicly owned land might not be allocated with the same attention to opportunity costs.

With private land ownership, portions of the economic rent can be redistributed using a land tax, which creates no deadweight loss when land is in fixed supply. Recall that many types of taxes cause deadweight loss by reducing the equilibrium quantity and eliminating some mutually beneficial exchanges. When the quantity of land is fixed, a tax on land does not decrease the quantity of land that is bought and sold, so there is no deadweight loss. The entire burden of the tax is placed on landowners in the form of a loss of economic rent. Although a land tax is appealing from an efficiency standpoint, there is no consensus on the level of taxation that is fair to landowners.

Economic rent is the payment to a factor of production in excess of the minimum payment necessary to employ that factor.

Dave Anderson

When a factor of production such as land would be available regardless of its price, the entire payment for that factor is economic rent.

TEACH Connect It

The equilibrium for rental rate and quantity in the land and capital markets is found at the intersection of supply and demand, as it was in other markets.

TEACH Connect It

Workers receive economic rent when the wage they obtain is actually higher than the wage they would be willing to work for.

Module 70 The Markets for Land and Capital **701**

TEACH Teach It

Economic rent is earned when the payment for a factor of production is higher than the cost to employ that factor. When the supply of land is fixed, the supply curve for land is vertical (perfectly inelastic) and the rental rate is determined by demand.

FOCUS Active Learning

TRM For students to gain practice understanding the graph of a fixed factor of production, assign **Worksheet 70.1 (Fixed Factors)** from the TRM.

Figure 70.2 Demand, the Rental Rate, and Economic Rent

When the supply of a factor of production is fixed, the rental rate is determined by the level of demand. For example, if the demand curve for land were D_1, the annual rental rate would be zero. If the demand curve were D_2, the rental rate would be \$1,000 per acre. And if the demand curve were D_3, the rental rate would be \$4,000 per acre. The shaded area of the graph represents the economic rent of \$4,000 × 512 = \$2,480,000 that exists when the rental rate is \$4,000 per acre.

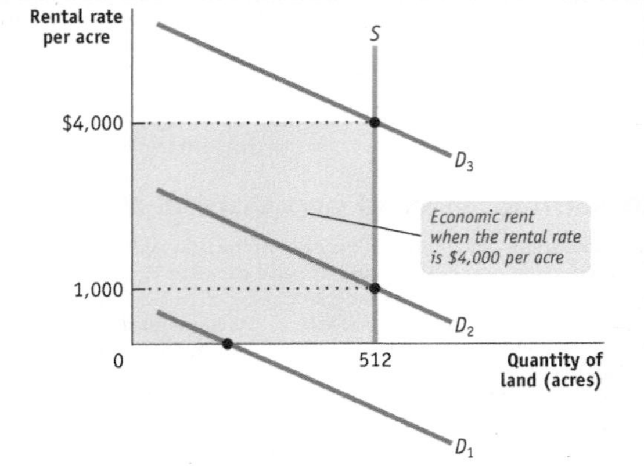

AP® Exam Tip

Economic rent is similar to producer surplus, except that economic rent applies in factor markets and producer surplus applies in the markets for goods and services.

Workers receive economic rent as well. If you earn \$12 per hour, but you would be willing to work for as little as \$8 per hour—perhaps because that's the most you could earn elsewhere—you receive \$4 of economic rent per hour. If you don't have any alternatives and you love your job so much that you would work for free, your income is pure economic rent.

Now that we know how equilibrium rental rates and quantities are determined in factor markets, we can learn how these markets influence the factor distribution of income. To do this, we look more closely at marginal productivity in factor markets.

Marginal Productivity Theory

According to the **marginal productivity theory of income distribution**, every factor of production is paid the equilibrium marginal revenue product.

The **marginal productivity theory of income distribution** sums up what we have learned about payments to factors when goods markets and factor markets are perfectly competitive. According to this theory, each factor is paid the value of the additional revenue generated by the last unit of that factor employed in the factor market as a whole—its equilibrium marginal revenue product. To understand why the marginal productivity theory of income distribution is important, look back at Figure 69.1, which shows the factor distribution of income in the United States, and ask yourself this question: who or what determined that labor would get 69.2% of total U.S. income? Why not 90% or 50%?

The answer, according to this theory, is that the division of income among the economy's factors of production isn't arbitrary: in the economy-wide factor market, the price paid for each factor is equal to the contribution to revenue made by the last unit of that factor hired. If a unit of labor is paid more than a unit of capital, it is because at the equilibrium quantity of each factor, the marginal revenue product of labor exceeds the marginal revenue product of capital.

So far we have treated factor markets as if every unit of each factor were identical. That is, as if all land were identical, all labor were identical, and all capital were identical.

702 Section 13 Factor Markets

But in reality factors differ considerably with respect to productivity. For instance, land resources differ in their ability to produce crops and workers have different skills and abilities. Rather than thinking of one land market for all land resources in an economy, and similarly one capital market and one labor market, we can instead think of different markets for different types of land, capital, and labor. For example, the market for computer programmers is different from the market for pastry chefs.

When we consider that there are separate factor markets for different types of factors, the marginal productivity theory of income distribution still holds. That is, when the labor market for computer programmers is in equilibrium, the wage rate earned by all computer programmers is equal to the market's equilibrium marginal revenue product—the marginal revenue product of the last computer programmer hired in that market. The marginal productivity theory can explain the distribution of income among different types of land, labor, and capital as well as the distribution of income among the factors of production. In Module 73 we look more closely at the distribution of income between different types of labor and the extent to which the marginal productivity theory of income distribution explains differences in workers' wages.

FYI Help Wanted!

Hamill Manufacturing of Pennsylvania makes precision components for military helicopters and nuclear submarines. Their highly skilled senior machinists are well paid compared to other workers in manufacturing, earning nearly $70,000 in 2011, excluding benefits. Like most skilled machinists in the United States, Hamill's machinists are very productive: according to the U.S. Census Annual Survey of Manufacturers, in 2010 the average skilled machinist generated approximately $137,000 in yearly revenue.

But there is a $67,000 difference between the salary paid to Hamill machinists and the revenue they generate. Does this mean that the marginal productivity theory of income distribution doesn't hold? Doesn't the theory imply that machinists should be paid $137,000, the average revenue that each one generates? The answer is no, for two reasons. First, the $137,000 figure is averaged over *all machinists currently employed.* The theory says that machinists will be paid the marginal revenue product of the *last machinist* hired, and due to diminishing returns to labor, that value will be lower than the average over all machinists currently employed. Second, a worker's equilibrium wage rate includes other costs, such as employee benefits, that have to be added to the $70,000 salary. The marginal productivity theory of income distribution says that workers are paid a wage rate, *including all benefits,* equal to the marginal revenue product. At Hamill, the machinists have job security and good benefits, which add to their salary. Including these benefits, machinists' total compensation will be equal to the marginal revenue product of the last machinist employed.

In Hamill's case, there is yet another factor that explains the $67,000 gap: there are not enough machinists at the current wage rate. Although the company increased the number of employees from 85 in 2004 to 125 in 2011, they would like to hire more.

Why doesn't Hamill raise its wages in order to attract more skilled machinists? The problem is that the work they do is so specialized that it is hard to hire from the outside, even when the company raises wages as an inducement. To address this problem, Hamill is now spending a significant amount of money training each new hire, approximately $125,000 plus the cost of benefits per trainee. In the end, it does appear that the marginal productivity theory of income distribution holds.

FOCUS In the News

TRM If time permits, assign the *Washington Post* article "Higher Productivity Used to Mean Higher Wages: Has That Broken Down?" by Jim Tankersley at http://www.washingtonpost.com/blogs/wonkblog/wp/2013/07/17/higher-productivity-used-to-mean-higher-wages-has-that-broken-down/. Ask students to complete **Worksheet 70.2 (Compensation)** in the TRM to extend the ideas from the FYI.

OPEN & CLOSE Exit Slip

TRM *Please see **Exit Slip: Module 70** in the TRM for formative multiple-choice questions to ask your students before finishing your lesson. These questions will help you quickly assess whether your students have mastered the module's concepts before moving on.*

Answers to the Exit Slip Questions

1. D
2. B
3. B

Module 70 The Markets for Land and Capital **703**

MODULE 70 Review

Check Your Understanding

1. Explain how each of the following events would affect the equilibrium rental rate and the equilibrium quantity in the land market.
   - **a.** Developers improve the process of filling in coastal waters with rocks and soil to form large new areas of land.
   - **b.** New fertilizers improve the productivity of each acre of farmland.
2. Explain the following statement: "When firms in different industries all compete for the same land, the marginal revenue product of the last unit of land rented will be equal across all firms, regardless of whether they are in different industries."

Tackle the Test: Multiple-Choice Questions

1. The implicit cost of capital that you own is
   - **a.** the rental rate.
   - **b.** greater than the rental rate.
   - **c.** the original purchase price of the capital.
   - **d.** greater than the original purchase price of the capital.
   - **e.** zero because you already own it.
2. Which of the following is true in relation to a very steep supply curve for land?
   - **I.** It is relatively elastic.
   - **II.** The quantity of land is very responsive to price changes.
   - **III.** Finding new supplies of land is relatively expensive and difficult.
   - **a.** I only
   - **b.** II only
   - **c.** III only
   - **d.** I and II only
   - **e.** I, II, and III
3. The explicit cost of land you don't own is equal to the
   - **a.** rental rate.
   - **b.** interest rate.
   - **c.** profit received from using that land.
   - **d.** market wage rate.
   - **e.** marginal product of land.
4. A firm will continue to employ more land until its marginal revenue product of land is
   - **a.** zero.
   - **b.** maximized.
   - **c.** equal to the rental rate.
   - **d.** equal to the wage rate.
   - **e.** equal to the marginal revenue product of labor and capital.
5. According to the marginal productivity theory of income distribution,
   - **a.** each unit of a factor will be paid its marginal revenue product.
   - **b.** as more of a factor is used, its marginal productivity increases.
   - **c.** factors that receive higher payments are less productive.
   - **d.** capital should receive the highest portion of factor income.
   - **e.** each factor is paid the equilibrium marginal revenue product.

Tackle the Test: Free-Response Questions

1. Refer to the table below. Assume that the price of the product is \$10 and the rental rate for capital is \$100 per unit.

Quantity of capital (units)	*Quantity of output*
0	0
1	30
2	55
3	70
4	78
5	85
6	89

   - **a.** What is the *MRP* of the 2nd unit of capital?
   - **b.** Will the firm employ the 2nd unit of capital? Explain.
   - **c.** How many units of capital will the firm hire? Explain.

Rubric for FRQ 1 (5 points)

1 point: $MRP = 25 \times \$10 = \$250$

1 point: Yes

1 point: Because the *MRP* of \$250 is greater than the rental rate of \$100

1 point: 3

1 point: Because the *MRP* exceeds the rental rate for the first 3 units

2. Draw a correctly labeled graph for a land market in which land is in fixed supply. Label each of the following on your graph: the axes, the supply and demand curves for land, the equilibrium rental rate, and the equilibrium quantity of land employed. Shade and label the area that represents economic rent. **(5 points)**

Answers to Module 70 Review Questions

Check Your Understanding

1. a. This would increase the supply of land, shifting the supply curve to the right and leading to a new equilibrium at a lower rental rate and a higher quantity.

b. This would increase the marginal product of land and thus the value of the marginal product of land. The *MRP* curve for land would shift to the right, leading to a new equilibrium at a higher rental rate and a higher quantity.

2. When firms from different industries compete for the same land, an interindustry land market develops and, other things being equal, each unit of land used by the various industries will rent for the same equilibrium rental rate, *R*. According to the marginal productivity theory of income distribution, *MRP* for land = *R* for the last unit of land rented. Because each industry rents until *MRP* for land = *R*, the last unit of land rented in each of these different industries will have the same marginal revenue product of land.

Tackle the Test: Multiple-Choice Questions

1. a
2. c
3. a
4. c
5. e

Tackle the Test: Free-Response Question

Rubric for FRQ 2 (5 points)

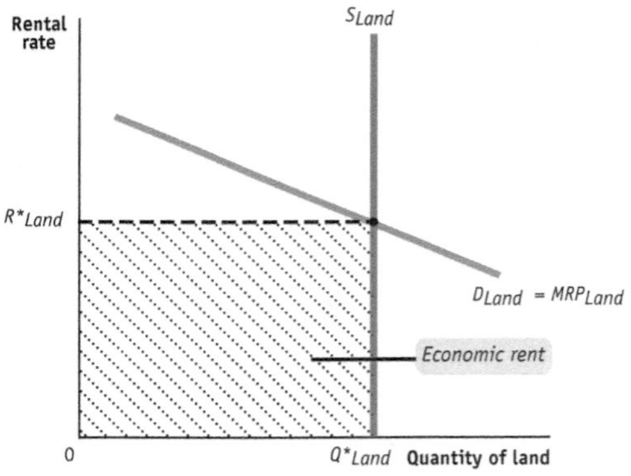

1 point: The vertical axis is labeled "Rental rate" and the horizontal axis is labeled "Quantity of land."

1 point: The land supply curve is vertical and labeled "S_{Land}."

1 point: The land demand curve is downward-sloping and labeled "D_{Land}" or "MRP_{Land}."

1 point: The equilibrium rental rate and the equilibrium quantity of land are labeled in the correct locations along the axes.

1 point: The area that represents economic rent is shaded and labeled.

704 **Section 13** Factor Markets

LOOK Die Bildagentur der Fotografen GmbH/Alamy

MODULE 71 The Market for Labor

In this Module, you will learn to:

- Describe how a worker's decision about time preference gives rise to labor supply
- Determine the equilibrium wage and level of employment in the labor market

In Module 69 we looked at the determinants of labor demand and how the wage rate influences the quantity of labor demanded by firms. Now we complete our development of the labor market model by adding the supply of labor and exploring the determination of equilibrium wage and quantity in the labor market.

The Supply of Labor

There are only 24 hours in a day, so to supply labor is to give up leisure, which presents a dilemma of sorts. For this and other reasons, as we'll see, the labor market looks different from markets for goods and services.

Work Versus Leisure

In the labor market, the roles of firms and households are the reverse of what they are in markets for goods and services. A good such as wheat is supplied by firms and demanded by households; labor, though, is demanded by firms and supplied by households. How do people decide how much labor to supply?

As a practical matter, most people have limited control over their work hours: sometimes a worker has little choice but to take a job for a set number of hours per week. However, there is often flexibility to choose among different careers and employment situations that involve varying numbers of work hours. There is a range of part-time and full-time jobs; some are strictly 9:00 A.M. to 5:00 P.M., others have much longer or shorter work hours. Some people work two jobs; others don't work at all. And self-employed people have many work-hour options. To simplify our study of labor supply, we will imagine an individual who can choose to work as many or as few hours as he or she likes.

PD To prepare for teaching this lesson, you may want to consult the **Module 71 Sample Lecture** in the TRM.

OPEN & CLOSE Start Here

Begin this module by asking your students if they have part-time jobs, or if they work during the summer. Ask them what determines whether they will work, and how many hours they will work. Explain that all of the things they consider when they decide how much to work are factors that affect the supply of labor.

TEACH Connect It

Students learned that when analyzing consumer choice, we study how a utility-maximizing consumer uses a marginal dollar. When analyzing labor supply, we study how an individual uses a marginal hour.

TEACH Teach It

The decision to allocate time to work is viewed as a choice between labor and leisure. Leisure is the time available for purposes other than earning wages. The opportunity cost of labor is the time lost for other purposes and the opportunity cost of leisure is the foregone wages. Individuals compare the opportunity cost of labor with the wage to determine how to best allocate their time.

Module 71 The Market for Labor 705

FOCUS Active Learning

Have students review the substitution effect and income effect. *The substitution effect—the quantity demanded of a good will change as a consumer substitutes in its place a good that has become relatively less expensive; the income effect—the quantity of a good purchased changes as does the income (purchasing power) of a consumer*

If a worker's wage increases, discuss how it will affect the quantity of leisure a worker demands. Have students identify whether each of the following represents the substitution effect or income effect:

- If the wage increases, the opportunity cost of taking an hour off from work rises, giving the worker an incentive to work more. *Substitution effect*
- If the wage increases, the amount paid for a given number of hours increases, giving the worker an incentive to work less. *Income effect*

TEACH Teach It

The substitution effect and income effect cause the quantity of labor supplied to move in opposite directions when the wage changes:

- When the substitution effect is greater than the income effect, an increase in wage rate causes the consumer to supply more hours of labor to the market. The incentive to work more dominates.
- When the income effect is greater than the substitution effect, an increase in wage rate causes the consumer to supply fewer hours of labor to the market. The incentive to work less dominates.

Decisions about labor supply result from decisions about **time allocation**: how many hours to spend on different activities.

Leisure is time available for purposes other than earning money to buy marketed goods.

Why wouldn't such an individual work as many hours as possible? Because workers are human beings, too, and have other uses for their time. An hour spent on the job is an hour not spent on other, presumably more pleasant, activities. So the decision about how much labor to supply involves making a decision about **time allocation**—how many hours to spend on different activities.

By working, people earn income that they can use to buy goods. The more hours an individual works, the more goods he or she can afford to buy. But this increased purchasing power comes at the expense of a reduction in **leisure**, the time spent not working. (Leisure doesn't necessarily mean time goofing off. It could mean time spent with one's family, pursuing hobbies, exercising, and so on.) And though purchased goods yield utility, so does leisure. Indeed, we can think of leisure itself as a normal good, which most people would like to consume more of as their incomes increase.

Focal Point/Shutterstock

How does a rational individual decide how much leisure to consume? By making a marginal comparison, of course. In analyzing consumer choice, we asked how a utility-maximizing consumer uses a marginal *dollar.* In analyzing labor supply, we ask how an individual uses a marginal *hour.*

Consider Clive, an individual who likes both leisure and the goods money can buy. Suppose that his wage rate is $10 per hour. In deciding how many hours he wants to work, he must compare the marginal utility of an additional hour of leisure with the additional utility he gets from $10 worth of goods. If $10 worth of goods adds more to his total utility than an additional hour of leisure, he can increase his total utility by giving up an hour of leisure in order to work an additional hour. If an extra hour of leisure adds more to his total utility than $10 worth of goods, he can increase his total utility by working one fewer hour in order to gain an hour of leisure.

At Clive's optimal level of labor supply, then, the marginal utility he receives from one hour of leisure is equal to the marginal utility he receives from the goods that his hourly wage can purchase. This is very similar to the *optimal consumption rule* we encountered previously, except that it is a rule about time rather than money.

Our next step is to ask how Clive's decision about time allocation is affected when his wage rate changes.

Wages and Labor Supply

Suppose that Clive's wage rate doubles, from $10 to $20 per hour. How will he change his time allocation?

You could argue that Clive will work longer hours because his incentive to work has increased: by giving up an hour of leisure, he can now gain twice as much money as before. But you could equally well argue that he will work less because he doesn't need to work as many hours to generate the income required to pay for the goods he wants.

As these opposing arguments suggest, the quantity of labor Clive supplies can either rise or fall when his wage rate rises. To understand why, let's recall the distinction between *substitution effects* and *income effects.* We have seen that a price change affects consumer choice in two ways: by changing the opportunity cost of a good in terms of other goods (the substitution effect) and by making the consumer richer or poorer (the income effect).

Now think about how a rise in Clive's wage rate affects his demand for leisure. The opportunity cost of leisure—the amount of money he gives up by taking an hour off instead of working—rises. Other things equal, that substitution effect gives him an incentive to consume less leisure and work longer hours. Conversely, a higher wage rate makes Clive richer—and, other things equal, this income effect leads him to want to consume *more* leisure and supply less labor because leisure is a normal good.

So in the case of labor supply, the substitution effect and the income effect work in opposite directions. If the substitution effect is so powerful that it dominates the income effect, an increase in Clive's wage rate leads him to supply *more* hours of labor. If the income effect is so powerful that it dominates the substitution effect, an increase in the wage rate leads him to supply *fewer* hours of labor.

706 Section 13 Factor Markets

Figure 71.1 The Individual Labor Supply Curve

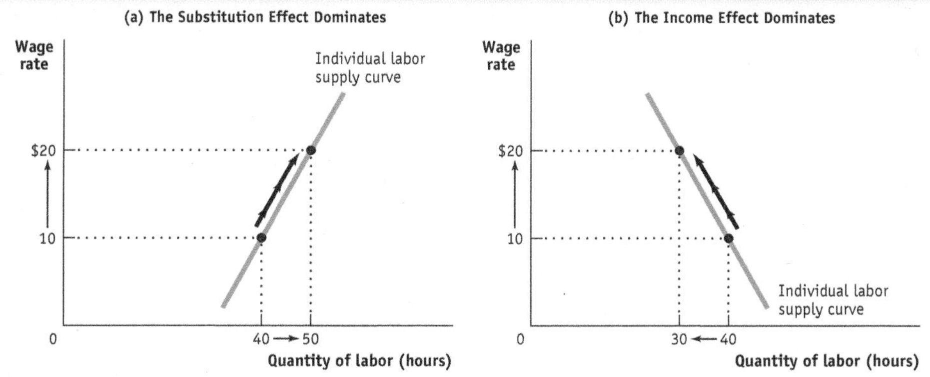

When the substitution effect of a wage increase dominates the income effect, the individual labor supply curve slopes upward, as in panel (a). Here a rise in the wage rate from $10 to $20 per hour increases the number of hours worked from 40 to 50. But when the income effect of a wage increase dominates the substitution effect, the individual labor supply curve slopes downward, as in panel (b). Here the same rise in the wage rate reduces the number of hours worked from 40 to 30.

We see, then, that the **individual labor supply curve**—the relationship between the wage rate and the number of hours of labor supplied by an individual worker—does not necessarily slope upward. If the income effect dominates, a higher wage rate will reduce the quantity of labor supplied.

The **individual labor supply curve** shows how the quantity of labor supplied by an individual depends on that individual's wage rate.

Figure 71.1 illustrates the two possibilities for labor supply. If the substitution effect dominates the income effect, the individual labor supply curve slopes upward; panel (a) shows an increase in the wage rate from $10 to $20 per hour leading to a *rise* in the number of hours worked from 40 to 50. However, if the income effect dominates, the quantity of labor supplied goes down when the wage rate increases. Panel (b) shows the same rise in the wage rate leading to a *fall* in the number of hours worked from 40 to 30.

Economists refer to an individual labor supply curve that contains both upward-sloping and downward-sloping segments as a "backward-bending labor supply curve." At lower wage rates, the substitution effect dominates the income effect. At higher wage rates, the income effect eventually dominates the substitution effect.

Is a backward-bending labor supply curve a real possibility? Yes: many labor economists believe that income effects on the supply of labor may be somewhat stronger than substitution effects at high wage rates. The most compelling piece of evidence for this belief comes from Americans' increasing consumption of leisure over the past century. At the end of the nineteenth century, wages adjusted for inflation were only about one-eighth what they are today; the typical work week was 70 hours, and very few workers retired at age 65. Today the typical work week is less than 40 hours, and most people retire at age 65 or earlier. So it seems that Americans have chosen to take advantage of higher wages in part by consuming more leisure.

Shifts of the Labor Supply Curve

Now that we have examined how income and substitution effects shape the individual labor supply curve, we can turn to the market labor supply curve. In any

FOCUS Graph It

Figure 71.1 shows that when the substitution effect is dominant, the individual supply curve slopes upward as an increase in the wage rate increases the number of hours worked. When the income effect is dominant, the individual supply curve slopes downward, indicating a reduction in hours worked as the wage rate increases.

TEACH Teach It

A backward-bending labor supply curve shows that, at some point, an increase in the wage will cause a worker to work less. At that point, the worker sees an increase in the wage as a way to earn the same income while working fewer hours. The wage at which a worker's supply curve bends backward depends on his or her preferences for labor and leisure. Some workers will pick leisure over labor at a relatively low wage and others will only cut back their hours worked at a relatively high wage.

TEACH Connect It

Point out that the development of the labor market model is similar to the supply and demand model students know so well. The main differences are that firms now demand while households supply, and price is the wage while quantity is measured in number of workers or hours. The wage is on the vertical axis in a labor market graph; therefore, a change in the wage rate will cause a movement along the supply or demand curve. Changes in other factors will cause a shift in the supply or demand curve.

TEACH Teach It

Module 69 discussed the changes that will lead to a shift in the labor demand curve. Changes in each of the following will lead to a shift in the supply curve for labor:

- preferences and social norms
- population
- opportunities
- wealth

FOCUS Active Learning

TRM Assign **Worksheet 71.1 (Thinking About the Supply of Labor)** from the TRM for questions relating to labor supply.

AP® Exam Tip

You may be asked to identify, graph, and analyze shifts of the labor supply curve for the AP® exam.

labor market, the market supply curve is the horizontal sum of the individual labor supply curves of all workers in that market. A change in any factor *other than the wage* that alters workers' willingness to supply labor causes a shift of the labor supply curve. A variety of factors can lead to such shifts, including changes in preferences and social norms, changes in population, changes in opportunities, and changes in wealth.

Changes in Preferences and Social Norms Changes in preferences and social norms can lead workers to increase or decrease their willingness to work at any given wage. A striking example of this phenomenon is the large increase in the number of employed women—particularly married, employed women—that has occurred in the United States since the 1960s. Until that time, women who could afford to largely avoided working outside the home. Changes in preferences and norms in post-World War II America (helped along by the invention of labor-saving home appliances such as washing machines, the trend for more people to live in cities, and higher female education levels) have induced large numbers of American women to join the workforce—a phenomenon often observed in other countries that experience similar social and technological changes.

Changes in Population Changes in the population size generally lead to shifts of the labor supply curve. A larger population tends to shift the labor supply curve rightward as more workers are available at any given wage; a smaller population tends to shift the labor supply curve leftward due to fewer available workers. Currently the size of the U.S. labor force grows by approximately 0.5% per year, a result of immigration from other countries and, in comparison to other developed countries, a relatively high birth rate. As a result, the labor supply curve in the United States is shifting to the right.

Bill Truslow/Photodisc/Getty Images

Women now choose among myriad careers.

Changes in Opportunities At one time, teaching was the only occupation considered suitable for well-educated women. However, as opportunities in other professions opened up to women starting in the 1960s, many women left teaching and chose other careers.

This generated a leftward shift of the supply curve for teachers, reflecting a fall in the willingness to work at any given wage and forcing school districts to pay more to maintain an adequate teaching staff. These events illustrate a general result: when superior alternatives arise for workers in another labor market, the supply curve in the original labor market shifts leftward as workers move to the new opportunities. Similarly, when opportunities diminish in one labor market—say, layoffs in the manufacturing industry due to increased foreign competition—the supply in alternative labor markets increases as workers move to these other markets.

Changes in Wealth A person whose wealth increases will buy more normal goods, including leisure. So when a class of workers experiences a general increase in wealth—say, due to a stock market boom—the income effect from the wealth increase will shift the labor supply curve associated with those workers leftward as workers consume more leisure and work less. Note that *the income effect caused by a change in wealth shifts the labor supply curve,* but *the income effect from a wage rate increase*—as we discussed in the case of the individual labor supply curve—*is a movement along the labor supply curve.* The following FYI illustrates how such a change in the wealth levels of many families during the late 1990s led to a shift of the market labor supply curve associated with their employable children.

Equilibrium in the Labor Market

Now that we have discussed the labor supply curve, we can use the supply and demand curves for labor to determine the equilibrium wage and level of employment in the labor market.

708 Section 13 Factor Markets

FYI The Decline of the Summer Job

Come summertime, resort towns along the New Jersey shore find themselves facing a recurring annual problem: a serious shortage of lifeguards. Traditionally, lifeguard positions, together with many other seasonal jobs, have been filled mainly by high school and college students. But in recent years a growing number of young Americans have chosen not to take summer jobs. In 1979, 71% of Americans between the ages of 16 and 19 were in the summer workforce. Twenty years later that number had fallen to 63%; and by 2013, it was 34.5%. Data show that young men in particular have become much less willing to take summer jobs.

One explanation for the decline in the summer labor supply is that more students feel they should devote their summers to additional study. But an important factor in the decline is increasing household affluence. As a result, many teenagers no longer feel pressured to contribute to household finances by taking a summer job; that is, the income effect leads to a reduced labor supply. Another factor points to the substitution effect: increased competition from immigrants, who are now doing the jobs typically done by teenagers (mowing lawns, delivering pizzas), has led to a decline in wages. So many teenagers forgo summer work and consume leisure instead.

Source: Bureau of Labor Statistics.

Figure 71.2 illustrates the labor market as a whole. The *market labor demand curve,* like the market demand curve for a good, is the horizontal sum of all the individual labor demand curves of all the firms that hire labor. And recall that a firm's labor demand curve is the same as its marginal revenue product of labor curve. As discussed above, the labor supply curve is upward-sloping.

The equilibrium wage rate is the wage rate at which the quantity of labor supplied is equal to the quantity of labor demanded. In Figure 71.2, this leads to an equilibrium wage rate of W^* and the corresponding equilibrium employment level of L^*. The equilibrium wage rate is also known as the market wage rate.

So far we have assumed that the labor market is perfectly competitive, but that isn't always the case. Next we'll examine the workings of an imperfectly competitive labor market.

Figure 71.2 Equilibrium in the Labor Market

The market labor demand curve is the horizontal sum of the individual labor demand curves of all producers. Here the equilibrium wage rate is W^*, the equilibrium employment level is L^*, and every producer hires labor up to the point at which $MRPL = W^*$. So labor is paid its equilibrium marginal revenue product, that is, the marginal revenue product of the last worker hired in the labor market as a whole.

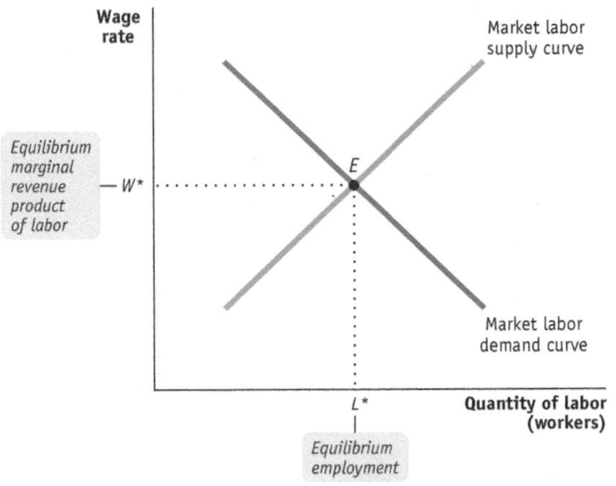

FOCUS Test It

Ask students if they agree with the material in the FYI. Do they work in the summer? Do they think the Great Recession has changed the dynamic of summer work for students? What do they see with their friends and in their neighborhoods? Are they planning on working the summer before college to earn some money? If so, remind them to save some as well! *Answers will vary and result in an interesting discussion.*

FOCUS Flip It

TRM Have students watch Jacob Clifford's video "5.2 Perfectly Competitive Labor Market and Firm" (see econextras video list with hyperlinks on the bcs and TRFD) and complete **Worksheet 71.2 (Perfectly Competitive Labor Markets)** from the TRM.

FOCUS Graph It

Figure 71.2 shows equilibrium in the labor market. Labor is paid the marginal revenue product of the last worker hired and firms hire the quantity of labor where the quantity supplied equals the quantity demanded.

FOCUS Flip It

TRM Assign Jacob Clifford's video "Micro 5.4 Resource Market, *MRP* and *MRC*" (see econextras video list with hyperlinks on the bcs and TRFD) and **Worksheet 71.3 (Resource Markets, *MRP*, and *MRC*)** from the TRM, which provides questions about the video.

St. Louis Federal Reserve Bank Resources

"The Labor Market," *The Economic Lowdown Podcast Series*, Episode 10

This episode provides an explanation of the supply of and demand for labor, while including the roles played by education, productivity, and government regulation.

"The Labor Market," *The Economic Lowdown Video Companion Series*, Episode 4

This episode teaches how the laws of supply and demand determine the wage and quantity of labor employed in various labor markets.

TEACH Teach It

The MFC_L is the additional cost of hiring another worker. For firms in a perfectly competitive labor market, the MFC_L is the wage. Since there are so many small firms hiring labor, each firm can hire as much labor as it wants without affecting the market wage rate.

For firms in imperfectly competitive labor markets, the marginal factor cost is above the market wage. Since there are few firms hiring labor (e.g., only one firm in a monopsony), the firm must raise the wage in order to hire more workers.

TEACH Connect It

The wage rate for a firm in a perfectly competitive labor market is determined in the market. Once the market wage is established, the labor supply curve for an individual firm is horizontal at the market wage. Have students recall that price was determined in a perfectly competitive product market, and once the price was determined, the demand curve for an individual firm was horizontal at the market price. The two processes are similar and shown using side-by-side graphs.

FOCUS Active Learning

TRM You may want to assign **Worksheet 71.4 (How Many Workers to Hire?)** from the TRM for practice on hiring workers in a perfectly competitive market.

When the Labor Market Is Not Perfectly Competitive

The **marginal factor cost** is the additional cost of employing an additional unit of a factor of production.

A **monopsonist** is a single buyer in a factor market. A market in which there is a monopsonist is a **monopsony**.

There are important differences when considering an imperfectly competitive factor market rather than a perfectly competitive market. One major difference is the *marginal factor cost*. The **marginal factor cost** is the additional cost of employing one more unit of a factor of production. For example, the marginal factor cost of labor (*MFCL*) is the additional cost of hiring one more unit of labor. With perfect competition in the labor market, each firm is so small that it can hire as much labor as it wants at the market wage. The firm's hiring decision does not affect the market. This means that with perfect competition in the labor market, the additional cost of hiring another worker (the *MFCL*) is always equal to the market wage, and each firm faces a horizontal labor supply curve, as shown in **Figure 71.3**.

A firm faces a very different labor supply curve in a labor market characterized by imperfect competition: it is upward-sloping and the marginal factor cost is above the market wage. Unlike a perfect competitor that is small and cannot affect the market, a firm in an imperfectly competitive labor market is large enough to affect the market wage. For example, a labor market in which there is only one firm hiring labor is called a **monopsony**. A **monopsonist** is the single buyer of a factor. Perhaps you've seen a small town where one firm, such as a meatpacking company or a lumber mill, hires most of the labor—that's an example of a monopsony. Since the firm already hires most of the available labor in the town, if it wants to hire more workers it has to offer higher wages to attract them. The higher wages go to all workers, not just the workers hired last. Therefore, the additional cost of hiring an additional worker (*MFCL*) is *higher* than the wage: it is the wage plus the raises paid to all workers. The calculation of *MFCL* is shown in **Table 71.1**.

The fact that a firm in an imperfectly competitive labor market must raise the wage to hire more workers means that the *MFCL* curve is *above* the labor supply curve, as

Figure 71.3 Firm Labor Supply in a Perfectly Competitive Labor Market

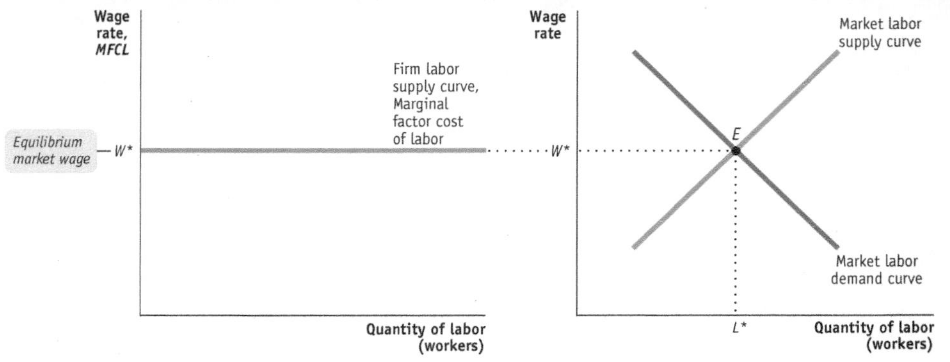

In a perfectly competitive labor market, an individual firm faces a labor supply curve that is horizontal at the market equilibrium wage because the firm is so small relative to the market that it can hire all the labor that it wants at the market wage. For this reason, the labor supply curve for a firm in a perfectly competitive labor market is equivalent to the marginal factor cost of labor curve.

FOCUS Graph It

Side-by-side graphs of the market and firm show how a perfectly competitive firm's supply curve for labor is horizontal at the market wage (established at equilibrium in the market). Because the wage is measured on the vertical axis on both graphs, the same wage can be shown across the graphs.

FOCUS Active Learning

TRM Assign **Worksheet 71.5 (Graphing Perfectly Competitive Labor Markets)** from the TRM for practice on the graphical analysis for perfectly competitive labor markets.

Table 71.1 Marginal Factor Cost of Labor with Imperfect Competition in the Labor Market

Quantity of Labor *L*	Wage *W*	Total Labor Cost = *L* × *W*	Marginal Factor Cost of Labor *MFCL*
0	$0	$0	
			$6
1	6	6	
			8
2	7	14	
			10
3	8	24	
			12
4	9	36	
			14
5	10	50	

shown in **Figure 71.4**. The explanation for this is similar to the explanation for why the monopolist's marginal revenue curve is below the demand curve. To sell one more, the monopolist has to lower the price, so the additional revenue is the price minus the losses on the units that would otherwise sell at the higher price. Here, to hire an additional worker, the monopolist has to raise the wage, so the marginal factor cost is the wage plus the wage increase for those workers who could otherwise be hired at the lower wage.

Equilibrium in the Imperfectly Competitive Labor Market

In a perfectly competitive labor market, firms hire labor until the marginal revenue product of labor equals the market wage. With imperfect competition in a factor market, a firm will hire additional workers until the marginal revenue product of labor equals the marginal factor cost of labor. Note that the marginal factor cost of labor in a

Figure 71.4 Supply of Labor and Marginal Factor Cost in an Imperfectly Competitive Market

The marginal factor cost of labor curve is above the market labor supply curve because, to hire more workers in an imperfectly competitive labor market (such as a monopsony), the firm must raise the wage and pay everyone more. This makes the additional cost of hiring another worker higher than the wage rate.

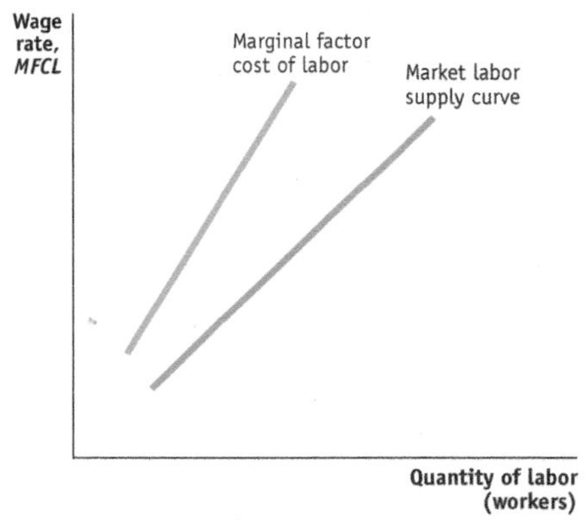

FOCUS Graph It

Figure 71.4 shows both the supply of labor and marginal factor cost curves for the imperfectly competitive firm. Ask students to explain why the curves are different for perfectly competitive labor markets and imperfectly competitive labor markets.

TEACH AP® Exam Tip

The AP® exam often asks students to draw side-by-side graphs showing the market and firm for a perfectly competitive labor market.

FOCUS Test It

Ask your students to complete Question 2 from the 2011 AP® Microeconomics exam at http://apcentral.collegeboard.com/apc/public/repository/ap11_frq_microeconomics.pdf.

This is a short free-response question and they should be able to complete it in less than 12½ minutes, as recommended by the College Board®. The rubric is available on AP® Central at http://apcentral.collegeboard.com/apc/public/repository/ap11_microecon_scoring_guidelines.pdf.

TEACH Connect It

The explanation of the *MFC* curve compared to the labor supply curve in an imperfectly competitive labor market is analogous to the explanation of the *MR* curve compared to the demand curve in monopoly product markets. A monopolist had to lower price *on all units* in order to sell one more unit of output, so *MR* was below *P*. A monopsonist has to raise the wage *for all workers* in order to hire one more worker, so the *MFC* is above *W*.

TEACH Teach It

A monopsony for labor is a labor market in which only one firm exists that is hiring labor. The firm buying the labor is called a monopsonist. Compare a monopsony market in which there is a single buyer to a monopoly market in which there is a single seller. Students may have a difficult time identifying a market in which only one firm hiring labor exists (the example of a small town with a dominant employer is given in the text). Professional sports leagues are another example of a single buyer of labor.

Module 71 The Market for Labor 711

TEACH Teach It

For the imperfectly competitive firm in a factor market, the firm will continue to hire additional workers as long as $MRP > MFC$. The firm will stop hiring labor when $MRP < MFC$.

FOCUS Graph It

Figure 71.5 shows equilibrium wage and level of employment for an imperfectly competitive labor market. The equilibrium quantity of labor is found where $MRP_L = MFC_L$.

- How is the equilibrium quantity determined? *Where* $MRP_L = MFC_L$
- How is the equilibrium wage rate determined? *At that quantity of labor, move up to the market supply curve.*
- The monopsonist finding the wage on the supply curve is analogous to the monopolist finding the price on the demand curve. A monopsonist will pay the lowest wage possible for the profit-maximizing quantity of labor (shown by the labor supply curve), just as a monopolist charged the highest price possible for the profit-maximizing level of output (shown by the demand curve).

perfectly competitive labor market is the market wage, so the term *marginal factor cost* is generally applicable to the analysis of hiring decisions in both perfectly competitive and imperfectly competitive labor markets. The term we used previously, *wage*, only applies in the specific case of perfect competition in the labor market. Thus, we can generalize and say that every firm hires workers up to the point at which the marginal revenue product of labor equals the marginal factor cost of labor:

(71-1) Hire workers until $MRPL = MFCL$

Equilibrium in the labor market with imperfect competition is shown in **Figure 71.5**. Once an imperfectly competitive firm has determined the optimal number of workers to hire, L^*, it finds the wage necessary to hire that number of workers by starting at the point on the labor supply curve above the optimal number of workers, and looking straight to the left to see the wage level at that point, W^*.

Let's put the information we just learned together, again referring to Figure 71.5: In an imperfectly competitive labor market, the firm must offer a higher wage to hire more workers, so the marginal factor cost curve is above the labor supply curve. The equilibrium quantity of labor is found where the marginal revenue product equals the marginal factor cost, as represented by L^* on the graph. The firm will pay the wage required to hire L^* workers, which is found on the supply curve above L^*. The labor supply curve shows that the quantity of labor supplied is equal to L^* at a wage of W^*. The equilibrium wage in the market is thus W^*. Note that, unlike the wage in a perfectly competitive labor market, the wage in the imperfectly competitive labor market is less than the marginal factor cost of labor.

In Modules 69–71 we have learned how firms determine the optimal amount of land, labor, or capital to hire in factor markets. But often there are different combinations of factors that a firm can use to produce the same level of output. In the next module, we look at how a firm chooses between alternative input combinations for producing a given level of output.

Figure 71.5 Equilibrium in the Labor Market with Imperfect Competition

The equilibrium quantity of labor is found where the marginal revenue product of labor equals the marginal factor cost, at L^*. The equilibrium wage, W^*, is found on the vertical axis at the height of the market supply curve directly above L^*.

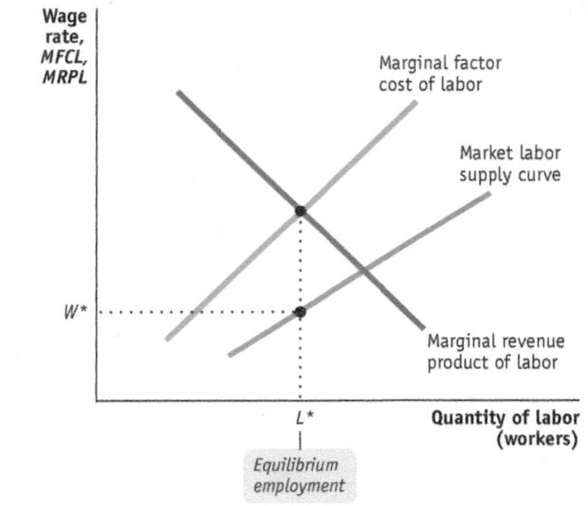

FOCUS Active Learning

TRM For practice on the graphical analysis for imperfectly competitive labor markets, assign **Worksheet 71.6 (Imperfectly Competitive Labor Markets)** from the TRM.

TEACH Connect It

Compare the way equilibrium is determined in an imperfectly competitive labor market with the way equilibrium quantity and price are determined in a monopoly. Have students recall how for the monopolist the equilibrium price was higher but the quantity was lower than the perfectly competitive market. Note that with a monopsonist the quantity of labor hired and the wage are lower.

FOCUS Test It

Have students draw a graph showing the equilibrium wage and employment in a monopsony labor market. Their answer should look like Figure 71.5.

MODULE 71 Review

Check Your Understanding

1. Formerly, Clive was free to work as many or as few hours per week as he wanted. But a new law limits the maximum number of hours he can work per week to 35. Explain under what circumstances, if any, he is made
   a. worse off.
   b. equally well off.
   c. better off.
2. Explain in terms of the income and substitution effects how a fall in Clive's wage rate can induce him to work more hours than before.

Tackle the Test: Multiple-Choice Questions

1. Which of the following is necessarily true if you work more when your wage rate increases?
   a. The income effect is large.
   b. The substitution effect is small.
   c. The income effect dominates the substitution effect.
   d. The substitution effect dominates the income effect.
   e. The income effect equals the substitution effect.
2. Which of the following will cause you to work more as your wage rate decreases?
   I. the income effect
   II. the substitution effect
   III. a desire for leisure
   a. I only
   b. II only
   c. III only
   d. I and II only
   e. I, II, and III
3. Which of the following will shift the supply curve for labor to the right?
   a. a decrease in the labor force participation rate of women
   b. a decrease in population
   c. an increase in wealth
   d. a decrease in the opportunity cost of leisure
   e. an increase in labor market opportunities for women
4. An increase in the wage rate will
   a. shift the labor supply curve to the right.
   b. shift the labor supply curve to the left.
   c. cause an upward movement along the labor supply curve.
   d. cause a downward movement along the labor supply curve.
   e. have no effect on the quantity of labor supplied.
5. The factor demand curve for a firm in an imperfectly competitive factor market is the same as which of the following curves?
   a. *MR*
   b. *MPP*
   c. *MFC*
   d. *MRP*
   e. *MP*

OPEN & CLOSE Exit Slip

TRM *Please see* ***Exit Slip: Module 71*** *in the TRM for formative multiple-choice questions to ask your students before finishing your lesson. These questions will help you quickly assess whether your students have mastered the module's concepts before moving on.*

Answers to the Exit Slip Questions

1. D
2. B
3. D

Answers to Module 71 Review Questions

Check Your Understanding

1. a. Clive is made worse off if, before the new law, he had preferred to work more than 35 hours per week. As a result of the law, he can no longer choose his preferred time allocation; he now consumes fewer goods and more leisure than he would like.

b. Clive's utility is unaffected by the law if, before the law, he had preferred to work 35 or fewer hours per week. The law has not changed his preferred time allocation.

c. Clive can never be made better off by a law that restricts the number of hours he can work. He can only be made worse off (case a) or equally as well off (case b).

2. The substitution effect would induce Clive to work fewer hours and consume more leisure after his wage rate falls—the fall in the wage rate means the price of an hour of leisure falls, leading Clive to consume more leisure. But a fall in his wage rate also generates a fall in Clive's income. The income effect of this is to induce Clive to consume less leisure and therefore work more hours, since he is now poorer and leisure is a normal good. If the income effect dominates the substitution effect, in the end Clive will work more hours than before.

Tackle the Test: Multiple-Choice Questions

1. d
2. a
3. e
4. c
5. d

Tackle the Test: Free-Response Questions

1. Assume the demand curve for a firm's product is as shown below and that the firm can hire as many workers as it wants for a wage of $80 per day.

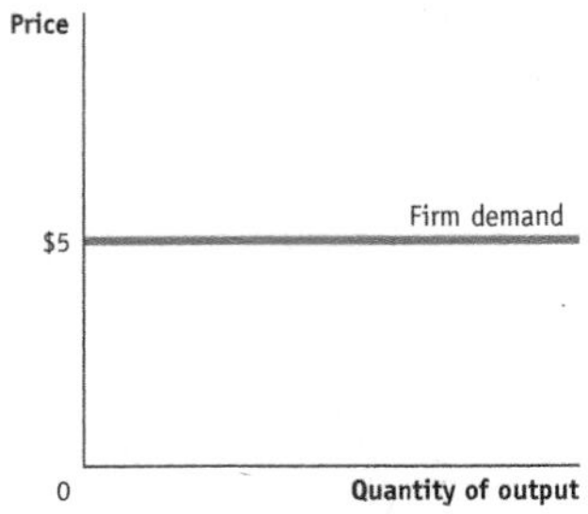

a. What is the market structure of the factor market in which the firm hires labor? Explain.
b. What is the market structure of the product market in which the firm sells its good? Explain.
c. Define marginal factor cost. What is the marginal factor cost of labor for this firm?
d. If the last worker hired produces an additional 20 units of output, what is the last worker's *MRPL*? Explain.

Rubric for FRQ 1 (8 points)

1 point: The firm hires labor in a perfectly competitive labor market.
1 point: The firm is a price-taker in the labor market. (It can hire all that it wants for $80 per day.)
1 point: The firm sells its good in a perfectly competitive product market.
1 point: The horizontal demand curve indicates that the firm is a price-taker in the product market (it can sell all the output it wants at the market price of $5).
1 point: the additional cost of hiring one more unit of a factor
1 point: $80
1 point: $100
1 point: $MRPL = MPL \times MR$, $MPL = 20$, $MR = \$5$, so $MRPL = 20 \times \$5 = \$100$.

2. Maggie's Pizzeria hires delivery drivers from a perfectly competitive labor market.
a. Draw correctly labeled side-by-side graphs of delivery driver supply and demand for Maggie's Pizzeria and for the entire delivery driver market.
b. On your graphs, show how an increase in the supply of delivery drivers would affect the equilibrium wage and the number of drivers hired, both by Maggie's Pizzeria and in the delivery driver market as a whole.
(8 points)

Tackle the Test: Free-Response Question

Rubric for FRQ 2 (8 points)

1 point: The vertical axes are labeled "Wage rate" and the horizontal axes are labeled "Quantity of labor."

1 point: The initial firm labor supply curve is labeled, horizontal, and at the level of the initial equilibrium wage.

1 point: The firm labor demand curve is labeled and downward-sloping.

1 point: The market labor supply curve is upward-sloping and the market labor demand curve is downward-sloping.

1 point: The initial equilibrium wage rate and quantities of labor are labeled in the correct locations along the axes for both the firm and market.

1 point: The market's new labor supply curve is to the right of its initial labor supply curve.

1 point: The firm's new labor supply curve is horizontal at the level of the new equilibrium wage.

1 point: The new equilibrium wage rate and quantities of labor are labeled in the correct locations along the axes for both the firm and market.

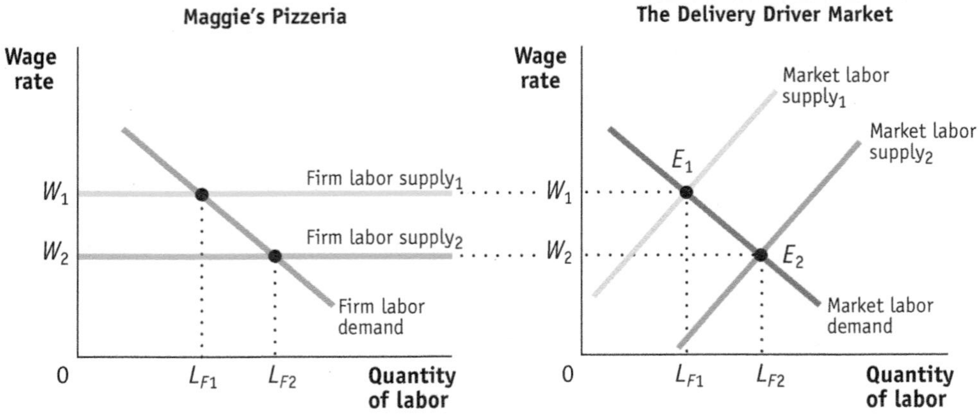

714 **Section 13** Factor Markets

© H. Lorren Au Jr/The Orange County Register/ZUMAPRESS.com

MODULE 72 The Cost-Minimizing Input Combination

In this Module, you will learn to:

- Explain how firms determine the optimal input mix
- Apply the cost-minimization rule for employing inputs

In the past three modules we discussed the markets for factors of production—land, capital, and labor—and how firms determine the optimal quantity of each factor to employ. But firms don't determine how much of each input to employ separately. Production requires multiple inputs, and firms must decide what *combination* of inputs to use to produce their output. In this module, we will look at how firms decide the optimal combination of factors for producing the desired level of output.

Alternative Input Combinations

In many instances a firm can choose among a number of alternative combinations of inputs that will produce a given level of output. For example, on George and Martha's wheat farm, the decision might involve labor and capital. To produce their optimal quantity of wheat, they could choose to have a relatively *capital-intensive* operation by investing in several tractors and other mechanized farm equipment and hiring relatively little labor. Alternatively, they could have a more *labor-intensive* operation by hiring a lot of workers to do much of the planting and harvesting by hand. The same amount of wheat can be produced using many different combinations of capital and labor. George and Martha must determine which combination of inputs will maximize their profits.

To begin our study of the optimal combination of inputs, we'll look at the relationship between two inputs used for production. Depending on the situation, inputs can be either substitutes or complements.

Substitutes and Complements in Factor Markets

In Section 2 we discussed substitutes and complements in the context of the supply and demand model. Two goods are *substitutes* if a rise in the price of one good makes

PD To prepare for teaching this lesson, you may want to consult the **Module 72 Sample Lecture** in the TRM.

OPEN & CLOSE **Start Here**

Previously students learned that inputs are hired to maximize profit and that firms employ an input up to the point where $MRP = MFC$. This module looks at the situation when there are different ways in which to produce the same output—that is, when a firm can choose between alternative combinations of labor and capital to produce the profit-maximizing level of output. For example, carpenters use tools to build houses, but with different combinations of labor and capital (carpenters and tools), the same house could be built. One carpenter with a nail gun could be more productive than several carpenters with hammers and nails. The firm must decide if the more expensive, but more productive, nail gun is a better choice than several carpenters with inexpensive hammers. Ask students to give other examples when a firm can choose from alternative combinations of capital and labor to produce the profit-maximizing level of output. Which combination will a firm choose? *The least-cost combination*

TEACH **Connect It**

Remind students that goods can be substitutes or complements. Extend this idea to explain that capital and labor can be either substitutes (you hire either capital or labor to produce) or complements (labor and capital are used together to produce). Assembly-line workers and robots are substitutes, and carpenters and hammers are complements.

Module 72 The Cost-Minimizing Input Combination 715

FOCUS **Test It**

Ask students for examples of capital and labor as substitutes or complements.

Capital can often substitute for labor, as when ATM machines substitute for bank tellers.

consumers more willing to buy the other good. For example, an increase in the price of oranges will cause some buyers to switch from purchasing oranges to purchasing tangerines. When buyers tend to consume two goods together, the goods are known as *complements*. For example, cereal and milk are considered complements because many people consume them together. If the price of cereal increases, people will buy less cereal and therefore need less milk. The decision about how much of a good to buy is influenced by the prices of related goods.

The concepts of substitutes and complements also apply to a firm's purchase of inputs. And just as the price of related goods affects consumers' purchasing decisions, the price of other inputs can affect a firm's decision about how much of an input it will use. In some situations, capital and labor are substitutes. For example, George and Martha can produce the same amount of wheat by substituting more tractors for fewer farm workers. Likewise, ATM machines can substitute for bank tellers.

Capital and labor can also be complements when more of one increases the marginal product of the other. For example, a farm worker is more productive when George and Martha buy a tractor, and each tractor requires a worker to drive it. Office workers are more productive when they can use faster computers, and doctors are more productive with modern X-ray machines. In these cases the quantity and quality of capital available affect the marginal product of labor, and thus the demand for labor. Given the relationship between inputs, how does a firm determine which of the possible combinations to use?

Determining the Optimal Input Mix

If several alternative input combinations can be used to produce the optimal level of output, a profit-maximizing firm will select the input combination with the lowest cost. This process is known as cost minimization.

AP® Exam Tip

Employers will hire a factor of production only up to the point at which the *MFC* is equal to the *MRP*. This is similar to the principle you learned in the product market.

Cost Minimization

How does a firm determine the combination of inputs that maximizes profit? Let's consider this question using an example.

Imagine you manage a grocery store chain and you need to decide the right combination of self-checkout stations and cashiers at a new store. **Table 72.1** shows the alternative combinations of capital (self-checkout stations) and labor (cashiers) you can hire to check out customers shopping at the store. If the store puts in 20 self-checkout stations, you will need to hire 1 cashier to monitor every 5 stations for a total of 4 cashiers. However, trained cashiers are faster than customers at scanning goods, so the store could check out the same number of customers using 10 cashiers and only 10 self-checkout stations.

If you can check out the same number of customers using either of these combinations of capital and labor, how do you decide which combination of inputs to use? By finding the input combination that costs the least—the cost-minimizing input combination.

Table 72.1 Cashiers and Self-Checkout Stations

	Capital (self-checkout stations)	**Labor (cashiers)**
	Rental rate = $1,000/month	Wage rate = $1,600/month
a.	20	4
b.	10	10

716 Section 13 Factor Markets

Assume that the cost to rent, operate, and maintain a self-checkout station for a month is $1,000 and hiring a cashier costs $1,600 per month. The cost of each input combination from Table 72.1 is shown below.

a. Cost of capital	$20 \times \$1{,}000 = \$20{,}000$	
Cost of labor	$4 \times \$1{,}600 = \underline{\$\ 6{,}400}$	
TOTAL	$26,400	
b. Cost of capital	$10 \times \$1{,}000 = \$10{,}000$	
Cost of labor	$10 \times \$1{,}600 = \underline{\$16{,}000}$	
TOTAL	$26,000	

Clearly, your grocery store chain would choose the lower cost combination, combination b, and hire 10 cashiers and put 10 self-checkout stations in the new store.

When firms must choose among alternative combinations of inputs, they evaluate the cost of each combination and select the one that minimizes the cost of production. This can be done by calculating the total cost of each alternative combination of inputs, as shown in this example. However, because the number of possible combinations can be very large, it is more practical to use marginal analysis to find the cost-minimizing level of output—which brings us to the cost-minimization rule.

© Irene MacDonald / Alamy

Many stores have replaced some of their cashiers with self-checkout stations.

The Cost-Minimization Rule

We already know that the additional output that results from employing an additional unit of an input is the marginal product (*MP*) of that input. Firms want to receive the highest possible marginal product from each dollar spent on inputs. To do this, firms adjust their combination of inputs until the marginal product per dollar is equal for all inputs. This is the **cost-minimization rule**. When the inputs are labor and capital, this amounts to equating the marginal product of labor (*MPL*) per dollar spent on wages to the marginal product of capital (*MPK*) per dollar spent to rent capital:

(72-1) $MPL/\text{Wage} = MPK/\text{Rental rate}$

To understand why cost minimization occurs when the marginal product per dollar is equal for all inputs, let's start by looking at two counterexamples. Consider a situation in which the marginal product of labor per dollar is greater than the marginal product of capital per dollar. This situation is described by Equation 72-2:

(72-2) $MPL/\text{Wage} > MPK/\text{Rental rate}$

Suppose the marginal product of labor is 20 units and the marginal product of capital is 100 units. If the wage is $10 and the rental rate for capital is $100, then the marginal product per dollar will be 20/$10 = 2 units of output per dollar for labor and 100/$100 = 1 unit of output per dollar for capital. The firm is receiving 2 additional units of output for each dollar spent on labor and only 1 additional unit of output for each dollar spent on capital. In this case, the firm gets more additional output for its money by hiring labor, so it should hire more labor and rent less capital. Because of diminishing returns, as the firm hires more labor, the marginal product of labor falls and as it rents less capital, the marginal product of capital rises. The firm will continue to substitute labor for capital until the falling marginal product of labor per dollar meets the rising marginal product of capital per dollar and the two are equivalent. That is, the firm will adjust its quantities of capital and labor until the marginal product per dollar spent on each input is equal, as in Equation 72-1.

Next, consider a situation in which the marginal product of capital per dollar is greater than the marginal product of labor per dollar. This situation is described by Equation 72-3:

(72-3) $MPL/\text{Wage} < MPK/\text{Rental rate}$

AP® Exam Tip

You should know the cost-minimization rule for the AP® exam. Remember, if asked to calculate the least cost combination of goods, you won't have a calculator, but the numbers will be easy to work with.

A firm determines the cost-minimizing combination of inputs using the **cost-minimization rule**: employ factors so that the marginal product per dollar spent on each factor is the same.

TEACH Teach It

The cost-minimization rule states that a firm should hire factors of production so that the marginal product per dollar spent on each factor is the same. When only capital and labor are employed, the rule is stated as follows:

$$\frac{MPL}{W} \times \frac{MPK}{R}$$

TEACH Connect It

The reasoning represented by the cost-minimization rule is analogous to the reasoning represented by the utility-maximizing rule. Help students see the similarity between equalizing the marginal product per dollar to maximize utility and equalizing the marginal product per dollar to minimize costs.

FOCUS Active Learning

TRM Assign **Worksheet 72.1 (Cost Minimization)** from the TRM for questions on this topic.

FOCUS Test It

What should a firm do to minimize cost if the marginal products of the last unit of capital and labor are 100 and 2,000, the wage is $10, and the rental rate is $50? *The firm should hire more capital and less labor because the MP/P is 10 for labor and 40 for capital. The firm receives 40 units of output per dollar spent on capital and only 10 units of output per dollar spent on labor.*

FOCUS Active Learning

Ask your students to complete Question 2 from the 2010 AP® exam at http://apcentral.collegeboard.com/apc/public/repository/ap10_frq_microecon.pdf. This is a short free-response question, and they should be able to complete it in less than 12½ minutes, as recommended by the College Board®. The rubric is available on AP® Central at http://apcentral.collegeboard.com/apc/public/repository/ap10_microeconomics_scoring_guidelines.pdf.

Module 72 The Cost-Minimizing Input Combination **717**

OPEN & CLOSE Exit Slip

TRM *Please see **Exit Slip: Module 72** in the TRM for formative multiple-choice questions to ask your students before finishing your lesson. These questions will help you quickly assess whether your students have mastered the module's concepts before moving on.*

Answers to the Exit Slip Questions

1. D
2. A
3. D

Answers to Module 72 Review Questions

Check Your Understanding

1. Yes, the firm is employing the cost-minimizing combination of inputs because the marginal product per dollar is equal for capital and labor: 500/\$100 = 1,000/\$200 = 5 units of output per dollar.

Tackle the Test: Multiple-Choice Questions

1. c
2. b
3. c
4. a

Let's continue with the assumption that the marginal product of labor for the last unit of labor hired is 20 units and the marginal product of capital for the last unit of capital rented is 100 units. If the wage is \$10 and the rental rate for capital is \$25, then the marginal product per dollar will be 20/\$10 = 2 units of output per dollar for labor and 100/\$25 = 4 units of output per dollar for capital. The firm is receiving 4 additional units of output for each dollar spent on capital and only 2 additional units of output for each dollar spent on labor. In this case, the firm gets more additional output for its money by renting capital, so it should rent more capital and hire less labor. Because of diminishing returns, as the firm rents more capital, the marginal product of capital falls, and as it hires less labor, the marginal product of labor rises. The firm will continue to rent more capital and hire less labor until the falling marginal product of capital per dollar meets the rising marginal product of labor per dollar to satisfy the cost-minimization rule. That is, the firm will adjust its quantities of capital and labor until the marginal product per dollar spent on each input is equal.

The cost-minimization rule is analogous to the optimal consumption rule (introduced in Module 51), which has consumers maximize their utility by choosing the combination of goods so that the marginal utility per dollar is equal for all goods.

So far in this section we have learned how factor markets determine the equilibrium price and quantity in the markets for land, labor, and capital and how firms determine the combination of inputs they will employ. But how well do these models of factor markets explain the distribution of factor incomes in our economy? In Module 70 we considered how the marginal productivity theory of income distribution explains the factor distribution of income. In the final module in this section we look at the distribution of income in *labor* markets and consider to what extent the marginal productivity theory of income distribution explains wage differences.

MODULE 72 Review

Check Your Understanding

1. A firm produces its output using only capital and labor. Labor costs \$100 per worker per day and capital costs \$200 per unit per day. If the marginal product of the last worker employed is 500 and the marginal product of the last unit of capital employed is 1,000, is the firm employing the cost-minimizing combination of inputs? Explain.

Tackle the Test: Multiple-Choice Questions

1. An automobile factory employs either assembly line workers or robotic arms to produce automobile engines. In this case, labor and capital are considered
   a. independent.
   b. complements.
   c. substitutes.
   d. supplements.
   e. human capital.

2. If an increase in the amount of capital employed by a firm leads to an increase in the marginal product of labor, labor and capital are considered
   a. independent.
   b. complements.
   c. substitutes.
   d. supplements.
   e. human capital.

3. If the marginal product of labor per dollar is greater than the marginal product of capital per dollar, which of the following is true? The firm should
   a. not change its employment of capital and labor.
   b. rent more capital.
   c. hire more labor.
   d. hire less labor.
   e. rent more capital and hire more labor.

4. The cost-minimization rule states that costs are minimized when
   a. *MP* per dollar is equal for all factors.
   b. ($MP \times P$) is equal for all factors.
   c. each factor's *MP* is the same.
   d. *MRP* is maximized.
   e. *MFC* is minimized.

5. A firm currently produces its desired level of output. Its marginal product of labor is 400, its marginal product of capital is 1,000, the wage rate is $20 and the rental rate of capital is $100. In this case, the firm should

a. employ more capital and more labor.
b. employ less labor and less capital.
c. employ less labor and more capital.
d. employ less capital and more labor.
e. not change its allocation of capital and labor.

Tackle the Test: Free-Response Questions

1. Answer the following questions under the assumption that firms use only two inputs and seek to maximize profit.

a. Would it be wise for a firm that does not have the cost-minimizing combination of inputs to employ more of the input with the highest marginal product and less of the input with the lowest marginal product? Explain.
b. What is the cost-minimization rule?
c. When a firm hires more labor and rents less capital, what happens to the marginal product of labor per dollar and the marginal product of capital per dollar? Explain.

Rubric for FRQ 1 (5 points)

1 point: No

1 point: The input with the highest marginal product might be much more expensive than the input with the lowest marginal product, making the marginal product per dollar higher for the input with the lowest marginal product. When that is the case, costs would be lower if the firm employed more of the input with the lowest marginal product (but the highest marginal product per dollar) and less of the input with the highest marginal product (but the lowest marginal product per dollar.)

1 point: The cost-minimization rule says that firms should adjust their combination of inputs to equalize the marginal product per dollar spent on each input.

1 point: The marginal product of labor per dollar decreases and the marginal product of capital per dollar increases.

1 point: Each factor has diminishing marginal returns. So when more labor is hired, the marginal product of labor (and thus the marginal product of labor per dollar) decreases. Likewise, when less capital is rented, the marginal product of capital (and thus the marginal product of capital per dollar) increases because the units of capital that are given up had a lower marginal product than those that remain.

2. Refer to the table below. Assume that the wage is $10 per day and the price of pencils is $1.

Quantity of labor (workers)	*Quantity of pencils produced*
0	0
1	40
2	90
3	120
4	140
5	150
6	160
7	166

a. What is the *MPL* of the 4th worker?
b. What is the *MPL* per dollar of the 5th worker?
c. How many workers would the firm hire if it hired every worker for whom the marginal product per dollar is greater than or equal to 1 pencil per dollar?
d. If the marginal product per dollar spent on labor is 1 pencil per dollar, the marginal product of the last unit of capital rented is 100 pencils per dollar, and the rental rate is $50 per day, is the firm minimizing its cost? Explain.

(5 points)

5. d

Tackle the Test: Free-Response Question Rubric for FRQ 2 (5 points)

1 point: 20

1 point: 10/$10 = 1 pencil per dollar

1 point: The firm would hire 6 workers.

1 point: No.

1 point: The marginal product per dollar spent on capital is 100/$50 = 2 pencils per dollar. Thus, the firm is not following the cost-minimization rule because the marginal product per dollar spent on labor (1) is less than the marginal product per dollar spent on capital (2).

Module 72 The Cost-Minimizing Input Combination 719

PD To prepare for teaching this lesson, you may want to consult the **Module 73 Sample Lecture** in the TRM.

OPEN & CLOSE Start Here

Break the class into groups of four or five students and give each group 3 minutes for introductions (if necessary) and to select a group leader. Give each group a bag of M&M's (or some other candy that is easily divisible). Tell them, "You are stranded on a desert island with nothing but fish, coconuts, and slugs to eat. One morning, you find candy on the beach. You have 5 minutes to determine what to do with it."

Virtually all groups eventually decide to divide the candy evenly. Ask them why they would divide it evenly. They generally say, "Because it's fair." Start there to discuss alternative methods of allocation. The following questions may help spark discussion: What if one member of your group was the best, most productive member? If we give everyone an equal share of the candy, are we removing the incentive to be a hard worker? What if a member of the group was not able to work? Does that person get any candy? Or receive a smaller share because he or she is not productive?

You can also extend the discussion and talk about how to assign grades for group work. Students usually have strong opinions about productivity, incentives, and rewards when it comes to grades and groups!

TEACH Connect It

Remind students of the definition of marginal productivity. It is the additional output produced as a result of hiring one more unit of an input. The marginal productivity theory of income distribution states that every factor of production is paid its equilibrium value of the marginal product.

Getty Images/Hola Images RF

MODULE 73 Theories of Income Distribution

In this Module, you will learn to:

- Explain the labor market applications of the marginal productivity theory of income distribution
- Identify and describe sources of wage disparities and the role of discrimination

In Module 70, we introduced the factor distribution of income and explained how the *marginal productivity theory of income distribution* helps to explain how income is divided among factors of production in an economy. We also considered how the markets for factors of production are broken down. There are different markets for different types of factors. For example, there are different labor markets for different types of labor, such as for computer programmers, pastry chefs, and economists. In this module, we look more closely at the marginal productivity theory of income distribution and the extent to which it explains wage disparities between workers.

The Marginal Productivity Theory of Income Distribution

According to the marginal productivity theory of income distribution, the division of income among the economy's factors of production is determined by each factor's marginal revenue product at the market equilibrium. If we consider an economy-wide factor market, the price paid for *all* factors in the economy is equal to the increase in revenue generated by the last unit of the factor employed in the market. But what about the distribution of income among different labor markets and workers? Does the marginal productivity theory of income distribution help to explain why some workers earn more than others?

AP® Exam Tip

Be prepared to identify and explain sources of income inequality for the AP® exam.

Marginal Productivity and Wage Inequality

A large part of the observed inequality in wages can be explained by considerations that are consistent with the marginal productivity theory of income distribution. In particular, there are three well-understood sources of wage differences across occupations and individuals.

The first is the existence of **compensating differentials**: across different types of jobs, wages are often higher or lower depending on how attractive or unattractive the job is. Workers in unpleasant or dangerous jobs receive a higher wage than workers in jobs that require the same skill, training, and effort but lack the unpleasant or dangerous qualities. For example, truckers who haul hazardous chemicals are paid more than truckers who haul bread. For any *particular* job, the marginal productivity theory of income distribution generally holds true. For example, hazardous-load truckers are paid a wage equal to the equilibrium marginal revenue product of those truckers, which is the contribution to revenue of the last person employed in the market for hazardous-load truckers.

Compensating differentials are wage differences across jobs that reflect the fact that some jobs are less pleasant or more dangerous than others.

A second reason for wage inequality that is clearly consistent with marginal productivity theory is differences in talent. People differ in their abilities: a high-ability person, by producing a better product that commands a higher price compared to a lower-ability person, generates a higher marginal revenue product. And these differences in the marginal revenue product translate into differences in earning potential. We all know that this is true in sports: practice is important, but 99.99% (at least) of the population just doesn't have what it takes to control a soccer ball like Lionel Messi or hit a tennis ball like Serena Williams. The same is true, though less obvious, in other fields of endeavor.

Arthur S. Aubry/Photodisc/Getty Images

A third, very important reason for wage differences is differences in the quantity of *human capital*. Recall that human capital—education and training—is at least as important in the modern economy as physical capital in the form of buildings and machines. Different people "embody" quite different quantities of human capital, and a person with more human capital typically generates a higher marginal revenue product by producing more or better products. So differences in human capital account for substantial differences in wages. People with high levels of human capital, such as surgeons or engineers, generally receive high wages.

The most direct way to see the effect of human capital on wages is to look at the relationship between education levels and earnings. **Figure 73.1** shows earnings differentials

Figure 73.1 Earnings Differentials by Education, Gender, and Ethnicity, 2013

It is clear that, regardless of gender or ethnicity, education pays: those with a high school diploma earn more than those without one, and those with a college degree earn substantially more than those with only a high school diploma. Other patterns are evident as well: for any given education level, white males earn more than every other group, and males earn more than females for any given ethnic group.

Source: Bureau of Labor Statistics.

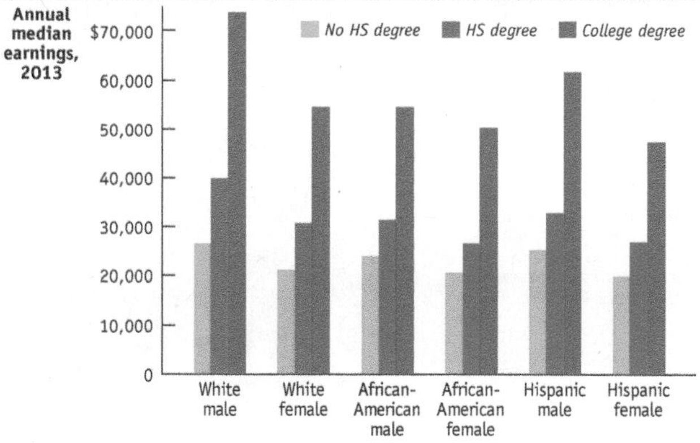

TEACH Teach It

There are three different sources of wage differences among occupations and individuals. Challenge students to list jobs that would fit these differences as you enumerate them.

- Compensating differentials are those differences among wages reflecting that some jobs are more dangerous or less liked by workers. *Railroad workers, trash collectors, mine workers, any hazardous or unpleasant job*
- Differences in worker talent. *Professional athletes, artists, movie and TV stars*
- Differences in the quantity of human capital (education and training). *Jobs that require college degrees or advanced training like that of surgeons or engineers*

FOCUS Graph It

Figure 73.1 illustrates the impact that education has on wages. Regardless of gender or ethnicity, greater education yields greater wages.

FOCUS Test It

Ask students the following questions regarding Figure 73.1:

- What is the salary range for Hispanic males? *$25,000–$60,000*
- What is the difference in salary in every case when comparing a person who has not completed a high school education and one who has completed a college education? *Salary at least doubles.*
- How can you explain that the salaries of women in every category are always less than those of men in the same ethnic class? *Answers will vary.*

St. Louis Federal Reserve Bank Resources

"Investing in Yourself: An Economic Approach to Education Decisions,"
***Page One Economics Classroom Edition* (February 2013)**

This article focuses on investing in education and training as a means to increase income and suffer fewer episodes of unemployment.

TEACH Connect It

The marginal productivity theory of income distribution assumes that markets are perfectly competitive. What other sources of wage inequality exist in labor markets that are not competitive?

1. *Unions organize workers in an attempt to raise wages and improve working conditions for those workers who are their members. They do so by collective bargaining. Employers can also organize to pay lower wages to their employees. This is known as collective action.*
2. *Employers use efficiency wages to motivate workers and decrease worker turnover.*
3. *Discrimination based on race, ethnicity, gender, or other characteristics unrelated to productivity can exist when markets are not competitive.*

by gender, ethnicity, and three education levels for people 25 years or older in 2013. As you can see, regardless of gender or ethnicity, higher education is associated with higher median earnings. For example, in 2013 white females with 9 to 12 years of schooling but without a high school diploma had median earnings 31% less than those with a high school diploma and 61% less than those with a college degree—and similar patterns exist for the other five groups. Additional data show that surgeons—an occupation that requires steady hands and many years of formal training—earned an average of $233,150 in 2013.

Because even now men typically have had more years of education than women and whites more years than non-whites, differences in education level are part of the explanation for earnings differences.

It's also important to realize that formal education is not the only source of human capital; on-the-job training and experience are also very important. This point was highlighted by a 2006 National Science Foundation report on earnings differences between male and female scientists and engineers. The study was motivated by concerns over the male-female earnings gap: the median salary for women in science and engineering is about 24% less than the median salary for men. The study found that, on average, women in these occupations are younger than men and have considerably less experience than their male counterparts. This difference in age and experience, according to the study, explained most of the earnings differential. Differences in job tenure and experience can partly explain one notable aspect of Figure 73.1: that, across all ethnicities, women's median earnings are less than men's median earnings for any given education level.

It's also important to emphasize that earnings differences arising from differences in human capital are not necessarily "fair." A society in which non-White children typically receive a poor education because they live in underfunded school districts, and then go on to earn low wages because they are poorly educated, may have labor markets that are well described by marginal productivity theory (and earnings consistent with the earnings differentials across ethnic groups shown in Figure 73.1). Yet many people would still consider the resulting distribution of income unfair.

Still, many observers think that actual wage differentials cannot be entirely explained by compensating differentials, differences in talent, and differences in human capital. They believe that market power, *efficiency wages*, and discrimination also play an important role. We will examine these forces next.

Market Power

The marginal productivity theory of income distribution is based on the assumption that factor markets are perfectly competitive. In such markets we can expect workers to be paid the equilibrium value of their marginal product, regardless of who they are. But how valid is this assumption?

AP® Exam Tip

Unions act like single sellers of labor. Through collective bargaining, they represent all the workers, making them a monopoly.

Unions are organizations of workers that try to raise wages and improve working conditions for their members by bargaining collectively.

STEPHANE DE SAKUTIN/AFP/Getty Images

Union members rally to demand higher wages.

We studied markets that are *not* perfectly competitive in previous modules; now let's touch briefly on the ways in which labor markets may deviate from the competitive assumption.

One undoubted source of differences in wages among otherwise similar workers is **unions**—organizations that try to raise wages and improve working conditions for their members. Labor unions, when successful, replace one-on-one wage deals between workers and employers with "collective bargaining," in which the employer negotiates wages with union representatives. Without question, this leads to higher wages for those workers who are represented by unions. In 2013, the median weekly earnings of union members in the United States were $950, compared with $750 for workers not represented by unions—about a 26% difference.

722 Section 13 Factor Markets

Just as workers can sometimes organize to demand higher wages than they would otherwise receive, employers can sometimes organize to pay *lower* wages than would result from competition. For example, health care workers—doctors, nurses, and so on—sometimes argue that health maintenance organizations (HMOs) are engaged in a collective effort to hold down their wages.

Collective action, either by workers or by employers, is less common in the United States than it used to be. Several decades ago, approximately 30% of U.S. workers were union members. Today, however, union membership in the United States is relatively limited: 6.7% of the employees of private businesses are represented by unions. And although there are fields like health care in which a few large firms account for a sizable share of employment in certain geographical areas, the sheer size of the U.S. labor market and the ease with which most workers can move in search of higher-paying jobs probably mean that concerted efforts to hold wages below the unrestrained market equilibrium level rarely occur and even more rarely succeed.

Efficiency Wages

A second source of wage inequality is the phenomenon of *efficiency wages*—a type of incentive scheme used by employers to motivate workers to work hard and to reduce worker turnover. Suppose a worker performs a job that is extremely important but that the employer can observe how well the job is being performed only at infrequent intervals. This would be true, for example, for childcare providers. Then it often makes sense for the employer to pay more than the worker could earn in an alternative job—that is, more than the equilibrium wage. Why? Because earning a premium makes losing this job and having to take the alternative job quite costly for the worker. So a worker who happens to be observed performing poorly and is therefore fired is now worse off for having to accept a lower-paying job. The threat of losing a job that pays a premium motivates the worker to perform well and avoid being fired. Likewise, paying a premium also reduces worker turnover—the frequency with which an employee leaves a job voluntarily. Despite the fact that it may take no more effort and skill to be a childcare provider than to be an office worker, efficiency wages show why it often makes economic sense for a parent to pay a caregiver more than the equilibrium wage of an office worker.

The **efficiency-wage model** explains why we may observe wages offered above their equilibrium level. Like the price floors we studied in Module 8—and, in particular, much like the minimum wage—this phenomenon leads to a surplus of labor in labor markets that are characterized by the efficiency-wage model. This surplus of labor translates into unemployment—some workers are actively searching for a high-paying efficiency-wage job but are unable to get one, and other more fortunate but no more deserving workers are able to find work. As a result, two workers with exactly the same profile—the same skills and job history—may earn different wages: the worker who is lucky enough to get an efficiency-wage job earns more than the worker who gets a standard job (or who remains unemployed while searching for a higher-paying job). Efficiency wages are a response to a type of market failure that arises from the fact that some employees don't always perform as well as they should and are able to hide that fact. As a result, employers use above-equilibrium wages to motivate their employees, leading to an inefficient outcome.

According to the **efficiency-wage model**, some employers pay an above-equilibrium wage as an incentive for better performance and loyalty.

Discrimination

It is an ugly fact that throughout history there has been discrimination against workers who are considered to be of the wrong race, ethnicity, gender, or other characteristics. How does this fit into our economic models?

The main insight economic analysis offers is that discrimination is *not* a natural consequence of market competition. On the contrary, market forces tend to work against discrimination. To see why, consider the incentives that would exist if social convention dictated that women be paid, say, 30% less than men with equivalent qualifications and

TEACH Teach It

The efficiency-wage model states that there are some employers who pay an above-equilibrium wage that serves as an incentive for better performance and loyalty from employees. Efficiency wages can result in employees working harder and also reduce worker turnover.

FOCUS Active Learning

TRM Have your students watch the partial video "Economics: The Theory of Efficiency Wages" by Steven Tomlinson (see econextras video list with hyperlinks on the bcs and TRFD). Then assign **Worksheet 73.1 (Efficiency Wages)** from the TRM for questions on efficiency wages.

experience. A company whose management was itself unbiased would then be able to reduce its costs by hiring women rather than men—and such companies would have an advantage over other companies that hired men despite their higher cost. The result would be to create an excess demand for female workers, which would tend to drive up their wages.

But if market competition works against discrimination, how is it that so much discrimination has taken place? The answer is twofold. First, when labor markets don't work well, employers may have the ability to discriminate without hurting their profits. For example, market interferences (such as unions or minimum-wage laws) or market failures (such as efficiency wages) can lead to wages that are above their equilibrium levels. In these cases, there are more job applicants than there are jobs, leaving employers free to discriminate among applicants. In research published in the *American Economic Review*, two economists, Marianne Bertrand and Sendhil Mullainathan, documented discrimination in hiring by sending fictitious résumés to prospective employers on a random basis. Applicants with "White-sounding" names such as Emily Walsh were 50% more likely to be contacted than applicants with "African-American-sounding" names such as Lakisha Washington. Also, applicants with White-sounding names and good credentials were much more likely to be contacted than those without such credentials. By contrast, potential employers seemed to ignore the credentials of applicants with African-American-sounding names.

Second, discrimination has sometimes been institutionalized in government policy. This institutionalization has made it easier to maintain discrimination against market pressure. For example, at one time in the United States, African-Americans were barred from attending "Whites-only" public schools and universities in many parts of the country and forced to attend inferior schools. Although market competition tends to work against *current* discrimination, it is not a remedy for past discrimination, which typically has had an impact on the education and experience of its victims and thereby reduces their income. The following FYI illustrates the way in which government policy enforced discrimination in the world's most famous racist regime, that of the former government of South Africa.

FYI The Economics of Apartheid

The Republic of South Africa is the richest nation in Africa, but it also has a harsh political history. Until the peaceful transition to majority rule in 1994, the country was controlled by its White minority, Afrikaners, the descendants of European (mainly Dutch) immigrants. This minority imposed an economic system known as apartheid, which overwhelmingly favored White interests over those of native Africans and other groups considered "non-White," such as Asians.

The origins of apartheid go back to the early years of the twentieth century, when large numbers of White farmers began moving into South Africa's growing cities. There they discovered, to their horror, that they did not automatically earn higher wages than other races. But they had the right to vote—and non-Whites did not. And so the South African government instituted "job-reservation" laws designed to ensure that only Whites got jobs that paid well. The government also set about creating jobs for Whites in government-owned industries. As Allister Sparks notes in *The Mind of South Africa* (1990), in its efforts to provide high-paying jobs for Whites, the country "eventually acquired the largest amount of nationalized industry of any country outside the Communist bloc."

In other words, racial discrimination was possible because it was backed by the power of the government, which prevented markets from following their natural course.

A postscript: in 1994, in one of the

political miracles of modern times, the White regime ceded power and South Africa became a full-fledged democracy. Apartheid was abolished. Unfortunately, large racial differences in earnings remain. The main reason is that apartheid created huge disparities in human capital, which will persist for many years to come.

TEACH Teach It

Discrimination is generally maintained through either problems in the labor markets or institutionalized government policies in areas of education or other opportunities. Students can read about the apartheid issue in the FYI and discuss how South Africa was able to practice discrimination for decades.

724 Section 13 Factor Markets

Wage Disparities in Practice

Wage rates in the United States cover a very wide range. In 2014, hundreds of thousands of workers received the legal federal minimum of $7.25 per hour. At the other extreme, the chief executives of several companies were paid more than $100 million for the year, which works out to $20,000 per hour even if they worked 100-hour weeks. Leaving out these extremes, there is still a huge range of wage rates. Are people really that different in their marginal productivities? Do workers really differ that much in their value to firms?

A particular source of concern is the existence of systematic wage differences across gender and ethnicity. **Figure 73.2** compares annual median earnings in 2013 of workers 25 years or older classified by gender and ethnicity. As a group, White males had the highest earnings. Women (averaging across all ethnicities) earned only about 79% as much; African-American workers (male and female combined) only 71% as much; and Hispanic workers only 65% as much.

We are a nation founded on the belief that all men are created equal—and if the Constitution were rewritten today, we would say that *all people* are created equal. So why do they receive such unequal pay? The pay differences may involve some differences in marginal productivity, but we also must allow for the possibility of other influences.

Figure 73.2 Median Earnings by Gender and Ethnicity, 2013

The U.S. labor market continues to show large differences across workers according to gender and ethnicity. Women are paid substantially less than men; African-American and Hispanic workers are paid substantially less than White male workers.

Source: Bureau of Labor Statistics.

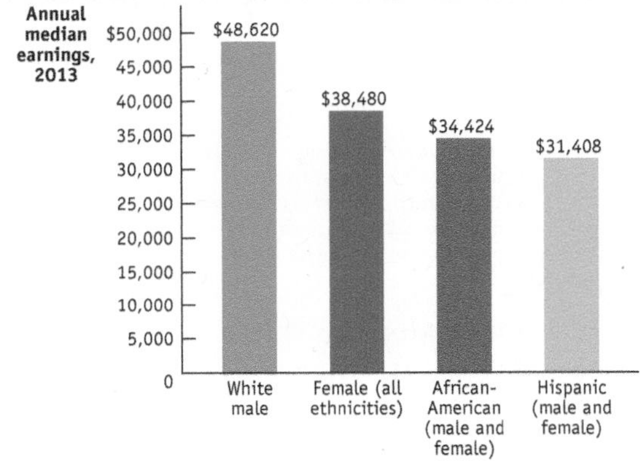

Is the Marginal Productivity Theory of Income Distribution Really True?

Although the marginal productivity theory of income distribution is a well-established part of economic theory, it is a source of some controversy. There are two main objections to it.

FOCUS Graph It

Figure 73.2 shows the median earnings by gender and ethnicity in 2013. Point out the interesting comparison to Figure 73.1 where the data include differences in education levels.

FOCUS Test It

Have students refer to Figures 73.1 and 73.2. For which groups does added education make the largest difference in annual median earnings? *The difference between the high school and college education bars on the graph is greatest for white males, Hispanic males, and white females.*

Module 73 Theories of Income Distribution 725

First, in the real world we see large disparities in income among workers who, in the eyes of some observers, should receive the same payment. Perhaps the most conspicuous examples in the United States are the large differences in the average wages between women and men and among various racial and ethnic groups. Do these wage differences really reflect differences in marginal productivity, or is something else going on?

Second, many people wrongly believe that the marginal productivity theory of income distribution gives a *moral* justification for the distribution of income, implying that the existing distribution is fair and appropriate. This misconception sometimes leads other people, who believe that the current distribution of income is unfair, to reject marginal productivity theory.

So Does Marginal Productivity Theory Hold?

The main conclusion you should draw from this discussion is that the marginal productivity theory of income distribution is not a perfect description of how factor incomes are determined but that it works pretty well. The deviations are important. But, by and large, in a modern economy with well-functioning labor markets, factors of production are paid the equilibrium marginal revenue product—the marginal revenue product of the last unit employed in the market as a whole.

It's important to emphasize, once again, that this does not mean that the factor distribution of income is morally justified.

MODULE 73 Review

Check Your Understanding

1. Assess each of the following statements. Do you think they are true, false, or ambiguous? Explain.
   a. The marginal productivity theory of income distribution is inconsistent with the presence of income disparities associated with gender, race, or ethnicity.
   b. Companies that engage in workplace discrimination but whose competitors do not are likely to earn less profit as a result of their actions.
   c. Workers who are paid less because they have less experience are not the victims of discrimination.

Tackle the Test: Multiple-Choice Questions

1. Which group of U.S. workers had the lowest median earnings in 2013?
   a. White males
   b. females (all ethnicities)
   c. African-Americans (males and female)
   d. Hispanics
   e. African-American males
2. Which of the following sources of wage differences is/are consistent with the marginal productivity theory of income distribution?
   I. talent
   II. compensating differentials
   III. efficiency wages
   a. I only
   b. II only
   c. III only
   d. I and II only
   e. I, II, and III
3. Compensating differentials mean that which of the following leads to higher wages for some jobs?
   a. danger
   b. discrimination
   c. marginal productivity
   d. market power
   e. a surplus of labor

OPEN & CLOSE Exit Slip

TRM *Please see* ***Exit Slip: Module 73*** *in the TRM for formative multiple-choice questions to ask before finishing your lesson. These questions will help you quickly assess whether your students have mastered the module's concepts before moving on.*

Answers to the Exit Slip Questions

1. D
2. B
3. C

Answers to Module 73 Review Questions

Check Your Understanding

1. a. False. Income disparities associated with gender, race, and ethnicity can be explained by the marginal productivity theory of income distribution, provided that differences in marginal productivity across people are correlated with gender, race, or ethnicity. One possible source for such correlation is past discrimination. For example, such discrimination can lower individuals' marginal productivity by preventing them from acquiring the human capital that would raise their productivity. Another possible source of the correlation is differences in work experience that are associated with gender, race, or ethnicity. For example, in jobs for which work experience or length of tenure is important, women may earn lower wages because, on average, more women than men take child-care-related absences from work.

b. True. Companies that discriminate when their competitors do not are likely to hire less able workers because they discriminate against more able workers who are considered to be of the wrong gender, race, ethnicity, or other characteristic. And with less able workers, such companies are likely to earn less profit than their competitors who don't discriminate.

c. Ambiguous. In general, workers who are paid less because they have less experience may or may not be the victims of discrimination. The answer depends on the reason for the lack of experience. If workers have less experience because they are young or have chosen to do something else rather than gain experience, then they are not victims of discrimination as long as the lower earnings are commensurate with the lower level of experience (as opposed, e.g., to earning a lot less while having just a little less experience). But if workers lack experience because previous job discrimination prevented them from gaining experience, then they are indeed victims of discrimination when they are paid less.

Tackle the Test: Multiple-Choice Questions

1. d
2. d
3. a

4. Which of the following is a result in the efficiency-wage model?
   a. compensating differentials
   b. surpluses of labor
   c. shortages of labor
   d. discrimination
   e. increased productivity
5. Which of the following statements regarding the marginal productivity theory of income distribution is correct?
   a. Each worker should earn a wage based on his or her marginal productivity.
   b. The wage rate should equal the rental rate.
   c. Workers with higher marginal products always receive a higher wage than workers with lower marginal products.
   d. The factor distribution of income is morally justified.
   e. With well-functioning labor markets, each factor is paid the equilibrium marginal revenue product of that factor.

Tackle the Test: Free-Response Questions

1. For each of the following situations in which similar workers are paid different wages, provide the most likely reason for the differences and explain why that reason applies.
   a. Test pilots for new jet aircraft earn higher wages than airline pilots.
   b. College graduates usually have higher earnings in their first year on the job than workers without college degrees have in their first year on the job.
   c. Experienced AP teachers command higher salaries than new AP teachers for teaching the same class.

Rubric for FRQ 1 (6 points)

1 point: Compensating differentials
1 point: Being a test pilot is more dangerous.
1 point: Differences in human capital
1 point: Education leads to higher productivity.
1 point: Differences in human capital
1 point: On-the-job experience increases the marginal product of experienced teachers.

2. List three different economic concepts that explain wage differences when the marginal productivity theory of income distribution does not. Explain each. **(6 points)**

SECTION 13 Review

Section 13 Review Video

Module 69

1. Just as there are markets for goods and services, there are markets for factors of production, including labor, land, and both **physical capital** and **human capital**. These markets determine the **factor distribution of income**.
2. A profit-maximizing firm hiring from a perfectly competitive factor market will keep employing more units of a factor until the factor's price is equal to the **marginal revenue product**—the marginal product of the factor multiplied by the marginal revenue of the output it produces. The **marginal revenue product curve** is therefore the firm's demand curve for a factor. Factor demand is often referred to as a **derived demand** because it is derived from the demand for the producer's output.
3. The market demand curve for labor is the horizontal sum of the individual demand curves of firms in that market. It shifts for three main reasons: changes in output price, changes in the supply of other factors, and technological changes.

4. b
5. e

Tackle the Test: Free-Response Question

Rubric for FRQ 2 (6 points)

1 point: Market power

1 point: Firms with market power can organize to pay lower wages than would result in a perfectly competitive labor market. Monopsonies pay less than the value of the marginal product of labor. And unions can organize to demand higher wages than would result in a perfectly competitive labor market.

1 point: Efficiency wages

1 point: Some firms pay high wages to boost worker performance and encourage loyalty.

1 point: Discrimination

1 point: Some firms pay workers differently solely on the basis of worker characteristics that do not affect marginal productivity.

FOCUS Flip It

Encourage your students to watch the **Section 13 Review Video**, which was created as a special student review tool and is linked into the e-Book or can be found on the book's companion website.

Module 70

4. When a perfectly competitive labor market is in equilibrium, the market wage is equal to the **equilibrium marginal revenue product** of labor, the additional revenue generated by the last worker hired in the labor market as a whole. The same principle applies to other factors of production: the **rental rate** of land or capital is equal to the equilibrium marginal revenue product. This insight leads to the **marginal productivity theory of income distribution**, according to which each factor is paid the marginal revenue product of the last unit of that factor employed in the factor market as a whole. The payment to a factor in excess of the minimum amount necessary to employ that factor is called **economic rent**.

Module 71

5. Labor supply is the result of decisions about **time allocation**, with each worker facing a trade-off between **leisure** and work. An increase in the hourly wage rate tends to increase work hours via the substitution effect but decrease work hours via the income effect. If the net result is that a worker increases the quantity of labor supplied in response to a higher wage, the **individual labor supply curve** slopes upward. If the net result is that a worker decreases work hours, the individual labor supply curve—unlike supply curves for goods and services—slopes downward.
6. The market labor supply curve is the horizontal sum of the individual labor supply curves of all workers in that market. It shifts for four main reasons: changes in preferences and social norms, changes in population, changes in opportunities, and changes in wealth.
7. When a firm is not a price-taker in a factor market due to imperfect competition, the firm will consider the marginal revenue product and the **marginal factor cost** when determining how much of a factor to employ. The marginal factor cost is equivalent to the wage (or the price of the factor) in a perfectly competitive market.
8. A **monopsonist** is the single buyer of a factor. A market in which there is a monopsonist is a **monopsony**.

Module 72

9. Firms will determine the optimal input combination using the **cost-minimization rule**: When a firm uses the cost-minimizing combination of inputs, the marginal product of labor divided by the wage rate is equal to the marginal product of capital divided by the rental rate.

Module 73

10. Large disparities in wages raise questions about the validity of the marginal productivity theory of income distribution. Many disparities can be explained by **compensating differentials** and by differences in talent, job experience, and human capital across workers. Market interference in the forms of **unions** and collective action by employers also creates wage disparities. The **efficiency-wage model**, which arises from a type of market failure, shows how wage disparities can result from employers' attempts to increase worker performance. Free markets tend to diminish discrimination, but discrimination remains a real source of wage disparity. Discrimination is typically maintained either through problems in labor markets or (historically) through institutionalization in government policies.

728 Section 13 Factor Markets

Key Terms

Physical capital, p. 688
Human capital, p. 688
Derived demand, p. 689
Factor distribution of income, p. 689
Marginal revenue product, p. 692
Marginal revenue product curve, p. 694
Rental rate, p. 700
Equilibrium marginal revenue product, p. 701
Economic rent, p. 701
Marginal productivity theory of income distribution, p. 702
Time allocation, p. 706
Leisure, p. 706
Individual labor supply curve, p. 707
Marginal factor cost, p. 710
Monopsonist, p. 710
Monopsony, p. 710
Cost-minimization rule, p. 717
Compensating differentials, p. 721
Unions, p. 722
Efficiency-wage model, p. 723

AP® Exam Practice Questions

Multiple-Choice Questions

1. The four principal classes of factors of production are
   a. money, capital, land, and labor.
   b. money, capital, labor, and entrepreneurship.
   c. money, labor, land, and entrepreneurship.
   d. land, labor, capital, and entrepreneurship.
   e. land, labor, entrepreneurship, and money.
2. Because it results from the demand for automobiles, the demand for automobile workers is a/an
   a. derived demand.
   b. irrational demand.
   c. elastic demand.
   d. inelastic demand.
   e. unit elastic demand.
3. In the United States, the percentage of factor income earned by labor is close to
   a. 10%.
   b. 30%.
   c. 50%.
   d. 70%.
   e. 90%.
4. For a perfectly competitive firm in both the product market and the factor market, the demand curve for labor slopes downward due to
   a. market power.
   b. economies of scale.
   c. diseconomies of scale.
   d. diminishing marginal returns.
   e. increasing marginal returns.
5. If marginal product is positive and falling as the firm hires more workers, then
   a. total product is rising at a decreasing rate.
   b. total product is falling at a decreasing rate.
   c. average product must be falling.
   d. the marginal revenue product of labor is increasing.
   e. the diminishing returns to labor are decreasing.

Use the following production data for a firm operating in both a perfectly competitive product market and a perfectly competitive factor market to answer Questions 6–8.

Number of workers	Total output/hour
1	10
2	22
3	30
4	36
5	40
6	43
7	45
8	46

6. Based on the production data above, at what level of employment does the firm begin to experience diminishing marginal returns?
   a. There are no diminishing marginal returns.
   b. 3 workers
   c. 4 workers
   d. 5 workers
   e. 6 workers
7. Assume the firm sells its product for $2 each and must pay each worker $8 per hour. What is the marginal revenue product of labor for the second worker?
   a. $10
   b. $22
   c. $24
   d. $60
   e. $176

Answers to Section 13 AP® Exam Practice Questions

Multiple-Choice Questions

1. d
2. a
3. d
4. d
5. a
6. b
7. c

Section 13 Review 729

8. c
9. c
10. b
11. d
12. d
13. b
14. a
15. d
16. d
17. c
18. c
19. b

8. Assume the firm sells its product for $2 each and must pay each worker $8 per hour. How many workers should the firm hire in order to maximize profit?
- **a.** 2
- **b.** 3
- **c.** 5
- **d.** 6
- **e.** 8

9. Which of the following would shift the demand curve for labor to the right?
- **a.** a decrease in the wage rate
- **b.** an increase in the wage rate
- **c.** an increase in labor productivity
- **d.** a decrease in the final price of the product produced
- **e.** a decrease in the availability of physical capital per worker

10. Suppose a firm produces coffee mugs in a perfectly competitive output market. Which of the following would shift the firm's demand curve for labor to the left?
- **a.** an increase in the demand for mugs
- **b.** a decrease in the price of mugs
- **c.** an increase in the price of mugs
- **d.** improvements in technology that increase the marginal product of labor
- **e.** an increase in the availability of physical capital per worker

11. Suppose a firm hires labor in a perfectly competitive labor market. If the marginal revenue product is less than the wage, the firm should definitely
- **a.** shut down in the short run.
- **b.** shut down in the long run.
- **c.** hire more workers.
- **d.** hire fewer workers.
- **e.** not change the number of workers it hires.

12. Compared to the supply curve for capital, the supply curve for land is
- **a.** flatter, more elastic, and more responsive to factor prices.
- **b.** flatter, less elastic, and less responsive to factor prices
- **c.** steeper, more elastic, and more responsive to factor prices.
- **d.** steeper, less elastic, and less responsive to factor prices.
- **e.** steeper, more elastic, and less responsive to factor prices.

13. The supply curve for labor slopes downward when
- **a.** the substitution effect outweighs the income effect.
- **b.** the income effect outweighs the substitution effect.
- **c.** the substitution effect equals the income effect.
- **d.** workers experience an overall decrease in wealth.
- **e.** wage rates are at very low levels.

14. The supply curve for labor may shift to the left due to
- **a.** an increase in wealth.
- **b.** an increase in the wage rate due to the income effect.
- **c.** a decrease in the wage rate due to the income effect.
- **d.** an increase in the wage rate due to the substitution effect.
- **e.** a decrease in the wage rate due to the substitution effect.

15. For a monopsony, the marginal factor cost of labor curve lies above the supply curve at every quantity of labor due to
- **a.** diminishing marginal returns.
- **b.** increasing marginal returns.
- **c.** different workers receiving different wage rates.
- **d.** all workers receiving the same wage rate.
- **e.** decreasing opportunity cost of leisure.

16. Compared to a competitive labor market, a firm with monopsony power in the labor market would pay a
- **a.** higher wage rate and hire more workers.
- **b.** higher wage rate and hire fewer workers.
- **c.** lower wage rate and hire more workers.
- **d.** lower wage rate and hire fewer workers.
- **e.** lower wage rate but hire the same amount of workers.

17. Assume an effective minimum wage is imposed on a monopsony labor market, and the minimum wage is set below the wage that would exist in a perfectly competitive market. Employment would
- **a.** decrease, and there would be unemployment.
- **b.** decrease, and there would be a shortage of workers.
- **c.** increase, but there would be a shortage of workers.
- **d.** increase, but there would be unemployment.
- **e.** increase, and there would be no shortages or surpluses of labor.

18. Assume a firm is operating as a monopolist in the product market and as a perfect competitor in the factor market. The firm's demand curve for labor will be
- **a.** horizontal due to the competitive labor market.
- **b.** horizontal due to the effects of market power.
- **c.** downward-sloping due to diminishing marginal returns and decreasing marginal revenue.
- **d.** downward-sloping due solely to diminishing marginal returns.
- **e.** downward-sloping due solely to decreasing marginal revenue.

19. If a former monopolist in the product market begins to face competition as firms enter the market, the firm's demand curve for labor would
- **a.** not change.
- **b.** become more elastic.
- **c.** become less elastic.
- **d.** show the effects of more rapidly diminishing marginal returns.
- **e.** show the effects of less rapidly diminishing marginal returns.

20. Suppose that a firm is currently producing its desired quantity of output and that the firm's marginal product of labor is 20, its marginal product of capital is 100, the wage rate for labor is $5, and the rent for capital is $25. All data are per hour. The firm should
 a. employ more labor and rent more capital.
 b. employ less labor and rent less capital.
 c. employ less labor and rent more capital.
 d. employ more labor and rent less capital.
 e. employ/rent the current amount of labor and capital.

21. According to marginal productivity theory, a factor of production will be paid based on the
 a. increase in revenue generated by the last unit of the factor employed in the market.
 b. increase in output generated by the last unit of the factor employed in the market.
 c. average revenue generated by the factor of production employed in the market.
 d. average output generated by the factor of production employed in the market.
 e. average revenue generated by all factors of production employed in the market.

22. According to marginal productivity theory, wage inequality in perfectly competitive markets can be attributed to
 a. compensating differentials.
 b. union activity.
 c. discrimination.
 d. efficiency wages.
 e. the similarity in quality and quantity of human capital among all workers.

23. An increase in which of the following practices would help to minimize wage inequality in labor markets?
 a. discrimination
 b. compensating differentials
 c. efficiency wages
 d. educational opportunities for the poor
 e. the wages paid to workers that produce a higher value of marginal product

24. Efficiency wages are wages that
 a. are below market equilibrium wages.
 b. are above market equilibrium wages.
 c. usually result in high turnover of employees.
 d. usually result in lower levels of output.
 e. usually necessitate greater amounts of worker supervision.

Free-Response Question

1. Quinn and Courtney manage a factory in the toy airplane industry, which is perfectly competitive in both the product market and the factor market. They have compiled the following per-day data on worker productivity:

Number of workers	0	1	2	3	4	5	6
Marginal product	–	6	5	4	3	2	1

 a. The price of toy airplanes is $100, the wage per worker is $200, and the rent per machine is $400. Assume the firm always produces the profit-maximizing quantity of airplanes using the cost-minimizing combination of inputs. If the marginal product of capital is 4, how many workers do Quinn and Courtney hire?
 b. Draw a graph of Quinn and Courtney's supply and demand curves for labor using the specific data from part a above. Be sure to indicate the equilibrium wage rate and the number of workers hired. Label all curves and axes.
 c. Explain why the demand curve for labor slopes the way it does.
 d. On your factor market graph from part b, show the effect of a decrease in the supply of workers in the toy airplane industry. Add the subscript "new" to the label of anything that changes.
 (7 points)

20. e
21. a
22. a
23. d
24. b

Rubric for Free-Response Questions

1 point: 5 workers

1 point: The horizontal axis is labeled "Quantity of labor," the vertical axis is labeled "Wage rate," and the firm's demand curve for labor is downward-sloping.

1 point: The firm's supply curve for labor is horizontal at a wage rate of $200.

1 point: The equilibrium quantity of 5 workers is labeled below the intersection of the firm's labor demand curve and its labor supply curve.

1 point: The demand curve for labor slopes downward due to diminishing marginal returns.

1 point: The new labor supply curve for the firm is labeled and lies above the original labor supply curve.

1 point: The new equilibrium wage rate is labeled above the initial wage rate of $200 and the new equilibrium quantity is labeled to the left of the initial equilibrium quantity.

Please see page SG-6 for a sample student graph for this Free-Response Question.

SECTION 14

Market Failure and the Role of Government

PD Section 14 Overview

Watch the video overview of Section 14 (for teachers), which is accessible through the Teacher's e-Book, the TR-flash drive, or the book's website, bcs.worthpublishers.com/krugmanap2e *(teacher log-in required).*

Section 14 introduces market failures. While earlier sections focused on market efficiency, this section looks at inefficiency in markets in the case of externalities and public goods. The inefficiency that results from market failure can be addressed by government intervention. This section considers the justification for government intervention created by market failures and some of the government policies designed to promote efficiency, including taxes, subsidies, provision of public goods, and antitrust policy. Finally, this section presents an overview of income inequality, its measurement, and policies to address it.

Topics that your students will study in Section 14 include:

- the definition of positive and negative externalities.
- the effect of externalities on efficiency in markets.
- the Coase theorem as a private solution to externalities.
- the use of the supply and demand model to explain and analyze externalities.
- government policy actions to address inefficiency resulting from externalities.
- the characteristics of public goods.
- why markets fail to provide public goods in efficient quantities.
- how common resources and artificially scarce goods are similar to public goods.
- the "free-rider" problem.
- determining the optimal level of government intervention.
- government regulation of natural monopoly markets.
- the use of marginal cost pricing and average cost pricing to regulate natural monopolies.
- the definition of poverty and its consequences.
- how income inequality has changed over time in the United States.
- using the Lorenz curve and Gini coefficient to measure a country's level of income inequality.
- how programs like Social Security and unemployment insurance affect income inequality.

Alignment to AP® Microeconomics Course Description

Microeconomics IV. Market Failure and the Role of Government: 12–18%

AP® Outline	Module
A. Externalities	74: Introduction to Externalities 75: Externalities and Public Policy
B. Public goods	76: Public Goods
C. Public policy to promote competition	77: Public Policy to Promote Competition
D. Income distribution	78: Income Inequality and Income Distribution

Pacing Guide

Module	Standard Teaching Days	Block Teaching Days
74	1	1
75	2	1½
76	2	1½
77	1	1
78	2	1
Section 14 Assessment	1	½
Total	**9**	**6½**

TRM Section Resources

All section resources may be accessed through the Teacher's e-Book, the TR-flash drive, or the book's website bcs.worthpublishers.com/krugmanap2e *(teacher log-in required).*

Section 14 PD Video (for teachers)

Module 74

Module 74 Sample Lecture
Worksheet 74.1: Notes: Coase Theorem
Worksheet 74.2: *MSC* and *MSB*
Exit Slip: Module 74

Module 75

Module 75 Sample Lecture
Worksheet 75.1: Emissions Tax
Worksheet 75.2: Positive Externalities
Worksheet 75.3: Negative Externalities
Worksheet 75.4: Externalities Practice
Exit Slip: Module 75

Module 76

Module 76 Sample Lecture
Worksheet 76.1: Types of Goods
Worksheet 76.2: Public Goods
Worksheet 76.3: Coca-Cola
Exit Slip: Module 76

Module 77

Module 77 Sample Lecture
Worksheet 77.1: Regulation
Exit Slip: Module 77

Module 78

Module 78 Sample Lecture
Worksheet 78.1: Poverty
Worksheet 78.2: Lorenz Curve and Gini Coefficient
Worksheet 78.3: Freedom and Equality
Exit Slip: Module 78
Section 14 Review Video (for students)

St. Louis Federal Reserve Bank Resources

Many of the Federal Reserve Banks have educational departments that offer helpful resources for studying economics. Members of the Educators Advisory Board of the St. Louis Federal Reserve Bank have handpicked some of their best resources for use with your AP® Economics students. References to these resources are included in the marginal notes. A complete list of the St. Louis Fed resources for each section with the corresponding URL (as of fall 2014) can be found in the TRM.

NOTE We have included a number of links to useful videos and articles in the margin notes in this section. Although all are active at the time of publication, we know that some may expire over the next few years. If a link is no longer active, you may wish to search for a similar article or video to illustrate the point. We may also periodically refresh resources on the book's companion website.

PD Section 14 Overview

Watch the video overview of Section 14 (for teachers), which is accessible through the Teacher's e-Book, the TR-flash drive, or the book's companion website bcs.worthpublishers.com/krugmanap2e (teacher log-in required).

FOCUS Active Learning

Have students read Chapter 11 of *Economics by Example* to discover more examples of market failure that hit close to home.

SECTION 14

Market Failure and the Role of Government

Incentives Matter, for Better or Worse

For many people in the northeastern United States, there is no better way to relax than to fish in one of the region's thousands of lakes. But in the 1960s, avid fishers noticed something alarming: lakes that had formerly teemed with fish were now almost empty. What had happened?

The answer was acid rain, caused mainly by coal-burning power plants. When coal is burned, it releases sulfur dioxide and nitric oxide into the atmosphere; these gases react with water, producing sulfuric acid and nitric acid. The result in the Northeast, downwind from the nation's industrial heartland, was rain sometimes as acidic as lemon juice. Acid rain didn't just kill fish; it also damaged trees and crops, and in time even began to dissolve limestone buildings.

You'll be glad to hear that the acid rain problem today is much less serious than it was in the 1960s. Power plants have reduced their emissions by switching to low-sulfur coal and installing scrubbers in their smokestacks. But they didn't do this out of the goodness of their hearts; they did it in response to government policy. Without such government intervention, power companies would have had no incentive to take the environmental effects of their actions into account.

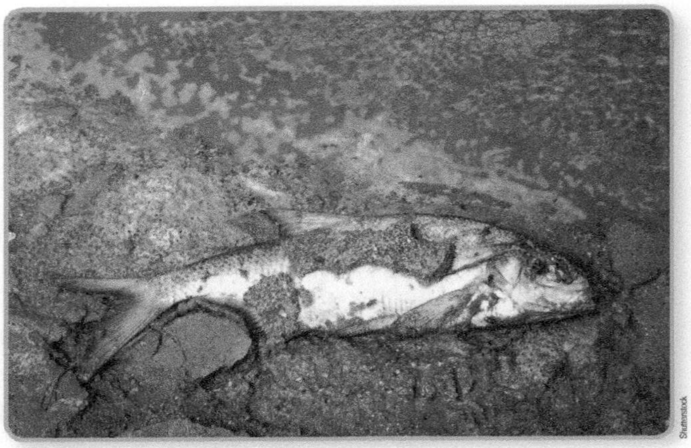

For many polluters, the damage is someone else's problem.

The Gulf of Mexico oil spill of 2010 is among the reminders that environmental problems persist. Neglected pollution is one of several reasons why markets sometimes fail to deliver efficient quantities of goods and services. We've already seen that inefficiency can arise from market power, which allows monopolists and colluding oligopolists to charge prices above marginal cost, thereby preventing mutually beneficial transactions from occurring. In this section we will consider other reasons for market failure. In Modules 74 and 75, we will see that inefficiency can arise from *externalities,* which create a conflict between the best interests of an individual or a firm and the best interests of society as a whole. In Module 76, we will focus on how the characteristics of goods often determine whether markets can deliver them efficiently. In Modules 77 and 78, we will look at the role of government in addressing market failures. The investigation of sources of inefficiency will deepen our understanding of the types of policy that can make society better off.

AVTG/E+/Getty Images

MODULE 74 Introduction to Externalities

In this Module, you will learn to:

- Explain what externalities are and why they can lead to inefficiency in a market economy
- Discuss why externalities often require government intervention
- Describe the difference between negative and positive externalities
- Explain how, according to the Coase theorem, private individuals can sometimes remedy externalities

The Economics of Pollution

Pollution is a bad thing. Yet most pollution is a side effect of activities that provide us with good things: our air is polluted by power plants generating the electricity that lights our cities, and our rivers are sullied by fertilizer runoff from farms that grow our food. Why shouldn't we accept a certain amount of pollution as the cost of a good life?

Actually, we do. Even highly committed environmentalists don't think that we can or should completely eliminate pollution—even an environmentally conscious society would accept *some* pollution as the cost of producing useful goods and services. What environmentalists argue is that unless there is a strong and effective environmental policy, our society will generate *too much* pollution—too much of a bad thing. And the great majority of economists agree.

To see why, we need a framework that lets us think about how much pollution a society *should* have. We'll then be able to see why a market economy, left to itself, will produce more pollution than it should. We'll start by adopting a framework to study the problem under the simplifying assumption that the amount of pollution emitted by a polluter is directly observable and controllable.

Costs and Benefits of Pollution

How much pollution should society allow? We learned previously that "how much" decisions always involve comparing the marginal benefit from an additional unit of something with the marginal cost of that additional unit. The same is true of pollution.

St. Louis Federal Reserve Bank Resources

"Externalities," *The Economic Lowdown Podcast Series* (Volume 1, Episode 11)

Do your students ever feel as if they are paying the price for someone else's "deal"? Perhaps they are choking on the pollution from a foundry where cheap widgets are made. That spillover effect is called an *externality*. There are positive ones, too.

PD To prepare for teaching this lesson, you may want to consult the **Module 74 Sample Lecture** in the TRM.

OPEN & CLOSE Start Here

Use *The Lorax* by Dr. Seuss to introduce externalities to your class. Students can read the book or watch the video, or you can read the book to the class, as in kindergarten (many high school students may appreciate a return to the read-aloud classes of yesteryear!). Discuss the negative effects of production on the environment and who bears those costs.

FOCUS Flip It

Watch the Jacob Clifford video "Micro Unit 6 Market Failures and the Government" to introduce the topics in this section (see econextras video list with hyperlinks on the bcs and TRFD).

TEACH Connect It

Section 2 presented the supply and demand model. At that point, external costs and benefits had not been introduced. The supply curve was the *MC* curve (Section 11), and the demand curve was the *MB* curve (Section 9). The supply and demand curves were actually *MPC* and *MPB* curves, but since external costs had yet to be discussed, there was no need to emphasize the "P." But now that we have introduced external costs and benefits, we need to distinguish between private costs and benefits, and also between social costs and benefits. When external costs exist, the *MSC* (which includes both private and external costs) is to the left of the *MPC* (supply) curve—remember that higher costs move the supply curve to the left. When external benefits exist, the *MSB* curve is to the right of the *MPB* (demand) curve—remember that increased benefits move the demand curve to the right.

Module 74 Introduction to Externalities 733

TEACH Connect It

The socially optimal quantity of pollution is the quantity of pollution that would maximize society's welfare. As is always the case, the socially optimal level occurs where $MC = MB$. In situations where there are external costs or benefits, we need to consider private AND external costs and benefits. So, the optimal level is where $MSC = MSB$.

FOCUS Graph It

Have students refer to Figure 74.1 and answer the following questions:

- What are some examples of the social costs of pollution? *For instance, examples of environmental damage*
- What are some examples of social benefits of pollution? *For example, that firms don't have to spend to reduce or eliminate pollution*
- Why is the socially optimal level of pollution above zero? *Because $MSC = MSB$ at a positive quantity*

FOCUS Active Learning

Ask students to make a list of three external costs and three external benefits they confer on others. Examples from the classroom might include talking or otherwise distracting fellow students (negative), or bringing up good examples or asking good questions (positive).

The **marginal social cost of pollution** is the additional cost imposed on society as a whole by an additional unit of pollution.

The **marginal social benefit of pollution** is the additional gain to society as a whole from an additional unit of pollution.

The **socially optimal quantity of pollution** is the quantity of pollution that society would choose if all the costs and benefits of pollution were fully accounted for.

AP® Exam Tip

Treat an externalities graph like a supply and demand graph with different labels. The equilibrium point indicates the socially optimal level of the externality.

The **marginal social cost of pollution** is the additional cost imposed on society as a whole by an additional unit of pollution. For example, acid rain harms fisheries, crops, and forests; and each additional ton of sulfur dioxide released into the atmosphere increases the harm.

The **marginal social benefit of pollution** is the additional benefit to society from an additional unit of pollution. This concept may seem counterintuitive—what's good about pollution? However, pollution avoidance requires the use of money and inputs that could otherwise be used for other purposes. For example, to reduce the quantity of sulfur dioxide they emit, power companies must either buy expensive low-sulfur coal or install special scrubbers to remove sulfur from their emissions. The more sulfur dioxide they are allowed to emit, the lower are these avoidance costs. If we calculated how much money the power industry would save if it were allowed to emit an additional ton of sulfur dioxide, that savings would be the marginal benefit to society of emitting that ton of sulfur dioxide.

Using hypothetical numbers, **Figure 74.1** shows how we can determine the **socially optimal quantity of pollution**—the quantity of pollution that makes society as well off as possible, taking all costs and benefits into account. The upward-sloping marginal social cost curve, labeled *MSC*, shows how the marginal cost to society of an additional ton of pollution emissions varies with the quantity of emissions. (An upward slope is likely because nature can often safely handle low levels of pollution but is increasingly harmed as pollution reaches high levels.) The marginal social benefit curve, labeled *MSB*, is downward-sloping because it is progressively harder, and therefore more expensive, to achieve a further reduction in pollution as the total amount of pollution falls—increasingly more expensive technology must be used. As a result, as pollution falls, the cost savings to a polluter of being allowed to emit one more ton rises.

The socially optimal quantity of pollution in this example isn't zero. It's Q_{OPT}, the quantity corresponding to point *O*, where the marginal social benefit curve crosses the marginal social cost curve. At Q_{OPT}, the marginal social benefit from an additional ton of emissions and its marginal social cost are equalized at $200.

But will a market economy, left to itself, arrive at the socially optimal quantity of pollution? No, it won't.

Figure 74.1 The Socially Optimal Quantity of Pollution

Pollution yields both costs and benefits. Here the curve *MSC* shows how the marginal cost to society as a whole from emitting one more ton of pollution emissions depends on the quantity of emissions. The curve *MSB* shows how the marginal benefit to society as a whole of emitting an additional ton of pollution emissions depends on the quantity of pollution emissions. The socially optimal quantity of pollution is Q_{OPT}; at that quantity, the marginal social benefit of pollution is equal to the marginal social cost, in this case $200.

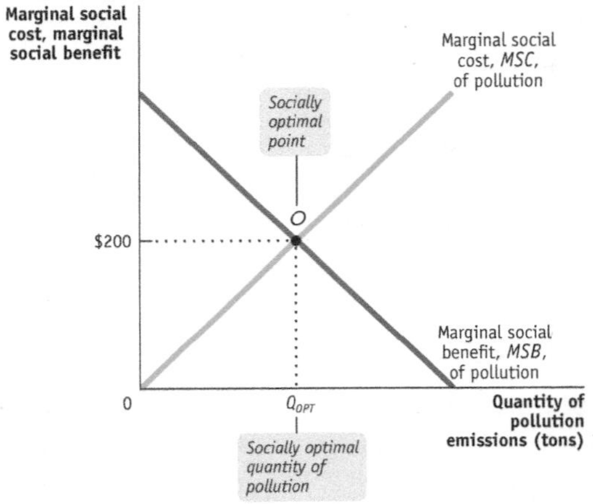

Pollution: An External Cost

Pollution yields both benefits and costs to society. But in a market economy without government intervention, those who benefit from pollution—like the owners of power companies—decide how much pollution occurs. They have no incentive to take into account the costs of pollution that they impose on others.

To see why, remember the nature of the benefits and costs from pollution. For polluters, the benefits take the form of monetary savings: by emitting an extra ton of sulfur dioxide, any given polluter saves the cost of buying expensive, low-sulfur coal or installing pollution-control equipment. So the benefits of pollution accrue directly to the polluters.

The costs of pollution, however, fall on people who have no say in the decision about how much pollution takes place: for example, people who fish in northeastern lakes do not control the decisions of power plants.

Figure 74.2 shows the result of this asymmetry between who reaps the benefits and who pays the costs. In a market economy without government intervention to protect the environment, only the benefits of pollution are taken into account in choosing the quantity of pollution. So the quantity of emissions won't be the socially optimal quantity Q_{OPT}; it will be Q_{MKT}, the quantity at which the marginal social benefit of an additional ton of pollution is zero, but the marginal social cost of that additional ton is much larger—\$400. The quantity of pollution in a market economy without government intervention will be higher than its socially optimal quantity.

The reason is that, in the absence of government intervention, those who derive the benefit from pollution—the owners of polluting firms—don't have to compensate those who bear the cost. So the marginal cost of pollution to any given polluter is zero (the assumption being that the polluter isn't also the pollution victim): polluters have no incentive to limit the amount of emissions. For example, before the Clean Air Act of 1970, midwestern power plants used the cheapest type of coal available, despite the fact that cheap coal generated more pollution, and they did nothing to scrub their emissions.

The environmental cost of pollution is perhaps the best-known and most important example of an **external cost**—an uncompensated cost that an individual or a firm imposes on others. There are many other examples of external costs besides pollution.

An **external cost** is an uncompensated cost that an individual or a firm imposes on others.

Figure 74.2 Why a Market Economy Produces Too Much Pollution

In the absence of government intervention, the quantity of pollution will be Q_{MKT}, the quantity at which the marginal social benefit of pollution equals the price polluters pay for each unit of pollution they emit: \$0. This is an inefficiently high quantity of pollution because the marginal social cost, \$400, greatly exceeds the marginal social benefit, \$0.

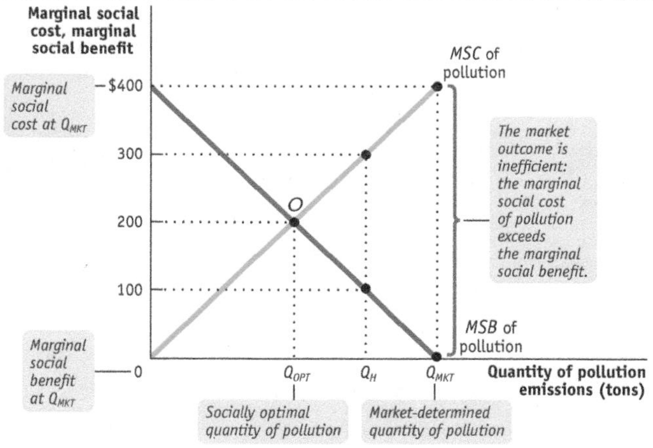

FOCUS Graph It

Have students refer to Figure 74.2 and answer the following questions:

- Without government intervention, what is the *MC* of pollution for the polluting firm? *\$0*
- Why does the market quantity equal Q_{MKT}? *Because that is where MSB = 0*
- Why is Q_{MKT} inefficient? *Because MSC > MSB*

FOCUS Active Learning

Show the Jacob Clifford video "Micro 6.2 Pollution, the Government, and *MSB = MSC*" (see econ-extras video list with hyperlinks on the bcs and TRFD). Students can discuss why "zero" pollution is not a smart idea (*economists think on the margin*). Then, discuss the examples given in the video (*air pollution and cigarettes, which impose harmful effects on people who are not part of the market*). Have one student redraw the graph titled Soda in Schools on the board. Is banning the sale of soda in schools a good solution? (*Questions to ask: Does the ban reduce the harmful effects, like higher taxes to treat obese students, on those who are not obese?*) Are there other solutions that may work to reduce youth obesity? (*Answers will vary, but subsidies to the obese to obtain medical care and using social media to inform the obese about the dangers of their condition are other options.*)

TEACH Teach It

External costs create a negative externality and external benefits create a positive externality.

Traffic congestion is a negative externality.

Another important, and certainly familiar, external cost is traffic congestion—an individual who chooses to drive during rush hour increases congestion and so increases the travel time of other drivers.

We'll see in the next module that there are also important examples of **external benefits**, benefits that individuals or firms confer on others without receiving compensation. External costs and external benefits are jointly known as **externalities**. External costs are called **negative externalities** and external benefits are called **positive externalities**.

As we've already suggested, externalities can lead to individual decisions that are not optimal for society as a whole. Let's take a closer look at why, focusing on the case of pollution.

An **external benefit** is a benefit that an individual or a firm confers on others without receiving compensation.

External costs and benefits are known as **externalities**.

External costs are **negative externalities**, and external benefits are **positive externalities**.

The Inefficiency of Excess Pollution

We have just shown that in the absence of government action, the quantity of pollution will be *inefficient*: polluters will pollute up to the point at which the marginal social benefit of pollution is zero, as shown by quantity Q_{MKT} in Figure 74.2. Recall that an outcome is inefficient if some people could be made better off without making others worse off. We have already seen why the equilibrium quantity in a perfectly competitive market with no externalities is the efficient quantity of the good, the quantity that maximizes total surplus. Here, we can use a variation of that analysis to show how the presence of a negative externality upsets that result.

Because the marginal social benefit of pollution is zero at Q_{MKT}, reducing the quantity of pollution by one ton would subtract very little from the total social benefit from pollution. In other words, the benefit to polluters from that last unit of pollution is very low—virtually zero. Meanwhile, the marginal social cost imposed on the rest of society of that last ton of pollution at Q_{MKT} is quite high—$400. So by reducing the quantity of pollution at Q_{MKT} by one ton, the total social cost of pollution falls by $400, but total social benefit falls by virtually zero. That is, total surplus rises by approximately $400 if the quantity of pollution at Q_{MKT} is reduced by one ton.

If the quantity of pollution is reduced further, there will be more gains in total surplus, though they will be smaller. For example, if the quantity of pollution is Q_H in

FYI Talking and Driving

Why is that woman in the car in front of us driving so erratically? Is she drunk? No, she's talking on her cell phone.

Traffic safety experts take the risks posed by driving while talking very seriously. Using hands-free, voice-activated phones doesn't seem to help much because the main danger is distraction. As one traffic safety consultant put it, "It's not where your eyes are; it's where your head is." And we're not talking about a trivial problem. One estimate suggests that people who talk on their cell phones while driving may be responsible for 600 or more traffic deaths each year.

The National Safety Council urges people not to use phones while driving. But a growing number of people say that voluntary standards aren't enough; they want the use of hand-held cell phones while driving made illegal, as it already is in fourteen states and the District of Columbia, as well as in Japan, Israel, and many other countries.

Why not leave the decision up to the driver? Because the risk posed by driving while talking isn't just a risk to the driver; it's also a safety risk to others—especially people in other cars. Even if you decide that the benefit to you of taking that call is worth the cost, you aren't taking into account the cost to other people. Driving while talking, in other words, generates a serious—sometimes fatal—negative externality.

FOCUS Active Learning

If your students have not already signed it, download the "Don't Text While Driving" pledge from http://www.att.com/Common/about_us/txting_driving/6_TWDToolKit_Pledge_form.pdf and distribute copies. They may even want to take copies home for their parents and siblings.

St. Louis Federal Reserve Bank Resources

"Externalities," *The Economic Lowdown Video Series*, Episode 5

Students will learn how costs and benefits sometimes affect bystanders and discover how taxes and subsidies can be used to "internalize" externalities.

Figure 74.2, the marginal social benefit of a ton of pollution is $100, but the marginal social cost is still much higher at $300. This means that reducing the quantity of pollution by one ton leads to a net gain in total surplus of approximately $300 – $100 = $200. Thus Q_H is still an inefficiently high quantity of pollution. Only if the quantity of pollution is reduced to Q_{OPT}, where the marginal social cost and the marginal social benefit of an additional ton of pollution are both $200, is the outcome efficient.

Private Solutions to Externalities

Can the private sector solve the problem of externalities without government intervention? Bear in mind that when an outcome is inefficient, there is potentially a deal that makes people better off. Why don't individuals find a way to make that deal?

In an influential 1960 article, economist and Nobel laureate Ronald Coase pointed out that in an ideal world the private sector could indeed deal with all externalities. According to the **Coase theorem**, even in the presence of externalities, an economy can reach an efficient solution, provided that the legal rights of the parties are clearly defined and the costs of making a deal are sufficiently low. In some cases it takes a lot of time, or even money, to bring the relevant parties together, negotiate a deal, and carry out the terms of the deal. The costs of making a deal are known as **transaction costs**.

To get a sense of Coase's argument, imagine two neighbors, Mick and Christina, who both like to barbecue in their backyards on summer afternoons. Mick likes to play golden oldies on his boombox while barbecuing, but this annoys Christina, who can't stand that kind of music.

Who prevails? You might think it depends on the legal rights involved in the case: if the law says that Mick has the right to play whatever music he wants, Christina just has to suffer; if the law says that Mick needs Christina's consent to play music in his backyard, Mick has to live without his favorite music while barbecuing.

But as Coase pointed out, the outcome need not be determined by legal rights, because Christina and Mick can make a private deal as long as the legal rights are clearly defined. Even if Mick has the right to play his music, Christina could pay him not to. Even if Mick can't play the music without an OK from Christina, he can offer to pay her to give that OK. These payments allow them to reach an efficient solution, regardless of who has the legal upper hand. If the benefit of the music to Mick exceeds its cost to Christina, the music will go on; if the benefit to Mick is less than the cost to Christina, there will be silence.

The implication of Coase's analysis is that externalities need not lead to inefficiency because individuals have an incentive to make mutually beneficial deals—deals that lead them to take externalities into account when making decisions. When individuals *do* take externalities into account when making decisions, economists say that they **internalize the externalities**. If externalities are fully internalized, as when Mick must forgo a payment from Christina *equal to the external cost he imposes on her* in order to play music, the outcome is efficient even without government intervention.

Why can't individuals always internalize externalities? Our barbecue example implicitly assumes the transaction costs are low enough for Mick and Christina to be able to make a deal. In many situations involving externalities, however, transaction costs prevent individuals from making efficient deals. Examples of transaction costs include the following:

- *The costs of communication among the interested parties.* Such costs may be very high if many people are involved.
- *The costs of making legally binding agreements.* Such costs may be high if expensive legal services are required.
- *Costly delays involved in bargaining.* Even if there is a potentially beneficial deal, both sides may hold out in an effort to extract more favorable terms, leading to increased effort and forgone utility.

AP® Exam Tip

For the AP® exam, be prepared to identify and explain the reasons the Coase theorem won't always work.

According to the **Coase theorem**, even in the presence of externalities, an economy can always reach an efficient solution as long as **transaction costs**—the costs to individuals of making a deal—are sufficiently low. When individuals take external costs or benefits into account, they **internalize the externalities**.

TEACH Teach It

Transaction costs are those involved in "making a deal" and include:

- the costs of communication among involved parties.
- the costs of making legally binding agreements.
- costly delays involved in bargaining.

TEACH Teach It

TRM To help students understand this solution to negative externalities, assign **Worksheet 74.1 (Notes: Coase Theorem)** from the TRM.

FOCUS Active Learning

TRM Ask your class to complete **Worksheet 74.2 (*MSC* and *MSB*)** from the TRM for practice with the concept that marginal social cost equals marginal social benefit.

OPEN & CLOSE Exit Slip

TRM *Please see* ***Exit Slip: Module 74*** *in the TRM for formative multiple-choice questions to ask your students before finishing your lesson. These questions will help you quickly assess whether your students have mastered the module's concepts before moving on.*

Answers to the Exit Slip Questions

1. D
2. C
3. E

Answers to Module 74 Review Questions

Check Your Understanding

1. a. This is an externality problem because the cost of wastewater runoff is imposed on the farms' neighbors with no compensation and no other way for the farms to internalize the cost.

b. Since the large poultry farmers do not take the external cost of their actions into account when making decisions about how much wastewater to generate, they will create more runoff than is socially optimal. They will produce runoff up to the point at which the marginal social benefit of an additional unit of runoff is zero; however, their neighbors experience a high, positive level of marginal social cost of runoff from this output level. So, the quantity of wastewater runoff is inefficient: reducing runoff by 1 unit would reduce total social benefit by less than it would reduce total social cost.

c. At the socially optimal quantity of wastewater runoff, the marginal social benefit is equal to the marginal social cost. This quantity is lower than the quantity of wastewater runoff that would be created in the absence of government intervention or a private deal.

2. Yasmin's reasoning is not correct:
Allowing some late returns of books is likely to be socially optimal. Although a marginal social cost is imposed on others every day they are late in returning a book, there is some positive marginal social benefit to returning a book late—one gets a longer period during which to use it for education and pleasure. If one needs it for a book report, the additional benefit from another day might be large indeed. The socially optimal number of days that a book is returned late is the number at which the marginal social benefit equals the marginal social cost. A fine so stiff that it prevents any late returns is likely to result in a situation in which people return books although the marginal social benefit of keeping them another day is greater than the marginal social cost—an inefficient outcome. In that case, allowing an overdue patron another day would increase total social benefit more than it would increase total social cost. Thus, it is appropriate to charge a moderate fine, one that leads to a reduction in the number of days books are returned late so that it is the same as the socially optimal number of days.

FYI Thank You for Not Smoking

New Yorkers call them the "shiver-and-puff people"—the smokers who stand outside their workplaces, even in the depths of winter, to take a cigarette break. Over the past couple of decades, rules against smoking in spaces shared by others have become ever stricter. This is partly a matter of personal dislike—nonsmokers really don't like to smell other people's cigarette smoke—but it also reflects concerns over the health risks of second-hand smoke. As the Surgeon General's warning on many packs says, "Smoking causes lung cancer, heart disease, emphysema, and may complicate pregnancy." And there's no question that being in the same room as someone who smokes exposes you to at least some health risk.

Second-hand smoke, then, is clearly an example of a negative externality. But how important is it? Putting a dollar-and-cents value on it—that is, measuring the marginal social cost of cigarette smoke—requires researchers to not only estimate the health effects but also to put a value on these effects. Despite the difficulty, economists have tried. A paper published in 1993 in the *Journal of Economic Perspectives* surveyed the research on the external costs of both cigarette smoking and alcohol consumption.

According to this paper, conclusions regarding the health costs of cigarettes depend on whether the costs imposed on members of smokers' families, including unborn children, are counted along with the costs borne by smokers. If not, the external costs of second-hand smoke have been estimated at about $0.19 per pack smoked. (Using this method of calculation, $0.19 corresponds to the *average* social cost of smoking per pack at the current level of smoking in society.) A 2005 study raised this estimate to $0.52 per pack smoked. If the effects on smokers' families are included, the number rises considerably—family members who live with smokers are exposed to a lot more smoke. (They are also exposed to the risk of fire, which alone is estimated at $0.09 per pack.) If you include the effects of smoking by pregnant women on their unborn children's future health, the cost is immense—$4.80 per pack, which is more than twice the wholesale price charged by cigarette manufacturers.

In some cases, transaction costs are low enough to allow individuals to resolve externality problems. For example, while filming *A League of Their Own* on location in a neighborhood ballpark, director Penny Marshall paid a man $100 to stop using his noisy chainsaw nearby. But in many other cases, transaction costs are too high to make it possible to deal with externalities through private action. For example, tens of millions of people are adversely affected by acid rain. It would be prohibitively expensive to try to make a deal among all those people and all those power companies.

When transaction costs prevent the private sector from dealing with externalities, it is time to look for government solutions—the subject of the next module.

MODULE 74 Review

Check Your Understanding

1. Wastewater runoff from large poultry farms adversely affects residents in neighboring homes. Explain the following:
   a. why this is considered an externality problem
   b. the efficiency of the outcome with neither government intervention nor a private deal
   c. how the socially optimal outcome is determined and how it compares with the no-intervention, no-deal outcome
2. According to Yasmin, any student who borrows a book from the university library and fails to return it on time imposes a negative externality on other students. She claims that rather than charging a modest fine for late returns, the library should charge a huge fine, so that borrowers will never return a book late. Is Yasmin's economic reasoning correct?

738 Section 14 Market Failure and the Role of Government

Tackle the Test: Multiple-Choice Questions

1. The socially optimal level of pollution is
   a. less than that created by the market, but not zero.
   b. more than that created by the market.
   c. whatever the market creates.
   d. determined by firms.
   e. zero.
2. Which of the following is a source of negative externalities?
   a. loud conversations in a library
   b. smokestack scrubbers
   c. a beautiful view
   d. national defense
   e. a decision to purchase dressy but uncomfortable shoes
3. Inefficiencies created by externalities can be dealt with through
   a. government actions only.
   b. private actions only.
   c. market outcomes only.
   d. either private or government actions.
   e. neither private nor government actions.
4. The Coase theorem asserts that, under the right circumstances, inefficiencies created by externalities can be dealt with through
   a. lawsuits.
   b. private bargaining.
   c. vigilante actions.
   d. government policies.
   e. mediation.
5. Which of the following makes it more likely that private solutions to externality problems will succeed?
   a. high transaction costs
   b. high prices for legal services
   c. delays in the bargaining process
   d. a small number of affected parties
   e. loosely defined legal rights

Tackle the Test: Free-Response Questions

1. Draw a correctly labeled graph showing the market-determined quantity of pollution, and explain why that quantity will be chosen in the absence of intervention and private deals. On the same graph, show the socially optimal level of pollution.

Rubric for FRQ 1 (6 points)

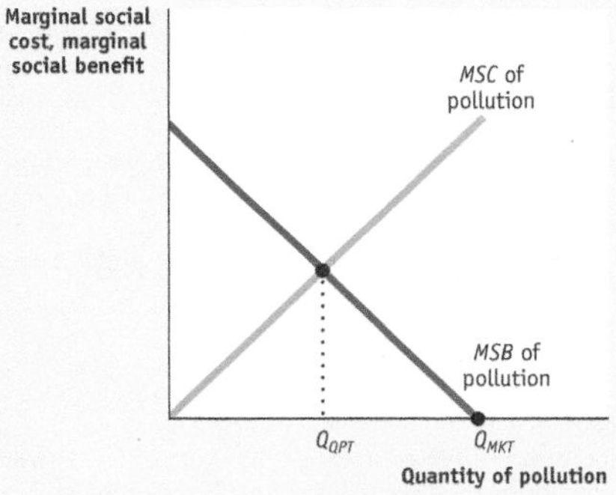

1 point: The vertical axis is labeled "Marginal social cost, marginal social benefit" or "Dollars per unit" and the horizontal axis is labeled "Quantity of pollution" or "Q."

1 point: The marginal social cost curve is labeled and upward-sloping.

1 point: The marginal social benefit curve is labeled and downward-sloping.

1 point: The market-determined level of pollution is shown on the horizontal axis where the marginal social benefit curve reaches the horizontal axis.

1 point: In the absence of intervention and private deals, the marginal cost to a polluter of polluting is zero. Thus, pollution will continue until the marginal social benefit (all of which goes to the polluter) equals the polluter's marginal cost of zero, which occurs at the horizontal intercept of the marginal social cost curve.

1 point: The socially optimal level of pollution is shown on the horizontal axis below the intersection of MSC and MSB.

2. a. Define the marginal social cost of pollution.
   b. Define the marginal social benefit of pollution, and explain why polluting more can provide benefits to a firm even when it could produce the same quantity of output without polluting as much.
   c. Define the socially optimal level of pollution.
   (4 points)

Tackle the Test: Multiple-Choice Questions

1. a
2. a
3. d
4. b
5. d

Tackle the Test: Free-Response Question

Rubric for FRQ 2 (4 points)

1 point: The marginal social cost of pollution is the additional cost imposed on society by an additional unit of pollution.

1 point: The marginal social benefit of pollution is the additional benefit to society from an additional unit of pollution.

1 point: Even when a firm could provide the same quantity of output without polluting as much, there is a benefit from polluting more because the firm can devote less money and resources to pollution avoidance.

1 point: The socially optimal level of pollution is that level at which the marginal social benefit of pollution equals the marginal social cost.

Module 74 Introduction to Externalities 739

PD To prepare for teaching this lesson, you may want to consult the **Module 75 Sample Lecture** in the TRM.

OPEN & CLOSE Start Here

The previous module presented texting while driving and smoking as examples of activities that create negative externalities. Choose one of those examples and have the class discuss and list the private costs of the activity and its external costs. Ask students to think of policies that have been used (or could be used) to internalize the external costs of the activity. Be sure that they identify the potential usefulness of taxing the behavior as a way to reduce it. You can assign students to do the same exercise on their own for the other example activity.

TEACH AP® Exam Tip

Pollution is likely the most common example of a negative externality used to teach about externalities, and you will find this example on many AP® exams. However, you should focus on the economic concepts rather than the environmental issues when preparing students for the AP® exam.

ekash/E+/Getty Images

MODULE 75 Externalities and Public Policy

In this Module, you will learn to:

- Address externality problems with specific public policies
- Explain why some government policies to deal with externalities, such as emissions taxes, tradable emissions permits, and Pigouvian subsidies, are efficient, although others, including environmental standards, are not

Policies Toward Pollution

Before 1970 there were no rules governing the amount of sulfur dioxide that power plants in the United States could emit—which is why acid rain got to be such a problem. In 1970, the Clean Air Act set rules about sulfur dioxide emissions; thereafter, the acidity of rainfall declined significantly. Economists argued, however, that a more flexible system of rules that exploited the effectiveness of markets could achieve lower pollution levels at a lower cost. In 1990 this theory was put into effect with a modified version of the Clean Air Act. And guess what? The economists were right!

In this section we'll look at the policies governments use to deal with pollution and at how economic analysis has been used to improve those policies.

AP® Exam Tip

Environmental standards are generally not the most effective way to combat negative externalities caused by pollution because they are inflexible and don't allow pollution reduction to occur in the least costly way.

Environmental Standards

Because the economy, and life itself, depend on a viable environment, external costs that threaten the environment—air pollution, water pollution, habitat destruction, and so on, are worthy of attention. Protection of the environment has become a major focus of government in every advanced nation. In the United States, the Environmental Protection Agency is the principal enforcer of environmental policies at the national level and is supported by the actions of state and local governments.

How does a country protect its environment? At present the main policy tools are **environmental standards**, rules that protect the environment by specifying limits for or actions by producers and consumers. A familiar example is the law that requires almost all vehicles to have catalytic converters, which reduce the emission of chemicals that can cause smog and lead to health problems. Other rules require communities to treat their sewage, factories to limit their pollution emissions, and homes to be painted with lead-free paint, among many other examples.

Environmental standards are rules that protect the environment by specifying limits for or actions by producers and consumers.

740 Section 14 Market Failure and the Role of Government

Environmental standards came into widespread use in the 1960s and 1970s with considerable success. Since the United States passed the Clean Air Act in 1970, for example, the emission of air pollutants has fallen by more than a third, even though the population has grown by a third and the size of the economy has more than doubled. Even in Los Angeles, still famous for its smog, the air has improved dramatically: in 1992 ozone levels in the surrounding South Coast Air Basin exceeded federal standards on 143 days; in 2012, on only 12 days.

© David Sims/iStockphoto

Environmental standards are helping to erase the Los Angeles smog.

Despite these successes, economists believe that when regulators can control a polluter's emissions directly, there are more efficient ways than environmental standards to deal with pollution. By using methods grounded in economic analysis, society can achieve a cleaner environment at lower cost. Most current environmental standards are inflexible and don't allow reductions in pollution to be achieved at the lowest possible cost. For example, two power plants—plant A and plant B—might be ordered to reduce pollution by the same percentage, even if their costs of achieving that objective are very different.

How does economic theory suggest that pollution should be controlled? We'll examine two approaches: taxes and tradable permits. As we'll see, either approach can achieve the efficient outcome at the minimum feasible cost.

Emissions Taxes

One way to deal with pollution directly is to charge polluters an **emissions tax**. Emissions taxes are taxes that depend on the amount of pollution a firm produces. For example, power plants might be charged $200 for every ton of sulfur dioxide they emit.

An **emissions tax** is a tax that depends on the amount of pollution a firm produces.

Consider the socially optimal quantity of pollution, Q_{OPT}, shown in **Figure 75.1**. At that quantity of pollution, the marginal social benefit and the marginal social cost of an additional ton of emissions are equal at $200. But in the absence of government

Figure 75.1 In Pursuit of the Efficient Quantity of Pollution

The market determined quantity of pollution, Q_{MKT}, is too high because polluters don't pay the marginal social cost, and thus pollute beyond the socially optimal quantity, Q_{OPT}, at which marginal social cost equals marginal social benefit. A Pigouvian tax of $200—the value of the marginal social cost of pollution when it equals the marginal social benefit of pollution—gives polluters the incentive to emit only the socially optimal quantity of pollution. Another solution is to provide permits for only the socially optimal quantity of pollution.

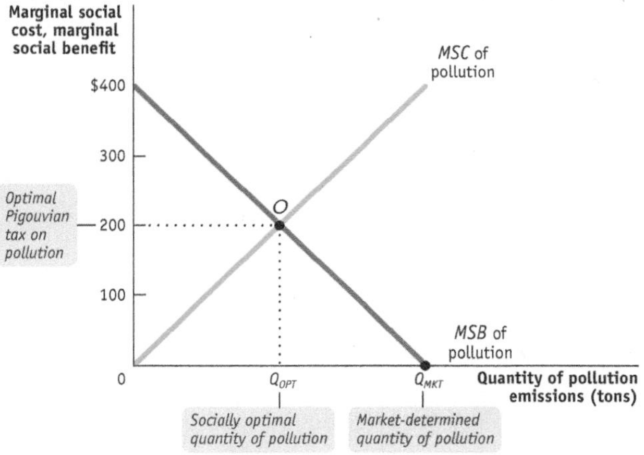

FOCUS Test It

Why do economists believe environmental standards are an inefficient way to reduce pollution to its optimal level? *Because they do not minimize the cost of pollution reduction by setting MC = MB*

FOCUS Graph It

Figure 75.1 shows the market-determined and socially optimal quantities of pollution. Have students refer to the illustrations and answer the following questions:

- Why is Q_{MKT} the market quantity of pollution? *Without government intervention, there is no cost for polluting and firms set MSB = MSC = 0.*
- Why is Q_{OPT} the optimal level of pollution (and not zero pollution)? *Q_{OPT} occurs where MSC = MSB; the optimal level is only zero if the cost of pollution cleanup is zero or the benefit of pollution is infinite.*
- How is the optimal level of the Pigouvian tax determined? *It is set equal to the MSC of pollution at the quantity where MSC = MSB so that the firm must internalize the MSC of its pollution.*

FOCUS Active Learning

TRM Assign **Worksheet 75.1 (Emissions Tax)** from the TRM for practice graphing the market-determined and socially optimal quantity of pollution.

intervention, power companies have no incentive to limit pollution to the socially optimal quantity Q_{OPT}; instead, they will push pollution up to the quantity Q_{MKT}, at which the marginal social benefit is zero.

It's now easy to see how an emissions tax can solve the problem. If power companies are required to pay a tax of $200 per ton of emissions, they face a marginal cost of $200 per ton and have an incentive to reduce emissions to Q_{OPT}, the socially optimal quantity. This illustrates a general result: an emissions tax equal to the marginal social cost at the socially optimal quantity of pollution induces polluters to internalize the externality—to take into account the true cost to society of their actions.

Why is an emissions tax an efficient way (that is, a cost-minimizing way) to reduce pollution but environmental standards generally are not? Because an emissions tax ensures that the marginal benefit of pollution is equal for all sources of pollution, but an environmental standard does not. **Figure 75.2** shows a hypothetical industry consisting of only two plants, plant A and plant B. We'll assume that plant A uses newer technology than plant B and so has a lower cost of reducing pollution. Reflecting this difference in costs, plant A's marginal benefit of pollution curve, MB_A, lies below plant B's marginal benefit of pollution curve, MB_B. Because it is more costly for plant B to

Figure 75.2 Environmental Standards Versus Emissions Taxes

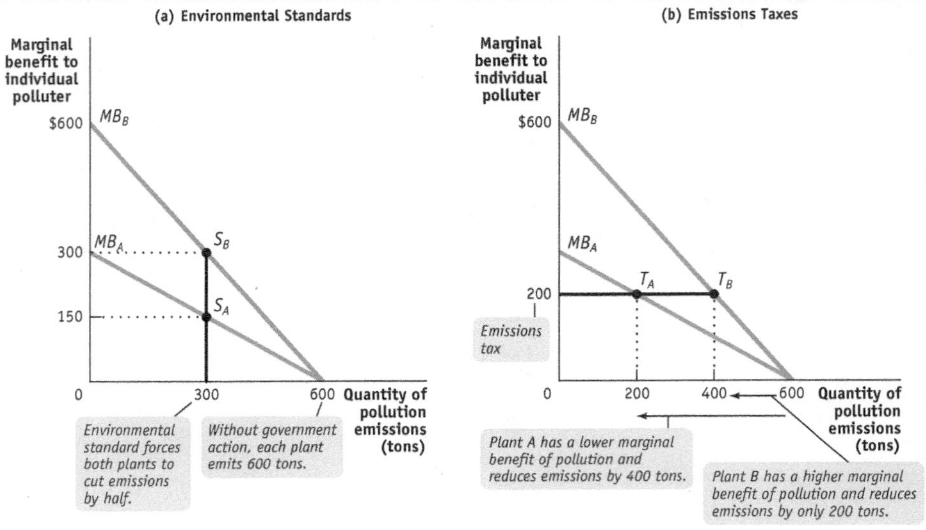

In both panels, MB_A shows the marginal benefit of pollution to plant A and MB_B shows the marginal benefit of pollution to plant B. In the absence of government intervention, each plant would emit 600 tons. However, the cost of reducing emissions is lower for plant A, as shown by the fact that MB_A lies below MB_B. Panel (a) shows the result of an environmental standard that requires both plants to cut emissions in half; this is inefficient, because it leaves the marginal benefit of pollution higher for plant B than for plant A. Panel (b) shows that an emissions tax achieves the same quantity of overall pollution efficiently: faced with an emissions tax of $200 per ton, both plants reduce pollution to the point where its marginal benefit is $200.

FOCUS Graph It

Figure 75.2 compares the efficiency of environmental standards and emissions taxes. Have students refer to the figure and answer the following questions:

- With an environmental standard of 300, what are the marginal benefits of plants A and B? *MB_A = $150 and MB_B = $300*
- If the marginal benefit of plant B is higher than the marginal benefit of plant A, how could total benefits be increased? *Since $MB_B > MB_A$, total benefits will increase by allowing plant B to pollute more since additional pollution from plant B adds more to total benefit than additional pollution from plant A.*
- With an emission tax of $200, how much pollution do plant A and plant B emit? *Plant A = 200 units and plant B = 400 units*
- Why does plant A emit less pollution than plant B with the emission tax? *Because plant A has a lower marginal benefit from polluting*
- Is the cost to achieve the socially optimal output the same for environmental standards and emission taxes? *No, the cost of using environmental standards is higher.*
- Why is an emissions tax more efficient than environmental standards? *An emissions tax allocates pollution cleanup based on each plant's marginal benefit of polluting.*

reduce its pollution at any output quantity, an additional ton of pollution is worth more to plant B than to plant A.

In the absence of government action, polluters will pollute until the marginal social benefit of an additional unit of emissions is equal to zero. Recall that the marginal social benefit of pollution is the cost savings, at the margin, to polluters of an additional unit of pollution. As a result, without government intervention each plant will pollute until its own marginal benefit of pollution is equal to zero. This corresponds to an emissions quantity of 600 tons each for plants A and B—the quantity of pollution at which MB_A and MB_B are each equal to zero. So although plant A and plant B value a ton of emissions differently, without government action they will each choose to emit the same amount of pollution.

Now suppose that the government decides that overall pollution from this industry should be cut in half, from 1,200 tons to 600 tons. Panel (a) of Figure 75.2 shows how this might be achieved with an environmental standard that requires each plant to cut its emissions in half, from 600 to 300 tons. The standard has the desired effect of reducing overall emissions from 1,200 to 600 tons but accomplishes it in an inefficient way. As you can see from panel (a), the environmental standard leads plant A to produce at point S_A, where its marginal benefit of pollution is \$150, but plant B produces at point S_B, where its marginal benefit of pollution is twice as high, \$300.

This difference in marginal benefits between the two plants tells us that the same quantity of pollution can be achieved at lower total cost by allowing plant B to pollute more than 300 tons but inducing plant A to pollute less. In fact, the efficient way to reduce pollution is to ensure that at the industry-wide outcome, the marginal benefit of pollution is the same for all plants. When each plant values a unit of pollution equally, there is no way to rearrange pollution reduction among the various plants that achieves the optimal quantity of pollution at a lower total cost.

We can see from panel (b) how an emissions tax achieves exactly that result. Suppose both plant A and plant B pay an emissions tax of \$200 per ton so that the marginal cost of an additional ton of emissions to each plant is now \$200 rather than zero. As a result, plant A produces at T_A and plant B produces at T_B. So plant A reduces its pollution more than it would under an inflexible environmental standard, cutting its emissions from 600 to 200 tons; meanwhile, plant B reduces its pollution less, going from 600 to 400 tons. In the end, total pollution—600 tons—is the same as under the environmental standard, but total surplus is higher. That's because the reduction in pollution has been achieved efficiently, allocating most of the reduction to plant A, the plant that can reduce emissions at lower cost.

The term *emissions tax* may convey the misleading impression that taxes are a solution to only one kind of external cost, pollution. In fact, taxes can be used to discourage any activity that generates negative externalities, such as driving during rush hour or operating a noisy bar in a residential area. In general, taxes designed to correct for the effects of external costs are known as **Pigouvian taxes**, after the economist A. C. Pigou, who emphasized their usefulness in a classic 1920 book, *The Economics of Welfare*. Look again at Figure 75.1. In our example, the optimal Pigouvian tax is \$200; as you can see from Figure 75.1, this tax causes power plants to internalize the external cost by paying the marginal social cost of pollution at the optimal output quantity, Q_{OPT}.

Are there any problems with emissions taxes? The main concern is that in practice government officials usually aren't sure at what level the tax should be set. If they set the tax too low, there will be too little improvement in the environment; if they set it too high, emissions will be reduced by more than is efficient. This uncertainty cannot be eliminated, but the nature of the risks can be changed by using an alternative strategy, issuing tradable emissions permits.

Tradable Emissions Permits

Tradable emissions permits are licenses to emit limited quantities of pollutants that can be bought and sold by polluters. They are usually issued to polluting firms according to some formula reflecting their history. For example, each power plant might be

AP® Exam Tip

Emissions taxes can be more efficient than environmental standards, but it is difficult to determine the level of taxation that leads to the socially optimal level of emissions.

Taxes designed to correct for the effects of external costs are known as **Pigouvian taxes**.

Tradable emissions permits are licenses to emit limited quantities of pollutants that can be bought and sold by polluters.

TEACH Teach It

A tax designed to internalize external costs is known as a Pigouvian tax. It is named after the economist A. C. Pigou who wrote about the usefulness of taxes for addressing externalities.

Module 75 Externalities and Public Policy 743

TEACH Connect It

Emission permits give their owner the right to emit a specified level of pollutants. The owner of a permit can either use the permit (e.g., emit pollution) or clean up its pollution and sell the permit to someone else. Firms without emission permits must either buy permits or not pollute (e.g., clean up). Permits are sold in a market with a fixed supply (equal to the optimal level of pollution) and a demand by polluting firms. A firm's demand for emission permits is based on its *MB* of polluting (which is its *MC* of cleanup since the alternative to polluting is cleaning up). The price of an emission permit will be determined by supply and demand, as it was for other goods.

issued permits equal to 50% of its emissions before the system went into effect. The more important point, however, is that these permits are *tradable*. Firms with differing costs of reducing pollution can now engage in mutually beneficial transactions: those that find it easier to reduce pollution will sell some of their permits to those that find it more difficult. In other words, firms will use transactions in permits to reallocate pollution reduction among themselves, so that in the end those with the lowest cost will reduce their pollution the most and those with the highest cost will reduce their pollution the least. Assume that the government issues 300 permits each to plant A and plant B, where one permit allows the emission of one ton of pollution. Under a system of tradable emissions permits, commonly known as a *cap and trade program*, plant A will find it profitable to sell 100 of its 300 government-issued permits to plant B. The effect of a cap and trade program is to create a market in rights to pollute.

AP® Exam Tip

Cap and trade programs reward producers who reduce emissions with the ability to create revenue for the firm by selling the emissions permits they no longer need.

Just like emissions taxes, tradable permits provide polluters with an incentive to take the marginal social cost of pollution into account. To see why, suppose that the market price of a permit to emit one ton of sulfur dioxide is $200. Then every plant has an incentive to limit its emissions of sulfur dioxide to the point where its marginal benefit of emitting another ton of pollution is $200. This is obvious for plants that buy rights to pollute: if a plant must pay $200 for the right to emit an additional ton of sulfur dioxide, it faces the same incentives as a plant facing an emissions tax of $200 per ton. But it's equally true for plants that have more permits than they plan to use: by *not* emitting a ton of sulfur dioxide, a plant frees up a permit that it can sell for $200, so the opportunity cost of a ton of emissions to the plant's owner is $200.

In short, tradable emissions permits have the same cost-minimizing advantage as emissions taxes over environmental standards: either system ensures that those who can reduce pollution most cheaply are the ones who do so. The socially optimal quantity of pollution shown in Figure 75.1 could be efficiently achieved either way: by imposing an emissions tax of $200 per ton of pollution or by issuing tradable permits to emit Q_{OPT} tons of pollution. If regulators choose to issue Q_{OPT} permits, where one permit allows the release of one ton of emissions, then the equilibrium market price of a permit among polluters will indeed be $200. Why? You can see from Figure 75.1 that at Q_{OPT}, only polluters with a marginal benefit of pollution of $200 or more will buy a permit. And the last polluter who buys—who has a marginal benefit of exactly $200—sets the market price.

It's important to realize that emissions taxes and tradable permits do more than induce polluting industries to reduce their output. Unlike rigid environmental standards, emissions taxes and tradable permits provide incentives to create and use technology that emits less pollution—new technology that lowers the socially optimal level of pollution. The main effect of the permit system for sulfur dioxide has been to change *how* electricity is produced rather than to reduce the nation's electricity output. For example, power companies have shifted to the use of alternative fuels such as low-sulfur coal and natural gas; they have also installed scrubbers that take much of the sulfur dioxide out of a power plant's emissions.

The main problem with tradable emissions permits is the flip-side of the problem with emissions taxes: because it is difficult to determine the optimal quantity of pollution, governments can find themselves either issuing too many permits (that is, they don't reduce pollution enough) or issuing too few (that is, they reduce pollution too much).

After first relying on environmental standards, the U.S. government has turned to a system of tradable permits to control acid rain. Current proposals would extend the system to other major sources of pollution. And in 2005 the European Union created an emissions-trading scheme with the purpose of controlling emissions of carbon dioxide, a greenhouse gas. The European Union scheme is part of a larger global market for the trading of greenhouse gas permits. The FYI that follows describes these two systems in greater detail.

744 Section 14 Market Failure and the Role of Government

FYI Cap and Trade

The tradable emissions permit systems for both acid rain in the United States and greenhouse gases in the European Union are examples of *cap and trade programs*: the government sets a *cap* (a total amount of pollution that can be emitted), issues tradable emissions permits, and enforces a yearly rule that a polluter must hold a number of permits equal to the amount of pollution emitted. The goal is to set the cap low enough to generate environmental benefits and, at the same time, to give polluters flexibility in meeting environmental standards and motivate them to adopt new technologies that will lower the cost of reducing pollution.

In 1994 the United States began a cap and trade system for the sulfur dioxide emissions that cause acid rain by issuing permits to power plants based on their historical consumption of coal. The cap of 8.95 million tons set for 2010 and beyond is about half the level of sulfur dioxide emissions in 1980. Economists who have analyzed the sulfur dioxide cap and trade system point to another reason for its success: it would have been a lot more expensive—80% more to be exact—to reduce emissions by this much using a non-market-based regulatory policy.

The European Union cap and trade scheme is the world's only mandatory trading scheme for greenhouse gases and covers all 27 member nations of the European Union. Available data indicate that within the system, 3,093 metric tons of emissions were transacted in 2008 and 6,326 metric tons in 2009, an astonishing increase of 105%. The U.S. Congress was suitably impressed by the results in the European Union to consider an American cap and trade system for greenhouse gases. The American Clean Energy and Security Act of 2009 and the American Power Act of 2010 contained cap and trade provisions, although no such act has become law at the time of this writing.

Despite the promising news from Europe, however, cap and trade systems are not silver bullets for the world's pollution problems. While they are appropriate for pollution that's geographically dispersed, like sulfur dioxide and greenhouse gases, they don't work for pollution that's localized, like mercury or lead contamination. In addition, the amount of overall reduction in pollution depends on the level of the cap. Under industry pressure, regulators run the risk of issuing too many permits, effectively eliminating the cap. Finally, there must be vigilant monitoring of compliance if the system is to work. Without oversight of how much a polluter is actually emitting, there is no way to know for sure that the rules are being followed.

Production, Consumption, and Externalities

Nobody imposes external costs like pollution out of malice. Pollution, traffic congestion, and other negative externalities are side effects of activities, like electricity generation, manufacturing, or driving, that are otherwise desirable. We've just learned how government regulators can move the market to the socially optimal quantity when the side effects can be directly controlled. But as we cautioned earlier, in some cases it's not possible to directly control the side effects—only the activities that cause them can be influenced. As we'll see shortly, government policies in these situations must instead be geared to changing the levels of production and consumption that create externalities, which in turn changes the levels of the externalities themselves.

This approach, although slightly more complicated, has several advantages. First, for activities that generate external *costs*, it gives us a clear understanding of how the desirable activity is affected by policies designed to manage its side effects. Second, it helps us think about a question that is different but related to the problem of external costs: what should be done when an activity generates external *benefits*. It's important to realize that not all externalities are negative. In fact, we encounter many positive externalities every day; for example, a neighbor's bird-feeder has the side effect of maintaining the local wild bird population for everyone's enjoyment. And a beautiful flower garden in front of a neighbor's house can be enjoyed by many passersby.

Using the approach of targeting the activity behind the externalities, we'll now turn our attention to the topic of positive externalities.

TEACH Teach It

Externalities can be negative (e.g., pollution) or positive. When the production and consumption of a good provide benefits to third parties, that good is said to offer positive externalities to society. Below are three examples of private versus external benefits:

- I consume a chocolate bar. This provides me with private benefit, but no one else receives any benefit from my action.
- I consume a flu shot or chickenpox vaccine, and everyone else receives a benefit because these two viruses are less likely to spread from me and affect them. There are external benefits.
- I spend money improving my home, so I receive a private benefit. But the improvement also provides an external benefit to my neighbors by raising the property value of their homes:

Total social benefit = Total private benefit + Total external benefit

On an incremental basis, $MSB = MPB + MEB$.

FOCUS **Active Learning**

TRM Assign Jacob Clifford's video "Micro 6.4 Positive Externalities" (see econextras video list with hyperlinks on the bcs and TRFD) and **Worksheet 75.2 (Positive Externalities)** from the TRM for questions about this video.

TEACH **AP® Exam Tip**

Figures 75.3 and 75.4 (on page 749) show the key graphs and analysis of externalities that students will see on the AP® exam. Make sure they understand these graphs and can draw them to illustrate the effect of a positive or negative externality example presented in an FRQ.

Private Versus Social Benefits

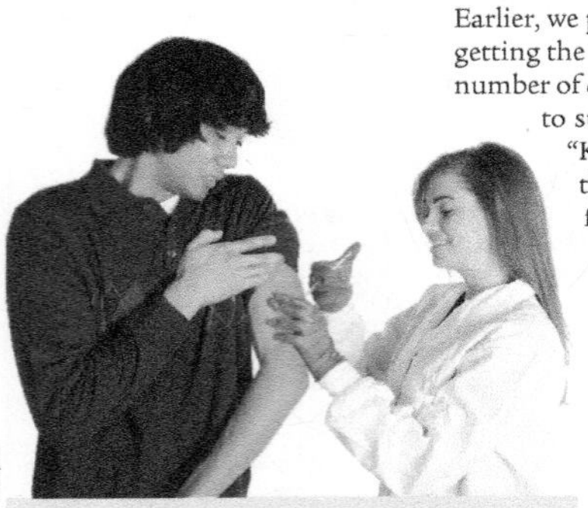

iStockphoto

Your flu shot provides positive externalities to those whom you would otherwise make sick.

Earlier, we pointed out that getting a flu shot has benefits to people beyond the person getting the shot. Under some conditions, getting a flu vaccination reduces the expected number of *other* people who get the flu by as much as 1.5. This prompted one economist to suggest a new T-shirt slogan, one particularly suited for the winter months: "Kiss Me, I'm Vaccinated!" When you get vaccinated against the flu, it's likely that you're conferring a substantial benefit on those around you—a benefit for others that you are not compensated for. In other words, getting a flu shot generates a positive externality.

The government can directly control the external costs of pollution because it can measure emissions. In contrast, it can't observe the reduction in flu cases caused by you getting a flu shot, so it can't directly control the external benefits—say, by rewarding you based on how many fewer people caught the flu because of your actions. So if the government wants to influence the level of external benefits from flu vaccinations, it must target the original activity—getting a flu shot.

From the point of view of society as a whole, a flu shot carries both costs (the price you pay for the shot, which compensates the vaccine maker and your health care provider for the inputs and factors of production necessary to grow the vaccine and deliver it to your bloodstream) and benefits. Those benefits include the private benefit that accrues to you from not getting the flu yourself, but they also include the external benefits that accrue to others from a lower likelihood of catching the flu. However, you have no incentive to take into account the beneficial side effects that are generated by your actions. As a result, in the absence of government intervention, too few people will choose to be vaccinated.

Panel (a) of **Figure 75.3** illustrates this point. The market demand curve for flu shots is represented by the curve *D*; the market, or industry, supply curve is given by the curve *S*. In the absence of government intervention, market equilibrium will be at point E_{MKT}, with Q_{MKT} flu shots being bought and sold at the market price of P_{MKT}. At that point, the marginal cost to society of another flu shot is equal to the marginal benefit *gained by the individual consumer who purchases that flu shot*, measured by the market price.

The **marginal private benefit** of a good is the marginal benefit that accrues to consumers of a good, not including any external benefits.

The **marginal social benefit of a good** is the marginal private benefit plus the marginal external benefit.

The **marginal external benefit** of a good is the addition to external benefits created by one more unit of the good.

So far we have studied goods in the absence of external benefits, so the marginal benefit to the consumer has been no different from the marginal benefit to society. When a good like flu shots creates positive externalities, there is a difference between the marginal benefit to the consumer, which we'll distinguish by calling it the **marginal private benefit**, and the marginal benefit to society, called the **marginal social benefit of a good** (or similarly, of a service or activity). The difference between the marginal private benefit (*MPB*) and the marginal social benefit (*MSB*) is the **marginal external benefit** (*MEB*) that indicates the increase in external benefits to society from an additional unit of the good:

$$\textbf{(75-1)} \quad MSB = MPB + MEB$$

The demand curve represents the marginal benefit that accrues to *consumers of the good*: the marginal private benefit. It does not incorporate the benefits to society as a whole from consuming the good—in this case, the reduction in the number of flu cases. As you can see from panel (a) of Figure 75.3, the marginal social benefit curve, *MSB*, corresponds to the demand curve, *D*, *shifted upward* by the amount of the marginal external benefit.

With the marginal social benefit curve and the supply curve, we can find the socially optimal quantity of a good or activity that generates external benefits: it is the quantity Q_{OPT} that corresponds to point *O* at which the marginal social benefit equals the marginal cost (as shown by the supply curve). Because the external benefit is not accounted for in market decisions, Q_{MKT} is less than Q_{OPT}. The yellow deadweight loss area represents the lost opportunities for net gains that could be achieved by producing Q_{OPT} rather than Q_{MKT}.

Figure 75.3 Positive Externalities and Consumption

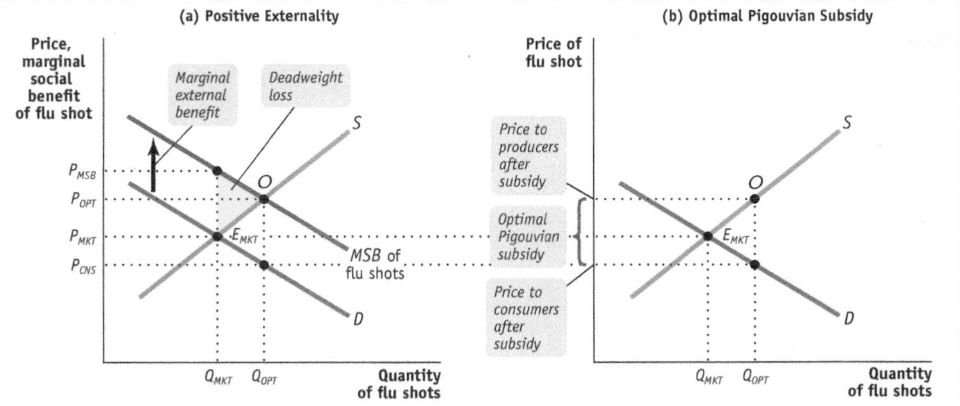

Consumption of flu shots generates external benefits, so the marginal social benefit curve, *MSB*, of flu shots, corresponds to the demand curve, *D*, shifted upward by the marginal external benefit. Panel (a) shows that without government action, the market produces Q_{MKT}. The market quantity is lower than the socially optimal quantity of consumption, Q_{OPT}, at which *MSB* crosses the supply curve, *S*. At Q_{MKT}, the marginal social benefit of another flu shot, P_{MSB}, is greater than the marginal private benefit to consumers of another flu shot, P_{MKT}. The yellow deadweight loss area represents the lost opportunities for net gains that could be achieved by producing Q_{OPT} rather than Q_{MKT}. Panel (b) shows how an optimal Pigouvian subsidy to consumers, equal to the marginal external benefit, moves consumption to Q_{OPT} by lowering the price paid by consumers to P_{CNS} and raising the price received by producers to P_{OPT}.

So, left to its own, a market will bring about too little production and consumption of a good or activity that generates external benefits. Correspondingly, without government action, the price to consumers of such a good or activity is too high: at the market output level Q_{MKT}, the unregulated market price is P_{MKT} and the marginal benefit to consumers of an additional flu shot is lower than P_{MSB}, the true marginal benefit to society of an additional flu shot.

How can the economy be induced to produce Q_{OPT}, the socially optimal level of flu shots shown in Figure 75.3? The answer is by a **Pigouvian subsidy**: a payment designed to correct for the effects of external benefits. The optimal Pigouvian subsidy, shown in panel (b) of Figure 75.3, is equal to the marginal external benefit of consuming another unit of flu shots. In this example, a Pigouvian subsidy works by lowering the price of consuming the good to P_{CNS} and raising the price producers receive to P_{OPT}: consumers pay a price for a flu shot that is equal to the price the producers receive *minus* the subsidy. In 2001, Japan began a program of subsidizing 71% of the cost of flu shots for the elderly in large cities. A 2005 study found that the subsidy significantly reduced the incidence of pneumonia, and influenza-caused mortality, at a net benefit to Japanese society of $1.08 billion dollars.

A **Pigouvian subsidy** is a payment designed to correct for the effects of external benefits.

The most important single source of external benefits in the modern economy is the creation of knowledge. In high-tech industries such as the semiconductor, software design, and bioengineering industries, innovations by one firm are quickly emulated by rival firms and put to use in the development of further advancements in related industries. This spreading of cutting-edge technological information among firms is

FOCUS Graph It

Figure 75.3 illustrates the effect of a positive externality using the supply and demand model and how a Pigouvian subsidy can be used to address the externality. Have students refer to the figure and answer the following questions:

- Where is the *MPB* curve on this graph? *It is the demand curve.*
- Where is the *MPC* curve on this graph? *It is the supply curve.*
- Where is the *MSC* curve on this graph? *If there are no external costs, the MPC curve is the same as the MSC curve—it is the supply curve.*
- How is the Q_{MKT} determined on this graph? *It is where S and D intersect.*
- How is the Q_{OPT} determined on this graph? *It is where MSB = MSC.*
- How is the optimal Piguovian subsidy determined? *It is the vertical distance between the MPB and MSB at the optimal output level—the amount of the MEB.*

St. Louis Federal Reserve Bank Resources

"Economics and the Environment," ***Page One Economics Classroom Edition*** **(September 2014)**

How are economics and the environment related? The quick answer is that environmental quality is a worthy goal, but there is an economic trade-off—a clean environment does not come without costs. This article provides some economic strategies for protecting the environment.

TEACH Teach It

When the production and consumption of a good put costs on third parties, that good is said to create a negative externality. As discussed in the previous module, most forms of production create pollution as a by-product, which creates an external cost to society.

So in the case of home electricity production, there is a difference between the private costs incurred by producers and the external costs that society bears. The total cost to society is equal to the sum of private and external costs:

Total social cost = Total private cost + Total external cost

On an incremental basis, $MSC = MPC + MEC$.

A **technology spillover** is an external benefit that results when new technological knowledge spreads among firms.

known as **technology spillover**. Such spillovers often take place through face-to-face contact. For example, bars and restaurants in California's Silicon Valley are famed for their technical chitchat. Workers know that the best way to keep up with the latest technological innovations is to hang around in the right places, have a drink, and gossip. Such informal contact helps to spread useful knowledge, which may also explain why so many high-tech firms are clustered close to one another.

Private Versus Social Costs

Now let's turn briefly to consider a case in which production of a good creates external costs—namely, the livestock industry. Whatever it is—cows, pigs, chicken, sheep, or salmon—livestock farming produces prodigious amounts of what is euphemistically known as "muck." But that's not all: scientists estimate that the amount of methane gas produced by livestock currently rivals the amount caused by the burning of fossil fuels in the creation of greenhouse gases. From the point of view of society as a whole, then, the cost of livestock farming includes both direct production costs (payments for factors of production and inputs) and the external environmental costs imposed as a by-product of farming.

Photodisc

The social cost of livestock production is felt beyond the farm.

When a good like pork involves negative externalities, there is a difference between the marginal cost to the *firm*, which we distinguish as the **marginal private cost**, and the marginal cost to *society*, the **marginal social cost of a good** (or likewise of a service or activity). The difference between the marginal private cost (*MPC*) and the marginal social cost (*MSC*) is the **marginal external cost** (*MEC*)—the increase in external costs to society from an additional unit of the good:

$$\textbf{(75-2)} \quad MSC = MPC + MEC$$

The **marginal private cost** of a good is the marginal cost of producing that good, not including any external costs.

The **marginal social cost of a good** is equal to the marginal private cost of production plus its marginal external cost.

The **marginal external cost** of a good is the increase in external costs to society created by one more unit of the good.

Panel (a) in **Figure 75.4** shows the marginal social cost curve, *MSC*, of livestock; it corresponds to the industry supply curve, *S*, *shifted upward* by the amount of the marginal external cost. (Recall that in a competitive industry, the industry supply curve is the horizontal sum of the individual firms' supply curves, which are the same as their marginal cost curves.) In the absence of government intervention, the market equilibrium will be at point E_{MKT}, yielding an equilibrium quantity of Q_{MKT} and an equilibrium price of P_{MKT}.

The ever-important socially optimal quantity of a good is the quantity at which *marginal social benefit equals marginal social cost.* In the livestock example, this criterion is met at point *O*, where the *MSC* and *D* curves cross. Why can we substitute the demand curve for marginal social benefit in this case? Because although the demand curve represents the marginal benefit to consumers—the marginal private benefit—there are no external benefits to separate the marginal private benefit from the marginal social benefit. That means that when $MSC = D$ and there are no external benefits, it is also true that $MSC = MPB = MSB$.

Unfortunately, the market equilibrium quantity Q_{MKT} is greater than Q_{OPT}, the socially optimal quantity of livestock. The yellow deadweight loss area represents society's net losses from producing Q_{OPT} rather than Q_{MKT}.

So left to its own, the market produces too much of a good that generates an external cost in production, and the price to consumers of such a good is too low: P_{MKT} is less than P_{MSC}, the true marginal cost to society of another unit of livestock. As panel (b) of Figure 75.4 shows, an optimal Pigouvian tax on livestock production, equal to the marginal external cost, moves the market to the socially optimal level of production, Q_{OPT}. The Pigouvian tax works by raising the price paid by consumers to P_{OPT} and lowering the price received by producers to P_{PRD}: the consumers pay a price equal to what the producers receive *plus* the tax.

AP® Exam Tip

When a positive externality exists, the marginal social benefit curve is above the demand curve. When a negative externality exists, the marginal social cost curve is above the supply curve.

In the flu shot example, we explained that the socially optimal quantity was found where the *MSB* and *S* curves crossed. That point met the $MSB = MSC$ criterion

748 Section 14 Market Failure and the Role of Government

Figure 75.4 Negative Externalities and Production

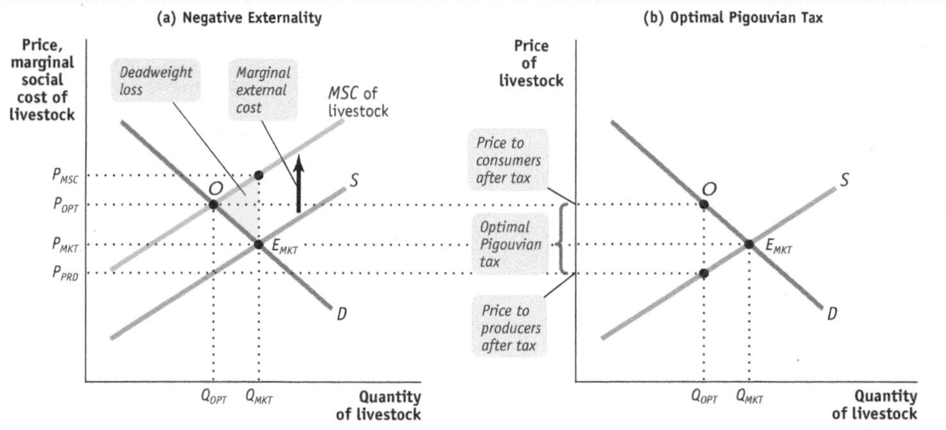

Livestock production generates external costs, so the marginal social cost curve, *MSC*, of livestock, corresponds to the supply curve, *S*, shifted upward by the marginal external cost. Panel (a) shows that without government action, the market produces the quantity Q_{MKT}. That market quantity is greater than the socially optimal quantity of livestock production, Q_{OPT}, at which *MSC* crosses the demand curve, *D*. At Q_{MKT}, the market price, P_{MKT}, is less than P_{MSC}, the true marginal cost to society of livestock production. The yellow deadweight loss area represents society's net losses from producing Q_{OPT} rather than Q_{MKT}. Panel (b) shows how an optimal Pigouvian tax on livestock production, equal to its marginal external cost, moves the production to Q_{OPT} by raising the price paid by consumers to P_{OPT} and lowering the price received by producers to P_{PRD}.

for the socially optimal quantity as well because in the absence of external costs, marginal social cost equals marginal private cost, which is indicated by the supply curve. That is, when $MSB = S$ and there are no external costs, it is also true that $MSB = MPC = MSC$.

At this point, you might ask whether a regulator would choose a method of control that targets pollution directly, such as a cap and trade program, or would prefer to control the production of the associated good with a Pigouvian tax. Generally, it is a good idea to target the pollution directly whenever feasible. The main reason is that this method creates incentives for the invention and adoption of production methods that create less pollution. For example, the AgCert company has found a way to capture greenhouse gases emitted from animal waste for use as tradable emissions reductions in a cap and trade program.

Network Externalities

There is one type of externality that has no inherently favorable or adverse effect on society at large, but it does affect other users of the associated good or service. Suppose you were the only user of Twitter in the world. What would it be worth to you? The answer, of course, is nothing. Twitter derives its value only from the fact that other people also use Twitter and you can send or receive tweets. In general, the more people who use Twitter, the more valuable it is to you.

FOCUS Active Learning

Figure 75.4 illustrates the effect of a negative externality using the supply and demand model and how a Pigouvian tax can be used to address the externality. Have students refer to the figure and answer the following questions:

- Where is the *MPC* curve on this graph? *It is the supply curve.*
- Where is the *MPB* curve on this graph? *It is the demand curve.*
- Where is the *MSB* curve on this graph? *If there are no external benefits, the MPB curve is the same as the MSB curve—it is the demand curve.*
- How is the Q_{MKT} determined on this graph? *It is where S and D intersect.*
- How is the Q_{OPT} determined on this graph? *It is where MSB = MSC.*
- How is the optimal Piguovian tax determined? *It is the vertical distance between the MPC and MSC at the optimal output level—the amount of the MEC.*

FOCUS Flip It

TRM Assign Jacob Clifford's video "Micro 6.3 Negative Externalities" (see econextras video list with hyperlinks on the bcs and TRFD) and **Worksheet 75.3 (Negative Externalities)** from the TRM for review questions.

TEACH Teach It

A network externality exists when the value of a good or service to an individual depends on how many other people use the same good or service. When more people use Facebook or Twitter, it becomes more valuable to you. When more people have cell phones with Verizon service, it means your Verizon phone can call more people at lower prices. If you buy an electric car, you will need recharging stations so that you can get a charged battery when yours is low. If there are more people driving electric cars, more of these recharging stations will emerge, making it more convenient for you (and the other drivers) to "fill up."

FOCUS Active Learning

TRM Conclude the module with **Worksheet 75.4 (Externalities Practice)** from the TRM to complete the study of externalities. Divide the class into groups of two or three to work through it; then share all answers on the board.

OPEN & CLOSE Exit Slip

TRM *Please see* ***Exit Slip: Module 75*** *in the TRM for formative multiple-choice questions to ask your students before finishing your lesson. These questions will help you quickly assess whether your students have mastered the module's concepts before moving on.*

Answers to the Exit Slip Questions

1. D
2. E
3. C

A good is subject to a **network externality** when the value of the good to an individual depends on how many other people also use the good.

A **network externality** exists when the value to an individual of a good or service depends on how many other people use the same good or service. Sometimes referred to as the "fax machine effect," the phenomenon of network externalities is so named because the classic examples involve networks of telephones, computers, and transportation systems. When it comes to sharing digital information, it helps to have more users of the same software, hardware, and online networking services. In other contexts, it's better to have more users of the same stock exchanges, gauges of railroad line, and sizes of electrical plugs, among many examples. Congestion creates a form of negative network externality: it can make things worse for you when more people use the same highway, elevator, or swimming pool.

MODULE 75 Review

Check Your Understanding

1. Some opponents of tradable emissions permits object to them on the grounds that polluters that sell their permits benefit monetarily from their involvement in polluting the environment. Assess this argument.
2. For each of the following cases, explain whether an external cost or an external benefit is created and identify an appropriate policy response.
   a. Trees planted in urban areas improve air quality and lower summer temperatures.
   b. Water-saving toilets reduce the need to pump water from rivers and aquifers. The cost of a gallon of water to homeowners is virtually zero.
   c. Old computer monitors contain toxic materials that pollute the environment when improperly disposed of.

Tackle the Test: Multiple-Choice Questions

1. Which of the following policy tools is inefficient even when correctly administered?
   a. environmental standards
   b. emissions taxes
   c. tradable emissions permits
   d. Pigouvian taxes
   e. cap and trade programs
2. An efficient Pigouvian subsidy for a good is set equal to the good's
   a. external cost.
   b. marginal social benefit.
   c. marginal external cost.
   d. marginal external benefit.
   e. price at which $MSC = MSB$.
3. Which of the following is true in the case of a positive externality?
   a. $MSC > MSB$
   b. $MPB > MSC$
   c. $MSB > MPB$
   d. $MPB > MSB$
   e. $MSC > MPC$
4. One example of a source of external benefits is
   a. technology spillover.
   b. traffic congestion.
   c. pollution.
   d. subsidies for polluters.
   e. taxes on environmental conservation.
5. Marginal social benefit equals marginal private benefit plus
   a. marginal external benefit.
   b. marginal private cost.
   c. total external benefit.
   d. total external cost.
   e. marginal social cost.

Answers to Module 75 Review Questions

Check Your Understanding

1. This is a misguided argument. Allowing polluters to sell emissions permits makes polluters face a cost of polluting: the opportunity cost of not being able to sell the permits that cover the pollution. If a polluter chooses not to reduce its emissions, it cannot sell its emissions permits. As a result, it forgoes the opportunity of making money from the sale of the permits. So, despite the fact that the polluter receives a monetary benefit from selling the permits, the scheme has the desired effect: to make polluters internalize the externality of their actions and reduce the total amount of pollution.

2. a. Planting trees imposes an external benefit: the marginal social benefit of planting trees is higher than the marginal private benefit to individual tree planters because many people (not just those who plant the trees) can enjoy the improved air quality and lower summer temperatures. The difference between the marginal social benefit and marginal private benefit to individual tree planters is the marginal external benefit. A Pigouvian subsidy equal to the marginal external benefit could be placed on each tree planted in urban areas in order to increase the marginal private benefit to individual tree planters to the same level as the marginal social benefit.

b. Water-saving toilets create an external benefit: the marginal private benefit to individual homeowners from replacing a traditional toilet with a water-saving toilet is almost zero because water is very inexpensive. But the marginal social benefit is large because fewer critical rivers and aquifers need to be pumped. Marginal external benefit can be calculated as described in part a, and a Pigouvian subsidy can be provided for installing water-saving toilets.

c. Disposing of old computer monitors imposes an external cost: the marginal private cost to those disposing of old computer monitors is lower than the marginal social cost, since environmental pollution is borne by people other than the person disposing of the monitor. The difference between the marginal social cost and marginal private cost to those disposing of old computer monitors is the marginal external cost. A Pigouvian tax on the disposal of computer monitors equal to the marginal external cost, or a system of tradable permits for their disposal, could raise the marginal private cost to those disposing of old computer monitors up to the level of the marginal social cost.

Tackle the Test: Multiple-Choice Questions

1. a
2. d
3. c
4. a
5. a

Tackle the Test: Free-Response Questions

1. The purchase of antivirus software by one person provides benefits to other people because they are less likely to receive a virus from the software purchaser. Draw a correctly labeled graph showing how the market will determine the quantity of antivirus software purchased. On the same graph, show the socially optimal quantity of antivirus software. Shade and label the area that represents deadweight loss. List two different government policies that could bring about the optimal quantity of antivirus software.

Rubric for FRQ 1 (9 points)

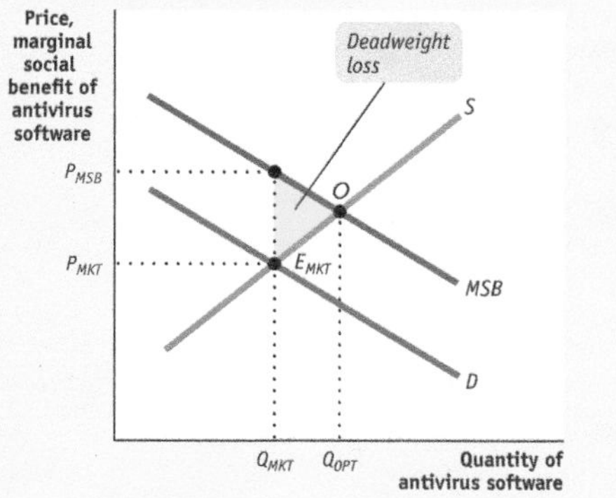

1 point: Vertical axis labeled "Price, marginal social benefit" or "Dollars per unit," horizontal axis labeled "Quantity of antivirus software" or "Q"

1 point: Upward-sloping supply (or equivalently, marginal cost) curve. (Note that with no external costs, marginal private cost equals marginal social cost.)

1 point: Downward-sloping demand (or equivalently, marginal private benefit) curve

1 point: The market quantity of antivirus software is found at the intersection of supply and demand and shown on the horizontal axis.

1 point: Downward-sloping marginal social benefit curve drawn above demand curve

1 point: The optimal quantity of antivirus software is found at the intersection of supply and marginal social benefit and shown on the horizontal axis.

1 point: The correct deadweight-loss area is shaded and labeled.

1 point: A Pigouvian subsidy equal to the marginal external benefit at the socially optimal quantity

1 point: A government regulation requiring the optimal quantity of antivirus software

2. The use of plastic water bottles creates external costs as the result of plastic production, bottle transportation, litter, and waste disposal. Draw a correctly labeled graph showing how the market will determine the quantity of water bottles purchased. On the same graph, show the marginal external cost, the socially optimal quantity of water bottles, and the size of a Pigouvian tax that could be used to achieve the socially optimal quantity of water bottles.
(6 points)

Tackle the Test: Free-Response Questions
Rubric for FRQ 2 (6 points)

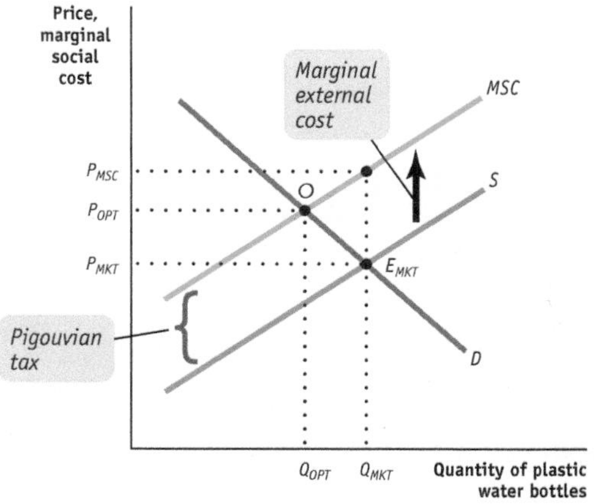

1 point: The vertical axis is labeled "Price, marginal social cost" and the horizontal axis is labeled "Quantity of plastic water bottles" or "Q."

1 point: The demand curve is downward-sloping and the supply curve is upward-sloping.

1 point: The market quantity is labeled on the horizontal axis directly below the intersection of the demand curve and supply curve.

1 point: The marginal social cost curve is above the supply curve.

1 point: The socially optimal quantity is labeled on the horizontal axis directly below the intersection of the marginal social cost curve and demand curve.

1 point: The Pigouvian tax is labeled as the vertical distance between the supply curve and marginal social cost curve.

Module 75 Externalities and Public Policy **751**

PD To prepare for teaching this lesson, you may want to consult the **Module 76 Sample Lecture** in the TRM.

OPEN & CLOSE Start Here

Introduce the concept of public goods by having students participate in an experiment. Several computerized and noncomputerized experiments for both small and large classes are provided by the Experimental Economics Center at Georgia State University (http://www.econport.org/content/teaching/modules/PublicGoods.html).

TEACH Teach It

The characteristics of a good that are used to identify whether it is public or private (or artificially scarce or common property) are the degree of rivalry and excludability. A good is rival if the good or service cannot be consumed by more than one person at the same time. A good is excludable if you can prevent nonpayers from consuming the good.

James Steidl/Shutterstock

MODULE 76 Public Goods

In this Module, you will learn to:

- Characterize public goods and explain why markets fail to supply efficient quantities of public goods
- Define common resources and explain why they are overused
- Define artificially scarce goods and explain why they are underconsumed
- Describe how government intervention in the production and consumption of these types of goods can make society better off
- Discuss why finding the right level of government intervention is often difficult

In this module, we take a somewhat different approach to the question of why markets sometimes fail. Here we focus on how the characteristics of goods often determine whether markets can deliver them efficiently. When goods have the "wrong" characteristics, the resulting market failures resemble those associated with externalities or market power. This alternative way of looking at sources of inefficiency deepens our understanding of why markets sometimes don't work well and how government can take actions that improve the welfare of society.

Private Goods—and Others

What's the difference between installing a new bathroom in a house and building a municipal sewage system? What's the difference between growing wheat and fishing in the open ocean?

These aren't trick questions. In each case there is a basic difference in the characteristics of the goods involved. Bathroom appliances and wheat have the characteristics necessary to allow markets to work efficiently. Public sewage systems and fish in the sea do not.

Let's look at these crucial characteristics and why they matter.

Characteristics of Goods

A good is **excludable** if the supplier of that good can prevent people who do not pay from consuming it.

Goods like bathroom fixtures and wheat have two characteristics that are essential if a good is to be provided in efficient quantities by a market economy.

- They are **excludable**: suppliers of the good can prevent people who don't pay from consuming it.

752 Section 14 Market Failure and the Role of Government

- They are **rival in consumption**: the same unit of the good cannot be consumed by more than one person at the same time.

When a good is both excludable and rival in consumption, it is called a **private good**. Wheat is an example of a private good. It is *excludable*: the farmer can sell a bushel to one consumer without having to provide wheat to everyone in the county. And it is *rival in consumption*: if I eat bread baked with a farmer's wheat, that wheat cannot be consumed by someone else.

Not all goods possess these two characteristics. Some goods are **nonexcludable**—the supplier cannot prevent consumption of the good by people who do not pay for it. Fire protection is one example: a fire department that puts out fires before they spread protects the whole city, not just people who have made contributions to the Firemen's Benevolent Association. An improved environment is another: pollution can't be ended for some users of a river while leaving the river foul for others.

Nor are all goods rival in consumption. Goods are **nonrival in consumption** if more than one person can consume the same unit of the good at the same time. TV programs are nonrival in consumption: your decision to watch a show does not prevent other people from watching the same show.

Because goods can be either excludable or nonexcludable, and either rival or nonrival in consumption, there are four types of goods, illustrated by the matrix in **Figure 76.1**:

- *Private goods*, which are excludable and rival in consumption, like wheat
- *Public goods*, which are nonexcludable and nonrival in consumption, like a public sewer system
- *Common resources*, which are nonexcludable but rival in consumption, like clean water in a river
- *Artificially scarce goods*, which are excludable but nonrival in consumption, like pay-per-view movies on cable TV

A good is **rival in consumption** if the same unit of the good cannot be consumed by more than one person at the same time.

A good that is both excludable and rival in consumption is a **private good**.

When a good is **nonexcludable**, the supplier cannot prevent consumption by people who do not pay for it.

A good is **nonrival in consumption** if more than one person can consume the same unit of the good at the same time.

AP® Exam Tip

Be prepared to classify goods according to the four different types for the AP® exam.

Figure 76.1 Four Types of Goods

There are four types of goods. The type of a good depends on (1) whether or not it is excludable—whether a producer can prevent someone from consuming it; and (2) whether or not it is rival in consumption—whether it is impossible for the same unit of a good to be consumed by more than one person at the same time.

	Rival in consumption	Nonrival in consumption
Excludable	**Private goods** • Wheat • Bathroom fixtures	**Artificially scarce goods** • Pay-per-view movies • Computer software
Non-excludable	**Common resources** • Clean water • Biodiversity	**Public goods** • Public sanitation • National defense

Of course there are many other characteristics that distinguish between types of goods—necessities versus luxuries, normal versus inferior, and so on. Why focus on whether goods are excludable and rival in consumption?

Why Markets Can Supply Only Private Goods Efficiently

As we learned in earlier modules, markets are typically the best means for a society to deliver goods and services to its members; that is, markets are efficient except in the case of market power, externalities, or other instances of market failure. One source of market

FOCUS Graph It

Figure 76.1 illustrates in table format the four types of goods. Ask students to list three additional examples of each of the four types of goods.

TEACH Teach It

Examples are the best way to make sure students really understand the two characteristics (rival and excludable).

Private goods are excludable and rival in consumption.

Example: A car dealership sells a car to Tom at a price of $20,000. Tom gets the car because he is willing and able to pay that price. The seller does not sell a car to Becky because Becky considers that price too high. The car is excludable. This means that the seller does not have to provide a car to Becky or the rest of the people in town who are unwilling and unable to pay the going price. Once Tom has purchased the car, Huck can't buy it from the car dealership. The car is rival because Huck and Tom can't both buy the same car.

Public goods are nonexcludable and nonrival in consumption.

Example: Cities have fire departments that protect all homes in the city and can't exclude anyone on the basis of payment. And more than one person can consume the fire protection at the same time. If a fire breaks out at Margaret's house, the fire department rushes to put it out. This prevents the fire from spreading to Melanie's store, so both people are consuming the same unit of fire protection.

Artificially scarce goods are excludable and nonrival in consumption.

Example: A college economics lecture is excludable because only students who have paid tuition can enroll in the course and attend the lecture. However, it is nonrival because many people can consume the same unit of the good at the same time. Other examples are pay-per-view movies or sporting events.

Common resources are nonexcludable but rival in consumption.

Example: The stock of salmon in the Pacific Ocean has historically been a common resource. If a person had a boat, he or she could harvest salmon from the ocean, or even scoop the fish from the bank of a river as the salmon headed upstream. This made the salmon nonexcludable. However, once a salmon is caught, it cannot be caught by a second person, which makes it rival.

St. Louis Federal Reserve Bank Resources

"Market Failures—Income Redistribution, and the Role of Government," ***Tools for Teaching the Arkansas Economics and Personal Finance Course*****, Session 10**

Students learn about the economic functions of government, public goods, and earning income.

FOCUS Active Learning

TRM For practice defining and learning the types of goods, assign **Worksheet 76.1 (Types of Goods)** from the TRM.

FOCUS Active Learning

TRM Assign Dr. Mary J. McGlasson's video "Episode 33: Public Goods" (see econextras video list with hyperlinks on the bcs and TRFD) and **Worksheet 76.2 (Public Goods)** from the TRM for accompanying questions.

TEACH Teach It

If a good is nonexcludable, it may have a free-rider problem. For goods that are nonexcludable, consumers are not excluded if they do not pay for them. Therefore, many people will let others pay so they can "free ride" (use them without paying for them). Because of free-riding behavior, markets do not produce an efficient quantity of public goods.

FOCUS Active Learning

Show the Jacob Clifford video "Micro 6.1 Public Goods and Free Riders" (see econextras video list with hyperlinks on the bcs and TRFD). Ask students why we have public goods in our market economy. *Most truly public goods are excludable and nonrival. There is no profit to be had by private firms providing these goods or service.*

failure is rooted in the nature of the good itself: markets cannot supply goods and services efficiently unless they are private goods—excludable and rival in consumption.

To see why excludability is crucial, suppose that a farmer had only two choices: either produce no wheat or provide a bushel of wheat to every resident of the county who wants it, whether or not that resident pays for it. It seems unlikely that anyone would grow wheat under those conditions.

Goods that are nonexcludable suffer from the **free-rider problem**: individuals have no incentive to pay for their own consumption and instead will take a "free ride" on anyone who does pay.

Yet the operator of a public sewage system consisting of pipes that anyone can dump sewage into faces pretty much the same problem as our hypothetical farmer. A sewage system makes the whole city cleaner and healthier—but that benefit accrues to all the city's residents, whether or not they pay the system operator. The general point is that if a good is nonexcludable, rational consumers won't be willing to pay for it—they will take a "free ride" on anyone who *does* pay. So there is a **free-rider problem**. Examples of the free-rider problem are familiar from daily life. One example you may have encountered happens when students are required to do a group project. There is often a tendency of some group members to shirk their responsibilities, relying on others in the group to get the work done. The shirkers *free-ride* on someone else's effort.

When the benefits from a group project are nonexcludable, there is a temptation to free-ride on the efforts of others.

Because of the free-rider problem, the forces of self-interest alone do not lead to an efficient level of production for a nonexcludable good. Even though consumers would benefit from increased production of the good, no one individual is willing to pay for more, and so no producer is willing to supply it. The result is that nonexcludable goods suffer from *inefficiently low production* in a market economy. In fact, in the face of the free-rider problem, self-interest may not ensure that any amount of the good—let alone the efficient quantity—is produced.

Goods that are excludable and nonrival in consumption, like pay-per-view movies, suffer from a different kind of inefficiency. As long as a good is excludable, it is possible to earn a profit by making it available only to those who pay. Therefore, producers are willing to supply an excludable good. But the marginal cost of letting an additional viewer watch a pay-per-view movie is zero because it is nonrival in consumption. So the efficient price to the consumer is also zero—or, to put it another way, individuals should watch TV movies up to the point where their marginal benefit is zero. But if the cable company actually charges viewers $4, viewers will consume the good only up to the point where their marginal benefit is $4. When consumers must pay a price greater than zero for a good that is nonrival in consumption, the price they pay is higher than the marginal cost of allowing them to consume that good, which is zero. So in a market economy goods that are nonrival in consumption suffer from *inefficiently low consumption*.

Now we can see why private goods are the only goods that will be produced and consumed in efficient quantities in a competitive market. (That is, a private good will be produced and consumed in efficient quantities in a market free of market power, externalities, and other sources of market failure.) Because private goods are excludable, producers can charge for them and so have an incentive to produce them. And because they are also rival in consumption, it is efficient for consumers to pay a positive price—a price equal to the marginal cost of production. If one or both of these characteristics are lacking, a market economy will lack the incentives to bring about efficient quantities of the good.

Yet there are crucial goods that don't meet these criteria—and in these cases, the government can offer assistance.

Public Goods

A **public good** is both nonexcludable and nonrival in consumption.

A **public good** is the exact opposite of a private good: it is both nonexcludable and nonrival in consumption. A public sewage system is an example of a public good: you can't keep a river clean without making it clean for everyone who lives near its banks, and my protection from sewage contamination does not prevent my neighbor from being protected as well.

Here are some other examples of public goods:

- *Disease prevention.* When a disease is stamped out, no one can be excluded from the benefit, and one person's health doesn't prevent others from being healthy.
- *National defense.* A strong military protects all citizens.
- *Scientific research.* In many cases new findings provide widespread benefits that are not excludable or rival.

Because these goods are nonexcludable, they suffer from the free-rider problem, so private firms would produce inefficiently low quantities of them. And because they are nonrival in consumption, it would be inefficient to charge people for consuming them. As a result, society must find nonmarket methods for providing these goods.

Providing Public Goods

Public goods are provided in a variety of ways. The government doesn't always get involved—in many cases a non-governmental solution has been found for the free-rider problem. But these solutions are usually imperfect in some way.

Some public goods are supplied through voluntary contributions. For example, private donations help support public radio and a considerable amount of scientific research. But private donations are insufficient to finance large programs of great importance, such as the Centers for Disease Control and Prevention and national defense.

Some public goods are supplied by self-interested individuals or firms because those who produce them are able to make money in an indirect way. The classic example is broadcast television, which in the United States is supported entirely by advertising. The downside of such indirect funding is that it skews the nature and quantity of the public goods that are supplied, while imposing additional costs on consumers. TV stations show the programs that yield the most advertising revenue (that is, programs best suited for selling antacids, hair-loss remedies, antihistamines, and the like to the segment of the population that buys them), which are not necessarily the programs people most want to see. And viewers must endure many commercials.

Some potentially public goods are deliberately made excludable and therefore subject to charge, like pay-per-view movies. In the United Kingdom, where most television programming is paid for by a yearly license fee assessed on every television owner (£145.50, or about \$244.50 in 2014), television viewing is made artificially excludable by the use of "television detection vans": vans that roam neighborhoods in an attempt to detect televisions in non-licensed households and fine them. However, as noted earlier, when suppliers charge a price greater than zero for a nonrival good, consumers will consume an inefficiently low quantity of that good.

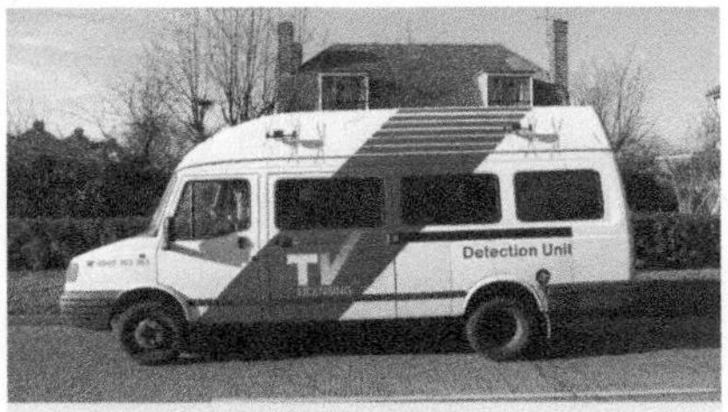

On the prowl: a British TV detection van at work.

In small communities, a high level of social encouragement or pressure can be brought to bear on people to contribute money or time to provide the efficient level of a public good. Volunteer fire departments, which depend both on the volunteered services of the firefighters themselves and on contributions from local residents, are a good example. But as communities grow larger and more anonymous, social pressure is increasingly difficult to apply, compelling larger towns and cities to tax residents and depend on salaried firefighters for fire protection services.

As this last example suggests, when other solutions fail, it is up to the government to provide public goods. Indeed, the most important public goods—national defense, the legal system, disease control, fire protection in large cities, and so on—are provided by the government and paid for by taxes. Economic theory tells us that the provision of public goods is one of the crucial roles of government.

TEACH Teach It

If a good is nonrival, the marginal cost of that good is zero. That is, it doesn't cost anything additional to allow one more person to consume the good. When $MC = 0$, the efficient quantity is found where $MC = MB = 0$. Anyone who receives a positive benefit from consuming the good should be allowed to consume it since $MC = 0$. So, charging anything for the good leads to an inefficiently low level of consumption.

Module 76 Public Goods 755

FOCUS In the News

TRM Have students read the article "Public Goods Go Better With Coca-Cola" by Kevin Williamson at http://www.nationalreview.com/articles/344249/public-goods-go-better-coca-cola-kevin-d-williamson. Assign **Worksheet 76.3 (Coca-Cola)** from the TRM for questions about this article.

TEACH Teach It

Marginal analysis is again used to determine the efficient amount of the public good. The optimal quantity of a public good occurs when the marginal social benefit equals the marginal social cost. Because public goods are nonexcludable and nonrival, the marginal social benefit of a unit of the good is equal to the sum of the marginal private benefits enjoyed by each of the individual consumers of that unit.

AP® Exam Tip

Like private goods, public goods should be produced until the marginal social cost is equal to the marginal social benefit. Remember that for a public good, the marginal social benefit of each unit is found by adding up the marginal private benefit received by each person who benefits from that unit.

How Much of a Public Good Should Be Provided?

In some cases, the provision of a public good is an "either-or" decision: a city can either have a sewage system—or not. But in most cases, governments must decide not only whether to provide a public good but also *how much* of that public good to provide. For example, street cleaning is a public good—but how often should the streets be cleaned? Once a month? Twice a month? Every other day?

Imagine a city with only two residents, Ted and Alice. Assume that the public good in question is street cleaning and that Ted and Alice truthfully tell the government how much they value a unit of the public good, one unit being one street cleaning per month. Specifically, each of them tells the government his or her *willingness to pay* for another unit of the public good supplied—an amount that corresponds to that individual's *marginal private benefit* from another unit of the public good.

Using this information along with information on the cost of providing the good, the government can use marginal analysis to find the efficient level of providing the public good: the level at which the *marginal social benefit* of the public good is equal to the marginal social cost of producing it. Recall that the marginal social benefit of a good is the benefit that accrues to society as a whole from the consumption of one additional unit of the good.

But what is the marginal social benefit of another unit of a public good—a unit that generates utility for *all* consumers, not just one consumer, because it is nonexcludable and nonrival in consumption? This question leads us to an important principle: *In the special case of a public good, the marginal social benefit of a unit of the good is equal to the sum of the marginal private benefits enjoyed by all consumers of that unit.* Or to consider it from a slightly different angle, if a consumer could be compelled to pay for a unit before consuming it (the good is made excludable), then the marginal social benefit of a unit is equal to the *sum* of each consumer's willingness to pay for that unit. Using this principle, the marginal social benefit of an additional street cleaning per month is equal to Ted's marginal private benefit from that additional cleaning *plus* Alice's marginal private benefit.

Why? Because a public good is nonrival in consumption—Ted's benefit from a cleaner street does not diminish Alice's benefit from that same clean street, and vice versa. Because Ted and Alice can simultaneously "consume" the same unit of street cleaning, the marginal social benefit is the *sum* of their marginal private benefits. And the efficient quantity of a public good is the quantity at which the marginal social benefit is equal to the marginal social cost of providing it.

Figure 76.2 illustrates the efficient provision of a public good, showing three marginal benefit curves. Panel (a) shows Ted's marginal private benefit curve from street cleaning, MPB_T: he would be willing to pay \$25 for the city to clean its streets once a month, an additional \$18 to have it done a second time, and so on. Panel (b) shows Alice's marginal private benefit curve from street cleaning, MPB_A. Panel (c) shows the marginal social benefit curve from street cleaning, *MSB:* it is the vertical sum of Ted's and Alice's marginal private benefit curves, MPB_T and MPB_A.

To maximize society's welfare, the government should increase the quantity of street cleanings until the marginal social benefit of an additional cleaning would fall below the marginal social cost. Suppose that the marginal social cost is \$6 per cleaning. Then the city should clean its streets 5 times per month, because the marginal social benefit of each of the first 5 cleanings is more than \$6, but going from 5 to 6 cleanings would yield a marginal social benefit of only \$2, which is less than the marginal social cost.

One fundamental rationale for the existence of government is that it provides a way for citizens to tax themselves in order to provide public goods—particularly a vital public good like national defense.

Figure 76.2 A Public Good

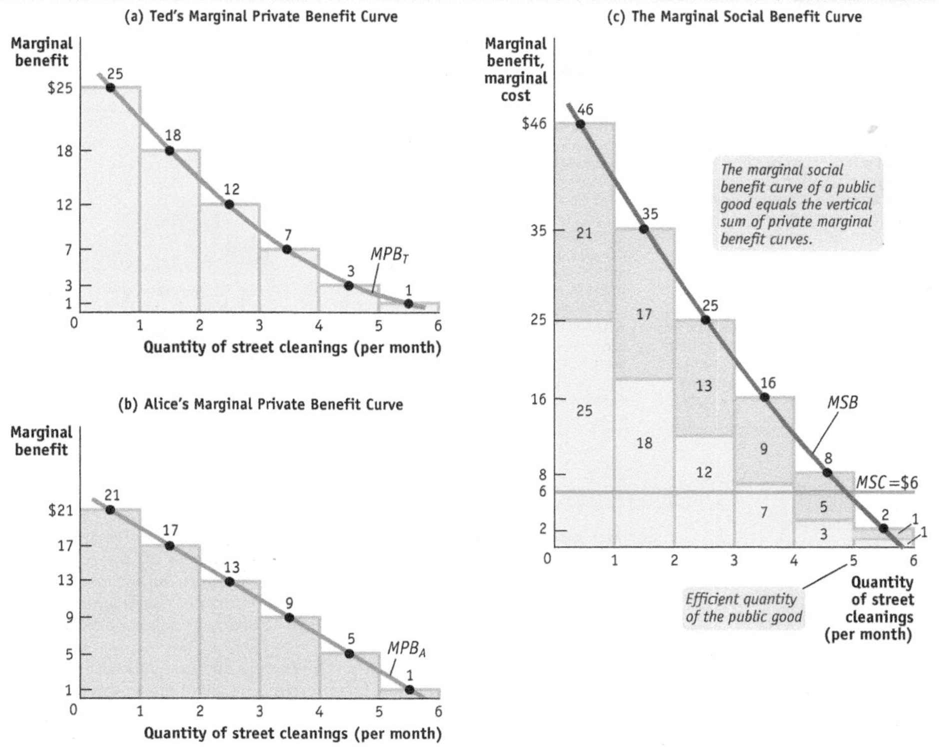

Panel (a) shows Ted's marginal private benefit curve, MPB_T, and panel (b) shows Alice's marginal private benefit curve, MPB_A. Panel (c) shows the marginal social benefit of the public good, equal to the *sum* of the marginal private benefits to all consumers (in this case, Ted and Alice). The marginal social benefit curve, *MSB*, is the vertical sum of the marginal private benefit curves MPB_T and MPB_A. At a constant marginal social cost of $6, there should be 5 street cleanings per month, because the marginal social benefit of going from 4 to 5 cleanings is $8 ($3 for Ted plus $5 for Alice), but the marginal social benefit of going from 5 to 6 cleanings is only $2.

Of course, if society really consisted of only two individuals, they would probably manage to strike a deal to provide the good. But imagine a city with a million residents, each of whose marginal private benefit from a good is only a tiny fraction of the marginal social benefit. It would be impossible for people to reach a voluntary agreement to pay for the efficient level of a good like street cleaning—the potential for free-riding would make it too difficult to make and enforce an agreement among so many people. But they could and would vote to tax themselves to pay for a citywide sanitation department.

FOCUS Graph It

Figure 76.2 shows individual marginal social benefit curves added together to form the marginal social benefit curve for a public good providing benefit to many consumers.

Have students refer to the illustration to answer the following questions:

- What benefit do Ted and Alice get from the first unit of street cleaning? *Ted = $25, Alice = $21*
- What is the social benefit of the first unit of street cleaning? *$25 + $21 = $46*
- What is the last unit for which the marginal social benefit exceeds the marginal cost of street cleaning, and what are the *MSB* and *MSC* at that quantity? *The 5th unit; MSB = $8 and MSC = $6*
- If the *MSC* was $20, how many units of street cleaning should there be? *3 because MSB ($25) > the MSC of $20; for the 4th unit, MSB ($16) is below the MSC of $10.*

TEACH Teach It

A common resource is nonexcludable but rival in consumption. For example, suppose I live in an area that gets its freshwater from an aquifer. If I drill a well, I can access this clean water for my own personal use; it's nonexcludable. However, every gallon that I pump for my own use is a gallon that someone else cannot use; it's rival. My consumption of water draws down the water in the aquifer and makes it more difficult (costly) for other people to get their water.

In the language of economics, my marginal private cost of the next gallon of water is lower than the marginal social cost. This tells us that a common resource will be overused. If rainfall is insufficient to recharge the aquifer, we will exhaust it.

The same is true of common resources like fish in the ocean. Every fish that I catch provides benefit only to me, while imposing a small, almost imperceptible, cost on everyone else. Since I don't really have to worry about those social costs, I will catch as many fish as I can. When everyone is doing that, the fish can't repopulate quickly enough and the fishery collapses. This concept was labeled the "Tragedy of the Commons" by Garrett Hardin (1968).

FYI Voting as a Public Good

It's a sad fact that many Americans who are eligible to vote don't bother to. As a result, their interests tend to be ignored by politicians. But what's even sadder is that this self-defeating behavior may be completely rational.

As the economist Mancur Olson pointed out in a famous book titled *The Logic of Collective Action*, voting is a public good, one that suffers from severe free-rider problems.

Imagine that you are one of a million people who would stand to gain the equivalent of $100 each if some plan is passed in a statewide referendum—say, a plan to improve public schools. And suppose that the opportunity cost of the time it would take you to vote is $10. Will you be sure to go to the polls and vote for the referendum? If you are rational, the answer is no! The reason is that it is very unlikely that your vote will decide the issue, either way. If the measure passes, you benefit, even if you didn't bother to vote—the benefits are nonexcludable. If the measure doesn't pass, your vote would not have changed the outcome. Either way, by not voting—by free-riding on those who do vote—you save $10.

Of course, many people do vote out of a sense of civic duty. But because political action is a public good, in general people devote too little effort to defending their own interests.

The result, Olson pointed out, is that when a large group of people share a common political interest, they are likely to exert too little effort promoting their cause and so will be ignored. Conversely, small, well-organized interest groups that act on issues narrowly targeted in their favor tend to have disproportionate power.

Is this a reason to distrust democracy? Winston Churchill said it best: "Democracy is the worst form of government, except for all the other forms that have been tried."

Cheryl Graham/Getty Images

Common Resources

A **common resource** is nonexcludable and rival in consumption: you can't stop others from consuming the good, and when they consume it, less of the good is available for you.

A **common resource** is a good that is nonexcludable but is rival in consumption. An example is the stock of fish in a fishing area, like the fisheries off the coast of New England. Traditionally, anyone who had a boat could go out to sea and catch fish—fish in the sea were a nonexcludable good. Yet the total number of fish is limited: the fish that one person catches are no longer available to be caught by someone else. So fish in the sea are rival in consumption.

Other examples of common resources include clean air, water, and the diversity of animal and plant species on the planet (biodiversity). In each of these cases the fact that the good is rival in consumption, and yet nonexcludable, poses a serious problem.

AP® Exam Tip

For the AP® exam, you should be able to explain and identify solutions to the overuse of common resources.

The Problem of Overuse

Overuse is the depletion of a common resource that occurs when individuals ignore the fact that their use depletes the amount of the resource remaining for others.

Because common resources are nonexcludable, individuals cannot be charged for their use. But the resources are rival in consumption, so an individual who uses a unit depletes the resource by making that unit unavailable to others. As a result, a common resource is subject to **overuse**: an individual will continue to use it until his or her marginal private benefit is equal to his or her marginal private cost, ignoring the cost that this action inflicts on society as a whole.

Fish are a classic example of a common resource. Particularly in heavily fished waters, each fisher's catch imposes a cost on others by reducing the fish population and making it harder for others to catch fish. But fishers have no personal incentive to take this cost into account. As a result, from society's point of view, too many fish are caught. Traffic congestion is another example of overuse of a common resource. A major highway during rush hour can accommodate only a certain number of vehicles per hour. Each person who decides to drive to work alone, rather than carpool or work at home, causes many other people to have a longer commute; but there is no incentive for individual drivers to take these consequences into account.

In the case of a common resource, as in the earlier examples involving marginal external costs, the *marginal social cost* of your use of that resource is higher than your *marginal*

St. Louis Federal Reserve Bank Resources

"Market Failures," *Tools for Teaching the Arkansas Economics and Personal Finance Course*, Session 9

Students will learn that market failures are caused by a problem within a market that can result in an inefficient use of resources. Policy makers may intervene in an attempt to correct market failures through laws that include regulations and/or programs to alleviate the failure.

Figure 76.3 A Common Resource

The supply curve *S*, which shows the marginal private cost of production of the fishing industry, is composed of the individual supply curves of the individual fishers. But each fisher's marginal private cost does not include the cost that his or her actions impose on others: the depletion of the common resource. As a result, the marginal social cost curve, *MSC*, lies above the supply curve; in an unregulated market, the quantity of the common resource used, Q_{MKT}, exceeds the efficient quantity of use, Q_{OPT}.

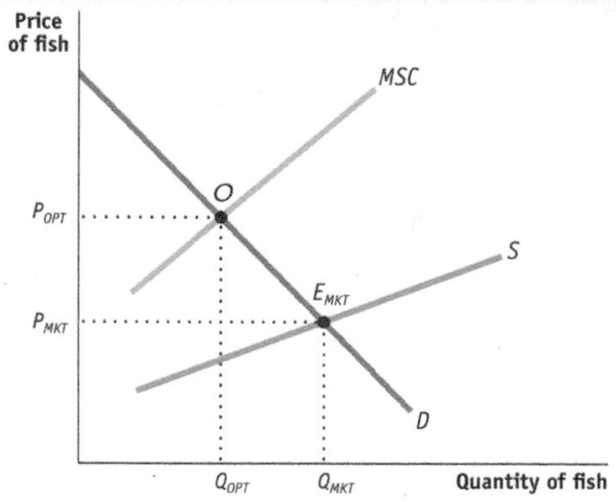

private cost, the cost to you of using an additional unit of the good. **Figure 76.3** illustrates this point. It shows the demand curve for fish, which measures the marginal private benefit of fish (as well as the marginal social benefit because there are no external benefits from catching and consuming fish). The figure also shows the supply curve for fish, which measures the marginal private cost of production in the fishing industry. We know that the industry supply curve is the horizontal sum of each individual fisher's supply curve—quivalent to his or her marginal private cost curve. The fishing industry supplies the quantity Q_{MKT} at which its marginal private cost equals the price. But the efficient quantity is Q_{OPT}, the quantity of fish that equates the marginal social benefit (as indicated by the demand curve) to the marginal social cost, not to the fishing industry's marginal private cost of production. Thus, the market outcome results in overuse of the common resource.

As we noted, there is a close parallel between the problem of managing a common resource and the problem posed by negative externalities. In the case of an activity that generates a negative externality, the marginal social cost of production is greater than the marginal private cost of production, the difference being the marginal external cost imposed on society. Here, the loss to society arising from a fisher's depletion of the common resource plays the same role as the external cost when there is a negative externality. In fact, many negative externalities (such as pollution) can be thought of as involving common resources (such as clean air).

The Efficient Use and Maintenance of a Common Resource

Because common resources pose problems similar to those created by negative externalities, the solutions are also similar. To ensure efficient use of a common resource, society must find a way to get individual users of the resource to take into account the costs they impose on others. This is the same principle as that of getting individuals to internalize a negative externality that arises from their actions.

There are three principal ways to induce people who use common resources to internalize the costs they impose on others:

- Tax or otherwise regulate the use of the common resource
- Create a system of tradable licenses for the right to use the common resource
- Make the common resource excludable and assign property rights to some individuals

FOCUS Graph It

Figure 76.3 illustrates the market for a common resource. Have students refer to the graph to answer the following questions:

- How is Q_{MKT} determined on the graph? *The intersection of supply and demand*
- How is Q_{OPT} determined on the graph? *The intersection of MSC and MSB. Note: MSB = MPB in this case because there are no external benefits.*
- This situation is similar to what other situation from the previous module? *Negative externality*

FOCUS Test It

What policies can be used to prevent depletion of common resources?

- *Regulate their use.*
- *Tax their use.*
- *Create a system of tradable licenses.*
- *Make the common resource excludable.*

TEACH Teach It

An artificially scarce good is excludable but nonrival in consumption. For example, a pay-per-view movie is artificially scarce because it is excludable but nonrival. The cable company can exclude me from watching the movie if I don't pay for it, but if I watch the movie, it doesn't mean someone else can't also watch the same movie.

The marginal cost of providing the movie to one more household is zero. The efficient quantity would be the quantity where the demand curve intersects the horizontal axis (i.e., the price is zero.) Of course, there is no way the firm can profit if the price is zero, so the firm sets a price above zero and excludes some of the potential customers. But if the price is above zero, fewer movies will be ordered than the efficient number. This is why the good is called "artificially scarce."

OPEN & CLOSE Exit Slip

TRM *Please see* ***Exit Slip: Module 76*** *in the TRM for formative multiple-choice questions to ask your students before finishing your lesson. These questions will help you quickly assess whether your students have mastered the module's concepts before moving on.*

Answers to the Exit Slip Questions

1. E
2. D
3. E

Jim Jurica/Getty Images

If it weren't for fees and restrictions, some common resources would be overrun.

The first two solutions overlap with the approaches to private goods with negative externalities. Just as governments use Pigouvian excise taxes to temper the consumption of alcohol, they use alternative forms of Pigouvian taxes to reduce the use of common resources. For example, in some countries there are "congestion charges" on those who drive during rush hour, in effect charging them for the use of highway space, a common resource. Likewise, visitors to national parks in the United States must pay an entry fee that is essentially a Pigouvian tax.

A second way to correct the problem of overuse is to create a system of tradable licenses for the use of the common resource, much like the tradable emissions permit systems designed to address negative externalities. The policy maker issues the number of licenses that corresponds to the efficient level of use of the good. For example, hundreds of fisheries around the world have adopted *individual transferable quotas* that are effectively licenses to catch a certain quantity of fish. Making the licenses tradable ensures that the right to use the good is allocated efficiently—that is, those who end up using the good (those willing to pay the most for a license) are those who gain the most from its use.

But when it comes to common resources, often the most natural solution is simply to assign property rights. At a fundamental level, common resources are subject to overuse because *nobody owns them*. The essence of ownership of a good—the *property right* over the good—is that you can limit who can and cannot use the good as well as how much of it can be used. When a good is nonexcludable, in a very real sense no one owns it because a property right cannot be enforced—and consequently no one has an incentive to use it efficiently. So one way to correct the problem of overuse is to make the good excludable and assign property rights over it to someone. The good now has an owner who has an incentive to protect the value of the good—to use it efficiently rather than overuse it. This solution is applicable when currently nonexcludable goods can be made excludable, as with the privatization of parks and even roads, but it cannot be applied to resources that are inherently nonexcludable, including the air and flowing water.

Artificially Scarce Goods

An **artificially scarce good** is a good that is excludable but nonrival in consumption.

An **artificially scarce good** is a good that is excludable but nonrival in consumption. As we've already seen, pay-per-view movies are a familiar example. The marginal cost to society of allowing an individual to watch a movie is zero because one person's viewing doesn't interfere with another person's viewing. Yet cable companies prevent an individual from seeing a movie if he or she hasn't paid. Goods like computer software and audio files, which are valued for the information they embody (and are sometimes called "information goods"), are also artificially scarce.

Markets will supply artificially scarce goods because their excludability allows firms to charge people for them. However, since the efficient price is equal to the marginal cost of zero and the actual price is something higher than that, the good is "artificially scarce" and consumption is inefficiently low. The problem is that, unless the producer can somehow earn revenue from producing and selling the good, none will be produced, which is likely to be worse than a positive but inefficiently low quantity.

We have seen that, in the cases of public goods, common resources, and artificially scarce goods, a market economy will not provide adequate incentives for efficient levels of production and consumption. Fortunately for the sake of market efficiency, most goods are private goods. Food, clothing, shelter, and most other desirable things in life are excludable and rival in consumption, so the types of market failure discussed in this module are important exceptions rather than the norm.

760 Section 14 Market Failure and the Role of Government

MODULE 76 Review

Check Your Understanding

1. For each of the following goods, indicate whether it is excludable, whether it is rival in consumption, and what kind of good it is.
   a. a public space such as a park
   b. a cheese burrito
   c. information from a website that is password-protected
   d. publicly announced information about the path of an incoming hurricane
2. Which of the goods in Question 1 will be provided by a private producer without government intervention? Which will not be? Explain your answer.

Tackle the Test: Multiple-Choice Questions

1. Which of the following types of goods are always nonrival in consumption?
   a. public goods
   b. private goods
   c. common resources
   d. inferior goods
   e. goods provided by the government
2. The free-rider problem occurs in the case of
   a. private goods.
   b. common resources.
   c. artificially scarce goods.
   d. motorcycles.
   e. all of the above.
3. Public goods are sometimes provided through which of the following means?
   I. voluntary contributions
   II. individual self-interest
   III. the government
   a. I only
   b. II only
   c. III only
   d. I and III only
   e. I, II, and III
4. Market provision of a public good will lead to
   a. the efficient quantity.
   b. the efficient price.
   c. an inefficiently high quantity of the good.
   d. an inefficiently low quantity of the good.
   e. none of the good being provided.
5. The overuse of a common resource can be reduced by which of the following?
   a. a Pigouvian tax
   b. government regulations
   c. tradable licenses
   d. the assignment of property rights
   e. all of the above

Answers to Module 76 Review Questions

Check Your Understanding

1. a. A public space is generally nonexcludable, but it may or may not be rival in consumption, depending on the level of congestion. For example, if you and I are the only users of a jogging path in the public park, then your use will not prevent my use—the path is nonrival in consumption. In this case, the public space is a public good. But the space is rival in consumption if there are many people trying to use the jogging path at the same time or if my use of the public tennis court prevents your use of the same court. In this case, the public space becomes a common resource.

b. A cheese burrito is both excludable and rival in consumption. Hence, it is a private good.

c. Information from a password-protected website is excludable but nonrival in consumption. So, it is an artificially scarce good.

d. Publicly announced information about the path of an incoming hurricane is nonexcludable and nonrival in consumption, so it is a public good.

2. A private producer will supply only a good that is excludable; otherwise, the producer won't be able to charge a price for it that covers the cost of production. Thus, a private producer would be willing to supply a cheese burrito and information from a password-protected website, but unwilling to supply a public park or publicly announced information about an incoming hurricane.

Tackle the Test: Multiple-Choice Questions

1. a
2. b
3. e
4. d
5. e

Tackle the Test: Free-Response Questions

1. Suppose Austin and Ally are the only soccer enthusiasts in a village where any number of public soccer clinics could be put on by visiting experts for $80 each. There are no external costs involved. Austin's marginal private benefit curve for soccer clinics is horizontal at $60. Ally's marginal private benefit curve is a straight line starting at $100 on the vertical axis and ending at 10 clinics on the horizontal axis. Draw a correctly labeled graph for soccer clinics showing the marginal social cost, the marginal social benefit, and each resident's marginal private benefit. Label the quantity of clinics that Austin would purchase if he were the only resident as Q_{Austin}. Label the quantity of clinics that Ally would purchase if she were the only resident as Q_{Ally}. Label the optimal quantity of clinics for society as $Q_{Optimal}$.

Rubric for FRQ 1 (6 points):

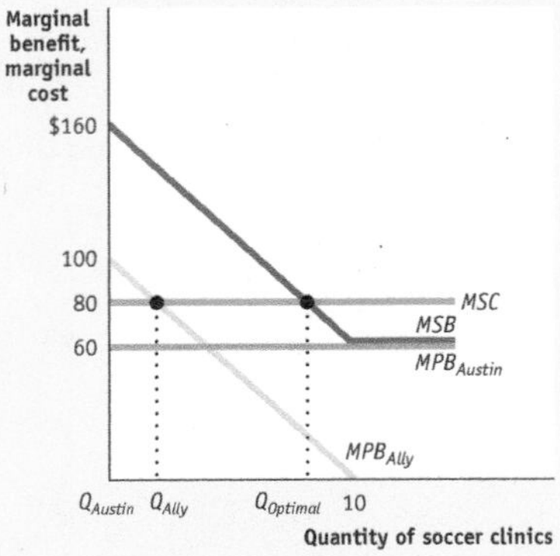

1 point: Correct axis labels ("Marginal benefit, marginal cost" or "Dollars per unit" on the vertical axis, "Quantity of soccer clinics" or "Q" on the horizontal axis)

1 point: *MSC* curve horizontal at a height of $80

1 point: *MSB* curve starts at a height of $160 where the quantity is zero, slopes downward to a height of $60 where the quantity is 10, and then coincides with MPB_{Austin}

1 point: Q_{Austin} labeled at a quantity of zero (because *MSC* exceeds MPB_{Austin} for every clinic)

1 point: Q_{Ally} found at the intersection of *MSC* and MPB_{Ally} and shown on the horizontal axis

1 point: $Q_{Optimal}$ found at the intersection of *MSC* and *MSB* and shown on the horizontal axis

2. Imagine that the city of Townville has 1,000 residents and pays $100,000 per year to rent a public good for the benefit of every member of the community.
   a. Identify and explain the two characteristics shared by every public good.
   b. Suppose a new resident moves to Townville. What is the additional cost of providing the public good to the new community member? Explain.
   (6 points)

Tackle the Test: Free-Response Question Rubric for FRQ 2 (6 points)

1 point: Nonrival in consumption

1 point: The same unit of the good can be consumed by more than one person at the same time.

1 point: Nonexcludable

1 point: Suppliers of the good can't prevent people who don't pay from consuming the good.

1 point: The additional cost is zero.

1 point: Public goods are nonrival, so the same unit can be provided to additional community members at no added cost.

762 Section 14 Market Failure and the Role of Government

myLoupe/Universal Images Group via Getty Images

MODULE 77 Public Policy to Promote Competition

In this Module, you will learn to:

- Identify the three major antitrust laws and describe how they are used to promote competition
- Explain how government regulation is used to prevent inefficiency in the case of natural monopoly
- Discuss the pros and cons of using marginal cost pricing and average cost pricing to regulate prices in natural monopolies

Promoting Competition

We have seen that, in general, equilibrium in a competitive market with no externalities is efficient. On the other hand, imperfectly competitive markets—for example, those with a monopoly or an oligopoly—generally create inefficient outcomes. Concern about the higher prices, lower quantities, and lower quality of goods that can result from imperfect competition has led to public policies to promote competition. These policies include antitrust laws and direct government regulation.

Public policy toward monopoly depends crucially on whether or not the industry in question is a natural monopoly. The most common approach to a natural monopoly is for the government to allow one firm to exist but to regulate that firm to increase the quantity and lower the price relative to the monopoly outcome.

In this module, we first focus on ways to promote competition in cases that don't involve natural monopolies. If the industry is *not* a natural monopoly, the best policy is to prevent a monopoly from arising or to break it up if it already exists. These policies are carried out through antitrust laws. Later in this module we will turn to the more difficult problem of dealing with a natural monopoly.

Antitrust Policy

As we discussed in Module 66, imperfect competition first became an issue in the United States during the second half of the nineteenth century when industrialists formed trusts to facilitate monopoly pricing. By having shareholders place their shares in the hands of a board of trustees, major companies in effect merged into a single firm. That is, they created monopolies.

PD To prepare for teaching this lesson, you may want to consult the **Module 77 Sample Lecture** in the TRM.

OPEN & CLOSE **Start Here**

Many students will recall the Sherman Antitrust Act and other antitrust laws from their study of U.S. history. Ask them the purpose of such laws. Some students will likely suggest that these laws are designed to promote competition (prevent monopoly). Help them tie what they know about antitrust laws from history to what they have learned about inefficiency and deadweight loss in the competition and monopoly models they have studied in this course.

TEACH AP® Exam Tip

Antitrust law policy to promote competition and to prevent monopoly is included on the AP® exam. However, the exam will not test the details, dates, or specifics of the antitrust laws.

Eventually, there was a public backlash, driven partly by concern about the economic effects of the trust movement and partly by fear that the owners of the trusts were simply becoming too powerful. The result was the Sherman Antitrust Act of 1890, which was intended both to prevent the creation of more monopolies and to break up existing ones. Following the Sherman Act, the government passed several other acts intended to clarify antitrust policy.

The Sherman Antitrust Act of 1890

AP® Exam Tip

You should be able to recognize the important pieces of antitrust legislation in case they appear in the multiple choice section of the AP® exam.

When Microsoft Corporation bundled its Internet Explorer web browser software with its Windows operating system, the makers of competing Netscape Navigator cried foul. Netscape advocates claimed the immediate availability of Internet Explorer to Windows users would create unfair competition. The plaintiffs sought protection under the cornerstone of U.S. antitrust policy (known in many other countries as "competition policy"), the Sherman Antitrust Act. This Act was the first of three major federal antitrust laws in the United States, followed by the Clayton Antitrust Act and the Federal Trade Commission Act, both passed in 1914. The Department of Justice, which has an Antitrust Division charged with enforcing antitrust laws, describes the goals of antitrust laws as protecting competition, ensuring lower prices, and promoting the development of new and better products. It emphasizes that firms in competitive markets attract consumers by cutting prices and increasing the quality of products or services. Competition and profit opportunities also stimulate businesses to find new and more efficient production methods.

The Sherman Antitrust Act of 1890 has two important provisions, each of which outlaws a particular type of activity. The first provision makes it illegal to create a contract, combination, or conspiracy that unreasonably restrains interstate trade. The second provision outlaws the monopolization of any part of interstate commerce. In addition, under the law, the Department of Justice is empowered to bring civil claims and criminal prosecutions when the law is violated. Indeed, it was the Department of Justice that filed suit against Microsoft in the web browser case. The initial court ruling, by the way, was that Microsoft should be broken up into one company that sold Windows and another that sold other software components. After that ruling was overturned on appeal, a final settlement kept Microsoft intact, but prohibited various forms of predatory behavior and practices that could create barriers to entry.

As the ambiguities of the Microsoft case suggest, the law provides little detail regarding what constitutes "restraining trade." And the law does not make it illegal to *be* a monopoly but to "monopolize," that is, to take illegal actions to become a monopoly. If you are the only firm in an industry because no other firm chooses to enter the market, you are not in violation of the Sherman Act.

The two provisions of the Sherman Act give very broad, general descriptions of the activities it makes illegal. The act does not provide details regarding specific actions or activities that it prohibits. The vague nature of the Sherman Act led to the subsequent passage of two additional major antitrust laws.

The Clayton Antitrust Act of 1914

The Clayton Antitrust Act of 1914 was intended to clarify the Sherman Act, which did not identify specific firm behaviors that were illegal. The Clayton Act outlaws four specific firm behaviors: price discrimination, anticompetitive practices, anticompetitive mergers and acquisitions, and interlocking directorates (two corporate boards of directors that share at least one director in common).

You are already familiar with the topic of price discrimination from our discussion of market structures. The Clayton Act makes it illegal to charge different prices to different customers for the same product. Obviously, there are exceptions to this rule that allow the price discrimination we see in practice, for example, at movie theaters where children pay a different price than adults.

764 Section 14 Market Failure and the Role of Government

By prohibiting the anticompetitive practice of *exclusive dealing*, the Clayton Act makes it illegal for a firm to refuse to do business with you just because you also do business with its competitors. If a firm had the dominant product in a given market, exclusive dealing could allow it to gain monopoly power in other markets. For example, a company that sells an extremely popular felt-tip marker—the only one of its kind—could set a condition that customers who want to purchase the marker must purchase all of their office supplies from the company. This would allow the marker company to expand its existing market power into the market for other office supplies.

The Clayton Act also outlaws *tying arrangements* because, otherwise, a firm could expand its monopoly power for a dominant product by "tying" the purchase of one product to the purchase of a dominant product in another market. Tying arrangements occur when a firm stipulates that it will sell you a specific product, say a printer, only if you buy something else, such as printer paper, at the same time. In this case, tying the printer and paper together expands the firm's printer market power into the market for paper. In this way, as with exclusive dealing, tying arrangements can lessen competition by allowing a firm to expand its market power from one market into another.

Mergers and acquisitions happen fairly often in the U.S. economy; most are not illegal despite the Clayton Act stipulations. The Justice Department regularly reviews proposed mergers between companies in the same industry and, under the Clayton Act, bars any that they determine would significantly reduce competition. To evaluate proposed mergers, they often use the measures we discussed in the oligopoly modules: *concentration ratios* and the *Herfindahl–Hirschman Index*. But the Justice Department is not the only agency responsible for enforcing antitrust laws. Another of our major antitrust laws created and empowers the Federal Trade Commission to enforce antitrust laws.

The Federal Trade Commission Act of 1914

Passed in 1914, the Federal Trade Commission Act prohibits unfair methods of competition in interstate commerce and created the Federal Trade Commission (FTC) to enforce the Act. The FTC Act outlaws unfair competition, including "unfair or deceptive acts." The FTC Act also outlaws some of the same practices included in the Sherman and Clayton Acts. In addition, it specifically outlaws price fixing (including the setting of minimum resale prices), output restrictions, and actions that prevent the entry of new firms. The FTC's goal is to promote lower prices, higher output, and free entry—all characteristics of competitive markets (as opposed to monopolies and oligopolies).

© Sandra Baker/Alamy

The Federal Trade Commission promotes fair practices, free entry by firms, and the virtues of competitive markets.

Dealing with Natural Monopoly

Antitrust laws are designed to promote competition by preventing business behaviors that concentrate market power. But what if a market is a natural monopoly? As you will recall, a natural monopoly occurs when economies of scale make it efficient to have only one firm in a market. Now we turn from promoting competition to establishing a monopoly, but seeking a public policy to prevent the relatively high prices and low quantities that result when there is only one firm.

Breaking up a monopoly that isn't natural is clearly a good idea: the gains to consumers outweigh the loss to the firm. But what about the situation in which a large firm has a lower average total cost than many small firms—the case of natural monopoly we discussed in Section 9? The goal in these circumstances is to retain the advantage of lower average total cost that results from a single producer and still curb the inefficiency associated with a monopoly. In Module 62, we presented two ways to do this—public ownership and price regulation.

While there are a few examples of public ownership in the United States, such as Amtrak, a provider of passenger rail service, the more common answer has been to leave the industry in private hands but subject it to regulation.

TEACH Connect It

Students learned about natural monopolies in Module 62. This module presents more detail related to price regulation in the case of natural monopoly. Regulation can set price equal to marginal cost (marginal cost pricing) or equal to average total cost (average cost pricing). Marginal cost pricing ($P = MC$) achieves allocative efficiency, but the firm would incur a loss without government subsidization. Average cost pricing ($P = ATC$) prevents a loss but is not allocatively efficient.

FOCUS Graph It

Figure 77.1 illustrates marginal cost and average cost pricing for a natural monopoly. Have students refer to the graph and answer the following questions:

- Which quantity is allocatively efficient and why? Q_1; $P = MC$
- Which quantity results in no economic profit or loss and why? Q_2; $P = ATC$
- What problem results from setting $P = MC$? *The firm loses money if it is not subsidized.*
- What problem results from setting $P = ATC$? *The resulting quantity is not allocatively efficient.*

FOCUS Active Learning

TRM Assign Dr. Mary J. McGlasson's video "Episode 28: Regulation" (see econextras video list with hyperlinks on the bcs and TRFD) and **Worksheet 77.1 (Regulation)** from the TRM for accompanying questions.

FOCUS Active Learning

As a quick review, Jacob Clifford provides a video "Micro Unit 4, Question 7—Regulating Natural Monopolies" (see econextras video list with hyperlinks on the bcs and TRFD). You may want to have a student draw the graph on the board and challenge other students to explain the logic of the marginal cost and average cost pricing solutions.

Price Regulation Most local utilities are natural monopolies with regulated prices. By having only one firm produce in the market, society benefits from increased efficiency. That is, the average cost of production is lower due to economies of scale. But without price regulation, the natural monopoly would be tempted to restrict its output and raise its price. How, then, do regulators determine an appropriate price?

Since the purpose of regulation is to achieve efficiency in the market, a logical place to set the price is at the level at which the marginal cost curve intersects the demand curve. This is called **marginal cost pricing**. (Because we are no longer discussing situations with externalities, we will refer to a single marginal cost that is both the marginal social cost and the marginal private cost.) We have seen that it is allocatively efficient for a firm to set its price equal to its marginal cost. So should regulators require marginal cost pricing?

Marginal cost pricing occurs when regulators set a monopoly's price equal to its marginal cost to achieve efficiency.

AP® Exam Tip

Understanding the different pricing options for a regulated natural monopoly is a key skill for the AP® exam. You may need to graph and explain marginal cost pricing and average cost pricing.

Figure 77.1 illustrates this situation. In the case of a natural monopoly, the firm is operating on the downward-sloping portion of its average total cost curve (it is experiencing economies of scale). When the average total cost is falling, it must be that the marginal cost is below the average total cost, pulling it down. If the firm had to set its price equal to its marginal cost and sell Q_1 units (the quantity demanded when $P = MC$), the price would be below the average total cost and the firm would incur a loss: for each unit sold, the firm would lose the difference between the average total cost and the price. The firm would not continue to operate at a loss in the long run unless it received a subsidy equal to the amount of the loss. The government could require the efficient price and subsidize the firm, resulting in an overall increase in efficiency for society. But firm subsidies funded from tax revenues are often politically unpopular. What other options do regulators have?

Figure 77.1 Price Setting for a Regulated Monopoly

This figure shows the marginal cost curve, *MC*, and the average total cost curve, *ATC*. When the price is set equal to the marginal cost (where the *MC* curve crosses the demand curve), the firm incurs a loss. When the price is set equal to the average total cost (where the *ATC* curve crosses the demand curve) the firm breaks even, but the quantity is below the allocatively efficient level.

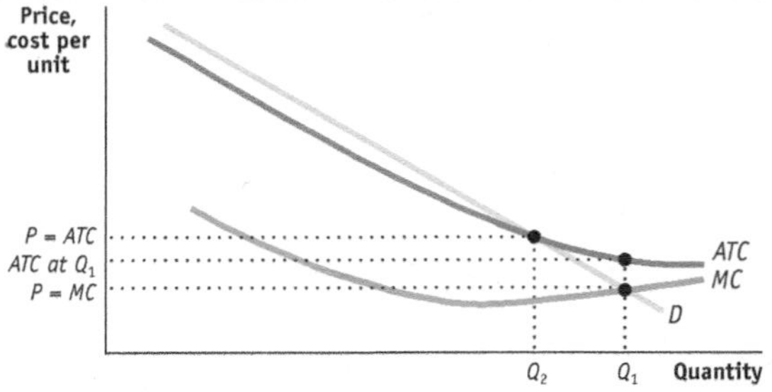

Average cost pricing occurs when regulators set a monopoly's price equal to its average cost to prevent the firm from incurring a loss.

If regulators want to set the price so that the firm does not require a subsidy, they can set the price at which the demand curve intersects the average total cost curve and the firm breaks even. This is called **average cost pricing**. As Figure 77.1 illustrates, average cost pricing results in output level Q_2. The result, a lower quantity at a higher price than with marginal cost pricing, seems to fly in the face of what antitrust regulation is all about. But remember that there are always trade-offs, and it may be best to avoid subsidizing a loss even if it results in less than the allocatively efficient quantity.

Allowing a natural monopoly to exist permits the firm to produce at a lower average total cost than if multiple firms produced in the same market. And price regulation seeks to prevent the inefficiency that results when an unregulated monopoly limits its output and raises its price. This all looks terrific: consumers are better off, monopoly profits are avoided, and overall welfare increases. Unfortunately, things are rarely that easy in practice. The main problem is that regulators don't always have the information required to set the price exactly at the level at which the demand curve crosses the average total cost curve. Sometimes they set it too low, creating shortages; at other times they set it too high, increasing inefficiency. Also, regulated monopolies, like publicly owned firms, tend to exaggerate their costs to regulators and to provide inferior quality to consumers.

FYI The Regulated Price of Power

Power doesn't come cheap, and we're not just talking about the nearly $2 billion spent on congressional races in 2012. By 2017, Georgia Power plans to add two 1,100-megawatt nuclear reactors to its Vogtle Electric Generating Plant in eastern Georgia at an estimated cost of $14 billion. In Kentucky, Louisville Gas and Electric will spend $1.2 billion to add a 750-megawatt coal-fired generating unit. With high start-up costs like these, power plants are natural monopolies. If many plants competed for customers in the same region, none would sell enough energy to warrant the cost of each plant. Here we see the spreading effect from Module 55 in action—having just one plant allows the production level to be relatively high and the average fixed cost to be tolerably low.

On October 6, 2010, U.S. Interior Secretary Ken Salazar and representatives from Cape Wind Associates signed the lease for a wind farm off the coast of Massachusetts. The $2.5 billion project will generate 468 megawatts of electricity. With lower output and higher start-up costs than the coal-fired power plant, the spreading effect is smaller, making the average fixed cost and the average total cost relatively high. If regulators set prices for this natural monopoly in accordance with average total cost, we would expect coal-fired plants to be held to a lower price per kilowatt-hour (kWh) than the relatively expensive wind power plants. Indeed, Cape Wind plans to charge 19 cents per kWh, more than twice the 8 cents per kWh allowed for electricity from coal-fired plants in Kentucky and Massachusetts.

Why the interest in generating energy from wind when energy from coal is cheaper for the consumer? The dynamics of supply and demand provide one reason: as supplies of coal decrease and energy demand increases, the equilibrium price for coal energy will rise, helping investments in wind energy to pay off. Another reason relates to the external costs discussed in Module 75: wind turbines create no emissions. The U.S. Department of Energy reports that if 20 percent of the nation's energy needs were satisfied with wind, carbon dioxide emissions would fall by 825 million metric tons annually. Like coal-fired power plants, wind farms do create some negative externalities. The potential for noise and obstructed views elicit cries of "not in my back yard (or even five miles off my coast)!" As with lunches, there's no such thing as a free kWh, which highlights the importance of cost-benefit analysis.

MODULE 77 Review

Check Your Understanding

1. Would each of the following business practices be legal under antitrust law? Explain.
   - **a.** You have a patent for a superior fax machine and therefore are the only person able to sell that type of fax machine. In order to buy your fax machine, you require the purchaser to buy a service contract from you (even though other firms provide excellent service for your machine).
   - **b.** You have invented a new type of correction fluid that does an amazing job covering up mistakes made on paper forms. In order to buy your correction fluid, you require purchasers to buy all of their office supplies from you.
   - **c.** You own a car dealership and plan to buy the dealership across the street and merge the two companies. There are several other car dealerships in town.
2. The FYI in this module discusses the possibility that regulators set prices for wind energy on the basis of average total cost. Explain why policymakers who don't want to pay subsidies would choose average cost pricing over marginal cost pricing in the market for wind energy.

FOCUS Test It

Assign Question 1 from the released 2013 AP® Microeconomics exam at http://media.collegeboard.com/digitalServices/pdf/ap/apcentral/ap13_frq_microeconomics.pdf. This question will provide a thorough review of all monopoly content. It is recommended that students take $12\frac{1}{2}$ minutes to answer this question to match the time suggested for the AP® exam. The rubric may be viewed at http://media.collegeboard.com/digitalServices/pdf/ap/apcentral/ap13_microeconomics_scoring_guidelines.pdf.

OPEN & CLOSE Exit Slip

*TRM Please see **Exit Slip: Module 77** in the TRM for formative multiple-choice questions to ask your students before finishing your lesson. These questions will help you quickly assess whether your students have mastered the module's concepts before moving on.*

Answers to the Exit Slip Questions

1. D
2. D
3. E

Answers to Module 77 Review Questions

Check Your Understanding

1. a. This practice would be illegal because it constitutes a tying arrangement.

b. This practice would be illegal because it constitutes exclusive dealing.

c. This is legal because the merger does not lead to monopolization.

2. Wind energy is created by a natural monopoly, which means that marginal cost is below average total cost in the relevant range of production. (In fact, the marginal cost of wind energy is virtually zero, because the wind itself is free.) Thus, a requirement to charge a price equal to marginal cost would result in a price below average total cost and cause the firm to incur a loss. Only with subsidies could the firm survive with marginal cost pricing. If policy makers chose average cost pricing instead, the operator of the wind farm would make a normal profit and no subsidy would be necessary.

Tackle the Test: Multiple-Choice Questions

1. e
2. b
3. b
4. c
5. c

Tackle the Test: Multiple-Choice Questions

1. The Sherman Antitrust Act of 1890 sought to do which of the following?
   - **a.** break up existing monopolies
   - **b.** prevent the creation of new monopolies
   - **c.** stop monopoly behavior engaged in by trusts
   - **d.** respond to the increasing power of trusts in the economy
   - **e.** all of the above
2. A natural monopoly exists when, over the relevant range, increasing the output level results in a lower
   - **a.** total cost.
   - **b.** average total cost.
   - **c.** average variable cost.
   - **d.** average fixed cost.
   - **e.** marginal cost.
3. Which of the following is the most common policy approach to a natural monopoly?
   - **a.** public ownership
   - **b.** price regulation
   - **c.** quantity regulation
   - **d.** quality regulation
   - **e.** a breakup of the monopoly into smaller firms

For questions 4 and 5, refer to the graph below.

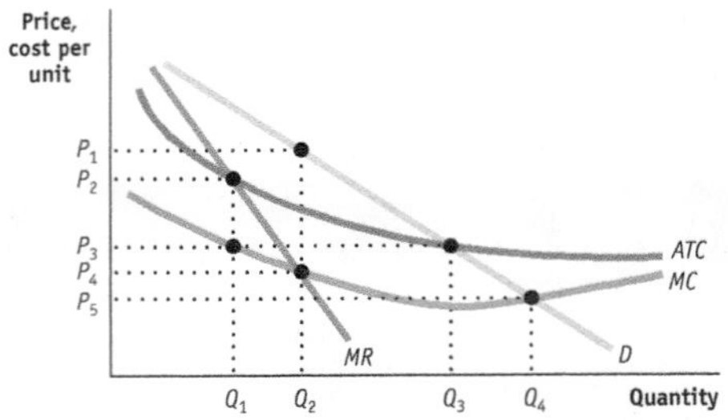

4. Without government intervention, a monopolist will produce ______ and charge ______
   - **a.** Q_3 P_3
   - **b.** Q_2 P_4
   - **c.** Q_2 P_1
   - **d.** Q_1 P_3
   - **e.** Q_1 P_2
5. The lowest regulated price the government could expect this monopolist to maintain in the long run is
   - **a.** P_1.
   - **b.** P_2.
   - **c.** P_3.
   - **d.** P_4.
   - **e.** P_5.

Tackle the Test: Free-Response Questions

1. **a.** Draw a correctly labeled graph showing a natural monopoly. On your graph, label the price and quantity the monopoly will choose if unregulated as P_U and Q_U.

   b. On the same graph, shade in and label consumer surplus and the firm's profit in the absence of regulation.

   c. On the same graph, label the lowest price that regulators could expect the monopoly to maintain in the long run as P_R and the resulting quantity as Q_R.

   d. What happens to the size of consumer surplus when the firm is required to charge P_R rather than P_U? What happens to the firm's profit?

768 Section 14 Market Failure and the Role of Government

Rubric for FRQ 1 (10 points)

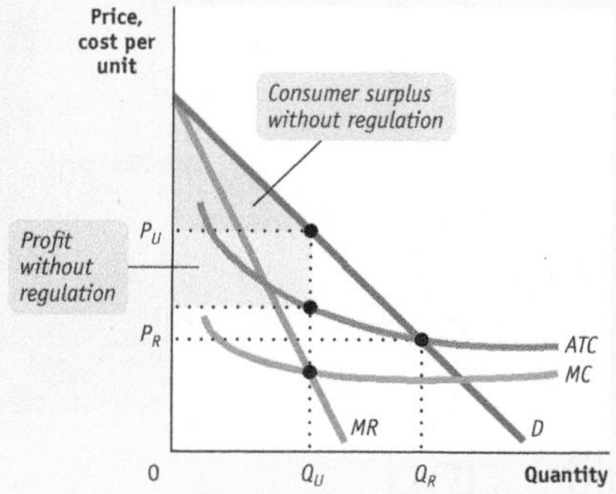

1 point: Correctly labeled axes ("Price, cost per unit" or "Dollars per unit" on the vertical axis, "Quantity" or "Q" on the horizontal axis)

1 point: Downward-sloping *ATC* curve

1 point: Downward-sloping *MC* curve below the *ATC* curve

1 point: Unregulated quantity Q_U shown on the horizontal axis where $MC = MR$

1 point: Unregulated price P_U found on a downward-sloping demand curve above Q_U and shown on the vertical axis

1 point: Correct profit rectangle

1 point: Consumer surplus triangle shown below the demand curve and above the price

1 point: Regulated price and quantity P_R and Q_R shown on the appropriate axes, corresponding to where the demand curve crosses the average total cost curve

1 point: Consumer surplus will increase

1 point: Profit will decrease to zero

2. List and explain three different public policy approaches to monopoly.
(6 points)

Tackle the Test: Free-Response Question

Rubric for FRQ 2 (6 points)

1 point: Antitrust policy

1 point: Prohibit practices that create monopolies and break up existing monopolies.

1 point: Public ownership

1 point: Have the government operate the monopoly with the goal of efficiency rather than profit.

1 point: Price regulation

1 point: Restrict price to the lowest price that does not cause losses, which is the price at which the average total cost curve intersects the demand curve.

Module 77 Public Policy to Promote Competition **769**

PD To prepare for teaching this lesson, you may want to consult the **Module 78 Sample Lecture** in the TRM.

OPEN & CLOSE Start Here

Ask students whether they are rich or poor. From their responses, make the point that it depends on how you define "rich" and how you define "poor." The U.S. government definition of poverty is the poverty threshold. That threshold is used to determine the poverty rate (the percentage of the population living below the poverty line). Provide students with the poverty threshold (http://aspe.hhs.gov/poverty/14poverty.cfm) and have them break down the amount to get a better understanding of what it means. First, the poverty threshold is set at three times the cost of a minimum food diet. That is, it is assumed that $\frac{1}{3}$ of the amount is spent on food. Have students divide the poverty threshold amount by 3 to obtain their food budget. Then have them divide by 52 to get a weekly amount for food and by 7 to get a daily amount for food. Ask students how they would budget to feed themselves from that amount. Also remind them that at this threshold they are NOT poor and would need to pay for everything else with the other $\frac{2}{3}$ of the amount.

TEACH Connect It

Positive economics provides statistics on the amount of poverty and the income distribution in a country. However, what (if anything) we should do about poverty and the distribution of income is normative (depends on our opinions and value judgments).

Lawrence Sawyer/Getty Images

MODULE **78**

Income Inequality and Income Distribution

In this Module, you will learn to:

- Define poverty and describe its causes and consequences
- Explain how income inequality in America has changed over time
- Discuss how Social Security and similar programs affect poverty and income inequality

The descriptive *positive* branch of economics offers information about the extent of poverty and income inequality. *Normative* questions about how to weigh equity in the distribution of income against associated losses in efficiency present greater challenges. For example, the redistribution of income from the rich to the poor reduces income inequality, but the taxes used to collect money for the poor generally cause deadweight loss. How much income redistribution is appropriate? That is a subject of debate, and although there may not be a single "right" answer, the tools of economics do much to inform the debate. In this module, we look at the problem of poverty and the issue of income distribution, and learn how public policy can affect them.

The Problem of Poverty

For at least the past 75 years, every U.S. president has promised to do his best to reduce poverty. In 1964 President Lyndon Johnson went so far as to declare a "war on poverty," creating a number of new programs to aid the poor. Antipoverty programs account for a significant part of the U.S. *welfare state*—the system whereby the government takes responsibility for the welfare of its citizens—although social insurance programs are an even larger part.

The **poverty threshold** is the annual income below which a family is officially considered poor.

What, exactly, do we mean by poverty? Any definition is somewhat arbitrary. Since 1965, however, the U.S. government has maintained an official definition of the **poverty threshold**, a minimum annual income that is considered adequate to purchase the necessities of life. Families whose incomes fall below the poverty threshold are considered poor.

The official poverty threshold depends on the size and composition of a family. In 2014 the poverty threshold for an adult living alone was $11,670; for a household consisting of two adults and two children, it was $23,850.

Trends in Poverty

Contrary to popular misconceptions, although the official poverty threshold is adjusted each year to reflect changes in the cost of living, it has *not* been adjusted upward over time to reflect the long-term rise in the standard of living of the average American family. As a result, as the economy grows and becomes more prosperous, and average incomes rise, you might expect the percentage of the population living below the poverty threshold to steadily decline.

Somewhat surprisingly, however, this hasn't happened. **Figure 78.1** shows the U.S. **poverty rate**—the percentage of the population living below the poverty threshold—from 1959 to 2012. As you can see, the poverty rate fell steeply during the 1960s and early 1970s. Since then, however, it has fluctuated up and down, with no clear trend. In fact, in 2012 the poverty rate was higher than it had been in 1973.

The **poverty rate** is the percentage of the population with incomes below the poverty threshold.

Figure 78.1 Trends in the U.S Poverty Rate, 1959–2012

The poverty rate fell sharply from the 1960s to the early 1970s but has not shown a clear trend since then.
Source: U.S. Census Bureau.

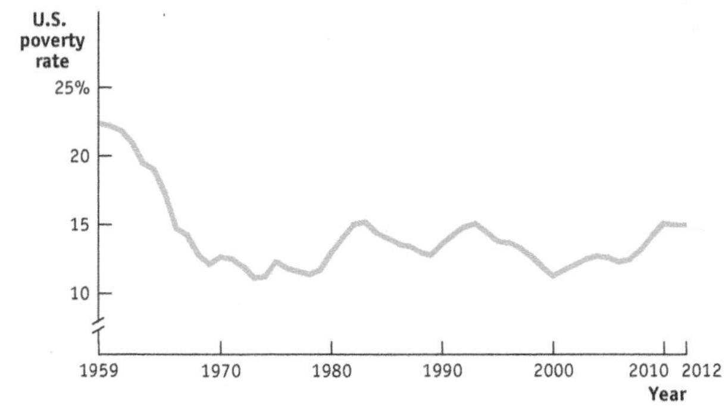

Who Are the Poor?

Many Americans probably hold a stereotyped image of poverty: an African-American or Hispanic family with no husband present and the female head of the household unemployed at least part of the time. This picture isn't completely off-base: poverty is disproportionately high among African-Americans and Hispanics as well as among female-headed households. But a majority of the poor don't fit the stereotype.

In 2012, about 46.5 million Americans were in poverty—15% of the population, or about one in seven persons. About one-quarter of the poor were African-American and a roughly equal number, Hispanic. Within these two groups, poverty rates were well above the national average: 27.2% of African-Americans and 25.6% of Hispanics. But there was also widespread poverty among non-Hispanic Whites, who had a poverty rate of 9.7%.

There is also a correlation between family makeup and poverty. Female-headed families with no husband present had a very high poverty rate: 33.9%. Married couples were much less likely to be poor, with a poverty rate of only 6.3%; still, about 39% of poor families were married couples.

What really stands out from the data, however, is the association between poverty and lack of adequate employment. Adults who work full time are very unlikely to be poor: only 2.9% of full-time workers were poor in 2012. Adults who worked part time or not at all during the year made up 85.4% of the poor in 2012. Many industries,

TEACH AP® Exam Tip

The distribution of income is an important topic on the AP® course outline. However, because much of the discussion of income distribution is normative, it is difficult to create questions on this area for the exam. Questions are much more likely to test positive aspects of the topic.

FOCUS Active Learning

TRM To extend the learning about the poverty guidelines, direct students to the Department of Health and Human Services website again at http://aspe.hhs.gov/poverty/14poverty.cfm and ask them to complete **Worksheet 78.1 (Poverty)** from the TRM.

FOCUS Graph It

Figure 78.1 shows the poverty rate in the United States from 1959 through 2012. Have students look at the illustration and describe changes in the poverty rate over this time period. *Students will observe that the poverty rate fell sharply from 1960 to early 1970, but has shown no clear trend. The rate of poverty floats around 12–15%.*

FOCUS Test It

Ask students the following questions:

- Which demographic characteristics are associated with higher rates of poverty? *African Americans and Hispanics, female-headed households*
- What characteristic is most associated with poverty? *Lack of adequate, full-time employment with benefits*

TEACH Teach It

Consequences of poverty impact children especially hard. Challenge students to consider ways in which poverty affects children and their development. *Homelessness, hunger that impacts learning, lack of stability, learning disabilities, lack of adequate health care, and reduced opportunities for higher education*

particularly in the retail and service sectors, now rely primarily on part-time workers. Part-time work typically lacks benefits such as health plans, paid vacation days, and retirement benefits, and it also usually pays a lower hourly wage than comparable full-time work. As a result, many of the poor are members of what analysts call the *working poor*: workers whose income falls at or below the poverty threshold.

AP® Exam Tip

Learn the causes of poverty, as they may show up in a question on the multiple choice section of the AP® exam.

What Causes Poverty?

Poverty is often blamed on lack of education, and educational attainment clearly has a strong positive effect on income level—on average, those with more education earn higher incomes than those with less education. For example, in 1979 the average hourly wage of men with a college degree was 38% higher than that of men with only a high school diploma; by 2013 the "college premium" had increased to 83%. Lack of proficiency in English is also a barrier to higher income. For example, Mexican-born male workers in the United States—two-thirds of whom have not graduated from high school and many of whom have poor English skills—earn less than half of what native-born men earn. And it's important not to overlook the role of racial and gender discrimination; although less pervasive today than 50 years ago, discrimination still erects formidable barriers to advancement for many Americans. Non-Whites earn less and are less likely to be employed than Whites with comparable levels of education. Studies find that African-American males suffer persistent discrimination by employers in favor of Whites, African-American women, and Hispanic immigrants. Women earn lower incomes than men with similar qualifications.

In addition, one important source of poverty that should not be overlooked is bad luck. Many families find themselves impoverished when a wage-earner loses a job or a family member falls seriously ill.

Consequences of Poverty

The consequences of poverty are often severe, particularly for children. Currently, 21.8% of children in the United States live in poverty. Poverty is often associated with a lack of access to health care, which can lead to further health problems that erode the ability to attend school and work later in life. Affordable housing is also frequently a problem, leading poor families to move often and disrupting school and work schedules. Recent medical studies have shown that children raised in severe poverty tend to suffer from lifelong learning disabilities. As a result, American children growing up in or near poverty don't have an equal chance at the starting line: they tend to be at a disadvantage throughout their lives. For example, even talented children who come from poor families are unlikely to finish college.

Table 78.1 shows the results of a long-term survey conducted by the U.S. Department of Education, which tracked a group of students who were in eighth grade in 1988. That year, the students took a mathematics test that the study used as an indicator of their innate ability; the study also scored students by the socioeconomic status of their families, a measure that took into account their parents' income and employment. As you can see, the results were disturbing: only 29% of students who were in the highest-scoring 25% on the test but whose parents were of low status finished college.

Table 78.1 Percent of Eighth-Graders from 1988 who Finished College

	Mathematics test score in bottom quartile	Mathematics test score in top quartile
Parents in bottom quartile	3%	29%
Parents in top quartile	30	74

Source: National Center for Education Statistics, *The Condition of Education 2003*, p. 47.

772 Section 14 Market Failure and the Role of Government

FYI The Impeccable Economic Logic of Early-Childhood Intervention Programs

One of the most vexing problems facing any society is how to break what researchers call the "cycle of poverty": children who grow up with disadvantaged socioeconomic backgrounds are far more likely to remain trapped in poverty as adults, even after we account for differences in ability. They are more likely to be unemployed or underemployed, to engage in crime, and to suffer chronic health problems.

Early childhood intervention has offered some hope of breaking the cycle. A 2006 study by the RAND Corporation found that high-quality early-childhood programs that focus on education and health care lead to significant social, intellectual, and financial advantages for kids who would otherwise be at risk of dropping out of high school and of engaging in criminal behavior. Children in programs like Head Start were less likely to engage in such destructive behaviors and more likely to end up with a job and to earn a high salary later in life. Another study by researchers at the University of Pittsburgh in 2003 looked at early-childhood intervention programs from a dollars-and-cents perspective, finding from $4 to $7 in benefits for every $1 spent on early-childhood intervention programs. The study also pointed to one program whose participants, by age 20, were 26% more likely to have finished high school, 35% less likely to have been charged in juvenile court, and 40% less likely to have repeated a grade compared to individuals of similar socio-economic background who did not attend preschool. The observed external benefits to society of these programs are so large that the Brookings Institution predicts that providing high-quality preschool education to every American child would result in an increase in GDP, the total value of a country's domestic output, by almost 2%, representing over 3 million more jobs.

By contrast, the equally talented children of high-status parents had a 74% chance of finishing college—and children of high-status parents had a 30% chance of finishing college even if they had low test scores. What this tells us is that poverty, to an important degree, is self-perpetuating: the children of the poor start at such a disadvantage relative to other Americans that it's very hard for them to achieve a better life.

Economic Inequality

The United States is a rich country. In 2012, the average U.S. household had an income of more than $71,000, far exceeding the poverty threshold. How is it possible, then, that so many Americans still live in poverty? The answer is that income is unequally distributed, with many households earning much less than the average and others earning much more.

Table 78.2 shows the distribution of pre-tax income among U.S. families in 2012—income before federal income taxes are paid—as estimated by the Census Bureau. Households are grouped into *quintiles*, each containing 20% or one-fifth of the population. The first, or bottom, quintile contains households whose income put them below the 20th percentile in income, the second quintile contains households whose income put them between the 20th and 40th percentiles, and so on. The Census Bureau also provides data on the 5% of families with the highest incomes.

Table 78.2 U.S. Income Distribution in 2012

Income group	Income range	Average income	Percent of total income
Bottom quintile	Less than $20,599	$11,490	3.2%
Second quintile	$20,599 to $39,764	29,696	8.3
Third quintile	$39,764 to $64,582	51,179	14.4
Fourth quintile	$64,582 to $104,096	82,098	23.0
Top quintile	More than $104,096	181,905	51.0
Top 5%	More than $191,156	318,052	22.3
Mean income = $71,274		**Median income = $51,017**	

Source: U.S. Census Bureau.

FOCUS Active Learning

Refer students to the FYI "The Impeccable Economic Logic of Early-Childhood Intervention Programs." Ask them to discuss how these programs might lead to decreased poverty. *The connection between education, especially early in the child's development of skills; employment; and poverty*

FOCUS Graph It

To study the distribution of income in an economy, households are often grouped into quintiles, each containing 20% of households. Table 78.2 shows the income distribution in the United States in 2012 by quintiles. The data provided show that the distribution of income is not equal. The bottom 5th of the population has only 3.2% of income, while the top 5th of the population has 51% of the total income. More striking are the data showing that the top 5% of income earners has 22.3% of total income.

TEACH Teach It

The Lorenz curve represents the distribution of income in an economy. The line of equality shows an exactly equal distribution of income. The closer the Lorenz curve is to the line of equality, the more equal the income distribution; the farther away the Lorenz curve is from the line of equality, the less equal the income distribution.

FOCUS Graph It

Figure 78.2 shows a Lorenz curve and the line of equality. Have students refer to the illustration and answer the following questions:

- Where would the Lorenz curve be if the income distribution were perfectly equal? *It would be the same as the line of equality.*
- What would it mean for the income distribution to be perfectly unequal? *One person has all the income.*
- Where would the Lorenz curve be if the income were perfectly unequal? *It would be equal to the horizontal axis (zero) until 100%, when it would be equal to the line up to 100%.*

For each group, Table 78.2 shows three numbers. The second column shows the range of incomes that define the group. For example, in 2012, the bottom quintile consisted of households with annual incomes of less than $20,599; the next quintile of households with incomes between $20,599 and $39,764; and so on. The third column shows the average income in each group, ranging from $11,490 for the bottom fifth to $318,052 for the top 5 percent. The fourth column shows the percentage of total U.S. income received by each group.

At the bottom of Table 78.2 are two useful numbers for thinking about the incomes of American households. **Mean household income**, also called average household income, is the total income of all U.S. households divided by the number of households. **Median household income** is the income of a household in the exact middle of the income distribution—the level of income at which half of all households have lower income and half have higher income. It's very important to realize that these two numbers do not measure the same thing. Economists often illustrate the difference by asking people first to imagine a room containing several dozen more or less ordinary wage-earners and then to think about what happens to the mean and median incomes of the people in the room if a billionaire Wall Street tycoon walks in. The mean income soars, because the tycoon's income pulls up the average, but median income hardly rises at all. This example helps explain why economists generally regard median income as a better guide to the economic status of typical American families than mean income: mean income is strongly affected by the incomes of a relatively small number of very-high-income Americans, who are not representative of the population as a whole; median income is not.

Mean household income is the average income across all households.

Median household income is the income of the household lying in the middle of the income distribution.

AP® Exam Tip

The *Course Description* published for AP® Economics teachers by the College Board recommends coverage of the Lorenz curve and the Gini coefficient. Although you will not need to calculate the Gini coefficient, you may need to interpret Gini coefficient values for the AP® exam.

What we learn from Table 78.2 is that income in the United States is quite unequally distributed. The average income of the poorest fifth of families is less than a quarter of the average income of families in the middle, and the richest fifth have an average income more than three times that of families in the middle. On average, the incomes of the richest fifth of the population are about 15 times as high as those of the poorest fifth. In fact, the distribution of income in America has become more unequal since 1980, rising to a level that has made it a significant political issue. The FYI at the end of this section discusses long-term trends in U.S. income inequality, which declined in the 1930s and 1940s, was stable for more than 30 years after World War II, but began rising again in the late 1970s.

We can visualize income inequality with the *Lorenz curve* as shown in **Figure 78.2**. The **Lorenz curve** indicates the percentage of all income received by the poorest members of the population, starting from the poorest 0% who receive 0% of the income and ending with the poorest 100% who receive 100% of the income. If income were equally distributed—that is, if the poorest 20% of the population received 20% of the income, the poorest 40%

The **Lorenz curve** shows the percentage of all income received by the poorest members of the population, from the poorest 0% to the poorest 100%.

Figure 78.2 The Lorenz Curve

The Lorenz curve indicates the percentage of all income received by the poorest members of the population, starting from the poorest 0% who receive 0% of the income and ending with the poorest 100% who receive 100% of the income. If everyone received the same income, the Lorenz curve would follow the line of equality. Income inequality causes the Lorenz curve to fall below the line of equality.

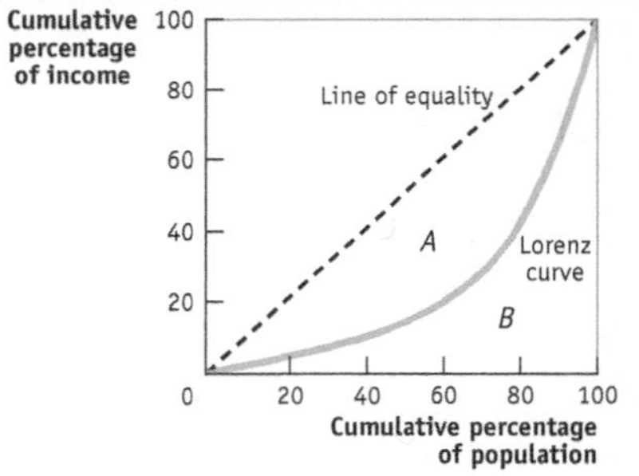

St. Louis Federal Reserve Bank Resources

"Gini in a Bottle: Some Facts on Income Inequality," ***Page One Economics Classroom Edition*** **(March 2012)**

Income inequality has been rising in the United States and other developed countries. This issue discusses income inequality, its causes, and some possible policy solutions.

of the population received 40% of the income, and so on—the Lorenz curve would coincide with the *line of equality*. However, from the data in Table 78.2, we know, for example, that the poorest 20% receive 3.2% of the income and the poorest 40% receive 3.2% + 8.4% = 11.6% percent of the income, so the Lorenz curve falls below the line of equality.

It's often convenient to have a single number that summarizes a country's level of income inequality. The **Gini coefficient**, the most widely used measure of inequality, is the ratio of area A in Figure 78.2, between the line of equality and the Lorenz curve, to area B, below the line of equality. So we have

$$\text{Gini coefficient} = A/(A + B)$$

The **Gini coefficient** is a number that summarizes a country's level of income inequality based on how unequally income is distributed.

A country with a perfectly equal distribution of income would have a Gini coefficient of 0, because the Lorenz curve would follow the line of equality, and area A would be zero. At the other extreme, the highest possible value for the Gini coefficient is 1—the level it would attain if all of a country's income went to just one person. In that case, area A would equal area $A + B$, because the Lorenz curve would lie along the horizontal axis until the richest person was included, at which point it would jump up to a height of 100%.

One way to get a sense of what Gini coefficients mean in practice is to look at international comparisons. **Figure 78.3** shows the most recent estimates of the Gini coefficient for many of the world's countries. Aside from a few countries in Africa, the highest levels of income inequality are found in Latin America; countries with a high degree

Figure 78.3 Income Inequality Around the World

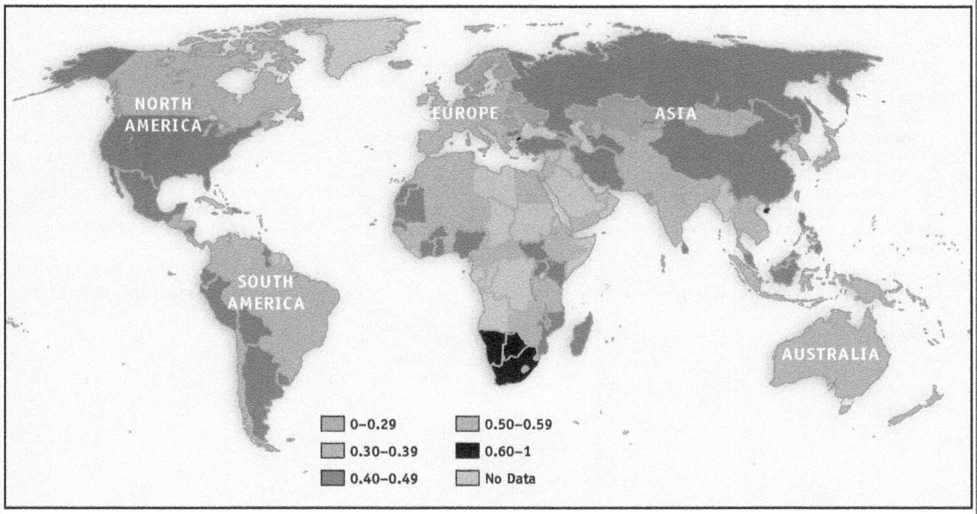

The highest levels of income inequality are found in Africa and Latin America. The most equal distributions of income are in Europe, especially in Scandinavia. Compared to other wealthy countries, the United States, with a Gini coefficient of 0.477 in 2012, has unusually high inequality.

Sources: World Bank, CIA World Factbook, various years depending on data availability.

TEACH Teach It

The Gini coefficient is a widely used measure of income distribution. It summarizes a country's level of income inequality based on how income is distributed across the population. A country with a perfectly equal distribution of income would have a Gini coefficient of 0 and all 5 quintiles of the country would each have 20% of the income. A country with a perfectly unequal distribution of income would have a Gini coefficient of 1, since the richest person has all the income.

- The most equal distributions of income occur in Scandinavian countries like Sweden.
- The most unequal distributions of income occur in Brazil and some African countries.
- The higher the income equality, the more a nation's people share in the country's prosperity.

FOCUS Graph It

Figure 78.2 shows how to use the Lorenz curve to calculate the Gini coefficient. The Gini coefficient is equal to area A divided by area A plus area B:

$$\text{Gini coefficient} = A/(A + B)$$

- As the Lorenz curve moves *farther* away from the line of equality, area A becomes larger, the income distribution is more unequal, and the Gini coefficient is larger.
- As the Lorenz curve moves *closer* to the line of equality, area A becomes smaller, the income distribution is more equal, and the Gini coefficient is smaller.

FOCUS Active Learning

TRM Have students watch the video "Lorenz Curve and Gini Coefficient" by Steve Lobsey (see econextras video list with hyperlinks on the bcs and TRFD). Then have them complete **Worksheet 78.2 (Lorenz Curve and Gini Coefficient)** from the TRM for further understanding of this concept.

FOCUS Test It

After students read the FYI, ask the following questions:

- What were some of the causes of the great increase in income inequality after 1970? *Rapid technological changes, increases in demand for highly skilled workers, wage gap increase, increases in U.S. imports of labor-intensive goods from low-wage countries, increases in immigration*
- What is interesting about the most recent type of income inequality? *It is happening among different groups of highly educated people—teachers versus executives versus entertainers—with an unknown cause.*
- What trend can you see in panel (b)? *The share of total income going to the top 10% of earners has risen sharply since the 1970s.* Can you think of a reason for this trend? *Changes in income tax rates, immigration policy, demand for highly skilled workers, and foreign trade*

FOCUS Active Learning

TRM Assign Professor Robert Lawson's video "Economic Freedom and Income Equality" (see econextras video list with hyperlinks on the bcs and TRFD) and **Worksheet 78.3 (Freedom and Equality)** from the TRM for corresponding questions.

FYI Long-Term Trends in Income Inequality in the United States

Does inequality tend to rise, fall, or stay the same over time? The answer is yes—all three. Over the course of the past century, the United States has gone through periods characterized by all three trends: an era of falling inequality during the 1930s and 1940s, an era of stable inequality for about 35 years after World War II, and an era of rising inequality over the past generation.

Detailed U.S. data on income by quintiles, as shown in Table 78.2, are only available starting in 1947. The figure shows the annual rate of growth of income, adjusted for inflation, for each quintile over two periods: from 1947 to 1980, and from 1980 to 2012. There's a clear difference between the two periods. In the first period, income within each group grew at about the same rate—that is, there wasn't much change in the inequality of income, just growing incomes across the board. After 1980, however, incomes grew much more quickly at the top than in the middle, and more quickly in the middle than at the bottom. So inequality has increased substantially since 1980. Overall, inflation-adjusted income for the top quintile rose 48% between 1980 and 2012, but it rose only 0.5% for the bottom quintile.

Although detailed data on income distribution aren't available before 1947, economists have instead used other information including income tax data to estimate the share of income going to the top 10% of the population all the way back to 1917. Panel (b) of the figure shows this measure from 1917 to 2012. These data, like the more detailed data available since 1947, show that American inequality was more or less stable between 1947 and the late 1970s but has risen substantially since. The longer-term data also show, however, that the relatively equal distribution of 1947 was something new. In the late nineteenth century, often referred to as the Gilded Age, American income was very unequally distributed; this high level of inequality persisted into the 1930s. But inequality declined sharply between the late 1930s and the end of World War II. In a famous paper, Claudia Goldin and Robert Margo, two economic historians, dubbed this narrowing of income inequality "the Great Compression."

The Great Compression roughly coincided with World War II, a period during which the U.S. government imposed special controls on wages and prices. Evidence indicates that these controls were applied in ways that reduced inequality—for example, it was much easier for employers to get approval to increase the wages of their lowest-paid employees than to increase executive salaries. What remains puzzling is that the equality imposed by wartime controls lasted for decades after those controls were lifted in 1946.

Since the 1970s, as we've already seen, inequality has increased substantially. In fact, pre-tax income appears to be as unequally distributed in America today as it was in the 1920s, prompting many commentators to describe the current state of the nation as a new Gilded Age—albeit one in which the effects of inequality are moderated by taxes and the existence of the welfare state. There is intense debate among economists about the causes of this widening inequality. The most popular explanation is rapid technological change, which has increased the demand for highly skilled or talented workers more rapidly than the demand for other workers, leading to a rise in the wage gap between the highly skilled and other workers. Growing international trade may also have contributed by allowing the United States to import labor-intensive products from low-wage countries rather than making them domestically, reducing the demand for less skilled American workers and depressing their wages. Rising immigration may be yet another source. On average, immigrants have lower education levels than native-born workers and increase the supply of low-skilled labor while depressing low-skilled wages.

All of these explanations, however, fail to account for one key feature: much of the rise in inequality doesn't reflect a rising gap between highly educated workers and those with less education, but rather growing differences among highly educated workers themselves. For example, schoolteachers and top business executives have similarly high levels of education, but executive paychecks have risen dramatically and teachers' salaries have not. For some reason, the economy now pays a few "superstars"—a group that includes literal superstars in the entertainment world but also such groups as Wall Street traders and top corporate executives—much higher incomes than it did a generation ago. It's still not entirely clear what caused the change.

(a) Rates of Income Growth Since 1947

(b) The Richest 10% of Americans, 1917–2012

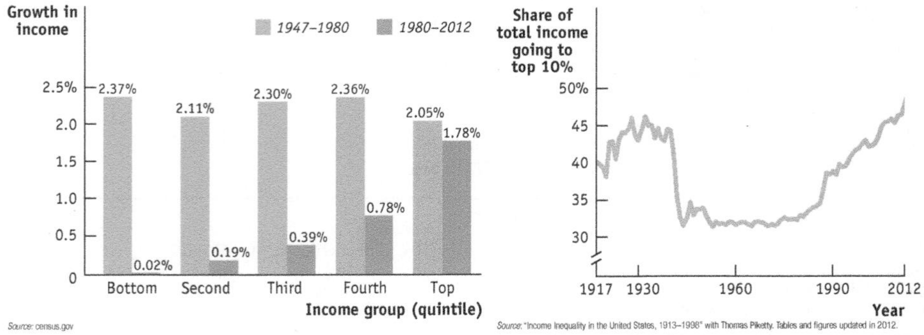

Source: census.gov

Source: "Income Inequality in the United States, 1913–1998" with Thomas Piketty. Tables and figures updated in 2012.

of inequality, such as Brazil, have Gini coefficients close to 0.6. The most equal distributions of income are in Europe, especially in Scandinavia; countries with very equal income distributions, such as Sweden, have Gini coefficients around 0.25. Compared to other wealthy countries, the United States, with a Gini coefficient of 0.477 in 2012, has unusually high inequality, though it isn't as unequal as in Latin America.

How serious an issue is income inequality? In a direct sense, high income inequality means that some people don't share in a nation's overall prosperity. As we've seen, rising inequality explains how it's possible that the U.S. poverty rate has failed to fall for the past 35 years even though the country as a whole has become considerably richer. Also, extreme inequality, as found in Latin America, is often associated with political instability, because of tension between a wealthy minority and the rest of the population.

It's important to realize, however, that the data shown in Table 78.2 overstate the true degree of inequality in America, for several reasons. One is that the data represent a snapshot for a single year, whereas the incomes of many individual families fluctuate over time. That is, many of those near the bottom in any given year are having an unusually bad year and many of those at the top are having an unusually good one. Over time, their incomes will revert to a more normal level. So a table showing average incomes within quintiles over a longer period, such as a decade, would not show as much inequality. Furthermore, a family's income tends to vary over its life cycle: most people earn considerably less in their early working years than they will later in life, and then experience a considerable drop in income when they retire. Consequently, the numbers in Table 78.2, which combine young workers, mature workers, and retirees, show more inequality than would a table that compares families of similar ages.

Despite these qualifications, there is a considerable amount of genuine inequality in the United States. Moreover, the fact that families' incomes fluctuate from year to year isn't entirely good news. Measures of inequality in a given year *do* overstate true inequality. But those year-to-year fluctuations are part of a problem that worries even affluent families—economic insecurity.

Economic Insecurity

The rationale for the welfare state rests in part on the benefits of reducing economic insecurity, which afflicts even relatively well-off families. One source of economic insecurity is the risk of a sudden loss of income, as occurs when a family member loses a job and either spends an extended period without work or is forced to take a new job that pays considerably less. In a given year, according to recent estimates, about one in six American families will see their income cut in half. Related estimates show that the percentage of people who find themselves below the poverty threshold for at least one year over the course of a decade is several times higher than the percentage of people below the poverty threshold in any given year.

Even if a family doesn't face a loss in income, it can face a surge in expenses. The most common reason for such surges is a medical problem that requires expensive treatment, such as heart disease or cancer. Many Americans have health insurance that covers a large share of their expenses in such cases, but a substantial number either do not have health insurance or rely on insurance provided by the government. In 2014, about 42 million Americans were uninsured. In the same year, several major provisions of the Affordable Care Act of 2010 went into effect, with the aim of expanding health insurance coverage to an additional 24 million citizens by 2023.

U.S. Antipoverty Programs

U.S. antipoverty programs include three huge programs—Social Security, Medicare, and Medicaid—several other fairly big programs, including Temporary Assistance for Needy Families, the Supplemental Nutrition Assistance Program, and the Earned Income Tax

Module 78 Income Inequality and Income Distribution 777

TEACH Teach It

There are three major U.S. programs intended to fight poverty (Social Security, Medicare, and Medicaid):

- Ask students to define means-tested programs. *Benefits are tied to income guidelines.*
  - Ask for examples. *Food stamps, Medicaid, Earned Income Tax Credit*
- Ask students to define in-kind benefit programs. *Benefits are given in the form of goods or services.*
  - Ask for examples. *Food giveaways, veterans' hospital care and services, senior lunch programs, free breakfast or lunch for schoolchildren*

TEACH Teach It

Means-tested programs include the following:

- Temporary Assistance for Needy Families is the current program that many will label "welfare." It is only available to those poor families with children. The Supplemental Nutrition Assistance Program helps low-income families buy food.
- The Supplemental Security Income program provides income for the disabled and those who cannot work.
- A negative income tax is a term used by economists that refers to programs that supplement the earnings of low-income workers by providing additional income. The Earned Income Tax Credit for low-income workers is one example.

Table 78.3 Major U.S. Welfare State Programs, 2013

	Monetary transfers	In-kind
Means - tested	Temporary Assistance for Needy Families: $21 billion Supplemental Security Income: $50.4 billion Earned Income Tax Credit: $83.4 billion	Supplemental Nutrition Assistance Program: $74.7 billion Medicaid: $441.1 billion
Not means - tested	Social Security: $799 billion Unemployment insurance: $62.2 billion	Medicare: $572.4 billion

Source: bea.gov

Credit, and a number of smaller programs. **Table 78.3** shows one useful way to categorize these programs, along with the amount spent on each listed program in 2013.

A **means-tested** program is available only to individuals or families whose incomes fall below a certain level.

First, the table distinguishes between programs that are **means-tested** and those that are not. In means-tested programs, benefits are available only to families or individuals whose income and/or wealth falls below some minimum. Basically, means-tested programs are poverty programs designed to help only those with low incomes. By contrast, non-means-tested programs provide their benefits to everyone, although, as we'll see, in practice they tend to reduce income inequality by increasing the incomes of the poor by a larger proportion than the incomes of the rich.

An **in-kind benefit** is a benefit given in the form of goods or services.

Second, the table distinguishes between programs that provide monetary transfers that beneficiaries can spend as they choose and those that provide **in-kind benefits**, which are given in the form of goods or services rather than money. As the numbers suggest, in-kind benefits are dominated by Medicare and Medicaid, which pay for health care.

Means-Tested Programs

When people use the term *welfare*, they're often referring to monetary aid to poor families. The main source of such monetary aid in the United States is Temporary Assistance for Needy Families, or TANF. This program does not aid everyone who is poor; it is available only to poor families with children and only for a limited period of time.

A **negative income tax** is a program that supplements the income of low-income workers.

TANF was introduced in the 1990s to replace a highly controversial program known as Aid to Families with Dependent Children, or AFDC. The older program was widely accused of creating perverse incentives for the poor, including encouraging family breakup. Partly as a result of the change in programs, the benefits of modern "welfare" are considerably less generous than those available a generation ago, once the data are adjusted for inflation. Also, TANF contains time limits, so welfare recipients—even single parents—must eventually seek work. As you can see from Table 78.3, TANF is a relatively small part of the modern U.S. welfare state.

The Supplemental Nutrition Assistance Program helps those with low-incomes put food on the table. Purchases are made using an electronic benefits transfer card that works like a debit card but can be used only to purchase food.

Other means-tested programs, though more expensive, are less controversial. The Supplemental Security Income program aids disabled Americans who are unable to work and have no other source of income. The Supplemental Nutrition Assistance Program (formerly known as the Food Stamp Program) helps low-income families and individuals to buy food staples.

Finally, economists use the term **negative income tax** for a program that supplements the earnings of low-income workers. For example, in the United States, the Earned Income Tax Credit (EITC) provides additional income to millions of workers. It has become more generous as traditional welfare has become less generous. As an incentive to work, only workers who earn income are eligible for the EITC. And as an incentive to work more, over a certain range of incomes, the more a worker earns, the higher the amount of EITC received. That is, the EITC acts as a negative income tax

St. Louis Federal Reserve Bank Resources

Government Spending and Taxes

Students engage in an activity that matches programs for low-income people with the type of economic inequity the program addresses and also observe another activity simulating tax payments and transfers.

for low-wage workers. In 2014, married couples with two children earning less than $13,650 per year received EITC payments equal to 40% of their earnings. Payments were slightly lower for single-parent families or workers without children. At higher incomes, the EITC is phased out, disappearing at an income of $49,186 in 2014.

Social Security and Unemployment Insurance

Social Security, the largest program in the U.S. welfare state, is a non-means-tested program that guarantees retirement income to qualifying older Americans. It also provides benefits to workers who become disabled and "survivor benefits" to family members of workers who die. Social Security is supported by a dedicated tax on wages: the Social Security portion of the payroll tax pays for Social Security benefits. The benefits workers receive on retirement depend on their taxable earnings during their working years: the more you earn up to the maximum amount subject to Social Security taxes ($117,000 in 2014), the more you receive in retirement. However, benefits are not strictly proportional to earnings. Instead, they're determined by a formula that gives high earners more than low earners, but with a sliding scale that makes the program relatively more generous for low earners.

Because most senior citizens don't receive pensions from their former employers, and most don't own enough assets to live off the income from their assets, Social Security benefits are an enormously important source of income for them. Fully 64% of Americans 65 and older rely on Social Security for more than half their income, and 35% of those 65 or older rely on Social Security for 90% or more of their income.

Unemployment insurance, although a much smaller amount of government transfers than Social Security, is another key social insurance program. It provides workers who lose their jobs with about 35% of their previous salary until they find a new job or until 26 weeks have passed. (This period is sometimes extended when the economy is in a slump.) Unemployment insurance is financed by a tax on employers.

The Effects of Programs on Poverty and Inequality

Because the people who receive government transfers tend to be different from those who are taxed to pay for those transfers, the U.S. welfare state has the effect of redistributing income from some people to others. Each year the Census Bureau estimates the effect of this redistribution in a report titled "The Effects of Government Taxes and Transfers on Income and Poverty." The report calculates only the *direct* effects of taxes and transfers, without taking into account changes in behavior that the taxes and transfers might cause. For example, the report doesn't try to estimate how many older Americans who are now retired would still be working if they weren't receiving Social Security checks. As a result, the estimates are only a partial indicator of the true effects of the welfare state. Nonetheless, the results are striking.

Table 78.4 shows how taxes and government transfers affected the poverty threshold for the population as a whole and for different age groups in 2009. It shows two numbers for each group: the percentage of the group that *would have had* incomes below

Table 78.4 Effects of Taxes and Transfers on the Poverty Rate, 2009

Group (by age)	Poverty rate without taxes and transfers	Poverty rate with taxes and transfers
All	23.7%	13.1%
Under 18	24.7	16.6
18 to 64	17.5	11.7
65 and over	48.0	9.8

Source: U.S. Census Bureau.

TEACH Teach It

- Social Security is the largest program in the U.S. welfare state. It is supported by a dedicated tax on wages. The amount of the benefit is determined by a formula that gives high earners more than low earners yet has built-in generosity with regard to low earners.
- Social Security also provides payments for the disabled and "survivor benefits" to family members of workers who die.
- Unemployment insurance is another key program. Workers who lose their jobs receive approximately 35% of their income until either they find work or 26 weeks elapse. This benefit is supported by taxes on employers.
- Figure 78.4 provides information on the effect of taxes and transfers on the poverty rate. Ask students which age group benefits the most from taxes and transfers. (*65 and older*) Why? (*Social Security and Medicare provide incomes and benefits, and are the largest programs in the U.S. welfare system.*)

the poverty threshold if the government neither collected taxes nor made transfers, and the percentage that actually fell below the poverty threshold once taxes and transfers were taken into account. (For technical reasons, the second number is somewhat lower than the standard measure of the poverty rate.) Overall, the combined effect of taxes and transfers is to cut the U.S. poverty rate nearly in half. The elderly derived the greatest benefits from redistribution, which reduced their potential poverty rate of 48.0% to an actual poverty rate of 9.8%.

TEACH Teach It

Table 78.5 uses the same concept of showing the effects of taxes and transfers but uses quintiles as the measure.

- Ask students which income group gains the most from taxes and transfers. *Bottom quintile*
- Ask students why the top quintile loses some share of aggregate income as taxes and transfers are applied. *The income tax is progressive and takes more income from this quintile and the means-tested transfers are not available to these income earners.*

Table 78.5 Effects of Taxes and Transfers on Income Distribution, 2009

Quintiles	Share of aggregate income without taxes and transfers	Share of aggregate income with taxes and transfers
Bottom quintile	0.7%	3.7%
Second quintile	6.9	9.8
Third quintile	14.0	15.9
Fourth quintile	24.1	24.2
Top quintile	54.3	46.4

Source: U.S. Census Bureau.

Table 78.5 shows the effects of taxes and transfers on the share of aggregate income going to each quintile of the income distribution in 2009. Like Table 78.4, it shows both what the distribution of income *would have been* if there were no taxes or government transfers and the actual distribution of income taking into account both taxes and transfers. The effect of government programs was to increase the share of income going to the poorest 80% of the population, especially the share going to the poorest 20%, while reducing the share of income going to the richest 20%.

The Debate Over Income Redistribution

The goals of income redistribution seem laudable: to help the poor, protect everyone from financial risk, and ensure that people can afford essential health care. But good intentions don't always make for good policy. There is an intense debate about how large the antipoverty programs should be, a debate that partly reflects differences in philosophy but also reflects concern about the possibly counterproductive effects of antipoverty programs. Disputes about the role of government in income redistribution are also one of the defining issues of modern politics.

Problems with Income Redistribution

There are two different lines of argument against antipoverty programs. One is based on philosophical concerns about the proper role of government. Some political theorists believe that governments should not redistribute income—that government's role should be limited to maintaining the rule of law, providing public goods, and managing externalities.

The more conventional argument against income redistribution involves the trade-off between efficiency and equity. A government with extensive antipoverty programs requires more revenue, and thus higher marginal tax rates, than one that limits itself mainly to the provision of public goods such as national defense. **Table 78.6** shows "social expenditure," a measure that roughly corresponds to welfare state spending, as a percentage of GDP in the United States, Britain, and France; it also compares this with an estimate of the marginal tax rate faced by an average wage-earner, including payroll taxes paid by employers and state and local taxes. As you can see, France's large welfare state goes along with a high marginal rate of taxation. Some, but not all, economists

St. Louis Federal Reserve Bank Resources

"Income Inequality: It's Not So Bad," *Inside the Vault* (Spring 2010)

The lead article in this issue discusses redistributing wealth through taxation. In this lesson, students will examine the ability-to-pay principle of taxation. They will compare a progressive tax system and a flat tax system by analyzing the same household scenarios using one system and then the other.

780 Section 14 Market Failure and the Role of Government

Table 78.6 Social Expenditure and Marginal Tax Rates

	Social expenditure in 2013 (% of GDP)	Marginal tax rate in 2013
US	20%	31.3%
UK	23.8	31.5
France	33.0	48.9

Sources: OECD Social Expenditure Database; OECD Taxing Wages Database.

believe that this high rate of taxation is a major reason the French work substantially fewer hours per year than Americans.

The trade-off between antipoverty programs and high marginal tax rates seems to suggest that we should try to hold down the cost of these programs. One way to do this is to means-test benefits: make them available only to those who need them. But means-testing, it turns out, creates a different kind of trade-off between equity and efficiency. Consider the following example: Suppose there is some means-tested benefit worth $2,000 per year that is available only to families with incomes of less than $20,000 per year. Now suppose that a family currently has an income of $19,500 but that one family member is deciding whether to take a new job that will raise the family's income to $20,500. Well, taking that job will actually make the family worse off because it will gain $1,000 in earnings but lose the $2,000 government benefit.

This situation, in which earning more actually leaves a family worse off through lost benefits, is known as a *notch*. It is a well-known problem with programs that aid the poor and behaves much like a high marginal tax rate on income. Most welfare state programs are designed to avoid creating a notch. This is typically done by setting a sliding scale for benefits such that they fall off gradually as the recipient's income rises. As long as benefits are reduced by less than a dollar for every additional dollar earned, there is an incentive to work more if possible. Current programs are not always successful in providing incentives for work. The combined effects of the major means-tested programs shown in Table 78.3, plus additional means-tested programs such as housing aid that are offered by some state and local governments, can create very high effective marginal tax rates. For example, one 2005 study found that a family consisting of two adults and two children that raised its annual income from $20,000—just above the poverty threshold in 2005—to $35,000 would find almost all of its increase in after-tax income offset by the loss of benefits such as those from the Supplemental Nutrition Assistance Program, the Earned Income Tax Credit, and Medicaid.

The Politics of Income Redistribution

In 1791, in the early phase of the French Revolution, France had a sort of congress, the National Assembly, in which representatives were seated according to social class: nobles, who pretty much liked the way things were, sat on the right; commoners, who wanted big changes, sat on the left. Ever since, it has been common in political discourse to talk about politicians as being on the "right" (more conservative) or on the "left" (more liberal).

But what do modern politicians on the left and right disagree about? In the modern United States, they mainly disagree about the appropriate size of antipoverty programs.

You might think that saying that political debate is really about just one thing—how big should government's involvement in income redistribution be—is a huge oversimplification. But political scientists have found that once you carefully rank members of Congress from right to left, a congressperson's position in that ranking does a very good job of predicting his or her votes on proposed legislation. Modern politics isn't completely one-dimensional—but it comes pretty close.

FOCUS Graph It

Table 78.6 shows welfare state spending as a percentage of GDP in the United States, France, and Britain; and it also compares it with the marginal tax rate of these countries. Have students refer to the data and answer the following questions:

- What explains the very large marginal tax rate for France? *A country with larger social expenditures requires more tax revenue.*
- Why do some economists believe that workers in France work fewer hours than workers in the United States? *Because of the very high marginal tax rate*
- What is a "notch"? *A situation where earning more actually leaves a family worse off—they would not qualify for assistance*

FOCUS Active Learning

As a class, watch the video "Wealth Inequality in America" (see econextras video list with hyperlinks on the bcs and TRFD). Created by Daily Conversation, it provides a candid visualization of the distribution of wealth in the United States. Review the difference between income and wealth with students. This video is a thought-provoking way to end this unit. Ask questions that center on how to change wealth inequality.

The same studies that show a strong left–right spectrum in U.S. politics also show strong polarization between the major parties on this spectrum. Thirty years ago there was a substantial overlap between the parties: some Democrats were to the right of some Republicans, or, if you prefer, some Republicans were to the left of some Democrats. Today, however, the rightmost Democrats appear to be to the left of the leftmost Republicans. There's nothing necessarily wrong with this. Although it's common to decry "partisanship," it's hard to see why members of different political parties shouldn't have different views about policy.

Can economic analysis help resolve this political conflict? Only up to a point.

Some of the political controversy over the welfare state involves differences in opinion about the trade-offs we have just discussed: if you believe that the disincentive effects of generous benefits and high taxes are very large, you're likely to look less favorably on welfare state programs than if you believe they're fairly small. Economic analysis, by improving our knowledge of the facts, can help resolve some of these differences.

To an important extent, however, differences of opinion on income redistribution reflect differences in values and philosophy. And those are differences economics can't resolve.

MODULE 78 Review

Check Your Understanding

1. Recall that the poverty threshold is not adjusted to reflect changes in the standard of living. As a result, is the poverty threshold a relative or an absolute measure of poverty? That is, does it define poverty according to how poor someone is relative to others or according to some fixed measure that doesn't change over time? Explain.

Tackle the Test: Multiple-Choice Questions

1. Which of the following is true of the U.S. poverty rate?
   a. It fell in the 1960s.
   b. There has been a clear upward trend since 1973.
   c. It was lower in 2012 than in 1973.
   d. It has remained unchanged since the mid 1970s.
   e. It has been steadily decreasing since 1959.
2. In 2012, the poorest 20% of households received approximately what percent of total income?
   a. 1%
   b. 3%
   c. 7%
   d. 10%
   e. 17%
3. If one person received all of the income in an economy, the Lorenz curve would
   a. rise steadily until the middle of the graph, and then fall.
   b. be upward-sloping.
   c. be downward-sloping.
   d. be vertical on the left side of the graph.
   e. lie along the horizontal axis except at the far right side of the graph.
4. Programs designed to help only those with low incomes are called
   a. welfare programs.
   b. in-kind programs.
   c. means-tested programs.
   d. income maintenance programs.
   e. social programs.
5. If a country has a perfectly equal distribution of income, its Gini coefficient equals
   a. 0.
   b. 1.
   c. 10.
   d. 50.
   e. 100.

OPEN & CLOSE Exit Slip

TRM *Please see **Exit Slip: Module 78** in the TRM for formative multiple-choice questions to ask your students before finishing your lesson. These questions will help you quickly assess whether your students have mastered the module's concepts before moving on.*

Answers to the Exit Slip Questions

1. C
2. D
3. B

Answers to Module 78 Review Questions

Check Your Understanding

1. The poverty threshold is an absolute measure of poverty. It defines individuals as poor if their incomes fall below a level that is considered adequate to purchase the necessities of life, irrespective of how well other people are doing. And that measure is fixed: in 2014, for instance, it took $11,670 for an individual living alone to purchase the necessities of life, regardless of how well off other Americans were. In particular, the poverty threshold is not adjusted for an increase in living standards: even if other Americans are becoming increasingly well off over time, in real terms (i.e., in terms of how many goods an individual at the poverty threshold can buy) the poverty threshold remains the same.

Tackle the Test: Multiple-Choice Questions

1. a
2. b
3. e
4. c
5. a

Tackle the Test: Free-Response Questions

1. There are 100 households in the economy of Equalor. Initially, 99 of them have an income of $10,000 each, and one household has an income of $1,010,000.
   a. What is the median income in this economy? What is the mean income?

   Through its antipoverty programs, the government of Equalor now redistributes income: it collects $990,000 from the richest household and distributes it equally among the remaining 99 households.

   b. What is the median income in this economy now? What is the mean income? Which indicator (mean or median household income) is a better indicator of the typical Equalorian household's income?

Rubric for FRQ 1 (5 points)

1 point: median income = $10,000
1 point: mean income = $20,000
1 point: median income = $20,000
1 point: mean income = $20,000
1 point: median

2. Again consider the economy of Equalor described in Question 1, in which the total income is $2 million.
   a. Draw a correctly labeled graph showing the points on the Lorenz curve for the poorest 0%, 20%, 40%, 60%, 80%, and 100% of the population before the redistribution of income.
   b. On the graph you have already drawn, repeat your answer to part a for the situation after the redistribution of income. Indicate the points that have changed with an "X".
   c. What is the Gini coefficient after the redistribution of income?
   (5 points)

SECTION 14 Review

Section 14 Review Video

Module 74

1. When pollution can be directly observed and controlled, government policies should be geared directly to producing the **socially optimal quantity of pollution**, the quantity at which the **marginal social cost of pollution** is equal to the **marginal social benefit of pollution**. In the absence of government intervention, a market produces too much pollution because polluters take only their benefit from polluting into account, not the costs imposed on others.
2. The cost to society of pollution from a power plant is an example of an **external cost**; the benefit to neighbors of beautiful flowers planted in your yard is an example of an **external benefit**. External costs and benefits are jointly known as **externalities**, with external costs called **negative externalities** and external benefits called **positive externalities**.
3. According to the **Coase theorem**, when externalities exist, bargaining will cause individuals to **internalize the externalities**, making government intervention unnecessary, as long as property rights are clearly defined and **transaction costs**—the costs of making a deal—are sufficiently low. However, in many cases transaction costs are too high to permit such deals.

Module 75

4. Governments often deal with pollution by imposing **environmental standards**, an approach, economists argue, that is usually inefficient. Two efficient (cost-minimizing) methods for reducing pollution are **emissions taxes**, a form of **Pigouvian tax**, and **tradable emissions permits**. The optimal Pigouvian tax on pollution causes the polluter to pay the marginal social cost at the socially optimal quantity of pollution. These methods also provide incentives for the creation and adoption of production technologies that cause less pollution.

Tackle the Test: Free-Response Question Rubric for FRQ 2 (5 points)

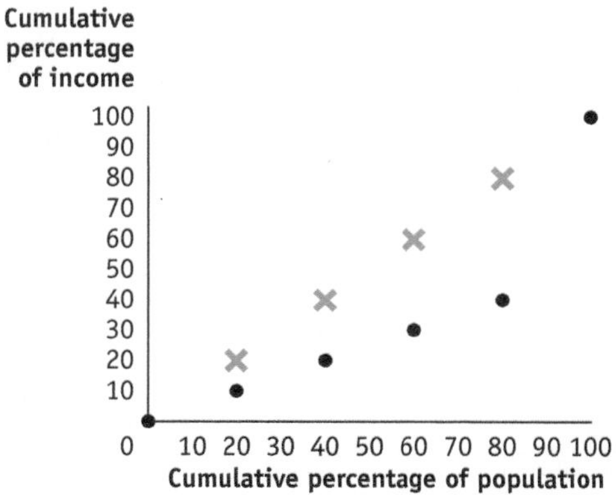

1 point: The vertical axis is labeled "Cumulative percentage of income" and the horizontal axis is labeled "Cumulative percentage of population."

1 point: The heights of the points at 0% and 100% of the population are 0% and 100% of the income, respectively.

1 point: The heights of the points at 20%, 40%, and 60% of the population are 10%, 20%, and 30% of the income, respectively.

1 point: The heights of the "X's" at 20%, 40%, and 60% of the population are 20%, 40%, and 60% of the income, respectively.

1 point: The Gini coefficient after the redistribution is zero.

FOCUS Flip It

Encourage your students to watch the **Section 14 Review Video**, which was created as a special student review tool and is linked into the e-Book or may be found on the book's companion website.

5. When a good yields external benefits, such as **technology spillovers**, the **marginal social benefit of the good** is equal to the **marginal private benefit** accruing to consumers plus its **marginal external benefit**. Without government intervention, the market produces too little of the good. An optimal **Pigouvian subsidy** to producers, equal to the marginal external benefit, moves the market to the socially optimal quantity of production. This yields higher output and a higher price to producers.
6. When there are external costs from production, the **marginal social cost of a good** exceeds its **marginal private cost** to producers, the difference being the **marginal external cost**. Without government action, the market produces too much of the good. The optimal Pigouvian tax on production of the good is equal to its marginal external cost, yielding lower output and a higher price to consumers. A system of tradable production permits for the right to produce the good can also achieve efficiency at minimum cost.
7. Communications, transportation, and high-technology goods are frequently subject to **network externalities**, which arise when the value of the good to an individual is greater when more people use the good.

Module 76

8. Goods may be classified according to whether or not they are **excludable**, meaning that people can be prevented from consuming them, and whether or not they are **rival in consumption**, meaning that one person's consumption of them affects another person's consumption of them.
9. Free markets can deliver efficient levels of production and consumption for **private goods**, which are both excludable and rival in consumption. When goods are **nonexcludable**, **nonrival in consumption**, or both, free markets cannot achieve efficient outcomes.
10. When goods are nonexcludable, there is a **free-rider problem**: consumers will not pay for the good, leading to inefficiently low production. When goods are nonrival in consumption, any positive price leads to inefficiently low consumption.
11. A **public good** is nonexcludable and nonrival in consumption. In most cases a public good must be supplied by the government. The marginal social benefit of a public good is equal to the sum of the marginal private benefits to each consumer. The efficient quantity of a public good is the quantity at which the marginal social benefit equals the marginal social cost of providing the good. As with a positive externality, the marginal social benefit is greater than any one individual's marginal private benefit, so no individual is willing to provide the efficient quantity.
12. One rationale for the presence of government is that it allows citizens to tax themselves in order to provide public goods. Governments use cost-benefit analysis to determine the efficient provision of a public good. Such analysis is difficult, however, because individuals have an incentive to overstate the good's value to them.
13. A **common resource** is rival in consumption but nonexcludable. It is subject to **overuse**, because an individual does not take into account the fact that his or her use depletes the amount available for others. This is similar to the problem with a negative externality: the marginal social cost of an individual's use of a common resource is always higher than his or her marginal private cost. Pigouvian taxes, the creation of a system of tradable licenses, and the assignment of property rights are possible solutions.
14. **Artificially scarce goods** are excludable but nonrival in consumption. Because no marginal cost arises from allowing another individual to consume the good, the efficient price is zero. A positive price compensates the producer for the cost of production but leads to inefficiently low consumption.

Module 77

15. Antitrust laws and regulation are used to promote competition. When the industry in question is a natural monopoly, price regulation is used.
16. The Sherman Act, the Clayton Act, and the Federal Trade Commission Act were the first major antitrust laws.
17. **Marginal cost pricing** and **average cost pricing** are examples of price regulation used in the case of natural monopoly to allow efficiencies from large scale production without allowing the deadweight loss that results from unregulated monopoly.

784 Section 14 Market Failure and the Role of Government

Module 78

18. Despite the fact that the **poverty threshold** is adjusted according to the cost of living but not according to the standard of living, and that the average income in the United States has risen substantially over the last 30 years, the **poverty rate**, the percentage of the population with an income below the poverty threshold, is no lower than it was 30 years ago. There are various causes of poverty: lack of education, the legacy of discrimination, and bad luck. The consequences of poverty are particularly harmful for children.

19. **Median household income**, the income of a family at the center of the income distribution, is a better indicator of the income of the typical household than **mean household income** because it is not distorted by the inclusion of a small number of very wealthy households. The **Lorenz curve** indicates the percentage of all income received by the poorest members of the population, starting with the poorest 0% and ending with the poorest 100%. The **Gini coefficient**, a number that summarizes a country's level of income inequality, is used to compare income inequality across countries.

20. **Means-tested** programs target aid to people whose income falls below a certain level. The major **in-kind benefits** programs are Medicare and Medicaid, which pay for medical care. Due to concerns about the effects on incentives to work and on family cohesion, aid to poor families has become significantly less generous even as the **negative income tax** has become more generous. Social Security, the largest U.S. welfare program, has significantly reduced poverty among the elderly. Unemployment insurance is another key social insurance program.

Key Terms

AP® Exam Practice Questions

Multiple-Choice Questions

1. The poverty rate is
   a. the total number of people who earn less than $23,850 annually.
   b. the percentage of households that file for bankruptcy in a year.
   c. the percentage of the population that earns less than the poverty threshold.
   d. the percentage of the labor force that is unemployed at some point during a year.
   e. the percentage of the population that is in the lowest income quintile.

Answers to Section 14 AP® Exam Practice Questions

Multiple-Choice Questions

1. c

2. e
3. c
4. e
5. d
6. a
7. b
8. a

2. Which of the following conditions contributes to the resolution of externality problems as suggested by the Coase theorem?
a. It is awkward for the parties involved to approach each other about the problem.
b. There is ambiguity about the legal rights of the parties involved.
c. There are many parties involved.
d. Transaction costs are high.
e. The legal rights of the parties involved are clearly defined.

3. When the production of a good creates negative externalities, which of the following leads to the socially optimal quantity of output?
a. a price ceiling set equal to the marginal external cost
b. a price floor set equal to the marginal private cost
c. a Pigouvian tax set equal to the marginal external cost
d. a Pigouvian subsidy set equal to the marginal external cost
e. average cost pricing

4. Which of the following policy changes would be the most likely to provide a gain in efficiency while achieving the same goal of reducing pollution?
a. environmental standards instead of emissions taxes
b. Pigouvian taxes instead of tradable emissions permits
c. emissions taxes instead of Pigouvian taxes
d. environmental standards instead of in-kind benefits
e. tradable emissions permits instead of environmental standards

5. When the economy is producing the socially optimal amount of pollution, it is necessarily true that
a. the marginal social benefit of pollution exceeds the marginal social cost.
b. the marginal external cost of pollution equals the marginal external benefit.
c. no pollution is being emitted.
d. the marginal social benefit of pollution equals the marginal social cost.
e. the marginal external cost of pollution is zero.

6. Market failure caused by a positive externality will involve
a. deadweight loss.
b. overconsumption.
c. pollution.
d. marginal external costs.
e. taxation.

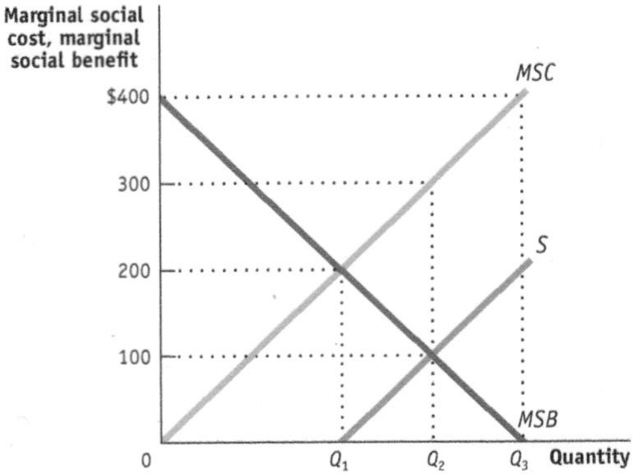

The graph above shows the marginal social cost, supply, and marginal social benefit in an industry that generates pollution. Use this graph to answer Questions 7 and 8.

7. Suppose the industry is currently producing the quantity Q_2 and the price is $100. If a Pigouvian tax equal to the marginal external cost is imposed, what will happen to society's total surplus and the deadweight loss in the industry?

	Total surplus	*Deadweight loss*
a.	decrease	stay the same
b.	increase	decrease
c.	increase	increase
d.	decrease	decrease
e.	increase	stay the same

8. The marginal social cost (*MSC*) and the marginal external cost (*MEC*) at the socially optimal equilibrium would be

	MSC	*MEC*
a.	$200	$200
b.	$100	$0
c.	$200	$100
d.	$100	$200
e.	$200	$0

786 Section 14 Market Failure and the Role of Government

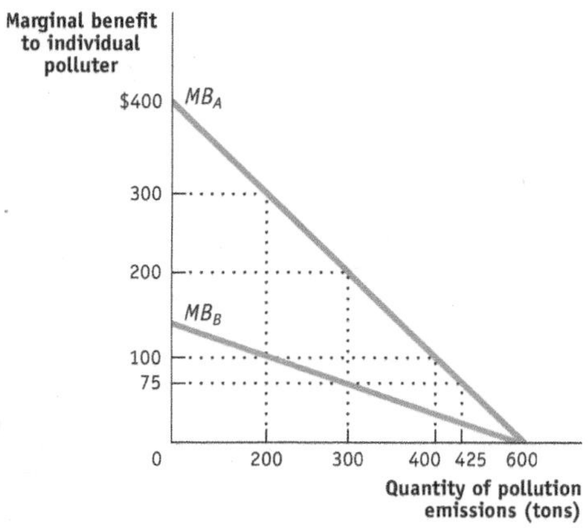

The graph above depicts the marginal benefit of pollution to plants A and B. Currently, each firm is emitting 600 tons of pollution. Use the graph to answer Questions 9 and 10.

9. An emissions tax of how much per ton would cut the total amount of pollution in half?
- **a.** $400
- **b.** $300
- **c.** $200
- **d.** $100
- **e.** $75

10. Instead of using taxes, if the government were to set environmental standards to cut the total amount of pollution in half, what would be the resulting marginal benefits to plants A and B?

	Marginal benefit for plant A	*Marginal benefit for plant B*
a.	$100	$100
b.	$75	$75
c.	$200	$100
d.	$100	$0
e.	$200	$75

11. Which of the following is accurate for goods provided by markets?
- **a.** Artificially scarce goods are likely to be produced in inefficiently large quantities.
- **b.** Common resources are likely to suffer from inefficiently low consumption levels.
- **c.** Private goods that are popular are likely to suffer from overuse problems.
- **d.** Public goods are likely to suffer from inefficiently low production.
- **e.** Artificially scarce goods are likely to suffer from the free-rider problem.

12. Which of the following is an example of market failure?
- **a.** Most people can't buy as many pairs of shoes as they would like.
- **b.** Most stores can't sell as much merchandise as they would like.
- **c.** Fishing in many waterways brings the quantity of fish below its socially optimal level.
- **d.** People typically pay more for a good than they would like to pay.
- **e.** Stores typically must charge a price that is less than they would like to charge.

13. Which of the following characteristics apply to private goods and common resources?

	Private goods	*Common resources*
a.	nonrival in consumption	nonexcludable
b.	rival in consumption	excludable
c.	nonexcludable	rival in consumption
d.	excludable	nonrival in consumption
e.	rival in consumption	nonexcludable

14. Based on economic analysis, why do so many people decide not to vote?
- **a.** The benefits of voting are nonexcludable.
- **b.** The costs of voting are nonrival.
- **c.** The benefits of voting are rival.
- **d.** The costs of voting are excludable.
- **e.** The benefits of voting outweigh the costs.

15. Which of the following statements regarding the passage of laws intended to promote competition in the marketplace is true?
- **a.** The Sherman Antitrust Act was intended to clarify the Clayton Act.
- **b.** The Clayton Antitrust Act made price discrimination illegal.
- **c.** The Federal Trade Commission Act made anticompetitive mergers illegal.
- **d.** The Sherman Antitrust Act outlawed price fixing.
- **e.** The Clayton Antitrust Act made it legal for two boards of directors to share a director in common.

16. Which of the following statements regarding a natural monopoly is accurate?
- **a.** The FTC will try to break up the natural monopoly because it is inefficient.
- **b.** Marginal cost pricing would lead to an efficient outcome and monopoly profits.
- **c.** The cost of producing any given quantity of the good produced by the natural monopoly would increase if multiple firms produced it.
- **d.** Regulators require the natural monopoly to produce the quantity that equates marginal cost and marginal benefit.
- **e.** The information required for average cost pricing is readily available to regulators.

9. d
10. e
11. d
12. c
13. e
14. a
15. b
16. c

17. b
18. d
19. b
20. a

Rubric for Free-Response Question

1 point: A positive externality

1 point: Every palm tree provides benefits to the purchaser and 99 other people, so the marginal social benefit is 100 times the marginal private benefit. The benefits that spill over to other people constitute a positive externality.

1 point: Graph with "Marginal social benefit, marginal social cost" or "$ per unit" on the vertical axis, "Quantity of palm trees" on the horizontal axis, and a downward-sloping marginal social benefit curve

1 point: Horizontal marginal social cost curve at a level of $200

1 point: Zero palm trees would be purchased in a private market because the most an individual would pay for a palm tree is $8, and in the private market the price would be at least $200, which is the marginal cost of producing palm trees.

1 point: The socially optimal quantity of palm trees is 3.

1 point: It is with the purchase of 3 palm trees that the marginal social cost equals the marginal social benefit.

1 point: In this situation, palm trees are a public good—everyone enjoys the benefits of each palm tree, so consumption is nonrival and nonexcludable.

1 point: A subsidy or direct government provision of the public good

1 point: A subsidy could bring the marginal private benefit up to the level of the marginal social benefit, or government provision of a public good could solve the free-rider problem.

Please see page SG-6 for sample student graphs for this Free-Response Question.

17. Which of the following welfare state programs provides in-kind benefits?
a. Temporary Assistance for Needy Families (TANF)
b. Medicaid
c. the Earned Income Tax Credit
d. Social Security
e. Supplemental Security Income

18. Which of the following welfare state programs is not means-tested?
a. Temporary Assistance for Needy Families (TANF)
b. Medicaid
c. the Earned Income Tax Credit
d. Social Security
e. Supplemental Security Income

19. A Gini coefficient of 0.5 would indicate
a. that the richest 50% of the population receives all of the income.
b. more income inequality than a Gini coefficient of 0.4.
c. that a country has perfect income equality.
d. that a country has perfect income inequality.
e. that the poorest 10% of the population receives half as much income as the richest 10% of the population.

20. Which of the following combinations correctly describes the changes since the 1970s in the poverty threshold and in the mean income as compared to the median income in the United States?

	Poverty threshold	*Mean income compared to median income*
a.	not adjusted for the standard of living	rose faster
b.	adjusted for the cost of living	declined
c.	adjusted for the standard of living	declined
d.	not adjusted for the cost of living	rose faster
e.	not adjusted for the standard of living	remained the same

Free-Response Question

Quantity of Palm trees	Total social cost = total private cost	Total private benefit per resident
0	$0	$0
1	200	8
2	400	12
3	600	14
4	800	15

1. Suppose there are 100 residents on the island of Mahalo. Whenever someone purchases a palm tree to plant on the island, everyone on the island receives the same benefits from the tree, which include beauty, shade, and erosion control. The table above shows the total social cost (which is also the total private cost) and the total private benefit received *per resident* depending on the quantity of palm trees purchased. Use this information to answer the questions below.
a. Does the purchase of palm trees create a negative externality, a positive externality, or no externality? Explain.
b. Draw a graph that depicts the marginal social cost and the marginal social benefit of palm trees.
c. What quantity of palm trees would be purchased if they were sold in a private market? Explain.
d. What is the socially optimal quantity of palm trees? Explain.
e. In this situation are palm trees a private good, a public good, or a common resource?
f. What could be an appropriate governmental policy response to this situation? Explain.
(10 points)

788 Section 14 Market Failure and the Role of Government

AP® Macroeconomics Exam Practice Test

Multiple-Choice Questions

Refer to the figure below to answer Question 1.

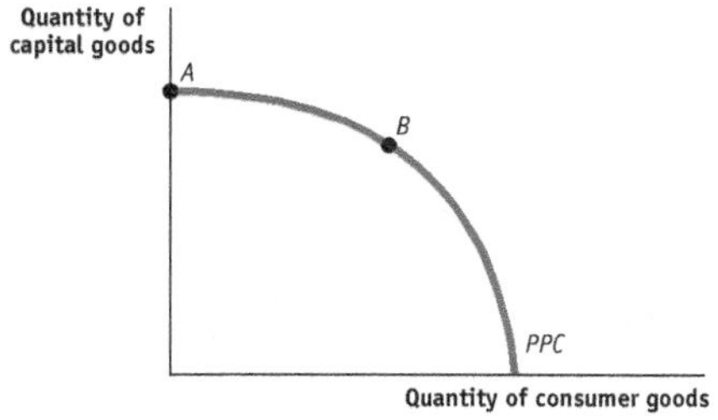

1. A movement from point *A* to point *B* illustrates which of the following?
   a. the opportunity cost of consumer goods
   b. an advance in technology
   c. an increase in available resources used to produce consumer goods
   d. an increase in the price of capital goods
   e. an increase in efficiency

Refer to the figure below to answer Question 2.

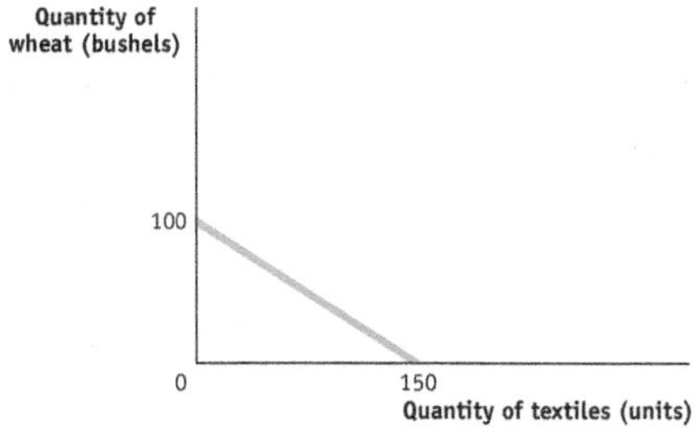

2. A country can produce either 100 bushels of wheat or 150 units of textiles, as shown on the graph above. If an advance in technology affects only the production of textiles, what happens to the slope of the production possibilities curve and the opportunity cost of wheat?

	Slope	*Opportunity cost of wheat*
a.	no change	no change
b.	decrease	decrease
c.	increase	increase
d.	no change	increase
e.	decrease	increase

3. According to the concept of comparative advantage, which of the following is true when countries specialize and trade?
   a. Each country obtains an absolute advantage.
   b. Total world output increases.
   c. The production possibilities curve for both countries shifts outward.
   d. Prices fall in both countries.
   e. Deadweight loss is created.

Refer to the figure below to answer Question 4.

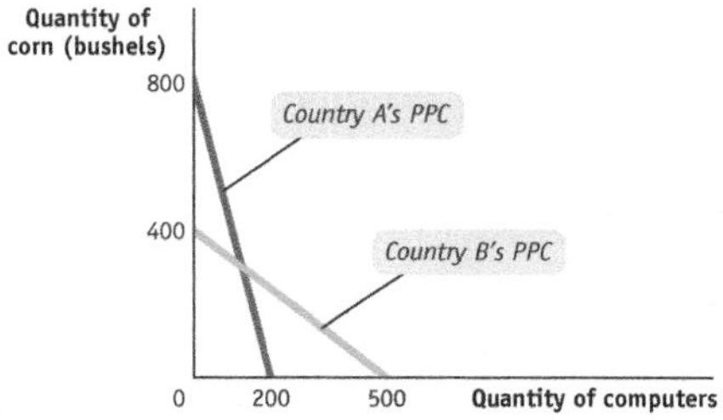

4. Using equal amounts of labor hours, two countries, Alpha and Beta, can produce corn and computers as shown. Based on the information provided, which of the following is true?
   a. Country A has an absolute advantage in the production of corn and computers.
   b. Country B has an absolute advantage in the production of corn and computers.
   c. Country A has a comparative advantage in the production of computers.
   d. Country B has a comparative advantage in the production of corn.
   e. Country A has an absolute advantage in the production of corn.

AP® Macroeconomics Practice Exam

Multiple-Choice Questions

1. a
2. e
3. b
4. e

AP® Macroeconomics Exam Practice Test PE-1

5. a
6. b
7. e
8. a
9. d
10. d
11. b
12. c
13. d
14. b
15. c
16. e
17. a

5. If the price of a substitute good increases, which of the following will happen to the price and the quantity sold in a market?

	Price	*Quantity sold*
a.	increase	increase
b.	increase	decrease
c.	decrease	increase
d.	decrease	decrease
e.	increase	no change

6. If the wages of workers producing a good increase, the price and quantity of the good sold will change in which of the following ways?

	Price	*Quantity*
a.	increase	increase
b.	increase	decrease
c.	decrease	increase
d.	decrease	decrease
e.	increase	no change

7. If real gross domestic product is declining, the economy is most likely experiencing which of the following?
a. declining unemployment
b. negative long-run economic growth
c. inflationary pressures
d. an increase in aggregate demand
e. a recession

8. In the circular-flow model of an economy, which of the following is a leakage?
a. savings
b. investment
c. wages
d. government spending
e. exports

9. Which of the following is not counted in a country's GDP?
a. goods exported to other countries
b. changes in inventories
c. domestically produced capital goods
d. financial assets, such as stocks and bonds
e. newly produced services

10. Which of the following is true of the relationship between real GDP and nominal GDP?
a. Real GDP is higher than nominal GDP when there is inflation in the economy.
b. Real GDP is equal to nominal GDP when the economy is at full employment.
c. Real GDP minus nominal GDP equals the rate of inflation.
d. Real GDP is nominal GDP adjusted for changes in the price level.
e. Real GDP increases when nominal GDP increases.

11. Which of the following transactions would be included in the calculation of GDP?
a. Lee buys a used car.
b. Kylie buys a new softball bat.
c. Eric mows his own lawn rather than paying someone else $25.
d. Ray resells his ticket to a football game.
e. Kumar volunteers for 3 hours per week as a tutor at the local high school.

12. If the real interest rate is 2% and the nominal interest rate is 6%, the expected rate of inflation is
a. 0%.
b. 2%.
c. 4%.
d. 6%.
e. 8%.

13. Suppose that last year the price level increased and the production of goods and services increased. Which of the following must be true? Nominal GDP
a. increased but real GDP decreased.
b. increased while the value of real GDP cannot be determined.
c. stayed the same while real GDP increased.
d. increased and real GDP increased.
e. decreased while real GDP increased.

14. Given the information provided below, what is the unemployment rate?

Population	1,000
Labor force	800
Employment	600

a. 20%
b. 25%
c. 33%
d. 40%
e. 50%

15. A worker laid off due to a recession is experiencing which type of unemployment?
a. temporary
b. frictional
c. cyclical
d. structural
e. seasonal

16. Which of the following could lead the unemployment rate to be overstated?
a. discouraged workers
b. teenage workers
c. part-time workers
d. retired workers
e. workers deciding which job offer to accept

17. Which of the following individuals is considered frictionally unemployed? A person who is not working and
a. is in the process of looking for a new job.
b. does not have the skills needed in the job market.
c. was laid off during a recession.
d. was laid off due to an increase in the minimum wage.
e. has given up looking for a job.

PE-2 AP® Macroeconomics Exam Practice Test

18. If the general price level doubles and at the same time a worker's real wage rate doubles, what must be true of the worker's nominal wage rate?
a. It doubled.
b. It increased by 50%.
c. It quadrupled.
d. It decreased.
e. It did not change.

19. Which of the following is true of the natural rate of unemployment?
a. It equals the actual rate of unemployment in short-run equilibrium.
b. It includes both frictional and structural unemployment.
c. It measures cyclical unemployment.
d. It changes with the business cycle.
e. It increases over time.

20. A Canadian recession will affect the United States' aggregate supply and demand in which of the following ways?

	Aggregate supply	*Aggregate demand*
a.	increase	increase
b.	increase	decrease
c.	decrease	increase
d.	decrease	decrease
e.	no change	decrease

21. Which of the following will shift the aggregate demand curve to the left?
a. expansionary monetary policy
b. an increase in the aggregate price level
c. an increase in the value of household assets
d. an increase in the consumer confidence index
e. a decrease in planned business investment

22. If the marginal propensity to consume in an economy is 0.9 and the government increases spending by $10 million, GDP will increase by how much?
a. $9 million
b. $10 million
c. $19 million
d. $90 million
e. $100 million

23. In the short run, an increase in aggregate demand will change the price level and aggregate output in which of the following ways?

	Price level	*Aggregate output*
a.	increase	increase
b.	increase	decrease
c.	decrease	increase
d.	decrease	decrease
e.	increase	no change

24. Which of the following is the most likely to cause a leftward shift in the long-run aggregate supply curve?
a. a decrease in the wage rate
b. a decrease in short-run aggregate supply
c. contractionary fiscal policy
d. a deadly disease that decreases the size of the labor force
e. a long-term decrease in demand

25. If an economy is in long-run equilibrium, how will an increase in aggregate demand affect real GDP and nominal wages in the long run?

	Real GDP	*Nominal wages*
a.	increase	increase
b.	increase	decrease
c.	decrease	increase
d.	decrease	decrease
e.	no change	increase

26. The long-run aggregate supply curve is always
a. vertical and below potential output.
b. horizontal and at potential output.
c. upward-sloping at all output levels.
d. vertical and at potential output.
e. horizontal at all output levels.

27. An economy experiences inflationary pressures when the equilibrium level of output is
a. too low.
b. above the full employment level of output.
c. equal to the full employment level of output.
d. decreasing.
e. in long-run equilibrium.

28. Which of the following policies might provide a remedy when the equilibrium output in an economy is below the potential level of output?
a. Decrease government spending.
b. Raise the federal funds rate.
c. Reduce transfer payments.
d. Cut taxes.
e. Sell more government securities.

29. Which of the following would cause the aggregate demand curve to shift to the left?
a. a decrease in taxes
b. an increase in consumer wealth
c. a decrease in consumer confidence
d. an increase in exports
e. a decrease in savings

30. Which of the following is a liability for a commercial bank?
a. deposits
b. loans
c. reserves
d. Treasury securities
e. its building and equipment

18. c
19. b
20. e
21. e
22. e
23. a
24. d
25. e
26. d
27. b
28. d
29. c
30. a

AP® Macroeconomics Exam Practice Test **PE-3**

31. a
32. b
33. c
34. e
35. d
36. e
37. b
38. c
39. a
40. a
41. b
42. c
43. c
44. b
45. b
46. a
47. c
48. d
49. a
50. e
51. d
52. b
53. d
54. c
55. d
56. b

31. If the interest rate is 2%, what is the present value of $1 paid to you in one year?
a. less than $1
b. $1
c. $1.02
d. $1.04
e. $1.20

32. Which of the following is a component of the M1 money supply?
a. gold
b. cash
c. savings deposits
d. Treasury bills
e. certificates of deposit

33. Which of the following will decrease the ability of the banking system to create money?
a. a decrease in the amount of cash people hold
b. a decrease in the reserve requirement
c. an increase in the amount of excess reserves held by banks
d. an increase in banks' willingness to make loans
e. a decrease in the discount rate

34. If the reserve ratio is 5%, what is the maximum amount of money that could be created by a new deposit of $1,000?
a. $1,000
b. $1,020
c. $1,050
d. $10,000
e. $20,000

35. Advances in information technology such as ATM machines have had what effect on the demand for money and the interest rate?

	Money demand	*Interest rate*
a.	increase	increase
b.	increase	decrease
c.	decrease	increase
d.	decrease	decrease
e.	no change	decrease

36. Which of the following will increase the demand for money?
a. a decrease in the aggregate price level
b. an increase in the use of mobile devices such as iPhones for payments
c. a decrease in the interest rate
d. an increase in the supply of money
e. an increase in real GDP

37. Which of the following will increase the interest rate in the market for loanable funds?
a. a decrease in the expected rate of return from investment spending
b. an increase in government budget deficits
c. an increase in the aggregate savings rate
d. a decrease in expected inflation
e. an increase in capital inflows

38. Which of the following is true of the money supply curve?
a. It shifts to the right when the interest rate increases.
b. It shifts to the left when the savings rate decreases.
c. It is vertical.
d. It shows a positive relationship between the interest rate and the quantity of loanable funds.
e. It shifts to the left when the Federal Reserve buys Treasury bills.

39. When government borrowing increases interest rates, it is known as
a. crowding out.
b. fiscal policy.
c. expansionary monetary policy.
d. contractionary monetary policy.
e. financial regulation.

40. According to the quantity theory of money, the money supply times the velocity of money is equal to
a. nominal GDP.
b. real GDP.
c. full employment real GDP.
d. the price level.
e. a constant value.

41. An open market sale of securities by the Federal Reserve will lead to which of the following?
a. an increase in the demand for money
b. an increase in interest rates
c. a decrease in investment demand
d. an increase in aggregate demand
e. an increase in the price level

42. The Federal Reserve will take actions that cause the federal funds rate to rise in an attempt to
a. increase unemployment.
b. increase the money supply.
c. reduce inflation.
d. increase real GDP.
e. encourage investment.

43. An increase in expected inflation is likely to have which of the following effects?
a. shift the long-run Phillips curve to the right
b. shift the short-run Phillips curve downward
c. increase the actual inflation rate
d. decrease the unemployment rate
e. shift the short-run aggregate supply curve to the right

44. Which of the following policies could the Federal Reserve implement to combat inflation created by expansionary fiscal policy?
a. Lower the reserve requirement.
b. Raise the discount rate.
c. Buy Treasury securities.
d. Raise taxes.
e. Reduce government spending.

PE-4 AP® Macroeconomics Exam Practice Test

45. Which of the following is a contractionary fiscal policy?
- **a.** raising the reserve requirement
- **b.** decreasing transfer payments
- **c.** decreasing taxes
- **d.** raising government spending
- **e.** increasing the federal funds rate

46. If a country currently has a positive national debt and a balanced budget, how would a decrease in taxes affect the country's deficit and debt?

	Deficit	*Debt*
a.	increase	increase
b.	increase	decrease
c.	decrease	increase
d.	decrease	decrease
e.	decrease	no change

47. A country's national debt is
- **a.** the amount the country owes to foreigners.
- **b.** the difference between the country's tax revenue and government spending in a given year.
- **c.** the sum of the country's past deficits and surpluses.
- **d.** always positive.
- **e.** higher when gross domestic product is increasing.

48. Which of the following is an example of expansionary monetary policy?
- **a.** decreasing taxes
- **b.** increasing government spending
- **c.** raising the discount rate
- **d.** lowering the reserve requirement
- **e.** selling Treasury securities

49. During a recession, the Federal Reserve might ________ its purchase of Treasury bills in order to ________ the Federal funds rate and ________ aggregate demand.

	Treasury bill purchases	*Federal funds rate*	*Aggregate demand*
a.	increase	decrease	increase
b.	increase	decrease	decrease
c.	decrease	decrease	increase
d.	decrease	increase	increase
e.	decrease	increase	decrease

50. The short-run Phillips curve shows a ________ relationship between the unemployment rate and the rate of ________.
- **a.** negative; interest
- **b.** positive; interest
- **c.** negative; employment
- **d.** positive; GDP growth
- **e.** negative; inflation

51. Which of the following is true of the long-run Phillips curve?
- **a.** It shows a negative relationship between the unemployment rate and the inflation rate.
- **b.** It shows a negative relationship between the unemployment rate and the interest rate.
- **c.** It shifts upward when expected inflation increases.
- **d.** It is vertical at the natural rate of unemployment.
- **e.** It shifts to the right when the Federal Reserve pursues expansionary monetary policy.

52. An increase in which of the following over time best describes economic growth?
- **a.** nominal GDP
- **b.** real GDP per capita
- **c.** nominal GDP per capita
- **d.** the labor force
- **e.** aggregate demand

53. Which of the following is true of an increase in labor productivity in an economy?
- **a.** It will shift the long-run aggregate supply curve to the left.
- **b.** It will decrease the wages of workers.
- **c.** It will reduce the size of the labor force.
- **d.** It will shift the production possibilities curve outward.
- **e.** It results from a decrease in the availability of capital.

54. Which of the following is most likely to lead to long-run economic growth?
- **a.** a more restrictive immigration policy
- **b.** higher trade barriers
- **c.** increased government funding of education
- **d.** contractionary fiscal policy
- **e.** negative net investment

55. Which of the following transactions will be recorded in the financial account of the United States?
- **a.** A U.S. firm sells $100 million worth of its product to Mexico.
- **b.** Chinese imports to the United States increase by $200 million.
- **c.** The wages paid by U.S. firms to workers in India increase by $20 million.
- **d.** Canada purchases $50 million of new U.S. Treasury bills.
- **e.** The United States' trade balance moves from deficit to surplus.

56. The exchange rate is the price of
- **a.** goods expressed in terms of another nation's currency.
- **b.** one nation's currency expressed in terms of another's.
- **c.** the same basket of goods purchased in two countries.
- **d.** exported goods, adjusted for inflation.
- **e.** imported goods expressed in the other country's currency.

(Answers to page PE-6 begin here.)

57. b
58. d
59. b
60. b

Free-Response Questions

Rubric for FRQ 1

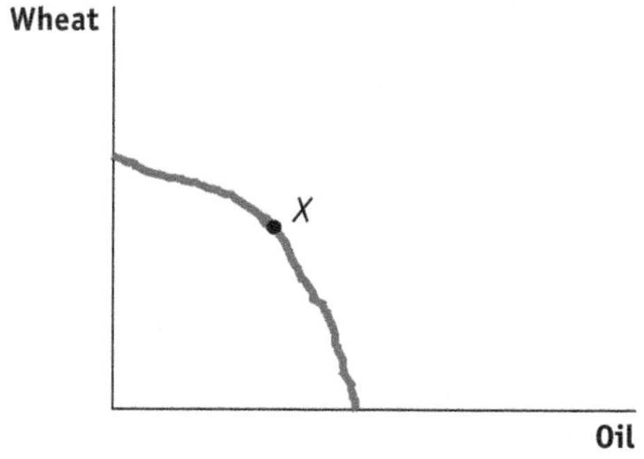

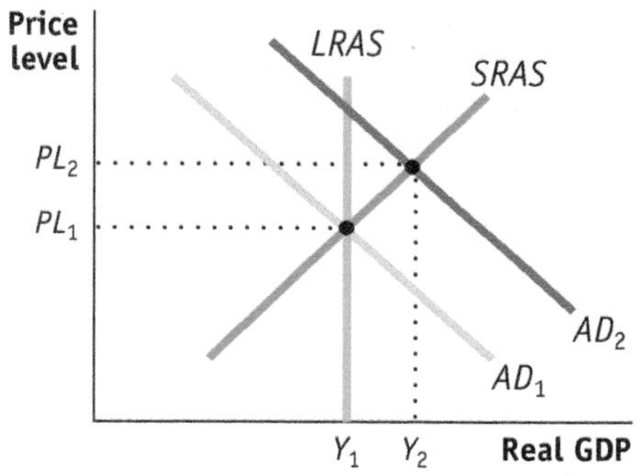

1 point: The axes are labeled "Wheat" and "Oil" and the production possibilities curve is negatively sloped.

1 point: Point *X* is shown on the production possibilities curve.

1 point: A graph with "Price level "on the vertical axis and "Real GDP" on the horizontal axis, upward-sloping short-run aggregate supply curve, downward-sloping aggregate demand curve, and PL_1 shown on the vertical axis where aggregate demand and aggregate supply cross

1 point: Long-run aggregate supply is vertical and crosses short-run aggregate supply and aggregate demand where they intersect. Y_1 is labeled where the long-run aggregate supply curve intersects the horizontal axis.

1 point: Apland will experience a budget deficit.

1 point: Aggregate demand is shown shifting to the right.

1 point: PL_2 and Y_2 are shown on the vertical and horizontal axis, respectively, where the new aggregate demand curve and the existing short-run aggregate supply curve intersect.

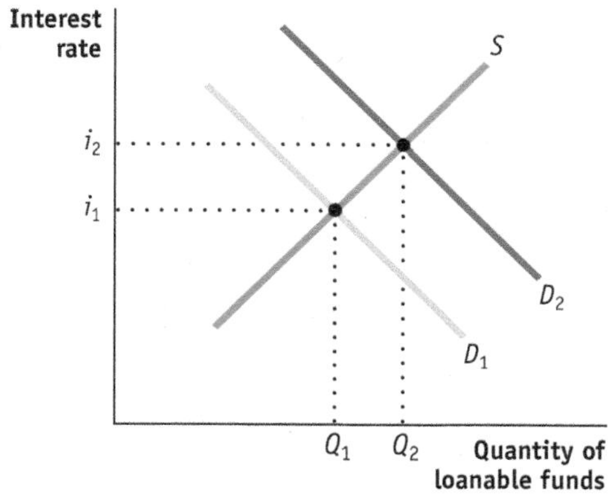

1 point: A graph of the loanable funds market with the vertical axis labeled "Interest rate," the horizontal axis labeled "Quantity of loanable funds," an upward-sloping supply curve, a downward-sloping demand curve, and the initial interest rate, i_1, labeled on the vertical axis where supply and demand intersect

1 point: The demand curve for loanable funds shifts to the right with the new interest rate, i_2, labeled on the vertical axis where the new demand curve and existing supply curve intersect.

1 point: The higher interest rate will reduce (crowd out) investment in capital, and with less capital, real GDP will decrease in the long run.

Rubric for FRQ 2

1 point: Mexico's current account balance will decrease (or move toward a deficit).

1 point: The U.S. current account balance will increase (or move toward a surplus).

1 point: Aggregate demand in Mexico will fall because net exports fall with an increase in imports.

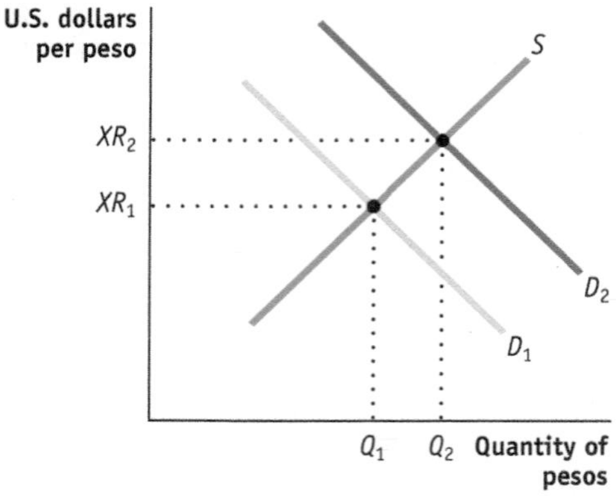

1 point: A foreign exchange market graph with "U.S. dollars per peso" on the vertical axis, "Quantity of pesos" on the horizontal axis, an upward-sloping and labeled supply curve, and a downward-sloping and labeled demand curve. The equilibrium exchange rate and the quantity of pesos are labeled on the axes where supply and demand intersect.

1 point: The demand curve for pesos shifts to the right, and a higher exchange rate and quantity of pesos are labeled on the axes at the intersection of the existing supply curve and the new demand curve.

1 point: The value of the Mexican peso appreciates relative to the dollar.

57. Which of the following would cause the U.S. dollar to appreciate relative to the Canadian dollar?
- **a.** a decrease in net capital flows from Canada to the United States
- **b.** a decrease in the real interest rate in Canada relative to the United States
- **c.** a decrease in the balance of payments on the current account in the United States
- **d.** a doubling of prices in both Canada and the United States
- **e.** an increase in exports from Canada to the United States

58. If a country's inflation rate rises, which of the following will happen to the demand for the country's currency and the value of the country's currency on the foreign exchange market?

	Demand	*Value*
a.	shift right	depreciate
b.	shift right	appreciate
c.	shift left	appreciate
d.	shift left	depreciate
e.	no change	depreciate

59. If foreign investors increase investment in the United States, what will happen to the value of the dollar in the foreign exchange market and U.S. net exports?

	Value of the U.S. dollar	*U.S. net exports*
a.	appreciate	increase
b.	appreciate	decrease
c.	depreciate	increase
d.	depreciate	decrease
e.	no change	no change

60. Which of the following is an example of U.S. direct foreign investment?
- **a.** a U.S. citizen spending while traveling abroad
- **b.** a U.S. manufacturer building a factory overseas
- **c.** a U.S. investor purchasing corporate bonds from a Mexican company
- **d.** a U.S. worker sending money to a family member living abroad
- **e.** a U.S. bank loaning money to an international company

Free-Response Questions

1. Assume the country of Apland is currently in long-run equilibrium.

(a) Draw a correctly labeled production possibilities curve if Apland produces only wheat and oil. On your graph, label point *X*, a point that illustrates a productively efficient output combination for Apland.

(b) Draw a correctly labeled aggregate supply and aggregate demand graph for Apland. Show each of the following:
- **(i)** equilibrium output, labeled Y_1
- **(ii)** equilibrium price level, labeled PL_1

(c) Assume the government of Apland has a balanced budget and decides to reduce income taxes.
- **(i)** What effect will the reduction in taxes have on Apland's budget?
- **(ii)** Show the short-run effect of the reduction in taxes on your graph from part (b), labeling the new equilibrium output and price level Y_2 and PL_2, respectively.

(d) Draw a correctly labeled graph of the loanable funds market. Suppose the government borrows money to pay for the tax cut. Show the effect of this borrowing on your graph from part (c).
- **(i)** Label the equilibrium interest rate before the government borrowing i_1.
- **(ii)** Label the equilibrium interest rate after the government borrowing i_2.

(e) How will the change in the interest rate depicted in your graph from part (d) affect real GDP in the long run? Explain.

(10 points)

2. Suppose a manufacturing firm in the United States sells $5 million worth of its output to consumers in Mexico.

(a) How will this transaction affect each of the following?
- **(i)** Mexico's current account balance
- **(ii)** the United States' current account balance
- **(iii)** aggregate demand in Mexico

(b) Suppose there is an increase in U.S. financial investment in Mexico.
- **(i)** Draw a correctly labeled graph of the foreign exchange market for Mexican pesos and show how an increase in U.S. financial investment in Mexico affects equilibrium in the market.
- **(ii)** What happens to the value of the Mexican peso relative to the U.S. dollar?

(6 points)

3. Assume the expected rate of inflation is zero.

(a) Draw a correctly labeled graph showing the short-run and long-run Phillips curves. On your graph, identify each of the following:
- **(i)** the nonaccelerating inflation rate of unemployment, labeled *N*
- **(ii)** a point on the short-run Phillips curve indicating an unemployment rate below the natural rate of unemployment, labeled *A*

(b) Now assume the inflation rate associated with point *A* in part (a) is incorporated into inflationary expectations. Show the effect of this change in expectations on your graph from part (a).

(5 points)

Rubric for FRQ 3

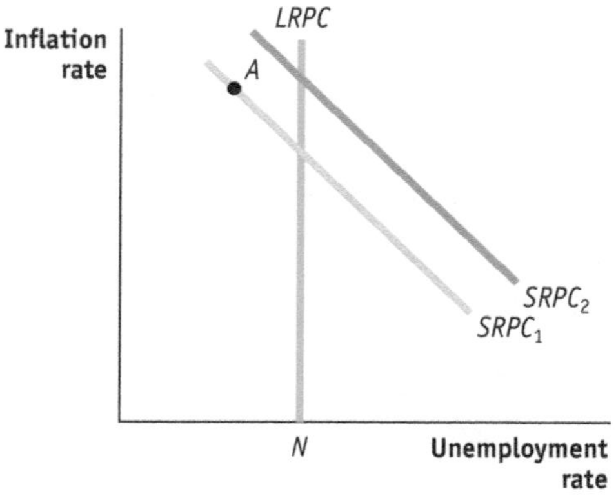

1 point: The axes are labeled "Unemployment rate" and "Inflation rate," and the short-run Phillips curve is downward-sloping and labeled.

1 point: The long-run Phillips curve is vertical and labeled.

1 point: A point *N* is shown at the intersection of the long-run Phillips curve and the horizontal axis.

1 point: A point *A* is labeled on the short-run Phillips curve to the left of point *N*.

1 point: A new short-run Phillips curve is shown above the existing short-run Phillips curve.

PE-6 AP® Macroeconomics Exam Practice Test

AP® Microeconomics Exam Practice Test

Multiple-Choice Questions

1. Which of the following would be considered a positive economic statement?
   a. The company should raise its prices.
   b. The company should lower its prices.
   c. Taxes should be raised on companies making high profits.
   d. Taxes should be lowered to attract more businesses to the city.
   e. If the company lowers its prices, total revenue will increase.
2. Which of the following statements best describes economic models?
   a. They are simplifications of the real world using the concept of *ceteris paribus*.
   b. They are simplifications of the real world using the concept of *caveat emptor*.
   c. They are simplifications of the real world using the concept of *laissez-faire*.
   d. They are exact replicas of the real world using the concept of *ceteris paribus*.
   e. They are exact replicas of the real world using the concept of *laissez-faire*.
3. A production possibilities curve that is bowed out from the origin throughout the range of production reflects what fact about the nature of the resources being used in production?
   a. The resources are equally transferable, causing increasing opportunity costs.
   b. The resources are equally transferable, causing decreasing opportunity costs.
   c. The resources are equally transferable, causing constant opportunity costs.
   d. The resources are not equally transferable, causing decreasing opportunity costs.
   e. The resources are not equally transferable, causing increasing opportunity costs.
4. Which of the following must a country possess in order to realize gains from trade?
   a. the absolute advantage
   b. more resources
   c. better technology
   d. a comparative advantage
   e. larger work force
5. Given a direct or positive relationship between two variables on a two-dimensional graph, what change in the variable on the vertical axis is associated with an increase in the variable on the horizontal axis?
   a. a decrease, as shown by a movement down along the curve
   b. a decrease, as shown by a movement up along the curve
   c. an increase, as shown by a movement down along the curve
   d. an increase, as shown by a movement up along the curve
   e. an increase, as shown by a shift of the curve to the right
6. Which of the following would cause an increase in the quantity demanded of coffee?
   a. an increase in the supply of tea, a substitute
   b. a decrease in the price of tea, a substitute
   c. a decrease in the price of coffee
   d. a decrease in the supply of bagels, a complement
   e. an increase in the price of bagels, a complement
7. Which of the following would occur in the market for street drugs if they were to increase in price?
   a. a shift of the demand curve to the left
   b. a shift of the supply curve to the right
   c. a movement down along the supply curve
   d. a movement up along the supply curve
   e. There would be no effect since the demand for street drugs is inelastic.
8. A new price ceiling set below the equilibrium price in a competitive market with relatively elastic supply and demand would result in which of the following?
   a. an increase in the quantity demanded and an increase in the quantity supplied
   b. an increase in the quantity demanded and no change in the quantity supplied
   c. an increase in the quantity demanded and a decrease in the quantity supplied
   d. a decrease in the quantity demanded and an increase in the quantity supplied
   e. a decrease in the quantity demanded and no change in the quantity supplied

AP® Microeconomics Practice Exam

Multiple-Choice Questions

1. e
2. a
3. e
4. d
5. d
6. c
7. d
8. c

9. a
10. a
11. d
12. c
13. d
14. a
15. d
16. c
17. c
18. e
19. d
20. a
21. c

9. Assuming relatively elastic supply and demand curves, which of the following would occur if the market quantity were to fall below the equilibrium quantity due to a quota in a competitive market?
   a. a deadweight loss
   b. a market surplus
   c. a violation of the law of demand
   d. a less elastic demand
   e. the development of a horizontal demand curve

10. Due to the fixed quantity of at least one input, what will happen in the short run as a firm increases production by hiring additional workers?
    a. Marginal product will decrease.
    b. Marginal cost will decrease.
    c. Total product will increase at an increasing rate.
    d. Marginal product will increase.
    e. Total cost will increase at a decreasing rate.

11. What will a firm experience when it adds a variable input to a fixed input to increase production?
    a. economies of scale
    b. diseconomies of scale
    c. increasing marginal returns
    d. diminishing marginal returns
    e. constant marginal returns

12. Which of the following is true when marginal product is decreasing?
    a. Average product is necessarily decreasing.
    b. Average product is necessarily increasing.
    c. Average product could be increasing or decreasing.
    d. Total cost is increasing at a decreasing rate.
    e. Marginal cost is decreasing.

13. Which item below best describes the result of the spreading effect?
    a. Marginal product initially rises and then falls.
    b. Marginal product initially falls and then rises.
    c. Marginal product remains constant at large levels of output.
    d. Average fixed cost falls.
    e. Average fixed cost rises.

14. Which of the following is true based on the relationship between average total cost and marginal cost?
    a. When marginal cost is below average total cost, average total cost is declining.
    b. When marginal cost is below average total cost, average total cost is rising.
    c. When marginal cost is above average total cost, average total cost is declining.
    d. When marginal cost is above average total cost, average total cost remains constant.
    e. When marginal cost is above average total cost, marginal cost is declining.

15. Which of the following curves always falls as quantity increases?
    a. the marginal cost curve
    b. the average variable cost curve
    c. the average total cost curve
    d. the average fixed cost curve
    e. the total fixed cost curve

16. A firm facing rising long-run average total costs is experiencing what condition?
    a. economies of scale
    b. economies of scope
    c. diseconomies of scale
    d. increasing marginal returns
    e. diminishing marginal returns

17. If a firm experiencing increasing returns to scale doubles all inputs, which of the following will occur?
    a. Output will double.
    b. Output will less than double.
    c. Output will more than double.
    d. Total cost will decrease.
    e. Sunk cost will decrease.

18. Each firm in a perfectly competitive industry
    a. has a large market share.
    b. sells a differentiated product.
    c. must advertise its product in order to compete with other firms.
    d. faces a downward-sloping demand curve.
    e. can easily enter or exit the industry.

19. What does the Herfindahl–Hirschman Index measure?
    a. the degree of comparative advantage one nation has relative to another
    b. the amount of specialization and trade between nations
    c. opportunity cost differences between firms
    d. the amount of market concentration in a given industry
    e. the amount of government intervention in a market

20. What is one way to distinguish implicit costs from explicit costs?
    a. Checks are only written for explicit costs.
    b. Checks are only written for implicit costs.
    c. All costs are implicit, but some are also explicit.
    d. All costs are explicit, but some are also implicit.
    e. All opportunity costs are implicit.

21. Which two market structures are characterized by free entry into and exit from the industry in the long run?
    a. monopolistic competition and monopoly
    b. monopolistic competition and oligopoly
    c. monopolistic competition and perfect competition
    d. oligopoly and perfect competition
    e. monopoly and perfect competition

PE-8 AP® Microeconomics Exam Practice Test

22. In a graph of a perfectly competitive market, which of the following is true regarding the market demand curve?
- **a.** It is downward-sloping, but marginal revenue is equal to price for the firm.
- **b.** It is horizontal, but marginal revenue is equal to price for the firm.
- **c.** It is vertical, but marginal revenue is equal to price for the firm.
- **d.** It is downward-sloping, but marginal revenue is lower than price for the firm.
- **e.** It is horizontal, but marginal revenue is lower than price for the firm.

23. Firms generally choose to produce the quantity that equates marginal revenue with
- **a.** price, because that minimizes average total cost.
- **b.** average total cost, because that minimizes total cost.
- **c.** average variable cost, because that stabilizes costs.
- **d.** marginal cost, because that minimizes average total cost.
- **e.** marginal cost, because that maximizes profit or minimizes loss.

24. For a competitive firm, if marginal revenue exceeds marginal cost at the current level of output and the firm is currently earning economic losses, what could the firm certainly do?
- **a.** increase output to ensure economic profits
- **b.** decrease output to ensure economic profits
- **c.** increase output to reduce economic losses
- **d.** decrease output to reduce economic losses
- **e.** shut down to reduce economic losses

25. The short-run shut-down point for a competitive firm is when price falls below which cost curve?
- **a.** marginal cost
- **b.** average total cost
- **c.** total cost
- **d.** average variable cost
- **e.** average fixed cost

26. The long-run shut-down point for a competitive firm is when price falls below which cost curve?
- **a.** marginal cost
- **b.** average total cost
- **c.** total cost
- **d.** average variable cost
- **e.** average fixed cost

27. Which of the following is true about fixed costs?
- **a.** They never change.
- **b.** In the short run they stay the same even when output changes.
- **c.** They are all implicit costs.
- **d.** They are all explicit costs.
- **e.** They do not include opportunity costs.

28. The long-run supply curve is flatter and therefore more elastic than the short-run supply curve for a competitive industry due to
- **a.** the availability of more substitutes.
- **b.** the availability of more complements.
- **c.** easy exit and entry of firms.
- **d.** economies of scale.
- **e.** diseconomies of scale.

29. Suppose the firms in a competitive industry are temporarily earning a positive economic profit due to an increase in demand. When the industry returns to a long-run equilibrium, each existing firm's output will
- **a.** increase and it will earn a normal profit.
- **b.** increase and it will earn a positive economic profit.
- **c.** increase and it will incur an economic loss.
- **d.** decrease and it will earn a normal profit.
- **e.** decrease and it will earn a positive economic profit.

30. For a monopolist, when marginal revenue is positive and decreasing, what is true about total revenue?
- **a.** It is increasing at a decreasing rate.
- **b.** It is increasing at an increasing rate.
- **c.** It is decreasing at the same rate as marginal revenue.
- **d.** It is decreasing faster than marginal revenue.
- **e.** It is decreasing slower than marginal revenue.

31. If a monopolist is currently operating in the inelastic range of its demand curve, it can increase its profit or reduce its loss by
- **a.** producing a larger quantity of output.
- **b.** producing the quantity that maximizes total revenue.
- **c.** raising its price.
- **d.** lowering its price.
- **e.** producing the quantity that minimizes average total cost.

32. What happens to the consumer surplus that is lost when a perfectly competitive market becomes a monopoly facing the same demand and costs?
- **a.** All of it is gained by the monopolist.
- **b.** Some of it is gained by the monopolist and the rest is part of the deadweight loss.
- **c.** It is all part of the deadweight loss.
- **d.** It is paid to the government in taxes.
- **e.** It is transferred to the Federal Trade Commission.

22. a
23. e
24. c
25. d
26. b
27. b
28. c
29. d
30. a
31. c
32. b

AP® Microeconomics Exam Practice Test PE-9

33. c
34. b
35. c
36. a
37. b
38. e
39. b
40. a

33. Which of the following is a distinguishing characteristic of a natural monopoly, assuming that it is capable of earning positive economic profit?
- **a.** Production is at the point where marginal revenue equals marginal cost.
- **b.** Production is at the point where price equals marginal cost.
- **c.** The average total cost curve crosses the demand curve twice in the economies of scale region.
- **d.** The average total cost curve crosses the demand curve in the diseconomies of scale region.
- **e.** The marginal cost curve crosses the average total cost curve at the minimum point of the average total cost curve.

34. If a regulatory agency wants to allow a natural monopoly to earn a normal profit, then the price charged should equal which of the following?
- **a.** marginal cost
- **b.** average total cost
- **c.** average variable cost
- **d.** average fixed cost
- **e.** total cost

35. If a regulatory agency selects marginal cost pricing to regulate a natural monopoly, what will be the result?
- **a.** The monopoly will earn a normal profit.
- **b.** The monopoly will produce the socially optimal amount assuming external benefits exist.
- **c.** The monopoly will require a subsidy since it will incur losses.
- **d.** The monopoly will require a tax since it will earn a greater than normal profit.
- **e.** The monopoly will require a subsidy since it will earn a greater than normal profit.

36. What is the result of perfect price discrimination?
- **a.** a gain in producer surplus
- **b.** a gain in consumer surplus
- **c.** less output overall
- **d.** marginal revenue less than price
- **e.** marginal revenue greater than price

37. Which of the following best describes an oligopoly?
- **a.** a Herfindahl–Hirschman Index higher than that for a monopoly, and the existence of interdependent firms
- **b.** a Herfindahl–Hirschman Index higher than that for a monopolistically competitive market, and the existence of interdependent firms
- **c.** a Herfindahl–Hirschman Index lower than that for a perfect competitor, and the existence of interdependent firms
- **d.** a Herfindahl–Hirschman Index lower than that for a monopoly, and the existence of independent firms
- **e.** a Herfindahl–Hirschman Index lower than that for a monopolistic competitor, and the existence of independent firms

38. The numbers in the following payoff matrix indicate profits for firms Alpha and Beta.

Beta's Price Policy

Alpha's Price Policy	High	Low
High	$20 / $20	$30 / $10
Low	$10 / $30	$15 / $15

Which of the following is true?
- **a.** Charging a high price is a dominant strategy for Alpha.
- **b.** Charging a high price is a dominant strategy for Beta.
- **c.** Beta will charge a high price if Alpha charges a high price.
- **d.** Alpha will charge a high price if Beta charges a high price.
- **e.** Charging a low price is a dominant strategy for Alpha.

39. In the long run, a monopolistically competitive firm will earn
- **a.** positive or negative economic profit, depending on the situation.
- **b.** normal profit.
- **c.** positive economic profit due to barriers to entry.
- **d.** positive economic profit due to a differentiated product.
- **e.** positive economic profit due to price discrimination.

40. If monopolistically competitive firms were earning positive economic profit in the short run, how would the existing firms' demand curves change after the long-run response in the industry?
- **a.** They would shift leftward.
- **b.** They would shift rightward.
- **c.** They would become perfectly inelastic.
- **d.** They would become perfectly elastic.
- **e.** They would become unit-elastic.

PE-10 AP® Microeconomics Exam Practice Test

41. The labor demand curve for a firm hiring in a perfectly competitive labor market is
    a. the firm's marginal revenue product curve.
    b. the firm's marginal product curve.
    c. horizontal.
    d. the firm's average product curve.
    e. the firm's marginal revenue curve.

42. A firm renting in a perfectly competitive capital market should definitely rent more capital if which condition is true?
    a. The marginal revenue product of capital is equal to the rental rate.
    b. The average revenue product of capital is equal to the rental rate.
    c. The marginal revenue product of capital is greater than the rental rate.
    d. The marginal revenue product of capital is less than the rental rate.
    e. The average revenue product of capital is less than the rental rate.

Use the following per day employment and output data for a bakery to answer Questions 43 and 44.

Number of bakers	Total number of pies
0	0
1	8
2	20
3	38
4	54
5	64
6	68

43. If pies sell in a perfectly competitive market for $5 per pie, what is the marginal revenue product of the third baker?
    a. $5
    b. $20
    c. $38
    d. $90
    e. $190

44. If pies sell in a perfectly competitive market for $5 per pie and bakers are paid $75 per day, how many bakers should be hired to maximize profit?
    a. 2
    b. 3
    c. 4
    d. 5
    e. 6

45. Which of the following is always horizontal?
    a. the demand curve facing a firm that sells its product in a perfectly competitive market
    b. the labor demand curve for a firm hiring in a perfectly competitive labor market
    c. the labor supply curve for a monopsony
    d. the demand curve for a monopoly
    e. the long-run industry supply curve in a goods market

46. If Jack's Lumber is the only employer in a small town, that firm is a
    a. monopolist.
    b. monopolistic competitor.
    c. perfectly competitive firm.
    d. Keynesian.
    e. monopsonist.

47. The marginal factor cost curve of labor for a monopsonist is
    a. upward-sloping and above the supply curve at every quantity of labor beyond one.
    b. downward-sloping and above the supply curve at every quantity of labor beyond one.
    c. upward-sloping and below the supply curve at every quantity of labor beyond one.
    d. downward-sloping and below the supply curve at every quantity of labor beyond one.
    e. upward-sloping and coincident with the supply curve of labor.

48. To maximize profit, a monopsonist will hire the quantity of labor at which the
    a. supply curve intersects the demand curve and pay a wage less than the competitive wage.
    b. supply curve intersects the demand curve and pay a wage more than the competitive wage.
    c. supply curve intersects the demand curve and pay a wage equal to the competitive wage.
    d. marginal factor cost is equal to the marginal revenue product.
    e. marginal factor cost curve intersects the supply curve.

49. In order to minimize the cost of producing a given quantity of output, how should a firm combine labor and capital resources?
    a. Make the marginal product of capital per dollar spent on capital equal to the marginal product of labor per dollar spent on labor.
    b. Make the total amount spent on labor equal to the total amount spent on capital.
    c. Make the marginal revenue product of capital per dollar spent on capital greater than the marginal revenue product of labor per dollar spent on labor.
    d. Make the marginal revenue product of capital per dollar spent on capital less than the marginal revenue product of labor per dollar spent on labor and equal to one.
    e. Hire mostly the factor of production that has the lowest cost per unit of the factor.

41. a
42. c
43. d
44. c
45. a
46. e
47. a
48. d
49. a

AP® Microeconomics Exam Practice Test PE-11

50. c
51. b
52. a
53. a
54. d
55. a
56. a
57. d
58. d
59. a
60. a

50. Higher wages paid in order to motivate hard work and reduce worker turnover are called
a. compensating differentials.
b. union wages.
c. efficiency wages.
d. equilibrium wages.
e. marginal productivity wages.

51. According to the Coase theorem, under the right conditions, an economy can achieve an efficient solution despite the existence of externalities using which of the following?
a. taxation
b. negotiations
c. subsidies
d. production quotas
e. public service announcements

52. A market with external costs and no external benefits will do which of the following?
a. produce too much output
b. produce too little output
c. have a price that is too high
d. experience deadweight gains
e. produce the socially optimal quantity

53. Which of the following is true of the deadweight loss caused by an excise tax?
a. It consists of lost producer and consumer surplus.
b. It results in gains to consumers but losses to producers.
c. It results in gains to producers but losses to consumers.
d. It results from overproduction.
e. It results from externalities.

54. Which theorem posits that solutions to externalities can be achieved in the private sector when transaction costs are low and property rights are clearly defined?
a. the Marshall theorem
b. the Keynesian theorem
c. the supply-side theorem
d. the Coase theorem
e. Okun's theorem

55. What taxes are designed to reduce external costs?
a. Pigouvian taxes
b. excise taxes
c. Okun's taxes
d. Keynesian taxes
e. Marshall taxes

56. What contributes to the efficiency of tradable emissions permit programs?
a. They reward firms that reduce pollution with the ability to create revenue by selling permits.
b. They reward firms that have a high cost of reducing pollution by allowing them to sell the rights to pollute.
c. They reward firms that have a low cost of reducing pollution by allowing them to buy the rights to pollute.
d. They require each firm to limit emissions to a set amount.
e. They require each firm to employ the latest pollution-control technology.

57. What is true if marginal social benefit exceeds marginal social costs at the market level of output?
a. A negative externality exists, and the government could correct for it with a Pigouvian tax.
b. A negative externality exists, and the government could correct for it with a Pigouvian subsidy.
c. A positive externality exists, and the government could correct for it with a Pigouvian tax.
d. A positive externality exists, and the government could correct for it with a Pigouvian subsidy.
e. The market outcome is ideal, since there are positive marginal benefits.

58. Which term applies to cases in which potential sellers know more about the quality of what they are selling than the potential buyers?
a. game theory
b. upper hand
c. moral hazard
d. adverse selection
e. prisoner's dilemma

59. What do you call the situation in which distorted incentives arise because an individual has private information about his or her own actions but someone else bears the costs of a lack of care or effort?
a. moral hazard
b. adverse selection
c. upper hand
d. game theory
e. prisoner's dilemma

60. Insurance companies deal with moral hazard by requiring that insured individuals pay a deductible. Which of the following items best defines the concept of a deductible?
a. The insured pays for the excess when the claim exceeds a certain dollar amount.
b. The insured pays a certain percentage of a claim before the insurance company must pay.
c. The insured pays lower premiums if the claim is denied.
d. The insured pays higher premiums if the claim is denied.
e. The insured pays higher premiums if the claim is honored.

PE-12 AP® Microeconomics Exam Practice Test

Free-Response Questions

1. Assume that the perfectly competitive housecleaning industry is in long-run equilibrium and that Sally's Clean Bowls is one of the typical firms in the industry.
   (a) Draw correctly labeled side-by-side graphs of the housecleaning industry and Sally's Clean Bowls showing the long-run equilibrium.
   (b) Explain what indicates that the industry is in long-run equilibrium.
   (c) Now assume the government imposes a one-time license fee to operate a housecleaning business. Show the short-run impact of this one-time fee on the side-by-side graphs in part (a). Add a subscript "1" to the label of anything that changes.
   (d) Given the change you show in part (c), explain (do not show) the long-run impact on the industry and identify any resulting changes in price and output.
   (e) Now assume that Sally's Clean Bowls obtains some degree of market power from the license fee. Draw a correctly labeled graph showing the demand, marginal revenue, marginal cost, and average total cost curves for Sally's Clean Bowls assuming that Sally's earns an economic profit.
   (11 points)

2. Assume that Clark's Pothole Repair firm uses both labor and capital such that the marginal product per hour of labor is 5 holes and the marginal product per hour of capital is 15 holes. The wage is $25 per hour and the capital rents for $75 per hour.
   (a) What should Clark do if he wants to minimize his cost at the current level of output? Explain.
   (b) Now assume that the wage rate rises to $30 per hour while the marginal product of labor rises to 6 holes and everything else remains the same. What should Clark do if he wants to minimize his cost? Explain.
   (c) Using the data from part (b) and assuming Clark buys his labor in a perfectly competitive labor market, draw a correctly labeled graph of Clark's labor supply and labor demand.
   (6 points)

3. Assume that the competitive meatpacking industry has no external benefits, but the plants in the industry emit a bad smell which can cause nausea and sickness for some people living nearby.
   (a) Draw a properly labeled graph of the meatpacking industry and label the marginal private benefit curve, the marginal private cost curve, the marginal social benefit curve, and the marginal social cost curve. Label the private market output Q_{Mkt}.
   (b) Label the socially optimal level of output Q_S.
   (c) Completely shade in the area of deadweight loss.
   (d) Suppose the government wants to impose a Pigouvian tax that brings meat output to the socially optimal quantity. The appropriate amount of the tax per unit would be determined by the vertical distance between which two curves on the graph?
   (7 points)

Free-Response Questions Rubric for FRQ 1

(The rubrics for FRQ 2 and FRQ 3 appear on page PE-14.)

a.

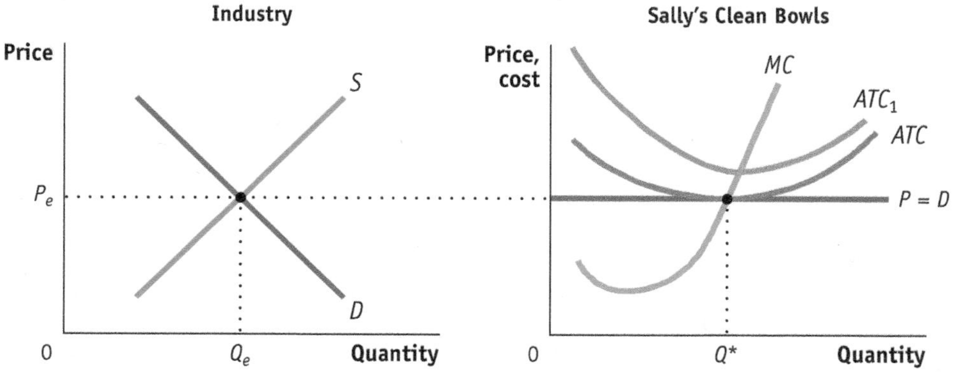

1 point: Correctly labeled axes, downward-sloping demand, and upward-sloping supply curves for the industry and a horizontal demand curve for the firm extending from the intersection of supply and demand in the industry

1 point: The *MC* curve intersects the *ATC* curve at the *ATC* minimum.

1 point: The *ATC* curve is tangent to the demand curve.

b. 1 point: The firm is making a normal profit or zero economic profit.

c. 1 point: The *ATC* curve is shifted up and labeled "ATC_1."

d. 1 point: Because firms are earning economic losses, some firms will leave the industry and the industry supply curve will shift to the left.

1 point: The price will rise and output will fall.

e.

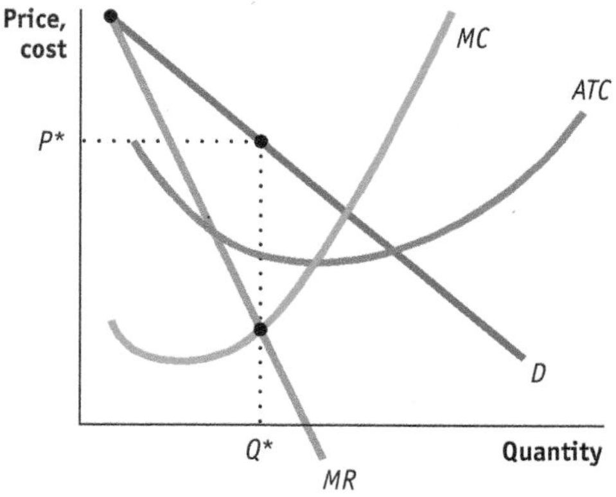

1 point: Correctly labeled axes and a downward-sloping demand curve

1 point: The *MR* curve is drawn below the demand curve.

1 point: The output level is found where *MC* equals *MR* and the price is found at the height of the demand curve above that quantity.

1 point: The price is above the *ATC* at the selected output level.

Rubric for FRQ 2

a. 1 point: Clark should employ the current levels of labor and capital.

1 point: The *MP* of labor per dollar spent on labor is equal to the *MP* of capital per dollar spent on capital, thus minimizing cost.

b. 1 point: Clark should continue to employ the same levels of labor and output.

1 point: The marginal product per dollar spent on each input has not changed, and as a result, Clark is still minimizing cost at the current level of output.

c.

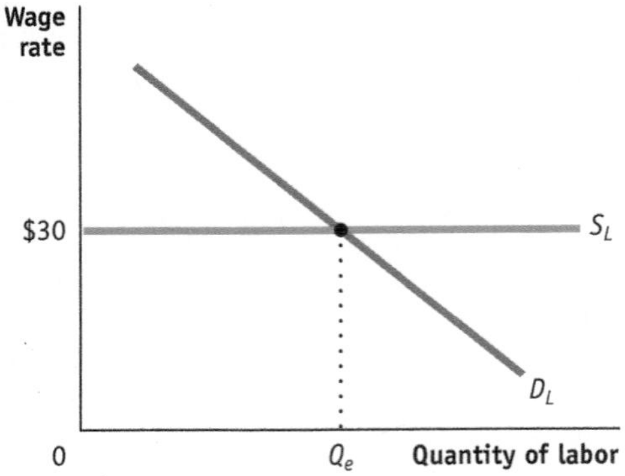

1 point: Correctly labeled axes and a horizontal supply curve at the wage rate of $30/hour

1 point: Downward-sloping demand curve intersecting the supply curve at the equilibrium level of employment

Rubric for FRQ 3

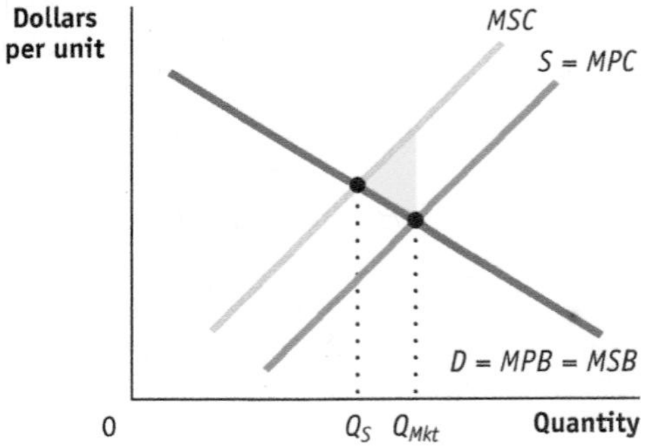

a. 1 point: Downward-sloping curve labeled "$MPB = MSB$"

1 point: Upward-sloping curve labeled "*MPC*"

1 point: The *MSC* curve is above the *MPC* curve and labeled.

1 point: The private market output where $MPC = MPB$ is labeled "Q_{Mkt}"

b. 1 point: The level of output where $MSC = MSB$ is labeled "Q_S"

c. 1 point: The deadweight loss is correctly shaded.

d. 1 point: The *MPC* curve and the *MSC* curve (both curves must be correct)

Enrichment Modules

Economics by Example:

"What Is the Role of Government?"

"How Can Economics Influence Your Choice of a Spouse?"

"How Gullible Are We?"

"Why Is Cash the Ultimate Gift?"

Hopefully this sampling of economics has kindled your interest in more than just exam content. If you've wondered what the recent financial crisis was all about, you'll enjoy Enrichment Module A, which tells the story of the Great Recession. Have you questioned the rationality of buyers or sellers? Enrichment Module B explains how economists deal with behavior that isn't so rational. If you've ever bought a used car, you know that even rational people sometimes don't have all the information they would like. Enrichment Module C explains how imperfect information affects markets and discusses related problems and remedies. In Enrichment Module D you will learn how economists use indifference curves to illustrate preferences and to model various aspects of consumer choice. Finally, the Financial Literacy Handbook that follows Enrichment Module D will help you navigate your own financial situation. While these Modules cover material in greater depth than is expected for the current AP® exams, they provide interesting background and insights for subsequent coursework, and they offer advice for making good economic decisions and developing sound financial habits.

TEACH Teach It

TRM The answers to the end-of-module questions are included in the margins for this module. Some additional support material may be found in the TRM.

Shutterstock

ENRICHMENT MODULE A Financial Markets and Crises

In this Module, you will learn to:

- Describe the importance of a well-functioning financial system
- List the causes of financial crises in the economy
- Identify the macroeconomic consequences of financial crises
- Explain the factors leading to the financial crisis of 2008

The Role of Financial Markets

These days, almost everyone is connected in some way to *financial markets*. When you receive a paycheck, pay a bill, borrow money, or use a credit card, the financial markets assist with the transaction. And a recent FDIC study found that about 91% of U.S. households have some form of checking or savings account.

In Module 22, we learned about the three tasks of a financial system: to reduce transactions costs, to reduce risk, and to provide liquidity. The financial system performs these tasks largely through financial intermediaries, such as banks and mutual funds. In Module 25, we looked at what banks do and how problems in the banking system can adversely affect the economy. Past problems have led to financial regulations that help to ensure a safe and efficient financial system. But what happens in an economy when its financial markets do not function well—or even worse, collapse? In this module we will take another look at the role of financial markets in the economy and the causes and consequences of financial crises, including the 2008 financial crisis.

The Importance of an Efficient Financial System

A well-functioning financial system promotes the saving and investing required for long-run economic growth. Depository institutions such as banks are a major part of an economy's financial system and are necessary to facilitate the flow of funds from lenders to borrowers. Let's take a look at the role the banking system and other **financial markets**—the markets that channel private saving into investment spending—play in an economy and how problems in the financial system can result in macroeconomic downturns.

Financial markets are the markets (banking, stock, and bond) that channel private saving into investment spending.

EM-2 Enrichment Modules

The Purpose of the Banking System

Banks and other depository institutions are financial intermediaries that use liquid assets in the form of deposits to finance the illiquid investments of borrowers. When individuals deposit their savings in a depository institution, they are providing that institution with a short-term loan. In turn, the depository institution uses those funds to make long-term loans to other borrowers. Depositors are paid interest on their deposits and lenders pay interest on their loans. Because depository institutions receive the difference between the lower interest rate paid to depositors and the higher interest rate received from borrowers, they earn profits by converting their short-term deposit liabilities into long-term loans. This conversion is known as **maturity transformation**. Because deposits are short-term loans, depositors can demand to be repaid at any time. However, the loans made by depository institutions are long-term, and borrowers cannot be forced to repay their loans until the end of the loan period.

Maturity transformation is the conversion of short-term liabilities into long-term assets.

A **shadow bank** is a financial institution that engages in maturity transformation but does not accept deposits.

Other financial institutions also engage in maturity transformation and are part of the banking system. But instead of taking deposits, these institutions—known as **shadow banks**—borrow funds in short-term credit markets in order to invest in longer-term assets. Like depository institutions, shadow banks can earn profits as a result of the difference between the amount paid to borrow in the short-term credit market and the return received from the long-term asset. Increasing profits in the shadow banking market since 1980 have led to a steady increase in shadow banking in the United States.

You may recall seeing the maturity transformation function of financial markets in the circular-flow diagram. Financial markets take private savings that would otherwise leak out of the circular flow and inject it back into the economy through loans. In this way, financial markets facilitate the investment that drives economic growth.

Depository institutions earn profits by turning short-term deposits into long-term loans.

Risks of the Banking System: Banking Crises

Because a well-functioning financial system is crucial to economic growth, we need to understand the risk to an economy of a banking system failure. Individual bank failures are not uncommon; banks fail every year, as shown in **Figure A.1**. In 2013, the Federal Deposit Insurance Corporation reported 24 bank failures, down from 51 failures in 2012. Like other businesses in the economy, banks can fail for a variety of reasons. However, there is a big difference between the failure of a single bank and the failure of the banking system.

Fears of a bank failure can lead many depositors to panic and attempt to withdraw their funds at the same time, a phenomenon described in Module 25 as a *bank run*. The U.S. economy has experienced two periods of widespread bank failures: the National Banking era and the Great Depression. **Table A-1** on the next page shows the number of failures that occurred during each of those periods of panic. Current banking regulations protect U.S. depositors and the economy as a whole against bank runs. So modern bank failures generally take place through an orderly process overseen by regulators and often go largely unnoticed by depositors or the general public.

A *banking crisis* is much less common, and far more dangerous to the economy, than individual bank failures.

Figure A.1 Bank Failures

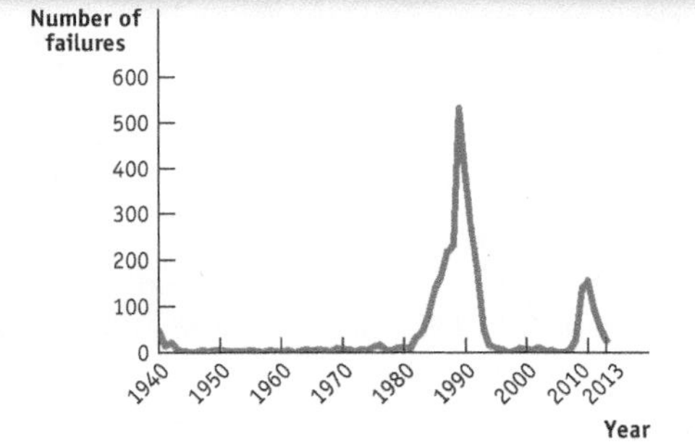

Module A Financial Markets and Crises EM-3

Table A.1 Bank Failures during the National Banking Era and the Great Depression

National Banking era (1883–1912)		Great Depression (1929–1941)	
Panic dates	**Number of failures**	**Panic dates**	**Number of failures**
September 1873	101	November–December 1930	806
May 1884	42	April–August 1931	573
November 1890	18	September–October 1931	827
May–August 1893	503	June–July 1932	283
October–December 1907	73*	February–March 1933	Bank Holiday

*This underestimates the scale of the 1907 crisis because it doesn't take into account the role of trusts.

A **banking crisis** occurs when a large part of the banking system fails.

A **banking crisis** occurs when a large part of the banking sector, either depository institutions or shadow banks, fails or threatens to fail. Banking crises that involve large segments of the banking system are comparatively rare. The failure of a large number of banks at the same time can occur either because many institutions make the same mistake or because mistakes from one institution spread to others through links in the financial system.

In an **asset bubble**, the price of an asset increases to a high level due to expectations of future price gains.

Banking crises often occur as a result of *asset bubbles*. In an **asset bubble**, the price of an asset, such as housing, is pushed above a reasonable level by investor expectations of future price increases. Eventually the market runs out of new buyers, the future price increases do not materialize, and the bubble bursts, leading to a decrease in the asset price. People who borrowed money to purchase the asset based on the expectation that prices would rise end up with a large debt when prices decrease instead. For example, individuals who borrow to purchase a house may find themselves "underwater," meaning that the value of their house is below the amount borrowed to purchase it.

Imagine that you purchase a house valued at $100,000 and pay for it with a $95,000 mortgage and a $5,000 down payment. At first, the value of your house increases, because investors demand more houses to resell at a profit after housing prices increase. In a few years, you have paid off some of your mortgage and you find yourself with a $93,000 mortgage on the same house; however, it is now worth $120,000! You have a more expensive house, but you didn't have to pay any more for it. You now have $27,000 of equity in your house. A few years later, the price increases that investors counted on for their profits end, so they stop buying houses. Demand in the housing market falls, and, with it, the value of your house. Now you find yourself living in the same house, but it is worth only $80,000. You have paid off more of your mortgage, but you still owe $90,000. You find yourself with a $90,000 mortgage on a house that is now worth $80,000. Your mortgage is underwater. If you stay in your house and continue to make your mortgage payments, being underwater may not make much difference to you. However, if you want or need to sell your house, it can become a real problem. The amount you would receive in the sale would not be enough to pay off your mortgage. You would actually have to *pay* to sell your house.

Andy Dean Photography/Shutterstock

The bursting of a housing bubble can cause the value of some homes to fall below the amount owed in loans for the homes. If the borrowers default on their loans, lenders take possession of the homes and sell them to recoup some of their losses.

The fall in asset prices from a bursting asset bubble exposes financial institutions to losses that can affect confidence in the financial system as a whole. For example, an economic downturn can cause people with underwater mortgages to default on them and abandon their houses rather than paying to sell them. When default rates on mortgages increase, financial institutions experience losses that undermine confidence in the financial system. If the loss in confidence is sufficiently severe, it can lead to an economy-wide banking crisis.

EM-4 Enrichment Modules

In an especially severe banking crisis, links in the financial system can increase the odds of even more bank failures. Bank failures can lead to a downward spiral; as each failure increases rumors and fears, thereby creating more bank failures. For example, when financial institutions have engaged in **leverage** by financing investments with borrowed funds, the institutions that loaned the funds may recall their loans if they are worried about default from failure of the borrowing institution. In addition, when financial institutions are in trouble, they try to reduce debt and raise cash by selling assets. When many banks try to sell similar assets at the same time, prices fall. The decrease in asset prices further hurts the financial position of banks, reinforcing the downward spiral in the banking system. Institutions in financial markets are linked to each other through their mutual dependence on confidence in the banking system and the value of long-term assets.

A financial institution engages in **leverage** when it finances its investments with borrowed funds.

As we have discussed, a well-developed financial system is a central part of a well-functioning economy. However, banking systems come with an inherent risk of banking crises. And banking crises, when left unchecked, can lead to a more widespread *financial crisis*.

Financial Crises: Consequences and Prevention

Some economists believe that to have a developed financial system is to face the risk of financial crises. Understanding the causes and consequences of financial crises is a key to understanding how they can be prevented.

What Is a Financial Crisis?

A **financial crisis** is a sudden and widespread disruption of financial markets. Such a crisis can occur when people suddenly lose faith in the ability of financial institutions to provide liquidity by bringing together those with cash to offer and those who need it. Since the banking system provides liquidity for buyers and sellers of everything from homes and cars to stocks and bonds, banking crises can easily turn into more widespread financial crises, as happened in 2008. In addition, an increase in the number and size of shadow banks in the economy can increase the scope and severity of financial crises, because shadow banks are not subject to the same regulations as depository institutions.

A **financial crisis** is a sudden and widespread disruption of financial markets.

The Consequences of Financial Crises

Financial crises have a significant negative effect on the economy and are closely associated with recessions. Historically, the origins of the worst economic downturns, such as the Great Depression, were tied to severe financial crises that led to decreased output and high unemployment (especially long-term unemployment). Recessions caused by financial crises tend to inflict sustained economic damage, and recovery from them can be very slow. **Figure A.2** on the next page shows the unemployment and duration associated with selected banking crises around the world.

When the financial system fails, there can be an economy-wide **credit crunch**, meaning that borrowers lose access to credit—either they cannot get credit at all, or they must pay high interest rates on loans. The lack of available or affordable credit in turn causes consumers and businesses to cut back on spending and investing, which leads to a recession. In addition, a financial crisis can lead to a recession because of a decrease in the price of assets. Decreases in housing prices are especially significant because real estate is often an individual's largest asset. Consumers who become poorer as a result of the decrease in the price of housing respond by reducing their spending to pay off debt and rebuild their assets, deepening the recession.

A **credit crunch** occurs when potential borrowers can't get credit or must pay very high interest rates.

Finally, financial crises can also lead to a decrease in the effectiveness of expansionary monetary policy intended to combat a recession. Typically, the Fed decreases the target interest rate to provide an incentive to increase spending during a recession.

Module A Financial Markets and Crises **EM-5**

Figure A.2 Episodes of Banking Crises and Unemployment

Economists Carmen Reinhart and Kenneth Rogoff have compared employment performance across several countries in the aftermath of a number of severe banking crises. For each country, the bar on the left shows the rise in the unemployment rate during and following the crisis, and the bar on the right shows how long it took for unemployment to begin to fall. On average, severe banking crises have been followed by a 7 percentage point rise in the unemployment rate, and in many cases it has taken four years or more before unemployment even begins to fall, let alone returns to precrisis levels.

Source: Carmen M. Reinhart and Kenneth S. Rogoff, "The Aftermath of Financial Crises," *American Economic Review* 99, no. 2 (2009): 466–472.

However, with a financial crisis, depositors, depository institutions, and borrowers all lose confidence in the system. As a result, even very low interest rates may not stimulate lending or borrowing in the economy.

Government Regulation of Financial Markets

Before the Great Depression, the government pursued a laissez-faire approach to banking. That is, the government let market forces determine the success or failure of banks, just as they did in other markets. However, since the Great Depression, considerable government regulation of financial markets has been implemented to prevent the severe economic downturns that can result from financial crises. Governments take three major actions to diminish the effects of banking crises: they act as a lender of last resort, guarantee deposits, and provide private credit market financing.

When governments act as a lender of last resort (usually through a central bank, such as the Federal Reserve), they provide funds to banks that are unable to borrow through private credit markets. Access to credit can help solvent banks—banks that have assets in excess of their liabilities—withstand bank runs without requiring them to sell off assets. In the case of financially unsound banks that are truly insolvent and will eventually go bankrupt, the government creates confidence in the banking system by guaranteeing the banks' liabilities. Deposit guarantees assure depositors that they will receive their deposits, preventing possible bank runs that would result from fear that deposits could be lost. Finally, governments have the ability to provide credit to shadow banks and to purchase private debt to keep the economy afloat when a banking crisis causes private credit markets to dry up.

The 2008 Financial Crisis

In 2008, the combination of a burst housing market bubble, a loss of faith in the liquidity of financial institutions, and an unregulated shadow banking system led to a widespread disruption of financial markets.

EM-6 Enrichment Modules

Causes of the 2008 Financial Crisis

The collapse of Lehman Brothers—a large shadow bank—set off the 2008 financial crisis, first in the United States and eventually across the globe. Although a number of factors led to the bank's collapse and the subsequent worldwide economic downturn, economists have identified four major causes of the 2008 financial crisis:

1. Macroeconomic conditions
2. A housing bubble
3. Financial system linkages
4. Failure of government regulation

The economy experienced a long period of low inflation, stable growth, and low global interest rates prior to the 2008 financial crisis. These macroeconomic conditions encouraged risk taking by shadow banks because they made it easy and cheap to borrow money. The banks searched for new ways to invest the funds they borrowed from short-term credit markets to earn higher returns in financial markets. One way to invest was through **securitization**, assembling a group of loans into a pool and selling shares of that pool to investors. Before the 2008 crisis, Lehman Brothers had been borrowing heavily in short-term credit markets and investing in subprime mortgages. **Subprime lending** had been a part of the banking industry for a long time, but subprime borrowing increased in the period leading up to the crisis. Subprime mortgages started to be packaged into so-called low-risk securities by pooling them together as **collateralized debt obligations**. These debt obligations are a type of financial **derivative**, a financial contract that has value based on the performance of another asset, index, or interest rate. Unfortunately, the shadow banks invested in these derivatives without accurately assessing their risk. When the real estate bubble burst, people began to default on their subprime mortgages and the value of the collateralized debt obligations fell. Because real estate markets represent a large part of the economy and shadow banks had invested heavily in subprime mortgages, the defaults quickly exposed the fragility of the financial system.

Securitization involves assembling a pool of loans and selling shares of that pool to investors.

Subprime lending involves lending to home-buyers who don't meet the usual criteria for being able to afford their payments.

A **collateralized debt obligation** is an asset-backed security tied to corporate debt or mortgages.

A **derivative** is a financial contract that has value based on the performance of another asset, index, or interest rate.

A **credit default swap** is an agreement that the seller will compensate the buyer in the event of a loan default.

In 2008, when rumors of Lehman's exposure in the housing market spread, the shadow bank was no longer able to borrow in short-term credit markets to finance its long-term obligations. Without access to credit, Lehman Brothers went bankrupt.

Chains of debt linked Lehman to other financial institutions. **Credit default swaps** had been created to spread the risk of default on loans, but in fact they concentrated that risk. AIG was a large insurance company that provided those swaps. When the housing bubble burst, the large number of defaults caused AIG to collapse soon after Lehman Brothers.

The 2008 crisis was like a traditional bank run—except that it was in the shadow banking system. The fall of Lehman Brothers led to a credit freeze, withdrawals of mutual funds, and a fall in derivative prices.

Finally, relaxed regulation of investment banks in the shadow banking sector failed to prevent the start and spread of the financial crisis. Prior to 2008, risk taking by shadow banks increased for several reasons. To begin with, given the vital importance of the financial system to the economy as a whole, many people thought the government would step in to prevent severe problems. That is, large financial institutions were considered "too big to fail." This led to the problem of **moral hazard**, which exists when a party takes excessive risks because it believes it will not bear all of the costs that could result. At the same time, the large profits earned by shadow banks further encouraged increased risk taking. Initially, the high-risk shadow banking activities were not a problem, because economic conditions were good. When the housing bubble burst, however, everything changed. It became clear that derivatives, which were thought to mitigate or eliminate default risk, only hid it. Because much of the existing government regulation did not apply to shadow banks, it could not prevent their activities from continuing to crisis.

Moral hazard involves a distortion of incentives when someone else bears the costs of lack of care or effort.

Module A Financial Markets and Crises EM-7

Figure A.3 Unemployment in the Aftermath of the 2008 Crisis

After 2008, the unemployment rate increased dramatically and remained high. Long-term unemployment, measured by the percentage of the unemployed who were out of work for 27 weeks or longer, increased at the same time. By 2011, almost half of all unemployed workers were long-term unemployed.

Source: Bureau of Labor Statistics.

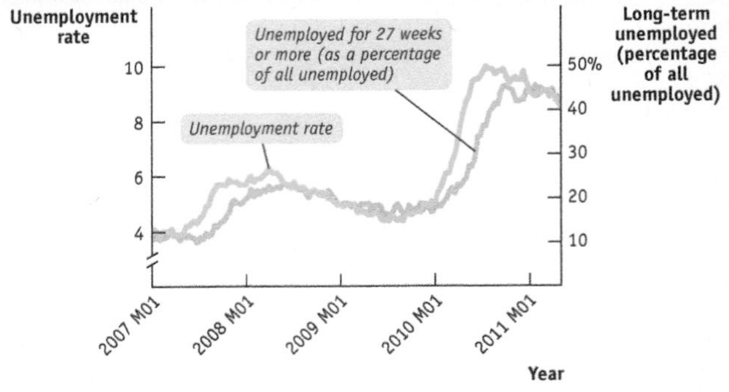

Consequences of the 2008 Financial Crisis

The 2008 financial crisis caused significant, prolonged damage to economies across the globe, with consequences that continued years later. For example, by the end of 2009, the United States' economy had lost over 7 million jobs, causing the unemployment rate to increase dramatically and remain high for years after, as shown in **Figure A.3**. In particular, the crisis led to an increase in long-term unemployment, which rose to almost half of the total unemployment in the economy.

The recession in the U.S. economy sent ripples throughout the world, and the years since the recession have seen only a weak recovery. For example, **Figure A.4** shows that it took more than five years for the United States to get back to the precrisis level of real GDP. In addition, in 2011–2012, fear of a second crisis related to public debt in Southern Europe and Ireland further hampered economic recovery from the crisis.

Figure A.4 Crisis and Recovery in the United States and the European Union

In the aftermath of the 2008 financial crisis, aggregate output in the European Union and in the United States fell dramatically. Real GDP, shown here as an index with each economy's peak precrisis quarter set to 100, declined by more than 5%. By late 2011, real GDP in the United States had only barely recovered to precrisis levels, and aggregate output in the European Union had still not reached its precrisis peak.

Sources: Bureau of Economic Analysis; Eurostat.

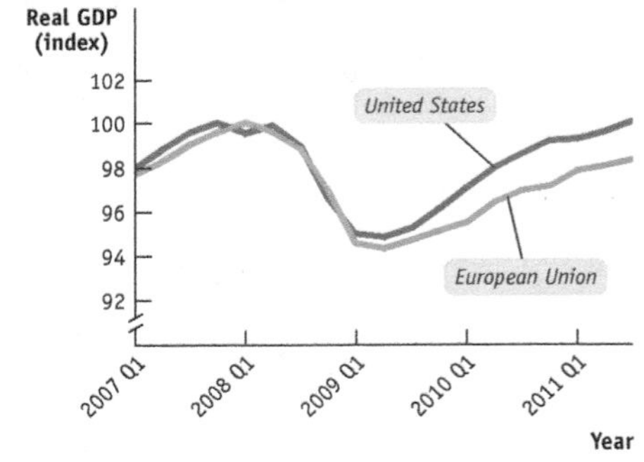

EM-8 Enrichment Modules

Government Response to the 2008 Financial Crisis

The intervention of the U.S. government and the Federal Reserve at the start of the financial crisis helped to calm financial markets. The federal government bailed out some failing financial institutions and instituted the Troubled Asset Relief Program (TARP), which involved the purchase of assets and equity from financial institutions to help strengthen the markets.

The Federal Reserve pursued an expansionary monetary policy, decreasing the federal funds rate to zero. The Fed also implemented programs to foster improved conditions in financial markets, significantly changing its own balance sheet. For example, the Fed acted as a lender of last resort by providing liquidity to financial institutions, it provided credit to borrowers and investors in key credit markets, and it put downward pressure on long-term interest rates by purchasing longer-term securities.

Financial Crises and the Future

The 2008 financial crisis highlighted the importance of financial markets and the need to ensure a well-functioning financial system. In 2010, the Wall Street Reform and Consumer Protection Act, known as the Dodd-Frank Act, was enacted to overhaul financial regulation in the aftermath of the crisis. The Dodd-Frank Act contains four main elements:

1. Consumer protection
2. Derivatives regulation
3. Shadow bank regulation
4. Resolution authority over nonbank financial institutions

Increases in the complexity of financial instruments played a large role in the financial crisis of 2008, as consumers purchased assets they either didn't understand or were not able to afford. The Consumer Financial Protection Bureau was created by the Dodd-Frank Act to protect borrowers from abusive practices that became prevalent due to the complexity of these instruments. The proliferation of derivatives was another important factor in the crisis, because derivatives, which had been designed to spread risk, worked to conceal risk prior to 2008. As a result, the new law also contains stipulations designed to make financial markets transparent so that asset risk is no longer concealed.

Shadow bank regulation and resolution authority extend government control during financial crises to cover nonbank financial institutions. The Dodd-Frank Act gives a special panel the ability to designate financial institutions that have the potential to create a banking crisis. These designated shadow banks are then subject to banklike regulation. In addition, the government now has the authority to seize control of financial institutions that require a bailout during a crisis, the way it already did with commercial banks. This power, called resolution authority, allows governments to guarantee a wide range of financial institution debts in a crisis.

Going forward, financial regulation faces several challenges. First of all, the idea that a financial institution can be "too big to fail" is still prevalent and the problem of moral hazard still exists. And, while new regulation has been put in place in the United States, it is not clear how these regulations can or will be applied in other countries. The 2008 financial crisis highlighted the global nature of financial markets and the worldwide linkages that must be acknowledged in order for regulation to be effective.

Finally, regulation that addresses what happened in 2008 may not be effective in addressing whatever financial crisis might loom in the future. World economies and world financial markets are ever changing; regulation must be dynamic and must be able to respond to the current situation, not merely the most recent crisis.

The Dodd-Frank Act created the Consumer Financial Protection Agency to protect borrowers from abusive practices that became more prevalent as financial instruments became more complex.

Module A Financial Markets and Crises EM-9

FYI The Day the Lights Went Out at Lehman

On Friday night, September 12, 2008, an urgent meeting was held in the New York Federal Reserve Bank's headquarters on Wall Street. In attendance were the outgoing Bush administration's Treasury secretary, Hank Paulson, and the then head of the New York Fed, Tim Geithner (later the Treasury secretary in the Obama administration), along with the heads of the country's largest investment banks. Lehman Brothers was rapidly imploding, and Paulson had called the meeting in the hope of pressing the investment bankers into a deal that would, like the LTCM bailout described in Module 26, avert a messy bankruptcy.

Since the forced sale six months earlier of the nearly bankrupt investment bank Bear Stearns to a healthier bank, Lehman had been under increasing pressure. Like Bear Stearns, Lehman had invested heavily in subprime mortgages and other assets tied to real estate. And when Bear Stearns fell as its creditors began calling in its loans and other banks refused to lend to it, many wondered if Lehman would fall next.

In July 2008, Lehman reported a \$2.8 billion loss for the second quarter of 2008 (the months April–June), precipitating a 54% fall in its stock price. As its share price fell, Lehman's sources of credit began to dry up and its trading operations withered. The CEO of Lehman, Richard Fuld, began a desperate search for a healthier bank to buy shares of Lehman and provide desperately needed funding. By early September 2008, Lehman's loss for the third quarter had risen to \$3.9 billion. On September 9, J.P. Morgan Chase, a far healthier investment bank that had been Lehman's major source of financing for its trades, demanded \$5 billion in cash as extra collateral or it would freeze Lehman's accounts and cut off its credit. Unable to come up with the cash, Lehman teetered on the edge of bankruptcy.

In the September 12 meeting, Treasury Secretary Paulson urged the investment bankers to put together a package to purchase Lehman's bad assets. But, fearing for their own survival in an extremely turbulent market, they refused unless Paulson would give them a government guarantee on the value of Lehman's assets. The Treasury had made the Bear Stearns sale possible by arranging a huge loan from the New York Fed to its purchaser. This time, facing a backlash from Congress over "bailing out profligate bankers," Paulson refused to provide government help. And in the wee hours of Monday morning, September 15, 2008, Lehman went down, declaring the most expensive bankruptcy in history.

Yet, as Fuld had earlier warned Paulson, the failure of Lehman unleashed the furies. That same day, the U.S. stock market fell 504 points, triggering an increase in bank borrowing costs and a run on money market funds and financial institutions around the world. By Tuesday, Paulson agreed to an \$85 billion bailout of another major corporation, the foundering AIG, at the time the world's largest insurer. Before the markets stabilized months later, the U.S. government made \$250 billion of capital infusions to bolster major U.S. banks. Whether or not Paulson made a catastrophic mistake by not acting to save Lehman is a matter likely to be debated for years to come.

Richard Fuld, the head of Lehman, testified before a congressional panel on how the collapse of Lehman precipitated a financial panic.

ENRICHMENT MODULE A Review

Check Your Understanding

1. Draw a circular-flow diagram that includes households, firms, factor markets, markets for goods and services, and financial markets. Circle the section of the diagram that illustrates maturity transformation and briefly explain the maturity transformation process.
2. What are the four major causes of the 2008 financial crisis? Briefly describe each one.
3. What are the four main elements of the Dodd-Frank Act? Briefly describe each one.

Discussion Starters

1. Explain why an efficient financial system is important.
2. What is a shadow bank? Give several specific examples of shadow banks.
3. Explain how an asset bubble can lead to an economy-wide banking crisis.
4. What are some of the possible consequences of a financial crisis?
5. Define moral hazard. Explain the role of moral hazard in the 2008 financial crisis.

Check Your Understanding

1.

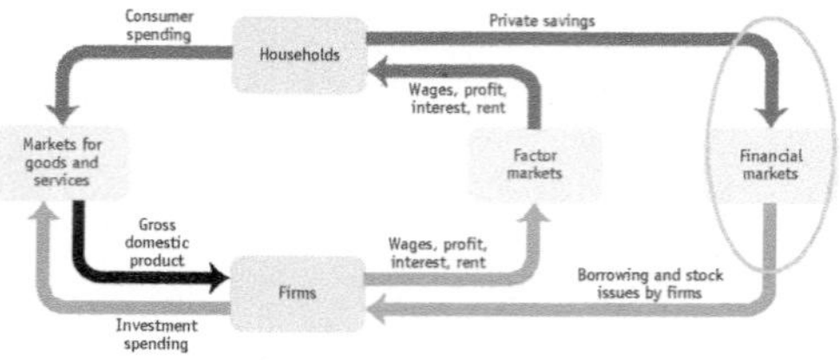

Financial markets take private savings in the form of short-term deposits and inject that money back into the economy through long-term loans.

2. Macroeconomic conditions: The economy experienced a long period of low inflation, stable growth, and low global interest rates prior to the 2008 financial crisis. These macroeconomic conditions encouraged risk-taking by shadow banks by making it easy and cheap to borrow money.

Housing bubble: Housing prices increased to a high level due to expectations of future price gains, creating a housing bubble. When the housing bubble burst, people began to default on their subprime mortgages and the value of the collateralized debt obligations fell.

Financial system linkages: When the housing bubble burst, the large number of defaults that resulted had the effect of a traditional bank run in the shadow banking system.

Failure of government regulation: Relaxed regulation of investment banks in the shadow banking sector failed to prevent the start and spread of the financial crisis.

3. Consumer protection: The Consumer Financial Protection Bureau was created by the Dodd-Frank Act to protect borrowers from abusive practices that became prevalent leading up to the crisis.

Derivatives regulation: The new law also contains stipulations designed to make financial markets transparent so that a derivative's risk is no longer concealed.

Shadow bank regulation: The shadow bank regulation extends government control during financial crises to cover nonbank financial institutions.

Resolution authority: The government now has the authority to seize control of financial institutions that require a bailout during a crisis, the way it already did with commercial banks. Resolution authority allows governments to guarantee a wide range of financial institutions' debts in a crisis.

Discussion Starters

Following are possible answers to the Discussion Starter questions:

1. The financial system improves efficiency and leads to long-run economic growth by reducing transaction costs, reducing risk, and providing liquidity.

2. A shadow bank is a financial institution that engages in maturity transformation but does not accept deposits. Examples include: JP Morgan Chase, Bank of America, Merrill Lynch, and Goldman Sachs.

3. When the price of an asset like housing is pushed above a reasonable level by investor expectations of future price increases, eventually the market runs out of new buyers and the future price increases do not materialize. This causes the bubble to burst, leading to a decrease in the asset price. People who borrowed money to purchase the asset based on the expectation that prices would rise instead end up with a large debt on an asset that is now worth much less when prices decrease. When many asset owners default on their loans, it can lead to an economy-wide crisis.

4. Domestic and possibly worldwide recession; reduced real GDP and high unemployment

5. Moral hazard involves a distortion of incentives when someone else bears the costs of a lack of care or effort. Banks may have taken excessive risks because some people believed the banks would be protected by the government because they were "too big to fail."

© KVA/TDW/Corbis

ENRICHMENT MODULE

B Behavioral Economics

In this Module, you will learn to:

- Identify barriers to rational decision making
- Discuss the role of psychology in consumer behavior
- Explain why assumptions of rationality are useful despite limits on the rationality of humans

Consumers and Rationality

During a recent promotion, Nytro Multisport sold the Felt B2 triathlon bike for $4,798.99. Aside from the question of whether it is rational for anyone to pay that much money for a bicycle, why would the retailer not simply charge $4,800? The difference, $1.01, is 1/4,751th of the price. Could that matter? TV ads routinely offer products for $19.95 rather than $20. Gasoline prices typically end in 9/10ths of a cent. And Steve Jobs arguably revived the music industry by charging 99 cents for iTunes music downloads. Traditional economic theory does nothing to explain the importance of shaving a price down from an even number to a substantially equivalent odd number, yet some 90% of advertised prices end in "9" or "5." Psychological influences clearly matter, whether or not those influences can be categorized as rational. A melding of psychology and economics, **behavioral economics** is the study of economic decision making as influenced by the limits of the human mind.

Behavioral economics is the study of economic decision making as influenced by the limits of the human mind.

Homo economicus

Economists have made great strides with models starring "economic man" or ***Homo economicus***, a fictional economic actor and amalgamation of all people, who makes self-interested, informed, rational judgments in pursuit of wealth and leisure. In neoclassical models, *Homo economicus* represents the typical member of society. *Homo economicus* is a reasonable facsimile of the average economic decision maker in many contexts, in that variations in behaviors either average out across people or are unimportant. In those cases, the neoclassical models form the basis for useful conclusions. For example, those models predict that people will buy more of a product when the price falls, work more when the wage rises, and prefer some money to none at all. This module, however, explains challenges to the traditional assumptions about *Homo economicus*, and explores the implications of irrationality among economic actors.

Homo economicus, a fictional economic actor who makes self-interested, informed, rational judgments in pursuit of wealth and leisure.

TEACH Teach It

TRM The answers to the end-of-module questions are included in the margins for this module. Some additional support material may be found in the TRM.

Behavioral economics unveils *Homo economicus* and finds an individual who is sensitive, flawed, and biased in ways that can disrupt the efficient allocation of resources. Human decisions can go awry due to the scarcity of time, intelligence, and information. The importance of the psychological side of economic behavior is still controversial, but acceptance of the field of behavioral economics has grown considerably over the past four decades. Herbert Simon and Daniel Kahneman won Nobel Prizes in economics in 1978 and 2002, respectively, for their research on behavioral economics. In addition, the *Journal of Behavioral Economics* was established in 1970. And a surge in popularity in the 1980s and 1990s led scholars at virtually every top economics department in North America to dive into the field of behavioral economics. Now it is your turn.

Homo misinformicus

There are differing schools of thought about the extent of information problems and behavioral anomalies. The work of neoclassical economists such as Milton Friedman, Arthur Pigou, and Gary Becker placed considerable reliance on *rational choice theory*, which holds that decision makers are able to compare all of their alternatives with full information about their choices. For example, based on this theory, one would predict that when Nytro Multisport lowers the price of the Felt B2 bicycle from the list price of $6,199.00 down to $4,798.99, it will sell more bikes. The assumption is that consumers are aware of the product, its virtues, and the price change. However, unless you are a bicycle enthusiast, chances are that you did not know much about the Felt B2 before reading this module. In reality, information is imperfect, and consumers do not know every product's availability, quality, or price. The large amounts of money people pay for Internet access, smartphones, and college educations exemplify the value placed on information. Yet the cost of perfect information is prohibitive—no one has the time or money to become all knowing. The result is ill-informed behavior, such as people paying the list price for a Felt B2 because they are unaware of the deals that are available at particular bike shops.

Researchers in the field of behavioral economics study the rationality of market participants under realistic constraints on time, information, and intelligence. Because information takes time and sometimes money to obtain, it is appropriate to continue seeking information until the marginal benefit of doing so no longer exceeds the marginal cost. This is why rational people often act on incomplete information. For example, if you live in a large city, you wouldn't want to call every shoe store in town to check prices before buying a new pair of shoes. After you call a few stores, the likely savings from additional calls falls below the value of your time.

It takes time to acquire information about the prices and products available to consumers: at some point, the marginal cost of information gathering exceeds the marginal benefit. So shoppers typically buy shoes and other goods on the basis of incomplete information.

Many uses of information are not so rational. In defiance of rationality, individuals often respond to the way in which information is presented. For example, would a half-empty glass of soda pop sound as appealing to you as a half-full glass of soda pop? In a related experiment, psychologists Daniel Kahneman and Amos Tversky found that respondents who were presented with four identical outcomes with differing descriptions overwhelmingly preferred a disease-control program that would save 200 out of 600 people to a program that would allow 400 out of 600 people to die. In other words, it is perceived as better to have one-third of a population live than to have two-thirds of a population die.

Descriptions also drive perceptions of products and policies. For example, New York Super Fudge Chunk ice cream is a top seller for Ben and Jerry's, whereas Bovinity Divinity and Dastardly Mash, though similarly chewy and chocolaty, were discontinued for lack of interest. Similarly, policies that environmentalists say would weaken current standards have gained steam due to appealing names such as the Clear Skies Initiative and the Healthy Forests Initiative. And, while the prospect of higher wages motivates employees to work harder, so does the prospect of loftier job titles, such as vice president or office manager.

EM-12 Enrichment Modules

Uninformed consumers may buy too much of products that have health risks, such as junk food; pay more for products or services than they are worth, such as counterfeit watches; or purchase products that are inferior in price or quality to those available elsewhere, such as full-priced triathlon bicycles. Uninformed managers face the same problems when purchasing from vendors. Incomplete information and irrational behavior also stab at the heart of *Homo economicus.* With perfect information and rationality at the foundation of efficient decision making in many economic models, there is reason to be concerned about errors, bias, and incomplete information.

Universal History Archive/UIG via Getty images

When decisions are made quickly, options can look better than they really are. Malcolm Gladwell calls this the *Warren Harding effect.* Warren Harding looked like a good presidential candidate while campaigning, but once he was in office, even Harding himself felt that he shouldn't have been elected.

Psychology and Economics

In *Blink: The Power of Thinking Without Thinking,* Malcolm Gladwell explains that by necessity or instinct, many decisions are made on the basis of first impressions. Snap judgments can lead to less-than-optimal choices when products—such as new cars—or people—such as potential employees, marital prospects, or presidential candidates—look better than they really are. Gladwell calls this the *Warren Harding effect* in reference to the twenty-ninth president of the United States, who looked winningly presidential to over 60% of the voters, but turned out to be a poor leader with a scandal-ridden administration. Harding reportedly said of himself, "I am not fit for this office and never should have been here." Clearly, Harding, and those who voted for him, made some mistakes due to limits on information and intelligence.

Bounded Rationality

Dubious about models based on rationality and full information, Nobel laureate Herbert Simon explained that rationality is bounded by limitations in the ability of decision makers to formulate and solve complex problems. In *Models of My Life,* Simon argued that even Albert Einstein could not match the mental gymnastics ascribed to the fictional "economic man." Simon coined the phrase **bounded rationality** to describe the limits on optimal decision making that result from imperfect intelligence and the scarcity of time and information. Bounded rationality causes missteps, as when a price that ends in "99" makes a consumer perceive the amount as being lower than it really is.

© Timothy Large/Alamy

Bounded rationality causes missteps, as when a price that ends in "99" makes a consumer perceive the amount as being lower than it really is.

Bounded rationality describes the limits on optimal decision making that result from imperfect intelligence and the scarcity of time and information.

Simon also studied the *judgmental heuristics*—rules of thumb—that people use to simplify decisions when constrained by time, information, or cognitive ability. Consumers and managers are like chess players: they cannot fully analyze every possible sequence of actions that will follow their move. Instead, they must rely on instincts, experience, advice, short-cuts, and guesswork. For example, rather than making pricing decisions by evaluating the consumer response and subsequent profit from every possible price point, many managers use the simple "keystone" technique of doubling the wholesale price of each good to establish the retail price. The next FYI box explains that people often stick with the way things are rather than exploring their options. Simon felt that such heuristics led to decisions that were satisfactory but not optimal, and described this type of decision making as *satisficing.*

Neoclassical theories rest on assumptions of rationality that are sometimes at odds with observed human behavior. For example, some theories of consumer choice are valid under the assumption that the amount an individual would be willing to pay for a good and the amount he or she would accept to give up an identical good are the same. However, researchers have found *endowment effects,* meaning that people place a

Module B Behavioral Economics **EM-13**

FYI Sticking with the Status Quo

Status quo bias causes people to stick with what they've got despite equally attractive alternatives. In *Smart Choices*, John Hammond, Ralph Keeney, and Howard Raiffa describe a natural experiment in which the state governments of New Jersey and Pennsylvania both adopted the same two options for automobile insurance, but each selected a different default plan. Under plan A, insurance premiums were lower but drivers had a limited right to litigate after an accident. Under plan B, the premiums were higher but litigation options were broader. In New Jersey, drivers received plan A unless they specified otherwise; Pennsylvania drivers were assigned to plan B unless they opted for plan A. The result was that the majority of drivers in each state stuck with the status quo, meaning that they felt the best plan was the plan they were given in the first place.

Do you experience status quo bias? Think about your family's choice of where to live, and your favorite sports teams, politicians, and brand names. In some cases, the choice might be clear. In other cases, perhaps you've stuck with the status quo despite the existence of equally attractive alternatives.

Lower premiums or broader options for litigation? Most drivers stuck with the status quo.

higher value on what they have than on what they don't have. In a famous example, Daniel Kahneman, Jack Knetsch, and Richard Thaler found that, after randomly selecting half the students in a class to receive coffee mugs, students without mugs were willing to pay less than half as much to buy one as the people with a mug had to be paid to give one up.

Behavioral economists use the concept of *loss aversion* to explain evidence that consumers consider sunk costs—those costs that have already been incurred and cannot be recovered—in their decision making. No matter how much money one has sunk into a project, it would be rational to abandon that project if the future benefits do not exceed the future costs. Yet some people choose to overeat in order to finish expensive meals, go to bad plays because they paid a lot for season tickets, or stick with a failing stock because they have invested so much money in it. An additional reason that people choose to stick with failing stocks is excessive optimism.

Excessive Optimism Crime provides an important example of bounded rationality in the form of excessive optimism. Neoclassical models treat crime as a rational activity, the price of which is the expected punishment. This implies that more severe punishments or higher rates of apprehension or conviction will deter crime. Yet a study of the knowledge and mindset of criminals found that most criminals do not have the information required to perform cost-benefit analysis before committing their crimes. Specifically, 76% of the convicted criminals in the study either had no thought that they might be caught or had no idea of the punishment for their crime, or both. Among the violent offenders, 89% lacked the information necessary to perform cost-benefit analysis. So in order to solve the crime problem, policy makers must go beyond the tenets of neoclassical economics and be open to solutions that address psychological problems and informational shortcomings.

Unfortunately, crime is just the tip of the iceberg of poor decisions caused by excessive optimism. Here are some additional examples:

- People underestimate the risks of common but unpublicized events such as work-related motor vehicle accidents and falls, and overestimate the risk of uncommon but dramatic, highly publicized events such as earthquakes, homicides, airplane

EM-14 Enrichment Modules

crashes, and rare types of cancer. The result is inadequate safety precautions against the large risks and overinvestment in precautions against the small risks.

- More than half of all new businesses fail within five years, which may indicate excessive optimism among entrepreneurs. It is also possible that the potential benefits of a successful business outweigh the high risks of failure, but decision makers who underestimate the risks are prone to overinvest.
- The majority of Americans believe they are smarter than average and have better-than-average chances of winning the lottery, being professionally successful, and avoiding disease and automobile accidents. In the business world, most managers think they are more capable than the average manager.
- A common reason that many lawsuits go to trial is unrealistic optimism on the part of one side or both sides about the strength of their case. In a representative study, the average plaintiff's attorney expected a jury award 27% higher than the amount anticipated by the average defense attorney.

Even when good information is available, people may not use it wisely. Because people are capable of stubbornness, bias, and misjudgment to their own downfall, the improper use of information can lead to unfortunate and inefficient resource allocations.

Framing It is standard procedure at several international hotel chains to place a card in the bathrooms of guest rooms with a message along the following lines:

> Save Our Planet. Every day millions of gallons of water are used to wash towels . . .
> A towel on the rack means "I will use again." Thank you for helping us conserve the Earth's vital resources.

If the hotels were really bent on saving Earth's resources, they would provide recycling bins, organic cotton sheets, and carpets made from recycled fibers. The pitch to avoid washing towels may have more to do with saving the financial resources of the hotels, but customer participation depends on how the appeal is framed.

Framing is the creation of context for a product or idea, and context matters. Richard Thaler found that a typical consumer would pay no more than $1.50 for a good brand of beer from a grocery store but would pay up to $2.65 for an identical beer from a fancy hotel, even if a friend was bringing that beer to the consumer to drink at the same beach either way. Brand managers spend millions of dollars to frame their brand names because, for example, consumers perceive apparel differently after seeing Maria Sharapova wear it, and they perceive a hotel differently knowing that Brad Pitt stays there. Consumers pay more for a cup of coffee at Starbucks than at McDonald's, not because the Starbucks coffee itself is necessarily better (a 2007 *Consumer Reports* taste test suggests that McDonald's coffee is actually better), but because of the image and ambiance in which Starbucks coffee is framed.

Framing is the creation of context for a product or idea.

The strategy of *odd* or *just-below* pricing—setting prices that end in an odd number or just below an even dollar amount—is about framing as well. In terms of damage to the pocketbook, there's little difference between paying $4.99 and paying $5.00. But the human mind finds it easier to accept a price of $4.99. Consumers subconsciously downplay the importance of the cents at the end of a price, and place more emphasis on the dollar amount at the beginning. Thus, $4.99 might seem close to $4.00, even though it is only a penny shy of $5.00. Also, prices ending in "99" or "95" convey the idea of a discount to bargain-hungry shoppers. Thomas Kibarian tested the influence of prices with odd-numbered endings by sending out three versions of a direct mail catalog for women's clothing. The catalogs were identical except for the prices, which ended with either 00, 99, or 88. The catalogs with prices ending in 99 generated 8% more sales volume and attracted more consumers than those with prices ending in the even numbers. Managers at upscale department stores such as Nordstrom are aware of the psychology of pricing as well, but they use the contrasting strategy of ending prices with even numbers, symbolic of their high-end brand image.

Module B Behavioral Economics **EM-15**

Bounded Willpower

It's rational to spend money, retire, or take vacations that decrease earnings, as long as the value of the resulting benefits exceeds the value of the money forgone. Yet sometimes people forgo money in irrational ways. **Bounded willpower**—willpower constrained by limits on the determination needed to do difficult things—can be the cause. The effects include spending too much money and earning too little money, but it isn't all about money. Bounded willpower can also explain decisions to do too little homework, procrastinate too much, overeat, or throw a career-ending temper tantrum in front of the boss.

Ann Heath

At Nordstrom, prices ending in even numbers convey an upscale image.

In the analysis of behavior, it is important not to categorize everything that causes problems as irrational. Economists Gary Becker and Kevin Murphy pointed out that even the use of potentially addictive substances can be rational if the benefits outweigh the costs. They showed that people who care more about the present than the future are more prone to addiction because they discount future problems related to health, relationships, and finances when weighing them against ongoing desires for addictive substances. Becker and Murphy argue that when heavy drinkers and smokers say they want to quit but cannot, it may be a matter of the long-term benefits of quitting falling below the short-term costs of making that adjustment.

Bounded willpower is willpower constrained by limits on the determination needed to do difficult things.

While some addictions may be rational, humans are subject to temptations and emotions that can lead them astray. Anger, jealousy, frustration, and embarrassment can overcome willpower and trigger irrational responses. Take, for example, the Wendy's customer who shot manager Renal Frage due to anger over not receiving enough packets of chili sauce. Similar examples appear frequently in the news.

Bounded Self-Interest

Neoclassical economic models rest on assumptions of self-interested behavior, which is seldom in short supply. But some behavior exhibits elements of altruism uncharacteristic of *Homo economicus*. Warren Buffet is apparently not *Homo economicus*, having donated $2.6 billion to charity in 2013. Americans recycled or composted almost 87 million tons of materials in 2011 to the benefit of the environment and future generations. And the Bureau of Labor Statistics estimates that in 2012, 26.5% of the U.S. population volunteered some of their time to help less fortunate individuals. Charitable efforts can be self-serving if they bring attention, gratitude, tax advantages, or other benefits to the donors. But to the extent that some decisions are made selflessly, **bounded self-interest**—self-interest that leaves room for concerns about the welfare of others—represents a third category of deviance from neoclassical economic models.

Bounded self-interest is self-interest that leaves room for concerns about the welfare of others.

Economists have examined the human struggle between self-interest and fairness with experiments involving *ultimatum games* and *dictator games*. In an ultimatum game, one person, whom we shall call *the divider*, has an amount of money, say $10, to divide between herself and another person, whom we shall call *the recipient*. After the divider makes the allocation, the recipient can either accept that division or reject it. If the allocation is rejected by the recipient, neither side gets anything. A rational, wealth-maximizing recipient will accept any positive share of the money, because some money is better than the alternative of no money. When working with such recipients, a rational, wealth-maximizing divider would allocate the smallest possible positive amount to the recipient: one cent. However, much experimentation has revealed strong interest in fair allocations, and punishment for those who make unfair allocations. Daniel Kahneman, Jack Knetsch, and Richard Thaler found that the typical recipient rejects anything less than a 23% share of the money to be divided, and that the average divider offers 45% of the money to the recipient.

kindy16/Shutterstock

Would you divide $20 evenly between you and an anonymous recipient if you didn't have to?

EM-16 Enrichment Modules

Related research has found fairness to be important even with changes in the culture of the participants, the amount of money at stake, and opportunities to learn from experience with the game.

In the dictator game, the recipient has no choice but to accept the divider's allocation. Thus, a rational, wealth-maximizing divider would give nothing to the recipient. Kahneman, Knetsch, and Thaler gave 161 students the option of dividing $20 evenly with an anonymous other student or giving the other student $2 while keeping $18. Even though the recipients had no say in the matter, 76% of the dividers gave half of the money to the recipient, again exhibiting substantial interest in fairness.

Clearly there is more to decision making than wealth maximization. Customers may pay more for a product that causes less harm to other people or the environment, as managers at Toyota discovered when their relatively expensive but environmentally friendly Prius Hybrid flew out of showrooms faster than the company could make more. Attracting a new employee by offering a salary that eclipses the salary of existing employees can cause considerable strife due to those employees' interests in fairness. And there may be no amount of money that can separate a parent from a needy child, as suggested by Derek Fisher's forfeiture of the remaining three years and $21 million in his NBA contract with the Utah Jazz to be with his ill daughter in 2007.

Evolving Models

Just as *Homo ergasters* may have evolved into modern men and women, in contemporary economic theory, the traditional model of *Homo economicus* is evolving into a modern conception of economic man and woman. Behavioral economists have adapted earlier notions of economic man to capture decision making under the constraints on human rationality, willpower, and self-interest. Some strange behaviors can be traced to rational foundations, but others are sufficiently suspect to warrant policy that addresses the possibility of misinformation, mistakes, and psychosis.

We've seen that the information that neoclassical theory treats as fully and freely available is often incomplete and costly. We've also seen that market participants do not always put the information they have to its best use. The salient question is whether problems with information justify an abandonment of neoclassical precepts, some revisions and expansions in rational choice theory, or none of the above. Most contemporary economists stake out a middle ground, leaning toward the neoclassical side. Despite their flaws, neoclassical models provide useful guidance and predictive power. Experiments demonstrate that people—not to mention rats, dolphins, and other decision makers broadly defined—generally respond to incentives in rational ways: they all tend to follow the money, cheese, or sardines. That being said, worthwhile improvements in theories and policy making can be achieved by acknowledging psychological influences beyond the desire for money and leisure. Consumers, managers, employees, and all other participants in an economy are more or less flawed, biased, emotional, benevolent, undisciplined, and uninformed, which helps to explain myriad behaviors that neoclassical models do not predict.

Module B Behavioral Economics EM-17

Check Your Understanding

1. a. Framing

b. Bounded willpower

c. Excessive optimism

d. Bounded self-interest

2. Strong interests in fairness, and a desire to punish those whose decisions seem unfair

Discussion Starters

Following are possible answers to the Discussion Starter questions:

1. Students might discuss situations in which they were led astray from rationality by emotions, framing, sunk costs, satisficing, excessive optimism, bounded willpower, or bounded self-interest. For example, a student might say that she or he broke something or hit someone in a fit of anger, only to regret the action shortly afterwards.

2. Students might discuss misinformation received online, false rumors heard from friends, or misleading information conveyed in political advertisements.

3. Students might discuss donations to charity, volunteer work, or tipping. Do they ever put money in a tip jar at a counter when the clerk isn't watching? Or do they make sure that receipt of the tip is observed, meaning that they might receive better treatment in return?

4. The opportunity cost of time and, in some cases, money weighs against the benefits of obtaining information. Seldom do we collect all the available information about a topic because at some point the marginal benefit of additional information outweighs the cost.

5. Students might say that they would set prices that end in 99 because consumers respond to the lower-seeming prices. Some students might find this unethical. Some students might say that the approach works on them, while others might say that they're not so easily fooled.

6. Students might discuss situations in which the scarcity of time, intelligence, or information affects consumer behavior. Perhaps competition among restaurants increased in their town, but did not result in lower prices in the restaurant market because not enough people knew what the new restaurants had to offer. Or perhaps students have seen urgent needs for medical care prevent consumers from comparing prices across care providers. Students might discuss how increases or decreases in gas prices affect their family's driving habits.

ENRICHMENT MODULE B Review

Check Your Understanding

1. Identify the cause of each of the following types of behavior:
   - **a.** Roberto will pay more for the same steak in a restaurant with fancy tablecloths than in a restaurant without them.
   - **b.** Karen knows she should stop eating chocolate, but she eats more anyway.
   - **c.** Alesia opens a new hardware store despite market research indicating insufficient consumer demand for the store's products.
   - **d.** Nelson employs a worker whose family desperately needs the income, even though the worker's wage exceeds the revenue that worker brings into Nelson's firm.
2. What do experiments with the ultimatum game reveal about the typical participant?

Discussion Starters

1. Which of your behaviors might be considered irrational? Do you consider sunk costs? Do emotions ever put you on an irrational path?
2. How gullible are you? Do you tend to believe what you hear from your friends and what you read on the Internet? Have you ever learned that you were fooled by these or other information sources?
3. Do you sometimes exhibit altruism? In what instances have you forgone money for the benefit of others?
4. Would a product's effects on the environment influence your decision to buy it? Can you name the greenhouse gases that cause global warming? What sorts of costs weigh against the benefits of obtaining this information?
5. As a manager, would you set prices so that they ended in "99"? Why or why not? Does this approach ever work on you as a consumer?
6. What evidence have you seen of the failure or success of neoclassical models? Have you noticed changes in the price or quality of goods as the number of competitors changed? Does the quantity of a good demanded decrease as its price increases?

iStockphoto/Getty Images

ENRICHMENT MODULE C

The Economics of Information

TEACH Teach It

TRM The answers to the end-of-module questions are included in the margins for this module. Some additional support material may be found in the TRM.

In this Module, you will learn to:

- Identify the special problems posed by information that some people have and other people do not, which is known as *private information* or *asymmetric information*
- Explain how information asymmetries can lead to the problem of adverse selection
- Discuss ways that firms can deal with imperfect information using screening and signaling
- Explain how information asymmetries can lead to the problem of moral hazard

Private Information: What You Don't Know Can Hurt You

Markets can handle situations in which nobody knows what is going to happen. However, markets have much more trouble with situations in which *some people know things that other people don't know*—situations involving **private information** (also known as "asymmetric information"). As we will see, private information can distort economic decisions and sometimes prevent mutually beneficial economic transactions from taking place.

Private information is information that some people have and others do not.

Why is some information private? The most important reason is that people generally know more about themselves than other people do. For example, you know whether or not you are a careful driver; but unless you have already been in several accidents, your auto insurance company does not. You are more likely to have a better estimate than your health insurance company of whether or not you will need an expensive medical procedure. And if you are selling your used car, you are more likely to be aware of any problems with it than the buyer is.

But why should such differences in who knows what be a problem? It turns out that there are two distinct sources of trouble: *adverse selection,* which arises from having private information about the way things are, and *moral hazard,* which arises from having private information about what people do.

Adverse Selection: The Economics of Lemons

Suppose that someone offers to sell you an almost brand-new car—purchased just three months ago, with only 2,000 miles on the odometer and no dents or scratches. Will you be willing to pay almost the same for it as for a car direct from the dealer?

Probably not, for one main reason: you cannot help but wonder why this car is being sold. Has the owner discovered that something is wrong with it—that it is a "lemon"? Having driven the car for a while, the owner knows more about it than you do—and people are more likely to sell cars that give them trouble.

You might think that the extra information held by sellers of used cars provides a distinct advantage to the sellers. But potential buyers know that potential sellers are likely to offer them lemons—they just don't know exactly which car is a lemon. Because potential buyers of a used car know that potential sellers are more likely to sell lemons than good cars, buyers will offer a lower price than they would if they had a guarantee of the car's quality. Worse yet, this poor opinion of used cars tends to be self-reinforcing, precisely because it depresses the prices that buyers offer. Used cars sell at a discount because buyers expect a disproportionate share of those cars to be lemons. Even a used car that is not a lemon would sell only at a large discount because buyers don't know whether it's a lemon or not. But potential sellers who have good cars are unwilling to sell them at a deep discount, except under exceptional circumstances. So it is relatively uncommon for good used cars to be offered for sale, and used cars that are offered for sale have a tendency to be lemons. (This is why people who have a compelling reason to sell a car, such as moving overseas, make a point of revealing that information to potential buyers—as if to say "This car is not a lemon!")

The end result, then, is not only that used cars sell for low prices but also that there are a large number of used cars with hidden problems. Equally important, many potentially beneficial transactions—sales of good used cars by people who would like to get rid of them to people who would like to buy them—end up being frustrated by the inability of potential sellers to convince potential buyers that their cars are actually worth the higher price demanded. So some mutually beneficial trades between those who want to sell used cars and those who want to buy them go unexploited.

Although economists sometimes refer to situations like this as the "lemons problem" (the issue was introduced in a famous 1970 paper by economist and Nobel laureate George Akerlof entitled "The Market for Lemons"), the more formal name of the problem is **adverse selection**. The reason for the name is obvious: because the potential sellers know more about the quality of what they are selling than the potential buyers, they have an incentive to select the worst things to sell.

Adverse selection occurs when one person knows more about the way things are than other people do. Adverse selection exists, for example, when sellers offer items of particularly low (hidden) quality for sale, and when the people with the greatest need for insurance are those most likely to purchase it.

Adverse selection applies to more than just used cars. It is a problem for many parts of the economy—notably for insurance companies, and most notably for health insurance companies. Suppose that a health insurance company were to offer a standard policy to everyone with the same premium. The premium would reflect the *average* risk of incurring a medical expense. But that would make the policy look very expensive to healthy people, who know that they are less likely than the average person to incur medical expenses. So healthy people would be less likely than less healthy people to buy the policy, leaving the health insurance company with exactly the customers it doesn't want: people with a higher-than-average risk of needing medical care, who would find the premium to be a good deal. In order to cover its expected losses from this sicker customer pool, the health insurance company is compelled to raise premiums, driving away more of the remaining healthier customers, and so on. Because the insurance company can't determine who is healthy and who is not, it must charge everyone the same premium, thereby discouraging healthy people from purchasing policies and encouraging unhealthy people to buy policies.

Adverse selection can lead to a phenomenon called an *adverse selection death spiral* as the market for health insurance collapses: insurance companies refuse to offer policies because there is no premium at which the company can cover its losses. Because of the severe adverse selection problems, governments in many advanced countries assume the role of providing health insurance to their citizens. The U.S. government, through

EM-20 Enrichment Modules

its various health insurance programs including Medicare, Medicaid, and the Children's Health Insurance Program, now disburses more than half the total payments for medical care in the United States.

In general, people or firms faced with the problem of adverse selection follow one of several well-established strategies for dealing with it. One strategy is **screening**: using observable information to make inferences about private information. If you apply to purchase health insurance, you'll find that the insurance company will demand documentation of your health status in an attempt to "screen out" sicker applicants, whom they will refuse to insure or will insure only at very high premiums. Auto insurance also provides a very good example. An insurance company may not know whether you are a careful driver, but it has statistical data on the accident rates of people who resemble your profile—and it uses those data in setting premiums. A 19-year-old male who drives a sports car and has already had a fender-bender is likely to pay a very high premium. A 40-year-old female who drives a minivan and has never had an accident is likely to pay much less. In some cases, this may be quite unfair: some adolescent males are very careful drivers, and some mature women drive their minivans as if they were fighter jets. But nobody can deny that the insurance companies are right on average.

Adverse selection can be reduced through **screening**: using observable information about people to make inferences about their private information.

Another strategy is for people who are good prospects to somehow *signal* their private information. **Signaling** involves taking some action that wouldn't be worth taking unless they were indeed good prospects. Reputable used-car dealers often offer warranties—promises to repair any problems with the cars they sell that arise within a given amount of time. This isn't just a way of insuring their customers against possible expenses; it's a way of credibly showing that they are not selling lemons. As a result, more sales occur and dealers can command higher prices for their used cars.

Finally, in the face of adverse selection, it can be very valuable to establish a good **reputation**: a used-car dealership will often advertise how long it has been in business to show that it has continued to satisfy its customers. As a result, new customers will be willing to purchase cars and to pay more for that dealer's cars.

Adverse selection can be diminished by people **signaling** their private information through actions that credibly reveal what they know.

A long-term **reputation** allows an individual to assure others that he or she isn't concealing adverse private information.

Moral Hazard

In the late 1970s, New York and other major cities experienced an epidemic of suspicious fires—fires that appeared to be deliberately set. Some of the fires were probably started by teenagers on a lark, others by gang members struggling over turf. But investigators eventually became aware of patterns in a number of the fires. Particular landlords who owned several buildings seemed to have an unusually large number of their buildings burn down. Although it was difficult to prove, police had few doubts that most of these fire-prone landlords were hiring professional arsonists to torch their own properties.

Why burn your own buildings? These buildings were typically in declining neighborhoods, where rising crime rates and middle-class flight had led to a decline in property values. But the insurance policies on the buildings were written to compensate owners based on historical property values, and so would pay the owner of a destroyed building more than the building was worth in the current market. For an unscrupulous landlord who knew the right people, this presented a profitable opportunity.

The arson epidemic became less severe during the 1980s, partly because insurance companies began making it difficult to over-insure properties and partly because a boom in real estate values made many previously arson-threatened buildings worth more unburned.

The arson episodes make it clear that it is a bad idea for insurance companies to let customers insure buildings for more than their value—it gives the customers some destructive incentives. However, you might think that the incentive problem would go away as long as the insurance is no more than 100% of the value of what is being insured.

But, unfortunately, anything close to 100% insurance still distorts incentives—it induces policyholders to behave differently from how they would in the absence of insurance. The reason is that preventing fires requires effort and cost on the part of a building's owner. Fire alarms and sprinkler systems have to be kept in good repair, fire safety rules have to be strictly enforced, and so on. All of this takes time and money—time and

Module C The Economics of Information EM-21

Would you be more careful with fire if you didn't have fire insurance?

Moral hazard arises when an individual knows more about his or her own actions than other people do. This leads to a distortion of incentives to take care or to exert effort when someone else bears the costs of the lack of care or effort.

A **deductible** is a sum specified in an insurance policy that the insured individuals must pay before being compensated for a claim; deductibles reduce moral hazard.

money that the owner may not find worth spending if the insurance policy will provide close to full compensation for any losses.

Of course, the insurance company could specify in the policy that it won't pay if basic safety precautions have not been taken. But it isn't always easy to tell how careful a building's owner has been—the owner knows, but the insurance company does not.

The point is that the building's owner has private information about his or her own actions; the owner knows whether he or she has really taken all appropriate precautions. As a result, the insurance company is likely to face greater claims than if it were able to determine exactly how much effort a building owner exerts to prevent a loss. The problem of distorted incentives arises when an individual has private information about his or her own actions but someone else bears the costs of a lack of care or effort. This problem is known as **moral hazard**.

To deal with moral hazard, it is necessary to give individuals with private information some personal stake in what happens, a stake that gives them a reason to exert effort even if others cannot verify that they have done so. Moral hazard is the reason salespeople in many stores receive a commission on sales: it's hard for managers to be sure how hard the salespeople are really working, and if they were paid only straight salary, they would not have an incentive to exert effort to make those sales. Similar logic explains why many stores and restaurants, even if they are part of national chains, are actually franchises, licensed outlets owned by the people who run them.

Insurance companies deal with moral hazard by requiring a **deductible**: they compensate for losses only above a certain amount, so that coverage is always less than 100%. The insurance on your car, for example, may pay for repairs only after the first $500 in loss. This means that a careless driver who gets into a fender-bender will end up paying $500 for repairs even if he is insured, which provides at least some incentive to be careful and reduces moral hazard.

In addition to reducing moral hazard, deductibles provide a partial solution to the problem of adverse selection. Your insurance premium often drops substantially if you are willing to accept a large deductible. This is an attractive option to people who know they are low-risk customers; it is less attractive to people who know they are high-risk—and so are likely to have an accident and end up paying the deductible. By offering a menu of policies with different premiums and deductibles, insurance companies can screen their customers, inducing them to sort themselves out on the basis of their private information.

As the example of deductibles suggests, moral hazard limits the ability of the economy to allocate risks efficiently. You generally can't get full (100%) insurance on your home or car, even though you would like to buy full insurance, and you bear the risk of large deductibles, even though you would prefer not to.

ENRICHMENT MODULE C Review

Check Your Understanding

1. Your car insurance premiums are lower if you have had no moving violations for several years. Explain how this feature tends to decrease the potential inefficiency caused by adverse selection.
2. A common feature of home construction contracts is that when it costs more to construct a building than was originally estimated, the contractor must absorb the additional cost. Explain how this feature reduces the problem of moral hazard but also forces the contractor to bear more risk than she would like.
3. True or false? Explain your answer, stating what concept discussed in this module accounts for the feature.

   People with higher deductibles on their auto insurance

   a. generally drive more carefully.

   b. pay lower premiums.

Check Your Understanding

1. The inefficiency caused by adverse selection is that an insurance policy with a premium based on the average risk of all drivers will attract only an adverse selection of bad drivers. Good (i.e., safe) drivers will find this insurance premium too expensive and so will remain uninsured. This is inefficient. However, safe drivers are also those drivers who have had fewer moving violations for several years. Lowering premiums for only those drivers allows the insurance company to screen its customers and sell insurance to safe drivers, too. This means that at least some of the good drivers now are also insured, which decreases the inefficiency that arises from adverse selection. In a way, having no moving violations for several years is a way of building a reputation as a safe driver.

2. The moral hazard problem in home construction arises from private information about what the contractor does: whether she takes care to reduce the cost of construction or allows costs to increase. The homeowner cannot, or can only imperfectly, observe the cost-reduction efforts of the contractor. If the contractor were fully reimbursed for all costs incurred during construction, she would have no incentive to reduce costs. Making the contractor responsible for any additional costs above the original estimate means that she now has an incentive to keep costs low. However, this imposes risk on the contractor. For instance, if the weather is bad, home construction will take longer, and will be more costly, than if the weather had been good. Since the contractor pays for any additional costs (such as weather-induced delays) above the original estimate, she now faces risk that she cannot control.

3. a. True. Drivers with higher deductibles have more incentive to take care in their driving in order to avoid paying the deductible. The high deductibles are a way of reducing problems with moral hazard.

b. True. Suppose you know that you are a safe driver. You have a choice of a policy with a high premium but a low deductible or one with a lower premium but a higher deductible. In this case, you would be more inclined to choose the cheap policy with the high deductible because you know that you will be unlikely to have to pay the deductible. When there is adverse selection, insurance companies use screening devices such as this to infer private information about how skillful people are as drivers.

We provide these review questions in addition to discussion starters in case you or the AP® program chooses a rigorous approach to this material.

Multiple-Choice Review Questions

1. Which of the following is true about private information?
   I. It has value.
   II. Everyone has access to it.
   III. It can distort economic decisions.
   a. I only
   b. II only
   c. III only
   d. I and III only
   e. I, II, and III
2. Due to adverse selection,
   a mutually beneficial trades go unexploited.
   b. people buy lemons rather than other fruit.
   c. sick people buy less insurance.
   d. private information is available to all.
   e. public information is available to no one.
3. When colleges use grade point averages to make admissions decisions, they are employing which strategy?
   a. signaling
   b. screening
   c. profit maximization
   d. marginal analysis
   e. adverse selection
4. Moral hazard is the result of
   a. asymmetric information.
   b. signaling.
   c. toxic waste.
   d. adverse selection.
   e. public information.
5. A deductible is used by insurance companies to
   a. allow customers to pay for insurance premiums using payroll deduction.
   b. deal with moral hazard.
   c. make public information private.
   d. compensate policyholders fully for their losses.
   e. avoid all payments to policyholders.

Free-Response Review Questions

1. Identify whether each of the following situations reflects moral hazard or adverse selection. Propose a potential solution to reduce the inefficiency that each situation creates.
   a. When you buy a second-hand car, you do not know whether it is a lemon (low quality) or a plum (high quality), but the seller knows.
   b. People with dental insurance might not brush their teeth as often, knowing that if they get cavities, the insurance will pay for the fillings.
   c. A company does not know whether individual workers on an assembly line are working hard or slacking off.
   d. When making a decision about hiring you, prospective employers do not know whether or not you are a productive worker.

Rubric for FRQ 1 (8 points)

1 point: Adverse selection

1 point: Sellers could offer a warranty with the car that pays for repair costs.

1 point: Moral hazard

1 point: Each insured person can be made to pay a co-payment of a certain dollar amount each time he or she gets a filling.

1 point: Moral hazard

1 point: Pay the workers "piece rates," that is, pay them according to how much they have produced each day.

1 point: Adverse selection

1 point: Provide potential employers with references from previous employers.

2. Suppose individuals or corporations (for example home-buyers or banks) believe that the government will "bail them out" in the event that their decisions lead to a financial collapse. This is an example of what problem created by asymmetric information? How does this situation lead to inefficiency? What is a possible remedy for the problem?
   (3 points)

Discussion Starters

1. In what situations have you experienced asymmetric information? What screening or signaling was involved?
2. Do you experience moral hazard by taking fewer precautions when the cost of damage would be at least partially someone else's problem? For example, this might be the case when a product is under warranty, a car or home is being rented, or insurance would cover the cost of damage.
3. Describe a case in which you used a seller's reputation to deal with asymmetric information.

Multiple-Choice Review Questions

1. d
2. a
3. b
4. a
5. b

Free-Response Review Question

Rubric for FRQ 2 (3 points)

1 point: This is an example of moral hazard.

1 point: The government bears the cost of any lack of care in the individual/corporate decisions. Distorted incentives lead the individual/corporation to make riskier decisions because, if a decision is bad, the cost falls on others.

1 point: The individuals/corporations must be given a personal stake in the result of their decisions. This could be achieved by making the individuals/corporations repay at least some portion of the bailout cost.

Discussion Starters

Following are possible answers to the Discussion Starter questions:

1. Students might discuss experiences with job seeking or the purchase of used goods or insurance. In a hiring situation, perhaps they took a screening test. When purchasing car insurance, they would have revealed information about their driving record. These are among many possible examples.
2. Students might take fewer precautions when their parents would pay for the damage, when they are insured, or when the personal property at risk belongs to someone else.
3. Answers might involve the purchase of concert tickets or other items online.

TEACH Teach It

TRM The answers to the end-of-module questions are included in the margins for this module. Some additional support material may be found in the TRM.

clickstock/iStock/Getty Images

ENRICHMENT MODULE

D Indifference Curves and Consumer Choice

In this Module, you will learn to:

- Explain why economists use indifference curves to illustrate a person's preferences
- Discuss the importance of the marginal rate of substitution, the rate at which a consumer is just willing to substitute one good for another
- Use indifference curves and the budget line to find a consumer's optimal consumption bundle

Mapping the Utility Function

Earlier we introduced the concept of a utility function, which determines a consumer's total utility, given his or her consumption bundle. Here we will extend the analysis by learning how to express total utility as a function of the consumption of two goods. This will deepen our understanding of the trade-offs involved when choosing the optimal consumption bundle. We will also see how the optimal consumption bundle itself changes in response to changes in the prices of goods. We begin by examining a different way of representing a consumer's utility function, based on the concept of *indifference curves*.

Indifference Curves

Ingrid is a consumer who buys only two goods: housing, measured by the number of rooms in her house or apartment, and restaurant meals. How can we represent her utility function in a way that takes account of her consumption of both goods?

One way is to draw a three-dimensional picture. **Figure D.1** shows a three-dimensional "utility hill." The distance along the horizontal axis measures the quantity of housing Ingrid consumes in terms of the number of rooms; the distance along the vertical axis measures the number of restaurant meals she consumes. The altitude or height of the hill at each point is indicated by a contour line, along which the height of the hill is constant. For example, point *A*, which corresponds to a consumption bundle of 3 rooms and 30 restaurant meals, and point *B*, which corresponds to a bundle of 6 rooms and 15 restaurant meals, lie on the contour line labeled 450. So the total utility Ingrid receives from consuming either of these bundles is 450 utils.

EM-24 Enrichment Modules

Figure D.1 Ingrid's Utility Function

The three-dimensional hill shows how Ingrid's total utility depends on her consumption of housing and restaurant meals. Point *A* corresponds to consumption of 3 rooms and 30 restaurant meals. That consumption bundle yields Ingrid 450 utils, corresponding to the height of the hill at point *A*. The lines running around the hill are contour lines, along which the height is constant. So point *B* and every other point along the same contour line as point *A* generates the same level of utility.

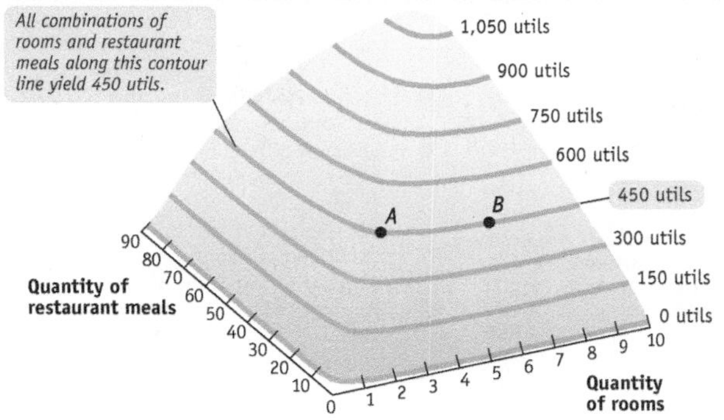

A three-dimensional picture like Figure D.1 helps us think about the relationship between consumption bundles and total utility. But anyone who has ever used a topographical map to plan a hiking trip knows that it is possible to represent a three-dimensional surface in only two dimensions. A topographical map doesn't offer a three-dimensional view of the terrain; instead, it conveys information about altitude solely through the use of contour lines.

The same principle can be applied to the representation of a utility function. In **Figure D.2**, Ingrid's consumption of rooms is measured on the horizontal axis and her consumption of restaurant meals on the vertical axis. The curve here corresponds to the contour line in Figure D.1, drawn at a total utility of 450 utils. This curve shows

Figure D.2 An Indifference Curve

An indifference curve is a contour line along which total utility is constant. In this case, we show all the consumption bundles that yield Ingrid 450 utils. Consumption bundle *A*, consisting of 3 rooms and 30 restaurant meals, yields the same total utility as bundle *B*, consisting of 6 rooms and 15 restaurant meals. That is, Ingrid is indifferent between bundle *A* and bundle *B*.

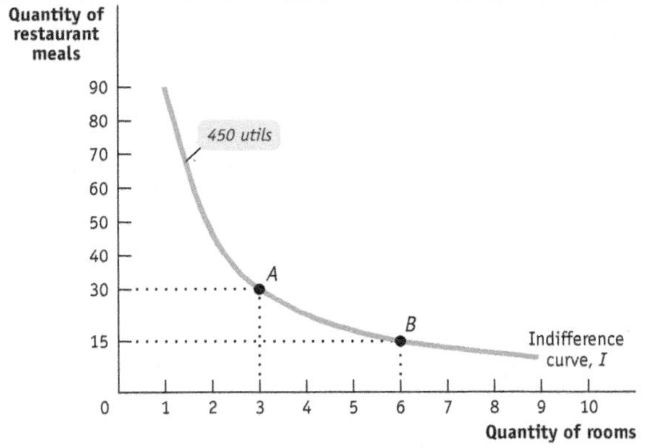

Module D Indifference Curves and Consumer Choice **EM-25**

all the consumption bundles that yield a total utility of 450 utils As we've seen, one point on that contour line is *A*, a consumption bundle consisting of 3 rooms and 30 restaurant meals. Another point on that contour line is *B*, a consumption bundle consisting of 6 rooms but only 15 restaurant meals. Because *B* lies on the same contour line, it yields Ingrid the same total utility—450 utils—as *A*. We say that Ingrid is *indifferent* between *A* and *B*: because bundles *A* and *B* yield the same total utility level, Ingrid is equally well off with either bundle.

An **indifference curve** shows all the consumption bundles that yield the same amount of total utility for an individual.

The entire utility function of an individual can be represented by an **indifference curve map**—a collection of indifference curves, each of which corresponds to a different total utility level.

A contour line that represents consumption bundles that give a particular individual the same amount of total utility is known as an **indifference curve**. An individual is always indifferent between any two bundles that lie on the same indifference curve. For a given consumer, there is an indifference curve corresponding to each possible level of total utility. For example, the indifference curve in Figure D.2 shows consumption bundles that yield Ingrid 450 utils; different indifference curves would show consumption bundles that yield Ingrid 400 utils, 500 utils, and so on.

A collection of indifference curves that represents a given consumer's entire utility function, with each indifference curve corresponding to a different level of total utility, is known as an **indifference curve map**. **Figure D.3** shows three indifference curves—I_1, I_2, and I_3—from Ingrid's indifference curve map, as well as several consumption bundles, *A*, *B*, *C*, and *D*. The accompanying table lists each bundle, its composition of rooms and restaurant meals, and the total utility it provides. Because bundles *A* and *B* generate the same number of utils, 450, they lie on the same indifference curve, I_2.

Although Ingrid is indifferent between *A* and *B*, she is certainly not indifferent between *A* and *C*: as you can see from the table, *C* generates only 391 utils, fewer than *A* or *B*. So Ingrid prefers consumption bundles *A* and *B* to bundle *C*. This is evident from the graph because *C* is on indifference curve I_1, and I_1 lies below I_2. Bundle *D*, though,

Figure D.3 An Indifference Curve Map

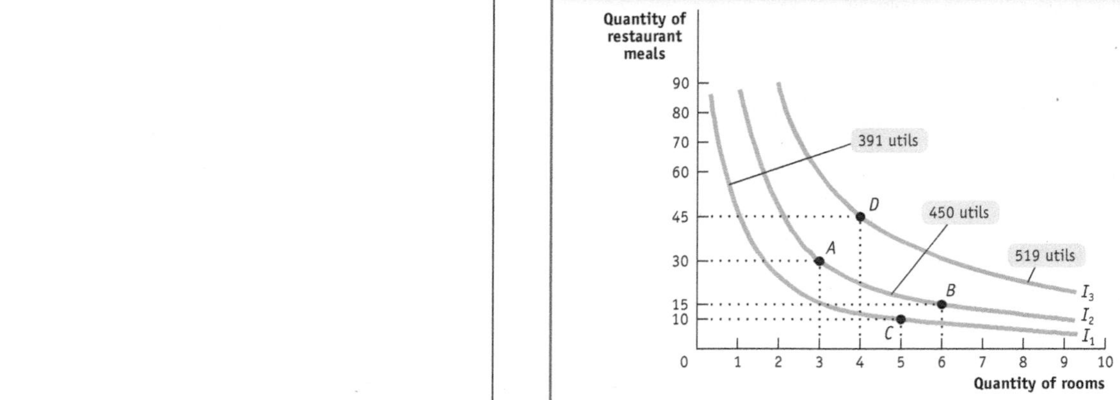

Consumption bundle	Quantity of rooms	Quantity of meals	Total utility (utils)
A	3	30	450
B	6	15	450
C	5	10	391
D	4	45	519

The utility function can be represented in greater detail by increasing the number of indifference curves drawn, each corresponding to a different level of total utility. In this figure, bundle *C* lies on an indifference curve corresponding to a total utility of 391 utils. As in Figure D.2, bundles *A* and *B* lie on an indifference curve corresponding to a total utility of 450 utils. Bundle *D* lies on an indifference curve corresponding to a total utility of 519 utils. Ingrid prefers any bundle on I_2 to any bundle on I_1, and she prefers any bundle on I_3 to any bundle on I_2.

EM-26 Enrichment Modules

FYI Are Utils Useful?

In the table that accompanies Figure D.3, we give the number of utils achieved on each of the indifference curves shown in the figure. But is this information actually needed?

The answer is no. As you will see shortly, the indifference curve map tells us all we need to know in order to find a consumer's optimal consumption bundle. That is, it's important that Ingrid has higher total utility along indifference curve I_2 than she does along I_1, but it doesn't matter *how much higher* her total utility is. In other words, we don't have to measure utils in order to understand how consumers make choices.

Economists say that consumer theory requires an *ordinal* measure of utility—one that ranks consumption bundles in terms of desirability—so that we can say that bundle *X* is better than bundle *Y*. The theory does not, however, require *cardinal* utility, which actually assigns a specific number to the total utility yielded by each bundle.

So why introduce the concept of utils at all? The answer is that it is much easier to understand the basis of rational choice by using the concept of measurable utility.

generates 519 utils, more than *A* and *B*. So bundle D is on indifference curve I_3, which lies above I_2. Clearly, Ingrid prefers *D* to either *A* or *B*. And, even more strongly, she prefers *D* to *C*.

Properties of Indifference Curves

No two individuals have the same indifference curve map because no two individuals have the same preferences. But economists believe that, regardless of the person, every indifference curve map has two general properties. These are illustrated in panel (a) of **Figure D.4** on the next page.

a. *Indifference curves never cross.* Suppose that we tried to draw an indifference curve map like the one depicted in the left diagram in panel (a), in which two indifference curves cross at *A*. What is the total utility at *A*? Is it 100 utils or 200 utils? Indifference curves cannot cross because each consumption bundle must correspond to one unique total utility level—not, as shown at *A*, two different total utility levels.

b. *The farther out an indifference curve lies—the farther it is from the origin—the higher the level of total utility it indicates.* The reason, illustrated in the right diagram in panel (a), is that we assume that more is better—we consider only the consumption bundles for which the consumer is not satiated. Bundle *B*, on the outer indifference curve, contains more of both goods than bundle *A* on the inner indifference curve. So *B*, because it generates a higher total utility level (200 utils), lies on a higher indifference curve than *A*.

Furthermore, economists believe that, for most goods, consumers' indifference curve maps also have two additional properties. They are illustrated in panel (b) of Figure D.4:

c. *Indifference curves slope downward.* Here, too, the reason is that more is better. The left diagram in panel (b) shows four consumption bundles on the same indifference curve: *W*, *X*, *Y*, and *Z*. By definition, these consumption bundles yield the same level of total utility. But as you move along the curve to the right, from *W* to *Z*, the quantity of rooms consumed increases. The only way a person can consume more rooms without gaining utility is by giving up some restaurant meals. So the indifference curve must slope downward.

d. *Indifference curves have a convex shape.* The right diagram in panel (b) shows that the slope of each indifference curve changes as you move down the curve to the right: the curve gets flatter. If you move up an indifference curve to the left, the curve gets steeper. So the indifference curve is steeper at *A* than it is at *B*. When this occurs, we say that an indifference curve has a *convex* shape—it is bowed-in toward the origin. This feature arises from diminishing marginal utility, a principle we discussed in

Module D Indifference Curves and Consumer Choice **EM-27**

Figure D.4 Properties of Indifference Curves

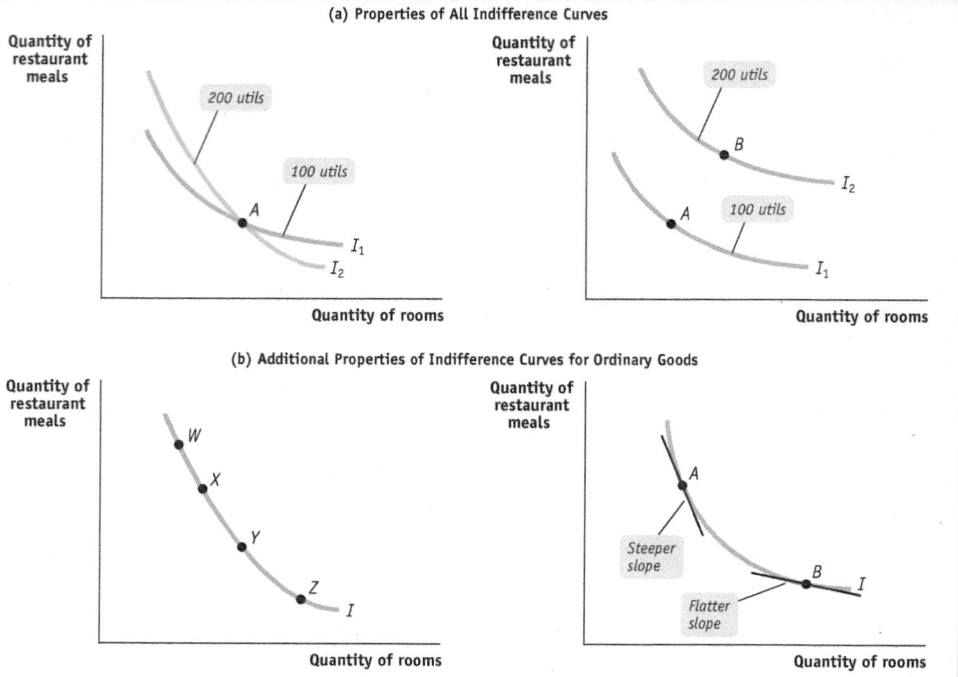

Panel (a) represents two general properties that all indifference curves share. The left diagram shows why indifference curves cannot cross: if they did, a consumption bundle such as *A* would yield both 100 and 200 utils, a contradiction. The right diagram of panel (a) shows that indifference curves that are farther out yield higher total utility: bundle *B*, which contains more of both goods than bundle *A*, yields higher total utility. Panel (b) depicts two additional properties of indifference curves for ordinary goods. The left diagram of panel (b) shows that indifference curves slope downward: as you move down the curve from bundle *W* to bundle *Z*, consumption of rooms increases. To keep total utility constant, this must be offset by a reduction in quantity of restaurant meals. The right diagram of panel (b) shows a convex-shaped indifference curve. The slope of the indifference curve gets flatter as you move down the curve to the right, a feature arising from diminishing marginal utility.

Module 51. Recall that when a consumer has diminishing marginal utility, consumption of another unit of a good generates a smaller increase in total utility than the previous unit consumed. Next we will examine in detail how diminishing marginal utility gives rise to convex-shaped indifference curves.

Goods that satisfy all four properties of indifference curve maps are called *ordinary goods*. The vast majority of goods in any consumer's utility function fall into this category. In the next section we will define ordinary goods more precisely and see the key role that diminishing marginal utility plays for them.

EM-28 Enrichment Modules

Indifference Curves and Consumer Choice

In the previous section we used indifference curves to represent the preferences of Ingrid, whose consumption bundles consist of rooms and restaurant meals. Our next step is to show how to use Ingrid's indifference curve map to find her utility-maximizing consumption bundle, given her budget constraint, which exists because she must choose a consumption bundle that costs no more than her total income.

It's important to understand how our analysis here relates to what we did in Module 51. We are not offering a new theory of consumer behavior in this module—consumers are assumed to maximize total utility as before. In particular, we know that consumers will follow the *optimal consumption rule*: the optimal consumption bundle lies on the budget line, and the marginal utility per dollar is the same for every good in the bundle.

But as we'll see shortly, we can derive this optimal consumer behavior in a somewhat different way—a way that yields deeper insights into consumer choice.

The Marginal Rate of Substitution

The first element of our approach is a new concept, the *marginal rate of substitution.* We'll see that this concept is tied closely to the shape of the indifference curve, which gets flatter moving from left to right, as illustrated in **Figure D.5**.

We have just seen that for most goods, consumers' indifference curves are downward-sloping and convex. Figure D.5 shows such an indifference curve. The points labeled *V*, *W*, *X*, *Y*, and *Z* all lie on this indifference curve—that is, they represent consumption bundles that yield Ingrid the same level of total utility. The table accompanying the figure shows the components of each of the bundles. As we move along the indifference

Figure D.5 The Changing Slope of an Indifference Curve

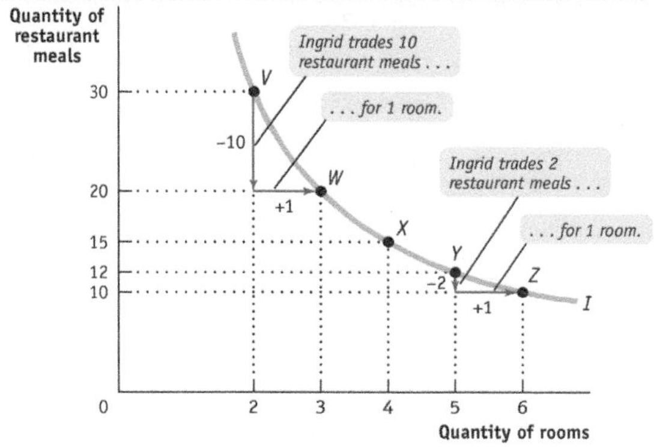

Consumption bundle	Quantity of rooms	Quantity of restaurant meals
V	2	30
W	3	20
X	4	15
Y	5	12
Z	6	10

This indifference curve is downward-sloping and convex, implying that restaurant meals and rooms are ordinary goods for Ingrid. As Ingrid moves down her indifference curve from *V* to *Z*, she gives up restaurant meals in exchange for a larger number of rooms. However, the terms of that trade-off change. As she moves from *V* to *W*, she is willing to give up 10 restaurant meals in return for 1 more room. As her consumption of rooms rises and her consumption of restaurant meals falls, she is willing to give up fewer restaurant meals in return for each additional room. The flattening of the slope as she moves from left to right arises from diminishing marginal utility.

Module D Indifference Curves and Consumer Choice **EM-29**

curve from V to Z, Ingrid's consumption of housing steadily increases from 2 rooms to 6 rooms, her consumption of restaurant meals steadily decreases from 30 meals to 10 meals, and her total utility is kept constant. As we move down the indifference curve, then, Ingrid is trading more of one good for less of the other, with the *terms* of that trade-off—the ratio of additional rooms consumed to restaurant meals sacrificed—chosen to keep her total utility constant.

Notice that the quantity of restaurant meals that Ingrid is willing to give up in return for an additional room changes along the indifference curve. As we move from V to W, housing consumption rises from 2 to 3 rooms and restaurant meal consumption falls from 30 to 20—a trade-off of 10 restaurant meals for 1 additional room. But as we move from Y to Z, housing consumption rises from 5 to 6 rooms and restaurant meal consumption falls from 12 to 10, a trade-off of only 2 restaurant meals for an additional room.

To put it in terms of slope, the slope of the indifference curve between V and W is −10: the change in restaurant meal consumption, −10, divided by the change in housing consumption, 1. Similarly, the slope of the indifference curve between Y and Z is −2. So the indifference curve gets flatter as we move down it to the right—that is, it has a convex shape, one of the four properties of an indifference curve for ordinary goods.

Why does the trade-off change in this way? Let's think about it intuitively and then work through it more carefully. When Ingrid moves down her indifference curve, whether from V to W or from Y to Z, she gains utility from her additional consumption of housing but loses an equal amount of utility from her reduced consumption of restaurant meals. But at each step, the initial position from which Ingrid begins is different. At V, Ingrid consumes only a small quantity of rooms; because of diminishing marginal utility, her marginal utility per room at that point is high. At V, then, an additional room adds a lot to Ingrid's total utility. But at V she already consumes a large quantity of restaurant meals, so her marginal utility of restaurant meals is low at that point. This means that it takes a large reduction in her quantity of restaurant meals consumed to offset the increased utility she gets from the extra room of housing.

At Y, in contrast, Ingrid consumes a much larger quantity of rooms and a much smaller quantity of restaurant meals than at V. This means that an additional room adds fewer utils, and a restaurant meal forgone costs more utils, than at V. So Ingrid is willing to give up fewer restaurant meals in return for another room of housing at Y (where she gives up 2 meals for 1 room) than she is at V (where she gives up 10 meals for 1 room).

Now let's express the same idea—that the trade-off Ingrid is willing to make depends on where she is starting from—by using a little math. We do this by examining how the slope of the indifference curve changes as we move down it. Moving down the indifference curve—reducing restaurant meal consumption and increasing housing consumption—will produce two opposing effects on Ingrid's total utility: lower restaurant meal consumption will reduce her total utility, but higher housing consumption will raise her total utility. And since we are moving down the indifference curve, these two effects must exactly cancel out:

Along the indifference curve:

(D-1) (Change in total utility due to lower restaurant meal consumption) + (Change in total utility due to higher housing consumption) = 0

or, rearranging terms,

Along the indifference curve:

(D-2) −(Change in total utility due to lower restaurant meal consumption) = (Change in total utility due to higher housing consumption)

Let's now focus on what happens as we move only a short distance down the indifference curve, trading off a small increase in housing consumption in place of a small

EM-30 Enrichment Modules

decrease in restaurant meal consumption. Following our notation from before, let's use MU_R and MU_M to represent the marginal utility of rooms and restaurant meals, respectively, and ΔQ_R and ΔQ_M to represent the changes in room and meal consumption, respectively. In general, the change in total utility caused by a small change in consumption of a good is equal to the change in consumption multiplied by the *marginal utility* of that good. This means that we can calculate the change in Ingrid's total utility generated by a change in her consumption bundle using the following equations:

(D-3) Change in total utility due to a change in restaurant meal consumption $= MU_M \times \Delta Q_M$

and

(D-4) Change in total utility due to a change in housing consumption $= MU_R \times \Delta Q_R$

So we can write Equation D-2 in symbols as:

Along the indifference curve:

(D-5) $-MU_M \times \Delta Q_M = MU_R \times \Delta Q_R$

Note that the left-hand side of Equation D-5 has a negative sign; it represents the loss in total utility from decreased restaurant meal consumption. This must equal the gain in total utility from increased room consumption, represented by the right-hand side of the equation.

What we want to know is how this translates into the slope of the indifference curve. To find the slope, we divide both sides of Equation D-5 by ΔQ_R, and again by $-MU_M$, in order to get the ΔQ_M, ΔQ_R terms on one side and the MU_R, MU_M terms on the other. This results in:

(D-6) *Along the indifference curve:* $\frac{\Delta Q_M}{\Delta Q_R} = -\frac{MU_R}{MU_M}$

The left-hand side of Equation D-6 is the slope of the indifference curve; it is the rate at which Ingrid is willing to trade rooms (the good on the horizontal axis) for restaurant meals (the good on the vertical axis) without changing her total utility level. The right-hand side of Equation D-6 is the negative of the ratio of the marginal utility of rooms to the marginal utility of restaurant meals—that is, the ratio of what she gains from one more room to what she gains from one more meal, with a negative sign in front.

Putting all this together, Equation D-6 shows that, along the indifference curve, the quantity of restaurant meals Ingrid is willing to give up in return for a room, $\frac{\Delta Q_M}{\Delta Q_R}$, is exactly equal to the negative of the ratio of the marginal utility of a room to that of a meal, $-\frac{MU_R}{MU_M}$. Only when this condition is met will her total utility level remain constant as she consumes more rooms and fewer restaurant meals.

Economists have a special name for the ratio of the marginal utilities found in the right-hand side of Equation D-6: it is called the **marginal rate of substitution**, or ***MRS***, of rooms (the good on the horizontal axis) in place of restaurant meals (the good on the vertical axis). That's because as we slide down Ingrid's indifference curve, we are substituting more rooms for fewer restaurant meals in her consumption bundle. As we'll see shortly, the marginal rate of substitution plays an important role in finding the optimal consumption bundle.

The **marginal rate of substitution**, or ***MRS***, of good *R* in place of good *M* is equal to $\frac{MU_R}{MU_M}$, the ratio of the marginal utility of *R* to the marginal utility of *M*.

Module D Indifference Curves and Consumer Choice **EM-31**

Recall that indifference curves get flatter as you move down them to the right. The reason, as we've just discussed, is diminishing marginal utility: as Ingrid consumes more housing and fewer restaurant meals, her marginal utility from housing falls and her marginal utility from restaurant meals rises. So her marginal rate of substitution, which is equal to the negative of the slope of her indifference curve, falls as she moves down the indifference curve.

The flattening of indifference curves as you slide down them to the right—which reflects the same logic as the principle of diminishing marginal utility—is known as the principle of **diminishing marginal rate of substitution**. It says that the more of one good an individual consumes in proportion to a second good, the less of the second good he or she is willing to give up in exchange for another unit of the first good.

The principle of **diminishing marginal rate of substitution** states that the more of one good a person consumes in proportion to a second good, the less of the second good he or she is willing to substitute for another unit of the first good.

Two goods are **ordinary goods** in a consumer's utility function when (1) the consumer requires additional units of one good to compensate for fewer units of the other; and (2) the consumer experiences a diminishing marginal rate of substitution when substituting one good for the other.

We can illustrate this point by referring back to Figure D.5. At point *V*, a bundle with a low proportion of rooms to restaurant meals, Ingrid is willing to forgo 10 restaurant meals in return for 1 room. But at point *Y*, a bundle with a high proportion of rooms to restaurant meals, she is willing to forgo only 2 restaurant meals in return for 1 room.

From this example we can see that, in Ingrid's utility function, rooms and restaurant meals possess the two additional properties that characterize ordinary goods. Ingrid requires additional rooms to compensate her for the loss of a meal, and vice versa; so her indifference curves for these two goods slope downward. And her indifference curves are convex: the slope of her indifference curve—*the negative of* the marginal rate of substitution—becomes flatter as we move down it. In fact, an indifference curve is convex only when it has a diminishing marginal rate of substitution—these two conditions are equivalent.

With this information, we can define *ordinary goods,* which account for the great majority of all goods. A pair of goods are **ordinary goods** in a consumer's utility function if they possess two properties: the consumer requires more of one good to compensate for less of the other, and the consumer experiences a diminishing marginal rate of substitution when substituting one good for the other.

Next we will see how to determine Ingrid's optimal consumption bundle using indifference curves.

The Tangency Condition

Now let's put some of Ingrid's indifference curves on the same diagram as her budget line to illustrate her optimal consumption choice. **Figure D.6** shows Ingrid's budget

Figure D.6 The Optimal Consumption Bundle

The budget line, *BL*, shows Ingrid's possible consumption bundles, given an income of $2,400 per month, when rooms cost $150 per month and restaurant meals cost $30 each. I_1, I_2, and I_3 are indifference curves. Consumption bundles such as *B* and *C* are not optimal because Ingrid can move to a higher indifference curve. The optimal consumption bundle is *A*, where the budget line is just tangent to the highest possible indifference curve.

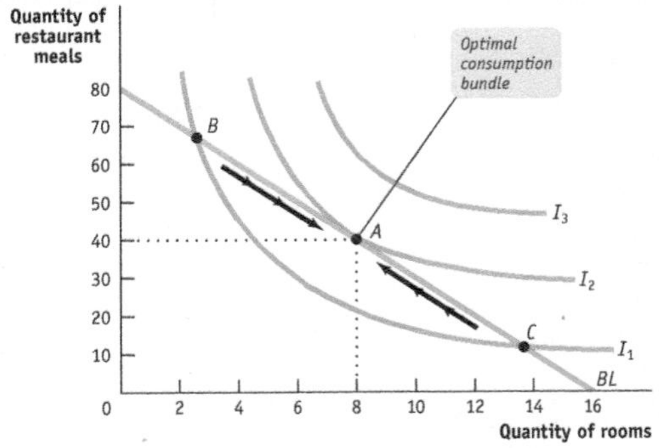

EM-32 Enrichment Modules

line, *BL*, when her income is $2,400 per month, housing costs $150 per room each month, and restaurant meals cost $30 each. What is her optimal consumption bundle?

To answer this question, we consider three of Ingrid's indifference curves: I_1, I_2, and I_3. Of these curves, I_3 represents the highest total utility level, but Ingrid cannot afford to reach that level because she is constrained by her income: no consumption bundle on her budget line yields that much total utility. But she shouldn't settle for the total utility level generated by *B*, which lies on I_1: there are other bundles on her budget line, such as *A*, that clearly yield more total utility than *B*.

In fact, *A*—a consumption bundle consisting of 8 rooms and 40 restaurant meals per month—is Ingrid's optimal consumption choice. The reason is that *A* lies on the highest indifference curve Ingrid can reach given her income.

At the optimal consumption bundle *A*, Ingrid's budget line *just touches* the relevant indifference curve—the budget line is *tangent* to the indifference curve. This **tangency condition** between the indifference curve and the budget line applies to the optimal consumption bundle when the indifference curves have the typical convex shape.

The **tangency condition** between the indifference curve and the budget line holds when the indifference curve and the budget line just touch. This condition determines the optimal consumption bundle when the indifference curves have the typical convex shape.

To see why, let's look more closely at how we know that a consumption bundle that *doesn't* satisfy the tangency condition can't be optimal. Reexamining Figure D.6, we can see that consumption bundles *B* and *C* are both affordable because they lie on the budget line. However, neither is optimal. Both of them lie on the indifference curve I_1, which cuts through the budget line at both points. But because I_1 cuts through the budget line, Ingrid can do better: she can move down the budget line from *B* or up the budget line from *C*, as indicated by the arrows. In each case, this allows her to get onto a higher indifference curve, I_2, which increases her total utility.

However, Ingrid cannot do any better than I_2: any other indifference curve either cuts through her budget line or doesn't touch it at all. And the bundle that allows her to achieve I_2, of course, is her optimal consumption bundle.

The Slope of the Budget Line

Figure D.6 shows us how to use a graph of the budget line and the indifference curves to find the optimal consumption bundle, the bundle at which the budget line and the indifference curve are tangent. But rather than rely on drawing graphs, we can determine the optimal consumption bundle by using a bit more math. As you can see from Figure D.6, the budget line and the indifference curve have the same slope at the optimal consumption bundle, *A*. Why? Because two curves can only be tangent to each other if they have the same slope at the point where they meet. Otherwise, they would cross each other at that point. And we know that if we are on an indifference curve that crosses the budget line (like I_1, in Figure D.6), we can't be on the indifference curve that contains the optimal consumption bundle (like I_2).

So we can use information about the slopes of the budget line and the indifference curve to find the optimal consumption bundle. To do that, we must first analyze the slope of the budget line, a fairly straightforward task. We know that Ingrid will get the highest possible utility by spending all of her income and consuming a bundle on her budget line. So we can represent Ingrid's budget line, made up of the consumption bundles available to her when she spends all of her income, with the equation:

$$\text{(D-7)} \qquad (Q_R \times P_R) + (Q_M \times P_M) = N$$

where *N* stands for Ingrid's income. To find the slope of the budget line, we divide its vertical intercept (where the budget line hits the vertical axis) by its horizontal intercept (where it hits the horizontal axis) and then add a negative sign. The vertical intercept is the point at which Ingrid spends all her income on restaurant meals and none on housing (that is, $Q_R = 0$). In that case the number of restaurant meals she consumes is:

$$\text{(D-8)} \quad Q_M = \frac{N}{P_M} = \$2{,}400/(\$30 \text{ per meal}) = 80 \text{ meals}$$

$$= \text{Vertical intercept of budget line}$$

Module D Indifference Curves and Consumer Choice EM-33

At the other extreme, Ingrid spends all her income on housing and none on restaurant meals (so that $Q_M = 0$). This means that at the horizontal intercept of the budget line, the number of rooms she consumes is:

$$\text{(D-9)} \qquad Q_R = \frac{N}{P_R} = \frac{\$2{,}400}{(\$150 \text{ per room})} = 16 \text{ rooms}$$
$$= \text{Horizontal intercept of budget line}$$

Now we have the information needed to find the slope of the budget line. It is:

$$\text{(D-10)} \qquad \text{Slope of budget line} = -\frac{\text{Vertical intercept}}{\text{Horizontal intercept}} = -\frac{\frac{N}{P_M}}{\frac{N}{P_R}} = -\frac{P_R}{P_M}$$

The **relative price** of good *R* in terms of good *M* is equal to $\frac{P_R}{P_M}$, the rate at which *R* trades for *M* in the market.

Notice the negative sign in Equation D-10; it's there because the budget line slopes downward. The quantity $\frac{P_R}{P_M}$ is known as the **relative price** of rooms in terms of restaurant meals, to distinguish it from an ordinary price in terms of dollars. Because buying one more room requires Ingrid to give up the quantity $\frac{P_R}{P_M}$ of restaurant meals, or 5 meals, we can interpret the relative price $\frac{P_R}{P_M}$ as the rate at which a room trades for restaurant meals in the market; it is the price—in terms of restaurant meals—Ingrid has to "pay" to get one more room.

Looking at this another way, the slope of the budget line—the negative of the relative price—tells us the opportunity cost of each good in terms of the other. The relative price illustrates the opportunity cost to an individual of consuming one more unit of one good in terms of how much of the other good in his or her consumption bundle must be forgone. This opportunity cost arises from the consumer's limited resources—his or her limited budget. It's useful to note that Equations D-8, D-9, and D-10 give us all the information we need about what happens to the budget line when relative price or income changes. From Equations D-8 and D-9 we can see that a change in income, *N*, leads to a parallel shift of the budget line: both the vertical and horizontal intercepts will shift. That is, how far out the budget line is from the origin depends on the consumer's income. If a consumer's income rises, the budget line moves outward. If the consumer's income shrinks, the budget line shifts inward. In each case, the slope of the budget line stays the same because the relative price of one good in terms of the other does not change.

In contrast, a change in the relative price $\frac{P_R}{P_M}$ will lead to a change in the slope of the budget line. We'll analyze these changes in the budget line and how the optimal consumption bundle changes when the relative price changes or when income changes in greater detail later in the module.

Prices and the Marginal Rate of Substitution

Now we're ready to bring together the slope of the budget line and the slope of the indifference curve to find the optimal consumption bundle. From Equation D-6, we know that the slope of the indifference curve at any point is equal to the negative of the marginal rate of substitution:

$$\text{(D-11)} \qquad \text{Slope of indifference curve} = -\frac{MU_R}{MU_M}$$

As we've already noted, at the optimal consumption bundle the slope of the budget line and the slope of the indifference curve are equal. We can write this formally by putting

EM-34 Enrichment Modules

Equations D-10 and D-11 together, which gives us the **relative price rule** for finding the optimal consumption bundle:

The **relative price rule** says that at the optimal consumption bundle, the marginal rate of substitution between two goods is equal to their relative price.

$$\text{(D-12)} \quad \textit{At the optimal consumption bundle: } -\frac{MU_R}{MU_M} = -\frac{P_R}{P_M}$$

$$\text{or, } \textit{cancelling the negative signs, } \frac{MU_R}{MU_M} = \frac{P_R}{P_M}$$

That is, at the optimal consumption bundle, the marginal rate of substitution between any two goods is equal to the ratio of their prices. To put it in a more intuitive way, starting with Ingrid's optimal consumption bundle, the rate at which she would trade a room for more restaurant meals along her indifference curve, $\frac{MU_R}{MU_M}$, is equal to the rate at which rooms are traded for restaurant meals in the market, $\frac{P_R}{P_M}$.

What would happen if this equality did not hold? We can see by examining **Figure D.7**. There, at point *B*, the slope of the indifference curve, $-\frac{MU_R}{MU_M}$, is greater in absolute value than the slope of the budget line, $-\frac{P_R}{P_M}$. This means that, at *B*, Ingrid values an additional room in place of meals *more* than it costs her to buy an additional room and forgo some meals. As a result, Ingrid would be better off moving down her budget line toward *A*, consuming more rooms and fewer restaurant meals—and because

Figure D.7 Understanding the Relative Price Rule

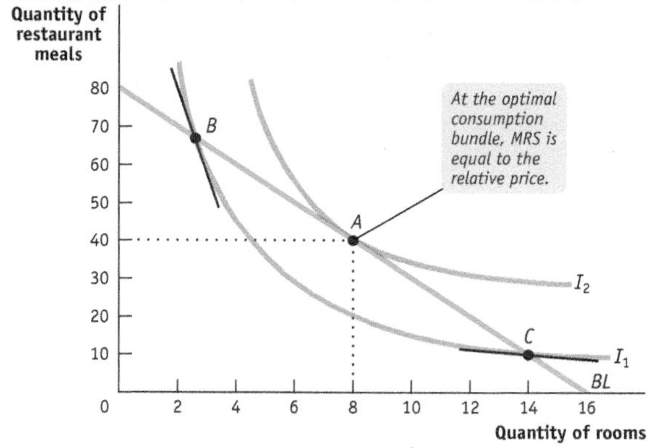

The *relative price* of rooms in terms of restaurant meals is equal to the negative of the slope of the budget line. The *marginal rate of substitution* of rooms for restaurant meals is equal to the negative of the slope of the indifference curve. The *relative price rule* says that at the optimal consumption bundle, the marginal rate of substitution must equal the relative price. This point can be demonstrated by considering what happens when the marginal rate of substitution is not equal to the relative price. At consumption bundle *B*, the marginal rate of substitution is larger than the relative price; Ingrid can increase her total utility by moving down her budget line, *BL*. At *C*, the marginal rate of substitution is smaller than the relative price, and Ingrid can increase her total utility by moving up the budget line. Only at *A*, where the relative price rule holds, is her total utility maximized, given her budget constraint.

Module D Indifference Curves and Consumer Choice **EM-35**

of that, B could not have been her optimal bundle! Likewise, at C, the slope of Ingrid's indifference curve is less in absolute value than the slope of the budget line. The implication is that, at C, Ingrid values additional meals in place of a room *more* than it costs her to buy additional meals and forgo a room. Again, Ingrid would be better off moving along her budget line—consuming more restaurant meals and fewer rooms—until she reaches A, her optimal consumption bundle.

But suppose we transform the last term of Equation D-12 in the following way: divide both sides by P_R and multiply both sides by MU_M. Then the relative price rule becomes the optimal consumption rule:

$$\textbf{(D-13)} \qquad \textit{Optimal consumption rule: } \frac{MU_R}{P_R} = \frac{MU_M}{P_M}$$

So using either the optimal consumption rule or the relative price rule, we find the same optimal consumption bundle.

Preferences and Choices

Now that we have seen how to represent the optimal consumption choice in an indifference curve diagram, we can turn briefly to the relationship between consumer preferences and consumer choices.

When we say that two consumers have different preferences, we mean that they have different utility functions. This in turn means that they will have indifference curve maps with different shapes. And those different maps will translate into different consumption choices, even among consumers with the same income and who face the same prices.

To see this, suppose that Ingrid's friend Lars also consumes only housing and restaurant meals. However, Lars has a stronger preference for restaurant meals and a weaker preference for housing. This difference in preferences is shown in **Figure D.8**, which shows *two* sets of indifference curves: panel (a) shows Ingrid's preferences and panel (b) shows Lars's preferences. Note the difference in their shapes.

Suppose, as before, that rooms cost \$150 per month and restaurant meals cost \$30. Let's also assume that both Ingrid and Lars have incomes of \$2,400 per month, giving them identical budget lines. Nonetheless, because they have different preferences, they will make different consumption choices, as shown in Figure D.8. Ingrid will choose 8 rooms and 40 restaurant meals, whereas Lars will choose 4 rooms and 60 restaurant meals.

EM-36 Enrichment Modules

Figure D.8 Differences in Preferences

Ingrid and Lars have different preferences, reflected in the different shapes of their indifference curve maps. So they will choose different consumption bundles even when they have the same options. Each has an income of $2,400 per month and faces prices of $30 per meal and $150 per room. Panel (a) shows Ingrid's consumption choice: 8 rooms and 40 restaurant meals. Panel (b) shows Lars's choice: even though he has the same budget line, he consumes fewer rooms (4) and more restaurant meals (60).

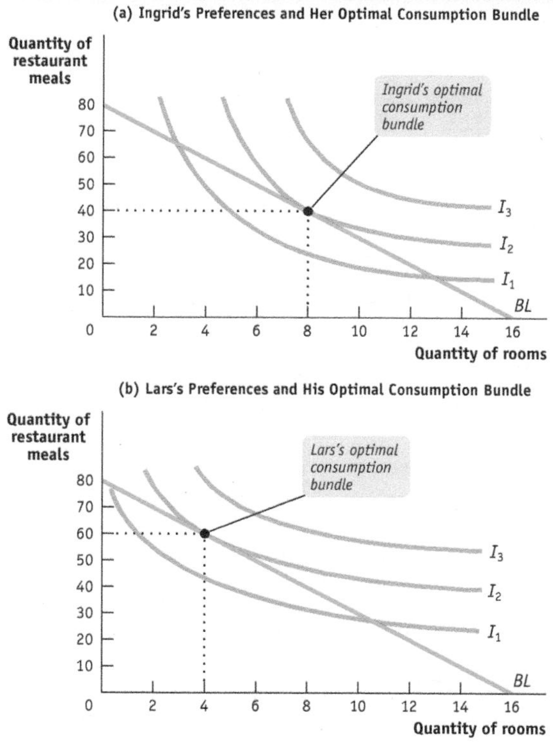

Module D Indifference Curves and Consumer Choice **EM-37**

ENRICHMENT MODULE D Review

Check Your Understanding

1. The accompanying table shows Samantha's preferences for consumption bundles composed of chocolate kisses and licorice drops.

Consumption bundle	Quantity of chocolate kisses	Quantity of licorice drops	Total utility (utils)
A	1	3	6
B	2	3	10
C	3	1	6
D	2	1	4

   a. With chocolate kisses on the horizontal axis and licorice drops on the vertical axis, draw hypothetical indifference curves for Samantha and locate the bundles on the curves. Assume that both items are ordinary goods.
   b. Suppose you don't know the number of utils provided by each bundle. Assuming that more is better, predict Samantha's ranking of each of the four bundles to the extent possible. Explain your answer.

2. On the left diagram in panel (a) of Figure D.4, draw a point *B* anywhere on the 200-util indifference curve and a point *C* anywhere on the 100-util indifference curve (but *not* at the same location as point *A*). By comparing the utils generated by bundles *A* and *B* and those generated by bundles *A* and *C*, explain why indifference curves cannot cross.
3. Lucinda and Kyle each consume 3 comic books and 6 video games. Lucinda's marginal rate of substitution of books for games is 2 and Kyle's is 5.
   a. For each person, find another consumption bundle that yields the same total utility as the current bundle. Who is less willing to trade games for books? In a diagram with books on the horizontal axis and games on the vertical axis, how would this be reflected in differences in the slopes of their indifference curves at their current consumption bundles?
   b. Find the relative price of books in terms of games at which Lucinda's current bundle is optimal. Is Kyle's bundle optimal given this relative price? If not, how should Kyle rearrange his consumption?

We provide these review questions in addition to discussion starters in case you or the AP® program chooses a rigorous approach to this material.

Multiple-Choice Review Questions

1. Which of the following is true along an individual's indifference curve for ordinary goods?
   a. The slope is constant.
   b. Total utility changes.
   c. The individual is indifferent between any two points.
   d. The slope is equal to the ratio of the prices of the consumption bundles.
   e. The individual doesn't care if utility is maximized.
2. Which of the following is/are true of indifference curves for ordinary goods?
   I. They cannot intersect.
   II. They have a negative slope.
   III. They are convex.
   a. I only
   b. II only
   c. III only
   d. I and II only
   e. I, II, and III
3. Moving from left to right along an indifference curve, which of the following increases?
   a. the marginal utility of the vertical axis good
   b. the marginal utility of the horizontal axis good
   c. the absolute value of the slope
   d. the marginal rate of substitution
   e. the demand for the vertical axis good
4. If the quantity of good *X* is measured on the horizontal axis and the quantity of good *Y* is measured on the vertical axis, the marginal rate of substitution is equal to
   a. $\frac{\Delta Q_X}{\Delta Q_Y}$.
   b. $\frac{MU_X}{MU_Y}$.
   c. $\frac{P_X}{P_Y}$.
   d. the ratio of the slope of the budget line and the slope of the indifference curve.
   e. 1 at the optimal level of consumption.
5. If the quantity of good *X* is again measured on the horizontal axis and the quantity of good *Y* is measured on the vertical axis, which of the following is true? The optimal consumption bundle is found where
   a. $\frac{MU_X}{MU_Y} = \frac{P_X}{P_Y}$.
   b. the slope of the indifference curve equals the slope of the budget line.
   c. the indifference curve is tangent to the budget line.
   d. $\frac{MU_X}{P_X} = \frac{MU_Y}{P_Y}$.
   e. all of the above are true.

Check Your Understanding

1. a. As you can see from the accompanying diagram, the four bundles are associated with three indifference curves: *B* on the 10-util indifference curve, *A* and *C* on the 6-util indifference curve, and *D* on the 4-util indifference curve.

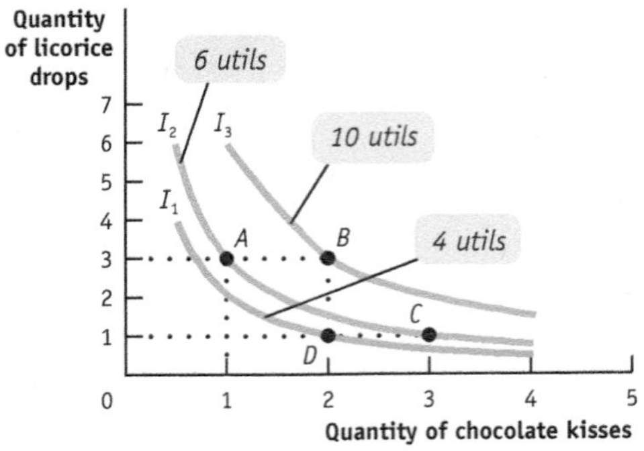

b. From comparing the quantities of chocolate kisses and licorice drops, you can predict that Samantha will prefer *B* to *A* because *B* gives her one more chocolate kiss and the same number of licorice drops as *A*. Next, you can predict that she will prefer *C* to *D* because *C* gives her one more chocolate kiss and the same number of licorice drops as *D*. You can also predict that she will prefer *B* to *D* because *B* gives her two more licorice drops and the same number of chocolate kisses as *D*. But without data about utils, you cannot predict how Samantha would rank *A* versus *C* or *D* because *C* and *D* have more chocolate kisses but fewer licorice drops than *A*. Nor can you rank *B* versus *C*, for the same reason.

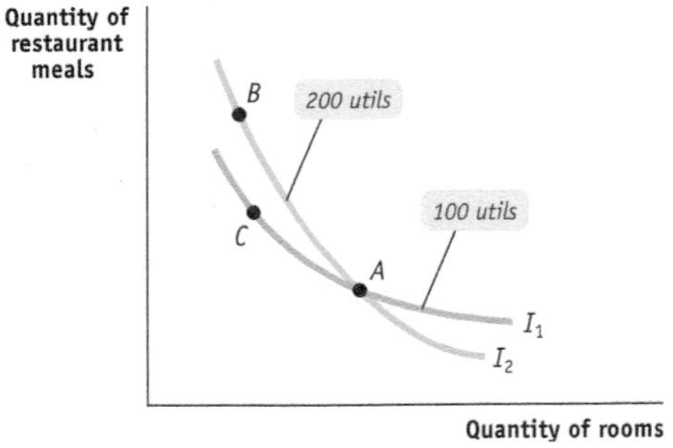

2. Bundles *A* and *B* each generate 200 utils since they both lie on the 200-util indifference curve. Likewise, bundles *A* and *C* each generate 100 utils since they both lie on the 100-util indifference curve. But this implies that *A* generates 100 utils and also that *A* generates 200 utils. This is a contradiction and so cannot be true. Therefore, indifference curves cannot cross.

3. a. The marginal rate of substitution of books for games, MU_B/MU_G, is 2 for Lucinda and 5 for Kyle. This implies that Lucinda is willing to trade 1 more book for 2 fewer games and Kyle is willing to trade 1 more book for 5 fewer games. So starting from a bundle of 3 books and 6 games, Lucinda would be equally content with a bundle of 4 books and 4 games and Kyle would be equally content with a bundle of 4 books and 1 game. Lucinda finds it more difficult to trade games for books: She is willing to give up only 2 games for a book, but Kyle is willing to give up 5 games for a book. If books are measured on the horizontal axis and games on the vertical axis, Kyle's indifference curve will be steeper than Lucinda's at the current consumption bundle.

b. Lucinda's current consumption bundle is optimal if P_B/P_G, the relative price of books in terms of games, is 2. Kyle's current consumption bundle is not optimal at this relative price; his bundle would be optimal only if the relative price of books in terms of games were 5. Since, for Kyle, $MU_B/MU_G = 5$, if $P_B/P_G = 2$, he should consume fewer games and more books to lower his MU_B/MU_G until it is equal to 2.

Free-Response Review Questions

1. Each of the combinations of song and movie downloads shown in the table below give Kathleen an equal level of utility.

Quantity of songs	*Quantity of movies*
0	8
1	6
2	4
3	2
4	0

a. Graph Kathleen's indifference curve.

b. Economists believe that each individual indifference curve for ordinary goods exhibits what two properties?

c. Does Kathleen's indifference curve exhibit the two properties from part b? Explain.

Rubric for FRQ 1 (8 points)

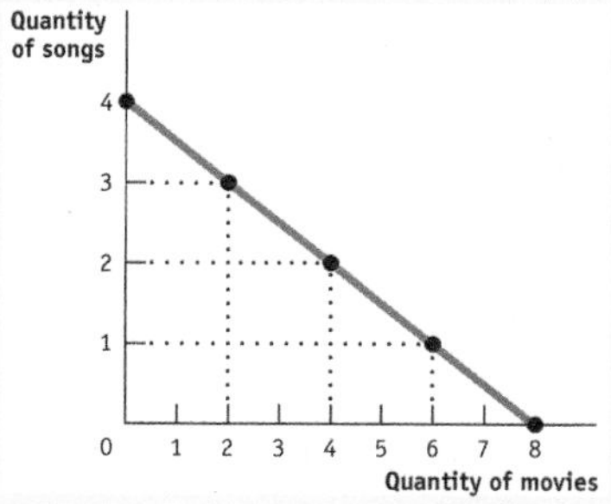

1 point: Axes labeled "Quantity of songs" and "Quantity of movies"

1 point: Correctly plotted indifference curve points

1 point: Negative slope

1 point: Convex shape

1 point: Negative slope—yes

1 point: As more movies are downloaded, there must be *fewer* song downloads to give Kathleen the same level of utility as before. This trade-off of more of one good for less of another gives the indifference curve a negative slope.

1 point: Convex shape—no

1 point: The indifference curve is a straight line with a constant slope, rather than being a convex line with a slope that decreases in absolute value from left to right.

2. Kathleen has $20 to spend on song and movie downloads each week. The price of a song download is $2 and the price of a movie download is $5.

a. Graph Kathleen's budget line.

b. Suppose all of Kathleen's indifference curves have the same shape and slope as the one in Question 1. How many song and movie downloads will Kathleen purchase to maximize her utility? Explain.

(4 points)

Discussion Starters

1. What would it indicate about your preferences for two items if your indifference curves were vertical? Can you think of examples of pairs of items for which this is the case?

2. Suppose that on a Saturday afternoon you must divide your time between studying and playing sports, and both activities are free. Could you use a budget constraint and indifference curves to model this decision? Explain your answer.

3. Consider the dilemma of how much money to spend now and how much to set aside for the future. Is this another trade-off that could be modeled with a budget constraint and indifference curves? What makes it possible to spend more now than you actually have? If you spend less than you have now, what can you do with your money so that the amount you have to spend in the future grows? What rate associated with these opportunities affects the slope of the budget constraint?

Multiple-Choice Review Questions

1. c
2. e
3. a
4. b
5. e

Free-Response Review Question

Rubric for FRQ 2 (4 points)

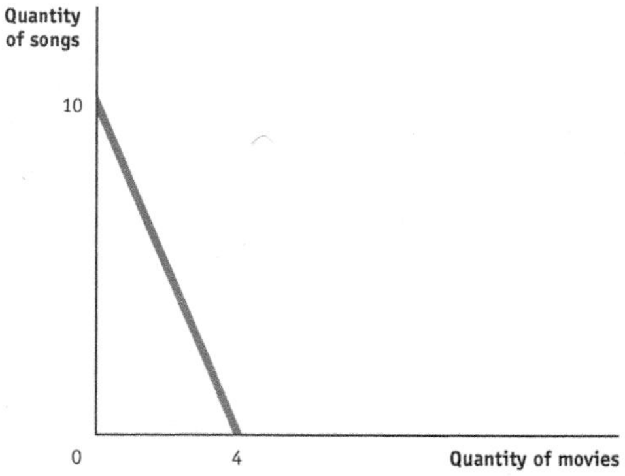

1 point: The vertical axis is labeled "Quantity of songs" and the horizontal axis is labeled "Quantity of movies."

1 point: The budget line is a straight line with the vertical intercept at 10 songs and the horizontal intercept at 4 movies.

1 point: Kathleen would purchase 10 songs and 0 movies.

1 point: We know that Kathleen wants to be on the highest indifference curve possible. We also know that there is no tangency point in this case because the indifference curve and the budget line are both straight lines with different slopes. Thus, the highest indifference curve that touches the budget line will touch it on one of the axes. Since the slope of the budget line is steeper than the slope of the indifference curve (–2.5 vs. –0.5), the highest indifference curve that can be afforded, given the budget line, is at the point 10 songs and 0 movies.

Discussion Starters

Following are possible answers to the Discussion Starter questions:

1. This would indicate that you didn't care at all about the good on the vertical axis, because as you get more of that good, you remain on the same indifference curve. Getting more of the good on the horizontal axis puts you on a different vertical indifference curve so that good would matter to you. For example, if the number of golf balls on the moon were measured on the vertical axis and the number of pairs of sunglasses you own were measured on the horizontal axis, you might have vertical indifference curves.

2. Yes, a budget constraint for time could be used to model this situation. The budget constraint would start at a point that represents spending all afternoon studying and end at a point that represents spending all afternoon playing sports. The indifference curves would have their usual shape.

3. Yes, this could be modeled with a budget constraint and indifference curves as well. Borrowing makes it possible to spend more now than you actually have. If you spend less than you have now, you can lend your money and have more to spend in the future when the loan is repaid. The interest rate at which money is borrowed and lent would affect the slope of the budget constraint.

Module D Indifference Curves and Consumer Choice **EM-39**

NOTES

Financial Literacy Handbook

By Laura Adams ("The Money Girl")

PART 1

Take It to the Bank

A bank account is a safe and convenient place to accumulate savings and to keep the money you need to pay bills and to make everyday cash purchases. Keeping a large amount of cash at home or in your wallet isn't as safe because your money could be lost or stolen.

Overview of Banks

Banks can be small community institutions that have just one or a few locations or they can be huge companies with thousands of branch locations all over the country. There are Internet-only banks with no physical location to visit and only a website address. In addition to holding your money, banks also offer a variety of services to help you manage your money.

Banks stay in business by using the money you deposit to make a profit by offering loans to other customers or businesses. They lend to customers who want to borrow money for big purchases like cars or homes. They also lend to small and large businesses for making purchases like inventory and equipment.

When you take a loan from a bank, you're charged interest, which is an additional charge on top of the amount you borrow. To stay profitable, a bank must receive more money in interest from borrowers than it pays out in the form of loans to customers.

Despite the benefits banking institutions offer, almost one-third of Americans are "unbanked" or "underbanked" and use no or few basic financial services. According to the Federal Deposit Insurance Corporation (FDIC), these individuals typically have low income. FDIC data shows that for households with annual income of less than $15,000 per year, 28% have no bank account and another 22% use less than a full range of banking services.

Consumers may not use banks for a variety of reasons, including the lack of a conveniently located branch office or the desire to avoid bank fees. However, some potential customers do not take advantage of the services banks offer because they don't understand how banks work or how much nonbank alternatives cost. In this section you'll learn why going without banking services is both expensive and inconvenient.

Finance Tip

You can use the Electronic Deposit Insurance Estimator (EDIE) at myfdicinsurance.gov to make sure your deposits in various bank accounts are fully covered by the FDIC.

Types of Financial Institutions

When you're ready to open a bank account, there are three main types of institutions to choose from: savings and loan associations, commercial banks, and credit unions.

Savings and Loan Associations and Commercial Banks

Savings and loan associations (S&Ls) and commercial banks operate under federal and state regulations. They specialize in taking deposits for checking and savings accounts, making home loans (known as mortgages) and other personal and business loans, facilitating the flow of money into and out of accounts, and providing various financial services for individuals and businesses.

Have you ever wondered what would happen to your money if your bank went out of business or failed? Most banks insure your deposits through the FDIC up to the maximum amount allowed by law, which is currently $250,000 per depositor per account type for each insured bank.

FDIC insurance means that if your bank closes for any reason, you won't lose your money. You'll know a bank is properly insured if it displays the FDIC logo at a local branch, on advertising materials, or online. To learn more, visit fdic.gov.

Credit Unions

Credit unions are nonprofit organizations owned by their customers, who are called members. Credit union members typically have something in common, like working for the same employer, working in the same profession, or living in the same geographic area. You must qualify to become a member of a credit union to be able to use its financial services.

Credit unions offer many of the same services as commercial banks and S&Ls. Most also offer insurance for your deposits through the National Credit Union Administration (NCUA), which gives the same coverage (up to $250,000 per depositor) as the FDIC. Just look for the official NCUA sign at credit union branches and websites. To learn more, visit ncua.gov.

Why Keep Money in a Bank?

While it's possible to keep your money at home and manage your personal finances using a cash-only system, here are five reasons why it's better to use an insured bank or credit union:

1. **Safety**: Money you deposit in a bank account is safe from loss, theft, or destruction. Even the best hiding places for money can be found by a thief or be susceptible to a flood or fire.
2. **Insurance**: Deposits covered by FDIC or NCUA insurance are protected by a fund backed by the full faith and credit of the U.S. government. So if your bank closes and can't return your money, the FDIC or NCUA will pay the insured portion of your deposits.
3. **Convenience**: Money in a bank account can be accessed in a variety of ways. You can make deposits by visiting a local branch or setting up electronic direct deposit. Some institutions have remote deposit services where you deposit a paper check by taking a picture of it with a mobile device or scanner and uploading it online. You can use online bill pay to send funds in the form of a paper check or electronic transfer.
4. **Low cost**: Different banks offer accounts with a variety of benefits, such as interest paid, debit cards, online banking, account alerts, bill pay, and overdraft protection. Many bank services are free, which makes using a bank to get cash or pay bills less expensive than alternatives, such as a check cashing service. Some check cashers charge a fee that's a percentage of the check value, plus an additional flat fee. For instance, cashing a $1,000 check at a check cashing service could cost 1.5%, or $15.
5. **Business relationship**: Building a relationship with a bank may give you the opportunity to qualify for premium banking services, loans, and credit cards that can improve your financial future.

Finance Tip

Did you know that funds deposited electronically into your bank account are available sooner than those deposited by a paper check?

Types of Bank Accounts

The two main types of bank accounts are deposit accounts and non-deposit accounts.

Deposit Accounts

Deposit accounts allow you to add money to or withdraw money from your account at any time. Examples of deposit accounts are checking, savings, and money market accounts.

Checking Account A checking account, also known as a payment account, is the most common type of bank account. It's a real workhorse that allows you to make purchases or pay bills using paper checks, a debit or check card, online bill pay, automatic transfer, or cash withdrawal from an automatic teller machine (**ATM**). The institution keeps a record of your deposits and withdrawals and sends you a monthly account statement. The best checking accounts offer no fees, no minimum balance requirement, and free checks.

Finance Tip

Rewards checking accounts pay a relatively high rate of interest when you follow certain requirements, such as receiving e-statements, having at least one direct deposit per month, and using a debit card for a certain number of purchases each month.

Savings Account A savings account is a safe place to keep money, and it earns you interest. It doesn't give you as much flexibility or access to your money as a checking account. While there's typically no limit on the number of deposits you can make into a savings account, you can only make up to six withdrawals or transfers per month. Savings accounts typically don't come with paper checks, but they may offer a debit or ATM card that you can use a maximum of three times per month.

Finance Tip

Use the power of the Internet to shop for the best bank accounts. Sites like checkingfinder.com and bankrate.com gather up-to-date information about the best offers nationwide.

If your balance dips below a certain amount, you may be charged a monthly fee. The institution keeps a record of your transactions and sends you a monthly account statement.

Savings accounts are perfect for your short-term savings goals, like a down payment on a car or holiday gift-giving. Interest rates on savings accounts vary, so it's important to shop around locally or online for the highest offers. Interest rates on savings accounts are variable, which means they're subject to change and can decrease after you open an account. (You'll learn more about compounded interest in Part 2 of this handbook.)

Money Market Account (MMA) A money market account has features of both a savings and a checking account. You can make up to six withdrawals or transfers per month, including payments by check, debit card, and online bill pay. You're paid relatively high interest rates, especially if you maintain a high minimum balance, such as $5,000 or more.

Money market accounts are a great choice when you start to accumulate more savings. Interest rates vary and are subject to change, so always do your research to find the best money market account offer.

There are also special types of deposit accounts known as *time deposits*, where you're restricted from withdrawing your money for a certain period of time.

Certificate of Deposit (CD) A certificate of deposit is a time deposit that requires you to give up the use of your money for a fixed term or period of time, such as 3 months, 12 months, or 5 years. In exchange for this restricted access, banks typically pay higher interest rates than for savings or money market accounts (where you can withdraw money on demand). In general, the longer the term of the CD, the higher the interest rate you receive.

For instance, a six-month CD might pay 1% interest and a five-year CD might pay 3.5%. If you take money out of a CD before the end of the term, or maturity date, you generally have to pay a penalty. So before putting money in a CD, be sure that you won't need it until after the maturity date and that you understand all the charges and fees associated with early withdrawals.

Non-deposit Accounts

Many banks offer non-deposit accounts that can be investments, such as stocks, bonds, or mutual funds. It's important to remember that non-deposit products are never insured by the FDIC or NCUA and may lose some or all of their value.

How Old Do You Have to Be to Open a Bank Account?

Many banks offer checking and savings accounts for young people. Some require you to open a joint account with a parent or guardian; however, some offer independent student accounts when you reach age 16.

The earlier you open up a bank account and start saving on a regular basis, the better. Having a checking and savings account established before you go to college will help you manage money and make necessary purchases. Money you earn from a job, get from a relative, or receive as a gift can be set aside for your future needs.

How to Maintain a Checking Account

It's important to maintain your checking account on a regular basis so you know exactly how much money you have at all times. You should reconcile each monthly statement's ending balance against your records so you never miss a transaction, such as an unexpected fee. Never write checks or make debit card purchases that exceed your balance.

Using ATM and Debit Cards

An ATM card allows you to use ATMs to make deposits, check your account balance, transfer funds between accounts, and make cash withdrawals 24 hours a day. You typically have to pay a fee for each ATM cash withdrawal at banks other than your own—unless your bank gives you free access to a network of ATMs or reimburses your ATM fees.

FYI What Is a Prepaid Card?

A prepaid card may look like a debit or credit card, but it isn't linked to a bank or credit account. Prepaid cards may come loaded with a set value or may require you to add money to the card. The card value goes down each time you make a purchase. Prepaid cards have many fees—such as a purchase fee, monthly fees, ATM withdrawal fees, transaction fees, balance inquiry fees, and more—which generally makes them more expensive to use than a bank debit card.

A debit card, also known as a check card, looks like a credit card because it typically has a MasterCard or VISA logo. A debit card can be used just like an ATM card or to make purchases where accepted by merchants. When you use a debit card, money is deducted immediately from your bank account and credited to the merchant's account. This reduces your available balance.

If you make a debit card purchase for more than your available balance, your transaction will be declined. However, if you enroll in overdraft protection, you authorize your bank to cover your transaction—but at the cost of a large service fee.

Writing Checks

With the popularity of debit cards and online banking, people don't use paper checks as much anymore. However, if you need to write one, it's easy to fill in the blanks. Always write clearly using dark ink and never cross out a mistake–it's better to start over with a fresh check.

Reconciling Your Checking Account

Each month you'll receive a statement that shows activity in your account. The statement

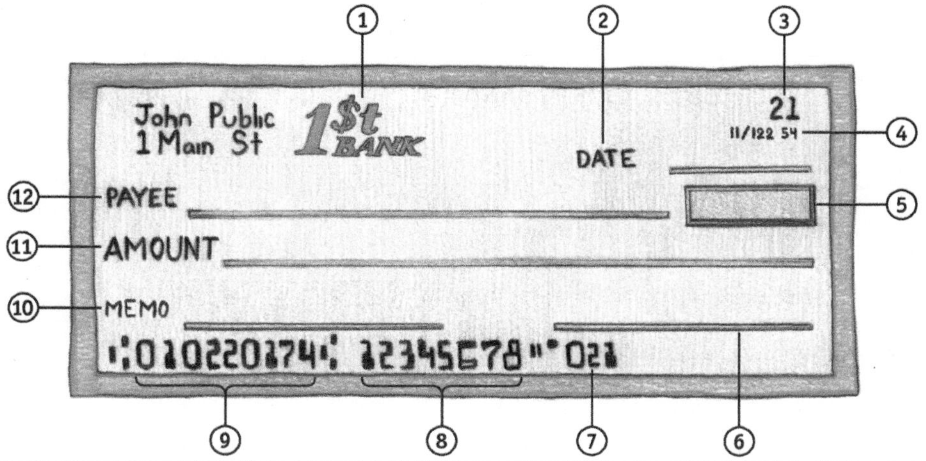

1. **Bank name**: This may be preprinted on each check.
2. **Date**: Enter the month, day, and year.
3. **Check number**: If your checks don't have preprinted numbers, label them with consecutive numbers.
4. **Bank ID numbers**: This may be preprinted on each check.
5. **Amount**: Enter the amount to pay in figures.
6. **Signature**: Sign your name exactly as you signed it on documents you completed when you opened the account.
7. **Check number**: This may be preprinted on each check.
8. **Account number**: This should be preprinted on each check.
9. **Bank routing number**: This should be preprinted on each check to identify your bank's unique routing number.
10. **Memo**: Write a quick note to remind yourself of the reason for the check.
11. **Amount**: Enter the amount to pay in words and draw a line over unused space so nothing can be added later.
12. **Payee**: Enter the person or company to pay.

Tips for Secure Mobile Banking

Online and mobile banking isn't particularly risky but it is important to be careful when making online transactions. Use these tips to avoid risk when you're making purchases or banking using a mobile device:

1. **Use a secured network** instead of public Wi-Fi so your personal information can't be exposed to a criminal. The web address of a secured network begins with "https" instead of "http."
2. **Guard your mobile device** like your wallet, because it may contain information to access your accounts if it were lost or stolen.
3. **Create strong passwords** for your devices (to turn them on or wake them from sleep mode) and for your online accounts that are at least 8 characters long and use a combination of letters, numbers, and symbols.
4. **Don't lend your mobile devices** or share your passwords with anyone you don't know or trust.
5. **Log off** from financial accounts and close the browser window or app when you finish using them.
6. **Only download trusted apps** from sources like your bank or other legitimate financial institutions.
7. **Delete text messages** from your bank once you've read them.
8. **Don't divulge personal information** such as your social security number or account number. A financial institution or authorized agency will never ask you for personal information over the Internet or even on the phone.

should include a reconciliation worksheet that you can follow. Reconciling or balancing your account is the process of making sure the information on the bank statement matches your records. Always keep track of your deposits, checks, debit card purchases, ATM withdrawals, and fees. You can use a paper or digital check register. Most financial software programs allow you to automatically download bank and credit card account transactions. Not having to enter each of your transactions manually saves time and makes account reconciliation simple.

Overdraft Protection

Having overdraft protection means your debit card purchases and ATM withdrawals will be processed, even if your bank account balance isn't high enough to cover them. You must give written permission for overdraft protection because using it comes with expensive nonsufficient funds (NSF) fees. However, you can opt out of overdraft protection and avoid the potential charges. This means that if you try to use your debit card and your account balance is too low, you will not be permitted to make the purchase.

How to Choose the Best Bank

Banks provide many financial services and may charge a fee for some of them. It's important to shop around to find a bank that charges the lowest fees for services you plan to use frequently and pays the highest rate of interest.

Common Banking Terms to Know

Banks use certain vocabulary that you should be familiar with so that you understand all you can about where your money is held. Here are several key banking terms to know:

account statement—a paper or electronic record of account activity, service charges, and fees, issued on a regular basis

bounced or **bad check**—slang for a check that is rejected due to insufficient funds in the account

check—a paper form that authorizes a bank to release funds from the payer's account to the payee

cleared or **canceled checks**—paper checks that have been processed and paid by a bank

deposit slip or **ticket**—a printed form you complete that lists cash and checks to be deposited into an account

direct deposit—an electronic payment method typically used by an employer or government agency

electronic payment or **transaction**—a deposit or charge to an account that happens without the use of a paper form

endorsement—the payee's signature on the back of a paper check that is required to deposit or to take cash out of an account

payee—the person or company to whom a check is made payable

payer—the person or company who writes a check or pays another party

reconciliation—the process of comparing a bank account statement to your records and resolving any differences until you determine an identical account balance

service charge (or maintenance charge)—a fee charged by a bank to maintain your account

Part 1 Review Questions

1. How do banks make money?
2. Describe the similarities and differences between commercial banks and credit unions. Why do you think someone would choose one over the other?
3. In your own words, describe why it's better to keep your money in a financial institution instead of holding large amounts of cash.
4. Give several reasons why someone would open more than one type of bank account.
5. Come up with at least five questions you should ask before deciding to put your money in a financial institution.

Project

Find and research several kinds of banks in your area. How many savings and loan associations, commercial banks, and credit unions are in your town? Speak to the manager of each financial institution. Approximately how many customers does each have? What services do they provide their customers? How do they attract new customers?

PART 2 Get Interested in Money Math

Whether you're shopping at the grocery store, choosing a car loan, or figuring out how much to invest for retirement, managing money comes down to the numbers. Making the best decisions for your personal finances always begins by doing some simple money math.

Pay Attention to Interest

When you borrow money by taking out a loan for college, a car, or any other loan, you'll be charged interest. Additionally, if you don't pay off a credit card balance in full by the statement due date, you'll also be charged interest on the balance owed. Lenders make money by charging interest to a borrower as a percentage of the amount of the loan, or the credit card balance due.

When you deposit money in a bank account that pays interest—for example, a savings account or CD—you become the lender and the bank is the borrower. The bank pays you interest for keeping money on deposit.

Interest is typically expressed as an annual percentage rate, or APR. To keep more of your money, it's wise to shop around and borrow at the lowest interest rates. Likewise, lend your money and deposit it in the bank that offers the highest possible interest rates, so you earn more.

How Simple and Compound Interest Work

But how does your money actually earn interest? There are two basic types of interest: simple interest and compound interest.

Simple Interest Simple interest is, well, pretty simple! That's because it's calculated on the original principal amount.

Say you borrow $100 from your friend John at a 5% annual rate of simple interest for a term of 3 years. Here's how the interest would be calculated for the loan:

Loan year	Principal amount (dollars)	APR (percent)	Annual interest earned (dollars)	Balance due (dollars)
1	$100	5%	$5	$105
2	100	5	5	110
3	100	5	5	115

Notice that the 5% APR is always calculated on the original principal amount of $100. At the end of the third year you have to pay $100 plus $15 in interest. In other words, your $100 loan cost a total of $115.

Compound Interest Compound interest is more complex because it's calculated on the original principal amount and also on the accumulated interest of a deposit or loan. Compound interest allows you to earn interest on a growing principal balance, which allows you to accumulate interest at a much faster rate. Interest can be compounded on any period of time, such as daily, monthly, semiannually, or annually.

Say you get the same loan of $100 for 3 years from your friend John, but this time he charges you 5% interest that compounds annually. Here's how the interest would be calculated:

Loan year	Principal amount (dollars)	APR (percent)	Annual interest earned (dollars)	Balance due (dollars)
1	$100	5%	$5	$105
2	105	5	5.25	110.25
3	110.25	5	5.51	115.76

Notice that the 5% APR is calculated on an increasing principal balance. At the end of the third year you'd owe the original

Table 1 Semiannual Compound Interest Calculation

Loan year	Principal amount (dollars)	Semiannual percentage rate (percent)	Annual interest earned (dollars)	Balance due (dollars)
1 (January)	$100	2.5%	$2.50	$102.50
1 (July)	102.50	2.5	2.56	105.06
2 (January)	105.06	2.5	2.63	107.69
2 (July)	107.69	2.5	2.69	110.38
3 (January)	110.38	2.5	2.76	113.14
3 (July)	113.14	2.5	2.83	115.97

amount of $100 plus interest of $15.76. Your $100 loan cost $115.76 with annual compounding interest. This table also shows you how much you'd earn if you deposited $100 in the bank and earned a 5% annual return that compounds annually.

Let's see how much you'd pay if John charged you 5% compounded semiannually, or every 6 months, shown in **Table 1**, above.

At the end of the third year you'd owe the original loan amount of $100 plus $15.97 of interest. With semiannual compounding your $100 loan would cost $115.97. Likewise, this table shows how much you could earn from $100 in savings if compounded semi-annually at a 5% annual rate of return.

Remember that the more frequent the compounding, the faster the interest grows.

Annual Percentage Yield (APY)

Annual percentage yield (APY) is the amount of interest you'll earn on an annual basis that includes the effect of compounding. APY is expressed as a percentage and will be higher the more often your money compounds.

What is the Rule of 72?

How long would it take you to double your money through savings and investments? It's easy to figure it out using a handy formula called the **Rule of 72**. If you divide 72 by the interest rate you earn, the answer is the number of years it will take for your initial savings amount to double in value.

For example, if you earn an average annual return of 1% on a bank savings account, dividing 1 into 72 tells you that your money will double in 72 years. But if you earn 6% on an investment, your money will take only 12 (72 ÷ 6 = 12) years to double.

You can also estimate the interest rate you'd need to earn to double your money within a set number of years by dividing 72 by the number of years. For instance, if you put $500 in an account that you want to grow to $1,000 in 12 years, you'll need an interest rate of 6% (72 ÷ 12 = 6).

Understand Credit Cards

Using credit cards without fully understanding the relevant money math is a recipe for financial disaster. Credit cards start charging interest the day you make a purchase, take a cash advance, or transfer a balance from another account.

You're typically charged a daily rate that's equal to the APR divided by 365 (the 365 days in a year). Rates may be different for each transaction category and depending on your credit rating. For instance, your APR could be 11.99% for new purchases, 23.99% for cash advances, and 5% for balance transfers. Balances accumulate day after day until you pay them off in full.

You can make a monthly minimum payment and carry over the remaining balance from month to month. But that's not a wise way to manage credit cards because the interest starts racking up. Additionally, if you make a late payment, you're charged a late fee that gets added to your outstanding balance—and interest is calculated on that amount too.

The bright spot in using a credit card wisely is that you're given a grace period for new purchases that allows you to avoid all

Finance Tip

Interest that you earn is considered income, and you may have to pay federal and state tax on it.

Finance Tip

When comparing different bank accounts, always compare APY instead of APR to know which one pays more interest on an annual basis.

Table 2 Amortization Schedule

Payment month	Loan balance (dollars)	Monthly payment (dollars)	Interest portion of payment (dollars)	Principal portion of payment (dollars)
1	$20,000	$617.54	$116.67	$500.88
2	19,499.12	617.54	113.74	503.80
3	18,995.32	617.54	110.81	506.74
4	18,488.58	617.54	107.85	509.69
5	17,978.89	617.54	104.88	512.67
6	17,466.22	617.54	101.89	515.66

interest charges—if you pay your balance in full by the billing statement due date. Note that there is generally no grace period for cash advances or balance transfers.

Credit cards are a powerful financial tool that can enhance your life if you use them responsibly. But abusing them by making purchases that you can't afford to pay off in full each month can be devastating to your financial future. It will also harm your credit report history if you make late payments. You'll learn more about how to establish and maintain a good credit history in Part 5.

Calculate Credit Card Payoff

Question: If you buy a TV for $2,000 using a credit card that charges 23.99% APR, how long would it take to pay off, if you only make minimum payments of 3% of your outstanding balance down to a minimum of $15 per month?

Answer: It would take over 16 years! So, if you're 17 years old right now, you'd celebrate your thirty-third birthday before you finally pay off the TV. Due to the high rate of credit card interest, the total cost of the TV would actually be $5,328. That's an increase of more than 266% on the TV's original purchase price. Only making minimum payments can easily double or triple the price of any item charged to a credit card, which is why it's so important to pay off credit card balances in full every month.

Finance Tip

To determine how long it would take to pay off a credit card if you only made the minimum payments, do a web search for "credit card minimum payment calculator" and enter your information.

Amortization

Gradually paying off a debt's principal and interest in regular installments over time is called amortization. Loans that amortize, such as a car loan or home mortgages, have fixed interest rates and charge equal monthly payments, though each payment is made up of a slightly different amount of principal and interest.

Take a look at **Table 2** to see how each payment is split up for the first six months on a three-year $20,000 car loan with an interest rate of 7%:

Notice that each month's beginning loan balance is reduced by the prior month's principal portion paid. The interest portion is slightly lower each month because it's calculated on an ever-decreasing principal balance.

How to Become a Millionaire

If you think that the only way to become a millionaire is to win the lottery, think again! Thanks to the power of compounding interest it's easy—if you get an early start. **Table 3** shows you how.

If you start saving and investing just $250 a month as soon as you get your first job, you could amass a million dollars by the time you're in your 60s. But if you wait until you're over 40 years old to get started and invest the same amount, you'd be close to 90 before becoming a millionaire!

Millionaire Case Study

Steve and Jessica are both 25 years old and work for the same company. They have the same financial goal: to retire at age 65 with one million dollars in savings. Steve starts contributing to his company's retirement plan right away, but Jessica waits 10 years, until she's 35 years old, to begin investing. Here's what happens: Steve can reach his million-dollar goal by contributing $400 a month and earning an average 7% annual

Table 3 At What Age Could You Become a Millionaire?

Age to begin saving	Amount to save each month (dollars)	Average APR (percent)	Years to become a millionaire	Age you're a millionaire!
18	$250	7%	46	64
20	250	7	46	66
25	250	7	45	70
30	250	7	45	75
40	250	7	45	86

return. But since Jessica gets a late start, she has to contribute much more than Steve. Jessica must contribute $850 a month with the same 7% rate of return to reach her million-dollar goal, as shown in **Figure 1**.

You'll notice that Steve only had to invest $192,000 over a 40-year period to amass over one million dollars. However, Jessica had to invest $306,000, or 60% more than Steve, over a 30-year period to accumulate approximately the same amount.

The Power of Saving Early Case Study

Sarah and Tom are both 25 years old, but they begin saving for retirement at different times. Sarah begins saving $200 per month right away, but Tom decides to buy a new car instead. Tom ends up delaying his retirement savings for 10 years. After his 35th birthday, he finally gets started and saves $300 per month. They both earn an average annual return of 8%.

Here's what happens: When Tom reaches age 65, he has almost $450,000. But Sarah has amassed close to $700,000. The benefit of choosing to invest earlier, rather than later, really pays off for Sarah because she has $250,000 more than Tom to spend during retirement, as demonstrated in **Figure 2** on the next page.

The sooner you start saving and investing, the more you will benefit from the power of compounding interest!

Figure 1 Saving To Be a Millionaire

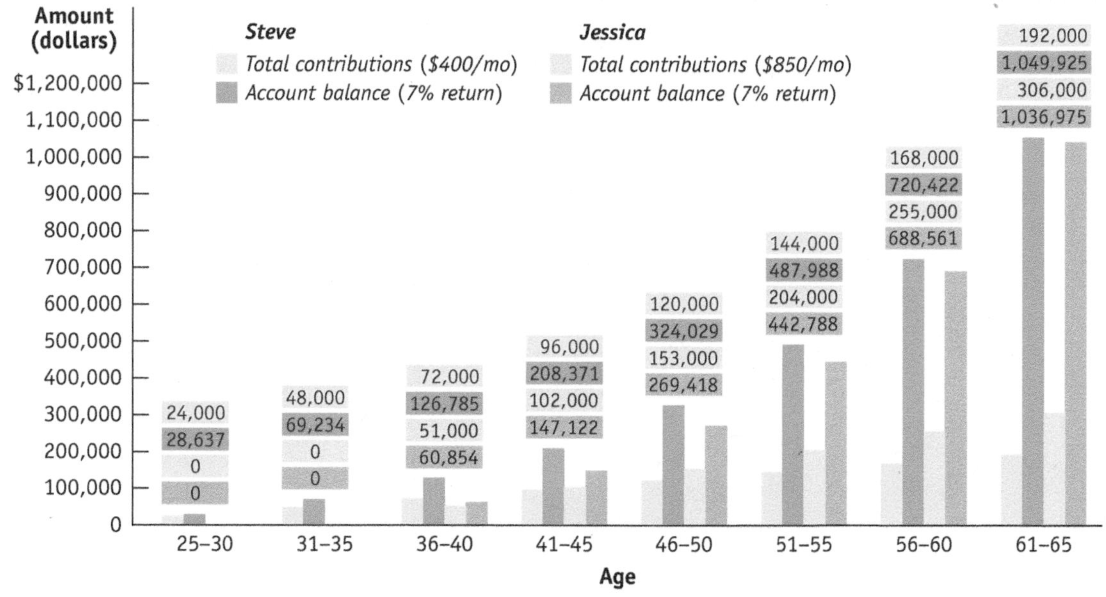

Figure 2 Saving for Retirement

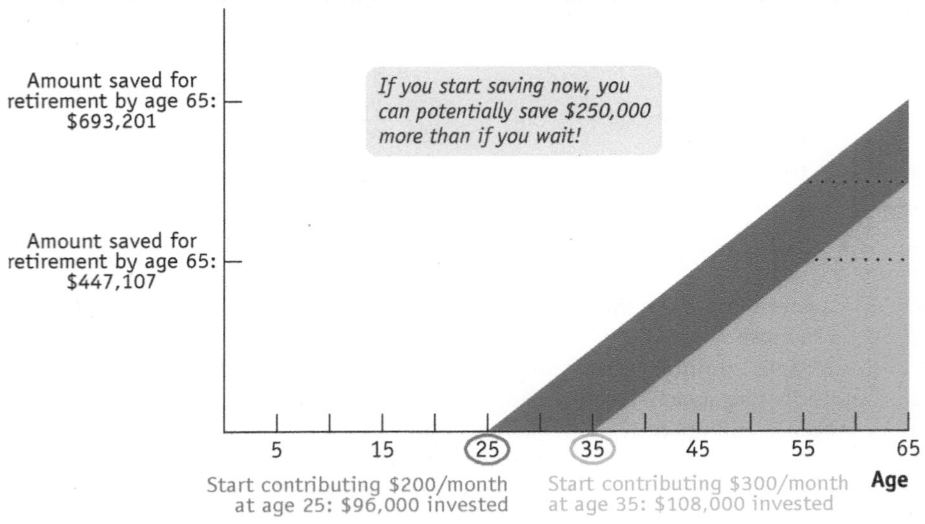

Part 2 Review Questions

1. What is the difference between simple and compound interest?
2. Using the Rule of 72, how long will it take you to double your savings if you have $3,200 in an account making 4% interest?
3. Why is it generally a bad idea to make only minimum payments on your credit card?

Project

Imagine you deposit $125 in a savings account each month. It pays 3% annually, which is compounded monthly. How much interest will you earn for the year?

PART 3 Learn to Earn

How can you earn enough money to cover your expenses and save for the future? It starts by having the education and skills to get a good job or to start your own business. Every work experience builds your level of knowledge, boosts your resume, helps you know what work you like best, and makes you more attractive to potential employers.

What Is a Resume?

A resume is a summary of your education, skills, and work experience—that you submit to a potential employer in person, through the mail, or online—that highlights many of your outstanding traits and experiences. It should be a one-page document that is succinct and well written.

Employers typically conduct a background check to verify data in your resume, so never include any false information. Lying on a resume or job application can disqualify you for a job or cause an employer to fire you later on.

At the top of a resume, list your name, address, phone number, and e-mail address. The body should include sections titled "Objective," "Experience," "Skills," "Education," and "Honors or Awards." Tailor each resume to the particular job you apply for so the employer knows you have the skills to be successful.

If you have trouble creating a resume, ask for help from family, friends, or a professional resume writer, who can help you articulate the skills and experiences you have to offer a potential employer. You can also use free online resources such as careeronestop.org and myfuture.com.

What Is a Job Application?

In addition to your resume, many potential employers require you to complete a job or employment application. The application can be customized by the employer, but it typically asks for personal information, references, and specifics about the job you're applying for. Submitting an impressive resume and application will make you stand out from other applicants.

There are certain questions that an employer is not allowed to ask applicants under federal and some state and local laws. These may include topics such as your age, race, religion, citizenship status, and whether you are disabled, pregnant, or married. You can learn more about employment laws at the U.S. Department of Labor website at www.dol.gov.

Types of Income

The money you make falls into one of two basic categories: earned income and passive income.

Earned Income

Earned income is the income you receive by working for a company or someone who pays you, or from a business that you own and run. Earned income includes your hourly wages, salaries, tips, commissions, and bonuses. This is the most common way to make money. Of course, if you stop working, you stop earning. However, if you save and invest your earned income wisely, you can turn it into passive income.

Passive Income

Passive income is generated from assets you buy or create, such as financial investments, rental real estate, or something you have created, such as a book or a song. If you buy a house and rent it for more than your mortgage and other expenses, the profit is passive income. If you write and publish a book or a song that pays royalties, that is intellectual property that pays passive income. The benefit of passive income is that you get paid with little or no additional work on your part. That makes it possible to retire and still receive money to pay your everyday living expenses.

Although you must have income to meet your financial needs, it doesn't give you lasting wealth unless you save or invest some amount of it on a regular basis. Even those with high incomes can live paycheck to paycheck and end up with no true wealth. Likewise, those with modest incomes can save small amounts of money over a long period of time and accumulate a nest egg for a healthy financial future.

Getting a Paycheck

It might surprise you to know that if you get a job earning $600 a week, you don't actually receive $600 a week. Although your gross income or pay will be $600, you'll have payroll taxes deducted from each paycheck before you receive it, which include federal, state, Medicare, and Social Security taxes. You may also have voluntary deductions for workplace benefits such as health insurance, life insurance, and contributions to a retirement account. The remaining amount that you'll have to spend after taxes and deductions is called your net income or net pay.

When you take a new job, one of the forms you must complete is the W-4. It tells your employer how much tax should be taken out, or withheld, from each of your paychecks. If too little tax is withheld during the year, you'll owe money to the government's Internal Revenue Service (IRS) on tax day (which is usually April 15 unless it falls on a weekend or holiday). If too much tax is withheld, the IRS will pay a refund, but you will lose the use of your money until the refund payment arrives. So it is good to have your payroll withholding match the actual amount of tax you'll owe.

Significant events—such as marriage, divorce, the birth or adoption of a child, buying a home, or taking an additional job—will affect how much tax you owe. Additionally, earning income from savings accounts or investments affects the tax you owe. Any time your personal situation changes, you can file a new W-4 with your employer to make sure the right amount of tax is withheld so you don't have any surprises on tax day. You can learn more by visiting the IRS website at irs.gov and searching for Publication 919, How Do I Adjust My Tax Withholding?

Finance Tip

Employers are required to pay 50% of FICA on behalf of their employees. If you become your own boss, you must pay self-employment tax, which includes 100% of the Social Security and Medicare tax owed.

How Payroll Withholding Works

Employers are required to withhold four different types of tax from your paycheck:

1. **Federal income tax** is paid to the IRS for expenses such as salaries of elected officials, the military, welfare assistance programs, public education, and interest on the national debt.
2. **State income tax** is generally paid to your state's revenue department for expenses such as salaries of state employees and maintenance of state highways and parks. Depending on where you live, there may also be payroll deductions for county and city tax.
3. **Social Security tax** provides income for eligible taxpayers who are retired or disabled, or who survive a relative who was receiving benefits. The program's official name is OASDI, which stands for Old-Age, Survivors, and Disability Insurance.
4. **Medicare tax** provides hospital insurance benefits to eligible individuals who are over the age of 65 or have certain medical conditions. Social Security and Medicare taxes are collectively called the Federal Insurance Contributions Act (FICA) tax.

Filing an Income Tax Return

By April 15th of each year you must complete and file, by mail or electronically, a federal tax return to the IRS for income from the prior year. Most states also require a state tax return at the same time. Whether you must file a tax return depends on your income, tax filing status, age, and whether or not you are a dependent. The filing requirements apply even if you don't owe any tax.

If you don't file taxes on time, you'll be charged a late payment penalty, plus interest on any amount owed. Willfully failing to file a return is a serious matter because it's against the law and may result in criminal prosecution.

If you are an unmarried dependent student, you must file a tax return if your earned or unearned income exceeds certain limits. You may also owe tax on certain scholarships and fellowships for education. Tax rules are subject to change each year, so be sure to visit irs.gov and review IRS Publication 501, Exemptions, Standard Deduction and Filing Information, for income limits and up-to-date information.

In January and February each year, you'll receive official forms, like the sample shown below, from institutions that paid you, such as your employer, bank, or investment brokerage or firm. These forms provide the data you need to complete your taxes. Even if you don't receive these official tax documents, you must still declare all your income on a tax return. So be sure to request any missing information.

Even if your income is below a threshold set by the IRS and you do not have to file, you should file a tax return each year if you may be owed a refund—for instance, if you had income tax withheld from your pay or you qualify for refundable tax benefits.

In addition to individuals and families, the IRS (and certain states) also tax corporations, trusts, and estates.

How Much Income Tax Do You Pay?

The United States has a marginal or progressive tax system, which means that people with more earned income pay tax at a higher rate or percentage. A tax bracket is a range of income that's taxed at a certain rate. Currently, there are seven federal tax brackets that range from 10% up to 39.6%. So, someone with very little income may pay 10% while someone with high income could pay as much as 39.6% on their highest range of income for just federal income tax.

Every year the IRS adjusts many tax provisions as the cost of living goes up or down. They use the Consumer Price Index (CPI) to calculate the prior year's inflation rate and adjust income limits for tax brackets, tax deduction amounts, and tax credit values

Mom and Pop's Pizza Shop
1234 Main Street
Longview, NJ 99229

First Bank
Positano, NJ

233

18-1-1010

PAY TO THE ORDER OF **Jennifer Adams** **$** 128.24

One hundred and twenty-eight and 24/100 ——— DOLLARS

MEMO ____________

Joseph Posentino

⑈000165⑈ ⑆123456789O⑆ 022⑈053304⑈

EMPLOYEE PAY STUB — POSENTINO PIZZA SHOP — CHECK NUMBER: 000233

Employee	SSN	Pay Period	Pay Date
Jennifer Adams	555-55-5555	04/06/2014–04/12/2014	04/18/2014

HOURS	Regular	OT
TP	20.00	0
YTD	160.00	0

EARNINGS	Regular	OT	Bonus	Other	Gross Pay
TP	$160.00	0	0	0	$160.00
YTD	$1,280.00	0	0	0	$1,280.00

DEDUCTIONS Pay	Social Security	Medicare	Federal	State	Retirement	Other	Net Pay
TP	$9.92	$2.24	$14.00	$5.60	0	0	$128.24
YTD	$79.36	$17.92	$112.00	$44.80	0	0	$1,025.92

Finance Tip

Use an online calculator at taxfoundation.org to find out how much federal tax you really pay (your effective tax rate) based on your income and tax filing status.

accordingly. All of these variables affect the net amount of tax you must pay.

Here's a table showing the federal income tax brackets and rates for 2014 for some different types of taxpayers:

2014 Federal Income Tax Brackets and Rates

Tax Rate	Single Filers	Married Joint Filers	Head Of Household Filers
10%	$0 - $9,075	$0 - $18,150	$0 - $12,950
15%	$9,076 - $36,900	$18,151 - $73,800	$12,951 - $49,400
25%	$36,901 - $89,350	$73,801 - $148,850	$49,401 - $127,550
28%	$89,351 - $186,350	$148,851 - $226,850	$127,551 - $206,600
33%	$186,351 - $405,100	$226,851 - $405,100	$206,601 - $405,100
35%	$405,101 - $406,750	$405,101 - $457,600	$405,101 - $432,200
39.6%	$406,751 +	$457,601 +	$432,201 +

You'll notice that if you're single and earn $40,000, you're in the 25% tax *bracket* for 2014. However, the following shows that your effective or net rate of federal tax rate would be only 15%:

Income Tax Bracket	Income Taxed	Federal Tax Rate	Federal Tax Due
$0 - $9,075	$9,075	10%	$908
$9,076 - $36,900	$27,825	15%	$4,174
$36,901 - $40,000	$3,100	25%	$775
Totals	$40,000		$5,857

Effective tax rate = $5,857 ÷ $40,000 = 15%

Although earning $40,000 means you're in the 25% tax bracket, your entire income is not taxed at this rate. A portion is taxed at 10%, another at 15%, and another at 25%, which generally makes your effective or net tax rate lower than your tax bracket rate.

There are four ways to file your federal and state tax returns:

1. Free File is tax preparation software provided free of charge at irs.gov for individuals with income below a certain amount. You're guided through a series of questions to calculate your tax liability, and your federal and state returns are filed electronically.
2. Fillable forms are free online tax forms at irs.gov that you can complete and file electronically without the help of software, regardless of your income. State tax forms are not included.
3. Tax software can be purchased to help you prepare your federal and state returns and file them electronically.
4. Tax preparers are tax professionals who prepare your federal and state returns and file electronically. Visit irs.gov for a list of authorized e-file providers or ask people you know to recommend a reputable tax accountant.

Not Every State Collects Income Tax

In addition to federal taxes, you may have to pay state tax on your income. Each state has its own tax system. The following nine states don't collect any tax from income that individuals earn: Alaska, Florida, Nevada, New Hampshire, South Dakota, Tennessee, Texas, Washington, and Wyoming.

Part 3 Review Questions

1. List several reasons that people work. What are some reasons people change jobs throughout their lifetime?
2. What are some "marketable skills" you possess? Think about skills you've developed and used in past jobs, volunteer opportunities, and even in school.
3. What are four different kinds of taxes withheld from your paycheck? What is the money ultimately used for?
4. Briefly describe the U.S. tax system.

Project

Research how the United States spent last year's tax dollars. What percentages went to discretionary spending, mandatory spending, and interest on federal debt? What does discretionary and mandatory spending pay for?

PART

4

Save and Invest Money

Going to college. Buying a car. Starting a business. Retiring from work. Any financial goal or dream that you have can become a reality if you get in the habit of consistently setting aside small amounts of money over time. Starting this routine at a young age will really pay off and allow you to control your financial future.

Though we tend to use the terms saving and investing interchangeably, they're not the same. The difference has to do with taking financial risk. Investors walk a line between wanting to make money and not wanting to lose money. Saving money in a bank keeps it completely safe but pays a lower rate of return than some other investments. Investments that pay higher rates of return come with higher risk—the chance you could lose some or all of your money.

It's important to understand that, most often, high-return investments come with higher risk. And low-return investments or savings usually come with low risk.

Types of Savings Accounts

You will probably earn only a small amount of interest on savings. But the purpose of having savings is to keep the funds completely safe and accessible. Money you need to spend in the short-term for planned purchases and emergencies should be kept in a federally-insured savings account, so you can't lose it.

There are three basic types of savings accounts you can open at most banks and credit unions: a savings account, a money market account, and a certificate of deposit. Review Part 1 of this handbook for an explanation of these accounts and the protection offered by the Federal Deposit Insurance Corporation, or FDIC.

Investing Basics

Looking at the period from 1928 to 2013, we see that investing money in the stock market has historically rewarded investors with average returns that exceed 11%. Even from 2004 to 2013—the decade that includes the most recent economic recession—investors earned approximately 9% on average.

So why would you put money in a bank savings account that might earn 0.1% to 2% instead? Because investing money always involves some amount of risk—the potential to lose money as well as the potential to make money.

Financial analysts make forecasts based on what happened in the past. But they include the disclaimer "Past performance does not guarantee future results." In other words, even the smartest analyst can't predict how much an investment will be worth in the future. Therefore, it's very important to invest with wisdom and caution.

The purpose of investing money is to increase your wealth over a long time period so you can achieve goals like paying for retirement or purchasing a home. Whether you should save or invest depends on your time horizon, which is the amount of time between now and when you'll actually need to spend the money. If you have a long time horizon—such as 10 years or more—investing makes sense. When you have a short time horizon—such as a year or less—many financial advisors recommend that you stick with an insured savings account.

What Is the Securities Investor's Protection Corporation (SIPC)?

Investments, or securities, are not guaranteed by any federal agency such as the FDIC. There is no insurance against losing money in an investment. However, the Securities

Investor Protection Corporation (SIPC) is a nongovernment entity that gives you limited protection in certain situations. They step in when an investment brokerage firm fails or fraud is the cause of investor loss. The SIPC replaces missing securities up to $500,000 per customer. You can learn more at sipc.org.

Types of Investments

The earlier you start investing, the more money you'll have to pay for your financial dreams and goals. There are four basic types of financial securities and products that you can purchase for your investment portfolio. They are stocks, bonds, mutual funds, and exchange-traded funds.

Stocks

Stocks are issued by companies—like Apple, Google, and Facebook—that want to raise money. When you buy shares of a stock, you purchase an ownership interest in a company and your shares can go up or down in value over time. Stocks are bought and sold on exchanges, like the New York Stock Exchange or the NASDAQ, and you can monitor their prices in real time online.

Stocks are one of the riskiest investments because the price per share can be volatile, swinging up or down in a short period of time. People can't be sure about which stocks will increase in value over the short or long term. However, historically, stocks have rewarded investors with higher returns than other major investment classes, like cash or bonds.

Bonds

Bonds are loans you give to a corporation or government entity, known as the issuer, who wants to raise money for a specific project. Projects paid for by a bond include things such as building a factory or a school. Bonds pay a fixed interest rate over a set period of time. The time can range from weeks to 30 years. In general, interest is higher for longer-term bond terms and for bonds issued by companies with better credit.

Bonds are also called fixed-income investments because the return is guaranteed. In return for a higher degree of safety than stocks, you receive a relatively low rate of return. (Remember that lower risk investments give you a lower return and higher risk investments typically offer higher returns.) But these conservative investments still have some risk. For example, a bond issuer can default on repayment. Agencies such as Standard and Poor's (standardandpoors.com) do research and offer a rating system of bond safety.

Mutual Funds

Mutual funds are products that bundle combinations of investments, such as stocks, bonds, and other securities. They're operated by professional money managers who invest the fund's money according to stated objectives, such as achieving maximum growth or earning fixed income. Mutual fund shares are purchased directly from the fund company or from investment brokers and can go up or down in value over time.

In general, mutual funds composed of stock have the greatest potential risk and reward; however, there's a wide range of risk within this category. Mutual funds composed of bonds also have a range of risk but are considered more conservative than stock funds.

Exchange-Traded Funds (ETFs)

Exchange-traded funds are products that bundle combinations of investments—just like mutual funds—but trade like a stock on an exchange throughout the day. These securities are growing in popularity due to their flexibility and low cost. The cost to operate an ETF is very low compared to many mutual funds.

Other Types of Investments

Other types of investments include real estate, precious metals (like gold and silver), and businesses, just to name a few. They generally require more expertise and skill to buy and sell than the four types of securities covered here. The drawback to alternative investments is that they aren't as liquid, or sold as easily, as mainstream investments.

Finance Tip

You can reduce risk by diversification, which means owning a variety of investments in your portfolio.

What Is Financial Risk?

To be a successful investor, you need to understand the financial risks of different types of investments and gauge your own tolerance for risk. Many brokerage firms offer a questionnaire that can help you determine this.

What seems safe to one person may be deemed very risky by another. Your tolerance for risk is how you react when your investments decline in value. Someone who doesn't like risk is considered risk averse. A risk-averse person is willing to miss out on higher rates of return in exchange for financial safety. A more risk-tolerant person is willing to accept investment losses in exchange for potential higher returns.

There is no right or wrong risk style that you should adopt. It just comes down to your personal feelings and preferences for how you want to manage your investments.

Ways to Invest

You have many choices when it comes to investing your money. The two most common are brokerage accounts and retirement accounts.

Brokerage Accounts

Brokerage accounts are available at local brokerage firms and firms that operate online that are licensed to place investment orders, such as buying or selling shares of a stock, a mutual fund, or an ETF. You own the assets in a brokerage account and must pay tax each year on the earnings, which are called capital gains.

Retirement Accounts

Retirement accounts are special accounts you can open at a variety of institutions, such as local or online banks and brokerage firms, that allow you to save for retirement. One of the advantages is that they allow you to pay less tax.

There are different kinds of retirement accounts available for individuals, as part of an employee benefit package at work, and for the self-employed. Investment options include many of the instruments already mentioned, such as stocks, bonds, mutual funds, ETFs, or even bank CDs.

When you invest through a retirement account—as opposed to a regular brokerage account—you defer, or avoid paying, tax on your earnings. That means you save money on taxes and have more money for retirement! However, if you withdraw funds from a retirement account that weren't previously taxed, you're typically subject to an early withdrawal penalty, in addition to ordinary income tax.

The most commonly used retirement accounts include individual retirement arrangements, the 401(k) plan, and the 403(b) plan. In order to have enough money to live comfortably for decades during retirement, it's important to get in the habit of saving money in a retirement account.

Individual Retirement Arrangement (IRA) The IRA is a personal account available to anyone, regardless of age, who has taxable income. You can begin making contributions to an IRA as soon as you get your first job. However, you're in charge of it, not your employer. With a traditional IRA you generally don't pay tax on contributions or earnings until after you retire and start taking withdrawals. In other words, taxes on the account are deferred until sometime in the future. With a Roth IRA, you pay tax on your contributions up front. However, you never pay tax on them again or on any amount of earnings. You get a huge tax benefit with a Roth because your entire account grows completely tax free.

401(k) Plan The 401(k) plan is a retirement account offered by many companies. You authorize a portion of your wages to be contributed to the plan before income tax is withheld from your paycheck. A 401(k) plan offers participants a set menu of investment choices. You can contribute amounts up to certain allowable limits each year.

403(b) Plan The 403(b) plan is a retirement account offered by certain organizations such as schools, churches, and hospitals. It's similar to a 401(k) in most aspects and also limits contributions each year.

Retirement Accounts for Employees

There are two main types of retirement programs found in the workplace: defined benefit plans and defined contribution plans.

- A **defined benefit plan** is funded and managed by an employer and is commonly known as a pension. Employees don't pay into the plan, pick investments, or manage the money in any way. Defined benefit plans give retired workers a specific, defined benefit, such as $800 per month for the rest of their life. The benefit paid depends on various factors, such as age, length of employment, and salary history. These plans have become rare in the workplace because they're expensive to operate. However, some large companies, government agencies, and labor unions offer them.
- A **defined contribution plan** is established by an employer but requires that the employee manage it. This type of plan includes the 401(k) and 403(b) plans. The retirement benefit that an employee will receive depends on the amount that's invested and the performance of the chosen investments over the years. Defined contribution plans are more common because they're less risky for an employer to administer.

What Is Employer Matching?

If you could earn a guaranteed 100% return on your money, would you be interested? Many employers match a certain amount of the money you put in a workplace retirement plan. Say your employer matches 100% of your contributions to a 401(k) up to 3% of your salary. If you earn $30,000 a year and contribute $75 a month or $900 a year, that's a contribution of 3% of your salary. With matching, your employer would also contribute $900. So you'd invest $900 and automatically get $900 from your company—an immediate 100% return on your money!

How Much Will Social Security Pay in Retirement?

As a young person, it's not possible to know exactly how much you'll receive in Social Security retirement benefits. They're calculated based on various factors, such as the current law, your future earnings, how long you pay payroll or self-employment taxes, the age you elect to start receiving benefits, and military service.

However, according to the Social Security Administration, the benefit replaces only about 40% of your preretirement earnings, if you have average income. As of June 2013, the average monthly benefit for a retired worker was $1,269. The maximum monthly benefit was $2,533; however, higher benefits may be possible if you choose to delay benefits and start receiving them after you reach full retirement age.

Therefore, it's important not to count on Social Security retirement benefits as your sole source of income during retirement. The program was created as a supplement for personal savings, not as a substitute for having a retirement plan.

Investing for Education

Just as there are special accounts that allow you to invest for retirement and pay less tax, there are two education savings accounts, or ESAs, to be familiar with: 529 plans and Coverdells.

- A **529 plan** is a savings or investment vehicle that allows you to contribute money to pay for a student's qualified expenses at a college, university, or vocational school. There are prepaid plans, where you prepay all or a portion of the future cost, and investment plans, where you choose specific investments. Contributions and earnings in a 529 plan grow tax free.
- A **Coverdell account** allows you to contribute money to pay for any level of education, from kindergarten through graduate school. It differs from a 529 plan in that it has more restrictions, such as how much can be contributed each year and the age of the student who will use the funds.

You can learn more about 529s and Coverdells at savingforcollege.com and finaid.org.

Part 4 Review Questions

1. What is the difference between *saving* and *investing*?
2. Briefly describe each of the four kinds of investments.
3. Briefly describe the different kinds of retirement accounts. Why is it a good idea to invest in retirement accounts as soon as you start working?

Project

What does it mean to "diversify" your savings plan? Research different kinds of savings and investments and come up with a plan that provides a good balance of both.

PART 5

Give Yourself Some Credit

How is it possible to make a major purchase, like a home, if you don't have the cash? The answer is credit. If you're "creditworthy," you can be trusted to borrow money and pay it back over time.

What Is Credit?

Credit is the ability to borrow money that you promise to repay with interest. Credit is an important part of your financial life because it allows you to do the following:

- **Make a large purchase and pay for it over time**. If you don't have enough money saved up to buy a car, having credit allows you to get a loan and repay it over a set period of time.
- **Stay safe in an emergency situation**. If your car breaks down and you don't have enough to pay for the repair, having a credit card or line of credit allows you to get back on the road and repay the balance over time.
- **Avoid having to carry cash or paper checks**. When you're making a large purchase, like a computer or furniture, using a credit card is safer than carrying around a large amount of cash or paper checks that could be stolen.
- **Make online purchases and reservations**. When you need to buy something over the Internet—like books, clothes, or travel reservations—it's convenient to use a credit card.

If you don't have credit, the only way to get a loan or credit card is to have someone with good credit cosign an account. A cosigner might be a family member or friend who guarantees to take full responsibility for the debt if you don't repay it.

How do you become creditworthy so a potential creditor—such as a bank or credit card company—will allow you to borrow money? While each institution has different guidelines for evaluating a potential borrower, the following five criteria are generally used:

1. **Credit score**: How likely are you to make on-time payments based on your credit history? In this section you'll learn more about what a credit score is.
2. **Income**: Do you have a steady job and have enough income to repay a debt?
3. **Debt**: Do you have existing debts? If so, will you have enough money to pay your current debt and make payments on a new debt?
4. **Financial ratios**: How much debt do you have relative to your income?
5. **Collateral**: Will you secure a debt by pledging property (like a car or home) that a lender could sell if you don't make payments?

Understanding Credit Reports

Your credit history is maintained by three major nationwide credit reporting agencies: Equifax (equifax.com), Experian (experian.com), and TransUnion (transunion.com). These agencies receive information about you from your creditors and list it on your credit report. They are interested in things such as whether you make payments on time, your outstanding debt balances, and your available credit limits. Credit reporting agencies don't make credit decisions; they simply report information provided to them on your credit reports.

Each of your credit reports from the three agencies is slightly different, but they generally contain the following four types of information:

1. **Personal information** includes your name, current and previous addresses, Social Security number, birth date, and employer.

2. **Account information** lists your open accounts and your closed accounts for up to a certain period of time.
3. **Credit inquiries** include a list of companies and employers that have made inquiries about you because you applied for a credit account or job.
4. **Public information** is data that's available in the public records about you, including bankruptcies, foreclosures, liens for unpaid income taxes, and legal judgments.

The information in your credit report sticks with you for a long time. Credit accounts with negative information (for example, late payments) remain on your credit report for seven years from the date your payment became past due, even after you close the account or pay it off in full. Credit accounts with positive information remain on your credit report for 10 years after you close the account or pay it off in full.

Understanding Credit Scores

Just as your schoolwork determines your final grade in various classes, the information in your credit reports is used to calculate your credit scores. One of the most confusing things about credit scores is that there isn't just one. Your credit score depends on the particular scoring model that's used to calculate it. Companies can create their own scoring systems or use brand-name scores calculated by other firms, like the FICO (Fair Isaac Corporation) Score or the VantageScore.

Your credit score is different from the final grade you receive for a class because it isn't figured once and filed away. Your credit score is calculated fresh every time it's requested. Therefore, it's a snapshot of your credit behavior up to that moment in time.

Poor credit may indicate that you've mismanaged your finances by making late payments or maxing out credit accounts. However, having too little credit history can also be a reason for having a low credit score.

Having poor credit means you'll be viewed as a risky customer who may not repay a debt. You'll either be turned down for credit or charged an interest rate that's higher than the rate offered to a customer with good credit. Why? In exchange for taking a financial risk on a customer with poor credit, lenders protect themselves financially by charging higher interest rates, which means you have to make higher monthly payments.

How Much Can Poor Credit Cost You?

Dora has excellent credit and goes to her bank to apply for a $15,000 car loan. After a few days the bank's lending representative calls her with good news—she's been approved! She can borrow $15,000 at 4% APR for a term of four years, which makes her monthly payment $338.69. The total amount of interest she'll pay on the loan principal is $1,256.92.

On the other hand, let's imagine Dora didn't have excellent credit and the bank charged her 12% APR instead of 4%. At this higher interest rate, her monthly payment would be $395.01. She'd pay a total of $3,960.36 in interest—or $2,703.44 more than if her credit was in good shape.

The larger a loan, the more poor credit costs you. **Table 1** below shows different scenarios for a home mortgage of $150,000 paid over 30 years. Not having excellent credit means you could pay an additional $127,493.41 in interest—on top of the original loan amount of $150,000.

Table 1 The Cost of Poor Credit

Credit status	APR (percent)	Monthly payment (dollars)	Total interest paid (dollars)	Cost of having poor credit (dollars)
Excellent	3.75%	$694.67	100,082.42	$0
Good	5.00	805.23	139,883.68	39,801.26
Average	7.50	1,048.82	227,575.83	127,493.41

Other Ways Having Poor Credit Hurts Your Finances

Did you know that having poor credit scores can cost you even if you don't want a loan or credit card? Here are five ways that having poor credit affects your personal finances:

1. **Paying high insurance premiums**: In most U.S. states, insurance companies are allowed to factor in your credit when setting car and home insurance rates. Having poor credit means you'll be quoted rates that could be double or triple the amount that someone with excellent credit would pay. That's because consumers with poor credit have been found to file more insurance claims.
2. **Paying high security deposits**: You may be asked to pay higher deposits for an apartment and for utilities such as power, gas, water, and phone accounts.
3. **Getting declined as a tenant**: You could be turned down for an apartment or house to rent because property managers prefer tenants who demonstrate good payment history.
4. **Getting turned down for government benefits**: You might not qualify for certain types of federal or state benefits that require a good credit history.
5. **Getting denied a job**: You might be turned down for a job by an employer who requires a credit check. Employers can't get your credit scores or see your entire credit report, but they can find out if you've had credit problems.

Finance Tip

To find out your credit score, you can visit the credit bureau websites mentioned earlier and purchase the information from them. You may also buy your FICO Score at myfico.com, or get several scores for free at creditkarma.com.

How to Establish Credit

The information in your credit report has a ripple effect throughout your entire financial life. How can you get started building good credit? Knowing how credit scores are calculated can help you improve them.

Each credit scoring model values the information in your credit report differently and uses a unique score range. The popular FICO Score uses a scale from 300 to 850 and values the following five factors:

1. **Payment history** (35%): making payments for bills and credit accounts on time
2. **Credit utilization** (30%): having lower amounts of debt relative to your available credit limits on credit cards and lines of credit
3. **Length of credit history** (15%): having credit accounts for a longer period of time
4. **Type of credit used** (10%): having a mix of credit types, including loans and credit cards
5. **Applications for credit** (10%): having fewer requests for new credit accounts

To build good credit, focus on actions within your control that have the biggest influence on typical scoring models. These include paying bills on time and not maxing out credit cards. But remember that it takes time to build good credit—it's a marathon, not a sprint.

Finance Tip

To stay on top of your credit more than once a year, space out your requests and get a free report from a different credit agency every four months at annualcreditreport.com.

How to Build Your Credit

It may be difficult to get approved for a credit card before you've established a good credit history. However, everyone over age 18 can get a secured credit card, which can help you build credit for the first time—as long as it reports payment transactions to the credit agencies. With a secured credit card, you must make a refundable upfront deposit (as little as $200) that serves as your credit limit.

How to Protect Your Credit

To protect the integrity of your credit, you should check your credit report on a regular basis. It's up to you to make sure that the information in your credit report is correct. Errors or fraudulent activity can hurt your credit scores without you knowing it.

Checking your credit reports is easy and it never hurts your credit scores. You can purchase your credit report from any of the three credit agencies, but you're entitled to a free report once a year at annualcreditreport.com. You can report inaccuracies or put a stop to fraud by placing a credit alert or credit freeze on your credit reports. The Fair Credit Reporting Act (FCRA) is a federal law that regulates how your credit information can be used and your consumer credit rights. You can learn more on the Federal Trade Commission website at ftc.gov.

Part 5 Review Questions

1. Briefly describe the criteria a creditor uses to evaluate a potential borrower.
2. Why is it important to maintain an excellent credit score? Name ways that bad credit can hurt someone. How can good credit help you achieve some of your own financial goals?
3. Why do you think lenders have an interest in your credit history?
4. Do you think it's fair that consumers with good credit scores typically pay less for credit accounts, such as credit cards and loans, and certain insurance products? Why or why not?

Project

Imagine that your best friend just got approved for a credit card with a $500 available credit limit. He or she is excited to use a credit card for the first time and wants to go on a shopping spree. If you know that he or she doesn't have much money to pay off the credit card bill, what advice would you offer?

PART 6

Borrow Without Sorrow

It can be easy to get into financial trouble if you borrow money that you can't repay. Getting behind on bills—such as payments for a car loan, student loan, or credit card—results in large late fees and long-term damage to your credit history. Therefore, it's important to know how to use debt responsibly and to make wise choices that are best for your financial future.

What to Know About Debt

Before you apply for credit or take on any amount of debt, ask yourself some important questions:

- Do I really need this item?
- Can I wait until I save enough cash to pay for it?
- What's the total cost of the credit, including interest and fees?
- Can I afford the monthly payments?

There are many different kinds of debt, but they fall into two main categories: installment loans and revolving credit.

Installment Loan Basics

An installment loan is an agreement you make with a creditor to borrow a certain amount of money and repay it in equal monthly payments, or installments, for a set period of time. The length or term of the loan could be very short or in excess of 30 years and may be secured or unsecured.

Secured loans are backed by collateral, which is something of value that you pledge to the lender. For instance, a car you finance is collateral for the car loan. And a house is collateral for a home loan, which is also known as a mortgage. Collateral protects lenders because they can sell it to repay your debt if you don't make payments as agreed.

Unsecured loans are not backed by any collateral. They're often called personal or signature loans because you sign an agreement where you promise to repay the debt. For instance, credit card debt and student loans are both forms of unsecured loans.

When you take an installment loan, your monthly payment will depend on three factors:

1. **Principal amount**: The less you borrow, the lower your monthly payment will be.
2. **Interest rate**: The lower the rate, the lower your monthly payment will be.
3. **Loan term**: The longer the term, the lower your monthly payment will be; however, this generally results in paying more total interest.

Common Types of Installment Loans

Installment loans give consumers money to buy many different products and services, like cars, homes, or a college education.

Consumer Loans

Consumer installment loans, also called personal or signature loans, are commonly used for small purchases, like buying a computer or paying for unexpected expenses. You can apply for an unsecured consumer loan from local banks, credit unions, or online lenders.

Auto Loans

Installment loans to buy a new or used vehicle are available from local banks, credit unions, online lenders, and some car dealers. You may be required to make a down payment on the purchase price—especially if you don't have good credit.

For example, if you want to buy a used car that costs $10,000, the lender may require that you pay 20% or $2,000 up front in order to borrow the remaining balance of $8,000.

As previously mentioned, a car you buy becomes collateral for the loan. If you don't make payments as agreed, the lender can repossess, or take back, the vehicle to pay off the outstanding loan balance. The lender typically holds the title of the car until the loan is paid off in full.

The term or repayment period for a car loan is typically 2 to 7 years. Choosing a longer loan term reduces the monthly payment but can significantly increase the amount of total interest you have to pay.

What's Being "Upside Down"? A new car depreciates, or loses its value, very quickly—especially in the first three years—depending on the make and model. For example, a $20,000 car might be worth only $15,000 after a year. But your outstanding loan balance could be over $16,000 if you made a low or no down payment (depending on the loan terms).

When you owe more for a car than it's worth, you're "upside down" on the loan. If you want to trade or sell the car, you have to pay extra out of pocket to pay off the loan. Making a down payment helps you avoid this common financial problem of being "upside down"—and helps reduce your monthly loan payment. So, even if you have good credit, it's wise to make a down payment on a car loan.

What's a Car Title? A car title is a document that shows who purchased a vehicle and lists information including the vehicle identification number (VIN), make, year of manufacture, purchase price, registered owner name and address, and the legal owner if any money is owed. When a car is sold, the title must be transferred to the new owner.

What's Vehicle Leasing? Instead of owning a car you can lease one for a set period of time. After the lease term (usually two, three, or four years) expires, you have to return the vehicle to the leasing company. Monthly lease payments may be less than a loan payment for the same vehicle and term. However, after you pay off a car loan the vehicle belongs to you. You can sell it for cash or continue to drive it for many years without having to make a car payment. Therefore, purchasing a car is more cost effective when you keep it for the long term.

Student Loans

Student loans are funds you can use for education expenses, such as tuition, books, room and board, and other living expenses while you attend college. There are two main types of unsecured installment loans that may be available to you or your parents: federal student loans and private student loans.

Federal student loans are issued by the federal government and most don't require a credit check for approval. Most students qualify for some type of federal loan, up to certain limits, depending on their income or their parents' financial qualifications. To apply, you must complete the Free Application for Federal Student Aid (FAFSA). You can submit it online at the U.S. Department of Education website at fafsa.ed.gov.

Here are three types of federal student loans:

- **Stafford Loan** is the main federal loan for students, which can be subsidized by the federal government or unsubsidized. To receive a subsidized Stafford Loan, you must demonstrate financial need. The government pays, or subsidizes, the interest on the loan while you're in school.

  Unsubsidized Stafford Loans require you to pay all the interest; however, you can defer making payments until after graduation. All students, regardless of financial need, can get an unsubsidized Stafford Loan.
- **Perkins Loan** is a subsidized federal loan given to students who have the most financial need. The government pays the loan interest during school and for a nine-month grace period.
- **Parent Loan for Undergraduate Students (PLUS)** is an unsubsidized federal loan for parents of students. A credit check is made to verify that the parents have no adverse credit history.

Private student loans originate from a private lender, such as an online institution, a local bank, or a credit union.

Finance Tip

The Kelley Blue Book at kbb.com is a guide that helps car buyers and sellers determine the market value of a new or used vehicle.

Finance Tip

Use the car loan calculator at dinkytown.com to find out how changing the down payment, loan amount, interest rate, and term of a loan results in different monthly payments.

Private education loans are generally used to bridge the gap between the cost of college and the amount you can borrow from the government.

Eligibility for a private loan depends on your or your parents' financial qualifications and credit scores. You submit an application directly to a private lender and don't have to complete any federal forms.

Private student loans typically have higher interest rates and less repayment flexibility than federal loans. Therefore, always apply for a federal student loan first.

Finance Tip

To learn more about completing the FAFSA and paying for college, finaid.org is a leading resource for financial aid—including loans, scholarships, grants, and fellowships.

Home Loans

You can get a home loan or mortgage from local banks, credit unions, or online lenders. They can be used to

- buy real estate, such as a house or condominium,
- buy a parcel of vacant land,
- build a home, or
- borrow against the equity or value of a home you already own.

There are three main types of home loans:

1. A **purchase loan** is used to buy a home and is secured by the property. You must make a down payment that's typically 5% to 20% of the purchase price. The loan term is typically 30 years, but 15- and 20-year mortgages are also common.
2. An **equity loan** is secured by your home and can be used for any purpose. **Equity** is the current market value of your property less the amount of outstanding debt you owe. For instance, if your home is worth $200,000 and your mortgage balance is $140,000, you have $60,000 in equity.
3. A **refinance loan** replaces an existing home loan by paying it off and creating a brand new loan that has better terms, such as a lower interest rate. Refinancing at a lower interest rate may allow you to lower your monthly payments and save money.

What Is Foreclosure? Foreclosure is a legal process a home lender uses to collect the balance of an unpaid debt when a borrower defaults or stops making loan payments as agreed. The lender can take legal title to the property, evict the borrower(s), and sell the property to pay off the debt, according to state laws.

Revolving Credit Basics

Revolving credit is different from an installment loan (such as a car or student loan) because it doesn't have a fixed number of payments or a final due date. The account revolves, or stays open indefinitely, as long as you make minimum monthly payments. The lender approves a maximum loan amount, or credit limit, to use at any time. Credit cards, retail store credit cards, and home equity lines of credit (HELOCs) are common types of revolving credit.

Applying for a Credit Card

If you're under age 21, you must show that you have income or an eligible cosigner to qualify for a credit card. The law requires that you receive a Federal Truth in Lending Disclosure Statement from any company that offers you credit. Be sure to read it carefully so you understand the terms and can compare cards based on these features:

- annual percentage rate (APR) for purchases, promotions, cash advances, and balance transfers
- your credit limit
- potential fees and penalties
- how balances are calculated
- rewards or rebates for purchases
- additional protections (such as travel insurance or extended warranties)

Managing a Credit Card

A credit card gives you the ability to make purchases now and pay for them later. For example, if you have a credit card with a $1,000 credit limit, you can use it to buy products or services, or take cash advances that total up to $1,000. However, you should never max out a credit card because that hurts your credit.

This flexibility makes credit cards powerful financial tools that can help you in an emergency situation. But credit cards can also devastate your finances if you get over your head in debt that you can't repay.

Because they're so convenient for consumers and come with unsecured risk for lenders, credit cards charge relatively high interest rates that can exceed 30%. Every time you make a credit card purchase, you're borrowing money that must be paid back. You'll also have to pay interest charges if you don't pay off your balance in full by the monthly statement due date.

Paying Your Credit Card

Credit cards issue an account statement each month that lists transactions from the previous month. The lowest amount you can pay—your "minimum payment"—varies depending on the card, but may range from 2% to 4% of your outstanding balance. For instance, if you owe $500, your minimum payment could be 3%, or $15. The remaining balance of $485 will continue to accrue interest, in addition to any new transactions you make or late fees that may apply.

However, if you pay off your entire credit card balance by the due date on your statement each month, you can use a credit card without paying any interest charges or late fees. That's because no interest charges accrue during this "grace period."

Tips to Reduce the Cost of Borrowing

The cost of borrowing money depends on several factors, such as the current interest rates, your credit rating, the APR you're offered, loan fees, and how long it takes you to repay the debt. Here are 10 tips to reduce the cost of borrowing:

1. **Shop around for the lowest APR** for a loan or credit card before you accept an offer.
2. **Finance an item based on the total price** (including interest) that you can afford—not just on a monthly payment amount.
3. **Repay loans over a shorter term** so you pay less total interest over the life of a loan.
4. **Pay off credit card purchases in full each month** so you're never charged interest or late fees.
5. **Make payments on time** so you're never penalized with expensive late fees or an increased APR on a credit card.
6. **Build a good credit history** so you have high credit scores and will be offered low interest rates by lenders and credit card companies. Establishing credit was covered in Part 5 of this handbook.
7. **Make a bigger down payment** so you'll owe less and receive lower APR offers from auto and home lenders.
8. **Take out federal student loans** before accepting private education loans so you qualify for the most favorable interest rates and repayment terms.
9. **Claim tax benefits** that come with education loans, such as the student loan interest tax deduction, which may allow you to reduce the amount of tax you owe.
10. **Never take a payday loan**, which is a short-term unsecured advance against your next paycheck. The interest rate for one of these loans can be over 15% for just two weeks—which translates into a sky-high APR that can exceed 400%!

Part 6 Review Questions

1. What do you think are the advantages and disadvantages of borrowing money?
2. What goals do you have that might require you to borrow money?
3. Briefly describe the different kinds of student loans. How can you be sure you don't borrow more than you can comfortably pay back, taking other lifetime financial burdens (such as buying a home or car, having children, etc.) into consideration?
4. What are some important rules to remember when it comes to managing a credit card the right way?
5. Why should credit cards and loans never be viewed as "free money"?

Project

Come up with five questions to ask when you are comparing different kinds of loans or credit. For example, one question can be "What is my minimum monthly payment?"

PART 7

Manage Your Money

Building wealth and creating financial security can be easy if you have a reliable income and manage your money wisely. Good money management starts with never spending more than you make each month. Your financial life will always be a balancing act between the short-term gratification of spending to fulfill your current wants versus the long-term benefit of saving. Striking the right balance will allow you to have enough money to fulfill your future wants and needs.

It's your job to have the willpower to resist unnecessary spending and get into the habit of saving for the future on a regular basis. If you use your financial resources responsibly, you'll be able to have a secure future and make your dreams a reality.

Setting Financial Goals

A financial goal is something you want to do with your money in a certain period of time. Goals can be short-term, like buying a car this year or taking a vacation next summer. Or goals can be long-term, like accumulating a large nest egg for retirement. Retirement is one of the most important goals for everyone. Why? Because as you grow older, you may neither want nor be able to work until the end of your life. The hope is that we save enough money so it's possible to enjoy life and pursue other interests besides work when desired.

In Part 3 you learned that Social Security benefits are likely to provide you with a small amount of income after you retire. However, you'll need additional savings for everyday expenses, such as housing, food, and medical costs—otherwise you won't have a comfortable lifestyle as you grow older.

Though you have many years to go, saving enough for retirement generally takes decades to achieve. That's why it's critical that you begin saving for the future as early as possible. Financial success doesn't happen overnight—so the earlier you start saving for retirement, the better.

What Is Social Security?

Social Security is a group of benefits paid to eligible taxpayers who are retired, disabled, or who survive a relative who was receiving benefits. The funds for Social Security come from taxes withheld from your paycheck. The amount you'll receive in retirement depends on how many years you work, how much payroll or self-employment tax you pay during your career, the age you elect to start receiving benefits, and the future financial health of the Social Security system. Visit ssa.gov for more information.

Creating a Budget

It's easy for everyday purchases like snacks, magazines, and music to get out of control if you're not watching them carefully. Keeping your expenses as low as possible can add up to huge savings over time. For instance, let's say bringing your lunch to work 4 days a week saves you $8 a day or $32 a week. If you invested $32 a week for 40 years at a moderate rate of return, that savings would grow to over $330,000.

The best way to take control of your money is to create a budget, also known as a spending plan. A spending plan helps you understand how much money you have and where it goes, so you can prioritize expenses and set objectives to achieve your short- and long-term financial goals.

Managing money the right way is all about making choices and sacrifices—like whether to spend money on a night out with friends or save it to buy a car. You'll always have many needs and wants competing for your limited financial resources.

You can apply an economic mindset to your financial planning too! It's up to you to choose your priorities and decide the best way to spend your money.

Four Steps to Preparing a Successful Budget

Knowing exactly how much you have to spend and where you spend it gives you power over your finances. You can keep track of your financial information on paper, using a computer spreadsheet or a mobile app, or by importing transactions from your bank or credit card accounts into a financial program like Quicken.

Here are four easy steps to creating a successful spending plan:

Step #1—Enter your net monthly income.

To stay in control of your money and reach your financial goals, you must know how much money you have coming in each month. Recall that net income, or take-home pay, is the amount you have left after taxes and other voluntary workplace deductions. Enter this amount at the top of your spending plan because it's what you actually have to spend each month.

Step #2—Enter your fixed and variable expenses.

Many people don't achieve financial success because they spend money carelessly. It's critical that you keep a close watch on your spending so it never exceeds your net income. Enter all your expenses below your income.

Fixed expenses don't change from month to month and may include your rent, insurance, phone, or a loan payment. Variable expenses can change each month or are discretionary, like dining out, transportation, or buying clothes.

Organize your expenses into major categories—such as rent, insurance, groceries, dining out, clothes, and entertainment—and enter the total amounts.

Step #3—Compare your income and expenses.

When you compare your total take-home pay to your total expenses, you may be pleased that you have money left over or be disappointed that there's none to spare. Discretionary income is the amount of money you have left over each month after all your essential living expenses are paid.

You must spend less than you make in order to have enough discretionary income to save and invest for your future. Living paycheck to paycheck may satisfy immediate wants and needs, but it won't empower you to achieve long-term financial success.

Step #4—Set priorities and make changes.

The final step is to create new spending guidelines. Decide how much you want to allocate toward each of your short- and long-term financial goals and enter them as separate categories in your spending plan. You may need to reduce spending in other categories or find ways to earn extra income to cover all your expenses.

It's up to you to figure out the best way to balance your spending and saving so you enjoy life today and put away enough money for a safe and secure tomorrow.

What Does "Pay Yourself First" Mean?

"Pay yourself first" is a common saying in personal finance that means saving money should be your top priority. Putting your savings on autopilot is the best way to remove the temptation to spend it! A portion of each paycheck can be deposited automatically in a savings or retirement account before you receive the balance. That way you pay yourself before paying your living expenses or making discretionary purchases.

Tracking Your Wealth

A spending plan is the perfect way to track your income and expenses. But to monitor the big picture of your finances, you need to know your net worth. Your net worth can be summed up in this simple equation:

$$\text{net worth} = \text{assets} - \text{liabilities}$$

Assets are items you own that have real value, such as cash in the bank, vehicles, investments, real estate, personal belongings, and money owed to you. Liabilities are your debts and financial obligations to others, such as a car loan, credit card debt, or money you borrowed from a friend.

If you have more assets than you owe in liabilities, your net worth will be a positive number. But if you owe more than you own, your net worth will be a negative number. The goal is to raise your net worth over time by increasing your assets or decreasing your liabilities, so you build wealth.

Paying Bills

Paying bills on time is one of the most important money management responsibilities. Late payments can result in expensive fees and damage to your credit. Thanks to online banking, it's never been easier to manage bills and pay them on time.

Most local and Internet-only banks offer free bill pay, which allows you to pay any company or individual with the click of a button. If a company you want to pay accepts electronic payments, your funds will transfer electronically. If not, the bill pay service prints and mails a paper check on your behalf to any payee in the United States that has a mailing address.

E-bills and e-statements can be sent to your e-mail, bill pay center, or both. You can set up a bill to be paid automatically on a certain date and e-mail you when the transaction is complete. Or you can log on to your bill pay center and manually initiate a payment for up to one year into the future. You can set up reminder alerts for all your recurring bills so no payment due date ever falls through the cracks.

Tips to Manage Money Like a Millionaire

One of the most surprising facts about wealthy people is that most of them weren't born that way. About 80% of the wealthiest people in the United States are first-generation millionaires. They accumulated wealth by working hard and saving and investing money. That means anyone who is disciplined with his or her money can achieve financial security. Here are 10 tips to manage your money like a millionaire:

1. **Live below your means**. Spending less than you make is a choice. Saving money, and not overspending, is how you build wealth.
2. **Know where your money goes**. If you don't have a spending plan to track your money, you won't know if you're making wise decisions. Getting ahead financially starts with taking control of your cash flow.
3. **Create an emergency fund**. Having money set aside for unexpected expenses is a safety net that you should never be without. That's how you'll make it through a financial rough patch, such as suddenly losing your job or having large unexpected expenses. Make a goal to accumulate at least six months' worth of your living expenses to keep on hand at all times.
4. **Focus on net worth instead of income**. No matter how much you earn, you can grow rich by slowly increasing your net worth over time. But even if you have a large income, you'll never grow rich if you don't get in the habit of setting aside money for the future.
5. **Have long-term financial goals**. Wealthy people know what they want to achieve and then work backward so they have a plan for what to do each year, month, week, or day to stay on track and meet their goals. Set objectives to achieve your goals.
6. **Begin saving for retirement early**. If you think you're too young to start saving for retirement, think again. Creating wealth for your future rarely happens overnight—unless you beat huge odds by having a winning lottery ticket or a big inheritance.
7. **Save and invest at least 15% of your income**. Make it a habit to save 15% to 20% of your income, starting with your first job, and adjust your lifestyle so you can easily live on the rest.
8. **Automate your savings and investments**. It's easier to save money that you never see. Participate in a workplace retirement account or have your paycheck split between a checking and savings account so your savings are on autopilot.
9. **View money as a tool**. Money is only as useful as what you do with it. So decide what's important to you and use money to achieve your needs and your dreams. Push away short-term gratification in favor of important, long-term goals like saving for retirement.
10. **Realize when you've made a money mistake**. Everyone makes mistakes with their money from time to time. If you overspend or make unwise decisions, stop and make the choice to get back on track right away.

Part 7 Review Questions

1. Do you think that writing down your goals and reviewing them on a regular basis could help increase your chances of accomplishing them? Why or why not?
2. What is the relationship between spending and the ability to build wealth?
3. Why does tracking how you spend money help you make better financial decisions?
4. What is the purpose of an emergency fund and how much should it be?

Project

Choose a savings goal that you'd like to achieve before the end of the summer. Create a savings plan and keep track of your progress over the next few months.

PART 8

Protect Yourself from Risk

Life is full of events that no one can predict. It's impossible to know if you'll get into a car accident, have your laptop stolen, or need to visit the emergency room for a broken bone. While you can't prevent these kinds of catastrophes, you can protect your personal finances by having enough of the right kinds of insurance.

Insurance is a special type of contract between you and an insurance company. The company agrees that when certain events occur, that are defined in an insurance policy, they'll meet certain expenses or provide a payout. For example, with a car insurance policy, the insurer agrees to pay some amount of the cost to repair it if you're in an accident. Health insurance pays a certain amount of your medical expenses if you need to go to the doctor.

Insurance eliminates or reduces the potential financial loss you could experience from an unforeseen event and protects the income and assets that you work hard for.

Types of Insurance

There are many different types of insurance products that can be purchased from an insurance company or a licensed insurance agent, either in person or online. The types you should have depend on your age and life circumstances. There are eight major types of insurance: health, disability, life, auto, homeowner's, renter's, long-term care, and umbrella.

Health Insurance

Without health insurance you could get stuck with a huge bill if you have any kind of medical need, from a broken bone to a chronic illness. Even a quick trip to the emergency room can cost thousands of dollars.

The Affordable Care Act (ACA), also known as Obamacare, is the nation's health reform law that was enacted in 2010. Starting in 2014, it requires most U.S. citizens and legal residents to purchase and maintain health insurance for themselves and their dependents, or to pay a penalty. The ACA may provide a financial subsidy, which reduces the monthly cost of health insurance, depending on your income and family size.

Many employers offer group health insurance, or you can purchase an individual policy on your own. You can stay on your parents' health policy until you're 26 years old—unless you're offered insurance at work.

Visit healthcare.gov to explore your health insurance options.

Disability Insurance

A disability is a physical or mental condition that limits your ability to perform various types of activities. If you're unable to work due to a disability, accident, or long-term illness, disability insurance replaces a portion of your income while you recuperate. Unless you have plenty of savings in an emergency fund, a disability could leave you unable to pay for everyday living expenses, such as housing or groceries. Remember that health insurance only covers a portion of your medical bills—not your everyday living expenses.

Many employers offer some type of disability coverage for employees, or if you're self-employed you can purchase an individual policy on your own. Professionals—like surgeons, athletes, or dancers—who want to protect their ability to do their job should always have disability coverage. Every disability policy is different, but there are two main types: short-term disability (STD) and long-term disability (LTD). A short-term policy usually pays you for a maximum of two years, while a long-term policy could provide benefits that last your entire life.

Life Insurance

Life insurance provides a lump-sum payment, known as a death benefit, to one or more named beneficiaries when the insured person dies. It's important to have life insurance when your death would cause a financial burden for those you leave behind—such as a spouse or child.

Many employers offer life insurance for employees, or you can purchase your own policy. There are two basic kinds of life insurance: term and permanent.

- **Term life insurance** provides less expensive coverage for a set period of time, such as 10 or 20 years, and pays the policy's death benefit amount to the beneficiary.
- **Permanent life insurance** provides lifetime coverage that pays a death benefit and accumulates a cash value that you can withdraw later in life. This type of policy is much more expensive that a term life policy.

A good rule of thumb is to purchase life insurance with a benefit that's 10 times your income. So if you make $50,000 a year, you might need coverage that would pay your beneficiary $500,000. However, factors such as your family size, debt, assets, and the lifetime income needs of a surviving partner, spouse, or child are critical considerations.

Auto Insurance

Most U.S. states require you to have some amount of insurance for vehicles such as cars, trucks, motorcycles, and recreational vehicles. The required insurance types and minimum amounts vary depending on the state in which you live.

Auto insurance is a package of coverages that may include the following:

- **Collision** pays for damage to your vehicle caused by getting into an accident with another vehicle, even if you are at fault.
- **Comprehensive** pays for damage to your vehicle due to something other than a collision, such as fire, hail, or theft.
- **Property damage liability** pays for damage you cause to someone else's property, such as their vehicle, a stop sign, or fence.
- **Bodily injury liability** pays for injuries you cause to another person. It's important to have enough liability because if you're involved in a serious accident, you could be sued for a large sum of money.
- **Personal injury protection** pays for medical expenses of the driver and passengers of the policyholder's car regardless of who's at fault, in certain states.
- **Uninsured and underinsured motorist coverage** pays when you're in an accident with an at-fault driver who has insufficient or no insurance to pay for your loss.

The cost of auto insurance varies depending on many factors, such as your age, driving record, credit history, vehicle, and the amount and type of coverage you choose. According to the most recent data, the Toyota Sienna is the least expensive car to insure, at $1,111 per year, and the Audi R8 Spyder Quattro Convertible is the most expensive, at $3,384 per year. So remember to factor in the cost of insurance when choosing a new ride.

Homeowner's Insurance

When you have a home mortgage, the lender requires you to purchase and maintain insurance for the property. Basic homeowner's insurance pays for damage to your property or personal belongings caused by a covered event, such as a natural disaster or theft. Homeowner's insurance also includes liability coverage that protects you if someone gets hurt while on your property.

Renter's Insurance

When you rent an apartment or home, your landlord's insurance doesn't cover your personal belongings or liability. Renter's insurance pays for damage to your possessions (such as clothes, jewelry, electronics, furniture, artwork, household goods, and sporting equipment) if they're damaged by a covered event, such as a natural disaster, wind storm, theft, or faulty plumbing. It can also reimburse your living expenses if you're forced to move out temporarily while repairs are being made. And as with homeowner's insurance, the liability protection keeps you safe if someone is injured on the property and involves you in a lawsuit.

If you rent a home or apartment, you should never go without renter's insurance. According to the National Association of Insurance Commissioners (NAIC), the national average cost of a renter's policy in 2011 was only $187. So it's a very inexpensive way to protect your finances from an unforeseen crisis!

Long-Term Care Insurance

If you have a long-term illness or disability that keeps you from taking care of yourself, long-term care (LTC) insurance pays a certain amount of day-to-day care that isn't covered by other types of insurance. Remember that disability insurance only replaces a portion of your lost income if you're unable to work due to a disability. And health insurance only pays for a portion of your medical bills.

Individuals who require long-term care may need help with activities of daily living, such as dressing, bathing, eating, and walking. Long-term care insurance generally covers care provided in your home by a visiting professional or in an assisted living facility.

Umbrella Insurance

As you build wealth, you may find that you need additional liability insurance protection to cover the total value of your assets. An umbrella policy gives you broad coverage from losses above the limits of your existing policies.

For instance, say you have $100,000 of auto insurance liability and a million dollar umbrella policy. If you were in a car accident that caused serious injuries to another driver that exceeded $100,000, your umbrella policy would give you protection up to one million dollars.

What Is an Insurance Deductible?

Many types of insurance—such as health, auto, renter's, and homeowner's—require you to pay a certain amount of expenses before the policy covers your remaining costs. This out-of-pocket expense is called your deductible. For example, if you have a medical bill for $2,000 and your deductible is $500, then you must pay $500 before the policy will pay all or a portion of the remaining $1,500 in covered benefits.

Extended Product Warranties

If you've ever purchased a product like a computer or a TV, the salesperson probably gave you a sales pitch for an extended product warranty. These warranties give you additional protection if something breaks after the manufacturer's warranty expires. They can also cover issues that the manufacturer doesn't.

While the added protection of an extended product warranty can come in handy, the cost can be very high. Product warranties are typically very profitable for retailers, who train salespeople to sell them aggressively. If the benefit isn't worth the cost, never let a salesperson talk you into buying something you don't need.

When to Purchase an Extended Product Warranty

Consider the following to know when you should purchase an extended product warranty:

- **Look at the price of the warranty versus the price of the product.** If you spend $100 for an MP3 player and the extended warranty is $40, that increases the price 40% for a relatively inexpensive product. However, spending $150 for a warranty on a $2,000 computer may be worthwhile, since it has many expensive parts that could break.
- **Consider the likelihood that you'll need extra coverage.** Will you use the product on a daily basis or in an environment where it could be damaged easily? Does the manufacturer have a reputation for making quality products?
- **Understand the coverage provided.** Does the warranty simply duplicate what's already available from the manufacturer, and how long does it

last? What about parts and labor? Are the rules of the warranty clear and do they make sense for your situation? If the coverage is thin or it's too difficult to file a claim, then the warranty would be useless.

- **Remember coverage offered by your credit card**. Many credit cards offer built-in extended warranty coverage as a card benefit. So it might make sense to purchase a product with your credit card to take advantage of the extra protection.

Identity Theft

Identity theft is a serious and growing crime. It happens when a criminal steals your personal information and uses it to commit fraud. A thief can use data—such as your name, date of birth, Social Security number, driver's license number, bank account number, or credit card number—to wreak havoc on your finances. An identity criminal can open new phone accounts, credit cards, or loans in your name, then go on a spending spree and leave you with a huge bill. Thieves have even filed fictitious tax returns and applied for driver's licenses in their victims' names.

Many insurance companies offer identity theft insurance to cover expenses that you may incur as a victim, such as lost wages, attorney fees, and certified mailing costs. You may have the option to add this protection to your homeowner's or renter's policy.

There are also companies that specialize in identity theft protection, credit monitoring, and identity restoration. These services may be sold through insurance agents, credit card companies, credit reporting agencies, or banks and credit unions. Be sure to read the fine print of these policies before signing up so you understand if do-it-yourself safeguards may be just as effective.

It's impossible to completely prevent identity theft; however, if you catch it early, you can stop it quickly and with less potential hassle and expense.

What To Do If You're the Victim of Identity Theft

Once your identity is jeopardized, getting it corrected can cost time and money. So be sure to keep an eye on your accounts and immediately take the following actions if you see any suspicious activity:

Step #1—Place an initial fraud alert on your credit report with one of the major credit reporting agencies (Equifax, Experian, TransUnion). They must inform the other two agencies on your behalf.

This makes it more difficult for a thief to open additional accounts in your name because a business must take additional steps to contact you directly to verify your identity. An initial fraud alert lasts for 90 days; however, you can renew it for free as needed.

Step #2—Request your credit reports from each of the three major credit reporting agencies. Placing a fraud alert also gives you access to free copies of your credit reports. It's a good idea to request copies that reveal only the last four digits of your Social Security number.

If you know which of your accounts have been compromised, contact those companies directly to discuss the fraudulent activity. Take notes about what actions are being taken and follow up in writing. Be sure to send all communication regarding an identity theft case by certified mail and ask for a return receipt. It's important to create a record that proves you have been diligent to resolve unauthorized charges on your account.

Step #3—Submit an identity theft report to the Federal Trade Commission (FTC) and then the local police. Having these formal reports will help you prove that you've been an identity theft victim to credit reporting agencies, businesses, and debt collectors. If a thief opened new accounts in your name and made large purchases, this could damage your credit history unless the creditor is willing to remove the account or the fraudulent charges from your report.

Visit the FTC website at consumer.ftc.gov to submit an identity theft report or to learn more.

Tips to Stay Safe from Identity Theft

Here are 10 tips to help you protect yourself and stay safe from identity theft:

1. **Never carry confidential information that you don't need.** Unless you plan to use them, remove your Social Security card, paper checks, and financial cards from your wallet and leave them at home so they can't be lost or stolen.
2. **Don't share your Social Security number.** There are only a few situations where you might need to provide it, such as for a new job, in tax-related matters, or when applying for credit or insurance. Never reveal your confidential information over the phone or Internet to any person or company that you don't trust entirely.
3. **Keep a close watch over your debit and credit cards.** When you hand a financial card to a store clerk or restaurant server, watch to make sure that it isn't copied and get it back as soon as possible. Also, never loan your financial cards to anyone.
4. **Shred all documents with personal information.** Make confetti out of receipts, financial account statements, and unwanted credit card offers before putting them in the garbage. Identity thieves dumpster dive for paperwork and can even use the last few digits of a confidential number against you.
5. **Check your credit reports once a year.** If an identity thief opens an account in your name, it will show up on your credit reports. That's why it's important to review them on a periodic basis at annualcreditreport.com.
6. **Resist clicking on links in e-mails.** Thieves can pose as a legitimate organization—such as the IRS, a bank, or PayPal—and send "phishing" e-mails with links to phony sites that ask for confidential information. Genuine companies never ask you for personal information over the phone or Internet. Instead of clicking on a hyperlink, enter a website address directly into an Internet browser.
7. **Use a secure Internet connection.** Don't access a website where you enter confidential information using a public computer or an open Wi-Fi connection. Hackers can track what you're doing over an unsecured Internet connection. Also, never send any personal information to a website unless the address begins with "https," which means that it's secure.
8. **Create strong online usernames and passwords.** Each password for your financial accounts should be unique, with no fewer than eight characters made up of uppercase and lowercase letters, numbers, and symbols. They should never include your Social Security number, name, address, or birth date.
9. **Opt for e-bills and e-statements when possible.** Criminals can change your mailing address so they receive your mail and have access to your personal information. Therefore, reducing the amount of paper documents you send and receive with confidential information is beneficial.
10. **Monitor your bank and credit card account activity.** Review your accounts online or view monthly statements to watch out for unauthorized transactions.

Part 8 Review Questions

1. Why do you think most U.S. states require drivers to have some amount of auto insurance for liability? Do you agree with this requirement? Why or why not?
2. Why does your driving record affect your auto insurance rates?
3. Imagine your best friend has enrolled in a photography program at a fine arts school. He was required to purchase nearly $3,000 worth of photography equipment for his courses and will be keeping it all in his new apartment. What kind of insurance would you suggest he get, if any, and why?
4. Who should have renter's insurance, and why is it a good idea?
5. Why do you think mortgage lenders require homeowners to have a certain amount of homeowner's insurance?
6. Describe several precautions you or your family take to stay safe from identity theft.

Project

Research health insurance plans online, taking into account your specific situation and needs. Start by making a list of how you use health insurance (frequency of doctor visits, need for special dental or vision services, etc.) and decide what kind of insurance policy would fit your needs best. Is it one with a high deductible but low monthly premium? Or is it different? Once you have selected the right fit, list the details of the plan and explain why this plan was the best fit for you.

Glossary

Italicized terms within definitions are key terms that are defined elsewhere in this glossary.

absolute advantage the advantage conferred by the ability to produce more of a good or service with a given amount of time and resources; not the same thing as *comparative advantage*. (p. 27)

absolute value the value of a number without a minus sign, whether or not the number was negative to begin with. (p. 42)

actual investment spending the sum of *planned investment spending* and *unplanned inventory investment*. (p. 168)

***AD–AS* model** *model* in which the *aggregate supply curve* and the *aggregate demand curve* are used together to analyze economic fluctuations. (p. 192)

administrative costs (of a tax) the resources used by the government to collect the tax, and by taxpayers to pay (or to evade) it, over and above the amount collected. (p. 511)

adverse selection when one person knows more about the way things are than other people do; for example, when sellers offer items of particularly low (hidden) quality for sale, and when the people with the greatest need for insurance are those most likely to purchase it. (p. EM-20)

aggregate consumption function the relationship for the *economy* as a whole between aggregate current *disposable income* and *aggregate consumer spending*. (p. 164)

aggregate demand curve shows the relationship between the *aggregate price level* and the quantity of *aggregate output* demanded by *households*, businesses, the government, and the rest of the world. (p. 172)

aggregate output the economy's total production of goods and services for a given time period. (pp. 12, 116)

aggregate price level a measure of the overall level of prices in the *economy*. (p. 146)

aggregate production function a hypothetical function that shows how *productivity* (output per worker) depends on the quantities of *physical capital* per worker and *human capital* per worker as well as the state of technology. (p. 373)

aggregate spending the total spending on domestically produced *final goods and services* in the *economy*; the sum of consumer spending, investment spending, government purchases of goods and services, and *exports* minus *imports*. (p. 109)

aggregate supply curve shows the relationship between the *aggregate price level* and the quantity of *aggregate output* supplied in the *economy*. (p. 180)

allocative efficiency achieved by an *economy* if it produces at the point along its *production possibilities curve* that makes consumers as well off as possible. (p. 18)

antitrust policy involves efforts by the government to prevent oligopolistic industries from becoming or behaving like monopolies. (p. 659)

appreciation occurs when a currency becomes more valuable in terms of other currencies. (p. 418)

artificially scarce good an artificially scarce good is a good that is excludable but nonrival in consumption. (p. 760)

asset bubble situation in which the price of an asset increases to a high level due to expectations of future price gains; can cause a *banking crisis*. (p. EM-4)

automatic stabilizers government spending and taxation rules that cause *fiscal policy* to be automatically expansionary when the *economy* contracts and automatically contractionary when the economy expands. (p. 215)

autonomous change in aggregate spending an initial rise or fall in *aggregate spending* that is the cause, not the result, of a series of income and spending changes. (p. 161)

autonomous consumer spending the amount of money a *household* would spend if it had no *disposable income*. (p. 163)

average cost pricing occurs when regulators set a monopoly's price equal to its average cost to prevent the firm from incurring a loss. (p. 766)

average fixed cost the fixed cost per unit of output. (p. 556)

average product the total product divided by the quantity of an input. (p. 562)

average product curve shows the relationship between the average product and the quantity of an input. (p. 562)

average total cost (average cost) *total cost* divided by quantity of output produced. (p. 556)

average variable cost the variable cost per unit of output. (p. 557)

balance of payments accounts a summary of a country's transactions with other countries. (p. 406)

balance of payments on goods and services the difference between the value of a country's exports and the value of its imports during a given period. (p. 409)

balance of payments on the current account (current account) a country's balance of payments on goods and services plus net international transfer payments and factor income. (p. 409)

balance of payments on the financial account (financial account) the difference between a country's sales of assets to foreigners and its purchases of assets from foreigners during a given period. (p. 409)

balanced budget multiplier the factor by which a change in both spending and taxes changes *real GDP*. (p. 213)

bank a *financial intermediary* that provides *liquid* assets in the form of *bank deposits* to lenders and uses those funds to finance borrowers' *investment spending* on *illiquid* assets. (p. 230)

bank deposit a claim on a bank that obliges the bank to give the depositor his or her cash when demanded. (p. 230)

bank reserves the currency that *banks* hold in their vaults plus their deposits at the Federal Reserve. (p. 244)

bank run a phenomenon in which many of a *bank's* depositors try to withdraw their funds due to fears of a bank failure. (p. 247)

banking crisis occurs when a large part of the banking system fails. (p. EM-4)

bar graph a graph that uses bars of various heights or lengths to indicate values of a variable. (p. 46)

barrier to entry protects a monopolist (and allows it to persist and earn economic profits) by preventing other firms from entering the industry. (p. 576)

behavioral economics the study of economic decision making as influenced by the limits of the human mind. (p. EM-11)

black market a market in which goods or services are bought and sold illegally—either because it is illegal to sell them at all or because the prices charged are legally prohibited by a price ceiling. (p. 84)

bond a loan in the form of an IOU that pays interest. (p. 107)

bounded rationality describes the limits on optimal decision making that result from imperfect intelligence and the scarcity of time and information. (p. EM-13)

bounded self-interest self-interest that leaves room for concerns about the welfare of others. (p. EM-16)

bounded willpower willpower constrained by limits on the determination needed to do difficult things. (p. EM-16)

brand name a name owned by a particular firm that distinguishes its products from those of other firms. (p. 680)

break-even price the minimum average total cost of a price-taking firm; the market price at which it earns zero profit. (p. 596)

budget balance the difference between tax revenue and government spending. (p. 224)

budget constraint limits the cost of a consumer's consumption bundle to no more than the consumer's income. (p. 517)

budget deficit the difference between tax revenue and government spending when government spending exceeds tax revenue. (p. 224)

budget line shows the consumption bundles available to a consumer who spends all of his or her income. (p. 518)

budget surplus the difference between tax revenue and government spending when tax revenue exceeds government spending. (p. 224)

business cycle the alternation between economic downturns, known as *recessions*, and economic upturns, known as *expansions*. (p. 11)

capital manufactured goods used to make other goods and services. (p. 3)

capital inflow the total inflow of foreign funds minus the total outflow of domestic funds to other countries. (p. 225)

cartel a group of producers that agree to restrict output in order to increase prices and their joint profits. (p. 643)

causal relationship a relationship between two *variables* in which the value taken by one variable directly influences or determines the value taken by the other variable. (p. 38)

central bank an institution that oversees and regulates the banking system and controls the *monetary base*. (p. 254)

chain-linking the method of calculating changes in *real GDP* using the average between the growth rate calculated using an early base year and the growth rate calculated using a late base year. (p. 118)

change in demand a shift of the demand curve, which changes the quantity demanded at any given price. (p. 52)

change in supply a shift of the supply curve, which changes the quantity supplied at any given price. (p. 61)

checkable bank deposits bank accounts on which people can write checks. (p. 233)

classical model of the price level *model* in which the real quantity of money is always at its *long-run equilibrium level*. (p. 319)

Coase theorem even in the presence of externalities, an economy can always reach an efficient solution as long as transaction costs are sufficiently low. (p. 737)

collateralized debt obligation an asset-backed security tied to corporate debt or mortgages. (p. EM-7)

collusion when sellers cooperate to raise their joint profits. (p. 643)

command economy an *economy* in which industry is publicly owned and a central authority makes production and consumption decisions. (p. 2)

commercial bank a depository *bank* that accepts deposits and is covered by *deposit insurance*. (p. 258)

commodity money a good used as a *medium of exchange* that has intrinsic value in other uses. (p. 234)

commodity-backed money a *medium of exchange* with no intrinsic value whose ultimate value is guaranteed by a promise that it can be converted into valuable goods. (p. 234)

common resource nonexcludable and rival in consumption; you can't stop others from consuming the good, and when they consume it, less of the good is available for you. (p. 758)

comparative advantage the advantage conferred by an individual if the *opportunity cost* of producing the good or service is lower for that individual than for other people. (p. 27)

compensating differentials wage differences across jobs that reflect the fact that some jobs are less pleasant or more dangerous than others. (p. 721)

competitive market a market in which there are many buyers and sellers of the same good or service, none of whom can influence the price at which the good or service is sold. (p. 49)

complements two goods (often consumed together) for which a rise in the price of one of the goods leads to a decrease in the demand for the other good. (p. 54)

concentration ratios measure the percentage of industry sales accounted for by the "X" largest firms, for example the four-firm concentration ratio or the eight-firm concentration ratio. (p. 578)

constant returns to scale when output increases directly in proportion to an increase in all inputs. (p. 568)

constant-cost industry an industry with a horizontal (perfectly elastic) *long-run supply curve*. (p. 608)

consumer price index (CPI) measures the cost of the *market basket* of a typical urban American family. (p. 148)

consumer spending *household* spending on goods and services. (p. 106)

consumer surplus the net gain received from purchasing a good or service. (p. 488)

consumption function shows how a *household's* consumer spending varies with the household's current *disposable income*. (p. 163)

consumption possibilities the set of all consumption bundles that are affordable, given a consumer's income and prevailing prices. (p. 517)

contractionary fiscal policy *fiscal policy* that reduces *aggregate demand*. (p. 207)

contractionary monetary policy *monetary policy* that reduces *aggregate demand.* (p. 307)

convergence hypothesis general principle stating that international differences in *real GDP* per capita tend to narrow over time. (p. 380)

copyright gives the creator of a literary or artistic work the sole right to profit from that work for a specified period of time. (p. 577)

cost the lowest price at which a seller is willing to sell a good. (p. 493)

cost-minimization rule a firm determines the cost-minimizing combination of inputs using the cost-minimization rule: employ factors so that the marginal product per dollar spent on each factor is the same. (p. 717)

cost-push inflation *inflation* that is caused by a significant increase in the price of an *input* with *economy*-wide importance. (p. 323)

credit crunch occurs when potential borrowers can't get credit or must pay very high interest rates. (p. EM-5)

credit default swap an agreement that the seller will compensate the buyer in the event of a loan default. (p. EM-7)

cross-price elasticity of demand measures the effect of the change in one good's price on the quantity demanded of another good; is equal to the percent change in the quantity demanded of one good divided by the percent change in the other good's price. (p. 478)

crowding out occurs when a government deficit drives up the *interest rate* and leads to reduced *investment spending.* (p. 280)

currency in circulation cash held by the public. (p. 233)

curve any line on a graph, regardless of whether it is a straight line or a curved line. (p. 38)

cyclical unemployment the deviation of the actual rate of *unemployment* from the natural rate. (p. 133)

cyclically adjusted budget balance an estimate of what the *budget balance* would be if *real GDP* were exactly equal to *potential output.* (p. 296)

deadweight loss (from a tax) the decrease in total surplus resulting from the tax, minus the tax revenues generated. (p. 509)

deadweight loss the value of foregone mutually beneficial transactions. (p. 96)

debt deflation the reduction in *aggregate demand* arising from the increase in the real burden of outstanding debt caused by *deflation.* (p. 337)

debt-GDP ratio the government's debt as a percentage of *GDP.* (p. 299)

decreasing returns to scale when output increases less than in proportion to an increase in all inputs. (p. 568)

decreasing-cost industry an industry with a downward-sloping long-run supply curve. (p. 609)

deductible a sum specified in an insurance policy that the insured individuals must pay before being compensated for a claim; reduces *moral hazard.* (p. EM-22)

default when a borrower fails to make payments as specified by a *loan* or *bond* contract. (p. 228)

deflation a falling overall price level. (p. 13)

demand curve a graphical representation of the demand schedule. It shows the relationship between quantity demanded and price. (p. 51)

demand price the price of a given quantity at which consumers will demand that quantity. (p. 93)

demand schedule shows how much of a good or service consumers will be willing and able to buy at different prices. (p. 50)

demand shock an event that shifts the *aggregate demand curve.* (p. 193)

demand-pull inflation *inflation* that is caused by an increase in *aggregate demand.* (p. 323)

dependent variable in a *causal relationship*, the variable that is determined by the *independent variable.* (p. 38)

deposit insurance guarantees that a *bank's* depositors will be paid even if the bank can't come up with the funds, up to a maximum amount per account. (p. 247)

depreciation occurs when the value of an asset is reduced by wear, age, or obsolescence or when a currency becomes less valuable in terms of other currencies. (pp. 398, 418)

depression a very deep and prolonged downturn. (p. 11)

derivative a financial contract that has value based on the performance of another asset, index, or interest rate. (p. EM-7)

derived demand demand for a factor is a derived demand. It results from (that is, it is derived from) the demand for the output being produced. (p. 689)

devaluation a reduction in the value of a currency that is set under a fixed *exchange rate regime.* (p. 431)

diminishing marginal rate of substitution the more of one good a person consumes in proportion to another good, the less of the second good he or she is willing to substitute for another unit of the first good. (p. EM-32)

diminishing returns to an input when an increase in the quantity of that input, holding the levels of all other inputs fixed, leads to a decline in the marginal product of that input. (p. 548)

diminishing returns to physical capital in an *aggregate production function* when, holding the amount of *human capital* per worker and the state of technology fixed, each successive increase in the amount of *physical capital* per worker leads to a smaller increase in productivity. (p. 374)

discount rate the *interest rate* the Fed charges on *loans* to *banks.* (p. 262)

discount window the channel through which the Federal Reserve lends money to *banks.* (p. 247)

discouraged workers nonworking people who are capable of working but have given up looking for a job due to the state of the job market. (p. 123)

discretionary fiscal policy *fiscal policy* that is the result of deliberate actions by policy makers rather than rules. (p. 215)

discretionary monetary policy the use of changes in the *interest rate* or the *money supply* by the *central bank* to stabilize the *economy.* (p. 346)

diseconomies of scale when long-run average total cost increases as output increases. (p. 567)

disinflation the process of bringing the *inflation rate* down. (p. 143)

disposable income income plus *government transfers* minus taxes; the total amount of *household* income available to spend on consumption and to save. (p. 108)

diversification investment in several different assets with unrelated, or independent, risks. (p. 226)

dominant strategy a player's best action regardless of the action taken by the other player. (p. 650)

duopolist each of the two firms in a *duopoly*. (p. 642)

duopoly an *oligopoly* consisting of only two firms. (p. 642)

economic aggregates economic measures that summarize data across many different markets. (p. 5)

economic growth an increase in the maximum amount of goods and services an *economy* can produce. (p. 13)

economic profit a business's total revenue minus the opportunity cost of its resources; usually less than the accounting profit. (p. 535)

economic rent the payment to a factor of production in excess of the minimum payment necessary to employ that factor. (p. 701)

economics the study of scarcity and choice. (p. 2)

economies of scale when long-run average total cost declines as output increases. (p. 567)

economy a system for coordinating a society's productive and consumptive activities. (p. 2)

efficiency wage model some employers pay an above-equilibrium wage as an incentive for better performance and loyalty. (p. 723)

efficiency wages wages that employers set above the equilibrium wage rate as an incentive for better employee performance. (p. 133)

efficient describes a market or *economy* in which there is no way to make anyone better off without making at least one person worse off. (p. 18)

elastic demand when the *price elasticity* of demand is greater than 1. (p. 468)

emissions tax a tax that depends on the amount of pollution a firm produces. (p 741)

employed people who are currently holding a job in the *economy*, either full time or part time. (p. 121)

employment the number of people who are currently working for pay in the *economy*. (p. 11)

entrepreneurship the efforts of entrepreneurs in organizing resources for production, taking risks to create new enterprises, and innovating to develop new products and production processes. (p. 3)

environmental standards rules that protect the environment by specifying limits for or actions by producers and consumers. (p. 740)

equilibrium an economic situation when no individual would be better off doing something different; a *competitive market* is in equilibrium when the price has moved to a level at which the quantity demanded of goods equals the quantity supplied of that good. (p. 69)

equilibrium exchange rate the exchange rate at which the quantity of a currency demanded in the foreign exchange market is equal to the quantity supplied. (p. 419)

equilibrium marginal revenue product the additional revenue generated by the last unit of that factor employed in the factor market as a whole. (p. 701)

equilibrium price (market-clearing price) the price of a good at which the quantity demanded of that good equals the quantity supplied of that good. (p. 70)

equilibrium quantity the quantity of a good bought and sold at its *equilibrium* price. (p. 70)

excess capacity when a monopolistically competitive industry's firms produce less than the output at which average total cost is minimized. (p. 673)

excess reserves a *bank's* reserves over and above its required reserves. (p. 250)

exchange market intervention government purchases or sales of currency in the *foreign exchange market*. (p. 429)

exchange rate regime a rule governing policy toward the exchange rate. (p. 427)

exchange rates the prices at which currencies trade. (p. 417)

excise tax a tax on sales of a particular good or service. (p. 503)

excludable a good is excludable if the supplier of that good can prevent people who do not pay from consuming it. (p. 752)

expansion a period of economic upturn in which output and employment are rising; also referred to as recovery. (p. 11)

expansionary fiscal policy *fiscal policy* that increases *aggregate demand*. (p. 207)

expansionary monetary policy *monetary policy* that increases *aggregate demand*. (p. 307)

expenditure approach an approach to calculating *GDP* by adding up *aggregate spending* on domestically produced *final goods and services* in the *economy*—the sum of consumer spending, investment spending, government purchases of goods and services, and *exports* minus *imports*. (p. 109)

explicit cost a cost that involves actually laying out money. (p. 534)

exports goods and services sold to other countries. (p. 108)

external benefit a benefit that an individual or a firm confers on others without receiving compensation. (p. 736)

external cost an uncompensated cost that an individual or a firm imposes on others. (p 735)

externalities external costs and benefits (p. 736)

factor distribution of income the division of total income among land, labor, capital, and entrepreneurship. (p. 689)

factor markets where *resources*, especially *capital* and *labor*, are bought and sold. (p. 106)

federal funds market allows *banks* that fall short of the *reserve requirement* to borrow funds from banks with *excess reserves*. (p. 262)

federal funds rate the *interest rate* that *banks* charge other banks for *loans*, as determined in the *federal funds market*. (p. 262)

fiat money a *medium of exchange* whose value derives entirely from its official status as a means of payment. (p. 235)

final goods and services goods and services sold to the final, or end, user. (p. 109)

financial asset a paper claim that entitles the buyer to future income from the seller. (p. 225)

financial crisis a sudden and widespread disruption of *financial markets*. (p. EM-5)

financial intermediary an institution that transforms the funds it gathers from many individuals into *financial assets*. (p. 229)

financial markets the markets (banking, *stock*, and *bond*) that channel *private savings* and foreign lending into *investment spending*, *government borrowing*, and foreign borrowing. (pp. 108, EM-2)

financial risk uncertainty about future outcomes that involve financial losses and gains. (p. 226)

firm an organization that produces goods and services for sale. (p. 106)

fiscal policy the use of government purchases of goods and services, government transfers, or tax policy to stabilize the *economy*. (p. 177)

fiscal year runs from October 1 to September 30 and is labeled according to the calendar year in which it ends. (p. 297)

Fisher effect the general principle that an increase in expected future *inflation* drives up the *nominal interest rate* by the same number of percentage points, leaving the expected *real interest rate* unchanged. (p. 282)

fixed cost a cost that does not depend on the quantity of output produced; the cost of the fixed input. (p. 552)

fixed exchange rate an *exchange rate regime* in which the government keeps the exchange rate against some other currency at or near a particular target. (p. 427)

fixed input an input whose quantity is fixed for a period of time and cannot be varied. (p. 545)

floating exchange rate an *exchange rate regime* in which the government lets the exchange rate go wherever the market takes it. (p. 427)

foreign exchange controls licensing systems that limit the right of individuals to buy foreign currency. (p. 429)

foreign exchange market the market in which currencies are traded. (p. 417)

foreign exchange reserves stocks of foreign currency that governments maintain to buy their own currency on the foreign exchange market. (p. 429)

framing the creation of context for a product or idea. (p. EM-15)

free entry and exit when new firms can easily enter into the industry and existing firms can easily leave the industry. (p. 575)

free-rider problem goods that are nonexcludable suffer from the free-rider problem. Individuals have no incentive to pay for their own consumption and instead will take a "free ride" on anyone who does pay. (p. 753)

frictional unemployment *unemployment* due to the time workers spend in *job search*. (p. 130)

future value the amount to which some current amount of money will grow as interest accumulates over a specified period of time. (p. 239)

gains from trade an economic principle that states that people can get more of what they want through *trade* than they could if they tried to be self-sufficient; this increase in *output* is due to *specialization*. (p. 24)

game theory the study of behavior in situations of *interdependence*. (p. 648)

GDP deflator (for a given year) 100 times the ratio of *nominal GDP* to *real GDP* in that year. (p. 150)

GDP per capita *GDP* divided by the size of the population; it is equivalent to the average *GDP* per person. (p. 118)

Gini coefficient a number that summarizes a country's level of income inequality based on how unequally income is distributed. (p. 775)

government borrowing the amount of funds borrowed by the government in the *financial markets*. (p. 108)

government debt the accumulation of past *budget deficits*, minus past *budget surpluses*. (p. 297)

government purchases of goods and services total expenditures on goods and services by federal, state, and local governments. (p. 108)

government transfers payments that the government makes to individuals without expecting a good or service in return. (p. 108)

gross domestic product (GDP) the total value of all final goods and services produced in the economy during a given year. (p. 109)

growth accounting estimates the contribution of each major factor in the *aggregate production function* to economic growth. (p. 375)

Herfindahl-Hirschman Index (HHI) is the square of each firm's share of market sales summed over the industry. It gives a picture of the industry market structure. (p. 578)

Homo economicus a fictional economic actor who makes self-interested, informed, rational judgments in pursuit of wealth and leisure. (p. EM-11)

horizontal intercept indicates the value of the x-variable when the value of the y-variable is zero. (p. 39)

household a person or group of people who share income. (p. 106)

human capital the improvement in labor created by the education and knowledge of members of the workforce. (pp. 371, 688)

illiquid describes an asset if it cannot be quickly converted into cash without much loss of value. (p. 227)

imperfect competition when no one firm has a *monopoly*, but producers nonetheless realize that they can affect market prices. (p. 578)

implicit cost a cost that does not require an outlay of money; it is measured by the value, in dollar terms, of benefits that are foregone. (p. 534)

implicit cost of capital the opportunity cost of the capital used by a business—the income the owner could have realized from that capital if it had been used in its next best alternative way. (p. 535)

implicit liabilities spending promises made by governments that are effectively a debt despite the fact that they are not included in the usual debt statistics. (p. 301)

import quota a limit on the quantity of a good that can be imported within a given period. (p. 440)

imports goods and services purchased from other countries. (p. 108)

incentives rewards or punishments that motivate particular choices. (p. 3)

income approach an approach to calculating *GDP* by adding up the total factor income earned by households from firms in the economy, including rent, wages, interest, and profit. (p. 109)

income effect the change in the quantity of a good demanded that results from a change in the consumer's purchasing power when the price of the good changes. (p. 460)

income elasticity of demand the percent change in the quantity of a good demanded when a consumer's income changes divided by the percent change in the consumer's income. (p. 478)

income-elastic demand when the *income elasticity of demand* for a good is greater than 1. (p. 479)

income-inelastic demand when the *income elasticity of demand* for a good is positive but less than 1. (p. 479)

increasing returns to scale when output increases more than in proportion to an increase in all inputs; for example, doubling all inputs would cause output to more than double. (p. 567)

increasing-cost industry an industry with an upward-sloping *long-run supply curve*. (p. 608)

independent variable in a *causal relationship*, the variable that determines the *dependent variable*. (p. 38)

indifference curve shows all the consumption bundles that yield the same amount of total utility for an individual. (p. EM-26)

indifference curve map a collection of *indifference curves*, each of which corresponds to a different total utility level; represents an individual's entire *utility function*. (p. EM-26)

individual choice decisions by individuals about what to do, which necessarily involve decisions about what not to do. (p. 2)

individual consumer surplus the net gain to an individual buyer from the purchase of a good; is equal to the difference between the buyer's willingness to pay and the price paid. (p. 487)

individual demand curve illustrates the relationship between quantity demanded and price for an individual consumer. (p. 56)

Individual labor supply curve shows how the quantity of labor supplied by an individual depends on that individual's wage rate. (p. 707)

individual producer surplus the net gain to an individual seller from selling a good; is equal to the difference between the price received and the seller's *cost*. (p. 493)

individual supply curve illustrates the relationship between quantity supplied and price for an individual producer. (p. 65)

industry supply curve shows the relationship between the price of a good and the total output of the industry as a whole. (p. 603)

inefficient allocation of sales among sellers a form of inefficiency resulting from *price floors* in which those who would be willing to sell the good at the lowest price are not always those who manage to sell it. (p. 87)

inefficient allocation to consumers a form of inefficiency often resulting from *price ceilings* in which people who want a good badly and are willing to pay a high price don't get it, and those who care relatively little about the good and are only willing to pay a relatively low price do get it. (p. 83)

inefficiently high quality a form of inefficiency resulting from *price floors* in which sellers offer high-quality goods at a high price, even though buyers would prefer a lower quality at a lower price. (p. 88)

inefficiently low quality a form of inefficiency resulting from *price ceilings* in which sellers offer low-quality goods at a low price even though buyers would prefer a higher quality at a higher price. (p. 84)

inelastic demand when the *price elasticity* of demand is less than 1. (p. 468)

inferior good when a rise in income decreases the demand for a good; usually considered less desirable than more expensive alternatives. (p. 55)

inflation a rising overall price level. (p. 13)

inflation rate the percentage increase in the overall level of prices per year. (p. 139)

inflation targeting occurs when the *central bank* sets an explicit target for the *inflation rate* and sets monetary policy in order to hit that target. (p. 309)

inflation tax a reduction in the value of money held by the public caused by *inflation*. (p. 322)

inflationary gap occurs when *aggregate output* is above *potential output*. (p. 198)

infrastructure roads, power lines, ports, information networks, and other underpinnings for economic activity. (p. 386)

in-kind benefit a benefit given in the form of goods or services (p. 778)

input a good or service that is used to produce another good or service. (p. 63)

interdependence when the outcome (profit) of each firm depends on the actions of the other firms in the market. (p. 642)

interest rate the price, calculated as a percentage of the amount borrowed, charged by lenders to borrowers for the use of their savings for one year. (p. 223)

interest rate effect of a change in the aggregate price level the change in investment and consumer spending caused by altered interest rates that result from changes in the demand for money. (p. 174)

intermediate goods and services goods and services bought from one firm by another firm to be used as inputs into the production of final goods and services. (p. 109)

internalize the externalities when individuals take external costs or benefits into account, they internalize the externalities. (p. 737)

inventories stocks of goods and raw materials held to facilitate business operations. (p. 109)

inventory investment the value of the change in total *inventories* held in the *economy* during a given period. (p. 168)

investment bank a *bank* that trades in *financial assets* and is not covered by *deposit insurance*. (p. 258)

investment spending spending on new productive physical capital, such as machinery and structures, and on changes in inventories. (p. 109)

job search when workers spend time looking for employment. (p. 130)

Keynesian economics a set of ideas that focuses on the ability of shifts in *aggregate demand* to influence *aggregate output* in the short run. (p. 343)

labor the effort of workers. (p. 3)

labor force the number of people who are either actively employed for pay or unemployed and actively looking for work; the sum of employment and unemployment. (pp. 12, 122)

labor force participation rate the percentage of the population aged 16 or older that is in the labor force. (p. 122)

labor productivity (productivity) output per worker. (p. 370)

land all *resources* that come from nature, such as minerals, timber, and petroleum. (p. 3)

law of demand the "law" that a higher price for a good or service, other things being equal, leads people to demand a smaller quantity of that good or service. (p. 51)

law of supply the "law" that, other things being equal, the price and quantity supplied of a good are positively related. (p. 61)

leisure time available for purposes other than earning money to buy marketed goods. (p. 706)

leverage the degree to which a financial institution is financing its investments with borrowed funds. (p. EM-5)

liability a requirement to pay money in the future. (p. 225)

license gives its owner the right to supply a good or service; a form of quantity control, as only those who are licensed can supply the good or service. (p. 92)

life insurance company sells policies that guarantee a payment to a policyholder's beneficiaries when the policyholder dies. (p. 230)

linear relationship the relationship between two *variables* when the *curve* that shows their relationship is a straight line, or linear. (p. 38)

liquid describes an asset if it can be quickly converted into cash without much loss of value. (p. 227)

liquidity preference model of the interest rate *model* that says that the *interest rate* is determined by the supply and demand for money. (p. 272)

liquidity trap a situation in which conventional monetary policy is ineffective because *nominal interest rates* are up against the *zero bound*. (p. 337)

loan a lending agreement between an individual lender and an individual borrower. (p. 227)

loanable funds market a hypothetical market that brings together those who want to lend money and those who want to borrow money. (p. 276)

loan-backed security an asset created by pooling individual *loans* and selling shares in that pool. (p. 228)

long run the time period in which all inputs can be varied. (p. 546)

long-run aggregate supply curve shows the relationship between the *aggregate price level* and the quantity of *aggregate output* supplied that would exist if all prices, including *nominal wages*, were fully flexible. (p. 186)

long-run average total cost curve shows the relationship between output and average total cost when fixed cost has been chosen to minimize average total cost for each level of output. (p. 566)

long-run industry supply curve shows how the quantity supplied responds to the price once producers have had time to enter or exit the industry. (p. 608)

long-run macroeconomic equilibrium when the point of *short-run macroeconomic equilibrium* is on the *long-run aggregate supply curve*. (p. 196)

long-run market equilibrium when the quantity supplied equals the quantity demanded, given that sufficient time has elapsed for entry into and exit from the industry to occur. (p. 606)

long-run Phillips curve (*LRPC*) shows the relationship between *unemployment* and *inflation* after expectations of inflation have had time to adjust to experience. (p. 334)

long-term interest rates *interest rates* on *financial assets* that mature a number of years in the future. (p. 269)

Lorenz curve shows the percentage of all income received by the poorest members of the population, from the poorest 0% to the poorest 100%. (p. 774)

lump-sum tax a tax of a fixed amount paid by all taxpayers, independent of the taxpayer's income. (pp. 213, 511)

macroeconomic policy activism the use of *monetary* and *fiscal policy* to smooth out the *business cycle*. (p. 344)

macroeconomics the branch of *economics* that is concerned with the overall ups and downs of the *economy*. (p. 5)

marginal analysis the study of the costs and benefits of doing a little bit more of an activity versus a little bit less. (p. 3)

marginal cost curve shows how the cost of producing one more unit depends on the quantity that has already been produced. (p. 541)

marginal cost pricing occurs when regulators set a monopoly's price equal to its marginal cost to achieve efficiency. (p. 766)

marginal external benefit the addition to external benefits created by one more unit of the good. (p. 746)

marginal external cost the marginal external cost of a good is the increase in external costs to society created by one more unit of the good. (p. 748)

marginal factor cost the additional cost of employing an additional unit of a factor of production. (p. 710)

marginal private benefit the marginal benefit that accrues to consumers of a good, not including any external benefits. (p. 746)

marginal private cost the marginal cost of producing that good, not including any external costs. (p. 748)

marginal product the additional quantity of output produced by using one more unit of an input. (p. 547)

marginal productivity theory of income distribution every *factor of production* is paid the *equilibrium marginal revenue product*. (p. 702)

marginal propensity to consume (*MPC*) the increase in consumer spending when *disposable income* rises by $1. (p. 160)

marginal propensity to save (*MPS*) the increase in household savings when *disposable income* rises by $1. (p. 160)

marginal rate of substitution (*MRS*) the ratio of the *marginal utility* of one good to the marginal utility of another. (p. EM-31)

marginal revenue the change in *total revenue* generated by an additional unit of output. (p. 540)

marginal revenue curve shows how marginal revenue varies as output varies. (p. 541)

marginal revenue product the additional revenue generated by employing one more unit of that factor. (p. 692)

marginal revenue product curve shows how the marginal revenue product of that factor depends on the quantity of the factor employed. (p. 694)

marginal social benefit of a good the marginal private benefit plus the marginal external benefit. (p. 746)

marginal social benefit of pollution the additional gain to society as a whole from an additional unit of pollution. (p. 734)

marginal social cost of a good equal to the marginal private cost of production plus its marginal external costs. (p. 748)

marginal social cost of pollution the additional cost imposed on society as a whole by an additional unit of pollution. (p. 734)

marginal utility the change in total utility generated by consuming one additional unit of a good or service. (p. 516)

marginal utility curve shows how *marginal utility* depends on the quantity of a good or service consumed. (p. 516)

marginal utility per dollar the additional *utility* from spending one more dollar on a good or service. (p. 521)

marginally attached workers would like to be employed and have looked for a job in the recent past but are not currently looking for work. (p. 123)

market basket a hypothetical set of consumer purchases of goods and services. (p. 147)

market economy an *economy* in which the decisions of individual producers and consumers largely determine what, how, and for whom to produce, with little government involvement in the decisions. (p. 2)

market share the fraction of the total industry output accounted for by a firm's output. (p. 574)

maturity transformation the conversion of short-term liabilities into long-term assets. (p. EM-3)

maximum the point along a *curve* with the largest value of *y*. (p. 42)

mean household income the average income across all households. (p. 774)

means-tested program available only to individuals or families whose incomes fall below a certain level. (p. 778)

median household income the income of the household lying in the middle of the income distribution. (p. 774)

medium of exchange an asset that individuals acquire for the purpose of trading for goods and services rather than for their own consumption. (p. 233)

menu costs the real costs of changing listed prices. (p. 140)

merchandise trade balance (trade balance) the difference between a country's exports and imports of goods. (p. 409)

microeconomics the branch of *economics* that studies how individuals, households, and firms make decisions and how those decisions interact. (p. 5)

midpoint method a technique for calculating the percent change by dividing the change in a variable by the average, or midpoint, of the initial and final values of that variable. (p. 463)

minimum the point along a *curve* with the smallest value of *y*. (p. 43)

minimum wage a legal floor on the hourly wage rate paid for a worker's labor. (p. 85)

minimum-cost output the quantity of output at which *average total cost* is lowest—it corresponds to the bottom of the *U-shaped average total cost curve*. (p. 559)

model a simplified representation used to better understand a real-life situation. (p. 14)

monetarism asserts that *GDP* will grow steadily if the *money supply* grows steadily. (p. 346)

monetary aggregate an overall measure of the *money supply*. (p. 236)

monetary base the sum of currency in circulation and *bank reserves*. (p. 251)

monetary neutrality the concept that changes in the *money supply* have no real effects on the *economy*. (p. 314)

monetary policy the central bank's use of changes in the quantity of money or the interest rate to stabilize the *economy*. (p. 177)

monetary policy rule a formula that determines the *central bank's* actions. (p. 347)

money any asset that can easily be used to purchase goods and services. (p. 232)

money demand curve shows the relationship between the quantity of money demanded and the *interest rate*. (p. 270)

money multiplier the ratio of the *money supply* to the *monetary base*; indicates the total number of dollars created in the banking system by each $1 addition to the monetary base. (p. 251)

money supply the total value of *financial assets* in the economy that are considered *money*. (p. 233)

money supply curve shows the relationship between the quantity of money supplied and the *interest rate*. (p. 272)

monopolist the only producer of a good that has no close substitutes. (p. 576)

monopolistic competition a market structure in which there are many competing firms in an industry, each firm sells a differentiated product, and there is free entry into and exit from the industry in the long run. (p. 580)

monopoly an industry controlled by a *monopolist*. (p. 576)

monopsonist a single buyer in a factor market. (p. 710)

monopsony a market in which there is a monopsonist is a monopsony. (p. 710)

moral hazard a distortion of incentives when someone else bears the costs of a lack of care or effort. (pp. EM-7, EM-22)

movement along the demand curve a change in the quantity demanded of a good that is the result of a change in that good's price. (p. 52)

movement along the supply curve a change in the quantity supplied of a good arising from a change in the good's price. (p. 62)

mutual fund a *financial intermediary* that creates a stock portfolio and then resells shares of this portfolio to individual investors. (p. 229)

Nash equilibrium (noncooperative equilibrium) the result when each player in a game chooses the action that maximizes his or her payoff, given the actions of other players. (p. 651)

national income and product accounts (national accounts) keep track of the flows of money among different sectors of the economy; calculated by the Bureau of Economic Analysis. (p. 105)

national savings the sum of private savings and the *budget balance*; the total amount of savings generated within the *economy*. (p. 224)

natural monopoly when economies of scale provide a large cost advantage to a single firm that produces all of an industry's output. (p. 576)

natural rate hypothesis to avoid accelerating *inflation* over time, the *unemployment rate* must be high enough that the actual *inflation rate* equals the expected inflation rate. (p. 348)

natural rate of unemployment the *unemployment rate* that arises from the effects of *frictional* plus *structural unemployment*. (p. 133)

near-moneys *financial assets* that can't be directly used as a *medium of exchange* but can be readily converted into cash or *checkable bank deposits*. (p. 236)

negative externalities external costs. (p. 736)

negative income tax a program that supplements the income of low-income workers. (p. 778)

negative relationship the relationship between two *variables* when an increase in one variable is associated with a decrease in the other variable. (p. 39)

net exports the difference between the value of *exports* and the value of *imports* ($X - IM$). (p. 111)

net present value the *present value* of current and future benefits minus the present value of current and future costs. (p. 241)

network externality a good is subject to a network externality when the value of the good to an individual depends on how many people also use the good. (p. 750)

new classical macroeconomics an approach to the *business cycle* that returns to the classical view that shifts in the *aggregate demand curve* affect only the *aggregate price level*, not *aggregate output*. (p. 349)

new Keynesian economics a set of ideas that argues that market imperfections can lead to price stickiness for the *economy* as a whole. (p. 350)

nominal GDP the total value of all *final goods and services* produced in the *economy* during a given year, calculated with the prices current in the year in which the *output* is produced. (p. 117)

nominal interest rate the interest rate actually paid for a loan. (p. 142)

nominal wage the dollar amount of the wage paid. (p. 181)

nonaccelerating inflation rate of unemployment (NAIRU) the *unemployment rate* at which *inflation* does not change over time. (p. 334)

noncooperative behavior when firms act in their own self-interest, ignoring the effects of their actions on each other's profits. (p. 644)

nonexcludable when a good is nonexcludable, the supplier cannot prevent consumption by people who do not pay for it. (p. 753)

nonlinear curve a *curve* along which the *slope* changes. (p. 41)

nonlinear relationship the relationship between two *variables* when the *curve* that shows their relationship is not a straight line, or is nonlinear. (p. 38)

nonprice competition when firms that have a tacit understanding not to compete on price use advertising and other means to try to increase their sales. (p. 664)

nonrival in consumption a good is nonrival in consumption if more than one person can consume the same unit of the good at the same time. (p. 753)

normal good when a rise in income increases the demand for a good; most goods are normal goods. (p. 55)

normal profit an economic profit equal to zero; an economic profit just high enough to keep a firm engaged in its current activity. (p. 536)

normative economics the branch of economic analysis that makes prescriptions about the way the economy should work. (p. 6)

oligopolist a producer in an *oligopoly*. (p. 577)

oligopoly an industry with only a small number of firms. (p. 577)

open-market operation a purchase or sale of government debt by the Fed. (p. 263)

opportunity cost the real cost of an item: what you must give up in order to get it. (p. 4)

optimal consumption bundle the consumption bundle that maximizes the consumer's total *utility* given his or her *budget constraint*. (p. 519)

optimal consumption rule says that in order to maximize utility, a consumer must equate the marginal utility per dollar spent on each good and service in the consumption bundle. (p. 523)

optimal output rule says that profit is maximized by producing the quantity of output at which the marginal revenue of the last unit produced is equal to its marginal cost. (p. 540)

ordinary goods in a consumer's *utility function*, those for which additional units of one good are required to compensate for fewer units of another, and vice versa; and for which the consumer experiences a *diminishing marginal rate of substitution* when substituting one good in place of another. (p. EM-32)

origin the point where the (horizontal) x-axis and (vertical) y-axis meet. (p. 37)

other things equal assumption in the development of a *model*, the assumption that all other relevant factors remain unchanged; also known as the *ceteris paribus* assumption. (p. 14)

output the quantity of goods and services produced. (p. 12)

output gap the percentage difference between actual *aggregate output* and *potential output*. (p. 198)

overuse the depletion of a common resource that occurs when individuals ignore the fact that their use depletes the amount of the resource remaining for others. (p. 758)

patent gives an inventor a temporary monopoly in the use or sale of an invention. (p. 577)

payoff the reward received by a player in a game, such as the profit earned by an *oligopolist*. (p. 648)

payoff matrix shows how the *payoff* to each of the participants in a two-player game depends on the actions of both. Such a matrix helps us analyze situations of *interdependence*. (p. 648)

pension fund a nonprofit institution that invests the savings of members and provides them with income when they retire. (p. 229)

perfect price discrimination when a *monopolist* charges each consumer his or her *willingness to pay*—the maximum that the consumer is willing to pay. (p. 633)

perfectly competitive industry an industry in which firms are price-takers. (p. 574)

perfectly competitive market a market in which all market participants are price-takers. (p. 573)

perfectly elastic demand when any price increase will cause the *quantity demanded* to drop to zero; the *demand curve* is a horizontal line. (p. 468)

perfectly elastic supply when the quantity supplied is zero below some price and infinite above that price; a perfectly elastic supply curve is a horizontal line. (p. 481)

perfectly inelastic demand when the *quantity demanded* does not respond at all to changes in the price; the *demand curve* is a vertical line. (p. 467)

perfectly inelastic supply when the price elasticity of supply is zero, so that changes in the price of the good have no effect on the quantity supplied; a perfectly inelastic supply curve is a vertical line. (p. 481)

physical asset a claim on a tangible object that gives the owner the right to dispose of the object as he or she wishes. (p. 225)

physical capital often referred to as simply as "capital"—consists of manufactured productive resources such as equipment, buildings, tools, and machines. (pp. 371, 688)

pie chart a chart that shows the share of a total amount that is accounted for by various components, usually expressed in percentages. (p. 45)

Pigouvian subsidy a payment designed to correct for the effects of external benefits. (p. 747)

Pigouvian taxes taxes designed to correct for the effects of external costs. (p. 743)

planned investment spending the investment spending that businesses intend to undertake during a given period. (p. 166)

political business cycle unnecessary instability in the *economy* resulting from when politicians use *macroeconomic* policy to serve political ends. (p. 349)

positive economics the branch of economic analysis that describes the way the *economy* actually works. (p. 6)

positive externalities external benefits. (p. 736)

positive relationship the relationship between two *variables* when an increase in one variable is associated with an increase in the other variable. (p. 39)

potential output the level of *real GDP* the *economy* would produce if all prices, including *nominal wages*, were fully flexible. (p. 187)

poverty rate the percentage of the population with incomes below the poverty threshold. (p. 771)

poverty threshold the annual income below which a family is officially considered poor. (p. 770)

present value (of \$1 realized one year from now) $\$1/(1 + r)$; the amount of money you must lend out today in order to have \$1 in one year. It is the value to you today of \$1 realized one year from now. (p. 240)

price ceiling a maximum price that sellers are allowed to charge for a good or service. (p. 80)

price controls legal restrictions on how high or low a market price may go; typically take the form of either a *price ceiling* or a *price floor*. (p. 80)

price discrimination when sellers charge different prices to different consumers for the same good. (p. 630)

price elasticity of demand the ratio of the percent change in the *quantity demanded* to the percent change in the price as we move along the demand curve (dropping the minus sign). (p. 461)

price elasticity of supply a measure of the responsiveness of the quantity of a good supplied to the price of that good; the ratio of the percent change in the quantity supplied to the percent change in the price as we move along the supply curve. (p. 480)

price floor a minimum price that buyers are required to pay for a good or service. (p. 80)

price index measures the cost of purchasing a given market basket in a given year; the index value is normalized so that it is equal to 100 in the selected base year. (p. 147)

price leadership one firm sets its price first, and other firms then follow. (p. 664)

price regulation limits the price that a *monopolist* is allowed to charge. (p. 625)

price stability when the overall price level is changing only slowly if at all. (p. 13)

price war when *tacit collusion* breaks down and aggressive price competition causes prices to collapse. (p. 663)

price-taking consumer a consumer whose actions have no effect on the market price of the good or service he or she buys. (p. 573)

price-taking firm a firm whose actions have no effect on the market price of the good or service it sells. (p. 573)

price-taking firm's optimal output rule says that a price-taking firm's profit is maximized by producing the quantity of output at which the market price is equal to the marginal cost of the last unit produced. (p. 589)

principle of diminishing marginal utility the idea that each successive unit of a good or service consumed adds less to total *utility* than does the previous unit. (p. 517)

principle of marginal analysis says that every activity should continue until marginal benefit equals marginal cost. (p. 540)

prisoners' dilemma a game based on two premises: (1) each player has an incentive to choose an action that benefits him- or herself at the other player's expense; and (2) when both players act in this way, both are worse off than if they had acted cooperatively. (p. 649)

private good a good that is both excludable and rival in consumption. (p. 753)

private information information that some people have and others do not. (p. EM-19)

private savings *disposable income* minus *consumer spending*; disposable income that is not spent on consumption but rather goes into *financial markets*. (p. 108)

producer price index (PPI) measures the prices of goods and services purchased by producers. (p. 150)

producer surplus refers to both *individual* and *total producer surplus*. (p. 493)

product differentiation an attempt by a firm to convince buyers that its product is different from the products of other firms in the industry. (p. 663)

product markets where goods and services are bought and sold. (p. 106)

production function the relationship between the quantity of inputs a firm uses and the quantity of output it produces. (p. 545)

production possibilities curve illustrates the *trade-offs* facing an *economy* that produces only two goods; shows the maximum quantity of one good that can be produced for each possible quantity of the other good produced. (p. 17)

productive efficiency achieved by an *economy* if it produces at a point on its *production possibilities curve*. (p. 18)

progressive tax a tax that rises more than in proportion to income. (p. 502)

property rights establish ownership and grant individuals the right to trade goods and services with each other. (p. 3)

proportional tax a tax that rises in proportion to income. (p. 503)

protectionism the practice of limiting trade to protect domestic industries. (p. 438)

public debt *government debt* held by individuals and institutions outside the government. (p. 297)

public good both nonexcludable and nonrival in consumption. (p. 754)

public ownership when a good is supplied by the government or by a firm owned by the government instead of by a *monopolist*. (p. 625)

purchasing power parity (between two countries' currencies) the nominal exchange rate at which a given basket of goods and services would cost the same amount in each country. (p. 423)

quantity control (quota) an upper limit on the quantity of some good that can be bought or sold. (p. 92)

quantity demanded the actual amount of a good or service consumers are willing and able to buy at some specific price. (p. 50)

quantity supplied the actual amount of a good or service people are willing to sell at some specific price. (p. 60)

Quantity Theory of Money emphasizes the positive relationship between the price level and the *money supply*; relies on the velocity equation ($M \times V = P \times Y$). (p. 347)

quota rent the earnings that accrue to the license-holder from ownership of the right to sell the good. (p. 95)

rate of return (on a project) is the profit earned on the project expressed as a percentage of its cost. (p. 277)

rational expectations the view that individuals and *firms* make decisions optimally, using all available information. (p. 350)

real business cycle theory claims that fluctuations in the rate of growth of total factor productivity cause the *business cycle*. (p. 350)

real exchange rates exchange rates adjusted for international differences in aggregate price levels. (p. 421)

real GDP the total value of all *final goods and services* produced in the *economy* during a given year, calculated using the prices of a selected base year in order to remove the effects of price changes. (p. 117)

real income income divided by the price level to adjust for the effects of inflation or deflation. (p. 139)

real interest rate the *nominal interest rate* minus the rate of *inflation*. (p. 142)

real wage the wage rate divided by the price level to adjust for the effects of inflation or deflation. (p. 139)

recession a period of economic downturn when output and employment are falling. (p. 11)

recessionary gap when *aggregate output* is below *potential output*. (p. 197)

regressive tax a tax that rises less than in proportion to income. (p. 503)

relative price the ratio of the price of one good to the price of another. (p. EM-34)

relative price rule at the *optimal consumption bundle*, the *marginal rate of substitution* between two goods is equal to their relative price. (p. EM-35)

rental rate either land or capital is the cost, explicit or implicit, of using a unit of that asset for a given period of time. (p. 700)

reputation long-term credibility that allows an individual to assure others that he or she isn't concealing adverse private information. (p. EM-21)

required reserve ratio the smallest fraction of deposits that the Federal Reserve allows *banks* to hold. (p. 245)

research and development (R & D) spending to create and implement new technologies. (p. 385)

reserve ratio the fraction of *bank deposits* that a *bank* holds as reserves. (p. 245)

reserve requirements rules set by the Federal Reserve that determine the *required reserve ratio* for *banks*. (p. 247)

resource anything that can be used to produce something else. (p. 3)

revaluation an increase in the value of a currency that is set under a fixed *exchange rate regime*. (p. 431)

rival in consumption a good is rival in consumption if the same unit of the good cannot be consumed by more than one person at the same time. (p. 753)

Rule of 70 a mathematical formula that tells us that the time it takes a variable that grows gradually over time to double is approximately 70 divided by that variable's annual growth rate. (p. 369)

savings and loan (thrift) a type of deposit-taking *bank*, usually specialized in issuing home *loans*. (p. 258)

savings-investment spending identity an accounting fact that states that savings and *investment spending* are always equal for the *economy* as a whole. (p. 224)

scarce in short supply; when a resource is not available in sufficient quantities to satisfy all the various ways a society wants to use it. (p. 3)

scatter diagram a diagram in which each point corresponds to an actual observation of the x-variable and the y-variable. (p. 45)

screening using observable information about people to make inferences about their *private information*; a way to reduce *adverse selection*. (p. EM-21)

securitization involves assembling a pool of loans and selling shares of that pool to investors. (p. EM-7)

self-correcting describes the *economy* when shocks to *aggregate demand* affect *aggregate output* in the short run, but not the long run. (p. 198)

shadow bank a financial institution that engages in *maturity transformation* but does not accept deposits. (p. EM-3)

shoe-leather costs the increased costs of transactions caused by *inflation*. (p. 140)

short run the time period in which at least one input is fixed. (p. 546)

shortage when the quantity of a good or service demanded exceeds the quantity supplied; occurs when the price is below its equilibrium level and is also known as *excess demand*. (p. 71)

short-run aggregate supply curve shows the relationship between the *aggregate price level* and the quantity of *aggregate output* supplied that exists in the short run, the time period when many production costs can be taken as fixed. (p. 182)

short-run equilibrium aggregate output the quantity of *aggregate output* produced in the *short-run macroeconomic equilibrium*. (p. 193)

short-run equilibrium aggregate price level the *aggregate price level* in the *short-run macroeconomic equilibrium*. (p. 193)

short-run individual supply curve shows how an individual firm's profit-maximizing level of output depends on the market price, taking the fixed cost as given. (p. 598)

short-run industry supply curve shows how the quantity supplied by an industry depends on the market price, given a fixed number of firms. (p. 604)

short-run macroeconomic equilibrium when the quantity of *aggregate output* supplied is equal to the quantity demanded. (p. 192)

short-run market equilibrium when the quantity supplied equals the quantity demanded, taking the number of producers as given. (p. 604)

short-run Phillips curve (*SRPC*) represents the negative short-run relationship between the *unemployment rate* and the *inflation rate*. (p. 328)

short-term interest rates the *interest rates* on *financial assets* that mature within a year. (p. 268)

shut-down price the price at which a firm ceases production in the short run; equal to minimum average variable cost. (p. 597)

signaling revealing *private information* through actions that establish credibility; a way to reduce *adverse selection*. (p. EM-21)

single-price monopolist charges all consumers the same price. (p. 630)

slope a measure of how steep a *curve* is; indicates how sensitive the *y*-variable is to a change in the *x*-variable. (p. 39)

social insurance government programs intended to protect families against economic hardship. (p. 205)

socially optimal quantity of pollution the quantity of pollution that society would choose if all the costs and benefits of pollution were fully accounted for. (p. 734)

specialization each person specializes in the task that he or she is good at performing. (p. 24)

spending multiplier the ratio of the total change in *real GDP* caused by an autonomous change in *aggregate spending* to the size of that autonomous change; indicates the total rise in *real GDP* that results from each $1 of an initial rise in spending. (p. 161)

stabilization policy the use of government policy to reduce the severity of *recessions* and rein in excessively strong expansions. (p. 201)

stagflation the combination of *inflation* and stagnating (or falling) *aggregate output*. (p. 195)

standardized product (commodity) describes a good when consumers regard the products of different firms as the same good. (p. 574)

sticky wages *nominal wages* that are slow to fall even in the face of high *unemployment* and slow to rise even in the face of *labor* shortages. (p. 181)

stock a share in the ownership of a company held by a shareholder. (p. 107)

store of value a means of holding purchasing power over time. (p. 234)

strategic behavior when a firm attempts to influence the future behavior of other firms. (p. 660)

structural unemployment *unemployment* that results when workers lack the skills required for the available jobs, or there are more people seeking jobs in a labor market than there are jobs available at the current wage rate. (p. 131)

subprime lending involves lending to home-buyers who don't meet the usual criteria for being able to afford their payments. (p. EM-7)

substitutes two goods for which a rise in the price of one of the goods leads to an increase in the demand for the other good. (p. 54)

substitution effect the change in the quantity of a good demanded as the consumer substitutes the good that has become relatively cheaper for the good that has become relatively more expensive. (p. 459)

sunk cost a cost that has already been incurred and is nonrecoverable; should be ignored in a decision about future actions. (p. 568)

supply and demand model a model of how a competitive market works. (p. 50)

supply curve shows the relationship between the quantity supplied and the price. (p. 60)

supply price the price of a given quantity at which producers will supply that quantity. (p. 94)

supply schedule shows how much of a good or service producers would supply at different prices. (p. 60)

supply shock an event that shifts the *short-run aggregate supply curve*. (p. 194)

surplus when the quantity supplied of a good or service exceeds the quantity demanded; occurs when the price is above its equilibrium level and is also known as *excess supply*. (p. 71)

sustainable describes *long-run economic growth* if it can continue in the face of the limited supply of natural resources and the impact of growth on the environment. (p. 388)

T-account a tool for analyzing a business's financial position by showing, in a single table, the business's assets (on the left) and *liabilities* (on the right). (p. 245)

tacit collusion when firms limit production and raise prices in a way that raises each other's profits, even though they have not made any formal agreement. (p. 661)

tangency condition on a graph of a consumer's *budget line* and available *indifference curves* of available *consumption bundles*, the point at which an indifference curve and the budget line just touch. This condition determines the *optimal consumption bundle* when the indifference curves have the typical convex shape. (p. EM-33)

target federal funds rate the Federal Reserve's desired level for the *federal funds rate*; the Federal Reserve can move the *interest rate* and achieve this target through open-market operations that shift the *money supply curve*. (p. 304)

tariffs taxes on imports. (p. 438)

tax incidence the distribution of the tax burden. (p. 505)

tax multiplier the factor by which a change in tax collections changes *real GDP*. (p. 213)

Taylor rule for monetary policy a rule for setting the *federal funds rate* that takes into account both the *inflation rate* and the *output gap*. (p. 308)

technology the technical means for producing goods and services. (pp. 21, 371)

technology spillover an external benefit that results when new technological knowledge spreads among firms. (p. 748)

terms of trade indicate the rate at which one good can be exchanged for another. (p. 28)

time allocation decisions about labor supply result from decisions about time allocation: how many hours to spend on different activities. (p. 706)

time-series graph a graph with successive dates on the *horizontal (x-) axis* and the values of a variable that occurred on those dates on the *vertical (y-) axis*. (p. 44)

tit for tat a strategy involving playing cooperatively at first, then doing whatever the other player did in the previous period. (p. 660)

total consumer surplus the sum of the *individual consumer surpluses* of all the buyers of a good in a market. (p. 487)

total cost the sum of the fixed cost and the variable cost of producing a given quantity of output. (p. 553)

total cost curve shows how *total cost* depends on the quantity of output. (p. 554)

total factor productivity the amount of output that can be achieved with a given amount of factor inputs. (p. 376)

total producer surplus the sum of the *individual producer surpluses* of all the sellers of a good in a market. (p. 493)

total product curve shows how the quantity of output depends on the quantity of the variable input, for a given quantity of the fixed input. (p. 547)

total revenue the total value of sales of a good or service; equal to the price multiplied by the quantity sold. (p. 470)

total surplus the total net gain to consumers and producers from trading in a market; the sum of producer and consumer surplus. (p. 498)

tradable emissions permits licenses to emit limited quantities of pollutants that can be bought and sold by polluters. (p. 743)

trade when individuals provide goods and services to others and receive goods and services in return. (p. 24)

trade-off when you give up something in order to have something else. (p. 16)

transaction costs the expenses of negotiating and executing a deal. (pp. 226, 737)

underemployed workers who would like to work more hours or who are overqualified for their jobs. (p. 123)

unemployed people who are actively looking for work but aren't currently employed. (p. 122)

unemployment the number of people who are actively looking for work but aren't currently employed. (p. 11)

unemployment rate the percentage of the labor force that is unemployed. (pp. 12, 122)

unions organizations of workers that try to raise wages and improve working conditions for their members by bargaining collectively. (p. 722)

unit of account a measure used to set prices and make economic calculations. (p. 234)

unit-elastic demand when the *price elasticity* of demand is exactly 1. (p. 468)

unit-of-account costs arise from the way *inflation* makes money a less reliable unit of measurement. (p. 142)

unplanned inventory investment occurs when actual sales are lower than businesses expected, leading to unplanned increases in inventories; sales in excess of expectations result in negative unplanned inventory investment. (p. 168)

U-shaped average total cost curve falls at low levels of output and then rises at higher levels. (p. 556)

util a unit of utility. (p. 515)

utility a measure of personal satisfaction. (p. 514)

value added (of a producer) the value of a producer's sales minus the value of its purchases of inputs. (p. 110)

value-added approach an approach to calculating *GDP* by surveying firms and adding up their contributions to the value of *final goods and services*. (p. 109)

variable a measure that can take on more than one value. (p. 36)

variable cost a cost that depends on the quantity of output produced. It is the cost of the variable input. (p. 553)

variable input an input whose quantity the firm can vary at any time. (p. 546)

velocity of money the ratio of *nominal GDP* to the *money supply*; a measure of the number of times the average dollar bill is spent per year. (p. 347)

vertical intercept indicates the value of the *y*-variable when the value of the *x*-variable is zero. (p. 39)

wasted resources a form of inefficiency in which people expend money, effort, and time to cope with the *shortages* caused by the *price ceiling* or *surpluses* caused by the *price floor*. (p. 83)

wealth the value of a *household's* accumulated savings. (p. 225)

wealth effect of a change in the aggregate price level the change in consumer spending caused by the altered purchasing power of consumers' assets. (p. 174)

wedge the difference between the *demand price* and the *supply price* of a good, often created by a quota. (p. 95)

willingness to pay the maximum price at which a consumer would buy a good. (p. 486)

***x*-axis** the solid horizontal line on a graph that intersects with the *y-axis* at the *origin*; also called the horizontal axis. (p. 37)

***y*-axis** the solid vertical line on a graph that intersects with the *x-axis* at the *origin*; also called the vertical axis. (p. 37)

zero bound the lower bound of zero on the nominal interest rate: it cannot go below zero. (p. 337)

zero-profit equilibrium when a monopolistically competitive industry's firms make zero profit at their profit-maximizing output quantities. (p. 670)

Sample Solution Graphs Section

Section 1 Review, page 35

Either of the following versions of the graph can be marked as correct:

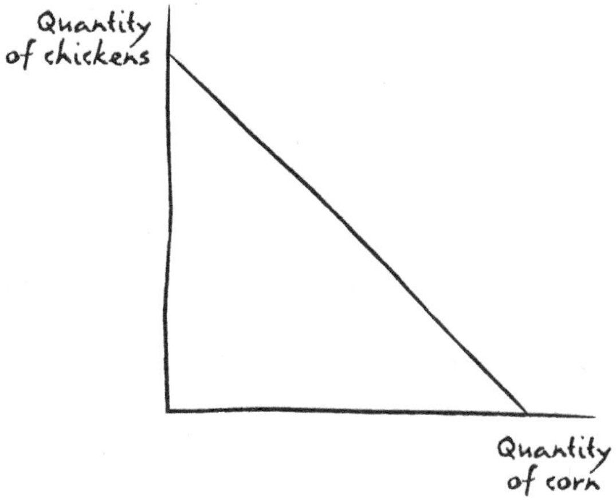

Section 2 Review, page 103

Either of the following versions of the graph can be marked as correct:

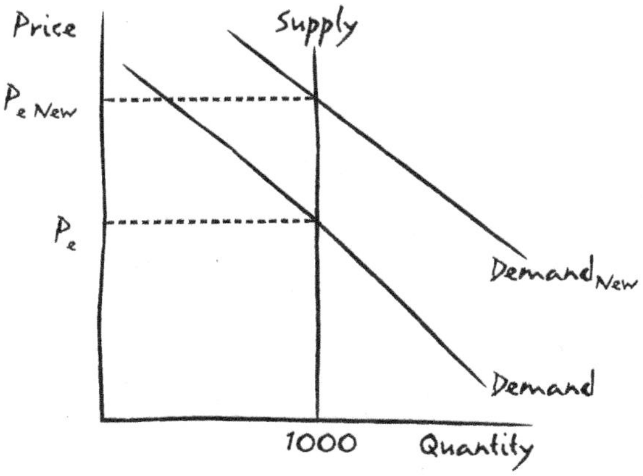

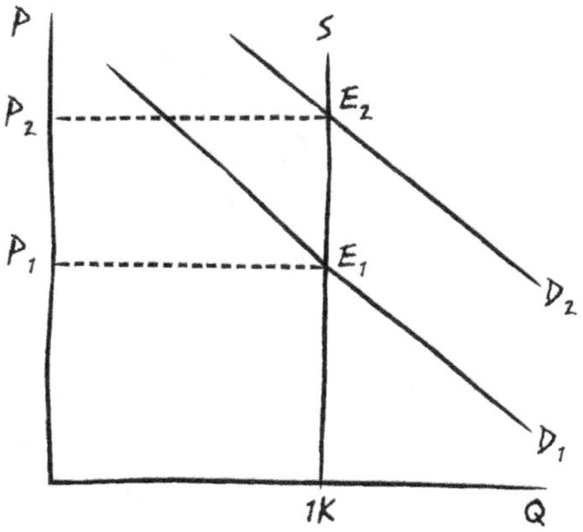

Section 3 Review, page 157

There are no graphs for Section 3's FRQ.

Section 4 Review, page 221

Either of the following versions of the graph can be marked as correct:

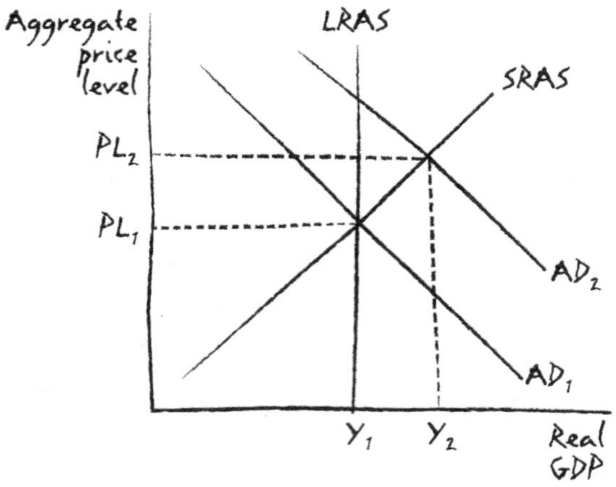

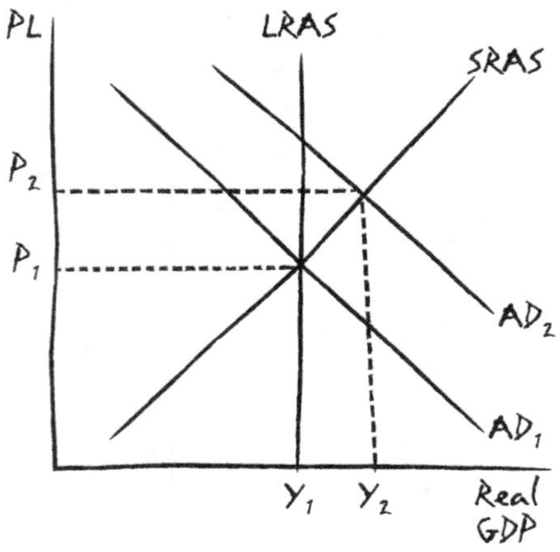

Section 5 Review, page 291

Either of the following versions of the graph can be marked as correct:

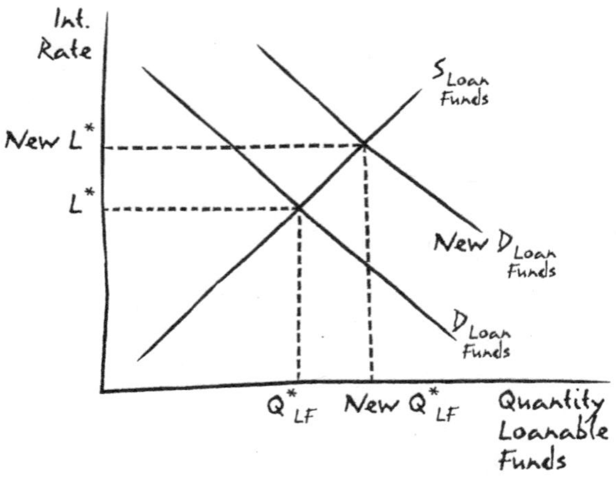

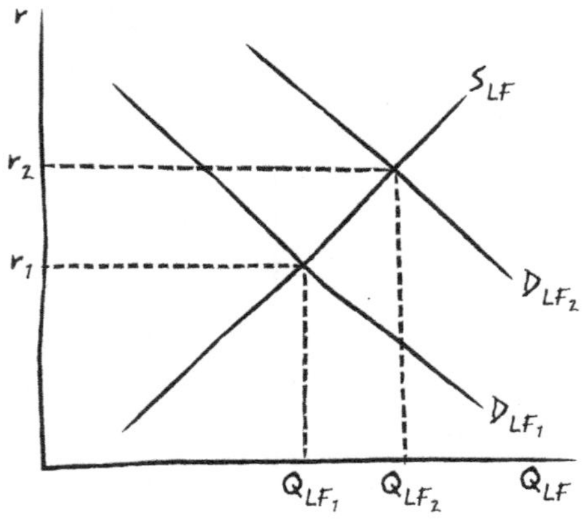

Section 6 Review, page 363

Either of the following versions of the graph can be marked as correct:

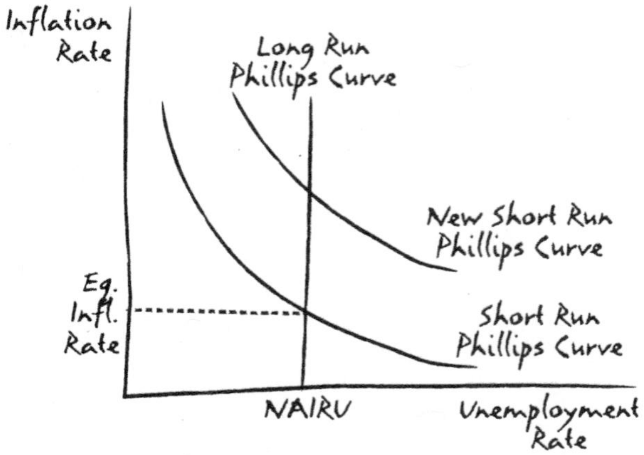

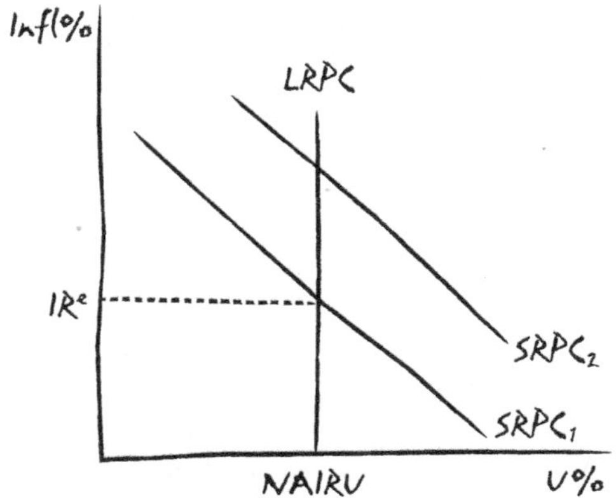

Section 7 Review, page 404

Either of the following versions of the graphs can be marked as correct:

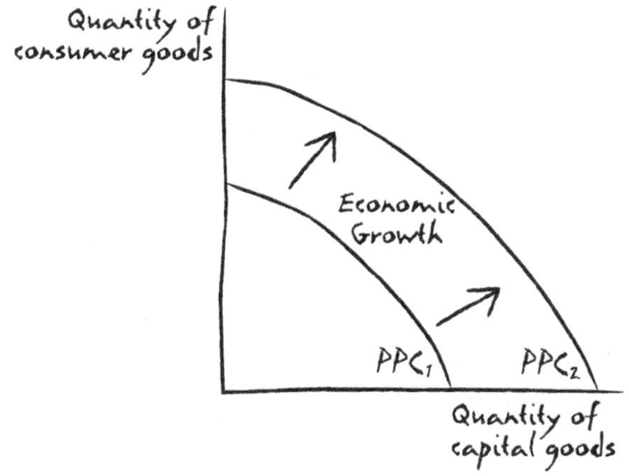

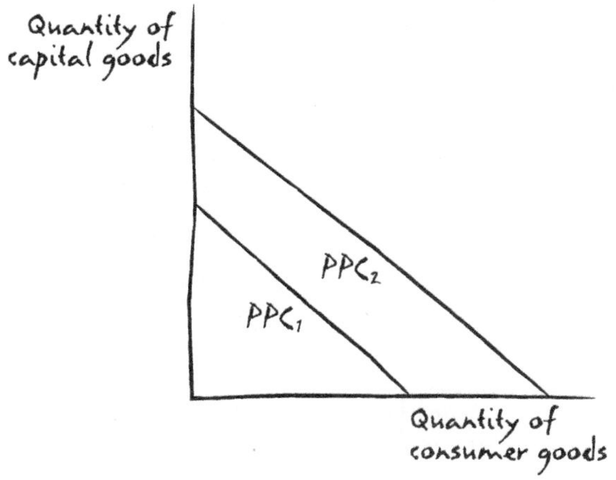

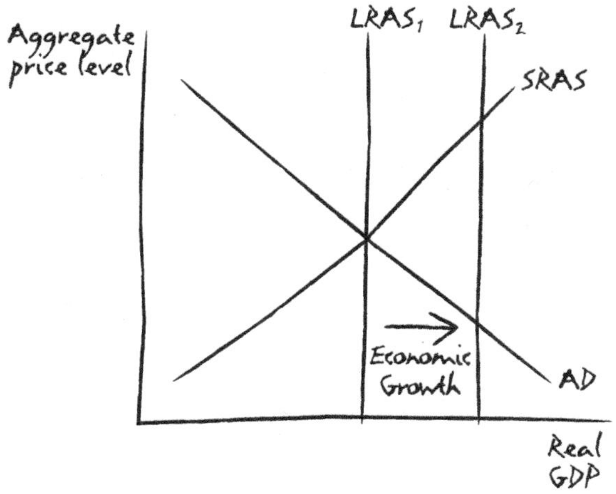

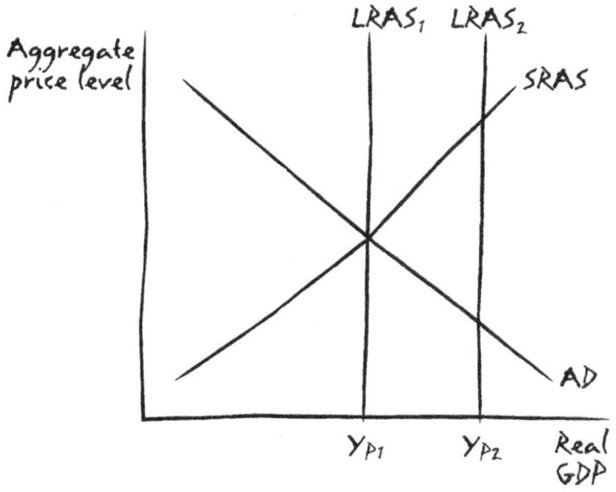

Section 8 Review, page 457

Either of the following versions of the graph can be marked as correct:

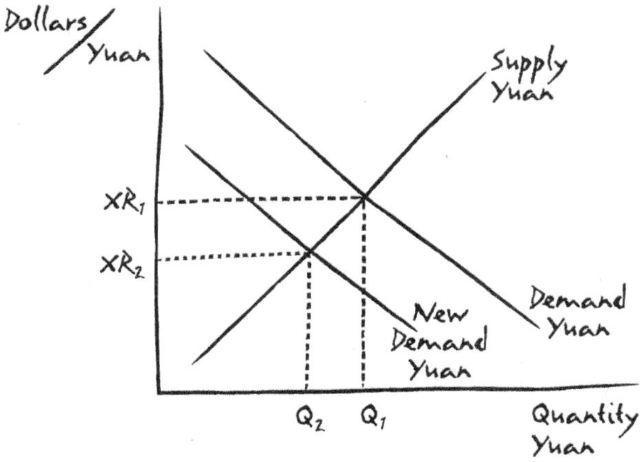

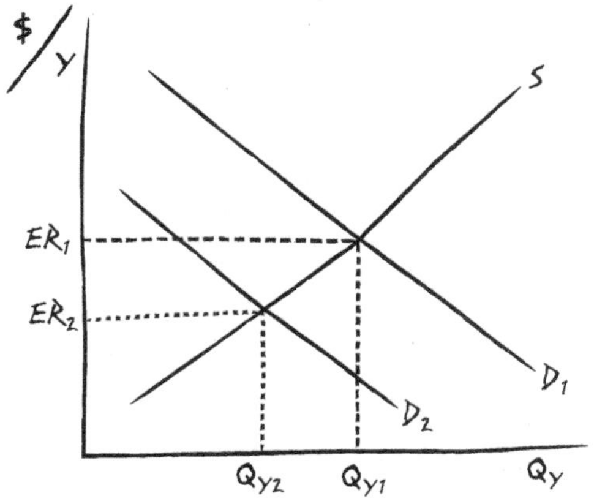

Section 9 Review, page 531

Either of the following versions of the graph can be marked as correct:

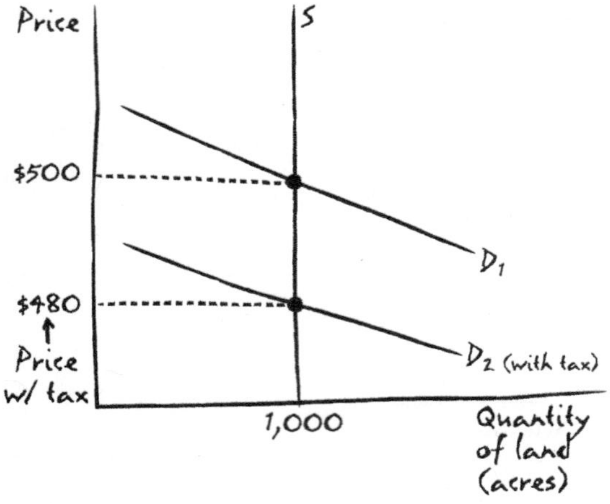

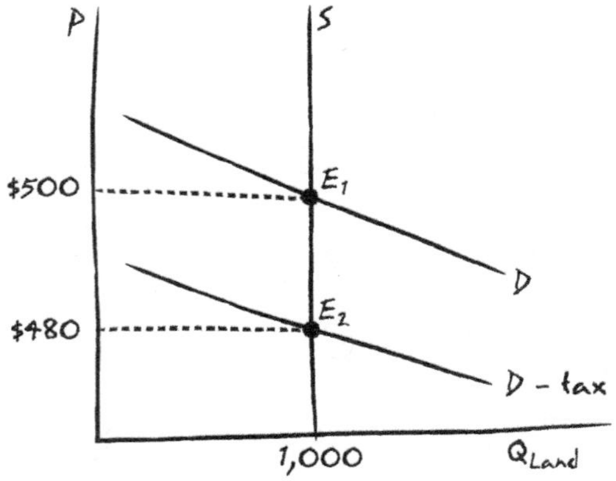

Section 10 Review page 586

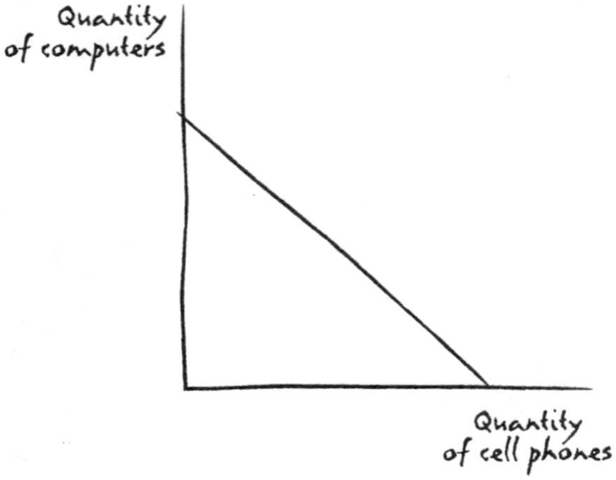

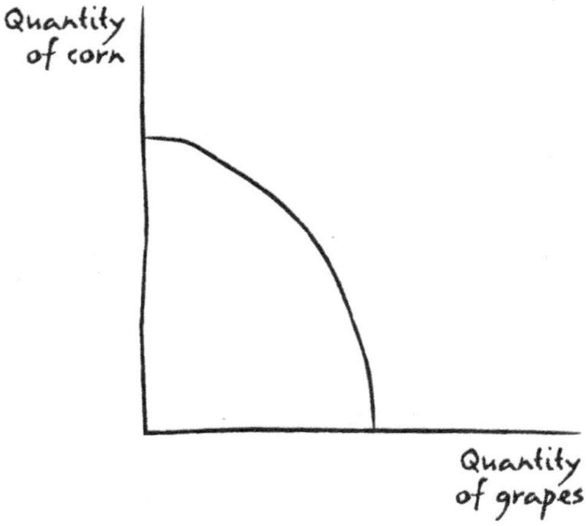

Section 11 Review, page 640

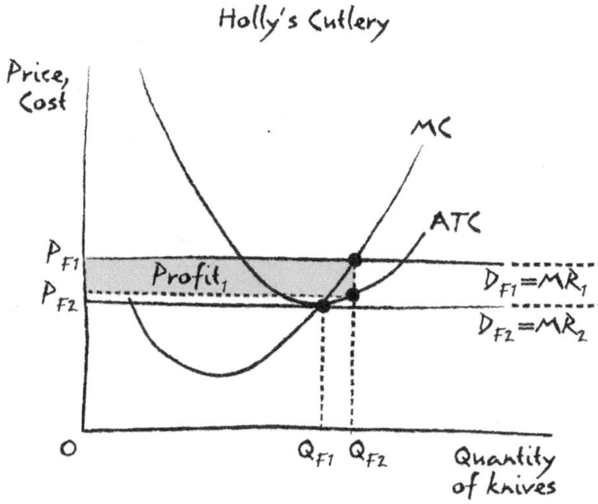

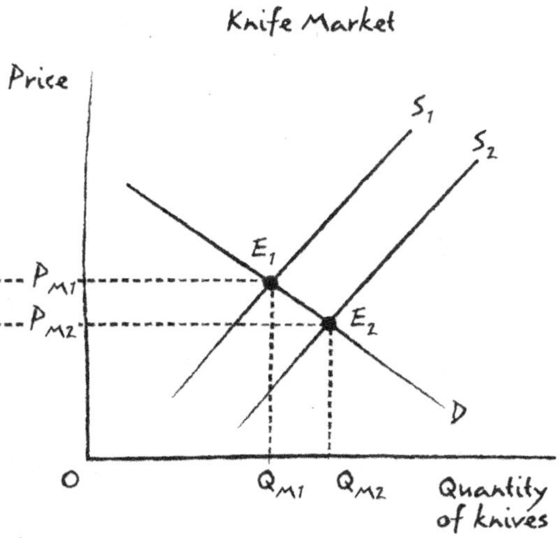

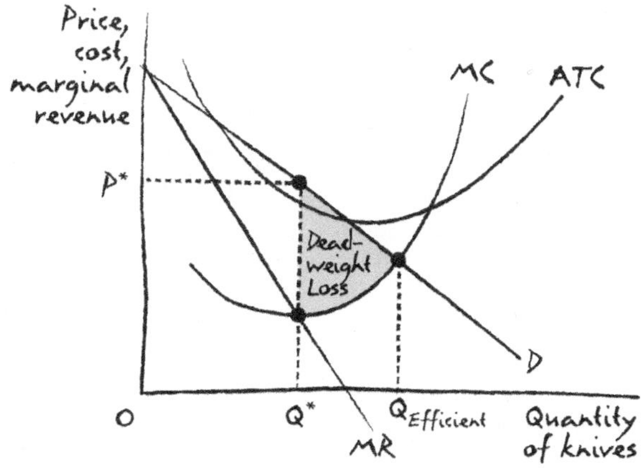

Section 12 Review, page 686

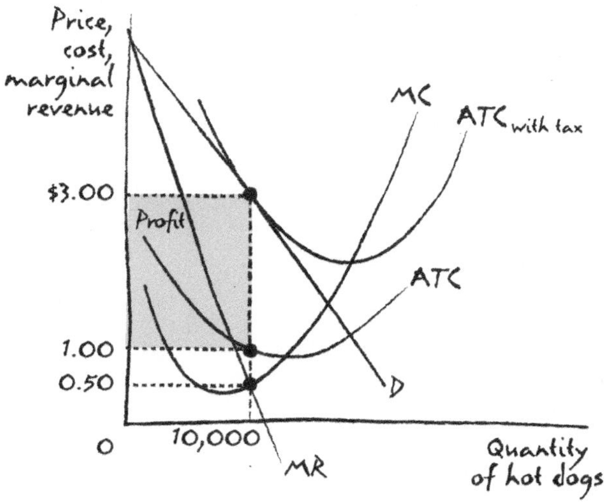

Section 13 Review, page 731

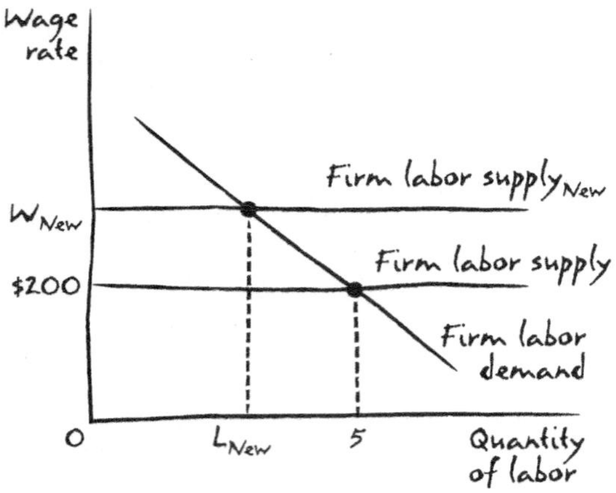

Section 14 Review, page 788

Either of the following versions of the graph can be marked as correct:

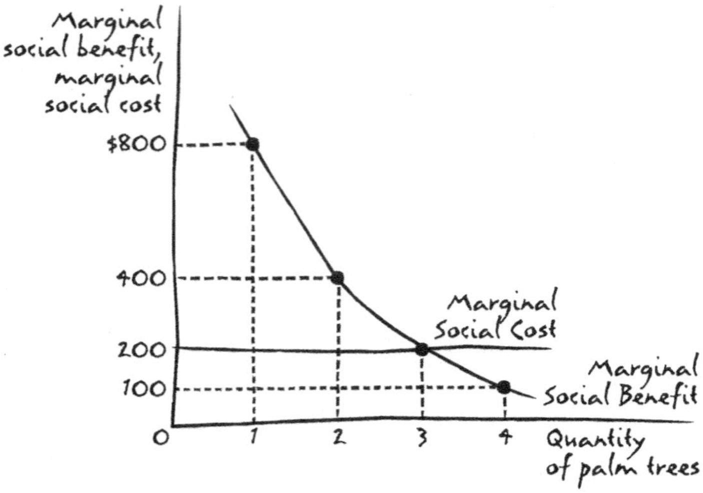

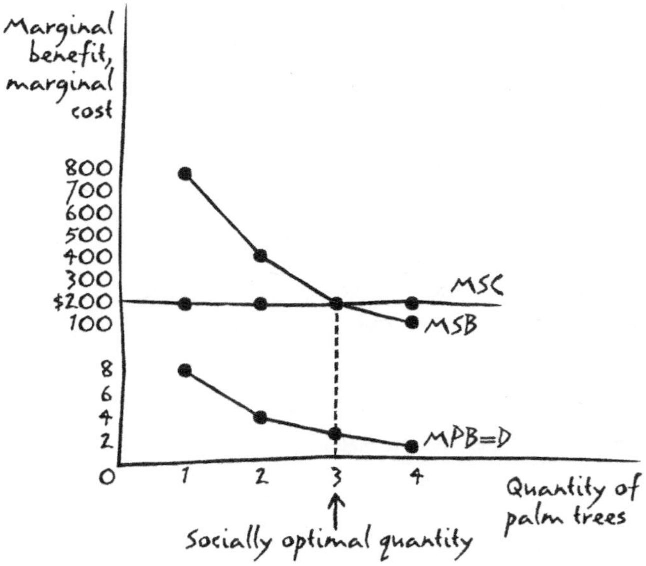

Index

Note: **Boldface** type indicates key terms.

N

T